This Bible belongs to: ______________________

no fears
no regrets
just a future
with a promise

Extreme™ Teen Bible

Given by: ______________________

Date: ______________________

Occasion: ______________________

Extreme Teen Bible™

The Holy Bible
New Century Version

THOMAS NELSON PUBLISHERS
Nashville

The preliminary research and development of the *New Century Version* was done by the World Bible Translation Center, Inc., Fort Worth, TX 76182.

Printed in the United States of America
1 2 3 4 5 6 7 8 9 – 05 04 03 02 01

Contents

Welcome
Extreme Teen™ Bible: Introduction

THIS IS A BOOK OF RISK-TAKERS

This Bible is about radical devotion and revolutionary people. It is a book that God breathed into the hearts and minds of people who were grappling with life and rising to the challenge of faith in the extreme.

The stories were written by and about dreamers and risk-takers—people who bet their lives on what they could only see through faith. They were people who took a chance on God and dared to believe that this world we live in is a *virtual world* compared to the reality of who God is and how he wants to connect with us.

They didn't pretty-up their lives. They told the truth even when it was raw. They admitted their mistakes. God inspired a book that reveals life with all its problems and all of humankind's frailties. He gave us a picture of the out-on-limb-life that is the life of faith.

THIS IS A BOOK ABOUT A REVOLUTIONARY

This whole Bible is really about God connecting to us through Jesus Christ. The Old Testament is the story of Jesus' ancestors and how they lived their lives while waiting for the Messiah to come. The New Testament is about Jesus' life and the universal shock waves from his death and resurrection.

Jesus was all-the-way man and all-the-way God. He was the truest revolutionary of all time. He wasn't afraid to blast the hypocritical religious leaders or to cry when his friend died. He lived through a life just like ours with its frustrations and hard times to do something no one else has done: die as a sacrifice for our sins. The truth he spoke and the fact that he beat death turned the world upside down.

WHAT MAKES READING THE BIBLE A CHALLENGE?

It was written for a different culture.

That's why some of the concepts and behaviors seem foreign to us. We have to figure out the feelings and convictions behind those concepts and behaviors and how they might work today.

It was translated from a different language.

That's why there are so many "versions" or "translations." As our language changes, we interpret the original Bible into our language again and again.

It was written in a different time.

That means different customs and attitudes. That means different names for the same things. That means understanding how faith worked in *that* time and *from that* figuring out how it should work today.

All of this means that we have to work a little harder to "translate" what the Bible says into our day and time. That's why we need extra notes and Bible helps. So take the plunge into all the great stuff packed in this Bible. It's worth it.

Welcome

THIS BIBLE IS A SURVIVAL GUIDE

The Bible is a lot of books strapped together. They are inspired by God, but written by all kinds of different people in all kinds of different circumstances and for all kinds of different reasons. These people weren't setting out to write a book of the Bible. They were facing life and surviving as best they could. Their stories teach us to survive as well by God's power. Because God inspired them, they're one hundred percent accurate and reliable.

Some of these books are stories, listings of events. Some of them are poetry. Some of them are song lyrics. Some are sermons. Some are biographies. Others are letters of introduction. One is a letter of reference. Another is a thank-you note. Some books were written to show God's presence in history. One book is a passionate love poem. Another is a health manual and a textbook for priests. Still another is a war saga. Several are heated letters written to set somebody straight. A few of them are visions of the future.

When you read the Bible, any part of it, understand the big picture. Understand why that book was written, what that writer was trying to accomplish. What were the people involved struggling with? What were they trying to make sense of? Each book has an **Introduction** written specifically to help answer these kinds of questions.

There are other special features to help you get as deep inside the Bible as you can.

People Profiles give you information about specific people who stood a head above the rest to change their world.

What's It Mean? notes give you byte-sized information on specific words or phrases you read about that might not be as obvious today as they were in the culture of Bible times.

Other notes point out **Promises** that God makes in the Bible and ways that he calls us to live **On the Edge** through faith that pushes us to trust God in the extreme. The **Extreme Index** at the back of this Bible indexes these features by subject and provides each note's page number.

The **Quick Reference Index** is the place to turn when you need God's answers to your questions. Look up your question by topic in the front of the Bible; then find the answer at the Bible book, chapter, verse location listed. The questions are also repeated in the Bible text next to their answer.

There are also **Reading Plans** in the back. These plans give you suggestions for what to read every day to cover the Bible in a year.

It's all here—truth, inspiration, bottom-line *actual reality*. Are you up for the challenge?

Production Design and Editorial Team

The Livingstone Corporation
Bruce B. Barton
Christopher D. Hudson
David R. Veerman

Associate Editors

Katie Gieser
Carol Ochs

Contributors

Ron Luce
Linda Washington
Randy Southern
Carol Smith
Neil Wilson

Quick Reference Finder

ABORTION

Does God care for the unborn? . . . . Exodus 21:22–25
Where are children from? . . . . Psalm 127:3
Are children formed by chance? . . . . Psalm 139:13–16
Does God know the unborn by name? . . . . Isaiah 49:1
What does God know about us before we're born? . . . . Jeremiah 1:5

ABUSE

Can intervention help? . . . . 2 Kings 11:1–3

ADOPTION

How does God treat us as his children? . . . . Deuteronomy 8:5
What are God's children called to do? . . . . Deuteronomy 26:18
Who does God discipline? . . . . 2 Samuel 7:14
Who can be called God's children? . . . . John 1:12

ADVICE

Where should we turn for advice? . . . . Joshua 3:9

ANGELS

Do angels work among people? . . . . Genesis 32:1
Who carries out God's judgment? . . . . 2 Samuel 24:16–17
Who do angels serve? . . . . Psalm 103:20–21
Who do angels praise? . . . . Psalm 148:1–2
What do some angels look like? . . . . Isaiah 6:2
Is the appearance of angels frightening? . . . . Ezekiel 1:27–28
How impressive are angels? . . . . Daniel 10:6
Do angels get married? . . . . Matthew 22:30
Can angels die? . . . . Luke 20:36
Who will judge the angels? . . . . 1 Corinthians 6:3

ANGER

Will anger be punished? . . . . Isaiah 14:5–6
What did Jesus get angry at? . . . . John 2:13–17
Can anger be sinful? . . . . Ephesians 4:26–27

ASSURANCE
- Does God hear our prayers? .... Psalm 17:1–2
- Does God always care for his children? .... Psalm 37:23–24
- How long do God's promises last? .... Jeremiah 32:40–41
- Is false assurance dangerous? .... Luke 18:18–30
- What are Christians assured of? .... John 5:24
- Will God ever disappoint his children? .... 2 Timothy 1:12

ATTITUDE
- How does our attitude affect decision making? .... Numbers 14:1–4

AUTHORITY
- Do laws help us live right? .... Judges 21:25

BELIEF
- What should accompany belief in God? .... Deuteronomy 27:10
- What happens if we reject God? .... 1 Samuel 15:26
- Is God's word reliable? .... Ezekiel 36:36

BIBLE
- Why should we obey the Bible? .... Joshua 23:6–7
- Is the Bible trustworthy? .... 2 Samuel 22:29–31
- How hard should we try to obey the Bible? .... 2 Chronicles 34:31
- Is it important to understand the Bible? .... Nehemiah 8:8
- Where did the Bible come from? .... Nehemiah 9:13–14
- What does the Bible give us? .... Psalm 119:99
- What does the Bible reveal? .... Acts 18:28

BLESSING
- Who does God bless? .... Leviticus 26:3–5; Psalm 112:1–3
- Is it wrong to ask God for blessings? .... Nehemiah 13:31
- How does God bless those who do right? .... Psalm 5:11–12
- When are we blessed? .... Psalm 24:3–6
- What brings us blessing (happiness)? .... James 1:25

CARING
- Who does God care for? .... Deuteronomy 7:9
- Does God care for needy people? .... Psalm 68:5
- How should we treat others? .... Zechariah 7:9–10
- Do we have to care for our enemies? .... Luke 6:27–28
- Should Christians care for the needy? .... Luke 14:13–14

CHARACTER
- Who is a good model of integrity? .... Job 1:1
- Does our integrity affect others? .... Jeremiah 7:5–11
- Where can we get strength of character? .... Ezekiel 3:4–9

DEVOTION

How should we be devoted? .... Joshua 24:14
Is it possible to forget about God? .... Isaiah 51:12–13
What does God require of us? .... Micah 6:8
What if we don't follow God? .... Malachi 3:14–18

DISCIPLINE

Is God's discipline good? .... Job 5:17
Why is instruction or discipline important to me? .... Proverbs 4:13
How will listening to instruction benefit me? .... Proverbs 6:20–23
What happens to the one who ignores discipline? .... Proverbs 15:10, 12

DISCOURAGEMENT

Who encourages us with victories? .... Joshua 8:1
Who should we bring our complaints to? ...... Psalm 142:1–7
How are we to respond to discouragement? ..... Proverbs 12:25

DISOBEDIENCE

Is God right to punish the disobedient? ...... Lamentations 1:18–22
Is it wrong to misuse God's name? .... Ezekiel 36:20
What if we neglect God's word? .... Hosea 4:6
What happened to the angels who followed Satan? ...... 2 Peter 2:4

DOUBT

Can our doubts be overcome? .... Psalm 42:5–6
Can we find refuge in God? .... Psalm 62:5–7

DRINKING

Is obsessive drinking bad for us? .... Isaiah 5:22
Is becoming drunk dangerous? .... Luke 21:34
Is drunkenness appropriate for a Christian? .... Romans 13:11–14
Is drunkenness associated with foolishness? .... Ephesians 5:17–18

EDUCATION

Who is responsible for teaching children? .... Deuteronomy 6:1–9
How can wise people increase their education? .... Proverbs 1:5
Is education for everybody? .... Proverbs 18:2
Should Christians ever stop learning about God? ..... Ephesians 4:14–15

EMBARRASSMENT

What causes embarrassment? .... Proverbs 29:23
What can embarrassment lead to? .... Matthew 14:1–12
Is the Good News a source of embarrassment? .... Romans 1:16

EMOTIONS

How should God's awesome acts make us feel? .... Joshua 2:8–13
Where can we find healing for a broken heart? .... Psalm 34:18
Did Jesus experience emotions? .... John 11:35

ENCOURAGEMENT

ENEMIES

ETERNAL LIFE

FAITH

FAMILY

FEAR

Quick Reference Finder

FEELINGS

What should we do when we are sad? . . . . . 1 Samuel 1:10; Nehemiah 1:4
Does God care when we hurt? . . . . Nehemiah 9:27

FOLLOWING GOD

What happens if we forget to follow God? . . . . Joshua 9:3–18
How should we follow God? . . . . . Joshua 22:5; 2 Chronicles 15:15; Job 23:11–12
What are Christians like? . . . . Judges 5:31
Who should we listen to? . . . . 1 Samuel 3:10
Does God put conditions on our obedience? . . . . . 2 Chronicles 7:17
Who will teach us to follow God? . . . . Nehemiah 9:20
What's the hope of a good person? . . . . Proverbs 10:24–25
Where will following God lead us? . . . . Isaiah 35:10
How can we have a changed life? . . . . Ezekiel 11:19–20

FORGIVENESS

What is God known for? . . . . Nehemiah 9:17
Why does God forgive us? . . . . Psalm 86:5
Is God's forgiveness possible? . . . . Ezekiel 37:23
How many times should I forgive someone before I stop? . . . . Matthew 18:21–35
Who can receive forgiveness? . . . . Acts 13:38–39

FRIENDSHIP

What's an example of good friendship? . . . . 1 Samuel 19:1–7
How can friendship outlast death? . . . . 2 Samuel 9:1
How should we care for our friends? . . . . 2 Samuel 19:33
How can friends pull you down? . . . . 2 Chronicles 10:1–14
What should we do to help hurting friends? . . . . Job 2:11
Can friends cause us pain? . . . . Psalm 55:12–14
Can standing up for a friend make a difference? . . . . . . Jeremiah 26:24
What is friendship marked by? . . . . John 15:13–15

FUTURE

How can our future be blessed? . . . . Deuteronomy 5:29
Does God put us in situations to make a difference? . . . . Esther 4:14
What's the future of someone who doesn't turn from sin? . . . Jeremiah 18:11
Is the future of Christians bright? . . . . Jeremiah 31:3–6

GIVING

What should be our attitude in giving? . . . . Exodus 35:22
Is the amount you give to God a personal decision? . . . . . 2 Kings 12:4–5
Who benefits when we give to the church? . . . . 2 Chronicles 31:4
What is the result of giving to others? . . . . Mark 9:41
What does giving help others to do? . . . . Acts 2:44–45
What's better than getting gifts? . . . . Acts 20:35
Who should we be mindful to support? . . . . Acts 28:7–10

GOD

Does God care about me? . . . . Genesis 8:1
What is God like? . . . . Exodus 15:3–4
Is God the only Lord? . . . . Deuteronomy 6:4
Is God trustworthy? . . . . Deuteronomy 7:9
How powerful is God? . . . . Joshua 4:23–24
Does God keep his promises? . . . . Joshua 23:5–10
What happens when we forget about God? . . . . Judges 3:7–8
Who is like God? . . . . 1 Samuel 2:2
How is God sovereign? . . . . 1 Samuel 2:6–7
Who can stand before God's holiness? . . . . 1 Samuel 6:19–20
Is God unique? . . . . 2 Samuel 7:22
Can we fully describe God? . . . . 1 Kings 8:27
Who else is like God? . . . . 2 Kings 5:15
How does God deal with his people? . . . . 2 Kings 20:4–6
Does God see people sin? . . . . Job 11:11
Is God perfect? . . . . Job 21:22
Do we have a right to correct God? . . . . Job 40:2
Is God eternal? . . . . Isaiah 41:4
Does God accomplish his plans? . . . . Lamentations 2:17
Will the world ever see God's greatness? . . . . Ezekiel 38:23
Does God love his people? . . . . Hosea 11:1

GOD'S WILL

What can we trust in when we are making decisions? . . . . . Psalm 16:7
Can Christians be hopeful about the future? . . . . Psalm 48:14
Can God turn something bad into good? . . . . Acts 7:9–10
Can we trust God with the events in our lives? . . . . Acts 16:6–7

GOOD NEWS

Who is the Good News for? . . . . Luke 24:46–47
How does believing in the Good News affect a person? . . . . 1 Thessalonians 1:4–5

GOSSIP

Does God command us not to gossip? . . . . Exodus 23:1
What should we be careful of when we're talking about other people? . . . . Leviticus 19:16
How should we resist gossip? . . . . Proverbs 4:24–27
What are some of the negative results of gossip? . . . . . Proverbs 16:27–28
What is one benefit found when gossip is stopped? . . . . . Proverbs 26:20

GREED

Is greed ever happy or satisfied? . . . . Isaiah 5:8–10
What does God think of greed? . . . . Jeremiah 8:10

GUIDANCE

Can we trust God to lead us? . . . . 1 Chronicles 14:10

HOPE

HUMILITY

HYPOCRISY

IDOLATRY

INTEGRITY

JEALOUSY

JESUS

LONELINESS

What does God do for lonely people? . . . . 1 Kings 19:14–18
Are we ever alone? . . . . Matthew 28:20

LOVE

Does God love me forever? . . . . Ezra 3:11
Do we have to love our enemies? . . . . Matthew 5:43–45
What is the most important command that God has given us? . . . . Mark 12:29–30
Is it important for Christians to love each other? . . . . John 13:34–35
Does true love ever quit? . . . . 1 Corinthians 13:4–8
What should Christians be known for? . . . . 2 John 5–6

LUST

Where can sexual lust lead? . . . . 2 Samuel 11:1–5
How should we maintain purity? . . . . Job 31:1
What will unchecked lust get us? . . . . Ezekiel 16:25–30

MARRIAGE

How can a spouse be a bad influence? . . . . 1 Kings 3:1–3
Can a spouse lead you away from God? . . . . 1 Kings 11:1–2
Can true love ever be quenched? . . . . Song of Solomon 8:6–7
What does God think of divorce? . . . . Malachi 2:16
Do angels get married? . . . . Matthew 22:30

MERCY

Why is kindness (mercy) important? . . . . Proverbs 3:3–4
Who do we honor by being merciful to the needy? . . . . . . Proverbs 14:31
What kind of limits are on God's mercy? . . . . Isaiah 63:7
Is Jesus merciful? . . . . 1 Timothy 1:2

MIND

What should a Christian's thoughts be characterized by? . . . . Romans 12:2

MONEY

What's a good way to spend some of the money we earn? . . . . 1 Chronicles 26:27
Will our possessions last forever? . . . . Job 1:21; Isaiah 31:6–7
What can our possessions distract us from? . . . . Isaiah 17:7–10
What's most important? . . . . Matthew 6:19–20
What can money do to our relationship with God? . . . . . . Mark 10:17–25
Can Christians serve both God and money? . . . . Luke 16:13
Should we share the resources that God has blessed us with? . . . . Acts 2:42–45

MURDER

Does God allow murder? . . . . Deuteronomy 5:17

Preface to the New Century Version

God intended for everyone to be able to understand his Word. Earliest Scriptures were in Hebrew, ideally suited for a barely literate society because of its economy of words, acrostic literary form and poetic parallelism. The New Testament was first written in the simple Greek of everyday life, not in the Latin of Roman courts or the classical Greek of the academies. Even Jesus, the Master Teacher, taught spiritual principles by comparing them to such familiar terms as pearls, seeds, rocks, trees, and sheep. Likewise, the *New Century Version* translates the Scriptures in familiar, everyday words of our times.

The *New Century Version* is a translation of God's Word from the original Hebrew and Greek languages. Several previous editions of the complete *New Century Version* have been published, such as the *International Children's Bible* (1986); *Time with God* (1991); *The Odyssey Bible* (1994); *The Answer* (1993); and *The Inspirational Study Bible* (1995), among others.

A TRUSTWORTHY TRANSLATION

Two basic premises guided the translation process of the *New Century Version.* The first concern was that the translation be faithful to the manuscripts in the original languages. A team composed of the World Bible Translation Center and fifty additional, highly qualified and experienced Bible scholars and translators was assembled. The team included people with translation experience on such accepted versions as the *New International Version,* the *New American Standard Bible,* and the *New King James Version.* The most recent scholarship and the best available Hebrew and Greek texts were used, principally the third edition of the United Bible Societies' Greek text and the latest edition of the Biblia Hebraica, along with the Septuagint.

A CLEAR TRANSLATION

The second concern was to make the language clear enough for anyone to read the Bible and understand it for himself. In maintaining clear language, several guidelines were followed. Vocabulary choice has been based upon *The Living Word Vocabulary* by Dr. Edgar Dale and Dr. Joseph O'Rourke (Worldbook-Childcraft International), which is the standard used by the editors of *The World Book Encyclopedia* to determine appropriate vocabulary. For difficult words which have no simpler synonyms, footnotes are provided. Footnotes appear at the bottom of the page and are indicated in the text by an *n* (for "note").

The *New Century Version* aids understanding by putting concepts into natural terms. Modern measurements and geographical locations have been used as much as possible. For instance, terms such as "shekels," cubits," "omer," and "hin" have been converted to modern equivalents of weights and measures. Where geographical references are identical, the modern name has been used, such as the "Mediterranean Sea" instead of "Great Sea" or "Western Sea." Also, to minimize confusion, the most familiar name for a place is used consistently, instead of using variant names for the same place. "Lake Galilee" is used throughout rather than its variant forms, "Sea of Kinnereth," "Lake Gennesaret," and "Sea of Tiberias."

Ancient customs are often unfamiliar to modern readers. Customs such as shaving a man's beard to shame him or walking between the halves of a dead animal to seal an agreement are meaningless to most people. So these are clarified either in the text or in a footnote.

Since *meanings* of words change with time, care has been taken to avoid potential misunderstandings. Frequently in the Old Testament God tells his people to "devote" something to him, as when he tells the Israelites to devote Jericho and everything in it to him. While we might understand this to mean he is telling them to keep it safe and holy, the exact opposite is true. He is telling them to destroy it totally as an offering to him. The *New Century Version* communicates the idea clearly by translating "devoted," in these situations, as "destroyed as an offering to the Lord."

Rhetorical questions have been stated according to their implied answers. The psalmist's question, "What god is so great as our God?" has been stated more directly as, "No god is as great as our God."

Figures of speech have been translated according to their meanings. For instance, the expression, "The Virgin Daughter of Zion," which is frequently used in the Old Testament, is simply translated "the people of Jerusalem."

Idiomatic expressions of the biblical languages are translated to communicate the same meaning to today's reader that would have been understood by the original audience. For example, the Hebrew idiom "he rested with his fathers" is translated by its corresponding meaning—"he died."

Obscure terms have been clarified. In the Old Testament God frequently condemns the people for their "high places" and "Asherah poles." The *New Century Version* translates these according to their meanings, which would have been understood by the Hebrews. "High places" is translated "places where gods were worshiped," and "Asherah poles" is translated "Asherah idols."

Gender language has also been translated with a concern for clarity. To avoid the misconception that "man" and "mankind" and "he" are exclusively masculine when they are being used in a generic sense, this translation has chosen to use less ambiguous language, such as "people" and "humans" and "human beings," and has prayerfully attempted throughout to choose gender language that would accurately convey the intent of the original writers. Specifically and exclusively masculine and feminine references in the text have been retained.

Following in the tradition of other English versions, the *New Century Version* indicates the divine name YHWH, the Tetragrammaton, by putting LORD, and sometimes GOD, in capital letters. This is to distinguish it from Adonai, another Hebrew word that is translated Lord.

Every attempt has been made to maintain proper English style, while clarifying concepts and communication. The beauty of the Hebrew parallelism in poetry and the word plays have been retained, and the images of the ancient languages have been captured in equivalent English images wherever possible.

OUR PRAYER

It is with great humility and prayerfulness that this Bible is presented. We acknowledge the infallibility of God's Word and yet our own human frailty. We pray that God has worked through us as his vessels so that we all might better learn his truth for ourselves and that it might richly grow in our lives. It is to his glory that this Bible is given.

THE PUBLISHER

THE OLD TESTAMENT

genesis

CONTENT Genesis is a bottom-line, this-is-how-it-is, no-sugarcoating kind of book. When we ask the big question, "Where do we come from?" Genesis gives the big answer, "We come from God. He made us and wants to be in relationship with us." When we ask the big question, "Who do we come from?" Genesis gives the honest answer, "This is who they are, but you might not like everything you see."

Genesis has loads of famous stories and people, from Adam to Noah to Abraham to Joseph. It's a who's who of the lightly populated days of the earth. What's amazing about this book though is that, unlike a who's who, Genesis tells us the real scoop on these people who established the original cultures of the world. We read about their failures, not just their successes. We read about their mess-ups and their doubts and their . . . well . . . flops.

From this very first book of the Bible, God lays a foundation. We are what he created when he chose to love and be loved. He is the God who embraces us humans, "warts" and all, and even uses us to make the world a better place.

Outline

1:1—2:25 .... The Story of Creation
3:1—4:15 .... The First Sin and the First Murder
4:16—5:32.......... Descendants of Adam Before the Flood
6:1—9:29 .... Noah and the Flood
10:1—11:32 .... The Descendants of Noah and the Tower of Babel
12:1—25:18 .... The Story of Abraham
25:19—36:43 ...... Isaac, Jacob, and Esau
37:1—50:26 .... The Story of Joseph

Purpose A living being—God—is the source of all things. He wants a personal relationship with us, based on our trust in his promises.

Theme Beginnings

Date of writing About 1446–1406 B.C.

"I will bless those who bless you, and I will place a curse on those who harm you. And all the people on earth will be blessed through you" (12:3).

Bible Talk

Creation

The story of creation, as simple and clear-cut as it is, has been the subject of a LOT of dispute. Was it literally seven days? Did God create everything as full-grown? If God created just one family, where did all the other families come from? Was it really an apple that Adam and Eve ate that ruined paradise for all of us?

No matter how much people disagree about all the things we *don't* know about how God created the world, Genesis gives us concrete information about what we *do* know. God did create the world from nothing. He did it miraculously through a process only he can understand or re-create. He did it with a plan and a purpose that we are now living out.

TOTAL TRUTH

What's up with all the wives?

If you've noticed any married couples around you lately, you're probably aware that one husband and one wife seems to be a challenge in terms of any long-term commitment. In Genesis things are even more complicated. Men often had more than one wife and sometimes had children by many wives and servants of those wives. Genesis gives us a window into an ancient world that can be wacky to say the least. Remember, though, that God never encouraged polygamy (multiple spouses) or commanded it or even honored it. Before Sarah died, Abraham had no other wives. As far as we know, Isaac only had one wife. And there seemed to be only one Mrs. Noah on the ark.

THE BEGINNING OF THE WORLD

[1]In the beginning God created the sky and
the earth. [2]The earth was empty and had no
form. Darkness covered the ocean, and God's
Spirit was moving over the water.
[3]Then God said, "Let there be light," and
there was light. [4]God saw that the light was
good, so he divided the light from the darkness. [5]God named the light "day" and the darkness "night." Evening passed, and morning
came. This was the first day.
[6]Then God said, "Let there be something to
divide the water in two." [7]So God made the air
and placed some of the water above the air
and some below it. [8]God named the air "sky."
Evening passed, and morning came. This was
the second day.
[9]Then God said, "Let the water under the
sky be gathered together so the dry land will
appear." And it happened. [10]God named the
dry land "earth" and the water that was gathered together "seas." God saw that this was
good.
[11]Then God said, "Let the earth produce
plants—some to make grain for seeds and
others to make fruits with seeds in them. Every
seed will produce more of its own kind of
plant." And it happened. [12]The earth produced
plants with grain for seeds and trees that made
fruits with seeds in them. Each seed grew its
own kind of plant. God saw that all this was
good. [13]Evening passed, and morning came.
This was the third day.

WHAT'S IT MEAN?

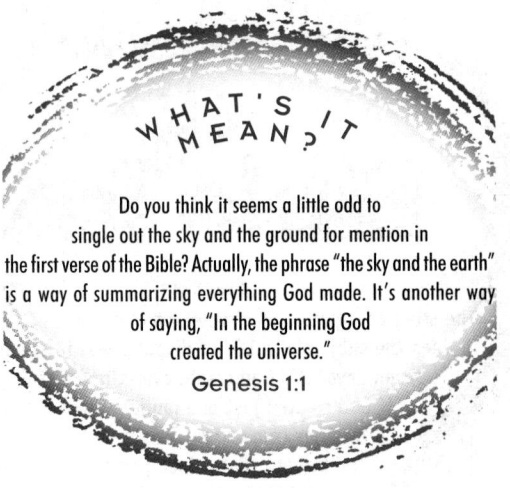

Do you think it seems a little odd to single out the sky and the ground for mention in the first verse of the Bible? Actually, the phrase "the sky and the earth" is a way of summarizing everything God made. It's another way of saying, "In the beginning God created the universe."

Genesis 1:1

On the Edge

In the beginning God created the sky and the earth (Gen. 1:1).

A common definition of the word *create* is "to make something out of nothing." That's exactly what God did when he created this world. He made this incredible planet out of absolutely nothing! That's what he did when he made you. Thirty years ago you didn't exist. Now you do. Just because the earth and lots of people have been created, it doesn't mean God is finished. He's still creating. He can create something out of nothing. You may look for confidence in your life and see nothing. You may look for joy in your life and see nothing. You may look for just one good thing anywhere in your life and see nothing. When you're looking at nothing, remember that God is the supreme Creator. Ask him to make something out of nothing for you.

SEE FOR YOURSELF:
Neh. 9:6;
Ps. 8; 93:1; 104

[14]Then God said, "Let there be lights in the
sky to separate day from night. These lights
will be used for signs, seasons, days, and years.
[15]They will be in the sky to give light to the
earth." And it happened.
[16]So God made the two large lights. He made
the brighter light to rule the day and made the
smaller light to rule the night. He also made the
stars. [17]God put all these in the sky to shine on
the earth, [18]to rule over the day and over the
night, and to separate the light from the darkness. God saw that all these things were good.
[19]Evening passed, and morning came. This was
the fourth day.
[20]Then God said, "Let the water be filled
with living things, and let birds fly in the air
above the earth."
[21]So God created the large sea animals and
every living thing that moves in the sea. The
sea is filled with these living things, with each
one producing more of its own kind. He also
made every bird that flies, and each bird produced more of its own kind. God saw that this
was good. [22]God blessed them and said, "Have
many young ones so that you may grow
in number. Fill the water of the seas, and let
the birds grow in number on the earth." [23]Eve-
ning passed, and morning came. This was the
fifth day.
[24]Then God said, "Let the earth be filled with
animals, each producing more of its own kind.

Let there be tame animals and small crawling
animals and wild animals, and let each produce more of its kind." And it happened.
[25]So God made the wild animals, the tame
animals, and all the small crawling animals to
produce more of their own kind. God saw that
this was good.
[26]Then God said, "Let us make human beings in our image and likeness. And let them
rule over the fish in the sea and the birds in the
sky, over the tame animals, over all the earth,
and over all the small crawling animals on the
earth."
[27]So God created human beings in his image. In the image of God he created them. He
created them male and female. [28]God blessed
them and said, "Have many children and grow
in number. Fill the earth and be its master. Rule
over the fish in the sea and over the birds in
the sky and over every living thing that moves
on the earth."
[29]God said, "Look, I have given you all the
plants that have grain for seeds and all the
trees whose fruits have seeds in them. They
will be food for you. [30]I have given all the
green plants as food for every wild animal,
every bird of the air, and every small crawling
animal." And it happened. [31]God looked at
everything he had made, and it was very good.
Evening passed, and morning came. This was
the sixth day.

WHAT'S IT MEAN?

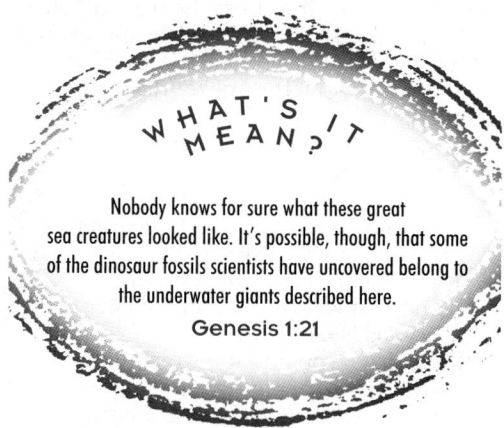

Nobody knows for sure what these great sea creatures looked like. It's possible, though, that some of the dinosaur fossils scientists have uncovered belong to the underwater giants described here.

Genesis 1:21

THE SEVENTH DAY—REST

2 [1]So the sky, the earth, and all that filled
them were finished. [2]By the seventh day God
finished the work he had been doing, so he
rested from all his work. [3]God blessed the seventh day and made it a holy day, because on
that day he rested from all the work he had
done in creating the world.

THE FIRST PEOPLE

[4]This is the story of the creation of the sky
and the earth. When the LORD God first made
the earth and the sky, [5]there were still no plants
on the earth. Nothing was growing in the fields
because the LORD God had not yet made it rain
on the land. And there was no person to care
for the ground, [6]but a mist would rise up from
the earth and water all the ground.

WHAT'S IT MEAN?

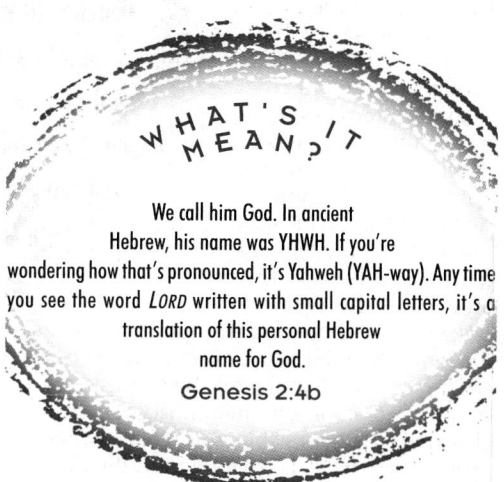

We call him God. In ancient Hebrew, his name was YHWH. If you're wondering how that's pronounced, it's Yahweh (YAH-way). Any time you see the word *LORD* written with small capital letters, it's a translation of this personal Hebrew name for God.

Genesis 2:4b

[7]Then the LORD God took dust from the
ground and formed a man from it. He breathed
the breath of life into the man's nose, and the
man became a living person. [8]Then the LORD
God planted a garden in the east, in a place
called Eden, and put the man he had formed
into it. [9]The LORD God caused every beautiful
tree and every tree that was good for food to
grow out of the ground. In the middle of the
garden, God put the tree that gives life and also
the tree that gives the knowledge of good and
evil.
[10]A river flowed through Eden and watered
the garden. From there the river branched out
to become four rivers. [11]The first river, named
Pishon, flows around the whole land of Havilah, where there is gold. [12]The gold of that land
is excellent. Bdellium and onyx[n] are also found
there. [13]The second river, named Gihon, flows
around the whole land of Cush. [14]The third
river, named Tigris, flows out of Assyria toward
the east. The fourth river is the Euphrates.
[15]The LORD God put the man in the garden
of Eden to care for it and work it. [16]The LORD

2:12 bdellium and onyx Bdellium is an expensive, sweet-smelling resin like myrrh, and onyx is a gem.

God commanded him, "You may eat the fruit
from any tree in the garden, [17]but you must
not eat the fruit from the tree which gives the
knowledge of good and evil. If you ever eat
fruit from that tree, you will die!"

THE FIRST WOMAN

[18]Then the LORD God said, "It is not good
for the man to be alone. I
will make a helper who is
right for him."
[19]From the ground
God formed every wild
animal and every bird
in the sky, and he
brought them to the
man so the man could
name them. Whatever
the man called each liv-
ing thing, that became its
name. [20]The man gave
names to all the tame animals, to the birds in the sky,
and to all the wild animals.
But Adam[n] did not find a helper that was right
for him. [21]So the LORD God caused the man to
sleep very deeply, and while he was asleep, God
removed one of the man's ribs. Then God
closed up the man's skin at the place where he
took the rib. [22]The LORD God used the rib from
the man to make a woman, and then he
brought the woman to the man.
[23]And the man said,

"Now, this is someone whose bones came
from my bones,
whose body came from my body.
I will call her 'woman,'
because she was taken out of man."

[24]So a man will leave his father and mother
and be united with his wife, and the two will
become one body.
[25]The man and his wife were naked, but
they were not ashamed.

THE BEGINNING OF SIN

3 [1]Now the snake was the most clever of all
the wild animals the LORD God had made. One
day the snake said to the woman, "Did God
really say that you must not eat fruit from any
tree in the garden?"
[2]The woman answered the snake, "We may
eat fruit from the trees in the garden. [3]But God
told us, 'You must not eat fruit from the tree
that is in the middle of the garden. You must
not even touch it, or you will die.' "
[4]But the snake said to the woman, "You will
not die. [5]God knows that if you eat the fruit
from that tree, you will learn about good and
evil and you will be like God!"
[6]The woman saw that the tree was beautiful, that its fruit was good to eat, and that it
would make her wise. So she took some of its
fruit and ate it. She also gave some of the fruit
to her husband, and he ate it.
[7]Then, it was as if their
eyes were opened. They
realized they were naked,
so they sewed fig leaves
together and made some-
thing to cover themselves.
[8]Then they heard the
LORD God walking in the
garden during the cool
part of the day, and the
man and his wife hid
from the LORD God
among the trees in the
garden. [9]But the LORD God
called to the man and said,
"Where are you?"
[10]The man answered, "I heard you walking
in the garden, and I was afraid because I was
naked, so I hid."
[11]God asked, "Who told you that you were
naked? Did you eat fruit from the tree from
which I commanded you not to eat?"
[12]The man said, "You gave this woman to me
and she gave me fruit from the tree, so I ate it."
[13]Then the LORD God said to the woman,
"How could you have done such a thing?"
She answered, "The snake tricked me, so I
ate the fruit."
[14]The LORD God said to the snake,

"Because you did this,
a curse will be put on you.
You will be cursed as no other animal,
tame or wild, will ever be.
You will crawl on your stomach,
and you will eat dust all the days of
your life.
[15]I will make you and the woman
enemies to each other.
Your descendants and her descendants
will be enemies.
One of her descendants will crush your
head,
and you will bite his heel."

[16]Then God said to the woman,
"I will cause you to have much trouble

> **"I will make you and the woman enemies to each other. Your descendants and her descendants will be enemies. One of her descendants will crush your head, and you will bite his heel."**
> **(Genesis 3:15)**

2:20 Adam This is the name of the first man. It also means "humans," including men and women.

when you are pregnant,
and when you give birth to children,
you will have great pain.
You will greatly desire your husband,
but he will rule over you."
17Then God said to the man, "You listened
to what your wife said, and you ate fruit from
the tree from which I commanded you not to
eat.
"So I will put a curse on the ground,
and you will have to work very hard
for your food.
In pain you will eat its food
all the days of your life.
18The ground will produce thorns and
weeds for you,
and you will eat the plants of the field.
19You will sweat and work hard
for your food.
Later you will return to the ground,
because you were taken from it.
You are dust,
and when you die, you will return to
the dust."
20The man named his wife Eve,[n] because she
is the mother of everyone who has ever lived.
21The LORD God made clothes from animal
skins for the man and his wife and dressed
them. 22Then the LORD God said, "The man has
become like one of us; he knows good and
evil. We must keep him from eating some of
the fruit from the tree of life, or he will live
forever." 23So the LORD God forced the man out
of the garden of Eden to work the ground from
which he was taken. 24After God forced the
man out of the garden, he placed angels and a
sword of fire that flashed around in every direction on its eastern border. This kept people
from getting to the tree of life.

THE FIRST FAMILY

4 1Adam had sexual relations with his wife
Eve, and she became pregnant and gave birth
to Cain.[n] Eve said, "With the LORD's help, I have
given birth to a man." 2After that, Eve gave
birth to Cain's brother Abel. Abel took care of
flocks, and Cain became a farmer.
3Later, Cain brought some food from the
ground as a gift to God. 4Abel brought the best
parts from some of the firstborn of his flock.
The LORD accepted Abel and his gift, 5but he
did not accept Cain and his gift. So Cain became very angry and felt rejected.
6The LORD asked Cain, "Why are you angry?

WHAT'S IT MEAN?

The Bible doesn't tell us exactly when or where animal sacrifice began. We do know that the practice has been going on since the earliest days of human history. The sacrifice ritual usually included killing the animal in a specific way, praying out loud, and burning incense. Jesus' death on the cross ended the need for animal sacrifice once and for all.

Genesis 4:4

Why do you look so unhappy? 7If you do
things well, I will accept you, but if you do not
do them well, sin is ready to attack you. Sin
wants you, but you must rule over it."
8Cain said to his brother Abel, "Let's go out
into the field." While they were out in the field,
Cain attacked his brother Abel and killed him.
9Later, the LORD said to Cain, "Where is your
brother Abel?"
Cain answered, "I don't know. Is it my job
to take care of my brother?"
10Then the LORD said, "What have you
done? Your brother's blood is crying out to me
from the ground. 11And now you will be
cursed in your work with the ground, the same
ground where your brother's blood fell and
where your hands killed him. 12You will work
the ground, but it will not grow good crops for
you anymore, and you will wander around on
the earth."
13Then Cain said to the LORD, "This punishment is more than I can stand! 14Today you
have forced me to stop working the ground,
and now I must hide from you. I must wander
around on the earth, and anyone who meets me
can kill me."
15The LORD said to Cain, "No! If anyone kills
you, I will punish that person seven times
more." Then the LORD put a mark on Cain
warning anyone who met him not to kill him.

CAIN'S FAMILY

16So Cain went away from the LORD and
lived in the land of Nod,[n] east of Eden. 17He

3:20 Eve This name sounds like the Hebrew word meaning "alive." **4:1 Cain** This name sounds like the Hebrew word for "I have given birth." **4:16 Nod** This name sounds like the Hebrew word for "wander."

ABEL made a difference

Abel compiled some unique "firsts" in his short lifetime: member of the first family, first little brother, first rancher. Other "firsts" were more tragic than unique: part of the first sibling rivalry; first to do something better than his big brother; first to die at his brother's hand.

While these facts make Abel interesting, they are not the way in which he made a difference. Abel invented worship. Because his parents Adam and Eve had turned away from God, Abel had to think about some way to approach God. Apparently Cain and Abel talked it over and both decided to offer God a sacrifice. Cain the farmer brought "some food from the ground as a gift to God"; Abel brought the best he had. He took "the best parts from some of the firstborn of his flock" and created a fat sacrifice. God accepted the attitude of Abel's worship. Jesus later called him righteous.

It doesn't seem as if Abel suspected his brother's intense jealousy and anger. He followed Cain out to a field where the older killed the younger. Though it ended unfairly and too soon, Abel's life left a legacy of faith. When the writer of Hebrews listed the Hall of Faith in the New Testament, the first inductee was Abel:

Cutting Edge

"It was by faith that Abel offered God a better sacrifice" (Heb. 11:4a).

YOU can, too!

If you've got brothers and/or sisters, here's a warning: don't try to make a difference by competing with them. That wasn't Abel's example. There's enough natural competition between siblings as it is. The question you can answer like Abel is, "How will I approach God?"

Cain and Abel "attended church" together, but their attitude was miles apart. One was there; the other was all there. Clarifying and participating in your relationship with God, not just going through the motions, will make a huge difference in your life . . . and in the lives of others.

Want to know more? Read about Abel's life in Genesis 4:1–8; Matthew 23:35; Hebrews 11:4; 12:24.

had sexual relations with his wife, and she became pregnant and gave birth to Enoch. At that time Cain was building a city, which he named after his son Enoch. 18Enoch had a son named Irad, Irad had a son named Mehujael, Mehujael had a son named Methushael, and Methushael had a son named Lamech.

19Lamech married two women, Adah and Zillah. 20Adah gave birth to Jabal, who became the first person to live in tents and raise cattle. 21Jabal's brother was Jubal, the first person to play the harp and flute. 22Zillah gave birth to Tubal-Cain, who made tools out of bronze and iron. The sister of Tubal-Cain was Naamah.

23Lamech said to his wives:

"Adah and Zillah, hear my voice!
You wives of Lamech, listen to what I say.
I killed a man for wounding me,
a young man for hitting me.
24If Cain's killer is punished seven times,
then Lamech's killer will be punished seventy-seven times."

ADAM AND EVE HAVE A NEW SON

25Adam had sexual relations with his wife Eve again, and she gave birth to a son. She named him Seth[n] and said, "God has given me another child. He will take the place of Abel, who was killed by Cain." 26Seth also had a son, and they named him Enosh. At that time people began to pray to the LORD.

ADAM'S FAMILY HISTORY

5 1This is the family history of Adam. When God created human beings, he made them in his own likeness. 2He created them male and female, and on that day he blessed them and named them human beings.

3When Adam was 130 years old, he became the father of another son in his likeness and image, and Adam named him Seth. 4After Seth was born, Adam lived 800 years and had other sons and daughters. 5So Adam lived a total of 930 years, and then he died.

6When Seth was 105 years old, he had a son named Enosh. 7After Enosh was born, Seth lived 807 years and had other sons and daughters. 8So Seth lived a total of 912 years, and then he died.

9When Enosh was 90 years old, he had a son named Kenan. 10After Kenan was born, Enosh lived 815 years and had other sons and daughters. 11So Enosh lived a total of 905 years, and then he died.

12When Kenan was 70 years old, he had a son named Mahalalel. 13After Mahalalel was born, Kenan lived 840 years and had other sons and daughters. 14So Kenan lived a total of 910 years, and then he died.

15When Mahalalel was 65 years old, he had a son named Jared. 16After Jared was born, Mahalalel lived 830 years and had other sons and daughters. 17So Mahalalel lived a total of 895 years, and then he died.

18When Jared was 162 years old, he had a son named Enoch. 19After Enoch was born, Jared lived 800 years and had other sons and daughters. 20So Jared lived a total of 962 years, and then he died.

21When Enoch was 65 years old, he had a son named Methuselah. 22After Methuselah was born, Enoch walked with God 300 years more and had other sons and daughters. 23So Enoch lived a total of 365 years. 24Enoch walked with God; one day Enoch could not be found, because God took him.

25When Methuselah was 187 years old, he had a son named Lamech. 26After Lamech was born, Methuselah lived 782 years and had other sons and daughters. 27So Methuselah lived a total of 969 years, and then he died.

WHAT'S IT MEAN?

Even by early biblical standards, where it was not unusual for people to live for hundreds of years, Methuselah was an old guy. At 969 years, he lived longer than anyone else mentioned in the Bible. Assuming his descendants all had children by their thirtieth birthday, Methuselah lived long enough to see his great-grandson!

Genesis 5:27

28When Lamech was 182, he had a son. 29Lamech named his son Noah[n] and said, "He will comfort us in our work, which comes from the ground the LORD has cursed." 30After

4:25 Seth This name sounds like the Hebrew word for "to give." **5:29 Noah** This name sounds like the Hebrew word for "rest."

Noah was born, Lamech lived 595 years and had other sons and daughters. [31]So Lamech lived a total of 777 years, and then he died.

[32]After Noah was 500 years old, he became the father of Shem, Ham, and Japheth.

THE HUMAN RACE BECOMES EVIL

6 [1]The number of people on earth began to grow, and daughters were born to them. [2]When the sons of God saw that these girls were beautiful, they married any of them they chose. [3]The LORD said, "My Spirit will not remain in human beings forever, because they are flesh. They will live only 120 years."

[4]The Nephilim were on the earth in those days and also later. That was when the sons of God had sexual relations with the daughters of human beings. These women gave birth to children, who became famous and were the mighty warriors of long ago.

[5]The LORD saw that the human beings on the earth were very wicked and that everything they thought about was evil. [6]He was sorry he had made human beings on the earth, and his heart was filled with pain. [7]So the LORD said, "I will destroy all human beings that I made on the earth. And I will destroy every animal and everything that crawls on the earth and the birds of the air, because I am sorry I have made them." [8]But Noah pleased the LORD.

NOAH AND THE GREAT FLOOD

[9]This is the family history of Noah. Noah was a good man, the most innocent man of his time, and he walked with God. [10]He had three sons: Shem, Ham, and Japheth.

[11]People on earth did what God said was evil, and violence was everywhere. [12]When God saw that everyone on the earth did only evil, [13]he said to Noah, "Because people have made the earth full of violence, I will destroy all of them from the earth. [14]Build a boat of cypress wood for yourself. Make rooms in it and cover it inside and outside with tar. [15]This is how big I want you to build the boat: four hundred fifty feet long, seventy-five feet wide, and forty-five feet high. [16]Make an opening around the top of the boat that is eighteen inches high from the edge of the roof down. Put a door in the side of the boat. Make an upper, middle, and lower deck in it. [17]I will bring a flood of water on the earth to destroy all living things that live under the sky, including everything that has the breath of life. Everything on the earth will die. [18]But I will make an agreement with you—you, your sons, your wife, and your sons' wives will all go into the boat. [19]Also, you must bring into the boat two of every living thing, male and female. Keep them alive with you. [20]Two of every kind of bird, animal, and crawling thing will come to you to be kept alive. [21]Also gather some of every kind of food and store it on the boat as food for you and the animals."

[22]Noah did everything that God commanded him.

WHAT'S IT MEAN?

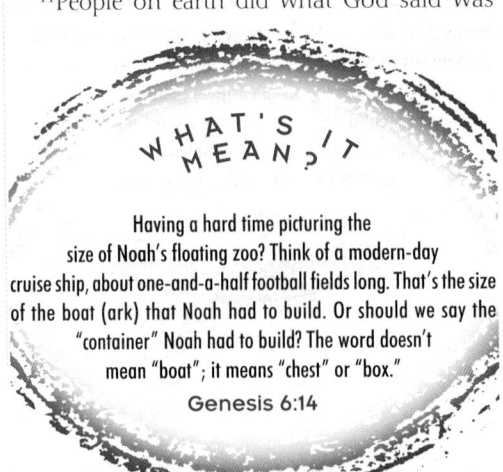

Having a hard time picturing the size of Noah's floating zoo? Think of a modern-day cruise ship, about one-and-a-half football fields long. That's the size of the boat (ark) that Noah had to build. Or should we say the "container" Noah had to build? The word doesn't mean "boat"; it means "chest" or "box."

Genesis 6:14

THE FLOOD BEGINS

7 [1]Then the LORD said to Noah, "I have seen that you are the best person among the people of this time, so you and your family can go into the boat. [2]Take with you seven pairs, each male with its female, of every kind of clean animal, and take one pair, each male with its female, of every kind of unclean animal. [3]Take seven pairs of all the birds of the sky, each male with its female. This will allow all these animals to continue living on the earth after the flood. [4]Seven days from now I will send rain on the earth. It will rain forty days and forty nights, and I will wipe off from the earth every living thing that I have made."

[5]Noah did everything the LORD commanded him.

[6]Noah was six hundred years old when the flood came. [7]He and his wife and his sons and their wives went into the boat to escape the waters of the flood. [8]The clean animals, the unclean animals, the birds, and everything that crawls on the ground [9]came to Noah. They went into the boat in groups of two, male and female, just as God had commanded Noah. [10]Seven days later the flood started.

[11]When Noah was six hundred years old,

the flood started. On the seventeenth day of the second month of that year the underground springs split open, and the clouds in the sky poured out rain. [12]The rain fell on the earth for forty days and forty nights.

WHAT'S IT MEAN?

God's rules for animal sacrifice were very strict. To "make the cut" as a sacrifice, an animal had to chew cud and have divided hooves. Sheep, which fit both of these categories, were among the most popular animals for sacrifice. Among our feathered friends, scavenging birds, including vultures, were unacceptable as sacrifices.

Genesis 7:2

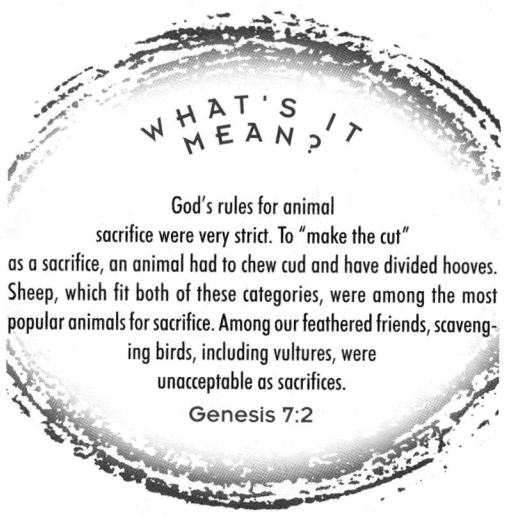

[13]On that same day Noah and his wife, his sons Shem, Ham, and Japheth, and their wives went into the boat. [14]They had every kind of wild and tame animal, every kind of animal that crawls on the earth, and every kind of bird. [15]Every creature that had the breath of life came to Noah in the boat in groups of two. [16]One male and one female of every living thing came, just as God had commanded Noah. Then the LORD closed the door behind them.

[17]Water flooded the earth for forty days, and as it rose it lifted the boat off the ground. [18]The water continued to rise, and the boat floated on it above the earth. [19]The water rose so much that even the highest mountains under the sky were covered by it. [20]It continued to rise until it was more than twenty feet above the mountains.

[21]All living things that moved on the earth died. This included all the birds, tame animals, wild animals, and creatures that swarm on the earth, as well as all human beings. [22]So everything on dry land that had the breath of life in it died. [23]God destroyed from the earth every living thing that was on the land—every man, animal, crawling thing, and bird of the sky. All that was left was Noah and what was with him in the boat. [24]And the waters continued to cover the earth for one hundred fifty days.

THE FLOOD ENDS

8 [1]But God remembered Noah and all the wild and tame animals with him in the boat. He made a wind blow over the earth, and the water went down. [2]The underground springs stopped flowing, and the clouds in the sky stopped pouring down rain. [3-4]The water that covered the earth began to go down. After one hundred fifty days it had gone down so much that the boat touched land again. It came to rest on one of the mountains of Ararat[n] on the seventeenth day of the seventh month. [5]The water continued to go down so that by the first day of the tenth month the tops of the mountains could be seen.

GOD
Does God care about me? (8:1)

[6]Forty days later Noah opened the window he had made in the boat, and [7]he sent out a raven. It flew here and there until the water had dried up from the earth. [8]Then Noah sent out a dove to find out if the water had dried up from the ground. [9]The dove could not find a place to land because water still covered the earth, so it came back to the boat. Noah reached out his hand and took the bird and brought it back into the boat.

[10]After seven days Noah again sent out the dove from the boat, [11]and that evening it came back to him with a fresh olive leaf in its mouth. Then Noah knew that the ground was almost dry. [12]Seven days later he sent the dove out again, but this time it did not come back.

[13]When Noah was six hundred and one years old, in the first day of the first month of

WHAT'S IT MEAN?

Where is Noah's ark today? Many people believe the boat can be found in the Ararat Mountains of eastern Turkey. Several explorers have attempted to find the ark's resting place. Some claim to have seen what could be the remnants of the boat, but nothing conclusive has been found yet.

Genesis 8:3–4

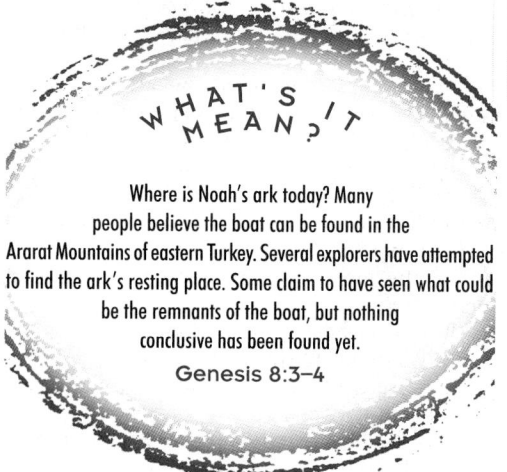

8:3-4 Ararat The ancient land of Urartu, an area in Eastern Turkey.

that year, the water was dried up from the
land. Noah removed the covering of the boat
and saw that the land was dry. 14By the twenty-
seventh day of the second month the land was
completely dry.
15Then God said to Noah, 16"You and your
wife, your sons, and their wives should go out
of the boat. 17Bring every animal out of the
boat with you—the birds, animals, and everything that crawls on the earth. Let them have
many young ones so that they might grow in
number."
18So Noah went out with his sons, his wife,
and his sons' wives. 19Every animal, everything
that crawls on the earth, and every bird went
out of the boat by families.
20Then Noah built an altar to the LORD. He
took some of all the clean birds and animals,
and he burned them on the altar as offerings to
God. 21The LORD was pleased with these sacrifices and said to himself, "I will never again
curse the ground because of human beings.
Their thoughts are evil even when they are
young, but I will never again destroy every living thing on the earth as I did this time.
22"As long as the earth continues,
planting and harvest,
cold and hot,
summer and winter,
day and night
will not stop."

THE NEW BEGINNING

9 1Then God blessed Noah and his sons and
said to them, "Have many children; grow in
number and fill the earth. 2Every animal on
earth, every bird in the sky, every animal that
crawls on the ground, and every fish in the sea
will respect and fear you. I have given them to
you.
3"Everything that moves, everything that is
alive, is yours for food. Earlier I gave you the
green plants, but now I give you everything for
food. 4But you must not eat meat that still has
blood in it, because blood gives life. 5I will demand blood for life. I will demand the life of
any animal that kills a person, and I will demand the life of anyone who takes another
person's life.
6"Whoever kills a human being
will be killed by a human being,
because God made humans
in his own image.
7"As for you, Noah, I want you and your
family to have many children, to grow in
number on the earth, and to become many."
8Then God said to Noah and his sons,
9"Now I am making my agreement with you
and your people who will live after you, 10and
with every living thing that is with you—the
birds, the tame and the wild animals, and
with everything that came out of the boat
with you—with every living thing on earth.
11I make this agreement with you: I will never
again destroy all living things by a flood. A
flood will never again destroy the earth."
12And God said, "This is the sign of the
agreement between me and you and every living creature that is with you. 13I am putting my
rainbow in the clouds as the sign of the agreement between me and the earth. 14When I bring
clouds over the earth and a rainbow appears in
them, 15I will remember my agreement between
me and you and every living thing. Floods will
never again destroy all life on the earth. 16When
the rainbow appears in the clouds, I will see it
and I will remember the agreement that continues forever between me and every living thing
on the earth."

WHAT'S IT MEAN?

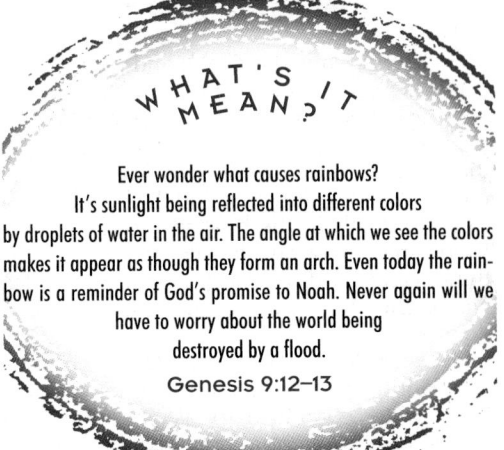

Ever wonder what causes rainbows? It's sunlight being reflected into different colors by droplets of water in the air. The angle at which we see the colors makes it appear as though they form an arch. Even today the rainbow is a reminder of God's promise to Noah. Never again will we have to worry about the world being destroyed by a flood.

Genesis 9:12–13

17So God said to Noah, "The rainbow is a
sign of the agreement that I made with all living things on earth."

NOAH AND HIS SONS

18The sons of Noah who came out of the
boat with him were Shem, Ham, and Japheth.
(Ham was the father of Canaan.) 19These three
men were Noah's sons, and all the people on
earth came from these three sons.
20Noah became a farmer and planted a
vineyard. 21When he drank wine made from
his grapes, he became drunk and lay naked in
his tent. 22Ham, the father of Canaan, looked at
his naked father and told his brothers outside.
23Then Shem and Japheth got a coat and,

WHAT'S IT MEAN?

How does grape juice become wine?
When grapes are crushed, the yeast on the outside of the fruit reaches the juice inside. In time, the yeast ferments, producing wine.

Genesis 9:20–21

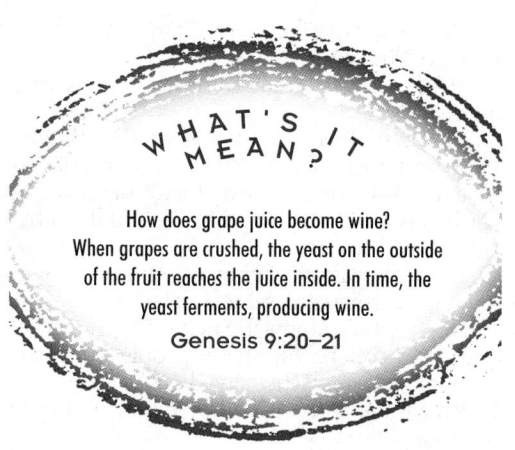

carrying it on both their shoulders, they
walked backwards into the tent and covered
their father. They turned their faces away so
that they did not see their father's nakedness.
24Noah was sleeping because of the wine.
When he woke up and learned what his youngest son, Ham, had done to him, 25he said,

"May there be a curse on Canaan!
May he be the lowest slave to his
brothers."

26Noah also said,

"May the LORD, the God of Shem, be
praised!
May Canaan be Shem's slave.
27May God give more land to Japheth.
May Japheth live in Shem's tents,
and may Canaan be their slave."

28After the flood Noah lived 350 years. 29He
lived a total of 950 years, and then he died.

NATIONS GROW AND SPREAD

10

1This is the family history of Shem, Ham,
and Japheth, the sons of Noah. After the flood
these three men had sons.

JAPHETH'S SONS

2The sons of Japheth were Gomer, Magog,
Madai, Javan, Tubal, Meshech, and Tiras.
3The sons of Gomer were Ashkenaz, Riphath, and Togarmah.
4The sons of Javan were Elishah, Tarshish,
Kittim,[n] and Rodanim. 5Those who lived in the
lands around the Mediterranean Sea came
from these sons of Japheth. All the families
grew and became different nations, each nation with its own land and its own language.

10:4 Kittim His descendants were the people of Cyprus.

Promise

HE PROMISES THE RAINBOW AS HIS SIGN.

I am putting my rainbow in the clouds as the sign of the agreement between me and the earth. When I bring clouds over the earth and a rainbow appears in them, I will remember my agreement between me and you and every living thing. Floods will never again destroy all life on the earth (Gen. 9:13–15).

God had just done something pretty amazing and probably pretty scary. He was so angry that he wiped out the whole world with a huge flood. Every person and every animal on earth drowned. Only the people and the animals on Noah's ark were saved. You can imagine what they might have been thinking. *Will he ever do this again? Maybe next time we won't live through it.* God calmed them down by promising that he would never destroy the world by flood again. To help them understand, he gave them something they could see. He put the rainbow in the sky as the sign of that promise.

Did God need the rainbow so he could remember what he'd said? No, the rainbow was for Noah and his family. It was for all his descendants who would live after him (Gen. 9:9). Today, it's for you. It lets you know that God does remember what he said. After all these years, God still remembers a promise he made to a group of people on an ark. He knew that as long as the sunlight hits the raindrops, people could see the rainbow and know that he remembers his promise.

SEE FOR YOURSELF:
Gen. 9:16–17

WHAT'S IT MEAN?

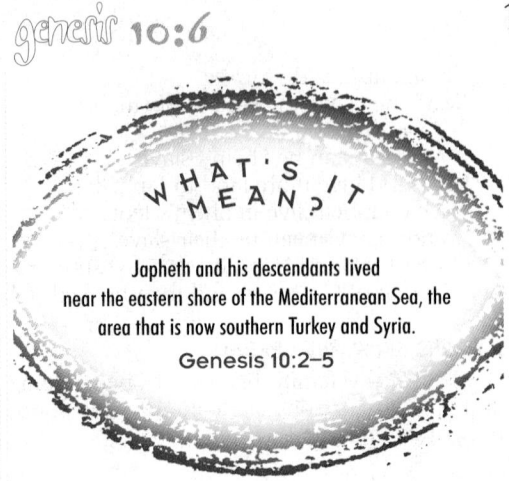

Japheth and his descendants lived near the eastern shore of the Mediterranean Sea, the area that is now southern Turkey and Syria.

Genesis 10:2–5

HAM'S SONS

6 The sons of Ham were Cush, Mizraim,[n] Put, and Canaan.

7 The sons of Cush were Seba, Havilah, Sabtah, Raamah, and Sabteca.

The sons of Raamah were Sheba and Dedan.

8 Cush also had a descendant named Nimrod, who became a very powerful man on earth. 9 He was a great hunter before the LORD, which is why people say someone is "like Nimrod, a great hunter before the LORD." 10 At first Nimrod's kingdom covered Babylon, Erech, Akkad, and Calneh in the land of Babylonia. 11 From there he went to Assyria, where he built the cities of Nineveh, Rehoboth Ir, and Calah. 12 He also built Resen, the great city between Nineveh and Calah.

13 Mizraim was the father of the Ludites, Anamites, Lehabites, Naphtuhites, 14 Pathrusites, Casluhites, and the people of Crete. (The Philistines came from the Casluhites.)

15 Canaan was the father of Sidon, his first son, and of Heth. 16 He was also the father of the Jebusites, Amorites, Girgashites, 17 Hivites, Arkites, Sinites, 18 Arvadites, Zemarites, and Hamathites. The families of the Canaanites scattered. 19 Their land reached from Sidon to Gerar as far as Gaza, and then to Sodom, Gomorrah, Admah, and Zeboiim, as far as Lasha.

20 All these people were the sons of Ham, and all these families had their own languages, their own lands, and their own nations.

SHEM'S SONS

21 Shem, Japheth's older brother, also had sons. One of his descendants was the father of all the sons of Eber.

22 The sons of Shem were Elam, Asshur, Arphaxad, Lud, and Aram.

23 The sons of Aram were Uz, Hul, Gether, and Meshech.

24 Arphaxad was the father of Shelah, who was the father of Eber. 25 Eber was the father of two sons—one named Peleg,[n] because the earth was divided during his life, and the other was named Joktan.

26 Joktan was the father of Almodad, Sheleph, Hazarmaveth, Jerah, 27 Hadoram, Uzal, Diklah, 28 Obal, Abimael, Sheba, 29 Ophir, Havilah, and Jobab. All these people were the sons of Joktan. 30 They lived in the area between Mesha and Sephar in the hill country in the East.

31 These are the people from the family of Shem, arranged by families, languages, countries, and nations.

32 This is the list of the families from the sons of Noah, arranged according to their nations. From these families came all the nations who spread across the earth after the flood.

WHAT'S IT MEAN?

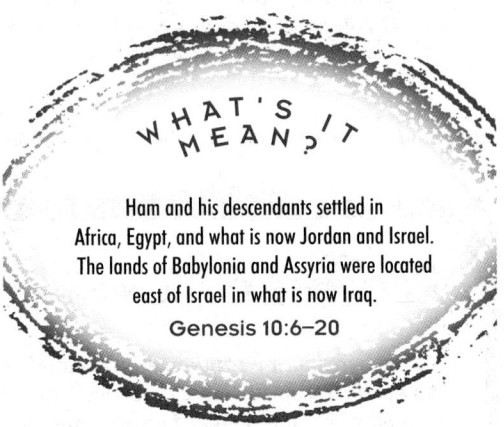

Ham and his descendants settled in Africa, Egypt, and what is now Jordan and Israel. The lands of Babylonia and Assyria were located east of Israel in what is now Iraq.

Genesis 10:6–20

THE LANGUAGES CONFUSED

11 1 At this time the whole world spoke one language, and everyone used the same words. 2 As people moved from the east, they found a plain in the land of Babylonia and settled there.

3 They said to each other, "Let's make bricks and bake them to make them hard." So they used bricks instead of stones, and tar instead of mortar. 4 Then they said to each other, "Let's build a city and a tower for ourselves, whose top will reach high into the sky. We will become famous. Then we will not be scattered over all the earth."

10:6 Mizraim This is another name for Egypt. **10:25 Peleg** This name sounds like the Hebrew word for "divided."

[5]The LORD came down to see the city and the tower that the people had built. [6]The LORD said, "Now, these people are united, all speaking the same language. This is only the beginning of what they will do. They will be able to do anything they want. [7]Come, let us go down and confuse their language so they will not be able to understand each other."

[8]So the LORD scattered them from there over all the earth, and they stopped building the city. [9]The place is called Babel[n] since that is where the LORD confused the language of the whole world. So the LORD caused them to spread out from there over the whole world.

> "The place is called Babel since that is where the LORD confused the language of the whole world."
> (Genesis 11:9a)

THE STORY OF SHEM'S FAMILY

[10]This is the family history of Shem. Two years after the flood, when Shem was 100 years old, his son Arphaxad was born. [11]After that, Shem lived 500 years and had other sons and daughters.

[12]When Arphaxad was 35 years old, his son Shelah was born. [13]After that, Arphaxad lived 403 years and had other sons and daughters.

[14]When Shelah was 30 years old, his son Eber was born. [15]After that, Shelah lived 403 years and had other sons and daughters.

[16]When Eber was 34 years old, his son Peleg was born. [17]After that, Eber lived 430 years and had other sons and daughters.

[18]When Peleg was 30 years old, his son Reu was born. [19]After that, Peleg lived 209 years and had other sons and daughters.

[20]When Reu was 32 years old, his son Serug was born. [21]After that, Reu lived 207 years and had other sons and daughters.

[22]When Serug was 30 years old, his son Nahor was born. [23]After that, Serug lived 200 years and had other sons and daughters.

[24]When Nahor was 29 years old, his son Terah was born. [25]After that, Nahor lived 119 years and had other sons and daughters.

[26]After Terah was 70 years old, his sons Abram, Nahor, and Haran were born.

THE STORY OF TERAH'S FAMILY

[27]This is the family history of Terah. Terah was the father of Abram, Nahor, and Haran. Haran was the father of Lot. [28]While his father, Terah, was still alive, Haran died in Ur in Babylonia, where he was born. [29]Abram and Nahor both married. Abram's wife was named Sarai, and Nahor's wife was named Milcah. She was the daughter of Haran, who was the father of both Milcah and Iscah. [30]Sarai was not able to have children.

[31]Terah took his son Abram, his grandson Lot (Haran's son), and his daughter-in-law Sarai (Abram's wife) and moved out of Ur of Babylonia. They had planned to go to the land of Canaan, but when they reached the city of Haran, they settled there.

[32]Terah lived to be 205 years old, and then he died in Haran.

WHAT'S IT MEAN?

Ever heard of the Promised Land? That's Canaan. The land was located east of the Mediterranean Sea, where Syria, Lebanon, and Israel are today.

Genesis 11:31

GOD CALLS ABRAM

12

[1]The LORD said to Abram, "Leave your country, your relatives, and your father's family, and go to the land I will show you.

[2]I will make you a great nation,
and I will bless you.
I will make you famous,
and you will be a blessing to others.
[3]I will bless those who bless you,
and I will place a curse on those who
harm you.
And all the people on earth
will be blessed through you."

[4]So Abram left Haran as the LORD had told him, and Lot went with him. At this time Abram was 75 years old. [5]He took his wife Sarai, his nephew Lot, and everything they owned, as

11:9 Babel This name sounds like the Hebrew word for "confused."

well as all the servants they had gotten in
Haran. They set out from Haran, planning to go
to the land of Canaan, and in time they arrived
there.
6Abram traveled through that land as far as
the great tree of Moreh at Shechem. The Canaanites were living in the land at that time.
7The LORD appeared to Abram and said, "I will
give this land to your descendants." So Abram
built an altar there to the LORD, who had appeared to him. 8Then he traveled from Shechem to the mountain east of Bethel and set up
his tent there. Bethel was to the west, and Ai
was to the east. There Abram built another altar to the LORD and worshiped him. 9After this,
he traveled on toward southern Canaan.

ABRAM GOES TO EGYPT

10At this time there was not much food in
the land, so Abram went down to Egypt to live
because there was so little food. 11Just before
they arrived in Egypt, he said to his wife Sarai,
"I know you are a very beautiful woman.
12When the Egyptians see you, they will say,
'This woman is his wife.' Then they will kill me
but let you live. 13Tell them you are my sister
so that things will go well with me and I may
be allowed to live because of you."
14When Abram came to Egypt, the Egyptians saw that Sarai was very beautiful. 15The
Egyptian officers saw her and told the king of
Egypt how beautiful she was. They took her
to the king's palace, and 16the king was kind to
Abram because he thought Abram was her
brother. He gave Abram sheep, cattle, male and
female donkeys, male and female servants, and
camels.
17But the LORD sent terrible diseases on the
king and all the people in his house because of
Abram's wife Sarai. 18So the king sent for
Abram and said, "What have you done to me?
Why didn't you tell me Sarai was your wife?

WHAT'S IT MEAN?

Shechem was located about halfway between the Dead Sea and the Sea of Galilee. The land lay between Mount Ebal and Mount Gerizim, both of which were about 3,000 feet high.

Genesis 12:6

Promise

HE PROMISES THAT EVERYONE ON EARTH WILL BE BLESSED.

I will make you a great nation, and I will bless you. I will make you famous, and you will be a blessing to others. I will bless those who bless you, and I will place a curse on those who harm you. And all the people on earth will be blessed through you (Gen. 12:2–3).

God had a plan for a man named Abram. God knew that Abram would believe him, and that Abram would live out his faith by his actions. Because God knew that, he promised Abram that the world would be blessed because of him.

God blessed the world through Abram in two ways. First, Abraham (the name God gave Abram later) became the prime example for everyone who would ever put their faith in God. His descendants were honored and proud to be called the "children of Abraham." Paul said that anyone who has the same kind of faith that Abraham did is a child of Abraham.

But the greatest blessing that God gave through Abraham—the thing God was specifically talking about here—is Jesus. Jesus was born on earth as a part of God's chosen nation—the children of Abraham. God redeemed all of the sin in your life through Jesus, a descendant of the man whose greatest claim to fame was the simple fact that he "believed the LORD" (Gen. 15:6a).

SEE FOR YOURSELF:
Gen. 15:4–5; 17:4–8; Luke 1:54–55; Gal. 3:14, 29

[19]Why did you say, 'She is my sister' so that I
made her my wife? Now, here is your wife.
Take her and leave!" [20]Then the king commanded his men to make Abram leave Egypt;
so Abram and his wife left with everything
they owned.

ABRAM AND LOT SEPARATE

13 [1]So Abram, his wife, and Lot left Egypt, taking everything they owned, and traveled to
southern Canaan. [2]Abram was very rich in
cattle, silver, and gold.
[3]He left southern Canaan and went back to
Bethel where he had camped before, between
Bethel and Ai, [4]and where he had built an altar.
So he worshiped the LORD there.
[5]During this time Lot was traveling with
Abram, and Lot also had flocks, herds, and
tents. [6]Abram and Lot had so many animals
that the land could not support both of them
together, [7]so Abram's herdsmen and Lot's
herdsmen began to argue. The Canaanites and
the Perizzites were living in the land at this
time.
[8]Abram said to Lot, "There should be no arguing between you and me, or between your
herdsmen and mine, because we are brothers.
[9]We should separate. The whole land is there
in front of you. If you go to the left, I will go to
the right. If you go to the right, I will go to
the left."
[10]Lot looked all around and saw the whole
Jordan Valley and that there was much water
there. It was like the LORD's garden, like the
land of Egypt in the direction of Zoar. (This
was before the LORD destroyed Sodom and
Gomorrah.) [11]So Lot chose to move east and
live in the Jordan Valley. In this way Abram
and Lot separated. [12]Abram lived in the land of
Canaan, but Lot lived among the cities in the
Jordan Valley, very near to Sodom. [13]Now the
people of Sodom were very evil and were always sinning against the LORD.
[14]After Lot left, the LORD said to Abram,
"Look all around you—to the north and south
and east and west. [15]All this land that you see I
will give to you and your descendants forever.
[16]I will make your descendants as many as the
dust of the earth. If anyone could count the
dust on the earth, he could count your people.
[17]Get up! Walk through all this land because I
am now giving it to you."
[18]So Abram moved his tents and went to
live near the great trees of Mamre at the city of
Hebron. There he built an altar to the LORD.

WHAT'S IT MEAN?

Hebron, which lies about twenty miles south of Jerusalem, was a very important city in Old Testament times. It is the final resting place of Abraham's wife Sarah.

Genesis 13:18

LOT IS CAPTURED

14 [1]Now Amraphel was king of Babylonia, Arioch was king of Ellasar, Kedorlaomer was king
of Elam, and Tidal was king of Goiim. [2]All
these kings went to war against several other
kings: Bera king of Sodom, Birsha king of Gomorrah, Shinab king of Admah, Shemeber king
of Zeboiim, and the king of Bela. (Bela is also
called Zoar.)
[3]These kings who were attacked united their
armies in the Valley of Siddim (now the Dead
Sea). [4]They had served Kedorlaomer for twelve
years, but in the thirteenth year, they all turned
against him. [5]Then in the fourteenth year, Kedorlaomer and the kings with him came and defeated the Rephaites in Ashteroth Karnaim, the
Zuzites in Ham, and the Emites in Shaveh
Kiriathaim. [6]They also defeated the Horites in
the mountains of Edom to El Paran (near the
desert). [7]Then they turned back and went to En
Mishpat (that is, Kadesh). They defeated all the
Amalekites, as well as the Amorites who lived
in Hazazon Tamar.
[8]At that time the kings of Sodom, Gomorrah, Admah, Zeboiim, and Bela went out to
fight in the Valley of Siddim. (Bela is called
Zoar.) [9]They fought against Kedorlaomer king
of Elam, Tidal king of Goiim, Amraphel king of
Babylonia, and Arioch king of Ellasar—four
kings fighting against five. [10]There were many
tar pits in the Valley of Siddim. When the kings
of Sodom and Gomorrah and their armies ran
away, some of the soldiers fell into the tar pits,
but the others ran away to the mountains.
[11]Now Kedorlaomer and his armies took
everything the people of Sodom and Gomorrah owned, including their food. [12]They took
Lot, Abram's nephew who was living in
Sodom, and everything he owned. Then they
left. [13]One of the men who was not captured
went to Abram, the Hebrew, and told him
what had happened. At that time Abram was

camped near the great trees of Mamre the
Amorite. Mamre was a brother of Eshcol and
Aner, and they had all made an agreement to
help Abram.

ABRAM RESCUES LOT

14 When Abram learned that Lot had been
captured, he called out his 318 trained men
who had been born in his camp. He led the
men and chased the enemy all the way to the
town of Dan. 15 That night he divided his men
into groups, and they made a surprise attack
against the enemy. They chased them all the
way to Hobah, north of Damascus. 16 Then
Abram brought back everything the enemy
had stolen, the women and the other people,
and Lot, and everything Lot owned.

WHAT'S IT MEAN?

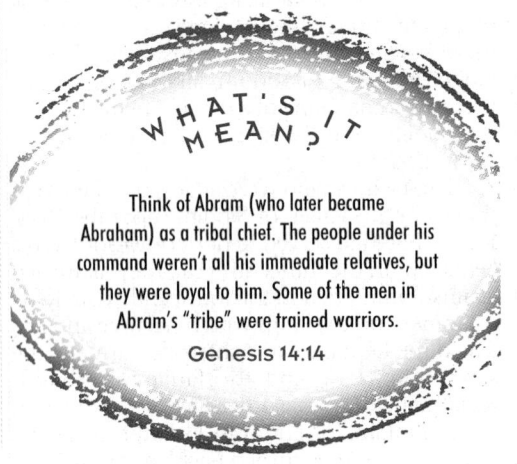

Think of Abram (who later became Abraham) as a tribal chief. The people under his command weren't all his immediate relatives, but they were loyal to him. Some of the men in Abram's "tribe" were trained warriors.

Genesis 14:14

17 After defeating Kedorlaomer and the kings
who were with him, Abram went home. As he
was returning, the king of Sodom came out to
meet him in the Valley of Shaveh (now called
King's Valley).
18 Melchizedek king of Salem brought out
bread and wine. He was a priest for God Most
High 19 and blessed Abram, saying,

"Abram, may you be blessed by God Most
High,
the God who made heaven and earth.
20 And we praise God Most High,
who has helped you to defeat your
enemies."

Then Abram gave Melchizedek a tenth of
everything he had brought back from the
battle.
21 The king of Sodom said to Abram, "You
may keep all these things for yourself. Just give
me my people who were captured."
22 But Abram said to the king of Sodom, "I
make a promise to the LORD, the God Most

WHAT'S IT MEAN?

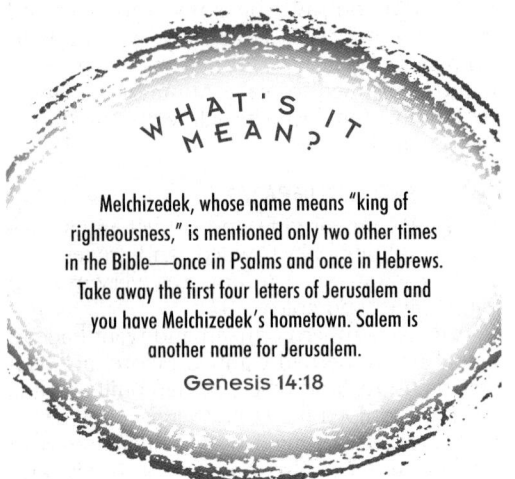

Melchizedek, whose name means "king of righteousness," is mentioned only two other times in the Bible—once in Psalms and once in Hebrews. Take away the first four letters of Jerusalem and you have Melchizedek's hometown. Salem is another name for Jerusalem.

Genesis 14:18

High, who made heaven and earth. 23 I promise
that I will not keep anything that is yours. I
will not keep even a thread or a sandal strap so
that you cannot say, 'I made Abram rich.' 24 I
will keep nothing but the food my young men
have eaten. But give Aner, Eshcol, and Mamre
their share of what we won, because they went
with me into battle."

GOD'S AGREEMENT WITH ABRAM

15
1 After these things happened, the LORD
spoke his word to Abram in a vision: "Abram,
don't be afraid. I will defend you, and I will
give you a great reward."
2 But Abram said, "Lord
GOD, what can you give me? I
have no son, so my slave Eliezer from Damascus will get
everything I own after I die."
3 Abram said, "Look, you have
given me no son, so a slave born
in my house will inherit everything I have."

PROTECTION
Who will protect me? (15:1)

4 Then the LORD spoke his word to Abram:
"He will not be the one to inherit what you
have. You will have a son of your own who
will inherit what you have."
5 Then God led Abram outside and said,
"Look at the sky. There are so many stars you
cannot count them. Your descendants also will
be too many to count."
6 Abram believed the LORD. And the LORD
accepted Abram's faith, and that faith made
him right with God.
7 God said to Abram, "I am the LORD who
led you out of Ur of Babylonia so that I could
give you this land to own."
8 But Abram said, "Lord GOD, how can I be
sure that I will own this land?"

9The LORD said to Abram, "Bring me a three-year-old cow, a three-year-old goat, a three-year-old male sheep, a dove, and a young pigeon."

10Abram brought them all to God. Then Abram killed the animals and cut each of them into two pieces, laying each half opposite the other half. But he did not cut the birds in half. 11Later, large birds flew down to eat the animals, but Abram chased them away.

12As the sun was going down, Abram fell into a deep sleep. While he was asleep, a very terrible darkness came. 13Then the LORD said to Abram, "You can be sure that your descendants will be strangers and travel in a land they don't own. The people there will make them slaves and be cruel to them for four hundred years. 14But I will punish the nation where they are slaves. Then your descendants will leave that land, taking great wealth with them. 15And you, Abram, will die in peace and will be buried at an old age. 16After your great-great-grandchildren are born, your people will come to this land again. It will take that long, because I am not yet going to punish the Amorites for their evil behavior."

17After the sun went down, it was very dark. Suddenly a smoking firepot and a blazing torch passed between the halves of the dead animals.[n] 18So on that day the LORD made an agreement with Abram and said, "I will give to your descendants the land between the river of Egypt and the great river Euphrates. 19This is the land of the Kenites, Kenizzites, Kadmonites, 20Hittites, Perizzites, Rephaites, 21Amorites, Canaanites, Girgashites, and Jebusites."

WHAT'S IT MEAN?

God's promise to give the land of Canaan to Abram is one of the most important events in the Old Testament. The modern conflict between the Palestinians and the Israelis can be traced back to this promise. As for the mysterious smoking firepot and blazing torch, we can only assume that they were symbols of the unusual meeting between God and Abram.

Genesis 15:17–21

ISHMAEL IS BORN

16 1Sarai, Abram's wife, had no children, but she had a slave girl from Egypt named Hagar. 2Sarai said to Abram, "Look, the LORD has not allowed me to have children, so have sexual relations with my slave girl. If she has a child, maybe I can have my own family through her."

WHAT'S IT MEAN?

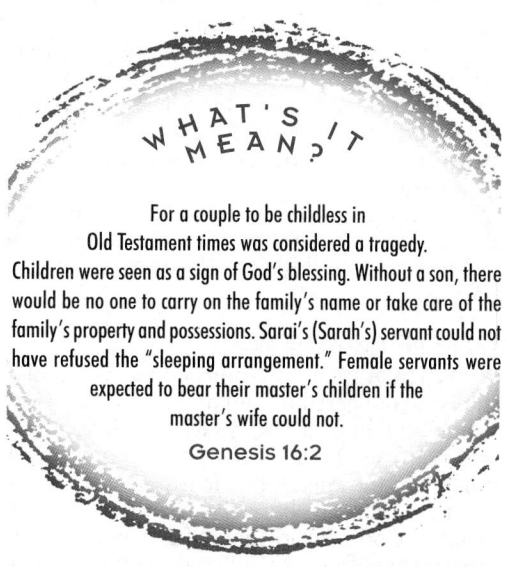

For a couple to be childless in Old Testament times was considered a tragedy. Children were seen as a sign of God's blessing. Without a son, there would be no one to carry on the family's name or take care of the family's property and possessions. Sarai's (Sarah's) servant could not have refused the "sleeping arrangement." Female servants were expected to bear their master's children if the master's wife could not.

Genesis 16:2

Abram did what Sarai said. 3It was after he had lived ten years in Canaan that Sarai gave Hagar to her husband Abram. (Hagar was her slave girl from Egypt.)

4Abram had sexual relations with Hagar, and she became pregnant. When Hagar learned she was pregnant, she began to treat her mistress Sarai badly. 5Then Sarai said to Abram, "This is your fault. I gave my slave girl to you, and when she became pregnant, she began to treat me badly. Let the LORD decide who is right—you or me."

6But Abram said to Sarai, "You are Hagar's mistress. Do anything you want to her." Then Sarai was hard on Hagar, and Hagar ran away.

7The angel of the LORD found Hagar beside a spring of water in the desert, by the road to Shur. 8The angel said, "Hagar, Sarai's slave girl, where have you come from? Where are you going?"

Hagar answered, "I am running away from my mistress Sarai."

9The angel of the LORD said to her, "Go

15:17 passed . . . animals This showed that God sealed the agreement between himself and Abram.

home to your mistress and obey her." 10The
angel also said, "I will give you so many descendants they cannot be counted."
11The angel added,
"You are now pregnant,
and you will have a son.
You will name him Ishmael,[n]
because the LORD has heard your cries.
12Ishmael will be like a wild donkey.
He will be against everyone,
and everyone will be against him.
He will attack all his brothers."
13The slave girl gave a name to the LORD
who spoke to her: "You are 'God who sees
me,' " because she said to herself, "Have I really
seen God who sees me?" 14So the well there,
between Kadesh and Bered, was called Beer
Lahai Roi.[n]
15Hagar gave birth to a son for Abram, and
Abram named him Ishmael. 16Abram was
eighty-six years old when Hagar gave birth to
Ishmael.

PROOF OF THE AGREEMENT

17 1When Abram was ninety-nine years old,
the LORD appeared to him and said, "I am God
Almighty. Obey me and do what is right. 2I will
make an agreement between us, and I will
make you the ancestor of many people."
3Then Abram bowed facedown on the
ground. God said to him, 4"I am making my
agreement with you: I will make you the father
of many nations. 5I am changing your name
from Abram[n] to Abraham[n] because I am making you a father of many nations. 6I will give
you many descendants. New nations will be
born from you, and kings will come from you.
7And I will make an agreement between me
and you and all your descendants from now
on: I will be your God and the God of all your
descendants. 8You live in the land of Canaan
now as a stranger, but I will give you and your
descendants all this land forever. And I will be
the God of your descendants."
9Then God said to Abraham, "You and your
descendants must keep this agreement from
now on. 10This is my agreement with you and
all your descendants, which you must obey:
Every male among you must be circumcised.
11Cut away your foreskin to show that you are
prepared to follow the agreement between me
and you. 12From now on when a baby boy is
eight days old, you will circumcise him. This
includes any boy born among your people or
any who is your slave, who is not one of your
descendants. 13Circumcise every baby boy
whether he is born in your family or bought as
a slave. Your bodies will be marked to show
that you are part of my agreement that lasts
forever. 14Any male who is not circumcised
will be cut off from his people, because he has
broken my agreement."

ISAAC—THE PROMISED SON

15God said to Abraham, "I will change the
name of Sarai,[n] your wife, to Sarah.[n] 16I will
bless her and give her a son, and you will be
the father. She will be the mother of many nations. Kings of nations will come from her."
17Abraham bowed facedown on the ground
and laughed. He said to himself, "Can a man
have a child when he is a hundred years old?
Can Sarah give birth to a child when she is
ninety?" 18Then Abraham said to God, "Please
let Ishmael be the son you promised."
19God said, "No, Sarah your wife will have a
son, and you will name him Isaac.[n] I will make
my agreement with him to be an agreement
that continues forever with all his descendants.
20"As for Ishmael, I have heard you. I will
bless him and give him many descendants.
And I will cause their numbers to grow greatly.
He will be the father of twelve great leaders,

WHAT'S IT MEAN?

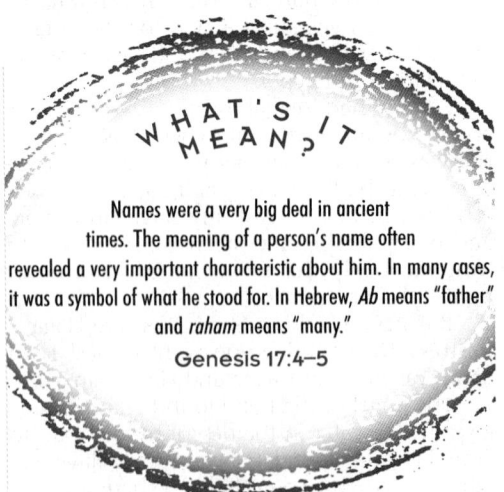

Names were a very big deal in ancient times. The meaning of a person's name often revealed a very important characteristic about him. In many cases, it was a symbol of what he stood for. In Hebrew, *Ab* means "father" and *raham* means "many."

Genesis 17:4–5

16:11 Ishmael The Hebrew words for "Ishmael" and "has heard" sound similar. **16:14 Beer Lahai Roi** This means "the well of the Living One who sees me." **17:5 Abram** This name means "honored father." **17:5 Abraham** The end of the Hebrew word for "Abraham" sounds like the beginning of the Hebrew word for "many." **17:15 Sarai** An Aramaic name meaning "princess." **17:15 Sarah** A Hebrew name meaning "princess." **17:19 Isaac** The Hebrew words for "he laughed" (v. 17) and "Isaac" sound the same.

and I will make him into a great nation. 21But I will make my agreement with Isaac, the son whom Sarah will have at this same time next year." 22After God finished talking with Abraham, God rose and left him.

23Then Abraham gathered Ishmael, all the males born in his camp, and the slaves he had bought. So that day Abraham circumcised every man and boy in his camp as God had told him to do. 24Abraham was ninety-nine years old when he was circumcised. 25And Ishmael, his son, was thirteen years old when he was circumcised. 26Abraham and his son were circumcised on the same day. 27Also on that day all the men in Abraham's camp were circumcised, including all those born in his camp and all the slaves he had bought from other nations.

THE THREE VISITORS

18

1Later, the LORD again appeared to Abraham near the great trees of Mamre. Abraham was sitting at the entrance of his tent during the hottest part of the day. 2He looked up and saw three men standing near him. When Abraham saw them, he ran from his tent to meet them. He bowed facedown on the ground before them 3and said, "Sir, if you think well of me, please stay awhile with me, your servant. 4I will bring some water so all of you can wash your feet. You may rest under the tree, 5and I will get some bread for you so you can regain your strength. Then you may continue your journey."

The three men said, "That is fine. Do as you said."

6Abraham hurried to the tent where Sarah was and said to her, "Hurry, prepare twenty quarts of fine flour, and make it into loaves of bread." 7Then Abraham ran to his herd and took one of his best calves. He gave it to a servant, who hurried to kill it and to prepare it for food. 8Abraham gave the three men the calf that had been cooked and milk curds and milk. While they ate, he stood under the tree near them.

9The men asked Abraham, "Where is your wife Sarah?"

"There, in the tent," said Abraham.

10Then the LORD said, "I will certainly return to you about this time a year from now. At that time your wife Sarah will have a son."

Sarah was listening at the entrance of the tent which was behind him. 11Abraham and Sarah were very old. Since Sarah was past the age when women normally have children, 12she laughed to herself, "My husband and I are too old to have a baby."

13Then the LORD said to Abraham, "Why did Sarah laugh? Why did she say, 'I am too old to have a baby'? 14Is anything too hard for the LORD? No! I will return to you at the right time a year from now, and Sarah will have a son."

15Sarah was afraid, so she lied and said, "I didn't laugh."

But the LORD said, "No. You did laugh."

16Then the men got up to leave and started out toward Sodom. Abraham walked along with them a short time to send them on their way.

"Abraham's children will certainly become a great and powerful nation, and all nations on earth will be blessed through him." (Genesis 18:18)

WHAT'S IT MEAN?

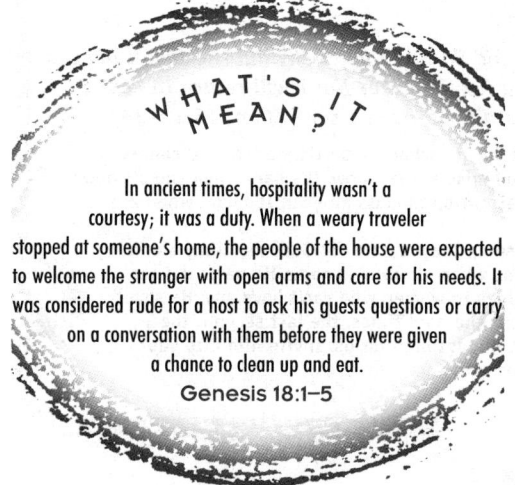

In ancient times, hospitality wasn't a courtesy; it was a duty. When a weary traveler stopped at someone's home, the people of the house were expected to welcome the stranger with open arms and care for his needs. It was considered rude for a host to ask his guests questions or carry on a conversation with them before they were given a chance to clean up and eat.

Genesis 18:1–5

ABRAHAM'S BARGAIN WITH GOD

17The LORD said, "Should I tell Abraham what I am going to do now? 18Abraham's children will certainly become a great and powerful nation, and all nations on earth will be blessed through him. 19I have chosen him so he would command his children and his descendants to live the way the LORD wants them to, to live right and be fair. Then I, the LORD, will give Abraham what I promised him."

20Then the LORD said, "I have heard many complaints against the people of Sodom and Gomorrah. They are very evil. 21I will go down and see if they are as bad as I have heard. If not, I will know."

[22]So the men turned and went toward Sodom, but Abraham stood there before the LORD. [23]Then Abraham approached him and asked, "Do you plan to destroy the good people along with the evil ones? [24]What if there are fifty good people in that city? Will you still destroy it? Surely you will save the city for the fifty good people living there. [25]Surely you will not destroy the good people along with the evil ones; then they would be treated the same. You are the judge of all the earth. Won't you do what is right?"

[26]The LORD said, "If I find fifty good people in the city of Sodom, I will save the whole city because of them."

[27]Then Abraham said, "Though I am only dust and ashes, I have been brave to speak to the Lord. [28]What if there are only forty-five good people in the city? Will you destroy the whole city for the lack of five good people?"

The LORD said, "If I find forty-five there, I will not destroy the city."

[29]Again Abraham said to him, "If you find only forty good people there, will you destroy the city?"

The LORD said, "If I find forty, I will not destroy it."

[30]Then Abraham said, "Lord, please don't be angry with me, but let me ask you this. If you find only thirty good people in the city, will you destroy it?"

He said, "If I find thirty good people there, I will not destroy the city."

[31]Then Abraham said, "I have been brave to speak to the Lord. But what if there are twenty good people in the city?"

He answered, "If I find twenty there, I will not destroy the city."

[32]Then Abraham said, "Lord, please don't be angry with me, but let me bother you this one last time. What if you find ten there?"

He said, "If I find ten there, I will not destroy it."

[33]When the LORD finished speaking to Abraham, he left, and Abraham returned home.

LOT LEAVES SODOM

19

[1]The two angels came to Sodom in the evening as Lot was sitting near the city gate. When he saw them, he got up and went to them and bowed facedown on the ground. [2]Lot said, "Sirs, please come to my house and spend the night. There you can wash your feet, and then tomorrow you may continue your journey."

The angels answered, "No, we will spend the night in the city's public square."

[3]But Lot begged them to come, so they agreed and went to his house. Then Lot prepared a meal for them. He baked bread without yeast, and they ate it.

[4]Before bedtime, men both young and old and from every part of Sodom surrounded Lot's house. [5]They called to Lot, "Where are the two men who came to you tonight? Bring them out to us so we can have sexual relations with them."

Promise

HE PROMISES NOTHING IS TOO HARD FOR HIM.

Then the LORD said to Abraham, "Why did Sarah laugh? Why did she say, 'I am too old to have a baby'? Is anything too hard for the LORD? No! I will return to you at the right time a year from now, and Sarah will have a son" (Gen. 18:13–14).

Hard. You know all about _hard_. It's hard to juggle school, a part-time job, and chores at home. It's hard when the game is tied and you miss a free throw. It's hard when you sit down to take a final and realize you should have paid attention in class all year. It's hard when a grandparent dies.

Sometimes, when things are hard for us, we assume they're hard for God, too. They aren't. Nothing is too hard for God. His best stuff happens when all hope is gone. He parts the sea for people who don't have a way out. He gives babies to women who can't have any. He saves the souls of people who deserve death. Think about the hard times, the last second, the darkest hour, the deepest hole. They are "mission impossible" for us. Invite him into your hard stuff. Every bit of it is "mission possible" for him.

SEE FOR YOURSELF:

Num. 11:23; Matt. 19:26; Mark 10:27

WHAT'S IT MEAN?

The city gate was like a commerce center and a courthouse rolled into one. It's where people conducted their business, judicial, and political matters. Judging by his position at the city gate, Lot apparently was an important man in Sodom. He saw it as his responsibility to welcome the two strangers to the city.
Genesis 19:1–2

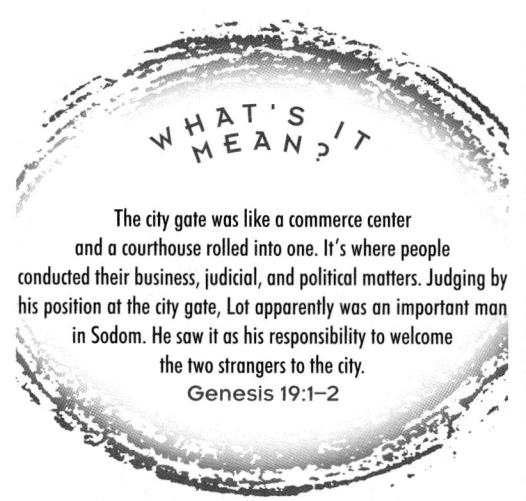

6Lot went outside to them, closing the door
behind him. 7He said, "No, my brothers! Do
not do this evil thing. 8Look! I have two
daughters who have never slept with a man. I
will give them to you, and you may do anything you want with them. But please don't do
anything to these men. They have come to my
house, and I must protect them."
9The men around the house answered,
"Move out of the way!" Then they said to each
other, "This man Lot came to our city as a
stranger, and now he wants to tell us what to
do!" They said to Lot, "We will do worse things
to you than to them." They started pushing him
back and were ready to break down the door.
10But the two men staying with Lot opened
the door, pulled him back inside the house,
and then closed the door. 11They struck those
outside the door with blindness, so the men,
both young and old, could not find the door.
12The two men said to Lot, "Do you have
any other relatives in this city? Do you have
any sons-in-law, sons, daughters, or any other
relatives? If you do, tell them to leave now,
13because we are about to destroy this city. The
LORD has heard of all the evil that is here, so he
has sent us to destroy it."
14So Lot went out and said to his future
sons-in-law who were pledged to marry his
daughters, "Hurry and leave this city! The LORD
is about to destroy it!" But they thought Lot
was joking.
15At dawn the next morning, the angels
begged Lot to hurry. They said, "Go! Take your
wife and your two daughters with you so you
will not be destroyed when the city is punished."
16But Lot delayed. So the two men took the
hands of Lot, his wife, and his two daughters
and led them safely out of the city. So the LORD
was merciful to Lot and his family. 17After they
brought them out of the city, one of the men
said, "Run for your lives! Don't look back or
stop anywhere in the valley. Run to the mountains, or you will be destroyed."
18But Lot said to one of them, "Sir, please
don't force me to go so far! 19You have been
merciful and kind to me and have saved my
life. But I can't run to the mountains. The disaster will catch me, and I will die. 20Look, that
little town over there is not too far away. Let
me run there. It's really just a little town, and
I'll be safe there."
21The angel said to Lot, "Very well, I will allow you to do this also. I will not destroy that
town. 22But run there fast, because I cannot destroy Sodom until you are safely in that town."
(That town is named Zoar,[n] because it is little.)

SODOM AND GOMORRAH ARE DESTROYED

23The sun had already come up when Lot
entered Zoar. 24The LORD sent a rain of burning
sulfur down from the sky on Sodom and Gomorrah 25and destroyed those cities. He also
destroyed the whole Jordan Valley, everyone
living in the cities, and even all the plants.
26At that point Lot's wife looked back.
When she did, she became a pillar of salt.
27Early the next morning, Abraham got up
and went to the place where he had stood
before the LORD. 28He looked down toward
Sodom and Gomorrah and all the Jordan Valley and saw smoke rising from the land, like
smoke from a furnace.
29God destroyed the cities in the valley, but
he remembered what Abraham had asked. So
God saved Lot's life, but he destroyed the city
where Lot had lived.

LOT AND HIS DAUGHTERS

30Lot was afraid to continue living in Zoar,
so he and his two daughters went to live in
the mountains in a cave. 31One day the older
daughter said to the younger, "Our father is
old. Everywhere on the earth women and
men marry, but there are no men around here
for us to marry. 32Let's get our father drunk
and have sexual relations with him. We can
use him to have children and continue our
family."
33That night the two girls got their father
drunk, and the older daughter went and had

19:22 Zoar This name sounds like the Hebrew word for "little."

sexual relations with him. But Lot did not
know when she lay down or when she got up.
34The next day the older daughter said to
the younger, "Last night I had sexual relations
with my father. Let's get him drunk again tonight so you can go and have sexual relations
with him, too. In this way we can use our father to have children to continue our family."
35So that night they got their father drunk
again, and the younger daughter went and had
sexual relations with him. Again, Lot did not
know when she lay down or when she got up.
36So both of Lot's daughters became pregnant by their father. 37The older daughter gave
birth to a son and named him Moab. He is the
ancestor of all the Moabite people who are still
living today. 38The younger daughter also gave
birth to a son and named him Ben-Ammi. He
is the father of all the Ammonite people who
are still living today.

ABRAHAM TRICKS ABIMELECH

20
1Abraham left Hebron and traveled to
southern Canaan where he stayed awhile between Kadesh and Shur. When he moved to
Gerar, 2he told people that his wife Sarah was
his sister. Abimelech king of Gerar heard this,
so he sent some servants to take her. 3But one
night God spoke to Abimelech in a dream and
said, "You will die. The woman you took is
married."
4But Abimelech had not gone near Sarah,
so he said, "Lord, would you destroy an innocent nation? 5Abraham himself told me,
'This woman is my sister,' and she also said,
'He is my brother.' I am innocent. I did not
know I was doing anything wrong."
6Then God said to Abimelech in the dream,
"Yes, I know you did not realize what you were
doing. So I did not allow you to sin against me
and touch her. 7Give Abraham his wife back.
He is a prophet. He will pray for you, and you
will not die. But if you do not give Sarah back,
you and all your family will surely die."
8So early the next morning, Abimelech
called all his officers and told them everything
that had happened in the dream. They were
very afraid. 9Then Abimelech called Abraham
to him and said, "What have you done to us?
What wrong did I do against you? Why did
you bring this trouble to my kingdom? You
should not have done these things to me.
10What were you thinking that caused you to
do this?"
11Then Abraham answered, "I thought no
one in this place respected God and that someone would kill me to get Sarah. 12And it is true
that she is my sister. She is the daughter of
my father, but she is not the daughter of my
mother. 13When God told me to leave my
father's house and wander in many different
places, I told Sarah, 'You must do a special favor for me. Everywhere we go tell people I am
your brother.' "
14Then Abimelech gave Abraham some
sheep, cattle, and male and female slaves. He
also gave Sarah, Abraham's wife, back to him
15and said, "Look around you at my land. You
may live anywhere you want."
16Abimelech said to Sarah, "I gave your
brother Abraham twenty-five pounds of silver
to make up for any wrong that people may
think about you. I want everyone to know that
you are innocent."
17Then Abraham prayed to God, and God
healed Abimelech, his wife, and his servant
girls so they could have children. 18The LORD
had kept all the women in Abimelech's house
from having children as a punishment on
Abimelech for taking Abraham's wife Sarah.

WHAT'S IT MEAN?

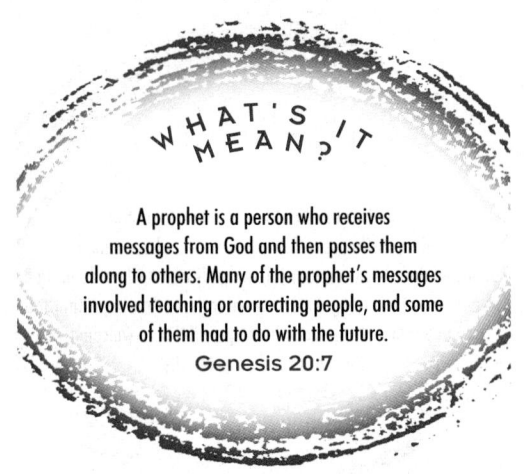

A prophet is a person who receives messages from God and then passes them along to others. Many of the prophet's messages involved teaching or correcting people, and some of them had to do with the future.
Genesis 20:7

A BABY FOR SARAH

21
1The LORD cared for Sarah as he had said
and did for her what he had promised. 2Sarah
became pregnant and gave birth to a son for
Abraham in his old age. Everything happened
at the time God had said it would. 3Abraham
named his son Isaac, the son Sarah gave birth
to. 4He circumcised Isaac when he was eight
days old as God had commanded.
5Abraham was one hundred years old
when his son Isaac was born. 6And Sarah said,
"God has made me laugh.[n] Everyone who

21:6 laugh The Hebrew words for "he laughed" and "Isaac" sound the same.

hears about this will laugh with me. 7No one thought that I would be able to have Abraham's child, but even though Abraham is old I have given him a son."

HAGAR AND ISHMAEL LEAVE

8Isaac grew, and when he became old enough to eat food, Abraham gave a great feast. 9But Sarah saw Ishmael making fun of Isaac. (Ishmael was the son of Abraham by Hagar, Sarah's Egyptian slave.) 10So Sarah said to Abraham, "Throw out this slave woman and her son. Her son should not inherit anything; my son Isaac should receive it all."

11This troubled Abraham very much because Ishmael was also his son. 12But God said to Abraham, "Don't be troubled about the boy and the slave woman. Do whatever Sarah tells you. The descendants I promised you will be from Isaac. 13I will also make the descendants of Ishmael into a great nation because he is your son, too."

14Early the next morning Abraham took some food and a leather bag full of water. He gave them to Hagar and sent her away. Carrying these things and her son, Hagar went and wandered in the desert of Beersheba.

15Later, when all the water was gone from the bag, Hagar put her son under a bush. 16Then she went away a short distance and sat down. She thought, "My son will die, and I cannot watch this happen." She sat there and began to cry.

17God heard the boy crying, and God's angel called to Hagar from heaven. He said, "What is wrong, Hagar? Don't be afraid! God has heard the boy crying there. 18Help him up and take him by the hand. I will make his descendants into a great nation."

19Then God showed Hagar a well of water. So she went to the well and filled her bag with water and gave the boy a drink.

20God was with the boy as he grew up. Ishmael lived in the desert and became an archer. 21He lived in the Desert of Paran, and his mother found a wife for him in Egypt.

ABRAHAM'S BARGAIN WITH ABIMELECH

22Then Abimelech came with Phicol, the commander of his army, and said to Abraham, "God is with you in everything you do. 23So make a promise to me here before God that you will be fair with me and my children and my descendants. Be kind to me and to this land where you have lived as a stranger—as kind as I have been to you."

24And Abraham said, "I promise." 25Then Abraham complained to Abimelech about Abimelech's servants who had seized a well of water.

26But Abimelech said, "I don't know who did this. You never told me about this before today."

27Then Abraham gave Abimelech some sheep and cattle, and they made an agreement. 28Abraham also put seven female lambs in front of Abimelech.

29Abimelech asked Abraham, "Why did you put these seven female lambs by themselves?"

30Abraham answered, "Accept these lambs from me to prove that you believe I dug this well."

31So that place was called Beersheba[n] because they made a promise to each other there.

32After Abraham and Abimelech made the agreement at Beersheba, Abimelech and Phicol, the commander of his army, went back to the land of the Philistines.

WHAT'S IT MEAN?

The Philistines, who lived along the coast of the Mediterranean Sea near Israel, were what you might call the archrivals of God's people. Abraham made the agreement with the Philistine king Abimelech so that he could live in Philistine land without any problems. Later, though, the Philistines proved to be a thorn in the side of Abraham's descendants.

Genesis 21:32

33Abraham planted a tamarisk tree at Beersheba and prayed to the LORD, the God who lives forever. 34And Abraham lived as a stranger in the land of the Philistines for a long time.

GOD TESTS ABRAHAM

22 1After these things God tested Abraham's faith. God said to him, "Abraham!"

And he answered, "Here I am."

2Then God said, "Take your only son, Isaac,

21:31 Beersheba This name means "well of the promise" or "well of seven."

the son you love, and go to the land of Moriah. Kill him there and offer him as a whole burnt offering on one of the mountains I will tell you about."

3Abraham got up early in the morning and saddled his donkey. He took Isaac and two servants with him. After he cut the wood for the sacrifice, they went to the place God had told them to go. 4On the third day Abraham looked up and saw the place in the distance. 5He said to his servants, "Stay here with the donkey. My son and I will go over there and worship, and then we will come back to you."

6Abraham took the wood for the sacrifice and gave it to his son to carry, but he himself took the knife and the fire. So he and his son went on together.

7Isaac said to his father Abraham, "Father!"

Abraham answered, "Yes, my son."

Isaac said, "We have the fire and the wood, but where is the lamb we will burn as a sacrifice?"

8Abraham answered, "God will give us the lamb for the sacrifice, my son."

So Abraham and his son went on together 9and came to the place God had told him about. Abraham built an altar there. He laid the wood on it and then tied up his son Isaac and laid him on the wood on the altar. 10Then Abraham took his knife and was about to kill his son.

11But the angel of the LORD called to him from heaven and said, "Abraham! Abraham!"

Abraham answered, "Yes."

WHAT'S IT MEAN?

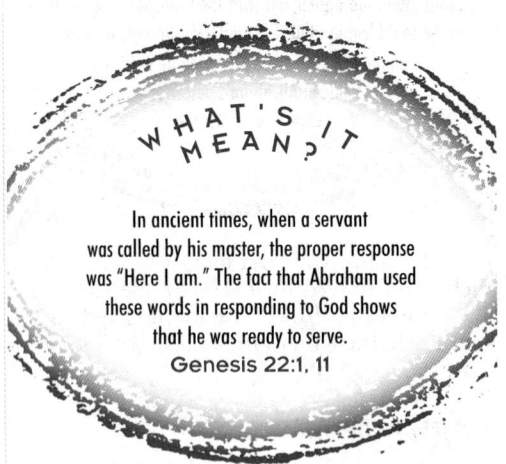

In ancient times, when a servant was called by his master, the proper response was "Here I am." The fact that Abraham used these words in responding to God shows that he was ready to serve.
Genesis 22:1, 11

12The angel said, "Don't kill your son or hurt him in any way. Now I can see that you trust God and that you have not kept your son, your only son, from me."

13Then Abraham looked up and saw a male sheep caught in a bush by its horns. So Abraham went and took the sheep and killed it. He offered it as a whole burnt offering to God, and his son was saved. 14So Abraham named that place The LORD Provides. Even today people say, "On the mountain of the LORD it will be provided."

15The angel of the LORD called to Abraham from heaven a second time 16and said, "The LORD says, 'Because you did not keep back your son, your only son, from me, I make you this promise by my own name: 17I will surely bless you and give you many descendants. They will be as many as the stars in the sky and the sand on the seashore, and they will capture the cities of their enemies. 18Through your descendants all the nations on the earth will be blessed, because you obeyed me.' "

19Then Abraham returned to his servants. They all traveled back to Beersheba, and Abraham stayed there.

20After these things happened, someone told Abraham: "Your brother Nahor and his wife Milcah have children now. 21The first son is Uz, and the second is Buz. The third son is Kemuel (the father of Aram). 22Then there are Kesed, Hazo, Pildash, Jidlaph, and Bethuel." 23Bethuel became the father of Rebekah. Milcah was the mother of these eight sons, and Nahor, Abraham's brother, was the father. 24Also Nahor had four other sons by his slave woman Reumah. Their names were Tebah, Gaham, Tahash, and Maacah.

SARAH DIES

23

1Sarah lived to be one hundred twenty-seven years old. 2She died in Kiriath Arba (that is, Hebron) in the land of Canaan. Abraham was very sad and cried because of her. 3After a while he got up from the side of his wife's body and went to talk to the Hittites. He said, 4"I am only a stranger and a foreigner here. Sell me some of your land so that I can bury my dead wife."

5The Hittites answered Abraham, 6"Sir, you are a great leader among us. You may have the best place we have to bury your dead. You may have any of our burying places that you want, and none of us will stop you from burying your dead wife."

7Abraham rose and bowed to the people of the land, the Hittites. 8He said to them, "If you truly want to help me bury my dead wife here, speak to Ephron, the son of Zohar for me. 9Ask him to sell me the cave of Machpelah at the edge of his field. I will pay him the full price.

You can be the witnesses that I am buying it as a burial place."

10Ephron was sitting among the Hittites at the city gate. He answered Abraham, 11"No, sir. I will give you the land and the cave that is in it, with these people as witnesses. Bury your dead wife."

12Then Abraham bowed down before the Hittites. 13He said to Ephron before all the people, "Please let me pay you the full price for the field. Accept my money, and I will bury my dead there."

14Ephron answered Abraham, 15"Sir, the land is worth ten pounds of silver, but I won't argue with you over the price. Take the land, and bury your dead wife."

16Abraham agreed and paid Ephron in front of the Hittite witnesses. He weighed out the full price, ten pounds of silver, and they counted the weight as the traders normally did.

17-18So Ephron's field in Machpelah, east of Mamre, was sold. Abraham became the owner of the field, the cave in it, and all the trees that were in the field. The sale was made at the city gate, with the Hittites as witnesses. 19After this, Abraham buried his wife Sarah in the cave in the field of Machpelah, near Mamre. (Mamre was later called Hebron in the land of Canaan.) 20So Abraham bought the field and the cave in it from the Hittites to use as a burying place.

A WIFE FOR ISAAC

24 1Abraham was now very old, and the LORD had blessed him in every way. 2Abraham said to his oldest servant, who was in charge of everything he owned, "Put your hand under my leg.[n] 3Make a promise to me before the LORD, the God of heaven and earth. Don't get a wife for my son from the Canaanite girls who live around here. 4Instead, go back to my country, to the land of my relatives, and get a wife for my son Isaac."

5The servant said to him, "What if this woman does not want to return with me to this land? Then, should I take your son with me back to your homeland?"

6Abraham said to him, "No! Don't take my son back there. 7The LORD, the God of heaven, brought me from the home of my father and the land of my relatives. And he promised me, 'I will give this land to your descendants.' The LORD will send his angel before you to help you get a wife for my son there. 8If the girl won't come back with you, you will be free from this promise. But you must not take my son back there." 9So the servant put his hand under his master's leg and made a promise to Abraham about this.

WHAT'S IT MEAN?

How do you feel about large families? In Old Testament times, the family unit included everyone from grandparents to multiple wives, from widowed daughters to servants. God used the family structure to spread his message from generation to generation. Abraham wanted Isaac's wife chosen from among his family in order to keep his family unified.

Genesis 24:4

10The servant took ten of Abraham's camels and left, carrying with him many different kinds of beautiful gifts. He went to Northwest Mesopotamia to Nahor's city. 11In the evening, when the women come out to get water, he made the camels kneel down at the well outside the city.

12The servant said, "LORD, God of my master Abraham, allow me to find a wife for his son today. Please show this kindness to my master Abraham. 13Here I am, standing by the spring, and the girls from the city are coming out to get water. 14I will say to one of them, 'Please put your jar down so I can drink.' Then let her say, 'Drink, and I will also give water to your camels.' If that happens, I will know she is the right one for your servant Isaac and that you have shown kindness to my master."

15Before the servant had finished praying, Rebekah, the daughter of Bethuel, came out of the city. (Bethuel was the son of Milcah and Nahor, Abraham's brother.) Rebekah was carrying her water jar on her shoulder. 16She was very pretty, a virgin; she had never had sexual relations with a man. She went down to the spring and filled her jar, then came back up. 17The servant ran to her and said, "Please give me a little water from your jar."

18Rebekah said, "Drink, sir." She quickly lowered the jar from her shoulder and gave him a drink. 19After he finished drinking, Rebekah said, "I will also pour some water for your

24:2 Put . . . leg This showed that a person would keep the promise.

camels." [20]So she quickly poured all the water from her jar into the drinking trough for the camels. Then she kept running to the well until she had given all the camels enough to drink.

[21]The servant quietly watched her. He wanted to be sure the LORD had made his trip successful. [22]After the camels had finished drinking, he gave Rebekah a gold ring weighing one-fifth of an ounce and two gold arm bracelets weighing about four ounces each. [23]He asked, "Who is your father? Is there a place in his house for me and my men to spend the night?"

[24]Rebekah answered, "My father is Bethuel, the son of Milcah and Nahor." [25]Then she said, "And, yes, we have straw for your camels and a place for you to spend the night."

[26]The servant bowed and worshiped the LORD [27]and said, "Blessed is the LORD, the God of my master Abraham. The LORD has been kind and truthful to him and has led me to my master's relatives."

[28]Then Rebekah ran and told her mother's family about all these things. [29]She had a brother named Laban, who ran out to Abraham's servant, who was still at the spring. [30]Laban had heard what she had said and had seen the ring and the bracelets on his sister's arms. So he ran out to the well, and there was the man standing by the camels at the spring. [31]Laban said, "Sir, you are welcome to come in; you don't have to stand outside. I have prepared the house for you and also a place for your camels."

[32]So Abraham's servant went into the house. After Laban unloaded the camels and gave them straw and food, he gave water to Abraham's servant so he and the men with him could wash their feet. [33]Then Laban gave the servant food, but the servant said, "I will not eat until I have told you why I came."

So Laban said, "Then tell us."

[34]He said, "I am Abraham's servant. [35]The LORD has greatly blessed my master in everything, and he has become a rich man. The LORD has given him many flocks of sheep, herds of cattle, silver and gold, male and female servants, camels, and horses. [36]Sarah, my master's wife, gave birth to a son when she was old, and my master has given everything he owns to that son. [37]My master had me make a promise to him and said, 'Don't get a wife for my son from the Canaanite girls who live around here. [38]Instead, you must go to my father's people and to my family. There you must get a wife for my son.' [39]I said to my master, 'What if the woman will not come back with me?' [40]But he said, 'I serve the LORD, who will send his angel with you and will help you. You will get a wife for my son from my family and my father's people. [41]Then you will be free from the promise. But if they will not give you a wife for my son, you will be free from this promise.'

[42]"Today I came to this spring. I said, 'LORD, God of my master Abraham, please make my trip successful. [43]I am standing by this spring. I will wait for a young woman to come out to get water, and I will say, "Please give me water from your jar to drink." [44]Then let her say, "Drink this water, and I will also get water for your camels." By this I will know the LORD has chosen her for my master's son.'

[45]"Before I finished my silent prayer, Rebekah came out of the city with her water jar on her shoulder. She went down to the spring and got water. I said to her, 'Please give me a drink.' [46]She quickly lowered the jar from her shoulder and said, 'Drink this. I will also get water for your camels.' So I drank, and she gave water to my camels too. [47]When I asked her, 'Who is your father?' she answered, 'My father is Bethuel son of Milcah and Nahor.' Then I put the ring in her nose and the bracelets on her arms, [48]and I bowed my head and thanked the LORD. I praised the LORD, the God of my master Abraham, because he led me on the right road to get the granddaughter of my master's brother for his son. [49]Now, tell me, will you be kind and truthful to my master? And if not, tell me so. Then I will know what I should do."

[50]Laban and Bethuel answered, "This is clearly from the LORD, and we cannot change what must happen. [51]Rebekah is yours. Take her and go. Let her marry your master's son as the LORD has commanded."

[52]When Abraham's servant heard these words, he bowed facedown on the ground before the LORD. [53]Then he gave Rebekah gold and silver jewelry and clothes. He also gave expensive gifts to her brother and mother. [54]The servant and the men with him ate and drank and spent the night there. When they got up the next morning, the servant said, "Now let me go back to my master."

[55]Rebekah's mother and her brother said, "Let Rebekah stay with us at least ten days. After that she may go."

[56]But the servant said to them, "Do not make me wait, because the LORD has made my trip successful. Now let me go back to my master."

[57]Rebekah's brother and mother said, "We will call Rebekah and ask her what she wants

WHAT'S IT MEAN?

Asking Rebekah's opinion about the marriage plans was an unusual courtesy. Marriages were generally arranged by young people's families. Very few women (and few men, for that matter) had the authority to go against their family's wishes.

Genesis 24:57

to do." [58]They called her and asked her, "Do you want to go with this man now?"

She said, "Yes, I do."

[59]So they allowed Rebekah and her nurse to go with Abraham's servant and his men. [60]They blessed Rebekah and said,

"Our sister, may you be the mother of
    thousands of people,
  and may your descendants capture the
    cities of their enemies."

[61]Then Rebekah and her servant girls got on the camels and followed the servant and his men. So the servant took Rebekah and left.

[62]At this time Isaac had left Beer Lahai Roi and was living in southern Canaan. [63]One evening when he went out to the field to think, he looked up and saw camels coming. [64]Rebekah also looked and saw Isaac. Then she jumped down from the camel [65]and asked the servant, "Who is that man walking in the field to meet us?"

The servant answered, "That is my master." So Rebekah covered her face with her veil.

[66]The servant told Isaac everything that had happened. [67]Then Isaac brought Rebekah into the tent of Sarah, his mother, and she became his wife. Isaac loved her very much, and so he was comforted after his mother's death.

ABRAHAM'S FAMILY

25

[1]Abraham married again, and his new wife was Keturah. [2]She gave birth to Zimran, Jokshan, Medan, Midian, Ishbak, and Shuah. [3]Jokshan was the father of Sheba and Dedan. Dedan's descendants were the people of Assyria, Letush, and Leum. [4]The sons of Midian were Ephah, Epher, Hanoch, Abida, and Eldaah. All these were descendants of Keturah. [5]Abraham left everything he owned to Isaac. [6]But before Abraham died, he did give gifts to the sons of his other wives, then sent them to the East to be away from Isaac.

[7]Abraham lived to be one hundred seventy-five years old. [8]He breathed his last breath and died at an old age, after a long and satisfying life. [9]His sons Isaac and Ishmael buried him in the cave of Machpelah in the field of Ephron east of Mamre. (Ephron was the son of Zohar the Hittite.) [10]So Abraham was buried with his wife Sarah in the same field that he had bought from the Hittites. [11]After Abraham died, God blessed his son Isaac. Isaac was now living at Beer Lahai Roi.

[12]This is the family history of Ishmael, Abraham's son. (Hagar, Sarah's Egyptian servant, was Ishmael's mother.) [13]These are the names of Ishmael's sons in the order they were born: Nebaioth, the first son, then Kedar, Adbeel, Mibsam, [14]Mishma, Dumah, Massa, [15]Hadad, Tema, Jetur, Naphish, and Kedemah. [16]These were Ishmael's sons, and these are the names of the tribal leaders listed according to their settlements and camps. [17]Ishmael lived one hundred thirty-seven years and then breathed his last breath and died. [18]His descendants lived from Havilah to Shur, which is east of Egypt stretching toward Assyria. They often attacked the descendants of his brothers.

ISAAC'S FAMILY

[19]This is the family history of Isaac. Abraham had a son named Isaac. [20]When Isaac was forty years old, he married Rebekah, who came from Northwest Mesopotamia. She was Bethuel's daughter and the sister of Laban the Aramean. [21]Isaac's wife could not have children, so Isaac prayed to the LORD for her. The LORD heard Isaac's prayer, and Rebekah became pregnant.

[22]While she was pregnant, the babies struggled inside her. She asked, "Why is this happening to me?" Then she went to get an answer from the LORD.

[23]The LORD said to her,

"Two nations are in your body,
  and two groups of people will be taken
    from you.
One group will be stronger than the other,
  and the older will serve the younger."

[24]When the time came, Rebekah gave birth to twins. [25]The first baby was born red. Since his skin was like a hairy robe, he was named Esau.[n] [26]When the second baby was born, he

25:25 Esau This name may mean "hairy."

WHAT'S IT MEAN?

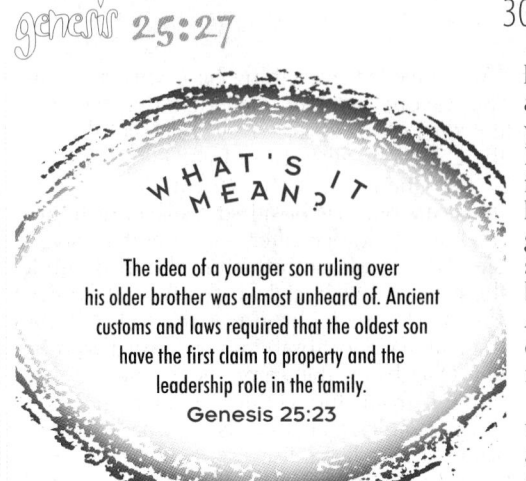

The idea of a younger son ruling over his older brother was almost unheard of. Ancient customs and laws required that the oldest son have the first claim to property and the leadership role in the family.
Genesis 25:23

was holding on to Esau's heel, so that baby was named Jacob.[n] Isaac was sixty years old when they were born.

27When the boys grew up, Esau became a skilled hunter. He loved to be out in the fields. But Jacob was a quiet man and stayed among the tents. 28Isaac loved Esau because he hunted the wild animals that Isaac enjoyed eating. But Rebekah loved Jacob.

29One day Jacob was boiling a pot of vegetable soup. Esau came in from hunting in the fields, weak from hunger. 30So Esau said to Jacob, "Let me eat some of that red soup, because I am weak with hunger." (That is why people call him Edom.[n])

31But Jacob said, "You must sell me your rights as the firstborn son."[n]

32Esau said, "I am almost dead from hunger. If I die, all of my father's wealth will not help me."

33But Jacob said, "First, promise me that you will give it to me." So Esau made a promise to Jacob and sold his part of their father's wealth to Jacob. 34Then Jacob gave Esau bread and vegetable soup, and he ate and drank, and then left. So Esau showed how little he cared about his rights as the firstborn son.

ISAAC LIES TO ABIMELECH

26 1Now there was a time of hunger in the land, besides the time of hunger that happened during Abraham's life. So Isaac went to the town of Gerar to see Abimelech king of the Philistines. 2The LORD appeared to Isaac and said, "Don't go down to Egypt, but live in the land where I tell you to live. 3Stay in this land, and I will be with you and bless you. I will give you and your descendants all these lands, and I will keep the oath I made to Abraham your father. 4I will give you many descendants, as hard to count as the stars in the sky, and I will give them all these lands. Through your descendants all the nations on the earth will be blessed. 5I will do this because your father Abraham obeyed me. He did what I said and obeyed my commands, my teachings, and my rules."

6So Isaac stayed in Gerar. 7His wife Rebekah was very beautiful, and the men of that place asked Isaac about her. Isaac said, "She is my sister," because he was afraid to tell them she was his wife. He thought they might kill him so they could have her.

8Isaac lived there a long time. One day as Abimelech king of the Philistines looked out his window, he saw Isaac holding his wife Rebekah tenderly. 9Abimelech called for Isaac and said, "This woman is your wife. Why did you say she was your sister?"

Isaac said to him, "I was afraid you would kill me so you could have her."

10Abimelech said, "What have you done to us? One of our men might have had sexual relations with your wife. Then we would have been guilty of a great sin."

11So Abimelech warned everyone, "Anyone who touches this man or his wife will be put to death."

ISAAC BECOMES RICH

12Isaac planted seed in that land, and that year he gathered a great harvest. The LORD blessed him very much, 13and he became rich. He gathered more wealth until he became a very rich man. 14He had so many slaves and flocks and herds that the Philistines envied him. 15So they stopped up all the wells the servants of Isaac's father Abraham had dug. (They had dug them when Abraham was alive.) The Philistines filled those wells with dirt. 16And Abimelech said to Isaac, "Leave our country because you have become much more powerful than we are."

17So Isaac left that place and camped in the Valley of Gerar and lived there. 18Long before this time Abraham had dug many wells, but after he died, the Philistines filled them with

25:26 Jacob This name sounds like the Hebrew word for "heel." "Grabbing someone's heel" is a Hebrew saying for tricking someone. **25:30 Edom** This name sounds like the Hebrew word for "red."
25:31 rights . . . son Usually the firstborn son had a high rank in the family. The firstborn son usually became the new head of the family.

dirt. So Isaac dug those wells again and gave them the same names his father had given them. 19 Isaac's servants dug a well in the valley, from which a spring of water flowed. 20 But the herdsmen of Gerar argued with them and said, "This water is ours." So Isaac named that well Argue because they argued with him. 21 Then his servants dug another well. When the people also argued about it, Isaac named that well Fight. 22 He moved from there and dug another well. No one argued about this one, so he named it Room Enough. Isaac said, "Now the LORD has made room for us, and we will be successful in this land."

WHAT'S IT MEAN?

When you consider the work that went into digging wells in ancient times, it's easy to understand why people argued over them. These wells weren't dug in soft dirt, or even clay. They were dug in solid limestone, using primitive tools. The job was time-consuming and backbreaking. With water in short supply in that region, it's no wonder that the diggers were eager to protect what they had worked for.

Genesis 26:17–20

23 From there Isaac went to Beersheba. 24 The LORD appeared to him that night and said, "I am the God of your father Abraham. Don't be afraid, because I am with you. I will bless you and give you many descendants because of my servant Abraham." 25 So Isaac built an altar and worshiped the LORD there. He also made a camp there, and his servants dug a well.

26 Abimelech came from Gerar to see Isaac. He brought with him Ahuzzath, who advised him, and Phicol, the commander of his army. 27 Isaac asked them, "Why have you come to see me? You were my enemy and forced me to leave your country."

28 They answered, "Now we know that the LORD is with you. Let us swear an oath to each other. Let us make an agreement with you 29 that since we did not hurt you, you will not hurt us. We were good to you and sent you away in peace. Now the LORD has blessed you."

30 So Isaac prepared food for them, and they all ate and drank. 31 Early the next morning the men swore an oath to each other. Then Isaac sent them away, and they left in peace.

32 That day Isaac's servants came and told him about the well they had dug, saying, "We found water in that well." 33 So Isaac named it Shibah[n] and that city is called Beersheba even now.

34 When Esau was forty years old, he married two Hittite women—Judith daughter of Beeri and Basemath daughter of Elon. 35 These women brought much sorrow to Isaac and Rebekah.

JACOB TRICKS ISAAC

27 1 When Isaac was old, his eyesight was poor, so he could not see clearly. One day he called his older son Esau to him and said, "Son."

Esau answered, "Here I am."

2 Isaac said, "I am old and don't know when I might die. 3 So take your bow and arrows and go hunting in the field for an animal for me to eat. 4 When you prepare the tasty food that I love, bring it to me, and I will eat. Then I will bless you before I die." 5 So Esau went out in the field to hunt.

WHAT'S IT MEAN?

Blessings were taken very seriously in Old Testament times. To bless someone was to call for God's favor and goodness in his life. What's more, the act of blessing someone somehow carried with it the power to make the blessing a reality. Once a blessing was spoken, it couldn't be taken back or changed.

Genesis 27:4

Rebekah was listening as Isaac said this to his son Esau. 6 She said to her son Jacob, "Listen, I heard your father saying to your brother Esau, 7 'Kill an animal and prepare some tasty food for me to eat. Then I will bless you in the presence of the LORD before I die.' 8 So obey me, my son, and do what I tell you. 9 Go out to our goats and bring me two of the best young ones. I will prepare them just the way your father likes them. 10 Then you will take the food

26:33 Shibah This name sounds like the Hebrew words for "seven" and "promise."

to your father, and he will bless you before he
dies."
11 But Jacob said to his mother Rebekah, "My
brother Esau is a hairy man, and I am smooth!
12 If my father touches me, he will know I am not
Esau. Then he will not bless me but will place a
curse on me because I tried to trick him."
13 So Rebekah said to him, "If your father
puts a curse on you, I will accept the blame. Just
do what I said and go, get the goats for me."
14 So Jacob went out and got two goats and
brought them to his mother, and she cooked
them in the special way Isaac enjoyed. 15 She
took the best clothes of her older son Esau that
were in the house and put them on the younger son Jacob. 16 She also took the skins of the
goats and put them on Jacob's hands and neck.
17 Then she gave Jacob the tasty food and the
bread she had made.
18 Jacob went in to his father and said, "Father."
And his father said, "Yes, my son. Who are
you?"
19 Jacob said to him, "I am Esau, your first
son. I have done what you told me. Now sit up
and eat some meat of the animal I hunted for
you. Then bless me."
20 But Isaac asked his son, "How did you
find and kill the animal so quickly?"
Jacob answered, "Because the LORD your
God helped me to find it."
21 Then Isaac said to Jacob, "Come near so I
can touch you, my son. Then I will know if
you are really my son Esau."
22 So Jacob came near to Isaac his father.
Isaac touched him and said, "Your voice
sounds like Jacob's voice, but your hands are
hairy like the hands of Esau." 23 Isaac did not
know it was Jacob, because his hands were
hairy like Esau's hands, so Isaac blessed him.
24 Isaac asked, "Are you really my son Esau?"
Jacob answered, "Yes, I am."
25 Then Isaac said, "Bring me the food, and I
will eat it and bless you." So Jacob gave him the
food, and he ate. Jacob gave him wine, and he
drank. 26 Then Isaac said to him, "My son, come
near and kiss me." 27 So Jacob went to his father
and kissed him. When Isaac smelled Esau's
clothes, he blessed him and said,

"The smell of my son
is like the smell of the field
that the LORD has blessed.
28 May God give you plenty of rain
and good soil
so that you will have plenty of grain
and new wine.
29 May nations serve you
and peoples bow down to you.
May you be master over your brothers,
and may your mother's sons bow down
to you.
May everyone who curses you be cursed,
and may everyone who blesses you be
blessed."

30 Isaac finished blessing Jacob. Then, just as
Jacob left his father Isaac, Esau came in from
hunting. 31 He also prepared some tasty food
and brought it to his father. He said, "Father,
rise and eat the food that your son killed for
you and then bless me."
32 Isaac asked, "Who are you?"
He answered, "I am your son—your firstborn son—Esau."
33 Then Isaac trembled greatly and said,
"Then who was it that hunted the animals and
brought me food before you came? I ate it, and
I blessed him, and it is too late now to take
back my blessing."
34 When Esau heard the words of his father,
he let out a loud and bitter cry. He said to his
father, "Bless me—me, too, my father!"
35 But Isaac said, "Your brother came and
tricked me. He has taken your blessing."
36 Esau said, "Jacob[n] is the right name for
him. He has tricked me these two times. He
took away my share of everything you own,
and now he has taken away my blessing." Then
Esau asked, "Haven't you saved a blessing
for me?"
37 Isaac answered, "I gave Jacob the power to
be master over you, and all his brothers will be
his servants. And I kept him strong with grain
and new wine. There is nothing left to give
you, my son."
38 But Esau continued, "Do you have only
one blessing, Father? Bless me, too, Father!"
Then Esau began to cry out loud.
39 Isaac said to him,

"You will live far away from the best land,
far from the rain.
40 You will live by using your sword,
and you will be a slave to your brother.
But when you struggle,
you will break free from him."

41 After that Esau hated Jacob because of the
blessing from Isaac. He thought to himself,
"My father will soon die, and I will be sad for
him. Then I will kill Jacob."

27:36 Jacob This name sounds like the Hebrew word for "heel." "Grabbing someone's heel" is a Hebrew saying for tricking someone.

42Rebekah heard about Esau's plan to kill Jacob. So she sent for Jacob and said to him, "Listen, your brother Esau is comforting himself by planning to kill you. 43So, my son, do what I say. My brother Laban is living in Haran. Go to him at once! 44Stay with him for a while, until your brother is not so angry. 45In time, your brother will not be angry, and he will forget what you did to him. Then I will send a servant to bring you back. I don't want to lose both of my sons on the same day."

46Then Rebekah said to Isaac, "I am tired of Hittite women. If Jacob marries one of these Hittite women here in this land, I want to die."

JACOB SEARCHES FOR A WIFE

28 1Isaac called Jacob and blessed him and commanded him, "You must not marry a Canaanite woman. 2Go to the house of Bethuel, your mother's father, in Northwest Mesopotamia. Laban, your mother's brother, lives there. Marry one of his daughters. 3May God Almighty bless you and give you many children, and may you become a group of many peoples. 4May he give you and your descendants the blessing of Abraham so that you may own the land where you are now living as a stranger, the land God gave to Abraham." 5So Isaac sent Jacob to Northwest Mesopotamia, to Laban the brother of Rebekah. Bethuel the Aramean was the father of Laban and Rebekah, and Rebekah was the mother of Jacob and Esau.

"May God Almighty bless you and give you many children. . . . May he give you and your descendants the blessing of Abraham." (Genesis 28:3–4)

6Esau learned that Isaac had blessed Jacob and sent him to Northwest Mesopotamia to find a wife there. He also learned that Isaac had commanded Jacob not to marry a Canaanite woman 7and that Jacob had obeyed his father and mother and had gone to Northwest Mesopotamia. 8So Esau saw that his father Isaac did not want his sons to marry Canaanite women. 9Now Esau already had wives, but he went to Ishmael son of Abraham, and he married Mahalath, Ishmael's daughter. Mahalath was the sister of Nebaioth.

JACOB'S DREAM AT BETHEL

10Jacob left Beersheba and set out for Haran. 11When he came to a place, he spent the night there because the sun had set. He found a stone and laid his head on it to go to sleep. 12Jacob dreamed that there was a ladder resting on the earth and reaching up into heaven, and he saw angels of God going up and coming down the ladder. 13Then Jacob saw the LORD standing above the ladder, and he said, "I am the LORD, the God of Abraham your grandfather, and the God of Isaac. I will give you and your descendants the land on which you are now sleeping. 14Your descendants will be as many as the dust of the earth. They will spread west and east, north and south, and all the families of the earth will be blessed through you and your descendants. 15I am with you and will protect you everywhere you go and will bring you back to this land. I will not leave you until I have done what I have promised you."

16Then Jacob woke from his sleep and said, "Surely the LORD is in this place, but I did not know it."

17He was afraid and said, "This place frightens me! It is surely the house of God and the gate of heaven."

18Jacob rose early in the morning and took the stone he had slept on and set it up on its end. Then he poured olive oil on the top of it. 19At first, the name of that city was Luz, but Jacob named it Bethel.[n]

20Then Jacob made a promise. He said, "I want God to be with me and to protect me on this journey. I want him to give me food to eat

WHAT'S IT MEAN?

Jacob took his dream seriously—and for good reason. The vision of the ladder, the bridge between heaven and earth, came straight from God. Jacob left his rock pillow behind as a memorial to God. To emphasize the point, he poured oil on the rock to symbolize that the land belonged to God in a special way.
Genesis 28:12–18

28:19 Bethel This name means "house of God."

and clothes to wear 21so I will be able to return in peace to my father's house. If the LORD does these things, he will be my God. 22This stone which I have set up on its end will be the house of God. And I will give God one-tenth of all he gives me."

JACOB ARRIVES IN NORTHWEST MESOPOTAMIA

29 1Then Jacob continued his journey and came to the land of the people of the East. 2He looked and saw a well in the field and three flocks of sheep lying nearby, because they drank water from this well. A large stone covered the mouth of the well. 3When all the flocks would gather there, the shepherds would roll the stone away from the well and water the sheep. Then they would put the stone back in its place.

4Jacob said to the shepherds there, "My brothers, where are you from?"

They answered, "We are from Haran."

5Then Jacob asked, "Do you know Laban, grandson of Nahor?"

They answered, "We know him."

6Then Jacob asked, "How is he?"

They answered, "He is well. Look, his daughter Rachel is coming now with his sheep."

7Jacob said, "But look, it is still the middle of the day. It is not time for the sheep to be gathered for the night, so give them water and let them go back into the pasture."

8But they said, "We cannot do that until all the flocks are gathered. Then we will roll away the stone from the mouth of the well and water the sheep."

9While Jacob was talking with the shepherds, Rachel came with her father's sheep, because it was her job to care for the sheep. 10When Jacob saw Laban's daughter Rachel and Laban's sheep, he went to the well and rolled the stone from its mouth and watered Laban's sheep. Now Laban was the brother of Rebekah, Jacob's mother. 11Then Jacob kissed Rachel and cried. 12He told her that he was from her father's family and that he was the son of Rebekah. So Rachel ran home and told her father.

13When Laban heard the news about his sister's son Jacob, he ran to meet him. Laban

Promise

HE PROMISES TO KEEP HIS PROMISES.

I am the LORD, the God of Abraham your grandfather, and the God of Isaac. I will give you and your descendants the land on which you are now sleeping. Your descendants will be as many as the dust of the earth. They will spread west and east, north and south, and all the families of the earth will be blessed through you and your descendants. I am with you and will protect you everywhere you go and will bring you back to this land. I will not leave you until I have done what I have promised you (Gen. 28:13b–15).

Jacob got off to a bad start in his spiritual life. First, he talked his older brother, Esau, out of the inheritance he was supposed to get as the firstborn. Later, he tricked his father, Isaac, into thinking he was Esau so that he could get the special blessing that Isaac wanted to give Esau. It didn't look like Jacob had much of a chance to do anything great for God. In fact, we might think his belief in God was kind of flimsy. But God had chosen Jacob. In spite of the sneaky things he'd done, the Lord appeared to Jacob in a dream and said, "I will not leave you until I have done what I have promised you."

There may be times when God's promises seem really out there—way beyond the realm of possibility—especially when you know you haven't kept up your end of the deal. Even when your faith is a lot stronger than Jacob's was, there may be days when you want to say, "No way. God isn't going to do *that*—not for me." Don't give in. Instead, listen with all your heart, with every ounce of your faith to hear God say, "I will not leave you until I have done what I have promised you."

SEE FOR YOURSELF:

2 Sam. 23:5; 1 Kin. 8:56; 2 Kin. 20:9

hugged him and kissed him and brought him
to his house, where Jacob told Laban everything that had happened.
[14]Then Laban said, "You are my own flesh
and blood."

JACOB IS TRICKED

Jacob stayed there a month. [15]Then Laban
said to Jacob, "You are my relative, but it is not
right for you to work for me without pay.
What would you like me to pay you?"
[16]Now Laban had two daughters. The older
was Leah, and the younger was Rachel. [17]Leah
had weak eyes, but Rachel was very beautiful.
[18]Jacob loved Rachel, so he said to Laban, "Let
me marry your younger daughter Rachel. If
you will, I will work seven years for you."

WHAT'S IT MEAN?

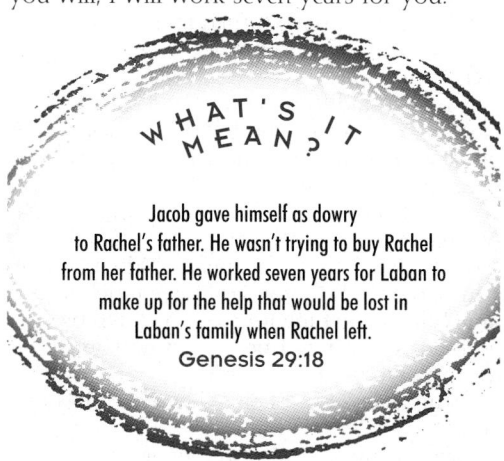

Jacob gave himself as dowry to Rachel's father. He wasn't trying to buy Rachel from her father. He worked seven years for Laban to make up for the help that would be lost in Laban's family when Rachel left.
Genesis 29:18

[19]Laban said, "It would be better for her to
marry you than someone else, so stay here
with me." [20]So Jacob worked for Laban seven
years so he could marry Rachel. But they
seemed like just a few days to him because he
loved Rachel very much.
[21]After seven years Jacob said to Laban,
"Give me Rachel so that I may marry her. The
time I promised to work for you is over."
[22]So Laban gave a feast for all the people
there. [23]That evening he brought his daughter
Leah to Jacob, and they had sexual relations.
[24](Laban gave his slave girl Zilpah to his
daughter to be her servant.) [25]In the morning
when Jacob saw that he had had sexual relations with Leah, he said to Laban, "What have
you done to me? I worked hard for you so that
I could marry Rachel! Why did you trick me?"
[26]Laban said, "In our country we do not allow the younger daughter to marry before the
older daughter. [27]But complete the full week of
the marriage ceremony with Leah, and I will
give you Rachel to marry also. But you must
serve me another seven years."
[28]So Jacob did this, and when he had completed the week with Leah, Laban gave him his
daughter Rachel as a wife. [29](Laban gave his
slave girl Bilhah to his daughter Rachel to be
her servant.) [30]So Jacob had sexual relations
with Rachel also, and Jacob loved Rachel more
than Leah. Jacob worked for Laban for another
seven years.

JACOB'S FAMILY GROWS

[31]When the LORD saw that Jacob loved Rachel more than Leah, he made it possible for
Leah to have children, but not Rachel. [32]Leah
became pregnant and gave birth to a son. She
named him Reuben,[n] because she said, "The
LORD has seen my troubles. Surely now my
husband will love me."
[33]Leah became pregnant again and gave
birth to another son. She named him Simeon[n]
and said, "The LORD has heard that I am not
loved, so he has given me this son."
[34]Leah became pregnant again and gave
birth to another son. She named him Levi[n] and
said, "Now, surely my husband will be close to
me, because I have given him three sons."
[35]Then Leah gave birth to another son. She
named him Judah,[n] because she said, "Now I
will praise the LORD." Then Leah stopped having children.

30

[1]When Rachel saw that she was not having
children for Jacob, she envied her sister Leah.
She said to Jacob, "Give me children, or I'll die!"
[2]Jacob became angry with her and said, "Can I
do what only God can do? He is the one who
has kept you from having children."
[3]Then Rachel said, "Here is my slave girl Bilhah. Have sexual relations with her so she can
give birth to a child for me. Then I can have
my own family through her."
[4]So Rachel gave Bilhah, her slave girl, to Jacob as a wife, and he had sexual relations with
her. [5]She became pregnant and gave Jacob a
son. [6]Rachel said, "God has judged me innocent. He has listened to my prayer and has
given me a son," so she named him Dan.[n]
[7]Bilhah became pregnant again and gave

29:32 Reuben This name sounds like the Hebrew word for "he has seen my troubles." **29:33 Simeon** This name sounds like the Hebrew word for "has heard." **29:34 Levi** This name sounds like the Hebrew word for "be close to." **29:35 Judah** This name sounds like the Hebrew word for "praise." **30:6 Dan** This name means "he has judged."

Jacob a second son. 8 Rachel said, "I have struggled hard with my sister, and I have won." So she named that son Naphtali.[n]

9 Leah saw that she had stopped having children, so she gave her slave girl Zilpah to Jacob as a wife. 10 When Zilpah had a son, 11 Leah said, "I am lucky," so she named him Gad.[n] 12 Zilpah gave birth to another son, 13 and Leah said, "I am very happy! Now women will call me happy," so she named him Asher.[n]

14 During the wheat harvest Reuben went into the field and found some mandrake[n] plants and brought them to his mother Leah. But Rachel said to Leah, "Please give me some of your son's mandrakes."

15 Leah answered, "You have already taken away my husband, and now you are trying to take away my son's mandrakes."

But Rachel answered, "If you will give me your son's mandrakes, you may sleep with Jacob tonight."

16 When Jacob came in from the field that night, Leah went out to meet him. She said, "You will have sexual relations with me tonight because I have paid for you with my son's mandrakes." So Jacob slept with her that night.

WHAT'S IT MEAN?

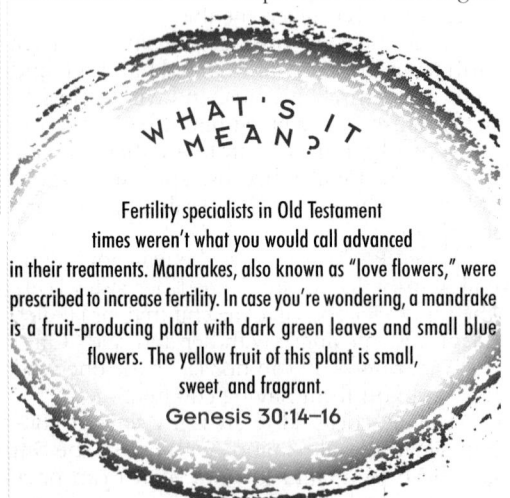

Fertility specialists in Old Testament times weren't what you would call advanced in their treatments. Mandrakes, also known as "love flowers," were prescribed to increase fertility. In case you're wondering, a mandrake is a fruit-producing plant with dark green leaves and small blue flowers. The yellow fruit of this plant is small, sweet, and fragrant.

Genesis 30:14–16

17 Then God answered Leah's prayer, and she became pregnant again. She gave birth to a fifth son 18 and said, "God has given me what I paid for, because I gave my slave girl to my husband." So Leah named her son Issachar.[n]

19 Leah became pregnant again and gave birth to a sixth son. 20 She said, "God has given me a fine gift. Now surely Jacob will honor me, because I have given him six sons," so she named him Zebulun.[n] 21 Later Leah gave birth to a daughter and named her Dinah.

22 Then God remembered Rachel and answered her prayer, making it possible for her to have children. 23 When she became pregnant and gave birth to a son, she said, "God has taken away my shame," 24 and she named him Joseph.[n] Rachel said, "I wish the LORD would give me another son."

JACOB TRICKS LABAN

25 After the birth of Joseph, Jacob said to Laban, "Now let me go to my own home and country. 26 Give me my wives and my children and let me go. I have earned them by working for you, and you know that I have served you well."

27 Laban said to him, "If I have pleased you, please stay. I know the LORD has blessed me because of you. 28 Tell me what I should pay you, and I will give it to you."

29 Jacob answered, "You know that I have worked hard for you, and your flocks have grown while I cared for them. 30 When I came, you had little, but now you have much. Every time I did something for you, the LORD blessed you. But when will I be able to do something for my own family?"

31 Laban asked, "Then what should I give you?"

Jacob answered, "I don't want you to give me anything. Just do this one thing, and I will come back and take care of your flocks. 32 Today let me go through all your flocks. I will take every speckled or spotted sheep, every black lamb, and every spotted or speckled goat. That will be my pay. 33 In the future you can easily see if I am honest. When you come to look at my flocks, if I have any goat that isn't speckled or spotted or any lamb that isn't black, you will know I stole it."

34 Laban answered, "Agreed! We will do what you ask." 35 But that day Laban took away all the male goats that had streaks or spots, all the speckled and spotted female goats (all those that had white on them), and all the black sheep. He told his sons to watch over them. 36 Then he took these animals to a place that

30:8 Naphtali This name sounds like the Hebrew word for "my struggle." **30:11 Gad** This name may mean "lucky." **30:13 Asher** This name may mean "happy." **30:14 mandrake** A plant which was believed to cause a woman to become pregnant. **30:18 Issachar** This name sounds like the Hebrew word for "paid for." **30:20 Zebulun** This name sounds like the Hebrew word for "honor." **30:24 Joseph** This name sounds like the Hebrew word for "he adds."

was three days' journey away from Jacob. Jacob took care of all the flocks that were left.

[37]So Jacob cut green branches from poplar, almond, and plane trees and peeled off some of the bark so that the branches had white stripes on them. [38]He put the branches in front of the flocks at the watering places. When the animals came to drink, they also mated there, [39]so the flocks mated in front of the branches. Then the young that were born were streaked, speckled, or spotted. [40]Jacob separated the young animals from the others, and he made them face the streaked and dark animals in Laban's flock. Jacob kept his animals separate from Laban's. [41]When the stronger animals in the flock were mating, Jacob put the branches before their eyes so they would mate near the branches. [42]But when the weaker animals mated, Jacob did not put the branches there. So the animals born from the weaker animals were Laban's, and those born from the stronger animals were Jacob's. [43]In this way Jacob became very rich. He had large flocks, many male and female servants, camels, and donkeys.

JACOB RUNS AWAY

31 [1]One day Jacob heard Laban's sons talking. They said, "Jacob has taken everything our father owned, and in this way he has become rich." [2]Then Jacob noticed that Laban was not as friendly as he had been before. [3]The LORD said to Jacob, "Go back to the land where your ancestors lived, and I will be with you."

[4]So Jacob told Rachel and Leah to meet him in the field where he kept his flocks. [5]He said to them, "I have seen that your father is not as friendly with me as he used to be, but the God of my father has been with me. [6]You both know that I have worked as hard as I could for your father, [7]but he cheated me and changed my pay ten times. But God has not allowed your father to harm me. [8]When Laban said, 'You can have all the speckled animals as your pay,' all the animals gave birth to speckled young ones. But when he said, 'You can have all the streaked animals as your pay,' all the flocks gave birth to streaked babies. [9]So God has taken the animals away from your father and has given them to me.

[10]"I had a dream during the season when the flocks were mating. I saw that the only male goats who were mating were streaked, speckled, or spotted. [11]The angel of God spoke to me in that dream and said, 'Jacob!' I answered, 'Yes!' [12]The angel said, 'Look! Only the streaked, speckled, or spotted male goats are mating. I have seen all the wrong things Laban has been doing to you. [13]I am the God who appeared to you at Bethel, where you poured olive oil on the stone you set up on end and where you made a promise to me. Now I want you to leave here and go back to the land where you were born.' "

[14]Rachel and Leah answered Jacob, "Our father has nothing to give us when he dies. [15]He has treated us like strangers. He sold us to you, and then he spent all of the money you paid for us. [16]God took all this wealth from our father, and now it belongs to us and our children. So do whatever God has told you to do."

[17]So Jacob put his children and his wives on camels, [18]and they began their journey back to Isaac, his father, in the land of Canaan. All the flocks of animals that Jacob owned walked ahead of them. He carried everything with him that he had gotten while he lived in Northwest Mesopotamia.

[19]While Laban was gone to cut the wool from his sheep, Rachel stole the idols that belonged to him. [20]And Jacob tricked Laban the Aramean by not telling him he was leaving. [21]Jacob and his family left quickly, crossed the Euphrates River, and traveled toward the mountains of Gilead.

[22]Three days later Laban learned that Jacob had run away, [23]so he gathered his relatives and began to chase him. After seven days Laban found him in the mountains of Gilead. [24]That night God came to Laban the Aramean in a dream and said, "Be careful! Do not say anything to Jacob, good or bad."

THE SEARCH FOR THE STOLEN IDOLS

[25]So Laban caught up with Jacob. Now Jacob had made his camp in the mountains, so Laban and his relatives set up their camp in the mountains of Gilead. [26]Laban said to Jacob, "What have you done? You cheated me and took my daughters as if you had captured them in a war. [27]Why did you run away secretly and trick me? Why didn't you tell me? Then I could have sent you away with joy and singing and with the music of tambourines and harps. [28]You did not even let me kiss my grandchildren and my daughters good-bye. You were very foolish to do this! [29]I have the power to harm you, but last night the God of your father spoke to me and warned me not to say anything to you, good or bad. [30]I know you want to go back to your home, but why did you steal my idols?"

[31]Jacob answered Laban, "I left without telling you, because I was afraid you would take your daughters away from me. [32]If you find

anyone here who has taken your idols, that person will be killed! Your relatives will be my witnesses. You may look for anything that belongs to you and take anything that is yours." (Now Jacob did not know that Rachel had stolen Laban's idols.)

[33]So Laban looked in Jacob's tent, in Leah's tent, and in the tent where the two slave women stayed, but he did not find his idols. When he left Leah's tent, he went into Rachel's tent. [34]Rachel had hidden the idols inside her camel's saddle and was sitting on them. Although Laban looked through the whole tent, he did not find them.

[35]Rachel said to her father, "Father, don't be angry with me. I am not able to stand up before you because I am having my monthly period." So Laban looked through the camp, but he did not find his idols.

[36]Then Jacob became very angry and said, "What wrong have I done? What law have I broken to cause you to chase me? [37]You have looked through everything I own, but you have found nothing that belongs to you. If you have found anything, show it to everyone. Put it in front of your relatives and my relatives, and let them decide which one of us is right. [38]I have worked for you now for twenty years. During all that time none of the lambs and kids died during birth, and I have not eaten any of the male sheep from your flocks. [39]Any time an animal was killed by wild beasts, I did not bring it to you, but made up for the loss myself. You made me pay for any animal that was stolen during the day or night. [40]In the daytime the sun took away my strength, and at night I was cold and could not sleep. [41]I worked like a slave for you for twenty years—the first fourteen to get your two daughters and the last six to earn your flocks. During that time you changed my pay ten times. [42]But the God of my father, the God of Abraham and the God of Isaac, was with me. Otherwise, you would have sent me away with nothing. But he saw the trouble I had and the hard work I did, and last night he corrected you."

JACOB AND LABAN'S AGREEMENT

[43]Laban said to Jacob, "These girls are my daughters. Their children belong to me, and these flocks are mine. Everything you see here belongs to me, but I can do nothing to keep my daughters and their children. [44]Let us make an agreement, and let us set up a pile of stones to remind us of it."

[45]So Jacob took a large rock and set it up on its end. [46]He told his relatives to gather rocks, so they took the rocks and piled them up; then they ate beside the pile. [47]Laban named that place in his language A Pile to Remind Us, and Jacob gave the place the same name in Hebrew.

[48]Laban said to Jacob, "This pile of rocks will remind us of the agreement between us." That is why the place was called A Pile to Remind Us. [49]It was also called Mizpah,[n] because Laban said, "Let the LORD watch over us while we are separated from each other. [50]Remember that God is our witness even if no one else is around us. He will know if you harm my daughters or marry other women. [51]Here is the pile of rocks that I have put between us and here is the rock I set up on end. [52]This pile of rocks and this rock set on end will remind us of our agreement. I will never go past this pile to hurt you, and you must never come to my side of them to hurt me. [53]Let the God of Abraham, who is the God of Nahor and the God of their fathers, punish either of us if we break this agreement."

WHAT'S IT MEAN?

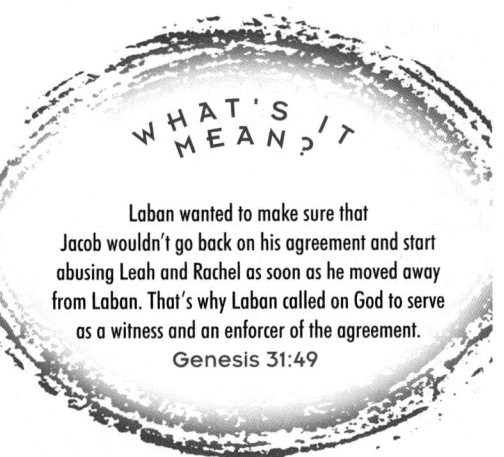

Laban wanted to make sure that Jacob wouldn't go back on his agreement and start abusing Leah and Rachel as soon as he moved away from Laban. That's why Laban called on God to serve as a witness and an enforcer of the agreement.

Genesis 31:49

So Jacob made a promise in the name of the God whom his father Isaac worshiped. [54]Then Jacob killed an animal and offered it as a sacrifice on the mountain, and he invited his relatives to share in the meal. After they finished eating, they spent the night on the mountain. [55]Early the next morning Laban kissed his grandchildren and his daughters and blessed them, and then he left to return home.

32

JACOB MEETS ESAU

[1]When Jacob also went his way, the angels of God met him. [2]When he saw them, he said,

31:49 Mizpah This name sounds like the Hebrew word for "watch."

ANGELS
Do angels work among people? (32:1)

"This is the camp of God!" So
he named that place Maha-
naim.[n]
3Jacob's brother Esau was
living in the area called Seir
in the country of Edom. Jacob sent messengers to Esau,
4telling them, "Give this message to my master
Esau: 'This is what Jacob, your servant, says: I
have lived with Laban and have remained
there until now. 5I have cattle, donkeys, flocks,
and male and female servants. I send this message to you and ask you to accept us.' "
6The messengers returned to Jacob and
said, "We went to your brother Esau. He is
coming to meet you and has four hundred
men with him."
7Then Jacob was very afraid and worried.
He divided the people who were with him and
all the flocks, herds, and camels into two
camps. 8Jacob thought, "Esau might come and
destroy one camp, but the other camp can run
away and be saved."
9Then Jacob said, "God of my father Abraham! God of my father Isaac! LORD, you told
me to return to my country and my family.
You said that you would treat me well. 10I am
not worthy of the kindness and continual
goodness you have shown me. The first time I
traveled across the Jordan River, I had only my
walking stick, but now I own enough to have
two camps. 11Please save me from my brother
Esau. I am afraid he will come and kill all of us,
even the mothers with the children. 12You said
to me, 'I will treat you well and will make your
children as many as the sand of the seashore.
There will be too many to count.' "
13Jacob stayed there for the night and prepared a gift for Esau from what he had with
him: 14two hundred female goats and twenty
male goats, two hundred female sheep and
twenty male sheep, 15thirty female camels and
their young, forty cows and ten bulls, twenty
female donkeys, and ten male donkeys. 16Jacob
gave each separate flock of animals to one of
his servants and said to them, "Go ahead of me
and keep some space between each herd." 17Ja-
cob gave them their orders. To the servant with
the first group of animals he said, "My brother
Esau will come to you and ask, 'Whose servant
are you? Where are you going and whose animals are these?' 18Then you will answer, 'They
belong to your servant Jacob. He sent them as
a gift to you, my master Esau, and he also is
coming behind us.' "
19Jacob ordered the second servant, the
third servant, and all the other servants to do
the same thing. He said, "Say the same thing to
Esau when you meet him. 20Say, 'Your servant
Jacob is coming behind us.' " Jacob thought, "If
I send these gifts ahead of me, maybe Esau will
forgive me. Then when I see him, perhaps he
will accept me." 21So Jacob sent the gifts to
Esau, but he himself stayed that night in the
camp.

JACOB WRESTLES WITH GOD

22During the night Jacob rose and crossed
the Jabbok River at the crossing, taking with
him his two wives, his two slave girls, and his
eleven sons. 23He sent his family and everything he had across the river. 24So Jacob was
alone, and a man came and wrestled with him
until the sun came up. 25When the man saw he
could not defeat Jacob, he struck Jacob's hip
and put it out of joint. 26Then he said to Jacob,
"Let me go. The sun is coming up."
But Jacob said, "I will let you go if you will
bless me."
27The man said to him, "What is your
name?"
And he answered, "Jacob."
28Then the man said, "Your name will no
longer be Jacob. Your name will now be Israel,[n]
because you have wrestled with God and with
people, and you have won."
29Then Jacob asked him, "Please tell me your
name."
But the man said, "Why do you ask my
name?" Then he blessed Jacob there.

WHAT'S IT MEAN?

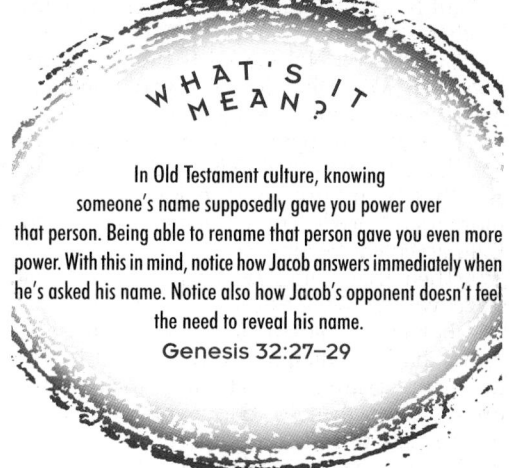

In Old Testament culture, knowing someone's name supposedly gave you power over that person. Being able to rename that person gave you even more power. With this in mind, notice how Jacob answers immediately when he's asked his name. Notice also how Jacob's opponent doesn't feel the need to reveal his name.

Genesis 32:27–29

32:2 Mahanaim This name means "two camps." **32:28 Israel** This name means "he wrestles with God."

30So Jacob named that place Peniel,[n] saying, "I have seen God face to face, but my life was saved." 31Then the sun rose as he was leaving that place, and Jacob was limping because of his leg. 32So even today the people of Israel do not eat the muscle that is on the hip joint of animals, because Jacob was touched there.

JACOB SHOWS HIS BRAVERY

33 1Jacob looked up and saw Esau coming, and with him were four hundred men. So Jacob divided his children among Leah, Rachel, and the two slave girls. 2Jacob put the slave girls with their children first, then Leah and her children behind them, and Rachel and Joseph last. 3Jacob himself went out in front of them and bowed down flat on the ground seven times as he was walking toward his brother.

4But Esau ran to meet Jacob and put his arms around him and hugged him. Then Esau kissed him, and they both cried. 5When Esau looked up and saw the women and children, he asked, "Who are these people with you?"

Jacob answered, "These are the children God has given me. God has been good to me, your servant."

6Then the two slave girls and their children came up to Esau and bowed down flat on the earth before him. 7Leah and her children also came up to Esau and also bowed down flat on the earth. Last of all, Joseph and Rachel came up to Esau, and they, too, bowed down flat before him.

8Esau said, "I saw many herds as I was coming here. Why did you bring them?"

Jacob answered, "They were to please you, my master."

9But Esau said, "I already have enough, my brother. Keep what you have."

10Jacob said, "No! Please! If I have pleased you, then accept the gift I give you. I am very happy to see your face again. It is like seeing the face of God, because you have accepted me. 11So I beg you to accept the gift I give you. God has been very good to me, and I have more than I need." And because Jacob begged, Esau accepted the gift.

12Then Esau said, "Let us be going. I will travel with you."

13But Jacob said to him, "My master, you know that the children are weak. And I must be careful with my flocks and their young ones. If I force them to go too far in one day, all the animals will die. 14So, my master, you go on ahead of me, your servant. I will follow you slowly and let the animals and the children set the speed at which we travel. I will meet you, my master, in Edom."

15So Esau said, "Then let me leave some of my people with you."

"No, thank you," said Jacob. "I only want to please you, my master." 16So that day Esau started back to Edom. 17But Jacob went to Succoth, where he built a house for himself and shelters for his animals. That is why the place was named Succoth.[n]

18Jacob left Northwest Mesopotamia and arrived safely at the city of Shechem in the land of Canaan. There he camped east of the city. 19He bought a part of the field where he had camped from the sons of Hamor father of Shechem for one hundred pieces of silver. 20He built an altar there and named it after God, the God of Israel.

WHAT'S IT MEAN?

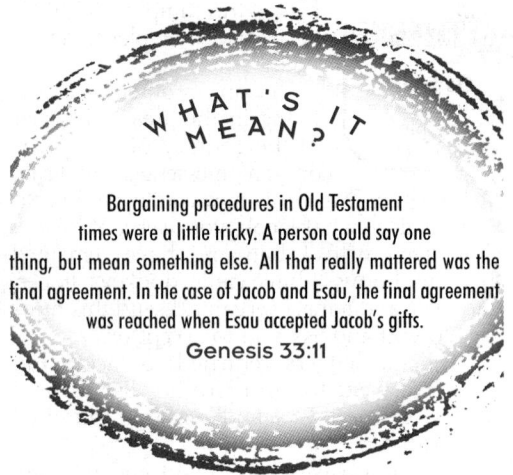

Bargaining procedures in Old Testament times were a little tricky. A person could say one thing, but mean something else. All that really mattered was the final agreement. In the case of Jacob and Esau, the final agreement was reached when Esau accepted Jacob's gifts.

Genesis 33:11

DINAH IS ATTACKED

34 1At this time Dinah, the daughter of Leah and Jacob, went out to visit the women of the land. 2When Shechem son of Hamor the Hivite, the ruler of the land, saw her, he took her and forced her to have sexual relations with him. 3Shechem fell in love with Dinah, and he spoke kindly to her. 4He told his father, Hamor, "Please get this girl for me so I can marry her."

5Jacob learned how Shechem had disgraced his daughter, but since his sons were out in the field with the cattle, Jacob said nothing until they came home. 6While he waited, Hamor father of Shechem went to talk with Jacob.

7When Jacob's sons heard what had happened, they came in from the field. They were very angry that Shechem had done such a

32:30 Peniel This name means "the face of God." **33:17 Succoth** This name means "shelters."

wicked thing to Israel. It was wrong for him to have sexual relations with Jacob's daughter; a thing like this should not be done.

WHAT'S IT MEAN?

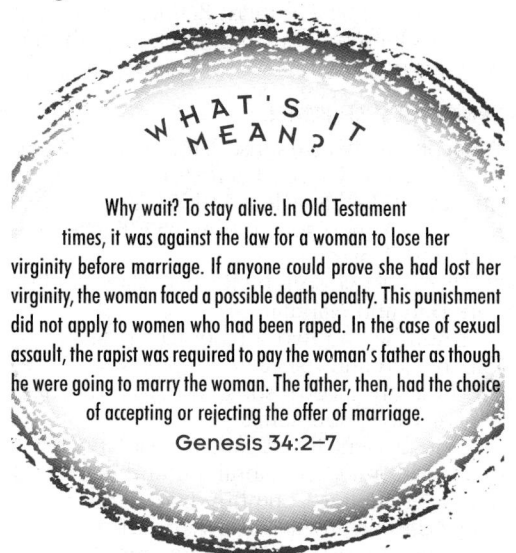

Why wait? To stay alive. In Old Testament times, it was against the law for a woman to lose her virginity before marriage. If anyone could prove she had lost her virginity, the woman faced a possible death penalty. This punishment did not apply to women who had been raped. In the case of sexual assault, the rapist was required to pay the woman's father as though he were going to marry the woman. The father, then, had the choice of accepting or rejecting the offer of marriage.

Genesis 34:2–7

8But Hamor talked to Dinah's brothers and said, "My son Shechem is deeply in love with Dinah. Please let him marry her. 9Marry our people. Give your women to our men as wives and take our women for your men as wives. 10You can live in the same land with us. You will be free to own land and to trade here."

11Shechem also talked to Jacob and to Dinah's brothers and said, "Please accept my offer. I will give anything you ask. 12Ask as much as you want for the payment for the bride, and I will give it to you. Just let me marry Dinah."

13Jacob's sons answered Shechem and his father with lies, because Shechem had disgraced their sister Dinah. 14The brothers said to them, "We cannot allow you to marry our sister, because you are not circumcised. That would be a disgrace to us. 15But we will allow you to marry her if you do this one thing: Every man in your town must be circumcised like us. 16Then your men can marry our women, and our men can marry your women, and we will live in your land and become one people. 17If you refuse to be circumcised, we will take Dinah and leave."

18What they asked seemed fair to Hamor and Shechem. 19So Shechem quickly went to be circumcised because he loved Jacob's daughter.

Now Shechem was the most respected man in his family. 20So Hamor and Shechem went to the gate of their city and spoke to the men of their city, saying, 21"These people want to be friends with us. So let them live in our land and trade here. There is enough land for all of us. Let us marry their women, and we can let them marry our women. 22But we must agree to one thing: All our men must be circumcised as they are. Then they will agree to live in our land, and we will be one people. 23If we do this, their cattle and their animals will belong to us. Let us do what they say, and they will stay in our land." 24All the people who had come to the city gate heard this. They agreed with Hamor and Shechem, and every man was circumcised.

25Three days later the men who were circumcised were still in pain. Two of Jacob's sons, Simeon and Levi (Dinah's brothers), took their swords and made a surprise attack on the city, killing all the men there. 26They killed Hamor and his son Shechem and then took Dinah out of Shechem's house and left. 27Jacob's sons came upon the dead bodies and stole everything that was in the city, to pay them back for what Shechem had done to their sister. 28So the brothers took the flocks, herds, and donkeys, and everything in the city and in the fields. 29They took every valuable thing the people owned, even their wives and children and everything in the houses.

30Then Jacob said to Simeon and Levi, "You have caused me a lot of trouble. Now the Canaanites and the Perizzites who live in the land will hate me. Since there are only a few of us, if they join together to attack us, my people and I will be destroyed."

31But the brothers said, "We will not allow our sister to be treated like a prostitute."

JACOB IN BETHEL

35 1God said to Jacob, "Go to the city of Bethel and live there. Make an altar to the God who appeared to you there when you were running away from your brother Esau."

2So Jacob said to his family and to all who were with him, "Put away the foreign gods you have, and make yourselves clean, and change your clothes. 3We will leave here and go to Bethel. There I will build an altar to God, who has helped me during my time of trouble. He has been with me everywhere I have gone." 4So they gave Jacob all the foreign gods they had, and the earrings they were wearing, and he hid them under the great tree near the town of Shechem. 5Then Jacob and his sons left there. But God caused the people in the nearby cities to be afraid, so they did not follow them. 6And Jacob and all the people who were with him

WHAT'S IT MEAN?

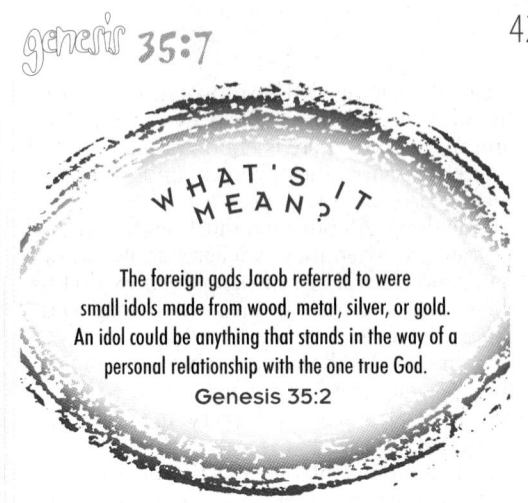

The foreign gods Jacob referred to were small idols made from wood, metal, silver, or gold. An idol could be anything that stands in the way of a personal relationship with the one true God.

Genesis 35:2

went to Luz, which is now called Bethel, in the land of Canaan. [7]There Jacob built an altar and named the place Bethel, after God, because God had appeared to him there when he was running from his brother.

[8]Deborah, Rebekah's nurse, died and was buried under the oak tree at Bethel, so they named that place Oak of Crying.

JACOB'S NEW NAME

[9]When Jacob came back from Northwest Mesopotamia, God appeared to him again and blessed him. [10]God said to him, "Your name is Jacob, but you will not be called Jacob any longer. Your new name will be Israel." So he called him Israel. [11]God said to him, "I am God Almighty. Have many children and grow in number as a nation. You will be the ancestor of many nations and kings. [12]The same land I gave to Abraham and Isaac I will give to you and your descendants." [13]Then God left him. [14]Jacob set up a stone on edge in that place where God had talked to him, and he poured a drink offering and olive oil on it to make it special for God. [15]And Jacob named the place Bethel.

RACHEL DIES GIVING BIRTH

[16]Jacob and his group left Bethel. Before they came to Ephrath, Rachel began giving birth to her baby, [17]but she was having much trouble. When Rachel's nurse saw this, she said, "Don't be afraid, Rachel. You are giving birth to another son." [18]Rachel gave birth to the son, but she herself died. As she lay dying, she named the boy Son of My Suffering, but Jacob called him Benjamin.[n]

[19]Rachel was buried on the road to Ephrath, a district of Bethlehem, [20]and Jacob set up a rock on her grave to honor her. That rock is still there. [21]Then Israel[n] continued his journey and camped just south of Migdal Eder.

[22]While Israel was there, Reuben had sexual relations with Israel's slave woman Bilhah, and Israel heard about it.

THE FAMILY OF ISRAEL

Jacob had twelve sons. [23]He had six sons by his wife Leah: Reuben, his first son, then Simeon, Levi, Judah, Issachar, and Zebulun.

[24]He had two sons by his wife Rachel: Joseph and Benjamin.

[25]He had two sons by Rachel's slave girl Bilhah: Dan and Naphtali.

[26]And he had two sons by Leah's slave girl Zilpah: Gad and Asher.

These are Jacob's sons who were born in Northwest Mesopotamia.

[27]Jacob went to his father Isaac at Mamre near Hebron, where Abraham and Isaac had lived. [28]Isaac lived one hundred eighty years. [29]So Isaac breathed his last breath and died when he was very old, and his sons Esau and Jacob buried him.

ESAU'S FAMILY

36 [1]This is the family history of Esau (also called Edom). [2]Esau married women from the land of Canaan: Adah daughter of Elon the Hittite; and Oholibamah daughter of Anah, the son of Zibeon the Hivite; [3]and Basemath, Ishmael's daughter, the sister of Nebaioth.

[4]Adah gave birth to Eliphaz for Esau. Basemath gave him Reuel, [5]and Oholibamah gave him Jeush, Jalam, and Korah. These were Esau's sons who were born in the land of Canaan.

[6]Esau took his wives, his sons, his daughters, and all the people who lived with him, his herds and other animals, and all the belongings he had gotten in Canaan, and he went to a land away from his brother Jacob. [7]Esau's and Jacob's belongings were becoming too many for them to live in the same land. The land where they had lived could not support both of them, because they had too many herds. [8]So Esau lived in the mountains of Edom. (Esau is also named Edom.)

[9]This is the family history of Esau. He is the ancestor of the Edomites, who live in the mountains of Edom.

[10]Esau's sons were Eliphaz, son of Adah and Esau, and Reuel, son of Basemath and Esau.

35:18 Benjamin This name means "right-hand son" or "favorite son." **35:21 Israel** Also called Jacob.

11 Eliphaz had five sons: Teman, Omar, Zepho, Gatam, and Kenaz. 12 Eliphaz also had a
slave woman named Timna, and Timna and
Eliphaz gave birth to Amalek. These were
Esau's grandsons by his wife Adah.

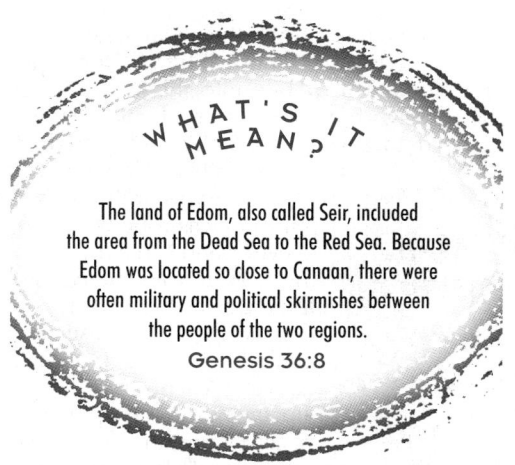

WHAT'S IT MEAN?

The land of Edom, also called Seir, included the area from the Dead Sea to the Red Sea. Because Edom was located so close to Canaan, there were often military and political skirmishes between the people of the two regions.

Genesis 36:8

13 Reuel had four sons: Nahath, Zerah,
Shammah, and Mizzah. These were Esau's
grandsons by his wife Basemath.
14 Esau's third wife was Oholibamah the
daughter of Anah. (Anah was the son of Zibeon.) Esau and Oholibamah gave birth to Jeush, Jalam, and Korah.
15 These were the leaders that came from
Esau: Esau's first son was Eliphaz. From him
came these leaders: Teman, Omar, Zepho,
Kenaz, 16 Korah, Gatam, and Amalek. These
were the leaders that came from Eliphaz in the
land of Edom. They were the grandsons of
Adah.
17 Esau's son Reuel was the father of these
leaders: Nahath, Zerah, Shammah, and Mizzah. These were the leaders that came from
Reuel in the land of Edom. They were the
grandsons of Esau's wife Basemath.
18 Esau's wife Oholibamah gave birth to
these leaders: Jeush, Jalam, and Korah. These
are the leaders that came from Esau's wife
Oholibamah the daughter of Anah. 19 These
were the sons of Esau (also called Edom), and
these were their leaders.
20 These were the sons of Seir the Horite,
who were living in the land: Lotan, Shobal,
Zibeon, Anah, 21 Dishon, Ezer, and Dishan.
These sons of Seir were the leaders of the Horites in Edom.
22 The sons of Lotan were Hori and Homam.
(Timna was Lotan's sister.)
23 The sons of Shobal were Alvan, Manahath, Ebal, Shepho, and Onam.
24 The sons of Zibeon were Aiah and Anah.
Anah is the man who found the hot springs in
the desert while he was caring for his father's
donkeys.
25 The children of Anah were Dishon and
Oholibamah daughter of Anah.
26 The sons of Dishon were Hemdan, Eshban, Ithran, and Keran.
27 The sons of Ezer were Bilhan, Zaavan, and
Akan.
28 The sons of Dishan were Uz and Aran.
29 These were the names of the Horite leaders: Lotan, Shobal, Zibeon, Anah, 30 Dishon,
Ezer, and Dishan.
These men were the leaders of the Horite
families who lived in the land of Edom.
31 These are the kings who ruled in the land
of Edom before the Israelites ever had a king:
32 Bela son of Beor was the king of Edom. He
came from the city of Dinhabah.
33 When Bela died, Jobab son of Zerah became king. Jobab was from Bozrah.
34 When Jobab died, Husham became king.
He was from the land of the Temanites.
35 When Husham died, Hadad son of Bedad,
who had defeated Midian in the country of
Moab, became king. Hadad was from the city
of Avith.
36 When Hadad died, Samlah became king.
He was from Masrekah.
37 When Samlah died, Shaul became king.
He was from Rehoboth on the Euphrates River.
38 When Shaul died, Baal-Hanan son of Acbor became king.
39 When Baal-Hanan son of Acbor died,
Hadad became king. He was from the city of
Pau. His wife's name was Mehetabel daughter of Matred, who was the daughter of Me-
Zahab.
40 These Edomite leaders, listed by their families and regions, came from Esau. Their names
were Timna, Alvah, Jetheth, 41 Oholibamah,
Elah, Pinon, 42 Kenaz, Teman, Mibzar, 43 Magdi-
el, and Iram. They were the leaders of Edom.
(Esau was the father of the Edomites.) The area
where each of these families lived was named
after that family.

JOSEPH THE DREAMER

37

1 Jacob lived in the land of Canaan, where
his father had lived. 2 This is the family history
of Jacob:
Joseph was a young man, seventeen years
old. He and his brothers, the sons of Bilhah
and Zilpah, his father's wives, cared for the
flocks. Joseph gave his father bad reports
about his brothers. 3 Since Joseph was born

when his father Israel[n] was old, Israel loved him more than his other sons. He made Joseph a special robe with long sleeves. 4When Joseph's brothers saw that their father loved him more than he loved them, they hated their brother and could not speak to him politely.

5One time Joseph had a dream, and when he told his brothers about it, they hated him even more. 6Joseph said, "Listen to the dream I had. 7We were in the field tying bundles of wheat together. My bundle stood up, and your bundles of wheat gathered around it and bowed down to it."

8His brothers said, "Do you really think you will be king over us? Do you truly think you will rule over us?" His brothers hated him even more because of his dreams and what he had said.

"My bundle stood up, and your bundles of wheat gathered around it and bowed down to it." (Genesis 37:7b)

9Then Joseph had another dream, and he told his brothers about it also. He said, "Listen, I had another dream. I saw the sun, moon, and eleven stars bowing down to me."

10Joseph also told his father about this dream, but his father scolded him, saying, "What kind of dream is this? Do you really believe that your mother, your brothers, and I will bow down to you?" 11Joseph's brothers were jealous of him, but his father thought about what all these things could mean.

12One day Joseph's brothers went to Shechem to graze their father's flocks. 13Israel said to Joseph, "Go to Shechem where your brothers are grazing the flocks."

Joseph answered, "I will go."

14His father said, "Go and see if your brothers and the flocks are all right. Then come back and tell me." So Joseph's father sent him from the Valley of Hebron.

When Joseph came to Shechem, 15a man found him wandering in the field and asked him, "What are you looking for?"

16Joseph answered, "I am looking for my brothers. Can you tell me where they are grazing the flocks?"

17The man said, "They have already gone. I heard them say they were going to Dothan." So Joseph went to look for his brothers and found them in Dothan.

JOSEPH SOLD INTO SLAVERY

18Joseph's brothers saw him coming from far away. Before he reached them, they made a plan to kill him. 19They said to each other, "Here comes that dreamer. 20Let's kill him and throw his body into one of the wells. We can tell our father that a wild animal killed him. Then we will see what will become of his dreams."

21But Reuben heard their plan and saved Joseph, saying, "Let's not kill him. 22Don't spill any blood. Throw him into this well here in the desert, but don't hurt him!" Reuben planned to save Joseph later and send him back to his father. 23So when Joseph came to his brothers, they pulled off his robe with long sleeves 24and threw him into the well. It was empty, and there was no water in it.

25While Joseph was in the well, the brothers sat down to eat. When they looked up, they saw a group of Ishmaelites traveling from Gilead to Egypt. Their camels were carrying spices, balm, and myrrh. 26Then Judah said to his brothers, "What will we gain if we kill our brother and hide his death? 27Let's sell him to these Ishmaelites. Then we will not be guilty of killing our own brother. After all, he is our brother, our own flesh and blood." And the other brothers agreed. 28So when the Midianite traders came by, the brothers took Joseph out of the well and sold him to the Ishmaelites for eight ounces of silver. And the Ishmaelites took him to Egypt.

WHAT'S IT MEAN?

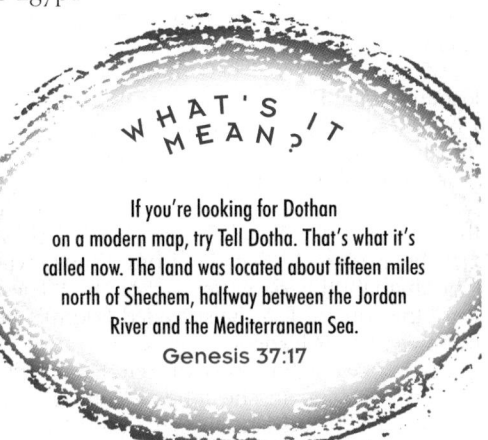

If you're looking for Dothan on a modern map, try Tell Dotha. That's what it's called now. The land was located about fifteen miles north of Shechem, halfway between the Jordan River and the Mediterranean Sea.

Genesis 37:17

29When Reuben came back to the well and Joseph was not there, he tore his clothes to show he was upset. 30Then he went back to his

37:3 Israel Also called Jacob.

brothers and said, "The boy is not there! What
shall I do?" 31The brothers killed a goat and
dipped Joseph's robe in its blood. 32Then they
brought the long-sleeved robe to their father
and said, "We found this robe. Look it over
carefully and see if it is your son's robe."
33Jacob looked it over and said, "It is my
son's robe! Some savage animal has eaten him.
My son Joseph has been torn to pieces!"
34Then Jacob tore his clothes and put on rough
cloth to show that he was upset, and he continued to be sad about his son for a long time.
35All of his sons and daughters tried to comfort
him, but he could not be comforted. He said, "I
will be sad about my son until the day I die."
So Jacob cried for his son Joseph.

WHAT'S IT MEAN?

The "rough cloth" that Jacob put on was a coarse material made from camel or goat hair. Because no one would wear such an uncomfortable cloth under normal conditions, it was an obvious sign of mourning. If you saw someone wearing this cloth, you knew that someone had died or that something bad had happened.

Genesis 37:34

36Meanwhile the Midianites who had
bought Joseph had taken him to Egypt. There
they sold him to Potiphar, an officer to the king
of Egypt and captain of the palace guard.

JUDAH AND TAMAR

38
1About that time, Judah left his brothers
and went to stay with a man named Hirah in
the town of Adullam. 2There Judah met a Canaanite girl, the daughter of a man named
Shua, and married her. Judah had sexual relations with her, 3and she became pregnant and
gave birth to a son, whom Judah named Er.
4Later she gave birth to another son and
named him Onan. 5Still later she had another
son and named him Shelah. She was at Kezib
when this third son was born.
6Judah chose a girl named Tamar to be the
wife of his first son Er. 7But Er, Judah's oldest
son, did what the LORD said was evil, so
the LORD killed him. 8Then Judah said to
Er's brother Onan, "Go and have sexual relations with your dead brother's wife.[n] It is
your duty to provide children for your brother
in this way."

WHAT'S IT MEAN?

If a man died before having children, it was his brother's personal responsibility to make sure that his widow would have a child. In other words, siblings were required to marry their own ex-sisters-in-law! The good news is that it helped continue the family bloodline. A child born of such a union was counted as a member of the family of the woman and her first husband.

Genesis 38:8

9But Onan knew that the children would
not belong to him, so when he was supposed
to have sexual relations with Tamar he did not
complete the sex act. This made it impossible
for Tamar to become pregnant and for Er to
have descendants. 10The LORD was displeased
by this wicked thing Onan had done, so the
LORD killed Onan also. 11Then Judah said to his
daughter-in-law Tamar, "Go back to live in
your father's house, and don't marry until my
young son Shelah grows up." Judah was afraid
that Shelah also would die like his brothers. So
Tamar returned to her father's home.
12After a long time Judah's wife, the daughter of Shua, died. After Judah had gotten over
his sorrow, he went to Timnah to his men who
were cutting the wool from his sheep. His
friend Hirah from Adullam went with him.
13Tamar learned that Judah, her father-in-law,
was going to Timnah to cut the wool from his
sheep. 14So she took off the clothes that
showed she was a widow and covered her face
with a veil to hide who she was. Then she sat
down by the gate of Enaim on the road to
Timnah. She did this because Judah's younger
son Shelah had grown up, but Judah had not
made plans for her to marry him.
15When Judah saw her, he thought she was
a prostitute, because she had covered her face

38:8 Go . . . wife It was a custom in Israel that if a man died without children, one of his brothers would marry the widow. If a child was born, it would be considered the dead man's child.

with a veil. [16]So Judah went to her and said, "Let me have sexual relations with you." He did not know that she was Tamar, his daughter-in-law.

She asked, "What will you give me if I let you have sexual relations with me?"

[17]Judah answered, "I will send you a young goat from my flock."

She answered, "First give me something to keep as a deposit until you send the goat."

[18]Judah asked, "What do you want me to give you as a deposit?"

WHAT'S IT MEAN?

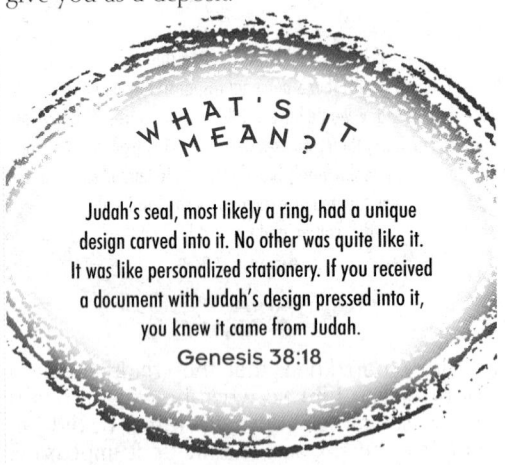

Judah's seal, most likely a ring, had a unique design carved into it. No other was quite like it. It was like personalized stationery. If you received a document with Judah's design pressed into it, you knew it came from Judah.

Genesis 38:18

Tamar answered, "Give me your seal and its cord,[n] and give me your walking stick." So Judah gave these things to her. Then Judah and Tamar had sexual relations, and Tamar became pregnant. [19]When Tamar went home, she took off the veil that covered her face and put on the clothes that showed she was a widow.

[20]Judah sent his friend Hirah with the young goat to find the woman and get back his seal and the walking stick he had given her, but Hirah could not find her. [21]He asked some of the people at the town of Enaim, "Where is the prostitute who was here by the road?"

They answered, "There has never been a prostitute here."

[22]So he went back to Judah and said, "I could not find the woman, and the people who lived there said, 'There has never been a prostitute here.' "

[23]Judah said, "Let her keep the things. I don't want people to laugh at us. I sent her the goat as I promised, but you could not find her."

[24]About three months later someone told Judah, "Tamar, your daughter-in-law, is guilty of acting like a prostitute, and now she is pregnant."

Then Judah said, "Bring her out and let her be burned to death."

[25]When the people went to bring Tamar out, she sent a message to her father-in-law that said, "The man who owns these things has made me pregnant. Look at this seal and its cord and this walking stick, and tell me whose they are."

[26]Judah recognized them and said, "She is more in the right than I. She did this because I did not give her to my son Shelah as I promised." And Judah did not have sexual relations with her again.

[27]When the time came for Tamar to give birth, there were twins in her body. [28]While she was giving birth, one baby put his hand out. The nurse tied a red string on his hand and said, "This baby came out first." [29]But he pulled his hand back in, so the other baby was born first. The nurse said, "So you are able to break out first," and they named him Perez.[n] [30]After this, the baby with the red string on his hand was born, and they named him Zerah.

JOSEPH IS SOLD TO POTIPHAR

39

[1]Now Joseph had been taken down to Egypt. An Egyptian named Potiphar was an officer to the king of Egypt and the captain of the palace guard. He bought Joseph from the Ishmaelites who had brought him down there. [2]The LORD was with Joseph, and he became a successful man. He lived in the house of his master, Potiphar the Egyptian.

[3]Potiphar saw that the LORD was with Joseph and that the LORD made Joseph successful in everything he did. [4]So Potiphar was very happy with Joseph and allowed him to be his personal servant. He put Joseph in charge of the house, trusting him with everything he owned. [5]When Joseph was put in charge of the house and everything Potiphar owned, the LORD blessed the people in Potiphar's house because of Joseph. And the LORD blessed everything that belonged to Potiphar, both in the house and in the field. [6]So Potiphar left Joseph in charge of everything he owned and was not concerned about anything except the food he ate.

JOSEPH IS PUT INTO PRISON

Now Joseph was well built and handsome. [7]After some time the wife of Joseph's master

38:18 seal . . . cord A seal was used like a rubber stamp, and people ran a string through it to tie around the neck. They wrote a contract, folded it, put wax or clay on the contract, and pressed the seal onto it as a signature. **38:29 Perez** This name means "breaking out."

began to desire Joseph, and one day she said to
him, "Have sexual relations with me."
8But Joseph refused and said to her, "My
master trusts me with everything in his house.
He has put me in charge of everything he
owns. 9There is no one in his house greater
than I. He has not kept anything from me except you, because you are his wife. How can I
do such an evil thing? It is a sin against God."
10The woman talked to Joseph every day,
but he refused to have sexual relations with
her or even spend time with her.
11One day Joseph went into the house to do
his work as usual and was the only man in the
house at that time. 12His master's wife grabbed
his coat and said to him, "Come and have sexual relations with me." But Joseph left his coat
in her hand and ran out of the house.
13When she saw that Joseph had left his
coat in her hands and had run outside, 14she
called to the servants in her house and said,
"Look! This Hebrew slave was brought here to
shame us. He came in and tried to have sexual
relations with me, but I screamed. 15My scream
scared him and he ran away, but he left his
coat with me." 16She kept his coat until her
husband came home, 17and she told him the
same story. She said, "This Hebrew slave you
brought here came in to shame me! 18When he
came near me, I screamed. He ran away, but he
left his coat."
19When Joseph's master heard what his wife
said Joseph had done, he became very angry.
20So Potiphar arrested Joseph and put him into
the prison where the king's prisoners were put.
And Joseph stayed there in the prison.
21But the LORD was with Joseph and
showed him kindness and caused the prison
warden to like Joseph. 22The prison warden
chose Joseph to take care of all the prisoners,
and he was responsible for whatever was done
in the prison. 23The warden paid no attention
to anything that was in Joseph's care because
the LORD was with Joseph and made him successful in everything he did.

JOSEPH INTERPRETS TWO DREAMS

40 1After these things happened, two of the
king's officers displeased the king—the man
who served wine to the king and the king's
baker. 2The king became angry with his officer
who served him wine and his baker, 3so he put
them in the prison of the captain of the guard,
the same prison where Joseph was kept. 4The
captain of the guard put the two prisoners in
Joseph's care, and they stayed in prison for
some time.
5One night both the king's officer who
served him wine and the baker had a dream.
Each had his own dream with its own meaning. 6When Joseph came to them the next
morning, he saw they were worried. 7He asked
the king's officers who were with him, "Why
do you look so unhappy today?"
8The two men answered, "We both had
dreams last night, but no one can explain their
meaning to us."
Joseph said to them, "God is the only One
who can explain the meaning of dreams. Tell
me your dreams."

WHAT'S IT MEAN?

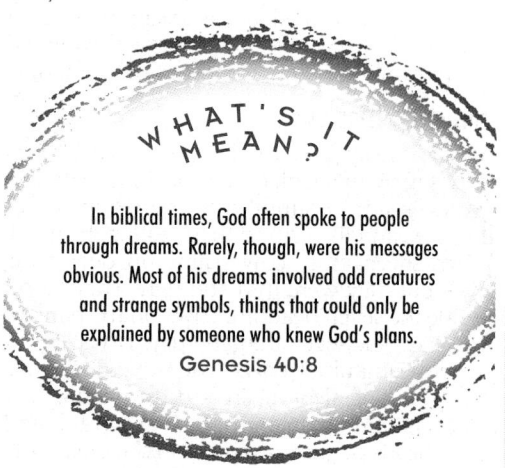

In biblical times, God often spoke to people through dreams. Rarely, though, were his messages obvious. Most of his dreams involved odd creatures and strange symbols, things that could only be explained by someone who knew God's plans.

Genesis 40:8

9So the man who served wine to the king
told Joseph his dream. He said, "I dreamed I
saw a vine, and 10on the vine were three
branches. I watched the branches bud and
blossom, and then the grapes ripened. 11I was
holding the king's cup, so I took the grapes and
squeezed the juice into the cup. Then I gave it
to the king."
12Then Joseph said, "I will explain the dream
to you. The three branches stand for three
days. 13Before the end of three days the king
will free you, and he will allow you to return
to your work. You will serve the king his wine
just as you did before. 14But when you are free,
remember me. Be kind to me, and tell the king
about me so I can get out of this prison. 15I was
taken by force from the land of the Hebrews,
and I have done nothing here to deserve being
put in prison."
16The baker saw that Joseph's explanation
of the dream was good, so he said to him, "I
also had a dream. I dreamed there were three
bread baskets on my head. 17In the top basket
were all kinds of baked food for the king, but
the birds were eating this food out of the basket on my head."

[18]Joseph answered, "I will tell you what the dream means. The three baskets stand for three days. [19]Before the end of three days, the king will cut off your head! He will hang your body on a pole, and the birds will eat your flesh."

[20]Three days later, on his birthday, the king gave a feast for all his officers. In front of his officers, he released from prison the chief officer who served his wine and the chief baker. [21]The king gave his chief officer who served wine his old position, and once again he put the king's cup of wine into the king's hand. [22]But the king hanged the baker on a pole. Everything happened just as Joseph had said it would, [23]but the officer who served wine did not remember Joseph. He forgot all about him.

THE KING'S DREAMS

41

[1]Two years later the king dreamed he was standing on the bank of the Nile River. [2]He saw seven fat and beautiful cows come up out of the river, and they stood there, eating the grass. [3]Then seven more cows came up out of the river, but they were thin and ugly. They stood beside the seven beautiful cows on the bank of the Nile. [4]The seven thin and ugly cows ate the seven beautiful fat cows. Then the king woke up. [5]The king slept again and dreamed a second time. In his dream he saw seven full and good heads of grain growing on one stalk. [6]After that, seven more heads of grain sprang up, but they were thin and burned by the hot east wind. [7]The thin heads of grain ate the seven full and good heads. Then the king woke up again, and he realized it was only a dream. [8]The next morning the king was troubled about these dreams, so he sent for all the magicians and wise men of Egypt. The king told them his dreams, but no one could explain their meaning to him.

[9]Then the chief officer who served wine to the king said to him, "Now I remember something I promised to do, but I forgot about it. [10]There was a time when you were angry with the baker and me, and you put us in prison in the house of the captain of the guard. [11]In prison we each had a dream on the same night, and each dream had a different meaning. [12]A young Hebrew man, a servant of the captain of the guard, was in the prison with us. When we told him our dreams, he explained their meanings to us. He told each man the meaning of his dream, and [13]things happened exactly as he said they would: I was given back my old position, and the baker was hanged."

[14]So the king called for Joseph. The guards quickly brought him out of the prison, and he shaved, put on clean clothes, and went before the king.

[15]The king said to Joseph, "I have had a dream, but no one can explain its meaning to me. I have heard that you can explain a dream when someone tells it to you."

[16]Joseph answered the king, "I am not able to explain the meaning of dreams, but God will do this for the king."

WISDOM
Where can I find wisdom? (41:16)

[17]Then the king said to Joseph, "In my dream I was standing on the bank of the Nile River. [18]I saw seven fat and beautiful cows that came up out of the river and ate the grass. [19]Then I saw seven more cows come out of the river that were thin and lean and ugly—the worst looking cows I have seen in all the land of Egypt. [20]And these thin and ugly cows ate the first seven fat cows, [21]but after they had eaten the seven cows, no one could tell they had eaten them. They looked just as thin and ugly as they did in the beginning. Then I woke up.

[22]"I had another dream. I saw seven full and good heads of grain growing on one stalk. [23]Then seven more heads of grain sprang up after them, but these heads were thin and ugly and were burned by the hot east wind. [24]Then the thin heads ate the seven good heads. I told this dream to the magicians, but no one could explain its meaning to me."

WHAT'S IT MEAN?

Ancient kings often used astrologers and magicians as advisors to help them make important decisions. Believe it or not, they tried to predict the future by "reading" the body parts of the animals they used for sacrifice. Can you imagine basing a major decision in your life on the way a sheep's liver looks?
Genesis 41:8

JOSEPH TELLS THE DREAMS' MEANING

[25]Then Joseph said to the king, "Both of these dreams mean the same thing. God is telling you what he is about to do. [26]The seven good cows stand for seven years, and the

seven good heads of grain stand for seven
years. Both dreams mean the same thing. 27The
seven thin and ugly cows stand for seven
years, and the seven thin heads of grain
burned by the hot east wind stand for seven
years of hunger. 28This will happen as I told
you. God is showing the king what he is about
to do. 29You will have seven years of good
crops and plenty to eat in all the land of Egypt.
30But after those seven years, there will come
seven years of hunger, and all the food that
grew in the land of Egypt will be forgotten. The
time of hunger will eat up the land. 31People
will forget what it was like to have plenty of
food, because the hunger that follows will be so
great. 32You had two dreams which mean the
same thing. This shows that God has firmly decided that this will happen, and he will make it
happen soon.

33"So let the king choose a man who is very
wise and understanding and set him over the
land of Egypt. 34And let the king also appoint
officers over the land, who should take one-
fifth of all the food that is grown during the
seven good years. 35They should gather all the
food that is produced during the good years
that are coming, and under the king's authority
they should store the grain in the cities and
guard it. 36That food should be saved to use
during the seven years of hunger that will
come on the land of Egypt. Then
the people in Egypt will not die
during the seven years of
hunger."

JOSEPH IS MADE RULER OVER EGYPT

37This seemed like a very
good idea to the king, and
all his officers agreed. 38And
the king asked them, "Can we
find a better man than Joseph to
take this job? God's spirit is truly in him!"

39So the king said to Joseph, "God has
shown you all this. There is no one as wise and
understanding as you are, so 40I will put you
in charge of my palace. All the people will
obey your orders, and only I will be greater
than you."

41Then the king said to Joseph, "Look! I have
put you in charge of all the land of Egypt."
42Then the king took off from his own finger
his ring with the royal seal on it, and he put it
on Joseph's finger. He gave Joseph fine linen
clothes to wear, and he put a gold chain
around Joseph's neck. 43The king had Joseph
ride in the second royal chariot, and people
walked ahead of his chariot calling, "Bow
down!" By doing these things, the king put Joseph in charge of all of Egypt.

44The king said to him, "I am the king, and I
say that no one in all the land of Egypt may lift
a hand or a foot without your permission."
45The king gave Joseph the name Zaphenath-
Paneah. He also gave Joseph a wife named Asenath, who was the daughter of Potiphera,
priest of On. So Joseph traveled through all the
land of Egypt.

46Joseph was thirty years old when he began serving the king of Egypt. And he left the
king's court and traveled through all the land
of Egypt. 47During the seven good years, the
crops in the land grew well. 48And Joseph
gathered all the food which was produced in
Egypt during those seven years of good crops
and stored the food in the cities. In every city
he stored grain that had been grown in the
fields around that city. 49Joseph stored much
grain, as much as the sand of the seashore—so
much that he could not measure it.

50Joseph's wife was Asenath daughter of
Potiphera, the priest of On. Before the years of
hunger came, Joseph and Asenath had two
sons. 51Joseph named the first son Manasseh[n]
and said, "God has made me
forget all the troubles I have
had and all my father's family." 52Joseph named the second son Ephraim[n] and said,
"God has given me children
in the land of my troubles."

53The seven years of
good crops came to an end
in the land of Egypt. 54Then
the seven years of hunger began, just as Joseph had said. In
all the lands people had nothing to
eat, but in Egypt there was food. 55The time of
hunger became terrible in all of Egypt, and the
people cried to the king for food. He said to all
the Egyptians, "Go to Joseph and do whatever
he tells you."

56The hunger was everywhere in that part
of the world. And Joseph opened the storehouses and sold grain to the people of Egypt,
because the time of hunger became terrible in
Egypt. 57And all the people in that part of the
world came to Joseph in Egypt to buy grain

> **"Can we find a better man than Joseph to take this job? God's spirit is truly in him!" (Genesis 41:38)**

41:51 Manasseh This name sounds like the Hebrew word for "made me forget." **41:52 Ephraim** This name sounds like the Hebrew word for "given me children."

because the hunger was terrible everywhere in
that part of the world.

THE DREAMS COME TRUE

42 1Jacob learned that there was grain in Egypt,
so he said to his sons, "Why are you just sitting
here looking at one another? 2I have heard
that there is grain in Egypt. Go down there and
buy grain for us to eat, so that we will live and
not die."
3So ten of Joseph's brothers went down to
buy grain from Egypt. 4But Jacob did not send
Benjamin, Joseph's brother, with them, because
he was afraid that something terrible might
happen to him. 5Along with many other people, the sons of Israel[n] went to Egypt to buy
grain, because the people in the land of Canaan were also hungry.
6Now Joseph was governor over Egypt. He
was the one who sold the grain to people who
came to buy it. So Joseph's brothers came to
him and bowed facedown on the ground before him. 7When Joseph saw his brothers, he
knew who they were, but he acted as if he
didn't know them. He asked unkindly, "Where
do you come from?"
They answered, "We have come from the
land of Canaan to buy food."
8Joseph knew they were his brothers, but
they did not know who he was. 9And Joseph
remembered his dreams about his brothers
bowing to him. He said to them, "You are spies!
You came to learn where the nation is weak!"
10But his brothers said to him, "No, my
master. We come as your servants just to buy
food. 11We are all sons of the same father. We
are honest men, not spies."
12Then Joseph said to them, "No! You have
come to learn where this nation is weak!"
13And they said, "We are ten of twelve
brothers, sons of the same father, and we live
in the land of Canaan. Our youngest brother is
there with our father right now, and our other
brother is gone."
14But Joseph said to them, "I can see I was
right! You are spies! 15But I will give you a way
to prove you are telling the truth. As surely as
the king lives, you will not leave this place until
your youngest brother comes here. 16One of
you must go and get your brother. The rest of
you will stay here in prison. We will see if you
are telling the truth. If not, as surely as the king
lives, you are spies." 17Then Joseph put them all
in prison for three days.
18On the third day Joseph said to them, "I
am a God-fearing man. Do this and I will let
you live: 19If you are honest men, let one of
your brothers stay here in prison while the rest
of you go and carry grain back to feed your
hungry families. 20Then bring your youngest
brother back here to me. If you do this, I will
know you are telling the truth, and you will
not die."
The brothers agreed to this. 21They said to
each other, "We are being punished for what
we did to our brother. We saw his trouble, and
he begged us to save him, but we refused to
listen. That is why we are in this trouble now."
22Then Reuben said to them, "I told you not
to harm the boy, but you refused to listen to
me. So now we are being punished for what
we did to him."
23When Joseph talked to his brothers, he
used an interpreter, so they did not know that
Joseph understood what they were saying.
24Then Joseph left them and cried. After a short
time he went back and spoke to them. He took
Simeon and tied him up while the other brothers watched. 25Joseph told his servants to fill
his brothers' bags with grain and to put the
money the brothers had paid for the grain
back in their bags. The servants were also to
give them what they would need for their trip
back home. And the servants did this.
26So the brothers put the grain on their donkeys and left. 27When they stopped for the
night, one of the brothers opened his sack to get
food for his donkey. Then he saw his money in
the top of the sack. 28He said to the other brothers, "The money I paid for the grain has been
put back. Here it is in my sack!"
The brothers were very frightened. They
said to each other, "What has God done to us?"

THE BROTHERS RETURN TO JACOB

29The brothers went to their father Jacob in
the land of Canaan and told him everything
that had happened. 30They said, "The master of
that land spoke unkindly to us. He accused us
of spying on his country, 31but we told him
that we were honest men, not spies. 32We told
him that we were ten of twelve brothers—sons
of one father. We said that one of our brothers
was gone and that our youngest brother was
with our father in Canaan.
33"Then the master of the land said to us,
'Here is a way I can know you are honest men:
Leave one of your brothers with me, and take
grain to feed your hungry families, and go.
34And bring your youngest brother to me so I

42:5 Israel Also called Jacob.

will know you are not spies but honest men. Then I will give you back your brother whom you leave with me, and you can move about freely in our land.' "

35As the brothers emptied their sacks, each of them found his money in his sack. When they and their father saw it, they were afraid.

36Their father Jacob said to them, "You are robbing me of all my children. Joseph is gone, Simeon is gone, and now you want to take Benjamin away, too. Everything is against me."

37Then Reuben said to his father, "You may put my two sons to death if I don't bring Benjamin back to you. Trust him to my care, and I will bring him back to you."

38But Jacob said, "I will not allow Benjamin to go with you. His brother is dead, and he is the only son left from my wife Rachel. I am afraid something terrible might happen to him during the trip to Egypt. Then I would be sad until the day I die."

THE BROTHERS GO BACK TO EGYPT

43 1Still no food grew in the land of Canaan. 2When Jacob's family had eaten all the grain they had brought from Egypt, Jacob said to them, "Go to Egypt again and buy a little more grain for us to eat."

3But Judah said to Jacob, "The governor of that country strongly warned us, 'If you don't bring your brother back with you, you will not be allowed to see me.' 4If you will send Benjamin with us, we will go down and buy food for you. 5But if you refuse to send Benjamin, we will not go. The governor of that country warned us that we would not see him if we didn't bring Benjamin with us."

6Israel[n] said, "Why did you tell the man you had another brother? You have caused me a lot of trouble."

7The brothers answered, "He questioned us carefully about ourselves and our family. He asked us, 'Is your father still alive? Do you have another brother?' We just answered his questions. How could we know he would ask us to bring our other brother to him?"

8Then Judah said to his father Jacob, "Send Benjamin with me, and we will go at once so that we, you, and our children may live and not die. 9I will guarantee you that he will be safe, and I will be personally responsible for him. If I don't bring him back to you, you can blame me all my life. 10If we had not wasted all this time, we could have already made two trips."

11Then their father Jacob said to them, "If it has to be that way, then do this: Take some of the best foods in our land in your packs. Give them to the man as a gift: some balm, some honey, spices, myrrh, pistachio nuts, and almonds. 12Take twice as much money with you this time, and take back the money that was returned to you in your sacks last time. Maybe it was a mistake. 13And take Benjamin with you. Now leave and go to the man. 14I pray that God Almighty will cause the governor to be merciful to you and that he will allow Simeon and Benjamin to come back with you. If I am robbed of my children, then I am robbed of them!"

15So the brothers took the gifts. They also took twice as much money as they had taken the first time, and they took Benjamin. They hurried down to Egypt and stood before Joseph.

16When Joseph saw Benjamin with them, he said to the servant in charge of his house, "Bring those men into my house. Kill an animal and prepare a meal. Those men will eat with me today at noon." 17The servant did as Joseph told him and brought the men to Joseph's house.

18The brothers were afraid when they were brought to Joseph's house and thought, "We were brought here because of the money that was put in our sacks on the first trip. He wants to attack us, make us slaves, and take our donkeys." 19So the brothers went to the servant in charge of Joseph's house and spoke to him at the door of the house. 20They said, "Master, we came here once before to buy food. 21While we were going home, we stopped for the night and when we opened our sacks each of us found all his money in his sack. We brought that money with us to give it back to you. 22And we have brought more money to pay for the food we want to buy this time. We don't know who put that money in our sacks."

23But the servant answered, "It's all right. Don't be afraid. Your God, the God of your father, must have put the money in your sacks. I got the money you paid me for the grain last time." Then the servant brought Simeon out to them.

24The servant led the men into Joseph's house and gave them water, and they washed their feet. Then he gave their donkeys food to eat. 25The men prepared their gift to give to Joseph when he arrived at noon, because they had heard they were going to eat with him there.

43:6 Israel Also called Jacob.

26When Joseph came home, the brothers gave him the gift they had brought into the house and bowed down to the ground in front of him. 27Joseph asked them how they were doing. He said, "How is your aged father you told me about? Is he still alive?"

28The brothers answered, "Your servant, our father, is well. He is still alive." And they bowed low before Joseph to show him respect.

29When Joseph saw his brother Benjamin, who had the same mother as he, Joseph asked, "Is this your youngest brother you told me about?" Then he said to Benjamin, "God be good to you, my son!" 30Then Joseph hurried off because he had to hold back the tears when he saw his brother Benjamin. So Joseph went into his room and cried there. 31Then he washed his face and came out. He controlled himself and said, "Serve the meal."

32So they served Joseph at one table, his brothers at another table, and the Egyptians who ate with him at another table. This was because Egyptians did not like Hebrews and never ate with them. 33Joseph's brothers were seated in front of him in order of their ages, from oldest to youngest. They looked at each other because they were so amazed. 34Food from Joseph's table was taken to them, but Benjamin was given five times more food than the others. Joseph's brothers ate and drank freely with him.

WHAT'S IT MEAN?

In biblical times, eating with another person was considered to be one of the highest forms of hospitality. The Egyptians, however, refused to eat at the same table as the Israelites because they saw the Israelites as a lower class of people. Notice that Joseph was following Egyptian custom by eating separately from his brothers. After all, his brothers still believed that he was an Egyptian.

Genesis 43:32

JOSEPH SETS A TRAP

44

1Then Joseph gave a command to the servant in charge of his house. He said, "Fill the men's sacks with as much grain as they can carry, and put each man's money into his sack with the grain. 2Put my silver cup in the sack of the youngest brother, along with his money for the grain." The servant did what Joseph told him.

3At dawn the brothers were sent away with their donkeys. 4They were not far from the city when Joseph said to the servant in charge of his house, "Go after the men. When you catch up with them, say, 'Why have you paid back evil for good? 5The cup you have stolen is the one my master uses for drinking and for explaining dreams. You have done a very wicked thing!' "

6So the servant caught up with the brothers and said to them what Joseph had told him to say.

7But the brothers said to the servant, "Why do you say these things? We would not do anything like that! 8We brought back to you from the land of Canaan the money we found in our sacks. So surely we would not steal silver or gold from your master's house. 9If you find that silver cup in the sack of one of us, then let him die, and we will be your slaves."

10The servant said, "We will do as you say, but only the man who has taken the cup will become my slave. The rest of you may go free."

11Then every brother quickly lowered his sack to the ground and opened it. 12The servant searched the sacks, going from the oldest brother to the youngest, and found the cup in Benjamin's sack. 13The brothers tore their clothes to show they were afraid. Then they put their sacks back on the donkeys and returned to the city.

14When Judah and his brothers went back to Joseph's house, Joseph was still there, so the brothers bowed facedown on the ground before him. 15Joseph said to them, "What have you done? Didn't you know that a man like me can learn things by signs and dreams?"

16Judah said, "Master, what can we say? And how can we show we are not guilty? God has uncovered our guilt, so all of us will be your slaves, not just Benjamin."

17But Joseph said, "I will not make you all slaves! Only the man who stole the cup will be my slave. The rest of you may go back safely to your father."

18Then Judah went to Joseph and said, "Master, please let me speak plainly to you, and please don't be angry with me. I know that you are as powerful as the king of Egypt himself. 19When we were here before, you asked us, 'Do you have a father or a brother?' 20And we answered you, 'We have an old father. And we have a younger brother, who was born when

our father was old. This youngest son's brother
is dead, so he is the only one of his mother's
children left alive, and our father loves him
very much.' 21Then you said to us, 'Bring that
brother to me. I want to see him.' 22And we
said to you, 'That young boy cannot leave his
father, because if he leaves him, his father
would die.' 23But you said to us, 'If you don't
bring your youngest brother, you will not be
allowed to see me again.' 24So we went back to
our father and told him what you had said.

25"Later, our father said, 'Go again and buy
us a little more food.' 26We said to our father,
'We cannot go without our youngest brother.
Without our youngest brother, we will not be
allowed to see the governor.' 27Then my father
said to us, 'You know that my wife Rachel gave
me two sons. 28When one son left me, I
thought, "Surely he has been torn apart by a
wild animal," and I haven't seen him since.
29Now you want to take this son away from
me also. But something terrible might happen
to him, and I would be miserable until the day
I die.' 30Now what will happen if we go home
to our father without our youngest brother?
He is so important in our father's life that
31when our father sees the young boy is not
with us, he will die. And it will be our fault. We
will cause the great sorrow that kills our father.

32"I gave my father a guarantee that the
young boy would be safe. I said to my father,
'If I don't bring him back to you, you can
blame me all my life.' 33So now, please allow
me to stay here and be your slave, and let the
young boy go back home with his brothers. 34I
cannot go back to my father if the boy is not
with me. I couldn't stand to see my father that
sad."

JOSEPH REVEALS WHO HE IS

45
1Joseph could not control himself in front
of his servants any longer, so he cried out,
"Have everyone leave me." When only the
brothers were left with Joseph, he told them
who he was. 2Joseph cried so loudly that the
Egyptians heard him, and the people in the
king's palace heard about it. 3He said to his
brothers, "I am Joseph. Is my father still alive?"
But the brothers could not answer him, because they were very afraid of him.

4So Joseph said to them, "Come close to me."
When the brothers came close to him, he said
to them, "I am your brother Joseph, whom you
sold as a slave to go to Egypt. 5Now don't be
worried or angry with yourselves because you
sold me here. God sent me here ahead of you
to save people's lives. 6No food has grown on
the land for two years now, and there will be
five more years without planting or harvest.
7So God sent me here ahead of you to make
sure you have some descendants left on earth
and to keep you alive in an amazing way. 8So it
was not you who sent me here, but God. God
has made me the highest officer of the king of
Egypt. I am in charge of his palace, and I am
the master of all the land of Egypt.

9"So leave quickly and go to my father. Tell
him, 'Your son Joseph says: God has made me
master over all Egypt. Come down to me
quickly. 10Live in the land of Goshen where
you will be near me. Your children, your
grandchildren, your flocks and herds, and all
that you have will also be near me. 11I will care
for you during the next five years of hunger so
that you and your family and all that you have
will not starve.'

12"Now you can see for yourselves, and so
can my brother Benjamin, that the one speaking to you is really Joseph. 13So tell my father
about how powerful I have become in Egypt.
Tell him about everything you have seen. Now
hurry and bring him back to me." 14Then Joseph hugged his brother Benjamin and cried,
and Benjamin cried also. 15And Joseph kissed
all his brothers and cried as he hugged them.
After this, his brothers talked with him.

16When the king of Egypt and his officers
learned that Joseph's brothers had come, they
were very happy. 17So the king said to Joseph,
"Tell your brothers to load their animals and
go back to the land of Canaan 18and bring their
father and their families back here to me. I will
give them the best land in Egypt, and they will
eat the best food we have here. 19Tell them to
take some wagons from Egypt for their children and their wives and to bring their father
back also. 20Tell them not to worry about
bringing any of their things with them, because
we will give them the best of what we have in
Egypt."

21So the sons of Israel did this. Joseph gave
them wagons as the king had ordered and
food for their trip. 22He gave each brother a
change of clothes, but he gave Benjamin five
changes of clothes and about seven and one-
half pounds of silver. 23Joseph also sent his father ten donkeys loaded with the best things
from Egypt and ten female donkeys loaded
with grain, bread, and other food for his father
on his trip back. 24Then Joseph told his brothers to go. As they were leaving, he said to them,
"Don't quarrel on the way home."

25So the brothers left Egypt and went to
their father Jacob in the land of Canaan. 26They

told him, "Joseph is still alive and is the ruler over all the land of Egypt." Their father was shocked and did not believe them. 27But when the brothers told him everything Joseph had said, and when Jacob saw the wagons Joseph had sent to carry him back to Egypt, he felt better. 28Israel[n] said, "Now I believe you. My son Joseph is still alive, and I will go and see him before I die."

JACOB GOES TO EGYPT

46 1So Israel[n] took all he had and started his trip. He went to Beersheba, where he offered sacrifices to the God of his father Isaac. 2During the night God spoke to Israel in a vision and said, "Jacob, Jacob."

And Jacob answered, "Here I am."

WHAT'S IT MEAN?

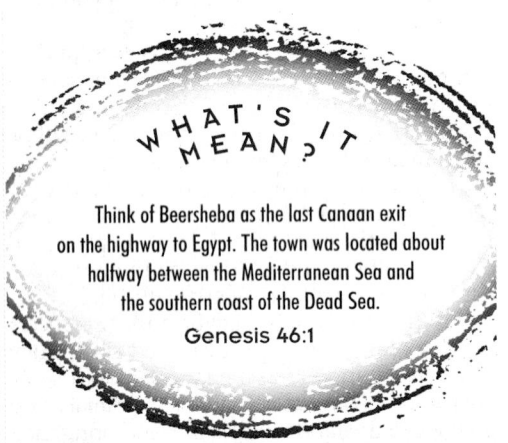

Think of Beersheba as the last Canaan exit on the highway to Egypt. The town was located about halfway between the Mediterranean Sea and the southern coast of the Dead Sea.

Genesis 46:1

3Then God said, "I am God, the God of your father. Don't be afraid to go to Egypt, because I will make your descendants a great nation there. 4I will go to Egypt with you, and I will bring you out of Egypt again. Joseph's own hands will close your eyes when you die."

5Then Jacob left Beersheba. The sons of Israel loaded their father, their children, and their wives in the wagons the king of Egypt had sent. 6They also took their farm animals and everything they had gotten in Canaan. So Jacob went to Egypt with all his descendants— 7his sons and grandsons, his daughters and granddaughters. He took all his family to Egypt with him.

JACOB'S FAMILY

8Now these are the names of the children of Israel who went into Egypt (Jacob and his descendants).

Reuben was Jacob's first son. 9Reuben's sons were Hanoch, Pallu, Hezron, and Carmi.

10Simeon's sons were Jemuel, Jamin, Ohad, Jakin, Zohar, and Shaul (Simeon's son by a Canaanite woman).

11Levi's sons were Gershon, Kohath, and Merari.

12Judah's sons were Er, Onan, Shelah, Perez, and Zerah (but Er and Onan had died in the land of Canaan). Perez's sons were Hezron and Hamul.

13Issachar's sons were Tola, Puah, Jashub, and Shimron.

14Zebulun's sons were Sered, Elon, and Jahleel.

15These are the sons of Leah and Jacob born in Northwest Mesopotamia, in addition to his daughter Dinah. There were thirty-three persons in this part of Jacob's family.

16Gad's sons were Zephon, Haggi, Shuni, Ezbon, Eri, Arodi, and Areli.

17Asher's sons were Imnah, Ishvah, Ishvi, and Beriah, and their sister was Serah. Beriah's sons were Heber and Malkiel.

18These are Jacob's sons by Zilpah, the slave girl whom Laban gave to his daughter Leah. There were sixteen persons in this part of Jacob's family.

19The sons of Jacob's wife Rachel were Joseph and Benjamin. 20In Egypt, Joseph became the father of Manasseh and Ephraim by his wife Asenath, the daughter of Potiphera, priest of On.

21Benjamin's sons were Bela, Beker, Ashbel, Gera, Naaman, Ehi, Rosh, Muppim, Huppim, and Ard.

22These are the sons of Jacob by his wife Rachel. There were fourteen persons in this part of Jacob's family.

23Dan's son was Hushim.

24Naphtali's sons were Jahziel, Guni, Jezer, and Shillem.

25These are Jacob's sons by Bilhah, the slave girl whom Laban gave to his daughter Rachel. There were seven persons in this part of Jacob's family.

26So the total number of Jacob's direct descendants who went to Egypt was sixty-six, not counting the wives of Jacob's sons. 27Joseph had two sons born in Egypt, so the total number in the family of Jacob in Egypt was seventy.

JACOB ARRIVES IN EGYPT

28Jacob sent Judah ahead of him to see Joseph in Goshen. When Jacob and his people came into the land of Goshen, 29Joseph pre-

45:28; 46:1 Israel Also called Jacob.

pared his chariot and went to meet his father Israel in Goshen. As soon as Joseph saw his father, he hugged him, and cried there for a long time.

[30]Then Israel said to Joseph, "Now I am ready to die, because I have seen your face and I know you are still alive."

[31]Joseph said to his brothers and his father's family, "I will go and tell the king you are here. I will say, 'My brothers and my father's family have left the land of Canaan and have come here to me. [32]They are shepherds and take care of farm animals, and they have brought their flocks and their herds and everything they own with them.' [33]When the king calls you, he will ask, 'What work do you do?' [34]This is what you should tell him: 'We, your servants, have taken care of farm animals all our lives. Our ancestors did the same thing.' Then the king will allow you to settle in the land of Goshen, away from the Egyptians, because they don't like to be near shepherds."

JACOB SETTLES IN GOSHEN

47 [1]Joseph went in to the king and said, "My father and my brothers have arrived from Canaan with their flocks and herds and everything they own. They are now in the land of Goshen." [2]Joseph chose five of his brothers to introduce to the king.

[3]The king said to the brothers, "What work do you do?"

And they said to him, "We, your servants, are shepherds, just as our ancestors were." [4]They said to the king, "We have come to live in this land, because there is no grass in the land of Canaan for our animals to eat, and the hunger is terrible there. So please allow us to live in the land of Goshen."

[5]Then the king said to Joseph, "Your father and your brothers have come to you, [6]and you may choose any place in Egypt for them to live. Give your father and your brothers the best land; let them live in the land of Goshen. And if any of them are skilled shepherds, put them in charge of my sheep and cattle."

[7]Then Joseph brought in his father Jacob and introduced him to the king, and Jacob blessed the king.

[8]Then the king said to Jacob, "How old are you?"

[9]Jacob said to him, "My life has been spent wandering from place to place. It has been short and filled with trouble—only one hundred thirty years. My ancestors lived much longer than I." [10]Then Jacob blessed the king and left.

[11]Joseph obeyed the king and gave his father and brothers the best land in Egypt, near the city of Rameses. [12]And Joseph gave his father, his brothers, and everyone who lived with them the food they needed.

JOSEPH BUYS LAND FOR THE KING

[13]The hunger became worse, and since there was no food anywhere in the land, Egypt and Canaan became very poor. [14]Joseph collected all the money that was to be found in Egypt and Canaan. People paid for the grain they were buying, and he brought that money to the king's palace. [15]After some time, when the people in Egypt and Canaan had no money left, they went to Joseph and said, "Please give us food. Our money is gone, and if we don't eat, we will die here in front of you."

[16]Joseph answered, "Since you have no money, give me your farm animals, and I will give you food in return." [17]So people brought their farm animals to Joseph, and he gave them food in exchange for their horses, sheep, goats, cattle, and donkeys. And he kept them alive by trading food for their farm animals that year.

[18]The next year the people came to Joseph and said, "You know we have no money left, and all our animals belong to you. We have nothing left except our bodies and our land. [19]Surely both we and our land will die here in front of you. Buy us and our land in exchange for food, and we will be slaves to the king, together with our land. Give us seed to plant so that we will live and not die, and the land will not become a desert."

[20]So Joseph bought all the land in Egypt for the king. Every Egyptian sold Joseph his field, because the hunger was very great. So the land became the king's, [21]and Joseph made the people slaves from one end of Egypt to the other. [22]The only land he did not buy was the land the priests owned. They did not need to sell their land because the king paid them for their work. So they had money to buy food.

[23]Joseph said to the people, "Now I have bought you and your land for the king, so I will give you seed and you can plant your fields. [24]At harvest time you must give one-fifth to the king. You may keep four-fifths for yourselves to use as seed for the field and as food for yourselves, your families, and your children."

[25]The people said, "You have saved our lives. If you like, we will become slaves of the king."

[26]So Joseph made a law in Egypt, which continues today: One-fifth of everything from

the land belongs to the king. The only land the
king did not get was the priests' land.

"DON'T BURY ME IN EGYPT"

27 The Israelites continued to live in the land
of Goshen in Egypt. There they got possessions
and had many children and grew in number.
28 Jacob[n] lived in Egypt seventeen years, so
he lived to be one hundred forty-seven years
old. 29 When Israel knew he soon would die, he
called his son Joseph to him and said to him,
"If you love me, put your hand under my leg.[n]
Promise me you will not bury me in Egypt.
30 When I die, carry me out of Egypt, and bury
me where my ancestors are buried."
Joseph answered, "I will do as you say."

WHAT'S IT MEAN?

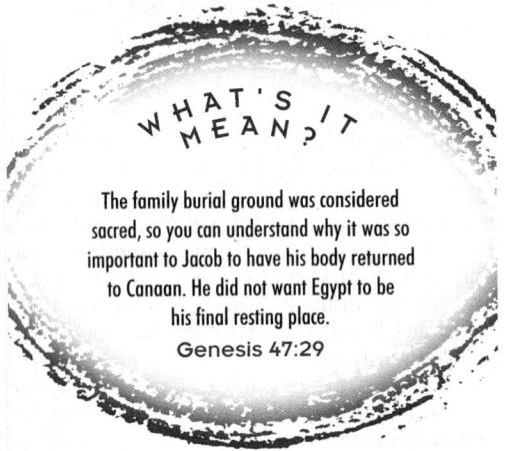

The family burial ground was considered sacred, so you can understand why it was so important to Jacob to have his body returned to Canaan. He did not want Egypt to be his final resting place.

Genesis 47:29

31 Then Jacob said, "Promise me." And Joseph
promised him that he would do this. Then Israel worshiped as he leaned on the top of his
walking stick.

BLESSINGS FOR MANASSEH AND EPHRAIM

48 1 Some time later Joseph learned that his father was very sick, so he took his two sons
Manasseh and Ephraim and went to his father.
2 When Joseph arrived, someone told Jacob,[n]
"Your son Joseph has come to see you." Jacob
was weak, so he used all his strength and sat
up on his bed.
3 Then Jacob said to Joseph, "God Almighty
appeared to me at Luz in the land of Canaan
and blessed me there. 4 He said to me, 'I will
give you many children. I will make you the
father of many peoples, and I will give your
descendants this land forever.' 5 Your two sons,
who were born here in Egypt before I came,
will be counted as my own sons. Ephraim and

WHAT'S IT MEAN?

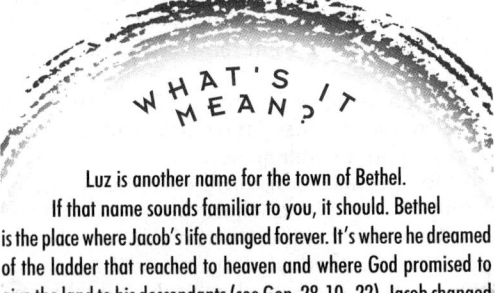

Luz is another name for the town of Bethel. If that name sounds familiar to you, it should. Bethel is the place where Jacob's life changed forever. It's where he dreamed of the ladder that reached to heaven and where God promised to give the land to his descendants (see Gen. 28:10–22). Jacob changed the name of the town from Luz to Bethel in honor of his dream. *Bethel* means "house of God."

Genesis 48:3

Manasseh will be my sons just as Reuben and
Simeon are my sons. 6 But if you have other
children, they will be your own, and their land
will be part of the land given to Ephraim and
Manasseh. 7 When I came from Northwest
Mesopotamia, Rachel died in the land of Canaan, as we were traveling toward Ephrath.
This made me very sad, and I buried her there
beside the road to Ephrath." (Today Ephrath is
Bethlehem.)
8 Then Israel saw Joseph's sons and said,
"Who are these boys?"
9 Joseph said to his father, "They are my sons
that God has given me here in Egypt."
Israel said, "Bring your sons to me so I may
bless them."
10 At this time Israel's eyesight was bad because he was old. So Joseph brought the boys
close to him, and Israel kissed the boys and put
his arms around them. 11 He said to Joseph, "I
thought I would never see you alive again, and
now God has let me see you and also your
children." 12 Then Joseph moved his sons off
Israel's lap and bowed facedown to the
ground. 13 He put Ephraim on his right side and
Manasseh on his left. (So Ephraim was near
Israel's left hand, and Manasseh was near
Israel's right hand.) Joseph brought the boys
close to Israel. 14 But Israel crossed his arms and
put his right hand on the head of Ephraim,
who was younger. He put his left hand on the
head of Manasseh, the firstborn son. 15 And Israel blessed Joseph and said,

"My ancestors Abraham and Isaac served
our God,

47:28; 48:2 Jacob Also called Israel. **47:29 put . . . leg** This showed that a person would keep a promise.

and like a shepherd God has led me all
my life.
16 He was the Angel who saved me from all
my troubles.
Now I pray that he will bless these
boys.
May my name be known through these
boys,
and may the names of my ancestors
Abraham and Isaac be known
through them.
May they have many descendants
on the earth."

17 When Joseph saw that his father put his
right hand on Ephraim's head, he didn't like it.
So he took hold of his father's hand, wanting
to move it from Ephraim's head to Manasseh's
head. 18 Joseph said to his father, "You are doing
it wrong, Father. Manasseh is the firstborn son.
Put your right hand on his head."

19 But his father refused and said, "I know,
my son, I know. Manasseh will be great and
have many descendants. But his younger
brother will be greater, and his descendants
will be enough to make a nation."

20 So Israel blessed them that day and said,
"When a blessing is given in Israel, they
will say:
'May God make you like Ephraim and
Manasseh.' "
In this way he made Ephraim greater than Manasseh.

21 Then Israel said to Joseph, "Look at me; I
am about to die. But God will be with you and
will take you back to the land of your fathers.
22 I have given you something that I did not
give your brothers—the land of Shechem that
I took from the Amorite people with my sword
and my bow."

JACOB BLESSES HIS SONS

49 1 Then Jacob called his sons to him. He said,
"Come here to me, and I will tell you what will
happen to you in the future.
2 "Come together and listen, sons of Jacob.
Listen to Israel, your father."

3 "Reuben, my first son, you are my
strength.
Your birth showed I could be a father.
You have the highest position among my
sons,
and you are the most powerful.
4 But you are uncontrolled like water,
so you will no longer lead your brothers.
This is because you got into your father's
bed
and shamed me by having sexual
relations with my slave girl.

5 "Simeon and Levi are brothers
who used their swords to do violence.
6 I will not join their secret talks,
and I will not meet with them to plan
evil.
They killed men because they were
angry,
and they crippled oxen just for fun.
7 May their anger be cursed, because it is
too violent.
May their violence be cursed, because it
is too cruel.
I will divide them up among the tribes of
Jacob
and scatter them through all the tribes
of Israel.

8 "Judah, your brothers will praise you.
You will grab your enemies by the neck,
and your brothers will bow down to
you.
9 Judah is like a young lion.
You have returned from killing, my son.
Like a lion, he stretches out and lies down
to rest,
and no one is brave enough to wake
him.
10 Kings will come from Judah's family;
someone from Judah will always be on
the throne.
Judah will rule until Shiloh comes,
and the nations will obey him.
11 He ties his donkey to a grapevine,
his young donkey to the best branch.
He can afford to use wine to wash his
clothes
and the best wine to wash his robes.
12 His eyes are dark like the color of wine,
and his teeth are as white as the color of
milk.

13 "Zebulun will live near the sea.
His shore will be a safe place for ships,
and his land will reach as far as Sidon.

14 "Issachar is like a strong donkey
who lies down while carrying his load.
15 When he sees his resting place is good
and how pleasant his land is,
he will put his back to the load
and become a slave.

16 "Dan will rule his own people
like the other tribes in Israel.

17 Dan will be like a snake by the side of the
road,
a dangerous snake lying near the path.
That snake bites a horse's leg,
and the rider is thrown off backward.

18 "LORD, I wait for your salvation.

19 "Robbers will attack Gad,
but he will defeat them and drive them
away.

20 "Asher's land will grow much good food;
he will grow food fit for a king.

21 "Naphtali is like a female deer that runs
free,
that has beautiful fawns.

22 "Joseph is like a grapevine that produces
much fruit,
a healthy vine watered by a spring,
whose branches grow over the wall.
23 Archers attack him violently
and shoot at him angrily,
24 but he aims his bow well.
His arms are made strong.
He gets his power from the Mighty God of
Jacob
and his strength from the Shepherd, the
Rock of Israel.
25 Your father's God helps you.
God Almighty blesses
you.
He blesses you with rain
from above,
with water from springs
below,
with many babies born to
your wives,
and many young ones born to your
animals.
26 The blessings of your father are greater
than the blessings of the oldest
mountains,
greater than the good things of the
long-lasting hills.
May these blessings rest on the head of
Joseph,
on the forehead of the one who was
separated from his brothers.

HELP

Who will help me? (49:25)

27 "Benjamin is like a hungry wolf.
In the morning he eats what he has
caught,
and in the evening he divides what he
has taken."

28 These are the twelve tribes of Israel, and
this is what their father said to them. He gave
each son the blessing that was right for him.
29 Then Israel gave them a command and said,
"I am about to die. Bury me with my ancestors
in the cave in the field of Ephron the Hittite.
30 That cave is in the field of Machpelah east of
Mamre in the land of Canaan. Abraham
bought the field and cave from Ephron the
Hittite for a burying place. 31 Abraham and
Sarah his wife are buried there. Isaac and Rebekah his wife are buried there, and I buried
my wife Leah there. 32 The field and the cave in
it were bought from the Hittite people." 33 After
Jacob finished talking to his sons, he lay down.
He put his feet back on the bed, took his last
breath, and died.

JACOB'S BURIAL

50
1 When Jacob died, Joseph hugged his father
and cried over him and kissed him. 2 He commanded the doctors who served him to prepare his father's body, so the doctors prepared
Jacob's body to be buried. 3 It took the doctors
forty days to prepare his body (the usual time
it took). And the Egyptians had a time of sorrow for Jacob that lasted seventy days.
4 When this time of sorrow had ended, Joseph spoke to the king's officers and said, "If
you think well of me, please tell this to the
king: 5 'When my father was near death, I made
a promise to him that I would bury him in a
cave in the land of Canaan, in a burial place
that he cut out for himself. So please let me go
and bury my father, and then I will return.' "
6 The king answered, "Keep your promise.
Go and bury your father."
7 So Joseph went to bury his father. All the

WHAT'S IT MEAN?

The Israelites had strict laws about touching dead bodies, so they rarely performed embalmings. In fact, Jacob and Joseph are the only two Old Testament people we know of who were embalmed. It may be that embalming was necessary for them because of the long journey back to Canaan that their corpses would have to endure.

Genesis 50:2

king's officers, the older leaders, and all the leading men of Egypt went with Joseph.
8Everyone who lived with Joseph and his brothers went with him, as well as everyone who lived with his father. They left only their children, their flocks, and their herds in the land of Goshen.
9They went with Joseph in chariots and on horses. It was a very large group.

10When they came to the threshing floor of Atad, near the Jordan River, they cried loudly and bitterly for his father. Joseph's time of sorrow continued for seven days.
11The people that lived in Canaan saw the sadness at the threshing floor of Atad and said, "Those Egyptians are showing great sorrow!" So now that place is named Sorrow of the Egyptians.

12So Jacob's sons did as their father commanded.
13They carried his body to the land of Canaan and buried it in the cave in the field of Machpelah near Mamre. Abraham had bought this cave and field from Ephron the Hittite to use as a burial place.
14After Joseph buried his father, he returned to Egypt, along with his brothers and everyone who had gone with him to bury his father.

THE BROTHERS FEAR JOSEPH

15After Jacob died, Joseph's brothers said, "What if Joseph is still angry with us? We did many wrong things to him. What if he plans to pay us back?"
16So they sent a message to Joseph that said, "Your father gave this command before he died.
17He said to us, 'You have done wrong and have sinned and done evil to Joseph. Tell Joseph to forgive you, his brothers.' So now, Joseph, we beg you to forgive our wrong. We are the servants of the God of your father." When Joseph received the message, he cried.

18And his brothers went to him and bowed low before him and said, "We are your slaves."

19Then Joseph said to them, "Don't be afraid. Can I do what only God can do?
20You meant to hurt me, but God turned your evil into good to save the lives of many people, which is being done.
21So don't be afraid. I will take care of you and your children." So Joseph comforted his brothers and spoke kind words to them.

22Joseph continued to live in Egypt with all his father's family. He died when he was one hundred ten years old.
23During Joseph's life Ephraim had children and grandchildren, and Joseph's son Manasseh had a son named Makir. Joseph accepted Makir's children as his own.

THE DEATH OF JOSEPH

24Joseph said to his brothers, "I am about to die, but God will take care of you. He will lead you out of this land to the land he promised to Abraham, Isaac, and Jacob."
25Then Joseph had the sons of Israel make a promise. He said, "Promise me that you will carry my bones with you out of Egypt."

26Joseph died when he was one hundred ten years old. Doctors prepared his body for burial, and then they put him in a coffin in Egypt.

exodus

CONTENT If Exodus was a movie, it would be action-adventure. You've got your miracles. You've got your spectacular events. You've got your special effects. You've got plenty of extras standing around with their mouths hanging open at the amazing things God does. And it's all true!

The bad guys in this scenario are the Egyptians, particularly the king, who (for longer than you would imagine) would *not* let those Hebrew people go, no matter what God did through Moses.

The good guys—well, the favored guys—are the Hebrews, led by Moses. After being enslaved by the Egyptians for generations, they were freed only to wander around in a desert, no—a *wilderness*. After reading about their travels, you may not be surprised that they sometimes wished for the comforts of captivity.

All through this adventure God does amazing things—more amazing than anything you've seen in a theater. Seas split in two. Food falls like dew. Boulders sprout fountains. The glory of God's presence becomes visible. Moses' face actually GLOWS.

So buckle your seat belts and prepare for a ride of a read.

Outline

1:1–22 .... The People of Israel Become Slaves
2:1–25 .... Moses Is Born and Grows Up
3:1—7:13 .... God Sends Moses to Speak to the Egyptian King
7:14—10:29 .... The First Nine Miracles
11:1—13:22 .... The Last Miracle and the First Passover
14:1—15:21 .... The People Cross the Sea
15:22—18:27 ...... Moses Leads the People to the Mountain of God
19:1—24:18 .... The Ten Commandments and Other Laws
25:1—27:21 .... Instructions for the Ark of the Agreement, the Holy Tent, and Its Furnishings
28:1—31:18 .... Instructions for the Priests, Sacrifices, and the Day of Rest
32:1-35 .... The People Make a Gold Calf
33:1—35:3.......... The Lord Makes Promises, Renews His Agreement, and Gives More Laws to Israel
35:4—36:7.......... Offerings and Gifts for the Holy Tent and the Priestly Clothes
36:8—38:31 .... Skilled Workers Make the Holy Tent and Its Furnishings
39:1-31 .... The Priestly Clothes Are Made
39:32—40:38 ...... The Holy Tent Is Set Up

Purpose God breaks our chains, then draws us to himself by teaching us wise ways and worship.

Theme Deliverance

Date of writing 1445–1440 B.C.

" 'So now if you obey me and keep my agreement, you will be my own possession, chosen from all nations. Even though the whole earth is mine, you will be my kingdom of priests and a holy nation.' You must tell the Israelites these words" (19:5–6).

Bible Talk

Passover

Have you heard of a Passover meal? It's a meal of very specific foods prepared a very specific way and eaten in a very specific order. When people eat a Passover meal, they are actually remembering the last miracle the Egyptians experienced because the king would not let the Hebrews leave.

On that last night, the Lord passed through Egypt and the oldest son of each household died as he passed . . . unless the family had spread the blood of a lamb on their doorframe. If the blood was on the doorframe, then the Lord *passed over* that home and the firstborn lived.

The Passover was a picture for the Hebrews, and anyone else watching, of what Jesus would do one day for all of us. He would spill his blood on a wooden cross to save us from certain death.

THE TEN COMMANDMENTS

Did you know that the first time the Ten Commandments were written, they were written by God himself? Did you know they had to be rewritten? Do you know why?

After Moses spent time up on Mt. Sinai with God, he came down the mountain carrying the stone tablets that God himself had written on. But when Moses saw that in his absence the people had *already* started worshiping idols, he basically pitched a fit. He threw down and broke the tablets that God had made and that God had written on.

It's amazing to think Moses would have done that, isn't it? There's no telling how many important things are lost when good men pitch fits.

JACOB'S FAMILY GROWS STRONG

1
1When Jacob[n] went to Egypt, he took his
sons, and each son took his own family with
him. These are the names of the sons of Israel:
2Reuben, Simeon, Levi, Judah, 3Issachar, Zebulun, Benjamin, 4Dan, Naphtali, Gad, and Asher.
5There was a total of seventy people who were
descendants of Jacob. Jacob's son Joseph was
already in Egypt.

WHAT'S IT MEAN?

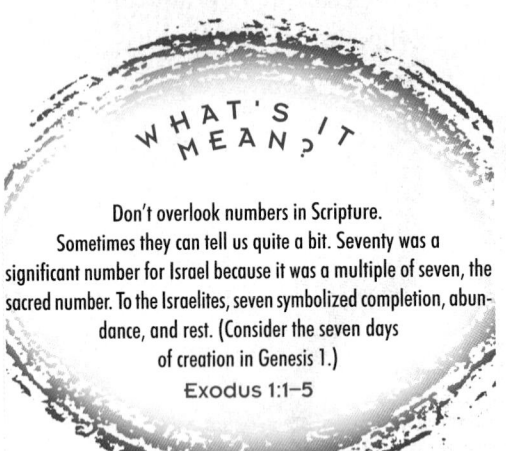

Don't overlook numbers in Scripture. Sometimes they can tell us quite a bit. Seventy was a significant number for Israel because it was a multiple of seven, the sacred number. To the Israelites, seven symbolized completion, abundance, and rest. (Consider the seven days of creation in Genesis 1.)

Exodus 1:1–5

6Some time later, Joseph and his brothers
died, along with all the people who had lived
at that same time. 7But the people of Israel had
many children, and their number grew greatly.
They became very strong, and the country of
Egypt was filled with them.

WHAT'S IT MEAN?

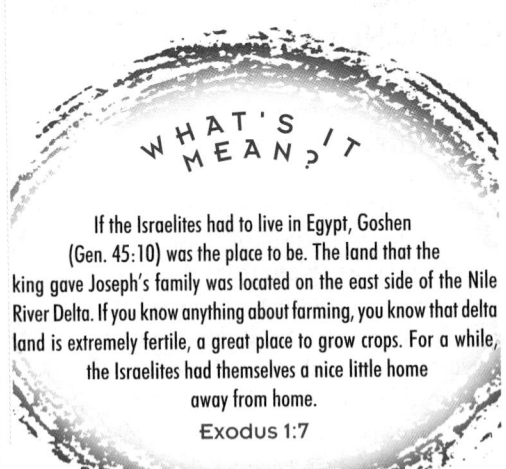

If the Israelites had to live in Egypt, Goshen (Gen. 45:10) was the place to be. The land that the king gave Joseph's family was located on the east side of the Nile River Delta. If you know anything about farming, you know that delta land is extremely fertile, a great place to grow crops. For a while, the Israelites had themselves a nice little home away from home.

Exodus 1:7

TROUBLE FOR THE PEOPLE OF ISRAEL

8Then a new king began to rule Egypt, who
did not know who Joseph was. 9This king said
to his people, "Look! The people of Israel are
too many and too strong for us to handle! 10If
we don't make plans against them, the number
of their people will grow even more. Then if
there is a war, they might join our enemies and
fight us and escape from the country!"
11So the Egyptians made life hard for the
Israelites. They put slave masters over them,
who forced the Israelites to build the cities Pi-
thom and Rameses as supply centers for the
king. 12But the harder the Egyptians forced the
Israelites to work, the more the Israelites grew
in number and spread out. So the Egyptians
became very afraid of them 13and demanded
even more of them. 14They made their lives
bitter. They forced the Israelites to work hard
to make bricks and mortar and to do all kinds
of work in the fields. The Egyptians were not
merciful to them in all their painful work.
15Two Hebrew nurses, named Shiphrah and
Puah, helped the Israelite women give birth to
their babies. The king of Egypt said to the
nurses, 16"When you are helping the Hebrew
women give birth to their babies, watch! If the
baby is a girl, let her live, but if it is a boy, kill
him!" 17But the nurses feared God, so they did
not do as the king told them; they let all the
boy babies live. 18Then the king of Egypt sent
for the nurses and said, "Why did you do this?
Why did you let the boys live?"
19The nurses said to him, "The Hebrew
women are much stronger than the Egyptian
women. They give birth to their babies before
we can get there." 20God was good to the
nurses. And the Hebrew people continued to
grow in number, so they became even stronger.
21Because the nurses feared God, he gave them
families of their own.
22So the king commanded all his people,
"Every time a boy is born to the Hebrews, you
must throw him into the Nile River, but let all
the girl babies live."

BABY MOSES

2
1Now a man from the family of Levi married a woman who was also from the family of
Levi. 2She became pregnant and gave birth to a
son. When she saw how wonderful the baby
was, she hid him for three months. 3But after
three months she was not able to hide the
baby any longer, so she got a basket made of
reeds and covered it with tar so that it would

1:1 Jacob Also called Israel.

float. She put the baby in the basket. Then she put the basket among the tall stalks of grass at the edge of the Nile River. 4The baby's sister stood a short distance away to see what would happen to him.

5Then the daughter of the king of Egypt came to the river to take a bath, and her servant girls were walking beside the river. When she saw the basket in the tall grass, she sent her slave girl to get it. 6The king's daughter opened the basket and saw the baby boy. He was crying, so she felt sorry for him and said, "This is one of the Hebrew babies."

7Then the baby's sister asked the king's daughter, "Would you like me to go and find a Hebrew woman to nurse the baby for you?"

8The king's daughter said, "Go!" So the girl went and got the baby's own mother.

9The king's daughter said to the woman, "Take this baby and nurse him for me, and I will pay you." So the woman took her baby and nursed him. 10When the child grew older, the woman took him to the king's daughter, and she adopted the baby as her own son. The king's daughter named him Moses,[n] because she had pulled him out of the water.

MOSES TRIES TO HELP

11Moses grew and became a man. One day he visited his people and saw that they were forced to work very hard. He saw an Egyptian beating a Hebrew man, one of Moses' own people. 12Moses looked all around and saw that no one was watching, so he killed the Egyptian and hid his body in the sand.

13The next day Moses returned and saw two Hebrew men fighting each other. He said to the one that was in the wrong, "Why are you hitting one of your own people?"

14The man answered, "Who made you our ruler and judge? Are you going to kill me as you killed the Egyptian?"

Moses was afraid and thought, "Now everyone knows what I did."

15When the king heard what Moses had done, he tried to kill him. But Moses ran away from the king and went to live in the land of Midian. There he sat down near a well.

MOSES IN MIDIAN

16There was a priest in Midian who had seven daughters. His daughters went to that well to get water to fill the water troughs for their father's flock. 17Some shepherds came and chased the girls away, but Moses defended the girls and watered their flock.

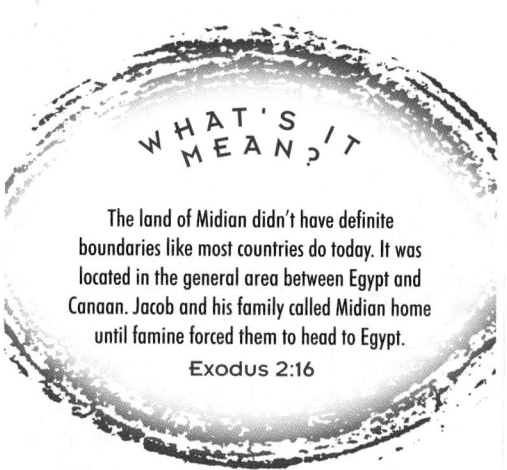

WHAT'S IT MEAN?

The land of Midian didn't have definite boundaries like most countries do today. It was located in the general area between Egypt and Canaan. Jacob and his family called Midian home until famine forced them to head to Egypt.

Exodus 2:16

18When they went back to their father Reuel,[n] he asked them, "Why have you come home early today?"

19The girls answered, "The shepherds chased us away, but an Egyptian defended us. He got water for us and watered our flock."

20He asked his daughters, "Where is this man? Why did you leave him? Invite him to eat with us."

21Moses agreed to stay with Jethro, and he gave his daughter Zipporah to Moses to be his wife. 22Zipporah gave birth to a son. Moses named him Gershom,[n] because Moses was a stranger in a land that was not his own.

"God heard their cries, and he remembered the agreement he had made with Abraham, Isaac, and Jacob. He saw the troubles of the people of Israel, and he was concerned about them." (Exodus 2:24–25)

23After a long time, the king of Egypt died. The people of Israel groaned, because they were forced to work very hard. When they cried for help, God heard them. 24God heard their cries, and he remembered the agreement

2:10 Moses The name "Moses" sounds like the Hebrew word for "to pull out." **2:18 Reuel** He was also called Jethro. **2:22 Gershom** This name sounds like the Hebrew word meaning "a stranger there."

he had made with Abraham, Isaac, and Jacob.
25 He saw the troubles of the people of Israel,
and he was concerned about them.

THE BURNING BUSH

3 1 One day Moses was taking care of Jethro's
flock. (Jethro was the priest of Midian and also
Moses' father-in-law.) When Moses led the
flock to the west side of the desert, he came to
Sinai, the mountain of God. 2 There the angel
of the LORD appeared to him in flames of fire
coming out of a bush. Moses saw that the
bush was on fire, but it was not burning up.
3 So he said, "I will go closer to this strange
thing. How can a bush continue burning without burning up?"
4 When the LORD saw Moses was coming to
look at the bush, God called to him from the
bush, "Moses, Moses!"
And Moses said, "Here I am."
5 Then God said, "Do not
come any closer. Take off your
sandals, because you are
standing on holy ground. 6 I
am the God of your ancestors—the God of Abraham,
the God of Isaac, and the God of
Jacob." Moses covered his face because he was
afraid to look at God.

RESPECT

Is God worthy of our respect? (3:5)

WHAT'S IT MEAN?

Sinai, the mountain of God, is in the peninsula of Sinai, which sits between Egypt and Arabia and is shaped like a triangle. Sinai Peninsula stretches from the Mediterranean Sea on the north to the Red Sea on the south. It is a dry, barren place, covered mostly by desert and mountains.

Exodus 3:1

7 The LORD said, "I have
seen the troubles my people
have suffered in Egypt, and I
have heard their cries when
the Egyptian slave masters
hurt them. I am concerned
about their pain, 8 and I have
come down to save them from the Egyptians. I
will bring them out of that land and lead them
to a good land with lots of room—a fertile

WORSHIP

Does worship include awe of God? (3:5–6)

Promise HE PROMISES TO SAVE HIS PEOPLE FROM EGYPT.

And I have come down to save them from the Egyptians. I will bring them out of that land and lead them to a good land with lots of room—a fertile land (Ex. 3:8).

The people of Israel had been saved from Egypt and had wandered in the desert for 40 years before entering the land God had promised them.

But you know what? Year number 41 came, and they didn't wander anymore. They left the desert and entered into the fertile land! Maybe it seems that you are in a desert period in your life. Maybe you feel like you've been stumbling around for 40 years. Don't worry, number 41 is on its way!

Look at these examples: Noah and his family were on the boat while it rained for 40 days and 40 nights—41 came, and the rain stopped. For 40 days Goliath showed up every morning and taunted Israel—41 came, and David killed him!

God has promised to bring you out of your Egypt as well—if you will hold on to your faith in him. Whatever situation you are going through right now, don't give up. God is on your side! So if it seems like trouble has been raining down on you, don't worry because 41 is on the way. The rain is going to stop. Whatever giant is in your life, 41 is coming and that giant's coming down! You are more than a victor through Christ Jesus (see Rom. 8:37). He will save you from your Egypt.

SEE FOR YOURSELF:

Gen. 7; 8; 1 Sam. 17; Ps. 34:17, 19

land. It is the land of the Canaanites, Hittites, Amorites, Perizzites, Hivites, and Jebusites. 9I have heard the cries of the people of Israel, and I have seen the way the Egyptians have made life hard for them. 10So now I am sending you to the king of Egypt. Go! Bring my people, the Israelites, out of Egypt!"

11But Moses said to God, "I am not a great man! How can I go to the king and lead the Israelites out of Egypt?"

12God said, "I will be with you. This will be the proof that I am sending you: After you lead the people out of Egypt, all of you will worship me on this mountain."

13Moses said to God, "When I go to the Israelites, I will say to them, 'The God of your fathers sent me to you.' What if the people say, 'What is his name?' What should I tell them?"

14Then God said to Moses, "I AM WHO I AM.[n] When you go to the people of Israel, tell them, 'I AM sent me to you.' "

15God also said to Moses, "This is what you should tell the people: 'The LORD is the God of your ancestors—the God of Abraham, the God of Isaac, and the God of Jacob. He sent me to you.' This will always be my name, by which people from now on will know me.

16"Go and gather the older leaders and tell them this: 'The LORD, the God of your ancestors Abraham, Isaac, and Jacob, has appeared to me. He said, I care about you, and I have seen what has happened to you in Egypt. 17I promised I would take you out of your troubles in Egypt. I will lead you to the land of the Canaanites, Hittites, Amorites, Perizzites, Hivites, and Jebusites—a fertile land.'

18"The older leaders will listen to you. And then you and the older leaders of Israel will go to the king of Egypt and tell him, 'The LORD, the God of the Hebrews, appeared to us. Let us travel three days into the desert to offer sacrifices to the LORD our God.'

19"But I know that the king of Egypt will not let you go. Only a great power will force him to let you go, 20so I will use my great power against Egypt. I will strike Egypt with all the miracles that will happen in that land. After I do that, he will let you go. 21I will cause the Egyptians to think well of the Israelites. So when you leave, they will give gifts to your people. 22Each woman should ask her Egyptian neighbor and any Egyptian woman living in her house for gifts—silver, gold, and clothing. You should put those gifts on your children when you leave Egypt. In this way you will take with you the riches of the Egyptians."

PROOF FOR MOSES

4 1Then Moses answered, "What if the people of Israel do not believe me or listen to me? What if they say, 'The LORD did not appear to you'?"

2The LORD said to him, "What is that in your hand?"

Moses answered, "It is my walking stick."

3The LORD said, "Throw it on the ground."

So Moses threw it on the ground, and it became a snake. Moses ran from the snake, 4but the LORD said to him, "Reach out and grab the snake by its tail." When Moses reached out and took hold of the snake, it again became a stick in his hand. 5The LORD said, "This is so that the Israelites will believe that the LORD appeared to you. I am the God of their ancestors, the God of Abraham, the God of Isaac, and the God of Jacob."

6Then the LORD said to Moses, "Put your hand inside your coat." So Moses put his hand inside his coat. When he took it out, it was white with a skin disease.

7Then he said, "Now put your hand inside your coat again." So Moses put his hand inside his coat again. When he took it out, his hand was healthy again, like the rest of his skin.

8Then the LORD said, "If the people do not believe you or pay attention to the first miracle, they may believe you when you show them this second miracle. 9After these two miracles, if

WHAT'S IT MEAN?

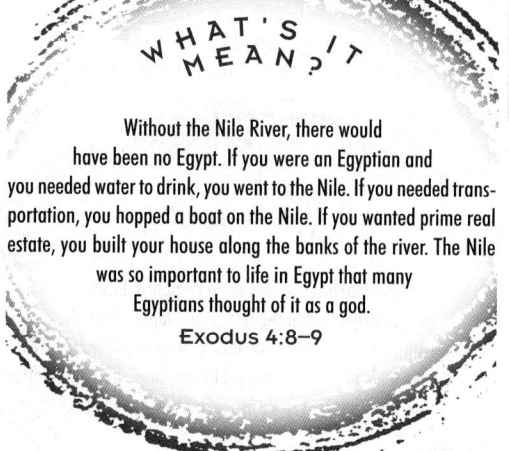

Without the Nile River, there would have been no Egypt. If you were an Egyptian and you needed water to drink, you went to the Nile. If you needed transportation, you hopped a boat on the Nile. If you wanted prime real estate, you built your house along the banks of the river. The Nile was so important to life in Egypt that many Egyptians thought of it as a god.

Exodus 4:8–9

3:14 I . . . I AM The Hebrew words are like the name "Yahweh." This Hebrew name for God, usually called "LORD," shows that God always lives and is always with his people.

they still do not believe or listen to you, take
some water from the Nile River and pour it on
the dry ground. The water will become blood
when it touches the ground."
10But Moses said to the LORD, "Please, Lord, I
have never been a skilled speaker. Even now,
after talking to you, I cannot speak well. I speak
slowly and can't find the best words."
11Then the LORD said to him, "Who made a
person's mouth? And who makes someone
deaf or not able to speak? Or who gives a person sight or blindness? It is I, the LORD. 12Now
go! I will help you speak, and I will teach you
what to say."
13But Moses said, "Please, Lord, send someone else."
14The LORD became angry with Moses and
said, "Your brother Aaron, from the family of
Levi, is a skilled speaker. He is already coming
to meet you, and he will be happy when he
sees you. 15You will speak to Aaron and tell
him what to say. I will help both of you to
speak and will teach you what to do. 16Aaron
will speak to the people for you. You will tell
him what God says, and he will speak for you.
17Take your walking stick with you, and use it
to do the miracles."

MOSES RETURNS TO EGYPT

18Moses went back to Jethro, his father-in-
law, and said to him, "Let me go back to my
people in Egypt. I want to see if they are still
alive."
Jethro said to Moses, "Go! I wish you well."
19While Moses was still in Midian, the LORD
said to him, "Go back to Egypt, because the
men who wanted to kill you are dead now."
20So Moses took his wife and his sons, put
them on a donkey, and started back to Egypt.
He took with him the walking stick of God.

WHAT'S IT MEAN?

The firstborn son had extra responsibilities and privileges. When the father of a family died, the firstborn son was responsible for taking care of the family. When it came time to divide up the family's inheritance, though, the first-born son received twice as much as everyone else.

Exodus 4:22

21The LORD said to Moses, "When you get
back to Egypt, do all the miracles I have given
you the power to do. Show them to the king of
Egypt. But I will make the king very stubborn,
and he will not let the people go. 22Then say to
the king, 'This is what the LORD says: Israel is
my firstborn son. 23I told you to let my son go
so he may worship me. But you refused to let
Israel go, so I will kill your firstborn son.' "
24As Moses was on his way to Egypt, he
stopped at a resting place for the night. The
LORD met him there and tried to kill him. 25But
Zipporah took a flint knife and circumcised her
son. Taking the skin, she touched Moses' feet
with it and said to him, "You are a bridegroom
of blood to me." 26She said, "You are a bridegroom of blood," because she had to circumcise her son. So the LORD let Moses alone.
27Meanwhile the LORD said to Aaron, "Go
out into the desert to meet Moses." When
Aaron went, he met Moses at Sinai, the mountain of God, and kissed him. 28Moses told
Aaron everything the LORD had said to him
when he sent him to Egypt. He also told him
about the miracles which the LORD had commanded him to do.

WHAT'S IT MEAN?

When friends or family members hadn't seen each other for a day or so, it was common for them to kiss when they met. It was also a common gesture for when two acquaintances said good-bye. Rarely is romantic kissing mentioned in the Bible.

Exodus 4:27

29Moses and Aaron gathered all the older
leaders of the Israelites, 30and Aaron told them
everything that the LORD had told Moses. Then
Moses did the miracles for all the people to see,
31and the Israelites believed. When they heard
that the LORD was concerned about them and
had seen their troubles, they bowed down and
worshiped him.

MOSES AND AARON BEFORE THE KING

5 1After Moses and Aaron talked to the people, they went to the king of Egypt and said,
"This is what the LORD, the God of Israel, says:

'Let my people go so they may hold a feast for
me in the desert.' "
[2]But the king of Egypt said, "Who is the
LORD? Why should I obey him and let Israel
go? I do not know the LORD, and I will not let
Israel go."
[3]Then Aaron and Moses said, "The God of
the Hebrews has met with us. Now let us travel
three days into the desert to offer sacrifices to
the LORD our God. If we don't do this, he may
kill us with a disease or in war."
[4]But the king said to them, "Moses and
Aaron, why are you taking the people away
from their work? Go back to your jobs! [5]There
are very many Hebrews, and now you want
them to quit working!"
[6]That same day the king gave a command
to the slave masters and foremen. [7]He said,
"Don't give the people straw to make bricks as
you used to do. Let them gather their own
straw. [8]But they must still make the same number of bricks as they did before. Do not accept
fewer. They have become lazy, and that is why
they are asking me, 'Let us go to offer sacrifices
to our God.' [9]Make these people work harder
and keep them busy; then they will not have
time to listen to the lies of Moses."

WHAT'S IT MEAN?

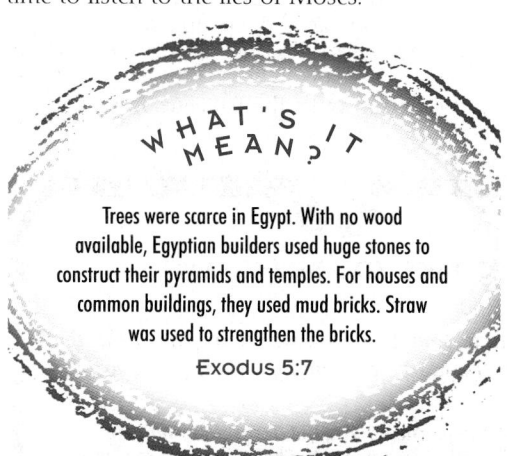

Trees were scarce in Egypt. With no wood available, Egyptian builders used huge stones to construct their pyramids and temples. For houses and common buildings, they used mud bricks. Straw was used to strengthen the bricks.

Exodus 5:7

[10]So the slave masters and foremen went to
the Israelites and said, "This is what the king
says: I will no longer give you straw. [11]Go and
get your own straw wherever you can find it.
But you must make as many bricks as you
made before." [12]So the people went everywhere
in Egypt looking for dry stalks to use for straw.
[13]The slave masters kept forcing the people to
work harder. They said, "You must make just as
many bricks as you did when you were given
straw." [14]The king's slave masters had made the
Israelite foremen responsible for the work the
people did. The Egyptian slave masters beat
these men and asked them, "Why aren't you
making as many bricks as you made in the
past?"
[15]Then the Israelite foremen went to the
king and complained, "Why are you treating
us, your servants, this way? [16]You give us no
straw, but we are commanded to make bricks.
Our slave masters beat us, but it is your own
people's fault."
[17]The king answered, "You are lazy! You
don't want to work! That is why you ask to
leave here and make sacrifices to the LORD.
[18]Now, go back to work! We will not give you
any straw, but you must make just as many
bricks as you did before."
[19]The Israelite foremen knew they were in
trouble, because the king had told them, "You
must make just as many bricks each day as you
did before." [20]As they were leaving the meeting
with the king, they met Moses and Aaron, who
were waiting for them. [21]So they said to Moses
and Aaron, "May the LORD punish you. You
caused the king and his officers to hate us. You
have given them an excuse to kill us."

MOSES COMPLAINS TO GOD

[22]Then Moses returned to the LORD and
said, "Lord, why have you brought this trouble
on your people? Is this why you sent me here?
[23]I went to the king and said what you told me
to say, but ever since that time he has made the
people suffer. And you have done nothing to
save them."
6 [1]Then the LORD said to Moses, "Now you
will see what I will do to the king of Egypt. I will
use my great power against him, and he will let
my people go. Because of my power, he will
force them out of his country."
[2]Then God said to Moses, "I am the LORD. [3]I
appeared to Abraham, Isaac, and Jacob by the
name God Almighty, but they did not know
me by my name, the LORD. [4]I also made my
agreement with them to give them the land of
Canaan. They lived in that land, but it was not
their own. [5]Now I have heard the cries of the
Israelites, whom the Egyptians are treating as
slaves, and I remember my agreement. [6]So tell
the people of Israel that I say to them, 'I am the
LORD. I will save you from the hard work the
Egyptians force you to do. I will make you free,
so you will not be slaves to the Egyptians. I
will free you by my great power, and I will
punish the Egyptians terribly. [7]I will make you
my own people, and I will be your God. You
will know that I am the LORD your God, the
One who saves you from the hard work the
Egyptians force you to do. [8]I will lead you to

the land that I promised to Abraham, Isaac,
and Jacob, and I will give you that land to
own. I am the LORD.' "
9So Moses told this to the Israelites, but they
would not listen to him. They were discouraged, and their slavery was hard.
10Then the LORD said to Moses, 11"Go tell the
king of Egypt that he must let the Israelites
leave his land."
12But Moses answered, "The Israelites will
not listen to me, so surely the king will not
listen to me either. I am not a good speaker."
13But the LORD spoke to Moses and Aaron
and gave them orders about the Israelites and
the king of Egypt. He commanded them to lead
the Israelites out of Egypt.

FAMILIES OF ISRAEL

14These are the leaders of the families of
Israel:

Israel's first son, Reuben, had four sons: Hanoch, Pallu, Hezron, and Carmi. These are the
family groups of Reuben.
15Simeon's sons were Jemuel, Jamin, Ohad,
Jakin, Zohar, and Shaul, the son of a Canaanite
woman. These are the family groups of Simeon.
16Levi lived one hundred thirty-seven years.
These are the names of his sons according to
their family history: Gershon, Kohath, and
Merari.
17Gershon had two sons, Libni and Shimei,
with their families.
18Kohath lived one hundred thirty-three
years. The sons of Kohath were Amram, Izhar,
Hebron, and Uzziel.
19The sons of Merari were Mahli and Mushi.
These are the family groups of Levi, according to their family history.
20Amram married his father's sister Jochebed, who gave birth to Aaron and Moses.
Amram lived one hundred thirty-seven years.
21Izhar's sons were Korah, Nepheg, and
Zicri.
22Uzziel's sons were Mishael, Elzaphan, and
Sithri.
23Aaron married Elisheba, the daughter of
Amminadab and the sister of Nahshon. Elisheba gave birth to Nadab, Abihu, Eleazar, and
Ithamar.
24The sons of Korah were Assir, Elkanah,
and Abiasaph. These are the family groups of
the Korahites.
25Eleazar son of Aaron married a daughter
of Putiel, and she gave birth to Phinehas.
These are the leaders of the family groups of
the Levites.
26This was the Aaron and Moses to whom
the LORD said, "Lead the people of Israel out of
Egypt by their divisions." 27Aaron and Moses
are the ones who talked to the king of Egypt
and told him to let the Israelites leave Egypt.

Promise HE PROMISES TO TAKE YOU AS HIS OWN.

I will make you my own people, and I will be your God. You will know that I am the LORD your God, the One who saves you from the hard work the Egyptians force you to do (Ex. 6:7).

In many ways, Israel's history is a symbol of the journey that all of Jesus' followers are making. That's one reason the Old Testament is still so important to Christians. You can look in the Old Testament to find wisdom for whatever you're going through and to find out what's coming next.

When God said, "I will make you my own people," he wasn't just talking to the Israelites. He was also looking out through time and speaking to Christians today. He knew you would be on earth at this moment, and he wanted to be sure you knew that he accepted you as his own. The people of Israel was God's own because of the faith and obedience of their father, Abraham. Today, you are a chosen person because of the love and obedience of Jesus.

Belonging to God makes you worth something. Your brains, your talent, your awesome sports ability—none of it impresses God. Even without all the cool things about you, you'd be worth something because God accepts you as his own.

SEE FOR YOURSELF:

Deut. 7:16; 14:2; Ps. 33:12; 1 Pet. 2:9

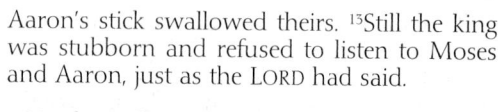

GOD REPEATS HIS CALL TO MOSES

28The LORD spoke to Moses in the land of Egypt 29and said, "I am the LORD. Tell the king of Egypt everything I tell you."

30But Moses answered, "I am not a good speaker. The king will not listen to me."

7 1The LORD said to Moses, "I have made you like God to the king of Egypt, and your brother Aaron will be like a prophet for you. 2Tell Aaron your brother everything that I command you, and let him tell the king of Egypt to let the Israelites leave his country. 3But I will make the king stubborn. I will do many miracles in Egypt, 4but he will still refuse to listen. So then I will punish Egypt terribly, and I will lead my divisions, my people the Israelites, out of that land. 5I will punish Egypt with my power, and I will bring the Israelites out of that land. Then they will know I am the LORD."

6Moses and Aaron did just as the LORD had commanded them. 7Moses was eighty years old and Aaron was eighty-three when they spoke to the king.

AARON'S WALKING STICK BECOMES A SNAKE

8The LORD said to Moses and Aaron, 9"Moses, when the king asks you to do a miracle, tell Aaron to throw his walking stick down in front of the king, and it will become a snake."

10So Moses and Aaron went to the king as the LORD had commanded. Aaron threw his walking stick down in front of the king and his officers, and it became a snake.

11So the king called in his wise men and his magicians, and with their tricks the Egyptian magicians were able to do the same thing. 12They threw their walking sticks on the ground, and their sticks became snakes. But Aaron's stick swallowed theirs. 13Still the king was stubborn and refused to listen to Moses and Aaron, just as the LORD had said.

WHAT'S IT MEAN?

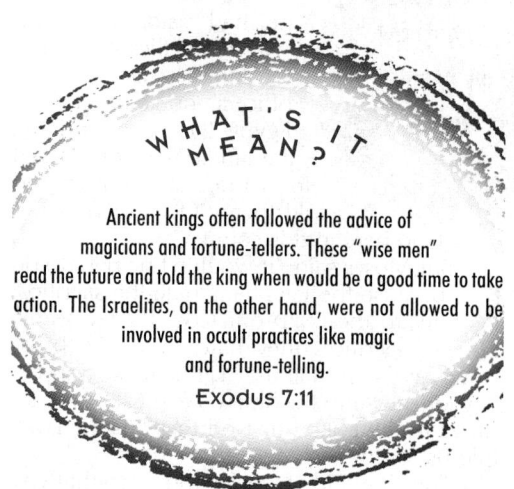

Ancient kings often followed the advice of magicians and fortune-tellers. These "wise men" read the future and told the king when would be a good time to take action. The Israelites, on the other hand, were not allowed to be involved in occult practices like magic and fortune-telling.

Exodus 7:11

THE WATER BECOMES BLOOD

14Then the LORD said to Moses, "The king is being stubborn and refuses to let the people go. 15In the morning the king will go out to the Nile River. Go meet him by the edge of the river, and take with you the walking stick that became a snake. 16Tell him: The LORD, the God of the Hebrews, sent me to you. He said, 'Let my people go worship me in the desert.' Until now you have not listened. 17This is what the LORD says: 'This is how you will know that I am the LORD. I will strike the water of the Nile River with this stick in my hand, and the water will change into blood. 18Then the fish in the Nile will die, and the river will begin to stink. The Egyptians will not be able to drink the water from the Nile.' "

19The LORD said to Moses, "Tell Aaron: 'Take the walking stick in your hand and stretch your hand over the rivers, canals, ponds, and pools in Egypt.' The water will become blood everywhere in Egypt, both in wooden buckets and in stone jars."

20So Moses and Aaron did just as the LORD had commanded. In front of the king and his officers, Aaron raised his walking stick and struck the water in the Nile River. So all the water in the Nile changed into blood. 21The fish in the Nile died, and the river began to stink, so the Egyptians could not drink water from it. Blood was everywhere in the land of Egypt.

22Using their tricks, the magicians of Egypt did the same thing. So the king was stubborn and refused to listen to Moses and Aaron, just as the LORD had said. 23The king turned and went into his palace and ignored what Moses and Aaron had done. 24The Egyptians could not drink the water from the Nile, so all of them dug along the bank of the river, looking for water to drink.

THE FROGS

25Seven days passed after the LORD changed the Nile River.

8 1Then the LORD told Moses, "Go to the king of Egypt and tell him, 'This is what the LORD says: Let my people go to worship me. 2If you refuse, I will punish Egypt with frogs. 3The Nile River will be filled with frogs. They will come up into your palace, into your bedroom, on your bed, into the houses of your officers, and onto your people. They will come into your ovens and into your baking pans. 4The frogs

will jump all over you, your people, and your officers.' "

[5]Then the LORD said to Moses, "Tell Aaron to hold his walking stick in his hand over the rivers, canals, and ponds. Make frogs come up out of the water onto the land of Egypt."

WHAT'S IT MEAN?

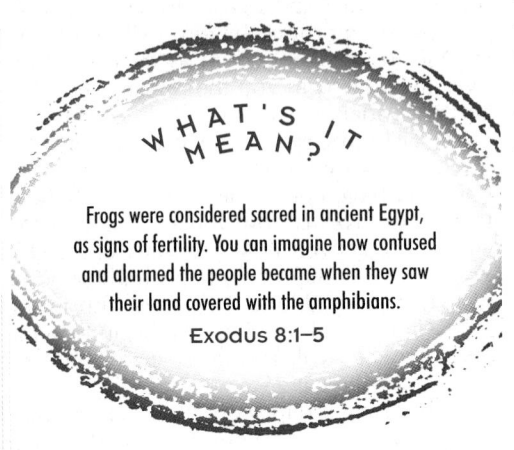

Frogs were considered sacred in ancient Egypt, as signs of fertility. You can imagine how confused and alarmed the people became when they saw their land covered with the amphibians.

Exodus 8:1–5

[6]So Aaron held his hand over all the waters of Egypt, and the frogs came up out of the water and covered the land of Egypt. [7]The magicians used their tricks to do the same thing, so even more frogs came up onto the land of Egypt.

[8]The king called for Moses and Aaron and said, "Pray to the LORD to take the frogs away from me and my people. I will let your people go to offer sacrifices to the LORD."

[9]Moses said to the king, "Please set the time when I should pray for you, your people, and your officers. Then the frogs will leave you and your houses and will remain only in the Nile."

[10]The king answered, "Tomorrow."

Moses said, "What you want will happen. By this you will know that there is no one like the LORD our God. [11]The frogs will leave you, your houses, your officers, and your people. They will remain only in the Nile."

[12]After Moses and Aaron left the king, Moses asked the LORD about the frogs he had sent to the king. [13]And the LORD did as Moses asked. The frogs died in the houses, in the yards, and in the fields. [14]The Egyptians put them in piles, and the whole country began to stink. [15]But when the king saw that they were free of the frogs, he became stubborn again. He did not listen to Moses and Aaron, just as the LORD had said.

"Then the LORD told Moses, 'Go to the king of Egypt and tell him, "This is what the LORD says: Let my people go to worship me." ' "
(Exodus 8:1)

THE GNATS

[16]Then the LORD said to Moses, "Tell Aaron to raise his walking stick and strike the dust on the ground. Then everywhere in Egypt the dust will change into gnats." [17]They did this, and when Aaron raised the walking stick that was in his hand and struck the dust on the ground, everywhere in Egypt the dust changed into gnats. The gnats got on the people and animals. [18]Using their tricks, the magicians tried to do the same thing, but they could not make the dust change into gnats. The gnats remained on the people and animals. [19]So the magicians told the king that the power of God had done this. But the king was stubborn and refused to listen to them, just as the LORD had said.

THE FLIES

[20]The LORD told Moses, "Get up early in the morning, and meet the king of Egypt as he goes out to the river. Tell him, 'This is what the LORD says: Let my people go so they can worship me. [21]If you don't let them go, I will send swarms of flies into your houses. The flies will be on you, your officers, and your people. The houses of Egypt will be full of flies, and they will be all over the ground, too. [22]But I will not treat the Israelites the same as the Egyptian people. There will not be any flies in the land of Goshen, where my people live. By this you will know that I, the LORD, am in this land. [23]I will treat my people differently from your people. This miracle will happen tomorrow.' "

[24]So the LORD did as he had said, and great swarms of flies came into the king's palace and his officers' houses. All over Egypt flies were ruining the land. [25]The king called for Moses and Aaron and told them, "Offer sacrifices to your God here in this country."

[26]But Moses said, "It wouldn't be right to do that, because the Egyptians hate the sacrifices we offer to the LORD our God. If they see us offering sacrifices they hate, they will throw stones at us and kill us. [27]Let us make a three-day journey into the desert. We must offer sacrifices to the LORD our God there, as the LORD told us to do."

[28]The king said, "I will let you go so that you

may offer sacrifices to the LORD your God in the desert, but you must not go very far away. Now go and pray for me."

[29]Moses said, "I will leave and pray to the LORD, and he will take the flies away from you, your officers, and your people tomorrow. But do not try to trick us again. Do not stop the people from going to offer sacrifices to the LORD."

[30]So Moses left the king and prayed to the LORD, [31]and the LORD did as he asked. He removed the flies from the king, his officers, and his people so that not one fly was left. [32]But the king became stubborn again and did not let the people go.

THE DISEASE ON THE FARM ANIMALS

9 [1]Then the LORD told Moses, "Go to the king of Egypt and tell him, 'This is what the LORD, the God of the Hebrews, says: Let my people go to worship me. [2]If you refuse to let them go and continue to hold them, [3]the LORD will punish you. He will send a terrible disease on your farm animals that are in the fields. He will cause your horses, donkeys, camels, cattle, goats, and sheep to become sick. [4]But the LORD will treat Israel's animals differently from the animals of Egypt. None of the animals that belong to the Israelites will die. [5]The LORD has set tomorrow as the time he will do this in the land.' " [6]The next day the LORD did as he promised. All the farm animals in Egypt died, but none of the animals belonging to Israelites died. [7]The king sent people to see what had happened to the animals of Israel, and they found that not one of them had died. But the king was still stubborn and did not let the people go.

THE BOILS

[8]The LORD said to Moses and Aaron, "Fill your hands with ashes from a furnace. Moses, throw the ashes into the air in front of the king of Egypt. [9]The ashes will spread like dust through all the land of Egypt. They will cause boils to break out and become sores on the skin of people and animals everywhere in the land."

[10]So Moses and Aaron took ashes from a furnace and went and stood before the king. Moses threw ashes into the air, which caused boils to break out and become sores on people and animals. [11]The magicians could not stand before Moses, because all the Egyptians had boils, even the magicians. [12]But the LORD made the king stubborn, so he refused to listen to Moses and Aaron, just as the LORD had said.

THE HAIL

[13]Then the LORD said to Moses, "Get up early in the morning and go to the king of Egypt. Tell him, 'This is what the LORD, the God of the Hebrews, says: Let my people go to worship me. [14]If you don't, this time I will punish you, your officers, and your people, with all my power. Then you will know there is no one in the whole land like me. [15]By now I could have used my power and caused a terrible disease that would have destroyed you and your people from the earth. [16]But I have let you live for this reason: to show you my power so that my name will be talked about in all the earth. [17]You are still against my people and do not want to let them go. [18]So at this time tomorrow, I will send a terrible hailstorm, the worst in Egypt since it became a nation. [19]Now send for your animals and whatever you have in the fields, and bring them into a safe place. The hail will fall on every person or animal that is still in the fields. If they have not been brought in, they will die.' " [20]Some of the king's officers respected the word of the LORD and hurried to bring their slaves and animals inside. [21]But others ignored the LORD's message and left their slaves and animals in the fields.

[22]The LORD told Moses, "Raise your hand toward the sky. Then the hail will start falling in all the land of Egypt. It will fall on people, animals, and on everything that grows in the fields of Egypt." [23]When Moses raised his walking stick toward the sky, the LORD sent thunder and hail, and lightning flashed down to the earth. So he caused hail to fall upon the land of Egypt. [24]There was hail, and lightning flashed as it hailed—the worst hailstorm in Egypt since it had become a nation. [25]The hail destroyed all the people and animals that were in the fields in all the land of Egypt. It also destroyed everything that grew in the fields and broke all the trees in the fields. [26]The only place it did not hail was in the land of Goshen, where the Israelites lived.

[27]The king sent for Moses and Aaron and told them, "This time I have sinned. The LORD is in the right, and I and my people are in the wrong. [28]Pray to the LORD. We have had enough of God's thunder and hail. I will let you go; you do not have to stay here any longer."

[29]Moses told the king, "When I leave the city, I will raise my hands to the LORD in prayer, and the thunder and hail will stop. Then you will know that the earth belongs to the LORD. [30]But I know that you and your officers do not yet fear the LORD God."

31The flax was in bloom, and the barley had
ripened, so these crops were destroyed. 32But
both wheat crops ripen later, so they were not
destroyed.
33Moses left the king and went outside the
city. He raised his hands to the LORD, and the
thunder and hail stopped. The rain also
stopped falling to the ground. 34When the king
saw that the rain, hail, and thunder had
stopped, he sinned again, and he and his officers became stubborn. 35So the king became
stubborn and refused to let the Israelites go,
just as the LORD had said through Moses.

THE LOCUSTS

10 1The LORD said to Moses, "Go to the king of
Egypt. I have made him and his officers stubborn so I could show them my powerful miracles. 2I also did this so you could tell your
children and your grandchildren how I was
hard on the Egyptians. Tell them about the
miracles I did among them so that all of you
will know that I am the LORD."
3So Moses and Aaron went to the king and
told him, "This is what the LORD, the God of
the Hebrews, says: 'How long will you refuse
to be sorry for what you have done? Let my
people go to worship me. 4If you refuse to let
my people go, tomorrow I will bring locusts
into your country. 5They will cover the land so
that no one will be able to see the ground.
They will eat anything that was left from the
hailstorm and the leaves from every tree growing in the field. 6They will fill your palaces and
all your officers' houses, as well as the houses
of all the Egyptians. There will be more locusts
than your fathers or ancestors have ever
seen—more than there have been since people
began living in Egypt.' " Then Moses turned
and walked away from the king.

WHAT'S IT MEAN?

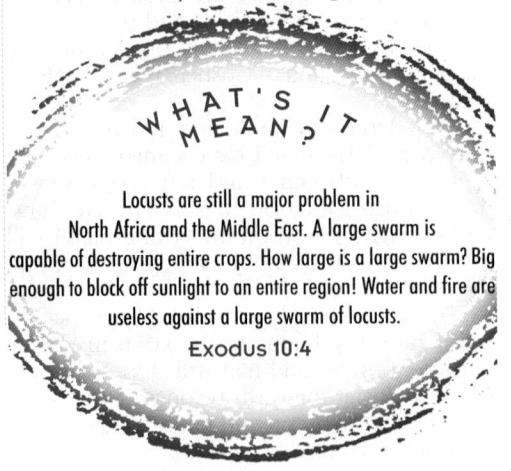

Locusts are still a major problem in North Africa and the Middle East. A large swarm is capable of destroying entire crops. How large is a large swarm? Big enough to block off sunlight to an entire region! Water and fire are useless against a large swarm of locusts.

Exodus 10:4

7The king's officers asked him, "How long
will this man make trouble for us? Let the Israelites go to worship the LORD their God. Don't
you know that Egypt is ruined?"
8So Moses and Aaron were brought back
to the king. He said to them, "Go and worship
the LORD your God. But tell me, just who is
going?"
9Moses answered, "We will go with our
young and old people, our sons and daughters, and our flocks and herds, because we are
going to have a feast to honor the LORD."
10The king said to them, "The LORD will
really have to be with you if ever I let you and
all of your children leave Egypt. See, you are
planning something evil! 11No! Only the men
may go and worship the LORD, which is what
you have been asking for." Then the king forced
Moses and Aaron out of his palace.
12The LORD told Moses, "Raise your hand
over the land of Egypt, and the locusts will
come. They will spread all over the land of
Egypt and will eat all the plants the hail did not
destroy."
13So Moses raised his walking stick over the
land of Egypt, and the LORD caused a strong
wind to blow from the east. It blew across the
land all that day and night, and when morning
came, the east wind had brought the locusts.
14Swarms of locusts covered all the land of
Egypt and settled everywhere. There were
more locusts than ever before or after, 15and
they covered the whole land so that it was
black. They ate everything that was left after
the hail—every plant in the field and all the
fruit on the trees. Nothing green was left on
any tree or plant anywhere in Egypt.
16The king quickly called for Moses and
Aaron. He said, "I have sinned against the LORD
your God and against you. 17Now forgive my
sin this time. Pray to the LORD your God, and
ask him to stop this punishment that kills."
18Moses left the king and prayed to the
LORD. 19So the LORD changed the wind. He
made a very strong wind blow from the west,
and it blew the locusts away into the Red Sea.
Not one locust was left anywhere in Egypt.
20But the LORD caused the king to be stubborn
again, and he did not let the Israelites go.

THE DARKNESS

21Then the LORD told Moses, "Raise your
hand toward the sky, and darkness will cover
the land of Egypt. It will be so dark you will be
able to feel it." 22Moses raised his hand toward
the sky, and total darkness was everywhere in
Egypt for three days. 23No one could see any-

one else, and no one could go anywhere for three days. But the Israelites had light where they lived.

24Again the king of Egypt called for Moses. He said, "All of you may go and worship the LORD. You may take your women and children with you, but you must leave your flocks and herds here."

25Moses said, "You must let us have animals to use as sacrifices and burnt offerings, because we have to offer them to the LORD our God. 26So we must take our animals with us; not a hoof will be left behind. We have to use some of the animals to worship the LORD our God. We won't know exactly what we will need to worship the LORD until we get there."

27But the LORD made the king stubborn again, so he refused to let them go. 28Then he told Moses, "Get out of here, and don't come again! The next time you see me, you will die."

29Then Moses told the king, "I'll do what you say. I will not come to see you again."

THE DEATH OF THE FIRSTBORN

11 1Now the LORD had told Moses, "I have one more way to punish the king and the people of Egypt. After this, the king will send all of you away from Egypt. When he does, he will force you to leave completely. 2Tell the men and women of Israel to ask their neighbors for things made of silver and gold." 3The LORD had caused the Egyptians to respect the Israelites, and both the king's officers and the Egyptian people considered Moses to be a great man.

4So Moses said to the king, "This is what the LORD says: 'About midnight tonight I will go through all Egypt. 5Every firstborn son in the land of Egypt will die—from the firstborn son of the king, who sits on his throne, to the firstborn of the slave girl grinding grain. Also the firstborn farm animals will die. 6There will be loud outcries everywhere in Egypt, worse than any time before or after this. 7But not even a dog will bark at the Israelites or their animals.' Then you will know that the LORD treats Israel differently from Egypt. 8All your officers will come to me. They will bow facedown to the ground before me and say, 'Leave and take all your people with you.' After that, I will leave." Then Moses very angrily left the king.

9The LORD had told Moses, "The king will not listen to you and Aaron so that I may do many miracles in the land of Egypt." 10Moses and Aaron did all these great miracles in front of the king. But the LORD made him stubborn, and the king would not let the Israelites leave his country.

THE FIRST PASSOVER

12 1The LORD spoke to Moses and Aaron in the land of Egypt: 2"This month will be the beginning of months, the first month of the year for you. 3Tell the whole community of Israel that on the tenth day of this month each man must get one lamb for the people in his house. 4If there are not enough people in his house to eat a whole lamb, he must share it with his closest neighbor, considering the number of people. There must be enough lamb for everyone to eat. 5The lamb must be a one-year-old male that has nothing wrong with it. This animal can be either a young sheep or a young goat. 6Take care of the animals until the fourteenth day of the month. On that day all the people of the community of Israel will kill them in the evening before dark. 7The people must take some of the blood and put it on the sides and tops of the doorframes of the houses where they eat the lambs. 8On this night they must roast the lamb over a fire. They must eat it with bitter herbs and bread made without yeast. 9Do not eat the lamb raw or boiled in water. Roast the whole lamb over a fire—with its head, legs, and inner organs. 10You must not leave any of it until morning, but if any of it is left over until morning, you must burn it with fire.

11"This is the way you must eat it: You must be fully dressed as if you were going on a trip. You must have your sandals on and your walking stick in your hand. You must eat it in a hurry; this is the LORD's Passover.

12"That night I will go through the land of Egypt and kill all the firstborn animals and people in the land of Egypt. I will also punish all the gods of Egypt. I am the LORD. 13But the blood will be a sign on the houses where you are. When I see the blood, I will pass over you. Nothing terrible will hurt you when I punish the land of Egypt.

14"You are always to remember this day and celebrate it with a feast to the LORD. Your descendants are to honor the LORD with this feast from now on. 15For this feast you must eat bread made without yeast for seven days. On the first day, you are to remove all the yeast from your houses. No one should eat any yeast for the full seven days of the feast, or that person will be cut off from Israel. 16You are to have holy meetings on the first and last days of the feast. You must not do any work on these days; the only work you may do is to prepare your meals. 17You must celebrate the Feast of Unleavened Bread, because on this very day I brought your divisions of people out of Egypt.

So all of your descendants must celebrate this
day. This is a law that will last from now on.
[18]In the first month of the year you are to eat
bread made without yeast, from the evening of
the fourteenth day until the evening of the
twenty-first day. [19]For seven days there must
not be any yeast in your houses. Anybody
who eats yeast during this time, either an Israelite or non-Israelite, must be cut off from the
community of Israel. [20]During this feast you
must not eat anything made with yeast. You
must eat only bread made without yeast wherever you live."
[21]Then Moses called all the older leaders of
Israel together and told them, "Get the animals
for your families and kill the lamb for the Passover. [22]Take a branch of the hyssop plant, dip it
into the bowl filled with blood, and then wipe
the blood on the sides and tops of the doorframes. No one may leave that house until
morning. [23]When the LORD goes through Egypt
to kill the Egyptians, he will see the blood on
the sides and tops of the doorframes, and he
will pass over that house. He will not let the
one who brings death come into your houses
and kill you.

WHAT'S IT MEAN?

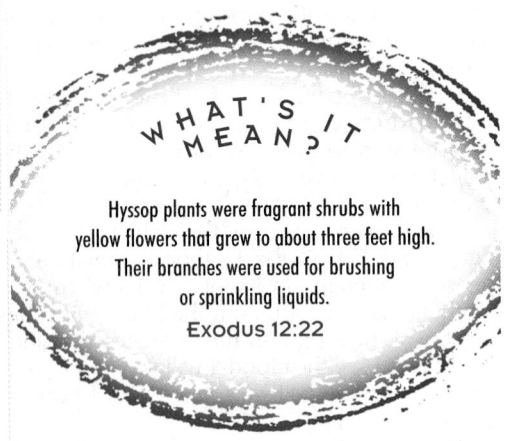

Hyssop plants were fragrant shrubs with yellow flowers that grew to about three feet high. Their branches were used for brushing or sprinkling liquids.

Exodus 12:22

[24]"You must keep this command as a law for
you and your descendants from now on. [25]Do
this when you go to the land the LORD has
promised to give you. [26]When your children
ask you, 'Why are we doing these things?'
[27]you will say, 'This is the Passover sacrifice to
honor the LORD. When we were in Egypt, the
LORD passed over the houses of Israel, and
when he killed the Egyptians, he saved our
homes.' " Then the people bowed down and
worshiped the LORD. [28]They did just as the
LORD commanded Moses and Aaron.
[29]At midnight the LORD killed all the firstborn sons in the land of Egypt—from the firstborn of the king who sat on the throne to the
firstborn of the prisoner in jail. Also, all the
firstborn farm animals died. [30]The king, his officers, and all the Egyptians got up during the
night because someone had died in every
house. So there was a loud outcry everywhere
in Egypt.

WHAT'S IT MEAN?

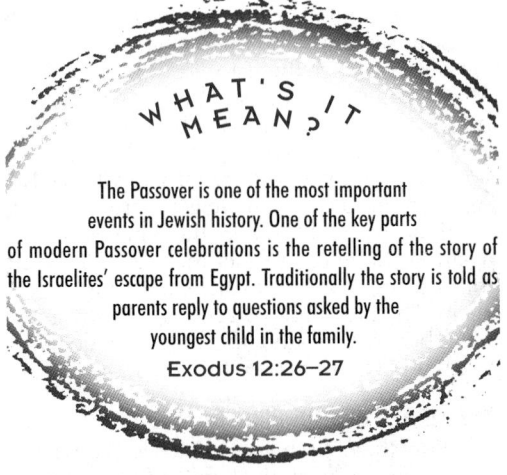

The Passover is one of the most important events in Jewish history. One of the key parts of modern Passover celebrations is the retelling of the story of the Israelites' escape from Egypt. Traditionally the story is told as parents reply to questions asked by the youngest child in the family.

Exodus 12:26–27

ISRAEL LEAVES EGYPT

[31]During the night the king called for Moses
and Aaron and said, "Get up and leave my
people. You and your people may do as you
have asked; go and worship the LORD. [32]Take
all of your flocks and herds as you have asked,
and go. And also bless me." [33]The Egyptians
also asked the Israelites to hurry and leave,
saying, "If you don't leave, we will all die!"
[34]So the people took their dough before the
yeast was added. They wrapped the bowls for
making dough in clothing and carried them on
their shoulders. [35]The Israelites did what Moses
told them to do and asked their Egyptian
neighbors for things made of silver and gold
and for clothing. [36]The LORD caused the Egyptians to think well of them, and the Egyptians
gave the people everything they asked for. So
the Israelites took rich gifts from them.
[37]The Israelites traveled from Rameses to
Succoth. There were about six hundred thousand men walking, not including the women
and children. [38]Many other people who were
not Israelites went with them, as well as a large
number of sheep, goats, and cattle. [39]The Israelites used the dough they had brought out of
Egypt to bake loaves of bread without yeast.
The dough had no yeast in it, because they had
been rushed out of Egypt and had no time to
get food ready for their trip.
[40]The people of Israel had lived in Egypt for

four hundred thirty years; 41on the very day the
four hundred thirty years ended, the LORD's
divisions of people left Egypt. 42That night the
LORD kept watch to bring them out of Egypt,
and so on this same night the Israelites are to
keep watch to honor the LORD from now on.
43The LORD told Moses and Aaron, "Here
are the rules for Passover: No foreigner is to eat
the Passover. 44If someone buys a slave and
circumcises him, the slave may eat the Passover. 45But neither a person who lives for a
short time in your country nor a hired worker
may eat it.
46"The meal must be eaten inside a house;
take none of the meat outside the house. Don't
break any of the bones. 47The whole community of Israel must take part in this feast. 48A
foreigner who lives with you may share in the
LORD's Passover if all the males in his house
become circumcised. Then, since he will be like
a citizen of Israel, he may share in the meal. But
a man who is not circumcised may not eat the
Passover meal. 49The same rules apply to an
Israelite born in the country or to a foreigner
living there."
50So all the Israelites did just as the LORD
had commanded Moses and Aaron. 51On that
same day the LORD led the Israelites out of
Egypt by their divisions.

THE LAW OF THE FIRSTBORN

13 1Then the LORD said to Moses, 2"Give every
firstborn male to me. Every firstborn male
among the Israelites belongs to me, whether
human or animal."
3Moses said to the people, "Remember this
day, the day you left Egypt. You were slaves in
that land, but the LORD with his great power
brought you out of it. You must not eat bread
made with yeast. 4Today, in the month of Abib,
you are leaving Egypt. 5The
LORD will lead you to the
land of the Canaanites,
Hittites, Amorites, Hi-
vites, and Jebusites. This
is the land he promised
your ancestors he
would give you, a fertile
land. There you must
celebrate this feast dur-
ing the first month of
every year. 6For seven
days you must eat bread
made without yeast, and
on the seventh day there will
be a feast to honor the LORD. 7So for seven
days you must not eat any bread made with
yeast. There must be no bread made with yeast
anywhere in your land. 8On that day you
should tell your son: 'We are having this feast
because of what the LORD did for me when I
came out of Egypt.' 9This feast will help you
remember, like a mark on your hand or a reminder on your forehead. This feast will remind you to speak the LORD's teachings,
because the LORD used his great power to
bring you out of Egypt. 10So celebrate this feast
every year at the right time.
11"And when the LORD takes you into the
land of the Canaanites, the land he promised
to give you and your ancestors, 12you must give
him every firstborn male. Also every firstborn
male animal must be given to the LORD. 13Buy
back every firstborn donkey by offering a lamb.
But if you don't want to buy the donkey back,
then break its neck. You must buy back from
the LORD every firstborn of your sons.

WHAT'S IT MEAN?

Donkeys were not considered clean animals, so they could not be used for food or sacrifices. They could be used for transportation, though. Donkeys were ideal for carrying people and possessions. They were also used by farmers to work the fields.

Exodus 13:13

14"From now on when your son asks you,
'What does this mean?' you will answer, 'With
his great power, the LORD
brought us out from
Egypt, the land where we
were slaves. 15The king of
Egypt was stubborn and
refused to let us leave.
But the LORD killed every
firstborn male in Egypt,
both human and ani-
mal. That is why I sacri-
fice every firstborn male
animal to the LORD, and
that is why I buy back
each of my firstborn sons
from the LORD.' 16This feast
is like a mark on your hand and a reminder on
your forehead to help you remember that the

"Moses said to the people, 'Remember this day, the day you left Egypt. You were slaves in that land, but the LORD with his great power brought you out of it. You must not eat bread made with yeast.'"
(Exodus 13:3)

LORD brought us out of Egypt with his great
power."

THE WAY OUT OF EGYPT

[17]When the king sent the people out of
Egypt, God did not lead them on the road
through the Philistine country, though that
was the shortest way. God said, "If they have to
fight, they might change their minds and go
back to Egypt." [18]So God led them through the
desert toward the Red Sea. The Israelites were
dressed for fighting when they left the land of
Egypt.
[19]Moses carried the bones of Joseph with
him, because before Joseph died, he had made
the Israelites promise to do this. He had said,
"When God saves you, remember to carry my
bones with you out of Egypt."
[20]The Israelites left Succoth and camped at
Etham, on the edge of the desert. [21]The LORD
showed them the way; during the day he went
ahead of them in a pillar of cloud, and during
the night he was in a pillar of fire to give them
light. In this way they could travel during the
day or night. [22]The pillar of cloud was always
with them during the day, and the pillar of fire
was always with them at night.

14
[1]Then the LORD said to Moses, [2]"Tell the Israelites to turn back to Pi Hahiroth and to
camp between Migdol and the Red Sea. Camp
across from Baal Zephon, on the shore of the
sea. [3]The king will think, 'The Israelites are lost,
trapped by the desert.' [4]I will make the king
stubborn again so he will chase after them, but
I will defeat the king and his army. This will
bring honor to me, and the Egyptians will
know that I am the LORD." The Israelites did
just as they were told.

THE KING CHASES THE ISRAELITES

[5]When the king of Egypt was told that the
Israelites had left, he and his officers changed
their minds about them. They said, "What have
we done? We have let the Israelites leave. We
have lost our slaves!" [6]So the king prepared his
war chariot and took his army with him. [7]He
took six hundred of his best chariots, together
with all the other chariots of Egypt, each with

WHAT'S IT MEAN?

The chariot was the vehicle of choice in ancient Egypt for good reason. The Egyptians were the Ferrari of chariot makers. Their models were built from wood held together by leather strips. This made the chariots light and gave them excellent shock absorbency. Chariots were designed to carry at least two people—one person to drive and one person, armed with a bow, to fight the enemy.

Exodus 14:6

Promise HE PROMISES TO FIGHT FOR YOU.

You only need to remain calm; the LORD will fight for you (Ex. 14:14).

Just as God fought for the Israelites when they were stuck between the raging sea and the advancing Egyptian army, Jesus has fought for you. He fought and defeated the power of sin in your life. Big deal, right? Right—that means you can do the right thing even when it's hard.

Even the apostle Paul said that he had a hard time doing the right thing because his selfish desires kept urging him to do something else. Everyone who wants to please God faces this problem. But Jesus went up against all of your selfishness and temptations. He went smack up against all the right things that you don't want to do. And he won.

Moses told the Israelites, "You only need to remain calm." That's true for you. You don't have to fight because Jesus has already won your battle. Does that mean you just sit around like mush? No, you just have to stay strong, stay close to him, and keep believing that he's already won.

SEE FOR YOURSELF:

Deut. 1:30–31; 2 Chr. 32:8; Neh. 4:20

an officer in it. [8]The LORD made the king of Egypt stubborn, so he chased the Israelites, who were leaving victoriously. [9]The Egyptians—with all the king's horses, chariot drivers, and army—chased the Israelites. They caught up with them while they were camped by the Red Sea, near Pi Hahiroth and Baal Zephon.

[10]When the Israelites saw the king and his army coming after them, they were very frightened and cried to the LORD for help. [11]They said to Moses, "What have you done to us? Why did you bring us out of Egypt to die in the desert? There were plenty of graves for us in Egypt. [12]We told you in Egypt, 'Let us alone; we will stay and serve the Egyptians.' Now we will die in the desert."

> "The LORD gives me strength and makes me sing; he has saved me. He is my God, and I will praise him. He is the God of my fathers, and I will honor him."
> (Exodus 15:2)

[13]But Moses answered, "Don't be afraid! Stand still and you will see the LORD save you today. You will never see these Egyptians again after today. [14]You only need to remain calm; the LORD will fight for you."

[15]Then the LORD said to Moses, "Why are you crying out to me? Command the Israelites to start moving. [16]Raise your walking stick and hold it over the sea so that the sea will split and the people can cross it on dry land. [17]I will make the Egyptians stubborn so they will chase the Israelites, but I will be honored when I defeat the king and all of his chariot drivers and chariots. [18]When I defeat the king, his chariot drivers, and chariots, the Egyptians will know that I am the LORD."

[19]Now the angel of God that usually traveled in front of Israel's army moved behind them. Also, the pillar of cloud moved from in front of the people and stood behind them. [20]So the cloud came between the Egyptians and the Israelites. This made it dark for the Egyptians but gave light to the Israelites. So the cloud kept the two armies apart all night.

[21]Then Moses held his hand over the sea. All that night the LORD drove back the sea with a strong east wind, making the sea become dry ground. The water was split, [22]and the Israelites went through the sea on dry land, with a wall of water on their right and on their left.

[23]Then all the king's horses, chariots, and chariot drivers followed them into the sea. [24]When morning came, the LORD looked down from the pillar of cloud and fire at the Egyptian army and made them panic. [25]He kept the wheels of the chariots from turning, making it hard to drive the chariots. The Egyptians shouted, "Let's get away from the Israelites! The LORD is fighting for them and against Egypt."

[26]Then the LORD told Moses, "Hold your hand over the sea so that the water will come back over the Egyptians, their chariots, and chariot drivers." [27]So Moses raised his hand over the sea, and at dawn the sea returned to its place. The Egyptians tried to run from it, but the LORD swept them away into the sea. [28]The water returned, covering the chariots, chariot drivers, and all the king's army that had followed the Israelites into the sea. Not one of them survived.

[29]But the Israelites crossed the sea on dry land, with a wall of water on their right and on their left. [30]So that day the LORD saved the Israelites from the Egyptians, and the Israelites saw the Egyptians lying dead on the seashore. [31]When the Israelites saw the great power the LORD had used against the Egyptians, they feared the LORD, and they trusted him and his servant Moses.

THE SONG OF MOSES

15

[1]Then Moses and the Israelites sang this song to the LORD:

"I will sing to the LORD,
because he is worthy of
great honor.
He has thrown the horse
and its rider
into the sea.
[2]The LORD gives me
strength and makes me
sing;
he has saved me.
He is my God,
and I will praise him.
He is the God of my fathers,
and I will honor him.
[3]The LORD is a warrior;
the LORD is his name.
[4]The chariots and soldiers
of the king of Egypt
he has thrown into the
sea.
The king's best officers
are drowned in the Red Sea.
[5]The deep waters covered them,
and they sank to the bottom like a rock.

MUSIC
What can music be used for? (15:1)

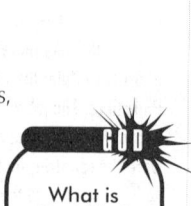

GOD
What is God like? (15:3–4)

6 Your right hand, LORD,
is amazingly strong.
LORD, your right hand
broke the enemy to pieces.
7 In your great victory
you destroyed those who were against
you.
Your anger destroyed them,
like fire burning straw.
8 Just a blast of your breath,
and the waters piled up.
The moving water stood like a wall;
the deep waters became solid in the
middle of the sea.

9 "The enemy bragged,
'I'll chase them and catch them.
I'll take all their riches;
I'll take all I want.
I'll pull out my sword,
and my hand will destroy them.'
10 But you blew on them with your breath
and covered them with the sea.
They sank like lead
in the raging water.

11 "Are there any gods like you, LORD?
There are no gods like you.
You are wonderfully holy,
amazingly powerful,
a worker of miracles.
12 You reached out with your right hand,
and the earth swallowed our enemies.
13 You keep your loving promise
and lead the people you have saved.
With your strength you will guide them
to your holy place.

14 "The other nations will hear this and
tremble with fear;
terror will take hold of the Philistines.
15 The leaders of the tribes of Edom will be
very frightened;
the powerful men of Moab will shake
with fear;
the people of Canaan will lose all their
courage.
16 Terror and horror will fall on them.
When they see your strength,
they will be as still as a rock.
They will be still until your people pass
by, LORD.
They will be still until the people you
have taken as your own pass by.
17 You will lead your people and place them
on your very own mountain,
the place that you, LORD, made for
yourself to live,
the temple, Lord, that your hands have
made.
18 The LORD will be king forever!"
19 The horses, chariot drivers, and chariots of
the king of Egypt went into the sea, and the
LORD covered them with water from the sea.
But the Israelites walked through the sea on
dry land.
20 Then Aaron's sister Miriam, a
prophetess, took a tambourine in her hand. All
the women followed her, playing tambourines
and dancing.
21 Miriam told them:
"Sing to the LORD,
because he is worthy of great honor;
he has thrown the horse and its rider
into the sea."

WHAT'S IT MEAN?

The Philistines happened to be living in the very place God had promised to the Israelites. In order to claim their land, the Israelites would have to "evict" the Philistines. The job would not be easy, though. The Philistines were known for making advanced weapons out of iron. Edom and Moab were the countries on the other side of the Jordan River, which ran to the east of the Philistines' land.

Exodus 15:14–15

BITTER WATER BECOMES GOOD

22 Moses led the Israelites away from the Red
Sea into the Desert of Shur. They traveled for
three days in the desert but found no water.
23 Then they came to Marah, where there was
water, but they could not drink it because it
was too bitter. (That is why the place was
named Marah.[n])
24 The people grumbled to
Moses and asked, "What will we drink?"
25 So Moses cried out to the LORD, and the
LORD showed him a tree. When Moses threw
the tree into the water, the water became good
to drink.

There the LORD gave the people a rule and a
law to live by, and there he tested their loyalty
to him.
26 He said, "You must obey the LORD

15:23 Marah This name means "bitter."

your God and do what he says is right. If you obey all his commands and keep his rules, I will not bring on you any of the sicknesses I brought on the Egyptians. I am the LORD who heals you."

[27]Then the people traveled to Elim, where there were twelve springs of water and seventy palm trees. So the people camped there near the water.

THE PEOPLE DEMAND FOOD

16 [1]The whole Israelite community left Elim and came to the Desert of Sin, which was between Elim and Sinai; they arrived there on the fifteenth day of the second month after they had left Egypt. [2]Then the whole Israelite community grumbled to Moses and Aaron in the desert. [3]They said to them, "It would have been better if the LORD had killed us in the land of Egypt. There we had meat to eat and all the food we wanted. But you have brought us into this desert to starve us to death."

[4]Then the LORD said to Moses, "I will cause food to fall like rain from the sky for all of you. Every day the people must go out and gather what they need for that day. I want to see if the people will do what I teach them. [5]On the sixth day of each week, they are to gather twice as much as they gather on other days. Then they are to prepare it."

WHAT'S IT MEAN?

This heavenly food that God sent to the Israelites was called manna. If you're wondering what it was, you're not alone. The word *manna* in Hebrew means "What is it?" Our best guess is that it was similar to a wafer.

Exodus 16:4

[6]So Moses and Aaron said to all the Israelites: "This evening you will know that the LORD is the one who brought you out of Egypt. [7]Tomorrow morning you will see the glory of the LORD, because he has heard you grumble against him. We are nothing, so you are not grumbling against us, but against the LORD." [8]And Moses said, "Each evening the LORD will give you meat to eat, and every morning he will give you all the bread you want, because he has heard you grumble against him. You are not grumbling against Aaron and me, because we are nothing; you are grumbling against the LORD."

[9]Then Moses said to Aaron, "Speak to the whole community of the Israelites, and say to them, 'Meet together in the presence of the LORD, because he has heard your grumblings.' "

[10]While Aaron was speaking to the whole community of the Israelites, they looked toward the desert. There the glory of the LORD appeared in a cloud.

[11]The LORD said to Moses, [12]"I have heard the grumblings of the people of Israel. So tell them, 'At twilight you will eat meat, and every morning you will eat all the bread you want. Then you will know I am the LORD your God.' "

[13]That evening quail came and covered the camp, and in the morning dew lay around the camp. [14]When the dew was gone, thin flakes like frost were on the desert ground. [15]When the Israelites saw it, they asked each other, "What is it?" because they did not know what it was.

So Moses told them, "This is the bread the LORD has given you to eat. [16]The LORD has commanded, 'Each one of you must gather what he needs, about two quarts for every person in your family.' "

[17]So the people of Israel did this; some people gathered much, and some gathered little. [18]Then they measured it. The person who gathered more did not have too much, nor did the person who gathered less have too little. Each person gathered just as much as he needed.

[19]Moses said to them, "Don't keep any of it to eat the next day." [20]But some of the people did not listen to Moses and kept part of it to eat the next morning. It became full of worms and began to stink, so Moses was angry with those people.

[21]Every morning each person gathered as much food as he needed, but when the sun became hot, it melted away.

[22]On the sixth day the people gathered twice as much food—four quarts for every person. When all the leaders of the community came and told this to Moses, [23]he said to them, "This is what the LORD commanded, because tomorrow is the Sabbath, the LORD's holy day of rest. Bake what you want to bake, and boil what you want to boil today. Save the rest of the food until tomorrow morning."

[24]So the people saved it until the next morning, as Moses had commanded, and none of it began to stink or have worms in it. [25]Moses told the people, "Eat the food you gathered

yesterday. Today is a Sabbath, the LORD's day
of rest; you will not find any out in the field
today. 26You should gather the food for six
days, but the seventh day is a Sabbath day. On
that day there will not be any food on the
ground."
27On the seventh day some of the people
went out to gather food, but they couldn't find
any. 28Then the LORD said to Moses, "How long
will you people refuse to obey my commands
and teachings? 29Look, the LORD has made the
Sabbath a day of rest for you. So on the sixth
day he will give you enough food for two
days, but on the seventh day each of you must
stay where you are. Do not go anywhere." 30So
the people rested on the seventh day.
31The people of Israel called the food manna.
It was like small white seeds and tasted like
wafers made with honey.
32Then Moses said, "The LORD said, 'Save
two quarts of this food for your descendants.
Then they can see the food I gave you to eat in
the desert when I brought you out of Egypt.' "
33Moses told Aaron, "Take a jar and fill it
with two quarts of manna. Then place it before
the LORD, and save it for your descendants."
34So Aaron did what the LORD had commanded
Moses. He put the jar of manna in front of the
Agreement to keep it safe. 35The Israelites ate
manna for forty years, until they came to the
land where they settled—the edge of the land of
Canaan. 36The measure they used for the manna was two quarts, or one-tenth of an ephah.[n]

WATER FROM A ROCK

17 1The whole Israelite community left the
Desert of Sin and traveled from place to place,
as the LORD commanded. They camped at
Rephidim, but there was no water there for the
people to drink. 2So they quarreled with Moses
and said, "Give us water to drink."

Moses said to them, "Why do you quarrel with me? Why are you testing the LORD?"

3But the people were very thirsty for water,
so they grumbled against Moses. They said,
"Why did you bring us out of Egypt? Was it to
kill us, our children, and our farm animals
with thirst?"
4So Moses cried to the LORD, "What can I do
with these people? They are almost ready to
stone me to death."
5The LORD said to Moses, "Go ahead of the
people, and take some of the older leaders of
Israel with you. Carry with you the walking
stick that you used to strike the Nile River.
Now go! 6I will stand in front of you on a rock
at Mount Sinai. Hit that rock with the stick,
and water will come out of it so that the people
can drink." Moses did these things as the older
leaders of Israel watched. 7He named that
place Massah,[n] because the Israelites tested the
LORD when they asked, "Is the LORD with us or
not?" He also named it Meribah,[n] because they
quarreled.

THE AMALEKITES FIGHT ISRAEL

8At Rephidim the Amalekites came and
fought the Israelites. 9So Moses said to Joshua,
"Choose some men and go and fight the Amalekites. Tomorrow I will stand on the top of the
hill, holding the walking stick of God in my
hands."

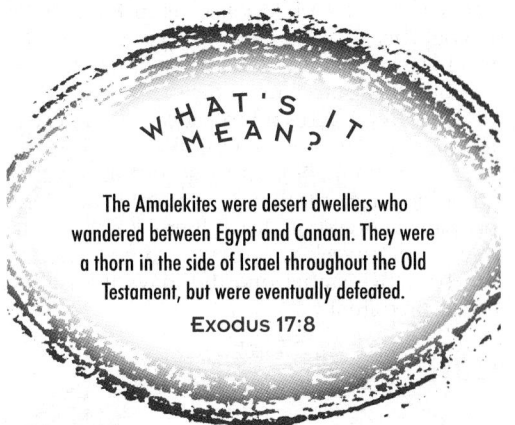

WHAT'S IT MEAN?

The Amalekites were desert dwellers who wandered between Egypt and Canaan. They were a thorn in the side of Israel throughout the Old Testament, but were eventually defeated.

Exodus 17:8

10Joshua obeyed Moses and went to fight
the Amalekites, while Moses, Aaron, and Hur
went to the top of the hill. 11As long as Moses
held his hands up, the Israelites would win the
fight, but when Moses put his hands down, the
Amalekites would win. 12Later, when Moses'
arms became tired, the men put a large rock
under him, and he sat on it. Then Aaron and
Hur held up Moses' hands—Aaron on one
side and Hur on the other. They kept his hands
steady until the sun went down. 13So Joshua
defeated the Amalekites in this battle.
14Then the LORD said to Moses, "Write about
this battle in a book so people will remember.
And be sure to tell Joshua, because I will completely destroy the Amalekites from the earth."
15Then Moses built an altar and named it
The LORD is my Banner. 16Moses said, "I lifted
my hands toward the LORD's throne. The LORD
will fight against the Amalekites forever."

16:36 ephah An ephah was a measure that equaled twenty quarts. **17:7 Massah** This name is the Hebrew word for "testing." **17:7 Meribah** This name is the Hebrew word for "quarrel."

WHAT'S IT MEAN?

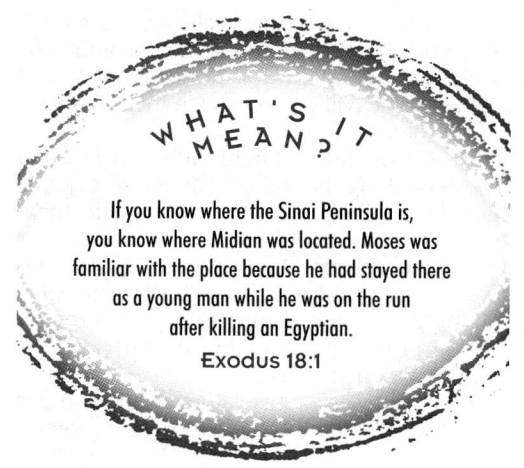

If you know where the Sinai Peninsula is, you know where Midian was located. Moses was familiar with the place because he had stayed there as a young man while he was on the run after killing an Egyptian.

Exodus 18:1

JETHRO VISITS MOSES

18 1Jethro, Moses' father-in-law, was the priest of Midian. He heard about everything that God had done for Moses and his people, the Israelites, and how the LORD had led the Israelites out of Egypt. 2Now Moses had sent his wife Zipporah to Jethro, his father-in-law, 3along with his two sons. The first son was named Gershom,[n] because when he was born, Moses said, "I am a stranger in a foreign country." 4The other son was named Eliezer,[n] because when he was born, Moses said, "The God of my father is my help. He saved me from the king of Egypt."

5So Jethro, Moses' father-in-law, took Moses' wife and his two sons and went to Moses. He was camped in the desert near the mountain of God. 6Jethro had sent a message ahead to Moses that said, "I, Jethro, your father-in-law, am coming to you with your wife and her two sons."

7So Moses went out to meet his father-in-law and bowed down and kissed him. After the two men asked about each other's health, they went into Moses' tent. 8Moses told his father-in-law everything the LORD had done to the king and the Egyptians to help Israel. He told about all the problems they had faced along the way and how the LORD had saved them.

9Jethro was very happy to hear all the good things the LORD had done for Israel when he had saved them from the Egyptians. 10He said, "Praise the LORD. He has saved you from the Egyptians and their king, and he has saved the people from the power of the Egyptians. 11Now I know the LORD is greater than all gods, because he did this to those who looked down on Israel." 12Then Jethro, Moses' father-in-law, gave a whole burnt offering and other sacrifices to God. Aaron and all the older leaders of Israel came to Moses' father-in-law to eat the holy meal together before God.

13The next day Moses solved disagreements among the people, and the people stood around him from morning until night. 14When Moses' father-in-law saw all that Moses was doing for the people, he asked, "What is all this you are doing for the people? Why are you the only one to solve disagreements? All the people are standing around you from morning until night!"

15Then Moses said to his father-in-law, "It is because the people come to me for God's help in solving their disagreements. 16When people have a disagreement, they come to me, and I decide who is right. I tell them God's laws and teachings."

WHAT'S IT MEAN?

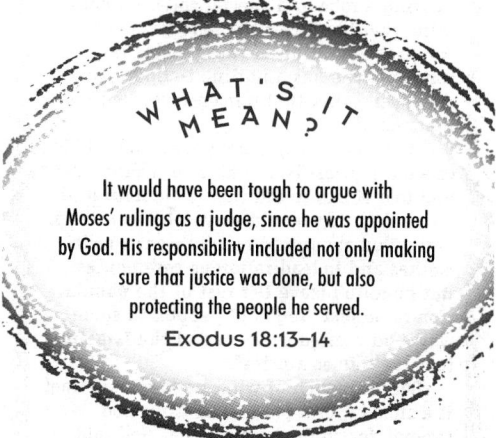

It would have been tough to argue with Moses' rulings as a judge, since he was appointed by God. His responsibility included not only making sure that justice was done, but also protecting the people he served.

Exodus 18:13–14

17Moses' father-in-law said to him, "You are not doing this right. 18You and the people who come to you will get too tired. This is too much work for you; you can't do it by yourself. 19Now listen to me, and I will give you some advice. I want God to be with you. You must speak to God for the people and tell him about their disagreements. 20Warn them about the laws and teachings, and teach them the right way to live and what they should do. 21But choose some capable men from among the people—men who respect God, who can be trusted, and who will

LEADERSHIP
What makes a good leader? (18:21)

18:3 Gershom This name sounds like the Hebrew word for "a stranger there." **18:4 Eliezer** This name sounds like the Hebrew words "My God is my help."

not change their decisions for money. Make
these men officers over the people, to rule over
groups of thousands, hundreds, fifties, and
tens. 22 Let these officers solve the disagreements
among the people all the time. They can bring
the hard cases to you, but they can decide the
simple cases themselves. That will make it easier for you, because they will share the work
with you. 23 If you do this as God commands
you, then you will be able to do your job, and
all the people will go home with their disagreements solved."
24 So Moses listened to his father-in-law and
did everything he said. 25 He chose capable
men from all the Israelites and made them
leaders over the people; they were officers over
groups of thousands, hundreds, fifties, and
tens. 26 These officers solved disagreements
among the people all the time. They brought
the hard cases to Moses, but they decided the
simple cases themselves.
27 So Moses sent his father-in-law on his
way, and Jethro went back to his own home.

ISRAEL CAMPS AT SINAI

19

1 Exactly three months after the Israelites
had left Egypt, they reached the Desert of Sinai.
2 When they left Rephidim, they came to the
Desert of Sinai and camped in the desert in
front of the mountain. 3 Then Moses went up
on the mountain to God. The LORD called to
him from the mountain and said, "Say this to
the family of Jacob, and tell the people of Israel:
4 'Every one of you has seen what I did to the
people of Egypt. You saw how I carried you
out of Egypt, as if on eagle's wings. And I
brought you here to me. 5 So now if you obey
me and keep my agreement, you will be my
own possession, chosen from all nations. Even
though the whole earth is mine, 6 you will be
my kingdom of priests and a holy nation.' You
must tell the Israelites these words."
7 So Moses went down and called the older
leaders of the people together. He told them all
the words the LORD had commanded him to
say. 8 All the people answered together, "We will
do everything he has said." Then Moses took
their answer back to the LORD.
9 And the LORD said to Moses, "I will come
to you in a thick cloud and speak to you. The
people will hear me speaking with you and
will always trust you." Then Moses told the
LORD what the people had said.
10 The LORD said to Moses, "Go to the people
and have them spend today and tomorrow
preparing themselves. They must wash their
clothes 11 and be ready by the day after tomorrow. On that day I, the LORD, will come down
on Mount Sinai, and all the people will see me.
12 But you must set a limit around the mountain that the people are not to cross. Tell them
not to go up on the mountain and not to touch
the foot of it. Anyone who touches the mountain must be put to death 13 with stones or shot

On the Edge

"'You will be my own possession, chosen from all nations. Even though the whole earth is mine, you will be my kingdom of priests and a holy nation.' You must tell the Israelites these words" (Ex. 19:5–6).

When you hear the word *priest*, what do you think of? Maybe you picture a person standing before a congregation wearing a robe or a special collar—something that identifies the person as holy. You probably think of that person as someone who has a hotline to God. You may even think that person loves God more than you do.

Since most people have this exalted idea of what a priest is, it's kind of a shock that God told Moses to tell the whole nation of Israel that they would serve him as priests. Later, God appointed men to wear special clothes and to lead religious ceremonies. But he didn't leave the rest of the population to be just "regular" people. In some way, God wanted every one of the Israelites to serve him as a priest.

Because much of what happens to Israel is a shadow, or a picture, of what God intends for all Christians, what God told Moses applies to you, too. In fact, 1 Peter 2:9 says, "You are a chosen people, royal priests." But don't think you have to go to seminary just yet. Being a priest isn't about wearing special clothes or conducting a religious service. It's about dedicating your whole life and heart to God, no matter what you decide to do for a living. It's about serving him out of a pure heart. It's about knowing that—because of Jesus—you've got your own hotline to heaven. So even if you don't become a pastor or a missionary, you still have the privilege of serving God as a priest.

SEE FOR YOURSELF:
1 Pet. 2:5, 9;
Rev. 1:6

with arrows. No one is allowed to touch him. Whether it is a person or an animal, he will not live. But the trumpet will make a long blast, and only then may the people go up on the mountain."

14 After Moses went down from the mountain to the people, he made them prepare themselves for service to God, and they washed their clothes. 15 Then Moses said to the people, "Be ready in three days. Do not have sexual relations during this time."

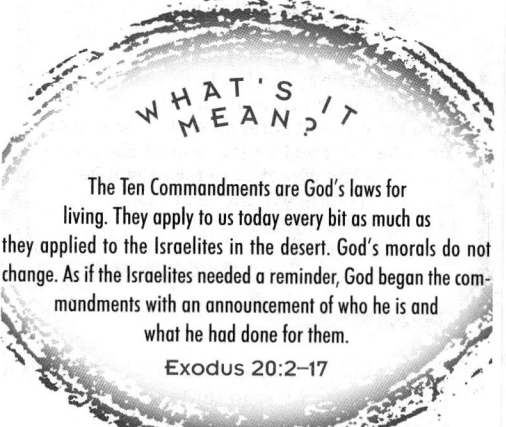

WHAT'S IT MEAN?

The Israelites wanted to do everything they could to make themselves clean before worshiping God. They believed that if their bodies were clean, their hearts would be clean, too. That's why they washed their clothes and refused to have sex for three days before the worship service.

Exodus 19:14–15

16 On the morning of the third day, there was thunder and lightning with a thick cloud on the mountain. There was a very loud blast from a trumpet, and all the people in the camp trembled. 17 Then Moses led the people out of the camp to meet God, and they stood at the foot of the mountain. 18 Mount Sinai was covered with smoke, because the LORD came down on it in fire. The smoke rose from the mountain like smoke from a furnace, and the whole mountain shook wildly. 19 The sound from the trumpet became louder. Then Moses spoke, and the voice of God answered him.

20 When the LORD came down on top of Mount Sinai, he called Moses to come up to the top of the mountain, and Moses went up. 21 The LORD said to Moses, "Go down and warn the people that they must not force their way through to see me. If they do, many of them will die. 22 Even the priests, who may come near me, must first prepare themselves. If they don't, I, the LORD, will punish them."

23 Moses told the LORD, "The people cannot come up on Mount Sinai, because you yourself told us, 'Set a limit around the mountain, and set it apart as holy.' "

24 The LORD said to him, "Go down and bring Aaron up with you, but don't allow the priests or the people to force their way through. They must not come up to the LORD, or I will punish them."

25 So Moses went down to the people and told them these things.

THE TEN COMMANDMENTS

20 1 Then God spoke all these words: 2 "I am the LORD your God, who brought you out of the land of Egypt where you were slaves.

3 "You must not have any other gods except me.

4 "You must not make for yourselves an idol that looks like anything in the sky above or on the earth below or in the water below the land. 5 You must not worship or serve any idol, because I, the LORD your God, am a jealous God. If you hate me, I will punish your children, and even your grandchildren and great-grandchildren. 6 But I show kindness to thousands who love me and obey my commands.

WHAT'S IT MEAN?

The Ten Commandments are God's laws for living. They apply to us today every bit as much as they applied to the Israelites in the desert. God's morals do not change. As if the Israelites needed a reminder, God began the commandments with an announcement of who he is and what he had done for them.

Exodus 20:2–17

7 "You must not use the name of the LORD your God thoughtlessly; the LORD will punish anyone who misuses his name.

8 "Remember to keep the Sabbath holy. 9 Work and get everything done during six days each week, 10 but the seventh day is a day of rest to honor the LORD your God. On that day no one may do any work: not you, your son or daughter, your male or female slaves, your animals, or the foreigners living in your cities. 11 The reason is that in six days the LORD made everything—the sky, the earth, the sea, and everything in them. On the seventh day he rested. So the LORD blessed the Sabbath day and made it holy.

12 "Honor your father and your mother so

On the Edge

Honor your father and your mother so that you will live a long time in the land that the LORD your God is going to give you (Ex. 20:12).

What do I do if my mom is always on my case about the way I dress? The answer to this question lies in the big principle of Exodus 20:12—honor your father and your mother. It's amazing how rational parents can be when you confront them with respect and honor instead of rebellion. The next time the clothes thing comes up with your mom, try something like this: "Mom, I know you don't like this outfit. This is what I like to wear when I'm around my friends. I want to honor you even with my clothes, so when we're going somewhere and it's really important to you that I dress less weird, just let me know." Major life events like weddings and funerals will probably rate pretty high on the "please dress less weird" list. Growing in your faith means that you're always trying to live your life according to the truth in the Bible. Go ahead and talk it through with your mom. You'll be surprised by the respect she'll give you when you give it to her. God will be honored because you honored her.

SEE FOR YOURSELF:
Eph. 6:1–3;
Col. 3:20

that you will live a long time in the land that
the LORD your God is going to give you.
13"You must not murder anyone.
14"You must not be guilty of adultery.
15"You must not steal.
16"You must not tell lies
about your neighbor.
17"You must not want to
take your neighbor's house.
You must not want his wife or
his male or female slaves, or
his ox or his donkey, or anything that belongs
to your neighbor."

HONESTY

Is honesty a command from God? (20:16)

18When the people heard the thunder and
the trumpet, and when they saw the lightning
and the smoke rising from the mountain, they
shook with fear and stood far away from the
mountain. 19Then they said to Moses, "Speak to
us yourself, and we will listen. But don't let
God speak to us, or we will die."
20Then Moses said to the people, "Don't be
afraid, because God has come to test you. He
wants you to respect him so you will not sin."
21The people stood far away from the
mountain while Moses went near the dark
cloud where God was. 22Then the LORD told
Moses to say these things to the Israelites: "You
yourselves have seen that I talked with you
from heaven. 23You must not use gold or silver
to make idols for yourselves; do not worship
these gods in addition to me.
24"Make an altar of dirt for me, and sacrifice
on it your whole burnt offerings and fellowship offerings, your sheep and your cattle.
Worship me in every place that I choose, and I
will come and bless you. 25If you use stones to
make an altar for me, don't use stones that you
have shaped with tools. When you use any
tools on them, you make them unsuitable for
use in worship. 26And you must not go up to
my altar on steps, or people will be able to see
under your clothes."

LAWS FOR LIVING

21
1Then God said to Moses, "These are the
laws for living that you will give to the Israelites:
2"If you buy a Hebrew slave, he will serve
you for six years. In the seventh year you are
to set him free, and he will have to pay nothing. 3If he is not married when he becomes
your slave, he must leave without a wife. But if
he is married when he becomes your slave, he
may take his wife with him. 4If the slave's master gives him a wife, and she gives birth to sons
or daughters, the woman and her children will
belong to the master. When the slave is set free,
only he may leave.
5"But if the slave says, 'I love my master, my
wife and my children, and I don't want to go

WHAT'S IT MEAN?

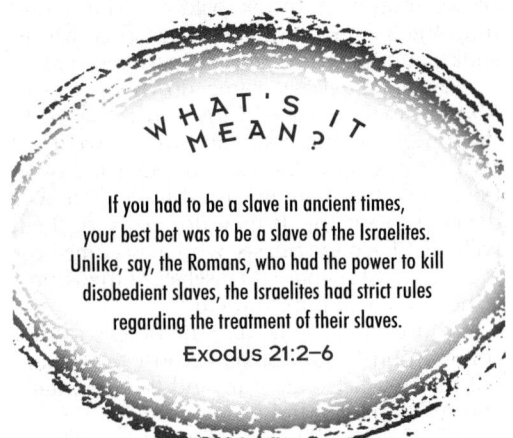

If you had to be a slave in ancient times, your best bet was to be a slave of the Israelites. Unlike, say, the Romans, who had the power to kill disobedient slaves, the Israelites had strict rules regarding the treatment of their slaves.

Exodus 21:2–6

free,' [6]then the slave's master must take him to God. The master is to take him to a door or doorframe and punch a hole through the slave's ear using a sharp tool. Then the slave will serve that master all his life.

[7]"If a man sells his daughter as a slave, the rules for setting her free are different from the rules for setting the male slaves free. [8]If the master wanted to marry her but then decided he was not pleased with her, he must let one of her close relatives buy her back. He has no right to sell her to foreigners, because he has treated her unfairly. [9]If the man who bought her promises to let the woman marry his son, he must treat her as a daughter. [10]If the man who bought her marries another woman, he must not keep his first wife from having food or clothing or sexual relations. [11]If he does not give her these three things, she may go free, and she owes him no money.

LAWS ABOUT INJURIES

[12]"Anyone who hits a person and kills him must be put to death. [13]But if a person kills someone accidentally, God allowed that to happen, so the person must go to a place I will choose. [14]But if someone plans and murders another person on purpose, put him to death, even if he has run to my altar for safety.

[15]"Anyone who hits his father or his mother must be put to death.

[16]"Anyone who kidnaps someone and either sells him as a slave or still has him when he is caught must be put to death.

[17]"Anyone who says cruel things to his father or mother must be put to death.

[18]"If two men argue, and one hits the other with a rock or with his fist, the one who is hurt but not killed might have to stay in bed. [19]Later if he is able to get up and walk around outside with his walking stick, the one who hit him is not to be punished. But he must pay the injured man for the loss of his time, and he must support the injured man until he is completely healed.

"You must not use gold or silver to make idols for yourselves; do not worship these gods in addition to me." (Exodus 20:23)

[20]"If a man beats his male or female slave with a stick, and the slave dies on the spot, the owner must be punished. [21]But if the slave gets well after a day or two, the owner will not be punished since the slave belongs to him.

[22]"Suppose two men are fighting and hit a pregnant woman, causing the baby to come out. If there is no further injury, the man who caused the accident must pay money—whatever amount the woman's husband says and the court allows. [23]But if there is further injury, then the punishment that must be paid is life for life, [24]eye for eye, tooth for tooth, hand for hand, foot for foot, [25]burn for burn, wound for wound, and bruise for bruise.

ABORTION
Does God care for the unborn? (21:22–25)

[26]"If a man hits his male or female slave in the eye, and the eye is blinded, the man is to free the slave to pay for the eye. [27]If a master knocks out a tooth of his male or female slave, the man is to free the slave to pay for the tooth.

[28]"If a man's bull kills a man or woman, you must kill that bull by throwing stones at it, and you should not eat the bull. But the owner of the bull is not guilty. [29]However, suppose the bull has hurt people in the past and the owner, though warned, did not keep it in a pen. Then if it kills a man or woman, the bull must be stoned to death, and the owner must also be put to death. [30]But if the family of the dead person accepts money, the one who owned the bull may buy back his life, but he must pay whatever is demanded. [31]Use this same law if the bull kills a person's son or daughter. [32]If the bull kills a male or female slave, the owner must pay the master the price for a new slave, or twelve ounces of silver, and the bull must also be stoned to death.

[33]"If a man takes the cover off a pit, or digs a pit and does not cover it, and another man's ox or donkey comes and falls into it, [34]the owner of the pit must pay the owner of the animal for the loss. The dead animal will belong to the one who pays.

[35]"If a man's bull kills another man's bull, they must sell the bull that is alive. Both men will get half of the money and half of the bull that was killed. [36]But if a person's bull has hurt other animals in the past and the owner did not keep it in a pen, that owner must pay bull for bull, and the dead animal is his.

PROPERTY LAWS

22

[1]"If a man steals a bull or a sheep and kills or sells it, he must pay back five bulls for the one bull he stole and four sheep for the one sheep he stole.

2-4"The robber who is caught must pay back
what he stole. If he owns nothing, he must be
sold as a slave to pay for what he stole. If
the stolen animal is found alive with the robber, he must give the owner two animals for
every animal he stole, whether it was a bull,
donkey, or sheep.
"If a thief is killed while breaking into a
house at night, the one who killed him is not
guilty of murder. But if this happens during the
day, he is guilty of murder.
5"If a man lets his farm animal graze in his
field or vineyard, and it wanders into another
man's field or vineyard, the owner of the animal
must pay back the loss from the best of his crop.
6"Suppose a man starts a fire that spreads
through the thornbushes to his neighbor's
field. If the fire burns his neighbor's growing
grain or grain that has been stacked, or if it
burns his whole field, the person who started
the fire must pay for what was burned.
7"Suppose a man gives his neighbor money
or other things to keep for him and those
things are stolen from the neighbor's house. If
the thief is caught, he must pay back twice as
much as he stole. 8But if the thief is never
found, the owner of the house must make a
promise before God that he has not stolen his
neighbor's things.
9"Suppose two men disagree about who
owns something—whether ox, donkey, sheep,
clothing, or something else that is lost. If each
says, 'This is mine,' each man must bring his
case to God. God's judges will decide who is
guilty, and that person must pay the other man
twice as much as the object is worth.
10"Suppose a man asks his neighbor to keep
his donkey, ox, sheep, or some other animal
for him, and that animal dies, gets hurt, or is
taken away, without anyone seeing what happened. 11That neighbor must promise before
the LORD that he did not harm or kill the other
man's animal, and the owner of the animal
must accept his promise made before God. The
neighbor does not have to pay the owner for
the animal. 12But if the animal was stolen from
the neighbor, he must pay the owner for it. 13If
wild animals killed it, the neighbor must bring
the body as proof, and he will not have to pay
for the animal that was killed.
14"If a man borrows an animal from his
neighbor, and it gets hurt or dies while the
owner is not there, the one who borrowed it
must pay the owner for the animal. 15But if the
owner is with the animal, the one who borrowed it does not have to pay. If the animal
was rented, the rental price covers the loss.

LAWS AND RELATIONSHIPS

16"Suppose a man finds a woman who is
not pledged to be married and has never had
sexual relations with a man. If he tricks her
into having sexual relations with him, he must
give her family the payment to marry her, and
she will become his wife. 17But if her father refuses to allow his daughter to marry him, the
man must still give the usual payment for a
bride who has never had sexual relations.
18"Put to death any woman who does evil
magic.
19"Put to death anyone who has sexual relations with an animal.
20"Destroy completely any person who
makes a sacrifice to any god except the LORD.
21"Do not cheat or hurt a foreigner, because
you were foreigners in the land of Egypt.

On the Edge

Put to death any woman who does evil magic (Ex. 22:18).

"You must not try to tell the future by signs or black magic"! That's what Leviticus 19:26 says. Don't even think about it. The world of witchcraft and black magic is very real and totally controlled by Satan. Experimenting with spells and curses is asking Satan to use his power for you. He will, but not without a trade. He'll want something from you in exchange for his power. People who experiment with witchcraft can really get messed up because they start out by just letting Satan have a tiny part of them. But the next time he requires a little more; then before they know it he's moved in and he's running the whole place. Stay away from witches, Satan worship, black magic, animal sacrifice, even "white witchcraft"—anything that promotes darkness and evil. Some forms are easy to spot, but others are sneaky. Check out movies, books, music—anything that goes into your head. Satan is happy if he can even get you to think about him. The old saying is still good: "Hear no evil. See no evil. Speak no evil."

SEE FOR YOURSELF:
Lev. 19:26; 20:6;
Phil. 4:8;
1 Thess. 5:21–22;
Rev. 21:8

WHAT'S IT MEAN?

The law was serious business among the Israelites, who considered all crimes to be against God. The people were responsible for treating each other fairly. Those who didn't were punished publicly.
Exodus 22:21–24

22"Do not cheat a widow or an orphan. 23If
you do, and they cry out to me for help, I certainly will hear their cry. 24And I will be very
angry and kill you in war. Then your wives
will become widows, and your children will
become orphans.
25"If you lend money to one of my people
who is poor, do not treat him as a moneylend-
er would. Charge him nothing for using your
money. 26If your neighbor gives you his coat as
a promise for the money he owes you, you
must give it back to him by sunset, 27because it
is the only cover to keep his body warm. He
has nothing else to sleep in. If he cries out to
me for help, I will listen, because I am merciful.
28"You must not speak against God or curse
a leader of your people.
29"Do not hold back your offering from the
first of your harvest and the first wine that you
make. Also, you must give me your firstborn
sons. 30You must do the same with your bulls
and your sheep. Let the firstborn males stay
with their mothers for seven days, and on the
eighth day you must give them to me.
31"You are to be my holy
people. You must not eat the
meat of any animal that has
been killed by wild animals.
Instead, give it to the dogs.

GOSSIP
Does God command us not to gossip? (23:1)

LAWS ABOUT FAIRNESS

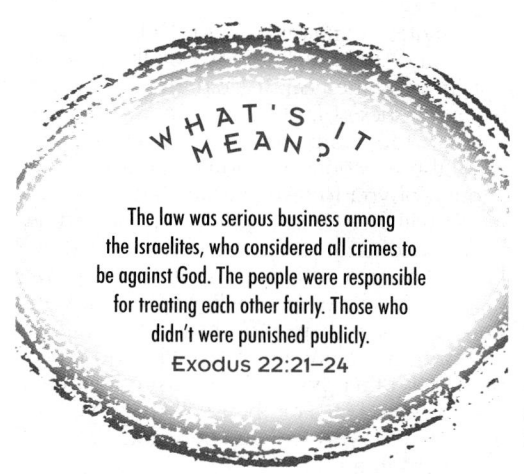

23
1"You must not tell lies. If you are a witness
in court, don't help a wicked person by telling
lies.
2"You must not do wrong just because
everyone else is doing it. If you are a witness in
court, you must not ruin a fair trial. You must
not tell lies just because everyone else is. 3If a
poor person is in court, you must not take his
side just because he is poor.
4"If you see your enemy's ox or donkey
wandering away, you must return it to him. 5If
you see that your enemy's donkey has fallen
because its load is too heavy, do not leave it
there. You must help your enemy get the donkey back on its feet.
6"You must not be unfair to a poor person
when he is in court. 7You must not lie when
you accuse someone in court. Never allow an
innocent or honest person to be put to death
as punishment, because I will not treat guilty
people as if they were innocent.
8"You must not accept money from a person who wants you to lie in court, because
such money will not let you see what is right.
Such money makes good people tell lies.
9"You must not mistreat a foreigner. You
know how it feels to be a foreigner, because
you were foreigners in Egypt.

LAWS FOR THE SABBATH

10"For six years you are to plant and harvest
crops on your land. 11Then during the seventh
year, do not plow or plant your land. If any
food grows there, allow the poor people to
have it, and let the wild animals eat what is left.
You should do the same with your vineyards
and your orchards of olive trees.
12"You should work six days a week, but on
the seventh day you must rest. This lets your
ox and your donkey rest, and it also lets the
slave born in your house and the foreigner be
refreshed.
13"Be sure to do all that I have said to you.
You must not even say the names of other
gods; those names must not come out of your
mouth.

THREE YEARLY FEASTS

14"Three times each year you must hold a
feast to honor me. 15You must celebrate the
Feast of Unleavened Bread in the way I commanded you. For seven days you must eat
bread that is made without yeast at the set time
during the month of Abib, the month when
you came out of Egypt. No one is to come to
worship me without bringing an offering.
16"You must celebrate the Feast of Weeks.
Offer to God the first things you harvest from
the crops you planted in your fields.
"You must celebrate the Feast of Shelters in
the fall, when you gather all the crops from
your fields.
17"So three times during every year all your
males must come to worship the LORD God.
18"You must not offer animal blood along
with anything that has yeast in it.

"You must not save any of the fat from the
sacrifice for the next day.
19"You must bring the best of the firstfruits
of your land to the Holy Tent[n] of the LORD
your God.
"You must not cook a young goat in its
mother's milk.

GOD WILL HELP ISRAEL

20"I am sending an angel ahead of you, who
will protect you as you travel. He will lead you
to the place I have prepared. 21Pay attention to
the angel and obey him. Do not turn against
him; he will not forgive such turning against
him because my power is in him. 22If you listen
carefully to all he says and do everything that I
tell you, I will be an enemy to your enemies. I
will fight all who fight against you. 23My angel
will go ahead of you and take you into the
land of the Amorites, Hittites, Perizzites, Canaanites, Hivites, and Jebusites, and I will destroy them.

WHAT'S IT MEAN?

The Amorites, Hittites, Perizzites, Canaanites, Hivites, and Jebusites all lived in the land God had promised to Abraham and his descendants. The Hittites lived as far north as modern-day Turkey. The Canaanites lived between the Jordan River and the Mediterranean Sea. The Jebusites could be found in what is now Jerusalem.
Exodus 23:23

24"You must not bow down to their gods or
worship them. You must not live the way those
people live. You must destroy their idols,
breaking into pieces the stone pillars they use
in worship. 25If you worship the LORD your
God, I will bless your bread and your water. I
will take away sickness from you. 26None of
your women will have her baby die before it is
born, and all women will have children. I will
allow you to live long lives.
27"I will make your enemies afraid of me. I
will confuse any people you fight against, and I
will make all your enemies run away from you.
28I will send terror ahead of you that will force
the Hivites, Canaanites, and Hittites out of
your way. 29But I will not force all those people
out in only one year. If I did, the land would
become a desert and the wild animals would
become too many for you. 30Instead, I will
force those people out slowly, until there are
enough of you to take over the land.
31"I will give you the land from the Red Sea
to the Mediterranean Sea, and from the desert
to the Euphrates River. I will give you power
over the people who now live in the land, and
you will force them out ahead of you. 32You
must not make an agreement with those people or with their gods. 33You must not let them
live in your land, or they will make you sin
against me. If you worship their gods, you will
be caught in a trap."

GOD AND ISRAEL MAKE THEIR AGREEMENT

24
1The LORD told Moses, "You, Aaron, Nadab,
Abihu, and seventy of the older leaders of Israel must come up to me and worship me from a
distance. 2Then Moses alone must come near
me; the others must not come near. The rest of
the people must not come up the mountain
with Moses."
3Moses told the people all the LORD's words
and laws for living. Then all of the people answered out loud together, "We will do all the
things the LORD has said." 4So Moses wrote
down all the words of the LORD. And he got up
early the next morning and built an altar near
the bottom of the mountain. He set up twelve
stones, one stone for each of the twelve tribes
of Israel. 5Then Moses sent young Israelite men
to offer whole burnt offerings and to sacrifice
young bulls as fellowship offerings to the
LORD. 6Moses put half of the blood of these
animals in bowls, and he sprinkled the other
half of the blood on the altar. 7Then he took
the Book of the Agreement and read it so the
people could hear him. And they said, "We will
do everything that the LORD has said; we will
obey."
8Then Moses took the blood from the
bowls and sprinkled it on the people, saying,
"This is the blood that begins the Agreement,
the Agreement which the LORD has made with
you about all these words."
9Moses, Aaron, Nadab, Abihu, and seventy
of the older leaders of Israel went up the
mountain 10and saw the God of Israel. Under
his feet was a surface that looked as if it were
paved with blue sapphire stones, and it was as
clear as the sky! 11These leaders of the Israelites

23:19 Holy Tent Literally, "house of the LORD your God." See Exodus 25:9.

WHAT'S IT MEAN?

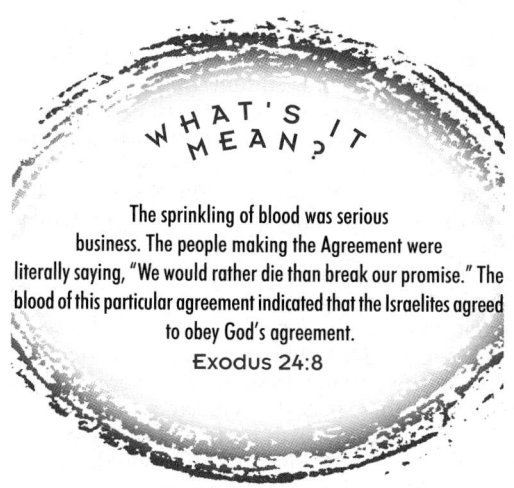

The sprinkling of blood was serious business. The people making the Agreement were literally saying, "We would rather die than break our promise." The blood of this particular agreement indicated that the Israelites agreed to obey God's agreement.

Exodus 24:8

saw God, but God did not destroy them. Then they ate and drank together.

GOD PROMISES MOSES THE STONE TABLETS

12The LORD said to Moses, "Come up the mountain to me. Wait there, and I will give you two stone tablets. On these are the teachings and the commands I have written to instruct the people."

13So Moses and his helper Joshua set out, and Moses went up to Sinai, the mountain of God. 14Moses said to the older leaders, "Wait here for us until we come back to you. Aaron and Hur are with you, and anyone who has a disagreement with others can take it to them."

MOSES MEETS WITH GOD

15When Moses went up on the mountain, the cloud covered it. 16The glory of the LORD came down on Mount Sinai, and the cloud covered it for six days. On the seventh day the LORD called to Moses from inside the cloud. 17To the Israelites the glory of the LORD looked like a fire burning on top of the mountain. 18Then Moses went into the cloud and went higher up the mountain. He was on the mountain for forty days and forty nights.

GIFTS FOR THE LORD

25

1The LORD said to Moses, 2"Tell the Israelites to bring me gifts. Receive for me the gifts each person wants to give. 3These are the gifts that you should receive from them: gold, silver, bronze; 4blue, purple, and red thread; fine linen, goat hair, 5sheepskins that are dyed red; fine leather; acacia wood; 6olive oil to burn in the lamps; spices for sweet-smelling incense, and the special olive oil poured on a person's head to make him a priest; 7onyx stones, and other jewels to be put on the holy vest and the chest covering.

8"The people must build a holy place for me so that I can live among them. 9Build this Holy Tent and everything in it by the plan I will show you.

THE ARK OF THE AGREEMENT

10"Use acacia wood and build an Ark forty-five inches long, twenty-seven inches wide, and twenty-seven inches high. 11Cover the Ark inside and out with pure gold, and put a gold strip all around it. 12Make four gold rings for the Ark and attach them to its four feet, two rings on each side. 13Then make poles from acacia wood and cover them with gold. 14Put the poles through the rings on the sides of the Ark, and use these poles to carry it. 15These poles must always stay in the rings of the Ark. Do not take them out. 16Then put in the Ark the Agreement which I will make with you.

WHAT'S IT MEAN?

Acacia wood was used because it's strong enough to withstand hungry insects and preserve the contents of the chest. If you'd like some acacia wood for your next building project, head for the Sinai Desert, southern Palestine, or Egypt. That's where the trees grow.

Exodus 25:10

17"Then make a lid of pure gold for the Ark; this is the mercy seat. Make it forty-five inches long and twenty-seven inches wide. 18Then hammer gold to make two creatures with wings, and put one on each end of the lid. 19Attach one creature on one end of the lid and the other creature on the other end. Make them to be one piece with the lid at the ends. 20The creatures' wings should be spread upward, covering the lid, and the creatures are to face each other across the lid. 21Put this lid on top of the Ark, and put in the Ark the Agreement which I will make with you. 22I will meet with you there, above the lid between the two winged creatures on the Ark of the Agreement. There I will give you all my commands for the Israelites.

THE TABLE

23"Make a table out of acacia wood, thirty-six inches long, eighteen inches wide, and twenty-seven inches high. 24Cover it with pure gold, and put a gold strip around it. 25Make a frame three inches high that stands up all around the edge, and put a gold strip around it. 26Then make four gold rings. Attach them to the four corners of the table where the four legs are. 27Put the rings close to the frame around the top of the table, because they will hold the poles for carrying it. 28Make the poles out of acacia wood, cover them with gold, and carry the table with these poles. 29Make the plates and bowls for the table, as well as the jars and cups, out of pure gold. They will be used for pouring out the drink offerings. 30On this table put the bread that shows you are in my presence so that it is always there in front of me.

THE LAMPSTAND

31"Hammer pure gold to make a lampstand. Its base, stand, flower-like cups, buds, and petals must all be joined together in one piece. 32The lampstand must have six branches going out from its sides—three on one side and three on the other. 33Each branch must have three cups shaped like almond flowers on it. Each cup must have a bud and a petal. Each of the six branches going out from the lampstand must be the same. 34And there must be four more cups made like almond flowers on the lampstand itself. These cups must also have buds and petals. 35Put a bud under each pair of branches that goes out from the lampstand. Each of the six branches going out from the lampstand must be the same. 36The branches, buds, and lampstand must be made of one piece, hammered out of pure gold.

37"Then make seven small oil lamps and put them on the lampstand so that they give light to the area in front of it. 38The wick trimmers and trays must be made of pure gold. 39Use seventy-five pounds of pure gold to make the lampstand and everything with it. 40Be very careful to make them by the plan I showed you on the mountain.

THE HOLY TENT

25

1"Make for the Holy Tent ten curtains of fine linen and blue, purple, and red thread. Have a skilled craftsman sew designs of creatures with wings on the pieces of cloth. 2Make each curtain the same size—forty-two feet long and six feet wide. 3Sew five curtains together for one set, and sew the other curtains together for the second set. 4Make loops of blue cloth on the edge of the end curtain of one set, and do the same for the end curtain of the other set. 5Make fifty loops on the end curtain of the first set and fifty loops on the end curtain of the second set. These loops must be opposite each other. 6And make fifty gold hooks to join the two sets of curtains so that the Holy Tent is one piece.

7"Then make another tent that will cover the Holy Tent, using eleven curtains made from goat hair. 8All these curtains must be the same size—forty-five feet long and six feet wide. 9Sew five of the curtains together into one set. Then sew the other six curtains together into the second set. Fold the sixth curtain double over the front of the Tent. 10Make fifty loops down the edge of the end curtain of one set, and do the same for the end curtain of the other set. 11Then make fifty bronze hooks and put them in the loops to join the tent together so that the covering is one piece. 12Let the extra half piece of cloth hang over the back of the Holy Tent. 13There will be eighteen inches hanging over the sides of the Holy Tent, to protect it. 14Make a covering for the Holy Tent from sheepskins colored red, and over that make a covering from fine leather.

15"Use acacia wood to make upright frames for the Holy Tent. 16Each frame must be fifteen feet long and twenty-seven inches wide, 17with two pegs side by side. Every frame must be made the same way. 18Make twenty frames for the south side of the Holy Tent. 19Each frame must have two silver bases to go under it, a peg fitting into each base. You must make forty silver bases for the frames. 20Make twenty more frames for the north side of the Holy Tent 21and forty silver bases for them—two bases for each frame. 22You must make six frames for the rear or west end of the Holy Tent 23and two frames for each corner at the rear. 24The two frames are to be doubled at the bottom and joined at the top with a metal ring. Both corner frames must be made this way. 25So there will be a total of eight frames at the rear of the Tent, and there will be sixteen silver bases—two bases under each frame.

26"Make crossbars of acacia wood to connect the upright frames of the Holy Tent. Make five crossbars to hold the frames together on one side 27and five to hold the frames together on the other side. Also make five crossbars to hold the frames together on the west end, at the rear. 28The middle crossbar is to be set halfway up the frames, and it is to run along the entire length of each side and rear. 29Make gold

rings on the sides of the frames to hold the
crossbars, and cover the frames and the crossbars with gold. 30 Set up the Holy Tent by the
plan shown to you on the mountain.

WHAT'S IT MEAN?

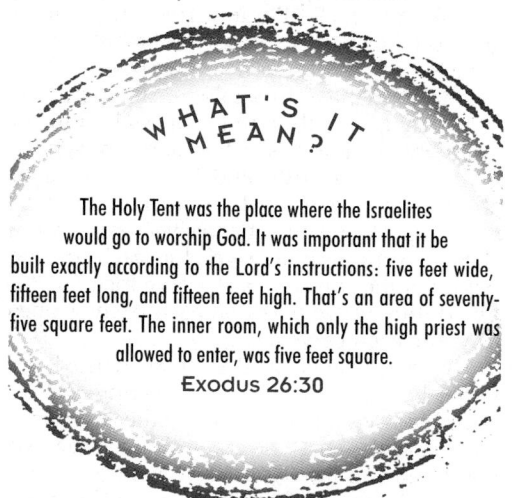

The Holy Tent was the place where the Israelites would go to worship God. It was important that it be built exactly according to the Lord's instructions: five feet wide, fifteen feet long, and fifteen feet high. That's an area of seventy-five square feet. The inner room, which only the high priest was allowed to enter, was five feet square.

Exodus 26:30

31 "Make a curtain of fine linen and blue,
purple, and red thread, and have a skilled
craftsman sew designs of creatures with wings
on it. 32 Hang the curtain by gold hooks on four
posts of acacia wood that are covered with
gold, and set them in four silver bases. 33 Hang
the curtain from the hooks in the roof, and put
the Ark of the Agreement containing the two
stone tablets behind it. This curtain will separate the Holy Place from the Most Holy Place.
34 Put the lid on the Ark of the Agreement in the
Most Holy Place.
35 "Outside the curtain, put the table on the
north side of the Holy Tent. Put the lampstand
on the south side of the Holy Tent across from
the table.

THE ENTRANCE OF THE HOLY TENT

36 "Then, for the entrance of the Tent, make a
curtain with fine linen and blue, purple, and
red thread. Someone who can sew well is to
sew designs on it. 37 Make five posts of acacia
wood covered with gold. Make gold hooks for
them on which to hang the curtain, and make
five bronze bases for them.

THE ALTAR FOR BURNT OFFERINGS

27 1 "Make an altar of acacia wood, four and
one-half feet high. It should be square—seven
and one-half feet long and seven and one-half
feet wide. 2 Make each of the four corners of the
altar stick out like a horn, in such a way that
the corners with their horns are all one piece.
Then cover the whole altar with bronze.
3 "Use bronze to make all the tools and
dishes that will be used on the altar: the pots to
remove the ashes, the shovels, the bowls for
sprinkling blood, the meat forks, and the pans
for carrying the burning wood.
4 "Make a large bronze screen to hold the
burning wood, and put a bronze ring at each
of the four corners of it. 5 Put the screen inside
the altar, under its rim, halfway up from the
bottom.
6 "Make poles of acacia wood for the altar,
and cover them with bronze. 7 Put the poles
through the rings on both sides of the altar to
carry it. 8 Make the altar out of boards and
leave the inside hollow. Make it as you were
shown on the mountain.

THE COURTYARD OF THE HOLY TENT

9 "Make a wall of curtains to form a courtyard around the Holy Tent. The south side
should have a wall of fine linen curtains one
hundred fifty feet long. 10 Hang the curtains
with silver hooks and bands on twenty bronze
posts with twenty bronze bases. 11 The north
side must also be one hundred fifty feet long.
Hang its curtains on silver hooks and bands
on twenty bronze posts with twenty bronze
bases.
12 "The west end of the courtyard must have
a wall of curtains seventy-five feet long, with
ten posts and ten bases on that wall. 13 The east
end of the courtyard must also be seventy-five
feet long. 14 On one side of the entry, there is to
be a wall of curtains twenty-two and one-half
feet long, held up by three posts on three bases.
15 On the other side of the entry, there is also to
be a wall of curtains twenty-two and one-half
feet long, held up by three posts on three bases.
16 "The entry to the courtyard is to be a curtain thirty feet wide, made of fine linen with
blue, purple, and red thread. Someone who
can sew well is to sew designs on it. It is to be
held up by four posts on four bases. 17 All the
posts around the courtyard must have silver
bands and hooks and bronze bases. 18 The
courtyard must be one hundred fifty feet long
and seventy-five feet wide, with a wall of curtains around it seven and one-half feet high,
made of fine linen. The bases in which the
posts are set must be bronze. 19 All the things
used in the Holy Tent and all the tent pegs for
the Holy Tent and the wall around the courtyard must be made of bronze.

OIL FOR THE LAMP

20 "Command the people of Israel to bring
you pure olive oil, made from pressed olives,

to keep the lamps on the lampstand burning.
21 Aaron and his sons must keep the lamps
burning before the LORD from evening till
morning. This will be in the Meeting Tent, outside the curtain which is in front of the Ark.
The Israelites and their descendants must obey
this rule from now on.

CLOTHES FOR THE PRIESTS

28
1 "Tell your brother Aaron to come to you,
along with his sons Nadab, Abihu, Eleazar, and
Ithamar. Separate them from the other Israelites to serve me as priests. 2 Make holy clothes
for your brother Aaron to give him honor and
beauty. 3 Tell all the skilled craftsmen to whom I
have given wisdom to make special clothes for
Aaron—clothes to show that he belongs to me
so that he may serve me as a priest. 4 These are
the clothes they must make: a chest covering, a
holy vest, an outer robe, a woven inner robe, a
turban, and a cloth belt. The craftsmen must
make these holy clothes for your brother
Aaron and his sons. Then they may serve me
as priests. 5 The craftsmen must use gold and
blue, purple and red thread, and fine linen.

THE HOLY VEST

6 "Use gold and blue, purple and red thread,
and fine linen to make the holy vest; skilled
craftsmen are to make it. 7 At each top corner of
this holy vest there will be a pair of shoulder
straps tied together over each shoulder.
8 "The craftsmen will very carefully weave a
belt on the holy vest that is made with the
same materials—gold and blue, purple and red
thread, and fine linen.
9 "Take two onyx stones and write the
names of the twelve sons of Israel on them,
10 six on one stone and six on the other. Write
the names in order, from the oldest son to the
youngest. 11 Carve the names of the sons of Israel on these stones in the same way a person
carves words and designs on a seal. Put gold
around the stones to hold them on the holy
vest. 12 Then put the two stones on the two
straps of the holy vest as reminders of the
twelve sons of Israel. Aaron is to wear their
names on his shoulders in the presence of the
LORD as reminders of the sons of Israel. 13 Make
two gold pieces to hold the stones 14 and two
chains of pure gold, twisted together like a
rope. Attach the chains to the two gold pieces
that hold the stones.

THE CHEST COVERING

15 "Make a chest covering to help in making
decisions. The craftsmen should make it as
they made the holy vest, using gold and blue,
purple and red thread, and fine linen. 16 The
chest covering must be square—nine inches
long and nine inches wide—and folded double
to make a pocket. 17 Put four rows of beautiful
gems on the chest covering: The first row must
have a ruby, topaz, and yellow quartz; 18 the
second must have turquoise, a sapphire, and
an emerald; 19 the third must have a jacinth, an
agate, and an amethyst; 20 the fourth must have
a chrysolite, an onyx, and a jasper. Put gold
around these jewels to attach them to the chest
covering. 21 There must be twelve jewels on the
chest covering—one jewel for each of the
names of the sons of Israel. Carve the name of
one of the twelve tribes on each of the stones
as you would carve a seal.
22 "Make chains of pure gold, twisted together like rope, for the chest covering. 23 Make
two gold rings and put them on the two upper
corners of the chest covering. 24 Attach the two
gold chains to the two rings at the upper corners of the chest covering. 25 Attach the other
ends of the two chains to the two gold pieces
on the shoulder straps in the front of the holy
vest.
26 "Make two gold rings and put them at the
two lower corners of the chest covering, on the
inside edge next to the holy vest. 27 Make two
more gold rings and attach them to the bottom
of the shoulder straps in the front of the holy
vest. Put them close to the seam above the woven belt of the holy vest. 28 Join the rings of the
chest covering to the rings of the holy vest
with blue ribbon, connecting it to the woven
belt so the chest covering will not swing out
from the holy vest.
29 "When Aaron enters the Holy Place, he
will wear the names of the sons of Israel over
his heart, on the chest covering that helps in
making decisions. This will be a continual reminder before the LORD. 30 And put the Urim
and Thummim inside the chest covering so
that they will be on Aaron's heart when he
goes before the LORD. They will help in making
decisions for the Israelites. So Aaron will always carry them with him when he is before
the LORD.
31 "Make the outer robe to be worn under the
holy vest, using only blue cloth. 32 Make a hole
in the center for Aaron's head, with a woven
collar around the hole so it will not tear. 33 Make
balls like pomegranates of blue, purple, and red
thread, and hang them around the bottom of
the outer robe with gold bells between them.
34 All around the bottom of the outer robe there
should be a gold bell and a pomegranate ball, a

gold bell and a pomegranate ball. 35 Aaron must
wear this robe when he serves as priest. The
ringing of the bells will be heard when he enters
and leaves the Holy Place before the LORD so
that Aaron will not die.

36 "Make a strip of pure gold and carve these
words on it as you would carve a seal: 'Holy to
the LORD.' 37 Use blue ribbon to tie it to the turban; put it on the front of the turban. 38 Aaron
must wear this on his forehead. In this way, he
will be blamed if anything is wrong with the
gifts of the Israelites. Aaron must always wear
this on his head so the LORD will accept the
gifts of the people.

39 "Make the woven inner robe of fine linen,
and make the turban of fine linen also. Make
the cloth belt with designs sewn on it. 40 Also
make woven inner robes, cloth belts, and
headbands for Aaron's sons, to give them
honor and beauty. 41 Put these clothes on your
brother Aaron and his sons, and pour olive oil
on their heads to appoint them as priests.
Make them belong to me so they may serve me
as priests.

WHAT'S IT MEAN?

Pouring oil on a person's head was a common way of preparing someone for a new job or a promotion. This ceremony was performed by a person acting with God's authority.

Exodus 28:41

42 "Make for them linen underclothes to
cover them from the waist to the upper parts
of the legs. 43 Aaron and his sons must wear
these underclothes when they enter the Meeting Tent and anytime they come near the altar
to serve as priests in the Holy Place. If they do
not wear these clothes, they will be guilty of
wrong, and they will die. This will be a law that
will last from now on for Aaron and all his
descendants.

APPOINTING THE PRIESTS

29
1 "This is what you must do to appoint
Aaron and his sons to serve me as priests. Take
one young bull and two male sheep that have
nothing wrong with them. 2 Use fine wheat
flour without yeast to make bread, cakes mixed
with olive oil, and wafers brushed with olive
oil. 3 Put these in one basket, and bring them
along with the bull and two male sheep. 4 Bring
Aaron and his sons to the entrance of the
Meeting Tent and wash them with water. 5 Take
the clothes and dress Aaron in the inner robe
and the outer robe of the holy vest. Then put
on him the holy vest and the chest covering,
and tie the holy vest on him with its skillfully
woven belt. 6 Put the turban on his head, and
put the holy crown on the turban. 7 Take the
special olive oil and pour it on his head to
make him a priest.

8 "Then bring his sons and put the inner
robes on them. 9 Put the headbands on their
heads, and tie cloth belts around their waists.
Aaron and his descendants will be priests in
Israel, according to a rule that will continue
from now on. This is how you will appoint
Aaron and his sons as priests.

10 "Bring the bull to the front of the Meeting
Tent, and Aaron and his sons must put their
hands on the bull's head. 11 Then kill the bull
before the LORD at the entrance to the Meeting
Tent. 12 Use your finger to put some of the bull's
blood on the corners of the altar, and then
pour the blood that is left at the bottom of the
altar. 13 Take all the fat that covers the inner organs, as well as the best part of the liver, both
kidneys, and the fat around them, and burn
them on the altar. 14 Take the bull's meat, skin,
and intestines, and burn them outside the
camp. This is an offering to take away sin.

15 "Take one of the male sheep, and have
Aaron and his sons put their hands on its
head. 16 Kill it, and take its blood and sprinkle it
on all four sides of the altar. 17 Then cut it into
pieces and wash its inner organs and its legs,
putting them with its head and its other pieces.
18 Burn the whole sheep on the altar; it is a
burnt offering made by fire to the LORD. Its
smell is pleasing to the LORD.

19 "Take the other male sheep, and have
Aaron and his sons put their hands on its
head. 20 Kill it and take some of its blood. Put
the blood on the bottom of the right ears of
Aaron and his sons and on the thumbs of their
right hands and on the big toes of their right
feet. Then sprinkle the rest of the blood against
all four sides of the altar. 21 Take some of the
blood from the altar, and mix it with the special oil used in appointing priests. Sprinkle this
on Aaron and his clothes and on his sons and
their clothes. This will show that Aaron and
his sons and their clothes are given to my service.

22"Then take the fat from the male sheep, the fat tail, and the fat that covers the inner organs. In addition, take the best part of the liver, both kidneys, and the fat around them, and the right thigh. (This is the male sheep to be used in appointing priests.)

23"Then take the basket of bread that you made without yeast, which you put before the LORD. From it take a loaf of bread, a cake made with olive oil, and a wafer. 24Put all of these in the hands of Aaron and his sons, and tell them to present them as an offering to the LORD. 25Then take them from their hands and burn them on the altar with the whole burnt offering. This is an offering made by fire to the LORD; its smell is pleasing to the LORD. 26Then take the breast of the male sheep used to appoint Aaron as priest, and present it before the LORD as an offering. This part of the animal will be your share. 27Set aside the breast and the thigh of the sheep that were used to appoint Aaron and his sons as priests. These parts belong to them. 28They are to be the regular share which the Israelites will always give to Aaron and his sons. It is the gift the Israelites must give to the LORD from their fellowship offerings.

29"The holy clothes made for Aaron will belong to his descendants so that they can wear these clothes when they are appointed as priests. 30Aaron's son, who will become high priest after Aaron, will come to the Meeting Tent to serve in the Holy Place. He is to wear these clothes for seven days.

31"Take the male sheep used to appoint priests and boil its meat in a place that is holy. 32Then at the entrance of the Meeting Tent, Aaron and his sons must eat the meat of the sheep and the bread that is in the basket. 33They should eat these offerings that were used to remove their sins and to make them holy when they were made priests. But no one else is to eat them, because they are holy things. 34If any of the meat from that sheep or any of the bread is left the next morning, it must be burned. It must not be eaten, because it is holy.

35"Do all these things that I commanded you to do to Aaron and his sons, and spend seven days appointing them. 36Each day you are to offer a bull to remove the sins of Aaron and his sons so they will be given for service to the LORD. Make the altar ready for service to the LORD, and pour oil on it to make it holy. 37Spend seven days making the altar ready for service to God and making it holy. Then the altar will become very holy, and anything that touches it must be holy.

THE DAILY SACRIFICES

38"Every day from now on, offer on the altar two lambs that are one year old. 39Offer one lamb in the morning and the other in the evening before dark. 40In the morning, when you offer the first lamb, offer also two quarts of fine flour mixed with one quart of oil from pressed olives. Pour out a quart of wine as a drink offering. 41Offer the second lamb in the evening with the same grain offering and drink offering as you did in the morning. This is an offering made by fire to the LORD, and its smell is pleasing to him.

42"You must burn these things as an offering to the LORD every day, from now on, at the entrance of the Meeting Tent before the LORD. When you make the offering, I, the LORD, will meet you there and speak to you. 43I will meet with the people of Israel there, and that place will be holy because of my glory.

44"So I will make the Meeting Tent and the altar holy; I will also make Aaron and his sons holy so they may serve me as priests. 45I will live with the people of Israel and be their God. 46And they will know that I am the LORD their God who led them out of Egypt so that I could live with them. I am the LORD their God.

THE ALTAR FOR BURNING INCENSE

30

1"Make an altar out of acacia wood for burning incense. 2Make it square—eighteen inches long and eighteen inches wide—and make it thirty-six inches high. The corners that stick out like horns must be one piece with the altar. 3Cover its top, its sides, and its corners with pure gold, and put a gold strip all around the altar. 4Make two gold rings beneath the gold strip on opposite sides of the altar, and slide poles through them to carry the altar.

WHAT'S IT MEAN?

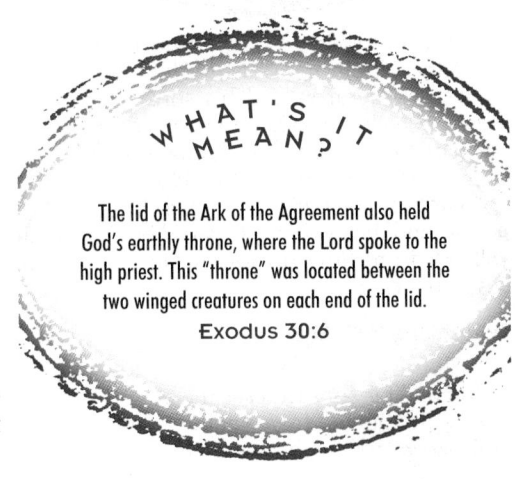

The lid of the Ark of the Agreement also held God's earthly throne, where the Lord spoke to the high priest. This "throne" was located between the two winged creatures on each end of the lid.

Exodus 30:6

5Make the poles from acacia wood and cover them with gold. 6Put the altar of incense in front of the curtain that is near the Ark of the Agreement, in front of the lid that covers that Ark. There I will meet with you.

7"Aaron must burn sweet-smelling incense on the altar every morning when he comes to take care of the oil lamps. 8He must burn incense again in the evening when he lights the lamps, so incense will burn before the LORD every day from now on. 9Do not use this altar for offering any other incense, or burnt offering, or any kind of grain offering, or drink offering. 10Once a year Aaron must make the altar ready for service to God by putting blood on its corners—the blood of the animal offered to remove sins. He is to do this once a year from now on. This altar belongs completely to the LORD's service."

THE TAX FOR THE MEETING TENT

11The LORD said to Moses, 12"When you count the people of Israel, every person must buy back his life from the LORD so that no terrible things will happen to the people when you number them. 13Every person who is counted must pay one-fifth of an ounce of silver. (This is set by using one-half of the Holy Place measure, which weighs two-fifths of an ounce.) This amount is a gift to the LORD. 14Every person who is counted and is twenty years old or older must give this amount to the LORD. 15A rich person must not give more than one-fifth of an ounce, and a poor person must not give less. You are paying this to the LORD to buy back your lives. 16Gather from the people of Israel this money paid to buy back their lives, and spend it on things for the service in the Meeting Tent. This payment will remind the LORD that the Israelites' lives have been bought back."

THE BRONZE BOWL

17The LORD said to Moses, 18"Make a bronze bowl, on a bronze stand, for washing. Put the bowl and stand between the Meeting Tent and the altar, and put water in the bowl. 19Aaron and his sons must wash their hands and feet with the water from this bowl. 20Each time they enter the Meeting Tent they must wash with water so they will not die. Whenever they approach the altar to serve as priests and offer a sacrifice to the LORD by fire, 21they must wash their hands and their feet so they will not die. This is a rule which Aaron and his descendants are to keep from now on."

OIL FOR APPOINTING

22Then the LORD said to Moses, 23"Take the finest spices: twelve pounds of liquid myrrh, half that amount (that is, six pounds) of sweet-smelling cinnamon, six pounds of sweet-smelling cane, 24and twelve pounds of cassia. Weigh all these by the Holy Place measure. Also take four quarts of olive oil, 25and mix all these things like a perfume to make a holy olive oil. This special oil must be put on people and things to make them ready for service to God. 26Put this oil on the Meeting Tent and the Ark of the Agreement, 27on the table and all its dishes, on the lampstand and all its tools, and on the incense altar. 28Also, put the oil on the altar for burnt offerings and on all its tools, as well as on the bowl and the stand under the bowl. 29You will prepare all these things for service to God, and they will be very holy. Anything that touches these things must be holy.

30"Put the oil on Aaron and his sons to give them for service to me, that they may serve me as priests. 31Tell the Israelites, 'This is to be my holy olive oil from now on. It is to be put on people and things to make them ready for service to God. 32Do not pour it on the bodies of ordinary people, and do not make perfume the same way you make this oil. It is holy, and you must treat it as holy. 33If anyone makes perfume like it or puts it on someone who is not a priest, that person must be cut off from his people.' "

INCENSE

34Then the LORD said to Moses, "Take these sweet-smelling spices: resin, onycha, galbanum, and pure frankincense. Be sure that you have

WHAT'S IT MEAN?

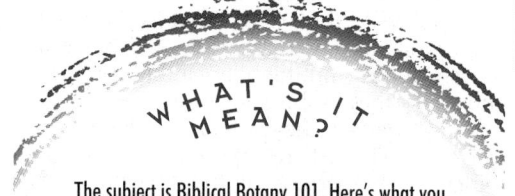

The subject is Biblical Botany 101. Here's what you will need to know for the test. The resin mentioned comes from the storax tree, a small shrub that can be found throughout Palestine. Onycha comes from the sweet-smelling rockrose or ladanum. Galbanum is a milky gum that comes from an herb. Frankincense comes from the Boswellia tree, with its white, star-shaped flowers.

Exodus 30:34–35

equal amounts of each. [35]Make incense as a
person who makes perfume would do. Add
salt to it to keep it pure and holy. [36]Beat some
of the incense into a fine powder, and put it in
front of the Ark of the Agreement in the Meeting Tent, where I will meet with you. You must
use this incense powder only for its very special purpose. [37]Do not make incense for yourselves the same way you make this incense.
Treat it as holy to the LORD. [38]Whoever makes
incense like this to use as perfume must be cut
off from his people."

BEZALEL AND OHOLIAB HELP

31
[1]Then the LORD said to Moses, [2]"See, I have
chosen Bezalel son of Uri from the tribe of Judah. (Uri was the son of Hur.)
[3]I have filled Bezalel with the
Spirit of God and have
given him the skill, ability,
and knowledge to do all
kinds of work. [4]He is
able to design pieces to
be made from gold, sil-
ver, and bronze, [5]to cut
jewels and put them in
metal, to carve wood,
and to do all kinds of
work. [6]I have also chosen
Oholiab son of Ahisamach
from the tribe of Dan to work
with Bezalel. I have given skills to all the
craftsmen, and they will be able to make all
these things I have commanded you: [7]the
Meeting Tent, the Ark of the Agreement, the lid
that covers the Ark, and everything in the Tent.
[8]This includes the table and everything on it,
the pure gold lampstand and everything with
it, the altar of incense, [9]the altar for burnt offerings and everything used with it, and the bowl
and the stand under it. [10]They will make the
woven clothes and the holy clothes for Aaron
and the clothes for his sons to wear when they
serve as priests. [11]They will also make the special olive oil used in appointing people and
things to the service of the LORD, and the
sweet-smelling incense for the Holy Place.
"These workers will make all these things
just as I have commanded you."

THE DAY OF REST

[12]Then the LORD said to Moses, [13]"Tell the
Israelites, 'You must keep the rules about my
Sabbaths, because they will be a sign between
you and me from now on. In this way you will
know that I, the LORD, make you holy.
[14]" 'Make the Sabbath a holy day. If anyone
treats the Sabbath like any other day, that person must be put to death; anyone who works
on the Sabbath day must be cut off from his
people. [15]There are six days for working, but the
seventh day is a day of rest, a day holy for the
LORD. Anyone who works during the Sabbath
day must be put to death. [16]The Israelites must
remember the Sabbath day as an agreement
between them and me that will continue from
now on. [17]The Sabbath day will be a sign between me and the Israelites forever, because in
six days I, the LORD, made the sky and the
earth. On the seventh day I did not work; I
rested.' "
[18]When the LORD finished speaking to Moses on Mount Sinai, he gave him the two stone
tablets with the Agreement
written on them, written by
the finger of God.

"When the LORD finished speaking to Moses on Mount Sinai, he gave him the two stone tablets with the Agreement written on them, written by the finger of God." (Exodus 31:18)

THE PEOPLE MAKE A GOLD CALF

32
[1]The people saw that a
long time had passed and
Moses had not come
down from the moun-
tain. So they gathered
around Aaron and said,
"Moses led us out of Egypt,
but we don't know what has
happened to him. Make us
gods who will lead us."
[2]Aaron said to the people, "Take off the gold
earrings that your wives, sons, and daughters
are wearing, and bring them to me." [3]So all the
people took their gold earrings and brought
them to Aaron. [4]He took the gold from the
people and formed it with a tool and made a
statue of a calf. Then the people said, "Israel,
these are your gods who brought you out of
the land of Egypt!"

WHAT'S IT MEAN?

Bulls were popular worship objects in the ancient world. Centuries-old images of bulls have been found everywhere from the palaces of Crete, an island in the Mediterranean Sea, to the temples of Egypt.

Exodus 32:2–4

BEZALEL made a difference

God creates creators. That's why God is the original Creator. The rest of us, creatures all, in one way or another simply imitate the One who made us. To make this point very clear, God sometimes fills a person with special abilities and calls them to do special work for him. Those people make a difference. One of them was a Bezalel.

God gave Moses, who may not have had an artistic bone in his body, the exact details of the Meeting Tent, that portable worship center the people of Israel would use in the wilderness. Then God gave Moses someone to do the work—Bezalel. God filled Bezalel with the Spirit of God. The results in this case meant two things in Bezalel's life: (1) he could do; (2) he could teach others to do. Bezalel was an artist's artist. He could cast, cut, shape, build, paint, design, sew, and weave objects of exquisite beauty. He helped others do the same. Imagine building a place in which God's presence would be so real that it would take on the form of a cloud or pillar of fire. So, how did Bezalel make a difference? He built a house for God. He helped create a beautiful space in which people could worship. His work touched the spiritual life of an entire nation.

Cutting Edge

YOU can, too!

Perhaps you are a Michelangelo, a da Vinci, a Bezalel in the wings—go for it! In any case, the most important lessons from Bezalel's life are not limited to artists. He was available to God. He was called by God. Bezalel was equipped by God; and he was filled by the Spirit of God. How many of these facts are already true in your Life? Notice that most of Bezalel's portfolio was up to God. The only aspect under his control was availability. Are you available to God? Do you remind yourself and God regularly that you want to serve him in the world? "God made us what we are. In Christ Jesus, God made us to do good works, which God planned in advance for us to live our lives doing" (Eph. 2:10).

Want to know more? Read about Bezalel's gifted work in Exodus 31:1–11; 35:30—36:3.

5When Aaron saw all this, he built an altar before the calf and announced, "Tomorrow there will be a special feast to honor the LORD." 6The people got up early the next morning and offered whole burnt offerings and fellowship offerings. They sat down to eat and drink, and then they got up and sinned sexually.

7Then the LORD said to Moses, "Go down from this mountain, because your people, the people you brought out of the land of Egypt, have ruined themselves. 8They have quickly turned away from the things I commanded them to do. They have made for themselves a calf covered with gold, and they have worshiped it and offered sacrifices to it. They have said, 'Israel, these are your gods who brought you out of Egypt.' "

9The LORD said to Moses, "I have seen these people, and I know that they are very stubborn. 10So now do not stop me. I am so angry with them that I am going to destroy them. Then I will make you and your descendants a great nation."

11But Moses begged the LORD his God and said, "LORD, don't let your anger destroy your people, whom you brought out of Egypt with your great power and strength. 12Don't let the people of Egypt say, 'The LORD brought the Israelites out of Egypt for an evil purpose. He planned to kill them in the mountains and destroy them from the earth.' So stop being angry, and don't destroy your people. 13Remember the men who served you—Abraham, Isaac, and Israel. You promised with an oath to them and said, 'I will make your descendants as many as the stars in the sky. I will give your descendants all this land that I have promised them, and it will be theirs forever.' " 14So the LORD changed his mind and did not destroy the people as he had said he might.

15Then Moses went down the mountain, and in his hands he had the two stone tablets with the Agreement on them. The commands were written on both sides of each stone, front and back. 16God himself had made the tablets, and God himself had written the commands on the tablets.

17When Joshua heard the sound of the people shouting, he said to Moses, "It sounds like war down in the camp."

18Moses answered:

"It is not a shout of victory;
it is not a cry of defeat.
It is the sound of singing that I hear."

19When Moses came close to the camp, he saw the gold calf and the dancing, and he became very angry. He threw down the stone tablets that he was carrying and broke them at the bottom of the mountain. 20Then he took the calf that the people had made and melted it in the fire. He ground it into powder. Then he threw the powder into the water and forced the Israelites to drink it.

21Moses said to Aaron, "What did these people do to you? Why did you cause them to do such a terrible sin?"

22Aaron answered, "Don't be angry, master. You know that these people are always ready to do wrong. 23The people said to me, 'Moses led us out of Egypt, but we don't know what has happened to him. Make us gods who will lead us.' 24So I told the people, 'Take off your gold jewelry.' When they gave me the gold, I threw it into the fire and out came this calf!"

25Moses saw that the people were acting wildly. Aaron had let them get out of control and become fools in front of their enemies. 26So Moses stood at the entrance to the camp and said, "Let anyone who wants to follow the LORD come to me." And all the people from the family of Levi gathered around Moses.

27Then Moses said to them, "The LORD, the God of Israel, says this: 'Every man must put on his sword and go through the camp from one end to the other. Each man must kill his brother, his friend, and his neighbor.' " 28The people from the family of Levi obeyed Moses, and that day about three thousand of the Israelites died. 29Then Moses said, "Today you have been given for service to the LORD. You were willing to kill your own sons and brothers, and God has blessed you for this."

30The next day Moses told the people, "You have done a terrible sin. But now I will go up to the LORD. Maybe I can do something so your sins will be removed." 31So Moses went back to the LORD and said, "How terribly these people have sinned! They have made for themselves gods from gold. 32Now, please forgive them of this sin. If you will not, then erase my name from the book in which you have written the names of your people."

33But the LORD told Moses, "I will erase from my book the names of the people who sin against me. 34So now, go. Lead the people where I have told you, and my angel will lead you. When the time comes to punish, I will punish them for their sin."

35So the LORD caused terrible things to happen to the people because of what they did with the calf Aaron had made.

SIN

Does sin have consequences? (32:33–34)

33 [1]Then the LORD said to Moses, "You and the people you brought out of Egypt must leave this place. Go to the land that I promised with an oath to give to Abraham, Isaac, and Jacob when I said, 'I will give that land to your descendants.' [2]I will send an angel to lead you, and I will force these people out of the land: the Canaanites, Amorites, Hittites, Perizzites, Hivites, and Jebusites. [3]Go up to a fertile land. But I will not go with you, because I might destroy you on the way, since you are such a stubborn people."

[4]When the people heard this bad news, they became very sad, and none of them put on jewelry. [5]This was because the LORD had said to Moses, "Tell the Israelites, 'You are a stubborn people. If I were to go with you even for a moment, I would destroy you. So take off all your jewelry, and I will decide what to do with you.' " [6]So the people of Israel took off their jewelry at Mount Sinai.

THE MEETING TENT

[7]Moses used to take a tent and set it up a long way outside the camp; he called it the "Meeting Tent." Anyone who wanted to ask the LORD about something would go to the Meeting Tent outside the camp. [8]Whenever Moses went out to the Tent, all the people would rise and stand at the entrances of their tents, watching him until he entered the Meeting Tent. [9]When Moses went into the Tent, the pillar of cloud would always come down and stay at the entrance of the Tent while the LORD spoke with Moses. [10]Whenever the people saw the pillar of cloud at the entrance of the Tent, they stood and worshiped, each person at the entrance of his own tent.

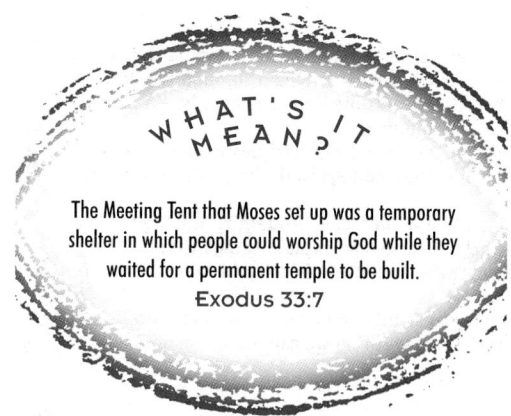

WHAT'S IT MEAN?

The Meeting Tent that Moses set up was a temporary shelter in which people could worship God while they waited for a permanent temple to be built.
Exodus 33:7

[11]The LORD spoke to Moses face to face as a man speaks with his friend. Then Moses would return to the camp, but Moses' young helper, Joshua son of Nun, did not leave the Tent.

[12]Moses said to the LORD, "You have told me to lead these people, but you did not say whom you would send with me. You have said to me, 'I know you very well, and I am pleased with you.' [13]If I have truly pleased you, show me your plans so that I may know you and continue to please you. Remember that this nation is your people."

[14]The LORD answered, "I myself will go with you, and I will give you victory."

[15]Then Moses said to him, "If you yourself don't go with us, then don't send us away from this place. [16]If you don't go with us, no one will know that you are pleased with me and with your people. These people and I will be no different from any other people on earth."

[17]Then the LORD said to Moses, "I will do what you ask, because I know you very well, and I am pleased with you."

MOSES SEES GOD'S GLORY

[18]Then Moses said, "Now, please show me your glory."

[19]The LORD answered, "I will cause all my goodness to pass in front of you, and I will announce my name, the LORD, so you can hear it. I will show kindness to anyone to whom I want to show kindness, and I will show mercy to anyone to whom I want to show mercy. [20]But you cannot see my face, because no one can see me and live.

[21]"There is a place near me where you may stand on a rock. [22]When my glory passes that place, I will put you in a large crack in the rock and cover you with my hand until I have passed by. [23]Then I will take away my hand, and you will see my back. But my face must not be seen."

MOSES GETS NEW STONE TABLETS

34 [1]The LORD said to Moses, "Cut two more stone tablets like the first two, and I will write the same words on them that were on the first two stones which you broke. [2]Be ready tomorrow morning, and then come up on Mount Sinai. Stand before me there on the top of the mountain. [3]No one may come with you or even be seen any place on the mountain. Not even the flocks or herds may eat grass near that mountain."

[4]So Moses cut two stone tablets like the first ones. Then early the next morning he went up Mount Sinai, just as the LORD had commanded him, carrying the two stone tablets with him. [5]Then the LORD came down in the cloud and

stood there with Moses, and the LORD called
out his name: the LORD.
6The LORD passed in front of Moses and
said, "I am the LORD. The LORD is a God who
shows mercy, who is kind, who doesn't become
angry quickly, who has great love and faithfulness 7and is kind to thousands of people. The
LORD forgives people for evil, for sin, and for
turning against him, but he does not forget to
punish guilty people. He will punish not only
the guilty people, but also their children, their
grandchildren, their great-grandchildren, and
their great-great-grandchildren."
8Then Moses quickly bowed to the ground
and worshiped. 9He said, "Lord, if you are
pleased with me, please go with us. I know that
these are stubborn people, but forgive our evil
and our sin. Take us as your own people."
10Then the LORD said, "I am making this
agreement with you. I will do miracles in front
of all your people—things that have never before been done for any other nation on earth—
and the people with you will see my work. I, the
LORD, will do wonderful things for you. 11Obey
the things I command you today, and I will
force out the Amorites, Canaanites, Hittites, Perizzites, Hivites, and Jebusites ahead of you. 12Be
careful that you don't make an agreement with
the people who live in the land where you are
going, because it will bring you trouble. 13De-
stroy their altars, break their stone pillars, and
cut down their Asherah idols. 14Don't
worship any other god, because I, the LORD, the Jealous
One, am a jealous God.
15"Be careful that you don't
make an agreement with the
people who live in that land.
When they worship their
gods, they will invite you to join
them. Then you will eat their sacrifices. 16If you

WHAT'S IT MEAN?

The Asherah idols were wooden images used in the worship of Asherah, who was similar to Venus, the Roman goddess of love. The Canaanites believed that Asherah, the wife of the fertility god Baal, had some special powers over fertility herself.
Exodus 34:13

WORSHIP

Is worship meant for anyone else except God? (34:14)

Promise HE PROMISES TO DO MIRACLES.

Then the LORD said, "I am making this agreement with you. I will do miracles in front of all your people—things that have never before been done for any other nation on earth (Ex. 34:10).

God said that he would do things "that have never before been done for any other nation on earth." He sure kept that promise to the Israelites. He cut a path for them through the Jordan River. He made the walls of Jericho fall down when the priests blew their trumpets. He kept the sun from going down one day. And that was just the beginning.

God did a lot of miracles in New Testament times, too. Jesus and his disciples healed people almost all the time. Jesus made blind eyes see. He made crippled legs walk. He made lepers whole. He even raised people from the dead.

Today, a lot of people have just quit expecting to see God do miracles. Modern technology has been able to do things that used to require a miracle. Science can explain things that no one understood many years ago. Sometimes even people who do believe in miracles aren't on the lookout for them anymore.

We live in a day of miracles. God's miracle-working power is alive and moving all over the world. Be on the lookout. He can do "much, much more than anything we can ask or imagine" (Eph. 3:20). He'll do miracles.

SEE FOR YOURSELF:

Ex. 11:9; Ps. 77:14; Dan. 6:27; Mic. 7:15; Gal. 3:5

choose some of their daughters as wives for your sons and those daughters worship gods, they will lead your sons to do the same thing.

[17]"Do not make gods of melted metal.

[18]"Celebrate the Feast of Unleavened Bread. For seven days you must eat bread made without yeast as I commanded you. Do this during the month I have chosen, the month of Abib, because in that month you came out of Egypt.

[19]"The firstborn of every mother belongs to me, including every firstborn male animal that is born in your flocks and herds. [20]You may buy back a donkey by paying for it with a lamb, but if you don't want to buy back a donkey, you must break its neck. You must buy back all your firstborn sons.

"No one is to come before me without a gift.

[21]"You must work for six days, but on the seventh day you must rest—even during the planting season and the harvest season.

[22]"Celebrate the Feast of Weeks when you gather the first grain of the wheat harvest. And celebrate the Feast of Shelters in the fall.

[23]"Three times each year all your males must come before the Lord GOD, the God of Israel. [24]I will force out nations ahead of you and expand the borders of your land. You will go before the LORD your God three times each year, and at that time no one will try to take your land from you.

[25]"Do not offer the blood of a sacrifice to me with anything containing yeast, and do not leave any of the sacrifice of the Feast of Passover until the next morning.

[26]"Bring the best first crops that you harvest from your ground to the Tent of the LORD your God.

"You must not cook a young goat in its mother's milk."

[27]Then the LORD said to Moses, "Write down these words, because with these words I have made an agreement with you and Israel."

[28]Moses stayed there with the LORD forty days and forty nights, and during that time he did not eat food or drink water. And Moses wrote the words of the Agreement—the Ten Commandments—on the stone tablets.

THE FACE OF MOSES SHINES

[29]Then Moses came down from Mount Sinai, carrying the two stone tablets of the Agreement in his hands. But he did not know that his face was shining because he had talked with the LORD. [30]When Aaron and all the people of Israel saw that Moses' face was shining, they were afraid to go near him. [31]But Moses called to them, so Aaron and all the leaders of the people returned to Moses, and he talked with them. [32]After that, all the people of Israel came near him, and he gave them all the commands that the LORD had given him on Mount Sinai.

[33]When Moses finished speaking to the people, he put a covering over his face. [34]Anytime Moses went before the LORD to speak with him, Moses took off the covering until he came out. Then Moses would come out and tell the Israelites what the LORD had commanded. [35]They would see that Moses' face was shining. So he would cover his face again until the next time he went in to speak with the LORD.

RULES ABOUT THE SABBATH

35

[1]Moses gathered all the Israelite community together and said to them, "These are the things the LORD has commanded you to do. [2]You are to work for six days, but the seventh day will be a holy day, a Sabbath of rest to honor the LORD. Anyone who works on that day must be put to death. [3]On the Sabbath day you must not light a fire in any of your houses."

[4]Moses said to all the Israelites, "This is what the LORD has commanded: [5]From what you have, take an offering for the LORD. Let everyone who is willing bring this offering to the LORD: gold, silver, bronze, [6]blue, purple and red thread, and fine linen, goat hair [7]and male sheepskins that are colored red. They may also bring fine leather, acacia wood, [8]olive oil for the lamps, spices for the special olive oil used for appointing priests and for the sweet-smelling incense, [9]onyx stones, and other jewels to be put on the holy vest and chest covering of the priests.

[10]"Let all the skilled workers come and make everything the LORD commanded: [11]the Holy Tent, its outer tent and its covering, the hooks, frames, crossbars, posts, and bases; [12]the Ark of the Agreement, its poles, lid, and the curtain in front of it; [13]the table, and its poles, all the things that go with the table, and the bread that shows we are in God's presence; [14]the lampstand for the light and all the things that go with it, the lamps, and olive oil for the light; [15]the altar of incense and its poles, the special oil and the sweet-smelling incense, the curtain for the entrance of the Meeting Tent; [16]the altar of burnt offering and its bronze screen, its poles and all its tools, the bronze bowl and its base; [17]the curtains around the courtyard, their posts and bases, and the curtain at the entry to the courtyard; [18]the pegs of the Holy Tent and of the courtyard and their ropes; [19]the special clothes

that the priest will wear in the Holy Place. These are the holy clothes for Aaron the priest and his sons to wear when they serve as priests."

20Then all the people of Israel went away from Moses. 21Everyone who wanted to give came and brought a gift to the LORD for making the Meeting Tent, all the things in the Tent, and the special clothes. 22All the men and women who wanted to give brought gold jewelry of all kinds—pins, earrings, rings, and bracelets. They all presented their gold to the LORD. 23Everyone who had blue, purple, and red thread, and fine linen, and anyone who had goat hair or male sheepskins colored red or fine leather brought them to the LORD. 24Everyone who could give silver or bronze brought that as a gift to the LORD, and everyone who had acacia wood to be used in the work brought it. 25Every skilled woman used her hands to make the blue, purple, and red thread, and fine linen, and they brought what they had made. 26All the women who were skilled and wanted to help made thread of the goat hair. 27The leaders brought onyx stones and other jewels to put on the holy vest and chest covering for the priest. 28They also brought spices and olive oil for the sweet-smelling incense, the special oil, and the oil to burn in the lamps. 29All the men and women of Israel who wanted to help brought gifts to the LORD for all the work the LORD had commanded Moses and the people to do.

GIVING
What should be our attitude in giving? (35:22)

30Then Moses said to the Israelites, "Look, the LORD has chosen Bezalel son of Uri the son of Hur, from the tribe of Judah. 31The LORD has filled Bezalel with the Spirit of God and has given him the skill, ability, and knowledge to do all kinds of work. 32He is able to design pieces to be made of gold, silver, and bronze, 33to cut stones and jewels and put them in metal, to carve wood, and to do all kinds of work. 34Also, the LORD has given Bezalel and Oholiab, the son of Ahisamach from the tribe of Dan, the ability to teach others. 35The LORD has given them the skill to do all kinds of work. They are able to cut designs in metal and stone. They can plan and sew designs in the fine linen with the blue, purple, and red thread. And they are also able to weave things.

36

1So Bezalel, Oholiab, and every skilled person will do the work the LORD has commanded, because he gave them the wisdom and understanding to do all the skilled work needed to build the Holy Tent."

2Then Moses called Bezalel, Oholiab, and all the other skilled people to whom the LORD had given skills, and they came because they wanted to help with the work. 3They received from Moses everything the people of Israel had brought as gifts to build the Holy Tent. The people continued to bring gifts each morning because they wanted to. 4So all the skilled workers left the work they were doing on the Holy Tent, 5and they said to Moses, "The people are bringing more than we need to do the work the LORD commanded."

6Then Moses sent this command throughout the camp: "No man or woman should make anything else as a gift for the Holy Tent." So the people were kept from giving more, 7because what they had was already more than enough to do all the work.

THE HOLY TENT

8Then the skilled workers made the Holy Tent. They made the ten curtains of blue, purple, and red cloth, and they sewed designs of creatures with wings on the curtains. 9Each curtain was the same size—forty-two feet long and six feet wide. 10Five of the curtains were fastened together to make one set, and the other five were fastened together to make another set. 11Then they made loops of blue cloth along the edge of the end curtain on the first set of five, and they did the same thing with the other set of five. 12There were fifty loops on one curtain and fifty loops on the other curtain, with the loops opposite each other. 13They made fifty gold hooks to join the two curtains together so that the Holy Tent was joined together as one piece.

"Everyone who wanted to give came and brought a gift to the LORD for making the Meeting Tent, all the things in the Tent, and the special clothes." (Exodus 35:21)

14Then the workers made another tent of eleven curtains made of goat hair, to put over the Holy Tent. 15All eleven curtains were the same size—forty-five feet long and six feet wide. 16The workers sewed five curtains together into one set and six together into another set. 17They made fifty loops along the edge of the outside curtain of one set and fifty loops along the edge of the outside curtain of the other set. [18]Then they made fifty bronze rings to join the two sets of cloth together and make the tent one piece. [19]They made two more coverings for the outer tent—one made of male sheepskins colored red and the other made of fine leather.

[20]Then they made upright frames of acacia wood for the Holy Tent. [21]Each frame was fifteen feet tall and twenty-seven inches wide, [22]and there were two pegs side by side on each one. Every frame of the Holy Tent was made this same way. [23]They made twenty frames for the south side of the Tent, [24]and they made forty silver bases that went under the twenty frames. There were two bases for every frame—one for each peg of each frame. [25]They also made twenty frames for the north side of the Holy Tent [26]and forty silver bases—two to go under each frame. [27]They made six frames for the rear or west end of the Holy Tent [28]and two frames for the corners at the rear of the Holy Tent. [29]These two frames were doubled at the bottom and joined at the top with a metal ring. They did this for each of these corners. [30]So there were eight frames and sixteen silver bases—two bases under each frame.

WHAT'S IT MEAN?

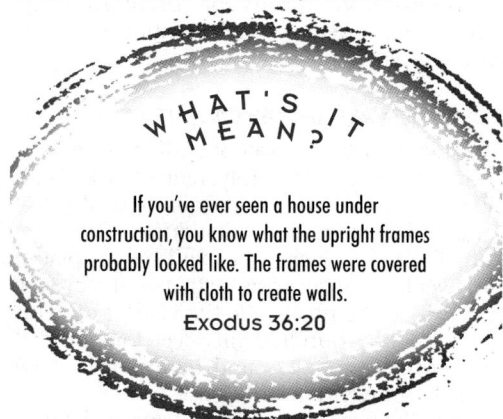

If you've ever seen a house under construction, you know what the upright frames probably looked like. The frames were covered with cloth to create walls.

Exodus 36:20

[31]Then they made crossbars of acacia wood to connect the upright frames of the Holy Tent. Five crossbars held the frames together on one side of the Tent, [32]and five held the frames together on the other side. Also, five crossbars held the frames together on the west end, at the rear of the Tent. [33]They made the middle crossbar run along the entire length of each side and rear of the Tent. It was set halfway up the frames. [34]They made gold rings on the sides of the frames to hold the crossbars, and they covered the frames and the crossbars with gold.

[35]Then they made the curtain of blue, purple, and red thread, and fine linen. A skilled craftsman sewed designs of creatures with wings on it. [36]They made four posts of acacia wood for it and covered them with gold. Then they made gold hooks for the posts, as well as four silver bases in which to set the posts. [37]For the entrance to the Tent, they made a curtain of blue, purple, and red thread, and fine linen. A person who sewed well sewed designs on it. [38]Then they made five posts and hooks for it. They covered the tops of the posts and their bands with gold, and they made five bronze bases for the posts.

THE ARK OF THE AGREEMENT

37

[1]Bezalel made the Ark of acacia wood; it was forty-five inches long, twenty-seven inches wide, and twenty-seven inches high. [2]He covered it, both inside and out, with pure gold, and he put a gold strip around it. [3]He made four gold rings for it and attached them to its four feet, with two rings on each side. [4]Then he made poles of acacia wood and covered them with gold. [5]He put the poles through the rings on each side of the Ark to carry it. [6]Then he made a lid of pure gold that was forty-five inches long and twenty-seven inches wide. [7]Then Bezalel hammered gold to make two creatures with wings and attached them to each end of the lid. [8]He made one creature on one end of the lid and the other creature on the other end. He attached them to the lid so that it would be one piece. [9]The creatures' wings were spread upward, covering the lid, and the creatures faced each other across the lid.

THE TABLE

[10]Then he made the table of acacia wood; it was thirty-six inches long, eighteen inches wide, and twenty-seven inches high. [11]He covered it with pure gold and put a gold strip around it. [12]He made a frame three inches high that stood up all around the edge, and he put a gold strip around it. [13]Then he made four gold rings for the table and attached them to the four corners of the table where the four legs were. [14]The rings were put close to the frame around the top of the table, because they held the poles for carrying it. [15]The poles for carrying the table were made of acacia wood and were covered with gold. [16]He made of pure gold all the things that were used on the table: the plates, bowls, cups, and jars used for pouring the drink offerings.

THE LAMPSTAND

[17]Then he made the lampstand of pure gold, hammering out its base and stand. Its

WHAT'S IT MEAN?

The lampstand had seven branches, with a lamp on each branch. The lamps themselves were small cups that were partially closed on top, with an opening just large enough for a wick. The lamp fuel of choice in ancient days was olive oil.
Exodus 37:17–18

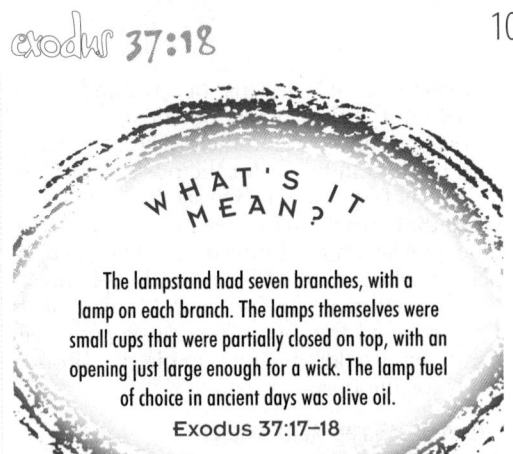

flower-like cups, buds, and petals were joined
together in one piece with the base and stand.
18Six branches went out from the sides of the
lampstand—three on one side and three on the
other. 19Each branch had three cups shaped
like almond flowers, and each cup had a bud
and a petal. Each of the six branches going out
from the lampstand was the same. 20There
were four more cups shaped like almond flowers on the lampstand itself, each with its buds
and petals. 21Three pairs of branches went out
from the lampstand. A bud was under the
place where each pair was attached to the
lampstand. Each of the six branches going out
from the lampstand was the same. 22The buds,
branches, and lampstand were all one piece of
pure, hammered gold. 23He made seven pure
gold lamps for this lampstand, and he made
pure gold wick trimmers and trays. 24He used
about seventy-five pounds of pure gold to
make the lampstand and all the things that go
with it.

THE ALTAR FOR BURNING INCENSE

25Then he made the altar of incense out of
acacia wood. It was square—eighteen inches
long and eighteen inches wide—and it was
thirty-six inches high. Each corner that stuck
out like a horn was joined into one piece with
the altar. 26He covered the top and all the sides
and the corners with pure gold, and he put
gold trim around the altar. 27He made two gold
rings and put them below the trim on opposite
sides of the altar; these rings held the poles for
carrying it. 28He made the poles of acacia wood
and covered them with gold.

29Then he made the holy olive oil for appointing the priests and the pure, sweet-smelling incense. He made them like a person who
mixes perfumes.

THE ALTAR FOR BURNT OFFERINGS

38
1Then he built the altar for burnt offerings
out of acacia wood. The altar was square—
seven and one-half feet long and seven and
one-half feet wide—and it was four and one-
half feet high. 2He made each corner stick out
like a horn so that the horns and the altar were
joined together in one piece. Then he covered
the altar with bronze. 3He made all the tools of
bronze to use on the altar: the pots, shovels,
bowls for sprinkling blood, meat forks, and
pans for carrying the fire. 4He made a large
bronze screen to hold the burning wood for
the altar and put it inside the altar, under its
rim, halfway up from the bottom. 5He made
bronze rings to hold the poles for carrying the
altar, and he put them at the four corners of the
screen. 6Then he made poles of acacia wood
and covered them with bronze. 7He put the
poles through the rings on both sides of the
altar, to carry it. He made the altar of boards
and left the inside hollow.

THE BRONZE BOWL

8He made the bronze bowl for washing,
and he built it on a bronze stand. He used
the bronze from mirrors that belonged to the
women who served at the entrance to the
Meeting Tent.

THE COURTYARD OF THE HOLY TENT

9Then he made a wall of curtains to form a
courtyard around the Holy Tent. On the south
side the curtains were one hundred fifty feet
long and were made of fine linen. 10The curtains hung on silver hooks and bands, placed
on twenty bronze posts with twenty bronze
bases. 11On the north side the wall of curtains
was also one hundred fifty feet long, and it
hung on silver hooks and bands on twenty
posts with twenty bronze bases.

12On the west side of the courtyard, the wall
of curtains was seventy-five feet long. It was
held up by silver hooks and bands on ten
posts with ten bases. 13The east side was also
seventy-five feet long. 14On one side of the entry there was a wall of curtains twenty-two
and one-half feet long, held up by three posts
and three bases. 15On the other side of the entry there was also a wall of curtains twenty-
two and one-half feet long, held up by three
posts and three bases. 16All the curtains around
the courtyard were made of fine linen. 17The
bases for the posts were made of bronze. The
hooks and the bands on the posts were made
of silver, and the tops of the posts were cov-

ered with silver also. All the posts in the courtyard had silver bands.
[18]The curtain for the entry of the courtyard
was made of blue, purple, and red thread, and
fine linen, sewn by a person who could sew
well. The curtain was thirty feet long and seven
and one-half feet high, the same height as the
curtains around the courtyard. [19]It was held up
by four posts and four bronze bases. The
hooks and bands on the posts were made of
silver, and the tops on the posts were covered
with silver. [20]All the tent pegs for the Holy Tent
and for the curtains around the courtyard
were made of bronze.
[21]This is a list of the materials used to make
the Holy Tent, where the Agreement was kept.
Moses ordered the Levites to make this list, and
Ithamar son of Aaron was in charge of keeping
it. [22]Bezalel son of Uri, the son of Hur of the
tribe of Judah, made everything the LORD commanded Moses. [23]Oholiab son of Ahisamach
of the tribe of Dan helped him. He could cut
designs into metal and stone; he was a designer
and also skilled at sewing the blue, purple, and
red thread, and fine linen.

WHAT'S IT MEAN?

The Holy Tent was the worship area. Only gold and silver, the finest and most expensive metals, were good enough to be used as decorations for the holy area. The outer area of the Meeting Tent was decorated with bronze, a less expensive metal.

Exodus 38:21–31

[24]The total amount of gold used to build the
Holy Tent was presented to the LORD. It
weighed over 2,000 pounds, as set by the Holy
Place measure.
[25]The silver was given by the members of
the community who were counted. It weighed
7,550 pounds, as set by the Holy Place measure. [26]All the men twenty years old or older
were counted. There were 603,550 men, and
each man had to pay one-fifth of an ounce of
silver, as set by the Holy Place measure. [27]Of
this silver, 7,500 pounds were used to make the
one hundred bases for the Holy Tent and for
the curtain—75 pounds of silver in each base.
[28]They used 50 pounds of silver to make the
hooks for the posts and to cover the tops of
the posts and to make the bands on them.
[29]The bronze which was presented to the
LORD weighed about 5,000 pounds. [30]They
used the bronze to make the bases at the entrance of the Meeting Tent, to make the altar
and the bronze screen, and to make all the
tools for the altar. [31]This bronze was also used
to make bases for the wall of curtains around
the courtyard and bases for curtains at the entry to the courtyard, as well as to make the tent
pegs for the Holy Tent and the curtains that
surrounded the courtyard.

CLOTHES FOR THE PRIESTS

39
[1]They used blue, purple, and red thread to
make woven clothes for the priests to wear
when they served in the Holy Place. They
made the holy clothes for Aaron as the LORD
had commanded Moses.
[2]They made the holy vest of gold, and blue,
purple, and red thread, and fine linen. [3]They
hammered the gold into sheets and then cut it
into long, thin strips. They worked the gold
into the blue, purple, and red thread, and fine
linen. This was done by skilled craftsmen.
[4]They made the shoulder straps for the holy
vest, which were attached to the top corners of
the vest and tied together over each shoulder.
[5]The skillfully woven belt was made in the
same way; it was joined to the holy vest as one
piece. It was made of gold, and blue, purple,
and red thread, and fine linen, the way the
LORD commanded Moses.
[6]They put gold around the onyx stones and
then wrote the names of the sons of Israel on
these gems, as a person carves words and designs on a seal. [7]Then they attached the gems
on the shoulder straps of the holy vest, as reminders of the twelve sons of Israel. This was
done just as the LORD had commanded Moses.
[8]The skilled craftsmen made the chest covering like the holy vest; it was made of gold,
and blue, purple, and red thread, and fine
linen. [9]The chest covering was square—nine
inches long and nine inches wide—and it was
folded double to make a pocket. [10]Then they
put four rows of beautiful jewels on it: In the
first row there was a ruby, a topaz, and a yellow quartz; [11]in the second there was a turquoise, a sapphire, and an emerald; [12]in the
third there was a jacinth, an agate, and an amethyst; [13]in the fourth there was a chrysolite,
an onyx, and a jasper. Gold was put around
these jewels to attach them to the chest covering, [14]and the names of the sons of Israel were

carved on these twelve jewels as a person carves a seal. Each jewel had the name of one of the twelve tribes of Israel.

15They made chains of pure gold, twisted together like a rope, for the chest covering. 16The workers made two gold pieces and two gold rings. They put the two gold rings on the two upper corners of the chest covering. 17Then they put two gold chains in the two rings at the ends of the chest covering, 18and they fastened the other two ends of the chains to the two gold pieces. They attached these gold pieces to the two shoulder straps in the front of the holy vest. 19They made two gold rings and put them at the lower corners of the chest covering on the inside edge next to the holy vest. 20They made two more gold rings on the bottom of the shoulder straps in front of the holy vest, near the seam, just above the woven belt of the holy vest. 21They used a blue ribbon and tied the rings of the chest covering to the rings of the holy vest, connecting it to the woven belt. In this way the chest covering would not swing out from the holy vest. They did all these things the way the LORD commanded.

22Then they made the outer robe to be worn under the holy vest. It was woven only of blue cloth. 23They made a hole in the center of the outer robe, with a woven collar sewn around it so it would not tear. 24Then they made balls like pomegranates of blue, purple, and red thread, and fine linen and hung them around the bottom of the outer robe. 25They also made bells of pure gold and hung these around the bottom of the outer robe between the balls. 26So around the bottom of the outer robe there was a bell and a pomegranate ball, a bell and a pomegranate ball. The priest wore this outer robe when he served as priest, just as the LORD had commanded Moses.

27They wove inner robes of fine linen for Aaron and his sons, 28and they made turbans, headbands, and underclothes of fine linen. 29Then they made the cloth belt of fine linen, and blue, purple, and red thread, and designs were sewn onto it, just as the LORD had commanded Moses.

30They made a strip of pure gold, which is the holy crown, and carved these words in the gold, as one might carve on a seal: "Holy to the LORD." 31Then they tied this flat piece to the turban with a blue ribbon, as the LORD had commanded Moses.

32So all the work on the Meeting Tent was finished. The Israelites did everything just as the LORD had commanded Moses. 33Then they brought the Holy Tent to Moses: the Tent and all its furniture, hooks, frames, crossbars, posts, and bases; 34the covering made of male sheepskins colored red, the covering made of fine leather, and the curtain that covered the entrance to the Most Holy Place; 35the Ark of the Agreement, its poles and lid; 36the table, all its containers, and the bread that showed they were in God's presence; 37the pure gold lampstand with its lamps in a row, all its tools, and the olive oil for the light; 38the gold altar, the special olive oil used for appointing priests, the sweet-smelling incense, and the curtain that covered the entrance to the Tent; 39the bronze altar and its screen, its poles and all its tools, the bowl and its stand; 40the curtains for the courtyard with their posts and bases, the curtain that covered the entry to the courtyard, the cords, pegs, and all the things in the Meeting Tent. 41They brought the clothes for the priests to wear when they served in the Holy Tent—the holy clothes for Aaron the priest and the clothes for his sons, which they wore when they served as priests.

42The Israelites had done all this work just as the LORD had commanded Moses. 43Moses looked closely at all the work and saw they had done it just as the LORD had commanded. So Moses blessed them.

WHAT'S IT MEAN?

Only big shots wore purple dye in ancient times. The dye came from a shellfish that lived in the Mediterranean Sea. Preparing it was difficult and expensive. Only royalty and other important people could afford it. Purple wasn't the only expensive dye, though. Red and blue dyes were also very valuable.

Exodus 39:24–26

SETTING UP THE HOLY TENT

40 1Then the LORD said to Moses: 2"On the first day of the first month, set up the Holy Tent, which is the Meeting Tent. 3Put the Ark of the Agreement in it and hang the curtain in front of the Ark. 4Bring in the table and arrange everything on the table that should be there. Then bring in the lampstand and set up its

lamps. 5Put the gold altar for burning incense in front of the Ark of the Agreement, and put the curtain at the entrance to the Holy Tent.

6"Put the altar of burnt offerings in front of the entrance of the Holy Tent, the Meeting Tent. 7Put the bowl between the Meeting Tent and the altar, and put water in it. 8Set up the courtyard around the Holy Tent, and put the curtain at the entry to the courtyard.

9"Use the special olive oil and pour it on the Holy Tent and everything in it, in order to give the Tent and all that is in it for service to the LORD. They will be holy. 10Pour the special oil on the altar for burnt offerings and on all its tools. Give the altar for service to God, and it will be very holy. 11Then pour the special olive oil on the bowl and the base under it so that they will be given for service to God.

> "Then the cloud covered the Meeting Tent, and the glory of the LORD filled the Holy Tent."
> (Exodus 40:34)

12"Bring Aaron and his sons to the entrance of the Meeting Tent, and wash them with water. 13Then put the holy clothes on Aaron. Pour the special oil on him, and give him for service to God so that he may serve me as a priest. 14Bring Aaron's sons and put the inner robes on them. 15Pour the special oil on them in the same way that you appointed their father as priest so that they may also serve me as priests. Pouring oil on them will make them a family of priests, they and their descendants from now on." 16Moses did everything that the LORD commanded him.

17So the Holy Tent was set up on the first day of the first month during the second year after they left Egypt. 18When Moses set up the Holy Tent, he put the bases in place, and he put the frames on the bases. Next he put the crossbars through the rings of the frames and set up the posts. 19After that, Moses spread the cloth over the Holy Tent and put the covering over it, just as the LORD commanded.

20Moses put the stone tablets that had the Agreement written on them into the Ark. He put the poles through the rings of the Ark and put the lid on it. 21Next he brought the Ark into the Tent and hung the curtain to cover the Ark, just as the LORD commanded him.

22Moses put the table in the Meeting Tent on the north side of the Holy Tent in front of the curtain. 23Then he put the bread on the table before the LORD, just as the LORD commanded him. 24Moses put the lampstand in the Meeting Tent on the south side of the Holy Tent across from the table. 25Then he put the lamps on the lampstand before the LORD, just as the LORD commanded him.

26Moses put the gold altar for burning incense in the Meeting Tent in front of the curtain. 27Then he burned sweet-smelling incense on it, just as the LORD commanded him. 28Then he hung the curtain at the entrance to the Holy Tent.

29He put the altar for burnt offerings at the entrance to the Holy Tent, the Meeting Tent, and offered a whole burnt offering and grain offerings on it, just as the LORD commanded him. 30Moses put the bowl between the Meeting Tent and the altar for burnt offerings, and he put water in it for washing. 31Moses, Aaron, and Aaron's sons used this water to wash their hands and feet. 32They washed themselves every time they entered the Meeting Tent and every time they went near the altar for burnt offerings, just as the LORD commanded Moses.

33Then Moses set up the courtyard around the Holy Tent and the altar, and he put up the curtain at the entry to the courtyard. So Moses finished the work.

THE CLOUD OVER THE HOLY TENT

34Then the cloud covered the Meeting Tent, and the glory of the LORD filled the Holy Tent. 35Moses could not enter the Meeting Tent, because the cloud had settled on it, and the glory of the LORD filled the Holy Tent.

36When the cloud rose from the Holy Tent, the Israelites would begin to travel, 37but as long as the cloud stayed on the Holy Tent, they did not travel. They stayed in that place until the cloud rose. 38So the cloud of the LORD was over the Holy Tent during the day, and there was a fire in the cloud at night. So all the Israelites could see the cloud while they traveled.

Leviticus

CONTENT When you hear someone say, "I never knew *that* was in the Bible!" they could very well be talking about the Book of Leviticus. Leviticus was a "Basic Holiness & Survival Guide" for the Hebrews as they wandered through the desert wilderness. It was an instruction manual for the priests. It discussed everything from mildew to baldness to skin disease to sacrifices to holiness.

Think about it. This group of people was living like gypsies. It was a forty-year camping trip. Who took out the garbage? How did they keep from passing around colds and infections? What about food poisoning? Just staying alive and well was a huge task, not to mention maintaining their faith and a right relationship with God.

So, God introduced the concept of clean and unclean. He applied it to their lifestyle and their lives. The Book of Leviticus is a housekeeping/faith-keeping kind of book. To us it can seem a bit nitpicky and a little pretentious, but to them it was new news.

Put yourself in the Hebrews' sandals before you read the Book of Leviticus. A little mildew on the bathroom wall might look different to you if your whole family could get exiled because of it.

Outline

1:1—7:38 .... Laws About Offerings
8:1-36 .... Appointing the Priests
9:1-24 .... Aaron's First Offerings
10:1-20 .... Two Priests Are Killed
11:1—15:33 .... Laws About What Is Clean and Unclean
16:1-34 .... Laws About the Day of Cleansing
17:1—20:27 .... Laws on Various Subjects
21:1—22:33 .... Rules for Priests to Follow
23:1—25:55 .... Instructions for Special Holidays
26:1-46 .... Rewards and Punishments
27:1-34 .... Laws About Promises and Offerings to the Lord

Purpose We worship God by the way we live as well as by celebrating his goodness.

Theme The Sanctity of God and Holiness in Everyday Life

Date of writing 1445-1440 B.C.

"Be my holy people. Be holy because I am the LORD your God. Remember and obey my laws. I am the LORD, and I have made you holy" (20:7–8).

Bible Talk

Sacrifices

You read a lot about sacrifices in the Old Testament books. In fact, the Meeting Tent and the Temple were both built around places where people slaughtered then barbecued animals, sacrificing them to God. Seem a little barbaric in a world filled with vegetarian bumper stickers, not to mention vegetarians? There are two things you might consider—

First, the sacrifices in the Temple were a picture of the sacrifice that Jesus eventually made for all of us. He basically put himself on that wooden altar that was a cross and spilled his blood and gave his life.

Second, as gross as a sacrifice might seem to you—that's how gross our sin is to a holy God. We should be just that repulsed by our own sin. It's something to think about.

KEEPING KOSHER

The laws in Leviticus regarding food are the very laws that people follow even today when they are "keeping Kosher." That means they are eating according to the Jewish laws. You can see items on almost every grocery store aisle that are kosher. Look for a *U* on the label or a *K*. (The letters may be in a circle as well.)

When you see those symbols, it means that food is considered clean and was prepared in a way that is considered clean according to the laws that originated in Leviticus.

Amazing, isn't it, that an ancient law in the Bible affects our food labels today?

THE BURNT OFFERING

1 1The LORD called to Moses and spoke to him from the Meeting Tent, saying, 2"Tell the people of Israel: 'When you bring an offering to the LORD, bring as your offering an animal from the herd or flock.

WHAT'S IT MEAN?

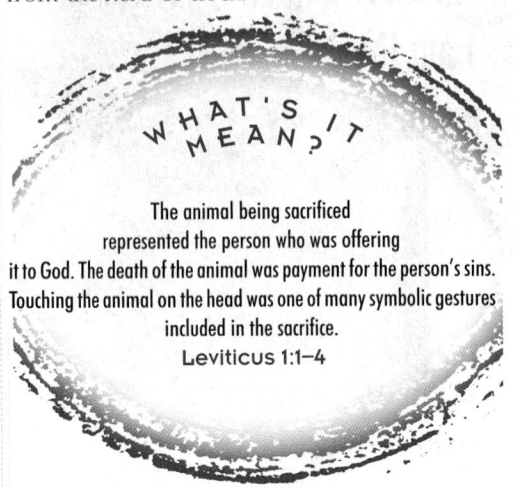

The animal being sacrificed represented the person who was offering it to God. The death of the animal was payment for the person's sins. Touching the animal on the head was one of many symbolic gestures included in the sacrifice.

Leviticus 1:1–4

3" 'If the offering is a whole burnt offering from the herd, it must be a male that has nothing wrong with it. The person must take the animal to the entrance of the Meeting Tent so that the LORD will accept the offering. 4He must put his hand on the animal's head, and the LORD will accept it to remove the person's sin so he will belong to God. 5He must kill the young bull before the LORD, and Aaron's sons, the priests, must bring its blood and sprinkle it on all sides of the altar at the entrance to the Meeting Tent. 6After that he will skin the animal and cut it into pieces. 7The priests, when they have put wood and fire on the altar, 8are to lay the head, the fat, and other pieces on the wood that is on the fire of the altar. 9The animal's inner organs and legs must be washed with water. Then the priest must burn all the animal's parts on the altar. It is a whole burnt offering, an offering made by fire, and its smell is pleasing to the LORD.

10" 'If the burnt offering is a sheep or a goat from the flock, it must be a male that has nothing wrong with it. 11The person must kill the animal on the north side of the altar before the LORD, and Aaron's sons, the priests, must sprinkle its blood on all sides of the altar. 12The person must cut the animal into pieces, and the priest must lay them, with the head and fat, on the wood that is on the fire of the altar. 13The person must wash the animal's inner organs and legs with water, and then the priest must burn all its parts on the altar. It is a whole burnt offering, an offering made by fire, and its smell is pleasing to the LORD.

14" 'If the whole burnt offering for the LORD is a bird, it must be a dove or a young pigeon. 15The priest will bring it to the altar and pull off its head, which he will burn on the altar; the bird's blood must be drained out on the side of the altar. 16The priest must remove the bird's crop[n] and its contents and throw them on the east side of the altar, where the ashes are. 17Then he must tear the bird open by its wings without dividing it into two parts. He must burn the bird on the altar, on the wood which is on the fire. It is a whole burnt offering, an offering made by fire, and its smell is pleasing to the LORD.

THE GRAIN OFFERING

2 1" 'When anyone offers a grain offering to the LORD, it must be made from fine flour. The person must pour oil on it, put incense on it, 2and then take it to Aaron's sons, the priests. The priest must take a handful of the fine flour and oil and all the incense, and burn it on the altar as a memorial portion. It is an offering made by fire, and its smell is pleasing to the LORD. 3The rest of the grain offering will belong to Aaron and the priests; it is a most holy part of the offerings made by fire to the LORD.

WHAT'S IT MEAN?

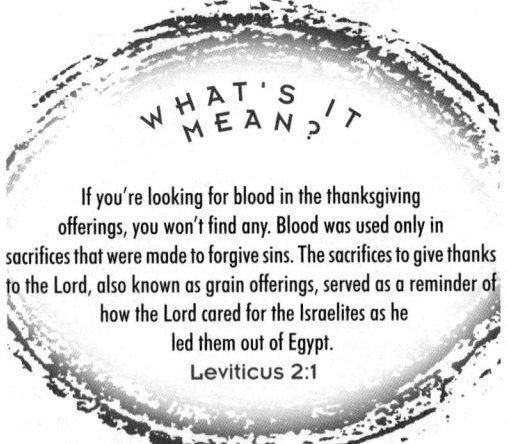

If you're looking for blood in the thanksgiving offerings, you won't find any. Blood was used only in sacrifices that were made to forgive sins. The sacrifices to give thanks to the Lord, also known as grain offerings, served as a reminder of how the Lord cared for the Israelites as he led them out of Egypt.

Leviticus 2:1

4" 'If you bring a grain offering that was baked in the oven, it must be made from fine flour. It may be loaves made without yeast and

1:16 crop A small bag inside a bird's throat. When a bird eats, its food goes into this part first. There, the food is made soft before it goes into the stomach.

mixed with oil, or it may be wafers made without yeast that have oil poured over them. 5If your grain offering is cooked on a griddle, it must be made, without yeast, of fine flour mixed with oil. 6Crumble it and pour oil over it; it is a grain offering. 7If your grain offering is cooked in a pan, it must be made from fine flour and oil. 8Bring the grain offering made of these things to the LORD. Give it to the priest, and he will take it to the altar. 9He will take out the memorial portion from the grain offering and burn it on the altar, as an offering made by fire. Its smell is pleasing to the LORD. 10The rest of the grain offering belongs to Aaron and the priests. It is a most holy part of the offerings made to the LORD by fire.

11" 'Every grain offering you bring to the LORD must be made without yeast, because you must not burn any yeast or honey in an offering made by fire to the LORD. 12You may bring yeast and honey to the LORD as an offering from the first harvest, but they must not be burned on the altar as a pleasing smell. 13You must also put salt on all your grain offerings. Salt stands for your agreement with God that will last forever; do not leave it out of your grain offering. You must add salt to all your offerings.

14" 'If you bring a grain offering from the first harvest to the LORD, bring crushed heads of new grain roasted in the fire. 15Put oil and incense on it; it is a grain offering. 16The priest will burn the memorial portion of the crushed grain and oil, with the incense on it. It is an offering by fire to the LORD.

THE FELLOWSHIP OFFERING

3

1" 'If a person's fellowship offering to the LORD is from the herd, it may be a male or female, but it must have nothing wrong with it. 2The person must put his hand on the animal's head and kill it at the entrance to the Meeting Tent. Then Aaron's sons, the priests, must sprinkle the blood on all sides of the altar. 3From the fellowship offering he must make a sacrifice by fire to the LORD. He must offer the fat of the animal's inner organs (both the fat that is in them and that covers them), 4both kidneys with the fat that is on them near the lower back muscle, and the best part of the liver, which he will remove with the kidneys. 5Then the priests will burn these parts on the altar, on the whole burnt offering that is on the wood of the fire. It is an offering made by fire, and its smell is pleasing to the LORD.

6" 'If a person's fellowship offering to the LORD is a lamb or a goat, it may be a male or female, but it must have nothing wrong with it. 7If he offers a lamb, he must bring it before the LORD 8and put his hand on its head. Then he must kill the animal in front of the Meeting Tent, and the priests must sprinkle its blood on all sides of the altar. 9From the fellowship offering the person must make a sacrifice by fire to the LORD. He must bring the fat, the whole fat tail cut off close to the backbone, the fat of the inner organs (both the fat that is in them and that covers them), 10both kidneys with the fat that is on them, near the lower back muscle, and the best part of the liver, which he will remove with the kidneys. 11Then the priest will burn these parts on the altar as food; it will be an offering made by fire to the LORD.

12" 'If a person's offering is a goat, he must offer it before the LORD 13and put his hand on its head. Then he must kill it in front of the Meeting Tent, and the priests must sprinkle its blood on all sides of the altar. 14From this offering the person must make a sacrifice by fire to the LORD. He must offer all the fat of the goat's inner organs (both the fat that is in them and that covers them), 15both kidneys with the fat that is on them near the lower back muscle, and the best part of the liver, which he will remove with the kidneys. 16The priest will burn these parts on the altar as food. It is an offering made by fire, and its smell is pleasing to the LORD. All the fat belongs to the LORD.

17" 'This law will continue for people from now on, wherever you live: You must not eat any fat or blood.' "

THE SIN OFFERING

4

1The LORD said to Moses, 2"Tell the people of Israel this: 'When a person sins by accident and does some things the LORD has commanded not to be done, that person must do these things:

3" 'If the appointed priest sins so that he brings guilt on the people, then he must offer a young bull to the LORD, one that has nothing wrong with it, as a sin offering for the sin he has done. 4He will bring the bull to the entrance of the Meeting Tent in front of the LORD, put his hand on its head, and kill it before the LORD. 5Then the appointed priest must bring some of the bull's blood into the Meeting Tent. 6The priest is to dip his finger into the blood and sprinkle it seven times before the LORD in front of the curtain of the Most Holy Place. 7The priest must also put some of the blood on the corners of the altar of incense that stands before the LORD in the Meeting Tent. The rest of the blood he must pour out at the bottom of

WHAT'S IT MEAN?

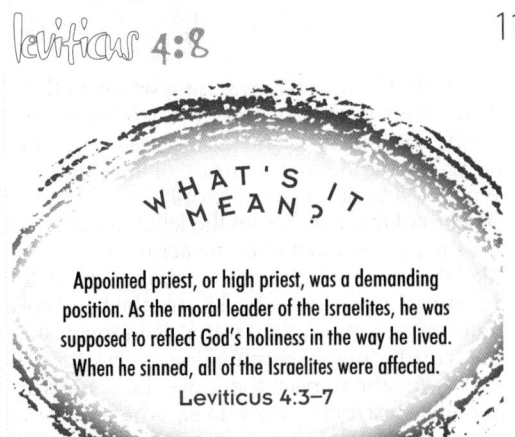

Appointed priest, or high priest, was a demanding position. As the moral leader of the Israelites, he was supposed to reflect God's holiness in the way he lived. When he sinned, all of the Israelites were affected.

Leviticus 4:3–7

the altar of burnt offering, which is at the entrance of the Meeting Tent. 8He must remove
all the fat from the bull of the sin offering—the
fat on and around the inner organs, 9both kidneys with the fat that is on them near the
lower back muscle, and the best part of the
liver which he will remove with the kidneys.
10(He must do this in the same way the fat is
removed from the bull of the fellowship offering.) Then the priest must burn the animal
parts on the altar of burnt offering. 11But the
priest must carry off the skin of the bull and all
its meat, along with the rest of the bull—its
head, legs, intestines, and other inner organs.
12He must take it outside the camp to the special clean place where the ashes are poured
out. He must burn it on a wood fire on the pile
of ashes.

13" 'If the whole nation of Israel sins accidentally without knowing it and does something the LORD has commanded not to be
done, they are guilty. 14When
they learn about the sin they
have done, they must offer a
young bull as a sin offering
and bring it before the
Meeting Tent. 15The older
leaders of the group of people must put their hands on
the bull's head before the
LORD, and it must be killed
before the LORD. 16Then the appointed priest must bring some of
the bull's blood into the Meeting Tent.
17Dipping his finger in the blood, he must
sprinkle it seven times before the LORD in front
of the curtain. 18Then he must put some of the
blood on the corners of the altar that is before
the LORD in the Meeting Tent. The priest must
pour out the rest of the blood at the bottom of
the altar of burnt offering, which is at the entrance to the Meeting Tent. 19He must remove
all the fat from the animal and burn it on the
altar; 20he will do the same thing with this bull
that he did with the first bull of the sin offering.
In this way the priest removes the sins of the
people so they will belong to the LORD and be
forgiven. 21Then the priest must carry the bull
outside the camp and burn it, just as he did
with the first bull. This is the sin offering for
the whole community.

22" 'If a ruler sins by accident and does
something the LORD his God has commanded
must not be done, he is guilty. 23When he
learns about his sin, he must bring a male goat
that has nothing wrong with it as his offering.
24The ruler must put his hand on the goat's
head and kill it in the place where they kill the
whole burnt offering before the LORD; it is a sin
offering. 25The priest must take some of the
blood of the sin offering on his finger and put
it on the corners of the altar of burnt offering.
He must pour out the rest of the blood at the
bottom of the altar of burnt offering. 26He must
burn all the goat's fat on the altar in the same
way he burns the fat of the fellowship offerings. In this way the priest removes the ruler's
sin so he belongs to the LORD, and the LORD
will forgive him.

27" 'If any person in the community sins by
accident and does something which the LORD
has commanded must not be done, he is guilty.
28When the person learns about his sin, he
must bring a female goat that has nothing
wrong with it as an offering for his sin. 29He
must put his hand on the animal's head and
kill it at the place of the whole burnt offering.
30Then the priest must take some of the goat's
blood on his finger and put it
on the corners of the altar of
burnt offering. He must pour
out the rest of the goat's
blood at the bottom of the
altar. 31Then the priest must
remove all the goat's fat in
the same way the fat is removed from the fellowship
offerings. He must burn it
on the altar as a smell pleasing
to the LORD. In this way the
priest will remove that person's sin
so he will belong to the LORD, and the LORD
will forgive him.

32" 'If this person brings a lamb as his offering for sin, he must bring a female that has
nothing wrong with it. 33He must put his hand
on the animal's head and kill it as a sin offering
in the place where the whole burnt offering is

"In this way the priest will remove that person's sins so he will belong to the LORD, and the LORD will forgive him." (Leviticus 4:35b)

killed. 34 The priest must take some of the blood
from the sin offering on his finger and put it
on the corners of the altar of burnt offering. He
must pour out the rest of the lamb's blood at
the bottom of the altar. 35 Then the priest must
remove all the lamb's fat in the same way that
the lamb's fat is removed from the fellowship
offerings. He must burn the pieces on the altar
on top of the offerings made by fire for the
LORD. In this way the priest will remove that
person's sins so he will belong to the LORD,
and the LORD will forgive him.

SPECIAL TYPES OF ACCIDENTAL SINS

5 1 " 'If a person is ordered to tell in court
what he has seen or what he knows and he
does not tell the court, he is guilty of sin.
2 " 'Or someone might touch something unclean, such as the dead body of an unclean
wild animal or an unclean farm animal or an
unclean crawling animal. Even if he does not
know that he touched it, he will still be unclean
and guilty of sin.
3 " 'Someone might touch human uncleanness—anything that makes someone unclean—and not know it. But when he learns
about it, he will be guilty.
4 " 'Or someone might make a promise before the LORD without thinking. It might be a
promise to do something bad or something
good; it might be about anything. Even if he
forgets about it, when he remembers, he will
be guilty.
5 " 'When anyone is guilty of any of these
things, he must tell how he sinned. 6 He must
bring an offering to the LORD as a penalty for
sin; it must be a female lamb or goat from the
flock. The priest will perform the acts to remove that person's sin so he will belong to the
LORD.
7 " 'But if the person cannot afford a lamb, he
must bring two doves or two young pigeons to
the LORD as the penalty for his sin. One bird
must be for a sin offering, and the other must
be for a whole burnt offering. 8 He must bring
them to the priest, who will first offer the one
for the sin offering. He will pull the bird's head
from its neck, but he will not pull it completely
off. 9 He must sprinkle the blood from the sin
offering on the side of the altar, and then he
must pour the rest of the blood at the bottom
of the altar; it is a sin offering. 10 Then the priest
must offer the second bird as a whole burnt
offering, as the law says. In this way the priest
will remove the person's sin so he will belong
to the LORD, and the LORD will forgive him.
11 " 'If the person cannot afford two doves or
two pigeons, he must bring about two quarts of
fine flour as an offering for sin. He must not put
oil or incense on the flour, because it is a sin
offering. 12 He must bring the flour to the priest.
The priest will take a handful of the flour as a
memorial offering and burn it on the altar on
top of the offerings made by fire to the LORD; it
is a sin offering. 13 In this way the priest will
remove the person's sins so he will belong to
the LORD, and the LORD will forgive him. What
is left of the sin offering belongs to the priest,
like the grain offering.' "

THE PENALTY OFFERING

14 The LORD said to Moses, 15 "If a person accidentally sins and does something against the
holy things of the LORD, he must bring from
the flock a male sheep that has nothing wrong
with it. This will be his penalty offering to the
LORD. Its value in silver must be correct as set
by the Holy Place measure. It is a penalty offering. 16 That person must pay for the sin he
did against the holy thing, adding one-fifth to
its value. Then he must give it all to the priest.
In this way the priest will remove the person's
sin so he will belong to the LORD, by using the
male sheep as the penalty offering. And the
LORD will forgive the person.

WHAT'S IT MEAN?

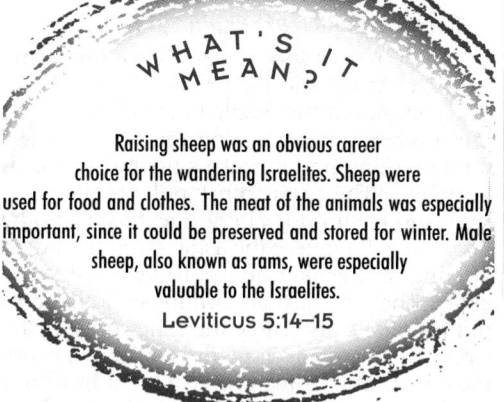

Raising sheep was an obvious career choice for the wandering Israelites. Sheep were used for food and clothes. The meat of the animals was especially important, since it could be preserved and stored for winter. Male sheep, also known as rams, were especially valuable to the Israelites.

Leviticus 5:14–15

17 "If a person sins and does something the
LORD has commanded not to be done, even if
he does not know it, he is still guilty. He is responsible for his sin. 18 He must bring the priest
a male sheep from the flock, one that has
nothing wrong with it and that is worth the
correct amount. It will be a penalty offering.
Though the person sinned without knowing it,
with this offering the priest will remove the sin
so the person will belong to the LORD, and the
LORD will forgive him. 19 The person is guilty of

doing wrong, so he must give the penalty offering to the LORD."

6 [1]The LORD said to Moses, [2]"A person might sin against the LORD by doing one of these sins: He might lie about what happened to something he was taking care of for someone else, or he might lie about a promise he made. He might steal something or cheat someone. [3]He might find something that had been lost and then lie about it. He might make a promise before the LORD about something and not mean it, or he might do some other sin. [4]If he does any of these things, he is guilty of sin. He must bring back whatever he stole or whatever he took by cheating. He must bring back the thing he took care of for someone else. He must bring back what he found and lied about [5]or what he made a false promise about. He must pay the full price plus an extra one-fifth of the value of what he took. He must give the money to the true owner on the day he brings his penalty offering. [6]He must bring his penalty to the priest—a male sheep from the flock, one that does not have anything wrong with it and that is worth the correct amount. It will be a penalty offering to the LORD. [7]Then the priest will perform the acts to remove that person's sin so he will belong to the LORD, and the LORD will forgive him for the sins that made him guilty."

THE WHOLE BURNT OFFERING

[8]The LORD said to Moses, [9]"Give this command to Aaron and the priests: 'These are the teachings about the whole burnt offering: The burnt offering must stay on the altar all night until morning, and the altar's fire must be kept burning. [10]The priest must put on his linen robe and linen underclothes next to his body. Then he will remove the ashes from the burnt offering on the altar and put them beside the altar. [11]Then he must take off those clothes and put on others and carry the ashes outside the camp to a special clean place. [12]But the fire must be kept burning on the altar; it must not be allowed to go out. The priest must put more firewood on the altar every morning, place the whole burnt offering on the fire, and burn the fat of the fellowship offerings. [13]The fire must be kept burning on the altar all the time; it must not go out.

THE GRAIN OFFERING

[14]" 'These are the teachings about the grain offering: The priests must bring it to the LORD in front of the altar. [15]The priest must take a handful of fine flour, with the oil and all of the incense on it, and burn the grain offering on the altar as a memorial offering to the LORD. Its smell is pleasing to him. [16]Aaron and the priests may eat what is left, but it must be eaten without yeast in a holy place. They must eat it in the courtyard of the Meeting Tent. [17]It must not be cooked with yeast. I have given it as their share of the offerings made to me by fire; it is most holy, like the sin offering and the penalty offering. [18]Any male descendant of Aaron may eat it as his share of the offerings made to the LORD by fire, and this will continue from now on. Whatever touches these offerings shall become holy.' "

[19]The LORD said to Moses, [20]"This is the offering Aaron and the priests must bring to the LORD on the day they appoint Aaron as high priest: They must bring two quarts of fine flour for a continual grain offering, half of it in the morning and half in the evening. [21]The fine flour must be mixed with oil and cooked on a griddle. Bring it when it is well mixed. Present the grain offering that is broken into pieces, and it will be a smell that is pleasing to the LORD. [22]One of the priests appointed to take Aaron's place as high priest must make the grain offering. It is a rule forever that the grain offering must be completely burned to the LORD. [23]Every grain offering made by a priest must be completely burned; it must not be eaten."

THE SIN OFFERING

[24]The LORD said to Moses, [25]"Tell Aaron and the priests: 'These are the teachings about the sin offering: The sin offering must be killed in front of the LORD in the same place the whole burnt offering is killed; it is most holy. [26]The priest who offers the sin offering must eat it in

WHAT'S IT MEAN?

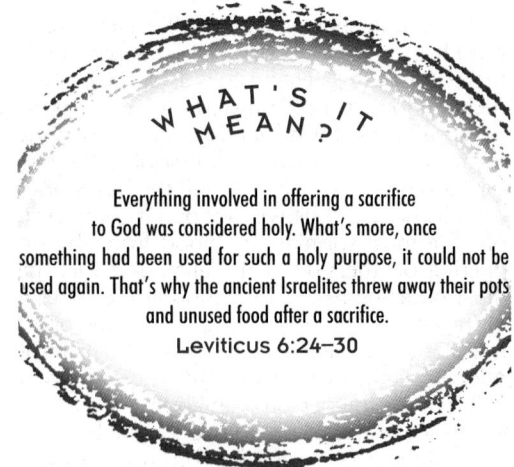

Everything involved in offering a sacrifice to God was considered holy. What's more, once something had been used for such a holy purpose, it could not be used again. That's why the ancient Israelites threw away their pots and unused food after a sacrifice.

Leviticus 6:24–30

a holy place, in the courtyard of the Meeting Tent. 27Whatever touches the meat of the sin offering must be holy, and if the blood is sprinkled on any clothes, you must wash them in a holy place. 28The clay pot the meat is cooked in must be broken, or if a bronze pot is used, it must be scrubbed and rinsed with water. 29Any male in a priest's family may eat the offering; it is most holy. 30But if the blood of the sin offering is taken into the Meeting Tent and used to remove sin in the Holy Place, that sin offering must be burned with fire. It must not be eaten.

THE PENALTY OFFERING

7 1" 'These are the teachings about the penalty offering, which is most holy: 2The penalty offering must be killed where the whole burnt offering is killed. Then the priest must sprinkle its blood on all sides of the altar. 3He must offer all the fat from the penalty offering—the fat tail, the fat that covers the inner organs, 4both kidneys with the fat that is on them near the lower back muscle, and the best part of the liver, which is to be removed with the kidneys. 5The priest must burn all these things on the altar as an offering made by fire to the LORD. It is a penalty offering. 6Any male in a priest's family may eat it. It is most holy, so it must be eaten in a holy place.

7" 'The penalty offering is like the sin offering in that the teachings are the same for both. The priest who offers the sacrifice to remove sins will get the meat for food. 8The priest who offers the burnt offering may also have the skin from it. 9Every grain offering that is baked in an oven, cooked on a griddle, or baked in a dish belongs to the priest who offers it. 10Every grain offering, either dry or mixed with oil, belongs to the priests, and all priests will share alike.

THE FELLOWSHIP OFFERING

11" 'These are the teachings about the fellowship offering a person may offer to the LORD: 12If he brings the fellowship offering to show his thanks, he should also bring loaves of bread made without yeast that are mixed with oil, wafers made without yeast that have oil poured over them, and loaves of fine flour that are mixed with oil. 13He must also offer loaves of bread made with yeast along with his fellowship offering, which he gives to show thanks. 14One of each kind of offering will be for the LORD; it will be given to the priest who sprinkles the blood of the fellowship offering. 15When the fellowship offering is given to thank the LORD, the meat from it must be eaten the same day it is offered; none of it must be left until morning.

WHAT'S IT MEAN?

The bread with leavening to lighten the batter was a change of pace for the Israelites. Most of the time they were instructed to make bread without leavening because that was the kind of bread served at the first Passover meal. Continuing to eat bread without leavening reminded them of how God had rescued and protected them.

Leviticus 7:13–14

16" 'If a person brings a fellowship offering just to give a gift to God or because of a special promise to him, the sacrifice should be eaten the same day he offers it. If there is any left, it may be eaten the next day. 17If any meat from this sacrifice is left on the third day, it must be burned up. 18Any meat of the fellowship offering eaten on the third day will not be accepted, nor will the sacrifice count for the person who offered it. It will become unclean, and anyone who eats the meat will be guilty of sin.

19" 'People must not eat meat that touches anything unclean; they must burn this meat with fire. Anyone who is clean may eat other meat. 20But if anyone is unclean and eats the meat from the fellowship offering that belongs to the LORD, he must be cut off from his people.

21" 'If anyone touches something unclean—uncleanness that comes from people, from an animal, or from some hated thing—touching it will make him unclean. If he then eats meat from the fellowship offering that belongs to the LORD, he must be cut off from his people.' "

22The LORD said to Moses, 23"Tell the people of Israel: 'You must not eat any of the fat from cattle, sheep, or goats. 24If an animal is found dead or torn by wild animals, you may use its fat for other things, but you must not eat it. 25If someone eats fat from an animal offering made by fire to the LORD, he must be cut off from his people. 26No matter where you live, you must not eat blood from any bird or animal. 27Anyone who eats blood must be cut off from his people.' "

THE PRIESTS' SHARE

28The LORD said to Moses, 29"Tell the people
of Israel: 'If someone brings a fellowship offering to the LORD, he must give part of it as his
sacrifice to the LORD. 30He must carry that part
of the gift in his own hands as an offering
made by fire to the LORD. He must bring the fat
and the breast of the animal to the priest, to be
presented to the LORD as the priests' share.
31Then the priest must burn the fat on the altar,
but the breast of the animal will belong to
Aaron and the priests. 32You must also give the
right thigh from the fellowship offering to the
priest as a gift; 33it will belong to the priest who
offers the blood and fat of the fellowship offering. 34I have taken the breast and the thigh
from the fellowship offerings of the Israelites,
and I have given these parts to Aaron and the
priests as their share for all time from the Israelites.'"

35This is the portion that belongs to Aaron
and his sons from the offerings made by fire to
the LORD. They were given this share on the
day they were presented to the LORD as priests.
36On the day the LORD appointed the priests,
he commanded Israel to give this share to
them, and it is to be given to the priests as their
share from now on.

37These are the teachings about the whole
burnt offering, the grain offering, the sin offering, the penalty offering, the offering for the
appointment of priests, and the fellowship offering. 38The LORD gave these teachings to Moses on Mount Sinai on the day he commanded
the Israelites to bring their offerings to the
LORD in the Sinai Desert.

AARON AND HIS SONS APPOINTED

8 1The LORD said to Moses, 2"Bring Aaron and
his sons and their clothes, the special olive oil
used in appointing people and things to the
service of the LORD, the bull of the sin offering
and the two male sheep, and the basket of
bread made without yeast. 3Then gather the
people together at the entrance to the Meeting
Tent." 4Moses did as the LORD commanded him,
and the people met together at the entrance to
the Meeting Tent.

5Then Moses spoke to the people and said,
"This is what the LORD has commanded to be
done." 6Bringing Aaron and his sons forward,
Moses washed them with water. 7He put the
inner robe on Aaron and tied the cloth belt
around him. Then Moses put the outer robe
on him and placed the holy vest on him. He
tied the skillfully woven belt around him so
that the holy vest was tied to Aaron. 8Then
Moses put the chest covering on him and put
the Urim and the Thummim in the chest covering. 9He also put the turban on Aaron's head.
He put the strip of gold, the holy crown, on the
front of the turban, as the LORD commanded
him to do.

WHAT'S IT MEAN?

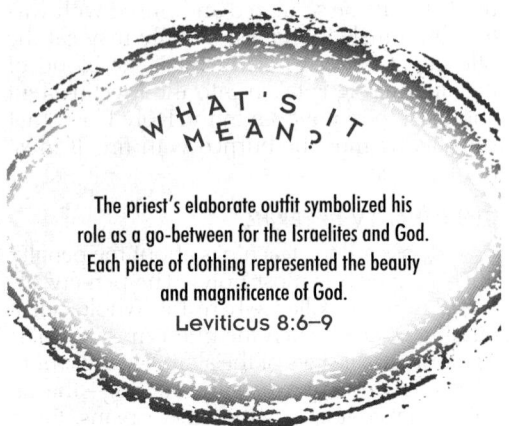

The priest's elaborate outfit symbolized his role as a go-between for the Israelites and God. Each piece of clothing represented the beauty and magnificence of God.
Leviticus 8:6–9

10Then Moses put the special oil on the
Holy Tent and everything in it, making them
holy for the LORD. 11He sprinkled some oil on
the altar seven times, sprinkling the altar and
all its tools and the large bowl and its base. In
this way he made them holy for the LORD. 12He
poured some of the special oil on Aaron's head
to make Aaron holy for the LORD. 13Then Moses brought Aaron's sons forward. He put the
inner robes on them, tied cloth belts around
them, and put headbands on them, as the LORD
had commanded him.

14Then Moses brought the bull for the sin
offering, and Aaron and his sons put their
hands on its head. 15Moses killed the bull, took
the blood, and with his finger put some of it on
all the corners of the altar, to make it pure.
Then he poured out the rest of the blood at the
bottom of the altar. In this way he made it holy
and ready for service to God. 16Moses took all
the fat from the inner organs of the bull, the
best part of the liver, and both kidneys with
the fat that is on them, and he burned them on
the altar. 17But he took the bull's skin, its meat,
and its intestines and burned them in a fire
outside the camp, as the LORD had commanded him.

18Next Moses brought the male sheep of the
burnt offering, and Aaron and his sons put
their hands on its head. 19Then Moses killed it
and sprinkled the blood on all sides of the altar. 20He cut the male sheep into pieces and
burned the head, the pieces, and the fat. 21He
washed the inner organs and legs with water
and burned the whole sheep on the altar as a

burnt offering made by fire to the LORD; its
smell was pleasing to the LORD. Moses did
these things as the LORD had commanded him.
22Then Moses brought the
other male sheep, the one used
in appointing Aaron and his
sons as priests, and Aaron
and his sons put their hands
on its head. 23Then Moses
killed the sheep and put
some of its blood on the bottom of Aaron's right ear,
some on the thumb of Aaron's
right hand, and some on the big
toe of his right foot. 24Then Moses
brought Aaron's sons close to the altar. He
put some of the blood on the bottom of their
right ears, some on the thumbs of their right
hands, and some on the big toes of their right
feet. Then he sprinkled blood on all sides of the
altar. 25He took the fat, the fat tail, all the fat on
the inner organs, the best part of the liver, both
kidneys with their fat, and the right thigh.
26From the basket of bread made without yeast
that is put before the LORD each day, Moses
took a loaf of bread, a loaf made with oil, and a
wafer. He put these pieces of bread on the fat
and right thigh of the male sheep. 27All these
things he put in the hands of Aaron and his
sons and presented them as an offering before
the LORD. 28Then Moses took them from their
hands and burned them on the altar on top of
the burnt offering. So this was the offering for
appointing Aaron and his sons as priests. It was
an offering made by fire to the LORD, and its
smell was pleasing to him. 29Moses also took
the breast and presented it as an offering before
the LORD. It was Moses' share of the male sheep
used in appointing the priests, as the LORD had
commanded him.

30Moses took some of the special oil and
some of the blood which was on the altar, and
he sprinkled them on Aaron and Aaron's
clothes and on Aaron's sons and their clothes.
In this way Moses made Aaron, his clothes, his
sons, and their clothes holy for the LORD.

31Then Moses said to Aaron and his sons, "I
gave you a command, saying, 'Aaron and his
sons will eat these things.' So take the meat and
basket of bread from the offering for appointing priests. Boil the meat at the door of the
Meeting Tent, and eat it there with the bread.
32If any of the meat or bread is left, burn it.
33The time of appointing will last seven days;
you must not go outside the entrance of the
Meeting Tent until that time is up. Stay there
until the time of your appointing is finished.
34The LORD commanded the things that were
done today to remove your sins so you will
belong to him. 35You must stay at the entrance
of the Meeting Tent day and night
for seven days. If you don't
obey the LORD's commands,
you will die. The LORD has
given me these commands."
36So Aaron and his sons
did everything the LORD had
commanded through Moses.

> **"Its smell was pleasing to the LORD. Moses did these things as the LORD had commanded him."**
> **(Leviticus 8:21b)**

AARON AND HIS SONS OFFER SACRIFICES

9 1On the eighth day after the
time of appointing, Moses called
for Aaron and his sons and for the older leaders of Israel. 2He said to Aaron, "Take a bull calf
and a male sheep that have nothing wrong
with them, and offer them to the LORD. The calf
will be a sin offering, and the male sheep will
be a whole burnt offering. 3Tell the people of
Israel, 'Take a male goat for a sin offering and a
calf and a lamb for a whole burnt offering;
each must be one year old, and it must have
nothing wrong with it. 4Also take a bull and a
male sheep for fellowship offerings, along with
a grain offering mixed with oil. Offer all these
things to the LORD, because the LORD will appear to you today.' "

5So all the people came to the front of the
Meeting Tent, bringing the things Moses had
commanded them to bring, and they stood
before the LORD. 6Moses said, "You have done
what the LORD commanded, so you will see the
LORD's glory."

7Then Moses told Aaron, "Go to the altar
and offer sin offerings and whole burnt offerings. Do this to remove your sins and the
people's sins so you will belong to God. Offer
the sacrifices for the people and perform the
acts to remove their sins for them so they will
belong to the LORD, as the LORD has commanded."

8So Aaron went to the altar and killed the
bull calf as a sin offering for himself. 9Then his
sons brought the blood to him, and he dipped
his finger in the blood and put it on the corners of the altar. He poured out the rest of the
blood at the bottom of the altar. 10Aaron took
the fat, the kidneys, and the best part of the
liver from the sin offering and burned them on
the altar, in the way the LORD had commanded
Moses. 11The meat and skin he burned outside
the camp.

12Then Aaron killed the animal for the
whole burnt offering. His sons brought the

blood to him, and he sprinkled it on all sides of the altar. [13]As they gave him the pieces and head of the burnt offering, Aaron burned them on the altar. [14]He also washed the inner organs and the legs of the burnt offering and burned them on top of the burnt offering on the altar.

[15]Then Aaron brought the offering that was for the people. He took the goat of the people's sin offering and killed it and offered it for the sin offering, just as he had done the first sin offering.

[16]Then Aaron brought the whole burnt offering and offered it in the way that the LORD had commanded. [17]He also brought the grain offering to the altar. He took a handful of the grain and burned it on the altar, in addition to the morning's burnt offering.

[18]Aaron also killed the bull and the male sheep as the fellowship offerings for the people. His sons brought him the blood, and he sprinkled it on all sides of the altar. [19]Aaron's sons also brought to Aaron the fat of the bull and the male sheep—the fat tail, the fat covering the inner organs, the kidneys, and the best part of the liver. [20]Aaron's sons put them on the breasts of the bull and the sheep. Then Aaron burned these fat parts on the altar. [21]He presented the breasts and the right thigh before the LORD as the priests' share of the offering, as Moses had commanded.

[22]Then Aaron lifted his hands toward the people and blessed them. When he had finished offering the sin offering, the burnt offering, and the fellowship offering, he stepped down from the altar.

[23]Moses and Aaron went into the Meeting Tent. Then they came out and blessed the people, and the LORD's glory came to all the people. [24]Fire came out from the LORD and burned up the burnt offering and fat on the altar. When the people saw this, they shouted with joy and bowed facedown on the ground.

GOD DESTROYS NADAB AND ABIHU

10 [1]Aaron's sons Nadab and Abihu took their pans for burning incense, put fire in them, and added incense; but they did not use the special fire Moses had commanded them to use in the presence of the LORD. [2]So fire came down from the LORD and destroyed Nadab and Abihu, and they died in front of the LORD. [3]Then Moses said to Aaron, "This is what the LORD was speaking about when he said,

'I must be respected as holy
by those who come near me;
before all the people
I must be given honor.' "

So Aaron did not say anything about the death of his sons.

[4]Aaron's uncle Uzziel had two sons named Mishael and Elzaphan. Moses said to them, "Come here and pick up your cousins' bodies. Carry them outside the camp away from the front of the Holy Place." [5]So Mishael and Elzaphan obeyed Moses and carried the bodies of Nadab and Abihu, still clothed in the special priest's inner robes, outside the camp.

[6]Then Moses said to Aaron and his other sons, Eleazar and Ithamar, "Don't show sadness by tearing your clothes or leaving your hair uncombed. If you do, you will die, and the LORD will be angry with all the people. All the people of Israel, your relatives, may cry loudly about the LORD burning Nadab and Abihu, [7]but you must not even leave the Meeting Tent. If you go out of the entrance, you will die, because the LORD has appointed you to his service." So Aaron, Eleazar, and Ithamar obeyed Moses.

WHAT'S IT MEAN?

Uncombed hair and torn clothes were signs of mourning in ancient Israel. The mourning began as soon as a loved one died and continued indefinitely. Both family members and neighbors alike joined in expressing their grief and sorrow.

Leviticus 10:6

[8]Then the LORD said to Aaron, [9]"You and your sons must not drink wine or beer when you go into the Meeting Tent. If you do, you will die. This law will continue from now on. [10]You must keep what is holy separate from what is not holy; you must keep what is clean separate from what is unclean. [11]You must teach the people all the laws that the LORD gave to them through Moses."

[12]Moses said to Aaron and his remaining sons, Eleazar and Ithamar, "Eat the part of the grain offering that is left from the sacrifices offered by fire to the LORD, but do not add yeast to it. Eat it near the altar because it is most holy. [13]You must eat it in a holy place, because this part of the offerings made by fire to the LORD belongs to you and your sons. I have been commanded to tell you this.

14"Also, you and your sons and daughters
may eat the breast and thigh of the fellowship
offering that was presented to the LORD. You
must eat them in a clean place; they are your
share of the fellowship offerings given by the
Israelites. 15The people must bring the fat from
their animals that was part of the offering
made by fire, and they must present it to the
LORD along with the thigh and the breast of the
fellowship offering. They will be the regular
share of the offerings for you and your children, as the LORD has commanded."

16Moses looked for the goat of the sin offering, but it had already been burned up. So he
became very angry with Eleazar and Ithamar,
Aaron's remaining sons. He said, 17"Why didn't
you eat that goat in a holy place? It is most
holy, and the LORD gave it to you to take away
the guilt of the people, to remove their sins so
they will belong to the LORD. 18You didn't bring
the goat's blood inside the Holy Place. You
were supposed to eat the goat in a holy place,
as I commanded!"

19But Aaron said to Moses, "Today they
brought their sin offering and burnt offering
before the LORD, but these terrible things have
still happened to me! Do you think the LORD
would be any happier if I ate the sin offering
today?" 20When Moses heard this, he was satisfied.

RULES ABOUT WHAT MAY BE EATEN

11 1The LORD said to Moses and Aaron, 2"Tell
the Israelites this: 'These are the land animals
you may eat: 3You may eat any animal that has
split hoofs completely divided and that chews
the cud.

4" 'Some animals only chew the cud or only
have split hoofs, and you must not eat them.
The camel chews the cud but does not have a
split hoof; it is unclean for you. 5The rock bad-
ger chews the cud but does not have a split
hoof; it is unclean for you. 6The rabbit chews
the cud but does not have a split hoof; it is
unclean for you. 7Now the pig has a split hoof
that is completely divided, but it does not chew
the cud; it is unclean for you. 8You must not eat
the meat from these animals or even touch their
dead bodies; they are unclean for you.

9" 'Of the animals that live in the sea or in a
river, if the animal has fins and scales, you may
eat it. 10But whatever lives in the sea or in a
river and does not have fins and scales—including the things that fill the water and all
other things that live in it—you should hate.
11You must not eat any meat from them or
even touch their dead bodies, because you
should hate them. 12You must hate any animal
in the water that does not have fins and scales.

13" 'Also, these are the birds you are to hate.
They are hateful and should not be eaten. You
must not eat eagles, vultures, black vultures,
14kites, any kind of falcon, 15any kind of raven,
16horned owls, screech owls, sea gulls, any
kind of hawk, 17little owls, cormorants, great
owls, 18white owls, desert owls, ospreys,
19storks, any kind of heron, hoopoes, or bats.

20" 'Don't eat insects that have wings and
walk on all four feet; they also are to be hated.

21" 'But you may eat certain insects that
have wings and walk on four feet. You may eat
those that have legs with joints above their feet
so they can jump. 22These are the insects you
may eat: all kinds of locusts, winged locusts,
crickets, and grasshoppers. 23But all other insects that have wings and walk on four feet
you are to hate. 24Those insects will make you
unclean, and anyone who touches the dead
body of one of these insects will become unclean until evening. 25Anyone who picks up
one of these dead insects must wash his
clothes and be unclean until evening.

26" 'Some animals have split hoofs, but the
hoofs are not completely divided; others do not
chew the cud. They are unclean for you, and
anyone who touches the dead body of one of
these animals will become unclean. 27Of all the
animals that walk on four feet, the animals that
walk on their paws are unclean for you. Anyone who touches the dead body of one of these
animals will become unclean until evening.
28Anyone who picks up their dead bodies must
wash his clothes and be unclean until evening;
these animals are unclean for you.

29" 'These crawling animals are unclean
for you: moles, rats, all kinds of great lizards,

WHAT'S IT MEAN?

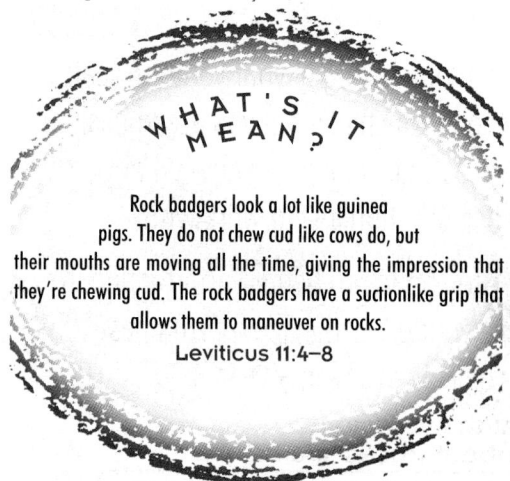

Rock badgers look a lot like guinea pigs. They do not chew cud like cows do, but their mouths are moving all the time, giving the impression that they're chewing cud. The rock badgers have a suctionlike grip that allows them to maneuver on rocks.

Leviticus 11:4–8

MOSES made a difference

Few doubt the amazing difference Moses made in his lifetime. Or in the millennia since. His is one of the few almost universally known names in history. But what about his youth? Were there signs of his later greatness in the events of his early years?

We don't know when Moses discovered his unique background, but perhaps his mother cared for him long enough to instill a strong sense of his heritage. Apparently his training in all the wisdom and knowledge of Egypt couldn't drive out of Moses his early education. He knew himself to be a Hebrew, and the Book of Hebrews describes Moses: "He chose to suffer with God's people instead of enjoying sin for a short time" (Heb. 11:25).

Moses was loyal to his people. When faced with an Egyptian guard beating a Hebrew slave, Moses did not hesitate. He intervened, killing the guard. This led to his escape into the wilderness and the second long phase of training in his life. When he eventually led his people out of Egypt, he led them into a desert that had become his backyard in the previous forty years.

Cutting Edge

Two large lessons from Moses' youth lurk behind the events of his life: (1) His faith in God and (2) his ability to write. He did not record the first five books of the Bible in his youth. They were actually more like a journal he kept during the years of travel. But he learned to write in Egypt. He remembered his ABCs. His elementary school tutors taught him well. And Moses made a difference for the world with the way he used the tools of faith and knowledge he was given as a child.

YOU can, too! Don't fall into the trap of thinking of your youthful years as marking time until you arrive at adulthood. Much of what you accomplish as an adult will be shaped by what you learn as a kid. You don't know what God will use from your past when you get older. Give him lots to work with.

Make the most of your opportunities to know God better. Pay attention in church. Read your Bible on your own. Take your educational opportunities seriously, but enjoy learning. Let God make a difference in your Life. He will take care of most of the rest.

Want to know more?
Read about Moses' life in
Exodus, Leviticus, Numbers, and Deuteronomy.

[30]geckos, crocodiles, lizards, sand reptiles, and chameleons. [31]These crawling animals are unclean for you; anyone who touches their dead bodies will be unclean until evening.

[32]" 'If an unclean animal dies and falls on something, that item will also become unclean. This includes anything made from wood, cloth, leather, or rough cloth, regardless of its use. Whatever the animal falls on must be washed with water and be unclean until evening; then it will become clean again. [33]If the dead, unclean animal falls into a clay bowl, anything in the bowl will become unclean, and you must break the bowl. [34]If water from the unclean clay bowl gets on any food, that food will become unclean. [35]If any dead, unclean animal falls on something, it becomes unclean. If it is a clay oven or a clay baking pan, it must be broken into pieces. These things will be unclean; they are unclean for you.

[36]" 'A spring or well that collects water will stay clean, but anyone who touches the dead body of any unclean animal will become unclean. [37]If a dead, unclean animal falls on a seed to be planted, that seed is still clean. [38]But if you put water on some seeds and a dead, unclean animal falls on them, they are unclean for you.

[39]" 'Also, if an animal which you use for food dies, anyone who touches its body will be unclean until evening. [40]Anyone who eats meat from this animal's dead body must wash his clothes and be unclean until evening. Anyone who picks up the animal's dead body must wash his clothes and be unclean until evening.

[41]" 'Every animal that crawls on the ground is to be hated; it must not be eaten. [42]You must not eat any of the animals that crawl on the ground, including those that crawl on their stomachs, that walk on all four feet, or on many feet. They are to be hated. [43]Do not make yourself unclean by these animals; you must not become unclean by them. [44]I am the LORD your God. Keep yourselves holy for me because I am holy. Don't make yourselves unclean with any of these crawling animals. [45]I am the LORD who brought you out of Egypt to be your God; you must be holy because I am holy.

[46]" 'These are the teachings about all of the cattle, birds, and other animals on earth, as well as the animals in the sea and those that crawl on the ground. [47]These teachings help people know the difference between unclean animals and clean animals; they help people

"I am the LORD your God. Keep yourselves holy for me because I am holy."
(Leviticus 11:44a)

Promise — HE PROMISES THAT HE IS HOLY.

I am the LORD your God. Keep yourselves holy for me because I am holy (Lev. 11:44a).

It's the bottom of the ninth inning, bases loaded, and your team's down 4—1. The best hitter's at bat with two outs and two strikes. The pitch . . . grand slam! Your team wins 5—4. "HOLY COW!" screams the announcer. "Holy cow!"

Holiness is taken lightly by a lot of people—not just sports announcers. Let's find out what God says about being holy.

First, we must know that we serve a holy God. Psalm 111:9 says, "He sets his people free. He made his agreement everlasting. He is holy and wonderful." Psalm 99:5 also tells us that the Lord is holy. Second, he wants us to strive to be holy as well, so we can be like him (see Eph. 5:1). Do you want to be like Jesus? Live like him? Talk like him? Act like him? Think like him? That's what being holy is: being devoted to God and obeying his Word.

As you spend time with God, he will make himself known to you. There's nothing greater than spending time in the presence of Almighty God! Spend time today praising him because he is the Holy One (see Ps. 71:22).

SEE FOR YOURSELF:
Lev. 20:7; 1 Pet. 1:15–16

know which animals may be eaten and which ones must not be eaten.' "

RULES FOR NEW MOTHERS

12 [1]The LORD said to Moses, [2]"Tell the people of Israel this: 'If a woman gives birth to a son, she will become unclean for seven days, as she is unclean during her monthly period. [3]On the eighth day the boy must be circumcised. [4]Then it will be thirty-three days before she becomes clean from her loss of blood. She must not touch anything that is holy or enter the Holy Tent until her time of cleansing is finished. [5]But if she gives birth to a daughter, the mother will be unclean for two weeks, as she is unclean during her monthly period. It will be sixty-six days before she becomes clean from her loss of blood.

WHAT'S IT MEAN?

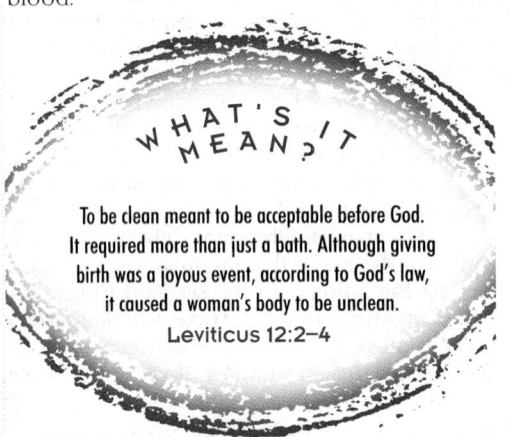

To be clean meant to be acceptable before God. It required more than just a bath. Although giving birth was a joyous event, according to God's law, it caused a woman's body to be unclean.

Leviticus 12:2–4

[6]" 'After she has a son or daughter and her days of cleansing are over, the new mother must bring certain sacrifices to the Meeting Tent. She must give the priest at the entrance a year-old lamb for a burnt offering and a dove or young pigeon for a sin offering. [7]He will offer them before the LORD to make her clean so she will belong to the LORD again; then she will be clean from her loss of blood. These are the teachings for a woman who gives birth to a boy or girl.

[8]" 'If she cannot afford a lamb, she is to bring two doves or two young pigeons, one for a burnt offering and one for a sin offering. In this way the priest will make her clean so she will belong to the LORD again, and she will be clean.' "

RULES ABOUT SKIN DISEASES

13 [1]The LORD said to Moses and Aaron, [2]"Someone might have on his skin a swelling or a rash or a bright spot. If the sore looks like a harmful skin disease, the person must be brought to Aaron the priest or to one of Aaron's sons, the priests. [3]The priest must look at the sore on the person's skin. If the hair in the sore has become white, and the sore seems deeper than the person's skin, it is a harmful skin disease. When he has finished looking at the person, the priest must announce that the person is unclean.

WHAT'S IT MEAN?

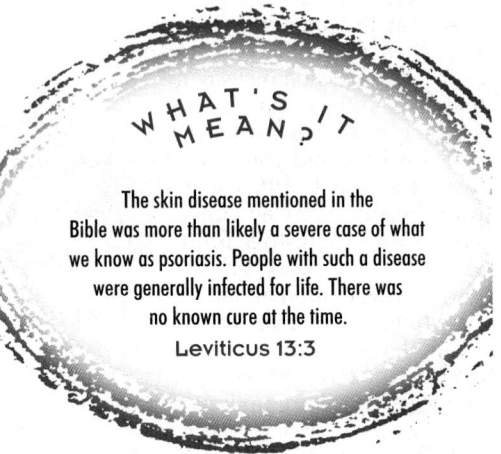

The skin disease mentioned in the Bible was more than likely a severe case of what we know as psoriasis. People with such a disease were generally infected for life. There was no known cure at the time.

Leviticus 13:3

[4]"If there is a white spot on a person's skin, but the spot does not seem deeper than the skin, and if the hair from the spot has not turned white, the priest must separate that person from other people for seven days. [5]On the seventh day the priest must look at the person again. If he sees that the sore has not changed and it has not spread on the skin, the priest must keep the person separated for seven more days. [6]On the seventh day the priest must look at the person again. If the sore has faded and has not spread on the skin, the priest must announce that the person is clean. The sore is only a rash. The person must wash his clothes, and he will become clean again.

[7]"But if the rash spreads again after the priest has announced him clean, the person must come again to the priest. [8]The priest must look at him, and if the rash has spread on the skin, the priest must announce that the person is unclean; it is a harmful skin disease.

[9]"If a person has a harmful skin disease, he must be brought to the priest, [10]and the priest must look at him. If there is a white swelling in the skin, and the hair has become white, and the skin looks raw in the swelling, [11]it is a harmful skin disease. It is one he has had for a long time. The priest must announce that the person is unclean. He will not need to separate that person from other people, because everyone already knows that the person is unclean.

12"If the skin disease spreads all over a person's body, covering his skin from his head to his feet, as far as the priest can see, the priest must look at the person's whole body. 13If the priest sees that the disease covers the whole body and has turned all of the person's skin white, he must announce that the person is clean.

14"But when the person has an open sore, he is unclean. 15When the priest sees the open sore, he must announce that the person is unclean. The open sore is not clean; it is a harmful skin disease. 16If the open sore becomes white again, the person must come to the priest. 17The priest must look at him, and if the sores have become white, the priest must announce that the person with the sores is clean. Then he will be clean.

18"Someone may have a boil on his skin that is healed. 19If in the place where the boil was, there is a white swelling or a bright red spot, this place on the skin must be shown to the priest. 20And the priest must look at it. If the spot seems deeper than the skin and the hair on it has become white, the priest must announce that the person is unclean. The spot is a harmful skin disease that has broken out from inside the boil. 21But if the priest looks at the spot and there are no white hairs in it and the spot is not deeper than the skin and it has faded, the priest must separate the person from other people for seven days. 22If the spot spreads on the skin, the priest must announce that the person is unclean; it is a disease that will spread. 23But if the bright spot does not spread or change, it is only the scar from the old boil. Then the priest must announce that the person is clean.

24"When a person gets a burn on his skin, if the open sore becomes white or red, 25the priest must look at it. If the white spot seems deeper than the skin and the hair at that spot has become white, it is a harmful skin disease. The disease has broken out in the burn, and the priest must announce that the person is unclean. It is a harmful skin disease. 26But if the priest looks at the spot and there is no white hair in the bright spot, and the spot is no deeper than the skin and has faded, the priest must separate the person from other people for seven days. 27On the seventh day the priest must look at him again. If the spot has spread on the skin, the priest must announce that the person is unclean. It is a harmful skin disease. 28But if the bright spot has not spread on the skin but has faded, it is the swelling from the burn. The priest must announce that the person is clean, because the spot is only a scar from the burn.

29"When a man or a woman gets a sore on the scalp or on the chin, 30a priest must look at the sore. If it seems deeper than the skin and the hair around it is thin and yellow, the priest must announce that the person is unclean. It is an itch, a harmful skin disease of the head or chin. 31But if the priest looks at it and it does not seem deeper than the skin and there is no black hair in it, the priest must separate the person from other people for seven days. 32On the seventh day the priest must look at the sore. If it has not spread, and there are no yellow hairs growing in it, and the sore does not seem deeper than the skin, 33the person must shave himself, but he must not shave the sore place. The priest must separate that person from other people for seven more days. 34On the seventh day the priest must look at the sore. If it has not spread on the skin and it does not seem deeper than the skin, the priest must announce that the person is clean. So the person must wash his clothes and become clean. 35But if the sore spreads on the skin after the person has become clean, 36the priest must look at him again. If the sore has spread on the skin, the priest doesn't need to look for the yellowish hair; the person is unclean. 37But if the priest thinks the sore has stopped spreading, and black hair is growing in it, the sore has healed. The person is clean, and the priest must announce that he is clean.

38"When a man or a woman has white spots on the skin, 39a priest must look at them. If the spots on the skin are dull white, the disease is only a harmless rash. That person is clean.

40"When anyone loses hair from his head and is bald, he is clean. 41If he loses hair from the front of his head and has a bald forehead, he is clean. 42But if there is a red-white sore on his bald head or forehead, it is a skin disease breaking out in those places. 43A priest must look at that person. If the swelling of the sore on his bald head or forehead is red-white, like a skin disease that spreads, 44that person has a skin disease. He is unclean. The priest must announce that the person is unclean because of the sore on his head.

45"If a person has a skin disease that spreads, he must warn other people by shouting, 'Unclean, unclean!' His clothes must be torn at the seams, he must let his hair stay uncombed, and he must cover his mouth. 46That person will be unclean the whole time he has the disease; he is unclean. He must live alone outside the camp.

RULES ABOUT MILDEW

47"Clothing might have mildew on it. It might be clothing made of linen or wool 48(either woven or knitted), or of leather, or something made from leather. 49If the mildew in the clothing, leather, or woven or knitted material is green or red, it is a spreading mildew. It must be shown to the priest. 50The priest must look at the mildew, and he must put that piece of clothing in a separate place for seven days. 51On the seventh day he must look at the mildew again. If the mildew has spread on the cloth (either woven or knitted) or the leather, no matter what the leather was used for, it is a mildew that destroys; it is unclean. 52The priest must burn the clothing. It does not matter if it is woven or knitted, wool or linen, or made of leather, because the mildew is spreading. It must be burned.

53"If the priest sees that the mildew has not spread in the cloth (either knitted or woven) or leather, 54he must order the people to wash that piece of leather or cloth. Then he must separate the clothing for seven more days. 55After the piece with the mildew has been washed, the priest must look at it again. If the mildew still looks the same, the piece is unclean, even if the mildew has not spread. You must burn it in fire; it does not matter if the mildew is on one side or the other.

56"But when the priest looks at that piece of leather or cloth, the mildew might have faded after the piece has been washed. Then the priest must tear the mildew out of the piece of leather or cloth (either woven or knitted). 57But if the mildew comes back to that piece of leather or cloth (either woven or knitted), the mildew is spreading. And whatever has the mildew must be burned with fire. 58When the cloth (either woven or knitted) or the leather is washed and the mildew is gone, it must be washed again; then it will be clean.

59"These are the teachings about mildew on pieces of cloth (either woven or knitted) or leather, to decide if they are clean or unclean."

RULES FOR CLEANSING FROM SKIN DISEASES

14 1The LORD said to Moses, 2"These are the teachings for the time at which people who had a harmful skin disease are made clean.

"The person shall be brought to the priest, 3and the priest must go outside the camp and look at the one who had the skin disease. If the skin disease is healed, 4the priest will command that two living, clean birds, a piece of cedar wood, a piece of red string, and a hyssop plant be brought for cleansing the person with the skin disease.

5"The priest must order one bird to be killed in a clay bowl containing fresh water. 6Then he will take the living bird, the piece of cedar wood, the red string, and the hyssop; all these he will dip into the blood of the bird that was killed over the fresh water. 7The priest will sprinkle the blood seven times on the person being cleansed from the skin disease. He must announce that the person is clean and then go to an open field and let the living bird go free.

8"The person to be cleansed must wash his clothes, shave off all his hair, and bathe in water. Then he will be clean and may go into the camp, though he must stay outside his tent for the first seven days. 9On the seventh day he must shave off all his hair—the hair from his head, his beard, his eyebrows, and the rest of his hair. He must wash his clothes and bathe his body in water, and he will be clean.

10"On the eighth day the person who had the skin disease must take two male lambs that have nothing wrong with them and a year-old female lamb that has nothing wrong with it. He must also take six quarts of fine flour mixed with oil for a grain offering and two-thirds of a pint of olive oil. 11The priest who is to announce that the person is clean must bring him and his sacrifices before the LORD at the entrance of the Meeting Tent. 12The priest will take one of the male lambs and offer it with the olive oil as a penalty offering; he will present them before the LORD as an offering. 13Then he will kill the male lamb in the holy place, where the sin offering and the whole burnt offering are killed. The penalty offering is like the sin offering—it belongs to the priest and it is most holy.

14"The priest will take some of the blood of the penalty offering and put it on the bottom

WHAT'S IT MEAN?

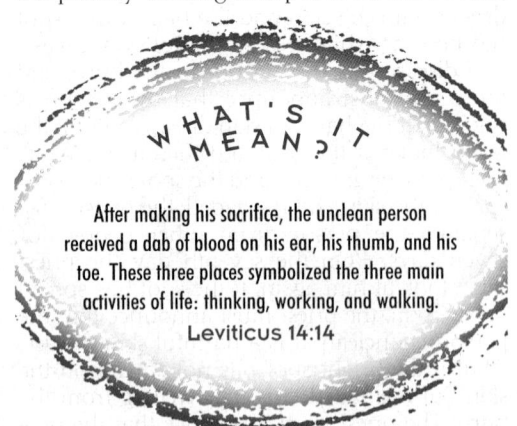

After making his sacrifice, the unclean person received a dab of blood on his ear, his thumb, and his toe. These three places symbolized the three main activities of life: thinking, working, and walking.

Leviticus 14:14

of the right ear of the person to be made clean.
He will also put some of it on the thumb of the
person's right hand and on the big toe of the
person's right foot. 15Then the priest will take
some of the oil and pour it into his own left
hand. 16He will dip a finger of his right hand
into the oil that is in his left hand, and with his
finger he will sprinkle some of the oil seven
times before the LORD. 17The priest will put
some oil from his hand on the bottom of the
right ear of the person to be made clean, some
on the thumb of the person's right hand, and
some on the big toe of the person's right foot.
The oil will go on these places on top of the
blood for the penalty offering. 18He will put the
rest of the oil that is in his left hand on the head
of the person to be made clean. In this way the
priest will make that person clean so he can
belong to the LORD again.

19"Next the priest will offer the sin offering
to make that person clean so he can belong to
the LORD again. After this the priest will kill the
animal for the whole burnt offering, 20and he
will offer the burnt offering and grain offering
on the altar. In this way he will make that person clean so he can belong to the LORD again.

21"But if the person is poor and unable to
afford these offerings, he must take one male
lamb for a penalty offering. It will be presented
to the LORD to make him clean so he can belong to the LORD again. The person must also
take two quarts of fine flour mixed with oil for
a grain offering. He must also take two-thirds
of a pint of olive oil 22and two doves or two
young pigeons, which he can afford. One bird
is for a sin offering and the other for a whole
burnt offering. 23On the eighth day the person
will bring them for his cleansing to the priest at
the entrance of the Meeting Tent, before the
LORD. 24The priest will take the lamb for the
penalty offering and the oil, and he will present
them as an offering before the LORD. 25Then he
will kill the lamb of the penalty offering, take
some of its blood, and put it on the bottom of
the right ear of the person to be made clean.
The priest will put some of this blood on the
thumb of the person's right hand and some on
the big toe of the person's right foot. 26He will
also pour some of the oil into his own left
hand. 27Then with a finger of his right hand, he
will sprinkle some of the oil from his left hand
seven times before the LORD. 28The priest will
take some of the oil from his hand and put it
on the bottom of the right ear of the person to
be made clean. He will also put some of it on
the thumb of the person's right hand and some
on the big toe of the person's right foot. The oil
will go on these places on top of the blood
from the penalty offering. 29The priest must
put the rest of the oil that is in his hand on the
head of the person to be made clean, to make
him clean so he can belong to the LORD again.
30Then the priest will offer one of the doves or
young pigeons, which the person can afford.
31He must offer one of the birds for a sin offering and the other for a whole burnt offering,
along with the grain offering. In this way the
priest will make the person clean so he can belong to the LORD again; he will become clean.

32"These are the teachings for making a person clean after he has had a skin disease, if he
cannot afford the regular sacrifices for becoming clean."

RULES FOR CLEANING MILDEW

33The LORD also said to Moses and Aaron,
34"I am giving the land of Canaan to your people. When they enter that land, if I cause mildew to grow in someone's house in that land,
35the owner of that house must come and tell
the priest. He should say, 'I have seen something like mildew in my house.' 36Then the
priest must order the people to empty the
house before he goes in to look at the mildew.
This is so he will not have to say that everything in the house is unclean. After this, the
priest will go in to look at it. 37He will look at
the mildew, and if the mildew on the walls of
the house is green or red and goes into the
wall's surface, 38he must go out and close up
the house for seven days. 39On the seventh day
the priest must come back and check the
house. If the mildew has spread on the walls of
the house, 40the priest must order the people to
tear out the stones with the mildew on them.
They should throw them away, at a certain unclean place outside the city. 41Then the priest
must have all the inside of the house scraped.
The people must throw away the plaster they
scraped off the walls, at a certain unclean place
outside the city. 42Then the owner must put
new stones in the walls, and he must cover the
walls with new clay plaster.

43"Suppose a person has taken away the
old stones and plaster and put in new stones
and plaster. If mildew again appears in his
house, 44the priest must come back and check
the house again. If the mildew has spread in the
house, it is a mildew that destroys things; the
house is unclean. 45Then the owner must tear
down the house, remove all its stones, plaster,
and wood, and take them to the unclean place
outside the city. 46Anyone who goes into that
house while it is closed up will be unclean

until evening. [47]Anyone who eats in that house or lies down there must wash his clothes.

[48]"Suppose after new stones and plaster have been put in a house, the priest checks it again and the mildew has not spread. Then the priest will announce that the house is clean, because the mildew is gone.

[49]"Then, to make the house clean, the priest must take two birds, a piece of cedar wood, a piece of red string, and a hyssop plant. [50]He will kill one bird in a clay bowl containing fresh water. [51]Then he will take the bird that is still alive, the cedar wood, the hyssop, and the red string, and he will dip them into the blood of the bird that was killed over the fresh water. The priest will sprinkle the blood on the house seven times. [52]He will use the bird's blood, the fresh water, the live bird, the cedar wood, the hyssop, and the red string to make the house clean. [53]He will then go to an open field outside the city and let the living bird go free. This is how the priest makes the house clean and ready for service to the LORD."

[54]These are the teachings about any kind of skin disease, [55]mildew on pieces of cloth or in a house, [56]swellings, rashes, or bright spots on the skin; [57]they help people decide when things are unclean and when they are clean. These are the teachings about all these kinds of diseases.

RULES ABOUT A PERSON'S BODY

15 [1]The LORD also said to Moses and Aaron, [2]"Say to the people of Israel: 'When a fluid comes from a person's body, the fluid is unclean. [3]It doesn't matter if the fluid flows freely or if it is blocked from flowing; the fluid will make him unclean. This is the way the fluid makes him unclean:

[4]" 'If the person who discharges the body fluid lies on a bed, that bed becomes unclean, and everything he sits on becomes unclean. [5]Anyone who touches his bed must wash his clothes and bathe in water, and the person will be unclean until evening. [6]Whoever sits on something that the person who discharges the fluid sat on must wash his clothes and bathe in water; he will be unclean until evening. [7]Anyone who touches the person who discharges the body fluid must wash his clothes and bathe in water; he will be unclean until evening.

[8]" 'If the person who discharges the body fluid spits on someone who is clean, that person must wash his clothes and bathe in water; he will be unclean until evening. [9]Everything on which the person who is unclean sits when riding will become unclean. [10]Anyone who touches something that was under him will be unclean until evening. And anyone who carries these things must wash his clothes and bathe in water; he will be unclean until evening.

[11]" 'If the person who discharges a body fluid has not washed his hands in water and touches another person, that person must wash his clothes and bathe in water; he will be unclean until evening.

[12]" 'If a person who discharges a body fluid touches a clay bowl, that bowl must be broken. If he touches a wooden bowl, that bowl must be washed in water.

[13]" 'When a person who discharges a body fluid is made clean, he must count seven days for himself for his cleansing. He must wash his clothes and bathe his body in fresh water, and he will be clean. [14]On the eighth day he must take two doves or two young pigeons before the LORD at the entrance of the Meeting Tent. He will give the two birds to the priest. [15]The priest will offer the birds, one for a sin offering and the other for a burnt offering. And the priest will make that person clean so he can belong to the LORD again.

[16]" 'If semen[n] goes out from a man, he must bathe in water; he will be unclean until evening. [17]If the fluid gets on any clothing or leather, it must be washed with water; it will be unclean until evening.

[18]" 'If a man has sexual relations with a woman and semen comes out, both people must bathe in water; they will be unclean until evening.

RULES ABOUT A WOMAN'S BODY

[19]" 'When a woman has her monthly period, she is unclean for seven days; anyone who touches her will be unclean until evening. [20]Anything she lies on during this time will be unclean, and everything she sits on during this time will be unclean. [21]Anyone who touches her bed must wash his clothes and bathe in water; that person will be unclean until evening. [22]Anyone who touches something she has sat on must wash his clothes and bathe in water; that person will be unclean until evening. [23]It does not matter if the person touched the woman's bed or something she sat on; he will be unclean until evening.

[24]" 'If a man has sexual relations with a woman and her monthly period touches him,

15:16 semen A man's body fluid by which he can make a woman pregnant.

he will be unclean for seven days; every bed he
lies on will be unclean.
25" 'If a woman has a loss of blood for
many days and it is not during her regular
monthly period, or if she continues to have a
loss of blood after her regular period, she will
be unclean, as she is during her monthly period. She will be unclean for as long as she continues to bleed. 26Any bed she lies on during all
the time of her bleeding will be like her bed
during her regular monthly period. Everything
she sits on will be unclean, as during her regular monthly period.
27" 'Whoever touches
those things will be
unclean and must wash
his clothes and bathe
in water; he will be
unclean until evening.
28When the woman
becomes clean from
her bleeding, she must
wait seven days, and
after this she will be
clean. 29Then on the
eighth day she must take
two doves or two young
pigeons and bring them to
the priest at the entrance of the Meeting
Tent. 30The priest must offer one bird for a sin
offering and the other for a whole burnt offering. In this way the priest will make her clean so
she can belong to the LORD again.
31" 'So you must warn the people of Israel to
stay separated from things that make them unclean. If you don't warn the people, they might
make my Holy Tent unclean, and then they
would have to die!' "
32These are the teachings for the person
who discharges a body fluid and for the man
who becomes unclean from semen coming out
of his body. 33These are the teachings for the
woman who becomes unclean from her
monthly period, for a man or woman who has
a discharge, and for a man who becomes unclean by having sexual relations with a woman who is unclean.

"So you must warn the people of Israel to stay separated from things that make them unclean. If you don't warn the people, they might make my Holy Tent unclean, and then they would have to die!" (Leviticus 15:31)

THE DAY OF CLEANSING

16
1Now two of Aaron's sons had died while
offering incense to the LORD, and after that
time the LORD spoke to Moses. 2The LORD said
to him, "Tell your brother Aaron that there are
times when he cannot go behind the curtain
into the Most Holy Place where the Ark is. If he
goes in when I appear in a cloud over the lid
on the Ark, he will die.
3"This is how Aaron may enter the Most
Holy Place: Before he enters, he must offer a
bull for a sin offering and a male sheep for a
whole burnt offering. 4He must put on the
holy linen inner robe, with the linen underclothes next to his body. His belt will be the
cloth belt, and he will wear the linen turban.
These are holy clothes, so he must bathe his
body in water before he puts them on.
5"Aaron must take from the people of Israel
two male goats for a sin offering and one male
sheep for a burnt offering. 6Then he will offer
the bull for the sin offering
for himself to remove
sins from him and his
family so they will be-
long to the LORD.
7"Next Aaron will
take the two goats and
bring them before the
LORD at the entrance
to the Meeting Tent.
8He will throw lots
for the two goats—
one will be for the
LORD and the other for
the goat that removes sin.
9Then Aaron will take the
goat that was chosen for the
LORD by throwing the lot, and he will offer it as
a sin offering. 10The other goat, which was
chosen by lot to remove the sin, must be
brought alive before the LORD. The priest will
use it to perform the acts that remove Israel's
sin so they will belong to the LORD. Then this
goat will be sent out into the desert as a goat
that removes sin.
11"Then Aaron will offer the bull as a sin
offering for himself, to remove the sins from

WHAT'S IT MEAN?

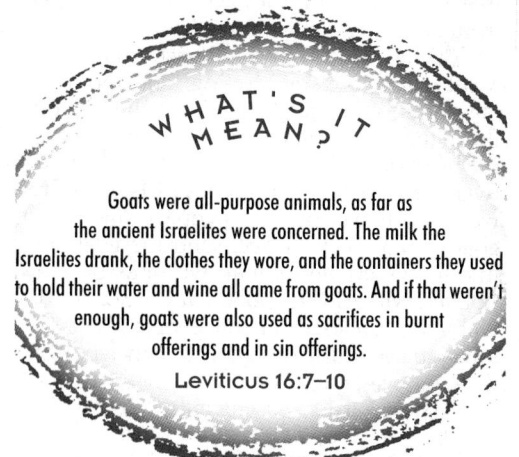

Goats were all-purpose animals, as far as the ancient Israelites were concerned. The milk the Israelites drank, the clothes they wore, and the containers they used to hold their water and wine all came from goats. And if that weren't enough, goats were also used as sacrifices in burnt offerings and in sin offerings.

Leviticus 16:7–10

him and his family so they will belong to the LORD; he will kill the bull for the sin offering for himself. 12Then he must take a pan full of burning coals from the altar before the LORD and two handfuls of sweet incense that has been ground into powder. He must bring it into the room behind the curtain. 13He must put the incense on the fire before the LORD so that the cloud of incense will cover the lid on the Ark. Then when Aaron comes in, he will not die. 14Also, he must take some of the blood from the bull and sprinkle it with his finger on the front of the lid; with his finger he will sprinkle the blood seven times in front of the lid.

15"Then Aaron must kill the goat of the sin offering for the people and bring its blood into the room behind the curtain. He must do with the goat's blood as he did with the bull's blood, sprinkling it on the lid and in front of the lid. 16Because the people of Israel have been unclean, Aaron will perform the acts to make the Most Holy Place ready for service to the LORD. Then it will be clean from the sins and crimes of the Israelites. He must also do this for the Meeting Tent, because it stays in the middle of unclean people. 17When Aaron makes the Most Holy Place ready for service to the LORD, no one is allowed in the Meeting Tent until he comes out. So Aaron will perform the acts to remove sins from himself, his family, and all the people of Israel, so they will belong to the LORD. 18Afterward he will go out to the altar that is before the LORD and will make it ready for service to the LORD. Aaron will take some of the bull's blood and some of the goat's blood and put it on the corners of the altar on all sides. 19Then, with his finger, he will sprinkle some of the blood on the altar seven times to make the altar holy for the LORD and clean from all the sins of the Israelites.

20"When Aaron has finished making the Most Holy Place, the Meeting Tent, and the altar ready for service to the LORD, he will offer the living goat. 21He will put both his hands on the head of the living goat, and he will confess over it all the sins and crimes of Israel. In this way Aaron will put the people's sins on the goat's head. Then he will send the goat away into the desert, and a man who has been appointed will lead the goat away. 22So the goat will carry on itself all the people's sins to a lonely place in the desert. The man who leads the goat will let it loose there.

23"Then Aaron will enter the Meeting Tent and take off the linen clothes he had put on before he went into the Most Holy Place; he must leave these clothes there. 24He will bathe his body in water in a holy place and put on his regular clothes. Then he will come out and offer the whole burnt offering for himself and for the people, to remove sins from himself and the people so they will belong to the LORD. 25Then he will burn the fat of the sin offering on the altar.

26"The person who led the goat, the goat to remove sins, into the desert must wash his clothes and bathe his body in water. After that, he may come back into the camp.

27"The bull and the goat for the sin offerings, whose blood was brought into the Most Holy Place to make it ready for service to the LORD, must be taken outside the camp; the animals' skins, bodies, and intestines will be burned in the fire. 28Then the one who burns them must wash his clothes and bathe his body in water. After that, he may come back into the camp.

29"This law will always continue for you: On the tenth day of the seventh month, you must not eat and you must not do any work. The travelers or foreigners living with you must not work either. 30It is on this day that the priests will make you clean so you will belong to the LORD again. All your sins will be removed. 31This is a very important day of rest for you, and you must not eat. This law will continue forever.

32"The priest appointed to take his father's place, on whom the oil was poured, will perform the acts for making things ready for service to the LORD. He must put on the holy linen clothes 33and make the Most Holy Place, the Meeting Tent, and the altar ready for service to the LORD. He must also remove the sins of the priests and all the people of Israel so they will belong to the LORD. 34That law for removing the sins of the Israelites so they will belong to the LORD will continue forever. You will do these things once a year."

So they did the things the LORD had commanded Moses.

OFFERING SACRIFICES

17 1The LORD said to Moses, 2"Speak to Aaron, his sons, and all the people of Israel. Tell them: 'This is what the LORD has commanded. 3If an Israelite kills an ox, a lamb, or a goat either inside the camp or outside it, 4when he should have brought the animal to the entrance of the Meeting Tent as a gift to the LORD in front of the LORD's Holy Tent, he is guilty of killing. He has killed, and he must be cut off from the people. 5This rule is so people will bring their sacrifices, which they have been sacrificing in

the open fields, to the LORD. They must bring those animals to the LORD at the entrance of the Meeting Tent; they must bring them to the priest and offer them as fellowship offerings. 6Then the priest will sprinkle the blood from those animals on the LORD's altar near the entrance of the Meeting Tent. And he will burn the fat from those animals on the altar, as a smell pleasing to the LORD. 7They must not offer any more sacrifices to their goat idols, which they have chased like prostitutes. These rules will continue for people from now on.'

8"Tell the people this: 'If any citizen of Israel or foreigner living with you offers a burnt offering or sacrifice, 9that person must take his sacrifice to the entrance of the Meeting Tent to offer it to the LORD. If he does not do this, he must be cut off from the people.

10" 'I will be against any citizen of Israel or foreigner living with you who eats blood. I will cut off that person from the people. 11This is because the life of the body is in the blood, and I have given you rules for pouring that blood on the altar to remove your sins so you will belong to the LORD. It is the blood that removes the sins, because it is life. 12So I tell the people of Israel this: "None of you may eat blood, and no foreigner living among you may eat blood."

13" 'If any citizen of Israel or foreigner living among you catches a wild animal or bird that can be eaten, that person must pour the blood on the ground and cover it with dirt. 14If blood is still in the meat, the animal's life is still in it. So I give this command to the people of Israel: "Don't eat meat that still has blood in it, because the animal's life is in its blood. Anyone who eats blood must be cut off."

15" 'If a person, either a citizen or a foreigner, eats an animal that died by itself or was killed by another animal, he must wash his clothes and bathe in water. He will be unclean until evening; then he will be clean. 16If he does not wash his clothes and bathe his body, he will be guilty of sin.' "

RULES ABOUT SEXUAL RELATIONS

18 1The LORD said to Moses, 2"Tell the people of Israel: 'I am the LORD your God. 3In the past you lived in Egypt, but you must not do what was done in that country. And you must not do as they do in the land of Canaan, where I am bringing you. Do not follow their customs. 4You must obey my rules and follow them. I am the LORD your God. 5Obey my laws and rules; a person who obeys them will live because of them. I am the LORD.

WHAT'S IT MEAN?

The Canaanites worshiped a fertility god named Baal. Male and female prostitutes lived in Baal's temple. Both the Egyptians and Canaanites believed that if they had sex with the temple prostitutes, they would be blessed with more children, animals, and crops. God wanted his people to have nothing to do with those kinds of practices.

Leviticus 18:3

6" 'You must never have sexual relations with your close relatives. I am the LORD.

7" 'You must not shame your father by having sexual relations with your mother. She is your mother; do not have sexual relations with her. 8You must not have sexual relations with your father's wife; that would shame your father.

9" 'You must not have sexual relations with your sister, either the daughter of your father or your mother. It doesn't matter if she was born in your house or somewhere else.

10" 'You must not have sexual relations with your son's daughter or your daughter's daughter; that would bring shame on you.

11" 'If your father and his wife have a daughter, she is your sister. You must not have sexual relations with her.

12" 'You must not have sexual relations with your father's sister; she is your father's close relative. 13You must not have sexual relations with your mother's sister; she is your mother's close relative. 14You must not have sexual relations with the wife of your father's brother, because this would shame him. She is your aunt.

15" 'You must not have sexual relations with your daughter-in-law; she is your son's wife. Do not have sexual relations with her.

16" 'You must not have sexual relations with your brother's wife. That would shame your brother.

17" 'You must not have sexual relations with both a woman and her daughter. And do not have sexual relations with this woman's granddaughter, either the daughter of her son or her daughter; they are her close relatives. It is evil to do this.

18“ ‘While your wife is still living, you must not take her sister as another wife. Do not have sexual relations with her.

19“ ‘You must not go near a woman to have sexual relations with her during her monthly period, when she is unclean.

20“ ‘You must not have sexual relations with your neighbor’s wife and make yourself unclean with her.

21“ ‘You must not give any of your children to be sacrificed to Molech, because this would show that you do not respect your God. I am the LORD.

HOMOSEXUALITY

What does God say about homosexual behavior? (18:22)

22“ ‘You must not have sexual relations with a man as you would a woman. That is a hateful sin.

23“ ‘You must not have sexual relations with an animal and make yourself unclean with it. Also a woman must not have sexual relations with an animal; it is not natural.

24“ ‘Don’t make yourself unclean by any of these wrong things. I am forcing nations out of their countries because they did these sins, and I am giving their land to you. 25The land has become unclean, and I punished it for its sins, so the land is throwing out those people who live there.

26“ ‘You must obey my laws and rules, and you must not do any of these hateful sins. These rules are for the citizens of Israel and for the people who live with you. 27The people who lived in the land before you did all these hateful things and made the land unclean. 28If you do these things, you will also make the land unclean, and it will throw you out as it threw out the nations before you. 29Anyone who does these hateful sins must be cut off from the people. 30Keep my command not to do these hateful sins that were done by the people who lived in the land before you. Don’t make yourself unclean by doing them. I am the LORD your God.’ ”

On the Edge

You must not have sexual relations with a man as you would a woman. That is a hateful sin (Lev. 18:22).

In the Old Testament and again in the New Testament, God calls homosexuality a sin that is disgusting to him. Sin always has its consequences. With homosexuality comes guilt, emotional scars, condemnation, and possibly disease and death—not to mention how it can impact the people around a person. If your friend does not know Jesus, that’s the first step. Introduce him or her to Jesus. Let your friend know that Jesus loves us *no matter what we do.* People who don’t know Jesus often live according to what *feels* right. Most of the time that gets folks in trouble. If your friend does know Jesus, remind him or her of some things. Remind him or her that our purpose is to live a life that pleases God and to do our best to stay away from sin. Remind him or her that in Jesus there is the power to break any bondage. Your friend may need counseling or other help. For sure he or she will need a good friend. Hang in there. God can do anything!

SEE FOR YOURSELF:
Lev. 20:13;
1 Cor. 6:9–10

OTHER LAWS

19

1The LORD said to Moses, 2“Tell all the people of Israel: ‘I am the LORD your God. You must be holy because I am holy.

RESPECT

Do we need to respect our parents? (19:3)

3“ ‘You must respect your mother and father, and you must keep my Sabbaths. I am the LORD your God.

4“ ‘Do not worship idols or make statues or gods for yourselves. I am the LORD your God.

5“ ‘When you sacrifice a fellowship offering to the LORD, offer it in such a way that will be accepted. 6You may eat it the same day you offer it or on the next day. But if any is left on the third day, you must burn it up. 7If any of it is eaten on the third day, it is unclean, and it will not be accepted. 8Anyone who eats it then will be guilty of sin, because he did not respect the holy things that belong to the LORD. He must be cut off from the people.

9“ ‘When you harvest your crops on your land, do not harvest all the way to the corners of your fields. If grain falls onto the ground, don’t gather it up. 10Don’t pick all the grapes in your vineyards, and don’t pick up the grapes that fall to the ground. You must leave those things for poor people and for people traveling through your country. I am the LORD your God.

11“ ‘You must not steal. You must not cheat people, and you must not lie to each other.

[12]You must not make a false promise by my name, or you will show that you don't respect your God. I am the LORD.

[13]" 'You must not cheat your neighbor or rob him. You must not keep a hired worker's salary all night until morning. [14]You must not curse a deaf person or put something in front of a blind person to make him fall. But you must respect your God. I am the LORD.

[15]" 'Be fair in your judging. You must not show special favor to poor people or great people, but be fair when you judge your neighbor. [16]You must not spread false stories against other people, and you must not do anything that would put your neighbor's life in danger. I am the LORD.

GOSSIP
What should we be careful of when we're talking about other people? (19:16)

[17]" 'You must not hate your fellow citizen in your heart. If your neighbor does something wrong, tell him about it, or you will be partly to blame. [18]Forget about the wrong things people do to you, and do not try to get even. Love your neighbor as you love yourself. I am the LORD.

REVENGE
Should God's people seek revenge? (19:18)

[19]" 'Obey my laws. You must not mate two different kinds of cattle or sow your field with two different kinds of seed. You must not wear clothing made from two different kinds of material mixed together.

[20]" 'If a man has sexual relations with a slave girl of another man, but this slave girl has not been bought or given her freedom, there must be punishment. But they are not to be put to death, because the woman was not free. [21]The man must bring a male sheep as his penalty offering to the LORD at the entrance to the Meeting Tent. [22]The priest will offer the sheep as a penalty offering before the LORD for the man's sin, to remove the sins of the man so he will belong to the LORD. Then he will be forgiven for his sin.

[23]" 'In the future, when you enter your country, you will plant many kinds of trees for food. After planting a tree, wait three years before using its fruit. [24]In the fourth year the fruit from the tree will be the LORD's, a holy offering of praise to him. [25]Then in the fifth year, you may eat the fruit from the tree. The tree will then produce more fruit for you. I am the LORD your God.

[26]" 'You must not eat anything with the blood in it.

" 'You must not try to tell the future by signs or black magic.

OCCULT
What does God think about fortune-telling? (19:26)

[27]" 'You must not cut the hair on the sides of your heads or cut the edges of your beard. [28]You must not cut your body to show sadness for someone who died or put tattoo marks on yourselves. I am the LORD.

[29]" 'Do not dishonor your daughter by making her become a prostitute. If you do this, the country will be filled with all kinds of sin.

[30]" 'Obey the laws about Sabbaths, and respect my Most Holy Place. I am the LORD.

[31]" 'Do not go to mediums or fortune-tellers

On the Edge

Forget about the wrong things people do to you, and do not try to get even. Love your neighbor as you love yourself. I am the LORD (Lev. 19:18).

Here's a great piece of advice from Leviticus. You can use it in all your relationships, not just friendships. Unfortunately, friendships can be tricky sometimes. They can be especially hard at times when you're growing so much so fast—like in your teenage years. People may treat you like their best buddy one day and not even speak to you the next. High schools are famous for cliques and clubs and sometimes even when you're "in" you get treated like you're "out."

God knows about high school. He knows what it's like to be tight with a group and have your back stabbed. Don't play those games. He says not to be angry and not to take revenge. Stuff hurts. So hurt, but don't be angry and don't start thinking about how you're going to get someone back. The Lord says love. Love that person as much as you love yourself. Whoa. That's big love. The cool thing is that God will help you. You may not be able to muster up one ounce of love on your own, but ask God to help you love and he will. Be quick to love and quick to forgive. That's God's good advice and you'll be happier and healthier if you live by it.

SEE FOR YOURSELF:
John 15:12; Eph. 4:31–32; 1 John 5:1–3

for advice, or you will become unclean. I am
the LORD your God.
32 "'Show respect to old people; stand up in
their presence. Show respect also to your God.
I am the LORD.
33 "'Do not mistreat foreigners living in your
country, 34 but treat them just as you treat your
own citizens. Love foreigners as you love
yourselves, because you were foreigners one
time in Egypt. I am the LORD your God.
35 "'Do not cheat when you measure the
length or weight or amount of something.
36 Your weights and balances should weigh
correctly, with your weighing baskets the right
size and your jars holding the right amount of
liquid. I am the LORD your God. I brought you
out of the land of Egypt.
37 "'Remember all my laws and rules, and
obey them. I am the LORD.'"

WARNINGS ABOUT VARIOUS SINS

20
1 The LORD said to Moses, 2 "You must also
tell the people of Israel these things: 'If a person
in your country gives one of his children to
Molech, that person must be killed. It doesn't
matter if he is a citizen or a foreigner living in
Israel; you must throw stones at him and kill
him. 3 I will be against him and cut him off
from his people, because he gave his children
to Molech. He showed that he did not respect
my holy name, and he made my Holy Place
unclean. 4 The people of the community might
ignore that person and not kill the one who
gave his children to Molech. 5 But I will be
against him and his family, and I will cut him
off from his people. I will do this to anyone
who follows him in being unfaithful to me by
worshiping Molech.
6 "'I will be against anyone who goes to mediums and fortune-tellers for advice, because
that person is being unfaithful to me. So I will
cut him off from his people.
7 "'Be my holy people. Be holy because I am
the LORD your God. 8 Remember and obey my
laws. I am the LORD, and I have made you holy.
9 "'Anyone who curses his father or mother
must be put to death. He has cursed his father
or mother, so he has brought his own death on
himself.

PUNISHMENTS FOR SEXUAL SINS

10 "'If a man has sexual relations with his
neighbor's wife, both the man and the woman

WHAT'S IT MEAN?

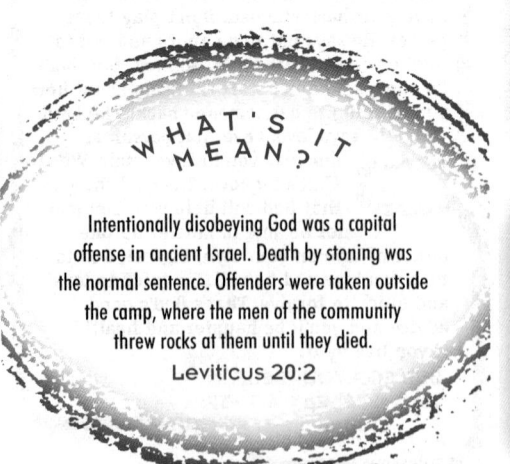

Intentionally disobeying God was a capital offense in ancient Israel. Death by stoning was the normal sentence. Offenders were taken outside the camp, where the men of the community threw rocks at them until they died.

Leviticus 20:2

On the Edge

I will be against anyone who goes to mediums and fortune-tellers for advice, because that person is being unfaithful to me. So I will cut him off from his people (Lev. 20:6).

How many times have you flipped through the channels to see somebody trying to convince you to call a 1-900 number that will put you in touch with your very own psychic?

We live in a world today that is fascinated with the supernatural, but rather than turning to God or his Word for answers, a lot of people want to turn to "mediums and fortune-tellers," that is, to psychics, witches, channelers, and others. God's Word calls this kind of stuff hateful; and in this particular verse, he says that he is against those who even visit someone like this. Don't even associate with such people. Instead, turn to Jesus. He really is the *only* answer!

You don't need to go looking to someone else for answers about your future. God speaks to you through his Word and through his Holy Spirit. Don't settle for a cheap imitation. All the answers you need are in the Bible, and if you read the end of it you'll see that you are a winner. In fact, you're more than a victor (Rom. 8:37), and God is on your side. Your power isn't counterfeit. It's real. "God's Spirit, who is in you, is greater than the devil, who is in the world" (1 John 4:4).

SEE FOR YOURSELF:
2 Chr. 33:6;
Gal. 5:19–21

are guilty of adultery and must be put to death. [11]If a man has sexual relations with his father's wife, he has shamed his father, and both the man and his father's wife must be put to death. They have brought it on themselves.

[12]" 'If a man has sexual relations with his daughter-in-law, both of them must be put to death. What they have done is not natural. They have brought their own deaths on themselves.

[13]" 'If a man has sexual relations with another man as a man does with a woman, these two men have done a hateful sin. They must be put to death. They have brought it on themselves.

[14]" 'If a man has sexual relations with both a woman and her mother, this is evil. The people must burn that man and the two women in fire so that your people will not be evil.

[15]" 'If a man has sexual relations with an animal, he must be put to death. You must also kill the animal. [16]If a woman approaches an animal and has sexual relations with it, you must kill the woman and the animal. They must be put to death. They have brought it on themselves.

[17]" 'It is shameful for a brother to marry his sister, the daughter of either his father or his mother, and to have sexual relations with her. In front of everyone they must both be cut off from their people. The man has shamed his sister, and he is guilty of sin.

[18]" 'If a man has sexual relations with a woman during her monthly period, both the woman and the man must be cut off from their people. They sinned because they showed the source of her blood.

[19]" 'Do not have sexual relations with your mother's sister or your father's sister, because that would shame a close relative. Both of you are guilty of this sin.

[20]" 'If a man has sexual relations with his uncle's wife, he has shamed his uncle. That man and his uncle's wife will die without children; they are guilty of sin.

[21]" 'It is unclean for a man to marry his brother's wife. That man has shamed his brother, and they will have no children.

[22]" 'Remember all my laws and rules, and obey them. I am leading you to your own land, and if you obey my laws and rules, that land will not throw you out. [23]I am forcing out ahead of you the people who live there. Because they did all these sins, I have hated them. Do not live the way those people lived.

[24]" 'I have told you that you will get their land, which I will give to you as your very own; it is a fertile land. I am the LORD your God, and I have set you apart from other people and made you my own. [25]So you must treat clean animals and birds differently from unclean animals and birds. Do not make yourselves unclean by any of these unclean birds or animals or things that crawl on the ground, which I have made unclean for you. [26]So you must be holy to me because I, the LORD, am holy, and I have set you apart from other people to be my own.

[27]" 'A man or woman who is a medium or a fortune-teller must be put to death. You must stone them to death; they have brought it on themselves.' "

> "I have told you that you will get their land, which I will give to you as your very own; it is a fertile land. I am the LORD your God, and I have set you apart from other people and made you my own."
> (Leviticus 20:24)

HOW PRIESTS MUST BEHAVE

21 [1]The LORD said to Moses, "Tell these things to Aaron's sons, the priests: 'A priest must not make himself unclean by touching a dead person. [2]But if the dead person was one of his close relatives, he may touch him. The priest may make himself unclean if the dead person is his mother or father, son or daughter, brother or [3]unmarried sister who is close to him because she has no husband. The priest may make himself unclean for her if she dies. [4]But a priest must not make himself unclean if the dead person was only related to him by marriage.

[5]" 'Priests must not shave their heads, or shave off the edges of their beards, or cut their bodies. [6]They must be holy to their God and show respect for God's name, because they present the offerings made by fire to the LORD, which is the food of their God. So they must be holy.

[7]" 'A priest must not marry an unclean prostitute or a divorced woman, because he is holy to his God. [8]Treat him as holy, because he offers up the food of your God. Think of him as holy; I am the LORD who makes you holy, and I am holy.

[9]" 'If a priest's daughter makes herself

unclean by becoming a prostitute, she shames
her father. She must be burned with fire.
10" 'The high priest, who was chosen from
among his brothers, had the special olive oil
poured on his head. He was also appointed to
wear the priestly clothes. So he must not show
his sadness by letting his hair go uncombed or
tearing his clothes. 11He must not go into a
house where there is a dead body. He must not
make himself unclean, even if it is for his own
father or mother. 12The high priest must not go
out of the Holy Place, because if he does and
becomes unclean, he will make God's Holy
Place unclean. The special oil used in appointing priests was poured on his head to separate
him from the rest of the people. I am the LORD.
13" 'The high priest must marry a woman
who is a virgin. 14He must not marry a widow,
a divorced woman, or a prostitute. He must
marry a virgin from his own people 15so the
people will respect his children as his own. I
am the LORD. I have set the high priest apart
for his special job.' "

WHAT'S IT MEAN?

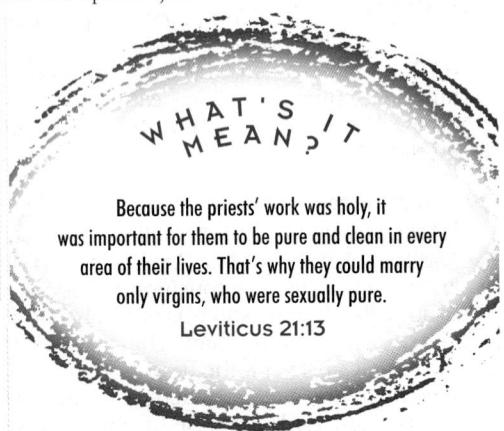

Because the priests' work was holy, it was important for them to be pure and clean in every area of their lives. That's why they could marry only virgins, who were sexually pure.

Leviticus 21:13

16The LORD said to Moses, 17"Tell Aaron: 'If
any of your descendants have something
wrong with them, they must never come near
to offer the special food of their God. 18Anyone
who has something wrong with him must not
come near: blind men, crippled men, men with
damaged faces, deformed men, 19men with a
crippled foot or hand, 20hunchbacks, dwarfs,
men who have something wrong with their
eyes, men who have an itching disease or a
skin disease, or men who have damaged sex
glands.
21" 'If one of Aaron's descendants has something wrong with him, he cannot come near to
make the offerings made by fire to the LORD.
He has something wrong with him; he cannot
offer the food of his God. 22He may eat the
most holy food and also the holy food. 23But
he may not go through the curtain into the
Most Holy Place, and he may not go near the
altar, because he has something wrong with
him. He must not make my Holy Place unfit. I
am the LORD who makes these places holy.' "
24So Moses told these things to Aaron,
Aaron's sons, and all the people of Israel.

22

1The LORD said to Moses, 2"Tell Aaron and
his sons: 'The people of Israel will give offerings to me. These offerings are holy, and they
are mine, so you must respect them to show
that you respect my holy name. I am the LORD.'
3Say to them: 'If any one of your descendants
from now on is unclean and comes near the
offerings that the Israelites made holy for me,
that person must be cut off from appearing
before me. I am the LORD.
4" 'If one of Aaron's descendants has a
harmful skin disease, or if he discharges a
body fluid, he cannot eat the holy offerings
until he becomes clean. He could also become
unclean from touching a dead body, from his
own semen,[n] 5from touching any unclean
crawling animal, or from touching an unclean
person (no matter what made the person unclean). 6Anyone who touches those things will
become unclean until evening. That person
must not eat the holy offerings unless he
washes with water. 7He will be clean only after
the sun goes down. Then he may eat the holy
offerings; the offerings are his food.
8" 'If a priest finds an animal that died by
itself or that was killed by some other animal,
he must not eat it. If he does, he will become
unclean. I am the LORD.
9" 'If the priests keep all the rules I have
given, they will not become guilty; if they are
careful, they will not die. I am the LORD who
has made them holy. 10Only people in a priest's
family may eat the holy offering. A visitor
staying with the priest or a hired worker must
not eat it. 11But if the priest buys a slave with
his own money, that slave may eat the holy
offerings; slaves who were born in his house
may also eat his food. 12If a priest's daughter
marries a person who is not a priest, she must
not eat any of the holy offerings. 13But if the
priest's daughter becomes widowed or divorced, with no children to support her, and if
she goes back to her father's house where she
lived as a child, she may eat some of her
father's food. But only people from a priest's
family may eat this food.

22:4 semen A man's body fluid by which he can make a woman pregnant.

[14]" 'If someone eats some of the holy offering by mistake, that person must pay back the
priest for that holy food, adding another one-
fifth of the price of that food.
[15]" 'When the Israelites give their holy offerings to the LORD, the priest must not treat these
holy things as though they were not holy.
[16]The priests must not allow those who are not
priests to eat the holy offerings. If they do, they
cause the ones who eat the holy offerings to
become guilty, and they will have to pay for it.
I am the LORD, who makes them holy.' "
[17]The LORD said to Moses, [18]"Tell Aaron and
his sons and all the people of Israel: 'A citizen of
Israel or a foreigner living in Israel might want
to bring a whole burnt offering, either for some
special promise he has made or for a special gift
he wants to give to the LORD. [19]If he does, he
must bring a male animal that has nothing
wrong with it—a bull, a sheep, or a goat—so it
might be accepted for him. [20]He must not bring
an animal that has something wrong with it, or
it will not be accepted for him.
[21]" 'If someone brings a fellowship offering
to the LORD, either as payment for a special
promise the person has made or as a special
gift the person wants to give the LORD, it might
be from the herd or from the flock. But it must
be healthy, with nothing wrong with it, so that
it will be accepted. [22]You must not offer to the
LORD any animal that is blind, that has broken
bones or is crippled, that has running sores or
any sort of skin disease. You must not offer
any animals like these on the altar as an offering by fire to the LORD.
[23]" 'If an ox or lamb is smaller than normal
or is not perfectly formed, you may give it as a
special gift to the LORD; it will be accepted. But
it will not be accepted as payment for a special
promise you have made.
[24]" 'If an animal has bruised, crushed, torn,
or cut sex glands, you must not offer it to the
LORD. You must not do this in your own land,
[25]and you must not take such animals from
foreigners as sacrifices to the LORD. Because the
animals have been hurt in some way and have
something wrong with them, they will not be
accepted for you.' "
[26]The LORD said to Moses, [27]"When an ox, a
sheep, or a goat is born, it must stay seven
days with its mother. But from the eighth day
on, this animal will be accepted as a sacrifice
by fire to the LORD. [28]But you must not kill the
animal and its mother on the same day, either
an ox or a sheep.
[29]"If you want to offer some special offering
of thanks to the LORD, you must do it in a way
that pleases him. [30]You must eat the whole animal that same day and not leave any of the
meat for the next morning. I am the LORD.
[31]"Remember my commands and obey
them; I am the LORD. [32]Show respect for my
holy name. You Israelites must remember that
I am holy; I am the LORD, who has made you
holy. [33]I brought you out of Egypt to be your
God. I am the LORD."

SPECIAL HOLIDAYS

23

[1]The LORD said to Moses, [2]"Tell the people
of Israel: 'You will announce the LORD's appointed feasts as holy meetings. These are my
special feasts.

THE SABBATH

[3]" 'There are six days for you to work, but
the seventh day will be a special day of rest. It
is a day for a holy meeting; you must not do
any work. It is a Sabbath to the LORD in all
your homes.

THE PASSOVER AND UNLEAVENED BREAD

[4]" 'These are the LORD's appointed feasts, the
holy meetings, which you will announce at the
times set for them. [5]The LORD's Passover is on
the fourteenth day of the first month, beginning at twilight. [6]The Feast of Unleavened
Bread begins on the fifteenth day of the same
month. You will eat bread made without yeast
for seven days. [7]On the first day of this feast
you will have a holy meeting, and you must
not do any work. [8]For seven days you will
bring an offering made by fire to the LORD.
There will be a holy meeting on the seventh

WHAT'S IT MEAN?

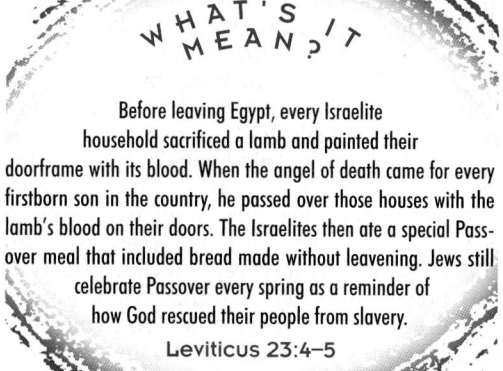

Before leaving Egypt, every Israelite household sacrificed a lamb and painted their doorframe with its blood. When the angel of death came for every firstborn son in the country, he passed over those houses with the lamb's blood on their doors. The Israelites then ate a special Passover meal that included bread made without leavening. Jews still celebrate Passover every spring as a reminder of how God rescued their people from slavery.

Leviticus 23:4–5

day, and on that day you must not do any
regular work.' "

THE FIRST OF THE HARVEST

9The LORD said to Moses, 10"Tell the people
of Israel: 'You will enter the land I will give you
and gather its harvest. At that time you must
bring the first bundle of grain from your harvest to the priest. 11The priest will present the
bundle before the LORD, and it will be accepted
for you; he will present the bundle on the day
after the Sabbath.

12" 'On the day when you present the bundle of grain, offer a male lamb, one year old,
that has nothing wrong with it, as a burnt offering to the LORD. 13You must also offer a
grain offering—four quarts of fine flour mixed
with olive oil as an offering made by fire to the
LORD; its smell will be pleasing to him. You
must also offer a quart of wine as a drink offering. 14Until the day you bring your offering
to your God, do not eat any new grain, roasted
grain, or bread made from new grain. This law
will always continue for people from now on,
wherever you live.

THE FEAST OF WEEKS

15" 'Count seven full weeks from the morning after the Sabbath. (This is the Sabbath that
you bring the bundle of grain to present as an
offering.) 16On the fiftieth day, the first day after
the seventh week, you will bring a new grain
offering to the LORD. 17On that day bring two
loaves of bread from your homes to be presented as an offering. Use yeast and four quarts
of flour to make those loaves of bread; they
will be your gift to the LORD from the first
wheat of your harvest.

18" 'Offer with the bread one young bull,
two male sheep, and seven male lambs that are
one year old and have nothing wrong with
them. Offer them with their grain offerings and
drink offerings, as a burnt offering to the LORD.
They will be an offering made by fire, and the
smell will be pleasing to the LORD. 19You must
also offer one male goat for a sin offering and
two male, one-year-old lambs as a fellowship
offering.

20" 'The priest will present the two lambs as
an offering before the LORD, along with the
bread from the first wheat of the harvest. They
are holy to the LORD, and they will belong to
the priest. 21On that same day you will call a
holy meeting; you must not do any work that
day. This law will continue for you from now
on, wherever you live.

22" 'When you harvest your crops on your
land, do not harvest all the way to the corners
of your field. If grain falls onto the ground,
don't gather it up. Leave it for poor people and
foreigners in your country. I am the LORD your
God.' "

THE FEAST OF TRUMPETS

23Again the LORD said to Moses, 24"Tell the
people of Israel: 'On the first day of the seventh
month you must have a special day of rest, a
holy meeting, when you blow the trumpet for
a special time of remembering. 25Do not do
any work, and bring an offering made by fire
to the LORD.' "

THE DAY OF CLEANSING

26The LORD said to Moses, 27"The Day of
Cleansing will be on the tenth day of the seventh month. There will be a holy meeting, and
you will give up eating and bring an offering
made by fire to the LORD. 28Do not do any
work on that day, because it is the Day of
Cleansing. On that day the priests will go before the LORD and perform the acts to make
you clean so you will belong to the LORD.

29"Anyone who refuses to give up food on
this day must be cut off from the people. 30If
anyone works on this day, I will destroy that
person from among the people. 31You must not
do any work at all; this law will continue for
people from now on wherever you live. 32It
will be a special day of rest for you, and you
must not eat. You will start this special day of
rest on the evening after the ninth day of the
month, and it will continue from that evening
until the next evening."

THE FEAST OF SHELTERS

33Again the LORD said to Moses, 34"Tell the
people of Israel: 'On the fifteenth day of the
seventh month is the Feast of Shelters. This
feast to the LORD will continue for seven days.
35There will be a holy meeting on the first day;
do not do any work. 36You will bring an offering made by fire to the LORD each day for
seven days. On the eighth day you will have
another holy meeting, and you will bring an
offering made by fire to the LORD. This will be a
holy meeting; do not do any work.

37(" 'These are the LORD's special feasts,
when there will be holy meetings and when
you bring offerings made by fire to the LORD.
You will bring whole burnt offerings, grain offerings, sacrifices, and drink offerings—each at
the right time. 38These offerings are in addition
to those for the LORD's Sabbath days, in addition to offerings you give as payment for spe-

cial promises, and in addition to special offerings you want to give to the LORD.)
39" 'So on the fifteenth day of the seventh
month, after you have gathered in the crops of
the land, celebrate the LORD's festival for seven
days. You must rest on the first day and the
eighth day. 40On the first day you will take
good fruit from the fruit trees, as well as
branches from palm trees, poplars, and other
leafy trees. You will celebrate before the LORD
your God for seven days. 41Celebrate this festival to the LORD for seven days each year. This
law will continue from now on; you will celebrate it in the seventh month.
42Live in shelters for seven days.
All the people born in Israel
must live in shelters 43so that
all your descendants will
know I made Israel live in
shelters during the time I
brought them out of Egypt.
I am the LORD your God.' "
44So Moses told the people of
Israel about all of the LORD's appointed feast days.

"So the people of Israel did as the LORD had commanded Moses." (Leviticus 24:23b)

THE LAMPSTAND AND THE HOLY BREAD

24 1The LORD said to Moses, 2"Command the
people of Israel to bring you pure oil from
crushed olives. That oil is for the lamps so that
these lamps may never go out. 3Aaron will keep
the lamps burning in the Meeting Tent from
evening until morning before the LORD; this is
in front of the curtain of the Ark of the Agreement. This law will continue from now on.
4Aaron must always keep the lamps burning on
the lampstands of pure gold before the LORD.

WHAT'S IT MEAN?

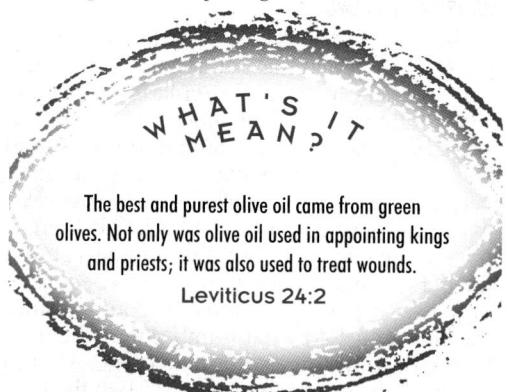

The best and purest olive oil came from green olives. Not only was olive oil used in appointing kings and priests; it was also used to treat wounds.

Leviticus 24:2

5"Take fine flour and bake twelve loaves of
bread with it, using four quarts of flour for
each loaf. 6Put them in two rows on the golden
table before the LORD, six loaves in each row.
7Put pure incense on each row as the memorial
portion to take the place of the bread. It is an
offering made by fire to the LORD. 8Every Sabbath day Aaron will put the bread in order
before the LORD, as an agreement with the people of Israel that will continue forever. 9That
bread will belong to Aaron and his sons. They
will eat it in a holy place, because it is a most
holy part of the offerings made by fire to the
LORD. That bread is their share forever."

THE MAN WHO CURSED GOD

10Now there was a son of an Israelite
woman and an Egyptian father who was
walking among the Israelites. A
fight broke out in the camp
between him and an Israelite.
11The son of the Israelite
woman began cursing and
speaking against the LORD, so
the people took him to Moses.
(The mother's name was Shelomith, the daughter of Dibri
from the family of Dan.) 12The
people held him as a prisoner
while they waited for the LORD's
command to be made clear to them.
13Then the LORD said to Moses, 14"Take the
one who spoke against me outside the camp.
Then all the people who heard him must put
their hands on his head, and all the people
must throw stones at him and kill him. 15Tell
the people of Israel this: 'If anyone curses his
God, he is guilty of sin. 16Anyone who speaks
against the LORD must be put to death; all the
people must kill him by throwing stones at
him. Foreigners must be punished just like the
people born in Israel; if they speak against the
LORD, they must be put to death.
17" 'Whoever kills another person must be
put to death. 18Whoever kills an animal that
belongs to another person must give that person another animal to take its place. 19And
whoever causes an injury to a neighbor must
receive the same kind of injury in return:
20Broken bone for broken bone, eye for eye,
tooth for tooth. Anyone who injures another
person must be injured in the same way in return. 21Whoever kills another person's animal
must give that person another animal to take
its place. But whoever kills another person
must be put to death.
22" 'The law will be the same for the foreigner as for those from your own country. I
am the LORD your God.' "
23Then Moses spoke to the people of Israel,
and they took the person who had cursed outside the camp and killed him by throwing

stones at him. So the people of Israel did as the
LORD had commanded Moses.

THE TIME OF REST FOR THE LAND

25 1The LORD said to Moses at Mount Sinai,
2"Tell the people of Israel this: 'When you enter
the land I will give you, let it have a special
time of rest, to honor the LORD. 3You may plant
seed in your field for six years, and you may
trim your vineyards for six years and bring in
their fruits. 4But during the seventh year, you
must let the land rest. This will be a special
time to honor the LORD. You must not plant
seed in your field or trim your vineyards. 5You
must not cut the crops that grow by themselves after harvest, or gather the grapes from
your vines that are not trimmed. The land will
have a year of rest.
6" 'You may eat whatever the land produces
during that year of rest. It will be food for your
men and women servants, for your hired
workers, and for the foreigners living in your
country. 7It will also be food for your cattle
and the wild animals of your land. Whatever
the land produces may be eaten.

THE YEAR OF JUBILEE

8" 'Count off seven groups of seven years, or
forty-nine years. During that time there will be
seven years of rest for the land. 9On the Day of
Cleansing, you must blow the horn of a male
sheep; this will be on the tenth day of the seventh month. You must blow the horn through
the whole country. 10Make the fiftieth year a
special year, and announce freedom for all the
people living in your country. This time will be
called Jubilee.[n] You will each go back to your
own property, each to your own family and
family group. 11The fiftieth year will be a special time for you to celebrate. Don't plant seeds,
or harvest the crops that grow by themselves,
or gather grapes from the vines that are not
trimmed. 12That year is Jubilee; it will be a holy
time for you. You may eat only the crops that
come from the field. 13In the year of Jubilee
you each must go back to your own property.
14" 'If you sell your land to your neighbor,
or if you buy land from your neighbor, don't
cheat each other. 15If you want to buy your
neighbor's land, count the number of years
since the last Jubilee, and use that number to
decide the right price. If your neighbor sells the
land to you, count the number of years left for
harvesting crops, and use that number to decide the right price. 16If there are many years,
the price will be high. But if there are only a
few years, lower the price, because your neighbor is really selling only a few crops to you.
17You must not cheat each other, but you must
respect your God. I am the LORD your God.
18" 'Remember my laws and rules, and obey
them so that you will live safely in the land.
19The land will give good crops to you, and
you will eat as much as you want and live
safely in the land.
20" 'But you might ask, "If we don't plant
seeds or gather crops, what will we eat the seventh year?" 21I will send you such a great blessing during the sixth year that the land will
produce enough crops for three years. 22When
you plant in the eighth year, you will still be
eating from the old crop; you will eat the old
crop until the harvest of the ninth year.

PROPERTY LAWS

23" 'The land really belongs to me, so you
can't sell it for all time. You are only foreigners
and travelers living for a while on my land.
24People might sell their land, but it must always be possible for the family to get its land
back. 25If a person in your country becomes
very poor and sells some land, then close relatives must come and buy it back. 26If there is
not a close relative to buy the land back, but if
the person makes enough money to be able to
buy it back, 27the years must be counted since
the land was sold. That number must be used
to decide how much the first owner should
pay back the one who bought it. Then the land
will belong to the first owner again. 28But if
there is not enough money to buy it back, the
one who bought it will keep it until the year of

WHAT'S IT MEAN?

The Year of Jubilee was designed to keep Israel from developing different classes among the people. Imagine having the opportunity to start over again economically and socially! God wanted his people to be free—including free from debt. The Year of Jubilee was a way of reminding the Israelites of this.

Leviticus 25:14–15

25:10 Jubilee This word comes from the Hebrew word for a horn of a male sheep.

Jubilee. During that celebration, the land will
go back to the first owner's family.
29" 'If someone sells a home in a walled city,
for a full year after it is sold, the person has the
right to buy it back. 30But if the owner does not
buy back the house before a full year is over, it
will belong to the one who bought it and to his
future sons. The house will not go back to the
first owner at Jubilee. 31But houses in small
towns without walls are like open country;
they can be bought back, and they must be
returned to their first owner at Jubilee.
32" 'The Levites may always buy back their
houses in the cities that belong to them. 33If
someone buys a house from a Levite, that
house in the Levites' city will again belong to
the Levites in the Jubilee. This is because
houses in Levite cities belong to the people of
Levi; the Israelites gave these cities to them.
34Also the fields and pastures around the Levites' cities cannot be sold, because those fields
belong to the Levites forever.

RULES FOR SLAVE OWNERS

35" 'If anyone from your country becomes
too poor to support himself, help him to live
among you as you would a stranger or foreigner. 36Do not charge him any interest on
money you loan to him, but respect your God;
let the poor live among you. 37Don't lend him
money for interest, and don't try to make a
profit from the food he buys. 38I am the LORD
your God, who brought you out of the land of
Egypt to give the land of Canaan to you and to
become your God.
39" 'If anyone from your country becomes
very poor and sells himself as a slave to you,
you must not make him work like a slave. 40He
will be like a hired worker and a visitor with
you until the year of Jubilee. 41Then he may
leave you, take his children, and go back to his
family and the land of his ancestors. 42This is
because the Israelites are my servants, and I
brought them out of slavery in Egypt. They
must not become slaves again. 43You must not
rule this person cruelly, but you must respect
your God.
44" 'Your men and women slaves must come
from other nations around you; from them
you may buy slaves. 45Also you may buy as
slaves children from the families of foreigners
living in your land. These child slaves will belong to you, 46and you may even pass them on
to your children after you die; you can make
them slaves forever. But you must not rule
cruelly over your own people, the Israelites.
47" 'Suppose a foreigner or visitor among
you becomes rich. If someone in your country
becomes so poor that he has to sell himself as
a slave to the foreigner living among you or to
a member of the foreigner's family, 48the poor
person has the right to be bought back and
become free. One of his relatives may buy him
back: 49His uncle, his uncle's son, or any one of
his close relatives may buy him back. Or, if he
gets enough money, he may pay the money to
free himself.
50" 'He and the one who bought him must
count the time from when he sold himself up
to the next year of Jubilee. Use that number to
decide the price, because the person really only
hired himself out for a certain number of years.
51If there are still many years before the year of
Jubilee, the person must pay back a large part
of the price. 52If there are only a few years left
until Jubilee, the person must pay a small part
of the first price. 53But he will live like a hired
person with the foreigner every year; don't let
the foreigner rule cruelly over him.
54" 'Even if no one buys him back, at the
year of Jubilee, he and his children will become
free. 55This is because the people of Israel are
servants to me. They are my servants, whom I
brought out of Egypt. I am the LORD your God.

REWARDS FOR OBEYING GOD

26
1" 'Don't make idols for yourselves or set up
statues or memorials. Don't put stone statues
in your land to bow down to, because I am the
LORD your God.
2" 'Remember my Sabbaths, and respect my
Holy Place. I am the LORD.
3" 'If you remember my laws and commands and obey them, 4I will give you rains at
the right season; the land will produce crops, and the trees of the
field will produce their fruit.
5Your threshing will continue
until the grape harvest, and
your grape harvest will continue until it is time to plant.
Then you will have plenty to
eat and live safely in your land. 6I will give
peace to your country; you will lie down in
peace, and no one will make you afraid. I will
keep harmful animals out of your country, and
armies will not pass through it.
7" 'You will chase your enemies and defeat
them, killing them with your sword. 8Five of
you will chase a hundred men; a hundred of
you will chase ten thousand men. You will defeat your enemies and kill them with your
sword.
9" 'Then I will show kindness to you and let

BLESSING
Who does God bless? (26:3–5)

you have many children; I will keep my agreement with you. 10You will have enough crops
to last for more than a year. When you harvest
the new crops, you will have to throw out the
old ones to make room for them. 11Also I will
place my Holy Tent among you, and I will not
turn away from you. 12I will walk with you
and be your God, and you will be my people.
13I am the LORD your God, who brought you
out of Egypt, where you were slaves. I broke
the heavy weights that were on your shoulders
and let you walk proudly again.

PUNISHMENT FOR NOT OBEYING GOD

14" 'But if you do not obey me and keep all
my commands, 15and if you turn away from
my rules and hate my laws, refusing to obey
all my commands, you have broken our agreement. 16As a result, I will do this to you: I will
cause terrible things to happen to you. I will
cause you to have disease and fever that
will destroy your eyes and slowly kill you. You
will not have success when you plant your
seed, and your enemy will eat your crops. 17I
will be against you, and your enemies will defeat you. These people who hate you will rule
over you, and you will run away even when
no one is chasing you.

18" 'If after all this you still do not obey me,
I will punish you seven times more for your
sins. 19I will break your great pride, and I will
make the sky like iron and the earth like
bronze.[n] 20You will work hard, but it will not
help. Your land will not grow any crops, and
your trees will not give their fruit.

21" 'If you still turn against me and refuse to
obey me, I will beat you seven times harder.
The more you sin, the more you will be punished. 22I will send wild animals to attack you,
and they will take your children away from
you and destroy your cattle. They will make
you so few in number the roads will be empty.

23" 'If you don't learn your lesson after all
these things, and if you still turn against me, 24I
will also turn against you. I will punish you
seven more times for your sins. 25You broke
my agreement, and I will punish you. I will
bring armies against you, and if you go into
your cities for safety, I will cause diseases to
spread among you so that your enemy will
defeat you. 26There will be very little bread to
eat; ten women will be able to cook all your
bread in one oven. They will measure each
piece of bread, and you will eat, but you will
still be hungry.

27" 'If you still refuse to listen to me and still

26:19 sky . . . bronze This means the sky will give no rain and the earth will produce no crops.

Promise HE PROMISES TO WALK ALONG WITH YOU.

I will walk with you and be your God, and you will be my people (Lev. 26:12).

You may have heard the story called "Footprints." It's the story of a man who had a dream. In his dream he was walking along the beach with the Lord. Scenes from his life flashed across the sky. For each scene, he noticed two sets of footprints in the sand—one belonging to him and the other to the Lord. When the last scene of his life flashed before him, he looked back at the footprints in the sand. He noticed that many times along the path of his life there was only one set of footprints. He also noticed that only one set appeared during the lowest and saddest times in his life. This really bothered him, and he questioned the Lord about it. "Lord, you said that once I decided to follow you, you'd walk with me all the way. But I have noticed that during the most troublesome times in my life, there is only one set of footprints. I don't understand why you weren't there when I needed you most. You said you would never leave me."

The Lord replied, "My son, my precious child, I love you and I would never leave you. During your times of trial and suffering, when you see only one set of footprints, it was then that I carried you."

Can you catch what this story is saying? No matter what kind of situation you go through, the Lord is going to be right there with you. Don't forget it. You never have to walk alone again. He's the One who walks with you.

SEE FOR YOURSELF:
Ps. 23:4; Prov. 3:23–26; Heb. 13:5b

turn against me, [28]I will show my great anger; I
will punish you seven more times for your
sins. [29]You will eat the bodies of your sons and
daughters. [30]I will destroy your places where
gods are worshiped and cut down your incense altars. I will pile your dead bodies on the
lifeless forms of your idols. I will hate you. [31]I
will destroy your cities and make your holy
places empty, and I will not smell the pleasing
smell of your offerings. [32]I will make the land
empty so that your enemies who come to live
in it will be shocked at it. [33]I will scatter you
among the nations, and I will pull out my
sword and destroy you. Your land will become
empty, your cities a waste. [34]When you are
taken to your enemy's country, your land will
finally get its rest. It will enjoy its time of rest all
the time it lies empty. [35]During the time the land
is empty, it will have the rest you should have
given it while you lived in it.
[36]" 'Those of you who are left alive will lose
their courage in the land of their enemies. They
will be frightened by the sound of a leaf being
blown by the wind. They will run as if someone were chasing them with a sword, and they
will fall even when no one is chasing them.
[37]They will fall over each other, as if someone
were chasing them with a sword, even though
no one is chasing them. You will not be strong
enough to stand up against your enemies.
[38]You will die among other nations and disappear in your enemies' countries. [39]So those
who are left alive will rot away in their enemies' countries because of their sins. They will
also rot away because of their ancestors' sins.

THERE IS ALWAYS HOPE

[40]" 'But maybe the people will confess their
sins and the sins of their ancestors; maybe they
will admit they turned against me and sinned
against me, [41]which made me turn against them
and send them into the land of their enemies. If
these disobedient people are sorry for what
they did and accept punishment for their sin, [42]I
will remember my agreement with Jacob, my
agreement with Isaac, and my agreement with
Abraham, and I will remember the land. [43]The
land will be left empty by its people, and it will
enjoy its time of rest as it lies bare without
them. Then those who are left alive will accept
the punishment for their sins. They will learn
that they were punished because they hated my
laws and refused to obey my rules. [44]But even
though this is true, I will not turn away from
them when they are in the land of their enemies. I will not hate them so much that I completely destroy them and break my agreement
with them, because I am the LORD their God.
[45]For their good I will remember the agreement
with their ancestors, whom I brought out of the
land of Egypt so I could become their God; the
other nations saw these things. I am the LORD.' "

Promise

HE PROMISES TO PUNISH SIN.

But if you do not obey me and keep all my commands, and if you turn away from my rules and hate my laws, refusing to obey all my commands, you have broken our agreement. As a result, I will do this to you: I will cause terrible things to happen to you. I will cause you to have disease and fever that will destroy your eyes and slowly kill you. . . . If after all this you still do not obey me, I will punish you seven times more for your sins (Lev. 26:14–18).

Wow! God really means business. He intends for us to obey his laws. He gave us laws in order to give us guidance and boundaries. God designed our lives, so he knows better than anyone how they need to operate. Think of him as the "manufacturer." The manufacturer has set the limits, knowing at what point the whole system will crash and burn. Breaking God's law is sin. God punishes sin for the same reason that a parent fairly punishes a child for disobedience. Sometimes, the consequence of the sin is the punishment. Other times, punishment may come in another form. The promise of punishment is enough to encourage some people to try to stay out of sin. For others, once they've been punished, they know they never want to make the same mistake again. Been there, done that, no thanks.

SEE FOR YOURSELF:
Ps. 89:32; Lam. 4:22; Hos. 9:9

[46]These are the laws, rules, and teachings the LORD made between himself and the Israelites through Moses at Mount Sinai.

PROMISES ARE IMPORTANT

27 [1]The LORD said to Moses, [2]"Speak to the people of Israel and tell them: 'If someone makes a special promise to give a person as a servant to the LORD by paying a price that is the same value as that person, [3]the price for a man twenty to sixty years old is about one and one-fourth pounds of silver. (You must use the measure as set by the Holy Place.) [4]The price for a woman twenty to sixty years old is about twelve ounces of silver. [5]The price for a man five to twenty years old is about eight ounces of silver; for a woman it is about four ounces of silver. [6]The price for a baby boy one month to five years old is about two ounces of silver; for a baby girl the price is about one and one-half ounces of silver. [7]The price for a man sixty years old or older is about six ounces of silver; for a woman it is about four ounces of silver.

[8]" 'If anyone is too poor to pay the price, bring him to the priest, and the priest will set the price. The priest will decide how much money the person making the vow can afford to pay.

WHAT'S IT MEAN?

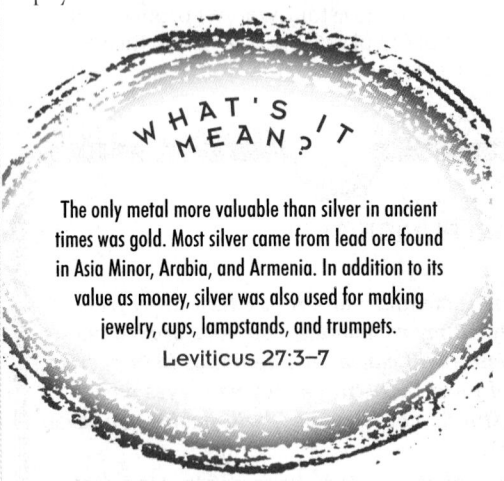

The only metal more valuable than silver in ancient times was gold. Most silver came from lead ore found in Asia Minor, Arabia, and Armenia. In addition to its value as money, silver was also used for making jewelry, cups, lampstands, and trumpets.

Leviticus 27:3–7

GIFTS TO THE LORD

[9]" 'Some animals may be used as sacrifices to the LORD. If someone promises to bring one of these to the LORD, it will become holy. [10]That person must not try to put another animal in its place or exchange it, a good animal for a bad one, or a bad animal for a good one. If this happens, both animals will become holy.

[11]" 'Unclean animals cannot be offered as sacrifices to the LORD, and if someone brings one of them to the LORD, that animal must be brought to the priest. [12]The priest will decide a price for the animal, according to whether it is good or bad; as the priest decides, that is the price for the animal. [13]If the person wants to buy back the animal, an additional one-fifth must be added to the price.

VALUE OF A HOUSE

[14]" 'If a person gives a house as holy to the LORD, the priest must decide its value, according to whether the house is good or bad; as the priest decides, that is the price for the house. [15]But if the person who gives the house wants to buy it back, an additional one-fifth must be added to the price. Then the house will belong to that person again.

VALUE OF LAND

[16]" 'If a person gives some family property to the LORD, the value of the fields will depend on how much seed is needed to plant them. It will cost about one and one-fourth pounds of silver for each six bushels of barley seed needed. [17]If the person gives a field at the year of Jubilee, its value will stay at what the priest has decided. [18]But if the person gives the field after the Jubilee, the priest must decide the exact price by counting the number of years to the next year of Jubilee. Then he will subtract that number from its value. [19]If the person who gave the field wants to buy it back, one-fifth must be added to that price, and the field will belong to the first owner again.

[20]" 'If the person does not buy back the field, or if it is sold to someone else, the first person cannot ever buy it back. [21]When the land is released at the year of Jubilee, it will become holy to the LORD, like land specially given to him. It will become the property of the priests.

[22]" 'If someone gives to the LORD a field he has bought, which is not a part of his family land, [23]the priest must count the years to the next Jubilee. He must decide the price for the land, and the price must be paid on that day. Then that land will be holy to the LORD. [24]At the year of Jubilee, the land will go back to its first owner, to the family who sold the land.

[25]" 'You must use the measure as set by the Holy Place in paying these prices; it weighs two-fifths of an ounce.

VALUE OF ANIMALS

[26]" 'If an animal is the first one born to its parent, it already belongs to the LORD, so people may not give it again. If it is a cow or a sheep, it is the LORD's. [27]If the animal is un-

clean, the person must buy it back for the price set by the priest, and the person must add one-fifth to that price. If it is not bought back, the priest must sell it for the price he had decided.

28 " 'There is a special kind of gift that people set apart to give to the LORD; it may be a person, animal, or field from the family property. That gift cannot be bought back or sold. Every special kind of gift is most holy to the LORD.

29 " 'If anyone is given for the purpose of being destroyed, he cannot be bought back; he must be put to death.

30 " 'One-tenth of all crops belongs to the LORD, including the crops from fields and the fruit from trees. That one-tenth is holy to the LORD. 31 If a person wants to get back that tenth, one-fifth must be added to its price.

"These are the commands the LORD gave to Moses at Mount Sinai for the people of Israel." (Leviticus 27:34)

32 " 'The priest will take every tenth animal from a person's herd or flock, and it will be holy to the LORD. 33 The owner should not pick out the good animals from the bad or exchange one animal for another. If that happens, both animals will become holy; they cannot be bought back.' "

34 These are the commands the LORD gave to Moses at Mount Sinai for the people of Israel.

numbers

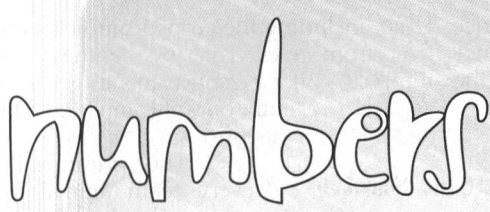

CONTENT First of all, this isn't just a book of numerals, Roman or otherwise. The book title refers to the two times that Moses took a census of the people (counted them). The book itself is really about the time period in between the two censuses.

The awful truth is this: After God miraculously brought the Israelites out of slavery in Egypt, they went directly to the Promised Land without delay. It took about twenty-four months, and they were about to pass "Go" and collect their heritage when—they freaked out and got afraid. After all God had done to get them there, they basically wimped out. The consequence for their lack of faith was that they put the camels in reverse and cruised the wilderness for almost forty long, hot, dry years.

The Book of Numbers is about the yucky parts of life that we bring on ourselves when we refuse to believe that God will come through for us. It's about the weak parts of our selves that don't believe even when God has been faithful. It's about the part of us that grumbles because we want God's blessings, but we want them the easy way; we don't want to work to keep our part of our agreement to worship him. It's about us learning from the Israelites' mistakes so that maybe we won't make the same ones.

Outline

1:1—4:49 .... The People of Israel Are Counted
5:1—8:26 .... Various Laws and the Cleansing of the Levites
9:1-23 .... Passover Is Celebrated and a Cloud Covers the Holy Tent
10:1-36 .... The People Begin Their Journey
11:1-35 .... The People Complain
12:1-16 .... Miriam and Aaron Speak Against Moses
13:1-33 .... The Spies Are Sent into Canaan
14:1-45 .... The People Complain Again and Are Punished
15:1-41 .... Laws and Punishments
16:1—17:13 .... The People Rebel
18:1-32 .... Priests and Levites
19:1-22 .... Becoming Clean
20:1—21:35 .... On the Way to Moab
22:1—24:25 .... The Messages of Balaam
25:1-18 .... The People Are Unfaithful
26:1-65 .... The People of Israel Are Counted a Second Time
27:1-11 .... The Daughters of Zelophehad Are Given Land
27:12-23 .... Joshua Is Appointed Israel's Leader
28:1—30:16 .... Various Laws and Offerings for Israel's Feasts
31:1—36:13 .... Israel Defeats Midian and Prepares to Cross the Jordan River

Purpose Actions have consequences that even the forgiven cannot escape.

Theme God's Guiding Presence for the Journey from Sinai Across the Jordan River

Date of writing 1445–1440 B.C.

"But the LORD said to Moses and Aaron, 'Because you did not believe me, and because you did not honor me as holy before the people, you will not lead them into the land I will give them' " (20:12).

Bible Talk

Complaining

You know what one of the main themes of Numbers is about? Plain old complaining. Mere grumbling. Simple crankiness.

The people had been under horrible stress in Egypt. They were literally worked to death! There was one period of time when a baby boy could be killed, just because he was a Hebrew. Make no mistake—the Hebrews wanted out.

Yet, when they ended up in the desert, they complained and grumbled. It wasn't that they were hungry. God sent manna every day. It wasn't that they needed new clothes. In forty years their shoes never even wore out! No, it was the inconvenience of it all. It was the boredom.

So they complained. We wouldn't be that way—would we?

CIVIL WARS AND FAMILY CONFLICTS

Sometimes when we retell the ancient stories, we gloss over them. Moses led the people out. . . . It was hard. . . . They finally got there. . . . End of story.

We forget that these were people, in many ways, just like us. They had opinions. They had family loyalties. They got ticked off. They wanted their way. They wanted control. Have you ever known a group of people *not* to have conflicts? Is there any way a group of 600,000+ wouldn't?

A man name Korah led a rebellion. Moses' own sister and brother picked a fight with him.

When you read these stories, remember that these are people like you and the guy who made you angry last week. Their stories are as true to life as your own.

THE PEOPLE OF ISRAEL ARE COUNTED

1 1The LORD spoke to Moses in the Meeting
Tent in the Desert of Sinai. This was on the first
day of the second month in the second year
after the Israelites left Egypt. He said to Moses:
2"You and Aaron must count all the people of
Israel by families and family groups, listing the
name of each man. 3You and Aaron must
count every man twenty years old or older
who will serve in the army of Israel, and list
them by their divisions. 4One man from each
tribe, the leader of his family, will help you.
5These are the names of the men who will help
you:

from the tribe of Reuben—Elizur son of Shedeur;
6from the tribe of Simeon—Shelumiel son of Zurishaddai;
7from the tribe of Judah—Nahshon son of Amminadab;
8from the tribe of Issachar—Nethanel son of Zuar;
9from the tribe of Zebulun—Eliab son of Helon;
10from the tribe of Ephraim son of Joseph—Elishama son of Ammihud;
from the tribe of Manasseh son of Joseph—Gamaliel son of Pedahzur;
11from the tribe of Benjamin—Abidan son of Gideoni;
12from the tribe of Dan—Ahiezer son of Ammishaddai;
13from the tribe of Asher—Pagiel son of Ocran;
14from the tribe of Gad—Eliasaph son of Deuel;
15from the tribe of Naphtali—Ahira son of Enan."

16These were the men chosen from the people to be leaders of their tribes, the heads of
Israel's family groups.

17Moses and Aaron took these men who
had been picked 18and called all the people of
Israel together on the first day of the second
month. Then the people were listed by their
families and family groups, and all the men
who were twenty years old or older were listed
by name. 19Moses did exactly what the LORD
had commanded and listed the people while
they were in the Desert of Sinai.

20The tribe of Reuben, the first son born to
Israel, was counted; all the men twenty years
old or older who were able to serve in the
army were listed by name with their families
and family groups. 21The tribe of Reuben totaled 46,500 men.

22The tribe of Simeon was counted; all the
men twenty years old or older who were able
to serve in the army were listed by name with
their families and family groups. 23The tribe of
Simeon totaled 59,300 men.

24The tribe of Gad was counted; all the men
twenty years old or older who were able to
serve in the army were listed by name with
their families and family groups. 25The tribe of
Gad totaled 45,650 men.

26The tribe of Judah was counted; all the
men twenty years old or older who were able
to serve in the army were listed by name with
their families and family groups. 27The tribe of
Judah totaled 74,600 men.

28The tribe of Issachar was counted; all the
men twenty years old or older who were able
to serve in the army were listed by name with
their families and family groups. 29The tribe of
Issachar totaled 54,400 men.

30The tribe of Zebulun was counted; all the
men twenty years old or older who were able
to serve in the army were listed by name with
their families and family groups. 31The tribe of
Zebulun totaled 57,400 men.

32The tribe of Ephraim, a son of Joseph, was
counted; all the men twenty years old or older
who were able to serve in the army were listed
by name with their families and family groups.
33The tribe of Ephraim totaled 40,500 men.

34The tribe of Manasseh, also a son of Joseph, was counted; all the men twenty years
old or older who were able to serve in the
army were listed by name with their families
and family groups. 35The tribe of Manasseh totaled 32,200 men.

WHAT'S IT MEAN?

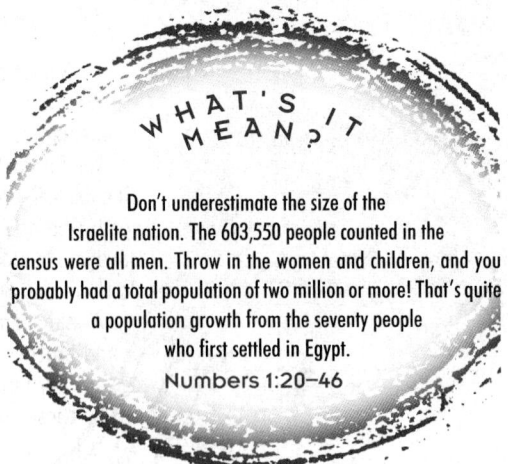

Don't underestimate the size of the Israelite nation. The 603,550 people counted in the census were all men. Throw in the women and children, and you probably had a total population of two million or more! That's quite a population growth from the seventy people who first settled in Egypt.

Numbers 1:20–46

36The tribe of Benjamin was counted; all the
men twenty years old or older who were able
to serve in the army were listed by name with

their families and family groups. 37The tribe of
Benjamin totaled 35,400 men.
38The tribe of Dan was counted; all the men
twenty years old or older who were able to
serve in the army were listed by name with
their families and family groups. 39The tribe of
Dan totaled 62,700 men.
40The tribe of Asher was counted; all the
men twenty years old or older who were able
to serve in the army were listed by name with
their families and family groups. 41The tribe of
Asher totaled 41,500 men.
42The tribe of Naphtali was counted; all the
men twenty years old or older who were able
to serve in the army were listed by name with
their families and family groups. 43The tribe of
Naphtali totaled 53,400 men.
44Moses, Aaron, and the twelve leaders of
Israel, one from each of the families, counted
these men. 45Every man of Israel twenty years
old or older who was able to serve in the army
was counted and listed with his family. 46The
total number of men was 603,550.
47The families from the tribe of Levi were
not listed with the others, because 48the LORD
had told Moses: 49"Do not count the tribe of
Levi or include them with the other Israelites.
50Instead put the Levites in charge of the Holy
Tent of the Agreement and everything that is
with it. They must carry the Holy Tent and
everything in it, and they must take care of it
and make their camp around it. 51Any time the
Holy Tent is moved, the Levites must take it
down, and any time it is set up, the Levites must
do it. Anyone else who goes near the Holy Tent
will be put to death. 52The Israelites will make
their camps in separate divisions, each family
near its flag. 53But the Levites must make their
camp around the Holy Tent of the Agreement
so that I will not be angry with the Israelites.
The Levites will take care of the Holy Tent of
the Agreement."
54So the Israelites did everything just as the
LORD commanded Moses.

THE CAMP ARRANGEMENT

2
1The LORD said to Moses and Aaron: 2"The
Israelites should make their camps around the
Meeting Tent, but they should not camp too
close to it. They should camp under their family flag and banners."
3The camp of Judah will be on the east side,
where the sun rises, and they will camp by divisions there under their flag. The leader of the
people of Judah is Nahshon son of Amminadab. 4There are 74,600 men in his division.
5Next to them the tribe of Issachar will
camp. The leader of the people of Issachar is
Nethanel son of Zuar. 6There are 54,400 men in
his division.

WHAT'S IT MEAN?

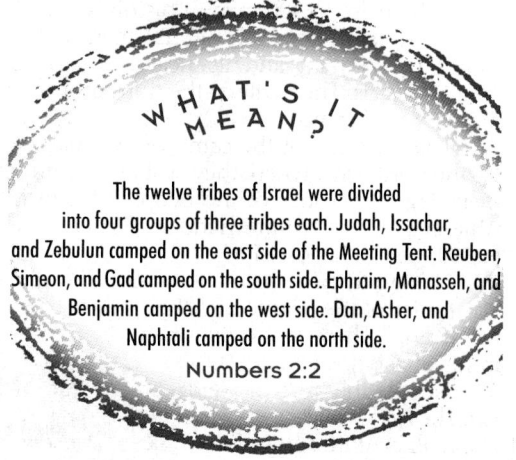

The twelve tribes of Israel were divided into four groups of three tribes each. Judah, Issachar, and Zebulun camped on the east side of the Meeting Tent. Reuben, Simeon, and Gad camped on the south side. Ephraim, Manasseh, and Benjamin camped on the west side. Dan, Asher, and Naphtali camped on the north side.

Numbers 2:2

7Next is the tribe of Zebulun. The leader of
the people of Zebulun is Eliab son of Helon.
8There are 57,400 men in his division.
9There are a total of 186,400 men in the
camps of Judah and its neighbors, in all their
divisions. They will be the first to march out of
camp.
10The divisions of the camp of Reuben will
be on the south side, where they will camp
under their flag. The leader of the people of
Reuben is Elizur son of Shedeur. 11There are
46,500 men in his division.
12Next to them the tribe of Simeon will
camp. The leader of the people of Simeon is
Shelumiel son of Zurishaddai. 13There are
59,300 men in his division.
14Next is the tribe of Gad. The leader of the
people of Gad is Eliasaph son of Deuel. 15There
are 45,650 men in his division.
16There are a total of 151,450 men in the
camps of Reuben and its neighbors, in all their
divisions. They will be the second group to
march out of camp.
17When the Levites march out with the
Meeting Tent, they will be in the middle of
the other camps. The tribes will march out in
the same order as they camp, each in its place
under its flag.
18The divisions of the camp of Ephraim will
be on the west side, where they will camp under their flag. The leader of the people of
Ephraim is Elishama son of Ammihud. 19There
are 40,500 men in his division.
20Next to them the tribe of Manasseh will
camp. The leader of the people of Manasseh is

Gamaliel son of Pedahzur. 21There are 32,200 men in his division.

22Next is the tribe of Benjamin. The leader of the people of Benjamin is Abidan son of Gideoni. 23There are 35,400 men in his division.

24There are a total of 108,100 men in the camps of Ephraim and its neighbors, in all their divisions. They will be the third group to march out of camp.

25The divisions of the camp of Dan will be on the north side, where they will camp under their flag. The leader of the people of Dan is Ahiezer son of Ammishaddai. 26There are 62,700 men in his division.

27Next to them the tribe of Asher will camp. The leader of the people of Asher is Pagiel son of Ocran. 28There are 41,500 men in his division.

29Next is the tribe of Naphtali. The leader of the people of Naphtali is Ahira son of Enan. 30There are 53,400 men in his division.

31There are 157,600 men in the camps of Dan and its neighbors. They will be the last to march out of camp, and they will travel under their own flag.

> "So the Israelites obeyed everything the LORD commanded Moses."
> (Numbers 2:34a)

32These are the Israelites who were counted by families. The total number of Israelites in the camps, counted by divisions, is 603,550. 33Moses obeyed the LORD and did not count the Levites among the other people of Israel.

34So the Israelites obeyed everything the LORD commanded Moses. They camped under their flags and marched out by families and family groups.

AARON'S FAMILY, THE PRIESTS

3 1This is the family history of Aaron and Moses at the time the LORD talked to Moses on Mount Sinai.

2Aaron had four sons: Nadab, the oldest, Abihu, Eleazar, and Ithamar. 3These were the names of Aaron's sons, who were appointed to serve as priests. 4But Nadab and Abihu died in the presence of the LORD when they offered the wrong kind of fire before the LORD in the Desert of Sinai. They had no sons. So Eleazar and Ithamar served as priests during the lifetime of their father Aaron.

5The LORD said to Moses, 6"Bring the tribe of Levi and present them to Aaron the priest to help him. 7They will help him and all the Israelites at the Meeting Tent, doing the work in the Holy Tent. 8The Levites must take care of everything in the Meeting Tent and serve the people of Israel by doing the work in the Holy Tent. 9Give the Levites to Aaron and his sons; of all the Israelites, the Levites are given completely to him. 10Appoint Aaron and his sons to serve as priests, but anyone else who comes near the holy things must be put to death."

11The LORD also said to Moses, 12"I am choosing the Levites from all the Israelites to take the place of all the firstborn children of Israel. The Levites will be mine, 13because the firstborn are mine. When you were in Egypt, I killed all the firstborn children of the Egyptians and took all the firstborn of Israel to be mine, both animals and children. They are mine. I am the LORD."

14The LORD again said to Moses in the Desert of Sinai, 15"Count the Levites by families and family groups. Count every male one month old or older." 16So Moses obeyed the LORD and counted them all.

17Levi had three sons, whose names were Gershon, Kohath, and Merari.

18The Gershonite family groups were Libni and Shimei.

19The Kohathite family groups were Amram, Izhar, Hebron, and Uzziel.

20The Merarite family groups were Mahli and Mushi.

These were the family groups of the Levites.

21The family groups of Libni and Shimei belonged to Gershon; they were the Gershonite family groups. 22The number that was counted was 7,500 males one month old or older. 23The Gershonite family groups camped on the west side, behind the Holy Tent. 24The leader of the families of Gershon was Eliasaph son of Lael. 25In the Meeting Tent the Gershonites were in charge of the Holy Tent, its covering, the curtain at the entrance to the Meeting Tent, 26the curtains in the courtyard, the curtain at the entry to the courtyard around the Holy Tent and the altar, the ropes, and all the work connected with these items.

27The family groups of Amram, Izhar, Hebron, and Uzziel belonged to Kohath; they were the Kohathite family groups. 28They had 8,600 males one month old or older, and they were responsible for taking care of the Holy Place. 29The Kohathite family groups camped south of the Holy Tent. 30The leader of the Kohathite families was Elizaphan son of Uzziel. 31They were responsible for the Ark, the table, the lampstand, the altars, the tools of the Holy Place which they were to use, the curtain, and

all the work connected with these items. [32]The
main leader of the Levites was Eleazar son of
Aaron, the priest, who was in charge of all
those responsible for the Holy Place.
[33]The family groups of Mahli and Mushi
belonged to Merari; they were the Merarite
family groups. [34]The number that was counted
was 6,200 males one month old or older. [35]The
leader of the Merari families was Zuriel son of
Abihail, and they were to camp north of the
Holy Tent. [36]The Merarites were responsible
for the frames of the Holy Tent, the braces, the
posts, the bases, and all the work connected
with these items. [37]They were also responsible
for the posts in the courtyard around the Holy
Tent and their bases, tent pegs, and ropes.
[38]Moses, Aaron, and his sons camped east
of the Holy Tent, toward the sunrise, in front of
the Meeting Tent. They were responsible for
the Holy Place for the Israelites. Anyone else
who came near the Holy Place was to be put to
death.
[39]Moses and Aaron counted the Levite men
by their families, as the LORD commanded,
and there were 22,000 males one month old or
older.

LEVITES TAKE THE PLACE OF THE FIRSTBORN SONS

[40]The LORD said to Moses, "Count all the
firstborn sons in Israel one month old or older,
and list their names. [41]Take the Levites for me
instead of the firstborn sons of Israel; take the
animals of the Levites instead of the firstborn
animals from the rest of Israel. I am the LORD."
[42]So Moses did what the LORD commanded
and counted all the firstborn sons of the Israelites. [43]When he listed all the firstborn sons one
month old or older, there were 22,273 names.
[44]The LORD also said to Moses, [45]"Take the
Levites instead of all the firstborn sons of the
Israelites, and take the animals of the Levites
instead of the animals of the other people. The
Levites are mine. I am the LORD. [46]Since there
are 273 more firstborn sons than Levites, [47]col-
lect two ounces of silver for each of the 273
sons. Use the measure as set by the Holy Place,
which is two-fifths of an ounce. [48]Give the silver to Aaron and his sons as the payment for
the 273 Israelites."
[49]So Moses collected the money for the people the Levites could not replace. [50]From the
firstborn of the Israelites, he collected thirty-
five pounds of silver, using the measure set by
the Holy Place. [51]Moses obeyed the command
of the LORD and gave the silver to Aaron and
his sons.

THE JOBS OF THE KOHATH FAMILY

4 [1]The LORD said to Moses and Aaron,
[2]"Count the Kohathites among the Levites by
family groups and families. [3]Count the men
from thirty to fifty years old, all who come to
serve in the Meeting Tent.
[4]"The Kohathites are responsible for the
most holy things in the Meeting Tent. [5]When
the Israelites are ready to move, Aaron and his
sons must go into the Holy Tent, take down the
curtain, and cover the Ark of the Agreement
with it. [6]Over this they must put a covering
made from fine leather, then spread the solid
blue cloth over that, and put the poles in place.
[7]"Then they must spread a blue cloth over
the table for the bread that shows a person is
in God's presence. They must put the plates,
pans, bowls, and the jars for drink offerings on
the table; they must leave the bread that is always there on the table. [8]Then they must put a
red cloth over all of these things, cover everything with fine leather, and put the poles in
place.
[9]"With a blue cloth they must cover the
lampstand, its lamps, its wick trimmers, its
trays, and all the jars for the oil used in the
lamps. [10]Then they must wrap everything in
fine leather and put all these things on a frame
for carrying them.
[11]"They must spread a blue cloth over the
gold altar, cover it with fine leather, and put the
poles in place.
[12]"They must gather all the things used for
serving in the Holy Place and wrap them in a
blue cloth. Then they must cover that with fine
leather and put these things on a frame for
carrying them.
[13]"They must clean the ashes off the bronze
altar and spread a purple cloth over it. [14]They
must gather all the things used for serving at
the altar—the pans for carrying the fire, the
meat forks, the shovels, and the bowls—and
put them on the bronze altar. Then they must
spread a covering of fine leather over it and
put the poles in place.
[15]"When the Israelites are ready to move,
and when Aaron and his sons have covered
the holy furniture and all the holy things, the
Kohathites may go in and carry them away. In
this way they won't touch the holy things and
die. It is the Kohathites' job to carry the things
that are in the Meeting Tent.
[16]"Eleazar son of Aaron, the priest, will be
responsible for the Holy Tent and for everything in it, for all the holy things it has: the
oil for the lamp, the sweet-smelling incense,
the continual grain offering, and the oil used to

appoint priests and things to the LORD's service."

17The LORD said to Moses and Aaron, 18"Don't let the Kohathites be cut off from the Levites. 19Do this for the Kohathites so that they may go near the Most Holy Place and not die: Aaron and his sons must go in and show each Kohathite what to do and what to carry. 20The Kohathites must not enter and look at the holy things, even for a second, or they will die."

THE JOBS OF THE GERSHON FAMILY

21The LORD said to Moses, 22"Count the Gershonites by families and family groups. 23Count the men from thirty to fifty years old, all who have a job to do in the Meeting Tent.

24"This is what the Gershonite family groups must do and what they must carry. 25They must carry the curtains of the Holy Tent, the Meeting Tent, its covering, and its outer covering made from fine leather. They must also carry the curtains for the entrance to the Meeting Tent, 26the curtains of the courtyard that go around the Holy Tent and the altar, the curtain for the entry to the courtyard, the ropes, and all the things used with the curtains. They must do everything connected with these things. 27Aaron and his sons are in charge of what the Gershonites do or carry; you tell them what they are responsible for carrying. 28This is the work of the Gershonite family group at the Meeting Tent. Ithamar son of Aaron, the priest, will direct their work.

THE JOBS OF THE MERARI FAMILY

29"Count the Merarite families and family groups. 30Count the men from thirty to fifty years old, all who work at the Meeting Tent. 31It is their job to carry the following as they serve in the Meeting Tent: the frames of the Holy Tent, the crossbars, the posts, and bases, 32in addition to the posts that go around the courtyard, their bases, tent pegs, ropes, and everything that is used with the poles around the courtyard. Tell each man exactly what to carry. 33This is the work the Merarite family group will do for the Meeting Tent. Ithamar son of Aaron, the priest, will direct their work."

THE LEVITE FAMILIES

34Moses, Aaron, and the leaders of Israel counted the Kohathites by families and family groups, 35the men from thirty to fifty years old who were to work at the Meeting Tent. 36There were 2,750 men in the family groups. 37This was the total of the Kohath family groups who worked at the Meeting Tent, whom Moses and Aaron counted as the LORD had commanded Moses.

38Also, the Gershonites were counted by families and family groups, 39the men from thirty to fifty years old who were given work at the Meeting Tent. 40The families and family groups had 2,630 men. 41This was the total of the Gershon family groups who worked at the Meeting Tent, whom Moses and Aaron counted as the LORD had commanded.

42Also, the men in the families and family groups of the Merari family were counted, 43the men from thirty to fifty years old who were to work at the Meeting Tent. 44The family groups had 3,200 men. 45This was the total of the Merari family groups, whom Moses and Aaron counted as the LORD had commanded Moses.

46So Moses, Aaron, and the leaders of Israel counted all the Levites by families and family groups. 47They counted the men from thirty to fifty who were given work at the Meeting Tent and who carried the Tent. 48The total number of these men was 8,580. 49Each man was counted as the LORD had commanded Moses; each man was given his work and told what to carry as the LORD had commanded Moses.

RULES ABOUT CLEANLINESS

5

1The LORD said to Moses, 2"Command the Israelites to send away from camp anyone with a harmful skin disease. Send away anyone who gives off body fluid or who has become unclean by touching a dead body. 3Send both men and women outside the camp so that they won't spread the disease there, where I am living among you." 4So Israel obeyed the LORD's command and sent those people outside the camp. They did just as the LORD had told Moses.

PAYING FOR DOING WRONG

5The LORD said to Moses, 6"Tell the Israelites: 'When a man or woman does something wrong to another person, that is really sinning against the LORD. That person is guilty 7and must admit the wrong that has been done. The person must fully pay for the wrong that has been done, adding one-fifth to it, and giving it to the person who was wronged. 8But if that person is dead and does not have any close relatives to receive the payment, the one who did wrong owes the LORD and must pay the priest. In addition, the priest must sacrifice a male sheep to remove the wrong so that the person will belong to the LORD. 9When an Israelite brings a holy gift, it should be given to the priest. [10]No one has to give these holy gifts, but if someone does give them, they belong to the priest.' "

SUSPICIOUS HUSBANDS

[11]Then the LORD said to Moses, [12]"Tell the Israelites: 'A man's wife might be unfaithful to him [13]and have sexual relations with another man. Her sin might be kept hidden from her husband so that he does not know about the wrong she did. Perhaps no one saw it, and she wasn't caught. [14]But if her husband has feelings of jealousy and suspects she has sinned—whether she has or not— [15]he should take her to the priest. The husband must also take an offering for her of two quarts of barley flour. He must not pour oil or incense on it, because this is a grain offering for jealousy, an offering of remembrance. It is to find out if she is guilty.

WHAT'S IT MEAN?

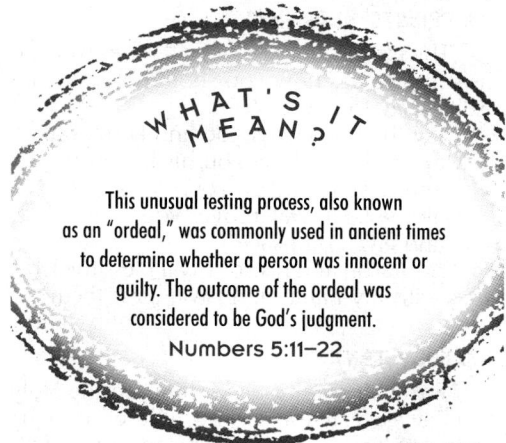

This unusual testing process, also known as an "ordeal," was commonly used in ancient times to determine whether a person was innocent or guilty. The outcome of the ordeal was considered to be God's judgment.

Numbers 5:11–22

[16]" 'The priest will bring in the woman and make her stand before the LORD. [17]He will take some holy water in a clay jar, and he will put some dirt from the floor of the Holy Tent into the water. [18]The priest will make the woman stand before the LORD, and he will loosen her hair. He will hand her the offering of remembrance, the grain offering for jealousy; he will hold the bitter water that brings a curse. [19]The priest will make her take an oath and ask her, "Has another man had sexual relations with you? Have you been unfaithful to your husband? If you haven't, this bitter water that brings a curse won't hurt you. [20]But if you have been unfaithful to your husband and have had sexual relations with a man besides him"— [21]the priest will then put on her the curse that the oath will bring—"the LORD will make the people curse and reject you. He will make your stomach get big, and he will make your body unable to give birth to another baby. [22]This water that brings a curse will go inside you and make your body unable to give birth to another baby."

" 'The woman must say, "I agree."

[23]" 'The priest should write these curses on a scroll, wash the words off into the bitter water, [24]and make the woman drink the bitter water that brings a curse. If she is guilty, the water will make her sick. [25]Then the priest will take the grain offering for jealousy from her. He will present it before the LORD and bring it to the altar. [26]He will take a handful of the grain, which is a memorial offering, and burn it on the altar. After that he will make the woman drink the water [27]to see if she is not pure and if she has sinned against her husband. When it goes into her, if her stomach gets big so that she is not able to have another baby, her people will reject her. [28]But if the woman has not sinned, she is pure. She is not guilty, and she will be able to have babies.

[29]" 'So this is the teaching about jealousy. This is what to do when a woman does wrong and is unfaithful while she is married to her husband. [30]It also should be done if the man gets jealous because he suspects his wife. The priest will have her stand before the LORD, and he will do all these things, just as the teaching commands. [31]In this way the husband can be proven correct, and the woman will suffer if she has done wrong.' "

RULES FOR THE NAZIRITES

6

[1]The LORD said to Moses, [2]"Tell the Israelites: 'If men or women want to promise to belong to the LORD in a special way, they will be called Nazirites. [3]During this time, they must not drink wine or beer, or vinegar made from wine or beer. They must not even drink grape juice or eat grapes or raisins. [4]While they are Nazirites, they must not eat anything that comes from the grapevine, even the seeds or the skin.

[5]" 'During the time they have promised to belong to the LORD, they must not cut their hair. They must be holy until this special time is over. They must let their hair grow long. [6]During their special time of belonging to the LORD, Nazirites must not go near a dead body. [7]Even if their own father, mother, brother, or sister dies, they must not touch them, or they will become unclean. They must still keep their promise to belong to God in a special way. [8]While they are Nazirites, they belong to the LORD in a special way.

[9]" 'If they are next to someone who dies suddenly, their hair, which was part of their

promise, has been made unclean. So they must shave their head seven days later to be clean. [10]Then on the eighth day, they must bring two doves or two young pigeons to the priest at the entrance to the Meeting Tent. [11]The priest will offer one as a sin offering and the other as a burnt offering. This removes sin so they will belong to the LORD. (They had sinned because they were near a dead body.) That same day they will again promise to let their hair grow [12]and give themselves to the LORD for another special time. They must bring a male lamb a year old as a penalty offering. The days of the special time before don't count, because they became unclean during their first special time.

WHAT'S IT MEAN?

The vow to become a Nazirite was like a contract to dedicate one's life specifically to serving God. All Israelites were free to make the vow. Most Nazirite vows were made for a certain period of time. The only people we know of in the Bible who were lifelong Nazirites were Samson (and he did not always live up to the vow's requirements), Samuel, and John the Baptist.

Numbers 6:2–12

[13]" 'This is the teaching for the Nazirites. When the promised time is over, they must go the entrance of the Meeting Tent [14]and give their offerings to the LORD. They must offer a year-old male lamb that has nothing wrong with it, as a burnt offering, a year-old female lamb that has nothing wrong with it, as a sin offering, and a male sheep that has nothing wrong with it, for a fellowship offering. [15]They must also bring the grain offerings and drink offerings that go with them. And they must bring a basket of bread made without yeast, loaves made with fine flour mixed with oil, and wafers made without yeast spread with oil.

[16]" 'The priest will give these offerings to the LORD and make the sin offering and the burnt offering. [17]Then he will kill the male sheep as a fellowship offering to the LORD; along with it, he will present the basket of bread made without yeast, the grain offering, and the drink offering.

[18]" 'The Nazirites must go to the entrance of the Meeting Tent and shave off their hair that they grew for their promise. The hair will be put in the fire that is under the sacrifice of the fellowship offering.

[19]" 'After the Nazirites cut off their hair, the priest will give them a boiled shoulder from the male sheep. From the basket he will also give a loaf and a wafer, both made without yeast. [20]Then the priest will present them to the LORD. They are holy and belong to the priest. Also, he is to present the breast and the thigh from the male sheep. After that, the Nazirites may drink wine.

[21]" 'This is the teaching for the Nazirites who make a promise. Everyone who makes the Nazirite promise must give all of these gifts to the LORD. If they promised to do more, they must keep their promise, according to the teaching of the Nazirites.' "

THE PRIESTS' BLESSINGS

[22]The LORD said to Moses, [23]"Tell Aaron and his sons, 'This is how you should bless the Israelites. Say to them:

[24]"May the LORD bless you and keep you.
[25]May the LORD show you his kindness
and have mercy on you.
[26]May the LORD watch over you
and give you peace." '

[27]"So Aaron and his sons will bless the Israelites with my name, and I will bless them."

THE HOLY TENT

7 [1]When Moses finished setting up the Holy Tent, he gave it for service to the LORD by pouring olive oil on the Tent and on everything used in it. He also poured oil on the altar and all its tools to prepare them for service to the LORD. [2]Then the leaders of Israel made offerings. These were the heads of the families, the leaders of each tribe who counted the people. [3]They brought to the LORD six covered carts and twelve oxen—each leader giving an ox, and every two leaders giving a cart. They brought these to the Holy Tent.

[4]The LORD said to Moses, [5]"Accept these gifts from the leaders and use them in the work of the Meeting Tent. Give them to the Levites as they need them."

[6]So Moses accepted the carts and the oxen and gave them to the Levites. [7]He gave two carts and four oxen to the Gershonites, which they needed for their work. [8]Then Moses gave four carts and eight oxen to the Merarites, which they needed for their work. Ithamar son of Aaron, the priest, directed the work of all of them. [9]Moses did not give any oxen or carts to

the Kohathites, because their job was to carry
the holy things on their shoulders.
10When the oil was poured on the altar, the
leaders brought their offerings to it to give it to
the LORD's service; they presented them in
front of the altar. 11The LORD told Moses, "Each
day one leader must bring his gift to make the
altar ready for service to me."
12-83Each of the twelve leaders brought these
gifts. Each leader brought one silver
plate that weighed about three
and one-fourth pounds, and one
silver bowl that weighed about
one and three-fourths pounds.
These weights were set by the
Holy Place measure. The bowl
and the plate were filled with
fine flour mixed with oil for a
grain offering. Each leader also
brought a large gold dish that weighed
about four ounces and was filled with incense.
In addition, each of the leaders brought one
young bull, one male sheep, and one male lamb
a year old for a burnt offering; one male goat
for a sin offering; and two oxen, five male
sheep, five male goats, and five male lambs a
year old for a fellowship offering.
On the first day Nahshon son of Amminadab brought his gifts. He was the leader of the
tribe of Judah.
On the second day Nethanel son of Zuar
brought his gifts. He was the leader of the tribe
of Issachar.
On the third day Eliab son of Helon
brought his gifts. He was the leader of the tribe
of Zebulun.
On the fourth day Elizur son of Shedeur
brought his gifts. He was the leader of the tribe
of Reuben.
On the fifth day Shelumiel son of Zurishaddai brought his gifts. He was the leader of the
tribe of Simeon.
On the sixth day Eliasaph son of Deuel
brought his gifts. He was the leader of the tribe
of Gad.
On the seventh day Elishama son of Ammihud brought his gifts. He was the leader of the
tribe of Ephraim.
On the eighth day Gamaliel son of Pedahzur brought his gifts. He was the leader of the
tribe of Manasseh.
On the ninth day Abidan son of Gideoni
brought his gifts. He was the leader of the tribe
of Benjamin.
On the tenth day Ahiezer son of Ammishaddai brought his gifts. He was the leader of
the tribe of Dan.
On the eleventh day Pagiel son of Ocran
brought his gifts. He was the leader of the tribe
of Asher.
On the twelfth day Ahira son of Enan
brought his gifts. He was the leader of the tribe
of Naphtali.
84So these were the gifts from the Israelite
leaders when oil was poured on the altar and it
was given for service to the LORD: twelve silver
plates, twelve silver bowls, and
twelve gold dishes. 85Each silver
plate weighed about three and
one-fourth pounds, and each
bowl weighed about one and
three-fourths pounds. All the
silver plates and silver bowls
together weighed about sixty
pounds according to a weight
set by the Holy Place measure.
86The twelve gold dishes filled with
incense weighed four ounces each, according
to the weight set by the Holy Place measure.
Together the gold dishes weighed about three
pounds. 87The total number of animals for
the burnt offering was twelve bulls, twelve
male sheep, and twelve male lambs a year old.
There was also a grain offering, and there were
twelve male goats for a sin offering. 88The total
number of animals for the fellowship offering
was twenty-four bulls, sixty male sheep, sixty
male goats, and sixty male lambs a year old. All
these offerings were for giving the altar to the
service of the LORD after the oil had been
poured on it.
89When Moses went into the Meeting Tent
to speak with the LORD, he heard the LORD
speaking to him. The voice was coming from
between the two gold creatures with wings
that were above the lid of the Ark of the Agreement. In this way the LORD spoke with him.

"May the LORD bless you and keep you. . . ." (Numbers 6:24–26)

WHAT'S IT MEAN?

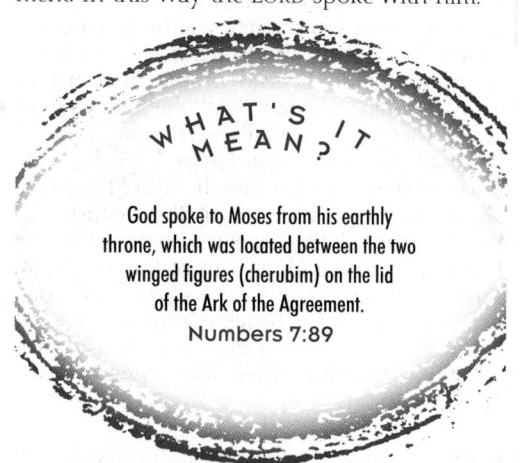

God spoke to Moses from his earthly throne, which was located between the two winged figures (cherubim) on the lid of the Ark of the Agreement.
Numbers 7:89

THE LAMPSTAND

8 1The LORD said to Moses, 2"Speak to Aaron
and tell him, 'Put the seven lamps where they
can light the area in front of the lampstand.' "
3Aaron did this, putting the lamps so they
lighted the area in front of the lampstand; he
obeyed the command the LORD gave Moses.
4The lampstand was made from hammered
gold, from its base to the flowers. It was made
exactly the way the LORD had showed Moses.

THE LEVITES ARE GIVEN TO GOD

5The LORD said to Moses, 6"Take the Levites
away from the other Israelites and make them
clean. 7This is what you should do to make
them clean: Sprinkle the cleansing water on
them, and have them shave their bodies and
wash their clothes so they will be clean. 8They
must take a young bull and the grain offering
of flour mixed with oil that goes with it. Then
take a second young bull for a sin offering.
9Bring the Levites to the front of the Meeting
Tent, and gather all the Israelites around.
10When you bring the Levites before the LORD,
the Israelites should put their hands on them.[n]
11Aaron will present the Levites before the
LORD as an offering presented from the Israelites. Then the Levites will be ready to do the
work of the LORD.
12"The Levites will put their hands on the
bulls' heads—one bull will be a sin offering to
the LORD, and the other will be a burnt offering, to remove the sins of the Levites so they
will belong to the LORD. 13Make the Levites
stand in front of Aaron and his sons and present the Levites as an offering to the LORD. 14In
this way you must set apart the Levites from
the other Israelites; the Levites will be mine.
15"Make the Levites pure, and present them
as an offering so that they may come to work
at the Meeting Tent. 16They will be given completely to me from the Israelites; I have taken
them for myself instead of the firstborn of
every Israelite woman. 17All the firstborn in
Israel—people or animals—are mine. When I
killed all the firstborn in Egypt, I set the firstborn in Israel aside for myself. 18But I have tak-
en the Levites instead of all the firstborn in
Israel. 19From all the Israelites I have given the
Levites to Aaron and his sons so that they may
serve the Israelites at the Meeting Tent. They
will help remove the Israelites' sins so they will
belong to the LORD and so that no disaster will
strike the Israelites when they approach the
Holy Place."
20So Moses, Aaron, and all the Israelites
obeyed and did with the Levites what the LORD
commanded Moses. 21The Levites made themselves clean and washed their clothes. Then
Aaron presented them as an offering to the
LORD. He also removed their sins so they
would be pure. 22After that, the Levites came to
the Meeting Tent to work, and Aaron and his
sons told them what to do. They did with the
Levites what the LORD commanded Moses.
23The LORD said to Moses, 24"This command
is for the Levites. Everyone twenty-five years
old or older must come to the Meeting Tent,
because they all have jobs to do there. 25At the
age of fifty, they must retire from their jobs and
not work again. 26They may help their fellow
Levites with their work at the Meeting Tent, but
they must not do the work themselves. This is
the way you are to give the Levites their jobs."

THE PASSOVER IS CELEBRATED

9 1The LORD spoke to Moses in the Desert of
Sinai in the first month of the second year after
the Israelites left Egypt. He said, 2"Tell the Israelites to celebrate the Passover at the appointed
time. 3That appointed time is the fourteenth
day of this month at twilight; they must obey
all the rules about it."
4So Moses told the Israelites to celebrate the
Passover, 5and they did; it was in the Desert of
Sinai at twilight on the fourteenth day of the
first month. The Israelites did everything just as
the LORD commanded Moses.
6But some of the people could not celebrate
the Passover on that day because they were
unclean from touching a dead body. So they
went to Moses and Aaron that day and 7said
to Moses, "We are unclean because of touching
a dead body. But why should we be kept from
offering gifts to the LORD at this appointed
time? Why can't we join the other Israelites?"
8Moses said to them, "Wait, and I will find
out what the LORD says about you."
9Then the LORD said to Moses, 10"Tell the
Israelites this: 'If you or your descendants become unclean because of a dead body, or if
you are away on a trip during the Passover,
you must still celebrate the LORD's Passover.
11But celebrate it at twilight on the fourteenth
day of the second month. Eat the lamb with
bitter herbs and bread made without yeast.
12Don't leave any of it until the next morning
or break any of its bones. When you celebrate
the Passover, follow all the rules. 13Anyone
who is clean and is not away on a trip but does

8:10 put . . . them This showed that the people had a part in giving the Levites their special work.

not eat the Passover must be cut off from the
people. That person did not give an offering to
the LORD at the appointed time and must be
punished for the sin.

14" 'Foreigners among you may celebrate the
LORD's Passover, but they must follow all the
rules. You must have the same rules for foreigners as you have for yourselves.' "

THE CLOUD ABOVE THE TENT

15On the day the Holy Tent, the Tent of the
Agreement, was set up, a cloud covered it.
From dusk until dawn the cloud above the
Tent looked like fire. 16The cloud stayed above
the Tent, and at night it looked like fire. 17When
the cloud moved from its place over the Tent,
the Israelites moved, and wherever the cloud
stopped, the Israelites camped. 18So the Israelites moved at the LORD's command, and they
camped at his command. While the cloud
stayed over the Tent, they remained camped.
19Sometimes the cloud stayed over the Tent for
a long time, but the Israelites obeyed the LORD
and did not move. 20Sometimes the cloud was
over it only a few days. At the LORD's command the people camped, and at his command
they moved. 21Sometimes the cloud stayed
only from dusk until dawn; when the cloud
lifted the next morning, the people moved.
When the cloud lifted, day or night, the people
moved. 22The cloud might stay over the Tent
for two days, a month, or a year. As long as it
stayed, the people camped, but when it lifted,
they moved. 23At the LORD's command the
people camped, and at his command they
moved. They obeyed the LORD's order that he
commanded through Moses.

THE SILVER TRUMPETS

10 1The LORD said to Moses, 2"Make two trumpets of hammered silver, and use them to call
the people together and to march out of camp.
3When both trumpets are blown, the people
should gather before you at the entrance to the
Meeting Tent. 4If you blow only one trumpet,
the leaders, the heads of the family groups of
Israel, should meet before you. 5When you
loudly blow the trumpets, the tribes camping
on the east should move. 6When you loudly
blow them again, the tribes camping on the
south should move; the loud sound will tell
them to move. 7When you want to gather the
people, blow the trumpets, but don't blow
them as loudly.

8"Aaron's sons, the priests, should blow the
trumpets. This is a law for you and your descendants from now on. 9When you are fighting an enemy who attacks you in your own
land, blow the trumpets loudly. The LORD your
God will take notice of you and will save you
from your enemies. 10Also blow your trumpets
at happy times and during your feasts and at
New Moon festivals. Blow them over your
burnt offerings and fellowship offerings, because they will help you remember your God.
I am the LORD your God."

WHAT'S IT MEAN?

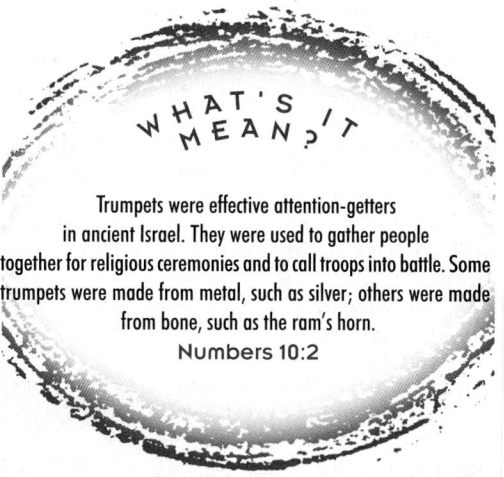

Trumpets were effective attention-getters in ancient Israel. They were used to gather people together for religious ceremonies and to call troops into battle. Some trumpets were made from metal, such as silver; others were made from bone, such as the ram's horn.

Numbers 10:2

THE ISRAELITES MOVE CAMP

11The cloud lifted from the Tent of the
Agreement on the twentieth day of the second
month of the second year. 12So the Israelites
moved from the Desert of Sinai and continued
until the cloud stopped in the Desert of Paran.
13This was their first time to move, and they
did it as the LORD had commanded Moses.

14The divisions from the camp of Judah
moved first under their flag. Nahshon son of
Amminadab was the commander. 15Nethanel
son of Zuar was over the division of the tribe
of Issachar. 16Eliab son of Helon was over the
division of the tribe of Zebulun. 17Then the
Holy Tent was taken down, and the Gershonites and Merarites, who carried it, moved next.

18Then came the divisions from the camp of
Reuben under their flag, and Elizur son of
Shedeur was the commander. 19Shelumiel son
of Zurishaddai was over the division of the
tribe of Simeon. 20Eliasaph son of Deuel was
over the division of the tribe of Gad. 21Then
came the Kohathites, who carried the holy
things; the Holy Tent was to be set up before
they arrived.

22Next came the divisions from the camp of
Ephraim under their flag, and Elishama son of
Ammihud was the commander. 23Gamaliel son
of Pedahzur was over the division of the tribe

of Manasseh, 24and Abidan son of Gideoni was over the division of the tribe of Benjamin.

25The last ones were the rear guard for all the tribes. These were the divisions from the camp of Dan under their flag, and Ahiezer son of Ammishaddai was the commander. 26Pagiel son of Ocran was over the division of the tribe of Asher; 27Ahira son of Enan was over the division of the tribe of Naphtali. 28This was the order the Israelite divisions marched in when they moved.

29Hobab was the son of Reuel the Midianite,[n] who was Moses' father-in-law. Moses said to Hobab, "We are moving to the land the LORD promised to give us. Come with us and we will be good to you, because the LORD has promised good things to Israel."

30But Hobab answered, "No, I will not go. I will go back to my own land where I was born."

31But Moses said, "Please don't leave us. You know where we can camp in the desert, and you can be our guide. 32Come with us. We will share with you all the good things the LORD gives us." 33So they left the mountain of the LORD and traveled for three days. The Ark of the LORD's Agreement went in front of the people for those three days, as they looked for a place to camp. 34The LORD's cloud was over them during the day when they left their camp.

> "Rise up, LORD! Scatter your enemies: make those who hate you run from you."
> (Numbers 10:35b)

35When the Ark left the camp, Moses said,

"Rise up, LORD!
Scatter your enemies:
make those who hate you run from you."

36And when the Ark was set down, Moses said,

"Return, LORD,
to the thousands of people of Israel."

FIRE FROM THE LORD

11 1Now the people complained to the LORD about their troubles, and when he heard them, he became angry. Then fire from the LORD burned among the people at the edge of the camp. 2The people cried out to Moses, and when he prayed to the LORD, the fire stopped burning. 3So that place was called Taberah,[n] because the LORD's fire had burned among them.

SEVENTY OLDER LEADERS HELP MOSES

4Some troublemakers among them wanted better food, and soon all the Israelites began complaining. They said, "We want meat! 5We remember the fish we ate for free in Egypt. We also had cucumbers, melons, leeks, onions, and garlic. 6But now we have lost our appetite; we never see anything but this manna!"

7The manna was like small white seeds. 8The people would go to gather it, and then grind it in handmills, or crush it between stones. After they cooked it in a pot or made cakes with it, it tasted like bread baked with olive oil. 9When the dew fell on the camp each night, so did the manna.

10Moses heard every family crying as they stood in the entrances of their tents. Then the LORD became very angry, and Moses got upset. 11He asked the LORD, "Why have you brought me, your servant, this trouble? What have I done wrong that you made me responsible for all these people? 12I am not the father of all these people, and I didn't give birth to them. So why do you make me carry them to the land you promised to our ancestors? Must I carry them in my arms as a nurse carries a baby? 13Where can I get meat for all these people? They keep crying to me, 'We want meat!' 14I can't take care of all these people alone. It is too much for me. 15If you are going to continue doing this to me, then kill me now. If you care about me, put me to death, and then I won't have any more troubles."

16The LORD said to Moses, "Bring me seventy of Israel's older leaders, men that you know are leaders among the people. Bring them to the Meeting Tent, and have them stand there with you. 17I will come down and speak with you there. I will take some of the Spirit that is in you, and I will give it to them. They will help you care for the people so that you will not have to care for them alone.

18"Tell the people this: 'Make yourselves holy for tomorrow, and you will eat meat. You cried to the LORD, "We want meat! We were better off in Egypt!" So now the LORD will give you meat to eat. 19You will eat it not for just one, two, five, ten, or even twenty days, 20but you will eat that meat for a whole month. You will eat it until it comes out your nose, and

10:29 Reuel the Midianite Also called Jethro. **11:3 Taberah** This name means "burning."

you will grow to hate it. This is because you have rejected the LORD, who is with you. You have cried to him, saying, "Why did we ever leave Egypt?" ' "
21Moses said, "LORD, here are six hundred thousand people standing around me, and you say, 'I will give them enough meat to eat for a month!' 22If we killed all the flocks and herds, that would not be enough. If we caught all the fish in the sea, that would not be enough."
23But the LORD said to Moses, "Do you think I'm weak? Now you will see if I can do what I say."
24So Moses went out to the people and told them what the LORD had said. He gathered seventy of the older leaders together and had them stand around the Tent. 25Then the LORD came down in the cloud and spoke to Moses. The LORD took some of the Spirit Moses had, and he gave it to the seventy leaders. With the Spirit in them, they prophesied, but just that one time.
26Two men named Eldad and Medad were also listed as leaders, but they did not go to the Tent. They stayed in the camp, but the Spirit was also given to them, and they prophesied in the camp. 27A young man ran to Moses and said, "Eldad and Medad are prophesying in the camp."
28Joshua son of Nun said, "Moses, my master, stop them!" (Ever since he was a young boy, Joshua had been Moses' assistant.)

WHAT'S IT MEAN?

A prophet was a person who received messages from God and passed them along to the people. Sometimes those messages told of future events. There was no use in arguing with a prophet, since his authority came directly from God. Rich people, poor people, young people, and old people alike delivered God's messages. No special training was necessary to become a prophet.

Numbers 11:26

29But Moses answered, "Are you jealous for me? I wish all the LORD's people could prophesy. I wish the LORD would give his Spirit to all

Promise HE PROMISES THAT HE CAN DO ANYTHING.

But the LORD said to Moses, "Do you think I'm weak? Now you will see if I can do what I say" (Num. 11:23).

This is a powerful chapter! It starts out with the Israelites complaining about their troubles. They were grumbling to Moses that they didn't have any meat to eat. They complained that they had all the fish they wanted in Egypt and that they were sick of having only manna to eat. God heard their cry and told Moses to tell them to purify themselves because he was going to send meat. Moses replied by asking God how such a feat was possible because there were more than 600,000 people to feed. Moses knew that all the meat from their animals wouldn't be enough to feed them. That's when the Lord replied, "Do you think I'm weak?" In other words, "I can do anything!"

Let this verse encourage you today. Nothing is beyond reach with God on your side, because he is the One who can do anything. What's your need today? Do you need a miracle? He's just waiting for you to bring that need to him.

In 2 Peter 1:3, God promises to give us "everything we need to live and to serve God." That includes things that pertain to our spiritual, physical, emotional, financial, and other needs. In fact, if something affects you, God wants to be right there. He is El Shaddai—the God who is more than enough! He is bigger than any problem you can encounter. Begin to seek him first and watch him give you everything you need. He promises that he can do anything!

SEE FOR YOURSELF:
Matt. 19:26; Mark 9:23; 10:27; Luke 18:27; Rom. 8:32

of them!" 30Then Moses and the leaders of Israel went back to the camp.

THE LORD SENDS QUAIL

31The LORD sent a strong wind from the sea,
and it blew quail into the area all around the
camp. The quail were about three feet deep on
the ground, and there were quail a day's walk
in any direction. 32The people went out and
gathered quail all that day, that night, and the
next day. Everyone gathered at least sixty
bushels, and they spread them around the
camp. 33But the LORD became very angry, and
he gave the people a terrible sickness that came
while the meat was still in their mouths. 34So
the people named that place Kibroth Hattaavah,[n] because there they buried those who
wanted other food.

35From Kibroth Hattaavah the people went
to stay at Hazeroth.

MIRIAM AND AARON SPEAK AGAINST MOSES

12
1Miriam and Aaron began to talk against
Moses because of his Cushite wife (he had
married a Cushite). 2They said, "Is Moses the
only one the LORD speaks through? Doesn't he
also speak through us?" And the LORD heard
this.

3(Now Moses was very humble. He was the
least proud person on earth.)

4So the LORD suddenly spoke to Moses,
Aaron, and Miriam and said, "All three of you
come to the Meeting Tent." So they went. 5The
LORD came down in a pillar of cloud and stood
at the entrance to the Tent. He called to Aaron
and Miriam, and they both came near. 6He
said, "Listen to my words:

When a prophet is among you,
  I, the LORD, will show myself to him in
    visions;
  I will speak to him in dreams.
7But this is not true with my servant
    Moses.
  I trust him to lead all my people.
8I speak face to face with him—
  clearly, not with hidden meanings.
  He has even seen the form of the LORD.
You should be afraid
  to speak against my servant Moses."

9The LORD was very angry with them, and
he left.

10When the cloud lifted from the Tent and
Aaron turned toward Miriam, she was as
white as snow; she had a skin disease. 11Aaron
said to Moses, "Please, my master, forgive us
for our foolish sin. 12Don't let her be like a
baby who is born dead. (Sometimes a baby is
born with half of its flesh eaten away.)"

13So Moses cried out to the LORD, "God,
please heal her!"

14The LORD answered Moses, "If her father
had spit in her face, she would have been
shamed for seven days, so put her outside the
camp for seven days. After that, she may come
back." 15So Miriam was put outside of the
camp for seven days, and the people did not
move on until she came back.

16After that, the people left Hazeroth and
camped in the Desert of Paran.

THE SPIES EXPLORE CANAAN

13
1The LORD said to Moses, 2"Send men to explore the land of Canaan, which I will give to
the Israelites. Send one leader from each tribe."

3So Moses obeyed the LORD's command
and sent the Israelite leaders out from the
Desert of Paran. 4These are their names: from
the tribe of Reuben, Shammua son of Zaccur;
5from the tribe of Simeon, Shaphat son of
Hori; 6from the tribe of Judah, Caleb son of
Jephunneh; 7from the tribe of Issachar, Igal son
of Joseph; 8from the tribe of Ephraim, Hoshea
son of Nun; 9from the tribe of Benjamin, Palti
son of Raphu; 10from the tribe of Zebulun,
Gaddiel son of Sodi; 11from the tribe of Manasseh (a tribe of Joseph), Gaddi son of Susi;
12from the tribe of Dan, Ammiel son of Ge-
malli; 13from the tribe of Asher, Sethur son of
Michael; 14from the tribe of Naphtali, Nahbi
son of Vophsi; 15from the tribe of Gad, Geuel
son of Maki.

16These are the names of the men Moses
sent to explore the land. (Moses gave Hoshea
son of Nun the new name Joshua.)

17Moses sent them to explore Canaan and
said, "Go through southern Canaan and then
into the mountains. 18See what the land looks
like. Are the people who live there strong or
weak? Are there a few or many? 19What kind
of land do they live in? Is it good or bad? What
about the towns they live in—are they open
like camps, or do they have walls? 20What
about the soil? Is it fertile or poor? Are there
trees there? Try to bring back some of the fruit
from that land." (It was the season for the first
grapes.)

21So they went up and explored the land,
from the Desert of Zin all the way to Rehob by
Lebo Hamath. 22They went through the southern area to Hebron, where Ahiman, Sheshai,

11:34 Kibroth Hattaavah This name in Hebrew means "graves of wanting."

MIRIAM made a difference

Older brothers or sisters find out sooner or later that they have an automatic job—watching younger brothers or sisters! Miriam lived during a time when the people of Israel were slaves in Egypt. As if that wasn't bad enough, the government decided that male children were to be killed at birth. That's when Miriam's little brother Moses was born.

Miriam and her mother worked out a plan they hoped would keep Moses alive. They put the baby in a floating basket near a place in the Nile River where wealthy Egyptian women came to bathe. As it turned out, as Miriam watched from the reeds, Moses was fished out and adopted by a daughter of the king of Egypt. Thinking quickly, Miriam approached the king's daughter and offered to get a nanny for the baby. She brought her mother, of course.

Cutting Edge

Miriam was part of God's plan to keep Moses alive. She made a difference by following through on her responsibilities. How could she have known her little brother would turn out to be such a large figure in history? She didn't have to know. She only had to do what she was asked to do.

YOU can, too! The younger you are, the less important your duties may seem sometimes. Don't worry about it. The shortest road to bigger jobs is doing little jobs very well. In fact, God tells us that those who show him they can be trusted with small things will be trusted with large ones. Besides, like Miriam, you probably won't know ahead of time what tasks in your Life will make the biggest difference. Your job is to carry out your responsibilities—whatever their size!

Want to know more? You can read this adventure in babysitting in Exodus 1:15—2:10.

and Talmai, the descendants of Anak lived. (The city of Hebron had been built seven years before Zoan in Egypt.) 23In the Valley of Eshcol, they cut off a branch of a grapevine that had one bunch of grapes on it and carried that branch on a pole between two of them. They also got some pomegranates and figs. 24That place was called the Valley of Eshcol,[n] because the Israelites cut off the bunch of grapes there. 25After forty days of exploring the land, the men returned to the camp.

WHAT'S IT MEAN?

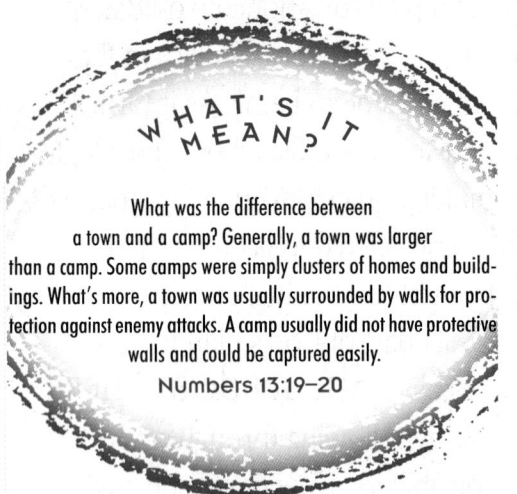

What was the difference between a town and a camp? Generally, a town was larger than a camp. Some camps were simply clusters of homes and buildings. What's more, a town was usually surrounded by walls for protection against enemy attacks. A camp usually did not have protective walls and could be captured easily.

Numbers 13:19–20

26They came back to Moses and Aaron and all the Israelites at Kadesh, in the Desert of Paran. The men reported to them and showed everybody the fruit from the land. 27They told Moses, "We went to the land where you sent us, and it is a fertile land! Here is some of its fruit. 28But the people who live there are strong. Their cities are walled and very large. We even saw some Anakites there. 29The Amalekites live in the southern area; the Hittites, Jebusites, and Amorites live in the mountains; and the Canaanites live near the sea and along the Jordan River."

30Then Caleb told the people near Moses to be quiet, and he said, "We should certainly go up and take the land for ourselves. We can certainly do it."

31But the men who had gone with him said, "We can't attack those people; they are stronger than we are." 32And those men gave the Israelites a bad report about the land they explored, saying, "The land that we explored is too large to conquer. All the people we saw are very tall. 33We saw the Nephilim people there. (The Anakites come from the Nephilim people.) We felt like grasshoppers, and we looked like grasshoppers to them."

THE PEOPLE COMPLAIN AGAIN

14 1That night all the people in the camp began crying loudly. 2All the Israelites complained against Moses and Aaron, and all the people said to them, "We wish we had died in Egypt or in this desert. 3Why is the LORD bringing us to this land to be killed with swords? Our wives and children will be taken away. We would be better off going back to Egypt." 4They said to each other, "Let's choose a leader and go back to Egypt."

ATTITUDE
How does our attitude affect decision making? (14:1–4)

5Then Moses and Aaron bowed facedown in front of all the Israelites gathered there. 6Joshua son of Nun and Caleb son of Jephunneh, who had explored the land, tore their clothes. 7They said to all of the Israelites, "The land we explored is very good. 8If the LORD is pleased with us, he will lead us into that land and give us that fertile land. 9Don't turn against the LORD! Don't be afraid of the people in that land! We will chew them up. They have no protection, but the LORD is with us. So don't be afraid of them."

10Then all the people talked about killing them with stones. But the glory of the LORD appeared at the Meeting Tent to all the Israelites. 11The LORD said to Moses, "How long will these people ignore me? How long will they not believe me in spite of the miracles I have done among them? 12I will give them a terrible sickness and get rid of them. But I will make you into a great nation that will be stronger than they are."

13Then Moses said to the LORD, "The Egyptians will hear about it! You brought these people from there by your great power, 14and the Egyptians will tell this to those who live in this land. They have already heard about you, LORD. They know that you are with your people and that you were seen face to face. They know that your cloud stays over your people and that you lead your people with that cloud during the day and with fire at night. 15If you put these people to death all at once, the nations who have heard about your power will say, 16'The LORD was not able to bring them into the land he promised them. So he killed them in the desert.'

17"So show your strength now, Lord. Do what you said: 18'The LORD doesn't become

13:24 Eshcol This name in Hebrew means "bunch."

angry quickly, but he has great love. He forgives sin and law breaking. But the LORD never
forgets to punish guilty people. When parents
sin, he will also punish their children, their
grandchildren, their great-grandchildren, and
their great-great-grandchildren.' 19By your great
love, forgive these people's sin, just as you have
forgiven them from the time they left Egypt
until now."
20The LORD answered, "I
have forgiven them as you
asked. 21But, as surely as I
live and as surely as my
glory fills the whole
earth, I make this prom-
ise: 22All these men saw
my glory and the mira-
cles I did in Egypt and in
the desert, but they dis-
obeyed me and tested me
ten times. 23So not one of
them will see the land I promised to their ancestors. No one
who rejected me will see that land. 24But my
servant Caleb thinks differently and follows
me completely. So I will bring him into the
land he has already seen, and his children will
own that land. 25Since the Amalekites and the
Canaanites are living in the valleys, leave tomorrow and follow the desert road toward the
Red Sea."

"The LORD doesn't become angry quickly, but he has great love. He forgives sin and law breaking. But the LORD never forgets to punish guilty people." (Numbers 14:18a)

THE LORD PUNISHES THE PEOPLE

26The LORD said to Moses and Aaron,
27"How long will these evil people complain
about me? I have heard the grumbling and
complaining of these Israelites. 28So tell them,
'This is what the LORD says. I heard what you
said, and as surely as I live, I will do those very
things to you: 29You will die in this desert.
Every one of you who is twenty years old or
older and who was counted with the people—
all of you who complained against me—will
die. 30Not one of you will enter the land where
I promised you would live; only Caleb son of
Jephunneh and Joshua son of Nun will go in.
31You said that your children would be taken
away, but I will bring them into the land to
enjoy what you refused. 32As for you, you will
die in this desert. 33Your children will be shepherds here for forty years. Because you were
not loyal, they will suffer until you lie dead in
the desert. 34For forty years you will suffer for
your sins—a year for each of the forty days
you explored the land. You will know me as
your enemy.' 35I, the LORD, have spoken, and I
will certainly do these things to all these evil
people who have come together against me. So
they will all die here in this desert."
36The men Moses had sent to explore the
land had returned and spread complaints
among all the people. They had given a bad
report about the land. 37The men who gave a
very bad report died; the LORD killed them
with a terrible sickness. 38Only two of the men
who explored the land did
not die—Joshua son of
Nun and Caleb son of
Jephunneh.
39When Moses told
these things to all the Israelites, they were very
sad. 40Early the next
morning they started to
go toward the top of the
mountains, saying, "We
have sinned. We will go
where the LORD told us."
41But Moses said, "Why
are you disobeying the LORD's
command? You will not win! 42Don't
go, because the LORD is not with you and you
will be beaten by your enemies. 43You will run
into the Amalekites and Canaanites, who will
kill you with swords. You have turned away
from the LORD, so the LORD will not be with
you."
44But they were proud. They went toward
the top of the mountains, but Moses and the
Ark of the Agreement with the LORD did not
leave the camp. 45The Amalekites and the Canaanites who lived in those mountains came
down and attacked the Israelites and beat them
back all the way to Hormah.

RULES ABOUT SACRIFICES

15
1The LORD said to Moses, 2"Speak to the
Israelites and say to them, 'When you enter
the land that I am giving you as a home, 3give
the LORD offerings made by fire. These may be
from your herds or flocks, as a smell pleasing
to the LORD. These may be burnt offerings or
sacrifices for special promises, or as gifts to
him, or as festival offerings. 4The one who
brings the offering shall also give the LORD a
grain offering. It should be two quarts of fine
flour mixed with one quart of olive oil. 5Each
time you offer a lamb as a burnt offering or
sacrifice, also prepare a quart of wine as a
drink offering.
6" 'If you are giving a male sheep, also prepare a grain offering of four quarts of fine flour
mixed with one and one-fourth quarts of olive
oil. 7Also prepare one and one-fourth quarts

of wine as a drink offering. Its smell will be pleasing to the LORD.

8" 'If you prepare a young bull as a burnt offering or sacrifice, whether it is for a special promise or a fellowship offering to the LORD, 9bring a grain offering with the bull. It should be six quarts of fine flour mixed with two quarts of olive oil. 10Also bring two quarts of wine as a drink offering. This offering is made by fire, and its smell will be pleasing to the LORD. 11Prepare each bull or male sheep, lamb or young goat this way. 12Do this for every one of the animals you bring.

13" 'All citizens must do these things in this way, and the smell of their offerings by fire will be pleasing to the LORD. 14From now on if foreigners who live among you want to make offerings by fire so the smell will be pleasing to the LORD, they must offer them the same way you do. 15The law is the same for you and for foreigners, and it will be from now on; you and the foreigners are alike before the LORD. 16The teachings and rules are the same for you and for the foreigners among you.' "

17The LORD said to Moses, 18"Tell the Israelites: 'You are going to another land, where I am taking you. 19When you eat the food there, offer part of it to the LORD. 20Offer a loaf of bread from the first of your grain, which will be your offering from the threshing floor. 21From now on offer to the LORD the first part of your grain.

22" 'Now what if you forget to obey any of these commands the LORD gave Moses? 23These are the LORD's commands given to you through Moses, which began the day the LORD gave them to you and will continue from now on. 24If the people forget to obey one of these commands, all the people must offer a young bull as a burnt offering, a smell pleasing to the LORD. By law you must also give the grain offering and the drink offering with it, and you must bring a male goat as a sin offering.

25" 'The priest will remove that sin for all the Israelites so they will belong to the LORD. They are forgiven, because they didn't know they were sinning. For the wrong they did they brought offerings to the LORD, an offering by fire and a sin offering. 26So all of the people of Israel and the foreigners living among them will be forgiven. No one meant to do wrong.

27" 'If just one person sins without meaning to, a year-old female goat must be brought for a sin offering. 28The priest will remove the sin of the person who sinned accidentally. He will remove it before the LORD, and the person will be forgiven. 29The same teaching is for everyone who sins accidentally—for those born Israelites and for foreigners living among you.

30" 'But anyone who sins on purpose is against the LORD and must be cut off from the people, whether it is someone born among you or a foreigner. 31That person has turned against the LORD's word and has not obeyed his commands. Such a person must surely be cut off from the others. He is guilty.' "

A MAN WORKED ON THE SABBATH

32When the Israelites were still in the desert, they found a man gathering wood on the Sabbath day. 33Those who found him gathering wood brought him to Moses and Aaron and all the people. 34They held the man under guard, because they did not know what to do with him. 35Then the LORD said to Moses, "The man must surely die. All the people must kill him by throwing stones at him outside the camp." 36So all the people took him outside the camp and stoned him to death, as the LORD commanded Moses.

WHAT'S IT MEAN?

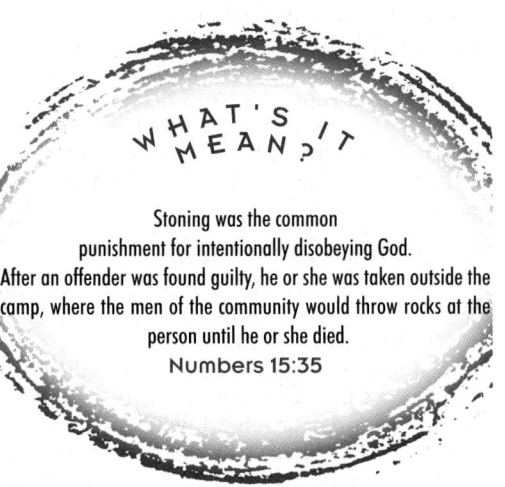

Stoning was the common punishment for intentionally disobeying God. After an offender was found guilty, he or she was taken outside the camp, where the men of the community would throw rocks at the person until he or she died.

Numbers 15:35

THE TASSELS

37The LORD said to Moses, 38"Speak to the Israelites and tell them this: 'Tie several pieces of thread together and attach them to the corners of your clothes. Put a blue thread in each one of these tassels. Wear them from now on. 39You will have these tassels to look at to remind you of all the LORD's commands. Then you will obey them and not be disloyal by following what your bodies and eyes want. 40Then you will remember to obey all my commands, and you will be God's holy people. 41I am the LORD your God, who brought you out of Egypt to be your God. I am the LORD your God.' "

KORAH, DATHAN, ABIRAM, AND ON

16 [1]Korah, Dathan, Abiram, and On turned
against Moses. (Korah was the son of Izhar,
the son of Kohath, the son of Levi; Dathan and
Abiram were brothers, the sons of Eliab;
and On was the son of Peleth; Dathan, Abiram,
and On were from the tribe of Reuben.) [2]These
men gathered two hundred fifty other Israelite
men, well-known leaders chosen by the community, and challenged Moses. [3]They came as
a group to speak to Moses and Aaron and
said, "You have gone too far. All the people are
holy, every one of them, and the LORD is
among them. So why do you put yourselves
above all the people of the LORD?"
[4]When Moses heard this, he bowed facedown. [5]Then he said to Korah and all his followers: "Tomorrow morning the LORD will
show who belongs to him. He will bring the
one who is holy near to him; he will bring to
himself the person he chooses. [6]So Korah, you
and all your followers do this: Get some pans
for burning incense. [7]Tomorrow put fire and
incense in them and take them before the
LORD. He will choose the man who is holy. You
Levites have gone too far."
[8]Moses also said to Korah, "Listen, you Levites. [9]The God of Israel has separated you
from the rest of the Israelites. He brought you
near to himself to do the work in the LORD's
Holy Tent and to stand before all the Israelites
and serve them. Isn't that enough? [10]He has
brought you and all your fellow Levites near to
himself, yet now you want to be priests. [11]You
and your followers have joined together
against the LORD. Your complaint is not against
Aaron."
[12]Then Moses called Dathan and Abiram,
the sons of Eliab, but they said, "We will not
come! [13]You have brought us out of a fertile
land to this desert to kill us, and now you want
to order us around. [14]You haven't brought us
into a fertile land; you haven't given us any
land with fields and vineyards. Will you put
out the eyes of these men? No! We will not
come!"
[15]Then Moses became very angry and said
to the LORD, "Don't accept their gifts. I have not
taken anything from them, not even a donkey,
and I have not done wrong to any of them."
[16]Then Moses said to Korah, "You and all
your followers must stand before the LORD tomorrow. And Aaron will stand there with you
and them. [17]Each of you must take your pan
and put incense in it; present these two hundred fifty pans before the LORD. You and
Aaron must also present your pans." [18]So each
man got his pan and put burning incense in it
and stood with Moses and Aaron at the entrance to the Meeting Tent. [19]Korah gathered all
his followers who were against Moses and
Aaron, and they stood at the entrance to the
Meeting Tent. Then the glory of the LORD appeared to everyone.
[20]The LORD said to Moses and Aaron,
[21]"Move away from these men so I can destroy
them quickly."
[22]But Moses and Aaron bowed facedown
and cried out, "God, you are the God over the
spirits of all people. Please don't be angry with
this whole group. Only one man has really
sinned."
[23]Then the LORD said to Moses, [24]"Tell
everyone to move away from the tents of Korah, Dathan, and Abiram."
[25]Moses stood and went to Dathan and
Abiram; the older leaders of Israel followed
him. [26]Moses warned the people, "Move away
from the tents of these evil men! Don't touch
anything of theirs, or you will be destroyed
because of their sins." [27]So they moved away
from the tents of Korah, Dathan, and Abiram.
Dathan and Abiram were standing outside
their tents with their wives, children, and little
babies.
[28]Then Moses said, "Now you will know
that the LORD has sent me to do all these
things; it was not my idea. [29]If these men die a
normal death—the way men usually die—then
the LORD did not really send me. [30]But if the
LORD does something new, you will know they
have insulted the LORD. The ground will open
and swallow them. They will be buried alive
and will go to the place of the dead, and everything that belongs to them will go with them."
[31]When Moses finished saying these things,
the ground under the men split open. [32]The
earth opened and swallowed them and all their
families. All Korah's men and everything they
owned went down. [33]They were buried alive,
going to the place of the dead, and everything
they owned went with them. Then the earth
covered them. They died and were gone from
the community. [34]The people of Israel around
them heard their screams and ran away, saying, "The earth will swallow us, too!"
[35]Then a fire came down from the LORD and
destroyed the two hundred fifty men who had
presented the incense.
[36]The LORD said to Moses, [37]"Tell Eleazar
son of Aaron, the priest, to take all the incense
pans out of the fire. Have him scatter the coals
a long distance away. But the incense pans are
still holy. [38]Take the pans of these men who

sinned and lost their lives, and hammer them into flat sheets that will be used to cover the altar. They are holy, because they were presented to the LORD, and they will be a sign to the Israelites."

[39]So Eleazar the priest gathered all the bronze pans that had been brought by the men who were burned up. He had the pans hammered into flat sheets to put on the altar, [40]as the LORD had commanded him through Moses. These sheets were to remind the Israelites that only descendants of Aaron should burn incense before the LORD. Anyone else would die like Korah and his followers.

AARON SAVES THE PEOPLE

[41]The next day all the Israelites complained against Moses and Aaron and said, "You have killed the LORD's people."

[42]When the people gathered to complain against Moses and Aaron, they turned toward the Meeting Tent, and the cloud covered it. The glory of the LORD appeared. [43]Then Moses and Aaron went in front of the Meeting Tent.

[44]The LORD said to Moses, [45]"Move away from these people so I can destroy them quickly." So Moses and Aaron bowed facedown.

[46]Then Moses said to Aaron, "Get your pan, and put fire from the altar and incense in it. Hurry to the people and remove their sin. The LORD is angry with them; the sickness has already started." [47]So Aaron did as Moses said. He ran to the middle of the people, where the sickness had already started among them. So Aaron offered the incense to remove their sin. [48]He stood between the dead and the living, and the sickness stopped there. [49]But 14,700 people died from that sickness, in addition to those who died because of Korah. [50]Then Aaron went back to Moses at the entrance to the Meeting Tent. The terrible sickness had been stopped.

AARON'S WALKING STICK BUDS

17 [1]The LORD said to Moses, [2]"Speak to the people of Israel and get twelve walking sticks from them—one from the leader of each tribe. Write the name of each man on his stick, and [3]on the stick from Levi, write Aaron's name. There must be one stick for the head of each tribe. [4]Put them in the Meeting Tent in front of the Ark of the Agreement, where I meet with you. [5]I will choose one man whose walking stick will begin to grow leaves; in this way I will stop the Israelites from always complaining against you."

[6]So Moses spoke to the Israelites. Each of the twelve leaders gave him a walking stick—one from each tribe—and Aaron's walking stick was among them. [7]Moses put them before the LORD in the Tent of the Agreement.

[8]The next day, when Moses entered the Tent, he saw that Aaron's stick (which stood for the family of Levi) had grown leaves. It had even budded, blossomed, and produced almonds. [9]So Moses brought out to the Israelites all the walking sticks from the LORD's presence. They all looked, and each man took back his stick.

WHAT'S IT MEAN?

Almond trees were popular with the Israelites because almonds were used to make medicine. The Hebrew word for almond means "awakening," probably due to the fact that the almond tree is the first to bloom in the spring. For the Israelites, the almond was a symbol of God's dependability.

Numbers 17:8

[10]Then the LORD said to Moses, "Put Aaron's walking stick back in front of the Ark of the Agreement. It will remind these people who are always turning against me to stop their complaining against me so they won't die." [11]So Moses obeyed what the LORD commanded him.

[12]The people of Israel said to Moses, "We are going to die! We are destroyed. We are all destroyed! [13]Anyone who even comes near the Holy Tent of the LORD will die. Will we all die?"

THE WORK OF THE PRIESTS AND LEVITES

18 [1]The LORD said to Aaron, "You, your sons, and your family are now responsible for any wrongs done against the Holy Place; you and your sons are responsible for any wrongs done against the priests. [2]Bring with you your fellow Levites from your tribe, and they will help you and your sons serve in the Tent of the Agreement. [3]They are under your control, to do all the work that needs to be done in the Tent. But they must not go near the things in the Holy Place or near the altar. If they do, both you and they will die. [4]They will join you in taking care of the Meeting Tent. They must

CAIN made a difference

Opportunities to make a positive difference are also opportunities to make a negative difference. The Bible includes many people who made a negative difference. There are two reasons for this: (1) we can learn from others' mistakes; and (2) we are more likely to recognize ourselves making negative differences than positive. Cain made a difference in the wrong way. As is true of many people in Scripture, God included their stories to help us learn from their mistakes. But even Cain had that opportunity. God warned him when danger approached. Cain chose not to listen.

When Abel and Cain agreed to worship God, they each had something different in mind. Their personal sacrifices came from their lives. But the Bible indicates a significant difference in their attitudes. Abel brought the best; Cain brought whatever. It was a careless mistake that Cain compounded by getting angry and jealous at his younger brother.

Cutting Edge

Until this point, the sin was between Cain and God. God warned Cain that he was quickly approaching a point of no return. God graciously granted Cain a second chance to get it right.

Attitudes like jealousy and anger can be rebuked and corrected. Murder cannot be undone. Cain chose to follow the guidance of his anger rather than to follow God. He killed his brother Abel and then offered God an arrogant denial— "Is it my job to take care of my brother?" (Gen. 4:9). Cain became a vivid example of the mess we create when anger is out of control.

YOU can, too!

What you do with anger will affect your Life in many ways. It will also make a big difference to others. As God pointed out to Cain, anger is like a huge billboard in our path which warns: What you do next matters! Anger is a reaction looking for a way to express itself. Anger doesn't think. That's why you have to think for it when you get angry. Without a master, anger hurts and destroys. Mastered, anger offers a forceful response to wrong.

If you have a problem with anger, listen carefully to God's warning to Cain. Letting God master your anger will make a difference for you and others.

Want to know more? Read about Cain's sin and the lessons the Bible teaches from it in Genesis 4:1–17; Hebrews 11:4; 1 John 3:12; Jude 11.

ISAAC made a difference

Isaac was the only child of Abraham and Sarah. Growing up as an only child carries with it certain benefits. For one thing, sharing is just a concept you learn, not a life-and-death struggle as in most families. Only childhood also includes special challenges. You get all the attention—sometimes too much. Isaac had the added factor of parents who were old enough to be his great-grandparents. No wonder he had some special problems later when he became father of twins.

Isaac was a promise as well as a person. He had to learn to live with that fact. He was the first installment in God's promise to create a nation through Abraham. For instance, one day his father told him they were going on a camping trip. The next thing he knew, Isaac found himself tied up on an altar about to be sacrificed as a burnt offering. Fortunately, this was only a test—a test of Abraham's trust in God. An alternative sacrifice was provided.

Cutting Edge

If Isaac didn't learn anything else about God while under the knife, he certainly realized faith was serious business. His life wasn't full of accomplishments, but he kept the faith, and he passed it on. He gave God's special blessing to Jacob and continued the generations, which became God's people, Israel.

YOU can, too!

Making a difference may not lead to greatness. Perhaps you will seem to do little more than be a faithful spouse, caring parent, growing disciple of Jesus—but these are the stuff from which God makes a difference in other people's lives. In God's hands, little differences become big.

Want to know more? Read about Isaac's life in Genesis 17:15—35:29. Romans 9:7–10; Hebrews 11:17–20; and James 2:21–24 also describe his significance.

REBEKAH made a difference

Even today in some cultures, marriages are arranged. Brides and grooms don't get to choose each other. We who see these choices as absolute rights find it hard to imagine a time when arranged marriages were the norm. Rebekah grew up in such a world. She lived in a large household ruled by her father and brother. They had the power to decide her marital fate. But God was also working in the background in her life.

One day when she went to the city well for water she met an old man named Eliezer, who was a servant of Abraham. Eliezer had just prayed for guidance in finding a suitable wife for Abraham's son Isaac. Rebekah turned out to be the answer to that prayer. Both Rebekah's timing and her attitude fit the servant's expectations. She didn't hesitate to be helpful, even before she found out he represented a distant relative.

After Eliezer met her family and explained his mission and the events at the well, Rebekah's father and brother realized God was arranging these events. They agreed to release Rebekah for marriage with Isaac. Gifts were presented. Return travel arrangements were made. Then, Rebekah was honored with final veto, "Do you want to go with this man now?" (Gen. 24:58). Her simple affirmation took God's plan for the world another step.

She made a difference.

YOU can, too!

Rebekah had a lot to learn. She made some major mistakes as a wife and mother. But her early and beautiful cooperation with God's work in her life was never undone. If we are going to make a difference in our tomorrows, and if we are going to cooperate with the difference God wants to make through us, it will hinge on what we do with our nows. What decisions and opportunities are before you now? In what ways are you seeking God's guidance about the choices you have? How ready are you to respond to his direction?

Want to know more? Read Rebekah's story in Genesis 24—27.

JOSEPH made a difference

Some young people seem to know exactly what they will accomplish in life. In Joseph's case, God gave him a vivid set of dreams that cast him in the role of ruler over his father and eleven brothers. The brothers, of course, thought their younger brother was being arrogant, rude, and silly. They were already upset by the fact that their father treated Joseph with special attention. Their jealousy and anger escalated to the point where they considered killing him but decided to sell him into slavery.

Little did the brothers know that they were working out God's plan. Still a teenager, Joseph found himself a slave in Egypt. His integrity, work ethic, and efforts earned him the trust of others. No matter where life landed him, Joseph immediately found a place to make a difference and worked at it. He practiced his considerable gifts and abilities. He made a difference in his master's home. Unfairly imprisoned, he made a difference in prison. Given an opportunity, he made a difference in a nation. With God's help, he set up a massive preparation for famine, which would save Egypt and her neighbors. Later, his dream came true when his entire family bowed before him, not recognizing him as a brother but appreciating his generosity as the governor of Egypt.

Cutting Edge

Joseph knew God's hand was on his life. He apparently never wavered in his confidence of that fact. He never let the immediate circumstances determine his view of God's power and ability to make a difference through his life.

YOU can, too!

Your vision of your future may not be as clear as Joseph's. That doesn't mean your confidence in God has to be less than his. The key is to remember that faith doesn't rest on a vision but on God. Your God must be big enough to work out his plans in your Life, no matter what the obstacles. Trust in such a God, and your life will make a difference.

Want to know more? Read about Joseph's amazing riches to rags to riches to rags to riches life in Genesis 37—50 and his listing in Hebrews 11:21–22.

do the work at the Tent, and no one else may
come near you.
5“You must take care of the Holy Place and
the altar so that I won’t become angry with the
Israelites again. 6I myself chose your fellow Levites from among the Israelites as a gift given
for you to the LORD, to work at the Meeting
Tent. 7But only you and your sons may serve
as priests. Only you may serve at the altar or
go behind the curtain. I am giving you this gift
of serving as a priest, and anyone else who
comes near the Holy Place will be put to death.”
8Then the LORD said to Aaron, “I myself
make you responsible for the
offerings given to me. All the
holy offerings that the Israelites give to me, I give to
you and your sons as
your share, your contin-
ual portion. 9Your share
of the holy offerings is
that part which is not
burned. When the peo-
ple bring me gifts as most
holy offerings, whether
they are grain or sin or penalty offerings, they will be set
apart for you and your sons.
10You must eat the offering in a most holy
place. Any male may eat it, but you must respect it as holy.
11“I also give you the offerings the Israelites
present to me. I give these to you and your
sons and daughters as your continual share.
Anyone in your family who is clean may eat it.
12“And I give you all the best olive oil and all
the best new wine and grain. This is what the
Israelites give to me, the LORD, from the first
crops they harvest. 13When they bring to the
LORD all the first things they harvest, they will
be yours. Anyone in your family who is clean
may eat these things.
14“Everything in Israel that is given to the
LORD is yours. 15The first one born to any family, whether people or animals, will be offered
to the LORD. And that will be yours. But you
must make a payment for every firstborn child
and every firstborn animal
that is unclean. 16When
they are one month old,
you must make a payment
for them of two ounces of
silver, as set by the Holy
Place measure.
17“But you must not
make a payment for the
firstborn ox or sheep or
goat. Those animals are
holy. Sprinkle their
blood on the altar and
burn their fat as an offering
made by fire. The smell is
pleasing to the LORD. 18But the meat will
be yours, just as the breast that is presented
and the right thigh will be yours. 19Anything
the Israelites present as holy gifts I, the LORD,
give to you, your sons and daughters as your
continual portion. This is a lasting agreement

“And I give you all the best olive oil and all the best new wine and grain. This is what the Israelites give to me, the LORD, from the first crops they harvest.” (Numbers 18:12)

Promise

HE PROMISES TO GIVE YOU EVERYTHING YOU NEED.

I will be yours. Out of all the Israelites, only you will inherit me (Num. 18:20b).

God is faithful. You can count on him. God has always been faithful to keep his word. He has supplied all of our needs. Most of the time we have much more than we could ever use or appreciate. We doubt God’s provision when we confuse our needs with our wants. Need says that you need clothes. Want says that you can only put the hippest, coolest things on your body. Need says that you need to eat lunch every day. Want says that you have to go out with your friends because they’d laugh if you ate in the cafeteria. We live in abundant times. A lot of people have a lot of stuff, and they want more. Think about your needs. Learn to separate them from the things you want. What do you really need in order to live? Has God provided? Take some time to thank him. He’s given you all you need.

SEE FOR YOURSELF:
Matt. 6:31–33; Luke 12:29–30; Phil. 4:19

of salt[n] before the LORD for you and your children forever."
20The LORD also said to Aaron, "You will not
inherit any of the land, and you will not own
any land among the other people. I will be
yours. Out of all the Israelites, only you will
inherit me.
21"When the people of Israel give me a tenth
of what they make, I will give that tenth to the
Levites. This is their payment for the work they
do serving at the Meeting Tent. 22But the other
Israelites must never go near the Meeting Tent,
or they will die for their sin. 23Only the Levites
should work in the Meeting Tent and be responsible for any sins against it. This is a rule
from now on. The Levites will not inherit any
land among the other Israelites, 24but when the
Israelites give a tenth of everything they make
to me, I will give that tenth to the Levites as a
reward. That is why I said about the Levites:
'They will not inherit any land among the Israelites.' "
25The LORD said to Moses, 26"Speak to the
Levites and tell them: 'You will receive a tenth
of everything the Israelites make, which I will
give to you. But you must give a tenth of that
back to the LORD. 27I will accept your offering
just as much as I accept the offerings from others, who give new grain or new wine. 28In this
way you will present an offering to the LORD as
the other Israelites do. When you receive a
tenth from the Israelites, you will give a tenth
of that to Aaron, the priest, as the LORD's share.
29Choose the best and holiest part from what
you are given as the portion you must give to
the LORD.'
30"Say to the Levites: 'When you present the
best, it will be accepted as much as the grain
and wine from the other people. 31You and
your families may eat all that is left anywhere,
because it is your pay for your work in the
Meeting Tent. 32And if you always give the best
part to the LORD, you will never be guilty. If
you do not sin against the holy offerings of the
Israelites, you will not die.' "

THE OFFERING FOR CLEANSING

19
1The LORD said to Moses and Aaron,
2"These are the teachings that the LORD commanded. Tell the Israelites to get a young red
cow that does not have anything wrong with
it and that has never been worked. 3Give the
cow to Eleazar the priest; he will take it outside
the camp and kill it. 4Then Eleazar the priest
must put some of its blood on his finger and
sprinkle it seven times toward the front of the
Meeting Tent. 5The whole cow must be burned
while he watches; the skin, the meat, the blood,
and the intestines must all be burned. 6Then
the priest must take a cedar stick, a hyssop
branch, and a red string and throw them onto
the burning cow. 7After the priest has washed
himself and his clothes with water, he may
come back into the camp, but he will be
unclean until evening. 8The man who burns
the cow must wash himself and his clothes in
water; he will be unclean until evening.
9"Then someone who is clean will collect
the ashes from the cow and put them in a
clean place outside the camp. The Israelites will
keep these ashes to use in the cleansing water,
in a special ceremony to cleanse away sin.
10The man who collected the cow's ashes must
wash his clothes and be unclean until evening.
This is a lasting rule for the Israelites and for
the foreigners among them.
11"Those who touch a dead person's body
will be unclean for seven days. 12They must
wash themselves with the cleansing water on
the third day and on the seventh day; then
they will be clean. But if they do not wash
themselves on the third day and the seventh
day, they cannot be clean. 13If those who touch
a dead person's body stay unclean and go to
the LORD's Holy Tent, it becomes unclean; they
must be cut off from Israel. If the cleansing
water is not sprinkled on them, they are unclean and will stay unclean.

WHAT'S IT MEAN?

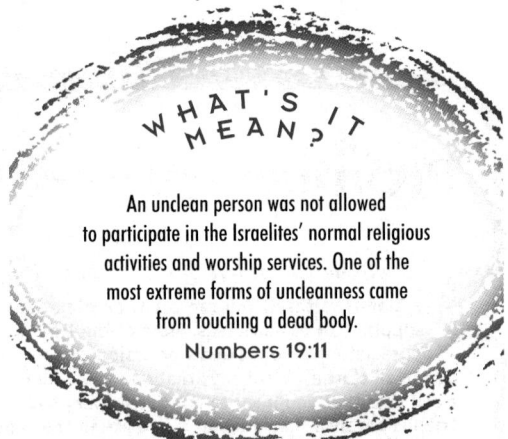

An unclean person was not allowed to participate in the Israelites' normal religious activities and worship services. One of the most extreme forms of uncleanness came from touching a dead body.
Numbers 19:11

14"This is the teaching about someone who
dies in a tent: Anyone in the tent or anyone
who enters it will be unclean for seven days.

18:19 agreement of salt The meaning is not clear, but Leviticus 2:13 says, "Salt stands for your agreement with God that will last forever."

15And every open jar or pot without a cover
becomes unclean. 16If anyone is outside and
touches someone who was killed by a sword
or who died a natural death, or if anyone
touches a human bone or a grave, that person
will be unclean for seven days.
17"So you must use the ashes from the burnt
offering to make that person clean again. Pour
fresh water over the ashes into a jar. 18A clean
person must take a hyssop branch and dip it
into the water, and then he must sprinkle it
over the tent and all its objects. He must also
sprinkle the people who were there, as well as
anyone who touched a bone, or the body of
someone who was killed, or a dead person, or
a grave. 19The person who is clean must sprinkle this water on the unclean people on the
third day and on the seventh day. On the seventh day they will become clean. They must
wash their clothes and take a bath, and they
will be clean that evening. 20If any who are unclean do not become clean, they must be cut
off from the community. Since they were not
sprinkled with the cleansing water, they stay
unclean, and they could make the LORD's Holy
Tent unclean. 21This is a lasting rule. Those
who sprinkle the cleansing water must also
wash their clothes, and anyone who touches
the water will be unclean until evening. 22Any-
thing an unclean person touches becomes unclean, and whoever touches it will be unclean
until evening."

MOSES DISOBEYS GOD

20
1In the first month all the people of Israel
arrived at the Desert of Zin, and they stayed at
Kadesh. There Miriam died and was buried.
2There was no water for the people, so they
came together against Moses and Aaron. 3They
argued with Moses and said, "We should have
died in front of the LORD as our brothers did.
4Why did you bring the LORD's people into
this desert? Are we and our animals to die
here? 5Why did you bring us from Egypt to
this terrible place? It has no grain, figs, grapevines, or pomegranates, and there's no water
to drink!"
6So Moses and Aaron left the people and
went to the entrance of the Meeting Tent. There
they bowed facedown, and the glory of the
LORD appeared to them. 7The LORD said to
Moses, 8"Take your walking stick, and you and
your brother Aaron should gather the people.
Speak to that rock in front of them so that its
water will flow from it. When you bring the
water out from that rock, give it to the people
and their animals."
9So Moses took the stick from in front of
the LORD, as he had said. 10Moses and Aaron
gathered the people in front of the rock, and
Moses said, "Now listen to me, you who turn
against God! Do you want us to bring water
out of this rock?" 11Then Moses lifted his hand
and hit the rock twice with his stick. Water
began pouring out, and the people and their
animals drank it.
12But the LORD said to Moses and Aaron,
"Because you did not believe me, and because
you did not honor me as holy before the people, you will not lead them into the land I will
give them."
13These are the waters of Meribah,[n] where
the Israelites argued with the LORD and where
he showed them he was holy.

EDOM WILL NOT LET ISRAEL PASS

14From Kadesh, Moses sent messengers to
the king of Edom. He said, "Your brothers, the
Israelites, say to you: You know about all the
troubles we have had, 15how our ancestors
went down into Egypt and we lived there for
many years. The people of Egypt were cruel to
us and our ancestors, 16but when we cried out
to the LORD, he heard us and sent us an angel to
bring us out of Egypt.
"Now we are here at Kadesh, a town on the
edge of your land. 17Please let us pass through
your country. We will not touch any fields of
grain or vineyards, and will not drink water
from the wells. We will travel only along the
king's road, not turning right or left until we
have passed through your country."
18But the king of Edom answered: "You may
not pass through here. If you try, I will come
and meet you with swords."
19The Israelites answered: "We will go along
the main road, and if we or our animals drink
any of your water, we will pay for it. We only
want to walk through. That's all."
20But he answered: "You may not pass
through here."
Then the Edomites went out to meet the Israelites with a large and powerful army. 21The
Edomites refused to let them pass through
their country, so the Israelites turned back.

AARON DIES

22All the Israelites moved from Kadesh to
Mount Hor, 23near the border of Edom. There
the LORD said to Moses and Aaron, 24"Aaron

20:13 Meribah This name in Hebrew means "argument."

will die. He will not enter the land that I'm giving to the Israelites, because you both acted
against my command at the waters of Meribah. 25Take Aaron and his son Eleazar up on
Mount Hor, 26and take off Aaron's special
clothes and put them on his son Eleazar. Aaron
will die there; he will join his ancestors."

WHAT'S IT MEAN?

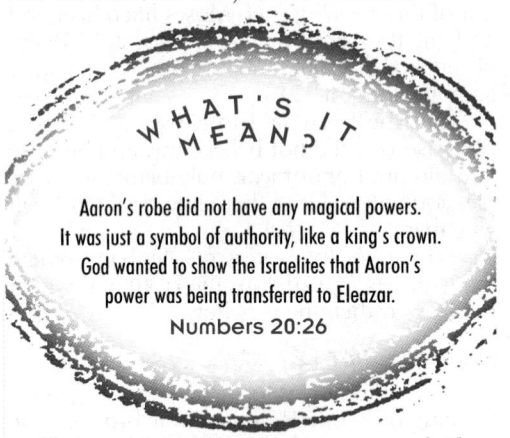

Aaron's robe did not have any magical powers. It was just a symbol of authority, like a king's crown. God wanted to show the Israelites that Aaron's power was being transferred to Eleazar.

Numbers 20:26

27Moses obeyed the LORD's command. They
climbed up Mount Hor, and all the people saw
them go. 28Moses took off Aaron's clothes and
put them on Aaron's son Eleazar. Then Aaron
died there on top of the mountain. Moses and
Eleazar came back down the mountain, 29and
when all the people learned that Aaron was
dead, everyone in Israel cried for him for thirty
days.

WAR WITH THE CANAANITES

21 1The Canaanite king of Arad lived in the
southern area. When he heard that the Israelites were coming on the road to Atharim, he
attacked them and captured some of them.
2Then the Israelites made this promise to the
LORD: "If you will help us defeat these people,
we will completely destroy their cities." 3The
LORD listened to the Israelites, and he let them
defeat the Canaanites. The Israelites completely
destroyed the Canaanites and their cities, so the
place was named Hormah.[n]

THE BRONZE SNAKE

4The Israelites left Mount Hor and went on
the road toward the Red Sea, in order to go
around the country of Edom. But the people
became impatient on the way 5and grumbled
at God and Moses. They said, "Why did you
bring us out of Egypt to die in this desert?
There is no bread and no water, and we hate
this terrible food!"

6So the LORD sent them poisonous snakes;
they bit the people, and many of the Israelites
died. 7The people came to Moses and said, "We
sinned when we grumbled at you and the
LORD. Pray that the LORD will take away these
snakes." So Moses prayed for the people.

8The LORD said to Moses, "Make a bronze
snake, and put it on a pole. When anyone who
is bitten looks at it, that person will live." 9So
Moses made a bronze snake and put it on a
pole. Then when a snake bit anyone, that person looked at the bronze snake and lived.

THE JOURNEY TO MOAB

10The Israelites went and camped at Oboth.
11They went from Oboth to Iye Abarim, in the
desert east of Moab. 12From there they went
and camped in the Zered Valley. 13From there
they went and camped across the Arnon, in
the desert just inside the Amorite country. The
Arnon is the border between the Moabites and
the Amorites. 14That is why the Book of the
Wars of the LORD says:

". . . and Waheb in Suphah, and the
ravines,
the Arnon, 15and the slopes of the
ravines
that lead to the settlement of Ar.
These places are at the border of Moab."

16The Israelites went from there to Beer; a
well is there where the LORD said to Moses,
"Gather the people and I will give them water."

17Then the Israelites sang this song:

"Pour out water, well!
Sing about it.
18Princes dug this well.
Important men made it.

WHAT'S IT MEAN?

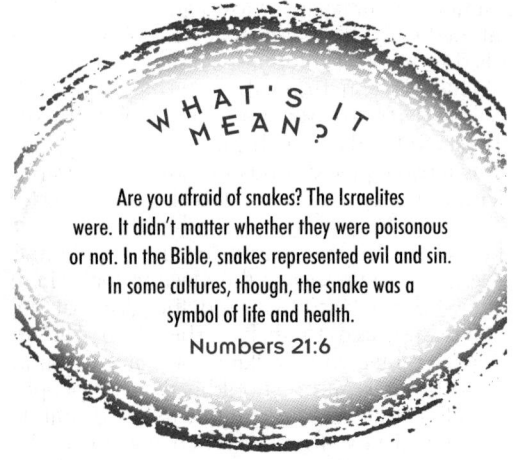

Are you afraid of snakes? The Israelites were. It didn't matter whether they were poisonous or not. In the Bible, snakes represented evil and sin. In some cultures, though, the snake was a symbol of life and health.

Numbers 21:6

21:3 Hormah This name in Hebrew means "completely destroyed."

With their scepters and poles, they dug
it."

The people went from the desert to Mattanah. [19]From Mattanah they went to Nahaliel and on to Bamoth. [20]From Bamoth they went to the valley of Moab where the top of Mount Pisgah looks over the desert.

ISRAEL KILLS SIHON AND OG

[21]The Israelites sent messengers to Sihon, king of the Amorites, saying, [22]"Let us pass through your country. We will not go through any fields of grain or vineyards, or drink water from the wells. We will travel only along the king's road until we have passed through your country."

[23]But King Sihon would not let the Israelites pass through his country. He gathered his whole army together, and they marched out to meet Israel in the desert. At Jahaz they fought the Israelites. [24]Israel killed the king and captured his land from the Arnon River to the Jabbok River. They took the land as far as the Ammonite border, which was strongly defended. [25]Israel captured all the Amorite cities and lived in them, taking Heshbon and all the towns around it. [26]Heshbon was the city where Sihon, the Amorite king, lived. In the past he had fought with the king of Moab and had taken all the land as far as the Arnon.

[27]That is why the poets say:

"Come to Heshbon
and rebuild it;
rebuild Sihon's city.
[28]A fire began in Heshbon;
flames came from Sihon's city.
It destroyed Ar in Moab,
and it burned the Arnon highlands.
[29]How terrible for you, Moab!
The people of Chemosh are ruined.
His sons ran away
and his daughters were captured
by Sihon, king of the Amorites.
[30]But we defeated those Amorites.
We ruined their towns from Heshbon to
Dibon,
and we destroyed them as far as
Nophah, near Medeba."

[31]So Israel lived in the land of the Amorites.

[32]After Moses sent spies to the town of Jazer, they captured the towns around it, forcing out the Amorites who lived there.

[33]Then the Israelites went up the road toward Bashan. Og king of Bashan and his whole army marched out to meet the Israelites, and they fought at Edrei.

[34]The LORD said to Moses, "Don't be afraid of him. I will hand him, his whole army, and his land over to you. Do to him what you did to Sihon, the Amorite king who lived in Heshbon."

[35]So the Israelites killed Og and his sons and all his army; no one was left alive. And they took his land.

"The LORD said to Moses, 'Don't be afraid of him. I will hand him, his whole army, and his land over to you.' "
(Numbers 21:34a)

BALAK SENDS FOR BALAAM

22 [1]Then the people of Israel went to the plains of Moab, and they camped near the Jordan River across from Jericho.

[2]Balak son of Zippor saw everything the Israelites had done to the Amorites. [3]And Moab was scared of so many Israelites; truly, Moab was terrified by them.

[4]The Moabites said to the older leaders of Midian, "These people will take everything around us like an ox eating grass."

Balak son of Zippor was the king of Moab at this time. [5]He sent messengers to Balaam son of Beor at Pethor, near the Euphrates River in his native land. Balak said, "A nation has come out of Egypt that covers the land. They have camped next to me, [6]and they are too powerful for me. So come and put a curse on them. Maybe then I can defeat them and make them leave the area. I know that if you bless someone, the

WHAT'S IT MEAN?

Sticking close to the water, the Israelites were traveling up the eastern side of the Dead Sea when they reached Heshbon. Twenty-five miles to the west of Heshbon was Jericho, the first city the Israelites came to when they entered Canaan.

Numbers 21:25

blessings happen, and if you put a curse on
someone, it happens."
7 The older leaders of Moab and Midian
went with payment in their hands. When they
found Balaam, they told him what Balak had
said.
8 Balaam said to them, "Stay here for the
night, and I will tell you what the LORD tells
me." So the Moabite leaders stayed with him.
9 God came to Balaam and asked, "Who are
these men with you?"
10 Balaam said to God, "The king of Moab,
Balak son of Zippor, sent them to me with this
message: 11 'A nation has come out of Egypt
that covers the land. So come and put a curse
on them, and maybe I can fight them and force
them out of my land.' "
12 But God said to Balaam, "Do not go with
them. Don't put a curse on those people, because I have blessed them."
13 The next morning Balaam awoke and said
to Balak's leaders, "Go back to your own country; the LORD has refused to let me go with
you."
14 So the Moabite leaders went back to Balak
and said, "Balaam refused to come with us."
15 So Balak sent other leaders—this time
there were more of them, and they were more
important. 16 They went to Balaam and said,
"Balak son of Zippor says this: Please don't let
anything stop you from coming to me. 17 I will
pay you very well, and I will do what you say.
Come and put a curse on these people for me."
18 But Balaam answered Balak's servants,
"King Balak could give me his palace full of
silver and gold, but I cannot disobey the LORD
my God in anything, great or small. 19 You stay
here tonight as the other men did, and I will
find out what more the LORD tells me."
20 That night God came to Balaam and said,
"These men have come to ask you to go with
them. Go, but only do what I tell you."

BALAAM'S DONKEY SPEAKS

21 Balaam got up the next morning and put
a saddle on his donkey. Then he went with the
Moabite leaders. 22 But God became angry because Balaam went, so the angel of the LORD
stood in the road to stop Balaam. Balaam was
riding his donkey, and he had two servants
with him. 23 When the donkey saw the angel of
the LORD standing in the road with a sword in
his hand, the donkey left the road and went
into the field. Balaam hit the donkey to force
her back on the road.
24 Later, the angel of the LORD stood on a narrow path between two vineyards, with walls on
both sides. 25 Again the donkey saw the angel of
the LORD, and she walked close to one wall,
crushing Balaam's foot against it. So he hit her
again.

WHAT'S IT MEAN?

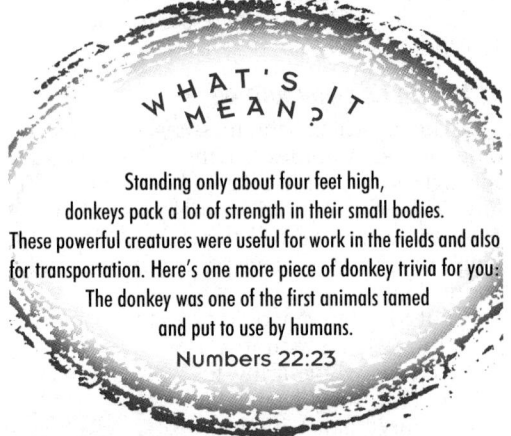

Standing only about four feet high, donkeys pack a lot of strength in their small bodies. These powerful creatures were useful for work in the fields and also for transportation. Here's one more piece of donkey trivia for you: The donkey was one of the first animals tamed and put to use by humans.

Numbers 22:23

26 The angel of the LORD went ahead again
and stood at a narrow place, too narrow to
turn left or right. 27 When the donkey saw the
angel of the LORD, she lay down under Balaam.
This made him so angry that he hit her with
his stick. 28 Then the LORD made the donkey
talk, and she said to Balaam, "What have I
done to make you hit me three times?"
29 Balaam answered the donkey, "You have
made me look foolish! I wish I had a sword in
my hand! I would kill you right now!"
30 But the donkey said to Balaam, "I am your
very own donkey, which you have ridden for
years. Have I ever done this to you before?"
"No," Balaam said.
31 Then the LORD let Balaam see the angel of
the LORD, who was standing in the road with
his sword drawn. Then Balaam bowed facedown on the ground.
32 The angel of the LORD asked Balaam,
"Why have you hit your donkey three times? I
have stood here to stop you, because what
you are doing is wrong. 33 The donkey saw me
and turned away from me three times. If she
had not turned away, I would have killed you
by now, but I would have let her live."
34 Then Balaam said to the angel of the LORD,
"I have sinned; I did not know you were
standing in the road to stop me. If I am wrong,
I will go back."
35 The angel of the LORD said to Balaam, "Go
with these men, but say only what I tell you."
So Balaam went with Balak's leaders.
36 When Balak heard that Balaam was coming, he went out to meet him at Ar in Moab,
which was beside the Arnon, at the edge of his

country. 37Balak said to Balaam, "I had asked
you before to come quickly. Why didn't you
come to me? I am able to reward you well."
38But Balaam answered, "I have come to
you now, but I can't say just anything. I can
only say what God tells me to say."
39Then Balaam went with Balak to Kiriath
Huzoth. 40Balak offered cattle and sheep as a
sacrifice and gave some meat to Balaam and
the leaders with him.
41The next morning Balak took Balaam to
Bamoth Baal; from there he could see the edge
of the Israelite camp.

BALAAM'S FIRST MESSAGE

23 1Balaam said to Balak, "Build me seven altars here, and prepare seven bulls and seven
male sheep for me." 2Balak did what Balaam
asked, and they offered a bull and a male sheep
on each of the altars.
3Then Balaam said to Balak, "Stay here beside your burnt offering and I will go. If the
LORD comes to me, I will tell you whatever he
shows me." Then Balaam went to a higher
place.
4God came to Balaam there, and Balaam
said to him, "I have prepared seven altars, and
I have offered a bull and a male sheep on each
altar."
5The LORD told Balaam what he should say.
Then the LORD said, "Go back to Balak and give
him this message."
6So Balaam went back to Balak. Balak and
all the leaders of Moab were still standing beside his burnt offering 7when Balaam gave
them this message:

"Balak brought me here from Aram;
the king of Moab brought me from the
eastern mountains.
Balak said, 'Come, put a curse on the
people of Jacob for me.
Come, call down evil on the people of
Israel.'
8But God has not cursed them,
so I cannot curse them.
The LORD has not called down evil on
them,
so I cannot call down evil on them.
9I see them from the top of the mountains;
I see them from the hills.
I see a people who live alone,
who think they are different from other
nations.
10No one can number the many people of
Jacob,
and no one can count a fourth of
Israel.
Let me die like good men,
and let me end up like them!"

11Balak said to Balaam, "What have you
done to me? I brought you here to curse my
enemies, but you have only blessed them!"
12But Balaam answered, "I must say what
the LORD tells me to say."

Promise

HE PROMISES NOT TO BE LIKE PEOPLE.

God is not a human being, and he will not lie. His is not a human, and he does not change his mind. What he says he will do, he does. What he promises, he makes come true (Num. 23:19).

Do you know anyone who has *never* broken a promise? It's a fact: Somewhere along the line, everyone is going to break a promise. Maybe they didn't mean to and they're terribly sorry, but for some reason they just couldn't keep their word. That can hurt. The Bible tells us that God is not like people. Aren't you glad that he doesn't break any of his promises?

God's Word tells us that Christ says yes to *all* his promises for you. And all we have to do is say Amen (or, literally, "Let it be") to that promise. If God said it, he'll do it. If he spoke it, he'll bring it to pass. God cannot lie. He is not human. He's not going to lie, and he's not going to change his mind. Do you know what that means? All the promises of the Bible are for you. He's not going to forget one of them. You've been promised not only eternal life, but also "everything we need to live and to serve God" here on earth (2 Pet. 1:3). Personalize every one of his promises for yourself because he is the One who always keeps his promises!

SEE FOR YOURSELF:

Josh. 23:15; 1 Kin. 8:56; 2 Cor. 1:20

BALAAM'S SECOND MESSAGE

13Then Balak said to him, "Come with me to
another place, where you can also see the people. But you can only see part of them, not all
of them. Curse them for me from there." 14So
Balak took Balaam to the field of Zophim, on
top of Mount Pisgah. There Balak built seven
altars and offered a bull and a male sheep on
each altar.
15So Balaam said to Balak, "Stay here by
your burnt offering, and I will meet with God
over there."
16So the LORD came to Balaam and told him
what to say. Then he said, "Go back to Balak
and say such and such."
17So Balaam went to Balak, where he and
the leaders of Moab were standing beside his
burnt offering. Balak asked him, "What did the
LORD say?"
18Then Balaam gave this message:
"Stand up, Balak, and listen.
Hear me, son of Zippor.
19God is not a human being, and he will not
lie.
He is not a human, and he does not
change his mind.
What he says he will do, he does.
What he promises, he makes come true.
20He told me to bless them,
so I cannot change the blessing.
21He has found no wrong in the people of
Jacob;
he saw no fault in Israel.
The LORD their God is with them,
and they praise their King.
22God brought them out of Egypt;
they are as strong as a wild ox.
23No tricks will work on the people of
Jacob,
and no magic will work against Israel.
People now say about them,
'Look what God has done for Israel!'
24The people rise up like a lioness;
they get up like a lion.
Lions don't rest until they have eaten,
until they have drunk their enemies'
blood."
25Then Balak said to Balaam, "You haven't
cursed these people, so at least, don't bless
them!"
26Balaam answered Balak, "I told you before
that I can only do what the LORD tells me."

BALAAM'S THIRD MESSAGE

27Then Balak said to Balaam, "Come, I will
take you to another place. Maybe God will
be pleased to let you curse them from there."
28So Balak took Balaam to the top of Peor, the
mountain that looks over the desert.
29Balaam told Balak, "Build me seven altars
here and prepare for me seven bulls and seven
male sheep." 30Balak did what Balaam asked,
and he offered a bull and a male sheep on each
altar.

24

1Balaam saw that the LORD wanted to bless
Israel, so he did not try to use any magic but
looked toward the desert. 2When Balaam saw
the Israelites camped in their tribes, the Spirit
of God took control of him, 3and he gave this
message:
"This is the message of Balaam son of Beor,
the message of a man who sees clearly;
4this is the message of a man who hears
the words of God.
I see a vision from the Almighty,
and my eyes are open as I fall before
him.
5Your tents are beautiful, people of Jacob!
So are your homes, Israel!
6Your tents spread out like valleys,
like gardens beside a river.
They are like spices planted by the LORD,
like cedar trees growing by the water.
7Israel's water buckets will always be full,
and their crops will have plenty of
water.
Their king will be greater than Agag;
their kingdom will be very great.
8God brought them out of Egypt;
they are as strong as a wild ox.
They will defeat their enemies
and break their enemies' bones;
they will shoot them with arrows.
9Like a lion, they lie waiting to attack;
like a lioness, no one would be brave
enough to wake them.
Anyone who blesses you will be blessed,
and anyone who curses you will be
cursed."
10Then Balak was angry with Balaam, and
he pounded his fist. He said to Balaam, "I called
you here to curse my enemies, but you have
continued to bless them three times. 11Now go
home! I said I would pay you well, but the
LORD has made you lose your reward."
12Balaam said to Balak, "When you sent
messengers to me, I told them, 13'Balak could
give me his palace filled with silver and gold,
but I still cannot go against the LORD's commands. I could not do anything, good or bad,
on my own, but I must say what the LORD
says.' 14Now I am going back to my own people, but I will tell you what these people will do
to your people in the future."

BALAAM'S FINAL MESSAGE

15Then Balaam gave this message:
"This is the message of Balaam son of
Beor,
the message of a man who sees clearly;
16this is the message of a man who hears
the words of God.
I know well the Most High God.
I see a vision from the Almighty,
and my eyes are open as I fall before
him.
17I see someone who will come some day,
someone who will come, but not soon.
A star will come from Jacob;
a ruler will rise from Israel.
He will crush the heads of the Moabites
and smash the skulls of the sons of
Sheth.
18Edom will be conquered;
his enemy Edom will be conquered,
but Israel will grow wealthy.
19A ruler will come from the descendants of
Jacob
and will destroy those left in the city."

20Then Balaam saw Amalek and gave this
message:
"Amalek was the most important nation,
but Amalek will be destroyed at last."

21Then Balaam saw the Kenites and gave
this message:
"Your home is safe,
like a nest on a cliff.
22But you Kenites will be burned up;
Assyria will keep you captive."

23Then Balaam gave this message:
"No one can live when God does this.
24 Ships will sail from the shores of Cyprus
and defeat Assyria and Eber,
but they will also be destroyed."

25Then Balaam got up and returned home,
and Balak also went on his way.

ISRAEL WORSHIPS BAAL AT PEOR

25 1While the people of Israel were still
camped at Acacia, the men began sinning sexually with Moabite women. 2The women invited them to their sacrifices to their gods, and
the Israelites ate food there and worshiped
these gods. 3So the Israelites began to worship
Baal of Peor, and the LORD was very angry
with them.
4The LORD said to Moses, "Get all the leaders
of the people and kill them in open daylight in
the presence of the LORD. Then the LORD will
not be angry with the people of Israel."
5So Moses said to Israel's judges, "Each of
you must put to death your people who have
become worshipers of Baal of Peor."
6Moses and the Israelites were gathered at
the entrance to the Meeting Tent, crying there.

WHAT'S IT MEAN?

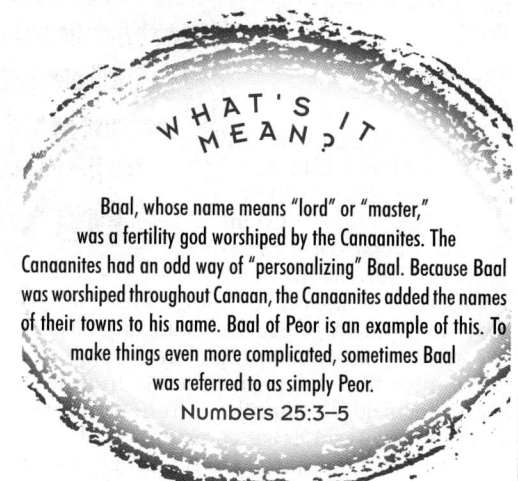

Baal, whose name means "lord" or "master," was a fertility god worshiped by the Canaanites. The Canaanites had an odd way of "personalizing" Baal. Because Baal was worshiped throughout Canaan, the Canaanites added the names of their towns to his name. Baal of Peor is an example of this. To make things even more complicated, sometimes Baal was referred to as simply Peor.

Numbers 25:3–5

Then an Israelite man brought a Midianite
woman to his brothers in plain sight of Moses
and all the people. 7Phinehas son of Eleazar,
the son of Aaron, the priest, saw this, so he left
the meeting and got his spear. 8He followed the
Israelite into his tent and drove his spear
through both the Israelite man and the Midianite woman. Then the terrible sickness among
the Israelites stopped.
9This sickness had killed twenty-four thousand people.
10The LORD said to Moses, 11"Phinehas son
of Eleazar, the son of Aaron, the priest, has
saved the Israelites from my anger. He hates sin
as much as I do. Since he tried to save my
honor among them, I will not kill them. 12So
tell Phinehas that I am making my peace
agreement with him. 13He and his descendants
will always be priests, because he had great
concern for the honor of his God. He removed
the sins of the Israelites so they would belong
to God."
14The Israelite man who was killed with the
Midianite woman was named Zimri son of
Salu. He was the leader of a family in the tribe
of Simeon. 15And the name of the Midianite
woman who was put to death was Cozbi
daughter of Zur, who was the chief of a Midianite family.
16The LORD said to Moses, 17"The Midianites
are your enemies, and you should kill them.

18They have already made you their enemies, because they tricked you at Peor and because of their sister Cozbi, the daughter of a Midianite leader. She was the woman who was killed when the sickness came because the people sinned at Peor."

> **"So tell Phinehas that I am making my peace agreement with him. He and his descendants will always be priests, because he had great concern for the honor of his God."**
> **(Numbers 25:12–13a)**

THE PEOPLE ARE COUNTED

26 1After the great sickness, the LORD said to Moses and Eleazar son of Aaron, the priest, 2"Count all the people of Israel by families. Count all the men who are twenty years old or older who will serve in the army of Israel." 3Moses and Eleazar the priest spoke to the people on the plains of Moab near the Jordan River, across from Jericho. They said, 4"Count the men twenty years old or older, as the LORD commanded Moses."

Here are the Israelites who came out of Egypt:

5The tribe of Reuben, the first son born to Israel, was counted. From Hanoch came the Hanochite family group; from Pallu came the Palluite family group; 6from Hezron came the Hezronite family group; from Carmi came the Carmite family group. 7These were the family groups of Reuben, and the total number of men was 43,730.

8The son of Pallu was Eliab, 9and Eliab's sons were Nemuel, Dathan, and Abiram. Dathan and Abiram were the leaders who turned against Moses and Aaron and followed Korah when he turned against the LORD. 10The earth opened up and swallowed them and Korah; they died at the same time the fire burned up the 250 men. This was a warning, 11but the children of Korah did not die.

12These were the family groups in the tribe of Simeon: From Nemuel came the Nemuelite family group; from Jamin came the Jaminite family group; from Jakin came the Jakinite family group; 13from Zerah came the Zerahite family group; from Shaul came the Shaulite family group. 14These were the family groups of Simeon, and the total number of men was 22,200.

15These were the family groups in the tribe of Gad: From Zephon came the Zephonite family group; from Haggi came the Haggite family group; from Shuni came the Shunite family group; 16from Ozni came the Oznite family group; from Eri came the Erite family group; 17from Arodi came the Arodite family group; from Areli came the Arelite family group. 18These were the family groups of Gad, and the total number of men was 40,500.

19Two of Judah's sons, Er and Onan, died in Canaan.

20These were the family groups in the tribe of Judah: From Shelah came the Shelanite family group; from Perez came the Perezite family group; from Zerah came the Zerahite family group. 21These were the family groups from Perez: From Hezron came the Hezronite family group; from Hamul came the Hamulite family group. 22These were the family groups of Judah, and the total number of men was 76,500.

23These were the family groups in the tribe of Issachar: From Tola came the Tolaite family group; from Puah came the Puite family group; 24from Jashub came the Jashubite family group; from Shimron came the Shimronite family group. 25These were the family groups of Issachar, and the total number of men was 64,300.

26These were the family groups in the tribe of Zebulun: From Sered came the Seredite family group; from Elon came the Elonite family group; from Jahleel came the Jahleelite family group. 27These were the family groups of Zebulun, and the total number of men was 60,500.

28These were the family groups of Joseph through Manasseh and Ephraim.

29These were the family groups of Manasseh: From Makir came the Makirite family group (Makir was the father of Gilead); from Gilead came the Gileadite family group. 30These were the family groups that came from Gilead: From Iezer came the Iezerite family group; from Helek came the Helekite family group; 31from Asriel came the Asrielite family group; from Shechem came the Shechemite family group; 32from Shemida came the Shemidaite family group; from Hepher came the Hepherite family group. 33(Zelophehad son of Hepher had no sons; he had only daughters, and their names were Mahlah, Noah, Hoglah, Milcah, and Tirzah.) 34These were the family groups of Manasseh, and the total number of men was 52,700.

35These were the family groups in the tribe

of Ephraim: From Shuthelah came the Shuthelahite family group; from Beker came the Bekerite family group; from Tahan came the Tahanite family group. [36]This was the family group from Shuthelah: From Eran came the Eranite family group. [37]These were the family groups of Ephraim, and the total number of men was 32,500. These are the family groups that came from Joseph.

[38]These were the family groups in the tribe of Benjamin: From Bela came the Belaite family group; from Ashbel came the Ashbelite family group; from Ahiram came the Ahiramite family group; [39]from Shupham came the Shuphamite family group; from Hupham came the Huphamite family group. [40]These were the family groups from Bela through Ard and Naaman: From Ard came the Ardite family group; from Naaman came the Naamite family group. [41]These were the family groups of Benjamin, and the total number of men was 45,600.

[42]This was the family group in the tribe of Dan: From Shuham came the Shuhamite family group. That was the family of Dan, [43]and the total number of men in the Shuhamite family group of Dan was 64,400.

[44]These were the family groups in the tribe of Asher: From Imnah came the Imnite family group; from Ishvi came the Ishvite family group; from Beriah came the Beriite family group. [45]These were the family groups that came from Beriah: From Heber came the Heberite family group; from Malkiel came the Malkielite family group. [46](Asher also had a daughter named Serah.) [47]These were the family groups of Asher, and the total number of men was 53,400.

[48]These were the family groups in the tribe of Naphtali: From Jahzeel came the Jahzeelite family group; from Guni came the Gunite family group; [49]from Jezer came the Jezerite family group; from Shillem came the Shillemite family group. [50]These were the family groups of Naphtali, and the total number of men was 45,400.

[51]So the total number of the men of Israel was 601,730.

[52]The LORD said to Moses, [53]"Divide the land among these people by the number of names. [54]A large tribe will get more land, and a small tribe will get less land; the amount of land each tribe gets will depend on the number of its people. [55]Divide the land by drawing lots, and the land each tribe gets will be named for that tribe. [56]Divide the land between large and small groups by drawing lots."

[57]The tribe of Levi was also counted. These were the family groups of Levi: From Gershon came the Gershonite family group; from Kohath came the Kohathite family group; from Merari came the Merarite family group. [58]These also were Levite family groups: the Libnite family group, the Hebronite family group, the Mahlite family group, the Mushite family group, and the Korahite family group. (Kohath was the ancestor of Amram, [59]whose wife was named Jochebed. She was from the tribe of Levi and she was born in Egypt. She and Amram had two sons, Aaron and Moses, and their sister Miriam. [60]Aaron was the father of Nadab, Abihu, Eleazar, and Ithamar. [61]But Nadab and Abihu died because they made an offering before the LORD with the wrong kind of fire.)

[62]The total number of male Levites one month old or older was 23,000. But these men were not counted with the other Israelites, because they were not given any of the land among the other Israelites.

[63]Moses and Eleazar the priest counted all these people. They counted the Israelites on the plains of Moab across the Jordan River from Jericho. [64]Moses and Aaron the priest had counted the Israelites in the Desert of Sinai, but no one Moses counted on the plains of Moab was in the first counting. [65]The LORD had told the Israelites they would all die in the desert, and the only two left were Caleb son of Jephunneh and Joshua son of Nun.

ZELOPHEHAD'S DAUGHTERS

27 [1]Then the daughters of Zelophehad came near. Zelophehad was the son of Hepher, the son of Gilead, the son of Makir, the son of Manasseh. Zelophehad's daughters belonged to the family groups of Manasseh son of Joseph. The daughters' names were Mahlah,

WHAT'S IT MEAN?

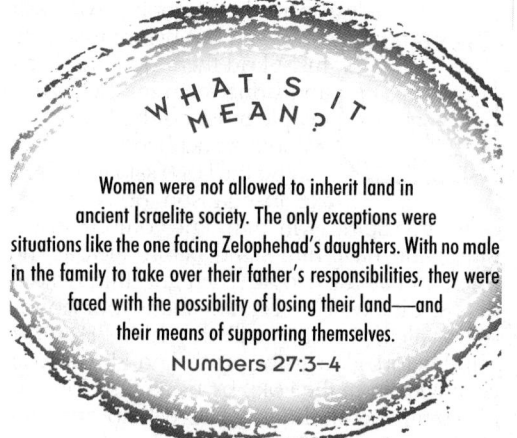

Women were not allowed to inherit land in ancient Israelite society. The only exceptions were situations like the one facing Zelophehad's daughters. With no male in the family to take over their father's responsibilities, they were faced with the possibility of losing their land—and their means of supporting themselves.

Numbers 27:3–4

Noah, Hoglah, Milcah, and Tirzah. 2They went to the entrance of the Meeting Tent and stood before Moses, Eleazar the priest, the leaders, and all the people. They said, 3"Our father died in the desert. He was not one of Korah's followers who came together against the LORD, but he died because of his own sin, and he had no sons. 4Our father's name will die out because he had no sons. Give us property among our father's relatives."

5So Moses brought their case to the LORD, 6and the LORD said to him, 7"The daughters of Zelophehad are right; they should certainly get what their father owned. Give them property among their father's relatives.

8"Tell the Israelites, 'If a man dies and has no son, then everything he owned should go to his daughter. 9If he has no daughter, then everything he owned should go to his brothers. 10If he has no brothers, then everything he owned should go to his father's brothers. 11And if his father had no brothers, then everything he owned should go to the nearest relative in his family group. This should be a rule among the people of Israel, as the LORD has given this command to Moses.' "

JOSHUA IS THE NEW LEADER

12Then the LORD said to Moses, "Climb this mountain in the Abarim Mountains, and look at the land I have given to the Israelites. 13After you have seen it, you will die and join your ancestors as your brother Aaron did, 14because you both acted against my command in the Desert of Zin. You did not honor me as holy before the people at the waters of Meribah." (This was at Meribah in Kadesh in the Desert of Zin.)

15Moses said to the LORD, 16"The LORD is the God of the spirits of all people. May he choose a leader for these people, 17who will go in and out before them. He must lead them out like sheep and bring them in; the LORD's people must not be like sheep without a shepherd."

LEADERSHIP

Who should leaders look out for? (27:16–17)

18So the LORD said to Moses, "Take Joshua son of Nun, because my Spirit is in him. Put your hand on him, 19and have him stand before Eleazar the priest and all the people. Then give him his orders as they watch. 20Let him share your honor so that all the Israelites will obey him. 21He must stand before Eleazar the priest, and Eleazar will get advice from the LORD by using the Urim. At his command all the Israelites will go out, and at his command they will all come in."

22Moses did what the LORD told him. He took Joshua and had him stand before Eleazar the priest and all the people, 23and he put his hands on him and gave him orders, just as the LORD had told him.

DAILY OFFERINGS

28 1The LORD said to Moses, 2"Give this command to the Israelites. Tell them: 'Bring me food offerings made by fire, for a smell that is pleasing to me, and be sure to bring them at the right time.' 3Say to them, 'These are the offerings you must bring to the LORD: two male lambs, a year old, as a burnt offering each day. They must have nothing wrong with them. 4Offer one lamb in the morning and the other lamb at twilight. 5Also bring a grain offering of two quarts of fine flour, mixed with one quart of oil from pressed olives. 6This is the daily

On the Edge

The LORD said to Moses, "Give this command to the Israelites. . . ." (Num. 28:1–2).

God told Moses to give lots of laws to the people of Israel. He did that because he wanted to bless the people. You're thinking *What? Why would he make them do all that stuff if all he wanted was to bless them? Why didn't he just bless them anyway?*

Think about it. God is holy. He has rules for living. He will not bless sin. He could not have a bunch of people running around doing whatever they wanted and then bless them in spite of it. The laws don't exist so that God can play "boss" and bark orders to people. They were necessary conditions for the blessing that comes from holy living.

Jewish law had 613 points, or rules, that had to be obeyed before a person could approach God. Imagine that. It would be impossible for anybody to meet all those demands. When Jesus came, he fulfilled the law—all 613 points. When Jesus lives in you, every rule is obeyed. The law is satisfied and you can approach God. You are free from having to live up to all those rules. Jesus has done it for you.

SEE FOR YOURSELF:
Ex. 20; Deut. 5:1–22; 1 Chr. 22:13; Rom. 10:4; Gal. 3—5

burnt offering which began at Mount Sinai; its smell is pleasing to the LORD. [7]Offer one quart of wine with each lamb as a drink offering; pour it out to the LORD at the Holy Place. [8]Offer the second lamb at twilight. As in the morning, also give a grain offering and a drink offering. This offering is made by fire, and its smell is pleasing to the LORD.

SABBATH OFFERINGS

[9]" 'On the Sabbath day you must give two male lambs, a year old, that have nothing wrong with them. Also give a drink offering and a grain offering; the grain offering must be four quarts of fine flour mixed with olive oil. [10]This is the burnt offering for every Sabbath, in addition to the daily burnt offering and drink offering.

MONTHLY OFFERINGS

[11]" 'On the first day of each month bring a burnt offering to the LORD. This will be two young bulls, one male sheep, and seven male lambs a year old, and they must have nothing wrong with them. [12]Give a grain offering with each bull of six quarts of fine flour mixed with olive oil. Also give a grain offering with the male sheep. It must be four quarts of fine flour mixed with olive oil. [13]And give a grain offering with each lamb of two quarts of fine flour mixed with olive oil. This is a burnt offering, and its smell is pleasing to the LORD. [14]The drink offering with each bull will be two quarts of wine, with the male sheep it will be one and one-third quarts, and with each lamb it will be one quart of wine. This is the burnt offering that must be offered each month of the year. [15]Besides the daily burnt offerings and drink offerings, bring a sin offering of one goat to the LORD.

THE PASSOVER

[16]" 'The LORD's Passover will be on the fourteenth day of the first month. [17]The Feast of Unleavened Bread begins on the fifteenth day of that month. For seven days, you may eat only bread made without yeast. [18]Have a holy meeting on the first day of the festival, and don't work that day. [19]Bring to the LORD an offering made by fire, a burnt offering of two young bulls, one male sheep, and seven male lambs a year old. They must have nothing wrong with them. [20]With each bull give a grain offering of six quarts of fine flour mixed with olive oil. With the male sheep it must be four quarts of fine flour mixed with oil. [21]With each of the seven lambs, it must be two quarts of fine flour mixed with oil. [22]Bring one goat as a sin offering, to remove your sins so you will belong to God. [23]Bring these offerings in addition to the burnt offerings you give every morning. [24]So bring food for the offering made by fire each day for seven days, for a smell that is pleasing to the LORD. Do it in addition to the daily burnt offering and its drink offering. [25]On the seventh day have a holy meeting, and don't work that day.

WHAT'S IT MEAN?

If you would like to mark Passover on your calendar, check late March or early April. If you have a Hebrew calendar, check Abib (or Nisan), the first month of the sacred year. Jewish people still celebrate Passover today because God commanded them to remember how he led them out of Egypt.

Numbers 28:16

THE FEAST OF WEEKS

[26]" 'On the day of firstfruits when you bring new grain to the LORD during the Feast of Weeks, have a holy meeting. Don't work that day. [27]Bring this burnt offering to the LORD: two young bulls, one male sheep, and seven male lambs a year old. This smell is pleasing to the LORD. [28]Also, with each bull give a grain offering of six quarts of fine flour mixed with oil. With the male sheep, it must be four quarts of flour, [29]and with each of the seven lambs offer two quarts of flour. [30]Offer one male goat to remove your sins so you will belong to God. [31]Bring these offerings and their drink offerings in addition to the daily burnt offering and its grain offering. The animals must have nothing wrong with them.

THE FEAST OF TRUMPETS

29 [1]" 'Have a holy meeting on the first day of the seventh month, and don't work on that day. That is the day you blow the trumpets. [2]Bring these burnt offerings as a smell pleasing to the LORD: one young bull, one male sheep, and seven male lambs a year old. They must have nothing wrong with them. [3]With the bull give a grain offering of six quarts of fine flour mixed with oil. With the male sheep offer four

quarts, 4and with each of the seven lambs offer two quarts. 5Offer one male goat for a sin offering to remove your sins so you will belong to God. 6These offerings are in addition to the monthly and daily burnt offerings. Their grain offerings and drink offerings must be done as you have been told. These offerings are made by fire to the LORD, and their smell is pleasing to him.

THE DAY OF CLEANSING

7" 'Have a holy meeting on the tenth day of the seventh month. On that day do not eat and do not work. 8Bring these burnt offerings as a smell pleasing to the LORD: one young bull, one male sheep, and seven male lambs a year old. They must have nothing wrong with them. 9With the bull give a grain offering of six quarts of fine flour mixed with oil. With the male sheep it must be four quarts, 10and with each of the seven lambs it must be two quarts. 11Offer one male goat as a sin offering. This will be in addition to the sin offering which removes your sins, the daily burnt offering with its grain offering, and the drink offerings.

> **"Moses told the Israelites everything the LORD had commanded him." (Numbers 29:40)**

THE FEAST OF SHELTERS

12" 'Have a holy meeting on the fifteenth day of the seventh month, and do not work on that day. Celebrate a festival to the LORD for seven days. 13Bring these burnt offerings, made by fire, as a smell pleasing to the LORD: thirteen young bulls, two male sheep, and fourteen male lambs a year old. They must have nothing wrong with them. 14With each of the thirteen bulls offer a grain offering of six quarts of fine flour mixed with oil. With each of the two male sheep it must be four quarts, 15and with each of the fourteen lambs it must be two quarts. 16Offer one male goat as a sin offering in addition to the daily burnt offering with its grain and drink offerings.

17" 'On the second day of this festival give an offering of twelve bulls, two male sheep, and fourteen male lambs a year old. They must have nothing wrong with them. 18Bring the grain and drink offerings for the bulls, sheep, and lambs, according to the number required. 19Offer one male goat as a sin offering, in addition to the daily burnt offering with its grain and drink offerings.

20" 'On the third day offer eleven bulls, two male sheep, and fourteen male lambs a year old. They must have nothing wrong with them. 21Bring the grain and drink offerings for the bulls, sheep, and lambs, according to the number required. 22Offer one male goat as a sin offering, in addition to the daily burnt offering with its grain and drink offerings.

23" 'On the fourth day offer ten bulls, two male sheep, and fourteen male lambs a year old. They must have nothing wrong with them. 24Bring the grain and drink offerings for the bulls, sheep, and lambs, according to the number required. 25Offer one male goat as a sin offering, in addition to the daily burnt offering with its grain and drink offerings.

26" 'On the fifth day offer nine bulls, two male sheep, and fourteen male lambs a year old. They must have nothing wrong with them. 27Bring the grain and drink offerings for the bulls, sheep, and lambs, according to the number required. 28Offer one male goat as a sin offering, in addition to the daily burnt offering with its grain and drink offerings.

29" 'On the sixth day offer eight bulls, two male sheep, and fourteen male lambs a year old. They must have nothing wrong with them. 30Bring the grain and drink offerings for the bulls, sheep, and lambs, according to the number required. 31Offer one male goat as a sin offering, in addition to the daily burnt offering with its grain and drink offerings.

32" 'On the seventh day offer seven bulls, two male sheep, and fourteen male lambs a year old. They must have nothing wrong with them. 33Bring the grain and drink offerings for the bulls, sheep, and lambs, according to the number required. 34Offer one male goat as a sin offering, in addition to the daily burnt offering with its grain and drink offerings.

35" 'On the eighth day have a closing meeting, and do not work on that day. 36Bring an offering made by fire, a burnt offering, as a smell pleasing to the LORD. Offer one bull, one male sheep, and seven male lambs a year old. They must have nothing wrong with them. 37Bring the grain and drink offerings for the bull, the male sheep, and the lambs, according to the number required. 38Offer one male goat as a sin offering, in addition to the daily burnt offering with its grain and drink offerings.

39" 'At your festivals you should bring these to the LORD: your burnt offerings, grain offerings, drink offerings and fellowship offerings. These are in addition to other promised offerings and special gifts you want to give to the LORD.' "

[40]Moses told the Israelites everything the LORD had commanded him.

RULES ABOUT SPECIAL PROMISES

30 [1]Moses spoke with the leaders of the Israelite tribes. He told them these commands from the LORD.

[2]"If a man makes a promise to the LORD or says he will do something special, he must keep his promise. He must do what he said. [3]If a young woman still living at home makes a promise to the LORD or pledges to do something special, [4]and if her father hears about the promise or pledge and says nothing, she must do what she promised. She must keep her pledge. [5]But if her father hears about the promise or pledge and does not allow it, then the promise or pledge does not have to be kept. Her father would not allow it, so the LORD will free her from her promise.

[6]"If a woman makes a pledge or a careless promise and then gets married, [7]and if her husband hears about it and says nothing, she must keep her promise or the pledge she made. [8]But if her husband hears about it and does not allow it, he cancels her pledge or the careless promise she made. The LORD will free her from keeping it.

[9]"If a widow or divorced woman makes a promise, she must do whatever she promised.

WHAT'S IT MEAN?

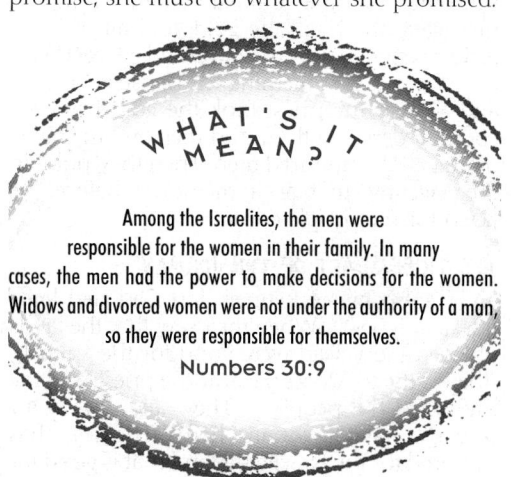

Among the Israelites, the men were responsible for the women in their family. In many cases, the men had the power to make decisions for the women. Widows and divorced women were not under the authority of a man, so they were responsible for themselves.

Numbers 30:9

[10]"If a woman makes a promise or pledge while she is married, [11]and if her husband hears about it but says nothing and does not stop her, she must keep her promise or pledge. [12]But if her husband hears about it and cancels it, she does not have to do what she said. Her husband has canceled it, so the LORD will free her from it. [13]A woman's husband may make her keep or cancel any promise or pledge she has made. [14]If he says nothing to her about it for several days, she must keep her promises. If he hears about them and says nothing, she must keep her promises. [15]But if he cancels them long after he heard about them, he is responsible if she breaks her promise."

[16]These are commands that the LORD gave to Moses for husbands and wives, and for fathers with daughters living at home.

ISRAEL ATTACKS THE MIDIANITES

31 [1]The LORD spoke to Moses and said, [2]"Pay back the Midianites for what they did to the Israelites; after that you will die."

[3]So Moses said to the people, "Get some men ready for war. The LORD will use them to pay back the Midianites. [4]Send to war a thousand men from each of the tribes of Israel." [5]So twelve thousand men got ready for war, a thousand men from each tribe. [6]Moses sent those men to war; Phinehas son of Eleazar the priest was with them. He took with him the holy things and the trumpets for giving the alarm. [7]They fought the Midianites as the LORD had commanded Moses, and they killed every Midianite man. [8]Among those they killed were Evi, Rekem, Zur, Hur, and Reba, who were the five kings of Midian. They also killed Balaam son of Beor with a sword.

[9]The Israelites captured the Midianite women and children, and they took all their flocks, herds, and goods. [10]They burned all the Midianite towns where they had settled and all their camps, [11]but they took all the people and animals and goods. [12]Then they brought the captives, the animals, and the goods back to Moses and Eleazar the priest and all the Israelites. Their camp was on the plains of Moab near the Jordan River, across from Jericho.

[13]Moses, Eleazar the priest, and all the leaders of the people went outside the camp to meet them. [14]Moses was angry with the army officers, the commanders over a thousand men, and those over a hundred men, who returned from war.

[15]He asked them, "Why did you let the women live? [16]They were the ones who followed Balaam's advice and turned the Israelites from the LORD at Peor. Then a terrible sickness struck the LORD's people. [17]Kill all the Midianite boys, and kill all the Midianite women who have had sexual relations. [18]But save for yourselves the girls who have not had sexual relations with a man.

[19]"All you men who killed anyone or

WHAT'S IT MEAN?

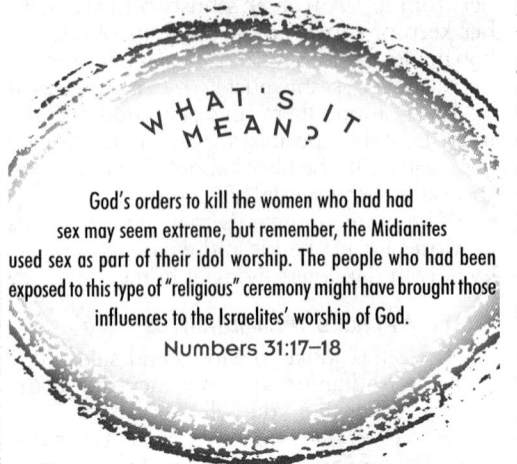

God's orders to kill the women who had had sex may seem extreme, but remember, the Midianites used sex as part of their idol worship. The people who had been exposed to this type of "religious" ceremony might have brought those influences to the Israelites' worship of God.

Numbers 31:17–18

touched a dead body must stay outside the
camp for seven days. On the third and seventh
days you and your captives must make yourselves clean. 20You must clean all your clothes
and anything made of leather, goat hair, or
wood."
21Then Eleazar the priest said to the soldiers
who had gone to war, "These are the teachings
that the LORD gave to Moses: 22Put any gold,
silver, bronze, iron, tin, or lead— 23anything
that will not burn—into the fire, and then it
will be clean. But also purify those things with
the cleansing water. Then they will be clean. If
something cannot stand the fire, wash it with
the water. 24On the seventh day wash your
clothes, and you will be clean. After that you
may come into the camp."

DIVIDING THE GOODS

25The LORD said to Moses, 26"You, Eleazar
the priest, and the leaders of the family groups
should take a count of the goods, the men, and
the animals that were taken. 27Then divide
those possessions between the soldiers who
went to war and the rest of the people. 28From
the soldiers who went to war, take a tax for the
LORD of one item out of every five hundred.
This includes people, cattle, donkeys, or sheep.
29Take it from the soldiers' half, and give it to
Eleazar the priest as the LORD's share. 30And
from the people's half, take one item out of
every fifty. This includes people, cattle, donkeys, sheep, or other animals. Give that to the
Levites, who take care of the LORD's Holy Tent."
31So Moses and Eleazar did as the LORD commanded Moses.
32There remained from what the soldiers
had taken 675,000 sheep, 3372,000 cattle, 3461,000
donkeys, 35and 32,000 women who had not
had sexual relations with a man. 36The soldiers
who went to war got 337,000 sheep, 37and they
gave 675 of them to the LORD. 38They got 36,000
cattle, and they gave 72 of them to the LORD.
39They got 30,500 donkeys, and they gave 61 of
them to the LORD. 40They got 16,000 people, and
they gave 32 of them to the LORD. 41Moses gave
the LORD's share to Eleazar the priest, as the
LORD had commanded him.
42Moses separated the people's half from
the soldiers' half. 43The people got 337,500
sheep, 4436,000 cattle, 4530,500 donkeys, 46and
16,000 people. 47From the people's half Moses
took one item out of every fifty for the LORD.
This included the animals and the people. Then
he gave them to the Levites, who took care of
the LORD's Holy Tent. This was what the LORD
had commanded Moses.
48Then the officers of the army, the commanders of a thousand men and commanders
of a hundred men, came to Moses. 49They told
Moses, "We, your servants, have counted our
soldiers under our command, and not one of
them is missing. 50So we have brought the
LORD a gift of the gold things that each of us
found: arm bands, bracelets, signet rings, earrings, and necklaces. These are to remove our
sins so we will belong to the LORD."
51So Moses and Eleazar the priest took the
gold from them, which had been made into all
kinds of objects. 52The commanders of a thousand men and the commanders of a hundred
men gave the LORD the gold, and all of it together weighed about 420 pounds; 53each soldier had taken something for himself. 54Moses
and Eleazar the priest took the gold from the
commanders of a thousand men and the commanders of a hundred men. Then they put it in
the Meeting Tent as a memorial before the
LORD for the people of Israel.

THE TRIBES EAST OF THE JORDAN

32

1The people of Reuben and Gad had large
flocks and herds. When they saw that the lands
of Jazer and Gilead were good for the animals,
2they came to Moses, Eleazar the priest, and the
leaders of the people. 3-4They said, "We, your
servants, have flocks and herds. The LORD has
captured for the Israelites a land that is good for
animals—the land around Ataroth, Dibon, Jazer, Nimrah, Heshbon, Elealeh, Sebam, Nebo,
and Beon. 5If it pleases you, we would like this
land to be given to us. Don't make us cross the
Jordan River."
6Moses told the people of Gad and Reuben,
"Shall your brothers go to war while you stay
behind? 7You will discourage the Israelites

from going over to the land the LORD has given them. [8]Your ancestors did the same thing. I sent them from Kadesh Barnea to look at the land. [9]They went as far as the Valley of Eshcol, and when they saw the land, they discouraged the Israelites from going into the land the LORD had given them. [10]The LORD became very angry that day and made this promise: [11]'None of the people who came from Egypt and who are twenty years old or older will see the land that I promised to Abraham, Isaac, and Jacob. These people have not followed me completely. [12]Only Caleb son of Jephunneh the Kenizzite and Joshua son of Nun followed the LORD completely.'

[13]"The LORD was angry with Israel, so he made them wander in the desert for forty years. Finally all the people who had sinned against the LORD died, [14]and now you are acting just like your ancestors! You sinful people are making the LORD even more angry with Israel. [15]If you quit following him, it will add to their stay in the desert, and you will destroy all these people."

[16]Then the Reubenites and Gadites came up to Moses and said, "We will build pens for our animals and cities for our children here. [17]Then our children will be in strong, walled cities, safe from the people who live in this land. Then we will prepare for war. We will help the other Israelites get their land, [18]and we will not return home until every Israelite has received his land. [19]We won't take any of the land west of the Jordan River; our part of the land is east of the Jordan."

[20]So Moses told them, "You must do these things. You must go before the LORD into battle [21]and cross the Jordan River armed, until the LORD forces out the enemy. [22]After the LORD helps us take the land, you may return home. You will have done your duty to the LORD and Israel, and you may have this land as your own.

[23]"But if you don't do these things, you will be sinning against the LORD; know for sure that you will be punished for your sin. [24]Build cities for your children and pens for your animals, but then you must do what you promised."

[25]The Gadites and Reubenites said to Moses, "We are your servants, and we will do what you, our master, command. [26]Our children, wives, and all our cattle will stay in the cities of Gilead, [27]but we, your servants, will prepare for battle. We will go over and fight for the LORD, as you, our master, have said."

[28]So Moses gave orders about them to Eleazar the priest, to Joshua son of Nun, and to the leaders of the tribes of Israel. [29]Moses said to them, "If the Gadites and Reubenites prepare for battle and cross the Jordan River with you, to go before the LORD and help you take the land, give them the land of Gilead for their own. [30]But if they do not go over armed, they will not receive it; their land will be in Canaan with you."

[31]The Gadites and Reubenites answered, "We are your servants, and we will do as the LORD said. [32]We will cross over into Canaan and go before the LORD ready for battle. But our land will be east of the Jordan River."

[33]So Moses gave that land to the tribes of Gad, Reuben, and East Manasseh. (Manasseh was Joseph's son.) That land had been the kingdom of Sihon, king of the Amorites, and the kingdom of Og, king of Bashan, as well as all the cities and the land around them.

[34]The Gadites rebuilt the cities of Dibon, Ataroth, Aroer, [35]Atroth Shophan, Jazer, Jogbehah, [36]Beth Nimrah, and Beth Haran. These were strong, walled cities. And they built sheep pens.

[37]The Reubenites rebuilt Heshbon, Elealeh, Kiriathaim, [38]Nebo, Baal Meon, and Sibmah. They renamed Nebo and Baal Meon when they rebuilt them.

[39]The descendants of Makir son of Manasseh went and captured Gilead and forced out the Amorites who were there. [40]So Moses gave Gilead to the family of Makir son of Manasseh, and they settled there. [41]Jair son of Manasseh went out and captured the small towns there, and he called them the Towns of Jair. [42]Nobah went and captured Kenath and the small towns around it; then he named it Nobah after himself.

ISRAEL'S JOURNEY FROM EGYPT

33 [1]These are the places the Israelites went as Moses and Aaron led them out of Egypt in divisions. [2]At the LORD's command Moses recorded the places they went, and these are the places they went.

[3]On the fifteenth day of the first month, the day after the Passover, the Israelites left Rameses and marched out boldly in front of all the Egyptians. [4]The Egyptians were burying their firstborn sons, whom the LORD had killed; the LORD showed that the gods of Egypt were false.

[5]The Israelites left Rameses and camped at Succoth.

[6]They left Succoth and camped at Etham, at the edge of the desert.

[7]They left Etham and went back to Pi Hahiroth, to the east of Baal Zephon, and camped near Migdol.

8 They left Pi Hahiroth and walked through
the sea into the desert. After going three days
through the Desert of Etham, they camped at
Marah.
9 They left Marah and went to Elim; there
were twelve springs of water and seventy palm
trees where they camped.
10 They left Elim and camped near the Red
Sea.
11 They left the Red Sea and camped in the
Desert of Sin.
12 They left the Desert of Sin and camped at
Dophkah.
13 They left Dophkah and camped at Alush.
14 They left Alush and camped at Rephidim,
where the people had no water to drink.
15 They left Rephidim and camped in the
Desert of Sinai.
16 They left the Desert of Sinai and camped
at Kibroth Hattaavah.
17 They left Kibroth Hattaavah and camped
at Hazeroth.
18 They left Hazeroth and camped at Rithmah.
19 They left Rithmah and camped at Rimmon Perez.
20 They left Rimmon Perez and camped at
Libnah.
21 They left Libnah and camped at Rissah.
22 They left Rissah and camped at Kehelathah.
23 They left Kehelathah and camped at
Mount Shepher.
24 They left Mount Shepher and camped at
Haradah.
25 They left Haradah and camped at Makheloth.
26 They left Makheloth and camped at Tahath.
27 They left Tahath and camped at Terah.
28 They left Terah and
camped at Mithcah.
29 They left Mithcah and
camped at Hashmonah.
30 They left Hashmo-
nah and camped at Mo-
seroth.
31 They left Moseroth
and camped at Bene Jaa-
kan.
32 They left Bene Jaakan
and camped at Hor Hag-
gidgad.
33 They left Hor Haggidgad and camped
at Jotbathah.
34 They left Jotbathah and camped at Abronah.
35 They left Abronah and camped at Ezion
Geber.
36 They left Ezion Geber and camped at Kadesh in the Desert of Zin.
37 They left Kadesh and camped at Mount
Hor, on the border of Edom. 38 Aaron the priest
obeyed the LORD and went up Mount Hor.
There he died on the first day of the fifth
month in the fortieth year after the Israelites
left Egypt. 39 Aaron was 123 years old when he
died on Mount Hor.
40 The Canaanite king of Arad, who lived in
the southern area of Canaan, heard that the
Israelites were coming.
41 The people left Mount Hor and camped at
Zalmonah.
42 They left Zalmonah and camped at Punon.
43 They left Punon and camped at Oboth.
44 They left Oboth and camped at Iye Abarim, on the border of Moab.
45 They left Iye Abarim and camped at Dibon Gad.
46 They left Dibon Gad and camped at Almon Diblathaim.
47 They left Almon Diblathaim and camped
in the mountains of Abarim, near Nebo.
48 They left the mountains of Abarim and
camped on the plains of Moab near the Jordan
River across from Jericho. 49 They camped
along the Jordan on the plains of Moab, and
their camp went from Beth Jeshimoth to Abel
Acacia.
50 On the plains of Moab by the Jordan
River across from Jericho, the LORD spoke to
Moses. He said, 51 "Speak to the Israelites and
tell them, 'When you cross the Jordan River
and go into Canaan, 52 force out all the people
who live there. Destroy all of their carved statues and metal idols. Wreck all of
their places of worship. 53 Take
over the land and settle
there, because I have given
this land to you to own.
54 Throw lots to divide up
the land by family groups,
giving larger portions to
larger family groups and
smaller portions to smaller family groups. The
land will be given as the
lots decide; each tribe will
get its own land.
55 " 'But if you don't force
those people out of the land, they will bring
you trouble. They will be like sharp hooks in
your eyes and thorns in your sides. They will

> **"Speak to the Israelites and tell them, 'When you cross the Jordan River and go into Canaan, force out all the people who live there.' " (Numbers 33:51–52a)**

bring trouble to the land where you live. 56Then I will punish you as I had planned to punish them.' "

THE BORDERS OF CANAAN

34 1The LORD said to Moses, 2"Give this command to the people of Israel: 'You will soon enter Canaan and it will be yours. These shall be the borders: 3On the south you will get part of the Desert of Zin near the border of Edom. On the east side your southern border will start at the south end of the Dead Sea, 4cross south of Scorpion Pass, and go through the Desert of Zin and south of Kadesh Barnea. Then it will go to Hazar Addar and over to Azmon. 5From Azmon it will go to the brook of Egypt, and it will end at the Mediterranean Sea.

6" 'Your western border will be the Mediterranean Sea.

7" 'Your northern border will begin at the Mediterranean Sea and go to Mount Hor. 8From Mount Hor it will go to Lebo Hamath, and on to Zedad. 9Then the border will go to Ziphron, and it will end at Hazar Enan. This will be your northern border.

10" 'Your eastern border will begin at Hazar Enan and go to Shepham. 11From Shepham the border will go east of Ain to Riblah and along the hills east of Lake Galilee. 12Then the border will go down along the Jordan River and end at the Dead Sea.

" 'These are the borders around your country.' "

13So Moses gave this command to the Israelites: "This is the land you will receive. Throw lots to divide it among the nine and one-half tribes, because the LORD commanded that it should be theirs. 14The tribes of Reuben, Gad, and East Manasseh have already received their land. 15These two and one-half tribes received land east of the Jordan River, across from Jericho."

16Then the LORD said to Moses, 17"These are the men who will divide the land: Eleazar the priest and Joshua son of Nun. 18Also take one leader from each tribe to help divide the land. 19These are the names of the leaders: from the tribe of Judah, Caleb son of Jephunneh; 20from the tribe of Simeon, Shemuel son of Ammihud; 21from the tribe of Benjamin, Elidad son of Kislon; 22from the tribe of Dan, Bukki son of Jogli; 23from the tribe of Manasseh son of Joseph, Hanniel son of Ephod; 24from the tribe of Ephraim son of Joseph, Kemuel son of Shiphtan; 25from the tribe of Zebulun, Elizaphan son of Parnach; 26from the tribe of Issachar, Paltiel son of Azzan; 27from the tribe of Asher, Ahihud son of Shelomi; 28from the tribe of Naphtali, Pedahel son of Ammihud."

29The LORD commanded these men to divide the land of Canaan among the Israelites.

THE LEVITES' TOWNS

35 1The LORD spoke to Moses on the plains of Moab across from Jericho by the Jordan River. He said, 2"Command the Israelites to give the Levites cities to live in from the land they receive. Also give the Levites the pastureland around these cities. 3Then the Levites will have cities where they may live and pastureland for their cattle, flocks, and other animals. 4The pastureland you give the Levites will extend fifteen hundred feet from the city wall. 5Also measure three thousand feet in each direction outside the city wall–three thousand feet east of the city, three thousand feet south of the city, three thousand feet west of the city, and three thousand feet north of the city, with the city in the center. This will be pastureland for the Levites' cities.

CITIES OF SAFETY

6"Six of the cities you give the Levites will be cities of safety. A person who accidentally kills someone may run to one of those cities for safety. You must also give forty-two other cities to the Levites; 7give the Levites a total of forty-eight cities and their pastures. 8The larger tribes of Israel must give more cities, and the smaller tribes must give fewer cities. Each tribe must give some of its cities to the Levites, but the number of cities they give will depend on the size of their land."

9Then the LORD said to Moses, 10"Tell the Israelites these things: 'When you cross the Jordan River and go into Canaan, 11you must choose cities to be cities of safety, so that a person who accidentally kills someone may run to them for safety. 12There the person will be safe from the dead person's relative who has the duty of punishing the killer. He will not die before he receives a fair trial in court. 13The six cities you give will be cities of safety. 14Give three cities east of the Jordan River and three cities in Canaan as cities of safety. 15These six cities will be places of safety for citizens of Israel, as well as for foreigners and other people living with you. Any of these people who accidentally kills someone may run to one of these cities.

16" 'Anyone who uses an iron weapon to kill someone is a murderer. He must be put to death. 17Anyone who takes a rock and kills a person with it is a murderer. He must be put to death. [18]Anyone who picks up a piece of wood and kills someone with it is a murderer. He must be put to death. [19]A relative of the dead person must put the murderer to death; when they meet, the relative must kill the murderer. [20]A person might shove someone or throw something at someone and cause death. [21]Or a person might hit someone with his hand and cause death. If it were done from hate, the person is a murderer and must be put to death. A relative of the dead person must kill the murderer when they meet.

[22]" 'But a person might suddenly shove someone, and not from hatred. Or a person might accidentally throw something and hit someone. [23]Or a person might drop a rock on someone he couldn't see and kill that person. There was no plan to hurt anyone and no hatred for the one who was killed. [24]If that happens, the community must judge between the relative of the dead person and the killer, according to these rules. [25]They must protect the killer from the dead person's relative, sending the killer back to the original city of safety, to stay there until the high priest dies (the high priest had the holy oil poured on him).

[26]" 'Such a person must never go outside the limits of the city of safety. [27]If a relative of the dead person finds the killer outside the city, the relative may kill that person and not be guilty of murder. [28]The killer must stay in the city of safety until the high priest dies. After the high priest dies, the killer may go home.

[29]" 'These laws are for you from now on, wherever you live.

> "These were the laws and commands that the LORD gave to the Israelites through Moses."
> (Numbers 36:13a)

[30]" 'If anyone kills a person, the murderer may be put to death only if there are witnesses. No one may be put to death with only one witness.

[31]" 'Don't take money to spare the life of a murderer who should be put to death. A murderer must be put to death.

[32]" 'If someone has run to a city of safety, don't take money to let the person go back home before the high priest dies.

[33]" 'Don't let murder spoil your land. The only way to remove the sin of killing an innocent person is for the murderer to be put to death. [34]I am the LORD, and I live among the Israelites. I live in that land with you, so do not spoil it with murder.' "

LAND FOR ZELOPHEHAD'S DAUGHTERS

36

[1]The leaders of Gilead's family group went to talk to Moses and the leaders of the families of Israel. (Gilead was the son of Makir, the son of Manasseh, the son of Joseph.) [2]They said, "The LORD commanded you, our master, to give the land to the Israelites by throwing lots, and the LORD commanded you to give the land of Zelophehad, our brother, to his daughters. [3]But if his daughters marry men from other tribes of Israel, then that land will leave our family, and the people of the other tribes will get that land. So we will lose some of our land. [4]When the time of Jubilee comes for the Israelites, their land will go to the tribes of the people they marry; their land will be taken away from us, the land we received from our fathers."

[5]Then Moses gave the Israelites this command from the LORD: "These men from the tribe of Joseph are right. [6]This is the LORD's command to Zelophehad's daughters: You may marry anyone you wish, as long as the person is from your own tribe. [7]In this way the Israelites' land will not pass from tribe to tribe, and each Israelite will keep the land in the tribe that belonged to his ancestors. [8]A woman who inherits her father's land may marry, but she must marry someone from her own tribe. In this way every Israelite will keep the land that belonged to his ancestors. [9]The land must not pass from tribe to tribe, and each Israelite tribe will keep the land it received from its ancestors."

[10]Zelophehad's daughters obeyed the LORD's command to Moses.

[11]So Zelophehad's daughters—Mahlah, Tirzah, Hoglah, Milcah, and Noah—married their cousins, their father's relatives. [12]Their husbands were from the tribe of Manasseh son of Joseph, so their land stayed in their father's family group and tribe.

[13]These were the laws and commands that the LORD gave to the Israelites through Moses on the plains of Moab by the Jordan River, across from Jericho.

deuteronomy

CONTENT You don't really understand Deuteronomy unless you understand that this book is really a dying man's last words. Let's recap. Moses had just led the Hebrews out of Egypt and then wandered around the desert for forty years, trying to get up the courage and the faith to cross the border.

By the time they finally get to the border, only three of the adults who had left Egypt survived. To make it worse, one of them was about to die—Moses.

So Moses did what any leader would do. He gathered all the people together, and he told them the story all over again. But he didn't just tell them the story, he told them why the story mattered and what they should do about it. It was his last chance, so he talked to them about *real stuff*, the *real-est*.

Imagine if your country had had the same president your whole life, and he was a great and wonderful leader. Imagine your leader said, "You go the rest of the way without me. But before you leave, let me tell you one last thing. . . ."

You'd listen to him, wouldn't you? Listen to Deuteronomy like that.

Outline

1:1—4:43 .... The First Message: Moses Reviews the Past
4:44—28:68 .... The Second Message: Moses Tells What the Lord Requires
29:1—30:20 .... The Third Message: Israel Must Keep Its Agreement with the Lord
31:1–14 .... Joshua Is Appointed Leader of Israel
31:15–29 .... Israel Will Reject the Lord
31:30—32:47 ...... The Song of Moses
32:48—33:29 ...... Moses Sees the Land and Blesses the People of Israel
34:1–12 .... The Death of Moses

Purpose Love is expressed in God's Word and in our response to God's Word.

Theme Obedience Brings Blessing; Disobedience Brings Cursing

Date of writing 1445–1440 B.C.

"Now, Israel, this is what the LORD your God wants you to do: Respect the LORD your God, and do what he has told you to do. Love him. Serve the LORD your God with your whole being, and obey the LORD's commands and laws that I am giving you today for your own good" (10:12–13).

Bible Talk

Biblical Welfare

There are a lot of directions in Deuteronomy about taking care of people who have less than you do. Sometimes those people were homeless. Sometimes they were poor. Every time they were less fortunate.

Deuteronomy doesn't let us off the hook by passing people's needs over to a church or an agency. Instead, Deuteronomy teaches us that if we pass someone in need we're responsible to at least help. Deuteronomy also has practical tips for helping people help themselves.

We think that's a modern lesson today—being a community. But it's not new. We just forgot that God had said it.

MOSES DIDN'T GO IN?

After all the effort Moses put into caring for the Hebrew people, he never got to set a foot into the land of Israel. Think about all he had done. He confronted the king of Egypt when it gave him the shivers. He wandered around for forty years with the worst grumblers he'd probably ever known. He faced God himself on several occasions. But, in the end, he only got to hike to the top of a mountain and look over the other side.

If you want the whole sad tale, check out Numbers 20:6–12 and Deuteronomy 32:48–52.

MOSES TALKS TO THE ISRAELITES

[1]This is the message Moses gave to all the people of Israel in the desert east of the Jordan River. They were in the desert area near Suph, between Paran and the towns of Tophel, Laban, Hazeroth, and Dizahab.

[2](The trip from Mount Sinai to Kadesh Barnea on the Mount Seir road takes eleven days.) [3]Forty years after the Israelites had left Egypt, on the first day of the eleventh month, Moses told the people of Israel everything the LORD had commanded him to tell them. [4]This was after the LORD had defeated Sihon and Og. Sihon was king of the Amorite people and lived in Heshbon. Og was king of Bashan and lived in Ashteroth and Edrei.

[5]Now the Israelites were east of the Jordan River in the land of Moab, and there Moses began to explain what God had commanded. He said:

> "See, I have given you this land, so go in and take it for yourselves. The LORD promised it to your ancestors—Abraham, Isaac, and Jacob and their descendants."
> (Deuteronomy 1:8)

[6]The LORD our God spoke to us at Mount Sinai and said, "You have stayed long enough at this mountain. [7]Get ready, and go to the mountain country of the Amorites, and to all the places around there—the Jordan Valley, the mountains, the western hills, the southern area, the seacoast, the land of Canaan, and Lebanon. Go as far as the great river, the Euphrates. [8]See, I have given you this land, so go in and take it for yourselves. The LORD promised it to your ancestors—Abraham, Isaac, and Jacob and their descendants."

MOSES APPOINTS LEADERS

[9]At that time I said, "I am not able to take care of you by myself. [10]The LORD your God has made you grow in number so that there are as many of you as there are stars in the sky. [11]I pray that the LORD, the God of your ancestors, will give you a thousand times more people and do all the wonderful things he promised. [12]But I cannot take care of your problems, your troubles, and your arguments by myself. [13]So choose some men from each tribe—wise men who have understanding and experience—and I will make them leaders over you."

[14]And you said, "That's a good thing to do."

[15]So I took the wise and experienced leaders of your tribes, and I made them your leaders. I appointed commanders over a thousand people, over a hundred people, over fifty people, and over ten people and made them officers over your tribes. [16]Then I told your leaders, "Listen to the arguments between your people. Judge fairly between two Israelites or between an Israelite and a foreigner. [17]When you judge, be fair to everyone; don't act as if one person is more important than another, and don't be afraid of anyone, because your decision comes from God. Bring the hard cases to me, and I will judge them." [18]At that time I told you everything you must do.

SPIES ENTER THE LAND

[19]Then, as the LORD our God commanded us, we left Mount Sinai and went toward the mountain country of the Amorite people. We went through that large and terrible desert you saw, and then we came to Kadesh Barnea. [20]I said to you, "You have now come to the mountain country of the Amorites, to the land the LORD our God will give us. [21]Look, here it is! Go up and take it. The LORD, the God of your ancestors, told you to do this, so don't be afraid and don't worry."

[22]Then all of you came to me and said, "Let's send men before us to spy out the land. They can come back and tell us about the way we should go and the cities we will find."

WHAT'S IT MEAN?

In most places in the ancient world, a foreigner had no legal rights. The land of the Israelites, however, was different. God's people were expected to treat foreigners just as they would treat each other. They were to show that God's law applied to everyone.

Deuteronomy 1:16

[23]I thought that was a good idea, so I chose twelve of your men, one for each tribe. [24]They left and went up to the mountains, and when they came to the Valley of Eshcol they explored it. [25]They took some of the fruit from

that land and brought it down to us, saying, "It is a good land that the LORD our God is giving us."

ISRAEL REFUSES TO ENTER

[26]But you refused to go. You would not obey the command of the LORD your God, [27]but grumbled in your tents, saying, "The LORD hates us. He brought us out of Egypt just to give us to the Amorites, who will destroy us. [28]Where can we go now? The spies we sent have made us afraid, because they said, 'The people there are stronger and taller than we are. The cities are big, with walls up to the sky. And we saw the Anakites there!' "

[29]Then I said to you, "Don't be frightened; don't be afraid of those people. [30]The LORD your God will go ahead of you and fight for you as he did in Egypt; you saw him do it. [31]And in the desert you saw how the LORD your God carried you, like one carries a child. And he has brought you safely all the way to this place."

[32]But you still did not trust the LORD your God, even though [33]he had always gone before you to find places for you to camp. In a fire at night and in a cloud during the day, he showed you which way to go.

[34]When the LORD heard what you said, he was angry and made an oath, saying, [35]"I promised a good land to your ancestors, but none of you evil people will see it. [36]Only Caleb son of Jephunneh will see it. I will give him and his descendants the land he walked on, because he followed the LORD completely."

[37]Because of you, the LORD was also angry with me and said, "You won't enter the land either, [38]but your assistant, Joshua son of Nun, will enter it. Encourage him, because he will lead Israel to take the land for their own.

[39]"Your little children that you said would be captured, who do not know right from wrong at this time, will go into the land. I will give the land to them, and they will take it for their own. [40]But you must turn around and follow the desert road toward the Red Sea."

[41]Then you said to me, "We have sinned against the LORD, but now we will go up and fight, as the LORD our God commanded us." Then all of you put on weapons, thinking it would be easy to go into the mountains.

[42]But the LORD said to me, "Tell the people, 'You must not go up there and fight. I will not be with you, and your enemies will defeat you.' "

[43]So I told you, but you would not listen. You would not obey the LORD's command. You were proud, so you went on up into the mountains, [44]and the Amorites who lived in those mountains came out and fought you. They chased you like bees and defeated you from Edom to Hormah. [45]So you came back and cried before the LORD, but the LORD did not listen to you; he refused to pay attention to you. [46]So you stayed in Kadesh a long time.

ISRAEL WANDERS IN THE DESERT

2 [1]Then we turned around, and we traveled on the desert road toward the Red Sea, as the LORD had told me to do. We traveled through the mountains of Edom for many days.

[2]Then the LORD said to me, [3]"You have traveled through these mountains long enough. Turn north [4]and give the people this command: 'You will soon go through the land that belongs to your relatives, the descendants of Esau who live in Edom. They will be afraid of you, but be very careful. [5]Do not go to war against them. I will not give you any of their land—not even a foot of it, because I have given the mountains of Edom to Esau as his own. [6]You must pay them in silver for any food you eat or water you drink.' "

[7]The LORD your God has blessed everything you have done; he has protected you while you traveled through this great desert. The LORD your God has been with you for the past forty years, and you have had everything you needed.

[8]So we passed by our relatives, the descendants of Esau who lived in Edom. We turned off the Jordan Valley road that comes from the towns of Elath and Ezion Geber and traveled along the desert road to Moab.

THE LAND OF AR

[9]Then the LORD said to me, "Don't bother the people of Moab. Don't go to war against them, because I will not give you any of their land as your own; I have given Ar to the descendants of Lot as their own." [10](The Emites, who lived in Ar before, were strong people, and there were many of them. They were very tall, like the Anakites. [11]The Emites were thought to be Rephaites, like the Anakites, but the Moabite people called them Emites. [12]The Horites also lived in Edom before, but the descendants of Esau forced them out and destroyed them, taking their place as Israel did in the land the LORD gave them as their own.)

[13]And the LORD said to me, "Now get up and cross the Zered Valley." So we crossed the valley. [14]It had been thirty-eight years from the

time we left Kadesh Barnea until we crossed the Zered Valley. By then, all the fighting men from that time had died, as the LORD had promised would happen. 15The LORD continued to work against them to remove them from the camp until they were all dead.

16When the last of those fighting men had died, 17the LORD said to me, 18"Today you will pass by Ar, on the border of Moab. 19When you come near the people of Ammon, don't bother them or go to war against them, because I will not give you any of their land as your own. I have given it to the descendants of Lot for their own."

20(That land was also thought to be a land of the Rephaites, because those people used to live there, but the Ammonites called them Zamzummites. 21They were strong people, and there were many of them; they were very tall, like the Anakites. The LORD destroyed the Zamzummites, and the Ammonites forced them out of the land and took their place. 22The LORD did the same thing for the descendants of Esau, who lived in Edom, when he destroyed the Horites. The Edomites forced them out of the land and took their place, and they live there to this day. 23The Cretan people came from Crete and destroyed the Avvites, who lived in towns all the way to Gaza; the Cretans destroyed them and took their place.)

FIGHTING THE AMORITES

24The LORD said, "Get up and cross the Arnon Ravine. See, I am giving you the power to defeat Sihon the Amorite, king of Heshbon, and I am giving you his land. So fight against him and begin taking his land. 25Today I will begin to make all the people in the world afraid of you. When they hear reports about you, they will shake with fear, and they will be terrified of you."

26I sent messengers from the desert of Kedemoth to Sihon king of Heshbon. They offered him peace, saying, 27"If you let us pass through your country, we will stay on the road and not turn right or left. 28We will pay you in silver for any food we eat or water we drink. We only want to walk through your country. 29The descendants of Esau in Edom let us go through their land, and so did the Moabites in Ar. We want to cross the Jordan River into the land the LORD our God has given us." 30But Sihon king of Heshbon would not let us pass, because the LORD your God had made him stubborn. The LORD wanted you to defeat Sihon, and now this has happened.

31The LORD said to me, "See, I have begun to give Sihon and his country to you. Begin taking the land as your own."

32Then Sihon and all his army came out and fought us at Jahaz, 33but the LORD our God gave Sihon to us. We defeated him, his sons, and all his army. 34We captured all his cities at that time and completely destroyed them, as well as the men, women, and children. We left no one alive. 35But we kept the cattle and valuable things from the cities for ourselves. 36We defeated Aroer on the edge of the Arnon Ravine, and we defeated the town in the ravine, and even as far as Gilead. No town was too strong for us; the LORD our God gave us all of them. 37But you did not go near the land of the Ammonites, on the shores of the Jabbok River, or the towns in the mountains, as the LORD our God had commanded.

THE BATTLE AT BASHAN

3 1When we turned and went up the road toward Bashan, Og king of Bashan and all his army came out to fight us at Edrei. 2The LORD said to me, "Don't be afraid of Og, because I will hand him, his whole army, and his land over to you. Do to him what you did to Sihon king of the Amorites, who ruled in Heshbon."

3So the LORD our God gave us Og king of Bashan and all his army; we defeated them and left no one alive. 4Then we captured all of Og's cities, all sixty of them, and took the whole area of Argob, Og's kingdom in Bashan. 5All these were strong cities, with high walls and gates with bars. And there were also many small towns with no walls. 6We completely destroyed them, just like the cities of Sihon king of Heshbon. We killed all the men, women, and children, 7but we kept all the cattle and valuable things from the cities for ourselves.

8So at that time we took the land east of the Jordan River, from the Arnon Ravine to Mount

WHAT'S IT MEAN?

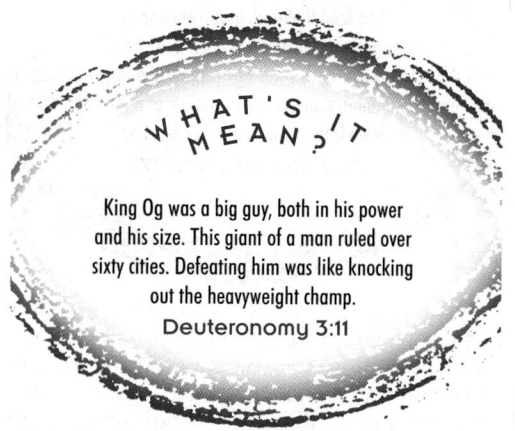

King Og was a big guy, both in his power and his size. This giant of a man ruled over sixty cities. Defeating him was like knocking out the heavyweight champ.

Deuteronomy 3:11

Hermon, from these two Amorite kings. [9](Hermon is called Sirion by the Sidonian people,
but the Amorites call it Senir.) [10]We captured all
the cities on the high plain and all of Gilead,
and we took all of Bashan as far as Salecah and
Edrei, towns in Og's kingdom of Bashan.
[11](Only Og king of Bashan was left of the few
Rephaites. His bed was made of iron, and it
was more than thirteen feet long and six feet
wide! It is still in the Ammonite city of Rabbah.)

THE LAND IS DIVIDED

[12]At that time we took this land to be our
own. I gave the people of Reuben and Gad the
land from Aroer by the Arnon Ravine, as well
as half of the mountain country of Gilead and
the cities in it. [13]To the people of East Manasseh I gave the rest of Gilead and all of Bashan,
the kingdom of Og. (The area of Argob in Bashan was called the land of the Rephaites.
[14]Jair, a descendant of Manasseh, took the
whole area of Argob, all the way to the border
of the Geshurites and Maacathites. So that land
was named for Jair, and even today Bashan is
called the Towns of Jair.) [15]I gave Gilead to Makir. [16]I gave the Reubenites and the Gadites the
land that begins at Gilead and goes from the
Arnon Ravine (the middle of the Arnon is
the border) to the Jabbok River, which is the
Ammonite border. [17]The border on the west
was the Jordan River in the Jordan Valley, and it
goes from Lake Galilee to the Dead Sea west of
Mount Pisgah.

WHAT'S IT MEAN?

The land that each group of people, or tribe, received was supposed to be held by that tribe for always. Each tribe was responsible for protecting its territory, maintaining control over its region, and passing the land down from generation to generation.

Deuteronomy 3:12–17

[18]At that time I gave you this command:
"The LORD your God has given you this land as
your own. Now your fighting men must take
their weapons, and you must lead the other
Israelites across the river. [19]Your wives, your
young children, and your cattle may stay here.
I know you have many cattle, and they may
stay here in the cities I have given you, [20]until
the LORD also gives your Israelite relatives a
place to rest. They will receive the land the
LORD your God has given them on the other
side of the Jordan River. After that, you may
each return to the land I have given you."

[21]Then I gave this command to Joshua: "You
have seen for yourself all that the LORD your
God has done to these two kings. The LORD
will do the same thing to all the kingdoms
where you are going. [22]Don't be afraid of them,
because the LORD your God will fight for you."

MOSES CANNOT ENTER THE LAND

[23]Then I begged the LORD: [24]"Lord GOD, you
have begun to show me, your servant, how
great you are. You have great strength, and no
other god in heaven or on earth can do the
powerful things you do. There is no other god
like you. [25]Please let me cross the Jordan River
so that I may see the good land by the Jordan.
I want to see the beautiful mountains and Lebanon."

[26]But the LORD was angry with me because
of you, and he would not listen to me. The
LORD said to me, "That's enough. Don't talk to
me anymore about it. [27]Climb to the top of
Mount Pisgah and look west, north, south, and
east. You can look at the land, but you will not
cross the Jordan River. [28]Appoint Joshua and
help him be brave and strong. He will lead the
people across the river and give them the land
that they are to inherit, but you can only look
at it." [29]So we stayed in the valley opposite Beth
Peor.

MOSES TELLS ISRAEL TO OBEY

4 [1]Now, Israel, listen to the laws and commands I will teach you. Obey them so that you
will live and so that you will go over and take
the land the LORD, the God of
your ancestors, is giving to
you. [2]Don't add to these
commands, and don't leave
anything out, but obey the
commands of the LORD your
God that I give you.

REPUTATION
How is a good reputation built? (4:1–14)

[3]You have seen for yourselves
what the LORD did at Baal Peor, how the LORD
your God destroyed everyone among you who
followed Baal in Peor. [4]But all of you who continued following the LORD your God are still
alive today.

[5]Look, I have taught you the laws and rules
the LORD my God commanded me. Now you

WHAT'S IT MEAN?

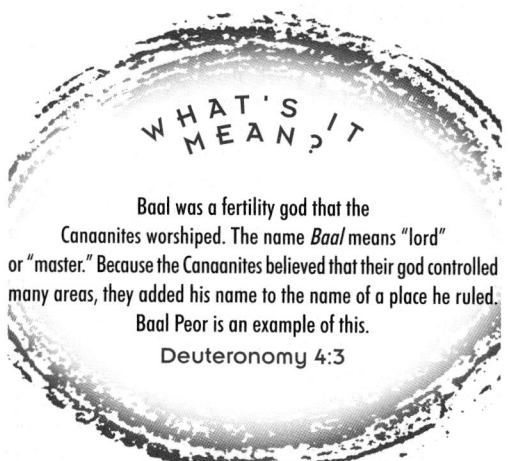

Baal was a fertility god that the Canaanites worshiped. The name *Baal* means "lord" or "master." Because the Canaanites believed that their god controlled many areas, they added his name to the name of a place he ruled. Baal Peor is an example of this.

Deuteronomy 4:3

can obey the laws in the land you are entering,
in the land you will take. [6]Obey these laws
carefully, in order to show the other nations
that you have wisdom and understanding.
When they hear about these laws, they will
say, "This great nation of Israel is wise and understanding." [7]No other nation is as great as we
are. Their gods do not come near them, but the
LORD our God comes near when we pray to
him. [8]And no other nation has such good
teachings and commands as those I am giving
to you today.
[9]But be careful! Watch out and don't forget
the things you have seen. Don't forget them as
long as you live, but teach them to your children and grandchildren. [10]Re-
member the day you stood
before the LORD your God
at Mount Sinai. He said
to me, "Bring the people
together so I can tell
them what I have to say.
Then they will respect
me as long as they live
in the land, and they
will teach these things to
their children." [11]When
you came and stood at the
bottom of the mountain, it
blazed with fire that reached to the sky,
and black clouds made it very dark. [12]The
LORD spoke to you from the fire. You heard the
sound of words, but you did not see him; there
was only a voice. [13]The LORD told you about
his Agreement, the Ten Commandments. He
told you to obey them, and he wrote them on
two stone tablets. [14]Then the LORD commanded me to teach you the laws and rules that you
must obey in the land you will take when you
cross the Jordan River.

"But be careful! Watch out and don't forget the things you have seen. Don't forget them as long as you live, but teach them to your children and grandchildren." (Deuteronomy 4:9)

LAWS ABOUT IDOLS

[15]Since the LORD spoke to you from the fire
at Mount Sinai, but you did not see him, watch
yourselves carefully! [16]Don't sin by making
idols of any kind, and don't make statues—of
men or women, [17]of animals on earth or birds
that fly in the air, [18]of anything that crawls on
the ground, or of fish in the water below.

WHAT'S IT MEAN?

Idol worship was very popular in ancient times. The Egyptians, Greeks, and Babylonians all had false gods of one kind or another. To give people something to look at when they worshiped, craftsmen often created idols to represent their gods. Most idols were given the form of a bird or animal. In a weird turn of events, then, people started worshiping the idols themselves, rather than the gods they represented. The Lord knew that if the Israelites started making and worshiping idols, they would stop worshiping him.

Deuteronomy 4:16–18

[19]When you look up at the sky, you see the
sun, moon, and stars, and everything in the
sky. But don't bow down and
worship them, because the
LORD your God has
made these things for all
people everywhere. [20]But
the LORD brought you
out of Egypt, which test-
ed you like a furnace for
melting iron, and he
made you his very own
people, as you are now.
[21]The LORD was an-
gry with me because of
you, and he swore that I
would not cross the
Jordan River to go into the
good land the LORD your
God is giving you as your
own. [22]I will die here in this
land and not cross the Jordan,
but you will soon go across
and take that good land.
[23]Be careful. Don't forget the

IDOLATRY
Is it okay to be more devoted to something than we are to God? (4:23)

Agreement of the LORD your God that he made with you, and don't make any idols for yourselves, as the LORD your God has commanded you not to
do. 24The LORD your God is a jealous God, like a fire that burns things up.

JEALOUSY Does God want to share our devotion? (4:24)

25Even after you have lived in the land a long time and have had children and grandchildren, don't do evil things. Don't make any kind of idol, and don't do what the LORD your God says is evil,
because that will make him angry. 26If you do, I
ask heaven and earth to speak against you this day that you will quickly be removed from this land that you are crossing the Jordan River to take. You will not live there long after that, but
you will be completely destroyed. 27The LORD
will scatter you among the other nations. Only a few of you will be left alive, and those few will be in other nations where the LORD will send
you. 28There you will worship gods made by people, gods made of wood and stone, that
cannot see, hear, eat, or smell. 29But even there you can look for the LORD your God, and you will find him if you look for him with your
whole being. 30It will be hard when all these things happen to you. But after that you will come back to the LORD your God and obey
him, 31because the LORD your God is a merciful God. He will not leave you or destroy you. He will not forget the Agreement with your ancestors, which he swore to them.

THE LORD IS GREAT

32Nothing like this has ever happened before! Look at the past, long before you were even born. Go all the way back to when God made humans on the earth, and look from one end of heaven to the other. Nothing like this
has ever been heard of! 33No other people have ever heard God speak from a fire and have still
lived. But you have. 34No other god has ever taken for himself one nation out of another. But the LORD your God did this for you in Egypt, right before your own eyes. He did it with tests, signs, miracles, war, and great sights, by his great power and strength.
35He showed you things so you would know that the LORD is God, and there is no
other God besides him. 36He spoke to you from heaven to teach you. He showed you his great fire on earth, and you heard him speak
from the fire. 37Because the LORD loved your ancestors, he chose you, their descendants, and he brought you out of Egypt himself by his
great strength. 38He forced nations out of their land ahead of you, nations that were bigger and stronger than you were. The LORD did this so he could bring you into their land and give it to you as your own, and this land is yours today.
39Know and believe today that the LORD is God. He is God in heaven above and on the
earth below. There is no other god! 40Obey his laws and commands that I am giving you today so that things will go well for you and

Promise

HE PROMISES TO REMEMBER HIS AGREEMENT.

The LORD your God is a merciful God. He will not leave you or destroy you. He will not forget the Agreement with your ancestors, which he swore to them (Deut. 4:31).

You promise to meet your friend for breakfast a week from Saturday. A family emergency takes you out of town until late Friday night. You remember that you've got a breakfast date, but will your friend remember? You decide to chance it and show up. Pulling into the restaurant parking lot, you see her. She remembered. Wow. No phone calls to say, "We're still on." You were so important to her that she couldn't forget. It made you feel special that she remembered this time with you.

You're even more important to God. Trust him when he promises to remember his promises. He won't lose his calendar or forget your phone number. He will never stand you up. It's a promise.

SEE FOR YOURSELF:
Josh. 23:15–16; 2 Sam. 23:5; 1 Kin. 8:56; Neh. 1:5

your children. Then you will live a long time in
the land that the LORD your God is giving to
you forever.

CITIES OF SAFETY

[41]Moses chose three cities east of the Jordan
River, [42]where a person who accidentally killed
someone could go. If the person was not killed
because of hatred, the murderer's life could be
saved by running to one of these cities. [43]These
were the cities: Bezer in the desert high plain
was for the Reubenites; Ramoth in Gilead was
for the Gadites; and Golan in Bashan was for
the Manassites.

THE LAWS MOSES GAVE

[44]These are the teachings Moses gave to the
people of Israel. [45]They are the rules, commands, and laws he gave them when they
came out of Egypt. [46]They were in the valley
near Beth Peor, east of the Jordan River, in the
land of Sihon. Sihon king of the Amorites ruled
in Heshbon and was defeated by Moses and
the Israelites as they came out of Egypt. [47]The
Israelites took his land and the land of Og king
of Bashan, the two Amorite kings east of the
Jordan River. [48]This land went from Aroer, on
the edge of the Arnon Ravine, to Mount Hermon. [49]It included all the Jordan Valley east of
the Jordan River, and it went as far as the Dead
Sea below Mount Pisgah.

THE TEN COMMANDMENTS

5 [1]Moses called all the people of Israel together and said: Listen, Israel, to the commands
and laws I am giving you today. Learn them
and obey them carefully. [2]The LORD our God
made an Agreement with us at Mount Sinai.

WHAT'S IT MEAN?

The Agreement between God and his people was very similar to a treaty between two political leaders. In ancient times, a leader seeking a treaty would identify himself, describe some of the things he had done, then present a list of regulations to be followed. After a treaty had been established, the two leaders would agree on how it would be written down and where copies of it would be kept.

Deuteronomy 5:2

Promise

HE PROMISES TO BE JEALOUS FOR YOU.

You must not worship or serve any idol, because I, the LORD your God, am a jealous God. If people sin against me and hate me, I will punish their children, even their grandchildren and great-grandchildren (Deut. 5:9).

God is a jealous God—that's the bottom line. He wants to be number one in your life above everything: your boyfriend/girlfriend, your job, your family, TV, music, your friends—the list goes on.

There's nothing wrong with having things, but *don't allow things to have you!* You may not bow down and worship a physical idol you've constructed in your bedroom, but once you've placed someone or something above God, that person, place, or thing becomes an article of worship—an idol. Be careful. That idol will eventually let you down. Nothing can fill the place of God in your life.

Remember the story of Abraham and how he put God first in his life. God was so important to him that he was willing to kill Isaac and sacrifice him to the Lord. God has that kind of love for you. You're that important to him.

Where is God on your priority list? Check your heart and make him first in your life today. He wants to be close to you. In fact, he created you to have fellowship with him. And his Word says that if you seek him first, he'll bless you. Be blessed today!

SEE FOR YOURSELF:

Gen. 22:1–18; Deut. 4:24; Josh. 24:19–20; Matt. 6:33; Mark 12:30

3He did not make this Agreement with our ancestors, but he made it with us, with all of us who are alive here today. 4The LORD spoke to you face to face from the fire on the mountain. 5(At that time I stood between you and the LORD in order to tell you what the LORD said; you were afraid of the fire, so you would not go up on the mountain.) The LORD said:

6"I am the LORD your God; I brought you out of the land of Egypt where you were slaves.

7"You must not have any other gods except me.

8"You must not make for yourselves any idols or anything to worship that looks like something in the sky above or on the earth below or in the water below the land. 9You must not worship or serve any idol, because I, the LORD your God, am a jealous God. If people sin against me and hate me, I will punish their children, even their grandchildren and great-grandchildren. 10But I will be very kind for a thousand lifetimes to those who love me and obey my commands.

11"You must not use the name of the LORD your God thoughtlessly, because the LORD will punish anyone who uses his name in this way.

12"Keep the Sabbath as a holy day, as the LORD your God has commanded you. 13You may work and get everything done during six days each week, 14but the seventh day is a day of rest to honor the LORD your God. On that day no one may do any work: not you, your son or daughter, your male or female slaves, your ox, your donkey, or any of your animals, or the foreigners living in your cities. That way your servants may rest as you do. 15Remember that you were slaves in Egypt and that the LORD your God brought you out of there by his great power and strength. So the LORD your God has commanded you to rest on the Sabbath day.

16"Honor your father and your mother as the LORD your God has commanded you. Then you will live a long time, and things will go well for you in the land that the LORD your God is going to give you.

MURDER

Does God allow murder? (5:17)

17"You must not murder anyone.

18"You must not be guilty of adultery.

19"You must not steal.

20"You must not tell lies about your neighbor.

21"You must not want to take your neighbor's wife. You must not want to take your neighbor's house or land, his male or female slaves, his ox or his donkey, or anything that belongs to your neighbor."

22The LORD spoke these commands to all of you on the mountain in a loud voice out of the fire, the cloud, and the deep darkness; he did not say anything else. Then he wrote them on two stone tablets, and he gave them to me.

23When you heard the voice from the darkness, as the mountain was blazing with fire, all your older leaders and leaders of your tribes came to me. 24And you said, "The LORD our God has shown us his glory and majesty, and we have heard his voice from the fire. Today we have seen that a person can live even if God speaks to him. 25But now, we will die! This great fire will burn us up, and we will die if we hear the LORD our God speak anymore. 26No human being has ever heard the living God speaking from a fire and still lived, but we have. 27Moses, you go near and listen to everything the LORD our God says. Then you tell us what the LORD our God tells you, and we will listen and obey."

28The LORD heard what you said to me, and he said to me, "I have heard what the people said to you. Everything they said was good. 29I wish their hearts would always respect me and that they would always obey my commands so that things would go well for them and their children forever!

FUTURE

How can our future be blessed? (5:29)

30"Go and tell the people to return to their tents, 31but you stay here with me so that I may give you all the commands, rules, and laws that you must teach the people to obey in the land I am giving them as their own."

32So be careful to do what the LORD your God has commanded you, and follow the commands exactly. 33Live the way the LORD your God has commanded you so that you may live and have what is good and have a long life in the land you will take.

THE COMMAND TO LOVE GOD

6 1These are the commands, rules, and laws that the LORD your God told me to teach you to obey in the land you are crossing the Jordan River to take. 2You, your children, and your grandchildren must respect the LORD your God as long as you live. Obey all his rules and commands I give you so that you will live a long time. 3Listen, Israel, and carefully obey these laws. Then all

EDUCATION

Who is responsible for teaching children? (6:1–9)

will go well for you, and you will become a
great nation in a fertile land, just as the LORD,
the God of your ancestors, has
promised you.
4Listen, people of Israel!
The LORD our
God is the
only LORD.
5Love the
LORD your God with all
your heart, all your soul,
and all your strength.
6Always remember these
commands I give you to-
day. 7Teach them to your
children, and talk about
them when you sit at home
and walk along the
road, when you
lie down and when you
get up. 8Write them down and
tie them to your hands as a
sign. Tie them on your forehead to remind you, 9and
write them on your doors and
gates.
10The LORD your God will bring you into
the land he promised to your ancestors, to
Abraham, Isaac, and Jacob, and he will give it
to you. The land has large, growing cities you
did not build, 11houses full of good things you
did not buy, wells you did not dig, and vineyards and olive trees you did not plant. You
will eat as much as you want.
12But be careful! Do not forget
the LORD, who brought
you out of the land of
Egypt where you were
slaves.
13Respect the LORD
your God. You must wor-
ship him and make your
promises only in his
name. 14Do not worship
other gods as the people
around you do, 15because
the LORD your God is a jealous
God. He is present with you, and
if you worship other gods, he will become angry with you and destroy you from the earth.
16Do not test the LORD your God as you did at
Massah. 17Be sure to obey the commands of
the LORD your God and the rules and laws he
has given you. 18Do what the LORD says is
good and right so that things will go well for
you. Then you may go in and take the good

GOD
Is God the only Lord? (6:4)

FAMILY
What can the members of a family do for each other? (6:4–9)

"Listen, people of Israel! The LORD our God is the only LORD. Love the LORD your God with all your heart, all your soul, and all your strength." (Deuteronomy 6:4–5)

Promise

HE PROMISES TO PUNISH THOSE WHO WORSHIP FALSE GODS.

Do not worship other gods as the people around you do, because the LORD your God is a jealous God. He is present with you, and if you worship other gods, he will become angry with you and destroy you from the earth (Deut. 6:14–15).

There are a lot of other religions out there and a lot of people who worship other gods, but you worship the only true God! You serve the Great I Am. You have something that isn't a fairy tale, that isn't phony, that isn't fake. You have the truth that will cause blinders to fall from the eyes of those who don't know God.

Why are so many people wrapped up in false religions and worshiping false gods? Because they want to live for a cause. They are searching for power. Because you are living for Jesus, you have the same power living in you that raised him from the dead (see Rom. 8:11). Now that's power! That's someone and something to live for! Don't settle for boring religion with a bunch of rules and regulations. You can have a radical relationship with Christ! You want to do the right thing because of your relationship with him. It's a relationship that brings freedom, a relationship that brings life, a relationship that brings power, and a relationship that brings every other good thing. Only Jesus will give you what you're looking for.

Embrace the true Christianity you have. You'll have everything you need, and you'll escape the punishment of those who worship false gods.

SEE FOR YOURSELF:

Ex. 3:14; Ezek. 23:49; Matt. 5:16; Rom. 1:19

land the LORD promised to your ancestors.
19He will force all your enemies out as you go
in, as the LORD has said.
20In the future when your children ask you,
"What is the meaning of the laws, commands,
and rules the LORD our God gave us?" 21tell
them, "We were slaves to the king of Egypt, but
the LORD brought us out of Egypt by his great
power. 22The LORD showed us great and terrible signs and miracles, which he did to Egypt,
the king, and his whole family. 23The LORD
brought us out of Egypt to lead us here and to
give us the land he promised our ancestors.
24The LORD ordered us to obey all these commands and to respect the LORD our God so
that we will always do well and stay alive, as
we are today. 25The right thing for us to do is
this: Obey all these rules in the presence of the
LORD our God, as he has commanded."

YOU ARE GOD'S PEOPLE

7 1The LORD your God will bring you into the
land that you are entering and that you will
have as your own. As you go in, he will force
out these nations: the Hittites, Girgashites, Amorites, Canaanites, Perizzites, Hivites, and Jebusites—seven nations that are stronger than
you. 2The LORD your God will hand these nations over to you, and when you defeat them,
you must destroy them completely. Do not
make a peace treaty with them or show them
any mercy. 3Do not marry any of them, or let
your daughters marry their sons, or let your
sons marry their daughters. 4If you do, those
people will turn your children away from me,
to begin serving other gods. Then the LORD will
be very angry with you, and he will quickly
destroy you. 5This is what you must do to
those people: Tear down their altars, smash
their holy stone pillars, cut down their Asherah idols, and burn their idols in the fire. 6You
are holy people who belong to the LORD your
God. He has chosen you from all the people on
earth to be his very own.
7The LORD did not care for you and choose
you because there were many of you—you are
the smallest nation of all. 8But the LORD chose
you because he loved you, and he kept
his promise to your ancestors. So
he brought you out of Egypt
by his great power and freed
you from the land of slavery,
from the power of the king of
Egypt. 9So know that the LORD
your God is God, the faithful
God. He will keep his agreement of love for a
thousand lifetimes for people who love him

CARING
Who does God care for? (7:9)

and obey his commands. 10But he will pay
back those people who hate him. He will destroy them, and he will not be
slow to pay back those who
hate him. 11So be careful to
obey the commands, rules,
and laws I give you today.
12If you pay attention to
these laws and obey them
carefully, the LORD your God will
keep his agreement and show his love to you,
as he promised your ancestors.
13He will love and bless you.
He will make the number of
your people grow; he will
bless you with children. He
will bless your fields with
good crops and will give you
grain, new wine, and oil. He will
bless your herds with calves and your flocks
with lambs in the land he promised your ancestors he would give you. 14You will be
blessed more than any other people. Every
husband and wife will have children, and all
your cattle will have calves. 15The LORD will
take away all disease from you; you will not
have the terrible diseases that were in Egypt,
but he will give them to all the people who
hate you. 16You must destroy all the people the
LORD your God hands over to you. Do not feel
sorry for them, and do not worship their gods,
or they will trap you.

GOD
Is God trustworthy? (7:9)

PAIN
Does God care for his people? (7:9)

WHAT'S IT MEAN?

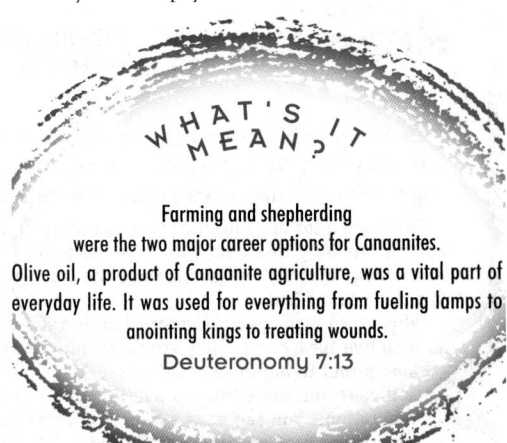

Farming and shepherding were the two major career options for Canaanites. Olive oil, a product of Canaanite agriculture, was a vital part of everyday life. It was used for everything from fueling lamps to anointing kings to treating wounds.
Deuteronomy 7:13

17You might say to yourselves, "Because
these nations are stronger than we are, we can't
force them out." 18But don't be afraid of them.
Remember what the LORD your God did to all
of Egypt and its king. 19You saw for yourselves
the troubles, signs, and miracles he did, how the
LORD's great power and strength brought you

out of Egypt. The LORD your God will do the
same thing to all the nations you now fear.
[20]The LORD your God will also send terror
among them so that even those who are alive
and hiding from you will die. [21]Don't be afraid
of them, because the LORD your God is with
you; he is a great God and people are afraid of
him. [22]When the LORD your God forces those
nations out of the land, he will do it little by
little ahead of you. You won't be able to destroy
them all at once; otherwise, the wild animals
will grow too many in number. [23]But the LORD
your God will hand those nations over to you,
confusing them until they are destroyed. [24]The
LORD will help you defeat their kings, and the
world will forget who they were. No one will be
able to stop you; you will destroy them all.
[25]Burn up their idols in the fire. Do not wish for
the silver and gold they have, and don't take it
for yourselves, or you will be trapped by it. The
LORD your God hates it. [26]Do not bring one of
those hateful things into your house, or you
will be completely destroyed along with it. Hate
and reject those things; they must be completely destroyed.

REMEMBER THE LORD

8 [1]Carefully obey every command I give you
today. Then you will live and grow in number,
and you will enter and take the land the LORD
promised your ancestors. [2]Remember how the
LORD your God has led you in the desert for
these forty years, taking away your pride and
testing you, because he wanted to know what
was in your heart. He wanted to know if you
would obey his commands. [3]He took away
your pride when he let you get hungry, and
then he fed you with manna, which neither
you nor your ancestors had ever seen. This
was to teach you that a person does not live
by eating only bread, but by everything the
LORD says. [4]During these forty years, your
clothes did not wear out, and your
feet did not swell. [5]Know in
your heart that the LORD your
God corrects you as a parent
corrects a child.
[6]Obey the commands of
the LORD your God, living as
he has commanded you and
respecting him. [7]The LORD your God is bringing you into a good land, a land with rivers

ADOPTION
How does God treat us as his children? (8:5)

On the Edge

But remember the LORD your God! It is he who gives you the power to become rich, keeping the agreement he promised to your ancestors, as it is today (Deut. 8:18).

We serve an awesome God! He is so practical. There's nothing that he will not or cannot do for you. It's a fact. God is concerned with every area of your life. Every area? Yes, every area. He's so concerned that he will even give you strength to make a living. He wants to give you creative ideas that will cause you to turn the corner financially. If anybody should be blessed, it should be God's children. Remember, God wants you blessed so you can be a blessing! You are his child, and he gets pleasure when his people prosper. Don't settle for second best. God has equipped you with the goods that you need to make a living.

We can learn from Solomon's example. God told Solomon that he could ask for whatever he wanted, and it would be granted. What did Solomon ask for? Money, wealth, power, fame? No! He asked for wisdom; and, boy, did he get it! He received the wisdom of God and this wisdom brought the money, wealth, fame, and the admiration of others. One thing is certain: Solomon didn't have a problem making a living, and neither should you. Begin asking God for godly wisdom today—and meaning it from your heart. He promises to give you the strength to make a living!

SEE FOR YOURSELF:
1 Kin. 3:5–14; Job 12:13; Ps. 35:27; Prov. 8:12; Phil. 4:19

WHAT'S IT MEAN?

The Hebrew name for the Israelites' heavenly food tells us a lot about their attitude toward it. *Manna* in Hebrew means "What is it?" The Israelites did not know what to make of the food that was also known as "bread from heaven."

Deuteronomy 8:3

and pools of water, with springs that flow in
the valleys and hills, [8]a land that has wheat
and barley, vines, fig trees, pomegranates, olive
oil, and honey. [9]It is a land where you will
have plenty of food, where you will have
everything you need, where the rocks are iron,
and where you can dig copper out of the hills.
[10]When you have all you want to eat, then
praise the LORD your God for giving you a
good land. [11]Be careful not to forget the LORD
your God so that you fail to obey his commands, laws, and rules that I am giving to you
today. [12]When you eat all you want and build
nice houses and live in them, [13]when your
herds and flocks grow large and your silver
and gold increase, when you have more of
everything, [14]then your heart will become
proud. You will forget the LORD your God,
who brought you out of the land of Egypt,
where you were slaves. [15]He led you through
the large and terrible desert that was dry and
had no water, and that had poisonous snakes
and stinging insects. He gave you water from a
solid rock [16]and manna to eat in the desert.
Manna was something your ancestors had
never seen. He did this to take away your pride
and to test you, so things would go well for
you in the end. [17]You might say to yourself, "I
am rich because of my own power and
strength," [18]but remember the LORD your God!
It is he who gives you the power to become
rich, keeping the agreement he promised to
your ancestors, as it is today.
[19]If you ever forget the LORD your God and
follow other gods and worship them and bow
down to them, I warn you today that you will
be destroyed. [20]Just as the LORD destroyed the
other nations for you, you can be destroyed if
you do not obey the LORD your God.

THE LORD WILL BE WITH ISRAEL

9 [1]Listen, Israel. You will soon cross the Jordan River to go in and force out nations that
are bigger and stronger than you. They have
large cities with walls up to the sky. [2]The people there are Anakites, who are strong and tall.
You know about them, and you have heard it
said: "No one can stop the Anakites." [3]But today remember that the LORD your God goes in
before you to destroy them like a fire that
burns things up. He will defeat them ahead of
you, and you will force them out and destroy
them quickly, just as the LORD has said.
[4]After the LORD your God has forced those
nations out ahead of you, don't say to yourself,
"The LORD brought me here to take this land
because I am so good." No! It is because these
nations are evil that the LORD will force them
out ahead of you. [5]You are going in to take the
land, not because you are good and honest,
but because these nations are evil. That is why
the LORD your God will force them out ahead
of you, to keep his promise to your ancestors,
to Abraham, Isaac, and Jacob. [6]The LORD your
God is giving you this good land to take as
your own. But know this: It is not because you
are good; you are a stubborn people.

REMEMBER THE LORD'S ANGER

[7]Remember this and do not forget it: You
made the LORD your God angry in the desert.
You would not obey the LORD from the day
you left Egypt until you arrived here. [8]At
Mount Sinai you made the LORD angry—angry enough to destroy you. [9]When I went up
on the mountain to receive the stone tablets,
the tablets with the Agreement the LORD had
made with you, I stayed on the mountain for
forty days and forty nights; I did not eat bread
or drink water. [10]The LORD gave me two stone
tablets, which God had written on with his
own finger. On them were all the commands
that the LORD gave to you on the mountain out
of the fire, on the day you were gathered there.
[11]When the forty days and forty nights
were over, the LORD gave me the two stone
tablets, the tablets with the Agreement on
them. [12]Then the LORD told me, "Get up and go
down quickly from here, because the people
you brought out from Egypt are ruining themselves. They have quickly turned away from
what I commanded and have made an idol for
themselves."
[13]The LORD said to me, "I have watched
these people, and they are very stubborn! [14]Get
away so that I may destroy them and make the
whole world forget who they are. Then I will
make another nation from you that will be
bigger and stronger than they are."
[15]So I turned and came down the mountain
that was burning with fire, and the two stone
tablets with the Agreement were in my hands.
[16]When I looked, I saw you had sinned against
the LORD your God and had made an idol in
the shape of a calf. You had quickly turned
away from what the LORD had told you to do.
[17]So I took the two stone tablets and threw
them down, breaking them into pieces right in
front of you.
[18]Then I again bowed facedown on the
ground before the LORD for forty days and forty nights; I did not eat bread or drink water.
You had sinned by doing what the LORD said
was evil, and you made him angry. [19]I was

afraid of the LORD's anger and rage, because he
was angry enough with you to destroy you,
but the LORD listened to me again. 20And the
LORD was angry enough with Aaron to destroy
him, but then I prayed for Aaron, too. 21I took
that sinful calf idol you had made and burned
it in the fire. I crushed it into a powder like dust
and threw the dust into a stream that flowed
down the mountain.
22You also made the LORD angry at Taberah,
Massah, and Kibroth Hattaavah.
23Then the LORD sent you away from Kadesh Barnea and said, "Go up and take the land
I have given you." But you rejected the command of the LORD your God. You did not trust
him or obey him. 24You have refused to obey
the LORD as long as I have known you.
25The LORD had said he would destroy you,
so I threw myself down in front of him for
those forty days and forty nights. 26I prayed to
the LORD and said, "Lord GOD, do not destroy
your people, your own people, whom you
freed and brought out of Egypt by your great
power and strength. 27Remember your servants Abraham, Isaac, and Jacob. Don't look at
how stubborn these people are, and don't look
at their sin and evil. 28Otherwise, Egypt will
say, 'It was because the LORD was not able to
take his people into the land he promised
them, and it was because he hated them that
he took them into the desert to kill them.' 29But
they are your people, LORD, your own people,
whom you brought out of Egypt with your
great power and strength."

NEW STONE TABLETS

10
1At that time the LORD said to me, "Cut two
stone tablets like the first ones and come up to
me on the mountain. Also make a wooden
Ark. 2I will write on the tablets the same words
that were on the first tablets, which you broke,
and you will put the new tablets in the Ark."
3So I made the Ark out of acacia wood, and
I cut out two stone tablets like the first ones.
Then I went up on the mountain with the two
tablets in my hands. 4The LORD wrote the same
things on these tablets he had written before—
the Ten Commandments that he had told you
on the mountain from the fire, on the day you
were gathered there. And the LORD gave them
to me. 5Then I turned and came down the
mountain; I put the tablets in the Ark I had
made, as the LORD had commanded, and they
are still there.
6(The people of Israel went from the wells of
the Jaakanites to Moserah. Aaron died there
and was buried; his son Eleazar became priest
in his place. 7From Moserah they went to Gudgodah, and from Gudgodah they went to Jotbathah, a place with streams of water. 8At that
time the LORD chose the tribe of Levi to carry
the Ark of the Agreement with the LORD. They

WHAT'S IT MEAN?

The acacia was a thorn tree that grew in the Sinai Desert, southern Canaan, and Egypt. Because its wood was hard enough to withstand insects, it was used to preserve the contents of the Ark of the Agreement. The Ark, or chest, itself was about the size of a small desk.

Deuteronomy 10:3

On the Edge

Now, Israel, this is what the LORD your God wants you to do: Respect the LORD your God, and do what he has told you to do. Love him. Serve the LORD your God with your whole being, and obey the LORD's commands and laws that I am giving you today for your own good (Deut. 10:12–13).

Your teacher gave you a final exam. One question—"What is the meaning of life?" You read it and feel sick. What does she want? An essay? A word? A drawing? You hate stuff like this. You look at the teacher for some kind of direction. She just gives you that "do your best" look.

God is not like that teacher. Life is not a test on which you just hope you get the right answer. God gives you the answers himself. He gives them over and over again. He even reminds you when you forget. Everybody wonders *What does he want?* What does God require from me? Read Deuteronomy 10:12–13 for yourself. He gives you the answer.

SEE FOR YOURSELF:
Mic. 6:8;
John 13:34–35

were to serve the LORD and to bless the people in his name, which they still do today. [9]That is why the Levites did not receive any land of their own; instead, they received the LORD himself as their gift, as the LORD your God told them.)

[10]I stayed on the mountain forty days and forty nights just like the first time, and the LORD listened to me this time also. He did not want to destroy you. [11]The LORD said to me, "Go and lead the people so that they will go in and take the land I promised their ancestors."

"Respect the LORD your God and serve him. Be loyal to him and make your promises in his name." (Deuteronomy 10:20)

WHAT THE LORD WANTS YOU TO DO

[12]Now, Israel, this is what the LORD your God wants you to do: Respect the LORD your God, and do what he has told you to do. Love him. Serve the LORD your God with your whole being, [13]and obey the LORD's commands and laws that I am giving you today for your own good.

[14]The LORD owns the world and everything in it—the heavens, even the highest heavens, are his. [15]But the LORD cared for and loved your ancestors, and he chose you, their descendants, over all the other nations, just as it is today. [16]Give yourselves completely to serving him, and do not be stubborn any longer. [17]The LORD your God is God of all gods and Lord of all lords. He is the great God, who is strong and wonderful. He does not take sides, and he will not be talked into doing evil. [18]He helps orphans and widows, and he loves foreigners and gives them food and clothes. [19]You also must love foreigners, because you were foreigners in Egypt. [20]Respect the LORD your God and serve him. Be loyal to him and make your promises in his name. [21]He is the one you should praise; he is your God, who has done great and wonderful things for you, which you have seen with your own eyes. [22]There were only seventy of your ancestors when they went down to Egypt, and now the LORD your God has made you as many as the stars in the sky.

WHAT'S IT MEAN?

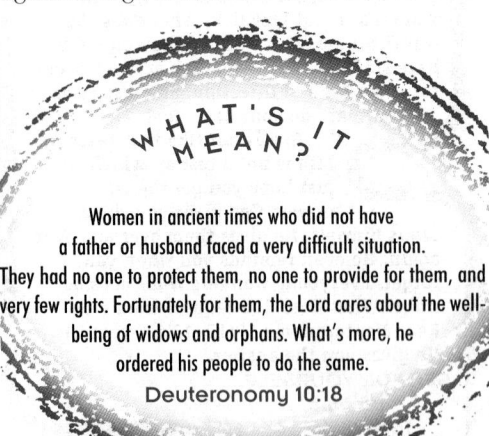

Women in ancient times who did not have a father or husband faced a very difficult situation. They had no one to protect them, no one to provide for them, and very few rights. Fortunately for them, the Lord cares about the well-being of widows and orphans. What's more, he ordered his people to do the same.

Deuteronomy 10:18

GREAT THINGS ISRAEL SAW

11

[1]Love the LORD your God and always obey his orders, rules, laws, and commands. [2]Remember today it was not your children who saw and felt the correction of the LORD your God. They did not see his majesty, his power, his strength, [3]or his signs and the things he did in Egypt to the king and his whole country. [4]They did not see what he did to the Egyptian army, its horses and chariots, when he drowned them in the Red Sea as they were chasing you. The LORD ruined them forever. [5]They did not see what he did for you in the desert until you arrived here. [6]They did not see what he did to Dathan and Abiram, the sons of Eliab the Reubenite, when the ground opened up and swallowed them, their families, their tents, and everyone who stood with them in Israel. [7]It was you who saw all these great things the LORD has done.

[8]So obey all the commands I am giving you today so that you will be strong and can go in and take the land you are going to take as your own. [9]Then you will live a long time in the land that the LORD promised to give to your ancestors and their descendants, a fertile land. [10]The land you are going to take is not like Egypt, where you were. There you had to plant your seed and water it, like a vegetable garden, by using your feet. [11]But the land that you will soon cross the Jordan River to take is a land of hills and valleys, a land that drinks rain from heaven. [12]It is a land the LORD your God cares for. His eyes are on it continually, and he watches it from the beginning of the year to the end.

[13]If you carefully obey the commands I am giving you today and love the LORD your God and serve him with your whole being, [14]then he will send rain on your land at the right time, in the fall and spring, and you will be able to

gather your grain, new wine, and oil. 15He will
put grass in the fields for your cattle, and you
will have plenty to eat.
16Be careful, or you will be fooled and will
turn away to serve and worship other gods.
17If you do, the LORD will become angry with
you and will shut the heavens so it will not
rain. Then the land will not grow crops, and
you will soon die in the good land the LORD is
giving you. 18Remember my words with your
whole being. Write them down and tie them to
your hands as a sign; tie them on your foreheads to remind you. 19Teach them well to
your children, talking about them when you
sit at home and walk along the road, when you
lie down and when you get up. 20Write them
on your doors and gates 21so that both you
and your children will live a long time in the
land the LORD promised your ancestors, as
long as the skies are above the earth.

WHAT'S IT MEAN?

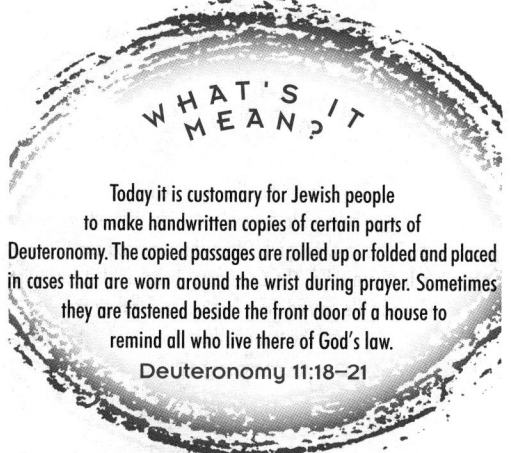

Today it is customary for Jewish people to make handwritten copies of certain parts of Deuteronomy. The copied passages are rolled up or folded and placed in cases that are worn around the wrist during prayer. Sometimes they are fastened beside the front door of a house to remind all who live there of God's law.

Deuteronomy 11:18–21

22If you are careful to obey every command
I am giving you to follow, and love the LORD
your God, and do what he has told you to do,
and are loyal to him, 23then the LORD will force
all those nations out of the land ahead of you,
and you will take the land from nations that
are bigger and stronger than you. 24Every-
where you step will be yours. Your land will go
from the desert to Lebanon and from the Euphrates River to the Mediterranean Sea. 25No
one will be able to stop you. The LORD your
God will do what he promised and will make
the people afraid everywhere you go.
26See, today I am letting you choose a blessing or a curse. 27You will be blessed if you obey
the commands of the LORD your God that I am
giving you today. 28But you will be cursed if
you disobey the commands of the LORD your
God. So do not disobey the commands I am
giving you today, and do not worship other
gods you do not know. 29When the LORD your
God brings you into the land you will take as
your own, you are to announce the blessings
from Mount Gerizim and the curses from
Mount Ebal. 30(These mountains are on the
other side of the Jordan River, to the west, toward the sunset. They are near the great trees
of Moreh in the land of the Canaanites who
live in the Jordan Valley opposite Gilgal.) 31You
will soon cross the Jordan River to enter and
take the land the LORD your God is giving you.
When you take it over and live there, 32be careful to obey all the commands and laws I am
giving you today.

THE PLACE FOR WORSHIP

12
1These are the commands and laws you
must carefully obey in the land the LORD, the
God of your ancestors, is giving you. Obey
them as long as you live in the land. 2When
you inherit the lands of these nations, you
must completely destroy all the places where
they serve their gods, on high mountains and
hills and under every green tree. 3Tear down
their altars, smash their holy stone pillars, and
burn their Asherah idols in the fire. Cut down
their idols and destroy their names from those
places.
4Don't worship the LORD your God that
way, 5but look for the place the LORD your
God will choose—a place among your tribes
where he is to be worshiped. Go there, 6and
bring to that place your burnt offerings and
sacrifices; bring a tenth of what you gain and
your special gifts; bring what you have promised and the special gifts you want to give the
LORD, and bring the first animals born to your
herds and flocks.
7There you will be together with the LORD
your God. There you and your families will
eat, and you will enjoy all the good things for
which you have worked, because the LORD
your God has blessed you.
8Do not worship the way we have been
doing today, each person doing what he thinks
is right. 9You have not yet come to a resting
place, to the land the LORD your God will give
you as your own. 10But soon you will cross the
Jordan River to live in the land the LORD your
God is giving you as your own, where he will
give you rest from all your enemies and you
will live in safety. 11Then the LORD your God
will choose a place where he is to be worshiped. To that place you must bring everything I tell you: your burnt offerings and
sacrifices, your offerings of a tenth of what you

gain, your special gifts, and all your best things
you promised to the LORD. 12There rejoice before the LORD your God. Everyone should rejoice: you, your sons and daughters, your male
and female servants, and the Levites from your
towns who have no land of their own. 13Be
careful that you don't sacrifice your burnt
offerings just anywhere you please. 14Offer
them only in the place the LORD will choose.
He will choose a place in one of your tribes,
and there you must do everything I am commanding you.

15But you may kill your animals in any of
your towns and eat as much of the meat as
you want, as if it were a deer or a gazelle; this is
the blessing the LORD your God is giving you.
Anyone, clean or unclean, may eat this meat,
16but do not eat the blood. Pour it out on the
ground like water. 17Do not eat in your own
towns what belongs to the LORD: one-tenth of
your grain, new wine, or oil; the first animals
born to your herds or flocks; whatever you
have promised to give; the special gifts you
want to give to the LORD, or any other gifts.
18Eat these things when you are together with
the LORD your God, in the place the LORD your
God chooses to be worshiped. Everyone must
do this: you, your sons and daughters, your
male and female servants, and the Levites from
your towns. Rejoice in the LORD your God's
presence about the things you have worked
for. 19Be careful not to forget the Levites as long
as you live in the land.

20When the LORD your God enlarges your
country as he has promised, and you want
some meat so you say, "I want some meat," you
may eat as much meat as you want. 21If the
LORD your God chooses a place where he is to
be worshiped that is too far away from you,
you may kill animals from your herds and
flocks, which the LORD has given to you. I have
commanded that you may do this. You may
eat as much of them as you want in your own
towns, 22as you would eat gazelle or deer meat.
Both clean and unclean people may eat this
meat, 23but be sure you don't eat the blood,
because the life is in the blood. Don't eat the
life with the meat. 24Don't eat the blood, but
pour it out on the ground like water. 25If you
don't eat it, things will go well for you and
your children, because you will be doing what
the LORD says is right.

26Take your holy things and the things you
have promised to give, and go to the place the
LORD will choose. 27Present your burnt offerings on the altar of the LORD your God, both
the meat and the blood. The blood of your
sacrifices should be poured beside the altar of
the LORD your God, but you may eat the meat.
28Be careful to obey all the rules I am giving
you so that things will always go well for you
and your children, and you will be doing what
the LORD your God says is good and right.

29You will enter the land and take it away
from the nations that the LORD your God will
destroy ahead of you. When you force them
out and live in their land, 30they will be destroyed for you, but be careful not to be
trapped by asking about their gods. Don't say,
"How do these nations worship? I will do the
same." 31Don't worship the LORD your God that
way, because the LORD hates the evil ways they
worship their gods. They even burn their sons
and daughters as sacrifices to their gods!

32Be sure to do everything I have commanded you. Do not add anything to it, and
do not take anything away from it.

WHAT'S IT MEAN?

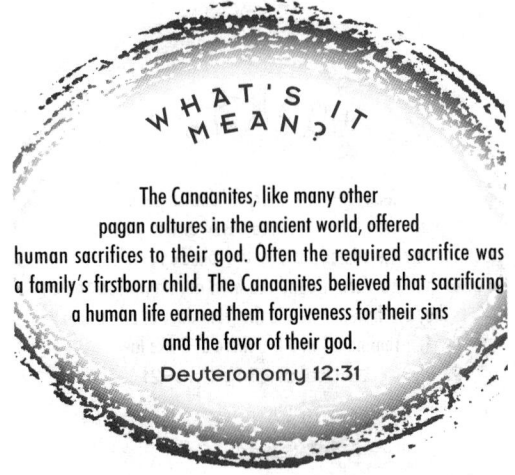

The Canaanites, like many other pagan cultures in the ancient world, offered human sacrifices to their god. Often the required sacrifice was a family's firstborn child. The Canaanites believed that sacrificing a human life earned them forgiveness for their sins and the favor of their god.

Deuteronomy 12:31

FALSE PROPHETS

13 1Prophets or those who tell the future with
dreams might come to you and say they will
show you a miracle or a sign. 2The miracle or
sign might even happen, and then they might
say, "Let's serve other gods" (gods you have not
known) "and let's worship them." 3But you
must not listen to those prophets or dreamers.
The LORD your God is testing you, to find out if
you love him with your whole being. 4Serve
only the LORD your God. Respect him, keep his
commands, and obey him. Serve him and be
loyal to him. 5The prophets or dreamers must
be killed, because they said you should turn
against the LORD your God, who brought you
out of Egypt and saved you from the land
where you were slaves. They tried to turn you
from doing what the LORD your God com-

On the Edge

Someone might try to lead you to serve other gods—it might be your brother, your son or daughter, the wife you love, or a close friend. The person might say, "Let's go and worship other gods." (These are gods that neither you nor your ancestors have known, gods of the people who live around you, either nearby or far away, from one end of the land to the other.) Do not give in to such people. Do not listen or feel sorry for them, and do not let them go free or protect them. You must put them to death (Deut. 13:6–9a).

Most Christians who experiment with other religions (Hinduism, Buddhism, the New Age, etc.) lack the maturity needed to learn about other faiths. When you're spiritually immature, you can easily get confused and "sucked in" to the deception of other religions. This can be especially true when those other religions claim to be "Christian based" or claim to believe in Jesus.

It takes maturity to discern spiritual things. Maturity comes from consistently walking with the Lord, communicating with him, growing in the knowledge of him and of his Word, and knowing that areas of your life are different because he is changing you. Some people have fallen into false religions because they weren't mature enough to tell good from "evil in disguise." Satan is the master of trickery. He is more than happy to make other religions look good to you, because he wants to pull you away from the truth. Do not experiment with other religions. You may fall into a well-set trap.

SEE FOR YOURSELF:
Ex. 20:3; Deut. 6:14; 1 Kin. 9:6–9; Jer. 35:15; John 14:6

manded you to do. You must get rid of the evil
among you.
[6]Someone might try to lead you to serve
other gods—it might be your brother, your
son or daughter, the wife you love, or a close
friend. The person might say, "Let's go and
worship other gods." (These are gods that neither you nor your ancestors have known,
[7]gods of the people who live around you, either nearby or far away, from one end of the
land to the other.) [8]Do not give in to such people. Do not listen or feel sorry for them, and do
not let them go free or protect them. [9]You must
put them to death. You must be the first one to
start to kill them, and then everyone else must
join in. [10]You must throw stones at them until
they die, because they tried to turn you away
from the LORD your God, who brought you
out of the land of Egypt, where you were
slaves. [11]Then everyone in Israel will hear
about this and be afraid, and no one among
you will ever do such an evil thing again.

CITIES TO DESTROY

[12]The LORD your God is giving you cities in
which to live, and you might hear something
about one of them. Someone might say [13]that
evil people have moved in among you. And
they might lead the people of that city away
from God, saying, "Let's go and worship other
gods." (These are gods you have not known.)
[14]Then you must ask about it, looking into the
matter and checking carefully whether it is
true. If it is proved that a hateful thing has
happened among you, [15]you must kill with a
sword everyone who lives in that city. Destroy
the city completely and kill everyone in it, as
well as the animals, with a sword. [16]Gather up
everything those people owned, and put it in
the middle of the city square. Then completely
burn the city and everything they owned as a
burnt offering to the LORD your God. That city
should never be rebuilt; let it be ruined forever.
[17]Don't keep for yourselves any of the things
found in that city, so the LORD will not be angry anymore. He will give you mercy and feel
sorry for you, and he will make your nation
grow larger, as he promised to your ancestors.
[18]You will have obeyed the LORD your God by
keeping all his commands that I am giving to
you today, and you will be doing what the
LORD says is right.

GOD'S SPECIAL PEOPLE

14

[1]You are the children of the LORD your God.
When someone dies, do not cut yourselves or
shave your heads to show your sadness. [2]You
are holy people, who belong to the LORD your
God. He has chosen you from all the people on
earth to be his very own.
[3]Do not eat anything the LORD hates. [4]These
are the animals you may eat: oxen, sheep,
goats, [5]deer, gazelle, roe deer, wild goats, ibex,
antelope, and mountain sheep. [6]You may eat

On the Edge

You are holy people, who belong to the LORD your God. He has chosen you from all the people on earth to be his very own (Deut. 14:2).

You know what it feels like to be chosen. Remember in grade school when your gym class picked teams for sports? Remember when you got chosen pretty close to the beginning? Or maybe you were the last one chosen and you remember that sting. Regardless of what happened to you then, God chose you. And he chose you first. He chose you for just one reason—he loves you. He's crazy about you. He wants you on his team because he doesn't want to be apart from you.

That's cool! It's awesome that God chose you. He can choose anybody he wants and he chose you. This shows you how much he wants you with him. He wants to be with you, too.

SEE FOR YOURSELF:
Ex. 22:31; 1 Chr. 16; Is. 49:7; 1 Pet. 2:9

any animal that has a split hoof and chews the
cud, 7but you may not eat camels, rabbits, or
rock badgers. These animals chew the cud, but
they do not have split hoofs, so they are unclean for you. 8Pigs are also unclean for you;
they have split hoofs, but they do not chew the
cud. Do not eat their meat or touch their dead
bodies.

9There are many things that live in the water. You may eat anything that has fins and
scales, 10but do not eat anything that does not
have fins and scales. It is unclean for you.

11You may eat any clean bird. 12But do not
eat these birds: eagles, vultures, black vultures,
13red kites, falcons, any kind of kite, 14any kind
of raven, 15horned owls, screech owls, sea gulls,
any kind of hawk, 16little owls, great owls,
white owls, 17desert owls, ospreys, cormorants,
18storks, any kind of heron, the hoopoes, or
bats.

19All insects with wings are unclean for you;
do not eat them. 20Other things with wings are
clean, and you may eat them.

21Do not eat anything you find that is already dead. You may give it to a foreigner living in your town, and he may eat it, or you
may sell it to a foreigner. But you are holy people, who belong to the LORD your God.

Do not cook a baby goat in its mother's
milk.

GIVING ONE-TENTH

22Be sure to save one-tenth of all your crops
each year. 23Take it to the place the LORD your
God will choose where he is to be worshiped.
There, where you will be together with the
LORD, eat the tenth of your grain, new wine,
and oil, and eat the animals born first to your
herds and flocks. Do this so that you will learn
to respect the LORD your God always. 24But if
the place the LORD will choose to be worshiped
is too far away and he has blessed you so
much you cannot carry a tenth, 25exchange
your one-tenth for silver. Then take the silver
with you to the place the LORD your God shall
choose. 26Use the silver to buy anything you
wish—cattle, sheep, wine, beer, or anything
you wish. Then you and your family will eat
and celebrate there before the LORD your God.
27Do not forget the Levites in your town, because they have no land of their own among
you.

28At the end of every third year, everyone
should bring one-tenth of that year's crop and
store it in your towns. 29This is for the Levites
so they may eat and be full. (They have no
land of their own among you.) It is also for
strangers, orphans, and widows who live in
your towns so that all of them may eat and be
full. Then the LORD your God will bless you
and all the work you do.

WHAT'S IT MEAN?

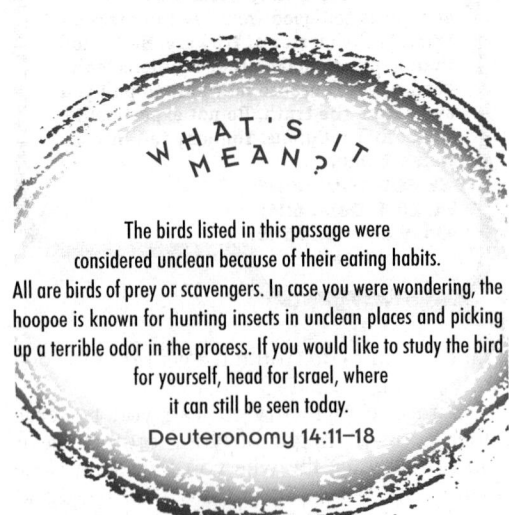

The birds listed in this passage were considered unclean because of their eating habits. All are birds of prey or scavengers. In case you were wondering, the hoopoe is known for hunting insects in unclean places and picking up a terrible odor in the process. If you would like to study the bird for yourself, head for Israel, where it can still be seen today.

Deuteronomy 14:11–18

THE SPECIAL SEVENTH YEAR

15 1At the end of every seven years, you must tell those who owe you anything that they do not have to pay you back. 2This is how you must do it: Everyone who has loaned money must cancel the loan and not make a neighbor or relative pay it back. This is the LORD's time for canceling what people owe. 3You may make a foreigner pay what is owed to you, but you must not collect what another Israelite owes you. 4But there should be no poor people among you, because the LORD your God will richly bless you in the land he is giving you as your own. 5He will bless you if you obey the LORD your God completely, but you must be careful to obey all the commands I am giving you today. 6The LORD your God will bless you as he promised, and you will lend to other nations, but you will not need to borrow from them. You will rule over many nations, but none will rule over you.

7If there are poor among you, in one of the towns of the land the LORD your God is giving you, do not be selfish or greedy toward them. 8But give freely to them, and freely lend them whatever they need. 9Beware of evil thoughts. Don't think, "The seventh year is near, the year to cancel what people owe." You might be mean to the needy and not give them anything. Then they will complain to the LORD about you, and he will find you guilty of sin. 10Give freely to the poor person, and do not wish that you didn't have to give. The LORD your God will bless your work and everything you touch. 11There will always be poor people in the land, so I command you to give freely to your neighbors and to the poor and needy in your land.

> "The LORD your God will bless you as he promised."
> (Deuteronomy 15:6a)

LETTING SLAVES GO FREE

12If one of your own people sells himself to you as a slave, whether it is a Hebrew man or woman, that person will serve you for six years. But in the seventh year you must let the slave go free. 13When you let slaves go, don't send them away without anything. 14Give them some of your flock, your grain, and your wine, giving to them as the LORD has given to you. 15Remember that you were slaves in Egypt, and the LORD your God saved you. That is why I am commanding this to you today.

16But if your slave says to you, "I don't want to leave you," because he loves you and your family and has a good life with you, 17stick an awl[n] through his ear into the door; he will be your slave for life. Also do this to a female slave.

18Do not think of it as a hard thing when you let your slaves go free. After all, they served you six years and did twice the work of a hired person. The LORD your God will bless you in everything you do.

RULES ABOUT FIRSTBORN ANIMALS

19Save all the first male animals born to your herds and flocks. They are for the LORD your God. Do not work the first calf born to your oxen, and do not cut off the wool from the first lamb born to your sheep. 20Each year you and your family are to eat these animals in the presence of the LORD your God, in the place he will choose to be worshiped. 21If an animal is crippled or blind or has something else wrong, do not sacrifice it to the LORD your God. 22But you may eat that animal in your own town. Both clean and unclean people may eat it, as they would eat a gazelle or a deer. 23But don't eat its blood; pour it out on the ground like water.

THE PASSOVER

16 1Celebrate the Passover of the LORD your God during the month of Abib, because it was during Abib that he brought you out of Egypt

WHAT'S IT MEAN?

Israelites were allowed to keep other Israelites as slaves, but only for six years. God's law required that all slaves be set free in the seventh year. The law was intended to prevent a class system from developing among the Israelites.

Deuteronomy 15:12

15:17 awl A tool like a big needle with a handle at one end.

at night. 2As the sacrifice for the Passover to
the LORD your God, offer an animal from your
flock or herd at the place the LORD will choose
to be worshiped. 3Do not eat it with bread
made with yeast. But for seven days eat bread
made without yeast, the bread of suffering,
because you left Egypt in a hurry. So all your
life you will remember the time you left Egypt.
4There must be no yeast anywhere in your
land for seven days. Offer the sacrifice on the
evening of the first day, and eat all the meat
before morning; do not leave it overnight.
5Do not offer the Passover sacrifice in just
any town the LORD your God gives you, 6but
offer it in the place he will choose to be worshiped. Offer it in the evening as the sun goes
down, which is when you left Egypt. 7Roast the
meat and eat it at the place the LORD your God
will choose. The next morning go back to your
tents. 8Eat bread made without yeast for six
days. On the seventh day have a special meeting for the LORD your God, and do not work
that day.

WHAT'S IT MEAN?

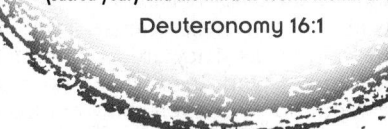

The Hebrew calendar is based on a week of seven days and a month of about four weeks, just like our calendar. One big difference is the names of the months. Passover is celebrated in the first month of the Hebrew calendar (sacred year) and the third or fourth month of ours.

Deuteronomy 16:1

THE FEAST OF WEEKS

9Count seven weeks from the time you begin
to harvest the grain, 10and then celebrate the
Feast of Weeks for the LORD your God. Bring an
offering as a special gift to him, giving to him
just as he has blessed you. 11Rejoice before the
LORD your God at the place he will choose to be
worshiped. Everybody should rejoice: you,
your sons and daughters, your male and female
servants, the Levites in your town, the strangers,
orphans, and widows living among you. 12Re-
member that you were slaves in Egypt, and
carefully obey all these laws.

THE FEAST OF SHELTERS

13Celebrate the Feast of Shelters for seven
days, after you have gathered your harvest
from the threshing floor and winepress. 14Every-
body should rejoice at your Feast: you, your
sons and daughters, your male and female servants, the Levites, strangers, orphans, and widows who live in your towns. 15Celebrate the
Feast to the LORD your God for seven days at
the place he will choose, because the LORD your
God will bless all your harvest and all the work
you do, and you will be completely happy.
16All your men must come before the LORD
three times a year to the place he will choose.
They must come at these times: the Feast of
Unleavened Bread, the Feast of Weeks, and the
Feast of Shelters. No man should come before
the LORD without a gift. 17Each of you must
bring a gift that will show how much the LORD
your God has blessed you.

JUDGES FOR THE PEOPLE

18Appoint judges and officers for your
tribes in every town the LORD your God is giving you; they must judge the people fairly. 19Do
not judge unfairly or take sides. Do not let people pay you to make wrong decisions, because
that kind of payment makes wise people seem
blind, and it changes the words of good people. 20Always do what is right so that you will
live and always have the land the LORD your
God is giving you.

GOD HATES IDOLS

21Do not set up a wooden Asherah idol
next to the altar you build for the LORD your
God, 22and do not set up holy stone pillars.
The LORD your God hates them.

17

1If an ox or sheep has something wrong
with it, do not offer it as a sacrifice to the LORD
your God. He would hate that.
2A man or woman in one of the towns the
LORD gave you might be found doing something evil and breaking the Agreement. 3That
person may have served other gods and
bowed down to them or to the sun or moon
or stars of the sky, which I have commanded
should not be done. 4If someone has told you
about it, you must look into the matter carefully. If it is true that such a hateful thing has
happened in Israel, 5take the man or woman
who has done the evil thing to the city gates
and throw stones at that person until he dies.
6There must be two or three witnesses that it is
true before the person is put to death; if there is
only one witness, the person should not be put
to death. 7The witnesses must be the first to
throw stones at the person, and then everyone
else will follow. You must get rid of the evil
among you.

COURTS OF LAW

[8]Some cases that come before you, such as murder, quarreling, or attack, may be too difficult to judge. Take these cases to the place the LORD your God will choose. [9]Go to the priests who are Levites and to the judge who is on duty at that time. Ask them about the case, and they will decide. [10]You must follow the decision they give you at the place the LORD your God will choose. Be careful to do everything they tell you. [11]Follow the teachings they give you, and do whatever they decide, exactly as they tell you. [12]The person who does not show respect for the judge or priest who is there serving the LORD your God must be put to death. You must get rid of that evil from Israel. [13]Then everyone will hear about this and will be afraid, and they will not show disrespect anymore.

WHAT'S IT MEAN?

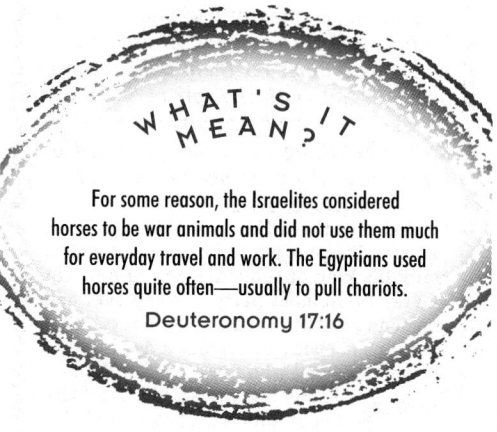

Stoning was the ancient equivalent of the electric chair or lethal injection. It was the death penalty handed down to convicted murderers. The only difference is there was no death row in ancient Israel. When a person was convicted, he was immediately taken outside the camp, where the men of the community threw rocks at him until he died.

Deuteronomy 17:5–7

CHOOSING A KING

[14]When you enter the land the LORD your God is giving you, taking it as your own and living in it, you will say, "Let's appoint a king over us like the nations all around us." [15]Be sure to appoint over you the king the LORD your God chooses. He must be one of your own people. Do not appoint as your king a foreigner who is not a fellow Israelite. [16]The king must not have too many horses for himself, and he must not send people to Egypt to get more horses, because the LORD has told you, "Don't return that way again." [17]The king must not have many wives, or his heart will be led away from God. He must not have too much silver and gold.

[18]When he becomes king, he should write a copy of the teachings on a scroll for himself, a copy taken from the priests and Levites. [19]He should keep it with him all the time and read from it every day of his life. Then he will learn to respect the LORD his God, and he will obey all the teachings and commands. [20]He should not think he is better than his fellow Israelites, and he must not stop obeying the law in any way so that he and his descendants may rule the kingdom for a long time.

WHAT'S IT MEAN?

For some reason, the Israelites considered horses to be war animals and did not use them much for everyday travel and work. The Egyptians used horses quite often—usually to pull chariots.

Deuteronomy 17:16

SHARES FOR PRIESTS AND LEVITES

18

[1]The priests are from the tribe of Levi, and that tribe will not receive a share of the land with the Israelites. They will eat the offerings made to the LORD by fire, which is their share. [2]They will not inherit any of the land like their brothers, but they will inherit the LORD himself, as he has promised them.

[3]When you offer a bull or sheep as a sacrifice, you must share with the priests, giving them the shoulder, the cheeks, and the inner organs. [4]Give them the first of your grain, new wine, and oil, as well as the first wool you cut from your sheep. [5]The LORD your God has chosen the priests and their descendants out of all your tribes to stand and serve the LORD always.

[6]If a Levite moves from one of your towns anywhere in Israel where he lives and comes to the place the LORD will choose, because he wants to serve the LORD there, [7]he may serve the LORD his God. He will be like his fellow Levites who serve there before the LORD. [8]They all will have an equal share of the food. That is separate from what he has received from the sale of family possessions.

DO NOT FOLLOW OTHER NATIONS

[9]When you enter the land the LORD your God is giving you, don't learn to do the hateful

On the Edge

Don't let anyone among you offer a son or daughter as a sacrifice in the fire. Don't let anyone use magic or witchcraft, or try to explain the meaning of signs. Don't let anyone try to control others with magic, and don't let them be mediums or try to talk with the spirits of dead people. The LORD hates anyone who does these things. . . . But you must be innocent in the presence of the LORD your God (Deut. 18:10–13).

God calls those things hateful. As a believer, it's your job to imitate God and to think his kind of thoughts. So the next time you're at a slumber party or sleep-over and someone wants to turn off the lights and levitate somebody or contact a dead person, be the brave one who says, "No. That's disgusting and stupid. It's fooling around with Satan; and if he's invited to this party, I'm outta here." That's what séances are—an invitation for Satan to come in and use his power on a game board or whatever else you ask him for. He'd love to come to your party and play tricks with a bunch of young people and hang out all night messing with you. Come on, there are plenty of other fun, innocent things to do at slumber parties. (We don't need to give you any ideas!)

SEE FOR YOURSELF:
Ex. 22:18;
Lev. 19:31; 20:6, 27

things the other nations do. 10Don't let anyone
among you offer a son or daughter as a sacrifice in the fire. Don't let anyone use magic or
witchcraft, or try to explain the meaning of
signs. 11Don't let anyone try to control others
with magic, and don't let them be mediums or
try to talk with the spirits of dead people. 12The
LORD hates anyone who does these things. Because the other nations do these things, the
LORD your God will force them out of the land
ahead of you. 13But you must be innocent in
the presence of the LORD your God.

THE LORD'S SPECIAL PROPHET

14The nations you will force out listen to
people who use magic and witchcraft, but the
LORD your God will not let you do those
things. 15The LORD your God will give you a
prophet like me, who is one of your own people. Listen to him. 16This is what you asked the
LORD your God to do when you were gathered
at Mount Sinai. You said, "Don't make us listen
to the voice of the LORD our God again, and
don't make us look at this terrible fire anymore, or we will die."
17So the LORD said to me, "What they have
said is good. 18So I will give them a prophet
like you, who is one of their own
people. I will tell him what to
say, and he will tell them
everything I command. 19This
prophet will speak for me;
anyone who does not listen
when he speaks will answer
to me. 20But if a prophet says
something I did not tell him to
say as though he were speaking for me, or if a prophet
speaks in the name of other
gods, that prophet must be killed."
21You might be thinking, "How can we
know if a message is not from the LORD?" 22If
what a prophet says in the name of the LORD
does not happen, it is not the LORD's message.
That prophet was speaking his own ideas.
Don't be afraid of him.

CULT
How does God feel about people who wrongly claim to be speaking for him? (18:20–22)

WHAT'S IT MEAN?

The Israelites had some bad neighbors, most of whom practiced witchcraft and magic. Witchcraft involved trying to see the future with the help of a pagan god. Magic involved trying to expand one's knowledge through mind-altering drugs. All forms of witchcraft, magic, and fortune-telling were strictly forbidden by God.

Deuteronomy 18:10–11

CITIES OF SAFETY

19
1When the LORD your God gives you land
that belongs to the other nations, nations that
he will destroy, you will force them out and
live in their cities and houses. 2Then choose
three cities in the middle of the land the LORD
your God is giving you as your own. 3Build

roads to these cities, and divide the land the LORD is giving you into three parts so that someone who kills another person may run to these cities.

4This is the rule for someone who kills another person and runs to one of these cities in order to save his life. But the person must have killed a neighbor without meaning to, not out of hatred. 5For example, suppose someone goes into the forest with a neighbor to cut wood and swings an ax to cut down a tree. If the ax head flies off the handle, hitting and killing the neighbor, the one who killed him may run to one of these cities to save his life. 6Otherwise, the dead person's relative who has the duty of punishing a murderer might be angry and chase him. If the city is far away, the relative might catch and kill the person, even though he should not be killed because there was no intent to kill his neighbor. 7This is why I command you to choose these three cities.

8-9Carefully obey all these laws I'm giving you today. Love the LORD your God, and always do what he wants you to do. Then the LORD your God will enlarge your land as he promised your ancestors, giving you the whole land he promised to them. After that, choose three more cities of safety 10so that innocent people will not be killed in your land, the land that the LORD your God is giving you as your own. By doing this you will not be guilty of allowing the death of innocent people.

11But if a person hates his neighbor and, after hiding and waiting, attacks and kills him and then runs to one of these cities for safety, 12the older leaders of his own city should send for the murderer. They should bring the person back from the city of safety and hand him over to the relative who has the duty of punishing the murderer. 13Show no mercy. You must remove from Israel the guilt of murdering innocent people so that things will go well for you.

14Do not move the stone that marks the border of your neighbor's land, which people long ago set in place. It marks what you inherit in the land the LORD your God is giving you as your own.

RULES ABOUT WITNESSES

15One witness is not enough to accuse a person of a crime or sin. A case must be proved by two or three witnesses.

16If a witness lies and accuses a person of a crime, 17the two people who are arguing must stand in the presence of the LORD before the priests and judges who are on duty. 18The judges must check the matter carefully. The witness who is a liar, lying about a fellow Israelite, 19must be punished. He must be punished in the same way the other person would have been punished. You must get rid of the evil among you. 20The rest of the people will hear about this and be afraid, and no one among you will ever do such an evil thing again. 21Show no mercy. A life must be paid for a life, an eye for an eye, a tooth for a tooth, a hand for a hand, a foot for a foot.

LAWS FOR WAR

20

1When you go to war against your enemies and you see horses and chariots and an army that is bigger than yours, don't be afraid of them. The LORD your God, who brought you out of Egypt, will be with you. 2The priest must come and speak to the army before you go into battle. 3He will say, "Listen, Israel! Today you are going into battle against your enemies. Don't lose your courage or be afraid. Don't panic or be frightened, 4because the LORD your God goes with you, to fight for you against your enemies and to save you."

> "The LORD your God, who brought you out of Egypt, will be with you." (Deuteronomy 20:1b)

5The officers should say to the army, "Has anyone built a new house but not given it to God? He may go home, because he might die in battle and someone else would get to give his house to God. 6Has anyone planted a vineyard and not begun to enjoy it? He may go home, because he might die in battle and someone else would enjoy his vineyard. 7Is any man engaged to a woman and not yet married to her? He may go home, because he might die in battle and someone else would marry her." 8Then the officers should also say, "Is anyone here afraid? Has anyone lost his courage? He may go home so that he will not cause others to lose their courage, too." 9When the officers finish speaking to the army, they should appoint commanders to lead it.

10When you march up to attack a city, first make them an offer of peace. 11If they accept your offer and open their gates to you, all the people of that city will become your slaves and work for you. 12But if they do not make peace with you and fight you in battle, you should surround that city. 13The LORD your God will give it to you. Then kill all the men with your swords, [14]and you may take everything else in the city for yourselves. Take the women, children, and animals, and you may use these things the LORD your God gives you from your enemies. [15]Do this to all the cities that are far away, that do not belong to the nations nearby.

[16]But leave nothing alive in the cities of the land the LORD your God is giving you. [17]Completely destroy these people: the Hittites, Amorites, Canaanites, Perizzites, Hivites, and Jebusites, as the LORD your God has commanded. [18]Otherwise, they will teach you what they do for their gods, and if you do these hateful things, you will sin against the LORD your God.

[19]If you surround and attack a city for a long time, trying to capture it, do not destroy its trees with an ax. You can eat the fruit from the trees, but do not cut them down. These trees are not the enemy, so don't make war against them. [20]But you may cut down trees that you know are not fruit trees and use them to build devices to attack the city walls, until the city is captured.

A PERSON FOUND MURDERED

21

[1]Suppose someone is found murdered, lying in a field in the land the LORD your God is giving you as your own, and no one knows who killed the person. [2]Your older leaders and judges should go to where the body was found, and they should measure how far it is to the nearby cities. [3]The older leaders of the city nearest the body must take a young cow that has never worked or worn a yoke, [4]and they must lead her down to a valley that has never been plowed or planted, with a stream flowing through it. There they must break the young cow's neck. [5]The priests, the sons of Levi, should come forward, because they have been chosen by the LORD your God to serve him and to give blessings in the LORD's name. They are the ones who decide cases of quarreling and attacks. [6]Then all the older leaders of the city nearest the murdered person should wash their hands over the young cow whose neck was broken in the valley. [7]They should declare: "We did not kill this person, and we did not see it happen. [8]LORD, remove this sin from your people Israel, whom you have saved. Don't blame your people, the Israelites, for the murder of this innocent person." And so the murder will be paid for. [9]Then you will have removed from yourselves the guilt of murdering an innocent person, because you will be doing what the LORD says is right.

CAPTIVE WOMEN AS WIVES

[10]When you go to war against your enemies, the LORD will help you defeat them so that you will take them captive. [11]If you see a beautiful woman among the captives and are attracted to her, you may take her as your wife. [12]Bring her into your home, where she must shave her head and cut her nails [13]and change the clothes she was wearing when you captured her. After she has lived in your house and cried for her parents for a month, you may marry her. You will be her husband, and she will be your wife. [14]But if you are not pleased with her, you must let her go anywhere she wants. You must not sell her for money or make her a slave, because you have taken away her honor.

THE OLDEST SON

[15]A man might have two wives, one he loves and one he doesn't. Both wives might have sons by him. If the older son belongs to the wife he does not love, [16]when that man wills his property to his sons he must not give the son of the wife he loves what belongs to the older son, the son of the wife he does not love. [17]He must agree to give the older son two shares of everything he owns, even though the older son is from the wife he does not love. That son was the first to prove his father could have children, so he has the rights that belong to the older son.

SONS WHO REFUSE TO OBEY

[18]If someone has a son who is stubborn, who turns against his father and mother and doesn't obey them or listen when they correct him, [19]his parents must take him to the older

WHAT'S IT MEAN?

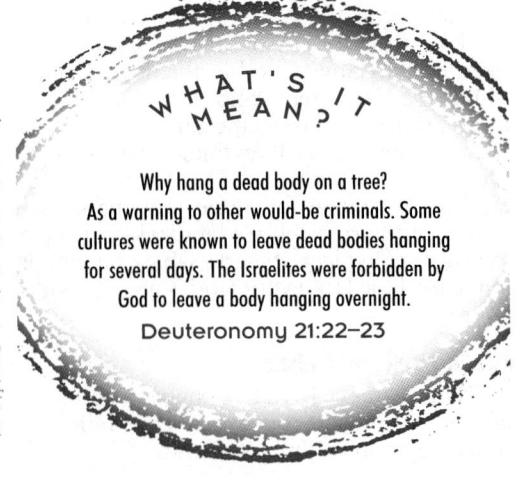

Why hang a dead body on a tree?
As a warning to other would-be criminals. Some cultures were known to leave dead bodies hanging for several days. The Israelites were forbidden by God to leave a body hanging overnight.
Deuteronomy 21:22–23

leaders at the city gate. 20They will say to the
leaders, "Our son is stubborn and turns against
us. He will not obey us. He eats too much, and
he is always drunk." 21Then all the men in his
town must throw stones at him until he dies.
Get rid of the evil among you, because then all
the people of Israel will hear about this and be
afraid.

OTHER LAWS

22If someone is guilty of a sin worthy of
death, he must be put to death and his body
displayed on a tree. 23But don't leave his body
hanging on the tree overnight; be sure to bury
him that same day, because anyone whose
body is displayed on a tree is cursed by God.
You must not ruin the land the LORD your God
is giving you as your own.

22 1If you see your fellow Israelite's ox or
sheep wandering away, don't ignore it. Take it
back to its owner. 2If the owner does not live
close to you, or if you do not know who the
owner is, take the animal home with you. Keep
it until the owner comes looking for it; then
give it back. 3Do the same thing if you find a
donkey or coat or anything someone lost.
Don't just ignore it.

4If you see your fellow Israelite's donkey or
ox fallen on the road, don't ignore it. Help the
owner get it up.

5A woman must not wear men's clothes, and
a man must not wear women's clothes. The
LORD your God hates anyone who does that.

6If you find a bird's nest by the road, either
in a tree or on the ground, and the mother bird
is sitting on the young birds or eggs, do not
take the mother bird with the young birds.
7You may take the young birds, but you must
let the mother bird go free. Then things will go
well for you, and you will live a long time.

8When you build a new house, build a low
wall around the edge of the roof*n* so you will
not be guilty if someone falls off the roof.

9Don't plant two different kinds of seeds in
your vineyard. Otherwise, both crops will be
ruined.

10Don't plow with an ox and a donkey tied
together.

11Don't wear clothes made of wool and linen
woven together.

12Tie several pieces of thread together; then
put these tassels on the four corners of your
coat.

On the Edge

A woman must not wear men's clothes, and a man must not wear women's clothes. The LORD your God hates anyone who does that (Deut. 22:5).

God made two types of people—men and women. He made us with different body shapes, different emotional makeups, and different strengths and weaknesses. He is disgusted when someone tries to go against his design. He has a plan and a purpose for both men and women, and it's sinful to dress up and pretend to be the opposite of what you are. People do it. Most often these people are confused—maybe rejected or angry or hurt, too. They need God's love. Cross-dressing is like shouting, "I know more than God does. I look better this way!" God hates cross-dressing. He loves every person on this earth. It is sin that he cannot stand.

Be glad that God made you the way you are. He has a plan for you as a strong, godly man or woman. He makes no mistakes.

SEE FOR YOURSELF:
1 Cor. 6:9–10

MARRIAGE LAWS

13If a man marries a girl and has sexual relations with her but then decides he does not
like her, 14he might talk badly about her and
give her a bad name. He might say, "I married
this woman, but when I had sexual relations
with her, I did not find that she was a virgin."
15Then the girl's parents must bring proof that
she was a virgin to the older leaders at the city
gate. 16The girl's father will say to the leaders, "I
gave my daughter to this man to be his wife,
but now he does not want her. 17This man has
told lies about my daughter. He has said, 'I did
not find your daughter to be a virgin,' but here
is the proof that my daughter was a virgin."
Then her parents are to show the sheet to the
city leaders, 18and the leaders must take the
man and punish him. 19They must make him
pay about two and one-half pounds of silver

22:8 roof In Bible times houses were built with flat roofs. The roof was used for drying things such as flax and fruit. And it was used as an extra room, as a place for worship, and as a cool place to sleep in the summer.

to the girl's father, because the man has given an Israelite virgin a bad name. The girl will continue to be the man's wife, and he may not divorce her as long as he lives.

[20]But if the things the husband said about his wife are true, and there is no proof that she was a virgin, [21]the girl must be brought to the door of her father's house. Then the men of the town must put her to death by throwing stones at her. She has done a disgraceful thing in Israel by having sexual relations before she was married. You must get rid of the evil among you.

[22]If a man is found having sexual relations with another man's wife, both the woman and the man who had sexual relations with her must die. Get rid of this evil from Israel.

[23]If a man meets a virgin in a city and has sexual relations with her, but she is engaged to another man, [24]you must take both of them to the city gate and put them to death by throwing stones at them. Kill the girl, because she was in a city and did not scream for help. And kill the man for having sexual relations with another man's wife. You must get rid of the evil among you.

[25]But if a man meets an engaged girl out in the country and forces her to have sexual relations with him, only the man who had sexual relations with her must be put to death. [26]Don't do anything to the girl, because she has not done a sin worthy of death. This is like the person who attacks and murders a neighbor; [27]the man found the engaged girl in the country and she screamed, but no one was there to save her.

[28]If a man meets a virgin who is not engaged to be married and forces her to have sexual relations with him and people find out about it, [29]the man must pay the girl's father about one and one-fourth pounds of silver. He must also marry the girl, because he has dishonored her, and he may never divorce her for as long as he lives.

[30]A man must not marry his father's wife; he must not dishonor his father in this way.

> "The LORD your God moves around through your camp to protect you and to defeat your enemies for you, so the camp must be holy. He must not see anything unclean among you so that he will not leave you."
> (Deuteronomy 23:14)

THE LORD'S PEOPLE

23

[1]No man who has had part of his sex organ cut off may come into the meeting to worship the LORD.

[2]No one born to parents who were forbidden by law to marry may come into the meeting to worship the LORD. The descendants for ten generations may not come in either.

[3]No Ammonite or Moabite may come into the meeting to worship the LORD, and none of their descendants for ten generations may come in. [4]This is because the Ammonites and Moabites did not give you bread and water when you came out of Egypt. And they hired Balaam son of Beor, from Pethor in Northwest Mesopotamia, to put a curse on you. [5]But the LORD your God would not listen to Balaam. He turned the curse into a blessing for you, because the LORD your God loves you. [6]Don't wish for their peace or success as long as you live.

[7]Don't hate Edomites; they are your close relatives. Don't hate Egyptians, because you were foreigners in their country. [8]The great-grandchildren of these two peoples may come into the meeting to worship the LORD.

KEEPING THE CAMP CLEAN

[9]When you are camped in time of war, keep away from unclean things. [10]If a man becomes unclean during the night, he must go outside the camp and not come back. [11]But when evening comes, he must wash himself, and at sunset he may come back into the camp.

[12]Choose a place outside the camp where people may go to relieve themselves. [13]Carry a tent peg with you, and when you relieve yourself, dig a hole and cover up your dung. [14]The LORD your God moves around through your camp to protect you and to defeat your enemies for you, so the camp must be holy. He must not see anything unclean among you so that he will not leave you.

OTHER LAWS

[15]If an escaped slave comes to you, do not hand over the slave to his master. [16]Let the slave live with you anywhere he likes, in any town he chooses. Do not mistreat him.

[17]No Israelite man or woman must ever become a temple prostitute. [18]Do not bring a male or female prostitute's pay to the Temple of the LORD your God to pay what you have prom-

WHAT'S IT MEAN?

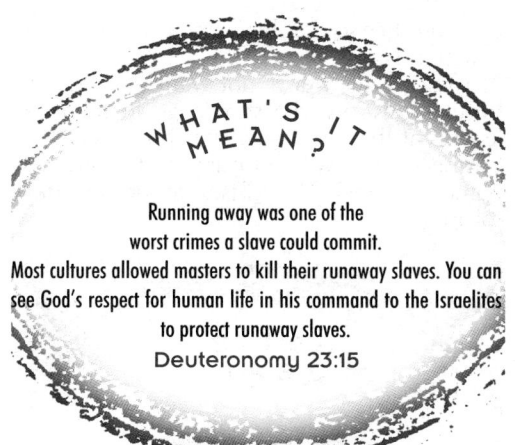

Running away was one of the worst crimes a slave could commit. Most cultures allowed masters to kill their runaway slaves. You can see God's respect for human life in his command to the Israelites to protect runaway slaves.

Deuteronomy 23:15

ised to the LORD, because the LORD your God
hates prostitution.
19If you loan your fellow Israelites money
or food or anything else, don't make them pay
back more than you loaned them. 20You may
charge foreigners, but not fellow Israelites.
Then the LORD your God will bless everything
you do in the land you are entering to take as
your own.
21If you make a promise to give something
to the LORD your God, do not be slow to pay it,
because the LORD your God demands it from
you. Do not be guilty of sin. 22But if you do not
make the promise, you will not be guilty. 23You
must do whatever you say you will do, because you chose to make the promise to the
LORD your God.
24If you go into your neighbor's vineyard,
you may eat as many grapes as you wish, but
do not put any grapes into your basket. 25If
you go into your neighbor's grainfield, you
may pick grain with your hands, but you must
not cut down your neighbor's grain with your
sickle.

24

1A man might marry a woman but later decide she doesn't please him because he has
found something bad about her. He writes out
divorce papers for her, gives them to her, and
sends her away from his house. 2After she
leaves his house, she goes and marries another
man, 3but her second husband does not like
her either. So he writes out divorce papers for
her, gives them to her, and sends her away
from his house. Or the second husband might
die. 4In either case, her first husband who divorced her must not marry her again, because
she has become unclean. The LORD would hate
this. Don't bring this sin into the land the LORD
your God is giving you as your own.
5A man who has just married must not be
sent to war or be given any other duty. He
should be free to stay home for a year to make
his new wife happy.
6If someone owes you something, do not
take his two stones for grinding grain—
not even the upper one—in place of what he
owes, because this is how the person makes a
living.
7If someone kidnaps a fellow Israelite, either
to make him a slave or sell him, the kidnapper
must be killed. You must get rid of the evil
among you.
8Be careful when someone has a skin disease. Do exactly what the priests, the Levites,
teach you, being careful to do what I have
commanded them. 9Remember what the LORD
your God did to Miriam on your way out of
Egypt.
10When you make a loan to your neighbors,
don't go into their homes to get something in

On the Edge

If a poor person gives you a coat to show he will pay the loan back, don't keep it overnight. Give the coat back at sunset, because your neighbor needs that coat to sleep in, and he will be grateful to you. And the LORD your God will see that you have done a good thing (Deut. 24:12–13).

We live in a society that notices everything that's wrong. The six o'clock news, organized protests, flyers on your windshield, newspapers, magazines—everything seems to highlight things that are bad. The world doesn't notice much when something really good happens.

Lots of times, kids in school say they act up just to get some attention. You can bet someone will notice when they break the rules, but there are few rewards for kids who do the right thing. We've forgotten that God promises to notice (see Heb. 6:10). He doesn't miss a thing. He isn't sleeping through your sacrifice. He isn't watching the bad kids when you're off doing good. He is pleased to watch you do the right thing. He's faithful to notice every good move you make.

SEE FOR YOURSELF: Ps. 33:13–15; Matt. 13:43; Mark 9:41

place of it. 11 Stay outside and let them go in and get what they promised you. 12 If a poor person gives you a coat to show he will pay the loan back, don't keep it overnight. 13 Give the coat back at sunset, because your neighbor needs that coat to sleep in, and he will be grateful to you. And the LORD your God will see that you have done a good thing.

14 Don't cheat hired servants who are poor and needy, whether they are fellow Israelites or foreigners living in one of your towns. 15 Pay them each day before sunset, because they are poor and need the money. Otherwise, they may complain to the LORD about you, and you will be guilty of sin.

16 Parents must not be put to death if their children do wrong, and children must not be put to death if their parents do wrong. Each person must die for his own sin.

17 Do not be unfair to a foreigner or an orphan. Don't take a widow's coat to make sure she pays you back. 18 Remember that you were slaves in Egypt, and the LORD your God saved you from there. That is why I am commanding you to do this.

19 When you are gathering your harvest in the field and leave behind a bundle of grain, don't go back and get it. Leave it there for foreigners, orphans, and widows so that the LORD your God can bless everything you do. 20 When you beat your olive trees to knock the olives off, don't beat the trees a second time. Leave what is left for foreigners, orphans, and widows. 21 When you harvest the grapes in your vineyard, don't pick the vines a second time. Leave what is left for foreigners, orphans, and widows. 22 Remember that you were slaves in Egypt; that is why I am commanding you to do this.

25

1 If two people have an argument and go to court, the judges will decide the case. They will declare one person right and the other guilty. 2 If the guilty person has to be punished with a beating, the judge will make that person lie down and be beaten in front of him. The number of lashes should match the crime. 3 But don't hit a person more than forty times, because more than that would disgrace him before others.

4 When an ox is working in the grain, do not cover its mouth to keep it from eating.

5 If two brothers are living together, and one of them dies without having a son, his widow must not marry someone outside her husband's family. Her husband's brother must marry her, which is his duty to her as a brother-in-law. 6 The first son she has counts as the son of the dead brother so that his name will not be forgotten in Israel.

7 But if a man does not want to marry his brother's widow, she should go to the older leaders at the town gate. She should say, "My brother-in-law will not carry on his brother's name in Israel. He refuses to do his duty for me."

WHAT'S IT MEAN?

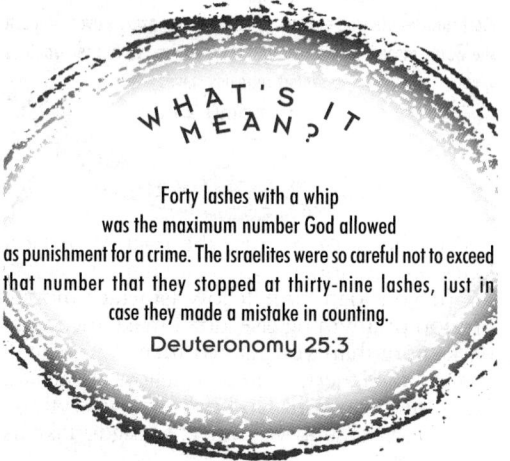

Forty lashes with a whip was the maximum number God allowed as punishment for a crime. The Israelites were so careful not to exceed that number that they stopped at thirty-nine lashes, just in case they made a mistake in counting.

Deuteronomy 25:3

8 Then the older leaders of the town must call for the man and talk to him. But if he is stubborn and says, "I don't want to marry her," 9 the woman must go up to him in front of the leaders. She must take off one of his sandals and spit in his face and say, "This is for the man who won't continue his brother's family!" 10 Then that man's family shall be known in Israel as the Family of the Unsandaled.

11 If two men are fighting and one man's wife comes to save her husband from his attacker, grabbing the attacker by his sex organs,

WHAT'S IT MEAN?

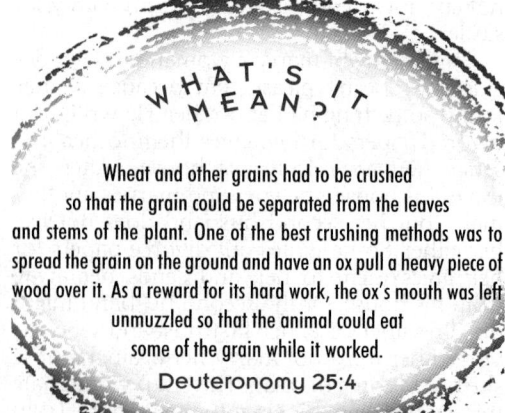

Wheat and other grains had to be crushed so that the grain could be separated from the leaves and stems of the plant. One of the best crushing methods was to spread the grain on the ground and have an ox pull a heavy piece of wood over it. As a reward for its hard work, the ox's mouth was left unmuzzled so that the animal could eat some of the grain while it worked.

Deuteronomy 25:4

[12]you must cut off her hand. Show her no mercy.

[13]Don't carry two sets of weights with you, one heavy and one light. [14]Don't have two different sets of measures in your house, one large and one small. [15]You must have true and honest weights and measures so that you will live a long time in the land the LORD your God is giving you. [16]The LORD your God hates anyone who is dishonest and uses dishonest measures.

[17]Remember what the Amalekites did to you when you came out of Egypt. [18]When you were tired and worn out, they met you on the road and attacked all those lagging behind. They were not afraid of God. [19]When the LORD your God gives you rest from all the enemies around you in the land he is giving you as your own, you shall destroy any memory of the Amalekites on the earth. Do not forget!

THE FIRST HARVEST

26 [1]When you go into the land the LORD your God is giving you as your own, to take it over and live in it, [2]you must take some of the first harvest of crops that grow from the land the LORD your God is giving you. Put the food in a basket and go to the place where the LORD your God will choose to be worshiped. [3]Say to the priest on duty at that time, "Today I declare before the LORD your God that I have come into the land the LORD promised our ancestors that he would give us." [4]The priest will take your basket and set it down in front of the altar of the LORD your God. [5]Then you shall announce before the LORD your God: "My father was a wandering Aramean. He went down to Egypt with only a few people, but they became a great, powerful, and large nation there. [6]But the Egyptians were cruel to us, making us suffer and work very hard. [7]So we prayed to the LORD, the God of our ancestors, and he heard us. When he saw our trouble, hard work, and suffering, [8]the LORD brought us out of Egypt with his great power and strength, using great terrors, signs, and miracles. [9]Then he brought us to this place and gave us this fertile land. [10]Now I bring part of the first harvest from this land that you, LORD, have given me." Place the basket before the LORD your God and bow down before him. [11]Then you and the Levites and foreigners among you should rejoice, because the LORD your God has given good things to you and your family.

[12]Bring a tenth of all your harvest the third year (the year to give a tenth of your harvest). Give it to the Levites, foreigners, orphans, and widows so that they may eat in your towns and be full. [13]Then say to the LORD your God, "I have taken out of my house the part of my harvest that belongs to God, and I have given it to the Levites, foreigners, orphans, and widows. I have done everything you commanded me; I have not broken your commands, and I have not forgotten any of them. [14]I have not eaten any of the holy part while I was in sorrow. I have not removed any of it while I was unclean, and I have not offered it for dead people. I have obeyed you, the LORD my God, and have done everything you commanded me. [15]So look down from heaven, your holy home. Bless your people Israel and bless the land you have given us, which you promised to our ancestors—a fertile land."

WHAT'S IT MEAN?

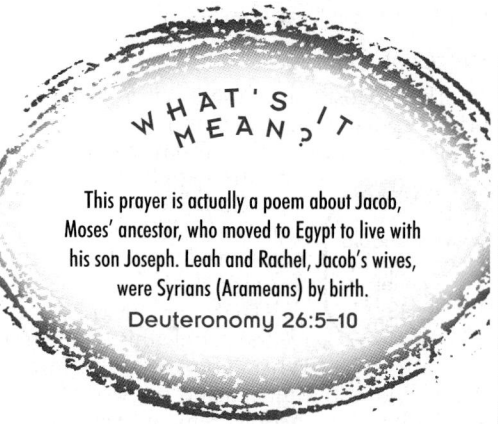

This prayer is actually a poem about Jacob, Moses' ancestor, who moved to Egypt to live with his son Joseph. Leah and Rachel, Jacob's wives, were Syrians (Arameans) by birth.

Deuteronomy 26:5–10

OBEY THE LORD'S COMMANDS

[16]Today the LORD your God commands you to obey all these rules and laws; be careful to obey them with your whole being. [17]Today you have said that the LORD is your God, and you have promised to do what he wants you to do—to keep his rules, commands, and laws. You have said you will obey him. [18]And today the LORD has said that you are his very own people, as he has promised you. But you must obey his commands. [19]He will make you greater than all the other nations he made. He will give you praise, fame, and honor, and you will be a holy people to the LORD your God, as he has said.

ADOPTION

What are God's children called to do? (26:18)

THE LAW WRITTEN ON STONES

27 [1]Then Moses, along with the older leaders of Israel, commanded the people, saying, "Keep all the commands I have given you today.

2 Soon you will cross the Jordan River to go into the land the LORD your God is giving you. On that day set up some large stones and cover them with plaster. 3 When you cross over, write all the words of these teachings on them. Then you may enter the land the LORD your God is giving you, a fertile land, just as the LORD, the God of your ancestors, promised. 4 After you have crossed the Jordan River, set up these stones on Mount Ebal, as I command you today, and cover them with plaster. 5 Build an altar of stones there to the LORD your God, but don't use any iron tool to cut the stones; 6 build the altar of the LORD your God with stones from the field. Offer burnt offerings on it to the LORD your God, 7 and offer fellowship offerings there, and eat them and rejoice before the LORD your God. 8 Then write clearly all the words of these teachings on the stones."

CURSES OF THE LAW

9 Then Moses and the Levites who were priests spoke to all Israel and said, "Be quiet, Israel. Listen! Today you have become the people of the LORD your God. 10 Obey the LORD your God, and keep his commands and laws that I give you today."

BELIEF

What should accompany belief in God? (27:10)

11 That day Moses also gave the people this command: 12 When you cross the Jordan River, these tribes must stand on Mount Gerizim to bless the people: Simeon, Levi, Judah, Issachar, Joseph and Benjamin. 13 And these tribes must stand on Mount Ebal to announce the curses: Reuben, Gad, Asher, Zebulun, Dan, and Naphtali.

14 The Levites will say to all the people of Israel in a loud voice:

15 "Anyone will be cursed who makes an idol or statue and secretly sets it up, because the LORD hates the idols people make."

Then all the people will say, "Amen!"

16 "Anyone will be cursed who dishonors his father or mother."

Then all the people will say, "Amen!"

17 "Anyone will be cursed who moves the stone that marks a neighbor's border."

Then all the people will say, "Amen!"

18 "Anyone will be cursed who sends a blind person down the wrong road."

Then all the people will say, "Amen!"

19 "Anyone will be cursed who is unfair to foreigners, orphans, or widows."

Then all the people will say, "Amen!"

20 "A man will be cursed who has sexual relations with his father's wife, because it is a dishonor to his father."

Then all the people will say, "Amen!"

21 "Anyone will be cursed who has sexual relations with an animal."

Then all the people will say, "Amen!"

22 "A man will be cursed who has sexual relations with his sister, whether she is his father's daughter or his mother's daughter."

Then all the people will say, "Amen!"

23 "A man will be cursed who has sexual relations with his mother-in-law."

Then all the people will say, "Amen!"

24 "Anyone will be cursed who kills a neighbor secretly."

Then all the people will say, "Amen!"

25 "Anyone will be cursed who takes money to murder an innocent person."

Then all the people will say, "Amen!"

26 "Anyone will be cursed who does not agree with the words of these teachings and does not obey them."

Then all the people will say, "Amen!"

BLESSINGS FOR OBEYING

28 1 You must completely obey the LORD your God, and you must carefully follow all his commands I am giving you today. Then the LORD your God will make you greater than any other nation on earth. 2 Obey the LORD your God so that all these blessings will come and stay with you:

3 You will be blessed in the city and blessed in the country.

4 Your children will be blessed, as well as your crops; your herds will be blessed with calves and your flocks with lambs.

5 Your basket and your kitchen will be blessed.

6 You will be blessed when you come in and when you go out.

7 The LORD will help you defeat the enemies that come to fight you.

"You must completely obey the LORD your God, and you must carefully follow all his commands I am giving you today. Then the LORD your God will make you greater than any other nation on earth." (Deuteronomy 28:1)

WHAT'S IT MEAN?

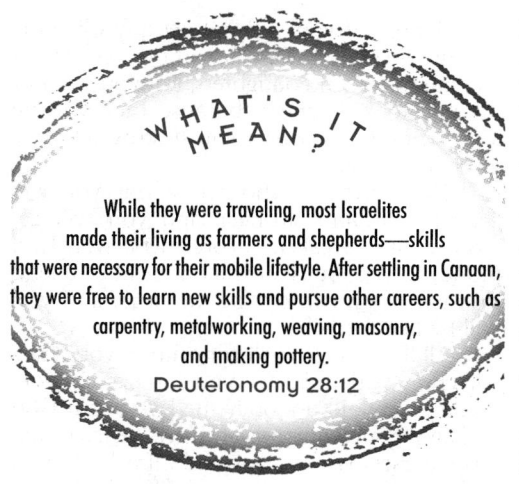

While they were traveling, most Israelites made their living as farmers and shepherds—skills that were necessary for their mobile lifestyle. After settling in Canaan, they were free to learn new skills and pursue other careers, such as carpentry, metalworking, weaving, masonry, and making pottery.

Deuteronomy 28:12

They will attack you from one direction, but they will run from you in seven directions.
8The LORD your God will bless you with full barns, and he will bless everything you do. He will bless the land he is giving you.
9The LORD will make you his holy people, as he promised. But you must obey his commands and do what he wants you to do.
10Then everyone on earth will see that you are the LORD's people, and they will be afraid of
you. 11The LORD will make you rich: You will have many children, your animals will have many young, and your land will give good crops. It is the land that the LORD promised your ancestors he would give to you.
12The LORD will open up his heavenly storehouse so that the skies send rain on your land at the right time, and he will bless everything you do. You will lend to other nations, but you
will not need to borrow from them. 13The LORD will make you like the head and not like the tail; you will be on top and not on bottom. But you must obey the commands of the LORD your God that I am giving you today, being
careful to keep them. 14Do not disobey anything I command you today. Do exactly as I command, and do not follow other gods or serve them.

CURSES FOR DISOBEYING

15But if you do not obey the LORD your God and carefully follow all his commands and laws I am giving you today, all these curses will come upon you and stay:
16You will be cursed in the city and cursed in the country.
17Your basket and your kitchen will be cursed.
18Your children will be cursed, as well as your crops; the calves of your herds and the lambs of your flocks will be cursed.
19You will be cursed when you go in and when you go out.
20The LORD will send you curses, confusion, and punishment in everything you do. You will be destroyed and suddenly ruined because you
did wrong when you left him. 21The LORD will give you terrible diseases and destroy you from
the land you are going to take. 22The LORD will
punish you with disease, fever, swelling, heat,

Promise

HE PROMISES TO MAKE YOU SUCCESSFUL IN YOUR WORK.

You will be blessed when you come in and when you go out (Deut. 28:6).

One of the blessings of obedience is that God will make you successful in your work (see Deut. 28:3–6). But be careful not to confuse God's kind of success with the world's version of success. The world deceives us into believing that we're successful if we wear the right clothes, drive an expensive car, live in a big house, have lots of people working for us, and carry a gold card. God says we have been successful in our work if we have been pleasing to him (see 2 Cor. 5:9). You've been successful to God today if you've brought glory to him. It's that simple. Rest easy tonight, knowing that you've been obedient to him. He'll make you successful in your work. You don't have to worry or wonder what he's going to do to make you look successful. He'll make you successful in his eyes.

SEE FOR YOURSELF:

Deut. 2:7; 15:10; 1 Chr. 28:20; Neh. 2:20; Ps. 1:3

lack of rain, plant diseases, and mildew until
you die. 23The sky above will be like bronze,[n]
and the ground below will be like iron. 24The
LORD will turn the rain into dust and sand,
which will fall from the skies until you are destroyed.
25The LORD will help your enemies defeat
you. You will attack them from one direction,
but you will run from them in seven directions. And you will become a thing of horror
among all the kingdoms on earth. 26Your dead
bodies will be food for all the birds and wild
animals, and there will be no one to scare them
away. 27The LORD will punish you with boils
like those the Egyptians had. You will have bad
growths, sores, and itches that can't be cured.
28The LORD will give you madness, blindness,
and a confused mind. 29You will have to feel
around in the daylight like a blind person. You
will fail in everything you do. People will hurt
you and steal from you every day, and no one
will save you.
30You will be engaged to a woman, but another man will force her to have sexual relations with him. You will build a house, but you
will not live in it. You will plant a vineyard, but
you will not get its grapes. 31Your ox will be
killed before your eyes, but you will not eat
any of it. Your donkey will be taken away from
you, and it will not be brought back. Your
sheep will be given to your enemies, and no
one will save you. 32Your sons and daughters
will be given to another nation, and you will
grow tired looking for them every day, but
there will be nothing you can do. 33People you
don't know will eat the crops your land and
hard work have produced. You will be mistreated and abused all your life. 34The things
you see will cause you to go mad. 35The LORD
will give you sore boils on your knees and legs
that cannot be cured, and they will go from the
soles of your feet to the tops of your heads.
36The LORD will send you and your king
away to a nation neither you nor your ancestors know, where you will serve other gods
made of wood and stone. 37You will become a
hated thing to the nations where the LORD
sends you; they will laugh at you and make
fun of you.
38You will plant much seed in your field, but
your harvest will be small, because locusts will
eat the crop. 39You will plant vineyards and
work hard in them, but you will not pick the
grapes or drink the wine, because the worms
will eat them. 40You will have olive trees in all
your land, but you will not get any olive oil,
because the olives will drop off the trees. 41You
will have sons and daughters, but you will not
be able to keep them, because they will be
taken captive. 42Locusts will destroy all your
trees and crops.
43The foreigners who live among you will
get stronger and stronger, and you will get
weaker and weaker. 44Foreigners will lend
money to you, but you will not be able to lend
to them. They will be like the head, and you
will be like the tail.
45All these curses will come upon you. They
will chase you and catch you and destroy you,
because you did not obey the LORD your God
and keep the commands and laws he gave you.
46The curses will be signs and miracles to you
and your descendants forever. 47You had plenty of everything, but you did not serve the
LORD your God with joy and a pure heart, 48so
you will serve the enemies the LORD sends
against you. You will be hungry, thirsty, naked,
and poor, and the LORD will put a load on you
until he has destroyed you.

WHAT'S IT MEAN?

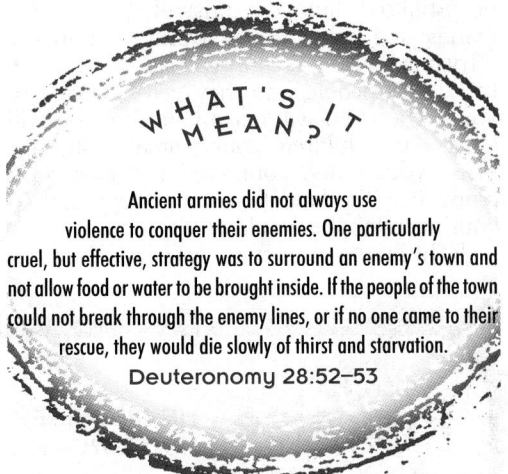

Ancient armies did not always use violence to conquer their enemies. One particularly cruel, but effective, strategy was to surround an enemy's town and not allow food or water to be brought inside. If the people of the town could not break through the enemy lines, or if no one came to their rescue, they would die slowly of thirst and starvation.

Deuteronomy 28:52–53

THE CURSE OF AN ENEMY NATION

49The LORD will bring a nation against you
from far away, from the end of the world, and
it will swoop down like an eagle. You won't
understand their language, 50and they will look
mean. They will not respect old people or feel
sorry for the young. 51They will eat the calves
from your herds and the harvest of your field,
and you will be destroyed. They will not leave
you any grain, new wine or oil, or any calves
from your herds or lambs from your flocks.
You will be ruined. 52That nation will surround

28:23 sky . . . bronze This means the sky will give no rain and the earth will produce no crops.

and attack all your cities. You trust in your
high, strong walls, but they will fall down. That
nation will surround all your cities everywhere
in the land the LORD your God is giving you.
53 Your enemy will surround you. Those
people will make you starve so that you will
eat your own babies, the bodies of the sons
and daughters the LORD your God gave you.
54 Even the most gentle and kind man among
you will become cruel to his brother, his wife
whom he loves, and his children who are still
alive. 55 He will not even give them any of the
flesh of his children he is eating, because it will
be all he has left. Your enemy will surround
you and make you starve in all your cities.
56 The most gentle and kind woman among
you, so gentle and kind she would hardly even
walk on the ground, will be cruel to her husband whom she loves and to her son and
daughter. 57 She will give birth to a baby, but
she will plan to eat the baby and what comes
after the birth itself. She will eat them secretly
while the enemy surrounds the city. Those
people will make you starve in all your cities.
58 Be careful to obey everything in these
teachings that are written in this book. You
must respect the glorious and wonderful name
of the LORD your God, 59 or the LORD will give
terrible diseases to you and your descendants.
You will have long and serious diseases, and
long and miserable sicknesses. 60 He will give
you all the diseases of Egypt that you dread,
and the diseases will stay with you. 61 The LORD
will also give you every disease and sickness
not written in this Book of the Teachings, until
you are destroyed. 62 You people may have
outnumbered the stars, but only a few of you
will be left, because you did not obey the LORD
your God. 63 Just as the LORD was once happy
with you and gave you good things and made
you grow in number, so then the LORD will be
happy to ruin and destroy you, and you will
be removed from the land you are entering to
take as your own.
64 Then the LORD will scatter you among the
nations—from one end of the earth to the
other. There you will serve other gods of wood
and stone, gods that neither you nor your ancestors have known. 65 You will have no rest
among those nations and no place that is
yours. The LORD will make your mind worried,
your sight weak, and your soul sad. 66 You will
live with danger and be afraid night and day.•
You will not be sure that you will live. 67 In the
morning you will say, "I wish it were evening,"
and in the evening you will say, "I wish it were
morning." Terror will be in your heart, and the
things you have seen will scare you. 68 The
LORD will send you back to Egypt in ships,
even though I, Moses, said you would never
go back to Egypt. And there you will try to sell
yourselves as slaves to your enemies, but no
one will buy you.

THE AGREEMENT IN MOAB

29
1 The LORD commanded Moses to make an
agreement with the Israelites in Moab in addition to the agreement he had made with them
at Mount Sinai. These are the words of that
agreement.
2 Moses called all the Israelites together and
said to them:
You have seen everything the LORD did before your own eyes to the king of Egypt and to
the king's leaders and to the whole country.
3 With your own eyes you saw the great troubles, signs, and miracles. 4 But to this day the
LORD has not given you a mind that understands; you don't really understand what you
see with your eyes or hear with your ears. 5 I
led you through the desert for forty years, and
during that time neither your clothes nor sandals wore out. 6 You ate no bread and drank no
wine or beer. This was so you would understand that I am the LORD your God.
7 When you came to this place, Sihon king
of Heshbon and Og king of Bashan came out
to fight us, but we defeated them. 8 We captured
their land and gave it to the tribes of Reuben,
Gad, and East Manasseh to be their own.

WHAT'S IT MEAN?

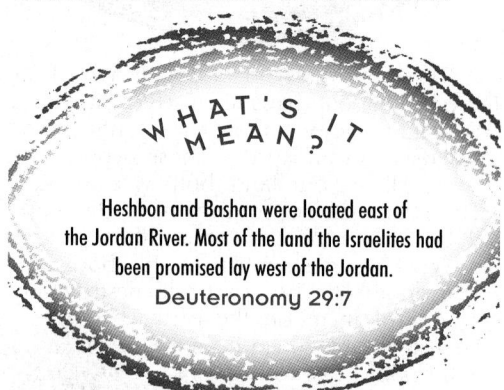

Heshbon and Bashan were located east of the Jordan River. Most of the land the Israelites had been promised lay west of the Jordan.
Deuteronomy 29:7

9 You must carefully obey everything in this
agreement so that you will succeed in everything you do. 10 Today you are all standing here
before the LORD your God—your leaders and
important men, your older leaders, officers,
and all the other men of Israel, 11 your wives
and children and the foreigners who live
among you, who chop your wood and carry
your water. 12 You are all here to enter into an

agreement and a promise with the LORD your God, an agreement the LORD your God is making with you today. 13This will make you today his own people. He will be your God, as he told you and as he promised your ancestors Abraham, Isaac, and Jacob. 14But I am not just making this agreement and its promises with you 15who are standing here before the LORD your God today, but also with those who are not here today.

16You know how we lived in Egypt and how we passed through the countries when we came here. 17You saw their hateful idols made of wood, stone, silver, and gold. 18Make sure no man, woman, family group, or tribe among you leaves the LORD our God to go and serve the gods of those nations. They would be to you like a plant that grows bitter, poisonous fruit.

WHAT'S IT MEAN?

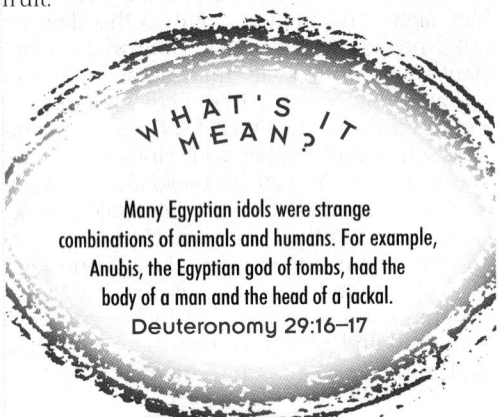

Many Egyptian idols were strange combinations of animals and humans. For example, Anubis, the Egyptian god of tombs, had the body of a man and the head of a jackal.
Deuteronomy 29:16–17

19These are the kind of people who hear these curses but bless themselves, thinking, "We will be safe even though we continue doing what we want to do." Those people may destroy all of your land, both wet and dry. 20The LORD will not forgive them. His anger will be like a burning fire against those people, and all the curses written in this book will come on them. The LORD will destroy any memory of them on the earth. 21He will separate them from all the tribes of Israel for punishment. All the curses of the Agreement that are written in this Book of the Teachings will happen to them.

22Your children who will come after you, as well as foreigners from faraway lands, will see the disasters that come to this land and the diseases the LORD will send on it. They will say, 23"The land is nothing but burning cinders and salt. Nothing is planted, nothing grows, and nothing blooms. It is like Sodom and Gomorrah, and Admah and Zeboiim, which the LORD destroyed because he was very angry." 24All the other nations will ask, "Why has the LORD done this to the land? Why is he so angry?"

25And the answer will be, "It is because the people broke the Agreement of the LORD, the God of their ancestors, which he made with them when he brought them out of Egypt. 26They went and served other gods and bowed down to gods they did not even know. The LORD did not allow that, 27so he became very angry at the land and brought all the curses on it that are written in this book. 28Since the LORD became angry and furious with them, he took them out of their land and put them in another land where they are today."

29There are some things the LORD our God has kept secret, but there are some things he has let us know. These things belong to us and our children forever so that we will do everything in these teachings.

THE ISRAELITES WILL RETURN

30

1When all these blessings and curses I have described happen to you, and the LORD your God has sent you away to other nations, think about these things. 2Then you and your children will return to the LORD your God, and you will obey him with your whole being in everything I am commanding you today. 3Then the LORD your God will give you back your freedom. He will feel sorry for you, and he will bring you back again from the nations where he scattered you. 4He may send you to the ends of the earth, but he will gather you and bring you back from there, 5back to the land that belonged to your ancestors. It will be yours. He will give you success, and there will be more of you than there were of your ancestors. 6The LORD your God will prepare you and your descendants to love him with your whole being so that you will live. 7The LORD your God will put all these curses on your enemies, who hate you and are cruel to you. 8And you will again obey the LORD, keeping all his commands that I give you today. 9The LORD your God will make you successful in everything you do. You will have many children, your cattle will have many calves, and your fields will produce good crops, because the LORD

"The LORD will again be happy with you, just as he was with your ancestors."
(Deuteronomy 30:9b)

will again be happy with you, just as he was
with your ancestors. 10But you must obey the
LORD your God by keeping all his commands
and rules that are written in this Book of the
Teachings. You must return to the LORD your
God with your whole being.

CHOOSE LIFE OR DEATH

11This command I give you today is not too
hard for you; it is not beyond what you can
do. 12It is not up in heaven. You do not have to
ask, "Who will go up to heaven and get it for us
so we can obey it and keep it?" 13It is not on the
other side of the sea. You do not have to ask,
"Who will go across the sea and get it? Who
will tell it to us so we can keep it?" 14No, the
word is very near you. It is in your mouth and
in your heart so you may obey it.

15Look, today I offer you life and success,
death and destruction. 16I command you today
to love the LORD your God, to do what he
wants you to do, and to keep his commands,
his rules, and his laws. Then you will live and
grow in number, and the LORD your God will
bless you in the land you are entering to take
as your own.

17But if you turn away from the LORD and
do not obey him, if you are led to bow and
serve other gods, 18I tell you today that you
will surely be destroyed. And you will not live
long in the land you are crossing the Jordan
River to enter and take as your own.

19Today I ask heaven and earth to be witnesses. I am offering you life or death, blessings
or curses. Now, choose life! Then you and
your children may live. 20To choose life is to
love the LORD your God, obey him, and stay
close to him. He is your life, and he will let you
live many years in the land, the land he promised to give your ancestors Abraham, Isaac,
and Jacob.

JOSHUA TAKES MOSES' PLACE

31 1Then Moses went and spoke these words to
all the Israelites: 2"I am now one hundred
twenty years old, and I cannot lead you anymore. The LORD told me I would not cross the
Jordan River; 3the LORD your God will lead
you across himself. He will destroy those nations for you, and you will take over their land.
Joshua will also lead you across, as the LORD
has said. 4The LORD will do to those nations
what he did to Sihon and Og, the kings of the
Amorites, when he destroyed them and their
land. 5The LORD will give those nations to you;
do to them everything I told you. 6Be strong
and brave. Don't be afraid of them and don't
be frightened, because the LORD your God will
go with you. He will not leave you or forget
you."

7Then Moses called Joshua and said to him
in front of the people, "Be strong and brave,
because you will lead these people into the
land the LORD promised to give their ancestors,
and help them take it as their own. 8The LORD
himself will go before you. He will be with
you; he will not leave you or forget you. Don't
be afraid and don't worry."

WHAT'S IT MEAN?

Joshua had experienced it all as an Israelite. He was born in Egypt while the Israelites were still captives, so he knew what it was like to be a slave. He was around for the first Passover, so he saw God's protection first-hand. He was one of the twelve spies Moses sent to check out the land of Canaan, so he knew what the Lord had waiting for the Israelites. He had faithfully served the Lord and followed Moses' instruction and now he was going to be the new leader of Israel.

Deuteronomy 31:7

MOSES WRITES THE TEACHINGS

9So Moses wrote down these teachings and
gave them to the priests and all the older leaders of Israel. (The priests are the sons of Levi,
who carry the Ark of the Agreement with the
LORD.) 10-11Then Moses commanded them:
"Read these teachings for all Israel to hear at
the end of every seven years, which is the year
to cancel what people owe. Do it during the
Feast of Shelters, when all the Israelites will
come to appear before the LORD your God and
stand at the place he will choose. 12Gather all
the people: the men, women, children, and foreigners living in your towns so that they can
listen and learn to respect the LORD your God
and carefully obey everything in this law.
13Since their children do not know this law,
they must hear it. They must learn to respect
the LORD your God for as long as they live in
the land you are crossing the Jordan River to
take for your own."

THE LORD CALLS MOSES AND JOSHUA

14The LORD said to Moses, "Soon you will
die. Get Joshua and come to the Meeting Tent

so that I may command him." So Moses and Joshua went to the Meeting Tent.

15The LORD appeared at the Meeting Tent in a cloud; the cloud stood over the entrance of the Tent. 16And the LORD said to Moses, "You will soon die. Then these people will not be loyal to me but will worship the foreign gods of the land they are entering. They will leave me, breaking the Agreement I made with them. 17Then I will become very angry at them, and I will leave them. I will turn away from them, and they will be destroyed. Many terrible things will happen to them. Then they will say, 'It is because God is not with us that these terrible things are happening.' 18I will surely turn away from them then, because they have done wrong and have turned to other gods.

19"Now write down this song and teach it to the Israelites. Then have them sing it, because it will be my witness against them. 20When I bring them into the land I promised to their ancestors, a fertile land, they will eat as much as they want and get fat. Then they will turn to other gods and serve them. They will reject me and break my Agreement. 21Then when many troubles and terrible things happen to them, this song will testify against them, because the song will not be forgotten by their descendants. I know what they plan to do, even before I take them into the land I promised them." 22So Moses wrote down the song that day, and he taught it to the Israelites.

23Then the LORD gave this command to Joshua son of Nun: "Be strong and brave, because you will lead the people of Israel to the land I promised them, and I will be with you."

24After Moses finished writing all the words of the teachings in a book, 25he gave a command to the Levites, who carried the Ark of the Agreement with the LORD. 26He said, "Take this Book of the Teachings and put it beside the Ark of the Agreement with the LORD your God. It must stay there as a witness against you. 27I know how stubborn and disobedient you are. You have disobeyed the LORD while I am alive and with you, and you will disobey even more after I die! 28Gather all the older leaders of your tribes and all your officers to me so that I may say these things for them to hear, and so that I may ask heaven and earth to testify against them. 29I know that after I die you will become completely evil. You will turn away from the commands I have given you. Terrible things will happen to you in the future when you do what the LORD says is evil, and you will make him angry with the idols you have made."

MOSES' SONG

30And Moses spoke this whole song for all the people of Israel to hear:

32

1Hear, heavens, and I will speak.
Listen, earth, to what I say.
2My teaching will drop like rain;
my words will fall like dew.

Promise

HE PROMISES NEVER TO LEAVE OR FORGET YOU.

The LORD himself will go before you. He will be with you; he will not leave you or forget you. Don't be afraid and don't worry (Deut. 31:8).

When you're about to go into unfamiliar territory—a new school, your first date, standing up for yourself for the first time—you probably feel a little shaky. Everyone understands that new situations can be a little scary. But if God told the Israelites not to be afraid of their enemies, you can bet he doesn't want you to be afraid of anything either. He certainly doesn't want you to be afraid of something just because you're not used to it.

He is with you all the time. You can't get rid of him. In these days of convenient relationships, children disowning their parents, divorce everywhere, it's easy to think that no one will ever be truly committed to you. God will. In the good times and the bad, in the familiar time and the new experiences, God is totally with you. No matter what you do or where you go, he is there. He doesn't take a break, doesn't blink for a split second. When God says he will not leave you or forget you, he is telling you he is with you all the time. You are never alone.

SEE FOR YOURSELF:

Josh. 1:5; Matt. 28:20; Heb. 13:5

They will be like showers on the grass;
they will pour down like rain on young plants.
3 I will announce the name of the LORD.
Praise God because he is great!
4 He is like a rock; what he does is perfect,
and he is always fair.
He is a faithful God who does no wrong,
who is right and fair.

5 They have done evil against him.
To their shame they are no longer his children;
they are an evil and lying people.
6 This is not the way to repay the LORD,
you foolish and unwise people.
He is your Father and Maker,
who made you and formed you.

7 Remember the old days.
Think of the years already passed.
Ask your father and he will tell you;
ask your older leaders and they will inform you.
8 God Most High gave the nations their lands,
dividing up the human race.
He set up borders for the people
and even numbered the Israelites.
9 The LORD took his people as his share,
the people of Jacob as his very own.

10 He found them in a desert,
a windy, empty land.
He surrounded them and brought them up,
guarding them as those he loved very much.
11 He was like an eagle building its nest
that flutters over its young.
It spreads its wings to catch them
and carries them on its feathers.
12 The LORD alone led them,
and there was no foreign god helping him.

13 The LORD brought them to the heights of the land
and fed them the fruit of the fields.
He gave them honey from the rocks,
bringing oil from the solid rock.
14 There were milk curds from the cows and milk from the flock;
there were fat sheep and goats.
There were sheep and goats from Bashan
and the best of the wheat.
You drank the juice of grapes.

15 Israel grew fat and kicked;
they were fat and full and firm.
They left the God who made them
and rejected the Rock who saved them.
16 They made God jealous with foreign gods
and angry with hateful idols.
17 They made sacrifices to demons, not God,
to gods they had never known,
new gods from nearby,
gods your ancestors did not fear.
18 You left God who is the Rock, your Father,
and you forgot the God who gave you birth.

19 The LORD saw this and rejected them;
his sons and daughters had made him angry.
20 He said, "I will turn away from them
and see what will happen to them.
They are evil people,
unfaithful children.
21 They used things that are not gods to make me jealous
and worthless idols to make me angry.
So I will use those who are not a nation to make them jealous;
I will use a nation that does not understand to make them angry.
22 My anger has started a fire
that burns down to the place of the dead.
It will burn up the ground and its crops,
and it will set fire to the base of the mountains.

23 "I will pile troubles upon them
and shoot my arrows at them.
24 They will be starved and sick,

WHAT'S IT MEAN?

Eagles and other birds of prey are like the stunt pilots of the bird world. If a young eagle falls out of its nest, the adult is capable of swooping down, catching the falling bird on its back before it hits the ground, and returning it to the nest.
Deuteronomy 32:11

destroyed by terrible diseases.
I will send them vicious animals
and gliding, poisonous snakes.
25 In the streets the sword will kill;
in their homes there will be terror.
Young men and women will die,
and so will babies and gray-haired men.
26 I will scatter them as I said,
and no one will remember them.
27 But I didn't want their enemy to brag;
their enemy might misunderstand
and say, 'We have won!
The LORD has done none of this.' "

28 Israel has no sense;
they do not understand.
29 I wish they were wise and understood this;
I wish they could see what will happen to them.
30 One person cannot chase a thousand people,
and two people cannot fight ten thousand
unless their Rock has sold them,
unless the LORD has given them up.
31 The rock of these people is not like our Rock;
our enemies agree to that.
32 Their vine comes from Sodom,
and their fields are like Gomorrah.
Their grapes are full of poison;
their bunches of grapes are bitter.
33 Their wine is like snake poison,
like the deadly poison of cobras.

34 "I have been saving this,
and I have it locked in my storehouses.
35 I will punish those who do wrong; I will repay them.
Soon their foot will slip,
because their day of trouble is near,
and their punishment will come quickly."

36 The LORD will defend his people
and have mercy on his servants.
He will see that their strength is gone,
that nobody is left, slaves or free.
37 Then he will say, "Where are their gods?
Where is the rock they trusted?
38 Who ate the fat from their sacrifices,
and who drank the wine of their drink offerings?
Let those gods come to help you!
Let them protect you!

39 "Now you will see that I am the one God!
There is no god but me.
I send life and death;
I can hurt, and I can heal.
No one can escape from me.
40 I raise my hand toward heaven and make this promise:
As surely as I live forever,
41 I will sharpen my flashing sword,

Promise

HE PROMISES TO PUNISH HIS ENEMIES.

I raise my hand toward heaven and make this promise: As surely as I live forever, I will sharpen my flashing sword, and I will take it in my hand to judge. I will punish my enemies and pay back those who hate me (Deut. 32:40–41).

Sometimes it seems like people can get away with anything. They cheat and steal and lie and curse God. They get other people to go along with them. Sometimes it goes on for years, and they just seem to be getting richer and more powerful by the minute. You look at them and think, *What good is it to obey God? I'm over here trying to live the Christian life, and I'm struggling day by day, and that guy is doing great!* Then BOOM, God takes revenge on his enemies. Everything goes to pieces for the other guy. You realize that God calls us to make choices for him. God calls us to be responsible for living his way. You see that he may tolerate stuff from his enemies for a while, but not forever. Read the Book of Revelation. You'll see that he will take revenge on his enemies. It is worth it to be on his side. He wins.

SEE FOR YOURSELF:
Is. 1:24; Ezek. 25:17; Nah. 1:2

and I will take it in my hand to judge.
I will punish my enemies
and pay back those who hate me.
42 My arrows will be covered with their blood;
my sword will eat their flesh.
The blood will flow from those who are killed and the captives.
The heads of the enemy leaders will be cut off."

43 Be happy, nations, with his people,
because he will repay you for the blood of his servants.
He will punish his enemies,
and he will remove the sin of his land and people.

44 Moses came with Joshua son of Nun, and
they spoke all the words of this song for the
people to hear. 45 When Moses finished speaking these words to all Israel, 46 he said to them:
"Pay careful attention to all the words I have
said to you today, and command your children to obey carefully everything in these
teachings. 47 These should not be unimportant
words for you, but rather they mean life for
you! By these words you will live a long time
in the land you are crossing the Jordan River
to take as your own."

MOSES GOES UP TO MOUNT NEBO

48 The LORD spoke to Moses again that same
day and said, 49 "Go up the Abarim Mountains,
to Mount Nebo in the country of Moab, across
from Jericho. Look at the land of Canaan that I
am giving to the Israelites as their own. 50 On
that mountain that you climb, you will die and
join your ancestors, just as your brother Aaron
died on Mount Hor and joined his ancestors.
51 You both sinned against me at the waters of
Meribah Kadesh in the Desert of Zin, and you
did not honor me as holy there among the Israelites. 52 So now you will only look at the
land from far away. You will not enter the land
I am giving the people of Israel."

MOSES BLESSES THE PEOPLE

33

1 Moses, the man of God, gave this blessing
to the Israelites before he died. 2 He said:

"The LORD came from Mount Sinai
and rose like the sun from Edom;
he showed his greatness from Mount Paran.
He came with thousands of angels
from the southern mountains.
3 The LORD surely loves his people
and takes care of all those who belong to him.
They bow down at his feet,
and they are taught by him.
4 Moses gave us the teachings
that belong to the people of Jacob.
5 The LORD became king of Israel
when the leaders of the people gathered,
when the tribes of Israel came together.

6 "Let the people of Reuben live and not die,
but let the people be few."

WHAT'S IT MEAN?

In ancient times, when a man reached the end of his life, it was common for him to pass along his visions or hopes for the future. In chapter 33's long poem, Moses shares his blessings for each of the twelve tribes of Israel.

Deuteronomy 33:1

7 Moses said this about the people of Judah:
"LORD, listen to Judah's prayer;
bring them back to their people.
They defend themselves with their hands.
Help them fight their enemies!"

8 Moses said this about the people of Levi:
"LORD, your Thummim and Urim belong
to Levi, whom you love.

WHAT'S IT MEAN?

Massah and Meribah weren't what you would call happy memories for the Israelites. These were the places God gave the Israelites water to stop their grumbling and complaining. They were remembered as places where the people of Israel had gone too far in questioning and challenging God.

Deuteronomy 33:8

LORD, you tested him at Massah
and argued with him at the waters of Meribah.
9 He said about his father and mother,
'I don't care about them.'
He did not treat his brothers as favorites
or give special favors to his children,
but he protected your word
and guarded your agreement.
10 He teaches your laws to the people of Jacob
and your teachings to the people of Israel.
He burns incense before you
and makes whole burnt offerings on your altar.
11 LORD, make them strong;
be pleased with the work they do.
Defeat those who attack them,
and don't let their enemies rise up again."

12 Moses said this about the people of Benjamin:
"The LORD's loved ones will lie down in safety,
because he protects them all day long.
The ones he loves rest with him."

> **"The LORD's loved ones will lie down in safety, because he protects them all day long. The ones he loves rest with him." (Deuteronomy 33:12)**

13 Moses said this about the people of Joseph:
"May the LORD bless their land with wonderful dew from heaven,
with water from the springs below,
14 with the best fruits that the sun brings,
and with the best fruits that the moon brings.
15 Let the old mountains give the finest crops,
and let the everlasting hills give the best fruits.
16 Let the full earth give the best fruits,
and let the LORD who lived in the burning bush be pleased.
May these blessings rest on the head of Joseph,
on the forehead of the one who was blessed among his brothers.
17 Joseph has the majesty of a firstborn bull;
he is as strong as a wild ox.
He will stab other nations,
even those nations far away.
These are the ten thousands of Ephraim,
and these are the thousands of Manasseh."

18 Moses said this about the people of Zebulun:
"Be happy when you go out, Zebulun,
and be happy in your tents, Issachar.
19 They will call the people to the mountain,
and there they will offer the right sacrifices.
They will do well from all that is in the sea,
and they will do well from the treasures hidden in the sand on the shore."

20 Moses said this about the people of Gad:
"Praise God who gives Gad more land!
Gad lives there like a lion,
who tears off arms and heads.
21 They chose the best land for themselves.
They received a large share, like that given to an officer.
When the leaders of the people gathered,
the people of Gad did what the LORD said was right,
and they judged Israel fairly."

22 Moses said this about the people of Dan:
"Dan is like a lion's cub,
who jumps out of Bashan."

23 Moses said this about the people of Naphtali:
"Naphtali enjoys special kindnesses,
and they are full of the LORD's blessings.
Take as your own the west and south."

24 Moses said this about the people of Asher:
"Asher is the most blessed of the sons;
let him be his brothers' favorite.
Let him bathe his feet in olive oil.
25 Your gates will have locks of iron and bronze,
and you will be strong as long as you live.

26 "There is no one like the God of Israel,
who rides through the skies to help you,
who rides on the clouds in his majesty.
27 The everlasting God is your place of safety,

and his arms will hold you up forever.
He will force your enemy out ahead of
you,
saying, 'Destroy the enemy!'
28The people of Israel will lie down in safety.
Jacob's spring is theirs alone.
Theirs is a land full of grain and new
wine,
where the skies drop their dew.
29Israel, you are blessed!
No one else is like you,
because you are a people saved by the
LORD.
He is your shield and helper,
your glorious sword.
Your enemies will be afraid of you,
and you will walk all over their holy
places."

MOSES DIES

34
1Then Moses climbed Mount Nebo from
the plains of Moab to the top of Mount Pisgah,
across from Jericho. From there the LORD
showed him all the land from Gilead to Dan,
2all of Naphtali and the lands of Ephraim and
Manasseh, all the land of Judah as far as the
Mediterranean Sea, 3as well as the southern
desert and the whole Valley of Jericho up to
Zoar. (Jericho is called the city of palm trees.)
4Then the LORD said to Moses, "This is the land
I promised to Abraham, Isaac, and Jacob when
I said to them, 'I will give this land to your
descendants.' I have let you look at it, Moses,
but you will not cross over there."
5Then Moses, the servant of the LORD, died
there in Moab, as the LORD had said. 6He buried Moses in Moab in the valley opposite Beth
Peor, but even today no one knows where his
grave is. 7Moses was one hundred twenty
years old when he died. His eyes were not
weak, and he was still strong. 8The Israelites
cried for Moses for thirty days, staying in the
plains of Moab until the time of sadness was
over.

WHAT'S IT MEAN?

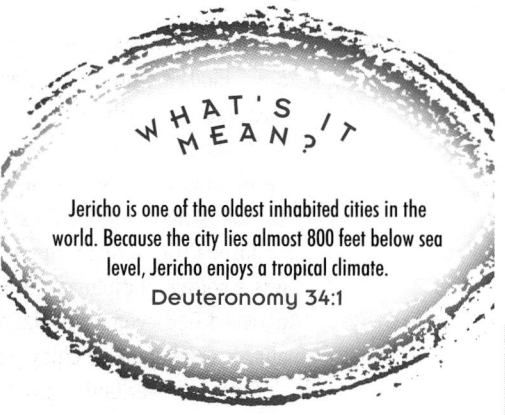

Jericho is one of the oldest inhabited cities in the world. Because the city lies almost 800 feet below sea level, Jericho enjoys a tropical climate.
Deuteronomy 34:1

9Joshua son of Nun was then filled with
wisdom, because Moses had put his hands on
him. So the Israelites listened to Joshua, and
they did what the LORD had commanded Moses.
10There has never been another prophet in
Israel like Moses. The LORD knew Moses face
to face 11and sent him to do signs and miracles
in Egypt—to the king, to all his officers, and to
the whole land of Egypt. 12Moses had great
power, and he did great and wonderful things
for all the Israelites to see.

Joshua

CONTENT If you want to read a war epic, Joshua is a book you'll enjoy. It's a "blood-and-guts" kind of story, too violent for a G-rating but too inspiring to pass up. Basically, while the Hebrews were slaves in Egypt, other people settled on their land. That meant the homeland was home to more than one inhabitant. That's never good news. So the Hebrews had to fight to get their land back. The Book of Joshua is the record of those battles.

Joshua was actually the name of the man who led the Hebrews into battles. He was a soldier, a diplomat, a negotiator, and a strategist. He was a good man who believed God even when the odds were stacked up so high against his people that almost everyone else chickened out. He was a real hero.

Over and over God showed the Hebrews that it takes as much courage to believe in the power of God as it does to fight under your own power. But when you believe, the results are better every time.

Outline

1:1-9 .... Joshua Becomes the Leader of Israel
1:10—6:27 .... Israel Crosses the Jordan River and Conquers Jericho
7:1-26 .... Achan Disobeys the Lord
8:1-35 .... The Battle at Ai
9:1-27 .... The People of Gibeon Trick the Leaders of Israel
10:1-15 .... Joshua Commands the Sun to Stand Still
10:16—12:24 ...... Israel Takes Over Much of the Land of Canaan
13:1-7 .... Land That Israel Did Not Take Over
13:8-33 .... Lands That Moses Had Assigned East of the Jordan
14:1—19:51 .... Lands Assigned West of the Jordan
20:1-9 .... Cities of Safety
21:1-45 .... Towns for the Levites
22:1-34 .... The Eastern Tribes Return Home
23:1—24:33 .... Joshua's Farewell Speeches and Death

Purpose Obedience to God is the key to a success-filled life.

Theme Possessing the Inheritance

Date of writing 1405–1390 B.C.

"Always remember what is written in the Book of the Teachings. Study it day and night to be sure to obey everything that is written there. If you do this, you will be wise and successful in everything" (1:8).

Bible Talk

Jericho

One of the most famous battles that Joshua faced was the battle of Jericho. This was the battle where the people marched around the city of Jericho for seven days. Just marched. That's all they did. On the seventh day, they marched seven times and then shouted. At this point, to everyone's amazement, the walls of the city fell right down. In went the Hebrews and down went the city.

God did these kinds of miracles for the Hebrews all the time as long as they were faithful. He did this because he wanted it to be oh so obvious that it was God's strength that won the battles, not the people's strength. Sometimes they got it and sometimes they didn't.

LIKE BATTLES WE FACE

The Book of Joshua matters to us today for several reasons. One of those reasons is because we face the same kind of battles that they faced. We face temptations that are too big for us to conquer alone. We face difficult times that feel like they are going to overwhelm us.

The lesson for us in our battles is the same as the lesson for the Hebrews. *Trust God to do your fighting for you. Keep your life clean and take it one step at a time.*

Joshua was pretty good at following this lesson. That's why he was known as a mighty warrior. He really and truly knew that it was God's strength that made the difference in the battles of life.

GOD'S COMMAND TO JOSHUA

1After Moses, the servant of the LORD, died,
the LORD spoke to Joshua son of Nun, Moses'
assistant. 2The LORD said, "My servant Moses is
dead. Now you and all these people go across
the Jordan River into the land I am giving to
the Israelites. 3I promised Moses I would give
you this land, so I will give you every place
you go in the land. 4All the land from the
desert in the south to Lebanon in the north
will be yours. All the land from the great river,
the Euphrates, in the east, to the Mediterranean
Sea in the west will be yours, too, including the
land of the Hittites. 5No one will be able to
defeat you all your life. Just as I was with Moses, so I will be with you. I will not leave you
or forget you.
6"Joshua, be strong and brave! You must
lead these people so they can take the land that
I promised their fathers I would give them. 7Be
strong and brave. Be sure to obey all the teachings my servant Moses gave you. If you follow
them exactly, you will be successful in everything you do. 8Always remember what is written in the Book of the Teachings. Study it day
and night to be sure to obey everything that is written there. If you
do this, you will be wise and
successful in everything. 9Re-
member that I commanded
you to be strong and brave.
Don't be afraid, because the
LORD your God will be with
you everywhere you go."

COURAGE
Why should we have courage? (1:9)

JOSHUA'S ORDERS TO THE PEOPLE

10Then Joshua gave orders to the officers of
the people: 11"Go through the camp and tell the
people, 'Get your supplies ready. Three days
from now you will cross the Jordan River and
take the land the LORD your God is giving
you.' "

WHAT'S IT MEAN?

Just in case you were wondering . . .
The Euphrates River is located 350 to 400 miles northeast of Jerusalem. At almost 1,780 miles, it is the longest river in western Asia. The Euphrates begins in Turkey, or Armenia, as the ancient Israelites called it. The ruins of the ancient cities of Babylon, Kish, and Ur can be found on the banks of the Euphrates.
Joshua 1:4

12Then Joshua said to the people of Reuben,
Gad, and East Manasseh, 13"Remember what
Moses, the servant of the LORD, told you. He
said the LORD your God would give you rest
and would give you this land. 14Now the LORD
has given you this land east of the Jordan
River. Your wives, children, and animals may
stay here, but your fighting men must dress for

Promise HE PROMISES TO HELP YOU WHEREVER YOU GO.

Remember that I commanded you to be strong and brave. Don't be afraid, because the LORD your God will be with you everywhere you go (Josh. 1:9).

Remember the last time you needed help? Not just help with your homework, but HELP. You were at the end of your rope, no more options; you'd done everything and nothing worked. You were confused, afraid, and lonely all at the same time. What do you do when the answers just don't seem to come? Joshua 1:9. God gives two positive commands here—be strong and brave. Don't be afraid. And then, the promise, "The LORD your God will be with you everywhere you go." That promise gives you strength to obey the two commands. You can rest in the fact that God promises to help. You are not alone. You may not get help at the exact second you think you need it, but he will help you. He knows exactly how much you can take. He'll be right on time.

SEE FOR YOURSELF:
Ps. 54:4; John 14:16; Heb. 13:6

war and cross the Jordan River ahead of your
brothers to help them. [15]The LORD has given
you a place to rest and will do the same for
your brothers. But you must help them until
they take the land the LORD their God is giving
them. Then you may return to your own land
east of the Jordan River, the land that Moses,
the servant of the LORD, gave you."
[16]Then the people answered Joshua, "Anything you command us to do, we will do. Any
place you send us, we will go. [17]Just as we fully
obeyed Moses, we will obey you. We ask only
that the LORD your God be with you just as he
was with Moses. [18]Whoever refuses to obey
your commands or turns against you will be
put to death. Just be strong and brave!"

SPIES SENT TO JERICHO

2 [1]Joshua son of Nun secretly sent out two
spies from Acacia and said to them, "Go and
look at the land, particularly at the city of Jericho."
So the men went to Jericho and stayed at
the house of a prostitute named Rahab.
[2]Someone told the king of Jericho, "Some
men from Israel have come here tonight to spy
out the land."
[3]So the king of Jericho sent this message to
Rahab: "Bring out the men who came to you
and entered your house. They have come to
spy out our whole land."
[4]But the woman had hidden the two men.
She said, "They did come here, but I didn't
know where they came from. [5]In the evening,
when it was time to close the city gate, they left.
I don't know where they went, but if you go
quickly, maybe you can catch them." [6](The
woman had taken the men up to the roof[n] and
had hidden them there under stalks of flax that
she had spread out.) [7]So the king's men went
out looking for the spies on the road that leads
to the crossings of the Jordan River. The city
gate was closed just after the king's men left the
city.
[8]Before the spies went to sleep for the night,
Rahab went up to the roof. [9]She said to them,
"I know the LORD has given this land to your
people. You frighten us very much. Everyone
living in this land is terribly afraid of you [10]be-
cause we have heard how the LORD dried up
the Red Sea when you came out of Egypt. We
have heard how you destroyed Sihon and Og,
two Amorite kings who lived east of the Jordan. [11]When we heard this, we were very
frightened. Now our men are afraid to fight
you because the LORD your God rules the
heavens above and the earth below! [12]So now, promise me
before the LORD that you will
show kindness to my family
just as I showed kindness to
you. Give me some proof that
you will do this. [13]Allow my
father, mother, brothers, sisters,
and all of their families to live. Save us from
death."
[14]The men agreed and said, "It will be our
lives for your lives if you don't tell anyone
what we are doing. When the LORD gives us
the land, we will be kind and true to you."
[15]The house Rahab lived in was built on the
city wall, so she used a rope to let the men
down through a window. [16]She said to them,
"Go into the hills so the king's men will not
find you. Hide there for three days. After the
king's men return, you may go on your way."
[17]The men said to her, "You must do as we
say. If not, we cannot be responsible for keeping this oath you have made us swear. [18]When
we return to this land, you must tie this red
rope in the window through which you let us
down. Bring your father, mother, brothers, and
all your family into your house. [19]If anyone
leaves your house and is killed, it is his own
fault. We cannot be responsible for him. If
anyone in your house is hurt, we will be responsible. [20]But if you tell anyone about this,
we will be free from the oath you made us
swear."

EMOTIONS
How should God's awesome acts make us feel? (2:8–13)

WHAT'S IT MEAN?

Ancient houses were built with flat roofs that were used like modern decks or porches. Crops and clothes were often laid out on the roof to dry. When visitors stopped by, extra beds were provided on the roof to accommodate them.
Joshua 2:3–7

2:6 roof In Bible times houses were built with flat roofs. The roof was used for drying things such as flax and fruit. And it was used as an extra room, as a place for worship, and as a cool place to sleep in the summer.

21 Rahab answered, "I agree to this." So she sent them away, and they left. Then she tied the red rope in the window.

22 The men left and went into the hills where they stayed for three days. The king's men looked for them all along the road, but after three days, they returned to the city without finding them. 23 Then the two men started back. They left the hills and crossed the river and came to Joshua son of Nun and told him everything that had happened to them. 24 They said, "The LORD surely has given us all of the land. All the people in that land are terribly afraid of us."

CROSSING THE JORDAN

3 1 Early the next morning Joshua and all the Israelites left Acacia. They traveled to the Jordan River and camped there before crossing it. 2 After three days the officers went through the camp 3 and gave orders to the people: "When you see the priests and Levites carrying the Ark of the Agreement with the LORD your God, leave where you are and follow it. 4 That way you will know which way to go since you have never been here before. But do not follow too closely. Stay about a thousand yards behind the Ark."

"Then Joshua told the people, 'Make yourselves holy, because tomorrow the LORD will do amazing things among you.'" (Joshua 3:5)

WHAT'S IT MEAN?

Carrying the Ark of the Agreement was no small task. It was about the size of a small desk. The Ark had rings on its sides so that the priests could put poles through them and carry the sacred container without actually touching it. The Israelites carried it into battle because they believed it gave them the power of God.

Joshua 3:3–4

5 Then Joshua told the people, "Make yourselves holy, because tomorrow the LORD will do amazing things among you."

6 Joshua said to the priests, "Take the Ark of the Agreement and go ahead of the people." So the priests lifted the Ark and carried it ahead of the people.

7 Then the LORD said to Joshua, "Today I will begin to make you great in the opinion of all the Israelites so the people will know I am with you just as I was with Moses. 8 Tell the priests who carry the Ark of the Agreement to go to the edge of the Jordan River and stand in the water."

ADVICE

Where should we turn for advice? (3:9)

9 Then Joshua said to the Israelites, "Come here and listen to the words of the LORD your God. 10 Here is proof that the living God is with you and that he will force out the Canaanites, Hittites, Hivites, Perizzites, Girgashites, Amorites, and Jebusites. 11 The Ark of the Agreement with the Lord of the whole world will go ahead of you into the Jordan River. 12 Now choose twelve men from among you, one from each of the twelve tribes of Israel. 13 The priests will carry the Ark of the LORD, the Master of the whole world, into the Jordan ahead of you. When they step into the water, it will stop. The river will stop flowing and will stand up in a heap."

14 So the people left the place where they had camped, and they followed the priests who carried the Ark of the Agreement across the Jordan River. 15 During harvest the Jordan overflows its banks. When the priests carrying the Ark came to the edge of the river and stepped into the water, 16 the water upstream stopped flowing. It stood up in a heap a great distance away at Adam, a town near Zarethan. The water flowing down to the Sea of Arabah (the Dead Sea) was completely cut off. So the people crossed the river near Jericho. 17 The priests carried the Ark of the Agreement with the LORD to the middle of the river and stood there on dry ground. They waited there while all the people of Israel walked across the Jordan River on dry land.

ROCKS TO REMIND THE PEOPLE

4 1 After all the people had finished crossing the Jordan, the LORD said to Joshua, 2 "Choose twelve men from among the people, one from each tribe. 3 Tell them to get twelve rocks from the middle of the river, from where the priests stood. Carry the rocks and put them down where you stay tonight."

4So Joshua chose one man from each tribe.
Then he called the twelve men together 5and
said to them, "Go out into the river where the
Ark of the LORD your God is. Each of you bring
back one rock, one for each tribe of Israel, and
carry it on your shoulder. 6They will be a sign
among you. In the future your children will
ask you, 'What do these rocks mean?' 7Tell
them the water stopped flowing in the Jordan
when the Ark of the Agreement with the LORD
crossed the river. These rocks will always remind the Israelites of this."
8So the Israelites obeyed Joshua and carried
twelve rocks from the middle of the Jordan
River, one rock for each of the twelve tribes of
Israel, just as the LORD had commanded
Joshua. They carried the rocks with them and
put them down where they made their camp.
9Joshua also put twelve rocks in the middle of
the Jordan River where the priests had stood
while carrying the Ark of the Agreement. These
rocks are still there today.
10The priests carrying the Ark continued
standing in the middle of the river until everything was done that the LORD had commanded
Joshua to tell the people, just as Moses had
told Joshua. The people hurried across the
river. 11After they finished crossing the river,
the priests carried the Ark of the LORD to the
other side as the people watched. 12The men
from the tribes of Reuben, Gad, and East Manasseh obeyed what Moses had told them.
They were dressed for war, and they crossed
the river ahead of the other people. 13About
forty thousand soldiers prepared for war
passed before the LORD as they marched across
the river, going toward the plains of Jericho.
14That day the LORD made Joshua great in
the opinion of all the Israelites. They respected
Joshua all his life, just as they had respected
Moses.
15Then the LORD said to Joshua, 16"Command the priests to bring the Ark of the Agreement out of the river."
17So Joshua commanded the priests, "Come
up out of the Jordan."
18Then the priests carried the Ark of the
Agreement with the LORD out of the river. As
soon as their feet touched dry land, the water
began flowing again. The river again overflowed its banks, just as it had before they
crossed.
19The people crossed the Jordan on the
tenth day of the first month and camped at
Gilgal, east of Jericho. 20They carried with them
the twelve rocks taken from the Jordan, and
Joshua set them up at Gilgal. 21Then he spoke
to the Israelites: "In the future your children
will ask you, 'What do these rocks mean?' 22Tell
them, 'Israel crossed the Jordan River on dry
land. 23The LORD your God caused the
water to stop flowing until you
finished crossing it, just as the
LORD did to the Red Sea. He
stopped the water until we
crossed it. 24The LORD did this
so all people would know he
has great power and so you
would always respect the LORD your God.' "

GOD
How powerful is God? (4:23–24)

5 1All the kings of the Amorites west of the
Jordan and the Canaanite kings living by the
Mediterranean Sea heard that the LORD dried
up the Jordan River until the Israelites had
crossed it. After that they were scared and too
afraid to face the Israelites.

THE ISRAELITES ARE CIRCUMCISED

2At that time the LORD said to Joshua,
"Make knives from flint stones and circumcise
the Israelites." 3So Joshua made knives from
flint stones and circumcised the Israelites at
Gibeath Haaraloth.
4This is why Joshua circumcised the men:
After the Israelites left Egypt, all the men old
enough to serve in the army died in the desert
on the way out of Egypt. 5The men who had
come out of Egypt had been circumcised, but
none of those who were born in the desert on
the trip from Egypt had been circumcised. 6The
Israelites had moved about in the desert for
forty years. During that time all the fighting
men who had left Egypt had died because they
had not obeyed the LORD. So the LORD swore
they would not see the land he had promised
their ancestors to give them, a fertile land.
7Their sons took their places. But none of the
sons born on the trip from Egypt had been
circumcised, so Joshua circumcised them. 8Af-
ter all the Israelites had been circumcised, they
stayed in camp until they were healed.
9Then the LORD said to Joshua, "As slaves in
Egypt you were ashamed, but today I have removed that shame." So Joshua named that
place Gilgal, which it is still named today.
10The people of Israel were camped at Gilgal
on the plains of Jericho. It was there, on the
evening of the fourteenth day of the month,
they celebrated the Passover Feast. 11The day
after the Passover, the people ate food grown
on that land: bread made without yeast and
roasted grain. 12The day they ate this food, the
manna stopped coming. The Israelites no longer
got the manna from heaven. They ate the food
grown in the land of Canaan that year.

13Joshua was near Jericho when he looked up and saw a man standing in front of him with a sword in his hand. Joshua went to him and asked, "Are you a friend or an enemy?"

14The man answered, "I am neither. I have come as the commander of the LORD's army."

Then Joshua bowed facedown on the ground and asked, "Does my master have a command for me, his servant?"

15The commander of the LORD's army answered, "Take off your sandals, because the place where you are standing is holy." So Joshua did.

WHAT'S IT MEAN?

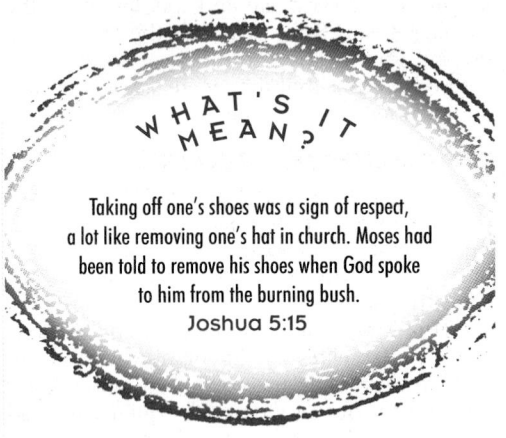

Taking off one's shoes was a sign of respect, a lot like removing one's hat in church. Moses had been told to remove his shoes when God spoke to him from the burning bush.

Joshua 5:15

THE FALL OF JERICHO

6 1The people of Jericho were afraid because the Israelites were near. They closed the city gates and guarded them. No one went into the city, and no one came out.

2Then the LORD said to Joshua, "Look, I have given you Jericho, its king, and all its fighting men. 3March around the city with your army once a day for six days. 4Have seven priests carry trumpets made from horns of male sheep and have them march in front of the Ark. On the seventh day march around the city seven times and have the priests blow the trumpets as they march. 5They will make one long blast on the trumpets. When you hear that sound, have all the people give a loud shout. Then the walls of the city will fall so the people can go straight into the city."

6So Joshua son of Nun called the priests together and said to them, "Carry the Ark of the Agreement. Tell seven priests to carry trumpets and march in front of it." 7Then Joshua ordered the people, "Now go! March around the city. The soldiers with weapons should march in front of the Ark of the Agreement with the LORD."

8When Joshua finished speaking to the people, the seven priests began marching before the LORD. They carried the seven trumpets and blew them as they marched. The priests carrying the Ark of the Agreement with the LORD followed them. 9Soldiers with weapons marched in front of the priests, and armed men walked behind the Ark. The priests were blowing their trumpets. 10But Joshua had told the people not to give a war cry. He said, "Don't shout. Don't say a word until the day I tell you. Then shout." 11So Joshua had the Ark of the LORD carried around the city one time. Then they went back to camp for the night.

12Early the next morning Joshua got up, and the priests carried the Ark of the LORD again. 13The seven priests carried the seven trumpets and marched in front of the Ark of the LORD, blowing their trumpets. Soldiers with weapons marched in front of them, and other soldiers walked behind the Ark of the LORD. All this time the priests were blowing their trumpets. 14So on the second day they marched around the city one time and then went back to camp. They did this every day for six days.

15On the seventh day they got up at dawn and marched around the city, just as they had on the days before. But on that day they marched around the city seven times. 16The seventh time around the priests blew their trumpets. Then Joshua gave the command: "Now, shout! The LORD has given you this city! 17The city and everything in it are to be destroyed as an offering to the LORD. Only Rahab the prostitute and everyone in her house should remain alive. They must not be killed, because Rahab hid the two spies we sent out. 18Don't take any of the things that are to be destroyed as an offering to the LORD. If you take them and bring them into our camp, you yourselves will be destroyed, and you will bring trouble to all of Israel. 19All the silver and gold and things made from bronze and iron belong to the LORD and must be saved for him."

20When the priests blew the trumpets, the people shouted. At the sound of the trumpets and the people's shout, the walls fell, and everyone ran straight into the city. So the Israelites defeated that city. 21They completely destroyed with the sword every living thing in the city—men and women, young and old, cattle, sheep, and donkeys.

22Joshua said to the two men who had spied out the land, "Go into the prostitute's house. Bring her out and bring out those who are with her, because of the promise you made to her." 23So the two men went into the house and brought out Rahab, her father, mother, brothers, and all those with her. They put all of her family in a safe place outside the camp of Israel.

24Then Israel burned the whole city and everything in it, but they did not burn the things made from silver, gold, bronze, and iron. These were saved for the LORD. 25Joshua saved Rahab the prostitute, her family, and all who were with her, because Rahab had helped the men he had sent to spy out Jericho. Rahab still lives among the Israelites today.

26Then Joshua made this oath:

"Anyone who tries to rebuild this city of Jericho
will be cursed by the LORD.
The one who lays the foundation of this city
will lose his oldest son,
and the one who sets up the gates
will lose his youngest son."

27So the LORD was with Joshua, and Joshua became famous through all the land.

SUCCESS

Who gives us success? (6:27)

THE SIN OF ACHAN

7 1But the Israelites did not obey the LORD. There was a man from the tribe of Judah named Achan. (He was the son of Carmi and grandson of Zabdi, who was the son of Zerah.) Because Achan kept some of the things that were to be given to the LORD, the LORD became very angry at the Israelites.

2Joshua sent some men from Jericho to Ai, which was near Beth Aven, east of Bethel. He told them, "Go to Ai and spy out the area." So the men went to spy on Ai.

3Later they came back to Joshua and said, "There are only a few people in Ai, so we will not need all our people to defeat them. Send only two or three thousand men to fight. There is no need to send all of our people." 4So about three thousand men went up to Ai, but the people of Ai beat them badly. 5The people of Ai killed about thirty-six Israelites and then chased the rest from the city gate all the way down to the canyon, killing them as they went down the hill. When the Israelites saw this, they lost their courage.

WHAT'S IT MEAN?

Ai was probably smaller than Jericho, which led the spies to believe it wouldn't take many soldiers to capture it. Big mistake.
Joshua 7:2–3

6Then Joshua tore his clothes in sorrow. He bowed facedown on the ground before the Ark of the LORD and stayed there until evening. The leaders of Israel did the same thing. They also threw dirt on their heads to show their sorrow. 7Then Joshua said, "Lord GOD, you brought our people across the Jordan River. Why did you bring us this far and then let the Amorites destroy us? We would have been happy to stay on the other side of the Jordan. 8Lord, there is nothing I can say now. Israel has been beaten by the enemy. 9The Canaanites and all the other people in this country will hear about this and will surround and kill us all! Then what will you do for your own great name?"

10The LORD said to Joshua, "Stand up! Why are you down on your face? 11The Israelites

On the Edge

So the LORD was with Joshua, and Joshua became famous through all the land (Josh. 6:27).

Jericho belonged to God, and it was time to reclaim it. So he sent Joshua and gave him the plan. "March slowly around the city every day for six days. On the seventh day, go around seven times, then blow the trumpets, and shout. The walls will fall down, and the soldiers can just walk in and take the city." Cool. What a plan! It worked. Do all good plans work? Nope. This plan worked because it was a God-plan. Joshua listened to God's plans, and God was with him to help in everything he did. The same is true for you. When you listen to God and obey his plan, he promises to help you. He will guide you every single day. His instruction will not be confusing. What wall is God calling you to conquer? Are you listening to him? Then start marching.

SEE FOR YOURSELF:
2 Chr. 14:11; Ps. 33:20; 46:1; Rom. 8:26

have sinned; they have broken the agreement I commanded them to obey. They took some of the things I commanded them to destroy. They have stolen and lied and have taken those things for themselves. 12That is why the Israelites cannot face their enemies. They turn away from the fight and run, because I have commanded that they be destroyed. I will not help you anymore unless you destroy everything as I commanded you.

WHAT'S IT MEAN?

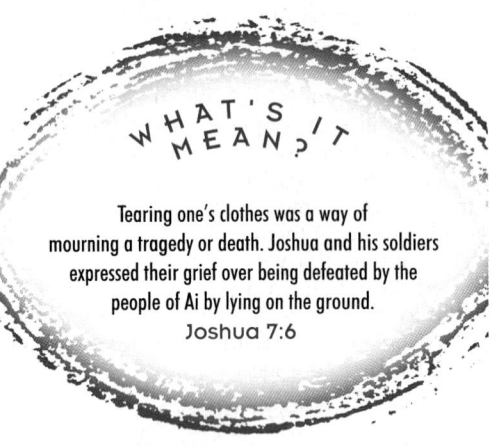

Tearing one's clothes was a way of mourning a tragedy or death. Joshua and his soldiers expressed their grief over being defeated by the people of Ai by lying on the ground.
Joshua 7:6

13"Now go! Make the people holy. Tell them, 'Set yourselves apart to the LORD for tomorrow. The LORD, the God of Israel, says some of you are keeping things he commanded you to destroy. You will never defeat your enemies until you throw away those things.

14" 'Tomorrow morning you must be present with your tribes. The LORD will choose one tribe to stand alone before him. Then the LORD will choose one family group from that tribe to stand before him. Then the LORD will choose one family from that family group to stand before him, person by person. 15The one who is keeping what should have been destroyed will himself be destroyed by fire. Everything he owns will be destroyed with him. He has broken the agreement with the LORD and has done a disgraceful thing among the people of Israel!' "

16Early the next morning Joshua led all of Israel to present themselves in their tribes, and the LORD chose the tribe of Judah. 17So the family groups of Judah presented themselves, and the LORD then chose the family group of Zerah. When all the families of Zerah presented themselves, the family of Zabdi was chosen. 18And Joshua told all the men in that family to present themselves. The LORD chose Achan son of Carmi. (Carmi was the son of Zabdi, who was the son of Zerah.)

19Then Joshua said to Achan, "My son, tell the truth. Confess to the LORD, the God of Israel. Tell me what you did, and don't try to hide anything from me."

20Achan answered, "It is true! I have sinned against the LORD, the God of Israel. This is what I did: 21Among the things I saw was a beautiful coat from Babylonia and about five pounds of silver and more than one and one-fourth pounds of gold. I wanted these things very much for myself, so I took them. You will find them buried in the ground under my tent, with the silver underneath."

22So Joshua sent men who ran to the tent and found the things hidden there, with the silver. 23The men brought them out of the tent, took them to Joshua and all the Israelites, and spread them out on the ground before the LORD. 24Then Joshua and all the people led Achan son of Zerah to the Valley of Trouble. They also took the silver, the coat, the gold, Achan's sons, daughters, cattle, donkeys, sheep, tent, and everything he owned. 25Joshua said, "I don't know why you caused so much trouble for us, but now the LORD will bring trouble to you." Then all the people threw stones at Achan and his family until they died. Then the people burned them. 26They piled rocks over Achan's body, and they are still there today. That is why it is called the Valley of Trouble. After this the LORD was no longer angry.

SIN
Does sin have consequences? (7:20–25)

AI IS DESTROYED

8

1Then the LORD said to Joshua, "Don't be afraid or give up. Lead all your fighting men to Ai. I will help you defeat the king of Ai, his people, his city, and his land. 2You will do to Ai and its king what you did to Jericho and its king. Only this time you may take all the wealth and keep it for yourselves. Now tell some of your soldiers to set up an ambush behind the city."

DISCOURAGEMENT
Who encourages us with victories? (8:1)

3So Joshua led his whole army toward Ai. Then he chose thirty thousand of his best fighting men and sent them out at night. 4Joshua gave them these orders: "Listen carefully. You must set up an ambush behind the city. Don't go far from it, but continue to watch and be ready. 5I and the men who are with me will march toward the city, and the men in the city will come out to fight us, just as they did before. Then we will turn

and run away from them. 6They will chase us
away from the city, thinking we are running
away from them as we did before. When we
run away, 7come out from your ambush and
take the city. The LORD your God will give you
the power to win. 8After you take the city, burn
it. See to it! You have your orders."
9Then Joshua sent them to
wait in ambush between Bethel and Ai, to the west of Ai.
But Joshua stayed the night
with his people.
10Early the next morning
Joshua gathered his men together. He and the older
leaders of Israel led them up
to Ai. 11All of the soldiers who
were with Joshua marched up to
Ai and stopped in front of the city and
made camp north of it. There was a valley between them and the city. 12Then Joshua chose
about five thousand men and set them in ambush in the area west of the city between Bethel and Ai. 13So the people took their positions;
the main camp was north of the city, and the
other men were hiding to the west. That night
Joshua went down into the valley.
14Now when the king of Ai saw the army of
Israel, he and his people got up early the next
morning and hurried out to fight them. They
went out to a place east of the city, but the king
did not know soldiers were waiting in ambush
behind the city. 15Joshua and all the men of Israel let the army of Ai push them back. Then
they ran toward the desert. 16The men in Ai
were called to chase Joshua and his men, so
they left the city and went after them. 17All the
men of Ai and Bethel chased the army of Israel.
The city was left open; not a man stayed to
protect it.
18Then the LORD said to Joshua, "Hold your
spear toward Ai, because I will give you that
city." So Joshua held his spear toward the city
of Ai. 19When the Israelites who were in ambush saw this, they quickly came out of their
hiding place and hurried toward the city. They
entered the city, took control of it, and quickly
set it on fire.
20When the men of Ai looked back, they
saw smoke rising from their city. At the same
time the Israelites stopped running and turned
against the men of Ai, who could not escape in
any direction. 21When Joshua and all his men
saw that the army had taken control of the city
and saw the smoke rising from it, they stopped
running and turned to fight the men of Ai.
22The men who were in ambush also came out
of the city to help with the fight. So the men of
Ai were caught between the armies of Israel.
None of the enemy escaped. The Israelites
fought until not one of the men of Ai was left
alive, except 23the king of Ai, and they brought
him to Joshua.

"Then the LORD said to Joshua, 'Don't be afraid or give up. Lead all your fighting men to Ai.' " (Joshua 8:1a)

A REVIEW OF THE FIGHTING

24During the fighting the
army of Israel chased the
men of Ai into the fields and
desert and killed all of them.
Then they went back to Ai
and killed everyone there.
25All the people of Ai died
that day, twelve thousand
men and women. 26Joshua
had held his spear toward Ai, as
a sign to destroy the city, and did
not draw it back until all the people of Ai were
destroyed. 27The people of Israel kept for themselves the animals and the other things the
people of Ai had owned, as the LORD had commanded Joshua to do.
28Then Joshua burned the city of Ai and
made it a pile of ruins. And it is still like that
today. 29Joshua hanged the king of Ai on a tree
and left him there until evening. At sunset
Joshua told his men to take the king's body
down from the tree and to throw it down at
the city gate. Then they covered it with a pile of
rocks, which is still there today.

WHAT'S IT MEAN?

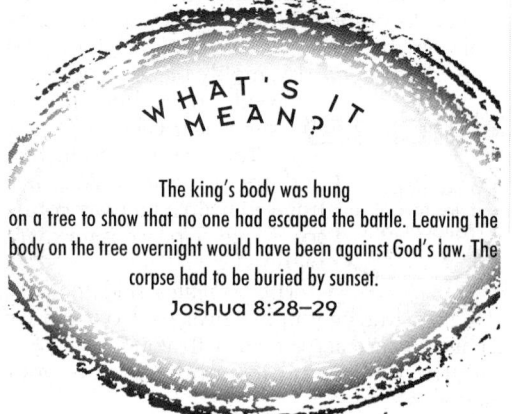

The king's body was hung on a tree to show that no one had escaped the battle. Leaving the body on the tree overnight would have been against God's law. The corpse had to be buried by sunset.

Joshua 8:28–29

30Joshua built an altar for the LORD, the God
of Israel, on Mount Ebal, as 31Moses, the
LORD's servant, had commanded. Joshua built
the altar as it was explained in the Book of the
Teachings of Moses. It was made from uncut
stones; no tool was ever used on them. On that
altar the Israelites offered burnt offerings to the
LORD and fellowship offerings. 32There Joshua

wrote the teachings of Moses on stones for all the people of Israel to see. 33The older leaders, officers, judges, and all the Israelites were there; Israelites and non-Israelites were all standing around the Ark of the Agreement with the LORD in front of the priests, the Levites who had carried the Ark. Half of the people stood in front of Mount Ebal, and half stood in front of Mount Gerizim. This was the way the LORD's servant Moses had earlier commanded the people to be blessed.

34Then Joshua read all the words of the teachings, the blessings and the curses, exactly as they were written in the Book of the Teachings. 35All the Israelites were gathered together—men, women, and children—along with the non-Israelites who lived among them. Joshua read every command that Moses had given.

THE GIBEONITE TRICKERY

9 1All the kings west of the Jordan River heard about these things: the kings of the Hittites, Amorites, Canaanites, Perizzites, Hivites, and Jebusites. They lived in the mountains and on the western hills and along the whole Mediterranean Sea coast. 2So all these kings gathered to fight Joshua and the Israelites.

3When the people of Gibeon heard how Joshua had defeated Jericho and Ai, 4they decided to trick the Israelites. They gathered old sacks and old leather wine bags that were cracked and mended, and they put them on the backs of their donkeys. 5They put old sandals on their feet and wore old clothes, and they took some dry, moldy bread. 6Then they went to Joshua in the camp near Gilgal.

FOLLOWING GOD

What happens if we forget to follow God? (9:3–18)

The men said to Joshua and the Israelites, "We have traveled from a faraway country. Make a peace agreement with us."

7The Israelites said to these Hivites, "Maybe you live near us. How can we make a peace agreement with you?"

8The Hivites said to Joshua, "We are your servants."

But Joshua asked, "Who are you? Where do you come from?"

9The men answered, "We are your servants who have come from a far country, because we heard of the fame of the LORD your God. We heard about what he has done and everything he did in Egypt. 10We heard that he defeated the two kings of the Amorites from the east side of the Jordan River—Sihon king of Heshbon and Og king of Bashan who ruled in Ashtaroth. 11So our older leaders and our people said to us, 'Take food for your journey and go and meet the Israelites. Tell them, "We are your servants. Make a peace agreement with us." '

12"Look at our bread. On the day we left home to come to you it was warm and fresh, but now it is dry and moldy. 13Look at our leather wine bags. They were new and filled with wine, but now they are cracked and old. Our clothes and sandals are worn out from the long journey."

14The men of Israel tasted the bread, but they did not ask the LORD what to do. 15So Joshua agreed to make peace with the Gibeonites and to let them live. And the leaders of the Israelites swore an oath to keep the agreement.

16Three days after they had made the agreement, the Israelites learned that the Gibeonites lived nearby. 17So the Israelites went to where they lived and on the third day came to their cities: Gibeon, Kephirah, Beeroth, and Kiriath Jearim. 18But the Israelites did not attack those cities, because they had made a promise to them before the LORD, the God of Israel.

All the Israelites grumbled against the leaders. 19But the leaders answered, "We have given our promise before the LORD, the God of Israel, so we cannot attack them now. 20This is what we must do. We must let them live. Otherwise, God's anger will be against us for breaking the oath we swore to them. 21So let them live, but they will cut wood and carry water for our people." So the leaders kept their promise to them.

22Joshua called for the Gibeonites and asked, "Why did you lie to us? Your land was near our camp, but you told us you were from a far country. 23Now, you will be placed under a curse to be our slaves. You will have to cut wood and carry water for the house of my God."

24The Gibeonites answered Joshua, "We lied to you because we were afraid you would kill us. We heard that the LORD your God commanded his servant Moses to give you all of this land and to kill all the people who lived in it. That is why we did this. 25Now you can decide what to do with us, whatever you think is right."

26So Joshua saved their lives by not allowing the Israelites to kill them, 27but he made the Gibeonites slaves. They cut wood and carried water for the Israelites, and they did it for the altar of the LORD—wherever he chose it to be. They are still doing this today.

THE SUN STANDS STILL

10 1At this time Adoni-Zedek king of Jerusalem heard that Joshua had defeated Ai and completely destroyed it, as he had also done to Jericho and its king. The king also learned that the Gibeonites had made a peace agreement with Israel and that they lived nearby. 2Adoni-Zedek and his people were very afraid because of this. Gibeon was not a little town like Ai; it was a large city, as big as a city that had a king, and all its men were good fighters. 3So Adoni-Zedek king of Jerusalem sent a message to Hoham king of Hebron, Piram king of Jarmuth, Japhia king of Lachish, and Debir king of Eglon. He begged them, 4"Come with me and help me attack Gibeon, which has made a peace agreement with Joshua and the Israelites."

"Joshua said to his men, 'Be strong and brave! Don't be afraid, because I will show you what the LORD will do.' " (Joshua 10:25a)

5Then these five Amorite kings—the kings of Jerusalem, Hebron, Jarmuth, Lachish, and Eglon—gathered their armies, went to Gibeon, surrounded it, and attacked it.

6The Gibeonites sent this message to Joshua in his camp at Gilgal: "Don't let us, your servants, be destroyed. Come quickly and help us! Save us! All the Amorite kings from the mountains have joined their armies and are fighting against us."

7So Joshua marched out of Gilgal with his whole army, including his best fighting men. 8The LORD said to Joshua, "Don't be afraid of those armies, because I will hand them over to you. None of them will be able to stand against you."

9Joshua and his army marched all night from Gilgal for a surprise attack. 10The LORD confused those armies when Israel attacked, so Israel defeated them in a great victory at Gibeon. They chased them along the road going up to Beth Horon and killed men all the way to Azekah and Makkedah. 11As they chased the enemy down the Beth Horon Pass to Azekah, the LORD threw large hailstones on them from the sky and killed them. More people were killed by the hailstones than by the Israelites' swords.

12On the day that the LORD gave up the Amorites to the Israelites, Joshua stood before all the people of Israel and said to the LORD:

"Sun, stand still over Gibeon.
Moon, stand still over the Valley of
Aijalon."

13So the sun stood still,
and the moon stopped
until the people defeated their enemies.

These words are written in the Book of Jashar.

The sun stopped in the middle of the sky and waited to go down for a full day. 14That has never happened at any time before that day or since. That was the day the LORD listened to a human being. Truly the LORD was fighting for Israel!

15After this, Joshua and his army went back to the camp at Gilgal.

16During the fight the five kings ran away and hid in a cave near Makkedah, 17but someone found them hiding in the cave at Makkedah and told Joshua. 18So he said, "Cover the opening of the cave with large rocks. Put some men there to guard it, 19but don't stay there yourselves. Continue chasing the enemy and attacking them from behind. Don't let them get to their cities, because the LORD your God will hand them over to you."

20So Joshua and the Israelites killed the enemy, but a few were able to get back to their strong, walled cities. 21After the fighting, Joshua's men came back safely to him at Makkedah. No one was brave enough to say a word against the Israelites.

22Joshua said, "Move the rocks that are covering the opening of the cave and bring those five kings out to me." 23So Joshua's men brought the five kings out of the cave—the kings of Jerusalem, Hebron, Jarmuth, Lachish, and Eglon. 24When they brought the five kings out to Joshua, he called for all his men. He said to the commanders of his army, "Come here! Put your feet on the necks of these kings." So they came close and put their feet on their necks.

ENEMIES
Who can defeat our enemies? (10:24–25)

25Joshua said to his men, "Be strong and brave! Don't be afraid, because I will show you what the LORD will do to the enemies you will fight in the future." 26Then Joshua killed the five kings and hung their bodies on five trees, where he left them until evening.

27At sunset Joshua told his men to take the bodies down from the trees. Then they threw them into the same cave where they had been hiding and covered the opening of the cave with large rocks, which are still there today.

28 That day Joshua defeated Makkedah. He killed the king and completely destroyed all the people in that city as an offering to the LORD; no one was left alive. He did the same thing to the king of Makkedah that he had done to the king of Jericho.

WHAT'S IT MEAN?

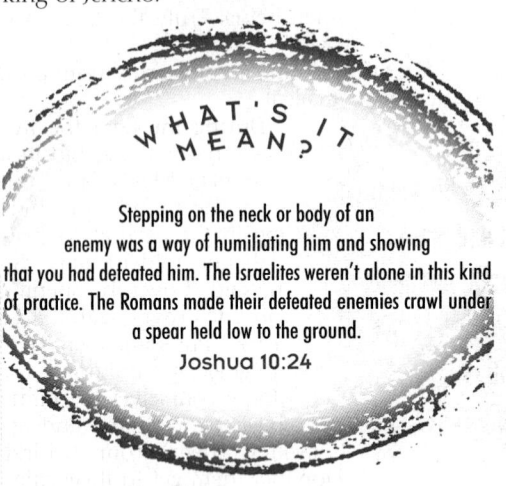

Stepping on the neck or body of an enemy was a way of humiliating him and showing that you had defeated him. The Israelites weren't alone in this kind of practice. The Romans made their defeated enemies crawl under a spear held low to the ground.

Joshua 10:24

DEFEATING SOUTHERN CITIES

29 Joshua and all the Israelites traveled from Makkedah to Libnah and attacked it. 30 The LORD handed over the city and its king. They killed every person in the city; no one was left alive. And they did the same thing to that king that they had done to the king of Jericho.

31 Then Joshua and all the Israelites left Libnah and went to Lachish, which they surrounded and attacked. 32 The LORD handed over Lachish on the second day. The Israelites killed everyone in that city just as they had done to Libnah. 33 During this same time Horam king of Gezer came to help Lachish, but Joshua also defeated him and his army; no one was left alive.

34 Then Joshua and all the Israelites went from Lachish to Eglon. They surrounded Eglon, attacked it, and 35 captured it the same day. They killed all its people and completely destroyed everything in it as an offering to the LORD, just as they had done to Lachish.

36 Then Joshua and the Israelites went from Eglon to Hebron and attacked it, 37 capturing it and all the little towns near it. The Israelites killed everyone in Hebron; no one was left alive there. Just as they had done to Eglon, they completely destroyed the city and all its people as an offering to the LORD.

38 Then Joshua and the Israelites went back to Debir and attacked it. 39 They captured that city, its king, and all the little towns near it, completely destroying everyone in Debir as an offering to the LORD; no one was left alive there. Israel did to Debir and its king just as they had done to Libnah and its king, just as they had done to Hebron.

40 So Joshua defeated all the kings of the cities of these areas: the mountains, southern Canaan, the western hills, and the slopes. The LORD, the God of Israel, had told Joshua to completely destroy all the people as an offering to the LORD, so he left no one alive in those places. 41 Joshua captured all the cities from Kadesh Barnea to Gaza, and from Goshen to Gibeon. 42 He captured all these cities and their kings on one trip, because the LORD, the God of Israel, was fighting for Israel.

43 Then Joshua and all the Israelites returned to their camp at Gilgal.

DEFEATING NORTHERN KINGS

11

1 When Jabin king of Hazor heard about all that had happened, he sent messages to Jobab king of Madon, to the king of Shimron, and to the king of Acshaph. 2 He sent messages to the kings in the northern mountains and also to the kings in the Jordan Valley south of Lake Galilee and in the western hills. He sent a message to the king of Naphoth Dor in the west 3 and to the kings of the Canaanites in the east and in the west. He sent messages to the Amorites, Hittites, Perizzites, and Jebusites in the mountains. Jabin also sent one to the Hivites, who lived below Mount Hermon in the area of Mizpah. 4 So the armies of all these kings came together with their horses and chariots. There were as many soldiers as grains of sand on the seashore.

WHAT'S IT MEAN?

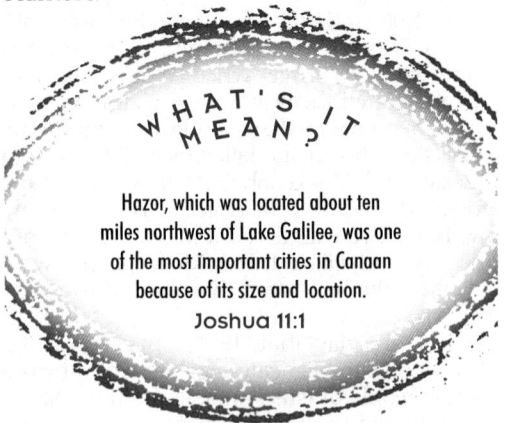

Hazor, which was located about ten miles northwest of Lake Galilee, was one of the most important cities in Canaan because of its size and location.

Joshua 11:1

5 All of these kings met together at the waters of Merom, joined their armies together

into one camp, and made plans to fight against the Israelites.

6 Then the LORD said to Joshua, "Don't be afraid of them, because at this time tomorrow I will give them to you. You will cripple their horses and burn all their chariots."

7 So Joshua and his whole army surprised the enemy by attacking them at the waters of Merom. 8 The LORD handed them over to Israel. They chased them to Greater Sidon, Misrephoth Maim, and the Valley of Mizpah in the east. Israel fought until none of the enemy was left alive. 9 Joshua did what the LORD said to do; he crippled their horses and burned their chariots.

10 Then Joshua went back and captured the city of Hazor and killed its king. (Hazor had been the leader of all the kingdoms that fought against Israel.) 11 Israel killed everyone in Hazor, completely destroying them; no one was left alive. Then they burned Hazor itself.

12 Joshua captured all of these cities, killed all of their kings, and completely destroyed everything in these cities. He did this just as Moses, the servant of the LORD, had commanded. 13 But the Israelites did not burn any cities that were built on their mounds, except Hazor; only that city was burned by Joshua. 14 The people of Israel kept for themselves everything they found in the cities, including all the animals. But they killed all the people there; they left no one alive. 15 Long ago the LORD had commanded his servant Moses to do this, and then Moses had commanded Joshua to do it. Joshua did everything the LORD had commanded Moses.

16 So Joshua defeated all the people in the land. He had control of the mountains and the area of southern Canaan, all the areas of Goshen, the western hills, and the Jordan Valley. He controlled the mountains of Israel and all the hills near them. 17 Joshua controlled all the land from Mount Halak near Edom to Baal Gad in the Valley of Lebanon, below Mount Hermon. Joshua also captured all the kings in the land and killed them. 18 He fought against them for many years. 19 The people of only one city in all the land had made a peace agreement with Israel—the Hivites living in Gibeon. All the other cities were defeated in war. 20 The LORD made those people stubborn so they would fight against Israel and he could completely destroy them without mercy. This is what the LORD had commanded Moses to do.

21 Now Joshua fought the Anakites who lived in the mountains of Hebron, Debir, Anab, Judah, and Israel, and he completely destroyed them and their towns. 22 There were no Anakites left living in the land of the Israelites and only a few were left in Gaza, Gath, and Ashdod. 23 Joshua took control of all the land of Israel as the LORD had told Moses to do long ago. He gave the land to Israel, because he had promised it to them. Then Joshua divided the land among the tribes of Israel, and there was peace in the land.

KINGS DEFEATED BY ISRAEL

12

1 The Israelites took control of the land east of the Jordan River from the Arnon Ravine to Mount Hermon and all the land along the eastern side of the Jordan Valley. These lands belonged to the kings whom the Israelites defeated.

2 Sihon king of the Amorites lived in the city of Heshbon and ruled the land from Aroer at the Arnon Ravine to the Jabbok River. His land started in the middle of the ravine, which was their border with the Ammonites. Sihon ruled over half the land of Gilead 3 and over the eastern side of the Jordan Valley from Lake Galilee to the Dead Sea. And he ruled from Beth Jeshimoth south to the slopes of Pisgah.

4 Og king of Bashan was one of the last of the Rephaites. He ruled the land in Ashtaroth and Edrei. 5 He ruled over Mount Hermon, Salecah, and all the area of Bashan up to where the people of Geshur and Maacah lived. Og also ruled half the land of Gilead up to the border of Sihon king of Heshbon.

6 The LORD's servant Moses and the Israelites defeated all these kings, and Moses gave that land to the tribes of Reuben and Gad and to East Manasseh as their own.

7 Joshua and the Israelites also defeated kings in the land west of the Jordan River. He gave the people the land and divided it among the twelve tribes to be their own. It was between Baal Gad in the Valley of Lebanon and Mount Halak near Edom. 8 This included the mountains, the western hills, the Jordan Valley, the slopes, the desert, and southern Canaan. This was the land where the Hittites, Amorites, Canaanites, Perizzites, Hivites, and Jebusites had lived. The Israelites defeated the king of each of the following cities: 9 Jericho, Ai (near Bethel), 10 Jerusalem, Hebron, 11 Jarmuth, Lachish, 12 Eglon, Gezer, 13 Debir, Geder, 14 Hormah, Arad, 15 Libnah, Adullam, 16 Makkedah, Bethel, 17 Tappuah, Hepher, 18 Aphek, Lasharon, 19 Madon, Hazor, 20 Shimron Meron, Acshaph, 21 Taanach, Megiddo, 22 Kedesh, Jokneam in Carmel, 23 Dor (in Naphoth Dor), Goyim in Gilgal, and 24 Tirzah.

The total number of kings was thirty-one.

LAND STILL TO BE TAKEN

13 1When Joshua was very old, the LORD said to him, "Joshua, you have grown old, but there is still much land for you to take. 2This is what is left: the regions of Geshur and of the Philistines; 3the area from the Shihor River at the border of Egypt to Ekron in the north, which belongs to the Canaanites; the five Philistine leaders at Gaza, Ashdod, Ashkelon, Gath, and Ekron; the Avvites, 4who live south of the Canaanite land; 5the Gebalites, and the area of Lebanon east of Baal Gad below Mount Hermon to Lebo Hamath.

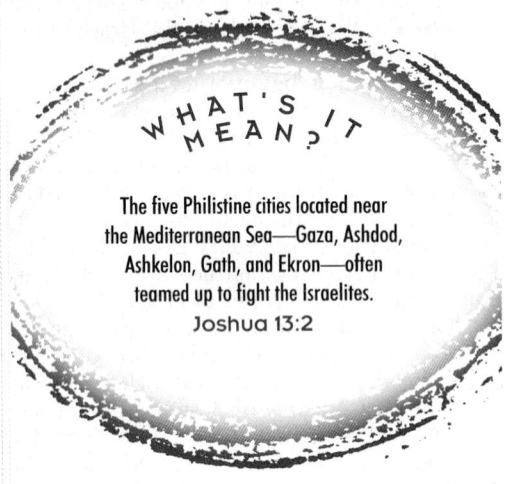

WHAT'S IT MEAN?

The five Philistine cities located near the Mediterranean Sea—Gaza, Ashdod, Ashkelon, Gath, and Ekron—often teamed up to fight the Israelites.
Joshua 13:2

6"The Sidonians are living in the hill country from Lebanon to Misrephoth Maim, but I will force all of them out ahead of the Israelites. Be sure to remember this land when you divide the land among the Israelites, as I told you.

7"Now divide the land among the nine tribes and West Manasseh."

DIVIDING THE LAND

8East Manasseh and the tribes of Reuben and Gad had received their land. The LORD's servant Moses had given them the land east of the Jordan River. 9Their land started at Aroer at the Arnon Ravine and continued to the town in the middle of the ravine, and it included the whole plain from Medeba to Dibon. 10All the towns ruled by Sihon king of the Amorites, who ruled in the city of Heshbon, were in that land. The land continued to the area where the Ammonites lived. 11Gilead was also there, as well as the area where the people of Geshur and Maacah lived, and all of Mount Hermon and Bashan as far as Salecah. 12All the kingdom of Og king of Bashan was in the land. Og was one of the last of the Rephaites, and in the past he ruled in Ashtaroth and Edrei. Moses had defeated them and had taken their land. 13Because the Israelites did not force out the people of Geshur and Maacah, they still live among the Israelites today.

14The tribe of Levi was the only one that did not get any land. Instead, they were given all the burned sacrifices made to the LORD, the God of Israel, as he had promised them.

15Moses had given each family group from the tribe of Reuben some land: 16Theirs was the land from Aroer near the Arnon Ravine to the town of Medeba, including the whole plain and the town in the middle of the ravine; 17Heshbon and all the towns on the plain: Dibon, Bamoth Baal, and Beth Baal Meon, 18Jahaz, Kedemoth, Mephaath, 19Kiriathaim, Sibmah, Zereth Shahar on the hill in the valley, 20Beth Peor, the hills of Pisgah, and Beth Jeshimoth. 21So that land included all the towns on the plain and all the area that Sihon king of the Amorites had ruled from the town of Heshbon. Moses had defeated him along with the leaders of the Midianites, including Evi, Rekem, Zur, Hur, and Reba. All these leaders fought together with Sihon and lived in that country. 22The Israelites killed many people during the fighting, including Balaam of Beor, who tried to use magic to tell the future. 23The land given to Reuben stopped at the shore of the Jordan River. So the land given to the family groups of Reuben included all these towns and their villages that were listed.

24This is the land Moses gave to the tribe of Gad, to all its family groups: 25the land of Jazer and all the towns of Gilead; half the land of the Ammonites that went as far as Aroer near Rabbah; 26the area from Heshbon to Ramath Mizpah and Betonim; the area from Mahanaim to the land of Debir; 27in the valley, Beth Haram, Beth Nimrah, Succoth, and Zaphon, the other land Sihon king of Heshbon had ruled east of the Jordan River and continuing to the end of Lake Galilee. 28All this land went to the family groups of Gad, including all these towns and their villages.

29This is the land Moses had given to East Manasseh. Half of all the family groups in the tribe of Manasseh were given this land: 30The land started at Mahanaim and included all of Bashan and the land ruled by Og king of Bashan; all the towns of Jair in Bashan, sixty cities in all; 31half of Gilead, Ashtaroth, and Edrei, the cities where Og king of Bashan had ruled. All this went to the family of Makir son of Manasseh, and half of all his sons were given this land.

[32]Moses had given this land to these tribes on the plains of Moab across the Jordan River east of Jericho. [33]But Moses had given no land to the tribe of Levi because the LORD, the God of Israel, promised that he himself would be the gift for the Levites.

14 [1]Eleazar the priest, Joshua son of Nun, and the leaders of all the tribes of Israel decided what land to give to the people in the land of Canaan. [2]The LORD had commanded Moses long ago how he wanted the people to choose their land. The people of the nine-and-a-half tribes threw lots to decide which land they would receive. [3]Moses had already given the two-and-a-half tribes their land east of the Jordan River. But the tribe of Levi was not given any land like the others. [4]The sons of Joseph had divided into two tribes—Manasseh and Ephraim. The tribe of Levi was not given any land. It was given only some towns in which to live and pastures for its animals. [5]The LORD had told Moses how to give the land to the tribes of Israel, and the Israelites divided the land.

"The other men who went with me frightened the people, but I fully believed the LORD would allow us to take the land." (Joshua 14:8)

CALEB'S LAND

[6]One day some men from the tribe of Judah went to Joshua at Gilgal. Among them was Caleb son of Jephunneh the Kenizzite. He said to Joshua, "You remember what the LORD said at Kadesh Barnea when he was speaking to the prophet Moses about you and me. [7]Moses, the LORD's servant, sent me to look at the land where we were going. I was forty years old then. When I came back, I told Moses what I thought about the land. [8]The other men who went with me frightened the people, but I fully believed the LORD would allow us to take the land. [9]So that day Moses promised me, 'The land where you went will become your land, and your children will own it forever. I will give you that land because you fully believed in the LORD, my God.'

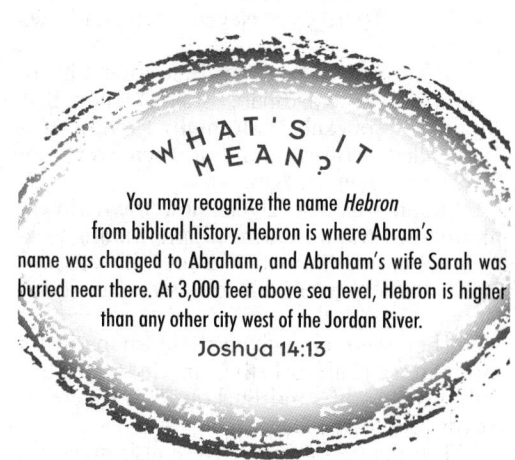

LIFE
Where do we get our strength? (14:10–12)

[10]"Now then, the LORD has kept his promise. He has kept me alive for forty-five years from the time he said this to Moses during the time we all wandered in the desert. Now here I am, eighty-five years old. [11]I am still as strong today as I was the day Moses sent me out, and I am just as ready to fight now as I was then. [12]So give me the mountain country the LORD promised me that day long ago. Back then you heard that the Anakite people lived there and the cities were large and well protected. But now with the LORD helping me, I will force them out, just as the LORD said."

[13]Joshua blessed Caleb son of Jephunneh and gave him the city of Hebron as his own. [14]Hebron still belongs to the family of Caleb son of Jephunneh the Kenizzite because he had faith and obeyed the LORD, the God of Israel. [15](In the past it was called Kiriath Arba, named for Arba, the greatest man among the Anakites.)

After this there was peace in the land.

WHAT'S IT MEAN?

You may recognize the name *Hebron* from biblical history. Hebron is where Abram's name was changed to Abraham, and Abraham's wife Sarah was buried near there. At 3,000 feet above sea level, Hebron is higher than any other city west of the Jordan River.
Joshua 14:13

LAND FOR JUDAH

15 [1]The land that was given to the tribe of Judah was divided among all the family groups. It went all the way to the Desert of Zin in the far south, at the border of Edom.

[2]The southern border of Judah's land started at the south end of the Dead Sea [3]and went south of Scorpion Pass to Zin. From there it passed to the south of Kadesh Barnea and continued past Hezron to Addar. From Addar it turned and went to Karka. [4]It continued to Azmon, the brook of Egypt, and then to the Mediterranean Sea. This was the southern border.

[5]The eastern border was the shore of the Dead Sea, as far as the mouth of the Jordan River.

The northern border started at the bay of

the sea at the mouth of the Jordan River. [6]Then
it went to Beth Hoglah and continued north of
Beth Arabah to the stone of Bohan son of Reuben. [7]Then the northern border went through
the Valley of Achor to Debir where it turned
toward the north and went to Gilgal. Gilgal is
across from the road that goes through Adummim Pass, on the south side of the ravine. The
border continued to the waters of En Shemesh
and stopped at En Rogel. [8]Then it went
through the Valley of Ben Hinnom, next to the
southern side of the Jebusite city (which is
called Jerusalem). There the border went to the
top of the hill on the west side of Hinnom Valley, at the northern end of the Valley of Giants.
[9]From there it went to the spring of the waters
of Nephtoah and then it went to the cities near
Mount Ephron. There it turned and went toward Baalah, which is called Kiriath Jearim.
[10]At Baalah the border turned west and went
toward Mount Seir. It continued along the
north side of Mount Jearim (also called Kesa-
lon) and came to Beth Shemesh. From there it
went past Timnah [11]to the hill north of Ekron.
Then it turned toward Shikkeron and went
past Mount Baalah and continued on to Jabneel, ending at the sea.

[12]The Mediterranean Sea was the western
border. Inside these borders lived the family
groups of Judah.

[13]The LORD had commanded Joshua to give
Caleb son of Jephunneh part of the land in Judah, so he gave Caleb the town of Kiriath Arba,
also called Hebron. (Arba was the father of
Anak.) [14]Caleb forced out the three Anakite
families living in Hebron: Sheshai, Ahiman,
and Talmai, the descendants of Anak. [15]Then
he left there and went to fight against the people living in Debir. (In the past Debir had been
called Kiriath Sepher.) [16]Caleb said, "I will give
Acsah, my daughter, as a wife to the man who
attacks and captures the city of Kiriath Sepher."
[17]Othniel son of Kenaz, Caleb's brother, captured the city, so Caleb gave his daughter Acsah to Othniel to be his wife. [18]When Acsah
came to Othniel, she told him to ask her father
for a field.

So Acsah went to her father. When she got
down from her donkey, Caleb asked her, "What
do you want?"

[19]Acsah answered, "Do me a special favor.
Since you have given me land in southern Canaan, also give me springs of water." So Caleb
gave her the upper and lower springs.

[20]The tribe of Judah got the land God had
promised them. Each family group got part of
the land.

[21]The tribe of Judah got all these towns in
the southern part of Canaan near the border of
Edom: Kabzeel, Eder, Jagur, [22]Kinah, Dimonah,
Adadah, [23]Kedesh, Hazor, Ithnan, [24]Ziph, Telem, Bealoth, [25]Hazor Hadattah, Kerioth Hezron (also called Hazor), [26]Amam, Shema,
Moladah, [27]Hazar Gaddah, Heshmon, Beth Pelet, [28]Hazar Shual, Beersheba, Biziothiah, [29]Ba-
alah, Iim, Ezem, [30]Eltolad, Kesil, Hormah,
[31]Ziklag, Madmannah, Sansannah, [32]Lebaoth,
Shilhim, Ain, and Rimmon. There were twenty-
nine towns and their villages.

[33]The tribe of Judah got these towns in the
western hills: Eshtaol, Zorah, Ashnah, [34]Za-
noah, En Gannim, Tappuah, Enam, [35]Jarmuth,
Adullam, Socoh, Azekah, [36]Shaaraim, Adithaim,
and Gederah (also called Gederothaim). There
were fourteen towns and their villages.

[37]Judah was also given these towns in the
western hills: Zenan, Hadashah, Migdal Gad,
[38]Dilean, Mizpah, Joktheel, [39]Lachish, Bozkath,
Eglon, [40]Cabbon, Lahmas, Kitlish, [41]Gederoth,
Beth Dagon, Naamah, and Makkedah. There
were sixteen towns and their villages.

[42]Judah was also given these towns in the
western hills: Libnah, Ether, Ashan, [43]Iphtah,
Ashnah, Nezib, [44]Keilah, Aczib, and Mareshah.
There were nine towns and their villages.

[45]The tribe of Judah was also given these
towns: Ekron and all the small towns and villages near it; [46]the area west of Ekron and all
the villages and small towns near Ashdod;
[47]Ashdod and the small towns and villages
around it; the villages and small towns around
Gaza as far as the brook of Egypt and along
the coast of the Mediterranean Sea.

[48]The tribe of Judah was also given these
towns in the mountains: Shamir, Jattir, Socoh,
[49]Dannah, Kiriath Sannah (also called Debir),
[50]Anab, Eshtemoh, Anim, [51]Goshen, Holon,
and Giloh. There were eleven towns and their
villages.

[52]They were also given these towns in the
mountains: Arab, Dumah, Eshan, [53]Janim, Beth
Tappuah, Aphekah, [54]Humtah, Kiriath Arba
(also called Hebron), and Zior. There were nine
towns and their villages.

[55]Judah was also given these towns in the
mountains: Maon, Carmel, Ziph, Juttah, [56]Jez-
reel, Jokdeam, Zanoah, [57]Kain, Gibeah, and
Timnah. There were ten towns and their villages.

[58]They were also given these towns in the
mountains: Halhul, Beth Zur, Gedor, [59]Maa-
rath, Beth Anoth, and Eltekon. There were six
towns and their villages.

[60]The people of Judah were also given the

JOSHUA made a difference

Some shoes are impossible to fill. Think about the person who amazes you the most, and then imagine what it would be like to hear you have to assume their role and responsibilities tomorrow. Joshua lived his youth in the shadow of Moses. He became Moses' military commander as well as his personal assistant. Joshua was trained and mentored more than forty years before stepping into Moses' sandals. His development demonstrates that big shoes can sometimes be grown into and sometimes have to be remade to fit new feet.

Joshua appears in the Bible story without introduction. By that point in the Exodus, Joshua was already a recognized soldier and leader. Only later (Ex. 33:11) do we discover two significant facts about Joshua: (1) he was young; (2) he spent most of his time at the Meeting Tent where Moses met with God. What shaped Joshua most were the times spent with his mentor, Moses, and the times he spent alone with God.

Cutting Edge

When God affirmed Joshua's role as Israel's new leader, the Lord used a revealing phrase to indicate his approval: "Just as I was with Moses, so I will be with you" (Josh. 1:5). Joshua was also promised that "the LORD your God will be with you everywhere you go" (Josh. 1:9). Joshua spent enough time with God to know that God would be with him all the time throughout his life.

YOU can, too! Not a moment you spend with God is wasted. No relationship in your life will turn out to be more significant than your relationship with God. Every other relationship you have will be affected by the development of your relationship with God. Here's the big secret. What God does in you will improve every other relationship you have. There's no real choice between God and everyone else. But when you choose God truly, everyone in your Life will benefit.

Want to know more? You can pick up hints of Joshua's life in Exodus, Numbers, and Deuteronomy. He is the central figure in the book that bears his name.

two towns of Rabbah and Kiriath Baal (also
called Kiriath Jearim) and their villages.
[61]Judah was given these towns in the desert:
Beth Arabah, Middin, Secacah, [62]Nibshan, the
City of Salt, and En Gedi. There were six towns
and all their villages.
[63]The army of Judah was not able to force
out the Jebusites living in Jerusalem, so the Jebusites still live among the people of Judah to
this day.

LAND FOR EPHRAIM AND MANASSEH

16
[1]This is the land the tribe of Joseph received.
It started at the Jordan River near Jericho and
continued to the waters of Jericho, just east of
the city. The border went up from Jericho to
the mountains of Bethel. [2]Then it continued
from Bethel (also called Luz) to the Arkite border at Ataroth. [3]From there it went west to the
border of the Japhletites and continued to the
area of the Lower Beth Horon. Then it went to
Gezer and ended at the sea.
[4]So Manasseh and Ephraim, sons of Joseph,
received their land.
[5]This is the land that was given to the family groups of Ephraim: Their border started at
Ataroth Addar in the east, went to Upper Beth
Horon, [6]and then to the sea. From Micmethath
it turned eastward toward Taanath Shiloh and
continued eastward to Janoah. [7]Then it went
down from Janoah to Ataroth and to Naarah.
It continued until it touched Jericho and
stopped at the Jordan River. [8]The border went
from Tappuah west to Kanah Ravine and ended at the sea. This is all the land that was given
to each family group in the tribe of the Ephraimites. [9]Many of the towns were actually within Manasseh's borders, but the people of
Ephraim got those towns and their villages.
[10]The Ephraimites could not force the Canaanites to leave Gezer, so the Canaanites still live
among the Ephraimites today, but they became
slaves of the Ephraimites.

17
[1]Then land was given to the tribe of Manasseh, Joseph's first son. Manasseh's first son
was Makir, the father of Gilead. Makir was a
great soldier, so the lands of Gilead and Bashan
were given to his family. [2]Land was also given
to the other family groups of Manasseh—Abiezer, Helek, Asriel, Shechem, Hepher, and Shemida. These were all the other sons of
Manasseh son of Joseph.
[3]Zelophehad was the son of Hepher, who
was the son of Gilead, who was the son of
Makir, who was the son of Manasseh. Zelophehad had no sons, but he had five daughters, named Mahlah, Noah, Hoglah, Milcah,
and Tirzah. [4]They went to Eleazar the priest
and to Joshua son of Nun and all the leaders.
They said, "The LORD told Moses to give us
land like the men received." So Eleazar obeyed
the LORD and gave the daughters some land,
just like the brothers of their father. [5]So the
tribe of Manasseh had ten sections of land
west of the Jordan River and two more sections, Gilead and Bashan, on the east side of
the Jordan River. [6]The daughters of Manasseh
received land just as the sons did. Gilead was
given to the rest of the families of Manasseh.

WHAT'S IT MEAN?

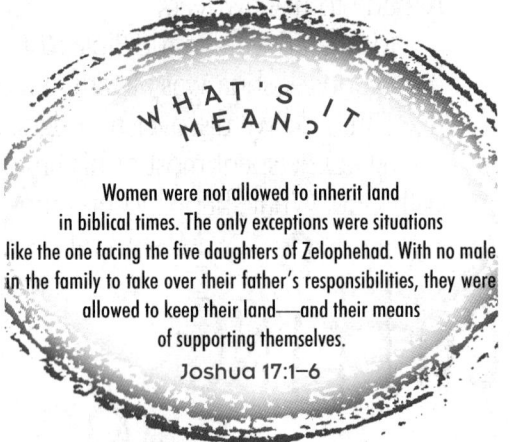

Women were not allowed to inherit land in biblical times. The only exceptions were situations like the one facing the five daughters of Zelophehad. With no male in the family to take over their father's responsibilities, they were allowed to keep their land—and their means of supporting themselves.

Joshua 17:1–6

[7]The lands of Manasseh were in the area
between Asher and Micmethath, near Shechem. The border went south to the En Tappuah area, [8]which belonged to Manasseh,
except for the town of Tappuah. It was along
the border of Manasseh's land and belonged
to the sons of Ephraim. [9]The border of Manasseh continued south to Kanah Ravine. The cities in this area of Manasseh belonged to
Ephraim. Manasseh's border was on the north
side of the ravine and went to the sea. [10]The
land to the south belonged to Ephraim, and
the land to the north belonged to Manasseh.
The Mediterranean Sea was the western border. The border touched Asher's land on the
north and Issachar's land on the east.
[11]In the areas of Issachar and Asher, the
people of Manasseh owned these towns: Beth
Shan and its small towns; Ibleam and its small
towns; the people who lived in Dor and its
small towns; the people in Naphoth Dor and
its small towns; the people who lived in Taanach and its small towns; the people in Megiddo and its small towns. [12]Manasseh was not
able to defeat those cities, so the Canaanites
continued to live there. [13]When the Israelites
grew strong, they forced the Canaanites to

work for them, although they did not force
them to leave the land.
14The people from the tribes of Joseph said
to Joshua, "You gave us only one area of land,
but we are many people. Why did you give us
only one part of all the land the LORD gave his
people?"
15And Joshua answered them, "If you have
too many people, go up to the forest and make
a place for yourselves to live there in the land
of the Perizzites and the Rephaites. The mountain country of Ephraim is too small for you."
16The people of Joseph said, "It is true. The
mountain country of Ephraim is not enough
for us, but the land where the Canaanites live
is dangerous. They are skilled fighters. They
have powerful weapons in Beth Shan and all
the small towns in that area, and they are also
in the Valley of Jezreel."

WHAT'S IT MEAN?

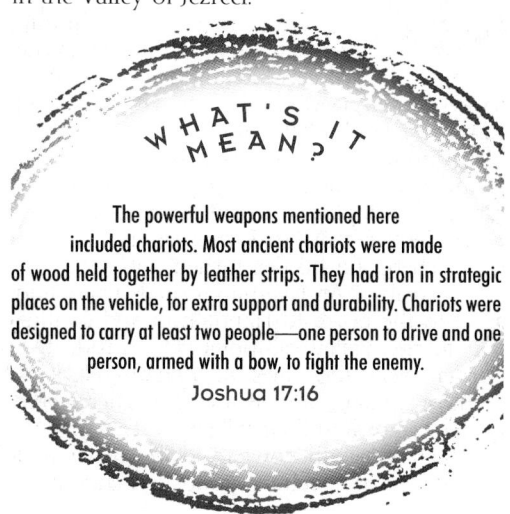

The powerful weapons mentioned here included chariots. Most ancient chariots were made of wood held together by leather strips. They had iron in strategic places on the vehicle, for extra support and durability. Chariots were designed to carry at least two people—one person to drive and one person, armed with a bow, to fight the enemy.

Joshua 17:16

17Then Joshua said to the people of Joseph—to Ephraim and Manasseh, "There are
many of you, and you have great power. You
should be given more than one share of land.
18You also will have the mountain country. It is
a forest, but you can cut down the trees and
make it a good place to live. You will own all of
it because you will force the Canaanites to
leave the land even though they have powerful
weapons and are strong."

THE REST OF THE LAND DIVIDED

18 1All of the Israelites gathered together at
Shiloh where they set up the Meeting Tent. The
land was now under their control. 2But there
were still seven tribes of Israel that had not yet
received their land.
3So Joshua said to the Israelites: "Why do
you wait so long to take your land? The LORD,

WHAT'S IT MEAN?

Shiloh, a city located about twenty miles north of Jerusalem, became an important religious center in Canaan after the Israelites set up their Meeting Tent there.

Joshua 18:1

the God of your ancestors, has given this land
to you. 4Choose three men from each tribe,
and I will send them out to study the land.
They will describe in writing the land their
tribe wants as its share, and then they will
come back to me. 5They will divide the land
into seven parts. The people of Judah will keep
their land in the south, and the people of Joseph will keep their land in the north. 6You
should describe the seven parts of land in
writing and bring what you have written to
me. Then I will throw lots in the presence of
the LORD our God. 7But the Levites do not get
any part of these lands, because they are
priests, and their work is to serve the LORD.
Gad, Reuben, and East Manasseh have received the land promised to them, which is
east of the Jordan River. Moses, the servant of
the LORD, gave it to them."
8So the men who were chosen to map the
land started out. Joshua told them, "Go and
study the land and describe it in writing. Then
come back to me, and I will throw lots in the
presence of the LORD here in Shiloh." 9So the
men left and went into the land. They described in a scroll each town in the seven parts
of the land. Then they came back to Joshua,
who was still at the camp at Shiloh. 10There
Joshua threw lots in the presence of the LORD
to choose the lands that should be given to
each tribe.

LAND FOR BENJAMIN

11The first part of the land was given to the
tribe of Benjamin. Each family group received
some land between the land of Judah and the
land of Joseph. This is the land chosen for Benjamin: 12The northern border started at the
Jordan River and went along the northern edge
of Jericho, and then it went west into the
mountains. That boundary continued until it

was just east of Beth Aven. 13From there it went south to Luz (also called Bethel) and then down to Ataroth Addar, which is on the hill south of Lower Beth Horon.

14At the hill to the south of Beth Horon, the border turned and went south near the western side of the hill. It went to Kiriath Baal (also called Kiriath Jearim), a town where people of Judah lived. This was the western border.

15The southern border started near Kiriath Jearim and went west to the waters of Nephtoah. 16Then it went down to the bottom of the hill, which was near the Valley of Ben Hinnom, on the north side of the Valley of Rephaim. The border continued down the Hinnom Valley just south of the Jebusite city to En Rogel. 17There it turned north and went to En Shemesh. It continued to Geliloth near the Adummim Pass. Then it went down to the great Stone of Bohan son of Reuben. 18The border continued to the northern part of Beth Arabah and went down into the Jordan Valley. 19From there it went to the northern part of Beth Hoglah and ended at the north shore of the Dead Sea, where the Jordan River flows into the sea. This was the southern border.

"There Joshua threw lots in the presence of the LORD to choose the lands that should be given to each tribe." (Joshua 18:10)

20The Jordan River was the border on the eastern side. So this was the land given to the family groups of Benjamin with the borders on all sides.

21The family groups of Benjamin received these cities: Jericho, Beth Hoglah, Emek Keziz, 22Beth Arabah, Zemaraim, Bethel, 23Avvim, Parah, Ophrah, 24Kephar Ammoni, Ophni, and Geba. There were twelve towns and all their villages.

25The tribe of Benjamin also received Gibeon, Ramah, Beeroth, 26Mizpah, Kephirah, Mozah, 27Rekem, Irpeel, Taralah, 28Zelah, Haeleph, the Jebusite city (Jerusalem), Gibeah, and Kiriath. There were fourteen towns and their villages. All these areas are the lands the family groups of Benjamin were given.

LAND FOR SIMEON

19 1The second part of the land was given to the tribe of Simeon. Each family group received some of the land inside the area of Judah. 2They received Beersheba (also called Sheba), Moladah, 3Hazar Shual, Balah, Ezem, 4Eltolad, Bethul, Hormah, 5Ziklag, Beth Marcaboth, Hazar Susah, 6Beth Lebaoth, and Sharuhen. There were thirteen towns and their villages.

7They received the towns of Ain, Rimmon, Ether, and Ashan, four towns and their villages. 8They also received all the very small areas with people living in them as far as Baalath Beer (this is the same as Ramah in southern Canaan). So these were the lands given to the family groups in the tribe of Simeon. 9The land of the Simeonites was taken from part of the land of Judah. Since Judah had much more land than they needed, the Simeonites received part of their land.

LAND FOR ZEBULUN

10The third part of the land was given to the tribe of Zebulun. Each family group of Zebulun received some of the land. The border of Zebulun went as far as Sarid. 11Then it went west to Maralah and came near Dabbesheth and then near Jokneam. 12Then it turned to the east. It went from Sarid to the area of Kisloth Tabor and on to Daberath and to Japhia. 13It continued eastward to Gath Hepher and Eth Kazin, ending at Rimmon. There the border turned and went toward Neah. 14At Neah it turned again and went to the north to Hannathon and continued to the Valley of Iphtah El. 15Inside this border were the cities of Kattath, Nahalal, Shimron, Idalah, and Bethlehem. There were twelve towns and their villages.

16So these are the towns and the villages that were given to the family groups of Zebulun.

LAND FOR ISSACHAR

17The fourth part of the land was given to the tribe of Issachar. Each family group of Issachar received some of the land. 18Their land included Jezreel, Kesulloth, Shunem, 19Hapharaim, Shion, Anaharath, 20Rabbith, Kishion, Ebez, 21Remeth, En Gannim, En Haddah, and Beth Pazzez.

22The border of their land touched the area called Tabor, Shahazumah, and Beth Shemesh and stopped at the Jordan River. There were sixteen towns and their villages.

23These cities and towns were part of the land that was given to the family groups of Issachar.

LAND FOR ASHER

24The fifth part of the land was given to the tribe of Asher. Each family group of Asher received some of the land. 25Their land included Helkath, Hali, Beten, Acshaph, 26Allammelech, Amad, and Mishal.

The western border touched Mount Carmel and Shihor Libnath. 27Then it turned east and went to Beth Dagon, touching Zebulun and the Valley of Iphtah El. Then it went north of Beth Emek and Neiel and passed north to Cabul. 28From there it went to Abdon, Rehob, Hammon, and Kanah and continued to Greater Sidon. 29Then the border went back south toward Ramah and continued to the strong, walled city of Tyre. There it turned and went toward Hosah, ending at the sea. This was in the area of Aczib, 30Ummah, Aphek, and Rehob. There were twenty-two towns and their villages.

31These cities and their villages were part of the land that was given to the family groups of Asher.

LAND FOR NAPHTALI

32The sixth part of the land was given to the tribe of Naphtali. Each family group of Naphtali received some of the land. 33The border of their land started at the large tree in Zaanannim, which is near Heleph. Then it went through Adami Nekeb and Jabneel, as far as Lakkum, and ended at the Jordan River. 34Then it went to the west through Aznoth Tabor and stopped at Hukkok. It went to the area of Zebulun on the south, Asher on the west, and Judah, at the Jordan River, on the east. 35The strong, walled cities inside these borders were called Ziddim, Zer, Hammath, Rakkath, Kinnereth, 36Adamah, Ramah, Hazor, 37Kedesh, Edrei, En Hazor, 38Iron, Migdal El, Horem, Beth Anath, and Beth Shemesh. There were nineteen towns and all their villages.

39The towns and the villages around them were in the land that was given to the family groups of Naphtali.

LAND FOR DAN

40The seventh part of the land was given to the tribe of Dan. Each family group of Dan received some of the land. 41Their land included Zorah, Eshtaol, Ir Shemesh, 42Shaalabbin, Aijalon, Ithlah, 43Elon, Timnah, Ekron, 44Eltekeh, Gibbethon, Baalath, 45Jehud, Bene Berak, Gath Rimmon, 46Me Jarkon, Rakkon, and the area near Joppa.

47(But the Danites had trouble taking their land. They went and fought against Leshem, defeated it, and killed the people who lived there. So the Danites moved into the town of Leshem and changed its name to Dan, because he was the father of their tribe.) 48All of these towns and villages were given to the family groups of Dan.

LAND FOR JOSHUA

49After the leaders finished dividing the land and giving it to the different tribes, the Israelites gave Joshua son of Nun his land also. 50They gave Joshua the town he asked for, Timnath Serah in the mountains of Ephraim, just as the LORD commanded. He built up the town and lived there.

51So these lands were given to the different tribes of Israel. Eleazar the priest, Joshua son of Nun, and the leaders of each tribe divided up the land by lots at Shiloh. They met in the presence of the LORD at the entrance to the Meeting Tent. Now they were finished dividing the land.

CITIES OF SAFETY

20

1Then the LORD said to Joshua: 2"Tell the Israelites to choose the special cities of safety, as I had Moses command you to do. 3If a person kills someone accidentally and without meaning to kill him, that person may go to a city of safety to hide. There the killer will be safe from the relative who has the duty of punishing a murderer.

4"When the killer runs to one of those cities, he must stop at the entrance gate, stand there, and tell the leaders of the people what happened. Then that person will be allowed to enter the city and will be given a place to live among them. 5But if the one who is chasing him follows him to that city, the leaders of the city must not hand over the killer. It was an accident. He did not hate him beforehand or kill him on purpose. 6The killer must stay in the city until a court comes to a decision and until the high priest dies. Then he may go back home to the town from which he ran away."

7So the Israelites chose these cities to be cities of safety: Kedesh in Galilee in the mountains of Naphtali; Shechem in the mountains of Ephraim; Kiriath Arba (also called Hebron) in the mountains of Judah; 8Bezer on the east side of the Jordan River near Jericho in the desert in the land of Reuben; Ramoth in Gilead in the land of Gad; and Golan in Bashan in the land of Manasseh. 9Any Israelite or anyone living among them who killed someone accidentally was to be allowed to run to one of these cities of safety. There he would not be killed, before he was judged, by the relative who had the duty of punishing a murderer.

TOWNS FOR THE LEVITES

21
[1]The heads of the Levite families went to
talk to Eleazar the priest, to Joshua son of Nun,
and to the heads of the families of all the tribes
of Israel. [2]At Shiloh in the land of Canaan, the
heads of the Levite families said to them, "The
LORD commanded Moses that you give us
towns where we may live and pastures for our
animals." [3]So the Israelites obeyed this command of the LORD and gave the Levite people
these towns and pastures for their own land:
[4]The Kohath family groups were part of the
tribe of Levi. Some of the Levites in the Kohath
family groups were from the family of Aaron
the priest. To these Levites were given thirteen
towns in the areas of Judah, Simeon, and Benjamin. [5]The other family groups of Kohath
were given ten towns in the areas of Ephraim,
Dan, and West Manasseh.

[6]The people from the Gershon family
groups were given thirteen towns in the land
of Issachar, Asher, Naphtali, and the East Manasseh in Bashan.

[7]The family groups of Merari were given
twelve towns in the areas of Reuben, Gad, and
Zebulun.

[8]So the Israelites gave the Levites these
towns and the pastures around them, just as
the LORD had commanded Moses.

[9]These are the names of the towns that
came from the lands of Judah and Simeon.
[10]The first choice of towns was given to the
Kohath family groups of the Levites. [11]They
gave them Kiriath Arba, also called Hebron,
and all its pastures in the mountains of Judah.
(Arba was the father of Anak.) [12]But the fields
and the villages around Kiriath Arba had been
given to Caleb son of Jephunneh.

[13]So they gave the city of Hebron to the descendants of Aaron (Hebron was a city of
safety). They also gave them the towns of Libnah, [14]Jattir, Eshtemoa, [15]Holon, Debir, [16]Ain,
Juttah, and Beth Shemesh, and all the pastures
around them. Nine towns were given from
these two tribes.

[17]They also gave the people of Aaron these
cities that belonged to the tribe of Benjamin:
Gibeon, Geba, [18]Anathoth, and Almon. They
gave them these four towns and the pastures
around them.

[19]So these thirteen towns with their pastures were given to the priests, who were from
the family of Aaron.

[20]The other Kohathite family groups of the
Levites were given these towns from the tribe
of Ephraim: [21]Shechem in the mountains of
Ephraim (which was a city of safety), Gezer,
[22]Kibzaim, and Beth Horon. There were four
towns and their pastures.

[23]The tribe of Dan gave them Eltekeh, Gibbethon, [24]Aijalon, and Gath Rimmon. There
were four towns and their pastures.

[25]West Manasseh gave them Taanach and
Gath Rimmon and the pastures around these
two towns.

[26]So these ten towns and the pastures
around them were given to the rest of the Kohathite family groups.

[27]The Gershonite family groups of the Levite tribe were given these towns: East Manasseh gave them Golan in Bashan, which was a
city of safety, and Be Eshtarah, and the pastures around these two towns.

[28]The tribe of Issachar gave them Kishion,
Daberath, [29]Jarmuth, and En Gannim, and the
pastures around these four towns.

[30]The tribe of Asher gave them Mishal, Abdon, [31]Helkath, and Rehob, and the pastures
around these four towns.

[32]The tribe of Naphtali gave them Kedesh in
Galilee (a city of safety), Hammoth Dor, and
Kartan, and the pastures around these three
towns.

[33]So the Gershonite family groups received
thirteen towns and the pastures around them.

[34]The Merarite family groups (the rest of the
Levites) were given these towns: The tribe of
Zebulun gave them Jokneam, Kartah, [35]Dim-
nah, and Nahalal, and the pastures around
these four towns.

[36]The tribe of Reuben gave them Bezer, Jahaz, [37]Kedemoth, and Mephaath, along with
the pastures around these four towns.

[38]The tribe of Gad gave them Ramoth in
Gilead (a city of safety), Mahanaim, [39]Hesh-
bon, and Jazer, and the pastures around these
four towns.

[40]So the total number of towns given to the
Merarite family groups was twelve.

[41]A total of forty-eight towns with their
pastures in the land of Israel were given to the
Levites. [42]Each town had pastures around it.

[43]So the LORD gave the people all the land
he had promised their ancestors. The people
took the land and lived there. [44]The LORD gave
them peace on all sides, as he had promised
their ancestors. None of their enemies defeated
them; the LORD handed all their enemies over
to them. [45]He kept every promise he had made
to the Israelites; each one came true.

THREE TRIBES GO HOME

22
[1]Then Joshua called a meeting of all the
people from the tribes of Reuben, Gad, and

East Manasseh. 2He said to them, "You have done everything Moses, the LORD's servant, told you to do. You have also obeyed all my commands. 3For a long time you have supported the other Israelites. You have been careful to obey the commands the LORD your God gave you. 4The LORD your God promised to give the Israelites peace, and he has kept his promise. Now you may go back to your homes, to the land that Moses, the LORD's servant, gave you, on the east side of the Jordan River. 5But be careful to obey the teachings and laws Moses, the LORD's servant, gave you: to love the LORD your God and obey his commands, to continue to follow him and serve him the very best you can."

FOLLOWING GOD

How should we follow God? (22:5)

6Then Joshua said good-bye to them, and they left and went away to their homes. 7Moses had given the land of Bashan to East Manasseh. Joshua gave land on the west side of the Jordan River to West Manasseh. And he sent them to their homes and he blessed them. 8He said, "Go back to your homes and your riches. You have many animals, silver, gold, bronze, and iron, and many beautiful clothes. Also, you have taken many things from your enemies that you should divide among yourselves."

9So the people from the tribes of Reuben, Gad, and East Manasseh left the other Israelites at Shiloh in Canaan and went back to Gilead. It was their own land, given to them by Moses as the LORD had commanded.

10The people of Reuben, Gad, and East Manasseh went to Geliloth, near the Jordan River in the land of Canaan. There they built a beautiful altar. 11The other Israelites still at Shiloh heard about the altar these three tribes built at the border of Canaan at Geliloth, near the Jordan River on Israel's side. 12All the Israelites became very angry at these three tribes, so they met together and decided to fight them.

13The Israelites sent Phinehas son of Eleazar the priest to Gilead to talk to the people of Reuben, Gad, and East Manasseh. 14They also sent one leader from each of the ten tribes at Shiloh. Each of them was a leader of his family group of Israelites.

15These leaders went to Gilead to talk to the people of Reuben, Gad, and East Manasseh. They said: 16"All the Israelites ask you: 'Why did you turn against the God of Israel by building an altar for yourselves? You know that this is against God's law. 17Remember what happened at Peor? We still suffer today because of that sin, for which God made many Israelites very sick. 18And now are you turning against the LORD and refusing to follow him?

" 'If you don't stop what you're doing today, the LORD will be angry with everyone in Israel tomorrow. 19If your land is unclean, come over into our land where the LORD's Tent is. Share it with us. But don't turn against the LORD and us by building another altar for the LORD our God. 20Remember how Achan son of Zerah refused to obey the command about what must be completely destroyed. That one man broke God's law, but all the Israelites were punished. Achan died because of his sin, but others also died.' "

WHAT'S IT MEAN?

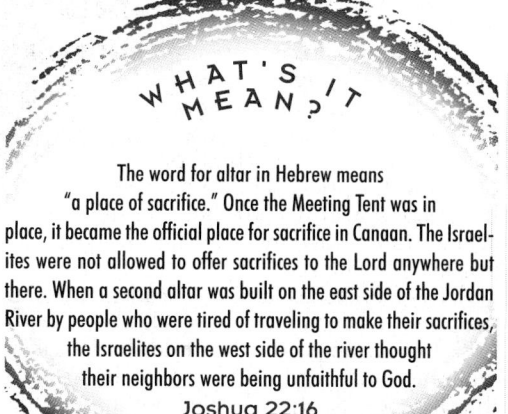

The word for altar in Hebrew means "a place of sacrifice." Once the Meeting Tent was in place, it became the official place for sacrifice in Canaan. The Israelites were not allowed to offer sacrifices to the Lord anywhere but there. When a second altar was built on the east side of the Jordan River by people who were tired of traveling to make their sacrifices, the Israelites on the west side of the river thought their neighbors were being unfaithful to God.

Joshua 22:16

21The people from Reuben, Gad, and East Manasseh answered, 22"The LORD is God of gods! The LORD is God of gods! God knows, and we want you to know also. If we have done something wrong, you may kill us. 23If we broke God's law, we ask the LORD himself to punish us. We did not build this altar to offer burnt offerings or grain and fellowship offerings.

24"We did not build it for that reason. We feared that some day your people would not accept us as part of your nation. Then they might say, 'You cannot worship the LORD, the God of Israel. 25The LORD made the Jordan River a border between us and you people of Reuben and Gad. You cannot worship the LORD.' So we feared that your children might make our children stop worshiping the LORD.

26"That is why we decided to build this altar. But it is not for burnt offerings and sacrifices.

27This altar is proof to you and us and to all
our children who will come after us that we
worship the LORD with our whole burnt offerings, grain, and fellowship offerings. This was
so your children would not say to our children, 'You are not the LORD's.'
28"In the future if your children say that, our
children can say, 'See the altar made by our
ancestors. It is exactly like the LORD's altar, but
we do not use it for sacrifices. It shows that we
are part of Israel.'
29"Truly, we don't want to be
against the LORD or to stop following him by building an altar for burnt offerings, grain
offerings, or sacrifices. We
know the only true altar to
the LORD our God is in
front of the Holy Tent."
30When Phinehas the
priest and the ten leaders
heard the people of Reuben,
Gad, and East Manasseh, they
were pleased. 31So Phinehas, son
of Eleazar the priest, said, "Now we know
the LORD is with us and that you didn't turn
against him. Now the Israelites will not be
punished by the LORD."
32Then Phinehas and the leaders left the
people of Reuben and Gad in Gilead and went
back to Canaan where they told the Israelites
what had happened. 33They were pleased and
thanked God. So they decided not to fight the
people of Reuben and Gad and destroy those
lands.
34And the people of Reuben and Gad
named the altar Proof That We Believe the
LORD Is God.

"If you don't stop what you're doing today, the LORD will be angry with everyone in Israel tomorrow." (Joshua 22:18b)

THE LAST WORDS OF JOSHUA

23

1The LORD gave Israel peace from their
enemies around them. Many years passed, and
Joshua grew very old. 2He called a meeting
of all the older leaders, heads of families,
judges, and officers of Israel. He said, "I am
now very old. 3You have seen what the LORD
has done to our enemies to help us. The LORD
your God fought for you. 4Re-
member that your people
have been given their land
between the Jordan River
and the Mediterranean Sea
in the west, the land I
promised to give you. 5The
LORD your God will force
out the people living there.
The LORD will push them
out ahead of you.
And you will
own the land,
as he has prom-
ised you.
6"Be strong. You must be
careful to obey everything
commanded in the Book of the
Teachings of Moses. Do exactly
as it says. 7Don't become
friends with the people living
among us who are not Israelites. Don't say the names of
their gods or make anyone
swear by them. Don't serve or

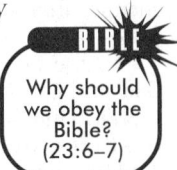

GOD
Does God keep his promises? (23:5–10)

BIBLE
Why should we obey the Bible? (23:6–7)

Promise HE DOES WHAT HE HAS PROMISED.

Every good promise that the LORD your God made has come true, and in the same way, his other promises will come true (Josh. 23:15a).

All through the Bible, God models what good character is, then calls us to be like him. Here, he promises to keep his word. You're a person of strong character if you do what you say you will do—if you keep your promises. Do you normally slide in after curfew? Do you keep people waiting for you? Do you really go where you tell your parents you'll be? If you find yourself always making excuses, it's time for a character adjustment. Look at God and imitate him. You can be successful at almost anything if you do what you've said you will do. Be dependable, trustworthy, faithful. Those are all attributes of God. He doesn't need to make any excuses.

SEE FOR YOURSELF:
Gen. 28:15; Num. 23:19; Deut. 4:31; 1 Kin. 8:56; Neh. 1:5

worship them. 8You must continue to follow the LORD your God, as you have done in the past.

9"The LORD has forced many great and powerful nations to leave ahead of you. No nation has been able to defeat you. 10With his help, one Israelite could defeat a thousand, because the LORD your God fights for you, as he promised to do. 11So you must be careful to love the LORD your God.

12"If you turn away from the way of the LORD and become friends with these people who are not part of Israel and marry them, 13the LORD your God will not help you defeat your enemies. They will be like traps for you, like whips on your back and thorns in your eyes, and none of you will be left in this good land the LORD your God has given you.

14"It's almost time for me to die. You know and fully believe that the LORD has done great things for you. You know that he has not failed to keep any of his promises. 15Every good promise that the LORD your God made has come true, and in the same way, his other promises will come true. He promised that evil will come to you and that he will destroy you from this good land that he gave you. 16This will happen if you don't keep your agreement with the LORD your God. If you go and serve other gods and worship them, the LORD will become very angry with you. Then none of you will be left in this good land he has given you."

24

1Joshua gathered all the tribes of Israel together at Shechem. He called the older leaders, heads of families, judges, and officers of Israel to stand before God.

2Then Joshua said to all the people, "Here's what the LORD, the God of Israel, says to you: 'A long time ago your ancestors lived on the other side of the Euphrates River. Terah, the father of Abraham and Nahor, worshiped other gods. 3But I, the LORD, took your ancestor Abraham from the other side of the river and led him through the land of Canaan. And I gave him many children, including his son Isaac. 4I gave Isaac two sons named Jacob and Esau. I gave the land around the mountains of Edom to Esau, but Jacob and his sons went down to Egypt. 5Then I sent Moses and Aaron to Egypt, where I brought many disasters on the Egyptians. Afterwards I brought you out. 6When I brought your ancestors out of Egypt, they came to the Red Sea, and the Egyptians chased them with chariots and men on horses. 7So the people called out to the LORD. And I brought darkness between you and the Egyptians and made the sea to cover them. You yourselves saw what I did to the army of Egypt. After that, you lived in the desert for a long time.

WHAT'S IT MEAN?

Shechem was a bustling city even before the Israelites lived there. Located near ancient highways and trade routes, the city drew travelers from all over. Shechem, the site of Joshua's farewell address, was located between Mount Gerizim and Mount Ebal. Mount Gerizim is the place where Moses blessed the Israelites for obeying God; Mount Ebal is where he cursed the people for their disobedience. Interestingly, today Mount Gerizim is covered with vegetation and Mount Ebal is bare, perhaps as reminders of the Lord's blessings and curses.

Joshua 24:1

8" 'Then I brought you to the land of the Amorites, east of the Jordan River. They fought against you, but I handed them over to you. I destroyed them before you, and you took control of that land. 9But the king of Moab, Balak son of Zippor, prepared to fight against the Israelites. The king sent for Balaam son of Beor to curse you, 10but I refused to listen to Balaam. So he asked for good things to happen to you! I saved you and brought you out of his power.

11" 'Then you crossed the Jordan River and came to Jericho, where the people of Jericho fought against you. Also, the Amorites, Perizzites, Canaanites, Hittites, Girgashites, Hivites, and Jebusites fought against you. But I handed them over to you. 12I sent terror ahead of you to force out two Amorite kings. You took the land without using swords and bows. 13I gave you that land where you did not have to work. I gave you cities that you did not have to build. And now you live in that land and in those cities, and you eat from vineyards and olive trees that you did not plant.' "

DEVOTION

How should we be devoted? (24:14)

14Then Joshua said to the people, "Now respect the LORD and serve him fully and sincerely. Throw away the gods that your ancestors worshiped on the other side of

the Euphrates River and in Egypt. Serve the
LORD. 15But if you don't want to serve the LORD,
you must choose for yourselves
today whom you will serve.
You may serve the gods that
your ancestors worshiped
when they lived on the other
side of the Euphrates River, or
you may serve the gods of the
Amorites who lived in this land. As for me and
my family, we will serve the LORD."

FAMILY
What should my family be like? (24:15)

16Then the people answered, "We will never
stop following the LORD to serve other gods!
17It was the LORD our God who brought our
ancestors out of Egypt. We were slaves in that
land, but the LORD did great things for us there.
He brought us out and protected us while we
traveled through other lands. 18Then he forced
out all the people living in these lands, even the
Amorites. So we will serve the LORD, because
he is our God."

19Then Joshua said, "You are not able to
serve the LORD, because he is a holy God and a
jealous God. If you turn against him and sin,
he will not forgive you. 20If you leave the LORD
and serve other gods, he will send you great
trouble. The LORD may have been good to you,
but if you turn against him, he will destroy
you."

21But the people said to Joshua, "No! We
will serve the LORD."

22Then Joshua said, "You are your own witnesses that you have chosen to serve the LORD."

The people said, "Yes, we are."

23Then Joshua said, "Now throw away the
gods that you have. Love the LORD, the God of
Israel, with all your heart."

24Then the people said to Joshua, "We will
serve the LORD our God, and we will obey
him."

25On that day at Shechem Joshua made an
agreement for the people. He made rules and
laws for them to follow. 26Joshua wrote these
things in the Book of the Teachings of God. Then he took a
large stone and set it up under the oak tree near the
LORD's Holy Tent.

27Joshua said to all the
people, "See this stone! It will remind you of what
we did today. It was here the LORD spoke to us today.
It will remind you of what happened so you will not turn
against your God."

On the Edge

Then Joshua said, "You are not able to serve the LORD, because he is a holy God and a jealous God. If you turn against him and sin, he will not forgive you" (Josh. 24:19).

Fake is in. Phony is fashionable: bodies that are beautiful because of plastic surgery; imitation foods that taste sweet—with no sugar. Virtual realities that are only pretend. Somewhere in the world of impostors we've lost our sense of what is true. God can restore the standard. He is not a fake. He is not pretending to be God. He is real, and pure, and holy, and awesome. So if you've been feeling like you can't figure out what's true anymore, get off the stage. Get with God. Some time in the presence of his truth will bring you back to reality.

SEE FOR YOURSELF:
Deut. 6:4; John 17:3; Eph. 4:5–6; 1 Tim. 2:5

JOSHUA DIES

28Then Joshua sent the people back to their
land.

29After that, Joshua son of Nun died at the
age of one hundred ten. 30They buried him in
his own land at Timnath Serah, in the mountains of Ephraim, north of Mount Gaash.

31The Israelites served the LORD during the
lifetime of Joshua and during the lifetimes of
the older leaders who lived after Joshua who
had seen what the LORD had done for Israel.

JOSEPH COMES HOME

32When the Israelites left Egypt, they carried
the bones of Joseph with them. They buried
them at Shechem, in the land Jacob had bought for a hundred pieces of silver from
the sons of Hamor (Hamor was the father of Shechem).
This land now belonged to Joseph's children.

33And Eleazar son of
Aaron died and was buried at Gibeah in the mountains
of Ephraim, which had been given to Eleazar's son
Phinehas.

"Then the people said to Joshua, 'We will serve the LORD our God, and we will obey him.'" (Joshua 24:24)

judges

CONTENT In their earliest days, the Hebrews were a family led by a dad named Jacob who had twelve sons. Then the descendants of those twelve sons grew to be a nation of slaves in Egypt, a country led by a king. Then they became exiles led by Moses. Then they became an army led by Joshua. Then came the Book of Judges.

The Book of Judges is about a time in the life of the Hebrews before they had a king. When they needed to make decisions, they went to a judge, a national leader. A judge was sort of like a king, but no castle or crown or bowing—just a leader.

During the time of the judges, the Hebrews went up and down like a morality yo-yo. They would obey God if they were listening to a good judge. Then that judge would die, and the people would fall away again. In fact, the phrase you'll most often read about in this book is "Everyone did what seemed right." When you read that in Judges, you know that it means, "Here they go again—doing their own thing no matter what God wants." Then another judge would come into leadership, and they'd clean up their act for a while.

Outline

1:1–36 .... Israel Captures Only Part of the Land
2:1—3:6 .... The Lord Chooses Judges for Israel
3:7–31 .... Othniel, Ehud, and Shamgar
4:1—5:31 .... Deborah, Barak, and Jael
6:1—8:35 .... Gideon
9:1–57 .... Abimelech
10:1—12:7 .... Tola, Jair, and Jephthah
12:8–15 .... Ibzan, Elon, and Abdon
13:1—16:31 .... Samson
17:1–13 .... Micah's Idols
18:1–31 .... The Tribe of Dan and Their Place of Worship
19:1—21:25 .... Civil War Against the Tribe of Benjamin

Purpose What we fail to learn from history we must often learn by painful experience.

Themes Apostasy, Oppression, Repentance, Deliverance

Date of writing 1043–1004 B.C.

"In those days Israel did not have a king. Everyone did what seemed right" (21:25).

Bible Talk

Deborah

You hear a lot about how women were second-class citizens in the culture that you read about in the Bible. It's important to notice, though, that women were not second-class citizens in God's eyes, ever. Deborah is a great example.

Deborah was a judge, a national leader, just like any male judge whom Israel recognized. She was even asked to go to battle. Know what she said? "I'll go as long as you realize that everyone is going to know that a woman did the winning."

SAMSON, NAZIRITE

Even if you've not been much of a churchgoer, you probably have heard of Samson with his long hair and supernatural strength. Sometimes the story can sound like Popeye with his spinach.

It's important to remember, though, that Samson's hair wasn't made of stuff different from yours. His hair just represented a promise he had made. He was a Nazirite (like Samuel and John the Baptist). That means he kept certain traditions (like not drinking wine) that kept him close to God.

When Samson let his hair be cut, it wasn't like some spell was broken. It was that a promise was broken. Samson was turning his back on a promise that he had made to God. When he did, he lost access to God's power, and you probably know the rest. If not, read on. . . .

JUDAH FIGHTS THE CANAANITES

1 1After Joshua died, the Israelites asked the LORD, "Who will be first to go and fight for us against the Canaanites?"

2The LORD said to them, "The tribe of Judah will go. I have handed the land over to them."

3The men of Judah said to the men of Simeon, their relatives, "Come and help us fight the Canaanites for our land. If you do, we will go and help you fight for your land." So the men of Simeon went with them.

4When Judah attacked, the LORD handed over the Canaanites and the Perizzites to them, and they defeated ten thousand men at the city of Bezek. 5There they found Adoni-Bezek, the ruler of the city, and fought him. The men of Judah defeated the Canaanites and the Perizzites, 6but Adoni-Bezek ran away. The men of Judah chased him, and when they caught him, they cut off his thumbs and big toes.

7Adoni-Bezek said, "Seventy kings whose thumbs and big toes had been cut off used to eat scraps that fell from my table. Now God has paid me back for what I did to them." The men of Judah took Adoni-Bezek to Jerusalem, and he died there.

8Then the men of Judah fought against Jerusalem and captured it. They attacked with their swords and burned the city.

9Later, they went down to fight the Canaanites who lived in the mountains, in the dry country to the south, and in the western hills. 10The men of Judah went to fight against the Canaanites in the city of Hebron (which used to be called Kiriath Arba). And they defeated Sheshai, Ahiman, and Talmai.

CALEB AND HIS DAUGHTER

11Then they left there and went to fight against the people living in Debir. (In the past Debir had been called Kiriath Sepher.) 12Before attacking the city, Caleb said, "I will give Acsah, my daughter, as a wife to the man who attacks and captures the city of Kiriath Sepher." 13Othniel son of Kenaz, Caleb's younger brother, captured the city, so Caleb gave his daughter Acsah to Othniel to be his wife. 14When Acsah came to Othniel, she told him to ask her father for a field. When she got down from her donkey, Caleb asked her, "What do you want?"

15Acsah answered him, "Do me a special favor. Since you have given me land in southern Canaan, also give me springs of water." So Caleb gave her the upper and lower springs.

FIGHTS WITH THE CANAANITES

16The Kenite people, who were from the family of Moses' father-in-law, left Jericho, the city of palm trees. They went with the men of Judah to the Desert of Judah to live with them there in southern Judah near the city of Arad.

17The men of Judah and the men of Simeon, their relatives, defeated the Canaanites who lived in Zephath. They completely destroyed the city, so they called it Hormah.[n] 18The men of Judah captured Gaza, Ashkelon, Ekron, and the lands around them.

19The LORD was with the men of Judah. They took the land in the mountains, but they could not force out the people living on the plain, because they had iron chariots. 20As Moses had promised, Hebron was given to Caleb, and Caleb forced out the three sons of Anak. 21But the people of Benjamin could not make the Jebusite people leave Jerusalem. Since that time the Jebusites have lived with the Benjaminites in Jerusalem.

WHAT'S IT MEAN?

Most chariots were made of wood and held together by leather strips. The deluxe models, the "iron chariots," probably weren't made completely of iron. They would have been too heavy to pull. Instead, they were probably reinforced with iron in certain spots to make them sturdier or to give their riders more protection. Though some chariots could carry as many as four passengers, most combat models were built to hold two—a driver and a fighter armed with a bow and arrows.

Judges 1:18–19

22The men of Joseph went to fight against the city of Bethel, and the LORD was with them. 23They sent some spies to Bethel (which used to be called Luz). 24The spies saw a man coming out of the city and said to him, "Show us a way into the city, and we will be kind to you." 25So the man showed them the way into the city. The men of Joseph attacked with swords the people in Bethel, but they let the man and his family go free. 26He went to the land where

1:17 Hormah Hormah sounds like the Hebrew word meaning "to destroy completely."

the Hittites lived and built a city. He named it Luz, which it is called even today.

27There were Canaanites living in the cities of Beth Shan, Taanach, Dor, Ibleam, Megiddo, and the small towns around them. The people of Manasseh did not force those people out of their towns, because the Canaanites were determined to stay there. 28Later, the Israelites grew strong and forced the Canaanites to work as slaves, but they did not make all the Canaanites leave their land. 29The people of Ephraim did not force out all of the Canaanites living in Gezer. So the Canaanites continued to live in Gezer with the people of Ephraim. 30The people of Zebulun did not force out the Canaanites living in the cities of Kitron and Nahalol. They stayed and lived with the people of Zebulun, but Zebulun made them work as slaves.

31The people of Asher did not force the Canaanites from the cities of Acco, Sidon, Ahlab, Aczib, Helbah, Aphek, and Rehob. 32Since the people of Asher did not force them out, the Canaanites continued to live with them. 33The people of Naphtali did not force out the people of the cities of Beth Shemesh and Beth Anath. So they continued to live with the Canaanites in those cities, and the Canaanites worked as slaves. 34The Amorites forced the Danites back into the mountains and would not let them come down to live in the plain. 35The Amorites were determined to stay in Mount Heres, Aijalon, and Shaalbim. But when the Israelites grew stronger, they made the Amorites work as slaves. 36The land of the Amorites was from Scorpion Pass to Sela and beyond.

THE ANGEL OF THE LORD AT BOKIM

2

1The angel of the LORD went up from Gilgal to Bokim and said, "I brought you up from Egypt and led you to the land I promised to give your ancestors. I said, 'I will never break my agreement with you. 2But you must not make an agreement with the people who live in this land. You must destroy their altars.' But you did not obey me. How could you do this? 3Now I tell you, 'I will not force out the people in this land. They will be your enemies, and their gods will be a trap for you.'"

4After the angel gave Israel this message from the LORD, they cried loudly. 5So they named the place Bokim.[n] There they offered sacrifices to the LORD.

"The people served the LORD during the lifetime of Joshua and during the lifetimes of the older leaders who lived after Joshua and who had seen what great things the LORD had done for Israel."
(Judges 2:7)

JOSHUA DIES

6Then Joshua sent the people back to their land. 7The people served the LORD during the lifetime of Joshua and during the lifetimes of the older leaders who lived after Joshua and who had seen what great things the LORD had done for Israel. 8Joshua son of Nun, the servant of the LORD, died at the age of one hundred ten. 9They buried him in his own land at Timnath Serah in the mountains of Ephraim, north of Mount Gaash.

THE PEOPLE DISOBEY

10After those people had died, their children grew up and did not know the LORD or what he had done for Israel. 11So they did what the LORD said was wrong, and they worshiped the Baal idols. 12They quit following the LORD, the God of their ancestors who had brought them out of Egypt. They began to worship the gods of the people who lived around them, and that made the LORD angry. 13The Israelites quit following the LORD and worshiped Baal and Ashtoreth. 14The LORD was angry with the people of Israel, so he handed them over to

WHAT'S IT MEAN?

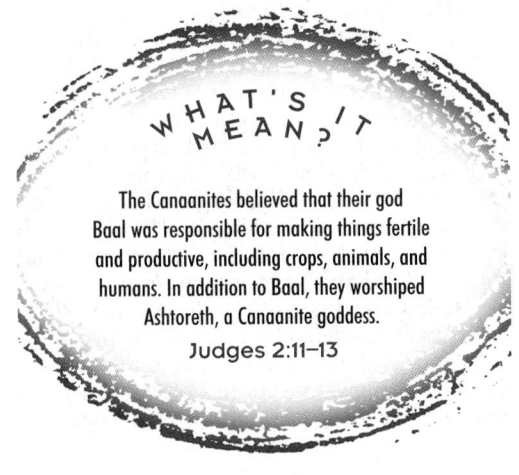

The Canaanites believed that their god Baal was responsible for making things fertile and productive, including crops, animals, and humans. In addition to Baal, they worshiped Ashtoreth, a Canaanite goddess.

Judges 2:11–13

2:5 Bokim This name means "crying."

robbers who took their possessions. He let their enemies who lived around them defeat them; they could not protect themselves. 15When the Israelites went out to fight, they always lost, because the LORD was not with them. The LORD had sworn to them this would happen. So the Israelites suffered very much.

GOD CHOOSES JUDGES

16Then the LORD chose leaders called judges,[n] who saved the Israelites from the robbers. 17But the Israelites did not listen to their judges. They were not faithful to God but worshiped other gods instead. Their ancestors had obeyed the LORD's commands, but they quickly turned away and did not obey. 18When their enemies hurt them, the Israelites cried for help. So the LORD felt sorry for them and sent judges to save them from their enemies. The LORD was with those judges all their lives. 19But when the judges died, the Israelites again sinned and worshiped other gods. They became worse than their ancestors. The Israelites were very stubborn and refused to change their evil ways.

WHAT'S IT MEAN?

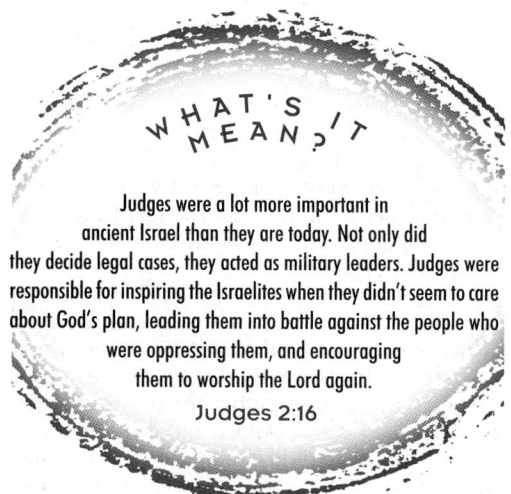

Judges were a lot more important in ancient Israel than they are today. Not only did they decide legal cases, they acted as military leaders. Judges were responsible for inspiring the Israelites when they didn't seem to care about God's plan, leading them into battle against the people who were oppressing them, and encouraging them to worship the Lord again.

Judges 2:16

20So the LORD became angry with the Israelites. He said, "These people have broken the agreement I made with their ancestors. They have not listened to me. 21I will no longer defeat the nations who were left when Joshua died. 22I will use them to test Israel, to see if Israel will keep the LORD's commands as their ancestors did." 23In the past the LORD had permitted those nations to stay in the land. He did not quickly force them out or help Joshua's army defeat them.

3

1These are the nations the LORD did not force to leave. He wanted to test the Israelites who had not fought in the wars of Canaan. 2(The only reason the LORD left those nations in the land was to teach the descendants of the Israelites who had not fought in those wars how to fight.) 3These are the nations: the five rulers of the Philistines, all the Canaanites, the people of Sidon, and the Hivites who lived in the Lebanon mountains from Mount Baal Hermon to Lebo Hamath. 4Those nations were in the land to test the Israelites—to see if they would obey the commands the LORD had given to their ancestors by Moses.

5The people of Israel lived with the Canaanites, Hittites, Amorites, Perizzites, Hivites, and Jebusites. 6The Israelites began to marry the daughters of those people, and they allowed their daughters to marry the sons of those people. Israel also served their gods.

OTHNIEL, THE FIRST JUDGE

7The Israelites did what the LORD said was wrong. They forgot about the LORD their God and served the idols of Baal and Asherah. 8So the LORD was angry with Israel and allowed Cushan-Rishathaim king of Northwest Mesopotamia to rule over the Israelites for eight years. 9When Israel cried to the LORD, the LORD sent someone to save them. Othniel son of Kenaz, Caleb's younger brother, saved the Israelites. 10The Spirit of the LORD entered Othniel, and he became Israel's judge. When he went to war, the LORD handed over to him Cushan-Rishathaim king of Northwest Mesopotamia. 11So the land was at peace for forty years. Then Othniel son of Kenaz died.

GOD
What happens when we forget about God? (3:7–8)

HELP
Who should we call for help? (3:9)

EHUD, THE JUDGE

12Again the people of Israel did what the LORD said was wrong. So the LORD gave Eglon king of Moab power to defeat Israel because of the evil Israel did. 13Eglon got the Ammonites and the Amalekites to join him. Then he attacked Israel and took Jericho, the city of palm trees. 14So the people of Israel were ruled by Eglon king of Moab for eighteen years.

15When the people cried to the LORD, he sent someone to save them. He was Ehud, son

2:16 judges They were not judges in courts of law, but leaders of the people in times of emergency.

of Gera from the people of Benjamin, who was left-handed. Israel sent Ehud to give Eglon king of Moab the payment he demanded. 16Ehud made himself a sword with two edges, about eighteen inches long, and he tied it to his right hip under his clothes. 17Ehud gave Eglon king of Moab the payment he demanded. Now Eglon was a very fat man. 18After he had given Eglon the payment, Ehud sent away the people who had carried it. 19When he passed the statues near Gilgal, he turned around and said to Eglon, "I have a secret message for you, King Eglon."

WHAT'S IT MEAN?

King Eglon was from Moab, across the Jordan River from Jericho. He used Joshua's old strategy for conquering Israel, crossing the Jordan from the east to attack and capture Jericho. Think of Gilgal as a suburb of Jericho. It was located about a mile and a half outside the city.

Judges 3:17–20

The king said, "Be quiet!" Then he sent all of his servants out of the room. 20Ehud went to King Eglon, as he was sitting alone in the room above his summer palace.

Ehud said, "I have a message from God for you." As the king stood up from his chair, 21Ehud reached with his left hand and took out the sword that was tied to his right hip. Then he stabbed the sword deep into the king's belly! 22Even the handle sank in, and the blade came out his back. The king's fat covered the whole sword, so Ehud left the sword in Eglon. 23Then he went out of the room and closed and locked the doors behind him.

24When the servants returned just after Ehud left, they found the doors to the room locked. So they thought the king was relieving himself. 25They waited for a long time. Finally they became worried because he still had not opened the doors. So they got the key and unlocked them and saw their king lying dead on the floor!

26While the servants were waiting, Ehud had escaped. He passed by the statues and went to Seirah. 27When he reached the mountains of Ephraim he blew the trumpet. The people of Israel heard it and went down from the hills with Ehud leading them.

28He said to them, "Follow me! The LORD has helped you to defeat your enemies, the Moabites." So Israel followed Ehud and captured the crossings of the Jordan River. They did not allow the Moabites to cross the Jordan River. 29Israel killed about ten thousand strong and able men from Moab; not one escaped. 30So that day Moab was forced to be under the rule of Israel, and there was peace in the land for eighty years.

SHAMGAR, THE JUDGE

31After Ehud, Shamgar son of Anath saved Israel. Shamgar killed six hundred Philistines with a sharp stick used to guide oxen.

DEBORAH, THE WOMAN JUDGE

4

1After Ehud died, the Israelites again did what the LORD said was wrong. 2So he let Jabin, a king of Canaan who ruled in the city of Hazor, defeat Israel. Sisera, who lived in Harosheth Haggoyim, was the commander of Jabin's army. 3Because he had nine hundred iron chariots and was very cruel to the people of Israel for twenty years, they cried to the LORD for help.

4A prophetess named Deborah, the wife of Lappidoth, was judge of Israel at that time. 5Deborah would sit under the Palm Tree of Deborah, which was between the cities of Ramah and Bethel, in the mountains of Ephraim. And the people of Israel would come to her to settle their arguments.

6Deborah sent a message to Barak son of Abinoam. Barak lived in the city of Kedesh, which is in the area of Naphtali. Deborah said to Barak, "The LORD, the God of Israel, commands you: 'Go and gather ten thousand men of Naphtali and Zebulun and lead them to Mount Tabor. 7I will make Sisera, the commander of Jabin's army, and his chariots, and his army meet you at the Kishon River. I will hand Sisera over to you.' "

8Then Barak said to Deborah, "I will go if you will go with me, but if you won't go with me, I won't go."

9"Of course I will go with you," Deborah answered, "but you will not get credit for the victory. The LORD will let a woman defeat Sisera." So Deborah went with Barak to Kedesh. 10At Kedesh, Barak called the people of Zebulun and Naphtali together. From them, he gathered ten thousand men to follow him, and Deborah went with him also.

11Now Heber the Kenite had left the other

Kenites, the descendants of Hobab, Moses'
brother-in-law. Heber had put up his tent by
the great tree in Zaanannim, near Kedesh.
[12]When Sisera was told that Barak son of
Abinoam had gone to Mount Tabor, [13]Sisera
gathered his nine hundred iron chariots and all
the men with him, from Harosheth Haggoyim
to the Kishon River.
[14]Then Deborah said to Barak, "Get up! Today is the day the LORD will hand over Sisera.
The LORD has already cleared the way for you."
So Barak led ten thousand men down Mount
Tabor. [15]As Barak approached, the LORD confused Sisera and his army and chariots. The
LORD defeated them with the sword, but Sisera
left his chariot and ran away on foot. [16]Barak
and his men chased Sisera's chariots and army
to Harosheth Haggoyim. With their swords
they killed all of Sisera's men; not one of them
was left alive.
[17]But Sisera himself ran away to the tent
where Jael lived. She was the wife of Heber, one
of the Kenite family groups. Heber's family was
at peace with Jabin king of Hazor. [18]Jael went
out to meet Sisera and said to him, "Come into
my tent, master! Come in. Don't be afraid." So
Sisera went into Jael's tent, and she covered
him with a rug.
[19]Sisera said to Jael, "I am thirsty. Please give
me some water to drink." So she opened a
leather bag of milk and gave him a drink. Then
she covered him up.
[20]He said to her, "Go stand at the entrance to
the tent. If anyone comes and asks you, 'Is
anyone here?' say, 'No.' "
[21]But Jael, the wife of Heber, took a tent peg
and a hammer and quietly went to Sisera.
Since he was very tired, he was in a deep sleep.
She hammered the tent peg through the side of
Sisera's head and into the ground. And so Sisera died.
[22]At that very moment Barak came by Jael's
tent, chasing Sisera. Jael went out to meet him
and said, "Come. I will show you the man you
are looking for." So Barak entered her tent, and
there Sisera lay dead, with the tent peg in his
head.
[23]On that day God defeated Jabin king of
Canaan in the sight of Israel.
[24]Israel became stronger and stronger
against Jabin king of Canaan until finally they
destroyed him.

THE SONG OF DEBORAH

5

[1]On that day Deborah and Barak son of
Abinoam sang this song:

[2]"The leaders led Israel.
The people volunteered to go to
battle.
Praise the LORD!
[3]Listen, kings.
Pay attention, rulers!
I myself will sing to the
LORD.
I will make music to the
LORD, the God of
Israel.

WORSHIP
Who should we worship? (5:3)

[4]"LORD, when you came from Edom,
when you marched from the land of
Edom,
the earth shook,
the skies rained,
and the clouds dropped water.
[5]The mountains shook before the LORD, the
God of Mount Sinai,
before the LORD, the God of Israel!

[6]"In the days of Shamgar son of Anath,
in the days of Jael, the main roads were
empty.
Travelers went on the back roads.
[7]There were no warriors in Israel
until I, Deborah, arose,
until I arose to be a mother to Israel.
[8]At that time they chose to follow new
gods.
Because of this, enemies fought us at our
city gates.
No one could find a shield or a spear
among the forty thousand people of
Israel.
[9]My heart is with the commanders of
Israel.
They volunteered freely from among the
people.
Praise the LORD!

WHAT'S IT MEAN?

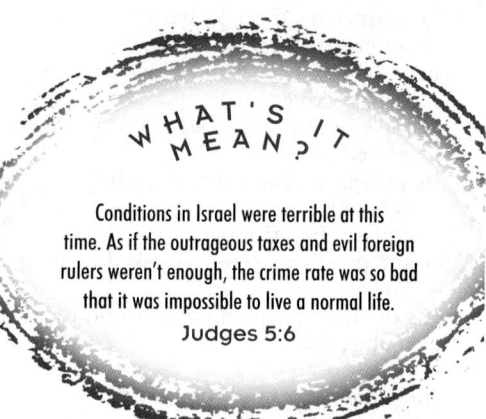

Conditions in Israel were terrible at this time. As if the outrageous taxes and evil foreign rulers weren't enough, the crime rate was so bad that it was impossible to live a normal life.
Judges 5:6

10 "You who ride on white donkeys
and sit on saddle blankets,
and you who walk along the road,
listen!
11 Listen to the sound of the singers
at the watering holes.
There they tell about the victories of the LORD,
the victories of the LORD's warriors in Israel.
Then the LORD's people went down to the city gates.

12 "Wake up, wake up, Deborah!
Wake up, wake up, sing a song!
Get up, Barak!
Go capture your enemies, son of Abinoam!

13 "Then those who were left came down to the important leaders.
The LORD's people came down to me with strong men.
14 They came from Ephraim in the mountains of Amalek.
Benjamin was among the people who followed you.
From the family group of Makir, the commanders came down.
And from Zebulun came those who lead.
15 The princes of Issachar were with Deborah.
The people of Issachar were loyal to Barak
and followed him into the valley.
The Reubenites thought hard
about what they would do.
16 Why did you stay by the sheepfold?
Was it to hear the music played for your sheep?
The Reubenites thought hard
about what they would do.
17 The people of Gilead stayed east of the Jordan River.
People of Dan, why did you stay by the ships?
The people of Asher stayed at the seashore,
at their safe harbors.
18 But the people of Zebulun risked their lives,
as did the people of Naphtali on the battlefield.

19 "The kings came, and they fought.
At that time the kings of Canaan fought
at Taanach, by the waters of Megiddo.
But they took away no silver or possessions of Israel.
20 The stars fought from heaven;
from their paths, they fought Sisera.
21 The Kishon River swept Sisera's men away,
that old river, the Kishon River.
March on, my soul, with strength!
22 Then the horses' hoofs beat the ground.
Galloping, galloping go Sisera's mighty horses.
23 'May the town of Meroz be cursed,' said the angel of the LORD.
'Bitterly curse its people,
because they did not come to help the LORD.
They did not fight the strong enemy.'

24 "May Jael, the wife of Heber the Kenite,
be blessed above all women who live in tents.
25 Sisera asked for water,
but Jael gave him milk.
In a bowl fit for a ruler,
she brought him cream.
26 Jael reached out and took the tent peg.
Her right hand reached for the workman's hammer.
She hit Sisera! She smashed his head!
She crushed and pierced the side of his head!
27 At Jael's feet he sank.
He fell, and he lay there.
At her feet he sank. He fell.
Where Sisera sank, there he fell, dead!

28 "Sisera's mother looked out through the window.

WHAT'S IT MEAN?

Have you ever heard the expression "To the winners go the spoils"? The spoils of war were whatever the victorious armies felt like taking from the cities they conquered. Not only did they take material possessions; they also captured women to be their wives, servants, or slaves.

Judges 5:30

She looked through the curtains and
cried out,
'Why is Sisera's chariot so late in coming?
Why are sounds of his chariots' horses
delayed?'
29 The wisest of her servant ladies answer
her,
and Sisera's mother says to herself,
30 'Surely they are robbing the people they
defeated!
Surely they are dividing those things
among themselves!
Each soldier is given a girl or two.
Maybe Sisera is taking pieces of dyed
cloth.
Maybe they are even taking
pieces of dyed, embroidered cloth for
the necks of the victors!'

FOLLOWING GOD
What are Christians like? (5:31)

31 "Let all your enemies
die this way, LORD!
But let all the people
who love you
be as strong as the
rising sun!"
Then there was peace in the land for forty
years.

THE MIDIANITES ATTACK ISRAEL

6
1 Again the Israelites did what the LORD said
was wrong. So for seven years the LORD handed them over to Midian. 2 Because the Midianites were very powerful and were cruel to
Israel, the Israelites made hiding places in the
mountains, in caves, and in safe places.
3 Whenever the Israelites planted
crops, the Midianites, Amalekites, and other peoples
from the east would come and
attack them. 4 They camped in
the land and destroyed the
crops that the Israelites had
planted as far away as Gaza. They
left nothing for Israel to eat, and
no sheep, cattle, or donkeys.
5 The Midianites came with their
tents and their animals like
swarms of locusts to ruin the
land. There were so many people and camels they could not
be counted. 6 Israel became very
poor because of the Midianites, so
they cried out to the LORD.
7 When the Israelites cried out to the LORD
against the Midianites, 8 the LORD sent a prophet
to them. He said, "This is what the LORD, the
God of Israel, says: I brought you out of Egypt,
the land of slavery. 9 I saved you from the Egyptians and from all those who were against you.
I forced the Canaanites out of their land and
gave it to you. 10 Then I said to you, 'I am the
LORD your God. Live in the land of the Amorites, but do not worship their gods.' But you
did not obey me."

DECISIONS
Do bad decisions have consequences? (6:1)

THE ANGEL OF THE LORD VISITS GIDEON

11 The angel of the LORD came and sat down
under the oak tree at Ophrah that belonged to
Joash, one of the Abiezrite people. Gideon,
Joash's son, was separating some wheat from
the chaff in a winepress to keep the wheat
from the Midianites. 12 The angel of the LORD
appeared to Gideon and said, "The LORD is
with you, mighty warrior!"
13 Then Gideon said, "Sir, if the LORD is with
us, why are we having so much trouble?
Where are the miracles our ancestors told us
he did when the LORD brought them out of
Egypt? But now he has left us and has handed
us over to the Midianites."
14 The LORD turned to Gideon and said, "Go
with your strength and save Israel from the
Midianites. I am the one who is sending you."
15 But Gideon answered, "Lord, how can I
save Israel? My family group is the weakest in
Manasseh, and I am the least important member of my family."
16 The LORD answered him, "I will be with
you. It will seem as if the Midianites you are
fighting are only one man."
17 Then Gideon said to the LORD, "If you are
pleased with me, give me proof that it is really
you talking with me. 18 Please wait here until I
come back to you. Let me bring my offering
and set it in front of you."
And the LORD said, "I will wait until you
return."
19 So Gideon went in and cooked a young
goat, and with twenty quarts of flour, made
bread without yeast. Then he put
the meat into a basket and the
broth into a pot. He brought
them out and gave them to the
angel under the oak tree.
20 The angel of God said to
Gideon, "Put the meat and the
bread without yeast on that
rock over there. Then pour the
broth on them." And Gideon did as
he was told. 21 The angel of the LORD
touched the meat and the bread with the end of
the stick that was in his hand. Then fire jumped
up from the rock and completely burned up the
meat and the bread! And the angel of the LORD

"Lord God! I have seen the angel of the Lord face to face!" (Judges 6:22b)

disappeared! 22Then Gideon understood he had been talking to the angel of the LORD. So Gideon cried out, "Lord GOD! I have seen the angel of the LORD face to face!"

23But the LORD said to Gideon, "Calm down! Don't be afraid! You will not die!"

24So Gideon built an altar there to worship the LORD and named it The LORD Is Peace. It still stands at Ophrah, where the Abiezrites live.

GIDEON TEARS DOWN THE ALTAR OF BAAL

25That same night the LORD said to Gideon, "Take the bull that belongs to your father and a second bull seven years old. Pull down your father's altar to Baal, and cut down the Asherah idol beside it. 26Then build an altar to the LORD your God with its stones in the right order on this high ground. Kill and burn a second bull on this altar, using the wood from the Asherah idol."

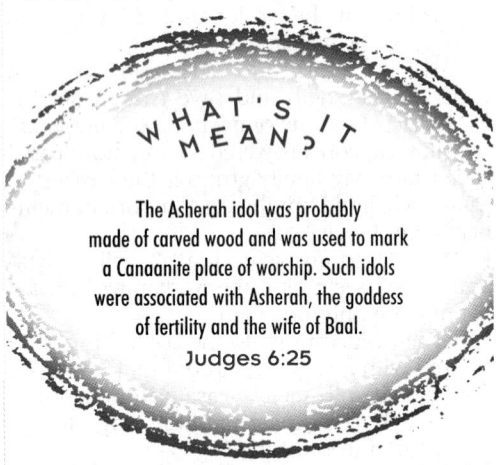

WHAT'S IT MEAN?

The Asherah idol was probably made of carved wood and was used to mark a Canaanite place of worship. Such idols were associated with Asherah, the goddess of fertility and the wife of Baal.

Judges 6:25

27So Gideon got ten of his servants and did what the LORD had told him to do. But Gideon was afraid that his family and the men of the city might see him, so he did it at night, not in the daytime.

28When the men of the city got up the next morning, they saw that the altar for Baal had been destroyed and that the Asherah idol beside it had been cut down! They also saw the altar Gideon had built and the second bull that had been sacrificed on it. 29The men of the city asked each other, "Who did this?"

After they asked many questions, someone told them, "Gideon son of Joash did this."

30So they said to Joash, "Bring your son out. He has pulled down the altar of Baal and cut down the Asherah idol beside it. He must die!"

31But Joash said to the angry crowd around him, "Are you going to take Baal's side? Are you going to defend him? Anyone who takes Baal's side will be killed by morning! If Baal is a god, let him fight for himself. It's his altar that has been pulled down." 32So on that day Gideon got the name Jerub-Baal, which means "let Baal fight against him," because Gideon pulled down Baal's altar.

GIDEON DEFEATS MIDIAN

33All the Midianites, the Amalekites, and other peoples from the east joined together and came across the Jordan River and camped in the Valley of Jezreel. 34But the Spirit of the LORD entered Gideon, and he blew a trumpet to call the Abiezrites to follow him. 35He sent messengers to all of Manasseh, calling them to follow him. He also sent messengers to the people of Asher, Zebulun, and Naphtali. So they also went up to meet Gideon and his men.

36Then Gideon said to God, "You said you would help me save Israel. 37I will put some wool on the threshing floor. If there is dew only on the wool but all of the ground is dry, then I will know that you will use me to save Israel, as you said." 38And that is just what happened. When Gideon got up early the next

On the Edge

But the Spirit of the LORD entered Gideon, and he blew a trumpet to call the Abiezrites to follow him (Judg. 6:34).

In this passage, the Holy Spirit "entered Gideon," giving him the divine power he needed to carry out God's plan. The assignment was big—rescue Israel. It required one faithful man and supernatural help from God's Spirit. One man plus God is mightier than any army and stronger than any opposition.

If God is calling you for a big job, you can bet that he will also send the power of his Spirit. You won't be alone. God goes before you to clear the way for you, and he sends his Spirit to take control of the situation—and of you. You'll know what to do. You'll know what to say. You can run to the battle with the total confidence that the Spirit of God is in control.

SEE FOR YOURSELF:
Judg. 14:19;
1 Sam. 10:6;
Ezek. 2:2

morning and squeezed the wool, he got a full bowl of water from it.

[39]Then Gideon said to God, "Don't be angry with me if I ask just one more thing. Please let me make one more test. Let only the wool be dry while the ground around it gets wet with dew." [40]That night God did that very thing. Just the wool was dry, but the ground around it was wet with dew.

7 [1]Early in the morning Jerub-Baal (also called Gideon) and all his men set up their camp at the spring of Harod. The Midianites were camped north of them in the valley at the bottom of the hill called Moreh. [2]Then the LORD said to Gideon, "You have too many men to defeat the Midianites. I don't want the Israelites to brag that they saved themselves. [3]So now, announce to the people, 'Anyone who is afraid may leave Mount Gilead and go back home.' " So twenty-two thousand men returned home, but ten thousand remained.

[4]Then the LORD said to Gideon, "There are still too many men. Take the men down to the water, and I will test them for you there. If I say, 'This man will go with you,' he will go. But if I say, 'That one will not go with you,' he will not go."

[5]So Gideon led the men down to the water. There the LORD said to him, "Separate them into those who drink water by lapping it up like a dog and those who bend down to drink." [6]There were three hundred men who used their hands to bring water to their mouths, lapping it as a dog does. All the rest got down on their knees to drink.

[7]Then the LORD said to Gideon, "Using the three hundred men who lapped the water, I will save you and hand Midian over to you. Let all the others go home." [8]So Gideon sent the rest of Israel to their homes. But he kept three hundred men and took the jars and the trumpets of those who left.

Now the camp of Midian was in the valley below Gideon. [9]That night the LORD said to Gideon, "Get up. Go down and attack the camp of the Midianites, because I will give them to you. [10]But if you are afraid to go down, take your servant Purah with you. [11]When you come to the camp of Midian, you will hear what they are saying. Then you will not be afraid to attack the camp."

"Get up! The LORD has handed the army of Midian over to you!" (Judges 7:15b)

GIDEON IS ENCOURAGED

So Gideon and his servant Purah went down to the edge of the enemy camp. [12]The Midianites, the Amalekites, and all the peoples from the east were camped in that valley. There were so many of them they seemed like locusts. Their camels could not be counted because they were as many as the grains of sand on the seashore!

[13]When Gideon came to the enemy camp, he heard a man telling his friend about a dream. He was saying, "I dreamed that a loaf of barley bread rolled into the camp of Midian. It hit the tent so hard that the tent turned over and fell flat!"

[14]The man's friend said, "Your dream is about the sword of Gideon son of Joash, a man of Israel. God will hand Midian and the whole army over to him!"

WHAT'S IT MEAN?

In ancient times, God spoke to people through their dreams, revealing his plans for them while they slept. Not all of these dreams made obvious sense at first. Sometimes the dreamers needed other people to help them understand what their nighttime visions meant.

Judges 7:13

[15]When Gideon heard about the dream and what it meant, he worshiped God. Then Gideon went back to the camp of Israel and called out to them, "Get up! The LORD has handed the army of Midian over to you!" [16]Gideon divided the three hundred men into three groups. He gave each man a trumpet and an empty jar with a burning torch inside.

[17]Gideon told the men, "Watch me and do what I do. When I get to the edge of the camp, do what I do. [18]Surround the enemy camp. When I and everyone with me blow our trumpets, you blow your trumpets, too. Then shout, 'For the LORD and for Gideon!' "

MIDIAN IS DEFEATED

[19]So Gideon and the one hundred men with him came to the edge of the enemy camp just after they had changed guards. It was during

the middle watch of the night. Then Gideon and his men blew their trumpets and smashed their jars. [20]All three groups of Gideon's men blew their trumpets and smashed their jars. They held the torches in their left hands and the trumpets in their right hands. Then they shouted, "A sword for the LORD and for Gideon!" [21]Each of Gideon's men stayed in his place around the camp, but the Midianites began shouting and running to escape.

[22]When Gideon's three hundred men blew their trumpets, the LORD made all the Midianites fight each other with their swords! The enemy army ran away to the city of Beth Shittah toward Zererah. They ran as far as the border of Abel Meholah, near the city of Tabbath. [23]Then men of Israel from Naphtali, Asher, and all of Manasseh were called out to chase the Midianites. [24]Gideon sent messengers through all the mountains of Ephraim, saying, "Come down and attack the Midianites. Take control of the Jordan River as far as Beth Barah before the Midianites can get to it."

So they called out all the men of Ephraim, who took control of the Jordan River as far as Beth Barah. [25]The men of Ephraim captured two princes of Midian named Oreb and Zeeb. They killed Oreb at the rock of Oreb and Zeeb at the winepress of Zeeb, and they continued chasing the Midianites. They brought the heads of Oreb and Zeeb to Gideon, who was east of the Jordan River.

WHAT'S IT MEAN?

A winepress was a place where ripe grapes were stomped for their juice. When that juice "fermented" for a certain period of time, it became wine. Not only was wine a common drink among the Israelites, it was also used as medicine and as part of their religious ceremonies.

Judges 7:25

8 [1]The men of Ephraim asked Gideon, "Why did you treat us this way? Why didn't you call us when you went to fight against Midian?" They argued angrily with Gideon.

[2]But he answered them, "I have not done as well as you! The small part you did was better than all that my people of Abiezer did. [3]God let you capture Oreb and Zeeb, the princes of Midian. How can I compare what I did with what you did?" When the men of Ephraim heard Gideon's answer, they were not as angry anymore.

GIDEON CAPTURES TWO KINGS

[4]When Gideon and his three hundred men came to the Jordan River, they were tired, but they chased the enemy across to the other side. [5]Gideon said to the men of Succoth, "Please give my soldiers some bread because they are very tired. I am chasing Zebah and Zalmunna, the kings of Midian."

[6]But the leaders of Succoth said, "Why should we give your soldiers bread? You haven't caught Zebah and Zalmunna yet."

[7]Then Gideon said, "The LORD will surrender Zebah and Zalmunna to me. After that, I will whip your skin with thorns and briers from the desert."

[8]Gideon left Succoth and went to the city of Peniel and asked them for food. But the people of Peniel gave him the same answer as the people of Succoth. [9]So Gideon said to the men of Peniel, "After I win the victory, I will return and pull down this tower."

[10]Zebah and Zalmunna and their army were in the city of Karkor. About fifteen thousand men were left of the armies of the peoples of the east. Already one hundred twenty thousand soldiers had been killed. [11]Gideon went up the road of those who live in tents east of Nobah and Jogbehah, and he attacked the enemy army when they did not expect it. [12]Zebah and Zalmunna, the kings of Midian, ran away, but Gideon chased and captured them and frightened away their army.

[13]Then Gideon son of Joash returned from the battle by the Pass of Heres. [14]Gideon captured a young man from Succoth and asked him some questions. So the young man wrote down for Gideon the names of seventy-seven officers and older leaders of Succoth.

GIDEON PUNISHES SUCCOTH

[15]When Gideon came to Succoth, he said to the people of that city, "Here are Zebah and Zalmunna. You made fun of me by saying, 'Why should we give bread to your tired men? You have not caught Zebah and Zalmunna yet.' " [16]So Gideon took the older leaders of the city and punished them with thorns and briers from the desert. [17]He also pulled down the tower of Peniel and killed the people in that city.

[18]Gideon asked Zebah and Zalmunna,

"What were the men like that you killed on Mount Tabor?"

They answered, "They were like you. Each one of them looked like a prince."

[19]Gideon said, "Those were my brothers, my mother's sons. As surely as the LORD lives, I would not kill you if you had spared them." [20]Then Gideon said to Jether, his oldest son, "Kill them." But Jether was only a boy and was afraid, so he did not take out his sword.

[21]Then Zebah and Zalmunna said to Gideon, "Come on. Kill us yourself. As the saying goes, 'It takes a man to do a man's job.'" So Gideon got up and killed Zebah and Zalmunna and took the decorations off their camels' necks.

"But Gideon told them, 'The LORD will be your ruler. I will not rule over you, nor will my son rule over you.'"
(Judges 8:23)

GIDEON MAKES AN IDOL

[22]The people of Israel said to Gideon, "You saved us from the Midianites. Now, we want you and your son and your grandson to rule over us."

[23]But Gideon told them, "The LORD will be your ruler. I will not rule over you, nor will my son rule over you." [24]He said, "I want you to do this one thing for me. I want each of you to give me a gold earring from the things you took in the fighting." (The Ishmaelites[n] wore gold earrings.)

WHAT'S IT MEAN?

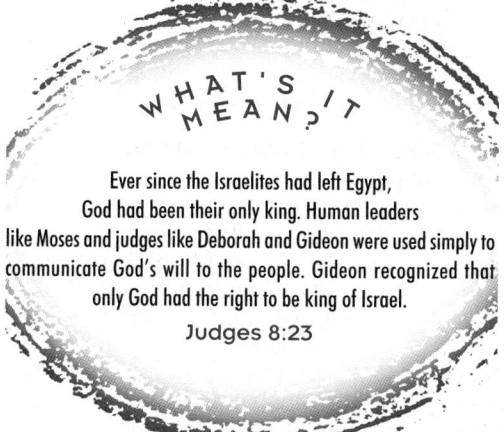

Ever since the Israelites had left Egypt, God had been their only king. Human leaders like Moses and judges like Deborah and Gideon were used simply to communicate God's will to the people. Gideon recognized that only God had the right to be king of Israel.

Judges 8:23

[25]They said, "We will gladly give you what you want." So they spread out a coat, and everyone threw down an earring from what he had taken. [26]The gold earrings weighed about forty-three pounds. This did not count the decorations, necklaces, and purple robes worn by the kings of Midian, nor the chains from the camels' necks. [27]Gideon used the gold to make a holy vest, which he put in his hometown of Ophrah. But all the Israelites were unfaithful to God and worshiped it, so it became a trap for Gideon and his family.

THE DEATH OF GIDEON

[28]So Midian was under the rule of Israel; they did not cause trouble anymore. And the land had peace for forty years, as long as Gideon was alive.

[29]Gideon[n] son of Joash went to his home to live. [30]He had seventy sons of his own, because he had many wives. [31]He had a slave woman who lived in Shechem, and he had a son by her, whom he named Abimelech. [32]So Gideon son of Joash died at a good old age. He was buried in the tomb of Joash, his father, in Ophrah, where the Abiezrites live.

[33]As soon as Gideon died, the people of Israel were again unfaithful to God and followed the Baals. They made Baal-Berith their god. [34]The Israelites did not remember the LORD their God, who had saved them from all their enemies living all around them. [35]And they were not kind to the family of Jerub-Baal, also called Gideon, for all the good he had done for Israel.

ABIMELECH BECOMES KING

9

[1]Abimelech son of Gideon went to his uncles in the city of Shechem. He said to his uncles and all of his mother's family group, [2]"Ask the leaders of Shechem, 'Is it better for the seventy sons of Gideon to rule over you or for one man to rule?' Remember, I am your relative."

[3]Abimelech's uncles spoke to all the leaders of Shechem about this. And they decided to follow Abimelech, because they said, "He is our relative." [4]So the leaders of Shechem gave Abimelech about one and three-quarter pounds of silver from the temple of the god Baal-Berith. Abimelech used the silver to hire some worthless, reckless men, who followed him wherever

8:24 Ishmaelites Another name for the Midianites. See Genesis 37:25–28. **8:29 Gideon** Also called Jerub-Baal.

WHAT'S IT MEAN?

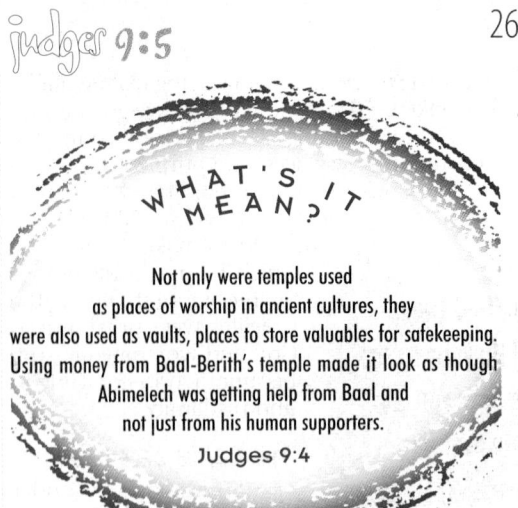

Not only were temples used as places of worship in ancient cultures, they were also used as vaults, places to store valuables for safekeeping. Using money from Baal-Berith's temple made it look as though Abimelech was getting help from Baal and not just from his human supporters.

Judges 9:4

he went. 5He went to Ophrah, the hometown of his father, and murdered his seventy brothers, the sons of Gideon. He killed them all on one stone. But Gideon's youngest son, Jotham, hid from Abimelech and escaped. 6Then all of the leaders of Shechem and Beth Millo gathered beside the great tree standing in Shechem. There they made Abimelech their king.

WHAT'S IT MEAN?

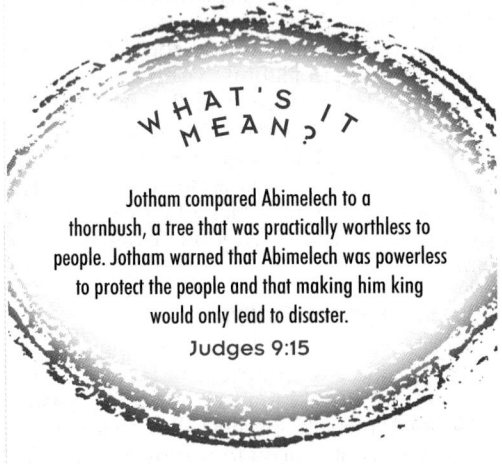

Jotham compared Abimelech to a thornbush, a tree that was practically worthless to people. Jotham warned that Abimelech was powerless to protect the people and that making him king would only lead to disaster.

Judges 9:15

JOTHAM'S STORY

7When Jotham heard this, he went and stood on the top of Mount Gerizim. He shouted to the people: "Listen to me, you leaders of Shechem, so that God will listen to you! 8One day the trees decided to appoint a king to rule over them. They said to the olive tree, 'You be king over us!'

9"But the olive tree said, 'Men and gods are honored by my oil. Should I stop making it and go and sway over the other trees?'

10"Then the trees said to the fig tree, 'Come and be king over us!'

11"But the fig tree answered, 'Should I stop making my sweet and good fruit and go and sway over the other trees?'

12"Then the trees said to the vine, 'Come and be king over us!'

13"But the vine answered, 'My new wine makes men and gods happy. Should I stop making it and go and sway over the trees?'

14"Then all the trees said to the thornbush, 'Come and be king over us.'

15"But the thornbush said to the trees, 'If you really want to appoint me king over you, come and find shelter in my shade! But if not, let fire come out of the thornbush and burn up the cedars of Lebanon!'

16"Now, were you completely honest and sincere when you made Abimelech king? Have you been fair to Gideon[n] and his family? Have you treated Gideon as you should? 17Remember, my father fought for you and risked his life to save you from the power of the Midianites. 18But now you have turned against my father's family and have killed his seventy sons on one stone. You have made Abimelech, the son of my father's slave girl, king over the leaders of Shechem just because he is your relative! 19So then, if you have been honest and sincere to Gideon and his family today, be happy with Abimelech as your king. And may he be happy with you! 20But if not, may fire come out of Abimelech and completely burn you leaders of Shechem and Beth Millo! Also may fire come out of the leaders of Shechem and Beth Millo and burn up Abimelech!"

21Then Jotham ran away and escaped to the city of Beer. He lived there because he was afraid of his brother Abimelech.

ABIMELECH FIGHTS AGAINST SHECHEM

22Abimelech ruled Israel for three years. 23Then God sent an evil spirit to make trouble between Abimelech and the leaders of Shechem so that the leaders of Shechem turned against him. 24Abimelech had killed Gideon's[n] seventy sons, his own brothers, and the leaders of Shechem had helped him. So God sent the evil spirit to punish them. 25The leaders of Shechem were against Abimelech then. They put men on the hilltops in ambush who robbed everyone going by. And Abimelech was told.

26A man named Gaal son of Ebed and his brothers moved into Shechem, and the leaders of Shechem trusted him. 27They went out to

9:16, 24 Gideon Also called Jerub-Baal.

the vineyards to pick grapes, and they squeezed the grapes. Then they had a feast in the temple of their god, where they ate and drank and cursed Abimelech. [28]Gaal son of Ebed said, "We are the men of Shechem. Who is Abimelech that we should serve him? Isn't he one of Gideon's sons, and isn't Zebul his officer? We should serve the men of Hamor, Shechem's father. Why should we serve Abimelech? [29]If you made me commander of these people, I would get rid of Abimelech. I would say to him, 'Get your army ready and come out to battle.' "

[30]Now when Zebul, the ruler of Shechem, heard what Gaal son of Ebed said, he was very angry. [31]He sent secret messengers to Abimelech, saying, "Gaal son of Ebed and Gaal's brothers have come to Shechem, and they are turning the city against you! [32]You and your men should get up during the night and hide in the fields outside the city. [33]As soon as the sun comes up in the morning, attack the city. When Gaal and his men come out to fight you, do what you can to them."

[34]So Abimelech and all his soldiers got up during the night and hid near Shechem in four groups. [35]Gaal son of Ebed went out and was standing at the entrance to the city gate. As he was standing there, Abimelech and his soldiers came out of their hiding places.

[36]When Gaal saw the soldiers, he said to Zebul, "Look! There are people coming down from the mountains!"

But Zebul said, "You are seeing the shadows of the mountains. The shadows just look like people."

[37]But again Gaal said, "Look, there are people coming down from the center of the land,

WHAT'S IT MEAN?

The "center of the land" probably refers to Mount Gerizim. This site was well known in Israelite history as the place where both Abraham and Jacob had built altars. In ancient times, most places of worship were built on hilltops.

Judges 9:37

and there is a group coming from the fortune-tellers' tree!"

[38]Zebul said to Gaal, "Where is your bragging now? You said, 'Who is Abimelech that we should serve him?' You made fun of these men. Now go out and fight them."

[39]So Gaal led the men of Shechem out to fight Abimelech. [40]Abimelech and his men chased them, and many of Gaal's men were killed before they could get back to the city gate. [41]While Abimelech stayed at Arumah, Zebul forced Gaal and his brothers to leave Shechem.

[42]The next day the people of Shechem went out to the fields. When Abimelech was told about it, [43]he separated his men into three groups and hid them in the fields. When he saw the people coming out of the city, he jumped up and attacked them. [44]Abimelech and his group ran to the entrance gate to the city. The other two groups ran out to the people in the fields and struck them down. [45]Abimelech and his men fought the city of Shechem all day until they captured it and killed its people. Then he tore it down and threw salt[n] over the ruins.

WHAT'S IT MEAN?

Throwing salt was Abimelech's way of cursing the land and destroying its ability to produce crops.

Judges 9:45

THE TOWER OF SHECHEM BURNS

[46]When the leaders who were in the Tower of Shechem heard what had happened to Shechem, they gathered in the safest room of the temple of El Berith. [47]Abimelech heard that all the leaders of the Tower of Shechem had gathered there. [48]So he and all his men went up Mount Zalmon, near Shechem. Abimelech took an ax and cut some branches and put them on his shoulders. He said to all those with him, "Hurry! Do what I have done!" [49]So all those men cut branches and followed Abimelech and piled them against the safest

9:45 salt The salt would keep crops from growing there.

room of the temple. Then they set them on fire and burned the people inside. So all the people who were at the Tower of Shechem also died—about a thousand men and women.

ABIMELECH'S DEATH

[50]Then Abimelech went to the city of Thebez. He surrounded the city, attacked it, and captured it. [51]But inside the city was a strong tower, so all the men, women, and leaders of that city ran to the tower. When they got inside, they locked the door behind them. Then they climbed up to the roof of the tower. [52]Abimelech came to the tower to attack it. He approached the door of the tower to set it on fire, [53]but as he came near, a woman dropped a grinding stone on his head, crushing his skull.

[54]He quickly called to the officer who carried his armor and said, "Take out your sword and kill me. I don't want people to say, 'A woman killed Abimelech.' " So the officer stabbed Abimelech, and he died. [55]When the people of Israel saw Abimelech was dead, they all returned home.

[56]In that way God punished Abimelech for all the evil he had done to his father by killing his seventy brothers. [57]God also punished the men of Shechem for the evil they had done. So the curse spoken by Jotham, the youngest son of Gideon,[n] came true.

TOLA, THE JUDGE

10

[1]After Abimelech died, another judge came to save Israel. He was Tola son of Puah, the son of Dodo. Tola was from the people of Issachar and lived in the city of Shamir in the mountains of Ephraim. [2]Tola was a judge for Israel for twenty-three years. Then he died and was buried in Shamir.

JAIR, THE JUDGE

[3]After Tola died, Jair from the region of Gilead became judge. He was a judge for Israel for twenty-two years. [4]Jair had thirty sons, who rode thirty donkeys. These thirty sons controlled thirty towns in Gilead, which are called the Towns of Jair to this day. [5]Jair died and was buried in the city of Kamon.

THE AMMONITES TROUBLE ISRAEL

[6]Again the Israelites did what the LORD said was wrong. They worshiped Baal and Ashtoreth, the gods of Aram, Sidon, Moab, and Ammon, and the gods of the Philistines. The Israelites left the LORD and stopped serving him. [7]So the LORD was angry with them and handed them over to the Philistines and the Ammonites. [8]In the same year those people destroyed the Israelites who lived east of the Jordan River in the region of Gilead, where the Amorites lived. So the Israelites suffered for eighteen years. [9]The Ammonites then crossed the Jordan River to fight the people of Judah, Benjamin, and Ephraim, causing much trouble to the people of Israel. [10]So the Israelites cried out to the LORD, "We have sinned against you. We left our God and worshiped the Baal idols."

[11]The LORD answered the Israelites, "When the Egyptians, Amorites, Ammonites, Philistines, [12]Sidonians, Amalekites, and Maonites were cruel to you, you cried out to me, and I saved you. [13]But now you have left me again and have worshiped other gods. So I refuse to save you again. [14]You have chosen those gods. So go call to them for help. Let them save you when you are in trouble."

[15]But the people of Israel said to the LORD, "We have sinned. Do to us whatever you want, but please save us today!" [16]Then the Israelites threw away the foreign gods among them, and they worshiped the LORD again. So he felt sorry for them when he saw their suffering.

[17]The Ammonites gathered for war and camped in Gilead. The Israelites gathered and camped at Mizpah. [18]The leaders of the people of Gilead said, "Who will lead us to attack the Ammonites? He will become the head of all those who live in Gilead."

WHAT'S IT MEAN?

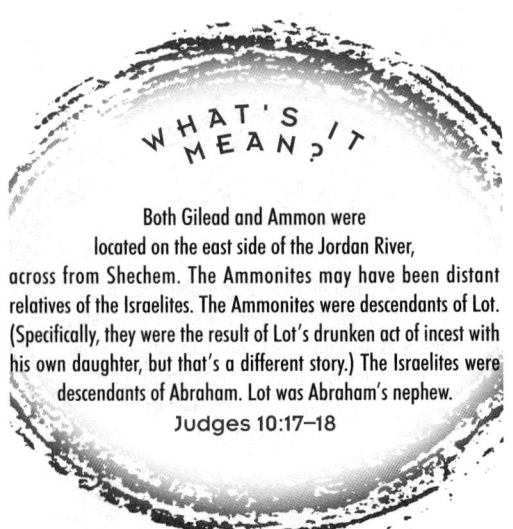

Both Gilead and Ammon were located on the east side of the Jordan River, across from Shechem. The Ammonites may have been distant relatives of the Israelites. The Ammonites were descendants of Lot. (Specifically, they were the result of Lot's drunken act of incest with his own daughter, but that's a different story.) The Israelites were descendants of Abraham. Lot was Abraham's nephew.

Judges 10:17–18

9:57 Gideon Also called Jerub-Baal.

JEPHTHAH IS CHOSEN AS LEADER

1Jephthah was a strong soldier from Gilead. His father was named Gilead, and his mother was a prostitute. 2Gilead's wife had several sons. When they grew up, they forced Jephthah to leave his home, saying to him, "You will not get any of our father's property, because you are the son of another woman." 3So Jephthah ran away from his brothers and lived in the land of Tob. There some worthless men began to follow him.

4After a time the Ammonites fought against Israel. 5When the Ammonites made war against Israel, the older leaders of Gilead went to Jephthah to bring him back from Tob. 6They said to him, "Come and lead our army so we can fight the Ammonites."

7But Jephthah said to them, "Didn't you hate me? You forced me to leave my father's house. Why are you coming to me now that you are in trouble?"

8The older leaders of Gilead said to Jephthah, "It is because of those troubles that we come to you now. Please come with us and fight against the Ammonites. You will be the ruler over everyone who lives in Gilead."

9Then Jephthah answered, "If you take me back to Gilead to fight the Ammonites and the LORD helps me win, I will be your ruler."

10The older leaders of Gilead said to him, "The LORD is listening to everything we are saying. We promise to do all that you tell us to do." 11So Jephthah went with the older leaders of Gilead, and the people made him their leader and commander of their army. Jephthah repeated all of his words in front of the LORD at Mizpah.

> "Then Jephthah went over to fight the Ammonites, and the LORD handed them over to him." (Judges 11:32)

JEPHTHAH SENDS MESSENGERS TO THE AMMONITE KING

12Jephthah sent messengers to the king of the Ammonites, asking, "What have you got against Israel? Why have you come to attack our land?"

13The king of the Ammonites answered the messengers of Jephthah, "We are fighting Israel because you took our land when you came up from Egypt. You took our land from the Arnon River to the Jabbok River to the Jordan River. Now give our land back to us peacefully."

14Jephthah sent the messengers to the Ammonite king again. 15They said:

"This is what Jephthah says: Israel did not take the land of the people of Moab or Ammon. 16When the Israelites came out of Egypt, they went into the desert to the Red Sea and then to Kadesh. 17Israel sent messengers to the king of Edom, saying, 'Let the people of Israel go across your land.' But the king of Edom refused. We sent the same message to the king of Moab, but he also refused. So the Israelites stayed at Kadesh.

18"Then the Israelites went into the desert around the borders of the lands of Edom and Moab. Israel went east of the land of Moab and camped on the other side of the Arnon River, the border of Moab. They did not cross it to go into the land of Moab.

19"Then Israel sent messengers to Sihon king of the Amorites, king of the city of Heshbon, asking, 'Let the people of Israel pass through your land to go to our land.' 20But Sihon did not trust the Israelites to cross his land. So he gathered all of his people and camped at Jahaz and fought with Israel.

21"But the LORD, the God of Israel, handed Sihon and his army over to Israel. All the land of the Amorites became the property of Israel. 22So Israel took all the land of the Amorites from the Arnon River to the Jabbok River, from the desert to the Jordan River.

23"It was the LORD, the God of Israel, who forced out the Amorites ahead of the people of Israel. So do you think you can make them leave? 24Take the land that your god Chemosh has given you. We will live in the land the LORD our God has given us!

25"Are you any better than Balak son of Zippor, king of Moab? Did he ever quarrel or fight with the people of Israel? 26For three hundred years the Israelites have lived in Heshbon and Aroer and the towns around them and in all the cities along the Arnon River. Why have you not taken these cities back in all that time? 27I have not sinned against you, but you are sinning against me by making war on me. May the LORD, the Judge, decide whether the Israelites or the Ammonites are right."

28But the king of the Ammonites ignored this message from Jephthah.

JEPHTHAH'S PROMISE

29Then the Spirit of the LORD entered Jephthah. Jephthah passed through Gilead and Manasseh and the city of Mizpah in Gilead to the land of the Ammonites. 30Jephthah made a

JEPHTHAH'S DAUGHTER made a difference

Jephthah was an Old Testament superhero. He had a daughter he loved. Unfortunately, Jephthah didn't always see how his job as a superhero might affect the life of his daughter. Jephthah got into trouble with a rash promise. He publicly announced he would sacrifice the first thing that came running out of his house if he returned from war victorious. His great victory march came to a halt when the first thing he saw from home was his daughter.

It appears that the sacrifice Jephthah made was to commit his only daughter to lifelong virginity. Jephthah rashly sacrificed his opportunity to have grandchildren. Though his daughter grieved over her loss, she honored her father's rash vow. That honor probably stung Jephthah deeply. Little hurts a loving parent more than when their mistakes cause their children to suffer. But Jephthah's daughter made a difference with her acceptance.

Cutting Edge

The dignity Jephthah's daughter displayed was so powerful that she is remembered. She offers an example of a costly obedience to the fifth commandment—to honor father and mother. She did so even when her father had made a mistake.

YOU can, too!

When parents make mistakes, children find out how difficult it is to honor and forgive. But dishonor and unforgiveness do not lead to freedom. Honoring and forgiving other people doesn't let them off the hook; it lets us off the hook. As long as we hold hurts against other people, we, too, are bound. Jephthah's daughter was free to grieve and play in the mountains because she forgave . . . because she honored. Do you have that freedom?

Want to know more? Read about Jephthah's daughter in Judges 11:1—12:7.

promise to the LORD, saying, "If you will hand
over the Ammonites to me, [31]I will give you as
a burnt offering the first thing that comes out
of my house to meet me when I return from
the victory. It will be the LORD's."

WHAT'S IT MEAN?

Did Jephthah really kill his own daughter as a sacrifice to God? Maybe not. First of all, human sacrifice was forbidden by the Law of Moses. Second, the passage seems to suggest that Jephthah may have "sacrificed" his daughter to the temple, meaning that she had to spend the rest of her life serving in God's house—never being able to marry or have a family of her own.

Judges 11:34–39

[32]Then Jephthah went over to fight the Ammonites, and the LORD handed them over to
him. [33]In a great defeat Jephthah struck them
down from the city of Aroer to the area of
Minnith, and twenty cities as far as the city of
Abel Keramim. So the Ammonites were defeated by the Israelites.

[34]When Jephthah returned to his home in
Mizpah, his daughter was the first one to come
out to meet him, playing a tambourine and
dancing. She was his only child; he had no
other sons or daughters. [35]When Jephthah saw
his daughter, he tore his clothes to show his
sorrow. He said, "My daughter! You have made
me so sad because I made a promise to the
LORD, and I cannot break it!"

[36]Then his daughter said, "Father, you made
a promise to the LORD. So do to me just what
you promised, because the LORD helped you
defeat your enemies, the Ammonites." [37]She
also said, "But let me do one thing. Let me be
alone for two months to go to the mountains.
Since I will never marry, let me and my friends
go and cry together."

[38]Jephthah said, "Go." So he sent her away
for two months. She and her friends stayed in
the mountains and cried for her because she
would never marry. [39]After two months she
returned to her father, and Jephthah did to her
what he had promised. Jephthah's daughter
never had a husband.

From this came a custom in Israel that
[40]every year the young women of Israel would
go out for four days to remember the daughter
of Jephthah from Gilead.

JEPHTHAH AND EPHRAIM

12

[1]The men of Ephraim called all their soldiers
together and crossed the river to the town of
Zaphon. They said to Jephthah, "Why didn't
you call us to help you fight the Ammonites?
We will burn your house down with you in it."

[2]Jephthah answered them, "My people and I
fought a great battle against the Ammonites.
I called you, but you didn't come to help me.
[3]When I saw that you would not help me, I
risked my own life and went against the Ammonites. The LORD handed them over to me. So
why have you come to fight against me today?"

[4]Then Jephthah called the men of Gilead together and fought the men of Ephraim. The
men of Gilead struck them down because the
Ephraimites had said, "You men of Gilead are
nothing but deserters from Ephraim—living
between Ephraim and Manasseh." [5]The men of
Gilead captured the crossings of the Jordan
River that led to the country of Ephraim. A
person from Ephraim trying to escape would
say, "Let me cross the river." Then the men of
Gilead would ask him, "Are you from Ephraim?" If he replied no, [6]they would say to him,
"Say the word 'Shibboleth.' " The men of
Ephraim could not say that word correctly. So
if the person from Ephraim said, "Sibboleth,"
the men of Gilead would kill him at the crossing. So forty-two thousand people from
Ephraim were killed at that time.

[7]Jephthah was a judge for Israel for six

WHAT'S IT MEAN?

Talk about a tough pop quiz! Imagine taking a one-question test to determine whether you live or die. That's the situation the men of Ephraim faced when they tried to escape. The men of Gilead used the word *Shibboleth* as a password. Those people who could pronounce it correctly were allowed to pass. Those who couldn't were killed on the spot. Seems easy enough, doesn't it? Not for the men of Ephraim, who apparently had problems making the "sh" sound. Forty-two thousand of them were killed because of their different dialect.

Judges 12:6

years. Then Jephthah, the man from Gilead, died and was buried in a town in Gilead.

IBZAN, THE JUDGE

8After Jephthah died, Ibzan from Bethlehem was a judge for Israel. 9He had thirty sons and thirty daughters. He let his daughters marry men who were not in his family group, and he brought thirty women who were not in his tribe to be wives for his sons. Ibzan judged Israel for seven years. 10Then he died and was buried in Bethlehem.

ELON, THE JUDGE

11After Ibzan died, Elon from the tribe of Zebulun was a judge for Israel. He judged Israel for ten years. 12Then Elon, the man of Zebulun, died and was buried in the city of Aijalon in the land of Zebulun.

ABDON, THE JUDGE

13After Elon died, Abdon son of Hillel from the city of Pirathon was a judge for Israel. 14He had forty sons and thirty grandsons, who rode on seventy donkeys. He judged Israel for eight years. 15Then Abdon son of Hillel died and was buried in Pirathon in the land of Ephraim, in the mountains where the Amalekites lived.

THE BIRTH OF SAMSON

13 1Again the people of Israel did what the LORD said was wrong. So he handed them over to the Philistines for forty years.

2There was a man named Manoah from the tribe of Dan, who lived in the city of Zorah. He had a wife, but she could not have children. 3The angel of the LORD appeared to Manoah's wife and said, "You have not been able to have children, but you will become pregnant and give birth to a son. 4Be careful not to drink wine or beer or eat anything that is unclean, 5because you will become pregnant and have a son. You must never cut his hair, because he will be a Nazirite, given to God from birth. He will begin to save Israel from the power of the Philistines."

6Then Manoah's wife went to him and told him what had happened. She said, "A man from God came to me. He looked like an angel from God; his appearance was frightening. I didn't ask him where he was from, and he didn't tell me his name. 7But he said to me, 'You will become pregnant and will have a son. Don't drink wine or beer or eat anything that is unclean, because the boy will be a Nazirite to God from his birth until the day of his death.' "

WHAT'S IT MEAN?

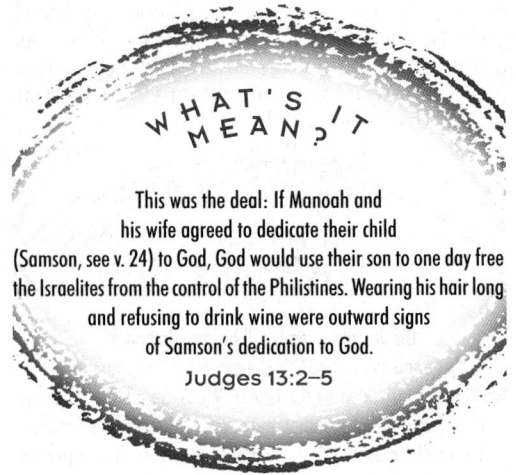

This was the deal: If Manoah and his wife agreed to dedicate their child (Samson, see v. 24) to God, God would use their son to one day free the Israelites from the control of the Philistines. Wearing his hair long and refusing to drink wine were outward signs of Samson's dedication to God.

Judges 13:2–5

8Then Manoah prayed to the LORD: "Lord, I beg you to let the man of God come to us again. Let him teach us what we should do for the boy who will be born to us."

9God heard Manoah's prayer, and the angel of God came to Manoah's wife again while she was sitting in the field. But her husband Manoah was not with her. 10So she ran to tell him, "He is here! The man who appeared to me the other day is here!"

11Manoah got up and followed his wife. When he came to the man, he said, "Are you the man who spoke to my wife?"

The man said, "I am."

12So Manoah asked, "When what you say happens, what kind of life should the boy live? What should he do?"

13The angel of the LORD said, "Your wife must be careful to do everything I told her to do. 14She must not eat anything that grows on a grapevine, or drink any wine or beer, or eat anything that is unclean. She must do everything I have commanded her."

15Manoah said to the angel of the LORD, "We would like you to stay awhile so we can cook a young goat for you."

16The angel of the LORD answered, "Even if I stay awhile, I would not eat your food. But if you want to prepare something, offer a burnt offering to the LORD." (Manoah did not understand that the man was really the angel of the LORD.)

17Then Manoah asked the angel of the LORD, "What is your name? Then we will honor you when what you have said really happens."

18The angel of the LORD said, "Why do you ask my name? It is too amazing for you to understand." 19So Manoah sacrificed a young goat on a rock and offered some grain as a gift to the LORD. Then an amazing thing happened as Manoah and his wife watched. 20The flames went up to the sky from the altar. As the fire burned, the angel of the LORD went up to heaven in the flame. When Manoah and his wife saw that, they bowed facedown on the ground. 21The angel of the LORD did not appear to them again. Then Manoah understood that the man was really the angel of the LORD. 22Manoah said, "We have seen God, so we will surely die."

WHAT'S IT MEAN?

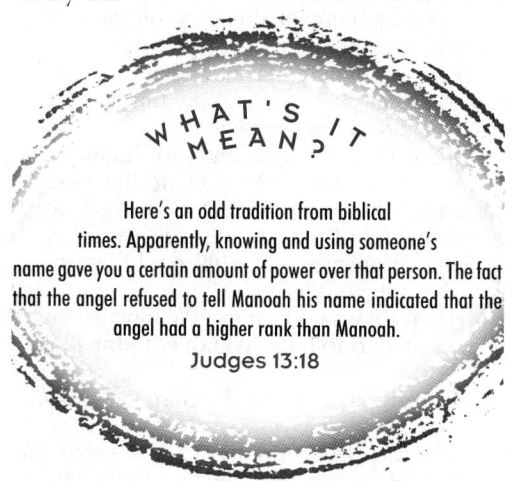

Here's an odd tradition from biblical times. Apparently, knowing and using someone's name gave you a certain amount of power over that person. The fact that the angel refused to tell Manoah his name indicated that the angel had a higher rank than Manoah.

Judges 13:18

23But his wife said to him, "If the LORD wanted to kill us, he would not have accepted our burnt offering or grain offering. He would not have shown us all these things or told us all this."

24So the woman gave birth to a boy and named him Samson. He grew, and the LORD blessed him. 25The Spirit of the LORD began to work in Samson while he was in the city of Mahaneh Dan, between the cities of Zorah and Eshtaol.

SAMSON'S FIRST MARRIAGE

14 1Samson went down to the city of Timnah where he saw a Philistine woman. 2When he returned home, he said to his father and mother, "I saw a Philistine woman in Timnah. I want you to get her for me so I can marry her."

3His father and mother answered, "Surely there is a woman from Israel you can marry. Do you have to marry a woman from the Philistines, who are not circumcised?"

But Samson said, "Get that woman for me! She is the one I want!" 4(Samson's parents did not know that the LORD wanted this to happen because he was looking for a way to challenge the Philistines, who were ruling over Israel at this time.) 5Samson went down with his father and mother to Timnah, as far as the vineyard near there. Suddenly, a young lion came roaring toward Samson! 6The Spirit of the LORD entered Samson with great power, and he tore the lion apart with his bare hands. For him it was as easy as tearing apart a young goat. But Samson did not tell his father or mother what he had done. 7Then he went down to the city and talked to the Philistine woman, and he liked her.

8Several days later Samson went back to marry her. On his way he went over to look at the body of the dead lion and found a swarm of bees and honey in it. 9Samson got some of the honey with his hands and walked along eating it. When he came to his parents, he gave some to them. They ate it, too, but Samson did not tell them he had taken the honey from the body of the dead lion.

10Samson's father went down to see the Philistine woman. And Samson gave a feast, as was the custom for the bridegroom. 11When the people saw him, they sent thirty friends to be with him.

SAMSON'S RIDDLE

12Samson said to them, "Let me tell you a riddle. Try to find the answer during the seven days of the feast. If you can, I will give you thirty linen shirts and thirty changes of clothes. 13But if you can't, you must give me thirty linen shirts and thirty changes of clothes."

WHAT'S IT MEAN?

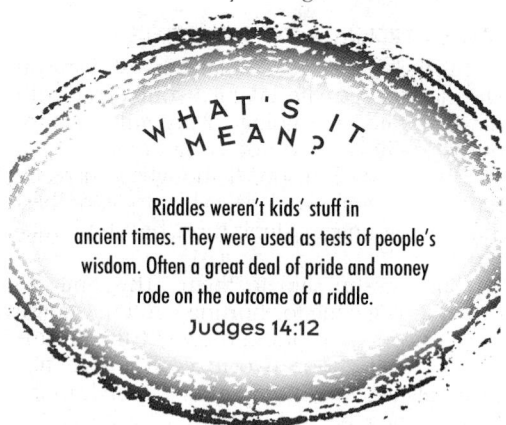

Riddles weren't kids' stuff in ancient times. They were used as tests of people's wisdom. Often a great deal of pride and money rode on the outcome of a riddle.

Judges 14:12

So they said, "Tell us your riddle so we can hear it."

14Samson said,

"Out of the eater comes something to eat.
Out of the strong comes something sweet."

After three days, they had not found the answer.

15 On the fourth[n] day they said to Samson's
wife, "Did you invite us here to make us poor?
Trick your husband into telling us the answer
to the riddle. If you don't, we will burn you
and everyone in your father's house."
16 So Samson's wife went to him, crying, and
said, "You hate me! You don't really love me!
You told my people a riddle, but you won't tell
me the answer."
Samson said, "I haven't even told my father
or mother. Why should I tell you?"
17 Samson's wife cried for the rest of the
seven days of the feast. So he finally gave her
the answer on the seventh day, because she
kept bothering him. Then she told her people
the answer to the riddle.
18 Before sunset on the seventh day of the
feast, the Philistine men had the answer. They
came to Samson and said,

"What is sweeter than honey?
  What is stronger than a lion?"

Then Samson said to them,

"If you had not plowed with my young
    cow,
  you would not have solved my riddle!"

19 Then the Spirit of the LORD entered Samson and gave him great power. Samson went
down to the city of Ashkelon and killed thirty
of its men and took all that they had and gave
the clothes to the men who had answered his
riddle. Then he went to his father's house very
angry. 20 And Samson's wife was given to his
best man.

SAMSON TROUBLES THE PHILISTINES

15
1 At the time of the wheat harvest, Samson
went to visit his wife, taking a young goat with
him. He said, "I'm going to my wife's room,"
but her father would not let him go in.
2 He said to Samson, "I thought you really
hated your wife, so I gave her to your best
man. Her younger sister is more beautiful. Take
her instead."
3 But Samson said to them, "This time no
one will blame me for hurting you Philistines!"
4 So Samson went out and caught three hundred foxes. He took two foxes at a time, tied
their tails together, and then tied a torch to the
tails of each pair of foxes. 5 After he lit the
torches, he let the foxes loose in the grainfields
of the Philistines so that he burned up their
standing grain, the piles of grain, their vineyards, and their olive trees.
6 The Philistines asked, "Who did this?"
Someone told them, "Samson, the son-in-
law of the man from Timnah, did because his
father-in-law gave his wife to his best man."
So the Philistines burned Samson's wife and
her father to death. 7 Then Samson said to the
Philistines, "Since you did this, I won't stop
until I pay you back!" 8 Samson attacked the
Philistines and killed many of them. Then he
went down and stayed in a cave in the rock of
Etam.
9 The Philistines went up and camped in the
land of Judah, near a place named Lehi. 10 The
men of Judah asked them, "Why have you
come here to fight us?"
They answered, "We have come to make
Samson our prisoner, to pay him back for
what he did to our people."
11 Then three thousand men of Judah went
to the cave in the rock of Etam and said to
Samson, "What have you done to us? Don't
you know that the Philistines rule over us?"
Samson answered, "I only paid them back
for what they did to me."
12 Then they said to him, "We have come to
tie you up and to hand you over to the Philistines."
Samson said to them, "Promise me you will
not hurt me yourselves."
13 The men from Judah said, "We agree. We
will just tie you up and give you to the Philistines. We will not kill you." So they tied Samson
with two new ropes and led him up from the
cave in the rock. 14 When Samson came to the
place named Lehi, the Philistines came to meet
him, shouting for joy. Then the Spirit of the
LORD entered Samson and gave him great
power. The ropes on him weakened like
burned strings and fell off his hands! 15 Samson

WHAT'S IT MEAN?

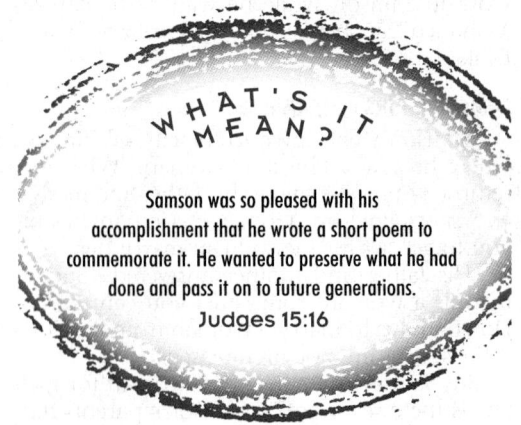

Samson was so pleased with his accomplishment that he wrote a short poem to commemorate it. He wanted to preserve what he had done and pass it on to future generations.

Judges 15:16

14:15 fourth The Hebrew word is "seventh." Some old translations say "fourth," which fits the order of events better.

found the jawbone of a dead donkey, took it, and killed a thousand men with it!

[16]Then Samson said,

"With a donkey's jawbone
I made donkeys out of them.
With a donkey's jawbone
I killed a thousand men!"

[17]When he finished speaking, he threw away the jawbone. So that place was named Ramath Lehi.[n]

[18]Samson was very thirsty, so he cried out to the LORD, "You gave me, your servant, this great victory. Do I have to die of thirst now? Do I have to be captured by people who are not circumcised?" [19]Then God opened up a hole in the ground at Lehi, and water came out. When Samson drank, he felt better; he felt strong again. So he named that spring Caller's Spring, which is still in Lehi.

[20]Samson judged Israel for twenty years in the days of the Philistines.

"So Delilah said to Samson, 'Tell me why you are so strong. How can someone tie you up and capture you?'" (Judges 16:6)

SAMSON GOES TO THE CITY OF GAZA

16

[1]One day Samson went to Gaza and saw a prostitute there. He went in to spend the night with her. [2]When the people of Gaza heard, "Samson has come here!" they surrounded the place and waited for him near the city gate all night. They whispered to each other, "When dawn comes, we will kill Samson!"

[3]But Samson only stayed with the prostitute until midnight. Then he got up and took hold of the doors and the two posts of the city gate and tore them loose, along with the bar. He put them on his shoulders and carried them to the top of the hill that faces the city of Hebron.

SAMSON AND DELILAH

[4]After this, Samson fell in love with a woman named Delilah, who lived in the Valley of Sorek. [5]The Philistine rulers went to Delilah and said, "Find out what makes Samson so strong. Trick him into telling you how we can overpower him and capture him and tie him up. If you do this, each one of us will give you twenty-eight pounds of silver."

[6]So Delilah said to Samson, "Tell me why you are so strong. How can someone tie you up and capture you?"

[7]Samson answered, "Someone would have to tie me up with seven new bowstrings that have not been dried. Then I would be as weak as any other man."

[8]The Philistine rulers brought Delilah seven new bowstrings that had not been dried, and she tied Samson with them. [9]Some men were hiding in another room. Delilah said to him, "Samson, the Philistines are here!" But Samson broke the bowstrings like pieces of burned string. So the Philistines did not find out the secret of Samson's strength.

[10]Then Delilah said to Samson, "You made a fool of me. You lied to me. Now tell me how someone can tie you up."

[11]Samson said, "They would have to tie me with new ropes that have not been used before. Then I would become as weak as any other man."

[12]So Delilah took new ropes and tied Samson. Some men were hiding in another room. She called out to him, "Samson, the Philistines are here!" But he broke the ropes as easily as if they were threads.

[13]Then Delilah said to Samson, "Again you have made a fool of me. You lied to me. Tell me how someone can tie you up."

He said, "Using the loom,[n] weave the seven braids of my hair into the cloth, and tighten it with a pin. Then I will be as weak as any other man."

While Samson slept, Delilah wove the seven braids of his hair into the cloth. [14]Then she fastened it with a pin.

Again she said to him, "Samson, the Philistines are here!" Samson woke up and pulled out the pin and the loom with the cloth.

WHAT'S IT MEAN?

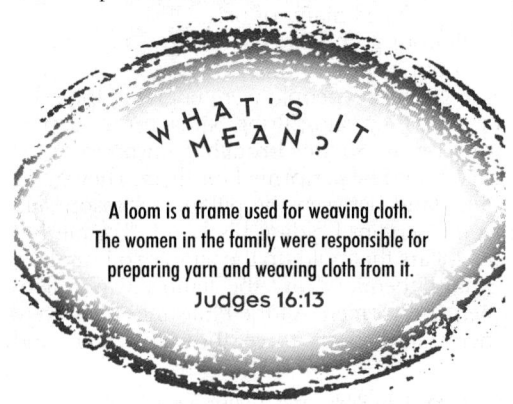

A loom is a frame used for weaving cloth. The women in the family were responsible for preparing yarn and weaving cloth from it.
Judges 16:13

15:17 Ramath Lehi This name means "Jawbone Hill."

16:13 loom A machine for making cloth from thread.

15Then Delilah said to him, "How can you
say, 'I love you,' when you don't even trust me?
This is the third time you have made a fool of
me. You haven't told me the secret of your
great strength." 16She kept bothering Samson
about his secret day after day until he felt he
was going to die!
17So he told her everything. He said, "I have
never had my hair cut, because I have been set
apart to God as a Nazirite since I was born. If
someone shaved my head, I would lose my
strength and be as weak as any other man."
18When Delilah saw that he had told her
everything sincerely, she sent a message to the
Philistine rulers. She said, "Come back one
more time, because he has told me everything."
So the Philistine rulers came back to Delilah
and brought the silver with them. 19Delilah got
Samson to sleep, lying in her lap. Then she
called in a man to shave off the seven braids of
Samson's hair. In this way she began to make
him weak, and his strength left him.
20Then she said, "Samson, the Philistines are
here!"

He woke up and thought, "I'll leave as I did
before and shake myself free." But he did not
know that the LORD had left him.
21Then the Philistines captured Samson and
tore out his eyes. They took him down to
Gaza, where they put bronze chains on him
and made him grind grain in the prison. 22But
his hair began to grow again.

SAMSON DIES

23The Philistine rulers gathered to celebrate
and to offer a great sacrifice to their god Dagon. They said, "Our god has handed Samson
our enemy over to us." 24When the people saw
him, they praised their god, saying,

"This man destroyed our country.
He killed many of us!
But our god handed over
our enemy to us."

25While the people were enjoying the celebration, they said, "Bring Samson out to perform for us." So they brought Samson from the
prison, and he performed for them. They made
him stand between the pillars. 26Samson said
to the servant holding his hand, "Let me feel
the pillars that hold up the temple so I can lean
against them." 27Now the temple was full of
men and women. All the Philistine rulers were
there, and about three thousand men and
women were on the roof[n] watching Samson
perform. 28Then Samson prayed to the LORD,
"Lord GOD, remember me. God, please give me
strength one more time so I can pay these Philistines back for putting out my two eyes!"
29Then Samson turned to the two center pillars
that supported the whole temple. He braced
himself between the two pillars, with his right
hand on one and his left hand on the other.
30Samson said, "Let me die with these Philistines!" Then he pushed as hard as he could,
causing the temple to fall on the rulers and all
the people in it. So Samson killed more of the
Philistines when he died than when he was
alive.
31Samson's brothers and his whole family
went down to get his body. They brought him
back and buried him in the tomb of Manoah,
his father, between the cities of Zorah and Eshtaol. Samson was a judge for the people of Israel for twenty years.

MICAH'S IDOLS

17
1There was a man named Micah who lived
in the mountains of Ephraim. 2He said to his
mother, "I heard you speak a curse about the
twenty-eight pounds of silver that were taken
from you. I have the silver with me; I took it."

His mother said, "The LORD bless you, my
son!"
3Micah gave the twenty-eight pounds of
silver to his mother. Then she said, "I will give

WHAT'S IT MEAN?

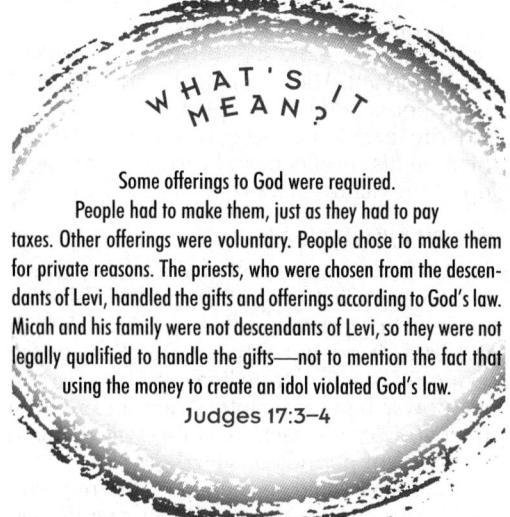

Some offerings to God were required. People had to make them, just as they had to pay taxes. Other offerings were voluntary. People chose to make them for private reasons. The priests, who were chosen from the descendants of Levi, handled the gifts and offerings according to God's law. Micah and his family were not descendants of Levi, so they were not legally qualified to handle the gifts—not to mention the fact that using the money to create an idol violated God's law.

Judges 17:3–4

16:27 roof In Bible times houses were built with flat roofs. The roof was used for drying things such as flax and fruit. And it was used as an extra room, as a place for worship, and as a cool place to sleep in the summer.

this silver to the LORD. I will have my son make
an idol and a statue. So I will give the silver
back to you."
[4]When he gave the silver back to his mother,
she took about five pounds and gave it to a
silversmith. With it he made an idol and a statue, which stood in Micah's house. [5]Micah had
a special holy place, and he made a holy vest
and some household idols. Then Micah chose
one of his sons to be his priest. [6]At that time
Israel did not have a king, so everyone did what
seemed right.
[7]There was a young man who was a Levite[n]
from the city of Bethlehem in Judah who was
from the people of Judah. [8]He left Bethlehem to
look for another place to live, and on his way
he came to Micah's house in the mountains of
Ephraim. [9]Micah asked him, "Where are you
from?"

He answered, "I'm a Levite from Bethlehem
in Judah. I'm looking for a place to live."
[10]Micah said to him, "Live with me and be
my father and my priest. I will give you four
ounces of silver each year and clothes and
food." So the Levite went in. [11]He agreed to live
with Micah and became like one of Micah's
own sons. [12]Micah made him a priest, and he
lived in Micah's house. [13]Then Micah said,
"Now I know the LORD will be good to me,
because I have a Levite as my priest."

DAN'S FAMILY CAPTURES LAISH

18 [1]At that time Israel did not have a king. And
at that time the tribe of Dan was still looking
for a land where they could live, a land of their
own. The Danites had not yet been given their
own land among the tribes of Israel. [2]So, from
their family groups, they chose five soldiers
from the cities of Zorah and Eshtaol to spy out
and explore the land. They were told, "Go, explore the land."

They came to the mountains of Ephraim, to
Micah's house, where they spent the night.
[3]When they came near Micah's house, they
recognized the voice of the young Levite.[n] So
they stopped there and asked him, "Who
brought you here? What are you doing here?
Why are you here?"
[4]He told them what Micah had done for
him, saying, "He hired me. I am his priest."
[5]They said to him, "Please ask God if our
journey will be successful."
[6]The priest said to them, "Go in peace. The
LORD is pleased with your journey."
[7]So the five men left. When they came to the
city of Laish, they saw that the people there
lived in safety, like the people of Sidon. They
thought they were safe and had plenty of
everything. They lived a long way from the Sidonians and had no dealings with anyone else.

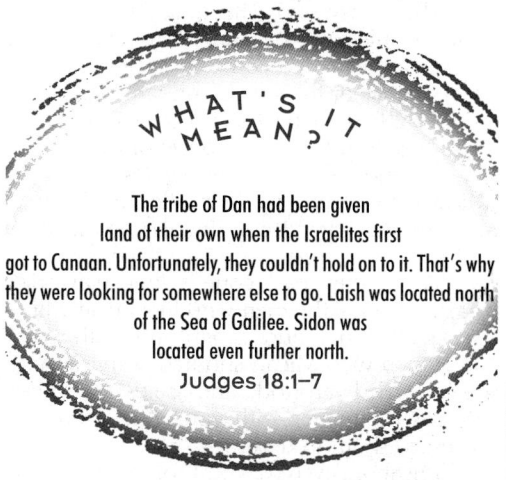

WHAT'S IT MEAN?

The tribe of Dan had been given land of their own when the Israelites first got to Canaan. Unfortunately, they couldn't hold on to it. That's why they were looking for somewhere else to go. Laish was located north of the Sea of Galilee. Sidon was located even further north.

Judges 18:1–7

[8]When the five men returned to Zorah and
Eshtaol, their relatives asked them, "What did
you find?"
[9]They answered, "We have seen the land,
and it is very good. We should attack them.
Aren't you going to do something? Don't wait!
Let's go and take that land! [10]When you go,
you will see there is plenty of land—plenty of
everything! The people are not expecting an
attack. Surely God has handed that land over
to us!"
[11]So six hundred Danites left Zorah and
Eshtaol ready for war. [12]On their way they set
up camp near the city of Kiriath Jearim in
Judah. That is why the place west of Kiriath
Jearim is named Mahaneh Dan[n] to this day.
[13]From there they traveled on to the mountains of Ephraim. Then they came to Micah's
house.
[14]The five men who had explored the land
around Laish said to their relatives, "Do you
know in one of these houses there are a holy
vest, household gods, an idol, and a statue?
You know what to do." [15]So they stopped at the
Levite's house, which was also Micah's house,
and greeted the Levite. [16]The six hundred Danites stood at the entrance gate, wearing their
weapons of war. [17]The five spies went into the
house and took the idol, the holy vest, the
household idols, and the statue. The priest and

17:7; 18:3 Levite The Levites were the only ones God had appointed as priests. **18:12 Mahaneh Dan** This name means "the camp of Dan."

the six hundred men armed for war stood by
the entrance gate.
18When the spies went into Micah's house
and took the image, the holy vest, the household idols, and the statue, the priest asked
them, "What are you doing?"
19They answered, "Be quiet! Don't say a
word. Come with us and be our father and
priest. Is it better for you to be a priest for one
man's house or for a tribe and family group in
Israel?" 20This made the priest happy. So he
took the holy vest, the household idols, and
the idol and went with the Danites. 21They left
Micah's house, putting their little children, their
animals, and everything they owned in front
of them.
22When they had gone a little way from
Micah's house, the men who lived near Micah
were called out and caught up with them.
23The men with Micah shouted at the Danites,
who turned around and said to Micah,
"What's the matter with you? Why have you
been called out to fight?"
24Micah answered, "You took my gods that
I made and my priest. What do I have left?
How can you ask me, 'What's the matter?' "
25The Danites answered, "You should not
argue with us. Some of our angry men might
attack you, killing you and your family." 26Then
the Danites went on their way. Micah knew
they were too strong for him, so he turned and
went back home.
27Then the Danites took what Micah had
made and his priest and went on to Laish.
They attacked those peaceful people and killed
them with their swords and then burned the
city. 28There was no one to save the people of
Laish. They lived too far from Sidon, and they
had no dealings with anyone else. Laish was in
a valley near Beth Rehob.
The people of Dan rebuilt the city and lived
there. 29They changed the name of Laish to
Dan, naming it for their ancestor Dan, one of
the sons of Israel.
30The people of Dan set up the idols in the
city of Dan. Jonathan son of Gershom, Moses'
son, and his sons served as priests for the tribe
of Dan until the land was captured. 31The people of Dan set up the idols Micah had made as
long as the Holy Tent of God was in Shiloh.

A LEVITE AND HIS SERVANT

19
1At that time Israel did not have a king.
There was a Levite who lived in the faraway
mountains of Ephraim. He had taken a slave
woman from the city of Bethlehem in the land
of Judah to live with him, 2but she was unfaithful to him. She left him and went back to
her father's house in Bethlehem in Judah and
stayed there for four months. 3Then her husband went to ask her to come back to him,
taking with him his servant and two donkeys.
When the Levite came to her father's house,
she invited him to come in, and her father was
happy to see him. 4The father-in-law, the
young woman's father, asked him to stay. So
he stayed for three days and ate, drank, and
slept there.
5On the fourth day they got up early in the
morning. The Levite was getting ready to leave,
but the woman's father said to his son-in-law,
"Refresh yourself by eating something. Then
go." 6So the two men sat down to eat and drink
together. After that, the father said to him,
"Please stay tonight. Relax and enjoy yourself."
7When the man got up to go, his father-in-law
asked him to stay. So he stayed again that
night. 8On the fifth day the man got up early in
the morning to leave. The woman's father said,
"Refresh yourself. Wait until this afternoon." So
the two men ate together.
9When the Levite, his slave woman, and his
servant got up to leave, the father-in-law, the
young woman's father, said, "It's almost night.
The day is almost gone. Spend the night here
and enjoy yourself. Tomorrow morning you
can get up early and go home." 10But the Levite
did not want to stay another night. So he took
his two saddled donkeys and his slave woman
and traveled toward the city of Jebus (also
called Jerusalem).
11As the day was almost over, they came
near Jebus. So the servant said to his master,
"Let's stop at this city of the Jebusites, and
spend the night here."

WHAT'S IT MEAN?

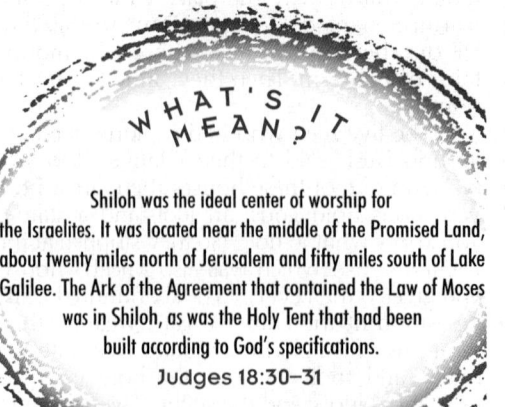

Shiloh was the ideal center of worship for the Israelites. It was located near the middle of the Promised Land, about twenty miles north of Jerusalem and fifty miles south of Lake Galilee. The Ark of the Agreement that contained the Law of Moses was in Shiloh, as was the Holy Tent that had been built according to God's specifications.

Judges 18:30–31

[12]But his master said, "No. We won't go inside a foreign city. Those people are not Israelites. We will go on to the city of Gibeah." [13]He said, "Come on. Let's try to make it to Gibeah or Ramah so we can spend the night in one of those cities." [14]So they went on. The sun went down as they came near Gibeah, which belongs to the tribe of Benjamin. [15]They stopped there to spend the night. They came to the public square of the city and sat down, but no one invited them home to spend the night.

[16]Finally, in the evening an old man came in from his work in the fields. His home was in the mountains of Ephraim, but now he was living in Gibeah. (The people of Gibeah were from the tribe of Benjamin.) [17]He saw the traveler in the public square and asked, "Where are you going? Where did you come from?"

[18]The Levite answered, "We are traveling from Bethlehem in Judah to my home in the mountains of Ephraim. I have been to Bethlehem in Judah, but now I am going to the Holy Tent of the LORD. No one has invited me to stay in his house. [19]We already have straw and food for our donkeys and bread and wine for me, the young woman, and my servant. We don't need anything."

[20]The old man said, "You are welcome to stay at my house. Let me give you anything you need, but don't spend the night in the public square." [21]So the old man took the Levite into his house, and he fed their donkeys. They washed their feet and had something to eat and drink.

WHAT'S IT MEAN?

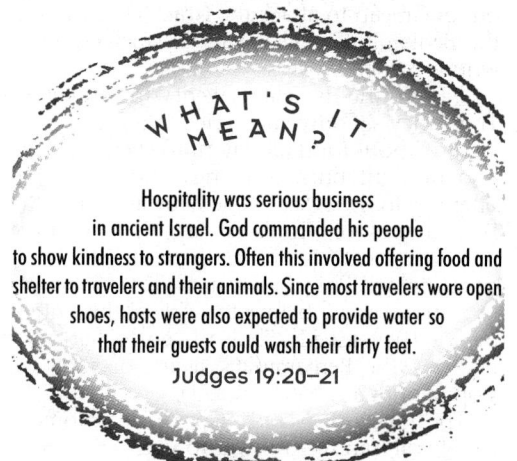

Hospitality was serious business in ancient Israel. God commanded his people to show kindness to strangers. Often this involved offering food and shelter to travelers and their animals. Since most travelers wore open shoes, hosts were also expected to provide water so that their guests could wash their dirty feet.

Judges 19:20–21

[22]While they were enjoying themselves, some wicked men of the city surrounded the house and beat on the door. They shouted to the old man who owned the house, "Bring out the man who came to your house. We want to have sexual relations with him."

HOMOSEXUALITY

When is sex perverted? (19:22)

[23]The owner of the house went outside and said to them, "No, my friends. Don't be so evil. This man is a guest in my house. Don't do this terrible thing! [24]Look, here are my daughter, who has never had sexual relations before, and the man's slave woman. I will bring them out to you now. Do anything you want with them, but don't do such a terrible thing to this man."

[25]But the men would not listen to him. So the Levite took his slave woman and sent her outside to them. They forced her to have sexual relations with them, and they abused her all night long. Then, at dawn, they let her go. [26]She came back to the house where her master was staying and fell down at the door and lay there until daylight.

[27]In the morning when the Levite got up, he opened the door of the house and went outside to go on his way. But his slave woman was lying at the doorway of the house, with her hands on the doorsill. [28]The Levite said to her, "Get up; let's go." But she did not answer. So he put her on his donkey and went home.

[29]When the Levite got home, he took a knife and cut his slave woman into twelve parts, limb by limb. Then he sent a part to each area of Israel. [30]Everyone who saw this said, "Nothing like this has ever happened before, not since the people of Israel came out of Egypt. Think about it. Tell us what to do."

THE WAR BETWEEN ISRAEL AND BENJAMIN

20

[1]So all the Israelites from Dan to Beersheba,[n] including the land of Gilead, joined together before the LORD in the city of Mizpah. [2]The leaders of all the tribes of Israel took their places in the meeting of the people of God. There were 400,000 soldiers with swords. [3](The people of Benjamin heard that the Israelites had gone up to Mizpah.) Then the Israelites said to the Levite, "Tell us how this evil thing happened."

[4]So the husband of the murdered woman answered, "My slave woman and I came to Gibeah in Benjamin to spend the night. [5]During the night the men of Gibeah came after me.

20:1 Dan . . . Beersheba Dan was the city farthest north in Israel. Beersheba was the city farthest south. So this means all the people of Israel.

They surrounded the house and wanted to kill me. They forced my slave woman to have sexual relations and she died. [6]I took her and cut her into parts and sent one part to each area of Israel because the people of Benjamin did this wicked and terrible thing in Israel. [7]Now, all you Israelites, speak up. What is your decision?"

[8]Then all the people stood up at the same time, saying, "None of us will go home. Not one of us will go back to his house! [9]Now this is what we will do to Gibeah. We will throw lots. [10]That way we will choose ten men from every hundred men from all the tribes of Israel, and we will choose a hundred men from every thousand, and a thousand men from every ten thousand. These will find supplies for the army. Then the army will go to the city of Gibeah of Benjamin to repay them for the terrible thing they have done in Israel." [11]So all the men of Israel were united and gathered against the city.

[12]The tribes of Israel sent men throughout the tribe of Benjamin demanding, "What is this evil thing some of your men have done? [13]Hand over the wicked men in Gibeah so that we can put them to death. We must remove this evil from Israel."

But the Benjaminites would not listen to their fellow Israelites. [14]The Benjaminites left their own cities and met at Gibeah to fight the Israelites. [15]In only one day the Benjaminites got 26,000 soldiers together who were trained with swords. They also had 700 chosen men from Gibeah. [16]Seven hundred of these trained soldiers were left-handed, each of whom could sling a stone at a hair and not miss!

[17]The Israelites, except for the Benjaminites, gathered 400,000 soldiers with swords.

[18]The Israelites went up to the city of Bethel and asked God, "Which tribe shall be first to attack the Benjaminites?"

The LORD answered, "Judah shall go first."

[19]The next morning the Israelites got up and made a camp near Gibeah. [20]The men of Israel went out to fight the Benjaminites and took their battle position at Gibeah. [21]Then the Benjaminites came out of Gibeah and killed 22,000 Israelites during the battle that day. [22-23]The Israelites went before the LORD and cried until evening. They asked the LORD, "Shall we go to fight our relatives, the Benjaminites, again?"

The LORD answered, "Go up and fight them." The men of Israel encouraged each other. So they took the same battle positions they had taken the first day.

[24]The Israelites came to fight the Benjaminites the second day. [25]The Benjaminites came out of Gibeah to attack the Israelites. This time, the Benjaminites killed 18,000 Israelites, all of whom carried swords.

[26]Then the Israelites went up to Bethel. There they sat down and cried to the LORD and went without food all day until evening. They also brought burnt offerings and fellowship offerings to the LORD. [27]The Israelites asked the LORD a question. (In those days the Ark of the Agreement with God was there at Bethel. [28]A priest named Phinehas son of Eleazar, the son of Aaron, served before the Ark of the Agreement.) They asked, "Shall we go to fight our relatives, the Benjaminites, again, or shall we stop fighting?"

The LORD answered, "Go, because tomorrow I will hand them over to you."

[29]Then the Israelites set up ambushes all around Gibeah. [30]They went to fight against the Benjaminites at Gibeah on the third day, getting into position for battle as they had done before. [31]When the Benjaminites came out to fight them, the Israelites backed up and

"So all the Israelites from Dan to Beersheba, including the land of Gilead, joined together before the LORD in the city of Mizpah."
(Judges 20:1)

WHAT'S IT MEAN?

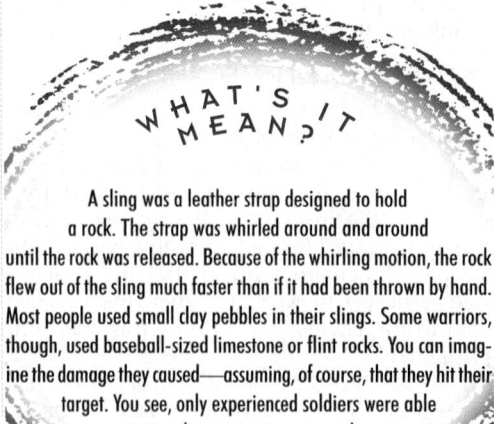

A sling was a leather strap designed to hold a rock. The strap was whirled around and around until the rock was released. Because of the whirling motion, the rock flew out of the sling much faster than if it had been thrown by hand. Most people used small clay pebbles in their slings. Some warriors, though, used baseball-sized limestone or flint rocks. You can imagine the damage they caused—assuming, of course, that they hit their target. You see, only experienced soldiers were able to use these weapons accurately.

Judges 20:16

led the Benjaminites away from the city. The Benjaminites began to kill some of the Israelites as they had done before. About thirty Israelites were killed—some in the fields and some on the roads leading to Bethel and to Gibeah.

[32]The Benjaminites said, "We are winning as before!"

But the Israelites said, "Let's run. Let's trick them into going farther away from their city and onto the roads."

[33]All the Israelites moved from their places and got into battle positions at a place named Baal Tamar. Then the Israelites ran out from their hiding places west of Gibeah. [34]Ten thousand of the best trained soldiers from all of Israel attacked Gibeah. The battle was very hard. The Benjaminites did not know disaster was about to come to them. [35]The LORD used the Israelites to defeat the Benjaminites. On that day the Israelites killed 25,100 Benjaminites, all armed with swords. [36]Then the Benjaminites saw that they were defeated.

The Israelites had moved back because they were depending on the surprise attack they had set up near Gibeah. [37]The men in hiding rushed into Gibeah, spread out, and killed everyone in the city with their swords. [38]Now the Israelites had set up a signal with the men in hiding. The men in the surprise attack were to send up a cloud of smoke from the city. [39]Then the army of Israel turned around in the battle.

The Benjaminites had killed about thirty Israelites. They were saying, "We are winning, as in the first battle!" [40]But then a cloud of smoke began to rise from the city. The Benjaminites turned around and saw that the whole city was going up in smoke. [41]Then the Israelites turned and began to fight. The Benjaminites were terrified because they knew that disaster was coming to them. [42]So the Benjaminites ran away from the Israelites toward the desert, but they could not escape the battle. And the Israelites who came out of the cities killed them. [43]They surrounded the Benjaminites and chased them and caught them in the area east of Gibeah. [44]So 18,000 brave Benjaminite fighters were killed. [45]The Benjaminites ran toward the desert to the rock of Rimmon, but the Israelites killed 5,000 Benjaminites along the roads. They chased them as far as Gidom and killed 2,000 more Benjaminites there.

[46]On that day 25,000 Benjaminites were killed, all of whom had fought bravely with swords. [47]But 600 Benjaminites ran to the rock of Rimmon in the desert, where they stayed for four months. [48]Then the Israelites went back to the land of Benjamin and killed the people in every city and also the animals and everything they could find. And they burned every city they found.

WIVES FOR THE MEN OF BENJAMIN

21 [1]At Mizpah the men of Israel had sworn, "Not one of us will let his daughter marry a man from the tribe of Benjamin."

[2]The people went to the city of Bethel and sat before God until evening, crying loudly. [3]They said, "LORD, God of Israel, why has this terrible thing happened to us so that one tribe of Israel is missing today?"

WHAT'S IT MEAN?

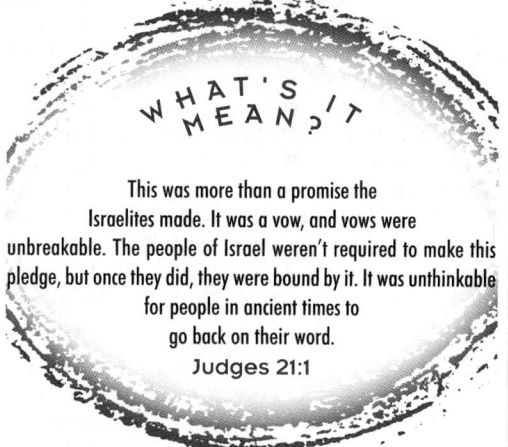

This was more than a promise the Israelites made. It was a vow, and vows were unbreakable. The people of Israel weren't required to make this pledge, but once they did, they were bound by it. It was unthinkable for people in ancient times to go back on their word.

Judges 21:1

[4]Early the next day the people built an altar and put burnt offerings and fellowship offerings to God on it.

[5]Then the Israelites asked, "Did any tribe of Israel not come here to meet with us in the presence of the LORD?" They asked this question because they had sworn that anyone who did not meet with them at Mizpah would be killed.

[6]The Israelites felt sorry for their relatives, the Benjaminites. They said, "Today one tribe has been cut off from Israel. [7]We swore before the LORD that we would not allow our daughters to marry a Benjaminite. How can we make sure that the remaining men of Benjamin will have wives?" [8]Then they asked, "Which one of the tribes of Israel did not come here to Mizpah?" They found that no one from the city of Jabesh Gilead had come. [9]The people of Israel counted everyone, but there was no one from Jabesh Gilead.

[10]So the whole group of Israelites sent twelve thousand soldiers to Jabesh Gilead to kill the people with their swords, even the women and children.

11"This is what you must do: Kill every
man in Jabesh Gilead and every married
woman." 12The soldiers found four hundred
young unmarried women in Jabesh Gilead,
so they brought them to the camp at Shiloh
in Canaan.
13Then the whole group of Israelites sent a
message to the men of Benjamin, who were at
the rock of Rimmon, offering to make peace
with them. 14So the men of Benjamin came
back at that time. The Israelites gave them the
women from Jabesh Gilead who had not been
killed, but there were not enough women.
15The people of Israel felt sorry for the Benjaminites because the LORD had separated the
tribes of Israel. 16The older leaders of the Israelites said, "The women of Benjamin have been
killed. Where can we get wives for the men of
Benjamin who are still alive? 17These men must
have children to continue their families so a
tribe in Israel will not die out. 18But we cannot
allow our daughters to marry them, because
we swore, 'Anyone who gives a wife to a man
of Benjamin is cursed.' 19We have an idea!
There is a yearly festival of the LORD at Shiloh,
which is north of the city of Bethel, east of the
road that goes from Bethel to Shechem, and
south of the city of Lebonah."
20So the older leaders told the men of Benjamin, "Go and hide in the vineyards. 21Watch for
the young women from Shiloh to come out to
join the dancing. Then run out from the vineyards and take one of the young Shiloh women
and return to the land of Benjamin. 22If their
fathers or brothers come to us and complain,
we will say: 'Be kind to the men of Benjamin.
We did not get wives for Benjamin during the
war, and you did not give the women to the
men from Benjamin. So you are not guilty.' "
23So that is what the Benjaminites did.
While the young women were dancing, each
man caught one of them, took her away, and
married her. Then they went back to the land
God had given them and rebuilt
their cities and lived there.
24Then the Israelites went
home to their own tribes and
family groups, to their own
land that God had given
them.
25In those days Israel did not
have a king. Everyone did what seemed right.

AUTHORITY

Do laws help us live right? (21:25)

ruth

CONTENT

The Book of Ruth is a story about a woman and, of all people, her mother-in-law. If it were a movie, you could call it a chick-flick. It has all the elements: drama, tragedy, danger, loyalty, flirtation, a love story, brave women, an honorable man, a marriage, and a baby. But it's not a flick at all, and it's not just for chicks.

This is actually a story that, first of all, shows us something about the Jewish culture. It also reveals an important link in the genetic chain that led to Jesus Christ. Finally, it tells us a lot about the kind of people we should be: people that stick by their families and ask for the love they need and honor their cultural traditions.

The Book of Ruth is about the kind of love that draws people together, then helps them stay that way. It's about the kind of love that you need in your life. The first key to finding it is recognizing the right kind of people to ask for it from. Ruth was one.

Outline

1:1–22 .... Ruth Is Loyal to Naomi
2:1–23 .... Ruth Meets Boaz
3:1–18 .... Naomi Makes Plans for Ruth
4:1–22 .... Ruth and Boaz Get Married

Purpose Faithful people live godly lives in the worst of times.

Theme God's Sovereign Intervention Brings Universal Redemption

Date of writing Uncertain

"But Ruth said, 'Don't beg me to leave you or to stop following you. Where you go, I will go. Where you live, I will live. Your people will be my people, and your God will be my God' " (1:16).

Bible Talk

Wheat Fields

Some important parts of this story take place in a field of wheat. When Ruth went out for groceries, a wheat field is one of the places she stopped. Boaz first noticed Ruth when she was gathering the leftover wheat in his fields.

So why was there leftover wheat? Because they didn't have automatic machines to harvest the wheat, some wheat would always be left behind. Ladies, usually from the poorer families, would go behind the harvesters and gather up the leftovers. This was one of the ways that society took care of its poor.

Boaz saw Ruth gathering the wheat, got a little crush on her, and told his guys to be sure and drop something extra for her to pick up. How's that for a move?

MARRIAGE CUSTOMS

Boaz was allowed, even obligated, to marry Ruth because of a particular family custom. In those days, women didn't *usually* have a career outside of the home. When a woman's husband died, she was up the creek. So there were a lot of provisions made for widows in Jewish customs.

If a widow was young, then she could go to the closest living male relative and expect him to take care of her, even marry her. Ruth wasn't related to Boaz; but her mother-in-law, Naomi, was. This put him in line to marry Ruth with only one person standing in line before him. Read chapter 4 to find out what he did about that.

[1]Long ago when the judges[n] ruled Israel, there was a shortage of food in the land. [2]So a man named Elimelech left the town of Bethlehem in Judah to live in the country of Moab with his wife and his two sons. His wife was named Naomi, and his two sons were named Mahlon and Kilion. They were Ephrathahites from Bethlehem in Judah. When they came to Moab, they settled there.

WHAT'S IT MEAN?

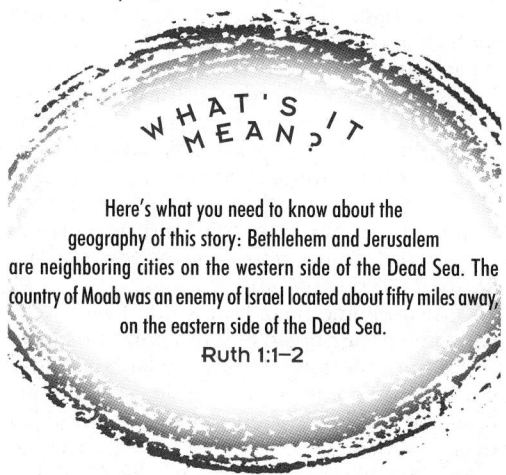

Here's what you need to know about the geography of this story: Bethlehem and Jerusalem are neighboring cities on the western side of the Dead Sea. The country of Moab was an enemy of Israel located about fifty miles away, on the eastern side of the Dead Sea.

Ruth 1:1–2

[3]Then Naomi's husband, Elimelech, died, and she was left with her two sons. [4]These sons married women from Moab. One was named Orpah, and the other was named Ruth. Naomi and her sons had lived in Moab about ten years [5]when Mahlon and Kilion also died. So Naomi was left alone without her husband or her two sons.

[6]While Naomi was in Moab, she heard that the LORD had come to help his people and had given them food again. So she and her daughters-in-law got ready to leave Moab and return home. [7]Naomi and her daughters-in-law left the place where they had lived and started back to the land of Judah. [8]But Naomi said to her two daughters-in-law, "Go back home, each of you to your own mother's house. May the LORD be as kind to you as you have been to me and my sons who are now dead. [9]May the LORD give you another happy home and a new husband."

When Naomi kissed the women good-bye, they began to cry out loud. [10]They said to her, "No, we want to go with you to your people."

[11]But Naomi said, "My daughters, return to your own homes. Why do you want to go with me? I cannot give birth to more sons to give you new husbands; [12]go back, my daughters, to your own homes. I am too old to have another husband. Even if I told myself, 'I still have hope' and had another husband tonight, and even if I had more sons, [13]should you wait until they were grown into men? Should you live for so many years without husbands? Don't do that, my daughters. My life is much too sad for you to share, because the LORD has been against me!"

[14]The women cried together out loud again. Then Orpah kissed her mother-in-law Naomi good-bye, but Ruth held on to her tightly.

[15]Naomi said to Ruth, "Look, your sister-in-law is going back to her own people and her own gods. Go back with her."

RUTH STAYS WITH NAOMI

[16]But Ruth said, "Don't beg me to leave you or to stop following you. Where you go, I will go. Where you live, I will live. Your people will be my people, and your God will be my God. [17]And where you die, I will die, and there I will be buried. I ask the LORD to punish me terribly if I do not keep this promise: Not even death will separate us."

FAMILY

What's a good example of family? (1:16)

[18]When Naomi saw that Ruth had firmly made up her mind to go with her, she stopped arguing with her. [19]So Naomi and Ruth went on until they came to the town of Bethlehem. When they entered Bethlehem, all the people became very excited. The women of the town said, "Is this really Naomi?"

"Where you go, I will go. Where you live, I will live. Your people will be my people, and your God will be my God."

(Ruth 1:16b)

[20]Naomi answered the people, "Don't call me Naomi.[n] Call me Mara,[n] because the Almighty has made my life very sad. [21]When I left, I had all I wanted, but now, the LORD has brought me home with nothing. Why should you call me Naomi when the LORD has spoken against me and the Almighty has given me so much trouble?"

[22]So Naomi and her daughter-in-law Ruth,

1:1 judges They were not judges in courts of law, but leaders of the people in times of emergency.
1:20 Naomi This name means "happy" or "pleasant." **1:20 Mara** This name means "bitter" or "sad."

the Moabite, returned from Moab and arrived at Bethlehem at the beginning of the barley harvest.

RUTH MEETS BOAZ

2

[1]Now Naomi had a rich relative named Boaz, from Elimelech's family.

[2]One day Ruth, the Moabite, said to Naomi, "I am going to the fields. Maybe someone will be kind enough to let me gather the grain he leaves behind."

Naomi said, "Go, my daughter."

[3]So Ruth went to the fields and gathered the grain that the workers cutting the grain had left behind. It just so happened that the field belonged to Boaz, from Elimelech's family.

WHAT'S IT MEAN?

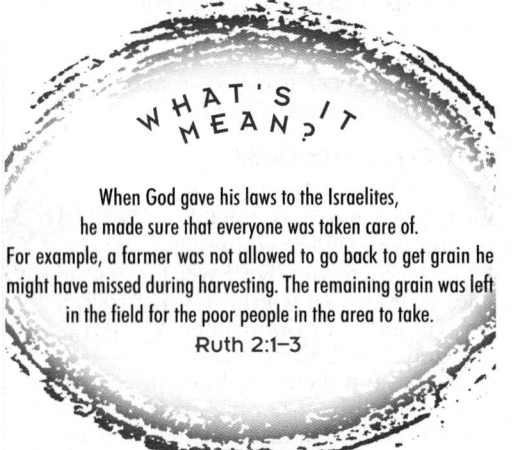

When God gave his laws to the Israelites, he made sure that everyone was taken care of. For example, a farmer was not allowed to go back to get grain he might have missed during harvesting. The remaining grain was left in the field for the poor people in the area to take.

Ruth 2:1–3

[4]Soon Boaz came from Bethlehem and greeted his workers, "The LORD be with you!"

And the workers answered, "May the LORD bless you!"

[5]Then Boaz asked his servant in charge of the workers, "Whose girl is that?"

[6]The servant answered, "She is the young Moabite woman who came back with Naomi from the country of Moab. [7]She said, 'Please let me follow the workers cutting grain and gather what they leave behind.' She came and has remained here, from morning until just now. She has stopped only a few moments to rest in the shelter."

[8]Then Boaz said to Ruth, "Listen, my daughter. Don't go to gather grain for yourself in another field. Don't even leave this field at all, but continue following closely behind my women workers. [9]Watch to see into which fields they go to cut grain and follow them. I have warned the young men not to bother you. When you are thirsty, you may go and drink from the water jugs that the young men have filled."

[10]Then Ruth bowed low with her face to the ground and said to him, "I am not an Israelite. Why have you been so kind to notice me?"

[11]Boaz answered her, "I know about all the help you have given your mother-in-law after your husband died. You left your father and mother and your own country to come to a nation where you did not know anyone. [12]May the LORD reward you for all you have done. May your wages be paid in full by the LORD, the God of Israel, under whose wings you have come for shelter."

[13]Then Ruth said, "I hope I can continue to please you, sir. You have said kind and encouraging words to me, your servant, though I am not one of your servants."

[14]At mealtime Boaz told Ruth, "Come here. Eat some of our bread and dip it in our sauce."

So Ruth sat down beside the workers. Boaz handed her some roasted grain, and she ate until she was full; she even had some food left over. [15]When Ruth rose and went back to work, Boaz commanded his workers, "Let her gather even around the piles of cut grain. Don't tell her to go away. [16]In fact, drop some full heads of grain for her from what you have in your hands, and let her gather them. Don't tell her to stop."

[17]So Ruth gathered grain in the field until evening. Then she separated the grain from the chaff, and there was about one-half bushel of barley. [18]Ruth carried the grain into town, and her mother-in-law saw how much she had gathered. Ruth also took out the food that was left over from lunch and gave it to Naomi.

[19]Naomi asked her, "Where did you gather all this grain today? Where did you work? Blessed be whoever noticed you!"

Ruth told her mother-in-law whose field she had worked in. She said, "The man I worked with today is named Boaz."

[20]Naomi told her daughter-in-law, "The LORD bless him! He continues to be kind to us—both the living and the dead!" Then Naomi told Ruth, "Boaz is one of our close relatives,[n] one who should take care of us."

[21]Then Ruth, the Moabite, said, "Boaz also told me, 'Keep close to my workers until they have finished my whole harvest.' "

2:20 close relatives In Bible times the closest relative could marry a widow without children so she could have children. He would care for this family, but they and their property would not belong to him. They would belong to the dead husband.

22But Naomi said to her daughter-in-law Ruth, "It is better for you to continue working with his women workers. If you work in another field, someone might hurt you." 23So Ruth continued working closely with the workers of Boaz, gathering grain until the barley harvest and the wheat harvest were finished. And she continued to live with Naomi, her mother-in-law.

NAOMI'S PLAN

3 1Then Naomi, Ruth's mother-in-law, said to her, "My daughter, I must find a suitable home for you, one that will be good for you. 2Now Boaz, whose young women you worked with, is our close relative.[n] Tonight he will be working at the threshing floor. 3Wash yourself, put on perfume, change your clothes, and go down to the threshing floor. But don't let him know you're there until he has finished his dinner. 4Watch him so you will know where he lies down to sleep. When he lies down, go and lift the cover off his feet[n] and lie down. He will tell you what you should do."

WHAT'S IT MEAN?

If you've never threshed grain, you may not know that it involves separating the grain itself from the stalk. In ancient times, this was done by beating the stalks or having animals walk over them. Afterward, the whole smashed mess was thrown into the air. The leaves and stalks were blown away by the wind, and the grain fell back to the ground. Threshing was hard work, but there was usually something special to look forward to when the work was done. Traditionally, the harvest and threshing season was a time of celebrations and fun.

Ruth 3:2

5Then Ruth answered, "I will do everything you say."

6So Ruth went down to the threshing floor and did all her mother-in-law told her to do. 7After his evening meal, Boaz felt good and went to sleep lying beside the pile of grain. Ruth went to him quietly and lifted the cover from his feet and lay down.

8About midnight Boaz was startled and rolled over. There was a woman lying near his feet! 9Boaz asked, "Who are you?"

She said, "I am Ruth, your servant girl. Spread your cover over me, because you are a relative who is supposed to take care of me."[n]

10Then Boaz said, "The LORD bless you, my daughter. This act of kindness is greater than the kindness you showed to Naomi in the beginning. You didn't look for a young man to marry, either rich or poor. 11Now, my daughter, don't be afraid. I will do everything you ask, because all the people in our town know you are a good woman. 12It is true that I am a relative who is to take care of you, but you have a closer relative than I. 13Stay here tonight, and in the morning we will see if he will take care of you. If he decides to take care of you, that is fine. But if he refuses, I will take care of you myself, as surely as the LORD lives. So stay here until morning."

14So Ruth stayed near his feet until morning but got up while it was still too dark to recognize anyone. Boaz thought, "People in town must not know that the woman came here to the threshing floor." 15So Boaz said to Ruth, "Bring me your shawl and hold it open."

So Ruth held her shawl open, and Boaz poured six portions of barley into it. Boaz then put it on her head and went back to the city.

16When Ruth went back to her mother-in-law, Naomi asked, "How did you do, my daughter?"

Ruth told Naomi everything that Boaz did for her. 17She said, "Boaz gave me these six portions of barley, saying, 'You must not go home without a gift for your mother-in-law.'"

18Naomi answered, "Ruth, my daughter, wait here until you see what happens. Boaz will not rest until he has finished doing what he should do today."

BOAZ MARRIES RUTH

4 1Boaz went to the city gate and sat there until the close relative he had mentioned passed by. Boaz called to him, "Come here, friend, and sit down." So the man came over and sat down. 2Boaz gathered ten of the older leaders of the city and told them, "Sit down here!" So they sat down.

3:2 close relative In Bible times the closest relative could marry a widow without children so she could have children. He would care for this family, but they and their property would not belong to him. They would belong to the dead husband. **3:4 lift . . . feet** This showed Ruth was asking him to be her husband. **3:9 Spread . . . me** By this, Ruth was asking Boaz to marry her.

WHAT'S IT MEAN?

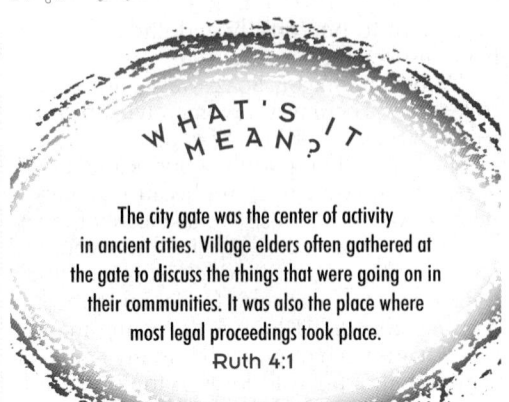

The city gate was the center of activity in ancient cities. Village elders often gathered at the gate to discuss the things that were going on in their communities. It was also the place where most legal proceedings took place.

Ruth 4:1

3Then Boaz said to the close relative, "Naomi,
who has come back from the country of
Moab, wants to sell the piece of land that belonged to our relative Elimelech. 4So I decided
to tell you about it: If you want to buy back
the land, then buy it in front of the people who
are sitting here and in front of the older leaders
of my people. But if you don't want to buy it,
tell me, because you are the only one who can
buy it, and I am next after you."

The close relative answered, "I will buy back
the land."

5Then Boaz explained, "When you buy the
land from Naomi, you must also marry Ruth,
the Moabite, the dead man's wife. That way,
the land will stay in the dead man's name."

6The close relative answered, "I can't buy
back the land. If I did, I might harm what I can
pass on to my own sons. I cannot buy the land
back, so buy it yourself."

7Long ago in Israel when people traded or
bought back something, one person took off
his sandal and gave it to the other person. This
was the proof of ownership in Israel.

8So the close relative said to Boaz, "Buy the
land yourself," and he took off his sandal.

9Then Boaz said to the older leaders and to
all the people, "You are witnesses today. I am
buying from Naomi everything that belonged
to Elimelech and Kilion and Mahlon. 10I am
also taking Ruth, the Moabite who was the
wife of Mahlon, as my wife. I am doing this so
her dead husband's property will stay in his
name and his name will not be separated from
his family and his hometown. You are witnesses today."

11So all the people and older leaders who
were at the city gate said, "We are witnesses.
May the LORD make this woman, who is coming into your home, like Rachel and Leah, who
had many children and built up the people of
Israel. May you become powerful in the district of Ephrathah and famous in Bethlehem.
12As Tamar gave birth to Judah's son Perez,[n]
may the LORD give you many children through
Ruth. May your family be great like his."

WHAT'S IT MEAN?

How would you like to be best known for the way you were born? That was the fate of Perez, an ancestor of Boaz. When it was time for Perez and his twin brother to be delivered, Perez's brother stuck his hand out first. After a few minutes, the hand disappeared back into the womb, and out popped Perez, followed by his older or younger brother (depending on how you look at it). Like Ruth, Perez's mother, Tamar, was an outsider who married into an Israelite family. Several kings of Israel, including David, descended from this family line.

Ruth 4:12

FAMILY

Where do kids come from? (4:13)

13So Boaz took Ruth home
as his wife and had sexual relations with her. The LORD let
her become pregnant, and she
gave birth to a son. 14The
women told Naomi, "Praise the
LORD who gave you this grandson. May he become famous in Israel. 15He will give you new
life and will take care of you in your old age
because of your daughter-in-law who loves
you. She is better for you than seven sons, because she has given birth to your grandson."

16Naomi took the boy, held him in her
arms, and cared for him. 17The neighbors gave
the boy his name, saying, "This boy was born
for Naomi." They named him Obed. Obed was
the father of Jesse, and Jesse was the father of
David.

18This is the family history of Perez, the father of Hezron. 19Hezron was the father of
Ram, who was the father of Amminadab.
20Amminadab was the father of Nahshon, who
was the father of Salmon. 21Salmon was the
father of Boaz, who was the father of Obed.
22Obed was the father of Jesse, and Jesse was
the father of David.

4:12 Perez One of Boaz's ancestors.

1 Samuel

CONTENT Reading 1 Samuel is like finding a home movie or home video of the Hebrew nation. It's a family history in real-time and with the skeletons all hanging out of the family closets.

The time line of this verbal "video" starts with one of the key players, Samuel, as a child being raised by the church. He grows up to be a national leader, a judge, and a prophet. His real claim to fame, though, is that he appointed the first king of Israel, King Saul.

Saul was a warrior kind of king. He protected his territory and fought off the bad guys. This time in history would have looked a little like an *Arabian Knights* episode with shields and horses and armor. Saul's downfall began when he got violently jealous of an up-and-coming leader named David.

Saul eventually lost his mind, then his life while he was losing his kingdom. He's an example to us of someone who failed to do things God's way and lost it all.

Outline

1:1—2:10 .... The Birth and Early Childhood of Samuel
2:11—3:21 .... Samuel at the House of the Lord
4:1—7:2 .... The Ark of God Is Captured and Returned
7:3–17 .... Samuel as the Leader of Israel
8:1—11:15 .... Saul, the First King of Israel
12:1–25 .... Samuel's Farewell Speech
13:1—15:35 .... Saul Disobeys the Lord, and the Lord Rejects Him as King
16:1–13 .... The Lord Chooses David to Be the Next King
16:14–23 .... David Plays a Harp for Saul
17:1–58 .... David Kills Goliath
18:1–30 .... Saul Fears David
19:1—21:9 .... Jonathan, Michal, Samuel, and Ahimelech Help David
21:10—22:5 .... David Runs from Saul
22:6–23 .... Saul Kills the Priests of the Lord
23:1—26:25 .... David Refuses to Kill Saul
27:1–12 .... David in Philistia
28:1–25 .... Saul Talks with Samuel's Ghost
29:1—30:31 .... David Rescues the Families of His Troops
31:1–13 .... Saul and His Sons Die in Battle Against the Philistines

Purpose In leaders, character and commitment do count.

Theme God Is Working in History

Date of writing 1050–750 B.C.

"But Samuel answered, 'What pleases the LORD more: burnt offerings and sacrifices or obedience to his voice? It is better to obey than to sacrifice. It is better to listen to God than to offer the fat of sheep' " (15:22).

Bible Talk

The First King Thing

Do you understand why this time in the Hebrews' history is so significant? The whole nation of Israel had never had a king before! That's like America not ever having had a president before. The Hebrews had been led by God through men like Moses and Joshua and then by judges, such as Samson and Deborah, but not by an official king.

Actually this system had worked well for them, but they did exactly what we do. They looked at the other nations around them, and said, "We want a king like *they've* got." Sometimes God gives us what we want even though he knows we won't like the consequences. That's what happened for the Hebrews.

TALK ABOUT AN INTERPERSONAL CONFLICT!

David and Saul's relationship was, at the *very* least, a difficult one. Saul was intimidated by David. He felt threatened because the people respected David. It's never a good thing for someone else in a kingdom to be respected more than the king.

Saul even put out a contract on David as if he were a criminal. David and his men had to hide out like Robin Hood's guys, but not because they had done anything wrong.

The amazing thing was that David didn't strike back at Saul. David realized that God had made Saul king and so Saul deserved respect. David also realized that in a conflict you can only control your own attitude, not the other person's.

Pretty smart guy.

SAMUEL'S BIRTH

[1]There was a man named Elkanah son of Jeroham from Ramathaim in the mountains of Ephraim. Elkanah was from the family of Zuph. (Jeroham was Elihu's son. Elihu was Tohu's son, and Tohu was the son of Zuph from the family group of Ephraim.) [2]Elkanah had two wives named Hannah and Peninnah. Peninnah had children, but Hannah had none.

[3]Every year Elkanah left his town of Ramah and went up to Shiloh to worship the LORD All-Powerful and to offer sacrifices to him. Shiloh was where Hophni and Phinehas, the sons of Eli, served as priests of the LORD. [4]When Elkanah offered sacrifices, he always gave a share of the meat to his wife Peninnah and to her sons and daughters. [5]But Elkanah always gave a special share of the meat to Hannah, because he loved Hannah and because the LORD had kept her from having children. [6]Peninnah would tease Hannah and upset her, because the LORD had made her unable to have children. [7]This happened every year when they went up to the house of the LORD at Shiloh. Peninnah would upset Hannah until Hannah would cry and not eat anything. [8]Her husband Elkanah would say to her, "Hannah, why are you crying and why won't you eat? Why are you sad? Don't I mean more to you than ten sons?"

[9]Once, after they had eaten their meal in Shiloh, Hannah got up. Now Eli the priest was sitting on a chair near the entrance to the LORD's house. [10]Hannah was so sad that she cried and prayed to the LORD. [11]She made a promise, saying, "LORD All-Powerful, see how sad I am. Remember me and don't forget me. If you will give me a son, I will give him back to you all his life, and no one will ever cut his hair with a razor."[n]

FEELINGS
What should we do when we are sad? (1:10)

[12]While Hannah kept praying, Eli watched her mouth. [13]She was praying in her heart so her lips moved, but her voice was not heard. Eli thought she was drunk [14]and said to her, "Stop getting drunk! Throw away your wine!"

[15]Hannah answered, "No, sir, I have not drunk any wine or beer. I am a deeply troubled woman, and I was telling the LORD about all my problems. [16]Don't think I am an evil woman. I have been praying because I have many troubles and am very sad."

[17]Eli answered, "Go! I wish you well. May the God of Israel give you what you asked of him."

[18]Hannah said, "May I always please you." When she left and ate something, she was not sad anymore.

PRAYER
Who answers prayer? (1:17)

[19]Early the next morning Elkanah's family got up and worshiped the LORD. Then they went back home to Ramah. Elkanah had sexual relations with his wife Hannah, and the LORD remembered her. [20]So Hannah became pregnant, and in time she gave birth to a son. She named him Samuel,[n] saying, "His name is Samuel because I asked the LORD for him."

WHAT'S IT MEAN?

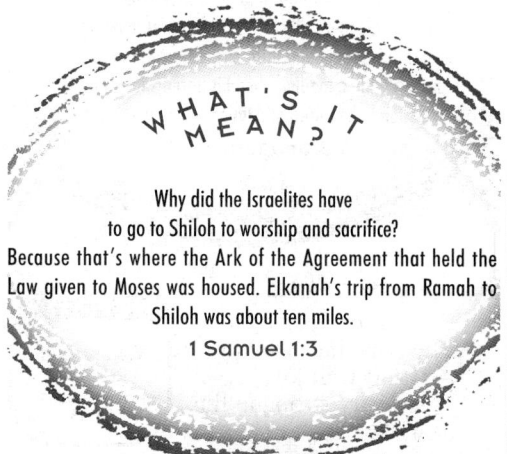

Why did the Israelites have to go to Shiloh to worship and sacrifice?

Because that's where the Ark of the Agreement that held the Law given to Moses was housed. Elkanah's trip from Ramah to Shiloh was about ten miles.

1 Samuel 1:3

HANNAH GIVES SAMUEL TO GOD

[21]Every year Elkanah went with his whole family to Shiloh to offer sacrifices and to keep the promise he had made to God. [22]But one time Hannah did not go with him. She told him, "When the boy is old enough to eat solid food, I will take him to Shiloh. Then I will give him to the LORD, and he will always live there."

[23]Elkanah, Hannah's husband, said to her, "Do what you think is best. You may stay home until the boy is old enough to eat. May the LORD do what you have said." So Hannah stayed at home to nurse her son until he was old enough to eat.

[24]When Samuel was old enough to eat, Hannah took him to the house of the LORD at Shiloh, along with a three-year-old bull, one-half bushel of flour, and a leather bag filled

1:11 cut . . . razor People who made special promises not to cut their hair or to drink wine or beer were called Nazirites. These people gave a specific time in their lives, or sometimes their entire lives, to the Lord. See Numbers 6:1-5. **1:20 Samuel** This name sounds like the Hebrew word for "God heard."

with wine. [25]After they had killed the bull for
the sacrifice, Hannah brought Samuel to Eli.
[26]She said to Eli, "As surely as you live, sir, I am
the same woman who stood near you praying
to the LORD. [27]I prayed for this child, and the
LORD answered my prayer and gave him to me.
[28]Now I give him back to the LORD. He will
belong to the LORD all his life." And he worshiped the LORD there.

WHAT'S IT MEAN?

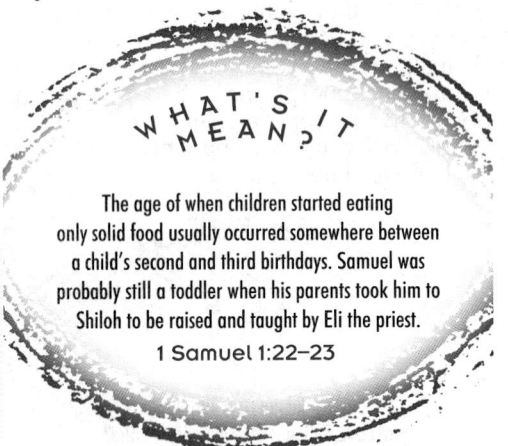

The age of when children started eating only solid food usually occurred somewhere between a child's second and third birthdays. Samuel was probably still a toddler when his parents took him to Shiloh to be raised and taught by Eli the priest.

1 Samuel 1:22–23

HANNAH GIVES THANKS

2 [1]Hannah prayed:
"The LORD has filled my
heart with joy;
I feel very strong in the
LORD.
I can laugh at my enemies;
I am glad because you have helped me!

HAPPINESS
Where can I find happiness? (2:1)

[2]"There is no one holy like the LORD.
There is no God but you;
there is no Rock like our
God.

GOD
Who is like God? (2:2)

[3]"Don't continue bragging,
don't speak proud
words.
The LORD is a God who
knows everything,
and he judges what people do.

[4]"The bows of warriors break,
but weak people become strong.
[5]Those who once had plenty of food now
must work for food,
but people who were hungry are
hungry no more.
The woman who could not have children
now has seven,
but the woman who had many children
now is sad.

[6]"The LORD sends death,
and he brings to life.
He sends people to the
grave,
and he raises them to
life again.
[7]The LORD makes some
people poor,
and others he makes rich.
He makes some people humble,
and others he makes great.
[8]The LORD raises the poor up from the
dust,
and he lifts the needy from the ashes.
He lets the poor sit with princes
and receive a throne of honor.

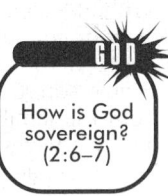

GOD
How is God sovereign? (2:6–7)

"The foundations of the earth belong to
the LORD,
and the LORD set the world upon them.
[9]He protects those who are loyal to him,
but evil people will be silenced in
darkness.
Power is not the key to success.
[10]The LORD destroys his enemies;
he will thunder in heaven against them.
The LORD will judge all the earth.
He will give power to his king
and make his appointed king strong."

ELI'S EVIL SONS

[11]Then Elkanah went home to Ramah, but
the boy continued to serve the LORD under Eli
the priest.
[12]Now Eli's sons were evil men; they did
not care about the LORD. [13]This is what the
priests would normally do to the people: Every
time someone brought a sacrifice, the meat
would be cooked in a pot. The priest's servant
would then come carrying a fork that had
three prongs. [14]He would plunge the fork into
the pot or the kettle. Whatever the fork
brought out of the pot belonged to the priest.
But this is how they treated all the Israelites
who came to Shiloh to offer sacrifices. [15]Even
before the fat was burned, the priest's servant
would come to the person offering sacrifices
and say, "Give the priest some meat to roast. He
won't accept boiled meat from you, only raw
meat."
[16]If the one who offered the sacrifice said,
"Let the fat be burned up first as usual, and
then take anything you want," the priest's servant would answer, "No, give me the meat
now. If you don't, I'll take it by force."
[17]The LORD saw that the sin of the servants

was very great because they did not show respect for the offerings made to the LORD.

SAMUEL GROWS UP

18But Samuel obeyed the LORD. As a boy he
wore a linen holy vest. 19Every
year Samuel's mother made a
little coat for him and took it
to him when she went with
her husband to Shiloh for
the sacrifice. 20When Eli
blessed Elkanah and his wife,
he would say, "May the
LORD repay you with chil-
dren through Hannah to take
the place of the boy Hannah
prayed for and gave back to the
LORD." Then Elkanah and Hannah would
go home. 21The LORD was kind to Hannah, so
she became the mother of three sons and two
daughters. And the boy Samuel grew up serving the LORD.

> **"There is no one holy like the LORD. There is no God but you; there is no Rock like our God."**
> **(1 Samuel 2:2)**

WHAT'S IT MEAN?

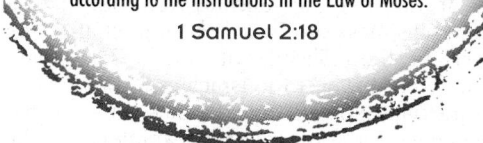

Linen, which was handwoven from the fibers of the hemp plant, was considered to be the highest-quality fabric in the ancient world. For the most part, only people of great wealth or power wore linen. Priests and those who served in the Temple were the exception. They, too, wore linen. The white linen uniforms that the priests wore were designed according to the instructions in the Law of Moses.

1 Samuel 2:18

22Now Eli was very old. He heard about
everything his sons were doing to all the Israelites and how his sons had sexual relations
with the women who served at the entrance to
the Meeting Tent. 23Eli said to his sons, "Why
do you do these evil things that the people tell
me about? 24No, my sons. The LORD's people
are spreading a bad report about you. 25If you
sin against someone, God can help you. But if
you sin against the LORD himself, no one can
help you!" But Eli's sons would not listen to
him, because the LORD had decided to put
them to death.

26The boy Samuel grew physically. He
pleased the LORD and the people.

27A man of God came to Eli and said, "This
is what the LORD says: 'I clearly showed myself
to the family of your ancestor Aaron when
they were slaves to the king of Egypt. 28I chose
them from all the tribes of Israel to be my
priests. I wanted them to go up to
my altar, to burn incense, and
to wear the holy vest. I also
let the family of your ancestor
have part of all the offerings
sacrificed by the Israelites.
29So why don't you respect
the sacrifices and gifts? You
honor your sons more than
me. You grow fat on the best
parts of the meat the Israelites
bring to me.'

30"So the LORD, the God of Is-
rael, says: 'I promised that your family and
your ancestor's family would serve me always.'
But now the LORD says: 'This must stop! I will
honor those who honor me, but I will dishon-
or those who ignore me. 31The time is coming
when I will destroy the descendants of both
you and your ancestors. No man will grow old
in your family. 32You will see trouble in my
house. No matter what good things happen
to Israel, there will never be an old man in
your family. 33I will not totally cut off your
family from my altar. But your eyes will cry
and your heart be sad, because all your descendants will die.

34" 'I will give you a sign. Both your sons,
Hophni and Phinehas, will die on the same
day. 35I will choose a loyal priest for myself
who will listen to me and do what I want. I
will make his family continue, and he will always serve before my appointed king. 36Then
everyone left in your family will come and
bow down before him. They will beg for a little
money or a little food and say, "Please give me
a job as priest so I can have food to eat." ' "

GOD CALLS SAMUEL

3

1The boy Samuel served the LORD under Eli.
In those days the LORD did not speak directly to
people very often; there were very few visions.

2Eli's eyes were so weak he was almost
blind. One night he was lying in bed. 3Samuel
was also in bed in the LORD's house, where the
Ark of the Agreement was. God's lamp was still
burning.

4Then the LORD called Samuel, and Samuel
answered, "I am here!" 5He ran to Eli and said,
"I am here. You called me."

But Eli said, "I didn't call you. Go back to
bed." So Samuel went back to bed.

[6]The LORD called again, "Samuel!"

Samuel again went to Eli and said, "I am here. You called me."

Again Eli said, "I didn't call you. Go back to bed."

[7]Samuel did not yet know the LORD, and the LORD had not spoken directly to him yet.

[8]The LORD called Samuel for the third time. Samuel got up and went to Eli and said, "I am here. You called me."

Then Eli realized the LORD was calling the boy. [9]So he told Samuel, "Go to bed. If he calls you again, say, 'Speak, LORD. I am your servant and I am listening.' " So Samuel went and lay down in bed.

[10]The LORD came and stood there and called as he had before, "Samuel, Samuel!"

FOLLOWING GOD

Who should we listen to? (3:10)

Samuel said, "Speak, LORD. I am your servant and I am listening."

[11]The LORD said to Samuel, "Watch, I am going to do something in Israel that will shock those who hear about it. [12]At that time I will do to Eli and his family everything I promised, from beginning to end. [13]I told Eli I would punish his family always, because he knew his sons were evil. They acted without honor, but he did not stop them. [14]So I swore to Eli's family, 'Your guilt will never be removed by sacrifice or offering.' "

[15]Samuel lay down until morning. Then he opened the doors of the house of the LORD. He was afraid to tell Eli about the vision, [16]but Eli called to him, "Samuel, my son!"

Samuel answered, "I am here."

[17]Eli asked, "What did the LORD say to you? Don't hide it from me. May God punish you terribly if you hide from me anything he said to you." [18]So Samuel told Eli everything and did not hide anything from him. Then Eli said, "He is the LORD. Let him do what he thinks is best."

[19]The LORD was with Samuel as he grew up; he did not let any of Samuel's messages fail to come true. [20]Then all Israel, from Dan to Beersheba,[n] knew Samuel was a true prophet of the LORD. [21]And the LORD continued to show himself at Shiloh, and he showed himself to Samuel through his word.

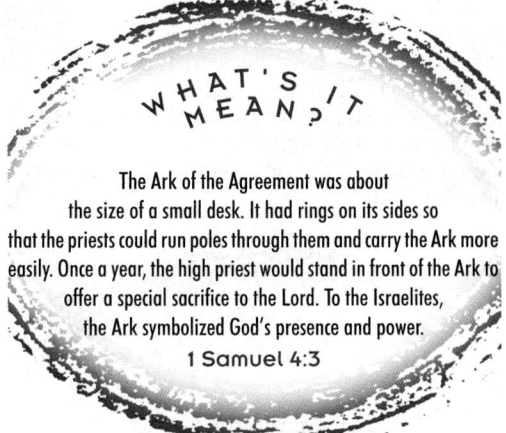

WHAT'S IT MEAN?

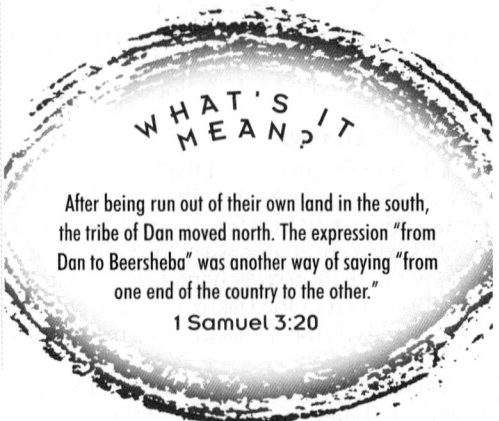

After being run out of their own land in the south, the tribe of Dan moved north. The expression "from Dan to Beersheba" was another way of saying "from one end of the country to the other."

1 Samuel 3:20

WHAT'S IT MEAN?

The Ark of the Agreement was about the size of a small desk. It had rings on its sides so that the priests could run poles through them and carry the Ark more easily. Once a year, the high priest would stand in front of the Ark to offer a special sacrifice to the Lord. To the Israelites, the Ark symbolized God's presence and power.

1 Samuel 4:3

4 [1]So, news about Samuel spread through all of Israel.

THE PHILISTINES CAPTURE THE ARK OF THE AGREEMENT

At that time the Israelites went out to fight the Philistines. The Israelites camped at Ebenezer and the Philistines at Aphek. [2]The Philistines went to meet the Israelites in battle. And as the battle spread, they defeated the Israelites, killing about four thousand soldiers on the battlefield. [3]When some Israelite soldiers went back to their camp, the older leaders of Israel asked, "Why did the LORD let the Philistines defeat us? Let's bring the Ark of the Agreement with the LORD here from Shiloh and take it with us into battle. Then God will save us from our enemies."

[4]So the people sent men to Shiloh. They brought back the Ark of the Agreement with the LORD All-Powerful, who sits between the gold creatures with wings. Eli's two sons, Hophni and Phinehas, were there with the Ark.

3:20 Dan to Beersheba Dan was the city farthest north in Israel, and Beersheba was the city farthest south. So this means all the people of Israel.

5When the Ark of the Agreement with the
LORD came into the camp, all the Israelites gave
a great shout of joy that made the ground
shake. 6When the Philistines heard Israel's
shout, they asked, "What's all this shouting in
the Hebrew camp?"
Then the Philistines found out that the Ark
of the LORD had come into the Hebrew camp.
7They were afraid and said, "A god has come
into the Hebrew camp! We're in trouble! This
has never happened before! 8How terrible it
will be for us! Who can save us from these
powerful gods? They are the ones who struck
the Egyptians with all kinds of disasters in the
desert. 9Be brave, Philistines! Fight like men! In
the past they were our slaves. So fight like men,
or we will become their slaves."
10So the Philistines fought hard and defeated the Israelites, and every Israelite soldier
ran away to his own home. It was a great defeat for Israel, because thirty thousand Israelite
soldiers were killed. 11The Ark of God was tak-
en by the Philistines, and Eli's two sons, Hophni and Phinehas, died.
12That same day a man from the tribe of
Benjamin ran from the battle. He tore his
clothes and put dust on his head to show his
great sadness. 13When he arrived in Shiloh, Eli
was by the side of the road. He was sitting
there in a chair, watching, because he was
worried about the Ark of God. When the
Benjaminite entered Shiloh, he told the bad
news. Then all the people in town cried loudly.
14Eli heard the crying and asked, "What's all
this noise?"
The Benjaminite ran to Eli and told him
what had happened. 15Eli was now ninety-
eight years old, and he was blind. 16The
Benjaminite told him, "I have come from the
battle. I ran all the way here today."
Eli asked, "What happened, my son?"
17The Benjaminite answered, "Israel ran
away from the Philistines, and the Israelite
army has lost many soldiers. Your two sons
are both dead, and the Philistines have taken
the Ark of God."
18When he mentioned the Ark of God, Eli
fell backward off his chair. He fell beside the
gate, broke his neck, and died, because he was
old and fat. He had led Israel for forty years.

THE GLORY IS GONE

19Eli's daughter-in-law, the wife of Phinehas, was pregnant and was about to give birth.
When she heard the news that the Ark of God
had been taken and that Eli, her father-in-law,
and Phinehas, her husband, were both dead,
she began to give birth to her child. The child
was born, but the mother had much trouble in
giving birth. 20As she was dying, the women
who helped her said, "Don't worry! You've
given birth to a son!" But she did not answer or
pay attention. 21She named the baby Ichabod,[n]
saying, "Israel's glory is gone." She said this because the Ark of God had been taken and her
father-in-law and husband were dead. 22She
said, "Israel's glory is gone, because the Ark of
God has been taken away."

TROUBLE FOR THE PHILISTINES

5
1After the Philistines had captured the Ark
of God, they took it from Ebenezer to Ashdod.
2They carried it into Dagon's temple and put it
next to Dagon. 3When the people of Ashdod
rose early the next morning, they found that
Dagon had fallen on his face on the ground
before the Ark of the LORD. So they put Dagon
back in his place. 4The next morning when
they rose, they again found Dagon fallen on
the ground before the Ark of the LORD. His
head and hands had broken off and were lying
in the doorway. Only his body was still in one
piece. 5So, even today, Dagon's priests and others who enter his temple at Ashdod refuse to
step on the doorsill.

WHAT'S IT MEAN?

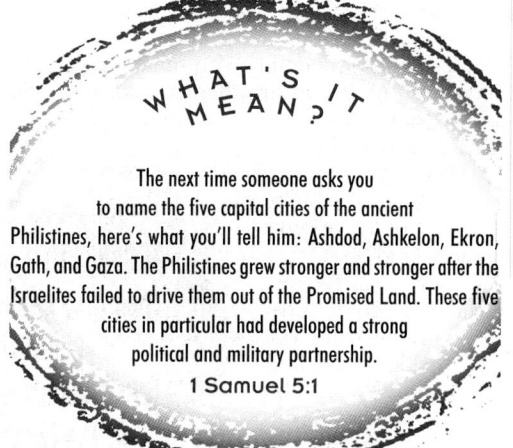

The next time someone asks you to name the five capital cities of the ancient Philistines, here's what you'll tell him: Ashdod, Ashkelon, Ekron, Gath, and Gaza. The Philistines grew stronger and stronger after the Israelites failed to drive them out of the Promised Land. These five cities in particular had developed a strong political and military partnership.

1 Samuel 5:1

6The LORD was hard on the people of Ashdod and their neighbors. He caused them to
suffer and gave them growths on their skin.
7When the people of Ashdod saw what was
happening, they said, "The Ark of the God of
Israel can't stay with us. God is punishing us

4:21 Ichabod This name means "no glory."

and Dagon our god." 8The people of Ashdod called all five Philistine kings together and asked them, "What should we do with the Ark of the God of Israel?"

The rulers answered, "Move the Ark of the God of Israel to Gath." So the Philistines moved it to Gath.

9But after they moved it to Gath, there was a great panic. The LORD was hard on that city also, and he gave both old and young people in Gath growths on their skin. 10Then the Philistines sent the Ark of God to Ekron.

But when it came into Ekron, the people of Ekron yelled, "Why are you bringing the Ark of the God of Israel to our city? Do you want to kill us and our people?" 11So they called all the kings of the Philistines together and said, "Send the Ark of the God of Israel back to its place before it kills us and our people!" All the people in the city were struck with terror because God was so hard on them there. 12The people who did not die were troubled with growths on their skin. So the people of Ekron cried loudly to heaven.

THE ARK OF GOD IS SENT HOME

6 1The Philistines kept the Ark of God in their land seven months. 2Then they called for their priests and magicians and said, "What should we do with the Ark of the LORD? Tell us how to send it back home!"

3The priests and magicians answered, "If you send back the Ark of the God of Israel, don't send it back empty. You must give a penalty offering. If you are then healed, you will know that it was because of the Ark that you had such trouble."

4The Philistines asked, "What kind of penalty offering should we send to Israel's God?"

They answered, "Make five gold models of the growths on your skin and five gold models of rats. The number of models must match the number of Philistine kings, because the same sickness has come on you and your kings. 5Make models of the growths and the rats that are ruining the country, and give honor to Israel's God. Then maybe he will stop being so hard on you, your gods, and your land. 6Don't be stubborn like the king of Egypt and the Egyptians. After God punished them terribly, they let the Israelites leave Egypt.

7"You must build a new cart and get two cows that have just had calves. These must be cows that have never had yokes on their necks. Hitch the cows to the cart, and take the calves home, away from their mothers. 8Put the Ark of the LORD on the cart and the gold models for the penalty offering in a box beside the Ark. Then send the cart straight on its way. 9Watch the cart. If it goes toward Beth Shemesh in Israel's own land, the LORD has given us this great sickness. But if it doesn't, we will know that Israel's God has not punished us. Our sickness just happened by chance."

WHAT'S IT MEAN?

The Philistines knew that under normal circumstances, the cows would not leave their calves behind. They also knew that if the cows left to carry the Ark back to the Israelites, it would be a sign that Israel's God was on the job—guiding, protecting, and avenging his people.

1 Samuel 6:7

10The Philistines did what the priests and magicians said. They took two cows that had just had calves and hitched them to the cart, but they kept their calves at home. 11They put the Ark of the LORD and the box with the gold rats and models of growths on the cart. 12Then the cows went straight toward Beth Shemesh. They stayed on the road, mooing all the way, and did not turn right or left. The Philistine kings followed the cows as far as the border of Beth Shemesh.

"The Philistines kept the Ark of God in their land seven months. Then they called for their priests and magicians and said, 'What should we do with the Ark of the LORD? Tell us how to send it back home!' "
(1 Samuel 6:1–2)

13Now the people of Beth Shemesh were harvesting their wheat in the valley. When they looked up and saw the Ark of the LORD, they were very happy. 14The cart came to the field belonging to Joshua of Beth Shemesh and stopped near a large rock. The people of Beth Shemesh chopped up the wood of the cart. Then they sacrificed the cows as burnt offerings to the LORD. [15]The Levites took down the Ark of the LORD and the box that had the gold models, and they put both on the large rock. That day the people of Beth Shemesh offered whole burnt offerings and made sacrifices to the LORD. [16]After the five Philistine kings saw this, they went back to Ekron the same day.

[17]The Philistines had sent these gold models of the growths as penalty offerings to the LORD. They sent one model for each Philistine town: Ashdod, Gaza, Ashkelon, Gath, and Ekron. [18]And the Philistines also sent gold models of rats. The number of rats matched the number of towns belonging to the Philistine kings, including both strong, walled cities and country villages. The large rock on which they put the Ark of the LORD is still there in the field of Joshua of Beth Shemesh.

[19]But some of the men of Beth Shemesh looked into the Ark of the LORD. So God killed seventy of them. The people of Beth Shemesh cried because the LORD had struck them down. [20]They said, "Who can stand before the LORD, this holy God? Whom will he strike next?"

GOD
Who can stand before God's holiness? (6:19–20)

[21]Then they sent messengers to the people of Kiriath Jearim, saying, "The Philistines have brought back the Ark of the LORD. Come down and take it to your city."

7 [1]The men of Kiriath Jearim came and took the Ark of the LORD to Abinadab's house on a hill. There they made Abinadab's son Eleazar holy for the LORD so he could guard the Ark of the LORD.

THE LORD SAVES THE ISRAELITES

[2]The Ark stayed at Kiriath Jearim a long time—twenty years in all. And the people of Israel began to follow the LORD again. [3]Samuel spoke to the whole group of Israel, saying, "If you're turning back to the LORD with all your hearts, you must remove your foreign gods and your idols of Ashtoreth. You must give yourselves fully to the LORD and serve only him. Then he will save you from the Philistines."

TRUTH
How does following truth help us? (7:3)

[4]So the Israelites put away their idols of Baal and Ashtoreth, and they served only the LORD.

[5]Samuel said, "All Israel must meet at Mizpah, and I will pray to the LORD for you." [6]So the Israelites met together at Mizpah. They drew water from the ground and poured it out before the LORD and did not eat that day. They confessed, "We have sinned against the LORD." And Samuel served as judge of Israel at Mizpah.

[7]The Philistines heard the Israelites were meeting at Mizpah, so the Philistine kings came up to attack them. When the Israelites heard they were coming, they were afraid. [8]They said to Samuel, "Don't stop praying to the LORD our God for us! Ask him to save us from the Philistines!" [9]Then Samuel took a baby lamb and offered it to the LORD as a whole burnt offering. He called to the LORD for Israel's sake, and the LORD answered him.

[10]While Samuel was burning the offering, the Philistines came near to attack Israel. But the LORD thundered against them with loud thunder. They were so frightened they became confused. So the Israelites defeated the Philistines in battle. [11]The men of Israel ran out of Mizpah and chased the Philistines almost to Beth Car, killing the Philistines along the way.

PEACE COMES TO ISRAEL

[12]After this happened Samuel took a stone and set it up between Mizpah and Shen. He named the stone Ebenezer,[n] saying, "The LORD has helped us to this point." [13]So the Philistines were defeated and did not enter the Israelites' land again.

The LORD was against the Philistines all Samuel's life. [14]Earlier the Philistines had taken

WHAT'S IT MEAN?

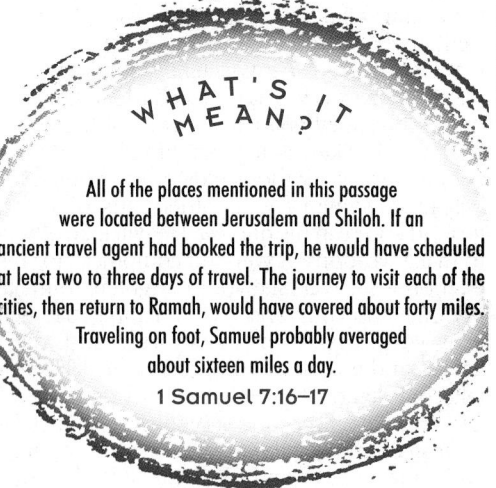

All of the places mentioned in this passage were located between Jerusalem and Shiloh. If an ancient travel agent had booked the trip, he would have scheduled at least two to three days of travel. The journey to visit each of the cities, then return to Ramah, would have covered about forty miles. Traveling on foot, Samuel probably averaged about sixteen miles a day.

1 Samuel 7:16–17

7:12 Ebenezer This name means "stone of help."

towns from the Israelites, but the Israelites won them back, from Ekron to Gath. They also took back from the Philistines the lands near these towns. There was peace also between Israel and the Amorites.

[15]Samuel continued as judge of Israel all his life. [16]Every year he went from Bethel to Gilgal to Mizpah and judged the Israelites in all these towns. [17]But Samuel always went back to Ramah, where his home was. There he judged Israel and built an altar to the LORD.

ISRAEL ASKS FOR A KING

8 [1]When Samuel was old, he made his sons judges for Israel. [2]His first son was named Joel, and his second son was named Abijah. Joel and Abijah were judges in Beersheba. [3]But Samuel's sons did not live as he did. They tried to get money dishonestly, and they accepted money secretly to make wrong judgments.

[4]So all the older leaders came together and met Samuel at Ramah. [5]They said to him, "You're old, and your sons don't live as you do. Give us a king to rule over us like all the other nations."

[6]When the older leaders said that, Samuel was not pleased. He prayed to the LORD, [7]and the LORD told Samuel, "Listen to whatever the people say to you. They have not rejected you. They have rejected me from being their king. [8]They are doing as they have always done. When I took them out of Egypt, they left me and served other gods. They are doing the same to you. [9]Now listen to the people, but warn them what the king who rules over them will do."

[10]So Samuel told those who had asked him for a king what the LORD had said. [11]Samuel said, "If you have a king ruling over you, this is what he will do: He will take your sons and make them serve with his chariots and his horses, and they will run in front of the king's chariot. [12]The king will make some of your sons commanders over thousands or over fifties. He will make some of your other sons plow his ground and reap his harvest. He will take others to make weapons of war and equipment for his chariots. [13]He will take your daughters to make perfume and cook and bake for him. [14]He will take your best fields, vineyards, and olive groves and give them to his servants. [15]He will take one-tenth of your grain and grapes and give it to his officers and servants. [16]He will take your male and female servants, your best cattle, and your donkeys and use them all for his own work. [17]He will take one-tenth of your flocks, and you yourselves will become his slaves. [18]When that time comes, you will cry out because of the king you chose. But the LORD will not answer you then."

[19]But the people would not listen to Samuel. They said, "No! We want a king to rule over us. [20]Then we will be the same as all the other nations. Our king will judge for us and go with us and fight our battles."

[21]After Samuel heard all that the people said, he repeated their words to the LORD. [22]The LORD answered, "You must listen to them. Give them a king."

Then Samuel told the people of Israel, "Go back to your towns."

SAUL LOOKS FOR HIS FATHER'S DONKEYS

9 [1]Kish, son of Abiel from the tribe of Benjamin, was an important man. (Abiel was the son of Zeror, who was the son of Becorath, who was the son of Aphiah of Benjamin.) [2]Kish had a son named Saul, who was a fine young man. There was no Israelite better than he. Saul stood a head taller than any other man in Israel.

[3]Now the donkeys of Saul's father, Kish, were lost. So Kish said to Saul, his son, "Take one of the servants, and go and look for the donkeys." [4]Saul went through the mountains of Ephraim and the land of Shalisha, but he and the servant could not find the donkeys. They went into the land of Shaalim, but the donkeys were not there. They went through the land of Benjamin, but they still did not find them. [5]When they arrived in the area of Zuph, Saul said to his servant, "Let's go back or my father will stop thinking about the donkeys and will start worrying about us."

[6]But the servant answered, "A man of God is in this town. People respect him because everything he says comes true. Let's go into the town now. Maybe he can tell us something about the journey we have taken."

[7]Saul said to his servant, "If we go into the town, what can we give him? The food in our bags is gone. We have no gift to give him. Do we have anything?"

[8]Again the servant answered Saul. "Look, I have one-tenth of an ounce of silver. Give it to the man of God. Then he will tell us about our journey." [9](In the past, if someone in Israel wanted to ask something from God, he would say, "Let's go to the seer." We call the person a prophet today, but in the past he was called a seer.)

[10]Saul said to his servant, "That's a good idea. Come, let's go." So they went toward the town where the man of God was.

11 As Saul and the servant were going up the
hill to the town, they met some young women
coming out to get water. Saul and the servant
asked them, "Is the seer here?"
12 The young women answered, "Yes, he's
here. He's ahead of you. Hurry now. He has
just come to our town today, because the people will offer a sacrifice at the place of worship.
13 As soon as you enter the town, you will find
him before he goes up to the place of worship
to eat. The people will not begin eating until
the seer comes, because he must bless the sacrifice. After that, the guests will eat. Go now,
and you should find him."

SAUL MEETS SAMUEL

14 Saul and the servant went up to the town.
Just as they entered it, they saw Samuel coming
toward them on his way up to the place of
worship.
15 The day before Saul came, the LORD had
told Samuel: 16 "About this time tomorrow I
will send you a man from the land of Benjamin. Appoint him to lead my people Israel. He
will save my people from the Philistines. I have
seen the suffering of my people, and I have
listened to their cry."

WHAT'S IT MEAN?

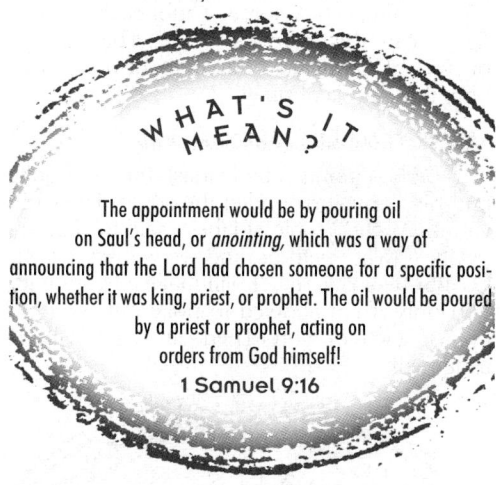

The appointment would be by pouring oil on Saul's head, or *anointing,* which was a way of announcing that the Lord had chosen someone for a specific position, whether it was king, priest, or prophet. The oil would be poured by a priest or prophet, acting on orders from God himself!

1 Samuel 9:16

17 When Samuel first saw Saul, the LORD said
to Samuel, "This is the man I told you about.
He will organize my people."
18 Saul approached Samuel at the gate and
said, "Please tell me where the seer's house is."
19 Samuel answered, "I am the seer. Go with
me to the place of worship. Today you and
your servant are to eat with me. Tomorrow
morning I will answer all your questions and
send you home. 20 Don't worry about the donkeys you lost three days ago, because they
have been found. Soon all the wealth of Israel
will belong to you and your family."
21 Saul answered, "But I am from the tribe of
Benjamin, the smallest tribe in Israel. And my
family group is the smallest in the tribe of Benjamin. Why are you saying such things?"
22 Then Samuel took Saul and his servant
into a large room and gave them a choice place
at the table. About thirty guests were there.
23 Samuel said to the cook, "Bring the meat I
gave you, the portion I told you to set aside."
24 So the cook took the thigh and put it on
the table in front of Saul. Samuel said, "This is
the meat saved for you. Eat it, because it was
set aside for you for this special time. As I said,
'I had invited the people.' " So Saul ate with
Samuel that day.
25 After they finished eating, they came
down from the place of worship and went to
the town. Then Samuel talked with Saul on the
roof[n] of his house. 26 At dawn they got up, and
Samuel called to Saul on the roof. He said, "Get
up, and I will send you on your way." So Saul
got up and went out of the house with Samuel.
27 As Saul, his servant, and Samuel were getting
near the edge of the city, Samuel said to Saul,
"Tell the servant to go on ahead of us, but you
stay, because I have a message from God
for you."

SAMUEL APPOINTS SAUL

10
1 Samuel took a jar of olive oil and poured it
on Saul's head. He kissed Saul and said, "The
LORD has appointed you to lead his people.
2 After you leave me today, you will meet two
men near Rachel's tomb on the border of Benjamin at Zelzah. They will say to you, 'The
donkeys you were looking for have been
found. But now your father has stopped thinking about his donkeys and is worrying about
you. He is asking, "What will I do about my
son?" '
3 "Then you will go on until you reach the
big tree at Tabor. Three men on their way to
worship God at Bethel will meet you there.
One man will be carrying three goats. Another
will be carrying three loaves of bread. And the
third will have a leather bag full of wine. 4 They
will greet you and offer you two loaves of
bread, which you must accept. 5 Then you will

9:25 roof In Bible times houses were built with flat roofs. The roof was used for drying things such as flax and fruit. And it was used as an extra room, as a place for worship, and as a cool place to sleep in the summer. See Deuteronomy 22:8.

go to Gibeah of God, where a Philistine camp is. When you approach this town, a group of prophets will come down from the place of worship. They will be playing harps, tambourines, flutes, and lyres, and they will be prophesying. [6]Then the Spirit of the LORD will rush upon you with power. You will prophesy with these prophets, and you will be changed into a different man. [7]After these signs happen, do whatever you find to do, because God will help you.

[8]"Go ahead of me to Gilgal. I will come down to you to offer whole burnt offerings and fellowship offerings. But you must wait seven days. Then I will come and tell you what to do."

SAUL MADE KING

[9]When Saul turned to leave Samuel, God changed Saul's heart. All these signs came true that day. [10]When Saul and his servant arrived at Gibeah, Saul met a group of prophets. The Spirit of God rushed upon him, and he prophesied with the prophets. [11]When people who had known Saul before saw him prophesying with the prophets, they asked each other, "What has happened to Kish's son? Is even Saul one of the prophets?"

> "When Saul turned to leave Samuel, God changed Saul's heart. All these signs came true that day."
> (1 Samuel 10:9)

[12]A man who lived there said, "Who is the father of these prophets?" So this became a famous saying: "Is even Saul one of the prophets?" [13]When Saul finished prophesying, he entered the place of worship.

[14]Saul's uncle asked him and his servant, "Where have you been?"

Saul said, "We were looking for the donkeys. When we couldn't find them, we went to talk to Samuel."

[15]Saul's uncle asked, "Please tell me. What did Samuel say to you?"

[16]Saul answered, "He told us the donkeys had already been found." But Saul did not tell his uncle what Samuel had said about his becoming king.

[17]Samuel called all the people of Israel to meet with the LORD at Mizpah. [18]He said, "This is what the LORD, the God of Israel, says: 'I led Israel out of Egypt. I saved you from Egypt's control and from other kingdoms that were troubling you.' [19]But now you have rejected your God. He saves you from all your troubles and problems, but you said, 'No! We want a king to rule over us.' Now come, stand before the LORD in your tribes and family groups."

[20]When Samuel gathered all the tribes of Israel, the tribe of Benjamin was picked. [21]Samuel had them pass by in family groups, and Matri's family was picked. Then he had each man of Matri's family pass by, and Saul son of Kish was picked. But when they looked for Saul, they could not find him. [22]They asked the LORD, "Has Saul come here yet?"

The LORD said, "Yes. He's hiding behind the baggage."

[23]So they ran and brought him out. When Saul stood among the people, he was a head taller than anyone else. [24]Then Samuel said to the people, "See the man the LORD has chosen. There is no one like him among all the people."

Then the people shouted, "Long live the king!"

[25]Samuel explained the rights and duties of the king and then wrote them in a book and put it before the LORD. Then he told the people to go to their homes.

[26]Saul also went to his home in Gibeah. God touched the hearts of certain brave men who went along with him. [27]But some troublemakers said, "How can this man save us?" They disapproved of Saul and refused to bring gifts to him. But Saul kept quiet.

NAHASH TROUBLES JABESH GILEAD

11 [1]About a month later Nahash the Ammonite and his army surrounded the city of Jabesh in Gilead. All the people of Jabesh said to Nahash, "Make a treaty with us, and we will serve you."

[2]But he answered, "I will make a treaty with you only if I'm allowed to poke out the right eye of each of you. Then all Israel will be ashamed!"

WHAT'S IT MEAN?

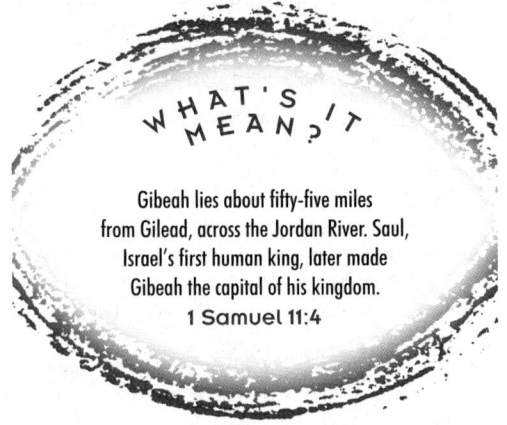

Gibeah lies about fifty-five miles from Gilead, across the Jordan River. Saul, Israel's first human king, later made Gibeah the capital of his kingdom.

1 Samuel 11:4

[3]The older leaders of Jabesh said to Nahash, "Give us seven days to send messengers through all Israel. If no one comes to help us, we will give ourselves up to you."

[4]When the messengers came to Gibeah where Saul lived and told the people the news, they cried loudly. [5]Saul was coming home from plowing the fields with his oxen when he heard the people crying. He asked, "What's wrong with the people that they are crying?" Then they told Saul what the messengers from Jabesh had said. [6]When Saul heard their words, God's Spirit rushed upon him with power, and he became very angry. [7]So he took a pair of oxen and cut them into pieces. Then he gave the pieces of the oxen to messengers and ordered them to carry them through all the land of Israel.

The messengers said, "This is what will happen to the oxen of anyone who does not follow Saul and Samuel." So the people became very afraid of the LORD. They all came together as if they were one person. [8]Saul gathered the people together at Bezek. There were three hundred thousand men from Israel and thirty thousand men from Judah.

WHAT'S IT MEAN?

Saul used the oxen as an attention-getter, not as a sacrifice. He wanted the people to understand that the situation was serious.

1 Samuel 11:7

[9]They said to the messengers who had come, "Tell the people at Jabesh Gilead this: 'Before the day warms up tomorrow, you will be saved.' " So the messengers went and reported this to the people at Jabesh, and they were very happy. [10]The people said to Nahash the Ammonite, "Tomorrow we will come out to meet you. Then you can do anything you want to us."

[11]The next morning Saul divided his soldiers into three groups. At dawn they entered the Ammonite camp and defeated them before the heat of the day. The Ammonites who escaped were scattered; no two of them were still together.

[12]Then the people said to Samuel, "Who didn't want Saul as king? Bring them here and we will kill them!"

[13]But Saul said, "No! No one will be put to death today. Today the LORD has saved Israel!"

[14]Then Samuel said to the people, "Come, let's go to Gilgal. There we will again promise to obey the king." [15]So all the people went to Gilgal, and there, before the LORD, the people made Saul king. They offered fellowship offerings to the LORD, and Saul and all the Israelites had a great celebration.

WHAT'S IT MEAN?

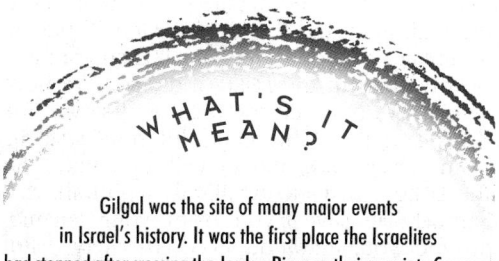

Gilgal was the site of many major events in Israel's history. It was the first place the Israelites had stopped after crossing the Jordan River on their way into Canaan. At their campsite in Gilgal, the Israelites had left twelve stones, one for each tribe, as a memorial to the help they had received from God during their long journey. Gilgal had also been Joshua's military headquarters during Israel's battles against the Canaanites. Finally, Gilgal was the place Saul had chosen as the central location for his war against the Philistines.

1 Samuel 11:14

SAMUEL'S FAREWELL SPEECH

12 [1]Samuel said to all Israel, "I have done everything you wanted me to do and have put a king over you. [2]Now you have a king to lead you. I am old and gray, and my sons are here with you. I have been your leader since I was young. [3]Here I am. If I have done anything wrong, you must testify against me before the LORD and his appointed king. Did I steal anyone's ox or donkey? Did I hurt or cheat anyone? Did I ever secretly accept money to pretend not to see something wrong? If I did any of these things, I will make it right."

[4]The Israelites answered, "You have not cheated us, or hurt us, or taken anything unfairly from anyone."

[5]Samuel said to them, "The LORD is a witness to what you have said. His appointed king is also a witness today that you did not find anything wrong in me."

"He is our witness," they said.

[6]Then Samuel said to the people, "It is the LORD who chose Moses and Aaron and

brought your ancestors out of Egypt. 7Now, stand there, and I will remind you of all the good things the LORD did for you and your ancestors.

8"After Jacob entered Egypt, his descendants cried to the LORD for help. So the LORD sent Moses and Aaron, who took your ancestors out of Egypt and brought them to live in this place.

9"But they forgot the LORD their God. So he handed them over as slaves to Sisera, the commander of the army of Hazor, and as slaves to the Philistines and the king of Moab. They all fought against your ancestors. 10Then your ancestors cried to the LORD and said, 'We have sinned. We have left the LORD and served the Baals and the Ashtoreths. But now save us from our enemies, and we will serve you.' 11So the LORD sent Gideon,[n] Barak, Jephthah, and Samuel. He saved you from your enemies around you, and you lived in safety. 12But when you saw Nahash king of the Ammonites coming against you, you said, 'No! We want a king to rule over us!'—even though the LORD your God was your king. 13Now here is the king you chose, the one you asked for. The LORD has put him over you. 14You must honor the LORD and serve him. You must obey his word and not turn against his commands. Both you and the king ruling over you must follow the LORD your God. If you do, it will be well with you. 15But if you don't obey the LORD, and if you turn against his commands, he will be against you. He will do to you what he did to your ancestors.

16"Now stand still and see the great thing the LORD will do before your eyes. 17It is now the time of the wheat harvest.[n] I will pray for the LORD to send thunder and rain. Then you will know what an evil thing you did against the LORD when you asked for a king."

18Then Samuel prayed to the LORD, and that same day the LORD sent thunder and rain. So the people were very afraid of the LORD and Samuel. 19They said to Samuel, "Pray to the LORD your God for us, your servants! Don't let us die! We've added to all our sins the evil of asking for a king."

20Samuel answered, "Don't be afraid. It's true that you did wrong, but don't turn away from the LORD. Serve the LORD with all your heart. 21Idols are of no use, so don't worship them. They can't help you or save you. They are useless! 22For his own sake, the LORD won't leave his people. Instead, he was pleased to make you his own people. 23I will surely not stop praying for you, because that would be sinning against the LORD. I will teach you what is good and right. 24You must honor the LORD and truly serve him with all your heart. Remember the wonderful things he did for you! 25But if you are stubborn and do evil, he will sweep you and your king away."

TRUTH
How are we to serve God? (12:24)

13 1Saul was thirty years old when he became king, and he was king over Israel forty-two years.[n] 2Saul chose three thousand men from Israel. Two thousand men stayed with him at Micmash in the mountains of Bethel, and one thousand men stayed with Jonathan at Gibeah in Benjamin. Saul sent the other men in the army back home.

3Jonathan attacked the Philistine camp in Geba, and the other Philistines heard about it. Saul said, "Let the Hebrews hear what happened." So he told the men to blow trumpets through all the land of Israel. 4All the Israelites heard the news. The men said, "Saul has defeated the Philistine camp. Now the Philistines will really hate us!" Then the Israelites were called to join Saul at Gilgal.

5The Philistines gathered to fight Israel with three thousand[n] chariots and six thousand men to ride in them. Their soldiers were as many as the grains of sand on the seashore. The Philistines went and camped at Micmash, which is east of Beth Aven. 6When the Israelites saw that they were in trouble, they went to hide in caves and bushes, among the rocks, and in pits and wells. 7Some Hebrews even went across the Jordan River to the land of Gad and Gilead.

But Saul stayed at Gilgal, and all the men in his army were shaking with fear. 8Saul waited seven days, because Samuel had said he would meet him then. But Samuel did not come to Gilgal, and the soldiers began to leave.

9So Saul said, "Bring me the whole burnt offering and the fellowship offerings." Then Saul offered the whole burnt offering. 10Just as he finished, Samuel arrived, and Saul went to greet him.

12:11 Gideon Also called Jerub-Baal. **12:17 time . . . harvest** This was a dry time in the summer when no rains fell. **13:1 Saul . . . years** This is how the verse is worded in some early Greek copies. The Hebrew is not clear here. **13:5 three thousand** Some Greek copies say three thousand. The Hebrew copies say thirty thousand.

SAMUEL made a difference

What would be your first words in response if you heard God speak to you? The first time God spoke to Samuel, the young man didn't even recognize the voice. Fortunately, Samuel knew someone who steered him in the right direction. After all, having God speak to you probably isn't as important in the long run as listening to what God has to say! So old Eli told Samuel if he heard the voice again to keep the conversation going.

That was one thing Eli got right. He didn't explain God to Samuel at that point. He might not even have been sure God was speaking to Samuel. But he helped Samuel let God settle the issue. The fact that Samuel learned at a young age to give attention to God indicates the central reason why Samuel's life made such a difference.

Samuel bridged the time in history between the judges and the prophets in Israel. He appointed the first two kings of Israel (Saul and David). He conveyed God's warnings to the people that, in begging for a king, they were not only asking for trouble; they were separating themselves from God's guidance. He held kings accountable in God's name for their behavior. Samuel listened to God and, as a result, was able to speak for God. But it all began when he was still very young. The conversation he began with God lasted a lifetime.

Cutting Edge

YOU can, too! You have a tremendous spiritual advantage over Samuel. God has not only spoken; he has made his Word available in writing. Samuel had Moses' inspired writings; you have God's complete Word. Eli's wisdom still applies. God's Word will not make a difference in your Life if you neither listen to nor obey it. But if you want your life to make a difference for God, pay attention to what your Creator has to say. Respond to the conversation he has begun with you!

Want to know more? Read the story of Samuel's effective life in 1 Samuel 1—28. He is also listed in the great Hall of Faith (Hebrews 11:32).

11Samuel asked, "What have you done?"
Saul answered, "I saw the soldiers leaving
me, and you were not here when you said you
would be. The Philistines were gathering at
Micmash. 12Then I thought, 'The Philistines
will come against me at Gilgal, and I haven't
asked for the LORD's approval.' So I forced myself to offer the whole burnt offering."
13Samuel said, "You acted foolishly! You
haven't obeyed the command of the LORD
your GOD. If you had obeyed him, the LORD
would have made your kingdom continue in
Israel always, 14but now your kingdom will
not continue. The LORD has looked for the kind
of man he wants. He has appointed him to rule
his people, because you haven't obeyed his
command."
15Then Samuel left Gilgal and went to Gibeah in Benjamin. Saul counted the men who
were still with him, and there were about six
hundred.

HARD TIMES FOR ISRAEL

16Saul and his son Jonathan and the soldiers with him stayed in Gibeah in the land of
Benjamin. The Philistines made their camp at
Micmash. 17Three groups went out from the
Philistine camp to make raids. One group went
on the Ophrah road in the land of Shual. 18The
second group went on the Beth Horon road.
The third group went on the border road that
overlooks the Valley of Zeboim toward the
desert.
19The whole land of Israel had no blacksmith because the Philistines had said, "The Hebrews might make swords and spears." 20So all
the Israelites had to go down to the Philistines
to have their plows, hoes, axes, and sickles
sharpened. 21The Philistine blacksmiths charged
about one-fourth of an ounce of silver for
sharpening plows and hoes. And they charged
one-eighth of an ounce of silver for sharpening
picks, axes, and the sticks used to guide oxen.
22So when the battle came, the soldiers with
Saul and Jonathan had no swords or spears.
Only Saul and his son Jonathan had them.

ISRAEL DEFEATS THE PHILISTINES

23A group from the Philistine army had
gone out to the pass at Micmash.
14 1One day Jonathan, Saul's son, said to the
officer who carried his armor, "Come, let's go
over to the Philistine camp on the other side."
But Jonathan did not tell his father.
2Saul was sitting under a pomegranate tree
at the threshing floor near Gibeah. He had
about six hundred men with him. 3One man
was Ahijah who was wearing the holy vest.
(Ahijah was a son of Ichabod's brother Ahitub.
Ichabod was the son of Phinehas, the son of
Eli, the LORD's priest in Shiloh.) No one knew
Jonathan had left.

WHAT'S IT MEAN?

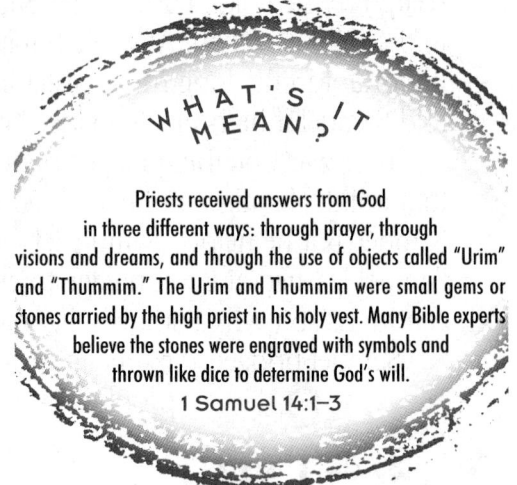

Priests received answers from God in three different ways: through prayer, through visions and dreams, and through the use of objects called "Urim" and "Thummim." The Urim and Thummim were small gems or stones carried by the high priest in his holy vest. Many Bible experts believe the stones were engraved with symbols and thrown like dice to determine God's will.

1 Samuel 14:1–3

4There was a steep slope on each side of the
pass that Jonathan planned to go through to
reach the Philistine camp. The cliff on one side
was named Bozez, and the cliff on the other
side was named Seneh. 5One cliff faced north
toward Micmash. The other faced south toward Geba.
6Jonathan said to his officer who carried his
armor, "Come. Let's go to the camp of those
men who are not circumcised. Maybe the
LORD will help us. The LORD can give us victory if we have many people, or just a few."
7The officer who carried Jonathan's armor
said to him, "Do whatever you think is best. Go
ahead. I'm with you."
8Jonathan said, "Then come. We will cross
over to the Philistines and let them see us. 9If
they say to us, 'Stay there until we come to
you,' we will stay where we are. We won't go
up to them. 10But if they say, 'Come up to us,'
we will climb up, and the LORD will let us defeat them. This will be the sign for us."
11When both Jonathan and his officer let
the Philistines see them, the Philistines said,
"Look! The Hebrews are crawling out of the
holes they were hiding in!" 12The Philistines in
the camp shouted to Jonathan and his officer,
"Come up to us. We'll teach you a lesson!"
Jonathan said to his officer, "Climb up behind me, because the LORD has given the Philistines to Israel!" 13So Jonathan climbed up,
using his hands and feet, and his officer
climbed just behind him. Jonathan struck

down the Philistines as he went, and his officer
killed them as he followed behind him. 14In
that first fight Jonathan and his officer killed
about twenty Philistines over a half acre of
ground.
15All the Philistine soldiers panicked—those
in the camp and those in the raiding party. The
ground itself shook! God had caused the panic.
16Saul's guards were at Gibeah in the land
of Benjamin when they saw the Philistine soldiers running in every direction. 17Saul said to
his army, "Check to see who has left our camp."
When they checked, they learned that Jonathan and his officer were gone.
18So Saul said to Ahijah the priest, "Bring
the Ark of God." (At that time it was with the
Israelites.) 19While Saul was talking to the
priest, the confusion in the Philistine camp was
growing. Then Saul said to Ahijah, "Put your
hand down!"
20Then Saul gathered his army and entered
the battle. They found the Philistines confused,
striking each other with their swords! 21Earlier,
there were Hebrews who had served the Philistines and had stayed in their camp, but now
they joined the Israelites with Saul and Jonathan. 22When all the Israelites hidden in the
mountains of Ephraim heard that the Philistine
soldiers were running away, they also joined
the battle and chased the Philistines. 23So the
LORD saved the Israelites that day, and the battle moved on past Beth Aven.

SAUL MAKES ANOTHER MISTAKE

24The men of Israel were miserable that day
because Saul had made an oath for all of them.
He had said, "No one should eat food before
evening and before I finish defeating my enemies. If he does, he will be cursed!" So no Israelite soldier ate food.
25Now the army went into the woods,
where there was some honey on the ground.
26They came upon some honey, but no one
took any because they were afraid of the oath.
27Jonathan had not heard the oath Saul had
put on the army, so he dipped the end of his
stick into the honey and lifted some out and
ate it. Then he felt better. 28Then one of the soldiers told Jonathan, "Your father made an oath
for all the soldiers. He said any man who eats
today will be cursed! That's why they are so
weak."
29Jonathan said, "My father has made trouble for the land! See how much better I feel
after just tasting a little of this honey! 30It
would have been much better for the men to
eat the food they took from their enemies today. We could have killed many more Philistines!"
31That day the Israelites defeated the Philistines from Micmash to Aijalon. After that, they
were very tired. 32They had taken sheep, cattle,
and calves from the Philistines. Now they were
so hungry they killed the animals on the
ground and ate them, without draining the
blood from them! 33Someone said to Saul,
"Look! The men are sinning against the LORD.
They're eating meat without draining the
blood from it!"

Saul said, "You have sinned! Roll a large
stone over here now!" 34Then he said, "Go to
the men and tell them that each person must
bring his ox and sheep to me and kill it here
and eat it. Don't sin against the LORD by eating
meat without draining the blood from it."

That night everyone brought his animals
and killed them there. 35Then Saul built an altar
to the LORD. It was the first altar he had built to
the LORD.
36Saul said, "Let's go after the Philistines tonight and rob them. We won't let any of them
live!"

The men answered, "Do whatever you think
is best."

But the priest said, "Let's ask God."
37So Saul asked God, "Should I chase the
Philistines? Will you let us defeat them?" But
God did not answer Saul at that time. 38Then
Saul said to all the leaders of his army, "Come
here. Let's find out what sin has been done today. 39As surely as the LORD lives who has
saved Israel, even if my son Jonathan did the
sin, he must die." But no one in the army spoke.
40Then Saul said to all the Israelites, "You
stand on this side. I and my son Jonathan will
stand on the other side."

The men answered, "Do whatever you think
is best."
41Then Saul prayed to the LORD, the God of
Israel, "Give me the right answer."

And Saul and Jonathan were picked; the
other men went free. 42Saul said, "Now let us
discover if it is I or Jonathan my son who is
guilty." And Jonathan was picked.
43Saul said to Jonathan, "Tell me what you
have done."

So Jonathan told Saul, "I only tasted a little
honey from the end of my stick. And must I
die now?"
44Saul said, "Jonathan, if you don't die, may
God punish me terribly."
45But the soldiers said to Saul, "Must Jonathan die? Never! He is responsible for saving
Israel today! As surely as the LORD lives, not

even a hair of his head will fall to the ground!
Today Jonathan fought against the Philistines
with God's help!" So the army saved Jonathan,
and he did not die.
[46]Then Saul stopped chasing the Philistines,
and they went back to their own land.

SAUL FIGHTS ISRAEL'S ENEMIES

[47]When Saul became king over Israel, he
fought against Israel's enemies all around. He
fought Moab, the Ammonites, Edom, the king
of Zobah, and the Philistines. Everywhere Saul
went he defeated Israel's enemies. [48]He fought
bravely and defeated the Amalekites. He saved
the Israelites from their enemies who had
robbed them.

WHAT'S IT MEAN?

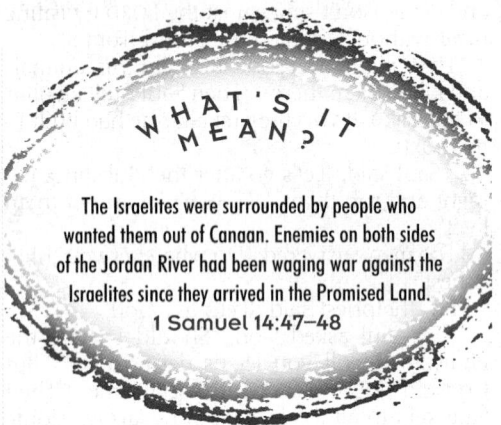

The Israelites were surrounded by people who wanted them out of Canaan. Enemies on both sides of the Jordan River had been waging war against the Israelites since they arrived in the Promised Land.

1 Samuel 14:47–48

[49]Saul's sons were Jonathan, Ishvi, and
Malki-Shua. His older daughter was named
Merab, and his younger daughter was named
Michal. [50]Saul's wife was Ahinoam daughter of
Ahimaaz. The commander of his army was
Abner son of Ner, Saul's uncle. [51]Saul's father
Kish and Abner's father Ner
were sons of Abiel.
[52]All Saul's life he fought
hard against the Philistines.
When he saw strong or
brave men, he took them
into his army.

SAUL REJECTED AS KING

15
[1]Samuel said to Saul,
"The LORD sent me to ap-
point you king over Israel.
Now listen to his message. [2]This
is what the LORD All-Powerful says:
'When the Israelites came out of Egypt, the
Amalekites tried to stop them from going to
Canaan. So I will punish them. [3]Now go, attack
the Amalekites and destroy everything they
own as an offering to the LORD. Don't let anything live. Put to death men and women, children and small babies, cattle and sheep, camels
and donkeys.' "

WHAT'S IT MEAN?

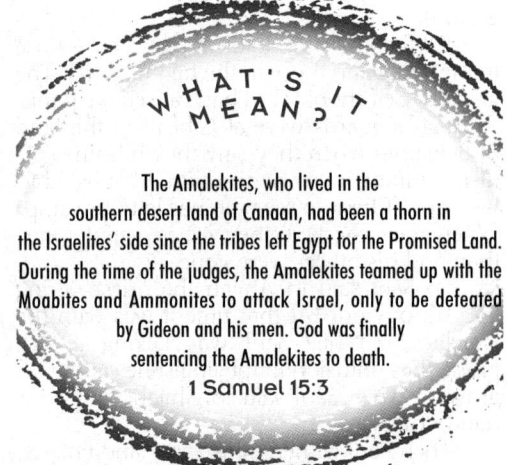

The Amalekites, who lived in the southern desert land of Canaan, had been a thorn in the Israelites' side since the tribes left Egypt for the Promised Land. During the time of the judges, the Amalekites teamed up with the Moabites and Ammonites to attack Israel, only to be defeated by Gideon and his men. God was finally sentencing the Amalekites to death.

1 Samuel 15:3

[4]So Saul called the army together at Telaim.
There were two hundred thousand foot soldiers and ten thousand men from Judah. [5]Then
Saul went to the city of Amalek and set up an
ambush in the ravine. [6]He said to the Kenites,
"Go away. Leave the Amalekites so that I won't
destroy you with them, because you showed
kindness to the Israelites when they came out
of Egypt." So the Kenites moved away from the
Amalekites.
[7]Then Saul defeated the Amalekites. He
fought them all the way from Havilah to Shur,
at the border of Egypt. [8]He took King Agag of
the Amalekites alive, but he killed all of Agag's
army with the sword. [9]Saul and the army let
Agag live, along with the best sheep, fat cattle,
and lambs. They let every good
animal live, because they did
not want to destroy them.
But when they found an animal that was weak or useless, they killed it.
[10]Then the LORD spoke
his word to Samuel: [11]"I am
sorry I made Saul king, because he has stopped fol-
lowing me and has not
obeyed my commands."
Samuel was upset, and he cried
out to the LORD all night long.
[12]Early the next morning Samuel got up
and went to meet Saul. But the people told
Samuel, "Saul has gone to Carmel, where he
has put up a monument in his own honor.
Now he has gone down to Gilgal."

"Samuel said to Saul, 'The LORD sent me to appoint you king over Israel. Now listen to his message.' " (1 Samuel 15:1)

[13]When Samuel came to Saul, Saul said, "May the LORD bless you! I have obeyed the LORD's commands."

[14]But Samuel said, "Then why do I hear cattle mooing and sheep bleating?"

[15]Saul answered, "The soldiers took them from the Amalekites. They saved the best sheep and cattle to offer as sacrifices to the LORD your God, but we destroyed all the other animals."

[16]Samuel said to Saul, "Stop! Let me tell you what the LORD said to me last night."

Saul answered, "Tell me."

[17]Samuel said, "Once you didn't think much of yourself, but now you have become the leader of the tribes of Israel. The LORD appointed you to be king over Israel. [18]And he sent you on a mission. He said, 'Go and destroy those evil people, the Amalekites. Make war on them until all of them are dead.' [19]Why didn't you obey the LORD? Why did you take the best things? Why did you do what the LORD said was wrong?"

[20]Saul said, "But I did obey the LORD. I did what the LORD told me to do. I destroyed all the Amalekites, and I brought back Agag their king. [21]The soldiers took the best sheep and cattle to sacrifice to the LORD your God at Gilgal."

[22]But Samuel answered,
"What pleases the LORD more:
burnt offerings and sacrifices
or obedience to his voice?
It is better to obey than to sacrifice.
It is better to listen to God than to offer the fat of sheep.
[23]Disobedience is as bad as the sin of sorcery.
Pride is as bad as the sin of worshiping idols.
You have rejected the LORD's command.
Now he rejects you as king."

OBEDIENCE
Is it better to obey or to ask forgiveness? (15:22)

[24]Then Saul said to Samuel, "I have sinned. I didn't obey the LORD's commands and your words. I was afraid of the people, and I did what they said. [25]Now, I beg you, forgive my sin. Come back with me so I may worship the LORD."

[26]But Samuel said to Saul, "I won't go back with you. You rejected the LORD's command, and now he rejects you as king of Israel."

BELIEF
What happens if we reject God? (15:26)

On the Edge

But Samuel answered, "What pleases the LORD more: burnt offerings and sacrifices or obedience to his voice? It is better to obey than to sacrifice. It is better to listen to God than to offer the fat of sheep" (1 Sam. 15:22).

The right thing is always to obey God. Saul proves in this passage that you can't just do whatever you want, even if it seems okay or harmless. God wants you to obey him. Saul thought he could just take over and revise God's instructions to suit himself. God was really disappointed with Saul's disobedience and took away his title as king. The Bible is God's word of instruction to us. It helps us live so that we can be safe, happy, and blessed. It is not up for revision. You can't just pick the parts you like. God wants you to obey him. All of him and all of his Word.

SEE FOR YOURSELF:
Ex. 19:5;
Deut. 10:12–13;
Is. 1:19

[27]As Samuel turned to leave, Saul caught his robe, and it tore. [28]Samuel said to him, "The LORD has torn the kingdom of Israel from you today and has given it to one of your neighbors who is better than you. [29]The LORD is the Eternal One of Israel. He does not lie or change his mind. He is not a human being, so he does not change his mind.

[30]Saul answered, "I have sinned. But please honor me in front of the older leaders of my people and in front of the Israelites. Come back with me so that I can worship the LORD your God." [31]So Samuel went back with Saul, and Saul worshiped the LORD.

[32]Then Samuel said, "Bring me King Agag of the Amalekites."

Agag came to Samuel in chains, but Agag thought, "Surely the threat of death has passed."

[33]Samuel said to him, "Your sword made other mothers lose their children. Now your mother will have no children." And Samuel cut Agag to pieces before the LORD at Gilgal.

[34]Then Samuel left and went to Ramah, but Saul went up to his home in Gibeah. [35]And Samuel never saw Saul again the rest of his life,

but he was sad for Saul. And the LORD was
very sorry he had made Saul king of Israel.

SAMUEL GOES TO BETHLEHEM

16 [1]The LORD said to Samuel, "How long will
you continue to feel sorry for Saul? I have rejected him as king of Israel. Fill your container
with olive oil and go. I am sending you to Jesse
who lives in Bethlehem, because I have chosen
one of his sons to be king."
[2]But Samuel said, "If I go, Saul will hear the
news and will try to kill me."
The LORD said, "Take a young calf with you.
Say, 'I have come to offer a sacrifice to the
LORD.' [3]Invite Jesse to the sacrifice. Then I will
tell you what to do. You must appoint the one
I show you."
[4]Samuel did what the LORD told him to do.
When he arrived at Bethlehem, the older leaders of Bethlehem shook with fear. They met
him and asked, "Are you coming in peace?"
[5]Samuel answered, "Yes, I come in peace. I
have come to make a sacrifice to the LORD. Set
yourselves apart to the LORD and come to the
sacrifice with me." Then he set Jesse and his
sons apart to the LORD, and he invited them to
come to the sacrifice.
[6]When they arrived, Samuel saw Eliab, and
he thought, "Surely the LORD has appointed
this person standing here before him."
[7]But the LORD said to Samuel,
"Don't look at how handsome
Eliab is or how tall he is, because I have not chosen him.
God does not see the same
way people see. People look at
the outside of a person, but
the LORD looks at the heart."
[8]Then Jesse called Abinadab and told him
to pass by Samuel. But Samuel said, "The LORD
has not chosen this man either." [9]Then Jesse
had Shammah pass by. But Samuel said, "No,
the LORD has not chosen this one." [10]Jesse had
seven of his sons pass by Samuel. But Samuel
said to him, "The LORD has not chosen any of
these."
[11]Then he asked Jesse, "Are these all the sons
you have?"
Jesse answered, "I still have the youngest
son. He is out taking care of the sheep."
Samuel said, "Send for him. We will not sit
down to eat until he arrives."
[12]So Jesse sent and had his youngest son
brought in. He was a fine boy, tanned, and
handsome.
The LORD said to Samuel, "Go, appoint him,
because he is the one."
[13]So Samuel took the container of olive oil
and poured it on Jesse's youngest son to appoint him in front of his brothers. From that

INTEGRITY

What's better: image or integrity? (16:7)

On the Edge

But the LORD said to Samuel, "Don't look at how handsome Eliab is or how tall he is, because I have not chosen him. God does not see the same way people see. People look at the outside of a person, but the LORD looks at the heart" (1 Sam. 16:7).

First impressions. Yuck. You look. They look. You shake hands; fake a smile. Yep, you've got this one figured out, wrapped up in a box, and slapped into category A, B, or C. He's either "hip, drip, or wanna-be." However you do it, you still label people. Everybody does, and we all do it based on the superficial. Looks determine the label—straight teeth, good haircut, right jeans—all the right stuff.

Guess what? God doesn't give a rip about jeans or haircuts. People's looks aren't even an issue for him. His radar locks on to the heart and makes an inspection there. He wants to know who you are way down deep inside. How do you really feel? Are you really mean as a yard dog, or do you cut other people down because your heart's been broken and really hurting? God knows the truth about people—good and bad. He always looks past all your stuff and sees your heart.

SEE FOR YOURSELF:
1 Chr. 28:9; 2 Chr. 6:30; Jer. 20:12; Acts 15:8–9

WHAT'S IT MEAN?

Sheepherding was a job often given to a son, a daughter, or a hired servant. Jesse gave this responsibility to David, his youngest son.

1 Samuel 16:11

day on, the LORD's Spirit worked in David.
Samuel then went back to Ramah.

DAVID SERVES SAUL

14But the LORD's Spirit had left Saul, and an
evil spirit from the LORD troubled him.
15Saul's servants said to him, "See, an evil
spirit from God is troubling you. 16Give us the
command to look for someone who can play
the harp. When the evil spirit from God troubles you, he will play, and you will feel better."
17So Saul said to his servants, "Find someone who can play well and bring him to me."
18One of the servants said, "I have seen a
son of Jesse of Bethlehem play the harp. He is
brave and courageous. He is a good speaker
and handsome, and the LORD is with him."
19Then Saul sent messengers to Jesse, saying,
"Send me your son David, who is with the
sheep." 20So Jesse loaded a donkey with bread,
a leather bag full of wine, and a young goat,
and he sent them with his son David to Saul.
21When David came to Saul, he began to
serve him. Saul liked David and made him the
officer who carried his armor. 22Saul sent a
message to Jesse, saying, "Let David stay and
serve me because I like him."
23When the evil spirit from God troubled
Saul, David would take his harp and play.
Then the evil spirit would leave him, and Saul
would feel better.

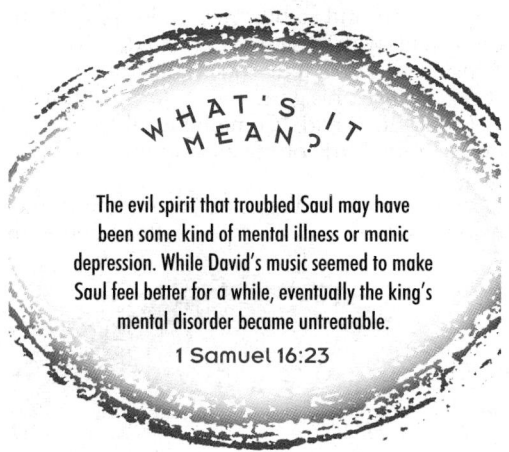

WHAT'S IT MEAN?

The evil spirit that troubled Saul may have been some kind of mental illness or manic depression. While David's music seemed to make Saul feel better for a while, eventually the king's mental disorder became untreatable.

1 Samuel 16:23

DAVID AND GOLIATH

17
1The Philistines gathered their armies for
war. They met at Socoh in Judah and camped
at Ephes Dammim between Socoh and Azekah. 2Saul and the Israelites gathered in the
Valley of Elah and camped there and took their
positions to fight the Philistines. 3The Philistines controlled one hill while the Israelites
controlled another. The valley was between
them.

WHAT'S IT MEAN?

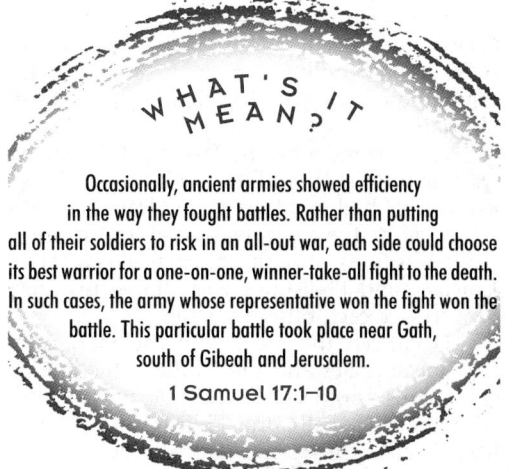

Occasionally, ancient armies showed efficiency in the way they fought battles. Rather than putting all of their soldiers to risk in an all-out war, each side could choose its best warrior for a one-on-one, winner-take-all fight to the death. In such cases, the army whose representative won the fight won the battle. This particular battle took place near Gath, south of Gibeah and Jerusalem.

1 Samuel 17:1–10

4The Philistines had a champion fighter from
Gath named Goliath. He was about nine feet,
four inches tall. He came out of the Philistine
camp 5with a bronze helmet on his head and a
coat of bronze armor that weighed about one
hundred twenty-five pounds. 6He wore bronze
protectors on his legs, and he had a bronze
spear on his back. 7The wooden part of his
larger spear was like a weaver's rod, and its
blade weighed about fifteen pounds. The officer
who carried his shield walked in front of him.
8Goliath stood and shouted to the Israelite
soldiers, "Why have you taken positions for
battle? I am a Philistine, and you are Saul's servants! Choose a man and send him to fight me.
9If he can fight and kill me, we will be your
servants. But if I can kill him, you will be our
servants." 10Then he said, "Today I stand and
dare the army of Israel! Send one of your men
to fight me!" 11When Saul and the Israelites
heard the Philistine's words, they were very
scared.
12Now David was the son of Jesse, an Eph-
rathite from Bethlehem in Judah. Jesse had
eight sons. In Saul's time Jesse was an old man.
13His three oldest sons followed Saul to the
war. The first son was Eliab, the second was
Abinadab, and the third was Shammah. 14Da-
vid was the youngest. Jesse's three oldest sons
followed Saul, 15but David went back and
forth from Saul to Bethlehem, where he took
care of his father's sheep.
16For forty days the Philistine came out
every morning and evening and stood before
the Israelite army.
17Jesse said to his son David, "Take this half

bushel of cooked grain and ten loaves of bread
to your brothers in the camp. [18]Also take ten
pieces of cheese to the commander and to your
brothers. See how your brothers are and bring
back some proof to show me that they are all
right. [19]Your brothers are with Saul and the
army in the Valley of Elah, fighting against the
Philistines."

[20]Early in the morning David left the sheep
with another shepherd. He took the food and
left as Jesse had told him. When David arrived
at the camp, the army was going out to their
battle positions, shouting their war cry. [21]The
Israelites and Philistines were lining up their
men to face each other in battle.

[22]David left the food with the man who
kept the supplies and ran to the battle line to
talk to his brothers. [23]While he was talking
with them, Goliath, the Philistine champion
from Gath, came out. He shouted things
against Israel as usual, and David heard him.
[24]When the Israelites saw Goliath, they were
very much afraid and ran away.

[25]They said, "Look at this man! He keeps
coming out to challenge Israel. The king will
give much money to whoever kills him. He
will also let whoever kills him marry his
daughter. And his father's family will not have
to pay taxes in Israel."

[26]David asked the men who stood near him,
"What will be done to reward the man who
kills this Philistine and takes away the shame
from Israel? Who does this uncircumcised Philistine think he is? Does he think he can speak
against the armies of the living God?"

[27]The Israelites told David what would be
done for the man who would kill Goliath.

[28]When David's oldest brother Eliab heard
David talking with the soldiers, he was angry
with David. He asked David, "Why did you
come here? Who's taking care of those few
sheep of yours in the desert? I know you are
proud and wicked at heart. You came down
here just to watch the battle."

[29]David asked, "Now what have I done
wrong? Can't I even talk?" [30]When he turned to
other people and asked the same questions,
they gave him the same answer as before. [31]Yet
what David said was told to Saul, and he sent
for David.

[32]David said to Saul, "Don't let anyone be
discouraged. I, your servant, will go and fight
this Philistine!"

[33]Saul answered, "You can't go out against
this Philistine and fight him. You're only a boy.
Goliath has been a warrior since he was a
young man."

[34]But David said to Saul, "I, your servant,
have been keeping my father's sheep. When a
lion or bear came and took a sheep from the
flock, [35]I would chase it. I would attack it and
save the sheep from its mouth. When it attacked me, I caught it by its fur and hit it and
killed it. [36]I, your servant, have killed both a
lion and a bear! This uncircumcised Philistine
will be like them, because he has spoken
against the armies of the living God. [37]The
LORD who saved me from a lion and a bear
will save me from this Philistine."

Saul said to David, "Go, and
may the LORD be with you."
[38]Saul put his own clothes on
David. He put a bronze helmet on his head and dressed
him in armor. [39]David put on
Saul's sword and tried to walk
around, but he was not used to
all the armor Saul had put on him.

TRIALS
Where can we find help in our trials? (17:37)

He said to Saul, "I can't go in this, because
I'm not used to it." Then David took it all off.
[40]He took his stick in his hand and chose five
smooth stones from a stream. He put them in
his shepherd's bag and grabbed his sling. Then
he went to meet the Philistine.

[41]At the same time, the Philistine was coming closer to David. The man who held his
shield walked in front of him. [42]When Goliath
looked at David and saw that he was only a
boy, tanned and handsome, he looked down
on David with disgust. [43]He said, "Do you
think I am a dog, that you come at me with a
stick?" He used his gods' names to curse David.
[44]He said to David, "Come here. I'll feed your
body to the birds of the air and the wild animals!"

[45]But David said to him, "You come to me
using a sword and two spears. But I come to

WHAT'S IT MEAN?

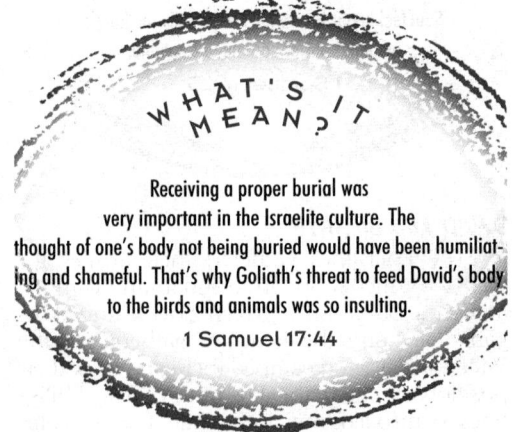

Receiving a proper burial was very important in the Israelite culture. The thought of one's body not being buried would have been humiliating and shameful. That's why Goliath's threat to feed David's body to the birds and animals was so insulting.

1 Samuel 17:44

you in the name of the LORD All-Powerful, the God of the armies of Israel! You have spoken against him. 46Today the LORD will hand you over to me, and I'll kill you and cut off your head. Today I'll feed the bodies of the Philistine soldiers to the birds of the air and the wild animals. Then all the world will know there is a God in Israel! 47Everyone gathered here will know the LORD does not need swords or spears to save people. The battle belongs to him, and he will hand you over to us."

48As Goliath came near to attack him, David ran quickly to meet him. 49He took a stone from his bag, put it into his sling, and slung it. The stone hit the Philistine and went deep into his forehead, and Goliath fell facedown on the ground.

WHAT'S IT MEAN?

A sling was a long-range weapon with a simple design: a pouch attached to long leather straps. The pouch held a rock, anywhere from the size of a pebble to the size of a baseball. When the straps were whirled around and released by an experienced warrior, the rock left the sling at an incredible speed. It took years and years of experience for a person to learn to sling rocks with any kind of accuracy. That's why David's victory against Goliath was so remarkable. David was a very young man.

1 Samuel 17:49

50So David defeated the Philistine with only a sling and a stone. He hit him and killed him. He did not even have a sword in his hand. 51Then David ran and stood beside him. He took Goliath's sword out of its holder and killed him by cutting off his head.

When the Philistines saw that their champion was dead, they turned and ran. 52The men of Israel and Judah shouted and chased the Philistines all the way to the entrance of the city of Gath and to the gates of Ekron.

The Philistines' bodies lay on the Shaaraim road as far as Gath and Ekron. 53The Israelites returned after chasing the Philistines and robbed their camp. 54David took Goliath's head to Jerusalem and put Goliath's weapons in his own tent.

55When Saul saw David go out to meet Goliath, Saul asked Abner, commander of the army, "Abner, who is that young man's father?"

Abner answered, "As surely as you live, my king, I don't know."

56The king said, "Find out whose son he is."

57When David came back from killing Goliath, Abner brought him to Saul. David was still holding Goliath's head.

58Saul asked him, "Young man, who is your father?"

David answered, "I am the son of your servant Jesse of Bethlehem."

SAUL FEARS DAVID

18

1When David finished talking with Saul, Jonathan felt very close to David. He loved David as much as he loved himself. 2Saul kept David with him from that day on and did not let him go home to his father's house. 3Jonathan made an agreement with David, because he loved David as much as himself. 4He took off his coat and gave it to David, along with his armor, including his sword, bow, and belt.

5Saul sent David to fight in different battles, and David was very successful. Then Saul put David over the soldiers, which pleased Saul's officers and all the other people.

6After David had killed the Philistine, he and the men returned home. Women came out from all the towns of Israel to meet King Saul. They sang songs of joy, danced, and played tambourines and stringed instruments. 7As they played, they sang,

"Saul has killed thousands of his enemies,
but David has killed tens of thousands."

WHAT'S IT MEAN?

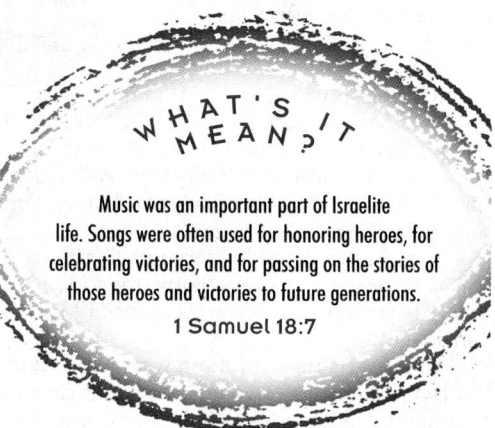

Music was an important part of Israelite life. Songs were often used for honoring heroes, for celebrating victories, and for passing on the stories of those heroes and victories to future generations.

1 Samuel 18:7

8The women's song upset Saul, and he became very angry. He thought, "The women say David has killed tens of thousands, but they say I have killed only thousands. The only thing left for him to have is the kingdom!" 9So Saul watched David closely from then on, because he was jealous.

10 The next day an evil spirit from God rushed upon Saul, and he prophesied in his house. David was playing the harp as he usually did, but Saul had a spear in his hand. 11 He threw the spear, thinking, "I'll pin David to the wall." But David escaped from him twice.

12 The LORD was with David but had left Saul. So Saul was afraid of David. 13 He sent David away and made him commander of a thousand soldiers. So David led them in battle. 14 He had great success in everything he did because the LORD was with him. 15 When Saul saw that David was very successful, he feared David even more. 16 But all the people of Israel and Judah loved David because he led them well in battle.

WHAT'S IT MEAN?

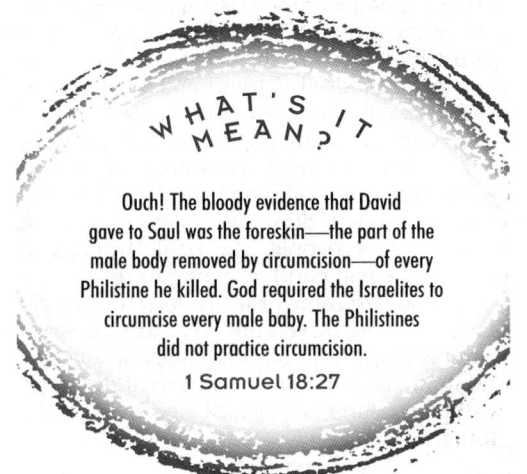

Ouch! The bloody evidence that David gave to Saul was the foreskin—the part of the male body removed by circumcision—of every Philistine he killed. God required the Israelites to circumcise every male baby. The Philistines did not practice circumcision.

1 Samuel 18:27

SAUL'S DAUGHTER MARRIES DAVID

17 Saul said to David, "Here is my older daughter Merab. I will let you marry her. All I ask is that you remain brave and fight the LORD's battles." Saul thought, "I won't have to kill David. The Philistines will do that."

18 But David answered Saul, saying, "Who am I? My family is not important enough for me to become the king's son-in-law." 19 So, when the time came for Saul's daughter Merab to marry David, Saul gave her instead to Adriel of Meholah.

20 Now Saul's other daughter, Michal, loved David. When they told Saul, he was pleased. 21 He thought, "I will let her marry David. Then she will be a trap for him, and the Philistines will defeat him." So Saul said to David a second time, "You may become my son-in-law."

22 And Saul ordered his servants to talk with David in private and say, "Look, the king likes you. His servants love you. You should be his son-in-law."

23 Saul's servants said these words to David, but David answered, "Do you think it is easy to become the king's son-in-law? I am poor and unimportant."

24 When Saul's servants told him what David had said, 25 Saul said, "Tell David, 'The king doesn't want money for the bride. All he wants is a hundred Philistine foreskins to get even with his enemies.' " Saul planned to let the Philistines kill David.

26 When Saul's servants told this to David, he was pleased to become the king's son-in-law. 27 So he and his men went out and killed two hundred Philistines. David brought all their foreskins to Saul so he could be the king's son-in-law. Then Saul gave him his daughter Michal for his wife. 28 Saul saw that the LORD was with David and that his daughter Michal loved David. 29 So he grew even more afraid of David, and he was David's enemy all his life.

30 The Philistine commanders continued to go out to fight the Israelites, but every time, David was more skillful than Saul's officers. So he became famous.

"Saul saw that the LORD was with David and that his daughter Michal loved David. So he grew even more afraid of David, and he was David's enemy all his life."
(1 Samuel 18:28–29)

SAUL TRIES TO KILL DAVID

19

1 Saul told his son Jonathan and all his servants to kill David, but Jonathan liked David very much. 2 So he warned David, "My father Saul is looking for a chance to kill you. Watch out in the morning. Hide in a secret place. 3 I will go out and stand with my father in the field where you are hiding, and I'll talk to him about you. Then I'll let you know what I find out."

4 When Jonathan talked to Saul his father, he said good things about David. Jonathan said, "The king should do no wrong to your servant David since he has done nothing wrong to you. What he has done has helped you greatly. 5 David risked his life when he killed Goliath

FRIENDSHIP
What's an example of good friendship? (19:1–7)

the Philistine, and the LORD won a great victory for all Israel. You saw it and were happy.
Why would you do wrong against David? He's
innocent. There's no reason to kill him!"
6Saul listened to Jonathan and then made
this promise: "As surely as the LORD lives, David won't be put to death."
7So Jonathan called to David and told him
everything that had been said. He brought David to Saul, and David was with Saul as before.
8When war broke out again, David went
out to fight the Philistines. He defeated them,
and they ran away from him.
9But once again an evil spirit from the LORD
rushed upon Saul as he was sitting in his
house with his spear in his hand. David was
playing the harp. 10Saul tried to pin David to
the wall with his spear, but David jumped out
of the way. So Saul's spear went into the wall,
and David ran away that night.
11Saul sent messengers to David's house to
watch it and to kill him in the morning. But
Michal, David's wife, warned him, saying, "Tonight you must run for your life. If you don't,
you will be dead in the morning." 12So she let
David down out of a window, and he ran
away and escaped. 13Then Michal took an idol,
laid it on the bed, covered it with clothes, and
put goats' hair at its head.
14Saul sent messengers to take David prisoner, but Michal said, "He is sick."
15Saul sent them back to see David, saying,
"Bring him to me on his bed so I can kill him."
16When the messengers entered David's
house, they found just an idol on the bed with
goats' hair on its head.
17Saul said to Michal, "Why did you trick
me this way? You let my enemy go so he could
run away!"
Michal answered Saul, "David told me if I
did not help him escape, he would kill me."
18After David had escaped from Saul, he
went to Samuel at Ramah and told him everything Saul had done to him. Then David and
Samuel went to Naioth and stayed there. 19Saul
heard that David was in Naioth at Ramah. 20So
he sent messengers to capture him. But they
met a group of prophets prophesying, with
Samuel standing there leading them. So the
Spirit of God entered Saul's men, and they also
prophesied.
21When Saul heard the news, he sent more
messengers, but they also prophesied. Then he
sent messengers a third time, but they also
prophesied. 22Finally, Saul himself went to Ramah, to the well at Secu. He asked, "Where are
Samuel and David?"
The people answered, "In Naioth at Ramah."
23When Saul went to Naioth at Ramah, the
Spirit of God also rushed upon him. And he
walked on, prophesying until he came to Naioth at Ramah. 24He took off his robes and
prophesied in front of Samuel. He lay that way
all day and all night. That is why people ask,
"Is even Saul one of the prophets?"

JONATHAN HELPS DAVID

20
1Then David ran away from Naioth in
Ramah. He went to Jonathan and asked, "What
have I done? What is my crime? How did I
sin against your father? Why is he trying to
kill me?"
2Jonathan answered, "No! You won't die!
See, my father doesn't do anything great or
small without first telling me. Why would he
keep this from me? It's not true!"
3But David took an oath, saying, "Your father knows very well that you like me. He says
to himself, 'Jonathan must not know about it,
or he will tell David.' As surely as the LORD lives
and as you live, I am only a step away from
death!"
4Jonathan said to David, "I'll do anything
you want me to do."
5So David said, "Look, tomorrow is the New
Moon festival. I am supposed to eat with the
king, but let me hide in the field until the third
evening. 6If your father notices I am gone, tell
him, 'David begged me to let him go to his
hometown of Bethlehem. Every year at this
time his family group offers a sacrifice.' 7If your
father says, 'Fine,' I am safe. But if he becomes
angry, you will know that he wants to hurt me.
8Jonathan, be loyal to me, your servant. You
have made an agreement with me before the
LORD. If I am guilty, you may kill me yourself!
Why hand me over to your father?"
9Jonathan answered, "No, never! If I learn
that my father plans to hurt you, I will warn
you!"
10David asked, "Who will let me know if
your father answers you unkindly?"
11Then Jonathan said, "Come, let's go out
into the field." So the two of them went out into
the field.
12Jonathan said to David, "I promise this
before the LORD, the God of Israel: At this same
time the day after tomorrow, I will find out
how my father feels. If he feels good toward
you, I will send word to you and let you know.
13But if my father plans to hurt you, I will let
you know and send you away safely. May the
LORD punish me terribly if I don't do this. And
may the LORD be with you as he has been with

my father. [14]But show me the kindness of the LORD as long as I live so that I may not die. [15]You must never stop showing your kindness to my family, even when the LORD has destroyed all your enemies from the earth."

[16]So Jonathan made an agreement with David. He said, "May the LORD hold David's enemies responsible." [17]And Jonathan asked David to repeat his promise of love for him, because he loved David as much as he loved himself.

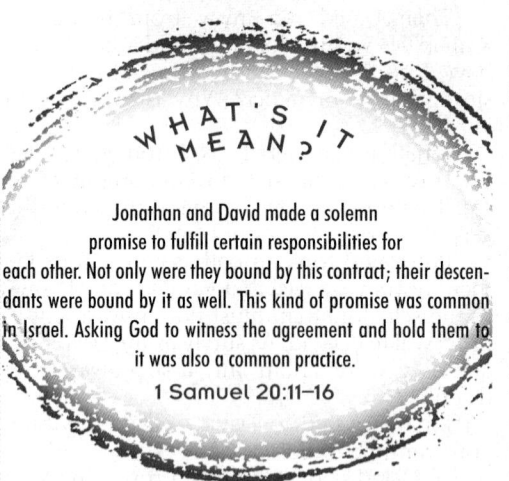

WHAT'S IT MEAN?

Jonathan and David made a solemn promise to fulfill certain responsibilities for each other. Not only were they bound by this contract; their descendants were bound by it as well. This kind of promise was common in Israel. Asking God to witness the agreement and hold them to it was also a common practice.

1 Samuel 20:11–16

[18]Jonathan said to David, "Tomorrow is the New Moon festival. Your seat will be empty, so my father will miss you. [19]On the third day go to the place where you hid when this trouble began. Wait by the rock Ezel. [20]On the third day I will shoot three arrows to the side of the rock as if I am shooting at a target. [21]Then I will send a boy to find the arrows. If I say to him, 'The arrows are near you; bring them here,' you may come out of hiding. You are safe. As the LORD lives, there is no danger. [22]But if I say to the boy, 'Look, the arrows are beyond you,' you must go, because the LORD is sending you away. [23]Remember what we talked about. The LORD is a witness between you and me forever."

[24]So David hid in the field. When the New Moon festival came, the king sat down to eat. [25]He sat where he always sat, near the wall. Jonathan sat across from him, and Abner sat next to Saul, but David's place was empty. [26]That day Saul said nothing. He thought, "Maybe something has happened to David so that he is unclean." [27]But the next day was the second day of the month, and David's place was still empty. So Saul said to Jonathan, "Why hasn't the son of Jesse come to the feast yesterday or today?"

[28]Jonathan answered, "David begged me to

WHAT'S IT MEAN?

Not just anyone could participate in a religious sacrifice or feast. People had to meet certain requirements; they had to be ceremonially "clean." Touching a dead body, for example, made a person "unclean." That person was not allowed to join in religious ceremonies until he had followed certain procedures to become clean again.

1 Samuel 20:24–26

let him go to Bethlehem. [29]He said, 'Let me go, because our family has a sacrifice in the town, and my brother has ordered me to be there. Now if I am your friend, please let me go to see my brothers.' That is why he has not come to the king's table."

[30]Then Saul became very angry with Jonathan. He said, "You son of a wicked, worthless woman! I know you are on the side of David son of Jesse! You bring shame on yourself and on your mother who gave birth to you. [31]As long as Jesse's son lives, you will never be king or have a kingdom. Now send for David and bring him to me. He must die!"

[32]Jonathan asked his father, "Why should David be killed? What wrong has he done?" [33]Then Saul threw his spear at Jonathan, trying to kill him. So Jonathan knew that his father really wanted to kill David. [34]Jonathan was very angry and left the table. That second day of the month he refused to eat. He was ashamed of his father and upset over David.

[35]The next morning Jonathan went out to the field to meet David as they had agreed. He had a young boy with him. [36]Jonathan said to the boy, "Run and find the arrows I shoot." When he ran, Jonathan shot an arrow beyond him. [37]The boy ran to the place where Jonathan's arrow fell, but Jonathan called, "The arrow is beyond you!" [38]Then he shouted, "Hurry! Go quickly! Don't stop!" The boy picked up the arrow and brought it back to his master. [39](The boy knew nothing about what this meant; only Jonathan and David knew.) [40]Then Jonathan gave his weapons to the boy and told him, "Go back to town."

[41]When the boy left, David came out from the south side of the rock. He bowed facedown

on the ground before Jonathan three times.
Then David and Jonathan kissed each other
and cried together, but David cried the most.
42Jonathan said to David, "Go in peace. We
have promised by the LORD that we will be
friends. We said, 'The LORD will be a witness
between you and me, and between our descendants always.' " Then David left, and Jonathan went back to town.

WHAT'S IT MEAN?

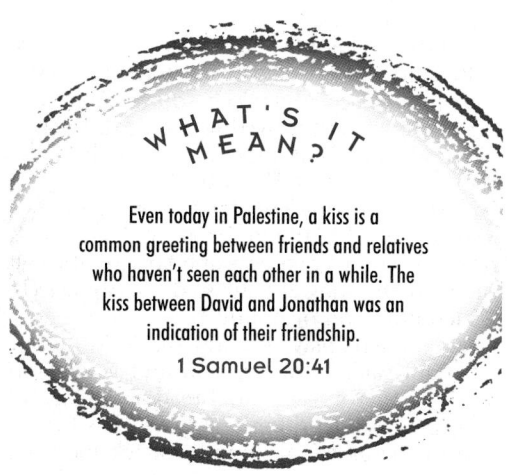

Even today in Palestine, a kiss is a common greeting between friends and relatives who haven't seen each other in a while. The kiss between David and Jonathan was an indication of their friendship.

1 Samuel 20:41

DAVID GOES TO SEE AHIMELECH

21 1David went to Nob to see Ahimelech the
priest. Ahimelech shook with fear when he
saw David, and he asked, "Why are you alone?
Why is no one with you?"
2David answered him, "The king gave me a
special order. He told me, 'No one must know
what I am sending you to do or what I told
you to do.' I told my men where to meet me.
3Now, what food do you have with you? Give
me five loaves of bread or anything you find."
4The priest said to David, "I don't have any
plain bread here, but I do have some holy
bread.[n] You may eat it if your men have kept
themselves from women."
5David answered, "No women have been
near us for days. My men always keep themselves holy, even when we do ordinary work.
And this is especially true when the work is
holy."
6So the priest gave David the holy bread
from the presence of God because there was
no other. Each day the holy bread was replaced with hot bread.
7One of Saul's servants happened to be
there that day. He had been held there before

WHAT'S IT MEAN?

The bread that was used for worship was replaced with a fresh loaf every seven days. Usually only priests were allowed to eat the old bread. Ahimelech wanted to make sure that David and his men were "clean" before he gave them the holy bread.

1 Samuel 21:1–6

the LORD. He was Doeg the Edomite, the chief
of Saul's shepherds.
8David asked Ahimelech, "Do you have a
spear or sword here? The king's business was
very important, so I left without my sword or
any other weapon."
9The priest answered, "The sword of Goliath
the Philistine, the one you killed in the Valley
of Elah, is here. It is wrapped in a cloth behind
the holy vest. If you want it, you may take it.
There's no other sword here but that one."
David said, "There is no other sword like it.
Give it to me."

DAVID GOES TO GATH

10That day David ran away from Saul and
went to Achish king of Gath. 11But the servants
of Achish said to him, "This is David, the king
of the Israelites. He's the man they dance and
sing about, saying:

WHAT'S IT MEAN?

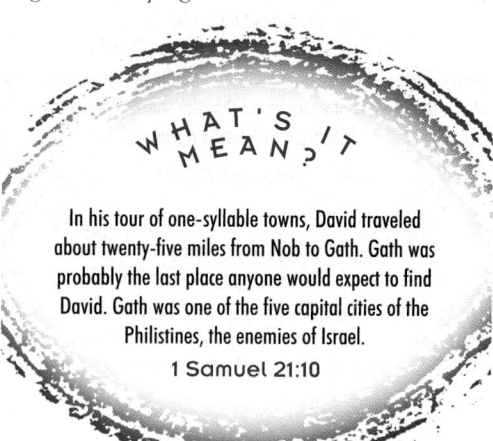

In his tour of one-syllable towns, David traveled about twenty-five miles from Nob to Gath. Gath was probably the last place anyone would expect to find David. Gath was one of the five capital cities of the Philistines, the enemies of Israel.

1 Samuel 21:10

21:4 holy bread This was the bread that showed the people were in the presence of God. Normally only the priests ate this bread.

'Saul has killed thousands of his enemies,
but David has killed tens of thousands.' "
12David paid attention to these words and
was very much afraid of Achish king of Gath.
13So he pretended to be crazy in front of
Achish and his servants. While he was with
them, he acted like a madman and clawed on
the doors of the gate and let spit run down his
beard.
14Achish said to his servants, "Look at the
man! He's crazy! Why do you bring him to
me? 15I have enough madmen. I don't need
you to bring him here to act like this in front of
me! Don't let him in my house!"

DAVID AT ADULLAM AND MIZPAH

22

1David left Gath and escaped to the cave of
Adullam. When his brothers and other relatives heard that he was there, they went to see
him. 2Everyone who was in trouble, or who
owed money, or who was unsatisfied gathered
around David, and he became their leader.
About four hundred men were with him.
3From there David went to Mizpah in
Moab and spoke to the king of Moab. He said,
"Please let my father and mother come and
stay with you until I learn what God is going
to do for me." 4So he left them with the king of
Moab, and they stayed with him as long as
David was hiding in the stronghold.

WHAT'S IT MEAN?

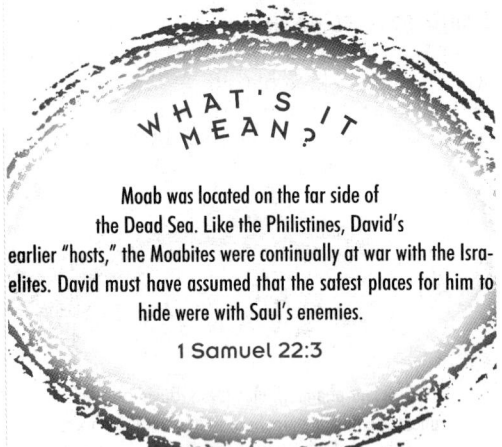

Moab was located on the far side of the Dead Sea. Like the Philistines, David's earlier "hosts," the Moabites were continually at war with the Israelites. David must have assumed that the safest places for him to hide were with Saul's enemies.

1 Samuel 22:3

5But the prophet Gad said to David, "Don't
stay in the stronghold. Go to the land of Judah." So David left and went to the forest of
Hereth.

SAUL DESTROYS AHIMELECH'S FAMILY

6Saul heard that David and his men had
been seen. Saul was sitting under the tamarisk
tree on the hill at Gibeah, and all his officers
were standing around him. He had a spear in
his hand. 7Saul said to them, "Listen, men of
Benjamin! Do you think the son of Jesse will
give all of you fields and vineyards? Will David
make you commanders over thousands of
men or hundreds of men? 8You have all made
plans against me! No one tells me when my
son makes an agreement with the son of Jesse!
No one cares about me! No one tells me when
my son has encouraged my servant to ambush
me this very day!"
9Doeg the Edomite, who was standing there
with Saul's officers, said, "I saw the son of Jesse.
He came to see Ahimelech son of Ahitub at
Nob. 10Ahimelech prayed to the LORD for David and gave him food and gave him the
sword of Goliath the Philistine."
11Then the king sent for the priest Ahimelech son of Ahitub and for all of Ahimelech's
relatives who were priests at Nob. And they all
came to the king. 12Saul said to Ahimelech,
"Listen now, son of Ahitub."
Ahimelech answered, "Yes, master."
13Saul said, "Why are you and Jesse's son
against me? You gave him bread and a sword!
You prayed to God for him. David has turned
against me and is waiting to attack me even
now!"
14Ahimelech answered, "You have no other
servant who is as loyal as David, your own
son-in-law and captain of your bodyguards.
Everyone in your house respects him. 15That
was not the first time I prayed to God for David. Don't blame me or any of my relatives. I,
your servant, know nothing about what is going on."
16But the king said, "Ahimelech, you and all
your relatives must die!" 17Then he told the
guards at his side, "Go and kill the priests of
the LORD, because they are on David's side.
They knew he was running away, but they
didn't tell me."
But the king's officers refused to kill the
priests of the LORD.
18Then the king ordered Doeg, "Go and kill
the priests." So Doeg the Edomite went and
killed the priests. That day he killed eighty-five
men who wore the linen holy vest. 19He also
killed the people of Nob, the city of the priests.
With the sword he killed men, women, children, babies, cattle, donkeys, and sheep.
20But Abiathar, a son of Ahimelech, who
was the son of Ahitub, escaped. He ran away
and joined David. 21He told David that Saul
had killed the LORD's priests. 22Then David told
him, "Doeg the Edomite was there at Nob that
day. I knew he would surely tell Saul. So I am

responsible for the death of all your father's
family. 23 Stay with me. Don't be afraid. The
man who wants to kill you also wants to kill
me. You will be safe with me."

DAVID SAVES THE PEOPLE OF KEILAH

23 1 Someone told David, "Look, the Philistines
are fighting against Keilah and stealing grain
from the threshing floors."
2 David asked the LORD, "Should I go and
fight these Philistines?"
The LORD answered him, "Go. Attack them,
and save Keilah."
3 But David's men said to him, "We're afraid
here in Judah. We will be more afraid if we go
to Keilah where the Philistine army is."
4 David again asked the LORD, and the LORD
answered, "Go down to Keilah. I will help you
defeat the Philistines." 5 So David and his men
went to Keilah and fought the Philistines and
took their cattle. David killed many Philistines
and saved the people of Keilah. 6 (Now Abiathar
son of Ahimelech had brought the holy vest
with him when he came to David at Keilah.)

SAUL CHASES DAVID

7 Someone told Saul that David was now at
Keilah. Saul said, "God has handed David over
to me! He has trapped himself, because he has
entered a town with gates and bars." 8 Saul
called all his army together for battle, and they
prepared to go down to Keilah to attack David
and his men.
9 David learned Saul was making evil plans
against him. So he said to Abiathar the priest,
"Bring the holy vest." 10 David
prayed, "LORD, God of Israel,
I have heard that Saul plans
to come to Keilah to de-
stroy the town because
of me. 11 Will the leaders
of Keilah hand me over
to Saul? Will Saul come
down to Keilah, as I
heard? LORD, God of Israel,
tell me, your servant!"
The LORD answered, "Saul
will come down."
12 Again David asked, "Will the leaders
of Keilah hand me and my men over to Saul?"
The LORD answered, "They will."
13 So David and his six hundred men left
Keilah and kept moving from place to place.
When Saul found out that David had escaped
from Keilah, he did not go there.
14 David stayed in the desert hideouts and in
the hills of the Desert of Ziph. Every day Saul
looked for David, but the LORD did not surrender David to him.

WHAT'S IT MEAN?

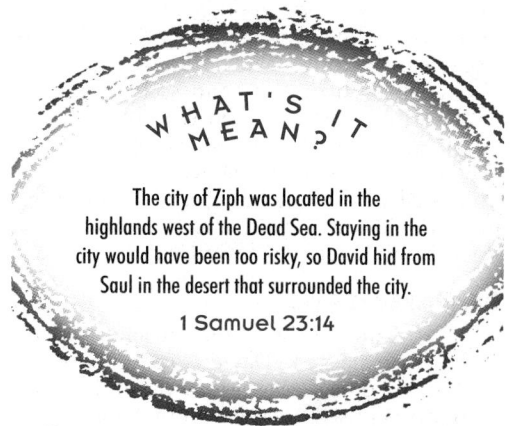

The city of Ziph was located in the highlands west of the Dead Sea. Staying in the city would have been too risky, so David hid from Saul in the desert that surrounded the city.

1 Samuel 23:14

15 While David was at Horesh in the Desert
of Ziph, he learned that Saul was coming to kill
him. 16 But Saul's son Jonathan went to David
at Horesh and strengthened his faith in God.
17 Jonathan told him, "Don't be afraid, because
my father won't touch you. You will be king of
Israel, and I will be second to you. Even my
father Saul knows this." 18 The two of them
made an agreement before the LORD. Then Jonathan went home, but David stayed at Horesh.
19 The people from Ziph went to Saul at Gibeah and told him, "David is hiding in our land.
He's at the hideouts of Horesh, on the hill of
Hakilah, south of Jeshimon. 20 Now, our king,
come down anytime you want. It's our duty to
hand David over to you."
21 Saul answered, "The
LORD bless you for helping
me. 22 Go and learn more
about him. Find out where
he is staying and who has
seen him there. I have
heard that he is clever.
23 Find all the hiding
places he uses, and come
back and tell me every-
thing. Then I'll go with you.
If David is in the area, I will
track him down among all the
families in Judah."
24 So they went back to Ziph ahead of Saul.
Now David and his men were in the Desert of
Maon[n] in the desert area south of Jeshimon.
25 Saul and his men went to look for David, but
David heard about it and went down to a rock

"David stayed in the desert hideouts and in the hills of the Desert of Ziph. Every day Saul looked for David, but the LORD did not surrender David to him." (1 Samuel 23:14)

23:24 Maon Some early Greek copies say "Maon." The Hebrew copies say "Paran."

and stayed in the Desert of Maon. When Saul heard that, he followed David into the Desert of Maon.

26 Saul was going along one side of the mountain, and David and his men were on the other side. They were hurrying to get away from Saul, because Saul and his men were closing in on them. 27 But a messenger came to Saul, saying, "Come quickly! The Philistines are attacking our land!" 28 So Saul stopped chasing David and went to challenge the Philistines. That is why people call this place Rock of Parting. 29 David also left the Desert of Maon and stayed in the hideouts of En Gedi.

WHAT'S IT MEAN?

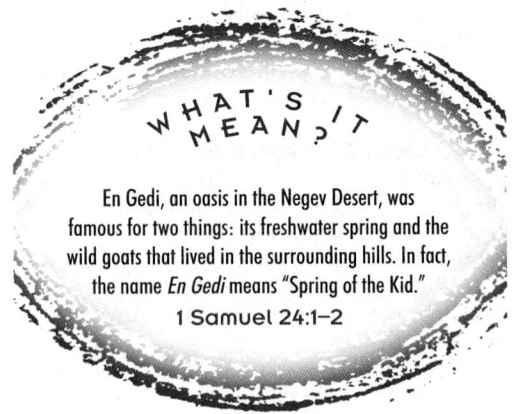

En Gedi, an oasis in the Negev Desert, was famous for two things: its freshwater spring and the wild goats that lived in the surrounding hills. In fact, the name *En Gedi* means "Spring of the Kid."

1 Samuel 24:1–2

DAVID SHAMES SAUL

24 1 After Saul returned from chasing the Philistines, he was told, "David is in the Desert of En Gedi." 2 So he took three thousand chosen men from all Israel and began looking for David and his men near the Rocks of the Wild Goats.

3 Saul came to the sheep pens beside the road. A cave was there, and he went in to relieve himself. Now David and his men were hiding far back in the cave. 4 The men said to David, "Today is the day the LORD spoke of when he said, 'I will give your enemy over to you. Do anything you want with him.' "

Then David crept up to Saul and quietly cut off a corner of Saul's robe. 5 Later David felt guilty because he had cut off a corner of Saul's robe. 6 He said to his men, "May the LORD keep me from doing such a thing to my master! Saul is the LORD's appointed king. I should not do anything against him, because he is the LORD's appointed king!" 7 David used these words to stop his men; he did not let them attack Saul. Then Saul left the cave and went his way.

LEADERSHIP
Why should we respect leaders? (24:1–6)

8 When David came out of the cave, he shouted to Saul, "My master and king!" Saul looked back, and David bowed facedown on the ground. 9 He said to Saul, "Why do you listen when people say, 'David wants to harm you'? 10 You have seen something with your own eyes today. The LORD put you in my power in the cave. They said I should kill you, but I was merciful. I said, 'I won't harm my master, because he is the LORD's appointed king.' 11 My father, look at this piece of your robe in my hand! I cut off the corner of your robe, but I didn't kill you. Now understand and know I am not planning any evil against you. I did nothing wrong to you, but you are hunting me to kill me. 12 May the LORD judge between us, and may he punish you for the wrong you have done to me! But I am not against you. 13 There is an old saying: 'Evil things come from evil people.' But I am not against you. 14 Whom is the king of Israel coming out against? Whom are you chasing? It's as if you are chasing a dead dog or a flea. 15 May the LORD be our judge and decide between you and me. May he support me and show that I am right. May he save me from you!"

REVENGE
Who is in charge of vengeance? (24:12)

16 When David finished saying these words, Saul asked, "Is that your voice, David my son?" And he cried loudly. 17 He said, "You are a better man than I am. You have been good to me, but I have done wrong to you. 18 You told me what good things you did. The LORD handed me over to you, but you did not kill me. 19 If a person finds his enemy, he doesn't just send him on his way, does he? May the LORD reward you because you were good to me today. 20 I know you will surely be king, and you will rule the kingdom of Israel. 21 Now swear to me by the LORD that you will not kill my descendants and that you won't wipe out my name from my father's family."

22 So David made the promise to Saul. Then Saul went back home, and David and his men went up to their hideout.

NABAL INSULTS DAVID

25 1 Now Samuel died, and all the Israelites met and had a time of sadness for him. Then they buried him at his home in Ramah.

David moved to the Desert of Maon.[n] 2 A

25:1 Maon Some early Greek copies say "Maon." The Hebrew copies say "Paran."

man in Maon who had land at Carmel was
very rich. He had three thousand sheep and a
thousand goats. He was cutting the wool off
his sheep at Carmel. 3His name was Nabal, and
he was a descendant of Caleb. His wife was
named Abigail. She was wise and beautiful, but
Nabal was cruel and mean.

WHAT'S IT MEAN?

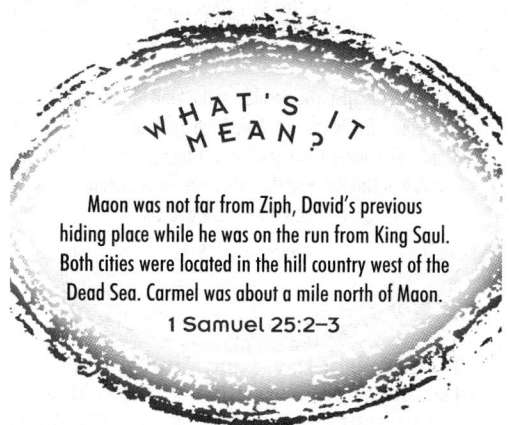

Maon was not far from Ziph, David's previous hiding place while he was on the run from King Saul. Both cities were located in the hill country west of the Dead Sea. Carmel was about a mile north of Maon.

1 Samuel 25:2–3

4While David was in the desert, he heard
that Nabal was cutting the wool from his
sheep. 5So he sent ten young men and told
them, "Go to Nabal at Carmel, and greet him
for me. 6Say to Nabal, 'May you and your family and all who belong to you have good
health! 7I have heard that you are cutting the
wool from your sheep. When your shepherds
were with us, we did not harm them. All the
time your shepherds were at Carmel, we stole
nothing from them. 8Ask your servants, and
they will tell you. We come at a happy time, so
be kind to my young men. Please give anything you can find for them and for your son
David.' "

9When David's men arrived, they gave the
message to Nabal, but Nabal insulted them.
10He answered them, "Who is David? Who is
this son of Jesse? Many slaves are running
away from their masters today! 11I have bread
and water, and I have meat that I killed for my
servants who cut the wool. But I won't give it
to men I don't know."

12David's men went back and told him all
Nabal had said. 13Then David said to them,
"Put on your swords!" So they put on their
swords, and David put on his also. About four
hundred men went with David, but two hundred men stayed with the supplies.

14One of Nabal's servants said to Abigail,
Nabal's wife, "David sent messengers from the
desert to greet our master, but Nabal insulted
them. 15These men were very good to us. They
did not harm us. They stole nothing from us
during all the time we were out in the field
with them. 16Night and day they protected us.
They were like a wall around us while we were
with them caring for the sheep. 17Now think
about it, and decide what you can do. Terrible
trouble is coming to our master and all his
family. Nabal is such a wicked man that no
one can even talk to him."

18Abigail hurried. She took two hundred
loaves of bread, two leather bags full of wine,
five cooked sheep, a bushel of cooked grain, a
hundred cakes of raisins, and two hundred
cakes of pressed figs and put all these on donkeys. 19Then she told her servants, "Go on. I'll
follow you." But she did not tell her husband.

20Abigail rode her donkey and came down
toward the mountain hideout. There she met
David and his men coming down toward her.

21David had just said, "It's been useless! I
watched over Nabal's property in the desert. I
made sure none of his sheep was missing. I did
good to him, but he has paid me back with
evil. 22May God punish my enemies even
more. I will not leave one of Nabal's men alive
until morning."

23When Abigail saw David, she quickly got
off her donkey and bowed facedown on the
ground before him. 24She fell at David's feet
and said, "My master, let the blame be on me!
Please let me talk to you. Listen to what I say.
25My master, don't pay attention to this worthless man Nabal. He is like his name. His name
means 'fool,' and he is truly a fool. But I, your
servant, didn't see the men you sent. 26The
LORD has kept you from killing and punishing
anyone. As surely as the LORD lives and as
surely as you live, may your enemies become
like Nabal! 27I have brought a gift to you for
the men who follow you. 28Please forgive my
wrong. The LORD will certainly let your family
have many kings, because you fight his battles.
As long as you live, may you do nothing bad.
29Someone might chase you to kill you, but the
LORD your God will keep you alive. He will
throw away your enemies' lives as he would
throw a stone from a sling. 30The LORD will
keep all his promises of good things for you.
He will make you leader over Israel. 31Then
you won't feel guilty or troubled because you
killed innocent people and punished them.
Please remember me when the LORD brings
you success."

32David answered Abigail, "Praise the LORD,
the God of Israel, who sent you to meet me.
33May you be blessed for your wisdom. You
have kept me from killing or punishing people
today. 34As surely as the LORD, the God of

Israel, lives, he has kept me from hurting you. If you hadn't come quickly to meet me, not one of Nabal's men would have lived until morning."

35 Then David accepted Abigail's gifts. He told her, "Go home in peace. I have heard your words, and I will do what you have asked."

NABAL'S DEATH

36 When Abigail went back to Nabal, he was in the house, eating like a king. He was very drunk and in a good mood. So she told him nothing until the next morning. 37 In the morning when he was not drunk, his wife told him everything. His heart stopped, and he became like stone. 38 About ten days later the LORD struck Nabal and he died.

39 When David heard that Nabal was dead, he said, "Praise the LORD! Nabal insulted me, but the LORD has supported me! He has kept me from doing wrong. The LORD has punished Nabal for his wrong."

Then David sent a message to Abigail, asking her to be his wife. 40 His servants went to Carmel and said to Abigail, "David sent us to take you so you can become his wife."

41 Abigail bowed facedown on the ground and said, "I am your servant. I'm ready to serve you and to wash the feet of my master's servants." 42 Abigail quickly got on a donkey and went with David's messengers, with her five maids following her. And she became David's wife.

43 David also had married Ahinoam of Jezreel. So they were both David's wives. 44 Saul's daughter Michal was also David's wife, but Saul had given her to Paltiel son of Laish, who was from Gallim.

DAVID SHAMES SAUL AGAIN

26 1 The people of Ziph went to Saul at Gibeah and said to him, "David is hiding on the hill of Hakilah opposite Jeshimon."

2 So Saul went down to the Desert of Ziph with three thousand chosen men of Israel to look for David there. 3 Saul made his camp beside the road on the hill of Hakilah opposite Jeshimon, but David stayed in the desert. When he heard Saul had followed him, 4 he sent out spies and learned for certain that Saul had come to Hakilah.

5 Then David went to the place where Saul had camped. He saw where Saul and Abner son of Ner, the commander of Saul's army, were sleeping. Saul was sleeping in the middle of the camp with all the army around him.

6 David asked Ahimelech the Hittite and Abishai son of Zeruiah, Joab's brother, "Who will go down into Saul's camp with me?"

Abishai answered, "I'll go with you."

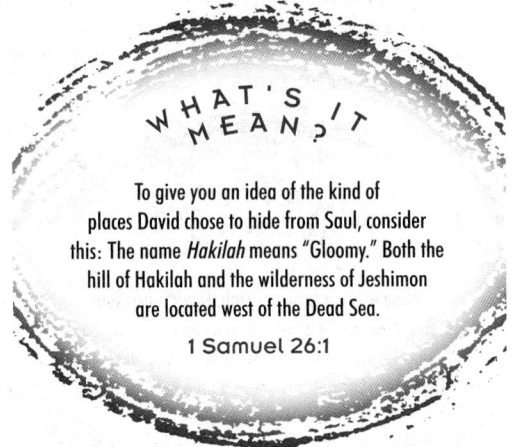

> **WHAT'S IT MEAN?**
>
> **To give you an idea of the kind of places David chose to hide from Saul, consider this: The name *Hakilah* means "Gloomy." Both the hill of Hakilah and the wilderness of Jeshimon are located west of the Dead Sea.**
>
> 1 Samuel 26:1

7 So that night David and Abishai went into Saul's camp. Saul was asleep in the middle of the camp with his spear stuck in the ground near his head. Abner and the army were sleeping around Saul. 8 Abishai said to David, "Today God has handed your enemy over to you. Let me pin Saul to the ground with my spear. I'll only have to do it once. I won't need to hit him twice."

9 But David said to Abishai, "Don't kill Saul! No one can harm the LORD's appointed king and still be innocent! 10 As surely as the LORD lives, the LORD himself will punish Saul. Maybe Saul will die naturally, or maybe he will go into battle and be killed. 11 But may the LORD keep me from harming his appointed king! Take the spear and water jug that are near Saul's head. Then let's go."

12 So David took the spear and water jug that were near Saul's head, and they left. No one saw them or knew about it or woke up, because the LORD had put them sound asleep.

13 David crossed over to the other side of the hill and stood on top of the mountain far from Saul's camp. They were a long way away from each other. 14 David shouted to the army and to Abner son of Ner, "Won't you answer me, Abner?"

Abner answered, "Who is calling for the king? Who are you?"

15 David said, "You're the greatest man in Israel. Isn't that true? Why didn't you guard your master the king? Someone came into your camp to kill your master the king! 16 You have not done well. As surely as the LORD lives, you and your men should die. You haven't guarded your master, the LORD's appointed

king. Look! Where are the king's spear and
water jug that were near his head?"
17Saul knew David's voice. He said, "Is that
your voice, David my son?"
David answered, "Yes, it is, my master and
king." 18David also said, "Why are you chasing
me, my master? What wrong have I done?
What evil am I guilty of? 19My master and
king, listen to me. If the LORD made you angry
with me, let him accept an
offering. But if people did it,
may the LORD curse them!
They have made me
leave the land the LORD
gave me. They have
told me, 'Go and serve
other gods.' 20Now
don't let me die far
away from the LORD's
presence. The king of Is-
rael has come out looking
for a flea! You're just hunting a bird in the mountains!"
21Then Saul said, "I have sinned.
Come back, David my son. Today you respected my life, so I will not try to hurt you. I
have been very stupid and foolish."

"The LORD rewards us for the things we do right and for our loyalty to him. The LORD handed you over to me today, but I wouldn't harm the LORD's appointed king." (1 Samuel 26:23)

WHAT'S IT MEAN?

Shiloh, the city where the Ark of the Agreement was kept, was considered the official worship site of the Israelites. Kicking someone out of Israel, then, prevented that person from officially worshiping God. Because worship was so important to the Israelites, depriving someone of the opportunity to worship was considered cruel punishment and was reserved for serious criminals.

1 Samuel 26:19

22David answered, "Here is your spear. Let
one of your young men come here and get it.
23The LORD rewards us for the things we do
right and for our loyalty to him. The LORD
handed you over to me today, but I wouldn't
harm the LORD's appointed king. 24As I respected your life today, may the LORD also respect my life and save me from all trouble."
25Then Saul said to David, "You are blessed,
my son David. You will do great things and
succeed."
So David went on his way, and Saul went
back home.

DAVID LIVES WITH THE PHILISTINES

27

1But David thought to himself, "Saul will
catch me someday. The best thing I can do is
escape to the land of the Philistines. Then he
will give up looking for me in Israel, and I can
get away from him."
2So David and his six
hundred men left Israel
and went to Achish son
of Maoch, king of Gath.
3David, his men, and
their families made their
home in Gath with
Achish. David had his
two wives with him—
Ahinoam of Jezreel and
Abigail of Carmel, the
widow of Nabal. 4When
Saul heard that David had
run away to Gath, he
stopped looking for him.
5Then David said to Achish, "If you are
pleased with me, give me a place in one of the
country towns where I can live. I don't need to
live in the royal city with you."
6That day Achish gave David the town of
Ziklag, and Ziklag has belonged to the kings of
Judah ever since. 7David lived in the Philistine
land a year and four months.
8David and his men raided the people of
Geshur, Girzi, and Amalek. (These people had
lived for a long time in the land that reached to
Shur and Egypt.) 9When David fought them, he
killed all the men and women and took their
sheep, cattle, donkeys, camels, and clothes.
Then he returned to Achish.

WHAT'S IT MEAN?

What's the biggest present you've ever received? David was given an entire city. Achish, the king of Gath, gave David the city of Ziklag in the south. David eventually used Ziklag as a military base for his attacks on the tribes of the desert nomads.

1 Samuel 27:6

10Achish would ask David, "Where did you go raiding today?" And David would tell him that he had gone to the southern part of Judah, or Jerahmeel, or to the land of the Kenites. 11David never brought a man or woman alive to Gath. He thought, "If we bring people alive, they may tell Achish, 'This is what David really did.' " David did this all the time he lived in the Philistine land. 12So Achish trusted David and said to himself, "David's own people, the Israelites, now hate him very much. He will serve me forever."

SAUL AND THE WITCH OF ENDOR

28 1Later, the Philistines gathered their armies to fight against Israel. Achish said to David, "You understand that you and your men must join my army."

2David answered, "You will see for yourself what I, your servant, can do!"

Achish said, "Fine, I'll make you my permanent bodyguard."

3Now Samuel was dead, and all the Israelites had shown their sadness for him. They had buried Samuel in his hometown of Ramah.

And Saul had forced out the mediums and fortune-tellers from the land.

OCCULT

Should we have anything to do with the occult? (28:3)

4The Philistines came together and made camp at Shunem. Saul gathered all the Israelites and made camp at Gilboa. 5When he saw the Philistine army, he was afraid, and his heart pounded with fear. 6He prayed to the LORD, but the LORD did not answer him through dreams, Urim, or prophets. 7Then Saul said to his servants, "Find me a woman who is a medium so I may go and ask her what will happen."

His servants answered, "There is a medium in Endor."

8Then Saul put on other clothes to disguise himself, and at night he and two of his men went to see the woman. Saul said to her, "Talk to a spirit for me. Bring up the person I name."

9But the woman said to him, "Surely you know what Saul has done. He has forced the mediums and fortune-tellers from the land. You are trying to trap me and get me killed."

10Saul made a promise to the woman in the name of the LORD. He said, "As surely as the LORD lives, you won't be punished for this."

11The woman asked, "Whom do you want me to bring up?"

He answered, "Bring up Samuel."

12When the woman saw Samuel, she screamed. She said, "Why have you tricked me? You are Saul!"

13The king said to the woman, "Don't be afraid! What do you see?"

The woman said, "I see a spirit coming up out of the ground."

14Saul asked, "What does he look like?"

The woman answered, "An old man wearing a coat is coming up."

Then Saul knew it was Samuel, and he bowed facedown on the ground.

15Samuel asked Saul, "Why have you disturbed me by bringing me up?"

Saul said, "I am greatly troubled. The Philistines are fighting against me, and God has left me. He won't answer me anymore, either by prophets or in dreams. That's why I called for you. Tell me what to do."

16Samuel said, "The LORD has left you and has become your enemy. So why do you call on me? 17He has done what he said he would do—the things he said through me. He has torn the kingdom out of your hands and given it to one of your neighbors, David. 18You did not obey the LORD; you did not show the Amalekites how angry he was with them. That's why he has done this to you today. 19The LORD will hand over both Israel and you to the Philistines. Tomorrow you and your sons will be with me. The LORD will hand over the army of Israel to the Philistines."

20Saul quickly fell flat on the ground and was afraid of what Samuel had said. He was also very weak because he had eaten nothing all that day and night.

21Then the woman came to Saul and saw that he was really frightened. She said, "Look, I, your servant, have obeyed you. I have risked my life and done what you told me to do. 22Now please listen to me. Let me give you

WHAT'S IT MEAN?

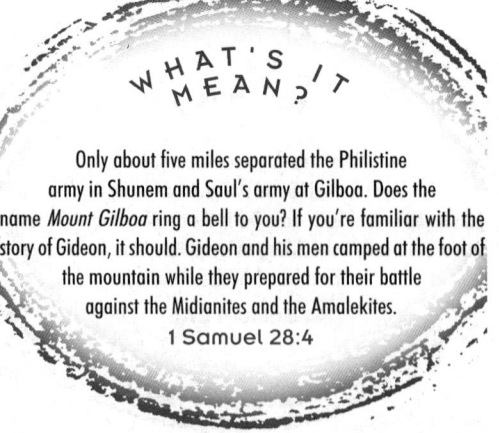

Only about five miles separated the Philistine army in Shunem and Saul's army at Gilboa. Does the name *Mount Gilboa* ring a bell to you? If you're familiar with the story of Gideon, it should. Gideon and his men camped at the foot of the mountain while they prepared for their battle against the Midianites and the Amalekites.

1 Samuel 28:4

some food so you may eat and have enough
strength to go on your way."
[23]But Saul refused, saying, "I won't eat."
His servants joined the woman in asking
him to eat, and he listened to them. So he got
up from the ground and sat on the bed.
[24]At the house the woman had a fat calf,
which she quickly killed. She took some flour
and mixed dough with her hands. Then she
baked some bread without yeast. [25]She put the
food before them, and they ate. That same
night they got up and left.

DAVID GOES BACK TO ZIKLAG

29 [1]The Philistines gathered all their soldiers at
Aphek. Israel camped by the spring at Jezreel.
[2]The Philistine kings were marching with their
groups of a hundred and a thousand men.
David and his men were marching behind
Achish. [3]The Philistine commanders asked,
"What are these Hebrews doing here?"
Achish told them, "This is David. He served
Saul king of Israel, but he has been with me for
over a year now. I have found nothing wrong
in David since the time he left Saul."

WHAT'S IT MEAN?

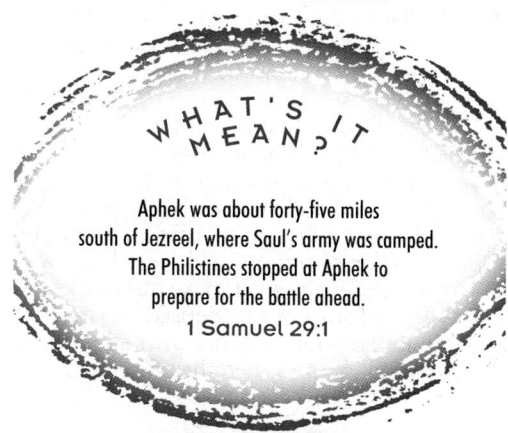

Aphek was about forty-five miles south of Jezreel, where Saul's army was camped. The Philistines stopped at Aphek to prepare for the battle ahead.

1 Samuel 29:1

[4]But the Philistine commanders were angry
with Achish and said, "Send David back to the
city you gave him. He cannot go with us into
battle. If he does, we'll have an enemy in our
own camp. He could please his king by killing
our own men. [5]David is the one the Israelites
dance and sing about, saying:
'Saul has killed thousands of his enemies,
but David has killed tens of thousands.' "
[6]So Achish called David and said to him, "As
surely as the LORD lives, you are loyal. I would
be pleased to have you serve in my army. Since
the day you came to me, I have found no
wrong in you. But the other kings don't trust
you. [7]Go back in peace. Don't do anything to
displease the Philistine kings."
[8]David asked, "What wrong have I done?
What evil have you found in me from the day
I came to you until now? Why can't I go fight
your enemies, my lord and king?"
[9]Achish answered, "I know you are as good
as an angel from God. But the Philistine commanders have said, 'David must not go with us
into battle.' [10]Early in the morning you and
your master's servants should leave. Get up as
soon as it is light and go."
[11]So David and his men got up early in the
morning and went back to the country of the
Philistines. And the Philistines went up to Jezreel.

DAVID'S WAR WITH THE AMALEKITES

30 [1]On the third day, when David and his men
arrived at Ziklag, he found that the Amalekites
had raided southern Judah and Ziklag, attacking Ziklag and burning it. [2]They captured the
women and everyone, young and old, but they
had not killed anyone. They had only taken
them away.
[3]When David and his men came to Ziklag,
they found the town had been burned and
their wives, sons, and daughters had been
taken as prisoners. [4]Then David and his army
cried loudly until they were too weak to cry
anymore. [5]David's two wives had also been
taken—Ahinoam of Jezreel and Abigail the
widow of Nabal from Carmel. [6]The men in the
army were threatening to kill David with
stones, which greatly upset David. Each man
was sad and angry because his sons and
daughters had been captured, but David found
strength in the LORD his God. [7]David said
to Abiathar the priest, "Bring me the holy
vest."
[8]Then David asked the LORD, "Should I
chase the people who took our families? Will I
catch them?"
The LORD answered, "Chase them. You will
catch them, and you will succeed in saving
your families."
[9]David and the six hundred men with him
came to the Besor Ravine, where some of the
men stayed. [10]David and four hundred men
kept up the chase. The other two hundred men
stayed behind because they were too tired to
cross the ravine.
[11]They found an Egyptian in a field and
brought him to David. They gave the Egyptian
some water to drink and some food to eat.
[12]And they gave him a piece of a fig cake and
two clusters of raisins. Then he felt better, because he had not eaten any food or drunk any
water for three days and nights.

13David asked him, "Who is your master?
Where do you come from?"
He answered, "I'm an Egyptian, the slave of
an Amalekite. Three days ago my master left
me, because I was sick. 14We had raided the
southern area of the Kerethites, the land of Judah, and the southern area of Caleb. We
burned Ziklag, as well."

WHAT'S IT MEAN?

The Amalekites were wanderers, roaming the desert between Israel and Egypt. They were bitter enemies of the Israelites from way back. The Kerethites, who were originally from the Mediterranean island of Crete, lived in the southern part of the Philistine territory. David later recruited some Kerethites for his own personal army.

1 Samuel 30:13–14

15David asked him, "Can you lead me to the
people who took our families?"
He answered, "Yes, if you promise me before
God that you won't kill me or give me back to
my master. Then I will take you to them."
16So the Egyptian led David to the Amalekites. They were lying around on the ground,
eating and drinking and celebrating with the
things they had taken from the land of the Philistines and from Judah. 17David fought them
from sunset until the evening of the next day.
None of them escaped, except four hundred
young men who rode off on their camels.
18David got his two wives back and everything
the Amalekites had taken. 19Nothing was missing. David brought back everyone, young and
old, sons and daughters. He recovered the
valuable things and everything the Amalekites
had taken. 20David took all the sheep and cattle, and his men made these animals go in
front, saying, "They are David's prize."
21Then David came to the two hundred
men who had been too tired to follow him,
who had stayed at the Besor Ravine. They
came out to meet David and the people with
him. When he came near, David greeted the
men at the ravine.
22But the evil men and troublemakers
among those who followed David said, "Since
these two hundred men didn't go with us, we
shouldn't give them any of the things we recovered. Just let each man take his wife and
children and go."
23David answered, "No, my brothers. Don't
do that after what the LORD has given us. He
has protected us and given us the enemy who
attacked us. 24Who will listen to what you say?
The share will be the same for the one who
stayed with the supplies as for the one who
went into battle. All will share alike." 25David
made this an order and rule for Israel, which
continues even today.
26When David arrived in Ziklag, he sent
some of the things he had taken from the Amalekites to his friends, the leaders of Judah. He
said, "Here is a present for you from the things
we took from the LORD's enemies."
27David also sent some things to the leaders
in Bethel, Ramoth in the southern part of
Judah, Jattir, 28Aroer, Siphmoth, Eshtemoa,
29Racal, the cities of the Jerahmeelites and the
Kenites, 30Hormah, Bor Ashan, Athach, 31He-
bron, and to the people in all the other places
where he and his men had been.

THE DEATH OF SAUL

31

1The Philistines fought against Israel, and the
Israelites ran away from them. Many Israelites
were killed on Mount Gilboa. 2The Philistines
fought hard against Saul and his sons, killing
his sons Jonathan, Abinadab, and Malki-Shua.
3The fighting was heavy around Saul. The archers shot him, and he was badly wounded.
4He said to the officer who carried his armor,
"Pull out your sword and kill me. Then those
uncircumcised men won't make fun of me and
kill me." But Saul's officer refused, because he
was afraid. So Saul took his own sword and
threw himself on it. 5When the officer saw that

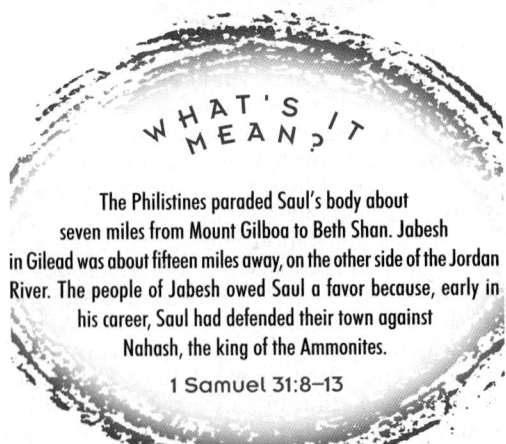

WHAT'S IT MEAN?

The Philistines paraded Saul's body about seven miles from Mount Gilboa to Beth Shan. Jabesh in Gilead was about fifteen miles away, on the other side of the Jordan River. The people of Jabesh owed Saul a favor because, early in his career, Saul had defended their town against Nahash, the king of the Ammonites.

1 Samuel 31:8–13

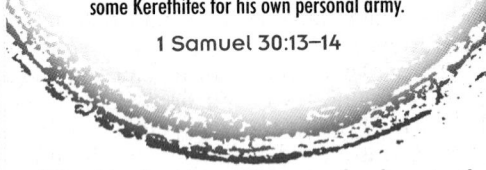

Saul was dead, he threw himself on his own
sword, and he died with Saul. 6So Saul, his three
sons, and the officer who carried his armor died
together that day.
7When the Israelites who lived across the
Jezreel Valley and those who lived across the
Jordan River saw how the Israelite army had
run away, and that Saul and his sons were
dead, they left their cities and ran away. Then
the Philistines came and lived there.
8The next day when the Philistines came to
take all the valuable things from the dead soldiers, they found Saul and his three sons dead
on Mount Gilboa. 9They cut off Saul's head
and took off his armor. Then they sent messengers through all the land of the Philistines to
tell the news in the temple of their idols and to
their people. 10They put Saul's armor in the
temple of the Ashtoreths and hung his body
on the wall of Beth Shan.
11When the people living in Jabesh Gilead
heard what the Philistines had done to Saul,
12the brave men of Jabesh marched all night
and came to Beth Shan. They removed the
bodies of Saul and his sons from the wall of
Beth Shan and brought them to Jabesh. There
they burned the bodies. 13They took their
bones and buried them under the tamarisk tree
in Jabesh. Then the people of Jabesh gave up
eating for seven days.

2 Samuel

CONTENT As you start on the second tape of this homegrown epic called 2 Samuel, King Saul's worst fears come true: David replaces Saul as king. You've probably heard of King David. He was an ancestor of Jesus. He planned the first Temple, and he wrote a lot of the Psalms. He was the original Renaissance man. There are more stories in the Bible about David than about anyone else except Jesus himself.

God called David a man after his own heart. That's why David's story is such an encouragement to us. He wasn't a perfect man, but he loved God and God was pleased with that.

There are a lot of sad tales and mishaps in 2 Samuel, but it's a book that shows us that God doesn't expect us to never foul up. His expectation is that we can keep coming back to him and starting over. David was a man who understood that.

Outline

1:1–27 .... David Mourns for Saul
2:1—4:12 .... David, King of Judah
5:1—6:23 .... David, King of All Israel
7:1–29 .... God's Promise to David
8:1—10:19 .... The Wars of King David
11:1—12:31 .... David's Affair with Bathsheba
13:1—14:33 .... Violence in David's Family: Tamar, Amnon, and Absalom
15:1—20:26 .... Absalom Leads a Rebellion
21:1-22 .... Other Events from David's Rule
22:1—23:7 .... Two Poems by David
23:8-39 .... David's Warriors
24:1-25 .... David Counts His Army, and Israel Is Punished

Purpose The most committed believer can fail and constantly needs God's grace.

Theme King David, Forerunner of the Messiah

Date of writing 1050–750 B.C.

"When you die and join your ancestors, I will make one of your sons the next king, and I will set up his kingdom. He will build a house for me, and I will let his kingdom rule always" (7:12–13).

Bible Talk

David: A Good Man, Except for One Thing

The Bible doesn't sugarcoat the truth, even for its heroes. Look at David more closely. He was one of the best. He loved God. He was a fantastic musician and writer. He was a good king. The Bible could have left it at that. God could have swept David's faults under a rug or into a closet.

That's not what God does, though. He accepts us and uses us as we are with all of our faults. David is famous for one *really* big blunder. He fell for a married woman. He even had her husband killed to try and clean up the mess.

David's story reminds us that the best of us make bad mistakes, but God never gives up on us.

TALK ABOUT A DYSFUNCTIONAL FAMILY

Families can be a great thing to have, but they can also be difficult. King David's family was . . . a mess. He had kids by several wives, and those kids mistreated each other. David didn't stand up to them when they did wrong, and so their wrongs got bigger and bigger.

Eventually David's own son tried to take the kingdom away from him. His daughter lived a life of shame after being raped by a half brother, who was killed by another brother in an act of retribution. David's youngest son, Solomon, did receive the kingdom from his father and, in many ways, succeeded greatly. Yet some of his most famous writings are writings of disillusionment with even the best things of life.

Families struggled in David's time, as they do now, with selfishness and greed and a lack of connection. Families needed, in David's time, what they need now—a connection to God that will heal them.

DAVID LEARNS ABOUT SAUL'S DEATH

1Now Saul was dead. After David had defeated the Amalekites, he returned to Ziklag
and stayed there two days. 2On the third day a
young man from Saul's camp came to Ziklag.
To show his sadness, his clothes were torn and
he had dirt on his head. He came and bowed
facedown on the ground before David.
3David asked him, "Where did you come
from?"

The man answered, "I escaped from the Israelite camp."

4David asked him, "What happened? Please
tell me!"

The man answered, "The people have run away from the battle, and many of them have fallen and are dead. Saul and his son Jonathan are dead also."

5David asked him, "How do you know Saul
and his son Jonathan are dead?"
6The young man answered, "I happened to
be on Mount Gilboa. There I saw Saul leaning
on his spear. The Philistine chariots and the
men riding in them were coming closer to Saul.
7When he looked back and saw me, he called
to me. I answered him, 'Here I am!'
8"Then Saul asked me, 'Who are you?'

"I told him, 'I am an Amalekite.'

9"Then Saul said to me, 'Please come here
and kill me. I am badly hurt and am almost
dead already.'
10"So I went over and killed him. He had
been hurt so badly I knew he couldn't live.
Then I took the crown from his head and the
bracelet from his arm, and I have brought
them here to you, my master."
11Then David tore his clothes to show his
sorrow, and all the men with him did also.
12They were very sad and cried and did not eat
until evening. They cried for Saul and his son
Jonathan and for all the people of the LORD
and for all the Israelites who had died in the
battle.

DAVID ORDERS THE AMALEKITE KILLED

13David asked the young man who brought
the report, "Where are you from?"

The young man answered, "I am the son of a foreigner, an Amalekite."

14David asked him, "Why were you not
afraid to kill the LORD's appointed
king?"
15Then David called one of
his men and told him, "Go!
Kill the Amalekite!" So the Israelite killed him. 16David had
said to the Amalekite, "You are
responsible for your own death. You confessed
by saying, 'I have killed the LORD's appointed
king.' "

LEADERSHIP
Are leaders ordained by God? (1:16)

DAVID'S SONG ABOUT SAUL AND JONATHAN

17David sang a funeral song about Saul and
his son Jonathan, 18and he ordered that the
people of Judah be taught this song. It is called
"The Bow," and it is written in the Book of Jashar:

19"Israel, your leaders have been killed on
the hills.
How the mighty have fallen in battle!
20Don't tell it in Gath.
Don't announce it in the streets of
Ashkelon.
If you do, the Philistine women will be
happy.
The daughters of the Philistines will
rejoice.

WHAT'S IT MEAN?

Don't bother looking for the Book of Jashar in your Bible or your local library or your nearest bookstore. You won't find it. This ancient book, which contained everything from Joshua's speech at the battle of Gibeon to David's tribute to Saul and Jonathan, has been lost for centuries. In case you're wondering, *Jashar* means "Upright" or "Righteous."

2 Samuel 1:18

21"May there be no dew or rain on the
mountains of Gilboa,
and may their fields produce no grain,
because there the mighty warrior's shield
was dishonored.
Saul's shield will no longer be rubbed
with oil.
22Jonathan's bow did not fail
to kill many soldiers.
Saul's sword did not fail
to wound many strong men.

23"We loved Saul and Jonathan
and enjoyed them while they lived.
They are together even in death.
They were faster than eagles.
They were stronger than lions.

[24] "You daughters of Israel, cry for Saul.
Saul clothed you with red dresses
and put gold decorations on them.

[25] "How the mighty have fallen in battle!
Jonathan is dead on Gilboa's hills.
[26] I cry for you, my brother Jonathan.
I enjoyed your friendship so much.
Your love to me was
wonderful,
better than the love of
women.

[27] "How the mighty have
fallen!
The weapons of war
are gone."

"May the LORD now be loyal and true to you. I will also treat you well because you have done this."
(2 Samuel 2:6)

DAVID IS MADE KING OF JUDAH

2

[1] Later, David prayed to the
LORD, saying, "Should I go up to any of the
cities of Judah?"
The LORD said to David, "Go."
David asked, "Where should I go?"
The LORD answered, "To Hebron."
[2] So David went up to Hebron with his two
wives: Ahinoam from Jezreel and Abigail, the
widow of Nabal from Carmel. [3] David also
brought his men and their families, and they
all made their homes in the cities of Hebron.
[4] Then the men of Judah came to Hebron and
appointed David king over Judah.
They told David that the men of Jabesh Gilead had buried Saul. [5] So David sent messengers to the men of Jabesh Gilead and said to
them, "The LORD bless you. You have shown
loyalty to your master Saul by burying him.
[6] May the LORD now be loyal and true to you. I

WHAT'S IT MEAN?

When a prophet or priest appointed someone to a special position, he poured olive oil on the person's head to indicate that the Lord had chosen that person for a special purpose. The same kind of presses that were used to make wine from grapes were used to make olive oil from green olives.

2 Samuel 2:4

will also treat you well because you have done
this. [7] Now be strong and brave. Saul your
master is dead, and the people of Judah have
appointed me their king."

WAR BETWEEN JUDAH AND ISRAEL

[8] Abner son of Ner was the commander of
Saul's army. Abner took Saul's son Ish-Bosheth
to Mahanaim [9] and made him
king of Gilead, Ashuri, Jezreel, Ephraim, Benjamin, and
all Israel. [10] Saul's son Ish-
Bosheth was forty years old
when he became king over
Israel, and he ruled two
years. But the people
of Judah followed David.
[11] David was king in Hebron for seven years and
six months.
[12] Abner son of Ner and the
servants of Ish-Bosheth son of
Saul left Mahanaim and went to Gibeon.
[13] Joab son of Zeruiah and David's men also
went there and met Abner and Ish-Bosheth's
men at the pool of Gibeon. Abner's group sat
on one side of the pool; Joab's group sat on the
other.

WHAT'S IT MEAN?

Both Saul and David believed in "keeping it in the family," when it came to appointing military leaders. Abner, the commander of Saul's army, was Saul's first cousin. Joab, the commander of David's army, was David's nephew. The gruesome game that Abner and Joab suggested was prompted by the rivalry between the tribe of Benjamin (Saul's tribe), which wanted the throne passed on to one of Saul's descendants, and the tribe of Judah (David's tribe), which had chosen David as its king.

2 Samuel 2:14–17

[14] Abner said to Joab, "Let the young men
have a contest here."
Joab said, "Yes, let them have a contest."
[15] Then the men got up and were counted—
twelve from the people of Benjamin for Ish-
Bosheth son of Saul, and twelve from David's
men. [16] Each man grabbed the one opposite
him by the head and stabbed him in the side

with a knife. So the men fell down together. For that reason, that place in Gibeon is called the Field of Knives. 17 That day there was a terrible battle, and David's men defeated Abner and the Israelites.

ABNER KILLS ASAHEL

18 Zeruiah's three sons, Joab, Abishai, and Asahel, were there. Now Asahel was a fast runner, as fast as a deer in the field. 19 Asahel chased Abner, going straight toward him. 20 Abner looked back and asked, "Is that you, Asahel?"

Asahel said, "Yes, it is."

21 Then Abner said to Asahel, "Turn to your right or left and catch one of the young men and take his armor." But Asahel refused to stop chasing him.

22 Abner again said to Asahel, "Stop chasing me! If you don't stop, I'll have to kill you! Then I won't be able to face your brother Joab again!"

23 But Asahel refused to stop chasing Abner. So using the back end of his spear, Abner stabbed Asahel in the stomach, and the spear came out of his back. Asahel died right there, and everyone stopped when they came to the place where Asahel's body lay.

24 But Joab and Abishai continued chasing Abner. As the sun was going down, they arrived at the hill of Ammah, near Giah on the way to the desert near Gibeon. 25 The men of Benjamin came to Abner, and all stood together at the top of the hill.

26 Abner shouted to Joab, "Must the sword kill forever? Surely you must know this will only end in sadness! Tell the people to stop chasing their own brothers!"

27 Then Joab said, "As surely as God lives, if you had not said anything, the people would have chased their brothers until morning." 28 Then Joab blew a trumpet, and his people stopped chasing the Israelites. They did not fight them anymore.

29 Abner and his men marched all night through the Jordan Valley. They crossed the Jordan River, and after marching all day, arrived at Mahanaim.

30 After he had stopped chasing Abner, Joab came back and gathered the people together. Asahel and nineteen of David's men were missing. 31 But David's men had killed three hundred sixty Benjaminites who had followed Abner. 32 David's men took Asahel and buried him in the tomb of his father at Bethlehem. Then Joab and his men marched all night. The sun came up as they reached Hebron.

3 1 There was a long war between the people who supported Saul's family and those who supported David's family. The supporters of David's family became stronger and stronger, but the supporters of Saul's family became weaker and weaker.

DAVID'S SONS

2 Sons were born to David at Hebron. The first was Amnon, whose mother was Ahinoam from Jezreel. 3 The second son was Kileab, whose mother was Abigail, the widow of Nabal from Carmel. The third son was Absalom, whose mother was Maacah daughter of Talmai, the king of Geshur. 4 The fourth son was Adonijah, whose mother was Haggith. The fifth son was Shephatiah, whose mother was Abital. 5 The sixth son was Ithream, whose mother was Eglah, David's wife. These sons were born to David at Hebron.

ABNER JOINS DAVID

6 During the war between the supporters of Saul's family and the supporters of David's family, Abner made himself a main leader among the supporters of Saul.

7 Saul once had a slave woman named Rizpah, who was the daughter of Aiah. Ish-Bosheth said to Abner, "Why did you have sexual relations with my father's slave woman?"

8 Abner was very angry because of what Ish-Bosheth said, and he replied, "I have been loyal to Saul and his family and friends! I didn't hand you over to David. I am not a traitor working for Judah! But now you are saying I did something wrong with this woman! 9 May God help me if I don't join David! I will make sure that what the LORD promised does happen! 10 I will take the kingdom from the family

WHAT'S IT MEAN?

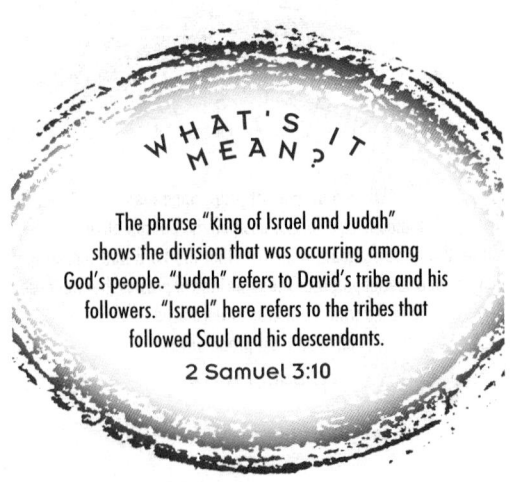

The phrase "king of Israel and Judah" shows the division that was occurring among God's people. "Judah" refers to David's tribe and his followers. "Israel" here refers to the tribes that followed Saul and his descendants.

2 Samuel 3:10

of Saul and make David king of Israel and Judah, from Dan to Beersheba!"[n]
11Ish-Bosheth couldn't say anything to Abner, because he was afraid of him.
12Then Abner sent messengers to ask David,
"Who is going to rule the land? Make an agreement with me, and I will help you unite all
Israel."
13David answered, "Good! I will make an
agreement with you, but I ask you one thing. I
will not meet with you unless you bring Saul's
daughter Michal to me." 14Then David sent
messengers to Saul's son Ish-Bosheth, saying,
"Give me my wife Michal. She was promised to
me, and I killed a hundred Philistines to get her."
15So Ish-Bosheth sent men to take Michal
from her husband Paltiel son of Laish.
16Michal's husband went with her, crying as he
followed her to Bahurim. But Abner said to
Paltiel, "Go back home." So he went home.
17Abner sent this message to the older leaders of Israel: "You have been wanting to make
David your king. 18Now do it! The LORD said of
David, 'Through my servant David, I will save
my people Israel from the Philistines and all
their enemies.' "
19Abner also said these things to the people
of Benjamin. He then went to Hebron to tell
David what the Benjaminites and Israel wanted
to do. 20Abner came with twenty men to David
at Hebron. There David prepared a feast for
them. 21Abner said to David, "My master and
king, I will go and bring all the Israelites to you.
Then they will make an agreement with you so
you will rule over all Israel as you wanted." So
David let Abner go, and he left in peace.

ABNER'S DEATH

22Just then Joab and David's men came
from a battle, bringing many valuable things
they had taken from the enemy. David had let
Abner leave in peace, so he was not with David
at Hebron. 23When Joab and all his army arrived at Hebron, the army said to Joab, "Abner
son of Ner came to King David, and David let
him leave in peace."
24Joab came to the king and said, "What
have you done? Abner came to you. Why did
you let him go? Now he's gone. 25You know
Abner son of Ner! He came to trick you! He
came to learn about everything you are doing!"
26After Joab left David, he sent messengers
after Abner, and they brought him back from
the well of Sirah. But David did not know this.
27When Abner arrived at Hebron, Joab took
him aside into the gateway. He acted as though
he wanted to talk with Abner in private, but
Joab stabbed him in the stomach, and Abner
died. Abner had killed Joab's brother Asahel,
so Joab killed Abner to pay him back.
28Later when David heard the news, he said,
"My kingdom and I are innocent forever of the
death of Abner son of Ner. The LORD knows
this. 29Joab and his family are responsible for
this. May his family always have someone
with sores or with a skin disease. May they
always have someone who must lean on a
crutch. May some of his family be killed in
war. May they always have someone without
food to eat."
30(Joab and his brother Abishai killed Abner, because he had killed their brother Asahel
in the battle at Gibeon.)
31Then David said to Joab and to all the
people with Joab, "Tear your clothes and put
on rough cloth to show how sad you are. Cry
for Abner." King David himself followed the
body of Abner. 32They buried Abner in Hebron, and David and all the people cried at
Abner's grave.

WHAT'S IT MEAN?

Grief was a much more public emotion in ancient times than it is today. People demonstrated their feelings of loss and sadness by tearing their clothes, putting ashes or dust in their hair, and wearing really uncomfortable clothes. These outward signs were used both for mourning a death and for repenting of sin, and they were often continued for several days.

2 Samuel 3:31

33King David sang this funeral song for
Abner.
"Did Abner die like a fool?
34 His hands were not tied.
His feet were not in chains.
He fell at the hands of evil men."
Then all the people cried again for Abner.
35They came to encourage David to eat while it
was still day. But he made a promise, saying,

3:10 Dan to Beersheba Dan was the city farthest north in Israel, and Beersheba was the city farthest south. So this means all the people of Israel.

MEPHIBOSHETH made a difference

Not long after David became king of Israel he made inquiries about the family of Saul, the previous king. His good friend Jonathan, Saul's son, had died with his father in battle. The news came back that Saul's entire family had been killed with one exception: Jonathan's son Mephibosheth. A nurse hurrying to save the orphan had dropped him, and Mephibosheth had grown up lame.

David honored and protected Mephibosheth out of respect for Jonathan. He guaranteed Mephibosheth's family property and welcomed the young man to the royal table. Later, Mephibosheth was betrayed by his servant Ziba who convinced a fleeing David that Mephibosheth still held hopes of reclaiming the crown for his family. In his words of humble reconciliation, Mephibosheth offers as fine an example of honesty and gratitude as found anywhere in Scripture.

Cutting Edge

Lame as he was, Mephibosheth was dependent on others. Some, like Ziba, took advantage of him. Others, like David, respected him in spite of his limitations. Mephibosheth understood where gratitude was due. When he was accused, he did everything he could to make the matter right and acted with dignity and integrity.

YOU can, too!

You may be frustrated by the limitations in your life. They come in all sizes and shapes. Some are physical; others are emotional, educational, or social. It will take self-control not to lobby for fairness or demand your own way. As with Mephibosheth, limitations don't have to become excuses. In the very act of persisting in spite of your limitations, you will be an example to others. Your efforts will make a difference.

Want to know more? Read about Mephibosheth's life in 2 Samuel 4; 9:1–13; 16:1–4; 19:24–30.

"May God punish me terribly if I eat bread or
anything else before the sun sets!"
36All the people saw what happened, and
they agreed with what the king was doing, just
as they agreed with everything he did. 37That
day all the people of Judah and Israel understood that David did not order the killing of
Abner son of Ner.
38David said to his officers, "You know that
a great man died today in Israel. 39Even though
I am the appointed king, I feel empty. These
sons of Zeruiah are too much for me. May the
LORD give them the punishment they should
have."

ISH-BOSHETH'S DEATH

4 1When Ish-Bosheth son of Saul heard that
Abner had died at Hebron, he was shocked
and all Israel became frightened. 2Two men
who were captains in Saul's army came to Ish-
Bosheth. One was named Baanah, and the
other was named Recab. They were the sons of
Rimmon of Beeroth, who was a Benjaminite.
(The town Beeroth belonged to the tribe of
Benjamin. 3The people of Beeroth ran away to
Gittaim, and they still live there as foreigners
today.)
4(Saul's son Jonathan had a son named Mephibosheth, who was crippled in both feet. He
was five years old when the news came from
Jezreel that Saul and Jonathan were dead.
Mephibosheth's nurse had picked him up and
run away. But as she hurried to leave, she
dropped him, and now he was lame.)
5Recab and Baanah, sons of Rimmon from
Beeroth, went to Ish-Bosheth's house in the afternoon while he was taking a nap. 6-7They
went into the middle of the house as if to get
some wheat. Ish-Bosheth was lying on his bed
in his bedroom. Then Recab and Baanah
stabbed him in the stomach, killed him, cut off
his head, and took it with them. They escaped
and traveled all night through the Jordan Valley. 8When they arrived at Hebron, they gave
his head to David and said to the king, "Here is
the head of Ish-Bosheth son of Saul, your enemy. He tried to kill you! Today the LORD has
paid back Saul and his family for what they
did to you!"
9David answered Recab and his brother
Baanah, the sons of Rimmon of Beeroth, "As
surely as the LORD lives, he has saved me from
all trouble! 10Once a man thought he was
bringing me good news. When he told me,
'Saul is dead!' I seized him and killed him at
Ziklag. That was the reward I gave him for his
news! 11So even more I must put you evil men
to death because you have killed an innocent
man on his own bed in his own house!"
12So David commanded his men
to kill Recab and Baanah. They
cut off the hands and feet of
Recab and Baanah and hung
them over the pool of He-
bron. Then they took Ish-
Bosheth's head and buried it
in Abner's tomb at Hebron.

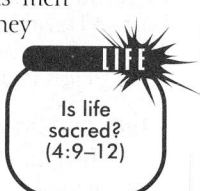

> **LIFE**
> Is life sacred? (4:9–12)

DAVID IS MADE KING OF ISRAEL

5 1Then all the tribes of Israel came to David
at Hebron and said to him, "Look, we are your
own family. 2Even when Saul was king, you
were the one who led Israel in battle. The LORD
said to you, 'You will be a shepherd for my
people Israel. You will be their leader.' "
3So all the older leaders of Israel came to
King David at Hebron, and he made an agreement with them in Hebron in the presence of
the LORD. Then they poured oil on David to
make him king over Israel.
4David was thirty years old when he became king, and he ruled forty years. 5He was
king over Judah in Hebron for seven years and
six months, and he was king over all Israel and
Judah in Jerusalem for thirty-three years.
6When the king and his men went to Jerusalem to attack the Jebusites who lived there,
the Jebusites said to David, "You can't get inside
our city. Even the blind and the crippled can
stop you." They thought David could not enter
their city. 7But David did take the city of Jerusalem with its strong walls, and it became the
City of David.
8That day David said to his men, "To defeat
the Jebusites you must go through the water
tunnel. Then you can reach those 'crippled'
and 'blind' enemies. This is why people say,
'The blind and the crippled may not enter the
palace.' "
9So David lived in the strong, walled city
and called it the City of David. David built
more buildings around it, beginning where
the land was filled in. He also built more buildings inside the city. 10He became stronger and
stronger, because the LORD God All-Powerful
was with him.
11Hiram king of the city of Tyre sent messengers to David, along with cedar logs, carpenters, and stonecutters. They built a palace
for David. 12Then David knew that the LORD
really had made him king of Israel and that the
LORD had made his kingdom great because the
LORD loved his people Israel.
13After he came from Hebron, David took

for himself more slave women and wives in Jerusalem. More sons and daughters were born to David. [14]These are the names of the sons born to David in Jerusalem: Shammua, Shobab, Nathan, Solomon, [15]Ibhar, Elishua, Nepheg, Japhia, [16]Elishama, Eliada, and Eliphelet.

DAVID DEFEATS THE PHILISTINES

[17]When the Philistines heard that David had been made king over Israel, all the Philistines went to look for him. But when David heard the news, he went down to the stronghold. [18]The Philistines came and camped in the Valley of Rephaim. [19]David asked the LORD, "Should I attack the Philistines? Will you hand them over to me?"

The LORD said to David, "Go! I will certainly hand them over to you."

[20]So David went to Baal Perazim and defeated the Philistines there. David said, "Like a flood of water, the LORD has broken through my enemies in front of me." So David named the place Baal Perazim.[n] [21]The Philistines left their idols behind at Baal Perazim, so David and his men carried them away.

[22]Once again the Philistines came and camped at the Valley of Rephaim. [23]When David prayed to the LORD, he answered, "Don't attack the Philistines from the front. Instead, go around and attack them in front of the balsam trees. [24]When you hear the sound of marching in the tops of the balsam trees, act quickly. I, the LORD, will have gone ahead of you to defeat the Philistine army." [25]So David did what the LORD commanded. He defeated the Philistines and chased them all the way from Gibeon to Gezer.

THE ARK IS BROUGHT TO JERUSALEM

6 [1]David again gathered all the chosen men of Israel—thirty thousand of them. [2]Then he and all his people went to Baalah in Judah[n] to bring back the Ark of God. The Ark is called by the Name, the name of the LORD All-Powerful, whose throne is between the gold creatures with wings. [3]They put the Ark of God on a new cart and brought it out of Abinadab's house on the hill. Uzzah and Ahio, sons of Abinadab, led the new cart [4]which had the Ark of God on it. Ahio was walking in front of it. [5]David and all the Israelites were celebrating in the presence of the LORD. They were playing wooden instruments: lyres, harps, tambourines, rattles, and cymbals.

WHAT'S IT MEAN?

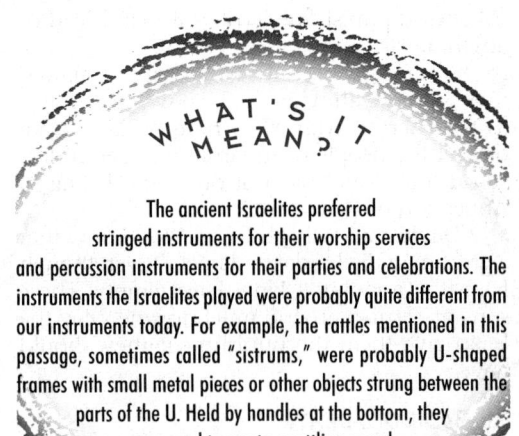

The ancient Israelites preferred stringed instruments for their worship services and percussion instruments for their parties and celebrations. The instruments the Israelites played were probably quite different from our instruments today. For example, the rattles mentioned in this passage, sometimes called "sistrums," were probably U-shaped frames with small metal pieces or other objects strung between the parts of the U. Held by handles at the bottom, they were used to create a rattling sound.

2 Samuel 6:5

[6]When David's men came to the threshing floor of Nacon, the oxen stumbled. So Uzzah reached out to steady the Ark of God. [7]The LORD was angry with Uzzah and killed him because of what he did. So Uzzah died there beside the Ark of God. [8]David was angry because the LORD had killed Uzzah. Now that place is called the Punishment of Uzzah.

[9]David was afraid of the LORD that day, and he said, "How can the Ark of the LORD come to me now?" [10]So David would not move the Ark of the LORD to be with him in Jerusalem. Instead, he took it to the house of Obed-Edom, a man from Gath. [11]The Ark of the LORD stayed in Obed-Edom's house for three months, and the LORD blessed Obed-Edom and all his family.

[12]The people told David, "The LORD has blessed the family of Obed-Edom and all that belongs to him, because the Ark of God is there." So David went and brought it up from Obed-Edom's house to Jerusalem with joy. [13]When the men carrying the Ark of the LORD had walked six steps, David sacrificed a bull and a fat calf. [14]Then David danced with all his might before the LORD. He had on a holy linen vest. [15]David and all the Israelites shouted with joy and blew the trumpets as they brought the Ark of the LORD to the city.

[16]As the Ark of the LORD came into the city, Saul's daughter Michal looked out the window. When she saw David jumping and dancing in the presence of the LORD, she hated him.

[17]David put up a tent for the Ark of the

5:20 Baal Perazim This name means "the Lord breaks through." **6:2 Baalah in Judah** Another name for Kiriath Jearim.

LORD, and then the Israelites put it in its place inside the tent. David offered whole burnt offerings and fellowship offerings before the LORD. [18]When David finished offering the whole burnt offerings and the fellowship offerings, he blessed the people in the name of the LORD All-Powerful. [19]David gave a loaf of bread, a cake of dates, and a cake of raisins to every Israelite, both men and women. Then all the people went home.

[20]David went back to bless the people in his home, but Saul's daughter Michal came out to meet him. She said, "With what honor the king of Israel acted today! You took off your clothes in front of the servant girls of your officers like one who takes off his clothes without shame!"

[21]Then David said to Michal, "I did it in the presence of the LORD. The LORD chose me, not your father or anyone from Saul's family. The LORD appointed me to be over Israel. So I will celebrate in the presence of the LORD. [22]Maybe I will lose even more honor, and maybe I will be brought down in my own opinion, but the girls you talk about will honor me!"

WORSHIP
How should we worship God? (6:21)

[23]And Saul's daughter Michal had no children to the day she died.

DAVID WANTS TO BUILD A TEMPLE

7 [1]King David was living in his palace, and the LORD had given him peace from all his enemies around him. [2]Then David said to Nathan the prophet, "Look, I am living in a palace made of cedar wood, but the Ark of God is in a tent!"

[3]Nathan said to the king, "Go and do what you really want to do, because the LORD is with you."

[4]But that night the LORD spoke his word to Nathan, [5]"Go and tell my servant David, 'This is what the LORD says: Will you build a house for me to live in? [6]From the time I brought the Israelites out of Egypt until now I have not lived in a house. I have been moving around all this time with a tent as my home. [7]As I have moved with the Israelites, I have never said to the tribes, whom I commanded to take care of my people Israel, "Why haven't you built me a house of cedar?" '

"Nathan said to the king, 'Go and do what you really want to do, because the LORD is with you.' " (2 Samuel 7:3)

[8]"You must tell my servant David, 'This is what the LORD All-Powerful says: I took you from the pasture and from tending the sheep and made you leader of my people Israel. [9]I have been with you everywhere you have gone and have defeated your enemies for you. I will make you as famous as any of the great people on the earth. [10]Also I will choose a place for my people Israel, and I will plant them so they can live in their own homes. They will not be bothered anymore. Wicked people will no longer bother them as they have in the past [11]when I chose judges for my people Israel. But I will give you peace from all your enemies. I also tell you that I will make your descendants kings of Israel after you.

[12]" 'When you die and join your ancestors, I will make one of your sons the next king, and I will set up his kingdom. [13]He will build a house for me, and I will let his kingdom rule always. [14]I will be his father, and he will be my son. When he sins, I will use other people to punish him. They will be my whips. [15]I took away my love from Saul, whom I removed before you, but I will never stop loving your son. [16]But your family and your kingdom will continue always before me. Your throne will last forever.' "

ADOPTION
Who does God discipline? (7:14)

[17]Nathan told David everything God had said in this vision.

DAVID PRAYS TO GOD

[18]Then King David went in and sat in front of the LORD. David said, "Lord GOD, who am I? What is my family? Why did you bring me to this point? [19]But even this is not enough for you, Lord GOD. You have also made promises about my future family. This is not normal, Lord GOD.

[20]"What more can I say to you, Lord GOD, since you know me, your servant, so well! [21]You have done this great thing because you said you would and because you wanted to, and you have let me know about it. [22]This is why you are great, Lord GOD! There is no one like you. There is no God except you. We have heard all this ourselves! [23]There is no nation like your people Israel. They are the only people on earth that God chose to be his own. You made your name well known. You did great and wonderful miracles

GOD
Is God unique? (7:22)

for them. You went ahead of them and forced
other nations and their gods out of the land.
You freed your people from slavery in Egypt.
24You made the people of Israel your very own
people forever, and, LORD, you are their God.
25"Now, LORD God, keep the promise forever that you made about my family and me,
your servant. Do what you have said. 26Then
you will be honored always, and people will
say, 'The LORD All-Powerful is God over Israel!'
And the family of your servant David will continue before you.
27"LORD All-Powerful, the God of Israel, you
have said to me, 'I will make your family great.'
So I, your servant, am brave enough to pray to
you. 28Lord GOD, you are God, and your
words are true. And you have promised these
good things to me, your servant. 29Please, bless
my family. Let it continue before you always.
Lord GOD, you have said so. With your blessing let my family always be blessed."

DAVID WINS MANY WARS

8 1Later, David defeated the Philistines, conquered them, and took the city of Metheg Ammah.
2He also defeated the people of Moab. He
made them lie on the ground, and then he used
a rope to measure them. Those who were measured within two rope lengths were killed, but
those who were within the next rope length
were allowed to live. So the people of Moab
became servants of David and gave him the
payment he demanded.
3David also defeated Hadadezer son of Rehob, king of Zobah, as he went to take control
again at the Euphrates River. 4David captured
one thousand chariots, seven thousand men
who rode in chariots, and twenty thousand
foot soldiers. He crippled all but a hundred of
the chariot horses.
5Arameans from Damascus came to help
Hadadezer king of Zobah, but David killed
twenty-two thousand of them. 6Then David
put groups of soldiers in Damascus in Aram.
The Arameans became David's servants and
gave him the payment he demanded. The LORD
gave David victory everywhere he went.
7David took the shields of gold that had belonged to Hadadezer's officers and brought
them to Jerusalem. 8David also took many
things made of bronze from Tebah and Bero-
thai, which had been cities under Hadadezer's
control.
9Toi king of Hamath heard that David had
defeated all the army of Hadadezer. 10So Toi
sent his son Joram to greet and congratulate
King David for defeating Hadadezer. (Hadadezer had been at war with Toi.) Joram
brought items made of silver, gold, and bronze.
11King David gave them to the LORD, along
with the silver and gold he had taken from the
other nations he had defeated. 12These nations
were Edom, Moab, Ammon, Philistia, and Amalek. David also gave the LORD what he had
taken from Hadadezer son of Rehob, king of
Zobah.

WHAT'S IT MEAN?

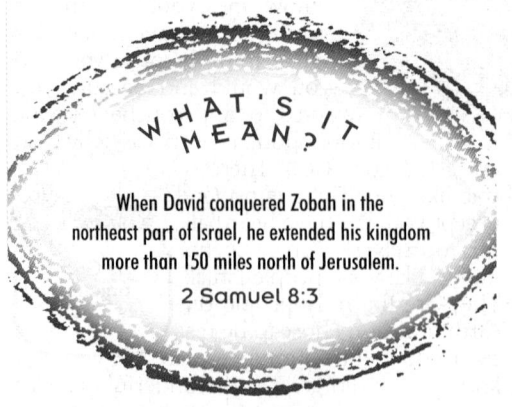

When David conquered Zobah in the northeast part of Israel, he extended his kingdom more than 150 miles north of Jerusalem.

2 Samuel 8:3

WHAT'S IT MEAN?

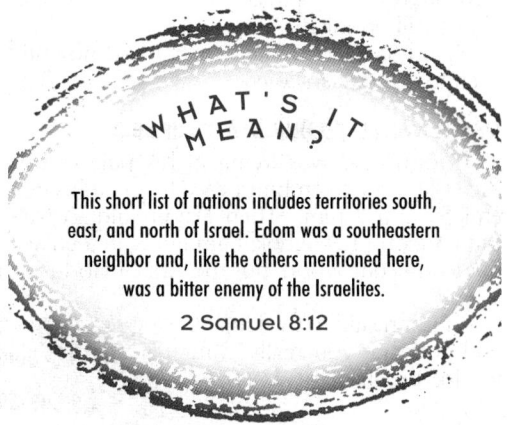

This short list of nations includes territories south, east, and north of Israel. Edom was a southeastern neighbor and, like the others mentioned here, was a bitter enemy of the Israelites.

2 Samuel 8:12

13David was famous after he returned from
defeating eighteen thousand Arameans in the
Valley of Salt. 14He put groups of soldiers all
over Edom, and all the Edomites became his
servants. The LORD gave David victory
everywhere he went.
15David was king over all
Israel, and he did what was
fair and right for all his people. 16Joab son of Zeruiah was
commander over the army.
Jehoshaphat son of Ahilud
was the recorder. 17Zadok son of Ahitub and
Abiathar son of Ahimelech were priests. Seraiah was the royal secretary. 18Benaiah son of

LEADERSHIP

What should leaders be known for? (8:15)

Jehoiada was over the Kerethites and Pelethites.[n] And David's sons were priests.

DAVID HELPS SAUL'S FAMILY

9 1David asked, "Is anyone still left in Saul's
family? I want to show kindness to that person
for Jonathan's sake!"
2Now there was a servant named Ziba from
Saul's family. So David's servants called Ziba to
him. King David said to him, "Are you
Ziba?"
He answered, "Yes, I am
your servant."
3The king asked, "Is any-
one left in Saul's family? I
want to show God's kindness
to that person."
Ziba answered the king, "Jonathan has a
son still living who is crippled in both feet."
4The king asked Ziba, "Where is this son?"
Ziba answered, "He is at the house of Makir
son of Ammiel in Lo Debar."
5Then King David had servants bring
Jonathan's son from the house of Makir son of
Ammiel in Lo Debar. 6Mephibosheth, Jonathan's son, came before David and bowed
facedown on the floor.
David said, "Mephibosheth!"
Mephibosheth said, "I am your servant."
7David said to him, "Don't be afraid. I will
be kind to you for your father Jonathan's sake.
I will give you back all the land of your grandfather Saul, and you will always eat at my table."
8Mephibosheth bowed to David again and
said, "You are being very kind to me, your servant! And I am no better than a dead dog!"
9Then King David called Saul's servant Ziba.
David said to him, "I have given your master's
grandson everything that belonged to Saul and
his family. 10You, your sons, and your servants
will farm the land and harvest the crops. Then
your family will have food to eat. But Mephibosheth, your master's grandson, will always eat
at my table."
(Now Ziba had fifteen sons and twenty servants.) 11Ziba said to King David, "I, your servant, will do everything my master, the king,
commands me."
So Mephibosheth ate at David's table as if he
were one of the king's sons. 12Mephibosheth
had a young son named Mica. Everyone in
Ziba's family became Mephibosheth's servants.
13Mephibosheth lived in Jerusalem, because he
always ate at the king's table. And he was crippled in both feet.

FRIENDSHIP

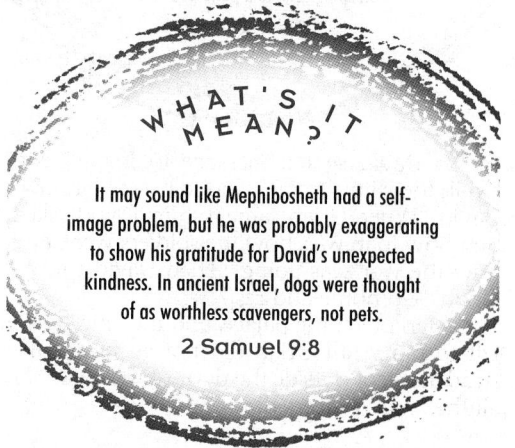

How can friendship outlast death? (9:1)

WHAT'S IT MEAN?

It may sound like Mephibosheth had a self-image problem, but he was probably exaggerating to show his gratitude for David's unexpected kindness. In ancient Israel, dogs were thought of as worthless scavengers, not pets.

2 Samuel 9:8

WAR WITH THE AMMONITES AND ARAMEANS

10 1When Nahash king of the Ammonites died,
his son Hanun became king after him. 2David
said, "Nahash was loyal to me, so I will be loyal
to his son Hanun." So David sent his messengers to comfort Hanun about his father's death.
David's officers went to the land of the Ammonites. 3But the Ammonite leaders said to
Hanun, their master, "Do you think David
wants to honor your father by sending men to
comfort you? No! David sent them to study the
city and spy it out and capture it!" 4So Hanun
arrested David's officers. To shame them he
shaved off half their beards and cut off their
clothes at the hips. Then he sent them away.
5When the people told David, he sent messengers to meet his officers because they were
very ashamed. King David said, "Stay in Jericho until your beards have grown back. Then
come home."
6The Ammonites knew that they had insulted David. So they hired twenty thousand
Aramean foot soldiers from Beth Rehob and
Zobah. They also hired the king of Maacah
with a thousand men and twelve thousand
men from Tob.
7When David heard about this, he sent Joab
with the whole army. 8The Ammonites came
out and prepared for battle at the city gate. The
Arameans from Zobah and Rehob and the men
from Tob and Maacah were out in the field by
themselves.
9Joab saw that there were enemies both in
front of him and behind him. So he chose

8:18 Kerethites and Pelethites These were probably special units of the army that were responsible for the king's safety, a kind of palace guard.

WHAT'S IT MEAN?

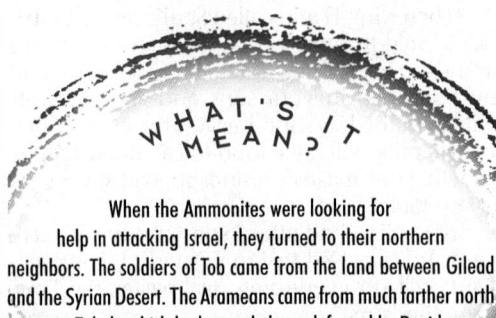

When the Ammonites were looking for help in attacking Israel, they turned to their northern neighbors. The soldiers of Tob came from the land between Gilead and the Syrian Desert. The Arameans came from much farther north in Zobah, which had recently been defeated by David.

2 Samuel 10:8

some of the best soldiers of Israel and sent them out to fight the Arameans. [10]Joab put the rest of the army under the command of Abishai, his brother. Then he sent them out to fight the Ammonites. [11]Joab said to Abishai, "If the Arameans are too strong for me, you must help me. Or, if the Ammonites are too strong for you, I will help you. [12]Be strong. We must fight bravely for our people and the cities of our God. The LORD will do what he thinks is right."

[13]Then Joab and the army with him went to attack the Arameans, and the Arameans ran away. [14]When the Ammonites saw that the Arameans were running away, they also ran away from Abishai and went back to their city. So Joab returned from the battle with the Ammonites and came to Jerusalem.

[15]When the Arameans saw that Israel had defeated them, they came together into one big army. [16]Hadadezer sent messengers to bring the Arameans from east of the Euphrates River, and they went to Helam. Their leader was Shobach, the commander of Hadadezer's army.

[17]When David heard about this, he gathered all the Israelites together. They crossed over the Jordan River and went to Helam. There the Arameans prepared for battle and attacked him. [18]But the Arameans ran away from the Israelites. David killed seven hundred Aramean chariot drivers and forty thousand Aramean horsemen. He also killed Shobach, the commander of the Aramean army.

[19]When the kings who served Hadadezer saw that the Israelites had defeated them, they made peace with the Israelites and served them. And the Arameans were afraid to help the Ammonites again.

DAVID SINS WITH BATHSHEBA

11 [1]In the spring, when the kings normally went out to war, David sent out Joab, his servants, and all the Israelites. They destroyed the Ammonites and attacked the city of Rabbah. But David stayed in Jerusalem. [2]One evening David got up from his bed and walked around on the roof[n] of his palace. While he was on the roof, he saw a woman bathing. She was very beautiful. [3]So David sent his servants to find out who she was. A servant answered, "That woman is Bathsheba daughter of Eliam. She is the wife of Uriah the Hittite." [4]So David sent messengers to bring Bathsheba to him. When she came to him, he had sexual relations with her. (Now Bathsheba had purified herself from her monthly period.) Then she went back to her house. [5]But Bathsheba became pregnant and sent word to David, saying, "I am pregnant."

LUST
Where can sexual lust lead? (11:1–5)

WHAT'S IT MEAN?

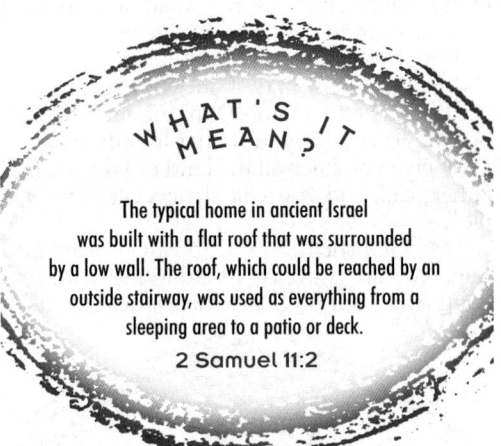

The typical home in ancient Israel was built with a flat roof that was surrounded by a low wall. The roof, which could be reached by an outside stairway, was used as everything from a sleeping area to a patio or deck.

2 Samuel 11:2

[6]So David sent a message to Joab: "Send Uriah the Hittite to me." And Joab sent Uriah to David. [7]When Uriah came to him, David asked him how Joab was, how the soldiers were, and how the war was going. [8]Then David said to Uriah, "Go home and rest."

So Uriah left the palace, and the king sent a gift to him. [9]But Uriah did not go home. Instead, he slept outside the door of the palace as all the king's officers did.

11:2 roof In Bible times houses were built with flat roofs. The roof was used for drying things such as flax and fruit. And it was used as an extra room, as a place for worship, and as a cool place to sleep in the summer.

10 The officers told David, "Uriah did not go home."

Then David said to Uriah, "You came from a long trip. Why didn't you go home?"

11 Uriah said to him, "The Ark and the soldiers of Israel and Judah are staying in tents. My master Joab and his officers are camping out in the fields. It isn't right for me to go home to eat and drink and have sexual relations with my wife!"

12 David said to Uriah, "Stay here today. Tomorrow I'll send you back to the battle." So Uriah stayed in Jerusalem that day and the next. 13 Then David called Uriah to come to see him, so Uriah ate and drank with David. David made Uriah drunk, but he still did not go home. That evening Uriah again slept with the king's officers.

14 The next morning David wrote a letter to Joab and sent it by Uriah. 15 In the letter David wrote, "Put Uriah on the front lines where the fighting is worst and leave him there alone. Let him be killed in battle."

16 Joab watched the city and saw where its strongest defenders were and put Uriah there. 17 When the men of the city came out to fight against Joab, some of David's men were killed. And Uriah the Hittite was one of them.

18 Then Joab sent David a complete account of the war. 19 Joab told the messenger, "Tell King David what happened in the war. 20 After you finish, the king may be angry and ask, 'Why did you go so near the city to fight? Didn't you know they would shoot arrows from the city wall? 21 Do you remember who killed Abimelech son of Jerub-Besheth?[n] It was a woman on the city wall. She threw a large stone for grinding grain on Abimelech and killed him there in Thebez. Why did you go so near the wall?' If King David asks that, tell him, 'Your servant Uriah the Hittite also died.' "

22 The messenger left and went to David and told him everything Joab had told him to say. 23 The messenger told David, "The men of Ammon were winning. They came out and attacked us in the field, but we fought them back to the city gate. 24 The archers on the city wall shot at your servants, and some of your men were killed. Your servant Uriah the Hittite also died."

25 David said to the messenger, "Say this to Joab: 'Don't be upset about this. The sword kills everyone the same. Make a stronger attack against the city and capture it.' Encourage Joab with these words."

26 When Bathsheba heard that her husband was dead, she cried for him. 27 After she finished her time of sadness, David sent servants to bring her to his house. She became David's wife and gave birth to his son, but the LORD did not like what David had done.

DAVID'S SON DIES

12 1 The LORD sent Nathan to David. When he came to David, he said, "There were two men in a city. One was rich, but the other was poor. 2 The rich man had many sheep and cattle. 3 But the poor man had nothing except one little female lamb he had bought. The poor man fed the lamb, and it grew up with him and his children. It shared his food and drank from his cup and slept in his arms. The lamb was like a daughter to him.

4 "Then a traveler stopped to visit the rich man. The rich man wanted to feed the traveler, but he didn't want to take one of his own sheep or cattle. Instead, he took the lamb from the poor man and cooked it for his visitor."

5 David became very angry at the rich man. He said to Nathan, "As surely as the LORD lives, the man who did this should die! 6 He must pay for the lamb four times for doing such a thing. He had no mercy!"

7 Then Nathan said to David, "You are the man! This is what the LORD, the God of Israel, says: 'I appointed you king of Israel and saved you from Saul. 8 I gave you his kingdom and his wives. And I made you king of Israel and Judah. And if that had not been enough, I would have given you even more. 9 So why did you ignore the LORD's

SIN

Does sin have consequences? (12:9–12)

WHAT'S IT MEAN?

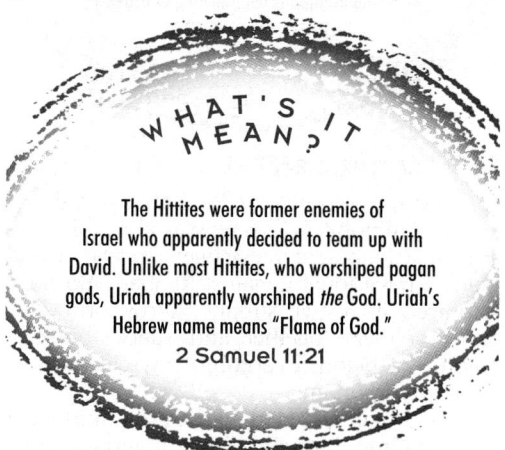

The Hittites were former enemies of Israel who apparently decided to team up with David. Unlike most Hittites, who worshiped pagan gods, Uriah apparently worshiped *the* God. Uriah's Hebrew name means "Flame of God."

2 Samuel 11:21

11:21 Jerub-Besheth Another name for Gideon.

command? Why did you do what he says is
wrong? You killed Uriah the Hittite with the
sword of the Ammonites and took his wife to
be your wife! [10]Now there will always be people in your family who will die by a sword,
because you did not respect me; you took the
wife of Uriah the Hittite for yourself!'
[11]"This is what the LORD
says: 'I am bringing trouble
to you from your own
family. While you watch,
I will take your wives
from you and give
them to someone who
is very close to you.
He will have sexual
relations with your
wives, and everyone
will know it. [12]You had
sexual relations with
Bathsheba in secret, but I
will do this so all the people
of Israel can see it.' "
[13]Then David said to Nathan, "I have sinned
against the LORD."
Nathan answered, "The LORD has taken
away your sin. You will not die. [14]But what
you did caused the LORD's enemies to lose all
respect for him. For this reason the son who
was born to you will die."
[15]Then Nathan went home. And the LORD
caused the son of David and Bathsheba,
Uriah's widow, to be very sick. [16]David prayed
to God for the baby. David refused to eat or
drink. He went into his house and stayed there,
lying on the ground all night. [17]The older leaders of David's family came to him and tried to
pull him up from the ground, but he refused to
get up or to eat food with them.
[18]On the seventh day the baby died. David's
servants were afraid to tell him that the baby
was dead. They said, "Look, we tried to talk to
David while the baby was alive, but he refused
to listen to us. If we tell him the baby is dead,
he may do something awful."
[19]When David saw his servants whispering,
he knew that the baby was dead. So he asked
them, "Is the baby dead?"
They answered, "Yes, he is dead."
[20]Then David got up from the floor, washed
himself, put lotions on, and changed his
clothes. Then he went into the LORD's house to
worship. After that, he went home and asked
for something to eat. His servants gave him
some food, and he ate.

"She became pregnant again and had another son, whom David named Solomon. The LORD loved Solomon. The LORD sent word through Nathan the prophet to name the baby Jedidiah, because the LORD loved the child." (2 Samuel 12:24b–25)

[21]David's servants said to him, "Why are
you doing this? When the baby was still alive,
you refused to eat and you cried. Now that the
baby is dead, you get up and eat food."
[22]David said, "While the baby was still alive,
I refused to eat, and I cried. I thought, 'Who
knows? Maybe the LORD will feel sorry for me
and let the baby live.' [23]But
now that the baby is dead,
why should I go with-
out food? I can't bring
him back to life. Some
day I will go to him, but
he cannot come back
to me."
[24]Then David com-
forted Bathsheba his
wife. He slept with her
and had sexual rela-
tions with her. She be-
came pregnant again and
had another son, whom Da-
vid named Solomon. The LORD
loved Solomon. [25]The LORD sent word through
Nathan the prophet to name the baby
Jedidiah,[n] because the LORD loved the child.

WHAT'S IT MEAN?

The name *Jedidiah* means "loved by the LORD." Nathan gave Solomon this name to indicate that God had forgiven David. Not only would Solomon live—unlike his older brother—he would eventually become king of Israel.

2 Samuel 12:25

DAVID CAPTURES RABBAH

[26]Joab fought against Rabbah, a royal city
of the Ammonites, and he was about to capture it. [27]Joab sent messengers to David and
said, "I have fought against Rabbah and have
captured its water supply. [28]Now bring the
other soldiers together and attack this city.
Capture it before I capture it myself and it is
called by my name!"
[29]So David gathered all the army and went
to Rabbah and fought against it and captured

12:25 Jedidiah This name means "loved by the LORD."

WHAT'S IT MEAN?

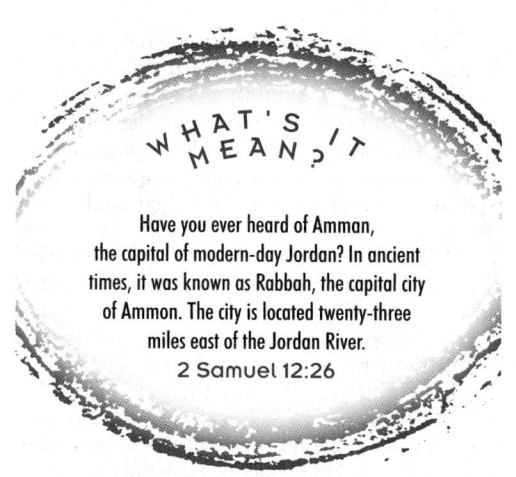

Have you ever heard of Amman, the capital of modern-day Jordan? In ancient times, it was known as Rabbah, the capital city of Ammon. The city is located twenty-three miles east of the Jordan River.

2 Samuel 12:26

it. 30David took the crown off their king's head
and had it placed on his own head. That gold
crown weighed about seventy-five pounds,
and it had valuable gems in it. And David took
many valuable things from the city. 31He also
brought out the people of the city and forced
them to work with saws, iron picks, and axes.
He also made them build with bricks. David
did this to all the Ammonite cities. Then David
and all his army returned to Jerusalem.

AMNON AND TAMAR

13
1David had a son named Absalom and a
son named Amnon. Absalom had a beautiful
sister named Tamar, and Amnon loved her.
2Tamar was a virgin. Amnon made himself sick
just thinking about her, because he could not
find any chance to be alone with her.

3Amnon had a friend named Jonadab son
of Shimeah, David's brother. Jonadab was a
very clever man. 4He asked Amnon, "Son of the
king, why do you look so sad day after day?
Tell me what's wrong!"

Amnon told him, "I love Tamar, the sister of
my half-brother Absalom."

5Jonadab said to Amnon, "Go to bed and
act as if you are sick. Then your father will
come to see you. Tell him, 'Please let my sister
Tamar come in and give me food to eat. Let her
make the food in front of me so I can watch
and eat it from her hand.' "

6So Amnon went to bed and acted sick.
When King David came in to see him, Amnon
said to him, "Please let my sister Tamar come
in. Let her make two of her special cakes for me
while I watch. Then I will eat them from her
hands."

7David sent for Tamar in the palace, saying,
"Go to your brother Amnon's house and make
some food for him." 8So Tamar went to her
brother Amnon's house, and he was in bed.
Tamar took some dough and pressed it together
with her hands. She made some special
cakes while Amnon watched. Then she baked
them. 9Next she took the pan and served him,
but he refused to eat.

He said to his servants, "All of you, leave me
alone!" So they all left him alone. 10Amnon said
to Tamar, "Bring the food into the bedroom so
I may eat from your hand."

Tamar took the cakes she had made and
brought them to her brother Amnon in the
bedroom. 11She went to him so he could eat
from her hands, but Amnon grabbed her. He
said, "Sister, come and have sexual relations
with me."

12Tamar said to him, "No, brother! Don't
force me! This should never be done in Israel!
Don't do this shameful thing! 13I could never
get rid of my shame! And you will be like the
shameful fools in Israel! Please talk with the
king, and he will let you marry me."

14But Amnon refused to listen to her. He
was stronger than she was, so he forced her to
have sexual relations with him. 15After that,
Amnon hated Tamar. He hated her more than
he had loved her before. Amnon said to her,
"Get up and leave!"

16Tamar said to him, "No! Sending me away
would be worse than what you've already
done!"

But he refused to listen to her. 17He called
his young servant back in and said, "Get this
woman out of here and away from me! Lock
the door after her." 18So his servant led her out
of the room and bolted the door after her.

Tamar was wearing a special robe with long
sleeves, because the king's virgin daughters

WHAT'S IT MEAN?

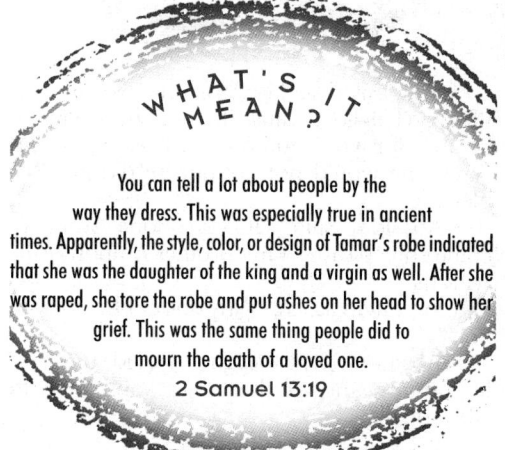

You can tell a lot about people by the way they dress. This was especially true in ancient times. Apparently, the style, color, or design of Tamar's robe indicated that she was the daughter of the king and a virgin as well. After she was raped, she tore the robe and put ashes on her head to show her grief. This was the same thing people did to mourn the death of a loved one.

2 Samuel 13:19

wore this kind of robe. 19To show how upset
she was, Tamar put ashes on her head and tore
her special robe and put her hand on her head.
Then she went away, crying loudly.
20Absalom, Tamar's brother, said to her,
"Has Amnon, your brother, forced you to have
sexual relations with him? For now, sister, be
quiet. He is your half-brother. Don't let this
upset you so much!" So Tamar lived in her
brother Absalom's house and was sad and
lonely.
21When King David heard the news, he was
very angry. 22Absalom did not say a word,
good or bad, to Amnon. But he hated Amnon
for disgracing his sister Tamar.

ABSALOM'S REVENGE

23Two years later Absalom had some men
come to Baal Hazor, near Ephraim, to cut the
wool from his sheep. Absalom invited all the
king's sons to come also. 24Absalom went to
the king and said, "I have men coming to cut
the wool. Please come with your officers and
join me."

WHAT'S IT MEAN?

Entertaining a king in ancient times was a pretty expensive job. Not only did the host have to feed and house the king himself; he had to take care of all the servants and officials who traveled with the king. King David did not want his son Absalom to have to pay for such a visit.

2 Samuel 13:25

25King David said to Absalom, "No, my son.
We won't all go, because it would be too much
trouble for you." Although Absalom begged
David, he would not go, but he did give his
blessing.
26Absalom said, "If you don't want to
come, then please let my brother Amnon come
with us."
King David asked, "Why should he go with
you?"
27Absalom kept begging David until he
let Amnon and all the king's sons go with
Absalom.
28Then Absalom instructed his servants,
"Watch Amnon. When he is drunk, I will tell
you, 'Kill Amnon.' Right then, kill him! Don't be
afraid, because I have commanded you! Be
strong and brave!" 29So Absalom's young men
killed Amnon as Absalom commanded, but all
of David's other sons got on their mules and
escaped.
30While the king's sons were on their way,
the news came to David, "Absalom has killed
all of the king's sons! Not one of them is left
alive!" 31King David tore his clothes and lay on
the ground to show his sadness. All his servants standing nearby tore their clothes also.
32Jonadab son of Shimeah, David's brother,
said to David, "Don't think all the young men,
your sons, are killed. No, only Amnon is dead!
Absalom has planned this ever since Amnon
forced his sister Tamar to have sexual relations
with him. 33My master and king, don't think
that all of the king's sons are dead. Only Amnon is dead!"
34In the meantime Absalom had run away.
A guard standing on the city wall saw
many people coming from the other side of the
hill. 35So Jonadab said to King David, "Look, I
was right! The king's sons are coming!"
36As soon as Jonadab had said this, the
king's sons arrived, crying loudly. David and
all his servants began crying also. 37David cried
for his son every day.
But Absalom ran away to Talmai[n] son of
Ammihud, the king of Geshur. 38After Absalom
ran away to Geshur, he stayed there for three
years. 39When King David got over Amnon's
death, he missed Absalom greatly.

WHAT'S IT MEAN?

Absalom had royal blood from both sides of his family. His mother, Maacah, was the daughter of King Talmai. Talmai's kingdom, Geshur, was a small Syrian country on the eastern shore of the Lake Galilee, about sixty miles from Jerusalem.

2 Samuel 13:37–38

13:37 Talmai He was Absalom's grandfather.

JOAB SENDS A WISE WOMAN TO DAVID

14
1Joab son of Zeruiah knew that King David
missed Absalom very much. 2So Joab sent
messengers to Tekoa to bring a wise woman
from there. He said to her, "Pretend to be very
sad. Put on funeral clothes and don't put lotion
on yourself. Act like a woman who has been
crying many days for someone who died.
3Then go to the king and say these words."
Then Joab told her what to say.
4So the woman from Tekoa spoke to the
king. She bowed facedown on the ground to
show respect and said, "My king, help me!"
5King David asked her, "What is the matter?"
The woman said, "I am a widow; my husband is dead. 6I had two sons. They were out in
the field fighting, and no one was there to stop
them. So one son killed the other son. 7Now all
the family group is against me. They said to me,
'Bring the son who killed his brother so we may
kill him for killing his brother. That way we will
also get rid of the one who would receive what
belonged to his father.' My son is like the last
spark of a fire. He is all I have left. If they kill
him, my husband's name and property will be
gone from the earth."
8Then the king said to the woman, "Go
home. I will take care of this for you."
9The woman of Tekoa said to him, "Let the
blame be on me and my father's family. My
master and king, you and your throne are innocent."
10King David said, "Bring me anyone who
says anything bad to you. Then he won't
bother you again."
11The woman said, "Please promise in the
name of the LORD your God. Then my relative
who has the duty of punishing a murderer
won't add to the destruction by killing my son."
David said, "As surely as the LORD lives, no
one will hurt your son. Not one hair from his
head will fall to the ground."
12The woman said, "Let me say something
to you, my master and king."
The king said, "Speak."
13Then the woman said, "Why have you decided this way against the people of God?
When you judge this way, you show that you
are guilty for not bringing back your son who
was forced to leave home. 14We will all die
some day. We're like water spilled on the
ground; no one can gather it back. But God
doesn't take away life. Instead, he plans ways
that those who have been sent away will not
have to stay away from him! 15My master and
king, I came to say this to you because the
people have made me afraid! I thought, 'Let me
talk to the king. Maybe he will do what I ask.
16Maybe he will listen. Perhaps he will save me
from those who want to keep both me and my
son from getting what God gave us.'
17"Now I say, 'May the words of my master
the king give me rest. Like an angel of God, you
know what is good and what is bad. May the
LORD your God be with you!' "
18Then King David said, "Do not hide the
truth. Answer me one question."
The woman said, "My master the king,
please ask your question."
19The king said, "Did Joab tell you to say all
these things?"
The woman answered, "As you live, my
master the king, no one could avoid that question. You are right. Your servant Joab did tell
me to say these things. 20Joab did it so you
would see things differently. My master, you
are wise like an angel of God who knows everything that happens on earth."

ABSALOM RETURNS TO JERUSALEM

21The king said to Joab, "Look, I will do
what I promised. Bring back the young man
Absalom."
22Joab bowed facedown on the ground and
blessed the king. Then he said, "Today I know
you are pleased with me, because you have
done what I asked."
23Then Joab got up and went to Geshur and
brought Absalom back to Jerusalem. 24But
King David said, "Absalom must go to his own
house. He may not come to see me." So Absalom went to his own house and did not go to
see the king.
25Absalom was greatly praised for his
handsome appearance. No man in Israel was
as handsome as he. No blemish was on him
from his head to his foot. 26At the end of every
year, Absalom would cut his hair, because it
became too heavy. When he weighed it, it
would weigh about five pounds by the royal
measure.
27Absalom had three sons and one daughter. His daughter's name was also Tamar, and
she was a beautiful woman.
28Absalom lived in Jerusalem for two full
years without seeing King David. 29Then Absalom sent for Joab so he could send him to the
king, but Joab would not come. Absalom sent
a message a second time, but Joab still refused
to come. 30Then Absalom said to his servants,
"Look, Joab's field is next to mine, and he has
barley growing there. Go burn it." So Absalom's servants set fire to Joab's field.
31Then Joab went to Absalom's house and

said to him, "Why did your servants burn my
field?"
32 Absalom said to Joab, "I sent a message to
you, asking you to come here. I wanted to send
you to the king to ask him why he brought me
home from Geshur. It would have been better
for me to stay there! Now let me see the king. If
I have sinned, he can put me to death!"
33 So Joab went to the king and told him
Absalom's words. Then the king called for Absalom. Absalom came and bowed facedown
on the ground before the king, and the king
kissed him.

ABSALOM PLANS TO TAKE DAVID'S KINGDOM

15 1 After this, Absalom got a chariot and
horses for himself and fifty men to run before
him. 2 Absalom would get up early and stand
near the city gate.[n] Anyone who had a problem for the king to settle would come here.
When someone came, Absalom would call out
and say, "What city are you from?"

WHAT'S IT MEAN?

Hebron, a city about twenty miles southwest of Jerusalem, was important in Israel's history. Abraham, Isaac, and Jacob were all buried there. Because Absalom was a hometown boy, he found many supporters in Hebron. One of these supporters, Ahithophel, may have been related to Bathsheba. He may have supported Absalom out of his disgust with King David for his sin with Bathsheba.

2 Samuel 15:10–12

The person would answer, "I'm from one of
the tribes of Israel."
3 Then Absalom would say, "Look, your
claims are right, but the king has no one to
listen to you." 4 Absalom would also say, "I wish
someone would make me judge in this land!
Then people with problems could come to me,
and I could help them get justice."
5 People would come near Absalom to bow
to him. When they did, Absalom would reach
out his hand and take hold of them and kiss
them. 6 Absalom did that to all the Israelites
who came to King David for decisions. In this
way, Absalom stole the hearts of all Israel.
7 After four years Absalom said to King David, "Please let me go to Hebron. I want to carry
out my promise that I made to the LORD 8 while
I was living in Geshur in Aram. I said, 'If the
LORD takes me back to Jerusalem, I will worship
him in Hebron.' "
9 The king said, "Go in peace."
So Absalom went to Hebron. 10 But he sent
secret messengers through all the tribes of Israel. They told the people, "When you hear the
trumpets, say this: 'Absalom is the king at Hebron!' "
11 Absalom had invited two hundred men to
go with him. So they went from Jerusalem
with him, but they didn't know what he was
planning. 12 While Absalom was offering sacrifices, he sent for Ahithophel, one of the people
who advised David, to come from his hometown of Giloh. So Absalom's plans were working very well. More and more people began to
support him.
13 A messenger came to David, saying, "The
Israelites are giving their loyalty to Absalom."
14 Then David said to all his officers who
were with him in Jerusalem, "We must leave
quickly! If we don't, we won't be able to get
away from Absalom. We must hurry before he
catches us and destroys us and kills the people
of Jerusalem."
15 The king's officers said to him, "We will do
anything you say."
16 The king set out with everyone in his
house, but he left ten slave women to take care
of the palace. 17 The king left with all his people
following him, and they stopped at a house far
away. 18 All the king's servants passed by him—

WHAT'S IT MEAN?

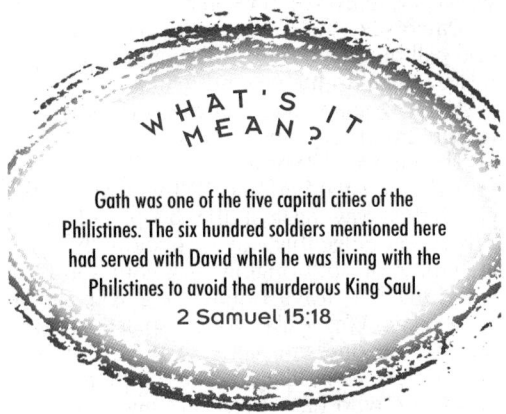

Gath was one of the five capital cities of the Philistines. The six hundred soldiers mentioned here had served with David while he was living with the Philistines to avoid the murderous King Saul.

2 Samuel 15:18

15:2 city gate People came here to conduct business. Public meetings and court cases were also held here.

the Kerethites and Pelethites,[n] all those from
Gath, and the six hundred men who had followed him.
[19]The king said to Ittai, a man from Gath,
"Why are you also going with us? Turn back
and stay with King Absalom because you are a
foreigner. This is not your homeland. [20]You
joined me only a short time ago. Should I make
you wander with us when I don't even know
where I'm going? Turn back and take your
brothers with you. May kindness and loyalty
be shown to you."
[21]But Ittai said to the king, "As surely as the
LORD lives and as you live, I will stay with you,
whether it means life or death."
[22]David said to Ittai, "Go, march on." So Ittai
from Gath and all his people with their children marched on. [23]All the people cried loudly
as everyone passed by. King David crossed the
Kidron Valley, and then all the people went on
to the desert. [24]Zadok and all the Levites with
him carried the Ark of the Agreement with
God. They set it down, and Abiathar offered
sacrifices until all the people had left the city.

WHAT'S IT MEAN?

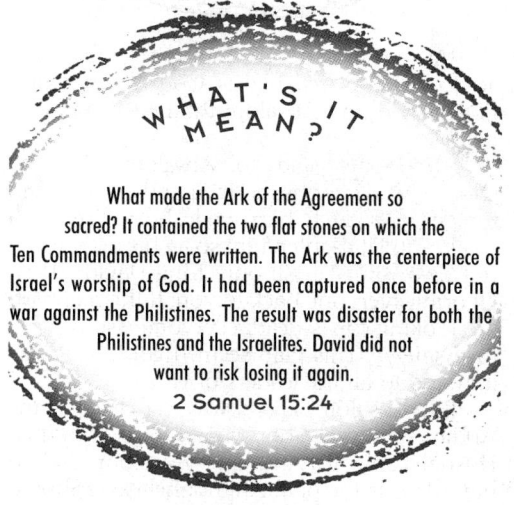

What made the Ark of the Agreement so sacred? It contained the two flat stones on which the Ten Commandments were written. The Ark was the centerpiece of Israel's worship of God. It had been captured once before in a war against the Philistines. The result was disaster for both the Philistines and the Israelites. David did not want to risk losing it again.
2 Samuel 15:24

[25]The king said to Zadok, "Take the Ark of
God back into the city. If the LORD is pleased
with me, he will bring me back and will let me
see both it and Jerusalem again. [26]But if the
LORD says he is not pleased with me, I am
ready. He can do what he wants with me."
[27]The king also said to Zadok the priest,
"Aren't you a seer? Go back to the city in peace
and take your son Ahimaaz and Abiathar's
son Jonathan with you. [28]I will wait near the
crossings into the desert until I hear from you."
[29]So Zadok and Abiathar took the Ark of God
back to Jerusalem and stayed there.
[30]David went up the Mount of Olives, crying as he went. He covered his head and went
barefoot. All the people with David covered
their heads also and cried as they went.
[31]Someone told David, "Ahithophel is one of
the people with Absalom who made secret
plans against you."
So David prayed, "LORD, please make
Ahithophel's advice foolish."
[32]When David reached the top of the
mountain where people used to worship God,
Hushai the Arkite came to meet him. Hushai's
coat was torn, and there was dirt on his head
to show how sad he was. [33]David said to Hushai, "If you go with me, you will be just one
more person for me to take care of. [34]But if you
return to the city, you can make Ahithophel's
advice useless. Tell Absalom, 'I am your servant, my king. In the past I served your father,
but now I will serve you.' [35]The priests Zadok
and Abiathar will be with you. Tell them
everything you hear in the royal palace.
[36]Zadok's son Ahimaaz and Abiathar's son
Jonathan are with them. Send them to tell me
everything you hear." [37]So David's friend Hushai entered Jerusalem just as Absalom arrived.

ZIBA MEETS DAVID

16 [1]When David had passed a short way over
the top of the Mount of Olives, Ziba,
Mephibosheth's servant, met him. Ziba had a
row of donkeys loaded with two hundred
loaves of bread, one hundred cakes of raisins,
one hundred cakes of figs, and leather bags full
of wine. [2]The king asked Ziba, "What are these
things for?"
Ziba answered, "The donkeys are for your
family to ride. The bread and cakes of figs are
for the servants to eat. And the wine is for anyone to drink who might become weak in the
desert."
[3]The king asked, "Where is Mephibosheth?"
Ziba answered him, "Mephibosheth is staying in Jerusalem because he thinks, 'Today the
Israelites will give my father's kingdom back
to me!' "
[4]Then the king said to Ziba, "All right.
Everything that belonged to Mephibosheth, I
now give to you!"
Ziba said, "I bow to you. I hope I will always be able to please you."

15:18 Kerethites and Pelethites These were probably special units of the army that were responsible for the king's safety, a kind of palace guard.

SHIMEI CURSES DAVID

5As King David came to Bahurim, a man
came out and cursed him. He was from Saul's
family group, and his name was Shimei son of
Gera. 6He threw stones at David and his officers, but the people and soldiers gathered all
around David. 7Shimei cursed David, saying,
"Get out, get out, you murderer, you troublemaker. 8The LORD is punishing you for the
people in Saul's family you killed! You took
Saul's place as king, but now the LORD has
given the kingdom to your son Absalom! Now
you are ruined because you are a murderer!"
9Abishai son of Zeruiah said to the king,
"Why should this dead dog curse you, the
king? Let me go over and cut off his head!"
10But the king answered, "This does not
concern you, sons of Zeruiah! If he is cursing
me because the LORD told him to, who can
question him?"
11David also said to Abishai and all his officers, "My own son is trying to kill me! This man
is a Benjaminite and has more right to kill me!
Leave him alone, and let him curse me because
the LORD told him to do this. 12Maybe the
LORD will see my misery and repay me with
something good for Shimei's curses today!"
13So David and his men went on down the
road, but Shimei followed on the nearby hillside. He kept cursing David and throwing
stones and dirt at him. 14When the king and all
his people arrived at the Jordan, they were
very tired, so they rested there.
15Meanwhile, Absalom, Ahithophel, and all
the Israelites arrived at Jerusalem. 16David's
friend Hushai the Arkite came to Absalom and
said to him, "Long live the king! Long live the
king!"
17Absalom asked, "Why are you not loyal to
your friend David? Why didn't you leave Jerusalem with your friend?"
18Hushai said, "I belong to the one chosen
by the LORD and by these people and everyone
in Israel. I will stay with you. 19In the past I
served your father. So whom should I serve
now? David's son! I will serve you as I served
him."

AHITHOPHEL'S ADVICE

20Absalom said to Ahithophel, "Tell us what
we should do."
21Ahithophel said, "Your father left behind
some of his slave women to take care of the
palace. Have sexual relations with them. Then
all Israel will hear that your father is your enemy, and all your people will be encouraged to
give you more support." 22So they put up a tent
for Absalom on the roof[n] of the palace where
everyone in Israel could see it. And Absalom
had sexual relations with his father's slave
women.

WHAT'S IT MEAN?

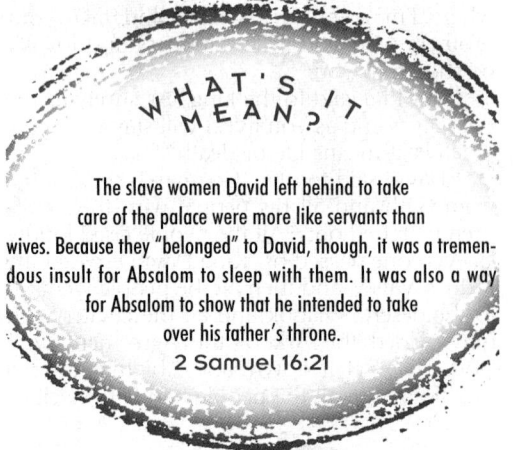

The slave women David left behind to take care of the palace were more like servants than wives. Because they "belonged" to David, though, it was a tremendous insult for Absalom to sleep with them. It was also a way for Absalom to show that he intended to take over his father's throne.

2 Samuel 16:21

23At that time people thought Ahithophel's
advice was as reliable as God's own word.
Both David and Absalom thought it was that
reliable.

17 1Ahithophel said to Absalom, "Let me
choose twelve thousand men and chase David
tonight. 2I'll catch him while he is tired and
weak, and I'll frighten him so all his people will
run away. But I'll kill only King David. 3Then
I'll bring everyone back to you. If the man you
are looking for is dead, everyone else will return safely." 4This plan seemed good to Absalom and to all the leaders of Israel.
5But Absalom said, "Now call Hushai the
Arkite, so I can hear what he says." 6When
Hushai came to Absalom, Absalom said to
him, "This is the plan Ahithophel gave. Should
we follow it? If not, tell us."
7Hushai said to Absalom, "Ahithophel's advice is not good this time." 8Hushai added, "You
know your father and his men are strong. They
are as angry as a bear that is robbed of its cubs.
Your father is a skilled fighter. He won't stay all
night with the army. 9He is probably already
hiding in a cave or some other place. If the first
attack fails, people will hear the news and
think, 'Absalom's followers are losing!' 10Then

16:22 roof In Bible times houses were built with flat roofs. The roof was used for drying things such as flax and fruit. And it was used as an extra room, as a place for worship, and as a cool place to sleep in the summer.

even the men who are as brave as lions will be
frightened, because all the Israelites know your
father is a fighter. They know his men are
brave!
11"This is what I suggest: Gather all the Israelites from Dan to Beersheba.[n] There will be as
many people as grains of sand by the sea. Then
you yourself must go into the battle. 12We will
go to David wherever he is hiding. We will fall
on him as dew falls on the ground. We will
kill him and all of his men so that no one
will be left alive. 13If David escapes into a city,
all the Israelites will bring ropes to that city
and pull it into the valley. Not a stone will be
left!"
14Absalom and all the Israelites said, "The
advice of Hushai the Arkite is better than that
of Ahithophel." (The LORD had planned to destroy the good advice of Ahithophel so the
LORD could bring disaster on Absalom.)
15Hushai told Zadok and Abiathar, the
priests, what Ahithophel had suggested to Absalom and the older leaders of Israel. He also
reported to them what he himself had suggested. Hushai said, 16"Quickly! Send a message
to David. Tell him not to stay tonight at the
crossings into the desert but to cross over
the Jordan River at once. If he crosses the river,
he and all his people won't be destroyed."
17Jonathan and Ahimaaz were waiting at En
Rogel. They did not want to be seen going into
the city, so a servant girl would go out to them
and give them messages. Then Jonathan and
Ahimaaz would go and tell King David.
18But a boy saw Jonathan and Ahimaaz and
told Absalom. So Jonathan and Ahimaaz left
quickly and went to a man's house in Bahurim. He had a well in his courtyard, and they
climbed down into it. 19The man's wife spread
a sheet over the opening of the well and covered it with grain. No one could tell that anyone was hiding there.
20Absalom's servants came to the woman at
the house and asked, "Where are Ahimaaz and
Jonathan?"

She said to them, "They have already
crossed the brook."

Absalom's servants then went to look for
Jonathan and Ahimaaz, but they could not
find them. So they went back to Jerusalem.
21After Absalom's servants left, Jonathan
and Ahimaaz climbed out of the well and went
to tell King David. They said, "Hurry, cross
over the river! Ahithophel has said these things
against you!" 22So David and all his people
crossed the Jordan River. By dawn, everyone
had crossed the Jordan.
23When Ahithophel saw that the Israelites
did not accept his advice, he saddled his donkey and went to his hometown. He left orders
for his family and property, and then he
hanged himself. He died and was buried in his
father's tomb.

WAR BETWEEN DAVID AND ABSALOM

24David arrived at Mahanaim. And Absalom and all his Israelites crossed over the Jordan River. 25Absalom had made Amasa
captain of the army instead of Joab. Amasa
was the son of a man named Jether the Ishmaelite. Amasa's mother was Abigail daughter of
Nahash and sister of Zeruiah, Joab's mother.
26Absalom and the Israelites camped in the
land of Gilead.
27Shobi, Makir, and Barzillai were at Mahanaim when David arrived. Shobi son of Nahash was from the Ammonite town of
Rabbah. Makir son of Ammiel was from Lo
Debar, and Barzillai was from Rogelim in Gilead. 28They brought beds, bowls, clay pots,
wheat, barley, flour, roasted grain, beans, small
peas, 29honey, milk curds, sheep, and cheese
made from cows' milk for David and his people. They said, "The people are hungry and
tired and thirsty in the desert."

18 1David counted his men and placed over
them commanders of thousands and commanders of hundreds. 2He sent the troops out
in three groups. Joab commanded one-third of
the men. Joab's brother Abishai son of Zeruiah
commanded another third. And Ittai from
Gath commanded the last third. King David
said to them, "I will also go with you."
3But the men said, "You must not go with
us! If we run away in the battle, Absalom's
men won't care. Even if half of us are killed,
Absalom's men won't care. But you're worth
ten thousand of us! You can help us most by
staying in the city."
4The king said to his people, "I will do what
you think is best." So the king stood at the side
of the gate as the army went out in groups of a
hundred and a thousand.
5The king commanded Joab, Abishai, and
Ittai, "Be gentle with young Absalom for my
sake." Everyone heard the king's orders to the
commanders about Absalom.
6David's army went out into the field

17:11 Dan to Beersheba Dan was the city farthest north in Israel, and Beersheba was the city farthest south. So this means all the people of Israel.

against Absalom's Israelites, and they fought in
the forest of Ephraim. 7There David's army defeated the Israelites. Many died that day—
twenty thousand men. 8The battle spread
through all the country, but that day more
men died in the forest than in the fighting.

ABSALOM DIES

9Then Absalom happened to meet David's
troops. As Absalom was riding his mule, it
went under the thick branches of a large oak
tree. Absalom's head got caught in the tree, and
his mule ran out from under him. So Absalom
was left hanging above the ground.
10When one of the men saw it happen, he
told Joab, "I saw Absalom hanging in an oak
tree!"
11Joab said to him, "You saw him? Why
didn't you kill him and let him fall to the
ground? I would have given you a belt and
four ounces of silver!"
12The man answered, "I wouldn't touch the
king's son even if you gave me twenty-five
pounds of silver. We heard the king command
you, Abishai, and Ittai, 'Be careful not to hurt
young Absalom.' 13If I had killed him, the king
would have found out, and you would not
have protected me!"
14Joab said, "I won't waste time here with
you!" Absalom was still alive in the oak tree, so
Joab took three spears and stabbed him in the
heart. 15Ten young men who carried Joab's armor also gathered around Absalom and struck
him and killed him.
16Then Joab blew the trumpet, so the troops
stopped chasing the Israelites. 17Then Joab's
men took Absalom's body and threw it into a
large pit in the forest and filled the pit with
many stones. All the Israelites
ran away to their homes.
18When Absalom was
alive, he had set up a pillar
for himself in the King's
Valley. He said, "I have no
son to keep my name
alive." So he named the pillar after himself, and it is
called Absalom's Monu-
ment even today.
19Ahimaaz son of Zadok
said to Joab, "Let me run and
take the news to King David. I'll tell him
the LORD has saved him from his enemies."
20Joab answered Ahimaaz, "No, you are not
the one to take the news today. You may do it
another time, but do not take it today, because
the king's son is dead."
21Then Joab said to a man from Cush, "Go,
tell the king what you have seen." The Cushite
bowed to Joab and ran to tell David.
22But Ahimaaz son of Zadok begged Joab
again, "No matter what happens, please let me
go along with the Cushite!"
Joab said, "Son, why do you want to carry
the news? You won't get any reward."
23Ahimaaz answered, "No matter what happens, I will run."
So Joab said to Ahimaaz, "Run!" Then
Ahimaaz ran by way of the Jordan Valley and
passed the Cushite.
24David was sitting between the inner and
outer gates of the city. The watchman went up
to the roof of the gate by the walls, and as he
looked up, he saw a man running alone. 25He
shouted the news to the king.
The king said, "If he is alone, he is bringing
good news!"
The man came nearer and nearer to the city.
26Then the watchman saw another man running, and he called to the gatekeeper, "Look!
Another man is running alone!"
The king said, "He is also bringing good
news!"
27The watchman said, "I think the first man
runs like Ahimaaz son of Zadok."
The king said, "Ahimaaz is a good man. He
must be bringing good news!"
28Then Ahimaaz called a greeting to the
king. He bowed facedown on the ground before the king and said, "Praise the LORD your
God! The LORD has defeated those who were
against you, my king."
29The king asked, "Is young Absalom all
right?"
Ahimaaz answered, "When Joab sent me, I
saw some great excitement,
but I don't know what it
was."
30The king said, "Step
over here and wait." So
Ahimaaz stepped aside and
stood there.
31Then the Cushite ar-
rived. He said, "Master and
king, hear the good news!
Today the LORD has pun-
ished those who were
against you!"
32The king asked the Cushite,
"Is young Absalom all right?"
The Cushite answered, "May your enemies
and all who come to hurt you be like that
young man!"
33Then the king was very upset, and he

> **"Then the Cushite arrived. He said, 'Master and king, hear the good news! Today the LORD has punished those who were against you!' "**
> **(2 Samuel 18:31)**

went to the room over the city gate and cried.
As he went, he cried out, "My son Absalom,
my son Absalom! I wish I had died and not
you. Absalom, my son, my son!"

JOAB SCOLDS DAVID

19 [1]People told Joab, "Look, the king is sad and
crying because of Absalom." [2]David's army had
won the battle that day. But it became a very
sad day for all the people, because they heard
that the king was very sad for his son. [3]The
people came into the city quietly that day. They
were like an army that had been
defeated in battle and had run
away. [4]The king covered his
face and cried loudly, "My son
Absalom! Absalom, my son,
my son!"
[5]Joab went into the king's
house and said, "Today you
have shamed all your men.
They saved your life and the lives of your sons,
daughters, wives, and slave women. [6]You have
shamed them because you love those who
hate you, and you hate those who love you.
Today you have made it clear that your commanders and men mean nothing to you. What
if Absalom had lived and all of us were dead? I
can see you would be pleased. [7]Now go out
and encourage your servants. I swear by the
LORD that if you don't go out, no man will be
left with you by tonight! That will be worse
than all the troubles you have had from your
youth until today."
[8]So the king went to the city gate.[n] When
the news spread that the king was at the gate,
everyone came to see him.

COMFORT
What should we do when comfort is hard to give? (19:5–7)

DAVID GOES BACK TO JERUSALEM

All the Israelites who had followed Absalom had run away to their homes. [9]People in
all the tribes of Israel began to argue, saying,
"The king saved us from the Philistines and our
other enemies, but he left the country because
of Absalom. [10]We appointed Absalom to rule
us, but now he has died in battle. We should
make David the king again."
[11]King David sent a message to Zadok and
Abiathar, the priests, that said, "Speak to the
older leaders of Judah. Say, 'Even in my house
I have heard what all the Israelites are saying.
So why are you the last tribe to bring the king
back to his palace? [12]You are my brothers, my
own family. Why are you the last tribe to bring
back the king?' [13]And say to Amasa, 'You are
part of my own family. May God punish me
terribly if I don't make you commander of the
army in Joab's place!' "
[14]David touched the hearts of all the people
of Judah at once. They sent a message to the
king that said, "Return with all your men."
[15]Then the king returned as far as the Jordan
River. The men of Judah came to Gilgal to meet
him and to bring him across the Jordan.
[16]Shimei son of Gera, a Benjaminite who
lived in Bahurim, hurried down with the men
of Judah to meet King David. [17]With Shimei
came a thousand Benjaminites. Ziba, the servant from Saul's family, also came, bringing his
fifteen sons and twenty servants with him.
They all hurried to the Jordan River to meet
the king. [18]The people went across the Jordan
to help bring the king's family back to Judah
and to do whatever the king wanted. As the
king was crossing the river, Shimei son of Gera
came to him and bowed facedown on the
ground in front of the king. [19]He said to the
king, "My master, don't hold me guilty. Don't
remember the wrong I did when you left Jerusalem! Don't hold it against me. [20]I know I
have sinned. That is why I am the first person
from Joseph's family to come down and meet
you today, my master and king!"
[21]But Abishai son of Zeruiah said, "Shimei
should die because he cursed you, the LORD's
appointed king!"
[22]David said, "This does not concern you,
sons of Zeruiah! Today you're against me! No
one will be put to death in Israel today. Today
I know I am king over Israel!" [23]Then the king
promised Shimei, "You won't die."
[24]Mephibosheth, Saul's grandson, also went
down to meet King David. Mephibosheth had
not cared for his feet, cut his beard, or washed
his clothes from the time the king had left Jerusalem until he returned safely. [25]When Mephibosheth came from Jerusalem to meet the
king, the king asked him, "Mephibosheth, why
didn't you go with me?"
[26]He answered, "My master, my servant
Ziba tricked me! I said to Ziba, 'I am crippled,
so saddle a donkey. Then I will ride it so I can
go with the king.' [27]But he lied about me to you.
You, my master and king, are like an angel
from God. Do what you think is good. [28]You
could have killed all my grandfather's family.
Instead, you put me with those people who eat
at your own table. So I don't have a right to
ask anything more from the king!"
[29]The king said to him, "Don't say anything

19:8 city gate People came here to conduct business. Public meetings and court cases were also held here.

more. I have decided that you and Ziba will
divide the land.”

30Mephibosheth said to the king, “Let Ziba
take all the land now that my master the king
has arrived safely home.”

31Barzillai of Gilead came down from Rogelim to cross the Jordan River with the king.
32Barzillai was a very old man, eighty years
old. He had taken care of the king when David
was staying at Mahanaim, because
Barzillai was a very rich man.
33David said to Barzillai,
“Cross the river with me.
Come with me to Jerusalem,
and I will take care of you.”

34But Barzillai answered
the king, “Do you know how old
I am? Do you think I can go with you to Jerusalem? 35I am eighty years old! I am too old to
taste what I eat or drink. I am too old to hear
the voices of men and women singers. Why
should you be bothered with me? 36I am not
worthy of a reward from you, but I will cross
the Jordan River with you. 37Then let me go
back so I may die in my own city near the
grave of my father and mother. But here is
Kimham, your servant. Let him go with you,
my master and king. Do with him whatever
you want.”

38The king answered, “Kimham will go with
me. I will do for him anything you wish, and I
will do anything for you that you wish.” 39The
king kissed Barzillai and blessed him. Then
Barzillai returned home, and the king and all
the people crossed the Jordan.

40When the king crossed over to Gilgal,
Kimham went with him. All the troops of Judah and half the troops of Israel led David
across the river.

41Soon all the Israelites came to the king and
said to him, “Why did our relatives, the people
of Judah, steal you away? Why did they bring
you and your family across the Jordan River
with your men?”

42All the people of Judah answered the Israelites, “We did this because the king is our close
relative. Why are you angry about it? We have
not eaten food at the king's expense or taken
anything for ourselves!”

43The Israelites answered the people of Judah, “We have ten tribes in the kingdom, so we
have more right to David than you do! But you
ignored us! We were the first ones to talk about
bringing our king back!”

But the people of Judah spoke even more
unkindly than the people of Israel.

FRIENDSHIP
How should we care for our friends? (19:33)

SHEBA LEADS ISRAEL AWAY FROM DAVID

20 1It happened that a troublemaker named
Sheba son of Bicri from the tribe of Benjamin
was there. He blew the trumpet and said:

“We have no share in David!
We have no part in the son of Jesse!
People of Israel, let's go home!”

2So all the Israelites left David and followed
Sheba son of Bicri. But the people of Judah
stayed with their king all the way from the Jordan River to Jerusalem.

3David came back to his palace in Jerusalem. He had left ten of his slave women there
to take care of the palace. Now he put them in
a locked house. He gave them food, but he did
not have sexual relations with them. So they
lived like widows until they died.

4The king said to Amasa, “Tell the men of
Judah to meet with me in three days, and you
must also be here.” 5So Amasa went to call the
men of Judah together, but he took more time
than the king had said.

6David said to Abishai, “Sheba son of Bicri
is more dangerous to us than Absalom was.
Take my men and chase him before he finds
walled cities and escapes from us.” 7So Joab's
men, the Kerethites and the Pelethites,[n] and all
the soldiers went with Abishai. They went out
from Jerusalem to chase Sheba son of Bicri.

8When Joab and the army came to the great
rock at Gibeon, Amasa came out to meet them.
Joab was wearing his uniform, and at his waist
he wore a belt that held his sword in its case.
As Joab stepped forward, his sword fell out of
its case. 9Joab asked Amasa, “Brother, is everything all right with you?” Then with his right
hand he took Amasa by the beard to kiss him.
10Amasa was not watching the sword in Joab's
hand. So Joab pushed the sword into Amasa's
stomach, causing Amasa's insides to spill onto
the ground. Joab did not have to stab Amasa
again; he was already dead. Then Joab and his
brother Abishai continued to chase Sheba son
of Bicri.

11One of Joab's young men stood by
Amasa's body and said, “Everyone who is for
Joab and David should follow Joab!” 12Amasa
lay in the middle of the road, covered with his
own blood. When the young man saw that
everyone was stopping to look at the body, he
dragged it from the road, laid it in a field, and

20:7 Kerethites and Pelethites These were probably special units of the army that were responsible for the king's safety, a kind of palace guard.

put a cloth over it. 13After Amasa's body was taken off the road, all the men followed Joab to chase Sheba son of Bicri.

14Sheba went through all the tribes of Israel to Abel Beth Maacah. All the Berites also came together and followed him. 15So Joab and his men came to Abel Beth Maacah and surrounded it. They piled dirt up against the city wall, and they began hacking at the walls to bring them down.

WHAT'S IT MEAN?

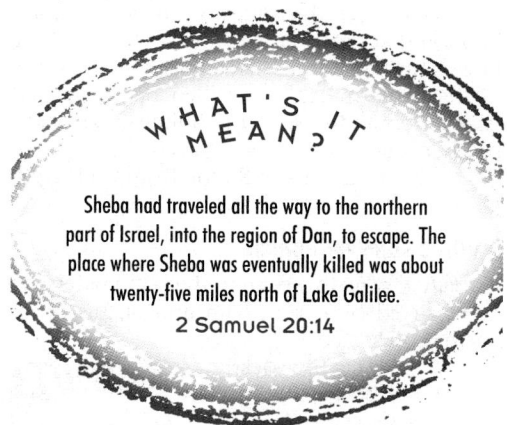

Sheba had traveled all the way to the northern part of Israel, into the region of Dan, to escape. The place where Sheba was eventually killed was about twenty-five miles north of Lake Galilee.

2 Samuel 20:14

16But a wise woman shouted out from the city, "Listen! Listen! Tell Joab to come here. I want to talk to him!"

17So Joab came near her. She asked him, "Are you Joab?"

He answered, "Yes, I am."

Then she said, "Listen to what I say."

Joab said, "I'm listening."

18Then the woman said, "In the past people would say, 'Ask for advice at Abel,' and the problem would be solved. 19I am one of the peaceful, loyal people of Israel. You are trying to destroy an important city of Israel. Why must you destroy what belongs to the LORD?"

20Joab answered, "I would prefer not to destroy or ruin anything! 21That is not what I want. But there is a man here from the mountains of Ephraim, who is named Sheba son of Bicri. He has turned against King David. If you bring him to me, I will leave the city alone."

The woman said to Joab, "His head will be thrown over the wall to you."

22Then the woman spoke very wisely to all the people of the city. They cut off the head of Sheba son of Bicri and threw it over the wall to Joab. So he blew the trumpet, and the army left the city. Every man returned home, and Joab went back to the king in Jerusalem.

23Joab was commander of all the army of Israel. Benaiah son of Jehoiada led the Kerethites and Pelethites. 24Adoniram was in charge of the men who were forced to do hard work. Jehoshaphat son of Ahilud was the recorder. 25Sheba was the royal secretary. Zadok and Abiathar were the priests, 26and Ira the Jairite was David's priest.

THE GIBEONITES PUNISH SAUL'S FAMILY

21 1During the time David was king, there was a shortage of food that lasted for three years. So David prayed to the LORD.

The LORD answered, "Saul and his family of murderers are the reason for this shortage, because he killed the Gibeonites." 2(Now the Gibeonites were not Israelites; they were a group of Amorites who were left alive. The Israelites had promised not to hurt the Gibeonites, but Saul had tried to kill them, because he was eager to help the people of Israel and Judah.)

King David called the Gibeonites together and spoke to them. 3He asked, "What can I do for you? How can I make up for the harm done so you can bless the LORD's people?"

4The Gibeonites said to David, "We cannot demand silver or gold from Saul or his family. And we don't have the right to kill anyone in Israel."

Then David asked, "What do you want me to do for you?"

5The Gibeonites said, "Saul made plans against us and tried to destroy all our people who are left in the land of Israel. 6So bring seven of his sons to us. Then we will kill them and hang them on stakes in the presence of the LORD at Gibeah, the hometown of Saul, the LORD's chosen king."

The king said, "I will give them to you." 7But the king protected Mephibosheth, the son of Jonathan, the son of Saul, because of the promise he had made to Jonathan in the LORD's name. 8The king did take Armoni and Mephibosheth,[n] sons of Rizpah and Saul. (Rizpah was the daughter of Aiah.) And the king took the five sons of Saul's daughter Merab. (Adriel son of Barzillai the Meholathite was the father of Merab's five sons.) 9David gave these seven sons to the Gibeonites. Then the Gibeonites killed them and hung them on stakes on a hill in the presence of the LORD. All seven sons died together. They were put to death during the first days of the harvest season at the beginning of barley harvest.

10Aiah's daughter Rizpah took the rough cloth that was worn to show sadness and put

21:8 Mephibosheth This is not Jonathan's son but another man with the same name.

it on a rock for herself. She stayed there from
the beginning of the harvest until the rain fell
on her sons' bodies. During the day she did
not let the birds of the sky touch her sons'
bodies, and during the night she did not let the
wild animals touch them.
11 People told David what Aiah's daughter
Rizpah, Saul's slave woman, was doing. 12 Then
David took the bones of Saul and Jonathan
from the men of Jabesh Gilead. (The Philistines
had hung the bodies of Saul and Jonathan in
the public square of Beth Shan after they had
killed Saul at Gilboa. Later the men of Jabesh
Gilead had secretly taken them from there.)
13 David brought the bones of Saul and his son
Jonathan from Gilead. Then the people gathered the bodies of Saul's seven sons who were
hanged on stakes. 14 The people buried the
bones of Saul and his son Jonathan at Zela in
Benjamin in the tomb of Saul's father Kish. The
people did everything the king commanded.
Then God answered the prayers for the
land.

WHAT'S IT MEAN?

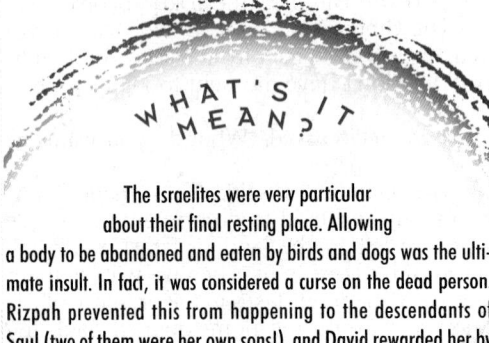

The Israelites were very particular about their final resting place. Allowing a body to be abandoned and eaten by birds and dogs was the ultimate insult. In fact, it was considered a curse on the dead person. Rizpah prevented this from happening to the descendants of Saul (two of them were her own sons!), and David rewarded her by having the bodies buried in the family tomb.

2 Samuel 21:13–14

WARS WITH THE PHILISTINES

15 Again there was war between the Philistines and Israel. David and his men went out to
fight the Philistines, but David became tired.
16 Ishbi-Benob, one of the sons of Rapha, had a
bronze spearhead weighing about seven and
one-half pounds and a new sword. He
planned to kill David, 17 but Abishai son of Zeruiah killed the Philistine and saved David's life.
Then David's men made a promise to him,
saying, "Never again will you go out with us to
battle. If you were killed, Israel would lose its
greatest leader."
18 Later, at Gob, there was another battle
with the Philistines. Sibbecai the Hushathite
killed Saph, another one of the sons of Rapha.
19 Later, there was another battle at Gob with
the Philistines. Elhanan son of Jaare-Oregim
from Bethlehem killed Goliath[n] from Gath. His
spear was as large as a weaver's rod.
20 At Gath another battle took place. A huge
man was there; he had six fingers on each
hand and six toes on each foot—twenty-four
fingers and toes in all. This man also was one
of the sons of Rapha. 21 When he challenged
Israel, Jonathan son of Shimeah, David's
brother, killed him.
22 These four sons of Rapha from Gath were
killed by David and his men.

DAVID'S SONG OF PRAISE

22

1 David sang this song to the LORD when the
LORD saved him from Saul and all his other
enemies. 2 He said:

"The LORD is my rock,
my protection, my
Savior.
3 My God is my rock.
I can run to him for
safety.
He is my shield and my
saving strength,
my defender and my place of safety.
The LORD saves me from those who
want to harm me.
4 I will call to the LORD, who
is worthy of praise,
and I will be saved
from my enemies.

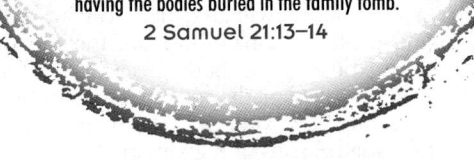

SALVATION
Who will deliver us? (22:2)

WORSHIP
Who is worthy of praise? (22:4)

5 "The waves of death came
around me;
the deadly rivers overwhelmed me.
6 The ropes of death wrapped around me.
The traps of death were before me.
7 In my trouble I called to the LORD;
I cried out to my God.
From his temple he heard
my voice;
my call for help
reached his ears.

HOPE
Why can we be hopeful? (22:7)

8 "The earth trembled and
shook.
The foundations of heaven began to
shake.

21:19 Goliath In 1 Chronicles 20:5 he is called Lahmi, brother of Goliath.

WHAT'S IT MEAN?

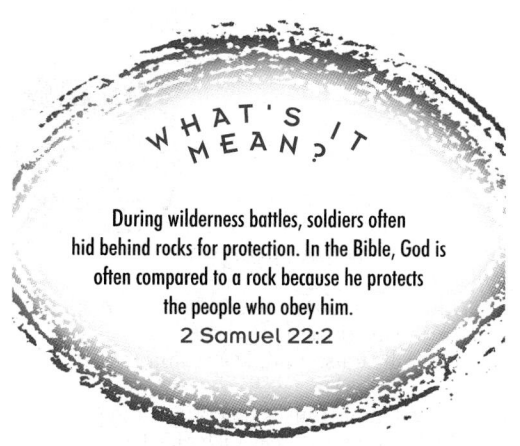

During wilderness battles, soldiers often hid behind rocks for protection. In the Bible, God is often compared to a rock because he protects the people who obey him.
2 Samuel 22:2

They trembled because the LORD was
angry.
9 Smoke came out of his nose,
and burning fire came out of his mouth.
Burning coals went before him.
10 He tore open the sky and came down
with dark clouds under his feet.
11 He rode a creature with wings and flew.
He raced on the wings of the wind.
12 He made darkness his shelter,
surrounded by fog and clouds.
13 Out of the brightness of his presence
came flashes of lightning.
14 The LORD thundered from heaven;
the Most High raised his voice.
15 He shot his arrows and scattered his
enemies.
His bolts of lightning confused them
with fear.
16 The LORD spoke strongly.
The wind blew from his nose.
Then the valleys of the sea appeared,
and the foundations of the earth were
seen.

17 "The LORD reached down from above and
took me;
he pulled me from the deep water.
18 He saved me from my powerful enemies,
from those who hated me, because they
were too strong for me.
19 They attacked me at my time of trouble,
but the LORD supported me.
20 He took me to a safe place.
Because he delights in me, he saved me.

21 "The LORD spared me because I did what
was right.
Because I have not done evil, he has
rewarded me.
22 I have followed the ways of the LORD;
I have not done evil by turning from
my God.
23 I remember all his laws
and have not broken his rules.
24 I am innocent before him;
I have kept myself from doing evil.
25 The LORD rewarded me because I did what
was right,
because I did what the LORD said was
right.

26 "LORD, you are loyal to those who are
loyal,
and you are good to those who are
good.
27 You are pure to those who are pure,
but you are against those
who are evil.
28 You save the humble,
but you bring down
those who are proud.
29 LORD, you give light to my
lamp.
The LORD brightens the darkness
around me.
30 With your help I can attack an army.
With God's help I can jump over a wall.

BIBLE
Is the Bible trustworthy?
(22:29–31)

WHAT'S IT MEAN?

"Loyal" and "good" can mean pretty much the same thing. Was David repeating himself? Well, yes, he was—but for a reason. David was writing a type of Hebrew poetry that used different words to make the same point.
2 Samuel 22:26

31 "The ways of God are without fault;
the LORD's words are pure.
He is a shield to those who trust him.
32 Who is God? Only the LORD.
Who is the Rock? Only our God.
33 God is my protection.
He makes my way free from fault.
34 He makes me like a deer that does not
stumble;
he helps me stand on the steep
mountains.

35 He trains my hands for battle
so my arms can bend a bronze bow.
36 You protect me with your saving shield.
You have stooped to make me great.
37 You give me a better way to live,
so I live as you want me to.
38 I chased my enemies and destroyed
them.
I did not quit till they were destroyed.
39 I destroyed and crushed them
so they couldn't rise up again.
They fell beneath my feet.
40 You gave me strength in battle.
You made my enemies bow before me.
41 You made my enemies turn back,
and I destroyed those who hated me.
42 They called for help,
but no one came to save them.
They called to the LORD,
but he did not answer them.
43 I beat my enemies into pieces,
like dust on the ground.
I poured them out and walked on them
like mud in the streets.

44 "You saved me when my people attacked
me.
You kept me as the leader of nations.
People I never knew serve me.
45 Foreigners obey me.
As soon as they hear me, they obey me.
46 They all become afraid
and tremble in their hiding places.
47 "The LORD lives!
May my Rock be praised!
Praise God, the Rock,
who saves me!
48 God gives me victory over
my enemies
and brings people
under my rule.
49 He frees me from my enemies.

SALVATION
Why should we praise God? (22:47–48)

"You set me over those who hate me.
You saved me from cruel men.
50 So I will praise you, LORD, among the
nations.
I will sing praises to your name.
51 The LORD gives great victories to his king.
He is loyal to his appointed king,
to David and his descendants forever."

DAVID'S LAST WORDS

23 1 These are the last words of David.

This is the message of David son of
Jesse.
The man made great by the Most High
God speaks.
He is the appointed king of the God of
Jacob;
he is the sweet singer of Israel:

2 "The LORD's Spirit spoke through me,
and his word was on my tongue.
3 The God of Israel spoke;

Promise

HE PROMISES TO NEVER BREAK HIS PROMISES.

This is how God has cared for my family. God made a lasting agreement with me, right and sure in every way. He will accomplish my salvation and satisfy all my desires (2 Sam. 23:5).

Broken promises. Nothing stings more. They tear you up and rip your heart out. Friends who tell your deepest secrets. Being stood up by the girl you finally ask out. Dads who walk out on moms. Promise made, promise broken, heartache. When someone breaks a promise, it feels like a punch in the gut—all the wind gets knocked out of you and all your energy is drained.

Because we've felt this pain so many times, we assume that God could treat us the same way. He might pull out at any turn. He might say he didn't really mean it—we just misunderstood him. Not a chance. He promises never to break his promise. He'll always keep your secrets, always be there when you need him, and always do what he says he will do. You can stake your heart on it.

See for Yourself:

Num. 23:19; Josh. 23:15–16; 1 Kin. 8:56

the Rock of Israel said to me:
'Whoever rules fairly over people,
who rules with respect for God,
4 is like the morning light at dawn,
like a morning without clouds.
He is like sunshine after a rain
that makes the grass sprout from the ground.'

5 "This is how God has cared for my family.
God made a lasting agreement with me,
right and sure in every way.
He will accomplish my salvation
and satisfy all my desires.

6 "But all evil people will be thrown away
like thorns
that cannot be held in a hand.
7 No one can touch them
except with a tool of iron or wood.
They will be thrown in the fire and
burned where they lie."

DAVID'S ARMY

8 These are the names of David's warriors:
Josheb-Basshebeth, the Tahkemonite, was
head of the Three.[n] He killed eight hundred
men at one time.
9 Next was Eleazar son of Dodai the Ahohite. Eleazar was one of the three soldiers who
were with David when they challenged the
Philistines. The Philistines were gathered for
battle, and the Israelites drew back. 10 But Eleazar stayed where he was and fought the Philistines until he was so tired his hand stuck to his
sword. The LORD gave a great victory for the
Israelites that day. The troops came back after
Eleazar had won the battle, but only to take
weapons and armor from the enemy.
11 Next there was Shammah son of Agee the
Hararite. The Philistines came together to fight
in a vegetable field. Israel's troops ran away
from the Philistines, 12 but Shammah stood in
the middle of the field and fought for it and
killed the Philistines. And the LORD gave a great
victory.
13 Once, three of the Thirty, David's chief
soldiers, came down to him at the cave of
Adullam during harvest. The Philistine army
had camped in the Valley of Rephaim. 14 At that
time David was in the stronghold, and some of
the Philistines were in Bethlehem.
15 David had a strong desire for some water.
He said, "Oh, I wish someone would get me
water from the well near the city gate of Bethlehem!" 16 So the three warriors broke through
the Philistine army and took water from the
well near the city gate of Bethlehem. Then they
brought it to David, but he refused to drink it.
He poured it out before the LORD, 17 saying,
"May the LORD keep me from drinking this
water! It would be like drinking the blood of
the men who risked their lives!" So David refused to drink it. These were the brave things
that the three warriors did.

WHAT'S IT MEAN?

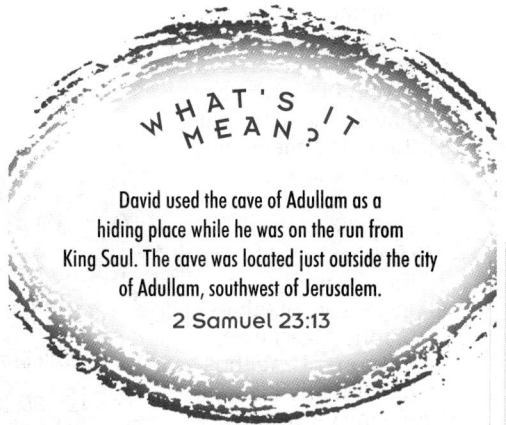

David used the cave of Adullam as a hiding place while he was on the run from King Saul. The cave was located just outside the city of Adullam, southwest of Jerusalem.

2 Samuel 23:13

18 Abishai, brother of Joab son of Zeruiah,
was captain of the Three. Abishai fought three
hundred soldiers with his spear and killed
them. He became as famous as the Three 19 and
was more honored than the Three. He became
their commander even though he was not one
of them.
20 Benaiah son of Jehoiada was a brave
fighter from Kabzeel who did mighty things.
He killed two of the best warriors from Moab.
He also went down into a pit and killed a lion
on a snowy day. 21 Benaiah killed a large Egyptian who had a spear in his hand. Benaiah had
a club, but he grabbed the spear from the
Egyptian's hand and killed him with his own
spear. 22 These were the things Benaiah son of
Jehoiada did. He was as famous as the Three.
23 He received more honor than the Thirty, but
he did not become a member of the Three.
David made him leader of his bodyguards.

THE THIRTY CHIEF SOLDIERS

24 The following men were among the Thirty:

Asahel brother of Joab;
Elhanan son of Dodo from Bethlehem;

23:8 Three These were David's most powerful soldiers. See 1 Chronicles 11:11.

25 Shammah the Harodite;
Elika the Harodite;
26 Helez the Paltite;
Ira son of Ikkesh from Tekoa;
27 Abiezer the Anathothite;
Mebunnai the Hushathite;
28 Zalmon the Ahohite;
Maharai the Netophathite;
29 Heled son of Baanah the Netophathite;
Ithai son of Ribai from Gibeah in Benjamin;
30 Benaiah the Pirathonite;
Hiddai from the ravines of Gaash;
31 Abi-Albon the Arbathite;
Azmaveth the Barhumite;
32 Eliahba the Shaalbonite;
the sons of Jashen;
Jonathan 33 son of Shammah the Hararite;
Ahiam son of Sharar the Hararite;
34 Eliphelet son of Ahasbai the Maacathite;
Eliam son of Ahithophel the Gilonite;
35 Hezro the Carmelite;
Paarai the Arbite;
36 Igal son of Nathan of Zobah;
the son of Hagri;
37 Zelek the Ammonite;
Naharai the Beerothite, who carried the armor of Joab son of Zeruiah;
38 Ira the Ithrite;
Gareb the Ithrite,
39 and Uriah the Hittite.

There were thirty-seven in all.

DAVID COUNTS HIS ARMY

24

1 The LORD was angry with Israel again, and
he caused David to turn against the Israelites.
He said, "Go, count the people of Israel and
Judah."
2 So King David said to Joab, the commander of the army, "Go through all the tribes
of Israel, from Dan to Beersheba,[n] and count
the people. Then I will know how many there
are."
3 But Joab said to the king, "May the LORD
your God give you a hundred times more people, and may my master the king live to see this
happen. Why do you want to do this?"
4 But the king commanded Joab and the
commanders of the army, so they left the king
to count the Israelites.
5 After crossing the Jordan River, they
camped near Aroer on the south side of the
city in the ravine. They went through Gad and
on to Jazer.
6 Then they went to Gilead and the
land of Tahtim Hodshi and to Dan Jaan and
around to Sidon.
7 They went to the strong,
walled city of Tyre and to all the cities of the
Hivites and Canaanites. Finally, they went to
southern Judah, to Beersheba.
8 After nine
months and twenty days, they had gone
through all the land. Then they came back to
Jerusalem.
9 Joab gave the list of the people to the king.
There were eight hundred thousand men in Israel who could use the sword
and five hundred thousand
men in Judah.
10 David felt ashamed after
he had counted the people.
He said to the LORD, "I have
sinned greatly by what I
have done. LORD, I beg you
to forgive me, your servant,
because I have been very
foolish."
11 When David got up in the
morning, the LORD spoke his
word to Gad, who was a prophet and David's
seer.
12 The LORD told Gad, "Go and tell David,
'This is what the LORD says: I offer you three
choices. Choose one of them and I will do it to
you.' "
13 So Gad went to David and said to him,
"Should three years of hunger come to you
and your land? Or should your enemies chase
you for three months? Or should there be
three days of disease in your land? Think
about it. Then decide which of these things I
should tell the LORD who sent me."
14 David said to Gad, "I am in great trouble.
Let the LORD punish us, because the LORD is
very merciful. Don't let my punishment come
from human beings!"
15 So the LORD sent a terrible
disease on Israel. It began in
the morning and continued
until the chosen time to stop.
From Dan to Beersheba seventy thousand people died.
16 When the angel raised his
arm toward Jerusalem to destroy it, the LORD
felt very sorry about the terrible things that

"The LORD lives!
May my Rock be praised!
Praise God, the Rock,
who saves me!"
(2 Samuel 22:47)

ANGELS
Who carries out God's judgment? (24:16–17)

24:2 Dan to Beersheba Dan was the city farthest north in Israel, and Beersheba was the city farthest south. So this means all the people of Israel.

had happened. He said to the angel who was
destroying the people, "That is enough! Put
down your arm!" The angel of the LORD was
then by the threshing floor of Araunah the
Jebusite.
17When David saw the angel that killed the
people, he said to the LORD, "I am the one who
sinned and did wrong. These people only followed me like sheep. They did nothing wrong.
Please punish me and my family."
18That day Gad came to David and said, "Go
and build an altar to the LORD on the threshing
floor of Araunah the Jebusite." 19So David did
what Gad told him to do, just as the LORD
commanded.
20Araunah looked and saw the king and his
servants coming to him. So he went out and
bowed facedown on the ground before the
king. 21He said, "Why has my master the king
come to me?"
David answered, "To buy the threshing
floor from you so I can build an altar to the
LORD. Then the terrible disease will stop."
22Araunah said to David, "My master and
king, you may take anything you want for a
sacrifice. Here are some oxen for the whole
burnt offering and the threshing boards and
the yokes for the wood. 23My king, I give
everything to you." Araunah also said to the
king, "May the LORD your God be pleased
with you."
24But the king answered Araunah, "No, I
will pay you for the land. I won't offer to the
LORD my God burnt offerings that cost me
nothing."

WHAT'S IT MEAN?

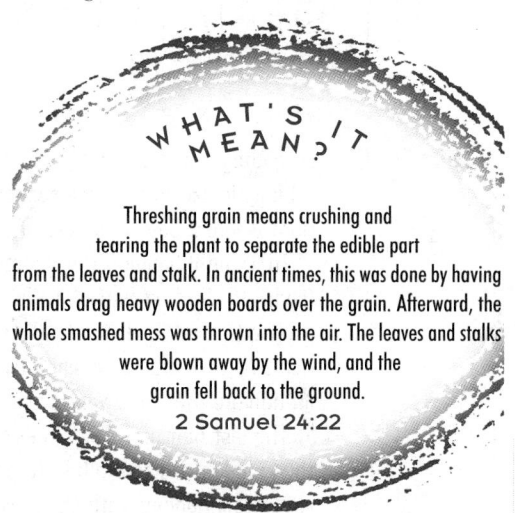

Threshing grain means crushing and tearing the plant to separate the edible part from the leaves and stalk. In ancient times, this was done by having animals drag heavy wooden boards over the grain. Afterward, the whole smashed mess was thrown into the air. The leaves and stalks were blown away by the wind, and the grain fell back to the ground.

2 Samuel 24:22

So David bought the threshing floor and
the oxen for one and one-fourth pounds of
silver. 25He built an altar to the LORD there and
offered whole burnt offerings and fellowship
offerings. Then the LORD answered his prayer
for the country, and the disease in Israel
stopped.

1 Kings

CONTENT If reading 1 and 2 Samuel is like watching a couple of home videos, then reading 1 Kings is like finding the sequel to those home videos. In fact, 1 Kings picks up right where 2 Samuel leaves off.

In 1 and 2 Samuel, the Hebrews got their first king, Saul, and their second king, David. In the first half of 1 Kings, David's son Solomon takes over the throne—and what a throne he made of it! King Solomon was like a superstar in Israel. He was as rich as a rock star, as glamorous as a movie star, and as smart as a Wall Street millionaire. He could wheel and deal and network and schmooze with the best.

The last half of 1 Kings tells the other side of the story. After Solomon's reign, the kingdom started falling to pieces. What was a united kingdom became two separate kingdoms with their own kings and their own *big* mistakes.

Outline

1:1-53 .... Solomon Becomes King
2:1-11 .... David's Final Words and His Death
2:12-46 .... Solomon Takes Control of the Kingdom
3:1—4:34 .... Solomon's Wisdom and His Officers
5:1—8:66 .... Building and Dedication of the Jerusalem Temple
9:1—10:29 .... Other Events During Solomon's Rule
11:1-43 .... Solomon's Unfaithfulness, Enemies, and Death
12:1-24 .... The Northern Tribes of Israel Rebel Against King Rehoboam
12:25-33 .... King Jeroboam of Israel Makes Two Gold Statues of Calves
13:1—14:20 .... Prophets Condemn Jeroboam
14:21—16:34 ...... Kings of Judah and Israel
17:1—19:21 .... Elijah the Prophet
20:1—22:40 .... King Ahab and Queen Jezebel
22:41-53 .... King Jehoshaphat of Judah and King Ahaziah of Israel

Purpose It is especially important for leaders to be fully committed to the Lord.

Theme Lessons from the Dividing of the Kingdom

Date of writing 590–570 B.C.

"So the LORD said to Solomon, 'Because you have chosen to break your agreement with me and have not obeyed my commands, I will tear your kingdom away from you and give it to one of your officers' "(11:11).

Bible Talk

King Solomon's Reign of Riches

Israel never enjoyed as much wealth or prestige as when King Solomon ruled. They also had to work way too hard to keep the riches flowing.

There was another problem as well. Solomon forgot where his wisdom and riches came from. He became disillusioned with "having it all" and failed to keep God in first place in his life. He even worshiped false gods before his life was over. (He wrote Ecclesiastes, a book of the Bible, about this very thing.) His country suffered for it. He is still known throughout the world as the person who had it all and found out that, without God, it's not good enough.

FALSE GODS AND IDOLS

The big problem with the Hebrews was always idolatry. In those days, there were temples to a lot of different gods. When the Hebrews moved back into their land (read about this in the Book of Joshua), they didn't do something that God had asked. They didn't get rid of everyone else who lived there. Instead they just moved in beside the people, their temples, and their idols.

So you can guess what happened. Slowly the Hebrews got to know these people. Eventually, these people would invite their new Hebrew friends to "church" with them. Finally, the Hebrews would start worshiping these fake-god-nothings.

To put it lightly, this was unacceptable to the one true God.

ADONIJAH TRIES TO BECOME KING

1 1At this time King David was very old, and although his servants covered him with blankets, he could not keep warm. 2They said to him, "We will look for a young woman to care for you. She will lie close to you and keep you warm." 3After searching everywhere in Israel for a beautiful young woman, they found a girl named Abishag from Shunam and brought her to the king. 4The girl was very beautiful, and she cared for the king and served him. But the king did not have sexual relations with her.

5Adonijah was the son of King David and Haggith, and he was very proud. "I will be the king," he said. So he got chariots and horses for himself and fifty men for his personal bodyguard. 6Now David had never interfered with Adonijah by questioning what he did. Born next after Absalom, Adonijah was a very handsome man.

7Adonijah spoke with Joab son of Zeruiah and Abiathar the priest, and they agreed to help him. 8But Zadok the priest, Benaiah son of Jehoiada, Nathan the prophet, Shimei, Rei, and King David's special guard did not join Adonijah.

9Then Adonijah killed some sheep, cows, and fat calves for sacrifices at the Stone of Zoheleth near the spring of Rogel. He invited all his brothers, the other sons of King David, to come, as well as all the men of Judah. 10But Adonijah did not invite Nathan the prophet, Benaiah, his father's special guard, or his brother Solomon.

11When Nathan heard about this, he went to Bathsheba, Solomon's mother. "Have you heard that Adonijah, Haggith's son, has made himself king?" Nathan asked. "Our real king, David, does not know it. 12I strongly advise you to save yourself and your sons. 13Go to King David and tell him, 'My master and king, you promised that my son Solomon would be king and would rule on your throne after you. Why then has Adonijah become king?' 14While you are still talking to the king, I will come in and tell him that what you have said about Adonijah is true."

15So Bathsheba went in to see the aged king in his bedroom, where Abishag, the girl from Shunam, was caring for him. 16Bathsheba bowed and knelt before the king. He asked, "What do you want?"

17She answered, "My master, you made a promise to me in the name of the LORD your God. You said, 'Your son Solomon will become king after me, and he will rule on my throne.' 18But now, unknown to you, Adonijah has become king. 19He has killed many cows, fat calves, and sheep for sacrifices. And he has invited all your sons, as well as Abiathar the priest and Joab the commander of the army, but he did not invite Solomon, who serves you. 20My master and king, all the Israelites are watching you, waiting for you to decide who will be king after you. 21As soon as you die, Solomon and I will be treated as criminals."

22While Bathsheba was still talking with the king, Nathan the prophet arrived. 23The servants told the king, "Nathan the prophet is here." So Nathan went to the king and bowed facedown on the ground before him.

24Nathan said, "My master and king, have you said that Adonijah will be the king after you and that he will rule on your throne? 25Today he has sacrificed many cows, fat calves, and sheep, and he has invited all your other sons, the commanders of the army, and Abiathar the priest. Right now they are eating and drinking with him. They are saying, 'Long live King Adonijah!' 26But he did not invite me, your own servant, or Zadok the priest, or Benaiah son of Jehoiada, or your son Solomon. 27Did you do this? Since we are your servants, why didn't you tell us who should be king after you?"

DAVID MAKES SOLOMON KING

28Then the king said, "Tell Bathsheba to come in!" So she came in and stood before the king.

29Then the king made this promise, "The LORD has saved me from all trouble. As surely as he lives, 30I will do today what I have promised you in the name of the LORD, the God of Israel. I promised that your son Solomon would be king after me and rule on my throne in my place."

31Then Bathsheba bowed facedown on the ground and knelt before the king and said, "Long live my master King David!"

32Then King David said, "Tell Zadok the priest, Nathan the prophet, and Benaiah son of Jehoiada to come in." When they came before the king, 33he said to them, "Take my servants with you and put my son Solomon on my own mule. Take him down to the spring called Gihon. 34There Zadok the priest and Nathan the prophet should pour olive oil on him and make him king over Israel. Blow the trumpet and shout, 'Long live King Solomon!' 35Then come back up here with him. He will sit on my throne and rule in my place, because he is the one I have chosen to be the ruler over Israel and Judah."

WHAT'S IT MEAN?

Gihon, which is located west of Jerusalem, still supplies water to the city today. The site had a great deal of significance to David and his family. David's soldiers had used a water shaft leading from the springs to sneak into the city and defeat the Jebusites. Years later, Gihon was the place David's son, Solomon, was declared king. Some Bible experts believe that later kings continued the tradition Solomon started by drinking from the spring during their coronation ceremonies.

1 Kings 1:33

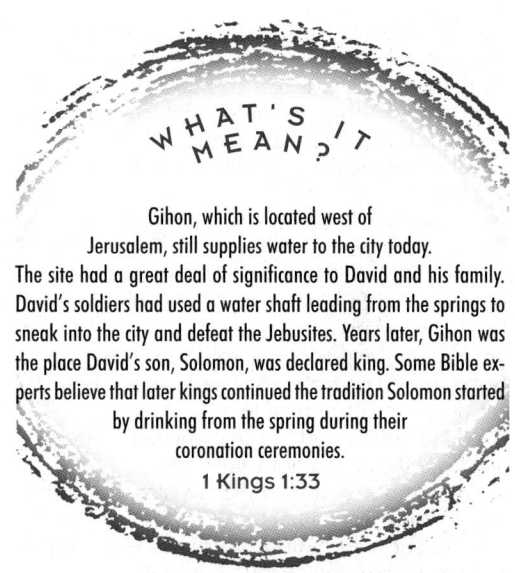

36 Benaiah son of Jehoiada answered the
king, "Amen! This is what the LORD, the God of
my master, has declared! 37 The LORD has always helped you, our king. May he also help
Solomon and make King Solomon's throne an
even greater throne than yours."
38 So Zadok the priest, Nathan the prophet,
and Benaiah son of Jehoiada left with the Kerethites and Pelethites.[n] They put Solomon on
King David's mule and took him to the spring
called Gihon. 39 Zadok the priest took the container of olive oil from the Holy Tent and
poured the oil on Solomon's head to show he
was the king. Then they blew the trumpet, and
all the people shouted, "Long live King Solomon!" 40 All the people followed Solomon into
the city. Playing flutes and shouting for joy,
they made so much noise the ground shook.
41 At this time Adonijah and all the guests
with him were finishing their meal. When he
heard the sound from the trumpet, Joab asked,
"What does all that noise from the city mean?"
42 While Joab was speaking, Jonathan son of
Abiathar the priest arrived. Adonijah said,
"Come in! You are an important man, so you
must be bringing good news."
43 But Jonathan answered, "No! Our master
King David has made Solomon the new king.
44 King David sent Zadok the priest, Nathan the
prophet, Benaiah son of Jehoiada, and all the
king's bodyguards with him, and they have put
Solomon on the king's own mule. 45 Then Zadok the priest and Nathan the prophet poured
olive oil on Solomon at Gihon to make him
king. After that they went into the city, shouting
with joy. Now the whole city is excited, and that
is the noise you hear. 46 Solomon has now become the king. 47 All the king's officers have
come to tell King David that he has done a
good thing. They are saying, 'May your God
make Solomon even more famous than you
and an even greater king than you.' " Jonathan
continued, "And King David bowed down on
his bed to worship God, 48 saying, 'Bless the
LORD, the God of Israel. Today he has made one
of my sons the king and allowed me to see it.' "
49 Then all of Adonijah's guests were afraid,
and they left quickly and scattered. 50 Adonijah
was also afraid of Solomon, so he went and
took hold of the corners of the altar.[n] 51 Then
someone told Solomon, "Adonijah is afraid of
you, so he is at the altar, holding on to its corners. He says, 'Tell King Solomon to promise
me today that he will not kill me.' "
52 So Solomon answered, "Adonijah must
show that he is a man of honor. If he does that,
I promise he will not lose even a single hair
from his head. But if he does anything wrong,
he will die." 53 Then King Solomon sent some
men to get Adonijah. When he was brought
from the altar, he came before King Solomon
and bowed down. Solomon told him, "Go
home."

THE DEATH OF DAVID

2 1 Since it was almost time for David to die,
he gave his son Solomon his last commands.
2 David said, "My time to die is near. Be a good
and strong leader. 3 Obey the LORD your God.
Follow him by obeying his demands, his commands, his laws, and his rules that are written
in the teachings of Moses. If you do these
things, you will be successful in all you do and
wherever you go. 4 And if you obey the LORD,
he will keep the promise he made to me. He
said: 'If your descendants live as I tell them and
have complete faith in me, a man from your
family will always be king over the people of
Israel.'
5 "Also, you remember what Joab son of Zeruiah did to me. He killed the two commanders
of Israel's armies: Abner son of Ner and Amasa
son of Jether. He did this as if he and they were

1:38 Kerethites and Pelethites These were probably special units of the army that were responsible for the king's safety, a kind of palace guard. **1:50 corners of the altar** If a person were innocent of a crime, he could run into the Holy Place where the altar was. If he held on to the corners of the altar, which looked like horns, he would be safe.

WHAT'S IT MEAN?

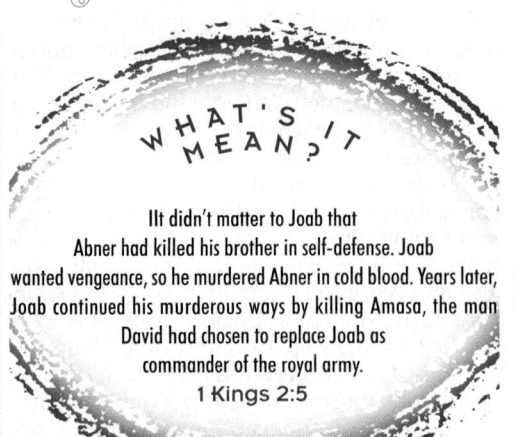

Ilt didn't matter to Joab that Abner had killed his brother in self-defense. Joab wanted vengeance, so he murdered Abner in cold blood. Years later, Joab continued his murderous ways by killing Amasa, the man David had chosen to replace Joab as commander of the royal army.

1 Kings 2:5

at war, although it was a time of peace. He put their blood on the belt around his waist and on his sandals on his feet. 6Punish him in the way you think is wisest, but do not let him die peacefully of old age.

KINDNESS

What should we do to those who have been kind to us? (2:7)

7"Be kind to the children of Barzillai of Gilead, and allow them to eat at your table. They welcomed me when I ran away from your brother Absalom.

8"And remember, Shimei son of Gera, the Benjaminite, is here with you. He cursed me the day I went to Mahanaim. But when he came down to meet me at the Jordan River, I promised him before the Lord, 'Shimei, I will not kill you.' 9But you should not leave him unpunished. You are a wise man, and you will know what to do to him, but you must be sure he is killed."

10Then David died and was buried with his ancestors in Jerusalem. 11He had ruled over Israel forty years—seven years in Hebron and thirty-three years in Jerusalem.

SOLOMON TAKES CONTROL AS KING

12Solomon became king after David, his father, and he was in firm control of his kingdom.

13At this time Adonijah son of Haggith went to Bathsheba, Solomon's mother. "Do you come in peace?" Bathsheba asked.

"Yes. This is a peaceful visit," Adonijah answered. 14"I have something to say to you."

"You may speak," she said.

15"You remember that at one time the kingdom was mine," Adonijah said. "All the people of Israel recognized me as their king, but things have changed. Now my brother is the king, because the LORD chose him. 16Now I have one thing to ask you; please do not refuse me."

Bathsheba answered, "What do you want?"

17"I know King Solomon will do anything you ask him," Adonijah continued. "Please ask him to give me Abishag the Shunammite to be my wife."

18"Very well," she answered. "I will speak to the king for you."

19So Bathsheba went to King Solomon to speak to him for Adonijah. When Solomon saw her, he stood up to meet her, then bowed down, and sat on the throne. He told some servants to bring another throne for his mother. Then she sat down at his right side.

20Bathsheba said, "I have one small thing to ask you. Please do not refuse me."

"Ask, mother," the king answered. "I will not refuse you."

21So she said, "Allow Abishag the Shunammite to marry your brother Adonijah."

22King Solomon answered his mother, "Why do you ask me to give him Abishag? Why don't you also ask for him to become the king since he is my older brother? Abiathar the priest and Joab son of Zeruiah would support him!"

23Then King Solomon swore by the name of the LORD, saying, "May God punish me terribly if this doesn't cost Adonijah his life! 24By the LORD who has given me the throne that belonged to my father David and who has kept his promise and given the kingdom to me and my people, Adonijah will die today!" 25Then King Solomon gave orders to Benaiah son of Jehoiada, and he went and killed Adonijah.

WHAT'S IT MEAN?

Abishag served as a nurse and a companion to David in his old age. Part of her responsibility was to help David stay warm at night. She slept with David, but did not have a physical relationship with him. Even so, she was considered to be one of David's concubines. Adonijah's request to marry Abishag was a way of claiming what had been David's. Solomon recognized Adonijah's plan to eventually claim something else of David's: the throne of Israel.

1 Kings 2:17–22

26King Solomon said to Abiathar the priest, "I should kill you too, but I will allow you to go back to your fields in Anathoth. I will not kill you at this time, because you helped carry the Ark of the Lord GOD while marching with my father David. And I know you shared in all the hard times with him." 27Then Solomon removed Abiathar from being the LORD's priest. This happened as the LORD had said it would, when he was speaking in Shiloh about the priest Eli and his descendants.

28When Joab heard about what had happened, he was afraid. He had supported Adonijah but not Absalom. So Joab ran to the Tent of the LORD and took hold of the corners of the altar.[n] 29Someone told King Solomon that Joab had run to the Tent of the LORD and was beside the altar. Then Solomon ordered Benaiah to go and kill him.

> "But there will be peace from the LORD for David, his descendants, his family, and his throne forever." (1 Kings 2:33b)

30Benaiah went into the Tent of the LORD and said to Joab, "The king says, 'Come out!' "

But Joab answered, "No, I will die here."

So Benaiah went back to the king and told him what Joab had said. 31Then the king ordered Benaiah, "Do as he says! Kill him there and bury him. Then my family and I will be free of the guilt of Joab, who has killed innocent people. 32Without my father knowing it, he killed two men who were much better than he was—Abner son of Ner, the commander of Israel's army, and Amasa son of Jether, the commander of Judah's army. So the LORD will pay him back for those deaths. 33Joab and his family will be forever guilty for their deaths, but there will be peace from the LORD for David, his descendants, his family, and his throne forever."

34So Benaiah son of Jehoiada killed Joab, and he was buried near his home in the desert. 35The king then made Benaiah son of Jehoiada commander of the army in Joab's place. He also made Zadok the new high priest in Abiathar's place.

36Next the king sent for Shimei. Solomon said to him, "Build a house for yourself in Jerusalem and live there. Don't leave the city. 37The very day you leave and cross the Kidron Valley, someone will kill you, and it will be your own fault."

38So Shimei answered the king, "I agree with what you say. I will do what you say, my master and king." So Shimei lived in Jerusalem for a long time.

39But three years later two of Shimei's slaves ran away to Achish king of Gath, who was the son of Maacah. Shimei heard that his slaves were in Gath, 40so he put his saddle on his donkey and went to Achish at Gath to find them. Then he brought them back from Gath.

41Someone told Solomon that Shimei had gone from Jerusalem to Gath and had returned. 42So Solomon sent for Shimei and said, "I made you promise in the name of the LORD not to leave Jerusalem. I warned you if you went out anywhere you would die, and you agreed to what I said. 43Why did you break your promise to the LORD and disobey my command?" 44The king also said, "You know the many wrong things you did to my father David, so now the LORD will punish you for those wrongs. 45But the LORD will bless me and make the rule of David safe before the LORD forever."

46Then the king ordered Benaiah to kill Shimei, and he did. Now Solomon was in full control of his kingdom.

SOLOMON ASKS FOR WISDOM

3 1Solomon made an agreement with the king of Egypt by marrying his daughter and bringing her to Jerusalem. At this time Solomon was still building his palace and the Temple of the LORD, as well as a wall around Jerusalem. 2The Temple for the worship of the LORD had not yet been finished, so people were still sacrificing at altars in many places of worship. 3Solomon showed he loved the LORD by following the commands his father David had given him, except many other places of worship were still used to offer sacrifices and to burn incense.

> **MARRIAGE**
> How can a spouse be a bad influence? (3:1–3)

4King Solomon went to Gibeon to offer a sacrifice, because it was the most important place of worship. He offered a thousand burnt offerings on that altar. 5While he was at Gibeon, the LORD appeared to him in a dream during

2:28 corners of the altar If a person were innocent of a crime, he could run into the Holy Place where the altar was. If he held on to the corners of the altar, which looked like horns, he would be safe.

WHAT'S IT MEAN?

Solomon went to Gibeon to offer sacrifices because that's where the bronze altar and Holy Tent were. These sacred items, which had been made during the time of Moses, were an important part of the Israelites' worship. Located about six miles northwest of Jerusalem, Gibeon (now known as El-Jib) had been the site of several bloody battles, including Joshua's victory over the Amorites and a deadly contest between the soldiers of David and Ish-Bosheth, Saul's son.

1 Kings 3:4

the night. God said, "Ask for whatever you want me to give you."

6 Solomon answered, "You were very kind to your servant, my father David. He obeyed you, and he was honest and lived right. You showed great kindness to him when you allowed his son to be king after him. 7 LORD my God, now you have made me, your servant, king in my father's place. But I am like a little child; I don't know how to do what must be done. 8 I, your servant, am here among your chosen people, and there are too many of them to count. 9 I ask that you give me an obedient heart so I can rule the people in the right way and will know the difference between right and wrong. Otherwise, it is impossible to rule this great people of yours."

10 The Lord was pleased that Solomon had asked this. 11 So God said to him, "You did not ask for a long life, or riches for yourself, or the death of your enemies. Since you asked for wisdom to make the right decisions, 12 I will do what you asked. I will give you wisdom and understanding that is greater than anyone has had in the past or will have in the future. 13 I will also give you what you did not ask for: riches and honor. During your life no other king will be as great as you. 14 If you follow me and obey my laws and commands, as your father David did, I will also give you a long life."

15 After Solomon woke up from the dream, he went to Jerusalem. He stood before the Ark of the Agreement with the LORD, where he made burnt offerings and fellowship offerings. After that, he gave a feast for all his leaders and officers.

SOLOMON MAKES A WISE DECISION

16 One day two women who were prostitutes came to Solomon. As they stood before him, 17 one of the women said, "My master, this woman and I live in the same house. I gave birth to a baby while she was there with me. 18 Three days later this woman also gave birth to a baby. No one else was in the house with us; it was just the two of us. 19 One night this woman rolled over on her baby, and he died. 20 So she took my son from my bed during the night while I was asleep, and she carried him to her bed. Then she put the dead baby in my bed. 21 The next morning when I got up to feed my baby, I saw that he was dead! When I looked at him more closely, I realized he was not my son."

22 "No!" the other woman cried. "The living baby is my son, and the dead baby is yours!"

But the first woman said, "No! The dead baby is yours, and the living one is mine!" So the two women argued before the king.

23 Then King Solomon said, "One of you says, 'My son is alive and your son is dead.' Then the other one says, 'No! Your son is dead and my son is alive.' "

24 The king sent his servants to get a sword. When they brought it to him, 25 he said, "Cut the living baby into two pieces, and give each woman half."

26 The real mother of the living child was full of love for her son. So she said to the king, "Please, my master, don't kill him! Give the baby to her!"

But the other woman said, "Neither of us will have him. Cut him into two pieces!"

27 Then King Solomon said, "Don't kill him. Give the baby to the first woman, because she is the real mother."

28 When the people of Israel heard about King Solomon's decision, they respected him very much. They saw he had wisdom from God to make the right decisions.

SOLOMON'S OFFICERS

4 1 King Solomon ruled over all Israel. 2 These are the names of his leading officers:

Azariah son of Zadok was the priest;

3 Elihoreph and Ahijah, sons of Shisha, recorded what happened in the courts;

Jehoshaphat son of Ahilud recorded the history of the people;

4 Benaiah son of Jehoiada was commander of the army;

Zadok and Abiathar were priests;

5 Azariah son of Nathan was in charge of the district governors;

Zabud son of Nathan was a priest and adviser to the king;

[6]Ahishar was responsible for everything in the palace;

Adoniram son of Abda was in charge of the labor force.

[7]Solomon placed twelve governors over the districts of Israel, who gathered food from their districts for the king and his family. Each governor was responsible for bringing food to the king one month of each year. [8]These are the names of the twelve governors:

Ben-Hur was governor of the mountain country of Ephraim.

[9]Ben-Deker was governor of Makaz, Shaalbim, Beth Shemesh, and Elon Bethhanan.

[10]Ben-Hesed was governor of Arubboth, Socoh, and all the land of Hepher.

[11]Ben-Abinadab was governor of Naphoth Dor. (He was married to Taphath, Solomon's daughter.)

[12]Baana son of Ahilud was governor of Taanach, Megiddo, and all of Beth Shan next to Zarethan. This was below Jezreel from Beth Shan to Abel Meholah across from Jokmeam.

[13]Ben-Geber was governor of Ramoth in Gilead. (He was governor of all the towns of Jair in Gilead. Jair was the son of Manasseh. Ben-Geber was also over the district of Argob in Bashan, which had sixty large, walled cities with bronze bars on their gates.)

[14]Ahinadab son of Iddo was governor of Mahanaim.

[15]Ahimaaz was governor of Naphtali. (He was married to Basemath, Solomon's daughter.)

[16]Baana son of Hushai was governor of Asher and Aloth.

[17]Jehoshaphat son of Paruah was governor of Issachar.

[18]Shimei son of Ela was governor of Benjamin.

[19]Geber son of Uri was governor of Gilead. Gilead had been the country of Sihon king of the Amorites and Og king of Bashan. But Geber was the only governor over this district.

SOLOMON'S KINGDOM

[20]There were as many people in Judah and Israel as grains of sand on the seashore. The people ate, drank, and were happy. [21]Solomon ruled over all the kingdoms from the Euphrates River to the land of the Philistines, as far as the border of Egypt. These countries brought Solomon the payments he demanded, and they were under his control all his life.

[22]Solomon needed much food each day to feed himself and all the people who ate at his table: one hundred ninety-five bushels of fine flour, three hundred ninety bushels of grain, [23]ten cows that were fed on good grain, twenty cows that were raised in the fields, one hundred sheep, three kinds of deer, and fattened birds.

[24]Solomon controlled all the countries west of the Euphrates River—the land from Tiphsah to Gaza. And he had peace on all sides of his kingdom. [25]During Solomon's life Judah and Israel, from Dan to Beersheba,[n] also lived in peace; all of his people were able to sit under their own fig trees and grapevines.

[26]Solomon had four thousand stalls for his chariot horses and twelve thousand horses. [27]Each month one of the district governors gave King Solomon all the food he needed—enough for every person who ate at the king's table. The governors made sure he had everything he needed. [28]They also brought enough barley and straw for Solomon's chariot and work horses; each person brought this grain to the right place.

SOLOMON'S WISDOM

[29]God gave Solomon great wisdom so he could understand many things. His wisdom was as hard to measure as the grains of sand on the seashore. [30]His wisdom was greater than any wisdom of the East, or any wisdom in Egypt. [31]He was wiser than anyone on earth.

WHAT'S IT MEAN?

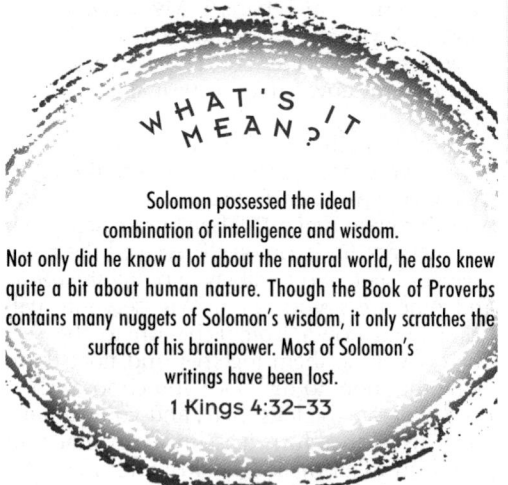

Solomon possessed the ideal combination of intelligence and wisdom. Not only did he know a lot about the natural world, he also knew quite a bit about human nature. Though the Book of Proverbs contains many nuggets of Solomon's wisdom, it only scratches the surface of his brainpower. Most of Solomon's writings have been lost.

1 Kings 4:32–33

4:25 Dan to Beersheba Dan was the city farthest north in Israel, and Beersheba was the city farthest south. So this means all the people of Israel.

He was even wiser than Ethan the Ezrahite, as well as Heman, Calcol, and Darda—the three sons of Mahol. King Solomon became famous in all the surrounding countries. 32During his life he spoke three thousand wise sayings and also wrote one thousand five songs. 33He taught about many kinds of plants—everything from the great cedar trees of Lebanon to the weeds that grow out of the walls. He also taught about animals, birds, crawling things, and fish. 34People from all nations came to listen to King Solomon's wisdom. The kings of all nations sent them to him, because they had heard of Solomon's wisdom.

PREPARING TO BUILD THE TEMPLE

5 1Hiram, the king of Tyre, had always been David's friend. When Hiram heard that Solomon had been made king in David's place, he sent his messengers to Solomon. 2Solomon sent this message back to King Hiram: 3"You remember my father David had to fight many wars with the countries around him, so he was never able to build a temple for worshiping the LORD his God. David was waiting until the LORD allowed him to defeat all his enemies. 4But now the LORD my God has given me peace on all sides of my country. I have no enemies now, and no danger threatens my people.

5"The LORD promised my father David, 'I will make your son king after you, and he will build a temple for worshiping me.' Now, I plan to build that temple for worshiping the LORD my God. 6So send your men to cut down cedar trees for me from Lebanon. My servants will work with yours, and I will pay them whatever wages you decide. We don't have anyone who can cut down trees as well as the people of Sidon."

7When Hiram heard what Solomon asked, he was very happy. He said, "Praise the LORD today! He has given David a wise son to rule over this great nation!" 8Then Hiram sent back this message to Solomon: "I received the message you sent, and I will give you all the cedar and pine trees you want. 9My servants will bring them down from Lebanon to the sea. There I will tie them together and float them along the shore to the place you choose. Then I will separate the logs there, and you can take them away. In return it is my wish that you give food to all those who live with me." 10So Hiram gave Solomon as much cedar and pine as he wanted. 11And Solomon gave Hiram about one hundred twenty-five thousand bushels of wheat each year to feed the people who lived with him. Solomon also gave him about one hundred fifteen thousand gallons of pure olive oil every year.

12The LORD gave Solomon wisdom as he had promised. And there was peace between Hiram and Solomon; these two kings made a treaty between themselves.

13King Solomon forced thirty thousand men of Israel to help in this work. 14He sent a group of ten thousand men each month to Lebanon. Each group worked in Lebanon one month, then went home for two months. A man named Adoniram was in charge. 15Solomon forced eighty thousand men to work in the hill country, cutting stone, and he had seventy thousand men to carry the stones. 16There were also thirty-three hundred men who directed the workers. 17King Solomon commanded them to cut large blocks of fine stone to be used for the foundation of the Temple. 18Solomon's and Hiram's builders and the men from Byblos carved the stones and prepared the stones and the logs for building the Temple.

FAMILY

What's more important: family or work? (5:13–14)

WHAT'S IT MEAN?

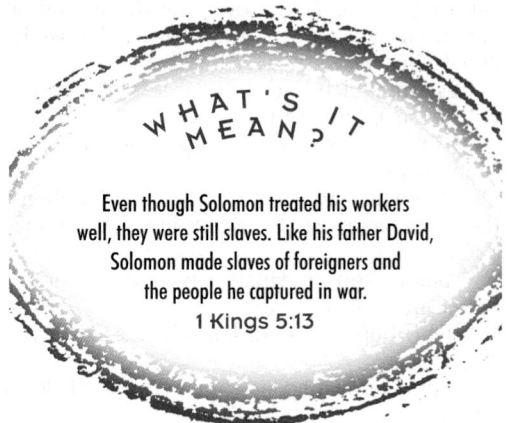

Even though Solomon treated his workers well, they were still slaves. Like his father David, Solomon made slaves of foreigners and the people he captured in war.

1 Kings 5:13

SOLOMON BUILDS THE TEMPLE

6 1Solomon began to build the Temple four hundred eighty years after the people of Israel had left Egypt. This was during the fourth year of King Solomon's rule over Israel. It was the second month, the month of Ziv.

2The Temple was ninety feet long, thirty feet wide, and forty-five feet high. 3The porch in front of the main room of the Temple was fifteen feet deep and thirty feet wide. This room ran along the front of the Temple itself. Its width was equal to that of the Temple. 4The Temple also had windows that opened and closed. 5Solomon also built some side rooms

against the walls of the main room and the inner room of the Temple. He built rooms all
around. 6The rooms on the bottom floor were
seven and one-half feet wide. Those on the middle floor were nine feet wide, and the rooms above them were ten and one-half feet wide. The Temple wall that formed the side of each room was thinner than the wall in the room below. These rooms were pushed against the Temple wall, but they did not have their main beams built into this wall.
7The stones were prepared at the same place where they were cut from the ground. Since these stones were the only ones used to build the Temple, there was no noise of hammers, axes, or any other iron tools at the Temple.
8The entrance to the lower rooms beside the Temple was on the south side. From there, stairs went up to the second-floor rooms. And from there, stairs went on to the third-floor
rooms. 9Solomon put a roof made from beams
and cedar boards on the Temple. So he finished building the Temple
10as well as the bottom floor that was beside the Temple. This bottom floor was seven and one-half feet high and was attached to the Temple by cedar beams.
11The LORD said to Solomon:
12"If you obey all my laws and commands, I will do for you what I promised your father David.
13I will live among the Israelites in this Temple, and I will never leave my people Israel."
14So Solomon finished building the Temple.

WHAT'S IT MEAN?

If the floor plan of the Temple seems familiar to you, it's because it's the same floor plan that was used for the Meeting Tent that Moses had built. The only difference was that the Temple was twice the size of the Meeting Tent. Notice that the Most Holy Place was designed to be a perfect cube, equal in length, width, and height.

1 Kings 6:16

15The inside walls were covered from floor to ceiling with cedar boards. The floor was made
from pine boards.
16A room thirty feet long was built in the back part of the Temple. This room, called the Most Holy Place, was separated from the rest of the Temple by cedar boards which reached from floor to ceiling.
17The main room, the one in front of the Most
Holy Place, was sixty feet long.
18Everything inside the Temple was covered with cedar, which was carved with pictures of flowers and plants. A person could not see the stones of the wall, only the cedar.
19Solomon prepared the inner room at the

Promise — HE PROMISES TO NEVER LEAVE YOU.

If you obey all my laws and commands, I will do for you what I promised your father David. I will live among the Israelites in this Temple, and I will never leave my people Israel (1 Kin. 6:12–13).

Do you remember the fears of your childhood? Monsters in the closet. Thunder in the night. Being left alone. You run through the house screaming, "Mommmmm!" Fearing that she has suddenly vanished, you begin to check everywhere, look in every room. Your heart is racing as your little imagination runs wild. Maybe everyone is gone. You've been deserted. You'll have to fend for yourself in this big old world. You'll have to cook and clean and earn money. Oh no. You're about to cry. Finally you hear her voice from the garage, "What is it, honey?" "Nothing, Mom," you reply in your calmest voice. "I just couldn't find you." "Well, I'm right here," she reassures you. And so is God. He will never desert you or leave you. Even when you're an adult and feel afraid, rest assured that God is as close as the air you breathe.

SEE FOR YOURSELF:

Ex. 33:14; Deut. 31:8; Ps. 37:28

back of the Temple to keep the Ark of the Agreement with the LORD. [20]This inner room was thirty feet long, thirty feet wide, and thirty feet high. He covered this room with pure gold, and he also covered the altar of cedar. [21]He covered the inside of the Temple with pure gold, placing gold chains across the front of the inner room, which was also covered with gold. [22]So all the inside of the Temple, as well as the altar of the Most Holy Place, was covered with gold.

[23]Solomon made two creatures from olive wood and placed them in the Most Holy Place. Each creature was fifteen feet tall [24]and had two wings. Each wing was seven and one-half feet long, so it was fifteen feet from the end of one wing to the end of the other. [25]The creatures were the same size and shape; [26]each was fifteen feet tall. [27]These creatures were put beside each other in the Most Holy Place with their wings spread out. One creature's wing touched one wall, and the other creature's wing touched the other wall with their wings touching each other in the middle of the room. [28]These two creatures were covered with gold.

"Solomon prepared the inner room at the back of the Temple to keep the Ark of the Agreement with the LORD." (1 Kings 6:19)

[29]All the walls around the Temple were carved with pictures of creatures with wings, as well as palm trees and flowers. This was true for both the main room and the inner room. [30]The floors of both rooms were covered with gold.

[31]Doors made from olive wood were placed at the entrance to the Most Holy Place. These doors had five-sided frames. [32]Creatures with wings, as well as palm trees and flowers, were also carved on the two olive wood doors that were covered with gold. The creatures and the palm trees on the doors were covered with gold as well. [33]At the entrance to the main room there was a square door frame made of olive wood. [34]Two doors were made from pine. Each door had two parts so the doors folded. [35]The doors were covered with pictures of creatures with wings, as well as palm trees and flowers. All of the carvings were covered with gold, which was evenly spread over them.

[36]The inner courtyard was enclosed by walls, which were made of three rows of cut stones and one row of cedar boards.

[37]Work began on the Temple in Ziv, the second month, during the fourth year Solomon was king over Israel. [38]The Temple was finished during the eleventh year he was king, in the eighth month, the month of Bul. It was built exactly as it was planned. Solomon had spent seven years building it.

WHAT'S IT MEAN?

Here's a brief history of the Temple in Jerusalem: Solomon began work on the first Temple around 967 B.C. and completed it seven years later. The Babylonians came along in 586 B.C. and destroyed the building completely. The Jewish people built a second Temple, but it was no longer standing when Jesus was born. The Temple that existed during Jesus' day had been built by Herod.

1 Kings 6:37

SOLOMON'S PALACE

7 [1]King Solomon also built a palace for himself; it took him thirteen years to finish it. [2]Built of cedars from the Forest of Lebanon, it was one hundred fifty feet long, seventy-five feet wide, and forty-five feet high. It had four rows of cedar columns which supported the cedar beams. [3]There were forty-five beams on the roof, with fifteen beams in each row, and the ceiling was covered with cedar above the beams. [4]Windows were placed in three rows facing each other. [5]All the doors were square, and the three doors at each end faced each other.

[6]Solomon also built the porch that had pillars. This porch was seventy-five feet long and forty-five feet wide. Along the front of the porch was a roof supported by pillars.

[7]Solomon also built a throne room where he judged people, called the Hall of Justice. This room was covered with cedar from the floor to the ceiling. [8]The palace where Solomon lived was built like the Hall of Justice, and it was behind this hall. Solomon also built the same kind of palace for his wife, who was the daughter of the king of Egypt.

[9]All these buildings were made with blocks

of fine stone. First they were carefully cut. Then
they were trimmed with a saw in the front and
back. These fine stones went from the foundations of the buildings to the top of the walls.
Even the courtyard was made with blocks of
stone. 10The foundations were made with large
blocks of fine stone, some as long as fifteen
feet. Others were twelve feet long. 11On top of
these foundation stones were other blocks of
fine stone and cedar beams. 12The palace
courtyard, the courtyard inside the Temple,
and the porch of the Temple were surrounded
by walls. All of these walls had three rows of
stone blocks and one row of cedar beams.

THE TEMPLE IS COMPLETED INSIDE

13King Solomon sent to Tyre and had Huram brought to him. 14Huram's mother was a
widow from the tribe of Naphtali. His father
was from Tyre and had been skilled in making
things from bronze. Huram was also very
skilled and experienced in bronze work. So he
came to King Solomon and did all the bronze
work.

15He made two bronze pillars, each one
twenty-seven feet tall and eighteen feet around.
16He also made two bronze capitals that were
seven and one-half feet tall, and he put them
on top of the pillars. 17Then he made a net of
seven chains for each capital, which covered
the capitals on top of the two pillars. 18He
made two rows of bronze pomegranates to go
on the nets. These covered the capitals at the
top of the pillars. 19The capitals on top of the
pillars in the porch were shaped like lilies, and
they were six feet tall. 20The capitals were on
top of both pillars, above the bowl-shaped
section and next to the nets. At that place there
were two hundred pomegranates in rows all
around the capitals. 21Huram put these two
bronze pillars at the porch of the Temple. He
named the south pillar He Establishes and the
north pillar In Him Is Strength. 22The capitals
on top of the pillars were shaped like lilies. So
the work on the pillars was finished.

23Then Huram made from bronze a large
round bowl, which was called the Sea. It was
forty-five feet around, fifteen feet across, and
seven and one-half feet deep. 24Around the
outer edge of the bowl was a rim. Under this
rim were two rows of bronze plants which
surrounded the bowl. There were ten plants
every eighteen inches, and these plants were
made in one piece with the bowl. 25The bowl
rested on the backs of twelve bronze bulls that
faced outward from the center of the bowl.
Three bulls faced north, three faced west, three
faced south, and three faced east. 26The sides of
the bowl were four inches thick, and it held
about eleven thousand gallons. The rim of the
bowl was like the rim of a cup or like a lily
blossom.

27Then Huram made ten bronze stands,
each one six feet long, six feet wide, and four
and one-half feet high. 28The stands were made
from square sides, which were put on frames.
29On the sides were bronze lions, bulls, and
creatures with wings. On the frames above and
below the lions and bulls were designs of
flowers hammered into the bronze. 30Each
stand had four bronze wheels with bronze axles. At the corners there were bronze supports
for a large bowl, and the supports had designs
of flowers. 31There was a frame on top of the
bowls, eighteen inches high above the bowls.
The opening of the bowl was round, twenty-
seven inches deep. Designs were carved into
the bronze on the frame, which was square,
not round. 32The four wheels, placed under the
frame, were twenty-seven inches high. The axles between the wheels were made as one piece
with the stand. 33The wheels were like a
chariot's wheels. Everything on the wheels—
the axles, rims, spokes, and hubs—were made
of bronze.

34The four supports were on the four corners of each stand. They were made as one
piece with the stand. 35A strip of bronze
around the top of each stand was nine inches
deep. It was also made as one piece with the
stand. 36The sides of the stand and the frames
were covered with carvings of creatures with
wings, as well as lions, palm trees, and flowers.
37This is the way Huram made the ten stands.
The bronze for each stand was melted and
poured into a mold, so all the stands were the
same size and shape.

38Huram also made ten bronze bowls, one
bowl for each of the ten stands. Each bowl was
six feet across and could hold about two hundred thirty gallons. 39Huram put five stands on
the south side of the Temple and five on the
north side. He put the large bowl in the southeast corner of the Temple. 40Huram also made
bowls, shovels, and small bowls.

So Huram finished all his work for King
Solomon on the Temple of the LORD:

41two pillars;
two large bowls for the capitals on top
of the pillars;
two nets to cover the two large bowls
for the capitals on top of the pillars;
42four hundred pomegranates for the
two nets (there were two rows of

pomegranates for each net covering the bowls for the capitals on
top of the pillars);
43 ten stands with a bowl on each stand;
44 the large bowl with twelve bulls under it;
45 the pots, shovels, small bowls, and all
the utensils for the Temple of the
LORD.

Huram made everything King Solomon
wanted from polished bronze. 46 The king had
these things poured into clay molds that
were made in the plain of the Jordan River between Succoth and Zarethan. 47 Solomon never
weighed the bronze used to make these things,
because there was too much to weigh. So the
total weight of all the bronze was never known.
48 Solomon also made all the items for the
Temple of the LORD:
the golden altar;
the golden table which held the bread
that shows God's people are in his
presence;
49 the lampstands of pure gold (five on
the right side and five on the left
side in front of the Most Holy
Place);
the flowers, lamps, and tongs of gold;
50 the pure gold bowls, wick trimmers,
small bowls, pans, and dishes used
to carry coals;
the gold hinges for the doors of the
Most Holy Place and the main
room of the Temple.

51 Finally the work King Solomon did for the
Temple of the LORD was finished. Solomon
brought in everything his father David had set
apart for the Temple—silver, gold, and other
articles. He put everything in the treasuries of
the Temple of the LORD.

THE ARK IS BROUGHT INTO THE TEMPLE

8
1 King Solomon called for the older leaders
of Israel, the heads of the tribes, and the leaders
of the families to come to him in Jerusalem. He
wanted them to bring the Ark of the Agreement with the LORD from the older part of the
city. 2 So all the Israelites came together with
King Solomon during the festival in the month
of Ethanim, the seventh month.
3 When all the older leaders of Israel arrived,
the priests lifted up the Ark. 4 They carried the
Ark of the LORD, the Meeting Tent, and the
holy utensils; the priests and the Levites
brought them up. 5 King Solomon and all the
Israelites gathered before the Ark and sacrificed
so many sheep and cattle no one could count
them all. 6 Then the priests put the Ark of the
Agreement with the LORD in its place inside the
Most Holy Place in the Temple, under the
wings of the golden creatures. 7 The wings of
these creatures were spread out over the place
for the Ark, covering it and its carrying poles.
8 The carrying poles were so long that anyone
standing in the Holy Place in front of the Most
Holy Place could see the ends of the poles, but
no one could see them from outside the Holy
Place. The poles are still there today. 9 The only
things inside the Ark were two stone tablets[n]
that Moses had put in the Ark at Mount Sinai.
That was where the LORD made his agreement
with the Israelites after they came out of Egypt.

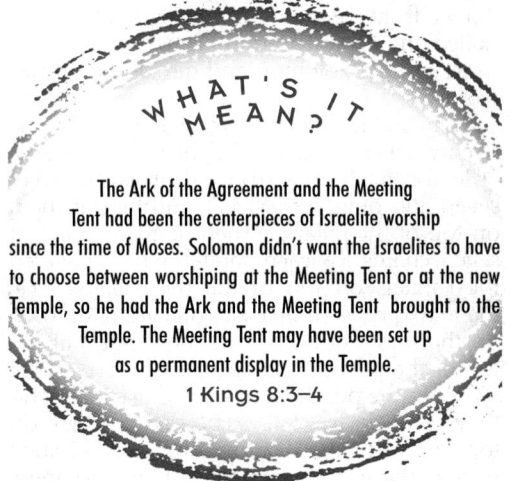

WHAT'S IT MEAN?

The Ark of the Agreement and the Meeting Tent had been the centerpieces of Israelite worship since the time of Moses. Solomon didn't want the Israelites to have to choose between worshiping at the Meeting Tent or at the new Temple, so he had the Ark and the Meeting Tent brought to the Temple. The Meeting Tent may have been set up as a permanent display in the Temple.

1 Kings 8:3–4

10 When the priests left the Holy Place, a
cloud filled the Temple of the LORD. 11 The
priests could not continue their work, because
the Temple was filled with the glory of the
LORD.

SOLOMON SPEAKS TO THE PEOPLE

12 Then Solomon said, "The LORD said he
would live in a dark cloud. 13 LORD, I have truly
built a wonderful Temple for you—a place for
you to live forever."
14 While all the Israelites were standing there,
King Solomon turned to them and blessed
them.
15 Then he said, "Praise the LORD, the God of
Israel. He has done what he promised to my
father David. The LORD said, 16 'Since the time I

8:9 stone tablets They were the two tablets on which God wrote the Ten Commandments.

brought my people Israel out of Egypt, I have
not chosen a city in any tribe of Israel where a
temple will be built for me. But I have chosen
David to lead my people Israel.'
17"My father David wanted to build a temple for the LORD, the God of Israel. 18But the
LORD said to my father David, 'It was good that
you wanted to build a temple for me. 19But you
are not the one to build it. Your son, who
comes from your own body, is the one who
will build my temple.'
20"Now the LORD has kept his promise. I am
the king now in place of David my father. Now
I rule Israel as the LORD promised, and I have
built the Temple for the LORD, the God of Israel.
21I have made a place there for the Ark, in
which is the Agreement the LORD made with
our ancestors when he brought them out of
Egypt."

SOLOMON'S PRAYER

22Then Solomon stood facing the LORD's altar, and all the Israelites were standing behind
him. He spread out his hands toward the sky
23and said:
"LORD, God of Israel, there is no god like
you in heaven above or on earth below. You
keep your agreement of love with your servants who truly follow you. 24You have kept
the promise you made to your servant David,
my father. You spoke it with your own mouth
and finished it with your hands today. 25Now
LORD, God of Israel, keep the promise you
made to your servant David, my father. You
said, 'If your sons are careful to obey me as
you have obeyed me, there will always be
someone from your family ruling Israel.'
26Now, God of Israel, please continue to keep
that promise you made to your servant David,
my father.

GOD

Can we fully describe God? (8:27)

27"But, God, can you really
live here on the earth? The
sky and the highest place in
heaven cannot contain you.
Surely this house which I
have built cannot contain
you. 28But please listen to my
prayer and my request, because I am your servant. LORD my God, hear this prayer your servant prays to you today. 29Night and day
please watch over this Temple where you have
said, 'I will be worshiped there.' Hear the prayer
I pray facing this Temple. 30Hear my prayers
and the prayers of your people Israel when we
pray facing this place. Hear from your home in
heaven, and when you hear, forgive us.
31"If someone wrongs another person, he
will be brought to the altar in this Temple. If he
swears an oath that he is not guilty, 32then hear
in heaven. Judge the case, punish the guilty, but
declare that the innocent person is not guilty.
33"When your people, the Israelites, sin
against you, their enemies will defeat them. But
if they come back to you and praise you and
pray to you in this Temple, 34then hear them in
heaven. Forgive the sins of your people Israel,
and bring them back to the land you gave to
their ancestors.
35"When they sin against you, you will stop
the rain from falling on their land. Then they
will pray, facing this place and praising you;
they will stop sinning when you make them
suffer. 36When this happens, please hear their
prayer in heaven, and forgive the sins of your
servants, the Israelites. Teach them to do what
is right. Then please send rain to this land you
have given particularly to them.
37"At times the land will become so dry that
no food will grow, or a great sickness will
spread among the people. Sometimes all the
crops will be destroyed by locusts or grasshoppers. Your people will be attacked in their
cities by their enemy or will become sick.
38When any of these things happen, the people
will become truly sorry. If your people spread
their hands in prayer toward this Temple,
39then hear their prayers from your home in
heaven. Forgive and treat each person as he
should be treated because you know what is in
a person's heart. Only you know what is in
everyone's heart. 40Then your people will respect you as long as they live in this land you
gave to our ancestors.
41-42"People who are not Israelites, foreigners

WHAT'S IT MEAN?

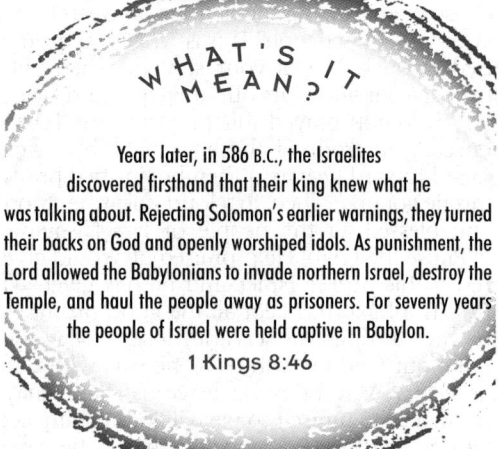

Years later, in 586 B.C., the Israelites discovered firsthand that their king knew what he was talking about. Rejecting Solomon's earlier warnings, they turned their backs on God and openly worshiped idols. As punishment, the Lord allowed the Babylonians to invade northern Israel, destroy the Temple, and haul the people away as prisoners. For seventy years the people of Israel were held captive in Babylon.

1 Kings 8:46

from other lands, will hear about your greatness and power. They will come from far away to pray at this Temple. 43Then hear from your home in heaven, and do whatever they ask you. Then people everywhere will know you and respect you, just as your people in Israel do. Then everyone will know I built this Temple as a place to worship you.

44"When your people go out to fight their enemies along some road on which you send them, your people will pray to you, facing the city which you have chosen and the Temple I have built for you. 45Then hear in heaven their prayers, and do what is right.

46"Everyone sins, so your people will also sin against you. You will become angry with them and hand them over to their enemies. Their enemies will capture them and take them away to their countries far or near. 47Your people will be sorry for their sins when they are held as prisoners in another country. They will be sorry and pray to you in the land where they are held as prisoners, saying, 'We have sinned. We have done wrong and acted wickedly.' 48They will truly turn back to you in the land of their enemies. They will pray to you, facing this land you gave their ancestors, this city you have chosen, and the Temple I have built for you. 49Then hear their prayers from your home in heaven, and do what is right. 50Forgive your people of all their sins and for turning against you. Make those who have captured them show them mercy. 51Remember, they are your special people. You brought them out of Egypt, as if you were pulling them out of a blazing furnace.

52"Give your attention to my prayers and the prayers of your people Israel. Listen to them anytime they ask you for help. 53You chose them from all the nations on earth to be your very own people. This is what you promised through Moses your servant when you brought our ancestors out of Egypt, Lord GOD."

54Solomon prayed this prayer to the LORD, kneeling in front of the altar with his arms raised toward heaven. When he finished praying, he got up. 55Then, in a loud voice, he stood and blessed all the people of Israel, saying: 56"Praise the LORD! He promised he would give rest to his people Israel, and he has given us rest. The LORD has kept all the good promises he gave through his servant Moses. 57May the LORD our God be with us as he was with our ancestors. May he never leave us, 58and may he turn us to himself so we will follow him. Let us obey all the laws and commands he gave our ancestors. 59May the LORD our God remember this prayer day and night and do what is right for his servant and his people Israel day by day. 60Then all the people of the world will know the LORD is the only true God. 61You must fully obey the LORD our God and follow all his laws and commands. Continue to obey in the future as you do now."

SACRIFICES ARE OFFERED

62Then King Solomon and all Israel with him offered sacrifices to the LORD. 63Solomon killed twenty-two thousand cattle and one hundred twenty thousand sheep as fellowship offerings. So the king and all the people gave the Temple to the LORD.

64On that day King Solomon made holy the middle part of the courtyard which is in front of the Temple of the LORD. There he offered whole burnt offerings, grain offerings, and the fat of the fellowship offerings. He offered them in the courtyard, because the bronze altar before the LORD was too small to hold all the burnt offerings, the grain offerings, and the fat of the fellowship offerings.

65Solomon and all the Israelites celebrated the other festival that came at that time. People came from as far away as Lebo Hamath and the brook of Egypt. A great many people celebrated before the LORD for seven days, then seven more days, for a total of fourteen days. 66On the following day Solomon sent the people home. They blessed the king as they went, happy because of all the good things the LORD had done for his servant David and his people Israel.

WORSHIP

How should we feel in our hearts when God is good to us? (8:66)

THE LORD APPEARS TO SOLOMON AGAIN

9

1Solomon finished building the Temple of the LORD and his royal palace and everything he wanted to build. 2Then the LORD appeared to him again just as he had done before, in Gibeon. 3The LORD said to him: "I have heard your prayer and what you have asked me to do. You built this Temple, and I have made it a holy place. I will be worshiped there forever and will watch over it and protect it always.

PRAYER

Does God hear our prayers? (9:3–5)

4"But you must serve me as your father David did; he was fair and sincere. You must obey all I have commanded and keep my laws and rules. 5If you do, I will make your kingdom strong. This is the promise I made to your fa-

ther David—that someone from his family
would always rule Israel.
6"But you and your children must follow
me and obey the laws and commands I have
given you. You must not serve or worship
other gods. 7If you do, I will force Israel to
leave the land I have given them, and I will
leave this Temple that I have made holy. All the
nations will make fun of Israel and speak evil
about them. 8If the Temple is destroyed, everyone who passes by will be shocked. They will
make fun of you and ask, 'Why did the LORD
do this terrible thing to this land and this Temple?' 9People will answer, 'This happened because they left the LORD their God. This was
the God who brought their ancestors out of
Egypt, but they decided to follow other gods.
They worshiped and served those gods, so the
LORD brought all this disaster on them.' "

SOLOMON'S OTHER ACHIEVEMENTS

10By the end of twenty years, King Solomon
had built two buildings—the Temple of the
LORD and the royal palace. 11At that time King
Solomon gave twenty towns in Galilee to Hiram king of Tyre, because Hiram had helped
with the buildings. Hiram
had given Solomon all the
cedar, pine, and gold he
wanted. 12So Hiram
traveled from Tyre to
see the towns Sol-
omon had given him,
but when he saw
them, he was not
pleased. 13He asked,
"What good are these
towns you have given
me, my brother?" So he
named them the Land of
Cabul,[n] and they are still
called that today. 14Hiram had
sent Solomon about nine thousand pounds of
gold.
15This is the account of the forced labor
Solomon used to build the Temple and the palace. He had them fill in the land and build the
wall around Jerusalem. He also had them rebuild the cities of Hazor, Megiddo, and Gezer.
16(In the past the king of Egypt had attacked
and captured Gezer. After burning it, he killed
the Canaanites who lived there. Then he gave it
as a wedding present to his daughter, who
married Solomon. 17So Solomon rebuilt it.) He
also built the cities of Lower Beth Horon 18and
Baalath, as well as Tadmor, which is in the
desert. 19King Solomon also built cities for
storing grain and supplies and cities for his
chariots and horses. He built whatever he
wanted in Jerusalem, Lebanon, and everywhere he ruled.
20There were other people in the land who
were not Israelites—Amorites, Hittites, Perizzites, Hivites, and Jebusites. 21They were descendants of people that the Israelites had not
destroyed. Solomon forced them to work for
him as slaves, as is still true today. 22But Solomon did not make slaves of the Israelites.
They were his soldiers, government leaders,
officers, captains, chariot commanders, and
drivers.
23These were his most important officers
over the work. There were five hundred fifty
supervisors over the people who did the work
on Solomon's projects.
24The daughter of the king of Egypt moved
from the old part of Jerusalem to the palace
that Solomon had built for her. Then Solomon
filled in the surrounding land.
25Three times each year Solomon offered
whole burnt offerings and fellowship offerings
on the altar he had built for
the LORD. He also burned
incense before the
LORD. So he finished the
work on the Temple.
26King Solomon also
built ships at Ezion Ge-
ber, a town near Elath
on the shore of the
Red Sea, in the land of
Edom. 27Hiram had
skilled sailors, so he
sent them to serve in
these ships with Sol-
omon's men. 28The ships
sailed to Ophir and brought
back about thirty-two thousand pounds of
gold to King Solomon.

"Three times each year Solomon offered whole burnt offerings and fellowship offerings on the altar he had built for the LORD. He also burned incense before the LORD. So he finished the work on the Temple."
(1 Kings 9:25)

THE QUEEN OF SHEBA VISITS SOLOMON

10 1When the queen of Sheba heard about
Solomon, she came to test him with hard questions. 2She traveled to Jerusalem with a large
group of servants and camels carrying spices,
jewels, and much gold. When she came to
Solomon, she talked with him about all she
had in mind, 3and Solomon answered all her
questions. Nothing was too hard for him to explain to her. 4The queen of Sheba learned that

9:13 Cabul This name sounds like the Hebrew word for "worthless."

Solomon was very wise. She saw the palace he had built, 5the food on his table, his many officers, the palace servants, and their good clothes. She saw the servants who served him at feasts and the whole burnt offerings he made in the Temple of the LORD. All these things amazed her.

WHAT'S IT MEAN?

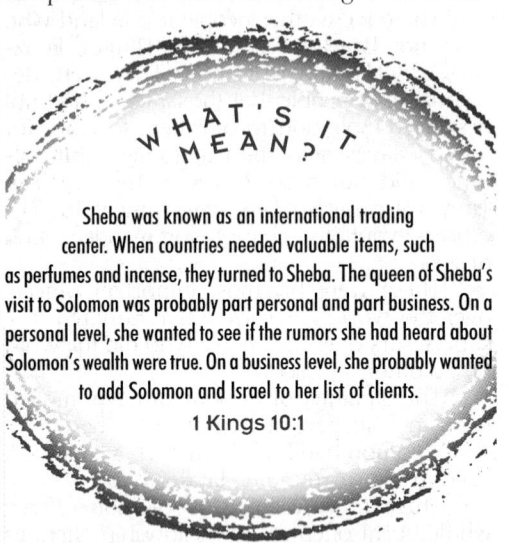

Sheba was known as an international trading center. When countries needed valuable items, such as perfumes and incense, they turned to Sheba. The queen of Sheba's visit to Solomon was probably part personal and part business. On a personal level, she wanted to see if the rumors she had heard about Solomon's wealth were true. On a business level, she probably wanted to add Solomon and Israel to her list of clients.

1 Kings 10:1

6So she said to King Solomon, "What I heard in my own country about your achievements and wisdom is true. 7I could not believe it then, but now I have come and seen it with my own eyes. I was not told even half of it! Your wisdom and wealth are much greater than I had heard. 8Your men and officers are very lucky, because in always serving you, they are able to hear your wisdom. 9Praise the LORD your God, who was pleased to make you king of Israel. The LORD has constant love for Israel, so he made you king to keep justice and to rule fairly."

10Then she gave the king about nine thousand pounds of gold and many spices and jewels. No one since that time has brought more spices than the queen of Sheba gave to King Solomon.

11(Hiram's ships brought gold from Ophir, as well as much juniper wood and jewels. 12Solomon used the juniper wood to build supports for the Temple of the LORD and the palace, and to make harps and lyres for the musicians. Such fine juniper wood has not been brought in or been seen since that time.)

13King Solomon gave the queen of Sheba everything she wanted and asked for, in addition to what he had already given her of his wealth. Then she and her servants returned to her own country.

SOLOMON'S WEALTH

14Every year King Solomon received about fifty thousand pounds of gold. 15Besides that, he also received gold from the traders and merchants, as well as from the kings of Arabia and governors of the land.

16King Solomon made two hundred large shields of hammered gold, each of which contained about seven and one-half pounds of gold. 17He also made three hundred smaller shields of hammered gold, each of which contained about four pounds of gold. The king put them in the Palace of the Forest of Lebanon.

18The king built a large throne of ivory and covered it with fine gold. 19The throne had six steps on it, and its back was round at the top. There were armrests on both sides of the chair, and each armrest had a lion beside it. 20Twelve lions stood on the six steps, one lion at each end of each step. Nothing like this had ever been made for any other kingdom. 21All of Solomon's drinking cups, as well as the dishes in the Palace of the Forest of Lebanon, were made of pure gold. Nothing was made from silver, because silver was not valuable in Solomon's time.

22King Solomon also had many trading ships at sea, along with Hiram's ships. Every three years the ships returned, bringing back gold, silver, ivory, apes, and baboons.

WHAT'S IT MEAN?

King Hiram was from Tyre, a seaport on the Mediterranean. If you'd like to visit Tyre today, head for Lebanon. If you'd like to visit Ophir, good luck! No one knows for sure where the city was located. Some guesses put it in west Arabia or east Africa, beyond the southern end of the Dead Sea. About all that is known for sure about Ophir is that it was a supplier of gold and precious stones.

1 Kings 10:11–13

23So Solomon had more riches and wisdom than all the other kings on earth. 24People everywhere wanted to see King Solomon and listen to the wisdom God had given him. 25Every year those who came brought gifts of silver and gold, clothes, weapons, spices, horses, and mules.

26Solomon had fourteen hundred chariots and twelve thousand horses. He kept some in special cities for the chariots, and others he kept with him in Jerusalem. 27In Jerusalem Solomon made silver as common as stones and cedar trees as common as the fig trees on the western hills. 28He imported horses from Egypt and Kue. His traders bought them in Kue. 29A chariot from Egypt cost about fifteen pounds of silver, and a horse cost nearly four pounds of silver. Solomon's traders also sold horses and chariots to all the kings of the Hittites and the Arameans.

SOLOMON'S MANY WIVES

11 1King Solomon loved many women who were not from Israel. He loved the daughter of the king of Egypt, as well as women of the Moabites, Ammonites, Edomites, Sidonians, and Hittites. 2The LORD had told the Israelites, "You must not marry people of other nations. If you do, they will cause you to follow their gods." But Solomon fell in love with these women. 3He had seven hundred wives who were from royal families and three hundred slave women who gave birth to his children. His wives caused him to turn away from God. 4As Solomon grew old, his wives caused him to follow other gods. He did not follow the LORD completely as his father David had done. 5Solomon worshiped Ashtoreth, the goddess of the people of Sidon, and Molech, the hated god of the Ammonites. 6So Solomon did what the LORD said was wrong and did not follow the LORD completely as his father David had done.

MARRIAGE
Can a spouse lead you away from God? (11:1–2)

7On a hill east of Jerusalem, Solomon built two places for worship. One was a place to worship Chemosh, the hated god of the Moabites, and the other was a place to worship Molech, the hated god of the Ammonites. 8Solomon did the same thing for all his foreign wives so they could burn incense and offer sacrifices to their gods.

9The LORD had appeared to Solomon twice, but the king turned away from following the LORD, the God of Israel. The LORD was angry with Solomon, 10because he had commanded Solomon not to follow other gods. But Solomon did not obey the LORD's command. 11So the LORD said to Solomon, "Because you have chosen to break your agreement with me and have not obeyed my commands, I will tear your kingdom away from you and give it to one of your officers. 12But I will not take it away while you are alive because of my love for your father David. I will tear it away from your son when he becomes king. 13I will not tear away all the kingdom from him, but I will leave him one tribe to rule. I will do this because of David, my servant, and because of Jerusalem, the city I have chosen."

SOLOMON'S ENEMIES

14The LORD caused Hadad the Edomite, a member of the family of the king of Edom, to become Solomon's enemy. 15Earlier, David had defeated Edom. When Joab, the commander of David's army, went into Edom to bury the dead, he killed all the males. 16Joab and all the Israelites stayed in Edom for six months and killed every male in Edom. 17At that time Hadad was only a young boy, so he ran away to Egypt with some of his father's officers. 18They left Midian and went to Paran, where they were joined by other men. Then they all went to Egypt to see the king, who gave Hadad a house, some food, and some land.

19The king liked Hadad so much he gave Hadad a wife—the sister of Tahpenes, the king's wife. 20They had a son named Genubath. Queen Tahpenes brought him up in the royal palace with the king's own children.

21While he was in Egypt, Hadad heard that David had died and that Joab, the commander of the army, was dead also. So Hadad said to the king, "Let me go; I will return to my own country."

22"Why do you want to go back to your own country?" the king asked. "What haven't I given you here?"

"Nothing," Hadad answered, "but please, let me go."

23God also caused another man to be Solomon's enemy—Rezon son of Eliada. Rezon had run away from his master, Hadadezer king of Zobah. 24After David defeated the army of Zobah, Rezon gathered some men and became the leader of a small army. They went to Damascus and settled there, and Rezon became king of Damascus. 25Rezon ruled Aram, and he hated Israel. So he was an enemy of Israel all the time Solomon was alive. Both Rezon and Hadad made trouble for Israel.

26Jeroboam son of Nebat was one of Solomon's officers. He was an Ephraimite from the town of Zeredah, and he was the son of a widow named Zeruah. Jeroboam turned against the king.

27This is the story of how Jeroboam turned against the king. Solomon was filling in the land and repairing the wall of Jerusalem, the

city of David, his father. [28]Jeroboam was a capable man, and Solomon saw that this young
man was a good worker. So Solomon put him
over all the workers from the tribes of Ephraim
and Manasseh.

WHAT'S IT MEAN?

Damascus just happens to be one of the oldest cities in the world. The city has been occupied continuously for over 4,000 years—though not by the same people, of course. In Arabic, the city is called "The Place." It's easy to understand why Damascus has been so popular for so long: Three major caravan routes pass right through it. The city, which also happens to be the capital of Syria, is located northeast of Lake Galilee, about 135 miles from Jerusalem.

1 Kings 11:24–25

[29]One day as Jeroboam was leaving Jerusalem, Ahijah, the prophet from Shiloh, who was
wearing a new coat, met him on the road. The
two men were alone out in the country. [30]Ahi-
jah took his new coat and tore it into twelve
pieces. [31]Then he said to Jeroboam, "Take ten
pieces of this coat for yourself. The LORD, the
God of Israel, says: 'I will tear the kingdom
away from Solomon and give you ten tribes.
[32]But I will allow him to control one tribe. I
will do this for the sake of my servant David
and for Jerusalem, the city I have chosen from
all the tribes of Israel. [33]I will do this because
Solomon has stopped following me and has
worshiped the Sidonian god Ashtoreth, the
Moabite god Chemosh, and the Ammonite
god Molech. Solomon has not obeyed me by
doing what I said is right and obeying my laws
and commands, as his father David did.
[34]" 'But I will not take all the kingdom away
from Solomon. I will let him rule all his life because of my servant David, whom I chose, who
obeyed all my commands and laws. [35]But I will
take the kingdom away from his son, and I will
allow you to rule over the ten tribes. [36]I will
allow Solomon's son to continue to rule over
one tribe so that there will always be a descendant of David, my servant, in Jerusalem,
the city where I chose to be worshiped. [37]But I
will make you rule over everything you want.
You will rule over all of Israel, [38]and I will always be with you if you do what I say is right.
You must obey all my commands. If you obey
my laws and commands as David did, I will be
with you. I will make your family a lasting family of kings, as I did for David, and give Israel to
you. [39]I will punish David's children because of
this, but I will not punish them forever.' "

SOLOMON'S DEATH

[40]Solomon tried to kill Jeroboam, but he ran
away to Egypt, to Shishak king of Egypt, where
he stayed until Solomon died.
[41]Everything else King Solomon did, and
the wisdom he showed, is written in the book
of the history of Solomon. [42]Solomon ruled in
Jerusalem over all Israel for forty years. [43]Then
he died and was buried in Jerusalem, the city
of David, his father. And his son Rehoboam
became king in his place.

ISRAEL TURNS AGAINST REHOBOAM

12

[1]Rehoboam went to Shechem, where all the
Israelites had gone to make him king. [2]Jerobo-
am son of Nebat was still in Egypt, where he
had gone to escape from Solomon. When Jeroboam heard about Rehoboam being made
king, he was living in Egypt. [3]After the people
sent for him, he and the people went to Rehoboam and said to him, [4]"Your father forced us
to work very hard. Now, make it easier for us,
and don't make us work as hard as he did.
Then we will serve you."
[5]Rehoboam answered, "Go away for three
days, and then come back to me." So the people
left.
[6]King Rehoboam asked the older leaders
who had advised Solomon during his lifetime,
"How do you think I should answer these people?"
[7]They said, "You should be like a servant to
them today. If you serve them and give them a
kind answer, they will serve you always."
[8]But Rehoboam rejected this advice. Instead,
he asked the young men who had grown up
with him and who served as his advisers. [9]Re-
hoboam asked them, "What is your advice?
How should we answer these people who said,
'Don't make us work as hard as your father
did'?"
[10]The young men who had grown up with
him answered, "Those people said to you,
'Your father forced us to work very hard. Now
make our work easier.' You should tell them,
'My little finger is bigger than my father's legs.
[11]He forced you to work hard, but I will make
you work even harder. My father beat you
with whips, but I will beat you with whips that
have sharp points.' "

12 Rehoboam had told the people, "Come back to me in three days." So after three days Jeroboam and all the people returned to Rehoboam. 13 King Rehoboam spoke cruel words to them, because he had rejected the advice the older leaders had given him. 14 He followed the advice of the young men and said to the people, "My father forced you to work hard, but I will make you work even harder. My father beat you with whips, but I will beat you with whips that have sharp points." 15 So the king did not listen to the people. The LORD caused this to happen to keep the promise he had made to Jeroboam son of Nebat through Ahijah, a prophet from Shiloh.

16 When all the Israelites saw that the new king refused to listen to them, they said to the king,

"We have no share in David!
    We have no part in the son of Jesse!
People of Israel, let's go to our own
        homes!
    Let David's son rule his own people!"

So the Israelites went home. 17 But Rehoboam still ruled over the Israelites who lived in the towns of Judah.

18 Adoniram was in charge of the forced labor. When Rehoboam sent him to the people of Israel, they threw stones at him until he died. But King Rehoboam ran to his chariot and escaped to Jerusalem. 19 Since then, Israel has been against the family of David.

20 When all the Israelites heard that Jeroboam had returned, they called him to a meeting and made him king over all Israel. Only the tribe of Judah continued to follow the family of David.

21 When Rehoboam arrived in Jerusalem, he gathered one hundred eighty thousand of the best soldiers from the tribes of Judah and Benjamin. As son of Solomon, Rehoboam wanted to fight the people of Israel to take back his kingdom.

22 But God spoke his word to Shemaiah, a man of God, saying, 23 "Speak to Solomon's son Rehoboam, the king of Judah, and to all the people of Judah and Benjamin and the rest of the people. Say to them, 24 'The LORD says you must not go to war against your brothers, the Israelites. Every one of you should go home, because I made all these things happen.' " So they obeyed the LORD's command and went home as the LORD had commanded.

25 Then Jeroboam made Shechem in the mountains of Ephraim a very strong city, and he lived there. He also went to the city of Peniel and made it stronger.

JEROBOAM BUILDS GOLDEN CALVES

26 Jeroboam said to himself, "The kingdom will probably go back to David's family. 27 If the people continue going to the Temple of the LORD in Jerusalem to offer sacrifices, they will want to be ruled again by Rehoboam. Then they will kill me and follow Rehoboam king of Judah."

28 King Jeroboam asked for advice. Then he made two golden calves. "It is too long a journey for you to go to Jerusalem to worship," he said to the people. "Israel, here are your gods who brought you out of Egypt." 29 Jeroboam put one golden calf in the city of Bethel and the other in the city of Dan. 30 This became a very great sin, because the people traveled as far as Dan to worship the calf there.

31 Jeroboam built temples on the places of worship. He also chose priests from all the people, not just from the tribe of Levi. 32 And he started a new festival on the fifteenth day of the eighth month, just like the festival in Judah. During that time the king offered sacrifices on the altar, along with sacrifices to the calves in Bethel he had made. He also chose priests in Bethel to serve at the places of worship he had made. 33 So Jeroboam chose his own time for a festival for the Israelites—the fifteenth day of the eighth month. During that time he offered sacrifices on the altar he had built in Bethel. He set up a festival for the Israelites and offered sacrifices on the altar.

THE MAN OF GOD SPEAKS AGAINST BETHEL

13 1 The LORD commanded a man of God from Judah to go to Bethel. When he arrived, Jeroboam was standing by the altar to offer a sacrifice. 2 The LORD had commanded the man of God to speak against the altar. The man said, "Altar, altar, the LORD says to you: 'David's family will have a son named Josiah. The priests for the places of worship now make their sacrifices on you, but Josiah will sacrifice those priests on you. Human bones will be burned on you.' " 3 That same day the man of God gave proof that these things would happen. "This is the LORD's sign that this will happen," he said. "This altar will break apart, and the ashes on it will fall to the ground."

4 When King Jeroboam heard what the man of God said about the altar in Bethel, the king raised his hand from the altar and pointed at the man. "Take him!" he said. But when the king said this, his arm was paralyzed, and he could not move it. 5 The altar also broke into pieces, and its ashes fell to the ground. This was the sign the LORD had told the man of God to give.

[6]Then the king said to the man of God,
"Please pray to the LORD your God for me, and
ask him to heal my arm."
So the man of God prayed to the LORD, and
the king's arm was healed, becoming as it was
before.
[7]Then the king said to the man of God,
"Please come home and eat with me, and I will
give you a gift."
[8]But the man of God answered the king,
"Even if you gave me half of your kingdom, I
would not go with you. I will not eat or drink
anything in this place. [9]The LORD commanded
me not to eat or drink anything nor to return
on the same road by which I came." [10]So he
took a different road and did not return on the
same road by which he had come to Bethel.
[11]Now an old prophet was living in Bethel.
His sons came and told him what the man of
God had done there that day. They also told
their father what he had said to King Jeroboam. [12]The father asked, "Which road did he use
when he left?" So his sons showed him the
road the man of God from Judah had taken.
[13]Then the prophet told his sons to put a saddle on his donkey. So they saddled the donkey,
and he left.
[14]He went after the man of God and found
him sitting under an oak tree. The prophet
asked, "Are you the man of God who came
from Judah?"
The man answered, "Yes, I am."
[15]The prophet said, "Please come home and
eat with me."
[16]"I can't go home with you," the man of
God answered. "I can't eat or drink with you in
this place. [17]The LORD said to me, 'Don't eat or
drink anything there or return on the same
road by which you came.' "
[18]Then the old prophet said, "But I also am a
prophet like you." Then he told a lie. He said,
"An angel from the LORD came to me and told
me to bring you to my home. He said you
should eat and drink with me." [19]So the man of
God went to the old prophet's house, and he
ate and drank with him there.
[20]While they were sitting at the table, the
LORD spoke his word to the old prophet. [21]The
old prophet cried out to the man of God from
Judah, "The LORD said you did not obey him!
He said you did not do what the LORD your
God commanded you. [22]The LORD commanded you not to eat or drink anything in this
place, but you came back and ate and drank.
So your body will not be buried in your family
grave."
[23]After the man of God finished eating and
drinking, the prophet put a saddle on his donkey for him, and the man left. [24]As he was
traveling home, a lion attacked and killed him.
His body lay on the road, with the donkey and
the lion standing nearby. [25]Some men who
were traveling on that road saw the body and
the lion standing nearby. So they went to the
city where the old prophet lived and told what
they had seen.
[26]The old prophet who had brought back
the man of God heard what had happened. "It
is the man of God who did not obey the
LORD's command," he said. "So the LORD sent a
lion to kill him, just as he said he would."
[27]Then the prophet said to his sons, "Put a
saddle on my donkey," which they did. [28]The
old prophet went out and found the body lying on the road, with the donkey and the lion
still standing nearby. The lion had not eaten
the body or hurt the donkey. [29]The prophet
put the body on his donkey and carried it back
to the city to have a time of sadness for him
and to bury him. [30]The prophet buried the
body in his own family grave, and they were
sad for the man of God and said, "Oh, my
brother."
[31]After the prophet buried the body, he said
to his sons, "When I die, bury me in this same
grave. Put my bones next to his. [32]Through
him the LORD spoke against the altar at Bethel
and against the places of worship in the towns
of Samaria. What the LORD spoke through him
will certainly come true."
[33]After this incident King Jeroboam did not
stop doing evil. He continued to choose priests
for the places of worship from among all the
people. Anyone who wanted to be a priest for
the places of worship was allowed to be one.
[34]In this way the family of Jeroboam sinned,
and this sin caused its ruin and destruction
from the earth.

JEROBOAM'S SON DIES

14

[1]At that time Jeroboam's son Abijah became
very sick. [2]So Jeroboam said to his wife, "Go to
Shiloh to see the prophet Ahijah. He is the one
who said I would become king of Israel. But
dress yourself so people won't know you are
my wife. [3]Take the prophet ten loaves of bread,
some cakes, and a jar of honey. Then ask him
what will happen to our son, and he will tell
you." [4]So the king's wife did as he said and
went to Ahijah's home in Shiloh.
Now Ahijah was very old and blind. [5]The
LORD said to him, "Jeroboam's son is sick, and
Jeroboam's wife is coming to ask you about
him. When she arrives, she will pretend to be

someone else." Then the LORD told Ahijah what
to say.
6When Ahijah heard her walking to the
door, he said, "Come in, wife of Jeroboam.
Why are you pretending to be someone else? I
have bad news for you. 7Go back and tell Jeroboam that this is what the LORD, the God of
Israel, says: 'Jeroboam, I chose you from
among all the people and made you the leader
of my people Israel. 8I tore the kingdom away
from David's family, and I gave it to you. But
you are not like my servant David, who always
obeyed my commands and followed me with
all his heart. He did only what I said was right.
9But you have done more evil than anyone
who ruled before you. You have quit following
me and have made other gods and idols of
metal. This has made me very angry, 10so I will
soon bring disaster to your family. I will kill all
the men in your family, both slaves and free
men. I will destroy your family as completely
as fire burns up manure. 11Anyone from your
family who dies in the city will be eaten by
dogs, and those who die in the fields will be
eaten by the birds. The LORD has spoken.' "
12Then Ahijah said to Jeroboam's wife, "Go
home now. As soon as you enter your city,
your son will die, 13and all Israel will be sad for
him and bury him. He is the only one of
Jeroboam's family who will be buried, because
he is the only one in the king's family who
pleased the LORD, the God of Israel.
14"The LORD will put a new king over Israel,
who will destroy Jeroboam's family, and this
will happen soon. 15Then
the LORD will punish Is-
rael, which will be like
grass moving in the
water. The LORD
will pull up Israel
from this good
land, the land he
gave their ances-
tors. He will scat-
ter Israel beyond
the Euphrates
River, because he
is angry with the
people. They made
the LORD angry when
they set up idols to
worship Asherah. 16Jero-
boam sinned, and then he
made the people of Israel sin. So the LORD will
let the people of Israel be defeated."
17Then Jeroboam's wife left and returned to
Tirzah. As soon as she entered her home, the
boy died. 18After they buried him, all Israel had
a time of sadness for him, just as the LORD had
said through his servant, the prophet Ahijah.

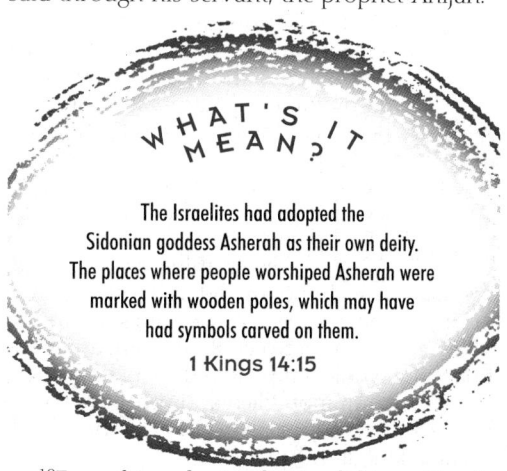

WHAT'S IT MEAN?

The Israelites had adopted the Sidonian goddess Asherah as their own deity. The places where people worshiped Asherah were marked with wooden poles, which may have had symbols carved on them.

1 Kings 14:15

19Everything else Jeroboam did is written in
the book of the history of the kings of Israel.
He fought wars and continued to rule the people, 20serving as king for twenty-two years.
Then he died, and his son Nadab became king
in his place.

THE DEATH OF REHOBOAM

21Solomon's son Rehoboam was forty-one
years old when he became king of Judah. His
mother was Naamah from Ammon. Rehoboam ruled in Jerusalem for seventeen years. (The
LORD had chosen that city from all the land of
Israel as the place where he would be worshiped.)
22The people of Ju-
dah did what the
LORD said was
wrong. Their sins
made the LORD very
angry, even more
angry than he had
been at their ances-
tors. 23The people
built stone pillars
and places to wor-
ship gods and
Asherah idols on
every high hill and
under every green
tree. 24There were even
male prostitutes in the
land. They acted like the
people who had lived in the land before the Israelites. They had done many evil things, and God
had taken the land away from them.
25During the fifth year Rehoboam was king,

"I chose you from among all the people and made you the leader of my people Israel. I tore the kingdom away from David's family, and I gave it to you. But you are not like my servant David, who always obeyed my commands and followed me with all his heart. He did only what I said was right."
(1 Kings 14:7b–8)

Shishak king of Egypt attacked Jerusalem. [26]He
took the treasures from the Temple of the LORD
and the king's palace. He took everything, even
the gold shields Solomon had made. [27]So King
Rehoboam made bronze shields to put in their
place and gave them to the commanders of the
guards for the palace gates. [28]When-
ever the king went to the Temple of the LORD, the guards
carried the shields. Later, they
would put them back in the
guardroom.
[29]Everything else King Rehoboam did is written in the
book of the history of the kings of Judah.
[30]There was war between Rehoboam and Jeroboam the whole time. [31]Rehoboam, son of Naamah from Ammon, died and was buried with
his ancestors in Jerusalem, and his son Abijah
became king in his place.

> **CULT**
> What does God think of worshiping other things? (14:21–28)

ABIJAH KING OF JUDAH

15 [1]Abijah became king of Judah during the
eighteenth year Jeroboam son of Nebat was
king of Israel. [2]Abijah ruled in Jerusalem for
three years. His mother was Maacah daughter
of Abishalom. [3]He did all the same sins his father before him had done. Abijah was not
faithful to the LORD his God as David, his
great-grandfather, had been. [4]Because the LORD
loved David, the LORD gave him a kingdom in
Jerusalem and allowed him to have a son to be
king after him. The LORD also kept Jerusalem
safe. [5]David always did what the LORD said
was right and obeyed his commands all his
life, except the one time when David sinned
against Uriah the Hittite.
[6]There was war between Abijah and Jeroboam during Abijah's lifetime. [7]Everything else
Abijah did is written in the book of the history
of the kings of Judah. During the time Abijah
ruled, there was war between Abijah and Jeroboam. [8]Abijah died and was buried in Jerusalem, and his son Asa became king in his place.

ASA KING OF JUDAH

[9]During the twentieth year Jeroboam was
king of Israel, Asa became king of Judah. [10]His
grandmother's name was Maacah, the daughter of Abishalom. Asa ruled in Jerusalem for
forty-one years.
[11]Asa did what the LORD said was right, as
his ancestor David had done. [12]He forced the
male prostitutes at the worship places to leave
the country. He also took away the idols that
his ancestors had made. [13]His grandmother
Maacah had made a terrible Asherah idol, so
Asa removed her from being queen mother. He
cut down that idol and burned it in the Kidron
Valley. [14]The places of worship to gods were
not removed. Even so, Asa was faithful to the
LORD all his life. [15]Asa brought into the Temple
of the LORD the gifts he and his father had
given: gold, silver, and utensils.
[16]There was war between Asa and Baasha
king of Israel all the time they were kings. [17]Ba-
asha attacked Judah, and he made the town of
Ramah strong so he could keep people from
leaving or entering Judah, Asa's country.
[18]Asa took the rest of the silver and gold
from the treasuries of the Temple of the LORD
and his own palace and gave it to his officers.
Then he sent them to Ben-Hadad son of Tabrim-
mon, who was the son of Hezion. Ben-Hadad
was the king of Aram and ruled in the city of
Damascus. Asa said, [19]"Let there be a treaty between you and me as there was between my
father and your father. I am sending you a gift
of silver and gold. Break your treaty with Baasha king of Israel so he will leave my land."
[20]Ben-Hadad agreed with King Asa, so he
sent the commanders of his armies to attack
the towns of Israel. They defeated the towns of
Ijon, Dan, and Abel Beth Maacah, as well as all
Galilee and the area of Naphtali. [21]When Baasha heard about these attacks, he stopped
building up Ramah and returned to Tirzah.
[22]Then King Asa gave an order to all the people
of Judah; everyone had to help. They carried
away all the stones and wood Baasha had
been using in Ramah, and they used them to
build up Geba and Mizpah in the land of Benjamin.
[23]Everything else Asa did—his victories and
the cities he built—is written in the book of the
history of the kings of Judah. When he became
old, he got a disease in his feet. [24]After Asa died,
he was buried with his ancestors in Jerusalem,
the city of David, his ancestor. Then Jehoshaphat, Asa's son, became king in his place.

NADAB KING OF ISRAEL

[25]Nadab son of Jeroboam became king of
Israel during the second year Asa was king of
Judah. Nadab was king of Israel for two years,
[26]and he did what the LORD said was wrong.
Jeroboam had led the people of Israel to sin,
and Nadab sinned in the same way as his father Jeroboam.
[27]Baasha son of Ahijah, from the tribe of
Issachar, made plans to kill Nadab. Nadab and
all Israel were attacking the Philistine town of
Gibbethon, so Baasha killed Nadab there.
[28]This happened during Asa's third year as

king of Judah, and Baasha became the next
king of Israel.

BAASHA KING OF ISRAEL

29As soon as Baasha became king, he killed
all of Jeroboam's family, leaving no one in
Jeroboam's family alive. He destroyed them all
as the LORD had said would happen through
his servant Ahijah from Shiloh. 30King Jeroboam had sinned very much and had led the
people of Israel to sin, so he made the LORD,
the God of Israel, very angry.
31Everything else Nadab did is written in the
book of the history of the kings of Israel.
32There was war between Asa king of Judah
and Baasha king of Israel all the time they
ruled.
33Baasha son of Ahijah became king of Israel during Asa's third year as king of Judah.
Baasha ruled in Tirzah for twenty-four years,
34and he did what the LORD said was wrong.
Jeroboam had led the people of Israel to sin,
and Baasha sinned in the same way as Jeroboam.
16 1Jehu son of Hanani spoke the word of the
LORD against King Baasha. 2The LORD said,
"You were nothing, but I took you and made
you a leader over my people Israel. But you
have followed the ways of Jeroboam and have
led my people Israel to sin. Their sins have
made me angry, 3so, Baasha, I will soon destroy you and your family. I will do to you
what I did to the family of Jeroboam son of
Nebat. 4Anyone from your family who dies in
the city will be eaten by dogs, and anyone
from your family who dies in the fields will be
eaten by birds."

WHAT'S IT MEAN?

The Israelites placed a high priority on proper burial for their dead. Allowing a body to be eaten by birds and animals was considered the ultimate insult to the deceased.

1 Kings 16:4

5Everything else Baasha did and all his victories are written down in the book of the history of the kings of Israel. 6So Baasha died and
was buried in Tirzah, and his son Elah became
king in his place.
7The LORD spoke his word against Baasha
and his family through the prophet Jehu son of
Hanani. Baasha had done many things the
LORD said were wrong, which made the LORD
very angry. He did the same evil deeds that
Jeroboam's family had done before him. The
LORD also spoke against Baasha because he
killed all of Jeroboam's family.

ELAH KING OF ISRAEL

8Elah son of Baasha became king of Israel
during Asa's twenty-sixth year as king of Judah, and Elah ruled in Tirzah for two years.
9Zimri, one of Elah's officers, commanded
half of Elah's chariots. Zimri made plans
against Elah while the king was in Tirzah, getting drunk at Arza's home. (Arza was in charge
of the palace at Tirzah.) 10Zimri went into
Arza's house and killed Elah during Asa's
twenty-seventh year as king of Judah. Then
Zimri became king of Israel in Elah's place.

ZIMRI KING OF ISRAEL

11As soon as Zimri became king, he killed all
of Baasha's family, not allowing any of
Baasha's family or friends to live. 12So Zimri
destroyed all of Baasha's family just as the
LORD had said it would happen through the
prophet Jehu. 13Baasha and his son Elah sinned
and led the people of Israel to sin, and they
made the LORD, the God of Israel, angry because of their worthless idols.
14Everything else Elah did is written in the
book of the history of the kings of Israel.
15So during Asa's twenty-seventh year as
king of Judah, Zimri became king of Israel and
ruled in Tirzah seven days.
The army of Israel was camped near Gibbethon, a Philistine town. 16The men in the camp
heard that Zimri had made secret plans against
King Elah and had killed him. So that day in
the camp they made Omri, the commander of
the army, king over Israel. 17So Omri and all
the Israelite army left Gibbethon and attacked
Tirzah. 18When Zimri saw that the city had
been captured, he went into the palace and set
it on fire, burning the palace and himself with
it. 19So Zimri died because he had sinned by
doing what the LORD said was wrong. Jeroboam had led the people of Israel to sin, and
Zimri sinned in the same way as Jeroboam.
20Everything else Zimri did and the story of
how he turned against King Elah are written
down in the book of the history of the kings of
Israel.

OMRI KING OF ISRAEL

21 The people of Israel were divided into two groups. Half of the people wanted Tibni son of Ginath to be king, while the other half wanted Omri. 22 Omri's followers were stronger than the followers of Tibni son of Ginath, so Tibni died, and Omri became king.

23 Omri became king of Israel during the thirty-first year Asa was king of Judah. Omri ruled Israel for twelve years, six of those years in the city of Tirzah. 24 He bought the hill of Samaria from Shemer for about one hundred fifty pounds of silver. Omri built a city on that hill and called it Samaria after the name of its earlier owner, Shemer.

WHAT'S IT MEAN?

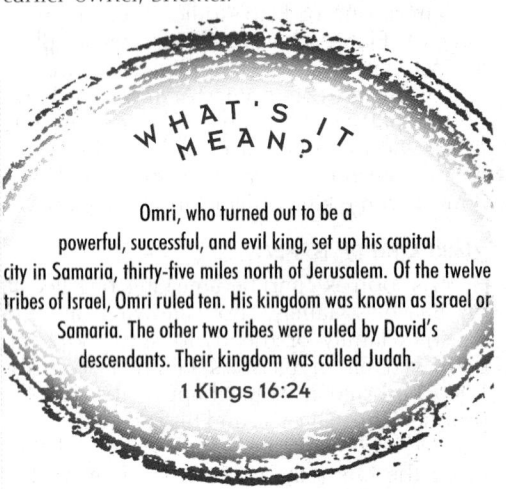

Omri, who turned out to be a powerful, successful, and evil king, set up his capital city in Samaria, thirty-five miles north of Jerusalem. Of the twelve tribes of Israel, Omri ruled ten. His kingdom was known as Israel or Samaria. The other two tribes were ruled by David's descendants. Their kingdom was called Judah.

1 Kings 16:24

25 But Omri did what the LORD said was wrong; he did more evil than all the kings who came before him. 26 Jeroboam son of Nebat had led the people of Israel to sin, and Omri sinned in the same way as Jeroboam. The Israelites made the LORD, the God of Israel, very angry because they worshiped worthless idols.

27 Everything else Omri did and all his successes are written in the book of the history of the kings of Israel. 28 So Omri died and was buried in Samaria, and his son Ahab became king in his place.

AHAB KING OF ISRAEL

29 Ahab son of Omri became king of Israel during Asa's thirty-eighth year as king of Judah, and Ahab ruled Israel in the city of Samaria for twenty-two years. 30 More than any king before him, Ahab son of Omri did many things the LORD said were wrong. 31 He sinned in the same ways as Jeroboam son of Nebat, but he did even worse things. He married Jezebel daughter of Ethbaal, the king of Sidon. Then Ahab began to serve Baal and worship him. 32 He built a temple in Samaria for worshiping Baal and put an altar there for Baal. 33 Ahab also made an idol for worshiping Asherah. He did more things to make the LORD, the God of Israel, angry than all the other kings before him.

34 During the time of Ahab, Hiel from Bethel rebuilt the city of Jericho. It cost Hiel the life of Abiram, his oldest son, to begin work on the city, and it cost the life of Segub, his youngest son, to build the city gates. This happened just as the LORD, speaking through Joshua son of Nun, said it would happen.[n]

ELIJAH STOPS THE RAIN

1 Now Elijah the Tishbite was a prophet from the settlers in Gilead. "I serve the LORD, the God of Israel," Elijah said to Ahab. "As surely as the LORD lives, no rain or dew will fall during the next few years unless I command it."

2 Then the LORD spoke his word to Elijah: 3 "Leave this place and go east and hide near Kerith Ravine east of the Jordan River. 4 You may drink from the stream, and I have commanded ravens to bring you food there." 5 So Elijah did what the LORD said; he went to Kerith Ravine, east of the Jordan, and lived there. 6 The birds brought Elijah bread and meat every morning and evening, and he drank water from the stream.

7 After a while the stream dried up because there was no rain. 8 Then the LORD spoke his

WHAT'S IT MEAN?

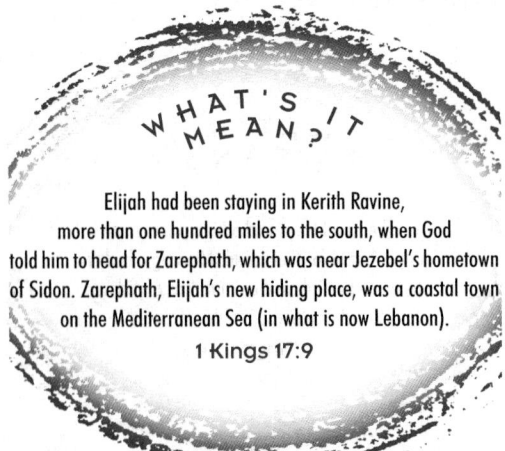

Elijah had been staying in Kerith Ravine, more than one hundred miles to the south, when God told him to head for Zarephath, which was near Jezebel's hometown of Sidon. Zarephath, Elijah's new hiding place, was a coastal town on the Mediterranean Sea (in what is now Lebanon).

1 Kings 17:9

16:34 the LORD . . . happen When Joshua destroyed Jericho, he said whoever rebuilt the city would lose his oldest and youngest sons. See Joshua 6:26.

word to Elijah, 9"Go to Zarephath in Sidon and
live there. I have commanded a widow there to
take care of you."
10So Elijah went to Zarephath. When he
reached the town gate, he saw a widow gathering wood for a fire. Elijah asked her, "Would
you bring me a little water in a cup so I may
have a drink?" 11As she was going to get his
water, Elijah said, "Please bring me a piece of
bread, too."
12The woman answered, "As surely as the
LORD your God lives, I have no bread. I have
only a handful of flour in a jar and only a little
olive oil in a jug. I came here to gather some
wood so I could go home and cook our last
meal. My son and I will eat it and then die
from hunger."
13"Don't worry," Elijah said to her. "Go home
and cook your food as you have said. But first
make a small loaf of bread from the
flour you have, and bring it to
me. Then cook something for
yourself and your son. 14The
LORD, the God of Israel, says,
'That jar of flour will never be
empty, and the jug will always
have oil in it, until the day the
LORD sends rain to the land.' "

OBEDIENCE
Does God reward obedience? (17:13–16)

15So the woman went home and did what
Elijah told her to do. And the woman and her
son and Elijah had enough food every day.
16The jar of flour and the jug of oil were never
empty, just as the LORD, through Elijah, had
promised.

ELIJAH BRINGS A BOY BACK TO LIFE

17Some time later the son of the woman
who owned the house became sick. He grew
worse and worse and finally stopped breathing. 18The woman said to Elijah, "Man of God,
what have you done to me? Did you come
here to remind me of my sin and to kill my
son?"
19Elijah said to her, "Give me your son." Elijah took the boy from her, carried him upstairs, and laid him on the bed in the room
where he was staying. 20Then he prayed to the
LORD: "LORD my God, this widow is letting me
stay in her house. Why have you done this
terrible thing to her and caused her son to die?"
21Then Elijah lay on top of the boy three times.
He prayed to the LORD, "LORD my God, let this
boy live again!"
22The LORD answered Elijah's prayer; the
boy began breathing again and was alive. 23Eli-
jah carried the boy downstairs and gave him
to his mother and said, "See! Your son is alive!"
24"Now I know you really are a man from
God," the woman said to Elijah. "I know that
the LORD truly speaks through you!"

ELIJAH KILLS THE PROPHETS OF BAAL

18
1During the third year without rain, the
LORD spoke his word to Elijah: "Go and meet
King Ahab, and I will soon send rain." 2So Elijah went to meet Ahab.
By this time there was no food in Samaria.
3King Ahab sent for Obadiah, who was in
charge of the king's palace. (Obadiah was a
true follower of the LORD. 4When Jezebel was
killing all the LORD's prophets, Obadiah hid a
hundred of them in two caves, fifty in one cave
and fifty in another. He also brought them
food and water.) 5Ahab said to Obadiah, "Let's
check every spring and valley in the land.
Maybe we can find enough grass to keep our
horses and mules alive and not have to kill our
animals." 6So each one chose a part of the
country to search; Ahab went in one direction
and Obadiah in another.
7While Obadiah was on his way, Elijah met
him. Obadiah recognized Elijah, so he bowed
down to the ground and said, "Elijah? Is it
really you, master?"
8"Yes," Elijah answered. "Go tell your master
that I am here."
9Then Obadiah said, "What wrong have I
done for you to hand me over to Ahab like
this? He will put me to death. 10As surely as the
LORD your God lives, the king has sent people
to every country to search for you. If the ruler
said you were not there, Ahab forced the ruler
to swear you could not be found in his country. 11Now you want me to go to my master
and tell him, 'Elijah is here'? 12The Spirit of the
LORD may carry you to some other place after
I leave. If I go tell King Ahab you are here, and
he comes and doesn't find you, he will kill me!
I have followed the LORD since I was a boy.
13Haven't you been told what I did? When Jezebel was killing the LORD's prophets, I hid a
hundred of them, fifty in one cave and fifty in
another. I brought them food and water.
14Now you want me to go and tell my master
you are here? He will kill me!"
15Elijah answered, "As surely as the LORD
All-Powerful lives, whom I serve, I will be seen
by Ahab today."
16So Obadiah went to Ahab and told him
where Elijah was. Then Ahab went to meet
Elijah.
17When he saw Elijah, he asked, "Is it you—
the biggest troublemaker in Israel?"
18Elijah answered, "I have not made trouble

in Israel. You and your father's family have made all this trouble by not obeying the LORD's commands. You have gone after the Baals. [19]Now tell all Israel to meet me at Mount Carmel. Also bring the four hundred fifty prophets of Baal and the four hundred prophets of Asherah, who eat at Jezebel's table."

WHAT'S IT MEAN?

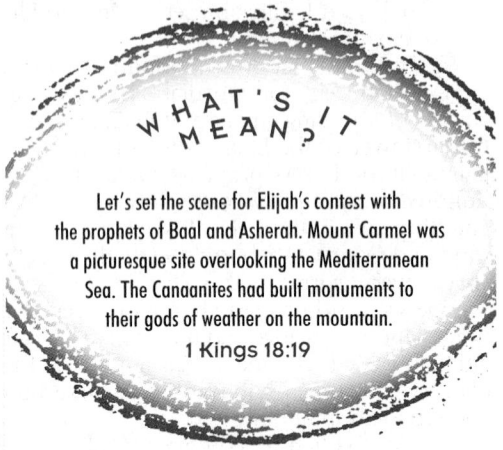

Let's set the scene for Elijah's contest with the prophets of Baal and Asherah. Mount Carmel was a picturesque site overlooking the Mediterranean Sea. The Canaanites had built monuments to their gods of weather on the mountain.

1 Kings 18:19

[20]So Ahab called all the Israelites and those prophets to Mount Carmel. [21]Elijah approached the people and said, "How long will you not decide between two choices? If the LORD is the true God, follow him, but if Baal is the true God, follow him!" But the people said nothing.

[22]Elijah said, "I am the only prophet of the LORD here, but there are four hundred fifty prophets of Baal. [23]Bring two bulls. Let the prophets of Baal choose one bull and kill it and cut it into pieces. Then let them put the meat on the wood, but they are not to set fire to it. I will prepare the other bull, putting the meat on the wood but not setting fire to it. [24]You prophets of Baal, pray to your god, and I will pray to the LORD. The god who answers by setting fire to his wood is the true God."

All the people agreed that this was a good idea.

[25]Then Elijah said to the prophets of Baal, "There are many of you, so you go first. Choose a bull and prepare it. Pray to your god, but don't start the fire."

[26]So they took the bull that was given to them and prepared it. They prayed to Baal from morning until noon, shouting "Baal, answer us!" But there was no sound, and no one answered. They danced around the altar they had built.

[27]At noon Elijah began to make fun of them. "Pray louder!" he said. "If Baal really is a god, maybe he is thinking, or busy, or traveling! Maybe he is sleeping so you will have to wake him!" [28]The prophets prayed louder, cutting themselves with swords and spears until their blood flowed, which was the way they worshiped. [29]The afternoon passed, and the prophets continued to act like this until it was time for the evening sacrifice. But no voice was heard; Baal did not answer, and no one paid attention.

[30]Then Elijah said to all the people, "Now come to me." So they gathered around him, and Elijah rebuilt the altar of the LORD, which had been torn down. [31]He took twelve stones, one stone for each of the twelve tribes, the number of Jacob's sons. (The LORD changed Jacob's name to Israel.) [32]Elijah used these stones to rebuild the altar in honor of the LORD. Then he dug a ditch around the altar that was big enough to hold about thirteen quarts of seed. [33]Elijah put the wood on the altar, cut the bull into pieces, and laid the pieces on the wood. [34]Then he said, "Fill four jars with water, and pour it on the meat and on the wood." Then Elijah said, "Do it again," and they did it again. Then he said, "Do it a third time," and they did it the third time. [35]So the water ran off the altar and filled the ditch.

[36]At the time for the evening sacrifice, the prophet Elijah went near the altar. "LORD, you are the God of Abraham, Isaac, and Israel," he prayed. "Prove that you are the God of Israel and that I am your servant. Show these people that you commanded me to do all these things. [37]LORD, answer my prayer so these people will know that you, LORD, are God and that you will change their minds."

[38]Then fire from the LORD came down and burned the sacrifice, the wood, the stones, and the ground around the altar. It also dried up the water in the ditch. [39]When all the people saw this, they fell down to the ground, crying, "The LORD is God! The LORD is God!"

[40]Then Elijah said, "Capture the prophets of Baal! Don't let any of them run away!" The people captured all the prophets. Then Elijah led them down to the Kishon Valley, where he killed them.

THE RAIN COMES AGAIN

[41]Then Elijah said to Ahab, "Now, go, eat, and drink, because a heavy rain is coming." [42]So King Ahab went to eat and drink. At the same time Elijah climbed to the top of Mount Carmel, where he bent down to the ground with his head between his knees.

[43]Then Elijah said to his servant, "Go and look toward the sea."

The servant went and looked. "I see nothing," he said.

Elijah told him to go and look again. This happened seven times. [44]The seventh time, the servant said, "I see a small cloud, the size of a human fist, coming from the sea."

Elijah told the servant, "Go to Ahab and tell him to get his chariot ready and go home now. Otherwise, the rain will stop him."

[45]After a short time the sky was covered with dark clouds. The wind began to blow, and soon a heavy rain began to fall. Ahab got in his chariot and started back to Jezreel. [46]The LORD gave his power to Elijah, who tightened his clothes around him and ran ahead of King Ahab all the way to Jezreel.

> **"Then fire from the LORD came down and burned the sacrifice, the wood, the stones, and the ground around the altar. It also dried up the water in the ditch. When all the people saw this, they fell down to the ground, crying, 'The LORD is God! The LORD is God!' "**
> **(1 Kings 18:38–39)**

ELIJAH RUNS AWAY

19

[1]King Ahab told Jezebel everything Elijah had done and how Elijah had killed all the prophets with a sword. [2]So Jezebel sent a messenger to Elijah, saying, "May the gods punish me terribly if by this time tomorrow I don't kill you just as you killed those prophets."

[3]When Elijah heard this, he was afraid and ran for his life, taking his servant with him. When they came to Beersheba in Judah, Elijah left his servant there. [4]Then Elijah walked for a whole day into the desert. He sat down under a bush and asked to die. "I have had enough, LORD," he prayed. "Let me die. I am no better than my ancestors." [5]Then he lay down under the tree and slept.

> **DEPRESSION**
> Can depression follow success? (19:1–4)

Suddenly an angel came to him and touched him. "Get up and eat," the angel said. [6]Elijah saw near his head a loaf baked over coals and a jar of water, so he ate and drank. Then he went back to sleep.

[7]Later the LORD's angel came to him a second time. The angel touched him and said, "Get up and eat. If you don't, the journey will be too hard for you." [8]So Elijah got up and ate and drank. The food made him strong enough to walk for forty days and nights to Mount Sinai, the mountain of God. [9]There Elijah went into a cave and stayed all night.

Then the LORD spoke his word to him: "Elijah! Why are you here?"

[10]He answered, "LORD God All-Powerful, I have always served you as well as I could. But the people of Israel have broken their agreement with you, destroyed your altars, and killed your prophets with swords. I am the only prophet left, and now they are trying to kill me, too."

[11]The LORD said to Elijah, "Go, stand in front of me on the mountain, and I will pass by you." Then a very strong wind blew until it caused the mountains to fall apart and large rocks to break in front of the LORD. But the LORD was not in the wind. After the wind, there was an earthquake, but the LORD was not in the earthquake. [12]After the earthquake, there was a fire, but the LORD was not in the fire. After the fire, there was a quiet, gentle sound. [13]When Elijah heard it, he covered his face with his coat and went out and stood at the entrance to the cave.

> **WHAT'S IT MEAN?**
> Remember the Ten Commandments—the two flat stones with God's law written on them? Mount Sinai is where God gave them to Moses while the rest of the Israelites waited at the base of the mountain.
> 1 Kings 19:8

Then a voice said to him, "Elijah! Why are you here?"

[14]He answered, "LORD God All-Powerful, I have always served you as well as I could. But the people of Israel have broken their agreement with you, destroyed your altars, and killed your prophets with swords. I am the only prophet left, and now they are trying to kill me, too."

15 The LORD said to him, "Go back on the
road that leads to the desert around Damascus.
Enter that city, and pour olive oil on Hazael to
make him king over Aram. 16 Then
pour oil on Jehu son of Nimshi to make him king over Israel. Next, pour oil on Elisha
son of Shaphat from Abel
Meholah to make him a
prophet in your place. 17 Jehu
will kill anyone who escapes
from Hazael's sword, and Elisha will kill anyone who escapes from Jehu's sword. 18 I have
seven thousand people left in Israel who have
never bowed down before Baal and whose
mouths have never kissed his idol."

LONELINESS
What does God do for lonely people? (19:14–18)

WHAT'S IT MEAN?

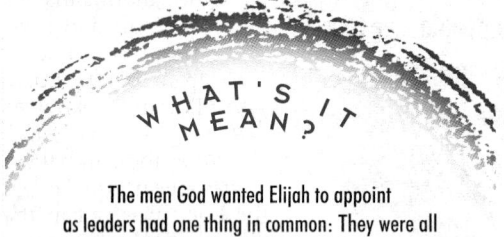

The men God wanted Elijah to appoint as leaders had one thing in common: They were all anti-Baal. Hazael and his fellow countrymen weren't particularly friendly toward either Israel or Judah. In fact, later in his reign, Hazael frequently attacked the Israelites. Jehu was a captain in Ahab's army when God gave these instructions to Elijah. During his reign, Jehu was responsible for many deaths, including a mass slaughter of Baal worshipers.

1 Kings 19:15

ELISHA BECOMES A PROPHET

19 So Elijah left that place and found Elisha
son of Shaphat plowing a field with a team of
oxen. He owned twelve teams of oxen and was
plowing with the twelfth team. Elijah came up
to Elisha, took off his coat, and put it on Elisha.
20 Then Elisha left his oxen and ran to follow
Elijah. "Let me kiss my father and my mother
good-bye," Elisha said. "Then I will go with you."
Elijah answered, "Go back. It does not matter to me."
21 So Elisha went back and took his pair of
oxen and killed them. He used their wooden
yoke for a fire. Then he cooked the meat and
gave it to the people. After they ate it, Elisha left
and followed Elijah and became his helper.

20

BEN-HADAD AND AHAB GO TO WAR

1 Ben-Hadad king of Aram gathered together
all his army. There were thirty-two kings with
their horses and chariots who went with him
and surrounded Samaria and attacked it. 2 The
king sent messengers into the city to Ahab king
of Israel.
This was his message: "Ben-Hadad says,
3 'Your silver and gold belong to me, as well as
the best of your wives and children.' "
4 Ahab king of Israel answered, "My master
and king, I agree to what you say. I and everything I have belong to you."
5 Then the messengers came to Ahab again.
They said, "Ben-Hadad says, 'I told you before
that you must give me your silver and gold,
your wives and your children. 6 About this time
tomorrow I will send my men, who will search
everywhere in your palace and in the homes
of your officers. Whatever they want they will
take and carry off.' "
7 Then Ahab called a meeting of all the older
leaders of his country. He said, "Ben-Hadad is
looking for trouble. First he said I had to give
him my wives, my children, my silver, and my
gold, and I have not refused him."
8 The older leaders and all the people said,
"Don't listen to him or agree to this."
9 So Ahab said to Ben-Hadad's messengers,
"Tell my master the king: 'I will do what you
said at first, but I cannot allow this second
command.' " And King Ben-Hadad's men carried the message back to him.
10 Then Ben-Hadad sent another message to
Ahab: "May the gods punish me terribly if I
don't completely destroy Samaria. There won't
be enough left for each of my men to get a
handful of dust!"
11 Ahab answered, "Tell Ben-Hadad, 'The
man who puts on his armor should not brag.
It's the man who lives to take it off who has the
right to brag.' "
12 Ben-Hadad was drinking in his tent with
the other rulers when the message came from
Ahab. Ben-Hadad commanded his men to
prepare to attack the city, and they moved into
place for battle.
13 At the same time a prophet came to Ahab
king of Israel. The prophet said, "Ahab, the
LORD says to you, 'Do you see that big army? I
will hand it over to you today so you will
know I am the LORD.' "
14 Ahab asked, "Who will you use to defeat
them?"
The prophet answered, "The LORD says, 'The
young officers of the district governors will
defeat them.' "
Then the king asked, "Who will command
the main army?"
The prophet answered, "You will."

[15]So Ahab gathered the young officers of the district governors, two hundred thirty-two of them. Then he called together the army of Israel, about seven thousand people in all.

[16]They marched out at noon, while Ben-Hadad and the thirty-two rulers helping him were getting drunk in their tents. [17]The young officers of the district governors attacked first. Ben-Hadad sent out scouts who told him that soldiers were coming from Samaria. [18]Ben-Hadad said, "They may be coming to fight, or they may be coming to ask for peace. In either case capture them alive."

[19]The young officers of the district governors led the attack, followed by the army of Israel. [20]Each officer of Israel killed the man who came against him. The men from Aram ran away as Israel chased them, but Ben-Hadad king of Aram escaped on a horse with some of his horsemen. [21]Ahab king of Israel led the army and destroyed the Arameans' horses and chariots. King Ahab thoroughly defeated the Aramean army.

[22]Then the prophet went to Ahab king of Israel and said, "The king of Aram will attack you again next spring. So go home now and strengthen your army and see what you need to do."

[23]Meanwhile the officers of Ben-Hadad king of Aram said to him, "The gods of Israel are mountain gods. Since we fought in a mountain area, Israel won. Let's fight them on the flat land, and then we will win. [24]This is what you should do. Don't allow the thirty-two rulers to command the armies, but put other commanders in their places. [25]Gather an army like the one that was destroyed and as many horses and chariots as before. We will fight the Israelites on flat land, and then we will win."

WHAT'S IT MEAN?

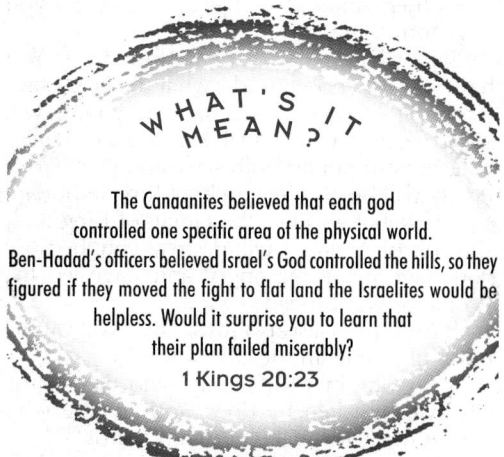

The Canaanites believed that each god controlled one specific area of the physical world. Ben-Hadad's officers believed Israel's God controlled the hills, so they figured if they moved the fight to flat land the Israelites would be helpless. Would it surprise you to learn that their plan failed miserably?

1 Kings 20:23

Ben-Hadad agreed with their advice and did what they said.

[26]The next spring Ben-Hadad gathered the army of Aram and went up to Aphek to fight against Israel.

[27]The Israelites also had prepared for war. They marched out to meet the Arameans and camped opposite them. The Israelites looked like two small flocks of goats, but the Arameans covered the area.

[28]A man of God came to the king of Israel with this message: "The LORD says, 'The people of Aram say that I, the LORD, am a god of the mountains, not a god of the valleys. So I will allow you to defeat this huge army, and then you will know I am the LORD.' "

[29]The armies were camped across from each other for seven days. On the seventh day the battle began. The Israelites killed one hundred thousand Aramean soldiers in one day. [30]The rest of them ran away to the city of Aphek, where a city wall fell on twenty-seven thousand of them. Ben-Hadad also ran away to the city and hid in a room.

[31]His officers said to him, "We have heard that the kings of Israel are trustworthy. Let's dress in rough cloth to show our sadness, and wear ropes on our heads. Then we will go to the king of Israel, and perhaps he will let you live."

[32]So they dressed in rough cloth and wore ropes on their heads and went to the king of Israel. They said, "Your servant Ben-Hadad says, 'Please let me live.' "

Ahab answered, "Is he still alive? He is my brother."

[33]Ben-Hadad's men had wanted a sign from Ahab. So when Ahab called Ben-Hadad his brother, they quickly said, "Yes! Ben-Hadad is your brother."

Ahab said, "Bring him to me." When Ben-Hadad came, Ahab asked him to join him in the chariot.

[34]Ben-Hadad said to him, "Ahab, I will give you back the cities my father took from your father. And you may put shops in Damascus, as my father did in Samaria."

Ahab said, "If you agree to this, I will allow you to go free." So the two kings made a peace agreement. Then Ahab let Ben-Hadad go free.

A PROPHET SPEAKS AGAINST AHAB

[35]One prophet from one of the groups of prophets told another, "Hit me!" He said this because the LORD had commanded it, but the other man refused. [36]The prophet said, "You did not obey the LORD's command, so a lion

will kill you as soon as you leave me." When
the man left, a lion found him and killed him.
[37]The prophet went to another man and
said, "Hit me, please!" So the man hit him and
hurt him. [38]The prophet wrapped his face in a
cloth so no one could tell who he was. Then he
went and waited by the road for the king. [39]As
Ahab king of Israel passed by, the prophet
called out to him. "I went to fight in the battle,"
the prophet said. "One of our men brought an
enemy soldier to me. Our man said, 'Guard
this man. If he runs away, you will have to give
your life in his place. Or, you will have to pay a
fine of seventy-five pounds of silver.' [40]But I
was busy doing other things, so the man ran
away."

The king of Israel answered, "You have already said what the punishment is. You must
do what the man said."

[41]Then the prophet quickly took the cloth
from his face. When the king of Israel saw him,
he knew he was one of the prophets. [42]The
prophet said to the king, "This is what the LORD
says: 'You freed the man I said should die, so
your life will be taken instead of his. The lives
of your people will also be taken instead of the
lives of his people.' "

[43]Then King Ahab went back to his palace
in Samaria, angry and upset.

AHAB TAKES NABOTH'S VINEYARD

21 [1]After these things had happened, this is
what followed. A man named Naboth owned
a vineyard in Jezreel, near the palace of Ahab
king of Israel. [2]One day Ahab said to Naboth,
"Give me your vineyard. It is near my palace,
and I want to make it into a vegetable garden. I
will give you a better vineyard in its place, or, if
you prefer, I will pay you what it is worth."

[3]Naboth answered, "May the LORD keep me
from ever giving my land to you. It belongs to
my family."

[4]Ahab went home angry and upset, because
he did not like what Naboth from Jezreel had
said. (Naboth had said, "I will not give you my
family's land.") Ahab lay down on his bed,
turned his face to the wall, and refused to eat.

[5]His wife, Jezebel, came in and asked him,
"Why are you so upset that you refuse to eat?"

[6]Ahab answered, "I talked to Naboth, the
man from Jezreel. I said, 'Sell me your vineyard, or, if you prefer, I will give you another
vineyard for it.' But Naboth refused."

[7]Jezebel answered, "Is this how you rule as
king over Israel? Get up, eat something, and
cheer up. I will get Naboth's vineyard for you."

[8]So Jezebel wrote some letters, signed
Ahab's name to them, and used his own seal to
seal them. Then she sent them to the older
leaders and important men who lived in
Naboth's town. [9]The letter she wrote said: "Declare a day during which the people are to give
up eating. Call the people together, and give
Naboth a place of honor among them. [10]Seat
two troublemakers across from him, and have
them say they heard Naboth speak against
God and the king. Then take Naboth out of the
city and kill him with stones."

[11]The older leaders and important men of
Jezreel obeyed Jezebel's command, just as she
wrote in the letters. [12]They declared a special
day on which the people were to give up eating. And they put Naboth in a place of honor
before the people. [13]Two troublemakers sat
across from Naboth and said in front of everybody that they had heard him speak against
God and the king. So the people carried Naboth out of the city and killed him with stones.
[14]Then the leaders sent a message to Jezebel,
saying, "Naboth has been killed."

[15]When Jezebel heard that Naboth had
been killed, she told Ahab, "Naboth of Jezreel is
dead. Now you may go and take for yourself
the vineyard he would not sell to you." [16]When
Ahab heard that Naboth of Jezreel was dead,
he got up and went to the vineyard to take it
for his own.

[17]At this time the LORD spoke his word to
the prophet Elijah the Tishbite. The LORD said,
[18]"Go to Ahab king of Israel in Samaria. He is at
Naboth's vineyard, where he has gone to take
it as his own. [19]Tell Ahab that I, the LORD, say
to him, 'You have murdered Naboth and taken
his land. So I tell you this: In the same place
the dogs licked up Naboth's blood, they will
also lick up your blood!' "

[20]When Ahab saw Elijah, he said, "So you
have found me, my enemy!"

Elijah answered, "Yes, I have found you. You
have always chosen to do what the LORD says
is wrong. [21]So the LORD says to you, 'I will
soon destroy you. I will kill you and every
male in your family, both slave and free. [22]Your
family will be like the family of King Jeroboam
son of Nebat and like the family of King Baasha son of Ahijah. I will destroy you, because
you have made me angry and have led the
people of Israel to sin.'

[23]"And the LORD also says, 'Dogs will eat the
body of Jezebel in the city of Jezreel.'

[24]"Anyone in your family who dies in the
city will be eaten by dogs, and anyone who
dies in the fields will be eaten by birds."

[25]There was no one like Ahab who had

chosen so often to do what the LORD said was
wrong, because his wife Jezebel influenced him
to do evil. 26Ahab sinned terribly by worshiping idols, just as the Amorite people did. And
the LORD had taken away their land and given
it to the people of Israel.
27After Elijah finished speaking, Ahab tore
his clothes. He put on rough cloth, refused to
eat, and even slept in the rough cloth to show
how sad and upset he was.
28The LORD spoke his word to Elijah the
Tishbite: 29"I see that Ahab is now sorry for
what he has done. So I will not cause the trouble to come to him during his life, but I will
wait until his son is king. Then I
will bring this trouble to Ahab's
family."

THE DEATH OF AHAB

22

1For three years there was
peace between Israel and
Aram. 2During the third year
Jehoshaphat king of Judah went
to visit Ahab king of Israel.
3At that time Ahab asked his officers, "Do you remember that the king of
Aram took Ramoth in Gilead from us? Why
have we done nothing to get it back?" 4So
Ahab asked King Jehoshaphat, "Will you go
with me to fight at Ramoth in Gilead?"
"I will go with you," Jehoshaphat answered.
"My soldiers are yours, and my horses are
yours." 5Jehoshaphat also said to Ahab, "But
first we should ask if this is the LORD's will."
6Ahab called about four hundred prophets
together and asked them, "Should I go to war
against Ramoth in Gilead or not?"
They answered, "Go, because the Lord will
hand them over to you."
7But Jehoshaphat asked, "Isn't there a
prophet of the LORD here? Let's ask him what
we should do."
8Then King Ahab said to Jehoshaphat,
"There is one other prophet. We could ask the
LORD through him, but I hate him. He never
prophesies anything good about me, but
something bad. He is Micaiah son of Imlah."
Jehoshaphat said, "King Ahab, you shouldn't
say that!"
9So Ahab king of Israel told one of his officers to bring Micaiah to him at once.
10Ahab king of Israel and Jehoshaphat king
of Judah had on their royal robes and were
sitting on their thrones at the threshing floor,
near the entrance to the gate of Samaria. All the
prophets were standing before them, speaking
their messages. 11Zedekiah son of Kenaanah
had made some iron horns. He said to Ahab,
"This is what the LORD says, 'You will use these
horns to fight the Arameans until they are destroyed.' "
12All the other prophets said the same thing.
"Attack Ramoth in Gilead and win, because the
LORD will hand the Arameans over to you."
13The messenger who had gone to get Micaiah said to him, "All the other prophets are
saying King Ahab will succeed. You should
agree with them and give the king a good answer."
14But Micaiah answered, "As surely as the
LORD lives, I can tell him only what the LORD
tells me."
15When Micaiah came to
Ahab, the king asked him, "Micaiah, should we attack Ramoth in Gilead or not?"
Micaiah answered, "Attack
and win! The LORD will hand
them over to you."
16But Ahab said to Micaiah,
"How many times do I have to
tell you to speak only the truth to
me in the name of the LORD?"
17So Micaiah answered, "I saw the army of
Israel scattered over the hills like sheep without
a shepherd. The LORD said, 'They have no leaders. They should go home and not fight.' "
18Then Ahab king of Israel said to Jehoshaphat, "I told you! He never prophesies anything good about me, but only bad."
19But Micaiah said, "Hear the message from
the LORD: I saw the LORD sitting on his throne
with his heavenly army standing near him on
his right and on his left. 20The LORD said, 'Who
will trick Ahab into attacking Ramoth in Gilead
where he will be killed?'
"Some said one thing; some said another.
21Then one spirit came and stood before the
LORD and said, 'I will trick him.'
22"The LORD asked, 'How will you do it?'
"The spirit answered, 'I will go to Ahab's
prophets and make them tell lies.'
"So the LORD said, 'You will succeed in tricking him. Go and do it.' "
23Micaiah said, "Ahab, the LORD has made
your prophets lie to you, and the LORD has
decided that disaster should come to you."
24Then Zedekiah son of Kenaanah went up
to Micaiah and slapped him in the face. Zedekiah said, "Has the LORD's spirit left me to
speak through you?"
25Micaiah answered, "You will find out on
the day you go to hide in an inside room."
26Then Ahab king of Israel ordered, "Take

> **"But Micaiah answered, 'As surely as the LORD lives, I can tell him only what the LORD tells me.' " (1 Kings 22:14)**

Micaiah and send him to Amon, the governor of the city, and to Joash, the king's son. 27 Tell them I said to put this man in prison and give him only bread and water until I return safely from the battle."

28 Micaiah said, "Ahab, if you come back safely from battle, the LORD has not spoken through me. Remember my words, all you people!"

29 So Ahab king of Israel and Jehoshaphat king of Judah went to Ramoth in Gilead. 30 King Ahab said to Jehoshaphat, "I will go into battle, but I will wear other clothes so no one will recognize me. But you wear your royal clothes." So Ahab wore other clothes and went into battle.

31 The king of Aram had ordered his thirty-two chariot commanders, "Don't fight with anyone—important or unimportant—except the king of Israel." 32 When these commanders saw Jehoshaphat, they thought he was certainly the king of Israel, so they turned to attack him. But Jehoshaphat began shouting. 33 When they saw he was not King Ahab, they stopped chasing him.

34 By chance, a soldier shot an arrow, but he hit Ahab king of Israel between the pieces of his armor. King Ahab said to his chariot driver, "Turn around and get me out of the battle, because I am hurt!" 35 The battle continued all day. King Ahab was held up in his chariot and faced the Arameans. His blood flowed down to the bottom of the chariot. That evening he died. 36 Near sunset a cry went out through the army of Israel: "Each man go back to his own city and land."

37 In that way King Ahab died. His body was carried to Samaria and buried there. 38 The men cleaned Ahab's chariot at a pool in Samaria where prostitutes bathed, and the dogs licked his blood from the chariot. These things happened as the LORD had said they would.

39 Everything else Ahab did is written in the book of the history of the kings of Israel. It tells about the palace Ahab built and decorated with ivory and the cities he built. 40 So Ahab died, and his son Ahaziah became king in his place.

WHAT'S IT MEAN?

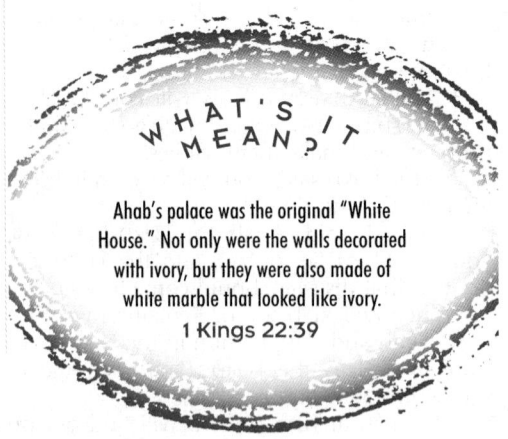

Ahab's palace was the original "White House." Not only were the walls decorated with ivory, but they were also made of white marble that looked like ivory.

1 Kings 22:39

JEHOSHAPHAT KING OF JUDAH

41 Jehoshaphat son of Asa became king of Judah during Ahab's fourth year as king of Israel. 42 Jehoshaphat was thirty-five years old when he became king, and he ruled in Jerusalem for twenty-five years. His mother's name was Azubah daughter of Shilhi. 43 Jehoshaphat was good, like his father Asa, and he did what the LORD said was right. But Jehoshaphat did not destroy the places where gods were worshiped, so the people continued offering sacrifices and burning incense there. 44 Jehoshaphat was at peace with the king of Israel. 45 Jehoshaphat fought many wars, and these wars and his successes are written in the book of the history of the kings of Judah. 46 There were male prostitutes still in the places of worship from the days of his father, Asa. So Jehoshaphat forced them to leave.

47 During this time the land of Edom had no king; it was ruled by a governor.

48 King Jehoshaphat built trading ships to sail to Ophir for gold. But the ships were wrecked at Ezion Geber, so they never set sail. 49 Ahaziah son of Ahab went to help Jehoshaphat, offering to give Jehoshaphat some men to sail with his men, but Jehoshaphat refused.

50 Jehoshaphat died and was buried with his ancestors in Jerusalem, the city of David, his ancestor. Then his son Jehoram became king in his place.

AHAZIAH KING OF ISRAEL

51 Ahaziah son of Ahab became king of Israel in Samaria during Jehoshaphat's seventeenth year as king over Judah. Ahaziah ruled Israel for two years, 52 and he did what the LORD said was wrong. He did the same evil his father Ahab, his mother Jezebel, and Jeroboam son of Nebat had done. All these rulers led the people of Israel into more sin. 53 Ahaziah worshiped and served the god Baal, and this made the LORD, the God of Israel, very angry. In these ways Ahaziah did what his father had done.

2 Kings

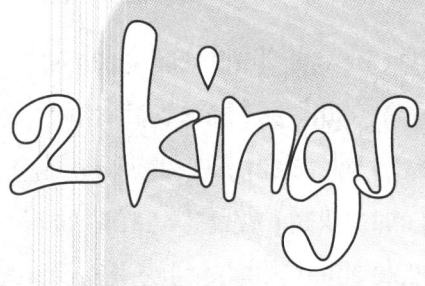

CONTENT Second Kings is the story of the divided kingdoms of the Hebrews: Israel and Judah. Each kingdom had its own kings and its own priests and its own prophets. But one thing they had in common: their governments went from bad to worse with only a few exceptions. The people continued to disregard God even though he sent prophets again and again to set them straight.

Through the years, each kingdom became a weakling spiritually and morally. After years of disobedience and struggle, they became sitting ducks for the larger nations around them. Assyria, a nation known for its cruelty in warfare, eventually attacked Israel. Babylon, a rich and strong nation from the east, attacked Judah. The Hebrew people were carried away from their countries to be slaves and prisoners in a foreign place.

The Hebrew people continued to lose their land because they wouldn't listen to God. They wouldn't listen to him about how to govern their land or how to treat each other. They wouldn't listen to him about *how* to worship and *who* to worship. This is their story so that we can learn from their mistakes.

Outline

1:1–18 .... Elijah the Prophet Condemns King Ahaziah of Israel
2:1—8:15 .... Elisha the Prophet
8:16—16:20 .... Kings of Judah and Israel
17:1–41 .... King Hoshea of Israel and the Defeat of the Northern Kingdom
18:1—20:21 .... King Hezekiah of Judah and the Assyrian Invasion
21:1–26 .... Two Evil Kings of Judah: Manasseh and Amon
22:1—23:30 .... The Rule of King Josiah and the Book of the Teachings
23:31—24:20 ...... The Last Kings of Judah
25:1–21 .... Jerusalem Is Destroyed, and the People Are Taken to Babylon
25:22–30 .... Gedaliah Is Made Governor, and King Jehoiachin Is Released from Prison

Purpose No nation marked by moral and spiritual decay can survive.

Theme Lessons from the Ruin of Israel and Judah

Date of writing 590–550 B.C.

"The LORD said, 'I will send Judah out of my sight, as I have sent Israel away. I will reject Jerusalem, which I chose. And I will take away the Temple about which I said, "I will be worshiped there" ' " (23:27).

Bible Talk

The Divided Kingdom

Readers of, particularly, 2 Kings have been known to get a little confused about the different kingdoms that Israel split into. You know how some movies skip back and forth between two story lines? Well, that's what 2 Kings does between kingdoms. So here's the scoop.

Israel divided into two kingdoms (get ready; this is gonna be tough): the northern kingdom and the southern kingdom. (Okay, not sooo tough.) What makes it confusing is that the northern kingdom is still called Israel. The southern kingdom is called Judah. Israel was bigger than Judah.

So when you're reading along and a new king is introduced, just remember to notice which kingdom he was in so you don't get mixed up.

WASN'T IT OBVIOUS?

Wasn't it obvious that the Hebrews needed to take God seriously? Don't you wonder sometimes what got in their way when they should have been listening to God and obeying him?

It's easy to wonder and even laugh at these people who seemed to avoid the obvious: Do what God says and things will go better for you! But the truth is, we do the same thing today. God told these people, "Worship only me; I am the true God." He tells us, "Worship only me. Don't trust anything else to get you through this life."

Yet they, and we, go our own way and worship and trust in other things to guide us and to rescue us from the difficult parts of life. Our world is not that far from theirs, is it?

ELIJAH AND KING AHAZIAH

1 1After Ahab died, Moab broke away from
Israel's rule. 2Ahaziah fell down through the
wooden bars in his upstairs room in Samaria
and was badly hurt. He sent messengers and
told them, "Go, ask Baal-Zebub, god of Ekron,
if I will recover from my injuries."

WHAT'S IT MEAN?

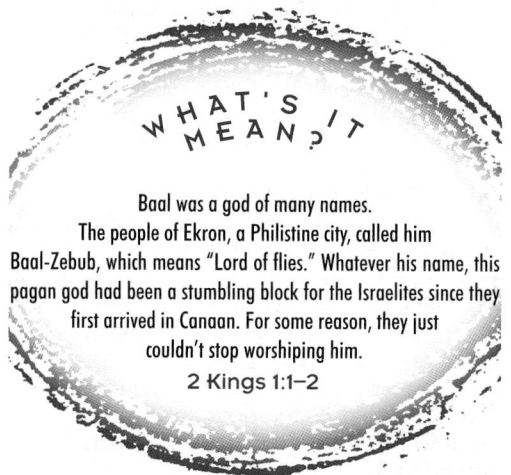

Baal was a god of many names. The people of Ekron, a Philistine city, called him Baal-Zebub, which means "Lord of flies." Whatever his name, this pagan god had been a stumbling block for the Israelites since they first arrived in Canaan. For some reason, they just couldn't stop worshiping him.

2 Kings 1:1–2

3But the LORD's angel said to Elijah the Tishbite, "Go up and meet the messengers sent by
the king of Samaria. Ask them, 'Why are you
going to ask questions of Baal-Zebub, god of
Ekron? Is it because you think there is no God
in Israel?' 4This is what the LORD says: 'You will
never get up from the bed you are lying on;
you will die.' " Then Elijah left.
5When the messengers returned to Ahaziah,
he asked them, "Why have you returned?"
6They said, "A man came to meet us. He
said, 'Go back to the king who sent you and
tell him what the LORD says: "Why do you
send messengers to ask questions of Baal-
Zebub, god of Ekron? Is it because you think
there is no God in Israel? You will never get up
from the bed you are lying on; you will die." ' "
7Ahaziah asked them, "What did the man
look like who met you and told you this?"
8They answered, "He was a hairy man and
wore a leather belt around his waist."
Ahaziah said, "It was Elijah the Tishbite."
9Then he sent a captain with his fifty men to
Elijah. The captain went to Elijah, who was sitting on top of the hill, and said to him, "Man of
God, the king says, 'Come down!' "
10Elijah answered the captain, "If I am a
man of God, let fire come down from heaven
and burn up you and your fifty men." Then fire
came down from heaven and burned up the
captain and his fifty men.
11Ahaziah sent another captain and fifty
men to Elijah. The captain said to him, "Man of
God, this is what the king says: 'Come down
quickly!' "
12Elijah answered, "If I am a man of God, let
fire come down from heaven and burn up you
and your fifty men!" Then fire came down
from heaven and burned up the captain and
his fifty men.
13Ahaziah then sent a third captain with his
fifty men. The third captain came and fell
down on his knees before Elijah and begged,
"Man of God, please respect my life and the
lives of your fifty servants. 14See, fire came
down from heaven and burned up the first
two captains of fifty with all their men. But
now, respect my life."
15The LORD's angel said to Elijah, "Go down
with him and don't be afraid of him." So Elijah
got up and went down with him to see the king.
16Elijah told Ahaziah, "This is what the
LORD says: 'You have sent messengers to ask
questions of Baal-Zebub, god of Ekron. Is it
because you think there is no God in Israel to
ask? Because of this, you will never get up from
your bed; you will die.' " 17So Ahaziah died, just
as the LORD, through Elijah, had said he would.
Joram became king in Ahaziah's place during the second year Jehoram son of Jehoshaphat was king of Judah. Joram ruled because
Ahaziah had no son to take his place. 18The
other things Ahaziah did are written in the
book of the history of the kings of Israel.

ELIJAH IS TAKEN TO HEAVEN

2 1It was almost time for the LORD to take Elijah by a whirlwind up into heaven. While Elijah
and Elisha were leaving Gilgal, 2Elijah said to
Elisha, "Please stay here. The LORD has told me
to go to Bethel."
But Elisha said, "As the LORD lives, and as
you live, I won't leave you." So they went
down to Bethel. 3The groups of prophets at
Bethel came out to Elisha and said to him, "Do
you know the LORD will take your master
away from you today?"
Elisha said, "Yes, I know, but don't talk
about it."
4Elijah said to him, "Stay here, Elisha, because the LORD has sent me to Jericho."
But Elisha said, "As the LORD lives, and as
you live, I won't leave you."
So they went to Jericho. 5The groups of
prophets at Jericho came to Elisha and said,
"Do you know that the LORD will take your
master away from you today?"
Elisha answered, "Yes, I know, but don't talk
about it."

[6]Elijah said to Elisha, "Stay here. The LORD
has sent me to the Jordan River."
Elisha answered, "As the LORD lives, and as
you live, I won't leave you."
So the two of them went on. [7]Fifty men of
the groups of prophets came and stood far
from where Elijah and Elisha were by the Jordan. [8]Elijah took off his coat, rolled it up, and
hit the water. The water divided to the right
and to the left, and Elijah and Elisha crossed
over on dry ground.
[9]After they had crossed over, Elijah said
to Elisha, "What can I do for you before I am
taken from you?"
Elisha said, "Leave me a double share of
your spirit."[n]
[10]Elijah said, "You have asked a hard thing.
But if you see me when I am taken from you,
it will be yours. If you don't, it won't happen."
[11]As they were walking and talking, a chariot and horses of fire appeared and separated
Elijah from Elisha. Then Elijah went up to
heaven in a whirlwind. [12]Elisha saw it and
shouted, "My father! My father! The chariots of
Israel and their horsemen!" And Elisha did not
see him anymore. Then Elisha grabbed his
own clothes and tore them to show how sad
he was.
[13]He picked up Elijah's coat that had fallen
from him. Then he returned and stood on the
bank of the Jordan. [14]Elisha hit the water with
Elijah's coat and said, "Where is the LORD, the
God of Elijah?" When he hit the water, it divided
to the right and to the left, and Elisha crossed
over.
[15]The groups of prophets at Jericho were
watching and said, "Elisha now has the spirit
Elijah had." And they came to meet him, bowing down to the ground before him. [16]They
said to him, "There are fifty strong men with
us. Please let them go and look for your master.
Maybe the Spirit of the LORD has taken Elijah
up and set him down on some mountain or in
some valley."
But Elisha answered, "No, don't send them."
[17]When the groups of prophets had begged
Elisha until he couldn't refuse them anymore,
he said, "Send them." So they sent fifty men
who looked for three days, but they could not
find him. [18]Then they came back to Elisha at
Jericho where he was staying. He said to them,
"I told you not to go, didn't I?"

ELISHA MAKES THE WATER PURE

[19]The people of the city said to Elisha,
"Look, master, this city is a nice place to live as
you can see. But the water is so bad the land
cannot grow crops."
[20]Elisha said, "Bring me a new bowl and put
salt in it." So they brought it to him.
[21]Then he went out to the spring and threw
the salt in it. He said, "This is what the LORD
says: 'I have healed this water. From now on it
won't cause death, and it won't keep the land
from growing crops.' " [22]So the water has been
healed to this day just as Elisha had said.

BOYS MAKE FUN OF ELISHA

[23]From there Elisha went up to Bethel. On
the way some boys came out of the city and
made fun of him. They said to him, "Go up too,
you baldhead! Go up too, you baldhead!" [24]Eli-
sha turned around, looked at them, and put a
curse on them in the name of the LORD. Then
two mother bears came out of the woods and
tore forty-two of the boys to pieces. [25]Elisha
went to Mount Carmel and from there he returned to Samaria.

WHAT'S IT MEAN?

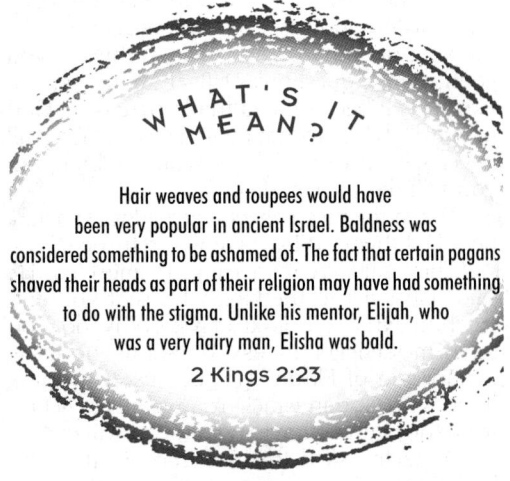

Hair weaves and toupees would have been very popular in ancient Israel. Baldness was considered something to be ashamed of. The fact that certain pagans shaved their heads as part of their religion may have had something to do with the stigma. Unlike his mentor, Elijah, who was a very hairy man, Elisha was bald.

2 Kings 2:23

WAR BETWEEN ISRAEL AND MOAB

3 [1]Joram son of Ahab became king over Israel
at Samaria in Jehoshaphat's eighteenth year as
king of Judah. And Joram ruled twelve years.
[2]He did what the LORD said was wrong, but he
was not like his father and mother; he removed
the stone pillars his father had made for Baal.
[3]But he continued to sin like Jeroboam son of

2:9 Leave . . . spirit By law, the first son in a family would inherit a double share of his father's possessions. Elisha is asking to inherit a share of his master's power as his follower. He is not asking for twice as much power as Elijah had.

ELISHA made a difference

As far as Elisha knew, his job that day was to take his father's twelve teams of oxen and plow the family fields. He was busy. Then the old prophet Elijah walked up to Elisha and put his own coat over Elisha's shoulders. Life was never the same again.

Elijah was following God's direction. God called Elisha through Elijah. But Elisha had to respond. He struggled. He ran after Elijah and asked for time to say a proper good-bye to his parents. Elijah's answer made it clear that this wasn't about following an old prophet but about following God's call. So Elisha sacrificed his oxen, used the yoke for firewood, shared the barbecue with the plowing crew, and placed the invisible yoke of service to God on his own shoulders.

Cutting Edge

As Elijah's helper, Elisha watched a man of God in action. He learned. Just before God took Elijah, Elisha had the opportunity to make a request. He asked for a double helping of the Spirit of God, which had been in Elijah. He didn't just want to be like his mentor; he wanted to be as available to God as his mentor had been. For more than fifty years, Elisha demonstrated in various ways what a difference a person can make when motivated and filled by the Spirit of God.

YOU can, too!

There's a lot we don't know about Elisha's story. Did he walk away from important responsibilities? He was one-twelfth of the workforce that day. His parents had a lot of help in the field. Perhaps they heard all the commotion and joined the party. The point is that when God's call required Elisha to walk away from all that was familiar to him, he did.

God's call in your Life may not require you to move somewhere else. But it will change the focus of your life. It may not change what you do, but it will definitely affect why you do it. Use Elisha's experience to word a prayer: Lord, help me know your call when the coat falls on my shoulders. Help me follow you.

Want to know more? Read about Elisha's life in 1 Kings 19:16—2 Kings 13:20.

Nebat who had led Israel to sin. Joram did not stop doing these same sins.

WHAT'S IT MEAN?

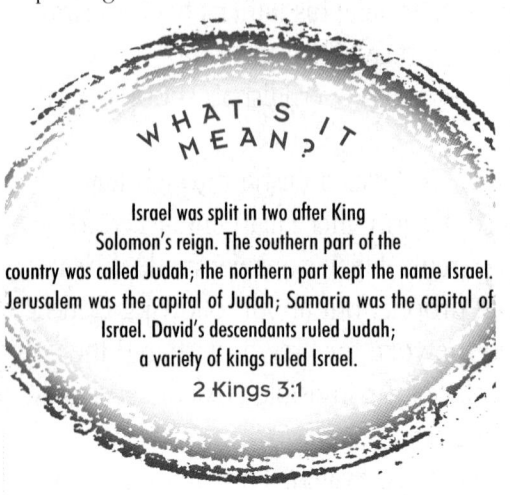

Israel was split in two after King Solomon's reign. The southern part of the country was called Judah; the northern part kept the name Israel. Jerusalem was the capital of Judah; Samaria was the capital of Israel. David's descendants ruled Judah; a variety of kings ruled Israel.

2 Kings 3:1

[4]Mesha king of Moab raised sheep. He paid the king of Israel one hundred thousand lambs and the wool of one hundred thousand sheep. [5]But when Ahab died, the king of Moab turned against the king of Israel. [6]So King Joram went out from Samaria and gathered Israel's army. [7]He also sent messengers to Jehoshaphat king of Judah. "The king of Moab has turned against me," he said. "Will you go with me to fight Moab?"

Jehoshaphat replied, "I will go with you. My soldiers and my horses are yours."

[8]Jehoshaphat asked, "Which way should we attack?"

Joram answered, "Through the Desert of Edom."

WHAT'S IT MEAN?

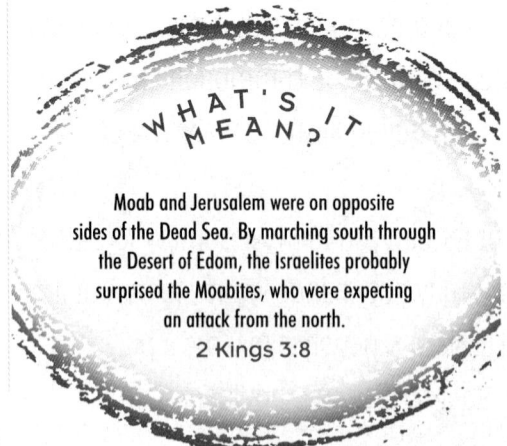

Moab and Jerusalem were on opposite sides of the Dead Sea. By marching south through the Desert of Edom, the Israelites probably surprised the Moabites, who were expecting an attack from the north.

2 Kings 3:8

[9]So the king of Israel went with the king of Judah and the king of Edom. After they had marched seven days, there was no more water for the army or for their animals that were with them. [10]The king of Israel said, "This is terrible! The LORD has called us three kings together to hand us over to the Moabites!"

[11]But Jehoshaphat asked, "Is there a prophet of the LORD here? We can ask the LORD through him."

An officer of the king of Israel answered, "Elisha son of Shaphat is here. He was Elijah's servant."

[12]Jehoshaphat said, "He speaks the LORD's truth." So the king of Israel and Jehoshaphat and the king of Edom went down to see Elisha.

[13]Elisha said to the king of Israel, "I have nothing to do with you. Go to the prophets of your father and to the prophets of your mother!"

The king of Israel said to Elisha, "No, the LORD has called us three kings together to hand us over to the Moabites."

[14]Elisha said, "As surely as the LORD All-Powerful lives, whom I serve, I tell you the truth. I wouldn't even look at you or notice you if Jehoshaphat king of Judah were not here. I respect him. [15]Now bring me someone who plays the harp."

While the harp was being played, the LORD gave Elisha power. [16]Then Elisha said, "The LORD says to dig holes in the valley. [17]The LORD says you won't see wind or rain, but the valley will be filled with water. Then you, your cattle, and your other animals can drink. [18]This is easy for the LORD to do; he will also hand Moab over to you. [19]You will destroy every strong, walled city and every important town. You will cut down every good tree and stop up all springs. You will ruin every good field with rocks."

[20]The next morning, about the time the sacrifice was offered, water came from the direction of Edom and filled the valley.

[21]All the Moabites heard that the kings had come up to fight against them. So they gathered everyone old enough to put on armor and waited at the border. [22]But when the Moabites got up early in the morning, the sun was shining on the water. They saw the water across from them, and it looked as red as blood. [23]Then they said, "This is blood! The kings must have fought and killed each other! Come, Moabites, let's take the valuables from the dead bodies!"

[24]When the Moabites came to the camp of Israel, the Israelites came out and fought them until they ran away. Then the Israelites went on into the land, killing the Moabites. [25]They

tore down the cities and threw rocks all over
every good field. They stopped up all the
springs and cut down all the good trees. Kir
Hareseth was the only city with its stones still
in place, but the men with slingshots surrounded it and conquered it, too.
[26]When the king of Moab saw that the battle was too much for him, he took seven hundred men with swords to try to break through
to the king of Edom. But they could not break
through. [27]Then the king of Moab took his
oldest son, who would have been king after
him, and offered him as a burnt offering on the
wall. So there was great anger against the Israelites, who left and went back to their own
land.

WHAT'S IT MEAN?

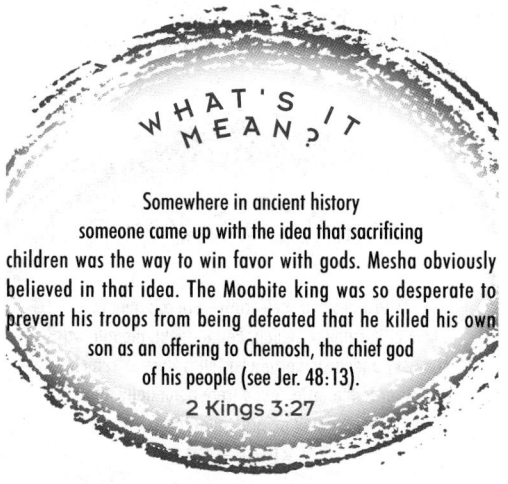

Somewhere in ancient history someone came up with the idea that sacrificing children was the way to win favor with gods. Mesha obviously believed in that idea. The Moabite king was so desperate to prevent his troops from being defeated that he killed his own son as an offering to Chemosh, the chief god of his people (see Jer. 48:13).

2 Kings 3:27

A WIDOW ASKS ELISHA FOR HELP

4 [1]The wife of a man from the groups of
prophets said to Elisha, "Your servant, my husband, is dead. You know he honored the LORD.
But now the man he owes money to is coming
to take my two boys as his slaves!"
[2]Elisha answered, "How can I help you? Tell
me, what do you have in your house?"
The woman said, "I don't have anything
there except a pot of oil."
[3]Then Elisha said, "Go and get empty jars
from all your neighbors. Don't ask for just a
few. [4]Then go into your house and shut the
door behind you and your sons. Pour oil into
all the jars, and set the full ones aside."
[5]So she left Elisha and shut the door behind
her and her sons. As they brought the jars to
her, she poured out the oil. [6]When the jars
were all full, she said to her son, "Bring me another jar."
But he said, "There are no more jars."
Then the oil stopped flowing.
[7]She went and told Elisha.
And the prophet said to her,
"Go, sell the oil and pay what
you owe. You and your sons
can live on what is left."

FAITH

What's a good example of faith? (4:1–7)

THE SHUNAMMITE WOMAN

[8]One day Elisha went to Shunem, where an
important woman lived. She begged Elisha to
stay and eat. So every time Elisha passed by, he
stopped there to eat. [9]The woman said to her
husband, "I know that this is a holy man of
God who passes by our house all the time.
[10]Let's make a small room on the roof[n] and put
a bed in the room for him. We can put a table,
a chair, and a lampstand there. Then when he
comes by, he can stay there."
[11]One day Elisha came to the woman's
house. After he went to his room and rested,
[12]he said to his servant Gehazi, "Call the Shunammite woman."
When the servant had called her, she stood
in front of him. [13]Elisha had told his servant,
"Now say to her, 'You have gone to all this trouble for us. What can I do for you? Do you want
me to speak to the king or the commander of
the army for you?' "
She answered, "I live among my own
people."
[14]Elisha said to Gehazi, "But what can we
do for her?"
He answered, "She has no son, and her husband is old."
[15]Then Elisha said to Gehazi, "Call her."
When he called her, she stood in the doorway.
[16]Then Elisha said, "About this time next year,
you will hold a son in your arms."
The woman said, "No, master, man of God,
don't lie to me, your servant!"
[17]But the woman became pregnant and
gave birth to a son at that time the next year,
just as Elisha had told her.
[18]The boy grew up and one day went out to
his father, who was with the grain harvesters.
[19]The boy said to his father, "My head! My
head!"
The father said to his servant, "Take him to
his mother!" [20]The servant took him to his
mother, and he lay on his mother's lap until

4:10 roof In Bible times houses were built with flat roofs. The roof was used for drying things such as flax and fruit. And it was used as an extra room, as a place for worship, and as a cool place to sleep in the summer.

noon. Then he died. 21So she took him up and
laid him on Elisha's bed. Then she shut the
door and left.
22She called to her husband, "Send me one
of the servants and one of the donkeys. Then I
can go quickly to the man of God and return."
23The husband said, "Why do you want to
go to him today? It isn't the New Moon or the
Sabbath day."
She said, "It will be all right."
24Then she saddled the donkey and said to
her servant, "Lead on. Don't slow down for me
unless I tell you." 25So she went to Elisha, the
man of God, at Mount Carmel.
When he saw her coming from far away, he
said to his servant Gehazi, "Look, there's the
Shunammite woman! 26Run to meet her and
ask, 'Are you all right? Is your husband all
right? Is the boy all right?' "
She answered, "Everything is all right."
27Then she came to Elisha at the hill and
grabbed his feet. Gehazi came near to pull her
away, but Elisha said to him, "Leave her alone.
She's very upset, and the LORD has not told me
about it. He has hidden it from me."
28She said, "Master, did I ask you for a son?
Didn't I tell you not to lie to me?"
29Then Elisha said to Gehazi, "Get ready.
Take my walking stick in your hand and go
quickly. If you meet anyone, don't say hello. If
anyone greets you, don't respond. Lay my
walking stick on the boy's face."
30The boy's mother said, "As surely as the
LORD lives and as you live, I won't leave you!"
So Elisha got up and followed her.
31Gehazi went on ahead and laid the walking stick on the boy's face, but the boy did not
talk or move. Then Gehazi went back to meet
Elisha. "The boy has not awakened," he said.
32When Elisha came into the house, the boy
was lying dead on his bed. 33Elisha entered the
room and shut the door, so only he and
the boy were in the room. Then he prayed to
the LORD. 34He went to the bed and lay on the
boy, putting his mouth on the boy's mouth,
his eyes on the boy's eyes, and his hands on
the boy's hands. He stretched himself out on
top of the boy. Soon the boy's skin became
warm. 35Elisha turned away and walked
around the room. Then he went back and put
himself on the boy again. The boy sneezed
seven times and opened his eyes.
36Elisha called Gehazi and said, "Call the
Shunammite!" So he did. When she came, Elisha said, "Pick up your son." 37She came in and
fell at Elisha's feet, bowing facedown to the
floor. Then she picked up her son and went out.

ELISHA AND THE STEW

38When Elisha returned to Gilgal, there was
a shortage of food in the land. While the
groups of prophets were sitting in front of him,
he said to his servant, "Put the large pot on the
fire, and boil some stew for these men."
39One of them went out into the field to
gather plants. Finding a wild vine, he picked
fruit from the vine and filled his robe with it.
Then he came and cut up the fruit into the pot.
But they didn't know what kind of fruit it was.
40They poured out the stew for the others to
eat. When they began to eat it, they shouted,
"Man of God, there's death in the pot!" And
they could not eat it.
41Elisha told them to bring some flour. He
threw it into the pot and said, "Pour it out for
the people to eat." Then there was nothing
harmful in the pot.

WHAT'S IT MEAN?

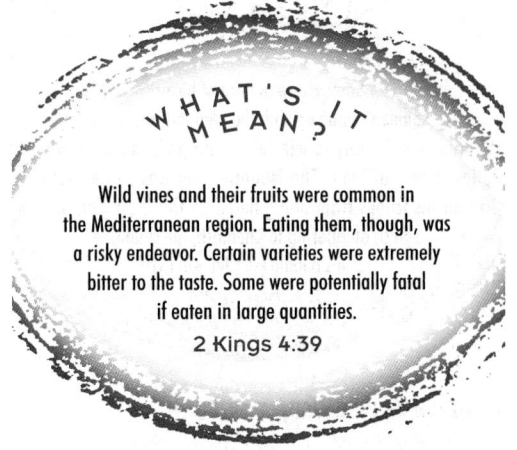

Wild vines and their fruits were common in the Mediterranean region. Eating them, though, was a risky endeavor. Certain varieties were extremely bitter to the taste. Some were potentially fatal if eaten in large quantities.

2 Kings 4:39

ELISHA FEEDS THE PEOPLE

42A man from Baal Shalishah came to Elisha, bringing him twenty loaves of barley
bread from the first harvest. He also brought
fresh grain in his sack. Elisha said, "Give it to
the people to eat."
43Elisha's servant asked, "How can I feed a
hundred people with so little?"
"Give the bread to the people to eat," Elisha
said. "This is what the LORD says: 'They will eat
and will have food left over.' " 44After he gave it
to them, the people ate and had food left over,
as the LORD had said.

NAAMAN IS HEALED

5
1Naaman was commander of the army of
the king of Aram. He was honored by his master, and he had much respect because the LORD
used him to give victory to Aram. He was a

mighty and brave man, but he had a skin disease.

[2]The Arameans had gone out to raid the Israelites and had taken a little girl as a captive. This little girl served Naaman's wife. [3]She said to her mistress, "I wish my master would meet the prophet who lives in Samaria. He would cure him of his disease."

WHAT'S IT MEAN?

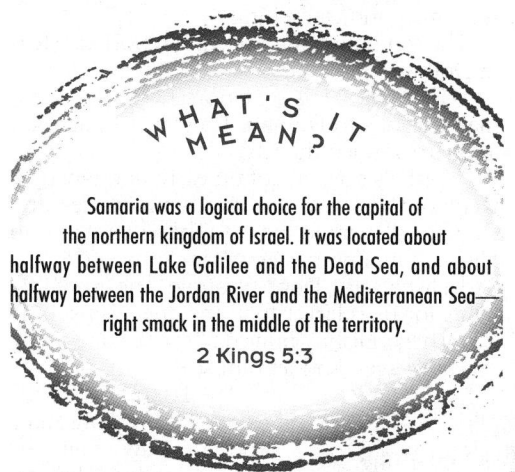

Samaria was a logical choice for the capital of the northern kingdom of Israel. It was located about halfway between Lake Galilee and the Dead Sea, and about halfway between the Jordan River and the Mediterranean Sea—right smack in the middle of the territory.

2 Kings 5:3

[4]Naaman went to the king and told him what the girl from Israel had said. [5]The king of Aram said, "Go ahead, and I will send a letter to the king of Israel." So Naaman left and took with him about seven hundred fifty pounds of silver, as well as one hundred fifty pounds of gold and ten changes of clothes. [6]He brought the letter to the king of Israel, which read, "I am sending my servant Naaman to you so you can heal him of his skin disease."

[7]When the king of Israel read the letter, he tore his clothes to show how upset he was. He said, "I'm not God! I can't kill and make alive again! Why does this man send someone with a skin disease for me to heal? You can see that the king of Aram is trying to start trouble with me."

[8]When Elisha, the man of God, heard that the king of Israel had torn his clothes, he sent the king this message: "Why have you torn your clothes? Let Naaman come to me. Then he will know there is a prophet in Israel." [9]So Naaman went with his horses and chariots to Elisha's house and stood outside the door.

[10]Elisha sent Naaman a messenger who said, "Go and wash in the Jordan River seven times. Then your skin will be healed, and you will be clean."

[11]Naaman became angry and left. He said, "I thought Elisha would surely come out and stand before me and call on the name of the LORD his God. I thought he would wave his hand over the place and heal the disease. [12]The Abana and the Pharpar, the rivers of Damascus, are better than all the waters of Israel. Why can't I wash in them and become clean?" So Naaman went away very angry.

[13]Naaman's servants came near and said to him, "My father, if the prophet had told you to do some great thing, wouldn't you have done it? Doesn't it make more sense just to do it? After all, he only told you, 'Wash, and you will be clean.'" [14]So Naaman went down and dipped in the Jordan seven times, just as Elisha had said. Then his skin became new again, like the skin of a child. And he was clean.

[15]Naaman and all his group returned to Elisha. He stood before Elisha and said, "Look, I now know there is no God in all the earth except in Israel. Now please accept a gift from me."

GOD

Who else is like God? (5:15)

[16]But Elisha said, "As surely as the LORD lives whom I serve, I won't accept anything." Naaman urged him to take the gift, but he refused.

[17]Then Naaman said, "If you won't take the gift, then please give me some soil—as much as two of my mules can carry. From now on I'll not offer any burnt offering or sacrifice to any other gods but the LORD. [18]But let the LORD pardon me for this: When my master goes into the temple of Rimmon[n] to worship, he leans on my arm. Then I must bow in that temple. May the LORD pardon me when I do that."

[19]Elisha said to him, "Go in peace."

Naaman left Elisha and went a short way. [20]Gehazi, the servant of Elisha the man of God, thought, "My master has not accepted what Naaman the Aramean brought. As surely as the LORD lives, I'll run after him and get something from him." [21]So Gehazi went after Naaman.

When Naaman saw someone running after him, he got off the chariot to meet Gehazi. He asked, "Is everything all right?"

[22]Gehazi said, "Everything is all right. My master has sent me. He said, 'Two young men from the groups of prophets in the mountains of Ephraim just came to me. Please give them seventy-five pounds of silver and two changes of clothes.'"

[23]Naaman said, "Please take one hundred fifty pounds," and he urged Gehazi to take it. He tied one hundred fifty pounds of silver in

5:18 temple of Rimmon The place where the Aramean people worshiped the god Rimmon.

two bags with two changes of clothes. Then he gave them to two of his servants to carry for Gehazi. 24When they came to the hill, Gehazi took these things from Naaman's servants and put them in the house. Then he let Naaman's servants go, and they left.

25When he came in and stood before his master, Elisha said to him, "Where have you been, Gehazi?"

"I didn't go anywhere," he answered.

26But Elisha said to him, "My spirit was with you. I knew when the man turned from his chariot to meet you. This isn't a time to take money, clothes, olives, grapes, sheep, oxen, male servants, or female servants. 27So Naaman's skin disease will come on you and your children forever." When Gehazi left Elisha, he had the disease and was as white as snow.

AN AXHEAD FLOATS

6

1The groups of prophets said to Elisha, "The place where we meet with you is too small for us. 2Let's go to the Jordan River. There everyone can get a log, and let's build a place there to live."

Elisha said, "Go."

3One of them said, "Please go with us."

Elisha answered, "I will go," 4so he went with them. When they arrived at the Jordan, they cut down some trees. 5As one man was cutting down a tree, the head of his ax fell into the water. He yelled, "Oh, my master! I borrowed that ax!"

6Elisha asked, "Where did it fall?" The man showed him the place. Then Elisha cut down a stick and threw it into the water, and it made the iron head float. 7Elisha said, "Pick up the axhead." Then the man reached out and took it.

ELISHA AND THE BLINDED ARAMEANS

8The king of Aram was at war with Israel. He had a council meeting with his officers and said, "I will set up my camp in this place."

9Elisha, the man of God, sent a message to the king of Israel, saying, "Be careful! Don't pass that place, because the Arameans are going down there!"

10The king of Israel checked the place about which Elisha had warned him. Elisha warned him several times, so the king protected himself there.

11The king of Aram was angry about this. He called his officers together and demanded, "Tell me who of us is working for the king of Israel."

12One of the officers said, "None, my master and king. It's Elisha, the prophet from Israel. He can tell you what you speak in your bedroom."

13The king said, "Go and find him so I can send men and catch him."

The servants came back and reported, "He is in Dothan."

14Then the king sent horses, chariots, and many troops to Dothan. They arrived at night and surrounded the city.

15Elisha's servant got up early, and when he went out, he saw an army with horses and chariots all around the city. The servant said to Elisha, "Oh, my master, what can we do?"

16Elisha said, "Don't be afraid. The army that fights for us is larger than the one against us."

17Then Elisha prayed, "LORD, open my servant's eyes, and let him see."

The LORD opened the eyes of the young man, and he saw that the mountain was full of horses and chariots of fire all around Elisha.

18As the enemy came down toward Elisha, he prayed to the LORD, "Make these people blind." So he made the Aramean army blind, as Elisha had asked.

19Elisha said to them, "This is not the right road or the right city. Follow me and I'll take you to the man you are looking for." Then Elisha led them to Samaria.

20After they entered Samaria, Elisha said, "LORD, open these men's eyes so they can see." So the LORD opened their eyes, and the Aramean army saw that they were inside the city of Samaria!

21When the king of Israel saw the Aramean army, he said to Elisha, "My father, should I kill them? Should I kill them?"

22Elisha answered, "Don't kill them. You wouldn't kill people whom you captured with your sword and bow. Give them food and water, and let them eat and drink and then go home to their master." 23So he prepared a great feast for the Aramean army. After they ate and drank, the king sent them away, and they went home to their master. The soldiers of Aram did not come anymore into the land of Israel.

> **"Elisha said, 'Don't be afraid. The army that fights for us is larger than the one against us.' Then Elisha prayed, 'LORD, open my servant's eyes, and let him see.' "**
> **(2 Kings 6:16–17a)**

A SHORTAGE OF FOOD

24Later, Ben-Hadad king of Aram gathered
his whole army and surrounded and attacked
Samaria. 25There was a shortage of food in Samaria. It was so bad that a donkey's head sold
for about two pounds of silver, and half of a
pint of dove's dung sold for about two ounces
of silver.
26As the king of Israel was passing by on the
wall, a woman yelled out to him, "Help me, my
master and king!"
27The king said, "If the LORD doesn't help
you, how can I? Can I get help from the
threshing floor or from the winepress?" 28Then
the king said to her, "What is your trouble?"

She answered, "This woman said to me,
'Give up your son so we can eat him today.
Then we will eat my son tomorrow.' 29So we
boiled my son and ate him. Then the next day
I said to her, 'Give up your son so we can eat
him.' But she had hidden him."
30When the king heard the woman's words,
he tore his clothes in grief. As he walked along
the wall, the people looked and saw he had on
rough cloth under his clothes to show his sadness. 31He said, "May God punish me terribly if
the head of Elisha son of Shaphat isn't cut off
from his body today!"

WHAT'S IT MEAN?

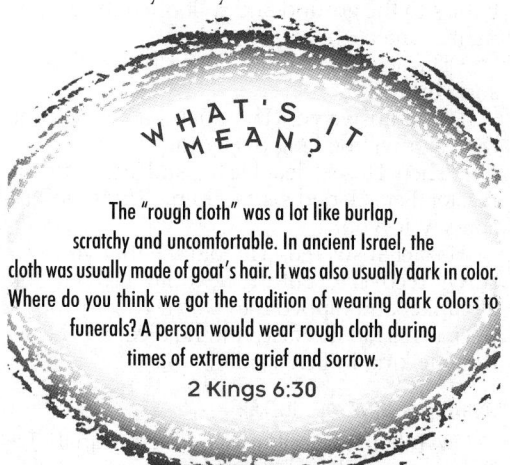

The "rough cloth" was a lot like burlap, scratchy and uncomfortable. In ancient Israel, the cloth was usually made of goat's hair. It was also usually dark in color. Where do you think we got the tradition of wearing dark colors to funerals? A person would wear rough cloth during times of extreme grief and sorrow.

2 Kings 6:30

32The king sent a messenger to Elisha, who
was sitting in his house with the older leaders.
But before the messenger arrived, Elisha said to
them, "See, this murderer is sending men to cut
off my head. When the messenger arrives, shut
the door and hold it; don't let him in. The
sound of his master's feet is behind him."
33Elisha was still talking with the leaders
when the messenger arrived. The king said,
"This trouble has come from the LORD. Why
should I wait for the LORD any longer?"

7 1Elisha said, "Listen to the LORD's word. This
is what the LORD says: 'About this time tomorrow seven quarts of fine flour will be sold for
two-fifths of an ounce of silver, and thirteen
quarts of barley will be sold for two-fifths of
an ounce of silver. This will happen at the gate
of Samaria.' "
2Then the officer who was close to the king
answered Elisha, "Even if the LORD opened
windows in the sky, that couldn't happen."

Elisha said, "You will see it with your eyes,
but you will not eat any of it."
3There were four men with a skin disease at
the entrance to the city gate. They said to each
other, "Why do we sit here until we die? 4There
is no food in the city. So if we go into the city,
we will die there. If we stay here, we will die. So
let's go to the Aramean camp. If they let us live,
we will live. If they kill us, we die."
5So they got up at twilight and went to the
Aramean camp, but when they arrived, no one
was there. 6The Lord had caused the Aramean
army to hear the sound of chariots, horses,
and a large army. They had said to each other,
"The king of Israel has hired the Hittite and
Egyptian kings to attack us!" 7So they got up
and ran away in the twilight, leaving their
tents, horses, and donkeys. They left the camp
standing and ran for their lives.
8When the men with the skin disease came
to the edge of the camp, they went into one of
the tents and ate and drank. They carried silver,
gold, and clothes out of the camp and hid them.
Then they came back and entered another tent.
They carried things from this tent and hid them,
also. 9Then they said to each other, "We're doing
wrong. Today we have good news, but we are
silent. If we wait until the sun comes up, we'll
be discovered. Let's go right now and tell the
people in the king's palace."
10So they went and called to the gatekeepers
of the city. They said, "We went to the Aramean
camp, but no one is there; we didn't hear anyone. The horses and donkeys were still tied up,
and the tents were still standing." 11Then the
gatekeepers shouted out and told the people in
the palace.
12The king got up in the night and said to
his officers, "I'll tell you what the Arameans are
doing to us. They know we are starving. They
have gone out of the camp to hide in the field.
They're saying, 'When the Israelites come out
of the city, we'll capture them alive. Then we'll
enter the city.' "
13One of his officers answered, "Let some
men take five of the horses that are still left in
the city. These men are like all the Israelites

who are left; they are also about to die. Let's send them to see what has happened."

14So the men took two chariots with horses. The king sent them after the Aramean army, saying, "Go and see what has happened." 15The men followed the Aramean army as far as the Jordan River. The road was full of clothes and equipment that the Arameans had thrown away as they had hurriedly left. So the messengers returned and told the king. 16Then the people went out and took valuables from the Aramean camp. So seven quarts of fine flour were sold for two-fifths of an ounce of silver, and thirteen quarts of barley were sold for two-fifths of an ounce of silver, just as the LORD had said.

17The king chose the officer who was close to him to guard the gate, but the people trampled the officer to death. This happened just as Elisha had told the king when the king came to his house. 18He had said, "Thirteen quarts of barley and seven quarts of fine flour will each sell for two-fifths of an ounce of silver about this time tomorrow at the gate of Samaria."

19But the officer had answered, "Even if the LORD opened windows in the sky, that couldn't happen." And Elisha had told him, "You will see it with your eyes, but you won't eat any of it." 20It happened to the officer just that way. The people trampled him in the gateway, and he died.

THE SHUNAMMITE REGAINS HER LAND

8 1Elisha spoke to the woman whose son he had brought back to life. He said, "Get up and go with your family. Stay any place you can, because the LORD has called for a time without food that will last seven years." 2So the woman got up and did as the man of God had said. She left with her family, and they stayed in the land of the Philistines for seven years. 3After seven years she returned from the land of the Philistines and went to beg the king for her house and land. 4The king was talking with Gehazi, the servant of the man of God. The king had said, "Please tell me all the great things Elisha has done." 5Gehazi was telling the king how Elisha had brought a dead boy back to life. Just then the woman whose son Elisha had brought back to life came and begged the king for her house and land.

Gehazi said, "My master and king, this is the woman, and this is the son Elisha brought back to life."

6The king asked the woman, and she told him about it. Then the king chose an officer to help her. "Give the woman everything that is hers," the king said. "Give her all the money made from her land from the day she left until now."

BEN-HADAD IS KILLED

7Then Elisha went to Damascus, where Ben-Hadad king of Aram was sick. Someone told him, "The man of God has arrived."

8The king said to Hazael, "Take a gift in your hand and go meet him. Ask the LORD through him if I will recover from my sickness."

9So Hazael went to meet Elisha, taking with him a gift of forty camels loaded with every good thing in Damascus. He came and stood before Elisha and said, "Your son Ben-Hadad king of Aram sent me to you. He asks if he will recover from his sickness."

10Elisha said to Hazael, "Go and tell Ben-Hadad, 'You will surely recover,' but the LORD has told me he will really die." 11Hazael stared at Elisha until he felt ashamed. Then Elisha cried.

12Hazael asked, "Why are you crying, master?"

Elisha answered, "Because I know what evil you will do to the Israelites. You will burn their strong, walled cities with fire and kill their young men with swords. You will throw their babies to the ground and split open their pregnant women."

13Hazael said, "Am I a dog? How could I do such things?"

Elisha answered, "The LORD has shown me that you will be king over Aram."

14Then Hazael left Elisha and came to his master. Ben-Hadad said to him, "What did Elisha say to you?"

Hazael answered, "He told me that you will surely recover." 15But the next day Hazael took a blanket and dipped it in water. Then he put it over Ben-Hadad's face, and he died. So Hazael became king in Ben-Hadad's place.

JEHORAM KING OF JUDAH

16While Jehoshaphat was king in Judah, Jehoram son of Jehoshaphat became king of Judah. This was during the fifth year Joram son of Ahab was king of Israel. 17Jehoram was thirty-two years old when he began to rule, and he ruled eight years in Jerusalem. 18He followed the ways of the kings of Israel, just as the family of Ahab had done, because he married Ahab's daughter. Jehoram did what the LORD said was wrong. 19But the LORD would not destroy Judah because of his servant David. The LORD had promised that one of David's descendants would always rule.

20In Jehoram's time Edom broke away from
Judah's rule and chose their own king. 21So Je-
horam and all his chariots went to Zair. The
Edomites surrounded him and his chariot
commanders. Jehoram got up and attacked the
Edomites at night, but his army ran away to
their tents. 22From then until now the country
of Edom has fought against the rule of Judah.
At the same time Libnah also broke away from
Judah's rule.

WHAT'S IT MEAN?

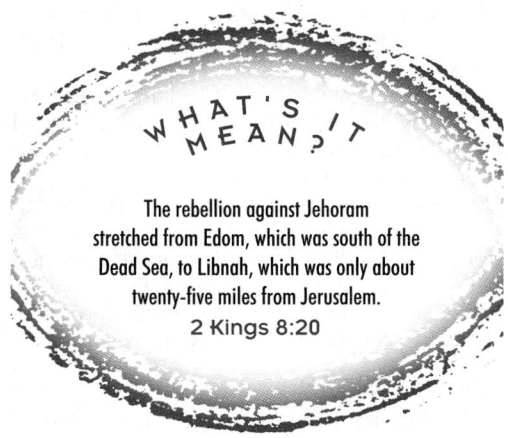

The rebellion against Jehoram stretched from Edom, which was south of the Dead Sea, to Libnah, which was only about twenty-five miles from Jerusalem.

2 Kings 8:20

23The other acts of Jehoram and all the
things he did are written in the book of the
history of the kings of Judah. 24Jehoram died
and was buried with his ancestors in Jerusalem, and Jehoram's son Ahaziah ruled in his
place.
25Ahaziah son of Jehoram became king of
Judah during the twelfth year Joram son of
Ahab was king of Israel. 26Ahaziah was twenty-
two years old when he became king, and he
ruled one year in Jerusalem. His mother's name
was Athaliah, a granddaughter of Omri king of
Israel. 27Ahaziah followed the ways of Ahab's
family. He did what the LORD said was wrong,
as Ahab's family had done, because he was a
son-in-law to Ahab.
28Ahaziah went with Joram son of Ahab to
Ramoth in Gilead, where they fought against
Hazael king of Aram. The Arameans wounded
Joram. 29So King Joram returned to Jezreel to
heal from the wound he had received from the
Arameans at Ramoth when he fought Hazael
king of Aram. Ahaziah son of Jehoram king of
Judah went down to visit Joram son of Ahab
at Jezreel, because he had been wounded.

WHAT'S IT MEAN?

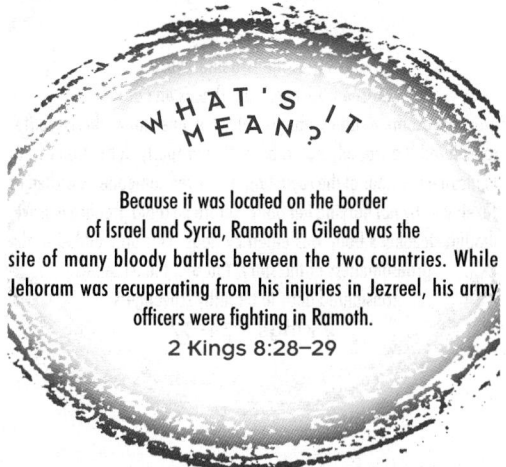

Because it was located on the border of Israel and Syria, Ramoth in Gilead was the site of many bloody battles between the two countries. While Jehoram was recuperating from his injuries in Jezreel, his army officers were fighting in Ramoth.

2 Kings 8:28–29

JEHU IS CHOSEN KING

9
1At the same time, Elisha the prophet called
a man from the groups of prophets. Elisha
said, "Get ready, and take this small bottle of
olive oil in your hand. Go to Ramoth in Gilead.
2When you arrive, find Jehu son of Jehoshaphat, the son of Nimshi. Go in and make Jehu
get up from among his brothers, and take him
to an inner room. 3Then take the bottle and
pour the oil on Jehu's head and say, 'This is
what the LORD says: I have appointed you king
over Israel.' Then open the door and run away.
Don't wait!"
4So the young man, the prophet, went to
Ramoth in Gilead. 5When he arrived, he saw
the officers of the army sitting together. He
said, "Commander, I have a message for you."
Jehu asked, "For which one of us?"
The young man said, "For you, commander."
6Jehu got up and went into the house. Then
the young prophet poured the olive oil on
Jehu's head and said to him, "This is what the
LORD, the God of Israel says: 'I have appointed
you king over the LORD's people Israel. 7You
must destroy the family of Ahab your master. I
will punish Jezebel for the deaths of my servants the prophets and for all the LORD's servants who were murdered. 8All of Ahab's
family must die. I will not let any male child in
Ahab's family live in Israel, whether slave or
free. 9I will make Ahab's family like the family
of Jeroboam son of Nebat and like the family
of Baasha son of Ahijah. 10The dogs will eat
Jezebel at Jezreel, and no one will bury her.' "
Then the young prophet opened the door
and ran away.
11When Jehu went back to his master's officers, one of them said to Jehu, "Is everything all
right? Why did this crazy man come to you?"
Jehu answered, "You know the man and
how he talks."
12They answered, "That's not true. Tell us."
Jehu said, "He said to me, 'This is what the

LORD says: I have appointed you to be king over Israel.' "

13 Then the officers hurried, and each man took off his own coat and put it on the stairs for Jehu. They blew the trumpet and shouted, "Jehu is king!"

JORAM AND AHAZIAH ARE KILLED

14 So Jehu son of Jehoshaphat, the son of Nimshi, made plans against Joram. Now Joram and all Israel had been defending Ramoth in Gilead from Hazael king of Aram. 15 But King Joram had to return to Jezreel to heal from the injuries the Arameans had given him when he fought against Hazael king of Aram.

Jehu said, "If you agree with this, don't let anyone leave the city. They might tell the news in Jezreel." 16 Then he got into his chariot and set out for Jezreel, where Joram was resting. Ahaziah king of Judah had gone down to see him.

17 The lookout was standing on the watchtower in Jezreel when he saw Jehu's troops coming. He said, "I see some soldiers!"

Joram said, "Take a horseman and send him to meet them. Tell him to ask, 'Is all in order?' "

18 The horseman rode out to meet Jehu, and he said, "This is what the king says: 'Is all in order?' "

Jehu said, "Why bother yourself with order? Come along behind me."

The lookout reported, "The messenger reached them, but he is not coming back."

19 Then Joram sent out a second horseman. This rider came to Jehu's group and said, "This is what the king says: 'Is all in order?' "

Jehu answered, "Why bother yourself with order? Come along behind me."

20 The lookout reported, "The second man reached them, but he is not coming back. The man in the chariot is driving like Jehu son of Nimshi. He drives as if he were crazy!"

21 Joram said, "Get my chariot ready." Then the servant got Joram's chariot ready. Joram king of Israel and Ahaziah king of Judah went out, each in his own chariot, to meet Jehu at the property of Naboth the Jezreelite.

22 When Joram saw Jehu, he said, "Is all in order, Jehu?"

Jehu answered, "There will never be any order as long as your mother Jezebel worships idols and uses witchcraft."

23 Joram turned the horses to run away and yelled to Ahaziah, "It's a trick, Ahaziah!"

24 Then Jehu drew his bow and shot Joram between his shoulders. The arrow went through Joram's heart, and he fell down in his chariot.

25 Jehu ordered Bidkar, his chariot officer, "Pick up Joram's body, and throw it into the field of Naboth the Jezreelite. Remember when you and I rode together with Joram's father Ahab. The LORD made this prophecy against him: 26 'Yesterday I saw the blood of Naboth and his sons, says the LORD, so I will punish Ahab in his field, says the LORD.' Take Joram's body and throw it into the field, as the LORD has said."

27 When Ahaziah king of Judah saw this, he ran away toward Beth Haggan. Jehu chased him, saying, "Shoot Ahaziah, too!" Ahaziah was wounded in his chariot on the way up to Gur near Ibleam. He got as far as Megiddo but died there. 28 Ahaziah's servants carried his body in a chariot to Jerusalem and buried him with his ancestors in his tomb in Jerusalem. 29 (Ahaziah had become king over Judah in the eleventh year Joram son of Ahab was king.)

DEATH OF JEZEBEL

30 When Jehu came to Jezreel, Jezebel heard about it. She put on her eye makeup and fixed her hair. Then she looked out the window. 31 When Jehu entered the city gate, Jezebel said, "Have you come in peace, you Zimri,[n] you who killed your master?"

32 Jehu looked up at the window and said, "Who is on my side? Who?" Two or three servants looked out the window at Jehu. 33 He said

WHAT'S IT MEAN?

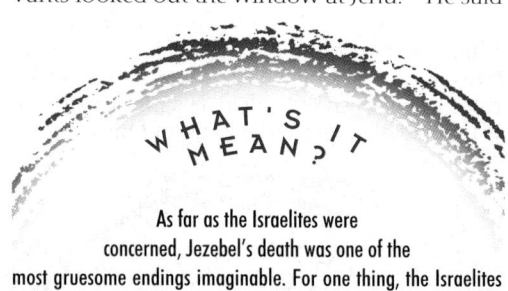

As far as the Israelites were concerned, Jezebel's death was one of the most gruesome endings imaginable. For one thing, the Israelites considered it a tragedy not to be buried properly. Jehu didn't want to insult a member of the royal family—even someone as wicked as Jezebel—by not burying her body. Before he could prepare a grave, though, Jezebel's body was eaten by dogs. This only added to the gruesomeness of the story. You see, the Israelites considered dogs to be filthy scavengers.

2 Kings 9:34–37

9:31 Zimri He was the man who killed Elah and the family of Baasha. Read 1 Kings 16:8-12.

to them, "Throw her down." So they threw Jezebel down, and the horses ran over her. Some
of her blood splashed on the wall and on the
horses.
34 Jehu went into the house and ate and
drank. Then he said, "Now see about this
cursed woman. Bury her, because she is a
king's daughter."
35 The men went to bury Jezebel, but they
could not find her. They found only her skull,
feet, and the palms of her hands. 36 When they
came back and told Jehu, he said, "The LORD
said this through his servant Elijah the Tishbite: 'The dogs will eat Jezebel at Jezreel. 37 Her
body will be like manure on the field in the
land at Jezreel. No one will be able to say that
this is Jezebel.' "

FAMILIES OF AHAB AND AHAZIAH KILLED

10
1 Ahab had seventy sons in Samaria. Jehu
wrote letters and sent them to Samaria to the
officers and older leaders of Jezreel and to the
guardians of the sons of Ahab. Jehu said, 2 "You
have your master's sons with you, and you
have chariots, horses, a city with strong walls,
and weapons. When you get this letter, 3 choose
the best and most worthy person among your
master's sons, and make him king. Then fight
for your master's family."
4 But the officers and leaders of Jezreel were
frightened. They said, "Two kings could not
stand up to Jehu, so how can we?"
5 The palace manager, the city governor, the
leaders, and the guardians sent a message to
Jehu. "We are your servants," they said. "We will
do everything you tell us to do. We won't make
any man king, so do whatever you think is
best."
6 Then Jehu wrote a second letter, saying, "If
you are on my side and will obey me, cut off
the heads of your master's sons and come to
me at Jezreel tomorrow about this time."
Now the seventy sons of the king's family
were with the leading men of the city who
were their guardians. 7 When the leaders received the letter, they took the king's sons and
killed all seventy of them. They put their heads
in baskets and sent them to Jehu at Jezreel.
8 The messenger came to Jehu and told him,
"They have brought the heads of the king's
sons."
Then Jehu said, "Lay the heads in two piles
at the city gate until morning."
9 In the morning, Jehu went out and stood
before the people and said to them, "You are
innocent. Look, I made plans against my master and killed him. But who killed all these?
10 You should know that everything the LORD
said about Ahab's family will come true. The
LORD has spoken through his servant Elijah,
and the LORD has done what he said." 11 So Jehu
killed everyone of Ahab's family in Jezreel who
was still alive. He also killed all Ahab's leading
men, close friends, and priests. No one who
had helped Ahab was left alive.
12 Then Jehu left and went to Samaria by
way of the road to Beth Eked of the Shepherds.
13 There Jehu met some relatives of Ahaziah
king of Judah. Jehu asked, "Who are you?"
They answered, "We are relatives of Ahaziah. We have come down to get revenge for
the families of the king and the king's mother."
14 Then Jehu said, "Take them alive!" So they
captured Ahaziah's relatives alive and killed
them at the well near Beth Eked—forty-two of
them. Jehu did not leave anyone alive.
15 After Jehu left there, he met Jehonadab
son of Recab, who was also on his way to meet
Jehu. Jehu greeted him and said, "Are you as
good a friend to me as I am to you?"
Jehonadab answered, "Yes, I am."
Jehu said, "If you are, then give me your
hand." So Jehonadab gave him his hand, and
Jehu pulled him into the chariot. 16 "Come with
me," Jehu said. "You can see how strong my
feelings are for the LORD." So Jehu had Jehonadab ride in his chariot.
17 When Jehu came to Samaria, he killed all
of Ahab's family in Samaria. He destroyed all
those who were left, just as the LORD had told
Elijah it would happen.

BAAL WORSHIPERS KILLED

18 Then Jehu gathered all the people together
and said to them, "Ahab served Baal a little, but
Jehu will serve Baal much. 19 Now call for me
all Baal's prophets and priests and all the people who worship Baal. Don't let anyone miss
this meeting, because I have a great sacrifice for
Baal. Anyone who is not there will not live."
But Jehu was tricking them so he could destroy
the worshipers of Baal. 20 He said, "Prepare a
holy meeting for Baal." So they announced the
meeting. 21 Then Jehu sent word through all Israel, and all the worshipers of Baal came; not
one stayed home. They came into the temple of
Baal, and the temple was filled from one side to
the other.
22 Jehu said to the man who kept the robes,
"Bring out robes for all the worshipers of Baal."
After he brought out robes for them, 23 Jehu
and Jehonadab son of Recab went into the
temple of Baal. Jehu said to the worshipers of
Baal, "Look around, and make sure there are

no servants of the LORD with you. Be sure there are only worshipers of Baal." [24]Then the worshipers of Baal went in to offer sacrifices and burnt offerings.

Jehu had eighty men waiting outside. He had told them, "Don't let anyone escape. If you do, you must pay with your own life."

[25]As soon as Jehu finished offering the burnt offering, he ordered the guards and the captains, "Go in and kill the worshipers of Baal. Don't let anyone come out." So the guards and captains killed the worshipers of Baal with the sword and threw their bodies out. Then they went to the inner rooms of the temple [26]and brought out the pillars of the temple of Baal and burned them. [27]They tore down the stone pillar of Baal, as well as the temple of Baal. And they made it into a sewage pit, as it is today.

[28]So Jehu destroyed Baal worship in Israel, [29]but he did not stop doing the sins Jeroboam son of Nebat had done. Jeroboam had led Israel to sin by worshiping the golden calves in Bethel and Dan.

[30]The LORD said to Jehu, "You have done well in obeying what I said was right. You have done to the family of Ahab as I wanted. Because of this, your descendants as far as your great-great-grandchildren will be kings of Israel." [31]But Jehu was not careful to follow the teachings of the LORD, the God of Israel, with all his heart. He did not stop doing the same sins Jeroboam had done, by which he had led Israel to sin.

[32]At that time the LORD began to make Israel smaller. Hazael defeated the Israelites in all the land of Israel, [33]taking all the land of the Jordan known as the land of Gilead. (It was the region of Gad, Reuben, and Manasseh.) He took land from Aroer by the Arnon Ravine through Gilead to Bashan.

[34]The other things Jehu did—everything he did and all his victories—are recorded in the book of the history of the kings of Israel. [35]Jehu died and was buried in Samaria, and his son Jehoahaz became king in his place. [36]Jehu was king over Israel in Samaria for twenty-eight years.

ATHALIAH AND JOASH

11 [1]When Ahaziah's mother, Athaliah, saw that her son was dead, she killed all the royal family. [2]But Jehosheba, King Jehoram's daughter and Ahaziah's sister, took Joash, Ahaziah's son. She stole him from among the other sons of the king who were about to be murdered. She put Joash and his nurse in a bedroom to hide him from Athaliah, so he was not killed. [3]He hid with her in the Temple of the LORD for six years. During that time Athaliah ruled the land.

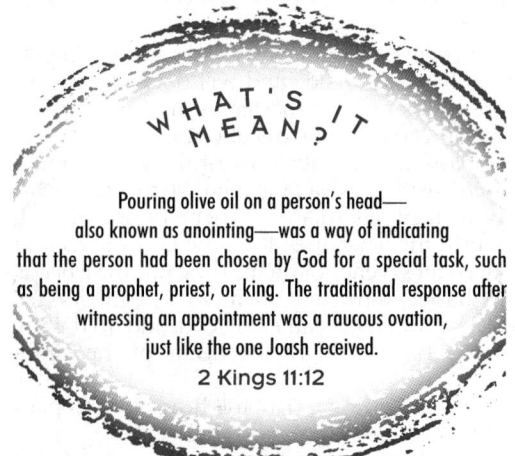

ABUSE
Can intervention help?
(11:1–3)

[4]In the seventh year Jehoiada sent for the commanders of groups of a hundred men, as well as the Carites.[n] He brought them together in the Temple of the LORD and made an agreement with them. There, in the Temple of the LORD, he made them promise loyalty, and then he showed them the king's son. [5]He commanded them, "This is what you must do. A third of you who go on duty on the Sabbath will guard the king's palace. [6]A third of you will be at the Sur Gate, and another third will be at the gate behind the guard. This way you will guard the Temple. [7]The two groups who go off duty on the Sabbath must protect the Temple of the LORD for the king. [8]All of you must stand around the king, each man with his weapons in his hand. If anyone comes near, kill him. Stay close to the king when he goes out and when he comes in."

[9]The commanders over a hundred men obeyed everything Jehoiada the priest had commanded. Each one took his men who came on duty on the Sabbath and those who went off duty on the Sabbath, and they came to Jehoiada the priest. [10]He gave the commanders the spears and shields that had belonged to King David and that were kept in the Temple of the LORD.

WHAT'S IT MEAN?

Pouring olive oil on a person's head—also known as anointing—was a way of indicating that the person had been chosen by God for a special task, such as being a prophet, priest, or king. The traditional response after witnessing an appointment was a raucous ovation, just like the one Joash received.

2 Kings 11:12

11:4 Carites This was probably a special unit of the army that was responsible for the king's safety, a kind of palace guard similar to the Kerethites and the Pelethites.

JOASH BECOMES KING

[11]Then each guard took his place with his weapons in his hand. There were guards from the south side of the Temple to the north side. They stood by the altar and the Temple and around the king. [12]Jehoiada brought out the king's son and put the crown on him and gave him a copy of the agreement. They appointed him king and poured olive oil on him. Then they clapped their hands and said, "Long live the king!"

[13]When Athaliah heard the noise of the guards and the people, she went to them at the Temple of the LORD. [14]She looked, and there was the king, standing by the pillar, as the custom was. The officers and trumpeters were standing beside him, and all the people of the land were very happy and were blowing trumpets. Then Athaliah tore her clothes and screamed, "Traitors! Traitors!"

[15]Jehoiada the priest gave orders to the commanders of a hundred men, who led the army. He said, "Surround her with soldiers and kill with a sword anyone who follows her." He commanded this because he had said, "Don't put Athaliah to death in the Temple of the LORD." [16]So they caught her when she came to the horses' entrance near the palace. There she was put to death.

[17]Then Jehoiada made an agreement between the LORD and the king and the people that they would be the LORD's special people. He also made an agreement between the king and the people. [18]All the people of the land went to the temple of Baal and tore it down, smashing the altars and idols. They also killed Mattan, the priest of Baal, in front of the altars.

Then Jehoiada the priest placed guards at the Temple of the LORD. [19]He took with him the commanders of a hundred men and the Carites, the royal bodyguards, as well as the guards and all the people of the land. Together they took the king out of the Temple of the LORD and went into the palace through the gate of the guards. Then the king sat on the royal throne. [20]So all the people of the land were very happy, and Jerusalem had peace, because Athaliah had been put to death with the sword at the palace.

[21]Joash was seven years old when he became king.

"Then Jehoiada made an agreement between the LORD and the king and the people that they would be the LORD's special people. He also made an agreement between the king and the people."
(2 Kings 11:17)

12

[1]Joash became king of Judah in Jehu's seventh year as king of Israel, and he ruled for forty years in Jerusalem. His mother's name was Zibiah, and she was from Beersheba. [2]Joash did what the LORD said was right as long as Jehoiada the priest taught him. [3]But the places where gods were worshiped were not removed; the people still made sacrifices and burned incense there.

JOASH REPAIRS THE TEMPLE

[4]Joash said to the priests, "Take all the money brought as offerings to the Temple of the LORD. This includes the money each person owes in taxes and the money each person promises or brings freely to the LORD. [5]Each priest will take the money from the people he serves. Then the priests must repair any damage they find in the Temple."

GIVING
Is the amount you give to God a personal decision? (12:4–5)

[6]But by the twenty-third year Joash was king, the priests still had not repaired the Temple. [7]So King Joash called for Jehoiada the priest and the other priests and said to them, "Why aren't you repairing the damage of the Temple? Don't take any more money from the people you serve, but hand over the money for the repair of the Temple." [8]The priests agreed not to take any more money

WHAT'S IT MEAN?

Once a year, every Israelite over the age of twenty donated a certain amount of money to be used for the Temple. Other people gave gold and silver as gifts to show how much they appreciated what the Lord had done for them. Since there was no such thing as the First National Bank of Israel, the money and other valuables were stored in the Temple.
2 Kings 12:4

from the people and not to repair the Temple themselves.

9Jehoiada the priest took a box and made a hole in the top of it. Then he put it by the altar, on the right side as the people came into the Temple of the LORD. The priests guarding the doorway put all the money brought to the Temple of the LORD into the box.

10Each time the priests saw that the box was full of money, the king's royal secretary and the high priest came. They counted the money that had been brought to the Temple of the LORD, and they put it into bags. 11Next they weighed the money and gave it to the people in charge of the work on the Temple. With it they paid the carpenters and the builders who worked on the Temple of the LORD, 12as well as the bricklayers and stonecutters. They also used the money to buy timber and cut stone to repair the damage of the Temple of the LORD. It paid for everything.

13The money brought into the Temple of the LORD was not used to make silver cups, wick trimmers, bowls, trumpets, or gold or silver vessels. 14They paid the money to the workers, who used it to repair the Temple of the LORD. 15They did not demand to know how the money was spent, because the workers were honest. 16The money from the penalty offerings and sin offerings was not brought into the Temple of the LORD, because it belonged to the priests.

JOASH SAVES JERUSALEM

17About this time Hazael king of Aram attacked Gath and captured it. Then he went to attack Jerusalem. 18Joash king of Judah took all the holy things given by his ancestors, the kings of Judah—Jehoshaphat, Jehoram, and Ahaziah. He also took his own holy things as well as the gold that was found in the treasuries of the Temple of the LORD and the gold from the palace. Joash sent all this treasure to Hazael king of Aram, who turned away from Jerusalem.

19Everything else Joash did is written in the book of the history of the kings of Judah. 20His officers made plans against him and killed him at Beth Millo on the road down to Silla. 21The officers who killed him were Jozabad son of Shimeath and Jehozabad son of Shomer. Joash was buried with his ancestors in Jerusalem, and Amaziah, his son, became king in his place.

13

JEHOAHAZ KING OF ISRAEL

1Jehoahaz son of Jehu became king over Israel in Samaria during the twenty-third year Joash son of Ahaziah was king of Judah. Jehoahaz ruled seventeen years, 2and he did what the LORD said was wrong. Jehoahaz did the same sins Jeroboam son of Nebat had done. Jeroboam had led Israel to sin, and Jehoahaz did not stop doing these same sins. 3So the LORD was angry with Israel and handed them over to Hazael king of Aram and his son Ben-Hadad for a long time.

4Then Jehoahaz begged the LORD, and the LORD listened to him. The LORD had seen the troubles of Israel; he saw how terribly the king of Aram was treating them. 5He gave Israel a man to save them, and they escaped from the Arameans. The Israelites then lived in their own homes as they had before, 6but they still did not stop doing the same sins that the family of Jeroboam had done. He had led Israel to sin, and they continued doing those sins. The Asherah idol also was left standing in Samaria.

7Nothing was left of Jehoahaz's army except fifty horsemen, ten chariots, and ten thousand foot soldiers. The king of Aram had destroyed them and made them like chaff.

8Everything else Jehoahaz did and all his victories are written in the book of the history of the kings of Israel. 9Jehoahaz died and was buried in Samaria, and his son Jehoash became king in his place.

JEHOASH KING OF ISRAEL

10Jehoash son of Jehoahaz became king of Israel in Samaria during Joash's thirty-seventh year as king of Judah. Jehoash ruled sixteen years, 11and he did what the LORD said was wrong. He did not stop doing the same sins Jeroboam son of Nebat had done. Jeroboam had led Israel to sin, and Jehoash continued to do the same thing. 12Everything else he did and all his victories, including his war against Amaziah king of Judah, are written in the book of the history of the kings of Israel. 13Jehoash died, and Jeroboam took his place on the throne. Jehoash was buried in Samaria with the kings of Israel.

THE DEATH OF ELISHA

14At this time Elisha became sick. Before he died, Jehoash king of Israel went to Elisha and cried for him. Jehoash said, "My father, my father! The chariots of Israel and their horsemen!"

15Elisha said to Jehoash, "Take a bow and arrows." So he took a bow and arrows. 16Then Elisha said to him, "Put your hand on the bow." So Jehoash put his hand on the bow. Then Elisha put his hands on the king's hands. 17Elisha said, "Open the east window." So Jehoash

opened the window. Then Elisha said, "Shoot,"
and Jehoash shot. Elisha said, "The LORD's arrow of victory over Aram! You will defeat the
Arameans at Aphek until you destroy them."
[18]Elisha said, "Take the arrows." So Jehoash
took them. Then Elisha said to him, "Strike the
ground." So Jehoash struck the ground three
times and stopped. [19]The man of God was angry with him. "You should have struck five or
six times!" Elisha said. "Then you would have
struck Aram until you had completely destroyed it. But now you will defeat it only three
times."
[20]Then Elisha died and was buried.
At that time groups of Moabites would rob
the land in the springtime. [21]Once as some Israelites were burying a man, suddenly they
saw a group of Moabites coming. The Israelites
threw the dead man into Elisha's grave. When
the man touched Elisha's bones, the man came
back to life and stood on his feet.

WAR WITH ARAM

[22]During all the days Jehoahaz was king,
Hazael king of Aram troubled Israel. [23]But the
LORD was kind to the Israelites; he had mercy
on them and helped them because of his
agreement with Abraham, Isaac, and Jacob. To
this day he has never wanted to destroy them
or reject them.
[24]When Hazael king of Aram died, his son
Ben-Hadad became king in his place. [25]During
a war Hazael had taken some cities from Jehoahaz, Jehoash's father. Now Jehoash took back
those cities from Hazael's son Ben-Hadad. He
defeated Ben-Hadad three times and took back
the cities of Israel.

AMAZIAH KING OF JUDAH

14 [1]Amaziah son of Joash became king of Judah during the second year Jehoash son of Jehoahaz was king of Israel. [2]Amaziah was
twenty-five years old when he became king,
and he ruled twenty-nine years in Jerusalem.
His mother was named Jehoaddin, and she
was from Jerusalem. [3]Amaziah did what the
LORD said was right. He did everything his father Joash had done, but he did not do as his
ancestor David had done. [4]The places where
gods were worshiped were not removed, so
the people still sacrificed and burned incense
there.
[5]As soon as Amaziah took control of the
kingdom, he executed the officers who had
murdered his father the king. [6]But he did not
put to death the children of the murderers because of the rule written in the Book of the
Teachings of Moses. The LORD had commanded: "Parents must not be put to death when
their children do wrong, and children must not
be put to death when their parents do wrong.
Each must die for his own sins."[n]
[7]In battle Amaziah killed ten thousand
Edomites in the Valley of Salt. He also took the
city of Sela. He called it Joktheel, as it is still
called today.
[8]Amaziah sent messengers to Jehoash son
of Jehoahaz, the son of Jehu, king of Israel.
They said, "Come, let's meet face to face."
[9]Then Jehoash king of Israel answered Amaziah king of Judah, "A thornbush in Lebanon
sent a message to a cedar tree in Lebanon. It
said, 'Let your daughter marry my son.' But
then a wild animal from Lebanon came by,
walking on and crushing the thornbush. [10]You
have defeated Edom, but you have become
proud. Stay at home and brag. Don't ask for
trouble, or you and Judah will be defeated."

WHAT'S IT MEAN?

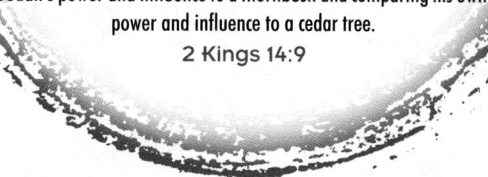

The cedar trees of Lebanon might be compared to the redwood trees of California. Some cedars grow up to one hundred feet tall, with trunks forty-five feet in diameter. Jehoash insulted Amaziah by comparing the king of Judah's power and influence to a thornbush and comparing his own power and influence to a cedar tree.

2 Kings 14:9

[11]But Amaziah would not listen, so Jehoash
king of Israel went to attack. He and Amaziah
king of Judah faced each other in battle at Beth
Shemesh in Judah. [12]Israel defeated Judah, and
every man of Judah ran away to his home. [13]At
Beth Shemesh Jehoash king of Israel captured
Amaziah king of Judah. (Amaziah was the son
of Joash, who was the son of Ahaziah.) Jehoash went up to Jerusalem and broke down the
wall of Jerusalem from the Gate of Ephraim to
the Corner Gate, which was about six hundred
feet. [14]He took all the gold and silver and all the
utensils in the Temple of the LORD, and he took

14:6 "Parents . . . sins." See Deuteronomy 24:16.

the treasuries of the palace and some hostages.
Then he returned to Samaria.
15The other acts of Jehoash and his victories, including his war against Amaziah king of
Judah, are written in the book of the history of
the kings of Israel. 16Jehoash died and was buried in Samaria with the kings of Israel, and his
son Jeroboam became king in his place.
17Amaziah son of Joash, the king of Judah,
lived fifteen years after the death of Jehoash son
of Jehoahaz, the king of Israel. 18The other
things Amaziah did are written in the book of
the history of the kings of Judah. 19The people
in Jerusalem made plans against him. So he ran
away to the town of Lachish, but they sent men
after him to Lachish and killed him. 20They
brought his body back on horses, and he was
buried with his ancestors in Jerusalem, in the
city of David.
21Then all the people of Judah made
Uzziah[n] king in place of his father Amaziah.
Uzziah was sixteen years old. 22He rebuilt the
town of Elath and made it part of Judah again
after Amaziah died.

JEROBOAM KING OF ISRAEL

23Jeroboam son of Jehoash became king of
Israel in Samaria during the fifteenth year Amaziah was king of Judah. (Amaziah was the son
of Joash.) Jeroboam ruled forty-one years,
24and he did what the LORD said was wrong.
Jeroboam son of Nebat had led Israel to sin,
and Jeroboam son of Jehoash did not stop doing the same sins. 25Jeroboam won back
Israel's border from Lebo Hamath to the Dead
Sea. This happened as the LORD, the God of
Israel, had said through his servant Jonah son
of Amittai, the prophet from Gath Hepher.
26The LORD had seen how the Israelites, both
slave and free, were suffering terribly. No one
was left who could help Israel. 27The LORD had
not said he would completely destroy Israel
from the world, so he saved the Israelites
through Jeroboam son of Jehoash.
28Everything else Jeroboam did is written
down—all his victories and how he won back
from Judah the towns of Damascus and Hamath for Israel. All this is written in the book
of the history of the kings of Israel. 29Jeroboam
died and was buried with his ancestors, the
kings of Israel. Jeroboam's son Zechariah became king in his place.

UZZIAH KING OF JUDAH

15
1Uzziah son of Amaziah became king of
Judah during Jeroboam's twenty-seventh year
as king of Israel. 2Uzziah was sixteen years old
when he became king, and he ruled fifty-two
years in Jerusalem. His mother was named
Jecoliah, and she was from Jerusalem. 3He did what the LORD
said was right, just as his father Amaziah had done. 4But
the places where gods were
worshiped were not removed,
so the people still made sacrifices and burned incense
there.
5The LORD struck Uzziah with a skin disease, which he had until the day he died. So
he had to live in a separate house. Jotham, the
king's son, was in charge of the palace, and he
governed the people of the land.
6All the other things Uzziah did are written
in the book of the history of the kings of Judah. 7Uzziah died and was buried near his ancestors in Jerusalem, and his son Jotham
became king in his place.

LEADERSHIP

Does God hold leaders accountable for how they lead? (15:3–5)

ZECHARIAH KING OF ISRAEL

8Zechariah son of Jeroboam was king over
Israel in Samaria. He ruled for six months during Uzziah's[n] thirty-eighth year as king of Judah. 9Zechariah did what the LORD said was
wrong, just as his ancestors had done. Jeroboam son of Nebat had led the people of Israel
to sin, and Zechariah did not stop doing the
same sins.
10Shallum son of Jabesh made plans against
Zechariah and killed him in front of the people.
Then Shallum became king in his place. 11The
other acts of Zechariah are written in the book
of the history of the kings of Israel. 12The LORD

WHAT'S IT MEAN?

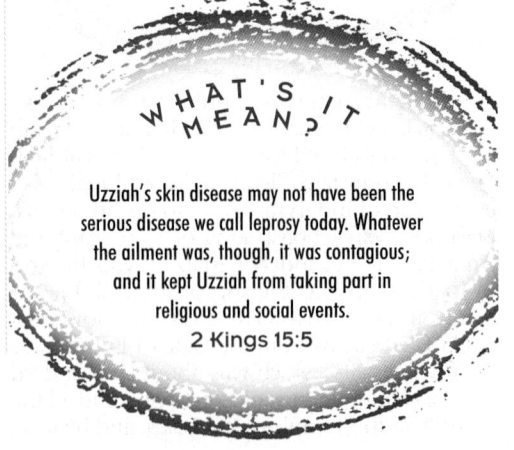

Uzziah's skin disease may not have been the serious disease we call leprosy today. Whatever the ailment was, though, it was contagious; and it kept Uzziah from taking part in religious and social events.
2 Kings 15:5

14:21; 15:8 Uzziah Also called Azariah.

had told Jehu: "Your sons down to your great-
great-grandchildren will be kings of Israel," and
the LORD's word came true.

SHALLUM KING OF ISRAEL

13 Shallum son of Jabesh became king dur-
ing Uzziah's thirty-ninth year as king of Judah.
Shallum ruled for a month in Samaria. 14 Then
Menahem son of Gadi came up from Tirzah to
Samaria and attacked Shallum son of Jabesh in
Samaria. He killed him and became king in
Shallum's place.
15 The other acts of Shallum and his secret
plans are written in the book of the history of
the kings of Israel.

MENAHEM KING OF ISRAEL

16 Menahem started out from Tirzah and attacked Tiphsah, destroying the city and the
area nearby. This was because the people had
refused to open the city gate for him. He defeated them and ripped open all their pregnant
women.

WHAT'S IT MEAN?

Tirzah had been the capital of Israel until King Omri moved the capital to Samaria. If you have a trip scheduled to Tiphsah, you'd better cancel it. No one knows where the city is today.

2 Kings 15:14–16

17 Menahem son of Gadi became king over
Israel during Uzziah's thirty-ninth year as king
of Judah. Menahem ruled ten years in Samaria,
18 and he did what the LORD said was wrong.
Jeroboam son of Nebat had led Israel to sin,
and all the time Menahem was king, he did not
stop doing the same sins.
19 Pul king of Assyria came to attack the
land. Menahem gave him about seventy-four
thousand pounds of silver so Pul would support him and make his hold on the kingdom
stronger. 20 Menahem taxed Israel to pay about
one and one-fourth pounds of silver to each
soldier of the king of Assyria. So the king left
and did not stay in the land.
21 Everything else Menahem did is written in
the book of the history of the kings of Israel.
22 Then Menahem died, and his son Pekahiah
became king in his place.

PEKAHIAH KING OF ISRAEL

23 Pekahiah son of Menahem became king
over Israel in Samaria during Uzziah's[n] fiftieth
year as king of Judah. Pekahiah ruled two
years, 24 and he did what the LORD said was
wrong. Jeroboam son of Nebat had led Israel
to sin, and Pekahiah did not stop doing the
same sins.
25 Pekah son of Remaliah was one of Pekahiah's captains, and he made plans against
Pekahiah. He took fifty men of Gilead with him
and killed Pekahiah, as well as Argob and
Arieh, in the palace at Samaria. Then Pekah
became king in Pekahiah's place.
26 Everything else Pekahiah did is written in
the book of the history of the kings of Israel.

PEKAH KING OF ISRAEL

27 Pekah son of Remaliah became king over
Israel in Samaria during Uzziah's[n] fifty-second
year as king of Judah. Pekah ruled twenty years,
28 and he did what the LORD said was wrong.
Jeroboam son of Nebat had led Israel to sin,
and Pekah did not stop doing the same sins.
29 Tiglath-Pileser[n] was king of Assyria. He
attacked while Pekah was king of Israel, capturing the cities of Ijon, Abel Beth Maacah, Janoah, Kedesh, and Hazor. He also captured
Gilead and Galilee and all the land of Naphtali
and carried the people away to Assyria. 30 Then
Hoshea son of Elah made plans against Pekah
son of Remaliah and attacked and killed
him. Then Hoshea became king in Pekah's
place during the twentieth year Jotham son of
Uzziah was king.
31 Everything else Pekah did is written in the
book of the history of the kings of Israel.

JOTHAM KING OF JUDAH

32 Jotham son of Uzziah became king of
Judah during the second year Pekah son of
Remaliah was king of Israel. 33 Jotham was
twenty-five years old when he became king,
and he ruled sixteen years in Jerusalem. His
mother's name was Jerusha daughter of Zadok.
34 Jotham did what the LORD said was right, just
as his father Uzziah had done. 35 But the places
where gods were worshiped were not removed, and the people still made sacrifices and
burned incense there. Jotham rebuilt the Upper
Gate of the Temple of the LORD.

15:23, 27 Uzziah Also called Azariah. **15:29 Tiglath-Pileser** Also called Pul.

36 The other things Jotham did while he was king are written in the book of the history of the kings of Judah. 37 At that time the LORD began to send Rezin king of Aram and Pekah son of Remaliah against Judah. 38 Jotham died and was buried with his ancestors in Jerusalem, the city of David, his ancestor. Then Jotham's son Ahaz became king in his place.

AHAZ KING OF JUDAH

16 1 Ahaz was the son of Jotham king of Judah. Ahaz became king of Judah in the seventeenth year Pekah son of Remaliah was king of Israel. 2 Ahaz was twenty years old when he became king, and he ruled sixteen years in Jerusalem. Unlike his ancestor David, he did not do what the LORD his God said was right. 3 Ahaz did the same things the kings of Israel had done. He even made his son pass through fire. He did the same hateful sins as the nations had done whom the LORD had forced out of the land ahead of the Israelites. 4 Ahaz offered sacrifices and burned incense at the places where gods were worshiped, on the hills, and under every green tree.

5 Rezin king of Aram and Pekah son of Remaliah, the king of Israel, came up to attack Jerusalem. They surrounded Ahaz but could not defeat him. 6 At that time Rezin king of Aram took back the city of Elath for Aram, and he forced out all the people of Judah. Then Edomites moved into Elath, and they still live there today.

7 Ahaz sent messengers to Tiglath-Pileser king of Assyria, saying, "I am your servant and your friend. Come and save me from the king of Aram and the king of Israel, who are attacking me." 8 Ahaz took the silver and gold that was in the Temple of the LORD and in the treasuries of the palace, and he sent these as a gift to the king of Assyria. 9 So the king of Assyria listened to Ahaz. He attacked Damascus and captured it and sent all its people away to Kir. And he killed Rezin.

10 Then King Ahaz went to Damascus to meet Tiglath-Pileser king of Assyria. Ahaz saw an altar at Damascus, and he sent plans and a pattern of this altar to Uriah the priest. 11 So Uriah the priest built an altar, just like the plans King Ahaz had sent him from Damascus. Uriah finished the altar before King Ahaz came back from Damascus. 12 When the king arrived from Damascus, he saw the altar and went near and offered sacrifices on it. 13 He burned his burnt offerings and grain offerings and poured out his drink offering. He also sprinkled the blood of his fellowship offerings on the altar.

14 Ahaz moved the bronze altar that was before the LORD at the front of the Temple. It was between Ahaz's altar and the Temple of the LORD, but he put it on the north side of his altar. 15 King Ahaz commanded Uriah the priest, "On the large altar burn the morning burnt offering, the evening grain offering, the king's burnt offering and grain offering, and the whole burnt offering, the grain offering, and the drink offering for all the people of the land. Sprinkle on the altar all the blood of the burnt offering and of the sacrifice. But I will use the bronze altar to ask questions of God." 16 So Uriah the priest did everything as King Ahaz commanded him.

17 Then King Ahaz took off the side panels from the bases and removed the washing bowls from the top of the bases. He also took the large bowl, which was called the Sea, off the bronze bulls that held it up, and he put it on a stone base. 18 Ahaz took away the platform for the royal throne, which had been built at the Temple of the LORD. He also took away the outside entrance for the king. He did these things because of the king of Assyria.

19 The other things Ahaz did as king are written in the book of the history of the kings of Judah. 20 Ahaz died and was buried with his ancestors in Jerusalem, and Ahaz's son Hezekiah became king in his place.

HOSHEA, LAST KING OF ISRAEL

17 1 Hoshea son of Elah became king over Israel during Ahaz's twelfth year as king of Judah. Hoshea ruled in Samaria nine years. 2 He did what the LORD said was wrong, but he was not as bad as the kings of Israel who had ruled before him.

3 Shalmaneser king of Assyria came to attack Hoshea. Hoshea had been Shalmaneser's servant and had made the payments to Shalmaneser that he had demanded. 4 But the king of Assyria found out that Hoshea had made plans against him by sending messengers to So, the king of Egypt. Hoshea had also stopped giving Shalmaneser the payments, which he had paid every year in the past. For that, the king put Hoshea in prison. 5 Then the king of Assyria came and attacked all the land of Israel. He surrounded Samaria and attacked it for three years. 6 He defeated Samaria in the ninth year Hoshea was king, and he took the Israelites away to Assyria. He settled them in Halah, in Gozan on the Habor River, and in the cities of the Medes.

ISRAELITES PUNISHED FOR SIN

7 All these things happened because the Israelites had sinned against the LORD their God.

WHAT'S IT MEAN?

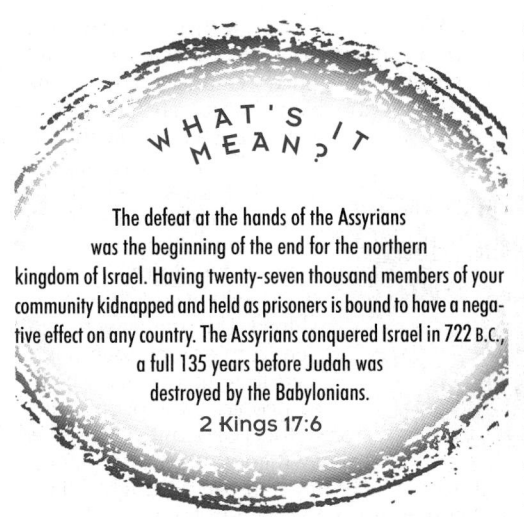

The defeat at the hands of the Assyrians was the beginning of the end for the northern kingdom of Israel. Having twenty-seven thousand members of your community kidnapped and held as prisoners is bound to have a negative effect on any country. The Assyrians conquered Israel in 722 B.C., a full 135 years before Judah was destroyed by the Babylonians.

2 Kings 17:6

He had brought them out of Egypt and had rescued them from the power of the king of Egypt, but the Israelites had honored other
gods. 8They lived like the nations the LORD had forced out of the land ahead of them. They lived as their evil kings had shown them, 9se-
cretly sinning against the LORD their God. They built places to worship gods in all their cities, from the watchtower to the strong, walled city.
10They put up stone pillars to gods and Asherah idols on every high hill and under every
green tree. 11The Israelites burned incense everywhere gods were worshiped, just as the nations who lived there before them had done, whom the LORD had forced out of the land. The Israelites did wicked things that made the
LORD angry. 12They served idols when the LORD had said, "You must not do this."
13The LORD used every prophet and seer to warn Israel and Judah. He said, "Stop your evil ways and obey my commands and laws. Follow all the teachings that I commanded your ancestors, the teachings that I gave you through my servants the prophets."

14But the people would not listen. They were stubborn, just as their ancestors had been who did not believe in the LORD their God.
15They rejected the LORD's laws and the agreement he had made with their ancestors. And they refused to listen to his warnings. They worshiped useless idols and became useless themselves. They did what the nations around them did, which the LORD had warned them not to do.

16The people rejected all the commands of the LORD their God. They molded statues of two calves, and they made an Asherah idol. They worshiped all the stars of the sky and
served Baal. 17They made their sons and daughters pass through fire and tried to find out the future by magic and witchcraft. They always chose to do what the LORD said was wrong, which
made him angry. 18Because he was very angry with the people of Israel, he removed them from his presence. Only the tribe of Judah was left.

OCCULT

How does God feel about occult practices? (17:17–18)

JUDAH IS ALSO GUILTY

19But even Judah did not obey the commands of the LORD their God. They did what
the Israelites had done, 20so the LORD rejected all the people of Israel. He punished them and let others destroy them; he threw them out of
his presence. 21When the LORD separated them from the family of David, the Israelites made Jeroboam son of Nebat their king. Jeroboam led the Israelites away from the LORD and led
them to sin greatly. 22So they continued to do all the sins Jeroboam did. They did not stop
doing these sins 23until the LORD removed the Israelites from his presence, just as he had said through all his servants the prophets. So the Israelites were taken out of their land to Assyria, and they have been there to this day.

WHAT'S IT MEAN?

Why bring in foreigners to replace the Israelites? To keep the Israelites from uniting and rebelling against Assyria.

2 Kings 17:24

THE BEGINNING OF THE SAMARITAN PEOPLE

24The king of Assyria brought people from Babylon, Cuthah, Avva, Hamath, and Sepharvaim and put them in the cities of Samaria to replace the Israelites. These people took over
Samaria and lived in the cities. 25At first they did not worship the LORD, so he sent lions
among them which killed some of them. 26The king of Assyria was told, "You sent foreigners into the cities of Samaria who do not know the law of the god of the land. This is why he has sent lions among them. The lions are killing

them because they don't know what the god
wants."
27 Then the king of Assyria commanded,
"Send back one of the priests you took away.
Let him live there and teach the
people what the god wants."
28 So one of the priests who
had been carried away from
Samaria returned to live in
Bethel. And he taught the
people how to honor the
LORD.
29 But each nation made
gods of its own and put them
in the cities where they lived
and in the temples where gods
were worshiped. These temples had been
built by the Samaritans. 30 The people from Babylon made Succoth Benoth their god. The people from Cuthah worshiped Nergal. The people
of Hamath worshiped Ashima. 31 The Avvites
worshiped Nibhaz and Tartak. The Sepharvites
burned their children in the fire,
sacrificing them to Adrammelech and Anammelech, the
gods of Sepharvaim. 32 They
also honored the LORD, but
they chose priests for the
places where gods were worshiped. The priests were chosen from among themselves,
and they made sacrifices for
the people. 33 The people honored the LORD but also served
their own gods, just as the nations
did from which they had been brought. 34 Even
today they do as they did in the past. They do
not worship the LORD nor obey his rules and
commands. They do not obey the teachings or
the commands of the LORD, which he gave to
the children of Jacob, whom he had named Israel. 35 The LORD had made an agreement with
them and had commanded them, "Do not
honor other gods. Do not bow down to them
or worship them or offer sacrifices to them.
36 Worship the LORD who brought you up out
of the land of Egypt with great power and
strength. Bow down to him and offer sacrifices
to him. 37 Always obey the rules, orders, teachings, and commands he wrote for you. Do not
honor other gods. 38 Do not forget the agreement I made with you, and do not honor other
gods. 39 Instead worship the LORD your God,
who will save you from all your enemies."
40 But the Israelites did not listen. They kept
on doing the same things they had done before.
41 So these nations honored the LORD but also
worshiped their idols, and their children and
grandchildren still do as their ancestors did.

"Do not honor other gods. Do not bow down to them or worship them or offer sacrifices to them."
(2 Kings 17:35b)

On the Edge

Do not honor other gods. Do not bow down to them or worship them or offer sacrifices to them. Worship the LORD who brought you up out of the land of Egypt with great power and strength. Bow down to him and offer sacrifices to him. Always obey the rules, orders, teachings, and commands he wrote for you. Do not honor other gods. Do not forget the agreement I made with you, and do not honor other gods (2 Kin. 17:35b–38).

God has revealed himself in mighty ways because he wants us to worship only him. He wants us to know that he is all-powerful and supremely wise. There is no one else who can even compare to God. No one else deserves our prayer or our praise. As the One who made us and saved us, only God is worthy of a life completely devoted to him. He is worshiped when we live our daily lives for his glory. How you spoke to your parents at breakfast, the way you acted at school, what you watch on TV—it all matters when you decide to live a life that worships God.

Don't let your friends trick you into believing that what they think counts—what God thinks matters most. Has your life been an act of worship today?

SEE FOR YOURSELF:
Ex. 20:5; Josh. 4:24; Ps. 115:12–13; Joel 2:32

HEZEKIAH KING OF JUDAH

18
1 Hezekiah son of Ahaz king of Judah became king during the third year Hoshea son of
Elah was king of Israel. 2 Hezekiah was twenty-
five years old when he became king, and he
ruled twenty-nine years in Jerusalem. His
mother's name was Abijah daughter of Zechariah. 3 Hezekiah did what the LORD said was
right, just as his ancestor David had done. 4 He
removed the places where gods were worshiped. He smashed the stone pillars and cut
down the Asherah idols. Also the Israelites
had been burning incense to Nehushtan, the
bronze snake Moses had made. But Hezekiah
broke it into pieces.

5Hezekiah trusted in the LORD, the God of Israel. There was no one like him among all the kings of Judah, either before him or after him. 6Hezekiah was loyal to the LORD and did not stop following him; he obeyed the commands the LORD had given Moses. 7And the LORD was with Hezekiah, so he had success in everything he did. He turned against the king of Assyria and stopped serving him. 8Hezekiah defeated the Philistines all the way to Gaza and its borders, including the watchtowers and the strong, walled cities.

THE ASSYRIANS CAPTURE SAMARIA

9Shalmaneser king of Assyria surrounded Samaria and attacked it in the fourth year Hezekiah was king. This was the seventh year Hoshea son of Elah was king of Israel. 10After three years the Assyrians captured Samaria. This was in the sixth year Hezekiah was king, which was Hoshea's ninth year as king of Israel. 11The king of Assyria took the Israelites away to Assyria and settled them in Halah, in Gozan on the Habor River, and in the cities of the Medes. 12This happened because they did not obey the LORD their God. They broke his agreement and did not obey all that Moses, the LORD's servant, had commanded. They would not listen to the commands or do them.

ASSYRIA ATTACKS JUDAH

13During Hezekiah's fourteenth year as king, Sennacherib king of Assyria attacked all the strong, walled cities of Judah and captured them. 14Then Hezekiah king of Judah sent a message to the king of Assyria at Lachish. He said, "I have done wrong. Leave me alone, and I will pay anything you ask." So the king of Assyria made Hezekiah pay about twenty-two thousand pounds of silver and two thousand pounds of gold. 15Hezekiah gave him all the silver that was in the Temple of the LORD and in the palace treasuries. 16Hezekiah stripped all the gold that covered the doors and doorposts of the Temple of the LORD. Hezekiah had put gold on these doors himself, but he gave it all to the king of Assyria.

17The king of Assyria sent out his supreme commander, his chief officer, and his field commander. They went with a large army from Lachish to King Hezekiah in Jerusalem. When they came near the waterway from the upper pool on the road where people do their laundry, they stopped. 18They called for the king, so the king sent Eliakim, Shebna, and Joah out to meet them. Eliakim son of Hilkiah was the palace manager, Shebna was the royal secretary, and Joah son of Asaph was the recorder.

19The field commander said to them, "Tell Hezekiah this:

" 'The great king, the king of Assyria, says: What can you trust in now? 20You say you have battle plans and power for war, but your words mean nothing. Whom are you trusting for help so that you turn against me? 21Look, you are depending on Egypt to help you, but Egypt is like a splintered walking stick. If you lean on it for help, it will stab your hand and hurt you. The king of Egypt will hurt all those who depend on him. 22You might say, "We are depending on the LORD our God," but Hezekiah destroyed the LORD's altars and the places of worship. Hezekiah told Judah and Jerusalem, "You must worship only at this one altar in Jerusalem."

23" 'Now make an agreement with my master, the king of Assyria: I will give you two thousand horses if you can find enough men to ride them. 24You cannot defeat one of my master's least important officers, so why do you depend on Egypt to give you chariots and horsemen? 25I have not come to attack and destroy this place without an order from the LORD. The LORD himself told me to come to this country and destroy it.' "

26Then Eliakim son of Hilkiah, Shebna, and Joah said to the field commander, "Please speak to us in the Aramaic language. We understand it. Don't speak to us in Hebrew, because the people on the city wall can hear you."

27"No," the commander said, "my master did not send me to tell these things only to you and your king. He sent me to speak also to those people sitting on the wall who will have to eat their own dung and drink their own urine like you."

WHAT'S IT MEAN?

Sennacherib, the king of Assyria, was so proud of his victory in Lachish that he had a scene of the battle recreated on one of the walls of his palace in Nineveh. The scene showed his Assyrian soldiers attacking with battering rams and other weapons while the inhabitants of Lachish tried to defend themselves with bows and arrows.

2 Kings 18:14

28Then the commander stood and shouted
loudly in the Hebrew language, "Listen to what
the great king, the king of Assyria, says! 29The
king says you should not let Hezekiah fool you,
because he can't save you from my power.
30Don't let Hezekiah talk you into trusting the
LORD by saying, 'The LORD will surely save us.
This city won't be handed over to the king of
Assyria.'

WHAT'S IT MEAN?

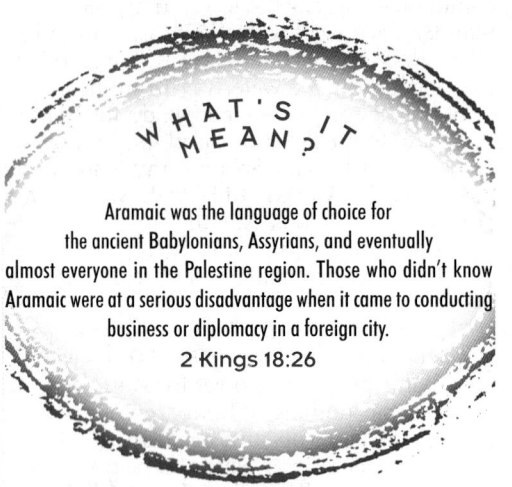

Aramaic was the language of choice for the ancient Babylonians, Assyrians, and eventually almost everyone in the Palestine region. Those who didn't know Aramaic were at a serious disadvantage when it came to conducting business or diplomacy in a foreign city.

2 Kings 18:26

31"Don't listen to Hezekiah. The king of Assyria says, 'Make peace with me, and come out
of the city to me. Then everyone will be free to
eat the fruit from his own grapevine and fig
tree and to drink water from his own well.
32After that I will come and take you to a land
like your own—a land with grain and new
wine, bread and vineyards, olives, and honey.
Choose to live and not to die!'

"Don't listen to Hezekiah. He is fooling you
when he says, 'The LORD will save us.' 33Has a
god of any other nation saved his people from
the power of the king of Assyria? 34Where are
the gods of Hamath and Arpad? Where are the
gods of Sepharvaim, Hena, and Ivvah? They
did not save Samaria from my power. 35Not
one of all the gods of these countries has saved
his people from me. Neither can the LORD save
Jerusalem from my power."

36The people were silent. They didn't answer the commander at all, because King Hezekiah had ordered, "Don't answer him."

37Then Eliakim, Shebna, and Joah tore their
clothes to show how upset they were. (Eliakim
son of Hilkiah was the palace manager, Shebna
was the royal secretary, and Joah son of Asaph
was the recorder.) The three men went to Hezekiah and told him what the field commander
had said.

JERUSALEM WILL BE SAVED

19 1When King Hezekiah heard the message,
he tore his clothes and put on rough cloth to
show how sad he was. Then he went into the
Temple of the LORD. 2Hezekiah sent Eliakim,
the palace manager, and Shebna, the royal secretary, and the older priests to Isaiah. They
were all wearing rough cloth when they came
to Isaiah the prophet, the son of Amoz. 3They
told Isaiah, "This is what Hezekiah says: Today
is a day of sorrow and punishment and disgrace, as when a child should be born, but the
mother is not strong enough to give birth to it.
4The king of Assyria sent his field commander
to make fun of the living God. Maybe the LORD
your God will hear what the commander said
and will punish him for it. So pray for the few
of us who are left alive."

5When Hezekiah's officers came to Isaiah,
6he said to them, "Tell your master this: The
LORD says, 'Don't be afraid of what you have
heard. Don't be frightened by the words the
servants of the king of Assyria have spoken
against me. 7Listen! I am going to put a spirit in
the king of Assyria. He will hear a report that
will make him return to his own country, and I
will cause him to die by the sword there.' "

8The field commander heard that the king
of Assyria had left Lachish. When he went
back, he found the king fighting against the city
of Libnah.

9The king received a report that Tirhakah,
the Cushite king of Egypt, was coming to attack
him. When the king of Assyria heard this, he
sent messengers to Hezekiah, saying, 10"Tell
Hezekiah king of Judah: Don't be fooled by the
god you trust. Don't believe him when he says
Jerusalem will not be handed over to the king
of Assyria. 11You have heard what the kings of
Assyria have done. They have completely defeated every country, so do not think you will
be saved. 12Did the gods of those people save
them? My ancestors destroyed them, defeating
the cities of Gozan, Haran, and Rezeph, and the
people of Eden living in Tel Assar. 13Where are
the kings of Hamath and Arpad? Where are the
kings of Sepharvaim, Hena, and Ivvah?"

HEZEKIAH PRAYS TO THE LORD

HOPE
What should you do when the situation is hopeless? (19:14–19)

14When Hezekiah received
the letter from the messengers
and read it, he went up to the
Temple of the LORD. He spread
the letter out before the LORD
15and prayed to the LORD:
"LORD, God of Israel, whose
throne is between the gold creatures with

wings, only you are God of all the kingdoms of
the earth. You made the heavens and the earth.
16Hear, LORD, and listen. Open your eyes, LORD,
and see. Listen to the words Sennacherib has
said to insult the living God. 17It is true, LORD,
that the kings of Assyria have destroyed these
countries and their lands. 18They have thrown
the gods of these nations into the fire, but they
were only wood and rock statues that people
made. So the kings have destroyed them.
19Now, LORD our God, save us from the king's
power so that all the kingdoms of the earth
will know that you, LORD, are the only God."

WHAT'S IT MEAN?

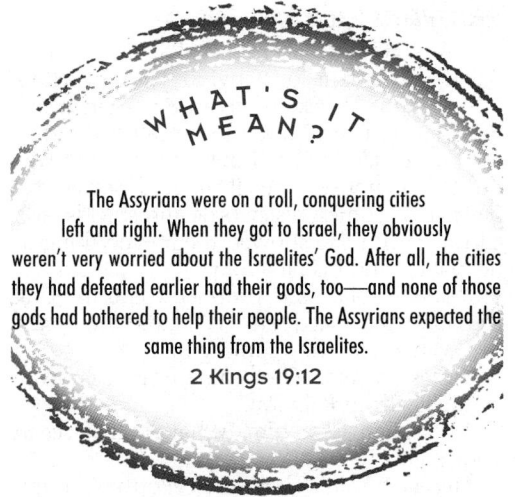

The Assyrians were on a roll, conquering cities left and right. When they got to Israel, they obviously weren't very worried about the Israelites' God. After all, the cities they had defeated earlier had their gods, too—and none of those gods had bothered to help their people. The Assyrians expected the same thing from the Israelites.

2 Kings 19:12

GOD ANSWERS HEZEKIAH

20Then Isaiah son of Amoz sent a message
to Hezekiah that said, "This is what the LORD,
the God of Israel, says: I have heard your
prayer to me about Sennacherib king of Assyria. 21This is what the LORD has said against
Sennacherib:

'The people of Jerusalem
hate you and make fun of you.
The people of Jerusalem
laugh at you as you run away.
22You have insulted me and spoken against me;
you have raised your voice against me.
You have a proud look on your face,
which is against me, the Holy One of Israel.
23You have sent your messengers to insult the Lord.
You have said, "With my many chariots
I have gone to the tops of the mountains,
to the highest mountains of Lebanon.
I have cut down its tallest cedars
and its best pine trees.
I have gone to its farthest places
and to its best forests.
24I have dug wells in foreign countries
and drunk water there.
By the soles of my feet,
I have dried up all the rivers of Egypt."

25" 'King of Assyria, surely you have heard.
Long ago I, the LORD, planned these things.
Long ago I designed them,
and now I have made them happen.
I allowed you to turn those strong, walled cities
into piles of rocks.
26The people in those cities were weak;
they were frightened and put to shame.
They were like grass in the field,
like tender, young grass,
like grass on the housetop
that is burned by the wind before it can grow.

27" 'I know when you rest,
when you come and go,
and how you rage against me.
28Because you rage against me,
and because I have heard your proud words,
I will put my hook in your nose
and my bit in your mouth.
Then I will force you to leave my country
the same way you came.'

PRIDE

What does God think of our pride? (19:27–28)

29"Then the LORD said, 'Hezekiah, I will give
you this sign:
This year you will eat the grain that grows wild,
and the second year you will eat what grows wild from that.
But in the third year, plant grain and harvest it.
Plant vineyards and eat their fruit.
30Some of the people in the family of Judah will escape.
Like plants that take root,
they will grow strong and have many children.
31A few people will come out of Jerusalem alive;
a few from Mount Zion will live.
The strong love of the LORD All-Powerful
will make this happen.'

32“So this is what the LORD says about the king of Assyria:

'He will not enter this city
    or even shoot an arrow here.
He will not fight against it with shields
    or build a ramp to attack the city walls.
33He will return to his country the same
        way he came,
    and he will not enter this city,'
    says the LORD.
34'I will defend and save this city
    for my sake and for the sake of David,
        my servant.' ”

35That night the angel of the LORD went out and killed one hundred eighty-five thousand men in the Assyrian camp. When the people got up early the next morning, they saw all the dead bodies. 36So Sennacherib king of Assyria left and went back to Nineveh and stayed there.

37One day as Sennacherib was worshiping in the temple of his god Nisroch, his sons Adrammelech and Sharezer killed him with a sword. Then they escaped to the land of Ararat. So Sennacherib's son Esarhaddon became king of Assyria.

HEZEKIAH'S ILLNESS

20 1At that time Hezekiah became so sick he almost died. The prophet Isaiah son of Amoz went to see him and told him, “This is what the LORD says: Make arrangements because you are not going to live, but die.”

2Hezekiah turned toward the wall and prayed to the LORD, 3“LORD, please remember that I have always obeyed you. I have given myself completely to you and have done what you said was right.” Then Hezekiah cried loudly.

4Before Isaiah had left the middle courtyard, the LORD spoke his word to Isaiah: 5“Go back and tell Hezekiah, the leader of my people: 'This is what the LORD, the God of your ancestor David, says: I have heard your prayer and seen your tears, so I will heal you. Three days from now you will go up to the Temple of the LORD. 6I will add fifteen years to your life. I will save you and this city from the king of Assyria; I will protect the city for my sake and for the sake of my servant David.' ”

> **GOD**
> How does God deal with his people? (20:4–6)

7Then Isaiah said, “Make a paste from figs.” So they made it and put it on Hezekiah's boil, and he got well.

8Hezekiah had asked Isaiah, “What will be the sign that the LORD will heal me and that I will go up to the Temple of the LORD on the third day?”

9Isaiah said, “The LORD will do what he says. This is the sign from the LORD to show you: Do you want the shadow to go forward ten steps or back ten steps?”

10Hezekiah answered, “It's easy for the shadow to go forward ten steps. Instead, let it go back ten steps.”

11Then Isaiah the prophet called to the LORD, and the LORD brought the shadow ten steps back up the stairway of Ahaz that it had gone down.

MESSENGERS FROM BABYLON

12At that time Merodach-Baladan son of Baladan was king of Babylon. He sent letters and a gift to Hezekiah, because he had heard that Hezekiah was sick. 13Hezekiah listened to the messengers, so he showed them what was in his storehouses: the silver, gold, spices, expensive perfumes, his swords and shields, and all his wealth. He showed them everything in his palace and his kingdom.

14Then Isaiah the prophet went to King Hezekiah and asked him, “What did these men say? Where did they come from?”

Hezekiah said, “They came from a faraway country—from Babylon.”

15So Isaiah asked him, “What did they see in your palace?”

Hezekiah said, “They saw everything in my palace. I showed them all my wealth.”

16Then Isaiah said to Hezekiah, “Listen to the words of the LORD: 17'In the future everything in your palace and everything your ancestors have stored up until this day will be taken away to Babylon. Nothing will be left,' says the LORD. 18'Some of your own children, those who will be born to you, will be taken away. And they will become servants in the palace of the king of Babylon.' ”

19Hezekiah told Isaiah, “These words from the LORD are good.” He said this because he thought, “There will be peace and security in my lifetime.”

20Everything else Hezekiah did—all his victories, his work on the pool, his work on the tunnel to bring water into the city—is written in the book of the history of the kings of Judah. 21Then Hezekiah died, and his son Manasseh became king in his place.

MANASSEH KING OF JUDAH

21 1Manasseh was twelve years old when he became king, and he was king fifty-five years in Jerusalem. His mother's name was Hephzibah.

CALEB made a difference

Anyone making a list of people who have successfully resisted peer pressure would have to include Caleb. He served on a special twelve-man unit sent into the Promised Land by Moses to spy and bring back a report. When the unit returned, they had a unanimous report; but they were seriously divided in their recommendations. They all agreed that the land was fertile, wonderful, and settled by powerful peoples. Ten of the spies concluded the invasion should be called off immediately. The enemy was simply too powerful to defeat. Caleb offered a minority opinion:

> "We should certainly go up and take the land for ourselves. We can certainly do it" (Num. 13:30b).

Cutting Edge

Short term, majorities often get their way. The people of Israel rejected Caleb and Joshua's confidence. They accepted the opinion of the ten. Then they discovered that God's plan included Caleb's perspective. The people's lack of trust led directly to forty years of wilderness wandering. Because he spoke the truth under intense pressure, Caleb was rewarded with one of only two permissions to enter the Promised Land given to his generation. From their peer group only Joshua and Caleb crossed the Jordan. The rest died in the desert.

Although they were right and were rewarded for their consistency, Caleb and Joshua shared forty years in the desert with everyone else. Even that disappointment didn't wear Caleb down. When he did receive his portion in the Promised Land (at age eighty-five!), he claimed to be fit, able, and trusting in God as he had been as a young man.

YOU can, too!

One of the important lessons from Caleb's life has to do with the purpose of standing alone. You can probably think of several people in your Life who are willing to stand alone for clothing styles, haircuts, and negative attitudes. Caleb's purpose wasn't to stand alone; it was to stand with God. Because Caleb wanted God's way, any other way didn't have much appeal to him.

Trusting in God and living for him will create minority situations. Taking God seriously in your life will quickly show you where the majority stands. Like Caleb's, your words may not seem to make a difference to those around you. But God hears. And eventually you will find that standing with God does make a difference!

Want to know more? Read about Caleb's adventures and his faithful attitude in Numbers 13 and 14 and in Joshua 14 and 15.

GIDEON made a difference

You can learn a lot from watching kids. Some sit in their playpens and randomly handle the blocks and toys around them. Others immediately try to build a skyscraper. Those are the resourceful ones. They grow up to be natural problem solvers. Gideon was just such a kid. God made good use of Gideon's skills when he called the boy to be a judge of Israel.

The Jewish people lived under crushing oppression by the Midianites. God had allowed it because Israel had ignored their unique role as God's people. But they had been calling out to God for relief. Meanwhile, Gideon was busy providing food for his family by using a winepress to thresh his wheat ("to keep the wheat from the Midianites," Judg. 6:11). This was a little like hiding a garden in a bathtub. It worked.

God called Gideon to lead the rebellion against Midian. But God used Gideon's creativity to emphasize who was behind the astounding victory. Gideon's band of three hundred—each armed with a clay jar, a torch, and a trumpet—routed an army of over one hundred and twenty thousand. God made a big difference! And Gideon had the wonderful honor of participating in God's plan.

Cutting Edge

YOU can, too! You may have some unusual skills, or you may be given an unusual opportunity to use what may seem like ordinary skills. Remember that God is behind the events of life. God gives us what we need; then he invites us to use it in his service. When you consider and pray about what God might want to do in your Life, remember this: God's plan will always include tasks that you will not be able to accomplish without his help. Making a difference isn't just about what you can do; it's even more about what God can do with you, in you, and through you!

Want to know more? Read about Gideon in Judges 6—8. He is also listed in the Hall of Faith Hebrews 11:32.

SAMSON made a difference

Samson never wore an *S* on his chest, but he was probably one of the few men who could claim the title of *superman*. His physical prowess astonished both friends and enemies. In battle, Samson proved lethal. There was little question that Samson had the basic qualifications to be a champion for his people. God had promised to give Samson unique gifts. He was designed with a special task in mind. Samson made a difference, all right, but far less than his potential promised.

Unfortunately, Samson made at least two errors in judgment early in his life, and they cost him dearly. He never learned to control the connection between his eyes and his heart. He failed to see the dangers in his relationship with Delilah. Not until he lost his eyes did he finally see the folly of much of his life. He also did not acknowledge the source of his amazing strength or take seriously the responsibilities that came with it. Though his long hair was a reminder of the source of his strength, Samson lost sight of God's presence in his life. His hair became his strength. He thought he was revealing his secret to Delilah; but he was actually revealing his failure. Once his hair was cut, Samson was faced with his true weaknesses.

Cutting Edge

Samson never regained his sight, but he learned to see the truth. His hair did grow back, but it was God to whom he turned for his final strength. Samson learned from his losses, but late. He represents so many other lives that might have made a big difference, but fell short. Others can avoid Samson's errors and gain insight from his lessons. **YOU can, too!**

youthful mistakes are part of the learning cycle. Hopefully, we learn from them. Fortunately, few of them prove to be fatal. But most of us could benefit from paying closer attention to our youthful lessons. We don't have to repeat the mistakes of others. When we see others receive painful and sometimes permanent consequences from their behaviors, we must resist the thought that such results cannot happen to us.

The more we seek to learn from our own mistakes, as well as from others' mistakes, the more we will be able to make a difference with our lives. Continually acknowledge God for your strengths and ask for his help with your mistakes.

Want to know more? Read about Samson's life in Judges 13—16.

RUTH made a difference

Moab and Israel were neighbors and enemies. They shared a history of conflicts. But hardship and famine sometimes change attitudes; and during an extreme food shortage in Israel, Naomi, her husband, and their two sons moved to Moab. There the boys eventually married local girls. One of those girls was Ruth.

Years later, after Naomi's husband and both boys died, she decided to return to her home in Bethlehem with her grief. Somewhat to her amazement, Ruth insisted on returning with her. They had not only become a family and friends; they had also grown to share a common faith.

The events that led up to Ruth's marriage to Boaz of Bethlehem were full of romance and excitement. God brought goodness out of grief. God grafted a foreign daughter into his own lineage. For we discover at the end of Ruth's story that she was an ancestor of King David. This fact also makes her part of the family tree of Jesus, the Savior and King.

Cutting Edge

In the relationship between Ruth and Naomi, we find a lovely example of the way young and old make a difference in each other's lives. Even mothers-in-law and daughters-in-law can be friends. They can also become sisters in their shared relationship with God. Ruth made a difference as she honored and cooperated with Naomi's wisdom. Her trust in God allowed him to make a difference through her and in her life.

YOU can, too!

Every relationship in your life offers God an opportunity to work. Relationships are his fertile ground. When God describes his highest purposes for us, he uses relationship language: "Love the Lord your God with all your heart, all your soul, all your mind, and all your strength" and "Love your neighbor as you love yourself" (Mark 12:30–31). Relationships are where God wants to make a difference. Shouldn't that be our goal, too?

Want to know more? Read Ruth's delightful story in the book that bears her name.

On the Edge

[Manasseh] practiced magic and told the future by explaining signs and dreams, and he got advice from mediums and fortune-tellers. He did many things the LORD said were wrong, which made the LORD angry (2 Kin. 21:6b).

Asking fortune-tellers for advice is listed here as a sinful thing that makes the Lord very angry. It is an insult to God to believe that a human being can look into the future and know the plans of the Lord. His ways and thoughts are so far above our thoughts. (See Isaiah 55:8–9.) Why pay money to speak to someone who will just give you his or her best guess?

Instead, get in touch with the Maker, the Master Designer, the One who *really* knows everything. Ask him for advice. He's been waiting to help you make sense of it all. His guidance will not be confusing or misleading. He will not stutter or fumble—he will clearly lead your steps. So go ahead, stop any time, any place, and ask God for his advice. Listen when he answers you through his Word or in your heart. Then follow through—do what he says, walk where he leads. You can count on him to know exactly what will happen in your future. He's never wrong.

SEE FOR YOURSELF:
Lev. 20:6; Deut. 18:10; Is. 40:13–14; Rom. 11:33

[2]He did what the LORD said was wrong. He did
the hateful things the other nations had done—
the nations that the LORD had forced out of the
land ahead of the Israelites. [3]Manasseh's father,
Hezekiah, had destroyed the places where gods
were worshiped, but Manasseh rebuilt them.
He built altars for Baal, and he made an Asherah idol as Ahab king of Israel had done. Manasseh also worshiped all the stars of the sky
and served them. [4]The LORD had said about the
Temple, "I will be worshiped in Jerusalem," but
Manasseh built altars in the Temple of the LORD.
[5]He built altars to worship the stars in the two
courtyards of the Temple of the LORD. [6]He made
his own son pass through fire. He practiced
magic and told the future by explaining signs
and dreams, and he got advice from mediums
and fortune-tellers. He did many things the
LORD said were wrong, which made the LORD
angry.

[7]Manasseh carved an
Asherah idol and put it in
the Temple. The LORD had
said to David and his son Solomon about the Temple, "I
will be worshiped forever in
this Temple and in Jerusalem,
which I have chosen from all
the tribes of Israel. [8]I will never again make the
Israelites wander out of the land I gave their
ancestors. But they must obey everything I
have commanded them and all the teachings
my servant Moses gave them." [9]But the people
did not listen. Manasseh led them to do more
evil than the nations the LORD had destroyed
ahead of the Israelites.

[10]The LORD said through his servants the
prophets, [11]"Manasseh king of Judah has done
these hateful things. He has done more evil
than the Amorites before him. He also has led
Judah to sin with his idols. [12]So this is what the
LORD, the God of Israel, says: 'I will bring so
much trouble on Jerusalem and Judah that
anyone who hears about it will be shocked. [13]I
will stretch the measuring line of Samaria over
Jerusalem, and the plumb line used against
Ahab's family will be used on Jerusalem. I will
wipe out Jerusalem as a person wipes a dish
and turns it upside down. [14]I will throw away
the rest of my people who are left. I will give
them to their enemies, and they will be robbed
by all their enemies, [15]because my people did
what I said was wrong. They have made me

TEMPTATION

What can you do to avoid temptation? (21:7–9)

WHAT'S IT MEAN?

Of all the kings who reigned in Israel and Judah, Manasseh held the throne longest. That's unfortunate, because Manasseh truly was an evil person. He built altars to pagan gods, reintroduced astrology to the Israelites, and personally practiced witchcraft. Along the way, he also put many innocent people to death. As if that weren't enough, Jewish tradition says Manasseh put Isaiah to death by ordering that the prophet be sawed in half.

2 Kings 21:16

angry from the day their ancestors left Egypt
until now.' "
16 Manasseh also killed many innocent people, filling Jerusalem from one end to the other
with their blood. This was besides the sin he
led Judah to do; he led Judah to do what the
LORD said was wrong.
17 The other things Manasseh did as king,
even the sin he did, are written in the book of
the history of the kings of Judah. 18 Manasseh
died and was buried in the garden of his own
palace, the garden of Uzza. Then Manasseh's
son Amon became king in his place.

AMON KING OF JUDAH

19 Amon was twenty-two years old when he
became king, and he was king for two years in
Jerusalem. His mother's name was Meshulle-
meth daughter of Haruz, who was from Jot-
bah. 20 Amon did what the LORD said was
wrong, as his father Manasseh had done. 21 He
lived in the same way his father had lived: he
worshiped the idols his father had worshiped,
and he bowed down before them. 22 Amon rejected the LORD, the God of his ancestors, and
did not follow the ways of the LORD.
23 Amon's officers made plans against him
and killed him in his palace. 24 Then the people
of the land killed all those who had made
plans to kill King Amon, and they made his
son Josiah king in his place.
25 Everything else Amon did is written in the
book of the history of the kings of Judah. 26 He
was buried in his grave in the garden of Uzza,
and his son Josiah became king in his place.

JOSIAH KING OF JUDAH

22
1 Josiah was eight years old when he became
king, and he ruled thirty-one years in Jerusalem. His mother's name was Jedidah daughter
of Adaiah, who was from Bozkath. 2 Josiah did
what the LORD said was right. He lived as his
ancestor David had lived, and he did not stop
doing what was right.
3 In Josiah's eighteenth year as king, he sent
Shaphan to the Temple of the LORD. Shaphan
son of Azaliah, the son of Meshullam, was the
royal secretary. Josiah said, 4 "Go up to Hilkiah
the high priest, and have him empty out the
money the gatekeepers have gathered from the
people. This is the money they have brought
into the Temple of the LORD. 5 Have him give
the money to the supervisors of the work on
the Temple of the LORD. They must pay the
workers who repair the Temple of the LORD—
6 the carpenters, builders, and bricklayers. Also
use the money to buy timber and cut stone to
repair the Temple. 7 They do not need to report
how they use the money given to them, because they are working honestly."

THE BOOK OF THE TEACHINGS IS FOUND

8 Hilkiah the high priest said to Shaphan the
royal secretary, "I've found the Book of the
Teachings in the Temple of the LORD." He gave it
to Shaphan, who read it.

WHAT'S IT MEAN?

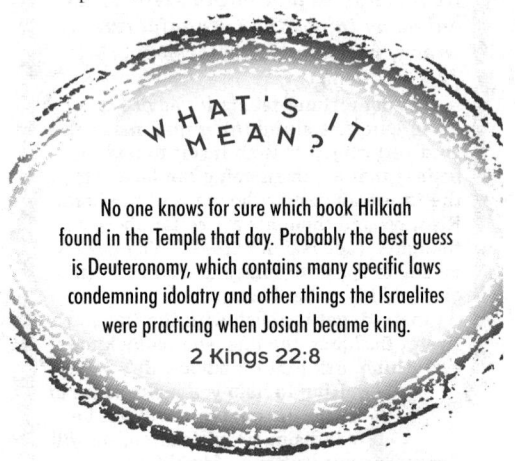

No one knows for sure which book Hilkiah found in the Temple that day. Probably the best guess is Deuteronomy, which contains many specific laws condemning idolatry and other things the Israelites were practicing when Josiah became king.

2 Kings 22:8

9 Then Shaphan the royal secretary went to
the king and reported to Josiah, "Your officers
have paid out the money that was in the Temple of the LORD. They have given it to the
workers and supervisors at the Temple." 10 Then
Shaphan the royal secretary told the king, "Hilkiah the priest has given me a book." And Shaphan read from the book to the king.
11 When the king heard the words of the
Book of the Teachings, he tore his clothes to
show how upset he was. 12 He gave orders to
Hilkiah the priest, Ahikam son of Shaphan, Acbor son of Micaiah, Shaphan the royal secretary, and Asaiah the king's servant. These were
the orders: 13 "Go and ask the LORD about the
words in the book that was found. Ask for me,
for all the people, and for all Judah. The LORD's
anger is burning against us, because our ancestors did not obey the words of this book; they
did not do all the things written for us to do."
14 So Hilkiah the priest, Ahikam, Acbor, Shaphan, and Asaiah went to talk to Huldah the
prophetess. She was the wife of Shallum son of
Tikvah, the son of Harhas, who took care of
the king's clothes. Huldah lived in Jerusalem, in
the new area of the city.
15 She said to them, "This is what the LORD,
the God of Israel, says: Tell the man who sent
you to me, 16 'This is what the LORD says: I will
bring trouble to this place and to the people
living here, as it is written in the book which

the king of Judah has read. 17The people of Judah have left me and have burned incense to other gods. They have made me angry by all that they have done. My anger burns against this place like a fire, and it will not be put out.' 18Tell the king of Judah, who sent you to ask the LORD, 'This is what the LORD, the God of Israel, says about the words you heard: 19When you heard my words against this place and its people, you became sorry for what you had done and humbled yourself before me. I said they would be cursed and would be destroyed. You tore your clothes to show how upset you were, and you cried in my presence. This is why I have heard you, says the LORD. 20So I will let you die, and you will be buried in peace. You won't see all the trouble I will bring to this place.' "

So they took her message back to the king.

"The king stood by the pillar and made an agreement in the presence of the LORD to follow the LORD and obey his commands, rules, and laws." (2 Kings 23:3a)

THE PEOPLE HEAR THE AGREEMENT

23 1Then the king gathered all the older leaders of Judah and Jerusalem together. 2He went up to the Temple of the LORD, and all the people from Judah and Jerusalem went with him. The priests, prophets, and all the people—from the least important to the most important—went with him. He read to them all the words of the Book of the Agreement that was found in the Temple of the LORD. 3The king stood by the pillar and made an agreement in the presence of the LORD to follow the LORD and obey his commands, rules, and laws with his whole being, and to obey the words of the agreement written in this book. Then all the people promised to obey the agreement.

LEADERSHIP
How can leaders influence their people for good? (23:3)

JOSIAH DESTROYS THE PLACES FOR IDOL WORSHIP

4The king commanded Hilkiah the high priest and the priests of the next rank and the gatekeepers to bring out of the Temple of the LORD everything made for Baal, Asherah, and all the stars of the sky. Then Josiah burned them outside Jerusalem in the open country of the Kidron Valley and carried their ashes to Bethel. 5The kings of Judah had chosen priests for these gods. These priests burned incense in the places where gods were worshiped in the cities of Judah and the towns around Jerusalem. They burned incense to Baal, the sun, the moon, the planets, and all the stars of the sky. But Josiah took those priests away. 6He removed the Asherah idol from the Temple of the LORD and took it outside Jerusalem to the Kidron Valley, where he burned it and beat it into dust. Then he threw the dust on the graves of the common people. 7He also tore down the houses of the male prostitutes who were in the Temple of the LORD, where the women did weaving for Asherah.

8King Josiah brought all the false priests from the cities of Judah. He ruined the places where gods were worshiped, where the priests had burned incense, from Geba to Beersheba. He destroyed the places of worship at the entrance to the Gate of Joshua, the ruler of the city, on the left side of the city gate. 9The priests at the places where gods were worshiped were not allowed to serve at the LORD's altar in Jerusalem. But they could eat bread made without yeast with their brothers.

10Josiah ruined Topheth, in the Valley of Ben Hinnom, so no one could sacrifice his son or daughter to Molech. 11Judah's kings had placed horses at the front door of the Temple of the LORD in the courtyard near the room of Nathan-Melech, an officer. These horses were for the worship of the sun. So Josiah removed them and burned the chariots that were for sun worship also.

12The kings of Judah had built altars on the

WHAT'S IT MEAN?

What in the world does a chariot have to do with the sun god? Good question. It seems that ancient people believed the sun was pulled across the sky by a horse-drawn chariot driven by—who else?—the sun god.
2 Kings 23:11

roof[n] of the upstairs room of Ahaz. Josiah broke down these altars and the altars Manasseh had made in the two courtyards of the Temple of the LORD. Josiah smashed them to pieces and threw their dust into the Kidron Valley. [13]King Josiah ruined the places where gods were worshiped east of Jerusalem, south of the Mount of Olives.[n] Solomon king of Israel had built these places. One was for Ashtoreth, the hated goddess of the Sidonians. One was for Chemosh, the hated god of Moab. And one was for Molech, the hated god of the Ammonites. [14]Josiah smashed to pieces the stone pillars they worshiped, and he cut down the Asherah idols. Then he covered the places with human bones.

[15]Josiah also broke down the altar at Bethel—the place of worship made by Jeroboam son of Nebat, who had led Israel to sin. Josiah burned that place, broke the stones of the altar into pieces, then beat them into dust. He also burned the Asherah idol. [16]When he turned around, he saw the graves on the mountain. He had the bones taken from the graves, and he burned them on the altar to ruin it. This happened as the LORD had said it would through the man of God.

[17]Josiah asked, "What is that monument I see?"

The people of the city answered, "It's the grave of the man of God who came from Judah. This prophet announced the things you have done against the altar of Bethel."

[18]Josiah said, "Leave the grave alone. No one may move this man's bones." So they left his bones and the bones of the prophet who had come from Samaria.

[19]The kings of Israel had built temples for worshiping gods in the cities of Samaria, which had caused the LORD to be angry. Josiah removed all those temples and did the same things as he had done at Bethel. [20]He killed all the priests of those places of worship; he killed them on the altars and burned human bones on the altars. Then he went back to Jerusalem.

JOSIAH CELEBRATES THE PASSOVER

[21]The king commanded all the people, "Celebrate the Passover to the LORD your God as it is written in this Book of the Agreement." [22]The Passover had not been celebrated like this since the judges led Israel. Nor had one like it happened while there were kings of Israel and kings of Judah. [23]This Passover was celebrated to the LORD in Jerusalem in the eighteenth year of King Josiah's rule.

[24]Josiah destroyed the mediums, fortunetellers, house gods, and idols. He also destroyed all the hated gods seen in the land of Judah and Jerusalem. This was to obey the words of the teachings written in the book Hilkiah the priest had found in the Temple of the LORD.

[25]There was no king like Josiah before or after him. He obeyed the LORD with all his heart, soul, and strength, following all the Teachings of Moses.

[26]Even so, the LORD did not stop his strong and terrible anger. His anger burned against Judah because of all Manasseh had done to make him angry. [27]The LORD said, "I will send Judah out of my sight, as I have sent Israel away. I will reject Jerusalem, which I chose. And I will take away the Temple about which I said, 'I will be worshiped there.' "

[28]Everything else Josiah did is written in the book of the history of the kings of Judah.

[29]While Josiah was king, Neco king of Egypt went to help the king of Assyria at the Euphrates River. King Josiah marched out to fight against Neco, but at Megiddo, Neco faced him and killed him. [30]Josiah's servants carried his body in a chariot from Megiddo to Jerusalem and buried him in his own grave. Then the people of Judah chose Josiah's son Jehoahaz and poured olive oil on him to make him king in his father's place.

WHAT'S IT MEAN?

Megiddo was located in a "high traffic" area on the road between Egypt and Syria. Its location made Megiddo an ideal military base. The battle mentioned in this verse was fought in 609 B.C.

2 Kings 23:29

JEHOAHAZ KING OF JUDAH

[31]Jehoahaz was twenty-three years old when he became king, and he was king in Jeru-

23:12 roof In Bible times houses were built with flat roofs. The roof was used for drying things such as flax and fruit. And it was used as an extra room, as a place for worship, and as a cool place to sleep in the summer. **23:13 Mount of Olives** Literally, "The Mountain of Ruin."

salem for three months. His mother's name was Hamutal, who was the daughter of Jeremiah from Libnah. 32 Jehoahaz did what the LORD said was wrong, just as his ancestors had done.

33 King Neco took Jehoahaz prisoner at Riblah in the land of Hamath so that Jehoahaz could not rule in Jerusalem. Neco made the people of Judah pay about seventy-five hundred pounds of silver and about seventy-five pounds of gold.

34 King Neco made Josiah's son Eliakim the king in place of Josiah his father. Then Neco changed Eliakim's name to Jehoiakim. But Neco took Jehoahaz to Egypt, where he died. 35 Jehoiakim gave King Neco the silver and gold he demanded. Jehoiakim taxed the land and took silver and gold from the people of the land to give to King Neco. Each person had to pay his share.

JEHOIAKIM KING OF JUDAH

36 Jehoiakim was twenty-five years old when he became king, and he was king in Jerusalem for eleven years. His mother's name was Zebidah daughter of Pedaiah, who was from Rumah. 37 Jehoiakim did what the LORD said was wrong, just as his ancestors had done.

24 1 While Jehoiakim was king, Nebuchadnezzar king of Babylon attacked the land of Judah. So Jehoiakim became Nebuchadnezzar's servant for three years. Then he turned against Nebuchadnezzar and broke away from his rule. 2 The LORD sent raiding parties from Babylon, Aram, Moab, and Ammon against Jehoiakim to destroy Judah. This happened as the LORD had said it would through his servants the prophets.

3 The LORD commanded this to happen to the people of Judah, to remove them from his presence, because of all the sins of Manasseh. 4 He had killed many innocent people and had filled Jerusalem with their blood. And the LORD would not forgive these sins.

5 The other things that happened while Jehoiakim was king and all he did are written in the book of the history of the kings of Judah. 6 Jehoiakim died, and his son Jehoiachin became king in his place.

7 The king of Egypt did not leave his land again, because the king of Babylon had captured all that belonged to the king of Egypt, from the brook of Egypt to the Euphrates River.

JEHOIACHIN KING OF JUDAH

8 Jehoiachin was eighteen years old when he became king, and he was king three months in Jerusalem. His mother's name was Nehushta daughter of Elnathan from Jerusalem. 9 Jehoiachin did what the LORD said was wrong, just as his father had done.

10 At that time the officers of Nebuchadnezzar king of Babylon came up to Jerusalem. When they reached the city, they attacked it. 11 Nebuchadnezzar himself came to the city while his officers were attacking it. 12 Jehoiachin king of Judah surrendered to the king of Babylon, along with Jehoiachin's mother, servants, older leaders, and officers. So Nebuchadnezzar made Jehoiachin a prisoner in the eighth year he was king of Babylon. 13 Nebuchadnezzar took all the treasures from the Temple of the LORD and from the palace. He cut up all the gold objects Solomon king of Israel had made for the Temple of the LORD. This happened as the LORD had said it would. 14 Nebuchadnezzar took away all the people of Jerusalem, including all the leaders, all the wealthy people, and all the craftsmen and metal workers. There were ten thousand prisoners in all. Only the poorest people in the land were left. 15 Nebuchadnezzar carried away Jehoiachin to Babylon, as well as the king's mother and his wives, the officers, and the leading men of the land. They were taken captive from Jerusalem to Babylon. 16 The king of Babylon also took all seven thousand soldiers, who were strong and able to fight in war, and about a thousand craftsmen and metal workers. Nebuchadnezzar took them as prisoners to Babylon. 17 Then he made Mattaniah, Jehoiachin's uncle, king in Jehoiachin's place. He also changed Mattaniah's name to Zedekiah.

WHAT'S IT MEAN?

Welcome to the Babylonian Exile. In 597 B.C., Babylon attacked and defeated Jerusalem and carried off thousands of people, including King Jehoiachin himself. These people were held captive for seventy years, until after the Persians conquered Babylon. It was the Persian king, Cyrus, who eventually allowed the Jewish people to return to their homeland and rebuild the temple.

2 Kings 24:11

ZEDEKIAH KING OF JUDAH

[18]Zedekiah was twenty-one years old when
he became king, and he was king in Jerusalem
for eleven years. His mother's name was Hamutal daughter of Jeremiah[n] from Libnah.
[19]Zedekiah did what the LORD said was wrong,
just as Jehoiakim had done. [20]All this happened in Jerusalem and Judah because the
LORD was angry with them. Finally, he threw
them out of his presence.

WHAT'S IT MEAN?

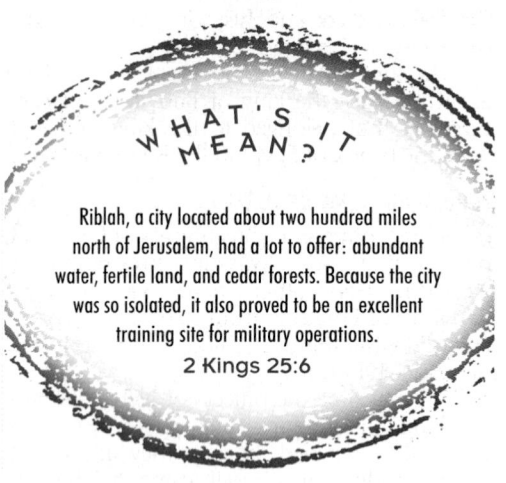

Riblah, a city located about two hundred miles north of Jerusalem, had a lot to offer: abundant water, fertile land, and cedar forests. Because the city was so isolated, it also proved to be an excellent training site for military operations.

2 Kings 25:6

THE FALL OF JERUSALEM

Zedekiah turned against the king of Babylon.
25 [1]Nebuchadnezzar king of Babylon marched
against Jerusalem with his whole army during
Zedekiah's ninth year as king, on the tenth day
of the tenth month. He made a camp around
the city and piled dirt against the city walls to
attack it. [2]The city was under attack until Zedekiah's eleventh year as king. [3]By the ninth day
of the fourth month, the hunger was terrible in
the city. There was no food for the people to eat.
[4]Then the city was broken into, and the whole
army ran away at night through the gate between the two walls by the king's garden. While
the Babylonians were still surrounding the city,
Zedekiah and his men ran away toward the
Jordan Valley. [5]But the Babylonian army
chased King Zedekiah and caught up with him
in the plains of Jericho. All of his army was
scattered from him, [6]so they captured Zedekiah
and took him to the king of Babylon at Riblah.
There he passed sentence on Zedekiah. [7]They
killed Zedekiah's sons as he watched. Then they
put out his eyes and put bronze chains on him
and took him to Babylon.

[8]Nebuzaradan was the commander of the
king's special guards. This officer of the king of
Babylon came to Jerusalem on the seventh day
of the fifth month, in Nebuchadnezzar's nineteenth year as king of Babylon. [9]Nebuzaradan
set fire to the Temple of the LORD and the palace and all the houses of Jerusalem. Every important building was burned.

[10]The whole Babylonian army, led by the
commander of the king's special guards, broke
down the walls around Jerusalem. [11]Nebuzar-
adan, the commander of the guards, captured
the people left in Jerusalem, those who had
surrendered to the king of Babylon, and the
rest of the people. [12]But the commander left
behind some of the poorest people of the land
to take care of the vineyards and fields.

[13]The Babylonians broke up the bronze pillars, the bronze stands, and the large bronze
bowl, which was called the Sea, in the Temple
of the LORD. Then they carried the bronze to
Babylon. [14]They also took the pots, shovels,
wick trimmers, dishes, and all the bronze objects used to serve in the Temple. [15]The commander of the king's special guards took away
the pans for carrying hot coals, the bowls, and
everything made of pure gold or silver. [16]There
were two pillars and the large bronze bowl
and the movable stands which Solomon had
made for the Temple of the LORD. There was so
much bronze that it could not be weighed.
[17]Each pillar was about twenty-seven feet high.
The bronze capital on top of the pillar was
about four and one-half feet high. It was decorated with a net design and bronze pomegranates all around it. The other pillar also had a
net design and was like the first pillar.

WHAT'S IT MEAN?

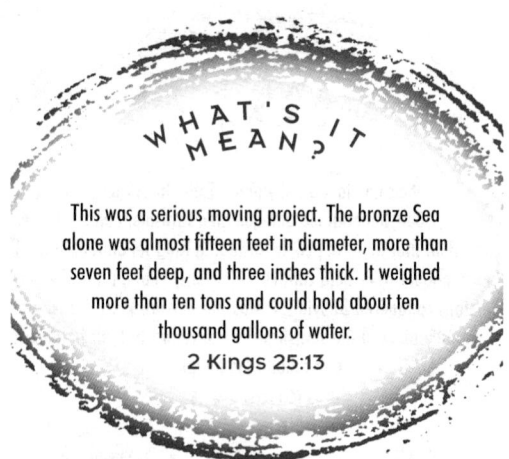

This was a serious moving project. The bronze Sea alone was almost fifteen feet in diameter, more than seven feet deep, and three inches thick. It weighed more than ten tons and could hold about ten thousand gallons of water.

2 Kings 25:13

24:18 Jeremiah This is not the prophet Jeremiah, but a different man with the same name.

JUDAH IS TAKEN PRISONER

18The commander of the guards took some prisoners—Seraiah the chief priest, Zephaniah the priest next in rank, and the three doorkeepers. 19Of the people who were still in the city, he took the officer in charge of the fighting men, as well as five people who advised the king. He took the royal secretary who selected people for the army and sixty other men who were in the city. 20Nebuzaradan, the commander, took all these people and brought them to the king of Babylon at Riblah. 21There at Riblah, in the land of Hamath, the king had them killed. So the people of Judah were led away from their country as captives.

GEDALIAH BECOMES GOVERNOR

22Nebuchadnezzar king of Babylon left some people in the land of Judah. He appointed Gedaliah son of Ahikam, the son of Shaphan, as governor.

23The army captains and their men heard that the king of Babylon had made Gedaliah governor, so they came to Gedaliah at Mizpah. They were Ishmael son of Nethaniah, Johanan son of Kareah, Seraiah son of Tanhumeth the Netophathite, Jaazaniah son of the Maacathite, and their men. 24Then Gedaliah promised these army captains and their men, "Don't be afraid of the Babylonian officers. Live in the land and serve the king of Babylon, and everything will go well for you."

25In the seventh month Ishmael son of Nethaniah, son of Elishama from the king's family, came with ten men and killed Gedaliah. They also killed the men of Judah and Babylon who were with Gedaliah at Mizpah. 26Then all the people, from the least important to the most important, along with the army leaders, ran away to Egypt, because they were afraid of the Babylonians.

JEHOIACHIN IS SET FREE

27Jehoiachin king of Judah was held in Babylon for thirty-seven years. In the thirty-seventh year Evil-Merodach became king of Babylon, and he let Jehoiachin out of prison on the twenty-seventh day of the twelfth month. 28Evil-Merodach spoke kindly to Jehoiachin and gave him a seat of honor above the seats of the other kings who were with him in Babylon. 29So Jehoiachin put away his prison clothes. For the rest of his life, he ate at the king's table. 30Every day, for as long as Jehoiachin lived, the king gave him an allowance.

1 Chronicles

CONTENT

You might remember that 1 and 2 Kings were the sequel to 1 and 2 Samuel. You might assume that 1 Chronicles would then be another sequel, but you would be wrong. First and 2 Chronicles present the same story line as 1 and 2 Kings but from a different perspective and by a different storyteller.

The books of the Kings tell the *facts* of the stories. "This king was good and the people followed God. That king was bad and the people fell away *again*." But the Chronicles tell the "whys." The people fell away because they were not wholehearted about obeying God. God did not bless them unless they became wholehearted again.

Having the benefit of another perspective is a good thing. Knowing the facts teaches us lessons, but knowing *why* the facts happened teaches us how to keep from making the same mistakes. When you read the 1 Chronicles, remember to look for the "whys." Remember to ask yourself how wholehearted you are. Remember that a kingdom falls for the same reason a person does—letting go of God's hand.

Outline

1:1—9:44 .... Descendants of Adam Until the Time of King Saul
10:1–14 .... The Death of Saul and His Sons
11:1–9 .... David Becomes King of Israel and Captures Jerusalem
11:10—12:40 ...... David's Warriors
13:1—16:43 .... The Ark Is Moved to Jerusalem
17:1–27 .... Solomon Will Build the Lord's Temple
18:1—20:8 .... David's Military Victories
21:1—28:21 .... David's Preparations for Building the Temple
29:1–20 .... The People Bring Gifts for Building the Temple
29:21–25 .... Solomon Is Crowned King
29:26–30 .... The Death of David

Purpose

God blesses those whose desire is to worship and to serve him.

Theme

Encouragement and Exhortation from Judah's Spiritual Heritage

Date of writing

430–425 B.C.

"LORD, you are great and powerful. You have glory, victory, and honor. Everything in heaven and on earth belongs to you. The kingdom belongs to you, LORD; you are the ruler over everything" (29:11).

Bible Talk

Genealogies

First of all, let's get this out of the way right here at the beginning: yes, there are a lot of lists of genealogies in the Chronicles. They aren't fun to read. You are allowed to skip some verses. But don't give up on both books because they have some lists in them.

Genealogies don't seem so important to us today. A lot of us don't know much about our great-great-great-grandfather. But to the Hebrews, family history was everything. One reason for this was that the Hebrews were looking forward to the Messiah (Jesus) being born. They knew he would be a descendant of Abraham and then of David. If they kept those families straight, they would have a better chance of spotting the Messiah when he made his appearance.

WHAT'S THE BIG DEAL WITH THE TEMPLE?

You'll read a lot in 1 Chronicles about David making preparations for the Temple. The important part of that is not how much gold David gathered or how many cedars of Lebanon (really nice lumber) he had brought in. The important part of that part of this story is that it was important for the Hebrews to honor God's presence in their lives. The Temple was their way of doing that.

Remember that Jesus hadn't come on the scene yet to help them understand that God resides *in* us. So they still felt like they had to go to a place to honor God. If you remember their history, then you remember that they needed all the reminders of God's presence that they could get. The Temple was a *very* big deal.

FROM ADAM TO ABRAHAM

1 [1]Adam was the father of Seth. Seth was the father of Enosh. Enosh was the father of Kenan. [2]Kenan was the father of Mahalalel. Mahalalel was the father of Jared. Jared was the father of Enoch. [3]Enoch was the father of Methuselah. Methuselah was the father of Lamech, and Lamech was the father of Noah.

[4]The sons of Noah were Shem, Ham, and Japheth.

WHAT'S IT MEAN?

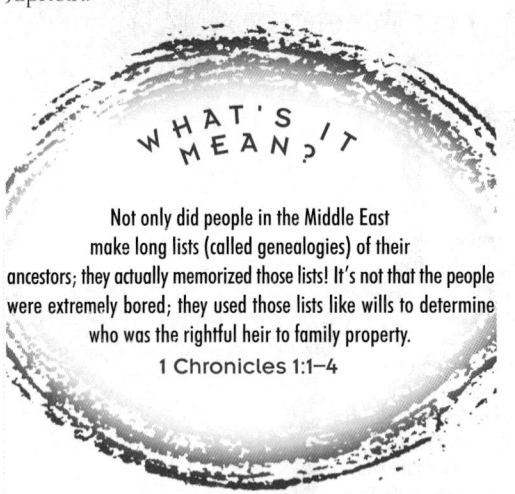

Not only did people in the Middle East make long lists (called genealogies) of their ancestors; they actually memorized those lists! It's not that the people were extremely bored; they used those lists like wills to determine who was the rightful heir to family property.

1 Chronicles 1:1–4

[5]Japheth's sons were Gomer, Magog, Madai, Javan, Tubal, Meshech, and Tiras.

[6]Gomer's sons were Ashkenaz, Riphath, and Togarmah.

[7]Javan's sons were Elishah, Tarshish, Kittim,[n] and Rodanim.

[8]Ham's sons were Cush, Mizraim,[n] Put, and Canaan.

[9]Cush's sons were Seba, Havilah, Sabta, Raamah, and Sabteca.

Raamah's sons were Sheba and Dedan.

[10]Cush was the father of Nimrod, who grew up to become a mighty warrior on the earth.

[11]Mizraim was the father of the Ludites, Anamites, Lehabites, and Naphtuhites, [12]Pathrusites, Casluhites, and Caphtorites. (The Philistines came from the Casluhites.)

[13]Canaan's first child was Sidon. He was also the father of the Hittites, [14]Jebusites, Amorites, Girgashites, [15]Hivites, Arkites, Sinites, [16]Arvadites, Zemarites, and Hamathites.

[17]Shem's sons were Elam, Asshur, Arphaxad, Lud, and Aram.

Aram's sons were Uz, Hul, Gether, and Meshech.

[18]Arphaxad was the father of Shelah, who was the father of Eber.

[19]Eber had two sons. One son was named Peleg,[n] because the people on the earth were divided into different languages during his life. Peleg's brother was named Joktan.

[20]Joktan was the father of Almodad, Sheleph, Hazarmaveth, Jerah, [21]Hadoram, Uzal, Diklah, [22]Obal, Abimael, Sheba, [23]Ophir, Havilah, and Jobab. All these were Joktan's sons. [24]The family line included Shem, Arphaxad, Shelah, [25]Eber, Peleg, Reu, [26]Serug, Nahor, Terah, [27]and Abram, who was called Abraham.

ABRAHAM'S FAMILY

[28]Abraham's sons were Isaac and Ishmael.

[29]These were the sons of Isaac and Ishmael. Ishmael's first son was Nebaioth. His other sons were Kedar, Adbeel, Mibsam, [30]Mishma, Dumah, Massa, Hadad, Tema, [31]Jetur, Naphish, and Kedemah. These were Ishmael's sons. [32]Keturah, Abraham's slave woman, gave birth to Zimran, Jokshan, Medan, Midian, Ishbak, and Shuah.

Jokshan's sons were Sheba and Dedan.

[33]Midian's sons were Ephah, Epher, Hanoch, Abida, and Eldaah. All these were descendants of Keturah.

[34]Abraham was the father of Isaac, and Isaac's sons were Esau and Israel.

[35]Esau's sons were Eliphaz, Reuel, Jeush, Jalam, and Korah.

[36]Eliphaz's sons were Teman, Omar, Zepho, Gatam, Kenaz, Timna, and Amalek.

[37]Reuel's sons were Nahath, Zerah, Shammah, and Mizzah.

WHAT'S IT MEAN?

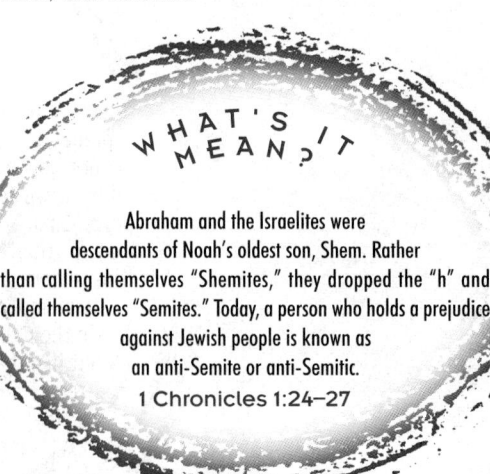

Abraham and the Israelites were descendants of Noah's oldest son, Shem. Rather than calling themselves "Shemites," they dropped the "h" and called themselves "Semites." Today, a person who holds a prejudice against Jewish people is known as an anti-Semite or anti-Semitic.

1 Chronicles 1:24–27

1:7 Kittim His descendants were the people of Cyprus. **1:8 Mizraim** This is another name for Egypt.
1:19 Peleg This name sounds like the Hebrew word for "divided."

THE EDOMITES FROM SEIR

38 Seir's sons were Lotan, Shobal, Zibeon,
Anah, Dishon, Ezer, and Dishan.
39 Lotan's sons were Hori and Homam, and
his sister was Timna.
40 Shobal's sons were Alvan, Manahath,
Ebal, Shepho, and Onam.
Zibeon's sons were Aiah and Anah.
41 Anah's son was Dishon.
Dishon's sons were Hemdan, Eshban, Ithran, and Keran.
42 Ezer's sons were Bilhan, Zaavan, and
Akan.
Dishan's sons were Uz and Aran.

THE KINGS OF EDOM

43 These kings ruled in Edom before there
were kings in Israel. Bela son of Beor was king
of Edom, and his city was named Dinhabah.
44 When Bela died, Jobab son of Zerah became king. He was from Bozrah.
45 When Jobab died, Husham became king.
He was from the land of the Temanites.
46 When Husham died, Hadad son of Bedad
became king, and his city was named Avith.
Hadad defeated Midian in the country of
Moab.
47 When Hadad died, Samlah became king.
He was from Masrekah.
48 When Samlah died, Shaul became king.
He was from Rehoboth by the river.
49 When Shaul died, Baal-Hanan son of Acbor became king.
50 When Baal-Hanan died, Hadad became
king, and his city was named Pau. Hadad's
wife was named Mehetabel, and she was the
daughter of Matred, who was the daughter of
Me-Zahab.
51 Then Hadad died.
The leaders of the family groups of Edom
were Timna, Alvah, Jetheth,
52 Oholibamah,
Elah, Pinon,
53 Kenaz, Teman, Mibzar,
54 Magdi-
el, and Iram. These were the leaders of Edom.

ISRAEL'S FAMILY

2
1 The sons of Israel[n] were Reuben, Simeon,
Levi, Judah, Issachar, Zebulun,
2 Dan, Joseph,
Benjamin, Naphtali, Gad, and Asher.

JUDAH'S FAMILY

SIN
How might God severely judge sin? (2:3)

3 Judah's sons were Er,
Onan, and Shelah. A Canaanite woman, the daughter of
Shua, was their mother.
Judah's first son, Er, did what
the LORD said was wicked, so
the LORD put him to death.
4 Judah's daughter-
in-law Tamar gave birth to Perez and Zerah.
Judah was the father, so Judah had five sons.
5 Perez's sons were Hezron and Hamul.
6 Zerah had five sons: Zimri, Ethan, Heman,
Calcol, and Darda.
7 Carmi's son was Achan, who caused trouble for Israel because he took things that had
been given to the LORD to be destroyed.
8 Ethan's son was Azariah.
9 Hezron's sons were Jerahmeel, Ram, and
Caleb.
10 Ram was Amminadab's father, and Amminadab was Nahshon's father. Nahshon was
the leader of the people of Judah.
11 Nahshon
was the father of Salmon, who was the father
of Boaz.
12 Boaz was the father of Obed, and
Obed was the father of Jesse.
13 Jesse's first son was Eliab. His second son
was Abinadab, his third was Shimea,
14 his
fourth was Nethanel, his fifth was Raddai,
15 his
sixth was Ozem, and his seventh son was David.
16 Their sisters were Zeruiah and Abigail.
Zeruiah's three sons were Abishai, Joab, and
Asahel.
17 Abigail was the mother of Amasa,
and his father was Jether, an Ishmaelite.

WHAT'S IT MEAN?

Read 1:1—2:15 carefully and you'll discover that David, who was of the tribe of Judah, was a direct descendant of Adam, Noah, and Abraham. As the genealogies of the Gospels of Matthew and Luke show, David was also a direct ancestor of Jesus.

1 Chronicles 2:13–15

CALEB'S FAMILY

18 Caleb son of Hezron had children by his
wife Azubah and by Jerioth. Caleb and
Azubah's sons were Jesher, Shobab, and Ar-
don.
19 When Azubah died, Caleb married Ephrath. They had a son named Hur,
20 who was
the father of Uri, who was the father of Bezalel.
21 Later, when Hezron was sixty years old,
he married the daughter of Makir, Gilead's father. Hezron had sexual relations with Makir's
daughter, and she had a son named Segub.

2:1 Israel Another name for Jacob.

22Segub was the father of Jair. Jair controlled twenty-three cities in the country of Gilead. 23(But Geshur and Aram captured the Towns of Jair, as well as Kenath and the small towns around it—sixty towns in all.) All these were descendants of Makir, the father of Gilead.

24After Hezron died in Caleb Ephrathah, his wife Abijah had his son, named Ashhur. Ashhur became the father of Tekoa.

JERAHMEEL'S FAMILY

25Hezron's first son was Jerahmeel. Jerahmeel's sons were Ram, Bunah, Oren, Ozem, and Ahijah. Ram was Jerahmeel's first son. 26Jerahmeel had another wife, named Atarah. She was the mother of Onam.

27Jerahmeel's first son, Ram, had sons. They were Maaz, Jamin, and Eker.

28Onam's sons were Shammai and Jada.

Shammai's sons were Nadab and Abishur.

29Abishur's wife was named Abihail, and their sons were Ahban and Molid.

30Nadab's sons were Seled and Appaim. Seled died without having children.

31Appaim's son was Ishi, who became the father of Sheshan.

Sheshan was the father of Ahlai.

32Jada was Shammai's brother, and Jada's sons were Jether and Jonathan. Jether died without having children.

33Jonathan's sons were Peleth and Zaza.

These were Jerahmeel's descendants.

34Sheshan did not have any sons, only daughters. He had a servant from Egypt named Jarha. 35Sheshan let his daughter marry his servant Jarha, and she had a son named Attai.

36Attai was the father of Nathan. Nathan was the father of Zabad. 37Zabad was the father of Ephlal. Ephlal was the father of Obed. 38Obed was the father of Jehu. Jehu was the father of Azariah. 39Azariah was the father of Helez. Helez was the father of Eleasah. 40Eleasah was the father of Sismai. Sismai was the father of Shallum. 41Shallum was the father of Jekamiah, and Jekamiah was the father of Elishama.

CALEB'S FAMILY

42Caleb was Jerahmeel's brother. Caleb's first son was Mesha. Mesha was the father of Ziph, and his son Mareshah was the father of Hebron.

43Hebron's sons were Korah, Tappuah, Rekem, and Shema. 44Shema was the father of Raham, who was the father of Jorkeam. Rekem was the father of Shammai. 45Shammai was the father of Maon, and Maon was the father of Beth Zur.

46Caleb's slave woman was named Ephah, and she was the mother of Haran, Moza, and Gazez. Haran was the father of Gazez.

47Jahdai's sons were Regem, Jotham, Geshan, Pelet, Ephah, and Shaaph.

48Caleb had another slave woman named Maacah. She was the mother of Sheber, Tirhanah, 49Shaaph, and Sheva. Shaaph was the father of Madmannah. Sheva was the father of Macbenah and Gibea. Caleb's daughter was Acsah.

50-51These were Caleb's descendants: Caleb's son Hur was the first son of his mother Ephrathah. Hur's sons were Shobal, Salma, and Hareph. Shobal was the father of Kiriath Jearim. Salma was the father of Bethlehem. And Hareph was the father of Beth Gader.

52Shobal was the father of Kiriath Jearim. Shobal's descendants were Haroeh, half the Manahathites, 53and the family groups of Kiriath Jearim: the Ithrites, Puthites, Shumathites, and Mishraites. The Zorathites and the Eshtaolites came from the Mishraite people.

54Salma's descendants were Bethlehem, the Netophathites, Atroth Beth Joab, half the Manahathites, and the Zorites. 55His descendants included the families who lived at Jabez, who wrote and copied important papers. They were called the Tirathites, Shimeathites, and Sucathites and were from the Kenite family group who came from Hammath. He was the father of the people living in Recab.

DAVID'S FAMILY

3 1These are David's sons who were born in Hebron. The first was Amnon, whose mother was Ahinoam from Jezreel. The second son was Daniel, whose mother was Abigail from Carmel. 2The third son was Absalom, whose mother was Maacah daughter of Talmai, the king of Geshur. The fourth son was Adonijah, whose mother was Haggith. 3The fifth son was Shephatiah, whose mother was Abital. The sixth son was Ithream, whose mother was Eglah. 4These six sons of David were born to him in Hebron, where David ruled for seven and one-half years.

David ruled in Jerusalem thirty-three years. 5These were his children who were born in Jerusalem: Shammua, Shobab, Nathan, and Solomon—the four children of David and Bathsheba, Ammiel's daughter. 6-8David's other nine children were Ibhar, Elishua, Eliphelet, Nogah, Nepheg, Japhia, Elishama, Eliada, and Eliphelet. 9These were all of David's sons, except for those born to his slave women. David also had a daughter named Tamar.

THE KINGS OF JUDAH

[10]Solomon's son was Rehoboam. Rehoboam's son was Abijah. Abijah's son was Asa. Asa's son was Jehoshaphat. [11]Jehoshaphat's son was Jehoram. Jehoram's son was Ahaziah. Ahaziah's son was Joash. [12]Joash's son was Amaziah. Amaziah's son was Azariah. Azariah's son was Jotham. [13]Jotham's son was Ahaz. Ahaz's son was Hezekiah. Hezekiah's son was Manasseh. [14]Manasseh's son was Amon, and Amon's son was Josiah.

[15]These were Josiah's sons: His first son was Johanan, his second was Jehoiakim, his third was Zedekiah, and his fourth was Shallum.

[16]Jehoiakim was followed by Jehoiachin, and he was followed by Zedekiah.

DAVID'S DESCENDANTS AFTER THE BABYLONIAN CAPTIVITY

[17]Jehoiachin was taken as a prisoner. His sons were Shealtiel, [18]Malkiram, Pedaiah, Shenazzar, Jekamiah, Hoshama, and Nedabiah.

WHAT'S IT MEAN?

The southern kingdom of Judah outlasted the northern kingdom of Israel by about 125 years. Samaria, the capital of the northern kingdom, was defeated by the Assyrians in 722 B.C. Jerusalem, the capital of the southern kingdom, was conquered by the Babylonians in 597 B.C. Jehoiachin, the king of Judah at the time of its defeat, was among the captives taken to Babylon.

1 Chronicles 3:17

[19]Pedaiah's sons were Zerubbabel and Shimei.

Zerubbabel's sons were Meshullam and Hananiah, and their sister was Shelomith. [20]Zerubbabel also had five other sons: Hashubah, Ohel, Berekiah, Hasadiah, and Jushab-Hesed.

[21]Hananiah's descendants were Pelatiah and Jeshaiah, and the sons of Rephaiah, Arnan, Obadiah, and Shecaniah.

[22]Shecaniah's son was Shemaiah. Shemaiah's sons were Hattush, Igal, Bariah, Neariah, and Shaphat. There were six in all.

[23]Neariah had three sons: Elioenai, Hizkiah, and Azrikam.

[24]Elioenai had seven sons: Hodaviah, Eliashib, Pelaiah, Akkub, Johanan, Delaiah, and Anani.

WHAT'S IT MEAN?

Zerubbabel led the first group of Jewish exiles back to Jerusalem after they had spent seventy years as captives in Babylon. (By the way, an exile is a person who has been separated from his country.) He became the governor of Judah and started the long, slow process of rebuilding the Temple, which had been completely destroyed. Haggai and Zechariah, two prophets of God, encouraged Zerubbabel in his work.

1 Chronicles 3:19

OTHER FAMILY GROUPS OF JUDAH

4

[1]Judah's descendants were Perez, Hezron, Carmi, Hur, and Shobal.

[2]Reaiah was Shobal's son. Reaiah was the father of Jahath, and Jahath was the father of Ahumai and Lahad. They were the family groups of the Zorathite people.

[3-4]Hur was the oldest son of Caleb and his wife Ephrathah. Hur was the leader of Bethlehem. His three sons were Etam, Penuel, and Ezer. Etam's sons were Jezreel, Ishma, and Idbash. They had a sister named Hazzelelponi. Penuel was the father of Gedor, and Ezer was the father of Hushah.

[5]Tekoa's father was Ashhur. Ashhur had two wives named Helah and Naarah.

[6]The sons of Ashhur and Naarah were Ahuzzam, Hepher, Temeni, and Haahashtari. These were the descendants of Naarah.

[7]Helah's sons were Zereth, Zohar, Ethnan, [8]and Koz. Koz was the father of Anub, Hazzobebah, and the Aharhel family group. Aharhel was the son of Harum.

[9]There was a man named Jabez, who was respected more than his brothers. His mother named him Jabez[n] because she said, "I was in much pain when I gave birth to him." [10]Jabez

4:9 Jabez This name in Hebrew sounds like the word for "pain."

prayed to the God of Israel, "Please do good things for me and give me more land. Stay with me, and don't let anyone hurt me. Then I won't have any pain." And God did what Jabez had asked.

[11]Kelub, Shuhah's brother, was the father of Mehir. Mehir was the father of Eshton. [12]Eshton was the father of Beth Rapha, Paseah, and Tehinnah. Tehinnah was the father of the people from the town of Nahash. These people were from Recah.

[13]The sons of Kenaz were Othniel and Seraiah.

Othniel's sons were Hathath and Meonothai. [14]Meonothai was the father of Ophrah.

Seraiah was the father of Joab. Joab was the ancestor of the people from Craftsmen's Valley, named that because the people living there were craftsmen.

[15]Caleb was Jephunneh's son. Caleb's sons were Iru, Elah, and Naam. Elah's son was Kenaz.

[16]Jehallelel's sons were Ziph, Ziphah, Tiria, and Asarel.

[17-18]Ezrah's sons were Jether, Mered, Epher, and Jalon. Mered married Bithiah, the daughter of the king of Egypt. The children of Mered and Bithiah were Miriam, Shammai, and Ishbah. Ishbah was the father of Eshtemoa. Mered also had a wife from Judah, who gave birth to Jered, Heber, and Jekuthiel. Jered became the father of Gedor. Heber became the father of Soco. And Jekuthiel became the father of Zanoah.

[19]Hodiah's wife was Naham's sister. The sons of Hodiah's wife were Eshtemoa and the father of Keilah. Keilah was from the Garmite people, and Eshtemoa was from the Maacathite people.

[20]Shimon's sons were Amnon, Rinnah, Ben-Hanan, and Tilon.

Ishi's sons were Zoheth and Ben-Zoheth.

[21-22]Shelah was Judah's son. Shelah's sons were Er, Laadah, Jokim, the men from Cozeba, Joash, and Saraph. Er was the father of Lecah. Laadah was the father of Mareshah and the family groups of linen workers at Beth Ashbea. Joash and Saraph ruled in Moab and Jashubi Lehem. The writings about this family are very old. [23]These sons of Shelah were potters. They lived in Netaim and Gederah and worked for the king.

SIMEON'S CHILDREN

[24]Simeon's sons were Nemuel, Jamin, Jarib, Zerah, and Shaul. [25]Shaul's son was Shallum. Shallum's son was Mibsam. Mibsam's son was Mishma.

[26]Mishma's son was Hammuel. Hammuel's son was Zaccur. Zaccur's son was Shimei. [27]Shimei had sixteen sons and six daughters, but his brothers did not have many children, so there were not as many people in their family group as there were in Judah.

[28]Shimei's children lived in Beersheba, Moladah, Hazar Shual, [29]Bilhah, Ezem, Tolad, [30]Bethuel, Hormah, Ziklag, [31]Beth Marcaboth, Hazar Susim, Beth Biri, and Shaaraim. They lived in these cities until David became king. [32]The five villages near these cities were Etam, Ain, Rimmon, Token, and Ashan. [33]There were also other villages as far away as Baalath. This is where they lived. And they wrote the history of their family.

WHAT'S IT MEAN?

When the land of Canaan was divided among the twelve tribes of Israel, Simeon received territory in the south, near the Edom border and the desert that led to Egypt. Despite the fact that Simeon's entire piece of land was located inside Judah's much larger territory, the Simeonites managed to maintain their own identity.

1 Chronicles 4:28–31

[34-38]The men in this list were leaders of their family groups: Meshobab, Jamlech, Joshah son of Amaziah, Joel, Jehu son of Joshibiah (Joshibiah was the son of Seraiah, who was the son of Asiel), Elioenai, Jaakobah, Jeshohaiah, Asaiah, Adiel, Jesimiel, Benaiah, and Ziza. (Ziza was the son of Shiphi, who was the son of Allon. Allon was the son of Jedaiah, who was the son of Shimri. And Shimri was the son of Shemaiah.)

These families grew very large. [39]They went outside the city of Gedor to the east side of the valley to look for pasture for their flocks. [40]They found good pastures with plenty of grass, and the land was open country and peaceful and quiet. Ham's descendants had lived there in the past.

[41]These men who were listed came to Gedor while Hezekiah was king of Judah. They fought against the Hamites, destroying their tents, and also against the Meunites who lived there, and completely destroyed them. So there are no Meunites there even today. Then these men

began to live there, because there was pasture for their flocks. 42 Ishi's sons, Pelatiah, Neariah, Rephaiah, and Uzziel, led five hundred of the Simeonites and attacked the people living in the mountains of Edom. 43 They killed the few Amalekites who were still alive. From that time until now these Simeonites have lived in Edom.

REUBEN'S CHILDREN

5 1 Reuben was Israel's first son. Reuben should have received the special privileges of the oldest son, but he had sexual relations with his father's slave woman. So those special privileges were given to Joseph's sons. (Joseph was a son of Israel.) In the family history Reuben's name is not listed as the first son. 2 Judah became stronger than his brothers, and a leader came from his family. But Joseph's family received the privileges that belonged to the oldest son. 3 Reuben was Israel's first son. Reuben's sons were Hanoch, Pallu, Hezron, and Carmi.

4 These were the children of Joel: Shemaiah was Joel's son. Gog was Shemaiah's son. Shimei was Gog's son. 5 Micah was Shimei's son. Reaiah was Micah's son. Baal was Reaiah's son. 6 Beerah was Baal's son. Beerah was a leader of the tribe of Reuben. Tiglath-Pileser king of Assyria captured him and took him away.

7 Joel's brothers and all his family groups are listed just as they are written in their family histories: Jeiel was the first, then Zechariah, 8 and Bela. (Bela was the son of Azaz. Azaz was the son of Shema, and Shema was the son of Joel.) They lived in the area of Aroer all the way to Nebo and Baal Meon. 9 Bela's people lived to the east—as far as the edge of the desert, which is beside the Euphrates River—because they had too many cattle for the land of Gilead.

10 When Saul was king, Bela's people fought a war against the Hagrite people and defeated them. Then Bela's people lived in the tents that had belonged to the Hagrites in all the area east of Gilead.

GAD'S CHILDREN

11 The people from the tribe of Gad lived near the Reubenites. The Gadites lived in the area of Bashan all the way to Salecah. 12 Joel was the main leader, Shapham was second, and then Janai and Shaphat were leaders in Bashan.

13 The seven relatives in their families were Michael, Meshullam, Sheba, Jorai, Jacan, Zia, and Eber. 14 They were the descendants of Abihail. Abihail was Huri's son. Huri was Jaroah's son. Jaroah was Gilead's son. Gilead was Michael's son. Michael was Jeshishai's son. Jeshishai was Jahdo's son, and Jahdo was the son of Buz. 15 Ahi was Abdiel's son, and Abdiel was Guni's son. Ahi was the leader of their family.

16 The Gadites lived in Gilead, Bashan and the small towns around it, and on all the pasturelands in the Plain of Sharon all the way to the borders.

17 All these names were written in the family history of Gad during the time Jotham was king of Judah and Jeroboam was king of Israel.

SOLDIERS SKILLED IN WAR

18 There were forty-four thousand seven hundred sixty soldiers from the tribes of Reuben and Gad and East Manasseh who carried shields and swords and bows. They were skilled in war. 19 They started a war against the Hagrites and the people of Jetur, Naphish, and Nodab. 20 The men from the tribes of Manasseh, Reuben, and Gad prayed to God during the war, asking him to help them. So he helped them because they trusted him. He handed over to them the Hagrites and all those who were with them. 21 They took the animals that belonged to the Hagrites: fifty thousand camels, two hundred fifty thousand sheep, and two thousand donkeys. They also captured one hundred thousand people. 22 Many Hagrites were killed because God helped the people of Reuben, Gad, and Manasseh. Then they lived there until Babylon captured them and took them away.

WHAT'S IT MEAN?

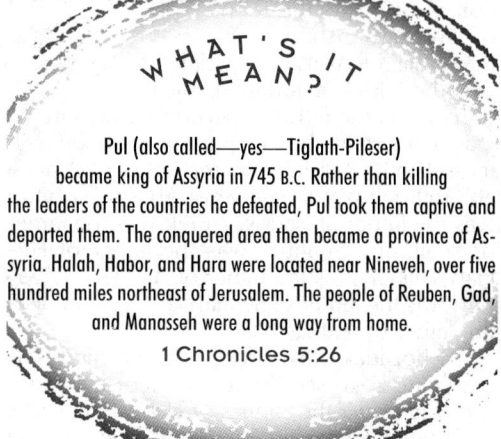

Pul (also called—yes—Tiglath-Pileser) became king of Assyria in 745 B.C. Rather than killing the leaders of the countries he defeated, Pul took them captive and deported them. The conquered area then became a province of Assyria. Halah, Habor, and Hara were located near Nineveh, over five hundred miles northeast of Jerusalem. The people of Reuben, Gad, and Manasseh were a long way from home.

1 Chronicles 5:26

EAST MANASSEH

23 There were many people in East Manasseh, and they lived in the area of Bashan all the way to Baal Hermon, Senir, and Mount Hermon.

24 These were the family leaders: Epher, Ishi, Eliel, Azriel, Jeremiah, Hodaviah, and Jahdiel. They were all strong, brave, and famous men, and leaders in their families. 25 But they sinned against the God that their ancestors had worshiped. They began worshiping the gods of the people in that land, and those were the people God was destroying. 26 So the God of Israel made Pul king of Assyria want to go to war. (Pul was also called Tiglath-Pileser.) He captured the people of Reuben, Gad, and East Manasseh, and he took them away to Halah, Habor, Hara, and near the Gozan River. They have lived there from that time until this day.

LEVI'S CHILDREN

6

1 Levi's sons were Gershon, Kohath, and Merari.

2 Kohath's sons were Amram, Izhar, Hebron, and Uzziel.

3 Amram's children were Aaron, Moses, and Miriam.

Aaron's sons were Nadab, Abihu, Eleazar, and Ithamar. 4 Eleazar was the father of Phinehas. Phinehas was the father of Abishua. 5 Abishua was the father of Bukki. Bukki was the father of Uzzi. 6 Uzzi was the father of Zerahiah. Zerahiah was the father of Meraioth. 7 Meraioth was the father of Amariah. Amariah was the father of Ahitub. 8 Ahitub was the father of Zadok. Zadok was the father of Ahimaaz. 9 Ahimaaz was the father of Azariah. Azariah was the father of Johanan. 10 Johanan was the father of Azariah. (Azariah was a priest in the Temple Solomon built in Jerusalem.) 11 Azariah was the father of Amariah. Amariah was the father of Ahitub. 12 Ahitub was the father of Zadok. Zadok was the father of Shallum. 13 Shallum was the father of Hilkiah. Hilkiah was the father of Azariah. 14 Azariah was the father of Seraiah, and Seraiah was the father of Jehozadak.

15 Jehozadak was forced to leave his home when the LORD sent Judah and Jerusalem into captivity under the control of Nebuchadnezzar.

16 Levi's sons were Gershon, Kohath, and Merari.

17 The names of Gershon's sons were Libni and Shimei.

18 Kohath's sons were Amram, Izhar, Hebron, and Uzziel.

19 Merari's sons were Mahli and Mushi.

This is a list of the family groups of Levi, listed by the name of the father of each group.

20 Gershon's son was Libni. Libni's son was Jehath. Jehath's son was Zimmah. 21 Zimmah's son was Joah. Joah's son was Iddo. Iddo's son was Zerah. And Zerah's son was Jeatherai.

22 Kohath's son was Amminadab. Amminadab's son was Korah. Korah's son was Assir. 23 Assir's son was Elkanah. Elkanah's son was Ebiasaph. Ebiasaph's son was Assir. 24 Assir's son was Tahath. Tahath's son was Uriel. Uriel's son was Uzziah, and Uzziah's son was Shaul.

25 Elkanah's sons were Amasai and Ahimoth. 26 Ahimoth's son was Elkanah. Elkanah's son was Zophai. Zophai's son was Nahath. 27 Nahath's son was Eliab. Eliab's son was Jeroham. Jeroham's son was Elkanah, and Elkanah's son was Samuel.

28 Samuel's sons were Joel, the first son, and Abijah, the second son.

29 Merari's son was Mahli. Mahli's son was Libni. Libni's son was Shimei. Shimei's son was Uzzah. 30 Uzzah's son was Shimea. Shimea's son was Haggiah, and Haggiah's son was Asaiah.

"David chose some people to be in charge of the music in the house of the LORD. They began their work after the Ark of the Agreement was put there." (1 Chronicles 6:31)

THE TEMPLE MUSICIANS

31 David chose some people to be in charge of the music in the house of the LORD. They began their work after the Ark of the Agreement was put there. 32 They served by making music at the Holy Tent (also called the Meeting Tent), and they served until Solomon built the Temple of the LORD in Jerusalem. They followed the rules for their work.

33 These are the musicians and their sons:

From Kohath's family there was Heman the singer. Heman was Joel's son. Joel was Samuel's son. 34 Samuel was Elkanah's son. Elkanah was Jeroham's son. Jeroham was Eliel's son. Eliel was Toah's son. 35 Toah was Zuph's son. Zuph was Elkanah's son. Elkanah was Mahath's son. Mahath was Amasai's son. 36 Amasai was Elkanah's son. Elkanah was Joel's son. Joel was Azariah's son. Azariah was Zephaniah's son. 37 Zephaniah was Tahath's son. Tahath was

Assir's son. Assir was Ebiasaph's son. Ebiasaph was Korah's son. 38Korah was Izhar's son. Izhar was Kohath's son. Kohath was Levi's son. Levi was Israel's son.

39There was Heman's helper Asaph, whose group stood by Heman's right side. Asaph was Berekiah's son. Berekiah was Shimea's son. 40Shimea was Michael's son. Michael was Baaseiah's son. Baaseiah was Malkijah's son. 41Malkijah was Ethni's son. Ethni was Zerah's son. Zerah was Adaiah's son. 42Adaiah was Ethan's son. Ethan was Zimmah's son. Zimmah was Shimei's son. 43Shimei was Jahath's son. Jahath was Gershon's son, and Gershon was Levi's son.

44Merari's family were the helpers of Heman and Asaph, and they stood by Heman's left side. In this group was Ethan son of Kishi. Kishi was Abdi's son. Abdi was Malluch's son. 45Malluch was Hashabiah's son. Hashabiah was Amaziah's son. Amaziah was Hilkiah's son. 46Hilkiah was Amzi's son. Amzi was Bani's son. Bani was Shemer's son. 47Shemer was Mahli's son. Mahli was Mushi's son. Mushi was Merari's son, and Merari was Levi's son.

OBEDIENCE
What's a good example of obeying God? (6:49)

48The other Levites served by doing their own special work in the Holy Tent, the house of God. 49Aaron and his descendants offered the sacrifices on the altar of burnt offering and burned the incense on the altar of incense. They offered the sacrifices that removed the Israelites' sins so they could belong to God. They did all the work in the Most Holy Place and followed all the laws that Moses, God's servant, had commanded.

50These were Aaron's sons: Eleazar was Aaron's son. Phinehas was Eleazar's son. Abishua was Phinehas' son. 51Bukki was Abishua's son. Uzzi was Bukki's son. Zerahiah was Uzzi's son. 52Meraioth was Zerahiah's son. Amariah was Meraioth's son. Ahitub was Amariah's son. 53Zadok was Ahitub's son, and Ahimaaz was Zadok's son.

WHAT'S IT MEAN?

The rules and procedures for entering the Holy Tent were extremely strict and extremely important to follow. Only the high priest was allowed to enter the inner room. Even he was allowed to enter only once a year, to ask God's forgiveness for Israel's sins. The only piece of furniture allowed in the inner room was the Ark of the Agreement, which the Israelites considered to be God's earthly throne. The Ark, which was made of acacia wood and covered with gold, contained the two flat stones on which the Law of Moses was written.

1 Chronicles 6:48

LAND FOR THE LEVITES

54These are the places where Aaron's descendants lived. His descendants from the Kohath family group received the first share of the land.

55They were given the city of Hebron in Judah and the pastures around it, 56but the fields farther from the city and the villages near Hebron were given to Caleb son of Jephunneh. 57So the descendants of Aaron were given Hebron, one of the cities of safety. They also received the towns and pastures of Libnah, Jattir, Eshtemoa, 58Hilen, Debir, 59Ashan, Juttah, and Beth Shemesh. 60They also received these towns and pastures from the tribe of Benjamin: Gibeon, Geba, Alemeth, and Anathoth.

The Kohath family groups received a total of thirteen towns.

61The rest of the Kohath family group was given ten towns from the family groups of West Manasseh. The towns were chosen by throwing lots.

62The Gershon family group received thirteen towns from the tribes of Issachar, Asher, Naphtali, and the part of Manasseh living in Bashan.

63The Merari family group received twelve towns from the tribes of Reuben, Gad, and Zebulun. Those towns were chosen by throwing lots.

64So the Israelites gave these towns and their pastures to the Levites. 65The towns from the tribes of Judah, Simeon, and Benjamin, which were named, were chosen by throwing lots.

66Some of the Kohath family groups received towns and pastures from the tribe of Ephraim. 67They received Shechem, one of the cities of safety,[n] with its pastures in the

6:67 cities of safety A person who had accidentally killed someone could go to one of the six cities of safety to receive protection and a fair trial.

mountains of Ephraim. They also received the
towns and pastures of Gezer, 68Jokmeam, Beth
Horon, 69Aijalon, and Gath Rimmon.

WHAT'S IT MEAN?

The Levites were the designated priests of Israel. They were responsible for taking care of the Meeting Tent, the altar, and the people's sacrifices. They were also responsible for meeting the spiritual needs of their fellow Israelites. Because their job was to take care of the various tribes, the Levites did not receive a specific area of land when they moved to Canaan. Instead, they were given forty-eight cities scattered throughout Israel.

1 Chronicles 6:64

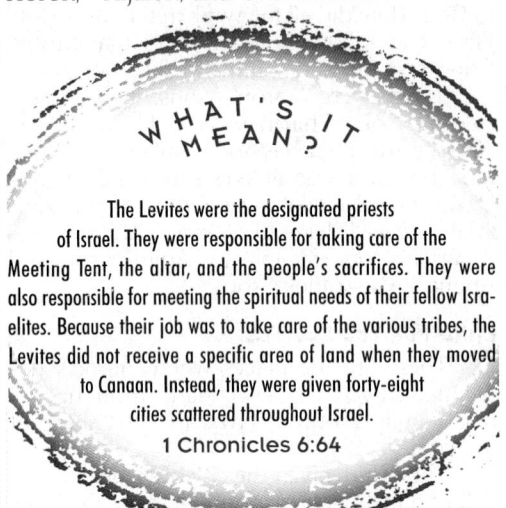

70The rest of the people in the Kohath family
group received the towns of Aner and Bileam
and their pastures from West Manasseh.
71From East Manasseh, the Gershon family
received the towns and pastures of Golan in
Bashan and Ashtaroth.
72-73From the tribe of Issachar, the Gershon
family received the towns and pastures of Kedesh, Daberath, Ramoth, and Anem.
74-75From the tribe of Asher, the Gershon
family received the towns and pastures of Mashal, Abdon, Hukok, and Rehob.
76From the tribe of Naphtali, the Gershon
family received the towns and pastures of Kedesh in Galilee, Hammon, and Kiriathaim.
77The rest of the Levites, the people from the
Merari family, received from the tribe of Zebulun the towns and pastures of Jokneam, Kartah, Rimmono, and Tabor.
78-79From the tribe of Reuben, the Merari
family received the towns and pastures of Bezer in the desert, Jahzah, Kedemoth, and
Mephaath. (The tribe of Reuben lived east of
the Jordan River, across from Jericho.)
80-81From the tribe of Gad, the Merari family
received the towns and pastures of Ramoth in
Gilead, Mahanaim, Heshbon, and Jazer.

ISSACHAR'S CHILDREN

7
1Issachar had four sons: Tola, Puah, Jashub,
and Shimron.
2Tola's sons were Uzzi, Rephaiah, Jeriel,
Jahmai, Ibsam, and Samuel, and they were
leaders of their families. In the family history of
Tola's descendants, twenty-two thousand six
hundred men were listed as fighting men during the time David was king.
3Uzzi's son was Izrahiah.
Izrahiah's sons were Michael, Obadiah,
Joel, and Isshiah. All five of them were leaders.
4Their family history shows they had thirty-six
thousand men ready to serve in the army, because they had many wives and children.
5The records of the family groups of Issachar show there were eighty-seven thousand
fighting men.

BENJAMIN'S CHILDREN

6Benjamin had three sons: Bela, Beker, and
Jediael.
7Bela had five sons: Ezbon, Uzzi, Uzziel,
Jerimoth, and Iri, and they were leaders of
their families. Their family history shows they
had twenty-two thousand thirty-four fighting
men.
8Beker's sons were Zemirah, Joash, Eliezer,
Elioenai, Omri, Jeremoth, Abijah, Anathoth,
and Alemeth. They all were Beker's sons. 9Their
family history listed the family leaders and
twenty thousand two hundred fighting men.
10Jediael's son was Bilhan.
Bilhan's sons were Jeush, Benjamin, Ehud,
Kenaanah, Zethan, Tarshish, and Ahishahar.
11All these sons of Jediael were leaders of their
families. They had seventeen thousand two
hundred fighting men ready to serve in the
army.
12The Shuppites and Huppites were descendants of Ir, and the Hushites were descendants
of Aher.

NAPHTALI'S CHILDREN

13Naphtali's sons were Jahziel, Guni, Jezer,
and Shillem. They were Bilhah's grandsons.

MANASSEH'S CHILDREN

14These are Manasseh's descendants. Manasseh had an Aramean slave woman, who
was the mother of Asriel and Makir. Makir was
Gilead's father. 15Makir took a wife from the
Huppites and Shuppites. His sister was named
Maacah. His second son was named Zelophehad, and he had only daughters. 16Makir's wife
Maacah had a son whom she named Peresh.
Peresh's brother was named Sheresh. Sheresh's
sons were Ulam and Rakem.
17Ulam's son was Bedan.
These were the sons of Gilead, who was the
son of Makir. Makir was Manasseh's son.
18Makir's sister Hammoleketh gave birth to
Ishhod, Abiezer, and Mahlah.

19 The sons of Shemida were Ahian, Shechem, Likhi, and Aniam.

WHAT'S IT MEAN?

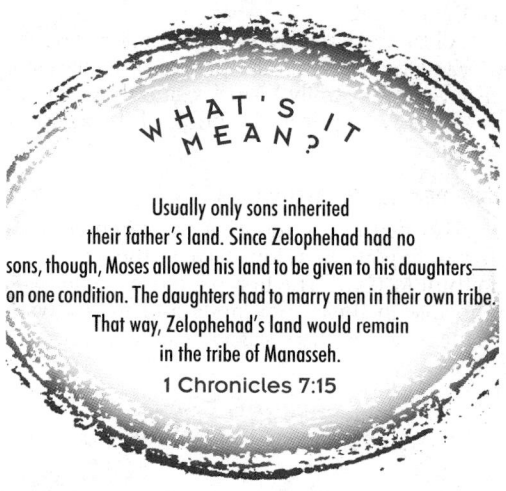

Usually only sons inherited their father's land. Since Zelophehad had no sons, though, Moses allowed his land to be given to his daughters—on one condition. The daughters had to marry men in their own tribe. That way, Zelophehad's land would remain in the tribe of Manasseh.

1 Chronicles 7:15

EPHRAIM'S CHILDREN

20 These are the names of Ephraim's descendants. Ephraim's son was Shuthelah. Shuthelah's son was Bered. Bered's son was Tahath. Tahath's son was Eleadah. Eleadah's son was Tahath. 21 Tahath's son was Zabad. Zabad's son was Shuthelah.

Ezer and Elead went to Gath to steal cows and sheep and were killed by some men who grew up in that city. 22 Their father Ephraim cried for them many days, and his family came to comfort him. 23 Then he had sexual relations with his wife again. She became pregnant and gave birth to a son whom Ephraim named Beriah[n] because of the trouble that had happened to his family. 24 Ephraim's daughter was Sheerah. She built Lower Beth Horon, Upper Beth Horon, and Uzzen Sheerah.

WHAT'S IT MEAN?

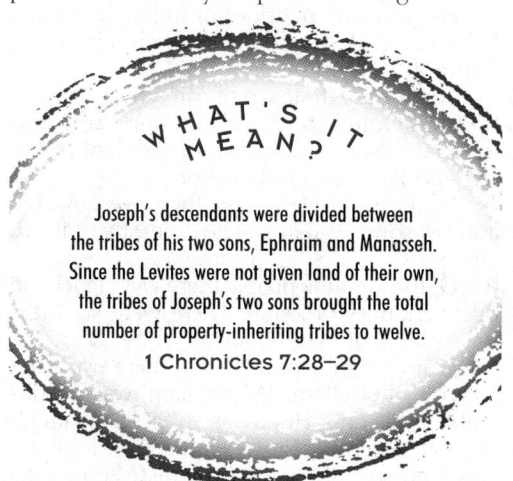

Joseph's descendants were divided between the tribes of his two sons, Ephraim and Manasseh. Since the Levites were not given land of their own, the tribes of Joseph's two sons brought the total number of property-inheriting tribes to twelve.

1 Chronicles 7:28–29

25 Rephah was Ephraim's son. Resheph was Rephah's son. Telah was Resheph's son. Tahan was Telah's son. 26 Ladan was Tahan's son. Ammihud was Ladan's son. Elishama was Ammihud's son. 27 Nun was Elishama's son, and Joshua was the son of Nun.

28 Ephraim's descendants lived in these lands and towns: Bethel and the villages near it, Naaran on the east, Gezer and the villages near it on the west, and Shechem and the villages near it. These villages went all the way to Ayyah and its villages. 29 Along the borders of Manasseh's land were the towns of Beth Shan, Taanach, Megiddo, and Dor, and the villages near them. The descendants of Joseph son of Israel lived in these towns.

ASHER'S CHILDREN

30 Asher's sons were Imnah, Ishvah, Ishvi, and Beriah. Their sister was Serah.

31 Beriah's sons were Heber and Malkiel. Malkiel was Birzaith's father.

32 Heber was the father of Japhlet, Shomer, Hotham, and their sister Shua.

33 Japhlet's sons were Pasach, Bimhal, and Ashvath. They were Japhlet's children.

34 Japhlet's brother was Shomer. Shomer's sons were Rohgah, Hubbah, and Aram.

35 Shomer's brother was Hotham. Hotham's sons were Zophah, Imna, Shelesh, and Amal.

36 Zophah's sons were Suah, Harnepher, Shual, Beri, Imrah, 37 Bezer, Hod, Shamma, Shilshah, Ithran, and Beera.

38 Jether's sons were Jephunneh, Pispah, and Ara.

39 Ulla's sons were Arah, Hanniel, and Rizia.

40 All these men were descendants of Asher and leaders of their families. They were powerful warriors and outstanding leaders. Their family history lists that they had twenty-six thousand soldiers ready to serve in the army.

THE FAMILY HISTORY OF KING SAUL

8

1 Benjamin was the father of Bela, his first son. Ashbel was his second son, Aharah was his third, 2 Nohah was his fourth, and Rapha was his fifth son.

3 Bela's sons were Addar, Gera, Abihud, 4 Abishua, Naaman, Ahoah, 5 Gera, Shephuphan, and Huram.

6 These were the descendants of Ehud and leaders of their families in Geba. They were forced to move to Manahath. 7 Ehud's

7:23 Beriah This name sounds like the Hebrew word for "trouble."

descendants were Naaman, Ahijah, and Gera. Gera forced them to leave. He was the father of Uzza and Ahihud.

[8-11]Shaharaim and his wife Hushim had sons named Abitub and Elpaal. In Moab, Shaharaim divorced his wives Hushim and Baara. Shaharaim and his wife Hodesh had these sons: Jobab, Zibia, Mesha, Malcam, Jeuz, Sakia, and Mirmah. They were leaders of their families.

[12-13]Elpaal's sons were Eber, Misham, Shemed, Beriah, and Shema. Shemed built the towns of Ono and Lod and the villages around them. Beriah and Shema were leaders of the families living in Aijalon, and they forced out the people who lived in Gath.

[14]Beriah's sons were Ahio, Shashak, Jeremoth, [15]Zebadiah, Arad, Eder, [16]Michael, Ishpah, and Joha.

[17]Elpaal's sons were Zebadiah, Meshullam, Hizki, Heber, [18]Ishmerai, Izliah, and Jobab.

[19]Shimei's sons were Jakim, Zicri, Zabdi, [20]Elienai, Zillethai, Eliel, [21]Adaiah, Beraiah, and Shimrath.

[22]Shashak's sons were Ishpan, Eber, Eliel, [23]Abdon, Zicri, Hanan, [24]Hananiah, Elam, Anthothijah, [25]Iphdeiah, and Penuel.

[26]Jeroham's sons were Shamsherai, Shehariah, Athaliah, [27]Jaareshiah, Elijah, and Zicri.

[28]The family histories show that all these men were leaders of their families and lived in Jerusalem.

[29]Jeiel lived in the town of Gibeon, where he was the leader. His wife was named Maacah. [30]Jeiel's first son was Abdon. His other sons were Zur, Kish, Baal, Ner, Nadab, [31]Gedor, Ahio, Zeker, [32]and Mikloth. Mikloth was the father of Shimeah. These sons also lived near their relatives in Jerusalem.

[33]Ner was the father of Kish. Kish was the father of Saul, and Saul was the father of Jonathan, Malki-Shua, Abinadab, and Esh-Baal.

[34]Jonathan's son was Merib-Baal, who was the father of Micah.

[35]Micah's sons were Pithon, Melech, Tarea, and Ahaz. [36]Ahaz was the father of Jehoaddah. Jehoaddah was the father of Alemeth, Azmaveth, and Zimri. Zimri was the father of Moza. [37]Moza was the father of Binea. Raphah was Binea's son. Eleasah was Raphah's son, and Azel was Eleasah's son.

[38]Azel had six sons: Azrikam, Bokeru, Ishmael, Sheariah, Obadiah, and Hanan. All these were Azel's sons.

[39]Azel's brother was Eshek. Eshek's first son was Ulam, his second was Jeush, and Eliphelet was his third. [40]Ulam's sons were mighty warriors and good archers. They had many sons and grandsons—one hundred fifty of them in all.

All these men were Benjamin's descendants.

9

[1]The names of all the people of Israel were listed in their family histories, and those family histories were put in the book of the kings of Israel.

THE PEOPLE IN JERUSALEM

The people of Judah were captured and forced to go to Babylon, because they were not faithful to God. [2]The first people to come back and live in their own lands and towns were some Israelites, priests, Levites, and Temple servants.

WHAT'S IT MEAN?

The kingdom of Babylon was a constant threat to the Israelites. This powerful city was located on the Euphrates River about 550 miles east of Jerusalem. Babylon conquered Jerusalem and the southern kingdom of Judah for the first time in 597 B.C. The Babylonians deported more than three thousand Jewish leaders after their victory. Recognizing a good thing when they saw it, the Babylonians came back for more captives in 587 and 581 B.C. Eventually, though, many of the captives were allowed to return.

1 Chronicles 9:1

[3]People from the tribes of Judah, Benjamin, Ephraim, and Manasseh lived in Jerusalem. This is a list of those people.

[4]There was Uthai son of Ammihud. (Ammihud was Omri's son. Omri was Imri's son. Imri was Bani's son. Bani was a descendant of Perez, and Perez was Judah's son.)

[5]Of the Shilonite people there were Asaiah and his sons. Asaiah was the oldest son in his family.

[6]Of the Zerahite people there were Jeuel and other relatives of Zerah. There were six hundred ninety of them in all.

[7]From the tribe of Benjamin there was Sallu son of Meshullam. (Meshullam was Hodaviah's son, and Hodaviah was Hassenuah's son.) [8]There was also Ibneiah son of Jeroham and Elah son of Uzzi. (Uzzi was Micri's son.) And there was Meshullam son of Shephatiah. (Shephatiah was Reuel's son, and Reuel was

Ibnijah's son.) [9]The family history of Benjamin lists nine hundred fifty-six people living in Jerusalem, and all these were leaders of their families.

[10]Of the priests there were Jedaiah, Jehoiarib, Jakin, and [11]Azariah son of Hilkiah. (Hilkiah was Meshullam's son. Meshullam was Zadok's son. Zadok was Meraioth's son. Meraioth was Ahitub's son. Ahitub was the officer responsible for the Temple of God.) [12]Also there was Adaiah son of Jeroham. (Jeroham was Pashhur's son, and Pashhur was Malkijah's son.) And there was Maasai son of Adiel. (Adiel was Jahzerah's son. Jahzerah was Meshullam's son. Meshullam was Meshillemith's son, and Meshillemith was Immer's son.) [13]There were one thousand seven hundred sixty priests. They were leaders of their families, and they were responsible for serving in the Temple of God.

[14]Of the Levites there was Shemaiah son of Hasshub. (Hasshub was Azrikam's son, and Azrikam was Hashabiah's son. Hashabiah was from the family of Merari.) [15]There were also Bakbakkar, Heresh, Galal, and Mattaniah son of Mica. (Mica was Zicri's son, and Zicri was Asaph's son.) [16]There was also Obadiah son of Shemaiah. (Shemaiah was Galal's son, and Galal was Jeduthun's son.) And there was Berekiah son of Asa. (Asa was the son of Elkanah, who lived in the villages of the Netophathites.)

[17]Of the gatekeepers there were Shallum, Akkub, Talmon, Ahiman, and their relatives. Shallum was their leader. [18]These gatekeepers from the tribe of Levi still stand next to the King's Gate on the east side of the city. [19]Shallum was Kore's son. Kore was Ebiasaph's son, and Ebiasaph was Korah's son. Shallum and his relatives from the family of Korah were gatekeepers and were responsible for guarding the gates of the Temple. Their ancestors had also been responsible for guarding the entrance to the Temple of the LORD. [20]In the past Phinehas, Eleazar's son, was in charge of the gatekeepers, and the LORD was with Phinehas. [21]Zechariah son of Meshelemiah was the gatekeeper at the entrance to the Temple.

[22]In all, two hundred twelve men were chosen to guard the gates, and their names were written in their family histories in their villages. David and Samuel the seer chose these men because they were dependable. [23]The gatekeepers and their descendants had to guard the gates of the Temple of the LORD. (The Temple took the place of the Holy Tent.) [24]There were gatekeepers on all four sides of the Temple: east, west, north, and south. [25]The gatekeepers' relatives who lived in the villages had to come and help them at times. Each time they came they helped the gatekeepers for seven days. [26]Because they were dependable, four gatekeepers were made the leaders of all the gatekeepers. They were Levites, and they were responsible for the rooms and treasures in the Temple of God. [27]They stayed up all night guarding the Temple of God, and they opened it every morning.

[28]Some of the gatekeepers were responsible for the utensils used in the Temple services. They counted these utensils when people took them out and when they brought them back. [29]Other gatekeepers were chosen to take care of the furniture and utensils in the Holy Place. They also took care of the flour, wine, oil, incense, and spices, [30]but some of the priests took care of mixing the spices. [31]There was a Levite named Mattithiah who was dependable and had the job of baking the bread used for the offerings. He was the first son of Shallum, who was from the family of Korah. [32]Some of the gatekeepers from the Kohath family had the job of preparing the special bread that was put on the table every Sabbath day.

[33]Some of the Levites were musicians in the Temple. The leaders of these families stayed in the rooms of the Temple. Since they were on duty day and night, they did not do other work in the Temple.

[34]These are the leaders of the Levite families. Their names were listed in their family histories, and they lived in Jerusalem.

THE FAMILY HISTORY OF KING SAUL

[35]Jeiel lived in the town of Gibeon, where he was the leader. His wife was named Maacah. [36]Jeiel's first son was Abdon. His other sons were Zur, Kish, Baal, Ner, Nadab, [37]Gedor, Ahio, Zechariah, and Mikloth. [38]Mikloth was Shimeam's father. Jeiel's family lived near their relatives in Jerusalem.

[39]Ner was Kish's father. Kish was Saul's father. Saul was the father of Jonathan, Malki-Shua, Abinadab, and Esh-Baal.

[40]Jonathan's son was Merib-Baal, who was the father of Micah.

[41]Micah's sons were Pithon, Melech, Tahrea, and Ahaz. [42]Ahaz was Jadah's father. Jadah was the father of Alemeth, Azmaveth, and Zimri. Zimri was Moza's father. [43]Moza was Binea's father. Rephaiah was Binea's son. Eleasah was Rephaiah's son, and Azel was Eleasah's son.

[44]Azel had six sons: Azrikam, Bokeru, Ishmael, Sheariah, Obadiah, and Hanan. They were Azel's sons.

THE DEATH OF KING SAUL

10 [1]The Philistines fought against Israel, and
the Israelites ran away from them. Many Israelites were killed on Mount Gilboa. [2]The Philistines fought hard against Saul and his sons,
killing his sons Jonathan, Abinadab, and Malki-
Shua. [3]The fighting was heavy around Saul,
and the archers shot him with their arrows
and wounded him.
[4]Then Saul said to the officer who carried
his armor, "Pull out your sword and stab me. If
you don't, these Philistines who are not circumcised will come and hurt me." But Saul's
officer refused, because he was afraid. So Saul
took his own sword and threw himself on it.
[5]When the officer saw that Saul was dead, he
threw himself on his own sword and died. [6]So
Saul and three of his sons died; all his family
died together.
[7]When the Israelites living in the valley saw
that their army had run away and that Saul
and his sons were dead, they left their towns
and ran away. Then the Philistines came and
settled in them.
[8]The next day when the Philistines came to
strip the dead soldiers, they found Saul and his
sons dead on Mount Gilboa. [9]The Philistines
stripped Saul's body and took his head and his
armor. Then they sent messengers through all
their country to tell the news to their idols and
to their people. [10]The Philistines put Saul's armor in the temple of their idols and hung his
head in the temple of Dagon.
[11]All the people in Jabesh Gilead heard
what the Philistines had done to Saul. [12]So the
brave men of Jabesh went and got the bodies
of Saul and his sons and brought them to Jabesh. They buried their bones under the large
tree in Jabesh. Then the people of Jabesh gave
up eating for seven days.
[13]Saul died because he was
not faithful to the LORD and
did not obey the LORD. He
even went to a medium and
asked her for advice [14]instead
of asking the LORD. This is
why the LORD put Saul to death
and gave the kingdom to Jesse's son David.

OCCULT

Does God judge occult practices? (10:13–14)

WHAT'S IT MEAN?

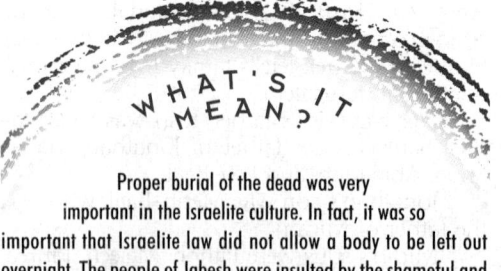

Proper burial of the dead was very important in the Israelite culture. In fact, it was so important that Israelite law did not allow a body to be left out overnight. The people of Jabesh were insulted by the shameful and degrading way the bodies of Saul and his sons were being treated. They showed courage and commitment in making sure the bodies received proper burial.

1 Chronicles 10:11–12

DAVID BECOMES KING

11 [1]Then the people of Israel came to David at
the town of Hebron and said, "Look, we are
your own family. [2]Even when Saul was king,
you were the one who led Israel in battle. The
LORD your God said to you, 'You will be the
shepherd for my people Israel. You will be
their leader.' "
[3]So all the older leaders of Israel came to
King David at Hebron. He made an agreement
with them in Hebron in the presence of the
LORD. Then they poured oil on David to make
him king over Israel. The LORD had promised
through Samuel that this would happen.

WHAT'S IT MEAN?

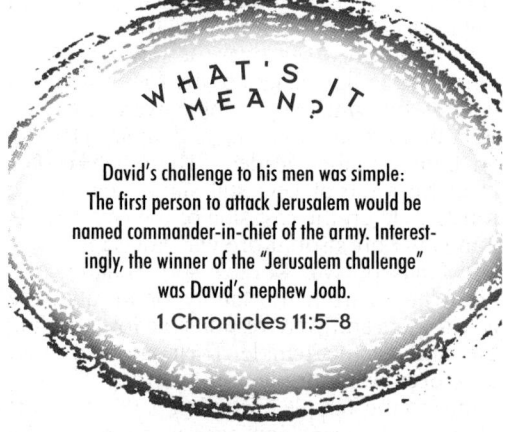

David's challenge to his men was simple: The first person to attack Jerusalem would be named commander-in-chief of the army. Interestingly, the winner of the "Jerusalem challenge" was David's nephew Joab.

1 Chronicles 11:5–8

DAVID CAPTURES JERUSALEM

[4]David and all the Israelites went to the city
of Jerusalem. At that time Jerusalem was called
Jebus, and the people living there were named
Jebusites. [5]They said to David, "You can't get
inside our city." But David did take the city of
Jerusalem with its strong walls, and it became
the City of David.
[6]David had said, "The person who leads the
attack against the Jebusites will become the
commander over all my army." Joab son of
Zeruiah led the attack, so he became the commander of the army.

[7]Then David made his home in the strong, walled city, which is why it was named the City of David. [8]David rebuilt the city, beginning where the land was filled in and going to the wall that was around the city. Joab repaired the other parts of the city. [9]David became stronger and stronger, and the LORD All-Powerful was with him.

DAVID'S MIGHTY WARRIORS

[10]This is a list of the leaders over David's warriors who helped make David's kingdom strong. All the people of Israel also supported David's kingdom. These heroes and all the people of Israel made David king, just as the LORD had promised.

> "This is a list of the leaders over David's warriors who helped make David's kingdom strong. All the people of Israel also supported David's kingdom. These heroes and all the people of Israel made David king, just as the LORD had promised."
> (1 Chronicles 11:10)

[11]This is a list of David's warriors:

Jashobeam was from the Hacmonite people. He was the head of the Three,[n] David's most powerful soldiers. He used his spear to fight three hundred men at one time, and he killed them all.

[12]Next was Eleazar, one of the Three. Eleazar was Dodai's son from the Ahohite people. [13]Eleazar was with David at Pas Dammim when the Philistines came there to fight. There was a field of barley at that place. The Israelites ran away from the Philistines, [14]but they stopped in the middle of that field and fought for it and killed the Philistines. The LORD gave them a great victory.

SUCCESS
Can we trust God for our success? (11:14)

[15]Once, three of the Thirty, David's chief soldiers, came down to him at the rock by the cave near Adullam. At the same time the Philistine army had camped in the Valley of Rephaim.

[16]At that time David was in a stronghold, and some of the Philistines were in Bethlehem. [17]David had a strong desire for some water. He said, "Oh, I wish someone would get me water from the well near the city gate of Bethlehem!" [18]So the Three broke through the Philistine army and took water from the well near the city gate in Bethlehem. Then they brought it to David, but he refused to drink it. He poured it out before the LORD, [19]saying, "May God keep me from drinking this water! It would be like drinking the blood of the men who risked their lives to bring it to me!" So David refused to drink it.

These were the brave things that the three warriors did.

[20]Abishai brother of Joab was the captain of the Three. Abishai fought three hundred soldiers with his spear and killed them. He became as famous as the Three [21]and was more honored than the Three. He became their commander even though he was not one of them.

[22]Benaiah son of Jehoiada was a brave fighter from Kabzeel who did mighty things. He killed two of the best warriors from Moab. He also went down into a pit and killed a lion on a snowy day. [23]Benaiah killed an Egyptian who was about seven and one-half feet tall and had a spear as large as a weaver's rod. Benaiah had a club, but he grabbed the spear from the Egyptian's hand and killed him with his own spear. [24]These were the things Benaiah son of Jehoiada did. He was as famous as the Three. [25]He received more honor than the Thirty, but he did not become a member of the Three. David made him leader of his bodyguards.

THE THIRTY CHIEF SOLDIERS

[26]These were also mighty warriors:
Asahel brother of Joab; Elhanan son of Dodo from Bethlehem;
[27]Shammoth the Harorite; Helez the Pelonite;
[28]Ira son of Ikkesh from Tekoa; Abiezer the Anathothite;
[29]Sibbecai the Hushathite; Ilai the Ahohite;
[30]Maharai the Netophathite; Heled son of Baanah the Netophathite;
[31]Ithai son of Ribai from Gibeah in Benjamin; Benaiah the Pirathonite;
[32]Hurai from the ravines of Gaash; Abiel the Arbathite;
[33]Azmaveth the Baharumite; Eliahba the Shaalbonite;

11:11 Three Or maybe "Thirty." These were David's most powerful soldiers. See 2 Samuel 23:8.

34 the sons of Hashem the Gizonite; Jonathan son of Shagee the Hararite;
35 Ahiam son of Sacar the Hararite; Eliphal son of Ur;
36 Hepher the Mekerathite; Ahijah the Pelonite;
37 Hezro the Carmelite; Naarai son of Ezbai;
38 Joel brother of Nathan; Mibhar son of Hagri;
39 Zelek the Ammonite; Naharai the Berothite, the officer who carried the armor for Joab son of Zeruiah;
40 Ira the Ithrite;
Gareb the Ithrite;
41 Uriah the Hittite;
Zabad son of Ahlai;
42 Adina son of Shiza the Reubenite, who was the leader of the Reubenites, and his thirty soldiers;
43 Hanan son of Maacah;
Joshaphat the Mithnite;
44 Uzzia the Ashterathite;
Shama and Jeiel sons of Hotham the Aroerite;
45 Jediael son of Shimri;
Joha, Jediael's brother, the Tizite;
46 Eliel the Mahavite;
Jeribai and Joshaviah, Elnaam's sons;
Ithmah the Moabite;
47 Eliel, Obed, and Jaasiel the Mezobaites.

WARRIORS JOIN DAVID

12 1 These were the men who came to David at
Ziklag when David was hiding from Saul son
of Kish. They were among the warriors who
helped David in battle. 2 They came with bows
for weapons and could use either their right or
left hands to shoot arrows or to sling rocks.
They were Saul's relatives from the tribe of
Benjamin. 3 Ahiezer was their leader, and there
was Joash. (Ahiezer and Joash were sons of
Shemaah, who was from the town of Gibeah.)
There were also Jeziel and Pelet, the sons of
Azmaveth. There were Beracah and Jehu from
the town of Anathoth. 4 And there was
Ishmaiah from the town of Gibeon; he was
one of the Thirty. In fact, he was the leader of
the Thirty. There were Jeremiah, Jahaziel, Johanan, and Jozabad from Gederah. 5 There were
Eluzai, Jerimoth, Bealiah, and Shemariah. There
was Shephatiah from Haruph. 6 There were Elkanah, Isshiah, Azarel, Joezer, and Jashobeam
from the family group of Korah. 7 And there
were Joelah and Zebadiah, the sons of Jeroham, from the town of Gedor.
8 Part of the people of Gad joined David at
his stronghold in the desert. They were brave
warriors trained for war and skilled with
shields and spears. They were as fierce as lions
and as fast as gazelles over the hills.
9 Ezer was the leader of Gad's army, and
Obadiah was second in command. Eliab was
third, 10 Mishmannah was fourth, Jeremiah was
fifth, 11 Attai was sixth, Eliel was seventh, 12 Johanan was eighth, Elzabad was ninth, 13 Jeremiah was tenth, and Macbannai was eleventh
in command.
14 They were the commanders of the army
from Gad. The least of these leaders was in
charge of a hundred soldiers, and the greatest
was in charge of a thousand. 15 They crossed
the Jordan River and chased away the people
living in the valleys, to the east and to the west.
This happened in the first month of the year
when the Jordan floods the valley.
16 Other people from the tribes of Benjamin
and Judah also came to David at his stronghold. 17 David went out to meet them and said
to them, "If you have come peacefully to help
me, I welcome you. Join me. But if you have
come to turn me over to my enemies, even
though I have done nothing wrong, the God of
our fathers will see this and punish you."
18 Then the Spirit entered Amasai, the leader
of the Thirty, and he said:

"We belong to you, David.
We are with you, son of Jesse.
Success, success to you.
Success to those who help you,
because your God helps you."

So David welcomed these men and made
them leaders of his army.
19 Some of the men from Manasseh also
joined David when he went with the Philistines
to fight Saul. But David and his men did not
really help the Philistines. After talking about it,

WHAT'S IT MEAN?

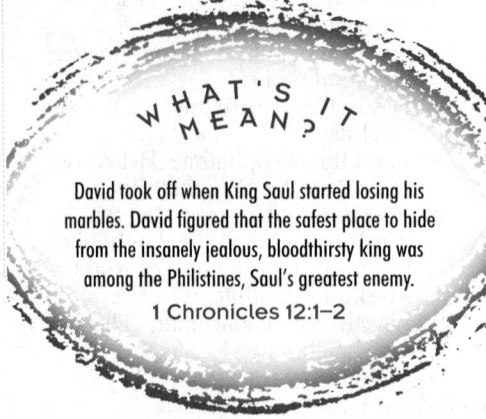

David took off when King Saul started losing his marbles. David figured that the safest place to hide from the insanely jealous, bloodthirsty king was among the Philistines, Saul's greatest enemy.

1 Chronicles 12:1–2

the Philistine leaders decided to send David away. They said, "If David goes back to his master Saul, we will be killed." [20]These are the men from Manasseh who joined David when he went to Ziklag: Adnah, Jozabad, Jediael, Michael, Jozabad, Elihu, and Zillethai. Each of them was a leader of a thousand men from Manasseh. [21]All these men of Manasseh were brave soldiers, and they helped David fight against groups of men who went around the country robbing people. These soldiers became commanders in David's army. [22]Every day more men joined David, and his army became large, like the army of God.

OTHERS JOIN DAVID AT HEBRON

[23]These are the numbers of the soldiers ready for battle who joined David at Hebron. They came to help turn the kingdom of Saul over to David, just as the LORD had said.

[24]There were sixty-eight hundred men with their weapons from Judah. They carried shields and spears.

[25]There were seventy-one hundred men from Simeon. They were warriors ready for war.

[26]There were forty-six hundred men from Levi. [27]Jehoiada, a leader from Aaron's family, was in that group. There were thirty-seven hundred with him. [28]Zadok was also in that group. He was a strong young warrior, and with him came twenty-two leaders from his family.

[29]There were three thousand men from Benjamin, who were Saul's relatives. Most of them had remained loyal to Saul's family until then.

[30]There were twenty thousand eight hundred men from Ephraim. They were brave warriors and were famous men in their own family groups.

[31]There were eighteen thousand men from West Manasseh. Each one was especially chosen to make David king.

[32]There were two hundred leaders from Issachar. They knew what Israel should do, and they knew the right time to do it. Their relatives were with them and under their command.

[33]There were fifty thousand men from Zebulun. They were trained soldiers and knew how to use every kind of weapon of war. They followed David completely.

[34]There were one thousand officers from Naphtali. They had thirty-seven thousand soldiers with them who carried shields and spears.

[35]There were twenty-eight thousand six hundred men from Dan, who were ready for war.

[36]There were forty thousand trained soldiers from Asher, who were ready for war.

[37]There were one hundred twenty thousand soldiers from the east side of the Jordan River from the people of Reuben, Gad, and East Manasseh. They had every kind of weapon.

[38]All these fighting men were ready to go to war. They came to Hebron fully agreed to make David king of all Israel. All the other Israelites also agreed to make David king. [39]They spent three days there with David, eating and drinking, because their relatives had prepared food for them. [40]Also, their neighbors came from as far away as Issachar, Zebulun, and Naphtali, bringing food on donkeys, camels, mules, and oxen. They brought much flour, fig cakes, raisins, wine, oil, cows, and sheep, because the people of Israel were very happy.

BRINGING BACK THE ARK

13 [1]David talked with all the officers of his army, the commanders of a hundred men and the commanders of a thousand men. [2]Then David called the people of Israel together and said, "If you think it is a good idea, and if it is what the LORD our God wants, let's send a message. Let's tell our fellow Israelites in all the areas of Israel and the priests and Levites living with them in their towns and pastures to come and join us. [3]Let's bring the Ark of our God back to us. We did not use it to ask God for help while Saul was king." [4]All the people agreed with David, because they all thought it was the right thing to do.

[5]So David gathered all the Israelites, from the Shihor River in Egypt to Lebo Hamath, to bring the Ark of God back from the town of Kiriath Jearim. [6]David and all the Israelites with him went to Baalah of Judah, which is Kiriath Jearim, to get the Ark of God the LORD. God's throne is between the golden, winged creatures on the Ark, and the Ark is called by his name.

[7]The people carried the Ark of God from Abinadab's house on a new cart, and Uzzah and Ahio guided it. [8]David and all the Israelites were celebrating in the presence of God. With all their strength they were singing and playing lyres, harps, tambourines, cymbals, and trumpets.

[9]When David's men came to the threshing floor of Kidon, the oxen stumbled, and Uzzah reached out his hand to steady the Ark. [10]The LORD was angry with Uzzah and killed him, because he had touched the Ark. So Uzzah died there in the presence of God.

11David was angry because the LORD had
punished Uzzah in his anger. Now that place is
called The Punishment of Uzzah.

WHAT'S IT MEAN?

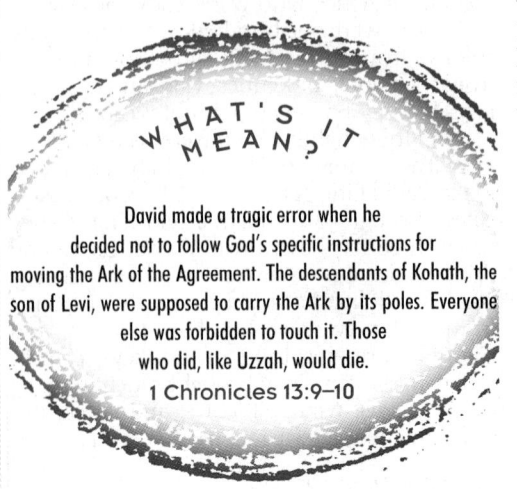

David made a tragic error when he decided not to follow God's specific instructions for moving the Ark of the Agreement. The descendants of Kohath, the son of Levi, were supposed to carry the Ark by its poles. Everyone else was forbidden to touch it. Those who did, like Uzzah, would die.

1 Chronicles 13:9–10

12David was afraid of God that day and
asked, "How can I bring the Ark of God home
to me?" 13So David did not take the Ark with
him to Jerusalem. Instead, he took it to the
house of Obed-Edom who was from Gath.
14The Ark of God stayed with Obed-Edom's
family in his house for three months, and the
LORD blessed Obed-Edom's family and everything he owned.

DAVID'S KINGDOM GROWS

14
1Hiram king of the city of Tyre sent messengers to David. He also sent cedar logs, bricklayers, and carpenters to build a palace for David.
2Then David knew that the LORD really had
made him king of Israel and that he had made
his kingdom great. The LORD did this because
he loved his people Israel.
3David married more women in Jerusalem
and had more sons and daughters. 4These are
the names of David's children born in Jerusalem: Shammua, Shobab, Nathan, Solomon,
5Ibhar, Elishua, Elpelet, 6Nogah, Nepheg, Japhia, 7Elishama, Beeliada, and Eliphelet.

DAVID DEFEATS THE PHILISTINES

8When the Philistines heard that David had
been made king of all Israel, they went to look
for him. But David heard about it and went out
to fight them. 9The Philistines had attacked and
robbed the people in the Valley of Rephaim.
10David asked God, "Should I go and attack the
Philistines? Will you hand them over to me?"
The LORD answered him, "Go,
I will hand them over to you."

GUIDANCE

Can we trust God to lead us? (14:10)

11So David and his men
went up to the town of Baal
Perazim and defeated the Philistines. David said, "Like a
flood of water, God has broken
through my enemies by using
me." So that place was named Baal Perazim.[n]
12The Philistines had left their idols there, so
David ordered his men to burn them.
13Soon the Philistines attacked the people in
the valley again. 14David prayed to God again,
and God answered him, saying, "Don't attack
the Philistines from the front. Instead, go
around them and attack them in front of the
balsam trees. 15When you hear the sound of
marching in the tops of the balsam trees, then
attack. I, God, will have gone out before you to
defeat the Philistine army." 16David did as God
commanded, and he and his men defeated the
Philistine army all the way from Gibeon to
Gezer.
17So David became famous in all the countries, and the LORD made all nations afraid
of him.

THE ARK IS BROUGHT TO JERUSALEM

15
1David built houses for himself in Jerusalem. Then he prepared a place for the Ark of
God, and he set up a tent for it. 2David said,
"Only the Levites may carry the Ark of God.
The LORD chose them to carry the Ark of the
LORD and to serve him forever."
3David called all the people of Israel to
come to Jerusalem. He wanted to bring the Ark
of the LORD to the place he had made for it.
4David called together the descendants of
Aaron and the Levites. 5There were one hundred twenty people from Kohath's family
group, with Uriel as their leader. 6There were
two hundred twenty people from Merari's
family group, with Asaiah as their leader.
7There were one hundred thirty people from
Gershon's family group, with Joel as their
leader. 8There were two hundred people from
Elizaphan's family group, with Shemaiah as
their leader. 9There were eighty people from
Hebron's family group, with Eliel as their
leader. 10And there were one hundred twelve
people from Uzziel's family group, with Amminadab as their leader.
11Then David asked the priests Zadok and
Abiathar and these Levites to come to him:
Uriel, Asaiah, Joel, Shemaiah, Eliel, and Am-

14:11 Baal Perazim This name means "the Lord breaks through."

minadab. 12David said to them, "You are the leaders of the families of Levi. You and the other Levites must give yourselves for service to the LORD. Bring up the Ark of the LORD, the God of Israel, to the place I have made for it. 13The last time we did not ask the LORD how to carry it. You Levites didn't carry it, so the LORD our God punished us."

WHAT'S IT MEAN?

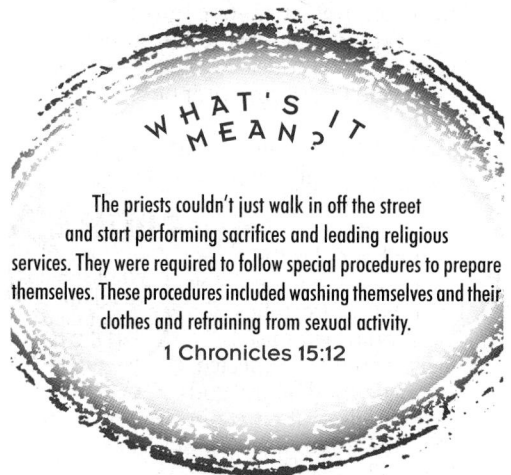

The priests couldn't just walk in off the street and start performing sacrifices and leading religious services. They were required to follow special procedures to prepare themselves. These procedures included washing themselves and their clothes and refraining from sexual activity.

1 Chronicles 15:12

14Then the priests and Levites prepared themselves for service to the LORD so they could carry the Ark of the LORD, the God of Israel. 15The Levites used special poles to carry the Ark of God on their shoulders, as Moses had commanded, just as the LORD had said they should.

16David told the leaders of the Levites to appoint their brothers as singers to play their lyres, harps, and cymbals and to sing happy songs.

17So the Levites appointed Heman and his relatives Asaph and Ethan. Heman was Joel's son. Asaph was Berekiah's son. And Ethan, from the Merari family group, was Kushaiah's son. 18There was also a second group of Levites: Zechariah, Jaaziel, Shemiramoth, Jehiel, Unni, Eliab, Benaiah, Maaseiah, Mattithiah, Eliphelehu, Mikneiah, Obed-Edom, and Jeiel. They were the Levite guards.

19The singers Heman, Asaph, and Ethan played bronze cymbals. 20Zechariah, Jaaziel, Shemiramoth, Jehiel, Unni, Eliab, Maaseiah, and Benaiah played the lyres. 21Mattithiah, Eliphelehu, Mikneiah, Obed-Edom, Jeiel, and Azaziah played the harps. 22The Levite leader Kenaniah was in charge of the singing, because he was very good at it.

23Berekiah and Elkanah were two of the guards for the Ark of the Agreement. 24The priests Shebaniah, Joshaphat, Nethanel, Amasai, Zechariah, Benaiah, and Eliezer had the job of blowing trumpets in front of the Ark of God. Obed-Edom and Jehiah were also guards for the Ark.

25David, the leaders of Israel, and the commanders of a thousand soldiers went to get the Ark of the Agreement with the LORD. They all went to bring the Ark from Obed-Edom's house with great joy. 26Because God helped the Levites who carried the Ark of the Agreement with the LORD, they sacrificed seven bulls and seven male sheep. 27All the Levites who carried the Ark, and Kenaniah, the man in charge of the singing, and all the singers wore robes of fine linen. David also wore a robe of fine linen and a holy vest of fine linen. 28So all the people of Israel brought up the Ark of the Agreement with the LORD. They shouted, blew horns and trumpets, and played cymbals, lyres, and harps.

29As the Ark of the Agreement with the LORD entered Jerusalem, Saul's daughter Michal watched from a window. When she saw King David dancing and celebrating, she hated him.

WHAT'S IT MEAN?

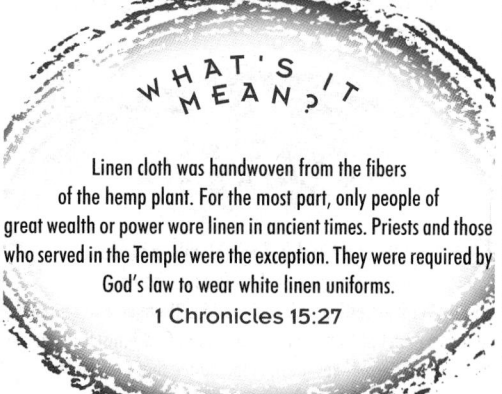

Linen cloth was handwoven from the fibers of the hemp plant. For the most part, only people of great wealth or power wore linen in ancient times. Priests and those who served in the Temple were the exception. They were required by God's law to wear white linen uniforms.

1 Chronicles 15:27

16

1They brought the Ark of God and put it inside the tent that David had set up for it. Then they offered burnt offerings and fellowship offerings to God. 2When David had finished giving the burnt offerings and fellowship offerings, he blessed the people in the name of the LORD. 3He gave a loaf of bread, some dates, and raisins to every Israelite man and woman.

4Then David appointed some of the Levites to serve before the Ark of the LORD. They had the job of leading the worship and giving thanks and praising the LORD, the God of Israel. 5Asaph, who played the cymbals, was the leader. Zechariah was second to him. The other

Levites were Jaaziel, Shemiramoth, Jehiel, Mattithiah, Eliab, Benaiah, Obed-Edom,
and Jeiel. They played the
lyres and harps. 6Benaiah
and Jahaziel were priests
who blew the trumpets regularly before the Ark of the
Agreement with God. 7That
day David first gave Asaph
and his relatives the job of
singing praises to the LORD.

THANKFULNESS
What should we do when we are thankful? (16:4–36)

DAVID'S SONG OF THANKS

8Give thanks to the LORD and pray to him.
Tell the nations what he has done.
9Sing to him; sing praises to him.
Tell about all his miracles.
10Be glad that you are his;
let those who seek the LORD be happy.
11Depend on the LORD and his strength;
always go to him for help.
12Remember the miracles he has done,
his wonders, and his decisions.
13You are the descendants of his servant, Israel;
you are the children of Jacob, his chosen people.

WHAT'S IT MEAN?

Don't get confused here. Jacob and Israel were the same person. *Israel* was the name given to Jacob after he wrestled with a mysterious stranger who turned out to be an angel of God—or perhaps even God himself. Later, the name *Israel* was given to the nation that was made up of Jacob's twelve sons and their descendants.
1 Chronicles 16:13

14He is the LORD our God.
His laws are for all the world.
15He will keep his agreement forever;
he will keep his promises always.
16He will keep the agreement he made with Abraham
and the promise he made to Isaac.
17He made it a law for the people of Jacob;
he made it an agreement with Israel to last forever.
18He said, "I will give the land of Canaan to you,
to belong to you."

19Then God's people were few in number,
and they were strangers in the land.
20They went from one nation to another,
from one kingdom to another.
21But he did not let anyone hurt them;
he warned kings not to harm them.
22He said, "Don't touch my chosen people,
and don't harm my prophets."

23Sing to the LORD, all the earth.
Every day tell how he saves us.
24Tell the nations about his glory;
tell all peoples the miracles he does.
25The LORD is great; he should be praised.
He should be respected more than all the gods.
26All the gods of the nations are only idols,
but the LORD made the skies.
27He has glory and majesty;
he has power and joy in his Temple.

WITNESSING
What should we tell others about God? (16:24)

28Praise the LORD, all nations on earth.
Praise the LORD's glory and power;
29 praise the glory of the LORD's name.
Bring an offering and come to him.
Worship the LORD because he is holy.
30Tremble before him, everyone on earth.
The earth is set, and it cannot be moved.
31Let the skies rejoice and the earth be glad.
Let people everywhere say, "The LORD is king!"
32Let the sea and everything in it shout;
let the fields and everything in them rejoice.
33Then the trees of the forest will sing
for joy before the LORD.
They will sing because he is coming to judge the world.

34Thank the LORD because he is good.
His love continues forever.
35Say to him, "Save us, God our Savior,
and bring us back and save us from other nations.
Then we will thank you
and will gladly praise you."

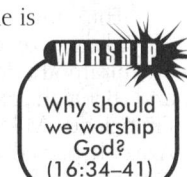

WORSHIP
Why should we worship God? (16:34–41)

36 Praise the LORD, the God of Israel.
He always was and always will be.
All the people said "Amen" and praised the
LORD.
37 Then David left Asaph and the other Levites there in front of the Ark of the Agreement
with the LORD. They were to serve there every
day. 38 David also left Obed-Edom and sixty-
eight other Levites to serve with them. Hosah
and Obed-Edom son of Jeduthun were guards.

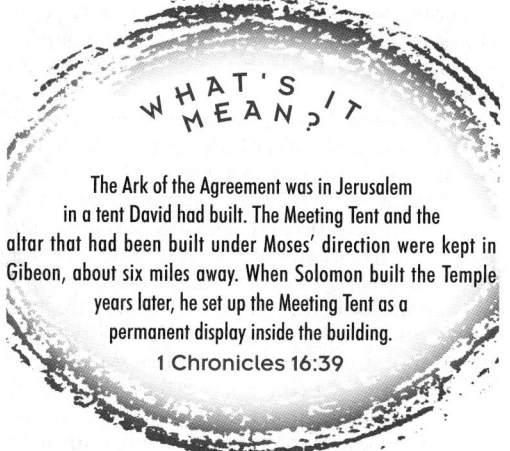

WHAT'S IT MEAN?

The Ark of the Agreement was in Jerusalem in a tent David had built. The Meeting Tent and the altar that had been built under Moses' direction were kept in Gibeon, about six miles away. When Solomon built the Temple years later, he set up the Meeting Tent as a permanent display inside the building.

1 Chronicles 16:39

39 David left Zadok the priest and the other
priests who served with him in front of the
Tent of the LORD at the place of worship in
Gibeon. 40 Every morning and evening they offered burnt offerings on the altar of burnt offerings, following the rules written in the
Teachings of the LORD, which he had given Israel. 41 With them were Heman
and Jeduthun and other Levites. They were chosen by
name to sing praises to the
LORD because his love continues forever. 42 Heman and
Jeduthun also had the job of
playing the trumpets and
cymbals and other musical
instruments when songs
were sung to God. Jeduthun's
sons guarded the gates.
43 Then all the people left. Each person
went home, and David also went home to
bless the people in his home.

"You made the people of Israel your very own people forever, and, LORD, you are their God." (1 Chronicles 17:22)

GOD'S PROMISE TO DAVID

17 1 When David moved into his palace, he said
to Nathan the prophet, "Look, I am living in a
palace made of cedar, but the Ark of the Agreement with the LORD sits in a tent."
2 Nathan said to David, "Do what you want
to do, because God is with you."
3 But that night God spoke his word to Nathan, saying, 4 "Go and tell David my servant,
'This is what the LORD says: You are not the
person to build a house for me to live in.
5 From the time I brought Israel out of Egypt
until now I have not lived in a house. I have
moved from one tent site to another and from
one place to another. 6 As I have moved with
the Israelites to different places, I have never
said to the leaders, whom I commanded to
take care of my people, "Why haven't you built
me a house of cedar?" '
7 "Now, tell my servant David: 'This is what
the LORD All-Powerful says: I took you from
the pasture and from tending the sheep and
made you king of my people Israel. 8 I have
been with you everywhere you have gone. I
have defeated your enemies for you. I will
make you as famous as any of the great people
on the earth. 9 I will choose a place for my people Israel, and I will plant them so they can live
in their own homes. They will not be bothered
anymore. Wicked people will no longer hurt
them as they have in the past 10 when I chose
judges for my people Israel. I will defeat all
your enemies.
" 'I tell you that the LORD will make your
descendants kings of Israel after you. 11 When
you die and join your ancestors, I will make
one of your sons the new king, and I will set
up his kingdom. 12 He will build a house for
me, and I will let his kingdom rule always. 13 I
will be his father, and he will be my son. I took
away my love from Saul, who ruled before
you, but I will never stop loving
your son. 14 I will put him in
charge of my house and
kingdom forever. His family
will rule forever.' "
15 Nathan told David
everything God had said in
this vision.

DAVID PRAYS TO GOD

16 Then King David went in
and sat in front of the LORD. David said, "LORD God, who am I?
What is my family? Why did you bring me to
this point? 17 But that was not enough for you,
God. You have also made promises about my
future family. LORD God, you have treated me
like a very important person.
18 "What more can I say to you for honoring
me, your servant? You know me so well.
19 LORD, you have done this wonderful thing

for my sake and because you wanted to. You
have made known all these great things.
20"There is no one like you, LORD. There is
no God except you. We have heard all this
ourselves! 21There is no nation like your people
Israel. They are the only people on earth that
God chose to be his own. You made your
name well known by the great and wonderful
things you did for them. You went ahead of
them and forced other nations out of the land.
You freed your people from slavery in Egypt.
22You made the people of Israel your very own
people forever, and, LORD, you are their God.
23"LORD, keep the promise forever that you
made about my family and me, your servant.
Do what you have said. 24Then you will be
honored always, and people will say, 'The LORD
All-Powerful, the God over Israel, is Israel's
God!' And the family of your servant David will
continue before you.
25"My God, you have told me that you
would make my family great. So I,
your servant, am brave enough
to pray to you. 26LORD, you
are God, and you have
promised these good things
to me, your servant. 27You
have chosen to bless my
family. Let it continue before
you always. LORD, you have
blessed my family, so it will always be blessed."

TRUST

Whose promises always come true? (17:26–27)

DAVID DEFEATS NATIONS

18 1Later, David defeated the Philistines, conquered them, and took the city of Gath and the
small towns around it.
2He also defeated the people of Moab. So
the people of Moab became servants of David
and gave him the payment he demanded.
3David also defeated Hadadezer king of Zobah all the way to the town of Hamath as he
tried to spread his kingdom to the Euphrates
River. 4David captured one thousand of his
chariots, seven thousand men who rode in
chariots, and twenty thousand foot soldiers.
He crippled all but a hundred of the chariot
horses.
5Arameans from Damascus came to help
Hadadezer king of Zobah, but David killed
twenty-two thousand of them. 6Then David
put groups of soldiers in Damascus in Aram.
The Arameans became David's servants and
gave him the payments he demanded. So the
LORD gave David victory everywhere he went.
7David took the shields of gold that had
belonged to Hadadezer's officers and brought
them to Jerusalem. 8David also took many
things made of bronze from Tebah and Cun,
which had been cities under Hadadezer's control. Later, Solomon used this bronze to make
things for the Temple: the large bronze bowl,
which was called the Sea, the pillars, and other
bronze utensils.
9Toi king of Hamath heard that David had

Promise

HE PROMISES THAT ISRAEL WILL BE HIS PEOPLE FOREVER.

You made the people of Israel your very own people forever, and, LORD, you are their God (1 Chr. 17:22).

Can you imagine belonging to someone forever—even way after you're dead? God has chosen Israel to belong to him forever. As a Christian, you are a part of Israel. One of the most awesome things about becoming a Christian is that "forever" becomes a real part of your life. Even though your body will eventually die, your spirit will live forever. When your life on earth is over, you will enter into a new kind of life in heaven. It's mind-blowing to think about, but you really will live forever with God. Just because you are a Christian, you won't always be perfect. You'll make mistakes, have regrets, and wish you'd made different choices. Through all those times, you still belong to God. When he says you belong to him forever, he means forever—even when you do stuff he wouldn't be pleased with. He's chosen you to be a part of Israel. And you'll belong to him from now on. Forever *never* ends.

SEE FOR YOURSELF:

Ex. 2:23–25; 1 Chr. 16:11–13; Is. 43:20–21; 1 Pet. 2:9–10

defeated all the army of Hadadezer king of Zobah. [10]So Toi sent his son Hadoram to greet
and congratulate King David for defeating
Hadadezer. (Hadadezer had been at war with
Toi.) Hadoram brought items made of gold, silver, and bronze. [11]King David gave them to the
LORD, along with the silver and gold he had
taken from these nations: Edom, Moab, the
Ammonites, the Philistines, and Amalek.

WHAT'S IT MEAN?

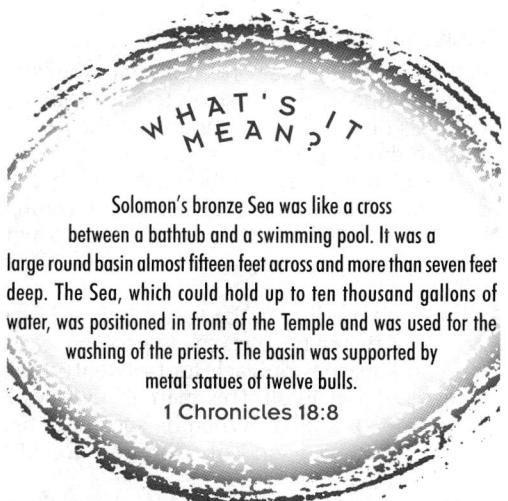

Solomon's bronze Sea was like a cross between a bathtub and a swimming pool. It was a large round basin almost fifteen feet across and more than seven feet deep. The Sea, which could hold up to ten thousand gallons of water, was positioned in front of the Temple and was used for the washing of the priests. The basin was supported by metal statues of twelve bulls.

1 Chronicles 18:8

[12]Abishai son of Zeruiah killed eighteen
thousand Edomites in the Valley of Salt. [13]Da-
vid put groups of soldiers in Edom, and all the
Edomites became his servants. The LORD gave
David victory everywhere he went.

DAVID'S IMPORTANT OFFICERS

[14]David was king over all of Israel, and he
did what was fair and right for all his people.
[15]Joab son of Zeruiah was commander over
the army. Jehoshaphat son of Ahilud was the
recorder. [16]Zadok son of Ahitub and Abiathar
son of Ahimelech were priests. Shavsha was
the royal secretary. [17]Benaiah son of Jehoiada
was over the Kerethites and Pelethites.[n] And
David's sons were important officers who
served at his side.

WAR WITH THE AMMONITES AND ARAMEANS

19 [1]When Nahash king of the Ammonites died,
his son became king after him. [2]David said,
"Nahash was loyal to me, so I will be loyal to
his son Hanun." So David sent messengers to
comfort Hanun about his father's death.
David's officers went to the land of the Ammonites to comfort Hanun. [3]But the Ammonite
leaders said to Hanun, "Do you think David
wants to honor your father by sending men to
comfort you? No! David sent them to study the
land and capture it and spy it out." [4]So Hanun
arrested David's officers. To shame them he
shaved their beards and cut off their clothes at
the hips. Then he sent them away.
[5]When the people told David what had
happened to his officers, he sent messengers to
meet them, because they were very ashamed.
King David said, "Stay in Jericho until your
beards have grown back. Then come home."
[6]The Ammonites knew that they had insulted David. So Hanun and the Ammonites
sent about seventy-four thousand pounds of
silver to hire chariots and chariot drivers from
Northwest Mesopotamia, Aram Maacah, and
Zobah. [7]The Ammonites hired thirty-two
thousand chariots and the king of Maacah and
his army. So they came and set up camp near
the town of Medeba. The Ammonites themselves came out of their towns and got ready
for battle.

WHAT'S IT MEAN?

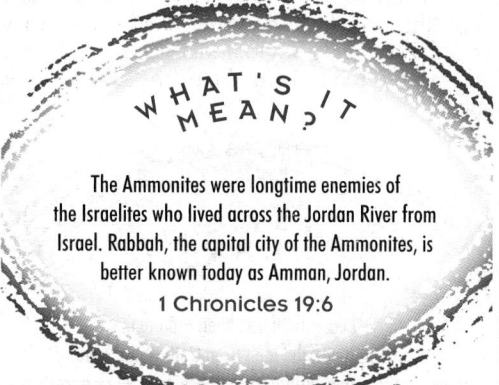

The Ammonites were longtime enemies of the Israelites who lived across the Jordan River from Israel. Rabbah, the capital city of the Ammonites, is better known today as Amman, Jordan.

1 Chronicles 19:6

[8]When David heard about this, he sent Joab
with the whole army. [9]The Ammonites came
out and prepared for battle at the city gate. The
kings who had come to help were out in the
field by themselves.
[10]Joab saw that there were enemies both in
front of him and behind him. So he chose
some of the best soldiers of Israel and sent
them out to fight the Arameans. [11]Joab put the
rest of the army under the command of Abishai, his brother. Then they went out to fight the
Ammonites. [12]Joab said to Abishai, "If the Arameans are too strong for me, you must help
me. Or, if the Ammonites are too strong for
you, I will help you. [13]Be strong. We must fight

18:17 Kerethites and Pelethites These were probably special units of the army that were responsible for the king's safety, a kind of palace guard.

bravely for our people and the cities of our God. The LORD will do what he thinks is right."

[14]Then Joab and the army with him went to attack the Arameans, and the Arameans ran away. [15]When the Ammonites saw that the Arameans were running away, they also ran away from Joab's brother Abishai and went back to their city. So Joab went back to Jerusalem.

[16]When the Arameans saw that Israel had defeated them, they sent messengers to bring other Arameans from east of the Euphrates River. Their leader was Shophach, the commander of Hadadezer's army.

[17]When David heard about this, he gathered all the Israelites, and they crossed over the Jordan River. He prepared them for battle, facing the Arameans. The Arameans fought with him, [18]but they ran away from the Israelites. David killed seven thousand Aramean chariot drivers and forty thousand Aramean foot soldiers. He also killed Shophach, the commander of the Aramean army.

[19]When those who served Hadadezer saw that the Israelites had defeated them, they made peace with David and served him. So the Arameans refused to help the Ammonites again.

WHAT'S IT MEAN?

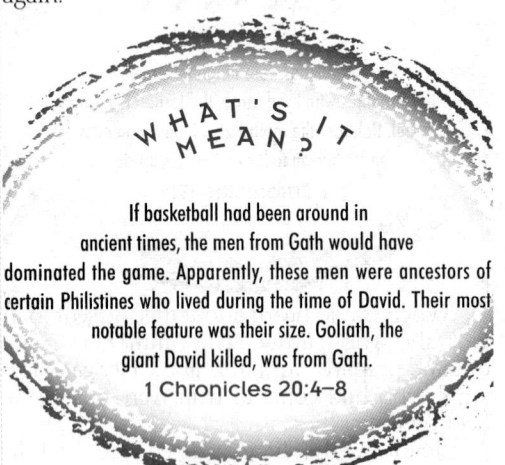

If basketball had been around in ancient times, the men from Gath would have dominated the game. Apparently, these men were ancestors of certain Philistines who lived during the time of David. Their most notable feature was their size. Goliath, the giant David killed, was from Gath.

1 Chronicles 20:4–8

JOAB DESTROYS THE AMMONITES

20 [1]In the spring, the time of year when kings normally went out to battle, Joab led out the army of Israel. But David stayed in Jerusalem. The army of Israel destroyed the land of Ammon and went to the city of Rabbah and attacked it. [2]David took the crown off the head of their king,[n] and had it placed on his own head. That gold crown weighed about seventy-five pounds, and it had valuable gems in it. And David took many valuable things from the city. [3]He also brought out the people of the city and forced them to work with saws, iron picks, and axes. David did this to all the Ammonite cities. Then David and all his army returned to Jerusalem.

PHILISTINE GIANTS ARE KILLED

[4]Later, at Gezer, war broke out with the Philistines. Sibbecai the Hushathite killed Sippai, who was one of the descendants of the Rephaites. So those Philistines were defeated.

[5]Later, there was another battle with the Philistines. Elhanan son of Jair killed Lahmi, the brother of Goliath, who was from the town of Gath. His spear was as large as a weaver's rod.

[6]At Gath another battle took place. A huge man was there; he had six fingers on each hand and six toes on each foot—twenty-four fingers and toes in all. This man also was one of the sons of Rapha. [7]When he spoke against Israel, Jonathan son of Shimea, David's brother, killed him.

[8]These descendants of Rapha from Gath were killed by David and his men.

DAVID COUNTS THE ISRAELITES

21 [1]Satan was against Israel, and he caused David to count the people of Israel. [2]So David said to Joab and the commanders of the troops, "Go and count all the Israelites from Beersheba to Dan.[n] Then tell me so I will know how many there are."

[3]But Joab said, "May the LORD give the nation a hundred times more people. My master the king, all the Israelites are your servants. Why do you want to do this, my master? You will make Israel guilty of sin."

[4]But the king commanded Joab, so Joab left and went through all Israel. Then he returned to Jerusalem. [5]Joab gave the list of the people to David. There were one million one hundred thousand men in all of Israel who could use the sword, and there were four hundred seventy thousand men in Judah who could use the sword. [6]But Joab did not count the tribes of Levi and Benjamin, because he didn't like King David's order. [7]David had done something God had said was wrong, so God punished Israel.

20:2 their king Or, "Milcom," the god of the Ammonite people. **21:2 Beersheba to Dan** Beersheba was the city farthest south in Israel. Dan was the city farthest north. So this means all the people of Israel.

8Then David said to God, "I have sinned
greatly by what I have done! Now, I
beg you to forgive me, your
servant, because I have been
very foolish."
9The LORD said to Gad,
who was David's seer, 10"Go
and tell David, 'This is what
the LORD says: I offer you three
choices. Choose one of them and I will do it.' "
11So Gad went to David and said to him,
"This is what the LORD says: 'Choose for yourself 12three years of hunger. Or choose three
months of running from your enemies as they
chase you with their swords. Or choose three
days of punishment from the LORD, in which a
terrible disease will spread through the country. The angel of the LORD will go through Israel destroying the people.' Now, David, decide
which of these things I should tell the LORD
who sent me."
13David said to Gad, "I am in great trouble.
Let the LORD punish me, because the LORD is
very merciful. Don't let my punishment come
from human beings."
14So the LORD sent a terrible disease on Israel, and seventy thousand people died. 15God
sent an angel to destroy Jerusalem, but when
the angel started to destroy it, the LORD saw it
and felt very sorry about the terrible things
that had happened. So he said to the angel
who was destroying, "That is enough! Put
down your arm!" The angel of the LORD was
then standing at the threshing floor of Araunah the Jebusite.
16David looked up and saw the angel of the
LORD in the sky, holding his sword drawn and
pointed at Jerusalem. Then David and the older
leaders bowed facedown on the ground. They
were wearing rough cloth to show their grief.
17David said to God, "I am the one who sinned
and did wrong. I gave the order for the people
to be counted. These people only followed me
like sheep. They did nothing wrong. LORD my
God, please punish me and my family, but stop
the terrible disease that is killing your people."
18Then the angel of the LORD told Gad to tell
David that he should build an altar to the LORD
on the threshing floor of Araunah the Jebusite.
19So David did what Gad told him to do, in the
name of the LORD.
20Araunah was separating the wheat from
the straw. When he turned around, he saw the
angel. Araunah's four sons who were with him
hid. 21David came to Araunah, and when Araunah saw him, he left the threshing floor and
bowed facedown on the ground before David.

SIN
How should we feel about our own sin? (21:7–8)

22David said to him, "Sell me your threshing
floor so I can build an altar to the LORD here.
Then the terrible disease will stop. Sell it to me
for the full price."
23Araunah said to David, "Take this threshing floor. My master the king, do anything you
want. Look, I will also give you oxen for the
whole burnt offerings, the threshing boards for
the wood, and wheat for the grain offering. I
give everything to you."
24But King David answered Araunah, "No, I
will pay the full price for the land. I won't take
anything that is yours and give it to the LORD. I
won't offer a burnt offering that costs me
nothing."
25So David paid Araunah about fifteen
pounds of gold for the place. 26David built an
altar to the LORD there and offered whole
burnt offerings and fellowship offerings. David
prayed to the LORD, and he answered him by
sending down fire from heaven on the altar of
burnt offering. 27Then the LORD commanded
the angel to put his sword back into its holder.
28When David saw that the LORD had answered him on the threshing floor of Araunah,
he offered sacrifices there. 29The Holy Tent that
Moses made while the Israelites were in the
desert and the altar of burnt offerings were in
Gibeon at the place of worship. 30But David
could not go to the Holy Tent to speak with
God, because he was afraid of the angel of the
LORD and his sword.

22
1David said, "The Temple of the LORD God
and the altar for Israel's burnt offerings will be
built here."

DAVID MAKES PLANS FOR THE TEMPLE

2So David ordered all foreigners living in Israel to gather together. From that group David
chose stonecutters to cut stones to be used in
building the Temple of God. 3David supplied a
large amount of iron to be used for making
nails and hinges for the gate doors. He also
supplied more bronze than could be weighed,
4and he supplied more cedar logs than could
be counted. Much of the cedar had been
brought to David by the people from Sidon
and Tyre.
5David said, "We should build a great Temple for the LORD, which will be famous everywhere for its greatness and beauty. But my son
Solomon is young. He hasn't yet learned what
he needs to know, so I will prepare for the
building of it." So David got many of the materials ready before he died.
6Then David called for his son Solomon
and told him to build the Temple for the LORD,

the God of Israel. 7David said to him, "My son, I wanted to build a temple for worshiping the LORD my God. 8But the LORD spoke his word to me, 'David, you have killed many people. You have fought many wars. You cannot build a temple for worship to me, because you have killed many people. 9But, you will have a son, a man of peace and rest. I will give him rest from all his enemies around him. His name will be Solomon,[n] and I will give Israel peace and quiet while he is king. 10Solomon will build a temple for worship to me. He will be my son, and I will be his father. I will make his kingdom strong; someone from his family will rule Israel forever.' "

11David said, "Now, my son, may the LORD be with you. May you build a temple for the LORD your God, as he said you would. 12He will make you the king of Israel. May the LORD give you wisdom and understanding so you will be able to obey the teachings of the LORD your God. 13Be careful to obey the rules and laws the LORD gave Moses for Israel. If you obey them, you will have success. Be strong and brave. Don't be afraid or discouraged.

14"Solomon, I have worked hard getting many of the materials for building the Temple of the LORD. I have supplied about seven and one-half million pounds of gold, about seventy-five million pounds of silver, so much bronze and iron it cannot be weighed, and wood and stone. You may add to them. 15You have many workmen—stonecutters, bricklayers, carpenters, and people skilled in every kind of work. 16They are skilled in working with gold, silver, bronze, and iron. You have more craftsmen than can be counted. Now begin the work, and may the LORD be with you."

17Then David ordered all the leaders of Israel to help his son Solomon. 18David said to them, "The LORD your God is with you. He has given you rest from our enemies. He has handed over to me the people living around us. The LORD and his people are in control of this land. 19Now give yourselves completely to obeying the LORD your God. Build the holy place of the LORD God; build the Temple for worship to the LORD. Then bring the Ark of the Agreement with the LORD and the holy items that belong to God into the Temple."

THE LEVITES

23

1After David had lived long and was old, he made his son Solomon the new king of Israel. 2David gathered all the leaders of Israel, along with the priests and Levites. 3He counted the Levites who were thirty years old and older. In all, there were thirty-eight thousand Levites. 4David said, "Of these, twenty-four thousand Levites will direct the work of the Temple of the LORD, six thousand Levites will be officers and judges, 5four thousand Levites will be gatekeepers, and four thousand Levites will praise the LORD with musical instruments I made for giving praise."

6David separated the Levites into three groups that were led by Levi's three sons: Gershon, Kohath, and Merari.

THE PEOPLE OF GERSHON

7From the people of Gershon, there were Ladan and Shimei.

8Ladan had three sons. His first son was Jehiel, and his other sons were Zetham and Joel.

9Shimei's sons were Shelomoth, Haziel, and Haran. These three sons were leaders of Ladan's families. 10Shimei had four sons: Jahath, Ziza, Jeush, and Beriah. 11Jahath was the first son, and Ziza was the second son. But Jeush and Beriah did not have many children, so they were counted as if they were one family.

THE PEOPLE OF KOHATH

12Kohath had four sons: Amram, Izhar, Hebron, and Uzziel.

13Amram's sons were Aaron and Moses. Aaron and his descendants were chosen to be special forever. They were chosen to prepare the holy things for the LORD's service, to offer sacrifices before the LORD, and to serve him as priests. They were to give blessings in his name forever.

14Moses was the man of God, and his sons were counted as part of the tribe of Levi. 15Moses' sons were Gershom and Eliezer. 16Gershom's first son was Shubael. 17Eliezer's first son was Rehabiah. Eliezer had no other sons, but Rehabiah had many sons.

18Izhar's first son was Shelomith.

19Hebron's first son was Jeriah, his second was Amariah, his third was Jahaziel, and his fourth was Jekameam.

20Uzziel's first son was Micah and his second was Isshiah.

THE PEOPLE OF MERARI

21Merari's sons were Mahli and Mushi. Mahli's sons were Eleazar and Kish. 22Eleazar died without sons; he had only daughters. Eleazar's daughters married their cousins, the

22:9 Solomon This name sounds like the Hebrew word for "peace."

sons of Kish. 23Mushi's three sons were Mahli,
Eder, and Jerimoth.

THE LEVITES' WORK

24These were Levi's descendants listed by
their families. They were the leaders of families.
Each person who was twenty years old or older was listed. They served in the LORD's Temple.
25David had said, "The LORD, the God of Israel, has given rest to his people. He has come
to live in Jerusalem forever. 26So the Levites
don't need to carry the Holy Tent or any of the
things used in its services anymore." 27David's
last instructions were to count the Levites who
were twenty years old and older.
28The Levites had the job of helping Aaron's
descendants in the service of the Temple of the
LORD. They cared for the Temple courtyard and
side rooms, and they made all the holy things
pure. Their job was to serve in the Temple of
God. 29They were responsible for putting the
holy bread on the table, for the flour in the
grain offerings, for the bread made without
yeast, for the baking and mixing, and for the
measuring. 30The Levites also stood every
morning and gave thanks and praise to the
LORD. They also did this every evening. 31The
Levites offered all the burnt offerings to the
LORD on the special days of rest, at the New
Moon festivals, and at all appointed feasts.
They served before the LORD every day. They
were to follow the rules for how many Levites
should serve each time. 32So the Levites took
care of the Meeting Tent and the Holy Place.
And they helped their relatives, Aaron's descendants, with the services at the Temple of
the LORD.

WHAT'S IT MEAN?

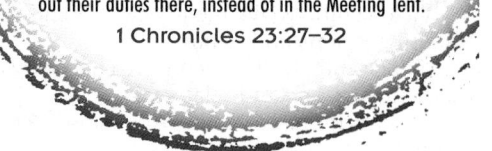

Only the direct descendants of Aaron were allowed to serve as priests. The other Levites assisted the priests in their work. The instructions for making sacrifices, worshiping God, and caring for the Meeting Tent and everything in it were spelled out by Moses in the Book of Leviticus. Once the Temple was built, the Levites would carry out their duties there, instead of in the Meeting Tent.

1 Chronicles 23:27–32

THE GROUPS OF THE PRIESTS

24 1These were the groups of Aaron's sons:
Aaron's sons were Nadab, Abihu, Eleazar, and
Ithamar. 2But Nadab and Abihu died before
their father did, and they had no sons. So Eleazar and Ithamar served as the priests. 3David,
with the help of Zadok, a descendant of Eleazar,
and Ahimelech, a descendant of Ithamar, separated their family groups into two different
groups. Each group had certain duties. 4There
were more leaders from Eleazar's family than
from Ithamar's—sixteen leaders from Eleazar's
family and eight leaders from Ithamar's family.
5Men were chosen from Eleazar's and Ithamar's
families by throwing lots. Some men from
each family were chosen to be in charge of the
Holy Place, and some were chosen to serve as
priests.
6Shemaiah son of Nethanel, from the tribe of
Levi, was the secretary. He recorded the names
of those descendants in front of King David, the
officers, Zadok the priest, Ahimelech son of
Abiathar, and the leaders of the families of the
priests and Levites. The work was divided by
lots among the families of Eleazar and Ithamar.
The following men with their groups were
chosen.
7The first one chosen was Jehoiarib. The
second was Jedaiah. 8The third was Harim. The
fourth was Seorim. 9The fifth was Malkijah.
The sixth was Mijamin. 10The seventh was
Hakkoz. The eighth was Abijah. 11The ninth
was Jeshua. The tenth was Shecaniah. 12The
eleventh was Eliashib. The twelfth was Jakim.
13The thirteenth was Huppah. The fourteenth
was Jeshebeab. 14The fifteenth was Bilgah. The
sixteenth was Immer. 15The seventeenth was
Hezir. The eighteenth was Happizzez. 16The
nineteenth was Pethahiah. The twentieth was
Jehezkel. 17The twenty-first was Jakin. The
twenty-second was Gamul. 18The twenty-third
was Delaiah. The twenty-fourth was Maaziah.
19These were the groups chosen to serve in
the Temple of the LORD. They obeyed the rules
given them by Aaron, just as the LORD, the God
of Israel, had commanded him.

THE OTHER LEVITES

20These are the names of the rest of Levi's
descendants:
Shubael was a descendant of Amram, and
Jehdeiah was a descendant of Shubael.
21Isshiah was the first son of Rehabiah.
22From the Izhar family group, there was
Shelomoth, and Jahath was a descendant of
Shelomoth.
23Hebron's first son was Jeriah, Amariah

was his second, Jahaziel was his third, and Jekameam was his fourth.

24Uzziel's son was Micah. Micah's son was Shamir. 25Micah's brother was Isshiah, and Isshiah's son was Zechariah.

26Merari's descendants were Mahli and Mushi. Merari's son was Jaaziah. 27Jaaziah son of Merari had sons named Shoham, Zaccur, and Ibri. 28Mahli's son was Eleazar, but Eleazar did not have any sons.

29Kish's son was Jerahmeel.

30Mushi's sons were Mahli, Eder, and Jerimoth.

These are the Levites, listed by their families. 31They were chosen for special jobs by throwing lots in front of King David, Zadok, Ahimelech, the leaders of the families of the priests, and the Levites. They did this just as their relatives, the priests, Aaron's descendants, had done. The families of the oldest brother and the youngest brother were treated the same.

THE MUSIC GROUPS

25 1David and the commanders of the army chose some of the sons of Asaph, Heman, and Jeduthun to preach and play harps, lyres, and cymbals. Here is a list of the men who served in this way:

WHAT'S IT MEAN?

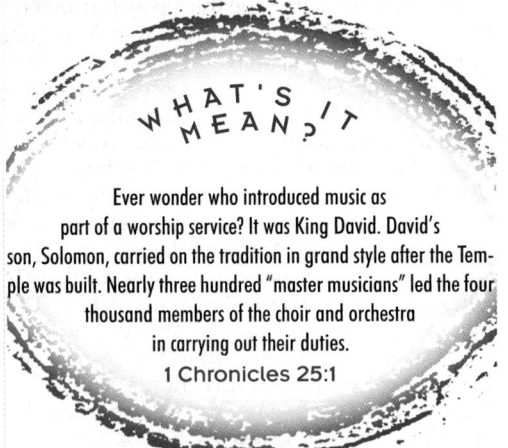

Ever wonder who introduced music as part of a worship service? It was King David. David's son, Solomon, carried on the tradition in grand style after the Temple was built. Nearly three hundred "master musicians" led the four thousand members of the choir and orchestra in carrying out their duties.

1 Chronicles 25:1

2Asaph's sons who served were Zaccur, Joseph, Nethaniah, and Asarelah. King David chose Asaph to preach, and Asaph directed his sons.

3Jeduthun's sons who served were Gedaliah, Zeri, Jeshaiah, Shimei, Hashabiah, and Mattithiah. There were six of them, and Jeduthun directed them. He preached and used a harp to give thanks and praise to the LORD.

4Heman's sons who served were Bukkiah, Mattaniah, Uzziel, Shubael, Jerimoth, Hananiah, Hanani, Eliathah, Giddalti, Romamti-Ezer, Joshbekashah, Mallothi, Hothir, and Mahazioth. 5All these were sons of Heman, David's seer. God promised to make Heman strong, so Heman had many sons. God gave him fourteen sons and three daughters. 6Heman directed all his sons in making music for the Temple of the LORD with cymbals, lyres, and harps; that was their way of serving in the Temple of God. King David was in charge of Asaph, Jeduthun, and Heman. 7These men and their relatives were trained and skilled in making music for the LORD. There were two hundred eighty-eight of them. 8Everyone threw lots to choose the time his family was to serve at the Temple. The young and the old, the teacher and the student, had to throw lots.

9First, the lot fell to Joseph, from the family of Asaph.

Second, twelve men were chosen from Gedaliah, his sons and relatives.

10Third, twelve men were chosen from Zaccur, his sons and relatives.

11Fourth, twelve men were chosen from Izri, his sons and relatives.

12Fifth, twelve men were chosen from Nethaniah, his sons and relatives.

13Sixth, twelve men were chosen from Bukkiah, his sons and relatives.

14Seventh, twelve men were chosen from Jesarelah, his sons and relatives.

15Eighth, twelve men were chosen from Jeshaiah, his sons and relatives.

16Ninth, twelve men were chosen from Mattaniah, his sons and relatives.

17Tenth, twelve men were chosen from Shimei, his sons and relatives.

18Eleventh, twelve men were chosen from Azarel, his sons and relatives.

19Twelfth, twelve men were chosen from Hashabiah, his sons and relatives.

20Thirteenth, twelve men were chosen from Shubael, his sons and relatives.

21Fourteenth, twelve men were chosen from Mattithiah, his sons and relatives.

22Fifteenth, twelve men were chosen from Jerimoth, his sons and relatives.

23Sixteenth, twelve men were chosen from Hananiah, his sons and relatives.

24Seventeenth, twelve men were chosen from Joshbekashah, his sons and relatives.

25Eighteenth, twelve men were chosen from Hanani, his sons and relatives.

26Nineteenth, twelve men were chosen from Mallothi, his sons and relatives.

27Twentieth, twelve men were chosen from Eliathah, his sons and relatives.

[28]Twenty-first, twelve men were chosen
from Hothir, his sons and relatives.
[29]Twenty-second, twelve men were chosen
from Giddalti, his sons and relatives.
[30]Twenty-third, twelve men were chosen
from Mahazioth, his sons and relatives.
[31]Twenty-fourth, twelve men were chosen
from Romamti-Ezer, his sons and relatives.

THE GATEKEEPERS

26 [1]These are the groups of the gatekeepers.
From the family of Korah, there was Meshelemiah son of Kore, who was from Asaph's family. [2]Meshelemiah had sons. Zechariah was his
first son, Jediael was second, Zebadiah was
third, Jathniel was fourth, [3]Elam was fifth, Jehohanan was sixth, and Eliehoenai was seventh.
[4]Obed-Edom had sons. Shemaiah was his
first son, Jehozabad was second, Joah was
third, Sacar was fourth, Nethanel was fifth,
[5]Ammiel was sixth, Issachar was seventh, and
Peullethai was eighth. God blessed Obed-
Edom with children.
[6]Obed-Edom's son Shemaiah also had
sons. They were leaders in their father's family
because they were capable men. [7]Shemaiah's
sons were Othni, Rephael, Obed, Elzabad, Elihu, and Semakiah. Elihu, and Semakiah were
skilled workers. [8]All these were Obed-Edom's
descendants. They and their sons and relatives
were capable men and strong workers. Obed-
Edom had sixty-two descendants in all.
[9]Meshelemiah had sons and relatives who
were skilled workers. In all, there were eighteen.
[10]From the Merari family, Hosah had sons.
Shimri was chosen to be in charge. Although
he was not the oldest son, his father chose him
to be in charge. [11]Hilkiah was his second son,
Tabaliah was third, and Zechariah was fourth.
In all, Hosah had thirteen sons and relatives.
[12]These were the leaders of the groups of
gatekeepers, and they served in the Temple of
the LORD. Their relatives also worked in the
Temple. [13]By throwing lots, each family chose a
gate to guard. Young and old threw lots.
[14]Meshelemiah was chosen by lot to guard
the East Gate. Then lots were thrown for
Meshelemiah's son Zechariah. He was a wise
counselor and was chosen for the North Gate.
[15]Obed-Edom was chosen for the South Gate,
and Obed-Edom's sons were chosen to guard
the storehouse. [16]Shuppim and Hosah were
chosen for the West Gate and the Shalleketh
Gate on the upper road.
Guards stood side by side with guards. [17]Six
Levites stood guard every day at the East Gate;
four Levites stood guard every day at the
North Gate; four Levites stood guard every
day at the South Gate; and two Levites at a
time guarded the storehouse. [18]There were two
guards at the western court and four guards
on the road to the court.
[19]These were the groups of the gatekeepers
from the families of Korah and Merari.

OTHER LEADERS

[20]Other Levites were responsible for guarding the treasuries of the Temple of God and for
the places where the holy items were kept.

WHAT'S IT MEAN?

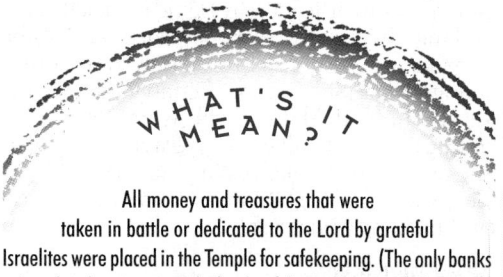

All money and treasures that were taken in battle or dedicated to the Lord by grateful Israelites were placed in the Temple for safekeeping. (The only banks in Israel at that time were the banks of the Jordan River.) The money was used to maintain the Temple and keep it properly furnished. For extra security, Solomon's Temple had a courtyard with a wall and gates around it.

1 Chronicles 26:20

[21]Ladan was Gershon's son and the ancestor of several family groups. Jehiel was a leader
of one of the family groups. [22]His sons were
Zetham and Joel his brother, and they were responsible for the treasuries of the Temple of the
LORD.
[23]Other leaders were chosen from the family groups of Amram, Izhar, Hebron, and Uzziel. [24]Shubael, the descendant of Gershom,
who was Moses' son, was the leader responsible for the treasuries. [25]These were Shubael's
relatives from Eliezer: Eliezer's son Rehabiah,
Rehabiah's son Jeshaiah, Jeshaiah's son Joram,
Joram's son Zicri, and Zicri's son Shelomith.
[26]Shelomith and his relatives were responsible for everything that
had been collected for the
Temple by King David, by the
heads of families, by the commanders of a thousand men
and of a hundred men, and
by other army commanders.
[27]They also gave some of the
things they had taken in wars to
be used in repairing the Temple of the LORD.

MONEY

What's a good way to spend some of the money we earn? (26:27)

[28]Shelomith and his relatives took care of all
the holy items. Some had been given by Samuel the seer, Saul son of Kish, Abner son of Ner,
and Joab son of Zeruiah.
[29]Kenaniah was from the Izhar family. He
and his sons worked outside the Temple as officers and judges in different places in Israel.
[30]Hashabiah was from the Hebron family.
He and his relatives were responsible for the
LORD's work and the king's business in Israel
west of the Jordan River. There were seventeen
hundred skilled men in Hashabiah's group.
[31]The history of the Hebron family shows that
Jeriah was their leader. In David's fortieth year
as king, the records were searched, and some
capable men of the Hebron family were found
living at Jazer in Gilead. [32]Jeriah had twenty-
seven hundred relatives who were skilled men
and leaders of families. King David gave them
the responsibility of directing the tribes of Reuben, Gad, and East Manasseh in God's work
and the king's business.

ARMY DIVISIONS

27
[1]This is the list of the Israelites who served
the king in the army. Each division was on
duty one month each year. There were leaders
of families, commanders of a hundred men,
commanders of a thousand men, and other officers. Each division had twenty-four thousand men.

WHAT'S IT MEAN?

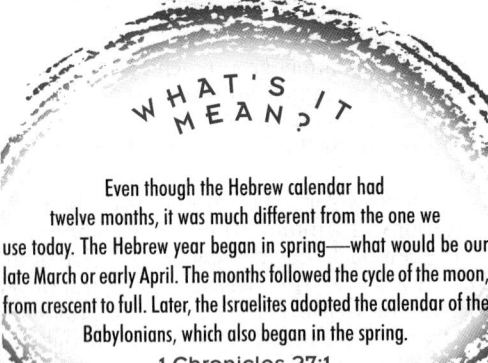

Even though the Hebrew calendar had twelve months, it was much different from the one we use today. The Hebrew year began in spring—what would be our late March or early April. The months followed the cycle of the moon, from crescent to full. Later, the Israelites adopted the calendar of the Babylonians, which also began in the spring.

1 Chronicles 27:1

[2]Jashobeam son of Zabdiel was in charge of
the first division for the first month. There
were twenty-four thousand men in his division. [3]Jashobeam, one of the descendants of
Perez, was leader of all the army officers for the
first month.
[4]Dodai, from the Ahohites, was in charge of
the division for the second month. Mikloth was
a leader in the division. There were twenty-four
thousand men in Dodai's division.
[5]The third commander, for the third month,
was Benaiah son of Jehoiada the priest. There
were twenty-four thousand men in his division. [6]He was the Benaiah who was one of the
Thirty[n] soldiers. Benaiah was a brave warrior
who led those men. Benaiah's son Ammizabad
was in charge of Benaiah's division.
[7]The fourth commander, for the fourth
month, was Asahel, the brother of Joab. Later,
Asahel's son Zebadiah took his place as commander. There were twenty-four thousand
men in his division.
[8]The fifth commander, for the fifth month,
was Shamhuth, from Izrah's family. There
were twenty-four thousand men in his division.
[9]The sixth commander, for the sixth month,
was Ira son of Ikkesh from the town of Tekoa.
There were twenty-four thousand men in his
division.
[10]The seventh commander, for the seventh
month, was Helez. He was from the Pelonites
and a descendant of Ephraim. There were
twenty-four thousand men in his division.
[11]The eighth commander, for the eighth
month, was Sibbecai. He was from Hushah and
was from Zerah's family. There were twenty-
four thousand men in his division.
[12]The ninth commander, for the ninth
month, was Abiezer. He was from Anathoth in
Benjamin. There were twenty-four thousand
men in his division.
[13]The tenth commander, for the tenth month,
was Maharai. He was from Netophah and was
from Zerah's family. There were twenty-four
thousand men in his division.
[14]The eleventh commander, for the eleventh
month, was Benaiah. He was from Pirathon in
Ephraim. There were twenty-four thousand
men in his division.
[15]The twelfth commander, for the twelfth
month, was Heldai. He was from Netophah
and was from Othniel's family. There were
twenty-four thousand men in his division.

LEADERS OF THE TRIBES

[16]These were the leaders of the tribes of Israel. Eliezer son of Zicri was over the tribe of
Reuben. Shephatiah son of Maacah was over
the tribe of Simeon. [17]Hashabiah son of Kemuel
was over the tribe of Levi. Zadok was over the

27:6 Thirty These were David's most powerful soldiers. See 2 Samuel 23:24.

people of Aaron. [18]Elihu, one of David's brothers, was over the tribe of Judah. Omri son of Michael was over the tribe of Issachar. [19]Ishmaiah son of Obadiah was over the tribe of Zebulun. Jerimoth son of Azriel was over the tribe of Naphtali. [20]Hoshea son of Azaziah was over the tribe of Ephraim. Joel son of Pedaiah was over West Manasseh. [21]Iddo son of Zechariah was over East Manasseh. Jaasiel son of Abner was over the tribe of Benjamin. [22]Azarel son of Jeroham was over the tribe of Dan.

These were the leaders of the tribes of Israel.

[23]The LORD had promised to make the Israelites as many as the stars in the sky. So David only counted the men who were twenty years old and older. [24]Joab son of Zeruiah began to count the people, but he did not finish. God became angry with Israel for counting the people, so the number of the people was not put in the history book about King David's rule.

THE KING'S DIRECTORS

[25]Azmaveth son of Adiel was in charge of the royal storehouses.

Jonathan son of Uzziah was in charge of the storehouses in the country, towns, villages, and towers.

[26]Ezri son of Kelub was in charge of the field workers who farmed the land.

[27]Shimei, from the town of Ramah, was in charge of the vineyards.

Zabdi, from Shapham, was in charge of storing the wine that came from the vineyards.

[28]Baal-Hanan, from Geder, was in charge of the olive trees and sycamore trees in the western hills.

Joash was in charge of storing the olive oil.

[29]Shitrai, from Sharon, was in charge of the herds that fed in the Plain of Sharon.

Shaphat son of Adlai was in charge of the herds in the valleys.

[30]Obil, an Ishmaelite, was in charge of the camels.

Jehdeiah, from Meronoth, was in charge of the donkeys.

[31]Jaziz, from the Hagrites, was in charge of the flocks.

All these men were the officers who took care of King David's property.

[32]Jonathan was David's uncle, and he advised David. Jonathan was a wise man and a teacher of the law. Jehiel son of Hacmoni took care of the king's sons. [33]Ahithophel advised the king. Hushai, from the Arkite people, was the king's friend. [34]Jehoiada and Abiathar later took Ahithophel's place in advising the king. Jehoiada was Benaiah's son. Joab was the commander of the king's army.

DAVID'S PLANS FOR THE TEMPLE

28 [1]David commanded all the leaders of Israel to come to Jerusalem. There were the leaders of the tribes, commanders of the divisions serving the king, commanders of a thousand men and of a hundred men, leaders who took care of the property and animals that belonged to the king and his sons, men over the palace, the powerful men, and all the brave warriors.

[2]King David stood up and said, "Listen to me, my relatives and my people. I wanted to build a place to keep the Ark of the Agreement with the LORD. I wanted it to be God's footstool. So I made plans to build a temple. [3]But God said to me, 'You must not build a temple for worshiping me, because you are a soldier and have killed many people.'

[4]"But the LORD, the God of Israel, chose me from my whole family to be king of Israel forever. He chose the tribe of Judah to lead, and from the people of Judah, he chose my father's family. From that family God was pleased to make me king of Israel. [5]The LORD has given me many sons, and from those sons he has chosen Solomon to be the new king of Israel. Israel is the LORD's kingdom. [6]The LORD said to me, 'Your son Solomon will build my Temple and its courtyards. I have chosen Solomon to be my son, and I will be his father. [7]He is obeying my laws and commands now. If he continues to obey them, I will make his kingdom strong forever.' "

"The LORD said to me, 'Your son Solomon will build my Temple and its courtyards. I have chosen Solomon to be my son, and I will be his father.' " (1 Chronicles 28:6)

[8]David said, "Now, in front of all Israel, the assembly of the LORD, and in the hearing of God, I tell you these things: Be careful to obey all the commands of the LORD your God. Then you will keep this good land and pass it on to your descendants forever.

FAMILY

What's a good legacy parents can leave their children? (28:8)

[9]"And you, my son Solomon, accept the God of your

father. Serve him completely and willingly, because the LORD knows what is in everyone's
mind. He understands everything you think. If
you go to him for help, you will get an answer.
But if you turn away from him, he will leave
you forever. [10]Solomon, you must understand
this. The LORD has chosen you to build the
Temple as his holy place. Be strong and finish
the job."
[11]Then David gave his son Solomon the
plans for building the Temple and the courtyard around the Temple. They included its
buildings, its storerooms, its upper rooms, its
inside rooms, and the place where the people's
sins were removed. [12]David gave him plans for
everything he had in mind: the courtyards
around the LORD's Temple and all the rooms
around it, the Temple treasuries, and the treasuries of the holy items used in the Temple.
[13]David gave Solomon directions for the
groups of the priests and Levites. David told
him about all the work of serving in the Temple of the LORD and about the items to be used
in the Temple service [14]that were made of gold
or silver. David told Solomon how much gold
or silver should be used to make each thing.
[15]David told him how much gold to use for
each gold lampstand and its lamps and how
much silver to use for each silver lampstand
and its lamps. The different lampstands were
to be used where needed. [16]David told how
much gold should be used for each table that
held the holy bread and how much silver
should be used for the silver tables. [17]He told
how much pure gold should be used to make
the forks, bowls, and pitchers and how much
gold should be used to make each gold dish.
He told how much silver should be used to
make each silver dish [18]and how much pure
gold should be used for the altar of incense. He
also gave Solomon the plans for the chariot of
the golden creatures that spread their wings
over the Ark of the Agreement with the LORD.
[19]David said, "All these plans were written
with the LORD guiding me. He helped me understand everything in the plans."
[20]David also said to his son Solomon, "Be
strong and brave, and do the work. Don't be
afraid or discouraged, because the LORD God,
my God, is with you. He will not fail you or
leave you until all the work for the Temple of
the LORD is finished. [21]The groups of the priests
and Levites are ready for all the work on the
Temple of God. Every skilled worker is ready
to help you with all the work. The leaders and
all the people will obey every command you
give."

GIFTS FOR BUILDING THE TEMPLE

29
[1]King David said to all the Israelites who
were gathered, "God chose my son Solomon,
who is young and hasn't yet learned what he
needs to know, but the work is important. This
palace is not for people; it is for the LORD God.
[2]I have done my best to prepare for building
the Temple of God. I have given gold for the
things made of gold and silver for the things
made of silver. I have given bronze for the
things made of bronze and iron for the things
made of iron. I have given wood for the things
made of wood and onyx for the settings. I
have given turquoise gems of many different
colors, valuable stones, and white marble. I
have given much of all these things. [3]I have
already given this for the Temple, but now I am
also giving my own treasures of gold and silver, because I really want the Temple of my
God to be built. [4]I have given about two hundred twenty thousand pounds of pure gold
from Ophir and about five hundred twenty
thousand pounds of pure silver. They will be
used to cover the walls of the buildings [5]and
for all the gold and silver work. Skilled men
may use the gold and silver to make things for
the Temple. Now, who is ready to give himself
to the service of the LORD today?"
[6]The family leaders and the leaders of the
tribes of Israel, the commanders of a thousand
men and of a hundred men, and the leaders
responsible for the king's work gave their valuable things. [7]They donated about three hundred eighty thousand pounds of gold, about
seven hundred fifty thousand pounds of silver,
about one million three hundred fifty thousand pounds of bronze, and about seven million five hundred thousand pounds of iron to
the Temple of God. [8]People who had valuable
gems gave them to the treasury of the Temple
of the LORD, and Jehiel, from the Gershon family, took care of the valuable gems. [9]The leaders
gave willingly and completely to the LORD. The
people rejoiced to see their leaders give so
gladly, and King David was also very happy.

DAVID'S PRAYER

[10]David praised the LORD in front of all the
people who were gathered. He said:
"We praise you, LORD,
God of our father Israel.
We praise you forever and ever.
[11]LORD, you are great and powerful.
You have glory, victory, and honor.
Everything in heaven and on earth
belongs to you.
The kingdom belongs to you, LORD;

you are the ruler over everything.
12 Riches and honor come from you.
You rule everything.
You have the power and
strength
to make anyone great
and strong.
13 Now, our God, we thank
you
and praise your glorious
name.

WORRY

Where should we find the confidence we need to survive? (29:12)

14 "These things did not really come from me
and my people.
Everything comes from you;
we have given you back what you gave
us.
15 We are like foreigners and strangers,
as our ancestors were.
Our time on earth is like a shadow.
There is no hope.
16 LORD our God, we have gathered all this
to build your Temple for worship to
you.
But everything has come from you;
everything belongs to you.
17 I know, my God, that you test people's
hearts.
You are happy when people do what is
right.
I was happy to give all these things,
and I gave with an honest heart.
Your people gathered here are happy to
give to you,
and I rejoice to see their giving.
18 LORD, you are the God of our ancestors,
the God of Abraham, Isaac, and Jacob.
Make your people want to serve you
always,
and make them want to obey you.
19 Give my son Solomon a desire to serve
you.
Help him always obey your commands,
laws, and rules.
Help him build the Temple
for which I have prepared."

20 Then David said to all the people who
were gathered, "Praise the LORD your God." So
they all praised the LORD, the God of their ancestors, and they bowed to the ground to give
honor to the LORD and the king.

SOLOMON BECOMES KING

21 The next day the people sacrificed to the
LORD. They offered burnt offerings to him of a
thousand bulls, a thousand male sheep, and a
thousand male lambs. They also brought drink
offerings. Many sacrifices were made for all the
people of Israel. 22 That day the people ate and
drank with much joy, and the LORD was with
them.

And they made David's son Solomon king
for the second time. They poured olive oil on
Solomon to appoint him king in the presence
of the LORD. And they poured oil on Zadok to
appoint him as priest. 23 Then Solomon sat on
the LORD's throne as king and took his father
David's place. Solomon was very successful,
and all the people of Israel obeyed him. 24 All
the leaders and soldiers and King David's sons
accepted Solomon as king and promised to
obey him. 25 The LORD made Solomon great
before all the Israelites and gave Solomon
much honor. No king of Israel before Solomon
had such honor.

WHAT'S IT MEAN?

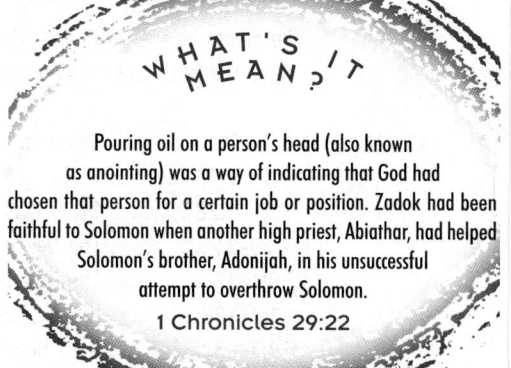

Pouring oil on a person's head (also known as anointing) was a way of indicating that God had chosen that person for a certain job or position. Zadok had been faithful to Solomon when another high priest, Abiathar, had helped Solomon's brother, Adonijah, in his unsuccessful attempt to overthrow Solomon.

1 Chronicles 29:22

DAVID'S DEATH

26 David son of Jesse was king over all Israel.
27 He had ruled over Israel forty years—seven
years in Hebron and thirty-three years in Jerusalem. 28 David died when he was old. He had
lived a good, long life and had received many
riches and honors. His son Solomon became
king after him.

29 Everything David did as king, from beginning to end, is recorded in the records of Samuel the seer, the records of Nathan the prophet,
and the records of Gad the seer. 30 Those writings tell what David did as king of Israel. They
tell about his power and what happened to
him and to Israel and to all the kingdoms
around them.

2 Chronicles

CONTENT When you read some of the previous books of the Bible, like 1 and 2 Kings and 1 Chronicles, you sometimes feel like you might hurt your neck! It can feel like you're watching a Ping-Pong tournament the way the Hebrews fall away from God, then return to God, then fall away from God, then return to God. Unfortunately, they fall away a few more times than they return.

But the Book of 2 Chronicles doesn't tell the story of all the kings and all the people. This book concentrates on the southern kingdom of Judah, and it concentrates on the stand-up kind of guys that rule. It tells the stories of kings like Josiah and Joash, who became kings when they were young, but really made a difference.

Second Chronicles reminds us that when we take a chance and stand up for God, he meets us every time. He doesn't hang us out to dry alone. He just wants us to have the faith to stand up and do the right thing.

Outline

1:1–17	Solomon's Wisdom and Wealth
2:1—7:22	Building and Dedication of the Jerusalem Temple
8:1—9:28	Other Events During Solomon's Rule
9:29–31	The Death of Solomon
10:1–19	The Northern Tribes of Israel Rebel Against King Rehoboam
11:1—28:27	Kings of Judah
29:1—32:33	King Hezekiah and the Assyrian Invasion
33:1–25	King Manasseh and King Amon
34:1—35:26–27	King Josiah and the Book of the Teachings
36:1–14	The Last Kings of Judah
36:15–21	Jerusalem Is Destroyed and the People Are Taken to Babylon
36:22–23	King Cyrus of Persia Lets the Jews Return to Judah

Purpose God is always faithful to those who put him first.

Theme Encouragement and Exhortation from Judah's Spiritual Heritage

Date of writing 430–425 B.C.

"Then if my people, who are called by my name, are sorry for what they have done, if they pray and obey me and stop their evil ways, I will hear them from heaven. I will forgive their sin, and I will heal their land" (7:14).

Bible Talk

Why?

Second Chronicles is that kind of book that prompts us to ask a lot of "why" questions. Why did the people keep falling away even though they saw God take care of them over and over? Why did they worship false gods, even though they should have known they were false? Why did they disobey God even after he clearly told them what to do? Why did they ignore the obvious and fall away again and again?

We have to ask ourselves the same questions. Why do we do what is wrong when we know what is right? Why do we get afraid even though God promises to take care of us? Why do we make friends with people who will push us farther away from God? Why do we ignore the obvious and fall away again and again?

WHAT'S WITH THE BLOOD AND GORE?

As you read through these historical books of the Old Testament, you might wonder after a while if all they did was fight. It really was a barbaric time in history.

Remember that Judah had become unbelievably wealthy during Solomon's rule. They weren't just wealthy; they were famous for being wealthy. So as the kingdom split and as the government weakened, the country became more of a target for invaders.

Keep in mind, too, that at this time, boundaries for land ownership were up for grabs to the strongest bully. There weren't any maps with black lines that showed who owned what. That was all being formed. It was definitely a different world.

SOLOMON ASKS FOR WISDOM

1
[1]Solomon, David's son, became a powerful
king, because the LORD his God was with him
and made him very great.
[2]Solomon spoke to all the people of Israel—
the commanders of a hundred men and of a
thousand men, the judges, every leader in all
Israel, and the leaders of the families. [3]Then
Solomon and all the people with him went to
the place of worship at the town of Gibeon.
God's Meeting Tent, which Moses the LORD's
servant had made in the desert, was there. [4]Da-
vid had brought the Ark of God from Kiriath
Jearim to Jerusalem, where he had made a
place for it and had set up a tent for it. [5]The
bronze altar that Bezalel son of Uri, who was
the son of Hur, had made was in Gibeon in
front of the Holy Tent. So Solomon and the
people worshiped there. [6]Solomon went up to
the bronze altar in the presence of the LORD at
the Meeting Tent and offered a thousand burnt
offerings on it.
[7]That night God appeared to Solomon and
said to him, "Ask for whatever you want me to
give you."
[8]Solomon answered, "You have been very
kind to my father David, and you have made
me king in his place. [9]Now, LORD God,
may your promise to my
father David come true. You
have made me king of a people who are as many as the
dust of the earth. [10]Now give
me wisdom and knowledge
so I can lead these people in
the right way, because no one can rule them
without your help."

PRAYER
What can we pray for? (1:9–10)

[11]God said to Solomon, "You have not
asked for wealth or riches or honor, or for the
death of your enemies, or for a long life. But
since you have asked for wisdom and knowledge to lead my people, over whom I have
made you king, [12]I will give you wisdom and
knowledge. I will also give you more wealth,
riches, and honor than any king who has lived
before you or any who will live after you."
[13]Then Solomon left the place of worship,
the Meeting Tent, at Gibeon and went back to
Jerusalem. There King Solomon ruled over Israel.

SOLOMON'S WEALTH

[14]Solomon had fourteen hundred chariots
and twelve thousand horses. He kept some in
special cities for the chariots, and others he
kept with him in Jerusalem. [15]In Jerusalem
Solomon made silver and gold as plentiful as
stones and cedar trees as plentiful as the fig
trees on the western hills. [16]He imported horses
from Egypt and Kue; his traders bought them
in Kue. [17]They imported chariots from Egypt
for about fifteen pounds of silver apiece, and
horses cost nearly four pounds of silver apiece.
Then they sold the horses and chariots to all
the kings of the Hittites and the Arameans.

WHAT'S IT MEAN?

Solomon recognized that the best way to strengthen Israel's military force was to invest in chariots, the most important piece of battle machinery available at that time. Ancient chariots came in all styles and sizes. Some were pulled by two horses, others by four. Some carried two riders; others carried four. The problem with chariots was the expense. Building, buying, and maintaining a fleet of chariots required more than a few ounces of silver. Only the wealthiest nations could afford to keep a strong chariot force. Later in Israel's history, as the kingdom declined in wealth and power, the use of chariots declined drastically. By the time King Jehoahaz came to power, Israel was down to ten measly chariots in their military. The rest had been destroyed in battle.

2 Chronicles 1:16–17

SOLOMON PREPARES FOR THE TEMPLE

2
[1]Solomon decided to build a temple as a
place to worship the LORD and also a palace
for himself. [2]He chose seventy thousand men
to carry loads, eighty thousand men to cut
stone in the hill country, and thirty-six hundred men to direct the workers.
[3]Solomon sent this message to Hiram king
of the city of Tyre: "Help me as you helped my
father David by sending him cedar logs so he
could build himself a palace to live in. [4]I will
build a temple for worshiping the LORD my
God, and I will give this temple to him. There
we will burn sweet-smelling spices in his presence. We will continually set out the holy
bread in God's presence. And we will burn
sacrifices every morning and evening, on Sabbath days and New Moons, and on the other
feast days commanded by the LORD our God.
This is a rule for Israel to obey forever.
[5]"The temple I build will be great, because
our God is greater than all gods. [6]But no one

can really build a house for our God. Not even
the highest of heavens can hold him. How then
can I build a temple for him except as a place
to burn sacrifices to him?
7"Now send me a man skilled in working
with gold, silver, bronze, and iron, and with
purple, red, and blue thread. He must also
know how to make engravings. He will work
with my skilled craftsmen in Judah and Jerusalem, whom my father David chose.
8"Also send me cedar, pine, and juniper logs
from Lebanon. I know your servants are experienced at cutting down the trees in Lebanon,
and my servants will help them. 9Send me a lot
of wood, because the temple I am going to
build will be large and wonderful. 10I will give
your servants who cut the wood one hundred
twenty-five thousand bushels of wheat, one
hundred twenty-five thousand bushels of barley, one hundred fifteen thousand gallons of
wine, and one hundred fifteen thousand gallons of oil."
11Then Hiram king of Tyre answered Solomon with this letter: "Solomon, because the
LORD loves his people, he chose you to be their
king." 12Hiram also said: "Praise the LORD, the
God of Israel, who made heaven and earth! He
has given King David a wise son, one with
wisdom and understanding, who will build a
temple for the LORD and a palace for himself.

WHAT'S IT MEAN?

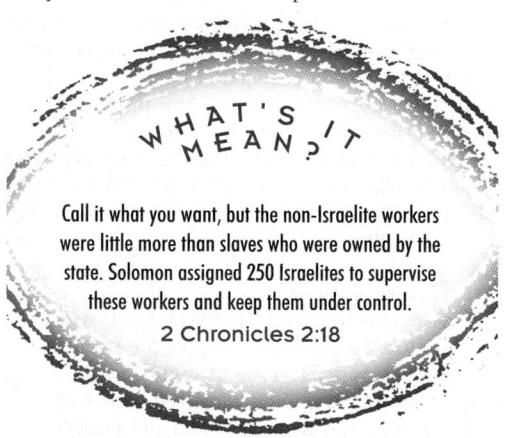

Call it what you want, but the non-Israelite workers were little more than slaves who were owned by the state. Solomon assigned 250 Israelites to supervise these workers and keep them under control.

2 Chronicles 2:18

13"I will send you a skilled and wise man
named Huram-Abi. 14His mother was from the
people of Dan, and his father was from Tyre.
Huram-Abi is skilled in working with gold, silver, bronze, iron, stone, and wood, and with
purple, blue, and red thread, and expensive
linen. He is skilled in making engravings and
can make any design you show him. He will
help your craftsmen and the craftsmen of your
father David.
15"Now send my servants the wheat, barley,
oil, and wine you promised. 16We will cut as
much wood from Lebanon as you need and
will bring it on rafts by sea to Joppa. Then you
may carry it to Jerusalem."
17Solomon counted all the foreigners living
in Israel. (This was after the time his father
David had counted the people.) There were
one hundred fifty-three thousand six hundred
foreigners in the country. 18Solomon chose
seventy thousand of them to carry loads,
eighty thousand of them to cut stone in the
mountains, and thirty-six hundred of them to
direct the workers and to keep the people
working.

WHAT'S IT MEAN?

How did Solomon know where to build his Temple? Years earlier, God had shown Solomon's father, David, the spot by lighting David's sacrifice with fire from heaven. The Temple Solomon had built was later destroyed by the Babylonians. In Jesus' day, another Temple—this one built by Herod the Great—sat on the site. If you were to go to Israel today, you would find a Moslem shrine known as the Dome of the Rock there.

2 Chronicles 3:1–2

SOLOMON BUILDS THE TEMPLE

3
1Then Solomon began to build the Temple
of the LORD in Jerusalem on Mount Moriah.
This was where the LORD had appeared to David, Solomon's father. Solomon built the Temple on the place David had prepared on the
threshing floor of Araunah the Jebusite. 2Sol-
omon began building in the second month of
the fourth year he ruled Israel.
3Solomon used these measurements for
building the Temple of God. It was ninety feet
long and thirty feet wide, using the old measurement. 4The porch in front of the main
room of the Temple was thirty feet long and
thirty feet high.
He covered the inside of the porch with
pure gold. 5He put panels of pine on the walls
of the main room and covered them with pure
gold. Then he put designs of palm trees and
chains in the gold. 6He decorated the Temple

with gems and gold from Parvaim.[n] 7He put
gold on the Temple's ceiling beams, doorposts,
walls, and doors, and he carved creatures with
wings on the walls.
8Then he made the Most Holy Place. It was
thirty feet long and thirty feet wide, as wide as
the Temple. He covered its walls with about
forty-six thousand pounds of pure gold. 9The
gold nails weighed over a pound. He also covered the upper rooms with gold.

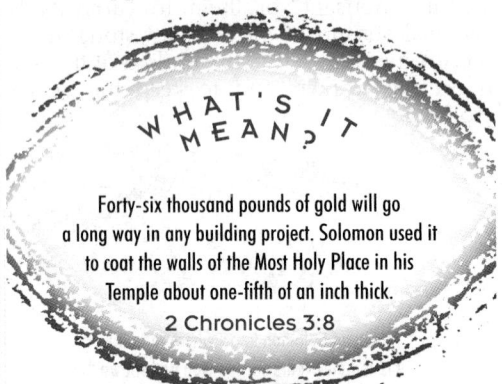

WHAT'S IT MEAN?

Forty-six thousand pounds of gold will go a long way in any building project. Solomon used it to coat the walls of the Most Holy Place in his Temple about one-fifth of an inch thick.

2 Chronicles 3:8

10He made two creatures with wings for the
Most Holy Place and covered them with gold.
11The wings of the gold creatures were thirty
feet across. One wing of one creature was
seven and one-half feet long and touched the
Temple wall. The creature's other wing was
also seven and one-half feet long, and it
touched a wing of the second creature. 12One
wing of the second creature touched the other
side of the room and was also seven and one-
half feet long. The second creature's other wing
touched the first creature's wing, and it was
also seven and one-half feet long. 13Together,
the creatures' wings were thirty feet across. The
creatures stood on their feet, facing the main
room.
14He made the curtain of blue, purple, and
red thread, and expensive linen, and he put designs of creatures with wings in it.
15He made two pillars to stand in front of
the Temple. They were about fifty-two feet tall,
and the capital of each pillar was over seven
feet tall. 16He made a net of chains and put
them on the tops of the pillars. He made a
hundred pomegranates and put them on the
chains. 17Then he put the pillars up in front of
the Temple. One pillar stood on the south side,
the other on the north. He named the south
pillar He Establishes and the north pillar In
Him Is Strength.

THINGS FOR THE TEMPLE

4
1He made a bronze altar thirty feet long,
thirty feet wide, and fifteen feet tall. 2Then he
made from bronze a large round bowl, which
was called the Sea. It was forty-five feet
around, fifteen feet across, and seven and one-
half feet deep. 3There were carvings of bulls
under the rim of the bowl—ten bulls every
eighteen inches. They were in two rows and
were made in one piece with the bowl.
4The bowl rested on the backs of twelve
bronze bulls that faced outward from the center of the bowl. Three bulls faced north, three
faced west, three faced south, and three faced
east. 5The sides of the bowl were four inches
thick, and it held about seventeen thousand
five hundred gallons. The rim of the bowl was
like the rim of a cup or like a lily blossom.
6He made ten smaller bowls and put five on
the south side and five on the north. They were
for washing the animals for the burnt offerings, but the large bowl was for the priests to
wash in.
7He made ten lampstands of gold, following
the plans. He put them in the Temple, five on
the south side and five on the north.
8He made ten tables and put them in the
Temple, five on the south side and five on the
north. And he used gold to make a hundred
other bowls.
9He also made the priests' courtyard and
the large courtyard. He made the doors that
opened to the courtyard and covered them
with bronze. 10Then he put the large bowl in
the southeast corner of the Temple.
11Huram also made bowls, shovels, and
small bowls. So he finished his work for King
Solomon on the Temple of God:
12two pillars;
two large bowls for the capitals on
top of the pillars;
two nets to cover the two large bowls
for the capitals on top of the pillars;
13four hundred pomegranates for the
two nets (there were two rows of
pomegranates for each net covering the bowls for the capitals on
top of the pillars);
14the stands with a bowl on each stand;
15the large bowl with twelve bulls under it;
16the pots, shovels, forks, and all the
things to go with them.
All the things that Huram-Abi made for
King Solomon for the Temple of the LORD were

3:6 Parvaim There was much gold there. It may have been in the country of Ophir.

made of polished bronze. [17]The king had these
things poured into clay molds that were made
in the plain of the Jordan River between Succoth and Zarethan. [18]Solomon had so many
things made that the total weight of all the
bronze was never known.
[19]Solomon also made all the things for
God's Temple: the golden altar; tables which
held the bread that shows God's people are in
his presence; [20]the lampstands and their lamps
of pure gold, to burn in front of the Most Holy
Place as planned; [21]the flowers, lamps, and
tongs of pure gold; [22]the pure gold wick trimmers, small bowls, pans, and dishes used to
carry coals, the gold doors for the Temple, and
the inside doors of the Most Holy Place and of
the main room.
5 [1]Finally all the work Solomon did for the
Temple of the LORD was finished. He brought
in everything his father David had set apart for
the Temple—all the silver and gold and other
articles. And he put everything in the treasuries
of God's Temple.

THE ARK IS BROUGHT INTO THE TEMPLE

[2]Solomon called for the older leaders of Israel, the heads of the tribes, and the leaders of
the families to come to him in Jerusalem. He
wanted them to bring the Ark of the Agreement with the LORD from the older part of the
city. [3]So all the Israelites came together with the
king during the festival in the seventh month.

WHAT'S IT MEAN?

The Levites' job description included taking care of the Ark of the Agreement, the Meeting Tent, and anything else used for worship. When the Temple was finished, the Ark of the Agreement was moved into the Most Holy Place. The Meeting Tent may have been set up as a permanent display inside the Temple as well.

2 Chronicles 5:4–5

[4]When all the older leaders of Israel arrived,
the Levites lifted up the Ark. [5]They carried the
Ark of the Agreement, the Meeting Tent, and
the holy utensils in it; the priests and the Levites brought them up. [6]King Solomon and all
the Israelites gathered before the Ark of the
Agreement and sacrificed so many sheep and
bulls no one could count them.
[7]Then the priests put the Ark of the Agreement with the LORD in its place inside the Most
Holy Place in the Temple, under the wings of
the golden creatures. [8]The wings of these creatures were spread out over the place for the
Ark, covering it and its carrying poles. [9]The
carrying poles were so long that anyone
standing in the Holy Place in front of the Most
Holy Place could see the ends of the poles. But
no one could see them from outside the Holy
Place. The poles are still there today. [10]The only
things inside the Ark were two stone tablets[n]
that Moses had put in the Ark at Mount Sinai.
That was where the LORD made his agreement
with the Israelites after they came out of Egypt.

WHAT'S IT MEAN?

When a treaty or agreement was made in ancient times, two copies of the contract were drawn up—one for each party. The two tablets inside the Ark of the Agreement may have been two copies of the same contract—one for God and one for the Israelites.

2 Chronicles 5:10

[11]Then all the priests left the Holy Place. (All
the priests from each group had made themselves ready to serve the LORD.) [12]All the Levite
musicians—Asaph, Heman, Jeduthun, and all
their sons and relatives—stood on the east side
of the altar. They were dressed in white linen
and played cymbals, harps, and lyres. With
them were one hundred twenty priests who
blew trumpets. [13]Those who blew the trumpets
and those who sang together sounded like one
person as they praised and thanked the LORD.
They sang as others played their trumpets,
cymbals, and other instruments. They praised
the LORD with this song:

"He is good;
his love continues forever."

Then the Temple of the LORD was filled with
a cloud. [14]The priests could not continue their

5:10 stone tablets They were the two stone tablets on which God wrote the Ten Commandments.

On the Edge

They sang as others played their trumpets, cymbals, and other instruments. They praised the LORD with this song: "He is good; his love continues forever" (2 Chr. 5:13b).

It's hard to imagine compassionate, loving concern that never ends. Your boyfriend loved you yesterday, but he loves someone else today. Your parents seem to love you more when your grades are good and your chores are done. You know someone whose dad just left because he doesn't love the mom anymore. Love seems to come and go very easily down here on earth. But there is Someone who is truly in love with you. He can't keep his eyes off of you. He is so proud that you belong to him. The love of God will never disappoint you. His commitment is forever. There will be no trial separations, no grounds for divorce. He is good, and you are the one he loves without end.

SEE FOR YOURSELF:
Rom. 5:8–11;
Eph. 2:4–7;
1 John 4:7–11

work because of the cloud, because the LORD's
glory filled the Temple of God.

SOLOMON SPEAKS TO THE PEOPLE

6

1Then Solomon said, "The LORD said he
would live in the dark cloud. 2LORD, I have
built a wonderful Temple for you—a place for
you to live forever."
3While all the Israelites were standing there,
King Solomon turned to them and blessed
them. 4Then he said, "Praise the LORD, the God
of Israel. He has done what he promised to my
father David. The LORD said, 5'Since the time I
brought my people out of Egypt, I have not
chosen a city in any tribe of Israel where a
temple will be built for me. I did not choose a
man to lead my people Israel. 6But now I have
chosen Jerusalem as the place I am to be worshiped, and I have chosen David to lead my
people Israel.'
7"My father David wanted to build a temple
for the LORD, the God of Israel. 8But the LORD
said to my father David, 'It was good that you
wanted to build a temple for me. 9But you are
not the one to build it. Your son, who comes from your own body, is the one who will build my temple.'
10"Now the LORD has kept his promise. I am
the king now in place of David my father. Now I rule Israel as the LORD promised, and I have built the Temple for the LORD, the God of Israel.
11There I have put the Ark, in which is the
Agreement the LORD made with the Israelites."

SOLOMON'S PRAYER

12Then Solomon stood facing the LORD's altar, and all the Israelites were standing behind
him. He spread out his hands. 13He had made a
bronze platform seven and one-half feet long, seven and one-half feet wide, and seven and one-half feet high, and he had placed it in the middle of the outer courtyard. Solomon stood on the platform. Then he kneeled in front of all the people of Israel gathered there, and he
spread out his hands toward the sky. 14He said,
"LORD, God of Israel, there is no god like you in heaven or on earth. You keep your agreement of love with your servants who truly follow
you. 15You have kept the promise you made to
your servant David, my father. You spoke it with your own mouth and finished it with your hands today.
16"Now, LORD, God of Israel, keep the promise you made to your servant David, my father. You said, 'If your sons are careful to obey my teachings as you have obeyed, there will always
be someone from your family ruling Israel.'
17Now, LORD, God of Israel, please continue to
keep that promise you made to your servant.
18"But, God, can you really live here on the
earth with people? The sky and the highest place in heaven cannot contain you. Surely this house which I have built cannot contain you.
19But please listen to my prayer and my request,
because I am your servant. LORD my God, hear
this prayer your servant prays to you. 20Day
and night please watch over this Temple where you have said you would be worshiped. Hear
the prayer I pray facing this Temple. 21Hear my
prayers and the prayers of your people Israel when we pray facing this place. Hear from your home in heaven, and when you hear, forgive us.
22"If someone wrongs another person, he
will be brought to the altar in this Temple. If he swears an oath that he is not
guilty, 23then hear in heaven.
Judge the case, punish the guilty, but declare that the innocent person is not guilty.
24"When your people, the
Israelites, sin against you, their

SIN
Do we really need to confess sin to God? (6:24–27)

enemies will defeat them. But if they come back
to you and praise you and pray to you in this
Temple, 25then listen from heaven. Forgive the
sin of your people Israel, and
bring them back to the land
you gave to them and their
ancestors.
26"When they sin
against you, you will stop
the rain from falling on
their land. Then they will
pray, facing this place and
praising you; they will
stop sinning when you
make them suffer. 27When this
happens, hear their prayer in
heaven, and forgive the sins of your servants, the Israelites. Teach them to do what is
right. Then please send rain to this land you
have given particularly to them.
28"At times the land will get so dry that no
food will grow, or a great sickness will spread
among the people. Sometimes the crops will be
destroyed by locusts or grasshoppers. Your
people will be attacked in their cities by their
enemies, or will become sick. 29When any of
these things happens, the people will become
truly sorry. If your people spread their hands in
prayer toward this Temple, 30then hear their
prayers from your home in heaven. Forgive
and treat each person as he should be treated
because you know what is in a person's heart.
Only you know what is in people's hearts.
31Then the people will respect and obey you as
long as they live in this land you gave our ancestors.
32"People who are not Israelites, foreigners
from other lands, will hear about your greatness and power. They will come from far away
to pray at this Temple. 33Then hear from your
home in heaven, and do whatever they ask
you. Then people everywhere will know you
and respect you, just as your people Israel do.
Then everyone will know that I built this Temple as a place to worship you.
34"When your people go out to fight their
enemies along some road on which you send
them, your people will pray to you, facing this
city which you have chosen and the Temple I
have built for you. 35Then hear in heaven their
prayers, and do what is right.
36"Everyone sins, so your people will also
sin against you. You will become angry with
them and will hand them over to their enemies. Their enemies will capture them and take
them away to a country far or near. 37Your
people will be sorry for their sins when they
are held as prisoners in another country. They
will be sorry and pray to you in the land
where they are held as prisoners, saying, 'We
have sinned. We have done
wrong and acted wickedly.'
38They will truly turn back
to you in the land where
they are captives. They will
pray, facing this land you
gave their ancestors, this
city you have chosen, and
the Temple I have built for
you. 39Then hear their
prayers from your home
in heaven and do what is
right. Forgive your people who
have sinned against you.
40"Now, my God, look at us. Listen to the
prayers we pray in this place.

"Hear my prayers and the prayers of your people Israel when we pray facing this place. . . . and when you hear, forgive us."
(2 Chronicles 6:21)

WHAT'S IT MEAN?

Here's the story of two kingdoms. See if you can identify the reason for their radically different endings. In 722 B.C., the Assyrians captured the city of Samaria and took the ten tribes of the northern kingdom of Israel into captivity. There is no indication that any of those tribes ever returned to Israel. In 586 B.C., the Babylonians captured the city of Jerusalem and took the two tribes of the southern kingdom of Judah into captivity. While they were captives in Babylon, the people of Judah asked God to forgive their sins. Years later, they were allowed to return to Jerusalem and rebuild their Temple.

2 Chronicles 6:36–39

41 Now, rise, LORD God, and come to your
resting place.
Come with the Ark of the Agreement
that shows your strength.
Let your priests receive your salvation,
LORD God,
and may your holy people be happy
because of your goodness.
42 LORD God, do not reject your appointed
one.
Remember your love for your servant
David."

THE TEMPLE IS GIVEN TO THE LORD

7 1When Solomon finished praying, fire came
down from the sky and burned up the burnt
offering and the sacrifices. The LORD's glory
filled the Temple. 2The priests could not enter
the Temple of the LORD, because the LORD's
glory filled it. 3When all the people of Israel
saw the fire come down from heaven and the
LORD's glory on the Temple, they bowed down
on the pavement with their faces to the
ground. They worshiped and thanked the
LORD, saying,

"He is good;
his love continues forever."

4Then King Solomon and all the people offered
sacrifices to the LORD. 5King Solomon offered a
sacrifice of twenty-two thousand cattle and
one hundred twenty thousand sheep. So the
king and all the people gave the Temple to God.
6The priests stood ready to do their work. The
Levites also stood with the instruments of the
LORD's music that King David had made for
praising the LORD. The priests and Levites were
saying, "His love continues forever." The priests,
who stood across from the Levites, blew their
trumpets, and all the Israelites were standing.
7Solomon made holy the middle part of the
courtyard, which is in front of the Temple of
the LORD. There he offered whole burnt offerings and the fat of the fellowship offerings. He
offered them in the courtyard, because the
bronze altar he had made could not hold the
burnt offerings, grain offerings, and fat.

WHAT'S IT MEAN?

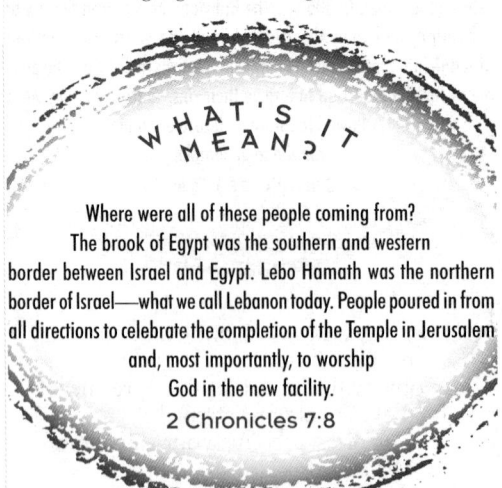

Where were all of these people coming from? The brook of Egypt was the southern and western border between Israel and Egypt. Lebo Hamath was the northern border of Israel—what we call Lebanon today. People poured in from all directions to celebrate the completion of the Temple in Jerusalem and, most importantly, to worship God in the new facility.

2 Chronicles 7:8

8Solomon and all the Israelites celebrated
the festival for seven days. There were many
people, and they came from as far away as
Lebo Hamath and the brook of Egypt. 9For
seven days they celebrated giving the altar for
the worship of God. Then they celebrated the
festival for seven days. On the eighth day they
had a meeting. 10On the twenty-third day of
the seventh month Solomon sent the people
home, full of joy. They were happy because the
LORD had been so good to David, Solomon,
and his people Israel.

THE LORD APPEARS TO SOLOMON

11Solomon finished the Temple of the LORD
and his royal palace. He had success in doing
everything he planned in the Temple of the
LORD and his own palace. 12Then the LORD appeared to Solomon at night and said to him, "I
have heard your prayer and have chosen this
place for myself to be a Temple for sacrifices.
13"I may stop the sky from sending rain. I
may command the locusts to destroy the land.
I may send sicknesses to my people. 14Then if
my people, who are called by my
name, are sorry for what they
have done, if they pray and
obey me and stop their evil
ways, I will hear them from
heaven. I will forgive their sin,
and I will heal their land.
15Now I will see them, and I
will listen to the prayers prayed in this place.
16I have chosen this Temple and made it holy.
So I will be worshiped there forever. Yes, I will
always watch over it and love it.

SUCCESS
How should we pray to obtain success? (7:14)

17"But you must serve me as your father
David did. You must obey all I have
commanded and keep
my laws and rules. 18If
you do, I will make your
kingdom strong. This is the
agreement I made with your
father David, saying, 'Someone from your family will always rule in Israel.'

FOLLOWING GOD
Does God put conditions on our obedience? (7:17)

19"But you must follow me and obey the
laws and commands I have given you. You
must not serve or worship other gods. 20If you
do, I will take the Israelites out of my land,
the land I have given them, and I will leave
this Temple that I have made holy. All the nations will make fun of it and speak evil about
it. 21This Temple is honored now, but then,
everyone who passes by will be shocked. They
will ask, 'Why did the LORD do this terrible
thing to this land and this Temple?' 22People
will answer, 'This happened because they left
the LORD, the God of their ancestors, the God
who brought them out of Egypt. They decided
to follow other gods and worshiped and

served them, so he brought all this disaster on
them.' "

SOLOMON'S OTHER ACHIEVEMENTS

8 1By the end of twenty years, Solomon had
built the Temple of the LORD and the royal palace. 2Solomon rebuilt the towns that Hiram
had given him, and Solomon sent Israelites to
live in them. 3Then he went to Hamath Zobah
and captured it. 4Solomon also built the town
of Tadmor in the desert, and he built all the
towns in Hamath as towns for storing grain
and supplies. 5He rebuilt the towns of Upper
Beth Horon and Lower Beth Horon, protecting
them with strong walls, gates, and bars in the
gates. 6He also rebuilt the town of Baalath. And
he built all the other towns for storage and all
the cities for his chariots and horses. He built
all he wanted in Jerusalem, Lebanon, and everywhere he ruled.
7There were other people in the land who
were not Israelites—the Hittites, Amorites, Perizzites, Hivites, and Jebusites. 8They were descendants of the people that the Israelites had
not destroyed. Solomon forced them to be
slave workers, as is still true today. 9But Solomon did not make slaves of the Israelites.
They were his soldiers, chief captains, commanders of his chariots, and his chariot drivers. 10These were his most important officers.
There were two hundred fifty of them to direct
the people.
11Solomon brought the daughter of the king
of Egypt from the older part of Jerusalem to
the palace he had built for her. Solomon said,
"My wife must not live in King David's palace,
because the places where the Ark of the Agreement has been are holy."
12Then Solomon offered burnt offerings to
the LORD on the altar he had built for the LORD
in front of the Temple porch. 13He offered sacrifices every day as Moses had commanded.
They were offered on the Sabbath days, New
Moons, and the three yearly feasts—the Feast
of Unleavened Bread, the Feast of Weeks, and
the Feast of Shelters. 14Solomon followed his
father David's instructions and chose the
groups of priests for their service and the Levites to lead the praise and to help the priests
do their daily work. And he chose the gatekeepers by their groups to serve at each gate, as
David, the man of God, had commanded.
15They obeyed all of Solomon's commands to
the priests and Levites, as well as his commands about the treasuries.
16All Solomon's work was done as he had
said from the day the foundation of the Temple
of the LORD was begun, until it was finished. So
the Temple was finished.

WHAT'S IT MEAN?

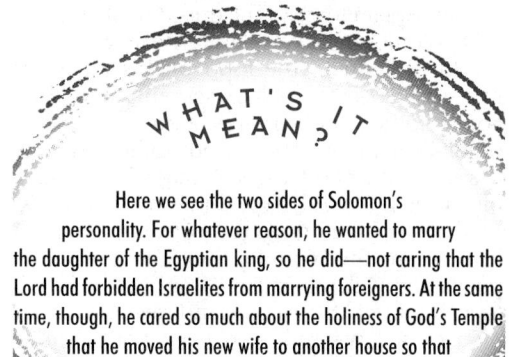

Here we see the two sides of Solomon's personality. For whatever reason, he wanted to marry the daughter of the Egyptian king, so he did—not caring that the Lord had forbidden Israelites from marrying foreigners. At the same time, though, he cared so much about the holiness of God's Temple that he moved his new wife to another house so that her idol worship wouldn't cause problems.

2 Chronicles 8:11

17Then Solomon went to the towns of Ezion
Geber and Elath near the Red Sea in the land of
Edom. 18Hiram sent ships to Solomon that
were commanded by his own men, who were
skilled sailors. Hiram's men went with Solomon's men to Ophir and brought back about
thirty-four thousand pounds of gold to King
Solomon.

WHAT'S IT MEAN?

Sheba was known as an international trading center. When countries needed valuable items, such as spices, perfumes, and precious stones, they turned to Sheba. The queen of Sheba's visit to Solomon was probably part personal and part business. On a personal level, she wanted to see if the rumors she had heard about Solomon's wealth were true. On a business level, she probably wanted to add Solomon and Israel to her list of clients.

2 Chronicles 9:1

THE QUEEN OF SHEBA VISITS

9 1When the queen of Sheba heard about
Solomon's fame, she came to Jerusalem to test
him with hard questions. She had a large
group of servants with her and camels carrying spices, jewels, and much gold. When she
came to Solomon, she talked with him about

all she had in mind, 2and Solomon answered all her questions. Nothing was too hard for him to explain to her. 3The queen of Sheba saw that Solomon was very wise. She saw the palace he had built, 4the food on his table, his many officers, the palace servants and their good clothes, the servants who served Solomon his wine and their good clothes. She saw the whole burnt offerings he made in the Temple of the LORD. All these things amazed her.

5So she said to King Solomon, "What I heard in my own country about your achievements and wisdom is true. 6I did not believe it then, but now I have come and seen it with my own eyes. I was not told even half of your great wisdom! You are much greater than I had heard. 7Your men and officers are very lucky, because in always serving you, they are able to hear your wisdom. 8Praise the LORD your God who was pleased to make you king. He has put you on his throne to rule for the LORD your God, because your God loves the people of Israel and supports them forever. He has made you king over them to keep justice and to rule fairly."

9Then she gave the king about nine thousand pounds of gold and many spices and jewels. No one had ever given such spices as the queen of Sheba gave to King Solomon.

10Hiram's men and Solomon's men brought gold from Ophir, juniper wood, and jewels. 11King Solomon used the juniper wood to build steps for the Temple of the LORD and the palace and to make lyres and harps for the musicians. No one in Judah had ever seen such beautiful things as these.

12King Solomon gave the queen of Sheba everything she wanted and asked for, even more than she had brought to him. Then she and her servants returned to her own country.

SOLOMON'S WEALTH

13Every year King Solomon received about fifty thousand pounds of gold. 14Besides that, he also received gold from traders and merchants. All the kings of Arabia and the governors of the land also brought gold and silver.

15King Solomon made two hundred large shields of hammered gold, each of which contained about seven and one-half pounds of hammered gold. 16He also made three hundred smaller shields of hammered gold, each of which contained about four pounds of gold. The king put them in the Palace of the Forest of Lebanon.

17The king built a large throne of ivory and covered it with pure gold. 18The throne had six steps on it and a gold footstool. There were armrests on both sides of the chair, and each armrest had a lion beside it. 19Twelve lions stood on the six steps, one lion at each end of each step. Nothing like this had ever been made for any other kingdom. 20All of Solomon's drinking cups, as well as the dishes in the Palace of the Forest of Lebanon, were made of pure gold. In Solomon's time people did not think silver was valuable.

21King Solomon had many ships that he sent out to trade, with Hiram's men as the crews. Every three years the ships returned, bringing back gold, silver, ivory, apes, and baboons.

22King Solomon had more riches and wisdom than all the other kings on earth. 23All the kings of the earth wanted to see Solomon and listen to the wisdom God had given him. 24Year after year everyone who came brought gifts of silver and gold, clothes, weapons, spices, horses, and mules.

25Solomon had four thousand stalls for horses and chariots, and he had twelve thousand horses. He kept some in special cities for the chariots, and others he kept with him in Jerusalem. 26Solomon ruled over all the kingdoms from the Euphrates River to the land of the Philistines, as far as the border of Egypt. 27In Jerusalem the king made silver as common as stones and cedar trees as plentiful as the fig trees on the western hills. 28Solomon imported horses from Egypt and all other countries.

WHAT'S IT MEAN?

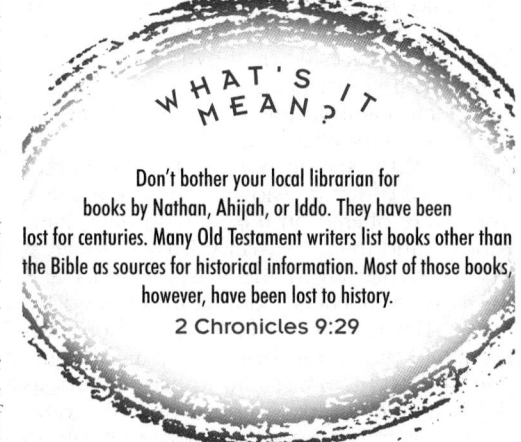

Don't bother your local librarian for books by Nathan, Ahijah, or Iddo. They have been lost for centuries. Many Old Testament writers list books other than the Bible as sources for historical information. Most of those books, however, have been lost to history.

2 Chronicles 9:29

SOLOMON'S DEATH

29Everything else Solomon did, from the beginning to the end, is written in the records of Nathan the prophet, and in the prophecy of Ahijah the Shilonite, and in the visions of Iddo the seer, who wrote about Jeroboam, Nebat's son. 30Solomon ruled in Jerusalem over all Israel for forty years. 31Then Solomon died and was buried in Jerusalem, the city of David, his father. And Solomon's son Rehoboam became king in his place.

ISRAEL TURNS AGAINST REHOBOAM

10 1Rehoboam went to Shechem, where all the Israelites had gone to make him king. 2Jeroboam son of Nebat was in Egypt, where he had gone to escape from King Solomon. When Jeroboam heard about Rehoboam being made king, he returned from Egypt. 3After the people sent for him, he and the people went to Rehoboam and said to him, 4"Your father forced us to work very hard. Now, make it easier for us, and don't make us work as he did. Then we will serve you."

WHAT'S IT MEAN?

Talk about being put in an awkward position! While Jeroboam was serving as a chief advisor to King Solomon, the prophet Ahijah told him that God was angry with Solomon for worshiping foreign gods. As a result, Solomon's kingdom was going to be torn apart. To demonstrate what was going to happen, Ahijah tore his coat into twelve pieces and gave ten of them to Jeroboam. He explained that Jeroboam would be given ten of the tribes of Israel to rule over. As you might imagine, Solomon was furious when he heard that his own advisor was going to replace him as king. Solomon was so furious, in fact, that he tried to kill Jeroboam. Jeroboam escaped and did not return to the kingdom until after Solomon's death.

2 Chronicles 10:2

5Rehoboam answered, "Come back to me in three days." So the people left.

6King Rehoboam asked the older leaders who had advised Solomon during his lifetime, "How do you think I should answer these people?"

7They answered, "Be kind to these people. If you please them and give them a kind answer, they will serve you always."

8But Rehoboam rejected this advice. Instead, he asked the young men who had grown up with him and who served as his advisers. 9Rehoboam asked them, "What is your advice? How should we answer these people who said, 'Don't make us work as hard as your father did'?"

10The young men who had grown up with him answered, "The people said to you, 'Your father forced us to work very hard. Now make our work easier.' You should tell them, 'My little finger is bigger than my father's legs. 11He forced you to work hard, but I will make you work even harder. My father beat you with whips, but I will beat you with whips that have sharp points.' "

FRIENDSHIP

How can friends pull you down? (10:1–14)

12Rehoboam had told the people, "Come back to me in three days." So after three days Jeroboam and all the people returned to Rehoboam. 13King Rehoboam spoke cruel words to them, because he had rejected the advice of the older leaders. 14He followed the advice of the young men and said, "My father forced you to work hard, but I will make you work even harder. My father beat you with whips, but I will beat you with whips that have sharp points." 15So the king did not listen to the people. God caused this to happen so that the LORD could keep the promise he had made to Jeroboam son of Nebat through Ahijah, a prophet from Shiloh.

16When all the Israelites saw that the king refused to listen to them, they said to the king,

"We have no share in David!
We have no part in the son of Jesse!
People of Israel, let's go to our own homes!
Let David's son rule his own people."

So all the Israelites went home. 17But Rehoboam still ruled over the Israelites who lived in the towns of Judah.

18Adoniram was in charge of the forced labor. When Rehoboam sent him to the people, they threw stones at him until he died. But King Rehoboam ran to his chariot and escaped to Jerusalem. 19Since then, Israel has been against the family of David.

11 1When Rehoboam arrived in Jerusalem, he gathered one hundred eighty thousand of the best soldiers from Judah and Benjamin. He wanted to fight Israel to take back his kingdom. 2But the LORD spoke his word to Shemaiah, a man of God, saying, 3"Speak to Solomon's son Rehoboam, the king of Judah, and to all the Israelites living in Judah and Benjamin. Say to them, 4'The LORD says you must not go to war against your brothers. Every one of you should go home, because I made all these things happen.' " So they obeyed the LORD's

command and turned back and did not attack Jeroboam.

REHOBOAM MAKES JUDAH STRONG

5Rehoboam lived in Jerusalem and built strong cities in Judah to defend it. 6He built up the cities of Bethlehem, Etam, Tekoa, 7Beth Zur, Soco, Adullam, 8Gath, Mareshah, Ziph, 9Adoraim, Lachish, Azekah, 10Zorah, Aijalon, and Hebron. These were strong, walled cities in Judah and Benjamin. 11When Rehoboam made those cities strong, he put commanders and supplies of food, oil, and wine in them. 12Also, Rehoboam put shields and spears in all the cities and made them very strong. Rehoboam kept the people of Judah and Benjamin under his control.

13The priests and the Levites from all over Israel joined Rehoboam. 14The Levites even left their pasturelands and property and came to Judah and Jerusalem, because Jeroboam and his sons refused to let them serve as priests to the LORD. 15Jeroboam chose his own priests for the places of worship and for the goat and calf idols he had made. 16There were people from all the tribes of Israel who wanted to obey the LORD, the God of Israel. So they went to Jerusalem with the Levites to sacrifice to the LORD, the God of their fathers. 17These people made the kingdom of Judah strong, and they supported Solomon's son Rehoboam for three years. During this time they lived the way David and Solomon had lived.

"These people made the kingdom of Judah strong, and they supported Solomon's son Rehoboam for three years. During this time they lived the way David and Solomon had lived."
(2 Chronicles 11:17)

REHOBOAM'S FAMILY

18Rehoboam married Mahalath, the daughter of Jerimoth and Abihail. Jerimoth was David's son, and Abihail was the daughter of Eliab, Jesse's son. 19Mahalath gave Rehoboam these sons: Jeush, Shemariah, and Zaham. 20Then Rehoboam married Absalom's daughter Maacah, and she gave Rehoboam these children: Abijah, Attai, Ziza, and Shelomith. 21Rehoboam loved Maacah more than his other wives and slave women. Rehoboam had eighteen wives and sixty slave women and was the father of twenty-eight sons and sixty daughters.

22Rehoboam chose Abijah son of Maacah to be the leader of his own brothers, because he planned to make Abijah king. 23Rehoboam acted wisely. He spread his sons through all the areas of Judah and Benjamin, sending them to every strong, walled city. He gave plenty of supplies to his sons, and he also found wives for them.

WHAT'S IT MEAN?

Jeroboam was afraid that if the people returned to Jerusalem to worship God, he would lose his control over them. To keep them away from Jerusalem, Jeroboam made goat and calf idols for the people to worship in Bethel and Dan. As if that weren't enough, Jeroboam appointed priests who were not from the tribe of Levi—another no-no, as far as God was concerned.

2 Chronicles 11:15

SHISHAK ATTACKS JERUSALEM

12

1After Rehoboam's kingdom was set up and he became strong, he and the people of Judah stopped obeying the teachings of the LORD. 2During the fifth year Rehoboam was king, Shishak king of Egypt attacked Jerusalem, because Rehoboam and the people were unfaithful to the LORD. 3Shishak had twelve hundred chariots and sixty thousand horsemen. He brought troops of Libyans, Sukkites, and Cushites from Egypt with him, so many they couldn't be counted. 4Shishak captured the strong, walled cities of Judah and came as far as Jerusalem.

SUCCESS

When can success be bad for us? (12:1)

5Then Shemaiah the prophet came to Rehoboam and the leaders of Judah who had gathered in Jerusalem because they were afraid of Shishak. Shemaiah said to them, "This is what the LORD says: 'You have left me, so now I will leave you to face Shishak alone.' "

6Then the leaders of Judah and King Reho-

boam were sorry for what they had done.
They said, "The LORD does what is right."
7When the LORD saw they were sorry for
what they had done, the LORD spoke his word
to Shemaiah, saying, "The king and the leaders
are sorry. So I will not destroy them but will
save them soon. I will not use Shishak to punish Jerusalem in my anger. 8But the people of
Jerusalem will become Shishak's servants so
they may learn that serving me is different
than serving the kings of other nations."
9Shishak king of Egypt attacked Jerusalem
and took the treasures from the Temple of the
LORD and the king's palace. He took everything, even the gold shields Solomon had
made. 10So King Rehoboam made bronze
shields to take their place and gave them to the
commanders of the guards for the palace gates.
11Whenever the king went to the Temple of the
LORD, the guards went with him, carrying the
shields. Later, they would put them back in the
guardroom.
12When Rehoboam was sorry for what he
had done, the LORD held his anger back and
did not fully destroy Rehoboam. There was
some good in Judah.
13King Rehoboam made himself a strong
king in Jerusalem. He was forty-one years old
when he became king, and he was king in Jerusalem for seventeen years. Jerusalem is the city
that the LORD chose from all the tribes of Israel
in which he was to be worshiped. Rehoboam's
mother was Naamah from the country of Ammon. 14Rehoboam did evil because he did not
want to obey the LORD.
15The things Rehoboam did as king, from
the beginning to the end, are written in the
records of Shemaiah the prophet and Iddo the
seer, in the family histories. There were wars
between Rehoboam and Jeroboam all the time
they ruled. 16Rehoboam died and was buried
in Jerusalem, and his son Abijah became king
in his place.

ABIJAH KING OF JUDAH

13 1Abijah became the king of Judah during
the eighteenth year Jeroboam was king of Israel. 2Abijah ruled in Jerusalem for three years.
His mother was Maacah daughter of Uriel
from the town of Gibeah.
And there was war between Abijah and Jeroboam. 3Abijah led an army of four hundred
thousand capable soldiers into battle, and Jeroboam prepared to fight him with eight hundred thousand capable soldiers.
4Abijah stood on Mount Zemaraim in the
mountains of Ephraim and said, "Jeroboam and
all Israel, listen to me! 5You should know that
the LORD, the God of Israel, gave David and his
sons the right to rule Israel forever by an agreement of salt. 6But Jeroboam son of Nebat, one
of the officers of Solomon, David's son, turned
against his master. 7Then worthless, evil men
joined Jeroboam against Rehoboam, Solomon's
son. He was young and didn't know what to
do, so he could not stop them.
8"Now you people are making plans against
the LORD's kingdom, which belongs to David's
sons. There are many of you, and you have the
gold calves Jeroboam made for you as gods.
9You have thrown out the Levites and the
LORD's priests, Aaron's sons. You have chosen
your own priests as people in other countries
do. Anyone who comes with a young bull and
seven male sheep can become a priest of idols
that are not gods.
10"But as for us, the LORD is our God; we
have not left him. The priests who serve the
LORD are Aaron's sons, and the Levites help
them. 11They offer burnt offerings and sweet-
smelling incense to the LORD every morning

On the Edge

We obey the command of the LORD our God, but you have left him. God himself is with us as our ruler. His priests blow the trumpet to call us to war against you (2 Chr. 13:11b–12a).

Remember choosing sides for kickball in the third grade? Whether you were the captain of the team or the last one chosen, it was always a huge relief to be on the team with the best kicker. Victory was sure. You could breathe easy—the best players were on your team. A win was in sight.

Well, you can take another deep breath and relax—God is with you, on your side, for life. He wants you to show up for the games, bring your best attitude, be committed to the coach, and play your heart out. The rest is up to him. He will carry the whole team. Your victory has already been decided. It's a sure thing. You've been warming up long enough; it's time to get in the game. Go for it!

SEE FOR YOURSELF:
2 Chr. 32:8; Ps. 118:5–9; Zech. 10:5

and evening. They put the bread on the special table in the Temple. And they light the lamps on the gold lampstand every evening. We obey the command of the LORD our God, but you have left him. 12God himself is with us as our ruler. His priests blow the trumpet to call us to war against you. Men of Israel, don't fight against the LORD, the God of your ancestors, because you won't succeed."

13But Jeroboam had sent some troops to sneak behind Judah's army. So while Jeroboam was in front of Judah's army, Jeroboam's soldiers were behind them. 14When the soldiers of Judah turned around, they saw Jeroboam's army attacking both in front and back. So they cried out to the LORD, and the priests blew the trumpets. 15Then the men of Judah gave a battle cry. When they shouted, God caused Jeroboam and the army of Israel to run away from Abijah and the army of Judah. 16When the army of Israel ran away from the men of Judah, God handed them over to Judah. 17Abijah's army struck Israel so that five hundred thousand of Israel's best men were killed. 18So at that time the people of Israel were defeated. And the people of Judah won, because they depended on the LORD, the God of their ancestors.

19Abijah's army chased Jeroboam's army and captured from him the towns of Bethel, Jeshanah, and Ephron, and the small villages near them. 20Jeroboam never became strong again while Abijah was alive. The LORD struck Jeroboam, and he died.

21But Abijah became strong. He married fourteen women and was the father of twenty-two sons and sixteen daughters. 22Everything else Abijah did—what he said and what he did—is recorded in the writings of the prophet Iddo.

14 1Abijah died and was buried in Jerusalem. His son Asa became king in his place, and there was peace in the country for ten years during Asa's time.

ASA KING OF JUDAH

2Asa did what the LORD his God said was good and right. 3He removed the foreign altars and the places where gods were worshiped. He smashed the stone pillars that honored other gods, and he tore down the Asherah idols. 4Asa commanded the people of Judah to follow the LORD, the God of their ancestors, and to obey his teachings and commandments. 5He also removed the places where gods were worshiped and the incense altars from every town in Judah. So the kingdom had peace while Asa was king. 6Asa built strong, walled cities in Judah during the time of peace. He had no war in these years, because the LORD gave him peace.

7Asa said to the people of Judah, "Let's build up these towns and put walls around them. Let's make towers, gates, and bars in the gates. This country is ours, because we have obeyed the LORD our God. We have followed him, and he has given us peace all around." So they built and had success.

8Asa had an army of three hundred thousand men from Judah and two hundred eighty thousand men from Benjamin. The men from Judah carried large shields and spears. The men from Benjamin carried small shields and bows and arrows. All of them were brave fighting men.

9Then Zerah from Cush came out to fight them with an enormous army and three hundred chariots. They came as far as the town of Mareshah. 10So Asa went out to fight Zerah and prepared for battle in the Valley of Zephathah at Mareshah.

WHAT'S IT MEAN?

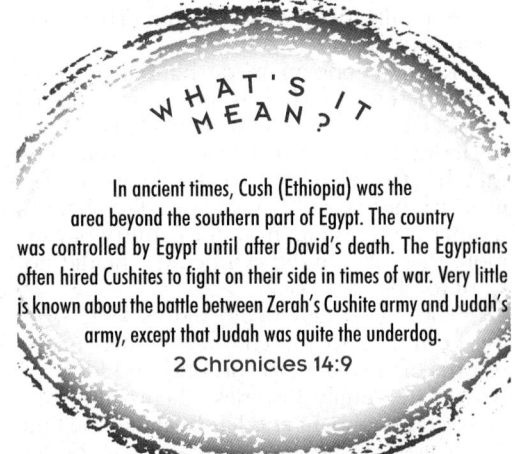

In ancient times, Cush (Ethiopia) was the area beyond the southern part of Egypt. The country was controlled by Egypt until after David's death. The Egyptians often hired Cushites to fight on their side in times of war. Very little is known about the battle between Zerah's Cushite army and Judah's army, except that Judah was quite the underdog.

2 Chronicles 14:9

11Asa called out to the LORD his God, saying, "LORD, only you can help weak people against the strong. Help us, LORD our God, because we depend on you. We fight against this enormous army in your name. LORD, you are our God. Don't let anyone win against you."

TRIALS

Where can we find rest? (14:11)

12So the LORD defeated the Cushites when Asa's army from Judah attacked them, and the Cushites ran away. 13Asa's army chased them as far as the town of Gerar. So many Cushites were killed that the army could not fight again; they were crushed by the LORD and his army. Asa and his army carried many valuable things away from the enemy. 14They destroyed all the towns near Gerar, because the people living in these towns were afraid of the LORD. Since these towns had many valuable things, Asa's army took them away. 15Asa's army also attacked the camps where the shepherds lived and took many sheep and camels. Then they returned to Jerusalem.

ASA'S CHANGES

15 1The Spirit of God entered Azariah son of Oded. 2Azariah went to meet Asa and said, "Listen to me, Asa and all you people of Judah and Benjamin. The LORD is with you when you are with him. If you obey him, you will find him, but if you leave him, he will leave you. 3For a long time Israel was without the true God and without a priest to teach them and without the teachings. 4But when they were in trouble, they turned to the LORD, the God of Israel. They looked for him and found him. 5In those days no one could travel safely. There was much trouble in all the nations. 6One nation would destroy another nation, and one city would destroy another city, because God troubled them with all kinds of distress. 7But you should be strong. Don't give up, because you will get a reward for your good work."

8Asa felt brave when he heard these words and the message from Azariah son of Oded the prophet. So he removed the hateful idols from all of Judah and Benjamin and from the towns he had captured in the hills of Ephraim. He repaired the LORD's altar that was in front of the porch of the Temple of the LORD.

9Then Asa gathered all the people from Judah and Benjamin and from the tribes of Ephraim, Manasseh, and Simeon who were living in Judah. Many people came to Asa even from Israel, because they saw that the LORD, Asa's God, was with him.

10Asa and these people gathered in Jerusalem in the third month of the fifteenth year of Asa's rule. 11At that time they sacrificed to the LORD seven hundred bulls and seven thousand sheep and goats from the valuable things Asa's army had taken from their enemies. 12Then they made an agreement to obey the LORD, the God of their ancestors, with their whole being. 13Anyone who refused to obey the LORD, the God of Israel, was to be killed. It did not matter if that person was important or unimportant, a man or woman. 14Then Asa and the people made a promise before the LORD, shouting with a loud voice and blowing trumpets and sheep's horns. 15All the people of Judah were happy about the promise, because they had promised with all their heart. They looked for God and found him. So the LORD gave them peace in all the country.

FOLLOWING GOD

How should we follow God? (15:15)

16King Asa also removed Maacah, his grandmother, from being queen mother, because she had made a terrible Asherah idol. Asa cut down that idol, smashed it into pieces, and burned it in the Kidron Valley. 17But the places of worship to gods were not removed from Judah. Even so, Asa was faithful all his life.

WHAT'S IT MEAN?

The Israelites had adopted several different Canaanite gods and goddesses as their own. Asherah, though, was one of their favorites. Shrines to Asherah were scattered throughout the land, especially on hilltops and in groves of trees. The shrines were easy to spot because they were marked by carved wooden poles.

2 Chronicles 15:16–17

18Asa brought into the Temple of God the gifts he and his father had given: silver, gold, and utensils.

19There was no more war until the thirty-fifth year of Asa's rule.

ASA'S LAST YEARS

16 1In the thirty-sixth year of Asa's rule, Baasha king of Israel attacked Judah. He made the town of Ramah strong so he could keep people from leaving or entering Judah, Asa's country.

2Asa took silver and gold from the treasuries of the Temple of the LORD and out of his own palace. Then he sent it with messengers to Ben-Hadad king of Aram, who lived in Damascus. Asa said, 3"Let there be a treaty between you and me as there was between my father and your father. I am sending you silver and gold. Break your treaty with Baasha king of Israel so he will leave my land."

4Ben-Hadad agreed with King Asa and sent the commanders of his armies to attack the towns of Israel. They defeated the towns of Ijon, Dan, and Abel Beth Maacah, and all the

towns in Naphtali where treasures were stored.
5When Baasha heard about this, he stopped
building up Ramah and left his work. 6Then
King Asa brought all the people of Judah to
Ramah, and they carried away the rocks and
wood that Baasha had used. And they used
them to build up Geba and Mizpah.
7At that time Hanani the seer came to Asa
king of Judah and said to him, "You depended
on the king of Aram to help you and not on the
LORD your God. So the king of Aram's army
escaped from you. 8The Cushites and Libyans
had a large and powerful army and many
chariots and horsemen. But you depended on
the LORD to help you, so he handed them over
to you. 9The LORD searches all the earth for
people who have given themselves completely
to him. He wants to make them strong. Asa,
you did a foolish thing, so from now on you
will have wars."
10Asa was angry with Hanani the seer because of what he had said; he was so angry
that he put Hanani in prison. And Asa was
cruel to some of the people at the same time.
11Everything Asa did as king, from the beginning to the end, is written in the book of the
kings of Judah and Israel. 12In the thirty-ninth
year of his rule, Asa got a disease in his feet.
Though his disease was very bad, he did not
ask for help from the LORD, but only from the
doctors. 13Then Asa died in the forty-first year
of his rule. 14The people buried Asa in the tomb
he had made for himself in Jerusalem. They laid
him on a bed filled with spices and different
kinds of mixed perfumes, and they made a large
fire to honor him.

JEHOSHAPHAT KING OF JUDAH

17
1Jehoshaphat, Asa's son, became king of Judah in his place. Jehoshaphat made Judah
strong so they could fight against Israel. 2He
put troops in all the strong, walled cities of Judah, in the land of Judah, and in the towns of
Ephraim that his father Asa had captured.
3The LORD was with Jehoshaphat, because
he lived as his ancestor David had lived when
he first became king. Jehoshaphat did not ask
for help from the Baal idols, 4but from the God
of his father. He obeyed God's commands and
did not live as the people of Israel lived. 5The
LORD made Jehoshaphat a strong king over Judah. All the people of Judah brought gifts to
Jehoshaphat, so he had much wealth and
honor. 6He wanted very much to obey the
LORD. He also removed the places for worshiping gods and the Asherah idols from Judah.
7During the third year of his rule, Jehoshaphat sent his officers to teach in the towns of
Judah. These officers were Ben-Hail, Obadiah,
Zechariah, Nethanel, and Micaiah. 8Jehosha-
phat sent with them these Levites: Shemaiah,
Nethaniah, Zebadiah, Asahel, Shemiramoth,
Jehonathan, Adonijah, Tobijah, and Tob-
Adonijah. He also sent the priests Elishama
and Jehoram. 9These leaders, Levites, and
priests taught the people in Judah. They took
the Book of the Teachings of the LORD and
went through all the towns of Judah and
taught the people.
10The nations near Judah were afraid of the
LORD, so they did not start a war against Jehoshaphat. 11Some of the Philistines brought
gifts and silver to Jehoshaphat as he demanded.

Promise

HE PROMISES TO KEEP AN EYE ON YOU CONSTANTLY.

The LORD searches all the earth for people who have given themselves completely to him. He wants to make them strong (2 Chr. 16:9a).

God watches you constantly. He's not peering down from heaven so he can whack you on the head when you blow it, but to give an extra measure of strength to people who are being faithful. He gives strength and support to those who are obedient—to those whose hearts belong to him. If you've ever tried to be obedient, you know that most of the time it takes more courage to do the right thing than to follow the crowd. He promises to see you and your efforts. He will make your weak knees strong. He will give your voice power and authority. He will sense your fear and cast it out. Your job is to be faithful. God promises to never miss a thing.

SEE FOR YOURSELF:
Ps. 34:15; 139:1–6; 1 Pet. 3:12

Some Arabs brought him flocks: seventy-seven hundred sheep and seventy-seven hundred goats.

WHAT'S IT MEAN?

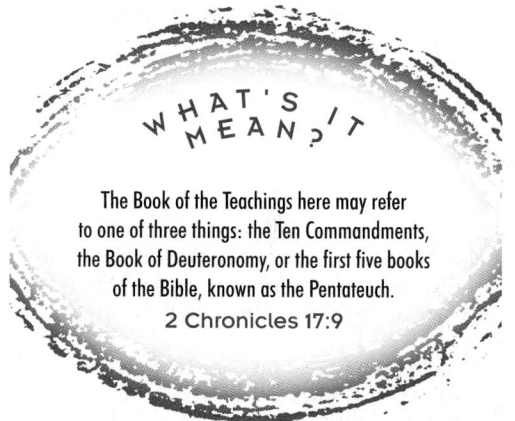

The Book of the Teachings here may refer to one of three things: the Ten Commandments, the Book of Deuteronomy, or the first five books of the Bible, known as the Pentateuch.

2 Chronicles 17:9

[12]Jehoshaphat grew more and more powerful. He built strong, walled cities and towns for storing supplies in Judah. [13]He kept many supplies in the towns of Judah, and he kept trained soldiers in Jerusalem. [14]These soldiers were listed by families. From the families of Judah, these were the commanders of groups of a thousand men: Adnah was the commander of three hundred thousand soldiers; [15]Jehohanan was the commander of two hundred eighty thousand soldiers; [16]Amasiah was the commander of two hundred thousand soldiers. Amasiah son of Zicri had volunteered to serve the LORD.

[17]These were the commanders from the families of Benjamin: Eliada, a brave soldier, had two hundred thousand soldiers who used bows and shields. [18]And Jehozabad had one hundred eighty thousand men armed for war.

[19]All these soldiers served King Jehoshaphat. The king also put other men in the strong, walled cities through all of Judah.

MICAIAH WARNS KING AHAB

18 [1]Jehoshaphat had much wealth and honor, and he made an agreement with King Ahab through marriage.[n] [2]A few years later Jehoshaphat went to visit Ahab in Samaria. Ahab sacrificed many sheep and cattle as a great feast to honor Jehoshaphat and the people with him. He encouraged Jehoshaphat to attack Ramoth in Gilead. [3]Ahab king of Israel asked Jehoshaphat king of Judah, "Will you go with me to attack Ramoth in Gilead?"

Jehoshaphat answered, "I will go with you, and my soldiers are yours. We will join you in the battle." [4]Jehoshaphat also said to Ahab, "But first we should ask if this is the LORD's will."

[5]So King Ahab called four hundred prophets together and asked them, "Should we go to war against Ramoth in Gilead or not?"

They answered, "Go, because God will hand them over to you."

[6]But Jehoshaphat asked, "Isn't there a prophet of the LORD here? Let's ask him what we should do."

[7]Then King Ahab said to Jehoshaphat, "There is one other prophet. We could ask the LORD through him, but I hate him. He never prophesies anything good about me, but always something bad. He is Micaiah son of Imlah."

Jehoshaphat said, "King Ahab, you shouldn't say that!"

[8]So Ahab king of Israel told one of his officers to bring Micaiah to him at once.

[9]Ahab king of Israel and Jehoshaphat king of Judah had on their royal robes and were sitting on their thrones at the threshing floor, near the entrance to the gate of Samaria. All the prophets were standing before them speaking their messages. [10]Zedekiah son of Kenaanah had made some iron horns. He said to Ahab, "This is what the LORD says: 'You will use these horns to fight the Arameans until they are destroyed.' "

WHAT'S IT MEAN?

Ramoth in Gilead was located near the border of Israel and Syria, about fifty to sixty miles from Samaria. Being that close to the border meant that Ramoth had seen its share of battles between the two nations. When the Israelites first arrived in Canaan, the city of Ramoth was given to the tribe of Gad and was declared a city of safety.

2 Chronicles 18:2

[11]All the other prophets said the same thing, "Attack Ramoth in Gilead and win, because the LORD will hand the Arameans over to you."

[12]The messenger who had gone to get Micaiah said to him, "All the other prophets are

18:1 agreement . . . through marriage Jehoshaphat's son Jehoram married Athaliah, Ahab's daughter. See 2 Chronicles 21:6.

saying King Ahab will win. You should agree with them and give the king a good answer."

[13]But Micaiah answered, "As surely as the LORD lives, I can tell him only what my God says."

[14]When Micaiah came to Ahab, the king asked him, "Micaiah, should we attack Ramoth in Gilead or not?"

Micaiah answered, "Attack and win! They will be handed over to you."

[15]But Ahab said to Micaiah, "How many times do I have to tell you to speak only the truth to me in the name of the LORD?"

[16]So Micaiah answered, "I saw the army of Israel scattered over the hills like sheep without a shepherd. The LORD said, 'They have no leaders. They should go home and not fight.' "

[17]Then Ahab king of Israel said to Jehoshaphat, "I told you! He never prophesies anything good about me, but only bad."

[18]But Micaiah said, "Hear the message from the LORD: I saw the LORD sitting on his throne with his heavenly army standing on his right and on his left. [19]The LORD said, 'Who will trick King Ahab of Israel into attacking Ramoth in Gilead where he will be killed?'

"Some said one thing; some said another. [20]Then one spirit came and stood before the LORD and said, 'I will trick him.'

"The LORD asked, 'How will you do it?'

[21]"The spirit answered, 'I will go to Ahab's prophets and make them tell lies.'

"So the LORD said, 'You will succeed in tricking him. Go and do it.' "

[22]Micaiah said, "Ahab, the LORD has made your prophets lie to you, and the LORD has decided that disaster should come to you."

[23]Then Zedekiah son of Kenaanah went up to Micaiah and slapped him in the face. Zedekiah said, "Has the LORD's Spirit left me to speak through you?"

[24]Micaiah answered, "You will find out on the day you go to hide in an inside room."

[25]Then Ahab king of Israel ordered, "Take Micaiah and send him to Amon, the governor of the city, and to Joash, the king's son. [26]Tell them I said to put this man in prison and give him only bread and water until I return safely from the battle."

[27]Micaiah said, "Ahab, if you come back safely from the battle, the LORD has not spoken through me. Remember my words, all you people!"

AHAB IS KILLED

[28]So Ahab king of Israel and Jehoshaphat king of Judah went to Ramoth in Gilead. [29]King Ahab said to Jehoshaphat, "I will go into battle, but I will wear other clothes so no one will recognize me. But you wear your royal clothes." So Ahab wore other clothes, and they went into battle.

[30]The king of Aram ordered his chariot commanders, "Don't fight with anyone—important or unimportant—except the king of Israel." [31]When these commanders saw Jehoshaphat, they thought he was the king of Israel, so they turned to attack him. But Jehoshaphat began shouting, and the LORD helped him. God made the chariot commanders turn away from Jehoshaphat. [32]When they saw he was not King Ahab, they stopped chasing him.

[33]By chance, a soldier shot an arrow which hit Ahab king of Israel between the pieces of his armor. King Ahab said to his chariot driver, "Turn around and get me out of the battle, because I am hurt!" [34]The battle continued all day. King Ahab held himself up in his chariot and faced the Arameans until evening. Then he died at sunset.

19

[1]Jehoshaphat king of Judah came back safely to his palace in Jerusalem. [2]Jehu son of Hanani, a seer, went out to meet him and said to the king, "Why did you help evil people? Why do you love those who hate the LORD? That is the reason the LORD is angry with you. [3]But there is some good in you. You took the Asherah idols out of this country, and you have tried to obey God."

WHAT'S IT MEAN?

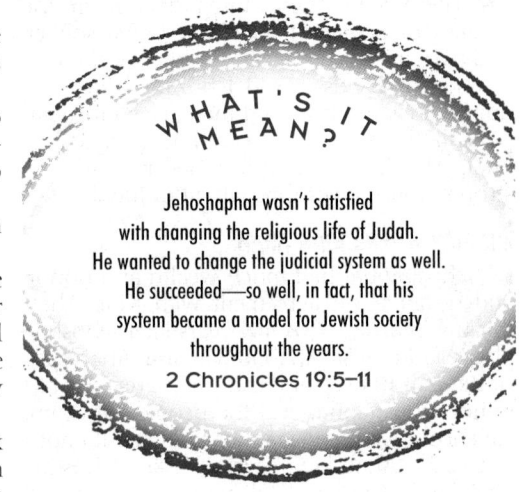

Jehoshaphat wasn't satisfied with changing the religious life of Judah. He wanted to change the judicial system as well. He succeeded—so well, in fact, that his system became a model for Jewish society throughout the years.

2 Chronicles 19:5–11

JEHOSHAPHAT CHOOSES JUDGES

[4]Jehoshaphat lived in Jerusalem. He went out again to be with the people, from Beersheba to the mountains of Ephraim, and he

turned them back to the LORD, the God of their ancestors. 5Jehoshaphat appointed judges in all the land, in each of the strong, walled cities of Judah. 6Jehoshaphat said to them, "Watch what you do, because you are not judging for people but for the LORD. He will be with you when you make a decision. 7Now let each of you fear the LORD. Watch what you do, because the LORD our God wants people to be fair. He wants all people to be treated the same, and he doesn't want decisions influenced by money."

LEADERSHIP
How should leaders make decisions? (19:5–7)

8And in Jerusalem Jehoshaphat appointed some of the Levites, priests, and leaders of Israelite families to be judges. They were to decide cases about the law of the LORD and settle problems between the people who lived in Jerusalem. 9Jehoshaphat commanded them, "You must always serve the LORD completely, and you must fear him. 10Your people living in the cities will bring you cases about killing, about the teachings, commands, rules, or some other law. In all these cases you must warn the people not to sin against the LORD. If you don't, he will be angry with you and your people. But if you warn them, you won't be guilty.

"Have courage. May the LORD be with those who do what is right." (2 Chronicles 19:11b)

11"Amariah, the leading priest, will be over you in all cases about the LORD. Zebadiah son of Ishmael, a leader in the tribe of Judah, will be over you in all cases about the king. Also, the Levites will serve as officers for you. Have courage. May the LORD be with those who do what is right."

JEHOSHAPHAT FACES WAR

20 1Later the Moabites, Ammonites, and some Meunites came to start a war with Jehoshaphat. 2Messengers came and told Jehoshaphat, "A large army is coming against you from Edom, from the other side of the Dead Sea. They are already in Hazazon Tamar!" (Hazazon Tamar is also called En Gedi.) 3Jehoshaphat was afraid, so he decided to ask the LORD what to do. He announced that no one in Judah should eat during this special time of prayer to God. 4The people of Judah came together to ask the LORD for help; they came from every town in Judah.

5The people of Judah and Jerusalem met in front of the new courtyard in the Temple of the LORD. Then Jehoshaphat stood up, 6and he said, "LORD, God of our ancestors, you are the God in heaven. You rule over all the kingdoms of the nations. You have power and strength, so no one can stand against you. 7Our God, you forced out the people who lived in this land as your people Israel moved in. And you gave this land forever to the descendants of your friend Abraham. 8They lived in this land and built a Temple for you. They said, 9'If trouble comes upon us, or war, punishment, sickness, or hunger, we will stand before you and before this Temple where you have chosen to be worshiped. We will cry out to you when we are in trouble. Then you will hear and save us.'

10"But now here are men from Ammon, Moab, and Edom. You wouldn't let the Israelites enter their lands when the Israelites came from Egypt. So the Israelites turned away and did not destroy them. 11But see how they repay us for not destroying them! They have come to force us out of your land, which you gave us as our own. 12Our God, punish those people. We have no power against this large army that is attacking us. We don't know what to do, so we look to you for help."

13All the men of Judah stood before the LORD with their babies, wives, and children. 14Then the Spirit of the LORD entered Jahaziel. (Jahaziel was Zechariah's son. Zechariah was Benaiah's son. Benaiah was Jeiel's son, and Jeiel was Mattaniah's son.) Jahaziel, a Levite and a descendant of Asaph, stood up in the meeting. 15He said, "Listen to me, King Jehoshaphat and all you people living in Judah and Jerusalem. The LORD says this to you: 'Don't be afraid or discouraged because

WHAT'S IT MEAN?

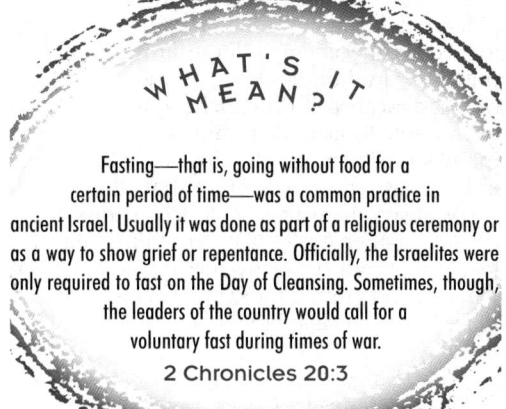

Fasting—that is, going without food for a certain period of time—was a common practice in ancient Israel. Usually it was done as part of a religious ceremony or as a way to show grief or repentance. Officially, the Israelites were only required to fast on the Day of Cleansing. Sometimes, though, the leaders of the country would call for a voluntary fast during times of war.

2 Chronicles 20:3

of this large army. The battle is not your battle,
it is God's. 16Tomorrow go down
there and fight those people.
They will come up through
the Pass of Ziz. You will find
them at the end of the ravine
that leads to the Desert of Je-
ruel. 17You won't need to fight
in this battle. Just stand strong
in your places, and you will see the LORD save
you. Judah and Jerusalem, don't be afraid or
discouraged, because the LORD is with you. So
go out against those people tomorrow.' "

FEAR

Why should we not be afraid? (20:15)

18Jehoshaphat bowed facedown on the
ground. All the people of Judah and Jerusalem
bowed down before the LORD and worshiped
him. 19Then some Levites from the Kohathite
and Korahite people stood up and praised the
LORD, the God of Israel, with very loud voices.
20Jehoshaphat's army went out into the
Desert of Tekoa early in the morning. As they
were starting out, Jehoshaphat stood and said,
"Listen to me, people of Judah and Jerusalem.
Have faith in the LORD your God, and you will
stand strong. Have faith in his prophets, and
you will succeed." 21Jehoshaphat listened to the
people's advice. Then he chose men to be singers to the LORD, to praise him because he is
holy and wonderful. As they marched in front
of the army, they said,

"Thank the LORD,
because his love continues forever."

22As they began to sing and praise God, the
LORD set ambushes for the people of Ammon,
Moab, and Edom who had come to attack Judah. And they were defeated. 23The Ammonites
and Moabites attacked the Edomites, destroying them completely. After they had killed the
Edomites, they killed each other.
24When the men from Judah came to a
place where they could see the desert, they
looked at the enemy's large army. But they
only saw dead bodies lying on the ground; no
one had escaped. 25When Jehoshaphat and his
army came to take their valuables, they found
many supplies, much clothing, and other valuable things. There was more than they could
carry away; there was so much it took three
days to gather it all. 26On the fourth day Jehoshaphat and his army met in the Valley of
Beracah and praised the LORD. That is why that
place has been called the Valley of Beracah[n] to
this day.
27Then Jehoshaphat led all the men from
Judah and Jerusalem back to Jerusalem. The
LORD had made them happy because their enemies were defeated. 28They entered Jerusalem
with harps, lyres, and trumpets and went to
the Temple of the LORD.
29When all the kingdoms of the lands
around them heard how the LORD had fought
Israel's enemies, they feared God. 30So
Jehoshaphat's kingdom was not at war. His
God gave him peace from all the countries
around him.

JEHOSHAPHAT'S RULE ENDS

31Jehoshaphat ruled over the country of Judah. He was thirty-five years old when he became king, and he ruled in Jerusalem for
twenty-five years. His mother's name was
Azubah daughter of Shilhi. 32Jehoshaphat was
good like his father Asa, and he did what the
LORD said was right. 33But the places where
gods were worshiped were not removed, and
the people did not really want to follow the
God of their ancestors.
34The other things Jehoshaphat did as king,
from the beginning to the end, are written in
the records of Jehu son of Hanani, which are in
the book of the kings of Israel.
35Later, Jehoshaphat king of Judah made a
treaty with Ahaziah king of Israel, which was a
wrong thing to do. 36Jehoshaphat agreed with
Ahaziah to build trading ships, which they
built in the town of Ezion Geber. 37Then Eliezer
son of Dodavahu from the town of Mareshah
spoke against Jehoshaphat. He said, "Jehoshaphat, because you joined with Ahaziah, the
LORD will destroy what you have made." The
ships were wrecked so they could not sail out
to trade.

21

1Jehoshaphat died and was buried with his
ancestors in Jerusalem, the city of David. Then
his son Jehoram became king in his place.
2Jehoram's brothers were Azariah, Jehiel, Zechariah, Azariahu, Michael, and Shephatiah. They
were the sons of Jehoshaphat king of Judah.
3Jehoshaphat gave his sons many gifts of silver,
gold, and valuable things, and he gave them
strong, walled cities in Judah. But Jehoshaphat
gave the kingdom to Jehoram, because he was
the first son.

JEHORAM KING OF JUDAH

4When Jehoram took control of his father's
kingdom, he killed all his brothers with a
sword and also killed some of the leaders of
Judah. 5He was thirty-two years old when he
began to rule, and he ruled eight years in Jeru-

20:26 Beracah This name means "blessing" or "praise."

salem. 6He followed in the ways of the kings of
Israel, just as the family of Ahab had done, because he married Ahab's daughter. Jehoram
did what the LORD said was wrong. 7But the
LORD would not destroy David's family because of the agreement he had made with
David. He had promised that one of David's
descendants would always rule.
8In Jehoram's time, Edom broke away from
Judah's rule and chose their own king. 9So Jehoram went to Edom with all his commanders
and chariots. The Edomites surrounded him
and his chariot commanders, but Jehoram got
up and attacked the Edomites at night. 10From
then until now the country of Edom has
fought against the rule of Judah. At the same
time the people of Libnah also broke away
from Jehoram because Jehoram left the LORD,
the God of his ancestors.

WHAT'S IT MEAN?

During David's reign, Israel had conquered the land of Edom and stationed military troops there. Later, Solomon built a port city on the Red Sea in Edom, which he still considered to be part of his kingdom. When Jehoshaphat was king, the Edomites started a rebellion, but couldn't finish it. They tried once more when Jehoram was king and finally succeeded in regaining control of their land.

2 Chronicles 21:10

11Jehoram also built places to worship gods
on the hills in Judah. He led the people of Jerusalem to sin, and he led the people of Judah
away from the LORD. 12Then Jehoram received
this letter from Elijah the prophet:

This is what the LORD, the God of
your ancestor David, says, "Jehoram, you
have not lived as your father Jehoshaphat lived and as Asa king of Judah
lived. 13But you have lived as the kings of
Israel lived, leading the people of Judah
and Jerusalem to sin against God, as
Ahab and his family did. You have killed
your brothers, and they were better than
you. 14So now the LORD is about to punish your people, your children, wives,
and everything you own. 15You will have
a terrible disease in your intestines that
will become worse every day. Finally it
will cause your intestines to come out."

16The LORD caused the Philistines and the
Arabs who lived near the Cushites to be angry
with Jehoram. 17So the Philistines and Arabs
attacked Judah and carried away all the wealth
of Jehoram's palace, as well as his sons and
wives. Only Jehoram's youngest son, Ahaziah,
was left.
18After these things happened, the LORD
gave Jehoram a disease in his intestines that
could not be cured. 19After he was sick for two
years, Jehoram's intestines came out because of
the disease, and he died in terrible pain. The
people did not make a fire to honor Jehoram as
they had done for his ancestors.
20Jehoram was thirty-two years old when
he became king, and he ruled eight years in
Jerusalem. No one was sad when he died. He
was buried in Jerusalem, but not in the graves
for the kings.

AHAZIAH KING OF JUDAH

22
1The people of Jerusalem chose Ahaziah,
Jehoram's youngest son, to be king in his place.
The robbers who had come with the Arabs to
attack Jehoram's camp had killed all of Jehoram's older sons. So Ahaziah began to rule
Judah. 2Ahaziah was twenty-two years old
when he became king, and he ruled one year in
Jerusalem. His mother's name was Athaliah, a
granddaughter of Omri. 3Ahaziah followed the
ways of Ahab's family, because his mother
encouraged him to do wrong. 4Ahaziah did
what the LORD said was wrong, as Ahab's family had done. They gave advice to Ahaziah after his father died, and their bad advice led to
his death. 5Following their advice, Ahaziah
went with Joram son of Ahab to Ramoth in
Gilead, where they fought against Hazael king
of Aram. The Arameans wounded Joram. 6So
Joram returned to Jezreel to heal from the
wounds he received at Ramoth when he
fought Hazael king of Aram.
Ahaziah son of Jehoram and king of Judah
went down to visit Joram son of Ahab at Jezreel because he had been wounded.
7God caused Ahaziah's death when he went
to visit Joram. Ahaziah arrived and went out
with Joram to meet Jehu son of Nimshi, whom
the LORD had appointed to destroy Ahab's
family. 8While Jehu was punishing Ahab's
family, he found the leaders of Judah and the
sons of Ahaziah's relatives who served Ahaziah, and Jehu killed them all. 9Then Jehu looked
for Ahaziah. Jehu's men caught him hiding in

Samaria, so they brought him to Jehu. Then they killed and buried him. They said, "Ahaziah is a descendant of Jehoshaphat, and Jehoshaphat obeyed the LORD with all his heart." No one in Ahaziah's family had the power to take control of the kingdom of Judah.

WHAT'S IT MEAN?

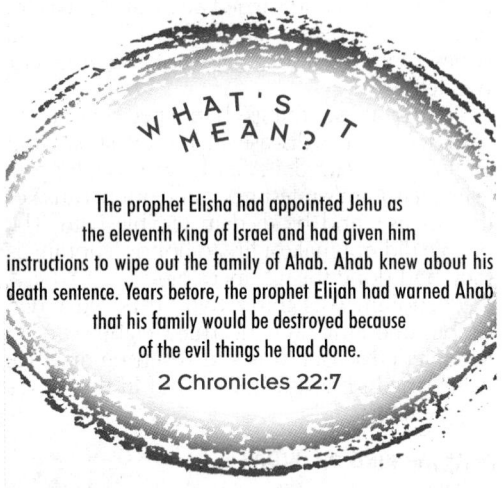

The prophet Elisha had appointed Jehu as the eleventh king of Israel and had given him instructions to wipe out the family of Ahab. Ahab knew about his death sentence. Years before, the prophet Elijah had warned Ahab that his family would be destroyed because of the evil things he had done.

2 Chronicles 22:7

ATHALIAH AND JOASH

10When Ahaziah's mother, Athaliah, saw that her son was dead, she killed all the royal family in Judah. 11But Jehosheba, King Jehoram's daughter, took Joash, Ahaziah's son. She stole him from among the other sons of the king who were going to be murdered and put him and his nurse in a bedroom. So Jehosheba, who was King Jehoram's daughter and Ahaziah's sister and the wife of Jehoiada the priest, hid Joash so Athaliah could not kill him. 12He hid with them in the Temple of God for six years. During that time Athaliah ruled the land.

23 1In the seventh year Jehoiada decided to do something. He made an agreement with the commanders of the groups of a hundred men: Azariah son of Jeroham, Ishmael son of Jehohanan, Azariah son of Obed, Maaseiah son of Adaiah, and Elishaphat son of Zicri. 2They went around in Judah and gathered the Levites from all the towns, and they gathered the leaders of the families of Judah. Then they went to Jerusalem. 3All the people together made an agreement with the king in the Temple of God.

Jehoiada said to them, "The king's son will rule, as the LORD promised about David's descendants. 4Now this is what you must do: You priests and Levites go on duty on the Sabbath. A third of you will guard the doors. 5A third of you will be at the king's palace, and a third of you will be at the Foundation Gate. All the other people will stay in the courtyards of the Temple of the LORD. 6Don't let anyone come into the Temple of the LORD except the priests and Levites who serve. They may come because they have been made ready to serve the LORD, but all the others must do the job the LORD has given them. 7The Levites must stay near the king, each man with his weapon in his hand. If anyone tries to enter the Temple, kill him. Stay close to the king when he goes in and when he goes out."

JOASH BECOMES KING

8The Levites and all the people of Judah obeyed everything Jehoiada the priest had commanded. He did not excuse anyone from the groups of the priests. So each commander took his men who came on duty on the Sabbath with those who went off duty on the Sabbath. 9Jehoiada gave the commanders of a hundred men the spears and the large and small shields that had belonged to King David and that were kept in the Temple of God. 10Then Jehoiada told the men where to stand, each man with his weapon in his hand. There were guards from the south side of the Temple to the north side. They stood by the altar and the Temple and around the king.

WHAT'S IT MEAN?

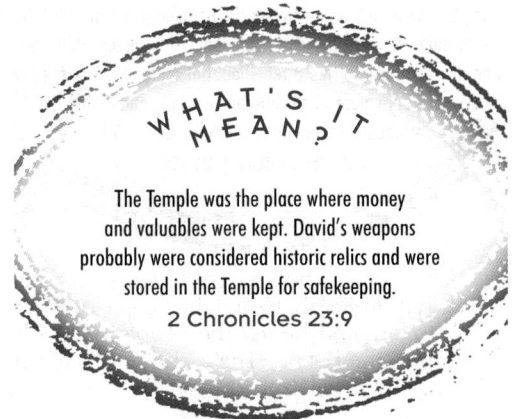

The Temple was the place where money and valuables were kept. David's weapons probably were considered historic relics and were stored in the Temple for safekeeping.

2 Chronicles 23:9

11Jehoiada and his sons brought out the king's son and put the crown on him and gave him a copy of the agreement. Then they appointed him king and poured olive oil on him and shouted, "Long live the king!"

12When Athaliah heard the noise of the people running and praising the king, she went to them at the Temple of the LORD. 13She looked, and there was the king standing by his pillar at the entrance. The officers and the trumpeters were standing beside him, and all the people of the land were happy and blowing trumpets. The singers were playing musical instruments and leading praises. Then Athaliah tore her clothes and screamed, "Traitors! Traitors!"

14Jehoiada the priest sent out the commanders of a hundred men, who led the army. He said, "Surround her with soldiers and take her out of the Temple area. Kill with a sword anyone who follows her." He had said, "Don't put Athaliah to death in the Temple of the LORD." 15So they caught her when she came to the entrance of the Horse Gate near the palace. There they put her to death.

16Then Jehoiada made an agreement with the people and the king that they would be the LORD's special people. 17All the people went to the temple of Baal and tore it down, smashing the altars and idols. They killed Mattan, the priest of Baal, in front of the altars.

18Then Jehoiada chose the priests, who were Levites, to be responsible for the Temple of the LORD. David had given them duties in the Temple of the LORD. They were to offer the burnt offerings to the LORD as the Teachings of Moses commanded, and they were to offer them with much joy and singing as David had commanded. 19Jehoiada put guards at the gates of the Temple of the LORD so that anyone who was unclean in any way could not enter.

20Jehoiada took with him the commanders of a hundred men, the important men, the rulers of the people, and all the people of the land to take the king out of the Temple of the LORD. They went through the Upper Gate into the palace, and then they seated the king on the throne. 21So all the people of the land were very happy, and Jerusalem had peace, because Athaliah had been put to death with the sword.

JOASH REPAIRS THE TEMPLE

24 1Joash was seven years old when he became king, and he ruled forty years in Jerusalem. His mother's name was Zibiah, and she was from Beersheba. 2Joash did what the LORD said was right as long as Jehoiada the priest was alive. 3Jehoiada chose two wives for Joash, and Joash had sons and daughters.

4Later, Joash decided to repair the Temple of the LORD. 5He called the priests and the Levites together and said to them, "Go to the towns of Judah and gather the money all the Israelites have to pay every year. Use it to repair the Temple of your God. Do this now." But the Levites did not hurry.

6So King Joash called for Jehoiada the leading priest and said to him, "Why haven't you made the Levites bring in from Judah and Jerusalem the tax money that Moses, the LORD's servant, and the people of Israel used for the Holy Tent?"

7In the past the sons of wicked Athaliah had broken into the Temple of God and used its holy things for worshiping the Baal idols.

8King Joash commanded that a box for contributions be made. They put it outside, at the gate of the Temple of the LORD. 9Then the Levites made an announcement in Judah and Jerusalem, telling people to bring to the LORD the tax money Moses, the servant of God, had made the Israelites give while they were in the desert. 10All the officers and people were happy to bring their money, and they put it in the box until the box was full. 11When the Levites would take the box to the king's officers, they would see that it was full of money. Then the king's royal secretary and the leading priest's officer would come and take out the money and return the box to its place. They did this often and gathered much money. 12King Joash and Jehoiada gave the money to the people who worked on the Temple of the LORD. And they hired stoneworkers and carpenters to repair the Temple of the LORD. They also hired people to work with iron and bronze to repair the Temple.

13The people worked hard, and the work to repair the Temple went well. They rebuilt the Temple of God to be as it was before, but even stronger. 14When the workers finished, they brought the money that was left to King Joash and Jehoiada. They used that money to make utensils for the Temple of the LORD, utensils for the service in the Temple and for the burnt offerings, and bowls and other utensils from gold and silver. Burnt offerings were given every day in the Temple of the LORD while Jehoiada was alive.

15Jehoiada grew old and lived many years. Then he died when he was one hundred thirty years old. 16Jehoiada was buried in Jerusalem with the kings, because he had done much good in Judah for God and his Temple.

JOASH DOES EVIL

17After Jehoiada died, the officers of Judah came and bowed down to King Joash, and he listened to them. 18The king and these leaders stopped worshiping in the Temple of the LORD, the God of their ancestors. Instead, they began to worship the Asherah idols and other idols. Because they did wrong, God was angry with the people of Judah and Jerusalem. 19Even though the LORD sent prophets to the people to turn them back to him and even though the prophets warned them, they refused to listen.

[20]Then the Spirit of God entered Zechariah son of Jehoiada the priest. Zechariah stood before the people and said, "This is what God says: 'Why do you disobey the LORD's commands? You will not be successful. Because you have left the LORD, he has also left you.' "

[21]But the king and his officers made plans against Zechariah. At the king's command they threw stones at him in the courtyard of the Temple of the LORD until he died. [22]King Joash did not remember Jehoiada's kindness to him, so Joash killed Zechariah, Jehoiada's son. Before Zechariah died, he said, "May the LORD see what you are doing and punish you."

[23]At the end of the year, the Aramean army came against Joash. They attacked Judah and Jerusalem, killed all the leaders of the people, and sent all the valuable things to their king in Damascus. [24]The Aramean army came with only a small group of men, but the LORD handed over to them a very large army from Judah, because the people of Judah had left the LORD, the God of their ancestors. So Joash was punished. [25]When the Arameans left, Joash was badly wounded. His own officers made plans against him because he had killed Zechariah son of Jehoiada the priest. So they killed Joash in his own bed. He died and was buried in Jerusalem but not in the graves of the kings.

[26]The officers who made plans against Joash were Jozabad and Jehozabad. Jozabad was the son of Shimeath, a woman from Ammon. And Jehozabad was the son of Shimrith, a woman from Moab. [27]The story of Joash's sons, the great prophecies against him, and how he repaired the Temple of God are written in the book of the kings. Joash's son Amaziah became king in his place.

AMAZIAH KING OF JUDAH

25

[1]Amaziah was twenty-five years old when he became king, and he ruled for twenty-nine years in Jerusalem. His mother's name was Jehoaddin, and she was from Jerusalem. [2]Amaziah did what the LORD said was right, but he did not really want to obey him. [3]As soon as Amaziah took strong control of the kingdom, he executed the officers who had murdered his father the king. [4]But Amaziah did not put to death their children. He obeyed what was written in the Book of Moses, where the LORD commanded, "Parents must not be put to death when their children do wrong, and children must not be put to death when their parents do wrong. Each must die for his own sins."[n]

> "Amaziah did what the LORD said was right, but he did not really want to obey him." (2 Chronicles 25:2)

[5]Amaziah gathered the people of Judah together. He grouped all the people of Judah and Benjamin by families, and he put commanders over groups of a thousand and over groups of a hundred. He counted the men who were twenty years old and older. In all there were three hundred thousand soldiers ready to fight and skilled with spears and shields. [6]Amaziah also hired one hundred thousand soldiers from Israel for about seventy-five hundred pounds of silver. [7]But a man of God came to Amaziah and said, "My king, don't let the army of Israel go with you. The LORD is not with Israel or the people from the tribe of Ephraim. [8]You can make yourself strong for war, but God will defeat you. He has the power to help you or to defeat you."

[9]Amaziah said to the man of God, "But what about the seventy-five hundred pounds of silver I paid to the Israelite army?"

The man of God answered, "The LORD can give you much more than that."

[10]So Amaziah sent the Israelite army back home to Ephraim. They were very angry with the people of Judah and went home angry.

[11]Then Amaziah became very brave and led his army to the Valley of Salt in the country of Edom. There Amaziah's army killed ten thousand Edomites. [12]The army of Judah also captured ten thousand and took them to the top of a cliff and threw them off so that they split open.

[13]At the same time the Israelite troops that Amaziah had not let fight in the war were robbing towns in Judah. From Samaria to Beth Horon they killed three thousand people and took many valuable things.

[14]When Amaziah came home after defeating the Edomites, he brought back the idols they worshiped and started to worship them himself. He bowed down to them and offered sacrifices to them. [15]The LORD was very angry with Amaziah, so he sent a prophet to him who said, "Why have you asked their gods for help? They could not even save their own people from you!"

[16]As the prophet spoke, Amaziah said to

25:4 "Parents . . . sins." See Deuteronomy 24:16.

him, "We never gave you the job of advising the king. Stop, or you will be killed."

The prophet stopped speaking except to say, "I know that God has decided to destroy you because you have done this. You did not listen to my advice."

[17]Amaziah king of Judah talked with those who advised him. Then he sent a message to Jehoash son of Jehoahaz, who was the son of Jehu king of Israel. Amaziah said to Jehoash, "Come, let's meet face to face."

[18]Then Jehoash king of Israel answered Amaziah king of Judah, "A thornbush in Lebanon sent a message to a cedar tree in Lebanon. It said, 'Let your daughter marry my son.' But then a wild animal from Lebanon came by, walking on and crushing the thornbush. [19]You say to yourself that you have defeated Edom, but you have become proud, and you brag. But you stay at home! Don't ask for trouble, or you and Judah will be defeated."

WHAT'S IT MEAN?

In the ancient Middle East, it was common for people to tell stories or to make odd comparisons to get their point across. These stories were known as parables. Jesus later used parables to illustrate heavenly truths. Jehoash compared himself to a strong, valuable cedar and Amaziah to a useless little thornbush. Jehoash was warning that Amaziah's pride was going to get him into trouble.

2 Chronicles 25:18

[20]But Amaziah would not listen. God caused this to happen so that Jehoash would defeat Judah, because Judah asked for help from the gods of Edom. [21]So Jehoash king of Israel went to attack. He and Amaziah king of Judah faced each other in battle at Beth Shemesh in Judah. [22]Israel defeated Judah, and every man of Judah ran away to his home. [23]At Beth Shemesh Jehoash king of Israel captured Amaziah king of Judah. (Amaziah was the son of Joash, who was the son of Ahaziah.) Then Jehoash brought him to Jerusalem. Jehoash broke down the wall of Jerusalem, from the Gate of Ephraim to the Corner Gate, about six hundred feet. [24]He took all the gold and silver and all the utensils from the Temple of God that Obed-Edom had taken care of. He also took the treasures from the palace and some hostages. Then he returned to Samaria.

[25]Amaziah son of Joash, the king of Judah, lived fifteen years after the death of Jehoash son of Jehoahaz, the king of Israel. [26]The other things Amaziah did as king, from the beginning to the end, are written in the book of the kings of Judah and Israel. [27]When Amaziah stopped obeying the LORD, the people in Jerusalem made plans against him. So he ran away to the town of Lachish, but they sent men after him to Lachish and killed him. [28]They brought his body back on horses, and he was buried with his ancestors in Jerusalem, the city of David.

UZZIAH KING OF JUDAH

26

[1]Then all the people of Judah made Uzziah[n] king in place of his father Amaziah. Uzziah was sixteen years old. [2]He rebuilt the town of Elath and made it part of Judah again after Amaziah died.

[3]Uzziah was sixteen years old when he became king, and he ruled fifty-two years in Jerusalem. His mother's name was Jecoliah, and she was from Jerusalem. [4]He did what the LORD said was right, just as his father Amaziah had done. [5]Uzziah obeyed God while Zechariah was alive, because he taught Uzziah how to respect and obey God. And as long as Uzziah obeyed the LORD, God gave him success.

INTEGRITY

What's someone look like who has integrity? (26:3–4)

[6]Uzziah fought a war against the Philistines. He tore down the walls around their towns of Gath, Jabneh, and Ashdod and built new

WHAT'S IT MEAN?

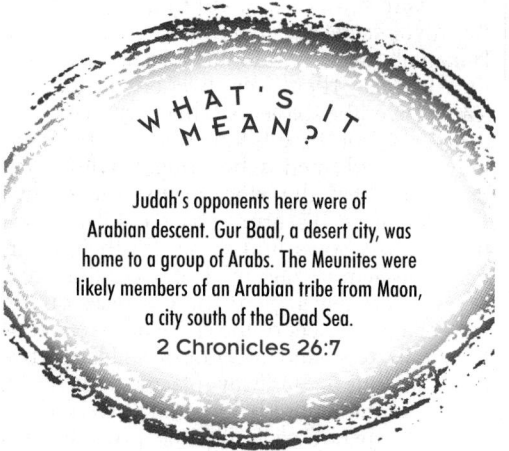

Judah's opponents here were of Arabian descent. Gur Baal, a desert city, was home to a group of Arabs. The Meunites were likely members of an Arabian tribe from Maon, a city south of the Dead Sea.

2 Chronicles 26:7

26:1 Uzziah Also called Azariah.

towns near Ashdod and in other places among
the Philistines. 7God helped Uzziah fight the
Philistines, the Arabs living in Gur Baal, and
the Meunites. 8Also, the Ammonites made the
payments Uzziah demanded. He was very
powerful, so his name became famous all the
way to the border of Egypt.
9Uzziah built towers in Jerusalem at the
Corner Gate, the Valley Gate, and where the
wall turned, and he made them strong. 10He
also built towers in the desert and dug many
wells, because he had many cattle on the western hills and in the plains. He had people who
worked his fields and vineyards in the hills and
in the fertile lands, because he loved the land.

WHAT'S IT MEAN?

It wasn't easy being a farmer in ancient Israel. If you weren't dealing with drought, you were probably trying to protect your crops from certain wandering tribes who made their living raiding farms. Some farmers built towers to provide defense against such raids. As for the drought, wells were the best solution to water shortage. Wells were large holes farmers dug—sometimes in solid rock—to hold rainwater. The water collected in the wells was used for the farmer's flocks of animals as well as his crops. A good rain could fill a very large well, if the collection system was properly designed.

2 Chronicles 26:10

11Uzziah had an army of trained soldiers.
They were counted and put in groups by Jeiel
the royal secretary and Maaseiah the officer.
Hananiah, one of the king's commanders, was
their leader. 12There were twenty-six hundred
leaders over the soldiers. 13They were in charge
of an army of three hundred seven thousand
five hundred men who fought with great
power to help the king against the enemy.
14Uzziah gave his army shields, spears, helmets, armor, bows, and stones for their slings.
15In Jerusalem Uzziah made devices that were
invented by clever men. These devices on the
towers and corners of the city walls were used
to shoot arrows and large rocks. So Uzziah became famous in faraway places, because he
had much help until he became powerful.
16But when Uzziah became powerful, his
pride led to his ruin. He was unfaithful to
the LORD his God; he went into the Temple of

WHAT'S IT MEAN?

The description of these war devices seems to suggest that they were like catapults. From about 800 B.C. to A.D. 1500, catapults were among the most feared weapons of war. They were capable of firing objects between 350 and 500 yards. (Imagine being hit with something that was fired almost five football fields away!) Of course, bows and arrows weren't exactly kids' toys. An arrow fired from a bow could travel up to 300 yards.

2 Chronicles 26:15

the LORD to burn incense on the altar for incense. 17Azariah and eighty other brave priests
who served the LORD followed Uzziah into the
Temple. 18They told him he was wrong and said
to him, "You don't have the right to burn incense to the LORD. Only the priests, Aaron's descendants, should burn the incense, because
they have been made holy. Leave this holy
place. You have been unfaithful, and the LORD
God will not honor you for this."
19Uzziah was standing beside the altar for
incense in the Temple of the LORD, and in his
hand was a pan for burning incense. He was
very angry with the priests. As he was standing
in front of the priests, a skin disease broke out
on his forehead. 20Azariah, the leading priest,
and all the other priests looked at him and saw
the skin disease on his forehead. So they hurried him out of the Temple. Uzziah also rushed

WHAT'S IT MEAN?

The Israelites treated certain skin conditions as serious diseases. People who suffered from those conditions were considered unacceptable for religious duties. Not only that, they were forced to live in isolation or with people who had similar afflictions until the disease cleared up.

2 Chronicles 26:21

out, because the LORD was punishing him. 21So
King Uzziah had the skin disease until the day
he died. He had to live in a separate house and
could not enter the Temple of the LORD. His
son Jotham was in charge of the palace, and he
governed the people of the land.
22The other things Uzziah did as king, from
beginning to end, were written down by the
prophet Isaiah son of Amoz. 23Uzziah died
and was buried near his ancestors in a grave-
yard that belonged to the kings. This was because people said, "He had a skin disease." And
his son Jotham became king in his place.

JOTHAM KING OF JUDAH

27
1Jotham was twenty-five years old when he
became king, and he ruled sixteen years in
Jerusalem. His mother's name was Jerusha
daughter of Zadok. 2Jotham did what the LORD
said was right, just as his father Uzziah had
done. But Jotham did not enter the Temple of
the LORD to burn incense as his father had. But
the people continued doing wrong. 3Jotham
rebuilt the Upper Gate of the Temple of the
LORD, and he added greatly to the wall at
Ophel. 4He also built towns in the hill country
of Judah, as well as walled cities and towers in
the forests.
5Jotham also fought the king of the Ammonites and defeated them. So each year for three
years they gave Jotham about seventy-five
hundred pounds of silver, about sixty-two
thousand bushels of wheat, and about sixty-
two thousand bushels of barley. 6Jotham became powerful, because he always obeyed the
LORD his God.
7The other things Jotham did while he was
king and all his wars are written in the book of
the kings of Israel and Judah. 8Jotham was
twenty-five years old when he became king,
and he ruled sixteen years in Jerusalem. 9Jo-
tham died and was buried in Jerusalem, the
city of David. Then Jotham's son Ahaz became
king in his place.

AHAZ KING OF JUDAH

28
1Ahaz was twenty years old when he became king, and he ruled sixteen years in Jerusalem. Unlike his ancestor David, he did not do
what the LORD said was right. 2Ahaz did the
same things the kings of Israel had done. He
made metal idols to worship Baal. 3He burned
incense in the Valley of Ben Hinnom and made
his children pass through the fire. He did the
same hateful sins as the nations had done
whom the LORD had forced out of the land
ahead of the Israelites. 4Ahaz offered sacrifices
and burned incense at the places where gods
were worshiped, and on the hills, and under
every green tree.

WHAT'S IT MEAN?

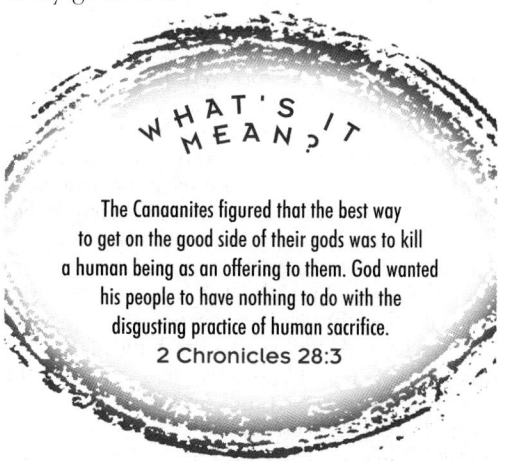

The Canaanites figured that the best way to get on the good side of their gods was to kill a human being as an offering to them. God wanted his people to have nothing to do with the disgusting practice of human sacrifice.
2 Chronicles 28:3

5So the LORD his God handed over Ahaz to
the king of Aram. The Arameans defeated Ahaz
and took many people of Judah as prisoners to
Damascus.
He also handed over Ahaz to Pekah king of
Israel, and Pekah's army killed many soldiers
of Ahaz. 6The army of Pekah son of Remaliah
killed one hundred twenty thousand brave
soldiers from Judah in one day. Pekah defeated
them because they had left the LORD, the God
of their ancestors. 7Zicri, a warrior from Ephraim, killed King Ahaz's son Maaseiah. He also
killed Azrikam, the officer in charge of the palace, and Elkanah, who was second in command to the king. 8The Israelite army captured
two hundred thousand of their own relatives.
They took women, sons and daughters, and
many valuable things from Judah and carried
them back to Samaria. 9But a prophet of the
LORD named Oded was there. He met the Israelite army when it returned to Samaria and
said to them, "The LORD, the God of your ancestors, handed Judah over to you, because he
was angry with those people. But God has seen
the cruel way you killed them. 10Now you plan
to make the people of Judah and Jerusalem
your slaves, but you also have sinned against
the LORD your God. 11Now listen to me. Send
back your brothers and sisters whom you captured, because the LORD is very angry with you."
12Then some of the leaders in Ephraim—
Azariah son of Jehohanan, Berekiah son of
Meshillemoth, Jehizkiah son of Shallum, and
Amasa son of Hadlai—met the Israelite soldiers coming home from war. 13They warned
the soldiers, "Don't bring the prisoners from
Judah here. If you do, we will be guilty of sin

against the LORD, and that will make our sin and guilt even worse. Our guilt is already so great that he is angry with Israel."

14 So the soldiers left the prisoners and valuable things in front of the officers and people there. 15 The leaders who were named took the prisoners and gave those who were naked the clothes that the Israelite army had taken. They gave the prisoners clothes, sandals, food, drink, and medicine. They put the weak prisoners on donkeys and took them back to their families in Jericho, the city of palm trees. Then they returned home to Samaria.

16-17 At that time the Edomites came again and attacked Judah and carried away prisoners. So King Ahaz sent to the king of Assyria for help. 18 The Philistines also robbed the towns in the western hills and in southern Judah. They captured the towns of Beth Shemesh, Aijalon, Gederoth, Soco, Timnah, and Gimzo, and the villages around them. Then the Philistines lived in those towns. 19 The LORD brought trouble on Judah because Ahaz their king led the people of Judah to sin, and he was unfaithful to the LORD. 20 Tiglath-Pileser king of Assyria came to Ahaz, but he gave Ahaz trouble instead of help. 21 Ahaz took some valuable things from the Temple of the LORD, from the palace, and from the princes, and he gave them to the king of Assyria, but it did not help.

22 During Ahaz's troubles he was even more unfaithful to the LORD. 23 He offered sacrifices to the gods of the people of Damascus, who had defeated him. He thought, "The gods of the kings of Aram helped them. If I offer sacrifices to them, they will help me also." But this brought ruin to Ahaz and all Israel.

24 Ahaz gathered the things from the Temple of God and broke them into pieces. Then he closed the doors of the Temple of the LORD. He made altars and put them on every street corner in Jerusalem. 25 In every town in Judah, Ahaz made places for burning sacrifices to worship other gods. So he made the LORD, the God of his ancestors, very angry.

26 The other things Ahaz did as king, from beginning to end, are written in the book of the kings of Judah and Israel. 27 Ahaz died and was buried in the city of Jerusalem, but not in the graves of the kings of Israel. Ahaz's son Hezekiah became king in his place.

HEZEKIAH PURIFIES THE TEMPLE

29 1 Hezekiah was twenty-five years old when he became king, and he ruled twenty-nine years in Jerusalem. His mother's name was Abijah daughter of Zechariah. 2 Hezekiah did what the LORD said was right, just as his ancestor David had done.

3 Hezekiah opened the doors of the Temple of the LORD and repaired them in the first month of the first year he was king. 4 Hezekiah brought in the priests and Levites and gathered them in the courtyard on the east side of the Temple. 5 Hezekiah said, "Listen to me, Levites. Make yourselves ready for the LORD's service, and make holy the Temple of the LORD, the God of your ancestors. Remove from the Temple everything that makes it impure. 6 Our ancestors were unfaithful to God and did what the LORD said was wrong. They left the LORD and stopped worshiping at the Temple where he lives. They rejected him. 7 They shut the doors of the porch of the Temple, and they let the fire go out in the lamps. They stopped burning incense and offering burnt offerings in the holy place to the God of Israel. 8 So the LORD became very angry with the people of Judah and Jerusalem, and he punished them. Other people are frightened and shocked by what he did to them. So they insult the people of Judah. You know these things are true. 9 That is why our ancestors were killed in battle and our sons, daughters, and wives were taken captive. 10 Now I, Hezekiah, have decided to make an agreement with the LORD, the God of Israel, so he will not be angry with us anymore. 11 My sons, don't waste any more time. The LORD chose you to stand before him, to serve him, to be his servants, and to burn incense to him."

12 These are the Levites who started to work. From the Kohathite family there were Mahath son of Amasai and Joel son of Azariah. From the Merarite family there were Kish son of Abdi and Azariah son of Jehallelel. From the Gershonite family there were Joah son of Zimmah and Eden son of Joah. 13 From Elizaphan's family there were Shimri and Jeiel. From Asaph's family there were Zechariah and Mattaniah. 14 From Heman's family there were Jehiel and Shimei. From Jeduthun's family there were Shemaiah and Uzziel.

15 These Levites gathered their brothers together and made themselves holy for service in the Temple. Then they went into the Temple of the LORD to purify it. They obeyed the king's command that had come from the LORD. 16 When the priests went into the Temple of the LORD to purify it, they took out all the unclean things they found in the Temple of the LORD and put them in the Temple courtyard. Then the Levites took these things out to the Kidron Valley. 17 Beginning on the first day of the first

month, they made the Temple holy for the LORD's service. On the eighth day of the month, they came to the porch of the Temple, and for eight more days they made the Temple of the LORD holy. So they finished on the sixteenth day of the first month.

[18]Then they went to King Hezekiah and said, "We have purified the entire Temple of the LORD, the altar for burnt offerings and its utensils, and the table for the holy bread and all its utensils. [19]When Ahaz was king, he was unfaithful to God and removed some things from the Temple. But we have put them back and made them holy for the LORD. They are now in front of the LORD's altar."

[20]Early the next morning King Hezekiah gathered the leaders of the city and went up to the Temple of the LORD. [21]They brought seven bulls, seven male sheep, seven lambs, and seven male goats. These animals were an offering to remove the sin of the people and the kingdom of Judah and to make the Temple ready for service to God. King Hezekiah commanded the priests, the descendants of Aaron, to offer these animals on the LORD's altar. [22]So the priests killed the bulls and sprinkled their blood on the altar. They killed the sheep and sprinkled their blood on the altar. Then they killed the lambs and sprinkled their blood on the altar. [23]Then the priests brought the male goats for the sin offering before the king and the people there. After the king and the people put their hands on the goats, [24]the priests killed them. With the goats' blood they made an offering on the altar to remove the sins of the Israelites so they would belong to God. The king had said that the burnt offering and sin offering should be made for all Israel.

[25]King Hezekiah put the Levites in the Temple of the LORD with cymbals, harps, and lyres, as David, Gad, and Nathan had commanded. (Gad was the king's seer, and Nathan was a prophet.) This command came from the LORD through his prophets. [26]So the Levites stood ready with David's instruments of music, and the priests stood ready with their trumpets.

[27]Then Hezekiah gave the order to sacrifice the burnt offering on the altar. When the burnt offering began, the singing to the LORD also began. The trumpets were blown, and the musical instruments of David king of Israel were played. [28]All the people worshiped, the singers sang, and the trumpeters blew their trumpets until the burnt offering was finished.

[29]When the sacrifices were completed, King Hezekiah and everyone with him bowed down and worshiped. [30]King Hezekiah and his officers ordered the Levites to praise the LORD, using the words David and Asaph the seer had used. So they praised God with joy and bowed down and worshiped.

[31]Then Hezekiah said, "Now that you people of Judah have given yourselves to the LORD, come near to the Temple of the LORD. Bring sacrifices and offerings, to show thanks to him." So the people brought sacrifices and thank offerings, and anyone who was willing also brought burnt offerings. [32]For burnt offerings they brought a total of seventy bulls, one hundred male sheep, and two hundred lambs; all these animals were sacrificed as burnt offerings to the LORD. [33]The holy offerings totaled six hundred bulls and three thousand sheep and goats. [34]There were not enough priests to skin all the animals for the burnt offerings. So their relatives the Levites helped them until the work was finished and other priests could be made holy. The Levites had been more careful to make themselves holy for the LORD's service than the priests. [35]There were many burnt offerings along with the fat of fellowship offerings and drink offerings. So the service in the Temple of the LORD began again. [36]And Hezekiah and the people were very happy that God had made it happen so quickly for his people.

WHAT'S IT MEAN?

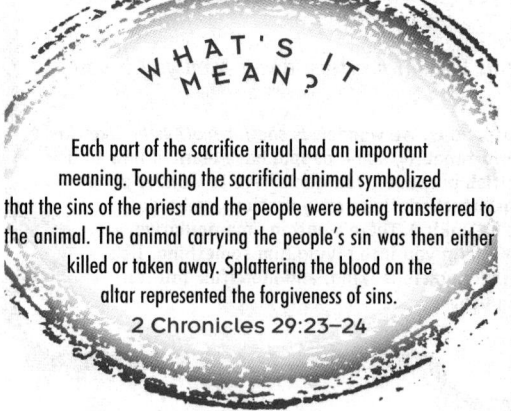

Each part of the sacrifice ritual had an important meaning. Touching the sacrificial animal symbolized that the sins of the priest and the people were being transferred to the animal. The animal carrying the people's sin was then either killed or taken away. Splattering the blood on the altar represented the forgiveness of sins.

2 Chronicles 29:23–24

THE PASSOVER CELEBRATION

30 [1]King Hezekiah sent messages to all the people of Israel and Judah, and he wrote letters to the people of Ephraim and Manasseh. Hezekiah invited all these people to come to the Temple of the LORD in Jerusalem to celebrate the Passover for the LORD, the God of Israel. [2]King Hezekiah, his officers, and all the people in Jerusalem agreed to celebrate the Passover in the second month. [3]They could not celebrate it

WHAT'S IT MEAN?

The Assyrians conquered Samaria, the capital of the northern kingdom of Israel, in 722 B.C. They destroyed the city and hauled the people away as captives. As a result, the ten tribes of the northern kingdom were never reunited.
2 Chronicles 30:6

at the normal time, because not enough priests
had made themselves ready to serve the LORD,
and the people had not yet gathered in Jerusalem. 4This plan satisfied King Hezekiah and all
the people. 5So they made an announcement everywhere in Israel, from Beersheba to Dan,[n]
telling the people to come to
Jerusalem to celebrate the
Passover for the LORD, the
God of Israel. For a long time
most of the people had not
celebrated the Passover as the
law commanded. 6At the king's
command, the messengers took
letters from him and his officers all
through Israel and Judah. This is what the letters said:

People of Israel, return to the LORD,
the God of Abraham, Isaac, and Israel.
Then God will return to you who are
still alive, who have escaped from the
kings of Assyria. 7Don't be like your ancestors or your relatives. They turned
against the LORD, the God of their ancestors, so he caused other people to be disgusted with them. You know this is true.
8Don't be stubborn as your ancestors
were, but obey the LORD willingly. Come
to the Temple, which he has made holy
forever. Serve the LORD your God so he
will not be angry with you. 9Come back
to the LORD. Then the people who captured your relatives and children will be
kind to them and will let them return to
this land. The LORD your God
is kind and merciful. He will
not turn away from you if
you return to him.

10The messengers went to
every town in Ephraim and
Manasseh, and all the way
to Zebulun, but the people
laughed at them and made
fun of them. 11But some men
from Asher, Manasseh, and
Zebulun were sorry for what they

> **"The LORD your God is kind and merciful. He will not turn away from you if you return to him."**
> **(2 Chronicles 30:9b)**

30:5 Beersheba to Dan Dan was the city farthest north in Israel, and Beersheba was the city farthest south. So this means all the people of Israel.

Promise HE PROMISES TO BE GRACIOUS AND MERCIFUL.

The LORD your God is kind and merciful. He will not turn away from you if you return to him (2 Chr. 30:9b).

Kindhearted people sometimes make us suspicious. We wonder, *Is she for real? Is he like this all the time? What does she want from me?* Unfortunately, some people have learned how to use kindness to manipulate and charm others for selfish purposes. You don't have to wonder about God's kindness. He *is* for real. There are no strings attached. He is truly gracious, generous, sympathetic, and tolerant toward you. He cannot be unkind. There's nothing manipulative about God. He owns the whole world, so he won't charm you into giving him something. He's always got your best interest at heart. He's genuinely gracious, kind, and merciful. You can trust him because he loves you so purely and so much.

SEE FOR YOURSELF:

Ps. 111:4; 145:8; Gal. 5:22–23; 2 Tim. 2:1

had done and went to Jerusalem. 12And God united all the people of Judah in obeying King Hezekiah and his officers, because their command had come from the LORD.

13In the second month a large crowd came together in Jerusalem to celebrate the Feast of Unleavened Bread. 14The people removed the altars and incense altars to gods in Jerusalem and threw them into the Kidron Valley.

15They killed the Passover lamb on the fourteenth day of the second month. The priests and the Levites were ashamed, so they made themselves holy and brought burnt offerings into the Temple of the LORD. 16They took their regular places in the Temple as the Teachings of Moses, the man of God, commanded. The Levites gave the blood of the sacrifices to the priests, who sprinkled it on the altar. 17Since many people in the crowd had not made themselves holy, the Levites killed the Passover lambs for everyone who was not clean. The Levites made each lamb holy for the LORD. 18-19Although many people from Ephraim, Manasseh, Issachar, and Zebulun had not purified themselves for the feast, they ate the Passover even though it was against the law. So Hezekiah prayed for them, saying, "LORD, you are good. You are the LORD, the God of our ancestors. Please forgive all those who try to obey you even if they did not make themselves clean as the rules of the Temple command." 20The LORD listened to Hezekiah's prayer, and he healed the people. 21The Israelites in Jerusalem celebrated the Feast of Unleavened Bread for seven days with great joy to the LORD. The Levites and priests praised the LORD every day with loud music. 22Hezekiah encouraged all the Levites who showed they understood well how to do their service for the LORD. The people ate the feast for seven days, offered fellowship offerings, and praised the LORD, the God of their ancestors.

23Then all the people agreed to stay seven more days, so they celebrated with joy for seven more days. 24Hezekiah king of Judah gave one thousand bulls and seven thousand sheep to the people. The officers gave one thousand bulls and ten thousand sheep to the people. Many priests made themselves holy. 25All the people of Judah, the priests, the Levites, those who came from Israel, the foreigners from Israel, and the foreigners living in Judah were very happy. 26There was much joy in Jerusalem, because there had not been a celebration like this since the time of Solomon son of David and king of Israel. 27The priests and Levites stood up and blessed the people, and God heard them because their prayer reached heaven, his holy home.

THE COLLECTION FOR THE PRIESTS

31 1When the Passover celebration was finished, all the Israelites in Jerusalem went out to the towns of Judah. There they smashed the stone pillars used to worship gods. They cut down the Asherah idols and destroyed the altars and places for worshiping gods in all of Judah, Benjamin, Ephraim, and Manasseh. After they had destroyed all of them, the Israelites returned to their own towns and homes.

WHAT'S IT MEAN?

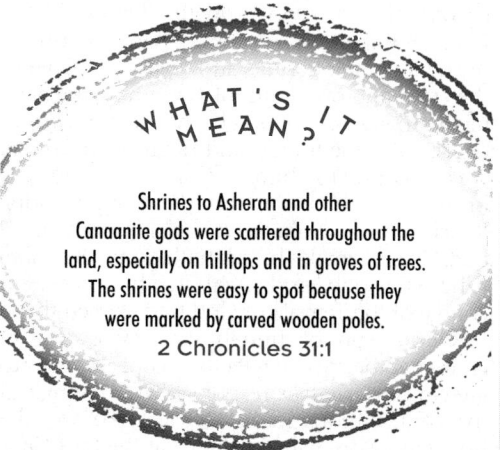

Shrines to Asherah and other Canaanite gods were scattered throughout the land, especially on hilltops and in groves of trees. The shrines were easy to spot because they were marked by carved wooden poles.
2 Chronicles 31:1

2King Hezekiah appointed groups of priests and Levites for their special duties. They were to offer burnt offerings and fellowship offerings, to worship, and to give thanks and praise at the gates of the LORD's house. 3Hezekiah gave some of his own animals for the burnt offerings, which were given every morning and evening, on Sabbath days, during New Moons, and at other feasts commanded in the LORD's Teachings.

4Hezekiah commanded the people living in Jerusalem to give the priests and Levites the portion that belonged to them. Then the priests and Levites could give all their time to the LORD's Teachings. 5As soon as the king's command went out to the Israelites, they gave freely of the first portion of their grain, new wine, oil, honey, and everything they grew in their fields. They brought a large amount, one-tenth of everything. 6The people of Israel and Judah who lived in Judah also brought one-tenth of their cattle and sheep and one-tenth of the holy things that were given to the LORD their God, and they put all of them in piles. 7The

GIVING
Who benefits when we give to the church? (31:4)

people began the piles in the third month and
finished in the seventh month. [8]When Hezekiah and his officers came and saw the piles,
they praised the LORD and his people, the people of Israel. [9]Hezekiah asked the priests and
Levites about the piles. [10]Azariah, the leading
priest from Zadok's family, answered Hezekiah,
"Since the people began to bring their offerings
to the Temple of the LORD, we have had plenty
to eat and plenty left over, because the LORD
has blessed his people. So we have all this left
over."

[11]Then Hezekiah commanded the priests to
prepare the storerooms in the Temple of the
LORD. So this was done. [12]Then the priests
brought in the offerings and the things given to
the LORD and one-tenth of everything the people had given. Conaniah the Levite was in
charge of these things, and his brother Shimei
was second to him. [13]Conaniah and his
brother Shimei were over these supervisors:
Jehiel, Azaziah, Nahath, Asahel, Jerimoth, Jozabad, Eliel, Ismakiah, Mahath, and Benaiah.
King Hezekiah and Azariah the officer in
charge of the Temple of God had chosen them.

[14]Kore son of Imnah the Levite was in
charge of the special gifts the people wanted to
give to God. He was responsible for giving out
the contributions made to the LORD and the
holy gifts. Kore was the guard at the East Gate.
[15]Eden, Miniamin, Jeshua, Shemaiah, Amariah,
and Shecaniah helped Kore in the towns
where the priests lived. They gave from what
was collected to the other groups of priests,
both young and old.

[16]From what was collected, these men also
gave to the males three years old and older who
had their names in the Levite family histories.
They were to enter the Temple of the LORD for
their daily service, each group having its own
responsibilities. [17]The priests were given their
part of the collection, by families, as listed in the
family histories. The Levites twenty years old
and older were given their part of the collection,
based on their responsibilities and their groups.
[18]The Levites' babies, wives, sons, and daughters also got part of the collection. This was
done for all the Levites who were listed in the
family histories, because they always kept
themselves ready to serve the LORD.

[19]Some of Aaron's descendants, the priests,
lived on the farmlands near the towns or in the
towns. Men were chosen by name to give part
of the collection to these priests. All the males
and those named in the family histories of the
Levites received part of the collection.

[20]This is what King Hezekiah did in Judah.
He did what was good and right and obedient
before the LORD his God. [21]Hezekiah tried to
obey God in his service of the Temple of God,
and he tried to obey God's teachings and commands. He gave himself fully to his work for
God. So he had success.

ASSYRIA ATTACKS JUDAH

32
[1]After Hezekiah did all these things to serve
the LORD, Sennacherib king of Assyria came
and attacked Judah. He and his army surrounded and attacked the strong, walled cities,
hoping to take them for himself. [2]Hezekiah
knew that Sennacherib had come to Jerusalem
to attack it. [3]So Hezekiah and his officers and
army commanders decided to cut off the water
from the springs outside the city. So the officers
and commanders helped Hezekiah. [4]Many
people came and cut off all the springs and the
stream that flowed through the land. They
said, "The king of Assyria will not find much
water when he comes here." [5]Then Hezekiah
made Jerusalem stronger. He rebuilt all the
broken parts of the wall and put towers on it.
He also built another wall outside the first one
and strengthened the area that was filled in on
the east side of the old part of Jerusalem. He
also made many weapons and shields.

WHAT'S IT MEAN?

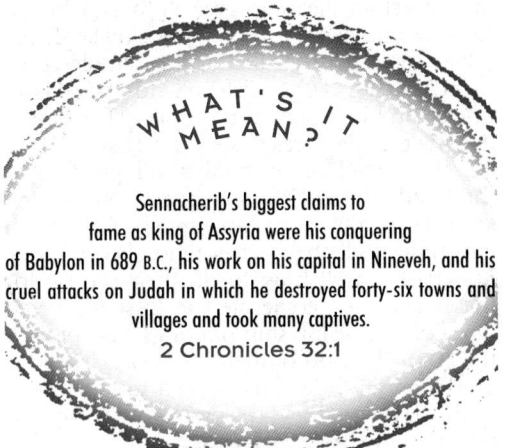

Sennacherib's biggest claims to fame as king of Assyria were his conquering of Babylon in 689 B.C., his work on his capital in Nineveh, and his cruel attacks on Judah in which he destroyed forty-six towns and villages and took many captives.
2 Chronicles 32:1

[6]Hezekiah put army commanders over the
people and met with them at the open place
near the city gate. Hezekiah encouraged them,
saying, [7]"Be strong and brave. Don't be afraid
or worried because of the king of Assyria or
his large army. There is a greater power with us
than with him. [8]He only has men, but we have
the LORD our God to help us and to fight our
battles." The people were encouraged by the
words of Hezekiah king of Judah.

[9]After this King Sennacherib of Assyria and

all his army surrounded and attacked Lachish. Then he sent his officers to Jerusalem with this message for King Hezekiah of Judah and all the people of Judah in Jerusalem:

10Sennacherib king of Assyria says this: "You have nothing to trust in to help you. It is no use for you to stay in Jerusalem under attack. 11Hezekiah says to you, 'The LORD our God will save us from the king of Assyria,' but he is fooling you. If you stay in Jerusalem, you will die from hunger and thirst. 12Hezekiah himself removed your LORD's places of worship and altars. He told you people of Judah and Jerusalem that you must worship and burn incense on only one altar.

13"You know what my ancestors and I have done to all the people in other nations. The gods of those nations could not save their people from my power. 14My ancestors destroyed those nations; none of their gods could save them from me. So your god cannot save you from my power. 15Do not let Hezekiah fool you or trick you, and do not believe him. No god of any nation or kingdom has been able to save his people from me or my ancestors. Your god is even less able to save you from me."

16Sennacherib's officers said worse things against the LORD God and his servant Hezekiah. 17King Sennacherib also wrote letters insulting the LORD, the God of Israel. They spoke against him, saying, "The gods of the other nations could not save their people from me. In the same way Hezekiah's god won't be able to save his people from me." 18Then the king's officers shouted in Hebrew, calling out to the people of Jerusalem who were on the city wall. The officers wanted to scare the people away so they could capture Jerusalem. 19They spoke about the God of Jerusalem as though he were like the gods the people of the world worshiped, which are made by human hands.

20King Hezekiah and the prophet Isaiah son of Amoz prayed to heaven about this. 21Then the LORD sent an angel who killed all the soldiers, leaders, and officers in the camp of the king of Assyria. So the king went back to his own country in disgrace. When he went into the temple of his god, some of his own sons killed him with a sword.

22So the LORD saved Hezekiah and the people in Jerusalem from Sennacherib king of Assyria and from all other people. He took care of them on every side. 23Many people brought gifts for the LORD to Jerusalem, and they also brought valuable gifts to King Hezekiah of Judah. From then on all the nations respected Hezekiah.

HEZEKIAH DIES

24At that time Hezekiah became so sick he almost died. When he prayed to the LORD, the

Promise

HE PROMISES TO FIGHT WITH YOU ON YOUR SIDE.

Be strong and brave. Don't be afraid or worried because of the king of Assyria or his large army. There is a greater power with us than with him. He only has men, but we have the LORD our God to help us and to fight our battles (2 Chr. 32:7–8a).

Ever had someone stick up for you? They walked right into the middle of your conflict and took your side? Awesome. Did you ever have someone decide to do more than watch? They cared enough to get involved, to actually stick their neck out and speak up for you. It's an incredible feeling to have someone help you fight your fight. All of a sudden you feel stronger, the enemy seems weaker, and your confidence gets a boost. God is ready to fight for you. He is on your side, ready to intervene and do battle. You are not fighting alone. All the power of the supernatural is right beside you. So look ahead with hope and assurance that the strongest Warrior fights for you.

SEE FOR YOURSELF:

2 Chr. 13:10–12; Zeph. 2:7; Zech. 10:5

LORD spoke to him and gave him a sign.[n] 25But
Hezekiah did not thank God for his kindness,
because he was so proud. So the LORD was
angry with him and the people of Judah and
Jerusalem. 26But later Hezekiah and the people
of Jerusalem were sorry and stopped being
proud, so the LORD did not punish them while
Hezekiah was alive.
27Hezekiah had many riches and much
honor. He made treasuries for his silver, gold,
gems, spices, shields, and other valuable things.
28He built storage buildings for grain, new
wine, and oil and stalls for all the cattle and
pens for the sheep. 29He also built many towns.
He had many flocks and herds, because God
had given Hezekiah much wealth.
30It was Hezekiah who cut off the upper
pool of the Gihon spring and made those waters flow straight down to the west side of the
older part of Jerusalem. And Hezekiah was
successful in everything he did. 31But one time
the leaders of Babylon sent messengers to
Hezekiah, asking him about a strange sign that
had happened in the land. When they came,
God left Hezekiah alone to test him so he could
know everything that was in Hezekiah's heart.[n]
32Hezekiah's love for God and the other
things he did as king are written in the vision
of the prophet Isaiah son of Amoz. This is in
the book of the kings of Judah and Israel.
33Hezekiah died and was buried on a hill,
where the graves of David's ancestors are. All
the people of Judah and Jerusalem honored
Hezekiah when he died, and his son Manasseh
became king in his place.

MANASSEH KING OF JUDAH

33
1Manasseh was twelve years old when he
became king, and he was king for fifty-five
years in Jerusalem. 2He did what the LORD said
was wrong. He did the hateful things the nations had done—the nations that the LORD had
forced out of the land ahead of the Israelites.
3Manasseh's father, Hezekiah, had torn down
the places where gods were worshiped, but
Manasseh rebuilt them. He also built altars for
the Baal gods, and he made Asherah idols and
worshiped all the stars of the sky and served
them. 4The LORD had said about the Temple, "I
will be worshiped in Jerusalem forever," but
Manasseh built altars in the Temple of the
LORD. 5He built altars to worship the stars in
the two courtyards of the Temple of the LORD.
6He made his children pass through fire in the
Valley of Ben Hinnom. He prac-
ticed magic and witchcraft and
told the future by explaining
signs and dreams. He got
advice from mediums and
fortune-tellers. He did many
things the LORD said were
wrong, which made the LORD
angry.

OCCULT

What does God think about witchcraft? (33:6)

7Manasseh carved an idol and put it in the
Temple of God. God had said to David and his
son Solomon about the Temple, "I will be worshiped forever in this Temple and in Jerusalem,
which I have chosen from all the tribes of Israel. 8I will never again make the Israelites leave
the land I gave to their ancestors. But they
must obey everything I have commanded
them in all the teachings, rules, and commands
I gave them through Moses." 9But Manasseh
led the people of Judah and Jerusalem to do
wrong. They did more evil than the nations the
LORD had destroyed ahead of the Israelites.

WHAT'S IT MEAN?

Manasseh apparently was determined to disobey as many of God's laws as he possibly could. Magic and witchcraft—attempting to do things outside the realm of nature—had been banned since the Agreement was handed down. Human sacrifice was detested by God. Putting an idol in the Temple was like a slap in the face to the Lord. As if all of that weren't enough, according to Jewish tradition, Manasseh was responsible for the murder of the prophet Isaiah. He was the one who gave the command to saw God's prophet in half.

2 Chronicles 33:6–7

10The LORD spoke to Manasseh and his
people, but they did not listen. 11So the LORD
brought the king of Assyria's army commanders to attack Judah. They captured Manasseh,
put hooks in him, placed bronze chains on his
hands, and took him to Babylon. 12As Manasseh suffered, he begged the LORD his God for
help and humbled himself before the God of
his ancestors. 13When Manasseh prayed, the
LORD heard him and had pity on him. So the

32:24 sign See Isaiah 38:1-8. It tells the story about the sign and how the Lord gave Hezekiah fifteen more years to live. **32:31 God . . . heart** See 2 Kings 20:12-19.

LORD let him return to Jerusalem and to his
kingdom. Then Manasseh knew that the LORD
is the true God.
14 After that happened, Manasseh rebuilt the
outer wall of Jerusalem and made it higher. It
was in the valley on the west side of the Gihon
spring and went to the entrance of the Fish
Gate and around the hill of Ophel. Then he put
commanders in all the strong, walled cities in
Judah.
15 Manasseh removed the idols of other nations, including the idol in the Temple of the
LORD. He removed all the altars he had built on
the Temple hill and in Jerusalem and threw
them out of the city. 16 Then he set up the
LORD's altar and sacrificed on it fellowship offerings and offerings to show thanks to God.
Manasseh commanded all the people of Judah
to serve the LORD, the God of Israel. 17 The people continued to offer sacrifices at the places of
worship, but their sacrifices were only to the
LORD their God. 18 The other things Manasseh
did as king, his prayer to his God, and what the
seers said to him in the name of the LORD, the
God of Israel—all are recorded in the book of
the history of the kings of Israel. 19 Manasseh's
prayer and God's pity for him, his sins, his
unfaithfulness, the places he built for worshiping gods and the Asherah idols before he
humbled himself—all are written in the book
of the seers. 20 Manasseh died and was buried
in his palace. Then Manasseh's son Amon became king in his place.

AMON KING OF JUDAH

21 Amon was twenty-two years old when he
became king, and he was king for two years in
Jerusalem. 22 He did what the LORD said was
wrong, as his father Manasseh had done.
Amon worshiped and offered sacrifices to all
the carved idols Manasseh had made. 23 Amon
did not humble himself before the LORD as his
father Manasseh had done. Instead, Amon
sinned even more.
24 King Amon's officers made plans against
him and killed him in his palace. 25 Then the
people of the land killed all those who had
made plans to kill King Amon, and they made
his son Josiah king in his place.

JOSIAH KING OF JUDAH

34
1 Josiah was eight years old when he became
king, and he ruled thirty-one years in Jerusalem. 2 He did what the LORD said was right. He
lived as his ancestor David had lived, and he
did not stop doing what was right.
3 In his eighth year as king while he was still
young, Josiah began to obey the God of his
ancestor David. In his twelfth year as king, Josiah began to remove from Judah and Jerusalem the gods, the places for worshiping gods,
the Asherah idols, and the wooden and metal
idols. 4 The people tore down the altars for the
Baal gods as Josiah directed. Then Josiah cut
down the incense altars that were above them.
He broke up the Asherah idols and the wood-
en and metal idols and beat them into powder.
Then he sprinkled the powder on the graves of
the people who had offered sacrifices to these
gods. 5 He burned the bones of their priests on
their own altars. So Josiah removed idol worship from Judah and Jerusalem, 6 and from the
towns in the areas of Manasseh, Ephraim, and
Simeon all the way to Naphtali, and in the ruins near these towns. 7 Josiah broke down the
altars and Asherah idols and beat the idols into
powder. He cut down all the incense altars in
all of Israel. Then he went back to Jerusalem.
8 In Josiah's eighteenth year as king, he made
Judah and the Temple pure again. He sent Shaphan son of Azaliah, Maaseiah the city leader,
and Joah son of Joahaz the recorder to repair
the Temple of the LORD, the God of Josiah.
9 These men went to Hilkiah the high priest and
gave him the money the Levite gatekeepers had
gathered from the people of Manasseh, Ephraim, and all the Israelites who were left alive,
and also from all the people of Judah, Benjamin, and Jerusalem. This is the money they
had brought into the Temple of God. 10 Then
the Levites gave it to the supervisors of the
work on the Temple of the LORD, and they paid
the workers who rebuilt and repaired the Temple. 11 They gave money to carpenters and
builders to buy cut stone and wood. The wood
was used to rebuild the buildings and to make
beams for them, because the kings of Judah
had let the buildings fall into ruin. 12 The men
did their work well. Their supervisors were Jahath and Obadiah, who were Levites from the
family of Merari, and Zechariah and Meshullam, who were from the family of Kohath.
These Levites were all skilled musicians. 13 They
were also in charge of the workers who carried
loads and all the other workers. Some Levites
worked as secretaries, officers, and gatekeepers.

THE BOOK OF THE TEACHINGS IS FOUND

14 The Levites brought out the money that
was in the Temple of the LORD. As they were
doing this, Hilkiah the priest found the Book of
the LORD's Teachings that had been given
through Moses. 15 Hilkiah said to Shaphan the
royal secretary, "I've found the Book of the

Teachings in the Temple of the LORD!" Then he
gave it to Shaphan.

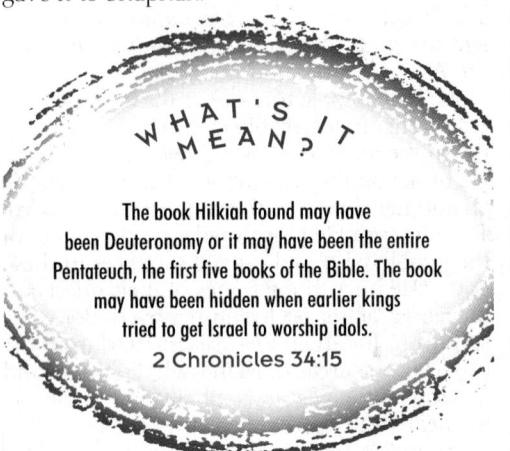

> **WHAT'S IT MEAN?**
>
> **The book Hilkiah found may have been Deuteronomy or it may have been the entire Pentateuch, the first five books of the Bible. The book may have been hidden when earlier kings tried to get Israel to worship idols.**
>
> 2 Chronicles 34:15

16Shaphan took the book to the king and
reported to Josiah, "Your officers are doing
everything you told them to do. 17They have
paid out the money that was in the Temple of
the LORD and have given it to the supervisors
and the workers." 18Then Shaphan the royal
secretary told the king, "Hilkiah the priest has
given me a book." And Shaphan read from the
book to the king.
19When the king heard the words of the
Teachings, he tore his clothes to show how
upset he was. 20He gave orders to Hilkiah, Ahikam son of Shaphan, Acbor son of Micaiah,
Shaphan the royal secretary, and Asaiah, the
king's servant. These were the orders: 21"Go
and ask the LORD about the words in the book
that was found. Ask for me and for the people
who are left alive in Israel and Judah. The LORD
is very angry with us, because our ancestors
did not obey the LORD's word; they did not do
everything this book says to do."
22So Hilkiah and those the king sent with
him went to talk to Huldah the prophetess. She
was the wife of Shallum son of Tikvah, the son
of Harhas, who took care of the king's clothes.
Huldah lived in Jerusalem, in the new area of
the city.
23She said to them, "This is what the LORD,
the God of Israel, says: Tell the man who sent
you to me, 24'This is what the LORD says: I will
bring trouble to this place and to the people
living here. I will bring all the curses that are
written in the book that was read to the king of
Judah. 25The people of Judah have left me and
have burned incense to other gods. They have
made me angry by all the evil things they have
made. So I will punish them in my anger,
which will not be put out.' 26Tell the king of
Judah, who sent you to ask the LORD, 'This is
what the LORD, the God of Israel, says about
the words you heard: 27When you heard my
words against this place and its people, you
became sorry for what you had done and you
humbled yourself before me. You tore your
clothes to show how upset you were, and you
cried in my presence. This is why I have heard
you, says the LORD. 28So I will let you die and
be buried in peace. You won't see all the trouble I will bring to this place and the people
living here.' "
So they took her message back to the king.
29Then the king gathered all the older leaders of Judah and Jerusalem together. 30He went
up to the Temple of the LORD, and all the people from Judah and from Jerusalem went with
him. The priests, the Levites, and all the people—from the most important to the least important—went with him. He read to them all
the words in the Book of the Agreement that
was found in the Temple of the LORD.
31The king stood by his pillar
and made an agreement in the
presence of the LORD to follow the LORD and obey his
commands, rules, and laws
with his whole being and to
obey the words of the agreement written in this book.

> **BIBLE**
>
> How hard should we try to obey the Bible? (34:31)

32Then Josiah made all the people in Jerusalem
and Benjamin promise to accept the agreement.
So the people of Jerusalem obeyed the agreement of God, the God of their ancestors.
33And Josiah threw out the hateful idols
from all the land that belonged to the Israelites.
He led everyone in Israel to serve the LORD
their God. While Josiah lived, the people
obeyed the LORD, the God of their ancestors.

JOSIAH CELEBRATES THE PASSOVER

35

1King Josiah celebrated the Passover to the
LORD in Jerusalem. The Passover lamb was
killed on the fourteenth day of the first month.
2Josiah chose the priests to do their duties, and
he encouraged them as they served in the Temple of the LORD. 3The Levites taught the Israelites and were made holy for service to the
LORD. Josiah said to them, "Put the Holy Ark in
the Temple that David's son Solomon, the king
of Israel, built. Do not carry it from place to
place on your shoulders anymore. Now serve
the LORD your God and his people Israel. 4Pre-
pare yourselves by your family groups for service, and do the jobs that King David and his
son Solomon gave you to do.
5"Stand in the holy place with a group of

the Levites for each family group of the people.
6Kill the Passover lambs, and make yourselves
holy to the LORD. Prepare the lambs for your
relatives, the people of Israel, as the LORD
through Moses commanded us to do."

WHAT'S IT MEAN?

The Ark of the Agreement was a wooden box covered with gold. The Ark had been built according to plans that God had given to Moses. It had rings on its sides so that priests could run poles through them and lift the box without actually touching it. Because the Israelites believed the Ark contained God's power, occasionally they carried it with them into battle.

2 Chronicles 35:3

7Josiah gave the Israelites thirty thousand
sheep and goats to kill for the Passover sacrifices, and he gave them three thousand cattle.
They were all his own animals.
8Josiah's officers also gave willingly to the
people, the priests, and the Levites. Hilkiah,
Zechariah, and Jehiel, the officers in charge of
the Temple, gave the priests twenty-six hundred lambs and goats and three hundred cattle
for Passover sacrifices. 9Conaniah, his brothers
Shemaiah and Nethanel, and Hashabiah, Jeiel,
and Jozabad gave the Levites five thousand
sheep and goats and five hundred cattle for
Passover sacrifices. These men were leaders of
the Levites.
10When everything was ready for the Passover service, the priests and Levites went to
their places, as the king had commanded. 11The
Passover lambs were killed. Then the Levites
skinned the animals and gave the blood to the
priests, who sprinkled it on the altar. 12Then
they gave the animals for the burnt offerings to
the different family groups so the burnt offerings could be offered to the LORD as was written in the book of Moses. They also did this
with the cattle. 13The Levites roasted the Passover sacrifices over the fire as they were commanded, and they boiled the holy offerings in
pots, kettles, and pans. Then they quickly gave
the meat to the people. 14After this was finished, the Levites prepared meat for themselves
and for the priests, the descendants of Aaron.
The priests worked until night, offering the
burnt offerings and burning the fat of the sacrifices.
15The Levite singers from Asaph's family
stood in the places chosen for them by King
David, Asaph, Heman, and Jeduthun, the king's
seer. The gatekeepers at each gate did not have
to leave their places, because their fellow Levites had prepared everything for them for the
Passover.
16So everything was done that day for the
worship of the LORD, as King Josiah commanded. The Passover was celebrated, and the
burnt offerings were offered on the LORD's altar. 17The Israelites who were there celebrated
the Passover and the Feast of Unleavened
Bread for seven days. 18The Passover had not
been celebrated like this in Israel since the
prophet Samuel was alive. None of the kings
of Israel had ever celebrated a Passover like it
was celebrated by King Josiah, the priests, the
Levites, the people of Judah and Israel who
were there, and the people of Jerusalem. 19This
Passover was celebrated in the eighteenth year
Josiah was king.

THE DEATH OF JOSIAH

20After Josiah did all this for the Temple,
Neco king of Egypt led an army to attack Carchemish, a town on the Euphrates River. And
Josiah marched out to fight against Neco. 21But
Neco sent messengers to Josiah, saying, "King
Josiah, there should not be war between us. I
did not come to fight you, but my enemies.
God told me to hurry, and he is on my side. So
don't fight God, or he will destroy you."
22But Josiah did not go away. He wore different clothes so no one would know who he
was. Refusing to listen to what Neco said at
God's command, Josiah went to fight on the
plain of Megiddo. 23In the battle King Josiah
was shot by archers. He told his servants, "Take
me away because I am badly wounded." 24So
they took him out of his chariot and put him
in another chariot and carried him to Jerusalem. There he died and was buried in the
graves where his ancestors were buried. All the
people of Judah and Jerusalem were very sad
because he was dead.
25Jeremiah wrote some sad songs about Josiah. Even to this day all the men and women
singers remember and honor Josiah with these
songs. It became a custom in Israel to sing
these songs that are written in the collection of
sad songs.
26-27The other things Josiah did as king,
from beginning to end, are written in the book
of the kings of Israel and Judah. It tells how he

loved what was written in the LORD's teachings.

JEHOAHAZ KING OF JUDAH

36 1The people of Judah chose Josiah's son Jehoahaz and made him king in Jerusalem in his father's place.

2Jehoahaz was twenty-three years old when he became king, and he was king in Jerusalem for three months. 3Then King Neco of Egypt removed Jehoahaz from being king in Jerusalem. Neco made the people of Judah pay about seventy-five hundred pounds of silver and about seventy-five pounds of gold. 4The king of Egypt made Jehoahaz's brother Eliakim the king of Judah and Jerusalem and changed his name to Jehoiakim. But Neco took his brother Jehoahaz to Egypt.

WHAT'S IT MEAN?

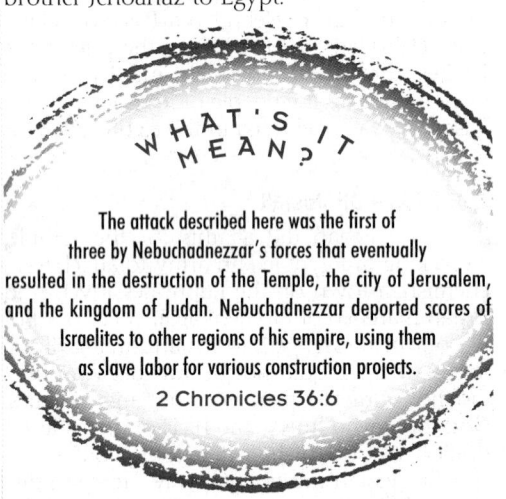

The attack described here was the first of three by Nebuchadnezzar's forces that eventually resulted in the destruction of the Temple, the city of Jerusalem, and the kingdom of Judah. Nebuchadnezzar deported scores of Israelites to other regions of his empire, using them as slave labor for various construction projects.

2 Chronicles 36:6

JEHOIAKIM KING OF JUDAH

5Jehoiakim was twenty-five years old when he became king, and he was king in Jerusalem for eleven years. He did what the LORD his God said was wrong. 6King Nebuchadnezzar of Babylon attacked Judah, captured Jehoiakim, put bronze chains on him, and took him to Babylon. 7Nebuchadnezzar removed some of the things from the Temple of the LORD, took them to Babylon, and put them in his own palace.

8The other things Jehoiakim did as king, the hateful things he did, and everything he was guilty of doing, are written in the book of the kings of Israel and Judah. And Jehoiakim's son Jehoiachin became king in his place.

JEHOIACHIN KING OF JUDAH

9Jehoiachin was eighteen years old when he became king of Judah, and he was king in Jerusalem for three months and ten days. He did what the LORD said was wrong. 10In the spring King Nebuchadnezzar sent for Jehoiachin and brought him and some valuable treasures from the Temple of the LORD to Babylon. Then Nebuchadnezzar made Jehoiachin's uncle Zedekiah the king of Judah and Jerusalem.

ZEDEKIAH KING OF JUDAH

11Zedekiah was twenty-one years old when he became king of Judah, and he was king in Jerusalem for eleven years. 12Zedekiah did what the LORD his God said was wrong. The prophet Jeremiah spoke messages from the LORD, but Zedekiah did not obey. 13Zedekiah turned against King Nebuchadnezzar, who had forced him to swear in God's name to be loyal to him. But Zedekiah became stubborn and refused to obey the LORD, the God of Israel. 14Also, all the leaders of the priests and the people of Judah became more wicked, following the evil example of the other nations. The LORD had made the Temple in Jerusalem holy, but the leaders made it unholy.

THE FALL OF JERUSALEM

15The LORD, the God of their ancestors, sent prophets again and again to warn his people, because he had pity on them and on his Temple. 16But they made fun of God's prophets and hated God's messages. They refused to listen to the prophets until, finally, the LORD became so angry with his people that he could not be stopped. 17So God brought the king of Babylon to attack them. The king killed the young men even when they were in the Temple. He had no mercy on the young men or women, the old

WHAT'S IT MEAN?

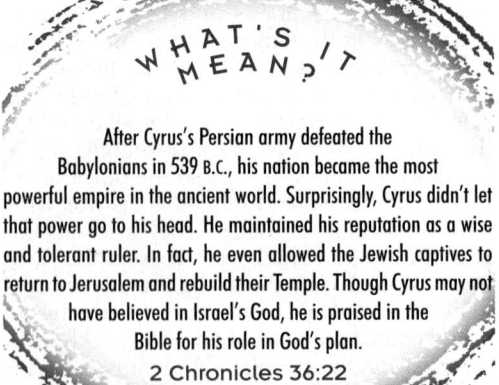

After Cyrus's Persian army defeated the Babylonians in 539 B.C., his nation became the most powerful empire in the ancient world. Surprisingly, Cyrus didn't let that power go to his head. He maintained his reputation as a wise and tolerant ruler. In fact, he even allowed the Jewish captives to return to Jerusalem and rebuild their Temple. Though Cyrus may not have believed in Israel's God, he is praised in the Bible for his role in God's plan.

2 Chronicles 36:22

men or those who were sick. God handed all
of them over to Nebuchadnezzar. 18Nebuchad-
nezzar carried away to Babylon all the things
from the Temple of God, both
large and small, and all the treasures from the Temple of the
LORD and from the king and
his officers. 19Nebuchadnez-
zar and his army set fire to
God's Temple and broke
down Jerusalem's wall and
burned all the palaces. They
took or destroyed every valuable thing in Jerusalem.

20Nebuchadnezzar took captive
to Babylon the people who were left alive,
and he forced them to be slaves for him and
his descendants. They remained there as slaves
until the Persian kingdom defeated Babylon.
21And so what the LORD had told Israel
through the prophet Jeremiah happened: The
country was an empty wasteland for seventy
years to make up for the years of Sabbath rest[n]
that the people had not kept.

22In the first year Cyrus was
king of Persia, the LORD had Cyrus send an announcement to
his whole kingdom. This happened so the LORD's message
spoken by Jeremiah would
come true. He wrote:

23This is what Cyrus king of
Persia says:

The LORD, the God of heaven, has given me all the kingdoms of the earth, and he has appointed me to build a Temple for him at Jerusalem in Judah. Now may the LORD your God be with all of you who are his people. You are free to go to Jerusalem.

"He has appointed me to build a Temple for him at Jerusalem in Judah."
(2 Chronicles 36:23b)

36:21 Sabbath rest The law said that every seventh year the land was not to be farmed. See Leviticus 25:1-7.

ezra

CONTENT Imagine . . . seventy years ago your parents and grandparents got dragged away from their homeland and resettled into a new country. You were born there, grew up and raised your kids there. Now your kids are grown, and you've got grandchildren there. One day, you get the news that a new king has taken over, and he has offered you the opportunity to move back to the land your parents left behind. You can move back home.

Home?

That was the dilemma that Ezra and his people faced in Babylon. Only a few of them made the choice to actually return to their hometown, Jerusalem. When they did, they found their city in ruins. All they could do was start over. They started rebuilding the Temple. They started rebuilding their homes. They started figuring out their cultural heritage.

Ezra returned to Jerusalem after the Temple was rebuilt, but before the people had renewed their relationship with God. He helped them see that the condition of the place of worship is important, but not as important as the condition of the hearts of the worshipers.

Outline

1:1—2:70 .... The Jews Return Home from Captivity
3:1—4:5 .... The Altar Is Rebuilt, and Work on the Temple Begins
4:6-24 .... Later Trouble Rebuilding Jerusalem
5:1—6:22 .... The Temple Is Rebuilt
7:1—8:36 .... Ezra Leads Many Jews Back to Jerusalem
9:1—10:44 .... Ezra Forces Men to Divorce Their Gentile Wives

Purpose God keeps the promises he makes to Israel, and he keeps his promises to us.

Theme Captives' Return to Jerusalem and Temple Reconstruction

Date of writing 457–444 B.C.

> "Ezra had worked hard to know and obey the Teachings of the LORD and to teach his rules and commands to the Israelites" (7:10).

Bible Talk

Intermarriage

One of the issues that Ezra addressed with the Jewish people was intermarriage, or marrying someone from another culture. Intermarriage wasn't a moral problem. People are people no matter what culture they are from. But intermarriage *was* a spiritual problem. All the surrounding cultures worshiped idols.

Marrying someone doesn't mean you will take on all their beliefs and practices, but it does mean that you will be influenced by them. The Hebrews already had a reputation for giving in to peer pressure, particularly where false gods were concerned. If the Hebrews married into one of the cultures that worshiped idols, it was almost a sure thing that they would embrace the worship of idols as well.

You really can't exaggerate how big a deal this idol worship stuff was to God. The first *and* second of the Ten Commandments (see Exodus 20) had to do with it.

THE TEMPLE

Restoring the Temple was one of the biggest tasks facing the people who had returned to Jerusalem. If you look back through the history of the Hebrews, you'll see that the way they treated the Temple almost *always* ran parallel with the respect they had for God. In the days before their exile to Babylon, getting the Temple back in shape after one of their irreligious "benders" wasn't as big of a deal. But by the time Ezra returned to Jerusalem, the Temple wasn't just in disrepair. It had been destroyed! This mirrored the faith of Ezra's people, and it broke his heart.

So when the people of Israel set about to rebuild the Temple, they were also setting about to restore their faith in and their relationship with God.

CYRUS HELPS THE CAPTIVES RETURN

1 [1]In the first year Cyrus was king of Persia, the LORD caused Cyrus to send an announcement to his whole kingdom and to put it in writing. This happened so the LORD's message spoken by Jeremiah would come true. He wrote:

> [2]This is what Cyrus king of Persia says:
>
> The LORD, the God of heaven, has given all the kingdoms of the earth to me, and he has appointed me to build a Temple for him at Jerusalem in Judah. [3]May God be with all of you who are his people. You are free to go to Jerusalem in Judah and build the Temple of the LORD, the God of Israel, who is in Jerusalem. [4]Those who stay behind, wherever they live, should support those who want to go. Give them silver and gold, supplies and cattle, and special gifts for the Temple of God in Jerusalem.

WHAT'S IT MEAN?

King Cyrus was killed in battle around 530 B.C. after a pretty successful career as ruler of Persia. Among the accomplishments that might have been included in his obituary was his conquering of the Medes, the Lydians, and the Babylonians. Unlike other ancient kings, Cyrus allowed the people he defeated to worship their own gods.

Ezra 1:2–3

[5]Then the family leaders of Judah and Benjamin and the priests and Levites got ready to go to Jerusalem—everyone God had caused to want to go to Jerusalem to build the Temple of the LORD. [6]All their neighbors helped them, giving them things made of silver and gold, along with supplies, cattle, valuable gifts, and special gifts for the Temple. [7]Also, King Cyrus brought out the bowls and pans that belonged in the Temple of the LORD, which Nebuchadnezzar had taken from Jerusalem and put in the temple of his own god. [8]Cyrus king of Persia had Mithredath the treasurer bring them and count them out for Sheshbazzar, the prince of Judah.

[9]He listed thirty gold dishes, one thousand silver dishes, twenty-nine pans, [10]thirty gold bowls, four hundred ten matching silver bowls, and one thousand other pieces.

[11]There was a total of fifty-four hundred pieces of gold and silver. Sheshbazzar brought all these things along when the captives went from Babylon to Jerusalem.

WHAT'S IT MEAN?

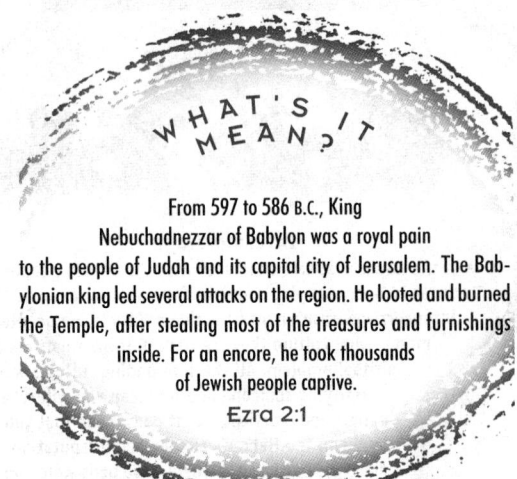

From 597 to 586 B.C., King Nebuchadnezzar of Babylon was a royal pain to the people of Judah and its capital city of Jerusalem. The Babylonian king led several attacks on the region. He looted and burned the Temple, after stealing most of the treasures and furnishings inside. For an encore, he took thousands of Jewish people captive.

Ezra 2:1

THE CAPTIVES WHO RETURNED

2 [1]These are the people of the area who returned from captivity, whom Nebuchadnezzar king of Babylon had taken away to Babylon. They returned to Jerusalem and Judah, each going back to his own town. [2]These people returned with Zerubbabel, Jeshua, Nehemiah, Seraiah, Reelaiah, Mordecai, Bilshan, Mispar, Bigvai, Rehum, and Baanah.

These are the people from Israel: [3]the descendants of Parosh—2,172; [4]the descendants of Shephatiah—372; [5]the descendants of Arah—775; [6]the descendants of Pahath-Moab (through the family of Jeshua and Joab)—2,812; [7]the descendants of Elam—1,254; [8]the descendants of Zattu—945; [9]the descendants of Zaccai—760; [10]the descendants of Bani—642; [11]the descendants of Bebai—623; [12]the descendants of Azgad—1,222; [13]the descendants of Adonikam—666; [14]the descendants of Bigvai—2,056; [15]the descendants of Adin—454; [16]the descendants of Ater (through the family of Hezekiah)—98; [17]the descendants of Bezai—323; [18]the descendants of Jorah—112; [19]the descendants of Hashum—223; [20]the descendants of Gibbar—95.

[21]These are the people from the towns: of Bethlehem—123; [22]of Netophah—56; [23]of An-

athoth—128; 24of Azmaveth—42; 25of Kiriath Jearim, Kephirah, and Beeroth—743; 26of Ramah and Geba—621; 27of Micmash—122; 28of Bethel and Ai—223; 29of Nebo—52; 30of Magbish—156; 31of the other town of Elam—1,254; 32of Harim—320; 33of Lod, Hadid and Ono—725; 34of Jericho—345; 35of Senaah—3,630.

36These are the priests: the descendants of Jedaiah (through the family of Jeshua)—973; 37the descendants of Immer—1,052; 38the descendants of Pashhur—1,247; 39the descendants of Harim—1,017.

40These are the Levites: the descendants of Jeshua and Kadmiel (through the family of Hodaviah)—74.

41These are the singers: the descendants of Asaph—128.

42These are the gatekeepers of the Temple: the descendants of Shallum, Ater, Talmon, Akkub, Hatita, and Shobai—139.

43These are the Temple servants: the descendants of Ziha, Hasupha, Tabbaoth, 44Keros, Siaha, Padon, 45Lebanah, Hagabah, Akkub, 46Hagab, Shalmai, Hanan, 47Giddel, Gahar, Reaiah, 48Rezin, Nekoda, Gazzam, 49Uzza, Paseah, Besai, 50Asnah, Meunim, Nephussim, 51Bakbuk, Hakupha, Harhur, 52Bazluth, Mehida, Harsha, 53Barkos, Sisera, Temah, 54Neziah, and Hatipha.

55These are the descendants of the servants of Solomon: the descendants of Sotai, Hassophereth, Peruda, 56Jaala, Darkon, Giddel, 57Shephatiah, Hattil, Pokereth-Hazzebaim, and Ami.

WHAT'S IT MEAN?

Because God had chosen the tribe of Levi to be priests—and because ancient priests had no need for real estate—the Levites were not able to inherit land like the other tribes. Instead, they were supported by the gifts they received at the Temple.

Ezra 2:59–63

58The Temple servants and the descendants of the servants of Solomon numbered 392.

59Some people came to Jerusalem from the towns of Tel Melah, Tel Harsha, Kerub, Addon, and Immer, but they could not prove that their ancestors came from Israel. 60They were the descendants of Delaiah, Tobiah, and Nekoda—652.

61Also these priests: the descendants of Hobaiah, Hakkoz, and Barzillai, who had married a daughter of Barzillai from Gilead and was called by her family name.

62These people searched for their family records but could not find them. So they could not be priests, because they were thought to be unclean. 63The governor ordered them not to eat any of the food offered to God until a priest had settled this matter by using the Urim and Thummim.

64The total number of those who returned was 42,360. 65This is not counting their 7,337 male and female servants and the 200 male and female singers they had with them. 66They had 736 horses, 245 mules, 67435 camels, and 6,720 donkeys.

68When they arrived at the Temple of the LORD in Jerusalem, some of the leaders of families gave offerings to rebuild the Temple of God on the same site as before. 69They gave as much as they could to the treasury to rebuild the Temple—about 1,100 pounds of gold, about 6,000 pounds of silver, and 100 pieces of clothing for the priests.

70All the Israelites settled in their hometowns. The priests, Levites, singers, gatekeepers, and Temple servants, along with some of the other people, settled in their own towns as well.

REBUILDING THE ALTAR

3

1In the seventh month, after the Israelites were settled in their hometowns, they met together in Jerusalem. 2Then Jeshua son of Jozadak and his fellow priests joined Zerubbabel son of Shealtiel and began to build the altar of the God of Israel where they could offer burnt offerings, just as it is written in the Teachings of Moses, the man of God. 3Even though they were afraid of the people living around them, they built the altar where it had been before. And they offered burnt offerings on it to the LORD morning and evening. 4Then, to obey what was written, they celebrated the Feast of Shelters. They offered the right number of sacrifices for each day of the festival. 5After the Feast of Shelters, they had regular sacrifices every day, as well as sacrifices for the New Moon and all the festivals commanded by the LORD. Also there were special offerings brought as gifts to the LORD. 6On the first day of the seventh month they began to bring burnt offerings to the LORD, but the foundation of the LORD's Temple had not yet been laid.

REBUILDING THE TEMPLE

7Then they gave money to the bricklayers
and carpenters. They also gave food, wine, and
oil to the cities of Sidon and Tyre so they
would float cedar logs from Lebanon to the
seacoast town of Joppa. Cyrus king of Persia
had given permission for this.

WHAT'S IT MEAN?

Lebanon was famous for its large, beautiful cedar trees. The wood from these trees was used to build everything from palaces and ships to coffins and musical instruments. Tyre and Sidon were Mediterranean port cities in Lebanon. After being cut down, the trees probably were taken to Tyre and Sidon, loaded onto rafts, and floated to Joppa. From there, they probably were hauled across land for the remaining thirty-five miles to Jerusalem.

Ezra 3:7

8In the second month of the second year
after their arrival at the Temple of God in Jerusalem, Zerubbabel son of Shealtiel, Jeshua son
of Jozadak, their fellow priests and Levites, and
all who had returned from captivity to Jerusalem began to work. They chose Levites twenty
years old and older to be in charge of the
building of the Temple of the LORD. 9These men
were in charge of the work of building the Temple of God: Jeshua and his sons and brothers;
Kadmiel and his sons who were the descendants of Hodaviah; and the sons of Henadad
and their sons and brothers. They were all Levites.

10The builders finished laying the foundation of the Temple of the LORD. Then the
priests, dressed in their robes, stood with their
trumpets, and the Levites, the
sons of Asaph, stood with
their cymbals. They all took
their places and praised the
LORD just as David king of Israel had said to do. 11With
praise and thanksgiving, they
sang to the LORD:

LOVE

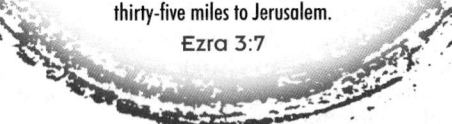

Does God love me forever? (3:11)

"He is good;
his love for Israel continues forever."

And then all the people shouted loudly, "Praise
the LORD! The foundation of his Temple has
been laid." 12But many of the older priests, Levites, and family leaders who had seen the first
Temple cried when they saw the foundation of
this Temple. Most of the other people were
shouting with joy. 13The people made so much
noise it could be heard far away, and no one
could tell the difference between the joyful
shouting and the sad crying.

On the Edge

"He is good; his love for Israel continues forever" (Ezra 3:11b).

"Good" can be a fleeting thing for us. Some days we think we have it, and sometimes it's hard to hold on to. A misunderstanding can turn really good friends into enemies overnight. We can have a good attitude toward one person and be totally rude to the next. Your favorite ice cream may taste really good, but after six scoops, it's gross. People can even get so confused that they believe that wrong and sinful things are good—like drugs, premarital sex, and pornography.

But God is nothing like we are. He is all good. He cannot change his mind because he misunderstood; he is not fickle with people. You can't get too much of his goodness.

He is good on every level, all the time. Let those words about God's goodness remind you that everything he does is for your good. You may struggle with good, but God never will.

SEE FOR YOURSELF: Ex. 33:19; 2 Sam. 7:28; Ps. 31:19; 100:5; Rom. 8:28

ENEMIES OF THE REBUILDING

4 1When the enemies of the people of Judah
and Benjamin heard that the returned captives
were building a Temple for the LORD, the God
of Israel, 2they came to Zerubbabel and the
leaders of the families. The enemies said, "Let us
help you build, because we are like you and
want to worship your God. We have been offering sacrifices to him since the time of Esarhaddon king of Assyria, who brought us here."

3But Zerubbabel, Jeshua, and the leaders of
Israel answered, "You will not help us build a
Temple to our God. We will build it ourselves
for the LORD, the God of Israel, as King Cyrus,
the king of Persia, commanded us to do."

4Then the people around them tried to
discourage the people of Judah by making
them afraid to build. 5Their enemies hired others to delay the building plans during the time
Cyrus was king of Persia. And it continued to
the time Darius was king of Persia.

WHAT'S IT MEAN?

When the northern kingdom of Israel was conquered by Assyria in 722 B.C., many Israelites were taken captive. At the same time, foreigners from many different regions were brought to live in Israel. The Israelites who remained in the land began to mingle with their new neighbors, eventually marrying them and adopting their idol worship. As a result, they were no longer a distinct people—either physically or spiritually.

Ezra 4:2

MORE PROBLEMS FOR THE BUILDERS

6When Xerxes first became king, those enemies wrote a letter against the people of Judah
and Jerusalem.
7When Artaxerxes became king of Persia,
Bishlam, Mithredath, Tabeel, and those with
them wrote a letter to Artaxerxes. It was written in the Aramaic language and translated.
8Rehum the governor and Shimshai the
governor's secretary wrote a letter against Jerusalem to Artaxerxes the king. It said:

WHAT'S IT MEAN?

The Assyrians were particularly good at preventing rebellion and revolt in the territories they conquered—without resorting to violence. They accomplished this by deporting most of the native citizens of the region and bringing in foreigners from several other countries. By maintaining an even mixture of ethnic groups, the Assyrians prevented any one group from becoming powerful enough to revolt. As it turned out, Ashurbanipal (who reigned from 669 to 627 B.C.) was the last powerful king of Assyria.

Ezra 4:8–10

9This letter is from Rehum the governor, Shimshai the secretary, and their
fellow workers—the judges and important officers over the men who came
from Tripolis, Persia, Erech, and Babylon,
the Elamite people of Susa, 10and those
whom the great and honorable Ashurbanipal forced out of their countries and
settled in the city of Samaria and in other
places of the Trans-Euphrates.

11(This is a copy of the letter they sent to
Artaxerxes.)

To King Artaxerxes.
From your servants who live in
Trans-Euphrates.

12King Artaxerxes, you should know
that the Jewish people who came to us
from you have gone to Jerusalem to rebuild that evil city that refuses to obey.
They are fixing the walls and repairing
the foundations of the buildings.
13Now, King Artaxerxes, you should
know that if Jerusalem is built and its
walls are fixed, Jerusalem will not pay
taxes of any kind. Then the amount of
money your government collects will be
less. 14Since we must be loyal to the government, we don't want to see the king
dishonored. So we are writing to let the
king know. 15We suggest you search the
records of the kings who ruled before
you. You will find out that the city of
Jerusalem refuses to obey and makes
trouble for kings and areas controlled by
Persia. Since long ago it has been a place
where disobedience has started. That is
why it was destroyed. 16We want you to
know, King Artaxerxes, that if this city is
rebuilt and its walls fixed, you will be left
with nothing in Trans-Euphrates.

17King Artaxerxes sent this answer:

To Rehum the governor and Shimshai
the secretary, to all their fellow workers
living in Samaria, and to those in other
places in Trans-Euphrates.

Greetings.
18The letter you sent to us has been
translated and read to me. 19I ordered the

records to be searched, and it was done.
We found that Jerusalem has a history of
disobedience to kings and has been a
place of problems and trouble. 20Jerusa-
lem has had powerful kings who have
ruled over the whole area of Trans-
Euphrates, and taxes of all kinds have
been paid to them. 21Now, give an order
for those men to stop work. The city of
Jerusalem will not be rebuilt until I say so.
22Make sure you do this, because if they
continue, it will hurt the government.

23A copy of the letter that King Artaxerxes
sent was read to Rehum and Shimshai the secretary and the others. Then they quickly went
to the Jewish people in Jerusalem and forced
them to stop building.
24So the work on the Temple of God in Jerusalem stopped until the second year Darius
was king of Persia.

TATTENAI'S LETTER TO DARIUS

5 1The prophets Haggai and Zechariah, a descendant of Iddo, prophesied to the Jewish
people in Judah and Jerusalem in the name of
the God of Israel, who was over them. 2Then
Zerubbabel son of Shealtiel and Jeshua son of
Jozadak started working again to rebuild the
Temple of God in Jerusalem. And the prophets
of God were there, helping them.
3At that time Tattenai, the governor of
Trans-Euphrates, and Shethar-Bozenai, and
their fellow workers went to the Jewish people
and asked, "Who gave you permission to rebuild this Temple and fix these walls?" 4They
also asked, "What are the names of the men
working on this building?" 5But their God was
watching over the older leaders of the Jewish
people. The builders were not stopped until a
report could go to King Darius and his written
answer could be received.
6This is a copy of the letter that was sent to
King Darius by Tattenai, the governor of
Trans-Euphrates, Shethar-Bozenai, and the
other important officers of Trans-Euphrates.
7This is what was said in the report they sent
to him:

To King Darius.

Greetings. May you have peace.
8King Darius, you should know that
we went to the district of Judah where
the Temple of the great God is. The people are building that Temple with large
stones, and they are putting timbers in
the walls. They are working very hard
and are building very fast.
9We asked their older leaders, "Who
gave you permission to rebuild this
Temple and these walls?" 10We also asked
for their names, and we wrote down the
names of their leaders so you would
know who they are.
11This is the answer they gave to
us: "We are the servants of the God of
heaven and earth. We are rebuilding the
Temple that a great king of Israel built
and finished many years ago. 12But our
ancestors made the God of heaven
angry, so he handed them over to Nebuchadnezzar king of Babylon, who destroyed this Temple and took the people
to Babylon as captives.
13"Later, in the first year Cyrus was
king of Babylon, he gave a special order
for this Temple to be rebuilt. 14Cyrus
brought out from the temple in Babylon
the gold and silver bowls and pans that
came from the Temple of God. Nebuchadnezzar had taken them from the
Temple in Jerusalem and had put them
in the temple in Babylon.
"Then King Cyrus gave them to
Sheshbazzar, his appointed governor.
15Cyrus said to him, 'Take these gold and
silver bowls and pans, and put them
back in the Temple in Jerusalem and rebuild the Temple of God where it was.'
16So Sheshbazzar came and laid the
foundations of the Temple of God in Jerusalem. From that day until now the
work has been going on, but it is not yet
finished."
17Now, if the king wishes, let a search
be made in the royal records of Babylon.
See if King Cyrus gave an order to rebuild this Temple in Jerusalem. Then let
the king write us and tell us what he has
decided.

THE ORDER OF DARIUS

6 1So King Darius gave an order to search the
records kept in the treasury in Babylon. 2A
scroll was found in Ecbatana, the capital city of
Media. This is what was written on it:

Note:

3King Cyrus gave an order about the
Temple of God in Jerusalem in the first
year he was king. This was the order:
"Let the Temple be rebuilt as a place to

present sacrifices. Let its foundations be
laid; it should be ninety feet high and
ninety feet wide. 4It must have three layers of large stones and then one layer of
timbers. The costs should be paid from
the king's treasury. 5The gold and silver
utensils from the Temple of God should
be put back in their places. Nebuchadnezzar took them from the Temple in Jerusalem and brought them to Babylon,
but they are to be put back in the Temple
of God in Jerusalem."
6Now then, Tattenai, governor of
Trans-Euphrates, Shethar-Bozenai, and
all the officers of that area, stay away
from there. 7Do not bother the work on
that Temple of God. Let the governor of
the Jewish people and the older Jewish
leaders rebuild this Temple where it was
before.
8Also, I order you to do this for those
older leaders of the Jewish people who
are building this Temple: The cost of the
building is to be fully paid from the royal treasury, from taxes collected from
Trans-Euphrates. Do this so the work
will not stop. 9Give those people anything they need—young bulls, male
sheep, or lambs for burnt offerings to the
God of heaven, or wheat, salt, wine, or
olive oil. Give the priests in Jerusalem
anything they ask for every day without
fail. 10Then they may offer sacrifices
pleasing to the God of heaven, and they
may pray for the life of the king and his
sons.
11Also, I give this order: If anyone
changes this order, a wood beam is to be
pulled from his house and driven
through his body. Because of his crime,
make his house a pile of ruins. 12God has
chosen Jerusalem as the place he is to be
worshiped. May he punish any king or
person who tries to change this order
and destroy this Temple.
I, Darius, have given this order. Let it
be obeyed quickly and carefully.

COMPLETION OF THE TEMPLE

13So, Tattenai, the governor of Trans-
Euphrates, Shethar-Bozenai, and their fellow
workers carried out King Darius' order quickly
and carefully. 14The older Jewish leaders continued to build and were successful because of
the preaching of Haggai the prophet and Zechariah, a descendant of Iddo. They finished
building the Temple as the God of Israel had
commanded and as kings Cyrus, Darius, and
Artaxerxes of Persia had ordered. 15The Temple
was finished on the third day of the month of
Adar in the sixth year Darius was king.

WHAT'S IT MEAN?

The new Temple was completed in 516 B.C., seventy years after Nebuchadnezzar had destroyed the original. Cyrus had given the okay to rebuild the Temple in 539 B.C., but the construction was delayed for fifteen years by the Samaritans, who opposed the rebuilding project. The new Temple was much smaller and less impressive than the original. What's more, many of the original furnishings, including the Ark of the Agreement, were never found.

Ezra 6:15

16Then the people of Israel celebrated and
gave the Temple to God to honor him. Everybody was happy: the priests, the Levites, and
the rest of the Jewish people who had returned
from captivity. 17They gave the Temple to God
by offering a hundred bulls, two hundred male
sheep, and four hundred lambs as sacrifices.
And as an offering to forgive the sins of all
Israel, they offered twelve male goats, one goat
for each tribe in Israel. 18Then they put the
priests and the Levites into their separate
groups. Each group had a certain time to serve
God in the Temple at Jerusalem as it is written
in the Book of Moses.

THE PASSOVER IS CELEBRATED

19The Jewish people who returned from
captivity celebrated the Passover on the fourteenth day of the first month. 20The priests and
Levites had made themselves clean. Then the
Levites killed the Passover lambs for all the
people who had returned from captivity, for
their relatives the priests, and for themselves.
21So all the people of Israel who returned from
captivity ate the Passover lamb. So did the
people who had given up the unclean ways of
their non-Jewish neighbors in order to worship the LORD, the God of Israel. 22For seven
days they celebrated the Feast of Unleavened
Bread in a very joyful way. The LORD had
made them happy by changing the mind of the
king of Assyria so that he helped them in the
work on the Temple of the God of Israel.

EZRA COMES TO JERUSALEM

[1]After these things[n] during the rule of Artaxerxes king of Persia, Ezra came up from Babylon. Ezra was the son of Seraiah, the son of Azariah, the son of Hilkiah, [2]the son of Shallum, the son of Zadok, the son of Ahitub, [3]the son of Amariah, the son of Azariah, the son of Meraioth, [4]the son of Zerahiah, the son of Uzzi, the son of Bukki, [5]the son of Abishua, the son of Phinehas, the son of Eleazar, the son of Aaron the high priest. [6]This Ezra came to Jerusalem from Babylon. He was a teacher and knew well the Teachings of Moses that had been given by the LORD, the God of Israel. Ezra received everything he asked for from the king, because the LORD his God was helping him. [7]In the seventh year of King Artaxerxes more Israelites came to Jerusalem. Among them were priests, Levites, singers, gatekeepers, and Temple servants.

WHAT'S IT MEAN?

The fact that Ezra was able to trace his family tree back to Aaron, the brother of Moses and the first high priest, gave him authority in the eyes of the Israelites. Genealogies were extremely important in ancient Israel. As far as the Israelites were concerned, Ezra's family background gave him the right to teach and preach the Teachings of Moses.

Ezra 7:1–6

[8]Ezra arrived in Jerusalem in the fifth month of Artaxerxes' seventh year as king. [9]Ezra had left Babylon on the first day of the first month, and he arrived in Jerusalem on the first day of the fifth month, because God was helping him. [10]Ezra had worked hard to know and obey the Teachings of the LORD and to teach his rules and commands to the Israelites.

"Ezra had worked hard to know and obey the Teachings of the LORD and to teach his rules and commands to the Israelites." (Ezra 7:10)

ARTAXERXES' LETTER TO EZRA

[11]King Artaxerxes had given a letter to Ezra, a priest and teacher who taught about the commands and laws the LORD gave Israel. This is a copy of the letter:

[12]From Artaxerxes, king of kings, to Ezra the priest, a teacher of the Law of the God of heaven.

Greetings.

[13]Now I give this order: Any Israelite in my kingdom who wishes may go with you to Jerusalem, including priests and Levites. [14]Ezra, you are sent by the king and the seven people who advise him to ask how Judah and Jerusalem are obeying the Law of your God, which you are carrying with you. [15]Also take with you the silver and gold that the king and those who advise him have given freely to the God of Israel, whose Temple is in Jerusalem. [16]Also take the silver and gold you receive from the area of Babylon. Take the offerings the Israelites and their priests have given as gifts for the Temple of your God in Jerusalem. [17]With this money buy bulls, male sheep, and lambs, and the grain offerings and drink offerings that go with those sacrifices. Then sacrifice them on the altar in the Temple of your God in Jerusalem.

[18]You and your fellow Jews may spend the silver and gold left over as you want and as God wishes. [19]Take to the God of Jerusalem all the utensils for worship in the Temple of your God, [20]which we have given you. Use the royal treasury to pay for anything else you need for the Temple of your God.

[21]Now I, King Artaxerxes, give this order to all the men in charge of the treasury of Trans-Euphrates: Give Ezra, a priest and a teacher of the Law of the God of heaven, whatever he asks for. [22]Give him up to seventy-five hundred pounds of silver, six hundred bushels of wheat, six hundred gallons of wine, and six hundred gallons of olive oil. And give him as much salt as he wants. [23]Carefully give him whatever the God of heaven wants for the Temple of the God of heaven. We do not want God to

7:1 After these things There is a time period of about sixty years between chapters six and seven.

be angry with the king and his sons. [24]Remember, you must not make these people pay taxes of any kind: priests, Levites, singers, gatekeepers, Temple servants, and other workers in this Temple of God.

[25]And you, Ezra, use the wisdom you have from your God to choose judges and lawmakers to rule the Jewish people of Trans-Euphrates. They know the laws of your God, and you may teach anyone who does not know them. [26]Whoever does not obey the law of your God or of the king must be punished. He will be killed, or sent away, or have his property taken away, or be put in jail.

[27]Praise the LORD, the God of our ancestors. He caused the king to want to honor the Temple of the LORD in Jerusalem. [28]The LORD has shown me, Ezra, his love in the presence of the king, those who advise the king, and the royal officers. Because the LORD my God was helping me, I had courage, and I gathered the leaders of Israel to return with me.

LEADERS WHO RETURNED WITH EZRA

8 [1]These are the leaders of the family groups and those who were listed with them who came back with me from Babylon during the rule of King Artaxerxes.

[2]From the descendants of Phinehas: Gershom.

From the descendants of Ithamar: Daniel.

From the descendants of David: Hattush [3]of the descendants of Shecaniah.

From the descendants of Parosh: Zechariah, with one hundred fifty men.

[4]From the descendants of Pahath-Moab: Eliehoenai son of Zerahiah, with two hundred men.

[5]From the descendants of Zattu: Shecaniah son of Jahaziel, with three hundred men.

[6]From the descendants of Adin: Ebed son of Jonathan, with fifty men.

[7]From the descendants of Elam: Jeshaiah son of Athaliah, with seventy men.

[8]From the descendants of Shephatiah: Zebadiah son of Michael, with eighty men.

[9]From the descendants of Joab: Obadiah son of Jehiel, with two hundred eighteen men.

[10]From the descendants of Bani: Shelomith son of Josiphiah, with one hundred sixty men.

[11]From the descendants of Bebai: Zechariah son of Bebai, with twenty-eight men.

[12]From the descendants of Azgad: Johanan son of Hakkatan, with one hundred ten men.

[13]From the descendants of Adonikam, these were the last ones: Eliphelet, Jeuel, and Shemaiah, with sixty men.

[14]From the descendants of Bigvai: Uthai and Zaccur, with seventy men.

Promise

HE PROMISES TO TAKE CARE OF THOSE WHO TRULY OBEY HIM.

Our God helps everyone who obeys him, but he is very angry with all who reject him (Ezra 8:22b).

Are you a genuine seeker? When you're with other people who are worshiping the Lord, where is your heart? In other words, do you *worship* when you worship? Is your mind participating in the things that are being said? Or are you just pretending? Eyes closed, mind wandering. Bible open, words blurry. Singing songs because you know them, not because you mean them. Don't answer these questions out loud, and don't start feeling guilty if you know that all the answers are "yes" in your life. God already knows the condition of your heart.

The point is that God takes care of everyone who truly worships him. Do you long to be cared for by God? Then worship him from your heart. Even if you don't feel superspiritual, tell him what you think and how you feel. Think about how awesome he is, and then tell him about it. When you sing a song, really pay attention to the words and sing them like you believe them. Pray a lot. Read the Bible so you can get to know God better. The more real he is to you, the more true your worship will be. Don't be lazy or distracted. No one can take care of you the way God can. Just be a genuine seeker.

SEE FOR YOURSELF:
Is. 29:13; John 4:23–24

THE RETURN TO JERUSALEM

15I called all those people together at the canal that flows toward Ahava, where we
camped for three days. I checked all the people
and the priests, but I did not find any Levites.
16So I called these leaders: Eliezer, Ariel, Shemaiah, Elnathan, Jarib, Elnathan, Nathan, Zechariah, and Meshullam. And I called Joiarib and
Elnathan, who were teachers. 17I sent these
men to Iddo, the leader at Casiphia, and told
them what to say to Iddo and his relatives,
who are the Temple servants in Casiphia. I sent
them to bring servants to us for the Temple of
our God. 18Our God was helping us, so Iddo's
relatives gave us Sherebiah, a wise man from
the descendants of Mahli son of Levi, who was
the son of Israel. And they brought Sherebiah's
sons and brothers, for a total of eighteen men.
19And they brought to us Hashabiah and Jeshaiah from the descendants of Merari, and his
brothers and nephews. In all there were twenty
men. 20They also brought two hundred twenty
of the Temple servants, a group David and the
officers had set up to help the Levites. All of
those men were listed by name.
21There by the Ahava Canal, I announced
we would all give up eating and humble ourselves before our God. We would ask God for a
safe trip for ourselves, our children, and all our
possessions. 22I was ashamed to ask the king
for soldiers and horsemen to protect us from
enemies on the road. We had said to the king,
"Our God helps everyone who obeys him, but
he is very angry with all who reject him." 23So
we gave up eating and prayed to our God
about our trip, and he answered our prayers.
24Then I chose twelve of the priests who
were leaders, Sherebiah, Hashabiah, and ten of
their relatives. 25I weighed the offering of silver
and gold and the utensils given for the Temple
of our God, and I gave them to the twelve
priests I had chosen. The king, the people who
advised him, his officers, and all the Israelites
there with us had given these things for the
Temple. 26I weighed out and gave them about
fifty thousand pounds of silver, about seventy-
five hundred pounds of silver objects, and
about seventy-five hundred pounds of gold.
27I gave them twenty gold bowls that weighed
about nineteen pounds and two fine pieces of
polished bronze that were as valuable as gold.
28Then I said to the priests, "You and these
utensils belong to the LORD for his service. The
silver and gold are gifts to the LORD, the God of
your ancestors. 29Guard these things carefully.
In Jerusalem, weigh them in front of the leading priests, Levites, and the leaders of the family groups of Israel in the rooms of the Temple
of the LORD." 30So the priests and Levites accepted the silver, the gold, and the utensils that
had been weighed to take them to the Temple
of our God in Jerusalem.

WHAT'S IT MEAN?

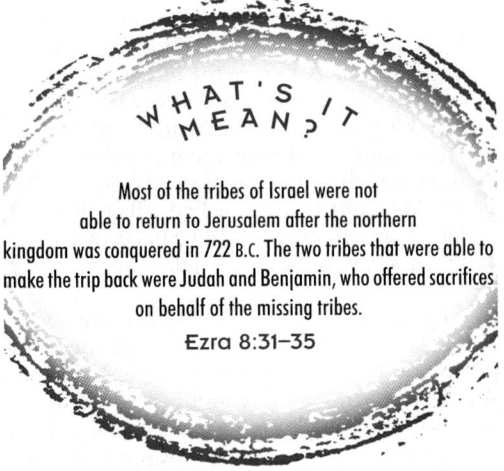

Most of the tribes of Israel were not able to return to Jerusalem after the northern kingdom was conquered in 722 B.C. The two tribes that were able to make the trip back were Judah and Benjamin, who offered sacrifices on behalf of the missing tribes.

Ezra 8:31–35

31On the twelfth day of the first month we
left the Ahava Canal and started toward Jerusalem. Our God helped us and protected us
from enemies and robbers along the way. 32Fi-
nally we arrived in Jerusalem where we rested
three days.
33On the fourth day we weighed out the silver, the gold, and the utensils in the Temple of
our God. We handed them to the priest Meremoth son of Uriah. Eleazar son of Phinehas
was with him, as were the Levites Jozabad son
of Jeshua and Noadiah son of Binnui. 34We
checked everything by number and by weight,
and the total weight was written down.
35Then the captives who returned made
burnt offerings to the God of Israel. They sacrificed twelve bulls for all Israel, ninety-six male
sheep, and seventy-seven lambs. For a sin offering there were twelve male goats. All this
was a burnt offering to the LORD. 36They took
King Artaxerxes' orders to the royal officers
and to the governors of Trans-Euphrates. Then
these men gave help to the people and the
Temple of God.

EZRA'S PRAYER

9
1After these things had been done, the leaders came to me and said, "Ezra, the Israelites,
including the priests and Levites, have not kept
themselves separate from the people around
us. Those neighbors do evil things, as the Canaanites, Hittites, Perizzites, Jebusites, Ammonites, Moabites, Egyptians, and Amorites did.
2The Israelite men and their sons have married

these women. They have mixed the people who belong to God with the people around them. The leaders and officers of Israel have led the rest of the Israelites to do this unfaithful thing."

LEADERSHIP
Can leaders' morals affect their people? (9:2)

3When I heard this, I angrily tore my robe and coat, pulled hair from my head and beard, and sat down in shock. 4Everyone who trembled in fear at the word of the God of Israel gathered around me because of the unfaithfulness of the captives who had returned. I sat there in shock until the evening sacrifice.

5At the evening sacrifice I got up from where I had shown my shame. My robe and coat were torn, and I fell on my knees with my hands spread out to the LORD my God. 6I prayed,

SIN
What should we do when we realize that we've sinned? (9:6)

"My God, I am too ashamed and embarrassed to lift up my face to you, my God, because our sins are so many. They are higher than our heads. Our guilt even reaches up to the sky. 7From the days of our ancestors until now, our guilt has been great. Because of our sins, we, our kings, and our priests have been punished by the sword and captivity. Foreign kings have taken away our things and shamed us, even as it is today.

8"But now, for a short time, the LORD our God has been kind to us. He has let some of us come back from captivity and has let us live in safety in his holy place. And so our God gives us hope and a little relief from our slavery. 9Even though we are slaves, our God has not left us. He caused the kings of Persia to be kind to us and has given us new life. We can rebuild the Temple and repair its ruins. And he has given us a wall to protect us in Judah and Jerusalem.

10"But now, our God, what can we say after you have done all this? We have disobeyed your commands 11that you gave through your servants the prophets. You said, 'The land you are entering to own is ruined; the people living there have spoiled it by the evil they do. Their evil filled the land with uncleanness from one end to the other. 12So do not let your daughters marry their sons, and do not let their daughters marry your sons. Do not wish for their peace or success. Then you will be strong and eat the good things of the land. Then you can leave this land to your descendants forever.'

13"What has happened to us is our own fault. We have done evil things, and our guilt is great. But you, our God, have punished us less than we deserve; you have left a few of us alive. 14We should not again break your commands by allowing marriages with these wicked people. If we did, you would get angry enough to destroy us, and none of us would be left alive. 15LORD, God of Israel, by your goodness a few of us are left alive today. We admit that we are guilty and none of us should be allowed to stand before you."

THE PEOPLE CONFESS SIN

10

1As Ezra was praying and confessing and crying and throwing himself down in front of the Temple, a large group of Israelite men, women, and children gathered around him who were also crying loudly. 2Then Shecaniah son of Jehiel the Elamite said to Ezra, "We have been unfaithful to our God by marrying women from the peoples around us. But even so, there is still hope for Israel. 3Now let us make an agreement before our God. We will send away all these women and their children as you and those who respect the commands of our God advise. Let it be done to obey God's Teachings. 4Get up, Ezra. You are in charge, and we will support you. Have courage and do it."

HOPE
Will God still love us even if we sin? (10:2)

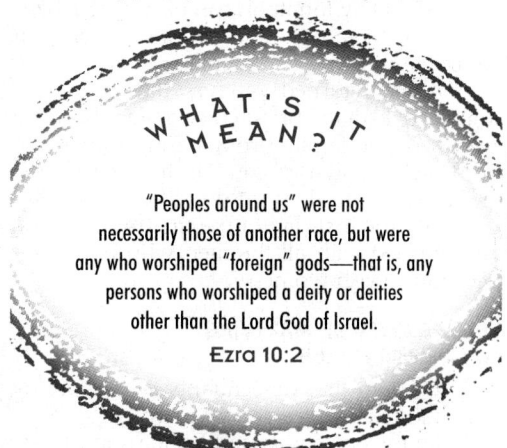

WHAT'S IT MEAN?

"Peoples around us" were not necessarily those of another race, but were any who worshiped "foreign" gods—that is, any persons who worshiped a deity or deities other than the Lord God of Israel.

Ezra 10:2

5So Ezra got up and made the priests, Levites, and all the people of Israel promise to do what was suggested; and they promised. 6Then Ezra left the Temple and went to the room of Jehohanan son of Eliashib. While Ezra was there, he did not eat or drink, because he was still sad about the unfaithfulness of the captives who had returned.

7 They sent an order in Judah and Jerusalem
for all the captives who had returned to meet
together in Jerusalem. 8 Whoever did not come
to Jerusalem within three days would lose
his property and would no longer be a member of the community of the returned captives.
That was the decision of the officers and older
leaders.

9 So within three days all the people of Judah and Benjamin gathered in Jerusalem. It
was the twentieth day of the ninth month. All
the people were sitting in the open place in
front of the Temple and were upset because of
the meeting and because it was raining. 10 Ezra
the priest stood up and said to them, "You
have been unfaithful and have married non-
Jewish women. You have made Israel more
guilty. 11 Now, confess it to the LORD, the God of
your ancestors. Do his will and separate yourselves from the people living around you and
from your non-Jewish wives."

12 Then the whole group answered Ezra with
a loud voice, "Ezra, you're right! We must do
what you say. 13 But there are many people here,
and it's the rainy season. We can't stand outside,
and this problem can't be solved in a day or
two, because we have sinned badly. 14 Let our
officers make a decision for the whole group.
Then let everyone in our towns who has married a non-Jewish woman meet with the older
leaders and judges of each town at a planned
time, until the hot anger of our God turns away
from us." 15 Only Jonathan son of Asahel, Jahze-
iah son of Tikvah, Meshullam, and Shabbethai
the Levite were against the plan.

16 So the returned captives did what was
suggested. Ezra the priest chose men who were
leaders of the family groups and named one
from each family division. On the first day of
the tenth month they sat down to study each
case. 17 By the first day of the first month, they
had finished with all the men who had married non-Jewish women.

THOSE GUILTY OF MARRYING NON-JEWISH WOMEN

18 These are the descendants of the priests
who had married foreign women:

From the descendants of Jeshua son of Jozadak and Jeshua's brothers: Maaseiah, Eliezer,
Jarib, and Gedaliah. 19 (They all promised to
divorce their wives, and each one brought a
male sheep from the flock as a penalty offering.)

20 From the descendants of Immer: Hanani
and Zebadiah.

21 From the descendants of Harim: Maaseiah, Elijah, Shemaiah, Jehiel, and Uzziah.

22 From the descendants of Pashhur: Elioenai, Maaseiah, Ishmael, Nethanel, Jozabad, and
Elasah.

23 Among the Levites: Jozabad, Shimei, Kela-
iah (also called Kelita), Pethahiah, Judah, and
Eliezer.

24 Among the singers: Eliashib.

Among the gatekeepers: Shallum, Telem,
and Uri.

25 And among the other Israelites, these
married non-Jewish women:

From the descendants of Parosh: Ramiah,
Izziah, Malkijah, Mijamin, Eleazar, Malkijah,
and Benaiah.

26 From the descendants of Elam: Mattaniah,
Zechariah, Jehiel, Abdi, Jeremoth, and Elijah.

27 From the descendants of Zattu: Elioenai,
Eliashib, Mattaniah, Jeremoth, Zabad, and
Aziza.

28 From the descendants of Bebai: Jehohanan, Hananiah, Zabbai, and Athlai.

29 From the descendants of Bani: Meshullam, Malluch, Adaiah, Jashub, Sheal, and Jeremoth.

30 From the descendants of Pahath-Moab:
Adna, Kelal, Benaiah, Maaseiah, Mattaniah,
Bezalel, Binnui, and Manasseh.

31 From the descendants of Harim: Eliezer,
Ishijah, Malkijah, Shemaiah, Shimeon, 32 Benjamin, Malluch, and Shemariah.

33 From the descendants of Hashum: Matte-
nai, Mattattah, Zabad, Eliphelet, Jeremai, Manasseh, and Shimei.

34 From the descendants of Bani: Maadai,
Amram, Uel, 35 Benaiah, Bedeiah, Keluhi, 36 Va-
niah, Meremoth, Eliashib, 37 Mattaniah, Matte-
nai, and Jaasu.

38 From the descendants of Binnui: Shimei,
39 Shelemiah, Nathan, Adaiah, 40 Macnadebai,
Shashai, Sharai, 41 Azarel, Shelemiah, Shemariah, 42 Shallum, Amariah, and Joseph.

43 From the descendants of Nebo: Jeiel, Mattithiah, Zabad, Zebina, Jaddai, Joel, and Benaiah.

44 All these men had married non-Jewish
women, and some of them had children by
these wives.

Nehemiah

CONTENT Nehemiah was the administrative assistant and *wine taster* for the king. That means one of his job responsibilities was to taste the king's wine to make sure it wasn't poisoned. If Nehemiah drank the wine and fell down dead, that was a big clue to the king that something might be amiss. Now that's a good job to highlight on career awareness day, huh?

Short of the possible poisoning scenario, Nehemiah really did have a lot of authority and prestige in his position as a government official. He asked for a leave of absence, though. Many Jews had traveled back to Jerusalem to rebuild the city. The Temple was rebuilt, but the city wall was still in ruins. Nehemiah wanted to help. Amazingly enough, the king let him go.

The Book of Nehemiah is famous for its down-to-earth story about organization. Nehemiah and his workers finished the wall in fifty-two days. That was a feat considering the wall was wide enough for the workmen to walk all the way around the city on top of it. It was even more of a feat considering they had to do a lot of the work with a tool in one hand and a weapon in the other.

Outline

1:1—2:10 .... King Artaxerxes Sends Nehemiah to Jerusalem
2:11—4:23 .... Rebuilding the Walls of Jerusalem
5:1–19 .... Nehemiah's Concern for the Poor
6:1—7:3 .... The Wall Is Finished, in Spite of Enemy Plots
7:4–73 .... The Captives Who Returned
8:1–18 .... Ezra Reads God's Teachings to the People, and They Celebrate the Feast of Shelters
9:1–37 .... The People Confess Their Sins
9:38—10:39 .... The People Sign an Agreement to Obey the Lord
11:1–36 .... The People Who Settled in Jerusalem and Judah
12:1–26 .... Priests and Levites Who Returned from Exile
12:27–47 .... Nehemiah Dedicates the City Wall
13:1–31 .... Changes Nehemiah Made

Purpose Leaders with vision and courage can set the direction of a society.

Themes Godly Leadership, Cooperation, Opposition to Success

Date of writing 457–444 B.C.

"They read from the Book of the Teachings of God and explained what it meant so the people understood what was being read" (8:8).

Bible Talk

God Uses People in All Professions

Sometimes we think that God will only use people whose job is in the church or in the pulpit. That is not true at all. God uses people who have faith in him wherever they are. Nehemiah is a great example of this. Nehemiah was a government official. God did change Nehemiah's place of work in the course of using him, but he didn't change him into a prophet or a priest. He just changed his place of operation from a palace to a city. Nehemiah's gift was still the gift of organization. God used that gift for his glory whether Nehemiah was serving a king or serving his people.

FEAST OF SHELTERS

If you've read much of the Old Testament, you know that the Jews had a lot of traditions. They had feasts. They had holy days. It could seem like they were always celebrating *something*.

God established most of those traditions. He established them as a kind of 3-D history book. Each of the Jewish feasts commemorated a big event in their history where God really pulled them through. Passover, for instance, was a feast that reminded the people how God brought them out of Egypt. The Feast of Shelters, which Nehemiah reinstated, reminded them of God's provision when they camped out in the wilderness for forty years.

In a world where books were scarce and video cameras were nonexistent, traditions helped the Hebrews remember their history and God's goodness.

NEHEMIAH'S PRAYER

1These are the words of Nehemiah son of
Hacaliah.
In the month of Kislev in the twentieth
year,[n] I, Nehemiah, was in the capital city of
Susa. 2One of my brothers named Hanani
came with some other men from Judah. I
asked them about Jerusalem and the Jewish
people who lived through the captivity.
3They answered me, "Those who are left
from the captivity are back in Judah, but they
are in much trouble and are full of shame. The
wall around Jerusalem is broken down, and its
gates have been burned."
4When I heard these things, I sat down and
cried for several days. I was sad and ate nothing. I prayed to the God of heaven,
5"LORD, God of heaven, you are
the great God who is to be
respected. You are loyal, and
you keep your agreement
with those who love you and
obey your commands. 6Look
and listen carefully. Hear the
prayer that I, your servant, am praying to you
day and night for your servants, the Israelites.
I confess the sins we Israelites have done
against you. My father's family and I have
sinned against you. 7We have been wicked toward you and have not obeyed the commands,
rules, and laws you gave your servant Moses.
8"Remember what you taught your servant
Moses, saying, 'If you are unfaithful, I will scatter you among the nations. 9But if you return
to me and obey my commands, I will gather
your people from the far ends of the earth.
And I will bring them from captivity to where
I have chosen to be worshiped.'
10"They are your servants and your people,
whom you have saved with your great
strength and power. 11Lord, listen carefully to
the prayer of your servant and the prayers of

FEELINGS

What should we do when we are sad? (1:4)

WHAT'S IT MEAN?

A quick word about the author: Nehemiah was a servant of the king of Persia. At the beginning of the story, he was in Susa (in what is now Iran), where Persian kings went for the winter. More importantly, Nehemiah was almost a thousand miles away from his homeland.

Nehemiah 1:1

1:1 twentieth year This is probably referring to the twentieth year King Artaxerxes I ruled Persia.

Promise

HE PROMISES YOU CAN ALWAYS RETURN TO HIM.

Remember what you taught your servant Moses, saying, "If you are unfaithful, I will scatter you among the nations. But if you return to me and obey my commands, I will gather your people from the far ends of the earth. And I will bring them from captivity to where I have chosen to be worshiped" (Neh. 1:8–9).

So you haven't spoken to God in a long time. Okay, a really long time. You made this big commitment, told all your family and friends, started going to church, went on a few retreats, sang around a campfire, bought a Bible with your name on it—the whole deal. Then you never followed through. You put the Bible in a drawer, slept in on Sundays, stopped talking to God, and eventually you just turned your back and walked away.

It's been a long time—years. The yearning that drew you to God is back, but even bigger, and now there's guilt—the guilt that comes from meeting the Maker of the universe and then trying to live like he doesn't exist. Is God disappointed? Probably. Has he given up on you? Nope. What's next? Return to God. He is kind and compassionate. He will welcome you home. Don't delay—every day lived apart from God is a totally wasted day.

SEE FOR YOURSELF:

Joel 2:12–13; Rom. 3:23–24

your servants who love to honor you. Give
me, your servant, success today; allow this
king to show kindness to me."
I was the one who served
wine to the king.

> "Lord, listen carefully to the prayer of your servant and the prayers of your servants who love to honor you." (Nehemiah 1:11a)

NEHEMIAH IS SENT TO JERUSALEM

2

1It was the month of
Nisan in the twentieth year
Artaxerxes was king. He
wanted some wine, so I took
some and gave it to the king. I
had not been sad in his presence
before. 2So the king said, "Why does your
face look sad even though you are not sick?
Your heart must be sad."
Then I was very afraid. 3I
said to the king, "May the
king live forever! My face is
sad because the city where
my ancestors are buried lies
in ruins, and its gates have
been destroyed by fire."

> **PRAYER**
> Can we pray anywhere at any time? (2:2–5)

4Then the king said to me, "What do you
want?"
First I prayed to the God of heaven. 5Then
I answered the king, "If you are willing and if
I have pleased you, send me to the city in Judah where my ancestors are buried so I can
rebuild it."
6The queen was sitting next to the king. He
asked me, "How long will your trip take, and
when will you get back?" It pleased the king to
send me, so I set a time.
7I also said to him, "If you are willing, give
me letters for the governors of Trans-Euphrates.
Tell them to let me pass safely through their
lands on my way to Judah. 8And may I have a
letter for Asaph, the keeper of the king's forest,
telling him to give me timber? I will need it to
make boards for the gates of the palace, which
is by the Temple, and for the city wall, and for
the house in which I will live." So the king gave
me the letters, because God was showing kindness to me. 9Then I went to the governors of
Trans-Euphrates and gave them the king's letters. The king had also sent army officers and
soldiers on horses with me.
10When Sanballat the Horonite and Tobiah
the Ammonite officer heard about this, they
were upset that someone had come to help the
Israelites.

NEHEMIAH INSPECTS JERUSALEM

11I went to Jerusalem and stayed there three
days. 12Then at night I started out with a few
men. I had not told anyone what God had
caused me to do for Jerusalem. There were no
animals with me except the
one I was riding.
13I went out at night
through the Valley Gate. I
rode toward the Dragon Well
and the Trash Gate, inspecting the walls of Jerusalem
that had been broken down
and the gates that had been
destroyed by fire. 14Then I
rode on toward the Fountain
Gate and the King's Pool, but
there was not enough room for the
animal I was riding to pass through. 15So I
went up the valley at night, inspecting the wall.
Finally, I turned and went back in through the
Valley Gate. 16The guards did not know where
I had gone or what I was doing. I had not yet
said anything to the Jewish people, the priests,
the important men, the officers, or any of the
others who would do the work.

> **WHAT'S IT MEAN?**
>
> Historical documents indicate that a man named Sanballat served as the governor of Samaria, the land to the north of Jerusalem—a region that had once been part of the Israelite kingdom. A devastating Assyrian attack in 722 B.C. led to the fall of Samaria. As was their custom with the territories they conquered, the Assyrians took many Israelites away as captives and brought in many foreigners to live in Canaan. It wasn't long before the Israelites who were left behind started getting involved with the new kids in town. Not only did the Israelites begin marrying and having kids with the foreigners, they also adopted their idol worship. This mingling continued generation after generation until the distinction between the Israelites and the foreigners disappeared altogether. The descendants of these mixed marriages were known as Samaritans.
>
> Nehemiah 2:10

17Then I said to them, "You can see the trouble we have here. Jerusalem is a pile of ruins,
and its gates have been burned. Come, let's rebuild the wall of Jerusalem so we won't be full
of shame any longer." 18I also told them how
God had been kind to me and what the king
had said to me.

Then they answered, "Let's start rebuilding."
So they began to work hard.
19But when Sanballat the Horonite, Tobiah
the Ammonite officer, and Geshem the Arab
heard about it, they made fun of us and
laughed at us. They said, "What are you doing?
Are you turning against the king?"
20But I answered them, "The God of heaven
will give us success. We, his servants, will start
rebuilding, but you have no share, claim, or
memorial in Jerusalem."

BUILDERS OF THE WALL

3
1Eliashib the high priest and his fellow
priests went to work and rebuilt the Sheep Gate.
They gave it to the Lord's service and set its
doors in place. They worked as far as the Tower
of the Hundred and gave it to the Lord's service.
Then they went on to the Tower of Hananel.
2Next to them, the men of Jericho built part of
the wall, and Zaccur son of Imri built next to
them.

WHAT'S IT MEAN?

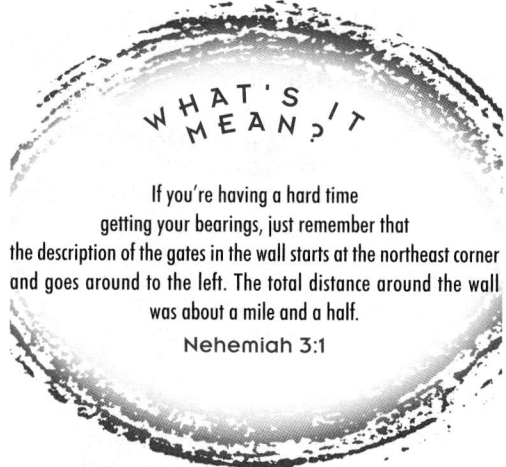

If you're having a hard time getting your bearings, just remember that the description of the gates in the wall starts at the northeast corner and goes around to the left. The total distance around the wall was about a mile and a half.

Nehemiah 3:1

3The sons of Hassenaah rebuilt the Fish
Gate, laying its boards and setting its doors,
bolts, and bars in place. 4Meremoth son of
Uriah, the son of Hakkoz, made repairs next to
them. Meshullam son of Berekiah, the son of
Meshezabel, made repairs next to Meremoth.
And Zadok son of Baana made repairs next to
Meshullam. 5The men from Tekoa made repairs next to them, but the leading men of Tekoa would not work under their supervisors.
6Joiada son of Paseah and Meshullam son of
Besodeiah repaired the Old Gate. They laid its
boards and set its doors, bolts, and bars in
place. 7Next to them, Melatiah from Gibeon,
other men from Gibeon and Mizpah, and Ja-
don from Meronoth made repairs. These places
were ruled by the governor of Trans-Euphrates.
8Next to them, Uzziel son of Harhaiah, a goldsmith, made repairs. And next to him, Hananiah, a perfume maker, made repairs. These
men rebuilt Jerusalem as far as the Broad Wall.
9The next part of the wall was repaired by Rephaiah son of Hur, the ruler of half of the district of Jerusalem. 10Next to him, Jedaiah son of
Harumaph made repairs opposite his own
house. And next to him, Hattush son of Hash-
abneiah made repairs. 11Malkijah son of Harim
and Hasshub son of Pahath-Moab repaired
another part of the wall and the Tower of the
Ovens. 12Next to them Shallum son of Hallo-
hesh, the ruler of half of the district of Jerusalem, and his daughters made repairs.
13Hanun and the people of Zanoah repaired
the Valley Gate, rebuilding it and setting its
doors, bolts, and bars in place. They also repaired the five hundred yards of the wall to the
Trash Gate.
14Malkijah son of Recab, the ruler of the
district of Beth Hakkerem, repaired the Trash
Gate. He rebuilt that gate and set its doors,
bolts, and bars in place.
15Shallun son of Col-Hozeh, the ruler of the
district of Mizpah, repaired the Fountain Gate.
He rebuilt it, put a roof over it, and set its
doors, bolts, and bars in place. He also repaired the wall of the Pool of Siloam next to
the King's Garden all the way to the steps that
went down from the older part of the city.
16Next to Shallun was Nehemiah[n] son of Az-
buk, the ruler of half of the district of Beth Zur.
He made repairs opposite the tombs of David
and as far as the man-made pool and the
House of the Heroes.
17Next to him, the Levites made repairs,
working under Rehum son of Bani. Next to
him, Hashabiah, the ruler of half of the district
of Keilah, for his district. 18Next to him, Binnui
son of Henadad and his Levites made repairs.
Binnui was the ruler of the other half of the
district of Keilah. 19Next to them, Ezer son of
Jeshua, the ruler of Mizpah, repaired another
part of the wall. He worked across from the
way up to the armory, as far as the bend.
20Next to him, Baruch son of Zabbai worked
hard on the wall that went from the bend to
the entrance to the house of Eliashib, the high
priest. 21Next to him, Meremoth son of Uriah,
the son of Hakkoz, repaired the wall that went
from the entrance to Eliashib's house to the far
end of it.

3:16 Nehemiah This is a different Nehemiah than the one who wrote this book.

22 Next to him worked the priests from the
surrounding area. 23 Next to them, Benjamin
and Hasshub made repairs in front of their
own house. Next to them, Azariah son of Maaseiah, the son of Ananiah, made repairs beside his own house. 24 Next to him, Binnui son
of Henadad repaired the wall that went from
Azariah's house to the bend and on to the corner. 25 Palal son of Uzai worked across from the
bend and by the tower on the upper palace,
which is near the courtyard of the king's guard.
Next to Palal, Pedaiah son of Parosh made repairs. 26 The Temple servants who lived on the
hill of Ophel made repairs as far as a point
opposite the Water Gate. They worked toward
the east and the tower that extends from the
palace. 27 Next to them, the people of Tekoa repaired the wall from the great tower that extends from the palace to the wall of Ophel.
28 The priests made repairs above the Horse
Gate, each working in front of his own house.
29 Next to them, Zadok son of Immer made repairs across from his own house. Next to him,
Shemaiah son of Shecaniah, the guard of the
East Gate, made repairs. 30 Next to him, Hananiah son of Shelemiah, and Hanun, the sixth
son of Zalaph, made repairs on another part of
the wall. Next to them, Meshullam son of Berekiah made repairs across from where he lived.
31 Next to him, Malkijah, one of the goldsmiths,
made repairs. He worked as far as the house of
the Temple servants and the traders, which is
across from the Inspection Gate, and as far as
the room above the corner of the wall. 32 The
goldsmiths and the traders made repairs between the room above the corner of the wall
and the Sheep Gate.

THOSE AGAINST THE REBUILDING

4
1 When Sanballat heard we were rebuilding
the wall, he was very angry, even furious. He
made fun of the Jewish people. 2 He said to his
friends and those with power in Samaria,
"What are these weak Jews doing? Will they rebuild the wall? Will they offer sacrifices? Can
they finish it in one day? Can they bring stones
back to life from piles of trash and ashes?"
3 Tobiah the Ammonite, who was next to
Sanballat, said, "If a fox climbed up on the
stone wall they are building, it would break it
down."
4 I prayed, "Hear us, our God. We are hated.
Turn the insults of Sanballat and Tobiah back
on their own heads. Let them be captured and
stolen like valuables. 5 Do not hide their guilt or
take away their sins so that you can't see them,
because they have insulted the builders."
6 So we rebuilt the wall to half its height, because the people were willing to work.
7 But Sanballat, Tobiah, the Arabs, the Ammonites, and the people from Ashdod were
very angry when they heard that the repairs to
Jerusalem's walls were continuing and that the
holes in the wall were being closed. 8 So they all
made plans to come to Jerusalem and fight and
stir up trouble. 9 But we prayed to our God and
appointed guards to watch for them day and
night.

WHAT'S IT MEAN?

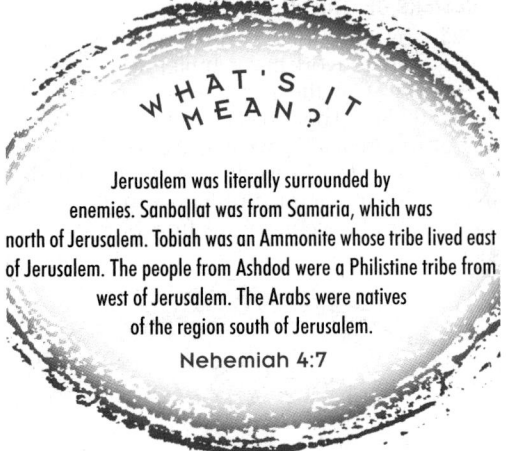

Jerusalem was literally surrounded by enemies. Sanballat was from Samaria, which was north of Jerusalem. Tobiah was an Ammonite whose tribe lived east of Jerusalem. The people from Ashdod were a Philistine tribe from west of Jerusalem. The Arabs were natives of the region south of Jerusalem.

Nehemiah 4:7

10 The people of Judah said, "The workers
are getting tired. There is so much trash we
cannot rebuild the wall."
11 And our enemies said, "The Jews won't
know or see anything until we come among
them and kill them and stop the work."
12 Then the Jewish people who lived near
our enemies came and told us ten times,
"Everywhere you turn, the enemy will attack
us." 13 So I put people behind the lowest places
along the wall—the open places—and I put
families together with their
swords, spears, and bows.
14 Then I looked around and
stood up and said to the important men, the leaders, and
the rest of the people: "Don't
be afraid of them. Remember
the Lord, who is great and
powerful. Fight for your brothers, your sons
and daughters, your wives, and your homes."
15 Then our enemies heard that we knew
about their plans and that God had ruined
their plans. So we all went back to the wall,
each to his own work.
16 From that day on, half my people worked
on the wall. The other half was ready with
spears, shields, bows, and armor. The officers

ENEMIES

Should we be afraid of our enemies? (4:14)

stood in back of the people of Judah 17who
were building the wall. Those who carried materials did their work with one hand and carried a weapon with the other. 18Each builder
wore his sword at his side as he worked. The
man who blew the trumpet to warn the people
stayed next to me.
19Then I said to the important men, the
leaders, and the rest of the people, "This is a
very big job. We are spreading out along the
wall so that we are far apart. 20Wherever you
hear the sound of the trumpet, assemble there.
Our God will fight for us."
21So we continued to work with half the
men holding spears from sunrise till the stars
came out. 22At that time I also said to the people, "Let every man and his helper stay inside
Jerusalem at night. They can be our guards at
night and workmen during the day." 23Neither
I, my brothers, my workers, nor the guards
with me ever took off our clothes. Each person
carried his weapon even when he went for
water.

NEHEMIAH HELPS POOR PEOPLE

5 1The men and their wives complained
loudly against their fellow Jews. 2Some of them
were saying, "We have many sons and daughters in our families. To eat and stay alive, we
need grain."
3Others were saying, "We are borrowing
money against our fields, vineyards, and
homes to get grain because there is not much
food."
4And still others were saying, "We are borrowing money to pay the king's tax on our
fields and vineyards. 5We are just like our fellow Jews, and our sons are like their sons. But
we have to sell our sons and daughters as
slaves. Some of our daughters have already
been sold. But there is nothing we can do, because our fields and vineyards already belong
to other people."
6When I heard their complaints about these
things, I was very angry. 7After I thought about
it, I accused the important people and the leaders, "You are charging your own brothers too
much interest." So I called a large meeting to
deal with them. 8I said to them, "As much as
possible, we have bought freedom for our fellow Jews who had been sold to foreigners.
Now you are selling your fellow Jews to us!"
The leaders were quiet and had nothing to say.
9Then I said, "What you are doing is not
right. Don't you fear God? Don't let our foreign
enemies shame us. 10I, my brothers, and my
men are also lending money and grain to the
people. But stop charging them so much for
this. 11Give back their fields, vineyards,
olive trees, and houses
right now. Also give
back the extra amount
you charged—the hundredth
part of the money, grain, new
wine, and oil."
12They said, "We will give it
back and not demand any-
thing more from them. We will
do as you say."
Then I called for the priests, and I made the
important men and leaders take an oath to do
what they had said. 13Also I shook out the
folds of my robe and said, "In this way may
God shake out everyone who does not keep
his promise. May God shake him out of his
house and out of the things that are his. Let
that person be shaken out and emptied!"
Then the whole group said, "Amen," and
they praised the LORD. So the people did what
they had promised.
14I was appointed governor in the land of
Judah in the twentieth year of King Artaxerxes'
rule. I was governor of Judah for twelve years,
until his thirty-second year. During that time
neither my brothers nor I ate the food that was
allowed for a governor. 15But the governors
before me had placed a heavy load on the
people. They took about one pound of silver
from each person, along with food and wine.
The governors' helpers before me also controlled the people, but I did not do that, because I feared God. 16I worked on the wall, as
did all my men who were gathered there. We
did not buy any fields.
17Also, I fed one hundred fifty Jewish people
and officers at my table, as well as those who
came from the nations around us. 18This is
what was prepared every day: one ox, six
good sheep, and birds. And every ten days
there were all kinds of wine. But I never demanded the food that was due a governor, because the people were already working very
hard.
19Remember to be kind to me, my God, for
all the good I have done for these people.

ENCOURAGEMENT

How should we stand up for those who need help? (5:7–11)

MORE PROBLEMS FOR NEHEMIAH

6 1Then Sanballat, Tobiah, Geshem the Arab,
and our other enemies heard that I had rebuilt
the wall and that there was not one gap in it.
But I had not yet set the doors in the gates. 2So
Sanballat and Geshem sent me this message:
"Come, Nehemiah, let's meet together in Kephi-
rim on the plain of Ono."

But they were planning to harm me. 3So I
sent messengers to them with this answer: "I
am doing a great work, and I can't come down.
I don't want the work to stop while I leave to
meet you." 4Sanballat and Geshem sent the
same message to me four times, and each time
I sent back the same answer.
5The fifth time Sanballat sent his helper to
me with the message, and in his hand was an
unsealed letter. 6This is what was written:

> A report is going around to all the
> nations, and Geshem says it is true, that
> you and the Jewish people are planning
> to turn against the king and that you are
> rebuilding the wall. They say you are go-
> ing to be their king 7and that you have
> appointed prophets to announce in Je-
> rusalem: "There is a king of Judah!" The
> king will hear about this. So come, let's
> discuss this together.

8So I sent him back this answer: "Nothing
you are saying is really happening. You are just
making it up in your own mind."
9Our enemies were trying to scare us, thinking, "They will get too weak to work. Then the
wall will not be finished."
But I prayed, "God, make me strong."
10One day I went to the house of Shemaiah
son of Delaiah, the son of Mehetabel. Shemaiah had to stay at home. He said, "Nehemiah,
let's meet in the Temple of God. Let's go inside
the Temple and close the doors, because men
are coming at night to kill you."
11But I said, "Should a man like me run
away? Should I run for my life into the Temple?
I will not go." 12I knew that God had not sent
him but that Tobiah and Sanballat had paid
him to prophesy against me. 13They paid him to
frighten me so I would do this and sin. Then
they could give me a bad name to shame me.
14I prayed, "My God, remember Tobiah and
Sanballat and what they have done. Also remember the prophetess Noadiah and the other
prophets who have been trying to frighten me."

THE WALL IS FINISHED

15The wall of Jerusalem was completed on
the twenty-fifth day of the month of Elul. It
took fifty-two days to rebuild. 16When all our
enemies heard about it and all the nations
around us saw it, they were shamed. They then
understood that the work had been done with
the help of our God.
17Also in those days the important men of
Judah sent many letters to Tobiah, and he answered them. 18Many Jewish people had
promised to be faithful to Tobiah, because he
was the son-in-law of Shecaniah son of Arah.
And Tobiah's son Jehohanan had married
the daughter of Meshullam son of Berekiah.
19These important men kept telling me about
the good things Tobiah was doing, and then
they would tell Tobiah what I said about him.
So Tobiah sent letters to frighten me.
7 1After the wall had been rebuilt and I had
set the doors in place, the gatekeepers, singers,
and Levites were chosen. 2I put my brother
Hanani, along with Hananiah, the commander
of the palace, in charge of Jerusalem. Hananiah
was honest and feared God more than most
people. 3I said to them, "The gates of Jerusalem
should not be opened until the sun is hot.
While the gatekeepers are still on duty, have
them shut and bolt the doors. Appoint people
who live in Jerusalem as guards, and put some
at guard posts and some near their own
houses."

THE CAPTIVES WHO RETURNED

4The city was large and roomy, but there
were few people in it, and the houses had not
yet been rebuilt. 5Then my God caused me to
gather the important men, the leaders, and the
common people so I could register them by
families. I found the family history of those
who had returned first. This is what I found
written there:
6These are the people of the area who returned from captivity, whom Nebuchadnezzar
king of Babylon had taken away. They returned to Jerusalem and Judah, each going
back to his own town. 7These people returned
with Zerubbabel, Jeshua, Nehemiah, Azariah,

WHAT'S IT MEAN?

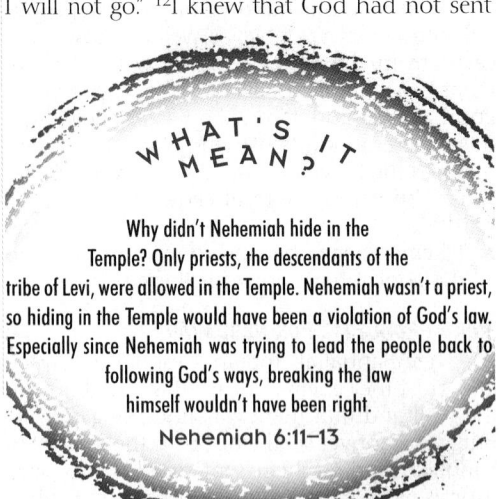

Why didn't Nehemiah hide in the Temple? Only priests, the descendants of the tribe of Levi, were allowed in the Temple. Nehemiah wasn't a priest, so hiding in the Temple would have been a violation of God's law. Especially since Nehemiah was trying to lead the people back to following God's ways, breaking the law himself wouldn't have been right.

Nehemiah 6:11–13

Raamiah, Nahamani, Mordecai, Bilshan, Mispereth, Bigvai, Nehum, and Baanah.

These are the people from Israel: 8the descendants of Parosh—2,172; 9the descendants of Shephatiah—372; 10the descendants of Arah—652; 11the descendants of Pahath-Moab (through the family of Jeshua and Joab)—2,818; 12the descendants of Elam—1,254; 13the descendants of Zattu—845; 14the descendants of Zaccai—760; 15the descendants of Binnui—648; 16the descendants of Bebai—628; 17the descendants of Azgad—2,322; 18the descendants of Adonikam—667; 19the descendants of Bigvai—2,067; 20the descendants of Adin—655; 21the descendants of Ater (through Hezekiah)—98; 22the descendants of Hashum—328; 23the descendants of Bezai—324; 24the descendants of Hariph—112; 25the descendants of Gibeon—95.

26These are the people from the towns of Bethlehem and Netophah—188; 27of Anathoth—128; 28of Beth Azmaveth—42; 29of Kiriath Jearim, Kephirah, and Beeroth—743; 30of Ramah and Geba—621; 31of Micmash—122; 32of Bethel and Ai—123; 33of the other Nebo—52; 34of the other Elam—1,254; 35of Harim—320; 36of Jericho—345; 37of Lod, Hadid, and Ono—721; 38of Senaah—3,930.

39These are the priests: the descendants of Jedaiah (through the family of Jeshua)—973; 40the descendants of Immer—1,052; 41the descendants of Pashhur—1,247; 42the descendants of Harim—1,017.

43These are the Levites: the descendants of Jeshua (through Kadmiel through the family of Hodaviah)—74.

44These are the singers: the descendants of Asaph—148.

45These are the gatekeepers: the descendants of Shallum, Ater, Talmon, Akkub, Hatita, and Shobai—138.

46These are the Temple servants: the descendants of Ziha, Hasupha, Tabbaoth, 47Keros, Sia, Padon, 48Lebana, Hagaba, Shalmai, 49Hanan, Giddel, Gahar, 50Reaiah, Rezin, Nekoda, 51Gazzam, Uzza, Paseah, 52Besai, Meunim, Nephussim, 53Bakbuk, Hakupha, Harhur, 54Bazluth, Mehida, Harsha, 55Barkos, Sisera, Temah, 56Neziah, and Hatipha.

57These are the descendants of the servants of Solomon: the descendants of Sotai, Sophereth, Perida, 58Jaala, Darkon, Giddel, 59Shephatiah, Hattil, Pokereth-Hazzebaim, and Amon.

60The Temple servants and the descendants of the servants of Solomon totaled 392 people.

61Some people came to Jerusalem from the towns of Tel Melah, Tel Harsha, Kerub, Addon, and Immer, but they could not prove that their ancestors came from Israel. Here are their names and their number: 62the descendants of Delaiah, Tobiah, and Nekoda—642.

63And these priests could not prove that their ancestors came from Israel: the descendants of Hobaiah, Hakkoz, and Barzillai. (He had married a daughter of Barzillai from Gilead and was called by her family name.)

64These people searched for their family records, but they could not find them. So they could not be priests, because they were thought to be unclean. 65The governor ordered them not to eat any of the holy food until a priest settled this matter by using the Urim and Thummim.

66The total number of those who returned was 42,360. 67This is not counting their 7,337 male and female servants and the 245 male and female singers with them. 68They had 736 horses, 245 mules, 69435 camels, and 6,720 donkeys.

70Some of the family leaders gave to the work. The governor gave to the treasury about 19 pounds of gold, 50 bowls, and 530 pieces of clothing for the priests. 71Some of the family leaders gave about 375 pounds of gold and about 2,660 pounds of silver to the treasury for the work. 72The total of what the other people gave was about 375 pounds of gold, about 2,250 pounds of silver, and 67 pieces of clothing for the priests. 73So these people all settled in their own towns: the priests, the Levites, the gatekeepers, the singers, the Temple servants, and all the other people of Israel.

EZRA READS THE TEACHINGS

By the seventh month the Israelites were settled in their own towns.

8

1All the people of Israel gathered together in the square by the Water Gate. They asked Ezra the teacher to bring out the Book of the Teachings of Moses, which the LORD had given to Israel.

2So on the first day of the seventh month, Ezra the priest brought out the Teachings for the crowd. Men, women, and all who could listen and understand had gathered. 3At the square by the Water Gate Ezra read the Teachings out loud from early morning until noon to the men, women, and everyone who could listen and understand. All the people listened carefully to the Book of the Teachings.

4Ezra the teacher stood on a high wooden platform that had been built just for this time. On his right were Mattithiah, Shema, Anaiah, Uriah, Hilkiah, and Maaseiah. And on his left

were Pedaiah, Mishael, Malkijah, Hashum,
Hashbaddanah, Zechariah, and Meshullam.
[5]Ezra opened the book in full view of
everyone, because he was above them. As he
opened it, all the people stood up.
[6]Ezra praised the LORD, the great
God, and all the people held up
their hands and said, "Amen!
Amen!" Then they bowed down
and worshiped the LORD with
their faces to the ground.
[7]These Levites explained the
Teachings to the people as they stood
there: Jeshua, Bani, Sherebiah, Jamin, Akkub,
Shabbethai, Hodiah, Maaseiah, Kelita,
Azariah, Jozabad, Hanan, and
Pelaiah. [8]They read from the
Book of the Teachings of God
and explained what it meant
so the people understood
what was being read.
[9]Then Nehemiah the gover-
nor, Ezra the priest and teacher, and the Levites
who were teaching said to all the people, "This
is a holy day to the LORD your God. Don't be
sad or cry." All the people had been crying as
they listened to the words of the Teachings.
[10]Nehemiah said, "Go and enjoy good food
and sweet drinks. Send some to people who
have none, because today is a holy day to the
Lord. Don't be sad, because the joy of the LORD
will make you strong."
[11]The Levites helped calm the people, saying, "Be quiet, because this is a holy day. Don't
be sad."
[12]Then all the people went away to eat and
drink, to send some of their food to others, and
to celebrate with great joy. They finally understood what they had been taught.
[13]On the second day of the month, the leaders of all the families, the priests, and the Levites
met with Ezra the teacher. They gathered to
study the words of the Teachings. [14]This is what
they found written in the Teachings: The LORD
commanded through Moses that the people of
Israel were to live in shelters during the feast of
the seventh month. [15]The people were supposed to preach this message and spread it
through all their towns and in Jerusalem: "Go
out into the mountains, and bring back
branches from olive and wild olive trees, myrtle
trees, palms, and shade trees. Make shelters
with them, as it is written."
[16]So the people went out and got tree
branches. They built shelters on their roofs,[n] in
their courtyards, in the courtyards of the Temple, in the square by the Water Gate, and in the
square next to the Gate of Ephraim.
[17]The whole group that had come
back from captivity built shelters
and lived in them. The Israelites
had not done this since the time
of Joshua son of Nun. And they
were very happy.
[18]Ezra read to them every day
from the Book of the Teachings,
from the first day to the last. The people of Israel celebrated the feast for seven days,
and then on the eighth day the people gathered as the law said.

"Ezra praised the LORD, the great God." (Nehemiah 8:6a)

BIBLE

Is it important to understand the Bible? (8:8)

WHAT'S IT MEAN?

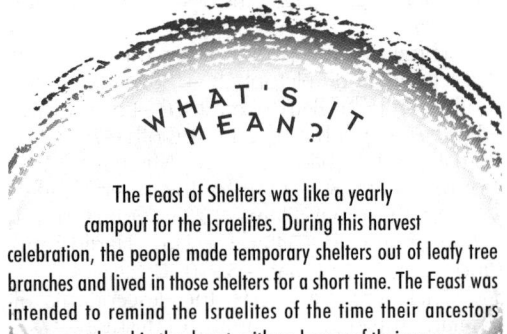

The Feast of Shelters was like a yearly campout for the Israelites. During this harvest celebration, the people made temporary shelters out of leafy tree branches and lived in those shelters for a short time. The Feast was intended to remind the Israelites of the time their ancestors wandered in the desert, with no homes of their own, after Moses led them out of Egypt.

Nehemiah 8:14

ISRAEL CONFESSES SINS

9 [1]On the twenty-fourth day of that same
month, the people of Israel gathered. They did
not eat, and they wore rough cloth and put
dust on their heads to show their sadness.
[2]Those people whose ancestors were from Israel had separated themselves from all foreigners. They stood and confessed their sins and
their ancestors' sins. [3]For a fourth of the day
they stood where they were and read from the
Book of the Teachings of the LORD their God.
For another fourth of the day they confessed
their sins and worshiped the LORD their God.
[4]These Levites were standing on the stairs:
Jeshua, Bani, Kadmiel, Shebaniah, Bunni, Sherebiah, Bani, and Kenani. They called out to the
LORD their God with loud voices. [5]Then these

8:16 roofs In Bible times houses were built with flat roofs. The roof was used for drying things such as flax and fruit. And it was used as an extra room, as a place for worship, and as a cool place to sleep in the summer.

Levites spoke: Jeshua, Kadmiel, Bani, Hashab-
neiah, Sherebiah, Hodiah, Shebaniah, and
Pethahiah. They said, "Stand up and praise the
LORD your God, who lives forever and ever."

THE PEOPLE'S PRAYER

"Blessed be your wonderful name.
It is more wonderful than all blessing
and praise.
6 You are the only LORD.
You made the heavens, even the highest
heavens,
with all the stars.
You made the earth and everything on it,
the seas and everything in them;
you give life to everything.
The heavenly army worships you.

7 "You are the LORD,
the God who chose Abram
and brought him out of Ur in Babylonia
and named him Abraham.
8 You found him faithful to you,
so you made an agreement with him
to give his descendants the land of the
Canaanites,
Hittites, Amorites,
Perizzites, Jebusites, and Girgashites.
You have kept your promise,
because you do what is right.

9 "You saw our ancestors suffering in Egypt
and heard them cry out at the Red Sea.
10 You did signs and miracles against the king
of Egypt,
and against all his officers and all his
people,
because you knew how proud they
were.
You became as famous as you are today.
11 You divided the sea in front of our
ancestors;
they walked through on dry ground.
But you threw the people chasing them
into the deep water,
like a stone thrown into mighty waters.
12 You led our ancestors with a pillar of
cloud by day
and with a pillar of fire at night.
It lit the way
they were supposed to go.
13 You came down to Mount
Sinai
and spoke from heaven
to our ancestors.
You gave them fair rules
and true teachings,
good orders and
commands.
14 You told them about your holy Sabbath
and gave them commands, orders, and
teachings
through your servant Moses.
15 When they were hungry, you gave them
bread from heaven.
When they were thirsty, you brought
them water from the rock.
You told them to enter and take over
the land you had promised to give them.

16 "But our ancestors were
proud and stubborn
and did not obey your
commands.
17 They refused to listen;
they forgot the miracles
you did for them.

On the Edge

You are the only LORD. You made the heavens, even the highest heavens, with all the stars. You made the earth and everything on it, the seas and everything in them; you give life to everything. The heavenly army worships you (Neh. 9:6).

God spoke everything you see into existence. Incredible. He made you and every person who has ever lived before you. He didn't copy someone else's idea. He didn't improve on an old design. The earth and the heavens and all things in them are totally original and straight from the mind of God. What a huge concept to process! Doing a science project can seem overwhelming to us, much less creating the whole world.

Because of his place as Creator, God deserves your respect and your honor. You don't just get physical life from him. You get spiritual life from him. He is the Source of the things that make you so alive—the ability to enjoy life, the capacity for love, laughter, peace, joy, work, play, rest. You can go to him and get replenished when you run low. He *is* your Life Preserver—life flows freely forever in him.

SEE FOR YOURSELF:
Gen. 1:1;
Ps. 95:3–7; 148:5–6;
Jer. 10:16; 51:15–16

BIBLE
Where did the Bible come from? (9:13–14)

FORGIVENESS
What is God known for? (9:17)

On the Edge

But you are a forgiving God. You are kind and full of mercy. You do not become angry quickly, and you have great love (Neh. 9:17b).

Patience should be put on the "endangered character trait" list. You rarely see patience anymore. Maybe everyone has already used up all their patience. No one wants to wait for anything—ever. Overnight mail moved too slowly, so someone invented the fax machine. But sometimes it takes a while for the fax to get through; so, thank goodness, someone invented e-mail. One push of a button, and your friend immediately has your message or very important document. Who knows what's next? Maybe think-mail, where you just have to think and your thoughts are instantly processed around the world.

So to say that God does "not become angry quickly" means he's patient with us—and we do try his patience! This is not to say that God is outdated in our fast-paced, we-need-to-know-now society. He's not. It's just that in our rush to know more and do more we have forgotten how to wait. God models the virtue for us. He is very patient, especially about important things, like waiting for the people he loves.

SEE FOR YOURSELF:
Neh. 9:30; Ps. 145:8; 2 Pet. 3:9

So they became stubborn and turned against you,
choosing a leader to take them back to slavery.
But you are a forgiving God.
You are kind and full of mercy.
You do not become angry quickly, and you have great love.
So you did not leave them.
18 Our ancestors even made an idol of a calf for themselves.
They said, 'This is your god, Israel, who brought you up out of Egypt.'
They spoke against you.

19 "You have great mercy,
so you did not leave them in the desert.
The pillar of cloud guided them by day,
and the pillar of fire led them at night,
lighting the way they were to go.
20 You gave your good Spirit to teach them.
You gave them manna to eat
and water when they were thirsty.
21 You took care of them for forty years in the desert;
they needed nothing.
Their clothes did not wear out,
and their feet did not swell.

FOLLOWING GOD

Who will teach us to follow God? (9:20)

22 "You gave them kingdoms and nations;
you gave them more land.
They took over the country of Sihon king of Heshbon
and the country of Og king of Bashan.
23 You made their children as many as the stars in the sky,
and you brought them into the land
that you told their fathers to enter and take over.
24 So their children went into the land and took over.
The Canaanites lived there, but you defeated them for our ancestors.
You handed over to them the Canaanites,
their kings, and the people of the land.
Our ancestors could do what they wanted with them.
25 They captured strong, walled cities and fertile land.
They took over houses full of good things,
wells that were already dug,
vineyards, olive trees, and many fruit trees.
They ate until they were full and grew fat;
they enjoyed your great goodness.

WHAT'S IT MEAN?

Sihon and Og were Amorite kings who ruled areas east of the Jordan River. In one of Israel's proudest victories, both kings were defeated by Moses and the Israelites, who were heading for the Promised Land.
Nehemiah 9:22

26 "But they were disobedient and turned
against you
and ignored your teachings.
Your prophets warned them to come back
to you,
but they killed those prophets
and spoke against you.
27 So you handed them over
to their enemies,
and their enemies
treated them badly.
But in this time of trouble
our ancestors cried
out to you,
and you heard from
heaven.
You had great mercy
and gave them saviors who saved them
from the power of their enemies.
28 But as soon as they had rest,
they again did what was evil.
So you left them to their enemies
who ruled over them.
When they cried out to you again,
you heard from heaven.
Because of your mercy, you saved them
again and again.
29 You warned them to return to your
teachings,
but they were proud and did not obey
your commands.
If someone obeys your laws, he will live,
but they sinned against your laws.
They were stubborn, unwilling, and
disobedient.
30 You were patient with them for many
years
and warned them by your Spirit
through the prophets,
but they did not pay attention.
So you handed them over to other
countries.
31 But because your mercy is great, you did
not kill them all or leave them.
You are a kind and merciful God.

FEELINGS
Does God care when we hurt? (9:27)

32 "And so, our God, you are the great and
mighty and wonderful God.
You keep your agreement of love.
Do not let all our trouble seem
unimportant to you.
This trouble has come to us, to our kings
and our leaders,
to our priests and prophets,
to our ancestors and all your people
from the days of the kings of Assyria until
today.
33 You have been fair in everything that has
happened to us;
you have been loyal, but we have been
wicked.
34 Our kings, leaders, priests, and ancestors
did not obey your teachings;
they did not pay attention to the
commands and warnings you gave
them.
35 Even when our ancestors were living in
their kingdom,
enjoying all the good things you had
given them,
enjoying the land that was fertile and
full of room,
they did not stop their evil ways.

36 "Look, we are slaves today
in the land you gave our ancestors.
They were to enjoy its fruit and its good
things,
but look, we are slaves here.
37 The land's great harvest belongs to the
kings you have put over us
because of our sins.
Those kings rule over us and our cattle as
they please,
so we are in much trouble.

THE PEOPLE'S AGREEMENT

38 "Because of all this, we are making an
agreement in writing, and our leaders, Levites,
and priests are putting their seals on it."

10 1 These are the men who sealed the agreement:
Nehemiah the governor, son of Hacaliah.
Zedekiah, 2 Seraiah, Azariah, Jeremiah,
3 Pashhur, Amariah, Malkijah, 4 Hattush, Shebaniah, Malluch, 5 Harim, Meremoth, Obadiah,
6 Daniel, Ginnethon, Baruch, 7 Meshullam, Abijah, Mijamin, 8 Maaziah, Bilgai, and Shemaiah.
These are the priests.
9 These are the Levites who sealed it: Jeshua
son of Azaniah, Binnui of the sons of Henadad, Kadmiel, 10 and their fellow Levites: Shebaniah, Hodiah, Kelita, Pelaiah, Hanan, 11 Mica,
Rehob, Hashabiah, 12 Zaccur, Sherebiah, Shebaniah, 13 Hodiah, Bani, and Beninu.
14 These are the leaders of the people who
sealed the agreement: Parosh, Pahath-Moab,
Elam, Zattu, Bani, 15 Bunni, Azgad, Bebai, 16 Adonijah, Bigvai, Adin, 17 Ater, Hezekiah, Azzur,
18 Hodiah, Hashum, Bezai, 19 Hariph, Anathoth,
Nebai, 20 Magpiash, Meshullam, Hezir, 21 Meshezabel, Zadok, Jaddua, 22 Pelatiah, Hanan,
Anaiah, 23 Hoshea, Hananiah, Hasshub, 24 Hal-
lohesh, Pilha, Shobek, 25 Rehum, Hashabnah,

Maaseiah, 26Ahiah, Hanan, Anan, 27Malluch, Harim, and Baanah.

28The rest of the people took an oath. They were the priests, Levites, gatekeepers, singers, Temple servants, all those who separated themselves from foreigners to keep the Teachings of God, and also their wives and their sons and daughters who could understand. 29They joined their fellow Israelites and their leading men in taking an oath, which was tied to a curse in case they broke the oath. They promised to follow the Teachings of God, which they had been given through Moses the servant of God, and to obey all the commands, rules, and laws of the LORD our God.

30They said:

We promise not to let our daughters marry foreigners nor to let our sons marry their daughters. 31Foreigners may bring goods or grain to sell on the Sabbath, but we will not buy on the Sabbath or any holy day. Every seventh year we will not plant, and that year we will forget all that people owe us.

32We will be responsible for the commands to pay for the service of the Temple of our God. We will give an eighth of an ounce of silver each year. 33It is for the bread that is set out on the table; the regular grain offerings and burnt offerings; the offerings on the Sabbaths, New Moon festivals, and special feasts; the holy offerings; the offerings to remove the sins of the Israelites so they will belong to God; and for the work of the Temple of our God.

34We, the priests, the Levites, and the people, have thrown lots to decide at what time of year each family must bring wood to the Temple. The wood is for burning on the altar of the LORD our God, and we will do this as it is written in the Teachings.

35We also will bring the first fruits from our crops and the first fruits of every tree to the Temple each year.

36We will bring to the Temple our firstborn sons and cattle and the firstborn of our herds and flocks, as it is written in the Teachings. We will bring them to the priests who are serving in the Temple.

37We will bring to the priests at the storerooms of the Temple the first of our ground meal, our offerings, the fruit from all our trees, and our new wine and oil. And we will bring a tenth of our crops to the Levites, who will collect these things in all the towns where we work. 38A priest of Aaron's family must be with the Levites when they receive the tenth of the people's crops. The Levites must bring a tenth of all they receive to the Temple of our God to put in the storerooms of the treasury. 39The people of Israel and the Levites are to bring to the storerooms the gifts of grain, new wine, and oil. That is where the utensils for the Temple are kept and where the priests who are serving, the gatekeepers, and singers stay.

We will not ignore the Temple of our God.

WHAT'S IT MEAN?

The Levites didn't have their own land or means of income. The rest of the Israelites supported them by giving them one-tenth of every harvest. The Levites, in turn, supported the priests by giving them one-tenth of everything they received. If this one-tenth stuff sounds familiar, it should. This system, called tithing, was established in the Teachings of Moses.

Nehemiah 10:38

NEW PEOPLE MOVE INTO JERUSALEM

11

1The leaders of Israel lived in Jerusalem. But the rest of the people threw lots to choose one person out of every ten to come and live in Jerusalem, the holy city. The other nine could stay in their own cities. 2The people blessed those who volunteered to live in Jerusalem.

3These are the area leaders who lived in Jerusalem. (Some people lived on their own land in the cities of Judah. These included Israelites, priests, Levites, Temple servants, and descendants of Solomon's servants. 4Others from the families of Judah and Benjamin lived in Jerusalem.)

These are the descendants of Judah who moved into Jerusalem. There was Athaiah son of Uzziah. (Uzziah was the son of Zechariah, the son of Amariah. Amariah was the son of Shephatiah, the son of Mahalalel. Mahalalel was a descendant of Perez.) 5There was also

Masseiah son of Baruch. (Baruch was the son of Col-Hozeh, the son of Hazaiah. Hazaiah was the son of Adaiah, the son of Joiarib. Joiarib was the son of Zechariah, a descendant of Shelah.) [6]All the descendants of Perez who lived in Jerusalem totaled 468 men. They were soldiers.

WHAT'S IT MEAN?

Only two of the twelve tribes of Israel—Judah and Benjamin—made it back to their homeland intact following the Babylonian captivity. The Levites were not counted as a tribe, even though they were descendants of one of Jacob's (or Israel's) sons. To replace Levi in the count, Joseph was divided into two tribes, Manasseh and Ephraim.

Nehemiah 11:4–6

[7]These are descendants of Benjamin who moved into Jerusalem. There was Sallu son of Meshullam. (Meshullam was the son of Joed, the son of Pedaiah. Pedaiah was the son of Kolaiah, the son of Maaseiah. Maaseiah was the son of Ithiel, the son of Jeshaiah.) [8]Following him were Gabbai and Sallai, for a total of 928 men. [9]Joel son of Zicri was appointed over them, and Judah son of Hassenuah was second in charge of the new area of the city.

[10]These are the priests who moved into Jerusalem. There was Jedaiah son of Joiarib, Jakin, [11]and Seraiah son of Hilkiah, the supervisor in the Temple. (Hilkiah was the son of Meshullam, the son of Zadok. Zadok was the son of Meraioth, the son of Ahitub.) [12]And there were others with them who did the work for the Temple. All together there were 822 men. Also there was Adaiah son of Jeroham. (Jeroham was the son of Pelaliah, the son of Amzi. Amzi was the son of Zechariah, the son of Pashhur. Pashhur was the son of Malkijah.) [13]And there were family heads with him. All together there were 242 men. Also there was Amashsai son of Azarel. (Azarel was the son of Ahzai, the son of Meshillemoth. Meshillemoth was the son of Immer.) [14]And there were brave men with Amashsai. All together there were 128 men. Zabdiel son of Haggedolim was appointed over them.

[15]These are the Levites who moved into Jerusalem. There was Shemaiah son of Hasshub. (Hasshub was the son of Azrikam, the son of Hashabiah. Hashabiah was the son of Bunni.) [16]And there were Shabbethai and Jozabad, two of the leaders of the Levites who were in charge of the work outside the Temple. [17]There was Mattaniah son of Mica. (Mica was the son of Zabdi, the son of Asaph.) Mattaniah was the director who led the people in thanksgiving and prayer. There was Bakbukiah, who was second in charge over his fellow Levites. And there was Abda son of Shammua. (Shammua was the son of Galal, the son of Jeduthun.) [18]All together 284 Levites lived in the holy city of Jerusalem.

[19]The gatekeepers who moved into Jerusalem were Akkub, Talmon, and others with them. There was a total of 172 men who guarded the city gates.

[20]The other Israelites, priests, and Levites lived on their own land in all the cities of Judah.

[21]The Temple servants lived on the hill of Ophel, and Ziha and Gishpa were in charge of them.

[22]Uzzi son of Bani was appointed over the Levites in Jerusalem. (Bani was the son of Hashabiah, the son of Mattaniah. Mattaniah was the son of Mica.) Uzzi was one of Asaph's descendants, who were the singers responsible for the service of the Temple. [23]The singers were under the king's orders, which regulated them day by day.

[24]Pethahiah son of Meshezabel was the king's spokesman. (Meshezabel was a descendant of Zerah, the son of Judah.)

[25]Some of the people of Judah lived in villages with their surrounding fields. They lived in Kiriath Arba and its surroundings, in Dibon and its surroundings, in Jekabzeel and its surroundings, [26]in Jeshua, Moladah, Beth Pelet, [27]Hazar Shual, Beersheba and its surroundings, [28]in Ziklag and Meconah and its surroundings, [29]in En Rimmon, Zorah, Jarmuth, [30]Zanoah, Adullam and their villages, in Lachish and the fields around it, and in Azekah and its surroundings. So they settled from Beersheba all the way to the Valley of Hinnom.

[31]The descendants of the Benjaminites from Geba lived in Micmash, Aija, Bethel and its surroundings, [32]in Anathoth, Nob, Ananiah, [33]Hazor, Ramah, Gittaim, [34]Hadid, Zeboim, Neballat, [35]Lod, Ono, and in the Valley of the Craftsmen.

[36]Some groups of the Levites from Judah settled in the land of Benjamin.

12

PRIESTS AND LEVITES

[1]These are the priests and Levites who returned with Zerubbabel son of Shealtiel and with Jeshua. There were Seraiah, Jeremiah, Ezra,

2Amariah, Malluch, Hattush, 3Shecaniah, Rehum, Meremoth, 4Iddo, Ginnethon, Abijah,
5Mijamin, Moadiah, Bilgah, 6Shemaiah, Joiarib,
Jedaiah, 7Sallu, Amok, Hilkiah, and Jedaiah.
They were the leaders of the priests and their
relatives in the days of Jeshua.
8The Levites were Jeshua, Binnui, Kadmiel,
Sherebiah, Judah, and Mattaniah. Mattaniah
and his relatives were in charge
of the songs of thanksgiving.
9Bakbukiah and Unni, their
relatives, stood across from
them in the services.
10Jeshua was the father
of Joiakim. Joiakim was
the father of Eliashib. Eliashib was the father of
Joiada. 11Joiada was the
father of Jonathan, and
Jonathan was the father of
Jaddua.
12In the days of Joiakim, these
priests were the leaders of the families of
priests: Meraiah, from Seraiah's family; Hananiah, from Jeremiah's family; 13Meshullam,
from Ezra's family; Jehohanan, from Amariah's
family; 14Jonathan, from Malluch's family; Joseph, from Shecaniah's family; 15Adna, from
Harim's family; Helkai, from Meremoth's family; 16Zechariah, from Iddo's family; Meshullam, from Ginnethon's family; 17Zicri, from
Abijah's family; Piltai, from Miniamin's and
Moadiah's families; 18Shammua, from Bilgah's
family; Jehonathan, from Shemaiah's family;
19Mattenai, from Joiarib's family; Uzzi, from
Jedaiah's family; 20Kallai, from Sallu's family;
Eber, from Amok's family; 21Hashabiah, from
Hilkiah's family; and Nethanel, from Jedaiah's
family.
22The leaders of the families of the Levites
and the priests were written down in the days
of Eliashib, Joiada, Johanan, and Jaddua, while
Darius the Persian was king. 23The family leaders among the Levites were written down in
the history book, but only up to the time of
Johanan son of Eliashib. 24The leaders of the
Levites were Hashabiah, Sherebiah, Jeshua son
of Kadmiel, and their relatives. Their relatives
stood across from them and gave praise and
thanksgiving to God. One group answered the
other group, as David, the man of God, had
commanded.
25These were the gatekeepers who guarded
the storerooms next to the gates: Mattaniah,
Bakbukiah, Obadiah, Meshullam, Talmon, and
Akkub. 26They served in the days of Joiakim
son of Jeshua, the son of Jozadak. They also
served in the days of Nehemiah the governor
and Ezra the priest and teacher.

THE WALL OF JERUSALEM

27When the wall of Jerusalem was offered as
a gift to God, they asked the Levites to come
from wherever they lived to Jerusalem to celebrate with joy the gift of the wall. They were to
celebrate with songs of thanks-
giving and with the music of
cymbals, harps, and lyres.
28They also brought to-
gether singers from all
around Jerusalem, from
the Netophathite villages,
29from Beth Gilgal, and
from the areas of Geba and
Azmaveth. The singers had
built villages for them-
selves around Jerusalem.
30The priests and Levites made
themselves pure, and they also
made the people, the gates, and the wall of
Jerusalem pure.

> **"They asked the Levites to come from wherever they lived to Jerusalem to celebrate with joy the gift of the wall."**
> **(Nehemiah 12:27b)**

WHAT'S IT MEAN?

The Israelites loved their music. They found reasons to sing for any occasion, whether it was a battle victory, a religious ceremony, or a death. Most of the time, though, they sang to worship the Lord. About the only time the Israelites didn't feel like singing was during their captivity in Babylon. According to Psalm 137, the Babylonians had commanded the Israelites to perform, but the Jewish captives were too heartbroken about the destruction of their Temple and their capital city.

Nehemiah 12:27

31I had the leaders of Judah go up on top of
the wall, and I appointed two large choruses to
give thanks. One chorus went to the right on
top of the wall, toward the Trash Gate. 32Be-
hind them went Hoshaiah and half the leaders
of Judah. 33Azariah, Ezra, Meshullam, 34Judah,
Benjamin, Shemaiah, and Jeremiah also went.
35Some priests with trumpets also went, along
with Zechariah son of Jonathan. (Jonathan
was the son of Shemaiah, the son of Mattaniah. Mattaniah was the son of Micaiah, the
son of Zaccur. Zaccur was the son of Asaph.)

[36]Zechariah's relatives also went. They were Shemaiah, Azarel, Milalai, Gilalai, Maai, Nethanel, Judah, and Hanani. These men played the musical instruments of David, the man of God, and Ezra the teacher walked in front of them. [37]They went from the Fountain Gate straight up the steps to the highest part of the wall by the older part of the city. They went on above the house of David to the Water Gate on the east.

[38]The second chorus went to the left, while I followed them on top of the wall with half the people. We went from the Tower of the Ovens to the Broad Wall, [39]over the Gate of Ephraim to the Old Gate and the Fish Gate, to the Tower of Hananel and the Tower of the Hundred. We went as far as the Sheep Gate and stopped at the Gate of the Guard.

[40]The two choruses took their places at the Temple. Half of the leaders and I did also. [41]These priests were there with their trumpets: Eliakim, Maaseiah, Miniamin, Micaiah, Elioenai, Zechariah, and Hananiah. [42]These people were also there: Maaseiah, Shemaiah, Eleazar, Uzzi, Jehohanan, Malkijah, Elam, and Ezer. The choruses sang, led by Jezrahiah. [43]The people offered many sacrifices that day and were happy because God had given them great joy. The women and children were happy. The sound of happiness in Jerusalem could be heard far away.

VICTORY

Who should we dedicate our victory to? (12:27, 43)

[44]At that time the leaders appointed men to be in charge of the storerooms. These rooms were for the gifts, the first fruits, and the ten percent that the people brought. The Teachings said they should bring a share for the priests and Levites from the fields around the towns. The people of Judah were happy to do this for the priests and Levites who served. [45]They performed the service of their God in making things pure. The singers and gatekeepers also did their jobs, as David had commanded his son Solomon. [46]Earlier, in the time of David and Asaph, there was a leader of the singers and of the songs of praise and thanksgiving to God. [47]So it was in the days of Zerubbabel and Nehemiah. All the people of Israel gave something to the singers and gatekeepers, and they also set aside part for the Levites. Then the Levites set aside part for the descendants of Aaron.

FOREIGN PEOPLE ARE SENT AWAY

13

[1]On that day they read the Book of Moses to the people, and they found that it said no Ammonite or Moabite should ever be allowed in the meeting to worship. [2]The Ammonites and Moabites had not welcomed the Israelites with food and water. Instead, they had hired Balaam to put a curse on Israel. (But our God turned the curse into a blessing.) [3]When the people heard this teaching, they separated all foreigners from Israel.

NEHEMIAH RETURNS TO JERUSALEM

[4]Before that happened, Eliashib the priest, who was in charge of the Temple storerooms, was friendly with Tobiah. [5]Eliashib let Tobiah use one of the large storerooms. Earlier it had been used for grain offerings, incense, the utensils, and the tenth offerings of grain, new wine, and olive oil that belonged to the Levites, singers, and gatekeepers. It had also been used for gifts for the priests.

[6]I was not in Jerusalem when this happened. I had gone back to Artaxerxes king of Babylon in the thirty-second year he was king. Finally I asked the king to let me leave. [7]When I returned to Jerusalem, I found out the evil Eliashib had done by letting Tobiah have a room in the Temple courtyard. [8]I was very upset at this, so I threw all of Tobiah's goods out of the room. [9]I ordered the rooms to be purified, and I brought back the utensils for God's Temple, the grain offerings, and the incense.

[10]Then I found out the people were not giving the Levites their shares. So the Levites and singers who served had gone back to their own farms. [11]I argued with the officers, saying, "Why haven't you taken care of the Temple?" Then I gathered the Levites and singers and put them back at their places.

[12]All the people of Judah then brought to the storerooms a tenth of their crops, new wine, and olive oil. [13]I put these men in charge of the storerooms: Shelemiah the priest, Zadok the teacher, and Pedaiah a Levite. I made Hanan son of Zaccur, the son of Mattaniah, their helper. Everyone knew they were honest men. They gave out the portions that went to their relatives.

[14]Remember me, my God, for this. Do not ignore my love for the Temple and its service.

[15]In those days I saw people in Judah working in the winepresses on the Sabbath day. They were bringing in grain and loading it on donkeys. And they were bringing loads of wine, grapes, and figs into Jerusalem on the Sabbath day. So I warned them about selling food on that day. [16]People from the city of Tyre who were living in Jerusalem brought in fish and other things and sold them there on the

WHAT'S IT MEAN?

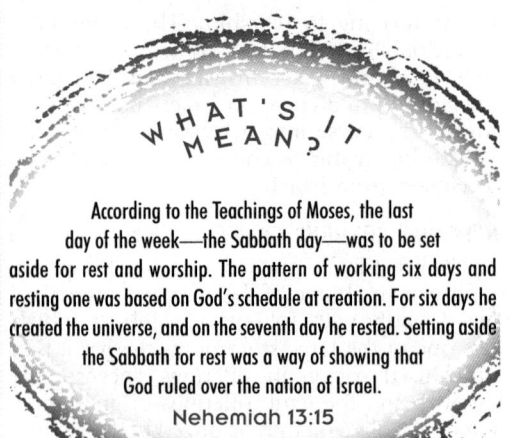

According to the Teachings of Moses, the last day of the week—the Sabbath day—was to be set aside for rest and worship. The pattern of working six days and resting one was based on God's schedule at creation. For six days he created the universe, and on the seventh day he rested. Setting aside the Sabbath for rest was a way of showing that God ruled over the nation of Israel.

Nehemiah 13:15

Sabbath day to the people of Judah. 17I argued
with the important men of Judah and said to
them, "What is this evil thing you are doing?
You are ruining the Sabbath day. 18This is just
what your ancestors did. So our God did terrible things to us and this city. Now you are making him even more angry at Israel by ruining the Sabbath day."

19So I ordered that the doors be shut at sunset before the Sabbath and not be opened until the Sabbath was over. I put my servants at the gates so no load could come in on the
Sabbath. 20Once or twice traders and sellers of
all kinds of goods spent the night outside Jerusalem. 21So I warned them, "Why are you spending the night by the wall? If you do it again, I will force you away." After that, they
did not come back on the Sabbath. 22Then I
ordered the Levites to purify themselves and to guard the city gates to make sure the Sabbath remained holy.

Remember me, my God, for this. Have mercy on me because of your great love.

23In those days I saw men of Judah who had married women from Ashdod, Ammon, and
Moab. 24Half their children were speaking the language of Ashdod or some other place, and
they couldn't speak the language of Judah. 25I
argued with those people, put curses on them, hit some of them, and pulled out their hair. I forced them to make a promise to God, saying, "Do not let your daughters marry the sons of foreigners, and do not take the daughters of foreigners as wives for your sons or yourselves.
26Foreign women made King Solomon of Israel
sin. There was never a king like him in any of the nations. God loved Solomon and made him king over all Israel, but foreign women made
him sin. 27And now you are not obedient when
you do this evil thing. You are unfaithful to our God when you marry foreign wives."

28Joiada was the son of Eliashib the high priest. One of Joiada's sons married a daughter of Sanballat the Horonite, so I sent him away from me.

29Remember them, my God, because they made the priesthood unclean and the agreement of the priests and Levites unclean.

30So I purified them of everything that was foreign. I appointed duties for the priests and Levites, giving each man his own
job. 31I also made sure wood
was brought for the altar at regular times and that the first fruits were brought.

Remember me, my God; be kind to me.

BLESSING
Is it wrong to ask God for blessings? (13:31)

esther

CONTENT

The story of Esther is a spy thriller if there ever was one. Think about it. A young woman changes her name. She then hides the fact that she is a part of a minority group treated with extreme prejudice in her culture. She enters a yearlong beauty contest in which the winner will become queen of the nation. She actually wins the contest and becomes the king's favorite. Then just when things are looking really good, she faces a situation where she has to reveal her identity to the king (risking her life) in order to catch the villain and save her people from destruction.

If you add in a walkie-talkie watch, you've got a movie script! But the important thing about Esther's story isn't the intrigue. The important thing is that God used Esther because she was willing to trust him and take some risks. Esther knew that God put her where she was for a reason, so when she saw the opportunity to make a difference she took it.

As it turned out, Esther did save her people. She also saved the life of a family member and saw that the bad guy was punished. There's nothing like a story with a happy ending, is there?

Outline

1:1—2:23 .... Esther Becomes Queen
3:1–15 .... Haman's Plot to Destroy the Jews
4:1–17 .... Mordecai Asks for Esther's Help
5:1—6:14 .... Mordecai Is Honored, Not Killed
7:1–10 .... Haman Is Put to Death
8:1—9:17 .... The Jews Defend Themselves and Kill Their Enemies
9:18–32 .... The Feast of Purim
10:1–3 .... The Greatness of Xerxes and Mordecai

Purpose

God works quietly through cause and effect to achieve his purposes in history and in our lives.

Theme

Teamwork That Shaped a Nation

Date of writing

464–435 B.C.

"If you keep quiet at this time, someone else will help and save the Jewish people, but you and your father's family will all die. And who knows, you may have been chosen queen for just such a time as this" (4:14).

Bible Talk

God Builds Our Platforms

Esther's role as queen gave her a platform. It gave her a place where her voice could be heard and she could make a difference. She didn't know it, though, until God asked her to speak up.

Has God given you a platform? Are you a leader in a group? Do you have younger brothers and sisters that listen to you? Do you help with younger kids at church or at school? Wherever you are, God can say something through your life. That is the platform that God has built for you.

Sometimes we don't know that we can do something that matters until God asks us to speak up. Then he uses us. Don't underestimate your opportunities to make a difference.

HAMAN

Haman was a bigot. He hated a group of people because of their race. Haman hated the Jews, and he was also power-hungry and deceitful. He used people to make himself look good.

There was one Jew that Haman really had it in for: Mordecai, Esther's cousin. Haman couldn't stand Mordecai because Mordecai had the one thing Haman didn't—people's respect.

If you like a story where the bad guy gets it in the end, read about Haman. He built a platform on which to hang his enemy Mordecai, but in the end the platform was used as the place to hang Haman and justice was done.

QUEEN VASHTI DISOBEYS THE KING

1

1This is what happened during the time of King Xerxes, the king who ruled the one hundred twenty-seven states from India to Cush. 2In those days King Xerxes ruled from his capital city of Susa. 3In the third year of his rule, he gave a banquet for all his important men and royal officers. The army leaders from the countries of Persia and Media and the important men from all Xerxes' empire were there.

WHAT'S IT MEAN?

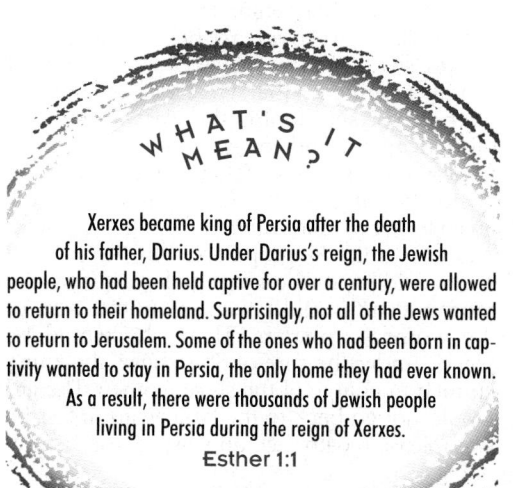

Xerxes became king of Persia after the death of his father, Darius. Under Darius's reign, the Jewish people, who had been held captive for over a century, were allowed to return to their homeland. Surprisingly, not all of the Jews wanted to return to Jerusalem. Some of the ones who had been born in captivity wanted to stay in Persia, the only home they had ever known. As a result, there were thousands of Jewish people living in Persia during the reign of Xerxes.

Esther 1:1

4The banquet lasted one hundred eighty days. All during that time King Xerxes was showing off the great wealth of his kingdom and his own great riches and glory. 5When the one hundred eighty days were over, the king gave another banquet. It was held in the courtyard of the palace garden for seven days, and it was for everybody in the palace at Susa, from the greatest to the least. 6The courtyard had fine white curtains and purple drapes that were tied to silver rings on marble pillars by white and purple cords. And there were gold and silver couches on a floor set with tiles of white marble, shells, and gems. 7Wine was served in gold cups of various kinds. And there was plenty of the king's wine, because he was very generous. 8The king commanded that the guests be permitted to drink as much as they wished. He told the wine servers to serve each person what he wanted.

9Queen Vashti also gave a banquet for the women in the royal palace of King Xerxes.

10On the seventh day of the banquet, King Xerxes was very happy, because he had been drinking much wine. He gave a command to the seven eunuchs who served him—Mehuman, Biztha, Harbona, Bigtha, Abagtha, Zethar, and Carcas. 11He commanded them to bring him Queen Vashti, wearing her royal crown. She was to come to show her beauty to the people and important men, because she was very beautiful. 12The eunuchs told Queen Vashti about the king's command, but she refused to come. Then the king became very angry; his anger was like a burning fire.

13It was a custom for the king to ask advice from experts about law and order. So King Xerxes spoke with the wise men who would know the right thing to do. 14The wise men the king usually talked to were Carshena, Shethar, Admatha, Tarshish, Meres, Marsena, and Memucan, seven of the important men of Persia and Media. These seven had special privileges to see the king and had the highest rank in the kingdom. 15The king asked them, "What does the law say must be done to Queen Vashti? She has not obeyed the command of King Xerxes, which the eunuchs took to her."

16Then Memucan said to the king and the other important men, "Queen Vashti has not done wrong to the king alone. She has also done wrong to all the important men and all the people in all the empire of King Xerxes. 17All the wives of the important men of Persia and Media will hear about the queen's actions. Then they will no longer honor their husbands. They will say, 'King Xerxes commanded Queen Vashti to be brought to him, but she refused to come.' 18Today the wives of the important men of Persia and Media have heard about the queen's actions. So they will speak in the same way to their husbands, and there will be no end to disrespect and anger.

19"So, our king, if it pleases you, give a royal order, and let it be written in the laws of Persia and Media, which cannot be changed. The law should say Vashti is never again to enter the presence of King Xerxes. Also let the king give her place as queen to someone who is better than she is. 20And let the king's order be announced everywhere in his enormous kingdom. Then all the women will respect their husbands, from the greatest to the least."

21The king and his important men were happy with this advice, so King Xerxes did as Memucan suggested. 22He sent letters to all the states of the kingdom in the writing of each state and in the language of each group of people. These letters announced that each man was to be the ruler of his own family.

ESTHER IS MADE QUEEN

2 1Later, when King Xerxes was not so angry,
he remembered Vashti and what she had done
and his order about her. 2Then the king's personal servants suggested, "Let a search be made
for beautiful young girls for the king. 3Let the
king choose supervisors in every state of his
kingdom to bring every beautiful young girl to
the palace at Susa. They should be taken to
the women's quarters and put under the care
of Hegai, the king's eunuch in charge of the
women. And let beauty treatments be given to
them. 4Then let the girl who most pleases the
king become queen in place of Vashti." The
king liked this idea, so he did as they said.
5Now there was a Jewish man in the palace
of Susa whose name was Mordecai son of Jair.
Jair was the son of Shimei, the son of Kish.
Mordecai was from the tribe of Benjamin,
6which had been taken captive from Jerusalem
by Nebuchadnezzar king of Babylon. They
were part of the group taken into captivity
with Jehoiachin king of Judah. 7Mordecai had
a cousin named Hadassah, who had no father
or mother, so Mordecai took care of her. Hadassah was also called Esther, and she had a
very pretty figure and face. Mordecai had
adopted her as his own daughter when her father and mother died.

WHAT'S IT MEAN?

Once was not enough for Nebuchadnezzar when it came to attacking Jerusalem. The first time his army invaded, they captured the king of Judah and took him back to Babylon. The second and third times the Babylonian army showed up, they took all of the wealthy people captive and destroyed the Temple.

Esther 2:6

8When the king's command and order had
been heard, many girls had been brought to
the palace in Susa and put under the care of
Hegai. Esther was also taken to the king's palace and put under the care of Hegai, who was
in charge of the women. 9Esther pleased Hegai,
and he liked her. So Hegai quickly began giving
Esther her beauty treatments and special food.
He gave her seven servant girls chosen from
the king's palace. Then he moved her and her
seven servant girls to the best part of the
women's quarters.
10Esther did not tell anyone
about her family or who her
people were, because Mordecai had told her not to.
11Every day Mordecai walked
back and forth near the courtyard where the king's women
lived to find out how Esther was
and what was happening to her.

FAMILY

What's a good example of love for family? (2:11)

12Before a girl could take her turn with King
Xerxes, she had to complete twelve months of
beauty treatments that were ordered for the
women. For six months she was treated with
oil and myrrh and for six months with perfumes and cosmetics. 13Then she was ready to
go to the king. Anything she asked for was
given to her to take with her from the women's
quarters to the king's palace. 14In the evening
she would go to the king's palace, and in the
morning she would return to another part of
the women's quarters. There she would be
placed under the care of Shaashgaz, the king's
eunuch in charge of the slave women. The girl
would not go back to the king again unless he
was pleased with her and asked for her by
name.
15The time came for Esther daughter of Abihail, Mordecai's uncle, who had been adopted
by Mordecai, to go to the king. She asked for
only what Hegai suggested she should take.
(Hegai was the king's eunuch who was in
charge of the women.) Everyone who saw Esther liked her. 16So Esther was taken to King
Xerxes in the royal palace in the tenth month,
the month of Tebeth, during Xerxes' seventh
year as king.
17And the king was pleased with Esther
more than with any of the other girls. He liked
her more than any of the other girls, so he put
a royal crown on her head and made her
queen in place of Vashti. 18Then the king gave a
great banquet for Esther and invited all his important men and royal officers. He announced
a holiday for all the empire and had the government give away gifts.

MORDECAI DISCOVERS AN EVIL PLAN

19Now Mordecai was sitting at the king's
gate when the girls were gathered the second
time. 20Esther still had not told anyone about
her family or who her people were, just as
Mordecai had commanded her. She obeyed
Mordecai just as she had done when she was
under his care.

21Now Bigthana and Teresh were two of the king's officers who guarded the doorway. While Mordecai was sitting at the king's gate, they became angry and began to make plans to kill King Xerxes. 22But Mordecai found out about their plans and told Queen Esther. Then Esther told the king how Mordecai had discovered the evil plan. 23When the report was investigated, it was found to be true, and the two officers who had planned to kill the king were hanged. All this was written down in the daily court record in the king's presence.

HAMAN PLANS TO DESTROY THE JEWISH PEOPLE

3 1After these things happened, King Xerxes honored Haman son of Hammedatha the Agagite. He gave him a new rank that was higher than all the important men. 2All the royal officers at the king's gate would bow down and kneel before Haman, as the king had ordered. But Mordecai would not bow down or show him honor.

3Then the royal officers at the king's gate asked Mordecai, "Why don't you obey the king's command?" 4And they said this to him every day. When he did not listen to them, they told Haman about it. They wanted to see if Haman would accept Mordecai's behavior because Mordecai had told them he was Jewish.

5When Haman saw that Mordecai would not bow down to him or honor him, he became very angry. 6He thought of himself as too important to try to kill only Mordecai. He had been told who the people of Mordecai were, so he looked for a way to destroy all of Mordecai's people, the Jews, in all of Xerxes' kingdom.

7It was in the first month of the twelfth year of King Xerxes' rule—the month of Nisan. Pur (that is, the lot) was thrown before Haman to choose a day and a month. So the twelfth month, the month of Adar, was chosen.

8Then Haman said to King Xerxes, "There is a certain group of people scattered among the other people in all the states of your kingdom. Their customs are different from those of all the other people, and they do not obey the king's laws. It is not right for you to allow them to continue living in your kingdom. 9If it pleases the king, let an order be given to destroy those people. Then I will pay seven hundred fifty thousand pounds of silver to those who do the king's business, and they will put it into the royal treasury."

10So the king took his signet ring off and gave it to Haman son of Hammedatha, the Agagite, the enemy of the Jewish people. 11Then the king said to Haman, "The money and the people are yours. Do with them as you please."

WHAT'S IT MEAN?

Authority figures in the ancient Middle East wore signet rings with their name or their own personal symbol on them. The rings were designed so that the raised name or symbol would make an impression on a seal made of moist clay or wet wax. The seal was used to indicate that a document was official. Putting one's ring on a seal was similar to signing one's name today. By allowing Haman to use his ring, Xerxes was giving his approval of the plan.

Esther 3:10

12On the thirteenth day of the first month, the royal secretaries were called, and they wrote out all of Haman's orders. They wrote to the king's governors and to the captains of the soldiers in each state and to the important men of each group of people. The orders were written in the writing of each state and in the language of each people. They were written in the name of King Xerxes and sealed with his signet ring. 13Letters were sent by messengers to all the king's empire ordering them to destroy, kill, and completely wipe out all the Jewish people. That meant young and old, women and little children, too. It was to happen on a single day—the thirteenth day of the twelfth month, which was Adar. And they could take everything the Jewish people owned. 14A copy of the order was given out as a law in every state so all the people would be ready for that day.

15The messengers set out, hurried by the king's command, as soon as the order was given in the palace at Susa. The king and Haman sat down to drink, but the city of Susa was in confusion.

MORDECAI ASKS ESTHER TO HELP

4 1When Mordecai heard about all that had been done, he tore his clothes, put on rough cloth and ashes, and went out into the city crying loudly and painfully. 2But Mordecai went only as far as the king's gate, because no one was allowed to enter that gate dressed in rough cloth. 3As the king's order reached every area, there was great sadness and loud crying among the Jewish people. They gave up eating

and cried out loud, and many of them lay down on rough cloth and ashes to show how sad they were.

WHAT'S IT MEAN?

People in ancient times wore clothes of rough cloth only in times of great sorrow or distress. If you'd ever felt it, you'd know why they didn't wear it more often. The cloth was a dark, scratchy material made of goat's hair. The outfit was usually topped off by ashes on the person's head. This odd combination symbolized the person's sadness about a specific situation and the sin that caused it. The tradition of wearing dark clothing to funerals came from the custom of wearing this rough cloth in times of sorrow.

Esther 4:1

[4]When Esther's servant girls and eunuchs came to her and told her about Mordecai, she was very upset and afraid. She sent clothes for Mordecai to put on instead of the rough cloth, but he would not wear them. [5]Then Esther called for Hathach, one of the king's eunuchs chosen by the king to serve her. Esther ordered him to find out what was bothering Mordecai and why.

[6]So Hathach went to Mordecai, who was in the city square in front of the king's gate. [7]Mordecai told Hathach everything that had happened to him, and he told Hathach about the amount of money Haman had promised to pay into the king's treasury for the killing of the Jewish people. [8]Mordecai also gave him a copy of the order to kill the Jewish people, which had been given in Susa. He wanted Hathach to show it to Esther and to tell her about it. And Mordecai told him to order Esther to go into the king's presence to beg for mercy and to plead with him for her people.

"Go and get all the Jewish people in Susa together. For my sake, give up eating." (Esther 4:16a)

[9]Hathach went back and reported to Esther everything Mordecai had said. [10]Then Esther told Hathach to tell Mordecai, [11]"All the royal officers and people of the royal states know that no man or woman may go to the king in the inner courtyard without being called. There is only one law about this: Anyone who enters must be put to death unless the king holds out his gold scepter. Then that person may live. And I have not been called to go to the king for thirty days."

[12]Esther's message was given to Mordecai. [13]Then Mordecai sent back word to Esther: "Just because you live in the king's palace, don't think that out of all the Jewish people you alone will escape. [14]If you keep quiet at this time, someone else will help and save the Jewish people, but you and your father's family will all die. And who knows, you may have been chosen queen for just such a time as this."

FUTURE

Does God put us in situations to make a difference? (4:14)

[15]Then Esther sent this answer to Mordecai: [16]"Go and get all the Jewish people in Susa together. For my sake, give up eating; do not eat or drink for three days, night and day. I and my servant girls will also give up eating. Then I will go to the king, even though it is against the law, and if I die, I die."

[17]So Mordecai went away and did everything Esther had told him to do.

ESTHER SPEAKS TO THE KING

5

[1]On the third day Esther put on her royal robes and stood in the inner courtyard of the king's palace, facing the king's hall. The king was sitting on his royal throne in the hall, facing the doorway. [2]When the king saw Queen Esther standing in the courtyard, he was pleased. He held out to her the gold scepter that was in his hand, so Esther went forward and touched the end of it.

[3]The king asked, "What is it, Queen Esther? What do you want to ask me? I will give you as much as half of my kingdom."

[4]Esther answered, "My king, if it pleases you, come today with Haman to a banquet that I have prepared for him."

[5]Then the king said, "Bring Haman quickly so we may do what Esther asks."

So the king and Haman went to the banquet Esther had prepared for them. [6]As they were drinking wine, the king said to Esther, "Now, what are you asking for? I will give it to you. What is it you want? I will give you as much as half of my kingdom."

[7]Esther answered, "This is what I want and what I ask for. [8]My king, if you are pleased with me and if it pleases you, give me what I

ask for and do what I want. Come with Haman
tomorrow to the banquet I will prepare for
you. Then I will answer your question about
what I want."

HAMAN'S PLANS AGAINST MORDECAI

9 Haman left the king's palace that day happy
and content. But when he saw Mordecai at the
king's gate and saw that Mordecai did not stand
up or tremble with fear before him, Haman became very angry with Mordecai. 10 But he controlled his anger and went home.
Then Haman called together his friends and
his wife, Zeresh. 11 He told them how wealthy
he was and how many sons he had. He also
told them all the ways the king had honored
him and how the king had placed him higher
than his important men and his royal officers.
12 He also said, "I'm the only person Queen Esther invited to come with the king to the banquet she gave. And tomorrow also the queen
has asked me to be her guest with the king.
13 But all this does not really make me happy
when I see that Jew Mordecai sitting at the
king's gate."
14 Then Haman's wife, Zeresh, and all his
friends said, "Have a seventy-five foot platform
built, and in the morning ask the king to have
Mordecai hanged on it. Then go to the banquet
with the king and be happy." Haman liked this
suggestion, so he ordered the platform to be
built.

WHAT'S IT MEAN?

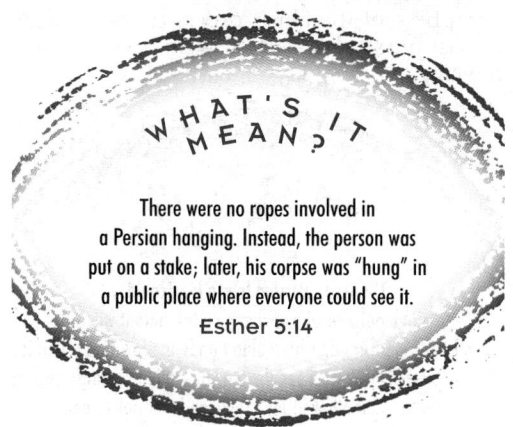

There were no ropes involved in a Persian hanging. Instead, the person was put on a stake; later, his corpse was "hung" in a public place where everyone could see it.

Esther 5:14

MORDECAI IS HONORED

6
1 That same night the king could not sleep.
So he gave an order for the daily court record
to be brought in and read to him. 2 It was found
recorded that Mordecai had warned the king
about Bigthana and Teresh, two of the king's
officers who guarded the doorway and who
had planned to kill the king.
3 The king asked, "What honor and reward
have been given to Mordecai for this?"
The king's personal servants answered,
"Nothing has been done for Mordecai."
4 The king said, "Who is in the courtyard?"
Now Haman had just entered the outer court
of the king's palace. He had come to ask the
king about hanging Mordecai on the platform
he had prepared.
5 The king's personal servants said, "Haman
is standing in the courtyard."
The king said, "Bring him in."
6 So Haman came in. And the king asked
him, "What should be done for a man whom
the king wants very much to honor?"
And Haman thought to himself, "Whom
would the king want to honor more than me?"
7 So he answered the king, "This is what you
could do for the man you want very much to
honor. 8 Have the servants bring a royal robe
that the king himself has worn. And also bring
a horse with a royal crown on its head, a horse
that the king himself has ridden. 9 Let the robe
and the horse be given to one of the king's
most important men. Let the servants put the
robe on the man the king wants to honor, and
let them lead him on the horse through the city
streets. As they are leading him, let them announce: 'This is what is done for the man
whom the king wants to honor!' "
10 The king commanded Haman, "Go quickly.
Take the robe and the horse just as you have
said, and do all this for Mordecai the Jew who
sits at the king's gate. Do not leave out anything
you have suggested."
11 So Haman took the robe and the horse,
and he put the robe on Mordecai. Then he led
him on horseback through the city streets, announcing before Mordecai: "This is what is
done for the man whom the king wants to
honor!"
12 Then Mordecai returned to the king's
gate, but Haman hurried home with his head
covered, because he was embarrassed and
ashamed. 13 He told his wife, Zeresh, and all his
friends everything that had happened to him.
Haman's wife and the men who gave him
advice said, "You are starting to lose power to
Mordecai. Since he is a Jew, you cannot win
against him. You will surely be ruined." 14 While
they were still talking, the king's eunuchs came
to Haman's house and made him hurry to the
banquet Esther had prepared.

HAMAN IS HANGED

7
1 So the king and Haman went in to eat with
Queen Esther. 2 As they were drinking wine on

the second day, the king asked Esther again, "What are you asking for? I will give it to you. What is it you want? I will give you as much as half of my kingdom."

[3]Then Queen Esther answered, "My king, if you are pleased with me, and if it pleases you, let me live. This is what I ask. And let my people live, too. This is what I want. [4]My people and I have been sold to be destroyed, to be killed and completely wiped out. If we had been sold as male and female slaves, I would have kept quiet, because that would not be enough of a problem to bother the king."

[5]Then King Xerxes asked Queen Esther, "Who is he, and where is he? Who has done such a thing?"

[6]Esther said, "Our enemy and foe is this wicked Haman!"

Then Haman was filled with terror before the king and queen. [7]The king was very angry, so he got up, left his wine, and went out into the palace garden. But Haman stayed inside to beg Queen Esther to save his life. He could see that the king had already decided to kill him.

[8]When the king returned from the palace garden to the banquet hall, he saw Haman falling on the couch where Esther was lying. The king said, "Will he even attack the queen while I am in the house?"

As soon as the king said that, servants came in and covered Haman's face. [9]Harbona, one of the eunuchs there serving the king, said, "Look, a seventy-five foot platform stands near Haman's house. This is the one Haman had prepared for Mordecai, who gave the warning that saved the king."

The king said, "Hang Haman on it!" [10]So they hanged Haman on the platform he had prepared for Mordecai. Then the king was not so angry anymore.

THE KING HELPS THE JEWISH PEOPLE

8 [1]That same day King Xerxes gave Queen Esther everything Haman, the enemy of the Jewish people, had left when he died. And Mordecai came in to see the king, because Esther had told the king how he was related to her. [2]Then the king took off his signet ring that he had taken back from Haman, and he gave it to Mordecai. Esther put Mordecai in charge of everything Haman left when he died.

[3]Once again Esther spoke to the king. She fell at the king's feet and cried and begged him to stop the evil plan that Haman the Agagite had planned against the Jews. [4]The king held out the gold scepter to Esther. So Esther got up and stood in front of him.

[5]She said, "My king, if you are pleased with me, and if it pleases you to do this, if you think it is the right thing to do, and if you are happy with me, let an order be written to cancel the letters Haman wrote. Haman the Agagite sent messages to destroy all the Jewish people in all of your kingdom. [6]I could not stand to see that terrible thing happen to my people. I could not stand to see my family killed."

[7]King Xerxes answered Queen Esther and Mordecai the Jew, "Because Haman was against the Jewish people, I have given his things to Esther, and my soldiers have hanged him. [8]Now, in the king's name, write another order to the Jewish people as it seems best to you. Then seal the order with the king's signet ring, because no letter written in the king's name and sealed with his signet ring can be canceled."

[9]At that time the king's secretaries were called. This was the twenty-third day of the third month, which is Sivan. The secretaries wrote out all of Mordecai's orders to the Jews, to the governors, to the captains of the soldiers in each state, and to the important men of the one hundred twenty-seven states that reached from India to Cush. They wrote in the writing of each state and in the language of each people. They also wrote to the Jewish people in their own writing and language. [10]Mordecai wrote orders in the name of King Xerxes and sealed the letters with the king's signet ring. Then he sent the king's orders by messengers on fast horses, horses that were raised just for the king.

WHAT'S IT MEAN?

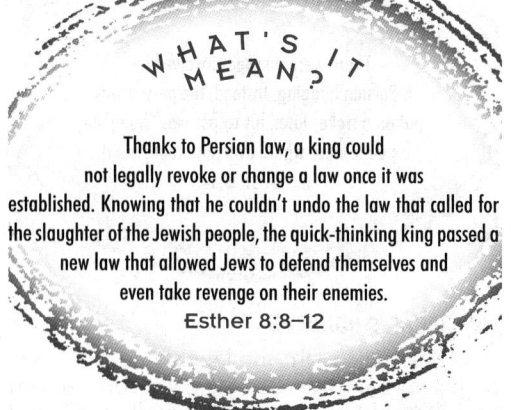

Thanks to Persian law, a king could not legally revoke or change a law once it was established. Knowing that he couldn't undo the law that called for the slaughter of the Jewish people, the quick-thinking king passed a new law that allowed Jews to defend themselves and even take revenge on their enemies.

Esther 8:8–12

[11]These were the king's orders: The Jewish people in every city have the right to gather together to protect themselves. They may destroy, kill, and completely wipe out the army of any

state or people who attack them. And they are
to do the same to the women and children of
that army. They may also take by force the
property of their enemies. 12 The one day set for
the Jewish people to do this in all the empire of
King Xerxes was the thirteenth day of the
twelfth month, the month of Adar. 13 A copy of
the king's order was to be sent out as a law in
every state. It was to be made known to the
people of every nation living in the kingdom so
the Jewish people would be ready on that set
day to strike back at their enemies.
14 The messengers hurried out, riding on the
royal horses, because the king commanded
those messengers to hurry. And the order was
also given in the palace at Susa.
15 Mordecai left the king's presence wearing
royal clothes of blue and white and a large
gold crown. He also had a purple robe made of
the best linen. And the people of Susa shouted
for joy. 16 It was a time of happiness, joy, gladness, and honor for the Jewish people. 17 As the
king's order went to every state and city, there
was joy and gladness among the Jewish people. In every state and city to which the king's
order went, they were having feasts and celebrating. And many people through all the empire became Jews, because they were afraid of
the Jewish people.

VICTORY FOR THE JEWISH PEOPLE

9
1 The order the king had commanded was to
be done on the thirteenth day of the twelfth
month, the month of Adar. That was the day
the enemies of the Jewish people had hoped to
defeat them, but that was changed. So the Jewish people themselves defeated those who hated them. 2 The Jews met in their cities in all the
empire of King Xerxes in order to attack those
who wanted to harm them. No one was strong
enough to fight against them, because all the
other people living in the empire were afraid of
them. 3 All the important men of the states, the
governors, captains of the soldiers, and the
king's officers helped the Jewish people, because they were afraid of Mordecai. 4 Mordecai
was very important in the king's palace. He
was famous in all the empire, because he was
becoming a leader of more and more people.
5 And, with their swords, the Jewish people
defeated all their enemies, killing and destroying them. And they did what they wanted with
those people who hated them. 6 In the palace at
Susa, they killed and destroyed five hundred
men. 7 They also killed: Parshandatha, Dal-
phon, Aspatha, 8 Poratha, Adalia, Aridatha,
9 Parmashta, Arisai, Aridai, and Vaizatha, 10 the
ten sons of Haman, son of Hammedatha, the
enemy of the Jewish people. But the Jewish
people did not take their belongings.
11 On that day the number killed in the palace at Susa was reported to the king. 12 The king
said to Queen Esther, "The Jewish people have
killed and destroyed five hundred people in the
palace at Susa, and they have also killed
Haman's ten sons. What have they done in the
rest of the king's empire! Now what else are
you asking? I will do it! What else do you
want? It will be done!"
13 Esther answered, "If it pleases the king,
give the Jewish people who are in Susa permission to do again tomorrow what the king
ordered for today. And let the bodies of
Haman's ten sons be hanged on the platform."
14 So the king ordered that it be done. A law
was given in Susa, and the bodies of the ten
sons of Haman were hanged. 15 The Jewish
people in Susa came together on the fourteenth day of the month of Adar. They killed
three hundred people in Susa, but they did not
take their belongings.
16 At that same time, all the Jewish people in
the king's empire also met to protect themselves and get rid of their enemies. They killed
seventy-five thousand of those who hated
them, but they did not take their belongings.
17 This happened on the thirteenth day of the
month of Adar. On the fourteenth day they
rested and made it a day of joyful feasting.

THE FEAST OF PURIM

18 But the Jewish people in Susa met on the
thirteenth and fourteenth days of the month of
Adar. Then they rested on the fifteenth day and
made it a day of joyful feasting.
19 This is why the Jewish people who live in
the country and small villages celebrate on the
fourteenth day of the month of Adar. It is a day
of joyful feasting and a day for exchanging
gifts.
20 Mordecai wrote down everything that
had happened. Then he sent letters to all the
Jewish people in all the empire of King Xerxes,
far and near. 21 He told them to celebrate every
year on the fourteenth and fifteenth days of the
month of Adar, 22 because that was when the
Jewish people got rid of their enemies. They
were also to celebrate it as the month their
sadness was turned to joy and their crying for
the dead was turned into celebration. He told
them to celebrate those days as days of joyful
feasting and as a time for giving food to each
other and presents to the poor.
23 So the Jewish people agreed to do what

Mordecai had written to them, and they agreed
to hold the celebration every year. 24Haman
son of Hammedatha, the Agagite, was the enemy of all the Jewish people. He had made an
evil plan against the Jewish people to destroy
them, and he had thrown the Pur (that is, the
lot) to choose a day to ruin and destroy them.
25But when the king learned of the evil plan, he
sent out written orders that the evil plans Haman had made against the Jewish people
would be used against him. And those orders
said that Haman and his sons should be
hanged on the platform. 26So these days were
called Purim, which comes from the word
"Pur" (the lot). Because of everything written in
this letter and what they had seen and what
happened to them, 27the Jewish people set up
this custom. They and their descendants and
all those who join them are always to celebrate
these two days every year. They should do it in
the right way and at the time Mordecai had
ordered them in the letter. 28These two days
should be remembered and celebrated from
now on in every family, in every state, and in
every city. These days of Purim should always
be celebrated by the Jewish people, and their
descendants should always remember to celebrate them, too.
29So Queen Esther daughter of Abihail,
along with Mordecai the Jew, wrote this second letter about Purim. Using the power they
had, they wrote to prove the first letter was
true. 30And Mordecai sent letters to all the Jewish people in the one hundred twenty-seven
states of the kingdom of Xerxes, writing them a
message of peace and truth. 31He wrote to set
up these days of Purim at the chosen times.
Mordecai the Jew and Queen Esther had sent
out the order for the Jewish people, just as they
had set up things for themselves and their descendants: On these two days the people
should give up eating and cry loudly. 32Esther's
letter set up the rules for Purim, and they were
written down in the records.

WHAT'S IT MEAN?

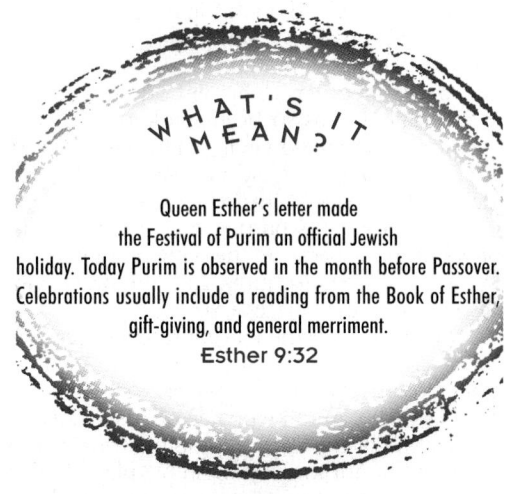

Queen Esther's letter made the Festival of Purim an official Jewish holiday. Today Purim is observed in the month before Passover. Celebrations usually include a reading from the Book of Esther, gift-giving, and general merriment.

Esther 9:32

THE GREATNESS OF MORDECAI

10
1King Xerxes demanded taxes everywhere,
even from the cities on the seacoast. 2And all
the great things Xerxes did by his power and
strength are written in the record books of the
kings of Media and Persia. Also written in
those record books are all the things done by
Mordecai, whom the king made great. 3Mor-
decai the Jew was second in
importance to King Xerxes,
and he was the most important man among the Jewish
people. His fellow Jews respected him very much, because he worked for the good
of his people and spoke up for
the safety of all the Jewish people.

LEADERSHIP

What's a good way to get your followers to like you? (10:3)

job

CONTENT The Book of Job is a really famous story about a man who suffered . . . *a lot*. He lost all his family except his nagging wife. He lost his wealth, his health, and his place in society. To make it worse, his three friends came to "console" him and ended up kicking him when he was down. Those are the obvious facts of the Book of Job as you can read them here.

On another level, though, Job is a story about the most difficult questions we face in life. Why do good people have bad things happen to them? If God sometimes intervenes in our lives, why doesn't he *always* intervene? If God is good, then why is there bad? If we obey God, why aren't we always rewarded for it? If something bad happens, does that mean we are being punished?

Job was a man who didn't just say "God is good" when good things happened. Instead, he said, "God is good and life is hard, but God is still good." That's pretty amazing, isn't it? The Book of Job reminds us that just because we can't always figure life out, that doesn't mean God is not who he says he is.

Outline

1:1-5 .... Righteous Job and His Family in Uz
1:6-12 .... Satan Attacks Job's Character
1:13—2:13 .... Job Loses His Wealth, Family, and Health
3:1-26 .... Job Curses the Day of His Birth
4:1—14:22 .... The First Round of the Debate
15:1—21:34 .... The Second Round of the Debate
22:1—26:14 .... The Third Round of the Debate
27:1—30:31 .... Job's Closing Statements
31:1-40 .... Job Swears That He Is Innocent
32:1—37:24 .... Elihu's Speeches
38:1—39:30 .... God's First Speech
40:1—42:6 .... God's Second Speech and Job's Responses
42:7-17 .... The Lord Again Blesses Job with Health, Wealth, and Family

Purpose We are to trust God's wisdom and his love when troubles come.

Theme The Suffering of the Godly and the Sovereignty of God

Date of writing Uncertain

"Even if God kills me, I have hope in him; I will still defend my ways to his face" (13:15).

Bible Talk

The Advice of Friends

Job was in a bad way. His wife knew it, and his friends knew it.

Job's friends heard about his troubles and did what friends do. They came to help. At first they did a pretty good job; but then, they started trying to fix the situation. They were convinced that Job had brought his troubles on himself. In the end they made him feel worse about it all because they tried to tell him it was all his fault.

Job listened to their long-winded speeches, but he just didn't believe that they were right. So even though he was miserable and worn out, he stood his ground. Sometimes friends are the hardest people to stand up to. Job gives us a good example of how to do this.

SATAN'S PLACE IN THE SCENARIO

The Book of Job gives us a major insight into the role of Satan in our world. Yes, he's real. No, he doesn't wear a red suit. Yes, he used to be an angel, a servant of God. Yes, he still has conversations with God. That's an amazing fact, isn't it?

When the Book of Job opens, Satan is having a conversation with God. God mentions Job and his faithfulness. Satan says something like, "Sure, he's a good man because he only knows good times. Give him some hard times and he'll turn his back on you."

Satan was wrong about Job. Doesn't that whole scenario make you wonder, though, what kind of conversation God and Satan would have about you?

JOB, THE GOOD MAN

1
[1]A man named Job lived in the land of Uz.
He was an honest and innocent man; he honored God and stayed away from evil. [2]Job had
seven sons and three daughters. [3]He owned
seven thousand sheep, three thousand
camels, five hundred teams of
oxen, and five hundred
female donkeys. He also had a
large number of servants. He
was the greatest man among
all the people of the East.
[4]Job's sons took turns
holding feasts in their homes and
invited their sisters to eat and drink with them.
[5]After a feast was over, Job would send and
have them made clean. Early in the morning
Job would offer a burnt offering for each of
them, because he thought, "My children may
have sinned and cursed God in their hearts."
Job did this every time.

CHARACTER
Who is a good model of integrity? (1:1)

SATAN APPEARS BEFORE THE LORD

[6]One day the angels came to show themselves before the LORD, and Satan was with
them. [7]The LORD said to Satan, "Where have
you come from?"
Satan answered the LORD, "I have been
wandering around the earth, going back and
forth in it."
[8]Then the LORD said to Satan, "Have you
noticed my servant Job? No one else on earth
is like him. He is an honest and innocent man,
honoring God and staying away from evil."
[9]But Satan answered the LORD, "Job honors
God for a good reason. [10]You have put a wall
around him, his family, and everything he
owns. You have blessed the things he has
done. His flocks and herds are so large they
almost cover the land. [11]But reach out your
hand and destroy everything he has, and he
will curse you to your face."
[12]The LORD said to Satan, "All right, then.
Everything Job has is in your power, but you
must not touch Job himself." Then Satan left
the LORD's presence.
[13]One day Job's sons and daughters were
eating and drinking wine together at the oldest
brother's house. [14]A messenger came to Job
and said, "The oxen were plowing and the
donkeys were eating grass nearby, [15]when the
Sabeans attacked and carried them away. They
killed the servants with swords, and I am the
only one who escaped to tell you!"
[16]The messenger was still speaking when
another messenger arrived and said, "Lightning
from God fell from the sky. It burned up the
sheep and the servants, and I am the only one
who escaped to tell you!"
[17]The second messenger was still speaking
when another messenger arrived and said,
"The Babylonians sent three groups of attack-
ers that swept down and stole your camels and
killed the servants. I am the only one who escaped to tell you!"

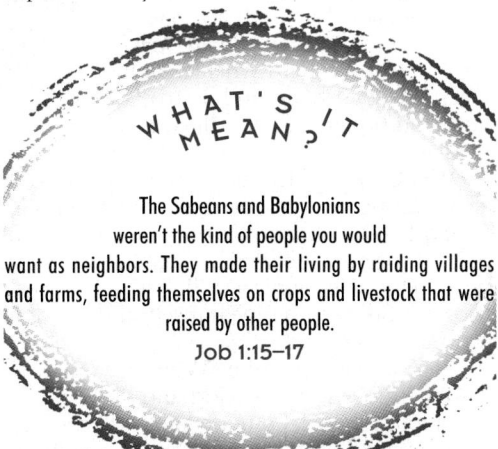

WHAT'S IT MEAN?
The Sabeans and Babylonians weren't the kind of people you would want as neighbors. They made their living by raiding villages and farms, feeding themselves on crops and livestock that were raised by other people.
Job 1:15–17

[18]The third messenger was still speaking
when another messenger arrived and said,
"Your sons and daughters were eating and
drinking wine together at the oldest brother's
house. [19]Suddenly a great wind came from the
desert, hitting all four corners of the house at
once. The house fell in on the young people,
and they are all dead. I am the only one who
escaped to tell you!"
[20]When Job heard this, he got up and tore
his robe and shaved his head to show how sad
he was. Then he bowed down to the ground to
worship God. [21]He said:

"I was naked when I was
born,
and I will be naked
when I die.
The LORD gave these
things to me,
and he has taken them away.
Praise the name of the LORD."

[22]In all this Job did not sin or blame God.

MONEY
Will our possessions last forever? (1:21)

SATAN APPEARS BEFORE THE LORD AGAIN

2
[1]On another day the angels came to show
themselves before the LORD, and Satan was
with them again. [2]The LORD said to Satan,
"Where have you come from?"
Satan answered the LORD, "I have been
wandering around the earth, going back and
forth in it."

3 Then the LORD said to Satan, "Have you
noticed my servant Job? No one else on earth
is like him. He is an honest and innocent man, honoring God and
staying away from evil. You
caused me to ruin him for no
good reason, but he continues
to be without blame."
4 "One skin for another!" Satan answered. "A man will give all
he has to save his own life. 5 But
reach out your hand and destroy his
flesh and bones, and he will curse you to your
face."
6 The LORD said to Satan, "All right, then. Job
is in your power, but you may not take his life."
7 So Satan left the LORD's presence. He put
painful sores on Job's body, from the top of his
head to the soles of his feet. 8 Job took a piece of
broken pottery to scrape himself, and he sat in
ashes in misery.
9 Job's wife said to him, "Why are you trying
to stay innocent? Curse God and die!"
10 Job answered, "You are talking like a foolish woman. Should we take only good things
from God and not trouble?" In spite of all this
Job did not sin in what he said.

"Should we take only good things from God and not trouble?" (Job 2:10b)

JOB'S THREE FRIENDS COME TO HELP

11 Now Job had three friends: Eliphaz the
Temanite, Bildad the Shuhite, and
Zophar the Naamathite.
When these friends heard
about Job's troubles, they
agreed to meet and visit him.
They wanted to show their
concern and to comfort him.
12 They saw Job from far away,
but he looked so different they almost didn't
recognize him. They began to cry loudly and
tore their robes and put dirt on their heads to
show how sad they were. 13 Then they sat on
the ground with Job seven days and seven
nights. No one said a word to him
because they saw how much he
was suffering.

FRIENDSHIP
What should we do to help hurting friends? (2:11)

WHAT'S IT MEAN?

The conversation that follows seems to suggest that Eliphaz was the oldest and most respected of Job's friends. That's not surprising. Teman, Eliphaz's hometown, was known for its wise men.
Job 2:11

JOB CURSES HIS BIRTH

3
1 After seven days Job cried
out and cursed the day he had
been born, 2 saying:

3 "Let the day I was born be
destroyed,
and the night it was said, 'A boy is
born!'
4 Let that day turn to darkness.
Don't let God care about it.
Don't let light shine on it.
5 Let darkness and gloom have that day.
Let a cloud hide it.
Let thick darkness cover its light.
6 Let thick darkness capture that night.
Don't count it among the days of the
year
or put it in any of the months.
7 Let that night be empty,
with no shout of joy to be heard.
8 Let those who curse days curse that day.
Let them prepare to wake up the sea
monster Leviathan.
9 Let that day's morning stars never appear;
let it wait for daylight that never comes.
Don't let it see the first light of dawn,
10 because it allowed me to be born
and did not hide trouble from my eyes.

11 "Why didn't I die as soon as I was born?
Why didn't I die when I came out of the
womb?
12 Why did my mother's knees receive me,
and my mother's breasts feed me?
13 If they had not been there,
I would be lying dead in peace;
I would be asleep and at rest
14 with kings and wise men of the earth
who built places for themselves that are
now ruined.
15 I would be asleep with rulers
who filled their houses with gold and
silver.
16 Why was I not buried like a child born
dead,
like a baby who never saw the light of
day?
17 In the grave the wicked stop making
trouble,
and the weary workers are at rest.

18 In the grave there is rest for the captives
who no longer hear the shout of the
slave driver.
19 People great and small are in the grave,
and the slave is freed from his master.

20 "Why is light given to those in misery?
Why is life given to those who are so
unhappy?
21 They want to die, but death does not
come.
They search for death more than for
hidden treasure.
22 They are very happy
when they get to the grave.
23 They cannot see where they are going.
God has hidden the road ahead.
24 I make sad sounds as I eat;
my groans pour out like water.
25 Everything I feared and dreaded
has happened to me.
26 I have no peace or quietness.
I have no rest, only trouble."

WHAT'S IT MEAN?

Job's "conversation" with his friends was probably a lot different from the talks you have with your friends. Job's friends spoke in what are called "cycles" of debate. Eliphaz, Bildad, and Zophar took turns talking to Job in three different cycles. (Though, for some reason, Zophar chose not to say anything in the third cycle.) After each of their speeches, Job was given a chance to reply.
Job 4:1

ELIPHAZ SPEAKS

4 1 Then Eliphaz the Temanite answered:

2 "If someone tried to speak with you,
would you be upset?
I cannot keep from speaking.
3 Think about the many people
you have taught
and the weak
hands you have
made strong.
4 Your words have
comforted those who
fell,

ENCOURAGEMENT
How can we encourage others? (4:3–4)

and you have strengthened those who
could not stand.
5 But now trouble comes to you, and you
are discouraged;
trouble hits you, and you are terrified.
6 You should have confidence because you
respect God;
you should have hope because you are
innocent.

WHAT'S IT MEAN?

Dreams were very important to people in ancient times. Awesome nighttime visions like the one Eliphaz experienced were thought to be messages from God. Sometimes those visions predicted the future; other times, they displayed important truths to people like Eliphaz.
Job 4:13

7 "Remember that the innocent will not die;
honest people will never be destroyed.
8 I have noticed that people who plow evil
and plant trouble, harvest it.
9 God's breath destroys them,
and a blast of his anger kills them.
10 Lions may roar and growl,
but when the teeth of a strong lion are
broken,
11 that lion dies of hunger.
The cubs of the mother lion are
scattered.

12 "A word was brought to me in secret,
and my ears heard a whisper of it.
13 It was during a nightmare
when people are in deep sleep.
14 I was trembling with fear;
all my bones were shaking.
15 A spirit glided past my face,
and the hair on my body stood on end.
16 The spirit stopped,
but I could not see what it was.
A shape stood before my eyes,
and I heard a quiet voice.
17 It said, 'Can a human be more right than
God?
Can a person be pure before his maker?
18 God does not trust his angels;

he blames them for mistakes.
[19]So he puts even more blame on people
who live in clay houses,[n]
whose foundations are made of dust,
who can be crushed like a moth.
[20]Between dawn and sunset many people
are broken to pieces;
without being noticed, they die and are
gone forever.
[21]The ropes of their tents are pulled up,
and they die without wisdom.'

5

[1]"Call if you want to, Job, but no one will
answer you.
You can't turn to any of the holy ones.
[2]Anger kills the fool,
and jealousy slays the stupid.
[3]I have seen a fool succeed,
but I cursed his home immediately.
[4]His children are far from safety
and are crushed in court with no
defense.
[5]The hungry eat his harvest,
even taking what grew among the
thorns,
and thirsty people want his wealth.
[6]Hard times do not come up from the
ground,
and trouble does not grow from the
earth.
[7]People produce trouble
as surely as sparks fly upward.
[8]"But if I were you, I would call on God
and bring my problem before him.
[9]God does wonders that cannot be
understood;
he does so many miracles they cannot
be counted.
[10]He gives rain to the earth
and sends water on the fields.
[11]He makes the humble person important
and lifts the sad to places of safety.
[12]He ruins the plans of those who trick
others
so they have no success.
[13]He catches the wise in their own clever
traps
and sweeps away the plans of those
who try to trick others.
[14]Darkness covers them up in the daytime;
even at noon they feel around in the
dark.
[15]God saves the needy from their lies
and from the harm done by powerful
people.
[16]So the poor have hope,
while those who are
unfair are silenced.

DISCIPLINE
Is God's discipline good? (5:17)

[17]"The one whom God
corrects is happy,
so do not hate being
corrected by the Almighty.
[18]God hurts, but he also bandages up;

4:19 clay houses This is probably talking about people's bodies.

Promise

HE PROMISES TO DELIVER YOU FROM HARM TIME AFTER TIME.

He will save you from six troubles; even seven troubles will not harm you (Job 5:19).

Only in heaven will we know how many times God has rescued us from harm. The list probably fills books: family car delayed in traffic to avoid three-car pileup; grounded from the big sophomore party and kept from the lure of drugs and a police raid; army of angels sent to protect unsuspecting students from attempted mugging on campus. Sometimes we can look back and know that God put his hand on us, directed our steps, and protected us. But most of the time we walk around totally unaware of his divine intervention on our behalf. Time after time he keeps us safe from things we can see, and even the things we can't. Take a minute to thank him for keeping watch over the big and the little things in your life and for guarding every move you make.

SEE FOR YOURSELF:

Ps. 7:10; Nah. 1:7; 2 Thess. 3:3

he injures, but his hands also heal.
19 He will save you from six troubles;
even seven troubles will not harm you.
20 God will buy you back from death in
times of hunger,
and in battle he will save you from the
sword.
21 You will be protected from the tongue that
strikes like a whip,
and you will not be afraid when
destruction comes.
22 You will laugh at destruction and hunger,
and you will not fear the wild animals,
23 because you will have an agreement with
the stones in the field,
and the wild animals will be at peace
with you.
24 You will know that your tent is safe,
because you will check the things you
own and find nothing missing.
25 You will know that you will have many
children,
and your descendants will be like the
grass on the earth.
26 You will come to the grave with all your
strength,
like bundles of grain gathered at the
right time.

WHAT'S IT MEAN?

A large family and a long, healthy life were considered to be rewards from God for living in a way that pleased him. You can imagine the kind of things that were said about people who lost their families and their health.

Job 5:25–26

27 "We have checked this, and it is true,
so hear it and decide what it means to
you."

JOB ANSWERS ELIPHAZ

6 1 Then Job answered:

2 "I wish my suffering could be weighed
and my misery put on scales.
3 My sadness would be heavier than the
sand of the seas.
No wonder my words seem careless.
4 The arrows of the Almighty are in me;
my spirit drinks in their poison;
God's terrors are gathered against me.
5 A wild donkey does not bray when it has
grass to eat,
and an ox is quiet when it has feed.
6 Tasteless food is not eaten without salt,
and there is no flavor in the white of an
egg.
7 I refuse to touch it;
such food makes me sick.

8 "How I wish that I might have what I ask
for
and that God would give me what I
hope for.
9 How I wish God would crush me
and reach out his hand to destroy me.
10 Then I would have this comfort
and be glad even in this unending pain,
because I would know I did not reject
the words of the Holy One.

11 "I do not have the strength to wait.
There is nothing to hope for,
so why should I be patient?
12 I do not have the strength of stone;
my flesh is not bronze.
13 I have no power to help myself,
because success has been taken away
from me.

14 "They say, 'A man's friends should be kind
to him when he is in trouble,
even if he stops fearing the Almighty.'
15 But my brothers cannot be counted on.
They are like streams that do not always
flow,
streams that sometimes run over.
16 They are made dark by melting ice
and rise with melting snow.
17 But they stop flowing in the dry season;
they disappear when it is hot.
18 Travelers turn away from their paths
and go into the desert and die.
19 The groups of travelers from Tema look
for water,
and the traders of Sheba look hopefully.
20 They are upset because they had been
sure;
when they arrive, they are disappointed.
21 You also have been no help.
You see something terrible, and you are
afraid.
22 I have never said, 'Give me a gift.
Use your wealth to pay my debt.

23 Save me from the enemy's power.
Buy me back from the clutches of cruel people.'

24 "Teach me, and I will be quiet.
Show me where I have been wrong.
25 Honest words are painful,
but your arguments prove nothing.
26 Do you mean to correct what I say?
Will you treat the words of a troubled man as if they were only wind?
27 You would even gamble for orphans
and would trade away your friend.

28 "But now please look at me.
I would not lie to your face.
29 Change your mind; do not be unfair;
think again, because my innocence is being questioned.
30 What I am saying is not wicked;
I can tell the difference between right and wrong.

7

1 "People have a hard task on earth,
and their days are like those of a laborer.
2 They are like a slave wishing for the evening shadows,
like a laborer waiting to be paid.
3 But I am given months that are empty,
and nights of misery have been given to me.
4 When I lie down, I think, 'How long until I get up?'
The night is long, and I toss until dawn.
5 My body is covered with worms and scabs,
and my skin is broken and full of sores.

6 "My days go by faster than a weaver's tool,
and they come to an end without hope.
7 Remember, God, that my life is only a breath.
My eyes will never see happy times again.
8 Those who see me now will see me no more;
you will look for me, but I will be gone.
9 As a cloud disappears and is gone,
people go to the grave and never return.
10 They will never come back to their houses again,
and their places will not know them anymore.

11 "So I will not stay quiet;
I will speak out in the suffering of my spirit.
I will complain because I am so unhappy.
12 I am not the sea or the sea monster.
So why have you set a guard over me?
13 Sometimes I think my bed will comfort me
or that my couch will stop my complaint.
14 Then you frighten me with dreams
and terrify me with visions.

WHAT'S IT MEAN?

Weaving involved a large frame (called a loom) with thread stretched across it. Using a tool called a shuttle, the weaver would then pull another piece of thread crosswise through the frame—in a quick back-and-forth rhythm—to create fabric.

Job 7:6

On the Edge

We were only born yesterday and know nothing. Our days on earth are only a shadow (Job 8:9).

Ever had anyone say, "You think you know everything"? They were being sarcastic, taking a jab at you. They were reminding you that your knowledge is limited. The Book of Job says the same thing—that you are only on this earth a short time and you know very little. Job says that you would be wise to learn from your parents and grandparents, and all the years they have already lived. Because of their age, we assume they couldn't possibly contribute anything to our generation. Not so. You'd be foolish to believe they haven't felt the emotions you deal with or struggled to make hard decisions. So lay down your stereotypes, listen to your ancestors, and learn from their understanding. The more you listen, the more you learn.

SEE FOR YOURSELF:
Prov. 4:1–5; 23:12

15 My throat prefers to be choked;
my bones welcome death.
16 I hate my life; I don't want to live forever.
Leave me alone, because my days have no meaning.

17 "Why do you make people so important
and give them so much attention?
18 You examine them every morning
and test them every moment.
19 Will you never look away from me
or leave me alone even long enough to swallow?
20 If I have sinned, what have I done to you,
you watcher of humans?
Why have you made me your target?
Have I become a heavy load for you?
21 Why don't you pardon my wrongs
and forgive my sins?
I will soon lie down in the dust of death.
Then you will search for me, but I will be no more."

BILDAD SPEAKS TO JOB

8 1 Then Bildad the Shuhite answered:

2 "How long will you say such things?
Your words are no more than wind.
3 God does not twist justice;
the Almighty does not make wrong what is right.
4 Your children sinned against God,
and he punished them for their sins.
5 But you should ask God for help
and pray to the Almighty for mercy.
6 If you are good and honest,
he will stand up for you
and bring you back where you belong.
7 Where you began will seem unimportant,
because your future will be so successful.

WHAT'S IT MEAN?

The papyrus plant grows in the water of swamps and marshes. Papyrus stalks are about the thickness of a person's wrist and can reach as high as twelve feet. More than anything else, papyrus resembles an over-size piece of grass. The Egyptians used papyrus to make paper, blankets, sandals, and rafts.

Job 8:11

8 "Ask old people;
find out what their ancestors learned,
9 because we were only born yesterday and know nothing.
Our days on earth are only a shadow.
10 Those people will teach you and tell you
and speak about what they know.

Promise — HE PROMISES TO GIVE YOU SOMETHING TO LAUGH ABOUT.

Surely God does not reject the innocent or give strength to those who do evil. God will yet fill your mouth with laughter and your lips with shouts of joy (Job 8:20–21).

Are you a smiler or a frowner? Do you naturally notice happy things, or are you a walking vessel of gloom and doom? How about laughing? Do you remember the last time you laughed until your sides hurt, and your eyes watered, and you begged for mercy—you just couldn't laugh anymore? However long it's been, whatever your natural disposition, God promises to give you something to laugh about. He promises to walk right into your most depressing day and turn things around. God didn't put you here to see how awful he could make you feel. He put you here to glorify him and to enjoy life. So invite him into your day and tell him you really need something to laugh about. Watch him do a miracle on your behalf. No heart is too hard, no day is too far gone, when the Maker of laughter keeps his promise.

SEE FOR YOURSELF:

1 Sam. 2:1; Ps. 126:1–3

[11]Papyrus plants cannot grow where there is no swamp,
and reeds cannot grow tall without water.
[12]While they are still growing and not yet cut,
they will dry up quicker than grass.
[13]That is what will happen to those who forget God;
the hope of the wicked will be gone.
[14]What they hope in is easily broken;
what they trust is like a spider's web.
[15]They lean on the spider's web, but it breaks.
They grab it, but it does not hold up.
[16]They are like well-watered plants in the sunshine
that spread their roots all through the garden.
[17]They wrap their roots around a pile of rocks
and look for a place among the stones.
[18]But if a plant is torn from its place,
then that place rejects it and says, 'I never saw you.'
[19]Now joy has gone away;
other plants grow up from the same dirt.

> "Surely God does not reject the innocent or give strength to those who do evil." (Job 8:20)

[20]"Surely God does not reject the innocent
or give strength to those who do evil.
[21]God will yet fill your mouth with laughter
and your lips with shouts of joy.
[22]Your enemies will be covered with shame,
and the tents of the wicked will be gone."

JOB ANSWERS BILDAD

9
[1]Then Job answered:

[2]"Yes, I know that this is true,
but how can anyone be right in the presence of God?
[3]Someone might want to argue with God,
but no one could answer God,
not one time out of a thousand.
[4]God's wisdom is deep, and his power is great;
no one can fight him without getting hurt.
[5]God moves mountains without anyone knowing it
and turns them over when he is angry.
[6]He shakes the earth out of its place
and makes its foundations tremble.
[7]He commands the sun not to shine
and shuts off the light of the stars.
[8]He alone stretches out the skies
and walks on the waves of the sea.
[9]It is God who made the Bear, Orion, and the Pleiades[n]
and the groups of stars in the southern sky.
[10]He does wonders that cannot be understood;
he does so many miracles they cannot be counted.
[11]When he passes me, I cannot see him;
when he goes by me, I do not recognize him.
[12]If he snatches something away, no one can stop him
or say to him, 'What are you doing?'
[13]God will not hold back his anger.
Even the helpers of the monster Rahab lie at his feet in fear.
[14]So how can I argue with God,
or even find words to argue with him?
[15]Even if I were right, I could not answer him;
I could only beg God, my Judge, for mercy.
[16]If I called to him and he answered,
I still don't believe he would listen to me.

WHAT'S IT MEAN?

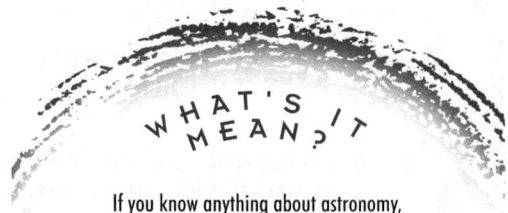

If you know anything about astronomy, you know that the Bear and Orion are bright formations of stars. You may even be able to find them on starry nights. Pleiades is a bit more difficult to spot. In fact, of the hundreds of stars that make up the constellation Pleiades, only six or seven are visible to the naked eye.
Job 9:9

9:9 Bear . . . Pleiades Names of well-known groups of stars.

On the Edge

Yes, I know that this is true, but how can anyone be right in the presence of God? (Job 9:2).

Most of us get into trouble by convincing ourselves that we're okay. Basically good people. No major sin happening. No blatant disrespect. Decent grades in school. Things at home are calm. So we're sailing along just fine.

But Job says that no human is right (innocent) in the sight of God—and that's true—before you get saved. When you become a Christian, God gives you a new heart. What you're dealing with is a sinful *nature,* not a sinful heart. In spite of the fact that you do (and will) sin, the great news is that God is more gracious than you could ever imagine, and you can be more accepted and loved than you ever hoped.

SEE FOR YOURSELF:
Rom. 3:23–24; Gal. 3:22; 1 John 1:8

17 He would crush me with a storm
and multiply my wounds for no reason.
18 He would not let me catch my breath
but would overwhelm me with misery.
19 When it comes to strength, God is stronger
than I;
when it comes to justice, no one can
accuse him.
20 Even if I were right, my own mouth
would say I was wrong;
if I were innocent, my mouth would say
I was guilty.

21 "I am innocent,
but I don't care about myself.
I hate my own life.
22 It is all the same. That is why I say,
'God destroys both the innocent and the
guilty.'
23 If the whip brings sudden death,
God will laugh at the suffering of the
innocent.
24 When the land falls into the hands of evil
people,
he covers the judges' faces so they can't
see it.
If it is not God who does this, then who
is it?

25 "My days go by faster than a runner;
they fly away without my seeing any
joy.
26 They glide past like paper boats.
They attack like eagles swooping down
to feed.
27 Even though I say, 'I will forget my
complaint;
I will change the look on my face and
smile,'
28 I still dread all my suffering.
I know you will hold me guilty.
29 I have already been found guilty,
so why should I struggle for no reason?
30 I might wash myself with soap
and scrub my hands with strong soap,
31 but you would push me into a dirty pit,
and even my clothes would hate me.

32 "God is not a man like me, so I cannot
answer him.
We cannot meet each other in court.
33 I wish there were someone to make peace
between us,

On the Edge

He does wonders that cannot be understood; he does so many miracles they cannot be counted. When he passes me, I cannot see him; when he goes by me, I do not recognize him (Job 9:10–11).

In this passage, Job ponders the hugeness of God. His miracles are beyond our understanding. His creativity is awesome, and we are part of it. His justice is supreme and fair. He is so amazing that he moves right past us, and we don't even know it. He is closer than we could imagine, so why do we doubt his wisdom and his power? We have mistakenly believed that God is up there somewhere, far away, looking down. He seems remote and out of touch. Distant. But God is here. Intimate. So close. He moves right past you. Are you willing to trust the One who is beside you to care for you and to love you? His presence is real. His patience is incredible. Since he has already been with you all this time, why keep ignoring him?

SEE FOR YOURSELF:
Ps. 119:151; 145:18

someone to decide our case.
34 Maybe he could remove God's
punishment
so his terror would no longer frighten
me.
35 Then I could speak without being afraid,
but I am not able to do that.

10

1 "I hate my life,
so I will complain without holding back;
I will speak because I am so unhappy.
2 I will say to God: Do not hold me guilty,
but tell me what you have against me.
3 Does it make you happy to trouble me?
Don't you care about me, the work of
your hands?
Are you happy with the plans of evil
people?
4 Do you have human eyes
that see as we see?
5 Are your days like the days of humans,
and your years like our years?
6 You look for the evil I have done
and search for my sin.
7 You know I am not guilty,
but no one can save me from your
power.

8 "Your hands shaped and made me.
Do you now turn around and destroy
me?
9 Remember that you molded me like a
piece of clay.
Will you now turn me back into dust?
10 You formed me inside my mother
like cheese formed from milk.
11 You dressed me with skin and flesh;
you sewed me together with bones and
muscles.
12 You gave me life and showed me kindness,
and in your care you watched over my
life.

13 "But in your heart you hid other plans.
I know this was in your mind.
14 If I sinned, you would watch me
and would not let my sin go
unpunished.
15 How terrible it will be for me if I am
guilty!
Even if I am right, I cannot lift my head.
I am full of shame
and experience only pain.
16 If I hold up my head, you hunt me like a
lion
and again show your terrible power
against me.
17 You bring new witnesses against me
and increase your anger against me.
Your armies come against me.

18 "So why did you allow me to be born?
I wish I had died before anyone saw me.
19 I wish I had never lived,
but had been carried straight from birth
to the grave.
20 The few days of my life are almost over.
Leave me alone so I can have a moment
of joy.
21 Soon I will leave; I will not return
from the land of darkness and gloom,
22 the land of darkest night,
from the land of gloom and confusion,
where even the light is darkness."

WHAT'S IT MEAN?

"The land of darkness and gloom" refers to Sheol, the place of the dead, according to ancient Hebrew beliefs. Sheol was pictured as a dark and gloomy underground world where the souls of both good and bad people lived after death. Sheol was also the place where people were thought to receive their eternal punishment or reward, according to how they lived.

Job 10:21–22

ZOPHAR SPEAKS TO JOB

11

1 Then Zophar the Naamathite answered:

2 "Should these words go unanswered?
Is this talker in the right?
3 Your lies do not make people quiet;
people should correct you when you
make fun of God.
4 You say, 'My teachings are right,
and I am clean in God's sight.'
5 I wish God would speak
and open his lips against you
6 and tell you the secrets of wisdom,
because wisdom has two sides.
Know this: God has even forgotten some
of your sin.

7 "Can you understand the secrets of God?
Can you search the limits of the
Almighty?

On the Edge

Can you understand the secrets of God? Can you search the limits of the Almighty? His limits are higher than the heavens; you cannot reach them! They are deeper than the grave; you cannot understand them! (Job 11:7–8).

To say that God is mysterious is to say that we don't fully understand him. We don't understand how he creates or how he makes decisions. His timing seems slow to us. Heaven is a big mystery; and all those miracles, well, we just don't get it. There are so many aspects of God that we can't totally grasp. That's where Colossians 2:2–3 comes in. Paul writes that Christ is the key to God's mystery. Jesus physically came to this earth and through his ministry began to unveil the mysteries of God. Paul also writes in 1 Corinthians 13:12 that now we see God as "a dim reflection, as if we were looking into a mirror, but then we shall see clearly." As you grow stronger in your relationship with the Lord, you'll begin to know him more and more. But even when you're 90 years old and have walked with him every day, there will still be magnificent mysteries about him. He's that big. Do you have faith, even in the mystery of God?

SEE FOR YOURSELF:
Deut. 29:29; 1 Cor. 2:7; 13:12; Col. 2:2–3

8 His limits are higher than the heavens; you
cannot reach them!
They are deeper than the grave; you
cannot understand them!
9 His limits are longer than the earth
and wider than the sea.

10 "If God comes along and puts
you in prison
or calls you into court,
no one can stop him.
11 God knows who is evil,
and when he sees evil,
he takes note of it.
12 A fool cannot become
wise
any more than a wild donkey can be
born tame.

GOD
Does God see people sin? (11:11)

13 "You must give your whole heart to him
and hold out your hands to him for
help.
14 Put away the sin that is in your hand;
let no evil remain in your tent.
15 Then you can lift up your face without
shame,
and you can stand strong without fear.
16 You will forget your trouble
and remember it only as water gone by.
17 Your life will be as bright as the noonday
sun,
and darkness will seem like morning.
18 You will feel safe because there is hope;
you will look around and rest in safety.
19 You will lie down, and no one will scare
you.
Many people will want favors from you.
20 But the wicked will not be able to see,
so they will not escape.
Their only hope will be to die."

JOB ANSWERS ZOPHAR

12

1 Then Job answered:

2 "You really think you are the only wise
people
and that when you die, wisdom will die
with you!
3 But my mind is as good as yours;
you are not better than I am.
Everyone knows all these things.
4 My friends all laugh at me
when I call on God and expect him to
answer me;
they laugh at me even though I am right
and innocent!
5 Those who are comfortable don't care that
others have trouble;
they think it right that those people
should have troubles.
6 The tents of robbers are not bothered,
and those who make God angry are
safe.
They have their god in their pocket.

7 "But ask the animals, and they will teach
you,
or ask the birds of the air, and they will
tell you.
8 Speak to the earth, and it will teach you,
or let the fish of the sea tell you.
9 Every one of these knows
that the hand of the LORD has done this.
10 The life of every creature
and the breath of all people are in God's
hand.

11 The ear tests words
as the tongue tastes food.
12 Older people are wise,
and long life brings understanding.

On the Edge

The ear tests words as the tongue tastes food. Older people are wise, and long life brings understanding (Job 12:11–12).

All those years your grandparents have lived have brought them much wisdom. They have watched several generations go through all the stuff of life, they've seen a lot of people grow up, they've seen people succeed, and they've seen people fail. They may or may not have made wise choices with their lives, but by now they've had lots of time to process the path they chose. They'd be happy to tell you about their successes and the things they would do over again. They'd be so honored that you cared enough to ask. By the time it's too late, and your grandparents are long gone, you'll realize how much they had to offer you. So take some time to get to know them. Ask them lots of questions. Ask about their childhood, their dreams, their disappointments. The smartest people are the ones who can learn from others—you could really learn a lot from your grandparents.

SEE FOR YOURSELF:
Prov. 17:6; 20:29

13 "But only God has wisdom and power,
good advice and understanding.
14 What he tears down cannot be rebuilt;
anyone he puts in prison cannot be let out.
15 If God holds back the waters, there is no rain;
if he lets the waters go, they flood the land.
16 He is strong and victorious;
both the one who fools others and the one who is fooled belong to him.
17 God leads the wise away as captives
and turns judges into fools.
18 He takes off chains that kings put on
and puts a garment on their bodies.
19 He leads priests away naked
and destroys the powerful.
20 He makes trusted people be silent
and takes away the wisdom of older leaders.
21 He brings disgrace on important people
and takes away the weapons of the strong.
22 He uncovers the deep things of darkness
and brings dark shadows into the light.
23 He makes nations great and then destroys them;
he makes nations large and then scatters them.
24 He takes understanding away from the leaders of the earth
and makes them wander through a pathless desert.
25 They feel around in darkness with no light;
he makes them stumble like drunks.

13

1 "Now my eyes have seen all this;
my ears have heard and understood it.
2 What you know, I also know.
You are not better than I am.
3 But I want to speak to the Almighty
and to argue my case with God.
4 But you smear me with lies.
You are worthless doctors, all of you!
5 I wish you would just stop talking;
then you would really be wise!
6 Listen to my argument,
and hear the pleading of my lips.
7 You should not speak evil in the name of God;
you cannot speak God's truth by telling lies.
8 You should not unfairly choose his side against mine;
you should not argue the case for God.
9 You will not do well if he examines you;
you cannot fool God as you might fool humans.
10 God would surely scold you
if you unfairly took one person's side.
11 His bright glory would scare you,
and you would be very much afraid of him.
12 Your wise sayings are worth no more than ashes,
and your arguments are as weak as clay.

13 "Be quiet and let me speak.
Let things happen to me as they will.
14 Why should I put myself in danger
and take my life in my own hands?
15 Even if God kills me, I have hope in him;
I will still defend my ways to his face.

16 This is my salvation.
The wicked cannot come before him.
17 Listen carefully to my words;
let your ears hear what I say.
18 See, I have prepared my case,
and I know I will be proved right.
19 No one can accuse me of doing wrong.
If someone can, I will be quiet and die.

20 "God, please just give me these two things,
and then I will not hide from you:
21 Take your punishment away from me,
and stop frightening me with your terrors.
22 Then call me, and I will answer,
or let me speak, and you answer.
23 How many evil things and sins have I done?
Show me my wrong and my sin.
24 Don't hide your face from me;
don't think of me as your enemy.
25 Don't punish a leaf that is blown by the wind;
don't chase after straw.
26 You write down cruel things against me
and make me suffer for my boyhood sins.
27 You put my feet in chains
and keep close watch wherever I go.
You even mark the soles of my feet.

28 "Everyone wears out like something rotten,
like clothing eaten by moths.

14

1 "All of us born to women
live only a few days and have lots of trouble.
2 We grow up like flowers
and then dry up and die.
We are like a passing
shadow that does not last.

TRIALS

Will we have problems in life? (14:1)

3 Lord, do you need to watch me like this?
Must you bring me before you to be judged?
4 No one can bring something clean from something dirty.
5 Our time is limited.
You have given us only so many months to live
and have set limits we cannot go beyond.
6 So look away from us and leave us alone
until we put in our time like a laborer.

7 "If a tree is cut down,
there is hope that it will grow again
and will send out new branches.
8 Even if its roots grow old in the ground,
and its stump dies in the dirt,
9 at the smell of water it will bud
and put out new shoots like a plant.
10 But we die, and our bodies are laid in the ground;
we take our last breath and are gone.
11 Water disappears from a lake,
and a river loses its water and dries up.
12 In the same way, we lie down and do not rise again;
we will not get up or be awakened
until the heavens disappear.

13 "I wish you would hide me in the grave;
hide me until your anger is gone.
I wish you would set a time
and then remember me!
14 If a person dies, will he live again?
All my days are a struggle;
I will wait until my change comes.
15 You will call, and I will answer you;
you will desire the creature your hands have made.
16 Then you will count my steps,
but you will not keep track of my sin.
17 My wrongs will be closed up in a bag,
and you will cover up my sin.

18 "A mountain washes away and crumbles;
and a rock can be moved from its place.
19 Water washes over stones and wears them down,
and rushing waters wash away the dirt.
In the same way, you destroy my hope.
20 You defeat a person forever, and he is gone;
you change his appearance and send him away.
21 His sons are honored, but he does not know it;
his sons are disgraced, but he does not see it.
22 He only feels the pain of his body
and feels sorry for himself."

ELIPHAZ ANSWERS JOB

15

1 Then Eliphaz the Temanite answered:

2 "A wise person would not answer with empty words
or fill his stomach with the hot east wind.
3 He would not argue with useless words
or make speeches that have no value.
4 But you even destroy respect for God

and limit the worship of him.
5 Your sin teaches your mouth what to say;
you use words to trick others.
6 It is your own mouth, not mine, that
shows you are wicked;
your own lips testify against you.

7 "You are not the first man ever born;
you are not older than the hills.
8 You did not listen in on God's secret
council.
But you limit wisdom to yourself.
9 You don't know any more than we know.
You don't understand any more than we
understand.
10 Old people with gray hair are on our side;
they are even older than your father.
11 Is the comfort God gives you
not enough for you,
even when words are
spoken gently to
you?
12 Has your heart carried
you away from God?
Why do your eyes
flash with anger?
13 Why do you speak out your
anger against God?
Why do these words pour out of
your mouth?

> "I have heard many things like these. You are all painful comforters!" (Job 16:2)

14 "How can anyone be pure?
How can someone born to a woman be
good?
15 God places no trust in his holy ones,
and even the heavens are not pure in
his eyes.
16 How much less pure is one who is terrible
and rotten
and drinks up evil as if it were water!

17 "Listen to me, and I will tell you about it;
I will tell you what I have seen.
18 These are things wise men have told;
their fathers told them, and they have
hidden nothing.
19 (The land was given to their fathers
only,
and no foreigner lived among them.)
20 The wicked suffer pain all their lives;
the cruel suffer during all the years
saved up for them.
21 Terrible sounds fill their ears,
and when things seem to be going well,
robbers attack them.
22 Evil people give up trying to escape from
the darkness;
it has been decided that they will die by
the sword.
23 They wander around and will become
food for vultures.
They know darkness will soon come.
24 Worry and suffering terrify them;
they overwhelm them, like a king ready
to attack,
25 because they shake their fists at God
and try to get their own way against the
Almighty.
26 They stubbornly charge at God
with thick, strong shields.

27 "Although the faces of the wicked are thick
with fat,
and their bellies are fat
with flesh,
28 they will live in towns
that are ruined,
in houses where no one
lives,
which are crumbling
into ruins.
29 The wicked will no longer
get rich,
and the riches they
have will not last;
the things they own will no longer
spread over the land.
30 They will not escape the darkness.
A flame will dry up their branches;
God's breath will carry the wicked
away.
31 The wicked should not fool themselves by
trusting what is useless.
If they do, they will get nothing in
return.
32 Their branches will dry up before they
finish growing
and will never turn green.
33 They will be like a vine whose grapes are
pulled off before they are ripe,
like an olive tree that loses its blossoms.
34 People without God can produce nothing.
Fire will destroy the tents of those who
take money to do evil,
35 who plan trouble and give birth to evil,
whose hearts plan ways to trick others."

JOB ANSWERS ELIPHAZ

16
1 Then Job answered:

2 "I have heard many things like these.
You are all painful comforters!
3 Will your long-winded speeches never
end?

What makes you keep on arguing?
4 I also could speak as you do
if you were in my place.
I could make great speeches against you
and shake my head at you.
5 But, instead, I would encourage you,
and my words would bring you relief.

6 "Even if I speak, my pain is not less,
and if I don't speak, it still does not go
away.
7 God, you have surely taken away my
strength
and destroyed my whole family.
8 You have made me thin and weak,
and this shows I have done wrong.
9 God attacks me and tears me with anger;
he grinds his teeth at me;
my enemy stares at me with his angry
eyes.
10 People open their mouths to make fun of
me
and hit my cheeks to insult me.
They join together against me.
11 God has turned me over to evil people
and has handed me over to the wicked.
12 Everything was fine with me,
but God broke me into pieces;
he held me by the neck and crushed me.
He has made me his target;
13 his archers surround me.
He stabs my kidneys without mercy;
he spills my blood on the ground.
14 Again and again God attacks me;
he runs at me like a soldier.

WHAT'S IT MEAN?

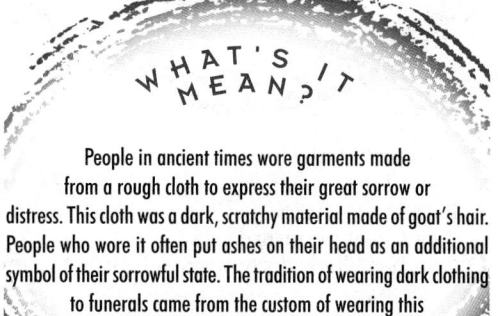

People in ancient times wore garments made from a rough cloth to express their great sorrow or distress. This cloth was a dark, scratchy material made of goat's hair. People who wore it often put ashes on their head as an additional symbol of their sorrowful state. The tradition of wearing dark clothing to funerals came from the custom of wearing this rough, dark cloth in times of sorrow.

Job 16:15–16

15 "I have sewed rough cloth over my skin to
show my sadness
and have buried my face in the dust.
16 My face is red from crying;
I have dark circles around my eyes.
17 Yet my hands have never done anything
cruel,
and my prayer is pure.

18 "Earth, please do not cover up my blood.
Don't let my cry ever stop being heard!
19 Even now I have one who speaks for me
in heaven;
the one who is on my side is high
above.
20 The one who speaks for me is my friend.
My eyes pour out tears to God.
21 He begs God on behalf of a human
as a person begs for his friend.

22 "Only a few years will pass
before I go on the journey of no return.

17

1 My spirit is broken;
the days of my life are almost gone.
The grave is waiting for me.
2 Those who laugh at me surround me;
I watch them insult me.

3 "God, make me a promise.
No one will make a pledge for me.
4 You have closed their minds to
understanding.
Do not let them win over me.
5 A person might speak against his friends
for money,
but if he does, the eyes of his children
go blind.

6 "God has made my name a curse word;
people spit in my face.
7 My sight has grown weak because of my
sadness,
and my body is as thin as a shadow.
8 Honest people are upset about this;
innocent people are upset with those
who do wrong.
9 But those who do right will continue to do
right,
and those whose hands are not dirty
with sin will grow stronger.

10 "But, all of you, come and try again!
I do not find a wise person among you.
11 My days are gone, and my plans have
been destroyed,
along with the desires of my heart.
12 These men think night is day;
when it is dark, they say, 'Light is near.'
13 If the only home I hope for is the grave,

if I spread out my bed in darkness,
14 if I say to the grave, 'You are my father,'
and to the worm, 'You are my mother'
or 'You are my sister,'
15 where, then, is my hope?
Who can see any hope for me?
16 Will hope go down to the gates of death?
Will we go down together into the
dust?"

BILDAD ANSWERS JOB

18

1 Then Bildad the Shuhite answered:

2 "When will you stop these speeches?
Be sensible, and then we can talk.
3 You think of us as cattle,
as if we are stupid.
4 You tear yourself to pieces in your anger.
Should the earth be vacant just for you?
Should the rocks move from their
places?

5 "The lamp of the wicked will be put out,
and the flame in their lamps will stop
burning.
6 The light in their tents will grow dark,
and the lamps by their sides will go out.
7 Their strong steps will grow weak;
they will fall into their own evil traps.
8 Their feet will be caught in a net
when they walk into its web.
9 A trap will catch them by the heel
and hold them tight.
10 A trap for them is hidden on the ground,
right in their path.
11 Terrible things startle them from every
side
and chase them at every step.
12 Hunger takes away their strength,
and disaster is at their side.
13 Disease eats away parts of their skin;
death gnaws at their arms and legs.
14 They are torn from the safety of their tents
and dragged off to Death, the King of
Terrors.
15 Their tents are set on fire,
and sulfur is scattered over their homes.
16 Their roots dry up below ground,
and their branches die above ground.
17 People on earth will not remember them;
their names will be forgotten in the
land.
18 They will be driven from light into
darkness
and chased out of the world.
19 They have no children or descendants
among their people,
and no one will be left alive where they
once lived.
20 People of the west will be shocked at what
has happened to them,
and people of the east will be very
frightened.
21 Surely this is what will happen to the
wicked;
such is the place of one who does not
know God."

JOB ANSWERS BILDAD

19

1 Then Job answered:

2 "How long will you hurt me
and crush me with your words?
3 You have insulted me ten times now
and attacked me without shame.
4 Even if I have sinned,
it is my worry alone.
5 If you want to make yourselves look
better than I,
you can blame me for my suffering.
6 Then know that God has wronged me
and pulled his net around me.

WHAT'S IT MEAN?

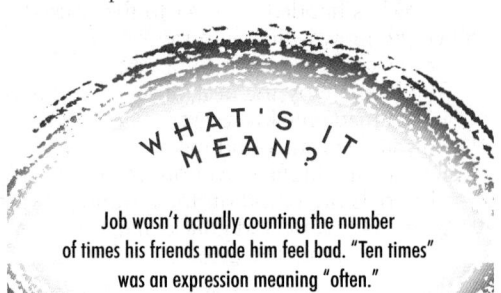

Job wasn't actually counting the number of times his friends made him feel bad. "Ten times" was an expression meaning "often."

Job 19:3

7 "I shout, 'I have been wronged!'
But I get no answer.
I scream for help
but I get no justice.
8 God has blocked my way so I cannot
pass;
he has covered my paths with darkness.
9 He has taken away my honor
and removed the crown from my head.
10 He beats me down on every side until I
am gone;
he destroys my hope like a fallen tree.
11 His anger burns against me,
and he treats me like an enemy.
12 His armies gather;

they prepare to attack me.
They camp around my tent.

13 "God has made my brothers my enemies,
and my friends have become strangers.
14 My relatives have gone away,
and my friends have forgotten me.
15 My guests and my female servants treat me like a stranger;
they look at me as if I were a foreigner.
16 I call for my servant, but he does not answer,
even when I beg him with my own mouth.
17 My wife can't stand my breath,
and my own family dislikes me.
18 Even the little boys hate me
and talk about me when I leave.
19 All my close friends hate me;
even those I love have turned against me.
20 I am nothing but skin and bones;
I have escaped by the skin of my teeth.
21 Pity me, my friends, pity me,
because the hand of God has hit me.
22 Why do you chase me as God does?
Haven't you hurt me enough?

23 "How I wish my words were written down,
written on a scroll.
24 I wish they were carved with an iron pen into lead,
or carved into stone forever.
25 I know that my Defender lives,
and in the end he will stand upon the earth.
26 Even after my skin has been destroyed,
in my flesh I will see God.
27 I will see him myself;
I will see him with my very own eyes.
How my heart wants that to happen!

28 "If you say, 'We will continue to trouble Job,
because the problem lies with him,'
29 you should be afraid of the sword yourselves.
God's anger will bring punishment by the sword.
Then you will know there is judgment."

WHAT'S IT MEAN?

Apparently Job believed that his body would be resurrected at some point after his death. Like many others in his culture, Job probably believed that God would one day rescue the souls of righteous people in Sheol, the place of the dead. They believed that God would then pair up those souls with their bodies and whisk them away to heaven.

Job 19:26

ZOPHAR ANSWERS

20

1 Then Zophar the Naamathite answered:

2 "My troubled thoughts cause me to answer,
because I am very upset.
3 You correct me and I am insulted,
but I understand how to answer you.

4 "You know how it has been for a long time,
ever since people were first put on the earth.
5 The happiness of evil people is brief,
and the joy of the wicked lasts only a moment.
6 Their pride may be as high as the heavens,
and their heads may touch the clouds,
7 but they will be gone forever, like their own dung.
People who knew them will say, 'Where are they?'
8 They will fly away like a dream
and not be found again;
they will be chased away like a vision in the night.
9 Those who saw them will not see them again;
the places where they lived will see them no more.
10 Their children will have to pay back the poor,
and they will have to give up their wealth.
11 They had the strength of their youth in their bones,
but it will lie with them in the dust of death.

12 "Evil may taste sweet in their mouths,
and they may hide it under their tongues.
13 They cannot stand to let go of it;

they keep it in their mouths.
14 But their food will turn sour in their stomachs,
like the poison of a snake inside them.
15 They have swallowed riches, but they will spit them out;
God will make them vomit their riches up.
16 They will suck the poison of snakes,
and the snake's fangs will kill them.
17 They will not admire the sparkling streams
or the rivers flowing with honey and cream.
18 They must give back what they worked for without eating it;
they will not enjoy the money they made from their trading,
19 because they troubled the poor and left them with nothing.
They have taken houses they did not build.

WHAT'S IT MEAN?

Though it may sound like a disgusting drink, the biblical phrase "honey and cream" actually symbolized wealth. Cream was a staple of everyday Hebrew life, a major food source for the Israelites. Honey, on the other hand, was considered a delicacy or a rare treat.

Job 20:17

20 "Evil people never lack an appetite,
and nothing escapes their selfishness.
21 But nothing will be left for them to eat;
their riches will not continue.
22 When they still have plenty, trouble will catch up to them,
and great misery will come down on them.
23 When the wicked fill their stomachs,
God will send his burning anger against them,
and blows of punishment will fall on them like rain.
24 The wicked may run away from an iron weapon,
but a bronze arrow will stab them.
25 They will pull the arrows out of their backs
and pull the points out of their livers.
Terrors will come over them;
26 total darkness waits for their treasure.
A fire not fanned by people will destroy them
and burn up what is left of their tents.
27 The heavens will show their guilt,
and the earth will rise up against them.
28 A flood will carry their houses away,
swept away on the day of God's anger.
29 This is what God plans for evil people;
this is what he has decided they will receive."

JOB ANSWERS ZOPHAR

21

1 Then Job answered:

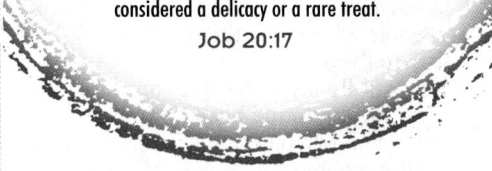

2 "Listen carefully to my words,
and let this be the way you comfort me.
3 Be patient while I speak.
After I have finished, you may continue to make fun of me.

4 "My complaint is not just against people;
I have reason to be impatient.
5 Look at me and be shocked;
put your hand over your mouth in shock.
6 When I think about this, I am terribly afraid
and my body shakes.
7 Why do evil people live a long time?
They grow old and become more powerful.
8 They see their children around them;
they watch them grow up.
9 Their homes are safe and without fear;
God does not punish them.
10 Their bulls never fail to mate;
their cows have healthy calves.
11 They send out their children like a flock;
their little ones dance about.
12 They sing to the music of tambourines and harps,
and the sound of the flute makes them happy.
13 Evil people enjoy successful lives
and then go peacefully to the grave.
14 They say to God, 'Leave us alone!
We don't want to know your ways.
15 Who is the Almighty that we should serve him?
What would we gain by praying to him?'

16 The success of the wicked is not their own
doing.
Their way of thinking is different from
mine.
17 Yet how often are the lamps of evil people
turned off?
How often does trouble come to them?
How often do they suffer God's angry
punishment?
18 How often are they like straw in the wind
or like chaff that is blown away by a
storm?
19 It is said, 'God saves up a person's
punishment for his children.'
But God should punish the wicked
themselves so they will know it.
20 Their eyes should see their own
destruction,
and they should suffer the anger of the
Almighty.
21 They do not care about the families they
leave behind
when their lives have come to an end.

22 "No one can teach
knowledge to God;
he is the one who
judges even the most
important people.
23 One person dies while he
still has all his strength,
feeling completely safe and comfortable.
24 His body was well fed,
and his bones were strong and healthy.
25 But another person dies with an unhappy
heart,
never enjoying any happiness.
26 They are buried next to each other,
and worms cover them both.

27 "I know very well your thoughts
and your plans to wrong me.
28 You ask about me, 'Where is this great
man's house?
Where are the tents where the wicked
live?'
29 Have you never asked those who travel?
Have you never listened to their stories?
30 On the day of God's anger and
punishment,
it is the wicked who are spared.
31 Who will accuse them to their faces?
Who will pay them back for the evil
they have done?
32 They are carried to their graves,
and someone keeps watch over their
tombs.
33 The dirt in the valley seems sweet to them.
Everybody follows after them,
and many people go before them.

34 "So how can you comfort me with this
nonsense?
Your answers are only lies!"

GOD

Is God perfect? (21:22)

ELIPHAZ ANSWERS

22

1 Then Eliphaz the Temanite answered:

2 "Can anyone be of real use to God?
Can even a wise person do him good?
3 Does it help the Almighty for you to be
good?
Does he gain anything if you are
innocent?
4 Does God punish you for respecting him?
Does he bring you into court for this?
5 No! It is because your evil is without
limits
and your sins have no end.
6 You took your brothers' things for a debt
they didn't owe;
you took clothes from people and left
them naked.
7 You did not give water to tired people,
and you kept food from the hungry.
8 You were a powerful man who owned
land;
you were honored and lived in the land.
9 But you sent widows away empty-handed,
and you mistreated orphans.
10 That is why traps are all around you
and sudden danger frightens you.
11 That is why it is so dark you cannot see
and a flood of water covers you.

WHAT'S IT MEAN?

The sins Eliphaz mentioned may not seem terrible today, but in ancient times they were pretty serious. The wealthy were expected to take care of poor people, orphans, and widows, without demanding or expecting anything in return. Homeowners were expected to welcome traveling guests and strangers alike, inviting them into their homes and treating them like family.

Job 22:6–9

12 "God is in the highest part of heaven.
See how high the highest stars are!
13 But you ask, 'What does God know?
Can he judge us through the dark clouds?
14 Thick clouds cover him so he cannot see us
as he walks around high up in the sky.'
15 Are you going to stay on the old path
where evil people walk?
16 They were carried away before their time was up,
and their foundations were washed away by a flood.
17 They said to God, 'Leave us alone!
The Almighty can do nothing to us.'
18 But it was God who filled their houses with good things.
Their way of thinking is different from mine.

19 "Good people can watch and be glad;
the innocent can laugh at them and say,
20 'Surely our enemies are destroyed,
and fire burns up their wealth.'

21 "Obey God and be at peace with him;
this is the way to happiness.
22 Accept teaching from his mouth,
and keep his words in your heart.
23 If you return to the Almighty, you will be blessed again.
So remove evil from your house.
24 Throw your gold nuggets into the dust
and your fine gold among the rocks in the ravines.
25 Then the Almighty will be your gold
and the best silver for you.
26 You will find pleasure in the Almighty,
and you will look up to him.
27 You will pray to him, and he will hear you,
and you will keep your promises to him.
28 Anything you decide will be done,
and light will shine on your ways.
29 When people are made humble and you say, 'Have courage,'
then the humble will be saved.
30 Even a guilty person will escape
and be saved because your hands are clean."

"Obey God and be at peace with him; this is the way to happiness." (Job 22:21)

JOB ANSWERS

23

1 Then Job answered:

2 "My complaint is still bitter today.
I groan because God's heavy hand is on me.

Promise

HE PROMISES TO HEAR AND ANSWER YOUR PRAYERS.

You will pray to him, and he will hear you, and you will keep your promises to him (Job 22:27).

Some high school kids meet once a week before school to pray. Last week they prayed for a job for one of their dads, for a grandmother to be healed of cancer, and for a friend who had a hard exam coming up. This week they met and as soon as they got together, the reports began: "My dad got a job the very morning we prayed!" "My grandmother's doctor can't find any trace of the cancer." "Our friend thinks he did well on his exam and thanks you for praying." They all were looking at each other in amazement. "Wow," someone said, "God really answered our prayers!" Sure, God answers our prayers, but we sometimes pray with so much doubt that we're totally shocked when he does.

Pray with assurance that God promises to answer. Expect him to work and watch for his action. Remember that God will answer in one of three ways—yes, no, or wait. Praying is not holy manipulation. God will choose in his wisdom how to respond.

SEE FOR YOURSELF:
Deut. 4:5–8; Ps. 28:6; 40:1–17

On the Edge

When he is at work in the north, I catch no sight of him; when he turns to the south, I cannot see him (Job 23:9).

Who blew the wind through your hair this morning? Who brought the sun over the horizon once again? Who changed the seasons while you weren't even looking? It was God! The One who is always at work. While you slept, he was preparing your day. While you haven't noticed, he is ordering your life. He is strengthening your gifts and giving you ideas about what you really have to do. We have downtime, unproductive days, and mental blocks. We take vacations, and naps, and study hall. We can go for days and not accomplish one thing. Not God. He is always at work. Always creating, always protecting, always loving.

SEE FOR YOURSELF:
Ps. 121:3–4;
John 5:17

3 I wish I knew where to find God
so I could go to where he lives.
4 I would present my case before him
and fill my mouth with arguments.
5 I would learn how he would answer me
and would think about what he would say.
6 Would he not argue strongly against me?
No, he would really listen to me.
7 Then an honest person could present his case to God,
and I would be saved forever by my judge.

8 "If I go to the east, God is not there;
if I go to the west, I do not see him.
9 When he is at work in the north, I catch no sight of him;
when he turns to the south, I cannot see him.
10 But God knows the way that I take,
and when he has tested me, I will come out like gold.
11 My feet have closely followed his steps;
I have stayed in his way;
I did not turn aside.
12 I have never left the commands he has spoken;
I have treasured his words more than my own.

FOLLOWING GOD

How should we follow God? (23:11–12)

13 "But he is the only God.
Who can come against him?
He does anything he wants.
14 He will do to me what he said he would do,
and he has many plans like this.
15 That is why I am frightened of him;
when I think of this, I am afraid of him.
16 God has made me afraid;
the Almighty terrifies me.
17 But I am not hidden by the darkness,
by the thick darkness that covers my face.

WHAT'S IT MEAN?

Here's a Bible lesson that might come in handy if you're planning to buy gold nuggets in the near future. After gold is mined, it must be refined. That means the ore must be heated to the point that the metal separates from the rock. People who bought gold in Job's day would test it first to see if the metal had been mixed with less valuable materials. They would have an expert metalsmith or smelter scrape, cut, and heat the gold as part of the testing process.

Job 23:10

24

1 "I wish the Almighty would set a time for judging.
Those who know God do not see such a day.
2 Wicked people take other people's land;
they steal flocks and take them to new pastures.
3 They chase away the orphan's donkey
and take the widow's ox when she has no money.
4 They push needy people off the path;
all the poor of the land hide from them.
5 The poor become like wild donkeys in the desert
who go about their job of finding food.
The desert gives them food for their children.

6 They gather hay and straw in the fields
and pick up leftover grapes from the
vineyard of the wicked.
7 They spend the night naked, because they
have no clothes,
nothing to cover themselves in the cold.
8 They are soaked from mountain rains
and stay near the large rocks because
they have no shelter.
9 The fatherless child is grabbed from its
mother's breast;
they take a poor mother's baby to pay
for what she owes.
10 So the poor go around naked without any
clothes;
they carry bundles of grain but still go
hungry;
11 they crush olives to get oil
and grapes to get wine, but they still go
thirsty.
12 Dying people groan in the city,
and the injured cry out for help,
but God accuses no one of doing
wrong.

WHAT'S IT MEAN?

In ancient times, stones were used to mark the boundaries of people's property. Moving those stones in order to extend one's property was a big-time no-no.

Job 24:2

13 "Those who fight against the light
do not know God's ways
or stay in his paths.
14 When the day is over, the murderers get
up
to kill the poor and needy.
At night they go about like thieves.
15 Those who are guilty of adultery watch
for the night,
thinking, 'No one will see us,'
and they keep their faces covered.
16 In the dark, evil people break into houses.
In the daytime they shut themselves up
in their own houses,
because they want nothing to do with
the light.
17 Darkness is like morning to all these evil
people
who make friends with the terrors of
darkness.

WHAT'S IT MEAN?

If light and daytime represented goodness and truth, what do you suppose darkness and night represented? If you said they symbolized sin, evil, and death, give yourself a pat on the back.

Job 24:13–17

18 "They are like foam floating on the water.
Their part of the land is cursed;
no one uses the road that goes by their
vineyards.
19 As heat and dryness quickly melt the snow,
so the grave quickly takes away the
sinners.
20 Their mothers forget them,
and worms will eat their bodies.
They will not be remembered,
so wickedness is broken in pieces like a
stick.
21 These evil people abuse women who
cannot have children
and show no kindness to widows.
22 But God drags away the strong by his
power.
Even though they seem strong, they do
not know how long they will live.
23 God may let these evil people feel safe,
but he is watching their ways.
24 For a little while they are important, and
then they die;
they are laid low and buried like
everyone else;
they are cut off like the heads of grain.
25 If this is not true, who can prove I am
wrong?
Who can show that my words are
worth nothing?"

BILDAD ANSWERS

25

1 Then Bildad the Shuhite answered:

2 "God rules and he must be honored;
he set up order in his high heaven.

3 No one can count God's armies.
His light shines on all
people.
4 So no one can be good in
the presence of God,
and no one born to a
woman can be pure.
5 Even the moon is not bright
and the stars are not pure in his eyes.
6 People are much less! They are like insects.
They are only worms!"

HUMILITY
How do people compare to God? (25:4–6)

JOB ANSWERS BILDAD

26

1 Then Job answered:

2 "You are no help to the helpless!
You have not aided the weak!
3 Your advice lacks wisdom!
You have shown little understanding!
4 Who has helped you say these words?
And where did you get these ideas?

5 "The spirits of the dead tremble,
those who are beneath and in the
waters.
6 Death is naked before God;
destruction is uncovered before him.
7 God stretches the northern sky out over
empty space
and hangs the earth on nothing.
8 He wraps up the waters in his thick
clouds,
but the clouds do not break under their
weight.
9 He covers the face of the moon,
spreading his clouds over it.
10 He draws the horizon like a circle on the
water
at the place where light and darkness
meet.
11 Heaven's foundations shake
when he thunders at them.
12 With his power he quiets the sea;
by his wisdom he destroys Rahab, the
sea monster.
13 He breathes, and the sky clears.
His hand stabs the fleeing snake.
14 And these are only a small part of God's
works.
We only hear a small whisper of him.
Who could understand God's
thundering power?"

27

1 And Job continued speaking:

2 "As surely as God lives, who has taken
away my rights,
the Almighty, who has made me
unhappy,
3 as long as I am alive
and God's breath of life is in my nose,
4 my lips will not speak evil,
and my tongue will not tell a lie.
5 I will never agree you are right;
until I die, I will never stop saying I am
innocent.
6 I will insist that I am right; I will not back
down.
My conscience will never bother me.

7 "Let my enemies be like evil people,
my foes like those who are wrong.
8 What hope do the wicked have when they
die,
when God takes their life away?
9 God will not listen to their cries
when trouble comes to them.
10 They will not find joy in the Almighty,
even though they call out to God all the
time.

11 "I will teach you about the power of God
and will not hide the ways of the
Almighty.
12 You have all seen this yourselves.
So why are we having all this talk that
means nothing?

13 "Here is what God has planned for evil
people,
and what the Almighty will give to cruel
people:
14 They may have many children, but the
sword will kill them.
Their children who are left will never
have enough to eat.
15 Then they will die of disease and be
buried,
and the widows will not even cry for
them.
16 The wicked may heap up silver like piles
of dirt
and have so many clothes they are like
piles of clay.
17 But good people will wear what evil
people have gathered,
and the innocent will divide up their
silver.
18 The houses the wicked build are like a
spider's web,
like a hut that a guard builds.
19 The wicked are rich when they go to
bed,
but they are rich for the last time;

when they open their eyes, everything is
gone.
20 Fears come over them like a flood,
and a storm snatches them away in the
night.
21 The east wind will carry them away, and
then they are gone,
because it sweeps them out of their
place.
22 The wind will hit them without mercy
as they try to run away from its power.
23 It will be as if the wind is clapping its
hands;
it will whistle at them as they run from
their place.

WHAT'S IT MEAN?

The people of the ancient Middle East were expert miners. Archaeologists have found that the Egyptians dug mining tunnels more than one hundred feet deep. They carried the ore they discovered to the surface in baskets. In addition to precious metals like gold, copper, and silver, the miners brought up valuable resources like gemstones.

Job 28:1–2

28

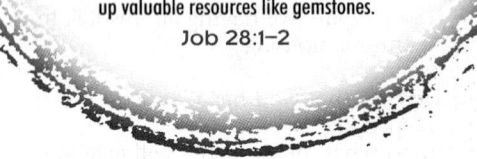

1 "There are mines where people dig silver
and places where gold is made pure.
2 Iron is taken from the ground,
and copper is melted out of rocks.
3 Miners bring lights
and search deep into the mines
for ore in thick darkness.
4 Miners dig a tunnel far from where people
live,
where no one has ever walked;
they work far from people, swinging
and swaying from ropes.
5 Food grows on top of the earth,
but below ground things are changed as
if by fire.
6 Sapphires are found in rocks,
and gold dust is also found there.
7 No hawk knows that path;
the falcon has not seen it.
8 Proud animals have not walked there,
and no lions cross over it.
9 Miners hit the rocks of flint
and dig away at the bottom of the
mountains.
10 They cut tunnels through the rock
and see all the treasures there.
11 They search for places where rivers begin
and bring things hidden out into the
light.

12 "But where can wisdom be found,
and where does understanding live?
13 People do not understand the value of
wisdom;
it cannot be found among those who
are alive.
14 The deep ocean says, 'It's not in me';
the sea says, 'It's not in me.'
15 Wisdom cannot be bought with gold,
and its cost cannot be weighed in silver.
16 Wisdom cannot be bought with fine gold
or with valuable onyx or sapphire gems.
17 Gold and crystal are not as valuable as
wisdom,
and you cannot buy it with jewels of
gold.
18 Coral and jasper are not worth talking
about,
and the price of wisdom is much greater
than rubies.
19 The topaz from Cush cannot compare to
wisdom;
it cannot be bought with the purest gold.

20 "So where does wisdom come from,
and where does understanding live?
21 It is hidden from the eyes of every living
thing,
even from the birds of the air.
22 The places of destruction and death say,
'We have heard reports about it.'
23 Only God understands the way to
wisdom,
and he alone knows where it lives,
24 because he looks to the farthest parts of
the earth
and sees everything under the sky.
25 When God gave power to the wind
and measured the water,
26 when he made rules for the rain
and set a path for a thunderstorm to
follow,
27 then he looked at wisdom and decided its
worth;
he set wisdom up and tested it.
28 Then he said to humans,
'The fear of the Lord is wisdom;
to stay away from evil is
understanding.' "

JOB CONTINUES

29 [1]Job continued to speak:

[2]"How I wish for the months that have passed
and the days when God watched over me.
[3]God's lamp shined on my head,
and I walked through darkness by his light.
[4]I wish for the days when I was strong,
when God's close friendship blessed my house.
[5]The Almighty was still with me,
and my children were all around me.
[6]It was as if my path were covered with cream
and the rocks poured out olive oil for me.
[7]I would go to the city gate
and sit in the public square.
[8]When the young men saw me, they would step aside,
and the old men would stand up in respect.
[9]The leading men stopped speaking
and covered their mouths with their hands.
[10]The voices of the important men were quiet,
as if their tongues stuck to the roof of their mouths.
[11]Anyone who heard me spoke well of me,
and those who saw me praised me,
[12]because I saved the poor who called out
and the orphan who had no one to help.
[13]The dying person blessed me,
and I made the widow's heart sing.
[14]I put on right living as if it were clothing;
I wore fairness like a robe and a turban.
[15]I was eyes for the blind
and feet for the lame.
[16]I was like a father to needy people,
and I took the side of strangers who were in trouble.
[17]I broke the fangs of evil people
and snatched the captives from their teeth.

[18]"I thought, 'I will live for as many days as there are grains of sand,
and I will die in my own house.
[19]My roots will reach down to the water.
The dew will lie on the branches all night.
[20]New honors will come to me continually,
and I will always have great strength.'
[21]"People listened to me carefully
and waited quietly for my advice.
[22]After I finished speaking, they spoke no more.
My words fell very gently on their ears.
[23]They waited for me as they would for rain
and drank in my words like spring rain.
[24]I smiled at them when they doubted,
and my approval was important to them.
[25]I chose the way for them and was their leader.
I lived like a king among his army,
like a person who comforts sad people.

30 [1]"But now men who are younger than I
make fun of me.
I would not have even let their fathers
sit with my sheep dogs.
[2]What use did I have for their strength
since they had lost their strength to work?
[3]They were thin from hunger
and wandered the dry and ruined land at night.
[4]They gathered desert plants among the brush
and ate the root of the broom tree.
[5]They were forced to live away from people;
people shouted at them as if they were thieves.
[6]They lived in dried up streambeds,
in caves, and among the rocks.
[7]They howled like animals among the bushes
and huddled together in the brush.
[8]They are worthless people without names
and were forced to leave the land.

[9]"Now they make fun of me with songs;
my name is a joke among them.
[10]They hate me and stay far away from me,
but they do not mind spitting in my face.
[11]God has taken away my strength and made me suffer,
so they attack me with all their anger.
[12]On my right side they rise up like a mob.
They lay traps for my feet
and prepare to attack me.
[13]They break up my road
and work to destroy me,
and no one helps me.
[14]They come at me as if through a hole in the wall,
and they roll in among the ruins.

15 Great fears overwhelm me.
They blow my honor away as if by a great wind,
and my safety disappears like a cloud.

16 "Now my life is almost over;
my days are full of suffering.
17 At night my bones ache;
gnawing pains never stop.
18 In his great power God grabs hold of my clothing
and chokes me with the collar of my coat.
19 He throws me into the mud,
and I become like dirt and ashes.

20 "I cry out to you, God, but you do not answer;
I stand up, but you just look at me.
21 You have turned on me without mercy;
with your powerful hand you attacked me.
22 You snatched me up and threw me into the wind
and tossed me about in the storm.
23 I know you will bring me down to death,
to the place where all living people must go.

WHAT'S IT MEAN?

What's wrong with wild dogs and ostriches? Most likely, Job was referring to the lonesome, disturbing sounds they make. Wild dogs and ostriches were considered unclean animals by the Israelites and were associated with desolation and despair.

Job 30:29

24 "Surely no one would hurt a ruined man
when he cries for help in his time of trouble.
25 I cried for those who were in trouble;
I have been very sad for poor people.
26 But when I hoped for good, only evil came to me;
when I looked for light, darkness came.
27 I never stop being upset;
days of suffering are ahead of me.
28 I have turned black, but not by the sun.
I stand up in public and cry for help.
29 I have become a brother to wild dogs
and a friend to ostriches.
30 My skin has become black and peels off,
as my body burns with fever.
31 My harp is tuned to sing a sad song,
and my flute is tuned to moaning.

31

1 "But I made an agreement with my eyes
not to look with desire at a girl.
2 What has God above promised for people?
What has the Almighty planned from on high?
3 It is ruin for evil people
and disaster for those who do wrong.
4 God sees my ways
and counts every step I take.

LUST

How should we maintain purity? (31:1)

5 "If I have been dishonest
or lied to others,
6 then let God weigh me on honest scales.
Then he will know I have done nothing wrong.
7 If I have turned away from doing what is right,
or my heart has been led by my eyes to do wrong,
or my hands have been made unclean,
8 then let other people eat what I have planted,
and let my crops be plowed up.

9 "If I have desired another woman
or have waited at my neighbor's door for his wife,

WHAT'S IT MEAN?

In the ancient Middle East, a person accused of a crime was required to take an oath of innocence. Job went one step further and submitted himself to the toughest polygraph test imaginable. He swore that he was innocent of all the accusations and called on God to punish him if he was lying.

Job 31:5–8

10 then let my wife grind another man's
grain,
and let other men have sexual relations
with her.
11 That would be shameful,
a sin to be punished.
12 It is like a fire that burns and destroys;
all I have done would be
plowed up.

> **"If I have been dishonest or lied to others, then let God weigh me on honest scales. Then he will know I have done nothing wrong." (Job 31:5–6)**

13 "If I have been unfair to
my male and
female slaves
when they had a
complaint against
me,
14 how could I tell God
what I did?
What will I answer when
he asks me to explain
what I've done?
15 God made me in my mother's womb, and
he also made them;
the same God formed both of us in our
mothers' wombs.

16 "I have never refused the appeals of the
poor
or let widows give up hope while
looking for help.
17 I have not kept my food to myself
but have given it to the orphans.
18 Since I was young, I have been like a
father to the orphans.
From my birth I guided the widows.
19 I have not let anyone die for lack of
clothes
or let a needy person go without a coat.
20 That person's heart blessed me,
because I warmed him with the wool of
my sheep.
21 I have never hurt an orphan
even when I knew I could win in court.
22 If I have, then let my arm fall off my
shoulder
and be broken at the joint.
23 I fear destruction from God,
and I fear his majesty, so I could not do
such things.

24 "I have not put my trust in gold
or said to pure gold, 'You are my
security.'
25 I have not celebrated my great wealth
or the riches my hands had gained.
26 I have not thought about worshiping the
sun in its brightness
nor admired the moon moving in glory
27 so that my heart was pulled away from
God.
My hand has never offered the sun and
moon a kiss of worship.
28 If I had, these also would have been sins
to be punished,
because I would have
been unfaithful to
God.

29 "I have not been happy
when my enemy fell
or laughed when he
had trouble.
30 I have not let my mouth
sin
by cursing my enemy's
life.
31 The men of my house
have always said,
'Everyone has eaten all he wants of Job's
food.'
32 No stranger ever had to spend the night in
the street,
because I always let travelers stay in my
home.
33 I have not hidden my sin as others do,
secretly keeping my guilt to myself.
34 I was not so afraid of the crowd
that I kept quiet and stayed inside
because I feared being hated by other
families.

35 ("How I wish a court would hear my case!
Here I sign my name to show I have
told the truth.
Now let the Almighty answer me;
let the one who accuses me write it
down.
36 I would wear the writing on my shoulder;
I would put it on like a crown.
37 I would explain to God every step I took,
and I would come near to him like a
prince.)

38 "If my land cries out against me
and its plowed rows are not wet with
tears,
39 if I have taken the land's harvest without
paying
or have broken the spirit of those who
worked the land,
40 then let thorns come up instead of wheat,
and let weeds come up instead of barley."

The words of Job are finished.

ELIHU SPEAKS

32 [1]These three men stopped trying to answer
Job, because he was so sure he was right. [2]But
Elihu son of Barakel the Buzite, from the family
of Ram, became very angry with Job, because
Job claimed he was right instead of God. [3]Elihu
was also angry with Job's three friends who
had no answer to show that Job was wrong,
yet continued to blame him. [4]Elihu had waited
before speaking to Job, because the three
friends were older than he was. [5]But when Elihu saw that the three men had nothing more
to say, he became very angry.
[6]So Elihu son of Barakel the Buzite said this:

"I am young,
and you are old.
That is why I was afraid
to tell you what I know.
[7]I thought, 'Older people should speak,
and those who have lived many years
should teach wisdom.'
[8]But it is the spirit in a person,
the breath of the Almighty, that gives
understanding.
[9]It is not just older people who are wise;
they are not the only ones who
understand what is right.
[10]So I say, listen to me.
I too will tell you what I know.
[11]I waited while you three spoke,
and listened to your explanations.
While you looked for words to use,
[12] I paid close attention to you.
But not one of you has proved Job
wrong;
none of you has answered his
arguments.
[13]Don't say, 'We have found wisdom;
only God will show Job to be wrong,
not people.'
[14]Job has not spoken his words against me,
so I will not use your arguments to
answer Job.

[15]"These three friends are defeated and have
no more to say;
words have failed them.
[16]Now they are standing there with no
answers for Job.
Now that they are quiet, must I wait to
speak?
[17]No, I too will speak
and tell what I know.
[18]I am full of words,
and the spirit in me causes me to speak.
[19]I am like wine that has been bottled up;
I am ready to burst like a new leather
wine bag.
[20]I must speak so I will feel relief;
I must open my mouth and answer.
[21]I will be fair to everyone
and not flatter anyone.
[22]I don't know how to flatter,
and if I did, my Maker would quickly
take me away.

33 [1]"Now, Job, listen to my words.
Pay attention to everything I say.
[2]I open my mouth
and am ready to speak.
[3]My words come from an honest heart,
and I am sincere in saying what I know.
[4]The Spirit of God created me,
and the breath of the Almighty gave me
life.
[5]Answer me if you can;
get yourself ready and stand before me.
[6]I am just like you before God;
I too am made out of clay.
[7]Don't be afraid of me;
I will not be hard on you.

[8]"But I heard what you have said;
I heard every word.
[9]You said, 'I am pure and without sin;
I am innocent and free from guilt.
[10]But God has found fault with me;
he considers me his enemy.
[11]He locks my feet in chains
and closely watches everywhere I go.'

[12]"But I tell you, you are not right in saying
this,
because God is greater than we are.
[13]Why do you accuse God
of not answering anyone?
[14]God does speak—sometimes one way and
sometimes another—
even though people may not
understand it.
[15]He speaks in a dream or a vision of the
night
when people are in a deep sleep,
lying on their beds.
[16]He speaks in their ears
and frightens them with warnings
[17]to turn them away from doing wrong
and to keep them from being proud.
[18]God does this to save a person from
death,
to keep him from dying.
[19]A person may be corrected while in bed in
great pain;

On the Edge

God does speak—sometimes one way and sometimes another—even though people may not understand it (Job 33:14).

God can speak to us in as many ways as he can imagine. He is very creative when it comes to getting our attention. He can whisper to us while we are still, or shout to us in our busyness. We can read the Bible and know that he has just spoken directly to our situation. A teacher may teach from the Scripture and God speaks through him or her. He uses billboards, phone calls, hugs from friends, successes, failures, and ordinary humdrum experiences. He will do whatever it takes, intervene whenever necessary to get you to look up and know that he is God. Do you have eyes to see? Do you have ears to hear God speaking to you?

SEE FOR YOURSELF:
1 Cor. 2:13; 2 Pet. 1:21; Rev. 2:7

he may have continual pain in his very
bones.
20 He may be in such pain that he even hates
food,
even the very best meal.
21 His body becomes so thin there is almost
nothing left of it,
and his bones that were hidden now
stick out.
22 He is near death,
and his life is almost over.

23 "But there may be an angel to speak for
him,
one out of a thousand, who will tell him
what to do.
24 The angel will beg for mercy and say:
'Save him from death.
I have found a way to pay for his life.'
25 Then his body is made new like a child's.
It will return to the way it was when he
was young.
26 That person will pray to God, and God
will listen to him.
He will see God's face and will shout
with happiness.
And God will set things right for him
again.
27 Then he will say to others,
'I sinned and twisted what was right,
but I did not receive the punishment I
should have received.
28 God bought my life back from death,
and I will continue to enjoy life.'

29 "God does all these things to a person
two or even three times
30 so he won't die as punishment for his sins
and so he may still enjoy life.

31 "Job, pay attention and listen to me;
be quiet, and I will speak.
32 If you have anything to say, answer me;
speak up, because I want to prove you
right.
33 But if you have nothing to say, then listen
to me;
be quiet, and I will teach you wisdom."

34

1 Then Elihu said:

2 "Hear my words, you wise men;
listen to me, you who know a lot.
3 The ear tests words

On the Edge

God does all these things to a person two or even three times (Job 33:29).

"Just one more chance, please, please. I promise to get it right this time." Ever said that to your parents, or to your teacher, or to God? While your parents or teacher may tire of saying, "Okay, one more time, give it a shot," God never will. Even when you are tired of trying, God will lift you up, give you a pep talk, and tell you to try again. When you don't deserve a second chance, God will let you have one. He loves you so much that he will never give up on you. He longs for you, and he delights in welcoming you back when you've blown it. So if you've given up on God, feel like you've used up all your chances, messed up really big this time—there is great news: You belong to the God who gives you chance after chance. Run to him.

SEE FOR YOURSELF:
Ps. 130:4; Hos. 14:4; Luke 7:48; 1 John 1:9

as the tongue tastes food.
[4]Let's decide for ourselves what is right,
and let's learn together what is good.

[5]"Job says, 'I am not guilty,
and God has refused me a fair trial.
[6]Instead of getting a fair trial,
I am called a liar.
I have been seriously hurt,
even though I have not sinned.'
[7]There is no other man like Job;
he takes insults as if he were drinking water.
[8]He keeps company with those who do evil
and spends time with wicked men,
[9]because he says, 'It is no use
to try to please God.'

[10]"So listen to me, you who can understand.
God can never do wrong!
It is impossible for the Almighty to do evil.
[11]God pays a person back for what he has done
and gives him what his actions deserve.
[12]Truly God will never do wrong;
the Almighty will never twist what is right.
[13]No one chose God to rule over the earth
or put him in charge of the whole world.
[14]If God should decide
to take away life and breath,
[15]then everyone would die together
and turn back into dust.

[16]"If you can understand, hear this;
listen to what I have to say.
[17]Can anyone govern who hates what is right?
How can you blame God who is both fair and powerful?
[18]God is the one who says to kings, 'You are worthless,'
or to important people, 'You are evil.'
[19]He is not nicer to princes than other people,
nor kinder to rich people than poor people,
because he made them all with his own hands.
[20]They can die in a moment, in the middle of the night.
They are struck down, and then they pass away;
powerful people die without help.

On the Edge

[God] is not nicer to princes than other people, nor kinder to rich people than poor people, because he made them all with his own hands (Job 34:19).

Imagine everyone different—but equal. No rich, no poor. No one more beautiful. No school better than your school. No house bigger than your house. No one chosen because they have more stuff. No favorites. Everyone accepted the same. Everyone loved completely. It's hard for us to imagine, but that's exactly the way it is with God. He loves the kid you can't stand to sit next to just as much as he loves you. He loves you as much as he loves the most popular kid in your school. The world uses labels like "VIP" or "Vice President." God is not impressed. He made each one of us different and unique, but loves us all the same.

SEE FOR YOURSELF:
Matt. 7:8;
Acts 13:38–39;
Gal. 2:6

[21]"God watches where people go;
he sees every step they take.
[22]There is no dark place or deep shadow
where those who do evil can hide from him.
[23]He does not set a time
for people to come before him for judging.
[24]Without asking questions, God breaks powerful people into pieces
and puts others in their place.
[25]Because God knows what people do,
he defeats them in the night, and they are crushed.
[26]He punishes them for the evil they do
so that everyone else can watch,
[27]because they stopped following God
and did not care about any of his ways.
[28]The cry of the poor comes to God;
he hears the cry of the needy.
[29]But if God keeps quiet, who can blame him?
If he hides his face, who can see him?
God still rules over both nations and persons alike.

30 He keeps the wicked from ruling
and from trapping others.

31 "But suppose someone says to God,
'I am guilty, but I will not sin anymore.
32 Teach me what I cannot see.
If I have done wrong, I will not do it again.'
33 So, Job, should God reward you as you want
when you refuse to change?
You must decide, not I,
so tell me what you know.

34 "Those who understand speak,
and the wise who hear me say,
35 'Job speaks without knowing what is true;
his words show he does not understand.'
36 I wish Job would be tested completely,
because he answered like an evil man!
37 Job now adds to his sin by turning against God.
He claps his hands in protest,
speaking more and more against God."

35

1 Then Elihu said:

2 "Do you think this is fair?
You say, 'God will show that I am right,'
3 but you also ask, 'What's the use?
I don't gain anything by not sinning.'

4 "I will answer you
and your friends who are with you.
5 Look up at the sky
and see the clouds so high above you.
6 If you sin, it does nothing to God;
even if your sins are many, they do nothing to him.
7 If you are good, you give nothing to God;
he receives nothing from your hand.
8 Your evil ways only hurt a man like yourself,
and the good you do only helps other human beings.

9 "People cry out when they are in trouble;
they beg for relief from powerful people.
10 But no one asks, 'Where is God, my Maker,
who gives us songs in the night,
11 who makes us smarter than the animals of the earth
and wiser than the birds of the air?'
12 God does not answer evil people when they cry out,
because the wicked are proud.
13 God does not listen to their useless begging;
the Almighty pays no attention to them.
14 He will listen to you even less
when you say that you do not see him,
that your case is before him,
that you must wait for him,
15 that his anger never punishes,
and that he doesn't notice evil.
16 So Job is only speaking nonsense,
saying many words without knowing what is true."

ELIHU'S SPEECH CONTINUES

36

1 Elihu continued:

2 "Listen to me a little longer, and I will show you
that there is more to be said for God.
3 What I know comes from far away.
I will show that my Maker is right.
4 You can be sure that my words are not false;
one who really knows is with you.

5 "God is powerful, but he does not hate people;

On the Edge

God is powerful, but he does not hate people; he is powerful and sure of what he wants to do (Job 36:5).

Why does God care about everyone? Because each one of us is his creation, fashioned by him, and completely loved. How does God care? He provides all that we need. He waits patiently for us to seek him. He is faithful to guide our steps and order our days. He pours grace all over us. What can we do to get God to care about us more? Nothing. We are already cared for completely just because we belong to him. When will his caring end? Never. He promises to be with us always. How can you be like God? Care about other people even more than you care about yourself.

SEE FOR YOURSELF:
John 13:34–35;
Gal. 2:20;
1 John 4:7–11

he is powerful and sure of what he
wants to do.
6 He will not keep evil people alive,
but he gives the poor their rights.
7 He always watches over those who do
right;
he sets them on thrones with kings
and they are honored forever.
8 If people are bound in chains,
or if trouble, like ropes, ties them up,
9 God tells them what they have done,
that they have sinned in their pride.
10 God makes them listen to his warning
and commands them to change from
doing evil.
11 If they obey and serve him,
the rest of their lives will be successful,
and the rest of their years will be happy.
12 But if they do not listen,
they will die by the sword,
and they will die without knowing why.

13 "Those who have wicked hearts hold on to
anger.
Even when God punishes them, they do
not cry for help.
14 They die while they are still young,
and their lives end in disgrace.
15 But God saves those who suffer through
their suffering;
he gets them to listen through their
pain.

16 "God is gently calling you from the jaws of
trouble
to an open place of freedom
where he has set your table full of the
best food.
17 But now you are being punished like the
wicked;
you are getting justice.
18 Be careful! Don't be led away from God by
riches;
don't let much money turn you away.
19 Neither your wealth nor all your great
strength
will keep you out of trouble.
20 Don't wish for the night
when people are taken from their
homes.
21 Be careful not to turn to evil,
which you seem to want more than
suffering.

22 "God is great and powerful;
no other teacher is like him.
23 No one has planned his ways for him;
no one can say to God, 'You have done
wrong.'
24 Remember to praise his work,
about which people have sung.
25 Everybody has seen it;
people look at it from far off.
26 God is so great, greater than we can
understand!
No one knows how old he is.

27 "He evaporates the drops of water from
the earth
and turns them into rain.
28 The rain then pours down from the
clouds,
and showers fall on people.
29 No one understands how God spreads out
the clouds
or how he sends thunder from where
he lives.
30 Watch how God scatters his lightning
around him,
lighting up the deepest parts of the sea.
31 This is the way God governs the nations;
this is how he gives us enough food.
32 God fills his hands with lightning
and commands it to strike its target.
33 His thunder announces the coming storm,
and even the cattle know it is near.

WHAT'S IT MEAN?

Electrical storms are pretty common in Palestine during the spring and fall. Not only do these storms bring lightning and thunder; they bring strong winds, dust clouds, heavy rains, and damaging hail. You can understand why the writers of the Bible used these storms to illustrate the power of God.

Job 36:32–33

37

1 "At the sound of his thunder, my heart
pounds
as if it will jump out of my chest.
2 Listen! Listen to the thunder of God's voice
and to the rumbling that comes from
his mouth.
3 He turns his lightning loose under the
whole sky

and sends it to the farthest parts of the
earth.
4 After that you can hear the roar
when he thunders with a great sound.
He does not hold back the flashing
when his voice is heard.
5 God's voice thunders in wonderful ways;
he does great things we cannot
understand.
6 He says to the snow, 'Fall on
the earth,'
and to the shower, 'Be a
heavy rain.'
7 With it, he stops everyone
from working
so everyone knows it is
the work of God.
8 The animals take cover from
the rain
and stay in their dens.
9 The storm comes from where it was
stored;
the cold comes with the strong winds.
10 The breath of God makes ice,
and the wide waters become frozen.
11 He fills the clouds with water
and scatters his lightning through them.
12 At his command they swirl around
over the whole earth,
doing whatever he commands.
13 He uses the clouds to punish people
or to water his earth and show his love.

"Job, listen to this: Stop and notice God's miracles." (Job 37:14)

14 "Job, listen to this:
Stop and notice God's
miracles.
15 Do you know how God
controls the clouds
and makes his lightning
flash?
16 Do you know how the
clouds hang in the sky?
Do you know the miracles of
God, who knows everything?
17 You suffer in your clothes
when the land is silenced by the hot,
south wind.
18 You cannot stretch out the sky like God
and make it look as hard as polished
bronze.
19 Tell us what we should say to him;
we cannot get our arguments ready
because we do not have enough
understanding.
20 Should God be told that I want to speak?
Would a person ask to be swallowed
up?
21 No one can look at the sun
when it is bright in the sky
after the wind has blown all the clouds
away.
22 God comes out of the north in golden
light,
in overwhelming greatness.
23 The Almighty is too high for us to reach.
He has great strength;
he is always right and never punishes
unfairly.
24 That is why people honor him;
he does not respect those who say they
are wise."

On the Edge

No one can look at the sun when it is bright in the sky after the wind has blown all the clouds away. God comes out of the north in golden light, in overwhelming greatness (Job 37:21–22).

Ever tried to look at the midday sun? You can't—and you're not even supposed to try. It will damage your eyes. The sun is millions of miles away from the earth, and yet you can't look at its brightness. If we were to travel to the sun, we would burn up long before we got there because of the intensity of the heat. There is nothing on this earth to compare with the power of the sun. Job says that the power of God is even brighter than the sun. Imagine that. To God the sun is probably like a nice campfire. It's a fire that God built himself and hung in the heavens. We sometimes forget how awesome God is. The next time you watch a sunset, think about God and remember that his power is even stronger.

SEE FOR YOURSELF:
Deut. 10:17;
1 Chr. 29:11–12;
Ps. 47:2

THE LORD QUESTIONS JOB

38 1 Then the LORD answered Job from the
storm. He said:

2 "Who is this that makes my purpose
unclear
by saying things that are not true?
3 Be strong like a man!

I will ask you questions,
and you must answer me.
4 Where were you when I made the earth's foundation?
Tell me, if you understand.
5 Who marked off how big it should be?
Surely you know!
Who stretched a ruler across it?
6 What were the earth's foundations set on,
or who put its cornerstone in place
7 while the morning stars sang together
and all the angels shouted with joy?

WHAT'S IT MEAN?

Here's a word you can throw around the next time you want to show someone how much you know about biblical things: *theophany*. It means a visible appearance of God. Job witnessed a theophany when the Lord came to him in the storm. As was true when Moses carried on a conversation with the burning bush, Job didn't actually see God; he saw the effects of God's presence.

Job 38:1

8 "Who shut the doors to keep the sea in
when it broke through and was born,
9 when I made the clouds like a coat for the sea
and wrapped it in dark clouds,
10 when I put limits on the sea
and put its doors and bars in place,
11 when I said to the sea, 'You may come this far, but no farther;
this is where your proud waves must stop'?

12 "Have you ever ordered the morning to begin,
or shown the dawn where its place was
13 in order to take hold of the earth by its edges
and shake evil people out of it?
14 At dawn the earth changes like clay being pressed by a seal;
the hills and valleys stand out like folds in a coat.
15 Light is not given to evil people;
their arm is raised to do harm, but it is broken.

16 "Have you ever gone to where the sea begins
or walked in the valleys under the sea?
17 Have the gates of death been opened to you?
Have you seen the gates of the deep darkness?
18 Do you understand how wide the earth is?
Tell me, if you know all these things.

19 "What is the path to light's home,
and where does darkness live?
20 Can you take them to their places?
Do you know the way to their homes?
21 Surely you know, if you were already born when all this happened!
Have you lived that many years?

22 "Have you ever gone into the storehouse of the snow
or seen the storehouses for hail,
23 which I save for times of trouble,
for days of war and battle?
24 Where is the place from which light comes?
Where is the place from which the east winds blow over the earth?
25 Who cuts a waterway for the heavy rains
and sets a path for the thunderstorm?
26 Who waters the land where no one lives,
the desert that has no one in it?
27 Who sends rain to satisfy the empty land
so the grass begins to grow?
28 Does the rain have a father?
Who is father to the drops of dew?
29 Who is the mother of the ice?
Who gives birth to the frost from the sky
30 when the water becomes hard as stone,
and even the surface of the ocean is frozen?

31 "Can you tie up the stars of the Pleiades
or loosen the ropes of the stars in Orion?
32 Can you bring out the stars on time
or lead out the stars of the Bear with its cubs?
33 Do you know the laws of the sky
and understand their rule over the earth?

34 "Can you shout an order to the clouds
and cover yourself with a flood of water?
35 Can you send lightning bolts on their way?

Do they come to you and say, 'Here we
are'?
36 Who put wisdom inside the mind
or understanding in the heart?
37 Who has the wisdom to count the clouds?
Who can pour water from the jars of
the sky
38 when the dust becomes hard
and the clumps of dirt stick together?

39 "Do you hunt food for the female lion
to satisfy the hunger of the young lions
40 while they lie in their dens
or hide in the bushes waiting to attack?
41 Who gives food to the birds
when their young cry out to God
and wander about without food?

39

1 "Do you know when the mountain goats
give birth?
Do you watch when the deer gives birth
to her fawn?
2 Do you count the months until they give
birth
and know the right time for them to
give birth?
3 They lie down, their young are born,
and then the pain of giving birth is
over.
4 Their young ones grow big and strong in
the wild country.
Then they leave their homes and do not
return.

5 "Who let the wild donkey go free?
Who untied its ropes?
6 I am the one who gave the donkey the
desert as its home;
I gave it the desert lands as a place to
live.
7 The wild donkey laughs at the confusion
in the city,
and it does not hear the drivers shout.
8 It roams the hills looking for pasture,
looking for anything green to eat.

9 "Will the wild ox agree to serve you
and stay by your feeding box at night?
10 Can you hold it to the plowed row with a
harness
so it will plow the valleys for you?
11 Will you depend on the wild ox for its
great strength
and leave your heavy work for it to do?
12 Can you trust the ox to bring in your
grain
and gather it to your threshing floor?

13 "The wings of the ostrich flap happily,
but they are not like the feathers of the
stork.
14 The ostrich lays its eggs on the ground
and lets them warm in the sand.
15 It does not stop to think that a foot might
step on them and crush them;
it does not care that some animal might
walk on them.
16 The ostrich is cruel to its young, as if they
were not even its own.
It does not care that its work is for
nothing,
17 because God did not give the ostrich
wisdom;
God did not give it a share of good
sense.
18 But when the ostrich gets up to run, it is
so fast
that it laughs at the horse and its rider.

WHAT'S IT MEAN?

Ostriches have a reputation for being dumb animals because of the way they treat their eggs. Rather than protect their young like most birds do, ostriches leave their eggs unattended, covered over with sand, throughout the day.

Job 39:13–17

19 "Job, are you the one who gives the horse
its strength
or puts a flowing mane on its neck?
20 Do you make the horse jump like a
locust?
It scares people with its proud snorting.
21 It paws wildly, enjoying its strength,
and charges into battle.
22 It laughs at fear and is afraid of nothing;
it does not run away from the sword.
23 The bag of arrows rattles against the
horse's side,
along with the flashing spears and
swords.
24 With great excitement, the horse races over
the ground;
and it cannot stand still when it hears
the trumpet.

25 When the trumpet blows, the horse snorts, 'Aha!'
It smells the battle from far away;
it hears the shouts of commanders and the battle cry.

26 "Is it through your wisdom that the hawk flies
and spreads its wings toward the south?
27 Are you the one that commands the eagle to fly
and build its nest so high?
28 It lives on a high cliff and stays there at night;
the rocky peak is its protected place.
29 From there it looks for its food;
its eyes can see it from far away.
30 Its young eat blood,
and where there is something dead, the eagle is there."

40

1 The LORD said to Job:

2 "Will the person who argues with the Almighty correct him?
Let the person who accuses God answer him."

GOD

Do we have a right to correct God? (40:2)

3 Then Job answered the LORD:

4 "I am not worthy; I cannot answer you anything,
so I will put my hand over my mouth.
5 I spoke one time, but I will not answer again;
I even spoke two times, but I will say nothing more."

6 Then the LORD spoke to Job from the storm:

7 "Be strong, like a man!
I will ask you questions,
and you must answer me.
8 Would you say that I am unfair?
Would you blame me to make yourself look right?
9 Are you as strong as God?
Can your voice thunder like his?
10 If so, then decorate yourself with glory and beauty;
dress in honor and greatness as if they were clothing.
11 Let your great anger punish;
look at the proud and bring them down.
12 Look at the proud and make them humble.
Crush the wicked wherever they are.
13 Bury them all in the dirt together;
cover their faces in the grave.
14 If you can do that, then I myself will praise you,
because you are strong enough to save yourself.

15 "Look at the behemoth,[n]
which I made just as I made you.
It eats grass like an ox.
16 Look at the strength it has in its body;
the muscles of its stomach are powerful.
17 Its tail is like a cedar tree;
the muscles of its thighs are woven together.
18 Its bones are like tubes of bronze;
its legs are like bars of iron.
19 It is one of the first of God's works,
but its Maker can destroy it.
20 The hills, where the wild animals play,
provide food for it.
21 It lies under the lotus plants,
hidden by the tall grass in the swamp.
22 The lotus plants hide it in their shadow;
the poplar trees by the streams surround it.
23 If the river floods, it will not be afraid;
it is safe even if the Jordan River rushes to its mouth.
24 Can anyone blind its eyes and capture it?
Can anyone put hooks in its nose?

41

1 "Can you catch the leviathan[n] on a fish hook
or tie its tongue down with a rope?
2 Can you put a cord through its nose
or a hook in its jaw?
3 Will it keep begging you for mercy
and speak to you with gentle words?
4 Will it make an agreement with you
and let you take it as your slave for life?
5 Can you make a pet of the leviathan as you would a bird
or put it on a leash for your girls?
6 Will traders try to bargain with you for it?
Will they divide it up among the merchants?

40:15 behemoth A large land animal. It could refer to the hippopotamus, the elephant, or a monster.
41:1 leviathan Possibly a crocodile or a sea monster.

On the Edge

No one has ever given me anything that I must pay back, because everything under the sky belongs to me (Job 41:11).

Ever feel like the world is out of control? People are doing the craziest things with the place God has given them. Abusing their bodies with any substance imaginable. Treating one another with total disrespect. Violent attitudes and behavior are rampant. It would be easy to think that God has turned his back and left. He has gotten fed up with the whole mess and just quit. Who would blame him? We would have quit a long time ago. But not God.

He is still in command of the world. His power has not been weakened. His plans have not been changed. He isn't even surprised at how badly we've messed up. He knows that when we choose not to follow him, we wander around, trying to fix everything ourselves, and finally make things worse. The Commander is still leading. The world still belongs to him. Will you follow, or will you join the chaos?

SEE FOR YOURSELF:
2 Sam. 23:5; Is. 9:7; Mark 1:27

7 Can you stick darts all over its skin
or fill its head with fishing spears?
8 If you put one hand on it,
you will never forget the battle,
and you will never do it again!
9 There is no hope of defeating it;
just seeing it overwhelms people.
10 No one is brave enough to make it angry,
so who would be able to stand up against me?
11 No one has ever given me anything that I must pay back,
because everything under the sky belongs to me.

12 "I will speak about Leviathan's arms and legs,
its great strength and well-formed body.
13 No one can tear off its outer hide
or poke through its double armor.
14 No one can force open its great jaws;
they are filled with frightening teeth.
15 It has rows of shields on its back
that are tightly sealed together.
16 Each shield is so close to the next one
that no air can go between them.
17 They are joined strongly to one another;
they hold on to each other and cannot be separated.
18 When it snorts, flashes of light are thrown out,
and its eyes look like the light at dawn.
19 Flames blaze from its mouth;
sparks of fire shoot out.
20 Smoke pours out of its nose,
as if coming from a large pot over a hot fire.
21 Its breath sets coals on fire,
and flames come out of its mouth.
22 There is great strength in its neck.
People are afraid and run away.
23 The folds of its skin are tightly joined;
they are set and cannot be moved.
24 Its chest is as hard as a rock,
even as hard as a grinding stone.
25 The powerful fear its terrible looks
and draw back in fear as it moves.
26 The sword that hits it does not hurt it,
nor the arrows, darts, and spears.
27 It treats iron as if it were straw
and bronze metal as if it were rotten wood.
28 It does not run away from arrows;
stones from slings are like chaff to it.
29 Clubs feel like pieces of straw to it,
and it laughs when they shake a spear at it.
30 The underside of its body is like broken pieces of pottery.
It leaves a trail in the mud like a threshing board.
31 It makes the deep sea bubble like a boiling pot;
it stirs up the sea like a pot of oil.
32 When it swims, it leaves a shining path in the water
that makes the sea look as if it had white hair.
33 Nothing else on earth is equal to it;
it is a creature without fear.
34 It looks down on all those who are too proud;
it is king over all proud creatures."

JOB ANSWERS THE LORD

42

1 Then Job answered the LORD:

2 "I know that you can do all things

and that no plan of yours can be ruined.
[3]You asked, 'Who is this that made my
purpose unclear by saying things that
are not true?'
Surely I spoke of things I did not
understand;
I talked of things too wonderful for me
to know.
[4]You said, 'Listen now, and I will speak.
I will ask you questions,
and you must answer me.'
[5]My ears had heard of you before,
but now my eyes have seen you.
[6]So now I hate myself;
I will change my heart and life.
I will sit in the dust and ashes."

END OF THE STORY

[7]After the LORD had said these things to Job,
he said to Eliphaz the Temanite, "I am angry
with you and your two friends, because you
have not said what is right about me, as my
servant Job did. [8]Now take seven bulls and
seven male sheep, and go to my servant Job,
and offer a burnt offering for yourselves. My
servant Job will pray for you, and I will listen
to his prayer. Then I will not punish you for
being foolish. You have not said what is right
about me, as my servant Job did." [9]So Eliphaz
the Temanite, Bildad the Shuhite, and Zophar
the Naamathite did as the LORD said, and the
LORD listened to Job's prayer.
[10]After Job had prayed for his friends, the
LORD gave him success again. The LORD gave
Job twice as much as he had owned before.
[11]Job's brothers and sisters came to his house,
along with everyone who had known him before, and they all ate with him there. They comforted him and made him feel better about the
trouble the LORD had brought on him, and each
one gave Job a piece of silver and a gold ring.
[12]The LORD blessed the last part of Job's life
even more than the first part. Job had fourteen
thousand sheep, six thousand camels, a thousand teams of oxen, and a thousand female
donkeys. [13]Job also had seven sons and three
daughters. [14]He named the first daughter Jemimah, the second daughter Keziah, and the
third daughter Keren-Happuch. [15]There were
no other women in all the land as beautiful as
Job's daughters. And their father Job gave them
land to own along with their brothers.

WHAT'S IT MEAN?

Do you know what your name means?
If you had lived in Bible times, you would have.
In the ancient world, a person's name was important because it revealed something about the person. The names of Job's daughters all reflect their beauty. *Jemimah* means "Turtledove." (Don't laugh—doves are used in the Bible as symbols of beauty, innocence, and gentleness.) *Keziah* means "Cinnamon," which was a plant that produced oil for perfumes. *Keren-Happuch* means "Horn, or Container, of Antimony." Antimony was a metal-gray mineral that was ground to powder and worn as eye makeup.

Job 42:13–14

[16]After this, Job lived one hundred forty
years. He lived to see his children, grandchildren, great-grandchildren, and great-great-
grandchildren. [17]Then Job died; he was old and
had lived many years.

psalms

CONTENT Music is a gift, but it is also a tool and a talent. Our society uses music to do everything from selling to inspiring to dancing to teaching. God uses music, too. The official roles in the early worship of the Jews included official musicians and song leaders. While their music was different from the music you hear today, it was just as important in worship.

Psalms is basically a book of lyric sheets. Some of the lyrics tell who wrote them. Some tell why the songs were written. They are a lot like a CD cover in that way. Some of the Psalms have musical notations like "Selah."

The topics of the psalms were like a mixture of hits from a contemporary Christian radio station. Worship was a hot topic, but it wasn't the only topic. Some psalms were about regret; some were about joy; some were about anger. Music did the same thing for those ancient songwriters that it does for songwriters today: it helped them process life. Some of the psalms were honest to the point of being raw, but all of them related to living a life of faith in a world that is sometimes faithless.

Outline

1—41 .... Book 1
42—72 .... Book 2
73—89 .... Book 3
90—106 .... Book 4
107—150 .... Book 5

Purpose We can come to God freely, whether our hearts are broken or filled with praise.

Theme Communion with God in Prayer and Praise

Date of writing About 1410–430 B.C.

"I hope my words and thoughts please you. LORD, you are my Rock, the one who saves me" (19:14).

Bible Talk

The Ancient Hebrew Worship Band

If you play in a worship band at church, you probably have drums, guitar, and a keyboard as your main instruments. If you play in an orchestra, you have a string section and some brass and woodwinds.

If you had played in an ancient Hebrew worship band of any kind, you would also have had instruments that you could blow into, or strum, or beat, but they would have looked a little different.

Your drums would have been called tambourines. The cymbals would have been small enough to fit on your fingers. The strings might have been laid down on your lap to play. The horns might have been made from animal horns rather than from metal.

HEBREW MUSIC AND POETRY

While the psalms are like lyric sheets, they don't rhyme like lyrics we learn today. Hebrew poetry was built on a concept instead of a rhyming scheme. The first line stated the concept. The second line built on it.

Hebrew poetry also used alphabetical structures. In its original language, one of the psalms is written so that each line starts with a letter of the alphabet . . . *in order* no less.

So, when you read a psalm, it won't be singsongy. And if you heard a psalm sung with its original tune, it wouldn't be catchy to your ear. But the truth of the psalm would fit today as surely as when it was written.

Book 1

TWO WAYS TO LIVE

1 [1]Happy are those who don't listen to the wicked,
who don't go where sinners go,
who don't do what evil people do.
[2]They love the LORD's teachings,
and they think about those teachings day and night.
[3]They are strong, like a tree planted by a river.
The tree produces fruit in season,
and its leaves don't die.
Everything they do will succeed.

"They love the LORD's teachings, and they think about those teachings day and night." (Psalm 1:2)

[4]But wicked people are not like that.
They are like chaff that the wind blows away.
[5]So the wicked will not escape God's punishment.
Sinners will not worship with God's people.
[6]This is because the LORD takes care of his people,
but the wicked will be destroyed.

On the Edge

They are strong, like a tree planted by a river. The tree produces fruit in season, and its leaves don't die. Everything they do will succeed (Ps. 1:3).

Think about a tree growing beside a river. Would it be a dry, ugly tree with brown, cracking leaves? No, that tree would always be alive and full with lush, green leaves. Even in the middle of a drought, that tree would thrive because the river would give it all the water it needed.

"They are strong, like a tree planted by a river." The word *they* refers to the godly people described in verses 1 and 2. These people don't listen to friends or others who tell them to go against what God wants. They don't make fun of God, even if it seems like everyone else does. They are delighted when they think about what God says, so they do what pleases him.

If you've made up your mind to follow Jesus, ask yourself if you fit that description. *You* are like that tree growing beside a river. God's Spirit is the river that flows by you and offers you all the life and strength you need. When you get your life from his Spirit, you're always able to succeed in God's eyes, even if everything around you seems out of control.

SEE FOR YOURSELF:
Num. 24:6–7; Ps. 52:8; Jer. 17:7–8; Zech. 14:8

THE LORD'S CHOSEN KING

2 [1]Why are the nations so angry?
Why are the people making useless plans?
[2]The kings of the earth prepare to fight,
and their leaders make plans together
against the LORD
and his appointed one.
[3]They say, "Let's break the chains that hold us back
and throw off the ropes that tie us down."

[4]But the one who sits in heaven laughs;
the LORD makes fun of them.
[5]Then the LORD warns them
and frightens them with his anger.

WHAT'S IT MEAN?

When David conquered Jerusalem around 1000 B.C., he got something extra in the process—an ancient Jebusite fortress known as Zion. The fortress itself, which was located in the highest part of the city, didn't amount to much. Its name, for some reason, did. Years later, when Solomon built the Temple on Mount Moriah, the entire area in and around Jerusalem came to be known as Zion. Eventually, Zion was used to refer to the entire nation of Israel.

Psalm 2:6

6 He says, "I have appointed my own king
to rule in Jerusalem on my holy
mountain, Zion."

7 Now I will tell you what the LORD has
declared:
He said to me, "You are my son.
Today I have become your father.
8 If you ask me, I will give you the
nations;
all the people on earth will be yours.
9 You will rule over them with an iron
rod.
You will break them into pieces like
pottery."

10 So, kings, be wise;
rulers, learn this lesson.
11 Obey the LORD with great fear.
Be happy, but tremble.
12 Show that you are loyal to his son,
or you will be destroyed by his anger,
because he can quickly become angry.
But happy are those who trust him for
protection.

A MORNING PRAYER

David sang this when he ran away
from his son Absalom.

3

1 LORD, I have many enemies!
Many people have turned against me.
2 Many are saying about me,
"God won't rescue him." *Selah*

3 But, LORD, you are my shield,
my wonderful God who gives me
courage.
4 I will pray to the LORD,
and he will answer me from his holy
mountain. *Selah*

5 I can lie down and go to sleep,
and I will wake up again,
because the LORD gives me strength.
6 Thousands of troops may surround me,
but I am not afraid.

7 LORD, rise up!
My God, come save me!
You have struck my enemies on the
cheek;
you have broken the teeth of the
wicked.
8 The LORD can save his people.
LORD, bless your people. *Selah*

AN EVENING PRAYER

For the director of music. With stringed
instruments. A psalm of David.

4

1 Answer me when I pray to you,
my God who does what is right.
Make things easier for me when I am in
trouble.
Have mercy on me and hear my prayer.

2 People, how long will you turn my honor
into shame?
How long will you love what is false
and look for new lies? *Selah*
3 You know that the LORD has chosen for
himself those who are loyal to him.
The LORD listens when I pray to him.
4 When you are angry, do not sin.
Think about these things quietly
as you go to bed. *Selah*
5 Do what is right as a sacrifice to the LORD
and trust the LORD.

WHAT'S IT MEAN?

The heart's not simply a hollow, muscular organ, as far as Bible writers were concerned. They considered the heart to be the center of a person's character, the source not only of emotions, but also of thoughts and decision making. They believed that both good and evil actions get their start in the heart.

Psalm 4:4

6 Many people ask,
"Who will give us anything good?"
LORD, be kind to us.
7 But you have made me very happy,
happier than they are,
even with all their grain and new wine.
8 I go to bed and sleep in peace,
because, LORD, only you keep me safe.

A MORNING PRAYER FOR PROTECTION

5

For the director of music. For flutes.
A psalm of David.

1 LORD, listen to my words.
Understand my sadness.

2 Listen to my cry for help, my King and
my God,
because I pray to you.
3 LORD, every morning you hear my voice.
Every morning, I tell you what I need,
and I wait for your answer.

4 You are not a God who is pleased with the
wicked;
you do not live with those who do evil.
5 Those people who make fun of you
cannot stand before you.
You hate all those who do evil.
6 You destroy liars;
the LORD hates those who kill and trick
others.

7 Because of your great love,
I can come into your Temple.
Because I fear and respect you,
I can worship in your holy Temple.
8 LORD, since I have many enemies,
show me the right thing to do.
Show me clearly how you want me to
live.

9 My enemies' mouths do not tell the truth;
in their hearts they want to destroy
others.
Their throats are like open graves;
they use their tongues for telling lies.
10 God, declare them guilty!
Let them fall into their own traps.
Send them away because their sins are
many;
they have turned against you.

11 But let everyone who trusts you be happy;
let them sing glad songs forever.
Protect those who love you
and who are happy
because of you.
12 LORD, you bless those
who do what is right;
you protect them like a
soldier's shield.

BLESSING
How does God bless those who do right? (5:11–12)

A PRAYER FOR MERCY IN TROUBLED TIMES

For the director of music. With stringed instruments. Upon the sheminith. A psalm of David.

6

1 LORD, don't correct me when you are
angry;
don't punish me when you are very
angry.
2 LORD, have mercy on me because I am
weak.
Heal me, LORD, because my bones ache.
3 I am very upset.
LORD, how long will it be?

4 LORD, return and save me;
save me because of your kindness.
5 Dead people don't remember you;
those in the grave don't praise you.

6 I am tired of crying to you.
Every night my bed is wet with tears;
my bed is soaked from my crying.
7 My eyes are weak from so much crying;
they are weak from crying about my
enemies.

8 Get away from me, all you who do evil,
because the LORD has heard my crying.
9 The LORD has heard my cry for help;
the LORD will answer my prayer.
10 All my enemies will be ashamed and
troubled.
They will turn and suddenly leave in
shame.

A PRAYER FOR FAIRNESS

A shiggaion of David which he sang to the LORD about Cush, from the tribe of Benjamin.

7

1 LORD my God, I trust in you for
protection.
Save me and rescue me
from those who are chasing me.

WHAT'S IT MEAN?

No one knows for sure who Cush was, but he may have been a buddy of Saul's since they both came from the tribe of Benjamin. Saul's jealous rages, which were fueled by his mental problems, prompted him to try to kill David on several occasions. Anyone wanting to get in good with the king, then, simply had to tell a lie about David to reinforce Saul's delusions. Some of Saul's supporters even tried to kill David themselves.

Psalm 7:1 and psalm title

On the Edge

God protects me like a shield; he saves those whose hearts are right (Ps. 7:10).

God protects the person whose heart is right toward him. Having your heart right toward him doesn't have anything to do with being perfect or knocking yourself out trying to do the right thing all the time. A person who has an upright heart knows that he or she isn't perfect. That person realizes that his only hope comes from the fact that Jesus died to make things right for him.

Admitting those things takes humility. That's a word that most people don't talk about very often, maybe because their picture of humility is a mealy-mouthed person who looks at the floor all the time. But for a real picture of humility, look at Jesus. It's one of the most outstanding parts of his personality.

A heart that's humble is the kind of heart God is looking for. That's the kind of person he can use to get the job done. He protects that person in a special way because he knows that person is ready to do what he wants.

SEE FOR YOURSELF:
Job 5:19; Ps. 121:7–8; 2 Thess. 3:3

2 Otherwise, like a lion they will tear me
apart.
They will rip me to pieces, and no one
can save me.

3 LORD my God, what have I done?
Have my hands done something wrong?
4 Have I done wrong to my friend
or stolen without reason from my
enemy?
5 If I have, let my enemy chase me and
capture me.
Let him trample me into the dust
and bury me in the ground. *Selah*

6 LORD, rise up in your anger;
stand up against my enemies' anger.
Get up and demand fairness.
7 Gather the nations around you
and rule them from above.
8 LORD, judge the people.
LORD, defend me because I am right,
because I have done no wrong, God
Most High.
9 God, you do what is right.
You know our thoughts and feelings.
Stop those wicked actions done by evil
people,
and help those who do what is right.

10 God protects me like a shield;
he saves those whose hearts are right.
11 God judges by what is right,
and God is always ready to punish the
wicked.
12 If they do not change their lives,
God will sharpen his sword;
he will string his bow and take aim.
13 He has prepared his deadly weapons;
he has made his flaming arrows.

14 There are people who think up evil
and plan trouble and tell lies.
15 They dig a hole to trap others,
but they will fall into it themselves.
16 They will get themselves into trouble;
the violence they cause will hurt only
themselves.

17 I praise the LORD because he does what is
right.
I sing praises to the LORD Most High.

THE LORD'S GREATNESS

For the director of music. On the gittith.
A psalm of David.

8

1 LORD our Lord,
your name is the most wonderful name
in all the earth!
It brings you praise in heaven above.
2 You have taught children and babies
to sing praises to you
because of your enemies.
And so you silence your enemies
and destroy those who try to get even.

3 I look at your heavens,
which you made with your fingers.
I see the moon and stars,
which you created.
4 But why are people important to you?
Why do you take care of human beings?
5 You made them a little lower than the
angels
and crowned them with glory and
honor.

On the Edge

You made them a little lower than the angels and crowned them with glory and honor (Ps. 8:5).

In this psalm, David is amazed that the awesome God of heaven would use people to rule the earth. David says that we seem like weaklings, not worthy of such a place of honor. Has anyone told you lately that you are worth a crown of glory? worth a place of honor? Well, you are. And David says that's the way God thinks of you. Sometimes it may seem like your worth comes from your report card or your batting average, but it doesn't. Accomplishments are great, but they don't make you more acceptable to God. You couldn't get God to love you more, even if you tried. He has loved you completely from the first time he thought of you. He's your biggest fan. He adores you. You hold a place of honor in his heart. He's so proud of you and so in love with you that he's put a crown of glory and honor on you.

SEE FOR YOURSELF: Luke 2:32; Rom. 2:10; 2 Tim. 2:10

6 You put them in charge of everything you
made.
You put all things under their control:
7 all the sheep, the cattle,
and the wild animals,
8 the birds in the sky,
the fish in the sea,
and everything that lives under water.

9 LORD our Lord,
your name is the most wonderful name
in all the earth!

THANKSGIVING FOR VICTORY

For the director of music. To the tune of "The Death of the Son." A psalm of David.

9

1 I will praise you, LORD, with all my heart.
I will tell all the miracles you have done.
2 I will be happy because of you;
God Most High, I will sing praises to
your name.
3 My enemies turn back;
they are overwhelmed and die because
of you.
4 You have heard my complaint;
you sat on your throne and judged by
what was right.
5 You spoke strongly against the foreign
nations and destroyed the wicked;
you wiped out their names forever and
ever.
6 The enemy is gone forever.
You destroyed their cities;
no one even remembers them.

7 But the LORD rules forever.
He sits on his throne to
judge,
8 and he will judge the
world in fairness;
he will decide what is
fair for the nations.
9 The LORD defends those
who suffer;
he defends them in times of trouble.
10 Those who know the LORD trust him,
because he will not leave those who
come to him.

JUDGMENT

Who is the ultimate authority? (9:7–8)

WHAT'S IT MEAN?

For the most part, the people who lived in the nations surrounding Israel were sinful and corrupt, enemies of God. That didn't mean they were hopeless, though. The miracles that God performed for the Israelites often caught the attention of other nations. Those who recognized the power of Israel's God were given an opportunity to serve him.

Psalm 9:11

11 Sing praises to the LORD who is king on
Mount Zion.
Tell the nations what he has done.
12 He remembers who the murderers are;
he will not forget the cries of those who
suffer.
13 LORD, have mercy on me.
See how my enemies hurt me.
Do not let me go through the gates of
death.

[14]Then, at the gates of Jerusalem, I will
praise you;
I will rejoice because you saved me.

[15]The nations have fallen into the pit they
dug.
Their feet are caught in the nets they
laid.
[16]The LORD has made himself known by his
fair decisions;
the wicked get trapped by what they do.
Higgaion. Selah
[17]Wicked people will go to the grave,
and so will all those who forget God.
[18]But those who have troubles will
not be forgotten.
The hopes of the poor
will never die.

HOPE
Who does God give hope? (9:18)

[19]LORD, rise up and judge
the nations.
Don't let people think they are strong.
[20]Teach them to fear you, LORD.
The nations must learn that they are
only human. *Selah*

A COMPLAINT ABOUT EVIL PEOPLE

10

[1]LORD, why are you so far away?
Why do you hide when there is trouble?
[2]Proudly the wicked chase down those
who suffer.
Let them be caught in their own traps.
[3]They brag about the things they want.
They bless the greedy but hate the LORD.
[4]The wicked people are too proud.
They do not look for God;
there is no room for God in their
thoughts.
[5]They always succeed.
They are far from keeping your laws;
they make fun of their enemies.
[6]They say to themselves, "Nothing bad will
ever happen to me;
I will never be ruined."
[7]Their mouths are full of curses, lies, and
threats;
they use their tongues for sin and evil.
[8]They hide near the villages.
They look for innocent people to kill;
they watch in secret for the helpless.
[9]They wait in hiding like a lion.
They wait to catch poor people;
they catch the poor in nets.
[10]The poor are thrown down and crushed;
they are defeated because the others are
stronger.
[11]The wicked think, "God has forgotten us.
He doesn't see what is happening."

[12]LORD, rise up and punish the wicked.
Don't forget those who need help.
[13]Why do wicked people hate God?
They say to themselves, "God won't
punish us."
[14]LORD, surely you see these cruel and evil
things;
look at them and do something.
People in trouble look to you for help.
You are the one who helps the orphans.
[15]Break the power of wicked people.
Punish them for the evil they have done.

[16]The LORD is King forever and ever.
Destroy from your land those nations
that do not worship you.
[17]LORD, you have heard what the poor
people want.
Do what they ask, and listen to them.
[18]Protect the orphans and put an end to
suffering
so they will no longer be afraid of evil
people.

WHAT'S IT MEAN?

Can you imagine having to worry about lion attacks while you travel? People in ancient Palestine faced that danger every day. Apparently the king of the jungle was a very real problem in Israel's territory. The animals were known to spring from their hiding places among the thickets near the Jordan River to pounce on people passing by. If you're planning a trip to the Holy Land, you can relax about lions—they're long gone.

Psalm 10:9

TRUST IN THE LORD

For the director of music. Of David.

11

[1]I trust in the LORD for protection.
So why do you say to me,
"Fly like a bird to your mountain.
[2]Like hunters, the wicked string their bows;
they set their arrows on the bowstrings.

They shoot from dark places
at those who are honest.
3 When all that is good falls apart,
what can good people do?"

WHAT'S IT MEAN?

Just as a metalsmith working with gold or silver uses fire to purify the good and get rid of the bad, God uses the fire of his judgment to purify us and get rid of the bad. Do the fiery coals and flaming brimstone in this passage remind you of any other Bible stories? The cities of Sodom and Gomorrah were destroyed by fireballs from heaven after God judged their wickedness.

Psalm 11:5–6

4 The LORD is in his holy temple;
the LORD sits on his throne in heaven.
He sees what people do;
he keeps his eye on them.
5 The LORD tests those who do right,
but he hates the wicked and those who
love to hurt others.
6 He will send hot coals and burning sulfur
on the wicked.
A whirlwind is what they will get.
7 The LORD does what is right, and he loves
justice,
so honest people will see his face.

A PRAYER AGAINST LIARS

For the director of music. Upon the sheminith. A psalm of David.

12

1 Save me, LORD, because the good people
are all gone;
no true believers are left on earth.
2 Everyone lies to his neighbors;
they say one thing and mean another.

3 The LORD will stop those flattering lips
and cut off those bragging tongues.
4 They say, "Our tongues will help us win.
We can say what we wish; no one is
our master."

5 But the LORD says,
"I will now rise up,
because the poor are
being hurt.
Because of the moans of
the helpless,
I will give them the help
they want."
6 The LORD's words are pure,
like silver purified by fire,
like silver purified seven times over.

PAIN

Who does God watch over? (12:5)

7 LORD, you will keep us safe;
you will always protect us from such
people.
8 But the wicked are all around us;
everyone loves what is wrong.

WHAT'S IT MEAN?

If you want to find silver, you've got to look in rocks made of lead ore. If you want to get silver from the rock, you've got to heat the rock to extreme temperatures. If you want to purify the silver and make it more valuable, you've got to repeat the heating process over and over again.

Psalm 12:6

A PRAYER FOR GOD TO BE NEAR

For the director of music.
A psalm of David.

13

1 How long will you forget me, LORD?
Forever?
How long will you hide from me?
2 How long must I worry
and feel sad in my heart all day?
How long will my enemy win over me?

3 LORD, look at me.
Answer me, my God;
tell me, or I will die.
4 Otherwise my enemy will
say, "I have won!"
Those against me will
rejoice that I've been
defeated.

LIGHT

Who enlightens us when we have questions? (13:3)

5 I trust in your love.
My heart is happy because you saved
me.

[6]I sing to the LORD
because he has taken care of me.

THE UNBELIEVING FOOL

14

For the director of music. Of David.

[1]Fools say to themselves,
"There is no God."
Fools are evil and do terrible things;
there is no one who does anything good.

WHAT'S IT MEAN?

A lack of respect for God and his laws was the worst kind of ignorance, as far as David was concerned. The person who rejected God was considered the biggest fool of them all.

Psalm 14:1

[2]The LORD looked down from heaven on all people
to see if anyone understood,
if anyone was looking to God for help.
[3]But all have turned away.
Together, everyone has become evil.
There is no one who does anything good,
not even one.

[4]Don't the wicked understand?
They destroy my people as if they were eating bread.
They do not ask the LORD for help.
[5]But the wicked are filled with terror,
because God is with those who do what is right.
[6]The wicked upset the plans of the poor,
but the LORD will protect them.

[7]I pray that victory will come to Israel from Mount Zion!
May the LORD bring them back.
Then the people of Jacob will rejoice,
and the people of Israel will be glad.

WHAT THE LORD DEMANDS

15

A psalm of David.

[1]LORD, who may enter your Holy Tent?
Who may live on your holy mountain?

[2]Only those who are innocent
and who do what is right.
Such people speak the truth from their hearts
[3] and do not tell lies about others.
They do no wrong to their neighbors
and do not gossip.
[4]They do not respect hateful people
but honor those who honor the LORD.
They keep their promises to their neighbors,
even when it hurts.
[5]They do not charge interest on money they lend
and do not take money to hurt innocent people.

Whoever does all these things will never be destroyed.

WHAT'S IT MEAN?

What made Zion such a holy mountain? David had brought the Ark of the Agreement there for safekeeping. What made the Ark of the Agreement so special? It contained the actual tablets of the Ten Commandments, which God himself had given to Moses.

Psalm 15:1

THE LORD TAKES CARE OF HIS PEOPLE

16

A miktam of David.

[1]Protect me, God,
because I trust in you.
[2]I said to the LORD, "You are my Lord.
Every good thing I have comes from you."
[3]As for the godly people in the world,
they are the wonderful ones I enjoy.
[4]But those who turn to idols

will have much pain.
I will not offer blood to those idols
or even speak their names.

5 No, the LORD is all I need.
He takes care of me.
6 My share in life has been pleasant;
my part has been beautiful.

7 I praise the LORD because he
advises me.
Even at night, I feel his
leading.
8 I keep the LORD before me
always.
Because he is close by
my side,
I will not be hurt.
9 So I rejoice and am glad.
Even my body has hope,
10 because you will not leave me in the
grave.
You will not let your holy one rot.
11 You will teach me how to live a holy life.
Being with you will fill me with joy;
at your right hand I will find pleasure
forever.

GOD'S WILL

What can we trust in when we are making decisions? (16:7)

WHAT'S IT MEAN?

Look carefully and you might spot Jesus in these verses. Who else do you know of who came back to life, rose out of the grave, and sits on God's right side?

Psalm 16:10–11

A PRAYER FOR PROTECTION

A prayer of David.

17

1 LORD, hear me begging for fairness;
listen to my cry for help.
Pay attention to my prayer,
because I speak the
truth.
2 You will judge that I am
right;
your eyes can see what
is true.

ASSURANCE

Does God hear our prayers? (17:1–2)

3 You have examined my heart;
you have tested me all night.
You questioned me without finding
anything wrong;
I have not sinned with my mouth.
4 I have obeyed your commands,
so I have not done what evil people do.
5 I have done what you told me;
I have not failed.

WHAT'S IT MEAN?

The eye, one of the most sensitive and precious parts of the human body, comes equipped with its own protector, the eyelid. The eyelid instinctively closes anytime it senses danger to the eye. It "shelters" this vital organ just as a mother hen shelters her chicks beneath her wings.

Psalm 17:8

6 I call to you, God,
and you answer me.
Listen to me now,
and hear what I say.
7 Your love is wonderful.
By your power you save those who
trust you
from their enemies.
8 Protect me as you would protect your
own eye.
Hide me under the shadow of your
wings.
9 Keep me from the wicked who attack me,
from my enemies who surround me.
10 They are selfish
and brag about themselves.
11 They have chased me until they have
surrounded me.
They plan to throw me to the ground.
12 They are like lions ready to kill;
like lions, they sit in hiding.

13 LORD, rise up, face the enemy, and throw
them down.
Save me from the wicked with your
sword.
14 LORD, save me by your power
from those whose reward is in this life.
They have plenty of food.

They have many sons
and leave much money to their children.

15 Because I have lived right, I will see your
face.
When I wake up, I will see your likeness
and be satisfied.

A SONG OF VICTORY

For the director of music. By the LORD's servant, David. David sang this song to the LORD when the LORD had saved him from Saul and all his other enemies.

18

1 I love you, LORD. You are my
strength.

2 The LORD is my rock, my
protection, my Savior.
My God is my rock.
I can run to him for safety.
He is my shield and my
saving strength, my
defender.

"I love you, LORD. You are my strength." (Psalm 18:1)

3 I will call to the LORD, who is worthy of
praise,
and I will be saved from my enemies.

4 The ropes of death came around me;
the deadly rivers overwhelmed me.
5 The ropes of death wrapped around me.
The traps of death were before me.
6 In my trouble I called to the LORD.
I cried out to my God for help.
From his temple he heard my voice;
my call for help reached his ears.

7 The earth trembled and shook.
The foundations of the mountains
began to shake.
They trembled because the LORD was
angry.
8 Smoke came out of his nose,
and burning fire came out of his mouth.
Burning coals went before him.
9 He tore open the sky and came down
with dark clouds under his feet.
10 He rode a creature with wings and flew.
He raced on the wings of the wind.
11 He made darkness his covering, his shelter
around him,
surrounded by fog and clouds.
12 Out of the brightness of his presence came
clouds
with hail and lightning.
13 The LORD thundered from heaven;
the Most High raised his voice,
and there was hail and lightning.
14 He shot his arrows and scattered his
enemies.
His many bolts of lightning confused
them with fear.
15 LORD, you spoke strongly.
The wind blew from your nose.
Then the valleys of the sea appeared,
and the foundations of the earth were
seen.

16 The LORD reached down from above and
took me;
he pulled me from the deep water.
17 He saved me from my
powerful enemies,
from those who hated me,
because they were too
strong for me.
18 They attacked me at my time
of trouble,
but the LORD supported
me.
19 He took me to a safe place.
Because he delights in me,
he saved me.

20 The LORD spared me because I did what
was right.
Because I have not done evil, he has
rewarded me.
21 I have followed the ways of the LORD;
I have not done evil by turning away
from my God.
22 I remember all his laws
and have not broken his rules.
23 I am innocent before him;
I have kept myself from doing evil.
24 The LORD rewarded me because I did what
was right,
because I did what the LORD said was
right.

25 LORD, you are loyal to those who are
loyal,
and you are good to those who are
good.
26 You are pure to those who are pure,
but you are against those who are bad.
27 You save the humble,
but you bring down those who are
proud.
28 LORD, you give light to my lamp.
My God brightens the darkness around
me.
29 With your help I can attack an army.

With God's help I can jump over a
wall.

WHAT'S IT MEAN?

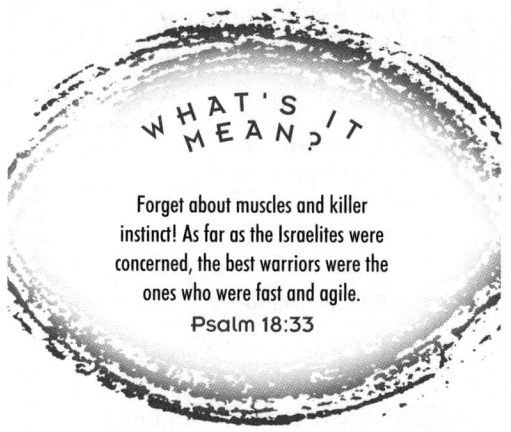

Forget about muscles and killer instinct! As far as the Israelites were concerned, the best warriors were the ones who were fast and agile.

Psalm 18:33

30 The ways of God are without fault.
The LORD's words are pure.
He is a shield to those who trust him.
31 Who is God? Only the LORD.
Who is the Rock? Only our God.
32 God is my protection.
He makes my way free from fault.
33 He makes me like a deer that does not
stumble;
he helps me stand on the steep
mountains.
34 He trains my hands for battle
so my arms can bend a bronze bow.
35 You protect me with your saving shield.
You support me with your right hand.
You have stooped to make me great.
36 You give me a better way to live,
so I live as you want me to.
37 I chased my enemies and caught them.

WHAT'S IT MEAN?

David knew what he was talking about when it came to being armed for battle. His life was filled with struggles and fights. He battled Goliath, he battled Saul, he battled Saul's family, he battled the Ammonites, he battled the Syrians, he battled the Philistines—he even battled his own son for control of Israel!

Psalm 18:39

I did not quit until they were destroyed.
38 I crushed them so they couldn't rise up
again.
They fell beneath my feet.
39 You gave me strength in battle.
You made my enemies bow before me.
40 You made my enemies turn back,
and I destroyed those who hated me.
41 They called for help,
but no one came to save them.
They called to the LORD,
but he did not answer them.
42 I beat my enemies into pieces, like dust in
the wind.
I poured them out like mud in the
streets.

43 You saved me when the people attacked
me.
You made me the leader of nations.
People I never knew serve me.
44 As soon as they hear me, they obey me.
Foreigners obey me.
45 They all become afraid
and tremble in their hiding places.

46 The LORD lives!
May my Rock be praised.
Praise the God who saves me!
47 God gives me victory over my enemies
and brings people under my rule.
48 He saves me from my enemies.

You set me over those who hate me.
You saved me from cruel men.
49 So I will praise you, LORD, among the
nations.
I will sing praises to your name.
50 The LORD gives great victories to his king.
He is loyal to his appointed king,
to David and his descendants forever.

GOD'S WORKS AND WORD

For the director of music.
A psalm of David.

19

1 The heavens tell the glory of God,
and the skies announce what his hands
have made.
2 Day after day they tell the story;
night after night they tell it again.
3 They have no speech or words;
they have no voice to be heard.
4 But their message goes out through all the
world;
their words go everywhere on earth.

The sky is like a home for the sun.
5 The sun comes out like a bridegroom
from his bedroom.
It rejoices like an athlete eager to run a
race.
6 The sun rises at one end of the sky
and follows its path to the other end.
Nothing hides from its heat.

7 The teachings of the LORD are perfect;
they give new strength.
The rules of the LORD can be trusted;
they make plain people wise.
8 The orders of the LORD are right;
they make people happy.
The commands of the LORD are pure;
they light up the way.
9 Respect for the LORD is good;
it will last forever.
The judgments of the LORD are true;
they are completely right.
10 They are worth more than gold,
even the purest gold.
They are sweeter than honey,
even the finest honey.
11 By them your servant is warned.
Keeping them brings great reward.

12 People cannot see their own mistakes.
Forgive me for my secret sins.
13 Keep me from the sins of
pride;
don't let them rule me.
Then I can be pure
and innocent of the
greatest of sins.

GUILT
Can we hide sins from God? (19:12–13)

14 I hope my words and
thoughts please you.
LORD, you are my Rock, the one who
saves me.

A PRAYER FOR THE KING

For the director of music.
A psalm of David.

20

1 May the LORD answer you in times of
trouble.
May the God of Jacob protect you.
2 May he send you help from his Temple
and support you from Mount Zion.
3 May he remember all your offerings
and accept all your sacrifices. *Selah*
4 May he give you what you want
and make all your plans succeed,
5 and we will shout for joy when you
succeed,
and we will raise a flag in the name of
our God.

Promise

HE PROMISES HE WILL BE WORSHIPED FOREVER.

Respect for the LORD is good; it will last forever (Ps. 19:9a).

Think about it. Some people worship their money. Some people worship their cars. Some people worship their careers. Maybe you don't see them bow down to these things, and maybe they don't call them "god"; but they think about them constantly, and all their effort and energy go into making them bigger or better or both. That's worship, or "fear," indicating what they hold to be most important in life. But the car eventually ends up in the junkyard. The money gets spent. The career ends in retirement.

Other people worship things that they think are God. They honor the forces of nature or the stars. Or they pray to a statue or a city. Their rituals make them feel better, but they're still worshiping *things*.

God is totally different. He is a Person. He will live forever. He doesn't rust, wear out, or run out. When everything on earth has decayed or burned up or blown away, he will still be running the show. And the people who chose to worship him (instead of their cars) will still be singing his praises.

Even when the earth has passed away, there will be worship in heaven for all of eternity. Awesome.

SEE FOR YOURSELF:
Ps. 22:27; Zeph. 2:11; Rev. 15:4

May the LORD give you all that you ask
for.

WHAT'S IT MEAN?

Large flags were used as "scoreboards" during battles. You could always tell which side was winning a skirmish by the flag that was raised. You can probably imagine how much those flags meant to the soldiers. Seeing their flag raised must have been a tremendous encouragement to the warriors. Seeing an opponent's flag raised, on the other hand, may have been an incentive to fight harder.

Psalm 20:5

6 Now I know the LORD helps his appointed
king.
He answers him from his holy heaven
and saves him with his strong right
hand.
7 Some trust in chariots, others in horses,
but we trust the LORD our God.
8 They are overwhelmed and defeated,
but we march forward and win.
9 LORD, save the king!
Answer us when we call for help.

THANKSGIVING FOR THE KING

For the director of music.
A psalm of David.

21

1 LORD, the king rejoices because of your
strength;
he is so happy when you save him!
2 You gave the king what he wanted
and did not refuse what he asked for.
Selah
3 You put good things before him
and placed a gold crown on his head.
4 He asked you for life,
and you gave it to him,
so his years go on and on.
5 He has great glory because you gave him
victories;
you gave him honor and praise.
6 You always gave him blessings;
you made him glad because you were
with him.
7 The king truly trusts the LORD.
Because God Most High always loves
him,
he will not be overwhelmed.
8 Your hand is against all your enemies;
those who hate you will feel your
power.
9 When you appear,
you will burn them as in a furnace.
In your anger you will swallow them up,
and fire will burn them up.
10 You will destroy their families from the
earth;
their children will not live.
11 They made evil plans against you,
but their traps won't work.
12 You will make them turn their backs
when you aim your arrows at them.
13 Be supreme, LORD, in your power.
We sing and praise your greatness.

WHAT'S IT MEAN?

"Eli, eli, lama sabachthani?" is the Aramaic translation of David's first question in this Psalm. Those foreign words may seem familiar to you even if you've never studied that language in your life. Jesus quoted them on the cross, after he had taken the responsibility of paying the price of death for the sins of the world.

Psalm 22:1

THE PRAYER OF A SUFFERING MAN

For the director of music. To the tune of
"The Doe of Dawn." A psalm of David.

22

1 My God, my God, why have you rejected
me?
You seem far from saving me,
far from the words of my groaning.
2 My God, I call to you during the day,
but you do not answer.
I call at night;
I am not silent.

3 You sit as the Holy One.
The praises of Israel are your throne.
4 Our ancestors trusted you;

they trusted, and you saved them.
5 They called to you for help
and were rescued.
They trusted you
and were not disappointed.

6 But I am like a worm instead of a man.
People make fun of me and hate me.
7 Those who look at me laugh.
They stick out their tongues and shake their heads.
8 They say, "Turn to the LORD for help.
Maybe he will save you.
If he likes you,
maybe he will rescue you."

9 You had my mother give birth to me.
You made me trust you
while I was just a baby.
10 I have leaned on you since the day I was born;
you have been my God since my mother gave me birth.
11 So don't be far away from me.
Now trouble is near,
and there is no one to help.
12 People have surrounded me like angry bulls.
Like the strong bulls of Bashan, they are on every side.
13 Like hungry, roaring lions
they open their mouths at me.

WHAT'S IT MEAN?

The dogs of ancient Israel certainly weren't man's best friend. In fact, they were more like scavengers than house pets. Traveling in packs, these wild creatures were known for attacking and killing the weak and the helpless. They ate discarded food and anything else they could find to stay alive.

Psalm 22:16

14 My strength is gone,
like water poured out onto the ground,
and my bones are out of joint.
My heart is like wax;
it has melted inside me.
15 My strength has dried up like a clay pot,
and my tongue sticks to the top of my mouth.
You laid me in the dust of death.
16 Evil people have surrounded me;
like dogs they have trapped me.
They have bitten my arms and legs.
17 I can count all my bones;
people look and stare at me.

Promise

HE PROMISES TO FILL YOU WITH HIS PRAISES.

LORD, I praise you in the great meeting of your people; these worshipers will see me do what I promised (Ps. 22:25).

When God's people come together, they usually praise him. That's what he expects. Because of that, people spend a lot of time trying hard to praise the Lord—with the right music, the right words, the right posture. You may even be sitting or standing in the pew trying to work up the frame of mind that will please God and make you feel good, too.

If that's the case, there's nothing wrong with your motives or the motives of the people who plan the songs and the prayers and the standing and sitting. But David had a different idea about how he was going to praise God. He was determined to praise God—no matter what. He knew that when he did his part by *choosing* to praise that God would fill him with praise. The happiness that David had in God's presence came straight from God.

So when you get together with other people who love God, make up your mind that you're going to praise God. Think about his goodness, his power, his awesome love. Ask him to fill your heart with praise like he did for David. And he will.

SEE FOR YOURSELF:
Ps. 4:7; Is. 61:11; Rom. 15:13

18 They divided my clothes among them,
and they threw lots for my clothing.

19 But, LORD, don't be far away.
You are my strength; hurry to help me.
20 Save me from the sword;
save my life from the dogs.
21 Rescue me from the lion's mouth;
save me from the horns of the bulls.

22 Then I will tell my fellow Israelites about
you;
I will praise you in the public meeting.
23 Praise the LORD, all you who respect him.
All you descendants of Jacob, honor
him;
fear him, all you Israelites.
24 He does not ignore those in trouble.
He doesn't hide from them
but listens when they call out to him.
25 LORD, I praise you in the great meeting of
your people;
these worshipers will see me do what I
promised.
26 Poor people will eat until they are full;
those who look to the LORD will praise
him.
May your hearts live forever!
27 People everywhere will remember
and will turn to the LORD.
All the families of the nations
will worship him
28 because the LORD is King,
and he rules the nations.

29 All the powerful people on earth will eat
and worship.
Everyone will bow down to him,
all who will one day die.
30 The people in the future will serve him;
they will always be told about the
Lord.
31 They will tell that he does what is right.
People who are not yet born
will hear what God has done.

THE LORD THE SHEPHERD

A psalm of David.

23

1 The LORD is my shepherd;
I have everything I need.
2 He lets me rest in green pastures.
He leads me to calm water.
3 He gives me new strength.
He leads me on paths that are right
for the good of his name.
4 Even if I walk through a very dark valley,
I will not be afraid,
because you are with me.

Promise

HE PROMISES YOU WILL NEVER WANT FOR ANYTHING.

The LORD is my shepherd; I have everything I need (Ps. 23:1).

David had a rock-solid confidence in God. He didn't wonder whether God was going to give him food to eat, clothes to wear, or a place to live. Part of that confidence came out of David's experiences. In spite of all the scrapes and tight places he found himself in, God had never let him be hurt or go hungry. And part of that confidence came from the fact that David knew God very well. He knew him like a best friend. He knew that God was—and is—kind, loving, and powerful.

There was another reason that David could say, "I have everything I need." All of David's hopes and dreams were caught up in the Lord. Even if he had been forced to go without some of the things that people consider necessities, he wouldn't have missed them much. David's relationship with God meant everything to him. As long as he knew that God was leading him and that their friendship was where it was supposed to be, David had the thing he wanted most. All the rest was extra.

As you grow toward having the same attitude that David did, you'll see—like David did—that God never lets you go without the things you really need. He is the one thing you need most.

SEE FOR YOURSELF:
Is. 49:10; Luke 12:29–31; John 6:35

WHAT'S IT MEAN?

All you needed to be a shepherd in ancient times were sheep (obviously) and a rod. A shepherd's rod was a stick with a hook at the end of it. With it, a shepherd could gently nudge a stray sheep back into line or, using the hook, pull a sheep from a dangerous spot. The rod was also used as a weapon to defend the flock against wolves and other invaders.

Psalm 23:4

Your rod and your walking stick[n]
comfort me.

[5]You prepare a meal for me
in front of my enemies.
You pour oil on my
head;[n]
you fill my cup to
overflowing.
[6]Surely your goodness
and love will be
with me
all my life,
and I will live in the house of
the LORD forever.

"The LORD is my shepherd; I have everything I need. He lets me rest in green pastures." (Psalm 23:1–2a)

A WELCOME FOR GOD INTO THE TEMPLE

A psalm of David.

24

[1]The earth belongs to the LORD, and
everything in it—
the world and all its people.
[2]He built it on the waters
and set it on the rivers.

BLESSING

When are we blessed? (24:3–6)

[3]Who may go up on the
mountain of the
LORD?
Who may stand in his holy Temple?
[4]Only those with clean hands and pure
hearts,
who have not worshiped idols,
who have not made promises in the
name of a false god.
[5]They will receive a blessing from the LORD;
the God who saves
them will declare
them right.
[6]They try to follow God;
they look to the God of
Jacob for help. *Selah*

[7]Gates, open all the way.
Open wide, aged doors
so the glorious King
will come in.
[8]Who is this glorious King?
The LORD, strong and
mighty.
The LORD, the powerful
warrior.
[9]Gates, open all the way.
Open wide, aged doors
so the glorious King will come in.
[10]Who is this glorious King?
The LORD All-Powerful—
he is the glorious King. *Selah*

WHAT'S IT MEAN?

Many Bible experts believe David wrote this psalm as part of the celebration for when he brought the Ark of the Lord to Jerusalem. Years before, the Ark had been captured during a battle with the Philistines. When David became king, he made Jerusalem his capital and had the recovered Ark moved there. Because the Ark contained the tablets on which God had written the Ten Commandments, it was a major part of the Israelites' worship.

Psalm 24:1

A PRAYER FOR GOD TO GUIDE

Of David.

25

[1]LORD, I give myself to you;
[2]my God, I trust you.
Do not let me be disgraced;
do not let my enemies laugh at me.
[3]No one who trusts you will be disgraced,
but those who sin without excuse will
be disgraced.

23:4 walking stick The stick a shepherd uses to guide and protect his sheep. **23:5 pour oil . . . head** This can mean that God gave him great wealth and blessed him.

4 LORD, tell me your ways.
Show me how to live.
5 Guide me in your truth,
and teach me, my God, my Savior.
I trust you all day long.
6 LORD, remember your mercy and love
that you have shown since long ago.
7 Do not remember the sins
and wrong things I did when I was
young.
But remember to love me always
because you are good, LORD.

WHAT'S IT MEAN?

The agreement between God and the Israelites was first made with Abraham, Isaac, and Jacob. After God led the Israelites out of Egypt, he confirmed the agreement with Moses and the people. The deal went like this: God would make Israel into a great nation and bless its people. In return, the Israelites would serve God faithfully, obeying and worshiping him as the only true God. The Israelites violated the agreement many times, but each time they renewed it, God held up his side of the agreement.

Psalm 25:10

8 The LORD is good and right;
he points sinners to the right way.
9 He shows those who are humble how to
do right,
and he teaches them his ways.
10 All the LORD's ways are loving and true
for those who follow the demands of
his agreement.
11 For the sake of your name,
LORD,
forgive my many sins.
12 Are there those who
respect the LORD?
He will point them to
the best way.
13 They will enjoy a good life,
and their children will inherit the land.
14 The LORD tells his secrets to those who
respect him;
he tells them about his agreement.
15 My eyes are always looking to the LORD
for help.

FEAR

Should Christians ever be afraid of God? (25:12–15)

He will keep me from any traps.
16 Turn to me and have mercy on me,
because I am lonely and hurting.
17 My troubles have grown larger;
free me from my problems.
18 Look at my suffering and troubles,
and take away all my sins.
19 Look at how many enemies I have!
See how much they hate me!
20 Protect me and save me.
I trust you, so do not let me be
disgraced.
21 My hope is in you,
so may goodness and honesty guard
me.
22 God, save Israel from all their troubles!

THE PRAYER OF AN INNOCENT BELIEVER

Of David.

26

1 LORD, defend me because I have lived an
innocent life.
I have trusted the LORD and never
doubted.
2 LORD, try me and test me;
look closely into my heart and mind.
3 I see your love,
and I live by your truth.
4 I do not spend time with liars,
nor do I make friends with those who
hide their sin.
5 I hate the company of evil people,
and I won't sit with the wicked.
6 I wash my hands to show I am innocent,
and I come to your altar, LORD.
7 I raise my voice in praise
and tell of all the miracles you have
done.

WHAT'S IT MEAN?

In Old Testament times, God occasionally showed his "glory," a visible symbol of his presence, to human beings. The best way to describe this glory is as a burning fire or a bright light. God's glory appeared in the Holy Tent over the lid of the Ark of the Agreement.

Psalm 26:8

8 LORD, I love the Temple where you live,
where your glory is.
9 Do not kill me with those sinners
or take my life with those murderers.
10 Evil is in their hands,
and they do wrong for money.
11 But I have lived an innocent life,
so save me and have mercy on me.
12 I stand in a safe place.
LORD, I praise you in the great meeting.

A SONG OF TRUST IN GOD

Of David.

27

1 The LORD is my light and
the one who saves
me.
I fear no one.
The LORD protects my life;
I am afraid of no one.
2 Evil people may try to destroy
my body.
My enemies and those who hate me
attack me,
but they are overwhelmed and defeated.
3 If an army surrounds me,
I will not be afraid.
If war breaks out,
I will trust the LORD.

4 I ask only one thing from the LORD.
This is what I want:
Let me live in the LORD's house
all my life.
Let me see the LORD's beauty
and look with my own eyes at his
Temple.

LIGHT

Is God ever called light? (27:1)

WHAT'S IT MEAN?

Before Solomon built the Temple, the Meeting Tent was the place the Israelites went to worship God. The tent was considered the house of God because his "glory," a symbol of his presence, appeared over the Ark of the Agreement, which was kept in the tent.

Psalm 27:4

On the Edge

LORD, hear me when I call; have mercy and answer me. My heart said of you, "Go, worship him." So I come to worship you, LORD. Do not turn away from me. Do not turn your servant away in anger; you have helped me. Do not push me away or leave me alone, God, my Savior. If my father and mother leave me, the LORD will take me in (Ps. 27:7–10).

If you've just found out that you're pregnant, you are probably feeling a multitude of emotions—disbelief, fear, confusion, loneliness, regret, and maybe anger, and others. Your life has changed forever. During the next months, you're going to have to make some very responsible decisions, so an important first step is to gather a support team. Hopefully your family and friends will be your team; but, if not, there are other options like a crisis pregnancy center, or other Christian agencies that assist pregnant women. As you begin to process everything and make decisions, the most important place you can look for guidance is to the Lord. You can cry out to God and ask him to take care of you. Keep reminding yourself of Psalm 27:14.

Do not be afraid to do the right thing. God has not abandoned you. He already has a plan and purpose for your baby's life. Take care of your body so that the baby will be healthy. And make sure that your child will be raised by godly parents in a safe and loving home. God will honor your faithfulness to him. He answers people when they cry out to him. He promises that he will take care of you.

SEE FOR YOURSELF:
Ps. 27:14; Is. 1:18–19; Jer. 29:11–12; Hos. 6:1–2; 14:1–9; Mark 3:28

5 During danger he will keep me safe in his
shelter.
He will hide me in his Holy Tent,
or he will keep me safe on a high
mountain.
6 My head is higher than my enemies
around me.

I will offer joyful sacrifices in his Holy
Tent.
I will sing and praise the LORD.

7 LORD, hear me when I call;
have mercy and answer me.
8 My heart said of you, "Go, worship him."
So I come to worship you, LORD.
9 Do not turn away from me.
Do not turn your servant away in
anger;
you have helped me.
Do not push me away or leave me alone,
God, my Savior.
10 If my father and mother leave me,
the LORD will take me in.
11 LORD, teach me your ways,
and guide me to do what is right
because I have enemies.
12 Do not hand me over to my enemies,
because they tell lies about me
and say they will hurt me.

13 I truly believe
I will live to see the LORD's goodness.
14 Wait for the LORD's help.
Be strong and brave,
and wait for the LORD's help.

A PRAYER IN TROUBLED TIMES

Of David.

28

1 LORD, my Rock, I call out to you for help.
Do not be deaf to me.
If you are silent,
I will be like those in the grave.
2 Hear the sound of my prayer,
when I cry out to you for help.
I raise my hands
toward your Most Holy Place.
3 Don't drag me away with the wicked,
with those who do evil.
They say "Peace" to their neighbors,
but evil is in their hearts.
4 Pay them back for what they have done,
for their evil deeds.
Pay them back for what they have done;
give them their reward.
5 They don't understand what the LORD has
done
or what he has made.
So he will knock them down
and not lift them up.

6 Praise the LORD,
because he heard my prayer for help.
7 The LORD is my strength and shield.
I trust him, and he helps me.
I am very happy,
and I praise him with my song.
8 The LORD is powerful;
he gives victory to his chosen one.
9 Save your people
and bless those who are your own.
Be their shepherd and carry them
forever.

WHAT'S IT MEAN?

Shields were as important to ancient soldiers as swords and spears were. Since few ancient armies wore body armor, shields were the only defense soldiers had against enemy arrows and swords. These shields came in all shapes and sizes, and could be made of leather, wood, or metal.

Psalm 28:7

GOD IN THE THUNDERSTORM

A psalm of David.

29

1 Praise the LORD, you
angels;
praise the LORD's glory
and power.
2 Praise the LORD for the
glory of his name;
worship the LORD
because he is holy.

WORSHIP

What should we give to the Lord during worship? (29:1–2)

3 The LORD's voice is heard over the sea.
The glorious God thunders;
the LORD thunders over the ocean.
4 The LORD's voice is powerful;
the LORD's voice is majestic.
5 The LORD's voice breaks the trees;
the LORD breaks the cedars of Lebanon.
6 He makes the land of Lebanon dance like
a calf
and Mount Hermon jump like a baby
bull.
7 The LORD's voice makes the lightning flash.
8 The LORD's voice shakes the desert;
the LORD shakes the Desert of Kadesh.

9 The LORD's voice shakes the oaks
and strips the leaves off the trees.
In his Temple everyone says, "Glory to God!"

10 The LORD controls the flood.
The LORD will be King forever.
11 The LORD gives strength to his people;
the LORD blesses his people with peace.

THANKSGIVING FOR ESCAPING DEATH

A psalm of David. A song for giving the Temple to the LORD.

30

1 I will praise you, LORD,
because you rescued me.
You did not let my enemies laugh at me.
2 LORD, my God, I prayed to you,
and you healed me.
3 You lifted me out of the grave;
you spared me from going down to the place of the dead.

4 Sing praises to the LORD, you who belong to him;
praise his holy name.
5 His anger lasts only a moment,
but his kindness lasts for a lifetime.
Crying may last for a night,
but joy comes in the morning.

6 When I felt safe, I said,
"I will never fear."
7 LORD, in your kindness you made my mountain safe.
But when you turned away, I was frightened.

8 I called to you, LORD,
and asked you to have mercy on me.
9 I said, "What good will it do if I die
or if I go down to the grave?
Dust cannot praise you;
it cannot speak about your truth.
10 LORD, hear me and have mercy on me.
LORD, help me."

11 You changed my sorrow into dancing.
You took away my clothes of sadness,
and clothed me in happiness.
12 I will sing to you and not be silent.
LORD, my God, I will praise you forever.

A PRAYER OF FAITH IN TROUBLED TIMES

For the director of music.
A psalm of David.

31

1 LORD, I trust in you;
let me never be disgraced.
Save me because you do what is right.
2 Listen to me
and save me quickly.
Be my rock of protection,
a strong city to save me.
3 You are my rock and my protection.
For the good of your name, lead me and guide me.
4 Set me free from the trap they set for me,
because you are my protection.
5 I give you my life.
Save me, LORD, God of truth.

6 I hate those who worship false gods.
I trust only in the LORD.
7 I will be glad and rejoice in your love,
because you saw my suffering;
you knew my troubles.
8 You have not handed me over to my enemies
but have set me in a safe place.

9 LORD, have mercy, because I am in misery.
My eyes are weak from so much crying,
and my whole being is tired from grief.
10 My life is ending in sadness,
and my years are spent in crying.
My troubles are using up my strength,
and my bones are getting weaker.
11 Because of all my troubles, my enemies hate me,
and even my neighbors look down on me.
When my friends see me,
they are afraid and run.
12 I am like a piece of a broken pot.
I am forgotten as if I were dead.
13 I have heard many insults.
Terror is all around me.
They make plans against me
and want to kill me.

14 LORD, I trust you.
I have said, "You are my God."
15 My life is in your hands.
Save me from my enemies
and from those who are chasing me.
16 Show your kindness to me, your servant.
Save me because of your love.

17 LORD, I called to you,
so do not let me be disgraced.
Let the wicked be disgraced
and lie silent in the grave.
18 With pride and hatred
they speak against those who do right.
So silence their lying lips.

19 How great is your goodness
that you have stored up for those who fear you,
that you have given to those who trust you.
You do this for all to see.
20 You protect them by your presence
from what people plan against them.
You shelter them from evil words.
21 Praise the LORD.
His love to me was wonderful
when my city was attacked.
22 In my distress, I said,
"God cannot see me!"
But you heard my prayer
when I cried out to you for help.
23 Love the LORD, all you who belong to him.
The LORD protects those who truly believe,
but he punishes the proud as much as they have sinned.
24 All you who put your hope in the LORD
be strong and brave.

IT IS BETTER TO CONFESS SIN

A maskil of David.

32

1 Happy is the person
whose sins are forgiven,
whose wrongs are pardoned.
2 Happy is the person
whom the LORD does not consider guilty
and in whom there is nothing false.

3 When I kept things to myself,
I felt weak deep inside me.
I moaned all day long.
4 Day and night you punished me.
My strength was gone as in the summer heat. *Selah*
5 Then I confessed my sins to you
and didn't hide my guilt.
I said, "I will confess my sins to the LORD,"
and you forgave my guilt. *Selah*

GUILT
What happens to our guilt when our sins are forgiven? (32:5)

6 For this reason, all who obey you
should pray to you while they still can.
When troubles rise like a flood,
they will not reach them.
7 You are my hiding place.
You protect me from my troubles
and fill me with songs of salvation. *Selah*

Promise

HE PROMISES TO TEACH YOU.

I will make you wise and show you where to go. I will guide you and watch over you (Ps. 32:8).

Who was your favorite teacher? Do you remember that person well? You probably do. Maybe he or she took a special interest in you; didn't let you get away with anything; believed in you more than you believed in yourself; made you want to learn; had high expectations of what you could do; actually made school fun. Whatever the reason, you remember that teacher well, and you're so glad he or she was a part of your growing up.

God promises to be your teacher—Life 101. He says that he will point out the road you should follow and that he will watch over you. He has the answers to all of your questions. By his Holy Spirit, he'll even guide you to what is true (see John 16:13). So if you were thinking about skipping God's class, don't. Listen to him and his wise instruction. He's the last guidance counselor you'll ever need.

SEE FOR YOURSELF:

Prov. 2:6; Is. 2:3; John 14:26; 16:13

8 The LORD says, "I will make you wise and
show you where to go.
I will guide you and watch over you.
9 So don't be like a horse or donkey,
that doesn't understand.
They must be led with bits and reins,
or they will not come near you."

10 Wicked people have many troubles,
but the LORD's love surrounds those
who trust him.
11 Good people, rejoice and be happy in the
LORD.
Sing all you whose hearts are right.

PRAISE GOD WHO CREATES AND SAVES

33

1 Sing to the LORD, you who do what is
right;
honest people should praise him.
2 Praise the LORD on the harp;
make music for him on a ten-stringed
lyre.
3 Sing a new song to him;
play well and joyfully.

WHAT'S IT MEAN?

The Israelites loved their music, especially when it came time to worship the Lord. Specific groups of Levites were assigned to sing in the choir or play in the orchestra that performed in or near the Holy Tent. The orchestra was made up of stringed instruments, such as guitars and harps, as well as percussion instruments, such as tambourines and cymbals.

Psalm 33:2

On the Edge

God's word is true, and everything he does is right (Ps. 33:4).

Who do you trust? Most people have a few friends who they think are trustworthy. Most people trust their parents and their brothers and sisters, at least to some extent. Maybe you have a favorite teacher or a coach you feel you can trust.

Has someone you trusted ever hurt you? That seems to happen to just about everybody at some point during their lives. Maybe you misjudged your friend and found out that person couldn't be trusted after all. More often, someone you've trusted for a long time makes a mistake that ends up hurting you. That doesn't mean you should stop trusting that person. It just means you need to accept the fact that that person isn't perfect—and forgive.

But trusting God isn't like that. He is perfect. He never lies, never misses the smallest details of any situation, never makes a mistake. You can count on every word he says. Everything he does is meant for something good in your life.

SEE FOR YOURSELF:
Is. 49:7; 1 Cor. 1:9;
2 Thess. 3:3

4 God's word is true,
and everything he does is right.
5 He loves what is right and fair;
the LORD's love fills the earth.

6 The sky was made at the LORD's
command.
By the breath from his mouth, he made
all the stars.
7 He gathered the water of the sea into a
heap.
He made the great ocean stay in its
place.
8 All the earth should worship the LORD;
the whole world should fear him.
9 He spoke, and it happened.
He commanded, and it appeared.
10 The LORD upsets the plans of nations;
he ruins all their plans.
11 But the LORD's plans will stand forever;
his ideas will last from now on.
12 Happy is the nation whose God is the
LORD,
the people he chose for his very own.
13 The LORD looks down from heaven
and sees every person.
14 From his throne he watches
all who live on earth.
15 He made their hearts
and understands everything they do.
16 No king is saved by his great army.

psalm 34:18

No warrior escapes by his great
strength.
17 Horses can't bring victory;
they can't save by their strength.
18 But the LORD looks after those who fear him,
those who put their hope in his love.
19 He saves them from death
and spares their lives in times of hunger.
20 So our hope is in the LORD.
He is our help, our shield to protect us.
21 We rejoice in him,
because we trust his holy name.
22 LORD, show your love to us
as we put our hope in you.

PRAISE GOD WHO JUDGES AND SAVES

David's song from the time he acted crazy so Abimelech would send him away, and David did leave.

34
1 I will praise the LORD at all times;
his praise is always on my lips.
2 My whole being praises the LORD.
The poor will hear and be glad.
3 Glorify the LORD with me,
and let us praise his name together.

4 I asked the LORD for help, and he
answered me.
He saved me from all that I feared.
5 Those who go to him for help are happy,
and they are never disgraced.
6 This poor man called, and the LORD heard
him
and saved him from all his troubles.
7 The angel of the LORD camps around those
who fear God,
and he saves them.

8 Examine and see how good the LORD is.
Happy is the person who trusts him.
9 You who belong to the LORD, fear him!
Those who fear him will have
everything they need.
10 Even lions may get weak and hungry,
but those who look to the LORD will
have every good thing.
11 Children, come and listen to me.
I will teach you to worship the LORD.
12 You must do these things
to enjoy life and have many happy
days.
13 You must not say evil things,
and you must not tell lies.
14 Stop doing evil and do good.
Look for peace and work for it.

15 The LORD sees the good people
and listens to their prayers.
16 But the LORD is against those who do
evil;
he makes the world forget them.
17 The LORD hears good
people when they cry
out to him,
and he saves them from
all their troubles.
18 The LORD is close to the
brokenhearted,

EMOTIONS
Where can we find healing for a broken heart? (34:18)

Promise HE PROMISES THAT HIS ADVICE AND PLANS WILL NEVER CHANGE.

But the LORD's plans will stand forever; his ideas will last from now on (Ps. 33:11).

Do you know what God thinks of you? He thinks you're the best. You belong to him and are like his prize. He has compassion toward you because he knows your weak places. He created you out of pure love. He *wanted* you to be alive. He has made plans for all of eternity—plans that will never change, because God's thoughts will never change. He's got a plan for you. Your heart, your mind, and your body were designed with his plan in mind. You can run from God's plan for the rest of your life, but you will never change his mind or mess with his plan. He knows what you would be great at and he built you to do it. Ask him to show you what he made you for. Invite him to remind you when you forget. Then go for it.

SEE FOR YOURSELF:
Jer. 29:11; Dan. 6:26; Mal. 3:6

and he saves those whose spirits have
been crushed.

19 People who do what is right may have
many problems,
but the LORD will solve them all.
20 He will protect their very bones;
not one of them will be broken.
21 Evil will kill the wicked;
those who hate good people will be
judged guilty.
22 But the LORD saves his servants' lives;
no one who trusts him will be judged
guilty.

On the Edge

You who belong to the LORD, fear him! Those who fear him will have everything they need (Ps. 34:9).

Ever feel like just one of the guys (or one of the girls)? You know, you go to the same school as all of your friends, hang out at the same places, like the same bands, wear the same style of clothing, watch the same movies, play the same sports, have the same tennis shoes . . . Maybe you have red hair and your friends have brown, but mostly you're all just about alike—regular kids.

The Lord doesn't see you as one of the guys. He says you are special—not in a cheesy way, but in the way that a treasure is special. You are rare, one-of-a-kind. When he looks at you, he goes, "Wow."

He feels that way about you all the time, not just when you pray or worship. That's one of the ways he honors you. Psalm 34:9 says that you are to honor (fear) him, too. You don't have to be all stuffy or religious to honor the Lord. You just have to think about him, consider what he wants, follow his direction, spend time with him. Thank him for making you his special treasure and feel the same about him—that he is your treasure. One of the best ways to honor him is to look at him and go, "Wow."

SEE FOR YOURSELF:
Deut. 26:18;
1 Cor. 1:30–31;
Heb. 2:11

A PRAYER FOR HELP

Of David.

35

1 LORD, battle with those who battle with
me.
Fight against those who fight against
me.
2 Pick up the shield and armor.
Rise up and help me.
3 Lift up your spears, both large and small,
against those who chase me.
Tell me, "I will save you."

4 Make those who want to kill me
be ashamed and disgraced.
Make those who plan to harm me
turn back and run away.
5 Make them like chaff blown by the
wind
as the angel of the LORD forces them
away.
6 Let their road be dark and slippery
as the angel of the LORD chases them.
7 For no reason they spread out their net to
trap me;
for no reason they dug a pit for me.
8 So let ruin strike them suddenly.
Let them be caught in their own nets;
let them fall into the pit and die.
9 Then I will rejoice in the LORD;
I will be happy when he saves me.
10 Even my bones will say,
"LORD, who is like you?
You save the weak from the strong,
the weak and poor from robbers."

11 Men without mercy stand up to testify.
They ask me things I do not know.
12 They repay me with evil for the good I
have done,
and they make me very sad.
13 Yet when they were sick, I put on clothes
of sadness
and showed my sorrow by going
without food.
But my prayers were not answered.
14 I acted as if they were my friends or
brothers.
I bowed in sadness as if I were crying for
my mother.
15 But when I was in trouble, they gathered
and laughed;
they gathered to attack before I knew it.
They insulted me without stopping.
16 They made fun of me and were cruel to
me
and ground their teeth at me in anger.

17 Lord, how long will you watch this
happen?
Save my life from their attacks;
save me from these people who are like
lions.
18 I will praise you in the great meeting.
I will praise you among crowds of
people.
19 Do not let my enemies laugh at me;
they hate me for no reason.
Do not let them make fun of me;
they have no cause to hate me.
20 Their words are not friendly
but are lies about peace-loving people.
21 They speak against me
and say, "Aha! We saw what you did!"

WHAT'S IT MEAN?

"Make fun" here is literally "wink with the eye." In ancient times, winking was commonly used as a signal between two people who were secretly planning to do something. Here, the winking was an expression of happiness because disaster had struck an enemy.

Psalm 35:19

22 LORD, you have been watching. Do not
keep quiet.
Lord, do not leave me alone.
23 Wake up! Come and defend me!
My God and Lord, fight for me!
24 LORD my God, defend me with your
justice.
Don't let them laugh at me.
25 Don't let them think, "Aha! We got what
we wanted!"
Don't let them say, "We destroyed
him."
26 Let them be ashamed and embarrassed,
because they were happy when I hurt.
Cover them with shame and disgrace,
because they thought they were better
than I was.
27 May my friends sing and shout for joy.
May they always say, "Praise the
greatness of the LORD,
who loves to see his servants do well."
28 I will tell of your goodness
and will praise you every day.

WICKED PEOPLE AND A GOOD GOD

For the director of music. Of David,
the servant of the LORD.

36

1 Sin speaks to the wicked in their hearts.
They have no fear of God.
2 They think too much of themselves
so they don't see their sin and hate it.
3 Their words are wicked lies;
they are no longer wise or good.
4 At night they make evil plans;
what they do leads to nothing good.
They don't refuse things that are evil.

5 LORD, your love reaches to the heavens,
your loyalty to the skies.
6 Your goodness is as high as the
mountains.
Your justice is as deep as the great
ocean.
LORD, you protect both people and
animals.
7 God, your love is so precious!
You protect people in the shadow of
your wings.
8 They eat the rich food in your house,
and you let them drink from your river
of pleasure.
9 You are the giver of life.
Your light lets us enjoy life.

WHAT'S IT MEAN?

Not much rain falls in Israel between May and September, which means that water is precious. Old Testament writers often used rain (here called "the giver of life") as a symbol of God's blessing and drought as a symbol of God's punishment.

Psalm 36:9

10 Continue to love those who know you
and to do good to those who are
good.
11 Don't let proud people attack me
and the wicked force me away.
12 Those who do evil have been defeated.
They are overwhelmed;
they cannot do evil any longer.

GOD WILL REWARD FAIRLY

Of David.

37

1 Don't be upset because of
evil people.
Don't be jealous of
those who do wrong,
2 because like the grass,
they will soon dry up.
Like green plants, they will
soon die away.

JEALOUSY
Can we ever envy evil people? (37:1)

3 Trust the LORD and do good.
Live in the land and feed on truth.
4 Enjoy serving the LORD,
and he will give you what you want.
5 Depend on the LORD;
trust him, and he will take care of you.
6 Then your goodness will shine like the
sun,
and your fairness like the noonday sun.

7 Wait and trust the LORD.
Don't be upset when others get rich
or when someone else's plans succeed.
8 Don't get angry.
Don't be upset; it only leads to trouble.
9 Evil people will be sent away,
but those who trust the LORD will
inherit the land.
10 In a little while the wicked will be no
more.
You may look for them, but they will be
gone.
11 People who are not proud will inherit the
land
and will enjoy complete peace.

12 The wicked make evil plans against good
people.
They grind their teeth at them in anger.
13 But the Lord laughs at the wicked,
because he sees that their day is
coming.
14 The wicked draw their swords
and bend their bows
to kill the poor and helpless,
to kill those who are honest.
15 But their swords will stab their own
hearts,
and their bows will break.

16 It is better to have little and be right
than to have much and be wrong.
17 The power of the wicked will be broken,
but the LORD supports those who do
right.
18 The LORD watches over the lives of the
innocent,
and their reward will last forever.
19 They will not be ashamed when trouble
comes.
They will be full in times of hunger.
20 But the wicked will die.
The LORD's enemies will be like the
flowers of the fields;
they will disappear like smoke.
21 The wicked borrow and don't pay back,
but those who do right give freely to
others.
22 Those whom the LORD blesses will inherit
the land,
but those he curses will be sent away.

23 When a person's steps follow the
LORD,
God is pleased with
his ways.
24 If he stumbles, he will
not fall,
because the LORD holds
his hand.

ASSURANCE
Does God always care for his children? (37:23–24)

25 I was young, and now I am old,
but I have never seen good people left
helpless
or their children begging for food.
26 Good people always lend freely to others,
and their children are a blessing.

27 Stop doing evil and do good,
so you will live forever.
28 The LORD loves justice
and will not leave those who worship
him.
He will always protect them,
but the children of the wicked will die.
29 Good people will inherit the land
and will live in it forever.

30 A good person speaks with wisdom,
and he says what is fair.
31 The teachings of his God are in his heart,
so he does not fail to keep them.
32 The wicked watch for good people
so that they may kill them.
33 But the LORD will not take away his
protection
or let good people be judged guilty.

34 Wait for the LORD's help
and follow him.
He will honor you and give you the land,
and you will see the wicked sent away.

35 I saw a wicked and cruel man
who looked strong like a healthy tree in good soil.
36 But he died and was gone;
I looked for him, but he couldn't be found.

37 Think of the innocent person,
and watch the honest one.
The man who has peace
will have children to live after him.
38 But sinners will be destroyed;
in the end the wicked will die.

39 The LORD saves good people;
he is their strength in times of trouble.
40 The LORD helps them and saves them;
he saves them from the wicked,
because they trust in him for protection.

A PRAYER IN TIME OF SICKNESS

A psalm of David to remember.

38

1 LORD, don't correct me when you are angry.
Don't punish me when you are furious.
2 Your arrows have wounded me,
and your hand has come down on me.
3 My body is sick from your punishment.
Even my bones are not healthy because of my sin.
4 My guilt has overwhelmed me;
like a load it weighs me down.

5 My sores stink and become infected
because I was foolish.
6 I am bent over and bowed down;
I am sad all day long.
7 I am burning with fever,
and my whole body is sore.
8 I am weak and faint.
I moan from the pain I feel.

9 Lord, you know everything I want;
my cries are not hidden from you.
10 My heart pounds, and my strength is gone.
I am losing my sight.
11 Because of my wounds, my friends and neighbors avoid me,
and my relatives stay far away.
12 Some people set traps to kill me.
Those who want to hurt me plan trouble;
all day long they think up lies.

13 I am like a deaf man; I cannot hear.
Like a mute, I cannot speak.
14 I am like a person who does not hear,
who has no answer to give.
15 I trust you, LORD.
You will answer, my LORD and God.

Promise — HE PROMISES HE'LL NEVER LEAVE YOU.

The LORD loves justice and will not leave those who worship him. He will always protect them, but the children of the wicked will die (Ps. 37:28).

Do you ever think the people who don't give a rip about God have really good lives? You probably know some people who don't give God a second thought, but they have nice clothes, good grades, lots of friends. There are definitely a lot of famous musicians, actors, athletes, and politicians who don't do a lot of good things, but they're living the "good life" all the same. It's easy to want what they have and to wonder why God let them have things he doesn't give to you. Sometimes when you compare your life to theirs, you think, *Man, where is God, anyway?*

Psalm 37 reminds you that the situation isn't always what it looks like. The people who don't care about God have what Jesus called a "house on the sand" (Matt. 7:26). It may be a really nice house, but it can't stand up for long. The people who refuse to obey God have nothing to show for their lives in the end. When it looks like God is blessing them and leaving you to fend for yourself, you need to know that he is still on your side. He will *never* forsake you. He won't collapse when a storm blows in or run away when things are rough. He's here to stay.

SEE FOR YOURSELF:

Deut. 31:6; Matt. 7:26; 18:12–14; 28:20

On the Edge

Lord, you know everything I want; my cries are not hidden from you (Ps. 38:9).

What do you secretly want to do with your life? Want to be an undertaker, but think all your friends would laugh? Want to be a chemist, but can't imagine how it could possibly happen? What does your heart long to do? God knows every one of your deepest desires. He put them there. He knows what makes you feel like time just flew by. He knows what fills you up and gives you a purpose. He knows what makes you so angry that you just have to do something. So trust him with your dreams and passions. He will not laugh. He is not surprised. He knows exactly how to make it all happen. His timing will be perfect.

SEE FOR YOURSELF:
Is. 66:18; Heb. 4:12

16 I said, "Don't let them laugh at me
or brag when I am defeated."
17 I am about to die,
and I cannot forget my pain.
18 I confess my guilt;
I am troubled by my sin.
19 My enemies are strong and healthy,
and many hate me for no reason.
20 They repay me with evil for the good I did.
They lie about me because I try to do good.

21 LORD, don't leave me;
my God, don't go away.
22 Quickly come and help me,
my Lord and Savior.

LIFE IS SHORT

For the director of music. For Jeduthun. A psalm of David.

39

1 I said, "I will be careful how I act
and will not sin by what I say.
I will be careful what I say
around wicked people."
2 So I kept very quiet.
I didn't even say anything good,
but I became even more upset.
3 I became very angry inside,
and as I thought about it, my anger burned.
So I spoke:
4 "LORD, tell me when the end will come
and how long I will live.
Let me know how long I have.
5 You have given me only a short life;
my lifetime is like nothing to you.
Everyone's life is only a breath.
Selah
6 People are like shadows moving about.
All their work is for nothing;
they collect things but don't know who will get them.

7 "So, Lord, what hope do I have?
You are my hope.
8 Save me from all my sins.
Don't let wicked fools make fun of me.

WHAT'S IT MEAN?

Jeduthun, the guy who gets billing at the beginning of this psalm, was appointed by David to serve as one of the three chief musicians in the Holy Tent. Jeduthun was also known as Ethan.

Psalm 39 title

WHAT'S IT MEAN?

Moths are mentioned several times in the Bible as symbols of destruction. Here's how the little critters are able to do so much damage. Female moths often lay their eggs in clothing. When the eggs hatch, the newborn larvae eat the fibers of the clothing. Because the larvae chew quietly, the owner of the clothing may not know that damage is being done until it's too late.

Psalm 39:11

[9] I am quiet; I do not open my mouth,
because you are the one who has done this.
[10] Quit punishing me;
your beating is about to kill me.
[11] You correct and punish people for their sins;
like a moth, you destroy what they love.
Everyone's life is only a breath. *Selah*

[12] "LORD, hear my prayer,
and listen to my cry.
Do not ignore my tears.
I am like a visitor with you.
Like my ancestors, I'm only here a short time.
[13] Leave me alone so I can be happy
before I leave and am no more."

PRAISE AND PRAYER FOR HELP

For the director of music.
A psalm of David.

40

[1] I waited patiently for the LORD.
He turned to me and heard my cry.
[2] He lifted me out of the pit of destruction,
out of the sticky mud.
He stood me on a rock
and made my feet steady.
[3] He put a new song in my mouth,
a song of praise to our God.
Many people will see this and worship him.
Then they will trust the LORD.

[4] Happy is the person
who trusts the LORD,
who doesn't turn to those who are proud
or to those who worship false gods.
[5] LORD my God, you have done many miracles.
Your plans for us are many.
If I tried to tell them all,
there would be too many to count.

[6] You do not want sacrifices and offerings.
But you have made a hole in my ear
to show that my body and life are yours.
You do not ask for burnt offerings
and sacrifices to take away sins.
[7] Then I said, "Look, I have come.
It is written about me in the book.
[8] My God, I want to do what you want.
Your teachings are in my heart."

[9] I will tell about your goodness in the great meeting of your people.
LORD, you know my lips are not silent.
[10] I do not hide your goodness in my heart;
I speak about your loyalty and salvation.
I do not hide your love and truth
from the people in the great meeting.

[11] LORD, do not hold back your mercy from me;
let your love and truth always protect me.
[12] Troubles have surrounded me;
there are too many to count.
My sins have caught me
so that I cannot see a way to escape.
I have more sins than hairs on my head,
and I have lost my courage.
[13] Please, LORD, save me.
Hurry, LORD, to help me.
[14] People are trying to kill me.
Shame them and disgrace them.
People want to hurt me.
Let them run away in disgrace.

PRAYER
Who should we go to for help? (40:13)

[15] People are making fun of me.
Let them be shamed into silence.
[16] But let those who follow you
be happy and glad.
They love you for saving them.
May they always say, "Praise the LORD!"

[17] Lord, because I am poor and helpless,
please remember me.
You are my helper and savior.
My God, do not wait.

A PRAYER IN TIME OF SICKNESS

For the director of music.
A psalm of David.

41

[1] Happy is the person who thinks about the poor.
When trouble comes, the LORD will save him.

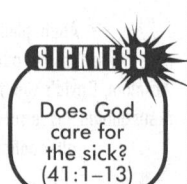

SICKNESS
Does God care for the sick? (41:1–13)

[2] The LORD will protect him
and spare his life
and will bless him in the land.
He will not let his enemies take him.

3 The LORD will give him strength when he
is sick,
and he will make him well again.

4 I said, "LORD, have mercy on me.
Heal me, because I have sinned against
you."
5 My enemies are saying evil things about
me.
They say, "When will he die and be
forgotten?"
6 Some people come to see me,
but they lie.
They just come to get bad news.
Then they go and gossip.
7 All my enemies whisper about me
and think the worst about me.
8 They say, "He has a terrible disease.
He will never get out of
bed again."
9 My best and truest friend,
who ate at my table,
has even turned
against me.

10 LORD, have mercy on me.
Give me strength so I
can pay them back.
11 Because my enemies do
not defeat me,
I know you are pleased with
me.
12 Because I am innocent, you support me
and will let me be with you forever.

13 Praise the LORD, the God of Israel.
He has always been,
and he will always be.
Amen and amen.

WHAT'S IT MEAN?

Ahithophel, who had been one of David's most trusted advisors, betrayed the king by helping Absalom, David's son, try to take over the throne. Centuries later, Jesus quoted this verse when he knew Judas was going to betray him after eating the Passover meal with him.

Psalm 41:9

Book 2

WISHING TO BE NEAR GOD

For the director of music.
A maskil of the sons of Korah.

42

1 As a deer thirsts for streams of water,
so I thirst for you, God.
2 I thirst for the living God.
When can I go to meet with him?
3 Day and night, my tears have been my
food.
People are always saying,
"Where is your God?"
4 When I remember these things,
I speak with a broken heart.
I used to walk with the crowd
and lead them to God's
Temple
with songs of praise.

"The LORD shows his true love every day. At night I have a song, and I pray to my living God." (Psalm 42:8)

5 Why am I so sad?
Why am I so upset?
I should put my hope in
God
and keep praising him,
my Savior and 6 my
God.

DOUBT

Can our doubts be overcome? (42:5–6)

I am very
sad.
So I remember you
where the Jordan
River begins,
near the peaks of Hermon
and Mount Mizar.
7 Troubles have come again and again,
sounding like waterfalls.
Your waves are crashing all around me.
8 The LORD shows his true love every day.
At night I have a song,
and I pray to my living God.
9 I say to God, my Rock,
"Why have you forgotten me?
Why am I sad
and troubled by my enemies?"
10 My enemies' insults make me feel
as if my bones were broken.
They are always saying,
"Where is your God?"

11 Why am I so sad?
Why am I so upset?
I should put my hope in God
and keep praising him,
my Savior and my God.

A PRAYER FOR PROTECTION

43

[1] God, defend me.
Argue my case against those who don't follow you.
Save me from liars and those who do evil.
[2] God, you are my strength.
Why have you rejected me?
Why am I sad
and troubled by my enemies?
[3] Send me your light and truth
to guide me.
Let them lead me to your holy mountain,
to where you live.
[4] Then I will go to the altar of God,
to God who is my joy and happiness.
I will praise you with a harp,
God, my God.

[5] Why am I so sad?
Why am I so upset?
I should put my hope in God
and keep praising him,
my Savior and my God.

WHAT'S IT MEAN?

God wanted every generation of Israelites to know what he had done for their ancestors. Though written records of past events were kept, few people had access to them. That's why it was important for the Israelites to tell their children and grandchildren about their history.

Psalm 44:1

A PRAYER FOR HELP

For the director of music.
A maskil of the sons of Korah.

44

[1] God, we have heard about you.
Our ancestors told us
what you did in their days,
in days long ago.
[2] With your power you forced the nations out of the land
and placed our ancestors here.
You destroyed those other nations,
but you made our ancestors grow strong.
[3] It wasn't their swords that took the land.
It wasn't their power that gave them victory.
But it was your great power and strength.
You were with them because you loved them.

Promise HE PROMISES TO BE YOUR GOD.

Why am I so sad? Why am I so upset? I should put my hope in God and keep praising him, my Savior and my God (Ps. 43:5).

Have you ever thought, *There are millions of people in the world. How can God keep up with all of us? How can he pay any attention to me? How can he hear my prayers when everybody else is talking to him, too?* Thoughts like that will blow your mind, but God is so much bigger than your mind. Psalm 43:5 has two words that will help put your mind at ease: "my God." In order to have a close and growing relationship with God, you have to make him personal. You have to know that he is *your* God. Here's a suggestion: When you pray, just say to the Lord, "You are *my* God." Put the emphasis on the word *my*. Even though there are lots of Christians in the world, your relationship with God is not like anybody else's. He made you to stand out from everybody else. Those things that set you apart from other people are the things that give you a unique place with him. When you feel like a dot in the middle of a swarm of Christians who need God's love and attention, just remember that he is *your* God.

SEE FOR YOURSELF:
Ps. 63:1; 118:28; Is. 25:1

4 My God, you are my King.
Your commands led Jacob's people to victory.
5 With your help we pushed back our enemies.
In your name we trampled those who came against us.
6 I don't trust my bow to help me,
and my sword can't save me.
7 You saved us from our foes,
and you made our enemies ashamed.
8 We will praise God every day;
we will praise your name forever. *Selah*

9 But you have rejected us and shamed us.
You don't march with our armies anymore.
10 You let our enemies push us back,
and those who hate us have taken our wealth.
11 You gave us away like sheep to be eaten
and have scattered us among the nations.
12 You sold your people for nothing
and made no profit on the sale.

13 You made us a joke to our neighbors;
those around us laugh and make fun of us.
14 You made us a joke to the other nations;
people shake their heads.
15 I am always in disgrace,
and I am covered with shame.
16 My enemy is getting even
with insults and curses.

17 All these things have happened to us,
but we have not forgotten you
or failed to keep our agreement with you.
18 Our hearts haven't turned away from you,
and we haven't stopped following you.
19 But you crushed us in this place where wild dogs live,
and you covered us with deep darkness.

20 If we had forgotten our God
or lifted our hands in prayer to foreign gods,
21 God would have known,
because he knows what is in our hearts.
22 But for you we are in danger of death all the time.
People think we are worth no more than sheep to be killed.

23 Wake up, Lord! Why are you sleeping?
Get up! Don't reject us forever.
24 Why do you hide from us?
Have you forgotten our pain and troubles?

25 We have been pushed down into the dirt;
we are flat on the ground.
26 Get up and help us.
Because of your love, save us.

A SONG FOR THE KING'S WEDDING

For the director of music. To the tune of "Lilies." A maskil. A love song of the sons of Korah.

45

1 Beautiful words fill my mind.
I am speaking of royal things.
My tongue is like the pen of a skilled writer.

2 You are more handsome than anyone,
and you are an excellent speaker,
so God has blessed you forever.
3 Put on your sword, powerful warrior.
Show your glory and majesty.
4 In your majesty win the victory
for what is true and right.
Your power will do amazing things.
5 Your sharp arrows will enter
the hearts of the king's enemies.
Nations will be defeated before you.
6 God, your throne will last forever and ever.
You will rule your kingdom with fairness.

WHAT'S IT MEAN?

The royal household must have shelled out quite a bit of money for the rare and expensive spices mentioned here. Myrrh was a plant used to make perfumes, among other things. It was also one of the presents the wise men brought to the baby Jesus. The aloes were not the plants we know today, but were actually trees whose fragrant wood was used for perfume and incense. Cassia plants smelled a lot like cinnamon. All three spices were associated with the oil used to anoint kings.
Psalm 45:8

[7]You love right and hate evil,
so God has chosen you from among your friends;
he has set you apart with much joy.
[8]Your clothes smell like myrrh, aloes, and cassia.
From palaces of ivory
music comes to make you happy.
[9]Kings' daughters are among your honored women.
Your bride stands at your right side
wearing gold from Ophir.

[10]Listen to me, daughter; look and pay attention.
Forget your people and your father's family.
[11]The king loves your beauty.
Because he is your master, you should obey him.
[12]People from the city of Tyre have brought a gift.
Wealthy people will want to meet you.

[13]The princess is very beautiful.
Her gown is woven with gold.
[14]In her beautiful clothes she is brought to the king.
Her bridesmaids follow behind her,
and they are also brought to him.
[15]They come with happiness and joy;
they enter the king's palace.

[16]You will have sons to replace your fathers.
You will make them rulers through all the land.
[17]I will make your name famous from now on,
so people will praise you forever and ever.

WHAT'S IT MEAN?

In ancient times, oceans and seas were thought of as things to be feared. Bible writers occasionally used the sea as a symbol of trouble. Rivers, on the other hand, were considered good and helpful. In this passage, the sea represents destruction and the river represents the blessings of God.
Psalm 46:2–4

GOD PROTECTS HIS PEOPLE

For the director of music. By alamoth.
A psalm of the sons of Korah.

46

[1]God is our protection and our strength.
He always helps in times of trouble.
[2]So we will not be afraid even if the earth shakes,
or the mountains fall into the sea,

Promise HE PROMISES TO BE READY TO HELP.

God is our protection and our strength. He always helps in times of trouble (Ps. 46:1).

God is always ready to help his children. When the nation of Israel found itself face-to-face with an enemy, God didn't have to go recruit an army and buy some weapons. He already had an army of angels—and enough power in his little finger to wipe out the enemy. Sometimes God used the men of Israel's army; sometimes he used a bunch of trumpets; but whatever he did, Israel came out on top—as long as they obeyed him.

Well, that same power, the "protection and strength," is for you, too. God is always ready to help you. When you ask for his help with a tough decision, he doesn't have to go research the problem. He's got more knowledge and wisdom than even Albert Einstein could get a handle on. If money is what you need, he doesn't have to go to the bank and get a loan. Everything on earth belongs to him anyway. Everything you need is wrapped up in God. He doesn't have to get it together before he can help. All he needs is for you to ask.

SEE FOR YOURSELF:

Josh. 1:9; Prov. 2:4–7; Is. 35:3–4

3 even if the oceans roar and foam,
or the mountains shake at the raging sea. *Selah*

4 There is a river that brings joy to the city of God,
the holy place where God Most High lives.
5 God is in that city, and so it will not be shaken.
God will help her at dawn.
6 Nations tremble and kingdoms shake.
God shouts and the earth crumbles.

7 The LORD All-Powerful is with us;
the God of Jacob is our defender. *Selah*

8 Come and see what the LORD has done,
the amazing things he has done on the earth.
9 He stops wars everywhere on the earth.
He breaks all bows and spears
and burns up the chariots with fire.
10 God says, "Be quiet and know that I am God.
I will be supreme over all the nations;
I will be supreme in the earth."

11 The LORD All-Powerful is with us;
the God of Jacob is our defender. *Selah*

GOD, THE KING OF THE WORLD

For the director of music.
A psalm of the sons of Korah.

47

1 Clap your hands, all you people.
Shout to God with joy.
2 The LORD Most High is wonderful.
He is the great King over all the earth!
3 He defeated nations for us
and put them under our control.
4 He chose the land we would inherit.
We are the children of Jacob, whom he loved. *Selah*

5 God has risen with a shout of joy;
the LORD has risen as the trumpets sounded.
6 Sing praises to God. Sing praises.
Sing praises to our King. Sing praises.
7 God is King of all the earth,
so sing a song of praise to him.
8 God is King over the nations.
God sits on his holy throne.
9 The leaders of the nations meet
with the people of the God of Abraham,
because the leaders of the earth belong to God.
He is supreme.

JERUSALEM, THE CITY OF GOD

A psalm of the sons of Korah.

48

1 The LORD is great; he should be praised
in the city of our God, on his holy mountain.
2 It is high and beautiful
and brings joy to the whole world.
Mount Zion is like the high mountains of the north;
it is the city of the Great King.
3 God is within its palaces;
he is known as its defender.
4 Kings joined together
and came to attack the city.
5 But when they saw it, they were amazed.
They ran away in fear.
6 Fear took hold of them;
they hurt like a woman having a baby.
7 You destroyed the large trading ships
with an east wind.

8 First we heard
and now we have seen
that God will always keep his city safe.
It is the city of the LORD All-Powerful,
the city of our God *Selah*

9 God, we come into your Temple
to think about your love.
10 God, your name is known everywhere;
all over the earth people praise you.
Your right hand is full of goodness.
11 Mount Zion is happy

WHAT'S IT MEAN?

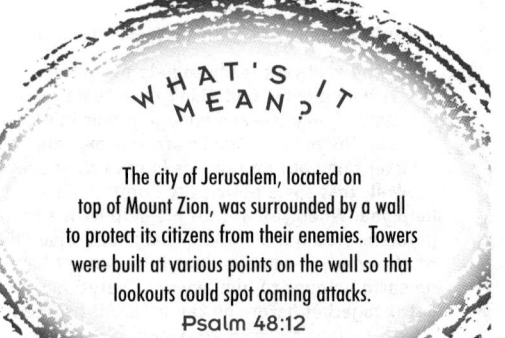

The city of Jerusalem, located on top of Mount Zion, was surrounded by a wall to protect its citizens from their enemies. Towers were built at various points on the wall so that lookouts could spot coming attacks.
Psalm 48:12

and all the towns of Judah rejoice,
because your decisions are fair.

12 Walk around Jerusalem
and count its towers.
13 Notice how strong they are.
Look at the palaces.
Then you can tell your
children about them.
14 This God is our God
forever and ever.
He will guide us from
now on.

GOD'S WILL

Can Christians be hopeful about the future? (48:14)

TRUSTING MONEY IS FOOLISH

For the director of music.
A psalm of the sons of Korah.

49

1 Listen to this, all you nations;
listen, all you who live on earth.
2 Listen, both great and small,
rich and poor together.
3 What I say is wise,
and my heart speaks with
understanding.
4 I will pay attention to a wise saying;
I will explain my riddle on the harp.

5 Why should I be afraid of bad days?
Why should I fear when evil men
surround me?
6 They trust in their money
and brag about their riches.
7 No one can buy back the life of another.
No one can pay God for his own life,
8 because the price of a life is high.
No payment is ever enough.
9 Do people live forever?
Don't they all face death?

10 See, even wise people die.
Fools and stupid people also die
and leave their wealth to others.
11 Their graves will always be their homes.
They will live there from now on,
even though they named places after
themselves.

WHAT'S IT MEAN?

Israelite poets were like folk singers. They often read their poems with musical accompaniment, usually from a stringed instrument. Greek poets, among others, also presented their work with a musical background.
Psalm 49:4

Promise

HE PROMISES TO RESCUE YOU FROM THE POWER OF DEATH.

But God will save my life and will take me from the grave (Ps. 49:15).

For the person who doesn't believe in Jesus, death has a lot of power. Death for them is the end of life on earth and the beginning of hell—forever. But Jesus promises to rescue his believers "from the grave." He is the One who drove death into the ground. He is more powerful than death. He has beaten death for you. All he asks is that you believe that he died just for you and that you let him redeem you. Then follow him. What that means is that you have to give up trying to save yourself. You will never be good enough, do enough good deeds, or accomplish enough great things to overcome death. You don't even have to try anymore.

Right now, right where you are, tell Jesus that you can't do it yourself; you are drowning in your own sin. Ask him to reach in and rescue you. Hold on tightly as he pulls you to shore and breathes new life into you. Then stand up and follow the One who has rescued you for eternity.

SEE FOR YOURSELF:
Is. 25:8; 1 Cor. 15:55; Rev. 21:4

On the Edge

Even rich people do not live forever; like the animals, people die (Ps. 49:12).

Justin was sixteen years old and a really awesome kid—the kind of guy everyone wanted to be around. He had such a great attitude—he even made work fun. One Tuesday night after supper, he hopped in his car to go to a Bible study. His mom kissed him and reminded him to buckle up and drive safely. Two miles from his house, Justin crossed the yellow line and hit another car. Justin died and so did the lady in the other car. No one could believe that Justin was gone. He had so much life ahead of him—he was really going to make a difference. A part of God's design is that we all die sometime. And even when we don't understand, we cling to the truth that God's timing is perfect. The coolest thing about Justin is that he really loved God and lived a life that proved it. When Justin left this earth and entered the presence of his Lord, the angels sang and the Savior surely said, "Well done, my son. I am so pleased with you."

SEE FOR YOURSELF:
Eccl. 2:15–16; 3:19–20; Matt. 25:23; 1 Cor. 15:21–22

12 Even rich people do not live forever;
like the animals, people die.

13 This is what will happen to those who trust in themselves
and to their followers who believe them. *Selah*
14 Like sheep, they must die,
and death will be their shepherd.
Honest people will rule over them in the morning,
and their bodies will rot in a grave far from home.
15 But God will save my life
and will take me from the grave. *Selah*

16 Don't be afraid of rich people
because their houses are more beautiful.
17 They don't take anything to the grave;
their wealth won't go down with them.
18 Even though they were praised when they were alive—
and people may praise you when you succeed—
19 they will go to where their ancestors are.
They will never see light again.
20 Rich people with no understanding
are just like animals that die.

GOD WANTS TRUE WORSHIP

A psalm of Asaph.

50

1 The God of gods, the LORD, speaks.
He calls the earth from the rising to the setting sun.
2 God shines from Jerusalem,
whose beauty is perfect.
3 Our God comes, and he will not be silent.
A fire burns in front of him,
and a powerful storm surrounds him.
4 He calls to the sky above and to the earth
that he might judge his people.
5 He says, "Gather around, you who worship me,
who have made an agreement with me, using a sacrifice."
6 God is the judge,
and even the skies say he is right. *Selah*

WHAT'S IT MEAN?

If you're keeping score at home, Asaph, who served as a chief musician in the Meeting Tent, is credited with writing twelve of the one hundred fifty psalms that appear in the Bible.
Psalm 50 title

7 God says, "My people, listen to me;
Israel, I will testify against you.
I am God, your God.
8 I do not scold you for your sacrifices.
You always bring me your burnt offerings.
9 But I do not need bulls from your stalls
or goats from your pens,
10 because every animal of the forest is already mine.
The cattle on a thousand hills are mine.

[11] I know every bird on the mountains,
and every living thing in the fields is mine.
[12] If I were hungry, I would not tell you,
because the earth and everything in it are mine.
[13] I don't eat the meat of bulls
or drink the blood of goats.
[14] Give an offering to show thanks to God.
Give God Most High what you have promised.
[15] Call to me in times of trouble.
I will save you, and you will honor me."

WHAT'S IT MEAN?

Some idol worshipers in ancient times believed that their gods got hungry and actually ate the animals that were sacrificed to them. They believed their gods needed the food to live. The God of Israel, on the other hand, did not need the sacrifices offered by his people; he found pleasure in the obedience of those who followed him.

Psalm 50:13

[16] But God says to the wicked,
"Why do you talk about my laws?
Why do you mention my agreement?
[17] You hate my teachings
and turn your back on what I say.
[18] When you see a thief, you join him.
You take part in adultery.
[19] You don't stop your mouth from speaking evil,
and your tongue makes up lies.
[20] You speak against your brother
and lie about your mother's son.
[21] I have kept quiet while you did these things,
so you thought I was just like you.
But I will scold you
and accuse you to your face.

[22] "Think about this, you who forget God.
Otherwise, I will tear you apart,
and no one will save you.
[23] Those people honor me
who bring me offerings to show thanks.
And I, God, will save those who do that."

A PRAYER FOR FORGIVENESS

For the director of music. A psalm of David when the prophet Nathan came to David after David's sin with Bathsheba.

51

[1] God, be merciful to me
because you are loving.
Because you are always ready to be merciful,
wipe out all my wrongs.
[2] Wash away all my guilt
and make me clean again.

TRUTH
How does God want us to live? (51:1–6)

[3] I know about my wrongs,
and I can't forget my sin.
[4] You are the only one I have sinned against;
I have done what you say is wrong.
You are right when you speak
and fair when you judge.
[5] I was brought into this world in sin.
In sin my mother gave birth to me.

[6] You want me to be completely truthful,
so teach me wisdom.
[7] Take away my sin, and I will be clean.
Wash me, and I will be whiter than snow.
[8] Make me hear sounds of joy and gladness;
let the bones you crushed be happy again.
[9] Turn your face from my sins
and wipe out all my guilt.

[10] Create in me a pure heart, God,
and make my spirit right again.
[11] Do not send me away from you
or take your Holy Spirit away from me.
[12] Give me back the joy of your salvation.
Keep me strong by giving me a willing spirit.
[13] Then I will teach your ways to those who do wrong,
and sinners will turn back to you.

[14] God, save me from the guilt of murder,
God of my salvation,
and I will sing about your goodness.
[15] Lord, let me speak
so I may praise you.
[16] You are not pleased by sacrifices, or I would give them.
You don't want burnt offerings.
[17] The sacrifice God wants is a broken spirit.

God, you will not reject a heart that is
broken and sorry for sin.

18 Do whatever good you wish for
Jerusalem.
Rebuild the walls of Jerusalem.
19 Then you will be pleased with right
sacrifices and whole burnt offerings,
and bulls will be offered on your altar.

GOD WILL PUNISH THE PROUD

For the director of music. A maskil of David.
When Doeg the Edomite came to Saul and said
to him, "David is in Ahimelech's house."

52

1 Mighty warrior, why do you brag about
the evil you do?
God's love will continue forever.
2 You think up evil plans.
Your tongue is like a sharp razor,
making up lies.
3 You love wrong more than right
and lies more than truth. *Selah*
4 You love words that bite
and tongues that lie.

5 But God will ruin you forever.
He will grab you and throw you out of
your tent;
he will tear you away from the land of
the living. *Selah*
6 Those who do right will see this and fear
God.
They will laugh at you and say,
7 "Look what happened to the man
who did not depend on God
but depended on his money.
He grew strong by his evil plans."

8 But I am like an olive tree
growing in God's Temple.
I trust God's love
forever and ever.
9 God, I will thank you forever for what
you have done.
With those who worship you, I will
trust you because you are good.

THE UNBELIEVING FOOL

53

For the director of music. By mahalath.
A maskil of David.

1 Fools say to themselves,
"There is no God."
Fools are evil and do terrible things;
none of them does anything good.

2 God looked down from heaven on all
people
to see if anyone was wise,
if anyone was looking to God for help.
3 But all have turned away.
Together, everyone has become evil;
none of them does anything good.
Not a single person.

4 Don't the wicked understand?
They destroy my people as if they were
eating bread.
They do not ask God for help.
5 The wicked are filled with terror
where there had been nothing to fear.
God will scatter the bones of your
enemies.
You will defeat them,
because God has rejected them.

6 I pray that victory will come to Israel from
Mount Zion!
May God bring them back.
Then the people of Jacob will rejoice,
and the people of Israel will be glad.

A PRAYER FOR HELP

For the director of music. With stringed
instruments. A maskil of David when the
Ziphites went to Saul and said, "We think
David is hiding among our people."

54

1 God, save me because of who you are.
By your strength show that I am
innocent.
2 Hear my prayer, God;

WHAT'S IT MEAN?

When David realized that King Saul was going to kill him, he ran away and hid in the desert surrounding the city of Ziph. The Ziphites, recognizing an opportunity to get in good with the king, told Saul where he could find David.

Psalm 54 title

listen to what I say.
3 Strangers turn against me,
and cruel men want to kill me.
They do not care about God. *Selah*

4 See, God will help me;
the Lord will support me.
5 Let my enemies be punished with their own evil.
Destroy them because you are loyal to me.

6 I will offer a sacrifice as a special gift to you.
I will thank you, LORD, because you are good.
7 You have saved me from all my troubles,
and I have seen my enemies defeated.

A PRAYER ABOUT A FALSE FRIEND

For the director of music. With stringed instruments. A maskil of David.

55

1 God, listen to my prayer
and do not ignore my cry for help.
2 Pay attention to me and answer me.
I am troubled and upset
3 by what the enemy says
and how the wicked look at me.
They bring troubles down on me,
and in anger they attack me.

4 I am frightened inside;
the terror of death has attacked me.
5 I am scared and shaking,
and terror grips me.
6 I said, "I wish I had wings like a dove.
Then I would fly away and rest.
7 I would wander far away
and stay in the desert. *Selah*
8 I would hurry to my place of escape,
far away from the wind and storm."

9 Lord, destroy and confuse their words,
because I see violence and fighting in the city.
10 Day and night they are all around its walls,
and evil and trouble are everywhere inside.
11 Destruction is everywhere in the city;
trouble and lying never leave its streets.

12 It was not an enemy insulting me.
I could stand that.
It was not someone who hated me.
I could hide from him.
13 But it is you, a person like me,
my companion and good friend.
14 We had a good friendship
and walked together to God's Temple.

FRIENDSHIP
Can friends cause us pain? (55:12–14)

15 Let death take away my enemies.
Let them die while they are still young
because evil lives with them.
16 But I will call to God for help,
and the LORD will save me.
17 Morning, noon, and night I am troubled and upset,
but he will listen to me.
18 Many are against me,
but he keeps me safe in battle.
19 God who lives forever
will hear me and punish them. *Selah*
But they will not change;
they do not fear God.

20 The one who was my friend attacks his friends
and breaks his promises.
21 His words are slippery like butter,
but war is in his heart.
His words are smoother than oil,
but they cut like knives.

22 Give your worries to the LORD,
and he will take care of you.
He will never let good people down.
23 But, God, you will bring down
the wicked to the grave.
Murderers and liars will live
only half a lifetime.
But I will trust in you.

TRUSTING GOD FOR HELP

For the director of music. To the tune of "The Dove in the Distant Oak." A miktam of David when the Philistines captured him in Gath.

56

1 God, be merciful to me because people are chasing me;
the battle has pressed me all day long.
2 My enemies have chased me all day;
there are many proud people fighting me.
3 When I am afraid,
I will trust you.
4 I praise God for his word.

I trust God, so I am not afraid.
What can human beings do to me?

5 All day long they twist my words;
all their evil plans are against me.
6 They wait. They hide.
They watch my steps,
hoping to kill me.
7 God, do not let them escape;
punish the foreign nations in your anger.
8 You have recorded my troubles.
You have kept a list of my tears.
Aren't they in your records?

On the Edge

You have recorded my troubles.
You have kept a list of my tears.
Aren't they in your records?
(Ps. 56:8).

Ever been through a time when it seemed like your heartache would never go away? The tears keep pouring out. The suffering seems endless. You're convinced you'll never be happy again. After a while you wonder if God even notices your broken heart. If he did, then surely he would do something—quick. God says that he has stored each one of your tears in a bottle. God knows you intimately, and he has not turned his back on your suffering. Even when you feel completely alone, God has not abandoned you. He sees your tear-stained pillow. He hears you cry yourself to sleep. It breaks his heart to see you hurt. Do not be afraid. He is there—close enough to catch each one of your tears.

SEE FOR YOURSELF:
Is. 38:5

9 On the day I call for help, my enemies will be defeated.
I know that God is on my side.
10 I praise God for his word to me;
I praise the LORD for his word.
11 I trust in God. I will not be afraid.
What can people do to me?

12 God, I must keep my promises to you.
I will give you my offerings to thank you,
13 because you have saved me from death.
You have kept me from being defeated.
So I will walk with God
in light among the living.

WHAT'S IT MEAN?

Throughout the Bible, wings are used as symbols of protection and safety. If that seems odd to you, consider the way a mother hen covers her babies with her wings. In the same way, God shelters his children from danger.

Psalm 57:1

A PRAYER IN TROUBLED TIMES

For the director of music. To the tune of "Do Not Destroy." A miktam of David when he escaped from Saul in the cave.

57

1 Be merciful to me, God; be merciful to me
because I come to you for protection.
Let me hide under the shadow of your wings
until the trouble has passed.

2 I cry out to God Most High,
to the God who does everything for me.
3 He sends help from heaven and saves me.
He punishes those who chase me. *Selah*
God sends me his love and truth.

4 Enemies, like lions, are all around me;
I must lie down among them.
Their teeth are like spears and arrows,
their tongues as sharp as swords.

5 God is supreme over the skies;
his majesty covers the earth.

6 They set a trap for me.
I am very worried.
They dug a pit in my path,
but they fell into it themselves. *Selah*

7 My heart is steady, God; my heart is steady.
I will sing and praise you.
8 Wake up, my soul.

Wake up, harp and lyre!
I will wake up the dawn.
9 Lord, I will praise you among the nations;
I will sing songs of praise about you to all the nations.
10 Your great love reaches to the skies,
your truth to the clouds.
11 God, you are supreme above the skies.
Let your glory be over all the earth.

UNFAIR JUDGES

58

For the director of music. To the tune of "Do Not Destroy." A miktam of David.

1 Do you rulers really say what is right?
Do you judge people fairly?
2 No, in your heart you plan evil;
you think up violent crimes in the land.
3 From birth, evil people turn away from God;
they wander off and tell lies as soon as they are born.
4 They are like poisonous snakes,
like deaf cobras that stop up their ears
5 so they cannot hear the music of the snake charmer
no matter how well he plays.

6 God, break the teeth in their mouths!
Tear out the fangs of those lions, LORD!
7 Let them disappear like water that flows away.
Let them be cut short like a broken arrow.
8 Let them be like snails that melt as they move.
Let them be like a child born dead who never saw the sun.
9 His anger will blow them away alive
faster than burning thorns can heat a pot.
10 Good people will be glad when they see him get even.
They will wash their feet in the blood of the wicked.
11 Then people will say,
"There really are rewards for doing what is right.
There really is a God who judges the world."

WHAT'S IT MEAN?

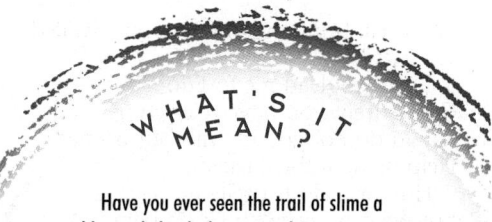

Have you ever seen the trail of slime a snail leaves behind when it crawls? In ancient times, people believed that the slime was actually part of the snail itself. They believed that as the snail traveled, it left behind more and more of itself, growing smaller and smaller, until it disappeared completely.

Psalm 58:8

A PRAYER FOR PROTECTION

59

For the director of music. To the tune of "Do Not Destroy." A miktam of David when Saul sent men to watch David's house to kill him.

1 God, save me from my enemies.
Protect me from those who come against me.
2 Save me from those who do evil
and from murderers.

3 Look, men are waiting to ambush me.
Cruel men attack me,
but I have not sinned or done wrong, LORD.
4 I have done nothing wrong, but they are ready to attack me.
Wake up to help me, and look.
5 You are the LORD God All-Powerful, the God of Israel.
Arise and punish those people.
Do not give those traitors any mercy. *Selah*

6 They come back at night.
Like dogs they growl and roam around the city.
7 Notice what comes from their mouths.
Insults come from their lips,
because they say, "Who's listening?"
8 But, LORD, you laugh at them;
you make fun of all of them.

9 God, my strength, I am looking to you,
because God is my defender.
10 My God loves me, and he goes in front of me.
He will help me defeat my enemies.
11 Lord, our protector, do not kill them, or my people will forget.
With your power scatter them and defeat them.
12 They sin by what they say;

they sin with their words.
They curse and tell lies,
so let their pride trap them.
13 Destroy them in your anger;
destroy them completely!
Then they will know
that God rules over Israel
and to the ends of the earth. *Selah*

WHAT'S IT MEAN?

Stray dogs in ancient Israel kept out of sight during the daytime. At night, however, they could be heard throughout the land, barking and scrounging for food. Dogs were extremely unpopular creatures with the Israelites.

Psalm 59:14

14 They come back at night.
Like dogs they growl
and roam around the city.
15 They wander about looking for food,
and they howl if they do not find enough.
16 But I will sing about your strength.
In the morning I will sing about your love.
You are my defender,
my place of safety in times of trouble.
17 God, my strength, I will sing praises to you.
God, my defender, you are the God who loves me.

A PRAYER AFTER A DEFEAT

For the director of music. To the tune of "Lily of the Agreement." A miktam of David. For teaching. When David fought the Arameans of Northwest Mesopotamia and Zobah, and when Joab returned and defeated twelve thousand Edomites at the Valley of Salt.

60

1 God, you have rejected us and scattered us.
You have been angry, but please come back to us.
2 You made the earth shake and crack.
Heal its breaks because it is shaking.
3 You have given your people trouble.
You made us unable to walk straight,
like people drunk with wine.
4 You have raised a banner to gather those who fear you.
Now they can stand up against the enemy. *Selah*

5 Answer us and save us by your power
so the people you love will be rescued.

6 God has said from his Temple,
"When I win, I will divide Shechem
and measure off the Valley of Succoth.
7 Gilead and Manasseh are mine.
Ephraim is like my helmet.
Judah holds my royal scepter.
8 Moab is like my washbowl.
I throw my sandals at Edom.
I shout at Philistia."

WHAT'S IT MEAN?

When David first became leader of Israel, he had to deal not only with the nation's enemies, but also with people in his own country who refused to accept him as king. Eventually, the territories mentioned in this passage recognized that God had chosen David as leader of Israel and submitted to his rule. What's more, the Lord gave David and his troops military victories over such longtime enemies as the Moabites, the Edomites, and the Philistines.

Psalm 60:6–8

9 Who will bring me to the strong, walled city?
Who will lead me to Edom?
10 God, surely you have rejected us;
you do not go out with our armies.
11 Help us fight the enemy.
Human help is useless,
12 but we can win with God's help.
He will defeat our enemies.

A PRAYER FOR PROTECTION

61

For the director of music. With stringed instruments. Of David.

1 God, hear my cry;
listen to my prayer.

2 I call to you from the ends of the earth
when I am afraid.
Carry me away to a high mountain.
3 You have been my protection,
like a strong tower against my enemies.

4 Let me live in your Holy Tent forever.
Let me find safety in the shelter of your
wings. *Selah*

5 God, you have heard my promises.
You have given me what belongs to
those who fear you.

6 Give the king a long life;
let him live many years.
7 Let him rule in the presence of God
forever.
Protect him with your love and truth.
8 Then I will praise your name forever,
and every day I will keep my
promises.

TRUST ONLY IN GOD

For the director of music. For Jeduthun.
A psalm of David.

62

1 I find rest in God;
only he can save me.
2 He is my rock and my salvation.
He is my defender;
I will not be defeated.

3 How long will you attack someone?
Will all of you kill that person?
Who is like a leaning wall, like a fence
ready to fall?
4 They are planning to make that person
fall.
They enjoy telling lies.
With their mouths they bless,
but in their hearts they curse. *Selah*

5 I find rest in God;
only he gives me hope.
6 He is my rock and my salvation.
He is my defender;
I will not be defeated.
7 My honor and salvation
come from God.
He is my mighty rock
and my protection.

DOUBT
Can we find refuge in God? (62:5–7)

8 People, trust God all the time.
Tell him all your problems,
because God is our protection. *Selah*

9 The least of people are only a breath,
and even the greatest are just a lie.
On the scales, they weigh nothing;
together they are only a breath.
10 Do not trust in force.
Stealing is of no use.
Even if you gain more riches,
don't put your trust in them.

11 God has said this,
and I have heard it over and over:
God is strong.
12 The Lord is loving.
You reward people for what they have
done.

On the Edge

The least of people are only a breath, and even the greatest are just a lie. On the scales, they weigh nothing; together they are only a breath (Ps. 62:9).

It seems weird for David to say that we humans are only a vapor, like a puff of air, and that none of us is truly great. After all, when he was a teenager, he killed the giant Goliath with a *slingshot!* Then he led Israel's army to defeat the mighty Philistines in battle after battle. He became the greatest warrior and king in Israel's history.

But David knew that everything he did was nothing compared to God. He had a grip on just how huge God is. Look at Psalm 62:11–12. David tells us that strength and lovingkindness belong to God. When a person begins to really understand (in his or her heart) how powerful and how kind the Lord is, it's impossible to be cocky. When you begin to see yourself as you really are before the Lord, you're amazed at how awesome he is and how little you are.

God uses little people. He uses humble people—people who are seeing how small they are compared to him. He doesn't want us to go around thinking we're dirt. He wants us to go around thinking about how enormous he is.

SEE FOR YOURSELF:
Job 14:2; Eccl. 6:12; Is. 40:6–8; James 4:14

WISHING TO BE NEAR GOD

A psalm of David when he was
in the desert of Judah.

63

1 God, you are my God.
I search for you.
I thirst for you
like someone in a dry, empty land
where there is no water.
2 I have seen you in the Temple
and have seen your strength and glory.
3 Because your love is better than life,
I will praise you.
4 I will praise you as long as I live.
I will lift up my hands in prayer to your name.
5 I will be content as if I had eaten the best foods.
My lips will sing, and my mouth will praise you.

6 I remember you while I'm lying in bed;
I think about you through the night.
7 You are my help.
Because of your protection, I sing.
8 I stay close to you;
you support me with your right hand.

9 Some people are trying to kill me,
but they will go down to the grave.
10 They will be killed with swords
and eaten by wild dogs.
11 But the king will rejoice in his God.
All who make promises in his name will praise him,
but the mouths of liars will be shut.

A PRAYER AGAINST ENEMIES

For the director of music.
A psalm of David.

64

1 God, listen to my complaint.
I am afraid of my enemies;
protect my life from them.
2 Hide me from those who plan wicked things,
from that gang who does evil.
3 They sharpen their tongues like swords
and shoot bitter words like arrows.
4 From their hiding places they shoot at innocent people;
they shoot suddenly and are not afraid.
5 They encourage each other to do wrong.
They talk about setting traps,
thinking no one will see them.
6 They plan wicked things and say,
"We have a perfect plan."
The mind of human beings is hard to understand.

7 But God will shoot them with arrows;
they will suddenly be struck down.
8 Their own words will be used against them.
All who see them will shake their heads.
9 Then everyone will fear God.
They will tell what God has done,
and they will learn from what he has done.
10 Good people will be happy in the LORD
and will find protection in him.
Let everyone who is honest praise the LORD.

A HYMN OF THANKSGIVING

For the director of music.
A psalm of David. A song.

65

1 God, you will be praised in Jerusalem.
We will keep our promises to you.
2 You hear our prayers.
All people will come to you.
3 Our guilt overwhelms us,
but you forgive our sins.
4 Happy are the people you choose
and invite to stay in your court.
We are filled with good things in your house,
your holy Temple.

5 You answer us in amazing ways,
God our Savior.
People everywhere on the earth
and beyond the sea trust you.
6 You made the mountains by your strength;
you are dressed in power.
7 You stopped the roaring seas,
the roaring waves,
and the uproar of the nations.
8 Even those people at the ends of the earth
fear your miracles.
You are praised from where the sun rises to where it sets.

9 You take care of the land and water it;
you make it very fertile.
The rivers of God are full of water.
Grain grows because you make it grow.
10 You send rain to the plowed fields;
you fill the rows with water.
You soften the ground with rain,

and then you bless it with crops.
11 You give the year a good harvest,
and you load the wagons with many
crops.
12 The desert is covered with grass
and the hills with happiness.
13 The pastures are full of flocks,
and the valleys are covered with grain.
Everything shouts and sings for joy.

PRAISE GOD FOR WHAT HE HAS DONE

For the director of music.
A song. A psalm.

66

1 Everything on earth, shout with joy to
God!
2 Sing about his glory!
Make his praise glorious!
3 Say to God, "Your works
are amazing!
Because your power is
great,
your enemies fall
before you.
4 All the earth worships
you
and sings praises to
you.
They sing praises to your
name." *Selah*

5 Come and see what God has done,
the amazing things he has done for
people.

"Everything on earth, shout with joy to God! Sing about his glory! Make his praise glorious!" (Psalm 66:1–2)

WHAT'S IT MEAN?

If you've ever seen the movie *The Ten Commandments*, you know the scene this verse is describing. The king of Egypt, after letting the Israelites leave his country, changed his mind and sent his army to bring them back. His plan was to trap the Israelites at the Red Sea, and it almost worked—almost. Just when things looked hopeless for the Israelites, God parted the waters of the sea, making a path of dry land through the middle of it. The Israelites were able to walk across to the other side. When the Egyptians tried to follow, the water collapsed on top of them, and they drowned.

Psalm 66:6

6 He turned the sea into dry land.
The people crossed the river on foot.
So let us rejoice because of what he did.
7 He rules forever with his power.
He keeps his eye on the nations,
so people should not turn against him.
Selah

8 You people, praise our God;
loudly sing his praise.
9 He protects our lives
and does not let us be defeated.
10 God, you have tested us;
you have purified us like silver.
11 You let us be trapped
and put a heavy load on us.
12 You let our enemies walk on our heads.
We went through fire
and flood,
but you brought us to a
place with good
things.

13 I will come to your
Temple with burnt
offerings.
I will give you what I
promised,
14 things I promised when I
was in trouble.
15 I will bring you offerings of fat animals,
and I will offer sheep, bulls, and goats.
Selah

16 All of you who fear God, come and listen,
and I will tell you what he has done for
me.
17 I cried out to him with my mouth
and praised him with my tongue.
18 If I had known of any sin in my heart,
the Lord would not have listened to me.
19 But God has listened;
he has heard my prayer.
20 Praise God,
who did not ignore my prayer
or hold back his love from me.

EVERYONE SHOULD PRAISE GOD

For the director of music. With stringed
instruments. A psalm. A song.

67

1 God, have mercy on us and bless us
and show us your kindness *Selah*
2 so the world will learn your ways,
and all nations will learn that you can
save.

3 God, the people should praise you;
all people should praise you.
4 The nations should be glad and sing
because you judge people fairly.
You guide all the nations on earth. *Selah*
5 God, the people should praise you;
all people should praise you.

6 The land has given its crops.
God, our God, blesses us.
7 God blesses us
so people all over the earth will fear
him.

WHAT'S IT MEAN?

The Israelites' neighbors worshiped many different gods and goddesses. They believed that each deity controlled one area of nature. For example, they believed one god controlled the sun, another controlled the rain, and so on. David wanted to make it clear that God not only ruled over all areas of nature, but he had actually created them.

Psalm 68:8–9

PRAISE GOD WHO SAVED THE NATION

For the director of music.
A psalm of David. A song.

68

1 Let God rise up and scatter his enemies;
let those who hate him run away from
him.
2 Blow them away as smoke
is driven away by the wind.
As wax melts before a fire,
let the wicked be destroyed before God.
3 But those who do right should be glad
and should rejoice before God;
they should be happy and glad.

4 Sing to God; sing praises to
his name.
Prepare the way for him
who rides through the
desert,
whose name is the LORD.
Rejoice before him.
5 God is in his holy Temple.

CARING
Does God care for needy people? (68:5)

He is a father to orphans,
and he defends the widows.
6 God gives the lonely a home.
He leads prisoners out with joy,
but those who turn against God will live
in a dry land.

7 God, you led your people out
when you marched through the desert.
Selah

8 The ground shook
and the sky poured down rain
before God, the God of Mount Sinai,
before God, the God of Israel.
9 God, you sent much rain;
you refreshed your tired land.
10 Your people settled there.
God, in your goodness
you took care of the poor.

11 The Lord gave the command,
and a great army told the news:
12 "Kings and their armies run away.
In camp they divide the wealth taken in
war.
13 Those who stayed by the campfires
will share the riches taken in battle."
14 The Almighty scattered kings
like snow on Mount Zalmon.

WHAT'S IT MEAN?

Mount Sinai, which is also known as Mount Horeb, is located in the desert area between Israel and Egypt. Its biggest claim to fame is that it was the place where God gave Moses the Ten Commandments. As for the millions of chariots mentioned in this verse, they may refer to the angels that surround the Lord.

Psalm 68:17

15 The mountains of Bashan are high;
the mountains of Bashan have many
peaks.
16 Why do you mountains with many peaks
look with envy
on the mountain that God chose for his
home?

The LORD will live there forever.
17 God comes with millions of chariots;
the Lord comes from Mount Sinai to his
holy place.
18 When you went up to the heights,
you led a parade of captives.
You received gifts from the people,
even from those who turned against you.
And the LORD God will live there.

19 Praise the Lord, God our Savior,
who helps us every day. *Selah*
20 Our God is a God who saves us;
the LORD God saves us from death.

21 God will crush his enemies' heads,
the hairy skulls of those who continue
to sin.
22 The Lord said, "I will bring the enemy
back from Bashan;
I will bring them back from the depths
of the sea.
23 Then you can stick your feet in their
blood,
and your dogs can lick their share."

WHAT'S IT MEAN?

Bashan, which was located east of the Jordan River, was a fertile area of land that belonged to the tribe of Manasseh. Later in Israel's history, the area became known as much for its selfish and arrogant inhabitants as for its plentiful harvests and choice livestock.
Psalm 68:22

24 God, people have seen your victory
march;
God my King marched into the holy
place.
25 The singers are in front and the
instruments are behind.
In the middle are the girls with the
tambourines.
26 Praise God in the meeting place;
praise the LORD in the gathering of
Israel.
27 There is the smallest tribe, Benjamin,
leading them.
And there are the leaders of Judah with
their group.
There also are the leaders of Zebulun
and of Naphtali.

28 God, order up your power;
show the mighty power you have used
for us before.
29 Kings will bring their wealth to you,
to your Temple in Jerusalem.
30 Punish Egypt, the beast in the tall grass
along the river.
Punish the leaders of nations, those
bulls among the cows.
Defeated, they will bring you their silver.
Scatter those nations that love war.
31 Messengers will come from Egypt;
the people of Cush will pray to God.

32 Kingdoms of the earth, sing to God;
sing praises to the Lord. *Selah*
33 Sing to the one who rides through the
skies, which are from long ago.
He speaks with a thundering voice.
34 Announce that God is powerful.
He rules over Israel,
and his power is in the skies.
35 God, you are wonderful in your Temple.
The God of Israel gives his people
strength and power.

Praise God!

A CRY FOR HELP

For the director of music. To the tune
of "Lilies." A psalm of David.

69

1 God, save me,
because the water has risen to my neck.
2 I'm sinking down into the mud,
and there is nothing to
stand on.
I am in deep water,
and the flood covers
me.
3 I am tired from calling for
help;
my throat is sore.
My eyes are tired from waiting
for God to help me.
4 There are more people who hate me for
no reason than hairs on my head;
powerful enemies want to destroy me
for no reason.
They make me pay back
what I did not steal.

WORRY
What should our response be in times of stress? (69:1–36)

5 God, you know what I have done wrong;
I cannot hide my guilt from you.
6 Lord GOD All-Powerful,
do not let those who hope in you be ashamed because of me.
God of Israel,
do not let your worshipers be disgraced because of me.
7 For you, I carry this shame,
and my face is covered with disgrace.
8 I am like a stranger to my closest relatives
and a foreigner to my mother's children.
9 My strong love for your Temple completely controls me.
When people insult you, it hurts me.
10 When I cry and go without food,
they make fun of me.
11 When I wear clothes of sadness,
they joke about me.
12 They make fun of me in public places,
and the drunkards make up songs about me.

13 But I pray to you, LORD, for favor.
God, because of your great love, answer me.
You are truly able to save.
14 Pull me from the mud,
and do not let me sink.
Save me from those who hate me
and from the deep water.
15 Do not let the flood drown me
or the deep water swallow me
or the grave close its mouth over me.
16 LORD, answer me because your love is so good.
Because of your great kindness, turn to me.
17 Do not hide from me, your servant.
I am in trouble. Hurry to help me!
18 Come near and save me;
rescue me from my enemies.

19 You see my shame and disgrace.
You know all my enemies and what they have said.
20 Insults have broken my heart
and left me weak.
I looked for sympathy, but there was none;
I found no one to comfort me.
21 They put poison in my food
and gave me vinegar to drink.

22 Let their own feasts cause their ruin;
let their feasts trap them and pay them back.
23 Let their eyes be closed so they cannot see
and their backs be forever weak from troubles.
24 Pour your anger out on them;
let your anger catch up with them.
25 May their place be empty;
leave no one to live in their tents.
26 They chase after those you have hurt,
and they talk about the pain of those you have wounded.
27 Charge them with crime after crime,
and do not let them have anything good.
28 Wipe their names from the book of life,
and do not list them with those who do what is right.

WHAT'S IT MEAN?

Forget the *Guinness Book of World Records*. This is the book you want your name mentioned in. Anyone whose name is erased from this book will not be able to spend eternity in heaven with the Lord. Obviously, the Lord doesn't need a book to remind him who his followers are—he is God, after all. The idea of a book of names may have come from the ancient practice of relying on written genealogies to determine who was supposed to receive an inheritance or serve as a priest or Levite.

Psalm 69:28

29 I am sad and hurting.
God, save me and protect me.

30 I will praise God in a song
and will honor him by giving thanks.
31 That will please the LORD more than offering him cattle,
more than sacrificing a bull with horns and hoofs.
32 Poor people will see this and be glad.
Be encouraged, you who worship God.
33 The LORD listens to those in need
and does not look down on captives.

34 Heaven and earth should praise him,
the seas and everything in them.
35 God will save Jerusalem
and rebuild the cities of Judah.

Then people will live there and own the land.
36 The descendants of his servants will inherit that land,
and those who love him will live there.

A CRY FOR GOD TO HELP QUICKLY

70

For the director of music. A psalm of David. To help people remember.

1 God, come quickly and save me.
LORD, hurry to help me.
2 Let those who are trying to kill me
be ashamed and disgraced.
Let those who want to hurt me
run away in disgrace.
3 Let those who make fun of me
stop because of their shame.
4 But let all those who worship you
rejoice and be glad.
Let those who love your salvation
always say, "Praise the greatness of God."
5 I am poor and helpless;
God, hurry to me.
You help me and save me.
LORD, do not wait.

71

AN OLD PERSON'S PRAYER

1 In you, LORD, is my protection.
Never let me be ashamed.
2 Because you do what is right, save and rescue me;
listen to me and save me.
3 Be my place of safety
where I can always come.
Give the command to save me,
because you are my rock and my strong, walled city.
4 My God, save me from the power of the wicked
and from the hold of evil and cruel people.
5 LORD, you are my hope.
LORD, I have trusted you since I was young.
6 I have depended on you since I was born;
you helped me even on the day of my birth.
I will always praise you.

7 I am an example to many people,
because you are my strong protection.
8 I am always praising you;
all day long I honor you.
9 Do not reject me when I am old;
do not leave me when my strength is gone.
10 My enemies make plans against me,
and they meet together to kill me.
11 They say, "God has left him.
Go after him and take him,
because no one will save him."

Promise HE PROMISES TO BE FAITHFUL.

I will praise you with the harp. I trust you, my God (Ps. 71:22a).

A mom and dad lose their only daughter two days before her fifteenth birthday. She was riding in a car that was hit by a drunk driver. Devastated, they start the long process of grieving for a child who wasn't supposed to die before they did. Several months later they come to your school and tell you how difficult the last few months have been. The pain has been incredible for them. Then they say something that grabs you. "All we have left is God. We couldn't have made it without him. He has been so faithful."

You begin to understand what his faithfulness is. He is helping those parents just make it from day to day. He is giving them hope that they won't hurt forever. He is sending them people to give them compassion. On days when they hurt so much they can hardly breathe, he stays right beside them. He carries them when they cannot walk and gives them smiles when they thought smiles were gone forever.

Don't wait for an emergency to find out how faithful he is. He's faithful in your good times, too. Be on the lookout for your faithful Father.

SEE FOR YOURSELF:
Neh. 1:5; Ps. 36:5

12 God, don't be far off.
My God, hurry to help me.
13 Let those who accuse me
be ashamed and destroyed.
Let those who are trying to hurt me
be covered with shame and disgrace.
14 But I will always have hope
and will praise you more and more.
15 I will tell how you do what is right.
I will tell about your salvation all day long,
even though it is more than I can tell.
16 I will come and tell about your powerful works, Lord GOD.
I will remind people that only you do what is right.

17 God, you have taught me since I was young.
To this day I tell about the miracles you do.
18 Even though I am old and gray,
do not leave me, God.
I will tell the children about your power;
I will tell those who live after me about your might.

19 God, your justice reaches to the skies.
You have done great things;
God, there is no one like you.
20 You have given me many troubles and bad times,
but you will give me life again.
When I am almost dead,
you will keep me alive.
21 You will make me greater than ever,
and you will comfort me again.

22 I will praise you with the harp.
I trust you, my God.
I will sing to you with the lyre,
Holy One of Israel.
23 I will shout for joy when I sing praises to you.
You have saved me.
24 I will tell about your justice all day long.
And those who want to hurt me
will be ashamed and disgraced.

A PRAYER FOR THE KING

Of Solomon.

72

1 God, give the king your good judgment
and the king's son your goodness.
2 Help him judge your people fairly
and decide what is right for the poor.
3 Let there be peace on the mountains
and goodness on the hills for the people.
4 Help him be fair to the poor
and save the needy
and punish those who hurt them.

5 May they respect you as long as the sun shines
and as long as the moon glows.
6 Let him be like rain on the grass,
like showers that water the earth.
7 Let goodness be plentiful while he lives.
Let peace continue as long as there is a moon.

8 Let his kingdom go from sea to sea,
and from the Euphrates River to the ends of the earth.
9 Let the people of the desert bow down to him,
and make his enemies lick the dust.
10 Let the kings of Tarshish and the faraway lands
bring him gifts.
Let the kings of Sheba and Seba
bring their presents to him.
11 Let all kings bow down to him
and all nations serve him.

12 He will help the poor when they cry out
and will save the needy when no one else will help.
13 He will be kind to the weak and poor,
and he will save their lives.
14 He will save them from cruel people who try to hurt them,
because their lives are precious to him.

15 Long live the king!
Let him receive gold from Sheba.
Let people always pray for him
and bless him all day long.
16 Let the fields grow plenty of grain
and the hills be covered with crops.
Let the land be as fertile as Lebanon,
and let the cities grow like the grass in a field.
17 Let the king be famous forever;
let him be remembered as long as the sun shines.
Let the nations be blessed because of him,
and may they all bless him.

18 Praise the LORD God, the God of Israel,
who alone does such miracles.
19 Praise his glorious name forever.

On the Edge

Praise the LORD God, the God of Israel, who alone does such miracles (Ps. 72:18).

A miracle is an event that happens in a way that nature doesn't normally work. A car is crushed from every angle, but the driver comes away unharmed. A kid walks in healed after doctors declare that there's no hope. The wildest troublemaker in town gets saved and starts telling everybody what God has done in his life. A Man dead three days in a grave gets up and appears to over 500 people.

If you've ever seen a miracle, you can be sure that you were witnessing the hand of God working. You experienced a supernatural event. Only God can do miracles. Sometimes he uses people in the process, but no man can work a miracle by his own power. You've got to have God for a miracle. The purpose of a miracle is to bring glory to God and to remind us of his amazing love toward us. Miracles force us to stop looking at ourselves and our limitations. We have to look up at God and his mighty power. A miracle is meant to get our attention and cause us to be amazed at our God.

SEE FOR YOURSELF:
Ex. 34:10; Mic. 7:15

Let his glory fill the whole world.
Amen and amen.

20 This ends the prayers of David son of Jesse.

Book 3

SHOULD THE WICKED BE RICH?

A psalm of Asaph.

JEALOUSY

Is it right to envy the prosperity of the wicked? (73:2–3)

73

1 God is truly good to
Israel,
to those who have pure
hearts.
2 But I had almost stopped
believing;
I had almost lost my
faith
3 because I was jealous of proud people.
I saw wicked people doing well.

4 They are not suffering;
they are healthy and strong.
5 They don't have troubles like the rest of
us;
they don't have problems like other
people.
6 They wear pride like a necklace
and put on violence as their clothing.
7 They are looking for profits
and do not control their selfish desires.
8 They make fun of others and speak evil;
proudly they speak of hurting others.
9 They brag to the sky.
They say that they own the earth.
10 So their people turn to them
and give them whatever they want.
11 They say, "How can God know?
What does God Most High know?"
12 These people are wicked,
always at ease, and getting richer.
13 So why have I kept my heart pure?
Why have I kept my hands from doing
wrong?
14 I have suffered all day long;
I have been punished every morning.

15 God, if I had decided to talk like this,
I would have let your people down.
16 I tried to understand all this,
but it was too hard for me to see
17 until I went to the Temple of God.
Then I understood what will happen to
them.
18 You have put them in danger;
you cause them to be destroyed.
19 They are destroyed in a moment;
they are swept away by terrors.
20 It will be like waking from a dream.
Lord, when you rise up, they will
disappear.

21 When my heart was sad
and I was angry,
22 I was senseless and stupid.
I acted like an animal toward you.
23 But I am always with you;
you have held my hand.
24 You guide me with your advice,
and later you will receive me in honor.
25 I have no one in heaven but you;
I want nothing on earth besides you.
26 My body and my mind may become
weak,
but God is my strength.
He is mine forever.

27 Those who are far from God will die;
you destroy those who are unfaithful.
28 But I am close to God, and that is good.
The Lord GOD is my protection.
I will tell all that you have done.

A NATION IN TROUBLE PRAYS

A maskil of Asaph.

74

1 God, why have you rejected us for so long?
Why are you angry with us, the sheep of your pasture?
2 Remember the people you bought long ago.
You saved us, and we are your very own.
After all, you live on Mount Zion.
3 Make your way through these old ruins;
the enemy wrecked everything in the Temple.

4 Those who were against you shouted in your meeting place
and raised their flags there.
5 They came with axes raised
as if to cut down a forest of trees.
6 They smashed the carved panels
with their axes and hatchets.
7 They burned your Temple to the ground;
they have made the place where you live unclean.
8 They thought, "We will completely crush them!"
They burned every place where God was worshiped in the land.
9 We do not see any signs.
There are no more prophets,
and no one knows how long this will last.
10 God, how much longer will the enemy make fun of you?
Will they insult you forever?
11 Why do you hold back your power?
Bring your power out in the open and destroy them!

12 God, you have been our king for a long time.
You bring salvation to the earth.
13 You split open the sea by your power
and broke the heads of the sea monster.
14 You smashed the heads of the monster Leviathan
and gave him to the desert creatures as food.
15 You opened up the springs and streams
and made the flowing rivers run dry.
16 Both the day and the night are yours;
you made the sun and the moon.
17 You set all the limits on the earth;
you created summer and winter.

18 LORD, remember how the enemy insulted you.
Remember how those foolish people made fun of you.
19 Do not give us, your doves, to those wild animals.
Never forget your poor people.
20 Remember the agreement you made with us,
because violence fills every dark corner of this land.
21 Do not let your suffering people be disgraced.
Let the poor and helpless praise you.

22 God, arise and defend yourself.
Remember the insults that come from those foolish people all day long.
23 Don't forget what your enemies said;
don't forget their roar as they rise against you always.

GOD THE JUDGE

For the director of music. To the tune of "Do Not Destroy." A psalm of Asaph. A song.

75

1 God, we thank you;
we thank you because you are near.
We tell about the miracles you do.

2 You say, "I set the time for trial,
and I will judge fairly.
3 The earth with all its people may shake,
but I am the one who holds it steady.
Selah
4 I say to those who are proud, 'Don't brag,'
and to the wicked, 'Don't show your power.
5 Don't try to use your power against heaven.
Don't be stubborn.' "

6 No one from the east or the west
or the desert can judge you.
7 God is the judge;
he judges one person as guilty and another as innocent.
8 The LORD holds a cup of anger in his hand;

it is full of wine mixed with spices.
He pours it out even to the last drop,
and the wicked drink it all.

[9] I will tell about this forever;
I will sing praise to the God of Jacob.
[10] He will take all power away from the wicked,
but the power of good people will grow.

THE GOD WHO ALWAYS WINS

For the director of music. With stringed instruments. A psalm of Asaph. A song.

76

[1] People in Judah know God;
his fame is great in Israel.
[2] His Tent is in Jerusalem;
his home is on Mount Zion.
[3] There God broke the flaming arrows,
the shields, the swords, and the weapons of war. *Selah*

WHAT'S IT MEAN?

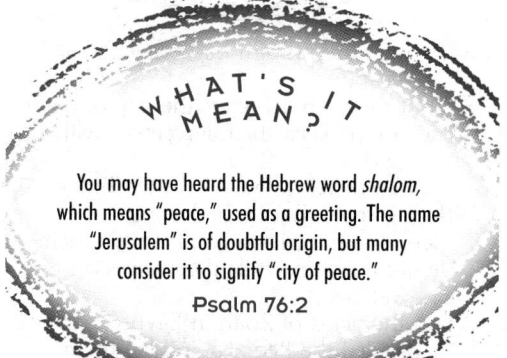

You may have heard the Hebrew word *shalom,* which means "peace," used as a greeting. The name "Jerusalem" is of doubtful origin, but many consider it to signify "city of peace."

Psalm 76:2

[4] God, how wonderful you are!
You are more splendid than the hills full of animals.
[5] The brave soldiers were stripped
as they lay asleep in death.
Not one warrior
had the strength to stop it.
[6] God of Jacob, when you spoke strongly,
horses and riders fell dead.
[7] You are feared;
no one can stand against you when you are angry.
[8] From heaven you gave the decision,
and the earth was afraid and silent.
[9] God, you stood up to judge
and to save the needy people of the earth. *Selah*
[10] People praise you for your anger against evil.
Those who live through your anger are stopped from doing more evil.

[11] Make and keep your promises to the LORD your God.
From all around, gifts should come to the God we worship.
[12] God breaks the spirits of great leaders;
the kings on earth fear him.

REMEMBERING GOD'S HELP

For the director of music. For Jeduthun. A psalm of Asaph.

77

[1] I cry out to God;
I call to God, and he will hear me.
[2] I look for the Lord on the day of trouble.
All night long I reach out my hands,
but I cannot be comforted.
[3] When I remember God, I become upset;
when I think, I become afraid. *Selah*

[4] You keep my eyes from closing.
I am too upset to say anything.
[5] I keep thinking about the old days,
the years of long ago.
[6] At night I remember my songs.
I think and I ask myself:
[7] "Will the Lord reject us forever?
Will he never be kind to us again?
[8] Is his love gone forever?
Has he stopped speaking for all time?
[9] Has God forgotten mercy?
Is he too angry to pity us?" *Selah*
[10] Then I say "This is what makes me sad:
For years the power of God Most High was with us."

WHAT'S IT MEAN?

This verse describes God's highly *visible* actions among his people during Old Testament times, such as the miracles he performed around the time of the Israelites' Exodus from Egypt.

Psalm 77:10

[11] I remember what the LORD did;
I remember the miracles you did long ago.
[12] I think about all the things you did
and consider your deeds.

[13] God, your ways are holy.
No god is as great as our God.
[14] You are the God who does miracles;
you have shown people your power.
[15] By your power you have saved your people,
the descendants of Jacob and Joseph. *Selah*

[16] God, the waters saw you;
they saw you and became afraid;
the deep waters shook with fear.
[17] The clouds poured down their rain.
The sky thundered.
Your lightning flashed back and forth like arrows.
[18] Your thunder sounded in the whirlwind.
Lightning lit up the world.
The earth trembled and shook.
[19] You made a way through the sea
and paths through the deep waters,
but your footprints were not seen.
[20] You led your people like a flock
by using Moses and Aaron.

GOD SAVED ISRAEL FROM EGYPT

A maskil of Asaph.

78

[1] My people, listen to my teaching;
listen to what I say.
[2] I will speak using stories;
I will tell secret things from long ago.
[3] We have heard them and known them
by what our ancestors have told us.
[4] We will not keep them from our children;
we will tell those who come later
about the praises of the LORD.
We will tell about his power
and the miracles he has done.

[5] The LORD made an agreement with Jacob
and gave the teachings to Israel,
which he commanded our ancestors
to teach to their children.
[6] Then their children would know them,
even their children not yet born.
And they would tell their children.
[7] So they would all trust God
and would not forget what he had done
but would obey his commands.
[8] They would not be like their ancestors
who were stubborn and disobedient.
Their hearts were not loyal to God,
and they were not true to him.

WHAT'S IT MEAN?

Ephraim had been the most important of the twelve tribes of Israel from the time of Joshua to the time Saul became king. Unfortunately, though, the Ephraimites eventually turned to idol worship and began to disobey God. Their descendants forgot about everything God had done for them. Interestingly, the specific incident referred to in this verse is not described anywhere else in Scripture.

Psalm 78:9

[9] The men of Ephraim had bows for weapons,
but they ran away on the day of battle.
[10] They didn't keep their agreement with God
and refused to live by his teachings.
[11] They forgot what he had done
and the miracles he had shown them.
[12] He did miracles while their ancestors watched,
in the fields of Zoan in Egypt.
[13] He divided the Red Sea and led them through.
He made the water stand up like a wall.
[14] He led them with a cloud by day
and by the light of a fire by night.
[15] He split the rocks in the desert

WHAT'S IT MEAN?

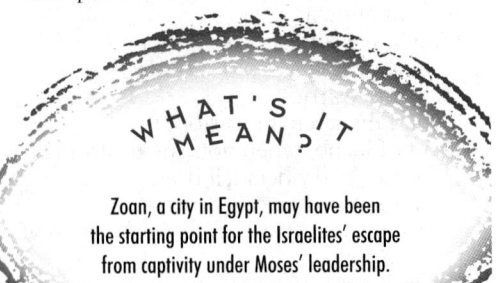

Zoan, a city in Egypt, may have been the starting point for the Israelites' escape from captivity under Moses' leadership.

Psalm 78:12

and gave them more than enough water,
as if from the deep ocean.
16 He brought streams out of the rock
and caused water to flow down like rivers.

17 But the people continued to sin against him;
in the desert they turned against God Most High.
18 They decided to test God
by asking for the food they wanted.
19 Then they spoke against God,
saying, "Can God prepare food in the desert?
20 When he hit the rock, water poured out
and rivers flowed down.
But can he give us bread also?
Will he provide his people with meat?"
21 When the LORD heard them, he was very angry.
His anger was like fire to the people of Jacob;
his anger grew against the people of Israel.
22 They had not believed God
and had not trusted him to save them.
23 But he gave a command to the clouds above
and opened the doors of heaven.
24 He rained manna down on them to eat;
he gave them grain from heaven.
25 So they ate the bread of angels.
He sent them all the food they could eat.
26 He sent the east wind from heaven
and led the south wind by his power.
27 He rained meat on them like dust.
The birds were as many as the sand of the sea.
28 He made the birds fall inside the camp,
all around the tents.
29 So the people ate and became very full.
God had given them what they wanted.
30 While they were still eating,
and while the food was still in their mouths,
31 God became angry with them.
He killed some of the healthiest of them;
he struck down the best young men of Israel.

32 But they kept on sinning;
they did not believe even with the miracles.
33 So he ended their days without meaning
and their years in terror.
34 Anytime he killed them, they would look to him for help;
they would come back to God and follow him.
35 They would remember that God was their Rock,
that God Most High had saved them.
36 But their words were false,
and their tongues lied to him.
37 Their hearts were not really loyal to God;
they did not keep his agreement.
38 Still God was merciful.
He forgave their sins
and did not destroy them.
Many times he held back his anger
and did not stir up all his anger.
39 He remembered that they were only human,
like a wind that blows and does not come back.

40 They turned against God so often in the desert
and grieved him there.
41 Again and again they tested God
and brought pain to the Holy One of Israel.
42 They did not remember his power
or the time he saved them from the enemy.
43 They forgot the signs he did in Egypt
and his wonders in the fields of Zoan.
44 He turned their rivers to blood
so no one could drink the water.
45 He sent flies that bit the people.
He sent frogs that destroyed them.
46 He gave their crops to grasshoppers
and what they worked for to locusts.
47 He destroyed their vines with hail
and their sycamore trees with sleet.
48 He killed their animals with hail
and their cattle with lightning.
49 He showed them his hot anger.
He sent his strong anger against them,
his destroying angels.
50 He found a way to show his anger.
He did not keep them from dying
but let them die by a terrible disease.
51 God killed all the firstborn sons in Egypt,
the oldest son of each family of Ham.[n]
52 But God led his people out like sheep

78:51 Ham The people in Egypt were descendants of Ham, one of Noah's sons. See Genesis 10:6.

and he guided them like a flock through
the desert.
53 He led them to safety so they had nothing
to fear,
but their enemies drowned in the sea.
54 So God brought them to his holy land,
to the mountain country he took with
his own power.
55 He forced out the other nations,
and he had his people inherit the
land.
He let the tribes of Israel settle there in
tents.

WHAT'S IT MEAN?

Joshua set up the Meeting Tent and the Ark of the Agreement in Shiloh, a city in Ephraim's territory. The city served as Israel's center of worship for many years.

Psalm 78:60

56 But they tested God
and turned against God Most High;
they did not keep his rules.
57 They turned away and were disloyal just
like their ancestors.
They were like a crooked bow that does
not shoot straight.
58 They made God angry by building places
to worship gods;
they made him jealous with their
idols.
59 When God heard them, he became very
angry
and rejected the people of Israel
completely.
60 He left his dwelling at Shiloh,
the Tent where he lived among the
people.
61 He let the Ark, his power, be captured;
he let the Ark, his glory, be taken by
enemies.
62 He let his people be killed;
he was very angry with his children.
63 The young men died by fire,
and the young women had no one to
marry.
64 Their priests fell by the sword,
but their widows were not allowed to
cry.

65 Then the Lord got up as if he had been
asleep;
he awoke like a man who had been
drunk with wine.
66 He struck down his enemies
and disgraced them forever.
67 But God rejected the family of Joseph;
he did not choose the tribe of Ephraim.
68 Instead, he chose the tribe of Judah
and Mount Zion, which he loves.
69 And he built his Temple high like the
mountains.
Like the earth, he built it to last forever.
70 He chose David to be his servant
and took him from the sheep pens.
71 He brought him from tending the
sheep
so he could lead the
flock, the people of
Jacob,
his own people, the
people of Israel.
72 And David led them with
an innocent heart
and guided them with skillful hands.

INTEGRITY

Is it important for leaders to have integrity? (78:72)

WHAT'S IT MEAN?

The events described in this verse took place in 597 B.C., when King Nebuchadnezzar and his Babylonian army conquered Jerusalem. Many Israelites were captured and taken to Babylon as prisoners. Others were simply killed, their bodies left to rot.

Psalm 79:1

THE NATION CRIES FOR JERUSALEM

A psalm of Asaph.

79

1 God, nations have come against your
chosen people.
They have ruined your holy Temple.
They have turned Jerusalem into ruins.
2 They have given the bodies of your
servants as food to the wild birds.

They have given the bodies of those who
worship you to the wild animals.
3 They have spilled blood like water all
around Jerusalem.
No one was left to bury the dead.
4 We are a joke to the other nations;
they laugh and make fun of us.

5 LORD, how long will this last?
Will you be angry forever?
How long will your jealousy burn like a
fire?
6 Be angry with the nations that do not
know you
and with the kingdoms that do not
honor you.
7 They have gobbled up the people of
Jacob
and destroyed their land.
8 Don't punish us for our past sins.
Show your mercy to us soon,
because we are helpless!
9 God our Savior, help us
so people will praise you.
Save us and forgive our sins
so people will honor you.
10 Why should the nations say,
"Where is their God?"
Tell the other nations in our presence
that you punish those who kill your
servants.
11 Hear the moans of the prisoners.
Use your great power
to save those sentenced to die.

12 Repay those around us seven times over
for their insults to you, Lord.
13 We are your people, the sheep of your
flock.
We will thank you always;
forever and ever we will praise you.

A PRAYER TO BRING ISRAEL BACK

For the director of music. To the tune
of "Lilies of the Agreement."
A psalm of Asaph.

80

1 Shepherd of Israel, listen to us.
You lead the people of Joseph like a
flock.
You sit on your throne between the gold
creatures with wings.
Show your greatness 2 to the people of
Ephraim, Benjamin, and Manasseh.
Use your strength,
and come to save us.

3 God, take us back.
Show us your kindness so we can be
saved.

4 LORD God All-Powerful,
how long will you be angry
at the prayers of your people?
5 You have fed your people with tears;
you have made them drink many
tears.
6 You made those around us fight over us,
and our enemies make fun of us.

7 God All-Powerful, take us back.
Show us your kindness so we can be
saved.

8 You brought us out of Egypt as if we were
a vine.
You forced out other nations and
planted us in the land.
9 You cleared the ground for us.
Like a vine, we took root and filled the
land.
10 We covered the mountains with our
shade.
We had limbs like the mighty cedar
tree.
11 Our branches reached the Mediterranean
Sea,
and our shoots went to the Euphrates
River.

12 So why did you pull down our walls?
Now everyone who passes by steals
from us.
13 Like wild pigs they walk over us;
like wild animals they feed on us.

14 God All-Powerful, come back.
Look down from heaven and see.
Take care of us, your vine.
15 You planted this shoot with your own
hands
and strengthened this child.
16 Now it is cut down and burned with fire;
you destroyed us by your angry looks.
17 With your hand,
strengthen the one you have chosen for
yourself.
18 Then we will not turn away from you.
Give us life again, and we will call to
you for help.

19 LORD God All-Powerful, take us back.
Show us your kindness so we can be
saved.

A SONG FOR A HOLIDAY

For the director of music. By the gittith.
A psalm of Asaph.

81

1 Sing for joy to God, our strength;
shout out loud to the God of Jacob.
2 Begin the music. Play the tambourines.
Play pleasant music on the harps and lyres.
3 Blow the trumpet at the time of the New Moon,
when the moon is full,
when our feast begins.
4 This is the law for Israel;
it is the command of the God of Jacob.
5 He gave this rule to the people of Joseph
when they went out of the land of Egypt.

MUSIC
How is music useful? (81:1–5)

"Sing for you to God, our strength; shout out loud to the God of Jacob." (Psalm 81:1)

I heard a language I did not know, saying:
6 "I took the load off their shoulders;
I let them put down their baskets.
7 When you were in trouble, you called, and I saved you.
I answered you with thunder.
I tested you at the waters of Meribah.
Selah
8 My people, listen. I am warning you.
Israel, please listen to me!
9 You must not have foreign gods;
you must not worship any false god.
10 I, the LORD, am your God,
who brought you out of Egypt.
Open your mouth and I will feed you.

11 "But my people did not listen to me;
Israel did not want me.
12 So I let them go their stubborn way
and follow their own advice.
13 I wish my people would listen to me;
I wish Israel would live my way.
14 Then I would quickly defeat their enemies
and turn my hand against their foes.
15 Those who hate the LORD would bow before him.
Their punishment would continue forever.
16 But I would give you the finest wheat
and fill you with honey from the rocks."

WHAT'S IT MEAN?

The "load" was the suffering the Israelites endured while they were slaves in Egypt. The "baskets" were the containers workers carried while making bricks for the Egyptians. Brick workers were often forced to carry wooden beams with a basket hanging from each end to hold materials or finished bricks.

Psalm 81:6

A CRY FOR JUSTICE

A psalm of Asaph.

82

1 God is in charge of the great meeting;
he judges among the "gods."
2 He says, "How long will you defend evil people?
How long will you show greater kindness to the wicked? *Selah*
3 Defend the weak and the orphans;
defend the rights of the poor and suffering.
4 Save the weak and helpless;
free them from the power of the wicked.

PROTECTION
Who should protect the helpless? (82:3–4)

5 "You know nothing. You don't understand.
You walk in the dark,
while the world is falling apart.
6 I said, 'You are "gods."
You are all sons of God Most High.'
7 But you will die like any other person;
you will fall like all the leaders."

8 God, come and judge the earth,
because you own all the nations.

A PRAYER AGAINST THE ENEMIES

83

A song. A psalm of Asaph.

1 God, do not keep quiet;
God, do not be silent or still.

2 Your enemies are making noises;
those who hate you are getting ready to attack.
3 They are making secret plans against your people;
they plot against those you love.
4 They say, "Come, let's destroy them as a nation.
Then no one will ever remember the name 'Israel.' "
5 They are united in their plan.
These have made an agreement against you:
6 the families of Edom and the Ishmaelites,
Moab and the Hagrites,
7 the people of Byblos, Ammon, Amalek,
Philistia, and Tyre.
8 Even Assyria has joined them
to help Ammon and Moab, the descendants of Lot. *Selah*

WHAT'S IT MEAN?

The one thing these enemies had in common was that they all had been defeated by the Israelites in an unlikely manner. The Midianites, who were led by Oreb and Zeeb and later by Zebah and Zalmunna (obviously "Z" names were popular with Midianite parents), put together an enormous army to fight the Israelites, yet were defeated by Gideon and his tiny band of soldiers. The army of Jabin, under the command of Sisera, lost to an Israelite army led by a woman, Deborah. Sisera escaped, but was later killed by another woman, Jael, who hammered a tent peg into his head while he slept. (Yes, you read that right.)

Psalm 83:9–11

9 God, do to them what you did to Midian,
what you did to Sisera and Jabin at the Kishon River.
10 They died at Endor,
and their bodies rotted on the ground.
11 Do to their important leaders what you did to Oreb and Zeeb.
Do to their princes what you did to Zebah and Zalmunna.
12 They said, "Let's take for ourselves
the pasturelands that belong to God."
13 My God, make them like tumbleweed,
like chaff blown away by the wind.
14 Be like a fire that burns a forest
or like flames that blaze through the hills.
15 Chase them with your storm,
and frighten them with your wind.
16 Cover them with shame.
Then people will look for you, LORD.
17 Make them afraid and ashamed forever.
Disgrace them and destroy them.
18 Then they will know that you are the LORD,
that only you are God Most High over all the earth.

WISHING TO BE IN THE TEMPLE

For the director of music. On the gittith.
A psalm of the sons of Korah.

84

1 LORD All-Powerful,
how lovely is your Temple!
2 I want more than anything
to be in the courtyards of the LORD's Temple.
My whole being wants
to be with the living God.
3 The sparrows have found a home,
and the swallows have nests.
They raise their young near your altars,
LORD All-Powerful, my King and my God.
4 Happy are the people who live at your Temple;
they are always praising you. *Selah*

5 Happy are those whose strength comes from you,
who want to travel to Jerusalem.
6 As they pass through the Valley of Baca,
they make it like a spring.
The autumn rains fill it with pools of water.
7 The people get stronger as they go,
and everyone meets with God in Jerusalem.

8 LORD God All-Powerful, hear my prayer;
God of Jacob, listen to me. *Selah*
9 God, look at our shield;
be kind to your appointed king.

10 One day in the courtyards of your Temple is better
than a thousand days anywhere else.
I would rather be a doorkeeper in the Temple of my God

than live in the homes of the wicked.
11 The LORD God is like a sun and shield;
the LORD gives us kindness and honor.
He does not hold back anything good
from those whose lives are innocent.
12 LORD All-Powerful,
happy are the people who trust you!

A PRAYER FOR THE NATION

For the director of music.
A psalm of the sons of Korah.

85

1 LORD, you have been kind to your land;
you brought back the people of Jacob.
2 You forgave the guilt of the people
and covered all their sins. *Selah*
3 You stopped all your anger;
you turned back from your strong
anger.

4 God our Savior, bring us back again.
Stop being angry with us.
5 Will you be angry with us forever?
Will you stay angry from now on?
6 Won't you give us life again?
Your people would rejoice in you.
7 LORD, show us your love,
and save us.

8 I will listen to God the LORD.
He has ordered peace for those who
worship him.
Don't let them go back to foolishness.
9 God will soon save those who respect
him,
and his glory will be seen in our
land.
10 Love and truth belong to God's people;
goodness and peace will be theirs.
11 On earth people will be loyal to God,
and God's goodness will shine down
from heaven.
12 The LORD will give his goodness,
and the land will give its crops.
13 Goodness will go before God
and prepare the way for him.

A CRY FOR HELP

A prayer of David.

86

1 LORD, listen to me and answer me.
I am poor and helpless.
2 Protect me, because I worship you.
My God, save me, your servant who
trusts in you.
3 Lord, have mercy on me,
because I have called to you
all day.
4 Give happiness to me,
your servant,
because I give my life
to you, Lord.
5 Lord, you are kind and
forgiving

FORGIVENESS

Why does God forgive us? (86:5)

Promise

HE PROMISES PEACE TO HIS FAITHFUL PEOPLE.

I will listen to God the LORD. He has ordered peace for those who worship him. Don't let them go back to foolishness (Ps. 85:8).

Faithfulness, the way God defines it, is not a stuck-like-glue observance of a bunch of rules you learn in Sunday school. What's going on inside you is more important to God than what you do. So the faithful person obeys, not because he has incredible willpower, but because his heart is turned toward God all the time. When a faithful person fails, he is quick to admit it, talk to Jesus about it, and accept his forgiveness. The faithful person is humble, meaning he doesn't think he can live his life—any part of it—without God.

This is the kind of person God promises peace to. Now, having peace doesn't mean everything that happens in your life will be wonderful and you won't ever be sad or get upset. The peace that God gives is a way-down-in-your-gut confidence that everything that happens to you, good or bad, is something he will use to bring you closer to him and make you more like him. As your friendship with Jesus grows, this peace will take root in your heart. He promises it will!

SEE FOR YOURSELF:
Mic. 5:4–5; John 14:27

and have great love for those who call
to you.
6 LORD, hear my prayer,
and listen when I ask for mercy.
7 I call to you in times of trouble,
because you will answer me.

8 Lord, there is no god like you
and no works like yours.
9 Lord, all the nations you have made
will come and worship you.
They will honor you.
10 You are great and you do miracles.
Only you are God.
11 LORD, teach me what you want me to do,
and I will live by your truth.
Teach me to respect you completely.
12 Lord, my God, I will praise you
with all my heart,
and I will honor your
name forever.
13 You have great love for
me.
You have saved me
from death.

HELL
Who will be saved from hell? (86:12–13)

14 God, proud men are attacking me;
a gang of cruel men is trying to kill me.
They do not respect you.
15 But Lord, you are a God who shows
mercy and is kind.
You don't become angry quickly.
You have great love and faithfulness.
16 Turn to me and have mercy.
Give me, your servant, strength.
Save me, the son of your female servant.
17 Show me a sign of your goodness.
When my enemies look, they will be
ashamed.
You, LORD, have helped me and
comforted me.

GOD LOVES JERUSALEM

87

A song. A psalm of the sons of Korah.

1 The LORD built Jerusalem on the holy
mountain.
2 He loves its gates more than any other
place in Israel.
3 City of God,
wonderful things are said about you.
Selah
4 God says, "I will put Egypt and Babylonia
on the list of nations that know me.
People from Philistia, Tyre, and Cush
will be born there."

5 They will say about Jerusalem,
"This one and that one were born there.
God Most High will strengthen her."
6 The LORD will keep a list of the nations.

Promise HE PROMISES TO READILY FORGIVE YOU.

Lord, you are kind and forgiving and have great love for those who call to you (Ps. 86:5).

In Luke 15, Jesus tells the story of a guy who wanted to live his own life. So he asked his dad for the money he was supposed to inherit later and left home. Of course, his money eventually ran out, and he had to get the worst job he could think of—feeding pigs. He was so hungry he wished he could eat some of what they were having. Finally, he got tired of living that way and decided to go home. He didn't expect things to be exactly like they were before he left, but he thought his dad might give him a job as a servant.

His dad surprised him. He saw him coming and ran down the road to meet him. His father was so excited to see him that he threw a big party.

Jesus told this story to give you a picture of just how ready God is to forgive you. He's like that dad, standing on the porch, looking down the road for you—*running* toward you when he sees you coming. He doesn't forgive you because he has to. He forgives you because, like that dad, he loves you; and what he wants more than anything else is to have you home with him.

SEE FOR YOURSELF:
Ps. 145:8; Mark 11:25; Luke 15:11–32; 1 John 1:9

He will note, "This person was born
there." *Selah*

7 They will dance and sing,
"All good things come from Jerusalem."

WHAT'S IT MEAN?

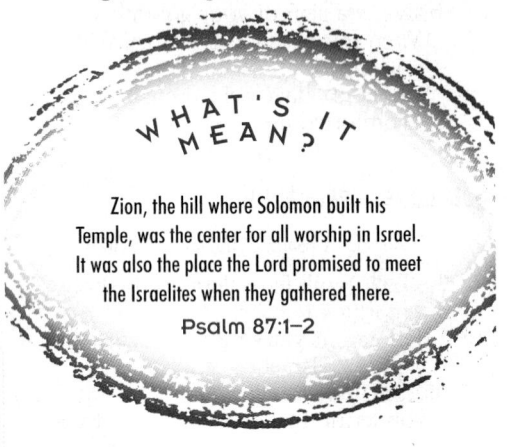

Zion, the hill where Solomon built his Temple, was the center for all worship in Israel. It was also the place the Lord promised to meet the Israelites when they gathered there.

Psalm 87:1–2

A SAD COMPLAINT

A song. A psalm of the sons of Korah. For the director of music. By the mahalath leannoth. A maskil of Heman the Ezrahite.

88

1 LORD, you are the God who saves me.
I cry out to you day and night.
2 Receive my prayer,
and listen to my cry.

3 My life is full of troubles,
and I am nearly dead.
4 They think I am on the way to my
grave.
I am like a man with no strength.
5 I have been left as dead,
like a body lying in a grave
whom you don't remember anymore,
cut off from your care.
6 You have brought me close to death;
I am almost in the dark place of the
dead.
7 You have been very angry with me;
all your waves crush me. *Selah*
8 You have taken my friends away from me
and have made them hate me.
I am trapped and cannot escape.
9 My eyes are weak from crying.
LORD, I have prayed to you every day;
I have lifted my hands in prayer to you.

10 Do you show your miracles for the dead?
Do their spirits rise up and praise you?
Selah

11 Will your love be told in the grave?
Will your loyalty be told in the place of
death?
12 Will your miracles be known in the dark
grave?
Will your goodness be known in the
land of forgetfulness?

13 But, LORD, I have called out to you for
help;
every morning I pray to you.
14 LORD, why do you reject me?
Why do you hide from me?
15 I have been weak and dying since I was
young.
I suffer from your terrors, and I am
helpless.
16 You have been angry with me,
and your terrors have destroyed me.
17 They surround me daily like a flood;
they are all around me.
18 You have taken away my loved ones and
friends.
Darkness is my only friend.

A SONG ABOUT GOD'S LOYALTY

A maskil of Ethan the Ezrahite.

89

1 I will always sing about the LORD's love;
I will tell of his loyalty from now on.
2 I will say, "Your love continues forever;
your loyalty goes on and on like the
sky."
3 You said, "I made an agreement with the
man of my choice;
I made a promise to my servant
David.
4 I told him, 'I will make your family
continue forever.
Your kingdom will go on and on.' " *Selah*

5 LORD, the heavens praise you for your
miracles
and for your loyalty in the meeting of
your holy ones.
6 Who in heaven is equal to the LORD?
None of the angels is like the LORD.
7 When the holy ones meet, it is God they
fear.
He is more frightening than all who
surround him.
8 LORD God All-Powerful, who is like you?
LORD, you are powerful and completely
trustworthy.
9 You rule the mighty sea
and calm the stormy waves.

10 You crushed the sea monster Rahab;
by your power you scattered your enemies.

11 The skies and the earth belong to you.
You made the world and everything in it.
12 You created the north and the south.
Mount Tabor and Mount Hermon sing for joy at your name.
13 Your arm has great power.
Your hand is strong; your right hand is lifted up.
14 Your kingdom is built on what is right and fair.
Love and truth are in all you do.

15 Happy are the people who know how to praise you.
LORD, let them live in the light of your presence.
16 In your name they rejoice
and continually praise your goodness.
17 You are their glorious strength,
and in your kindness you honor our king.
18 Our king, our shield, belongs to the LORD,
to the Holy One of Israel.

19 Once, in a vision, you spoke
to those who worship you.
You said, "I have given strength to a warrior;
I have raised up a young man from my people.
20 I have found my servant David;
I appointed him by pouring holy oil on him.
21 I will steady him with my hand
and strengthen him with my arm.
22 No enemy will make him give forced payments,
and wicked people will not defeat him.
23 I will crush his enemies in front of him;
I will defeat those who hate him.
24 My loyalty and love will be with him.
Through me he will be strong.
25 I will give him power over the sea
and control over the rivers.
26 He will say to me, 'You are my father,
my God, the Rock, my Savior.'
27 I will make him my firstborn son,
the greatest king on earth.
28 My love will watch over him forever,
and my agreement with him will never end.
29 I will make his family continue,
and his kingdom will last as long as the skies.

30 "If his descendants reject my teachings
and do not follow my laws,
31 if they ignore my demands
and disobey my commands,
32 then I will punish their sins with a rod
and their wrongs with a whip.
33 But I will not hold back my love from David,
nor will I stop being loyal.
34 I will not break my agreement
nor change what I have said.
35 I have promised by my holiness,
I will not lie to David.
36 His family will go on forever.
His kingdom will last before me like the sun.
37 It will continue forever, like the moon,
like a dependable witness in the sky." *Selah*

38 But now you have refused and rejected your appointed king.
You have been angry with him.
39 You have abandoned the agreement with your servant
and thrown his crown to the ground.
40 You have torn down all his city walls;
you have turned his strong cities into ruins.
41 Everyone who passes by steals from him.
His neighbors insult him.
42 You have given strength to his enemies
and have made them all happy.
43 You have made his sword useless;
you did not help him stand in battle.
44 You have kept him from winning
and have thrown his throne to the ground.
45 You have cut his life short
and covered him with shame. *Selah*

46 LORD, how long will this go on?
Will you ignore us forever?
How long will your anger burn like a fire?

DEATH
Who will face death? (89:46–48)

47 Remember how short my life is.
Why did you create us? For nothing?
48 What person alive will not die?
Who can escape the grave? *Selah*

49 Lord, where is your love from times past,

which in your loyalty you promised to
David?
50 Lord, remember how they insulted your
servant;
remember how I have suffered the
insults of the nations.
51 LORD, remember how your enemies
insulted you
and how they insulted your appointed
king wherever he went.

52 Praise the LORD forever!
Amen and amen.

Book 4

GOD IS ETERNAL, AND WE ARE NOT

A prayer of Moses, the man of God.

90

1 Lord, you have been our home
since the beginning.
2 Before the mountains were born
and before you created the earth and
the world,
you are God.
You have always been, and you will
always be.

WHAT'S IT MEAN?

Notice anything special about this psalm? It's the only one written by Moses. Not only that, but it's probably the oldest one in the entire collection. Written near the end of the Israelites' forty years of wandering in the wilderness, the psalm offers a prayer for the new generation of Israelites who were about to enter and conquer the land God had promised to them.

Psalm 90:1 and psalm title

3 You turn people back into dust.
You say, "Go back into dust, human
beings."
4 To you, a thousand years
is like the passing of a day,
or like a few hours in the night.

On the Edge

While people sleep, you take their lives. They are like grass that grows up in the morning. In the morning they are fresh and new, but by evening they dry up and die (Ps. 90:5–6).

Compared to God, who was never born and will never die, your life is like a blade of grass that grows up at dawn and withers by sunset. Our time on earth is short, so the really important question is, "How are you going to spend your life?" Are you going to waste most of it, hoping to make the last few years count, or will you max out your days to the glory of God?

Don't waste any more time. It's time to lock on to the things that you really love to do and pursue them with all your heart. It's time to get serious about your relationship with God. Before you know it, you'll be standing in his presence, giving an account of what you did on earth. It's time to love the people you need to forgive. It's time to plug in to your family. It's time to stop whining and look for the good in your life. The matter is urgent. A blink of the eye and you'll be gone.

SEE FOR YOURSELF:
Job 14:2; Eccl. 6:12; Is. 40:6–8

5 While people sleep, you take their lives.
They are like grass that grows up in the
morning.
6 In the morning they are fresh and new,
but by evening they dry up and die.

7 We are destroyed by your anger;
we are terrified by your hot anger.
8 You have put the evil we have done right
in front of you;
you clearly see our secret sins.
9 All our days pass while you are angry.
Our years end with a moan.
10 Our lifetime is seventy years
or, if we are strong, eighty years.
But the years are full of hard work and
pain.
They pass quickly, and then we are
gone.

[11] Who knows the full power of your anger?
Your anger is as great as our fear of you should be.
[12] Teach us how short our lives really are
so that we may be wise.

[13] LORD, how long before you return
and show kindness to your servants?
[14] Fill us with your love every morning.
Then we will sing and rejoice all our lives.
[15] We have seen years of trouble.
Now give us as much joy as you gave us sorrow.
[16] Show your servants the wonderful things you do;
show your greatness to their children.
[17] Lord our God, treat us well.
Give us success in what we do;
yes, give us success in what we do.

SAFE IN THE LORD

91

[1] Those who go to God Most High for safety
will be protected by the Almighty.
[2] I will say to the LORD, "You are my place of safety and protection.
You are my God and I trust you."

[3] God will save you from hidden traps
and from deadly diseases.
[4] He will cover you with his feathers,
and under his wings you can hide.
His truth will be your shield and protection.
[5] You will not fear any danger by night
or an arrow during the day.
[6] You will not be afraid of diseases that come in the dark
or sickness that strikes at noon.
[7] At your side one thousand people may die,
or even ten thousand right beside you,
but you will not be hurt.

FEAR

What two things does God tell us that we do not need to fear? (91:5–6)

WHAT'S IT MEAN?

The Hebrew day was divided into four sections: midnight or night, which was 12 A.M. to 6 A.M.; morning, which was 6 A.M. to 12 P.M.; midday or noonday, which was 12 P.M. to 6 P.M.; and evening, which was 6 P.M. to 12 A.M. The point of these verses is that the Lord offers round-the-clock protection.

Psalm 91:5–6

Promise

HE PROMISES TO COMMAND HIS ANGELS TO DEFEND AND PROTECT YOU.

He has put his angels in charge of you to watch over you wherever you go. They will catch you in their hands so that you will not hit your foot on a rock (Ps. 91:11–12).

A lot of people seem to be confused about angels. They like the idea of angels, their protection and presence, but they haven't paid much attention to the Commander of angels. We wear angel pins, read angel books, and hang little angels on everything. Maybe it's just easier to believe in them than in God. They don't ask you for a commitment. They don't convict you of sin. But here's the kicker—angels can't save you either. Angels belong to God. And God uses angels to protect his believers. He can deploy them at any time to defend his followers. They do as they are commanded by him. So rest secure, knowing that angels hover around those who love God—but loving God is the key.

SEE FOR YOURSELF:

Ps. 34:7; Matt. 4:6; Luke 4:10–11

8 You will only watch
and see the wicked punished.

9 The LORD is your protection;
you have made God Most High your place of safety.
10 Nothing bad will happen to you;
no disaster will come to your home.
11 He has put his angels in charge of you
to watch over you wherever you go.
12 They will catch you in their hands
so that you will not hit your foot on a rock.
13 You will walk on lions and cobras;
you will step on strong lions and snakes.

14 The LORD says, "Whoever loves me, I will save.
I will protect those who know me.
15 They will call to me, and I will answer them.
I will be with them in trouble;
I will rescue them and honor them.
16 I will give them a long, full life,
and they will see how I can save."

THANKSGIVING FOR GOD'S GOODNESS

A psalm. A song for the Sabbath day.

92

1 It is good to praise you, LORD,
to sing praises to God Most High.
2 It is good to tell of your love in the morning
and of your loyalty at night.
3 It is good to praise you with the ten-stringed lyre
and with the soft-sounding harp.

4 LORD, you have made me happy by what you have done;
I will sing for joy about what your hands have done.
5 LORD, you have done such great things!
How deep are your thoughts!
6 Stupid people don't know these things,
and fools don't understand.
7 Wicked people grow like the grass.
Evil people seem to do well,
but they will be destroyed forever.
8 But, LORD, you will be honored forever.

9 LORD, surely your enemies,
surely your enemies will be destroyed,
and all who do evil will be scattered.
10 But you have made me as strong as an ox.
You have poured fine oils on me.
11 When I looked, I saw my enemies;
I heard the cries of those who are against me.

WHAT'S IT MEAN?

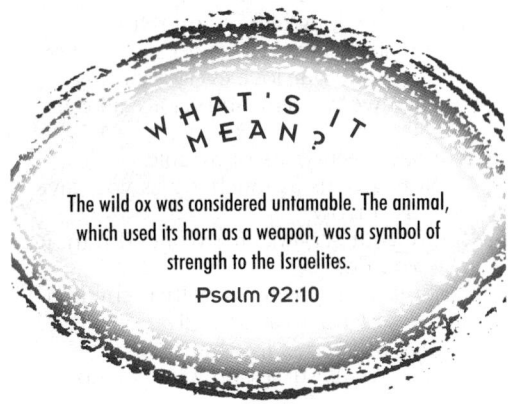

The wild ox was considered untamable. The animal, which used its horn as a weapon, was a symbol of strength to the Israelites.

Psalm 92:10

12 But good people will grow like palm trees;
they will be tall like the cedars of Lebanon.
13 Like trees planted in the Temple of the LORD,
they will grow strong in the courtyards of our God.
14 When they are old, they will still produce fruit;
they will be healthy and fresh.
15 They will say that the LORD is good.
He is my Rock, and there is no wrong in him.

THE MAJESTY OF THE LORD

93

1 The LORD is king. He is clothed in majesty.
The LORD is clothed in majesty
and armed with strength.
The world is set,
and it cannot be moved.
2 LORD, your kingdom was set up long ago;
you are everlasting.

3 LORD, the seas raise,
the seas raise their voice.
The seas raise up their pounding waves.
4 The sound of the water is loud;
the ocean waves are powerful,
but the LORD above is much greater.

5 LORD, your laws will stand forever.
Your Temple will be holy forevermore.

GOD WILL PAY BACK HIS ENEMIES

94
[1]The LORD is a God who punishes.
God, show your greatness and punish!
[2]Rise up, Judge of the earth,
and give the proud what they deserve.
[3]How long will the wicked be happy?
How long, LORD?

[4]They are full of proud words;
those who do evil brag about what they have done.
[5]LORD, they crush your people
and make your children suffer.
[6]They kill widows and foreigners
and murder orphans.
[7]They say, "The LORD doesn't see;
the God of Jacob doesn't notice."

[8]You stupid ones among the people, pay attention.
You fools, when will you understand?
[9]Can't the creator of ears hear?
Can't the maker of eyes see?
[10]Won't the one who corrects nations punish you?
Doesn't the teacher of people know everything?
[11]The LORD knows what people think.
He knows their thoughts are just a puff of wind.

[12]LORD, those you correct are happy;
you teach them from your law.
[13]You give them rest from times of trouble
until a pit is dug for the wicked.
[14]The LORD won't leave his people
nor give up his children.
[15]Judgment will again be fair,
and all who are honest will follow it.

[16]Who will help me fight against the wicked?
Who will stand with me against those who do evil?
[17]If the LORD had not helped me,
I would have died in a minute.
[18]I said, "I am about to fall,"
but, LORD, your love kept me safe.
[19]I was very worried,
but you comforted me and made me happy.

[20]Crooked leaders cannot be your friends.
They use the law to cause suffering.
[21]They join forces against people who do right
and sentence to death the innocent.
[22]But the LORD is my defender;
my God is the rock of my protection.
[23]God will pay them back for their sins
and will destroy them for their evil.
The LORD our God will destroy them.

A CALL TO PRAISE AND OBEDIENCE

95
[1]Come, let's sing for joy to the LORD.
Let's shout praises to the Rock who saves us.
[2]Let's come to him with thanksgiving.
Let's sing songs to him,
[3]because the LORD is the great God,
the great King over all gods.
[4]The deepest places on earth are his,
and the highest mountains belong to him.
[5]The sea is his because he made it,
and he created the land with his own hands.

[6]Come, let's worship him and bow down.
Let's kneel before the LORD who made us,
[7]because he is our God
and we are the people he takes care of
and the sheep that he tends.

On the Edge

He is our God and we are the people he takes care of and the sheep that he tends (Ps. 95:7).

Sheep are the only animals that need a shepherd for outside care. They would wander off, starve to death, or fall off a cliff if it weren't for the shepherd. The Lord calls us his sheep because, in the same way, we need him to guide us, to protect us, and to provide for our needs. Sometimes a shepherd will carry a helpless lamb in his arms, and a wonderful thing happens during that bonding process—the lamb finds security and learns to trust his shepherd. When the lamb begins to walk, he will never stray from the shepherd's side again. Are you a wandering sheep? God as your shepherd will coax you back into the flock time and again, and he will hold you close to encourage you to stay with him.

SEE FOR YOURSELF: Ps. 100:3; Is. 53:6; John 10:1–16

Today listen to what he says:
8 "Do not be stubborn, as your ancestors were at Meribah,
as they were that day at Massah in the desert.
9 There your ancestors tested me
and tried me even though they saw what I did.
10 I was angry with those people for forty years.
I said, 'They are not loyal to me
and have not understood my ways.'
11 I was angry and made a promise,
'They will never enter my rest.' "

PRAISE FOR THE LORD'S GLORY

96

1 Sing to the LORD a new song;
sing to the LORD, all the earth.
2 Sing to the LORD and praise his name;
every day tell how he saves us.
3 Tell the nations of his glory;
tell all peoples the miracles he does,

4 because the LORD is great; he should be praised at all times.
He should be honored more than all the gods,
5 because all the gods of the nations are only idols,
but the LORD made the heavens.
6 The LORD has glory and majesty;
he has power and beauty in his Temple.

7 Praise the LORD, all nations on earth;
praise the LORD's glory and power.
8 Praise the glory of the LORD's name.
Bring an offering and come into his Temple courtyards.
9 Worship the LORD because he is holy.
Tremble before him, everyone on earth.
10 Tell the nations, "The LORD is king."
The earth is set, and it cannot be moved.
He will judge the people fairly.
11 Let the skies rejoice and the earth be glad;
let the sea and everything in it shout.
12 Let the fields and everything in them rejoice.
Then all the trees of the forest will sing for joy
13 before the LORD, because he is coming.
He is coming to judge the world;
he will judge the world with fairness
and the peoples with truth.

A HYMN ABOUT THE LORD'S POWER

97

1 The LORD is king. Let the earth rejoice;
faraway lands should be glad.
2 Thick, dark clouds surround him.
His kingdom is built on what is right and fair.
3 A fire goes before him
and burns up his enemies all around.
4 His lightning lights up the world;
when the people see it, they tremble.
5 The mountains melt like wax before the LORD,
before the Lord of all the earth.
6 The heavens tell about his goodness,
and all the people see his glory.

7 Those who worship idols should be ashamed;
they brag about their gods.
All the gods should worship the LORD.
8 When Jerusalem hears this, she is glad,
and the towns of Judah rejoice.
They are happy because of your judgments, LORD.
9 You are the LORD Most High over all the earth;
you are supreme over all gods.

10 People who love the LORD hate evil.
The LORD watches over those who follow him
and frees them from the power of the wicked.
11 Light shines on those who do right;
joy belongs to those who are honest.
12 Rejoice in the LORD, you who do right.
Praise his holy name.

THE LORD OF POWER AND JUSTICE

A psalm.

98

1 Sing to the LORD a new song,
because he has done miracles.
By his right hand and holy arm
he has won the victory.
2 The LORD has made known his power to save;
he has shown the other nations his victory for his people.
3 He has remembered his love
and his loyalty to the people of Israel.
All the ends of the earth have seen
God's power to save.

4 Shout with joy to the LORD, all the earth;
burst into songs and make music.

5 Make music to the LORD with harps,
with harps and the sound of singing.
6 Blow the trumpets and the sheep's horns;
shout for joy to the LORD the King.

WHAT'S IT MEAN?

The horns used by musicians in ancient Israel were quite different from the horns used today. Whereas today's horns are made of highly polished brass, the horns of ancient Israel were commonly made of . . . well, horns—animal horns, that is. After removing the horn from an animal such as an ox or ram, the musician would cut off the end of it, and blow through it. These horns, which were also known as shophars, were used by priests and Levites for religious events. They were also used to sound an attack during wartime.

Psalm 98:6

7 Let the sea and everything in it shout;
let the world and everyone in it sing.
8 Let the rivers clap their hands;
let the mountains sing together for joy.
9 Let them sing before the LORD,
because he is coming to judge the world.
He will judge the world fairly;
he will judge the peoples with fairness.

THE LORD, THE FAIR AND HOLY KING

99

1 The LORD is king.
Let the peoples shake with fear.
He sits between the gold creatures with wings.
Let the earth shake.
2 The LORD in Jerusalem is great;
he is supreme over all the peoples.
3 Let them praise your name;
it is great, holy and to be feared.

4 The King is powerful and loves justice.
LORD, you made things fair;
you have done what is fair and right
for the people of Jacob.
5 Praise the LORD our God,
and worship at the Temple, his footstool.
He is holy.

6 Moses and Aaron were among his priests,
and Samuel was among his worshipers.
They called to the LORD,
and he answered them.
7 He spoke to them from the pillar of cloud.

Promise HE PROMISES TO BE A FAIR AND EQUAL JUDGE.

He is coming to judge the world. He will judge the world fairly; he will judge the peoples with fairness (Ps. 98:9).

How many times have you complained to someone, "Hey, that's not fair"? When someone who didn't study half as long as you did for a history test gets a better grade. When you have to be home at eleven but all your friends get to stay out till midnight. When your little sister gets to wear makeup a couple of years before you did.

Life doesn't seem fair, especially when you look at the world around you—murderers who don't go to jail because of legal technicalities, innocent little kids who are hurt by people they trust, people killed by drunk drivers. Sometimes you can think that God doesn't care about justice.

But, of course, he does. It's just that when he looks at these things, he sees a much bigger picture than you do. He sees from the beginning of time to the end of time in one glance. He knows what's in store for people who choose to hurt others and for the innocent people who suffer because of them. And he isn't going to play favorites, either. The only thing that will prevent people from getting exactly what they deserve will be the mercy that Jesus gives. That mercy will only be available to those who have trusted in him.

See for Yourself:

Ps. 7:9; 119:137; Is. 30:18; Zeph. 3:5

WHAT'S IT MEAN?

Moses and Aaron, who led the Israelites out of Egypt, were leaders when Israel became a nation. Samuel was a leader when Israel became a kingdom. He appointed Saul as the first king and David as the second king of Israel.

Psalm 99:6

They kept the rules and laws he gave
them.

8 LORD our God, you answered them.
You showed them that you are a
forgiving God,
but you punished them for their
wrongs.
9 Praise the LORD our God,
and worship at his holy mountain,
because the LORD our God is holy.

A CALL TO PRAISE THE LORD

A psalm of thanks.

100

1 Shout to the LORD, all the earth.
2 Serve the LORD with joy;
come before him with singing.
3 Know that the LORD is God.
He made us, and we belong to him;
we are his people, the sheep he tends.

4 Come into his city with songs of
thanksgiving
and into his courtyards with songs of
praise.
Thank him and praise his name.
5 The LORD is good. His love is forever,
and his loyalty goes on and on.

A PROMISE TO RULE WELL

A psalm of David.

101

1 I will sing of your love and fairness;
LORD, I will sing praises to you.
2 I will be careful to live an innocent life.
When will you come to me?
I will live an innocent life in my house.
3 I will not look at anything wicked.
I hate those who turn against you;
they will not be found
near me.
4 Let those who want to do
wrong stay away
from me;
I will have nothing to
do with evil.
5 If anyone secretly says
things against his neighbor,
I will stop him.
I will not allow people
to be proud and look down on others.

6 I will look for trustworthy people
so I can live with them in the land.
Only those who live innocent lives
will be my servants.

INTEGRITY

Does integrity take effort? (101:3–8)

On the Edge

The LORD is good. His love is forever, and his loyalty goes on and on (Ps. 100:5).

Goodness is not a product of God. It is an attribute of God. In other words, it is not something God does; it is something God is. It will never change. Think about it this way. If you were born Hispanic, that's what you are. No matter what you do, you will always be Hispanic. God will always be good. Because he is eternally good, everything that comes from him is good, too. His will is goodness. He shows us goodness, and he expects it from us.

What's good about you? There's nothing geeky about being good. In fact, it takes a really strong and disciplined person to be good. Do other people see goodness in you? Do you give goodness freely? If you do, keep it up. If you don't, it's never too late to start. What's the worst that could happen? Someone could throw it back in your face, but at least you gave some goodness. Maybe it'll have its impact months or years from now. Someone could return your goodness . . . and the world would be better for a moment. Give it a shot.

SEE FOR YOURSELF:
Ezra 3:11; Ps. 145:9; Jer. 33:11; Mark 10:18

On the Edge

I will not look at anything wicked. I hate those who turn against you; they will not be found near me (Ps. 101:3).

A club's initiation is like a test to see if you are worthy of the club. The greater test in this case is the test of your character. At many times in your walk as a believer, you will be tested, most of the time in your weakest places. A character test puts all your talk on the line. You may have been talking "Jesus talk" for a long time, but it's time to walk the talk. If your club asks you to do something illegal, or immoral, or offensive—don't. Don't even try to rationalize it. Just walk away. If they won't allow you to join—their loss. Why associate yourself with people who look cool on the outside but encourage evil on the inside? Doing the right thing may cost you. It may cost you the club, or some friends, or some status thing. But God promises to honor your right decisions. He will bless you for choosing well.

SEE FOR YOURSELF:
Ps. 1:1; Rom. 12:9; 1 Cor. 15:33–34; Phil. 4:8

7 No one who is dishonest will live in my
house;
no liars will stay around me.
8 Every morning I will destroy the wicked in
the land.
I will rid the LORD's city of people who
do evil.

A CRY FOR HELP

A prayer of a person who is suffering when he is discouraged and tells the LORD his complaints.

102

1 LORD, listen to my prayer;
let my cry for help come to you.
2 Do not hide from me
in my time of trouble.
Pay attention to me.
When I cry for help, answer me quickly.

3 My life is passing away like smoke,
and my bones are burned up with fire.
4 My heart is like grass
that has been cut and dried.
I forget to eat.
5 Because of my grief,
my skin hangs on my bones.
6 I am like a desert owl,
like an owl living among the ruins.
7 I lie awake.
I am like a lonely bird on a housetop.
8 All day long enemies insult me;
those who make fun of me use my
name as a curse.
9 I eat ashes for food,
and my tears fall into my drinks.
10 Because of your great anger,
you have picked me up and thrown me
away.
11 My days are like a passing shadow;
I am like dried grass.

12 But, LORD, you rule forever,
and your fame goes on and on.
13 You will come and have mercy on
Jerusalem,
because the time has now come to be
kind to her;
the right time has come.
14 Your servants love even her stones;
they even care about her dust.
15 Nations will fear the name of the LORD,
and all the kings on earth will honor
you.
16 The LORD will rebuild Jerusalem;
there his glory will be seen.
17 He will answer the prayers of the needy;
he will not reject their prayers.

WHAT'S IT MEAN?

The Babylonians weren't content with attacking Jerusalem once. In 586 B.C., they returned to finish the job. Led by Nebuchadnezzar, the Babylonian forces looted and destroyed Solomon's Temple. For fifty years the Temple lay in ruins, until a group of Jews returned home from captivity to rebuild the structure. The job was finished around 515 B.C. Like the Temple, the walls of Jerusalem lay in shambles until Nehemiah led a reconstruction project in 445 B.C.

Psalm 102:13–14

18 Write these things for the future
so that people who are not yet born will
praise the LORD.
19 The LORD looked down from his holy
place above;
from heaven he looked down at the
earth.
20 He heard the moans of the prisoners,
and he freed those sentenced to die.
21 The name of the LORD will be heard in
Jerusalem;
his praise will be heard
there.
22 People will come together,
and kingdoms will serve
the LORD.

23 God has made me tired of
living;
he has cut short my life.
24 So I said, "My God, do not
take me in the middle of
my life.
Your years go on and on.
25 In the beginning you made the earth,
and your hands made the skies.
26 They will be destroyed, but you will
remain.
They will all wear out like clothes.
And, like clothes, you will change them
and throw them away.
27 But you never change,
and your life will never end.
28 Our children will live in your presence,
and their children will remain with you."

"LORD, listen to my prayer; let my cry for help come to you." (Psalm 102:1)

PRAISE TO THE LORD OF LOVE

Of David.

103

1 My whole being, praise the LORD;
all my being, praise his holy name.
2 My whole being, praise the LORD
and do not forget all his kindnesses.
3 He forgives all my sins
and heals all my diseases.
4 He saves my life from the grave
and loads me with love and mercy.
5 He satisfies me with good things
and makes me young again, like the
eagle.

6 The LORD does what is right and fair
for all who are wronged by others.
7 He showed his ways to Moses
and his deeds to the people of Israel.
8 The LORD shows mercy and is kind.
He does not become angry quickly, and
he has great love.
9 He will not always accuse us,
and he will not be angry forever.
10 He has not punished us as our sins should
be punished;
he has not repaid us for the evil we
have done.
11 As high as the sky is above the earth,
so great is his love for those who
respect him.
12 He has taken our sins away
from us
as far as the east is from
west.
13 The LORD has mercy on
those who respect him,
as a father has mercy on
his children.
14 He knows how we were
made;
he remembers that we
are dust.

15 Human life is like grass;
we grow like a flower in the field.
16 After the wind blows, the flower is gone,
and there is no sign of where it was.
17 But the LORD's love for those who respect
him
continues forever and ever,
and his goodness continues to their
grandchildren
18 and to those who keep his agreement
and who remember to obey his orders.

WHAT'S IT MEAN?

Here are three things you may not have known about eagles. One, they can stay in the air for hours at a time. Two, they use their powerful claws to grab and kill their prey. Three, they can live for thirty years in the wild.

Psalm 103:5

19 The LORD has set his throne in heaven,
and his kingdom rules over everything.
20 You who are his angels, praise the LORD.
You are the mighty warriors who do
what he says

and who obey his voice.
[21]You, his armies, praise the
LORD;
you are his servants
who do what he
wants.
[22]Everything the LORD has
made
should praise him in all the
places he rules.
My whole being, praise the LORD.

ANGELS
Who do angels serve? (103:20–21)

PRAISE TO GOD WHO MADE THE WORLD

104

[1]My whole being, praise the LORD.
LORD my God, you are very great.
You are clothed with glory and majesty;
[2]you wear light like a robe.
You stretch out the skies like a tent.
[3]You build your room above the clouds.
You make the clouds your chariot,
and you ride on the wings of the wind.
[4]You make the winds your messengers,
and flames of fire are your servants.

[5]You built the earth on its foundations
so it can never be moved.
[6]You covered the earth with oceans;
the water was above the mountains.
[7]But at your command, the water rushed
away.
When you thundered your orders, it
hurried away.
[8]The mountains rose; the valleys sank.
The water went to the places you made
for it.
[9]You set borders for the seas that they
cannot cross,
so water will never cover the earth
again.

[10]You make springs pour into the ravines;
they flow between the mountains.
[11]They water all the wild animals;
the wild donkeys come there to drink.
[12]Wild birds make nests by the water;
they sing among the tree branches.
[13]You water the mountains from above.
The earth is full of the things you made.
[14]You make the grass for cattle
and vegetables for the people.
You make food grow from the earth.
[15]You give us wine that makes happy hearts
and olive oil that makes our faces
shine.
You give us bread that gives us strength.
[16]The LORD's trees have plenty of water;
they are the cedars of Lebanon, which
he planted.
[17]The birds make their nests there;
the stork's home is in the fir trees.
[18]The high mountains belong to the wild
goats.
The rocks are hiding places for the
badgers.

[19]You made the moon to mark the seasons,
and the sun always knows when to set.
[20]You make it dark, and it becomes night.
Then all the wild animals creep around.
[21]The lions roar as they attack.
They look to God for food.
[22]When the sun rises, they leave
and go back to their dens to lie down.
[23]Then people go to work
and work until evening.

[24]LORD, you have made many things;
with your wisdom you made them all.
The earth is full of your riches.
[25]Look at the sea, so big and wide,
with creatures large and small that
cannot be counted.
[26]Ships travel over the ocean,
and there is the sea monster Leviathan,
which you made to play there.

[27]All these things depend on you
to give them their food at the right time.
[28]When you give it to them,
they gather it up.
When you open your hand,
they are filled with good food.
[29]When you turn away from them,
they become frightened.
When you take away their breath,
they die and turn to dust.
[30]When you breathe on them,
they are created,
and you make the land new again.

[31]May the glory of the LORD be forever.
May the LORD enjoy what he has made.
[32]He just looks at the earth, and it shakes.
He touches the mountains, and they
smoke.

[33]I will sing to the LORD all my life;
I will sing praises to my God as long as
I live.
[34]May my thoughts please him;
I am happy in the LORD.
[35]Let sinners be destroyed from the earth,
and let the wicked live no longer.

My whole being, praise the LORD.
Praise the LORD.

GOD'S LOVE FOR ISRAEL

105

1 Give thanks to the LORD and pray to him.
Tell the nations what he has done.
2 Sing to him; sing praises to him.
Tell about all his miracles.
3 Be glad that you are his;
let those who seek the LORD be happy.
4 Depend on the LORD and his strength;
always go to him for help.
5 Remember the miracles he has done;
remember his wonders and his
decisions.
6 You are descendants of his servant
Abraham,
the children of Jacob, his chosen people.
7 He is the LORD our God.
His laws are for all the world.

8 He will keep his agreement forever;
he will keep his promises always.
9 He will keep the agreement he made with
Abraham
and the promise he made to Isaac.
10 He made it a law for the people of Jacob;
he made it an agreement with Israel to
last forever.
11 The LORD said, "I will give you the land of
Canaan,
and it will belong to you."

12 Then God's people were few in number.
They were strangers in the land.
13 They went from one nation to another,
from one kingdom to another.
14 But the LORD did not let anyone hurt
them;
he warned kings not to harm them.
15 He said, "Don't touch my chosen people,
and don't harm my prophets."

16 God ordered a time of hunger in the
land,
and he destroyed all the food.
17 Then he sent a man ahead of them—
Joseph, who was sold as a slave.
18 They put chains around his feet
and an iron ring around his neck.
19 Then the time he had spoken of came,
and the LORD's words proved that
Joseph was right.
20 The king of Egypt sent for Joseph and
freed him;
the ruler of the people set him free.
21 He made him the master of his house;
Joseph was in charge of his riches.
22 He could order the princes as he wished.
He taught the older men to be wise.
23 Then his father Israel came to Egypt;
Jacob[n] lived in Egypt.[n]
24 The LORD made his people grow in
number,
and he made them stronger than their
enemies.
25 He caused the Egyptians to hate his people
and to make plans against his servants.
26 Then he sent his servant Moses,
and Aaron, whom he had chosen.
27 They did many signs among the Egyptians
and worked wonders in Egypt.
28 The LORD sent darkness and made the
land dark,
but the Egyptians turned against what
he said.
29 So he changed their water into blood
and made their fish die.
30 Then their country was filled with frogs,
even in the bedrooms of their rulers.
31 The LORD spoke and flies came,
and gnats were everywhere in the
country.
32 He made hail fall like rain
and sent lightning through their land.
33 He struck down their grapevines and fig
trees,
and he destroyed every tree in the
country.
34 He spoke and grasshoppers came;
the locusts were too many to count.
35 They ate all the plants in the land
and everything the earth produced.
36 The LORD also killed all the firstborn sons
in the land,
the oldest son of each family.

37 Then he brought his people out,
and they carried with them silver and
gold.
Not one of his people stumbled.
38 The Egyptians were glad when they left,
because the Egyptians were afraid of
them.
39 The LORD covered them with a cloud
and lit up the night with fire.
40 When they asked, he brought them quail

105:23 Jacob Also called Israel. **105:23 Egypt** Literally, "the land of Ham." Also in verse 27. The people in Egypt were descendants of Ham, one of Noah's sons. See Genesis 10:6.

and filled them with bread from heaven.
41 God split the rock, and water flowed out;
it ran like a river through the desert.
42 He remembered his holy promise
to his servant Abraham.

43 So God brought his people out with joy,
his chosen ones with singing.
44 He gave them lands of other nations,
so they received what others had
worked for.
45 This was so they would keep his orders
and obey his teachings.

Praise the LORD!

ISRAEL'S FAILURE TO TRUST GOD

106

1 Praise the LORD!

Thank the LORD because he is good.
His love continues forever.
2 No one can tell all the mighty things the
LORD has done;
no one can speak all his praise.
3 Happy are those who do right,
who do what is fair at all times.

4 LORD, remember me when you are kind to
your people;
help me when you save them.
5 Let me see the good things you do for
your chosen people.
Let me be happy along with your happy
nation;
let me join your own people in praising
you.

6 We have sinned just as our ancestors did.
We have done wrong; we have done
evil.
7 Our ancestors in Egypt
did not learn from your miracles.
They did not remember all your
kindnesses,
so they turned against you at the Red
Sea.
8 But the LORD saved them for his own
sake,
to show his great power.
9 He commanded the Red Sea, and it dried
up.
He led them through the deep sea as if it
were a desert.
10 He saved them from those who hated
them.
He saved them from their enemies,
11 and the water covered their foes.
Not one of them escaped.
12 Then the people believed what the LORD
said,
and they sang praises to him.

13 But they quickly forgot what he had done;
they did not wait for his advice.
14 They became greedy for food in the desert,
and they tested God there.
15 So he gave them what they wanted,
but he also sent a terrible disease among
them.

16 The people in the camp were jealous of
Moses
and of Aaron, the holy priest of the
LORD.
17 Then the ground opened up and
swallowed Dathan
and closed over Abiram's group.
18 A fire burned among their followers,
and flames burned up the wicked.

WHAT'S IT MEAN?

As descendants of Reuben, Jacob's firstborn son, Dathan and Abiram believed that they and their tribe—and not Moses—should have been the political leaders of Israel. Their punishment for challenging Moses' authority was as unusual and severe as it was unexpected. The earth beneath the rebels' feet opened up, and Dathan and Abiram, along with all of their belongings, disappeared into the earth. God took care of the other people who joined in the rebellion with a fireball from heaven.

Psalm 106:17–18

19 The people made a gold calf at
Mount Sinai
and worshiped a metal
statue.
20 They exchanged their
glorious God
for a statue of a bull
that eats grass.
21 They forgot the God who
saved them,
who had done great things
in Egypt,

IDOLATRY

In what circumstances are we prone to give in to idolatry? (106:19–22)

22 who had done miracles in Egypt[n]
and amazing things by the Red Sea.
23 So God said he would destroy them.
But Moses, his chosen one, stood before him
and stopped God's anger from destroying them.

24 Then they refused to go into the beautiful land of Canaan;
they did not believe what God promised.
25 They grumbled in their tents
and did not obey the LORD.
26 So he swore to them
that they would die in the desert.
27 He said their children would be killed by other nations
and that they would be scattered among other countries.

28 They joined in worshiping Baal at Peor
and ate meat that had been sacrificed to lifeless statues.
29 They made the LORD angry by what they did,
so many people became sick with a terrible disease.
30 But Phinehas prayed to the LORD,
and the disease stopped.
31 Phinehas did what was right,
and it will be remembered from now on.

32 The people also made the LORD angry at Meribah,
and Moses was in trouble because of them.
33 The people turned against the Spirit of God,
so Moses spoke without stopping to think.

34 The people did not destroy the other nations
as the LORD had told them to do.
35 Instead, they mixed with the other nations
and learned their customs.
36 They worshiped other nations' idols
and were trapped by them.

DEMONS
Does idol worship have anything to do with demons? (106:34–38)

37 They even killed their sons and daughters
as sacrifices to demons.
38 They killed innocent people,
their own sons and daughters,
as sacrifices to the idols of Canaan.
So the land was made unholy by their blood.
39 The people became unholy by their sins;
they were unfaithful to God in what they did.

40 So the LORD became angry with his people
and hated his own children.
41 He handed them over to other nations
and let their enemies rule over them.
42 Their enemies were cruel to them
and kept them under their power.
43 The LORD saved his people many times,
but they continued to turn against him.
So they became even more wicked.

44 But God saw their misery
when he heard their cry.
45 He remembered his agreement with them,
and he felt sorry for them because of his great love.
46 He caused them to be pitied
by those who held them captive.

47 LORD our God, save us
and bring us back from other nations.
Then we will thank you
and will gladly praise you.

48 Praise the LORD, the God of Israel.
He always was and always will be.
Let all the people say, "Amen!"

Praise the LORD!

Book 5

GOD SAVES FROM MANY DANGERS

107

1 Thank the LORD because he is good.
His love continues forever.
2 That is what those whom the LORD has saved should say.
He has saved them
from the enemy
3 and has gathered them
from other lands,
from east and west,
north and south.

THANKFULNESS
Why should we thank the Lord? (107:1–3)

106:22 Egypt Literally, "the land of Ham." The people in Egypt were descendants of Ham, one of Noah's sons. See Genesis 10:6.

4 Some people had wandered in the desert
lands.
They found no city in which to live.
5 They were hungry and thirsty,
and they were
discouraged.
6 In their misery they cried
out to the LORD,
and he saved them
from their troubles.
7 He led them on a straight
road
to a city where they
could live.
8 Let them give thanks to the
LORD for his love
and for the miracles he does for people.
9 He satisfies the thirsty
and fills up the hungry.

"Thank the LORD because he is good. His love continues forever." (Psalm 107:1)

10 Some sat in gloom and
darkness;
they were prisoners
suffering in chains.
11 They had turned against
the words of God
and had refused the
advice of God Most
High.
12 So he broke their pride by
hard work.
They stumbled, and no one helped.
13 In their misery they cried out to the LORD,
and he saved them from their troubles.
14 He brought them out of their gloom and
darkness
and broke their chains.
15 Let them give thanks to the LORD for his
love
and for the miracles he does for people.
16 He breaks down bronze gates
and cuts apart iron bars.

17 Some fools turned against God
and suffered for the evil they did.
18 They refused to eat anything,
so they almost died.
19 In their misery they cried out to the LORD,
and he saved them from their troubles.
20 God gave the command and healed them,
so they were saved from dying.
21 Let them give thanks to the LORD for his
love
and for the miracles he does for people.
22 Let them offer sacrifices to thank him.
With joy they should tell what he has
done.

23 Others went out to sea in ships
and did business on the great oceans.
24 They saw what the LORD could do,
the miracles he did in the deep oceans.
25 He spoke, and a storm came up,
which blew up high waves.
26 The ships were tossed as high as the sky
and fell low to the depths.
The storm was so bad that they lost
their courage.
27 They stumbled and fell like people who
were drunk.
They did not know what to do.
28 In their misery they cried out to the LORD,
and he saved them from their troubles.

On the Edge

He brought them out of their gloom and darkness and broke their chains (Ps. 107:14).

In the Bible, the word *darkness* refers to ignorance, hiding, and sin. *Light* indicates truth, openness, and the presence of God. Jesus told Nicodemus, "They are judged by this fact: The Light has come into the world, but they did not want light. They wanted darkness, because they were doing evil things. All who do evil hate the light and will not come to the light, because it will show all the evil things they do" (John 3:19–20). Because people loved the darkness—their evil way of life—they rejected the Light, Jesus.

When you made Jesus your Lord, he rescued you from darkness. You are no longer ignorant of the wrong things you do or of God's love for you in spite of them. You don't have to be ashamed of anything. Even sin doesn't have to hold you back from God's love. Instead, Jesus has revealed his truth to you. He's given you the peace and confidence you need to share yourself with others. Most of all, he's become your Friend.

Look back to the time before you were a Christian. Look how far you've come. You've come out of the darkness of sin into the light and love of Jesus.

SEE FOR YOURSELF:
Is. 9:2; Eph. 5:8; 1 Pet. 2:9; 1 John 1:5

29 He stilled the storm
and calmed the waves.
30 They were happy that it was quiet,
and God guided them to the port they wanted.
31 Let them give thanks to the LORD for his love
and for the miracles he does for people.
32 Let them praise his greatness in the meeting of the people;
let them praise him in the meeting of the older leaders.

33 He changed rivers into a desert
and springs of water into dry ground.
34 He made fertile land salty,
because the people there did evil.
35 He changed the desert into pools of water
and dry ground into springs of water.
36 He had the hungry settle there
so they could build a city in which to live.
37 They planted seeds in the fields and vineyards,
and they had a good harvest.
38 God blessed them, and they grew in number.
Their cattle did not become fewer.

39 Because of disaster, troubles, and sadness,
their families grew smaller and weaker.
40 He showed he was displeased with their leaders
and made them wander in a pathless desert.
41 But he lifted the poor out of their suffering
and made their families grow like flocks of sheep.
42 Good people see this and are happy,
but the wicked say nothing.

43 Whoever is wise will remember these things
and will think about the love of the LORD.

A PRAYER FOR VICTORY

A song. A psalm of David.

108

1 God, my heart is steady.
I will sing and praise you with all my being.
2 Wake up, harp and lyre!
I will wake up the dawn.
3 LORD, I will praise you among the nations;
I will sing songs of praise about you to all the nations.
4 Your great love reaches to the skies,
your truth to the heavens.
5 God, you are supreme above the skies.
Let your glory be over all the earth.

6 Answer us and save us by your power
so the people you love will be rescued.
7 God has said from his Temple,
"When I win, I will divide Shechem
and measure off the Valley of Succoth.
8 Gilead and Manasseh are mine.
Ephraim is like my helmet.
Judah holds my royal scepter.
9 Moab is like my washbowl.
I throw my sandals at Edom.
I shout at Philistia."

10 Who will bring me to the strong, walled city?
Who will lead me to Edom?
11 God, surely you have rejected us;
you do not go out with our armies.
12 Help us fight the enemy.
Human help is useless,
13 but we can win with God's help.
He will defeat our enemies.

A PRAYER AGAINST AN ENEMY

For the director of music.
A psalm of David.

109

1 God, I praise you.
Do not be silent.
2 Wicked people and liars have spoken against me;
they have told lies about me.

WHAT'S IT MEAN?

If David had made a list of the people who lied about him or spread false rumors to make him look bad, here are three names that would have topped the list: King Saul, his one-time friend and predecessor to the throne; Shimei, a member of Saul's family; and Absalom, David's overly ambitious son.

Psalm 109:2

3 They have said hateful things about me
and attack me for no reason.
4 They attacked me, even though I loved them
and prayed for them.
5 I was good to them, but they repay me with evil.
I loved them, but they hate me in return.

6 They say about me, "Have an evil person work against him,
and let an accuser stand against him.
7 When he is judged, let him be found guilty,
and let even his prayers show his guilt.
8 Let his life be cut short,
and let another man replace him as leader.
9 Let his children become orphans
and his wife a widow.
10 Make his children wander around, begging for food.
Let them be forced out of the ruins in which they live.
11 Let the people to whom he owes money take everything he owns,
and let strangers steal everything he has worked for.
12 Let no one show him love
or have mercy on his orphaned children.
13 Let all his descendants die
and be forgotten by those who live after him.
14 LORD, remember how wicked his ancestors were,
and don't let the sins of his mother be wiped out.
15 LORD, always remember their sins.
Then make people forget about them completely.

16 "He did not remember to be loving.
He hurt the poor, the needy, and those who were sad
until they were nearly dead.
17 He loved to put curses on others,
so let those same curses fall on him.
He did not like to bless others,
so do not let good things happen to him.
18 He cursed others as often as he wore clothes.
Cursing others filled his body and his life,
like drinking water and using olive oil.
19 So let curses cover him like clothes
and wrap around him like a belt."
20 May the LORD do these things to those who accuse me,
to those who speak evil against me.

21 But you, Lord GOD,
be kind to me so others will know you are good.
Because your love is good, save me.
22 I am poor and helpless
and very sad.
23 I am dying like an evening shadow;
I am shaken off like a locust.
24 My knees are weak from hunger,
and I have grown thin.
25 My enemies insult me;
they look at me and shake their heads.

26 LORD my God, help me;
because you are loving, save me.
27 Then they will know that your power has done this;
they will know that you have done it, LORD.
28 They may curse me, but you bless me.
They may attack me, but they will be disgraced.
Then I, your servant, will be glad.
29 Let those who accuse me be disgraced
and covered with shame like a coat.

30 I will thank the LORD very much;
I will praise him in front of many people.
31 He defends the helpless
and saves them from those who accuse them.

THE LORD APPOINTS A KING

A psalm of David.

110

1 The LORD said to my Lord,
"Sit by me at my right side
until I put your enemies under your control."
2 The LORD will enlarge your kingdom beyond Jerusalem,
and you will rule over your enemies.
3 Your people will join you on your day of battle.
You have been dressed in holiness from birth;
you have the freshness of a child.

4 The LORD has made a promise
and will not change his mind.
He said, "You are a priest forever,
a priest like Melchizedek."

WHAT'S IT MEAN?

This is what Bible experts call a "messianic psalm," meaning that it predicts something about Jesus Christ, the Messiah. You might be interested to know that this psalm holds the record for being quoted more often in the New Testament than any other psalm in the Bible.

Psalm 110:1

5 The Lord is beside you to help you.
When he becomes angry, he will crush kings.
6 He will judge those nations, filling them with dead bodies;
he will defeat rulers all over the world.
7 The king will drink from the brook on the way.
Then he will be strengthened.

WHAT'S IT MEAN?

Melchizedek is one of the most mysterious figures in the Bible. Here's what we know about him. During the time of Abraham, Melchizedek reigned as the king of Salem, a city whose name was later changed to Jerusalem. When Abraham met Melchizedek, he gave the king ten percent of what he had just won in battle. That would seem to indicate that Abraham viewed Melchizedek as having the authority of a priest. Many Bible experts believe that Melchizedek was an Old Testament preview of Christ, who is also described in the Bible as both a king and a priest.

Psalm 110:4

PRAISE THE LORD'S GOODNESS

111

1 Praise the LORD!

I will thank the LORD with all my heart
in the meeting of his good people.
2 The LORD does great things;
those who enjoy them seek them.
3 What he does is glorious and splendid,
and his goodness continues forever.
4 His miracles are unforgettable.
The LORD is kind and merciful.
5 He gives food to those who fear him.
He remembers his agreement forever.
6 He has shown his people his power
when he gave them the lands of other nations.

7 Everything he does is good and fair;
all his orders can be trusted.
8 They will continue forever.
They were made true and right.
9 He sets his people free.
He made his agreement everlasting.
He is holy and wonderful.

10 Wisdom begins with respect for the LORD;
those who obey his orders have good understanding.
He should be praised forever.

HONEST PEOPLE ARE BLESSED

112

1 Praise the LORD!

Happy are those who respect the LORD,
who want what he commands.
2 Their descendants will be powerful in the land;
the children of honest people will be blessed.

BLESSING
Who does God bless? (112:1–3)

3 Their houses will be full of wealth and riches,
and their goodness will continue forever.
4 A light shines in the dark for honest people,
for those who are merciful and kind and good.
5 It is good to be merciful and generous.
Those who are fair in their business
6 will never be defeated.
Good people will always be remembered.

FEAR
Should we fear bad news? (112:7)

7 They won't be afraid of bad news;

their hearts are steady because they trust
the LORD.
8 They are confident and will not be afraid;
they will look down on their enemies.
9 They give freely to the poor.
The things they do are right and will
continue forever.
They will be given great honor.

10 The wicked will see this and become
angry;
they will grind their teeth in anger and
then disappear.
The wishes of the wicked will come to
nothing.

PRAISE FOR THE LORD'S KINDNESS

113

1 Praise the LORD!

Praise him, you servants of the LORD;
praise the name of the LORD.
2 The LORD's name should be praised
now and forever.
3 The LORD's name should be praised
from where the sun rises to where it
sets.
4 The LORD is supreme over all the
nations;
his glory reaches to the skies.

WHAT'S IT MEAN?

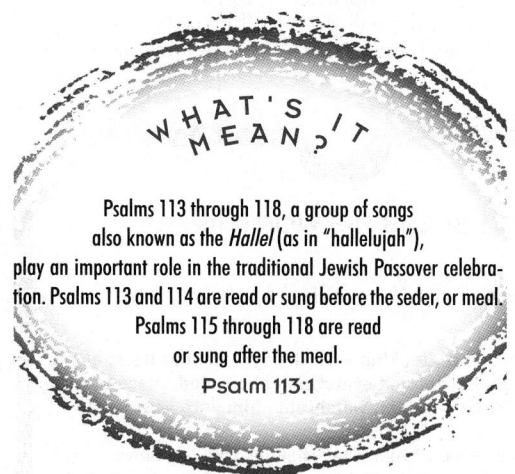

Psalms 113 through 118, a group of songs also known as the *Hallel* (as in "hallelujah"), play an important role in the traditional Jewish Passover celebration. Psalms 113 and 114 are read or sung before the seder, or meal. Psalms 115 through 118 are read or sung after the meal.

Psalm 113:1

5 No one is like the LORD our God,
who rules from heaven,
6 who bends down to look
at the skies and the earth.
7 The LORD lifts the poor from the dirt
and takes the helpless from the ashes.
8 He seats them with princes,
the princes of his people.
9 He gives children to the woman who has
none
and makes her a happy mother.

Praise the LORD!

GOD BROUGHT ISRAEL FROM EGYPT

114

1 When the Israelites went out of Egypt,
the people of Jacob left that foreign
country.
2 Then Judah became God's holy place;
Israel became the land he ruled.

3 The Red Sea looked and ran away;
the Jordan River turned back.
4 The mountains danced like sheep
and the hills like little lambs.
5 Sea, why did you run away?
Jordan, why did you turn back?
6 Mountains, why did you dance like
sheep?
Hills, why did you dance like little
lambs?

7 Earth, shake with fear before the Lord,
before the God of Jacob.
8 He turned a rock into a pool of water,
a hard rock into a spring of water.

THE ONE TRUE GOD

115

1 It does not belong to us, LORD.
The glory belongs to you
because of your love and loyalty.

2 Why do the nations ask,
"Where is their God?"
3 Our God is in heaven.
He does what he pleases.
4 Their idols are made of silver and gold,
the work of human hands.
5 They have mouths, but they cannot speak.
They have eyes, but they cannot see.
6 They have ears, but they cannot hear.
They have noses, but they cannot smell.
7 They have hands, but they cannot feel.
They have feet, but they cannot walk.
No sounds come from their throats.
8 People who make idols will be like them,
and so will those who trust them.

9 Family of Israel, trust the LORD;
he is your helper and your protection.
10 Family of Aaron, trust the LORD;
he is your helper and your protection.

11 You who respect the LORD should trust him;
he is your helper and your protection.

12 The LORD remembers us and will bless us.
He will bless the family of Israel;
he will bless the family of Aaron.
13 The LORD will bless those who respect him,
from the smallest to the greatest.

14 May the LORD give you success,
and may he give you and your children success.
15 May you be blessed by the LORD,
who made heaven and earth.

16 Heaven belongs to the LORD,
but he gave the earth to people.
17 Dead people do not praise the LORD;
those in the grave are silent.
18 But we will praise the LORD
now and forever.

Praise the LORD!

THANKSGIVING FOR ESCAPING DEATH

116

1 I love the LORD,
because he listens to my prayers for help.
2 He paid attention to me,
so I will call to him for help as long as I live.

3 The ropes of death bound me,
and the fear of the grave took hold of me.
I was troubled and sad.
4 Then I called out the name of the LORD.
I said, "Please, LORD, save me!"

5 The LORD is kind and does what is right;
our God is merciful.
6 The LORD watches over the foolish;
when I was helpless, he saved me.
7 I said to myself, "Relax,
because the LORD takes care of you."
8 LORD, you saved me from death.
You stopped my eyes from crying;
you kept me from being defeated.
9 So I will walk with the LORD
in the land of the living.
10 I believed, so I said,
"I am completely ruined."
11 In my distress I said,
"All people are liars."

12 What can I give the LORD
for all the good things he has given to me?
13 I will lift up the cup of salvation,
and I will pray to the LORD.
14 I will give the LORD what I promised
in front of all his people.

DEATH
Should Christians be afraid of death? (116:1–15)

Promise HE PROMISES TO BLESS HIS WORSHIPERS.

The LORD will bless those who respect him, from the smallest to the greatest (Ps. 115:13).

Worshiping the Lord involves being in his presence, looking with the eyes of your heart at his awesome greatness. Although you can't possibly understand everything about God, piece by piece he'll reveal himself to you as you keep looking at him, worshiping him with your whole heart, living your life in his presence.

There is a power in his presence, in continually looking at him, that changes you way down deep. Paul described it this way: "Our faces, then, are not covered," meaning there's no veil blocking our view of him. "We all show the Lord's glory, and we are being changed to be like him" (2 Cor. 3:18).

This is the blessing that he promises to his worshipers—change from the inside out. This blessing allows you to accomplish what God had in mind when he made you—to have a growing friendship with him and to become like his Son.

SEE FOR YOURSELF:
Ezra 8:22–23; Ps. 103:13; 115:12

15 The death of one that belongs to the LORD
is precious in his sight.
16 LORD, I am your servant;
I am your servant and the son of your female servant.
You have freed me from my chains.
17 I will give you an offering to show thanks to you,
and I will pray to the LORD.
18 I will give the LORD what I promised
in front of all his people,
19 in the Temple courtyards
in Jerusalem.

Praise the LORD!

A HYMN OF PRAISE

117

1 All you nations, praise the LORD.
All you people, praise him
2 because the LORD loves us very much,
and his truth is everlasting.

Praise the LORD!

THANKSGIVING FOR VICTORY

118

1 Thank the LORD because he is good.
His love continues forever.
2 Let the people of Israel say,
"His love continues forever."
3 Let the family of Aaron say,
"His love continues forever."
4 Let those who respect the LORD say,
"His love continues forever."

5 I was in trouble, so I called to the LORD.
The LORD answered me and set me free.
6 I will not be afraid, because the LORD is with me.
People can't do anything to me.
7 The LORD is with me to help me,
so I will see my enemies defeated.
8 It is better to trust the LORD
than to trust people.
9 It is better to trust the LORD
than to trust princes.

10 All the nations surrounded me,
but I defeated them in the name of the LORD.
11 They surrounded me on every side,
but with the LORD's power I defeated them.
12 They surrounded me like a swarm of bees,
but they died as quickly as thorns burn.
By the LORD's power, I defeated them.
13 They chased me until I was almost defeated,
but the LORD helped me.
14 The LORD gives me strength and a song.
He has saved me.

15 Shouts of joy and victory
come from the tents of those who do right:
"The LORD has done powerful things."
16 The power of the LORD
has won the victory;
with his power the LORD has done mighty things.

"I will not be afraid, because the LORD is with me. People can't do anything to me."
(Psalm 118:6)

17 I will not die, but live,
and I will tell what the LORD has done.
18 The LORD has taught me a hard lesson,
but he did not let me die.

19 Open for me the Temple gates.
Then I will come in and thank the LORD.
20 This is the LORD's gate;
only those who are good may enter through it.
21 LORD, I thank you for answering me.
You have saved me.

22 The stone that the builders rejected
became the cornerstone.
23 The LORD did this,
and it is wonderful to us.
24 This is the day that the LORD has made.
Let us rejoice and be glad today!

25 Please, LORD, save us;
please, LORD, give us success.
26 God bless the one who comes in the name of the LORD.
We bless all of you from the Temple of the LORD.
27 The LORD is God,
and he has shown kindness to us.
With branches in your hands, join the feast.
Come to the corners of the altar.

28 You are my God, and I will thank you;
you are my God, and I will praise your greatness.

29 Thank the LORD because he is good.
His love continues forever.

WHAT'S IT MEAN?

This Psalm, which also happens to be the longest chapter in the Bible, is an acrostic. What that means is, in the original Hebrew, each of the psalm's twenty-two sections begins with a corresponding letter of the Hebrew alphabet—from *aleph* to *tau*. (If it were written in English, the first line of the first section would begin with *A*, the second section would begin with *B*, and so on.) Each section is made up of eight verses. To make matters more interesting, the eight verses of each section are formed by couplets. The first letter of each couplet matches the first letter of the section.

Psalm 119:1

THE WORD OF GOD

119

1 Happy are those who live pure lives,
who follow the LORD's teachings.
2 Happy are those who keep his rules,
who try to obey him with their whole
heart.
3 They don't do what is wrong;
they follow his ways.
4 LORD, you gave your orders
to be obeyed completely.
5 I wish I were more loyal
in obeying your demands.
6 Then I would not be ashamed
when I study your commands.
7 When I learned that your laws are fair,
I praised you with an honest heart.
8 I will obey your demands,
so please don't ever leave me.

9 How can a young person live a pure life?
By obeying your word.
10 With all my heart I try to obey you.
Don't let me break your commands.
11 I have taken your words to heart
so I would not sin against you.
12 LORD, you should be praised.
Teach me your demands.
13 My lips will tell about
all the laws you have spoken.
14 I enjoy living by your rules
as people enjoy great riches.
15 I think about your orders
and study your ways.
16 I enjoy obeying your demands,
and I will not forget your word.

17 Do good to me, your servant, so I
can live,
so I can obey your
word.
18 Open my eyes to see
the miracles in your
teachings.
19 I am a stranger on earth.
Do not hide your
commands from me.
20 I wear myself out with desire
for your laws all the time.
21 You scold proud people;
those who ignore your commands are
cursed.
22 Don't let me be insulted and hated
because I keep your rules.
23 Even if princes speak against me,
I, your servant, will think about your
demands.
24 Your rules give me pleasure;
they give me good advice.

PURITY
How can we remain pure? (119:1–20)

25 I am about to die.
Give me life, as you have promised.
26 I told you about my life, and you
answered me.
Teach me your demands.
27 Help me understand your orders.
Then I will think about your miracles.
28 I am sad and tired.
Make me strong again as you have
promised.
29 Don't let me be dishonest;
have mercy on me by helping me obey
your teachings.
30 I have chosen the way of truth;
I have obeyed your laws.
31 I hold on to your rules.
LORD, do not let me be disgraced.
32 I will quickly obey your commands,
because you have made me happy.

33 LORD, teach me your demands,
and I will keep them until the end.
34 Help me understand, so I can keep your
teachings,
obeying them with all my heart.
35 Lead me in the path of your commands,
because that makes me happy.
36 Make me want to keep your rules
instead of wishing for riches.

[37]Keep me from looking at worthless things.
Let me live by your word.
[38]Keep your promise to me, your servant,
so you will be respected.
[39]Take away the shame I fear,
because your laws are good.
[40]How I want to follow your orders.
Give me life because of your goodness.

[41]LORD, show me your love,
and save me as you have promised.
[42]I have an answer for people who insult me,
because I trust what you say.
[43]Never keep me from speaking your truth,
because I depend on your fair laws.
[44]I will obey your teachings
forever and ever.
[45]So I will live in freedom,
because I want to follow your orders.
[46]I will discuss your rules with kings
and will not be ashamed.
[47]I enjoy obeying your commands,
which I love.
[48]I praise your commands, which I love,
and I think about your demands.

[49]Remember your promise to me, your servant;
it gives me hope.
[50]When I suffer, this comforts me:
Your promise gives me life.
[51]Proud people always make fun of me,
but I do not reject your teachings.
[52]I remember your laws from long ago,
and they comfort me, LORD.
[53]I become angry with wicked people
who do not keep your teachings.
[54]I sing about your demands
wherever I live.
[55]LORD, I remember you at night,
and I will obey your teachings.
[56]This is what I do:
I follow your orders.

[57]LORD, you are my share in life;
I have promised to obey your words.
[58]I prayed to you with all my heart.
Have mercy on me as you have promised.
[59]I thought about my life,
and I decided to follow your rules.
[60]I hurried and did not wait
to obey your commands.
[61]Wicked people have tied me up,
but I have not forgotten your teachings.
[62]In the middle of the night, I get up to thank you
because your laws are right.
[63]I am a friend to everyone who fears you,
to anyone who obeys your orders.
[64]LORD, your love fills the earth.
Teach me your demands.

[65]You have done good things for your servant,
as you have promised, LORD.
[66]Teach me wisdom and knowledge
because I trust your commands.
[67]Before I suffered, I did wrong,
but now I obey your word.
[68]You are good, and you do what is good.
Teach me your demands.
[69]Proud people have made up lies about me,

Promise HE PROMISES TO STRENGTHEN YOU.

I am sad and tired. Make me strong again as you have promised (Ps. 119:28).

Having one of those blacker than black days? Just make the world stop—you want to get off? No one is making sense. Nothing helps. You keep fighting back tears. You are overcome with sorrow and pain. No one could possibly understand. Maybe no one can understand—no one but God.

God promises to encourage you in your darkest hour. If you will seek him with all of your heart, he will come to you. He will show you the path that leads out of your situation. He will conduct a holy pep rally just for you. He will wipe away your tears. He will carry your heavy load. He is much better at all this than you are, so let him take it from here. Climb up into his strong arms. Lay your head down. And rest.

SEE FOR YOURSELF:
Matt. 11:28–30; Rom. 15:4

but I will follow your orders with all
my heart.
70 Those people have no feelings,
but I love your teachings.
71 It was good for me to suffer
so I would learn your demands.
72 Your teachings are worth more to me
than thousands of pieces of gold and
silver.

73 You made me and formed me with your
hands.
Give me understanding so I can learn
your commands.
74 Let those who respect you rejoice when
they see me,
because I put my hope in your
word.
75 LORD, I know that your laws are right
and that it was right for you to punish
me.
76 Comfort me with your love,
as you promised me, your servant.
77 Have mercy on me so that I may live.
I love your teachings.
78 Make proud people ashamed because they
lied about me.
But I will think about your orders.
79 Let those who respect you return to me,
those who know your rules.
80 Let me obey your demands perfectly
so I will not be ashamed.
81 I am weak from waiting for you to save
me,
but I hope in your word.
82 My eyes are tired from looking for your
promise.
When will you comfort me?
83 Even though I am like a wine bag going
up in smoke,
I do not forget your demands.
84 How long will I live?
When will you judge those who are
hurting me?
85 Proud people have dug pits to trap me.
They have nothing to do with your
teachings.
86 All of your commands can be trusted.
Liars are hurting me. Help me!
87 They have almost put me in the grave,
but I have not rejected your orders.
88 Give me life by your love
so I can obey your rules.

89 LORD, your word is everlasting;
it continues forever in heaven.
90 Your loyalty will go on and on;
you made the earth, and it still stands.
91 All things continue to this day because of
your laws,
because all things serve you.
92 If I had not loved your teachings,
I would have died from my sufferings.
93 I will never forget your orders,

Promise HE PROMISES TO COMFORT YOU WITH HIS LOVE.

Comfort me with your love, as you promised me, your servant (Ps. 119:76).

You studied your brains out for the chemistry exam. The teacher handed it back to you with a big fat "D" on it. All your friends and their parents went camping last weekend, but your family wasn't invited. You were laughed out of the locker room for refusing to take some pills that were supposed to help you train better. The coolest guy in school asked you out and then only wanted you to write his research paper.

Disappointment. Rejection. Failure. Sometimes it seems unbearable. You need someone to hear your story and say they understand. You need someone to let you cry and give you a big hug. You need someone to comfort you. Where do you go?

There are lots of places to run to, but most of them will leave you empty. God promises to be there and to really comfort you. His love brings faith for the moment and hope for the future. He gives you strength when you don't have any. He looks into your heart and sees how you're feeling and what you need. Then he pours out comfort by his Holy Spirit. No wonder they call him the Comforter.

SEE FOR YOURSELF:
Is. 49:13; John 14:15–18; 2 Cor. 1:3

because you have given me life by them.
94 I am yours. Save me.
I want to obey your orders.
95 Wicked people are waiting to destroy me,
but I will think about your rules.
96 Everything I see has its limits,
but your commands have none.

97 How I love your teachings!
I think about them all day long.
98 Your commands make me wiser than my
enemies,
because they are mine
forever.
99 I am wiser than all my
teachers,
because I think about
your rules.
100 I have more understanding
than the older leaders,
because I follow your orders.
101 I have avoided every evil way
so I could obey your word.
102 I haven't walked away from your laws,
because you yourself are my teacher.
103 Your promises are sweet to me,
sweeter than honey in my mouth!
104 Your orders give me understanding,
so I hate lying ways.

BIBLE
What does the Bible give us? (119:99)

105 Your word is like a lamp
for my feet
and a light for my path.
106 I will do what I have
promised
and obey your fair laws.
107 I have suffered for a long time.
LORD, give me life by your word.
108 LORD, accept my willing praise
and teach me your laws.
109 My life is always in danger,
but I haven't forgotten your teachings.
110 Wicked people have set a trap for me,
but I haven't strayed from your orders.
111 I will follow your rules forever,
because they make me happy.
112 I will try to do what you demand
forever, until the end.
113 I hate disloyal people,
but I love your teachings.
114 You are my hiding place and my shield;
I hope in your word.
115 Get away from me, you who do evil,
so I can keep my God's commands.
116 Support me as you promised so I can live.
Don't let me be embarrassed because of
my hopes.

DECISIONS
What helps us make decisions? (119:105)

117 Help me, and I will be saved.
I will always respect your demands.
118 You reject those who ignore your demands,
because their lies mislead them.
119 You throw away the wicked of the world
like trash.
So I will love your rules.
120 I shake in fear of you;
I respect your laws.

121 I have done what is fair and right.
Don't leave me to those who wrong me.
122 Promise that you will help me, your
servant.
Don't let proud people wrong me.
123 My eyes are tired from looking for your
salvation
and for your good promise.
124 Show your love to me, your servant,
and teach me your demands.
125 I am your servant. Give me wisdom
so I can understand your rules.
126 LORD, it is time for you to do something,
because people have disobeyed your
teachings.
127 I love your commands
more than the purest gold.
128 I respect all your orders,
so I hate lying ways.

129 Your rules are wonderful.
That is why I keep them.
130 Learning your words gives wisdom
and understanding for the foolish.
131 I am nearly out of breath.
I really want to learn your commands.
132 Look at me and have mercy on me
as you do for those who love you.
133 Guide my steps as you promised;
don't let any sin control me.
134 Save me from harmful people
so I can obey your orders.
135 Show your kindness to me, your servant.
Teach me your demands.
136 Tears stream from my eyes,
because people do not obey your
teachings.

137 LORD, you do what is right,
and your laws are fair.
138 The rules you commanded are right
and completely trustworthy.
139 I am so upset I am worn out,
because my enemies have forgotten
your words.
140 Your promises are proven,
so I, your servant, love them.

141 I am unimportant and hated,
but I have not forgotten your orders.
142 Your goodness continues forever,
and your teachings are true.
143 I have had troubles and misery,
but I love your commands.
144 Your rules are always good.
Help me understand so I can live.

145 LORD, I call to you with all my heart.
Answer me, and I will keep your demands.
146 I call to you.
Save me so I can obey your rules.
147 I wake up early in the morning and cry out.
I hope in your word.
148 I stay awake all night
so I can think about your promises.
149 Listen to me because of your love;
LORD, give me life by your laws.
150 Those who love evil are near,
but they are far from your teachings.
151 But, LORD, you are also near,
and all your commands are true.
152 Long ago I learned from your rules
that you made them to continue forever.

> **"LORD, I call to you with all my heart. Answer me, and I will keep your demands." (Psalm 119:145)**

153 See my suffering and rescue me,
because I have not forgotten your teachings.
154 Argue my case and save me.
Let me live by your promises.
155 Wicked people are far from being saved,
because they do not want your demands.
156 LORD, you are very kind;
give me life by your laws.
157 Many enemies are after me,
but I have not rejected your rules.
158 I see those traitors, and I hate them,
because they do not obey what you say.
159 See how I love your orders.
LORD, give me life by your love.
160 Your words are true from the start,
and all your laws will be fair forever.

161 Leaders attack me for no reason,
but I fear your law in my heart.
162 I am as happy over your promises
as if I had found a great treasure.
163 I hate and despise lies,
but I love your teachings.
164 Seven times a day I praise you
for your fair laws.
165 Those who love your teachings will find true peace,
and nothing will defeat them.
166 I am waiting for you to save me, LORD.
I will obey your commands.
167 I obey your rules,
and I love them very much.
168 I obey your orders and rules,
because you know everything I do.

169 Hear my cry to you, LORD.
Let your word help me understand.
170 Listen to my prayer;
save me as you promised.
171 Let me speak your praise,
because you have taught me your demands.
172 Let me sing about your promises,
because all your commands are fair.
173 Give me your helping hand,
because I have chosen your commands.
174 I want you to save me, LORD.
I love your teachings.
175 Let me live so I can praise you,
and let your laws help me.
176 I have wandered like a lost sheep.
Look for your servant, because I have not forgotten your commands.

A PRAYER OF SOMEONE FAR FROM HOME

A psalm for going up to worship.

120

1 When I was in trouble, I called to the LORD,
and he answered me.
2 LORD, save me from liars
and from those who plan evil.

3 You who plan evil, what will God do to you?
How will he punish you?
4 He will punish you with the sharp arrows of a warrior
and with burning coals of wood.

5 How terrible it is for me to live in the land of Meshech,

to live among the people of Kedar.
6 I have lived too long
with people who hate peace.
7 When I talk peace,
they want war.

WHAT'S IT MEAN?

Other nations were free to mistreat slaves and foreigners, but Israel was expected—by God himself, no less—to respect the foreigners who came to their land. Apparently, Meshech and Kedar were cities on the edge of the desert whose citizens were known for their violence.

Psalm 120:5

THE LORD GUARDS HIS PEOPLE

A song for going up to worship.

121

1 I look up to the hills,
but where does my help come from?
2 My help comes from the LORD,
who made heaven and earth.

3 He will not let you be defeated.
He who guards you never sleeps.
4 He who guards Israel
never rests or sleeps.
5 The LORD guards you.
The LORD is the shade that protects you
from the sun.
6 The sun cannot hurt you during the day,
and the moon cannot hurt you at night.
7 The LORD will protect you from all
dangers;
he will guard your life.
8 The LORD will guard you as you come and
go,
both now and forever.

HAPPY PEOPLE IN JERUSALEM

A song for going up to worship.
Of David.

122

1 I was happy when they said to me,
"Let's go to the Temple of the LORD."
2 Jerusalem, we are standing
at your gates.

3 Jerusalem is built as a city
with the buildings close together.
4 The tribes go up there,
the tribes who belong to the LORD.
It is the rule in Israel
to praise the LORD at Jerusalem.
5 There the descendants of David
set their thrones to judge the people.

6 Pray for peace in Jerusalem:
"May those who love her be safe.
7 May there be peace within her walls
and safety within her strong towers."
8 To help my relatives and friends,

Promise **HE PROMISES NOT TO FALL ASLEEP ON YOU.**

He who guards Israel never rests or sleeps (Ps. 121:4).

The Lord is the protector of Israel—and of everyone who puts his or her trust in him. He protects you from the enemy of his people, Satan. Satan hates the fact that you want to live for God. He will throw whatever he can at you to get you off track. But as long as you stand under God's protection—trusting him and obeying him—Satan's plans don't have a lot of effect.

And God doesn't ever let his guard down. He doesn't get bored or tired. Unlike humans, he doesn't need rest to renew his mind and body. That means you can call on him anytime you feel the enemy's attack. If Satan needles you with doubt at midnight, if he attacks you with fear at three A.M., if he throws you a temptation at high noon—whatever and whenever—the Lord can hear you call him and will rescue you.

SEE FOR YOURSELF:

Deut. 11:12; Ps. 11:4; Is. 40:28

I say, "Let Jerusalem have peace."
9 For the sake of the Temple of the LORD our God,
I wish good for her.

A PRAYER FOR MERCY

A song for going up to worship.

123

1 LORD, I look upward to you,
you who live in heaven.
2 Slaves depend on their masters,
and a female servant depends on her mistress.
In the same way, we depend on the LORD our God;
we wait for him to show us mercy.

3 Have mercy on us, LORD. Have mercy on us,
because we have been insulted.
4 We have suffered many insults from lazy people
and much cruelty from the proud.

On the Edge

I was happy when they said to me, "Let's go to the Temple of the LORD" (Ps. 122:1).

Going to church is important for several reasons. First, the church is something God wanted and established on earth. It's the place he's made for his people to come together and learn about him and serve him and worship him. Second, it's a place for you to find Christian friends and people you can look up to. Third, it's a place for you to get to know God and his Word and a place where you can be encouraged.

You may be thinking, *Yeah, but those things don't really happen. The church is full of hypocrites.* You're right. It is. It's full of humans—imperfect people who blow it, just like you. Jesus came to help imperfect people. What's important is that there are also some incredible people in church, people whose hearts are really longing to be like Jesus. These people can be awesome friends and role models for you.

You may be thinking, *Okay, but church is stuffy and boring.* But there are so many kinds of churches today—some with forms of music (even electric guitars and drums!) and worship that may really appeal to you. Or that are led by young, energetic pastors who really know how to relate to you.

Give church a chance. Look around at different ones; just make sure you find one that confesses Jesus Christ as the only Lord and Savior. Pray about your decision and ask him to help you find your place. Get involved and grow with other Christians. You'll be glad you did.

SEE FOR YOURSELF:
Ps. 26:8; John 2:17; Acts 2:46–47; Heb. 10:25

WHAT'S IT MEAN?

Being a servant in ancient times was hard work. Servants were expected to sit quietly in a corner, watching carefully for even the slightest indication that their master needed something.
Psalm 123:2

THE LORD SAVES HIS PEOPLE

A song for going up to worship.
Of David.

124

1 What if the LORD had not been on our side?
(Let Israel repeat this.)
2 What if the LORD had not been on our side
when we were attacked?
3 When they were angry with us,
they would have swallowed us alive.
4 They would have been like a flood drowning us;
they would have poured over us like a river.
5 They would have swept us away like a mighty stream.

6 Praise the LORD,
who did not let them chew us up.
7 We escaped like a bird
from the hunter's trap.
The trap broke,
and we escaped.
8 Our help comes from the LORD,
who made heaven and earth.

GOD PROTECTS THOSE WHO TRUST HIM

A song for going up to worship.

125
1 Those who trust the LORD are like Mount Zion,
which sits unmoved forever.
2 As the mountains surround Jerusalem,
the LORD surrounds his people
now and forever.

3 The wicked will not rule
over those who do right.
If they did, the people who do right
might use their power to do evil.

4 LORD, be good to those who are good,
whose hearts are honest.
5 But, LORD, when you remove those who do evil,
also remove those who stop following you.

Let there be peace in Israel.

On the Edge

Those who trust in the LORD are like Mount Zion, which sits unmoved forever (Ps. 125:1).

Real trust goes a lot deeper than being able to say, "Yeah, sure, I believe in God." James said, "You believe there is one God. Good! But the demons believe that, too, and they tremble with fear" (James 2:19). Real trust means letting go of your life and your heart and giving God control of them. It means obeying him. James used Abraham as an example: "So you see that Abraham's faith and the things he did worked together. His faith was made perfect by what he did" (James 2:22).

People who trust God in this way are like Mount Zion. They're immovable, unshakable. The way a mountain stands up against the forces of nature, they are able, by God's Spirit, to stand against all the stuff that life throws at them.

But Mount Zion isn't just any mountain. This is the spot in Jerusalem God chose for his Temple, the place where he would live among his people. Now that you've put your trust in him, he makes his home in you.

SEE FOR YOURSELF:
Heb. 12:22–29

WHAT'S IT MEAN?

Jerusalem was a fairly well-protected city. The mountains that surrounded Jerusalem sloped into valleys on the eastern and western sides of the city, making it difficult for opposing armies to attack from those directions. The ravines that lay south of the city made it difficult for an enemy to approach from that direction as well.

Psalm 125:2

LORD, BRING YOUR PEOPLE BACK

A song for going up to worship.

126
1 When the LORD brought the prisoners back to Jerusalem,
it seemed as if we were dreaming.
2 Then we were filled with laughter,
and we sang happy songs.
Then the other nations said,
"The LORD has done great things for them."
3 The LORD has done great things for us,
and we are very glad.

4 LORD, return our prisoners again,
as you bring streams to the desert.
5 Those who cry as they plant crops

WHAT'S IT MEAN?

This psalm celebrates the return of the Israelites from seventy years of captivity in Babylon, five hundred miles away from Jerusalem. Judah, the southern kingdom of Israel, was first defeated by the Babylonians in 597 B.C. King Nebuchadnezzar led two more attacks against the city in 586 and 581 B.C. As a result of the three attacks, more than forty-five hundred Jews were taken captive to Babylon. After the Persians conquered Babylon, the Jews were allowed to return to Jerusalem and rebuild their Temple.

Psalm 126:1

will sing at harvest time.
6 Those who cry
as they carry out the seeds
will return singing
and carrying bundles of grain.

ALL GOOD THINGS COME FROM GOD

A song for going up to worship.
Of Solomon.

127

1 If the LORD doesn't build the house,
the builders are working for nothing.
If the LORD doesn't guard the city,
the guards are watching for nothing.
2 It is no use for you to get up early
and stay up late,
working for a living.
The LORD gives sleep to
those he loves.
3 Children are a gift from
the LORD;
babies are a reward.
4 Children who are born to
a young man
are like arrows in the hand
of a warrior.
5 Happy is the man
who has his bag full of arrows.
They will not be defeated
when they fight their enemies at the city
gate.

ABORTION
Where are children from?
(127:3)

THE HAPPY HOME

A song for going up to worship.

128

1 Happy are those who respect the LORD
and obey him.
2 You will enjoy what you work for,
and you will be blessed with good
things.
3 Your wife will give you many children,
like a vine that produces much fruit.
Your children will bring you much good,
like olive branches that produce many
olives.
4 This is how the man who respects the
LORD
will be blessed.
5 May the LORD bless you from Mount
Zion;
may you enjoy the good things of
Jerusalem all your life.
6 May you see your grandchildren.

Let there be peace in Israel.

A PRAYER AGAINST THE ENEMIES

A song for going up to worship.

129

1 They have treated me badly all my life.
(Let Israel repeat this.)
2 They have treated me badly all my life,
but they have not defeated me.
3 Like farmers plowing, they plowed over
my back,
making long wounds.
4 But the LORD does what is right;
he has set me free from those wicked
people.

5 Let those who hate Jerusalem
be turned back in shame.

On the Edge

But the LORD does what is right; he has set me free from those wicked people (Ps. 129:4).

God always does what is right. That doesn't just mean that he follows the rules. Of course he does—they're his rules. But he goes beyond that. He does what is right for you. He knows you inside and out, and everything that comes into your life from his hand is the very best thing that could happen in your life. He gives you what you need to become the person he wants you to be—someone who's more and more like his Son. But don't think that everything that happens to you is something God does. When you or someone close to you sins, that has an effect on your life—but sin is *never* God's will. Or sometimes Satan hurts you. God allowed that with Job—the bad things that happened to Job did not come from him, but he knew what Job was going through.

Here's what's cool—God can even take people's mistakes and Satan's wicked plans and turn them into something good. Romans 8:28 says, "We know that in everything God works for the good of those who love him. They are the people he called, because that was his plan." He is so good at doing right, he takes even the crummy stuff in your life and turns it into something great—something that makes you stronger and brings you closer to him.

SEE FOR YOURSELF:
Ps. 7:9; 119:137; Is. 30:18

JONATHAN made a difference

Perhaps the most powerful way in which people make a difference in one another's lives has to do with friendship. Jonathan's friendship wasn't cheap. It cost him his father's trust, though he never betrayed his father. Jonathan made a difference in David's life because he recognized God's hand on David. Jonathan was an able and courageous leader in his own right. If his father hadn't turned from God, Jonathan would have made a good king. Instead, he accepted the role of David's loyal friend.

Jonathan made a difference because he understood the difference between blind and open-eyed loyalty. He had his priorities straight. He knew that loyalty doesn't justify helping someone do wrong. Jonathan's father, King Saul, wanted to kill David. Jonathan neither helped nor prevented his father's plans, but he warned his friend David. Jonathan remained with his father. He died with his father. Jonathan was able to be a loyal son and a loyal friend—to the death.

Cutting Edge

How did Jonathan keep his loyalties straight? He had an ultimate loyalty to God and his ways. His human loyalties were always controlled by his loyalty to his heavenly Father. That made the difference. That ultimate loyalty allowed Jonathan to make a difference.

YOU can, too! You have probably found that loyalties at the human level compete for attention. How do you decide between family and friends? The choices can be heartbreaking. They will be practically impossible until you establish a higher, single loyalty. No one deserves your ultimate loyalty but God. Have you established that ultimate loyalty?

Want to know more? Read about Jonathan in 1 Samuel 13—31. Note also 2 Samuel 1 and 9.

DAVID made a difference

Like little brothers often do, David got the jobs no one else wanted. His big brothers got to play soldier while David played shepherd with real sheep. But he turned what others didn't want into an adventure. He did so well tending his father's flock that his heavenly Father entrusted him with a kingdom. What David learned from the sheep made a difference in many people's lives.

The youthful David made good use of his time. He developed his abilities to sing and sling. He practiced singing and playing the harp to the sheep and was later a powerful comfort to King Saul when he played. He became a marksman with his sling as he protected the flock. Later, he made quite an impression on Goliath the giant with that same sling. Goliath didn't see the truth of what God can do with a committed young person until it hit him right between the eyes.

Cutting Edge

We don't know when David actually wrote Psalm 23, the Shepherd's Psalm. But everything in that psalm David learned when he was young. Those early experiences made him. Growing up is not just the passing of a certain number of years; it is the construction of a character. People and places had a big part in creating David's character. But David was also open to God's work in his life. As long as David lived the truth of his words, "The LORD is my shepherd; I have everything I need," he made the right kind of difference with his life.

YOU can, too!

The difference you can make may not be apparent right now, but you can be sure it is being constructed. What you are doing these days at home and school may not seem any greater a project than watching a bunch of sheep. You can imagine defeating a giant like Goliath, but what you face is a geometry quiz tomorrow. You want to sing for the multitudes, but you're struggling with piano lessons. When you're having days that aren't so great, it's hard to feel you're on your way to greatness.

Here's the point: Until you can discover God's part in the little, boring things in your life, you will not understand God's part in the big things of life. The more you allow God to make a difference each day in your life, the more your Life will make a difference in other's lives.

Want to know more? David's life is recounted in 1 Samuel 16—1 Kings 2. Read Psalm 23 and identify "places" in your life right now that are like the "places" in that psalm (that is, green pastures, calm water, dark valleys, and so on).

SOLOMON made a difference

Solomon turned out to be an example of almost everything he preached for and against! He should have listened better to himself. His wisest act was to humbly ask God for wisdom; his most foolish act was to live as if he were exempt from the very truths he taught others. So, for example, he published many proverbs on marriage, but violated every one of them himself.

In his unusual autobiography, Ecclesiastes, Solomon gives indication that he realized what a mess he had made out of his life. The book reveals a man who had the unusual circumstance of having the resources and opportunity to have and to try anything. So he did. Years later Jesus said this about lives like Solomon's: "It is worth nothing for them to have the whole world if they lose their souls" (Matt. 16:26). Solomon reported that such a man ends up chasing wind.

Cutting Edge

Solomon certainly made a difference in history. He built a great Temple for God in Jerusalem. He enlarged the borders of the kingdom of Israel. He applied wisdom to a system of public works and foreign diplomacy. The treasury of his kingdom overflowed with riches. From a worldly point of view, Solomon was an outstanding success. But his internal life decayed away as he failed to faithfully follow his own advice: "Trust the LORD with all your heart, and don't depend on your own understanding. Remember the LORD in all you do, and he will give you success" (Prov. 3:5–6).

YOU can, too!

The Bible includes many examples of people who started out well but finished poorly. You can probably think of some examples in our own times. Those who make the best kind of difference are those who don't give up once they begin to live for God.

We don't know how long the race called life will be, but we will fail and fall if we expect it to be a short sprint. The account of the difference you make in your life for God will not be over until God puts the final touches on your story.

Want to know more? In order to get a perspective on Solomon, you should read not only the history of his life and times in 2 Sam. 12:24—1 Kin. 11:43 but also his own writings in Proverbs, Ecclesiastes, and Song of Solomon.

NAAMAN'S WIFE'S SERVANT GIRL made a difference

Some heroes in God's great story make a difference while remaining anonymous. Their nameless role highlights God's work. And God always knows who they are. Naaman was a Syrian soldier during the ministry of Elisha the prophet. He contracted a horrible skin disease. His wife's servant was a young Jewish girl who had been kidnapped during a Syrian raid on Israel.

The only things we know about this young woman are that both her faith and her compassion were genuine. Instead of resenting her situation, she offered hope of healing to Naaman by suggesting he consult with God's prophet. Her timing was perfect. Naaman was desperate enough to try almost anything. His pride still had to be crushed, but his decision to seek help from God eventually led to his healing.

Cutting Edge

That young girl represents the most numerous category of God's servants. They are in this life unnamed and often overlooked. Their all-too-brief stories hint that God always has a lot more going on in this world than any one of us can keep under observation. But God sees it all. No act of kindness or gesture of faith goes unnoticed. The God who keeps track of sparrows won't miss the brief suggestions, the words of wisdom, and those moments when a true believer gives another person a reason to consider God. In the end, we will find out that many more made a bigger difference than we ever expected.

YOU can, too!

When you Live to serve God, you will often find yourself an anonymous participant in his plans. If you insist on recognition, you will probably experience frustration. If you settle for service, with your attention fixed on your divine Master, you can anticipate hearing the word, "Excellent! You are a good servant" (Luke 19:17). You will be surprised by what a difference that will make!

Want to know more? This young girl's story is told in 2 Kings 5:1–27.

6 Let them be like the grass on the roof
that dries up before it has grown.
7 There is not enough of it to fill a hand
or to make into a bundle to fill one's arms.
8 Let those who pass by them not say,
"May the LORD bless you.
We bless you by the power of the LORD."

A PRAYER FOR MERCY

A song for going up to worship.

130

1 LORD, I am in great trouble,
so I call out to you.
2 Lord, hear my voice;
listen to my prayer for help.
3 LORD, if you punished people for all their sins,
no one would be left, Lord.
4 But you forgive us,
so you are respected.

5 I wait for the LORD to help me,
and I trust his word.
6 I wait for the Lord to help me
more than night watchmen wait for the dawn,
more than night watchmen wait for the dawn.

7 People of Israel, put your hope in the LORD
because he is loving
and able to save.
8 He will save Israel
from all their sins.

CHILDLIKE TRUST IN THE LORD

A song for going up to worship.
Of David.

131

1 LORD, my heart is not proud;
I don't look down on others.
I don't do great things,
and I can't do miracles.
2 But I am calm and quiet,
like a baby with its mother.
I am at peace, like a baby with its mother.

3 People of Israel, put your hope in the LORD
now and forever.

IN PRAISE OF THE TEMPLE

A song for going up to worship.

132

1 LORD, remember David
and all his suffering.
2 He made an oath to the LORD,
a promise to the Mighty God of Jacob.
3 He said, "I will not go home to my house,
or lie down on my bed,
4 or close my eyes,
or let myself sleep
5 until I find a place for the LORD.
I want to provide a home for the Mighty God of Jacob."

6 We heard about the Ark in Bethlehem.
We found it at Kiriath Jearim.
7 Let's go to the LORD's house.
Let's worship at his footstool.
8 Rise, LORD, and come to your resting place;
come with the Ark that shows your strength.
9 May your priests do what is right.
May your people sing for joy.

WHAT'S IT MEAN?

The name translated here as "Bethlehem" is actually "Ephrathah." If the town's name had not been changed somewhere along the line, we might be singing "O Little Town of Ephrathah" at Christmastime.

Psalm 132:6

10 For the sake of your servant David,
do not reject your appointed king.
11 The LORD made a promise to David,
a sure promise that he will not take back.
He promised, "I will make one of your descendants
rule as king after you.
12 If your sons keep my agreement
and the rules that I teach them,
then their sons after them will rule
on your throne forever and ever."

13 The LORD has chosen Jerusalem;
he wants it for his home.

[14]He says, "This is my resting place forever.
Here is where I want to stay.
[15]I will bless her with plenty;
I will fill her poor with food.
[16]I will cover her priests with salvation,
and those who worship me will really
sing for joy.

[17]"I will make a king come from the family
of David.
I will provide my appointed one
descendants to rule after him.
[18]I will cover his enemies with shame,
but his crown will shine."

THE LOVE OF GOD'S PEOPLE

A song for going up to worship.
Of David.

133

[1]It is good and pleasant
when God's people live together in
peace!
[2]It is like perfumed oil poured on the
priest's head
and running down his beard.
It ran down Aaron's beard
and on to the collar of his robes.
[3]It is like the dew of Mount Hermon
falling on the hills of Jerusalem.
There the LORD gives his blessing
of life forever.

TEMPLE GUARDS, PRAISE THE LORD

A song for going up to worship.

134

[1]Praise the LORD, all you servants of the
LORD,
you who serve at night in the Temple of
the LORD.
[2]Raise your hands in the Temple
and praise the LORD.

[3]May the LORD bless you from Mount
Zion,
he who made heaven and earth.

THE LORD SAVES, IDOLS DO NOT

135

[1]Praise the LORD!

Praise the name of the LORD;
praise him, you servants of the LORD,
[2]you who stand in the LORD's Temple
and in the Temple courtyards.
[3]Praise the LORD, because he is good;
sing praises to him, because it is
pleasant.

[4]The LORD has chosen the people of Jacob
for himself;
he has chosen the people of Israel for
his very own.
[5]I know that the LORD is great.
Our Lord is greater than all the gods.
[6]The LORD does what he pleases,
in heaven and on earth,
in the seas and the deep oceans.
[7]He brings the clouds from the ends of the
earth.
He sends the lightning with the rain.
He brings out the wind from his
storehouses.

[8]He destroyed the firstborn sons in Egypt
the firstborn of both people and
animals.
[9]He did many signs and miracles in Egypt
against the king and his servants.
[10]He defeated many nations
and killed powerful kings:
[11]Sihon king of the Amorites,
Og king of Bashan,

On the Edge

The LORD does what he pleases, in heaven and on earth, in the seas and the deep oceans (Ps. 135:6).

The most reassuring thing you could know about God is that he is in control. Totally in charge. Doing as he pleases. Our sin has not thrown a wrench in his plans. He is not stressed out by our foolishness. He is not confused about which way to go. He still sits on the throne of heaven. If you think that the world is spinning out of control and that all hope is long gone, then you don't know about the sovereignty of God. He is working in and through what seems like craziness to accomplish his divine purposes. His plans will not be changed. You do not have to be nervous or wonder. God is in charge, both in the world and in the lives of his believers.

SEE FOR YOURSELF:
Ps. 115:3; Jer. 10:13; Rom. 8:28

and all the kings of Canaan.
12 Then he gave their land as a gift,
a gift to his people, the Israelites.

13 LORD, your name is everlasting;
LORD, you will be remembered forever.
14 The LORD defends his people
and has mercy on his servants.

15 The idols of other nations are made of
silver and gold,
the work of human hands.
16 They have mouths, but they cannot speak.
They have eyes, but they cannot see.
17 They have ears, but they cannot hear.
They have no breath in their mouths.
18 People who make idols will be like them,
and so will those who trust them.

19 Family of Israel, praise the LORD.
Family of Aaron, praise the LORD.
20 Family of Levi, praise the LORD.
You who respect the LORD should praise
him.
21 You people of Jerusalem, praise the LORD
on Mount Zion.
Praise the LORD!

GOD'S LOVE CONTINUES FOREVER

136

1 Give thanks to the LORD because he is
good.
His love continues forever.
2 Give thanks to the God of gods.
His love continues forever.
3 Give thanks to the Lord of lords.
His love continues forever.

4 Only he can do great miracles.
His love continues forever.
5 With his wisdom he made the skies.
His love continues forever.
6 He spread out the earth on the seas.
His love continues forever.
7 He made the sun and the moon.
His love continues forever.
8 He made the sun to rule the day.
His love continues forever.
9 He made the moon and stars to rule the
night.
His love continues forever.

10 He killed the firstborn sons of the
Egyptians.
His love continues forever.
11 He brought the people of Israel out of
Egypt.

On the Edge

Give thanks to the LORD because he is good. His love continues forever (Ps. 136:1).

This whole chapter in Psalm 136 tells about God's enduring love. He loves us with a merciful, unconditional love. It doesn't matter what you look like, what your breath smells like, how much money you have, or what your past is like. God loves you anyway! Regardless of anything, God loves you just the same. That's the kind of love we need to have for each other. We need to look at the world through Jesus' eyes.

There's a story in Mark 2 about four men who brought a paralyzed man to Jesus for healing. There was not enough room for them, so they ripped a hole in the roof where Jesus was teaching and lowered the man down through the hole. Now that's compassion. When Jesus saw their faith, he healed the man.

These four men loved their friend with an unconditional love. They were willing to rip off a roof to get him healed. Even though they probably had needs themselves, the only thing they were concerned about was getting their friend to Jesus! Unconditional love.

Next time you've failed and feel like nobody cares, remember that God loves you unconditionally. Like those friends, he's willing to rip a roof off in order to show you the love and mercy you need.

SEE FOR YOURSELF:
John 14:21; Rom. 5:5; 1 John 4:10, 16

His love continues forever.
12 He did it with his great power and
strength.
His love continues forever.
13 He parted the water of the Red Sea.
His love continues forever.
14 He brought the Israelites through the
middle of it.
His love continues forever.
15 But the king of Egypt and his army
drowned in the Red Sea.
His love continues forever.

16 He led his people through the desert.
His love continues forever.

17 He defeated great kings.
His love continues forever.
18 He killed powerful kings.
His love continues forever.
19 He defeated Sihon king of the Amorites.
His love continues forever.
20 He defeated Og king of Bashan.
His love continues forever.
21 He gave their land as a gift.
His love continues forever.
22 It was a gift to his servants, the Israelites.
His love continues forever.

23 He remembered us when we were in trouble.
His love continues forever.
24 He freed us from our enemies.
His love continues forever.
25 He gives food to every living creature.
His love continues forever.

26 Give thanks to the God of heaven.
His love continues forever.

137

ISRAELITES IN CAPTIVITY

1 By the rivers in Babylon we sat and cried
when we remembered Jerusalem.
2 On the poplar trees nearby
we hung our harps.
3 Those who captured us asked us to sing;
our enemies wanted happy songs.
They said, "Sing us a song about Jerusalem!"

4 But we cannot sing songs about the LORD
while we are in this foreign country!
5 Jerusalem, if I forget you,
let my right hand lose its skill.
6 Let my tongue stick to the roof of my mouth
if I do not remember you,
if I do not think about Jerusalem
as my greatest joy.

7 LORD, remember what the Edomites did
on the day Jerusalem fell.
They said, "Tear it down!
Tear it down to its foundations!"

8 People of Babylon, you will be destroyed.
The people who pay you back for what you did to us will be happy.
9 They will grab your babies
and throw them against the rocks.

Promise HE PROMISES ALWAYS TO LOVE YOU.

LORD, you do everything for me. LORD, your love continues forever. Do not leave us, whom you made (Ps. 138:8).

Some people have this idea of God as the "Big Guy" sitting up in heaven with a giant paddle just waiting for someone to step out of line so he can use it. Well, it's obvious that God isn't pleased when you do something you know you shouldn't. But he's not the guy with the paddle. His discipline comes out of his love. Everything he does, even if it's not so pleasant to you at the time, has your best interest at heart.

Look at how Jesus talked to Martha when she complained to him about her sister: "Martha, Martha, you are worried and upset about many things. Only one thing is important. Mary has chosen the better thing, and it will never be taken away from her" (Luke 10:41–42). He didn't scream at her; he just gently pointed her in the right way. He treated Thomas the same way. When Thomas wouldn't believe that Jesus had risen from the dead until he saw and touched Jesus' wounded hands, Jesus didn't refuse to show him what he needed to see. He did say, "You believe because you see me. Those who believe without seeing me will be truly happy" (John 20:29).

You can count on God to treat you gently and mercifully, even when he's letting you know you're out of line.

SEE FOR YOURSELF:
2 Chr. 30:9; Lam. 3:22

A HYMN OF THANKSGIVING

A psalm of David.

138

1 LORD, I will thank you with all my heart;
I will sing to you before the gods.
2 I will bow down facing your
holy Temple,
and I will thank you
for your love and
loyalty.
You have made your
name and your word
greater than anything.
3 On the day I called to you,
you answered me.
You made me strong and brave.

THANKFULNESS

What should we be thankful for? (138:1–8)

4 LORD, let all the kings of the earth praise
you
when they hear the words you speak.
5 They will sing about what the LORD has
done,
because the LORD's glory is great.

6 Though the LORD is supreme,
he takes care of those who are humble,
but he stays away from the proud.
7 LORD, even when I have trouble all around
me,
you will keep me alive.
When my enemies are angry,
you will reach down and save me by
your power.
8 LORD, you do everything for me.
LORD, your love continues forever.
Do not leave us, whom you made.

GOD KNOWS EVERYTHING

For the director of music.
A psalm of David.

139

1 LORD, you have examined me
and know all about me.
2 You know when I sit down and when I
get up.
You know my thoughts before I think
them.
3 You know where I go and where I lie down.
You know thoroughly everything I do.
4 LORD, even before I say a word,
you already know it.
5 You are all around me—in front and in
back—
and have put your hand on me.
6 Your knowledge is amazing to me;
it is more than I can understand.
7 Where can I go to get away from your
Spirit?
Where can I run from you?
8 If I go up to the heavens, you are there.
If I lie down in the grave, you are there.
9 If I rise with the sun in the east
and settle in the west beyond the sea,
10 even there you would guide me.
With your right hand you would hold
me.

11 I could say, "The darkness will hide me.
Let the light around me turn into
night."
12 But even the darkness is not dark to you.
The night is as light as the day;
darkness and light are the same to you.

13 You made my whole being;
you formed me in my mother's body.

On the Edge

If I go up to the heavens, you are there. If I lie down in the grave, you are there (Ps. 139:8).

Do you ever wish you could hide from God? Maybe you really want to do something you know he wouldn't approve of. Is it easier to go against your conscience if you pretend that God doesn't know what you're up to?

But the truth is, you can't hide from God. When you run a red light, he's there. He's there when you sneak a look at someone else's paper during a test. If you stick out your tongue (or worse) behind the back of someone who made you mad, he sees it. If you talk bad about someone when they're not around, he hears you.

You can't even hide from God what's going on inside you. He's spirit, and he's everywhere—even inside your head and heart. He knows what you think and feel. He sees it when you're jealous or angry. He knows when you're lonely or sad. You can't get away from him. And once you realize what he's all about, how much he loves you, why would you want to? It's okay for him to see all about you. He knows you're not perfect, and he's working on you.

SEE FOR YOURSELF:
Jer. 23:23

[14]I praise you because you
made me in an
amazing and
wonderful way.
What you have done is
wonderful.
I know this very well.
[15]You saw my bones being
formed
as I took shape in my
mother's body.
When I was put together
there,
[16] you saw my body as it
was formed.
All the days planned for me
were written in your book
before I was one day old.

LIFE
Does God create each person carefully? (139:13–14)

ABORTION
Are children formed by chance? (139:13–16)

[17]God, your thoughts are precious to me.
They are so many!
[18]If I could count them,
they would be more than all the grains
of sand.
When I wake up,
I am still with you.

[19]God, I wish you would kill the wicked!
Get away from me, you murderers!
[20]They say evil things about you.
Your enemies use your name
thoughtlessly.
[21]LORD, I hate those who hate you;
I hate those who rise up against you.
[22]I feel only hate for them;
they are my enemies.

[23]God, examine me and know my heart;
test me and know my nervous
thoughts.
[24]See if there is any bad thing in me.
Lead me on the road to everlasting life.

On the Edge

You saw my bones being formed as I took shape in my mother's body. When I was put together there, you saw my body as it was formed. All the days planned for me were written in your book before I was one day old (Ps. 139:15–16).

Read all of Psalm 139 to find out how God knows you. Totally. There's nothing you can ever think or do that God doesn't know about. He even knows what you're going to do before you do it. That could be scary if you think of God as the "Man Upstairs" who's just sitting around waiting to catch you doing something wrong.

Relax. God isn't like that. Because you're one of his children, you can be glad that God knows you inside and out. He knows and appreciates what you're good at. He knows exactly what he's got planned for your life. He understands the things that are hard for you. He won't let you face a temptation that you can't stand up to. Since God knows you so completely, you don't ever have to be afraid to share your whole heart with him. He won't laugh at you or reject you. The fact that God knows you says a lot about his enormous mind and his limitless love. But it also says something about you. It says that you are so important that *God* spends his time thinking about you. He's in love with you!

SEE FOR YOURSELF: 1 Chr. 28:9; Job 23:9–10; Acts 15:8; Rom. 8:27

A PRAYER FOR PROTECTION

140

For the director of music.
A psalm of David.

[1]LORD, rescue me from evil people;
protect me from cruel people
[2]who make evil plans,
who always start fights.
[3]They make their tongues sharp as a
snake's;
their words are like snake poison. *Selah*

[4]LORD, guard me from the power of wicked
people;
protect me from cruel people
who plan to trip me up.
[5]The proud hid a trap for me.
They spread out a net beside the
road;
they set traps for me. *Selah*

[6]I said to the LORD, "You are my God."
LORD, listen to my prayer for help.
[7]LORD God, my mighty savior,
you protect me in battle.
[8]LORD, do not give the wicked what they
want.

Don't let their plans succeed,
or they will become proud. *Selah*

9 Those around me have planned trouble.
Now let it come to them.
10 Let burning coals fall on them.
Throw them into the fire
or into pits from which they cannot escape.
11 Don't let liars settle in the land.
Let evil quickly hunt down cruel people.

12 I know the LORD will get justice for the poor
and will defend the needy in court.
13 Good people will praise his name;
honest people will live in his presence.

A PRAYER NOT TO SIN

A psalm of David.

141

1 LORD, I call to you. Come quickly.
Listen to me when I call to you.
2 Let my prayer be like incense placed before you,
and my praise like the evening sacrifice.

3 LORD, help me control my tongue;
help me be careful about what I say.
4 Take away my desire to do evil
or to join others in doing wrong.
Don't let me eat tasty food
with those who do evil.

5 If a good person punished me, that would be kind.
If he corrected me, that would be like perfumed oil on my head.
I shouldn't refuse it.
But I pray against those who do evil.
6 Let their leaders be thrown down the cliffs.
Then people will know that I have spoken correctly:
7 "The ground is plowed and broken up.
In the same way, our bones have been scattered at the grave."

8 GOD, I look to you for help.
I trust in you, LORD. Don't let me die.
9 Protect me from the traps they set for me
and from the net that evil people have spread.
10 Let the wicked fall into their own nets,
but let me pass by safely.

A PRAYER FOR SAFETY

A maskil of David when he was in the cave. A prayer.

142

1 I cry out to the LORD;
I pray to the LORD for mercy.
2 I pour out my problems to him;
I tell him my troubles.
3 When I am afraid,
you, LORD, know the way out.
In the path where I walk,
a trap is hidden for me.
4 Look around me and see.
No one cares about me.
I have no place of safety;
no one cares if I live.

DISCOURAGEMENT

Who should we bring our complaints to? (142:1–7)

WHAT'S IT MEAN?

Apparently David wrote this psalm while he was on the run from the murderous King Saul. To escape Saul's jealous rage and mental instability, David spent some time hiding out in the cave of Adullam (or En Gedi). That may be the place where this psalm was written.

Psalm 142 title

5 LORD, I cry out to you.
I say, "You are my protection.
You are all I want in this life."
6 Listen to my cry,
because I am helpless.
Save me from those who are chasing me,
because they are too strong for me.
7 Free me from my prison,
and then I will praise your name.
Then good people will surround me,
because you have taken care of me.

A PRAYER NOT TO BE KILLED

A psalm of David.

143

1 LORD, hear my prayer;
listen to my cry for mercy.
Answer me
because you are loyal and good.

2 Don't judge me, your servant,
because no one alive is right before you.
3 My enemies are chasing me;
they crushed me to the ground.
They made me live in darkness
like those long dead.
4 I am afraid;
my courage is gone.

5 I remember what happened long ago;
I consider everything you have done.
I think about all you have made.
6 I lift my hands to you in prayer.
As a dry land needs rain, I thirst for
you. *Selah*

7 LORD, answer me quickly,
because I am getting weak.
Don't turn away from me,
or I will be like those who are dead.
8 Tell me in the morning about your love,
because I trust you.
Show me what I should do,
because my prayers go up to you.
9 LORD, save me from my enemies;
I hide in you.
10 Teach me to do what you want,
because you are my God.
Let your good Spirit
lead me on level ground.

11 LORD, let me live
so people will praise you.
In your goodness
save me from my troubles.
12 In your love defeat my enemies.
Destroy all those who trouble me,
because I am your servant.

A PRAYER FOR VICTORY

Of David.

144

1 Praise the LORD, my Rock,
who trains me for war,
who trains me for battle.
2 He protects me like a strong, walled city,
and he loves me.
He is my defender and my Savior,
my shield and my protection.
He helps me keep my people under
control.

3 LORD, why are people important to you?
Why do you even think about human
beings?

On the Edge

People are like a breath; their lives are like passing shadows (Ps. 144:4).

Sometimes on a cloudy day, there's a tiny break in the clouds that the sun tries to shine through. Just for a second you can see your shadow—just barely—on the sidewalk. When the clouds shift, your shadow disappears.

David said your life is like that shadow—it shows up for just a short moment, and then it's gone. It sure doesn't seem that way right now. Right now, it seems like your life stretches out forever in front of you. In a lot of ways, your life is just beginning. The important thing to do is to make the things you're doing count. The old saying "Time flies when you're having fun" is true. One day you'll wake up and wonder how you got so old. God gives you life one day at a time. When a day or a moment is gone, it's history. Pay attention to your life every day. Don't waste it by wanting to be older or smarter or better-looking. Make it count.

SEE FOR YOURSELF:
Job 14:12; Ps. 62:9; Eccl. 6:12

4 People are like a breath;
their lives are like passing shadows.

5 LORD, tear open the sky and come down.
Touch the mountains so they will
smoke.
6 Send the lightning and scatter my enemies.
Shoot your arrows and force them
away.
7 Reach down from above.
Save me and rescue me out of this sea
of enemies,
from these foreigners.
8 They are liars;
they are dishonest.

9 God, I will sing a new song to you;
I will play to you on the ten-stringed
harp.
10 You give victory to kings.
You save your servant David from cruel
swords.

11 Save me, rescue me from these foreigners.
They are liars; they are dishonest.

12 Let our sons in their youth
grow like plants.
Let our daughters be
like the decorated stones in the Temple.
13 Let our barns be filled
with crops of all kinds.
Let our sheep in the fields have
thousands and tens of thousands of
lambs.
14 Let our cattle be strong.
Let no one break in.
Let there be no war,
no screams in our streets.

15 Happy are those who are like this;
happy are the people whose God is the
LORD.

PRAISE TO GOD THE KING

A psalm of praise. Of David.

145

1 I praise your greatness, my God the King;
I will praise you forever and ever.
2 I will praise you every day;
I will praise you forever and ever.
3 The LORD is great and worthy of our
praise;
no one can understand how great he is.

WHAT'S IT MEAN?

This psalm was written as an acrostic. In its original Hebrew form, each of the psalm's sections begins with a corresponding letter of the Hebrew alphabet—from *aleph* to *tau.* (If it were written in English, the first line of the first section would begin with *A*, the second section would begin with *B*, and so on.)

Psalm 145:1

4 Parents will tell their children what you
have done.
They will retell your mighty acts,
5 wonderful majesty, and glory.
And I will think about your miracles.

On the Edge

The LORD is great and worthy of our praise; no one can understand how great he is (Ps. 145:3).

It seems the apostle Paul knew God better than anyone. But even he found God too awesome to imagine. "Yes, God's riches are very great, and his wisdom and knowledge have no end! No one can explain the things God decides or understand his ways," he wrote to the Romans (Rom. 11:33). In another letter he wrote, "Now we see a dim reflection, as if we were looking into a mirror, but then we shall see clearly. Now I know only a part, but then I will know fully, as God has known me" (1 Cor. 13:12).

Trying to understand God all at once is like trying to count the stars in the sky. It's just too big of a job. The more you learn of his power to create, to save, to change; the more you see of his forgiveness, his grace, his love; the more you understand of his incredible intelligence (after all, the principles of math and physics were all his ideas)—the more you realize that you have a long way to go. Knowing him is a journey that takes a lifetime. It's worth it.

SEE FOR YOURSELF:
2 Chr. 2:5; Job 33:12; John 14:28; 1 John 3:19–20

6 They will tell about the amazing things
you do,
and I will tell how great you are.
7 They will remember your great goodness
and will sing about your fairness.

8 The LORD is kind and shows mercy.
He does not become angry quickly but
is full of love.
9 The LORD is good to everyone;
he is merciful to all he has made.
10 LORD, everything you have made will
praise you;
those who belong to you will bless
you.
11 They will tell about the glory of your
kingdom
and will speak about your power.
12 Then everyone will know the mighty
things you do

and the glory and majesty of your
kingdom.
13 Your kingdom will go on and on,
and you will rule forever.

The LORD will keep all his promises;
he is loyal to all he has made.
14 The LORD helps those who have been
defeated
and takes care of those who are in
trouble.
15 All living things look to you for food,
and you give it to them at the right time.
16 You open your hand,
and you satisfy all living things.

17 Everything the LORD does is right.
He is loyal to all he has made.
18 The LORD is close to everyone who prays
to him,
to all who truly pray to him.
19 He gives those who respect him what they
want.
He listens when they cry, and he saves
them.
20 The LORD protects everyone who loves
him,
but he will destroy the wicked.

21 I will praise the LORD.
Let everyone praise his holy name
forever.

PRAISE GOD WHO HELPS THE WEAK

146

1 Praise the LORD!

My whole being, praise the LORD.
2 I will praise the LORD all my life;
I will sing praises to my God as long as
I live.

3 Do not put your trust in princes
or other people, who cannot save you.
4 When people die, they are buried.
Then all of their plans come to an end.
5 Happy are those who are helped by the
God of Jacob.
Their hope is in the LORD their God.
6 He made heaven and earth,
the sea and everything in it.
He remains loyal forever.
7 He does what is fair for those who have
been wronged.
He gives food to the hungry.
The LORD sets the prisoners free.
8 The LORD gives sight to the blind.
The LORD lifts up people who are in
trouble.
The LORD loves those who do right.
9 The LORD protects the foreigners.
He defends the orphans and widows,
but he blocks the way of the wicked.

10 The LORD will be King forever.
Jerusalem, your God is everlasting.

Praise the LORD!

PRAISE GOD WHO HELPS HIS PEOPLE

147

1 Praise the LORD!

It is good to sing praises to our God;
it is good and pleasant to praise him.
2 The LORD rebuilds Jerusalem;
he brings back the captured Israelites.
3 He heals the brokenhearted
and bandages their wounds.

4 He counts the stars
and names each one.
5 Our Lord is great and very powerful.
There is no limit to what he knows.
6 The LORD defends the humble,

On the Edge

Our Lord is great and very powerful. There is no limit to what he knows (Ps. 147:5).

What tests your limits of understanding? Advanced calculus? Some basketball star's gravity-defying slam dunks? Italian opera? The creation of the world in six days? At some point, we just don't get it. It's beyond us. We can't get our arms around it. Our brain won't process any more. Our capacity to understand is limited, but God understands everything. Sometimes we don't even understand why we do things. But God does. He has infinite understanding. He sees into our souls very clearly. So when you're feeling confused and the way seems fuzzy, turn to the One who understands everything infinitely. He gives flawless directions, and his advice is perfect.

SEE FOR YOURSELF: **Ps. 139; Heb. 4:13; 1 John 3:19–20**

but he throws the wicked to the
ground.

7 Sing praises to the LORD;
praise our God with harps.
8 He fills the sky with clouds
and sends rain to the earth
and makes grass grow on the hills.
9 He gives food to cattle
and to the little birds that call.

10 He does not enjoy the strength of a horse
or the strength of a man.
11 The LORD is pleased with those who
respect him,
with those who trust his love.

12 Jerusalem, praise the LORD;
Jerusalem, praise your God.
13 He makes your city gates strong
and blesses your children inside.
14 He brings peace to your country
and fills you with the finest grain.

15 He gives a command to the earth,
and it quickly obeys him.
16 He spreads the snow like wool
and scatters the frost like ashes.
17 He throws down hail like rocks.
No one can stand the cold he sends.
18 Then he gives a command, and it melts.
He sends the breezes, and the waters
flow.

19 He gave his word to Jacob,
his laws and demands to Israel.
20 He didn't do this for any other nation.
They don't know his laws.

Praise the LORD!

THE WORLD SHOULD PRAISE THE LORD

148

1 Praise the LORD!

Praise the LORD from the
skies.
Praise him high above
the earth.
2 Praise him, all you angels.
Praise him, all you armies
of heaven.
3 Praise him, sun and moon.
Praise him, all you shining stars.
4 Praise him, highest heavens
and you waters above the sky.
5 Let them praise the LORD,
because they were created by his
command.
6 He put them in place forever and ever;
he made a law that will never change.

> **ANGELS**
> Who do angels praise? (148:1–2)

7 Praise the LORD from the earth,
you large sea animals and all the oceans,
8 lightning and hail, snow and mist,
and stormy winds that obey him,
9 mountains and all hills,
fruit trees and all cedars,
10 wild animals and all cattle,
crawling animals and birds,
11 kings of the earth and all nations,
princes and all rulers of the earth,
12 young men and women,
old people and children.

13 Praise the LORD,
because he alone is great.
He is more wonderful than heaven and
earth.
14 God has given his people a king.
He should be praised by all who belong
to him;
he should be praised by the Israelites,
the people closest to his heart.

Praise the LORD!

PRAISE THE GOD OF ISRAEL

149

1 Praise the LORD!

Sing a new song to the LORD;
sing his praise in the meeting of his
people.

2 Let the Israelites be happy because of God,
their Maker.
Let the people of Jerusalem rejoice
because of their King.
3 They should praise him with dancing.
They should sing praises to him with
tambourines and harps.
4 The LORD is pleased with his people;
he saves the humble.
5 Let those who worship him rejoice in his
glory.
Let them sing for joy even in bed!

6 Let them shout his praise
with their two-edged swords in their
hands.
7 They will punish the nations
and defeat the people.
8 They will put those kings in chains

and those important men in iron bands.
9 They will punish them as God has written.
God is honored by all who worship him.

Praise the LORD!

WHAT'S IT MEAN?

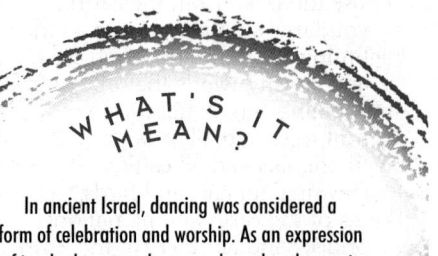

In ancient Israel, dancing was considered a form of celebration and worship. As an expression of joy, both men and women danced to the music of tambourines and stringed instruments.
Psalm 149:3

PRAISE THE LORD WITH MUSIC

150

1 Praise the LORD!

Praise God in his Temple;
praise him in his mighty heaven.
2 Praise him for his strength;
praise him for his greatness.
3 Praise him with trumpet blasts;
praise him with harps and lyres.
4 Praise him with tambourines and dancing;
praise him with stringed instruments
and flutes.
5 Praise him with loud cymbals;
praise him with crashing cymbals.
6 Let everything that breathes praise the
LORD.

Praise the LORD!

proverbs

CONTENT It seems like everyone speaks a proverb at some time in their lives: "Don't count your chickens before they're hatched." "Look before you leap." "Give him an inch and he'll take a mile." Proverbs are colorful ways to say something wise. They are little pieces of truth wrapped up in something sweet so we can swallow them more easily.

The problem with human proverbs is that they often contradict:

"Look before you leap" (be cautious), but "he who hesitates is lost" (don't be too cautious).

"Absence makes the heart grow fonder" (your sweetie will like you *more* after summer break), but "out of sight, out of mind" (your sweetie won't like you at all after summer break).

The Book of Proverbs is different in that it is *God's* wisdom. Some of Proverbs is lighthearted. Some is even downright funny. Don't be fooled, though. It is God's truth.

Reading Proverbs is like sitting on the porch of heaven and listening to the wisest, most famous of the saints telling us what they have learned about life. Better than that, though, the proverbs are like God himself giving us everyday advice about everyday situations.

Outline

1:1–7 .... Introduction: How Proverbs Can Be Used
1:8—7:27 .... Parental Advice on the Importance of Seeking Wisdom and Not Being Foolish
8:1–36 .... In Praise of Wisdom
9:1–18 .... Wisdom's Invitation to Feast
10:1—24:34 .... Solomon's Wise Sayings
25:1—29:27 .... More Wise Sayings of Solomon
30:1–33 .... Wise Words from Agur
31:1–31 .... The Words King Lemuel's Mother Taught Him

Purpose The wise person makes choices that are both godly and practical.

Theme Universal Principles for Living

Date of writing 950–700 B.C.

"Trust the LORD with all your heart, and don't depend on your own understanding. Remember the LORD in all you do, and he will give you success" (3:5–6).

Bible Talk

A Proverb a Day Keeps the* What *Away?

Here's a thought. There are thirty-one chapters in Proverbs. There are thirty or thirty-one days in most months. If you want a new Bible reading plan, just read a chapter of Proverbs every day. You don't have to worry about losing your place or remembering where you are. Just look at the date!

The great thing about reading in Proverbs is the variety. Each time you read a chapter, something different can jump right off the page and tap you on the shoulder.

A chapter in Proverbs every day may not keep the doctor away, or be worth two chapters in the bush, but it will remind you that God calls us to choose wisdom over foolishness and it takes his help to do it.

PRACTICAL DIRECTION FROM GOD

Sometimes the Bible gets the reputation for not being practical . . . particularly by people who never read it. For so long, the only Bible we had to read in English was a Bible that used old English and so was hard for some to understand.

But whether the Bible is written in modern English, old English, or not English at all, the truth is that the Bible was written by God. He wrote it through the minds and experiences of real people who faced life just like we do—by faith.

Proverbs is a great example of how practical the Bible is. A whole book on making good choices—not being lazy, loving your parents, being a good friend. This is real-life stuff. This is the stuff we care about. This is the stuff that God helps us with.

THE IMPORTANCE OF PROVERBS

1 1 These are the wise words of Solomon son of David, king of Israel.

2 They teach wisdom and self-control;
they will help you understand wise words.
3 They will teach you how to be wise and self-controlled
and will teach you to do what is honest and fair and right.
4 They make the uneducated smarter
and give knowledge and sense to the young.
5 Wise people can also listen and learn;
even smart people can find good advice in these words.
6 Then anyone can understand wise words and stories,
the words of the wise and their riddles.

EDUCATION

How can wise people increase their education? (1:5)

WHAT'S IT MEAN?

Solomon was a young guy, perhaps no more than twenty years old, when he became the third king of Israel. During his forty-year reign, from about 970 to 930 B.C., Solomon became so famous for his wisdom that people from other nations traveled to Jerusalem just to hear him speak.

Proverbs 1:1

7 Knowledge begins with respect for the LORD,
but fools hate wisdom and self-control.

WARNINGS AGAINST EVIL

8 My child, listen to your father's teaching
and do not forget your mother's advice.
9 Their teaching will be like flowers in your hair
or a necklace around your neck.

10 My child, if sinners try to lead you into sin,
do not follow them.
11 They will say, "Come with us.
Let's ambush and kill someone;
let's attack some innocent people just for fun.
12 Let's swallow them alive, as death does;
let's swallow them whole, as the grave does.
13 We will take all kinds of valuable things
and fill our houses with stolen goods.
14 Come join us,
and we will share with you stolen goods."
15 My child, do not go along with them;
do not do what they do.
16 They are eager to do evil
and are quick to kill.
17 It is useless to spread out a net
right where the birds can see it.
18 But sinners will fall into their own traps;
they will only catch themselves!
19 All greedy people end up this way;
greed kills selfish people.

WISDOM SPEAKS

20 Wisdom is like a woman shouting in the street;
she raises her voice in the city squares.
21 She cries out in the noisy street
and shouts at the city gates:
22 "You fools, how long will you be foolish?
How long will you make fun of wisdom
and hate knowledge?
23 If only you had listened when I corrected you,
I would have told you what's in my heart;
I would have told you what I am thinking.
24 I called, but you refused to listen;
I held out my hand, but you paid no attention.
25 You did not follow my advice
and did not listen when I corrected you.
26 So I will laugh when you are in trouble.
I will make fun when disaster strikes you,
27 when disaster comes over you like a storm,
when trouble strikes you like a whirlwind,
when pain and trouble overwhelm you.

28 "Then you will call to me,
but I will not answer.
You will look for me,
but you will not find me.
29 It is because you rejected knowledge
and did not choose to respect the LORD.
30 You did not accept my advice,

and you rejected my correction.
[31] So you will get what you deserve;
you will get what you planned for others.
[32] Fools will die because they refuse to listen;
they will be destroyed because they do not care.
[33] But those who listen to me will live in safety
and be at peace, without fear of injury."

REWARDS OF WISDOM

2

[1] My child, listen to what I say
and remember what I command you.
[2] Listen carefully to wisdom;
set your mind on understanding.
[3] Cry out for wisdom,
and beg for understanding.
[4] Search for it like silver,
and hunt for it like hidden treasure.
[5] Then you will understand respect for the LORD,
and you will find that you know God.
[6] Only the LORD gives wisdom;
he gives knowledge and understanding.
[7] He stores up wisdom for those who are honest.
Like a shield he protects the innocent.
[8] He makes sure that justice is done,
and he protects those who are loyal to him.
[9] Then you will understand what is honest and fair
and what is the good and right thing to do.
[10] Wisdom will come into your mind,
and knowledge will be pleasing to you.
[11] Good sense will protect you;
understanding will guard you.
[12] It will keep you from the wicked,
from those whose words are bad,
[13] who don't do what is right
but what is evil.
[14] They enjoy doing wrong
and are happy to do what is crooked and evil.
[15] What they do is wrong,
and their ways are dishonest.

[16] It will save you from the unfaithful wife
who tries to lead you into adultery with pleasing words.
[17] She leaves the husband she married when she was young.
She ignores the promise she made before God.
[18] Her house is on the way to death;
those who took that path are now all dead.

TEMPTATION

How do we guard against temptation? (2:10–14)

Promise

HE PROMISES TO GIVE YOU HELPFUL WISDOM AND UNDERSTANDING.

Only the LORD gives wisdom; he gives knowledge and understanding. He stores up wisdom for those who are honest. Like a shield he protects the innocent (Prov. 2:6–7).

Has anyone ever given you bad advice? Maybe they told you to take psychology because it was a breeze and then the year you take it, a new teacher makes it the hardest class in school. Maybe someone gave you some bad directions that told you to turn left instead of right. Forty miles later, when you run out of civilization, you realize that you've probably gone the wrong way. Bad advice—when you lack the wisdom to know the advice is bad—can ruin a day, a year, or an entire life.

God promises to give you wisdom and common sense. He says that you just have to search for him, take time to ask him, obey him, and he will be faithful to give you the help you need. He is the Source of all that is wise and helpful. He waits patiently for you to stop fumbling around and ask him for his helpful advice.

SEE FOR YOURSELF:

Mic. 7:7; Luke 11:10; 2 Thess. 3:3; James 1:5

WHAT'S IT MEAN?

Ancient Israelites believed that when people died, their souls went to a dark underground region called Sheol. Though Sheol was not what we would call hell, it wasn't exactly a day in the park, either. The souls that existed in this world of the dead could not eat, drink, work, worship, or experience joy like they could when they were alive.

Proverbs 2:18

19 No one who goes to her comes back
or walks the path of life again.

20 But wisdom will help you be good
and do what is right.
21 Those who are honest will live in the land,
and those who are innocent will remain in it.
22 But the wicked will be removed from the land,
and the unfaithful will be thrown out of it.

ADVICE TO CHILDREN

3 1 My child, do not forget my teaching,
but keep my commands in mind.
2 Then you will live a long time,
and your life will be successful.

3 Don't ever forget kindness and truth.
Wear them like a necklace.
Write them on your heart as if on a tablet.
4 Then you will be respected
and will please both God and people.

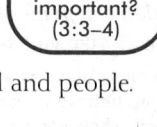

MERCY
Why is kindness (mercy) important? (3:3–4)

5 Trust the LORD with all your heart,
and don't depend on your own understanding.
6 Remember the LORD in all you do,
and he will give you success.

TRUST
How are we to trust God? (3:5–6)

7 Don't depend on your own wisdom.
Respect the LORD and refuse to do wrong.
8 Then your body will be healthy,
and your bones will be strong.

9 Honor the LORD with your wealth
and the firstfruits from all your crops.
10 Then your barns will be full,
and your wine barrels will overflow with new wine.

11 My child, do not reject the LORD's discipline,

On the Edge

My child, do not forget my teaching, but keep my commands in mind. Then you will live a long time, and your life will be successful. Don't ever forget kindness and truth. Wear them like a necklace. Write them on your heart as if on a tablet. Then you will be respected and will please both God and people (Prov. 3:1–4).

Good people usually make good friends, but one trait that sticks out in great friendships is loyalty. People get to the end of their lives and look back at the friends they've had. The ones they treasure are the ones who have stuck by them all the way. Being a loyal friend can be hard work. It means that you're committed even when it's tough. You look past the little things. You forgive and forgive and forgive. You go the extra mile.

Being interruptible is part of being loyal. Good friends are the ones you can call in the middle of the night, the ones who will come pick you up when your car dies, and the ones who would drop everything and rush right over if you needed them. Being loyal means that you keep quiet when others want to gossip, and you defend your friend's honor and integrity. If you choose your friends wisely, being loyal to them will be easy, and your loyalty will be returned. According to Proverbs 3, people will see your loyalty and admire you for it.

SEE FOR YOURSELF:
Prov. 17:17; 18:24; 27:5

WHAT'S IT MEAN?

Here's how tithing worked in ancient times: The Israelites were commanded to give ten percent of everything they had—including crops, livestock, and money—to God. The Israelites gave their tithes to the Levites, the people who worked in the Temple. The Levites, in turn, gave ten percent of everything they received to the priests. The priests offered a sacrifice to the Lord for their tithe. Tithing is a way for people to acknowledge that everything they receive comes from and belongs to God.

Proverbs 3:9

and don't get angry when
he corrects you.
12 The LORD corrects those
he loves,
just as parents correct
the child they
delight in.

13 Happy is the person who
finds wisdom,
the one who gets
understanding.
14 Wisdom is worth more than silver;
it brings more profit than gold.
15 Wisdom is more precious than rubies;
nothing you could want is equal to it.
16 With her right hand wisdom offers you a
long life,
and with her left hand she gives you
riches and honor.
17 Wisdom will make your life pleasant
and will bring you peace.
18 As a tree produces fruit, wisdom gives life
to those who use it,
and everyone who uses it will be happy.

19 The LORD made the earth, using his
wisdom.
He set the sky in place, using his
understanding.
20 With his knowledge, he made springs flow
into rivers
and the clouds drop rain on the earth.

"The LORD made the earth, using his wisdom. He set the sky in place, using his understanding." (Proverbs 3:19)

21 My child, hold on to
wisdom and good
sense.
Don't let them out of
your sight.
22 They will give you life
and beauty like a
necklace around your
neck.
23 Then you will go your
way in safety,
and you will not get
hurt.
24 When you lie down, you won't be afraid;

Promise

HE PROMISES TO GIVE YOU A STRAIGHT, SMOOTH PATH.

Trust the LORD with all your heart, and don't depend on your own understanding. Remember the LORD in all you do, and he will give you success (Prov. 3:5–6).

In this passage, "give you success" is literally "give you a straight, smooth path." If you trust in the Lord with all your heart—not just saying you believe in him, but really living a godly life—then he promises to do two things. First, he will show you what you are supposed to do with your life, what turns to make, when to stop, when to go. He promises to give clear directions to people who are seeking and trusting him. Second, he will clear the path of obstacles, making it smooth for you. So, not only will he show you the way to walk, but he also promises to go before you and clear away the things that could trip you up. He will fill up the holes you could fall into. He will straighten the road so the walk is easier. He will make the journey more enjoyable for those who trust in him.

SEE FOR YOURSELF:
John 16:13; 2 Cor. 2:14; Rev. 7:17

when you lie down, you will sleep in peace.
25 You won't be afraid of sudden trouble;
you won't fear the ruin that comes to the wicked,
26 because the LORD will keep you safe.
He will keep you from being trapped.

27 Whenever you are able,
do good to people who need help.
28 If you have what your neighbor asks for,
don't say, "Come back later.
I will give it to you tomorrow."
29 Don't make plans to hurt your neighbor
who lives nearby and trusts you.
30 Don't accuse a person for no good reason;
don't accuse someone who has not harmed you.

31 Don't be jealous of those who use violence,
and don't choose to be like them.
32 The LORD hates those who do wrong,
but he is a friend to those who are honest.
33 The LORD will curse the evil person's house,
but he will bless the home of those who do right.
34 The LORD laughs at those who laugh at him,
but he gives grace to those who are not proud.
35 Wise people will receive honor,
but fools will be disgraced.

WISDOM IS IMPORTANT

4

1 My children, listen to your father's teaching;
pay attention so you will understand.
2 What I am telling you is good,
so do not forget what I teach you.
3 When I was a young boy in my father's house
and like an only child to my mother,
4 my father taught me and said,
"Hold on to my words with all your heart.
Keep my commands and you will live.
5 Get wisdom and understanding.
Don't forget or ignore my words.
6 Hold on to wisdom, and it will take care of you.
Love it, and it will keep you safe.
7 Wisdom is the most important thing; so get wisdom.
If it costs everything you have, get understanding.
8 Treasure wisdom, and it will make you great;
hold on to it, and it will bring you honor.
9 It will be like flowers in your hair
and like a beautiful crown on your head."

10 My child, listen and accept what I say.
Then you will have a long life.
11 I am guiding you in the way of wisdom,
and I am leading you on the right path.
12 Nothing will hold you back;
you will not be overwhelmed.
13 Always remember what you have been taught,
and don't let go of it.
Keep all that you have learned;
it is the most important thing in life.

DISCIPLINE

Why is instruction or discipline important to me? (4:13)

14 Don't follow the ways of the wicked;
don't do what evil people do.
15 Avoid their ways, and don't follow them.
Stay away from them and keep on going,
16 because they cannot sleep until they do evil.
They cannot rest until they harm someone.
17 They feast on wickedness and cruelty
as if they were eating bread and drinking wine.

18 The way of the good person is like the light of dawn,
growing brighter and brighter until full daylight.
19 But the wicked walk around in the dark;
they can't even see what makes them stumble.

20 My child, pay attention to my words;
listen closely to what I say.
21 Don't ever forget my words;
keep them always in mind.
22 They are the key to life for those who find them;
they bring health to the whole body.
23 Be careful what you think,
because your thoughts run your life.
24 Don't use your mouth to tell lies;
don't ever say things that are not true.
25 Keep your eyes focused on what is right,

On the Edge

The way of the good person is like the light of dawn, growing brighter and brighter until full daylight (Prov. 4:18).

A match is struck inside the heart of each believer at the very moment he or she decides to trust in Jesus Christ as the One who delivers him or her from sin. For some, the flame burns dimly for a while. And for others, it's the match that sets the forest on fire. As you begin to learn more about the Lord—his forgiveness and grace—the flame begins to burn brighter. At some point you decide to begin living what you believe—giving forgiveness and grace to others. The flame burns brighter still. You grow in knowledge and in truth. You begin to understand why they call grace amazing. Then one day you realize that you look more like Jesus today than you did this time last year. You decide that that's a great goal—each year looking more like Jesus than you ever have before. The fire has become a blaze, and your lifestyle keeps getting brighter and brighter.

SEE FOR YOURSELF:
Judg. 5:31; Dan. 12:3; Luke 11:36

and look straight ahead to what
is good.
26 Be careful what you do,
and always do what is
right.
27 Don't turn off the road of
goodness;
keep away from evil
paths.

GOSSIP
How should we resist gossip? (4:24–27)

WARNING ABOUT ADULTERY

5

1 My son, pay attention to my wisdom;
listen to my words of understanding.
2 Be careful to use good sense,
and watch what you say.
3 The words of another man's wife may
seem sweet as honey;
they may be as smooth as olive oil.
4 But in the end she will bring you sorrow,
causing you pain like a two-edged
sword.
5 She is on the way to death;
her steps are headed straight to the
grave.
6 She gives little thought to life.
She doesn't even know that her ways
are wrong.

7 Now, my sons, listen to me,
and don't ignore what I say.
8 Stay away from such a woman.
Don't even go near the door of her
house,
9 or you will give your riches to others,
and the best years of your life will be
given to someone cruel.
10 Strangers will enjoy your wealth,
and what you worked so hard for will
go to someone else.
11 You will groan at the end of your life
when your health is gone.
12 Then you will say, "I hated being told
what to do!
I would not listen to correction!
13 I would not listen to my teachers
or pay attention to my instructors.
14 I came close to being completely ruined
in front of a whole group of people."

15 Be faithful to your own wife,
just as you drink water from your own
well.
16 Don't pour your water in the streets;
don't give your love to just any
woman.
17 These things are yours alone
and shouldn't be shared with
strangers.
18 Be happy with the wife you married when
you were young.
She gives you joy, as your fountain
gives you water.
19 She is as lovely and graceful as a deer.
Let her love always make you happy;
let her love always hold you captive.
20 My son, don't be held captive by a
woman who takes part in adultery.
Don't hug another man's wife.

21 The LORD sees everything you do,
and he watches where you go.
22 An evil man will be caught in his wicked
ways;
the ropes of his sins will tie him up.
23 He will die because he does not control
himself,
and he will be held captive by his
foolishness.

DANGERS OF BEING FOOLISH

6
1 My child, be careful about giving a
guarantee for somebody else's loan,
about promising to pay what someone
else owes.
2 You might get trapped by what you say;
you might be caught by your own
words.
3 My child, if you have done this and are
under your neighbor's control,
here is how to get free.
Don't be proud. Go to your neighbor
and beg to be free from your promise.
4 Don't go to sleep
or even rest your eyes,
5 but free yourself like a deer running from
a hunter,
like a bird flying away from a trapper.

WHAT'S IT MEAN?

Here's something you probably didn't know: There are more than one hundred types of ants in Palestine. The type the author singles out in this passage is the harvester ant. Harvester ants build their nests near fields or places where grain is separated from chaff. The ants collect fallen grain one seed at a time, carrying it back to their nest and storing it for cold weather.

Proverbs 6:6

6 Go watch the ants, you lazy person.
Watch what they do and be wise.
7 Ants have no commander,
no leader or ruler,
8 but they store up food in the summer
and gather their supplies at harvest.
9 How long will you lie there, you lazy
person?
When will you get up from sleeping?
10 You sleep a little; you take a nap.
You fold your hands and lie down to
rest.
11 So you will be as poor as if you had been
robbed;
you will have as little as if you had been
held up.

12 Some people are wicked and no good.
They go around telling lies,
13 winking with their eyes, tapping with their
feet,
and making signs with their fingers.
14 They make evil plans in their hearts
and are always starting arguments.
15 So trouble will strike them in an instant;
suddenly they will be so hurt no one
can help them.

16 There are six things the
LORD hates.
There are seven things
he cannot stand:
17 a proud look,
a lying tongue,
hands that kill
innocent people,
18 a mind that thinks up evil plans,
feet that are quick to do evil,
19 a witness who lies,
and someone who starts arguments
among families.

MURDER

How does the Lord feel about murder? (6:16–19)

WARNING ABOUT ADULTERY

20 My son, keep your father's
commands,
and don't forget your
mother's teaching.
21 Keep their words in mind
forever
as though you had
them tied around
your neck.
22 They will guide you when
you walk.
They will guard you when you sleep.
They will speak to you when you are
awake.
23 These commands are like a lamp;
this teaching is like a light.
And the correction that comes from them
will help you have life.
24 They will keep you from sinful women
and from the pleasing words of another
man's unfaithful wife.
25 Don't desire her because she is beautiful.
Don't let her capture you by the way
she looks at you.
26 A prostitute will treat you like a loaf of
bread,
and a woman who takes part in
adultery may cost you your life.
27 You cannot carry hot coals against your
chest
without burning your clothes,
28 and you cannot walk on hot coals
without burning your feet.

DISCIPLINE

How will listening to instruction benefit me? (6:20–23)

On the Edge

My son, keep your father's commands, and don't forget your mother's teaching (Prov. 6:20).

In the military, new recruits are taught that above everything else they must respect their commanders. They may disagree with their decisions or their lifestyles, but they are required to respect their positions of leadership. In much the same way, God requires that you respect your parents. He chose them to lead your family and to train you. In his wisdom, he made a perfect decision. Even when you disagree with your parents, you are called to respect them just because they are your mom and dad. Respect means that you obey their instruction—let it guide you and protect you. God influences your life directly through the leadership of your parents. It's the way he set things in order. It's the design that works best. It glorifies God when you respect your parents.

SEE FOR YOURSELF:
Matt. 15:4;
Eph. 6:1–3

29 The same is true if you have sexual
relations with another man's wife.
Anyone who does so will be punished.

30 People don't hate a thief
when he steals because he is hungry.
31 But if he is caught, he must pay back
seven times what he stole,
and it may cost him everything he
owns.
32 A man who takes part in adultery has no
sense;
he will destroy himself.
33 He will be beaten up and disgraced,
and his shame will never go away.
34 Jealousy makes a husband very angry,
and he will have no pity when he gets
revenge.
35 He will accept no payment for the wrong;
he will take no amount of money.

THE WOMAN OF ADULTERY

7

1 My son, remember what I say, and
treasure my commands.
2 Obey my commands, and you will live.
Guard my teachings as you would your
own eyes.
3 Remind yourself of them;
write them on your heart as if on a
tablet.
4 Treat wisdom as a sister,
and make understanding your closest
friend.
5 Wisdom and understanding will keep you
away from adultery,
away from the unfaithful wife and her
pleasing words.

6 Once while I was at the window of my
house
I looked out through the shutters
7 and saw some foolish, young men.
I noticed one of them had no wisdom.
8 He was walking down the street near the
corner
on the road leading to her house.
9 It was the twilight of the evening;
the darkness of the night was just
beginning.
10 Then the woman approached him,
dressed like a prostitute
and planning to trick him.
11 She was loud and stubborn
and never stayed at home.
12 She was always out in the streets or in the
city squares,
waiting around on the corners of the
streets.
13 She grabbed him and kissed him.
Without shame she said to him,

WHAT'S IT MEAN?

According to God's Law, after the priest had taken his portion of a fellowship offering, the person who offered the sacrifice was given the rest of the meat to take home. The only stipulation was that it all had to be eaten within two days. That meant the person usually ended up inviting his friends and neighbors over to help him finish the sacrificial food. Since meat wasn't served very often in ancient times, these post-sacrifice meals usually turned into festive events—celebrations of God's forgiveness.

Proverbs 7:14

14 "I made my fellowship offering and took
some of the meat home.
Today I have kept my special promises.
15 So I have come out to meet you;
I have been looking for you and have
found you.
16 I have covered my bed
with colored sheets from Egypt.
17 I have made my bed smell sweet
with myrrh, aloes, and cinnamon.
18 Come, let's make love until morning.
Let's enjoy each other's love.
19 My husband is not home;
he has gone on a long trip.
20 He took a lot of money with him
and won't be home for weeks."
21 By her clever words she made him give in;
by her pleasing words she led him into
doing wrong.
22 All at once he followed her,
like an ox led to the butcher,
like a deer caught in a trap
23 and shot through the liver with an
arrow.
Like a bird caught in a trap,
he didn't know what he did would kill
him.

24 Now, my sons, listen to me;
pay attention to what I say.
25 Don't let yourself be tricked by such a
woman;
don't go where she leads you.
26 She has ruined many good men,
and many have died because of her.
27 Her house is on the road to death,
the road that leads down to the grave.

LISTEN TO WISDOM

8 1 Wisdom calls to you like someone
shouting;
understanding raises her voice.
2 On the hilltops along the road
and at the crossroads, she stands calling.
3 Beside the city gates,
at the entrances into the city, she calls
out:
4 "Listen, everyone, I'm calling out to you;
I am shouting to all people.
5 You who are uneducated, be smarter.
You who are foolish, get understanding.
6 Listen, because I have important things to
say,
and what I tell you is right.
7 What I say is true,
I refuse to speak evil.
8 Everything I say is honest;
nothing I say is crooked or false.
9 People with good sense know what I say
is true;
and those with knowledge know my
words are right.
10 Choose my teachings instead of silver,
and knowledge rather than the finest
gold.
11 Wisdom is more precious than rubies.
Nothing you could want is equal to it.

12 "I am wisdom, and I am smart.
I also have knowledge and
good sense.
13 If you respect the LORD,
you will also hate
evil.
I hate pride and
bragging,
evil ways and lies.

WISDOM
What comes with wisdom? (8:12–14)

14 I have good sense and advice,
and I have understanding and power.
15 I help kings to govern
and rulers to make fair laws.
16 Princes use me to lead,
and so do all important people who
judge fairly.
17 I love those who love me,
and those who seek me find me.
18 Riches and honor are mine to give.
So are wealth and lasting success.
19 What I give is better than the finest gold,
better than the purest silver.
20 I do what is right
and follow the path of justice.
21 I give wealth to those who love me,
filling their houses with treasures.

22 "I, wisdom, was with the LORD when he
began his work,
long before he made anything else.
23 I was created in the very beginning,
even before the world began.
24 I was born before there were oceans,
or springs overflowing with water,
25 before the hills were there,
before the mountains were put in place.
26 God had not made the earth or fields,
not even the first dust of the earth.
27 I was there when God put the skies in
place,
when he stretched the horizon over the
oceans,
28 when he made the clouds above
and put the deep underground springs
in place.
29 I was there when he ordered the sea

not to go beyond the borders he had
set.
I was there when he laid the earth's
foundation.
30 I was like a child by his side.
I was delighted every day,
enjoying his presence all the time,
31 enjoying the whole world,
and delighted with all its people.

32 "Now, my children, listen to me,
because those who follow my ways are
happy.
33 Listen to my teaching, and you will be
wise;
do not ignore it.
34 Happy are those who listen to me,
watching at my door every day,
waiting at my open doorway.
35 Those who find me find life,
and the LORD will be pleased with them.
36 Those who do not find me hurt
themselves.
Those who hate me love death."

BEING WISE OR FOOLISH

9

1 Wisdom has built her house;
she has made its seven columns.
2 She has prepared her food
and wine;
she has set her table.
3 She has sent out her
servant girls,
and she calls out
from the highest
place in the city.
4 She says to those who
are uneducated,
"Come in here, you
foolish people!
5 Come and eat my food
and drink the wine I have prepared.
6 Stop your foolish ways, and you will live;
take the road of understanding.

7 "If you correct someone who makes fun of
wisdom, you will be insulted.
If you correct an evil person, you will
get hurt.
8 Do not correct those who make fun of
wisdom, or they will hate you.
But correct the wise, and they will love
you.
9 Teach the wise, and they will become even
wiser;
teach good people, and they will learn
even more.

WHAT'S IT MEAN?

Seven was a very important number to the ancient Israelites, who believed the numeral represented holiness or perfection. The number's history can be traced all the way back to Creation, when God worked six days and rested on the seventh. The number seven pops up throughout the Bible in dreams, visions, and rituals.

Proverbs 9:1

10 "Wisdom begins with respect for the LORD,
and understanding begins with knowing
the Holy One.
11 If you live wisely, you will live a long time;
wisdom will add years to your life.
12 The wise person is rewarded by wisdom,
but whoever makes fun of wisdom will
suffer for it."

"Wisdom begins with respect for the LORD, and understanding begins with knowing the Holy One." (Proverbs 9:10)

13 Foolishness is like a loud
woman;
she does not have
wisdom or
knowledge.
14 She sits at the door of her
house
at the highest place in
the city.
15 She calls out to those who
are passing by,
who are going along,
minding their own
business.
16 She says to those who are uneducated,
"Come in here, you foolish people!
17 Stolen water is sweeter,
and food eaten in secret tastes better."
18 But these people don't know that everyone
who goes there dies,
that her guests end up deep in the grave.

THE WISE WORDS OF SOLOMON

10

1 These are the wise words of Solomon:
A wise son makes his father happy,
but a foolish son makes his mother sad.

2 Riches gotten by doing wrong have no
value,

On the Edge

"Wisdom begins with respect for the Lord, and understanding begins with knowing the Holy One" (Prov. 9:10).

Ever get in a situation where your back's against the wall and you have no clue what to do? Ever need to make an important decision about your circumstances, but the problem is bigger than you are? Those are the times you need wisdom. You need to look at things from God's perspective and know what to do—that's wisdom. You know you need it, but how do you get it?

Proverbs 9:10 says that "wisdom begins with respect for the Lord." The more you learn to respect and obey the Lord, the more wisdom you'll gain. Remember that respect and obedience are two separate actions. To respect the Lord is to know that he knows best and to care about what he thinks. It is to consult him when you're in a tough spot. Obedience is a step beyond respect. To obey the Lord is to act on what he's told you.

The verse goes on to say that to have understanding, you need knowledge of the Holy One. Knowing God is much deeper than knowing *about* God. Knowing him won't happen overnight, and no one will ever know him completely; but as you spend time with him, you'll eventually begin to know him more and more. He will give you wisdom. Just respect him, obey him, and know him.

SEE FOR YOURSELF:
Dan. 2:21; Eph. 1:17; James 3:17

but right living will save you from
death.

3 The Lord does not let good people go
hungry,
but he keeps evil people from getting
what they want.

4 A lazy person will end up poor,
but a hard worker will become rich.

5 Those who gather crops on time are wise,
but those who sleep through the harvest
are a disgrace.

6 Good people will have rich blessings,
but the wicked will be overwhelmed by
violence.

7 Good people will be remembered as a
blessing,
but evil people will soon be forgotten.

8 The wise do what they are told,
but a talkative fool will be ruined.

9 The honest person will live in safety,
but the dishonest will be caught.

10 A wink may get you into trouble,
and foolish talk will lead to your ruin.

11 The words of a good person give life, like
a fountain of water,
but the words of the wicked contain
nothing but violence.

12 Hatred stirs up trouble,
but love forgives all wrongs.

On the Edge

Hatred stirs up trouble, but love forgives all wrongs (Prov. 10:12).

It's going to happen just by virtue of being sisters. Maybe the next time it'll be you. You're running late for school. Nothing is ironed. You look over at her closet, and there's the perfect shirt to throw on. You put it on and think, *I'll explain later. I'm sure she wouldn't mind.* Some things in life are worth getting upset about. And some things are best overlooked. Borrowed clothes between sisters is not a big deal—even when she didn't ask, even when you don't ask.

You could do the mature thing next time and say, "It's okay if you wear my clothes. But when it's not an emergency, I'd really appreciate it if you would ask me." Give your sister the same respect. Build bridges toward her. A sister is an awesome gift from God, even when she gets on your nerves. Love her and try to overlook the little stuff.

SEE FOR YOURSELF:
Rom. 12:9–10; 1 Cor. 13:4; Eph. 4:1–3; 1 John 4:7

13 Smart people speak wisely,
but people without wisdom should be punished.

14 The wise don't tell everything they know,
but the foolish talk too much and are ruined.

15 Having lots of money protects the rich,
but having no money destroys the poor.

16 Good people are rewarded with life,
but evil people are paid with punishment.

17 Whoever accepts correction is on the way to life,
but whoever ignores correction will lead others away from life.

18 Whoever hides hate is a liar.
Whoever tells lies is a fool.

19 If you talk a lot, you are sure to sin;
if you are wise, you will keep quiet.

20 The words of a good person are like pure silver,
but an evil person's thoughts are worth very little.

21 Good people's words will help many others,
but fools will die because they don't have wisdom.

22 The LORD's blessing brings wealth,
and no sorrow comes with it.

23 A foolish person enjoys doing wrong,
but a person with understanding enjoys doing what is wise.

24 Evil people will get what they fear most,
but good people will get what they want most.

FOLLOWING GOD
What's the hope of a good person? (10:24–25)

25 A storm will blow the evil person away,
but a good person will always be safe.

26 A lazy person affects the one he works for
like vinegar on the teeth or smoke in the eyes.

27 Whoever respects the LORD will have a long life,
but the life of an evil person will be cut short.

28 A good person can look forward to happiness,
but an evil person can expect nothing.

29 The LORD will protect good people
but will ruin those who do evil.

30 Good people will always be safe,
but evil people will not remain in the land.

31 A good person says wise things,
but a liar's tongue will be stopped.

32 Good people know the right thing to say,
but evil people only tell lies.

11

1 The LORD hates dishonest scales,
but he is pleased with honest weights.

2 Pride leads only to shame;
it is wise to be humble.

3 Good people will be guided by honesty;
dishonesty will destroy those who are not trustworthy.

4 Riches will not help when it's time to die,
but right living will save you from death.

5 The goodness of the innocent makes life easier,
but the wicked will be destroyed by their wickedness.

6 Doing right brings freedom to honest people,
but those who are not trustworthy will be caught by their own desires.

7 When the wicked die, hope dies with them;
their hope in riches will come to nothing.

8 The good person is saved from trouble;
it comes to the wicked instead.

9 With words an evil person can destroy a neighbor,

On the Edge

The LORD hates dishonest scales, but he is pleased with honest weights (Prov. 11:1).

Cheating has to do with integrity. A great way to define integrity is to think of it as "what you do when no one's looking." What do you do when no one is looking? The Lord says that he hates cheating (dishonest scales). That covers the answers you saw and used from the test next to you, all the homework you copied from your friend before school, the money you secretly "borrowed" from your mom's purse, and the gum you accidentally forgot to pay for but kept anyway. Cheating only brings some small momentary rewards. In the long run, it all catches up to you. God sees the whole thing. Even worse, he sees inside your heart and knows all about your selfish motives. The next time you are tempted to look and think, *It would be only one time* or *It might even help my grade*, listen to the siren that goes off in your head. It's the Holy Spirit saying, "Don't!" You may forfeit some correct answers, but the God who sees everything will not overlook your integrity. His rewards are more valuable than a test grade, and they last for eternity.

SEE FOR YOURSELF:
1 Cor. 13:6;
Eph. 4:15, 28

but a good person will
escape by being
smart.

10 When good people
succeed, the city is
happy.
When evil people die,
there are shouts of
joy.

11 Good people bless and build up their city,
but the wicked can destroy it with their
words.

12 People without good sense find fault with
their neighbors,
but those with understanding keep
quiet.

HYPOCRISY

What effect does the hypocrite have on those around him? (11:9)

13 Gossips can't keep secrets,
but a trustworthy person can.

14 Without leadership a nation falls,
but lots of good advice will save it.

15 Whoever guarantees to pay somebody
else's loan will suffer.
It is safer to avoid such promises.

16 A kind woman gets respect,
but cruel men get only wealth.

17 Kind people do themselves a favor,
but cruel people bring trouble on
themselves.

18 An evil person really earns nothing,
but a good person will surely be
rewarded.

19 Those who are truly good will live,
but those who chase after evil will die.

20 The LORD hates those with evil hearts
but is pleased with those who are
innocent.

21 Evil people will certainly be punished,
but those who do right will be set free.

22 A beautiful woman without good sense
is like a gold ring in a pig's snout.

23 Those who do right only wish for good,
but the wicked can expect to be defeated
by God's anger.

WHAT'S IT MEAN?

Pigs were among the least popular animals in ancient Israel. They were considered "unclean" and were unsuitable for food, according to God's Law. Throughout the Bible, pigs are used to symbolize greed, filth, or shame.

Proverbs 11:22

24 Some people give much but get back even
more.
Others don't give what they should and
end up poor.
25 Whoever gives to others will get richer;
those who help others will themselves
be helped.

26 People curse those who keep all the grain,
but they bless the one who is willing to
sell it.

27 Whoever looks for good will find kindness,
but whoever looks for evil will find
trouble.

28 Those who trust in riches will be ruined,
but a good person will be healthy like a
green leaf.

29 Whoever brings trouble to his family
will be left with nothing but the wind.
A fool will be a servant to the wise.

30 A good person gives life to others;
the wise person teaches others how to
live.

31 Good people will be rewarded on earth,
and the wicked and the sinners will be
punished.

12

1 Anyone who loves learning accepts
correction,
but a person who hates being corrected
is stupid.

2 The LORD is pleased with a good person,
but he will punish anyone who plans
evil.

3 Doing evil brings no safety at all,
but a good person has safety and
security.

4 A good wife is like a crown for her
husband,
but a disgraceful wife is like a disease in
his bones.

5 The plans that good people make are fair,
but the advice of the wicked will trick
you.

6 The wicked talk about killing people,
but the words of good people will save
them.

7 Wicked people die and they are no more,
but a good person's family continues.

8 The wisdom of the wise wins praise,
but there is no respect for the stupid.

9 A person who is not important but has a
servant is better off
than someone who acts important but
has no food.

10 Good people take care of their animals,
but even the kindest acts of the wicked
are cruel.

11 Those who work their land will have
plenty of food,
but the one who chases empty dreams
is not wise.

12 The wicked want what other evil people
have stolen,
but good people want to give what they
have to others.

13 Evil people are trapped by their evil talk,
but good people stay out of trouble.

14 People will be rewarded for what they say,
and they will also be rewarded for what
they do.

15 Fools think they are doing right,
but the wise listen to advice.

16 Fools quickly show that they are upset,
but the wise ignore insults.

17 An honest witness tells the truth,
but a dishonest witness tells lies.

18 Careless words stab like a sword,
but wise words bring healing.

19 Truth will continue forever,
but lies are only for a moment.

20 Those who plan evil are full of lies,
but those who plan peace are happy.

21 No harm comes to a good person,
but an evil person's life is full of
trouble.

22 The LORD hates those who tell lies
but is pleased with those who keep their
promises.

On the Edge

Hard workers will become leaders, but those who are lazy will be slaves (Prov. 12:24).

Forty algebra problems, a paper on the people of the Congo, Spanish vocabulary words—every night another pile of homework. Even though you may get tired of having work to do at home, the sacrifice will be worth it in the end. Verse 24 says that hard workers become leaders, and the lazy are made slaves. You may not become a slave in the full sense of the word, but you *will* become a slave to your lack of knowledge. Without hard work, there won't be success in a career. It will be hard to progress past low-paying jobs, and the lack of discipline will make it hard to hold on to good jobs. If you have goals and if you want to make a difference with your life, then you really need to do your homework. Even when you can't imagine how you will ever use the information, just press on. Know that each little accomplishment is building your character. You will be stronger, wiser, and more disciplined—all because you were faithful to do your homework.

SEE FOR YOURSELF:
Prov. 24:33–34;
Eccl. 9:10;
Gal. 6:4

23 Wise people keep what they know to
themselves,
but fools can't keep from showing how
foolish they are.

24 Hard workers will become leaders,
but those who are lazy will be slaves.

25 Worry is a heavy load,
but a kind word
cheers you up.

DISCOURAGEMENT

How are we to respond to discouragement? (12:25)

26 Good people take advice
from their friends,
but an evil person is
easily led to do wrong.

27 The lazy catch no food to cook,
but a hard worker will have great
wealth.

28 Doing what is right is the way to life,
but there is another way that leads to
death.

13

1 Wise children take their parents' advice,
but whoever makes fun of wisdom
won't listen to correction.

2 People will be rewarded for what they
say,
but those who can't be trusted want
only violence.

On the Edge

Wise children take their parents' advice, but whoever makes fun of wisdom won't listen to correction (Prov. 13:1).

The difference between what you want and what your parents want is all about perspective. You see what everyone else is doing and long to be a part of the fun. Your parents see a much bigger picture—the part that you don't want to think about—the stuff you know will never happen to you. When you say, "Why can't my curfew be one hour later; what's the big deal?" they see the reality—the later it gets, the more drunk drivers on the road, violent crimes increase, fatigue causes people to make poor decisions, and the list goes on.

Your parents' years have brought them wisdom. And God has given them you to be responsible for. Proverbs says that wise sons and daughters heed their parents' instructions. Your parents are the instruments through which God builds your life and gives you direction. Even if you have a hard time accepting their judgment, learn to respect their authority. Do not be the stubborn child who ignores his parents and grows up to be a fool.

SEE FOR YOURSELF:
Prov. 12:1, 15;
13:10; 20:20

3 Those who are careful about what they
say protect their lives,
but whoever speaks without thinking
will be ruined.

4 The lazy will not get what they
want,
but those who work
hard will.

LAZINESS

If diligence brings wealth, what does laziness bring? (13:4)

5 Good people hate what is
false,
but the wicked do
shameful and disgraceful
things.

6 Doing what is right protects the honest
person,
but doing evil ruins the sinner.

7 Some people pretend to be rich but really
have nothing.
Others pretend to be poor but really are
wealthy.

8 The rich may have to pay a ransom for
their lives,
but the poor will face no such danger.

9 Good people can look forward to a bright
future,
but the future of the wicked is like a
flame going out.

10 Pride only leads to arguments,
but those who take advice are wise.

11 Money that comes easily disappears
quickly,
but money that is gathered little by little
will grow.

12 It is sad not to get what you hoped for.
But wishes that come true are like eating
fruit from the tree of life.

13 Those who reject what they are taught will
pay for it,
but those who obey what they are told
will be rewarded.

14 The teaching of a wise person gives life.
It is like a fountain that can save people
from death.

15 People with good understanding will be
well liked,
but the lives of those who are not
trustworthy are hard.

16 Every wise person acts with good sense,
but fools show how foolish they are.

17 A wicked messenger brings nothing but
trouble,
but a trustworthy one makes everything
right.

18 A person who refuses correction will end
up poor and disgraced,
but the one who accepts correction will
be honored.

19 It is so good when wishes come true,
but fools hate to stop doing evil.

20 Spend time with the wise and you will
become wise,
but the friends of fools will suffer.

21 Trouble always comes to sinners,
but good people enjoy success.

22 Good people leave their wealth to their
grandchildren,
but a sinner's wealth is stored up for
good people.

23 A poor person's field might produce
plenty of food,
but others often steal it away.

24 If you do not punish your children, you
don't love them,
but if you love your children, you will
correct them.

25 Good people have enough to eat,
but the wicked will go hungry.

14

1 A wise woman strengthens her family,
but a foolish woman destroys hers by
what she does.

2 People who live good lives respect the
LORD,
but those who live evil lives don't.

3 Fools will be punished for their proud
words,
but the words of the wise will protect
them.

4 When there are no oxen, no food is in the
barn.
But with a strong ox, much grain can be
grown.

5 A truthful witness does not lie,
but a false witness tells nothing but lies.

6 Those who make fun of wisdom look for it and do not find it,
but knowledge comes easily to those with understanding.

7 Stay away from fools,
because they can't teach you anything.

8 A wise person will understand what to do,
but a foolish person is dishonest.

9 Fools don't care if they sin,
but honest people work at being right.

10 No one else can know your sadness,
and strangers cannot share your joy.

11 The wicked person's house will be destroyed,
but a good person's tent will still be standing.

12 Some people think they are doing right,
but in the end it leads to death.

13 Someone who is laughing may be sad inside,
and joy may end in sadness.

14 Evil people will be paid back for their evil ways,
and good people will be rewarded for their good ones.

15 Fools will believe anything,
but the wise think about what they do.

16 Wise people are careful and stay out of trouble,
but fools are careless and quick to act.

17 Someone with a quick temper does foolish things,
but someone with understanding remains calm.

18 Fools are rewarded with nothing but more foolishness,
but the wise are rewarded with knowledge.

19 Evil people will bow down to those who are good;
the wicked will bow down at the door of those who do right.

20 The poor are rejected, even by their neighbors,
but the rich have many friends.

21 It is a sin to hate your neighbor,
but being kind to the needy brings happiness.

22 Those who make evil plans will be ruined,
but those who plan to do good will be loved and trusted.

23 Those who work hard make a profit,
but those who only talk will be poor.

24 Wise people are rewarded with wealth,
but fools only get more foolishness.

"Those who respect the LORD will have security, and their children will be protected." (Proverbs 14:26)

25 A truthful witness saves lives,
but a false witness is a traitor.

26 Those who respect the LORD will have security,
and their children will be protected.

27 Respect for the LORD gives life.
It is like a fountain that can save people from death.

28 A king is honored when he has many people to rule,
but a prince is ruined if he has none.

29 Patient people have great understanding,
but people with quick tempers show their foolishness.

30 Peace of mind means a healthy body,
but jealousy will rot your bones.

31 Whoever mistreats the poor insults their Maker,
but whoever is kind to the needy honors God.

MERCY
Who do we honor by being merciful to the needy? (14:31)

32 The wicked are ruined by their own evil,
but those who do right are protected even in death.

33 Wisdom lives in those with understanding,
and even fools recognize it.

34 Doing what is right makes a nation great,
but sin will bring disgrace to any people.

35 A king is pleased with a wise servant,
but he will become angry with one who causes him shame.

15

1 A gentle answer will calm a person's anger,
but an unkind answer will cause more anger.

2 Wise people use knowledge when they speak,
but fools pour out foolishness.

WHAT'S IT MEAN?

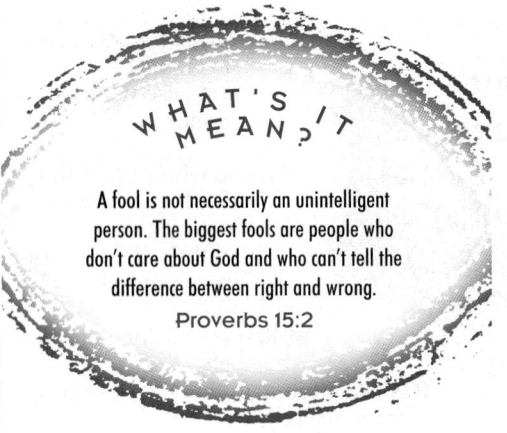

A fool is not necessarily an unintelligent person. The biggest fools are people who don't care about God and who can't tell the difference between right and wrong.

Proverbs 15:2

3 The LORD's eyes see everything;
he watches both evil and good people.

4 As a tree gives fruit, healing words give life,
but dishonest words crush the spirit.

5 Fools reject their parents' correction,
but anyone who accepts correction is wise.

6 Much wealth is in the houses of good people,
but evil people get nothing but trouble.

7 Wise people use their words to spread knowledge,
but there is no knowledge in the thoughts of fools.

8 The LORD hates the sacrifice that the wicked offer,
but he likes the prayers of honest people.

9 The LORD hates what evil people do,
but he loves those who do what is right.

10 The person who quits doing what is right will be punished,
and the one who hates to be corrected will die.

DISCIPLINE

What happens to the one who ignores discipline? (15:10, 12)

11 The LORD knows what is happening in the world of the dead,
so he surely knows the thoughts of the living.

12 Those who make fun of wisdom don't like to be corrected;
they will not ask the wise for advice.

13 Happiness makes a person smile,
but sadness can break a person's spirit.

14 People with understanding want more knowledge,
but fools just want more foolishness.

15 Every day is hard for those who suffer,
but a happy heart is like a continual feast.

16 It is better to be poor and respect the LORD
than to be wealthy and have much trouble.

WHAT'S IT MEAN?

In most ancient Israelite families, meat was served only on special occasions, such as when they were entertaining guests or celebrating a religious festival. Only the wealthiest people in the land could afford to eat meat regularly. The rest ate mostly fruits, vegetables, and grains.

Proverbs 15:17

17 It is better to eat vegetables with those
who love you
than to eat meat with those who hate
you.

18 People with quick tempers cause trouble,
but those who control their tempers
stop a quarrel.

19 A lazy person's life is like a patch of
thorns,
but an honest person's life is like a
smooth highway.

20 A wise son makes his father happy,
but a foolish son disrespects his mother.

21 A person without wisdom enjoys being
foolish,
but someone with understanding does
what is right.

22 Plans fail without good advice,
but they succeed with the advice of
many others.

On the Edge

Plans fail without good advice, but they succeed with the advice of many others (Prov. 15:22).

When it comes to making decisions, it doesn't matter how old you are. The smartest thing to do is to consult with wise people and think about their counsel when you make your plans. It's just that when you are younger, you live with your wise counsel—your parents. As long as you are in your parents' home, God has made them the guardians of your decisions. They are responsible to him for the freedoms they give to you and for the decisions they let you make on your own. Little by little, as you get older, more things will be left up to you. As you choose wisely, you will be given even more freedom. Your day is coming—all the decisions will be yours. In all your independence, don't be surprised if you find yourself calling home just to ask, "What do you think about this?"

SEE FOR YOURSELF:
Eph. 6:1–3; Col. 3:20; 1 Pet. 5:5

23 People enjoy giving good advice.
Saying the right word at the right time is
so pleasing.

24 Wise people's lives get better and better.
They avoid whatever would cause their
death.

25 The LORD will tear down the proud
person's house,
but he will protect the widow's property.

26 The LORD hates evil thoughts
but is pleased with kind words.

27 Greedy people bring trouble to their
families,
but the person who can't be paid to do
wrong will live.

28 Good people think before they answer,
but the wicked simply pour out evil.

29 The LORD does not listen to the wicked,
but he hears the prayers of those who
do right.

30 Good news makes you feel better.
Your happiness will show in your eyes.

31 If you listen to correction to improve your
life,
you will live among the wise.

32 Those who refuse correction hate
themselves,
but those who accept correction gain
understanding.

33 Respect for the LORD will teach you
wisdom.
If you want to be honored, you must be
humble.

16

1 People may make plans in their minds,
but only the LORD can make them come
true.

2 You may believe you are doing
right,
but the LORD will judge
your reasons.

3 Depend on the LORD in
whatever you do,
and your plans will
succeed.

TRUST

What is a result of trusting God? (16:3)

On the Edge

People may make plans in their minds, but only the LORD can make them come true. You may believe you are doing right, but the LORD will judge your reasons. Depend on the LORD in whatever you do, and your plans will succeed (Prov. 16:1–3).

Choosing a college is a big decision, but not too big for God. As you and your parents begin to narrow the field, make sure you are continually covering the whole process in prayer. If God directs your steps, Proverbs 16:3 says you'll succeed ("your plans will succeed"). Your plans have no strength if they're not from God. Begin by choosing the schools that interest you and have a curriculum in your field of study. Then "depend on the LORD" by taking time to pray. Visit some campuses. Take time to pray. Apply for scholarships and grants. Take time to pray. Talk over finances with your parents. Take time to pray. Go through the acceptance letters and ask yourself, "Can I honor God and live a life that glorifies him at any of these schools?" If the answer is yes, then pick the one you like. If the answer is no, then throw out the losers, and choose from the remainder. Between you and God and your parents, you are sure to make a wise decision and have a great life in college.

SEE FOR YOURSELF:
Ps. 37:5; Prov. 3:6; Matt. 6:33

4 The LORD makes everything go as he
pleases.
He has even prepared a day of disaster
for evil people.

5 The LORD hates those who are proud.
They will surely be punished.

6 Love and truth bring forgiveness of sin.
By respecting the LORD you will avoid
evil.

7 When people live so that they please the
LORD,
even their enemies will make peace with
them.

8 It is better to be poor and right
than to be wealthy and dishonest.

9 People may make plans in their minds,
but the LORD decides what they will do.

10 The words of a king are like a message
from God,
so his decisions should be fair.

11 The LORD wants honest balances and
scales;
all the weights are his work.

12 Kings hate those who do wrong,
because governments only continue if
they are fair.

13 Kings like honest people;
they value someone who speaks the
truth.

14 An angry king can put someone to death,
so a wise person will try to make him
happy.

15 A smiling king can give people life;
his kindness is like a spring shower.

WHAT'S IT MEAN?

Because it's located in a desert region, the land of Israel experiences frequent droughts. Because the ancient Israelites relied on farming for so many of their basic needs, they considered rain a precious gift from God. Long droughts were thought by many people to be God's judgment on the sins of the people.

Proverbs 16:15

16 It is better to get wisdom than gold,
and to choose understanding rather
than silver!

17 Good people stay away from evil.
By watching what they do, they protect
their lives.

18 Pride will destroy a person;
a proud attitude leads to ruin.

19 It is better to be humble and be with those
who suffer
than to share stolen property with the
proud.

20 Whoever listens to what is taught will
succeed,
and whoever trusts the LORD will be
happy.

21 The wise are known for their
understanding.
Their pleasant words make them better
teachers.

22 Understanding is like a fountain which
gives life to those who use it,
but foolishness brings punishment to
fools.

23 Wise people's minds tell them what to
say,
and that helps them be better teachers.

24 Pleasant words are like a honeycomb,
making people happy and healthy.

25 Some people think they are doing right,
but in the end it leads to death.

26 The workers' hunger helps them,
because their desire to eat makes them
work.

27 Useless people make evil
plans,
and their words are like
a burning fire.

GOSSIP
What are some of the negative results of gossip? (16:27–28)

28 A useless person causes
trouble,
and a gossip ruins
friendships.

29 Cruel people trick their neighbors
and lead them to do wrong.

30 Someone who winks is planning evil,
and the one who grins is planning
something wrong.

31 Gray hair is like a crown of honor;
it is earned by living a good life.

32 Patience is better than strength.
Controlling your temper is better than
capturing a city.

33 People throw lots to make a decision,
but the answer comes from the LORD.

17

1 It is better to eat a dry crust of bread in
peace
than to have a feast where there is
quarreling.

2 A wise servant will rule over the master's
disgraceful child
and will even inherit a share of what the
master leaves his children.

3 A hot furnace tests silver and gold,
but the LORD tests hearts.

4 Evil people listen to evil words.
Liars pay attention to cruel words.

5 Whoever mistreats the poor insults their
Maker;
whoever enjoys someone's trouble will be
punished.

6 Old people are proud of their
grandchildren,
and children are proud of their
parents.

7 Fools should not be proud,
and rulers should not be liars.

8 Some people think they can pay others to
do anything they ask.
They think it will work every time.

9 Whoever forgives
someone's sin makes
a friend,
but gossiping about the
sin breaks up
friendships.

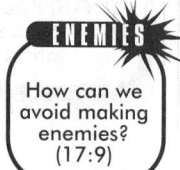

ENEMIES
How can we avoid making enemies? (17:9)

10 A wise person will learn
more from a warning
than a fool will learn from a hundred
lashings.

11 Disobedient people look only for
trouble,
so a cruel messenger will be sent against
them.

12 It is better to meet a bear robbed of her
cubs
than to meet a fool doing foolish
things.

On the Edge

Whoever forgives someone's sin makes a friend, but gossiping about the sin breaks up friendships (Prov. 17:9).

If you've been hurt by a friend, you've probably got some big scars. The truth is, you've only got a couple of options about how to handle your pain. You can look at your scars every day and let them remind you how hurt you've been. You can think about them all the time. You can spend hours plotting revenge or deciding what kind of snide remark to make the next time you see your friend. You can tell everybody else how badly you were treated. You can hold a grudge. Eventually that grudge will turn to hatred and bitterness. And you won't ever be satisfied. You'll just end up rehearsing your pain day after day, and it will finally eat you up. You'll regret how much of your life was spent wallowing in misery.

The other option is a combination of two powerful expressions: grace and forgiveness. Grace means forgiving a friend even when he or she doesn't deserve it. After that, live your forgiveness. Your words and your actions will show that you have truly forgiven.

The first option keeps you in chains. The second one sets you free. Forgiveness frees your heart to love your friend the way God loves you.

SEE FOR YOURSELF:
Eph. 4:32; Col. 3:13; 1 John 4:7

13 Whoever gives evil in return for good
will always have trouble at home.

14 Starting a quarrel is like a leak in a dam,
so stop it before a fight breaks out.

15 The LORD hates both of these things:
freeing the guilty and punishing the innocent.

16 It won't do a fool any good to try to buy wisdom,
because he doesn't have the ability to be wise.

17 A friend loves you all the time,
and a brother helps in time of trouble.

18 It is not wise to promise
to pay what your neighbor owes.

19 Whoever loves to argue loves to sin.
Whoever brags a lot is asking for trouble.

20 A person with an evil heart will find no success,
and the person whose words are evil will get into trouble.

21 It is sad to have a foolish child;
there is no joy in being the parent of a fool.

22 A happy heart is like good medicine,
but a broken spirit drains your strength.

23 When the wicked accept money to do wrong
there can be no justice.

24 The person with understanding is always looking for wisdom,
but the mind of a fool wanders everywhere.

25 A foolish son makes his father sad
and causes his mother great sorrow.

26 It is not good to punish the innocent
or to beat leaders for being honest.

27 The smart person says very little,
and one with understanding stays calm.

28 Even fools seem to be wise if they keep quiet;
if they don't speak, they appear to understand.

18

1 Unfriendly people are selfish
and hate all good sense.

2 Fools do not want to
understand anything.
They only want to tell
others what they
think.

EDUCATION

Is education for everybody? (18:2)

3 Do something evil, and people won't like you.

Do something shameful, and they will
make fun of you.

4 Spoken words can be like deep water,
but wisdom is like a flowing stream.

5 It is not good to honor the wicked
or to be unfair to the innocent.

6 The words of fools start quarrels.
They make people want to beat them.

7 The words of fools will ruin them;
their own words will trap them.

8 The words of a gossip are like tasty bits of
food.
People like to gobble them up.

9 A person who doesn't work hard
is just like someone who destroys
things.

10 The LORD is like a strong tower;
those who do right can run to him for
safety.

11 Rich people trust their wealth to protect
them.
They think it is like the high walls of a
city.

12 Proud people will be ruined,
but the humble will be honored.

13 Anyone who answers without listening
is foolish and confused.

14 The will to live can get you through
sickness,
but no one can live with a broken
spirit.

15 The mind of a person with understanding
gets knowledge;
the wise person listens to learn more.

16 Taking a gift to an important man
will help get you in to see him.

17 The person who tells one side of a story
seems right,
until someone else comes and asks
questions.

18 Throwing lots can settle arguments
and keep the two sides from fighting.

WHAT'S IT MEAN?

"Throwing lots" was a lot like flipping a coin or drawing straws to determine who's going to do something. Many Israelites believed God influenced the outcome when lots were cast. Therefore, it was his will, and not blind luck, that determined the results.

Proverbs 18:18

19 A brother who has been insulted is harder
to win back than a walled city,
and arguments separate people like the
barred gates of a palace.

20 People will be rewarded for what they say;
they will be rewarded by how they speak.

21 What you say can mean life or death.
Those who speak with care will be
rewarded.

22 When a man finds a wife, he finds
something good.
It shows that the LORD is pleased with
him.

23 The poor beg for mercy,
but the rich give rude answers.

24 Some friends may ruin you,
but a real friend will be more loyal than
a brother.

19

1 It is better to be poor and honest
than to be foolish and tell lies.

2 Enthusiasm without knowledge is not
good.
If you act too quickly, you might make a
mistake.

3 People's own foolishness ruins their lives,
but in their minds they blame the LORD.

4 Wealthy people are always finding more
friends,
but the poor lose all theirs.

5 A witness who lies will not go free;
liars will never escape.

6 Many people want to please a leader,
and everyone is friends with those who give gifts.

7 Poor people's relatives avoid them;
even their friends stay far away.
They run after them, begging,
but they are gone.

8 Those who get wisdom do themselves a favor,
and those who love learning will succeed.

On the Edge

Those who get wisdom do themselves a favor, and those who love learning will succeed (Prov. 19:8).

Josh was fourteen years old. After he died, people talked about his football ability, his great personality, his good looks, and his love for God. One night he was at home and accidentally killed himself by "huffing" fluorocarbons. His friends said he was just experimenting and wasn't a habitual user. He didn't mean to do it. He was just "messing around." Josh didn't use good sense. Getting a "buzz" from huffing seemed pretty harmless. He probably didn't even think it was dangerous. But it was a tragically unwise choice that ended his life after fourteen short years.

Whether it's huffing, or drag racing, you have to separate yourself from the potential "thrill" and ask, "Is this wise? What could the consequences be? What is the absolute worst thing that could happen? Could I hurt myself or someone else?" Make sure you know how much damage could be done to yourself or other people. The Holy Spirit will give you direction. But you have to follow through and do the right thing. It takes guts not to follow the crowd. God will provide the guts—all you have to do is ask him.

SEE FOR YOURSELF:
1 Cor. 6:19–20;
Col. 3:5;
1 Pet. 1:13–16

9 A witness who lies will not go free,
liars will die.

10 A fool should not live in luxury.
A slave should not rule over princes.

11 Smart people are patient;
they will be honored if they ignore insults.

12 An angry king is like a roaring lion,
but his kindness is like the dew on the grass.

13 A foolish son will ruin his father,
and a quarreling wife is like dripping water.

14 Houses and wealth are inherited from parents,
but a wise wife is a gift from the LORD.

LAZINESS

If you are lazy, what can you expect? (19:15)

15 Lazy people sleep a lot,
and idle people will go hungry.

16 Those who obey the commands protect themselves,
but those who are careless will die.

17 Being kind to the poor is like lending to the LORD;
he will reward you for what you have done.

18 Correct your children while there is still hope;
do not let them destroy themselves.

19 People with quick tempers will have to pay for it.
If you help them out once, you will have to do it again.

20 Listen to advice and accept correction,
and in the end you will be wise.

21 People can make all kinds of plans,
but only the LORD's plan will happen.

22 People want others to be loyal,
so it is better to be poor than to be a liar.

23 Those who respect the LORD will live
and be satisfied, unbothered by trouble.

24 Though the lazy person puts his hand in the dish,
he won't lift the food to his mouth.

25 Whip those who make fun of wisdom,
and perhaps foolish people will gain some wisdom.
Correct those with understanding, and they will gain knowledge.

26 A son who robs his father and sends away his mother
brings shame and disgrace on himself.

27 Don't stop listening to correction, my child,
or you will forget what you have already learned.

28 An evil witness makes fun of fairness,
and wicked people love what is evil.

29 People who make fun of wisdom will be punished,
and the backs of foolish people will be beaten.

"Smart people are patient; they will be honored if they ignore insults." (Proverbs 19:11)

20

1 Wine and beer make people loud and uncontrolled;
it is not wise to get drunk on them.

2 An angry king is like a roaring lion.
Making him angry may cost you your life.

3 Foolish people are always fighting,
but avoiding quarrels will bring you honor.

4 Lazy farmers don't plow when they should;
they expect a harvest, but there is none.

5 People's thoughts can be like a deep well,
but someone with understanding can find the wisdom there.

6 Many people claim to be loyal,
but it is hard to find a trustworthy person.

7 The good people who live honest lives
will be a blessing to their children.

8 When a king sits on his throne to judge,
he knows evil when he sees it.

9 No one can say, "I am innocent;
I have never done anything wrong."

10 The LORD hates both these things:
dishonest weights and dishonest measures.

HYPOCRISY

What does God think of a person with double standards? (20:10)

11 Even children are known by their behavior;
their actions show if they are innocent and good.

12 The LORD has made both these things:
ears to hear and eyes to see.

13 If you love to sleep, you will be poor.
If you stay awake, you will have plenty of food.

14 Buyers say, "This is bad. It's no good."
Then they go away and brag about what they bought.

15 There is gold and plenty of rubies,
but only a few people speak with knowledge.

16 Take the coat of someone who promises to pay a stranger's debts,
and keep it until he pays what the stranger owes.

17 Stolen food may taste sweet at first,
but later it will feel like a mouth full of gravel.

18 Get advice if you want your plans to work.
If you go to war, get the advice of others.

19 Gossips can't keep secrets,
so avoid people who talk too much.

20 Those who curse their father or mother
will be like a light going out in darkness.

21 Wealth inherited quickly in the beginning
will do you no good in the end.

On the Edge

Those who curse their father or mother will be like a light going out in darkness. . . . Don't say, "I'll pay you back for the wrong you did." Wait for the Lord, and he will make things right (Prov. 20:20, 22).

Ashley's mom got this new device that you put on your car. It plays forty different songs through your horn. One day in the junior high carpool line, Ashley's mom decide to play "parking lot DJ" and started playing songs through the horn. They were old songs, geeky songs—"Oh Susanna" and "Tea for Two." Really hip stuff *cannot* be played through a car horn. Mom thought it was a riot. Ashley thought it was the most humiliating thing that could possibly happen. Ashley tried to figure out what she could do that would be equally embarrassing to her mother, but nothing came close to that musical horn.

Finally, Ashley decided to take the high road. She sat down and told her mom how mortified she was, that it was not funny, and that she wanted her to stop. Mom apologized for being so goofy. She really had thought it was funny. Now she just entertains construction workers as she drives by and the school parking lot is quiet.

Parents can be really embarrassing, intentionally or without even knowing it. When it gets to you, work through it. Talk it out. Tell them how you feel. Be honest and don't try to get even. Your parents will appreciate your maturity.

SEE FOR YOURSELF:
Matt. 5:9;
1 Cor. 13:4–7

22 Don't say, "I'll pay you back for the wrong you did."
Wait for the LORD, and he will make things right.

23 The LORD hates dishonest weights,
and dishonest scales do not please him.

24 The LORD decides what a person will do;
no one understands what his life is all about.

25 It's dangerous to promise something to God too quickly.
After you've thought about it, it may be too late.

26 A wise king sorts out the evil people,
and he punishes them as they deserve.

27 The LORD looks deep inside people
and searches through their thoughts.

28 Loyalty and truth keep a king in power;
he continues to rule if he is loyal.

29 Young men glory in their strength,
and old men are honored for their gray hair.

30 Hard punishment will get rid of evil,
and whippings can change an evil heart.

21

1 The LORD can control a king's mind as he controls a river;
he can direct it as he pleases.

2 You may believe you are doing right,
but the LORD judges your reasons.

3 Doing what is right and fair
is more important to the LORD than sacrifices.

4 Proud looks, proud thoughts,
and evil actions are sin.

5 The plans of hard-working people earn a profit,

WHAT'S IT MEAN?

The roof was one of the main features of ancient Israelite houses. Some people used their roof as a deck or terrace. Others covered it with a layer of grass to keep rain from soaking through into the house. Still others used it to dry foods such as figs and corn in the sun. Usually people reached the roof via an outside staircase. A railing or low wall usually ran around the perimeter of the roof to keep people from falling off.

Proverbs 21:9

but those who act too quickly become
poor.

6 Wealth that comes from telling lies
vanishes like a mist and leads to death.

7 The violence of the wicked will destroy
them,
because they refuse to do what is right.

8 Guilty people live dishonest lives,
but honest people do right.

9 It is better to live in a corner on the roof[n]
than inside the house with a quarreling
wife.

On the Edge

God, who is always right, watches the house of the wicked and brings ruin on every evil person (Prov. 21:12).

As children, we continually watch our brothers and sisters, making sure they never get more than we do. A bigger scoop of ice cream could launch a full-fledged attack of whining. We grow up and hang onto that attitude. In our eyes, no one is entitled to more. No one should be able to get away with anything. The teams should always be equal—the best players evenly distributed. The problem is that we don't always have the whole story. That's where God comes in. He shows up and levels the playing field. He is always fair. He always does what is right. He always rewards those who deserve it. It's just that his ways are different from ours. His timing is perfect. Sometimes you'll get rewarded on earth, and sometimes you won't see the reward until you're in heaven. Next time you think you're being shortchanged, take it up with the Lord. Allow him to calm your heart and give you eyes to see his fairness.

SEE FOR YOURSELF:
Ezek. 18:20; Amos 5:24; Matt. 25:26

10 Evil people only want to harm others.
Their neighbors get no mercy from
them.

11 If you punish those who make fun of
wisdom, a foolish person may gain
some wisdom.
But if you teach the wise, they will get
knowledge.

12 God, who is always right, watches the
house of the wicked
and brings ruin on every evil person.

13 Whoever ignores the poor when they cry
for help
will also cry for help and not be
answered.

14 A secret gift will calm an angry person;
a present given in secrecy will quiet
great anger.

15 When justice is done, good people are
happy,
but evil people are ruined.

16 Whoever does not use good sense
will end up among the dead.

17 Whoever loves pleasure will become poor;
whoever loves wine and perfume will
never be rich.

18 Wicked people will suffer instead of good
people,
and those who cannot be trusted will
suffer instead of those who do right.

19 It is better to live alone in the desert
than with a quarreling and complaining
wife.

20 Wise people's houses are full of the best
foods and olive oil,
but fools waste everything they have.

21 Whoever tries to live right and be loyal
finds life, success, and honor.

22 A wise person can defeat a city full of
warriors
and tear down the defenses they trust in.

21:9 roof In Bible times houses were built with flat roofs. The roof was used for drying things such as flax and fruit. And it was used as an extra room, as a place for worship, and as a cool place to sleep in the summer.

23 Those who are careful about what they say
keep themselves out of trouble.

24 People who act with stubborn pride
are called "proud," "bragger," and "mocker."

25 Lazy people's desire for sleep will kill them,
because they refuse to work.
26 All day long they wish for more,
but good people give without holding back.

27 The LORD hates sacrifices brought by evil people,
particularly when they offer them for the wrong reasons.

28 A lying witness will be forgotten,
but a truthful witness will speak on.

29 Wicked people are stubborn,
but good people think carefully about what they do.

30 There is no wisdom, understanding, or advice
that can succeed against the LORD.

31 You can get the horses ready for battle,
but it is the LORD who gives the victory.

On the Edge

Being respected is more important than having great riches. To be well thought of is better than silver or gold (Prov. 22:1).

Don't ever let anyone else make decisions about your reputation or your character. So, someone wants you to do something you don't want to do—they plead with you, they promise you the moon, they charm you, they tell you they love you. Your mind is screaming "No!" Your heart is racing. Your gut tells you to run. That's the Holy Spirit speaking to you. Don't miss him. Do not be deceived! Do not fall into Satan's trap. Protect your integrity. Muster up all your courage and say, "No." Then remove yourself from temptation. Go home. Send (or take) your date home. Get a ride home. Just get away from the pressure to make a bad decision. To have a good name and to be respected is more valuable than silver and gold. You are building your character when you make hard decisions that are right and strong. God sees your faithfulness, and he will honor it.

SEE FOR YOURSELF:
Prov. 12:3; 15:21;
Eph. 6:10–17

22

1 Being respected is more important than having great riches.
To be well thought of is better than silver or gold.

2 The rich and the poor are alike
in that the LORD made them all.

3 The wise see danger ahead
and avoid it,
but fools keep going
and get into trouble.

HUMILITY
Does God bless a humble person? (22:4)

4 Respecting the LORD and not being proud
will bring you wealth, honor, and life.

5 Evil people's lives are like paths covered with thorns and traps.
People who guard themselves don't have such problems.

6 Train children how to live right,
and when they are old, they will not change.

7 The rich rule over the poor,
and borrowers are servants to lenders.

8 Those who plan evil will receive trouble.
Their cruel anger will come to an end.

9 Generous people will be blessed,
because they share their food with the poor.

10 Get rid of the one who makes fun of wisdom.
Then fighting, quarrels, and insults will stop.

11 Whoever loves pure thoughts and kind words
will have even the king as a friend.

[12]The LORD guards knowledge,
but he destroys false words.

[13]The lazy person says, "There's a lion outside!
I might get killed out in the street!"

[14]The words of an unfaithful wife are like a deep trap.
Those who make the LORD angry will get caught by them.

[15]Every child is full of foolishness,
but punishment can get rid of it.

[16]Whoever gets rich by mistreating the poor,
and gives presents to the wealthy, will become poor.

OTHER WISE SAYINGS

[17]Listen carefully to what wise people say;
pay attention to what I am teaching you.
[18]It will be good to keep these things in mind
so that you are ready to repeat them.
[19]I am teaching them to you now
so that you will put your trust in the LORD.
[20]I have written thirty sayings for you,
which give knowledge and good advice.
[21]I am teaching you true and reliable words
so that you can give true answers to anyone who asks.

[22]Do not abuse poor people because they are poor,
and do not take away the rights of the needy in court.
[23]The LORD will defend them in court
and will take the life of those who take away their rights.

[24]Don't make friends with quick-tempered people
or spend time with those who have bad tempers.
[25]If you do, you will be like them.
Then you will be in real danger.

[26]Don't promise to pay what someone else owes,
and don't guarantee anyone's loan.
[27]If you cannot pay the loan,
your own bed may be taken right out from under you.

[28]Don't move an old stone that marks a border,
because those stones were set up by your ancestors.

[29]Do you see people skilled in their work?
They will work for kings, not for ordinary people.

23

[1]If you sit down to eat with a ruler,
notice the food that is in front of you.
[2]Control yourself
if you have a big appetite.
[3]Don't be greedy for his fine foods,
because that food might be a trick.

[4]Don't wear yourself out trying to get rich;
be wise enough to control yourself.
[5]Wealth can vanish in the wink of an eye.
It can seem to grow wings
and fly away like an eagle.

[6]Don't eat the food of selfish people;
don't be greedy for their fine foods.
[7]Selfish people are always worrying
about how much the food costs.
They tell you, "Eat and drink,"
but they don't really mean it.
[8]You will throw up the little you have eaten,
and you will have wasted your kind words.

[9]Don't speak to fools;
they will only ignore your wise words.

[10]Don't move an old stone that marks a border,

WHAT'S IT MEAN?

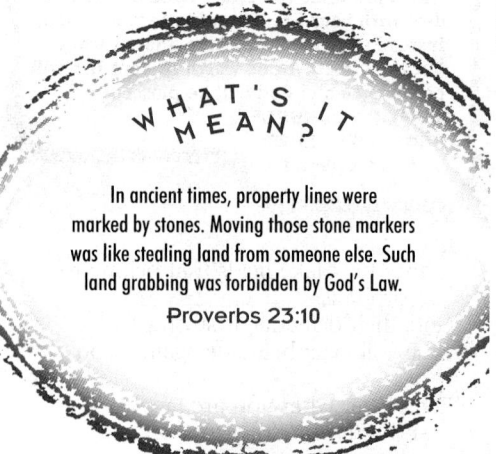

In ancient times, property lines were marked by stones. Moving those stone markers was like stealing land from someone else. Such land grabbing was forbidden by God's Law.

Proverbs 23:10

On the Edge

Notice the food that is in front of you. Control yourself if you have a big appetite. Don't be greedy for his fine foods, because that food might be a trick (Prov. 23:1b–3).

To binge for any reason is to abuse the intended use of food. A variety of emotions could trigger the desire to binge—a great report card, an awful report card, someone really cool asks you out, or everyone leaves you out. Depression, celebration, loneliness, frustration, and anger are some of the feelings that can trigger a massive pig-out. So if any emotion can be a potential reason to eat, then bingeing has to do with self-control.

You can't live your life running from one binge to the next for comfort. Self-control comes from the Holy Spirit. And the Holy Spirit resides in the heart of every believer. You may have already established some really deep patterns in regard to bingeing. If so, a medical professional or counselor may be the best route to understanding how you got to this place and how the Holy Spirit can restore control.

You shouldn't binge because it's harmful to the temple God gave you and because you are using food to insulate yourself from reality. When you eat instead of dealing with the issues in your life, you stick your head in the sand and hope it'll all go away. When you look up again, the issues are still there, and you still haven't learned to deal with life. Food is a poor substitute for the love and power of God, which are what you really need in order to deal with your life. Learning to run to God instead of to food may take a lot of work. But the effort will be worth it. Your life will be changed and God will be pleased.

SEE FOR YOURSELF:
Prov. 13:25; 23:20;
1 Cor. 6:19–20

and don't take fields that belong to
orphans.
11 God, their defender, is strong;
he will take their side against you.

12 Remember what you are taught,
and listen carefully to words of
knowledge.
13 Don't fail to punish children.
If you spank them, they won't die.
14 If you spank them,
you will save them from death.

15 My child, if you are wise,
then I will be happy.
16 I will be so pleased
if you speak what is right.

17 Don't envy sinners,
but always respect the LORD.
18 Then you will have hope for the future,
and your wishes will come true.

19 Listen, my child, and be wise.
Keep your mind on what is right.
20 Don't drink too much wine
or eat too much food.
21 Those who drink and eat too much
become poor.
They sleep too much and end up
wearing rags.

22 Listen to your father, who gave you life,
and do not forget your mother when
she is old.
23 Learn the truth and never reject it.
Get wisdom, self-control, and
understanding.
24 The father of a good child is very happy;
parents who have wise children are glad
because of them.
25 Make your father and mother happy;
give your mother a reason to be glad.

26 My son, pay attention to me,
and watch closely what I do.
27 A prostitute is as dangerous as a deep pit,
and an unfaithful wife is like a narrow
well.
28 They ambush you like robbers
and cause many men to be unfaithful to
their wives.

29 Who has trouble? Who has pain?
Who fights? Who complains?
Who has unnecessary bruises?
Who has bloodshot eyes?
30 It is people who drink too much wine,
who try out all different kinds of strong
drinks.
31 Don't stare at the wine when it is red,
when it sparkles in the cup,
when it goes down smoothly.
32 Later it bites like a snake
with poison in its fangs.

33 Your eyes will see strange sights,
and your mind will be confused.
34 You will feel dizzy as if you're in a storm on the ocean,
as if you're on top of a ship's sails.
35 You will think, "They hit me, but I'm not hurt.
They beat me up, but I don't remember it.
I wish I could wake up.
Then I would get another drink."

On the Edge

Who has trouble? . . . Who has bloodshot eyes? It is people who drink too much wine, who try out all different kinds of strong drinks. Don't stare at the wine when it is red, when it sparkles in the cup, when it goes down smoothly. Later it bites like a snake with poison in its fangs. Your eyes will see strange sights, and your mind will be confused. You will feel dizzy as if you're in a storm on the ocean, as if you're on top of a ship's sails. You will think, . . . "I wish I could wake up. Then I would get another drink" (Prov. 23:29–35).

The problem with drinking is that it's so easily abused. Most people don't stop with a glass of wine at dinner; they continue to drink until they are either lightheaded and confused, or drunk and totally disoriented. Either way, their judgment is impaired. They can harm themselves or anyone else in their path.

A lot of believers have decided to just stay clear of alcohol. Proverbs says it seems attractive, but eventually it is as devastating and as painful as a snakebite.

Drinking may cause you to make decisions that seem fun at the time, but stupid the next morning. In fact, it's entirely possible that you could do something that you have to pay for the rest of your life. People tell you not to drink because they care that you make wise decisions and that you live a long and healthy life. You'd be smart to take their advice. Don't let a chemical control you.

SEE FOR YOURSELF: Prov. 13:15; 14:18; 20:1; 31:4–5

24

1 Don't envy evil people
or try to be friends with them.
2 Their minds are always planning violence,
and they always talk about making trouble.

WISDOM

Why is wisdom important? (24:3–4)

3 It takes wisdom to have a good family,
and it takes understanding to make it strong.
4 It takes knowledge to fill a home
with rare and beautiful treasures.

5 Wise people have great power,
and those with knowledge have great strength.
6 So you need advice when you go to war.
If you have lots of good advice, you will win.

7 Foolish people cannot understand wisdom.
They have nothing to say in a discussion.

8 Whoever makes evil plans
will be known as a troublemaker.
9 Making foolish plans is sinful,
and making fun of wisdom is hateful.

10 If you give up when trouble comes,
it shows that you are weak.

11 Save those who are being led to their death;
rescue those who are about to be killed.
12 If you say, "We don't know anything about this,"
God, who knows what's in your mind, will notice.
He is watching you, and he will know.
He will reward each person for what he has done.

13 My child, eat honey because it is good.
Honey from the honeycomb tastes sweet.
14 In the same way, wisdom is pleasing to you.
If you find it, you have hope for the future,
and your wishes will come true.

15 Don't be wicked and attack a good family's house;

don't rob the place where they live.
16 Even though good people may be
bothered by trouble seven times, they
are never defeated,
but the wicked are overwhelmed by
trouble.

17 Don't be happy when your enemy is
defeated;
don't be glad when he is overwhelmed.
18 The LORD will notice and be displeased.
He may not be angry with them
anymore.

19 Don't envy evil people,
and don't be jealous of the wicked.
20 An evil person has nothing to hope for;
the wicked will die like a flame that is
put out.

21 My child, respect the LORD and the king.
Don't join those people who refuse to
obey them.
22 The LORD and the king will quickly
destroy such people.
Those two can cause great disaster!

WHAT'S IT MEAN?

The first three kings of Israel were all appointed by a prophet before they were officially crowned. This involved pouring olive oil on the head of the king-to-be. The ritual was important, because it indicated that the king had been chosen by God himself. Questioning the king's authority was like questioning God's authority. David recognized that when King Saul was trying to kill him. He refused to retaliate against the king because Saul had been appointed by God.

Proverbs 24:21

MORE WORDS OF WISDOM

23 These are also sayings of the wise:
It is not good to take sides when you are
the judge.
24 Don't tell the wicked that they are
innocent;
people will curse you, and nations will
hate you.
25 But things will go well if you punish the
guilty,
and you will receive rich blessings.

26 An honest answer is as pleasing
as a kiss on the lips.

27 First, finish your outside work
and prepare your fields.
After that, you can build your house.

28 Don't testify against your neighbor for no
good reason.
Don't say things that are false.
29 Don't say, "I'll get even;
I'll do to him what he did to me."

30 I passed by a lazy person's field
and by the vineyard of someone with
no sense.
31 Thorns had grown up everywhere.
The ground was covered with weeds,
and the stone walls had fallen down.
32 I thought about what I had seen;
I learned this lesson from what I saw.
33 You sleep a little; you take a nap.
You fold your hands and lie down to
rest.
34 Soon you will be as poor as if you had
been robbed;
you will have as little as if you had been
held up.

MORE WISE SAYINGS OF SOLOMON

25

1 These are more wise sayings of Solomon,
copied by the men of Hezekiah king of Judah.
2 God is honored for what he keeps
secret.
Kings are honored for what they can
discover.

3 No one can measure the height of the
skies or the depth of the earth.
So also no one can understand the mind
of a king.

4 Remove the scum from the silver,
so the silver can be used by the
silversmith.
5 Remove wicked people from the king's
presence;
then his government will be honest and
last a long time.

6 Don't brag to the king
and act as if you are great.

7 It is better for him to give you a higher
position
than to bring you down in front of the
prince.

Because of something you have seen,
8 do not quickly take someone to court.
What will you do later
when your neighbor proves you
wrong?

On the Edge

When you lie about your neighbors, it hurts them as much as a club, a sword, or a sharp arrow. Trusting unfaithful people when you are in trouble is like eating with a broken tooth or walking with a crippled foot. . . . If your enemy is hungry, feed him. If he is thirsty, give him a drink. Doing this will be like pouring burning coals on his head, and the LORD will reward you (Prov. 25:18–19, 21–22).

Here in Proverbs and later in the New Testament, the writers give us some wisdom about friends who tell lies or treat us badly. The advice is to do exactly the opposite of what your friends do. Even in your disappointment and anger, you are supposed to be Christlike. Luke 6:28 says to "bless those who curse you, pray for those who are cruel to you." By loving those who hurt you, you will pour "burning coals on his head." Wow, that's pretty hard advice. Your reputation has been shattered. Your pride has been wounded. Your tender heart is broken. And God wants you to do what? Yes, he says to love them anyway—even give food to them if they are hungry. Oh yeah, and pray for them, too. By doing so, you prove the strength of your character. That's God's way.

SEE FOR YOURSELF:
Matt. 18:21–22;
Luke 6:28; 17:3–4;
Col. 3:13

9 If you have an argument with your
neighbor,
don't tell other people what was said.
10 Whoever hears it might shame you,
and you might not ever be respected
again.

11 The right word spoken at the right
time
is as beautiful as gold apples in a silver
bowl.

12 A wise warning to someone who will
listen
is as valuable as gold earrings or fine
gold jewelry.

13 Trustworthy messengers refresh those who
send them,
like the coolness of snow in the
summertime.

14 People who brag about gifts they never
give
are like clouds and wind that give no
rain.

15 With patience you can convince a
ruler,
and a gentle word can get through to
the hard-headed.

16 If you find honey, don't eat too much,
or it will make you throw up.
17 Don't go to your neighbor's house too
often;
too much of you will make him hate
you.

18 When you lie about your neighbors,
it hurts them as much as a club, a
sword, or a sharp arrow.

19 Trusting unfaithful people when you are
in trouble
is like eating with a broken tooth or
walking with a crippled foot.

20 Singing songs to someone who is sad
is like taking away his coat on a cold
day
or pouring vinegar on soda.

21 If your enemy is hungry, feed him.
If he is thirsty, give him a drink.
22 Doing this will be like pouring burning
coals on his head,
and the LORD will reward you.

23 As the north wind brings rain,
telling gossip brings angry looks.

24 It is better to live in a corner on the roof[n]
than inside the house with a quarreling wife.

25 Good news from a faraway place
is like a cool drink when you are tired.

26 A good person who gives in to evil
is like a muddy spring or a dirty well.

27 It is not good to eat too much honey,
nor does it bring you honor to brag about yourself.

28 Those who do not control themselves
are like a city whose walls are broken down.

26

1 It shouldn't snow in summer or rain at harvest.
Neither should a foolish person ever be honored.

2 Curses will not harm someone who is innocent;
they are like sparrows or swallows that fly around and never land.

3 Whips are for horses, and harnesses are for donkeys,
so paddles are good for fools.

4 Don't give fools a foolish answer,
or you will be just like them.

5 But answer fools as they should be answered,
or they will think they are really wise.

6 Sending a message by a foolish person
is like cutting off your feet or drinking poison.

7 A wise saying spoken by a fool
is as useless as the legs of a crippled person.

8 Giving honor to a foolish person
is like tying a stone in a slingshot.

9 A wise saying spoken by a fool
is like a thorn stuck in the hand of a drunk.

10 Hiring a foolish person or anyone just passing by
is like an archer shooting at just anything.

11 A fool who repeats his foolishness
is like a dog that goes back to what it has thrown up.

12 There is more hope for a foolish person
than for those who think they are wise.

13 The lazy person says, "There's a lion in the road!
There's a lion in the streets!"

14 Like a door turning back and forth on its hinges,
the lazy person turns over and over in bed.

15 Lazy people may put their hands in the dish,
but they are too tired to lift the food to their mouths.

16 The lazy person thinks he is wiser
than seven people who give sensible answers.

17 Interfering in someone else's quarrel as you pass by
is like grabbing a dog by the ears.

18 Like a madman shooting
deadly, burning arrows
19 is the one who tricks a neighbor
and then says, "I was just joking."

20 Without wood, a fire will go out,
and without gossip, quarreling will stop.

21 Just as charcoal and wood keep a fire going,
a quarrelsome person keeps an argument going.

GOSSIP
What is one benefit found when gossip is stopped? (26:20)

22 The words of a gossip are like tasty bits of food;
people like to gobble them up.

25:24 roof In Bible times houses were built with flat roofs. The roof was used for drying things such as flax and fruit. And it was used as an extra room, as a place for worship, and as a cool place to sleep in the summer.

On the Edge

Interfering in someone else's quarrel as you pass by is like grabbing a dog by the ears (Prov. 26:17).

Your friends are arguing? Get out. Hurry. Proverbs 26:17 says it would be better to grab a dog by the ears than to take part in your friends' argument. The middle of your friends' argument is a lose-lose situation. The best that could happen is that they will make up, and only one of them will be mad at you. Politely tell them that you love them both too much to be pulled into their disagreement. No matter what you think, it's best to keep your mouth shut. They have to resolve things themselves. You can't relay information. Refuse to take sides. Let them both know that you want to spend time with them, but until this whole thing blows over, you have to step aside. Let them work it out. You will be spared lots of time and heartache if you quickly get out of the picture.

SEE FOR YOURSELF: Prov. 11:12; 13:3; 17:27; 27:12

23 Kind words from a wicked mind
are like a shiny coating on a clay pot.

24 Those who hate you may try to fool you with their words,
but in their minds they are planning evil.
25 People's words may be kind, but don't believe them,
because their minds are full of evil thoughts.
26 Lies can hide hate,
but the evil will be plain to everyone.

27 Whoever digs a pit for others will fall into it.
Whoever tries to roll a boulder down on others will be crushed by it.

28 Liars hate the people they hurt,
and false praise can ruin others.

27

1 Don't brag about tomorrow;
you don't know what may happen then.

2 Don't praise yourself. Let someone else do it.
Let the praise come from a stranger and not from your own mouth.

3 Stone is heavy, and sand is weighty,
but a complaining fool is worse than either.

4 Anger is cruel and destroys like a flood,
but no one can put up with jealousy!

5 It is better to correct someone openly
than to have love and not show it.

6 The slap of a friend can be trusted to help you,
but the kisses of an enemy are nothing but lies.

7 When you are full, not even honey tastes good,
but when you are hungry, even something bitter tastes sweet.

8 A person who leaves his home
is like a bird that leaves its nest.

9 The sweet smell of perfume and oils is pleasant,
and so is good advice from a friend.

10 Don't forget your friend or your parent's friend.
Don't always go to your family for help when trouble comes.
A neighbor close by is better than a family far away.

11 Be wise, my child, and make me happy.
Then I can respond to any insult.

12 The wise see danger ahead and avoid it,
but fools keep going and get into trouble.

13 Take the coat of someone who promises to pay a stranger's loan,
and keep it until he pays what the stranger owes.

14 If you loudly greet your neighbor early in the morning,
he will think of it as a curse.

15 A quarreling wife is as bothersome
as a continual dripping on a rainy day.

16 Stopping her is like stopping the wind
or trying to grab oil in your hand.

17 As iron sharpens iron,
so people can improve each other.

18 Whoever tends a fig tree gets to eat its
fruit,
and whoever takes care of his master
will receive honor.

19 As water reflects your face,
so your mind shows what kind of
person you are.

20 People will never stop dying and being
destroyed,
and they will never stop wanting more
than they have.

WHAT'S IT MEAN?

The Hebrew of this verse refers to "Death" and "Destruction" as living beings. The ancient Hebrews pictured death as a monster with an enormous mouth and an appetite that was never satisfied. No matter how many people it "ate," it always wanted more.

Proverbs 27:20

21 A hot furnace tests silver and gold,
and people are tested by the praise they
receive.

22 Even if you ground up a foolish person
like grain in a bowl,
you couldn't remove the foolishness.

23 Be sure you know how your sheep are
doing,
and pay attention to the condition of
your cattle.
24 Riches will not go on forever,
nor do governments go on forever.
25 Bring in the hay, and let the new grass
appear.
Gather the grass from the hills.
26 Make clothes from the lambs' wool,
and sell some goats to buy a field.
27 There will be plenty of goat's milk
to feed you and your family
and to make your servant girls healthy.

28

1 Evil people run even though no one is
chasing them,
but good people are as brave as a lion.

2 When a country is lawless, it has one ruler
after another;
but when it is led by a man with
understanding and knowledge, it
continues strong.

3 Rulers who mistreat the poor
are like a hard rain that destroys the
crops.

4 Those who disobey what they have been
taught praise the wicked,
but those who obey what they have
been taught are against them.

5 Evil people do not understand justice,
but those who follow the LORD
understand it completely.

6 It is better to be poor and innocent
than to be rich and wicked.

7 Children who obey what they have been
taught are smart,
but friends of troublemakers disgrace
their parents.

8 Some people get rich by overcharging
others,

WHAT'S IT MEAN?

One common form of overcharging was interest on loans. Banking rules in ancient Israel were pretty strict. God's Law prohibited people from charging interest on loans made to poor people. Borrowers could not be forced to give up their coats as collateral for loans. Lenders were not allowed to use force to collect payment.

Proverbs 28:8

but their wealth will be given to those
who are kind to the poor.

9 If you refuse to obey what you have been
taught,
your prayers will not be heard.

10 Those who lead good people to do wrong
will be ruined by their own evil,
but the innocent will be rewarded with
good things.

11 Rich people may think they
are wise,
but the poor with
understanding will
prove them wrong.

12 When good people
triumph, there is
great happiness,
but when the wicked
get control,
everybody hides.

"Innocent people will be kept safe, but those who are dishonest will suddenly be ruined." (Proverbs 28:18)

13 If you hide your sins, you will not
succeed.
If you confess and reject them, you will
receive mercy.

14 Those who are always respectful will be
happy,
but those who are stubborn will get into
trouble.

WHAT'S IT MEAN?

Believe it or not, lions and bears were serious problems in ancient Israel. Lions often hid in the tall grass beside the Jordan River or in the surrounding forests and attacked unsuspecting people. The Asian black bears in the area were a threat not only to humans, but also to livestock and even crops.

Proverbs 28:15

15 A wicked ruler is as dangerous to poor
people
as a roaring lion or a charging bear.

16 A ruler without wisdom will be cruel,
but the one who refuses to take
dishonest money will rule a long time.

17 Don't help those who are guilty of
murder;
let them run until they die.

18 Innocent people will be kept safe,
but those who are dishonest will
suddenly be ruined.

19 Those who work their
land will have plenty
of food,
but the ones who chase
empty dreams instead
will end up poor.

20 A truthful person will
have many blessings,
but those eager to get
rich will be punished.

21 It is not good for a judge
to take sides,
but some will sin for only a piece of
bread.

22 Selfish people are in a hurry to get rich
and do not realize they soon will be
poor.

23 Those who correct others will later be
liked
more than those who give false praise.

24 Whoever robs his father or mother
and says, "It's not wrong,"
is just like someone who destroys
things.

25 A greedy person causes
trouble,
but the one who trusts
the LORD will succeed.

26 Those who trust in
themselves are
foolish,
but those who live wisely will be kept
safe.

TRUST

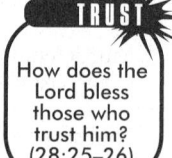

How does the Lord bless those who trust him? (28:25–26)

27 Whoever gives to the poor will have
everything he needs,
but the one who ignores the poor will
receive many curses.

28 When the wicked get control, everybody
hides,
but when they die, good people do well.

29

1 Whoever is stubborn after being corrected
many times
will suddenly be hurt beyond cure.

2 When good people do well, everyone is
happy,
but when evil people rule, everyone
groans.

3 Those who love wisdom make their
parents happy,
but friends of prostitutes waste their
money.

4 If a king is fair, he makes his country
strong,
but if he takes gifts dishonestly, he tears
his country down.

5 Those who give false praise to their
neighbors
are setting a trap for them.

6 Evil people are trapped by their own sin,
but good people can sing and be
happy.

7 Good people care about justice for the
poor,
but the wicked are not concerned.

8 People who make fun of wisdom cause
trouble in a city,
but wise people calm anger down.

9 When a wise person takes a foolish person
to court,
the fool only shouts or laughs, and
there is no peace.

10 Murderers hate an honest person
and try to kill those who do right.

11 Foolish people lose their tempers,
but wise people control theirs.

12 If a ruler pays attention to lies,
all his officers will become wicked.

13 The poor person and the cruel person are
alike
in that the LORD gave eyes to both of
them.

14 If a king judges poor people fairly,
his government will continue forever.

15 Correction and punishment make children
wise,
but those left alone will disgrace their
mother.

16 When there are many wicked people, there
is much sin,
but those who do right will see them
destroyed.

17 Correct your children, and you will be
proud;
they will give you satisfaction.

18 Where there is no word from God, people
are uncontrolled,
but those who obey what they have
been taught are happy.

19 Words alone cannot correct a servant,
because even if he understands, he
won't respond.

20 Do you see people who speak too
quickly?
There is more hope for a foolish person
than for them.

21 If you spoil your servants when they are
young,
they will bring you grief later on.

22 An angry person causes trouble;
a person with a quick temper
sins a lot.

23 Pride will ruin
people,
but those who are
humble will be
honored.

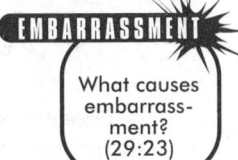

EMBARRASSMENT

What causes embarrassment? (29:23)

24 Partners of thieves are their own worst
enemies.
If they have to testify in court, they are
afraid to say anything.

25 Being afraid of people can get you into
trouble,
but if you trust the LORD, you will be
safe.

26 Many people want to speak to a ruler,
but justice comes only from the LORD.

27 Good people hate those who are
dishonest,
and the wicked hate those who are
honest.

WISE WORDS FROM AGUR

30

1 These are the words of Agur son of Jakeh.
This is his message to Ithiel and Ucal:

2 "I am the most stupid person there is,
and I have no understanding.
3 I have not learned to be wise,
and I don't know much about God, the
Holy One.
4 Who has gone up to heaven and come
back down?
Who can hold the wind in his hand?
Who can gather up the waters in his coat?
Who has set in place the ends of the
earth?
What is his name or his son's name?
Tell me, if you know!

5 "Every word of God is true.
He guards those who come to him for
safety.
6 Do not add to his words,
or he will correct you and prove you
are a liar.

7 "I ask two things from you, LORD.
Don't refuse me before I die.
8 Keep me from lying and being dishonest.
And don't make me either rich or poor;
just give me enough food for each day.
9 If I have too much, I might reject you
and say, 'I don't know the LORD.'
If I am poor, I might steal
and disgrace the name of my God.

10 "Do not say bad things about servants to
their masters,
or they will curse you, and you will
suffer for it.

11 "Some people curse their fathers
and do not bless their mothers.
12 Some people think they are pure,
but they are not really free from evil.
13 Some people have such a proud look!
They look down on others.
14 Some people have teeth like swords;
their jaws seem full of knives.
They want to remove the poor from the
earth
and the needy from the land.

15 "Greed has two daughters
named 'Give' and 'Give.'
There are three things that are never
satisfied,
really four that never say, 'I've had
enough!':
16 the cemetery, the childless mother,

Promise

HE PROMISES THAT EVERYTHING HE SAYS IS TRUE.

Every word of God is true. He guards those who come to him for safety (Prov. 30:5).

Have you ever told "a little white lie"? You know, what you said was not quite true, but it didn't hurt anybody and it got you out of a tight spot. Or maybe your skill is telling your mom something that is *technically* true. When you've finished explaining, what she thinks happened and what really happened are two different things. That's the way human beings are—they shade the truth this way and that, turning what's black and white into shades of gray.

But God isn't like that. Everything he says is pure and true, not barely sliding by on a variation of the truth. His honesty doesn't depend on technicalities. And God isn't just honest. He's also right. You might make a statement that you thought was true, only to find out later that you were wrong. But God doesn't make mistakes.

His word is so reliable that you can use it for a shield. That's what Jesus did when Satan tempted him (see Matt. 4:1–11). He used God's words to protect his heart. It's good to know that there are no cracks in the shield. Everything he says is true.

SEE FOR YOURSELF:
Prov. 12:19; Matt. 4:1–11

the land that never gets enough rain,
and fire that never says, 'I've had enough!'

17 "If you make fun of your father
and refuse to obey your mother,
the birds of the valley will peck out your eyes,
and the vultures will eat them.

18 "There are three things that are too hard for me,
really four I don't understand:
19 the way an eagle flies in the sky,
the way a snake slides over a rock,
the way a ship sails on the sea,
and the way a man and a woman fall in love.

20 "This is the way of a woman who takes part in adultery:
She acts as if she had eaten and washed her face;
she says, 'I haven't done anything wrong.'

21 "There are three things that make the earth tremble,
really four it cannot stand:
22 a servant who becomes a king,
a foolish person who has plenty to eat,
23 a hated woman who gets married,
and a maid who replaces her mistress.

24 "There are four things on earth that are small,
but they are very wise:
25 Ants are not very strong,
but they store up food in the summer.
26 Rock badgers are not very powerful,
but they can live among the rocks.
27 Locusts have no king,
but they all go forward in formation.
28 Lizards can be caught in the hand,
but they are found even in kings' palaces.

29 "There are three things that strut proudly,
really four that walk as if they were important:
30 a lion, the proudest animal,
which is strong and runs from nothing,
31 a rooster, a male goat,
and a king when his army is around him.

32 "If you have been foolish and proud,
or if you have planned evil, shut your mouth.
33 Just as stirring milk makes butter,
and twisting noses makes them bleed,
so stirring up anger causes trouble."

WISE WORDS OF KING LEMUEL

31

1 These are the words of King Lemuel, the
message his mother taught him:
2 "My son, I gave birth to you.
You are the son I prayed for.
3 Don't waste your strength on women
or your time on those who ruin kings.

4 "Kings should not drink wine, Lemuel,
and rulers should not desire beer.
5 If they drink, they might forget the law
and keep the needy from getting their rights.
6 Give beer to people who are dying
and wine to those who are sad.
7 Let them drink and forget their need
and remember their misery no more.

8 "Speak up for those who cannot speak for themselves;
defend the rights of all those who have nothing.
9 Speak up and judge fairly,
and defend the rights of the poor and needy."

THE GOOD WIFE

10 It is hard to find a good wife,
because she is worth more than rubies.
11 Her husband trusts her completely.
With her, he has everything he needs.
12 She does him good and not harm
for as long as she lives.
13 She looks for wool and flax
and likes to work with her hands.
14 She is like a trader's ship,
bringing food from far away.
15 She gets up while it is still dark
and prepares food for her family
and feeds her servant girls.
16 She inspects a field and buys it.
With money she earned, she plants a vineyard.
17 She does her work with energy,
and her arms are strong.
18 She knows that what she makes is good.

RESPECT
Is respect easily gained? (31:10–11, 18–23)

Her lamp burns late into the night.
19 She makes thread with her hands
and weaves her own cloth.
20 She welcomes the poor
and helps the needy.
21 She does not worry about her family
when it snows,
because they all have fine clothes to
keep them warm.
22 She makes coverings for herself;
her clothes are made of linen and other
expensive material.
23 Her husband is known at the city
meetings,
where he makes decisions as one of the
leaders of the land.
24 She makes linen clothes and sells them
and provides belts to the merchants.
25 She is strong and is respected by the
people.
She looks forward to the future with joy.
26 She speaks wise words
and teaches others to be kind.
27 She watches over her family
and never wastes her time.
28 Her children speak well of her.
Her husband also praises her,
29 saying, "There are many fine women,
but you are better than all of them."
30 Charm can fool you, and beauty can trick
you,
but a woman who respects the LORD
should be praised.
31 Give her the reward she has earned;
she should be praised in public for what
she has done.

ecclesiastes

CONTENT Ecclesiastes was written by a man who had it all and found out it wasn't enough.

You've got to understand that he *literally* had it all. He had all the money you could imagine. He had the possessions of the richest man on earth. He had wives and wannabe-wives at every turn. He had unlimited power. He had prestige. He had superstardom and fame. Everything his society could make available was his.

He also did everything. He tried every kind of recreation. Every form of entertainment and amusement was his for the bidding. What a life!

After he had it all and did it all, he wrote this book to leave a legacy of what he thought about having it all. He said, "Without God, none of it matters."

Some people think Ecclesiastes is a little depressing. After all, we spend our lives wanting the things this man, King Solomon, had. It's not much fun to think that everything we dream about won't really bring us happiness. On the other hand, though, putting our lives in perspective with God out in front should mean we'll enjoy our lives more because everything we do means something.

Outline

1:1—2:26 .... The Search for Meaning in Life
3:1–8 .... Everything Has Its Time
3:9—6:12 .... Life Isn't Always Fair, So Live Wisely
7:1—8:17 .... Practical Wisdom
9:1—11:6 .... No One Knows What the Future Will Bring
11:7—12:14 .... Respect and Obey God

Purpose Apart from God, life can have no meaning.

Theme A Quest for Something of True Value in This Life

Date of writing 935 B.C.

"Now, everything has been heard, so I give my final advice: Honor God and obey his commands, because this is all people must do. God will judge everything, even what is done in secret, the good and the evil" (12:13–14).

Bible Talk

Solomon's Wealth

It is true that in Solomon's day he didn't have all the conveniences that we have today. He didn't have electricity or computers or automobiles. But don't let that fool you. Solomon had stuff that would turn the heads of people in any age. The Bible says that he made silver as common as stones. He was surrounded by gold. He had hundreds of wives. He lived in an extravagant, beautiful palace. There was nothing that he might want that he couldn't have.

He had all this because, when God came to him in a dream and said he would give Solomon anything he asked for, Solomon asked for wisdom. He didn't ask for riches or wives or horses. God honored Solomon's wisdom by giving it all to him.

CELEBRITIES

We look at a lot of celebrities today like Solomon's people would have looked at him. We assume that because they *have* a lot of things and money to buy more things that they must be happy. We assume that, if we had everything a celebrity has, then we would be happy. Ecclesiastes tells us otherwise.

We don't often get to sit down and have a heart-to-heart with superstars. But that's exactly what Ecclesiastes is. It seems like he would be saying, "Come on over to money, fame, and fortune! The water's nice and warm!" Instead he's saying, "If you are not connected to God, if he's not the source of your joy, you won't find it here any more than you find it right where you are."

1 These are the words of the Teacher, a son of
David, king in Jerusalem.
2 The Teacher says,
"Useless! Useless!
Completely useless!
Everything is useless."

3 What do people really gain
from all the hard work they do here on
earth?

On the Edge

Everything is boring, so boring that you don't even want to talk about it. Words come again and again to our ears, but we never hear enough, nor can we ever really see all we want to see (Eccl. 1:8).

A lot of people spend all their lives trying to get satisfied. Cars, clothes, tattoos, body piercing, drugs—whatever the latest thing is to make you feel like somebody. Solomon says in Ecclesiastes that nothing this world has to offer will ever do it. Nothing will ever make you feel satisfied. New clothes may fill you up for a few days. And then you're empty again. The high doesn't last long enough.

The fact is that, without Jesus, nothing matters. There is no purpose in life, and even the coolest stuff only brings momentary pleasure. Apart from Jesus you will never enjoy your time on earth or the things you've been given. It's all meaningless without the Savior. Without Jesus, this is all there is—no future, no eternity to look forward to. So when your heart is aching, your life seems empty, and you feel lost, go to Jesus to be filled up and satisfied. He will not disappoint you.

SEE FOR YOURSELF:
1 Cor. 15:58; Gal. 6:8; Phil. 3:7, 12–14

THINGS NEVER CHANGE

4 People live, and people die,
but the earth continues forever.
5 The sun rises, the sun sets,
and then it hurries back to where it rises
again.
6 The wind blows to the south;
it blows to the north.
It blows from one direction and then
another.
Then it turns around and repeats the
same pattern, going nowhere.
7 All the rivers flow to the sea,
but the sea never becomes full.
8 Everything is boring,
so boring that you don't even want to
talk about it.
Words come again and again to our ears,
but we never hear enough,
nor can we ever really see all we want
to see.
9 All things continue the way they have
been since the beginning.
What has happened will happen again;
there is nothing new here on earth.
10 Someone might say,
"Look, this is new,"
but really it has always been here.
It was here before we were.
11 People don't remember what happened
long ago,
and in the future people will not
remember what happens now.
Even later, other people will not
remember what was done before
them.

DOES WISDOM BRING HAPPINESS?

12 I, the Teacher, was king over Israel in Jerusalem. 13 I decided to use my wisdom to learn
about everything that happens on earth. I
learned that God has given us terrible things to
face. 14 I looked at everything done on earth
and saw that it is all useless, like chasing the
wind.
15 If something is crooked,

WHAT'S IT MEAN?

Solomon was something of a celebrity during his lifetime. During his forty-year reign as king, people would come to Jerusalem from faraway countries just to hear Solomon say something wise. Not only did Solomon know a lot about human nature and the scientific world, he is also considered to be the most important and influential philosopher of the ancient Near East.
Ecclesiastes 1:16

you can't make it straight.
If something is missing,
you can't say it is there.
16 I said to myself, "I have become very wise
and am now wiser than anyone who ruled Jerusalem before me. I know what wisdom and
knowledge really are." 17 So I decided to find out
about wisdom and knowledge and also about
foolish thinking, but this turned out to be like
chasing the wind.
18 With much wisdom comes much
disappointment;
the person who gains more knowledge
also gains more sorrow.

DOES "HAVING FUN" BRING HAPPINESS?

2 1 I said to myself, "I will try having fun. I will
enjoy myself." But I found that this is also
useless. 2 It is foolish to laugh all the time, and
having fun doesn't accomplish anything. 3 I decided to cheer myself up with wine while my
mind was still thinking wisely. I wanted to find
a way to enjoy myself and see what was good
for people to do during their few days of life.

WHAT'S IT MEAN?

Times were good in Israel when Solomon was king. In fact, the nation's economy was so strong that Solomon began importing rare and exotic items such as ivory, apes, and peacocks. His vast orchards may have produced such fruits as pomegranates, mulberries, apricots, figs, and apples, as well as almonds and sycamores.

Ecclesiastes 2:4–5

DOES HARD WORK BRING HAPPINESS?

4 Then I did great things: I built houses and
planted vineyards for myself. 5 I made gardens
and parks, and I planted all kinds of fruit trees
in them. 6 I made pools of water for myself and
used them to water my growing trees. 7 I
bought male and female slaves, and slaves
were also born in my house. I had large herds
and flocks, more than anyone in Jerusalem
had ever had before. 8 I also gathered silver and
gold for myself, treasures from kings and other
areas. I had male and female singers and all the
women a man could ever want. 9 I became very
famous, even greater than anyone who had
lived in Jerusalem before me. My wisdom
helped me in all this.

WHAT'S IT MEAN?

Most women received very little respect in ancient times. In fact, they were often treated more like possessions than people. Some women were even given as gifts! For example, when two countries signed a treaty, it was customary for the less powerful nation to present women to the leader of the more powerful nation. That's how Solomon, the leader of the very powerful Israelite nation, came to have hundreds of wives and concubines, women who were little more than possessions to him. Many of Solomon's wives came from foreign countries and worshiped foreign gods.

Ecclesiastes 2:8

10 Anything I saw and wanted, I got for
myself;
I did not miss any pleasure I desired.
I was pleased with everything I did,
and this pleasure was the reward for all
my hard work.
11 But then I looked at what I had done,
and I thought about all the hard work.
Suddenly I realized it was useless, like
chasing the wind.
There is nothing to gain from anything
we do here on earth.

MAYBE WISDOM IS THE ANSWER

12 Then I began to think again about being
wise,
and also about being foolish and doing
crazy things.
But after all, what more can anyone do?
He can't do more than what the other
king has already done.
13 I saw that being wise is certainly better
than being foolish,
just as light is better than darkness.
14 Wise people see where they are going,
but fools walk around in the dark.
Yet I saw that
both wise and foolish people end the
same way.

15 I thought to myself,
"What happens to a fool will happen to
me, too,

so what is the reward for being wise?"
I said to myself,
"Being wise is also useless."
[16]The wise person and the fool
will both die,
and no one will remember either one for
long.
In the future, both will be forgotten.

IS THERE REAL HAPPINESS IN LIFE?

[17]So I hated life. It made me sad to think
that everything here on earth is useless, like
chasing the wind. [18]I hated all the things I had
worked for here on earth, because I must leave
them to someone who will live after me.
[19]Someone else will control everything for
which I worked so hard here on earth, and I
don't know if he will be wise or foolish. This is
also useless. [20]So I became sad about all the
hard work I had done here on earth. [21]People
can work hard using all their wisdom, knowledge, and skill, but they will die, and other
people will get the things for which they
worked. They did not do the work, but they
will get everything. This is also unfair and useless. [22]What do people get for all their work
and struggling here on earth? [23]All of their lives
their work is full of pain and sorrow, and even
at night their minds don't rest. This is also useless.

[24]The best that people can do is eat, drink,
and enjoy their work. I saw that even this
comes from God, [25]because no one can eat or
enjoy life without him. [26]If people please God,
God will give them wisdom, knowledge, and
joy. But sinners will get only the work of gathering and storing wealth that they will have to
give to the ones who please God. So all their
work is useless, like chasing the wind.

THERE IS A TIME FOR EVERYTHING

3

[1]There is a time for everything,
and everything on earth has its special
season.
[2]There is a time to be born
and a time to die.
There is a time to plant
and a time to pull up plants.
[3]There is a time to kill
and a time to heal.
There is a time to destroy
and a time to build.
[4]There is a time to cry
and a time to laugh.
There is a time to be sad
and a time to dance.
[5]There is a time to throw away stones
and a time to gather them.
There is a time to hug
and a time not to hug.

Promise

HE PROMISES TO MAKE EVERYTHING HAPPEN JUST RIGHT AND ON TIME.

God has given them a desire to know the future. He does everything just right and on time, but people can never completely understand what he is doing (Eccl. 3:11).

You're walking down the hall thinking about the two brand-new five-dollar bills in your wallet, and a guy you owe three bucks to comes around the corner. You're really tempted to cheat on a test, but the smart girl who sits next to you is absent that day. You're thinking about sending a card to a girl who looks like she needs cheering up, and when you find your student directory in the bottom of your locker, it's opened to the page that has her address on it.

Coincidences? If you've been hanging out with God for very long, you probably don't think so. He has a way of bringing even these little things together at the right time. It's one of the ways he reminds us that he's got everything under control.

That's his way with the big things in life, too. The list that Solomon put together in Ecclesiastes 3:1–8 includes some things that don't sound too good. But everything God allows in your life—even sadness—has a purpose, and he has worked out the timing perfectly. He can do that because he knows you better than you do. And he knows what's coming next, too. If the timing seems lousy to you, trust that God knows something you don't know.

SEE FOR YOURSELF:
Acts 4:28; Rom. 8:28; 2 Tim. 1:9

6 There is a time to look for something
and a time to stop looking
for it.
There is a time to keep
things
and a time to throw
things away.
7 There is a time to tear
apart
and a time to sew
together.
There is a time to be silent
and a time to speak.
8 There is a time to love
and a time to hate.
There is a time for war
and a time for peace.

"There is a time for everything, and everything on earth has its special season." (Ecclesiastes 3:1)

GOD CONTROLS HIS WORLD

9 Do people really gain anything from their
work? 10 I saw the hard work God has given
people to do. 11 God has given them a desire to
know the future. He does everything just right
and on time, but people can never completely
understand what he is doing. 12 So I realize that
the best thing for them is to be happy and enjoy themselves as long as they live. 13 God
wants all people to eat and drink and be happy
in their work, which are gifts from God. 14 I
know that everything God does will continue
forever. People cannot add anything to what
God has done, and they cannot take anything
away from it. God does it this way to make
people respect him.

15 What happens now has happened in the
past,
and what will happen in the future has
happened before.
God makes the same things happen
again and again.

UNFAIRNESS ON EARTH

16 I also saw this here on earth:
Where there should have been justice,
there was evil;
where there should have been right,
there was wrong.
17 I said to myself,
God has planned a time for every thing
and every action,
so he will judge both good people and
bad.

18 I decided that God leaves it the way it is to
test people and to show them they are just like
animals. 19 The same thing happens to animals
and to people; they both have the same breath,
so they both die. People are no better off than
the animals, because everything is
useless. 20 Both end up the same
way; both came from dust and
both will go back to dust.
21 Who can be sure that the
human spirit goes up to God
and that the spirit of an animal goes down into the
ground? 22 So I saw that the
best thing people can do is to
enjoy their work, because that
is all they have. No one can help
another person see what will happen in the future.

IS IT BETTER TO BE DEAD?

4 1 Again I saw all the people who were mistreated here on earth.
I saw their tears
and that they had no one to comfort
them.
Cruel people had all the power,
and there was no one to comfort those
they hurt.
2 I decided that the dead
are better off than the living.
3 But those who have never been born
are better off still;
they have not seen the evil
that is done here on earth.

WHY WORK SO HARD?

4 I realized the reason people work hard and
try to succeed: They are jealous of each other.
This, too, is useless, like chasing the wind.
5 Some say it is foolish to fold your hands
and do nothing,

WHAT'S IT MEAN?

In ancient times, true success was measured by the size of a person's family. The more kids a person had, the more successful—and favored by God—he was thought to be. Women who were unable to bear children were thought to be cursed by God. Since parents were expected to provide for their kids' needs, it made sense that they would work hard.

Ecclesiastes 4:8

because you will starve to death.
6 Maybe so, but I say it is better to be content
with what little you have.
Otherwise, you will always be struggling for more,
and that is like chasing the wind.

7 Again I saw something here on earth that was useless:
8 I saw a man who had no family,
no son or brother.
He always worked hard
but was never satisfied with what he had.
He never asked himself, "For whom am I working so hard?
Why don't I let myself enjoy life?"
This also is very sad and useless.

On the Edge

Two people are better than one, because they get more done by working together. If one falls down, the other can help him up. But it is bad for the person who is alone and falls, because no one is there to help (Eccl. 4:9–10).

Chances are, your parents are more concerned that you get hooked up with a good group of friends than about your passionate commitment to the Latin Club. It's important for you to do things you enjoy with people you enjoy. Activities at school or church offer opportunities for you to develop the ability to get along with other people and to build your leadership skills. They give you a place to focus your energy and increase your talents and abilities. They're great practice for life later on.

Life is all about living and working with other people. Some of the most successful people in the workforce are those who were very involved in high school. On the other hand, kids who isolate themselves or spend a lot of time alone often get into trouble. Get involved. Learn to be a part of a group. Learn to work with other people. You'll be glad you did.

SEE FOR YOURSELF:
Prov. 22:24–25;
1 Cor. 15:33

FRIENDS AND FAMILY GIVE STRENGTH

9 Two people are better than one,
because they get more done by working together.
10 If one falls down,
the other can help him up.
But it is bad for the person who is alone and falls,
because no one is there to help.
11 If two lie down together, they will be warm,
but a person alone will not be warm.
12 An enemy might defeat one person,
but two people together can defend themselves;
a rope that is woven of three strings is hard to break.

FAME AND POWER ARE USELESS

13 A poor but wise boy is better than a foolish but old king who doesn't listen to advice.
14 A boy became king. He had been born poor
in the kingdom and had even gone to prison
before becoming king. 15 I watched all the people who live on earth follow him and make
him their king. 16 Many followed him at first,
but later, they did not like him, either. So fame
and power are useless, like chasing the wind.

BE CAREFUL ABOUT MAKING PROMISES

5 1 Be careful when you go to worship at the
Temple. It is better to listen than to offer foolish
sacrifices without even knowing you are doing
wrong.
2 Think before you speak,
and be careful about what you say to God.
God is in heaven,
and you are on the earth,
so say only a few words to God.
3 The saying is true: Bad dreams come from too much worrying,
and too many words come from foolish people.
4 If you make a promise to God, don't be
slow to keep it. God is not happy with fools, so
give God what you promised. 5 It is better not
to promise anything than to promise something and not do it. 6 Don't let your words
cause you to sin, and don't say to the priest at
the Temple, "I didn't mean what I promised." If
you do, God will become angry with your
words and will destroy everything you have
worked for. 7 Many useless promises are like so
many dreams; they mean nothing. You should
respect God.

WHAT'S IT MEAN?

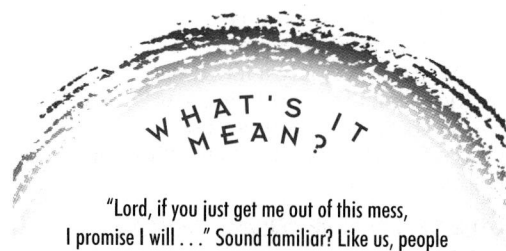

"Lord, if you just get me out of this mess, I promise I will . . ." Sound familiar? Like us, people in ancient times made all kinds of promises to God about what they would do if he helped them. For example, a person might have promised to make a certain kind of sacrifice if God heard his prayer. This verse serves as a reminder that God doesn't take such promises lightly.

Ecclesiastes 5:4

OFFICERS CHEAT EACH OTHER

8 In some places you will see poor people mistreated. Don't be surprised when they are not treated fairly or given their rights. One officer is cheated by a higher officer who in turn is cheated by even higher officers. 9 The wealth of the country is divided up among them all. Even the king makes sure he gets his share of the profits.

WEALTH CANNOT BUY HAPPINESS

10 Whoever loves money
will never have enough money;
Whoever loves wealth
will not be satisfied with it.
This is also useless.
11 The more wealth people have,
the more friends they have to help spend it.
So what do people really gain?
They gain nothing except to look at their riches.
12 Those who work hard sleep in peace;
it is not important if they eat little or much.
But rich people worry about their wealth
and cannot sleep.

13 I have seen real misery here on earth:
Money saved is a curse to its owners.
14 They lose it all in a bad deal
and have nothing to give to their children.
15 People come into this world with nothing,
and when they die they leave with nothing.
In spite of all their hard work,
they leave just as they came.
16 This, too, is real misery:
They leave just as they came.
So what do they gain from chasing the wind?
17 All they get are days full of sadness and sorrow,
and they end up sick, defeated, and angry.

ENJOY YOUR LIFE'S WORK

18 I have seen what is best for people here on earth. They should eat and drink and enjoy their work, because the life God has given

On the Edge

Don't let your words cause you to sin, and don't say to the priest at the Temple, "I didn't mean what I promised." If you do, God will become angry with your words and will destroy everything you have worked for (Eccl. 5:6).

How many times have you heard it? "Don't let your words cause you to sin," or, "Don't let your mouth get you in trouble." How many times have you let it? You were sassy to your mom, and she washed your mouth out with soap. You called your brother a name, and he punched you in the nose. You said something unkind about someone, and it got back to them.

Solomon, the writer of Ecclesiastes, is considered one of the wisest men ever. You'd be wise to take his advice. He knew that once you say something to somebody, you can never take it back. If you get angry and scream something you don't really mean, it could still hurt someone. You could say something innocent that gets twisted around and makes you look really bad. Proverbs 18:21 says that "what you say can mean life or death." It's true. Your words are powerful. They can encourage, inspire, comfort, or explain; or they can hurt, bite, sting, or devastate. Choose your words carefully and make them good. Count to ten before you spout off a bunch of insults you'll later regret. Your words can be life or death!

SEE FOR YOURSELF: Prov. 10:14; 18:6–7, 21; 21:23; Luke 6:45; Eph. 4:29

them on earth is short. 19 God gives some people the ability to enjoy the wealth and property
he gives them, as well as the ability to accept
their state in life and enjoy their work. 20 They do
not worry about how short life is, because God
keeps them busy with what they love to do.

6 1 I have seen something else wrong here on
earth that causes serious problems for people.
2 God gives great wealth, riches, and honor to
some people; they have everything they want.
But God does not let them enjoy such things; a
stranger enjoys them instead. This is useless
and very wrong. 3 A man might have a hundred children and live a long time, but what
good is it if he can't enjoy the good God gives
him or have a proper burial? I say a baby born
dead is better off than he is. 4 A baby born dead
is useless. It returns to darkness without even a
name. 5 That baby never saw the sun and never
knew anything, but it finds more rest than that
man. 6 Even if he lives two thousand years, he
doesn't enjoy the good God gives him. Everyone is going to the same place.

WHAT'S IT MEAN?

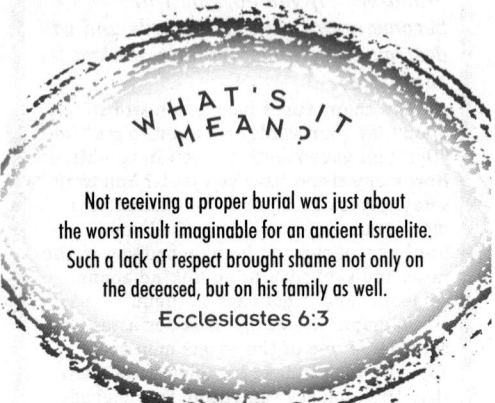

Not receiving a proper burial was just about the worst insult imaginable for an ancient Israelite. Such a lack of respect brought shame not only on the deceased, but on his family as well.

Ecclesiastes 6:3

7 People work just to feed themselves,
but they never seem to get enough to eat.
8 In this way a wise person
is no better off than a fool.
Then, too, it does a poor person little good
to know how to get along in life.
9 It is better to see what you have
than to want more.
Wanting more is useless—
like chasing the wind.

WHO CAN UNDERSTAND GOD'S PLAN?

10 Whatever happens was planned long ago.
Everyone knows what people are like.
No one can argue with God,
who is stronger than anyone.
11 The more you say,
the more useless it is.
What good does it do?

12 People have only a few useless days of life
on the earth; their short life passes like a shadow. Who knows what is best for them while
they live? Who can tell them what the future
will bring?

SOME BENEFITS OF SERIOUS THINKING

7 1 It is better to have respect than good perfume.
The day of death is better than the day of birth.
2 It is better to go to a funeral
than to a party.
We all must die,
and everyone living should think about this.
3 Sorrow is better than laughter,
and sadness has a good influence on you.
4 A wise person thinks about death,
but a fool thinks only about having a good time.
5 It is better to be criticized by a wise person
than to be praised by a fool.
6 The laughter of fools
is like the crackling of thorns in a cooking fire.
Both are useless.

7 Even wise people are fools
if they let money change their thinking.

8 It is better to finish something
than to start it.
It is better to be patient
than to be proud.
9 Don't become angry quickly,
because getting angry is foolish.

10 Don't ask, "Why was life better in the 'good old days'?"
It is not wise to ask such questions.

11 Wisdom is better when it comes with money.
They both help those who are alive.
12 Wisdom is like money:
they both help.
But wisdom is better,
because it can save whoever has it.

13 Look at what God has done:
No one can straighten what he has bent.
14 When life is good, enjoy it.

But when life is hard, remember:
God gives good times and hard times,
and no one knows what tomorrow will bring.

On the Edge

Surely there is not a good person on earth who always does good and never sins (Eccl. 7:20).

A woman was being harassed because of the bad things she had done. People yelled and jeered at her because her sin was so ugly. They were going to stone her to death. But Jesus said, "Anyone here who has never sinned can throw the first stone at her" (John 8:7). The angry crowd, one by one, dropped their stones and walked away. When each person had looked at his own life, he realized that his sin was just as ugly as hers.

As hard as you may try, you aren't sinless. You don't always do the right thing. You're human and you're not perfect. Into the pit of sin Jesus comes and gently shows you that you can't do it by yourself. You desperately need a Savior. There is no one alive who doesn't. Don't beat yourself up about your sin. Turn to the One who can save you from it.

SEE FOR YOURSELF:
Ps. 51; John 8:7; Rom. 3:23; Heb. 12:1–2

IT IS IMPOSSIBLE TO BE TRULY GOOD

15 In my useless life I have seen both of these:
I have seen good people die in spite of their goodness
and evil people live a long time in spite of their evil.
16 Don't be too right,
and don't be too wise.
Why destroy yourself?
17 Don't be too wicked,
and don't be foolish.
Why die before your time?
18 It is good to grab the one and not let go of the other;
those who honor God will hold them both.

19 Wisdom makes a person stronger
than ten leaders in a city.

20 Surely there is not a good person on earth
who always does good and never sins.

21 Don't listen to everything people say,
or you might hear your servant insulting you.
22 You know that many times
you have insulted others.

23 I used wisdom to test all these things.
I wanted to be wise,
but it was too hard for me.
24 I cannot understand why things are as they are.
It is too hard for anyone to understand.
25 I studied and tried very hard to find wisdom,
to find some meaning for everything.
I learned that it is foolish to be evil,
and it is crazy to act like a fool.

26 I found that some women are worse than death
and are as dangerous as traps.
Their love is like a net,
and their arms hold men like chains.
A man who pleases God will be saved from them,
but a sinner will be caught by them.

27 The Teacher says, "This is what I learned:
I added all these things together
to find some meaning for everything.
28 While I was searching,
I did not find one man among the thousands I found.
Nor did I find a woman among all these.
29 One thing I have learned:
God made people good,
but they have found all kinds of ways to be bad."

OBEY THE KING

8

1 No one is like the wise person
who can understand what things mean.
Wisdom brings happiness;
it makes sad faces happy.
2 Obey the king's command, because you
made a promise to God. 3 Don't be too quick
to leave the king. Don't support something
that is wrong, because the king does whatever he pleases. 4 What the king says is law;
no one tells him what to do.

5 Whoever obeys the king's command will
be safe.
A wise person does the right thing at the
right time.
6 There is a right time and a right way for
everything,
yet people often have many troubles.
7 They do not know what the future
holds,
and no one can tell them what will
happen.
8 No one can control the wind
or stop his own death.
No soldier is released in times of war,
and evil does not set free those who do
evil.

On the Edge

No one can control the wind or stop his own death. No soldier is released in times of war, and evil does not set free those who do evil (Eccl. 8:8).

You control your own destiny. You've heard that before, right? It's true to a certain extent. What you put into your life now will impact what you get out of it later. That's true of how hard you work at school or in your job. It's true of how you treat your parents. It's true of the kind of people you pick to be your friends.

But there's a whole lot in life that you can't control. You can't decide whether there's going to be a flood or a drought this year. You can't control how many people get hired for a summer job. You can't control the price of a soda. You can't control what other people do. But all these things can have an effect on you.

Does that mean you should get really scared worrying about all the things that _could_ happen without your being able to stop them? That wasn't Jesus' advice. He said don't sweat it. Let God take care of all that stuff that's out of your hands. You just concentrate on doing the things he wants you to do. You'll be a lot less frustrated if you quit worrying about things you can't control.

SEE FOR YOURSELF:
Matt. 6:34;
Luke 12:29–31;
1 Pet. 5:7

JUSTICE, REWARDS, AND PUNISHMENT

9 I saw all of this as I considered all that is
done here on earth. Sometimes men harm
those they control. 10 I saw the funerals of evil
people who used to go in and out of the holy
place. They were honored in the same towns
where they had done evil. This is useless, too.
11 When evil people are not punished right
away, it makes others want to do evil, too.
12 Though a sinner might do a hundred evil
things and might live a long time, I know it will
be better for those who honor God. 13 I also
know it will not go well for evil people, because they do not honor God. Like a shadow,
they will not last. 14 Sometimes something useless happens on earth. Bad things happen to
good people, and good things happen to bad
people. I say that this is also useless. 15 So I decided it was more important to enjoy life. The
best that people can do here on earth is to eat,
drink, and enjoy life, because these joys will
help them do the hard work God gives them
here on earth.

WE CANNOT UNDERSTAND ALL GOD DOES

16 I tried to understand all that happens on
earth. I saw how busy people are, working day
and night and hardly ever sleeping. 17 I also
saw all that God has done. Nobody can understand what God does here on earth. No
matter how hard people try to understand it,
they cannot. Even if wise people say they understand, they cannot; no one can really understand it.

IS DEATH FAIR?

9 1 I thought about all this and tried to understand it. I saw that God controls good people
and wise people and what they do, but no one
knows if they will experience love or hate.
2 Good and bad people end up the
same—
those who are right and those who are
wrong,
those who are good and those who are
evil,
those who are clean and those who are
unclean,
those who sacrifice and those who do
not.
The same things happen to a good person
as happen to a sinner,
to a person who makes promises to God
and to one who does not.
3 This is something wrong that happens
here on earth: What happens to one happens
to all. So people's minds are full of evil and

foolish thoughts while they live. After that,
they join the dead. 4But anyone still alive has
hope; even a live dog is better off than a dead
lion!

5 The living know they will die,
but the dead know nothing.
Dead people have no more reward,
and people forget them.
6 After people are dead,
they can no longer love or hate or envy.
They will never again share
in what happens here on earth.

WHAT'S IT MEAN?

In ancient Israel, the dog and the lion were on opposite ends of the popularity spectrum. The dogs of that era were wild creatures that traveled in packs, preyed on the weak, ate garbage, and stole food from the villages. You can imagine how popular they were with the Israelites. Lions, on the other hand, were respected for their size and strength. Although they were a very real danger to the Israelites, they also served as symbols of majesty and courage. Calling someone a dog in ancient Israel was an extremely offensive insult. Calling someone a lion was an extremely high compliment.

Ecclesiastes 9:4

On the Edge

Put on nice clothes and make yourself look good (Eccl. 9:8).

Why not? Solomon says that life is too short to not enjoy it. He says, "Put on nice clothes and make yourself look good." In other words, always be clean and look your best. Too soon you'll be at the end of your life, and you won't want to have looked like a bum all the way through it. God has given you a gift in your body. Even if you're not the most handsome or most beautiful, everybody appreciates your efforts to do the best with what you've got. Neat and clean doesn't mean "hippest and most expensive." It means clean clothes, combed hair, brushed teeth. All of those things will show the world that you have dignity and self-respect. Think of it as a "thank you" to God for making you as you are. After all, if you look like you care about yourself and take yourself seriously, other people will, too.

SEE FOR YOURSELF:
Num. 8:6; Zech. 3; Rev. 19:7–8

ENJOY LIFE WHILE YOU CAN

7 So go eat your food and enjoy it;
drink your wine and be happy,
because that is what God wants you to do.
8 Put on nice clothes
and make yourself look good.

9Enjoy life with the wife you love. Enjoy all
the useless days of this useless life God has
given you here on earth, because it is all you
have. So enjoy the work you do here on earth.
10Whatever work you do, do your best, because you are going to the grave, where there is
no working, no planning, no knowledge, and
no wisdom.

TIME AND CHANCE

11 I also saw something else here on earth:
The fastest runner does not always win
the race,
the strongest soldier does not always
win the battle,
the wisest does not always have food,
the smartest does not always become
wealthy,
and the talented one does not always
receive praise.
Time and chance happen to everyone.
12 No one knows what will happen next.
Like a fish caught in a net,
or a bird caught in a trap,
people are trapped by evil
when it suddenly falls on them.

WISDOM DOES NOT ALWAYS WIN

13I also saw something wise here on earth
that impressed me. 14There was a small town
with only a few people in it. A great king
fought against it and put his armies all around
it. 15Now there was a poor but wise man in the
town who used his wisdom to save his town.
But later on, everyone forgot about him. 16I still
think wisdom is better than strength. But those
people forgot about the poor man's wisdom
and stopped listening to what he said.

17 The quiet words of a wise person are
better

than the shouts of a foolish ruler.
18 Wisdom is better than weapons of war,
but one sinner can destroy much good.

10

1 Dead flies can make even perfume stink.
In the same way, a little
foolishness can spoil
wisdom.
2 The heart of the wise
leads to right,
but the heart of a fool
leads to wrong.
3 Even in the way fools
walk along the road,
they show they are not
wise;
they show everyone how
stupid they are.
4 Don't leave your job
just because your boss is angry with
you.
Remaining calm solves great problems.

"The quiet words of a wise person are better than the shouts of a foolish ruler." (Ecclesiastes 9:17)

WHAT'S IT MEAN?

Perfumes and ointments were very expensive in Solomon's day, many of them because they had to be imported from other countries. These fragrances were used not only for religious ceremonies, but also to cover up body odor. Add together a warm climate and an infrequent bathing schedule, and you'll come up with some nasty smells.

Ecclesiastes 10:1

5 There is something else wrong that
happens here on earth.
It is the kind of mistake rulers make:
6 Fools are given important positions
while gifted people are given lower
ones;
7 I have seen servants ride horses
while princes walk like servants on foot.
8 Anyone who digs a pit might fall into it;
anyone who knocks down a wall might
be bitten by a snake;
9 anyone who moves boulders might be
hurt by them;
and anyone who cuts logs might be
harmed by them.
10 A dull ax means
harder work.
Being wise will make it easier.
11 If a snake bites the tamer before it is
tamed,
what good is the tamer?

12 The words of the wise
bring them praise,
but the words of a fool
will destroy them.
13 A fool begins by saying
foolish things
and ends by saying
crazy and wicked
things.
14 A fool talks too much.
No one knows the
future,
and no one can tell what will happen
after death.
15 Work wears fools out;
they don't even know how to get home.

THE VALUE OF WORK

16 How terrible it is for a country whose king
is a child
and whose leaders eat all morning.
17 How lucky a country is whose king comes
from a good family,
whose leaders eat only at mealtime
and for strength, not to get drunk.

18 If someone is lazy, the roof will begin to
fall.
If he doesn't fix it, the house will leak.

19 A party makes you feel good,
wine makes you feel happy,
and money buys anything.

20 Don't make fun of the king,
and don't make fun of rich people, even
in your bedroom.
A little bird might carry your words;
a bird might fly and tell what you said.

BOLDLY FACE THE FUTURE

11

1 Invest what you have,
because after a while you will get a
return.
2 Invest what you have in several different
businesses,
because you don't know what disasters
might happen.

3 If clouds are full of rain,
they will shower on the earth.
A tree can fall to the north or south,

but it will stay where it falls.
4 Those who wait for perfect weather
will never plant seeds;
those who look at every cloud
will never harvest crops.

5 You don't know where the wind will blow,
and you don't know how a baby grows
inside the mother.
In the same way, you don't know what
God is doing,
or how he created everything.
6 Plant early in the morning,
and work until evening,
because you don't know if this or that will
succeed.
They might both do well.

SERVE GOD WHILE YOU ARE YOUNG

7 Sunshine is sweet;
it is good to see the light of day.
8 People ought to enjoy every day of their
lives,
no matter how long they live.
But they should also remember this:
You will be dead a long time.
Everything that happens then is useless.
9 Young people, enjoy yourselves while you
are young;
be happy while you are young.
Do whatever your heart desires,
whatever you want to do.
But remember that God will judge you
for everything you do.
10 Don't worry,
and forget the troubles of your body,
because youth and childhood are
useless.

THE PROBLEMS OF OLD AGE

12
1 Remember your Creator
while you are young,
before the days of trouble come
and the years when you say,
"I find no pleasure in them."
2 When you get old,
the light from the sun, moon, and stars
will grow dark;
the rain clouds will never seem to go
away.
3 At that time your arms will shake
and your legs will become weak.
Your teeth will fall out so you cannot
chew,
and your eyes will not see clearly.
4 Your ears will be deaf to the noise in the
streets,
and you will barely hear the millstone
grinding grain.
You'll wake up when a bird starts
singing,
but you will barely hear singing.
5 You will fear high places
and will be afraid to go for a walk.
Your hair will become white like the
flowers on an almond tree.
You will limp along like a grasshopper
when you walk.
Your appetite will be gone.
Then you will go to your everlasting
home,
and people will go to your funeral.

6 Soon your life will snap like a silver chain
or break like a golden bowl.
You will be like a broken pitcher at a
spring,
or a broken wheel at a well.

On the Edge

People ought to enjoy every day of their lives, no matter how long they live. But they should also remember this: You will be dead a long time. Everything that happens then is useless (Eccl. 11:8).

The past is long gone. Tomorrow is a dream, and right now is the only moment you have to enjoy. Are you wishing your life away, hoping that the next thing will make you happy? When I get my driver's license. When I graduate. When I get to college. When I get married. The wish list could go on forever. One day you'll be old and realize you missed the whole thing. God has given you every moment of your life as a gift.

How are you living this gift? Are you hoping someone will come into your life and give it meaning? Are you wanting your teenage years to be over so you can be an adult? Are you wishing it would just all go away? Are you just numb to the passage of time? If so, ask the Lord to restore your joy, to give you eyes to see your purpose, and to help you make the most of these once-in-a-lifetime days.

SEE FOR YOURSELF:
Prov. 27:1;
Eccl. 3:11–13;
1 Pet. 4:7

[7]You will turn back into the dust of the
earth again,
but your spirit will return to God who
gave it.

[8]Everything is useless!
The Teacher says that everything is
useless.

CONCLUSION: HONOR GOD

[9]The Teacher was very wise and taught the people what he knew. He very carefully thought about, studied, and set in order many wise teachings.
[10]The Teacher looked for just the right words to write what is dependable and true.

[11]Words from wise people are like sharp sticks used to guide animals. They are like nails that have been driven in firmly. Altogether they are wise teachings that come from one Shepherd.
[12]So be careful, my son, about other teachings. People are always writing books, and too much study will make you tired.

[13]Now, everything has been heard,
so I give my final advice:
Honor God and obey his commands,
because this is all people must do.
[14]God will judge everything,
even what is done in secret,
the good and the evil.

Promise

HE PROMISES TO JUDGE ALL THE WORK WE DO.

God will judge everything, even what is done in secret, the good and the evil (Eccl. 12:14).

Your mom asks you to take out the trash. You get an attitude, moan and complain, and finally take it out after you're both upset. You casually take some cash from your brother's dresser. You need it; he's got it. You're family. So what? Each situation seems kind of harmless—a bad attitude and "borrowing" some money. But God promises to judge all we do. He saw a kid who dishonored his mom and hasn't caught onto the idea of doing "everything without complaining" (Phil. 2:14). He saw stealing instead of "borrowing." You may choose to whitewash your life and pretend you're an okay guy—not a lot of sin to deal with, no major infractions. But God sees things as they really are. Ask him to give you his perspective, so that you can begin to clean up the stuff you've been pretending isn't so bad. Then you can walk clean before him.

SEE FOR YOURSELF:

1 Sam. 2:10; Ps. 9:7–8; 50:6; 2 Tim. 4:8

Song of Solomon

CONTENT A good word to describe Song of Solomon might be . . . *mushy*. Basically, this book of the Bible is a love poem. It's a poetic story about a young man (Solomon) and a young woman (his bride). They are infatuated. They are in love. They are caught up in romance. They are *crazy* about each other!

Their story tells us something important about God. He created us to need each other. He created romance. He created sex. All of that is good in its place.

You know how it is: Sometimes adults get very cautious with you about getting too serious too early and making mistakes. Sometimes they get so cautious that it can seem like anything that has to do with "the birds and bees" is a bad thing. Those adults have every reason to be cautious. Sexuality is a powerful force, one that requires a lot of maturity and self-control (even for the over-30 crowd!). But it's also true that the chemistry between men and women and all that it leads to was created by God. In the right place it is exciting and wonderful—and important enough for God to dedicate a whole book to it in his Word.

Outline

1:1–17 .... Love Is Better Than Wine
2:1—3:4 .... Love Makes Everything Beautiful
3:5—5:1 .... The Wedding
5:2—7:13 .... Why Is the One You Love More Special Than Others?
8:1–14 .... If Only You and I . . .

Purpose The true meaning and joy of sex is found only in marriage.

Theme The Quest for Authentic Love

Date of writing 965 B.C.

"I belong to my lover, and he desires only me" (7:10).

Bible Talk

The Lure of the Human Body

People talk a lot these days about private zones and inappropriate touch. In our culture we are having to redefine the boundaries. At what point does physical attraction toward someone overstep proper bounds and become sexual harassment? Can we be too attentive to another person—physically?

The characters in the poem we know as the Song of Solomon talk a lot about different parts of the body. They admire each other. This book of the Bible reminds us that God made the human body to be beautiful to our eyes. He made us to want to touch and be touched.

God also gives us the responsibility to give ourselves only to the person that we commit to for life before God, like Solomon and his bride.

WHY POETRY?

Why would God include a love poem in the very Book that he uses to call us to faith? Why not just say "sex is good in the right context" and leave it at that? Why not just point out the right and wrong and be done with it?

Because that's not what God is about. He doesn't just want our obedience; he wants our faith and love. He doesn't just communicate to us in do's and don'ts; he communicates to us within the context of our humanity. Whether that means a love poem, or putting on actual human flesh, that is what God does to connect with us, his creations.

Song of Solomon

1
1 Solomon's Greatest Song.

THE WOMAN SPEAKS TO THE MAN SHE LOVES

2 Kiss me with the kisses of your mouth,
because your love is better than wine.
3 The smell of your perfume is pleasant,
and your name is pleasant like
expensive perfume.
That's why the young women love you.
4 Take me with you; let's run together.
The king takes me into his rooms.

FRIENDS SPEAK TO THE MAN

We will rejoice and be happy with you;
we praise your love more than wine.
With good reason, the young women
love you.

THE WOMAN SPEAKS

5 I'm dark but lovely,
women of Jerusalem,
dark like the tents of Kedar,
like the curtains of Solomon.
6 Don't look at how dark I am,
at how dark the sun has made me.
My brothers were angry with me
and made me tend the vineyards,
so I haven't tended my own vineyard!
7 Tell me, you whom I love,
where do you feed your sheep?
Where do you let them rest at noon?
Why should I look for you near your
friend's sheep,
like a woman who wears a veil?[n]

THE MAN SPEAKS TO THE WOMAN

8 You are the most beautiful of women.
Surely you know to follow the sheep
and feed your young goats
near the shepherds' tents.
9 My darling, you are like a mare
among the king's stallions.
10 Your cheeks are beautiful with
ornaments,
and your neck with jewels.
11 We will make for you gold earrings
with silver hooks.

THE WOMAN SPEAKS

12 The smell of my perfume spreads out
to the king on his couch.
13 My lover is like a bag of myrrh
that lies all night between my breasts.
14 My lover is like a bunch of flowers
from the vineyards at En Gedi.

THE MAN SPEAKS

15 My darling, you are beautiful!
Oh, you are beautiful,
and your eyes are like doves.

WHAT'S IT MEAN?

You may be wondering why the author would compare his beloved to a dove, of all things. The ancient Israelites appreciated the faithfulness, the beauty, and especially the gentleness of the bird. A dove is one of the few creatures that will not attempt to defend itself when it's attacked. Instead, it will simply call out in distress.

Song of Solomon 1:15

THE WOMAN ANSWERS THE MAN

16 You are so handsome, my lover,
and so pleasant!
Our bed is the grass.
17 Cedar trees form our roof;
our ceiling is made of juniper wood.

2

THE WOMAN SPEAKS AGAIN

1 I am a rose in the Plain of Sharon,
a lily in the valleys.

WHAT'S IT MEAN?

The Plain of Sharon was a fertile coastal region in Israel known for its beautiful flowers. The rose mentioned in this verse probably wasn't what we know as a rose. Instead, it may have been a mountain tulip, an anemone, or a saffron. Since those flowers grew in abundance in Sharon, the woman was implying that she is nothing special.

Song of Solomon 2:1

1:7 veil This was the way a prostitute usually dressed.

THE MAN SPEAKS AGAIN

2 Among the young women, my darling
is like a lily among thorns!

THE WOMAN ANSWERS

3 Among the young men, my lover
is like an apple tree in the woods!
I enjoy sitting in his shadow;
his fruit is sweet to my taste.
4 He brought me to the banquet room,
and his banner over me is love.
5 Strengthen me with raisins,
and refresh me with apples,
because I am weak with love.
6 My lover's left hand is under my head,
and his right arm holds me tight.

THE WOMAN SPEAKS TO THE FRIENDS

7 Women of Jerusalem, promise me
by the gazelles and the deer
not to awaken
or excite my feelings of love
until it is ready.

THE WOMAN SPEAKS AGAIN

8 I hear my lover's voice.
Here he comes jumping across the mountains,
skipping over the hills.
9 My lover is like a gazelle or a young deer.
Look, he stands behind our wall
peeking through the windows,
looking through the blinds.
10 My lover spoke and said to me,
"Get up, my darling;
let's go away, my beautiful one.
11 Look, the winter is past;
the rains are over and gone.
12 Blossoms appear through all the land.
The time has come to sing;
the cooing of doves is heard in our land.
13 There are young figs on the fig trees,
and the blossoms on the vines smell sweet.
Get up, my darling;
let's go away, my beautiful one."

THE MAN SPEAKS

14 My beloved is like a dove hiding in the cracks of the rock,
in the secret places of the cliff.
Show me your face,
and let me hear your voice.
Your voice is sweet,
and your face is lovely.
15 Catch the foxes for us—
the little foxes that ruin the vineyards
while they are in blossom.

THE WOMAN SPEAKS

16 My lover is mine, and I am his.
He feeds among the lilies
17 until the day dawns
and the shadows disappear.
Turn, my lover.
Be like a gazelle or a young deer
on the mountain valleys.

THE WOMAN DREAMS

3
1 At night on my bed,
I looked for the one I love;
I looked for him, but I could not find him.
2 I got up and went around the city,
in the streets and squares,
looking for the one I love.
I looked for him, but I could not find him.
3 The watchmen found me as they patrolled the city,
so I asked, "Have you seen the one I love?"
4 As soon as I had left them,
I found the one I love.
I held him and would not let him go
until I brought him to my mother's house,
to the room where I was born.

THE WOMAN SPEAKS TO THE FRIENDS

5 Women of Jerusalem, promise me
by the gazelles and the deer
not to awaken
or excite my feelings of love
until it is ready.
6 Who is this coming out of the desert
like a cloud of smoke?
Who is this that smells like myrrh, incense,
and other spices?
7 Look, it's Solomon's couch[n]
with sixty soldiers around it,
the finest soldiers of Israel.
8 These soldiers all carry swords
and have been trained in war.
Every man wears a sword at his side
and is ready for the dangers of the night.
9 King Solomon had a couch made for himself

3:7 couch Something like a bed carried by slaves on which the king lay or sat while traveling.

of wood from Lebanon.
10 He made its posts of silver
and its braces of gold.
The seat was covered with purple cloth
that the women of Jerusalem wove with love.
11 Women of Jerusalem, go out and see King Solomon.
He is wearing the crown his mother put on his head
on his wedding day,
when his heart was happy!

THE MAN SPEAKS TO THE WOMAN

4 1 How beautiful you are, my darling!
Oh, you are beautiful!
Your eyes behind your veil are like doves.
Your hair is like a flock of goats
streaming down Mount Gilead.
2 Your teeth are white like newly sheared sheep
just coming from their bath.
Each one has a twin,
and none of them is missing.
3 Your lips are like red silk thread,
and your mouth is lovely.
Your cheeks behind your veil
are like slices of a pomegranate.
4 Your neck is like David's tower,
built with rows of stones.
A thousand shields hang on its walls;
each shield belongs to a strong soldier.
5 Your breasts are like two fawns,
like twins of a gazelle,
feeding among the lilies.
6 Until the day dawns
and the shadows disappear,
I will go to that mountain of myrrh
and to that hill of incense.
7 My darling, everything about you is beautiful,
and there is nothing at all wrong with you.
8 Come with me from Lebanon, my bride.
Come with me from Lebanon,
from the top of Mount Amana,
from the tops of Mount Senir and Mount Hermon.
Come from the lions' dens
and from the leopards' hills.
9 My sister, my bride,
you have thrilled my heart;
you have thrilled my heart
with a glance of your eyes,
with one sparkle from your necklace.
10 Your love is so sweet, my sister, my bride.
Your love is better than wine,
and your perfume smells better than any spice.
11 My bride, your lips drip honey;
honey and milk are under your tongue.
Your clothes smell like the cedars of Lebanon.
12 My sister, my bride, you are like a garden locked up,
like a walled-in spring, a closed-up fountain.
13 Your limbs are like an orchard
of pomegranates with all the best fruit,
filled with flowers and nard,
14 nard and saffron, calamus, and cinnamon,
with trees of incense, myrrh, and aloes—
all the best spices.
15 You are like a garden fountain—
a well of fresh water
flowing down from the mountains of Lebanon.

WHAT'S IT MEAN?

Some people in the ancient Near East closed their gardens to visitors in order to protect their privacy and preserve their water supply. Because of the frequent droughts in the area, water in Israel was tough to come by.

Song of Solomon 4:12

THE WOMAN SPEAKS

16 Awake, north wind.
Come, south wind.
Blow on my garden,
and let its sweet smells flow out.
Let my lover enter the garden
and eat its best fruits.

THE MAN SPEAKS

5 1 I have entered my garden, my sister, my bride.
I have gathered my myrrh with my spice.
I have eaten my honeycomb and my honey.
I have drunk my wine and my milk.

THE FRIENDS SPEAK

Eat, friends, and drink;
yes, drink deeply, lovers.

THE WOMAN DREAMS

2 I sleep, but my heart is awake.
I hear my lover knocking.
"Open to me, my sister, my darling,
my dove, my perfect one.
My head is wet with dew,
and my hair with the dampness of the night."
3 I have taken off my garment
and don't want to put it on again.
I have washed my feet
and don't want to get them dirty again.
4 My lover put his hand through the opening,
and I felt excited inside.
5 I got up to open the door for my lover.
Myrrh was dripping from my hands
and flowing from my fingers,
onto the handles of the lock.
6 I opened the door for my lover,
but my lover had left and was gone.
When he spoke, he took my breath away.
I looked for him, but I could not find him;
I called for him, but he did not answer.
7 The watchmen found me
as they patrolled the city.
They hit me and hurt me;
the guards on the wall took away my veil.
8 Promise me, women of Jerusalem,
if you find my lover,
tell him I am weak with love.

THE FRIENDS ANSWER THE WOMAN

9 How is your lover better than other lovers,
most beautiful of women?
How is your lover better than other lovers?
Why do you want us to promise this?

THE WOMAN ANSWERS THE FRIENDS

10 My lover is healthy and tan,
the best of ten thousand men.
11 His head is like the finest gold;
his hair is wavy and black like a raven.
12 His eyes are like doves
by springs of water.
They seem to be bathed in cream
and are set like jewels.
13 His cheeks are like beds of spices;
they smell like mounds of perfume.
His lips are like lilies
flowing with myrrh.
14 His hands are like gold hinges,
filled with jewels.
His body is like shiny ivory
covered with sapphires.
15 His legs are like large marble posts,
standing on bases of fine gold.
He is like a cedar of Lebanon,
like the finest of the trees.
16 His mouth is sweet to kiss,
and I desire him very much.
Yes, daughters of Jerusalem,
this is my lover
and my friend.

WHAT'S IT MEAN?

At one time, Lebanon was covered with cedar trees, which were known for their size and beauty. The Phoenicians, who inhabited the land, cut down the trees and sold the wood to other nations for use in constructing ships, buildings, and other things.

Song of Solomon 5:15

THE FRIENDS SPEAK TO THE WOMAN

6
1 Where has your lover gone,
most beautiful of women?
Which way did your lover turn?
We will look for him with you.

THE WOMAN ANSWERS THE FRIENDS

2 My lover has gone down to his garden,
to the beds of spices,
to feed in the gardens
and to gather lilies.
3 I belong to my lover,
and my lover belongs to me.
He feeds among the lilies.

THE MAN SPEAKS TO THE WOMAN

4 My darling, you are as beautiful as the city of Tirzah,
as lovely as the city of Jerusalem,
like an army flying flags.
5 Turn your eyes from me,
because they excite me too much.
Your hair is like a flock of goats
streaming down Mount Gilead.

6 Your teeth are white like sheep
just coming from their bath;
each one has a twin,
and none of them is missing.
7 Your cheeks behind your veil
are like slices of a pomegranate.
8 There may be sixty queens and eighty slave women
and so many girls you cannot count them,
9 but there is only one like my dove, my perfect one.
She is her mother's only daughter,
the brightest of the one who gave her birth.
The young women saw her and called her happy;
the queens and the slave women also praised her.

WHAT'S IT MEAN?

Mount Gilead, located east of the Jordan River, was an upland region known for its lush plant life. The land was an ideal grazing place for sheep, goats, and other livestock. Speaking of actual goats, did you know that the ones raised in the ancient Near East had long, silky black hair?

Song of Solomon 6:5

THE YOUNG WOMEN PRAISE THE WOMAN

10 Who is that young woman
that shines out like the dawn?
She is as pretty as the moon,
as bright as the sun,
as wonderful as an army flying flags.

THE MAN SPEAKS

11 I went down into the orchard of nut trees
to see the blossoms of the valley,
to look for buds on the vines,
to see if the pomegranate trees had bloomed.
12 Before I realized it, my desire for you made me feel
like a prince in a chariot.

THE FRIENDS CALL TO THE WOMAN

13 Come back, come back, woman of Shulam.
Come back, come back,
so we may look at you!

THE WOMAN ANSWERS THE FRIENDS

Why do you want to look at the woman of Shulam
as you would at the dance of two armies?

THE MAN SPEAKS TO THE WOMAN

7

1 Your feet are beautiful in sandals,
you daughter of a prince.
Your round thighs are like jewels
shaped by an artist.
2 Your navel is like a round drinking cup
always filled with wine.
Your stomach is like a pile of wheat
surrounded with lilies.
3 Your breasts are like two fawns,
like twins of a gazelle.
4 Your neck is like an ivory tower.
Your eyes are like the pools in Heshbon
near the gate of Bath Rabbim.
Your nose is like the mountain of Lebanon
that looks down on Damascus.
5 Your head is like Mount Carmel,
and your hair is like purple cloth;
the king is captured in its folds.
6 You are beautiful and pleasant;
my love, you are full of delights.
7 You are tall like a palm tree,
and your breasts are like its bunches of fruit.
8 I said, "I will climb up the palm tree
and take hold of its fruit."
Let your breasts be like bunches of grapes,
the smell of your breath like apples,
9 and your mouth like the best wine.

THE WOMAN SPEAKS TO THE MAN

Let this wine go down sweetly for my lover;
may it flow gently past the lips and teeth.
10 I belong to my lover,
and he desires only me.
11 Come, my lover,
let's go out into the country
and spend the night in the fields.
12 Let's go early to the vineyards
and see if the buds are on the vines.
Let's see if the blossoms have already opened
and if the pomegranates have bloomed.
There I will give you my love.
13 The mandrake flowers give their sweet smell,

and all the best fruits are at our gates.
I have saved them for you, my lover,
the old delights and the new.

8 [1] I wish you were like my brother
who fed at my mother's breasts.
If I found you outside,
I would kiss you,
and no one would look down on me.
[2] I would lead you and bring you
to my mother's house;
she is the one who taught me.
I would give you a drink of spiced wine
from my pomegranates.

"Love is as strong as death; jealousy is as strong as the grave. Love bursts into flames and burns like a hot fire." (Song of Solomon 8:6b)

THE WOMAN SPEAKS TO THE FRIENDS

[3] My lover's left hand is under my head,
and his right arm holds me tight.
[4] Women of Jerusalem,
promise not to awaken
or excite my feelings of love
until it is ready.

THE FRIENDS SPEAK

[5] Who is this coming out of the desert,
leaning on her lover?

THE MAN SPEAKS TO THE WOMAN

I woke you under the apple tree
where you were born;
there your mother gave birth to you.
[6] Put me like a seal on your heart,
like a seal on your arm.
Love is as strong as death;
jealousy is as strong as the grave.
Love bursts into flames
and burns like a hot fire.
[7] Even much water cannot put out the flame of love;
floods cannot drown love.
If a man offered everything in his house for love,
people would totally reject it.

MARRIAGE
Can true love ever be quenched? (8:6–7)

THE WOMAN'S BROTHERS SPEAK

[8] We have a little sister,
and her breasts are not yet grown.
What should we do for our sister
on the day she becomes engaged?
[9] If she is a wall,
we will put silver towers on her.
If she is a door,
we will protect her with cedar boards.

THE WOMAN SPEAKS

[10] I am a wall,
and my breasts are like towers.
So I was to him,
as one who brings happiness.
[11] Solomon had a vineyard at Baal Hamon.
He rented the vineyards for others to tend,
and everyone who rented had to pay
twenty-five pounds of silver for the fruit.
[12] But my own vineyard is mine to give.
Solomon, the twenty-five pounds of silver are for you,
and five pounds are for those who tend the fruit.

THE MAN SPEAKS TO THE WOMAN

[13] You who live in the gardens,
my friends are listening for your voice;
let me hear it.

THE WOMAN SPEAKS TO THE MAN

[14] Hurry, my lover,
be like a gazelle
or a young deer
on the mountains where spices grow.

WHAT'S IT MEAN?

According to ancient tradition, a woman's family was responsible for her welfare until she got married. The idea was that the women needed the protection of their family while they searched for a husband who would care for them.
Song of Solomon 8:8

isaiah

CONTENT Isaiah was a big fish in the prophet pond. He was well educated and a good communicator. He was known for being the most evangelistic of the prophets. That means instead of preaching only to God's people, he invited people to know God. He was also respected by government officials of his day and was able to influence Israel's government from the top on down.

Imagine Isaiah as a street preacher walking around town wearing a big sandwich sign. (You know those signs that hang from your shoulders with a message hanging down in front of you and behind you.) If that had been the case, Isaiah's sign on the front would have said, "STOP SINNING!" That wouldn't be unusual for a prophet to say. All the prophets said that. But Isaiah's prophetic sign had a flip side. On the back side it would have said, "GOD WILL SAVE YOU." Isaiah talked about salvation more than any other prophet.

Isaiah was convinced that salvation was possible if only people would repent of their sins and put their faith in God's goodness instead of their own. This truth was his passion. Sharing it was his life's mission.

Outline

1:1–31 .... Introduction
2:1—5:30 .... Messages About Judah and Israel
6:1—9:7 .... Events from Isaiah's Ministry
9:8—12:6 .... More Messages About Judah and Israel
13:1—23:18 .... God Will Punish Other Nations
24:1—27:13 .... Messages of Hope for the Lord's People Who Are Suffering
28:1—31:9 .... The Lord Will Punish His Rebellious People
32:1—35:10 .... The Lord Will Punish Edom and Bless Jerusalem
36:1—39:8 .... Assyria, Babylon, King Hezekiah, and Isaiah
40:1—48:22 .... The Lord Will Rescue His People
49:1—53:12 .... The Lord's Servant
54:1—55:13 .... The Lord Will Keep All His Promises
56:1–8 .... All Nations Will Be Part of God's People
56:9—59:21 .... Leaders Unfaithful to God Will Be Punished
60:1—62:12 .... The Future Glory of Jerusalem
63:1—66:24 .... God's Wonderful New Creation

Purpose God firmly intends to bless humanity.

Theme Salvation

Date of writing 740–680 B.C.

"We all have wandered away like sheep; each of us has gone his own way. But the LORD has put on him the punishment for all the evil we have done" (53:6).

Bible Talk

Isaiah's Vision

What do you think heaven would look like if you could peel back the layers of reality-as-we-know-it and see right in? Isaiah got a glimpse of heaven. He saw a throne and a Temple. He saw six-winged creatures worshiping God. These creatures sang a song you might recognize. It starts out, "Holy, Holy, Holy." If you go to church a lot, you probably have heard some songs that are based on Isaiah's vision.

When Isaiah was faced with God's holiness, he became so painfully aware of his own unholiness. It's like if you go to a party and stand by somebody who is dressed fancier than you've ever seen before, you suddenly evaluate how you are dressed. When Isaiah compared himself to God, he realized that he needed to be forgiven and cleaned up.

GOD AND SIN

Have you ever seen those shock collars for dogs that are used to teach them not to bark or not to cross over an invisible fence (made of electrical currents)? Sometimes it seems like it would be easier to learn not to sin if God used those electronic collars on us. How easy would it be to stop lying if every time you lied you felt an electric current run through your body?

God doesn't give us collars, though. He just gives us a conscience. He also gives us people, like Isaiah, who understand that God is holy and we are not. These people remind us that understanding God's holiness should affect how we live our lives.

Isaiah

1 1This is the vision Isaiah son of Amoz
saw about what would happen to Judah and
Jerusalem. Isaiah saw these things while Uzziah, Jotham, Ahaz, and Hezekiah were kings
of Judah.

WHAT'S IT MEAN?

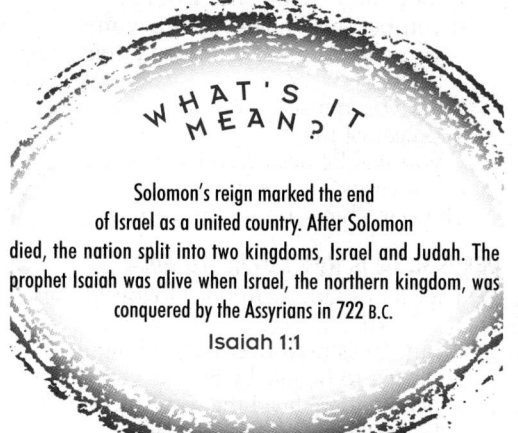

Solomon's reign marked the end of Israel as a united country. After Solomon died, the nation split into two kingdoms, Israel and Judah. The prophet Isaiah was alive when Israel, the northern kingdom, was conquered by the Assyrians in 722 B.C.

Isaiah 1:1

GOD'S CASE AGAINST HIS CHILDREN

2 Heaven and earth, listen,
because the LORD is speaking:
"I raised my children and helped them
grow up,
but they have turned against me.
3 An ox knows its master,
and a donkey knows where its owner
feeds it,
but the people of Israel do not know me;
my people do not understand."

4 How terrible! Israel is a nation of sin,
a people loaded down with guilt,
a group of children doing evil,
children who are full of evil.
They have left the LORD;
they hate God, the Holy One of Israel,
and have turned away from him as if he
were a stranger.

5 Why should you continue to be punished?
Why do you continue to turn against
him?
Your whole head is hurt,
and your whole heart is sick.
6 There is no healthy spot
from the bottom of your foot to the top
of your head;
you are covered with wounds, hurts,
and open sores
that are not cleaned and covered,
and no medicine takes away the pain.
7 Your land is ruined;
your cities have been burned with fire.
While you watch,
your enemies are stealing everything
from your land;
it is ruined like a country destroyed by
enemies.
8 Jerusalem is left alone
like an empty shelter in a vineyard,
like a hut left in a field of melons,
like a city surrounded by enemies.
9 The LORD All-Powerful
allowed a few of our people to live.
Otherwise we would have been
completely destroyed
like the cities of Sodom and Gomorrah.

WHAT'S IT MEAN?

The last thing a city wanted to be compared to was Sodom and Gomorrah. These two towns, which may have been located near the southern end of the Dead Sea, were destroyed by fire and sulfur from heaven. God handed down the "death penalty" for Sodom and Gomorrah because of their extreme wickedness.

Isaiah 1:9

10 Jerusalem, your rulers are like those of
Sodom,
and your people are like those of
Gomorrah.
Hear the word of the LORD;
listen to the teaching of our God!
11 The LORD says,
"I do not want all these sacrifices.
I have had enough of your burnt sacrifices
of male sheep and fat from fine animals.
I am not pleased
by the blood of bulls, lambs, and goats.
12 You come to meet with me,
but who asked you to do
all this running in and out of my
Temple's rooms?
13 Don't continue bringing me worthless
sacrifices!
I hate the incense you burn.
I can't stand your New Moons, Sabbaths,
and other feast days;

I can't stand the evil you do in your
holy meetings.
14 I hate your New Moon feasts
and your other yearly feasts.
They have become a heavy weight on
me,
and I am tired of carrying it.
15 When you raise your arms to me in
prayer,
I will refuse to look at you.
Even if you say many prayers,
I will not listen to you,
because your hands are full of blood.
16 Wash yourselves and make yourselves
clean.
Stop doing the evil things I
see you do.
Stop doing wrong.
17 Learn to do good.
Seek justice.
Punish those who hurt
others.
Help the orphans.
Stand up for the rights of widows."

SIN

What should we do about sin in our lives? (1:16–18)

On the Edge

The LORD says, "Come, let us talk about these things. Though your sins are like scarlet, they can be as white as snow. Though your sins are deep red, they can be white like wool" (Is. 1:18).

You've got a personal invitation to a private dinner with a king. What? Sure you do. It's right here in Isaiah 1:18. God invites you to come and reason things out. He's letting you know that he really wants you to talk over your life with him. It's not that he doesn't already know exactly what's going on—he just wants the pleasure of knowing you care enough about him to share it.

Specifically, this verse is referring to sin. The Lord invites people to confess their sin to him and turn their lives around. With God, it's that simple. All you've got to do to get your life headed in the right direction is talk it over with him. He'll take it from there.

SEE FOR YOURSELF:
Ps. 51:9; 62:8;
Is. 43:25

18 The LORD says,
"Come, let us talk about these things.
Though your sins are like scarlet,
they can be as white as snow.
Though your sins are deep red,
they can be white like wool.
19 If you become willing and obey me,
you will eat good crops from the
land.
20 But if you refuse to obey and if you turn
against me,
you will be destroyed by your enemies'
swords."
The LORD himself said these things.

JERUSALEM IS NOT LOYAL TO GOD

21 The city of Jerusalem once followed the
LORD,
but she is no longer loyal to him.
She used to be filled with fairness;
people there lived the way God wanted.
But now, murderers live there.
22 Jerusalem, you have become like the scum
left when silver is purified;
you are like wine mixed with water.
23 Your rulers are rebels
and friends of thieves.
They all accept money for doing wrong,
and they are paid to cheat people.
They don't seek justice for the orphans
or listen to the widows' needs.
24 So the Lord GOD All-Powerful,
the Mighty One of Israel, says:
"You, my enemies, will not cause me any
more trouble.
I will pay you back for what you did.
25 I will turn against you
and clean away all your wrongs as if
with soap;
I will take all the worthless things out of
you.
26 I will bring back judges as you had long
ago;
your counselors will be like those you
had in the beginning.
Then you will be called the City That Is
Right with God,
the Loyal City."

27 By doing what is fair,
Jerusalem will be free again.
By doing what is right,
her people who come back to the LORD
will have freedom.
28 But sinners and those who turn against
him will be destroyed;
those who have left the LORD will die.

29 "You will be ashamed,
because you have worshiped gods
under the oak trees.
You will be disgraced,
because you have worshiped idols in
your gardens.
30 You will be like an oak whose leaves are
dying
or like a garden without water.
31 Powerful people will be like small, dry
pieces of wood,
and their works will be like sparks.
They will burn together,
and no one will be able to put out that
fire."

THE MESSAGE ABOUT JERUSALEM

2 1 Isaiah son of Amoz saw this message
about Judah and Jerusalem:
2 In the last days
the mountain on which the LORD's Temple
stands
will become the most important of all
mountains.
It will be raised above the hills,
and people from all nations will come
streaming to it.
3 Many nations will come and say,
"Come, let us go up to the mountain of
the LORD,
to the Temple of the God of Jacob.
Then God will teach us his ways,
and we will obey his teachings."
His teachings will go out from Jerusalem;
the message of the LORD will go out
from Jerusalem.
4 He will settle arguments among the
nations
and will make decisions for many
nations.
Then they will make their swords into
plows
and their spears into hooks for
trimming trees.
Nations will no longer fight other nations,
nor will they train for war anymore.

5 Come, family of Jacob,
and let us follow the way of the LORD.

WHAT'S IT MEAN?

Here's a quick review of Israel's early history: Jacob, who was also called Israel, had twelve sons. From those sons came the twelve tribes of Israel. During Isaiah's time, the Temple where the Israelites worshiped God was located on Moriah in Jerusalem, in the territory that belonged to the tribe of Judah.

Isaiah 2:3

WHAT'S IT MEAN?

The Philistines, who lived along the coast of the Mediterranean Sea, had been among the Israelites' most notorious enemies. Over the years, though, the hatred between the two nations cooled and old grudges were forgotten. The Israelites even began to allow their children to marry Philistines, despite the fact that such marriages went against God's Law.

Isaiah 2:6

A TERRIBLE DAY IS COMING

6 LORD, you have left your people,
the family of Jacob,
because they have become filled with
wrong ideas from people in the East.
They try to tell the future like the
Philistines,
and they have completely accepted
those foreign ideas.
7 Their land has been filled with silver and
gold;
there are a great many treasures there.
Their land has been filled with horses;
there are many chariots there.
8 Their land is full of idols.
The people worship these idols they
made with their own hands
and shaped with their own fingers.
9 People will not be proud any longer
but will bow low with shame.
God, do not forgive them.

10 Go into the caves of the cliffs;
dig holes and hide in the ground
from the anger of the LORD
and from his great power!

[11]Proud people will be made humble,
and they will bow low with shame.
At that time only the LORD will still be
praised.

[12]The LORD All-Powerful has a certain day
planned
when he will punish the proud and
those who brag,
and they will no longer be important.
[13]He will bring down the tall cedar trees
from Lebanon
and the great oak trees of Bashan,
[14]all the tall mountains
and the high hills,
[15]every tall tower
and every high, strong wall,
[16]all the trading ships
and the beautiful ships.
[17]At that time proud people will be made
humble,
and they will bow low with shame.
At that time only the LORD will be praised,
[18] but all the idols will be gone.

[19]People will run to caves in the rocky cliffs
and will dig holes and hide in the
ground
from the anger of the LORD
and his great power,
when he stands to shake the earth.
[20]At that time people will throw away
their gold and silver idols,
which they made for themselves to
worship;
they will throw them away to the bats
and moles.
[21]Then the people will hide in caves
and cracks in the rocks
from the anger of the LORD
and his great power,
when he stands to shake the earth.

[22]You should stop trusting in people to save
you,
because people are only human;
they aren't able to help you.

GOD WILL PUNISH JUDAH AND JERUSALEM

3 [1]Understand this:
The Lord GOD All-Powerful
will take away everything Judah and
Jerusalem need—
all the food and water,
[2]the heroes and great soldiers,
the judges and prophets,
people who do magic and older leaders,
[3]the military leaders and government
leaders,
the counselors, the skilled craftsmen, and
those who try to tell the future.
[4]The LORD says, "I will cause young boys to
be your leaders,
and foolish children will rule over you.
[5]People will be against each other; everyone
will be against his neighbor.
Young people will not respect older
people,
and common people will not respect
important people."
[6]At that time a man will grab one of his
brothers
from his own family and say,
"You have a coat, so you will be our
leader.
These ruins will be under your control."
[7]But that brother will stand up and say,
"I cannot help you,
because I do not have food or clothes in
my house.
You will not make me your leader."
[8]This will happen because Jerusalem has
stumbled,
and Judah has fallen.
The things they say and do are against the
LORD;
they turn against him.
[9]The look on their faces shows they are
guilty;
like the people of Sodom, they are
proud of their sin.
They don't care who sees it.
How terrible it will be for them,
because they have brought much
trouble on themselves.

[10]Tell those who do what is right that things
will go well for them,
because they will receive a reward for
what they do.
[11]But how terrible it will be for the wicked!
They will be punished for all the wrong
they have done.
[12]Children treat my people cruelly,
and women rule over them.
My people, your guides lead you in the
wrong way
and turn you away from what is right.

[13]The LORD takes his place in court
and stands to judge the people.
[14]The LORD presents his case
against the older leaders and other
leaders of his people:

"You have burned the vineyard.
Your houses are full of what you took from the poor.
15 What gives you the right to crush my people
and grind the faces of the poor into the dirt?"
The Lord GOD All-Powerful says this.

A WARNING TO WOMEN OF JERUSALEM

16 The LORD says,
"The women of Jerusalem are proud.
They walk around with their heads held high,
and they flirt with their eyes.
They take quick, short steps,
making noise with their ankle bracelets."
17 So the Lord will put sores on the heads of those women in Jerusalem,
and he will make them lose their hair.
18 At that time the Lord will take away everything that makes them proud: their beautiful
ankle bracelets, their headbands, their necklaces
shaped like the moon, 19 their earrings, bracelets,
and veils, 20 their scarves, ankle chains, the
cloth belts worn around their waists, their bottles of perfume, and charms, 21 their signet rings,
nose rings, 22 their fine robes, capes, shawls, and
purses, 23 their mirrors, linen dresses, turbans,
and long shawls.

VANITY

What does God think about vanity? (3:16–18)

24 Instead of wearing sweet-smelling perfume, they will stink.
Instead of fine cloth belts, they will wear the ropes of captives.
Instead of having their hair fixed in fancy ways, they will be bald.
Instead of fine clothes, they will wear clothes of sadness.
Instead of being beautiful, they will wear the brand of a captive.
25 At that time your men will be killed with swords,
and your heroes will die in war.
26 There will be crying and sadness near the city gates.
Jerusalem will be like a woman who has lost everything and sits on the ground.

4

1 At that time seven women will grab one man
and say, "We will eat our own bread
and make our own clothes,
but please marry us!
Please, take away our shame."

THE BRANCH OF THE LORD

2 At that time the LORD's branch will be very
beautiful and great. The people still living in
Israel will be proud of what the land grows.
3 Those who are still living in Jerusalem will be
called holy; their names are recorded among
the living in Jerusalem. 4 The Lord will wash
away the filth from the women of Jerusalem.
He will wash the bloodstains out of Jerusalem
and clean the city with the spirit of fairness and
the spirit of fire. 5 Then the LORD will cover
Mount Zion and the people who meet there
with a cloud of smoke during the day and with
a bright, flaming fire at night. There will be a
covering over every person. 6 This covering will
protect the people from the heat of the sun and
will provide a safe place to hide from the storm
and rain.

ISRAEL, THE LORD'S VINEYARD

5

1 Now I will sing for my friend a song about his vineyard.
My friend had a vineyard
on a hill with very rich soil.
2 He dug and cleared the field of stones
and planted the best grapevines there.
He built a tower in the middle of it
and cut out a winepress as well.
He hoped good grapes would grow there,
but only bad ones grew.

WHAT'S IT MEAN?

Why would someone build a tower in the middle of a vineyard? To prevent people from stealing grapes. From the tower, a guard could spot thieves attempting a fruit heist. He could also defend the vineyard from that vantage point with a bow and arrow or a slingshot. The more the grapes ripened, the more the vineyard owner would step up his security.

Isaiah 5:2

3 My friend says, "You people living in Jerusalem,
and you people of Judah,
judge between me and my vineyard.
4 What more could I have done for my vineyard

than I have already done?
Although I expected good grapes to grow,
why were there only bad ones?
5 Now I will tell you
what I will do to my vineyard:
I will remove the hedge,
and it will be burned.
I will break down the stone wall,
and it will be walked on.
6 I will ruin my field.
It will not be trimmed or hoed,
and weeds and thorns will grow there.
I will command the clouds
not to rain on it."

7 The vineyard belonging to the LORD All-Powerful
is the nation of Israel;
the garden that he loves
is the people of Judah.
He looked for justice, but there was only killing.
He hoped for right living, but there were only cries of pain.

8 How terrible it will be for you who add more houses to your houses
and more fields to your fields
until there is no room left for other people.
Then you are left alone in the land.

GREED
Is greed ever happy or satisfied? (5:8–10)

9 The LORD All-Powerful said this to me:
"The fine houses will be destroyed;
the large and beautiful houses will be left empty.
10 At that time a ten-acre vineyard will make only six gallons of wine,
and ten bushels of seed will grow only half a bushel of grain."

11 How terrible it will be for people who rise early in the morning
to look for strong drink,
who stay awake late at night,
becoming drunk with wine.
12 At their parties they have lyres, harps,
tambourines, flutes, and wine.
They don't see what the LORD has done
or notice the work of his hands.
13 So my people will be captured and taken away,
because they don't really know me.
All the great people will die of hunger,
and the common people will die of thirst.
14 So the place of the dead wants more and more people,
and it opens wide its mouth.
Jerusalem's important people and common people will go down into it,
with their happy and noisy ones.
15 So the common people and the great people will be brought down;
those who are proud will be humbled.
16 The LORD All-Powerful will receive glory by judging fairly;
the holy God will show himself holy by doing what is right.
17 Then the sheep will go anywhere they want,
and lambs will feed on the land that rich people once owned.

18 How terrible it will be for those people!
They pull their guilt and sins behind them
as people pull wagons with ropes.
19 They say, "Let God hurry;
let him do his work soon
so we may see it.
Let the plan of the Holy One of Israel happen soon
so that we will know what it is."

20 How terrible it will be for people who call good things bad
and bad things good,
who think darkness is light
and light is darkness,
who think sour is sweet
and sweet is sour.

21 How terrible it will be for people who think they are wise
and believe they are clever.

22 How terrible it will be for people who are famous for drinking wine
and are champions at mixing drinks.

DRINKING
Is obsessive drinking bad for us? (5:22)

23 They take money to set the guilty free
and don't allow good people to be judged fairly.
24 They will be destroyed
just as fire burns straw or dry grass.
They will be destroyed
like a plant whose roots rot

and whose flower dies and blows away
like dust.
They have refused to obey the teachings of
the LORD All-Powerful
and have hated the message
from the Holy God of
Israel.
25 So the LORD has become
very angry with his
people,
and he has raised his
hand to punish them.
Even the mountains are
frightened.
Dead bodies lie in the
streets like garbage.

But the LORD is still angry;
his hand is still raised to strike down the
people.

26 He raises a banner for the nations far
away.
He whistles to call those people from the
ends of the earth.
Look! The enemy comes quickly!
27 Not one of them becomes tired or falls
down.
Not one of them gets sleepy and falls
asleep.
Their weapons are close at hand,
and their sandal straps are not broken.
28 Their arrows are sharp,
and all of their bows are ready to shoot.
The horses' hoofs are hard as rocks,
and their chariot wheels move like a
whirlwind.
29 Their shout is like the roar of a lion;
it is loud like a young lion.
They growl as they grab their captives.
There is no one to stop them from
taking their captives away.
30 On that day they will roar
like the waves of the sea.
And when people look at the land,
they will see only darkness and pain;
all light will become dark in this thick
cloud.

"Holy, holy, holy is the LORD All-Powerful. His glory fills the whole earth." (Isaiah 6:3)

ISAIAH BECOMES A PROPHET

6 1 In the year that King Uzziah
died, I saw the Lord sitting on
a very high throne. His long
robe filled the Temple. 2 Heavenly creatures of fire stood
above him. Each creature had
six wings: It used two wings to
cover its face, two wings to cover its feet, and
two wings for flying. 3 Each creature was calling
to the others:

"Holy, holy, holy is the LORD All-Powerful.
His glory fills the whole earth."

4 Their calling caused the frame
around the door to shake, as
the Temple filled with smoke.
5 I said, "Oh, no! I will be destroyed. I am not pure, and I
live among people who are
not pure, but I have seen the
King, the LORD All-Powerful."
6 One of the heavenly creatures used a pair of tongs to take
a hot coal from the altar. Then he
flew to me with the hot coal in his hand. 7 The
creature touched my mouth with the hot coal
and said, "Look, your guilt is taken away, because this hot coal has touched your lips. Your
sin is taken away."
8 Then I heard the Lord's voice, saying,
"Whom can I send? Who will go for us?"
So I said, "Here I am. Send me!"
9 Then the Lord said, "Go and tell this to the
people:

'You will listen and listen, but you will not
understand.
You will look and look, but you will not
learn.'
10 Make the minds of these people dumb.
Shut their ears. Cover their eyes.
Otherwise, they might really understand
what they see with their eyes
and hear with their ears.
They might really understand in their
minds
and come back to me and be healed."

11 Then I asked, "Lord, how long should I do
this?"
He answered,

"Until the cities are destroyed
and the people are gone,
until there are no people left in the
houses,
until the land is destroyed and left
empty.
12 The LORD will send the people far away,
and the land will be left empty.
13 One-tenth of the people will be left in the
land,
but it will be destroyed again.
These people will be like an oak tree
whose stump is left when the tree is
chopped down.
The people who remain will be like a
stump that will sprout again."

ANGELS
What do some angels look like? (6:2)

TROUBLE WITH ARAM

7 1Now Ahaz was the son of Jotham, who was the son of Uzziah. When Ahaz was king of Judah, Rezin king of Aram and Pekah son of Remaliah, the king of Israel, went up to Jerusalem to fight against it. But they were not able to defeat the city.

2Ahaz king of Judah received a message saying, "The armies of Aram and Israel[n] have joined together."

When Ahaz heard this, he and the people were frightened. They shook with fear like trees of the forest blown by the wind.

3Then the LORD told Isaiah, "You and your son Shear-Jashub[n] should go and meet Ahaz at the place where the water flows into the upper pool, on the road where people do their laundry. 4Tell Ahaz, 'Be careful. Be calm and don't worry. Don't let those two men, Rezin and Pekah son of Remaliah, scare you. Don't be afraid of their anger or Aram's anger, because they are like two barely burning sticks that are ready to go out. 5They have made plans against you, saying, 6"Let's fight against Judah and tear it apart. We will divide the land for ourselves and make the son of Tabeel the new king of Judah." 7But I, the Lord GOD, say,

" 'Their plan will not succeed;
it will not happen,
8because Aram is led by the city of Damascus,
and Damascus is led by its weak king, Rezin.
Within sixty-five years Israel will no longer be a nation.
9Israel is led by the city of Samaria,
and Samaria is led by its weak king, the son of Remaliah.
If your faith is not strong,
you will not have strength enough to last.' "

IMMANUEL—GOD IS WITH US

10Then the LORD spoke to Ahaz again, saying, 11"Ask for a sign from the LORD your God to prove to yourself that these things are true. It may be a sign from as deep as the place of the dead or as high as the heavens."

12But Ahaz said, "I will not ask for a sign or test the LORD."

13Then Isaiah said, "Ahaz, descendant of David, listen carefully! Isn't it bad enough that you wear out the patience of people? Do you also have to wear out the patience of my God? 14The Lord himself will give you a sign: The virgin[n] will be pregnant. She will have a son, and she will name him Immanuel.[n] 15He will be eating milk curds and honey when he learns to reject what is evil and to choose what is good. 16You are afraid of the kings of Israel and Aram now. But before the child learns to choose good and reject evil, the lands of Israel and Aram will be empty. 17The LORD will bring troubled times to you, your people, and to the people of your father's family. They will be worse than anything that has happened since Israel separated from Judah. The LORD will bring the king of Assyria to fight against you.

JESUS
Was Jesus born of a virgin? (7:14)

18"At that time the LORD will whistle for the Egyptians, and they will come like flies from Egypt's faraway streams. He will call for the Assyrians, and they will come like bees. 19These enemies will camp in the deep ravines and in the cliffs, by the thornbushes and watering holes. 20The Lord will hire Assyria and use it like a razor to punish Judah. It will be as if the Lord is shaving the hair from Judah's head and legs and removing Judah's beard.

WHAT'S IT MEAN?

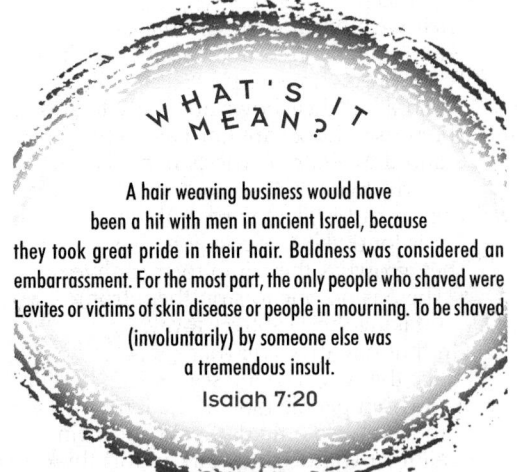

A hair weaving business would have been a hit with men in ancient Israel, because they took great pride in their hair. Baldness was considered an embarrassment. For the most part, the only people who shaved were Levites or victims of skin disease or people in mourning. To be shaved (involuntarily) by someone else was a tremendous insult.

Isaiah 7:20

21"At that time a person will be able to keep only one young cow and two sheep alive. 22There will be only enough milk for that person to eat milk curds. All who remain in the

7:2 Israel Literally, "Ephraim." Isaiah often uses "Ephraim" to mean all of Israel. **7:3 Shear-Jashub** This name means "a part of the people will come back." **7:14 virgin** The Hebrew word means "a young woman." Often this meant a girl who was not married and had not yet had sexual relations with anyone. **7:14 Immanuel** This name means "God is with us."

land will go back to eating just milk curds and
honey. 23 In this land there are now vineyards
that have a thousand grapevines, which are
worth about twenty-five pounds of silver. But
these fields will become full of weeds and
thorns. 24 The land will become wild and useful
only as a hunting ground. 25 People once worked
and grew food on these hills, but at that time
people will not go there, because the land will
be filled with weeds and thorns. Only sheep
and cattle will go to those places."

ASSYRIA WILL COME SOON

8 1 The LORD told me, "Take a large scroll
and write on it with an ordinary pen: 'Maher-
Shalal-Hash-Baz.' 2 I will gather some men to
be reliable witnesses: Uriah the priest and
Zechariah son of Jeberekiah."
3 Then I went to the prophetess, and she became pregnant and had a son. The LORD told
me, "Name the boy Maher-Shalal-Hash-Baz,ⁿ
4 because the king of Assyria will take away all
the wealth and possessions of Damascus and
Samaria before the boy learns to say 'my father' or 'my mother.' "
5 Again the LORD spoke to me, saying,

6 "These people refuse to accept
the slow-moving waters of the pool of Shiloah
and are terrified of Rezin
and Pekah son of Remaliah.
7 So I, the Lord, will bring
the king of Assyria and all his power against them,
like a powerful flood of water from the Euphrates River.
The Assyrians will be like water rising over the banks of the river,
flowing over the land.
8 That water will flow into Judah and pass through it,
rising to Judah's throat.
Immanuel, this army will spread its wings like a bird
until it covers your whole country."

9 Be broken, all you nations,
and be smashed to pieces.
Listen, all you faraway countries.
Prepare for battle and be smashed to pieces!
Prepare for battle and be smashed to pieces!
10 Make your plans for the fight,
but they will be defeated.
Give orders to your armies,
but they will be useless,
because God is with us.

WARNINGS TO ISAIAH

11 The LORD spoke to me with his great
power and warned me not to follow the lead
of the rest of the people. He said,

12 "People are saying that others make plans against them,
but you should not believe them.
Don't be afraid of what they fear;
do not dread those things.
13 But remember that the LORD All-Powerful is holy.
He is the one you should fear;
he is the one you should dread.
14 Then he will be a place of safety for you.
But for the two families of Israel,
he will be like a stone that causes people to stumble,
like a rock that makes them fall.
He will be like a trap for the people of Jerusalem,
and he will catch them in his trap.
15 Many people will fall over this rock.
They will fall and be broken;
they will be trapped and caught."

16 Make an agreement.
Seal up the teaching while my followers are watching.
17 I will wait for the LORD to help us,
the LORD who is ashamed of the family of Israel.
I will wait for him.

18 I am here, and with me are the children
the LORD has given me. We are signs and
proofs for the people of Israel from the LORD
All-Powerful, who lives on Mount Zion.
19 Some people say, "Ask the mediums and
fortune-tellers, who whisper and mutter, what
to do." But I tell you that people should ask
their God for help. Why should people who
are still alive ask something from the dead?
20 You should follow the teachings and the
agreement with the LORD. The mediums and
fortune-tellers do not speak the word of the
LORD, so their words are worth nothing.
21 People will wander through the land
troubled and hungry. When they become hungry, they will become angry and will look up
and curse their king and their God. 22 They will

8:3 Maher-Shalal-Hash-Baz This name means "there will soon be looting and stealing."

look around them at their land and see only trouble, darkness, and awful gloom. And they will be forced into the darkness.

A NEW DAY IS COMING

9 [1]But suddenly there will be no more gloom for the land that suffered. In the past God made the lands of Zebulun and Naphtali hang their heads in shame, but in the future those lands will be made great. They will stretch from the road along the Mediterranean Sea to the land beyond the Jordan River and north to Galilee, the land of people who are not Israelites.

[2]Before those people lived in darkness,
but now they have seen a great light.
They lived in a dark land,
but a light has shined on them.
[3]God, you have caused the nation to grow
and made the people happy.
And they have shown their happiness to you,
like the joy during harvest time,
like the joy of people
taking what they have won in war.
[4]Like the time you defeated Midian,
you have taken away their heavy load
and the heavy pole from their backs
and the rod the enemy used to punish them.
[5]Every boot that marched in battle
and every uniform stained with blood
has been thrown into the fire.
[6]A child has been born to us;
God has given a son to us.
He will be responsible for
leading the people.
His name will be
Wonderful Counselor,
Powerful God,
Father Who Lives
Forever, Prince of
Peace.
[7]Power and peace will be in his kingdom
and will continue to grow forever.
He will rule as king on David's throne
and over David's kingdom.
He will make it strong
by ruling with justice and goodness
from now on and forever.
The LORD All-Powerful will do this
because of his strong love for his
people.

JESUS

What is Jesus known for? (9:6)

GOD WILL PUNISH ISRAEL

[8]The Lord sent a message against the
people of Jacob;
it says that God will judge Israel.
[9]Then everyone in Israel, even the leaders
in Samaria,
will know that God has sent it.
Those people are proud and brag by
saying,
[10]"These bricks have fallen,
but we will build again with cut stones.
These small trees have been chopped
down,
but we will put great cedars there."
[11]But the LORD has brought the enemies of
Rezin against them;
he has stirred up their enemies against
them.
[12]The Arameans came from the east
and the Philistines from the west,
and they ate up Israel with their armies.

On the Edge

A child has been born to us; God has given a son to us. He will be responsible for leading the people. His name will be Wonderful Counselor, Powerful God, Father Who Lives Forever, Prince of Peace (Is. 9:6).

Seems like everybody is looking for a little peace and quiet these days. There's so much happening so fast in your life and in the world. There's so much to be confused about and you've got a really busy life—school, sports, church, friends, family. Whatever is going on in your life, it can get pretty hectic trying to figure it all out. But stop. It's time for some peace in your life. Jesus is the One who gives you peace. He whispers calm into your crazy situation. He gives you a break from the frantic worry that sometimes overwhelms you. When you get into his presence, there is peace.

When you take your eyes off of your circumstances long enough to turn them toward him, you immediately find relief. Remember, Jesus refuses to panic. No matter how hurried or confused your life may be, take a second to put the Prince of Peace on the throne of your life. Then you won't panic either.

SEE FOR YOURSELF:
John 14:27;
Acts 10:36;
Col. 3:15

But the LORD was still angry;
his hand was still raised to punish the people.

13 But the people did not return to the one who had struck them;
they did not follow the LORD All-Powerful.
14 So the LORD cut off Israel's head and tail,
taking away both the branch and stalk in one day.
15 The older leaders and important men were the head,
and the prophets who speak lies were the tail.
16 Those who led the people led them in the wrong direction,
and those who followed them were destroyed.
17 So the Lord is not happy with the young people,
nor will he show mercy to the orphans and widows.
All the people are separated from God and are very evil;
they all speak lies.

But the LORD is still angry;
his hand is still raised to strike down the people.

18 Evil is like a small fire.
First, it burns weeds and thorns.
Next, it burns the larger bushes in the forest,
and they all go up in a column of smoke.
19 The LORD All-Powerful is angry,
so the land will be burned.
The people are like fuel for the fire;
no one will try to save his brother or sister.
20 People will grab something on the right,
but they will still be hungry.
They will eat something on the left,
but they will not be filled.
Then they will each turn and eat their own children.
21 The people of Manasseh will fight against the people of Ephraim,
and Ephraim will fight against Manasseh.
Then both of them will turn against Judah.

But the LORD is still angry;
his hand is still raised to strike down the people.

10

1 How terrible it will be for those who make unfair laws,
and those who write laws that make life hard for people.
2 They are not fair to the poor,
and they rob my people of their rights.
They allow people to steal from widows
and to take from orphans what really belongs to them.
3 How will you explain the things you have done?
What will you do when your destruction comes from far away?
Where will you run for help?
Where will you hide your riches then?
4 You will have to bow down among the captives
or fall down among the dead bodies.
But the LORD is still angry;
his hand is still raised to strike down the people.

GOD WILL PUNISH ASSYRIA

5 God says, "How terrible it will be for the king of Assyria.
I use him like a rod to show my anger;
in anger I use Assyria like a club.
6 I send it to fight against a nation that is separated from God.
I am angry with those people,
so I command Assyria to fight against them,
to take their wealth from them,
to trample them down like dirt in the streets.
7 But Assyria's king doesn't understand that I am using him;
he doesn't know he is a tool for me.
He only wants to destroy other people
and to defeat many nations.
8 The king of Assyria says to himself,
'All of my commanders are like kings.
9 The city Calno is like the city Carchemish.
The city Hamath is like the city Arpad.
The city Samaria is like the city Damascus.
10 I defeated those kingdoms that worship idols,
and those idols were more than the idols of Jerusalem and Samaria.
11 As I defeated Samaria and her idols,
I will also defeat Jerusalem and her idols.' "

12 When the Lord finishes doing what he
planned to Mount Zion and Jerusalem, he will
punish Assyria. The king of Assyria is very
proud, and his pride has made him do these

evil things, so God will punish him. 13The king
of Assyria says this:
"By my own power I have done these
things;
by my wisdom I have defeated many
nations.
I have taken their wealth,
and, like a mighty one, I have taken
their people.
14I have taken the riches of all these people,
like a person reaching into a bird's nest.
I have taken these nations,
like a person taking eggs.
Not one raised a hand
or opened its mouth to stop me."

15An ax is not better than the person who
swings it.
A saw is not better than the one who
uses it.
A stick cannot control the person who
picks it up.
A club cannot pick up the person!
16So the Lord GOD All-Powerful
will send a terrible disease upon
Assyria's soldiers.
The strength of Assyria will be burned up
like a fire burning until everything is
gone.
17God, the Light of Israel, will be like a fire;
the Holy One will be like a flame.
He will be like a fire
that suddenly burns the weeds and
thorns.
18The fire burns away the great trees and
rich farmlands,
destroying everything.
It will be like a sick person who wastes
away.
19The trees left standing will be so few
that even a child could count them.

20At that time some people will be left alive
in Israel
from the family of Jacob.
They will not continue to depend
on the person who defeated them.
They will learn truly to depend on the
LORD,
the Holy One of Israel.
21Those who are left alive in Jacob's family
will again follow the powerful God.
22Israel, your people are many,
like the grains of sand by the sea.
But only a few of them will be left alive
to return to the LORD.
God has announced that he will destroy
the land
completely and fairly.
23The Lord GOD All-Powerful will certainly
destroy this land,
as he has announced.
24This is what the Lord GOD All-Powerful
says:
"My people living in Jerusalem,
don't be afraid of the Assyrians,
who beat you with a rod
and raise a stick against you, as Egypt
did.
25After a short time my anger against you
will stop,
and then I will turn my anger to
destroying them."

26Then the LORD All-Powerful will beat the
Assyrians with a whip
as he defeated Midian at the rock of
Oreb.
He will raise his stick over the waters
as he did in Egypt.
27Then the troubles that Assyria puts on
you
will be removed,
and the load they make you carry
will be taken away.

WHAT'S IT MEAN?

The Midianites were longtime enemies of the Israelites. Gideon, who had been appointed by God as a "judge" or leader of the Israelites (long before the nation had a king), led a small band of soldiers in battle against an enormous army of Midianites. God fought on the side of the Israelites. Guess who won the battle? Two Midianite leaders were captured during the fight. One was put to death at the rock of Oreb, the other at a nearby winepress.

Isaiah 10:26

ASSYRIA INVADES ISRAEL

28The army of Assyria will enter near Aiath.
Its soldiers will walk through Migron.
They will store their food in Micmash.
29The army will go over the pass.
The soldiers will sleep at Geba.
The people of Ramah will be afraid,

and the people at Gibeah of Saul will
run away.
30 Cry out, Bath Gallim!
Laishah, listen!
Poor Anathoth!
31 The people of Madmenah are running
away;
the people of Gebim are
hiding.
32 This day the army will
stop at Nob.
They will shake
their fist at
Mount Zion,
at the hill of
Jerusalem.

33 Watch! The Lord GOD
All-Powerful
with his great power
will chop them down
like a great tree.
Those who are great will be cut down;
those who are important will fall to the
ground.
34 He will cut them down
as a forest is cut down with an ax.
And the great trees of Lebanon
will fall by the power of the Mighty
One.

THE KING OF PEACE IS COMING

11

1 A new branch will grow
from a stump of a tree;
so a new king will come
from the family of Jesse.[n]
2 The Spirit of the LORD will rest upon that
king.
The Spirit will give
him wisdom and
understanding,
guidance and
power.
The Spirit will teach
him to know
and respect the
LORD.
3 This king will be glad to
obey the LORD.
He will not judge by
the way things
look
or decide by what he
hears.
4 But he will judge the poor honestly;
he will be fair in his decisions for the
poor people of the land.
At his command evil people will be
punished,
and by his words the wicked will be put
to death.

"The Spirit of the LORD will rest upon that king. The Spirit will give him wisdom and understanding, guidance and power. The Spirit will teach him to know and respect the LORD." (Isaiah 11:2)

11:1 Jesse King David's father.

Promise

HE PROMISES TO GIVE YOU UNDERSTANDING, WISDOM, AND KNOWLEDGE.

The Spirit of the LORD will rest upon that king. The Spirit will give him wisdom and understanding, guidance and power. The Spirit will teach him to know and respect the LORD (Is. 11:2).

This verse is talking specifically about a king who will arise from David's family. This king would be Jesus and he would receive understanding, wisdom, knowledge, and power from the Spirit of the Lord. But does that mean the Spirit won't give those gifts to anyone else? No, of course not. The Spirit of God gives understanding, wisdom, and knowledge to anyone who asks. He is the Source of those things. Read John 14—16 to see what the Holy Spirit's jobs are. You'll see some things that remind you of this verse. When you get in situations that call for understanding, wisdom, or knowledge, ask the Holy Spirit for his help. He'll always be there for you.

SEE FOR YOURSELF:

**Prov. 2:6; Luke 24:45; John 14—16;
Col. 1:9; James 3:17**

5 Goodness and fairness will give him
strength,
like a belt around his waist.

6 Then wolves will live in peace with lambs,
and leopards will lie down to rest with
goats.
Calves, lions, and young bulls will eat
together,
and a little child will lead them.
7 Cows and bears will eat together in peace.
Their young will lie down to rest
together.
Lions will eat hay as oxen do.
8 A baby will be able to play near a cobra's
hole,
and a child will be able to put his hand
into the nest of a poisonous snake.
9 They will not hurt or destroy each other
on all my holy mountain,
because the earth will be full of the
knowledge of the LORD,
as the sea is full of water.

10 At that time the new king from the family
of Jesse will stand as a banner for all peoples.
The nations will come together around him,
and the place where he lives will be filled with
glory. 11 At that time the Lord will again reach
out and take his people who are left alive in
Assyria, North Egypt, South Egypt, Cush, Elam,
Babylonia, Hamath, and all the islands of the
sea.

12 God will raise a banner as a sign for all
nations,
and he will gather the people of Israel
who were forced from their country.
He will gather the scattered people of
Judah
from all parts of the earth.
13 At that time Israel will not be jealous
anymore,
and Judah will have no more enemies.
Israel will not be jealous of Judah,
and Judah will not hate Israel.
14 But Israel and Judah will attack the
Philistines on the west.
Together they will take the riches from
the people of the east.
They will conquer Edom and Moab,
and the people of Ammon will be under
their control.
15 The LORD will dry up
the Red Sea of Egypt.
He will wave his arm over the Euphrates
River
and dry it up with a scorching wind.
He will divide it into seven small rivers
so that people can walk across them
with their sandals on.
16 So God's people who are left alive
will have a way to leave Assyria,
just like the time the Israelites
came out of Egypt.

A SONG OF PRAISE TO GOD

12 1 At that time you will say:
"I praise you, LORD!
You were angry with me,
but you are not angry with me now!
You have comforted me.
2 God is the one who saves
me;
I will trust him and not
be afraid.
The LORD, the LORD gives
me strength and
makes me sing.
He has saved me."

COURAGE
Where can we get courage? (12:2)

3 You will receive your salvation with joy
as you would draw water from a well.
4 At that time you will say,
"Praise the LORD and worship him.
Tell everyone what he has done
and how great he is.
5 Sing praise to the LORD, because he has
done great things.
Let all the world know what he has
done.
6 Shout and sing for joy, you people of
Jerusalem,
because the Holy One of Israel does
great things before your eyes."

GOD'S MESSAGE TO BABYLON

13 1 God showed Isaiah son of Amoz this message about Babylon:
2 Raise a flag on the bare mountain.
Call out to the men.
Raise your hand to signal them
to enter through the gates for important
people.
3 I myself have commanded those people
whom I have separated as mine.
I have called those warriors to carry out
my anger.
They rejoice and are glad to do my will.

4 Listen to the loud noise in the mountains,
the sound of many people.
Listen to the noise among the kingdoms,
the sound of nations gathering together.
The LORD All-Powerful is calling
his army together for battle.
5 This army is coming from a faraway land,

On the Edge

Shout and sing for joy, you people of Jerusalem, because the Holy One of Israel does great things before your eyes (Is. 12:6).

God has a pretty good track record when it comes to helping his children. He helped the Hebrew people escape from Egypt by dividing the water of the Red Sea. He helped David kill Goliath with just a slingshot. He helped Peter by sending an angel to lead him out of jail.

Of course, the list could go on and on. God *wants* to help his people. He wants to show the world his power through the lives of the people who love him. Has he helped you lately? He's not waiting for you to get into a life-or-death situation before he helps you. He's just waiting for you to ask him. He wants you to know that you need him. He wants you to admit that he can do a better job with your life than you can. Remember, his help might come in an unexpected way, but it will always be the best thing that could happen to you.

SEE FOR YOURSELF:
Ex. 33:14; Josh 1:9; Hos. 14:8–9; Zech. 1:2–3

from the edge of the horizon.
In anger the LORD is using this army like a weapon
to destroy the whole country.

6 Cry, because the LORD's day of judging is near;
the Almighty is sending destruction.
7 People will be weak with fear,
and their courage will melt away.
8 Everyone will be afraid.
Pain and hurt will grab them;
they will hurt like a woman giving birth to a baby.
They will look at each other in fear,
with their faces red like fire.

GOD'S JUDGMENT AGAINST BABYLON

9 Look, the LORD's day of judging is coming—
a terrible day, a day of God's anger.
He will destroy the land
and the sinners who live in it.
10 The stars will not show their light;
the skies will be dark.
The sun will grow dark as it rises,
and the moon will not give its light.

11 The LORD says, "I will punish the world for its evil
and wicked people for their sins.
I will cause proud people to lose their pride,
and I will destroy the pride of those who are cruel to others.
12 People will be harder to find than pure gold;
there will be fewer people than there is fine gold in Ophir.
13 I will make the sky shake,
and the earth will be moved from its place
by the anger of the LORD All-Powerful
at the time of his burning anger.

14 "Then the people from Babylon will run away like hunted deer
or like sheep who have no shepherd.
Everyone will turn back to his own people;
each will run back to his own land.
15 Everyone who is captured will be killed;
everyone who is caught will be killed with a sword.
16 Their little children will be beaten to death in front of them.
Their houses will be robbed
and their wives raped.

17 "Look, I will cause the armies of Media to attack Babylon.
They do not care about silver
or delight in gold.
18 Their soldiers will shoot the young men with arrows;
they will show no mercy on children,
nor will they feel sorry for little ones.
19 Babylon is the most beautiful of all kingdoms,
and the Babylonians are very proud of it.
But God will destroy it
like Sodom and Gomorrah.
20 No one will ever live there
or settle there again.
No Arab will put a tent there;
no shepherd will bring sheep there.
21 Only desert animals will live there,

WHAT'S IT MEAN?

The city of Babylon, located between the Tigris and Euphrates Rivers, was a site to behold. For starters, the city, which was spread over six square miles, was protected by walls eighty-five feet thick. Eight major gates led to the city, each one named for a Babylonian god. The main temple, which was dedicated to Marduk, the god of war, featured a seven-story tower built with nearly sixty million bricks. To top it all off, the royal palace contained the hanging gardens of Babylon—one of the seven wonders of the ancient world.

Isaiah 13:19

and their houses will be full of wild
dogs.
Owls will live there,
and wild goats will leap about in the
houses.
22 Wolves will howl within the strong walls,
and wild dogs will bark in the beautiful
buildings.
The end of Babylon is near;
its time is almost over."

ISRAEL WILL RETURN HOME

14
1 The LORD will show mercy to the people of
Jacob, and he will again choose the people of
Israel. He will settle them in their own land.
Then non-Israelite people will join the Israelites and will become a part of the family of
Jacob. 2 Nations will take the Israelites back to
their land. Then those men and women from
the other nations will become slaves to Israel
in the LORD's land. In the past the Israelites
were their slaves, but now the Israelites will
defeat those nations and rule over them.

THE KING OF BABYLON WILL FALL

3 The LORD will take away the Israelites' hard
work and will comfort them. They will no
longer have to work hard as slaves. 4 On that
day Israel will sing this song about the king of
Babylon:
The cruel king who ruled
us is finished;
his angry rule is
finished!
5 The LORD has broken the
scepter of evil rulers
and taken away their power.
6 The king of Babylon struck people in
anger
again and again.
He ruled nations in anger
and continued to hurt them.
7 But now, the whole world rests and is
quiet.
Now the people begin to sing.
8 Even the pine trees are happy,
and the cedar trees of Lebanon rejoice.
They say, "The king has fallen,
so no one will ever cut us down again."

ANGER
Will anger be punished? (14:5–6)

9 The place of the dead is excited
to meet you when you come.
It wakes the spirits of the dead,
the leaders of the world.
It makes kings of all nations
stand up from their thrones to greet
you.
10 All these leaders will make fun of you
and will say,
"Now you are weak, as we are.
Now you are just like us."
11 Your pride has been sent down to the
place of the dead.
The music from your harps goes with it.
Flies are spread out like your bed beneath
you,
and worms cover your body like a
blanket.
12 King of Babylon, morning star, you have
fallen from heaven,
even though you were as bright as the
rising sun!
In the past all the nations on earth bowed
down before you,
but now you have been cut down.
13 You told yourself,
"I will go up to heaven.
I will put my throne
above God's stars.
I will sit on the mountain of the gods,
on the slopes of the sacred mountain.
14 I will go up above the tops of the clouds.
I will be like God Most High."
15 But you were brought down to the grave,
to the deep places where the dead are.

16 Those who see you stare at you.
They think about what has happened to
you
and say, "Is this the same man who caused
great fear on earth,
who shook the kingdoms,
17 who turned the world into a desert,

who destroyed its cities,
who captured people in war
and would not let them go home?"

18 Every king of the earth has been buried
with honor,
each in his own grave.
19 But you are thrown out of your grave,
like an unwanted branch.
You are covered by bodies
that died in battle,
by bodies to be buried in a rocky pit.
You are like a dead body other soldiers
walk on.
20 You will not be buried with those
bodies,
because you ruined your own country
and killed your own people.
The children of evil people
will never be mentioned again.

21 Prepare to kill his children,
because their father is guilty.
They will never again take control of the
earth;
they will never again fill the world with
their cities.

22 The LORD All-Powerful says this:
"I will fight against those people;
I will destroy Babylon and its people,
its children and their descendants," says
the LORD.
23 "I will make Babylon fit only for owls
and for swamps.
I will sweep Babylon as with a broom of
destruction,"
says the LORD All-Powerful.

GOD WILL PUNISH ASSYRIA

24 The LORD All-Powerful has made this
promise:

WHAT'S IT MEAN?

At the height of its power, the Assyrian Empire stretched from Babylon in the east to the Mediterranean Sea in the west. Check it out on a map—that's a big chunk of land. The capital of the empire was Nineveh, located about three hundred miles north of Babylon on the Tigris River. The Assyrian Empire eventually fell when Babylon rebelled against it.

Isaiah 14:25

Promise

HE PROMISES THAT EVERYTHING WILL HAPPEN AS HE HAS PLANNED.

The LORD All-Powerful has made this promise: "These things will happen exactly as I planned them; they will happen exactly as I set them up" (Is. 14:24).

Isaiah gave the nation of Israel a message from God. Much of his message had to do with a Person called "the Messiah," who would bring the nation back to God and restore peace. Isaiah's prophecy came true when Jesus came to live on the earth—even though it didn't happen the way most of the Israelites thought it would. Still, God's plan had been written out, through Isaiah and others, so that they could see it.

In fact, all through the Bible, God tells you about his plans. Many of his plans have to do with you. You have a God-planned purpose in life, which is to know him and to love him like a best friend. He plans for you to become like his perfect Son. He plans for you to win out over that part of you that really likes to be selfish. He plans for you to be part of a group of people who love him and want to see things go his way on planet Earth. He plans for you to change the world, at least your little corner of it.

What he plans is going to happen. Let him use you to get the job done.

SEE FOR YOURSELF:

Is. 42:9; 46:10–11; Ezek. 12:25; Dan. 4:35

"These things will happen exactly as I
planned them;
they will happen exactly as I set them
up.
25 I will destroy the king of Assyria in my
country;
I will trample him on my mountains.
He placed a heavy load on my people,
but that weight will be removed.

26 "This is what I plan to do for all the earth.
And this is the hand that I have raised
over all nations."

27 When the LORD All-Powerful makes a plan,
no one can stop it.
When the LORD raises his hand to punish
people,
no one can stop it.

GOD'S MESSAGE TO PHILISTIA

28 This message was given in the year that
King Ahaz died:
29 Country of Philistia, don't be happy
that the king who struck you is now
dead.
He is like a snake that will give birth to
another dangerous snake.
The new king will be like a quick,
dangerous snake to bite you.
30 Even the poorest of my people will be able
to eat safely,
and people in need will be able to lie
down in safety.
But I will kill your family with hunger,
and all your people who are left will die.

31 People near the city gates, cry out!
Philistines, be frightened,
because a cloud of dust comes from the
north.
It is an army, full of men ready to fight.
32 What shall we tell the messengers from
Philistia?
Say that the LORD has made Jerusalem
strong
and that his poor people will go there
for safety.

15

GOD'S MESSAGE TO MOAB

1 This is a message about Moab:
In one night armies took the wealth from
Ar in Moab,
and it was destroyed.
In one night armies took the wealth from
Kir in Moab,
and it was destroyed.
2 The people of Dibon go to the places of
worship to cry.
The people of Moab cry for the cities of
Nebo and Medeba.
Every head and beard has been shaved to
show how sad Moab is.
3 In the streets they wear rough cloth to
show their sadness.
On the roofs[n] and in the public squares,
they are crying loudly.
4 People in the cities Heshbon and Elealeh
cry out loud.
You can hear their voices far away in
the city Jahaz.
Even the soldiers are frightened;
they are shaking with fear.

5 My heart cries with sorrow for Moab.
Its people run away to Zoar for safety;
they run to Eglath Shelishiyah.
People are going up the mountain road to
Luhith,
crying as they go.
People are going on the road to Horonaim,
crying over their destruction.
6 But the water of Nimrim has dried up.
The grass has dried up,
and all the plants are dead;
nothing green is left.
7 So the people gather up what they have
saved
and carry it across the Ravine of the
Poplars.
8 Crying is heard everywhere in Moab.
Their crying is heard as far away as the
city Eglaim;
it is heard as far away as Beer Elim.
9 The water of the city Dibon is full of
blood,
and I, the LORD, will bring even more
troubles to Dibon.
A few people living in Moab have escaped
the enemy,
but I will send lions to kill them.

16

1 Send the king of the land
the payment he demands.
Send a lamb from Sela through the desert
to the mountain of Jerusalem.

15:3 roofs In Bible times houses were built with flat roofs. The roof was used for drying things such as flax and fruit. And it was used as an extra room, as a place for worship, and as a cool place to sleep in the summer.

2 The women of Moab
try to cross the river Arnon
like little birds
that have fallen from their nest.

3 They say: "Help us.
Tell us what to do.
Protect us from our enemies
as shade protects us from the noon sun.
Hide us, because we are running for
safety!
Don't give us to our enemies.
4 Let those of us who were forced out of
Moab live in your land.
Hide us from our enemies."

The robbing of Moab will stop.
The enemy will be defeated;
those who hurt others will disappear
from the land.
5 Then a new loyal king will come;
this faithful king will be from the family
of David.
He will judge fairly
and do what is right.

6 We have heard that the people of Moab
are proud
and very conceited.
They are very proud and angry,
but their bragging means nothing.
7 So the people of Moab will cry;
they will all be sad.
They will moan and groan
for the raisin cakes they had in Kir
Hareseth.
8 But the fields of Heshbon and the vines of
Sibmah cannot grow grapes;
foreign rulers have destroyed
the grapevines.
The grapevines once spread
as far as the city of
Jazer and into the
desert;
they had spread as far
as the sea.
9 I cry with the people of
Jazer
for the grapevines of
Sibmah.
I will cry with the people of
Heshbon and Elealeh.
There will be no shouts of joy,
because there will be no harvest or ripe
fruit.
10 There will be no joy and happiness in the
orchards
and no songs or shouts of joy in the
vineyards.
No one makes wine in the winepresses,
because I have put an end to shouts of
joy.
11 My heart cries for Moab like a harp
playing a funeral song;
I am very sad for Kir Hareseth.
12 The people of Moab will go to their places
of worship
and will try to pray.
But when they go to their temple to pray,
they will not be able.

13 Earlier the LORD said these things about
Moab. 14 Now the LORD says, "In three years all
those people and what they take pride in will
be hated. (This is three years as a hired helper
would count time.) There will be a few people
left, but they will be weak."

"At that time people will look to God, their Maker; their eyes will see the Holy One of Israel." (Isaiah 17:7)

GOD'S MESSAGE TO ARAM

17

1 This is a message about Damascus:
"The city of Damascus will be destroyed;
only ruins will remain.
2 People will leave the cities of Aroer.
Flocks will wander freely in those empty
towns,
and there will be no one to bother
them.
3 The strong, walled cities of Israel will be
destroyed.
The government in Damascus will end.
Those left alive of Aram will be
like the glory of Israel," says the LORD
All-Powerful.

4 "At that time Israel's wealth will all be
gone.
Israel will be like
someone who has
lost much weight
from sickness.
5 That time will be like
the grain harvest in
the Valley of
Rephaim.
The workers cut the
wheat.
Then they cut the heads
of grain from the
plants
and collect the grain.
6 That time will also be like the olive
harvest,
when a few olives are left.
Two or three olives are left in the top
branches.

Four or five olives are left on full
branches," says the LORD, the God of
Israel.

7 At that time people will look to God, their
Maker;
their eyes will see the Holy One of
Israel.
8 They will not trust the altars they have
made,
nor will they trust what their hands
have made,
not even the Asherah idols and altars.

WHAT'S IT MEAN?

The altars described here were used in the worship of Asherah, a Canaanite goddess who had been adopted by the Israelites. Wooden poles, possibly carved into some kind of statues, marked the spots where Asherah was worshiped.

Isaiah 17:8

9 In that day all their strong cities will be
empty. They will be like the cities the Hivites
and the Amorites left when the Israelites came
to take the land. Everything will be ruined.
10 You have forgotten the God who saves
you;
you have not
remembered that God
is your place of
safety.
You plant the finest
grapevines
and grapevines from
faraway places.

MONEY

What can our possessions distract us from? (17:7–10)

11 You plant your grapevines one day and
try to make them grow,
and the next day you make them
blossom.
But at harvest time everything will be
dead;
a sickness will kill all the plants.

12 Listen to the many people!
Their crying is like the noise from the
sea.
Listen to the nations!
Their crying is like the crashing of great
waves.
13 The people roar like the waves,
but when God speaks harshly to them,
they will run away.
They will be like chaff on the hills being
blown by the wind,
or like tumbleweeds blown away by a
storm.
14 At night the people will be very frightened.
Before morning, no one will be left.
So our enemies will come to our land,
but they will become nothing.

GOD'S MESSAGE TO CUSH

18

1 How terrible it will be for the land beyond
the rivers of Cush.
It is filled with the sound of wings.
2 That land sends messengers across the sea;
they go on the water in boats made of
reeds.

WHAT'S IT MEAN?

The Nile River flows from two sources, one of them in Cush. In the Bible, Cush refers to the land south of Egypt, including portions of modern-day Ethiopia and Sudan.

Isaiah 18:1

Go, quick messengers,
to a people who are tall and smooth-
skinned,
who are feared everywhere.
They are a powerful nation that defeats
other nations.
Their land is divided by rivers.

3 All you people of the world, look!
Everyone who lives in the world, look!
You will see a banner raised on a
mountain.
You will hear a trumpet sound.
4 The LORD said to me,
"I will quietly watch from where I live,
like heat in the sunshine,
like the dew in the heat of harvest time."
5 The time will come, after the flowers have
bloomed and before the harvest,

when new grapes will be budding and
growing.
The enemy will cut the plants with knives;
he will cut down the vines and take
them away.
6 They will be left for the birds of the
mountains
and for the wild animals.
Birds will feed on them all summer,
and wild animals will eat them that
winter."

7 At that time a gift will be brought to the
LORD All-Powerful
from the people who are tall and
smooth-skinned,
who are feared everywhere.
They are a powerful nation that defeats
other nations.
Their land is divided by rivers.
These gifts will be brought to the place of
the LORD All-Powerful,
to Mount Zion.

GOD'S MESSAGE TO EGYPT

19 1 This is a message about Egypt:
Look, the LORD is coming on a fast cloud
to enter Egypt.
The idols of Egypt will tremble before him,
and Egypt's courage will melt away.

2 The LORD says, "I will cause the Egyptians
to fight against themselves.
People will fight with their relatives;
neighbors will fight neighbors;
cities will fight cities;
kingdoms will fight kingdoms.
3 The Egyptians will be afraid,
and I will ruin their plans.
They will ask advice from their idols and
spirits of the dead,
from their mediums and fortune-tellers."
4 The Lord GOD All-Powerful says,
"I will hand Egypt over to a hard master,
and a powerful king will rule over
them."

5 The sea will become dry,
and the water will disappear from the
Nile River.
6 The canals will stink;
the streams of Egypt will decrease and
dry up.
All the water plants will rot;
7 all the plants along the banks of the Nile
will die.
Even the planted fields by the Nile
will dry up, blow away, and disappear.
8 The fishermen, all those who catch fish
from the Nile,
will groan and cry;
those who fish in the Nile will be sad.
9 All the people who make cloth from flax
will be sad,
and those who weave linen will lose
hope.
10 Those who weave cloth will be broken.
All those who work for money will be
sad.

WHAT'S IT MEAN?

Because Egypt receives very little rainfall, its people rely on the Nile for their water. The Nile floods its banks nearly every year, watering the soil and creating a fertile farmland in the midst of a desert region. In those years when the Nile did not flood, the Egyptians experienced drought and famine. Today the Aswan Dam and the High Dam allow Egyptian officials to control the flooding and preserve water.

Isaiah 19:5

11 The officers of the city of Zoan are fools;
the wise men who advise the king of
Egypt give wrong advice.
How can you say to him, 'I am wise'?
How can you say, 'I am from the old
family of the kings'?
12 Egypt, where are your wise men?
Let them show you
what the LORD All-Powerful has planned
for Egypt.
13 The officers of Zoan have been fooled;
the leaders of Memphis have believed
false things.
So the leaders of Egypt
lead that nation the wrong way.
14 The LORD has made the leaders confused.
They have led Egypt to wander in the
wrong ways,
like drunk people stumbling in their
own vomit.
15 There is nothing Egypt can do;
no one there can help.
16 In that day the Egyptians will be like

women. They will be afraid of the LORD All-
Powerful, because he will raise his hand to
strike them down. [17]The land of Judah will
bring fear to Egypt. Anyone there who hears
the name Judah will be afraid, because the
LORD All-Powerful has planned terrible things
for them. [18]At that time five cities in Egypt will
speak Hebrew, the language of Canaan, and
they will promise to be loyal to the LORD All-
Powerful. One of these cities will be named the
City of Destruction. [19]At that time there will be
an altar for the LORD in the middle of Egypt
and a monument to the LORD at the border of
Egypt. [20]This will be a sign and a witness to the
LORD All-Powerful in the land of Egypt. When
the people cry to the LORD for help, he will
send someone to save and defend them. He
will rescue them from those who hurt them.
[21]So the LORD will show himself to the
Egyptians, and then they will know he is the
LORD. They will worship God and offer many
sacrifices. They will make promises to the LORD
and will keep them. [22]The LORD will punish the
Egyptians, but then he will heal them. They
will come back to the LORD, and he will listen
to their prayers and heal them.
[23]At that time there will be a highway from
Egypt to Assyria, and the Assyrians will go to
Egypt, and the Egyptians will go to Assyria.
The Egyptians and Assyrians will worship God
together. [24]At that time Israel, Assyria, and
Egypt will join together, which will be a blessing for the earth. [25]The LORD All-Powerful will
bless them, saying, "Egypt, you are my people.
Assyria, I made you. Israel, I own you. You are
all blessed!"

ASSYRIA WILL DEFEAT EGYPT AND CUSH

20
[1]Sargon king of Assyria sent a military
commander to Ashdod to attack that city. So
the commander attacked and captured it.
[2]Then the LORD spoke through Isaiah son of
Amoz, saying, "Take the rough cloth off your
body, and take your sandals off your feet." So
Isaiah obeyed and walked around naked and
barefoot.
[3]Then the LORD said, "Isaiah my servant has
walked around naked and barefoot for three
years as a sign against Egypt and Cush. [4]The
king of Assyria will carry away prisoners from
Egypt and Cush. Old people and young people
will be led away naked and barefoot, with their
buttocks bare. So the Egyptians will be
shamed. [5]People who looked to Cush for help
will be afraid, and those who were amazed by
Egypt's glory will be shamed. [6]People who live
near the sea will say, 'Look at those countries.
We trusted them to help us. We ran to them so
they would save us from the king of Assyria.
So how will we be able to escape?' "

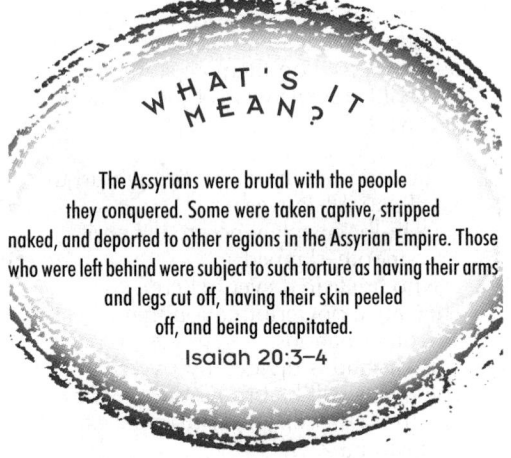

WHAT'S IT MEAN?

The Assyrians were brutal with the people they conquered. Some were taken captive, stripped naked, and deported to other regions in the Assyrian Empire. Those who were left behind were subject to such torture as having their arms and legs cut off, having their skin peeled off, and being decapitated.

Isaiah 20:3–4

GOD'S MESSAGE TO BABYLON

21
[1]This is a message about the Desert by the
Sea:[n]

Disaster is coming from the desert
like wind blowing in the south.
It is coming from a terrible country.
[2]I have seen a terrible vision.
I see traitors turning against you
and people taking your wealth.

Elam, attack the people!
Media, surround the city and attack it!
I will bring an end to the pain the city
causes.

[3]I saw those terrible things, and now I am
in pain;
my pains are like the pains of giving
birth.
What I hear makes me very afraid;
what I see causes me to shake with fear.
[4]I am worried,
and I am shaking with fear.
My pleasant evening
has become a night of fear.

[5]They set the table;
they spread the rugs;
they eat and drink.
Leaders, stand up.
Prepare the shields for battle!

21:1 Desert by the Sea Probably Babylon.

6 The Lord said to me,
"Go, place a lookout for the city
and have him report what he sees.
7 If he sees chariots and teams of horses,
donkeys, or camels,
he should pay very close attention."

8 Then the lookout called out,
"My master, each day I stand in the watchtower watching;
every night I have been on guard.
9 Look, I see a man coming in a chariot
with a team of horses."
The man gives back the answer,
"Babylon has fallen. It has fallen!
All the statues of her gods
lie broken on the ground."
10 My people are crushed like grain on the threshing floor.
My people, I tell you what I have heard
from the LORD All-Powerful,
from the God of Israel.

GOD'S MESSAGE TO EDOM

11 This is a message about Dumah:[n]
Someone calls to me from Edom,
"Watchman, how much of the night is left?
Watchman, how much longer will it be night?"
12 The watchman answers,
"Morning is coming, but then night will come again.
If you have something to ask,
then come back and ask."

GOD'S MESSAGE TO ARABIA

13 This is a message about Arabia:
A group of traders from Dedan
spent the night near some trees in Arabia.
14 They gave water to thirsty travelers;
the people of Tema gave food
to those who were escaping.
15 They were running from swords,
from swords ready to kill,
from bows ready to shoot,
from a hard battle.
16 This is what the Lord said to me: "In one
year all the glory of the country of Kedar will
be gone. (This is a year as a hired helper counts
time.) 17 At that time only a few of the archers,
the soldiers of Kedar, will be left alive." The
LORD, the God of Israel, has spoken.

GOD'S MESSAGE TO JERUSALEM

22

1 This is a message about the Valley of
Vision:[n]
What is wrong with you people?
Why are you on your roofs?[n]
2 This city was a very busy city,
full of noise and wild parties.
Now your people have been killed,
but not with swords,
nor did they die in battle.
3 All your leaders ran away together,
but they have been captured without using a bow.
All you who were captured
tried to run away before the enemy came.
4 So I say, "Don't look at me.
Let me cry loudly.
Don't hurry to comfort me
about the destruction of Jerusalem."
5 The Lord GOD All-Powerful has chosen a special day
of riots and confusion.
People will trample each other in the Valley of Vision.
The city walls will be knocked down,
and the people will cry out to the mountain.
6 The soldiers from Elam will gather their arrows
and their chariots and men on horses.
Kir will prepare their shields.
7 Your nicest valleys will be filled with chariots.
Horsemen will be ordered to guard the gates of the city.
8 The walls protecting Judah will fall.

At that time the people of Jerusalem depended on
the weapons kept at the Palace of the Forest.
9 You saw that the walls of Jerusalem
had many cracks that needed repairing.
You stored up water in the lower pool.
10 You counted the houses of Jerusalem,
and you tore down houses to repair the walls with their stones.
11 You made a pool between the two walls

21:11 Dumah Another name for Edom. **22:1 Valley of Vision** This probably means a valley near Jerusalem. **22:1 roofs** In Bible times houses were built with flat roofs. The roof was used for drying things such as flax and fruit. And it was used as an extra room, as a place for worship, and as a cool place to sleep in the summer.

to save water from the old pool,
but you did not trust the God who made these things;
you did not respect the One who planned them long ago.

12 The Lord GOD All-Powerful told the people
to cry and be sad,
to shave their heads and wear rough cloth.
13 But look, the people are happy
and are having wild parties.
They kill the cattle and the sheep;
they eat the food and drink the wine.
They say, "Let us eat and drink,
because tomorrow we will die."
14 The LORD All-Powerful said to me: "You people will die before this guilt is forgiven." The Lord GOD All-Powerful said this.

GOD'S MESSAGE TO SHEBNA

15 This is what the Lord GOD All-Powerful says:
"Go to this servant Shebna,
the manager of the palace.
16 Say to him, 'What are you doing here?
Who said you could cut out a tomb for your self here?
Why are you preparing your tomb in a high place?
Why are you carving out a tomb from the rock?
17 Look, mighty one! The LORD will throw you away.

WHAT'S IT MEAN?

When ordinary people died in ancient times, they were buried in shallow graves covered with stone slabs. The wealthy and powerful, on the other hand, often built elaborate tombs for themselves. These tombs were either created from natural caves or carved out of stone. The person's possessions were usually buried along with his body, in case he "needed" them in the afterlife. Shebna was an official in the government of Judah who tried to make himself like the king by building a custom tomb for himself.

Isaiah 22:15–19

He will take firm hold of you
18 and roll you tightly into a ball
and throw you into another country.
There you will die,
and there your fine chariots will remain.
You are a disgrace to your master's house.
19 I will force you out of your important job,
and you will be thrown down from your important place.'
20 "At that time I will call for my servant Eliakim son of Hilkiah. 21 I will take your robe and
put it on him and give him your belt. I will
hand over to him the important job you have,
and he will be like a father to the people of
Jerusalem and the family of Judah. 22 I will put
the key to the house of David around his neck.
If he opens a door, no one will be able to close
it; if he closes a door, no one will be able to
open it. 23 He will be like an honored chair in his
father's house. I will make him strong like a peg
that is hammered into a strong board. 24 All the
honored and important things of his family
will depend on him; all the adults and little
children will depend on him. They will be like
bowls and jars hanging on him.
25 "At that time," says the LORD All-Powerful,
"the peg hammered into the strong board will
weaken. It will break and fall, and everything
hanging on it will be destroyed." The LORD says
this.

GOD'S MESSAGE TO LEBANON

23 1 This is a message about Tyre:
You trading ships, cry!
The houses and harbor of Tyre are destroyed.
This news came to the ships
from the land of Cyprus.
2 Be silent, you who live on the island of Tyre;
you merchants of Sidon, be silent.
Sailors have made you rich.
3 They traveled the sea to bring grain from Egypt;
the sailors of Tyre brought grain from the Nile Valley
and sold it to other nations.

4 Sidon, be ashamed.
Strong city of the sea, be ashamed,
because the sea says:
"I have not felt the pain of giving birth;
I have not reared young men or women."
5 Egypt will hear the news about Tyre,

and it will make Egypt hurt with
sorrow.

[6]You ships should return to Tarshish.
You people living near the sea should be sad.
[7]Look at your once happy city!
Look at your old, old city!
People from that city have traveled
far away to live.
[8]Who planned Tyre's destruction?
Tyre made others rich.
Its merchants were treated like princes,
and its traders were greatly respected.
[9]It was the LORD All-Powerful who planned this.
He decided to make these proud people unimportant;
he decided to disgrace those who were greatly respected.
[10]Go through your land, people of Tarshish,
like the Nile goes through Egypt.
There is no harbor for you now!
[11]The LORD has stretched his hand over the sea
and made its kingdoms tremble.
He commands that Canaan's
strong, walled cities be destroyed.
[12]He said, "Sidon, you will not rejoice any longer,
because you are destroyed.
Even if you cross the sea to Cyprus,
you will not find a place to rest."
[13]Look at the land of the Babylonians;
it is not a country now.
Assyria has made it a place for wild animals.
Assyria built towers to attack it;
the soldiers took all the treasures from its cities,
and they turned it into ruins.
[14]So be sad, you trading ships,
because your strong city is destroyed.

[15]At that time people will forget about Tyre
for seventy years, which is the length of a
king's life. After seventy years, Tyre will be like
the prostitute in this song:

[16]"Oh woman, you are forgotten.
Take your harp and walk through the city.
Play your harp well. Sing your song often.
Then people will remember you."

[17]After seventy years the LORD will deal
with Tyre, and it will again have trade. It will
be like a prostitute for all the nations of the
earth. [18]The profits will be saved for the LORD.
Tyre will not keep the money she earns but
will give them to the people who serve the
LORD, so they will have plenty of food and nice
clothes.

THE LORD WILL PUNISH THE WORLD

24 [1]Look! The LORD will destroy the earth and leave it empty;
he will ruin the surface of the land and scatter its people.
[2]At that time the same thing will happen to everyone:
to common people and priests,
to slaves and masters,
to women slaves and their women masters,
to buyers and sellers,
to those who borrow and those who lend,
to bankers and those who owe the bank.
[3]The earth will be completely empty.
The wealth will all be taken,
because the LORD has commanded it.
[4]The earth will dry up and die;
the world will grow weak and die;
the great leaders in this land will become weak.
[5]The people of the earth have ruined it,
because they do not follow God's teachings
or obey God's laws
or keep their agreement with God that was to last forever.
[6]So a curse will destroy the earth.
The people of the world are guilty,
so they will be burned up;
only a few will be left.
[7]The new wine will be bad, and the grapevines will die.
People who were happy will be sad.
[8]The happy music of the tambourines will end.
The happy sounds of wild parties will stop.
The joyful music from the harps will end.
[9]People will no longer sing while they drink their wine.
The beer will taste bitter to those who drink it.
[10]The ruined city will be empty,
and people will hide behind closed doors.
[11]People in the streets will ask for wine,
but joy will have turned to sadness;
all the happiness will have left.
[12]The city will be left in ruins,

and its gates will be smashed to pieces.
13 This is what will happen all over the earth
and to all the nations.
The earth will be like an olive tree after the harvest
or like the few grapes left on a vine after harvest.

14 The people shout for joy.
From the west they praise the greatness of the LORD.
15 People in the east, praise the LORD.
People in the islands of the sea,
praise the name of the LORD, the God of Israel.
16 We hear songs from every part of the earth
praising God, the Righteous One.

"The people shout for joy. From the west they praise the greatness of the LORD." (Isaiah 24:14)

But I said, "I am dying! I am dying!
How terrible it will be for me!
Traitors turn against people;
with their dishonesty, they turn against people."
17 There are terrors, holes, and traps
for the people of the earth.
18 Anyone who tries to escape from the sound of terror
will fall into a hole.
Anyone who climbs out of the hole
will be caught in a trap.
The clouds in the sky will pour out rain,
and the foundations of the earth will shake.
19 The earth will be broken up;
the earth will split open;
the earth will shake violently.
20 The earth will stumble around like someone who is drunk;
it will shake like a hut in a storm.
Its sin is like a heavy weight on its back;
it will fall and never rise again.

21 At that time the LORD will punish
the powers in the sky above
and the rulers on earth below.
22 They will be gathered together
like prisoners thrown into a dungeon;
they will be shut up in prison.
After much time they will be punished.
23 The moon will be embarrassed,
and the sun will be ashamed,
because the LORD All-Powerful will rule as king
on Mount Zion in Jerusalem.
Jerusalem's leaders will see his greatness.

A SONG OF PRAISE TO GOD

25

1 LORD, you are my God.
I honor you and praise you,
because you have done amazing things.
You have always done what you said you would do;
you have done what you planned long ago.
2 You have made the city a pile of rocks
and have destroyed her walls.
The city our enemies built with strong walls is gone;
it will never be built again.
3 People from powerful nations will honor you;
cruel people from strong cities will fear you.
4 You protect the poor;
you protect the helpless when they are in danger.
You are like a shelter from storms,
like shade that protects them from the heat.
The cruel people attack
like a rainstorm beating against the wall,
5 like the heat in the desert.
But you, God, stop their violent attack.
As a cloud cools a hot day,
you silence the songs of those who have no mercy.

GOD'S BANQUET FOR HIS SERVANTS

6 The LORD All-Powerful will prepare a feast
on this mountain for all people.
It will be a feast with all the best food and wine,
the finest meat and wine.
7 On this mountain God will destroy
the veil that covers all nations,
the veil that stretches over all peoples;
8 he will destroy death forever.
The Lord GOD will wipe away every tear from every face.
He will take away the shame of his people from the earth.
The LORD has spoken.

HEAVEN
What will be missing in heaven? (25:8)

9 At that time people will say,
"Our God is doing this!
We have waited for him, and he has come to save us.
This is the LORD. We waited for him,
so we will rejoice and be happy when he saves us."
10 The LORD will protect Jerusalem,
but he will crush our enemy Moab
like straw that is trampled down in the manure.
11 They will spread their arms in it
like a person who is swimming.
But God will bring down their pride,
and all the clever things they have made will mean nothing.
12 Moab's high walls protect them,
but God will destroy these walls.
He will throw them down to the ground,
even to the dust.

A SONG OF PRAISE TO GOD

26 1 At that time people will sing this song in Judah:
We have a strong city.
God protects us with its strong walls and defenses.
2 Open the gates,
and the good people will enter,
those who follow God.
3 You, LORD, give true peace
to those who depend on you,
because they trust you.
4 So, trust the LORD always,
because he is our Rock forever.
5 He will destroy the proud city,
and he will punish the people living there.
He will bring that high city down to the ground
and throw it down into the dust.
6 Then those who were hurt by the city will walk on its ruins;
those who were made poor by the city will trample it under their feet.

7 The path of life is level for those who are right with God;
LORD, you make the way of life smooth for those people.
8 But, LORD, we are waiting
for your way of justice.
Our souls want to remember
you and your name.
9 My soul wants to be with you at night,
and my spirit wants to be with you at the dawn of every day.
When your way of justice comes to the land,

Promise HE PROMISES TO DESTROY DEATH AND TEARS.

He will destroy death forever. The Lord GOD will wipe away every tear from every face. He will take away the shame of his people from the earth. The LORD has spoken (Is. 25:8).

When Jesus died and came back to life, he dealt death a mortal blow. He gave notice to anyone who would believe in him that there was a power greater than death. His friends don't have to be afraid of death because they know that their physical death is not the end. And there will come a day when no one dies anymore.

Something else happened when Jesus died on the cross. He did battle with the spiritual death that had cast a shadow over planet Earth since Adam and Eve had left the Garden of Eden. If you put your confidence in Jesus' goodness rather than your own, the seemingly irresistible urge to go your own way (instead of God's way) doesn't have to run your life.

And Jesus promises that your tears will come to an end, too. That's because all the things that make you sad—someone's parents getting a divorce, people getting sick, even natural disasters—are part of a world that's not perfect because of sin. Jesus has already beat sin; and just like death, sin's days of having any say in our lives are coming to an end. Then we'll see what Revelation 21:4 reports: "All the old ways are gone."

SEE FOR YOURSELF:
Rom. 8:2; 2 Tim. 1:10; Rev. 21:4

people of the world will learn the right
way of living.
10 Evil people will not learn to do good
even if you show them kindness.
They will continue doing evil, even if they
live in a good world;
they never see the LORD's greatness.
11 LORD, you are ready to punish those
people,
but they do not see that.
Show them your strong love for your
people.
Then those who are evil will be
ashamed.
Burn them in the fire
you have prepared for your enemies.
12 LORD, all our success is because of what
you have done,
so give us peace.
13 LORD, our God, other masters besides you
have ruled us,
but we honor only you.
14 Those masters are now dead;
their ghosts will not rise from death.
You punished and destroyed them
and erased any memory of them.
15 LORD, you multiplied the number of your
people;
you multiplied them and brought honor
to yourself.
You made the borders of the land wide.
16 LORD, people remember you when they
are in trouble;
they say quiet prayers to you when you
punish them.
17 LORD, when we are with you,
we are like a woman giving birth to a
baby;
she cries and has pain from the birth.
18 In the same way, we had pain.
We gave birth, but only to wind.
We don't bring salvation to the land
or make new people for the world.
19 Your people have died, but they will live
again;
their bodies will rise from death.
You who lie in the ground,
wake up and be happy!
The dew covering you is like the dew of a
new day;
the ground will give birth to the dead.

JUDGMENT: REWARD OR PUNISHMENT

20 My people, go into your rooms
and shut your doors behind you.
Hide in your rooms for a short time
until God's anger is finished.
21 The LORD will leave his place
to punish the people of the world for
their sins.
The earth will show the blood of the
people who have been killed;
it will not cover the dead any longer.

27

1 At that time the LORD will punish
Leviathan, the gliding snake.
He will punish Leviathan, the coiled
snake;
with his great and hard and powerful
sword.
He will kill the monster in the sea.

2 At that time
people will sing about the pleasant
vineyard.
3 "I, the LORD, will care for that vineyard;
I will water it at the right time.
No one will hurt it,
because I will guard it day and night.
4 I am not angry.
If anyone builds a wall of thornbushes in
war,
I will march to it and burn it.
5 But if anyone comes to me for safety
and wants to make peace with me,
he should come and make peace with
me."
6 In the days to come, the people of Jacob
will be like a plant with good roots;
Israel will grow like a plant beginning to
bloom.
Then the world will be filled with their
children.

THE LORD WILL SEND ISRAEL AWAY

7 The LORD has not hurt his people as he
hurt their enemies;
his people have not been killed like
those who tried to kill them.
8 He will settle his argument with Israel by
sending it far away.
Like a hot desert wind, he will drive it
away.
9 This is how Israel's guilt will be forgiven;
this is how its sins will be taken away:
Israel will crush the rocks of the altar to
dust,
and no statues or altars will be left
standing for the Asherah idols.
10 At that time the strong, walled city will be
empty
like a desert.
Calves will eat grass there.
They will lie down there
and eat leaves from the branches.

11 The limbs will become dry and break off,
so women will use them for firewood.
The people refuse to understand,
so God will not comfort them;
their Maker will not be kind to them.
12 At that time the LORD will begin gathering
his people one by one from the Euphrates
River to the brook of Egypt. He will separate
them from others as grain is separated from
chaff. 13 Many of my people are now lost in
Assyria. Some have run away to Egypt. But at
that time a great trumpet will be blown, and all
those people will come and worship the LORD
on that holy mountain in Jerusalem.

WHAT'S IT MEAN?

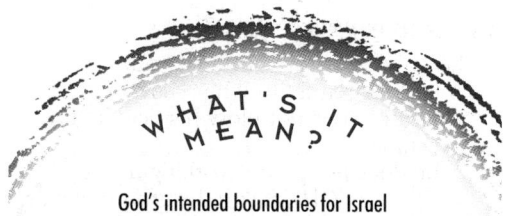

God's intended boundaries for Israel were Egypt on the west and the Euphrates River on the east. The Lord had promised to give all of the land in between to the descendants of Abraham, Isaac, and Jacob. The Israelites, though, never claimed all of what was rightfully theirs. They allowed other nations to live in the land that God had given to them.

Isaiah 27:12

WARNINGS TO ISRAEL

28

1 How terrible it will be for Samaria, the
pride of Israel's drunken people!
That beautiful crown of flowers is just a
dying plant
set on a hill above a rich valley where
drunkards live.
2 Look, the Lord has someone who is strong
and powerful.
Like a storm of hail and strong wind,
like a sudden flood of water pouring over
the country,
he will throw Samaria down to the
ground.
3 That city, the pride of Israel's drunken
people,
will be trampled underfoot.
4 That beautiful crown of flowers is just a
dying plant
set on a hill above a rich valley.
That city will be like the first fig of
summer.
Anyone who sees it
quickly picks it and eats it.

5 At that time the LORD All-Powerful
will be like a beautiful crown,
like a wonderful crown of flowers
for his people who are left alive.
6 Then he will give wisdom to the judges
who must decide cases
and strength to those who battle at the
city gate.
7 But now those leaders are drunk with
wine;
they stumble from drinking too much
beer.
The priests and prophets are drunk with
beer
and are filled with wine.
They stumble from too much beer.
The prophets are drunk when they see
their visions;
the judges stumble when they make
their decisions.
8 Every table is covered with vomit,
so there is not a clean place anywhere.

9 The LORD is trying to teach the people a
lesson;
he is trying to make them understand
his teachings.
But the people are like babies too old for
breast milk,
like those who no longer nurse at their
mother's breast.
10 So they make fun of the LORD's prophet
and say:
"A command here, a command there.
A rule here, a rule there.
A little lesson here, a little lesson there."
11 So the LORD will use strange words and
foreign languages
to speak to these people.
12 God said to them,
"Here is a place of rest;
let the tired people come and rest.
This is the place of peace."
But the people would not listen.
13 So the words of the LORD will be,
"A command here, a command there.
A rule here, a rule there.
A little lesson here, a little lesson there."
They will fall back and be defeated;
they will be trapped and captured.

14 So listen to the LORD's message, you who
brag,
you leaders in Jerusalem.

15 You say, "We have made an agreement
with death;
we have a contract with death.
When terrible punishment passes by,
it won't hurt us.
Our lies will keep us safe,
and our tricks will hide us."
16 Because of these things,
this is what the Lord GOD says:
"I will put a stone in the
ground in Jerusalem,
a tested stone.
Everything will be built
on this important and
precious rock.
Anyone who trusts in it will never be
disappointed.
17 I will use justice as a measuring line
and goodness as the standard.
The lies you hide behind will be destroyed
as if by hail.
They will be washed away as
if in a flood.
18 Your agreement with death
will be erased;
your contract with death
will not help you.
When terrible punishment
comes,
you will be crushed by it.
19 Whenever punishment comes,
it will take you away.
It will come morning after morning;
it will defeat you by day and by night.
Those who understand this punishment
will be terrified."
20 You will be like the person who tried to
sleep
on a bed that was too short
and with a blanket that was too narrow
to wrap around himself.
21 The LORD will fight as he did at Mount
Perazim.
He will be angry as he was in the Valley
of Gibeon.
He will do his work, his strange work.
He will finish his job, his strange job.
22 Now, you must not make fun of these
things,
or the ropes around you will become
tighter.
The Lord GOD All-Powerful has told me
how the whole earth will be destroyed.

COMFORT

Where can we find stress-relief (28:16)

"Listen closely to what I tell you; listen carefully to what I say." (Isaiah 28:23)

WHAT'S IT MEAN?

The word translated "Jerusalem" in this passage is "Zion." When David conquered Jerusalem around 1000 B.C., he set up his capital in an ancient fortress known as Zion. Years later, when Solomon built the Temple on Mount Moriah, the entire area in and around Jerusalem came to be known as Zion. Eventually, Zion was used to refer to the entire nation of Israel.

Isaiah 28:16

THE LORD PUNISHES FAIRLY

23 Listen closely to what I tell you;
listen carefully to what I say.
24 A farmer does not plow his field all the
time;
he does not go on working the soil.
25 He makes the ground flat and
smooth.
Then he plants the dill and
scatters the cumin.
He plants the wheat in rows,
the barley in its special
place,
and other wheat as a
border around the field.
26 His God teaches him
and shows him the right
way.
27 A farmer doesn't use heavy boards to
crush dill;
he doesn't use a wagon wheel to crush
cumin.
He uses a small stick to break open the
dill,
and with a stick he opens the cumin.
28 The grain is ground to make bread.
People do not ruin it by crushing it
forever.
The farmer separates the wheat from the
chaff with his cart,
but he does not let his horses grind it.
29 This lesson also comes from the LORD All-
Powerful,
who gives wonderful advice, who is
very wise.

WARNINGS TO JERUSALEM

29

1 How terrible it will be for you, Jerusalem,
the city where David camped.
Your festivals have continued
year after year.
2 I will attack Jerusalem,

and that city will be filled with sadness
and crying.
It will be like an altar to me.
3 I will put armies all around you,
Jerusalem;
I will surround you with towers
and with devices to attack you.
4 You will be pulled down and will speak
from the ground;
I will hear your voice rising from the
ground.
It will sound like the voice of a ghost;
your words will come like a whisper
from the dirt.

5 Your many enemies will become like fine
dust;
the many cruel people will be like chaff
that is blown away.
Everything will happen very quickly.
6 The LORD All-Powerful will come
with thunder, earthquakes, and great
noises,
with storms, strong winds, and a fire
that destroys.
7 Then all the nations that fight against
Jerusalem
will be like a dream;
all the nations that attack her
will be like a vision in the night.
8 They will be like a hungry man who
dreams he is eating,
but when he awakens, he is still hungry.
They will be like a thirsty man who
dreams he is drinking,
but when he awakens, he is still weak
and thirsty.
It will be the same way with all the
nations
who fight against Mount Zion.

9 Be surprised and amazed.
Blind yourselves so that you cannot see.
Become drunk, but not from wine.
Trip and fall, but not from beer.
10 The LORD has made you go into a deep
sleep.
He has closed your eyes. (The prophets
are your eyes.)
He has covered your heads. (The seers
are your heads.)

11 This vision is like the words of a book that
is closed and sealed. You may give the book to
someone who can read and tell that person to
read it. But he will say, "I can't read the book,
because it is sealed."
12 Or you may give the
book to someone who cannot read and tell
him to read it. But he will say, "I don't know
how to read."

13 The Lord says:
"These people say they
love me;
they show honor to me
with words,
but their hearts are far
from me.
The honor they show me
is nothing but human rules.
14 So I will continue to amaze these people
by doing more and more miracles.
Their wise men will lose their wisdom;
their wise men will not be able to
understand."

HYPOCRISY

What is hypocrisy? (29:13)

WARNINGS ABOUT OTHER NATIONS

15 How terrible it will be for those who try
to hide things from the LORD
and who do their work in darkness.
They think no one will see them or
know what they do.
16 You are confused.
You think the clay is equal to the potter.
You think that an object can tell the one
who made it,
"You didn't make me."
This is like a pot telling its maker,
"You don't know anything."

A BETTER TIME IS COMING

17 In a very short time, Lebanon will become
rich farmland,
and the rich farmland will seem like a
forest.
18 At that time the deaf will hear the words
in a book.
Instead of having darkness and gloom,
the blind will see.
19 The LORD will make the poor people
happy;
they will rejoice in the Holy One of
Israel.
20 Then the people without mercy will come
to an end;
those who do not respect God will
disappear.
Those who enjoy doing evil will be gone:
21 those who lie about others in court,
those who trap people in court,
those who lie and take justice from
innocent people in court.

22 This is what the LORD who set Abraham
free says to the family of Jacob:
"Now the people of Jacob will not be
ashamed

or disgraced any longer.
23 When they see all their children,
the children I made with my hands,
they will say my name is holy.
They will agree that the Holy One of Jacob is holy,
and they will respect the God of Israel.
24 People who do wrong will now understand.
Those who complain will accept being taught."

WARNINGS TO THE STUBBORN NATION

30 1 The LORD said,
"How terrible it will be for these stubborn children.
They make plans, but they don't ask me to help them.
They make agreements with other nations, without asking my Spirit.
They are adding more and more sins to themselves.
2 They go down to Egypt for help
without asking me about it first.
They hope they will be saved by the king of Egypt;
they want Egypt to protect them.
3 But hiding in Egypt will bring you only shame;
Egypt's protection will only disappoint you.
4 Your officers have gone to Zoan,
and your messengers have gone to Hanes,
5 but they will be put to shame,
because Egypt is useless to them.
It will give no help and will be of no use;
it will cause them only shame and embarrassment."

GOD'S MESSAGE TO JUDAH

6 This is a message about the animals in
southern Judah:
Southern Judah is a dangerous place
full of lions and lionesses,
poisonous snakes and darting snakes.
The messengers travel through there with their wealth on the backs of donkeys
and their treasure on the backs of camels.
They carry them to a nation that cannot help them,
7 to Egypt whose help is useless.
So I call that country Rahab the Do-Nothing.

8 Now write this on a sign for the people,
write this on a scroll,
so that for the days to come
this will be a witness forever.
9 These people are like children who lie and refuse to obey;
they refuse to listen to the LORD's teachings.
10 They tell the seers,
"Don't see any more visions!"
They say to the prophets,
"Don't tell us the truth!
Say things that will make us feel good;
see only good things for us.
11 Stop blocking our path.
Get out of our way.
Stop telling us
about God, the Holy One of Israel."
12 So this is what the Holy One of Israel
says:
"You people have refused to accept this message
and have depended on cruelty and lies to help you.
13 You are guilty of these things.
So you will be like a high wall with cracks in it
that falls suddenly and breaks into small pieces.
14 You will be like a clay jar that breaks,
smashed into many pieces.
Those pieces will be too small
to take coals from the fire
or to get water from a well."

15 This is what the Lord GOD,
the Holy One of Israel, says:
"If you come back to me
and trust me, you will be saved.
If you will be calm and
trust me, you will be strong."
But you don't want to do that.

COURAGE
Where should we go to find courage? (30:15)

16 You say, "No, we need horses to run away on."
So you will run away on horses.
You say, "We will ride away on fast horses."
So those who chase you will be fast.
17 One enemy will make threats,
and a thousand of your men will run away.
Five enemies will make threats,
and all of you will run from them.
You will be left alone like a flagpole on a hilltop,
like a banner on a hill.
18 The LORD wants to show his mercy to you.

He wants to rise and comfort you.
The LORD is a fair God,
and everyone who waits for his help
will be happy.

THE LORD WILL HELP HIS PEOPLE

19You people who live on Mount Zion in
Jerusalem will not cry anymore. The LORD will
hear your crying, and he will comfort you.
When he hears you, he will help you. 20The
Lord has given you sorrow and hurt like the
bread and water you ate every day. He is your
teacher; he will not continue to hide from you,
but you will see your teacher with your own
eyes. 21If you go the wrong way—to the right
or to the left—you will hear a voice behind
you saying, "This is the right way. You should
go this way." 22You have statues covered with
silver and gold, but you will ruin them for further use. You will throw them away like filthy
rags and say, "Go away!"

WHAT'S IT MEAN?

A season of drought was devastating to the Israelites, who relied on agriculture for their living. A season of rain, on the other hand, was a powerful symbol of hope.

Isaiah 30:23

23At that time the LORD will send rain for
the seeds you plant in the ground, and the
ground will grow food for you. The harvest
will be rich and great, and you will have plenty
of food in the fields for your animals. 24Your
oxen and donkeys that work the soil will have
all the food they need. You will have to use
shovels and pitchforks to spread all their food.
25Every mountain and hill will have streams
filled with water. These things will happen after
many people are killed and the towers are
pulled down. 26At that time the light from the
moon will be bright like the sun, and the light
from the sun will be seven times brighter than
now, like the light of seven days. These things
will happen when the LORD bandages his broken people and heals the hurts he gave them.

27Look! The LORD comes from far away.
His anger is like a fire with thick clouds
of smoke.
His mouth is filled with anger,
and his tongue is like a burning fire.
28His breath is like a rushing river,
which rises to the throat.
He will judge the nations as if he is sifting
them through the strainer of
destruction.
He will place in their mouths a bit that
will lead them the wrong way.
29You will sing happy songs
as on the nights you begin a festival.
You will be happy like people listening to
flutes
as they come to the mountain of the
LORD,
to the Rock of Israel.
30The LORD will cause all people to hear his
great voice
and to see his powerful arm come down
with anger,
like a great fire that burns everything,
like a great storm with much rain and
hail.
31Assyria will be afraid when it hears the
voice of the LORD,
because he will strike Assyria with a
rod.
32When the LORD punishes Assyria with a
rod,
he will beat them to the music of
tambourines and harps;
he will fight against them with his
mighty weapons.
33Topheth[n] has been made ready for a long
time;
it is ready for the king.
It was made deep and wide
with much wood and fire.
And the LORD's breath will come
like a stream of burning sulfur and set it
on fire.

WARNINGS ABOUT RELYING ON EGYPT

31

1How terrible it will be for those people
who go down to Egypt for help.
They think horses will save them.
They think their many chariots
and strong horsemen will save them.
But they don't trust God, the Holy One of
Israel,
or ask the LORD for help.

30:33 Topheth Gehenna; the Valley of Hinnom. Here people burned the bodies of criminals and animals, along with garbage.

[2]But he is wise and can bring them disaster.
He does not change his warnings.
He will rise up and fight against the evil people
and against those who try to help evil people.
[3]The Egyptians are only people and are not God.
Their horses are only animals and are not spirit.
The LORD will stretch out his arm,
and the one who helps will stumble,
and the people who wanted help will fall.
All of them will be destroyed together.
[4]The LORD says this to me:
"When a lion or a lion's cub kills an animal to eat,
it stands over the dead animal and roars.
A band of shepherds
may be assembled against it,
but the lion will not be afraid of their yelling
or upset by their noise.
So the LORD All-Powerful will come down
to fight on Mount Zion and on its hill.
[5]The LORD All-Powerful will defend Jerusalem
like birds flying over their nests.
He will defend and save it;
he will 'pass over' and save Jerusalem."

[6]You children of Israel, come back to the God you fought against. [7]The time is coming when each of you will stop worshiping idols of gold and silver, which you sinned by making.

MONEY
Will our possessions last forever? (31:6–7)

[8]"Assyria will be defeated by a sword, but not the sword of a person;
Assyria will be destroyed, but not by a person's sword.
Assyria will run away from the sword of God,
but its young men will be caught and made slaves.
[9]They will panic, and their protection will be destroyed.
Their commanders will be terrified when they see God's battle flag,"
says the LORD,
whose fire is in Jerusalem
and whose furnace is in Jerusalem.

A GOOD KINGDOM IS COMING

32

[1]A king will rule in a way that brings justice,
and leaders will make fair decisions.
[2]Then each ruler will be like a shelter from the wind,
like a safe place in a storm,
like streams of water in a dry land,
like a cool shadow from a large rock in a hot land.

[3]People will look to the king for help,
and they will truly listen to what he says.
[4]People who are now worried will be able to understand.
Those who cannot speak clearly now
will then be able to speak clearly and quickly.
[5]Fools will not be called great,
and people will not respect the wicked.
[6]A fool says foolish things,
and in his mind he plans evil.
A fool does things that are wicked,
and he says wrong things about the LORD.
A fool does not feed the hungry
or let thirsty people drink water.
[7]The wicked person uses evil like a tool.
He plans ways to take everything from the poor.
He destroys the poor with lies,
even when the poor person is in the right.
[8]But a good leader plans to do good,
and those good things make him a good leader.

HARD TIMES ARE COMING

[9]You women who are calm now,
stand up and listen to me.
You women who feel safe now,
hear what I say.
[10]You women feel safe now,
but after one year you will be afraid.
There will be no grape harvest
and no summer fruit to gather.
[11]Women, you are calm now, but you should shake with fear.
Women, you feel safe now, but you should tremble.
Take off your nice clothes
and put rough cloth around your waist
to show your sadness.
[12]Beat your breasts in grief, because the fields that were pleasant are now empty.

Cry, because the vines that once had
fruit now have no more grapes.
13 Cry for the land of my people,
in which only thorns and weeds now
grow.
Cry for the city that once was happy
and for all the houses that once were
filled with joy.
14 The palace will be empty;
people will leave the noisy city.
Strong cities and towers will be empty.
Wild donkeys will love to live there, and
sheep will go there to eat.

THINGS WILL GET BETTER

15 This will continue until
God pours his Spirit
from above upon us.
Then the desert will be
like a fertile field
and the fertile field like
a forest.
16 Justice will be found even in
the desert,
and fairness will be found in the
fertile fields.
17 That fairness will bring peace,
and it will bring calm and safety forever.
18 My people will live in peaceful places
and in safe homes
and in calm places of rest.
19 Hail will destroy the forest,
and the city will be completely
destroyed.
20 But you will be happy as you plant seeds
near every stream
and as you let your cattle and donkeys
wander freely.

"That fairness will bring peace, and it will bring calm and safety forever." (Isaiah 32:17)

WARNINGS TO ASSYRIA AND PROMISES TO GOD'S PEOPLE

33
1 How terrible it will be for you who
destroy others
but have not been destroyed yet.
How terrible it will be for you, traitor,
whom no one has turned against yet.
When you stop destroying,
others will destroy you.
When you stop turning against others,
they will turn against you.

2 LORD, be kind to us.
We have waited for your help.
Give us strength every morning.
Save us when we are in trouble.
3 Your powerful voice makes people run
away in fear;
your greatness causes the nations to run
away.
4 Like locusts, your enemies will take away
the things you stole in war.
Like locusts rushing about, they will take
your wealth.
5 The LORD is very great, and he lives in a
high place.
He fills Jerusalem with fairness and
justice.
6 He will be your safety.
He is full of salvation, wisdom, and
knowledge.
Respect for the LORD is
the greatest treasure.

7 See, brave men are crying
out in the streets;
those who tried to bring
peace are crying loudly.
8 There is no one on the
roads,
no one walking in the
paths.
People have broken the
agreements they made.
They refuse to believe the proof from
witnesses.
No one respects other people.
9 The land is sick and dying;
Lebanon is ashamed and dying.
The Plain of Sharon is dry like the desert,
and the trees of Bashan and Carmel are
dying.

WHAT'S IT MEAN?

The one thing these areas had in common was natural beauty. Mount Lebanon towered over the region and produced majestic cedar trees. The fertile Plain of Sharon was known for its breathtaking variety of flowers and plant life. Bashan was famous for its abundant wheat fields and vast herds of livestock. Mount Carmel was a beautiful, wooded mountain overlooking the Mediterranean Sea.
Isaiah 33:9

10 The LORD says, "Now, I will stand up
and show my greatness.
Now, I will become important to the
people.

[11] You people do useless things
that are like hay and straw.
A destructive wind will burn you like fire.
[12] People will be burned until their bones become like lime;
they will burn quickly like dry thornbushes."

[13] You people in faraway lands, hear what I have done.
You people who are near me, learn about my power.
[14] The sinners in Jerusalem are afraid;
those who are separated from God shake with fear.
They say, "Can any of us live through this fire that destroys?
Who can live near this fire that burns on and on?"
[15] A person who does what is right
and speaks what is right,
who refuses to take money unfairly,
who refuses to take money to hurt others,
who does not listen to plans of murder,
who refuses to think about evil—
[16] this is the kind of person who will be safe.
He will be protected as he would be in a high, walled city.
He will always have bread,
and he will not run out of water.
[17] Your eyes will see the king in his beauty.
You will see the land that stretches far away.
[18] You will think about the terror of the past:
"Where is that officer?
Where is the one who collected the taxes?
Where is the officer in charge of our defense towers?"
[19] No longer will you see those proud people from other countries,
whose strange language you couldn't understand.

GOD WILL PROTECT JERUSALEM

[20] Look at Jerusalem, the city of our festivals.
Look at Jerusalem, that beautiful place of rest.
It is like a tent that will never be moved;
the pegs that hold her in place will never be pulled up,
and her ropes will never be broken.
[21] There the LORD will be our Mighty One.
That land is a place with streams and wide rivers,
but there will be no enemy boats on those rivers;
no powerful ship will sail on them.
[22] This is because the LORD is our judge.
The LORD makes our laws.
The LORD is our king.
He will save us.
[23] You sailors from other lands, hear:
The ropes on your boats hang loose.
The mast is not held firm.
The sails are not spread open.
Then your great wealth will be divided.
There will be so much wealth that even the crippled people will carry off a share.
[24] No one living in Jerusalem will say, "I am sick."
The people who live there will have their sins forgiven.

GOD WILL PUNISH HIS ENEMIES

34

[1] All you nations, come near and listen.
Pay attention, you peoples!
The earth and all the people in it should listen,
the world and everything in it.
[2] The LORD is angry with all the nations;
he is angry with their armies.
He will destroy them and kill them all.
[3] Their bodies will be thrown outside.
The stink will rise from the bodies,
and the blood will flow down the mountains.
[4] The sun, moon, and stars will dissolve,
and the sky will be rolled up like a scroll.
The stars will fall
like dead leaves from a vine
or dried-up figs from a fig tree.
[5] The LORD's sword in the sky is covered with blood.
It will cut through Edom
and destroy those people as an offering to the LORD.
[6] The LORD's sword will be covered with blood;
it will be covered with fat,
with the blood from lambs and goats,
with the fat from the kidneys of sheep.
This is because the LORD decided there will be a sacrifice in Bozrah
and much killing in Edom.
[7] The oxen will be killed,
and the cattle and the strong bulls.
The land will be filled with their blood,
and the dirt will be covered with their fat.

8 The LORD has chosen a time for punishment.
He has chosen a year when people must pay for the wrongs they did to Jerusalem.
9 Edom's rivers will be like hot tar.
Its dirt will be like burning sulfur.
Its land will be like burning tar.
10 The fires will burn night and day;
the smoke will rise from Edom forever.
Year after year that land will be empty;
no one will ever travel through that land again.
11 Birds and small animals will own that land,
and owls and ravens will live there.
God will make it an empty wasteland;
it will have nothing left in it.
12 The important people will have no one left to rule them;
the leaders will all be gone.
13 Thorns will take over the strong towers,
and wild bushes will grow in the walled cities.
It will be a home for wild dogs
and a place for owls to live.
14 Desert animals will live with the hyenas,
and wild goats will call to their friends.
Night animals will live there
and find a place of rest.
15 Owls will nest there and lay eggs.
When they hatch open, the owls will gather their young under their wings.
Hawks will gather
with their own kind.

16 Look at the LORD's scroll and read what is written there:
None of these will be missing;
none will be without its mate.
God has given the command,
so his Spirit will gather them together.
17 God has divided the land among them,
and he has given them each their portion.
So they will own that land forever
and will live there year after year.

GOD WILL COMFORT HIS PEOPLE

35

1 The desert and dry land will become happy;
the desert will be glad and will produce flowers.
Like a flower, 2 it will have many blooms.
It will show its happiness, as if it were shouting with joy.
It will be beautiful like the forest of Lebanon,
as beautiful as the hill of Carmel and the Plain of Sharon.
Everyone will see the glory of the LORD
and the splendor of our God.
3 Make the weak hands strong
and the weak knees steady.
4 Say to people who are frightened,
"Be strong. Don't be afraid.
Look, your God will come,
and he will punish your enemies.
He will make them pay for the wrongs they did,
but he will save you."

5 Then the blind people will see again,
and the deaf will hear.
6 Crippled people will jump like deer,
and those who can't talk now will shout with joy.
Water will flow in the desert,
and streams will flow in the dry land.
7 The burning desert will have pools of water,
and the dry ground will have springs.
Where wild dogs once lived,
grass and water plants will grow.
8 A road will be there;
this highway will be called "The Road to Being Holy."
Evil people will not be allowed to walk on that road;
only good people will walk on it.
No fools will go on it.
9 No lions will be there,
nor will dangerous animals be on that road.
They will not be found there.
That road will be for the people God saves;
10 the people the LORD has freed will return there.
They will enter Jerusalem with joy,
and their happiness will last forever.
Their gladness and joy will fill them completely,
and sorrow and sadness will go far away.

FOLLOWING GOD
Where will following God lead us? (35:10)

THE ASSYRIANS INVADE JUDAH

36

1 During Hezekiah's fourteenth year as king,
Sennacherib king of Assyria attacked all the
strong, walled cities of Judah and captured
them. 2 The king of Assyria sent out his field
commander with a large army from Lachish to

King Hezekiah in Jerusalem. When the commander came near the waterway from the upper pool on the road where people do their laundry, he stopped. [3]Eliakim, Shebna, and Joah went out to meet him. Eliakim son of Hilkiah was the palace manager, Shebna was the royal secretary, and Joah son of Asaph was the recorder.

[4]The field commander said to them, "Tell Hezekiah this:

" 'The great king, the king of Assyria, says: What can you trust in now? [5]You say you have battle plans and power for war, but your words mean nothing. Whom are you trusting for help so that you turn against me? [6]Look, you are depending on Egypt to help you, but Egypt is like a splintered walking stick. If you lean on it for help, it will stab your hand and hurt you. The king of Egypt will hurt all those who depend on him. [7]You might say, "We are depending on the LORD our God," but Hezekiah destroyed the LORD's altars and the places of worship. Hezekiah told Judah and Jerusalem, "You must worship only at this one altar."

[8]" 'Now make an agreement with my master, the king of Assyria: I will give you two thousand horses if you can find enough men to ride them. [9]You cannot defeat one of my master's least important officers, so why do you depend on Egypt to give you chariots and horsemen? [10]I have not come to attack and destroy this country without an order from the LORD. The LORD himself told me to come to this country and destroy it.' "

[11]Then Eliakim, Shebna, and Joah said to the field commander, "Please speak to us in the Aramaic language. We understand it. Don't speak to us in Hebrew, because the people on the city wall can hear you."

[12]But the commander said, "My master did not send me to tell these things only to you and your king. He sent me to speak also to those people sitting on the wall who will have to eat their own dung and drink their own urine like you."

WHAT'S IT MEAN?

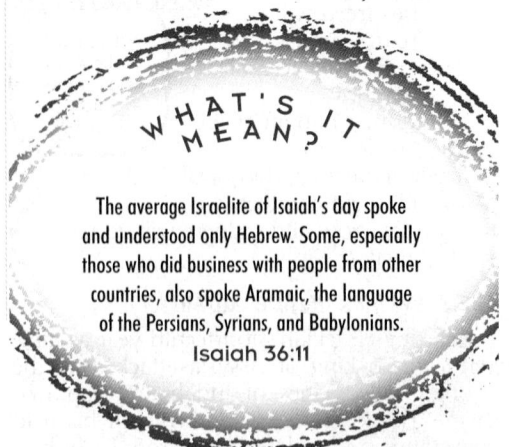

The average Israelite of Isaiah's day spoke and understood only Hebrew. Some, especially those who did business with people from other countries, also spoke Aramaic, the language of the Persians, Syrians, and Babylonians.

Isaiah 36:11

[13]Then the commander stood and shouted loudly in the Hebrew language, "Listen to what the great king, the king of Assyria says, [14]The king says you should not let Hezekiah fool you, because he can't save you. [15]Don't let Hezekiah talk you into trusting the LORD by saying, 'The LORD will surely save us. This city won't be handed over to the king of Assyria.'

[16]"Don't listen to Hezekiah. The king of Assyria says, 'Make peace with me, and come out of the city to me. Then everyone will be free to eat the fruit from his own grapevine and fig tree and to drink water from his own well. [17]After that I will come and take you to a land like your own—a land with grain and new wine, bread and vineyards.'

[18]"Don't let Hezekiah fool you, saying, 'The LORD will save us.' Has a god of any other nation saved his people from the power of the king of Assyria? [19]Where are the gods of Hamath and Arpad? Where are the gods of Sepharvaim? They did not save Samaria from my power. [20]Not one of all the gods of these countries has saved his people from me. Neither can the LORD save Jerusalem from my power."

WHAT'S IT MEAN?

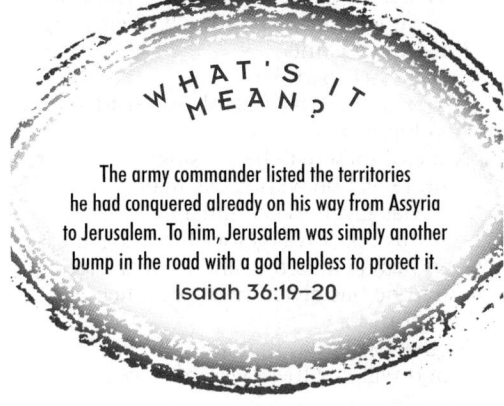

The army commander listed the territories he had conquered already on his way from Assyria to Jerusalem. To him, Jerusalem was simply another bump in the road with a god helpless to protect it.

Isaiah 36:19–20

[21]The people were silent. They didn't answer the commander at all, because King Hezekiah had ordered, "Don't answer him."

[22]Then Eliakim, Shebna, and Joah tore their clothes to show how upset they were. (Eliakim son of Hilkiah was the palace manager, Shebna was the royal secretary, and Joah son of Asaph was the recorder.) The three men went to Hezekiah and told him what the field commander had said.

HEZEKIAH ASKS GOD TO HELP

37

1When King Hezekiah heard the message,
he tore his clothes and put on rough cloth to
show how sad he was. Then he went into the
Temple of the LORD. 2Hezekiah sent Eliakim,
the palace manager, and Shebna, the royal secretary, and the older priests to Isaiah. They
were all wearing rough cloth when they came
to Isaiah the prophet, the son of Amoz. 3They
told Isaiah, "This is what Hezekiah says: Today
is a day of sorrow and punishment and disgrace, as when a child should be born, but the
mother is not strong enough to give birth to it.
4The king of Assyria sent his field commander
to make fun of the living God. Maybe the LORD
your God will hear what the commander said
and will punish him for it. So pray for the few
of us who are left alive."
5When Hezekiah's officers came to Isaiah,
6he said to them, "Tell your master this: The
LORD says, 'Don't be afraid of what you have
heard. Don't be frightened by the words the
servants of the king of Assyria have spoken
against me. 7Listen! I am going to put a spirit in
the king of Assyria. He will hear a report that
will make him return to his own country, and I
will cause him to die by the sword there.' "
8The field commander heard that the king
of Assyria had left Lachish. When he went
back, he found the king fighting against the city
of Libnah.
9The king received a report that Tirhakah,
the Cushite king of Egypt, was coming to attack
him. When the king of Assyria heard this, he
sent messengers to Hezekiah, saying, 10"Tell
Hezekiah king of Judah: Don't be fooled by the
god you trust. Don't believe him when he says
Jerusalem will not be handed over to the king
of Assyria. 11You have heard what the kings of
Assyria have done. They have completely defeated every country, so do not think you will
be saved. 12Did the gods of those people save
them? My ancestors destroyed them, defeating
the cities of Gozan, Haran, and Rezeph, and the
people of Eden living in Tel Assar. 13Where are
the kings of Hamath and Arpad? Where are the
kings of Sepharvaim, Hena, and Ivvah?"

HEZEKIAH PRAYS TO THE LORD

14When Hezekiah received the letter from
the messengers and read it, he went up to the
Temple of the LORD. He spread the letter out
before the LORD 15and prayed to the LORD:
16"LORD All-Powerful, you are the God of Israel, whose throne is between the gold creatures with wings, only you are God of all the
kingdoms of the earth. You made the heavens
and the earth. 17Hear, LORD, and listen. Open
your eyes, LORD, and see. Listen to all the
words Sennacherib has said to insult the living
God.
18"It is true, LORD, that the kings of Assyria
have destroyed all these countries and their
lands. 19They have thrown the gods of these
nations into the fire, but they were
only wood and rock statues
that people made. So the kings
have destroyed them. 20Now,
LORD our God, save us from
the king's power so that all the
kingdoms of the earth will
know that you, LORD, are the
only God."

TRIALS

Who will help us overcome our problems? (37:20)

THE LORD ANSWERS HEZEKIAH

21Then Isaiah son of Amoz sent a message
to Hezekiah that said, "This is what the LORD,
the God of Israel, says: 'You prayed to me
about Sennacherib king of Assyria. 22So this is
what the LORD has said against Sennacherib:

The people of Jerusalem
hate you and make fun of you;
the people of Jerusalem
laugh at you as you run away.
23You have insulted me and spoken against
me;
you have raised your voice against me.
You have a proud look on your face,
which is against me, the Holy One of
Israel!
24You have sent your messengers to insult
the Lord.
You have said, "With my many chariots
I have gone to the tops of the mountains,
to the highest mountains of Lebanon.
I have cut down its tallest cedars

WHAT'S IT MEAN?

The Nile River, which flows from central Africa to the Mediterranean region, is over 3,500 miles long. The Nile is big enough to provide water for the entire nation of Egypt. Do you suppose Sennacherib really believed that he was more powerful than the Nile?

Isaiah 37:25

and its best pine trees.
I have gone to its greatest heights
and its best forests.
25 I have dug wells in foreign countries
and drunk water there.
By the soles of my feet,
I have dried up all the rivers of Egypt."

26 " 'King of Assyria, surely you have heard.
Long ago I, the LORD, planned these
things.
Long ago I designed them,
and now I have made them happen.
I allowed you to turn those strong, walled
cities
into piles of rocks.
27 The people in those cities were weak;
they were frightened and put to shame.
They were like grass in the field,
like tender, young grass,
like grass on the housetop
that is burned by the wind before it can
grow.

28 " 'I know when you rest,
when you come and go,
and how you rage against me.
29 Because you rage against me,
and because I have heard your proud
words,
I will put my hook in your nose
and my bit in your mouth.
Then I will force you to leave my country
the same way you came.'
30 "Then the LORD said, 'Hezekiah, I will give
you this sign:
This year you will eat the grain that grows
wild,
and the second year you will eat what
grows wild from that.
But in the third year, plant
grain and harvest it.
Plant vineyards and
eat their fruit.
31 Some of the people in
the family of Judah
will escape.
Like plants that take root,
they will grow strong
and have many children.
32 A few people will come out of
Jerusalem alive;
a few from Mount Zion will live.
The strong love of the LORD All-Powerful
will make this happen.'
33 "So this is what the LORD says about the
king of Assyria:
'He will not enter this city
or even shoot an arrow here.
He will not fight against it with shields
or build a ramp to attack the city walls.
34 He will return to his country the same
way he came,
and he will not enter this city,'
says the LORD.
35 'I will defend and save this city
for my sake and for David, my servant.' "
36 Then the angel of the LORD went out and
killed one hundred eighty-five thousand men
in the Assyrian camp. When the people got up
early the next morning, they saw all the dead
bodies. 37 So Sennacherib king of Assyria left
and went back to Nineveh and stayed there.
38 One day as Sennacherib was worshiping
in the temple of his god Nisroch, his sons
Adrammelech and Sharezer killed him with a
sword. Then they escaped to the land of Ararat. So Sennacherib's son Esarhaddon became
king of Assyria.

"I will defend and save this city for my sake and for David, my servant." (Isaiah 37:35)

HEZEKIAH'S ILLNESS

38
1 At that time Hezekiah became very sick; he
was almost dead. The prophet Isaiah son of
Amoz went to see him and told
him, "This is what the LORD
says: Make arrangements, because you are not going to
live, but die."
2 Hezekiah turned toward
the wall and prayed to the
LORD, 3 "LORD, please remember
that I have always obeyed you. I
have given myself completely to you and have
done what you said was right." Then Hezekiah
cried loudly.

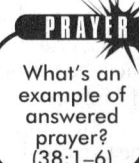

PRAYER
What's an example of answered prayer? (38:1–6)

4 Then the LORD spoke his word to Isaiah:
5 "Go to Hezekiah and tell him:
'This is what the LORD, the
God of your ancestor David,
says: I have heard your
prayer and seen your tears.
So I will add fifteen years to
your life. 6 I will save you and
this city from the king of Assyria; I will defend this city.
7 " 'The LORD will do what
he says. This is the sign from
the LORD to show you: 8 The sun
has made a shadow go down the stairway of
Ahaz, but I will make it go back ten steps.' " So
the shadow made by the sun went back up the
ten steps it had gone down.
9 After Hezekiah king of Judah got well, he
wrote this song:

WHAT'S IT MEAN?

A pillar or column may have cast the shadow that served as a sundial. As the shadow moved, it indicated the passing of time. Unfortunately, because the exact design of the sundial is unknown, it's impossible to tell how much time was lost.

Isaiah 38:8

10 I said, "I am in the middle of my life.
Do I have to go through the gates of death?
Will I have the rest of my life taken away from me?"
11 I said, "I will not see the LORD
in the land of the living again.
I will not again see the people
who live on the earth.
12 Like a shepherd's tent,
my home has been pulled down and taken from me.
I am finished
like the cloth a weaver rolls up and cuts from the loom.[n]
In one day you brought me to this end.
13 All night I cried loudly.
Like a lion, he crushed all my bones.
In one day you brought me to this end.
14 I cried like a bird
and moaned like a dove.
My eyes became tired as I looked to the heavens.
Lord, I have troubles. Please help me."

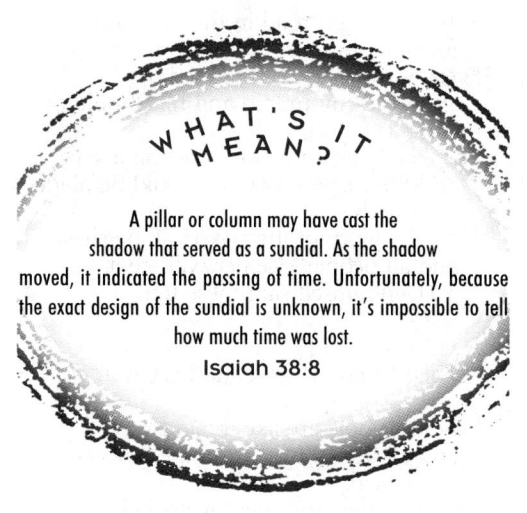

15 What can I say?
The Lord told me what would happen
and then made it happen.
I have had these troubles in my soul,
so now I will be humble all my life.
16 Lord, because of you, people live.
Because of you, my spirit also lives;
you made me well and let me live.
17 It was for my own good
that I had such troubles.
Because you love me very much,
you did not let me die
but threw my sins
far away.
18 People in the place of the dead cannot praise you;
those who have died cannot sing praises to you;
those who die don't trust you
to help them.
19 The people who are alive are the ones who praise you.
They praise you as I praise you today.
A father should tell his children
that you provide help.
20 The LORD saved me,
so we will play songs on stringed instruments
in the Temple of the LORD
all the days of our lives.

21 Then Isaiah said, "Make a paste from figs
and put it on Hezekiah's boil. Then he will get
well." 22 Hezekiah then asked Isaiah, "What will
be the sign? What will show that I will go up to
the Temple of the LORD?"

WHAT'S IT MEAN?

Ever wonder how people in ancient times made clothes? The only things they needed were thread and a loom. What's a loom, you ask? It's a large frame with threads stretched across it. Weavers threaded yarn back and forth across the loom to make fabric. The loom held the cloth tight until the weaver cut the threads of the material. The Bible describes life as a cloth woven by God, its pattern showing the events and experiences that made up a person's existence.

Isaiah 38:12

MESSENGERS FROM BABYLON

39 1 At that time Merodach-Baladan son of Baladan was king of Babylon. He sent letters and a
gift to Hezekiah, because he had heard that
Hezekiah had been sick and was now well.
2 Hezekiah was pleased and showed the messengers what was in his storehouses: the silver,
gold, spices, expensive perfumes, his swords

38:12 loom A machine for making cloth from thread.

and shields, and all his wealth. He showed
them everything in his palace and in his kingdom.
[3]Then Isaiah the prophet went to King Hezekiah and asked him, "What did these men
say? Where did they come from?"
Hezekiah said, "They came from a faraway
country—from Babylon."
[4]So Isaiah asked him, "What did they see in
your palace?"
Hezekiah said, "They saw everything in my
palace. I showed them all my wealth."
[5]Then Isaiah said to Hezekiah: "Listen to the
words of the LORD All-Powerful: [6]'In the future
everything in your palace and everything your
ancestors have stored up until this day will be
taken away to Babylon. Nothing will be left,'
says the LORD. [7]Some of your own children,
those who will be born to you, will be taken
away, and they will become servants in the
palace of the king of Babylon."

WHAT'S IT MEAN?

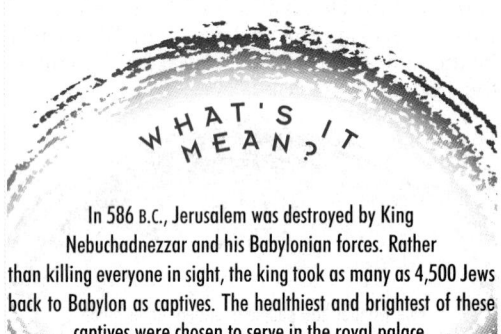

In 586 B.C., Jerusalem was destroyed by King Nebuchadnezzar and his Babylonian forces. Rather than killing everyone in sight, the king took as many as 4,500 Jews back to Babylon as captives. The healthiest and brightest of these captives were chosen to serve in the royal palace.

Isaiah 39:7

[8]Hezekiah told Isaiah, "These words from
the LORD are good." He said this because he
thought, "There will be peace and security in
my lifetime."

ISRAEL'S PUNISHMENT WILL END

40 [1]Your God says,
"Comfort, comfort my people.
[2]Speak kindly to the people of Jerusalem
and tell them
that their time of service is finished,
that they have paid for their sins,
that the LORD has punished Jerusalem
twice for every sin they did."
[3]This is the voice of one who calls out:
"Prepare in the desert
the way for the LORD.
Make a straight road in the dry lands
for our God.
[4]Every valley should be raised up,
and every mountain and hill should be
made flat.
The rough ground should be made level,
and the rugged ground should be made
smooth.
[5]Then the glory of the LORD will be shown,
and all people together will see it.
The LORD himself said these things."

[6]A voice says, "Cry out!"
Then I said, "What shall I cry out?"

"Say all people are like the grass,
and all their glory is like the flowers of
the field.
[7]The grass dies and the flowers fall
when the breath of the LORD blows on
them.
Surely the people are like grass.
[8]The grass dies and the flowers fall,
but the word of our God will live
forever."
[9]Jerusalem, you have good news to tell.
Go up on a high mountain.
Jerusalem, you have good news to tell.
Shout out loud the good news.
Shout it out and don't be afraid.
Say to the towns of Judah,
"Here is your God."
[10]Look, the Lord GOD is coming with power
to rule all the people.
Look, he will bring reward for his people;
he will have their payment with him.
[11]He takes care of his people like a shepherd.
He gathers them like lambs in his arms
and carries them close to him.
He gently leads the mothers of the lambs.

GOD IS SUPREME

[12]Who has measured the oceans in the palm
of his hand?
Who has used his hand to measure the
sky?
Who has used a bowl to measure all the
dust of the earth
and scales to weigh the mountains and
hills?
[13]Who has known the mind of the LORD
or been able to give him advice?
[14]Whom did he ask for help?
Who taught him the right way?
Who taught him knowledge
and showed him the way to
understanding?

15 The nations are like one small drop in a
bucket;
they are no more than the dust on his
measuring scales.
To him the islands are no more than
fine dust on his scales.
16 All the trees in Lebanon are not enough
for the altar fires,
and all the animals in Lebanon are not
enough for burnt offerings.
17 Compared to the LORD all the nations are
worth nothing;
to him they are less than nothing.

18 Can you compare God to anything?
Can you compare him to an image of
anything?
19 An idol is formed by a craftsman,
and a goldsmith covers it with gold
and makes silver chains for it.
20 A poor person cannot buy those
expensive statues,
so he finds a tree that will not rot.
Then he finds a skilled craftsman
to make it into an idol that will not fall
over.

21 Surely you know. Surely you have
heard.
Surely from the beginning someone told
you.
Surely you understand how the earth
was created.
22 God sits on his throne above the circle of
the earth,
and compared to him, people are like
grasshoppers.
He stretches out the skies like a piece of
cloth
and spreads them out like a tent to sit
under.
23 He makes rulers unimportant
and the judges of this world worth
nothing.
24 They are like plants that are placed in the
ground,
like seeds that are planted.
As soon as they begin to grow strong,
he blows on them and they die,
and the wind blows them away
like chaff.

25 God, the Holy One, says,
"Can you compare me
to anyone?
Is anyone equal to me?"
26 Look up to the skies.
Who created all these stars?
He leads out the army of heaven one by
one
and calls all the stars by name.
Because he is strong and powerful,
not one of them is missing.

27 People of Jacob, why do you complain?
People of Israel, why do you say,

On the Edge

Surely you know. Surely you have heard. The LORD is the God who lives forever, who created all the world. He does not become tired or need to rest. No one can understand how great his wisdom is. He gives strength to those who are tired and more power to those who are weak. Even children become tired and need to rest, and young people trip and fall. But the people who trust the LORD will become strong again. They will rise up as an eagle in the sky; they will run and not need rest; they will walk and not become tired (Is. 40:28–31).

Everyone goes through times in life when they feel like nothing is happening. Working hard with very few accomplishments. Nothing's new on the horizon. Each day looks the same and feels the same. Goals are just as far away as they've always been. It gets tiring to work so hard, be so committed, and see no fruit.

Isaiah says that even young people get tired and weary, so tired that they can stumble and fall. But hope for tired people comes from the Lord, who says that if you trust in him, he will give you a new strength—not just the ability to survive another day, but new strength that lifts you up and makes you soar. It's the difference between just surviving tomorrow and soaring above the day with the strength and presence of an eagle. You don't have to figure out how to be the eagle. That's God's gift to those who trust in him and who call on him on the days when life seems to be going nowhere.

SEE FOR YOURSELF:
Ps. 65:3, 5; Jer. 15:20; Hab. 3:19

TRUST
Why can we trust God? (40:25–28)

WHAT'S IT MEAN?

Many people in ancient times believed that the destiny of their nation was controlled by heavenly bodies—stars, planets, the sun, the moon, and so forth. Professional astrologers were in constant demand to help kings and their officials keep track of what was going on in the sky and to interpret what it meant. These astrologers claimed to be able to predict the future based on the movement of the planets and stars.

Isaiah 40:26

"The LORD does not see what happens to me;
he does not care if I am treated fairly"?
28 Surely you know.
Surely you have heard.
The LORD is the God who lives forever,
who created all the world.
He does not become tired or need to rest.
No one can understand how great his wisdom is.
29 He gives strength to those who are tired
and more power to those who are weak.
30 Even children become tired and need to rest,
and young people trip and fall.
31 But the people who trust the LORD will become strong again.
They will rise up as an eagle in the sky;
they will run and not need rest;
they will walk and not become tired.

STRENGTH
Will God help us soar to new heights? (40:29–31)

THE LORD WILL HELP ISRAEL

41 1 The LORD says, "Faraway countries, listen to me.
Let the nations become strong.
Come to me and speak;
we will meet together to decide who is right.

2 "Who caused the one to come from the east?
Who gives him victories everywhere he goes?
The one who brought him gives nations over to him
and defeats kings.
He uses his sword, and kings become like dust.
He uses his bow, and they are blown away like chaff.
3 He chases them and is never hurt,
going places he has never been before.
4 Who caused this to happen?
Who has controlled history since the beginning?
I, the LORD, am the one. I was here at the beginning,
and I will be here when all things are finished."

GOD
Is God eternal? (41:4)

5 All you faraway places, look and be afraid;
all you places far away on the earth, shake with fear.
Come close and listen to me.
6 The workers help each other
and say to each other, "Be strong!"
7 The craftsman encourages the goldsmith,
and the workman who smooths the metal with a hammer encourages the one who shapes the metal.
He says, "This metal work is good."
He nails the statue to a base so it can't fall over.

ONLY THE LORD CAN SAVE US

8 The LORD says, "People of Israel, you are my servants.
People of Jacob, I chose you.
You are from the family of my friend Abraham.
9 I took you from places far away on the earth
and called you from a faraway country.
I said, 'You are my servants.'
I have chosen you and have not turned against you.
10 So don't worry, because I am with you.
Don't be afraid, because I am your God.
I will make you strong and will help you;
I will support you with my right hand that saves you.

11 "All those people who are angry with you
will be ashamed and disgraced.
Those who are against you
will disappear and be lost.
12 You will look for your enemies,

On the Edge

I am the LORD your God, who holds your right hand, and I tell you, "Don't be afraid. I will help you" (Is. 41:13).

Remember the story of Shadrach, Meshach, and Abednego (Dan. 3)? The king had them thrown into the fire because they wouldn't bow to him. But the fire didn't burn them up; and when people looked into the flames, they saw *four* men. Well, the fourth person was Jesus. Because he was with those guys, they didn't burn. In fact, they didn't even smell like smoke when they came out!

Well, Jesus is with you in the same way. In Isaiah, he says he is holding your hand. He goes with you through the fire of hard times in your life, preventing the flames from injuring you but letting the heat melt away some of the things about you that are not godly. With your hand in his, he can calm you down when things aren't going so well. If you won't let go of him, he can lead you to the place he wants you to be.

SEE FOR YOURSELF:
Ps. 37:24; Prov. 2:7; Hab. 3:19; Rom. 8:26; Heb. 13:6

but you will not find them.
Those who fought against you
will vanish completely.
13 I am the LORD your God,
who holds your right hand,
and I tell you, 'Don't be afraid.
I will help you.'
14 You few people of Israel who are left,
do not be afraid even though you are
weak as a worm.
I myself will help you," says the LORD.
"The one who saves you is the Holy
One of Israel.
15 Look, I have made you like a new
threshing board
with many sharp teeth.
So you will walk on mountains and crush
them;
you will make the hills like chaff.
16 You will throw them into the air, and the
wind will carry them away;
a windstorm will scatter them.
Then you will be happy in the LORD;
you will be proud of the Holy One of
Israel.

17 "The poor and needy people look for
water,
but they can't find any.
Their tongues are dry with thirst.
But I, the LORD, will answer their prayers;
I, the God of Israel, will not leave them
to die.
18 I will make rivers flow on the dry hills
and springs flow through the valleys.
I will change the desert into a lake of
water
and the dry land into fountains of water.
19 I will make trees grow in the desert—
cedars, acacia, myrtle, and olive trees.
I will put pine, fir, and cypress trees
growing together in the desert.
20 People will see these things and
understand;
they will think carefully about these
things and learn
that the LORD's power did this,
that the Holy One of Israel made these
things."

THE LORD CHALLENGES FALSE GODS

21 The LORD says, "Present your case."
The King of Jacob says, "Tell me your
arguments.
22 Bring in your idols to tell us
what is going to happen.
Have them tell us what happened in the
beginning.
Then we will think about these things,

WHAT'S IT MEAN?

The next time you need to thresh grain but don't have any modern equipment for the job, do what the ancient Israelites did. Embed some sharp stones or metal spikes in a log, then drag that log over the grain to crush it and tear the kernels from the stalks. Once that's finished, throw the entire mess in the air and let wind blow away the useless husks.

Isaiah 41:15–16

and we will know how they will turn
out.
Or tell us what will happen in the future.
23 Tell us what is coming next
so we will believe that you are gods.
Do something, whether it is good or bad,
and make us afraid.
24 You gods are less than nothing;
you can't do anything.
Those who worship you should be
hated.

WHAT'S IT MEAN?

Who was this mysterious ruler from the north? Why, none other than Cyrus, the king of Persia! After Cyrus conquered Babylon in 538 B.C., he allowed the Jewish people to return to their homeland of Judah. Unlike the kings of Babylon, Cyrus encouraged people to worship whatever gods they wished and in whatever way they wanted. When the Jews wanted to rebuild their destroyed Temple in Jerusalem, Cyrus even provided the supplies.

Isaiah 41:25

25 "I have brought someone to come out of
the north.[n]
I have called by name a man from the
east, and he knows me.
He walks on kings as if they were mud,
just as a potter walks on the clay.
26 Who told us about this before it
happened?
Who told us ahead of time so we could
say, 'He was right'?
None of you told us anything;
none of you told us before it happened;
no one heard you tell about it.
27 I, the LORD, was the first one to tell
Jerusalem that the people were
coming home.
I sent a messenger to Jerusalem with the
good news.
28 I look at the idols, but there is not one
that can answer.
None of them can give advice;
none of them can answer my questions.
29 Look, all these idols are false.
They cannot do anything;
they are worth nothing.

THE LORD'S SPECIAL SERVANT

42

1 "Here is my servant, the one I support.
He is the one I chose, and I am pleased
with him.
I have put my Spirit upon him,
and he will bring justice to all nations.
2 He will not cry out or yell
or speak loudly in the streets.
3 He will not break a crushed blade of grass
or put out even a weak flame.
He will truly bring justice;
4 he will not lose hope or give up
until he brings justice to the world.
And people far away will trust his
teachings."

5 God, the LORD, said these things.
He created the skies and stretched them
out.
He spread out the earth and everything
on it.
He gives life to all people on earth,
to everyone who walks on the earth.
6 The LORD says, "I, the LORD, called you to
do right,
and I will hold your hand
and protect you.
You will be the sign of my agreement
with the people,
a light to shine for all people.
7 You will help the blind to see.
You will free those who are in prison,
and you will lead those who live in
darkness out of their prison.

8 "I am the LORD. That is my name.
I will not give my glory to another;
I will not let idols take the praise that
should be mine.
9 The things I said would happen have
happened,
and now I tell you about new things.
Before those things happen,
I tell you about them."

A SONG OF PRAISE TO THE LORD

10 Sing a new song to the LORD;
sing his praise everywhere on the
earth.
Praise him, you people who sail on the
seas and you animals who live in
them.

41:25 someone . . . north This probably means Cyrus, a king of Persia.

Praise him, you people living in faraway places.
11 The deserts and their cities should praise him.
The settlements of Kedar should praise him.
The people living in Sela should sing for joy;
they should shout from the mountaintops.
12 They should give glory to the LORD.
People in faraway lands should praise him.
13 The LORD will march out like a strong soldier;
he will be excited like a man ready to fight a war.
He will shout out the battle cry
and defeat his enemies.

"Sing a new song to the LORD; sing his praise everywhere on the earth." (Isaiah 42:10a)

14 The LORD says, "For a long time I have said nothing;
I have been quiet and held myself back.
But now I will cry out
and strain like a woman giving birth to a child.
15 I will destroy the hills and mountains
and dry up all their plants.
I will make the rivers become dry land
and dry up the pools of water.
16 Then I will lead the blind along a way they never knew;
I will guide them along paths they have not known.
I will make the darkness become light for them,
and the rough ground smooth.
These are the things I will do;
I will not leave my people.
17 But those who trust in idols,
who say to their statues,
'You are our gods'
will be rejected in disgrace.

ISRAEL REFUSED TO LISTEN TO THE LORD

18 "You who are deaf, hear me.
You who are blind, look and see.
19 No one is more blind than my servant Israel
or more deaf than the messenger I send.
No one is more blind than the person I own
or more blind than the servant of the LORD.
20 Israel, you have seen much, but you have not obeyed.
You hear, but you refuse to listen."
21 The LORD made his teachings wonderful,
because he is good.
22 These people have been defeated and robbed.
They are trapped in pits
or locked up in prison.
Like robbers, enemies have taken them away,
and there is no one to save them.
Enemies carried them off,
and no one said, "Bring them back."

23 Will any of you listen to this?
Will you listen carefully in the future?
24 Who let the people of Jacob be carried off?
Who let robbers take Israel away?
The LORD allowed this to happen,
because we sinned against him.
We did not live the way he wanted us to live
and did not obey his teaching.
25 So he became very angry with us
and brought terrible wars against us.
It was as if the people of Israel had fire all around them,
but they didn't know what was happening.
It was as if they were burning,
but they didn't pay any attention.

GOD IS ALWAYS WITH HIS PEOPLE

43
1 Now this is what the LORD says.
He created you, people of Jacob;
he formed you, people of Israel.
He says, "Don't be afraid, because I have saved you.
I have called you by name, and you are mine.
2 When you pass through the waters, I will be with you.
When you cross rivers, you will not drown.
When you walk through fire, you will not be burned,
nor will the flames hurt you.
3 This is because I, the LORD, am your God,
the Holy One of Israel, your Savior.
I gave Egypt to pay for you,

and I gave Cush and Seba to make you
mine.
4 Because you are precious to me,
because I give you honor and love you,
I will give other people in your place;
I will give other nations to save your
life.
5 Don't be afraid, because I am with you.
I will bring your children from the east
and gather you from the west.
6 I will tell the north: Give my people to me.
I will tell the south: Don't keep my
people in prison.
Bring my sons from far away
and my daughters from faraway places.
7 Bring to me all the people who are mine,
whom I made for my glory,
whom I formed and made."

JUDAH IS GOD'S WITNESS

8 Bring out the people who have eyes but
don't see
and those who have ears but don't hear.
9 All the nations gather together,
and all the people come together.
Which of their gods said this would
happen?
Which of their gods can tell what
happened in the beginning?
Let them bring their witnesses to prove
they were right.
Then others will say, "It is true."
10 The LORD says, "You are my witnesses
and the servant I chose.
I chose you so you would know and
believe me,
so you would understand that I am the
true God.
There was no God before me,
and there will be no God after me.
11 I myself am the LORD;
I am the only Savior.
12 I myself have spoken to you, saved you,
and told you these things.
It was not some foreign god among you.
You are my witnesses, and I am God,"
says the LORD.
13 "I have always been God.
No one can save people from my power;
when I do something, no one can
change it."

14 This is what the LORD, who saves you,
the Holy One of Israel, says:
"I will send armies to Babylon for you,
and I will knock down all its locked
gates.

On the Edge

The LORD says, "Forget what happened before, and do not think about the past. Look at the new thing I am going to do. It is already happening. Don't you see it? I will make a road in the desert and rivers in the dry land" (Is. 43:18–19).

One of the few things that you can count on in this lifetime is change. Just when you have everything kind of figured out, boom—it's time to go in a different direction. So many things happen that throw us off balance—new schools every few years, best friends move away, divorce, new teachers with new expectations, Dad gets transferred and the whole family has to move, new stepparents with stepsiblings, the death of someone you love. Life is continually changing.

Isaiah says not to look back and long for what used to be, that God is creating something new—new roads in the desert and new rivers in the dry land. You may be a creature of habit, and change may make you uncomfortable. But one measure of your success will be how easily you adapt to change—to the new things God is doing in your life. You will miss all the blessing he has for you in this day if you continue to long for the past. Set your eyes toward the future and welcome the new paths that God is making for you.

SEE FOR YOURSELF:
Is. 42:16; Jer. 29:11; 2 Cor. 5:17

The Babylonians will shout their cries of
sorrow.
15 I am the LORD, your Holy One,
the Creator of Israel, your King."

GOD WILL SAVE HIS PEOPLE AGAIN

16 This is what the LORD says.
He is the one who made a road through
the sea
and a path through rough waters.
17 He is the one who defeated the chariots
and horses
and the mighty armies.
They fell together and will never rise again.
They were destroyed as a flame is put
out.

WHAT'S IT MEAN?

The king of Egypt, after letting the Israelites leave his country, changed his mind and sent his army to bring them back. His plan was to trap the Israelites at the Red Sea. Just when things looked hopeless for the Israelites, God parted the waters of the sea to make a path of dry land through the middle of it. The Israelites were able to walk across to the other side. When the Egyptians tried to follow, the water collapsed on top of them, and they drowned.

Isaiah 43:16–17

18 The LORD says, "Forget what happened
before,
and do not think about the past.
19 Look at the new thing I am going to do.
It is already happening. Don't you see it?
I will make a road in the desert
and rivers in the dry land.
20 Even the wild animals will be thankful to
me—
the wild dogs and owls.
They will honor me when I put water in
the desert
and rivers in the dry land
to give water to my people, the ones I
chose.
21 The people I made
will sing songs to praise me.

22 "People of Jacob, you have not called to
me;
people of Israel, you have become tired
of me.
23 You have not brought me your sacrifices
of sheep
nor honored me with your sacrifices.
I did not weigh you down with sacrifices
to offer
or make you tired with incense to burn.
24 So you did not buy incense for me;
you did not freely bring me fat from
your sacrifices.
Instead you have weighed me down with
your many sins;
you have made me tired of your many
wrongs.

25 "I, I am the One who forgives all your sins,
for my sake;
I will not remember your sins.
26 But you should remind me.
Let's meet and decide what is right.
Tell what you have done and show you
are right.
27 Your first father sinned,
and your leaders have turned against
me.

Promise HE PROMISES TO FORGET YOUR PAST SINS.

I, I am the One who forgives all your sins, for my sake; I will not remember your sins (Is. 43:25).

What kind of past do you have? Decent? Wild? Funny? Tragic? Wonderful? Boring? Whatever the case, everybody has a past. No one just sprouts up on earth at forty years old. Everyone you know either has grown up or will grow up.

Sometimes people have a hard time with the Lord because of things they've done or said or thought (or things they haven't) in the past. Guess what? It doesn't matter.

When you confess your sins to God and ask him to forgive you, he does. Forever. He doesn't hide them in a book under his mattress. He totally forgets what you've done. When you pray to him, he thinks of you as totally innocent. It's as if you never did anything wrong. Never be afraid to go to the Lord because of your past. He's in the business of making bad things turn out good, ugly things turn out beautiful, and of making hurts heal. Start fresh with him.

SEE FOR YOURSELF:

Is. 54:4; 65:17; 2 Cor. 5:17; Heb. 10:17; 1 John 1:9; Rev. 21:5

28 So I will make your holy rulers unholy.
I will bring destruction on the people of Jacob,
and I will let Israel be insulted."

THE LORD IS THE ONLY GOD

44

1 The LORD says, "People of Jacob, you are my servants. Listen to me!
People of Israel, I chose you."
2 This is what the LORD says, who made you,
who formed you in your mother's body,
who will help you:
"People of Jacob, my servants, don't be afraid.
Israel, I chose you.

On the Edge

The LORD says, "People of Jacob, you are my servants. Listen to me! People of Israel, I chose you." This is what the LORD says, who made you, who formed you in your mother's body, who will help you: "People of Jacob, my servants, don't be afraid. Israel, I chose you" (Is. 44:1–2).

Does your teacher have a favorite student—someone she has chosen to be teacher's pet? Does your coach have an athlete who's obviously his choice for MVP? Do you see favoritism in choices made in your church or in your family? Sometimes, the same person will be the favorite everywhere they go. If you're the favored person, you can get to feeling pretty special. If you're not, it can be the pits.

God says *you* are his favorite—his chosen one. There's nobody else on earth he loves more than he loves you. When he sees you coming to pray or to worship him, he's so glad you want to be with him. He wants to be with you, too. You aren't just his favorite when you're down or left out and nobody else will give you a second glance. You're his favorite even when your ego doesn't need that kind of boost. No matter where you go or what you go through, you're always God's chosen one.

SEE FOR YOURSELF:
Job 34:19; Jer. 9:24; John 3:16; Acts 10:34

3 I will pour out water for the thirsty land
and make streams flow on dry land.
I will pour out my Spirit into your children
and my blessing on your descendants.
4 Your children will grow like a tree in the grass,
like poplar trees growing beside streams of water.
5 One person will say, 'I belong to the LORD,'
and another will use the name Jacob.
Another will sign his name 'I am the LORD's,'
and another will use the name Israel."

6 The LORD, the king of Israel,
is the LORD All-Powerful, who saves Israel.
This is what he says: "I am the beginning and the end.
I am the only God.
7 Who is a god like me?
That god should come and prove it.
Let him tell and explain all that has happened since I set up my ancient people.
He should also tell what will happen in the future.
8 Don't be afraid! Don't worry!
I have always told you what will happen.
You are my witnesses.
There is no other God but me.
I know of no other Rock; I am the only One."

IDOLS ARE USELESS

9 Some people make idols, but they are worth nothing.
People treasure them, but they are useless.
Those people are witnesses for the statues,
but those people cannot see.
They know nothing, so they will be ashamed.
10 Who made these gods?
Who made these useless idols?
11 The workmen who made them will be ashamed,
because they are only human.
If they all would come together,
they would all be ashamed and afraid.

12 One workman uses tools to heat iron,
and he works over hot coals.
With his hammer he beats the metal and makes a statue,

using his powerful arms.
But when he becomes hungry, he loses his power.
If he does not drink water, he becomes tired.

13 Another workman uses a line and a compass
to draw on the wood.
Then he uses his chisels to cut a statue
and his calipers to measure the statue.
In this way, the workman makes the wood look exactly like a person,
and this statue of a person sits in the house.
14 He cuts down cedars
or cypress or oak trees.
Those trees grew by their own power in the forest.
Or he plants a pine tree, and the rain makes it grow.
15 Then he burns the tree.
He uses some of the wood for a fire to keep himself warm.
He also starts a fire to bake his bread.
But he uses part of the wood to make a god, and then he worships it!
He makes the idol and bows down to it!
16 The man burns half of the wood in the fire.
He uses the fire to cook his meat,
and he eats the meat until he is full.
He also burns the wood to keep himself warm. He says,
"Good! Now I am warm. I can see because of the fire's light."
17 But he makes a statue from the wood that is left and calls it his god.
He bows down to it and worships it.
He prays to it and says,
"You are my god. Save me!"
18 Those people don't know what they are doing. They don't understand!
It is as if their eyes are covered so they can't see.
Their minds don't understand.
19 They have not thought about these things;
they don't understand.
They have never thought to themselves,
"I burned half of the wood in the fire
and used the hot coals to bake my bread.
I cooked and ate my meat.
And I used the wood that was left to make this hateful thing.
I am worshiping a block of wood!"
20 He doesn't know what he is doing;
his confused mind leads him the wrong way.
He cannot save himself
or say, "This statue I am holding is a false god."

THE LORD IS THE TRUE GOD

21 "People of Jacob, remember these things!
People of Israel, remember you are my servants.
I made you, and you are my servants.
So Israel, I will not forget you.
22 I have swept away your sins like a big cloud;
I have removed your sins like a cloud that disappears into the air.
Come back to me because I saved you."

23 Skies, sing for joy because the LORD did great things!
Earth, shout for joy, even in your deepest parts!
Sing, you mountains, with thanks to God.
Sing, too, you trees in the forest!
The LORD saved the people of Jacob!
He showed his glory when he saved Israel.
24 This is what the LORD says, who saved you,
who formed you in your mother's body:
"I, the LORD, made everything,
stretching out the skies by myself
and spreading out the earth all alone.
25 I show that the lying prophets' signs are false;
I make fools of those who do magic.
I confuse even wise men;
they think they know much, but I make them look foolish.
26 I make the messages of my servants come true;
I make the advice of my messengers come true.
I say to Jerusalem,
'People will live in you again!'
I say to the towns of Judah,
'You will be built again!'
I say to Jerusalem's ruins,
'I will repair you.'
27 I tell the deep waters, 'Become dry!
I will make your streams become dry!'
28 I say of Cyrus,[n] 'He is my shepherd

44:28 Cyrus A king of Persia who ruled from about 550–530 B.C.

and will do all that I want him to do.
He will say to Jerusalem, "You will be built again!"
He will tell the Temple, "Your foundations will be rebuilt." ' "

WHAT'S IT MEAN?

Cyrus was a sneaky monarch. Before his Persian forces attacked Babylon, Cyrus and his men built dams and redirected the water that flowed into the city. While the Babylonian king, Belshazzar, was throwing a wild party, Cyrus led his men through the empty water tunnels. Caught by surprise, the Babylonian forces surrendered immediately and Belshazzar was put to death.

Isaiah 45:1

GOD CHOOSES CYRUS TO FREE ISRAEL

45 [1]This is what the LORD says to Cyrus, his appointed king:
"I hold your right hand
and will help you defeat nations
and take away other kings' power.
I will open doors for you
so city gates will not stop you.
[2]I will go before you
and make the mountains flat.
I will break down the bronze gates of the cities
and cut through their iron bars.
[3]I will give you the wealth that is stored away
and the hidden riches
so you will know I am the LORD,
the God of Israel, who calls you by name.
[4]I do these things for my servants, the people of Jacob,
and for my chosen people, the Israelites.
Cyrus, I call you by name,
and I give you a title of honor even though you don't know me.
[5]I am the LORD. There is no other God;
I am the only God.
I will make you strong,
even though you don't know me,
[6]so that everyone will know
there is no other God.
From the east to the west they will know
I alone am the LORD.
[7]I made the light and the darkness.
I bring peace, and I cause troubles.
I, the LORD, do all these things.

[8]"Sky above, make victory fall like rain;
clouds, pour down victory.
Let the earth receive it,
and let salvation grow,
and let victory grow with it.
I, the LORD, have created it.

[9]"How terrible it will be for those who argue with the God who made them.
They are like a piece of broken pottery among many pieces.
The clay does not ask the potter,
'What are you doing?'
The thing that is made doesn't say to its maker,
'You have no hands.'
[10]How terrible it will be for the child who says to his father,
'Why are you giving me life?'
How terrible it will be for the child who says to his mother,
'Why are you giving birth to me?' "

[11]This is what the LORD,
the Holy One of Israel, and its Maker, says:
"You ask me about what will happen.
You question me about my children.
You give me orders about what I have made.

"I am the LORD. There is no other God; I am the only God." (Isaiah 45:5a)

[12]I made the earth
and all the people living on it.
With my own hands I stretched out the skies,
and I commanded all the armies in the sky.
[13]I will bring Cyrus to do good things,
and I will make his work easy.
He will rebuild my city
and set my people free
without any payment or reward.
The LORD All-Powerful says this."

[14]The LORD says,
"The goods made in Egypt and Cush

and the tall people of Seba
will come to you
and will become yours.
The Sabeans will walk behind you,
coming along in chains.
They will bow down before you
and pray to you, saying,
'God is with you,
and there is no other God.' "

15 God and Savior of Israel,
you are a God that people cannot see.
16 All the people who make idols will be put
to great shame;
they will go off together in disgrace.
17 But Israel will be saved by the LORD,
and that salvation will continue forever.
Never again will Israel be put to shame.

18 The LORD created the heavens.
He is the God who formed the earth
and made it.
He did not want it to be empty,
but he wanted life on the earth.
This is what the LORD says:
"I am the LORD. There is no other God.
19 I did not speak in secret
or hide my words in some dark place.
I did not tell the family of Jacob
to look for me in empty places.
I am the LORD, and I speak the truth;
I say what is right.

20 "You people who have escaped from other
nations,
gather together and come before me;
come near together.
People who carry idols of wood don't
know what they are doing.
They pray to a god who cannot save
them.
21 Tell these people to come to me.
Let them talk about these things
together.
Who told you long ago that this would
happen?
Who told about it long ago?
I, the LORD, said these things.
There is no other God besides me.
I am the only good God. I am the Savior.
There is no other God.

22 "All people everywhere,
follow me and be saved.
I am God. There is no other God.
23 I will make a promise by my own
power,
and my promise is true;
what I say will not be changed.
I promise that everyone will bow before
me
and will promise to follow me.
24 People will say about me, 'Goodness and
power
come only from the LORD.' "
Everyone who has been angry with him
will come to him and be ashamed.
25 But with the LORD's help, the people of
Israel
will be found to be good,
and they will praise him.

FALSE GODS ARE USELESS

46

1 Bel and Nebo bow down.
Their idols are carried by animals.
The statues are only heavy loads that must
be carried;
they only make people tired.
2 These gods will all bow down.
They cannot save themselves
but will all be carried away like
prisoners.

WHAT'S IT MEAN?

Bel (who was also known as Marduk) and Nebo were two of the Babylonians' favorite gods. Bel, the god of war, was the main deity of Babylon. Nebo, the god of education and wisdom, was thought to be Bel's son. Remember King Nebuchadnezzar, the guy who destroyed Jerusalem and took the Israelites captive? It's no coincidence that the first part of his name sounds an awful lot like the name of Nebo.

Isaiah 46:1

3 "Family of Jacob, listen to me!
All you people from Israel who are still
alive, listen!
I have carried you since you were born;
I have taken care of you from your
birth.
4 Even when you are old, I will be the
same.
Even when your hair has turned gray, I
will take care of you.
I made you and will take care of you.
I will carry you and save you.

5 "Can you compare me to anyone?
No one is equal to me or like me.
6 Some people are rich with gold
and weigh their silver on the scales.
They hire a goldsmith, and he makes it
into a god.
Then they bow down and worship it.
7 They put it on their shoulders and carry it.
They set it in its place, and there it
stands;
it cannot move from its place.
People may yell at it, but it cannot answer.
It cannot save them from their troubles.

8 "Remember this, and do not forget it!
Think about these things, you who turn
against God.
9 Remember what happened long ago.
Remember that I am God, and there is
no other God.
I am God, and there is no one like me.
10 From the beginning I told you what
would happen in the end.
A long time ago I told you things that
have not yet happened.
When I plan something, it happens.
What I want to do, I will do.
11 I am calling a man from the east to carry
out my plan;
he will come like a hawk from a country
far away.
I will make what I have said come true;
I will do what I have planned.
12 Listen to me, you stubborn people,
who are far from what is right.
13 I will soon do the things that are right.
I will bring salvation soon.
I will save Jerusalem
and bring glory to Israel."

GOD WILL DESTROY BABYLON

47

1 The LORD says, "City of Babylon,
go down and sit in the dirt.
People of Babylon, sit on the ground.
You are no longer the ruler.
You will no longer be called
tender or beautiful.
2 You must use large stones to grind grain
into flour.
Remove your veil and your nice skirts.
Uncover your legs and cross the rivers.
3 People will see your nakedness;
they will see your shame.
I will punish you;
I will punish every one of you."

4 Our Savior is named the LORD All-
Powerful;
he is the Holy One of Israel.

5 "Babylon, sit in darkness and say nothing.
You will no longer be called the queen
of kingdoms.
6 I was angry with my people,

Promise

HE PROMISES TO BE THERE WHEN YOU'RE OLD.

Even when you are old, I will be the same. Even when your hair has turned gray, I will take care of you. I made you and will take care of you. I will carry you and save you (Is. 46:4).

It can be a little scary to think about getting old. To you, getting old may mean losing some of the things that are very important to you right now: your good looks, your sharp mind, your athletic ability. You may picture yourself struggling to survive on a monthly Social Security check or wandering through the halls of a nursing home.

It's true that, as you get older, your body, your income, and even your address will probably go through a lot of changes. Some of these changes will be your idea; some won't.

So where's your security? Is it in these things that change from year to year? Or is it in the person who is "the same yesterday, today, and forever" (Heb. 13:8)? Jesus says that he will take care of you and keep you safe when you're old. He will be just as strong, just as trustworthy, just as loving then as he is now. And when you've been his friend for sixty years, you'll still be discovering how awesome he is.

SEE FOR YOURSELF:
Rom. 8:38–39; Heb. 1:12; 13:8; 1 Pet. 1:5

On the Edge

You are tired of the advice you have received. So let those who study the sky—those who tell the future by looking at the stars and the new moons—let them save you from what is about to happen to you. But they are like straw; fire will quickly burn them up. They cannot save themselves from the power of the fire. They are not like coals that give warmth nor like a fire that you may sit beside (Is. 47:13–14).

"You will be lucky in love toward the end of the month." "Be careful when you choose new friends." "What's your sign?" Sound familiar? You can find phrases like these in almost every popular fashion magazine and daily newspaper. There are people who trust astrology so much that they actually make decisions based on their horoscopes. Whoa. If you're a Christian, you can use the astrology pages to line your garbage can. You've got something so much greater—and someone you can totally depend on—the Holy Spirit. His job is to guide you, to help you make good decisions, and to give you insight about your future (see John 16:13).

Isaiah 47:14 says that people who consult the stars are helpless. John 14:16–17 says that God sent his Spirit to help you. Always put your trust in God, who knows everything. Never put your trust in a psychic or an astrologer. God says, "They cannot save themselves from the power of the fire." In other words, they can't save themselves, so they certainly can't save you. Only he can.

SEE FOR YOURSELF:
2 Kin. 21:6; Jer. 33:3

so I rejected those who belonged to me.
I gave them to you,
but you showed them no mercy.
You even made the old people
work very hard.
7 You said, 'I will live forever
as the queen.'
But you did not think about these things
or consider what would happen.

8 "Now, listen, you lover of pleasure.
You think you are safe.
You tell yourself,
'I am the only important person.
I will never be a widow
or lose my children.'
9 Two things will happen to you suddenly,
in a single day.
You will lose your children and your
husband.
These things will truly happen to you,
in spite of all your magic,
in spite of your powerful tricks.
10 You do evil things, but you feel safe
and say, 'No one sees what I do.'
Your wisdom and knowledge
have fooled you.
You say to yourself,
'I am God, and no one is equal to me.'
11 But troubles will come to you,
and you will not know how to stop
them.
Disaster will fall on you,
and you will not be able to keep it away.
You will be destroyed quickly;
you will not even see it coming.

12 "Keep on using your tricks
and doing all your magic
that you have used since you were
young.
Maybe they will help you;
maybe you will be able to scare
someone.
13 You are tired of the advice you have
received.
So let those who study the sky—
those who tell the future by looking at the
stars and the new moons—
let them save you from what is about to
happen to you.
14 But they are like straw;
fire will quickly burn them up.
They cannot save themselves
from the power of the fire.
They are not like coals that give warmth
nor like a fire that you may sit beside.
15 You have worked with these people,
and they have been with you since you
were young,
but they will not be able to help you.
Everyone will go his own way,
and there will be no one left to save
you."

GOD CONTROLS THE FUTURE

48
1 The LORD says, "Family of Jacob, listen to
me.
You are called Israel,

and you come from the family of Judah.
You swear by the LORD's name
and praise the God of Israel,
but you are not honest or sincere.
2 You call yourselves people of the holy city,
and you depend on the God of Israel,
who is named the LORD All-Powerful.
3 Long ago I told you what would happen.
I said these things and made them known;
suddenly I acted, and these things happened.
4 I knew you were stubborn;
your neck was like an iron muscle,
and your head was like bronze.
5 So a long time ago I told you about these things;
I told you about them before they happened
so you couldn't say, 'My idols did this,
and my wooden and metal statues made these things happen.'

6 "You heard and saw everything that happened,
so you should tell this news to others.
Now I will tell you about new things,
hidden things that you don't know yet.
7 These things are happening now, not long ago;
you have not heard about them before today.
So you cannot say, 'We already knew about that.'
8 But you have not heard me; you have not understood.
Even long ago you did not listen to me.
I knew you would surely turn against me;
you have fought against me since you were born.
9 But for my own sake I will be patient.
People will praise me for not becoming angry
and destroying you.
10 I have made you pure, but not by fire, as silver is made pure.
I have purified you by giving you troubles.
11 I do this for myself, for my own sake.
I will not let people speak evil against me,
and I will not let some god take my glory.

ISRAEL WILL BE FREE

12 "People of Jacob, listen to me.
People of Israel, I have called you to be my people.
I am God;
I am the beginning and the end.
13 I made the earth with my own hands.
With my right hand I spread out the skies.
When I call them,
they come together before me."

14 All of you, come together and listen.
None of the gods said these things would happen.
The LORD has chosen someone
to attack the Babylonians;
he will carry out his wishes against Babylon.

15 "I have spoken; I have called him.[n]
I have brought him, and I will make him successful.
16 Come to me and listen to this.
From the beginning I have spoken openly.
From the time it began, I was there."

Now, the Lord GOD
has sent me with his Spirit.

17 This is what the LORD, who saves you,
the Holy One of Israel, says:
"I am the LORD your God,
who teaches you to do what is good,
who leads you in the way you should go.
18 If you had obeyed me,
you would have had peace like a full-flowing river.
Good things would have flowed to you
like the waves of the sea.
19 You would have had many children,
as many as the grains of sand.
They would never have died out
nor been destroyed."

20 My people, leave Babylon!
Run from the Babylonians!
Tell this news with shouts of joy to the people;
spread it everywhere on earth.
Say, "The LORD has saved his servants, the people of Jacob."
21 They did not become thirsty when he led them through the deserts.

48:15 him This probably refers to Cyrus king of Persia.

He made water flow from a rock for
them.
He split the rock,
and water flowed out.

22 "There is no peace for evil people," says the
LORD.

WHAT'S IT MEAN?

God took care of the thirsty
Israelites in the desert by giving them
water to drink from an ordinary rock. The Israelites remembered that
period—just after their ancestors' escape from Egypt—as a time
when God was especially close to them.

Isaiah 48:21

On the Edge

All of you people in faraway places, listen to me. Listen, all you nations far away. Before I was born, the LORD called me to serve him. The LORD named me while I was still in my mother's body. He made my tongue like a sharp sword. He hid me in the shadow of his hand. He made me like a sharp arrow. He hid me in the holder for his arrows (Is. 49:1–2).

Remember when you were in kindergarten and you made plaster imprints of your hands or a sculpture out of pipe cleaners? Remember how excited you were? When you made something you were proud of, you couldn't wait to show it off. You were so careful until you got it home and put it in a safe place. And every once in a while you'd take a look at it and grin. You loved it.

God made you and that's why he loves you. You were his idea. You have his eyes, his hands, because you are made in his likeness. Even though you may not always act like your Father, the truth is that you are his child and his love for you will never end. Just as you carefully created your kindergarten masterpiece, God crafted each part of your being just exactly the way he wanted it. He made you a certain way so that you could be everything wonderful that he wants you to be. You're a part of his heart because he thought of you and then gave those thoughts life and created you. He's in love with you. He thinks you're awesome. And you are, because you're his.

SEE FOR YOURSELF:
Gen. 1:27; Is. 43:7; 44:2; 1 John 3:1

GOD CALLS HIS SPECIAL SERVANT

49

1 All of you people in faraway
places, listen to me.
Listen, all you nations
far away.
Before I was born, the
LORD called me to
serve him.
The LORD named me
while I was still in my mother's body.

ABORTION
Does God know the unborn by name? (49:1)

2 He made my tongue like a sharp sword.
He hid me in the shadow of his hand.
He made me like a sharp arrow.
He hid me in the holder for his arrows.
3 He told me, "Israel, you are my servant.
I will show my glory through you."
4 But I said, "I have worked hard for
nothing;
I have used all my power, but I did
nothing useful.
But the LORD will decide what my work is
worth;
God will decide my reward."
5 The LORD made me in the body of my
mother
to be his servant,
to lead the people of Jacob back to him
so that Israel might be gathered to him.
The LORD will honor me,
and I will get my strength from my God.
6 Now he told me,
"You are an important servant to me
to bring back the tribes of Jacob,
to bring back the people of Israel who
are left alive.
But, more importantly, I will make you a
light for all nations
to show people all over the world the
way to be saved."

7 The LORD who saves you
is the Holy One of Israel.

He speaks to the one who is hated by the
people,
to the servant of rulers.
This is what he says: "Kings will see you
and stand to honor you;
great leaders will bow down before you,
because the LORD can be trusted.
He is the Holy One of Israel, who has
chosen you."

THE DAY OF SALVATION

8 This is what the LORD says:
"At the right time I will hear your prayers.
On the day of salvation I will help you.
I will protect you,
and you will be the sign of my
agreement with the people.
You will bring back the people to the land
and give the land that is now ruined
back to its owners.
9 You will tell the prisoners, 'Come out of
your prison.'
You will tell those in darkness, 'Come
into the light.'
The people will eat beside the roads,
and they will find food even on bare
hills.
10 They will not be hungry or thirsty.
Neither the hot sun nor the desert wind
will hurt them.
The God who comforts them will lead
them
and guide them by springs of water.
11 I will make my mountains into roads,
and the roads will be raised up.
12 Look, people are coming to me from far
away,
from the north and from
the west,
from Aswan in
southern Egypt."

13 Heavens and earth, be
happy.
Mountains, shout with
joy,
because the LORD comforts
his people
and will have pity on those who
suffer.

"The LORD comforts
his people and will
have pity on those
who suffer."
(Isaiah 49:13b)

JERUSALEM AND HER CHILDREN

14 But Jerusalem said, "The LORD has left me;
the Lord has forgotten me."

15 The LORD answers, "Can a woman forget
the baby she nurses?
Can she feel no kindness for the child to
which she gave birth?
Even if she could forget her children,
I will not forget you.
16 See, I have written your name on my
hand.
Jerusalem, I always think about your
walls.
17 Your children will soon return to you,
and the people who defeated you and
destroyed you will leave.
18 Look up and look around you.
All your children are gathering to return
to you."
The LORD says, "As surely as I live,
your children will be like jewels
that a bride wears proudly.

19 "You were destroyed and defeated,
and your land was made useless.
But now you will have more people than
the land can hold,
and those people who destroyed you
will be far away.
20 Children were born to you while you were
sad,
but they will say to you,
'This place is too small for us.
Give us a bigger place to live.'
21 Then you will say to yourself,
'Who gave me all these children?
I was sad and lonely,
defeated and separated from my people.
So who reared these children?
I was left all alone.
Where did all these
children come
from?' "

22 This is what the Lord GOD
says:
"See, I will lift my hand to
signal the nations;
I will raise my banner
for all the people to
see.
Then they will bring your
sons back to you in
their arms,
and they will carry your daughters on
their shoulders.
23 Kings will teach your children,
and daughters of kings will take care of
them.
They will bow down before you
and kiss the dirt at your feet.
Then you will know I am the LORD.

Anyone who trusts in me will not be
disappointed."

24 Can the wealth a soldier wins in war be
taken away from him?
Can a prisoner be freed from a powerful
soldier?
25 This is what the LORD says:
"The prisoners will be taken from the
strong soldiers.
What the soldiers have taken will be
saved.
I will fight your enemies,
and I will save your children.
26 I will force those who trouble you to eat
their own flesh.
Their own blood will be the wine that
makes them drunk.
Then everyone will know
I, the LORD, am the One who saves you;
I am the Powerful One of Jacob who
saves you."

ISRAEL WAS PUNISHED FOR ITS SIN

50
1 This is what the LORD says:
"People of Israel, you say I divorced your
mother.
Then where is the paper that proves it?
Or do you think I sold you
to pay a debt?
Because of the evil things you did, I sold
you.
Because of the times she turned against
me, your mother was sent away.
2 I came home and found no one there;
I called, but no one answered.
Do you think I am not able to save you?
Do I not have the power to save you?
Look, I need only to shout and the sea
becomes dry.
I change rivers into a desert,
and their fish rot because there is no
water;
they die of thirst.
3 I can make the skies dark;
I can make them black like clothes of
sadness."

GOD'S SERVANT OBEYS

4 The Lord GOD gave me the ability to teach
so that I know what to say to make the
weak strong.
Every morning he wakes me.
He teaches me to listen like a student.
5 The Lord GOD helps me learn,
and I have not turned against him
nor stopped following him.
6 I offered my back to those who beat me.
I offered my cheeks to those who pulled
my beard.
I won't hide my face from them
when they make fun of me and spit at
me.
7 The Lord GOD helps me,
so I will not be ashamed.
I will be determined,
and I know I will not be disgraced.
8 He shows that I am innocent, and he is
close to me.
So who can accuse me?
If there is someone, let us go to court
together.
If someone wants to prove I have done
wrong,
he should come and tell me.
9 Look! It is the Lord GOD who helps me.
So who can prove me guilty?
Look! All those who try will become
useless like old clothes;
moths will eat them.

10 Who among you fears the LORD
and obeys his servant?
That person may walk in the dark
and have no light.
Then let him trust in the LORD
and depend on his God.
11 But instead, some of you want to light
your own fires
and make your own light.
So, go, walk in the light of your fires,
and trust your own light to guide you.
But this is what you will receive from me:
You will lie down in a place of pain.

WHAT'S IT MEAN?

People in ancient times wore rough cloth in times of great sorrow or distress. If you've ever felt this cloth, you know why they didn't wear it more often. The cloth was a dark, scratchy material made of goat's hair. The modern tradition of wearing dark clothing to funerals and memorial services is based on the ancient custom of wearing this rough cloth in times of sorrow.

Isaiah 50:3

JERUSALEM WILL BE SAVED

51

1The LORD says, "Listen to me,
those of you who try to live right and follow the LORD.
Look at the rock from which you were cut;
look at the stone quarry from which you were dug.
2Look at Abraham, your ancestor,
and Sarah, who gave birth to your ancestors.
Abraham had no children when I called him,
but I blessed him and gave him many descendants.
3So the LORD will comfort Jerusalem;
he will show mercy to those who live in her ruins.
He will change her deserts into a garden like Eden;
he will make her empty lands like the garden of the LORD.
People there will be very happy;
they will give thanks and sing songs.

4"My people, listen to me;
my nation, pay attention to me.
I will give the people my teachings,
and my decisions will be like a light to all people.
5I will soon show that I do what is right.
I will soon save you.
I will use my power and judge all nations.
All the faraway places are waiting for me;
they wait for my power to help them.
6Look up to the heavens.
Look around you at the earth below.
The skies will disappear like clouds of smoke.
The earth will become useless like old clothes,
and its people will die like flies.
But my salvation will continue forever,
and my goodness will never end.

7"You people who know what is right
should listen to me;
you people who follow my teachings
should hear what I say.
Don't be afraid of the evil things people say,
and don't be upset by their insults.
8Moths will eat those people as if they were clothes,
and worms will eat them as if they were wool.
But my goodness will continue forever,
and my salvation will continue from now on."

9Wake up, wake up, and use your strength,
powerful LORD.
Wake up as you did in the old times,
as you did a long time ago.
With your own power, you cut Rahab into pieces
and killed that sea monster.
10You dried up the sea
and the waters of the deep ocean.
You made the deepest parts of the sea into a road
for your people to cross over and be saved.
11The people the LORD has freed will return
and enter Jerusalem with joy.
Their happiness will last forever.
They will have joy and gladness,
and all sadness and sorrow will be gone far away.

WHAT'S IT MEAN?

According to a popular ancient myth, a dragonlike creature named Rahab tried to prevent God from creating the world. Needless to say, God defeated Rahab and her followers. Later, the name *Rahab* came to symbolize Egypt and the years the Israelites spent there.

Isaiah 51:9

12The LORD says, "I am the one who comforts you.
So why should you be afraid of people, who die?
Why should you fear
people who die like the grass?

DEVOTION
Is it possible to forget about God? (51:12–13)

13Have you forgotten the LORD who made you,
who stretched out the skies
and made the earth?
Why are you always afraid

of those angry people who trouble you
and who want to destroy?
But where are those angry people now?
14 People in prison will soon be set free;
they will not die in prison,
and they will have enough food.
15 I am the LORD your God,
who stirs the sea and makes the waves roar.
My name is the LORD All-Powerful.
16 I will give you the words I want you to say.
I will cover you with my hands and protect you.
I made the heavens and the earth,
and I say to Jerusalem, 'You are my people.' "

WHAT'S IT MEAN?

A cup that came from God's hand was a common symbol in ancient times for a person's (or a nation's) destiny. A cup of his fury symbolized punishment for a sin. A cup of his blessing symbolized a bright future.

Isaiah 51:17

GOD PUNISHED ISRAEL

17 Awake! Awake!
Get up, Jerusalem.
The LORD was very angry with you;
your punishment was like wine in a cup.
The LORD made you drink that wine;
you drank the whole cup until you stumbled.
18 Jerusalem had many people,
but there was not one to lead her.
Of all the people who grew up there,
no one was there to guide her.
19 Troubles came to you two by two,
but no one will feel sorry for you.
There was ruin and disaster, great hunger and fighting.
No one can comfort you.
20 Your people have become weak.
They fall down and lie on every street corner,
like animals caught in a net.
They have felt the full anger of the LORD
and have heard God's angry shout.

21 So listen to me, poor Jerusalem,
you who are drunk but not from wine.
22 Your God will defend his people.
This is what the LORD your God says:
"The punishment I gave you is like a cup of wine.
You drank it and could not walk straight.
But I am taking that cup of my anger away from you,
and you will never be punished by my anger again.
23 I will now give that cup of punishment to those who gave you pain,
who told you,
'Bow down so we can walk over you.'
They made your back like dirt for them to walk on;
you were like a street for them to travel on."

JERUSALEM WILL BE SAVED

52
1 Wake up, wake up, Jerusalem! Become strong!
Be beautiful again,
holy city of Jerusalem.
The people who do not worship God and who are not pure
will not enter you again.
2 Jerusalem, you once were a prisoner.
Now shake off the dust and stand up.
Jerusalem, you once were a prisoner.
Now free yourself from the chains around your neck.
3 This is what the LORD says:
"You were not sold for a price,
so you will be saved without cost."
4 This is what the Lord GOD says:
"First my people went down to Egypt to live.
Later Assyria made them slaves.

5 "Now see what has happened," says the LORD.
"Another nation has taken away my people for nothing.
This nation who rules them makes fun of me," says the LORD.
"All day long they speak against me.
6 This has happened so my people will know who I am,
and so, on that future day, they will know

that I am the one speaking to them.
It will really be me."

7 How beautiful is the person
who comes over themountains to bring good news,
who announces peace
and brings good news,
who announces salvation
and says to Jerusalem,
"Your God is King."
8 Listen! Your guards are shouting.
They are all shouting for joy!
They all will see with their own eyes
when the LORD returns to Jerusalem.
9 Jerusalem, your buildings are destroyed now,
but shout and rejoice together,
because the LORD has comforted his people.
He has saved Jerusalem.
10 The LORD will show his holy power
to all the nations.
Then everyone on earth
will see the salvation of our God.

11 You people, leave, leave; get out of Babylon!
Touch nothing that is unclean.
You men who carry the LORD's things used in worship,
leave there and make yourselves pure.
12 You will not be forced to leave Babylon quickly;
you will not be forced to run away,
because the LORD will go before you,
and the God of Israel will guard you from behind.

THE LORD'S SUFFERING SERVANT

13 The LORD says, "See, my servant will act wisely.
People will greatly honor and respect him.
14 Many people were shocked when they saw him.
His appearance was so changed he did not look like a man;
his form was changed so much they could barely tell he was human.
15 But now he will surprise many nations.
Kings will be amazed and shut their mouths.
They will see things they had not been told about him,
and they will understand things they had not heard."

53

1 Who would have believed what we heard?
Who saw the LORD's power in this?
2 He grew up like a small plant before the LORD,
like a root growing in a dry land.
He had no special beauty or form to make us notice him;
there was nothing in his appearance to make us desire him.
3 He was hated and rejected by people.
He had much pain and suffering.
People would not even look at him.
He was hated, and we didn't even notice him.

4 But he took our suffering on him
and felt our pain for us.
We saw his suffering
and thought God was punishing him.
5 But he was wounded for the wrong we did;
he was crushed for the evil we did.
The punishment, which made us well, was given to him,
and we are healed because of his wounds.
6 We all have wandered away like sheep;
each of us has gone his own way.
But the LORD has put on him the punishment
for all the evil we have done.

SIN
What happens to the sin of Christians? (53:6)

7 He was beaten down and punished,
but he didn't say a word.
He was like a lamb being led to be killed.
He was quiet, as a sheep is quiet while its wool is being cut;
he never opened his mouth.
8 Men took him away roughly and unfairly.
He died without children to continue his family.
He was put to death;
he was punished for the sins of my people.
9 He was buried with wicked men,
and he died with the rich.
He had done nothing wrong,
and he had never lied.

10 But it was the LORD who decided
to crush him and make him suffer.
The LORD made his life a penalty offering,

On the Edge

We all have wandered away like sheep; each of us has gone his own way. But the LORD has put on him the punishment for all the evil we have done (Is. 53:6).

God had a purpose in mind when he made you. His idea was that you would be his friend, love him, and do things his way. Somehow, though, it seemed better to you to do things your way. Eventually you found yourself a long way from God.

A sheep who wanders astray from the shepherd is in big trouble because the shepherd is the one who keeps him safe and makes sure he has all the things he needs. God is your Shepherd; and when you decided to go your way instead of his, you put some distance between you and the Person who has everything you need.

It seemed important to God for you to understand that you have wandered away from him: "*We all* have wandered away like sheep." That could be a downer. But this verse is actually part of a very hopeful passage telling what Jesus is like and what he did for the "sheep" who had walked away from God. "He carried away the sins of many people and asked forgiveness for those who sinned" (53:12). Now you can find your way back to the Shepherd.

SEE FOR YOURSELF:
Ps. 95:7; Is. 53:12; Jer. 50:6; Ezek. 34:12

but he will still see his descendants and
live a long life.
He will complete the things the LORD
wants him to do.
11 "After his soul suffers many things,
he will see life and be satisfied.
My good servant will make many people
right with God;
he will carry away their sins.
12 For this reason I will make him a great
man among people,
and he will share in all things with
those who are strong.
He willingly gave his life
and was treated like a criminal.
But he carried away the sins of many
people
and asked forgiveness for those who
sinned."

PEOPLE WILL RETURN TO JERUSALEM

54

1 The LORD says, "Sing, Jerusalem.
You are like a woman who never gave
birth to children.
Start singing and shout for joy.
You never felt the pain of giving birth,
but you will have more children
than the woman who has a husband.
2 Make your tent bigger;
stretch it out and make it wider.
Do not hold back.
Make the ropes longer
and its stakes stronger,
3 because you will spread out to the right
and to the left.
Your children will take over other
nations,
and they will again live in cities that
once were destroyed.

4 "Don't be afraid, because you will not be
ashamed.
Don't be embarrassed, because you will
not be disgraced.
You will forget the shame you felt
earlier;
you will not remember the shame you
felt when you lost your husband.
5 The God who made you is like your
husband.
His name is the LORD All-Powerful.
The Holy One of Israel is the one who
saves you.
He is called the God of all the earth.
6 You were like a woman whose husband
left her,
and you were very sad.
You were like a wife who married young
and then her husband left her.
But the LORD called you to be his,"
says your God.
7 God says, "I left you for a short time,
but with great kindness I will bring you
back again.
8 I became very angry
and hid from you for a time,
but I will show you mercy with kindness
forever,"
says the LORD who saves you.

9 The LORD says, "This day is like the time of
Noah to me.
I promised then that I would never
flood the world again.

In the same way, I promise I will not be angry with you
or punish you again.
10 The mountains may disappear,
and the hills may come to an end,
but my love will never disappear;
my promise of peace will not come to an end,"
says the LORD who shows mercy to you.

11 "You poor city. Storms have hurt you,
and you have not been comforted.
But I will rebuild you with turquoise stones,
and I will build your foundations with sapphires.
12 I will use rubies to build your walls
and shining jewels for the gates
and precious jewels for all your outer walls.
13 All your children will be taught by the LORD,
and they will have much peace.
14 I will build you using fairness.
You will be safe from those who would hurt you,
so you will have nothing to fear.
Nothing will come to make you afraid.
15 I will not send anyone to attack you,
and you will defeat those who do attack you.

"The Holy One of Israel is the one who saves you. He is called the God of all the earth." (Isaiah 54:5b)

16 "See, I made the blacksmith.
He fans the fire to make it hotter,
and he makes the kind of tool he wants.
In the same way I have made the destroyer to destroy.
17 So no weapon that is used against you will defeat you.
You will show that those who speak against you are wrong.
These are the good things my servants receive.
Their victory comes from me," says the LORD.

GOD GIVES WHAT IS GOOD

55

1 The LORD says, "All you who are thirsty, come and drink.
Those of you who do not have money, come, buy and eat!
Come buy wine and milk
without money and without cost.
2 Why spend your money on something that is not real food?
Why work for something that doesn't really satisfy you?
Listen closely to me, and you will eat what is good;
your soul will enjoy the rich food that satisfies.
3 Come to me and listen;
listen to me so you may live.

Promise HE PROMISES TO LOVE YOU FOREVER.

Come to me and listen; listen to me so you may live. I will make an agreement with you that will last forever. I will give you the blessings I promised to David (Is. 55:3).

Can you imagine having someone be eternally loyal to you, someone who loves you forever? For most of us, even the thought that there is an eternity just blows our mind. We can't imagine being eighty years old—much less living forever and ever and ever. God loves you so much that he promises not only to let you live with him forever, but also to love you and be loyal to you. That's the ultimate friendship!

God has so much confidence in who you are, who he made you to be, that he wants to spend forever with you. Even if every friend you ever had were to desert you, he would still be there loving you. If you did something and hacked off everyone you know, he would be loyal to you. God hasn't committed himself to you for the length of your life, but for the length of *his* life—for all eternity.

SEE FOR YOURSELF:

Jer. 31:3–4; Hos. 14:4; Rom. 8:35–39

I will make an agreement with you that will last forever.
I will give you the blessings I promised to David.
4 I made David a witness of my power for all nations,
a ruler and commander of many nations.
5 You will call for nations that you don't yet know.
And these nations that do not know you will run to you
because of the LORD your God,
because of the Holy One of Israel who honors you."

6 So you should look for the LORD before it is too late;
you should call to him while he is near.
7 The wicked should stop doing wrong,
and they should stop their evil thoughts.
They should return to the LORD so he may have mercy on them.
They should come to our God, because he will freely forgive them.

8 The LORD says, "My thoughts are not like your thoughts.
Your ways are not like my ways.
9 Just as the heavens are higher than the earth,
so are my ways higher than your ways
and my thoughts higher than your thoughts.
10 Rain and snow fall from the sky
and don't return without watering the ground.
They cause the plants to sprout and grow,
making seeds for the farmer
and bread for the people.
11 The same thing is true of the words I speak.
They will not return to me empty.
They make the things happen that I want to happen,
and they succeed in doing what I send them to do.

12 "So you will go out with joy
and be led out in peace.
The mountains and hills will burst into song before you,
and all the trees in the fields will clap their hands.
13 Large cypress trees will grow where thornbushes were.
Myrtle trees will grow where weeds were.
These things will be a reminder of the LORD's promise,
and this reminder will never be destroyed."

ALL NATIONS WILL OBEY THE LORD

56 1 This is what the LORD says:
"Give justice to all people,
and do what is right,
because my salvation will come to you soon.
Soon everyone will know that I do what is right.
2 The person who obeys the law about the Sabbath
will be blessed,
and the person who does no evil
will be blessed."

3 Foreigners who have joined the LORD should not say,
"The LORD will not accept me with his people."
The eunuch should not say,
"Because I cannot have children, the LORD will not accept me."
4 This is what the LORD says:
"The eunuchs should obey the law about the Sabbath
and do what I want
and keep my agreement.
5 If they do, I will make their names remembered
within my Temple and its walls.
It will be better for them than children.

WHAT'S IT MEAN?

The Sabbath is the seventh day of the week—Saturday, not Sunday. God instructed his people to set aside the seventh day of each week for him. All forms of normal work were forbidden on the Sabbath. Only acts of kindness, worship, and emergency were allowed. Keeping one's Saturday schedule free from work was a way of showing submission to God.

Isaiah 56:4

I will give them a name that will last
forever,
that will never be forgotten.
6 Foreigners will join the LORD
to worship him and love him,
to serve him,
to obey the law about the Sabbath,
and to keep my agreement.
7 I will bring these people to my holy
mountain
and give them joy in my house of
prayer.
The offerings and sacrifices
they place on my altar will please me,
because my Temple will be called
a house for prayer for people from all
nations."
8 The Lord GOD says—
he who gathers the Israelites that were
forced to leave their country:
"I will bring together other people
to join those who are already gathered."

ISRAEL'S LEADERS ARE EVIL

9 All you animals of the field,
all you animals of the forest, come to
eat.
10 The leaders who are to guard the people
are blind;
they don't know what they are doing.
All of them are like quiet dogs
that don't know how to bark.
They lie down and dream
and love to sleep.
11 They are like hungry dogs
that are never satisfied.
They are like shepherds
who don't know what they are doing.
They all have gone their own way;
all they want to do is satisfy
themselves.
12 They say, "Come, let's drink some wine;
let's drink all the beer we want.
And tomorrow we will do this again,
or, maybe we will have an even better
time."

ISRAEL DOES NOT FOLLOW GOD

57

1 Those who are right with God may die,
but no one pays attention.
Good people are taken away,
but no one understands.
Those who do right are being taken away
from evil
2 and are given peace.
Those who live as God wants
find rest in death.

3 "Come here, you magicians!
Come here, you sons of prostitutes and
those who take part in adultery!
4 Of whom are you making fun?
Whom are you insulting?
At whom do you stick out your tongue?
You turn against God,
and you are liars.
5 You have sexual relations under every
green tree
to worship your gods.
You kill children in the ravines
and sacrifice them in the rocky places.
6 You take the smooth rocks from the
ravines
as your portion.
You pour drink offerings on them to
worship them,
and you give grain offerings to them.
Do you think this makes me want to
show you mercy?
7 You make your bed on every hill and
mountain,
and there you offer sacrifices.
8 You have hidden your idols
behind your doors and doorposts.
You have left me, and you have uncovered
yourself.
You have pulled back the covers and
climbed into bed.
You have made an agreement with those
whose beds you love,
and you have looked at their
nakedness.
9 You use your oils and perfumes
to look nice for Molech.
You have sent your messengers to faraway
lands;

WHAT'S IT MEAN?

For some reason, the pagans in and around Israel preferred to worship their idols on hilltops or in groves of trees. Many of their so-called worship ceremonies were actually little more than sexual orgies. Some ceremonies called for children to be sacrificed. God despised such pagan rituals and specifically told the Israelites not to get involved in them.

Isaiah 57:5

you even tried to send them to the place
of the dead.
10 You were tired from doing these things,
but you never gave up.
You found new strength,
so you did not quit.

11 "Whom were you so afraid of
that you lied to me?
You have not remembered me
or even thought about me.
I have been quiet for a long time.
Is that why you are not afraid of me?
12 I will tell about your 'goodness' and what
you do,
and those things will do you no good.
13 When you cry out for help,
let the gods you have gathered help you.
The wind will blow them all away;
just a puff of wind will take them away.
But the person who depends on me will
receive the land
and own my holy mountain."

THE LORD WILL SAVE HIS PEOPLE

14 Someone will say, "Build a road! Build a
road! Prepare the way!
Make the way clear for my people."
15 And this is the reason: God lives forever
and is holy.
He is high and lifted up.
He says, "I live in a high and holy place,
but I also live with people who are sad
and humble.
I give new life to those who are humble
and to those whose hearts are broken.
16 I will not accuse forever,
nor will I always be angry,
because then human life would grow
weak.
Human beings, whom I created, would
die.
17 I was angry because they were dishonest
in order to make money.
I punished them and turned away from
them in anger,
but they continued to do evil.
18 I have seen what they have done, but I
will heal them.
I will guide them and comfort them and
those who felt sad for them.
They will all praise me.
19 I will give peace, real peace, to those far
and near,
and I will heal them," says the LORD.
20 But evil people are like the angry sea,
which cannot rest,
whose waves toss up waste and mud.
21 "There is no peace for evil people," says my
God.

HOW TO HONOR GOD

58

1 The LORD says, "Shout out loud. Don't
hold back.
Shout out loud like a trumpet.
Tell my people what they have done
against their God;
tell the family of Jacob about their sins.
2 They still come every day looking for me
and want to learn my ways.
They act just like a nation that does what
is right,
that obeys the commands of its God.
They ask me to judge them fairly.
They want God to be near them.
3 They say, 'To honor you we had special
days when we gave up eating,
but you didn't see.
We humbled ourselves to honor you,
but you didn't notice.' "
But the LORD says, "You do what pleases
yourselves on these special days,
and you are unfair to your workers.
4 On these special days when you do not
eat, you argue and fight
and hit each other with your fists.
You cannot do these things as you do now
and believe your prayers are
heard in heaven.
5 This kind of special day is
not what I want.
This is not the way I
want people to be
sorry for what they
have done.
I don't want people just to
bow their heads like a plant
and wear rough cloth and lie in ashes to
show their sadness.
This is what you do on your special days
when you do not eat,
but do you think this is what the LORD
wants?

HYPOCRISY
How is religion more than occasional actions? (58:5–7)

6 "I will tell you the kind of special day I
want:
Free the people you have put in prison
unfairly
and undo their chains.
Free those to whom you are unfair
and stop their hard labor.
7 Share your food with the hungry
and bring poor, homeless people into
your own homes.

When you see someone who has no
clothes, give him yours,
and don't refuse to help your own
relatives.
8 Then your light will shine like the dawn,
and your wounds will quickly heal.
Your God will walk before you,
and the glory of the LORD will protect
you from behind.
9 Then you will call out, and the LORD will
answer.
You will cry out, and he will say, 'Here I
am.'

"If you stop making trouble for others,
if you stop using cruel words and
pointing your finger at others,
10 if you feed those who are hungry
and take care of the needs of those who
are troubled,
then your light will shine in the darkness,
and you will be bright like sunshine at
noon.
11 The LORD will always lead you.
He will satisfy your needs in dry lands
and give strength to your bones.
You will be like a garden that has much
water,
like a spring that never runs dry.
12 Your people will rebuild the old cities that
are now in ruins;
you will rebuild their foundations.
You will be known for repairing the
broken places
and for rebuilding the roads and
houses.

13 "You must obey God's law about the
Sabbath
and not do what pleases yourselves on
that holy day.
You should call the Sabbath a joyful day
and honor it as the LORD's holy day.
You should honor it by not doing
whatever you please
nor saying whatever you please on that
day.
14 Then you will find joy in the LORD,
and I will carry you to the high places
above the earth.
I will let you eat the crops of the land
your ancestor Jacob had."
The LORD has said these things.

59

THE EVIL THAT PEOPLE DO

1 Surely the LORD's power is enough to save
you.
He can hear you when you ask him for
help.
2 It is your evil that has separated
you from your God.
Your sins cause him to turn away from
you,
so he does not hear you.
3 With your hands you have killed others,
and with your fingers you have done
wrong.
With your lips you have lied,
and with your tongue you say evil
things.
4 People take each other to court unfairly,
and no one tells the truth in arguing his
case.
They accuse each other falsely and tell lies.
They cause trouble and create more evil.
5 They hatch evil like eggs from poisonous
snakes.
If you eat one of those eggs, you will
die,
and if you break one open, a poisonous
snake comes out.
People tell lies as they would spin a
spider's web.
6 The webs they make cannot be used for
clothes;
you can't cover yourself with those
webs.
The things they do are evil,
and they use their hands to hurt others.
7 They eagerly run to do evil,
and they are always ready to kill
innocent people.
They think evil thoughts.
Everywhere they go they cause ruin and
destruction.
8 They don't know how to live in peace,
and there is no fairness in their lives.
They are dishonest.
Anyone who lives as they live will never
have peace.

ISRAEL'S SIN BRINGS TROUBLE

9 Fairness has gone far away;
goodness is nowhere to be found.
We wait for the light, but there is only
darkness now.
We hope for a bright light, but all we
have is darkness.
10 We are like the blind feeling our way along
a wall.
We feel our way as if we had no eyes.
In the brightness of day we trip as if it
were night.
We are like dead men among the strong.

11 All of us growl like the bears.
We call out sadly like the doves.
We look for justice, but there isn't any.
We want to be saved, but salvation is far away.

12 We have done many wrong things against our God;
our sins show we are wrong.
We know we have turned against God;
we know the evil things we have done:
13 sinning and rejecting the LORD,
turning away from our God,
planning to hurt others and to disobey God,
planning and speaking lies.
14 So we have driven away justice,
and we have kept away from what is right.
Truth is not spoken in the streets;
what is honest is not allowed to enter the city.
15 Truth cannot be found anywhere,
and people who refuse to do evil are attacked.

The LORD looked and could not find any justice,
and he was displeased.
16 He could not find anyone to help the people,
and he was surprised that there was no one to help.
So he used his own power to save the people;
his own goodness gave him strength.
17 He covered himself with goodness like armor.
He put the helmet of salvation on his head.
He put on the clothes of punishment
and wrapped himself in the coat of his strong love.
18 The LORD will pay back his enemies for what they have done.
He will show his anger to those who were against him;
he will punish the people in faraway places as they deserve.
19 Then people from the west will fear the LORD,
and people from the east will fear his glory.
The LORD will come quickly like a fast-flowing river,
driven by the breath of the LORD.

20 "Then a Savior will come to Jerusalem
and to the people of Jacob who have turned from sin,"
says the LORD.
21 The LORD says, "This is my agreement
with these people: My Spirit and my words
that I give you will never leave you or your
children or your grandchildren, now and forever."

> "Then a Savior will come to Jerusalem and to the people of Jacob who have turned from sin," says the LORD. (Isaiah 59:20)

JERUSALEM WILL BE GREAT

60

1 "Jerusalem, get up and shine, because your light has come,
and the glory of the LORD shines on you.
2 Darkness now covers the earth;
deep darkness covers her people.
But the LORD shines on you,
and people see his glory around you.
3 Nations will come to your light;
kings will come to the brightness of your sunrise.

4 "Look around you.
People are gathering and coming to you.
Your sons are coming from far away,
and your daughters are coming with them.
5 When you see them, you will shine with happiness;
you will be excited and full of joy,
because the wealth of the nations across the seas will be given to you;
the riches of the nations will come to you.
6 Herds of camels will cover your land,
young camels from Midian and Ephah.
People will come from Sheba
bringing gold and incense,
and they will sing praises to the LORD.
7 All the sheep from Kedar will be given to you;
the sheep from Nebaioth will be brought to you.
They will be pleasing sacrifices on my altar,
and I will make my beautiful Temple more beautiful.

8 "The people are returning to you like
clouds,
like doves flying to their nests.
9 People in faraway lands are waiting for
me.
The great trading ships will come first,
bringing your children from faraway
lands,
and with them silver and gold.
This will honor the LORD your God,
the Holy One of Israel,
who does wonderful things for you.

10 "Jerusalem, foreigners will rebuild your
walls,
and their kings will serve you.
When I was angry, I hurt you,
but now I want to be kind to you and
comfort you.
11 Your gates will always be open;
they will not be closed day or night
so the nations can bring their wealth to
you,
and their kings will be led to you.
12 The nation or kingdom that doesn't serve
you will be destroyed;
it will be completely ruined.

WHAT'S IT MEAN?

Many ancient cities were protected on all sides by enormous walls. Under normal circumstances, the gates in those walls were closed at night to keep out thieves and enemy armies.

Isaiah 60:11

13 "The great trees of Lebanon will be given
to you:
its pine, fir, and cypress trees together.
You will use them to make my Temple
beautiful,
and I will give much honor to this place
where I rest my feet.
14 The people who have hurt you will bow
down to you;
those who hated you will bow down at
your feet.
They will call you The City of the LORD,
Jerusalem, city of the Holy One of Israel.

15 "You have been hated and left empty
with no one passing through.
But I will make you great from now on;
you will be a place of happiness forever
and ever.
16 You will be given what you need from the
nations,
like a child drinking milk from its
mother.
Then you will know that it is I, the LORD,
who saves you.
You will know that the Powerful One of
Jacob protects you.
17 I will bring you gold in place of bronze,
silver in place of iron,
bronze in place of wood,
iron in place of rocks.
I will change your punishment into
peace,
and you will be ruled by what is right.
18 There will be no more violence in your
country;
it will not be ruined or destroyed.
You will name your walls Salvation
and your gates Praise.
19 The sun will no longer be your light
during the day
nor will the brightness from the moon
be your light,
because the LORD will be your light
forever,
and your God will be your glory.
20 Your sun will never set again,
and your moon will never be dark,
because the LORD will be your light
forever,
and your time of sadness will end.
21 All of your people will do what is right.
They will receive the earth forever.
They are the plant I have planted,
the work of my own hands
to show my greatness.
22 The smallest family will grow to a
thousand.
The least important of you will become
a powerful nation.
I am the LORD,
and when it is time, I will make these
things happen quickly."

THE LORD'S MESSAGE OF FREEDOM

61
1 The Lord GOD has put his Spirit in me,
because the LORD has appointed me to
tell the good news to the poor.
He has sent me to comfort those whose
hearts are broken,
to tell the captives they are free,

On the Edge

The Lord God has put his Spirit in me, because . . . he has sent me . . . to help the sorrowing people of Jerusalem. I will give them a crown to replace their ashes, and the oil of gladness to replace their sorrow, and clothes of praise to replace their spirit of sadness. Then they will be called Trees of Goodness, trees planted by the LORD to show his greatness (Is. 61:1–3).

Throughout the Bible, trees symbolize people. So it makes sense that you would be planted by the Lord. Think of a farmer. Why does he plant a crop? He plants so that the seeds will grow strong and eventually produce a harvest for him. But he doesn't just throw the seeds in a hole and hope they produce. He takes care of them and does all he can to help them grow.

The Lord does the same thing with you. He plants you and gives you life. Then as you grow, he helps you and does all he can to make you strong. He helps your roots go deep, so you won't be easily destroyed. He gives you living water—the life of Jesus. He gives you his Word—almost like a fertilizer—to help you be more than you would be without it. Then, one day you are part of his harvest. You are one of the people who has produced well for him and honored his name.

SEE FOR YOURSELF:
Ps. 1:1–3; Jer. 17:7–8; 24:6; Amos 9:15

and to tell the prisoners they are
released.
2 He has sent me to announce the time
when the LORD will show his kindness
and the time when our God will punish
evil people.
He has sent me to comfort all those who
are sad
3 and to help the sorrowing people of
Jerusalem.
I will give them a crown to replace their
ashes,
and the oil of gladness to replace their
sorrow,
and clothes of praise to replace their
spirit of sadness.
Then they will be called Trees of
Goodness,
trees planted by the LORD to show his
greatness.

4 They will rebuild the old ruins
and restore the places destroyed long
ago.
They will repair the ruined cities
that were destroyed for so long.

5 My people, foreigners will come to tend
your sheep.
People from other countries will tend
your fields and vineyards.
6 You will be called priests of the LORD;
you will be named the servants of our
God.
You will have riches from all the nations
on earth,
and you will take pride in them.
7 Instead of being ashamed, my people will
receive twice as much wealth.
Instead of being disgraced, they will be
happy because of what they receive.
They will receive a double share of the
land,
so their happiness will continue forever.
8 "I, the LORD, love justice.
I hate stealing and everything that is
wrong.
I will be fair and give my people what
they should have,
and I will make an agreement with them
that will continue forever.
9 Everyone in all nations will know the
children of my people,
and their children will be known among
the nations.
Anyone who sees them will know
that they are people the LORD has
blessed."

10 The LORD makes me very happy;
all that I am rejoices in my God.
He has covered me with clothes of
salvation
and wrapped me with a coat of
goodness,
like a bridegroom dressed for his
wedding,
like a bride dressed in jewels.
11 The earth causes plants to grow,
and a garden causes the seeds planted in
it to grow.

In the same way the Lord GOD will make
goodness and praise
come from all the nations.

NEW JERUSALEM

62

1 Because I love Jerusalem, I will continue to
speak for her;
for Jerusalem's sake I will not stop
speaking
until her goodness shines like a bright
light,
until her salvation burns bright like a
flame.
2 Jerusalem, the nations will see your
goodness,
and all kings will see your glory.
Then you will have a new name,
which the LORD himself will give you.
3 You will be like a beautiful crown in the
LORD's hand,
like a king's crown in your God's hand.
4 You will never again be called the People
that God Left,
nor your land the Land that God
Destroyed.
You will be called the People God Loves,
and your land will be called the Bride of
God,
because the LORD loves you.
And your land will belong to him as a
bride belongs to her
husband.
5 As a young man
marries a woman,
so your children will
marry your land.
As a man rejoices over his
new wife,
so your God will rejoice over you.

THANKFULNESS

Is God thankful for you? (62:5)

6 Jerusalem, I have put guards on the walls
to watch.
They must not be silent day or night.
You people who remind the LORD of your
needs in prayer
should never be quiet.
7 You should not stop praying to him until
he builds up Jerusalem
and makes it a city all people will
praise.

8 The LORD has made a promise,
and by his power he will keep his
promise.
He said, "I will never again give your grain
as food to your enemies.
I will not let your enemies drink the new
wine
that you have worked to make.
9 The person who gathers food will eat it,
and he will praise the LORD.
The person who gathers the grapes will
drink the wine
in the courts of my Temple."
10 Go through, go through the gates!
Make the way ready for the people.
Build up, build up the road!
Move all the stones off the road.
Raise the banner as a sign for the people.

11 The LORD is speaking
to all the faraway lands:
"Tell the people of Jerusalem,
'Look, your Savior is coming.
He is bringing your reward to you;
he is bringing his payment with him.'"
12 His people will be called the Holy
People,
the Saved People of the LORD,
and Jerusalem will be called the City God
Wants,
the City God Has Not Rejected.

On the Edge

You will be like a beautiful crown in the LORD's hand, like a king's crown in your God's hand (Is. 62:3).

Christians talk a lot about the things God gives them—faith, peace, forgiveness—everything they need, really. That's okay. It's good to think about all the good stuff God has given you and to say thanks.

But have you ever wondered what's in it for Jesus? He left the greatest place you can imagine (heaven) to spend years on planet Earth. It was definitely not a step up for him. And he didn't exactly get the royal treatment while he was here, either. So what's his reward—what does he get out of the deal?

You are his reward. You are what he wants for his trouble. You are his crown—which means your relationship with him brings him glory. After everything he gave up to make that happen, he deserves his crown. He deserves you. Let him have more of your life every day.

SEE FOR YOURSELF:
2 Tim. 4:8;
Rev. 14:14

THE LORD JUDGES HIS PEOPLE

63
[1]Who is this coming from Edom,
from the city of Bozrah, dressed in red?
Who is this dressed in fine clothes
and marching forward with his great power?

He says, "I, the LORD, speak what is right.
I have the power to save you."

[2]Someone asks, "Why are your clothes bright red
as if you had walked on the grapes to make wine?"

[3]The LORD answers, "I have walked in the winepress alone,
and no one among the nations helped me.

WHAT'S IT MEAN?

It was easy to spot people who pressed grapes for a living in ancient times. Because they literally had to stomp on the grapes with their bare feet to make juice, these vineyard workers developed stains on their legs and clothes that would not go away.

Isaiah 63:2

I was angry and walked on the nations
and crushed them because of my anger.
Blood splashed on my clothes,
and I stained all my clothing.
[4]I chose a time to punish people,
and the time has come for me to save.
[5]I looked around, but I saw no one to help me.
I was surprised that no one supported me.
So I used my own power to save my people;
my own anger supported me.
[6]While I was angry, I walked on the nations.
In my anger I punished them
and poured their blood on the ground."

On the Edge

But they turned against him and made his Holy Spirit very sad. So he became their enemy, and he fought against them (Is. 63:10).

God is always ready and willing to forgive you when you admit to him that you've done something wrong. He's so quick to do that for you that it's easy sometimes to take his forgiveness for granted, to treat it as automatic. After all, he promised he would forgive you, and he does what he promises.

But what you need to understand—to feel way down deep in your heart—is how it makes God feel when you decide not to do the right thing. When you sin, it hurts God—just like it hurts you when one of your friends does something that makes you think they don't care about your friendship anymore. It's important for you to realize that when you choose the wrong way, it hurts the Person who gave you everything good that's in your life. That doesn't mean that you should spend a week or two feeling guilty. But being aware of what you've done can help you to truly repent instead of quickly saying "I'm sorry" and then almost as quickly doing it again.

Know that your sin hurts God. Be quick to repent. After all, he's the best Friend you've got.

SEE FOR YOURSELF:
Eph. 4:30;
1 Thess. 5:19

THE LORD'S KINDNESS TO HIS PEOPLE

MERCY
What kind of limits are on God's mercy? (63:7)

[7]I will tell about the LORD's kindness
and praise him for everything he has done.
I will praise the LORD for the many good things he has given us
and for his goodness to the people of Israel.
He has shown great mercy to us
and has been very kind to us.
[8]He said, "These are my people;
my children will not lie to me."
So he saved them.
[9]When they suffered, he suffered also.
He sent his own angel to save them.
Because of his love and kindness, he saved them.

Since long ago he has picked them up
and carried them.
10 But they turned against him
and made his Holy Spirit very sad.
So he became their enemy,
and he fought against them.

11 But then his people remembered what
happened long ago,
in the days of Moses and the Israelites
with him.
Where is the LORD who brought the
people through the sea,
with the leaders of his people?
Where is the one
who put his Holy Spirit among them,
12 who led Moses by the right
hand
with his wonderful
power,
who divided the water
before them
to make his name
famous forever,
13 who led the people
through the deep
waters?
Like a horse walking
through a desert,
the people did not stumble.
14 Like cattle that go down to the valley,
the Spirit of the LORD gave the people a
place to rest.
LORD, that is the way you led your people,
and by this you won for yourself
wonderful fame.

A PRAYER FOR HELP

15 LORD, look down from the heavens and
see;
look at us from your wonderful and
holy home in heaven.
Where is your strong love and power?
Why are you keeping your love and
mercy from us?
16 You are our father.
Abraham doesn't know we are his
children,
and Israel doesn't recognize us.
LORD, you are our father.
You are called "the one who has always
saved us."
17 LORD, why are you making us wander
from your ways?
Why do you make us stubborn so that
we don't honor you?
For our sake come back to us,
your servants, who belong to you.
18 Your people had your Temple for a while,
but now our enemies have walked on
your holy place and crushed it.
19 We have become like people you never
ruled over,
like those who have never worn your
name.

64

1 Tear open the skies and come down to
earth
so that the mountains will tremble
before you.
2 Like a fire that burns twigs,
like a fire that makes water boil,
let your enemies know who you are.
Then all nations will
shake with fear when
they see you.
3 You have done amazing
things we did not
expect.
You came down, and
the mountains
trembled before you.
4 From long ago no one has
ever heard of a God
like you.
No one has ever seen a
God besides you,
who helps the people who trust you.
5 You help those who enjoy doing good,
who remember how you want them to
live.
But you were angry because we sinned.
For a long time we disobeyed,
so how can we be saved?
6 All of us are dirty with sin.
All the right things we have done are
like filthy pieces of cloth.
All of us are like dead leaves,
and our sins, like the wind, have carried
us away.
7 No one worships you
or even asks you to help us.
That is because you have turned away
from us
and have let our sins destroy us.

8 But LORD, you are our father.
We are like clay, and you are the potter;
your hands made us all.
9 LORD, don't continue to be angry with us;
don't remember our sins forever.
Please, look at us,
because we are your people.
10 Your holy cities are empty like the desert.
Jerusalem is like a desert;

"But LORD, you are our father. We are like clay, and you are the potter; your hands made us all." (Isaiah 64:8)

On the Edge

But LORD, you are our father. We are like clay, and you are the potter; your hands made us all (Is. 64:8).

God makes you who you are. He gave you the talents you were born with. Your personality came from him, too. All the things that happen to you he uses to help you become the person he wants you to be. He also gives you some discipline and a lot of gentle leading.

But God needs your cooperation. If you won't listen to him or if you're always complaining every time your life isn't going the way you planned, then it's going to take a long time for you to change. But if you let him do what he needs to do, the change will come quicker.

That's the key—let *him* do it. You can make yourself more patient, more loving, or more thoughtful only by letting God change the way you think (see Rom. 12:2). You can decide to change your actions ("I will not yell, I will not yell, I will not yell"), but unless you change on the inside, it'll fall apart after a while. Changing your actions is not a bad idea. But ask him to make the real change. That's his job.

SEE FOR YOURSELF:
Rom. 12:2; 1 Cor. 7:7; 1 Pet. 4:10

it is destroyed.
11 Our ancestors worshiped you
in our holy and wonderful Temple,
but now it has been burned with fire,
and all our precious things have been destroyed.
12 When you see these things, will you hold yourself back from helping us, LORD?
Will you be silent and punish us beyond what we can stand?

ALL PEOPLE WILL LEARN ABOUT GOD

65

1 The LORD says, "I made myself known to people who were not looking for me.
I was found by those who were not asking me for help.
I said, 'Here I am. Here I am,'
to a nation that was not praying to me.
2 All day long I stood ready to accept
people who turned against me,
but the way they continue to live is not good;
they do anything they want to do.
3 Right in front of me
they continue to do things that make me angry.
They offer sacrifices to their gods in their gardens,
and they burn incense on altars of brick.
4 They sit among the graves
and spend their nights waiting to get messages from the dead.
They eat the meat of pigs,
and their pots are full of soup made from meat that is wrong to eat.
5 But they tell others, 'Stay away, and don't come near me.
I am too holy for you.'
These people are like smoke in my nose.
Like a fire that burns all the time, they continue to make me angry.

6 "Look, it is written here before me.
I will not be quiet; instead, I will repay you in full.
I will punish you for what you have done.
7 I will punish you for your sins and your ancestors' sins,"
says the LORD.
"They burned incense to gods on the mountains
and shamed me on those hills.
So I will punish them as they should be punished
for what they did."

8 This is what the LORD says:
"When there is juice left in the grapes,

WHAT'S IT MEAN?

There were certain foods that God did not want his people to eat. Pork was one of them. Shellfish was another. Not only did the Israelites not eat these foods themselves; they were disgusted by anyone who did.
Isaiah 65:4

people do not destroy them,
because they know there is good left in them.
So I will do the same thing to my servants—
I will not completely destroy them.
9 I will leave some of the children of Jacob,
and some of the people of Judah will receive my mountain.
I will choose the people who will live there;
my servants will live there.
10 Then the Plain of Sharon will be a field for flocks,
and the Valley of Achor will be a place for herds to rest.
They will be for the people who want to follow me.

11 "But as for you who left the LORD,
who forgot about my holy mountain,
who worship the god Luck,
who hold religious feasts for the god Fate,
12 I decide your fate, and I will punish you with my sword.
You will all be killed,
because I called you, but you refused to answer.
I spoke to you, but you wouldn't listen.
You did the things I said were evil
and chose to do things that displease me."

13 So this is what the Lord GOD says:
"My servants will eat,
but you evil people will be hungry.
My servants will drink,
but you evil people will be thirsty.
My servants will be happy,
but you evil people will be shamed.
14 My servants will shout for joy
because of the goodness of their hearts,
but you evil people will cry,
because you will be sad.
You will cry loudly, because your spirits will be broken.
15 Your names will be like curses to my servants,
and the Lord GOD will put you to death.
But he will call his servants by another name.
16 People in the land who ask for blessings
will ask for them from the faithful God.
And people in the land who make a promise
will promise in the name of the faithful God,
because the troubles of the past will be forgotten.
I will make those troubles go away.

A NEW TIME IS COMING

17 "Look, I will make new heavens and a new earth,
and people will not remember the past
or think about those things.
18 My people will be happy forever
because of the things I will make.
I will make a Jerusalem that is full of joy,
and I will make her people a delight.
19 Then I will rejoice over Jerusalem
and be delighted with my people.
There will never again be heard in that city
the sounds of crying and sadness.
20 There will never be a baby from that city
who lives only a few days.
And there will never be an older person
who doesn't have a long life.
A person who lives a hundred years will be called young,
and a person who dies before he is a hundred will be thought of as a sinner.
21 In that city those who build houses will live there.
Those who plant vineyards will get to eat their grapes.
22 No more will one person build a house
and someone else live there.
One person will not plant a garden and someone else eat its fruit.
My people will live a long time,
as trees live long.
My chosen people will live there
and enjoy the things they make.
23 They will never again work for nothing.
They will never again give birth to children who die young.
All my people will be blessed by the LORD;
they and their children will be blessed.
24 I will provide for their needs before they ask,
and I will help them while they are still asking for help.
25 Wolves and lambs will eat together in peace.
Lions will eat hay like oxen,
and a snake on the ground will not hurt anyone.
They will not hurt or destroy each other
on all my holy mountain,"
says the LORD.

THE LORD WILL JUDGE ALL NATIONS

66 [1]This is what the LORD says:
"Heaven is my throne,
and the earth is my footstool.
So do you think you can build a house for me?
Do I need a place to rest?
[2]My hand made all things.
All things are here
because I made them,"
says the LORD.

WORSHIP
How should we respond to God? (66:2)

"These are the people I am pleased with:
those who are not proud or stubborn
and who fear my word.
[3]But those people who kill bulls as a sacrifice to me
are like those who kill people.
Those who kill sheep as a sacrifice
are like those who break the necks of dogs.
Those who give me grain offerings
are like those who offer me the blood of pigs.[n]
Those who burn incense
are like those who worship idols.
These people choose their own ways, not mine,
and they love the terrible things they do.
[4]So I will choose their punishments,
and I will punish them with what they fear most.
This is because I called to them, but they did not listen.
I spoke to them, but they did not hear me.
They did things I said were evil;
they chose to do things I did not like."

[5]You people who obey the words of the LORD,

WHAT'S IT MEAN?

According to God's Law, both pigs and dogs were unclean. Their flesh was unacceptable as food for the Israelites and was certainly unacceptable for sacrifices to God.
Isaiah 66:3

66:3 dogs . . . pigs God did not want his people to offer dogs and pigs as sacrifices because they were unclean animals.

Promise HE PROMISES TO ANSWER YOUR PRAYERS.

I will provide for their needs before they ask, and I will help them while they are still asking for help (Is. 65:24).

Your best friend is lying in a hospital bed. She was in a car wreck over the weekend and the doctors have said she probably won't live through the night. You remember when your parents used to make you go to Sunday school. You remember God. You pray, for the first time in years, and beg God to let your friend live. He does.

Do you believe God answers your prayers? Not "Do you believe because you think you're supposed to?" but do you really believe it? When you pray, do you just hope your prayer makes it all the way up to heaven, or do you know in your heart that God is listening to you? God says he will answer your prayers before you even get through praying. Now that is awesome! He knows you so well that he gets to work on your request before it even gets out of your mouth. Remember, not all prayers have the same "yes" answer. God is totally wise, and he knows exactly what's best for you. It's important for you to pray according to God's will, and you can find that in his Word. Sometimes he says, "Not yet." Whether your answer is yes, no, or not yet, he hears you and goes to work before you finish praying.

SEE FOR YOURSELF:
Deut. 4:5–8; Job 22:27; Ps. 28:6; 91:15

listen to what he says:
"Your brothers hated you
and turned against you because you
followed me.
Your brothers said, 'Let the LORD be
honored
so we may see you rejoice,'
but they will be punished.
6 Listen to the loud noise coming from the
city;
hear the noise from the Temple.
It is the LORD punishing his enemies,
giving them the punishment they should
have.

7 "A woman does not give birth before she
feels the pain;
she does not give birth to a son before
the pain starts.
8 No one has ever heard of that
happening;
no one has ever seen that happen.
In the same way no one ever saw a
country begin in one day;
no one has ever heard of a new nation
beginning in one moment.
But Jerusalem will give birth to her
children
just as soon as she feels the birth
pains.
9 In the same way I will not cause pain
without allowing something new to be
born," says the LORD.
"If I cause you the pain,
I will not stop you from giving birth to
your new nation," says your God.
10 "Jerusalem, rejoice.
All you people who love Jerusalem, be
happy.
Those of you who felt sad for Jerusalem
should now feel happy with her.
11 You will take comfort from her and be
satisfied,
as a child is nursed by its mother.
You will receive her good things
and enjoy her wealth."
12 This is what the LORD says:
"I will give her peace that will flow to her
like a river.
The wealth of the nations will come to
her like a river overflowing its banks.
Like babies you will be nursed and held in
my arms
and bounced on my knees.
13 I will comfort you
as a mother comforts her child.
You will be comforted in Jerusalem."

14 When you see these things, you will be
happy,
and you will grow like the grass.
The LORD's servants will see his power,
but his enemies will see his anger.
15 Look, the LORD is coming with fire
and his armies with clouds of dust.
He will punish those people with his
anger;
he will punish them with flames of fire.
16 The LORD will judge the people with fire,
and he will destroy many people with
his sword;
he will kill many people.

17 "These people make themselves holy and
pure to go to worship their gods in their gardens. Following each other into their special
gardens, they eat the meat of pigs and rats and
other hateful things. But they will all be destroyed together," says the LORD.
18 "I know they have evil thoughts and do
evil things, so I am coming to punish them. I
will gather all nations and all people, and they
will come together and see my glory.
19 "I will put a mark on some of the people,
and I will send some of these saved people to
the nations: to Tarshish, Libya, Lud (the land of
archers), Tubal, Greece, and all the faraway
lands. These people have never heard about
what I have done nor seen my glory. So the
saved people will tell the nations about my
glory. 20 And they will bring all your fellow Israelites from all nations to my holy mountain
in Jerusalem. Your fellow Israelites will come
on horses, donkeys, and camels and in chariots
and wagons. They will be like the grain offerings that the people bring in clean containers
to the Temple," says the LORD. 21 "And I will
choose even some of these people to be priests
and Levites," says the LORD.
22 "I will make new heavens and the new
earth, which will last forever," says the LORD.
"In the same way, your names and your children will always be with me. 23 All people will
come to worship me every Sabbath and every
New Moon," says the LORD. 24 "They will go out
and see the dead bodies of the people who
sinned against me. The worms that eat them
will never die, and the fires that burn them will
never stop, and everyone will hate to see those
bodies."

jeremiah

CONTENT

Jeremiah was not what you would call a diplomat. He didn't spend a lot of energy trying to find the softest way to say something. He just blurted out the truth and let his listeners deal with it in whatever way they wanted to. Because of this he wasn't a particularly loved prophet.

He wasn't a particularly happy prophet either. Jeremiah's heart was broken over the sin of his people. He knew that, if they didn't stay strong spiritually, they would eventually lose everything. He kept telling them, but they didn't listen.

Jeremiah is called the weeping prophet. What a reputation! But when you think about it, people cry because they are sad. People are sad because they have lost something whether it's a possession or a friend. Jeremiah knew that his people were going to be destroyed eventually because of their sin. That was something to be sad about. His tears showed his people a picture of how God felt about their lifestyle.

Outline

1:1–19 .... God Chooses Jeremiah to Speak for Him
2:1—26:24 .... God Will Punish the People of Judah and Jerusalem
27:1—29:32 .... Jeremiah Against the Lying Prophets
30:1—33:26 .... God Will Someday Bring His People Back to Their Land
34:1—38:28 .... Scenes from Jeremiah's Ministry
39:1—42:22 .... The Fall of Jerusalem and Later Events in Judah
43:1—44:30 .... Jeremiah in Egypt
45:1–5 .... A Message for Baruch
46:1—51:64 .... The Lord Speaks About the Nations
52:1–34 .... Another Account of the Fall of Jerusalem

Purpose

It is wise to heed God's warnings and honor his messengers.

Theme

Failure to Repent Will Lead to Destruction

Date of writing

626–586 B.C.

"I also gave them this command: Obey me, and I will be your God and you will be my people. Do all that I command so that good things will happen to you. But your ancestors did not listen or pay attention to me. They were stubborn and did whatever their evil hearts wanted. They went backward, not forward" (7:23–24).

Bible Talk

This Is Your Brain . . .

Have you seen those commercials where someone takes an egg and says, "This is your brain"? Then they break the egg into a hot frying pan and say, "This is your brain on drugs."

Jeremiah actually did an ancient version of that commercial. He got a clay pot and stood in front of his people. He basically told them, "This is your life." Then he threw the pot to the ground and it broke, of course, into little pieces. Then he told them, "This is your life without obeying God's Law."

Whether it's a frying egg or a broken clay pot, the truth is still the same. God teaches us how to live. When we don't live the way he has designed, destruction is going to come one way or another, sooner or later.

CONSEQUENCES

The Book of Jeremiah is really about consequences. Jeremiah's people were living their lives as if God didn't matter at all. The consequences for that was that when they needed God's protection they didn't get it. Eventually they were taken away like prisoners to a foreign country. They lost everything. How's that for consequences?

We deal with consequences, too. When we live our lives the way God wants us to, it's easier to find his guidance and direction. But if we live our lives as if God doesn't matter, then we don't even recognize his voice when he gives us direction. If we disregard God long enough, we don't recognize his help at all. We might not become exiles, but we'll be alone just the same.

1 [1]These are the words of Jeremiah son of
Hilkiah. He belonged to the family of priests
who lived in the town of Anathoth in the land
of Benjamin. [2]The LORD spoke his word to Jeremiah during the thirteenth year that Josiah
son of Amon was king of Judah. [3]The LORD
also spoke to Jeremiah while Jehoiakim son of
Josiah was king of Judah and during the eleven
years that Zedekiah son of Josiah was king of
Judah. In the fifth month of his last year, the
people of Jerusalem were taken away as captives.

WHAT'S IT MEAN?

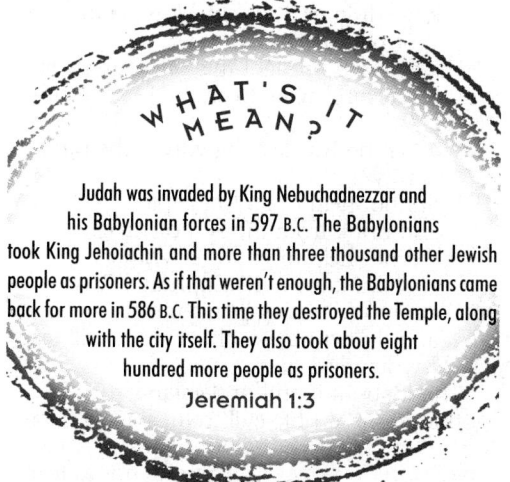

Judah was invaded by King Nebuchadnezzar and his Babylonian forces in 597 B.C. The Babylonians took King Jehoiachin and more than three thousand other Jewish people as prisoners. As if that weren't enough, the Babylonians came back for more in 586 B.C. This time they destroyed the Temple, along with the city itself. They also took about eight hundred more people as prisoners.

Jeremiah 1:3

THE LORD CALLS JEREMIAH

[4]The LORD spoke his word to me,
saying:

[5]"Before I made you in
your mother's womb,
I chose you.
Before you were born, I
set you apart for a
special work.
I appointed you as a
prophet to the nations."

ABORTION
What does God know about us before we're born? (1:5)

[6]Then I said, "But Lord GOD, I don't know
how to speak. I am only a boy."
[7]But the LORD said to me, "Don't say, 'I am
only a boy.' You must go everywhere I send
you, and you must say everything I tell you to
say. [8]Don't be afraid of anyone, because I am
with you to protect you," says the LORD.
[9]Then the LORD reached out his hand and
touched my mouth. He said to me, "See, I am
putting my words in your mouth. [10]Today I
have put you in charge of nations and kingdoms. You will pull up and tear down, destroy
and overthrow, build up and plant."

JEREMIAH SEES TWO VISIONS

[11]The LORD spoke his word to me, saying:
"Jeremiah, what do you see?"
I answered, "I see a stick of almond wood."
[12]The LORD said to me, "You have seen correctly, because I am watching to make sure my
words come true."
[13]The LORD spoke his word to me again:
"What do you see?"
I answered, "I see a pot of boiling water, tip-
ping over from the north."
[14]The LORD said to me, "Disaster will come
from the north and strike all the people who
live in this country. [15]In a short time I will call
all of the people in the northern kingdoms,"
said the LORD.

"Those kings will come and set up their
thrones
near the entrance of the gates of
Jerusalem.
They will attack all the city walls around
Jerusalem
and all the cities in Judah.
[16]And I will announce my judgments
against my people
because of their evil in turning away
from me.
They offered sacrifices to other gods
and worshiped idols they had made
with their own hands.

[17]"Jeremiah, get ready. Stand up and tell
them everything I command you to say. Don't
be afraid of the people, or I will give you good
reason to be afraid of them. [18]Today I am going
to make you a strong city, an iron pillar, a
bronze wall. You will be able to stand against
everyone in the land: Judah's kings, officers,
priests, and the people of the land. [19]They will
fight against you, but they will not defeat you,
because I am with you to protect you!" says
the LORD.

ISRAEL TURNS FROM GOD

2 [1]The LORD spoke his word to me, saying:
[2]"Go and speak to the people of Jerusalem,
saying: This is what the LORD says:

'I remember how faithful you were to me
when you were a young nation.
You loved me like a young bride.
You followed me through the desert,
a land that had never been planted.
[3]The people of Israel were holy to the
LORD,
like the first fruits from his harvest.
Those who tried to hurt Israel were judged
guilty.
Disasters struck them,' " says the LORD.

4 Hear the word of the LORD, family of
Jacob,
all you family groups of Israel.
5 This is what the LORD says:
"I was fair to your ancestors,
so why did they turn away from me?
Your ancestors worshiped useless idols
and became useless themselves.
6 Your ancestors didn't say,
'Where is the LORD who brought us out
of Egypt?
He led us through the desert,
through a dry and rocky land,
through a dark and dangerous land.
He led us where no one travels or lives.'
7 I brought you into a fertile land
so you could eat its fruit and produce.
But you came and made my land unclean;
you made it a hateful place.
8 The priests didn't ask,
'Where is the LORD?'
The people who know the teachings didn't
know me.
The leaders turned against me.
The prophets prophesied in the name of
Baal
and worshiped useless idols.

9 "So now I will again tell what I have
against you," says the LORD.
"And I will tell what I
have against your
grandchildren.
10 Go across the sea to
the island of
Cyprus and see.
Send someone to
the land of Kedar
to look closely.
See if there has ever
been anything like
this.
11 Has a nation ever exchanged
its gods?
(Of course, its gods are not really gods
at all.)
But my people have exchanged their
glorious God
for idols worth nothing.
12 Skies, be shocked at the things that have
happened
and shake with great fear!" says the
LORD.
13 "My people have done two evils:
They have turned away from me,
the spring of living water.
And they have dug their own wells,
which are broken wells that cannot hold
water.
14 Have the people of Israel become slaves?
Have they become like someone who
was born a slave?
Why were they taken captive?
15 Enemies have roared like lions at Israel;
they have growled at Israel.
They have destroyed the land of Israel.
The cities of Israel lie in ruins,
and all the people have left.
16 The men from the cities of Memphis and
Tahpanhes
have disgraced you by shaving the top
of your head.
17 Haven't you brought this on yourselves
by turning away from the LORD your
God
when he was leading you in the right
way?
18 It did not help to go to Egypt
and drink from the Shihor River.
It did not help to go to Assyria
and drink from the Euphrates River.
19 Your evil will bring punishment to you,
and the wrong you have done will teach
you a lesson.
Think about it and understand
that it is a terrible evil to turn away from
the LORD your God.
It is wrong not to fear
me,"
says the Lord GOD All-
Powerful.

> **" 'So now I will again tell what I have against you,' says the LORD. 'And I will tell what I have against your grandchildren.' "**
> **(Jeremiah 2:9)**

20 "Long ago you refused
to obey me as an ox
breaks its yoke.
You broke the ropes I
used to hold you
and said, 'I will not
serve you!'
In fact, on every high hill
and under every green
tree
you lay down as a prostitute.
21 But I planted you as a special vine,
as a very good seed.
How then did you turn
into a wild vine that grows bad fruit?
22 Although you wash yourself with cleanser
and use much soap,
I can still see the stain of your guilt,"
says the Lord GOD.
23 "How can you say to me, 'I am not guilty.
I have not worshiped the Baal idols'?
Look at the things you did in the valley.

Think about what you have done.
You are like a she-camel in mating season
that runs from place to place.
24 You are like a wild donkey that lives in the desert
and sniffs the wind at mating time.
At that time who can hold her back?
Any male who chases her will easily catch her;
at mating time, it is easy to find her.
25 Don't run until your feet are bare
or until your throat is dry.
But you say, 'It's no use!
I love those other gods,
and I must chase them!'

WHAT'S IT MEAN?

Baal worship is a little hard to explain, so pay attention. The Canaanites, the people who lived in the land God had promised to the Israelites, worshiped Baal as their chief god. Apparently, though, Baal assumed many different forms. The one that was most important to the Canaanites and their neighbors was the god of crops and livestock. Many people seemed to "customize" Baal to fit their specific needs. He was known by different names in different places.

Jeremiah 2:23

26 "A thief is ashamed when someone catches him stealing.
In the same way, the family of Israel is ashamed—
they, their kings, their officers,
their priests, and their prophets.
27 They say to things of wood, 'You are my father,'
and to idols of stone, 'You gave birth to me.'
Those people won't look at me;
they have turned their backs to me.
But when they get into trouble, they say,
'Come and save us!'
28 Where are the idols you made for yourselves?
Let them come and save you
when you are in trouble!
People of Judah, you have as many idols
as you have towns!

29 "Why do you complain to me?
All of you have turned against me," says the LORD.
30 "I punished your people, but it did not help.
They didn't come back when they were punished.
With your swords you killed your prophets
like a hungry lion.

31 "People of Judah, pay attention to the
word of the LORD:
Have I been like a desert to the people of Israel
or like a dark and dangerous land?
Why do my people say, 'We are free to wander.
We won't come to you anymore'?
32 A young woman does not forget her jewelry,
and a bride does not forget the decorations for her dress.
But my people have forgotten me
for more days than can be counted.
33 You really know how to chase after love.
Even the worst women can learn evil ways from you.
34 Even on your clothes you have the blood
of poor and innocent people,
but they weren't thieves you caught breaking in.
You do all these things,
35 but you say, 'I am innocent.
God is not angry with me.'
But I will judge you guilty of lying,
because you say, 'I have not sinned.'
36 It is so easy for you to change your mind.
Even Egypt will let you down,
as Assyria let you down.
37 You will eventually leave that place
with your hands on your head, like captives.
You trusted those countries,
but you will not be helped by them,
because the LORD has rejected them.

JUDAH IS UNFAITHFUL

3 1 "If a man divorces his wife
and she leaves him and marries another man,
should her first husband come back to her again?
If he went back to her, wouldn't the land become completely unclean?
But you have acted like a prostitute with many lovers,

and now you want to come back to
me?" says the LORD.
2"Look up to the bare hilltops, Judah.
Is there any place where you have not
been a prostitute?
You have sat by the road waiting for
lovers,
like an Arab in the desert.
You made the land unclean,
because you did evil and were like a
prostitute.
3So the rain has not come,
and there have not been any spring
rains.
But your face still looks like the face of a
prostitute.
You refuse even to be ashamed of what
you did.
4Now you are calling to me,
'My father, you have been my friend
since I was young.
5Will you always be angry at me?
Will your anger last forever?'
Judah, you said this,
but you did as much evil as you
could!"

JUDAH AND ISRAEL ARE LIKE SISTERS

6When King Josiah was ruling Judah, the
LORD said to me, "Did you see what unfaithful
Israel did? She was like a prostitute with her
idols on every hill and under every green tree.
7I said to myself, 'Israel will come back to me
after she does this evil,' but she didn't come
back. And Israel's wicked sister Judah saw

WHAT'S IT MEAN?

After Solomon died, Israel split into two separate nations. Ten of the twelve tribes formed the northern kingdom of Israel; the other two—Judah and Benjamin, for those of you interested in specifics—formed the southern kingdom of Judah. The capital of Israel was Samaria; the capital of Judah was Jerusalem. Because the Temple in Jerusalem was the center of worship for the Israelites, the Levites, who took care of priestly responsibilities, were associated with the southern kingdom.

Jeremiah 3:7–8

what she did. 8Judah saw that I divorced unfaithful Israel because of her adultery, but that
didn't make Israel's wicked sister Judah afraid.
She also went out and acted like a prostitute!
9And she didn't care that she was acting like a
prostitute. So she made her country unclean
and was guilty of adultery, because she worshiped idols made of stone and wood. 10Israel's
wicked sister didn't even come back to me with
her whole heart, but only pretended," says the
LORD.

11The LORD said to me, "Unfaithful Israel
had a better excuse than wicked Judah. 12Go
and speak this message toward the north:
'Come back, unfaithful people of Israel,'
says the LORD.
'I will stop being angry at you,
because I am full of mercy,' says the LORD.
'I will not be angry with you forever.
13All you have to do is admit your sin—
that you turned against the LORD your
God
and worshiped gods under every green
tree
and didn't obey me,' " says the LORD.

14"Come back to me, you unfaithful children," says the LORD, "because I am your master. I will take one person from every city and
two from every family group, and I will bring
you to Jerusalem. 15Then I will give you new
rulers who will be faithful to me, who will lead
you with knowledge and understanding. 16In
those days there will be many of you in the
land," says the LORD. "At that time people will
no longer say, 'I remember the Ark of the
Agreement.' They won't think about it anymore or remember it or miss it or make another one. 17At that time people will call
Jerusalem The Throne of the LORD, and all nations will come together in Jerusalem to show
respect to the LORD. They will not follow their
stubborn, evil hearts anymore. 18In those days
the family of Judah will join the family of Israel. They will come together from a land in
the north to the land I gave their ancestors.

19"I, the LORD, said,
'How happy I would be to treat you as
my own children
and give you a pleasant land,
a land more beautiful than that of any
other nation.'
I thought you would call me 'My Father'
and not turn away from me.
20But like a woman who is unfaithful to her
husband,
family of Israel, you have been
unfaithful to me," says the LORD.

21 You can hear crying on the bare hilltops.
It is the people of Israel crying and praying for mercy.
They have become very evil
and have forgotten the LORD their God.
22 "Come back to me, you unfaithful children,
and I will forgive you for being unfaithful."

On the Edge

I thought you would call me "My Father" and not turn away from me (Jer. 3:19b).

Though it might be easy to skip over this verse and just keep going, God is trying to show us a powerful truth. Notice here that God wants to be your Father. What does that really mean? You are his child. Just think about that for a moment. You are a child of God! The God who created the heavens and earth, and every living, breathing thing, is your Dad!

Your natural father may not be a good role model; in fact, many people don't even know who their natural father is. Whatever the case, God wants to fill that empty spot.

He has promised not to turn away from anyone fatherless! Remember, your earthly parents aren't perfect. They may let you down, but God never will. He's never going to hurt you. He's never going to break a promise. He's never going to be a bad example. God will never leave you nor turn his back on you. In other words, he's with you for the long haul, all the way to the end. Now that's a *great* Dad!

SEE FOR YOURSELF:
Ps. 2:7; 68:5; Is. 64:8; Matt. 5:48; 2 Cor. 6:18; Eph. 5:1

"Yes, we will come to you,
because you are the LORD our God.
23 It was foolish to worship idols on the hills
and on the mountains.
Surely the salvation of Israel
comes from the LORD our God.
24 Since our youth, shameful gods have eaten up in sacrifice
everything our ancestors worked for—
their flocks and herds,
their sons and daughters.
25 Let us lie down in our shame,
and let our disgrace cover us like a blanket.
We have sinned against the LORD our God,
both we and our ancestors.
From our youth until now,
we have not obeyed the LORD our God."

4

1 "If you will return, Israel,
then return to me," says the LORD.
"If you will throw away your idols that I hate,
then don't wander away from me.
2 If you say when you make a promise,
'As surely as the LORD lives,'
and you can say it in a truthful, honest, and right way,
then the nations will be blessed by him,
and they will praise him for what he has done."

3 This is what the LORD says to the people of Judah and to Jerusalem:
"Plow your unplowed fields,
and don't plant seeds among thorns.
4 Give yourselves to the service of the LORD,
and decide to obey him,
people of Judah and people of Jerusalem.
If you don't, my anger will spread among you like a fire,
and no one will be able to put it out,
because of the evil you have done.

TROUBLE FROM THE NORTH

5 "Announce this message in Judah and say it in Jerusalem:
'Blow the trumpet throughout the country!'
Shout out loud and say,
'Come together!
Let's all escape to the strong, walled cities!'
6 Raise the signal flag toward Jerusalem!
Run for your lives, and don't wait,
because I am bringing disaster from the north
There will be terrible destruction."

7 A lion has come out of his den;
a destroyer of nations has begun to march.
He has left his home
to destroy your land.
Your towns will be destroyed
with no one left to live in them.
8 So put on rough cloth,
show how sad you are, and cry loudly.

The terrible anger of the LORD
has not turned away from us.

WHAT'S IT MEAN?

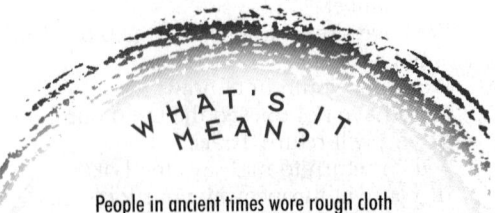

People in ancient times wore rough cloth in times of great distress or grief. If you've ever felt this cloth, you know why it wasn't a popular clothing choice. The cloth was a dark, scratchy material made of goat's hair. The modern tradition of wearing dark clothing to funerals and memorial services is based on the ancient custom of wearing this rough cloth in times of sorrow.

Jeremiah 4:8

9 "When this happens," says the LORD,
"the king and officers will lose their
courage.
The priests will be terribly afraid,
and the prophets will be shocked!"
10 Then I said, "Lord GOD, you have tricked
the people of Judah and Jerusalem. You said,
'You will have peace,' but now the sword is
pointing at our throats!"
11 At that time this message will be given to
Judah and Jerusalem: "A hot wind blows from
the bare hilltops of the desert toward the
LORD's people. It is not a gentle wind to separate grain from chaff. 12 I feel a stronger wind
than that. Now even I will announce judgments against the people of Judah."
13 Look! The enemy rises up like a cloud,
and his chariots come like a tornado.
His horses are faster than eagles.
How terrible it will be for us! We are
ruined!
14 People of Jerusalem, clean the evil from
your hearts so that you can be
saved.
Don't continue making evil plans.
15 A voice from Dan makes an
announcement
and brings bad news from the
mountains of Ephraim.
16 "Report this to the nations.
Spread this news in Jerusalem:
'Invaders are coming from a faraway
country,
shouting words of war against the cities
of Judah.
17 The enemy has surrounded Jerusalem as
men guard a field,
because Judah turned against me,' " says
the LORD.
18 "The way you have lived and acted
has brought this trouble to you.
This is your punishment.
How terrible it is!
The pain stabs your heart!"

JEREMIAH'S CRY

19 Oh, how I hurt! How I hurt!
I am bent over in pain.
Oh, the torture in my heart!
My heart is pounding inside me.
I cannot keep quiet,
because I have heard the sound of the
trumpet.
I have heard the shouts of war.
20 Disaster follows disaster;
the whole country has been destroyed.
My tents are destroyed in only a moment.
My curtains are torn down quickly.
21 How long must I look at the war flag?
How long must I listen to the war
trumpet?

22 The LORD says, "My people are foolish.
They do not know me.
They are stupid children;
they don't understand.
They are skillful at doing evil,
but they don't know how to do good."

DISASTER IS COMING

23 I looked at the earth,
and it was empty and had no shape.
I looked at the sky,
and its light was gone.
24 I looked at the mountains,
and they were shaking.
All the hills were trembling.
25 I looked, and there were no people.
Every bird in the sky had flown away.
26 I looked, and the good, rich land had
become a desert.
All its towns had been destroyed
by the LORD and his great anger.
27 This is what the LORD says:
"All the land will be ruined,
but I will not completely destroy it.
28 So the people in the land will cry loudly,
and the sky will grow dark,
because I have spoken and will not
change my mind.
I have made a decision, and I will not
change it."

29 At the sound of the horsemen and the
archers,
all the people in the towns run away.
They hide in the thick bushes
and climb up into the rocks.
All of the cities of Judah are empty;
no one lives in them.
30 Judah, you destroyed nation, what are you
doing?
Why do you put on your finest dress
and decorate yourself with gold
jewelry?
Why do you put color around your eyes?
You make yourself beautiful, but it is all
useless.
Your lovers hate you;
they want to kill you.

31 I hear a cry like a woman having a baby,
distress like a woman having her first
child.
It is the sound of Jerusalem gasping for
breath.
She lifts her hands in prayer and says,
"Oh! I am about to faint
before my murderers!"

NO ONE IS RIGHT

5
1 The LORD says, "Walk up and down the
streets of Jerusalem.
Look around and discover these things.
Search the public squares of the city.
If you can find one person who does
honest things,
who searches for the truth,
I will forgive this city.
2 Although the people say, 'As surely as the
LORD lives!'
they don't really mean it."

3 LORD, don't you look for truth in people?
You struck the people of Judah,
but they didn't feel any pain.
You crushed them,
but they refused to learn what is right.
They became more stubborn than a rock;
they refused to turn back to God.
4 But I thought,
"These are only the poor, foolish people.
They have not learned the way of the
LORD
and what their God wants them to do.
5 So I will go to the leaders of Judah
and talk to them.
Surely they understand the way of the
LORD
and know what God wants them to do."
But even the leaders had all joined
together to break away from the
LORD;
they had broken their ties with him.
6 So a lion from the forest will attack them.
A wolf from the desert will kill them.
A leopard is waiting for them near their
towns.
It will tear to pieces anyone who comes
out of the city,
because the people of Judah have sinned
greatly.
They have wandered away from the
LORD many times.

WHAT'S IT MEAN?

Lions and leopards and wolves—oh my! Believe it or not, lions were a common danger for people in ancient Israel. Travelers who passed by the tall, grassy areas near the Jordan River were wise to keep their eyes open for lions. Leopards and wolves weren't necessarily threats to human life, but they did attack livestock, threatening people's livelihood. All three animals are used throughout the Bible as symbols of God's judgment.

Jeremiah 5:6

7 The LORD said, "Tell me why I should
forgive you.
Your children have left me
and have made promises to idols that
are not gods at all.
I gave your children everything they
needed,
but they still were like an unfaithful wife
to me.
They spent much time in houses of
prostitutes.
8 They are like well-fed horses filled with
sexual desire;
each one wants another man's wife.
9 Shouldn't I punish the people of Judah for
doing these things?" says the LORD.
"Shouldn't I give a nation such as this
the punishment it deserves?

10 "Go along and cut down Judah's
vineyards,
but do not completely destroy them.

Cut off all her people as if they were
branches,
because they do not belong to the LORD.
11 The families of Israel and Judah
have been completely
unfaithful to me," says
the LORD.

12 Those people have lied
about the LORD
and said, "He will not
do anything to us!
Nothing bad will happen
to us!
We will never see war or
hunger!
13 The prophets are like an empty wind;
the word of God is not in them.
Let the bad things they say happen to
them."

14 So this is what the LORD God All-Powerful
says:
"The people said I would not punish them.
So, the words I give you will be like fire,
and these people will be like wood that
it burns up.
15 Listen, family of Israel," says the LORD,
"I will soon bring a nation from far
away to attack you.
It is an old nation that has lasted a long
time.
The people there speak a language you
do not know;
you cannot understand what they say.
16 Their arrows bring death.
All their people are strong warriors.
17 They will eat your crops and your food.
They will eat your sons and daughters.
They will eat your flocks and herds.
They will eat your grapes and figs.
They will destroy with their swords
the strong, walled cities you trust.

18 "Yet even then," says the LORD, "I will not
destroy you completely. 19 When the people of
Judah ask, 'Why has the LORD our God done
all these terrible things to us?' then give them
this answer: 'You have left the LORD and served
foreign idols in your own land. So now you
will serve foreigners in a land that does not
belong to you.'

20 "Announce this message to the family of
Jacob,
and tell it to the nation of Judah:
21 Hear this message, you foolish people who
have no sense.
They have eyes, but they don't really
see.
They have ears, but they don't really
listen.
22 Surely you are afraid of me," says the
LORD.

" 'Surely you are afraid of me,' says the LORD. 'You should shake with fear in my presence.' " (Jeremiah 5:22a)

"You should shake with
fear in my presence.
I am the one who made
the beaches to be a
border for the sea,
a border the water can
never go past.
The waves may pound
the beach, but they
can't win over it.
They may roar, but they
cannot go beyond it.
23 But the people of Judah
are stubborn and
have turned against
me.
They have turned aside and gone away
from me.
24 They do not say to themselves,
'We should fear the LORD our God,
who gives us autumn and spring rains in
their seasons,
who makes sure we have the harvest at
the right time.'
25 But your evil has kept away both rain and
harvest.
Your sins have kept you from enjoying
good things.
26 There are wicked men among my people.
Like those who make nets for catching
birds,
they set their traps to catch people.
27 Like cages full of birds,
their houses are full of lies.
They have become rich and powerful.
28 They have grown big and fat.
There is no end to the evil things they do.
They won't plead the case of the
orphan
or help the poor be judged fairly.
29 Shouldn't I punish the people of Judah for
doing these things?" says the LORD.
"Shouldn't I give a nation such as this
the punishment it deserves?

30 "A terrible and shocking thing
has happened in the land of Judah:
31 The prophets speak lies,
and the priests take power into their
own hands,
and my people love it this way.
But what will you do when the end
comes?

JERUSALEM IS SURROUNDED

6

[1]"Run for your lives, people of Benjamin!
Run away from Jerusalem!
Blow the war trumpet in the town of Tekoa!
Raise the warning flag over the town of Beth Hakkerem!
Disaster is coming from the north;
terrible destruction is coming to you.
[2]Jerusalem, I will destroy you,
you who are fragile and gentle.
[3]Shepherds with their flocks will come against Jerusalem.
They will set up their tents all around her,
each shepherd taking care of his own section."
[4]They say, "Get ready to fight against Jerusalem!
Get up! We will attack at noon!
But it is already getting late;
the evening shadows are growing long.
[5]So get up! We will attack at night.
We will destroy the strong towers of Jerusalem!"
[6]This is what the LORD All-Powerful says:
"Cut down the trees around Jerusalem,
and build an attack ramp to the top of its walls.
This city must be punished.
Inside it is nothing but slavery.
[7]Jerusalem pours out her evil
as a well pours out its water.
The sounds of violence and destruction are heard within her.
I can see the sickness and hurts of Jerusalem.
[8]Listen to this warning, Jerusalem,
or I will turn my back on you
and make your land an empty desert
where no one can live."
[9]This is what the LORD All-Powerful says:
"Gather the few people of Israel who are left alive,
as you would gather the last grapes on a grapevine.
Check each vine again,
like someone who gathers grapes."

[10]To whom can I speak? Whom can I warn?
Who will listen to me?
The people of Israel have closed ears,
so they cannot hear my warnings.
They don't like the word of the LORD;
they don't want to listen to it!
[11]But I am full of the anger of the LORD,
and I am tired of holding it in.
"Pour out my anger on the children who play in the street
and on the young men gathered together.
A husband and his wife will both be caught in his anger,
as will the very old.
[12]Their houses will be turned over to others,
along with their fields and wives,
because I will raise my hand
and punish the people of Judah," says the LORD.
[13]"Everyone, from the least important to the greatest,
is greedy for money.
Even the prophets and priests
all tell lies.
[14]They tried to heal my people's serious injuries
as if they were small wounds.
They said, 'It's all right, it's all right.'
But really, it is not all right.
[15]They should be ashamed of the terrible way they act,
but they are not ashamed at all.
They don't even know how to blush about their sins.
So they will fall, along with everyone else.
They will be thrown to the ground
when I punish them," says the LORD.
[16]This is what the LORD says:
"Stand where the roads cross and look.
Ask where the old way is,
where the good way is, and walk on it.
If you do, you will find rest for yourselves.
But they have said, 'We will not walk on the good way.'
[17]I set watchmen over you
and told you, 'Listen for the sound of the war trumpet!'
But they said, 'We will not listen.'
[18]So listen, all you nations,
and pay attention, you witnesses.
Watch what I will do to the people of Judah.
[19]Hear this, people of the earth:
I am going to bring disaster to the people of Judah
because of the evil they plan.
They have not listened to my messages
and have rejected my teachings.

GUILT

Are consequences to sin severe even if we don't realize our guilt? (6:15)

20 Why do you bring me offerings of incense
from the land of Sheba?
Why do you bring me sweet-smelling
cane from a faraway land?
Your burnt offerings will not be accepted;
your sacrifices do not please me."
21 So this is what the LORD says:
"I will put problems in front of Judah.
Fathers and sons will stumble over them
together.
Neighbors and friends will die."
22 This is what the LORD says:
"Look, an army is coming
from the land of the north;
a great nation is coming
from the far sides of the earth.
23 The soldiers carry bows and spears.
They are cruel and show no mercy.
They sound like the roaring ocean
when they ride their horses.
That army is coming lined up for battle,
ready to attack you, Jerusalem."

24 We have heard the news about that army
and are helpless from fear.
We are gripped by our pain,
like a woman having a baby.
25 Don't go out into the fields
or walk down the roads,
because the enemy has swords.
There is terror on every side.
26 My people, put on rough cloth
and roll in the ashes to show how sad
you are.
Cry loudly for those who are dead,
as if your only son were dead,
because the destroyer
will soon come against us.
27 "Jeremiah, I have made you like a worker
who tests metal,
and my people are like the ore.
You must observe their ways
and test them.
28 All my people have turned against me and
are stubborn.
They go around telling lies about
others.
They are like bronze and iron
that became covered with rust.
They all act dishonestly.
29 The fire is fanned to make it hotter,
but the lead does not melt.
The pure metal does not come out;
the evil is not removed from my
people.
30 My people will be called rejected silver,
because the LORD has rejected them."

JEREMIAH'S TEMPLE MESSAGE

7 1 This is the word that the LORD spoke to
Jeremiah: 2 "Stand at the gate of the Temple and
preach this message there:
" 'Hear the word of the LORD, all you people
of the nation of Judah! All you who come
through these gates to worship the LORD, listen
to this message! 3 This is what the LORD All-
Powerful, the God of Israel, says: Change your
lives and do what is right! Then I will let you
live in this place. 4 Don't trust the lies of people
who say, "This is the Temple of the LORD. This
is the Temple of the LORD. This is the
Temple of the LORD!" 5 You must
change your lives and do
what is right. Be fair to each
other. 6 You must not be hard
on strangers, orphans, and
widows. Don't kill innocent
people in this place! Don't fol-
low other gods, or they will ruin your lives. 7 If
you do these things, I will let you live in this
land that I gave to your ancestors to keep forever.
8 " 'But look, you are trusting lies, which is
useless. 9 Will you steal and murder and be
guilty of adultery? Will you falsely accuse
other people? Will you burn incense to the god
Baal and follow other gods you have not
known? 10 If you do that, do you think you can
come before me and stand in this place where
I have chosen to be worshiped? Do you think
you can say, "We are safe!" when you do all
these hateful things? 11 This place where I have
chosen to be worshiped is nothing more to
you than a hideout for robbers. I have been
watching you, says the LORD.
12 " 'You people of Judah, go now to the
town of Shiloh, where I first made a place to be

CHARACTER

Does our integrity affect others? (7:5–11)

WHAT'S IT MEAN?

When Joshua first arrived in the Promised Land, he set up the Meeting Tent and the Ark of the Agreement in Shiloh, a town twenty miles north of Jerusalem. That's where they stayed until around 1050 B.C., when the Philistines destroyed Shiloh and captured the Ark. Eventually, the Ark was recovered and placed in the Temple in Jerusalem.

Jeremiah 7:12

worshiped. See what I did to it because of the evil things the people of Israel had done. 13You people of Judah have done all these evil things too, says the LORD. I spoke to you again and again, but you did not listen to me. I called you, but you did not answer. 14So I will destroy the place where I have chosen to be worshiped in Jerusalem. You trust in that place, which I gave to you and your ancestors, but I will destroy it just as I destroyed Shiloh. 15I will push you away from me just as I pushed away your relatives, the people of Israel!'

16"As for you, Jeremiah, don't pray for these people. Don't cry out for them or ask anything for them or beg me to help them, because I will not listen to you. 17Don't you see what they are doing in the towns of Judah and in the streets of Jerusalem? 18The children gather wood, and the fathers use the wood to make a fire. The women make the dough for cakes of bread, and they offer them to the Queen Goddess. They pour out drink offerings to other gods to make me angry. 19But I am not the one the people of Judah are really hurting, says the LORD. They are only hurting themselves and bringing shame upon themselves.

20" 'So this is what the Lord GOD says: I will pour out my anger on this place, on people and animals, on the trees in the field and the crops in the ground. My anger will be like a hot fire that no one can put out.

OBEDIENCE IS MORE THAN SACRIFICE

21" 'This is what the LORD All-Powerful, the God of Israel, says: Offer burnt offerings along with your other sacrifices, and eat the meat yourselves! 22When I brought your ancestors out of Egypt, I did not speak to them and give them commands only about burnt offerings and sacrifices. 23I also gave them this command: Obey me, and I will be your God and you will be my people. Do all that I command so that good things will happen to you. 24But your ancestors did not listen or pay attention to me. They were stubborn and did whatever their evil hearts wanted. They went backward, not forward. 25Since the day your ancestors left Egypt, I have sent my servants, the prophets, again and again to you. 26But your ancestors did not listen or pay attention to me. They were very stubborn and did more evil than their ancestors.'

27"Jeremiah, you will tell all these things to the people of Judah, but they will not listen to you. You will call to them, but they will not answer you. 28So say to them, 'This is the nation that has not obeyed the LORD its God. These people do nothing when I correct them. They do not tell the truth; it has disappeared from their lips.

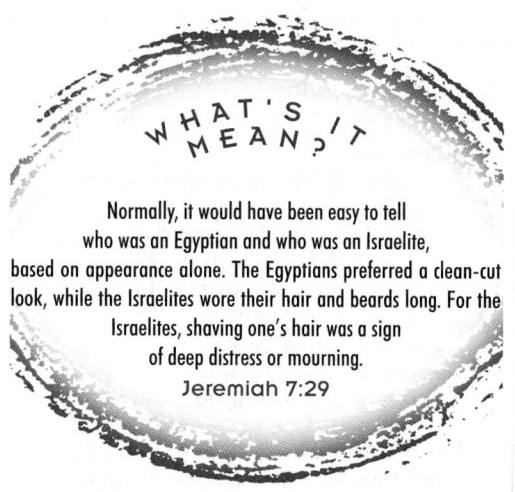

WHAT'S IT MEAN?

Normally, it would have been easy to tell who was an Egyptian and who was an Israelite, based on appearance alone. The Egyptians preferred a clean-cut look, while the Israelites wore their hair and beards long. For the Israelites, shaving one's hair was a sign of deep distress or mourning.

Jeremiah 7:29

THE VALLEY OF KILLING

29" 'Cut off your hair and throw it away. Go up to the bare hilltop and cry out, because the LORD has rejected these people. He has turned his back on them, and in his anger will punish them. 30The people of Judah have done what I said was evil, says the LORD. They have set up their hateful idols in the place where I have chosen to be worshiped and have made it unclean. 31The people of Judah have built places of worship at Topheth in the Valley of Ben Hinnom. There they burned their own sons and daughters as sacrifices, something I never commanded. It never even entered my mind. 32So, I warn you. The days are coming, says the LORD, when people will not call this place Topheth or the Valley of Ben Hinnom anymore. They will call it the Valley of Killing. They will bury the dead in Topheth until there is no room to bury anyone else. 33Then the bodies of the dead will become food for the birds of the sky and for the wild animals. There will be no one left alive to chase them away. 34I will end the happy sounds of the bride and bridegroom. There will be no happy sounds in the cities of Judah or in the streets of Jerusalem, because the land will become an empty desert!

8 1" 'The LORD says: At that time they will remove from their tombs the bones of Judah's kings and officers, priests and prophets, and the people of Jerusalem. 2The bones will be spread on the ground under the sun, moon, and stars that the people loved and served and went after and searched for and worshiped.

No one will gather up the bones and bury
them. So they will be like dung thrown on the
ground. 3I will force the people of Judah to
leave their homes and their land. Those of this
evil family who are not dead will wish they
were, says the LORD All-Powerful.'

SIN AND PUNISHMENT

4"Say to the people of Judah: 'This is what
the LORD says:
When people fall down, don't they get up
again?
And when someone goes the wrong
way, doesn't he turn back?
5Why, then, have the people of Jerusalem
gone the wrong way
and not turned back?
They believe their own lies
and refuse to turn around and come
back.
6I have listened to them very carefully,
but they do not say what is right.
They do not feel sorry about their wicked
ways,
saying, "What have I done?"
Each person goes his own way,
like a horse charging into a battle.
7Even the birds in the sky
know the right times to do things.
The storks, doves, swifts, and thrushes
know when it is time to migrate.
But my people don't know
what the LORD wants them to do.

8" 'You keep saying, "We are wise,
because we have the teachings of the
LORD."
But actually, those who explain the
Scriptures
have written lies with their pens.
9These wise men refused to listen to the
word of the LORD,
so they are not really wise at all.
They will be ashamed.
They will be shocked and trapped.
10So I will give their wives to other men
and their fields to new owners.
Everyone, from the least
important to the
greatest,
is greedy for money.
Even the prophets and
priests
all tell lies.

GREED
What does God think of greed? (8:10)

11They tried to heal my people's serious
injuries
as if they were small wounds.
They said, "It's all right, it's all right."
But really, it is not all right.
12They should be ashamed of the terrible
way they act,
but they are not ashamed at all.
They don't even know how to blush
about their sins.
So they will fall, along with everyone else.
They will be thrown to the ground
when I punish them, says the LORD.

13" 'I will take away their crops, says the LORD.
There will be no grapes on the vine
and no figs on the fig tree.
Even the leaves will dry up and die.
I will take away what I gave them.' "

14"Why are we just sitting here?
Let's get together!
We have sinned against the LORD,
so he has given us poisoned water to
drink.
Come, let's run to the strong, walled cities.
The LORD our God has decided that we
must die,
so let's die there.
15We hoped to have peace,
but nothing good has come.
We hoped for a time when he would heal
us,
but only terror has come.
16From the land of Dan,
the snorting of the enemy's horses is
heard.
The ground shakes from the neighing of
their large horses.
They have come and destroyed
the land and everything in it,
the city and all who live there."

17"Look! I am sending poisonous snakes to
attack you.
These snakes cannot be charmed,
and they will bite you," says the LORD.

JEREMIAH'S SADNESS

18God, you are my comfort when I am very
sad
and when I am afraid.
19Listen to the sound of my people.
They cry from a faraway land:
"Isn't the LORD still in Jerusalem?
Isn't Jerusalem's king still there?"

But God says, "Why did the people make
me angry by worshiping idols,
useless foreign idols?"

20 And the people say, "Harvest time is over;
summer has ended,
and we have not been saved."

21 Because my people are crushed, I am
crushed.
I cry loudly and am afraid for them.
22 Isn't there balm in the land of Gilead?
Isn't there a doctor there?
So why aren't the hurts of my people
healed?

9

1 I wish my head were like a spring of water
and my eyes like a fountain of tears!
Then I could cry day and night
for my people who have been killed.
2 I wish I had a place in the desert—
a house where travelers spend the
night—
so I could leave my people.
I could go away from them,
because they are all unfaithful to God;
they are all turning against him.

JUDAH'S FAILURES

3 "They use their tongues like a bow,
shooting lies from their mouths like
arrows.
Lies, not truth,
have grown strong in the land.
They go from one evil thing to another.
They do not know who I am," says the
LORD.
4 "Watch out for your friends,
and don't trust your own relatives,
because every relative is a cheater,
and every friend tells lies about you.
5 Everyone lies to his friend,
and no one speaks the truth.
The people of Judah have taught their
tongues to lie.
They have become tired from sinning.
6 Jeremiah, you live in the middle of lies.
With their lies the people refuse to know
me," says the LORD.
7 So this is what the LORD All-Powerful
says:
"I will test the people of
Judah as a person
tests metal in a fire.
I have no other choice,
because my people
have sinned.

VALUES
Are our values important? (9:7–9)

8 Their tongues are like sharp
arrows.
Their mouths speak lies.
Everyone speaks nicely to his neighbor,
but he is secretly planning to attack him.
9 Shouldn't I punish the people for doing
this?" says the LORD.
"Shouldn't I give a nation like this the
punishment it deserves?"

10 I, Jeremiah, will cry loudly for the
mountains
and sing a funeral song for the empty
fields.
They are empty, and no one passes
through.

Promise

HE PROMISES TO PURIFY YOUR HEART.

So this is what the LORD All-Powerful says: "I will test the people of Judah as a person tests metal in a fire. I have no other choice, because my people have sinned" (Jer. 9:7).

Sometimes we get paralyzed in our daily walk with God. We wake up one morning, take a look in the mirror, see our sin and its ugliness, and push God away. We might spend the next weeks or months trying to figure out how to make ourselves more presentable. But you can't refine and purify your own heart. What you can do is stay hooked up to God through prayer, and you can constantly renew your mind by memorizing and meditating on Scripture. God can make the unclean holy and restore beauty to the unlovely. No matter how ugly your heart or how sinful your life has been, God can clean and restore. Ask him daily to purify your heart. If you're continually allowing God in to remove your sin, your walk with him stays fresh, and you stay acceptable to him.

SEE FOR YOURSELF:
Zech. 13:9; Acts 15:9; Titus 2:14

The mooing of cattle cannot be heard.
The birds have flown away,
and the animals are gone.

11 "I, the LORD, will make the city of
Jerusalem a heap of ruins,
a home for wild dogs.
I will destroy the cities of Judah
so no one can live there."

12 What person is wise enough to understand these things? Is there someone who has
been taught by the LORD who can explain
them? Why was the land ruined? Why has it
been made like an empty desert where no one
goes?
13 The LORD answered, "It is because Judah
quit following my teachings that I gave them.
They have not obeyed me or done what I told
them to do. 14 Instead, they were stubborn and
followed the Baals, as their ancestors taught
them to do. 15 So this is what the LORD All-
Powerful, the God of Israel, says: "I will soon
make the people of Judah eat bitter food and
drink poisoned water. 16 I will scatter them
through other nations that they and their ancestors never knew about. I will chase the people of Judah with the sword until they are all
killed."

17 This is what the LORD All-Powerful says:
"Now, think about these things!
Call for the women who cry at funerals
to come.
Send for those women who are good at
that job.
18 Let them come quickly
and cry loudly for us.
Then our eyes will fill with tears,
and streams of water will flow from our
eyelids.
19 The sound of loud crying is heard from
Jerusalem:
'We are truly ruined!
We are truly ashamed!
We must leave our land,
because our houses are in ruins.' "

20 Now, women of Judah, listen to the word
of the LORD;
open your ears to hear the words of his
mouth.
Teach your daughters how to cry loudly.
Teach one another a funeral song.
21 Death has climbed in through our
windows
and has entered our strong cities.
Death has taken away our children who
play in the streets
and the young men who meet in the
city squares.

22 Say, "This is what the LORD says:
'The dead bodies of people will lie
in the open field like dung.
They will lie like grain a farmer has cut,
but there will be no one to gather
them.' "
23 This is what the LORD says:
"The wise must not brag about their
wisdom.
The strong must not brag about their
strength.
The rich must not brag about their
money.
24 But if someone wants to brag, let him brag
that he understands and knows me.
Let him brag that I am the LORD,
and that I am kind and fair,
and that I do things that are right on
earth.
This kind of bragging pleases me," says the
LORD.

25 The LORD says, "The time is coming when I
will punish all those who are circumcised only
in the flesh: 26 the people of Egypt, Judah, Edom,
Ammon, Moab, and the desert people who cut
their hair short. The men in all those countries
are not circumcised. And the whole family of
Israel does not give itself to serving me."

WHAT'S IT MEAN?

Circumcision is a minor operation performed on the sex organ of male babies, usually within a few days after birth. For the Israelites, circumcision was an outward sign of their Agreement with God. Other nations in the Near East also practiced circumcision, but waited until the young man was entering adulthood.

Jeremiah 9:25–26

THE LORD AND THE IDOLS

10 1 Family of Israel, listen to what the LORD
says to you. 2 This is what he says:
"Don't live like the people from other
nations,
and don't be afraid of special signs in
the sky,

even though the other nations are afraid
of them.
3 The customs of other people are worth
nothing.
Their idols are just wood cut from the
forest,
shaped by a worker with his chisel.
4 They decorate their idols with silver and
gold.
With hammers and nails they fasten
them down
so they won't fall over.
5 Their idols are like scarecrows in melon
fields;
they cannot talk.
Since they cannot walk,
they must be carried.
Do not be afraid of those idols,
because they can't hurt you,
and they can't help you either."

6 LORD, there is no one like you.
You are great,
and your name is great and powerful.
7 Everyone should respect you, King of the
nations;
you deserve respect.
Of all the wise people among the nations
and in all the kingdoms,
none of them is as wise as you.
8 Those wise people are stupid
and foolish.
Their teachings come
from worthless
wooden idols.
9 Hammered silver is
brought from
Tarshish
and gold from Uphaz,
so the idols are made by
craftsmen and
goldsmiths.
They put blue and purple clothes on the
idols.
All these things are made by skilled
workers.
10 But the LORD is the only true God.
He is the only living God, the King
forever.
The earth shakes when he is angry,
and the nations cannot stand up to his
anger.

> "LORD, there is no one like you. . . . Everyone should respect you, King of the nations." (Jeremiah 10:6–7a)

11 "Tell them this message: 'These gods did
not make heaven and earth; they will be destroyed and disappear from heaven and
earth.' "
12 God made the earth by his power.
He used his wisdom to build the world
and his understanding to stretch out the
skies.
13 When he thunders, the waters in the skies
roar.
He makes clouds rise in the sky all over
the earth.
He sends lightning with the rain
and brings out the wind from his
storehouses.

14 People are so stupid and know so little.
Goldsmiths are made ashamed by their
idols,
because those statues are only false gods.
They have no breath in them.
15 They are worth nothing; people make fun
of them.
When they are judged, they will be
destroyed.
16 But God, who is Jacob's Portion, is not like
the idols.
He made everything,
and he chose Israel to be his special
people.
The LORD All-Powerful is his name.

DESTRUCTION IS COMING

17 Get everything you own and prepare to
leave,
you people who are
trapped by your
enemies.
18 This is what the LORD
says:
"At this time I will
throw out the people
who live in this land.
I will bring trouble to
them
so that they may be
captured."

19 How terrible it will be for me because of
my injury.
My wound cannot be healed.
Yet I told myself,
"This is my sickness; I must suffer
through it."
20 My tent is ruined,
and all its ropes are broken.
My children have gone away and left me.
No one is left to put up my tent again
or to set up a shelter for me.
21 The shepherds are stupid
and don't ask the LORD for advice.
So they do not have success,

JEREMIAH made a difference

Our superficial impression of prophets makes it difficult to imagine what they were like as kids. Did they thunder judgment as five-year-olds? Were they prematurely bearded? The Bible (as usual) has a way of correcting our impressions. Prophets came in all shapes and sizes. Usually, they were normal. Often, the idea of being called as God's prophet came as just as much a shock to them as it would to us. Jeremiah was probably typical.

When God called Jeremiah to be a prophet, Jeremiah's immediate answer admitted insecurity and inexperience. He felt he couldn't speak, and he claimed he was too young. God didn't tell Jeremiah he was wrong. In fact, God agreed with Jeremiah. The newly appointed prophet was a tongue-tied beginner. God told him to stop thinking of himself that way and to start thinking about how God was going to make up for those obvious weaknesses. God gave Jeremiah three unforgettable promises as part of his commission: (1) God's guidance (1:7); (2) God's words (v. 7); (3) God's companionship (v. 8). God also gave Jeremiah three commands: (1) Don't use your youth as an excuse (v. 7); (2) Go where I send you (v. 7); (3) Don't be afraid (v. 8).

Cutting Edge

Jeremiah didn't have an easy life. He may have been the least popular prophet. He spent time in prison. Some of his writings were burned. He was even dropped in the bottom of a well. God kept his promise. We know Jeremiah always knew God was with him, because he complained to God constantly! They had a continual conversation, no matter what Jeremiah was doing or where he was.

One of the ways Jeremiah made a difference was by demonstrating a faith that expressed genuine feelings to God. Jeremiah didn't edit his prayers. He didn't tell God what he thought God wanted to hear. He told God what God already knew. Honest prayer changes the person who prays.

YOU can, too! God knows you inside out. God designed you. Like Jeremiah, you will discover that the more you are open to God's direction, the more you will find God using both your abilities and your inabilities to accomplish his purposes. God will make a difference with you as you are and in spite of the way you are. He will make a difference in you as he is making a difference through you. As God told Jeremiah, "I am with you to protect you" (Jer. 1:8).

Want to know more? You can read Jeremiah's writings and about his life in Jeremiah and Lamentations.

and all their flocks are scattered and lost.
[22]Listen! The news is coming.
A loud noise comes from the north
to make the towns of Judah an empty
desert
and a home for wild dogs!

WHAT'S IT MEAN?

Wild dogs were desert creatures that fed on garbage. They were especially unpopular with the Israelites not only because they destroyed crops, but also because they smelled bad.

Jeremiah 10:22

JEREMIAH'S PRAYER

[23]LORD, I know that a person's life doesn't
really belong to him.
No one can control his own life.
[24]LORD, correct me, but be fair.
Don't punish me in your anger,
or you will destroy me.
[25]Pour out your anger on other nations
that do not know you
and do not pray to you.
Those nations have destroyed Jacob's
family.
They have eaten him up completely
and destroyed his homeland.

THE AGREEMENT IS BROKEN

11 [1]These are the words that the LORD spoke to
Jeremiah: [2]"Listen to the words of this agreement and tell them to the people of Judah and
those living in Jerusalem. [3]Tell them this is
what the LORD, the God of Israel, says: 'Cursed
is the person who does not obey the words of
this agreement [4]that I made with your ancestors when I brought them out of Egypt. Egypt
was like a furnace for melting iron!' I told them,
'Obey me and do everything I command you.
Then you will be my people, and I will be your
God. [5]Then I will keep the promise I made to
your ancestors to give them a fertile land.' And
you are living in that country today."
I answered, "Amen, LORD."
[6]The LORD said to me, "Announce this message in the towns of Judah and in the streets of
Jerusalem: 'Listen to the words of this agreement and obey them. [7]I warned your ancestors
to obey me when I brought them out
of Egypt. I have warned them
again and again to this very
day: "Obey me!" [8]But your
ancestors did not listen to me.
They were stubborn and did
what their own evil hearts
wanted. So I made all the
curses of this agreement come
upon them. I commanded them to obey the
agreement, but they did not.' "

OBEDIENCE

How important is it to obey God? (11:6–8)

[9]Then the LORD said to me, "I know the
people of Judah and those living in Jerusalem
have made secret plans. [10]They have gone back
to the same sins their ancestors did. Their ancestors refused to listen to my message and
followed and worshiped other gods instead.
The families of Israel and Judah have broken
the agreement I made with their ancestors. [11]So
this is what the LORD says: 'I will soon bring a
disaster on the people of Judah which they will
not be able to escape. They will cry to me for
help, but I will not listen to them. [12]The people
living in the towns of Judah and the city of
Jerusalem will pray to their idols to whom they
burn incense. But those idols will not be able
to help when disaster comes. [13]Look, people of
Judah, you have as many idols as there are
towns in Judah. You have built as many altars
to burn incense to that shameful god Baal as
there are streets in Jerusalem.'
[14]"As for you, Jeremiah, don't pray for these
people or cry out for them or ask anything for
them. I will not listen when they call to me in
the time of their trouble.
[15]"What is my beloved Judah doing in my
Temple
when she makes many evil plans?
Do you think animal sacrifices will stop
your punishment?
When you do your evil, then you are
happy."
[16]The LORD called you "a leafy olive tree,
with beautiful fruit and shape."
But with the roar of a strong storm
he will set that tree on fire,
and its branches will be burned up.
[17]The LORD All-Powerful, who planted you,
has announced that disaster will come to you.
This is because the families of Israel and Judah
have done evil and have made him angry by
burning incense to Baal.

EVIL PLANS AGAINST JEREMIAH

[18]The LORD showed me that men were
making plans against me. Because he showed

me what they were doing, I knew they were
against me. [19]Before this, I was like a gentle
lamb waiting to be butchered. I did not know
they had made plans against me, saying:

"Let us destroy the tree and its fruit.
Let's kill him so people will forget him."

[20]But, LORD All-Powerful, you are a fair
judge.
You know how to test peoples' hearts
and minds.
I have told you what I have against them.
So let me see you give them the
punishment they deserve.

[21]So the LORD speaks about the men from
Anathoth who plan to kill Jeremiah and say,
"Don't prophesy in the name of the LORD, or
we will kill you!" [22]So this is what the LORD
All-Powerful says: "I will soon punish the men
from Anathoth. Their young men will die in
war. Their sons and daughters will die from
hunger. [23]No one from the city of Anathoth
will be left alive, because I will cause a disaster
to happen to them that year."

JEREMIAH'S FIRST COMPLAINT

12

[1]LORD, when I bring my case to you,
you are always right.
But I want to ask you about the justice
you give.
Why are evil people successful?
Why do dishonest people have such
easy lives?
[2]You have put the evil people here
like plants with strong roots.
They grow and produce fruit.
With their mouths they speak well of you,
but their hearts are really far away from
you.
[3]But you know my heart, LORD.
You see me and test my thoughts about
you.
Drag the evil people away like sheep to be
butchered.
Set them aside for the day of killing.
[4]How much longer will the land stay dried
up
and the grass in every field be dead?
The animals and birds in the land have
died,
because the people are evil.
Yes, they are even saying,
"God does not see what happens to us."

THE LORD'S ANSWER TO JEREMIAH

[5]"If you get tired while racing against
people,
how can you race against horses?
If you stumble in a country that is safe,
what will you do in the thick
thornbushes along the Jordan River?
[6]Even your own brothers and members of
your own family
are making plans against you.
They are crying out against you.
Don't trust them,
even when they say nice things to you!

WHAT'S IT MEAN?

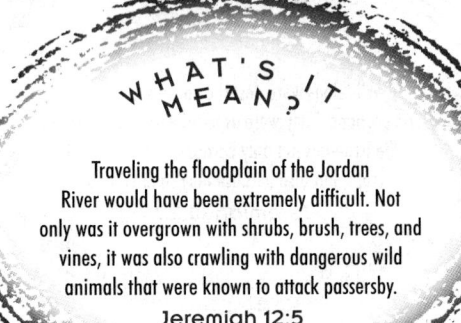

Traveling the floodplain of the Jordan River would have been extremely difficult. Not only was it overgrown with shrubs, brush, trees, and vines, it was also crawling with dangerous wild animals that were known to attack passersby.

Jeremiah 12:5

[7]"I have left Israel;
I have left my people.
I have given the people I love
over to their enemies.
[8]My people have become to me
like a lion in the forest.
They roar at me,
so I hate them.
[9]My people have become to me
like a speckled bird attacked on all sides
by hawks.
Go, gather the wild animals.
Bring them to get something to eat.
[10]Many shepherds have ruined my
vineyards
and trampled the plants in my field.
They have turned my beautiful field
into an empty desert.
[11]They have turned my field into a desert
that is wilted and dead.
The whole country is an empty desert,
because no one who lives there cares.
[12]Many soldiers have marched over those
barren hills.
The LORD is using the armies to punish
that land
from one end to the other.
No one is safe.
[13]The people have planted wheat,
but they have harvested only thorns.

They have worked hard until they were
very tired,
but they have nothing for all their work.
They are ashamed of their poor harvest,
because the LORD's terrible
anger has caused this."
14This is what the LORD said
to me: "Here is what I will do
to all my wicked neighbors
who take the land I gave my
people Israel. I will pull them
up and throw them out of
their land. And I will pull up
the people of Judah from
among them. 15But after I pull
them up, I will feel sorry for them
again. I will bring each person back to his
own property and to his own land. 16I want
them to learn their lessons well. In the past they
taught my people to swear by Baal's name. But
if they will now learn to swear by my name,
saying, 'As surely as the LORD lives . . .' I will
allow them to rebuild among my people. 17But
if a nation will not listen to my message, I will
pull it up completely and destroy it," says the
LORD.

"Give glory to the LORD your God before he brings darkness and before you slip and fall." (Jeremiah 13:16a)

JEREMIAH'S LINEN BELT

13
1This is what the LORD said to me: "Go and
buy a linen belt and put it around your waist.
Don't let the belt get wet."
2So I bought a linen belt, just as the LORD
told me, and put it around my waist. 3Then the
LORD spoke his word to me a second time:
4"Take the belt you bought and are wearing,
and go to Perath. Hide the belt there in a crack
in the rocks." 5So I went to Perath and hid the
belt there, just as the LORD told me.
6Many days later the LORD said to me, "Now
go to Perath and get the belt I told you to hide
there." 7So I went to Perath and dug up the belt
and took it from where I had hidden it. But
now it was ruined; it was good for nothing.
8Then the LORD spoke his word to me. 9This
is what the LORD said: "In the same way I will
ruin the pride of the people of Judah and the
great pride of Jerusalem. 10These evil people refuse to listen to my warnings. They stubbornly
do only what they want to do, and they follow
other gods to serve and worship them. So they
will become like this linen belt—good for
nothing. 11As a belt is wrapped tightly around
a person's waist, I wrapped the families of Israel and Judah around me," says the LORD. "I
did that so they would be my people and bring
fame, praise, and honor to me. But my people
would not listen.

WARNINGS ABOUT LEATHER WINE BAGS

12"Say to them: 'This is what the LORD, the
God of Israel, says: All leather bags for holding
wine should be filled with wine.' People will
say to you: 'Of course, we know
all wine bags should be filled
with wine.' 13Then you will
say to them, 'This is what the
LORD says: I will make everyone in this land like a
drunken person—the kings
who sit on David's throne,
the priests and the prophets,
and all the people who live in
Jerusalem. 14I will make them
smash against one another, fathers
and sons alike, says the LORD. I will not feel
sorry or have pity on them or show mercy
that would stop me from destroying them.' "

THREAT OF SLAVERY

15Listen and pay attention.
Don't be too proud,
because the LORD has spoken to you.
16Give glory to the LORD your God
before he brings darkness
and before you slip and fall
on the dark hills.
You hope for light,
but he will turn it into thick darkness;
he will change it into deep gloom.
17If you don't listen to him,
I will cry secretly
because of your pride.
I will cry painfully,
and my eyes will overflow with tears,
because the LORD's people will be
captured.

18Tell this to the king and the queen mother:
"Come down from your thrones,
because your beautiful crowns
have fallen from your heads."
19The cities of southern Judah are locked up,
and no one can open them.
All Judah will be taken as captives to a
foreign land;
they will be carried away
completely.

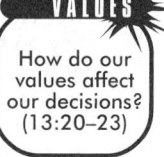

VALUES
How do our values affect our decisions? (13:20–23)

20Jerusalem, look up and
see
the people coming from
the north.
Where is the flock God
gave you to care for,
the flock you bragged about?

[21] What will you say when they appoint as your heads
those you had thought were your friends?
Won't you have much pain and trouble,
like a woman giving birth to a baby?
[22] You might ask yourself,
"Why has this happened to me?"
It happened because of your many sins.
Because of your sins, your skirt was torn off
and your body has been treated badly.
[23] Can a person from Cush change the color of his skin?
Can a leopard change his spots?
In the same way, Jerusalem, you cannot change and do good,
because you are accustomed to doing evil.

[24] "I will scatter you like chaff that is blown away by the desert wind.
[25] This is what will happen to you;
this is your part in my plans," says the LORD.
"Because you forgot me
and trusted in false gods,
[26] I will pull your skirts up over your face
so everyone will see your shame.
[27] I have seen the terrible things you have done:
your acts of adultery and your snorting,
your prostitution,
your hateful acts
on the hills and in the fields.
How terrible it will be for you, Jerusalem.
How long will you continue being unclean?"

A TIME WITHOUT RAIN

14

[1] These are the words that the LORD spoke to Jeremiah about the time when there was no rain:
[2] "The nation of Judah cries as if someone has died,
and her cities are very sad.
They are distressed over the land.
A cry goes up to God from Jerusalem.
[3] The important men send their servants to get water.
They go to the wells,
but they find no water.
So they return with empty jars.
They are ashamed and embarrassed
and cover their heads in shame.
[4] The ground is dry and cracked open,
because no rain falls on the land.
The farmers are upset and sad,
so they cover their heads in shame.
[5] Even the mother deer in the field
leaves her newborn fawn to die,
because there is no grass.
[6] Wild donkeys stand on the bare hills
and sniff the wind like wild dogs.
But their eyes go blind,
because there is no food."

[7] We know that we suffer because of our sins.
LORD, do something to help us for the good of your name.
We have left you many times;
we have sinned against you.
[8] God, the Hope of Israel,
you have saved Israel in times of trouble.
Why are you like a stranger in the land,
or like a traveler who only stays one night?
[9] Why are you like someone who has been attacked by surprise,
like a warrior who is not able to save anyone?
But you are among us, LORD,
and we are called by your name
so don't leave us without help!

[10] This is what the LORD says about the people of Judah:
"They really love to wander from me;
they don't stop themselves from leaving me.
So now the LORD will not accept them.
He will now remember the evil they do
and will punish them for their sins."

[11] Then the LORD said, "Don't pray for good things to happen to the people of Judah.
[12] Even if they give up eating, I will not listen to their prayers. Even if they offer burnt offerings and grain offerings to me, I will not accept them. Instead, I will destroy the people of Judah with war, hunger, and terrible diseases."

[13] But I said, "Oh, Lord GOD, the prophets keep telling the people, 'You will not suffer from an enemy's sword or from hunger. I, the LORD, will give you peace in this land.' "

[14] Then the LORD said to me, "Those prophets are prophesying lies in my name. I did not send them or appoint them or speak to them. They have been prophesying false visions, idolatries, worthless magic, and their own wishful thinking.
[15] So this is what I say about the prophets who are prophesying in my name. I did not send them. They say, 'No enemy will attack this country with swords. There will never be hun-

ger in this land.' So those prophets will die from
hunger and from an enemy's sword. 16And the
people to whom the prophets speak will be
thrown into the streets of Jerusalem. There they
will die from hunger and from an enemy's
sword. And no one will be there to bury them,
or their wives, or their sons, or their daughters.
I will punish them.
17"Jeremiah, speak this message to the people of Judah:

'Let my eyes be filled with tears
night and day, without stopping.
My people have received a terrible
blow;
they have been hurt badly.
18 If I go into the country,
I see people killed by swords.
If I go into the city,
I see much sickness, because the people
have no food.
Both the priests and the prophets
have been taken to a foreign land.' "

19 LORD, have you completely rejected the
nation of Judah?
Do you hate Jerusalem?
Why have you hurt us so badly
that we cannot be made well again?
We hoped for peace,
but nothing good has come.
We looked for a time of healing,
but only terror came.
20 LORD, we admit that we are wicked
and that our ancestors did evil things.
We have sinned against you.
21 For your sake, do not hate us.
Do not take away the honor from your
glorious throne.
Remember your agreement with us,
and do not break it.
22 Do foreign idols have the power to bring
rain?
Does the sky itself have the power to
send down showers?
No, it is you, LORD our God.
You are our only hope,
because you are the one who made all
these things.

15
1Then the LORD said to me: "I would not feel
sorry for the people of Judah even if Moses
and Samuel prayed for them. Send them away
from me! Tell them to go! 2When they ask you,
'Where will we go?' tell them: 'This is what the
LORD says:

Those who are meant to die
will die.
Those who are meant to die in war
will die in war.
Those who are meant to die from hunger
will die from hunger.
Those who are meant to be taken captive
will be taken captive.'

3"I will send four kinds of destroyers against
them," says the LORD. "I will send war to kill,
dogs to drag the bodies away, and the birds
of the air and wild animals to eat and destroy
the bodies. 4I will make the people of Judah
hated by everyone on earth because of what
Manasseh did in Jerusalem. (Manasseh son of
Hezekiah was king of the nation of Judah.)

5 "Who will feel sorry for you, Jerusalem?
Who will be sad and cry for you?
Who will go out of his way to ask how
you are?
6 Jerusalem, you have left me," says the
LORD.
"You keep going farther and farther
away,
so I have taken hold of you and destroyed
you.
I was tired of holding back my anger.
7 I have separated the people of Judah with
my pitchfork
and scattered them at the city gates of
the land.
My people haven't changed their ways.
So I have destroyed them
and taken away their children.
8 There are more widows than grains of
sand in the sea.
I brought a destroyer at noontime
against the mothers of the young men
of Judah.
I suddenly brought pain and fear
on the people of Judah.

WHAT'S IT MEAN?

Of all the kings of Judah, Manasseh was the worst. We're talking about an unbelievably wicked guy, one who sacrificed his own son to the pagan god Molech. To seal his reputation as an enemy of God, it's likely that Manasseh executed the prophet Isaiah by having him sawn in half.

Jeremiah 15:4

9 When the enemy attacked, a woman with
seven sons felt faint because they
would all die.
She became weak and unable to breathe.
Her bright day became dark from sadness.
She felt shame and disgrace.
And everyone else left alive in Judah
I will hand over to the enemies, too!"
says the LORD.

JEREMIAH'S SECOND COMPLAINT

10 Mother, I am sorry that you gave birth to
me
since I must accuse and criticize the
whole land.
I have not loaned or borrowed anything,
but everyone curses me.
11 The LORD said,
"I have saved you for a good reason.
I have made your enemies beg you
in times of disaster and trouble.
12 No one can smash a piece of iron or
bronze
that comes from the north.
13 Your wealth and treasures
I will give to others free of charge,
because the people of Judah have sinned
throughout the country.
14 I will make you slaves to your enemies
in a land you have never known.
My anger is like a hot fire,
and it will burn against you."

15 LORD, you understand.
Remember me and take care of me.
Punish for me those who are hurting
me.
Don't destroy me while you remain
patient with them.
Think about the shame I suffer for you.
16 Your words came to me, and I listened
carefullyto them.
Your words made me very happy,
because I am called by your name,
LORD God All-Powerful.
17 I never sat with the crowd
as they laughed and had fun.
I sat by myself, because you were there,
and you filled me with anger at the evil
around me.
18 I don't understand why my pain has no
end.
I don't understand why my injury is not
cured or healed.
Will you be like a brook that goes dry?
Will you be like a spring that stops
flowing?

19 So this is what the LORD says:
"If you change your heart and return to
me, I will take you back.
Then you may serve me.
And if you speak things that have worth,
not useless words,
then you may speak for me.
Let the people of Judah turn to you,
but you must not change and be like
them.
20 I will make you as strong as a wall to this
people,
as strong as a wall of bronze.
They will fight against you,
but they will not defeat you,
because I am with you.
I will rescue you and save you," says the
LORD.
21 "I will save you from these wicked people
and rescue you from these cruel people."

THE DAY OF DISASTER

16
1 Then the LORD spoke his word to me:
2 "You must not get married or have sons or
daughters in this place."
3 The LORD says this about the sons and
daughters born in this land and their mothers
and fathers: 4 "They will die of terrible diseases,
and no one will cry for them or bury them.
Their bodies will lie on the ground like dung.
They will die in war, or they will starve to
death. Their bodies will be food for the birds of
the sky and for the wild animals."
5 So this is what the LORD says: "Jeremiah,
do not go into a house where there is a funeral
meal. Do not go there to cry for the dead or to
show your sorrow for them, because I have
taken back my blessing, my love, and my pity
from these people," says the LORD. 6 "Important

WHAT'S IT MEAN?

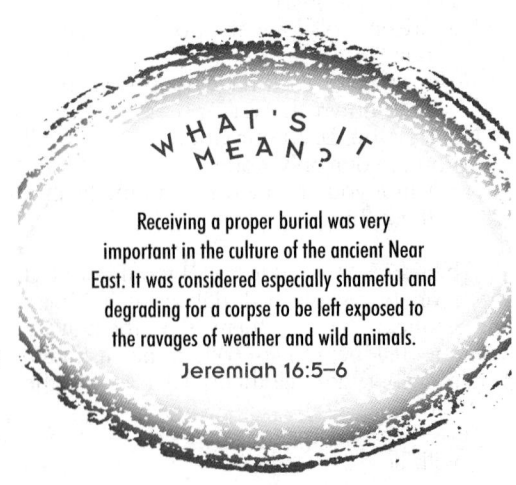

Receiving a proper burial was very important in the culture of the ancient Near East. It was considered especially shameful and degrading for a corpse to be left exposed to the ravages of weather and wild animals.

Jeremiah 16:5–6

people and common people will die in the land
of Judah. No one will bury them or cry for
them or cut himself or shave his head to show
sorrow for them. 7No one will bring food to
comfort those who are crying for the dead. No
one will offer a drink to comfort someone
whose mother or father has died.
8"Do not go into a house where the people
are having a feast to sit down to eat and drink,
9because this is what the LORD All-Powerful,
the God of Israel, says: I will soon stop the
sounds of joy and gladness and the happy
sounds of brides and bridegrooms in this
place. This will happen during your lifetime.
10"When you tell the people of Judah these
things, they will ask you, 'Why has the LORD
said these terrible things to us? What have we
done wrong? What sin have we done against
the LORD our God?'
11"Then say to them: 'This is because your
ancestors quit following me,' says the LORD.
'And they followed other gods and served and
worshiped them. Your ancestors left me and
quit obeying my teaching. 12But you have
done even more evil than your ancestors. You
are very stubborn and do only what you want
to do; you have not obeyed me. 13So I will
throw you out of this country and send you
into a land that you and your ancestors never
knew. There you can serve other gods day and
night, because I will not help you or show you
any favors.'

WHAT'S IT MEAN?

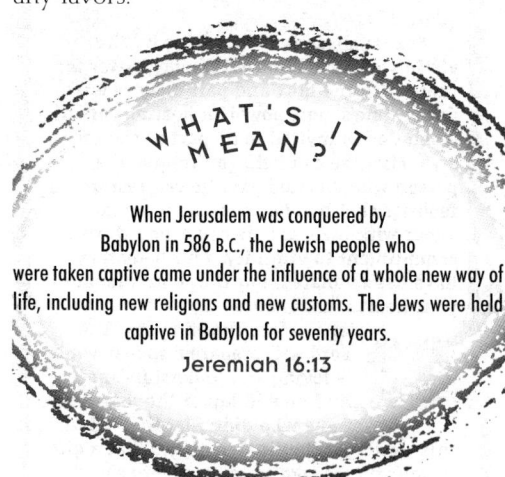

When Jerusalem was conquered by Babylon in 586 B.C., the Jewish people who were taken captive came under the influence of a whole new way of life, including new religions and new customs. The Jews were held captive in Babylon for seventy years.

Jeremiah 16:13

14"People say, 'As surely as the LORD lives,
who brought the people of Israel out of
Egypt . . .' But the time is coming," says the
LORD, "when people will not say this anymore.
15They will say instead, 'As surely as the LORD
lives, who brought the Israelites from the
northern land and from all the countries
where he had sent them . . .' And I will bring
them back to the land I gave to their ancestors.
16"I will soon send for many fishermen to
come to this land," says the LORD. "And they
will catch the people of Judah. After that, I will
send for many hunters to come to this land.
And they will hunt the people of Judah on
every mountain and hill and in the
cracks of the rocks. 17I see everything they do. They cannot
hide from me the things they
do; their sin is not hidden
from my eyes. 18I will pay back
the people of Judah twice for
every one of their sins, because
they have made my land unclean. They have
filled my country with their hateful idols."

SIN

Can we hide sin from God? (16:17)

19LORD, you are my strength and my
protection,
my safe place in times of trouble.
The nations will come to you from all
over the world
and say, "Our ancestors had only false
gods,
useless idols that didn't help them.
20Can people make gods for themselves?
They will not really be gods!"
21The LORD says, "So I will teach those who
make idols.
This time I will teach them
about my power and my strength.
Then they will know
that my name is the LORD.

JUDAH'S GUILTY HEART

17 1"The sin of the people of Judah is written
with an iron tool.
Their sins were cut with a hard point
into the stone that is their hearts.
Their sins were cut into the corners of
their altars.
2Even their children remember
their altars to idols and their Asherah
idols
beside the green trees
and on the high hills.
3My mountain in the open country
and your wealth and treasures
I will give away to other people.
I will give away the places of worship in
your country,
because you sinned by worshiping
there.
4You will lose the land I gave you,
and it is your own fault.
I will let your enemies take you as their
slaves

WHAT'S IT MEAN?

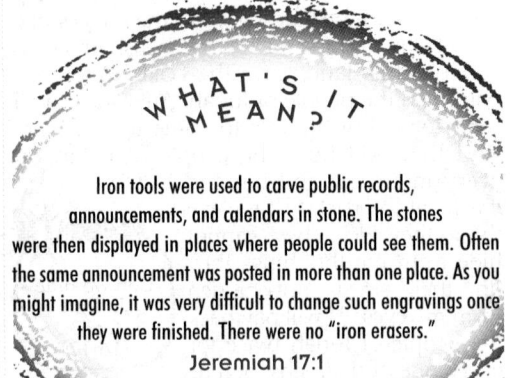

Iron tools were used to carve public records, announcements, and calendars in stone. The stones were then displayed in places where people could see them. Often the same announcement was posted in more than one place. As you might imagine, it was very difficult to change such engravings once they were finished. There were no "iron erasers."

Jeremiah 17:1

to a land you have never known.
This is because you have made my anger
burn like a hot fire,
and it will burn forever."

TRUSTING IN HUMANS OR GOD

5 This is what the LORD says:
"A curse is placed on those who trust
other people,
who depend on humans for strength,
who have stopped trusting the LORD.
6 They are like a bush in a desert
that grows in a land where no one lives,
a hot and dry land with bad soil.
They don't know about the good things
God can give.

7 "But the person who trusts in the LORD
will be blessed.
The LORD will show him that he can be
trusted.
8 He will be strong, like a tree planted near
water
that sends its roots by a stream.
It is not afraid when the days are hot;
its leaves are always green.
It does not worry in a year when no rain
comes;
it always produces fruit.
9 "More than anything else, a person's mind
is evil
and cannot be healed.
No one truly understands it.
10 But I, the LORD, look into a person's heart
and test the mind.
So I can decide what each one deserves;
I can give each one the right payment
for what he does."

11 Like a bird hatching an egg it did not lay,
so are the people who get rich by
cheating.
When their lives are half finished, they will
lose their riches.
At the end of their lives, it will be clear
they were fools.

12 From the beginning, our Temple has been
honored
as a glorious throne for God.
13 LORD, hope of Israel,
those who leave you will be shamed.
People who quit following the LORD will
be like a name written in the dust,
because they have left the LORD, the
spring of living water.

JEREMIAH'S THIRD COMPLAINT

14 LORD, heal me, and I will truly be healed.
Save me, and I will truly be saved.
You are the one I praise.

On the Edge

LORD, heal me, and I will truly be healed. Save me, and I will truly be saved. You are the one I praise (Jer. 17:14).

Sexual abuse is such a tragedy. The victims who are left behind may suffer for years with the hurt and pain they've endured. One's most powerful healing comes when God is invited to be part of the process. First, he can help you forgive the person who violated you. He can restore feelings that had become numb, replace anger with love, and he can even return a commitment to virginity. Your body may have been violated, but the commitment of your heart must endure—to wait on marriage before choosing sex. The Lord will prepare a spouse who is loving and understanding. And he will honor the marriage of one who didn't let the evil of this world get the final victory. What a gift to your future spouse to be able to say, "I may have been sexually abused, and I was powerless against it, but in every choice I've made, I have chosen to wait for you."

SEE FOR YOURSELF:
Ps. 40:1–3; 116:5–7; Is. 41:13; 57:18–19; Hos. 14:4

15The people of Judah keep asking me,
"Where is the word from the LORD?
Let's see that message come true!"

16LORD, I didn't run away from being the
shepherd you wanted.
I didn't want the terrible day to come.
You know everything I have said;
you see all that is happening.
17Don't be a terror to me.
I run to you for safety in times of
trouble.
18Make those who are hurting me be
ashamed,
but don't bring shame to me.
Let them be terrified,
but keep me from terror.
Bring the day of disaster on my enemies.
Destroy them, and destroy them again.

KEEPING THE SABBATH HOLY

19This is what the LORD said to me: "Go and
stand at the People's Gate of Jerusalem, where
the kings of Judah go in and out. And then go
to all the other gates of Jerusalem. 20Say to
them there: 'Hear the word of the LORD, kings
of Judah, all you people of Judah, and all who
live in Jerusalem, who come through these
gates into the city. 21This is what the LORD says:
Be careful not to carry a load on the Sabbath
day or bring it through the gates of Jerusalem.
22Don't take a load out of your houses on the
Sabbath or do any work on that day. But keep
the Sabbath as a holy day, as I commanded
your ancestors. 23But your ancestors did not
listen or pay attention to me. They were very
stubborn and did not listen. I punished them,
but it didn't do any good. 24But you must be
careful to obey me, says the LORD. You must
not bring a load through the gates of Jerusalem
on the Sabbath, but you must keep the Sabbath as a holy day and not do any work on
that day.
25" 'If you obey this command, kings who
sit on David's throne will come through the
gates of Jerusalem with their officers. They will
come riding in chariots and on horses, along
with the people of Judah and Jerusalem. And
the city of Jerusalem will have people living in
it forever. 26People will come to Jerusalem from
the villages around it, from the towns of Judah,
from the land of Benjamin, from the western
hills, from the mountains, and from southern
Judah. They will all bring to the Temple of the
LORD burnt offerings, sacrifices, grain offerings,
incense, and offerings to show thanks to God.
27But you must obey me and keep the Sabbath
day as a holy day. You must not carry any
loads into Jerusalem on the Sabbath. If you
don't obey me, I will start a fire at the gates of
Jerusalem, and it will burn until it burns even
the strong towers. And it will not be put out.' "

WHAT'S IT MEAN?

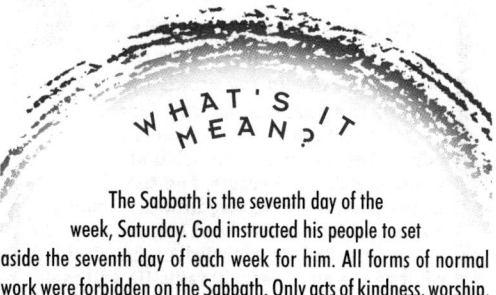

The Sabbath is the seventh day of the week, Saturday. God instructed his people to set aside the seventh day of each week for him. All forms of normal work were forbidden on the Sabbath. Only acts of kindness, worship, and emergency were allowed. Keeping one's Saturday schedule free from work was a way of showing submission to God. Refusing to observe the Sabbath was a way of showing rebellion against God.

Jeremiah 17:21–24

THE POTTER AND THE CLAY

18

1This is the word the LORD spoke to Jeremiah: 2"Go down to the potter's house, and I will
give you my message there." 3So I went down
to the potter's house and saw him working at
the potter's wheel. 4He was using his hands to
make a pot from clay, but something went
wrong with it. So he used that clay to make
another pot the way he wanted it to be.

WHAT'S IT MEAN?

A pottery wheel is a small round disk that the potter moves by turning a connected disk with his foot. While the wheel spins, the potter shapes a piece of clay sitting on the disk. Even the best potters find it hard to shape the clay precisely. Sometimes they have to start over again if the clay won't cooperate.

Jeremiah 18:3

5Then the LORD spoke his word to me:
6"Family of Israel, can't I do the same thing
with you?" says the LORD. "You are in my
hands like the clay in the potter's hands. 7There

On the Edge

"Family of Israel, can't I do the same thing with you?" says the Lord. "You are in my hands like the clay in the potter's hands" (Jer. 18:6).

You are like clay in the hands of the potter. The potter decides what shape he wants the clay to become, and then he molds and forms the clay into that shape. If he finds a flaw in the bowl he's making—he starts over. God, in his wisdom, has decided what shape our lives will take. He will mold us until we have become what he has envisioned. Did you know that you are just clay? Think about the job of clay—to rest in the potter's hands and to hold the shape he forms. If you sense that God is molding your life into one that pleases him, then do the job of clay—rest in his hands and trust him. The clay cannot argue with the potter. The potter's wisdom is greater and he ultimately decides on the shapes that please him. Trust God; he will lovingly mold you like a lump of clay. He will work out the flaws, and he may even start over, but the result will be pleasing to his eyes.

SEE FOR YOURSELF:
Is. 64:8;
Rom. 9:20–21

may come a time when I will speak about a nation or a kingdom that I will pull up by its roots or that I will pull down to destroy it.
8But if the people of that nation stop doing the evil they have done, I will change my mind and not carry out my plans to bring disaster to them.
9There may come another time when I will speak about a nation that I will build up and plant.
10But if I see it doing evil by not obeying me, I will change my mind and not carry out my plans to do good for them.

FUTURE
What's the future of someone who doesn't turn from sin? (18:11)

11"So, say this to the people of Judah and those who live in Jerusalem: 'This is what the Lord says: I am preparing disaster for you and making plans against you. So stop doing evil. Change your ways and do what is right.'
12But the people of Judah will answer, 'It won't do any good to try! We will continue to do what we want. Each of us will do what his stubborn, evil heart wants!' "

13So this is what the Lord says:
"Ask the people in other nations this
 question:
 'Have you ever heard anything like this?'
 The people of Israel have done a
 horrible thing.
14The snow on the mountains of Lebanon
 never melts from the rocks.
Its cool, flowing streams
 do not dry up.
15But my people have forgotten me.
 They burn incense to worthless idols
and have stumbled in what they do
 and in the old ways of their ancestors.
They walk along back roads
 and on poor highways.
16So Judah's country will become an empty
 desert.
 People will not stop making fun of it.
They will shake their heads as they pass
 by;
 they will be shocked at how the country
 was destroyed.
17Like a strong east wind,
 I will scatter them before their enemies.
At that awful time they will not see me
 coming to help them;
 they will see me leaving."

JEREMIAH'S FOURTH COMPLAINT

18Then the people said, "Come, let's make plans against Jeremiah. Surely the teaching of the law by the priest will not be lost. We will still have the advice from the wise men and the words of the prophets. So let's ruin him by telling lies about him. We won't pay attention to anything he says."

19Lord, listen to me.
 Listen to what my accusers are saying!
20Good should not be paid back with evil,
 but they have dug a pit in order to kill
 me.
Remember that I stood before you
 and asked you to do good things for
 these people
 and to turn your anger away from
 them.
21So now, let their children starve,
 and let their enemies kill them with
 swords.
Let their wives lose their children and
 husbands.
 Let the men from Judah be put to death
 and the young men be killed with
 swords in battle.

22 Let them cry out in their houses
when you bring an enemy against them
suddenly.
Let all this happen, because my enemies
have dug
a pit to capture me and have hidden
traps for my feet.
23 LORD, you know
about all their plans to kill me.
Don't forgive their crimes
or erase their sins from your mind.
Make them fall from their places;
punish them while you are angry.

JUDAH IS LIKE A BROKEN JAR

19
1 This is what the LORD said to me: "Go and
buy a clay jar from a potter. 2 Take some of the
older leaders of the people and the priests, and
go out to the Valley of Ben Hinnom, near the
front of the Potsherd Gate. There speak the
words I tell you. 3 Say, 'Kings of Judah and people of Jerusalem, listen to this message from
the LORD. This is what the LORD All-Powerful,
the God of Israel, says: I will soon bring a disaster on this place that will amaze and fright-
en everyone who hears about it. 4 The people of
Judah have quit following me. They have
made this a place for foreign gods. They have
burned sacrifices to other gods that neither
they, nor their ancestors, nor the kings of Judah had ever known before. They filled this
place with the blood of innocent people. 5 They
have built places on hilltops to worship Baal,
where they burn their children in the fire to
Baal. That is something I did not command or
speak about; it never even entered my mind.
6 Now people call this place the Valley of Ben
Hinnom or Topheth, but the days are coming,
says the LORD, when people will call it the Valley of Killing.
7 " 'At this place I will ruin the plans of the
people of Judah and Jerusalem. The enemy will
chase them, and I will have them killed with
swords. I will make their dead bodies food for
the birds and wild animals. 8 I will completely
destroy this city. People will make fun of it and
shake their heads when they pass by. They will
be shocked when they see how the city was
destroyed. 9 An enemy army will surround the
city and will not let anyone go out to get food.
I will make the people so hungry that they will
eat the bodies of their own sons and daughters, and then they will begin to eat each other.'
10 "While the people with you are watching,
break that jar. 11 Then say this: 'The LORD All-
Powerful says: I will break this nation and this
city just as someone breaks a clay jar that cannot be put back together again. The dead people will be buried here in Topheth, because
there is no other place for them. 12 This is what
I will do to these people and to this place, says
the LORD. I will make this city like Topheth.
13 The houses in Jerusalem and the king's palaces will become as unclean as this place, Topheth, because the people worshiped gods on
the roofs[n] of their houses. They worshiped the
stars and burned incense to honor them and
gave drink offerings to gods.' "
14 When Jeremiah left Topheth where the
LORD had sent him to prophesy, he went to the
LORD's Temple, stood in the courtyard, and
said to all the people: 15 "This is what the LORD
All-Powerful, the God of Israel, says: 'I will
soon bring disaster to Jerusalem and the villages around it, as I said I would. This will
happen because the people are very stubborn
and do not listen at all to what I say.' "

PASHHUR WILL BE CAPTURED

20
1 Pashhur son of Immer was a priest and
the highest officer in the Temple of the LORD.
When he heard Jeremiah prophesying in the
Temple courtyard, 2 he had Jeremiah the
prophet beaten. And he locked Jeremiah's
hands and feet between large blocks of
wood at the Upper Gate of Benjamin of the
LORD's Temple. 3 The next day when Pashhur
took Jeremiah out of the blocks of wood,
Jeremiah said to him, "The LORD's name for
you is not Pashhur. Now his name for you is
Terror on Every Side. 4 This is what the LORD
says: 'I will soon make you a terror to yourself and to all your friends. You will watch
enemies killing your friends with swords.
And I will give all the people of Judah to the
king of Babylon, who will take them away as
captives to Babylon and then will kill them
with swords. 5 I will give all the wealth of this
city to its enemies—its goods, its valuables,
and the treasures of the kings of Judah. The
enemies will carry all those valuables off to
Babylon. 6 And Pashhur, you and everyone in
your house will be taken captive. You will be
forced to go to Babylon, where you will die
and be buried, you and your friends to
whom you have prophesied lies.' "

19:13 roofs In Bible times houses were built with flat roofs. The roof was used for drying things such as flax and fruit. And it was used as an extra room, as a place for worship, and as a cool place to sleep in the summer.

JEREMIAH'S FIFTH COMPLAINT

7 LORD, you tricked me, and I was fooled.
You are stronger than I am, so you won.
I have become a joke;
everyone makes fun of me all day long.
8 Every time I speak, I shout.
I am always shouting about violence
and destruction.
I tell the people about the message I
received from the LORD,
but this only brings me insults.
The people make fun of me all day long.
9 Sometimes I say to myself,
"I will forget about the LORD.
I will not speak anymore in his name."
But then his message becomes like a
burning fire inside me,
deep within my bones.
I get tired of trying to hold it inside of me,
and finally, I cannot hold it in.
10 I hear many people whispering about me:
"Terror on every side!
Tell on him! Let's tell the rulers about
him."
My friends are all just waiting for me to
make some mistake.
They are saying,
"Maybe we can trick him
so we can defeat him
and pay him back."

11 But the LORD is with me like a strong
warrior,
so those who are chasing me will trip
and fall;
they will not defeat me.
They will be ashamed because they have
failed,
and their shame will never be forgotten.

12 LORD All-Powerful, you test good
people;
you look deeply into
the heart and mind of
a person.
I have told you my
arguments against
these people,
so let me see you give them
the punishment they deserve.

JUDGMENT
Does God judge motives? (20:12)

13 Sing to the LORD!
Praise the LORD!
He saves the life of the poor
from the power of the wicked.

JEREMIAH'S SIXTH COMPLAINT

14 Let there be a curse on the day I was
born;
let there be no blessing on the day when
my mother gave birth to me.
15 Let there be a curse on the man
who brought my father the news:

On the Edge

LORD All-Powerful, you test good people; you look deeply into the heart and mind of a person (Jer. 20:12a).

There is a huge difference between a test and a temptation! God will never *tempt* you with evil (see James 1:13). However, you will encounter testings from God. It works sort of like school. Just like a teacher, God will test you to help you see if you've truly learned what he's been teaching you.

You are sitting in class, and you find out your former best friend is going through a tough time. His dad has run off with his secretary, leaving your friend and his mom to fend for themselves. Now, the reason he is your former best friend is because you found out he was spreading some false rumors about you. What are you going to do?

(a) Rejoice under your breath, thinking he got what he deserved, while spreading the news about what his dad has done all around the school.

(b) Feel bad for him, but let him work through this all on his own.

(c) Look past your own hurts and see a friend who really needs somebody to encourage him through this situation with the Word of God, as well as with plenty of love and understanding.

If you answered "c," you passed the test! If your answer was "a" or "b," you are probably going to have to take the same test, or one just like it, over again before long.

Pass the test the first time, and you won't have to keep taking it. There's a big difference between knowing what to do and doing what you know! The difference is between passing or failing. Get in God's Word, find out what to do, and do the right thing. Pass the test!

SEE FOR YOURSELF: Ps. 7:9; 26:2; Jer. 17:10; James 1:12–15

"You have a son!"
This made my father very glad.
16 Let that man be like the towns
the LORD destroyed without pity.
Let him hear loud crying in the morning
and battle cries at noon,
17 because he did not kill me before I was born.
Then my mother would have been my grave;
she would have stayed pregnant forever.
18 Why did I have to come out of my mother's body?
All I have known is trouble and sorrow,
and my life will end in shame.

GOD REJECTS KING ZEDEKIAH'S REQUEST

21 1This is the word that the LORD spoke to
Jeremiah. It came when Zedekiah king of Judah
sent Pashhur son of Malkijah and the priest
Zephaniah son of Maaseiah to Jeremiah. 2They
said, "Ask the LORD for us what will happen,
because Nebuchadnezzar king of Babylon is
attacking us. Maybe the LORD will do miracles
for us as he did in the past so Nebuchadnezzar
will stop attacking us and leave."

WHAT'S IT MEAN?

Nebuchadnezzar was a hero to the Babylonians and an enemy to the Israelites. During his forty-year reign as king of Babylon, Nebuchadnezzar extended the borders of his country and collected heavy taxes from the people of Judah. When King Hezekiah of Judah started refusing to pay taxes, Nebuchadnezzar and his forces attacked Jerusalem and held the city in siege until 586 B.C., when the people of Judah finally surrendered. Nebuchadnezzar then destroyed the Temple and took many Jews back to Babylon as prisoners.

Jeremiah 21:2

3But Jeremiah answered them, "Tell King
Zedekiah this: 4'Here is what the LORD, the God
of Israel, says: You have weapons of war in
your hands to defend yourselves against the
king of Babylon and the Babylonians, who are
all around the city wall. But I will make those
weapons useless. Soon I will bring them into
the center of this city. 5In my anger, my very
great anger, I myself will fight against you with
my great power and strength. 6I will kill everything living in Jerusalem—both people and
animals. They will die from terrible diseases.
7Then, says the LORD, I'll hand over Zedekiah
king of Judah, his officers, and the people in
Jerusalem who do not die from the terrible diseases or battle or hunger, to Nebuchadnezzar
king of Babylon. I will let those win who want
to kill the people of Judah, so the people of
Judah and Jerusalem will be killed in war. Nebuchadnezzar will not show any mercy or pity
or feel sorry for them!'

8"Also tell this to the people of Jerusalem:
'This is what the LORD says: I will let you
choose to live or die. 9Anyone who stays in
Jerusalem will die in war or from hunger or
from a terrible disease. But anyone who goes
out of Jerusalem and surrenders to the Babylonians who are attacking you will live. Anyone
who leaves the city will save his life as if it were
a prize won in war. 10I have decided to make
trouble for this city and not to help it, says the
LORD. I will give it to the king of Babylon, and
he will burn it with fire.'

11"Say to Judah's royal family: 'Hear the
word of the LORD. 12Family of David, this is
what the LORD says:
You must judge people fairly every morning.
Save the person who has been robbed
from the power of his attacker.
If you don't, I will become very angry.
My anger will be like a fire that no one can put out,
because you have done evil things.

13 " 'Jerusalem, I am against you,
you who live on top of the mountain
over this valley, says the LORD.
You say, "No one can attack us
or come into our strong city."
14 But I will give you the punishment you deserve, says the LORD.
I will start a fire in your forests
that will burn up everything around you!' "

JUDGMENT AGAINST EVIL KINGS

22 1This is what the LORD says: "Go down to
the palace of the king of Judah and prophesy
this message there: 2'Hear the word of the
LORD, king of Judah, who rules from David's
throne. You and your officers, and your people
who come through these gates, listen! 3This is
what the LORD says: Do what is fair and right.
Save the one who has been robbed from the
power of his attacker. Don't mistreat or hurt
the foreigners, orphans, or widows. Don't kill

innocent people here. 4If you carefully obey
these commands, kings who sit on David's
throne will come through the gates of this palace with their officers and people, riding in
chariots and on horses. 5But if you don't obey
these commands, says the LORD, I swear by my
own name that this king's palace will become a
ruin.' "

6This is what the LORD says about the palace where the king of Judah lives:

"You are tall like the forests of Gilead,
like the mountaintops of Lebanon.
But I will truly make you into a desert,
into towns where no one lives.
7I will send men to destroy the palace,
each with his weapons.
They will cut up your strong, beautiful
cedar beams
and throw them into the fire.

8"People from many nations will pass by
this city and ask each other, 'Why has the
LORD done such a terrible thing to Jerusalem,
this great city?' 9And the answer will be: 'Because the people of Judah quit following the
agreement with the LORD their God. They worshiped and served other gods.' "

JUDGMENT AGAINST JEHOAHAZ

10Don't cry for the dead king or be sad
about him.
But cry painfully for the king who is
being taken away,
because he will never return
or see his homeland again.

11This is what the LORD says about Jehoahaz son of Josiah who became king of Judah
after his father died and who has left this place:
"He will never return. 12He will die where he has
been taken captive, and he will not see this land
again."

JUDGMENT AGAINST JEHOIAKIM

13"How terrible it will be for one who builds
his palace by doing evil,
who cheats people so he can build its
upper rooms.
He makes his own people work for
nothing
and does not pay them.
14He says, 'I will build a great palace for
myself
with large upper rooms.'
So he builds it with large windows
and uses cedar wood for the walls,
which he paints red.
15"Does having a lot of cedar in your house
make you a great king?
Your father was satisfied to have food and
drink.
He did what was right and fair,
so everything went well for him.
16He helped those who were poor and
needy,
so everything went well for him.
That is what it means to know God,"
says the LORD.
17"But you only look for and think about
what you can get dishonestly.
You are even willing to kill innocent
people to get it.
You feel free to hurt people and to steal
from them."

18So this is what the LORD says to Jehoiakim
son of Josiah king of Judah:

"The people of Judah will not cry when
Jehoiakim dies,
saying: 'Oh, my brother,' or 'Oh, my
sister.'
They will not cry for him, saying:
'Oh, master,' or 'Oh, my king.'
19They will bury him like a donkey,
dragging his body away
and throwing it outside the gates of
Jerusalem.

20"Judah, go up to Lebanon and cry out.
Let your voice be heard in Bashan.
Cry out from Abarim,
because all your friends are destroyed!
21Judah, when you were successful, I
warned you,
but you said, 'I won't listen.'
You have acted like this since you were
young;
you have not obeyed me.
22Like a storm, my punishment will blow all
your shepherds away
and send your friends into captivity.
Then you will really be ashamed and
disgraced
because of all the wicked things you did.
23King, you live in your palace,
cozy in your rooms of cedar.
But when your punishment comes, how
you will groan
like a woman giving birth to a baby!

JUDGMENT UPON JEHOIACHIN

24"As surely as I live," says the LORD, "Jehoiachin son of Jehoiakim king of Judah, even if
you were a signet ring on my right hand, I

WHAT'S IT MEAN?

Authority figures in the ancient Near East often wore rings with their name or their own personal symbol on them. The rings were designed so that the raised name or symbol would make an impression on a seal made of wet clay or soft wax. The seal was used to indicate that a document was official, that it had been authorized personally by the owner of the ring. Putting one's ring on a seal was similar to signing one's name today. Because of their importance, such rings were highly valued as symbols of power.

Jeremiah 22:24

would still pull you off. 25I will hand you over
to Nebuchadnezzar king of Babylon and to the
Babylonians—those people you fear because
they want to kill you. 26I will throw you and
your mother into another country. Neither of
you was born there, but both of you will die
there. 27They will want to come back, but they
will never be able to return."

28Jehoiachin is like a broken pot someone
threw away;
he is like something no one wants.
Why will Jehoiachin and his children be
thrown out
and sent into a foreign land?
29Land, land, land of Judah,
hear the word of the LORD!
30This is what the LORD says:
"Write this down in the record about
Jehoiachin:
He is a man without children,
a man who will not be
successful in his
lifetime.
And none of his
descendants will be
successful;
none will sit on the
throne of David
or rule in Judah."

"He will be a king who will rule in a wise way; he will do what is fair and right in the land." (Jeremiah 23:5b)

THE EVIL LEADERS OF JUDAH

23

1"How terrible it will be for the leaders
of Judah, who are scattering and destroying
my people," says the LORD.
2They are responsible for the people, so the
LORD, the God of Israel, says to them: "You
have scattered my people and forced them
away and not taken care of them. So I will
punish you for the evil things you have done,"
says the LORD. 3"I sent my people to other
countries, but I will gather those who are left
alive and bring them back to their own country. Then they will have many children and
grow in number. 4I will place new leaders over
my people, who will take care of them. And
my people will not be afraid or terrified again,
and none of them will be lost," says the LORD.

THE GOOD BRANCH WILL COME

5"The days are coming," says the LORD,
"when I will raise up a good branch in
David's family.
He will be a king who will rule in a wise
way;
he will do what is fair and right in the
land.
6In his time Judah will be saved,
and Israel will live in safety.
This will be his name:
The LORD Does What Is Right.

7"So the days are coming," says the LORD, "when
people will not say again: 'As surely as the LORD
lives, who brought Israel out of Egypt . . .' 8But
people will say something new: 'As surely as
the LORD lives, who brought the descendants
of Israel from the land of the north and from
all the countries where he had sent them
away . . .' Then the people of Israel will live in
their own land."

FALSE PROPHETS WILL BE PUNISHED

9A message to the prophets:
My heart is broken.
All my bones shake.
I'm like someone who is drunk,
like someone who has been overcome
with wine.
This is because of the LORD
and his holy words.
10The land of Judah is full of
people who are guilty
of adultery.
Because of this, the LORD
cursed the land.
It has become a very sad
place,
and the pastures have
dried up.
The people are evil
and use their power in the wrong way.

11"Both the prophets and the priests live as if
there were no God.

I have found them doing evil things
even in my own Temple," says the
LORD.
12 "So they will be in danger.
They will be forced into darkness
where they will be defeated.
I will bring disaster on them
in the year I punish them," says the
LORD.

13 "I saw the prophets of Samaria
do something wrong.
Those prophets prophesied by Baal
and led my people Israel away.
14 And I have seen the prophets of Jerusalem
do terrible things.
They are guilty of adultery
and live by lies.
They encourage evil people to keep on
doing evil,
so the people don't stop sinning.
All of those people are like the city of
Sodom.
The people of Jerusalem are like the city
of Gomorrah to me!"
15 So this is what the LORD All-Powerful says
about the prophets:
"I will make those prophets eat bitter food
and drink poisoned water,
because the prophets of Jerusalem spread
wickedness
through the whole country."
16 This is what the LORD All-Powerful says:
"Don't pay attention to what those
prophets are saying to you.
They are trying to fool
you.
They talk about visions
their own minds
made up,
not about visions from
me.

HOPE

Can our hope be misplaced? (23:16)

17 They say to those who hate me:
'The LORD says: You will have peace.'
They say to all those who are stubborn
and do as they please:
'Nothing bad will happen to you.'
18 But none of these prophets has stood in
the meeting of angels
to see or hear the message of the LORD.
None of them has paid close attention
to his message.
19 Look, the punishment from the LORD
will come like a storm.
His anger will be like a hurricane.
It will come swirling down on the heads
of those wicked people.
20 The LORD's anger will not stop
until he finishes what he plans to do.
When that day is over,
you will understand this clearly.
21 I did not send those prophets,
but they ran to tell their message.
I did not speak to them,
but they prophesied anyway.
22 But if they had stood in the meeting of
angels,
they would have told my message to
my people.
They would have turned the people from
their evil ways
and from doing evil.

23 "I am a God who is near," says the LORD.
"I am also a God who is far away."
24 "No one can hide
where I cannot see him," says the LORD.
"I fill all of heaven and earth," says the
LORD.
25 "I have heard the prophets who prophesy
lies in my name. They say, 'I have had a dream!
I have had a dream!' 26 How long will this continue in the minds of these lying prophets?
They prophesy from their own wishful thinking. 27 They are trying to make the people of
Judah forget me by telling each other these
dreams. In the same way, their ancestors forgot
me and worshiped Baal. 28 Is straw the same
thing as wheat?" says the LORD. "If a prophet
wants to tell about his dreams, let him! But let
the person who hears my message speak it
truthfully! 29 Isn't my message like a fire?" says
the LORD. "Isn't it like a hammer that smashes a
rock?
30 "So I am against the false prophets," says
the LORD. "They keep stealing words from each
other and say they are from me. 31 I am against
the false prophets," says the LORD. "They use
their own words and pretend it is a message
from me. 32 I am against the prophets who
prophesy false dreams," says the LORD. "They
mislead my people with their lies and false
teachings! I did not send them or command
them to do anything for me. They can't help
the people of Judah at all," says the LORD.

THE SAD MESSAGE FROM THE LORD

33 "Suppose the people of Judah, a prophet,
or a priest asks you: 'Jeremiah, what is the
message from the LORD?' You will answer them
and say, 'You are a heavy load to the LORD, and
I will throw you down, says the LORD.' 34 A
prophet or a priest or one of the people might
say, 'This is a message from the LORD.' That

person has lied, so I will punish him and his
whole family. 35This is what you will say to
each other: 'What did the LORD answer?' or
'What did the LORD say?' 36But you will never
again say, 'The message of the LORD,' because
the only message you speak is your own
words. You have changed the words of our
God, the living God, the LORD All-Powerful.
37This is how you should speak to the prophets: 'What answer did the LORD give you?' or
'What did the LORD say?' 38But don't say, 'The
message from the LORD.' If you use these
words, this is what the LORD says: Because you
called it a 'message from the LORD,' though I
told you not to use those words, 39I will pick
you up and throw you away from me, along
with Jerusalem, which I gave to your ancestors
and to you. 40And I will make a disgrace of you
forever; your shame will never be forgotten."

THE GOOD AND BAD FIGS

24
1Nebuchadnezzar king of Babylon captured
Jehoiachin son of Jehoiakim and king of Judah,
his officers, and all the craftsmen and metalworkers of Judah. He took them away from
Jerusalem and brought them to Babylon. It
was then that the LORD showed me two baskets of figs arranged in front of the Temple of
the LORD. 2One of the baskets had very good
figs in it, like figs that ripen early in the season.
But the other basket had figs too rotten to eat.
3The LORD said to me, "What do you see,
Jeremiah?"

I answered, "I see figs. The good figs are
very good, but the rotten figs are too rotten
to eat."

4Then the LORD spoke his word to me:
5"This is what the LORD, the God of Israel, says:
'I sent the people of Judah out of their country
to live in the country of Babylon. I think of
those people as good, like these good figs. 6I
will look after them and bring them back to the
land of Judah. I will not tear them down, but I
will build them up. I will not pull them up, but
I will plant them so they can grow. 7I will make
them want to know me, that I am the LORD.
They will be my people, and I will be their
God, because they will return to me with their
whole hearts.

8" 'But the bad figs are too rotten to eat.' So
this is what the LORD says: 'Zedekiah king of
Judah, his officers, and all the people from Jerusalem who are left alive, even those who live
in Egypt, will be like those rotten figs. 9I will
make those people hated as an evil people by
all the kingdoms of the earth. People will make
fun of them and tell jokes about them and
point fingers at them and curse them everywhere I scatter them. 10I will send war, hunger,
and disease against them. I will attack them
until they have all been killed. Then they will
no longer be in the land I gave to them and
their ancestors.' "

A SUMMARY OF JEREMIAH'S PREACHING

25
1This is the message that came to Jeremiah
concerning all the people of Judah. It came in
the fourth year that Jehoiakim son of Josiah
was king of Judah and the first year Nebuchadnezzar was king of Babylon. 2This is the
message Jeremiah the prophet spoke to all the
people of Judah and Jerusalem:

3The LORD has spoken his word to me again
and again for these past twenty-three years. I
have been a prophet since the thirteenth year
of Josiah son of Amon king of Judah. I have
spoken messages from the LORD to you from
that time until today, but you have not listened.

4The LORD has sent all his servants the
prophets to you over and over again, but you
have not listened or paid any attention to
them. 5Those prophets have said, "Stop your
evil ways. Stop doing what is wrong so you
can stay in the land that the LORD gave to you
and your ancestors to live in forever. 6Don't
follow other gods to serve them or to worship
them. Don't make me, the LORD, angry by worshiping idols that are the work of your own
hands, or I will punish you."

7"But you people of Judah did not listen to
me," says the LORD. "You made me angry by
worshiping idols that were the work of your
own hands, so I punished you."

8So this is what the LORD All-Powerful says:
"Since you have not listened to my messages, 9I
will send for all the peoples of the north," says
the LORD, "along with my servant Nebuchadnezzar king of Babylon. I will bring them all
against Judah, those who live there, and all
the nations around you, too. I will completely
destroy all those countries and leave them in
ruins forever. People will be shocked when
they see how badly I have destroyed those
countries. 10I will bring an end to the sounds of
joy and happiness, the sounds of brides and
bridegrooms, and the sound of people grinding meal. And I will take away the light of the
lamp. 11That whole area will be an empty
desert, and these nations will be slaves of the
king of Babylon for seventy years.

12"But when the seventy years have passed,
I will punish the king of Babylon and his entire
nation for their evil," says the LORD. "I will

make that land a desert forever. [13]I will make happen all the terrible things I said about Babylonia—everything Jeremiah prophesied about all those foreign nations, the warnings written in this book. [14]Even the Babylonians will have to serve many nations and many great kings. I will give them the punishment they deserve for all their own hands have done."

JUDGMENT ON THE NATIONS

[15]The LORD, the God of Israel, said this to me: "My anger is like the wine in a cup. Take it from my hand and make all the nations, to whom I am sending you, drink all of my anger from this cup. [16]They will drink my anger and stumble about and act like madmen because of the war I am going to send among them."

[17]So I took the cup from the LORD's hand and went to those nations and made them drink from it. [18]I served this wine to the people of Jerusalem and the towns of Judah, and the kings and officers of Judah, so they would become a ruin. Then people would be shocked and would insult them and speak evil of them. And so it has been to this day. [19]I also made these people drink of the LORD's anger: the king of Egypt, his servants, his officers, all his people, [20]and all the foreigners there; all the kings of the land of Uz; all the kings of the Philistines (the kings of the cities of Ashkelon, Gaza, Ekron, and the people left at Ashdod); [21]the people of Edom, Moab, and Ammon; [22]all the kings of Tyre and Sidon; all the kings of the coastal countries to the west; [23]the people of Dedan and Tema and Buz; all who cut their hair short; [24]all the kings of Arabia; and the kings of the people who live in the desert; [25]all the kings of Zimri, Elam, and Media; [26]and all the kings of the north, near and far, one after the other. I made all the kingdoms on earth drink from the cup of the LORD's anger, but the king of Babylon will drink from this cup after all the others.

[27]"Then say to them, 'This is what the LORD All-Powerful, the God of Israel, says: Drink this cup of my anger. Get drunk from it and vomit. Fall down and don't get up because of the war I am sending among you!'

[28]"If they refuse to take the cup from your hand and drink, say to them, 'The LORD All-Powerful says this: You must drink from this cup. [29]Look! I am already bringing disaster on Jerusalem, the city that is called by my name. Do you think you will not be punished? You will be punished! I am sending war on all the people of the earth, says the LORD All-Powerful.'

[30]"You, Jeremiah, will prophesy against them with all these words. Say to them:

'The LORD will roar from heaven
and will shout from his Holy Temple.
He will roar loudly against his land.
He will shout like people who walk on grapes to make wine;
he will shout against all who live on the earth.
[31]The noise will spread all over the earth,
because the LORD will accuse all the nations.
He will judge and tell what is wrong with all people,
and he will kill the evil people with a sword,' " says the LORD.

[32]This is what the LORD All-Powerful says:

"Disasters will soon spread
from nation to nation.
They will come like a powerful storm
from the faraway places on earth."

[33]At that time those killed by the LORD will reach from one end of the earth to the other. No one will cry for them or gather up their bodies and bury them. They will be left lying on the ground like dung.

[34]Cry, you leaders! Cry out loud!
Roll around in the dust, leaders of the people!
It is now time for you to be killed.
You will fall and be scattered,
like pieces of a broken jar.
[35]There will be no place for the leaders to hide;
they will not escape.
[36]I hear the sound of the leaders shouting.
I hear the leaders of the people crying loudly,
because the LORD is destroying their land.
[37]Those peaceful pastures will be like an empty desert,
because the LORD is very angry.
[38]Like a lion, he has left his den.
Their land has been destroyed
because of the terrible war he brought,
because of his fierce anger.

JEREMIAH'S LESSON AT THE TEMPLE

26

[1]This message came from the LORD soon after Jehoiakim son of Josiah became king of Judah. [2]This is what the LORD said: "Jeremiah, stand in the courtyard of the Temple of the LORD. Give this message to all the people of the towns of Judah who are coming to worship at the Temple of the LORD. Tell them everything I

tell you to say; don't leave out a word. 3 Maybe they will listen and stop their evil ways. If they will, I will change my mind about bringing on them the disaster that I am planning because of the evil they have done. 4 Say to them: 'This is what the LORD says: You must obey me and follow my teachings that I gave you. 5 You must listen to what my servants the prophets say to you. I have sent them to you again and again, but you did not listen. 6 If you don't obey me, I will destroy my Temple in Jerusalem as I destroyed my Holy Tent at Shiloh. When I do, people all over the world will curse Jerusalem.' "

WHAT'S IT MEAN?

In Jeremiah's day, Jerusalem was the official center of worship for the Jewish people. It hadn't always been, though. When Joshua first led the Israelites into the Promised Land, he set up the Ark of the Agreement and the Meeting Tent in the city of Shiloh. Years later, the Philistines destroyed Shiloh and left with the Ark of the Agreement. The Ark was later recovered and moved to Jerusalem, where King David established the new center of Jewish worship.

Jeremiah 26:6

7 The priests, the prophets, and all the people heard Jeremiah speaking these words in the Temple of the LORD. 8 When Jeremiah finished speaking everything the LORD had commanded him to say, the priests, prophets, and all the people grabbed Jeremiah. They said, "You must die! 9 How dare you prophesy in the name of the LORD that this Temple will be destroyed like the one at Shiloh! How dare you say that Jerusalem will become a desert without anyone to live in it!" And all the people crowded around Jeremiah in the Temple of the LORD.

10 Now when the officers of Judah heard about what was happening, they came out of the king's palace and went up to the Temple of the LORD and took their places at the entrance of the New Gate. 11 Then the priests and prophets said to the officers and all the other people, "Jeremiah should be killed. He prophesied against Jerusalem, and you heard him yourselves."

12 Then Jeremiah spoke these words to all the officers of Judah and all the other people: "The LORD sent me to say everything you have heard about this Temple and this city. 13 Now change your lives and start doing good and obey the LORD your God. Then he will change his mind and not bring on you the disaster he has told you about. 14 As for me, I am in your power. Do to me what you think is good and right. 15 But be sure of one thing. If you kill me, you will be guilty of killing an innocent person. You will make this city and everyone who lives in it guilty, too! The LORD truly sent me to you to give you this message."

16 Then the officers and all the people said to the priests and the prophets, "Jeremiah must not be killed. What he told us comes from the LORD our God."

17 Then some of the older leaders of Judah stood up and said to all the people, 18 "Micah, from the city of Moresheth, was a prophet during the time Hezekiah was king of Judah. Micah said to all the people of Judah, 'This is what the LORD All-Powerful says:

Jerusalem will be plowed like a field.
  It will become a pile of rocks,
  and the hill where the Temple stands
    will be covered with bushes.'

19 "Hezekiah king of Judah and the people of Judah did not kill Micah. You know that Hezekiah feared the LORD and tried to please the LORD. So the LORD changed his mind and did not bring on Judah the disaster he had promised. If we hurt Jeremiah, we will bring a terrible disaster on ourselves!"

20 (Now there was another man who prophesied in the name of the LORD. His name was Uriah son of Shemaiah from the city of Kiriath Jearim. He preached the same things against Jerusalem and the land of Judah that Jeremiah did. 21 When King Jehoiakim, all his army officers, and all the leaders of Judah heard Uriah preach, King Jehoiakim wanted to kill Uriah. But Uriah heard about it and was afraid. So he escaped to Egypt. 22 Then King Jehoiakim sent Elnathan son of Acbor and some other men to Egypt, 23 and they brought Uriah back from Egypt. Then they took him to King Jehoiakim, who had Uriah killed with a sword. His body was thrown into the burial place where poor people are buried.)

24 Ahikam son of Shaphan supported Jeremiah. So Ahikam did not hand Jeremiah over to be killed by the people.

FRIENDSHIP

Can standing up for a friend make a difference? (26:24)

NEBUCHADNEZZAR IS MADE RULER

27 1The LORD spoke his word to Jeremiah soon
after Zedekiah son of Josiah was made king of
Judah. 2This is what the LORD said to me:
"Make a yoke out of straps and poles, and put
it on the back of your neck. 3Then send messages to the kings of Edom, Moab, Ammon,
Tyre, and Sidon by their messengers who have
come to Jerusalem to see Zedekiah king of Judah. 4Tell them to give this message to their
masters: 'The LORD All-Powerful, the God of
Israel, says: "Tell your masters: 5I made the
earth, its people, and all its animals with my
great power and strength. I can give the earth
to anyone I want. 6Now I have given all these
lands to Nebuchadnezzar king of Babylon, my
servant. I will make even the wild animals
obey him. 7All nations will serve Nebuchadnezzar and his son and grandson. Then the
time will come for Babylon to be defeated, and
many nations and great kings will make Babylon their servant.

8" ' "But if some nations or kingdoms refuse
to serve Nebuchadnezzar king of Babylon and
refuse to be under his control, I will punish
them with war, hunger, and terrible diseases,
says the LORD. I will use Nebuchadnezzar to
destroy them. 9So don't listen to your false
prophets, those who use magic to tell the future, those who explain dreams, the mediums,
or magicians. They all tell you, 'You will not be
slaves to the king of Babylon.' 10They are telling
you lies that will cause you to be taken far
from your homeland. I will force you to leave
your homes, and you will die in another land.
11But the nations who put themselves under
the control of the king of Babylon and serve
him I will let stay in their own country, says
the LORD. The people from those nations will
live in their own land and farm it." ' "

12I gave the same message to Zedekiah king
of Judah. I said, "Put yourself under the control
of the king of Babylon and serve him, and you
will live. 13Why should you and your people
die from war, hunger, or disease, as the LORD
said would happen to those who do not serve
the king of Babylon? 14But the false prophets
are saying, 'You will never be slaves to the king
of Babylon.' Don't listen to them because they
are prophesying lies to you! 15'I did not send
them,' says the LORD. 'They are prophesying lies
and saying the message is from me. So I will
send you away, Judah. And you and those
prophets who prophesy to you will die.' "

16Then I, Jeremiah, said to the priests and all
the people, "This is what the LORD says: Those
false prophets are saying, 'The Babylonians
will soon return what they took from the Temple of the LORD.' Don't listen to them! They are
prophesying lies to you. 17Don't listen to those
prophets. But serve the king of Babylon, and
you will live. There is no reason for you to
cause Jerusalem to become a ruin. 18If they are
prophets and have the message from the LORD,
let them pray to the LORD All-Powerful. Let
them ask that the items which are still in the
Temple of the LORD and in the king's palace
and in Jerusalem not be taken away to Babylon.

WHAT'S IT MEAN?

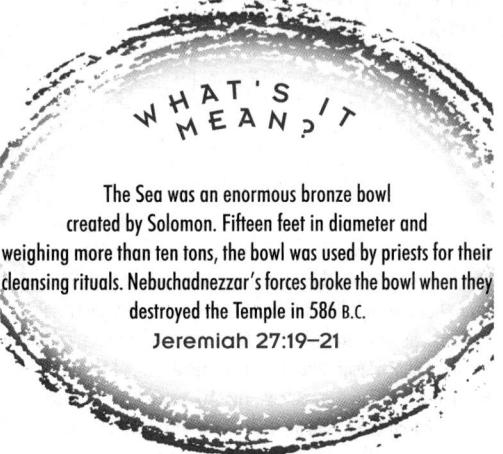

The Sea was an enormous bronze bowl created by Solomon. Fifteen feet in diameter and weighing more than ten tons, the bowl was used by priests for their cleansing rituals. Nebuchadnezzar's forces broke the bowl when they destroyed the Temple in 586 B.C.

Jeremiah 27:19–21

19"This is what the LORD All-Powerful says
about those items left in Jerusalem: the pillars,
the large bronze bowl, which is called the Sea,
the stands that can be moved, and other
things. 20Nebuchadnezzar king of Babylon did
not take these away when he took as captives
Jehoiachin son of Jehoiakim king of Judah and
all the other important people from Judah and
Jerusalem to Babylon. 21This is what the LORD
All-Powerful, the God of Israel, says about the
items left in the Temple of the LORD and in the
king's palace and in Jerusalem: 22'All of them
will also be taken to Babylon. And they will
stay there until the day I go to get them,' says
the LORD. 'Then I will bring them back and return them to this place.' "

THE FALSE PROPHET HANANIAH

28 1It was in that same year, in the fifth month
of Zedekiah's fourth year as king of Judah,
soon after he began to rule. The prophet Hananiah son of Azzur, from the town of Gibeon,
spoke to me in the Temple of the LORD in front
of the priests and all the people. He said: 2"The
LORD All-Powerful, the God of Israel, says: 'I
have broken the yoke the king of Babylon has
put on Judah. 3Before two years are over, I will

bring back everything that Nebuchadnezzar
king of Babylon took to Babylon from the
LORD's Temple. 4I will also bring back Jehoiachin son of Jehoiakim king of Judah and all the
other captives from Judah who went to Babylon,' says the LORD. 'So I will break the yoke
the king of Babylon put on Judah.' "
5Then the prophet Jeremiah spoke to the
prophet Hananiah in front of the priests and
all the people who were standing in the Temple
of the LORD. 6He said, "Amen! Let the LORD
really do that! May the LORD make the message
you prophesy come true. May he bring back
here everything from the LORD's Temple and all
the people who were taken as captives to Babylon.
7"But listen to what I am going to say to you
and all the people. 8There were prophets long
before we became prophets, Hananiah. They
prophesied that war, hunger, and terrible diseases would come to many countries and great
kingdoms. 9But if a prophet prophesies that we
will have peace and that message comes true,
he can be recognized as one truly sent by the
LORD."
10Then the prophet Hananiah took the yoke
off Jeremiah's neck and broke it. 11Hananiah
said in front of all the people, "This is what the
LORD says: 'In the same way I will break the
yoke of Nebuchadnezzar king of Babylon. He
put that yoke on all the nations of the world,
but I will break it before two years are over.' "
After Hananiah had said that, Jeremiah left the
Temple.
12The LORD spoke his word to Jeremiah after the prophet Hananiah had broken the yoke
off of the prophet Jeremiah's neck. 13The LORD
said, "Go and tell Hananiah, 'This is what the
LORD says: You have broken a wooden yoke,
but I will make a yoke of iron in its place! 14The
LORD All-Powerful, the God of Israel, says: I
will put a yoke of iron on the necks of all these
nations to make them serve Nebuchadnezzar
king of Babylon, and they will be slaves to him.
I will even give Nebuchadnezzar control over
the wild animals.' "
15Then the prophet Jeremiah said to the
prophet Hananiah, "Listen, Hananiah! The
LORD did not send you, and you have made
the people of Judah trust in lies. 16So this is
what the LORD says: 'Soon I will remove you
from the earth. You will die this year, because
you taught the people to turn against the
LORD.' "
17Hananiah died in the seventh month of
that same year.

A LETTER TO THE CAPTIVES IN BABYLON

29 1This is the letter that Jeremiah the prophet
sent from Jerusalem to the older leaders who
were among the captives, the priests, and the
prophets. He sent it to all the other people
Nebuchadnezzar had taken as captives from
Jerusalem to Babylon. 2(This letter was sent after all these people were taken away: Jehoiachin the king and the queen mother; the
officers and leaders of Judah and Jerusalem;
and the craftsmen and metalworkers from Jerusalem.) 3Zedekiah king of Judah sent Elasah
son of Shaphan and Gemariah son of Hilkiah
to Babylon to Nebuchadnezzar king of Babylon. So Jeremiah gave them this letter to carry
to Babylon:
4This is what the LORD All-Powerful, the
God of Israel, says to all those people I sent
away from Jerusalem as captives to Babylon:
5"Build houses and settle in the land. Plant gardens and eat the food they grow. 6Get married
and have sons and daughters. Find wives for
your sons, and let your daughters be married
so they also may have sons and
daughters. Have many children
in Babylon; don't become
fewer in number. 7Also do
good things for the city where
I sent you as captives. Pray to
the LORD for the city where
you are living, because if good
things happen in the city,
good things will happen to you
also." 8The LORD All-Powerful, the God of Israel, says: "Don't let the prophets among you
and the people who do magic fool you. Don't
listen to their dreams. 9They are prophesying
lies to you, saying that their message is from

WHAT'S IT MEAN?

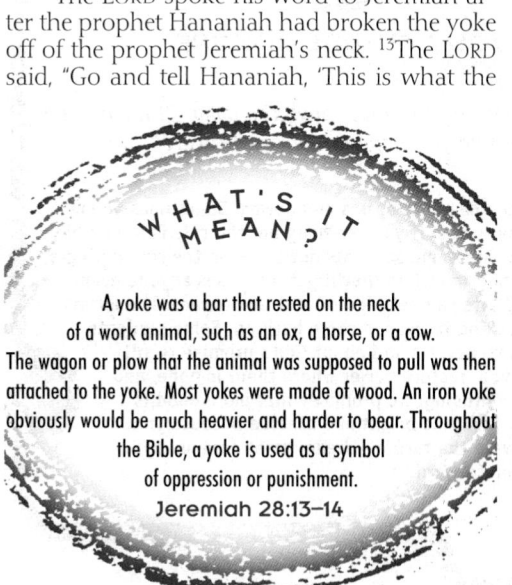

A yoke was a bar that rested on the neck of a work animal, such as an ox, a horse, or a cow. The wagon or plow that the animal was supposed to pull was then attached to the yoke. Most yokes were made of wood. An iron yoke obviously would be much heavier and harder to bear. Throughout the Bible, a yoke is used as a symbol of oppression or punishment.

Jeremiah 28:13–14

PRAYER

Why should I pray for people or places I don't like? (29:7)

me. But I did not send them," says the LORD.
10This is what the LORD says: "Babylon will
be powerful for seventy years. After that time I
will come to you, and I will keep my promise
to bring you back to Jerusalem. 11I say this because I know what I am planning for you,"
says the LORD. "I have good plans for you, not
plans to hurt you. I will give you hope and a
good future. 12Then you will call my name.
You will come to me and pray to me, and I will
listen to you. 13You will search for me. And
when you search for me with all your heart,
you will find me! 14I will let you find me," says
the LORD. "And I will bring you back from your
captivity. I forced you to leave this place, but I
will gather you from all the nations, from the
places I have sent you as captives," says the
LORD. "And I will bring you back to this place."
15You might say, "The LORD has given us
prophets here in Babylon."
16But the LORD says this about the king who
is sitting on David's throne now and all the
other people still in Jerusalem, your relatives
who did not go as captives to Babylon with
you. 17The LORD All-Powerful says: "I will soon
send war, hunger, and terrible diseases against
those still in Jerusalem. I will make them like
bad figs that are too rotten to eat. 18I will chase
them with war, hunger, and terrible diseases. I
will make them hated by all the kingdoms of
the earth. People will curse them and be
shocked and will use them as a shameful example wherever I make them go. 19This is because they have not listened to my message,"
says the LORD. "I sent my message to them
again and again through my servants, the
prophets, but they did not listen," says the
LORD.
20You captives, whom I forced to leave Jerusalem and go to Babylon, listen to the message
from the LORD. 21The LORD All-Powerful, the
God of Israel, says this about Ahab son of Kolaiah and Zedekiah son of Maaseiah: "These
two men have been prophesying lies to you,
saying that their message is from me. But soon
I will hand over those two prophets to Nebuchadnezzar king of Babylon, and he will kill
them in front of you. 22Because of them, all the
captives from Judah in Babylon will use this
curse: 'May the LORD treat you like Zedekiah
and Ahab, whom the king of Babylon burned
in the fire.' 23They have done evil things among
the people of Israel. They are guilty of adultery
with their neighbors' wives. They have also
spoken lies and said those lies were a message
from me. I did not tell them to do that. I know
what they have done; I am a witness to it," says
the LORD.
24Also give a message to Shemaiah from the
Nehelamite family. 25The LORD All-Powerful,
the God of Israel, says: "Shemaiah, you sent
letters in your name to all the people in Jerusa-

Promise HE PROMISES YOU A FUTURE OF HOPE.

"I say this because I know what I am planning for you," says the LORD. "I have good plans for you, not plans to hurt you. I will give you hope and a good future" (Jer. 29:11).

A student's life can feel like a roller-coaster ride—lots of ups and downs. Sometimes you're upside down in a tunnel, wondering which way is out. If you can hang on, the ride is incredible and is a time you'll look back on and smile at. But some students get stuck on the ride during a power failure. They're sitting in the tunnel wondering when they'll get out. Does anyone even know they're there? When will this ride be over? Life can get kind of dark sometimes. The downs seem to hang around too long, and the power is taking forever to come back on. Some students lose their hope in these scary places. Maybe they've never heard about God's promise to fill their future with hope. He promises to ride with you, restore power where there is none, and return order when things seem upside down and confusing. He promises that more good is ahead of you. There is everything to live for. Your future is bright and blessed because you belong to him. Stand on his promise and look toward the future—dream great dreams, and hope against the odds. You have everything to look forward to.

SEE FOR YOURSELF:

Prov. 23:17–18; 2 Thess. 2:16–17; 1 Tim. 1:1; 1 Pet. 1:3

lem, to the priest Zephaniah son of Maaseiah,
and to all the priests. 26You said to Zephaniah,
'The LORD has made you priest in place of Jehoiada. You are to be in charge of the Temple
of the LORD. You should arrest any madman
who acts like a prophet. Lock his hands and
feet between wooden blocks, and put iron
rings around his neck. 27Now Jeremiah from
Anathoth is acting like a prophet. So why
haven't you arrested him? 28Jeremiah has sent
this message to us in Babylon: You will be
there for a long time, so build houses and settle
down. Plant gardens and eat what they grow.' "
29Zephaniah the priest read the letter to Jeremiah the prophet. 30Then the LORD spoke his
word to Jeremiah: 31"Send this message to all
the captives in Babylon: 'This is
what the LORD says about Shemaiah the Nehelamite: Shemaiah has prophesied to
you, but I did not send him.
He has made you believe a
lie. 32So the LORD says, I will
soon punish Shemaiah the
Nehelamite and his family.
He will not see the good
things I will do for my people,
says the LORD. None of his family
will be left alive among the people, because
he has taught the people to turn against me.' "

"They will serve the LORD their God and David their king, whom I will send to them." (Jeremiah 30:9)

PROMISES OF HOPE

30 1These are the words that the LORD spoke to
Jeremiah. 2The LORD, the God of Israel, said:
"Jeremiah, write in a book all the words I have
spoken to you. 3The days will come when I
will bring Israel and Judah back from captivity," says the LORD. "I will return them to the
land I gave their ancestors, and they will own
it!" says the LORD.
4The LORD spoke this message about the
people of Israel and Judah: 5This is what the
LORD said:

"We hear people crying from fear.
They are afraid; there is no peace.
6Ask this question, and consider it:
A man cannot have a baby.
So why do I see every strong man
holding his stomach in pain like a
woman having a baby?
Why is everyone's face turning white
like a dead man's face?
7This will be a terrible day!
There will never be
another time like this.
This is a time of great
trouble for the people
of Jacob,
but they will be saved
from it."

8The LORD All-Powerful
says, "At that time
I will break the yoke
from their necks
and tear off the ropes that
hold them.
Foreign people will never again make
my people slaves.
9They will serve the LORD their God
and David their king,
whom I will send to them.

10"So people of Jacob, my servants, don't be
afraid.
Israel, don't be frightened," says the
LORD.
"I will soon save you from that faraway
place where you are captives.
I will save your family from that land.
The people of Jacob will be safe and have
peace again;
there will be no enemy to frighten them.
11I am with you and will save you,"
says the LORD.
"I will completely destroy all those nations
where I scattered you,
but I will not completely destroy you.
I will punish you fairly,
but I will still punish you."
12This is what the LORD said:
"You people have a wound that cannot be
cured;
your injury will not heal.

WHAT'S IT MEAN?

Before books were created in the second or third century A.D., documents were written on an early form of paper called papyrus or on pieces of smooth, thin leather. The pieces were then glued or sewn together to make a scroll. Most ancient scrolls were about eight inches wide and about fifteen to twenty feet long. Some were as long as thirty-five feet. To read a scroll, a person held it with one hand and unrolled it with the other.

Jeremiah 30:1–2

13 There is no one to argue your case
and no cure for your sores.
So you will not be healed.
14 All those nations who were your friends
have forgotten you.
They don't care about you.
I have hurt you as an enemy would.
I punished you very hard,
because your guilt was so great
and your sins were so many.
15 Why are you crying out about your
injury?
There is no cure for your pain.
I did these things to you because of your
great guilt,
because of your many sins.
16 But all those nations that destroyed you
will now be destroyed.
All your enemies will become captives
in other lands.
Those who stole from you will have their
own things stolen.
Those who took things from you in war
will have their own things taken.
17 I will bring back your health
and heal your injuries," says the LORD,
"because other people forced you away.
They said about you, 'No one cares
about Jerusalem!' "
18 This is what the LORD said:
"I will soon make the tents of Jacob's
people as they used to be,
and I will have pity on Israel's houses.
The city will be rebuilt on its hill of ruins,
and the king's palace will stand in its
proper place.
19 People in those places will sing songs of
praise.
There will be the sound of laughter.

WHAT'S IT MEAN?

The people of Judah were held captive by the Babylonians for seventy years. Their captivity ended when Babylon was conquered by Persia. Cyrus, the king of Persia, allowed the Jewish people to return to their homeland and rebuild their Temple.

Jeremiah 30:18

I will give them many children
so their number will not be small.
I will bring honor to them
so no one will look down on them.
20 Their descendants will be as they were in
the old days.
I will set them up as a strong people
before me,
and I will punish the nations who have
hurt them.
21 One of their own people will lead them;
their ruler will come from among them.
He will come near to me when I invite
him.
Who would dare to come to me
uninvited?" says the LORD.
22 "So you will be my people,
and I will be your God."

23 Look! It is a storm from the LORD!
He is angry and has gone out to punish
the people.
Punishment will come like a storm
crashing down on the evil people.
24 The LORD will stay angry
until he finishes punishing the people.
He will stay angry
until he finishes the punishment he
planned.
When that day comes,
you will understand this.

THE NEW ISRAEL

31 1 The LORD says, "At that time I will be God
of all Israel's family groups, and they will be
my people."
2 This is what the LORD says:
"The people who were not killed by the
enemy's sword
found help in the desert.
I came to give rest to Israel."
3 And from far away the LORD appeared to
his people and said,
"I love you people
with a love that will last
forever.
That is why I have
continued
showing you kindness.
4 People of Israel, I will
build you up again,
and you will be rebuilt.
You will pick up your tambourines again
and dance with those who are joyful.
5 You will plant vineyards again
on the hills around Samaria.
The farmers will plant them

FUTURE

Is the future of Christians bright? (31:3–6)

and enjoy their fruit.
6 There will be a time when watchmen in
the mountains of Ephraim shout this
message:
'Come, let's go up to Jerusalem to
worship the LORD our God!' "

7 This is what the LORD says:
"Be happy and sing for the people of
Jacob.
Shout for Israel, the greatest of the
nations.
Sing your praises and shout this:
'LORD, save your people,
those who are left alive from the nation
of Israel!'
8 Look, I will soon bring Israel from the
country in the north,
and I will gather them from the faraway
places on earth.
Some of the people are blind and crippled.
Some of the women are pregnant, and
some are ready to give birth.
A great many people will come back.
9 They will be crying as they come,
but they will pray as I bring them back.
I will lead those people by streams of
water
on an even road where they will not
stumble.
I am Israel's father,
and Israel is my firstborn son.

10 "Nations, listen to the message from the
LORD.
Tell this message in the faraway lands
by the sea:
'The one who scattered the people of Israel
will bring them back,
and he will watch over his people like a
shepherd.'
11 The LORD will pay for the people of Jacob
and will buy them back from people
stronger than they were.
12 The people of Israel will come to the high
points of Jerusalem
and shout for joy.
Their faces will shine with happiness
about all the good things from the
LORD:
the grain, new wine, oil, young sheep,
and young cows.
They will be like a garden that has plenty
of water,
and they will not be troubled anymore.
13 Then young women of Israel will be
happy and dance,
the young men and old men also.
I will change their sadness into
happiness;

Promise

HE PROMISES TO TURN YOUR SORROW INTO JOY.

Then young women of Israel will be happy and dance, the young men and old men also. I will change their sadness into happiness; I will give them comfort and joy instead of sadness (Jer. 31:13).

God can use things that seem bad to make you glad. You may think you're doomed, but later find out that God had a good purpose in the situation. Think about how you feel when you and your dad have a disagreement and then you finally straighten things out. Or when you're about to fail algebra, but you work really hard and pull your grade up to a B. You feel relieved and happy when a bad situation comes to an end.

Sometimes there are habits or friendships you have to let go of because you know that God doesn't approve. That can be tough. But there's satisfaction you get from obedience that replaces that sad feeling after a while. God is on your side! He's for you! He wants to see you joyful, healthy, and strong. He cares about you even more than you do! He is God, and he can do anything. He's especially good at turning your hardest times into your greatest blessings.

Look at what he did for Joseph: Joseph's brothers sold him into slavery and thought he'd probably live a miserably hard life. Instead, God made him a strong and successful leader. His brothers even bowed down to him! What they had meant for bad, God meant for good (see Gen. 37—50). Hard times will come. Hang in there with God and watch what he will do!

SEE FOR YOURSELF:

Gen. 50:20; Ps. 30:11–12; Is. 61:3

I will give them comfort and joy instead of sadness.
14 The priests will have more than enough sacrifices,
and my people will be filled with the good things I give them!" says the LORD.
15 This is what the LORD says:
"A voice was heard in Ramah
of painful crying and deep sadness:
Rachel crying for her children.
She refused to be comforted,
because her children are dead!"
16 But this is what the LORD says:
"Stop crying;
don't let your eyes fill with tears.
You will be rewarded for your work!" says the LORD.
"The people will return from their enemy's land.
17 So there is hope for you in the future," says the LORD.
"Your children will return to their own land.

18 "I have heard Israel moaning:
'LORD, you punished me, and I have learned my lesson.
I was like a calf that had never been trained.
Take me back so that I may come back.
You truly are the LORD my God.
19 LORD, after I wandered away from you,
I changed my heart and life.
After I understood,
I beat my breast with sorrow.
I was ashamed and disgraced,
because I suffered for the foolish things I did when I was young.'

20 "You know that Israel is my dear son,
The child I love.
Yes, I often speak against Israel,
but I still remember him.
I love him very much,
and I want to comfort him," says the LORD.

21 "People of Israel, fix the road signs.
Put up signs to show you the way home.
Watch the road.
Pay attention to the road on which you travel.
People of Israel, come home,
come back to your towns.
22 You are an unfaithful daughter.
How long will you wander before you come home?
The LORD has made something new happen in the land:
A woman will go seeking a man."
23 The LORD All-Powerful, the God of Israel,
says: "I will again do good things for the people of Judah. At that time the people in the land
of Judah and its towns will again use these
words: 'May the LORD bless you, home of what
is good, holy mountain.' 24 People in all the
towns of Judah will live together in peace.
Farmers and those who move around with
their flocks will live together in peace. 25 I will
give rest and strength to those who are weak
and tired."
26 After hearing that, I, Jeremiah, woke up
and looked around. My sleep had been very
pleasant.
27 The LORD says, "The time is coming when
I will help the families of Israel and Judah and
their children and animals to grow. 28 In the
past I watched over Israel and Judah, to pull
them up and tear them down, to destroy them
and bring them disaster. But now I will watch
over them to build them up and make them
strong," says the LORD.
29 "At that time people will no longer say:
'The parents have eaten sour grapes,
and that caused the children to grind their teeth from the sour taste.'
30 Instead, each person will die for his own sin;
the person who eats sour grapes will grind his
own teeth.

THE NEW AGREEMENT

31 "Look, the time is coming," says the LORD,
"when I will make a new agreement
with the people of Israel
and the people of Judah.
32 It will not be like the agreement
I made with their ancestors
when I took them by the hand
to bring them out of Egypt.
I was a husband to them,
but they broke that agreement," says the LORD.
33 "This is the agreement I will make
with the people of Israel at that time," says the LORD:
"I will put my teachings in their minds
and write them on their hearts.
I will be their God,
and they will be my people.
34 People will no longer have to teach their neighbors and relatives
to know the LORD,

On the Edge

"This is the agreement I will make with the people of Israel at that time," says the Lord: "I will put my teachings in their minds and write them on their hearts. I will be their God, and they will be my people" (Jer. 31:33).

God made an Agreement with the people of Israel after he miraculously rescued them from slavery in Egypt. Under the Agreement, they had to perform a lot of rituals and make sacrifices in order to please him. God said that he would bless them as long as they obeyed the laws he had given them. But they couldn't do it. They were constantly breaking their Agreement with God.

God spoke to Jeremiah and asked him to tell the Jewish people that he (God) was going to make a new agreement with them. That new agreement was put in place when Jesus died on the cross as a one-time perfect sacrifice for everybody's sins. But this time the agreement wasn't just for Jews. Jesus specifically gave the apostle Paul the job of telling Gentiles, or non-Jews, about him (see Acts 9:15). So whether you're Jewish or not, God's new agreement with his people is for you, too.

"I will put my teachings in their minds and write them on their hearts." That's part of God's new agreement. This time, it has nothing to do with sacrifices or rituals. Instead, you just have to get your heart right with Jesus. Trust Jesus and obey him with all of your heart.

SEE FOR YOURSELF:
Matt. 26:26–28;
Heb. 8:10; 12:24

because all people will know me,
from the least to the most important,"
says the LORD.
"I will forgive them for the wicked things
they did,
and I will not remember their sins
anymore."

THE LORD WILL NEVER LEAVE ISRAEL

35 The LORD makes the sun shine in the day
and the moon and stars to shine at
night.
He stirs up the sea so that its waves crash
on the shore.
The LORD All-Powerful is his name.
This is what the LORD says:
36 "Only if these laws should ever fail,"
says the LORD,
"will Israel's descendants ever stop
being a nation before me."
37 This is what the LORD says:
"Only if people can measure the sky above
and learn the secrets of the earth below,
will I reject all the descendants of Israel
because of what they have done," says
the LORD.

THE NEW JERUSALEM

38 The LORD says, "The time is coming when
Jerusalem will be rebuilt for me—everything
from the Tower of Hananel to the Corner Gate.
39 The measuring line will stretch from the Corner Gate straight to the hill of Gareb. Then it
will turn to the place named Goah. 40 The
whole valley where dead bodies and ashes are
thrown, and all the terraces out to the Kidron
Valley on the east as far as the corner of the
Horse Gate—all that area will be holy to the
LORD. The city of Jerusalem will never again be
torn down or destroyed."

WHAT'S IT MEAN?

God made his Agreement with the people of Israel shortly after he led them out of captivity in Egypt. On Mount Sinai, he gave Moses two pieces of stone. These stones contained specific instructions on Israel's part of the Agreement. God spelled out in detail how the Israelites were supposed to live. In return for obeying God's rules for living, the Israelites would be blessed above all other nations on earth. Disobeying his rules, however, would result in severe punishment.

Jeremiah 31:32

JEREMIAH BUYS A FIELD

32

1 This is the word the LORD spoke to Jeremiah in the tenth year Zedekiah was king of Judah, which was the eighteenth year of
Nebuchadnezzar. 2 At that time the army of the
king of Babylon was surrounding Jerusalem.
Jeremiah the prophet was under arrest in the

courtyard of the guard, which was at the palace of the king of Judah.

[3]Zedekiah king of Judah had put Jeremiah in prison there. Zedekiah had asked, "Why have you prophesied the things you have?" (Jeremiah had said, "This is what the LORD says: 'I will soon hand the city of Jerusalem over to the king of Babylon, and he will capture it. [4]Zedekiah king of Judah will not escape from the Babylonian army, but he will surely be handed over to the king of Babylon. And he will speak to the king of Babylon face to face and see him with his own eyes. [5]The king will take Zedekiah to Babylon, where he will stay until I have punished him,' says the LORD. 'If you fight against the Babylonians, you will not succeed.' ")

[6]While Jeremiah was in prison, he said, "The LORD spoke this word to me: [7]Your cousin Hanamel, son of your uncle Shallum, will come to you soon. Hanamel will say to you, 'Jeremiah, you are my nearest relative, so buy my field near the town of Anathoth. It is your right and your duty to buy that field.'

[8]"Then it happened just as the LORD had said. My cousin Hanamel came to me in the courtyard of the guard and said to me, 'Buy for yourself my field near Anathoth in the land of Benjamin. It is your right and duty to buy it and own it.' So I knew this was a message from the LORD.

[9]"I bought the field at Anathoth from my cousin Hanamel, weighing out seven ounces of silver for him. [10]I signed the record and sealed it and had some people witness it. I also weighed out the silver on the scales. [11]Then I took both copies of the record of ownership—the one that was sealed that had the demands and limits of ownership, and the one that was not sealed. [12]And I gave them to Baruch son of Neriah, the son of Mahseiah. My cousin Hanamel, the other witnesses who signed the record of ownership, and many Jews sitting in the courtyard of the guard saw me give the record of ownership to Baruch.

[13]"With all the people watching, I told Baruch, [14]'This is what the LORD All-Powerful, the God of Israel, says: Take both copies of the record of ownership—the sealed copy and the copy that was not sealed—and put them in a clay jar so they will last a long time. [15]This is what the LORD All-Powerful, the God of Israel, says: In the future my people will once again buy houses and fields for grain and vineyards in the land of Israel.'

[16]"After I gave the record of ownership to Baruch son of Neriah, I prayed to the LORD, [17]Oh, Lord GOD, you made the skies and the earth with your very great power. There is nothing too hard for you to do. [18]You show love and kindness to thousands of people, but you also bring punishment to children for their parents' sins. Great and powerful God, your name is the LORD All-Powerful. [19]You plan and do great things. You see everything that people do, and you reward people for the way they live and for what they do. [20]You did miracles and wonderful things in the land of Egypt. You have continued doing them in Israel and among the other nations even until today. So you have become well known. [21]You brought your people, the Israelites, out of Egypt using signs and miracles and your great power and strength. You brought great terror on everyone. [22]You gave them this land that you promised to their ancestors long ago, a fertile land. [23]They came into this land and took it for their own, but they did not obey you or follow your teachings. They did not do everything you commanded. So you made all these terrible things happen to them.

[24]"Look! The enemy has surrounded the city and has built roads to the top of the walls to capture it. Because of war, hunger, and terrible diseases, the city will be handed over to the Babylonians who are attacking it. You said this would happen, and now you see it is happening. [25]But now, Lord GOD, you tell me, 'Buy the field with silver and call in witnesses.' You tell me this while the Babylonian army is ready to capture the city."

[26]Then the LORD spoke this word to Jeremiah: [27]"I am the LORD, the God of every person on the earth. Nothing is impossible for me. [28]So this is what the LORD says: I will soon hand over the city of Jerusalem to the Babylonian army and to Nebuchadnezzar king of Babylon, who will capture it. [29]The Babylonian army is already attacking the city of Jerusalem. They will soon enter it and start a fire to burn down the city and its houses. The people of Jerusalem offered sacrifices to Baal on the roofs[n] of those same houses and poured out drink offerings to other idols to make me angry. [30]From their youth, the people of Israel and Judah have done only the things I said

32:29 roofs In Bible times houses were built with flat roofs. The roof was used for drying things such as flax and fruit. And it was used as an extra room, as a place for worship, and as a cool place to sleep in the summer.

were wrong. They have made me angry by
worshiping idols made with their own hands,"
says the LORD. 31"From the day Jerusalem was
built until now, this city has made me angry, so
angry that I must remove it from my sight. 32I
will destroy it, because of all the evil the people
of Israel and Judah have done. The people,
their kings and officers, their priests and
prophets, all the people of Judah, and the people of Jerusalem have made me angry. 33They
turned their backs to me, not their faces. I tried
to teach them again and again, but they
wouldn't listen or learn. 34They put their hateful idols in the place where I have chosen to be
worshiped, so they made it unclean. 35In the
Valley of Ben Hinnom they built places to
worship Baal so they could burn their sons
and daughters as sacrifices to Molech. But I
never commanded them to do such a hateful
thing. It never entered my mind that they
would do such a thing and cause Judah to sin.
36"You are saying, 'Because of war, hunger,
and terrible diseases, the city will be handed
over to the king of Babylon.' But the LORD, the
God of Israel, says about Jerusalem: 37I forced
the people of Israel and Judah to leave their
land, because I was furious and very angry
with them. But soon I will gather them from
all the lands where I forced them to go, and I
will bring them back to this place, where they
may live in safety. 38The people of Israel and
Judah will be my people, and I will be their
God. 39I will make them truly want to be one
people with one goal. They will truly want to
worship me all their lives, for their own good
and for the good of their children after them.
40"I will make an agreement with
them that will last forever. I
will never turn away from
them; I will always do good to
them. I will make them want
to respect me so they will
never turn away from me. 41I
will enjoy doing good to them.
And with my whole being I will surely plant
them in this land and make them grow."
42This is what the LORD says: "I have
brought this great disaster to the people of Israel and Judah. In the same way I will bring the
good things that I promise to do for them.
43You are saying, 'This land is an empty desert,
without people or animals. It has been handed
over to the Babylonians.' But in the future, people will again buy fields in this land. 44They will

ASSURANCE

How long do God's promises last? (32:40–41)

Promise

HE PROMISES TO DO GOOD THINGS FOR YOU FOREVER.

The people of Israel and Judah will be my people, and I will be their God. I will make them truly want to be one people with one goal. They will truly want to worship me all their lives, for their own good and for the good of their children after them. I will make an agreement with them that will last forever. I will never turn away from them; I will always do good to them. I will make them want to respect me so they will never turn away from me. I will enjoy doing good to them. And with my whole being I will surely plant them in this land and make them grow (Jer. 32:38–41).

On this earth, the good stuff always runs out. Things we look forward to finally arrive and then they're over. You open your last birthday present. You have to go home from vacation. The lights have to come off of the Christmas tree. All the anticipation is over, the event has taken place, you've got memories and some snapshots.

Have you ever heard anyone say, "I can't help anymore. I'm worn out. I've done all I can do. I just don't have anything left to give"? Maybe they've run out of time or money or energy or enthusiasm. That's just life as a human. Our resources are limited. Our passions change.

But the Lord never gets to the end of his goodness or his ability to help. He promises to always do good things for you. He won't whine when you ask for his help or get worn out and need a break. He is at work in your most awesome days, doing what is best for you. He will be excited about you *forever*. And he'll be doing good things for you all the while.

SEE FOR YOURSELF:

Rom. 8:28

use their money to buy fields. They will sign
and seal their agreements and call in witnesses.
They will again buy fields in the land of Benjamin, in the area around Jerusalem, in the towns
of Judah and in the mountains, in the western
hills, and in southern Judah. I will make everything as good for them as it once was," says the
LORD.

THE PROMISE OF THE LORD

33

1 While Jeremiah was still
locked up in the courtyard of
the guards, the LORD spoke
his word to him a second
time: 2 "These are the words of
the LORD, who made the
earth, shaped it, and gave it order, whose name is the LORD:
3 'Judah, pray to me, and I will answer you. I will tell you important secrets
you have never heard before.' 4 This is what the
LORD, the God of Israel, says about the houses
in Jerusalem and the royal palaces of Judah
that have been torn down to be used in defense of the attack by the Babylonian army:
5 'Some people will come to fight against the
Babylonians. They will fill these houses with
the bodies of people I killed in my hot anger. I
have turned away from this city because of all
the evil its people have done.

6 " 'But then I will bring health and healing to
the people there. I will heal them and let them
enjoy great peace and safety. 7 I will bring Judah
and Israel back from captivity and make them
strong countries as in the past. 8 They sinned
against me, but I will wash away that sin. They
did evil and turned away from me, but I will
forgive them. 9 Then "Jerusalem"
will be to me a name that brings
joy! And people from all nations of the earth will praise it
when they hear about the
good things I am doing there.
They will be surprised and
shocked at all the good things
and the peace I will bring to
Jerusalem.'

10 "You are saying, 'Our
country is an empty desert, with-
out people or animals.' But this is what the
LORD says: It is now quiet in the streets of Jerusalem and in the towns of Judah, without people or animals, but it will be noisy there soon!
11 There will be sounds of joy and gladness and
the happy sounds of brides and bridegrooms.
There will be the sounds of people bringing to
the Temple of the LORD their offerings of
thanks to the LORD. They will say,

'Praise the LORD All-Powerful,
because the LORD is good!

> "Praise the LORD All-Powerful, because the LORD is good! His love continues forever!" (Jeremiah 33:11b)

Promise

HE PROMISES TO CLEANSE YOU FROM YOUR SIN.

They sinned against me, but I will wash away that sin. They did evil and turned away from me, but I will forgive them (Jer. 33:8).

When Jeremiah gave God's message to the people of Israel, the whole country was seriously messed up. The people were doing some things that you would be shocked to hear about even in these days, and God was pretty mad about it. Jeremiah warned them that God was going to punish them, but they didn't change their ways. Jeremiah began to think they were pretty hopeless.

But God knew better. He knew that the people were not going to turn things around soon and that he would have to follow through with his punishment. But he also knew that after the people lived through all the terrible things that were going to happen, a lot of them would come to their senses. Then, in spite of all the awful things they had done, God said he would wash away their sin.

That's God's promise to everyone who will come to his senses and turn to God. That's his promise to you—even if you think that what you've done is too horrible to mention. Jesus has declared you "not guilty." He's already taken your punishment. Turn around, face him, repent, ask forgiveness, and he will take your guilt away.

SEE FOR YOURSELF:

Is. 43:25; Jer. 31:34; 1 John 1:9

His love continues forever!'
They will say this because I will again do good
things for Judah, as I did in the beginning," says
the LORD.
12This is what the LORD All-Powerful says:
"This place is empty now, without people or animals. But there will be shepherds in all the
towns of Judah and pastures where they let
their flocks rest. 13Shepherds will again count
their sheep as the sheep walk in front of them.
They will count them in the mountains and in
the western hills, in southern Judah and the
land of Benjamin, and around Jerusalem and
the other towns of Judah!" says the LORD.

THE GOOD BRANCH

14The LORD says, "The time is coming when
I will do the good thing I promised to the people of Israel and Judah.
15In those days and at that time,
I will make a good branch sprout from
David's family.
He will do what is fair and right in the
land.
16At that time Judah will be saved,
and the people of Jerusalem will live in
safety.
The branch will be named:
The LORD Does What Is Right."
17This is what the LORD says: "Someone from
David's family will always sit on the throne of
the family of Israel. 18And there will always be
priests from the family of Levi. They will always
stand before me to offer burnt offerings and
grain offerings and sacrifices to me."
19The LORD spoke his word to Jeremiah,
saying: 20"This is what the LORD says: I have an
agreement with day and night that they will
always come at the right times. If you could
change that agreement, 21only then could you
change my agreement with David and Levi.
Only then would my servant David not have a
descendant ruling as king on David's throne.
And only then would the family of Levi not be
priests serving me in the Temple. 22But I will
give many descendants to my servant David
and to the family group of Levi who serve me
in the Temple. They will be as many as the
stars in the sky that no one can count. They
will be as many as the grains of sand on the
seashore that no one can measure."
23The LORD spoke his word to Jeremiah,
saying: 24"Jeremiah, have you heard what the
people are saying? They say: 'The LORD turned
away from the two families of Israel and Judah
that he chose.' Now they don't think of my
people as a nation anymore!"
25This is what the LORD says: "If I had not
made my agreement with day and night, and
if I had not made the laws for the sky and
earth, 26only then would I turn away from
Jacob's descendants. And only then would I
not let the descendants of David my servant
rule over the descendants of Abraham, Isaac,
and Jacob. But I will be kind to them and cause
good things to happen to them again."

A WARNING TO ZEDEKIAH

34
1The LORD spoke his word to Jeremiah
when Nebuchadnezzar king of Babylon was
fighting against Jerusalem and all the towns
around it. Nebuchadnezzar had with him all
his army and the armies of all the kingdoms
and peoples he ruled. 2This is what the LORD,
the God of Israel, said: "Jeremiah, go to Zedekiah king of Judah and tell him: 'This is what
the LORD says: I will soon hand the city of Jerusalem over to the king of Babylon, and he
will burn it down! 3You will not escape from
the king of Babylon; you will surely be captured and handed over to him. You will see the
king of Babylon with your own eyes, and he
will talk to you face to face. And you will go to
Babylon. 4But, Zedekiah king of Judah, listen to
the promise of the LORD. This is what the LORD
says about you: You will not be killed with a
sword. 5You will die in a peaceful way. As people made funeral fires to honor your ancestors,
the kings who ruled before you, so people will
make a funeral fire to honor you. They will cry
for you and sadly say, "Ah, master!" I myself
make this promise to you, says the LORD.' "
6So Jeremiah the prophet gave this message
to Zedekiah in Jerusalem. 7This was while the
army of the king of Babylon was fighting
against Jerusalem and the cities of Judah that
had not yet been taken—Lachish and Azekah.
These were the only strong, walled cities left in
the land of Judah.

SLAVES ARE MISTREATED

8The LORD spoke his word to Jeremiah. This
was after King Zedekiah had made an agreement with all the people in Jerusalem to free all
the Hebrew slaves. 9Everyone was supposed to
free his Hebrew slaves, both male and female.
No one was to keep a fellow Jew as a slave.
10All the officers and all the people accepted
this agreement; they agreed to free their male
and female slaves and no longer keep them as
slaves. So all the slaves were set free. 11But after
that, the people who had slaves changed their
minds. So they took back the people they had
set free and made them slaves again.

[12]Then the LORD spoke his word to Jeremiah: [13]"This is what the LORD, the God of Israel, says: I brought your ancestors out of Egypt where they were slaves and made an agreement with them. [14]I said to your ancestors: 'At the end of every seven years, each one of you must set his Hebrew slaves free. If a fellow Hebrew has sold himself to you, you must let him go free after he has served you for six years.' But your ancestors did not listen or pay attention to me. [15]A short time ago you changed your hearts and did what I say is right. Each of you gave freedom to his fellow Hebrews who were slaves. And you even made an agreement before me in the place where I have chosen to be worshiped. [16]But now you have changed your minds. You have shown you do not honor me. Each of you has taken back the male and female slaves you had set free, and you have forced them to become your slaves again.

WHAT'S IT MEAN?

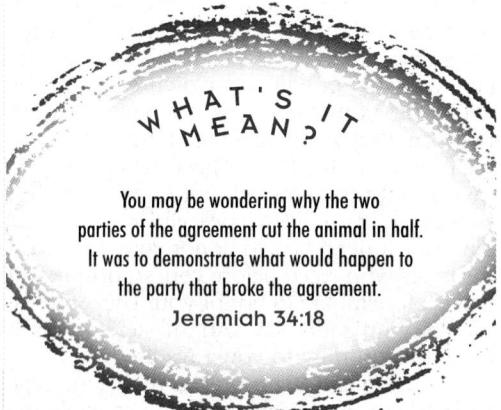

You may be wondering why the two parties of the agreement cut the animal in half. It was to demonstrate what would happen to the party that broke the agreement.

Jeremiah 34:18

[17]"So this is what the LORD says: You have not obeyed me. You have not given freedom to your fellow Hebrews, neither relatives nor friends. But now I will give freedom, says the LORD, to war, to terrible diseases, and to hunger. I will make you hated by all the kingdoms of the earth. [18]I will hand over the men who broke my agreement, who have not kept the promises they made before me. They cut a calf into two pieces before me and walked between the pieces.[n] [19]These people made the agreement before me by walking between the pieces of the calf: the leaders of Judah and Jerusalem, the officers of the court, the priests, and all the people of the land. [20]So I will hand them over to their enemies and to everyone who wants to kill them. Their bodies will become food for the birds of the air and for the wild animals of the earth. [21]I will hand Zedekiah king of Judah and his officers over to their enemies, and to everyone who wants to kill them, and to the army of the king of Babylon, even though they have left Jerusalem. [22]I will give the order, says the LORD, to bring the Babylonian army back to Jerusalem. It will fight against Jerusalem, capture it, set it on fire, and burn it down. I will destroy the towns in Judah so that they become ruins where no one lives!"

THE RECABITE FAMILY OBEYS GOD

35 [1]When Jehoiakim son of Josiah was king of Judah, the LORD spoke his word to Jeremiah, saying: [2]"Go to the family of Recab. Invite them to come to one of the side rooms of the Temple of the LORD, and offer them wine to drink."

[3]So I went to get Jaazaniah son of Jeremiah,[n] the son of Habazziniah. And I gathered all of Jaazaniah's brothers and sons and the whole family of the Recabites together. [4]Then I brought them into the Temple of the LORD. We went into the room of the sons of Hanan son of Igdaliah, who was a man of God. The room was next to the one where the officers stay and above the room of Maaseiah son of Shallum, the doorkeeper in the Temple. [5]Then I put some bowls full of wine and some cups before the men of the Recabite family. And I said to them, "Drink some wine."

[6]But the Recabite men answered, "We never drink wine. Our ancestor Jonadab son of Recab gave us this command: 'You and your descendants must never drink wine. [7]Also you

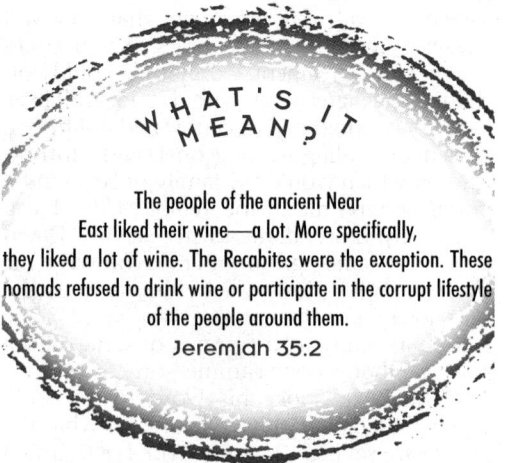

WHAT'S IT MEAN?

The people of the ancient Near East liked their wine—a lot. More specifically, they liked a lot of wine. The Recabites were the exception. These nomads refused to drink wine or participate in the corrupt lifestyle of the people around them.

Jeremiah 35:2

34:18 They . . . pieces. This showed that the men were willing to be killed, like this animal, if they did not keep their agreement. **35:3 Jeremiah** Not the prophet Jeremiah, but a different man with the same name.

must never build houses, plant seeds, or plant vineyards, or do any of those things. You must live only in tents. Then you will live a long time in the land where you are wanderers.' [8]So we Recabites have obeyed everything Jonadab our ancestor commanded us. Neither we nor our wives, sons, or daughters ever drink wine. [9]We never build houses in which to live, or own fields or vineyards, or plant crops. [10]We have lived in tents and have obeyed everything our ancestor Jonadab commanded us. [11]But when Nebuchadnezzar king of Babylon attacked Judah, we said to each other, 'Come, we must enter Jerusalem so we can escape the Babylonian army and the Aramean army.' So we have stayed in Jerusalem."

[12]Then the LORD spoke his word to Jeremiah: [13]"This is what the LORD All-Powerful, the God of Israel, says: Jeremiah, go and tell the men of Judah and the people of Jerusalem: 'You should learn a lesson and obey my message,' says the LORD. [14]'Jonadab son of Recab ordered his descendants not to drink wine, and that command has been obeyed. Until today they have obeyed their ancestor's command; they do not drink wine. But I, the LORD, have given you messages again and again, but you did not obey me. [15]I sent all my servants the prophets to you again and again, saying, "Each of you must stop doing evil. You must change and be good. Do not follow other gods to serve them. If you obey me, you will live in the land I have given to you and your ancestors." But you have not listened to me or paid attention to my message. [16]The descendants of Jonadab son of Recab obeyed the commands their ancestor gave them, but the people of Judah have not obeyed me.'

[17]"So the LORD God All-Powerful, the God of Israel, says: 'I will soon bring every disaster I said would come to Judah and to everyone living in Jerusalem. I spoke to those people, but they refused to listen. I called out to them, but they did not answer me.' "

[18]Then Jeremiah said to the Recabites, "This is what the LORD All-Powerful, the God of Israel, says: 'You have obeyed the commands of your ancestor Jonadab and have followed all of his teachings; you have done everything he commanded.' [19]So this is what the LORD All-Powerful, the God of Israel, says: 'There will always be a descendant of Jonadab son of Recab to serve me.' "

36

JEHOIAKIM BURNS JEREMIAH'S SCROLL

[1]The LORD spoke this word to Jeremiah during the fourth year that Jehoiakim son of Josiah was king of Judah: [2]"Get a scroll. Write on it all the words I have spoken to you about Israel and Judah and all the nations. Write everything from when I first spoke to you, when Josiah was king, until now. [3]Maybe the family of Judah will hear what disasters I am planning to bring on them and will stop doing wicked things. Then I would forgive them for the sins and the evil things they have done."

[4]So Jeremiah called for Baruch son of Neriah. Jeremiah spoke the messages the LORD had given him, and Baruch wrote those messages on the scroll. [5]Then Jeremiah commanded Baruch, "I cannot go to the Temple of the LORD. I must stay here. [6]So I want you to go to the Temple of the LORD on a day when the people are giving up eating. Read from the scroll to all the people of Judah who come into Jerusalem from their towns. Read the messages from the LORD, which are the words you wrote on the scroll as I spoke them to you. [7]Perhaps they will ask the LORD to help them. Perhaps each one will stop doing wicked things, because the LORD has announced that he is very angry with them." [8]So Baruch son of Neriah did everything Jeremiah the prophet told him to do. In the LORD's Temple he read aloud the scroll that had the LORD's messages written on it.

[9]In the ninth month of the fifth year that Jehoiakim son of Josiah was king, a special time to give up eating was announced. All the people of Jerusalem and everyone who had come into Jerusalem from the towns of Judah were supposed to give up eating to honor the LORD. [10]At that time Baruch read to all the people there the scroll containing Jeremiah's words. He read the scroll in the Temple of the LORD in the room of Gemariah son of Shaphan, a royal secretary. That room was in the upper courtyard at the entrance of the New Gate of the Temple.

[11]Micaiah son of Gemariah, the son of Shaphan, heard all the messages from the LORD that were on the scroll. [12]Micaiah went down to the royal secretary's room in the king's palace where all of the officers were sitting: Elishama the royal secretary; Delaiah son of Shemaiah; Elnathan son of Acbor; Gemariah son of Shaphan; Zedekiah son of Hananiah; and all the other officers. [13]Micaiah told those officers everything he had heard Baruch read to the people from the scroll.

[14]Then the officers sent a man named Jehudi son of Nethaniah to Baruch. (Nethaniah was the son of Shelemiah, who was the son of Cushi.) Jehudi said to Baruch, "Bring the scroll that you read to the people and come with me."

So Baruch son of Neriah took the scroll and went with Jehudi to the officers. 15Then the officers said to Baruch, "Please sit down and read the scroll to us."

So Baruch read the scroll to them. 16When the officers heard all the words, they became afraid and looked at each other. They said to Baruch, "We must certainly tell the king about these words." 17Then the officers asked Baruch, "Tell us, please, where did you get all these words you wrote on the scroll? Did you write down what Jeremiah said to you?"

18"Yes," Baruch answered. "Jeremiah spoke them all to me, and I wrote them down with ink on this scroll."

19Then the officers said to Baruch, "You and Jeremiah must go and hide, and don't tell anyone where you are."

WHAT'S IT MEAN?

You may be surprised to learn that Jerusalem has its share of cold spells in the winter—and even receives occasional snow. In ancient Judah, people who lived in two-story homes usually stayed on the first floor in the winter, then moved to the better-ventilated second floor in the summer.
Jeremiah 36:20–22

20The officers put the scroll in the room of Elishama the royal secretary. Then they went to the king in the courtyard and told him all about the scroll. 21So King Jehoiakim sent Jehudi to get the scroll. Jehudi brought the scroll from the room of Elishama the royal secretary and read it to the king and to all the officers who stood around the king. 22It was the ninth month of the year, so King Jehoiakim was sitting in the winter apartment. There was a fire burning in a small firepot in front of him. 23After Jehudi had read three or four columns, the king cut those columns off of the scroll with a penknife and threw them into the firepot. Finally, the whole scroll was burned in the fire. 24King Jehoiakim and his servants heard everything that was said, but they were not frightened! They did not tear their clothes to show their sorrow. 25Elnathan, Delaiah, and Gemariah even tried to talk King Jehoiakim out of burning the scroll, but he would not listen to them. 26Instead, the king ordered Jerahmeel son of the king, Seraiah son of Azriel, and Shelemiah son of Abdeel to arrest Baruch the secretary and Jeremiah the prophet. But the LORD had hidden them.

27So King Jehoiakim burned the scroll where Baruch had written all the words Jeremiah had spoken to him. Then the LORD spoke his word to Jeremiah: 28"Get another scroll. Write all the words on it that were on the first scroll that Jehoiakim king of Judah burned up. 29Also say this to Jehoiakim king of Judah: 'This is what the LORD says: You burned up that scroll and said, "Why, Jeremiah, did you write on it 'the king of Babylon will surely come and destroy this land and the people and animals in it'?" 30So this is what the LORD says about Jehoiakim king of Judah: Jehoiakim's descendants will not sit on David's throne. When Jehoiakim dies, his body will be thrown out on the ground. It will be left out in the heat of the day and in the cold frost of the night. 31I will punish Jehoiakim and his children and his servants, because they have done evil things. I will bring disasters upon them and upon all the people in Jerusalem and Judah—everything I promised but which they refused to hear.' "

32So Jeremiah took another scroll and gave it to Baruch son of Neriah, his secretary. As Jeremiah spoke, Baruch wrote on the scroll the same words that were on the scroll Jehoiakim king of Judah had burned in the fire. And many similar words were added to the second scroll.

JEREMIAH IN PRISON

37 1Nebuchadnezzar king of Babylon had appointed Zedekiah son of Josiah to be king of Judah. Zedekiah took the place of Jehoiachin son of Jehoiakim. 2But Zedekiah, his servants, and the people of Judah did not listen to the words the LORD had spoken through Jeremiah the prophet.

3Now King Zedekiah sent Jehucal son of Shelemiah and the priest Zephaniah son of Maaseiah with a message to Jeremiah the prophet. This was the message: "Jeremiah, please pray to the LORD our God for us."

4At that time Jeremiah had not yet been put into prison. So he was free to go anywhere he wanted. 5The army of the king of Egypt had marched from Egypt toward Judah. Now the Babylonian army had surrounded the city of Jerusalem. When they heard about the Egyptian army marching toward them, the Babylonian army left Jerusalem.

6The LORD spoke his word to Jeremiah the prophet: 7"This is what the LORD, the God of Israel, says: Jehucal and Zephaniah, I know Zedekiah king of Judah sent you to seek my help. Tell this to King Zedekiah: 'The army of the king of Egypt came here to help you, but they will go back to Egypt. 8After that, the Babylonian army will return and attack Jerusalem and capture it and burn it down.'

9"This is what the LORD says: People of Jerusalem, do not fool yourselves. Don't say, 'The Babylonian army will surely leave us alone.' They will not! 10Even if you defeated all of the Babylonian army that is attacking you and there were only a few injured men left in their tents, they would come from their tents and burn down Jerusalem!"

11So the Babylonian army left Jerusalem to fight the army of the king of Egypt. 12Now Jeremiah tried to travel from Jerusalem to the land of Benjamin to get his share of the property that belonged to his family. 13When Jeremiah got to the Benjamin Gate of Jerusalem, the captain in charge of the guards arrested him. The captain's name was Irijah son of Shelemiah son of Hananiah. Irijah said, "You are leaving us to join the Babylonians!"

14But Jeremiah said to Irijah, "That's not true! I am not leaving to join the Babylonians." Irijah refused to listen to Jeremiah, so he arrested Jeremiah and took him to the officers of Jerusalem. 15Those rulers were very angry with Jeremiah and beat him. Then they put him in jail in the house of Jonathan the royal secretary, which had been made into a prison. 16So those people put Jeremiah into a cell in a dungeon, and Jeremiah was there for a long time.

17Then King Zedekiah sent for Jeremiah and had him brought to the palace. Zedekiah asked him in private, "Is there any message from the LORD?"

Jeremiah answered, "Yes, there is. Zedekiah, you will be handed over to the king of Babylon." 18Then Jeremiah said to King Zedekiah, "What crime have I done against you or your officers or the people of Jerusalem? Why have you thrown me into prison? 19Where are your prophets that prophesied this message to you: 'The king of Babylon will not attack you or this land of Judah?' 20But now, my master, king of Judah, please listen to me, and please do what I ask of you. Do not send me back to the house of Jonathan the royal secretary, or I will die there!"

21So King Zedekiah gave orders for Jeremiah to be put under guard in the courtyard of the guard and to be given bread each day from the street of the bakers until there was no more bread in the city. So he stayed under guard in the courtyard of the guard.

JEREMIAH IS THROWN INTO A WELL

38

1Shephatiah son of Mattan, Gedaliah son of Pashhur, Jehucal son of Shelemiah, and Pashhur son of Malkijah heard what Jeremiah was telling all the people. He said: 2"This is what the LORD says: 'Everyone who stays in Jerusalem will die from war, or hunger, or terrible diseases. But everyone who surrenders to the Babylonian army will live; they will escape with their lives and live.' 3And this is what the LORD says: 'This city of Jerusalem will surely be handed over to the army of the king of Babylon. He will capture this city!' "

4Then the officers said to the king, "Jeremiah must be put to death! He is discouraging the soldiers who are still in the city, and all the people, by what he is saying to them. He does not want good to happen to us; he wants to ruin us."

5King Zedekiah said to them, "Jeremiah is in your control. I cannot do anything to stop you."

6So the officers took Jeremiah and put him into the well of Malkijah, the king's son, which was in the courtyard of the guards. The officers used ropes to lower Jeremiah into the well, which did not have any water in it, only mud. And Jeremiah sank down into the mud.

WHAT'S IT MEAN?

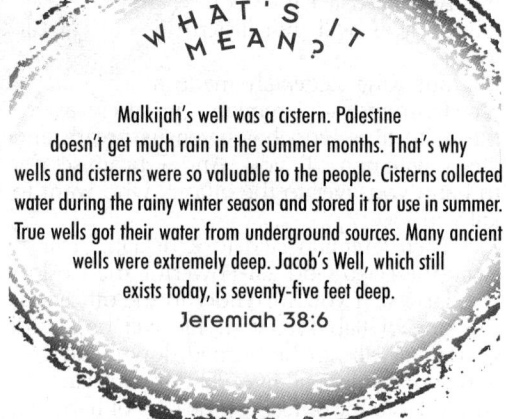

Malkijah's well was a cistern. Palestine doesn't get much rain in the summer months. That's why wells and cisterns were so valuable to the people. Cisterns collected water during the rainy winter season and stored it for use in summer. True wells got their water from underground sources. Many ancient wells were extremely deep. Jacob's Well, which still exists today, is seventy-five feet deep.

Jeremiah 38:6

7But Ebed-Melech, a Cushite and a servant in the palace, heard that the officers had put Jeremiah into the well. As King Zedekiah was sitting at the Benjamin Gate, 8Ebed-Melech left the palace and went to the king. Ebed-Melech said to him, 9"My master and king, these rulers have acted in an evil way. They have treated Jeremiah the prophet badly. They have thrown him into a well and left him there to die! When there is no more bread in the city, he will starve to death."

10Then King Zedekiah commanded Ebed-Melech the Cushite, "Take thirty men from the palace and lift Jeremiah the prophet out of the well before he dies."

11So Ebed-Melech took the men with him and went to a room under the storeroom in the palace. He took some old rags and worn-out clothes from that room. Then he let those rags down with some ropes to Jeremiah in the well. 12Ebed-Melech the Cushite said to Jeremiah, "Put these old rags and worn-out clothes under your arms to be pads for the ropes." So Jeremiah did as Ebed-Melech said. 13The men pulled Jeremiah up with the ropes and lifted him out of the well. And Jeremiah stayed under guard in the courtyard of the guard.

ZEDEKIAH QUESTIONS JEREMIAH

14Then King Zedekiah sent someone to get Jeremiah the prophet and bring him to the third entrance to the Temple of the LORD. The king said to Jeremiah, "I am going to ask you something. Do not hide anything from me, but tell me everything honestly."

15Jeremiah said to Zedekiah, "If I give you an answer, you will surely kill me. And even if I give you advice, you will not listen to me."

> "Obey the LORD by doing what I tell you. Then things will go well for you, and your life will be saved." (Jeremiah 38:20b)

16But King Zedekiah made a secret promise to Jeremiah, "As surely as the LORD lives who has given us breath and life, I will not kill you. And I promise not to hand you over to the officers who want to kill you."

17Then Jeremiah said to Zedekiah, "This is what the LORD God All-Powerful, the God of Israel, says: 'If you surrender to the officers of the king of Babylon, your life will be saved. Jerusalem will not be burned down, and you and your family will live. 18But if you refuse to surrender to the officers of the king of Babylon, Jerusalem will be handed over to the Babylonian army, and they will burn it down. And you yourself will not escape from them.' "

19Then King Zedekiah said to Jeremiah, "I'm afraid of some Jews who have already gone over to the side of the Babylonian army. If the Babylonians hand me over to them, they will treat me badly."

20But Jeremiah answered, "The Babylonians will not hand you over to the Jews. Obey the LORD by doing what I tell you. Then things will go well for you, and your life will be saved. 21But if you refuse to surrender to the Babylonians, the LORD has shown me what will happen. 22All the women left in the palace of the king of Judah will be brought out and taken to the important officers of the king of Babylon. Your women will make fun of you with this song:

'Your good friends misled you
and were stronger than you.
While your feet were stuck in the mud,
they left you.'

23"All your wives and children will be brought out and given to the Babylonian army. You yourself will not even escape from them. You will be taken prisoner by the king of Babylon, and Jerusalem will be burned down."

24Then Zedekiah said to Jeremiah, "Do not tell anyone that I have been talking to you, or you will die. 25If the officers find out I talked to you, they will come to you and say, 'Tell us what you said to King Zedekiah and what he said to you. Don't keep any secrets from us. If you don't tell us everything, we will kill you.' 26If they ask you, tell them, 'I was begging the king not to send me back to Jonathan's house to die.' "

27All the officers did come to question Jeremiah. So he told them everything the king had ordered him to say. Then the officers said no more to Jeremiah, because no one had heard what Jeremiah and the king had discussed.

28So Jeremiah stayed under guard in the courtyard of the guard until the day Jerusalem was captured.

THE FALL OF JERUSALEM

39 1This is how Jerusalem was captured: Nebuchadnezzar king of Babylon marched against Jerusalem with his whole army and surrounded the city to attack it. This was during the tenth month of the ninth year Zedekiah was king of Judah. 2This lasted until the ninth day of the fourth month in Zedekiah's eleventh year. Then the city wall was broken through. 3And all these officers of the king of Babylon came into Jerusalem and sat down at the Mid-

dle Gate: Nergal-Sharezer of the district of Samgar; Nebo-Sarsekim, a chief officer; Nergal-Sharezer, an important leader; and all the other important officers.

[4]When Zedekiah king of Judah and all his soldiers saw them, they ran away. They left Jerusalem at night and went out from the king's garden. They went through the gate that was between the two walls and then headed toward the Jordan Valley. [5]But the Babylonian army chased them and caught up with Zedekiah in the plains of Jericho. They captured him and took him to Nebuchadnezzar king of Babylon, who was at the town of Riblah in the land of Hamath. There Nebuchadnezzar passed his sentence on Zedekiah. [6]At Riblah the king of Babylon killed Zedekiah's sons and all the important officers of Judah as Zedekiah watched. [7]Then he put out Zedekiah's eyes. He put bronze chains on Zedekiah and took him to Babylon.

[8]The Babylonians set fire to the palace and to the houses of the people, and they broke down the walls around Jerusalem. [9]Nebuzaradan, commander of the king's special guards, took the people left in Jerusalem, those captives who had surrendered to him earlier, and the rest of the people of Jerusalem, and he took them all away to Babylon. [10]But Nebuzaradan, commander of the guard, left some of the poorest people of Judah behind. They owned nothing, but that day he gave them vineyards and fields.

[11]Nebuchadnezzar king of Babylon had given these orders about Jeremiah through Nebuzaradan, commander of the guard: [12]"Find Jeremiah and take care of him. Do not hurt him, but do for him whatever he asks you." [13]So Nebuchadnezzar sent these men for Jeremiah: Nebuzaradan, commander of the guards; Nebushazban, a chief officer; Nergal-Sharezer, an important leader; and all the other officers of the king of Babylon. [14]They had Jeremiah taken out of the courtyard of the guard. Then they turned him over to Gedaliah son of Ahikam son of Shaphan, who had orders to take Jeremiah back home. So they took him home, and he stayed among the people left in Judah.

[15]While Jeremiah was guarded in the courtyard, the LORD spoke his word to him: [16]"Jeremiah, go and tell Ebed-Melech the Cushite this message: 'This is what the LORD All-Powerful, the God of Israel, says: Very soon I will make my words about Jerusalem come true through disaster, not through good times. You will see everything come true with your own eyes. [17]But I will save you on that day, Ebed-Melech, says the LORD. You will not be handed over to the people you fear. [18]I will surely save you, Ebed-Melech. You will not die from a sword, but you will escape and live. This will happen because you have trusted in me, says the LORD.' "

JEREMIAH IS SET FREE

40 [1]The LORD spoke his word to Jeremiah after Nebuzaradan, commander of the guards, had set Jeremiah free at the city of Ramah. He had found Jeremiah in Ramah bound in chains with all the captives from Jerusalem and Judah who were being taken away to Babylon. [2]When commander Nebuzaradan found Jeremiah, Nebuzaradan said to him, "The LORD your God announced this disaster would come to this place. [3]And now the LORD has done everything he said he would do. This disaster happened because the people of Judah sinned against the LORD and did not obey him. [4]But today I am freeing you from the chains on your wrists. If you want to, come with me to Babylon, and I will take good care of you. But if you don't want to come, then don't. Look, the whole country is open to you. Go wherever you wish." [5]Before Jeremiah turned to leave, Nebuzaradan said, "Or go back to Gedaliah son of Ahikam, the son of Shaphan. The king of Babylon has chosen him to be governor over the towns of Judah. Go and live with Gedaliah among the people, or go anywhere you want."

Then Nebuzaradan gave Jeremiah some food and a present and let him go. [6]So Jeremiah went to Gedaliah son of Ahikam at Mizpah and stayed with him there. He lived among the people who were left behind in Judah.

THE SHORT RULE OF GEDALIAH

[7]Some officers and their men from the army of Judah were still out in the open country. They heard that the king of Babylon had put Gedaliah son of Ahikam in charge of the people who were left in the land: the men, women, and children who were the poorest. They were the ones who were not taken to Babylon as captives. [8]So these soldiers came to Gedaliah at Mizpah: Ishmael son of Nethaniah, Johanan and Jonathan sons of Kareah, Seraiah son of Tanhumeth, the sons of Ephai the Netophathite, Jaazaniah son of the Maacathite, and their men.

[9]Gedaliah son of Ahikam, the son of Shaphan, made a promise to them, saying, "Do not be afraid to serve the Babylonians. Stay in the

land and serve the king of Babylon. Then everything will go well for you. [10]I myself will live in Mizpah and will speak for you before the Babylonians who come to us here. Harvest the wine, the summer fruit, and the oil, and put what you harvest in your storage jars. Live in the towns you control."

[11]The Jews in Moab, Ammon, Edom, and other countries also heard that the king of Babylon had left a few Jews alive in the land. And they heard the king of Babylon had chosen Gedaliah as governor over them. (Gedaliah was the son of Ahikam, the son of Shaphan.) [12]When the people of Judah heard this news, they came back to Judah from all the countries where they had been scattered. They came to Gedaliah at Mizpah and gathered a large harvest of wine and summer fruit.

[13]Johanan son of Kareah and all the army officers of Judah still in the open country came to Gedaliah at Mizpah. [14]They said to him, "Don't you know that Baalis king of the Ammonite people wants you dead? He has sent Ishmael son of Nethaniah to kill you." But Gedaliah son of Ahikam did not believe them.

[15]Then Johanan son of Kareah spoke to Gedaliah in private at Mizpah. He said, "Let me go and kill Ishmael son of Nethaniah. No one will know anything about it. We should not let Ishmael kill you. Then all the Jews gathered around you would be scattered to different countries again, and the few people of Judah who are left alive would be lost."

[16]But Gedaliah son of Ahikam said to Johanan son of Kareah, "Do not kill Ishmael! The things you are saying about Ishmael are not true."

41 [1]In the seventh month Ishmael son of Nethaniah and ten of his men came to Gedaliah son of Ahikam at Mizpah. (Nethaniah was the son of Elishama.) Now Ishmael was a member of the king's family and had been one of the officers of the king of Judah. While they were eating a meal with Gedaliah at Mizpah, [2]Ishmael and his ten men got up and killed Gedaliah son of Ahikam, the son of Shaphan, with a sword. (Gedaliah was the man the king of Babylon had chosen as governor over Judah.) [3]Ishmael also killed all the Jews and the Babylonian soldiers who were there with Gedaliah at Mizpah.

[4]The day after Gedaliah was murdered, before anyone knew about it, [5]eighty men came to Mizpah bringing grain offerings and incense to the Temple of the LORD. Those men from Shechem, Shiloh, and Samaria had shaved off their beards, torn their clothes, and cut themselves.[n] [6]Ishmael son of Nethaniah went out from Mizpah to meet them, crying as he walked. When he met them, he said, "Come with me to meet Gedaliah son of Ahikam." [7]So they went into Mizpah. Then Ishmael son of Nethaniah and his men killed seventy of them and threw the bodies into a deep well. [8]But the ten men who were left alive said to Ishmael, "Don't kill us! We have wheat and barley and oil and honey that we have hidden in a field." So Ishmael let them live and did not kill them with the others. [9]Now the well where he had thrown all the bodies had been made by King Asa as a part of his defenses against Baasha king of Israel. But Ishmael son of Nethaniah put dead bodies in it until it was full.

[10]Ishmael captured all the other people in Mizpah: the king's daughters and all the other people who were left there. They were the ones whom Nebuzaradan commander of the guard had chosen Gedaliah son of Ahikam to take care of. So Ishmael son of Nethaniah captured those people, and he started to cross over to the country of the Ammonites.

[11]Johanan son of Kareah and all his army officers with him heard about all the evil things Ishmael son of Nethaniah had done. [12]So they took their men and went to fight Ishmael son of Nethaniah and caught him near the big pool of water at Gibeon. [13]When the captives Ishmael had taken saw Johanan and the army officers, they were glad. [14]So all the people Ishmael had taken captive from Mizpah turned around and ran to Johanan son of Kareah. [15]But Ishmael son of Nethaniah and eight of his men escaped from Johanan and ran away to the Ammonites.

[16]So Johanan son of Kareah and all his army officers saved the captives that Ishmael son of Nethaniah had taken from Mizpah after he murdered Gedaliah son of Ahikam. Among those left alive were soldiers, women, children, and palace officers. And Johanan brought them back from the town of Gibeon.

THE ESCAPE TO EGYPT

[17-18]Johanan and the other army officers were afraid of the Babylonians. Since the king of Babylon had chosen Gedaliah son of Ahikam to be governor of Judah but Ishmael son of Nethaniah had murdered him, Johanan was

41:5 shaved . . . themselves The men did this to show they were sad about the Temple in Jerusalem being destroyed.

afraid that the Babylonians would be angry. So
they decided to run away to Egypt. On the way
they stayed at Geruth Kimham, near the town
of Bethlehem.

42

1While there, Johanan son of Kareah and
Jezaniah son of Hoshaiah went to Jeremiah the
prophet. All the army officers and all the people, from the least important to the greatest,
went along, too. 2They said to him, "Jeremiah,
please listen to what we ask. Pray to the LORD
your God for all the people left alive from the
family of Judah. At one time there were many
of us, but you can see that there are few of
us now. 3So pray that the LORD your God will
tell us where we should go and what we
should do."
4Then Jeremiah the prophet answered, "I
understand what you want me to do. I will
pray to the LORD your God as you
have asked. I will tell you
everything he says and not
hide anything from you."
5Then the people said to
Jeremiah, "May the LORD be a
true and loyal witness against
us if we don't do everything
the LORD your God sends you to tell us. 6It
does not matter if we like the message or not.
We will obey the LORD our God, to whom we
are sending you. We will obey what he says so
good things will happen to us."

OBEDIENCE
What will obeying God get us? (42:6)

7Ten days later the LORD spoke his word to
Jeremiah. 8Then Jeremiah called for Johanan
son of Kareah, the army officers with him, and
all the other people, from the least important to
the greatest. 9Jeremiah said to them, "You sent
me to ask the LORD for what you wanted. This
is what the God of Israel says: 10'If you will
stay in Judah, I will build you up and not tear
you down. I will plant you and not pull you
up, because I am sad about the disaster I
brought on you. 11Now you fear the king of
Babylon, but don't be afraid of him. Don't be
afraid of him,' says the LORD, 'because I am
with you. I will save you and rescue you from
his power. 12I will be kind to you, and he will
also treat you with mercy and let you stay in
your land.'
13"But if you say, 'We will not stay in Judah,' you will disobey the LORD your God.
14Or you might say, 'No, we will go and live
in Egypt. There we will not see war, or hear
the trumpets of war, or be hungry.' 15If you
say that, listen to the message of the LORD,
you who are left alive from Judah. This is
what the LORD All-Powerful, the God of Israel, says: 'If you make up your mind to go
and live in Egypt, these things will happen:
16You are afraid of war, but it will find you in
the land of Egypt. And you are worried
about hunger, but it will follow you into
Egypt, and you will die there. 17Everyone
who goes to live in Egypt will die in war or
from hunger or terrible disease. No one who
goes to Egypt will live; no one will escape the
terrible things I will bring to them.'
18"This is what the LORD All-Powerful, the
God of Israel, says: 'I showed my anger against
the people of Jerusalem. In the same way I will
show my anger against you when you go to
Egypt. Other nations will speak evil of you.
People will be shocked by what will happen to
you. You will become a curse word, and people will insult you. And you will never see Judah again.'
19"You who are left alive in Judah, the LORD
has told you, 'Don't go to Egypt.' Be sure you
understand this; I warn you today 20that you
are making a mistake that will cause your
deaths. You sent me to the LORD your God,
saying, 'Pray to the LORD our God for us. Tell
us everything the LORD our God says, and we
will do it.' 21So today I have told you, but you
have not obeyed the LORD your God in all that
he sent me to tell you. 22So now be sure you
understand this: You want to go to live in
Egypt, but you will die there by war, hunger, or
terrible diseases."

43

1So Jeremiah finished telling the people the
message from the LORD their God; he told
them everything the LORD their God had sent
him to tell them.
2Azariah son of Hoshaiah, Johanan son of
Kareah, and some other men were too proud.
They said to Jeremiah, "You are lying! The
LORD our God did not send you to say, 'You
must not go to Egypt to live there.' 3Baruch son
of Neriah is causing you to be against us. He
wants you to hand us over to the Babylonians
so they can kill us or capture us and take us to
Babylon."
4So Johanan, the army officers, and all the
people disobeyed the LORD's command to stay
in Judah. 5But Johanan son of Kareah and the
army officers led away those who were left
alive from Judah. They were the people who
had run away from the Babylonians to other
countries but then had come back to live in
Judah. 6They led away the men, women, and
children, and the king's daughters. Nebuzaradan commander of the guard had put Gedaliah son of Ahikam son of Shaphan in charge
of those people. Johanan also took Jeremiah
the prophet and Baruch son of Neriah. 7These

people did not listen to the LORD. So they all
went to Egypt to the city of Tahpanhes.
8In Tahpanhes the LORD spoke his word to
Jeremiah: 9"Take some large stones. Bury them
in the clay in the brick pavement in front of the
king of Egypt's palace in Tahpanhes. Do this
while the Jews are watching you. 10Then say to
them, 'This is what the LORD All-Powerful, the
God of Israel, says: I will soon send for my
servant, Nebuchadnezzar king of Babylon. I
will set his throne over these stones I have
buried, and he will spread his covering for
shade above them. 11He will come here and
attack Egypt. He will bring death to those who
are supposed to die. He will make prisoners of
those who are to be taken captive, and he will
bring war to those who are to be killed with a
sword. 12Nebuchadnezzar will set fire to the
temples of the gods of Egypt and burn them.
And he will take the idols away as captives. As
a shepherd wraps himself in his clothes, so
Nebuchadnezzar will wrap Egypt around him.
Then he will safely leave Egypt. 13He will destroy the stone pillars in the temple of the sun
god in Egypt, and he will burn down the temples of the gods of Egypt.' "

DISASTER IN EGYPT

44

1Jeremiah received a message from the LORD
for all the Jews living in Egypt—in the cities of
Migdol, Tahpanhes, Memphis, and in southern
Egypt. This was the message: 2"The LORD All-
Powerful, the God of Israel, says: You saw all
the terrible things I brought on Jerusalem and
the towns of Judah, which are ruins today
with no one living in them. 3It is because the
people who lived there did evil. They made me
angry by burning incense and worshiping
other gods that neither they nor you nor your
ancestors ever knew. 4I sent all my servants,
the prophets, to you again and again. By them
I said to you, 'Don't do this terrible thing that I
hate.' 5But they did not listen or pay attention.
They did not stop doing evil things and burning incense to other gods. 6So I showed my
great anger against them. I poured out my anger in the towns of Judah and the streets of
Jerusalem so they are only ruins and piles of
stones today.
7"Now the LORD All-Powerful, the God of
Israel, says: Why are you doing such great
harm to yourselves? You are cutting off the
men and women, children and babies from the
family of Judah, leaving yourselves without
anyone from the family of Judah. 8Why do
you want to make me angry by making idols?
Why do you burn incense to the gods of
Egypt, where you have come to live? You will
destroy yourselves. Other nations will speak
evil of you and make fun of you. 9Have you
forgotten about the evil things your ancestors
did? And have you forgotten the evil the kings
and queens of Judah did? Have you forgotten
about the evil you and your wives did? These
things were done in the country of Judah and
in the streets of Jerusalem. 10Even to this day
the people of Judah are still too proud. They
have not learned to respect me or to follow my
teachings. They have not obeyed the laws I
gave you and your ancestors.
11"So this is what the LORD All-Powerful, the
God of Israel, says: I am determined to bring
disasters on you. I will destroy the whole family of Judah. 12The few who were left alive from
Judah were determined to go to Egypt and settle there, but they will all die in Egypt. They
will be killed in war or die from hunger. From
the least important to the greatest, they will be
killed in war or die from hunger. Other nations
will speak evil about them. People will be
shocked by what has happened to them. They
will become a curse word, and people will insult them. 13I will punish those people who
have gone to live in Egypt, just as I punished
Jerusalem, using swords, hunger, and terrible
diseases. 14Of the people of Judah who were
left alive and have gone to live in Egypt, none
will escape my punishment. They want to return to Judah and live there, but none of them
will live to return to Judah, except a few people
who will escape."
15A large group of the people of Judah who
lived in southern Egypt were meeting together.
Among them were many women of Judah
who were burning incense to other gods, and
their husbands knew it. All these people said to
Jeremiah, 16"We will not listen to the message
from the LORD that you spoke to us. 17We

WHAT'S IT MEAN?

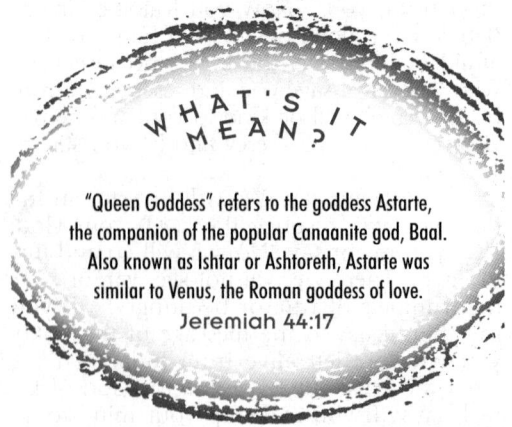

"Queen Goddess" refers to the goddess Astarte, the companion of the popular Canaanite god, Baal. Also known as Ishtar or Ashtoreth, Astarte was similar to Venus, the Roman goddess of love.

Jeremiah 44:17

promised to make sacrifices to the Queen Goddess, and we will certainly do everything we promised. We will burn incense and pour out drink offerings to worship her, just as we, our ancestors, kings, and officers did in the past. All of us did these things in the towns of Judah and in the streets of Jerusalem. At that time we had plenty of food and were successful, and nothing bad happened to us. [18]But since we stopped making sacrifices to the Queen Goddess and stopped pouring out drink offerings to her, we have had great problems. Our people have also been killed in war and by hunger."

[19]The women said, "Our husbands knew what we were doing. We had their permission to burn incense to the Queen Goddess and to pour out drink offerings to her. Our husbands knew we were making cakes that looked like her and were pouring out drink offerings to her."

[20]Then Jeremiah spoke to all the people—men and women—who answered him. [21]He said to them, "The LORD remembered that you and your ancestors, kings and officers, and the people of the land burned incense in the towns of Judah and in the streets of Jerusalem. He remembered and thought about it. [22]Then he could not be patient with you any longer. He hated the terrible things you did. So he made your country an empty desert, where no one lives. Other people curse that country. And so it is today. [23]All this happened because you burned incense to other gods. You sinned against the LORD. You did not obey him or follow his teachings or the laws he gave you. You did not keep your part of the agreement with him. So this disaster has happened to you. It is there for you to see."

[24]Then Jeremiah said to all those men and women, "People of Judah who are now in Egypt, hear the word of the LORD: [25]The LORD All-Powerful, the God of Israel, says: You and your wives did what you said you would do. You said, 'We will certainly keep the promises we made. We promised to make sacrifices to the Queen Goddess and to pour out drink offerings to her.' So, go ahead. Do the things you promised, and keep your promises. [26]But hear the word of the LORD. Listen, all you Jews living in Egypt. The LORD says, 'I have sworn by my great name: The people of Judah now living in Egypt will never again use my name to make promises. They will never again say in Egypt, "As surely as the Lord GOD lives . . ." [27]I am watching over them, not to take care of them, but to hurt them. The Jews who live in Egypt will die from swords or hunger until they are all destroyed. [28]A few will escape being killed by the sword and will come back to Judah from Egypt. Then, of the people of Judah who came to live in Egypt, those who are left alive will know if my word or their word came true. [29]I will give you a sign that I will punish you here in Egypt,' says the LORD. 'When you see it happen, you will know that my promises to hurt you will really happen.' [30]This is what the LORD says: 'Hophra king of Egypt has enemies who want to kill him. Soon I will hand him over to his enemies just as I handed Zedekiah king of Judah over to Nebuchadnezzar king of Babylon, who wanted to kill him.' "

"Then Jeremiah said to all those men and women, 'People of Judah who are now in Egypt, hear the word of the LORD.' " (Jeremiah 44:24)

A MESSAGE TO BARUCH

45

[1]It was the fourth year that Jehoiakim son of Josiah was king of Judah. Jeremiah the prophet told these things to Baruch son of Neriah, and Baruch wrote them on a scroll: [2]"This is what the LORD, the God of Israel, says to you, Baruch: [3]You have said, 'How terrible it is for me! The LORD has given me sorrow along with my pain. I am tired because of my suffering and cannot rest.' "

WHAT'S IT MEAN?

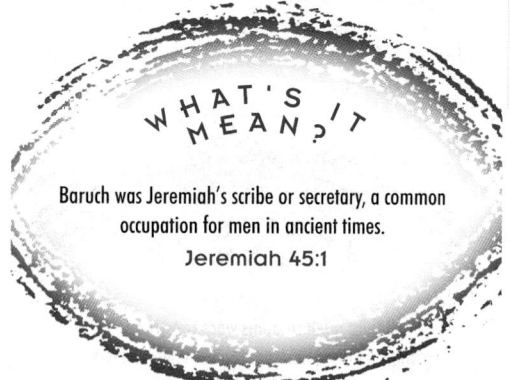

Baruch was Jeremiah's scribe or secretary, a common occupation for men in ancient times.

Jeremiah 45:1

[4]The LORD said, "Say this to Baruch: 'This is what the LORD says: I will soon tear down what I have built, and I will pull up what I have planted everywhere in Judah. [5]Baruch, you are looking for great things for yourself.

Don't look for them, because I will bring disaster on all the people, says the LORD. You will have to go many places, but I will let you escape alive wherever you go.' "

MESSAGES TO THE NATIONS

46
[1]The LORD spoke this word to Jeremiah the
prophet about the nations:
[2]This message is to Egypt. It is about the
army of Neco king of Egypt, which was defeated at the city of Carchemish on the Euphrates River by Nebuchadnezzar king of Babylon. This was in the fourth year that Jehoiakim son of Josiah was king of Judah. This is the LORD's message to Egypt:

[3]"Prepare your shields, large and small,
and march out for battle!
[4]Harness the horses
and get on them!
Go to your places for battle
and put on your helmets!
Polish your spears.
Put on your armor!
[5]What do I see?
That army is terrified,
and the soldiers are running away.
Their warriors are defeated.
They run away quickly
without looking back.
There is terror on every side!" says the LORD.
[6]"The fast runners cannot run away;
the strong soldiers cannot escape.
They stumble and fall
in the north, by the Euphrates River.
[7]Who is this, rising up like the Nile River,
like strong, fast rivers?
[8]Egypt rises up like the Nile River,
like strong, fast rivers.
Egypt says, 'I will rise up and cover the earth.

WHAT'S IT MEAN?

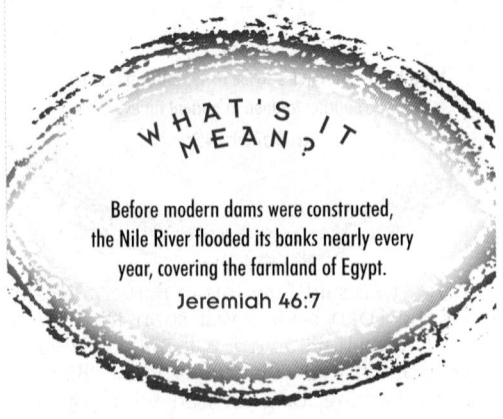

Before modern dams were constructed, the Nile River flooded its banks nearly every year, covering the farmland of Egypt.

Jeremiah 46:7

I will destroy cities and the people in them!'
[9]Horsemen, charge into battle!
Chariot drivers, drive hard!
March on, brave soldiers—
soldiers from the countries of Cush and Put who carry shields,
soldiers from Lydia who use bows.

WHAT'S IT MEAN?

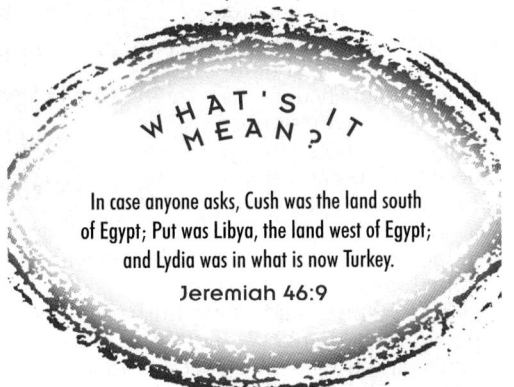

In case anyone asks, Cush was the land south of Egypt; Put was Libya, the land west of Egypt; and Lydia was in what is now Turkey.

Jeremiah 46:9

[10]"But that day belongs to the Lord GOD All-Powerful.
At that time he will give those people
the punishment they deserve.
The sword will kill until it is finished,
until it satisfies its thirst for their blood.
The Lord GOD All-Powerful will offer a sacrifice
in the land of the north, by the Euphrates River.

[11]"Go up to Gilead and get some balm,
people of Egypt!
You have prepared many medicines,
but they will not work;
you will not be healed.
[12]The nations have heard of your shame,
and your cries fill all the earth.
One warrior has run into another;
both of them have fallen down together!"

[13]This is the message the LORD spoke to Jer-
emiah the prophet about Nebuchadnezzar king of Babylon's coming to attack Egypt:

[14]"Announce this message in Egypt, and preach it in Migdol.
Preach it also in the cities of Memphis and Tahpanhes:
'Get ready for war,
because the battle is all around you.'
[15]Egypt, why were your warriors killed?
They could not stand because the LORD pushed them down.

16 They stumbled again and again
and fell over each other.
They said, 'Get up. Let's go back
to our own people and our homeland.
We must get away from our enemy's
sword!'
17 In their homelands those soldiers called
out,
'The king of Egypt is only a lot of noise.
He missed his chance for glory!' "
18 The King's name is the LORD All-Powerful.
He says, "As surely as I live,
a powerful leader will come.
He will be like Mount Tabor among the
mountains,
like Mount Carmel by the sea.
19 People of Egypt, pack your things
to be taken away as captives,
because Memphis will be destroyed.
It will be a ruin, and no one will live
there.

20 "Egypt is like a beautiful young cow,
but a horsefly is coming
from the north to attack her.
21 The hired soldiers in Egypt's army
are like fat calves,
because even they all turn and run away
together;
they do not stand strong against the
attack.
Their time of destruction is coming;
they will soon be punished.
22 Egypt is like a hissing snake that is trying
to escape.
The enemy comes closer and closer.
They come against Egypt with axes
like men who cut down trees.
23 They will chop down Egypt's army
as if it were a great forest," says the
LORD.
"There are more enemy soldiers than
locusts;
there are too many to count.
24 The people of Egypt will be ashamed.
They will be handed over to the enemy
from the north."

25 The LORD All-Powerful, the God of Israel,
says: "Very soon I will punish Amon, the god
of the city of Thebes. And I will punish Egypt,
her kings, her gods, and the people who depend on the king. 26 I will hand those people
over to their enemies, who want to kill them. I
will give them to Nebuchadnezzar king of
Babylon and his officers. But in the future,
Egypt will live in peace as it once did," says the
LORD.

A MESSAGE TO ISRAEL

27 "People of Jacob, my servants, don't be
afraid;
don't be frightened, Israel.
I will surely save you from
those faraway places
and your children from
the lands where they
are captives.
The people of Jacob will
have peace and safety
again,
and no one will make them afraid.
28 People of Jacob, my servants, do not be
afraid,
because I am with you," says the LORD.
"I will completely destroy the many
different nations
where I scattered you.
But I will not completely destroy you.
I will punish you fairly,
but I will not let you escape your
punishment."

FEAR

Who can conquer our fears? (46:27–28)

A MESSAGE TO THE PHILISTINES

47

1 Before the king of Egypt attacked the city
of Gaza, the LORD spoke his word to Jeremiah
the prophet. This message is to the Philistine
people.
2 This is what the LORD says:
"See, the enemy is gathering in the north
like rising waters.
They will become like an overflowing
stream
and will cover the whole country like a
flood,
even the towns and the people living in
them.
Everyone living in that country
will cry for help;
the people will cry painfully.
3 They will hear the sound of the running
horses
and the noisy chariots
and the rumbling chariot wheels.
Parents will not help their children to
safety,
because they will be too weak to help.
4 The time has come
to destroy all the Philistines.
It is time to destroy all who are left alive
who could help the cities of Tyre and
Sidon.
The LORD will soon destroy the Philistines,
those left alive from the island of Crete.
5 The people from the city of Gaza will be
sad and shave their heads.

The people from the city of Ashkelon
will be made silent.
Those left alive from the valley,
how long will you cut yourselves?[n]

6 "You cry, 'Sword of the LORD,
how long will you keep fighting?
Return to your holder.
Stop and be still.'
7 But how can his sword rest
when the LORD has given it a
command?
He has ordered it
to attack Ashkelon and the seacoast."

A MESSAGE TO MOAB

48 1 This message is to the country of Moab.

This is what the LORD All-Powerful, the God of Israel, says:
"How terrible it will be for the city of
Nebo,
because it will be ruined.
The town of Kiriathaim will be disgraced
and captured;
the strong city will be disgraced and
shattered.
2 Moab will not be praised again.
Men in the town of Heshbon plan
Moab's defeat.
They say, 'Come, let us put an end to
that nation!'
Town of Madmen,[n] you will also be
silenced.
The sword will chase you.
3 Listen to the cries from the town of
Horonaim,
cries of much confusion and
destruction.
4 Moab will be broken up.
Her little children will cry for help.
5 Moab's people go up the path to the town
of Luhith,
crying loudly as they go.
On the road down to Horonaim,
cries of pain and suffering can be heard.
6 Run! Run for your lives!
Go like a bush being blown through the
desert.
7 You trust in the things you do and in your
wealth,
so you also will be captured.
The god Chemosh will go into captivity
and his priests and officers with him.
8 The destroyer will come against every
town;
not one town will escape.
The valley will be ruined,
and the high plain will be destroyed,
as the LORD has said.
9 Give wings to Moab,
because she will surely leave her land.
Moab's towns will become empty,
with no one to live in them.

10 "A curse will be on anyone who doesn't
do what the LORD says,
and a curse will be on anyone who
holds back his sword from killing.

WHAT'S IT MEAN?

To understand Jeremiah's description of Moab, you have to know that when wine was made in ancient times, the bottles were left in places where they would not be touched. The winemakers wanted the grape juice to ferment and the sediment to settle at the bottom of the bottle. The wine was not considered fit for drinking until it had been poured to remove the sediment.

Jeremiah 48:11

11 "The people of Moab have never known
trouble.
They are like wine left to settle;
they have never been poured from one jar
to another.
They have not been taken into captivity.
So they taste as they did before,
and their smell has not changed.
12 A time is coming," says the LORD,
"When I will send people to pour you
from your jars.
They will empty Moab's jars
and smash her jugs.
13 The people of Israel trusted that god in the
town of Bethel,
and they were ashamed when there was
no help.
In the same way Moab will be ashamed
of their god Chemosh.

47:5 sad and . . . yourselves The people did these things to show their sadness. **48:2 Madmen** This name sounds like the Hebrew word for "be silenced."

14"You cannot say, 'We are warriors!
We are brave men in battle!'
15The destroyer of Moab and her towns has arrived.
Her best young men will be killed!" says the King,
whose name is the LORD All-Powerful.
16"The end of Moab is near,
and she will soon be destroyed.
17All you who live around Moab,
all you who know her, cry for her.
Say, 'The ruler's power is broken;
Moab's power and glory are gone.'

18"You people living in the town of Dibon,
come down from your place of honor
and sit on the dry ground,
because the destroyer of Moab has come against you.
And he has destroyed your strong, walled cities.
19You people living in the town of Aroer,
stand next to the road and watch.
See the man running away and the woman escaping.
Ask them, 'What happened?'
20Moab is filled with shame, because she is ruined.
Cry, Moab, cry out!
Announce at the Arnon River
that Moab is destroyed.
21People on the high plain have been punished.
Judgment has come to these towns:
Holon, Jahzah, and Mephaath;
22 Dibon, Nebo, and Beth Diblathaim;
23 Kiriathaim, Beth Gamul, and Beth Meon;
24 Kerioth and Bozrah.
Judgment has come to all the towns of Moab, far and near.
25Moab's strength has been cut off,
and its arm broken!" says the LORD.

26"The people of Moab thought they were greater than the LORD,
so punish them until they act as if they are drunk.
Moab will fall and roll around in its own vomit,
and people will even make fun of it.
27Moab, you made fun of Israel.
Israel was caught in the middle of a gang of thieves.
When you spoke about Israel,
you shook your head and acted as if you were better than it.
28People in Moab, leave your towns empty
and go live among the rocks.
Be like a dove that makes its nest
at the entrance of a cave.

29"We have heard that the people of Moab are proud,
very proud.
They are proud, very proud,
and in their hearts they think they are important."
30The LORD says,
"I know Moab's great pride, but it is useless.
Moab's bragging accomplishes nothing.
31So I cry sadly for Moab,
for everyone in Moab.
I moan for the people from the town of Kir Hareseth.
32I cry with the people of the town of Jazer
for you, the grapevines of the town of Sibmah.
In the past your vines spread all the way to the sea,
as far as the sea of Jazer.
But the destroyer has taken over
your fruit and grapes.
33Joy and happiness are gone
from the large, rich fields of Moab.
I have stopped the flow of wine from the winepresses.
No one walks on the grapes with shouts of joy.
There are shouts,
but not shouts of joy.

34"Their crying can be heard from Moabite towns,
from Heshbon to Elealeh and Jahaz.
It can be heard from Zoar as far away as Horonaim and Eglath Shelishiyah.
Even the waters of Nimrim are dried up.
35I will stop Moab
from making burnt offerings at the places of worship
and from burning incense to their gods,"
says the LORD.

36"My heart cries sadly for Moab like a flute playing a funeral song.
It cries like a flute for the people from Kir Hareseth.
The money they made has all been taken away.
37Every head has been shaved
and every beard cut off.
Everyone's hands are cut,

and everyone wears rough cloth around
his waist.[n]
38 People are crying on every roof[n] in Moab
and in every public square.
There is nothing but sadness,
because I have broken Moab
like a jar no one wants," says the LORD.
39 "Moab is shattered! The people are
crying!
Moab turns away in shame!
People all around her make fun of her.
The things that happened fill them with
great fear."

40 This is what the LORD says:
"Look! Someone is coming, like an eagle
diving down from the sky
and spreading its wings over Moab.
41 The towns of Moab will be captured,
and the strong, walled cities will be
defeated.
At that time Moab's warriors will be
frightened,
like a woman who is having a baby.
42 The nation of Moab will be destroyed,
because they thought they were greater
than the LORD.
43 Fear, deep pits, and traps wait for you,
people of Moab," says the LORD.
44 "People will run from fear,
but they will fall into the pits.
Anyone who climbs out of the pits
will be caught in the traps.
I will bring the year of punishment to
Moab," says the LORD.

45 "People have run from the powerful
enemy
and have gone to Heshbon for safety.
But fire started in Heshbon;
a blaze has spread from the hometown
of Sihon king of Moab.
It burned up the leaders of Moab
and destroyed those proud people.
46 How terrible it is for you, Moab!
The people who worship Chemosh have
been destroyed.
Your sons have been taken captive,
and your daughters have been taken
away.
47 "But in days to come,
I will make good things happen again to
Moab," says the LORD.

This ends the judgment on Moab.

WHAT'S IT MEAN?

Sihon blew his big chance to help the Israelites when he refused Moses' request to let God's people pass through the land of the Amorites. He then made matters worse by attacking the Israelites. Needless to say, he was killed and his army was defeated. The Israelite tribes of Gad and Reuben took control of the land that had belonged to the Amorites.

Jeremiah 48:45

A MESSAGE TO AMMON

49
1 This message is to the Ammonite people.

This is what the LORD says:
"Do you think that Israel has no children?
Do you think there is no one to take the
land when the parents die?
If that were true, why did Molech take
Gad's land
and why did Molech's people settle in
Gad's towns?"
2 The LORD says,
"The time will come when I will make
Rabbah,
the capital city of the Ammonites, hear
the battle cry.
It will become a hill covered with ruins,
and the towns around it will be burned.
Those people forced Israel out of that land,
but now Israel will force them out!" says
the LORD.
3 "People in the town of Heshbon, cry sadly
because the town of Ai is destroyed!
Those who live in Rabbah, cry out!
Put on your rough cloth to show your
sadness, and cry loudly.

48:37 Every head . . . waist. The people did these things to show their sadness for those who had died.
48:38 roof In Bible times houses were built with flat roofs. The roof was used for drying things such as flax and fruit. And it was used as an extra room, as a place for worship, and as a cool place to sleep in the summer.

Run here and there for safety inside the walls,
because Molech will be taken captive
and his priests and officers with him.
4 You brag about your valleys
and about the fruit in your valleys.
You are like an unfaithful child
who believes his treasures will save him.
You think, 'Who would attack me?'
5 I will soon bring terror on you
from everyone around you,"
says the Lord GOD All-Powerful.
"You will all be forced to run away,
and no one will be able to gather you.

6 "But the time will come
when I will make good things happen to the Ammonites again,"
says the LORD.

WHAT'S IT MEAN?

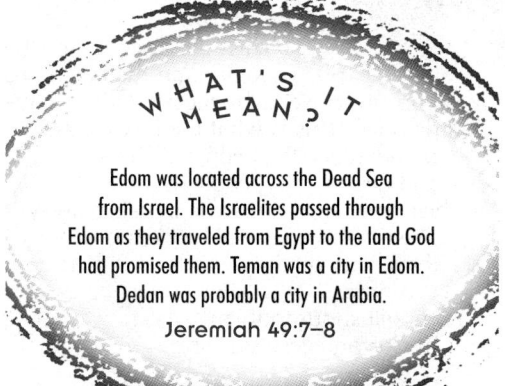

Edom was located across the Dead Sea from Israel. The Israelites passed through Edom as they traveled from Egypt to the land God had promised them. Teman was a city in Edom. Dedan was probably a city in Arabia.

Jeremiah 49:7–8

A MESSAGE TO EDOM

7 This message is to Edom. This is what the
LORD All-Powerful says:
"Is there no more wisdom in the town of Teman?
Can the wise men of Edom no longer give good advice?
Have they lost their wisdom?
8 You people living in the town of Dedan,
run away and hide in deep caves,
because I will bring disaster on the people of Esau.
It is time for me to punish them.
9 If workers came and picked the grapes from your vines,
they would leave a few grapes behind.
If robbers came at night,
they would steal only enough for themselves.
10 But I will strip Edom bare.
I will find all their hiding places,
so they will not be able to hide from me.
The children, relatives, and neighbors will die,
and Edom will be no more.
11 Leave the orphans, and I will take care of them.
Your widows also can trust in me."

12 This is what the LORD says: "Some people
did not deserve to be punished, but they had
to drink from the cup of suffering anyway.
People of Edom, you deserve to be punished,
so you will not escape punishment. You must
certainly drink from the cup of suffering." 13 The
LORD says, "I swear by my own name that the
city of Bozrah will become a pile of ruins! People will be shocked by what happened there.
They will insult that city and speak evil of it.
And all the towns around it will become ruins
forever."

14 I have heard a message from the LORD.
A messenger has been sent among the nations, saying,
"Gather your armies to attack it!
Get ready for battle!"

15 "Soon I will make you the smallest of nations,
and you will be greatly hated by everyone.
16 Edom, you frightened other nations,
but your pride has fooled you.
You live in the hollow places of the cliff
and control the high places of the hills.
Even if you build your home as high as an eagle's nest,
I will bring you down from there," says the LORD.
17 "Edom will be destroyed.
People who pass by will be shocked to see the destroyed cities,
and they will be amazed at all her injuries.
18 Edom will be destroyed like the cities of Sodom and Gomorrah
and the towns around them," says the LORD.
"No one will live there!
No one will stay in Edom."

19 "Like a lion coming up from the thick bushes near the Jordan River
to attack a strong pen for sheep,
I will suddenly chase Edom from its land.
Who is the one I have chosen to do this?

There is no one like me,
no one who can take me to court.
None of their leaders can stand up against me."

20 So listen to what the LORD has planned to do against Edom.
Listen to what he has decided to do to the people in the town of Teman.
He will surely drag away the young ones of Edom.
Their hometowns will surely be shocked at what happens to them.
21 At the sound of Edom's fall, the earth will shake.
Their cry will be heard all the way to the Red Sea.

"So listen to what the LORD has planned to do against Edom. Listen to what he has decided to do to the people in the town of Teman."
(Jeremiah 49:20a)

22 The LORD is like an eagle swooping down and spreading its wings over the city of Bozrah.
At that time Edom's soldiers will become very frightened,
like a woman having a baby.

A MESSAGE TO DAMASCUS

23 This message is to the city of Damascus:
"The towns of Hamath and Arpad are put to shame,
because they have heard bad news.
They are discouraged.
They are troubled like the tossing sea.
24 The city of Damascus has become weak.
The people want to run away;

WHAT'S IT MEAN?

Damascus, Hamath, and Arpad were all important cities in Syria. Damascus, the capital, is located about 140 miles northeast of the Dead Sea. Not only is Damascus one of the oldest cities in the world; it is still an important part of the region today.

Jeremiah 49:23

they are ready to panic.
The people feel pain and suffering,
like a woman giving birth to a baby.
25 Damascus was a city of my joy.
Why have the people not left that famous city yet?
26 Surely the young men will die in the city squares,
and all her soldiers will be killed at that time," says the LORD All-Powerful.
27 "I will set fire to the walls of Damascus,
and it will completely burn the strong cities of King Ben-Hadad."

A MESSAGE TO KEDAR AND HAZOR

28 This message is to the tribe of Kedar and the kingdoms of Hazor, which Nebuchadnezzar king of Babylon defeated. This is what the LORD says:
"Go and attack the people of Kedar,
and destroy the people of the East.
29 Their tents and flocks will be taken away.
Their belongings will be carried off—
their tents, all their goods, and their camels.
Men will shout to them,
'Terror on every side!'

30 "Run away quickly!
People in Hazor, find a good place to hide!" says the LORD.
"Nebuchadnezzar king of Babylon has made plans against you
and wants to defeat you.

31 "Get up! Attack the nation that is comfortable,
that is sure no one will defeat it," says the LORD.
"It does not have gates or fences to protect it.
Its people live alone.
32 The enemy will steal their camels
and their large herds of cattle as war prizes.
I will scatter the people who cut their hair short to every part of the earth,
and I will bring disaster on them from everywhere," says the LORD.
33 "The city of Hazor will become a home for wild dogs;

it will be an empty desert forever.
No one will live there,
and no one will stay in it."

A MESSAGE TO ELAM

34Soon after Zedekiah became king of Judah, the LORD spoke this word to Jeremiah the
prophet. This message is to the nation of Elam.
35This is what the LORD All-Powerful says:

"I will soon break Elam's bow,
its greatest strength.
36I will bring the four winds against Elam
from the four corners of the skies.
I will scatter its people everywhere the
four winds blow;
its captives will go to every nation.
37I will terrify Elam in front of their enemies,
who want to destroy them.
I will bring disaster to Elam
and show them how angry I am!" says
the LORD.
"I will send a sword to chase Elam
until I have killed them all.
38I will set up my throne in Elam to show
that I am king,
and I will destroy its king and its
officers!" says the LORD.

WHAT'S IT MEAN?

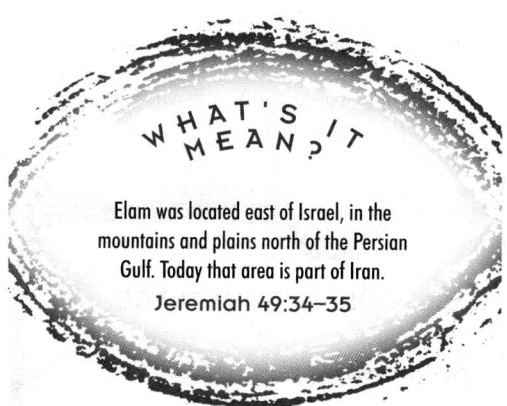

Elam was located east of Israel, in the mountains and plains north of the Persian Gulf. Today that area is part of Iran.

Jeremiah 49:34–35

39"But I will make good things happen to
Elam again
in the future," says the LORD.

A MESSAGE TO BABYLON

50

1This is the message the LORD spoke to Babylon and the Babylonian people through Jeremiah the prophet.

2"Announce this to the nations.
Lift up a banner and tell them.
Speak the whole message and say:
'Babylon will be captured.
The god Bel will be put to shame,
and the god Marduk will be afraid.
Babylon's gods will be put to shame,
and her idols will be afraid!'
3A nation from the north will attack
Babylon
and make it like an empty desert.
No one will live there;
both people and animals will run away."

WHAT'S IT MEAN?

Marduk was the chief god of the Babylonians. The people of Babylon believed that Marduk created the world, and they looked to him to protect their kingdom.

Jeremiah 50:2

4The LORD says, "At that time
the people of Israel and Judah will come
together.
They will cry and look for the LORD
their God.
5Those people will ask how to go to
Jerusalem
and will start in that direction.
They will come and join themselves to the
LORD.
They will make an agreement with him
that will last forever,
an agreement that will never be
forgotten.

6"My people have been like lost sheep.
Their leaders have led them in the
wrong way
and made them wander around in the
mountains and hills.
They forgot where their resting place
was.
7Whoever saw my people hurt them.
And those enemies said, 'We did nothing
wrong.
Those people sinned against the LORD,
their true resting place,
the God their fathers trusted.'

8"Run away from Babylon,
and leave the land of the Babylonians.
Be like the goats that lead the flock.

9 I will soon bring against Babylon
many great nations from the north.
They will take their places for war against
it,
and it will be captured by people from
the north.
Their arrows are like trained soldiers
who do not return from war with
empty hands.
10 The enemy will take all the wealth from
the Babylonians.
Those enemy soldiers will get all they
want," says the LORD.

11 "Babylon, you are excited and happy,
because you took my land.
You dance around like a young cow in the
grain.
Your laughter is like the neighing of
male horses.
12 Your mother will be very ashamed;
the woman who gave birth to you will
be disgraced.
Soon Babylonia will be the least important
of all the nations.
She will be an empty, dry desert.
13 Because of the LORD's anger,
no one will live there.
She will be completely empty.
Everyone who passes by Babylon will be
shocked.
They will shake their heads when they
see all her injuries.

14 "Take your positions for war against
Babylon,
all you soldiers with bows.
Shoot your arrows at Babylon! Do not
save any of them,
because Babylon has sinned against the
LORD.
15 Soldiers around Babylon, shout the war
cry!
Babylon has surrendered, her towers
have fallen,
and her walls have been torn down.
The LORD is giving her people the
punishment they deserve.
You nations should give her what she
deserves;
do to her what she has done to others.
16 Don't let the people from Babylon plant
their crops
or gather the harvest.
The soldiers treated their captives cruelly.
Now, let everyone go back home.
Let everyone run to his own country.

17 "The people of Israel are like a flock of
sheep that are scattered
from being chased by lions.
The first lion to eat them up
was the king of Assyria.
The last lion to crush their bones
was Nebuchadnezzar king of Babylon."
18 So this is what the LORD All-Powerful, the
God of Israel, says:

Promise

HE PROMISES TO BE YOUR RESTING PLACE.

Those people sinned against the LORD, their true resting place, the God their fathers trusted (Jer. 50:7b).

You're thinking, *Resting place, what's so great about a resting place?* Back in Bible days, people's wealth was wrapped up in their land—the place where they lived and rested in security. It was a place where their sheep could graze on plenty and in complete protection from the wild animals.

God has promised that he will be our "resting place"—*our true home.* He is the One who is our Protector and our Provider. He is our safe place in the middle of the jungle! He is the One who gives hope. When we learn to stop worrying and put our hope in God, our hearts are surrounded by an intense peace, which can't be penetrated by anything the Enemy throws our way (see Phil. 4:6–7). It's easy to put our hope in other people and other things, but remember that people and things will never provide a good place to "rest." God is our true resting place, and he won't fail us!

SEE FOR YOURSELF:
Ps. 16:1; 64:1; John 10:10; 17:11

"I will punish the king of Babylon and his
country
as I punished the king of Assyria.
19 But I will bring the people of Israel back to
their own pasture.
They will eat on Mount Carmel and in
Bashan.
They will eat and be full
on the hills of Ephraim and Gilead."
20 The LORD says,
"At that time people will try to find
Israel's guilt,
but there will be no guilt.
People will try to find Judah's sins,
but no sins will be found,
because I will leave a few people alive
from Israel and Judah,
and I will forgive their sins.

21 "Attack the land of Merathaim.
Attack the people who live in Pekod.
Chase them, kill them, and completely
destroy them.
Do everything I commanded you!" says
the LORD.

22 "The noise of battle can be heard all over
the country;
it is the noise of much destruction.
23 Babylon was the hammer of the whole
earth,
but how broken and shattered that
hammer is now.
It is truly the most ruined
of all the nations.
24 Babylon, I set a trap for you,
and you were caught before you knew
it.
You fought against the LORD,
so you were found and taken prisoner.
25 The LORD has opened up his storeroom
and brought out the weapons of his
anger,
because the Lord GOD All-Powerful has
work to do
in the land of the Babylonians.
26 Come against Babylon from far away.
Break open her storehouses of grain.
Pile up her dead bodies like heaps of
grain.
Completely destroy Babylon
and do not leave anyone alive.
27 Kill all the young men in Babylon;
let them be killed like animals.
How terrible it will be for them, because
the time has come for their defeat;
it is time for them to be punished.
28 Listen to the people running to escape the
country of Babylon!
They are telling Jerusalem
how the LORD our God is punishing
Babylon as it deserves
for destroying his Temple.

29 "Call for the archers
to come against Babylon.
Tell them to surround the city,
and let no one escape.
Pay her back for what she has done;
do to her what she has done to other
nations.
Babylon acted with pride against the LORD,
the Holy One of Israel.
30 So her young men will be killed in her
streets.
All her soldiers will die on that day,"
says the LORD.
31 "Babylon, you are too proud, and I am
against you,"
says the Lord GOD All-Powerful.
"The time has come
for you to be punished.
32 Proud Babylon will
stumble and fall,
and no one will help
her get up.
I will start a fire in her
towns,
and it will burn up
everything around her."

PRIDE
What is the reward of arrogant people? (50:31–32)

33 This is what the LORD All-Powerful says:
"The people of Israel
and Judah are slaves.
The enemy took them as prisoners
and won't let them go.
34 But God is strong and will buy them back.
His name is the LORD All-Powerful.
He will surely defend them with power
so he can give rest to their land.
But he will not give rest to those living
in Babylon."
35 The LORD says,
"Let a sword kill the people living in
Babylon
and her officers and wise men!
36 Let a sword kill her false prophets,
and they will become fools.
Let a sword kill her warriors,
and they will be full of terror.
37 Let a sword kill her horses and chariots
and all the soldiers hired from other
countries!
Then they will be like frightened
women.

Let a sword attack her treasures,
so they will be taken away.
38 Let a sword attack her waters
so they will be dried up.
She is a land of idols,
and the people go crazy with fear over them.

39 "Desert animals and hyenas will live there,
and owls will live there,
but no people will ever live there again.
She will never be filled with people again.
40 God completely destroyed the cities of Sodom and Gomorrah
and the towns around them," says the LORD.
"In the same way no people will live in Babylon,
and no human being will stay there.

41 "Look! An army is coming from the north.
A powerful nation and many kings
are coming together from all around the world.
42 Their armies have bows and spears.
The soldiers are cruel and have no mercy.
As the soldiers come riding on their horses,
the sound is loud like the roaring sea.
They stand in their places, ready for battle.
They are ready to attack you, city of Babylon.
43 The king of Babylon heard about those armies,
and he became helpless with fear.
Distress has gripped him.
His pain is like that of a woman giving birth to a baby.

44 "Like a lion coming up from the thick bushes near the Jordan River
to attack a strong pen for sheep,
I will suddenly chase the people of Babylon from their land.
Who is the one I have chosen to do this?
There is no one like me,
no one who can take me to court.
None of their leaders can stand up against me."

45 So listen to what the LORD has planned to do against Babylon.
Listen to what he has decided to do to the people in the city of Babylon.
He will surely drag away the young ones of Babylon.
Their hometowns will surely be shocked at what happens to them.
46 At the sound of Babylon's capture, the earth will shake.
People in all nations will hear Babylon's cry of distress.

51

1 This is what the LORD says:
"I will soon cause a destroying wind to blow
against Babylon and the Babylonian people.
2 I will send foreign people to destroy Babylon
like a wind that blows chaff away.
They will destroy the land.
Armies will surround the city
when the day of disaster comes upon her.
3 Don't let the Babylonian soldiers prepare their bows to shoot.
Don't even let them put on their armor.
Don't feel sorry for the young men of Babylon,
but completely destroy her army.
4 They will be killed in the land of the Babylonians
and will die in her streets.
5 The Lord GOD All-Powerful
did not leave Israel and Judah,
even though they were completely guilty
in the presence of the Holy One of Israel.
6 "Run away from Babylon
and save your lives!
Don't stay and be killed because of Babylon's sins.
It is time for the LORD to punish Babylon;
he will give Babylon the punishment she deserves.

WHAT'S IT MEAN?

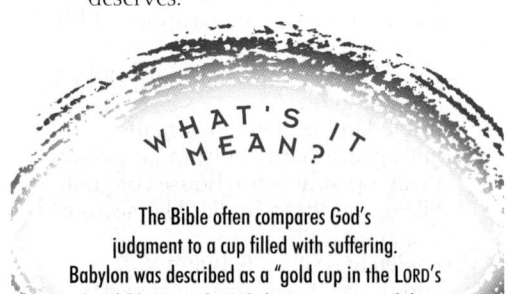

The Bible often compares God's judgment to a cup filled with suffering. Babylon was described as a "gold cup in the LORD's hand," because the Babylonians conquered the countries God wanted to punish.

Jeremiah 51:7

7 Babylon was like a gold cup in the LORD's hand
that made the whole earth drunk.
The nations drank Babylon's wine,
so they went crazy.
8 Babylon has suddenly fallen and been broken.
Cry for her!
Get balm for her pain,
and maybe she can be healed.

9 "Foreigners in Babylon say, 'We tried to heal Babylon,
but she cannot be healed.
So let us leave her and each go to his own country.
Babylon's punishment is as high as the sky;
it reaches to the clouds.'

10 "The people of Judah say,
'The LORD has shown us to be right.
Come, let us tell in Jerusalem
what the LORD our God has done.'

> "The LORD has shown us to be right. Come, let us tell in Jerusalem what the LORD our God has done." (Jeremiah 51:10)

11 "Sharpen the arrows!
Pick up your shields!
The LORD has stirred up the kings of the Medes,
because he wants to destroy Babylon.
The LORD will punish them as they deserve
for destroying his Temple.
12 Lift up a banner against the walls of Babylon!
Bring more guards.
Put the watchmen in their places,
and get ready for a secret attack!
The LORD will certainly do what he has planned
and what he said he would do against the people of Babylon.
13 People of Babylon, you live near much water
and are rich with many treasures,
but your end as a nation has come.
It is time to stop you from robbing other nations.
14 The LORD All-Powerful has promised in his own name:
'Babylon, I will surely fill you with so many enemy soldiers they will be like a swarm of locusts.
They will stand over you and shout their victory.'

15 "The LORD made the earth by his power.
He used his wisdom to build the world
and his understanding to stretch out the skies.
16 When he thunders, the waters in the skies roar.
He makes clouds rise in the sky all over the earth.
He sends lightning with the rain
and brings out the wind from his storehouses.

17 "People are so stupid and know so little.
Goldsmiths are made ashamed by their idols,
because those statues are only false gods.
They have no breath in them.
18 They are worth nothing;
people make fun of them.
When they are judged,
they will be destroyed.
19 But God, who is Jacob's Portion, is not like the idols.
He made everything,
and he chose Israel to be his special people.
The LORD All-Powerful is his name.

20 "You are my war club,
my battle weapon.
I use you to smash nations.
I use you to destroy kingdoms.
21 I use you to smash horses and riders.
I use you to smash chariots and drivers.
22 I use you to smash men and women.
I use you to smash old people and young people.
I use you to smash young men and young women.
23 I use you to smash shepherds and flocks.
I use you to smash farmers and oxen.
I use you to smash governors and officers.

24 "But I will pay back Babylon and all the
Babylonians for all the evil things they did to
Jerusalem in your sight," says the LORD.
25 The LORD says,
"Babylon, you are a destroying mountain,
and I am against you.

You have destroyed the whole land.
I will put my hand out against you.
I will roll you off the cliffs,
and I will make you a burned-out mountain.
26 People will not find any rocks in Babylon big enough for cornerstones.
People will not take any rocks from Babylon to use for the foundation of a building,
because your city will be just a pile of ruins forever," says the LORD.

27 "Lift up a banner in the land!
Blow the trumpet among the nations!
Get the nations ready for battle against Babylon.
Call these kingdoms of Ararat, Minni, and Ashkenaz to fight against her.
Choose a commander to lead the army against Babylon.
Send so many horses that they are like a swarm of locusts.
28 Get the nations ready for battle against Babylon—
the kings of the Medes,
their governors and all their officers,
and all the countries they rule.
29 The land shakes and moves in pain,
because the LORD will do what he has planned to Babylon.
He will make Babylon an empty desert,
where no one will live.
30 Babylon's warriors have stopped fighting.
They stay in their protected cities.
Their strength is gone,
and they have become like frightened women.
Babylon's houses are burning.
The bars of her gates are broken.
31 One messenger follows another;
messenger follows messenger.
They announce to the king of Babylon
that his whole city has been captured.
32 The river crossings have been captured,
and the swamplands are burning.
All of Babylon's soldiers are terribly afraid."
33 This is what the LORD All-Powerful, the God of Israel, says:
"The city of Babylon is like a threshing floor,
where people crush the grain at harvest time.
The time to harvest Babylon is coming soon."

34 "Nebuchadnezzar king of Babylon has defeated and destroyed us.
In the past he took our people away,
and we became like an empty jar.
He was like a giant snake that swallowed us.
He filled his stomach with our best things.
Then he spit us out.
35 Babylon did terrible things to hurt us.
Now let those things happen to Babylon,"
say the people of Jerusalem.
"The people of Babylon killed our people.
Now let them be punished for what they did," says Jerusalem.
36 So this is what the LORD says:
"I will soon defend you, Judah,
and make sure that Babylon is punished.
I will dry up Babylon's sea
and make her springs become dry.
37 Babylon will become a pile of ruins,
a home for wild dogs.
People will be shocked by what happened there.
No one will live there anymore.
38 Babylon's people roar like young lions;
they growl like baby lions.
39 While they are stirred up,
I will give a feast for them
and make them drunk.
They will shout and laugh.
And they will sleep forever and never wake up!" says the LORD.
40 "I will take the people of Babylon to be killed.
They will be like lambs,
like sheep and goats waiting to be killed.

41 "How Babylon has been defeated!
The pride of the whole earth has been taken captive.
People from other nations are shocked at what happened to Babylon,
and the things they see make them afraid.
42 The sea has risen over Babylon;
its roaring waves cover her.
43 Babylon's towns are ruined and empty.
It has become a dry, desert land,
a land where no one lives.
People do not even travel through Babylon.
44 I will punish the god Bel in Babylon.
I will make him spit out what he has swallowed.

Nations will no longer come to Babylon;
even the wall around the city will fall.

45 "Come out of Babylon, my people!
Run for your lives!
Run from the LORD's great anger.
46 Don't lose courage;
rumors will spread through the land,
but don't be afraid.
One rumor comes this year, and another
comes the next year.
There will be rumors of terrible fighting
in the country,
of rulers fighting against rulers.
47 The time will surely come
when I will punish the idols of Babylon,
and the whole land will be disgraced.
There will be many dead people lying all
around.
48 Then heaven and earth and all that is in
them
will shout for joy about Babylon.
They will shout because the army comes
from the north
to destroy Babylon," says the LORD.

49 "Babylon must fall, because she killed
people from Israel.
She killed people from everywhere on
earth.
50 You who have escaped being killed with
swords,
leave Babylon! Don't wait!
Remember the LORD in the faraway land
and think about Jerusalem."

51 "We people of Judah are disgraced,
because we have been insulted.
We have been shamed,
because strangers have gone into
the holy places of the LORD's Temple!"

52 So the LORD says, "The time is coming soon
when I will punish the idols of Babylon.
Wounded people will cry with pain
all over that land.
53 Even if Babylon grows until she touches
the sky,
and even if she makes her highest cities
strong,
I will send people to destroy her," says
the LORD.
54 "Sounds of people crying are heard in
Babylon.
Sounds of people destroying things
are heard in the land of the
Babylonians.
55 The LORD is destroying Babylon
and making the loud sounds of the city
become silent.
Enemies come roaring in like ocean waves.
The roar of their voices is heard all
around.
56 The army has come to destroy Babylon.
Her soldiers have been captured,
and their bows are broken,
because the LORD is a God who punishes
people for the evil they do.
He gives them the full punishment they
deserve.
57 I will make Babylon's rulers and wise men
drunk,
and her governors, officers, and soldiers,
too.
Then they will sleep forever and never
wake up," says the King,
whose name is the LORD All-Powerful.
58 This is what the LORD All-Powerful says:
"Babylon's thick wall will be completely
pulled down
and her high gates burned.
The people will work hard, but it won't
help;
their work will only become fuel for the
flames!"

A MESSAGE TO BABYLON

59 This is the message that Jeremiah the
prophet gave to the officer Seraiah son of Neriah, who was the son of Mahseiah. Seraiah
went to Babylon with Zedekiah king of Judah
in the fourth year Zedekiah was king of Judah.
His duty was to arrange the king's food and
housing on the trip. 60 Jeremiah had written on
a scroll all the terrible things that would happen
to Babylon, all these words about Babylon.
61 Jeremiah said to Seraiah, "As soon as you
come to Babylon, be sure to read this message
so all the people can hear you. 62 Then say,
'LORD, you have said that you will destroy this
place so that no people or animals will live in it.
It will be an empty ruin forever.' 63 After you finish reading this scroll, tie a stone to it and throw
it into the Euphrates River. 64 Then say, 'In the
same way Babylon will sink and will not rise
again because of the terrible things I will make
happen here. Her people will fall.' "
The words of Jeremiah end here.

52

THE FALL OF JERUSALEM

1 Zedekiah was twenty-one years old when
he became king, and he was king in Jerusalem for eleven years. His mother's name was

Hamutal daughter of Jeremiah,[n] and she was from Libnah. [2]Zedekiah did what the LORD said was wrong, just as Jehoiakim had done. [3]All this happened in Jerusalem and Judah because the LORD was angry with them. Finally, he threw them out of his presence.

Zedekiah turned against the king of Babylon. [4]Then Nebuchadnezzar king of Babylon marched against Jerusalem with his whole army. They made a camp around the city and built devices all around the city walls to attack it. This happened on Zedekiah's ninth year, tenth month, and tenth day as king. [5]And the city was under attack until Zedekiah's eleventh year as king.

[6]By the ninth day of the fourth month, the hunger was terrible in the city; there was no food for the people to eat. [7]Then the city wall was broken through, and the whole army of Judah ran away at night. They left the city through the gate between the two walls by the king's garden. Even though the Babylonians were surrounding the city, Zedekiah and his men headed toward the Jordan Valley.

WHAT'S IT MEAN?

The attack mentioned here was a siege. Ancient armies would besiege a city by surrounding it to prevent anyone from going in or out. During such a siege, the attacking army would keep food and water from entering the city, causing the people inside to die of hunger and thirst, if they did not surrender. Some sieges lasted months—even years. Jerusalem fell after a siege in 586 B.C.

Jeremiah 52:5–6

[8]But the Babylonian army chased King Zedekiah and caught him in the plains of Jericho. All of his army was scattered from him. [9]So the Babylonians captured Zedekiah and took him to the king of Babylon at the town of Riblah in the land of Hamath. There he passed sentence on Zedekiah. [10]At Riblah the king of Babylon killed Zedekiah's sons as he watched. The king also killed all the officers of Judah. [11]Then he put out Zedekiah's eyes, and put bronze chains on him, and took him to Babylon. And the king kept Zedekiah in prison there until the day he died.

[12]Nebuzaradan, commander of the king's special guards and servant of the king of Babylon, came to Jerusalem on the tenth day of the fifth month. This was in Nebuchadnezzar's nineteenth year as king of Babylon. [13]Nebuzaradan set fire to the Temple of the LORD, the palace, and all the houses of Jerusalem; every important building was burned. [14]The whole Babylonian army, led by the commander of the king's special guards, broke down all the walls around Jerusalem. [15]Nebuzaradan, the commander of the king's special guards, took captive some of the poorest people, those who were left in Jerusalem, those who had surrendered to the king of Babylon, and the skilled craftsmen who were left in Jerusalem. [16]But Nebuzaradan left behind some of the poorest people of the land to take care of the vineyards and fields.

[17]The Babylonians broke into pieces the bronze pillars, the bronze stands, and the large bronze bowl, called the Sea, which were in the Temple of the LORD. Then they carried all the bronze pieces to Babylon. [18]They also took the pots, shovels, wick trimmers, bowls, dishes, and all the bronze objects used to serve in the Temple. [19]The commander of the king's special guards took away bowls, pans for carrying hot coals, large bowls, pots, lampstands, pans, and bowls used for drink offerings. He took everything that was made of pure gold or silver.

[20]There was so much bronze that it could not be weighed: two pillars, the large bronze bowl called the Sea with the twelve bronze bulls under it, and the movable stands, which King Solomon had made for the Temple of the LORD.

[21]Each of the pillars was about twenty-seven feet high, eighteen feet around, and hollow inside. The wall of each pillar was three inches thick. [22]The bronze capital on top of the one pillar was about seven and one-half feet high. It was decorated with a net design and bronze pomegranates all around it. The other pillar also had pomegranates and was like the first pillar. [23]There were ninety-six pomegranates on the sides of the pillars. There was a total of a hundred pomegranates above the net design.

[24]The commander of the king's special guards took as prisoners Seraiah the chief

52:1 Jeremiah This is not the prophet Jeremiah but a different man with the same name.

priest, Zephaniah the priest next in rank, and the three doorkeepers. 25He also took from the city the officer in charge of the soldiers, seven people who advised the king, the royal secretary who selected people for the army, and sixty other men from Judah who were in the city when it fell. 26Nebuzaradan, the commander, took these people and brought them to the king of Babylon at the town of Riblah. 27There at Riblah, in the land of Hamath, the king had them killed.

So the people of Judah were led away from their country as captives. 28This is the number of the people Nebuchadnezzar took away as captives: in the seventh year, 3,023 Jews; 29in Nebuchadnezzar's eighteenth year, 832 people from Jerusalem; 30in Nebuchadnezzar's twenty-third year, Nebuzaradan, commander of the king's special guards, took 745 Jews as captives.

In all 4,600 people were taken captive.

JEHOIACHIN IS SET FREE

31Jehoiachin king of Judah was in prison in Babylon for thirty-seven years. The year Evil-Merodach became king of Babylon he let Jehoiachin king of Judah out of prison. He set Jehoiachin free on the twenty-fifth day of the twelfth month. 32Evil-Merodach spoke kindly to Jehoiachin and gave him a seat of honor above the seats of the other kings who were with him in Babylon. 33So Jehoiachin put away his prison clothes, and for the rest of his life, he ate at the king's table. 34Every day the king of Babylon gave Jehoiachin an allowance. This lasted as long as he lived, until the day Jehoiachin died.

Lamentations

CONTENT You might remember the prophet, Jeremiah, who wrote the book named after him. He talked and preached and cried and warned his people that if they didn't straighten up something bad was going to happen. Something bad *did* happen. The people were taken away from their land and held captive in Babylon. It was during this time that Jeremiah wrote Lamentations.

You can think of Lamentations as being like somebody singing the blues. The music we call "the blues" is music about the most difficult parts of life. It originated from a people and in a time that was hopeless and hard. When these people put music to their sorrow, it gave them a way to express their feelings. That's what the Lamentations did for the Hebrews.

Lamentations is actually a book of five songs. In that day they were sung as funeral dirges, which would be an appropriate thing to sing if the life of your whole nation was falling apart.

The name *Lamentations* comes from the word *lament*. A lament is a mournful cry. The whole Book of Lamentations is a mournful cry about the horrible situation the Hebrews got into because they didn't pay attention to the way God wanted them to live their lives.

Outline

1:1–22 .... First Lament: The Sorrows of Captive Jerusalem
2:1–22 .... Second Lament: The Lord's Anger with Jerusalem
3:1–66 .... Third Lament: Hope Through God's Mercy
4:1–22 .... Fourth Lament: Jerusalem Punished
5:1–22 .... Fifth Lament: A Prayer for Restoration

Purpose Persistent sin brings judgment that crushes the spirit.

Theme Suffering as Punishment for Sin

Date of writing 586–584 B.C.

JERUSALEM CRIES OVER HER LOSS

1 [1]Jerusalem once was full of people,
but now the city is empty.
Jerusalem once was a great city among the nations,
but now she[n] is like a widow.
She was like a queen of all the other cities,
but now she is a slave.

[2]She cries loudly at night,
and tears are on her cheeks.
There is no one to comfort her;
all who loved her are gone.
All her friends have turned against her
and are now her enemies.

[3]Judah has gone into captivity
where she suffers and works hard.
She lives among other nations,
but she has found no rest.
Those who chased her caught her
when she was in trouble.

[4]The roads to Jerusalem are sad,
because no one comes for the feasts.
No one passes through her gates.
Her priests groan,
her young women are suffering,
and Jerusalem suffers terribly.

[5]Her foes are now her masters.
Her enemies enjoy the wealth they have taken.
The LORD is punishing her
for her many sins.
Her children have gone away
as captives of the enemy.

[6]The beauty of Jerusalem
has gone away.
Her rulers are like deer
that cannot find food.
They are weak
and run from the hunters.

[7]Jerusalem is suffering and homeless.
She remembers all the good things
from the past.
But her people were defeated by the enemy,
and there was no one to help her.
When her enemies saw her,
they laughed to see her ruined.

[8]Jerusalem sinned terribly,
so she has become unclean.
Those who honored her now hate her,
because they have seen her nakedness.
She groans
and turns away.

[9]She made herself dirty by her sins
and did not think about what would happen to her.
Her defeat was surprising,
and no one could comfort her.
She says, "LORD, see how I suffer,
because the enemy has won."

[10]The enemy reached out and took
all her precious things.
She even saw foreigners
enter her Temple.
The LORD had commanded foreigners

"Jerusalem once was full of people, but now the city is empty. Jerusalem once was a great city among the nations, but now she is like a widow. She was like a queen of all the other cities, but now she is a slave." (Lamentations 1:1)

WHAT'S IT MEAN?

Abandoned city gates in ancient times would have seemed as unusual as empty freeways during rush hour today. Usually the gates of ancient cities were crowded with people and bustling with activity. The city gates were where most business and legal transactions took place. In addition, there was the constant flow of caravan traffic in and out of the city.
Lamentations 1:4

1:1 she In this poem the city of Jerusalem is described as a woman.

never to enter the meeting place of his
people.

11 All of Jerusalem's people groan,
looking for bread.
They are trading their precious things for
food
so they can stay alive.
The city says, "Look, LORD, and see.
I am hated."

12 Jerusalem says, "You who pass by on the
road don't seem to care.
Come, look at me and see:
Is there any pain like mine?
Is there any pain like that he has caused
me?
The LORD has punished me
on the day of his great anger.

13 "He sent fire from above
that went down into my bones.
He stretched out a net for my feet
and turned me back.
He made me so sad and lonely
that I am weak all day.

14 "He has noticed my sins;
they are tied together by his hands;
they hang around my neck.
He has turned my strength into
weakness.
The Lord has handed me over
to those who are stronger than I.

15 "The Lord has rejected
all my mighty men inside my walls.
He brought an army against me
to destroy my young men.
As if in a winepress, the Lord has crushed
the capital city of Judah.

16 "I cry about these things;
my eyes overflow with tears.
There is no one near to comfort me,
no one who can give me strength
again.
My children are left sad and lonely,
because the enemy has won."

17 Jerusalem reaches out her hands,
but there is no one to comfort her.
The LORD commanded the people of
Jacob
to be surrounded by their enemies.
Jerusalem is now unclean
like those around her.

18 Jerusalem says, "The LORD is
right,
but I refused to obey
him.
Listen, all you people,
and look at my pain.
My young women and
men
have gone into captivity.

DISOBEDIENCE

Is God right to punish the disobedient? (1:18–22)

19 "I called out to my friends,
but they turned against me.
My priests and my older leaders
have died in the city
while looking for food
to stay alive.

20 "Look at me, LORD. I am upset
and greatly troubled.
My heart is troubled,
because I have been so stubborn.
Out in the streets, the sword kills;
inside the houses, death destroys.

21 "People have heard my groaning,
and there is no one to comfort me.
All my enemies have heard of my trouble,
and they are happy you have done this
to me.
Now bring that day you have announced
so that my enemies will be like me.

22 "Look at all their evil.
Do to them what you have done to me
because of all my sins.
I groan over and over again,
and I am afraid."

WHAT'S IT MEAN?

The greatness of Israel was shown in the Temple that Solomon had built in Jerusalem, and in the Ark of the Agreement, which contained the Ten Commandments, God's instructions for living. That splendor was marred when King Nebuchadnezzar and his Babylonian forces captured Jerusalem and burned the Temple.

Lamentations 2:1

THE LORD DESTROYED JERUSALEM

2 [1]Look how the Lord in his anger
has brought Jerusalem to shame.
He has thrown down the greatness of Israel
from the sky to the earth;
he did not remember the Temple, his footstool,
on the day of his anger.

[2]The Lord swallowed up without mercy
all the houses of the people of Jacob;
in his anger he pulled down
the strong places of Judah.
He threw her kingdom and its rulers
down to the ground in dishonor.

[3]In his anger he has removed
all the strength of Israel;
he took away his power from Israel
when the enemy came.
He burned against the people of Jacob like a flaming fire
that burns up everything around it.

[4]Like an enemy, he prepared to shoot his bow,
and his hand was against us.
Like an enemy, he killed
all the good-looking people;
he poured out his anger like fire
on the tents of Jerusalem.

[5]The Lord was like an enemy;
he swallowed up Israel.
He swallowed up all her palaces
and destroyed all her strongholds.
He has caused more moaning and groaning
for Judah.

[6]He cut down his Temple like a garden;
he destroyed the meeting place.
The LORD has made Jerusalem forget
the set feasts and Sabbath days.
He has rejected the king and the priest
in his great anger.

[7]The Lord has rejected his altar
and abandoned his Temple.
He has handed over to the enemy
the walls of Jerusalem's palaces.
Their uproar in the LORD's Temple
was like that of a feast day.

[8]The LORD planned to destroy
the wall around Jerusalem.
He measured the wall
and did not stop himself from destroying it.
He made the walls and defenses sad;
together they have fallen.

WHAT'S IT MEAN?

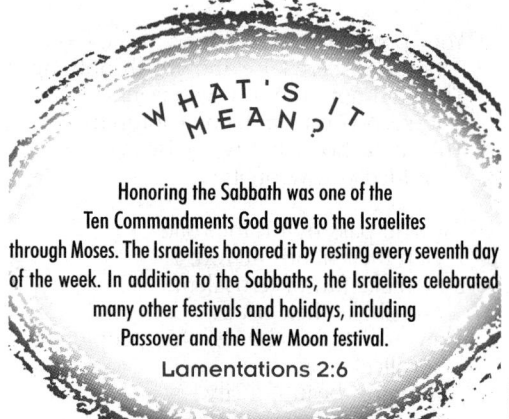

Honoring the Sabbath was one of the Ten Commandments God gave to the Israelites through Moses. The Israelites honored it by resting every seventh day of the week. In addition to the Sabbaths, the Israelites celebrated many other festivals and holidays, including Passover and the New Moon festival.

Lamentations 2:6

[9]Jerusalem's gates have fallen to the ground;
he destroyed and smashed the bars of the gates.
Her king and her princes are among the nations.
The teaching of the LORD has stopped,
and the prophets do not have
visions from the LORD.

[10]The older leaders of Jerusalem
sit on the ground in silence.
They throw dust on their heads
and put on rough cloth to show their sadness.
The young women of Jerusalem
bow their heads to the ground in sorrow.

[11]My eyes have no more tears,
and I am sick to my stomach.
I feel empty inside,
because my people have been destroyed.
Children and babies are fainting
in the streets of the city.

[12]They ask their mothers,
"Where is the grain and wine?"
They faint like wounded soldiers
in the streets of the city
and die in their mothers' arms.

13 What can I say about you, Jerusalem?
What can I compare you to?
What can I say you are like?
How can I comfort you, Jerusalem?
Your ruin is as deep as the sea.
No one can heal you.

14 Your prophets saw visions,
but they were false and worth nothing.
They did not point out your sins
to keep you from being captured.
They preached what was false
and led you wrongly.

15 All who pass by on the road
clap their hands at you;
they make fun of Jerusalem
and shake their heads.
They ask, "Is this the city that people called
the most beautiful city,
the happiest place on earth?"

16 All your enemies open their mouths
to speak against you.
They make fun and grind their teeth in anger.
They say, "We have swallowed you up.
This is the day we were waiting for!
We have finally seen it happen."

17 The LORD has done what he planned;
he has kept his word
that he commanded long ago.
He has destroyed without mercy,
and he has let your enemies laugh at you.
He has strengthened your enemies.

GOD
Does God accomplish his plans? (2:17)

18 The people cry out to the Lord.
Wall of Jerusalem,
let your tears flow
like a river day and night.
Do not stop
or let your eyes rest.

19 Get up, cry out in the night,
even as the night begins.
Pour out your heart like water
in prayer to the Lord.
Lift up your hands in prayer to him
for the life of your children
who are fainting with hunger
on every street corner.

20 Jerusalem says: "Look, LORD, and see
to whom you have done this.
Women eat their own babies,
the children they have cared for.
Priests and prophets are killed
in the Temple of the Lord.

21 "People young and old
lie outside on the ground.
My young women and young men
have been killed by the sword.
You killed them on the day of your anger;
you killed them without mercy.

22 "You invited terrors to come against me on every side,
as if you were inviting them to a feast.
No one escaped or remained alive
on the day of the LORD's anger.
My enemy has killed
those I cared for and brought up."

THE MEANING OF SUFFERING

3

1 I am a man who has seen the suffering
that comes from the rod of the LORD's anger.
2 He led me
into darkness, not light.
3 He turned his hand against me
again and again, all day long.

4 He wore out my flesh and skin
and broke my bones.
5 He surrounded me with sadness
and attacked me with grief.
6 He made me sit in the dark,
like those who have been dead a long time.

7 He shut me in so I could not get out;
he put heavy chains on me.
8 I cry out and beg for help,
but he ignores my prayer.
9 He blocked my way with a stone wall
and led me in the wrong direction.

10 He is like a bear ready to attack me,
like a lion in hiding.
11 He led me the wrong way and let me stray
and left me without help.
12 He prepared to shoot his bow
and made me the target for his arrows.

13 He shot me in the kidneys
with the arrows from his bag.
14 I was a joke to all my people,

who make fun of me with songs all day
long.
15 The LORD filled me with misery;
he made me drunk with suffering.

WHAT'S IT MEAN?

And they say junk food is bad for you. . . . Some tribes in the ancient Near East used to mix sand, gravel, and other solid substances in the food they gave to their prisoners. You can imagine the digestive problems that resulted from this diet, but don't forget about the dental nightmares it caused as well. The hard objects wore down and broke the teeth of the prisoners, causing them tremendous pain.

Lamentations 3:16

16 He broke my teeth with gravel
and trampled me into the dirt.
17 I have no more peace.
I have forgotten what happiness is.
18 I said, "My strength is gone,
and I have no hope in the LORD."

19 LORD, remember my suffering and my
misery,
my sorrow and trouble.
20 Please remember me
and think about me.
21 But I have hope
when I think of this:

HOPE

Can we have hope in bad situations? (3:19–23)

22 The LORD's love never
ends;
his mercies never stop.
23 They are new every morning;
LORD, your loyalty is great.
24 I say to myself, "The LORD is mine,
so I hope in him."

25 The LORD is good to those who hope in
him,
to those who seek him.
26 It is good to wait quietly
for the LORD to save.
27 It is good for someone to work hard
while he is young.

28 He should sit alone and be quiet;
the LORD has given him hard work to
do.
29 He should bow down to the ground;
maybe there is still hope.
30 He should let anyone slap his cheek;
he should be filled with shame.

31 The Lord will not reject
his people forever.
32 Although he brings sorrow,
he also has mercy and great love.
33 He does not like to punish people
or make them sad.

Promise

HE PROMISES TO SHOW YOU NEW MERCIES EACH MORNING.

The LORD's love never ends; his mercies never stop. They are new every morning; LORD, your loyalty is great (Lam. 3:22–23).

You lay your head on your pillow tonight and know it's been a terrible day. Your sin got the best of you all day long. Where did your self-control go? Guilt and shame begin to swallow you. You feel so far away from God. *He must really be disappointed,* you think. All you want to do is hide—hide from your friends and yourself, but mostly from God. But the right thing to do is to run to him. He is tender and loving. His forgiveness is pure and cleansing. His compassion brings comfort. His mercy grants freedom; his lovingkindness lets you open your eyes in the morning and be glad for the new day. It's a start-over day. It's a clean-slate day. It's a new day, with new compassion from the God of new beginnings.

SEE FOR YOURSELF:

Ps. 90:14; 118:1–4; 2 Cor. 1:3

34 He sees if any prisoner of the earth
is crushed under his feet;
35 he sees if someone is treated unfairly
before the Most High God;
36 the Lord sees
if someone is cheated in his case in
court.

37 Nobody can speak and have it happen
unless the Lord commands it.
38 Both bad and good things
come by the command of the Most
High God.
39 No one should complain
when he is punished for his sins.

40 Let us examine and see what we have done
and then return to the LORD.
41 Let us lift up our hands and pray from
our hearts
to God in heaven:
42 "We have sinned and turned against you,
and you have not forgiven us.

43 "You wrapped yourself in anger and
chased us;
you killed us without mercy.
44 You wrapped yourself in a cloud,
and no prayer could get through.
45 You made us like scum and trash
among the other nations.

46 "All of our enemies
open their mouths and speak against us.
47 We have been frightened and fearful,
ruined and destroyed."
48 Streams of tears flow from my eyes,
because my people are destroyed.

49 My tears flow continually,
without stopping,
50 until the LORD looks down
and sees from heaven.
51 I am sad when I see
what has happened to all the women of
my city.

52 Those who are my enemies for no reason
hunted me like a bird.
53 They tried to kill me in a pit;
they threw stones at me.
54 Water came up over my head,
and I said, "I am going to die."
55 I called out to you, LORD,
from the bottom of the pit.
56 You heard me calling, "Do not close your
ears
and ignore my gasps and shouts."
57 You came near when I called to you;
you said, "Don't be afraid."

58 Lord, you have taken my case
and given me back my life.
59 LORD, you have seen how I have been
wronged.
Now judge my case for me.
60 You have seen how my enemies took
revenge on me
and made evil plans against me.

61 LORD, you have heard their insults
and all their evil plans against me.
62 The words and thoughts of my enemies
are against me all the time.
63 Look! In everything they do
they make fun of me with songs.

64 Pay them back, LORD,
for what they have done.
65 Make them stubborn,
and put your curse on them.
66 Chase them in anger, LORD,
and destroy them from under your
heavens.

THE ATTACK ON JERUSALEM

4

1 See how the gold has lost its shine,
how the pure gold has dulled!
The stones of the Temple are scattered
at every street corner.

2 The precious people of Jerusalem
were more valuable than gold,
but now they are thought of as clay jars
made by the hands of a potter.

3 Even wild dogs give their milk
to feed their young,
but my people are cruel
like ostriches in the desert.

4 The babies are so thirsty
their tongues stick to the roofs of their
mouths.
Children beg for bread,
but no one gives them any.

5 Those who once ate fine foods
are now starving in the streets.
People who grew up wearing nice clothes
now pick through trash piles.

6 My people have been punished
more than Sodom was.

WHAT'S IT MEAN?

The female ostrich is never going to win any "mother of the year" awards in the animal kingdom. Most birds build nests to protect their young ones. The ostrich simply drops her eggs in the sand and takes off, letting the heat of the sun warm them. Things don't improve much after the eggs have hatched, either. If the mother ostrich feels threatened, she won't hesitate to abandon her young ones to save her own skin. The Israelites considered the ostrich's "parenting" style to be cruel.

Lamentations 4:3

Sodom was destroyed suddenly,
and no hands reached out to help her.

7 Our princes were purer than snow,
and whiter than milk.
Their bodies were redder than rubies;
they looked like sapphires.

8 But now they are blacker than coal,
and no one recognizes them in the streets.
Their skin hangs on their bones;
it is as dry as wood.

9 Those who were killed in the war were better off
than those killed by hunger.
They starve in pain and die,
because there is no food from the field.

10 With their own hands kind women
cook their own children.
They became food
when my people were destroyed.

11 The LORD turned loose all of his anger;
he poured out his strong anger.
He set fire to Jerusalem,
burning it down to the foundations.

12 Kings of the earth and people of the world
could not believe
that enemies and foes
could enter the gates of Jerusalem.

13 It happened because her prophets sinned
and her priests did evil.
They killed in the city
those who did what was right.

14 They wandered in the streets
as if they were blind.
They were dirty with blood,
so no one would touch their clothes.

15 "Go away! You are unclean," people shouted at them.
"Get away! Get away! Don't touch us!"
So they ran away and wandered.
Even the other nations said, "Don't stay here."

16 The LORD himself scattered them
and did not look after them anymore.
No one respects the priests
or honors the older leaders.

17 Also, our eyes grew tired,
looking for help that never came.
We kept watch from our towers
for a nation to save us.

18 Our enemies hunted us,
so we could not even walk in the streets.
Our end is near. Our time is up.
Our end has come.

19 Those who chased us
were faster than eagles in the sky.
They ran us into the mountains
and ambushed us in the desert.

20 The LORD's appointed king, who was our very breath,
was caught in their traps.
We had said about him, "We will be protected by him
among the nations."

21 Be happy and glad, people of Edom,
you who live in the land of Uz.
The cup of God's anger will come to you;
then you will get drunk and go naked.

22 Your punishment is complete, Jerusalem.
He will not send you into captivity again.
But the LORD will punish the sins of Edom;
he will uncover your evil.

5

A PRAYER TO THE LORD

1 Remember, LORD, what happened to us.
Look and see our disgrace.

2 Our land has been turned over to
strangers;
our houses have been given to
foreigners.
3 We are like orphans with no father;
our mothers are like widows.
4 We have to buy the water we drink;
we must pay for the firewood.
5 Those who chase after us want to catch us
by the neck.
We are tired and find no rest.
6 We made an agreement with Egypt
and with Assyria to get enough food.
7 Our ancestors sinned against you, but they
are gone;
now we suffer because of their sins.
8 Slaves have become our rulers,
and no one can save us from them.
9 We risk our lives to get our food;
we face death in the desert.
10 Our skin is hot like an oven;
we burn with starvation.
11 The enemy abused the
women of Jerusalem
and the girls in the
cities of Judah.
12 Princes were hung by the
hands;
they did not respect our
older leaders.
13 The young men ground grain
at the mill,
and boys stumbled under loads of
wood.
14 The older leaders no longer sit at the city
gates;
the young men no longer sing.
15 We have no more joy in our hearts;
our dancing has turned
to sadness.
16 The crown has fallen from
our head.
How terrible it is
because we sinned.
17 Because of this we are
afraid,
and now our eyes are dim.
18 Mount Zion is empty,
and wild dogs wander around it.

19 But you rule forever, LORD.
You will be King from now on.
20 Why have you forgotten
us for so long?
Have you left us forever?
21 Bring us back to you,
LORD, and we will
return.
Make our days as they
were before,
22 or have you completely
rejected us?
Are you so angry with
us?

TRIALS
What causes some trials? (5:15–16)

"Bring us back to you, LORD, and we will return. . . . or have you completely rejected us?" (Lamentations 5:21–22a)

ezekiel

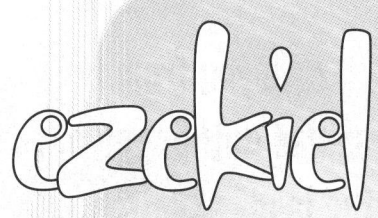

CONTENT Imagine trying to explain something that you have never seen before, that is made out of substances that don't exist and that functions in dimensions that are not a part of your world. Your explanation might turn out a bit confusing, don't you think? And don't you think that you would end up making a lot of comparisons? "It was like this, except . . ." "It was sort of like that, only it didn't . . ." If you can imagine that kind of explanation, then you are ready to read the Book of Ezekiel.

Ezekiel preached his message while his people were being held captive in Babylon. The other prophets, for years, had told these people that if they didn't change their ways they would self-destruct as a culture. Now they were facing that very destruction and they were *still* disregarding God. It was at this point that God called Ezekiel to give them one more chance to repent.

Ezekiel was preaching to people who were in a mess. He encouraged them by reminding them that there was a brighter future waiting. He also confronted their sin, which was the reason for the mess in the first place.

Outline

1:1—3:27 .... Ezekiel Sees the Lord's Glory and Is Chosen to Be His Prophet
4:1—5:17 .... Ezekiel Acts Out the Coming Destruction of Judah and Jerusalem
6:1—7:27 .... Disaster Is Near
8:1—11:25 .... The Lord's Glory Leaves Sinful Jerusalem
12:1—24:27 .... Messages of Doom for Judah and Jerusalem
25:1—32:32 .... Judgment on Foreign Nations
33:1-20 .... Ezekiel Must Warn the People to Turn from Their Sinful Ways
33:21-33 .... The Fall of Jerusalem and Judah
34:1—37:28 .... The Lord Promises to Bring the People Home and to Restore Judah
38:1—39:29 .... Gog Will Be Defeated, and Israel Will Be Restored
40:1—46:24 .... Ezekiel Sees the Future Temple in Jerusalem
47:1-12 .... The Stream Flowing from the Temple
47:13—48:35 ...... The Borders of the Restored Land and Its Division Among the Tribes

Purpose Count on God to judge sin as well as to bless.

Theme Destruction of Jerusalem and Its Restoration

Date of writing 593–571 B.C.

"I will take you from the nations and gather you out of all the lands and bring you back into your own land" (36:24).

Bible Talk

The Dry Bones

One of the most famous visions of Ezekiel is the vision of a whole valley of skeletons. An old spiritual calls them "dry bones." It must have looked like something out of an Indiana Jones-kind of story. But if it was amazing to see that valley of skeletons, imagine how amazing it must have been to see them reconnect and be brought back to life: a whole valley of old bones suddenly rattling together, gathering some skin on them, and becoming an army.

God's point in giving Ezekiel this vision was that we are never so far gone that God can't give us new life if we'll just turn to him and repent. That's good news, isn't it? No matter where we are or what a mess we've made, we are never too far gone.

WHY DIDN'T PEOPLE LISTEN?

When you review the history of the Hebrew people, it's sort of exasperating that by the time of Ezekiel they still hadn't learned to trust God and obey him. God had been working miracles among these people since their very first forefather, Abraham. God had saved this nation from death time after time. God had proved himself. What made these people keep missing the point?

We can't really and truly answer that question. But if we look at our own lives, we can get a big clue to the answer. It seems to be our human nature to choose our own way rather than God's way. We still do it today, even after God has proven himself. When we look at ourselves, the Hebrews aren't so hard to understand.

ezekiel

Ezekiel's Vision of Living Creatures

1It was the thirtieth year, on the fifth day of the fourth month of our captivity. I was by the Kebar River among the people who had been carried away as captives. The sky opened, and I saw visions of God.

2It was the fifth day of the month of the fifth year that King Jehoiachin had been a prisoner. 3The LORD spoke his word to Ezekiel son of Buzi in the land of the Babylonians by the Kebar River. There he felt the power of the LORD.

4When I looked, I saw a stormy wind coming from the north. There was a great cloud with a bright light around it and fire flashing out of it. Something that looked like glowing metal was in the center of the fire. 5Inside the cloud was what looked like four living creatures, who were shaped like humans, 6but each of them had four faces and four wings. 7Their legs were straight. Their feet were like a calf's hoofs and sparkled like polished bronze. 8The living creatures had human hands under their wings on their four sides. All four of them had faces and wings, 9and their wings touched each other. The living creatures did not turn when they moved, but each went straight ahead.

WHAT'S IT MEAN?

The bizarre appearance of these angels shows us just how powerful they are. You see, each of their four faces looks like one of the most powerful creatures on earth—a man, a lion, an ox (a bull), and an eagle. Think about it. Human beings rule over every creature on earth. The lion is the king of the jungle. Bulls are the strongest tame animals. Eagles are the fastest, strongest birds. If the angels that surround God are so powerful, imagine how mighty he is!

Ezekiel 1:10

10Their faces looked like this: Each living creature had a human face and the face of a lion on the right side and the face of an ox on the left side. And each one also had the face of an eagle. 11That was what their faces looked like. Their wings were spread out above. Each had two wings that touched one of the other living creatures and two wings that covered its body. 12Each went straight ahead. Wherever the spirit would go, the living creatures would also go, without turning. 13The living creatures looked like burning coals of fire or like torches. Fire went back and forth among the living creatures. It was bright, and lightning flashed from it. 14The living creatures ran back and forth like bolts of lightning.

15Now as I looked at the living creatures, I saw a wheel on the ground by each of the living creatures with its four faces. 16The wheels and the way they were made were like this: They looked like sparkling chrysolite. All four of them looked the same, like one wheel crossways inside another wheel. 17When they moved, they went in any one of the four directions, without turning as they went. 18The rims of the wheels were high and frightening and were full of eyes all around.

19When the living creatures moved, the wheels moved beside them. When the living creatures were lifted up from the ground, the wheels also were lifted up. 20Wherever the spirit would go, the living creatures would go. And the wheels were lifted up beside them, because the spirit of the living creatures was in the wheels. 21When the living creatures moved, the wheels moved. When the living creatures stopped, the wheels stopped. And when the living creatures were lifted from the ground, the wheels were lifted beside them, because the spirit of the living creatures was in the wheels.

22Now, over the heads of the living creatures was something like a dome that sparkled like ice and was frightening. 23And under the dome the wings of the living creatures were stretched out straight toward one another. Each living creature also had two wings covering its body. 24I heard the sound of their wings, like the roaring sound of the sea, as they moved. It was like the voice of God Almighty, a roaring sound like a noisy army. When the living creatures stopped, they lowered their wings.

25A voice came from above the dome over the heads of the living creatures. When the living creatures stopped, they lowered their wings. 26Now above the dome there was something that looked like a throne. It looked like a sapphire gem. And on the throne was a shape like a human. 27Then I noticed that from the waist up the shape looked like glowing metal with fire inside. From the waist down it looked like fire, and a bright light was all around. 28The surrounding glow looked like the rainbow in the clouds on a rainy day. It seemed to look like

ANGELS
Is the appearance of angels frightening? (1:27–28)

the glory of the LORD. So when I saw it, I
bowed facedown on the ground and heard a
voice speaking.

THE LORD SPEAKS TO EZEKIEL

2 [1]He said to me, "Human, stand up on your
feet so I may speak with you." [2]While he spoke
to me, the Spirit entered me and put me on my
feet. Then I heard the LORD speaking to me.
[3]He said, "Human, I am sending you to the
people of Israel. That nation has turned against
me and broken away from me. They and their
ancestors have sinned against me until this
very day. [4]I am sending you to people who are
stubborn and who do not obey. You will say
to them, 'This is what the Lord GOD says.'
[5]They may listen, or they may not, since they
are a people who have turned against me. But
they will know that a prophet has been among
them. [6]You, human, don't be afraid of the people or their words. Even though they may be
like thorny branches and stickers all around
you, and though you may feel like you live
with poisonous insects, don't be afraid. Don't
be afraid of their words or their looks, because
they are a people who turn against me. [7]But
speak my words to them. They may listen,
or they may not, because they turn against
me. [8]But you, human, listen to what I say
to you. Don't turn against me as those people
do. Open your mouth and eat what I am giving you."
[9]Then I looked and saw a hand stretched
out to me, and a scroll was in it. [10]He opened
the scroll in front of me. Funeral songs, sad
writings, and words about troubles were written on the front and back.
3 [1]Then the LORD said to me, "Human, eat
what you find; eat this scroll. Then go and
speak to the people of Israel." [2]So I opened my
mouth, and he gave me the scroll to eat.
[3]He said to me, "Human, eat this scroll
which I am giving you, and fill your stomach
with it." Then I ate it, and it was as sweet as
honey in my mouth.
[4]Then he said to me, "Human, go to the
people of Israel, and speak my words to them.
[5]You are not being sent to people whose
speech you can't understand,
whose language is difficult.
You are being sent to Israel.
[6]You are not being sent to
many nations whose speech
you can't understand, whose
language is difficult, whose
words you cannot under-
stand. If I had sent you to them, they would
have listened to you. [7]But the people of Israel
will not be willing to listen to you, because
they are not willing to listen to me. Yes, all the
people of Israel are stubborn and will not
obey. [8]See, I now make you as stubborn and as
hard as they are. [9]I am making you as hard as
a diamond, harder than stone. Don't be afraid
of them or be frightened by them, though they
are a people who turn against me."

CHARACTER

Where can we get strength of character? (3:4–9)

WHAT'S IT MEAN?

If someone ever tries to sell you a book from Old Testament times, don't buy it—it's a fake. Documents that old were not written in book form; they were written on long pieces of paper or leather called scrolls. Since most scrolls were usually thirty-five pages or longer, ancient librarians discovered that the best way to store them was to roll them up on a stick. A tag with the title written on it was attached to the scroll.

Ezekiel 2:9

[10]Also, he said to me, "Human, believe all
the words I will speak to you, and listen carefully to them. [11]Then go to the captives, your
own people, and say to them, 'The Lord GOD
says this.' Tell them this whether they listen
or not."
[12]Then the Spirit lifted me up, and I heard a
loud rumbling sound behind me, saying,
"Praise the glory of the LORD in heaven." [13]I
heard the wings of the living creatures touching each other and the sound of the wheels by
them. It was a loud rumbling sound. [14]So the
Spirit lifted me up and took me away. I was
unhappy and angry, and I felt the great power
of the LORD. [15]I came to the captives from Judah, who lived by the Kebar River at Tel Abib.
I sat there seven days where these people lived,
feeling shocked.

ISRAEL'S WARNING

[16]After seven days the LORD spoke his word
to me again. He said, [17]"Human, I now make
you a watchman for Israel. Any time you hear
a word from my mouth, warn them for me.
[18]When I say to the wicked, 'You will surely
die,' you must warn them so they may live. If
you don't speak out to warn the wicked to

stop their evil ways, they will die in their sin.
But I will hold you responsible for their death.
19If you warn the wicked and they do not turn
from their wickedness or their evil ways, they
will die because of their sin. But you will have
saved your life.

WHAT'S IT MEAN?

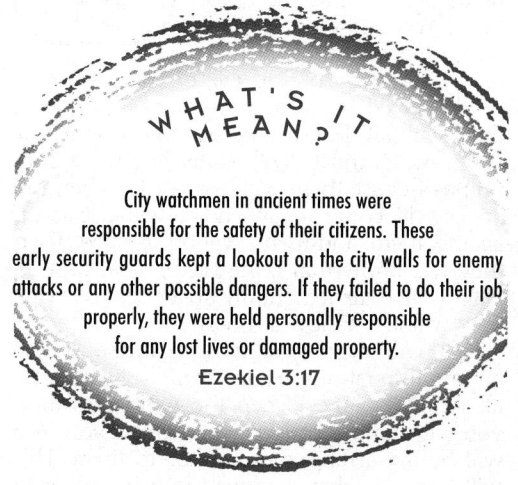

City watchmen in ancient times were responsible for the safety of their citizens. These early security guards kept a lookout on the city walls for enemy attacks or any other possible dangers. If they failed to do their job properly, they were held personally responsible for any lost lives or damaged property.

Ezekiel 3:17

20"Again, those who do right may turn away
from doing good and do evil. If I make something bad happen to them, they will die. Because you have not warned them, they will die
because of their sin, and the good they did will
not be remembered. But I will hold you responsible for their deaths. 21But if you have
warned those good people not to sin, and they
do not sin, they will surely live, because they
believed the warning. And you will have saved
your life."

22Then I felt the power of the LORD there. He
said to me, "Get up and go out to the plain.
There I will speak to you." 23So I got up and
went out to the plain. I saw the glory of the
LORD standing there, like the glory I saw by
the Kebar River, and I bowed facedown on the
ground.

24Then the Spirit entered me and made me
stand on my feet. He spoke to me and said,
"Go, shut yourself up in your house. 25As for
you, human, the people will tie you up with
ropes so that you will not be able to go out
among them. 26Also, I will make your tongue
stick to the roof of your mouth so you will be
silent. You will not be able to argue with the
people, even though they turn against me.
27But when I speak to you, I will open your
mouth, and you will say to them, 'The Lord
GOD says this.' Those who will listen, let them
listen. Those who refuse, let them refuse, because they are a people who turn against me.

THE MAP OF JERUSALEM

4 1"Now, human, get yourself a brick, put it in
front of you, and draw a map of Jerusalem on
it. 2Then surround it with an army. Build battle
works against the city and a dirt road to the
top of the city walls. Set up camps around it,
and put heavy logs in place to break down the
walls. 3Then get yourself an iron plate and set it
up like an iron wall between you and the city.
Turn your face toward the city as if to attack it
and then attack. This is a sign to Israel.

4"Then lie down on your left side, and take
the guilt of Israel on yourself. Their guilt will be
on you for the number of days you lie on your
left side. 5I have given you the same number of
days as the years of the people's sin. So you
will have the guilt of Israel's sin on you for
three hundred ninety days.

6"After you have finished these three hundred ninety days, lie down a second time, on
your right side. You will then have the guilt of
Judah on you. I will give it to you for forty
days, a day for each year of their sin. 7Then
you will look toward Jerusalem, which is being
attacked. With your arm bare, you will prophesy against Jerusalem. 8I will put ropes on you
so you cannot turn from one side to the other
until you have finished the days of your attack
on Jerusalem.

9"Take wheat, barley, beans, small peas, and
millet seeds, and put them in one bowl, and
make them into bread for yourself. You will eat
it the three hundred ninety days you lie on
your side. 10You will eat eight ounces of food
every day at set times. 11You will drink about
two-thirds of a quart of water every day at set
times. 12Eat your food as you would eat a barley cake, baking it over human dung where the
people can see." 13Then the LORD said, "In the
same way Israel will eat unclean food among
the nations where I force them to go."

14But I said, "No, Lord GOD! I have never
been made unclean. From the time I was
young until now I've never eaten anything that
died by itself or was torn by animals. Unclean
meat has never entered my mouth."

15"Very well," he said. "Then I will give you
cow's dung instead of human dung to use for
your fire to bake your bread."

16He also said to me, "Human, I am going to
cut off the supply of bread to Jerusalem. They
will eat the bread that is measured out to them,
and they will worry as they eat. They will
drink water that is measured out to them, and
they will be in shock as they drink it. 17This is
because bread and water will be hard to find.
The people will be shocked at the sight of each

other, and they will become weak because of their sin.

EZEKIEL CUTS HIS HAIR

5 1"Now, human, take a sharp sword, and use it like a barber's razor to shave your head and beard. Then take scales and weigh and divide the hair. 2Burn one-third with fire in the middle of the city when the days of the attack on Jerusalem are over. Then take one-third and cut it up with the knife all around the city. And scatter one-third to the wind. This is how I will chase them with a sword. 3Also take a few of these hairs and tie them in the folds of your clothes. 4Take a few more and throw them into the fire and burn them up. From there a fire will spread to all the people of Israel.

5"This is what the Lord GOD says: This is Jerusalem. I have put her at the center of the nations with countries all around her. 6But she has refused to obey my laws and has been more evil than the nations. She has refused to obey my rules, even more than nations around her. The people of Jerusalem have rejected my laws and have not lived by my rules.

7"So this is what the Lord GOD says: You have caused more trouble than the nations around you. You have not followed my rules or obeyed my laws. You have not even obeyed the laws of the nations around you.

8"So this is what the Lord GOD says: I myself am against you, and I will punish you as the nations watch. 9I will do things among you that I have not done before and that I will never do anything like again, because you do the things I hate. 10So parents among you will eat their children, and children will eat their parents. I will punish you and will scatter to the winds all who are left alive.

11So the Lord GOD says: You have made my Temple unclean with all your evil idols and the hateful things you do. Because of this, as surely as I live, I will cut you off. I will have no pity, and I will show no mercy. 12A third of you will die by disease or be destroyed by hunger inside your walls. A third will fall dead by the sword outside your walls. And a third I will scatter in every direction as I chase them with a sword. 13Then my anger will come to an end. I will use it up against them, and then I will be satisfied. Then they will know that I, the LORD, have spoken. After I have carried out my anger against them, they will know how strongly I felt.

WORSHIP

Why is pure worship important? (5:11)

14"I will make you a ruin and a shame among the nations around you, to be seen by all who pass by. 15Then the nations around you will shame you and make fun of you. You will be a warning and a terror to them. This will happen when I punish you in my great anger. I, the LORD, have spoken. 16I will send a time of hunger to destroy you, and then I will make your hunger get even worse, and I will cut off your supply of food. 17I will send a time of hunger and wild animals against you, and they will kill your children. Disease and death will sweep through your people, and I will bring the sword against you to kill you. I, the LORD, have spoken."

WHAT'S IT MEAN?

Instead of fighting, ancient armies would besiege a city by surrounding it to prevent anyone from going in or out. During such a siege, the attacking army would keep food and water from entering the city, causing the people inside to die of hunger and thirst. Some sieges lasted months—even years. You can imagine how desperate and horrible conditions became inside the city after such a long period of time. Jerusalem fell after Nebuchadnezzar besieged it in 586 B.C.

Ezekiel 5:10

PROPHECIES AGAINST THE MOUNTAINS

6 1Again the LORD spoke his word to me, saying: 2"Human, look toward the mountains of Israel, and prophesy against them. 3Say, 'Mountains of Israel, listen to the word of the Lord GOD. The Lord GOD says this to the mountains, the hills, the ravines, and the valleys: I will bring a sword against you, and I will destroy your places of idol worship. 4Your altars will be destroyed and your incense altars broken down. Your people will be killed in front of your idols. 5I will lay the dead bodies of the Israelites in front of their idols, and I will scatter your bones around your altars. 6In all the places you live, cities will become empty. The places of idol worship will be ruined; your altars will become lonely ruins. Your idols will be broken and brought to an end. Your incense altars will be cut down, and the things you made will be wiped out. 7Your people will be killed and fall among you. Then you will know that I am the LORD.

8" 'But I will leave some people alive; some will not be killed by the nations when you are scattered among the foreign lands. 9Then those who have escaped will remember me, as they live among the nations where they have been taken as captives. They will remember how I was hurt because they were unfaithful to me and turned away from me and desired to worship their idols. They will hate themselves because of the evil things they did that I hate. 10Then they will know that I am the LORD. I did not bring this terrible thing on them for no reason.

WHAT'S IT MEAN?

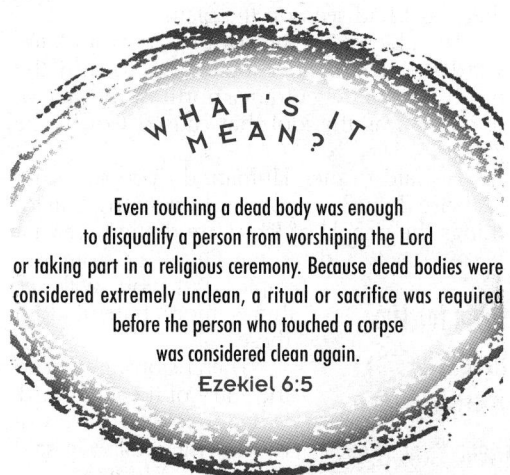

Even touching a dead body was enough to disqualify a person from worshiping the Lord or taking part in a religious ceremony. Because dead bodies were considered extremely unclean, a ritual or sacrifice was required before the person who touched a corpse was considered clean again.

Ezekiel 6:5

11" 'This is what the Lord GOD says: Clap your hands, stamp your feet, and groan because of all the hateful, evil things the people of Israel have done. They will die by war, hunger, and disease. 12The person who is far away will die by disease. The one who is nearby will die in war. The person who is still alive and has escaped these will die from hunger. So I will carry out my anger on them. 13Their people will lie dead among their idols around the altars, on every high hill, on all the mountain tops, and under every green tree and leafy oak—all the places where they offered sweet-smelling incense to their idols. Then you will know that I am the LORD. 14I will use my power against them to make the land empty and wasted from the desert to Diblah, wherever they live. Then they will know that I am the LORD.' "

EZEKIEL TELLS OF THE END

7 1Again the LORD spoke his word to me, saying: 2"Human, the Lord GOD says this to the land of Israel: An end! The end has come on the four corners of the land. 3Now the end has come for you, and I will send my anger against you. I will judge you for the way you have lived, and I will make you pay for all your actions that I hate. 4I will have no pity on you; I will not hold back punishment from you. Instead, I will make you pay for the way you have lived and for your actions that I hate. Then you will know that I am the LORD.

JUDGMENT

Who will judge us? (7:3–4)

5"This is what the Lord GOD says: Disaster on top of disaster is coming. 6The end has come! The end has come! It has stirred itself up against you! Look! It has come! 7Disaster has come for you who live in the land! The time has come; the day of confusion is near. There will be no happy shouting on the mountains. 8Soon I will pour out my anger against you; I will carry out my anger against you. I will judge you for the way you have lived and will make you pay for everything you have done that I hate. 9I will show no pity, and I will not hold back punishment. I will pay you back for the way you have lived and the things you have done that I hate. Then you will know that I am the LORD who punishes.

10"Look, the day is here. It has come. Disaster has come, violence has grown, and there is more pride than ever. 11Violence has grown into a weapon for punishing wickedness. None of the people will be left—none of that crowd, none of their wealth, and nothing of value. 12The time has come; the day has arrived. Don't let the buyer be happy or the seller be sad, because my burning anger is against the whole crowd. 13Sellers will not return to the land they have sold as long as they live, because the vision against all that crowd will not be changed. Because of their sins, they will not save their lives. 14They have blown the trumpet, and everything is ready. But no one is going to the battle, because my anger is against all that crowd.

15"The sword is outside, and disease and hunger are inside. Whoever is in the field will die by the sword. Hunger and disease will destroy those in the city. 16Those who are left alive and who escape will be on the mountains, moaning like doves of the valleys about their own sin. 17All hands will hang weakly with fear, and all knees will become weak as water. 18They will put on rough cloth to show how sad they are. They will tremble all over with fear. Their faces will show their shame, and all their heads will be shaved. 19The people will throw their silver into the streets, and their gold will be like trash. Their silver and gold will not save them from the LORD's anger. It will not

WHAT'S IT MEAN?

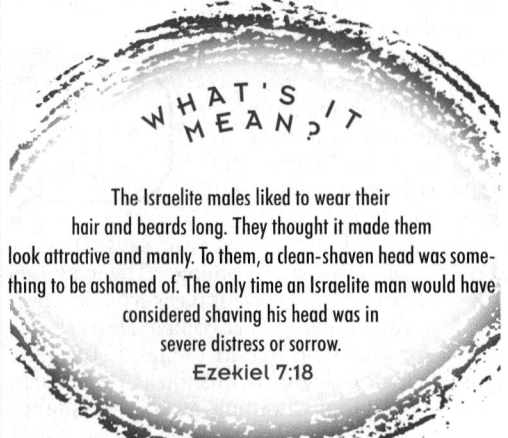

The Israelite males liked to wear their hair and beards long. They thought it made them look attractive and manly. To them, a clean-shaven head was something to be ashamed of. The only time an Israelite man would have considered shaving his head was in severe distress or sorrow.

Ezekiel 7:18

satisfy their hunger or fill their stomachs, because it caused them to fall into sin. 20They were proud of their beautiful jewelry and used it to make their idols and their evil statues, which I hate. So I will turn their wealth into trash. 21I will give it to foreigners as loot from war and to the most evil people in the world as treasure, and they will dishonor it. 22I will also turn away from the people of Israel, and they will dishonor my treasured place. Then robbers will enter and dishonor it.

> **"I will punish them for the way they have lived. The way they have judged others is the way I will judge them. Then they will know that I am the LORD."**
> **(Ezekiel 7:27b)**

23"Make chains for captives, because the land is full of bloody crimes and the city is full of violence. 24So I will bring the worst of the nations to take over the people's houses. I will also end the pride of the strong, and their holy places will be dishonored. 25When the people are suffering greatly, they will look for peace, but there will be none. 26Disaster will come on top of disaster, and rumor will be added to rumor. Then they will try to get a vision from a prophet; the teachings of God from the priest and the advice from the older leaders will be lost. 27The king will cry greatly, the prince will give up hope, and the hands of the people who own land will shake with fear. I will punish them for the way they have lived. The way they have judged others is the way I will judge them. Then they will know that I am the LORD."

8

EZEKIEL'S VISION OF JERUSALEM

1It was the sixth year, on the fifth day of the sixth month of our captivity. I was sitting in my house with the older leaders of Judah in front of me. There I felt the power of the Lord GOD. 2I looked and saw something that looked like a human. From the waist down it looked like fire, and from the waist up it looked like bright glowing metal. 3It stretched out the shape of a hand and caught me by the hair on my head. The Spirit lifted me up between the earth and the sky. He took me in visions of God to Jerusalem, to the entrance to the north gate of the inner courtyard of the Temple. In the courtyard was the idol that caused God to be jealous. 4I saw the glory of the God of Israel there, as I had seen on the plain.

5Then he said to me, "Human, now look toward the north." So I looked up toward the north, and in the entrance north of the gate of the altar was the idol that caused God to be jealous.

6He said to me, "Human, do you see what they are doing? Do you see how many hateful things the people of Israel are doing here that drive me far away from my Temple? But you will see things more hateful than these."

7Then he brought me to the entry of the courtyard. When I looked, I saw a hole in the wall. 8He said to me, "Human, dig through the wall." So I dug through the wall and saw an entrance.

9Then he said to me, "Go in and see the hateful, evil things they are doing here." 10So I entered and

WHAT'S IT MEAN?

The Lord had the Israelites on a very strict diet. He identified certain animals as clean and others as unclean. The Israelites were free to eat all of the clean animals they could get their hands on, but unclean animals were off-limits. Here are just some of the animals that were on the "clean" menu: cattle, goats, sheep, fish with scales, and many kinds of birds. Animals considered unclean included snails, pigs, vultures, shellfish, and dogs.

Ezekiel 8:10

looked, and I saw every kind of crawling thing
and hateful beast and all the idols of the people
of Israel, carved on the wall all around.
[11]Standing in front of these carvings and idols
were seventy of the older leaders of Israel and
Jaazaniah son of Shaphan. Each man had his
pan for burning incense in his hand, and a
sweet-smelling cloud of incense was rising.
[12]Then he said to me, "Human, have you
seen what the older leaders of Israel are doing
in the dark? Have you seen each man in the
room of his own idol? They say, 'The LORD
doesn't see us. The LORD has left the land.'"
[13]He also said to me, "You will see even more
hateful things that they are doing."
[14]Then he brought me to the entrance of the
north gate of the Temple of the LORD, where I
saw women sitting and crying for Tammuz.[n]
[15]He said to me, "Do you see, human? You will
see things even more hateful than these."
[16]Then he brought me into the inner courtyard of the Temple. There I saw about twenty-
five men at the entrance to the Temple of the
LORD, between the porch and the altar. With
their backs turned to the Temple of the LORD,
they faced east and were worshiping the sun in
the east.
[17]He said to me, "Do you see, human? Is it
unimportant that the people of Judah are doing the hateful things they have done here?
They have filled the land with violence and
made me continually angry. Look, they are
insulting me every way they can. [18]So I will act
in anger. I will have no pity, nor will I show
mercy. Even if they shout in my ears, I won't
listen to them."

VISION OF THE ANGELS

9 [1]Then he shouted with a loud voice in my
ears, "You who are chosen to punish this city,
come near with your weapon in your hand."
[2]Then six men came from the direction of the
upper gate, which faces north, each with his
powerful weapon in his hand. Among them
was a man dressed in linen with a writing case
at his side. The men went in and stood by the
bronze altar.
[3]Then the glory of the God of Israel went up
from above the creatures with wings, where it
had been, to the place in the Temple where the
door opened. He called to the man dressed in
linen who had the writing case at his side. [4]He
said to the man, "Go through Jerusalem and
put a mark on the foreheads of the people who
groan and cry about all the hateful things being done among them."

WHAT'S IT MEAN?

Linen, which was handwoven from the fibers of the hemp plant, was considered to be the highest-quality fabric in the ancient world. For the most part, only people of great wealth or power wore linen. Priests and those who served in the Temple were the exception. They, too, wore linen. The white linen uniforms that the priests wore were designed according to the instructions in the Teachings of Moses.
Ezekiel 9:2

[5]As I listened, he said to the other men, "Go
through the city behind the man dressed in
linen and kill. Don't pity anyone, and don't
show mercy. [6]Kill and destroy old men, young
men and women, little children, and older
women, but don't touch any who have the
mark on them. Start at my Temple." So they
started with the older leaders who were in
front of the Temple.
[7]Then he said to the men, "Make the Temple
unclean, and fill the courtyards with those
who have been killed. Go out!" So the men
went out and killed the people in the city.
[8]While the men were killing the people, I was
left alone. I bowed facedown on the ground
and I cried out, "Oh, Lord GOD! Will you destroy everyone left alive in Israel when
you turn loose your anger
on Jerusalem?"
[9]Then he said to me,
"The sin of the people of Israel
and Judah is very great. The
land is filled with people who
murder, and the city is full of
people who are not fair. The
people say, 'The LORD has left the land, and the
LORD does not see.' [10]But I will have no pity,
nor will I show mercy. I will bring their evil
back on their heads."
[11]Then the man dressed in linen with the
writing case at his side reported, "I have done
just as you commanded me."

RESPONSIBILITY
What are we responsible for? (9:9–10)

8:14 Tammuz Tammuz was a god in Babylon. Every year people thought this god died when the plants died. After they cried for him, they believed he came back to life, and the plants lived again.

THE COALS OF FIRE

10 1Then I looked and saw in the dome above the heads of the living creatures something like a sapphire gem which looked like a throne. 2The LORD said to the man dressed in linen, "Go in between the wheels under the living creatures, fill your hands with coals of fire from between the living creatures, and scatter the coals over the city."

As I watched, the man with linen clothes went in. 3Now the living creatures were standing on the south side of the Temple when the man went in. And a cloud filled the inner courtyard. 4Then the glory of the LORD went up from the living creatures and stood over the door of the Temple. The Temple was filled with the cloud, and the courtyard was full of the brightness from the glory of the LORD. 5The sound of the wings of the living creatures was heard all the way to the outer courtyard. It was like the voice of God Almighty when he speaks.

6When the LORD commanded the man dressed in linen, "Take fire from between the wheels, from between the living creatures," the man went in and stood by a wheel. 7One living creature put out his hand to the fire that was among them, took some of the fire, and put it in the hands of the man dressed in linen. Then the man took the fire and went out.

THE WHEELS AND THE CREATURES

8Something that looked like a human hand could be seen under the wings of the living creatures. 9I saw the four wheels by the living creatures, one wheel by each living creature. The wheels looked like shining chrysolite. 10All four wheels looked alike: Each looked like a wheel crossways inside another wheel. 11When the wheels moved, they went in any of the directions that the four living creatures faced. The wheels did not turn about, and the living creatures did not turn their bodies as they went. 12All their bodies, their backs, their hands, their wings, and the wheels were full of eyes all over. Each of the four living creatures had a wheel. 13I heard the wheels being called "whirling wheels." 14Each living creature had four faces. The first face was the face of a creature with wings. The second face was a human face, the third was the face of a lion, and the fourth was the face of an eagle.

15Then the living creatures flew up. They were the same living creatures I had seen by the Kebar River. 16When the living creatures moved, the wheels moved beside them. When the living creatures lifted their wings to fly up from the ground, the wheels did not leave their place beside them. 17When the living creatures stopped, the wheels stopped. When the creatures went up, the wheels went up also, because the spirit of the living creatures was in the wheels.

18Then the glory of the LORD left the door of the Temple and stood over the living creatures. 19As I watched, the living creatures spread their wings and flew up from the ground, with the wheels beside them. They stood where the east gate of the Temple of the LORD opened, and the glory of the God of Israel was over them.

20These were the living creatures I had seen under the God of Israel by the Kebar River. I knew they were called cherubim. 21Each one had four faces and four wings, and under their wings were things that looked like human hands. 22Their faces looked the same as the ones I had seen by the Kebar River. They each went straight ahead.

PROPHECIES AGAINST EVIL LEADERS

11 1The Spirit lifted me up and brought me to the front gate of the Temple of the LORD, which faces east. I saw twenty-five men where the gate opens, among them Jaazaniah son of Azzur and Pelatiah son of Benaiah, who were leaders of the people. 2Then the LORD said to me, "Human, these are the men who plan evil and give wicked advice in this city of Jerusalem. 3They say, 'It is almost time for us to build houses. This city is like a cooking pot, and we are like the best meat.' 4So prophesy against them, prophesy, human."

5Then the Spirit of the LORD entered me and told me to say: "This is what the LORD says: You have said these things, people of Israel, and I know what you are thinking. 6You have killed many people in this city, filling its streets with their bodies.

7"So this is what the Lord GOD says: Those people you have killed and left in the middle of the city are like the best meat, and this city is like the cooking pot. But I will force you out of the city. 8You have feared the sword, but I will bring a sword against you, says the Lord GOD. 9I will force you out of the city and hand you over to strangers and punish you. 10You will die by the sword. I will punish you at the border of Israel so you will know that I am the LORD. 11This city will not be your cooking pot, and you will not be the best meat in the middle of it. I will punish you at the border of Israel. 12Then you will know that I am the

DECISIONS

When is peer pressure bad? (11:12)

LORD. You did not live by my rules or obey my laws. Instead, you did the same things as the nations around you."
13As I prophesied, Pelatiah son of Benaiah died. Then I bowed facedown on the ground and shouted with a loud voice, "Oh no, Lord GOD! Will you completely destroy the Israelites who are left alive?"

PROMISE TO THOSE REMAINING

14The LORD spoke his word to me, saying,
15"Human, the people still in Jerusalem have spoken about your own relatives and all the people of Israel who are captives with you, saying, 'They are far from the LORD. This land has been given to us as our property.'
16"So say, 'This is what the Lord GOD says: I sent the people far away among the nations and scattered them among the countries. But for a little while I have become a Temple to them in the countries where they have gone.'
17"So say: 'This is what the Lord GOD says: I will gather you from the nations and bring you together from the countries where you have been scattered. Then I will give you back the land of Israel.'
18"When they come to this land, they will remove all the evil idols and all the hateful images.
19I will give them a desire to respect me completely, and I will put inside them a new way of thinking. I will take out the stubborn heart of stone from their bodies, and I will give them an obedient heart of flesh.
20Then they will live by my rules and obey my laws and keep them. They will be my people, and I will be their God.
21But those who want to serve their evil statues and hateful idols, I will pay back for their evil ways, says the Lord GOD."

FOLLOWING GOD

How can we have a changed life? (11:19–20)

EZEKIEL'S VISION ENDS

22Then the living creatures lifted their wings with the wheels beside them, and the glory of the God of Israel was above them.
23The glory of the LORD went up from inside Jerusalem

Promise

HE PROMISES TO BE YOUR HOME-AWAY-FROM-HOME.

So say, "This is what the Lord God says: I sent the people far away among the nations and scattered them among the countries. But for a little while I have become a Temple to them in the countries where they have gone." So say: "This is what the Lord God says: I will gather you from the nations and bring you together from the countries where you have been scattered. Then I will give you back the land of Israel" (Ezek. 11:16–17).

Around 600 B.C., an enemy king took the prophet Daniel and some other strong young men away from Jerusalem, where God's Temple was, to the city of Babylon. But Daniel was faithful to God, and God showed that he was with Daniel by protecting him and allowing the king to notice him and give him lots of authority.

Ezekiel was one of the men taken to Babylon with Daniel. The people who were left in Jerusalem were saying that God had not gone to Babylon with them. But the things that happened to them there told a different story. And Ezekiel had God's word on it: "But for a little while I have become a Temple to them in the countries where they have gone." In other words, "I am your home-away-from-home."

As you try to do what God wants you to do, you may find yourself in a place that seems really far from him—a state university, a job you can't stand, maybe even a city or country where people don't seem to care about God. But he promises to be where your home-away-from-home is because his Spirit lives inside of you.

SEE FOR YOURSELF:

Ex. 33:14; Lev. 26:12; Deut. 31:8; Ps. 37:28; Matt. 28:19–20

On the Edge

I will give them a desire to respect me completely, and I will put inside them a new way of thinking. I will take out the stubborn heart of stone from their bodies, and I will give them an obedient heart of flesh (Ezek. 11:19).

You may have a heart to obey God down deep inside, but he still requires you to make a choice. You can choose to obey him or to disobey him. The rewards are great if you choose to obey. In fact, the Holy Spirit will give you warning signs. Has there ever been a time where you were about to sin, and WHAM! There was this still, small voice that was saying, "Don't do it!" Well, that was the voice of the Holy Spirit. At that moment you had to make a choice to listen to that voice and obey, or to block out that voice and sin.

Your heart starts out as a heart of flesh. The more you continue to disobey the Holy Spirit, your heart of flesh turns hard into stone, and that can and will lead to problems. Once your heart is hard, you won't be able to hear the still, small voice. Then what? You will walk blindly into all sorts of trouble that could have otherwise been avoided by obeying the promptings of the Holy Spirit.

God is a loving God. Never forget it. He wants to take away any stubbornness or hardness and give you a heart of flesh. If your heart has become hard, ask God to forgive you and take away your stubbornness. But even after you ask him to give you a heart to obey him, the actual choice is up to you. Choose obedience, and tap into God's blessings today!

SEE FOR YOURSELF:
Ezek. 36:26; Matt. 5:8; Luke 8:15; Heb. 10:22

and stopped on the mountain on the east side
of the city. 24The Spirit lifted me up and
brought me to the captives who had been
taken from Judah to Babylonia. This happened
in a vision given by the Spirit of God, and then
the vision I had seen ended. 25And I told the
captives from Judah all the things the LORD
had shown me.

EZEKIEL MOVES OUT

12

1Again the LORD spoke his word to me, saying: 2"Human, you are living among a people
who refuse to obey. They have eyes to see, but
they do not see, and they have ears to hear, but
they do not hear, because they are a people
who refuse to obey.
3"So, human, pack your things as if you will
be taken away captive, and walk away like a
captive in the daytime with the people watching. Move from your place to another with the
people watching. Maybe they will understand,
even though they are a people who refuse to
obey. 4During the day when the people are
watching, bring out the things you would pack
as captive. At evening, with the people watching, leave your place like those who are taken
away as captives from their country. 5Dig a
hole through the wall while they watch, and
bring your things out through it. 6Lift them
onto your shoulders with the people watching,
and carry them out in the dark. Cover your
face so you cannot see the ground, because I
have made you a sign to the people of Israel."
7I did these things as I was commanded. In
the daytime I brought what I had packed as if I
were being taken away captive. Then in the evening I dug through the wall with my hands. I
brought my things out in the dark and carried
them on my shoulders as the people watched.
8Then in the morning the LORD spoke his
word to me, saying: 9"Human, didn't Israel,
who refuses to obey, ask you, 'What are you
doing?'
10"Say to them, 'This is what the Lord GOD
says: This message is about the king in Jerusalem and all the people of Israel who live there.'
11Say, 'I am a sign to you.'
"The same things I have done will be done
to the people in Jerusalem. They will be taken
away from their country as captives. 12The
king among them will put his things on his
shoulder in the dark and will leave. The people
will dig a hole through the wall to bring him
out. He will cover his face so he cannot see the
ground. 13But I will spread my net over him,
and he will be caught in my trap. Then I will
bring him to Babylon in the land of the Babylonians. He will not see that land, but he will
die there. 14All who are around the king—his
helpers and all his army—I will scatter in every
direction, and I will chase them with a sword.
15"They will know that I am the LORD when
I scatter them among the nations and spread
them among the countries. 16But I will save a
few of them from the sword and from hunger
and disease. Then they can tell about their hate-

ful actions among the nations where they go.
Then they will know that I am the LORD."

WHAT'S IT MEAN?

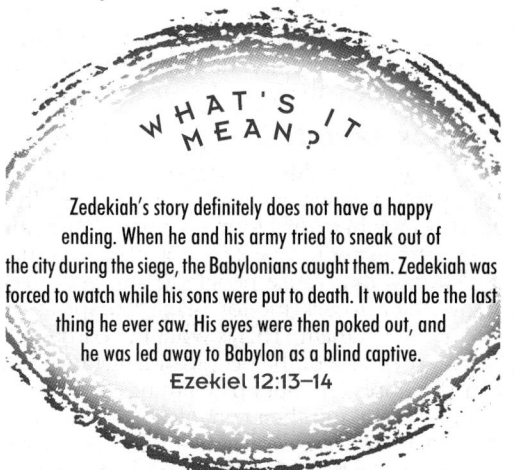

Zedekiah's story definitely does not have a happy ending. When he and his army tried to sneak out of the city during the siege, the Babylonians caught them. Zedekiah was forced to watch while his sons were put to death. It would be the last thing he ever saw. His eyes were then poked out, and he was led away to Babylon as a blind captive.
Ezekiel 12:13–14

THE LESSON OF EZEKIEL'S SHAKING

17The LORD spoke his word to me, saying:
18"Human, tremble as you eat your food, and
shake with fear as you drink your water.
19Then say to the people of the land: 'This is
what the Lord GOD says about the people who
live in Jerusalem in the land of Israel: They will
eat their food with fear and drink their water
in shock, because their land will be stripped
bare because of the violence of the people who
live in it. 20The cities where people live will become ruins, and the land will become empty.
Then you will know that I am the LORD.' "

THE VISIONS WILL COME TRUE

21The LORD spoke his word to me, saying:
22"Human, what is this saying you have in the
land of Israel: 'The days go by and
every vision comes to nothing'? 23So say to them, 'This is
what the Lord GOD says: I will
make them stop saying this,
and nobody in Israel will use
this saying anymore.' But tell
them, 'The time is near when
every vision will come true. 24There will be no
more false visions or pleasing prophecies inside
the nation of Israel, 25but I, the LORD, will speak.
What I say will be done, and it will not be delayed. You refuse to obey, but in your time I will
say the word and do it, says the Lord GOD.' "
26The LORD spoke his word to me, saying:
27"Human, the people of Israel are saying, 'The
vision that Ezekiel sees is for a time many years
from now. He is prophesying about times far
away.'
28"So say to them: 'The Lord GOD says this:
None of my words will be delayed anymore.
What I have said will be done, says the Lord
GOD.' "

IDOLATRY
Does God condemn idolatry? (12:21–25)

EZEKIEL SPEAKS AGAINST FALSE PROPHETS

13
1The LORD spoke his word to me, saying:
2"Human, prophesy against the prophets of Israel. Say to those who make up their own
prophecies: 'Listen to the word of the LORD.
3This is what the Lord GOD says: How terrible
it will be for the foolish prophets
who follow their own ideas
and have not seen a vision
from me! 4People of Israel,
your prophets have been like
wild dogs hunting to kill and
eat among ruins. 5Israel is like
a house in ruins, but you have
not gone up into the broken places or repaired
the wall. So how can Israel hold back the enemy in the battle on the LORD's day of judging?
6Your prophets see false visions and prophesy
lies. They say, "This is the message of the LORD,"
when the LORD has not sent them. But they still
hope their words will come true. 7You said,
"This is the message of the LORD," but that is a
false vision. Your prophecies are lies, because I
have not spoken.
8" 'So this is what the Lord GOD says: Because you prophets spoke things that are false
and saw visions that do not come true, I am
against you, says the Lord GOD. 9I will punish
the prophets who see false visions and prophesy lies. They will have no place among my
people. Their names will not be written on the
list of the people of Israel, and they will not
enter the land of Israel. Then you will know
that I am the Lord GOD.
10" 'It is because they lead my people the
wrong way by saying, "Peace!" when there is
no peace. When the people build a weak wall,
the prophets cover it with whitewash to make
it look strong. 11So tell those who cover a weak
wall with whitewash that it will fall down.
Rain will pour down, hailstones will fall, and a
stormy wind will break the wall down. 12When
the wall has fallen, people will ask you, "Where
is the whitewash you used on the wall?"
13" 'So this is what the Lord GOD says: I will
break the wall with a stormy wind. In my anger rain will pour down, and hailstones will
destroy the wall. 14I will tear down the wall on
which you put whitewash. I will level it to the
ground so that people will see the wall's foundation. And when the wall falls, you will be
destroyed under it. Then you will know that I

CULT
Why are cults dangerous? (13:3–7)

am the LORD. 15So I will carry out my anger on
the wall and against those who covered it with
whitewash. Then I will tell you, "The wall is
gone, and those who covered it with whitewash are gone. 16The prophets of Israel who
prophesy to Jerusalem and who see visions of
peace for the city, when there is no peace, will
be gone, says the Lord GOD." '

WHAT'S IT MEAN?

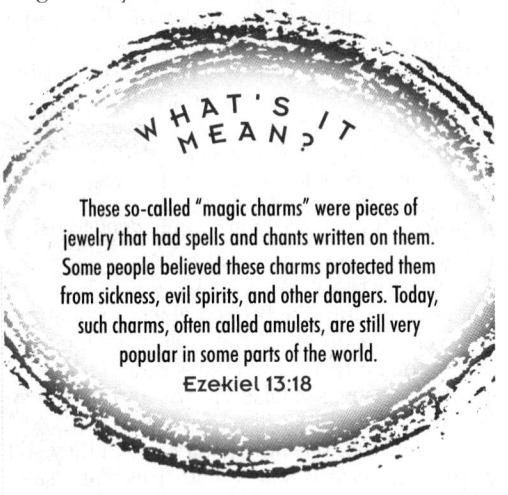

These so-called "magic charms" were pieces of jewelry that had spells and chants written on them. Some people believed these charms protected them from sickness, evil spirits, and other dangers. Today, such charms, often called amulets, are still very popular in some parts of the world.

Ezekiel 13:18

FALSE WOMEN PROPHETS

17"Now, human, look toward the women
among your people who make up their own
prophecies. Prophesy against
them. 18Say, 'This is what the
Lord GOD says: How terri-
ble it will be for women
who sew magic charms
on their wrists and make
veils of every length to
trap people! You ruin the
lives of my people but try
to save your own lives.
19For handfuls of barley
and pieces of bread, you
have dishonored me among
my people. By lying to my peo-
ple, who listen to lies, you have killed people who should not die, and you have kept
alive those who should not live.

20" 'So this is what the Lord GOD says: I am
against your magic charms, by which you trap
people as if they were birds. I will tear those
charms off your arms, and I will free those
people you have trapped like birds. 21I will also
tear off your veils and save my people from
your hands. They will no longer be trapped by
your power. Then you will know that I am the
LORD. 22By your lies you have caused those
who did right to be sad, when I did not make
them sad. And you have encouraged the wicked not to stop being wicked, which would
have saved their lives. 23So you will not see
false visions or prophesy anymore, and I will
save my people from your power so you will
know that I am the LORD.' "

"So say to the people of Israel, 'This is what the Lord GOD says: Change your hearts and lives, and stop worshiping idols. Stop doing all the things I hate.' "

(Ezekiel 14:6)

STOP WORSHIPING IDOLS

14

1Some of the older leaders of Israel came to
me and sat down in front of me. 2Then the
LORD spoke his word to me, saying: 3"Human,
these men want to worship idols. They put up
evil things that cause people to sin. Should I
allow them to ask me for help? 4So speak to
them and tell them, 'This is what the Lord GOD
says: When any of the people of Israel want to
worship idols and put up evil things that cause
people to sin and then come to the prophet, I,
the LORD, will answer them myself for worshiping idols. 5Then I will win back my people
Israel, who have left me because of all their
idols.'

6"So say to the people of Israel, 'This is what
the Lord GOD says: Change your hearts and
lives, and stop worshiping idols. Stop doing all
the things I hate. 7Any of the Israelites or foreigners in Israel can separate themselves from
me by wanting to worship idols or by putting
up the things that cause people to sin. Then if
they come to the prophet to ask me questions,
I, the LORD, will answer them
myself. 8I will reject them. I
will make them a sign and
an example, and I will separate them from my peo-
ple. Then you will know
that I am the LORD.

9" 'But if the prophet is
tricked into giving a
prophecy, it is because I,
the LORD, have tricked
that prophet to speak. Then
I will use my power against
him and destroy him from
among my people Israel. 10The prophet will
be as guilty as the one who asks him for help;
both will be responsible for their guilt. 11Then
the nation of Israel will not leave me anymore
or make themselves unclean anymore with all
their sins. They will be my people, and I will be
their GOD, says the Lord GOD.' "

JERUSALEM WILL NOT BE SPARED

12The LORD spoke his word to me, saying:
13"Human, if the people of a country sin
against me by not being loyal, I will use my
power against them. I will cut off their supply

JOSIAH made a difference

Among all the kings of Judah and Israel, including David and Solomon, God's Word gives a unique place to Josiah. "There was no king like Josiah before or after him. He obeyed the LORD with all his heart, soul, and strength, following all the Teachings of Moses" (2 Kin. 23:25).

Josiah became king of Judah when he was eight years old. His wicked father had been assassinated. Scripture tells us little of Josiah's adolescence. If he had a royal hero, it was probably his godly great-grandfather Hezekiah. By the time Josiah reached his mid-twenties, he was anxious to make a difference in his nation for God. He organized the renovation of the Temple in Jerusalem, which had been neglected. In the process, an even greater neglect was discovered. A book containing God's Teachings was delivered to the king. Confronted with the promises and warnings of God's Word, Josiah humbled himself before God. That attitude of responsiveness to God—of wanting to act wholeheartedly on any truthful information discovered about God—made Josiah stand out.

Cutting Edge

Under Josiah's leadership, there was a national revival of true worship. The king aggressively removed the evidences of paganism from the land. And he reinstituted the joyful celebration of Passover, remembering the faithfulness of God. Josiah made a difference because he demonstrated that even a king can live by the great commandment! (see Mark 12:28–34).

YOU can, too! What is your immediate response when you gain a new insight about God? Most of what we learn will change our view of God or our view of ourselves. Too often, young people will acknowledge that what they have learned about God is true, but they probably won't act on that truth until later in life. Can you hear yourself saying, "Sure, I know God wants my undivided commitment, and someday I plan to give him that. But for now, I've got other plans. . . ." Postponing or rejecting God's guidance will insure that your Life will make the wrong kind of difference. Josiah didn't wait to turn his life over to God.

Want to know more? Josiah's reign is told twice in Scripture: 2 Kings 21:24—23:30; 2 Chronicles 33:25—35:27. Jeremiah also mentions him in Jeremiah 1:1–3; 22:11, 18.

ESTHER made a difference

Young people often get frustrated over decisions made by others, which affect their lives. Esther would have understood. Most of the important decisions in her life—where to live, who would raise her, whom she would marry, how she would be treated—were all made by others. She grew up in a foreign land. Her parents died and she was raised by a cousin. She was picked for a beauty contest and found herself a queen. Even that position, surrounded by countless beautiful women, had little job security. That left her the most important decision of all: how she would respond to the situations in her life.

Esther didn't have to look for an opportunity to make a difference—it came looking for her. A man named Haman who hated Jewish people decided to wipe them out. He managed to convince the king that Jews were different and should be destroyed. Suddenly, Esther became the central figure in a life-and-death struggle. Her cousin reminded her, "And who knows, you may have been chosen queen for just such a time as this" (Esther 4:14b).

Cutting Edge

Esther's courage and wisdom in making the most of her situation offer an inspiring example. She turned the tables on Haman and gave her people a fighting chance. She risked her life, but Haman paid for his hatred with his life. Esther did not choose the size or the shape of the biggest challenge in her life, but she did choose her response well. Her choice made a difference for her people.

YOU can, too! You very well may feel surrounded and crushed by the decisions others have made. You may be in a good place or a bad place where you don't want to be. Trouble may be knocking at your door. You can still make a difference! In fact, you will. How you respond and the choices you make will determine a lot of the future.

You may not know exactly what the future holds, but make your choices today deliberate ones. Choose to ask God for help. God does know what the future holds. Make decisions relying on him. God can sort out what's happened and give you a way to go on. He will make a difference so you can make the right kind of difference with your Life.

Want to know more? Esther's story carries her name in the Bible.

SHADRACH, MESHACH, AND ABEDNEGO made a difference

You can tell who your real friends are when the heat is on! Standing together with a couple of friends against a death threat takes both courage and confidence in one another. These three backed each other up and made a difference. Their boldness provided an opportunity for God to confront a king.

Shadrach, Meshach, and Abednego spoke and lived as one. They were wise men in the service of King Nebuchadnezzar, but their higher allegiance was to God. Their work did not usually conflict with their faith. But those who hated them maneuvered the king into a prideful act—creating a huge statue, which everyone was required to worship. As expected, Shadrach, Meshach, and Abednego refused. No insult to the king was intended. They simply refused to go along with the idea that Nebuchadnezzar was any kind of god.

Cutting Edge

Whenever individuals take a stand on principle, they can expect resistance. For our three heroes, it came in the form of a roaring furnace. The heat got turned up. Shadrach, Meshach, and Abednego came up with one of the finest and boldest statements of faith recorded in Scripture: "If you throw us into the blazing furnace, the God we serve is able to save us from the furnace. He will save us from your power, O king. But even if God does not save us, we want you, O king, to know this: We will not serve your gods or worship the gold statue you have set up" (Dan. 3:17–18). They entrusted their lives to God and left the results in God's hands. They stood together—with God. God stood together with them in the furnace. Their faith made a difference. YOU can, too!

Furnaces come in many shapes and sizes. Often they are nothing more than the heat of public ridicule or rejection. We are tempted every day to avoid the elevated heat of conflict by compromising our faith as well as God's truth. When we learn God's truth and make it a point to practice faithfulness when the heat goes up, we will see that God can do amazing things in our lives, too. You won't always be able to pick your furnaces; be sure to pick some good friends who can stand with you and with God.

Want to know more? You can read about Shadrach, Meshach, and Abednego's friendship and service to God in Daniel.

MARY, THE MOTHER OF JESUS, made a difference

We can learn a lot about ourselves and other people by the way we act when we're surprised. The unexpected doesn't give us time to pretend or to slip into our disguises. Fear, confidence, courage, and cowardice are frequently revealed by the sudden. We know little about the character of Mary, the mother of Jesus, other than what we see through her responses. It was through her responses that she made a difference.

An angel's visit ranks high on the list of the unexpected. Mary was startled. She listened to Gabriel. Her initial response was a single question of amazement, "How will this happen since I am a virgn?" (Luke 1:34). Mary knew how things worked. She was a child of a culture whose history was filled with women who gave birth with God's help. But husbands had always been involved. She didn't have one yet. So, how was this to come about?

Cutting Edge

Gabriel's instructions were very specific. Mary was not to do anything. God's Spirit would do it all. Again, we are not told what Mary thought or how she felt. We only know her servantlike response: "Let this happen to me as you say!" (Luke 1:38). As soon as God let her know she didn't have to worry about the details, Mary left things in God's hands. That's how she made a difference. She participated and cooperated in God's wonderful plan. She didn't try to take control.

YOU can, too! One lesson you can take from Mary involves thinking about how you react to surprises. You may have to ask other people to help you see yourself. If you are responding well to the unexpected, congratulations! You are on track. You will probably find, though, that sometimes your responses will indicate an area in which you need to grow. Do you get angry, discouraged, doubtful, or completely confused by the unexpected? What do these responses tell you about your Life?

Assume that God wants to make a difference in and through your life. Expect God to guide you. Consider that his guidance may come in surprising or unexpected ways. Are you training your responses?

Want to know more? Mary was part of the scene in all four accounts of the Good News. She takes center stage in Luke 1:26—2:52.

of food and send a time of hunger, destroying
both people and animals. 14Even if three great
men like Noah, Daniel, and Job were in that
country, their goodness could save only themselves, says the Lord GOD.
15"Or I might send wild animals into that
land, leaving the land empty and without children. Then no one would pass through it because of the animals. 16As surely as I live, says
the Lord GOD, even if Noah, Daniel, and Job
were in the land, they could not save their own
sons or daughters. They could save only themselves, but that country would become empty.
17"Or I might bring a war against that country. I might say, 'Let a war be fought in that
land,' in this way destroying its people and its
animals. 18As surely as I live, says the Lord
GOD, even if those three men were in the land,
they could not save their sons or daughters.
They could save only themselves.
19"Or I might cause a disease to spread in
that country. I might pour out my anger
against it, destroying and killing people and
animals. 20As surely as I live, says the Lord
GOD, even if Noah, Daniel, and Job were in the
land, they could not save their son or daughter. They could save only themselves because
they did what was right.
21"This is what the Lord GOD says: My plans
for Jerusalem are much worse! I will send my
four terrible punishments against it—war,
hunger, wild animals, and disease—to destroy
its people and animals. 22But some people will
escape; some sons and daughters will be led
out. They will come out to you, and you will
see what happens to people who live as they
did. Then you will be comforted after the disasters I have brought against Jerusalem, after
all the things I have brought against it. 23You
will be comforted when you see what happens
to them for living as they did, because you will
know there was a good reason for what I did
to Jerusalem, says the Lord GOD."

STORY OF THE VINE

15
1The LORD spoke his word to me, saying:
2"Human, is the wood of the vine better than
the wood of any tree in the forest? 3Can wood
be taken from the vine to make anything? Can
you use it to make a peg on which to hang
something? 4If the vine is thrown into the fire
for fuel, and the fire burns up both ends and
starts to burn the middle, is it useful for anything? 5When the vine was whole, it couldn't
be made into anything. When the fire has
burned it completely, it certainly cannot be
made into anything."
6So this is what the Lord GOD says: "Out of
all the trees in the forest, I have given the wood
of the vine as fuel for fire. In the same way I
have given up the people who live in Jerusalem 7and will turn against them. Although they
came through one fire, fire will still destroy
them. When I turn against them, you will
know that I am the LORD. 8So I will make the
land empty, because the people have not been
loyal, says the Lord GOD."

THE LORD'S KINDNESS TO JERUSALEM

16
1The LORD spoke his word to me, saying:
2"Human, tell Jerusalem about her hateful actions. 3Say, 'This is what the Lord GOD says to
Jerusalem: Your beginnings and your ancestors
were in the land of the Canaanites. Your father
was an Amorite, and your mother was a Hittite. 4On the day you were born, your cord[n]
was not cut. You were not washed with water
to clean you. You were not rubbed with salt or
wrapped in cloths. 5No one felt sorry enough
for you to do any of these things for you. No,
you were thrown out into the open field, because you were hated on the day you were
born.
6" 'When I passed by and saw you kicking
about in your blood, I said to you, "Live!" 7I
made you grow like a plant in the field. You
grew up and became tall and became like a
beautiful jewel. Your breasts formed, and your
hair grew, but you were naked and without
clothes.
8" 'Later when I passed by you and looked
at you, I saw that you were old enough for

WHAT'S IT MEAN?

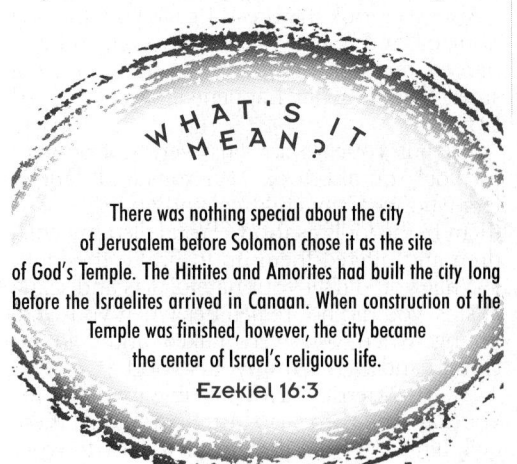

There was nothing special about the city of Jerusalem before Solomon chose it as the site of God's Temple. The Hittites and Amorites had built the city long before the Israelites arrived in Canaan. When construction of the Temple was finished, however, the city became the center of Israel's religious life.

Ezekiel 16:3

16:4 cord The umbilical cord that gives the unborn baby food and air from its mother.

love. So I spread my robe over you and covered your nakedness. I also made a promise to you and entered into an agreement with you so that you became mine, says the Lord GOD.

9" 'Then I bathed you with water, washed all the blood off of you, and put oil on you. 10I put beautiful clothes made with needlework on you and put sandals of fine leather on your feet. I wrapped you in fine linen and covered you with silk. 11I put jewelry on you: bracelets on your arms, a necklace around your neck, 12a ring in your nose, earrings in your ears, and a beautiful crown on your head. 13So you wore gold and silver. Your clothes were made of fine linen, silk, and beautiful needlework. You ate fine flour, honey, and olive oil. You were very beautiful and became a queen. 14Then you became famous among the nations, because you were so beautiful. Your beauty was perfect, because of the glory I gave you, says the Lord GOD.

JERUSALEM BECOMES A PROSTITUTE

15" 'But you trusted in your beauty. You became a prostitute, because you were so famous. You had sexual relations with anyone who passed by. 16You took some of your clothes and made your places of worship colorful. There you carried on your prostitution. These things should not happen; they should never occur. 17You also took your beautiful jewelry, made from my gold and silver I had given you, and you made for yourselves male idols so you could be a prostitute with them. 18Then you took your clothes with beautiful needlework and covered the idols. You gave my oil and incense as an offering to them. 19Also, you took the bread I gave you, the fine flour, oil, and honey I gave you to eat, and you offered them before the gods as a pleasing smell. This is what happened, says the Lord GOD.

20" 'But your sexual sins were not enough for you. You also took your sons and daughters who were my children, and you sacrificed them to the idols as food. 21You killed my children and offered them up in fire to the idols. 22While you did all your hateful acts and sexual sins, you did not remember when you were young, when you were naked and had no clothes and were left in your blood.

23" 'How terrible! How terrible it will be for you, says the Lord GOD. After you did all these evil things, 24you built yourself a place to worship gods. You made for yourself a place of worship in every city square. 25You built a place of worship at the beginning of every street. You made your beauty hateful, offering your body for sex to anyone who passed by, so your sexual sins became worse and worse. 26You also had sexual relations with the Egyptians, who were your neighbors and partners in sexual sin. Your sexual sins became even worse, and they caused me to be angry. 27So then, I used my power against you and took away some of your land. I let you be defeated by those who hate you, the Philistine women, who were ashamed of your evil ways. 28Also, you had sexual relations with the Assyrians, because you could not be satisfied. Even though you had sexual relations with them, you still were not satisfied. 29You did many more sexual sins in Babylonia, the land of traders, but even this did not satisfy you.

LUST
What will unchecked lust get us? (16:25–30)

30" 'Truly your will is weak, says the Lord GOD. You do all the things a stubborn prostitute does. 31You built your place to worship gods at the beginning of every street, and you made places of worship in every city square. But you were not like a prostitute when you refused to accept payment.

32" 'You are a wife who is guilty of adultery. You desire strangers instead of your husband. 33Men pay prostitutes, but you pay all your lovers to come to you. And they come from all around for sexual relations. 34So you are different from other prostitutes. No man asks you to be a prostitute, and you pay money instead of having money paid to you. Yes, you are different.

THE PROSTITUTE IS JUDGED

35" 'So, prostitute, hear the word of the LORD. 36This is what the Lord GOD says: You showed your nakedness to other countries. You uncovered your body in your sexual sins with them as your lovers and with all your hateful idols. You killed your children and offered their blood to your idols. 37So I will gather all your lovers with whom you found pleasure. Yes, I will gather all those you loved and those you hated. I will gather them against you from all around, and I will strip you naked in front of them so they can see your nakedness. 38I will punish you as women guilty of adultery or as murderers are punished. I will put you to death because I am angry and jealous. 39I will also hand you over to your lovers. They will tear down your places of worship and destroy other places where you worship gods. They will tear off your clothes and take

away your jewelry, leaving you naked and
bare. [40]They will bring a crowd against you to
throw stones at you and to cut you into pieces
with their swords. [41]They will burn down your
houses and will punish you in front of many
women. I will put an end to your sexual sins,
and you will no longer pay your lovers. [42]Then
I will rest from my anger against you, and I
will stop being jealous. I will be quiet and not
angry anymore.

[43]" 'Because you didn't remember when you
were young, but have made me angry in all
these ways, I will repay you for what you have
done, says the Lord GOD. Didn't you add sexual sins to all your other acts which I hate?

[44]" 'Everyone who uses wise sayings will
say this about you: "The daughter is like her
mother." [45]You are like your mother, who hated
her husband and children. You are also like
your sisters, who hated their husbands and
children. Your mother was a Hittite, and your
father was an Amorite. [46]Your older sister is
Samaria, who lived north of you with her
daughters; your younger sister is Sodom, who
lived south of you with her daughters. [47]You
not only followed their ways and did the hateful things they did, but you were soon worse
than they were in all your ways. [48]As surely as
I live, says the Lord GOD, this is
true. Your sister Sodom and
her daughters never did what
you and your daughters have
done.

PRIDE

Does God condemn arrogance? (16:48–50)

[49]" 'This was the sin of
your sister Sodom: She and
her daughters were proud and had plenty of
food and lived in great comfort, but she did
not help the poor and needy. [50]So Sodom and
her daughters were proud and did things I
hate in front of me. So I got rid of them when
I saw what they did. [51]Also, Samaria did not
do half the sins you do; you have done more
hateful things than they did. So you make your
sisters look good because of all the hateful
things you have done. [52]You will suffer disgrace, because you have provided an excuse
for your sisters. They are better than you are.
Your sins were even more terrible than theirs.
Feel ashamed and suffer disgrace, because you
made your sisters look good.

[53]" 'But I will give back to Sodom and her
daughters the good things they once had. I will
give back to Samaria and her daughters the
good things they once had. And with them I
will also give back the good things you once
had [54]so you may suffer disgrace and feel
ashamed for all the things you have done. You
even gave comfort to your sisters in their sins.
[55]Your sisters, Sodom with her daughters and
Samaria with her daughters, will return to
what they were before. You and your daughters will also return to what you were before.
[56]You humiliated your sister Sodom when you
were proud, [57]before your evil was uncovered.
And now the Edomite women and their neighbors humiliate you. Even the Philistine women
humiliate you. Those around you hate you.
[58]This is your punishment for your terrible sins
and for actions that I hate, says the LORD.

GOD KEEPS HIS PROMISES

[59]" 'This is what the Lord GOD says: I will do
to you what you have done. You hated and
broke the agreement you promised to keep.
[60]But I will remember my agreement I made
with you when you were young, and I will
make an agreement that will continue forever
with you. [61]Then you will remember what you
have done and feel ashamed when you receive
your sisters—both your older and your younger sisters. I will give them to you like daughters, but not because they share in my
agreement with you. [62]I will set up my agreement with you, and you will know that I am
the LORD. [63]You will remember what you did
and feel ashamed. You will not open your
mouth again because of your shame, when I
forgive you for all the things you have done,
says the Lord GOD.' "

THE EAGLE AND THE VINE

17 [1]The LORD spoke his word to me, saying:
[2]"Human, give a riddle and tell a story to the
people of Israel. [3]Say, 'This is what the Lord
GOD says: A giant eagle with big wings and
long feathers of many different colors came to
Lebanon and took hold of the top of a cedar
tree. [4]He pulled off the top branch and brought
it to a land of traders, where he planted it in a
city of traders.

[5]" 'The eagle took some seed from the land
and planted it in a good field near plenty of
water. He planted it to grow like a willow tree.
[6]It sprouted and became a low vine that
spread over the ground. The branches turned
toward the eagle, but the roots were under the
eagle. So the seed became a vine, and its
branches grew, sending out leaves.

[7]" 'But there was another giant eagle with
big wings and many feathers. The vine then
bent its roots toward this eagle. It sent out its
branches from the area where it was planted
toward the eagle so he could water it. [8]It had
been planted in a good field by plenty of water

so it could grow branches and give fruit. It
could have become a fine vine.'
9"Say to them, 'This is what the Lord GOD
says: The vine will not continue to grow. The
first eagle will pull up the vine's roots and strip
off its fruit. Then the vine and all its new leaves
will dry up and die. It will not take a strong
arm or many people to pull the vine up by its
roots. 10Even if it is planted again, it will not
continue to grow. It will completely dry up
and die when the east wind hits it in the area
where it grew.' "

ZEDEKIAH AGAINST NEBUCHADNEZZAR

11Then the LORD spoke his word to me, saying: 12"Say now to the people who refuse to
obey: 'Do you know what these things mean?'
Say: 'The king of Babylon came to Jerusalem
and took the king and important men of Jerusalem and brought them to Babylon. 13Then he
took a member of the family of the king of
Judah and made an agreement with him, forcing him to take an oath. The king also took
away the leaders of Judah 14to make the kingdom weak so it would not be strong again.
Then the kingdom of Judah could continue
only by keeping its agreement with the king of
Babylon. 15But the king of Judah turned against
the king of Babylon by sending his messengers
to Egypt and asking them for horses and many
soldiers. Will the king of Judah succeed? Will
the one who does such things escape? He cannot break the agreement and escape.
16" 'As surely as I live, says the Lord GOD, he
will die in Babylon, in the land of the king who
made him king of Judah. The king of Judah
hated his promise to the king of Babylon and
broke his agreement with him. 17The king of
Egypt with his mighty army and many people
will not help the king of Judah in the war. The
Babylonians will build devices to attack the
cities and to kill many people. 18The king of
Judah showed that he hated the promise by
breaking the agreement. He promised to support Babylon, but he did all these things. So he
will not escape.
19" 'So this is what the Lord GOD says: As
surely as I live, this is true: I will pay back the
king of Judah for hating my promise and
breaking my agreement. 20I will spread my net
over him, and he will be caught in my trap.
Then I will bring him to Babylon, where I will
punish him for the unfaithful acts he did
against me. 21All the best of his soldiers who
escape will die by the sword, and those who
live will be scattered to every wind. Then you
will know that I, the LORD, have spoken.
22" 'This is what the Lord GOD says: I myself
will also take a young branch from the top of a
cedar tree, and I will plant it. I will cut off a
small twig from the top of the tree's young
branches, and I will plant it on a very high
mountain. 23I will plant it on the high mountain of Israel. Then it will grow branches and
give fruit and become a great cedar tree. Birds
of every kind will build nests in it and live in
the shelter of the tree's branches. 24Then all the
trees in the countryside will know that I am
the LORD. I bring down the high tree and make
the low tree tall. I dry up the green tree and
make the dry tree grow. I am the LORD. I have
spoken, and I will do it.' "

WHAT'S IT MEAN?

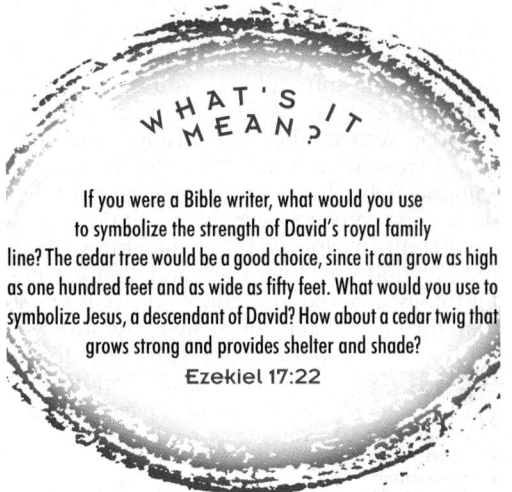

If you were a Bible writer, what would you use to symbolize the strength of David's royal family line? The cedar tree would be a good choice, since it can grow as high as one hundred feet and as wide as fifty feet. What would you use to symbolize Jesus, a descendant of David? How about a cedar twig that grows strong and provides shelter and shade?

Ezekiel 17:22

GOD IS FAIR

18

1The LORD spoke his word to me, saying:
2"What do you mean by using this saying
about the land of Israel:
'The parents have eaten sour grapes,
and that caused the children to grind
their teeth from the sour taste'?
3"As surely as I live, says the Lord GOD, this
is true: You will not use this saying in Israel
anymore. 4Every living thing belongs to me.
The life of the parent is mine, and the life of the
child is mine. The person who sins is the one
who will die.
5"Suppose a person is good and does what
is fair and right. 6He does not eat at the mountain places of worship. He does not look to the
idols of Israel for help. He does not have sexual
relations with his neighbor's wife or with a
woman during her time of monthly bleeding.
7He does not mistreat anyone but returns what
was given as a promise for a loan. He does not
rob other people. He gives bread to the hungry

and clothes to those who have none. [8]He does not lend money to get too much interest or profit. He keeps his hand from doing wrong. He judges fairly between one person and another. [9]He lives by my rules and obeys my laws faithfully. Whoever does these things is good and will surely live, says the Lord GOD.

[10]"But suppose this person has a wild son who murders people and who does any of these other things. [11](But the father himself has not done any of these things.) This son eats at the mountain places of worship. He has sexual relations with his neighbor's wife. [12]He mistreats the poor and needy. He steals and refuses to return what was promised for a loan. He looks to idols for help. He does things which I hate. [13]He lends money for too much interest and profit. Will this son live? No, he will not live! He has done all these hateful things, so he will surely be put to death. He will be responsible for his own death.

"He lives by my rules and obeys my laws faithfully. Whoever does these things is good and will surely live, says the Lord GOD." (Ezekiel 18:9)

FAMILY
Can children break the chain of sin and disobedience in a family? (18:14–19)

[14]"Now suppose this son has a son who has seen all his father's sins, but after seeing them does not do those things. [15]He does not eat at the mountain places of worship. He does not look to the idols of Israel for help. He does not have sexual relations with his neighbor's wife. [16]He does not mistreat anyone or keep something promised for a loan or steal. He gives bread to the hungry and clothes to those who have none. [17]He keeps his hand from doing wrong. He does not take too much interest or profit when he lends money. He obeys my laws and lives by my rules. He will not die for his father's sin; he will surely live. [18]But his father took other people's money unfairly and robbed his brother and did what was wrong among his people. So he will die for his own sin.

[19]"But you ask, 'Why is the son not punished for the father's sin?' The son has done what is fair and right. He obeys all my rules, so he will surely live. [20]The person who sins is the one who will die. A child will not be punished for a parent's sin, and a parent will not be punished for a child's sin. Those who do right will enjoy the results of their own goodness; evil people will suffer the results of their own evil.

[21]"But suppose the wicked stop doing all the sins they have done and obey all my rules and do what is fair and right. Then they will surely live; they will not die. [22]Their sins will be forgotten. Because they have done what is right, they will live. [23]I do not really want the wicked to die, says the Lord GOD. I want them to stop their bad ways and live.

[24]"But suppose good people stop doing good and do wrong and do the same hateful things the wicked do. Will they live? All their good acts will be forgotten, because they became unfaithful. They have sinned, so they will die because of their sins.

[25]"But you say, 'What the Lord does isn't fair.' Listen, people of Israel. I am fair. It is what you do that is not fair! [26]When good people stop doing good and do wrong, they will die because of it. They will die, because they did wrong. [27]When the wicked stop being wicked and do what is fair and right, they will save their lives. [28]Because they thought about it and stopped doing all the sins they had done, they will surely live; they will not die. [29]But the people of Israel still say, 'What the Lord does isn't fair.' People of Israel, I am fair. It is what you do that is not fair.

[30]"So I will judge you, people of Israel; I will judge each of you by what you do, says the Lord GOD. Change your hearts and stop all your sinning so sin will not bring your ruin. [31]Get rid of all the sins you have done, and get for yourselves a new heart and a new way of thinking. Why do you want to die, people of Israel? [32]I do not want anyone to die, says the Lord GOD, so change your hearts and lives so you may live.

A SAD SONG FOR ISRAEL

19

[1]"Sing a funeral song for the leaders of Israel. [2]Say:

'Your mother was like a female lion.
She lay down among the young lions.
  She had many cubs.
[3]When she brought up one of her cubs,
  he became a strong lion.
He learned to tear the animals he hunted,
  and he ate people.
[4]The nations heard about him.

He was trapped in their pit,
and they brought him with hooks
to the land of Egypt.

5" 'The mother lion waited and saw
that there was no hope for her cub.
So she took another one of her cubs
and made him a strong lion.
6This cub roamed among the lions.
He was now a strong lion.
He learned to tear the animals he hunted,
and he ate people.
7He tore down their strong places
and destroyed their cities.
The land and everything in it
were terrified by the sound of his roar.
8Then the nations came against him
from areas all around,
and they spread their net over him.
He was trapped in their pit.
9Then they put him into a cage with chains
and brought him to the king of Babylon.
They put him into prison
so his roar could not be heard again
on the mountains of Israel.

WHAT'S IT MEAN?

If someone were to write a song in your memory after your death, how would you want to be described or portrayed? In this funeral song (or lamentation), the nation of Israel is portrayed as a female lion. Two kings of Israel, Jehoahaz and Jehoiachin, are portrayed as lion cubs. Jehoahaz reigned for only three months before he was taken as a prisoner to Egypt in 609 B.C. Jehoiachin's story is practically the same. He reigned for only three months before being captured and taken to Babylon in 597 B.C.

Ezekiel 19:1–9

10" 'Your mother was like a vine in your
vineyard,
planted beside the water.
The vine had many branches and gave
much fruit,
because there was plenty of water.
11The vine had strong branches,
good enough for a king's scepter.
The vine became tall
among the thick branches.
And it was seen, because it was tall
with many branches.
12But it was pulled up by its roots in anger
and thrown down to the ground.
The east wind dried it up.
Its fruit was torn off.
Its strong branches were broken off
and burned up.
13Now the vine is planted in the desert,
in a dry and thirsty land.
14Fire spread from the vine's main branch,
destroying its fruit.
There is not a strong branch left on it
that could become a scepter for a king.'

This is a funeral song; it is to be used as a funeral song."

WHAT'S IT MEAN?

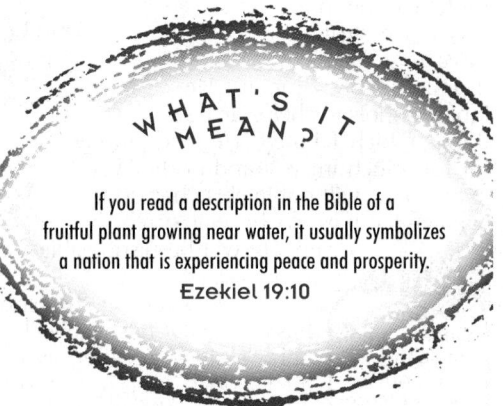

If you read a description in the Bible of a fruitful plant growing near water, it usually symbolizes a nation that is experiencing peace and prosperity.

Ezekiel 19:10

ISRAEL HAS REFUSED GOD

20 1It was the seventh year of our captivity, in
the fifth month, on the tenth day of the month.
Some of the older leaders of Israel came to ask
about the LORD and sat down in front of me.
2The LORD spoke his word to me, saying:
3"Human, speak to the older leaders of Israel
and say to them: 'This is what the Lord GOD
says: Did you come to ask me questions? As
surely as I live, I will not let you ask me questions.'
4"Will you judge them? Will you judge them,
human? Let them know the hateful things their
ancestors did. 5Say to them: 'This is what the
Lord GOD says: When I chose Israel, I made a
promise to the descendants of Jacob. I made
myself known to them in Egypt, and I promised them, "I am the LORD your God." 6At that
time I promised them I would bring them out
of Egypt into a land I had found for them, a
fertile land, the best land in the world. 7I said to
them, "Each one of you must throw away the
hateful idols you have seen and liked. Don't

make yourselves unclean with the idols of
Egypt. I am the LORD your God."
[8]" 'But they turned against me and refused to
listen to me. They did not throw away the hateful idols which they saw and liked; they did not
give up the idols of Egypt. Then I decided to
pour out my anger against them while they
were still in Egypt. [9]But I acted for the sake of
my name so it would not be dishonored in full
view of the nations where the Israelites lived. I
made myself known to the Israelites with a
promise to bring them out of Egypt while the
nations were watching. [10]So I took them out of
Egypt and brought them into the desert. [11]I gave
them my rules and told them about my laws,
by which people will live if they obey them. [12]I
also gave them my Sabbaths to be a sign between us so they would know that I am the
LORD who made them holy.
[13]" 'But in the desert Israel turned against
me. They did not follow my rules, and they
rejected my laws, by which people will live if
they obey them. They dishonored my Sabbaths. Then I decided to pour out my anger
against them and destroy them in the desert.
[14]But I acted for the sake of my name so it
would not be dishonored in full view of the
nations who watched as I had brought the Israelites out of Egypt. [15]And in the desert I
swore to the Israelites that I would not bring
them into the land I had given them. It is a
fertile land, the best land in the world. [16]This
was because they rejected my laws and did not
follow my rules. They dishonored my Sabbaths and wanted to worship their idols. [17]But
I had pity on them. I did not destroy them or
put an end to them in the desert. [18]I said to
their children in the desert, "Don't live by the
rules of your parents, or obey their laws. Don't
make yourselves unclean with their idols. [19]I
am the LORD your God. Live by my rules, obey
my laws, and follow them. [20]Keep my Sabbaths holy, and they will be a sign between me
and you. Then you will know that I am the
LORD your God."
[21]" 'But the children turned against me. They
did not live by my rules, nor were they careful
to obey my laws, by which people will live if
they obey them. They dishonored my Sabbaths. So I decided to pour out my anger
against them in the desert. [22]But I held back my
anger. I acted for the sake of my name so it
would not be dishonored in full view of the
nations who watched as I brought the Israelites out. [23]And in the desert I swore to the Israelites that I would scatter them among the
nations and spread them among the countries,
[24]because they had not obeyed my laws. They
had rejected my rules and dishonored my Sabbaths and worshiped the idols of their parents.
[25]I also allowed them to follow rules that were
not good and laws by which they could not
live. [26]I let the Israelites make themselves unclean by the gifts they brought to their gods
when they sacrificed their first children in the
fire. I wanted to terrify them so they would
know that I am the LORD.'
[27]"So, human, speak to the people of Israel.
Say to them, 'This is what the Lord GOD says:
Your ancestors spoke against me by being unfaithful to me in another way. [28]When I had
brought them into the land I promised to give
them, they saw every high hill and every leafy
tree. There they offered their sacrifices to gods.
They brought offerings that made me angry
and burned their incense and poured out their
drink offerings. [29]Then I said to them: What is
this high place where you go to worship?' " (It
is still called High Place today.)
[30]"So say to the people of Israel: 'This is
what the Lord GOD says: Are you going to
make yourselves unclean as your ancestors
did? Are you going to be unfaithful and desire
their hateful idols? [31]When you offer your children as gifts and sacrifice them in the fire, you
are making yourselves unclean with all your
idols even today. So, people of Israel, should I
let you ask me questions? As surely as I live,
says the Lord GOD, I will not accept questions
from you.
[32]" 'What you want will not come true. You
say, "We want to be like the other nations, like
the people in other lands. We want to worship
idols made of wood and stone." [33]As surely as I
live, says the Lord GOD, I will use my great
power and strength and anger to rule over
you. [34]I will bring you out from the foreign
nations. With my great power and strength
and anger I will gather you from the lands
where you are scattered. [35]I will bring you
among the nations as I brought your ancestors
into the desert with Moses. There I will judge
you face to face. [36]I will judge you the same
way I judged your ancestors in the desert of
the land of Egypt, says the Lord GOD. [37]I will
count you like sheep and will bring you into
line with my agreement. [38]I will get rid of those
who refuse to obey me and who turn against
me. I will bring them out of the land where
they are now living, but they will never enter
the land of Israel. Then you will know that I
am the LORD.
[39]" 'This is what the Lord GOD says: People
of Israel, go serve your idols for now. But later

you will listen to me; you will not continue to
dishonor my holy name with your gifts and
gods. 40On my holy mountain, the high mountain of Israel, all Israel will serve me in the land,
says the Lord GOD. There I will accept you.
There I will expect your offerings, the first harvest of your offerings, and all your holy gifts.
41I will accept you like the pleasing smell of
sacrifices when I bring you out from the foreign nations and gather you from the lands
where you are scattered. Then through you I
will show how holy I am so the nations will
see. 42When I bring you into the land of Israel,
the land I promised your ancestors, you will
know that I am the LORD. 43There you will remember everything you did that made you
unclean, and then you will hate yourselves for
all the evil things you have done. 44I will deal
with you for the sake of my name, not because
of your evil ways or unclean actions. Then you
will know I am the LORD, people of Israel, says
the Lord GOD.' "

BABYLON, THE LORD'S SWORD

45Now the LORD spoke his word to me, saying: 46"Human, look toward the south. Prophesy against the south and against the forest of
the southern area. 47Say to that forest: 'Hear the
word of the LORD. This is what
the Lord GOD says: I am ready
to start a fire in you that will
destroy all your green trees
and all your dry trees. The
flames that burn will not
be put out. Every face from
south to north will feel
their heat. 48Then all the
people will see that I, the
LORD, have started the fire. It
will not be put out.' "

49Then I said, "Ah, Lord GOD!
The people are saying about me, 'He is only
telling stories.' "

"Those who are important now will be made unimportant, and those who are unimportant now will be made important." (Ezekiel 21:26b)

21
1Then the LORD spoke his word to me, saying: 2"Human, look toward Jerusalem and
speak against the holy place. Prophesy against
the land of Israel. 3Say to Israel: 'This is what
the LORD says: I am against you. I will pull my
sword out of its holder, and I will cut off from
you both the wicked and those who do right.
4Because I am going to cut off the wicked and
those who do right, my sword will come out
from its holder and attack all people from
south to north. 5Then all people will know that
I, the LORD, have pulled my sword out from its
holder. My sword will not go back in again.'

6"So, human, groan with breaking heart and
great sadness. Groan in front of the people.
7When they ask you, 'Why are you groaning?'
you will say, 'Because of what I have heard is
going to happen. When it happens, every heart
will melt with fear, and all hands will become
weak. Everyone will be afraid; all knees will
become weak as water. Look, it is coming, and
it will happen, says the Lord GOD.' "

8The LORD spoke his word to me, saying:
9"Human, prophesy and say, 'This is what the
Lord says:

A sword, a sword,
made sharp and polished.
10It is made sharp for the killing.
It is polished to flash like lightning.

" 'You are not happy about this horrible
punishment by the sword. But my son Judah,
you did not change when you were only beat-
en with a rod.

11The sword should be polished.
It is meant to be held in the hand.
It is made sharp and polished,
ready for the hand of a killer.
12Shout and yell, human,
because the sword is meant for my people,
for all the rulers of Israel.
They will be killed by the sword,
along with my people.
So beat your chest in sadness.

13" 'The test will come.
And Judah, who is hated by
the armies of Babylon, will
not last, says the Lord GOD.'

14"So, human, prophesy
and clap your hands.
Let the sword strike
two or three times.
It is a sword meant for killing,
a sword meant for much killing.
This sword surrounds the people to be killed.
15Their hearts will melt with fear,
and many people will die.
I have placed the killing sword
at all their city gates.
Oh! The sword is made to flash like lightning.
It is held, ready for killing.
16Sword, cut on the right side;
then cut on the left side.
Cut anywhere your blade is turned.
17I will also clap my hands
and use up my anger.
I, the LORD, have spoken."

JERUSALEM TO BE DESTROYED

18 The LORD spoke his word to me, saying:
19 "Human, mark two roads that the king of
Babylon and his sword can follow. Both of
these roads will start from the same country.
And make signs where the road divides and
one way goes toward the city. 20 Mark one sign
to show the road he can take with his sword to
Rabbah in the land of the Ammonites. Mark
the other sign to show the road to Judah and
Jerusalem, which is protected with strong
walls. 21 The king of Babylon has come to
where the road divides, and he is using magic.
He throws lots with arrows and asks questions
of his family idols. He looks at the liver of a
sacrificed animal to learn where he should go.
22 The lot in his right hand tells him to go to
Jerusalem. It tells him to use logs to break
down the city gates, to shout the battle cry and
give the order to kill, and to build a dirt road to
the top of the walls and devices to attack the
walls. 23 The people of Jerusalem have made
agreements with other nations to help them
fight Babylon. So they will think this prediction
is wrong, but it is really proof of their sin, and
they will be captured.

WHAT'S IT MEAN?

If the Magic Eight Ball had been around in ancient times, the Babylonians probably would have used it to try to predict their future. After all, they used practically every other method you can imagine (and some you couldn't imagine in a million years) to find out what lay ahead for them. For example, when they were trying to decide which city to attack, Babylonian officials would drop arrows with names written on them. The officials would then plan their military strategy based on the way the arrows landed. Some Babylonians tried to consult the dead using idols. Others cut open sheep livers—yes, sheep livers—and predicted the future based on the shape and condition of the animals' internal organs.

Ezekiel 21:21

24 "So this is what the Lord GOD says: 'You
have shown how sinful you are by turning
against the LORD. Your sins are seen in all the
things you do. Because of this proof against
you, you will be taken captive by the enemy.
25 " 'You unclean and evil leader of Israel,
you will be killed! The time of your final punishment has come. 26 This is what the Lord GOD
says: Take off the royal turban, and remove the
crown. Things will change. Those who are important now will be made unimportant, and
those who are unimportant now will be made
important. 27 A ruin! A ruin! I will make it a
ruin! This place will not be rebuilt until the one
comes who has a right to be king. Then I will
give him that right.'

THE PUNISHMENT OF AMMON

28 "And you, human, prophesy and say: 'This
is what the Lord GOD says about the people of
Ammon and their insults:

A sword, a sword
  is pulled out of its holder.
It is polished to kill and destroy,
  to flash like lightning!
29 Prophets see false visions about you
  and prophesy lies about you.
The sword will be put on the necks
  of these unclean and evil people.
Their day of judging has come;
  the time of final punishment has come.
30 Put the sword back in its holder.
  I will judge you
in the place where you were created,
  in the land where you were born.
31 I will pour out my anger against you
  and blast you with the fire of my anger.
I will hand you over to cruel men,
  experts in destruction.
32 You will be like fuel for the fire;
  you will die in the land.
You will not be remembered,
  because I, the LORD, have spoken.' "

THE SINS OF JERUSALEM

22
1 The LORD spoke his word to me, saying:
2 "And you, human, will you judge? Will you
judge the city of murderers? Then tell her
about all her hateful acts. 3 You are to say: 'This
is what the Lord GOD says: You are a city that
kills those who come to live there. You make
yourself unclean by making idols. 4 You have
become guilty of murder and have become
unclean by your idols which you have made.
So you have brought your time of punishment
near; you have come to the end of your years.
That is why I have made you a shame to the
nations and why all lands laugh at you. 5 Those
near and those far away laugh at you with
your bad name, you city full of confusion.
6 " 'Jerusalem, see how each ruler of Israel in
you has been trying to kill people. 7 The people
in you hate their fathers and mothers. They

mistreat the foreigners in you and wrong the orphans and widows in you. [8]You hate my holy things and dishonor my Sabbaths. [9]The men in you tell lies to cause the death of others. The people in you eat food offered to idols at the mountain places of worship, and they take part in sexual sins. [10]The men in you have sexual relations with their fathers' wives and with women who are unclean, during their time of monthly bleeding. [11]One man in you does a hateful act with his neighbor's wife, while another has shamefully made his daughter-in-law unclean sexually. And another forces his half sister to have sexual relations with him. [12]The people in you take money to kill others. You take unfair interest and profits and make profits by mistreating your neighbor. And you have forgotten me, says the Lord GOD.

SEX

Does God care about sexual purity? (22:10–16)

[13]" 'So, Jerusalem, I will shake my fist at you for stealing money and for murdering people. [14]Will you still be brave and strong when I punish you? I, the LORD, have spoken, and I will act. [15]I will scatter you among the nations and spread you through the countries. That is how I will get rid of your uncleanness. [16]But you, yourself, will be dishonored in the sight of the nations. Then you will know that I am the LORD.' "

ISRAEL IS WORTHLESS

[17]The LORD spoke his word to me, saying: [18]"Human, the people of Israel have become useless like scum to me. They are like the copper, tin, iron, and lead left in the furnace when silver is purified. [19]So this is what the Lord GOD says: 'Because you have become useless like scum, I am going to put you together inside Jerusalem. [20]People put silver, copper, iron, lead, and tin together inside a furnace to melt them down in a blazing fire. In the same way I will gather you in my hot anger and put you together in Jerusalem and melt you down. [21]I will put you together and make you feel the heat of my anger. You will be melted down inside Jerusalem. [22]As silver is melted in a furnace, you will be melted inside the city. Then you will know that I, the LORD, have poured out my anger on you.' "

SINS OF THE PEOPLE

[23]The LORD spoke his word to me, saying: [24]"Human, say to the land, 'You are a land that has not had rain or showers when God is angry.' [25]Like a roaring lion that tears the animal it has caught, Israel's rulers make evil plans. They have destroyed lives and have taken treasure and valuable things. They have caused many women to become widows. [26]Israel's priests do cruel things to my teachings and do not honor my holy things. They make no difference between holy and unholy things, and they teach there is no difference between clean and unclean things. They do not remember my Sabbaths, so I am dishonored by them. [27]Like wolves tearing a dead animal, Jerusalem's leaders have killed people for profit. [28]And the prophets try to cover this up by false visions and by lying messages. They say, 'This is what the Lord GOD says' when the LORD has not spoken. [29]The people cheat others and steal. They hurt people who are poor and needy. They cheat foreigners and do not treat them fairly.

[30]"I looked for someone to build up the walls and to stand before me where the walls are broken to defend these people so I would not have to destroy them. But I could not find anyone. [31]So I let them see my anger. I destroyed them with an anger that was like fire because of all the things they have done, says the Lord GOD."

WHAT'S IT MEAN?

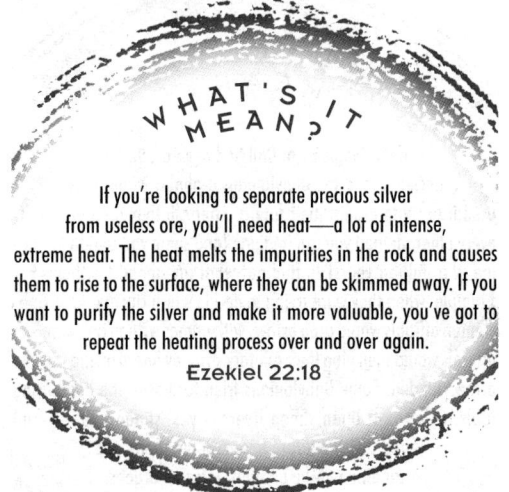

If you're looking to separate precious silver from useless ore, you'll need heat—a lot of intense, extreme heat. The heat melts the impurities in the rock and causes them to rise to the surface, where they can be skimmed away. If you want to purify the silver and make it more valuable, you've got to repeat the heating process over and over again.

Ezekiel 22:18

SAMARIA AND JERUSALEM

23 [1]The LORD spoke his word to me, saying: [2]"Human, a woman had two daughters. [3]While they were young, they went to Egypt and became prostitutes. They let men touch and hold their breasts. [4]The older girl was named Oholah, and her sister was named Oholibah. They became my wives and had

sons and daughters. Oholah is Samaria, and Oholibah is Jerusalem.[n]

[5]"While still my wife, Samaria had sexual relations with other men. She had great sexual desire for her lovers, men from Assyria. The Assyrians were warriors and [6]wore blue uniforms. They were all handsome young captains and lieutenants riding on horseback. [7]Samaria became a prostitute for all the important men in Assyria and made herself unclean with all the idols of everyone she desired. [8]She continued the prostitution she began in Egypt. When she was young, she had slept with men, and they touched her breasts and had sexual relations with her.

[9]"So I handed her over to her lovers, the Assyrians, that she wanted so badly. [10]They stripped her naked and took away her sons and daughters. Then they killed her with a sword. Women everywhere began talking about how she had been punished.

[11]"Her sister Jerusalem saw what happened, but she became worse than her sister in her sexual desire and prostitution. [12]She also desired the Assyrians, who were all soldiers in beautiful uniforms—handsome young captains and lieutenants riding horses. [13]I saw that both girls were alike; both were prostitutes.

[14]"But Jerusalem went even further. She saw carvings of Babylonian men on a wall. They wore red [15]and had belts around their waists and turbans on their heads. They all looked like chariot officers born in Babylonia. [16]When she saw them, she wanted to have sexual relations with them and sent messengers to them in Babylonia. [17]So these Babylonian men came and had sexual relations with her and made her unclean. After that, she became sick of them. [18]But she continued her prostitution so openly that everyone knew about it. And I finally became sick of her, as I had her sister. [19]But she remembered how she was a young prostitute in Egypt, so she took part in even more prostitution. [20]She wanted men who behaved like animals in their sexual desire. [21]In the same way you desired to do the sinful things you had done in Egypt. There men touched and held your young breasts.

GOD'S JUDGMENT ON JERUSALEM

[22]"So, Jerusalem, this is what the Lord GOD says: You are tired of your lovers. So now I will make them angry with you and have them attack you from all sides. [23]Men from Babylon and all Babylonia and men from Pekod, Shoa, and Koa will attack you. All the Assyrians will attack you: handsome young captains and lieutenants, all of them important men and all riding horses. [24]Those men will attack with great armies and with their weapons, chariots, and wagons. They will surround you with large and small shields and with helmets. And I will give them the right to punish you, and they will give you their own kind of punishment. [25]Then you will see how strong my anger can be when they punish you in their anger. They will cut off your noses and ears. They will take away your sons and daughters, and those who are left will be burned. [26]They will take off your clothes and steal your jewelry. [27]I will put a stop to the sinful life you began when you were in Egypt so that you will not desire it or remember Egypt anymore.

[28]"This is what the Lord GOD says: You became tired of your lovers, but I am going to hand you over to those men you now hate. [29]They will treat you with hate and take away everything you worked for, leaving you empty and naked. Everyone will know about the sinful things you did. Your sexual sins [30]have brought this on you. You have had sexual relations with the nations and made yourselves unclean by worshiping their idols. [31]You did the same things your sister did, so you will get the same punishment, like a bitter cup to drink.

[32]"This is what the Lord GOD says:
You will drink the same cup your sister did,
and that cup is deep and wide.
Everyone will make fun of you,
because the cup is full.
[33]It will make you miserable and drunk.
It is the cup of fear and ruin.
It is the cup of your sister Samaria.
[34]You will drink everything in it,
and then you will smash it
and tear at your breasts.
I have spoken, says the Lord GOD.

[35]"So this is what the Lord GOD says: You have forgotten me and turned your back on me. So you will be punished for your sexual sins."

JUDGMENT ON SAMARIA AND JERUSALEM

[36]The LORD said to me: "Human, will you judge Samaria and Jerusalem, showing them their hateful acts? [37]They are guilty of adultery and murder. They have taken part in adultery

23:4 Oholah . . . Jerusalem Throughout this chapter Samaria is used in place of Oholah, and Jerusalem is used in place of Oholibah.

with their idols. They even offered our children
as sacrifices in the fire to be food for these
idols. 38They have also done this to me: They
made my Temple unclean at the same time
they dishonored my Sabbaths. 39They sacrificed their children to their idols. Then they
entered my Temple at that very time to dishon-
or it. That is what they did inside my Temple!

40"They even sent for men from far away,
who came after a messenger was sent to them.
The two sisters bathed themselves for them,
painted their eyes, and put on jewelry. 41They
sat on a fine bed with a table set before it, on
which they put my incense and my oil.

42"There was the noise of a reckless crowd
in the city. Common people gathered, and
drunkards were brought from the desert. They
put bracelets on the wrists of the two sisters
and beautiful crowns on their heads. 43Then I
said about the one who was worn out by her
acts of adultery, 'Let them continue their sexual
sins with her. She is nothing but a prostitute.'
44They kept going to her as they would go to a
prostitute. So they continued to go to Samaria
and Jerusalem, these shameful women. 45But
men who do right will punish them as they
punish women who take part in adultery and
who murder people, because they are guilty of
adultery and murder.

46"This is what the Lord GOD says: Bring together a mob against Samaria and Jerusalem,
and hand them over to be frightened and
robbed. 47Let the mob kill them by throwing
stones at them, and let them cut them down
with their swords. Let them kill their sons and
daughters and burn their houses down.

48"So I will put an end to sexual sins in the
land. Then all women will be warned, and they
will not do the sexual sins you have done.
49You will be punished for your sexual sins
and the sin of worshiping idols. Then you will
know that I am the Lord GOD."

THE POT AND THE MEAT

24 1The LORD spoke his word to me in the
ninth year of our captivity, in the tenth month,
on the tenth day of the month. He said: 2"Human, write down today's date, this very date.
The king of Babylon has surrounded Jerusalem
this very day. 3And tell a story to the people
who refuse to obey me. Say to them: 'This is
what the Lord GOD says:

Put on the pot; put it on
and pour water in it.
4 Put in the pieces of meat,
the best pieces—the legs and the shoulders.
Fill it with the best bones.
5 Take the best of the flock,
and pile wood under the pot.
Boil the pieces of meat
until even the bones are cooked.

6" 'This is what the Lord GOD says:
How terrible it will be for the city of murderers!
How terrible it will be for the rusty pot
whose rust will not come off!
Take the meat out of it, piece by piece.
Don't choose any special piece.

7" 'The blood from her killings is still in the city.
She poured the blood on the bare rock.
She did not pour it on the ground
where dust would cover it.
8 To stir up my anger and revenge,
I put the blood she spilled on the bare rock
so it will not be covered.
9" 'So this is what the Lord GOD says:
How terrible it will be for the city of murderers!
I myself will pile the wood high for burning.
10 Pile up the wood
and light the fire.
Finish cooking the meat.
Mix in the spices,
and let the bones burn.
11 Then set the empty pot on the coals
so it may become hot and its copper sides glow.
The dirty scum stuck inside it may then melt
and its rust burn away.
12 But efforts to clean the pot have failed.
Its heavy rust cannot be removed,
even in the fire.

13" 'By your sinful action you have become
unclean. I wanted to cleanse you, but you are
still unclean. You will never be cleansed from
your sin until my anger against you is carried
out.

14" 'I, the LORD, have spoken. The time has
come for me to act. I will not hold back punishment or feel pity or change my mind. I will
judge you by your ways and actions, says the
Lord GOD.' "

THE DEATH OF EZEKIEL'S WIFE

15Then the LORD spoke his word to me, saying: 16"Human, I am going to take your wife
from you, the woman you look at with love.
She will die suddenly, but you must not be sad

or cry loudly for her or shed any tears. 17Groan
silently; do not cry loudly for the dead. Tie on
your turban, and put your sandals on your feet.
Do not cover your face, and do not eat the food
people eat when they are sad about a death."
18So I spoke to the people in the morning,
and my wife died in the evening. The next
morning I did as I had been commanded.
19Then the people asked me, "Tell us, what
do the things you are doing mean for us?"
20Then I said to them, "The LORD spoke his
word to me. He said,
21'Say to the people of Israel, This is what the
Lord GOD says: I am
going to dishonor
my Temple. You
think it gives you
strength. You are
proud of it, and
you look at it with
love and tender-
ness. But your sons
and daughters that
you left behind in Je-
rusalem will fall dead
by the sword. 22When that
happens, you are to act as I
have: you are not to cover your face, and you
are not to eat the food people eat when they are
sad about a death. 23Your turbans must stay on
your heads, and your sandals on your feet. You
must not cry loudly, but you must rot away in
your sins and groan to each other. 24So Ezekiel
is to be an example for you. You must do all the
same things he did. When all this happens, you
will know that I am the Lord GOD.'
25"And as for you, human, this is how it will
be. I will take away the Temple that gives them
strength and joy, that makes them proud. They
look at it with love, and it makes them happy.
And I will take away their sons and daughters
also. 26At that time a person who escapes will
come to you with information for you to hear.
27At that very time your mouth will be opened.
You will speak and be silent no more. So you
will be a sign for them, and they will know that
I am the LORD."

PROPHECY AGAINST AMMON

25
1The LORD spoke his word to me, saying:
2"Human, look toward the people of Ammon
and prophesy against them. 3Say to them,
'Hear the word of the Lord GOD. This is what
the Lord GOD says: You were glad when my
Temple was dishonored, when the land of Israel was ruined, and when the people of Judah
were taken away as captives. 4So I am going to
give you to the people of the East to be theirs.
They will set up their camps among you and
make their homes among you. They will eat
your fruit and drink your milk. 5I will make the
city of Rabbah a pasture for camels and the
land of Ammon a resting place for sheep. Then
you will know that I am the LORD. 6This is
what the Lord GOD says: You have clapped
your hands and stamped your feet; you have
laughed about all the insults you made against
the land of Israel. 7So I will
use my power against
you. I will give you to
the nations as if you
were treasures taken
in war. I will wipe
you out of the lands
so you will no longer
be a nation, and I will
destroy you. Then
you will know that I
am the LORD.'

> "This is what the Lord GOD says: You have clapped your hands and stamped your feet; you have laughed about all the insults you made against the land of Israel. So I will use my power against you. I will give you to the nations as if you were treasures taken in war."
> (Ezekiel 25:6–7a)

PROPHECY AGAINST MOAB AND EDOM

8"This is what the
Lord GOD says: 'Moab and
Edom say, "The people of Ju-
dah are like all the other nations." 9So I am going to take away the cities that protect Moab's
borders, the best cities in that land: Beth Jeshimoth, Baal Meon, and Kiriathaim. 10Then I will
give Moab, along with the Ammonites, to the
people of the East as their possession. Then,
along with the Ammonites, Moab will not be a
nation anymore. 11So I will punish the people
of Moab, and they will know that I am the
LORD.'

PROPHECY AGAINST EDOM

12"This is what the Lord GOD says: 'Edom
took revenge on the people of Judah, and the
Edomites became guilty because of it. 13So this
is what the Lord GOD says: I will use my
power against Edom, killing every human and
animal in it. And I will destroy Edom all the
way from Teman to Dedan as they die in battle.
14I will use my people Israel to take revenge on
Edom. So the Israelites will do to Edom what
my hot anger demands. Then the Edomites will
know what my revenge feels like, says the Lord
GOD.'

PROPHECY AGAINST PHILISTIA

15"This is what the Lord GOD says: 'The Philistines have taken revenge with hateful hearts.

Because of their strong hatred, they have tried
to destroy Judah. [16]So this is what the Lord
GOD says: I will use my power against the Philistines. I will kill the Kerethites, and I will destroy those people still alive on the coast of the
Mediterranean Sea. [17]I will punish them in my
anger and do great acts of revenge to them.
They will know that I am the LORD when I take
revenge on them.' "

PROPHECY AGAINST TYRE

26 [1]It was the eleventh year of our captivity, on
the first day of the month. The LORD spoke his
word to me, saying: [2]"Human, the city of Tyre
has spoken against Jerusalem: 'The city that
traded with the nations is destroyed. Now we
can be the trading center. Since the city of Jerusalem is ruined, we can make money.' [3]So this
is what the Lord GOD says: I am against you,
Tyre. I will bring many nations against you,
like the sea beating its waves on your island
shores. [4]They will destroy the walls of Tyre and
pull down her towers. I will also scrape away
her ruins and make her a bare rock. [5]Tyre will
be an island where fishermen dry their nets. I
have spoken, says the Lord GOD. The nations
will steal treasures from Tyre. [6]Also, her villages on the shore across from the island will
be destroyed by war. Then they will know that
I am the LORD.

WHAT'S IT MEAN?

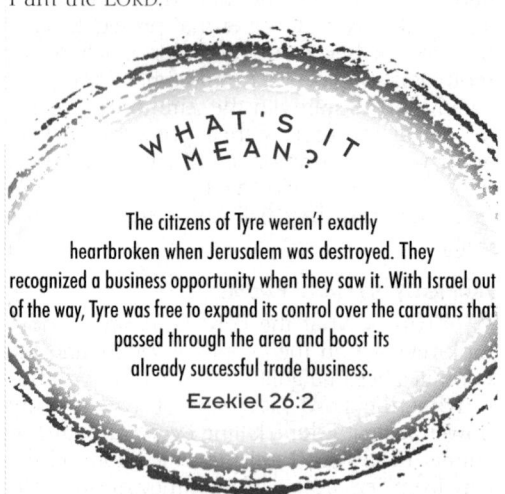

The citizens of Tyre weren't exactly heartbroken when Jerusalem was destroyed. They recognized a business opportunity when they saw it. With Israel out of the way, Tyre was free to expand its control over the caravans that passed through the area and boost its already successful trade business.

Ezekiel 26:2

NEBUCHADNEZZAR TO ATTACK TYRE

[7]"This is what the Lord GOD says: I will
bring a king from the north against Tyre. He is
Nebuchadnezzar king of Babylon, the greatest
king, with his horses, chariots, horsemen, and
a great army. [8]He will fight a battle and destroy
your villages on the shore across from the island. He will set up devices to attack you. He
will build a road of earth to the top of the
walls. He will raise his shields against you. [9]He
will bring logs to pound through your city
walls, and he will break down your towers
with his iron bars. [10]His horses will be so
many that they will cover you with their dust.
Your walls will shake at the noise of horsemen,
wagons, and chariots. The king of Babylon will
enter your city gates as men enter a city where
the walls are broken through. [11]The hoofs of
his horses will run over your streets. He will kill
your army with the sword, and your strong pillars will fall down to the ground. [12]Also, his
men will take away your riches and will steal
the things you sell. They will break down your
walls and destroy your nice houses. They will
throw your stones, wood, and trash into the
sea. [13]So I will stop your songs; the music of
your harps will not be heard anymore. [14]I will
make you a bare rock, and you will be a place
for drying fishing nets. You will not be built
again, because I, the LORD, have spoken, says
the Lord GOD.

[15]"This is what the Lord GOD says to Tyre:
The people who live along the seacoast will
shake with fear when they hear about your
defeat. Those of you who are injured and dying will groan. [16]Then all the leaders of the seacoast will get down from their thrones, take off
their beautiful needlework clothes, and show
how afraid they are. They will sit on the
ground and tremble all the time. When they
see you, they will be shocked. [17]They will begin
singing a funeral song about you and will say
to you:

'Tyre, you famous city, you have been
destroyed!
You have lost your sea power!
You and your people
had great power on the seas.
You made everyone around you
afraid of you.
[18]Now the people who live by the coast
tremble,
now that you have fallen.
The islands of the sea
are afraid because you have been
defeated.'

[19]"This is what the Lord GOD says: I will
make you an empty city, like cities that have no
people living in them. I will bring the deep
ocean waters over you, and the Mediterranean
Sea will cover you. [20]At that time I will send
you down to the place of the dead to join those
who died long ago. I will make you live with
the dead below the earth in places that are like
old ruins. You will not come back from there

or have any place in the world of the living
again. 21 Other people will be afraid of what
happened to you, and it will be the end of you.
People will look for you, but they will never
find you again, says the Lord GOD."

A FUNERAL SONG FOR TYRE

27 1 The LORD spoke his word to me, saying:
2 "Human, sing a funeral song for the city of
Tyre. 3 Speak to Tyre, which has ports for the
Mediterranean Sea and is a place for trade for
the people of many lands along the seacoast.
'This is what the Lord GOD says:

Tyre, you have said,
"I am like a beautiful ship."
4 You were at home on the high seas.
Your builders made your beauty perfect.
5 They made all your boards
of fir trees from Mount Hermon.
They took a cedar tree from Lebanon
to make a ship's mast for you.
6 They made your oars
from oak trees from Bashan.
They made your deck
from cypress trees from the coast of Cyprus
and set ivory into it.
7 Your sail of linen with designs sewed on it came from Egypt
and became like a flag for you.
Your cloth shades over the deck were blue and purple
and came from the island of Cyprus.
8 Men from Sidon and Arvad used oars to row you.
Tyre, your skilled men were the sailors on your deck.
9 Workers of Byblos were with you,
putting caulk[n] in your ship's seams.
All the ships of the sea and their sailors
came alongside to trade with you.

10 " 'Men of Persia, Lydia, and Put
were warriors in your navy
and hung their shields and helmets on your sides.
They made you look beautiful.
11 Men of Arvad and Cilicia
guarded your city walls all around.
Men of Gammad
were in your watchtowers
and hung their shields around your walls.
They made your beauty perfect.

12 " 'People of Tarshish became traders for
you because of your great wealth. They traded
your goods for silver, iron, tin, and lead.

13 " 'People of Greece, Tubal, and Meshech
became merchants for you. They traded your
goods for slaves and items of bronze.

14 " 'People of Beth Togarmah traded your
goods for work horses, war horses, and mules.

15 " 'People of Rhodes became merchants for
you, selling your goods on many coastlands.
They brought back ivory tusks and valuable
black wood as your payment.

16 " 'People of Aram became traders for you,
because you had so many good things to sell.
They traded your goods for turquoise, purple
cloth, cloth with designs sewed on, fine linen,
coral, and rubies.

17 " 'People of Judah and Israel became merchants for you. They traded your goods for
wheat from Minnith, and for honey, olive oil,
and balm.

18-19 " 'People of Damascus became traders
for you because you have many good things
and great wealth. They traded your goods for
wine from Helbon, wool from Zahar, and barrels of wine from Izal. They received wrought
iron, cassia, and sugar cane in payment for
your good things.

20 " 'People of Dedan became merchants for
you, trading saddle blankets for riding.

21 " 'People of Arabia and all the rulers of
Kedar became traders for you. They received
lambs, male sheep, and goats in payment for
you.

22 " 'The merchants of Sheba and Raamah
became merchants for you. They traded your
goods for all the best spices, valuable gems,
and gold.

23 " 'People of Haran, Canneh, Eden, and the
traders of Sheba, Asshur, and Kilmad became
merchants for you. 24 They were paid with the
best clothes, blue cloth, cloth with designs
sewed on, carpets of many colors, and tightly
wound ropes.

25 " 'Trading ships
carried the things you sold.
You were like a ship full of heavy cargo
in the middle of the sea.
26 The men who rowed you
brought you out into the high seas,
but the east wind broke you to pieces
in the middle of the sea.
27 Your wealth, your trade, your goods,
your seamen, your sailors, your workers,
your traders, your warriors,

27:9 caulk Something like tar put between the boards of a ship to make it waterproof.

and everyone else on board
sank into the sea
on the day your ship was wrecked.
28 The people on the shore shake with fear
when your sailors cry out.
29 All the men who row
leave their ships;
the seamen and the sailors of other ships
stand on the shore.
30 They cry loudly about you;
they cry very much.
They throw dust on their heads
and roll in ashes to show they are sad.
31 They shave their heads for you,
and they put on rough cloth to show
they are upset.
They cry and sob for you;
they cry loudly.
32 And in their loud crying
they sing a funeral song for you:
"No one was ever destroyed like Tyre,
surrounded by the sea."
33 When the goods you traded went out over
the seas,
you met the needs of many nations.
With your great wealth and goods,
you made kings of the earth rich.
34 But now you are broken by the sea
and have sunk to the bottom.
Your goods and all the people on board
have gone down with you.
35 All those who live along the shore
are shocked by what happened to you.
Their kings are terribly afraid,
and their faces show their fear.
36 The traders among the nations hiss at you.
You have come to a terrible end,
and you are gone forever.' "

PROPHECY AGAINST THE KING OF TYRE

28 1 The LORD spoke his word to
me, saying: 2 "Human, say to the
ruler of Tyre: 'This is what the
Lord GOD says:
Because you are proud,
you say, "I am a god.
I sit on the throne of a god
in the middle of the seas."
You think you are as wise as a god,
but you are a human, not a god.
3 You think you are wiser than Daniel.
You think you can find out all secrets.
4 Through your wisdom and understanding
you have made yourself rich.
You have gained gold and silver
and have saved it in your storerooms.
5 Through your great skill in trading,
you have made your riches grow.
You are too proud
because of your riches.
6 " 'So this is what the Lord GOD says:
You think you are wise
like a god,
7 but I will bring foreign people against
you,
the cruelest nation.
They will pull out their swords
and destroy all that your wisdom has
built,
and they will dishonor your greatness.
8 They will kill you;
you will die a terrible death
like those who are killed at sea.
9 While they are killing you,
you will not be able to say anymore, "I
am a god."
You will be only a human, not a god,
when your murderers kill you.
10 You will die like an unclean person;
foreigners will kill you.
I have spoken, says the Lord GOD.' "
11 The LORD spoke his word to me, saying:
12 "Human, sing a funeral song for the king of
Tyre. Say to him: 'This is what the Lord GOD
says:
You were an example of what was perfect,
full of wisdom and perfect in beauty.
13 You had a wonderful life,
as if you were in Eden, the garden of
God.
Every valuable gem was on you:
ruby, topaz, and emerald,
yellow quartz, onyx, and jasper,

TALENTS

Can our gifts lead to pride? (28:1–5)

WHAT'S IT MEAN?

Daniel, a captive Jew in Babylon, had been blessed with some talents that made him an extremely useful young man. You probably know that people took dreams very seriously in ancient times. Daniel had the ability to explain dreams (often without even hearing them described first) and, in some cases, to predict the future based on those dreams. Because of his ability, he landed a job as an advisor to the king of Babylon.

Ezekiel 28:3

sapphire, turquoise, and chrysolite.
Your jewelry was made of gold.
It was prepared on the day you were created.
14 I appointed a living creature to guard you.
I put you on the holy mountain of God.
You walked among the gems that shined like fire.
15 Your life was right and good
from the day you were created,
until evil was found in you.
16 Because you traded with countries far away,
you learned to be cruel, and you sinned.
So I threw you down in disgrace from the mountain of God.
And the living creature who guarded you
forced you out from among the gems that shined like fire.
17 You became too proud
because of your beauty.
You ruined your wisdom
because of your greatness.
I threw you down to the ground.
Your example taught a lesson to other kings.
18 You dishonored your places of worship
through your many sins and dishonest trade.
So I set on fire the place where you lived,
and the fire burned you up.
I turned you into ashes on the ground
for all those watching to see.
19 All the nations who knew you
are shocked about you.
Your punishment was so terrible,
and you are gone forever.' "

PROPHECY AGAINST SIDON

20 The LORD spoke his word to me, saying:
21 "Human, look toward the city of Sidon and
prophesy against her. 22 Say: 'This is what the
Lord GOD says:
I am against you, Sidon,
and I will show my glory among you.
People will know that I am the LORD
when I have punished Sidon;
I will show my holiness by defeating her.
23 I will send diseases to Sidon,
and blood will flow in her streets.
Those who are wounded in Sidon will fall dead,
attacked from all sides.
Then they will know that I am the LORD.

GOD WILL HELP ISRAEL

24 " 'No more will neighboring nations be
like thorny branches or sharp stickers to hurt
Israel. Then they will know that I am the Lord
GOD.
25 " 'This is what the Lord GOD says: I will
gather the people of Israel from the nations
where they are scattered. I will show my holiness when the nations see what I do for my
people. Then they will live in their own land—
the land I gave to my servant Jacob. 26 They will
live safely in the land and will build houses
and plant vineyards. They will live in safety
after I have punished all the nations around
who hate them. Then they will know that I am
the LORD their God.' "

PROPHECY AGAINST EGYPT

29

1 It was the tenth year of our captivity, in the
tenth month, on the twelfth day of the month.
The LORD spoke his word to me, saying: 2 "Human, look toward the king of Egypt, and
prophesy against him and all Egypt. 3 Say: 'This
is what the Lord GOD says:
I am against you, king of Egypt.
You are like a great crocodile that lies in the Nile River.
You say, "The Nile is mine;
I made it for myself."
4 But I will put hooks in your jaws,
and I will make the fish of the Nile stick to your sides.
I will pull you up out of your rivers,
with all the fish sticking to your sides.
5 I will leave you in the desert,
you and all the fish from your rivers.
You will fall onto the ground;
you will not be picked up or buried.
I have given you to the wild animals
and to the birds of the sky for food.
6 Then all the people who live in Egypt will
know that I am the LORD.
" 'Israel tried to lean on you for help, but
you were like a crutch made out of a weak
stalk of grass. 7 When their hands grabbed you,
you splintered and tore open their shoulders.
When they leaned on you, you broke and
made all their backs twist.
8 " 'So this is what the Lord GOD says: I will
cause an enemy to attack you and kill your
people and animals. 9 Egypt will become an
empty desert. Then they will know that I am
the LORD.
" 'Because you said, "The Nile River is mine,
and I have made it," 10 I am against you and
your rivers. I will destroy the land of Egypt
and make it an empty desert from Migdol in

the north to Aswan in the south, all the way to
the border of Cush. 11No person or animal will
walk through it, and no one will live in Egypt
for forty years. 12I will make the land of Egypt
the most deserted country of all. Her cities will
be the most deserted of all ruined cities for
forty years. I will scatter the Egyptians among
the nations, spreading them among the countries.
13" 'This is what the Lord GOD says: After
forty years I will gather Egypt from the nations
where they have been scattered. 14I will bring
back the Egyptian captives and make them return to southern Egypt, to the land they came
from. They will become a weak kingdom there.
15It will be the weakest kingdom, and it will
never again rule other nations. I will make it so
weak it will never again rule over the nations.
16The Israelites will never again depend on
Egypt. Instead, Egypt's punishment will remind
the Israelites of their sin in turning to Egypt for
help. Then they will know that I am the Lord
GOD.' "

EGYPT IS GIVEN TO BABYLON

17It was the twenty-seventh year of our
captivity, in the first month, on the first day of
the month. The LORD spoke his word to me,
saying: 18"Human, Nebuchadnezzar king of
Babylon made his army fight hard against
Tyre. Every soldier's head was rubbed bare,
and every shoulder was rubbed raw. But Nebuchadnezzar and his army gained nothing
from fighting Tyre. 19So this is
what the Lord GOD says: I will
give the land of Egypt to Nebuchadnezzar king of Babylon.
He will take away Egypt's
people and its wealth and its
treasures as pay for his army.
20I am giving Nebuchadnezzar the land of Egypt as a reward for working hard for me,
says the Lord GOD.
21"At that time I will make Israel
grow strong again, and I will let you, Ezekiel,
speak to them. Then they will know that I am
the LORD."

> "Those who fight on Egypt's side will fall. The power she is proud of will be lost." (Ezekiel 30:6a)

EGYPT WILL BE PUNISHED

30 1The LORD spoke his word to me, saying:
2"Human, prophesy and say, 'This is what the
Lord GOD says:

Cry and say,
"The terrible day is coming."
3The day is near;
the LORD's day of judging is near.
It is a cloudy day
and a time when the nations will be judged.
4An enemy will attack Egypt,
and Cush will tremble with fear.
When the killing begins in Egypt,
her wealth will be taken away,
and her foundations will be torn down.

5Cush, Put, Lydia, Arabia, Libya, and some of
my people who had made an agreement with
Egypt will fall dead in war.
6" 'This is what the LORD says:

Those who fight on Egypt's side will fall.
The power she is proud of will be lost.
The people in Egypt will fall dead in war
from Migdol in the north to Aswan in the south,
says the Lord GOD.
7They will be the most deserted lands.
Egypt's cities will be the worst of cities
that lie in ruins.
8Then they will know that I am the LORD
when I set fire to Egypt
and when all those nations on her side
are crushed.

9" 'At that time I will send messengers in
ships to frighten Cush, which now feels safe.
The people of Cush will tremble with fear
when Egypt is punished. And that time is sure
to come.
10" 'This is what the Lord GOD says:

I will destroy great numbers of people in Egypt
through the power of Nebuchadnezzar king of Babylon.
11Nebuchadnezzar and his army,
the cruelest army of any nation,
will be brought in to destroy the land.
They will pull out their swords against Egypt
and will fill the land with those they kill.
12I will make the streams of the Nile River
become dry land,
and then I will sell the land to evil people.
I will destroy the land and everything in it
through the power of foreigners.
I, the LORD, have spoken.

EGYPT'S IDOLS ARE DESTROYED

13" 'This is what the Lord GOD says:

I will destroy the idols

and take away the statues of gods from
the city of Memphis.
There will no longer be a leader in Egypt,
and I will spread fear through the land
of Egypt.
14 I will make southern Egypt empty
and start a fire in Zoan
and punish Thebes.
15 And I will pour out my anger against
Pelusium,
the strong place of Egypt.
I will destroy great numbers of people
in Thebes.
16 I will set fire to Egypt.
Pelusium will be in great pain.
The walls of Thebes will be broken open,
and Memphis will have troubles every
day.
17 The young men of Heliopolis and Bubastis
will fall dead in war,
and the people will be taken away as
captives.
18 In Tahpanhes the day will be dark
when I break Egypt's power.
Then she will no longer be proud of her
power.
A cloud will cover Egypt,
and her villages will be captured and
taken away.
19 So I will punish Egypt,
and they will know I am the LORD.' "

EGYPT BECOMES WEAK

20 It was in the eleventh year of our captivity, in the first month, on the seventh day of the
month. The LORD spoke his word to me, saying: 21 "Human, I have broken the powerful
arm of the king of Egypt. It has not been tied
up, so it will not get well. It has not been
wrapped with a bandage, so it will not be
strong enough to hold a sword in war. 22 So
this is what the Lord GOD says: I am against
the king of Egypt. I will break his arms, both
the strong arm and the broken arm, and I will
make the sword fall from his hand. 23 I will
scatter the Egyptians among the nations,
spreading them among the countries. 24 I will
make the arms of the king of Babylon strong
and put my sword in his hand. But I will break
the arms of the king of Egypt. Then when he
faces the king of Babylon, he will cry out in
pain like a dying person. 25 So I will make the
arms of the king of Babylon strong, but the
arms of the king of Egypt will fall. Then people
will know that I am the LORD when I put my
sword into the hand of the king of Babylon
and he uses it in war against Egypt. 26 Then I
will scatter the Egyptians among the nations,
spreading them among the countries. Then
they will know that I am the LORD."

A CEDAR TREE

31

1 It was in the eleventh year of our captivity,
in the third month, on the first day of the
month. The LORD spoke his word to me, saying: 2 "Human, say to the king of Egypt and his
people:
'No one is like you in your greatness.
3 Assyria was once like a cedar tree in
Lebanon
with beautiful branches that shaded the
forest.
It was very tall;
its top was among the clouds.
4 Much water made the tree grow;
the deep springs made it tall.
Rivers flowed
around the bottom of the tree
and sent their streams
to all other trees in the countryside.
5 So the tree was taller
than all the other trees in the
countryside.
Its limbs became long and big
because of so much water.
6 All the birds of the sky
made their nests in the tree's limbs.
And all the wild animals
gave birth under its branches.
All great nations
lived in the tree's shade.
7 So the tree was great and beautiful,
with its long branches,
because its roots reached down to much
water.
8 The cedar trees in the garden of God
were not as great as it was.
The pine trees
did not have such great limbs.
The plane trees
did not have such branches.
No tree in the garden of God
was as beautiful as this tree.
9 I made it beautiful
with many branches,
and all the trees of Eden in the garden of
God
wanted to be like it.

10 " 'So this is what the Lord GOD says: The
tree grew tall. Its top reached the clouds, and it
became proud of its height. 11 So I handed it
over to a mighty ruler of the nations for him to
punish it. Because it was evil, I got rid of it.
12 The cruelest foreign nation cut it down and

left it. The tree's branches fell on the mountains and in all the valleys, and its broken limbs were in all the ravines of the land. All the nations of the earth left the shade of that tree. 13 The birds of the sky live on the fallen tree. The wild animals live among the tree's fallen branches. 14 So the trees that grow by the water will not be proud to be tall; they will not put their tops among the clouds. None of the trees that are watered well will grow that tall, because they all are meant to die and go under the ground. They will be with people who have died and have gone down to the place of the dead.

15 " 'This is what the Lord GOD says: On the day when the tree went down to the place of the dead, I made the deep springs cry loudly. I covered them and held back their rivers, and the great waters stopped flowing. I dressed Lebanon in black to show her sadness about the great tree, and all the trees in the countryside were sad about it. 16 I made the nations shake with fear at the sound of the tree falling when I brought it down to the place of the dead. It went to join those who have gone down to the grave. Then all the trees of Eden and the best trees of Lebanon, all the well-watered trees, were comforted in the place of the dead below the earth. 17 These trees had also gone down with the great tree to the place of the dead. They joined those who were killed in war and those among the nations who had lived under the great tree's shade.

18 " 'So no tree in Eden is equal to you, Egypt, in greatness and honor, but you will go down to join the trees of Eden in the place below the earth. You will lie among unclean people, with those who were killed in war.

" 'This is about the king of Egypt and all his people, says the Lord GOD.' "

A FUNERAL SONG

32

1 It was in the twelfth year of our captivity, in the twelfth month, on the first day of the month. The LORD spoke his word to me, saying: 2 "Human, sing a funeral song about the king of Egypt. Say to him:

'You are like a young lion among the nations.
You are like a crocodile in the seas.
You splash around in your streams
and stir up the water with your feet,
making the rivers muddy.

3 " 'This is what the Lord GOD says:
I will spread my net over you,
and I will use a large group of people
to pull you up in my net.
4 Then I will throw you on the land
dropping you onto the ground.
I will let the birds of the sky rest on you
and all the animals of the earth eat you
until they are full.
5 I will scatter your flesh on the mountains
and fill the valleys with what is left of you.
6 I will drench the land with your flowing blood
as far as the mountains,
and the ravines will be full of your flesh.
7 When I make you disappear,
I will cover the sky and make the stars dark.
I will cover the sun with a cloud,
and the moon will not shine.
8 I will make all the shining lights in the sky
become dark over you;
I will bring darkness over your land,
says the Lord GOD.
9 I will cause many people to be afraid
when I bring you as a captive into other nations,
to lands you have not known.
10 I will cause many people to be shocked about you.
Their kings will tremble with fear
because of you
when I swing my sword in front of them.
They will shake every moment
on the day you fall;
each king will be afraid for his own life.
11 " 'So this is what the Lord GOD says:
The sword of the king of Babylon
will attack you.

WHAT'S IT MEAN?

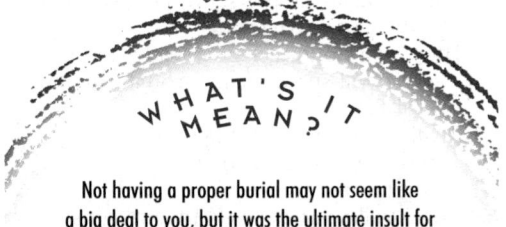

Not having a proper burial may not seem like a big deal to you, but it was the ultimate insult for people in the ancient Near East. Egyptian kings were especially concerned about their afterlife accommodations. Not only did they build elaborate tombs for themselves, they also stocked those tombs with their favorite treasures and anything else they thought they needed for the hereafter.

Ezekiel 32:4

12 I will cause your people to fall
by the swords of mighty soldiers,
the most terrible in the world.
They will destroy the pride of Egypt
and all its people.
13 I will also destroy all Egypt's cattle
which live alongside much water.
The foot of a human will not stir the
water,
and the hoofs of cattle will not muddy it
anymore.
14 So I will let the Egyptians' water become
clear.
I will cause their rivers to run as
smoothly as olive oil,
says the Lord GOD.
15 When I make the land of Egypt empty
and take everything that is in the land,
when I destroy all those who live in Egypt,
then they will know that I am the LORD.'
16 "This is the funeral song people will sing
for Egypt. The women of the nations will sing
it; they will sing a funeral song for Egypt and
all its people, says the Lord GOD."

EGYPT TO BE DESTROYED

17 It was in the twelfth year of our captivity,
on the fifteenth day of the month. The LORD
spoke his word to me, saying: 18 "Human, cry
for the people of Egypt. Bring down Egypt, together with the women of the powerful nations; bring them down to the place of the
dead below the earth to join those who go to
the place of the dead. 19 Say to them: 'Are you
more beautiful than others? Go lie down in
death with those who are unclean.' 20 The Egyptians will fall among those killed in war. The
sword is ready; the enemy will drag Egypt and
all her people away. 21 From the place of the
dead the leaders of the mighty ones will speak
about the king of Egypt and the nations which
help him: 'The unclean, those killed in war,
have come down here and lie dead.'
22 "Assyria and all its army lie dead there.
The graves of their soldiers are all around. All
were killed in war, 23 and their graves were put
in the deepest parts of the place of the dead.
Assyria's army lies around its grave. When
they lived on earth, they frightened people, but
now all of them have been killed in war.
24 "The nation of Elam is there with all its
army around its grave. All of them were killed
in war. They had frightened people on earth
and were unclean, so they went down to the
lowest parts of the place of the dead. They
must carry their shame with those who have
gone down to the place of the dead. 25 A bed
has been made for Elam with all those killed in
war. The graves of her soldiers are all around
her. All Elam's people are unclean, killed in war.
They frightened people when they lived on
earth, but now they must carry their shame
with those who have gone down to the place
of the dead. Their graves are with the rest who
were killed.

WHAT'S IT MEAN?

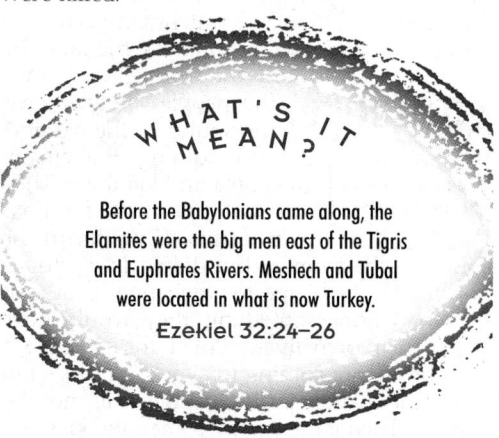

Before the Babylonians came along, the Elamites were the big men east of the Tigris and Euphrates Rivers. Meshech and Tubal were located in what is now Turkey.

Ezekiel 32:24–26

26 "Meshech and Tubal are there with the
graves of all their soldiers around them. All of
them are unclean and have been killed in war.
They also frightened people when they lived
on earth. 27 But they are not buried with the
other soldiers who were killed in battle long
ago, those who went with their weapons of
war to the place of the dead. These soldiers had
their swords laid under their heads and their
shields on their bodies. These mighty soldiers
used to frighten people when they lived on
earth.
28 "You, king of Egypt, will be broken and lie
among those who are unclean, who were
killed in war.
29 "Edom is there also, with its kings and all
its leaders. They were mighty, but now they lie
in death with those killed in war, with those
who are unclean, with those who have gone
down to the place of the dead.
30 "All the rulers of the north and all the Sidonians are there. Their strength frightened
people, but they have gone down in shame
with those who were killed. They are unclean,
lying with those killed in war. They carry their
shame with those who have gone down to the
place of the dead.
31 "The king of Egypt and his army will see
these who have been killed in war. Then he will
be comforted for all his soldiers killed in war,
says the Lord GOD. 32 I made people afraid of
the king of Egypt while he lived on earth. But
he and all his people will lie among those who

are unclean, who were killed in war, says the
Lord GOD."

EZEKIEL IS WATCHMAN FOR ISRAEL

33 1 The LORD spoke his word to me, saying:
2 "Human, speak to your people and say to
them: 'Suppose I bring a war against a land.
The people of the land may choose one of their
men and make him their watchman. 3 When he
sees the enemy coming to attack the land, he
will blow the trumpet and warn
the people. 4 If they hear
the sound of the trumpet
but do nothing, the enemy
will come and kill them. They
will be responsible for their
own deaths. 5 They heard the
sound of the trumpet but didn't do anything.
So they are to blame for their own deaths. If
they had done something, they would have
saved their own lives. 6 But if the watchman
sees the enemy coming to attack and does not
blow the trumpet, the people will not be
warned. Then if the enemy comes and kills any
of them, they have died because of their own
sin. But I will punish the watchman for their
deaths.'

RESPONSIBILITY

Are we responsible to help others? (33:1–6)

7 "You, human, are the one I have made a
watchman for Israel. If you hear a word from
my mouth, you must warn them for me. 8 Suppose I say to the wicked: 'Wicked people, you
will surely die,' but you don't speak to warn the
wicked to stop doing evil. Then they will die
because they were sinners, but I will punish
you for their deaths. 9 But if you warn the
wicked to stop doing evil and they do not stop,
they will die because they were sinners. But
you have saved your life.

10 "So you, human, say to Israel: 'You have
said: Surely our law-breaking and sins are
hurting us. They will kill us. What can we do
so we will live?' 11 Say to them: 'The Lord GOD
says: As surely as I live, I do not want any who
are wicked to die. I want them to stop doing
evil and live. Stop! Stop your wicked ways! You
don't want to die, do you, people of Israel?'

12 "Human, say to your people: 'The goodness of those who do right will not save them
when they sin. The evil of wicked people will
not cause them to be punished if they stop
doing it. If good people sin, they will not be
able to live by the good they did earlier.' 13 If I
tell good people, 'You will surely live,' they
might think they have done enough good and
then do evil. Then none of the good things
they did will be remembered. They will die because of the evil they have done. 14 Or, if I say
to the wicked people, 'You will surely die,' they
may stop sinning and do what is right and
honest. 15 For example, they may return what
somebody gave them as a promise to repay a
loan, or pay back what they stole. If they live
by the rules that give life and do not sin, then
they will surely live, and they will not die.
16 They will not be punished for any of their
sins. They now do what is right and fair, so
they will surely live.

17 "Your people say: 'The way of the Lord is
not fair.' But it is their own ways that are not
fair. 18 When the good people stop doing good
and do evil, they will die for their evil. 19 But
when the wicked stop doing evil and do what
is right and fair, they will live. 20 You still say:
'The way of the Lord is not fair.' Israel, I will
judge all of you by your own ways."

THE FALL OF JERUSALEM EXPLAINED

21 It was in the twelfth year of our captivity,
on the fifth day of the tenth month. A person
who had escaped from Jerusalem came to me
and said, "Jerusalem has been captured." 22 Now
I had felt the power of the LORD on me the
evening before. He had made me able to talk
again before this person came to me. I could
speak; I was not without speech anymore.

23 Then the LORD spoke his word to me, saying: 24 "Human, people who live in the ruins in
the land of Israel are saying: 'Abraham was
only one person, yet he was given the land as
his own. Surely the land has been given to us,
who are many, as our very own.' 25 So say to
them: 'This is what the Lord GOD says: You eat
meat with the blood still in it, you ask your
idols for help, and you murder people. Should

WHAT'S IT MEAN?

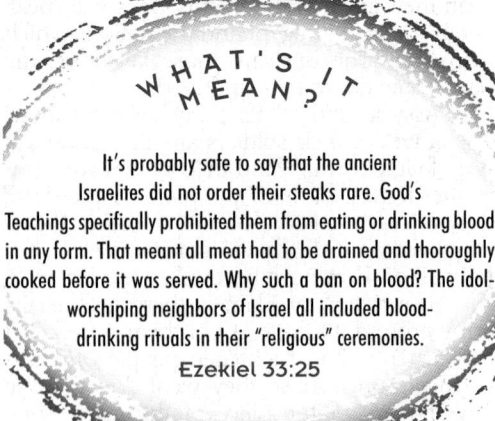

It's probably safe to say that the ancient Israelites did not order their steaks rare. God's Teachings specifically prohibited them from eating or drinking blood in any form. That meant all meat had to be drained and thoroughly cooked before it was served. Why such a ban on blood? The idol-worshiping neighbors of Israel all included blood-drinking rituals in their "religious" ceremonies.

Ezekiel 33:25

you then have the land as your very own? 26You depend on your sword and do terrible things which I hate. Each of you has sexual relations with his neighbor's wife. So should you have the land?'

27"Say to them: 'This is what the Lord GOD says: As surely as I live, those who are among the city ruins in Israel will be killed in war. I will cause those who live in the country to be eaten by wild animals. People hiding in the strongholds and caves will die of disease. 28I will make the land an empty desert. The people's pride in the land's power will end. The mountains of Israel will become empty so that no one will pass through them. 29They will know that I am the LORD when I make the land an empty desert because of the things they have done that I hate.'

30"But as for you, human, your people are talking about you by the walls and in the doorways of houses. They say to each other: 'Come now, and hear the message from the LORD.' 31So they come to you in crowds as if they were really ready to listen. They sit in front of you as if they were my people and hear your words, but they will not obey them. With their mouths they tell me they love me, but their hearts desire their selfish profits. 32To your people you are nothing more than a singer who sings love songs and has a beautiful voice and plays a musical instrument well. They hear your words, but they will not obey them.

33"When this comes true, and it surely will happen, then the people will know that a prophet has been among them."

THE LEADERS ARE LIKE SHEPHERDS

34

1The LORD spoke his word to me, saying: 2"Human, prophesy against the leaders of Israel, who are like shepherds. Prophesy and say to them: 'This is what the Lord GOD says: How terrible it will be for the shepherds of Israel who feed only themselves! Why don't the shepherds feed the flock? 3You eat the milk curds, and you clothe yourselves with the wool. You kill the fat sheep, but you do not feed the flock. 4You have not made the weak strong. You have not healed the sick or put bandages on those that were hurt. You have not brought back those who strayed away or searched for the lost. But you have ruled the sheep with cruel force. 5The sheep were scattered, because there was no shepherd, and they became food for every wild animal. 6My flock wandered over all the mountains and on every high hill. They were scattered all over the face of the earth, and no one searched or looked for them.

WHAT'S IT MEAN?

Quick, name the animal that is mentioned in the Bible more often than any other animal. If you guessed "sheep," you're correct! Sheep have been an especially important part of Israel's history, providing the Israelites with wool for clothes and meat for food and sacrifices. Because sheep are nearly helpless by themselves, they depend on a shepherd to guide and protect them. A good shepherd knows when and where to lead his flock to water and is willing to risk his life for the animals.

Ezekiel 34:2

7" 'So, you shepherds, hear the word of the LORD. This is what the Lord GOD says: 8As surely as I live, my flock has been caught and eaten by all the wild animals, because the flock has no shepherd. The shepherds did not search for my flock. No, they fed themselves instead of my flock. 9So, you shepherds, hear the word of the LORD. 10This is what the Lord GOD says: I am against the shepherds. I will blame them for what has happened to my sheep and will not let them tend the flock anymore. Then the shepherds will stop feeding themselves, and I will take my flock from their mouths so they will no longer be their food.

"As a shepherd takes care of his scattered flock when it is found, I will take care of my sheep. I will save them from all the places where they were scattered on a cloudy and dark day." (Ezekiel 34:12)

11" 'This is what the Lord GOD says: I, myself, will search for my sheep and take care of them. 12As a shepherd takes care of his scattered flock when it is found, I will take care of

my sheep. I will save them from all the places
where they were scattered on a cloudy and
dark day.
13 I will bring them out from the nations and gather them from the countries. I will
bring them to their own land and pasture
them on the mountains of Israel, in the ravines,
and in all the places where people live in the
land.
14 I will feed them in a good pasture, and
they will eat grass on the high mountains of
Israel. They will lie down on good ground
where they eat grass, and they will eat in rich
grassland on the mountains of Israel.
15 I will
feed my flock and lead them to rest, says the
Lord GOD.
16 I will search for the lost, bring
back those that strayed away, put bandages on
those that were hurt, and make the weak
strong. But I will destroy those sheep that are
fat and strong. I will tend the sheep with fairness.

17 " 'This is what the Lord GOD says: As for
you, my flock, I will judge between one sheep
and another, between the male sheep and the
male goats.
18 Is it not enough for you to eat
grass in the good land? Must you crush the
rest of the grass with your feet? Is it not
enough for you to drink clear water? Must you
make the rest of the water muddy with your
feet?
19 Must my flock eat what you crush, and
must they drink what you make muddy with
your feet?

20 " 'So this is what the Lord GOD says to
them: I, myself, will judge between the fat
sheep and the thin sheep.
21 You push with
your side and with your shoulder, and you
knock down all the weak sheep with your
horns until you have forced them away.
22 So I
will save my flock; they will not be hurt anymore. I will judge between one sheep and another.
23 Then I will put over them one
shepherd, my servant David. He will feed them

Promise — HE PROMISES TO BE YOUR SHEPHERD.

I will make an agreement of peace with my sheep and will remove harmful animals from the land. Then the sheep will live safely in the desert and sleep in the woods. I will bless them and let them live around my hill. I will cause the rains to come when it is time; there will be showers to bless them. Also the trees in the countryside will give their fruit, and the land will give its harvest. And the sheep will be safe on their land. Then they will know that I am the LORD when I break the bars of their captivity and save them from the power of those who made them slaves. They will not be led captive by the nations again. The wild animals will not eat them, but they will live safely, and no one will make them afraid. I will give them a place famous for its good crops, so they will no longer suffer from hunger in the land. They will not suffer the insults of other nations anymore. They they will know that I, the LORD their God, am with them. The nation of Israel will know that they are my people, says the Lord GOD. You, my human sheep, are the sheep I care for, and I am your God, says the Lord GOD (Ezek. 34:25–31).

Can you remember being two or three years old? Were you expected to buy your own groceries, pay your own bills, and build your own house at that age? Of course not! A two-year-old child is unable to do much without proper help or guidance. Even when you grow up, God says you will still be helpless. He calls us his flock because sheep are the most helpless of all animals. They don't know how to find new fields to graze. They can't protect themselves from wild animals. They are so fearful that they would just huddle together and die if they didn't have a shepherd. The shepherd is the one who keeps them fed and watered and safe.

The Lord promises to be your Shepherd. He will rescue lost people. He will bandage and heal us when we're wounded. He will make sure that we have all we need. He will calm our fears and protect us from our enemies. When you feel like a little lost sheep, wandering around aimlessly, remember that the Shepherd is waiting for you. He's calling your name. Run to him.

SEE FOR YOURSELF:
Ps. 23; Is. 53:6; Ezek. 34:11–15

and tend them and be their shepherd. 24Then I,
the LORD, will be their God, and my servant
David will be a ruler among them. I, the LORD,
have spoken.
25" 'I will make an agreement of peace with
my sheep and will remove harmful animals
from the land. Then the sheep will live safely in
the desert and sleep in the woods. 26I will bless
them and let them live around my hill. I will
cause the rains to come when it is time; there
will be showers to bless them. 27Also the trees
in the countryside will give their fruit, and the
land will give its harvest. And the sheep will be
safe on their land. Then they will know that I
am the LORD when I break the bars of their
captivity and save them from the power of
those who made them slaves. 28They will not
be led captive by the nations again. The wild
animals will not eat them, but they will live
safely, and no one will make them afraid. 29I
will give them a place famous for its good
crops, so they will no longer suffer from hunger in the land. They will not suffer the insults
of other nations anymore. 30Then they will
know that I, the LORD their God, am with them.
The nation of Israel will know that they are my
people, says the Lord GOD. 31You, my human
sheep, are the sheep I care for, and I am your
God, says the Lord GOD.' "

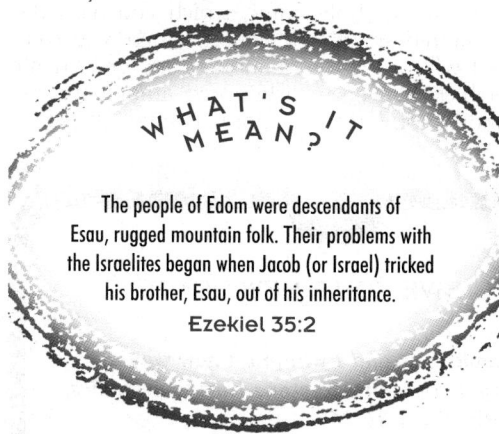

WHAT'S IT MEAN?

The people of Edom were descendants of Esau, rugged mountain folk. Their problems with the Israelites began when Jacob (or Israel) tricked his brother, Esau, out of his inheritance.

Ezekiel 35:2

PROPHECY AGAINST EDOM

35
1The LORD spoke his word to me, saying:
2"Human, look toward Edom and prophesy
against it. 3Say to it: 'This is what the Lord GOD
says: I am against you, Edom. I will stretch out
my hand against you and make you an empty
desert. 4I will destroy your cities, and you will
become empty. Then you will know that I am
the LORD.
5" 'You have always been an enemy of Israel. You let them be defeated in war when
they were in trouble at the time of their final
punishment. 6So the Lord GOD says, as surely
as I live, I will let you be murdered. Murder
will chase you. Since you did not hate murdering people, murder will chase you. 7I will make
Edom an empty ruin and destroy everyone
who goes in or comes out of it. 8I will fill its
mountains with those who are killed. Those
killed in war will fall on your hills, in your valleys, and in all your ravines. 9I will make you a
ruin forever; no one will live in your cities.
Then you will know that I am the LORD.
10" 'You said, "These two nations, Israel and
Judah, and these two lands will be ours. We
will take them for our own." But the
LORD was there. 11So this is
what the Lord GOD says: As
surely as I live, I will treat you
just as you treated them. You
were angry and jealous because you hated them. So I
will punish you and show the
Israelites who I am. 12Then you
will know that I, the LORD, have heard all your
insults against the mountains of Israel. You
said, "They have been ruined. They have
been given to us to eat." 13You
have not stopped your proud
talk against me. I have heard
you. 14This is what the Lord
GOD says: All the earth will be
happy when I make you an
empty ruin. 15You were happy
when the land of Israel was ruined, but I will
do the same thing to you. Mount Seir and all
Edom, you will become an empty ruin. Then
you will know that I am the LORD.' "

HATRED
What will God hold us accountable to? (35:11–12)

PRIDE
What can boasting bring? (35:13–15)

ISRAEL TO COME HOME

36
1"Human, prophesy to the mountains of Israel and say: 'Mountains of Israel, hear the
word of the LORD. 2This is what the Lord GOD
says: The enemy has said about you, "Now the
old places to worship gods have become
ours." ' 3So prophesy and say: 'This is what the
Lord GOD says: They have made you an empty
ruin and have crushed you from all around. So
you became a possession of the other nations.
People have talked and whispered against you.
4So, mountains of Israel, hear the word of the
Lord GOD. The Lord GOD speaks to the mountains, hills, ravines, and valleys, to the empty
ruins and abandoned cities that have been
robbed and laughed at by the other nations.
5This is what the Lord GOD says: I speak in hot
anger against the other nations. I speak against
the people of Edom, who took my land for

themselves with joy and with hate in their
hearts. They forced out the people and took
their pastureland.' 6So prophesy about the land
of Israel and say to the mountains, hills, ravines, and valleys: 'This is what the Lord GOD
says: I speak in my jealous anger, because you
have suffered the insults of the nations. 7So
this is what the Lord GOD says: I promise that
the nations around you will also have to suffer
insults.

8" 'But you, mountains of Israel, will grow
branches and fruit for my people, who will
soon come home. 9I am concerned about you;
I am on your side. You will be plowed, and
seed will be planted in you. 10I will increase the
number of people who live on you, all the
people of Israel. The cities will have people living in them, and the ruins will be rebuilt. 11I
will increase the number of people and animals living on you. They will grow and have
many young. You will have people living on
you as you did before, and I will make you
better off than at the beginning. Then you will
know that I am the LORD. 12I will cause my
people Israel to walk on you and own you,
and you will belong to them. You will never
again take their children away from them.

13" 'This is what the Lord GOD says: People
say about you, "You eat people and take children from your nation." 14But you will not eat
people anymore or take away the children,
says the Lord GOD. 15I will not make you listen
to insults from the nations anymore; you will
not suffer shame from them anymore. You will
not cause your nation to fall anymore, says the
Lord GOD.' "

THE LORD ACTS FOR HIMSELF

16The LORD spoke his word to me again,
saying: 17"Human, when the nation of Israel
was living in their own land, they made it unclean by their ways and the things they did.
Their ways were like a woman's uncleanness
in her time of monthly bleeding. 18So I poured
out my anger against them, because they murdered in the land and because they made the
land unclean with their idols. 19I scattered
them among the nations, and they
were spread through the
countries. I punished them
for how they lived and what
they did. 20They dishonored
my holy name in the nations
where they went. The nations
said about them 'These are the
people of the LORD, but they had to leave the
land which he gave them.' 21But I had concern
for my holy name, which the nation of Israel
had dishonored among the nations where they
went.

DISOBEDIENCE
Is it wrong to misuse God's name? (36:20)

22"So say to the people of Israel, 'This is
what the Lord GOD says: Israel, I am going to
act, but not for your sake. I will do something
to help my holy name, which you have dishonored among the nations where you went.
23I will prove the holiness of my great name,
which has been dishonored among the nations. You have dishonored it among these na-

Promise

HE PROMISES TO GIVE YOU A NEW HEART.

Also, I will teach you to respect me completely, and I will put a new way of thinking inside you. I will take out the stubborn hearts of stone from your bodies, and I will give you obedient hearts of flesh (Ezek. 36:26).

God didn't say he would just repair your old, dirty heart. He says he is going to perform a complete transplant, taking the old stubborn heart away and giving you a brand-new one. Doctors have come to the conclusion that some people's hearts are beyond repair, and the only way for them to survive is for them to receive a heart transplant. The same is true spiritually; the only way for us to live life the way God wants us to is to get a fresh start. He exchanges the old for the new. When God gives us this transplant, things don't look the same to us. It's not just a different attitude, but a brand-new life! We don't need to settle for a repair job when God has a whole new, wonderful life for each one of us.

SEE FOR YOURSELF:

Ps. 51:10; Jer. 32:39; Ezek. 11:19; John 3:3; 2 Cor. 5:17; Rev. 21:5

tions, but the nations will know that I am the
LORD when I prove myself holy before their
eyes, says the Lord GOD.
24" 'I will take you from the nations and
gather you out of all the lands and bring you
back into your own land. 25Then I will sprinkle
clean water on you, and you will be clean. I
will cleanse you from all your uncleanness and
your idols. 26Also, I will teach you to respect
me completely, and I will put a new way of
thinking inside you. I will take out the stubborn hearts of stone from your bodies, and I
will give you obedient hearts of flesh. 27I will
put my Spirit inside you and help you live by
my rules and carefully obey my laws. 28You
will live in the land I gave to your ancestors,
and you will be my people, and I will be your
God. 29So I will save you from all your uncleanness. I will command the grain to come
and grow; I will not allow a time of hunger to
hurt you. 30I will increase the harvest of the
field so you will never again suffer shame
among the nations because of hunger. 31Then
you will remember your evil ways and actions
that were not good, and you will hate yourselves because of your sins and your terrible
acts that I hate. 32I want you to know that I am
not going to do this for your sake, says the
Lord GOD. Be ashamed and embarrassed about
your ways, Israel.
33" 'This is what the Lord GOD says: This is
what will happen on the day I cleanse you
from all your sins: I will cause the cities to have
people living in them again, and the destroyed
places will be rebuilt. 34The empty land will be
plowed so it will no longer be a ruin for everyone who passes by to see. 35They will say, "This
land was ruined, but now it has become like
the garden of Eden. The cities were destroyed,
empty, and ruined, but now they are protected
and have people living in them." 36Then
those nations still around you
will know that I, the LORD,
have rebuilt what was de-
stroyed and have planted
what was empty. I, the LORD,
have spoken, and I will do it.'
37"This is what the Lord GOD
says: I will let myself be asked by the people of
Israel to do this for them again: I will make
their people grow in number like a flock.
38They will be as many as the flocks brought to
Jerusalem during her holy feasts. Her ruined
cities will be filled with flocks of people. Then
they will know that I am the LORD."

BELIEF

Is God's word reliable? (36:36)

THE VISION OF DRY BONES

37
1I felt the power of the LORD on me, and he
brought me out by the Spirit of the LORD and
put me down in the middle of a valley. It was
full of bones. 2He led me around among the
bones, and I saw that there were many bones
in the valley and that they were very dry. 3Then
he asked me, "Human, can these bones live?"

Promise HE PROMISES THAT YOU WILL LIVE.

And I will put my Spirit inside you, and you will come to life. Then I will put you in your own land. And you will know that I, the LORD, have spoken and done it, says the LORD (Ezek. 37:14).

How many times have you said, "This is killin' me!"? Maybe it was a term paper, a hard soccer practice in the beating sun, your little brother's trumpet practice, or being grounded when all the best parties are going on. All kinds of things can make you feel "like you're gonna die."

Sometimes there are serious situations that really do "kill" you emotionally, or that can make you feel like your heart really is dead. You may really feel like your life is over. Your parents divorce. Someone you love dies. A friend stabs you in the back. You're diagnosed with a chronic disease. You suffer a major disappointment.

God says, "I will put my Spirit in you, and you shall live." Hang on to that verse. You *will* live. The Spirit of God breathes new life into you. When you can't go on, he puts fresh life into you. He knows when something is "killin' " you. He knows when you need a boost. The Spirit of God is more powerful than you know. Ask him, and he'll help you live again.

SEE FOR YOURSELF:

Jer. 49:6; Zeph. 3:20; Zech. 10:6

I answered, "Lord GOD, only you know."
4He said to me, "Prophesy to these bones
and say to them, 'Dry bones, hear the word of
the LORD. 5This is what the Lord GOD says to
the bones: I will cause breath to enter you
so you will come to life. 6I will put muscles on
you and flesh on you and cover you with skin.
Then I will put breath in you so you will come
to life. Then you will know that I am the
LORD.' "
7So I prophesied as I was commanded.
While I prophesied, there was a noise and a
rattling. The bones came together, bone to
bone. 8I looked and saw muscles come on the
bones, and flesh grew, and skin covered the
bones. But there was no breath in them.
9Then he said to me, "Prophesy to the
wind.[n] Prophesy, human, and say to the wind,
'This is what the Lord GOD says: Wind, come
from the four winds, and breathe on these
people who were killed so they can come back
to life.' " 10So I prophesied as the LORD commanded me. And the breath came into them,
and they came to life and stood on their feet, a
very large army.
11Then he said to me, "Human, these bones
are like all the people of Israel. They say, 'Our
bones are dried up, and our hope has gone. We
are destroyed.' 12So, prophesy and say to them,
'This is what the Lord GOD says: My people, I
will open your graves and cause you to come
up out of your graves. Then I will bring you
into the land of Israel. 13My people, you will
know that I am the LORD when I open your
graves and cause you to come up from them.
14And I will put my Spirit inside you, and you
will come to life. Then I will put you in your
own land. And you will know that I, the LORD,
have spoken and done it, says the LORD.' "

JUDAH AND ISRAEL BACK TOGETHER

15The LORD spoke his word to me, saying,
16"Human, take a stick and write on it, 'For Judah and all the Israelites with him.' Then take
another stick and write on it, 'The stick of
Ephraim, for Joseph and all the Israelites with
him.' 17Then join them together into one stick
so they will be one in your hand.
18"When your people say to you, 'Explain to
us what you mean by this,' 19say to them, 'This
is what the Lord GOD says: I will take the stick
for Joseph and the tribes of Israel with him,
which is in the hand of Ephraim, and I will put
it with the stick of Judah. I will make them into
one stick, and they will be one in my hand.'
20Hold the sticks on which you wrote these
names in your hand so the people can see
them. 21Say to the people, 'This is what the
Lord GOD says: I am going to take the people
of Israel from among the nations where they
have gone. I will gather them from all around
and bring them into their own land. 22I will
make them one nation in the land, on the
mountains of Israel. One king will rule all of
them. They will never again be two nations;
they will not be divided into
two kingdoms anymore.
23They will not continue to
make themselves unclean by
their idols, their statues of
gods which I hate, or by their
sins. I will save them from all
the ways they sin and turn
against me, and I will make them clean. Then
they will be my people, and I will be their God.

FORGIVENESS
Is God's forgiveness possible? (37:23)

24" 'My servant David will be their king, and
they will all have one shepherd. They will live
by my rules and obey my laws. 25They will live
on the land I gave to my servant Jacob, the
land in which your ancestors lived. They will
all live on the land forever: they, their children,
and their grandchildren. David my servant will
be their king forever. 26I will make an agreement of peace with them, an agreement that
continues forever. I will put them in their land
and make them grow in number. Then I will
put my Temple among them forever. 27The
place where I live will be with them. I will be
their God, and they will be my people. 28When
my Temple is among them forever, the nations
will know that I, the LORD, make Israel holy.' "

PROPHECY AGAINST GOG

38
1The LORD spoke his word to me, saying,
2"Human, look toward Gog of the land of Magog, the chief ruler of the nations of Meshech
and Tubal. Prophesy against him 3and say, 'The
Lord GOD says this: I am against you, Gog,
chief ruler of Meshech and Tubal. 4I will turn
you around and put hooks in your jaws. And I
will bring you out with all your army, horses,
and horsemen, all of whom will be dressed in
beautiful uniforms. They will be a large army
with large and small shields and all having
swords. 5Persia, Cush, and Put will be with
them, all of them having shields and helmets.
6There will also be Gomer with all its troops
and the nation of Togarmah from the far north
with all its troops—many nations with you.
7" 'Be prepared. Be prepared, you and all the

37:9 wind This Hebrew word could also mean "breath" or "spirit."

armies that have come together to make you
their commander. 8After a long time you will
be called for service. After those years you will
come into a land that has been rebuilt from
war. The people in the land will have been
gathered from many nations to the mountains
of Israel, which were empty for a long time.
These people were brought out from the nations, and they will all be living in safety. 9You
will come like a storm. You, all your troops,
and the many nations with you will be like a
cloud covering the land.
10" 'This is what the Lord GOD says: At that
time ideas will come into your mind, and you
will think up an evil plan. 11You will say, "I will
march against a land of towns without walls. I
will attack those who are at rest and live in
safety. All of them live without city walls or
gate bars or gates. 12I will capture treasures and
take loot. I will turn my power against the rebuilt ruins that now have people living in
them. I will attack these people who have been
gathered from the nations, who have become
rich with farm animals and property, who live
at the center of the world." 13Sheba, Dedan, and
the traders of Tarshish, with all its villages, will
say to you, "Did you come to capture treasure?
Did you bring your troops together to take
loot? Did you bring them to carry away silver
and gold and to take away farm animals and
property?" '
14"So prophesy, human, and say to Gog,
'This is what the Lord GOD says: Now that my
people Israel are living in safety, you will know
about it. 15You will come with many people
from your place in the far north. You will have
a large group with you, a mighty army, all riding on horses. 16You will attack my people Israel like a cloud that covers the land. This will
happen in the days to come when I bring you
against my land. Gog, then the nations will
know me when they see me prove how holy I
am in what I do through you.
17" 'This is what the Lord GOD says: You are
the one about whom I spoke in past days. I
spoke through my servants, the prophets of Israel, who prophesied for many years that I
would bring you against them. 18This is what
will happen: On the day Gog attacks the land
of Israel, I will become very angry, says the
Lord GOD. 19With jealousy and great anger I tell
you that at that time there will surely be a great
earthquake in Israel. 20The fish of the sea, the
birds of the sky, the wild animals, everything
that crawls on the ground, and all the people
on the earth will shake with fear before me.
Also the mountains will be thrown down, the
cliffs will fall, and every wall will fall to the
ground. 21Then I will call for a war against Gog
on all my mountains, says the Lord GOD.
Everyone's sword will attack the soldier next to
him. 22I will punish Gog with disease and
death. I will send a heavy rain with hailstones
and burning sulfur on Gog, his army, and the
many nations with him. 23Then
I will show how great I am. I
will show my holiness, and I
will make myself known to
the many nations that watch.
Then they will know that I am
the LORD.'

GOD
Will the world ever see God's greatness? (38:23)

THE DEATH OF GOG AND HIS ARMY

39 1"Human, prophesy against Gog and say,
'This is what the Lord GOD says: I am against
you, Gog, chief ruler of Meshech and Tubal. 2I
will turn you around and lead you. I will bring
you from the far north and send you to attack
the mountains of Israel. 3I will knock your
bow out of your left hand and throw down
your arrows from your right hand. 4You, all
your troops, and the nations with you will fall
dead on the mountains of Israel. I will let you
be food for every bird that eats meat and for
every wild animal. 5You will lie fallen on the
ground, because I have spoken, says the Lord
GOD. 6I will send fire on Magog and those who
live in safety on the coastlands. Then they will
know that I am the LORD.
7" 'I will make myself known among my
people Israel, and I will not let myself be dishonored anymore. Then the nations will know
that I am the LORD, the Holy One in Israel. 8It is
coming! It will happen, says the Lord GOD. The
time I talked about is coming.
9" 'Then those who live in the cities of Israel
will come out and make fires with the enemy's
weapons. They will burn them, both large and
small shields, bows and arrows, war clubs, and
spears. They will use the weapons to burn in
their fires for seven years. 10They will not need
to take wood from the field or chop firewood
from the forests, because they will make fires
with the weapons. In this way they will take
the treasures of those who took their treasures;
they will take the loot of those who took their
loot, says the Lord GOD.
11" 'At that time I will give Gog a burial place
in Israel, in the Valley of the Travelers, east of
the Dead Sea. It will block the road for travelers. Gog and all his army will be buried there,
so people will call it The Valley of Gog's Army.
12" 'The people of Israel will be burying
them for seven months to make the land clean

again. 13All the people in the land will bury them, and they will be honored on the day of my victory, says the Lord GOD.

14" 'The people of Israel will choose men to work through the land to make it clean. Along with others, they will bury Gog's soldiers still lying dead on the ground. After the seven months are finished, they will still search. 15As they go through the land, anyone who sees a human bone is to put a marker by it. The sign will stay there until the gravediggers bury the bone in The Valley of Gog's Army. 16A city will be there named Hamonah. So they will make the land clean again.'

17"Human, this is what the Lord GOD says: Speak to every kind of bird and wild animal: 'Come together, come! Come together from all around to my sacrifice, a great sacrifice which I will prepare for you on the mountains of Israel. Eat flesh and drink blood! 18You are to eat the flesh of the mighty and drink the blood of the rulers of the earth as if they were fat animals from Bashan: male sheep, lambs, goats, and bulls. 19You are to eat and drink from my sacrifice which I have prepared for you, eating fat until you are full and drinking blood until you are drunk. 20At my table you are to eat until you are full of horses and riders, mighty men and all kinds of soldiers,' says the Lord GOD.

21"I will show my glory among the nations. All the nations will see my power when I punish them. 22From that time onward the people of Israel will know that I am the LORD their God. 23The nations will know Israel was taken away captive because they turned against me. So I turned away from them and handed them over to their enemies until all of them died in war. 24Because of their uncleanness and their sins, I punished them and turned away from them.

25"So this is what the Lord GOD says: Now I will bring the people of Jacob back from captivity, and I will have mercy on the whole nation of Israel. I will not let them dishonor me. 26The people will forget their shame and how they rejected me when they live again in safety on their own land with no one to make them afraid. 27I will bring the people back from other lands and gather them from the lands of their enemies. So I will use my people to show many nations that I am holy. 28Then my people will know that I am the LORD their God, because I sent them into captivity among the nations, but then I brought them back to their own land, leaving no one behind. 29I will not turn away from them anymore, because I will put my Spirit into the people of Israel, says the Lord GOD."

> **"I will show my glory among the nations. All the nations will see my power when I punish them. From that time onward the people of Israel will know that I am the LORD their God."**
> **(Ezekiel 39:21–22)**

THE NEW TEMPLE

40

1It was the twenty-fifth year of our captivity, at the beginning of the year, on the tenth day of the month. It was in the fourteenth year after Jerusalem was captured. On that same day I felt the power of the LORD, and he brought me to Jerusalem. 2In the visions of God he brought me to the land of Israel and put me down on a very high mountain. On the south of the mountain there were some buildings that looked like a city. 3He took me closer to the buildings, and I saw a man who looked as if he were made of bronze, standing in the gateway. He had a cord made of linen and a stick in his hand, both for measuring. 4The man said to me, "Human, look with your eyes and hear with your ears. Pay attention to all that I will show you, because that's why you have been brought here. Tell the people of Israel all that you see."

THE EAST GATEWAY

5I saw a wall that surrounded the Temple area. The measuring stick in the man's hand was ten and one-half feet long. So the man measured the wall, which was ten and one-half feet thick and ten and one-half feet high.

6Then the man went to the east gateway. He went up its steps and measured the opening of the gateway. It was ten and one-half feet deep. 7The rooms for the guards were ten and one-half feet long and ten and one-half feet wide. The walls that came out between the guards' rooms were about nine feet thick. The opening of the gateway next to the porch that faced the Temple was ten and one-half feet deep.

8Then the man measured the porch of the gateway. 9It was about fourteen feet deep, and its side walls were three and one-half feet thick. The porch of the gateway faced the Temple.

10On each side of the east gateway were

three rooms, which measured the same on each side. The walls between each room were the same thickness. 11The man measured the width of the entrance to the gateway, which was seventeen and one-half feet wide. The width of the gate was about twenty-three feet. 12And there was a low wall about twenty-one inches high in front of each room. The rooms were ten and one-half feet on each side. 13The man measured the gateway from the roof of one room to the roof of the opposite room. It was about forty-four feet from one door to the opposite door. 14The man also measured the porch, which was about thirty-five feet wide. The courtyard was around the porch. 15From the front of the outer side of the gateway to the front of the porch of the inner side of the gateway was eighty-seven and one-half feet. 16The rooms and porch had small windows on both sides. The windows were narrower on the side facing the gateway. Carvings of palm trees were on each side wall of the rooms.

THE OUTER COURTYARD

17Then the man brought me into the outer courtyard where I saw rooms and a pavement of stones all around the court. Thirty rooms were along the edge of the paved walkway. 18The pavement ran alongside the gates and was as deep as the gates were wide. This was the lower pavement. 19Then the man measured from the outer wall to the inner wall. The outer court between these two walls was one hundred seventy-five feet on the east and on the north.

THE NORTH GATEWAY

20The man measured the length and width of the north gateway leading to the outer courtyard. 21Its three rooms on each side, its inner walls, and its porch measured the same as the first gateway. It was eighty-seven and one-half feet long and forty-four feet wide. 22Its windows, porch, and carvings of palm trees measured the same as the east gateway. Seven steps went up to the gateway, and the gateway's porch was at the inner end. 23The inner courtyard had a gateway across from the northern gateway like the one on the east. The man measured it and found it was one hundred seventy-five feet from inner gateway to outer gateway.

THE SOUTH GATEWAY

24Then the man led me south where I saw a gateway facing south. He measured its inner walls and its porch, and they measured the same as the other gateways. 25The gateway and its porch had windows all around like the other gateways. It was eighty-seven and one-half feet long and forty-four feet wide. 26Seven steps went up to this gateway. Its porch was at the inner end, and it had carvings of palm trees on its inner walls. 27The inner courtyard had a gateway on its south side. The man measured from gate to gate on the south side, which was one hundred seventy-five feet.

THE INNER COURTYARD

28Then the man brought me through the south gateway into the inner courtyard. The inner south gateway measured the same as the gateways in the outer wall. 29The inner south gateway's rooms, inner walls, and porch measured the same as the gateways in the outer wall. There were windows all around the gateway and its porch. The gateway was eighty-seven and one-half feet long and forty-four feet wide. 30Each porch of each inner gateway was about forty-four feet long and about nine feet wide. 31The inner south gateway's porch faced the outer courtyard. Carvings of palm trees were on its side walls, and its stairway had eight steps.

32The man brought me into the inner courtyard on the east side. He measured the inner east gateway, and it was the same as the other gateways. 33The inner east gateway's rooms, inside walls, and porch measured the same as the other gateways. Windows were all around the gateway and its porch. The inner east gateway was eighty-seven and one-half feet long and forty-four feet wide. 34Its porch faced the outer courtyard. Carvings of palm trees were on its inner walls on each side, and its stairway had eight steps.

35Then the man brought me to the inner north gateway. He measured it, and it was the same as the other gateways. 36Its rooms, inner walls, and porch measured the same as the other gateways. There were windows all around the gateway, which was eighty-seven and one-half feet long and forty-four feet wide. 37Its porch faced the outer courtyard. Carvings of palm trees were on its inner walls on each side, and its stairway had eight steps.

ROOMS FOR PREPARING SACRIFICES

38There was a room with a door that opened onto the porch of the inner north gateway. In this room the priests washed animals for the burnt offerings. 39There were two tables on each side of the porch, on which animals for burnt offerings, sin offerings, and penalty offerings were killed. 40Outside, by each side wall of the porch, at the entrance to the north gateway, were two more tables. 41So there were four tables inside the gateway, and four tables outside. In all there were eight tables on which the priests killed animals for sacrifices. 42There were four tables made of cut stone for the burnt offering. These tables were about three feet long, three feet wide, and about two feet high. On these tables the priests put their tools which they used to kill animals for burnt offerings and the other sacrifices. 43Double shelves three inches wide were put up on all the walls. The flesh for the offering was put on the tables.

THE PRIESTS' ROOMS

44There were two rooms in the inner courtyard. One was beside the north gateway and faced south. The other room was beside the south gateway and faced north. 45The man said to me, "The room which faces south is for the priests who serve in the Temple area, 46while the room that faces north is for the priests who serve at the altar. This second group of priests are descendants of Zadok, the only descendants of Levi who can come near the LORD to serve him."

WHAT'S IT MEAN?

When David was on his deathbed, Abiathar, the high priest, made a terrible decision that ultimately cost him his job. He tried to help Adonijah, one of David's sons, seize the throne from Solomon, the rightful heir to the kingdom. Zadok, another priest, remained loyal to Solomon. When Solomon became king, then, he kicked the disloyal Abiathar out of office and replaced him with Zadok. Zadok's descendants were put in charge of offering sacrifices.

Ezekiel 40:46

47The man measured the inner courtyard. It was a square—one hundred seventy-five feet long and one hundred seventy-five feet wide. The altar was in front of the Temple.

THE TEMPLE PORCH

48The man brought me to the porch of the Temple and measured each side wall of the porch. Each was about nine feet thick. The doorway was twenty-four and one-half feet wide. The side walls of the doorway were each about five feet wide. 49The porch was thirty-five feet long and twenty-one feet wide, with ten steps leading up to it. Pillars were by the side walls, one on each side of the entrance.

WHAT'S IT MEAN?

If this floor plan seems familiar, it's because it's similar to the one Solomon used when he built the original Temple—as well as the one Moses used when he constructed the original Meeting Tent. The Most Holy Place, where the Ark of the Agreement and the tablets that contained the Ten Commandments were located, was a perfect cube, equal in length, width, and height. If you're wondering where to go to see such a magnificent structure, don't bother. The Temple whose plans Ezekiel saw has not yet been built.

Ezekiel 41:3–4

THE HOLY PLACE OF THE TEMPLE

41 1The man brought me to the Holy Place and measured its side walls, which were each ten and one-half feet thick. 2The entrance was seventeen and one-half feet wide. The walls alongside the entrance were each about nine feet wide. The man measured the Holy Place, which was seventy feet long and thirty-five feet wide.

3Then the man went inside and measured the side walls of the next doorway. Each was three and one-half feet thick. The doorway was ten and one-half feet wide, and the walls next to it were each more than twelve feet thick. 4Then the man measured the room at the end of the Holy Place. It was thirty-five feet long and thirty-five feet wide. The man said to me, "This is the Most Holy Place."

5Then the man measured the wall of the Temple, which was ten and one-half feet thick. There were side rooms seven feet wide all around the Temple. 6The side rooms were on three different stories, each above the other, with thirty rooms on each story. All around the Temple walls there were ledges for the side rooms. The upper rooms rested on the ledges but were not attached to the Temple walls. 7The side rooms around the Temple were wider on each higher story, so rooms were wider on the top story. A stairway went up from the lowest story to the highest through the middle story.

8I also saw that the Temple had a raised base all around. Its edge was the foundation for the side rooms, and it was ten and one-half feet thick. 9The outer wall of the side rooms was about nine feet thick. There was an open area between the side rooms of the Temple 10and some other rooms. It was thirty-five feet wide and went all around the Temple. 11The side rooms had doors which led to the open area around the outside of the Temple. One door faced north, and the other faced south. The open area was about nine feet wide all around.

12The building facing the private area at the west side was one hundred twenty-two and one-half feet wide. The wall around the building was about nine feet thick and one hundred fifty-seven and one-half feet long.

13Then the man measured the Temple. It was one hundred seventy-five feet long. The private area, including the building and its walls, was in all one hundred seventy-five feet long. 14Also the front of the Temple and the private area on its east side were one hundred seventy-five feet wide.

15The man measured the length of the building facing the private area on the west side, and it was one hundred seventy-five feet from one wall to the other.

The Holy Place, the Most Holy Place, and the outer porch 16had wood panels on the walls. By the doorway, the Temple had wood panels on the walls. The wood covered all the walls from the floor up to the windows, 17up to the part of the wall above the entrance.

All the walls inside the Most Holy Place and the Holy Place, and on the outside, in the porch, 18had carvings of creatures with wings and palm trees. A palm tree was between each carved creature, and every creature had two faces. 19One was a human face looking toward the palm tree on one side. The other was a lion's face looking toward the palm tree on the other side. They were carved all around the Temple walls. 20From the floor to above the entrance, palm trees and creatures with wings were carved. The walls of the Holy Place 21had square doorposts. In front of the Most Holy Place was something that looked like 22an altar of wood. It was more than five feet high and three feet wide. Its corners, base, and sides were wood. The man said to me, "This is the table that is in the presence of the LORD." 23Both the Holy Place and the Most Holy Place had double doors. 24Each of the doors had two pieces that would swing open. 25Carved on the doors of the Holy Place were palm trees and creatures with wings, like those carved on the walls. And there was a wood roof over the front Temple porch. 26There were windows and palm trees on both side walls of the porch. The side rooms of the Temple were also covered by a roof over the stairway.

THE PRIESTS' ROOMS

42 1Then the man led me north out into the outer courtyard and to the rooms across from the private area and the building. 2These rooms on the north side were one hundred seventy-five feet long and eighty-seven and one-half feet wide. 3There was thirty-five feet of the inner courtyard between them and the Temple. On the other side, they faced the stone pavement of the outer courtyard. The rooms were built in three stories like steps and had balconies. 4There was a path on the north side of the rooms, which was seventeen and one-half feet wide and one hundred seventy-five feet long. Doors led into the rooms from this path. 5The top rooms were narrower, because the balconies took more space from them. The rooms on the first and second stories of the building were wider. 6The rooms were on three stories. They did not have pillars like the pillars of the courtyards. So the top rooms were farther back than those on the first and second stories. 7There was a wall outside parallel to the rooms and to the outer courtyard. It ran in front of the rooms for eighty-seven and one-half feet. 8The row of rooms along the outer courtyard was eighty-seven and one-half feet long, and the rooms that faced the Temple were about one hundred seventy-five feet long. 9The lower rooms had an entrance on the east side so a person could enter them from the outer courtyard, 10at the start of the wall beside the courtyard.

There were rooms on the south side, which were across from the private area and the building. 11These rooms had a path in front of them. They were like the rooms on the north with the same length and width and the same doors. 12The doors of the south rooms were like the doors of the north rooms. There was an entrance at the open end of a path beside the wall, so a person could enter at the east end.

13The man said to me, "The north and south rooms across from the private area are holy rooms. There the priests who go near the LORD will eat the most holy offerings. There they will put the most holy offerings: the grain offerings, sin offerings, and the penalty offerings, because the place is holy. 14The priests who enter the Holy Place must leave their serving clothes there before they go into the outer courtyard, because these clothes are holy. After they put on other clothes, they may go to the part of the Temple area which is for the people."

OUTSIDE THE TEMPLE AREA

15When the man finished measuring inside the Temple area, he brought me out through the east gateway. He measured the area all around. 16The man measured the east side with the measuring stick; it was eight hundred seventy-five feet by the measuring stick. 17He measured the north side; it was eight hundred seventy-five feet by the measuring stick. 18He measured the south side; it was eight hundred seventy-five feet by the measuring stick. 19He went around to the west side; it measured eight hundred seventy-five feet by the measuring stick. 20So he measured the Temple area on all four sides. The Temple area had a wall all around it that was eight hundred seventy-five feet long and eight hundred seventy-five feet wide. It separated what was holy from that which was not holy.

THE LORD AMONG HIS PEOPLE

43 1Then the man led me to the outer east gateway, 2and I saw the glory of the God of Israel coming from the east. It sounded like the roar of rushing water, and its brightness made the earth shine. 3The vision I saw was like the vision I had seen when the LORD came to destroy the city and also like the vision I had seen by the Kebar River. I bowed facedown on the ground. 4The glory of the LORD came into the Temple area through the east gateway.

5Then the Spirit picked me up and brought me into the inner courtyard. There I saw the LORD's glory filling the Temple. 6As the man stood at my side, I heard someone speaking to me from inside the Temple. 7The voice from the Temple said to me, "Human, this is my throne and the place where my feet rest. I will live here among the Israelites forever. The people of Israel will not make my holy name unclean again. Neither the people nor their kings will make it unclean with their sexual sins or with the dead bodies of their kings. 8The kings made my name unclean by putting their doorway next to my doorway, and their doorpost next to my doorpost so only a wall separated me from them. When they did their acts that I hate, they made my holy name unclean, and so I destroyed them in my anger. 9Now let them stop their sexual sins and take the dead bodies of their kings far away from me. Then I will live among them forever.

10"Human, tell the people of Israel about the Temple so they will be ashamed of their sins. Let them think about the plan of the Temple. 11If they are ashamed of all they have done, let them know the design of the Temple and how it is built. Show them its exits and entrances, all its designs, and also all its rules and teachings. Write the rules as they watch so they will obey all the teachings and rules about the Temple. 12This is the teaching about the Temple: All the area around the top of the mountain is most holy. This is the teaching about the Temple.

THE ALTAR

13"These are the measurements of the altar, using the measuring stick. The altar's gutter is twenty-one inches high and twenty-one inches wide, and its rim is about nine inches around its edge. And the altar is this tall: 14From the ground up to the lower ledge, it measures three and one-half feet. It is twenty-one inches wide. It measures seven feet from the smaller ledge to the larger ledge and is twenty-one inches wide. 15The place where the sacrifice is burned on the altar is seven feet high, with its four corners shaped like horns and reaching up above it. 16It is square, twenty-one feet long and twenty-one feet wide. 17The upper ledge is also square, twenty-four and one-half feet long and twenty-four and one-half feet wide. The rim around the altar is ten and one-half inches wide, and its gutter is twenty-one inches wide all around. Its steps are on the east side."

18Then the man said to me, "Human, this is what the Lord GOD says: These are the rules for the altar. When it is built, use these rules to offer burnt offerings and to sprinkle blood on it. 19You must give a young bull as a sin offering to the priests, the Levites who are from the family of Zadok and who come near me to serve me, says the Lord GOD. 20Take some of the bull's blood and put it on the four corners of the altar, on the four corners of the ledge, and all around the rim. This is how you will make the altar pure and ready for God's service. 21Then take the bull for the sin offering and burn it in the proper place in the Temple area, outside the Temple building.

22"On the second day offer a male goat that has nothing wrong with it for a sin offering. The priests will make the altar pure and ready for God's service as they did with the young bull. 23When you finish making the altar pure

and ready, offer a young bull and a male sheep
from the flock, which have nothing wrong
with them. 24You must offer them in the presence of the LORD, and the priests are to throw
salt on them and offer them as a burnt offering
to the LORD.

25"You must prepare a goat every day for
seven days as a sin offering. Also, the priests
must prepare a young bull and male sheep
from the flock, which have nothing wrong
with them. 26For seven days the priests are to
make the altar pure and ready for God's service. Then they will give the altar to God. 27Af-
ter these seven days, on the eighth day, the
priests must offer your burnt offerings and
your fellowship offerings on the altar. Then I
will accept you, says the Lord GOD."

THE OUTER EAST GATE

44

1Then the man brought me back to the outer
east gateway of the Temple area, but the gate
was shut. 2The LORD said to me, "This gate will
stay shut; it will not be opened. No one may
enter through it, because the LORD God of Israel
has entered through it. So it must stay shut.
3Only the ruler himself may sit in the gateway
to eat a meal in the presence of the LORD. He
must enter through the porch of the gateway
and go out the same way."

4Then the man brought me through the
outer north gate to the
front of the Temple. As I
looked, I saw the glory
of the LORD filling
the Temple of the
LORD, and I
bowed facedown
on the ground.

5The LORD said
to me, "Human,
pay attention. Use
your eyes to see,
and your ears to
hear. See and hear
everything I tell you
about all the rules and
teachings of the Temple of
the LORD. Pay attention to
the entrance to the Temple and to all the
exits from the Temple area. 6Then speak to
those who refuse to obey. Say to the people of
Israel, 'This is what the Lord GOD says: Stop
doing all your acts that I hate, Israel! 7You
brought foreigners into my Holy Place who
were not circumcised in the flesh and had not
given themselves to serving me. You dishonored my Temple when you offered me food,

> "The LORD said to me, 'Human, pay attention. Use your eyes to see, and your ears to hear. See and hear everything I tell you about all the rules and teachings of the Temple of the LORD. Pay attention to the entrance to the Temple and to all the exits from the Temple area.' "
> (Ezekiel 44:5)

fat, and blood. You broke my agreement by all
the things you did that I hate. 8You did not take
care of my holy things yourselves but put foreigners in charge of my Temple. 9This is what
the Lord GOD says: Foreigners who are not circumcised in flesh and who do not give themselves to serving me may not enter my Temple.
Not even a foreigner living among the people
of Israel may enter.

10" 'But the Levites who stopped obeying me
when Israel left me and who followed their
idols must be punished for their sin. 11These
Levites are to be servants in my Holy Place.
They may guard the gates of the Temple and
serve in the Temple area. They may kill the animals for the burnt offering and the sacrifices
for the people. They may stand before the people to serve them. 12But these Levites helped
the people worship their idols and caused the
people of Israel to fall, so I make this promise:
They will be punished for their sin, says the
Lord GOD. 13They will not come near me to
serve as priests, nor will they come near any of
my holy things or the most holy offerings. But
they will be made ashamed of the things they
did that I hate. 14I will put them in charge of
taking care of the Temple area, all the work that
must be done in it.

15" 'But the priests who are Levites and descendants of Zadok took care of my Holy Place
when Israel left me, so
they may come near to
serve me. They may
stand in my pres-
ence to offer me
the fat and blood
of the animals they
sacrifice, says the
Lord GOD. 16They
are the only ones
who may enter my
Holy Place. Only
they may come
near my table to
serve me and take
care of the things I
gave them to do.

17" 'When they enter the
gates of the inner courtyard,
they must wear linen robes. They must not
wear wool to serve at the gates of the inner
courtyard or in the Temple. 18They will wear
linen turbans on their heads and linen underclothes. They will not wear anything that
makes them perspire. 19When they go out into
the outer courtyard to the people, they must
take off their serving clothes before they go.

They must leave these clothes in the holy
rooms and put on other clothes. Then they will
not let their holy clothes hurt the people.

WHAT'S IT MEAN?

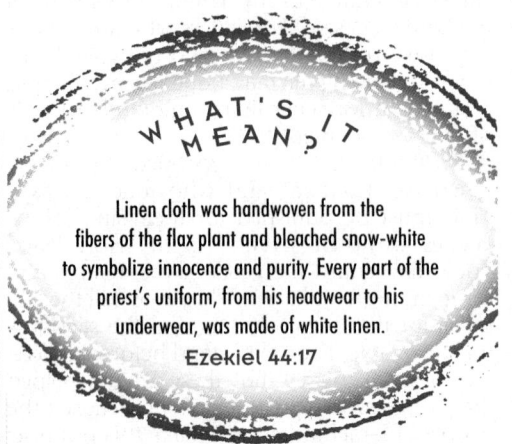

Linen cloth was handwoven from the fibers of the flax plant and bleached snow-white to symbolize innocence and purity. Every part of the priest's uniform, from his headwear to his underwear, was made of white linen.

Ezekiel 44:17

20" 'They must not shave their heads or let
their hair grow long but must keep the hair of
their heads trimmed. 21 None of the priests may
drink wine when they enter the inner courtyard. 22 The priests must not marry widows or
divorced women. They may marry only virgins from the people of Israel or widows of
priests. 23 They must teach my people the difference between what is holy and what is not
holy. They must help my people know what is
unclean and what is clean.
24" 'In court they will act as judges. When
they judge, they will follow my teachings. They
must obey my laws and my rules at all my
special feasts and keep my Sabbaths holy.
25" 'They must not go near a dead person,
making themselves unclean. But they are allowed to make themselves unclean if the dead
person is their father, mother, son, daughter,
brother, or a sister who has not married. 26 After a priest has been made clean again, he must
wait seven days. 27 Then he may go into the
inner courtyard to serve in the Temple, but he
must offer a sin offering for himself, says the
Lord GOD.
28" 'These are the rules about the priests and
their property: They will have me instead of
property. You will not give them any land to
own in Israel; I am what they will own. 29 They
will eat the grain offerings, sin offerings, and
penalty offerings. Everything Israel gives to me
will be theirs. 30 The best fruits of all the first
harvests and all the special gifts offered to me
will belong to the priests. You will also give to
the priests the first part of your grain that you
grind and so bring a blessing on your family.
31 The priests must not eat any bird or animal
that died a natural death or one that has been
torn by wild animals.

THE LAND IS DIVIDED

45
1" 'When you divide the land for the Israelite tribes by throwing lots, you must give a
part of the land to belong to the LORD. It will
be about seven miles long and about six miles
wide; all of this land will be holy. 2 From this
land, an area eight hundred seventy-five feet
square will be for the Temple. There will be an
open space around the Temple that is eighty-
seven and one-half feet wide. 3 In the holy area
you will measure a part about seven miles long
and three miles wide, and in it will be the Most
Holy Place. 4 This holy part of the land will be
for the priests who serve in the Temple, who
come near to the LORD to serve him. It will be a
place for the priests' houses and for the Temple. 5 Another area about seven miles long and
more than three miles wide will be for the Levites, who serve in the Temple area. It will belong to them so they will have cities in which
to live.
6" 'You must give the city an area that is
about one and one-half miles wide and about
seven miles long, along the side of the holy
area. It will belong to all the people of Israel.
7" 'The ruler will have land on both sides of
the holy area and the city. On the west of the
holy area, his land will reach to the Mediterranean Sea. On the east of the holy area, his land
will reach to the eastern border. It will be as
long as the land given to each tribe. 8 Only this
land will be the ruler's property in Israel. So
my rulers will not be cruel to my people anymore, but they will let each tribe in the nation
of Israel have its share of the land.
9" 'This is what the Lord GOD says: You have
gone far enough, you rulers of Israel! Stop being cruel and hurting people, and do what is
right and fair. Stop forcing my
people out of their homes, says
the Lord GOD. 10 You must
have honest scales, an honest
dry measurement and an
honest liquid measurement.
11 The dry measure and the
liquid measure will be the same:
The liquid measure will always be a tenth of a
homer,[n] and the ephah will always be a tenth

HONESTY
What does God require of us? (45:9–11)

45:11 homer The Hebrew word means "donkey-load." It measured about five dry bushels or one hundred seventy-five liquid quarts. So an ephah was about one-half bushel, and a bath was about eighteen quarts.

of a homer. The measurement they follow will
be the homer. 12The shekel[n] will be worth
twenty gerahs, and a mina will be worth sixty
shekels.

OFFERINGS AND HOLY DAYS

13" 'This is the gift you should offer: a sixth of
an ephah from every homer of wheat, and a
sixth of an ephah from every homer of barley.
14The amount of oil you are to offer is a tenth of
a bath from each cor. (Ten baths make a homer
and also make a cor.) 15You should give one
sheep from each flock of two hundred from the
watering places of Israel. All these are to be offered for the grain offerings, burnt offerings,
and fellowship offerings to remove sins so you
will belong to God, says the Lord GOD. 16All
people in the land will give this special offering
to the ruler of Israel. 17It will be the ruler's responsibility to supply the burnt offerings, grain
offerings, and drink offerings. These offerings
will be given at the feasts, at the New Moons,
on the Sabbaths, and at all the other feasts of
Israel. The ruler will supply the sin offerings,
grain offerings, and fellowship offerings to pay
for the sins of Israel.
18" 'This is what the Lord GOD says: On the
first day of the first month take a young bull
that has nothing wrong with it. Use it to make
the Temple pure and ready for God's service.
19The priest will take some of the blood from
this sin offering and put it on the doorposts of
the Temple, on the four corners of the ledge of
the altar, and on the posts of the gate to the
inner courtyard. 20You will do the same thing
on the seventh day of the month for anyone
who has sinned by accident or without knowing it. This is how you make the Temple pure
and ready for God's service.

PASSOVER FEAST OFFERINGS

21" 'On the fourteenth day of the first month
you will celebrate the Feast of Passover. It will
be a feast of seven days when you eat bread
made without yeast. 22On that day the ruler
must offer a bull for himself and for all the
people of the land as a sin offering. 23During
the seven days of the feast he must offer seven
bulls and seven male sheep that have nothing
wrong with them. They will be burnt offerings
to the LORD, which the ruler will offer every
day of the seven days of the feast. He must also
offer a male goat every day as a sin offering.
24The ruler must give as a grain offering one-
half bushel for each bull and one-half bushel
for each sheep. He must give a gallon of olive
oil for each half bushel.

WHAT'S IT MEAN?

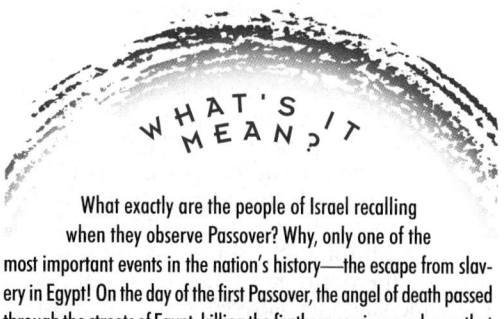

What exactly are the people of Israel recalling when they observe Passover? Why, only one of the most important events in the nation's history—the escape from slavery in Egypt! On the day of the first Passover, the angel of death passed through the streets of Egypt, killing the firstborn son in every house that was not marked with blood. Because the Israelites had smeared blood on their doorposts, the death angel "passed over" their homes and their sons were spared.

Ezekiel 45:21

25" 'Beginning on the fifteenth day of the
seventh month, when you celebrate the Feast
of Shelters, the ruler will supply the same
things for seven days: the sin offerings, burnt
offerings, grain offerings, and the olive oil.

RULES FOR WORSHIP

46

1" 'This is what the Lord GOD says: The east
gate of the inner courtyard will stay shut on
the six working days, but it will be opened on
the Sabbath day and on the day of the New
Moon. 2The ruler will enter from outside
through the porch of the gateway and stand
by the gatepost, while the priests offer the
ruler's burnt offering and fellowship offering.
The ruler will worship at the entrance of the
gateway, and then he will go out. But the gate
will not be shut until evening. 3The people of
the land will worship at the entrance of that
gateway in the presence of the LORD on the
Sabbaths and New Moons. 4This is the burnt
offering the ruler will offer to the LORD on the
Sabbath day: six male lambs that have nothing
wrong with them and a male sheep that has
nothing wrong with it. 5He must give a half-
bushel grain offering with the male sheep, but
he may give as much grain offering with the
lambs as he pleases. He must also give a gallon
of olive oil for each half bushel of grain. 6On the
day of the New Moon he must offer a young
bull that has nothing wrong with it. He must
also offer six lambs and a male sheep that have
nothing wrong with them. 7The ruler must give

45:12 shekel In Ezekiel's time a shekel weighed about two-fifths of an ounce.

a half-bushel grain offering with the bull and
one-half bushel with the male sheep. With the
lambs, he may give as much grain as he pleases.
But he must give a gallon of olive oil for each
half bushel of grain. 8When the ruler enters, he
must go in through the porch of the gateway,
and he must go out the same way.

9" 'When the people of the land come into
the LORD's presence at the special feasts, those
who enter through the north gate to worship
must go out through the south gate. Those
who enter through the south gate must go out
through the north gate. They must not return
the same way they entered; everyone must go
out the opposite way. 10The ruler will go in
with the people when they go in and go out
with them when they go out.

11" 'At the feasts and regular times of worship one-half bushel of grain must be offered
with a young bull, and one-half bushel of
grain must be offered with a male sheep. But
with an offering of lambs, the ruler may give as
much grain as he pleases. He should give a gallon of olive oil for each half bushel of grain.
12The ruler may give an offering as a special
gift to the LORD; it may be a burnt offering or
fellowship offering. When he gives it to the
LORD, the inner east gate is to be opened for
him. He must offer his burnt offering or his
fellowship offering as he does on the Sabbath
day. Then he will go out, and the gate will be
shut after he has left.

13" 'Every day you will give a year-old lamb
that has nothing wrong with it for a burnt offering to the LORD. Do it every morning. 14Also,
you must offer a grain offering with the lamb
every morning. For this you will give three and
one-third quarts of grain and one and one-
third quarts of olive oil, to make the fine flour
moist, as a grain offering to the LORD. This is a
rule that must be kept from now on. 15So you
must always give the lamb, together with the
grain offering and the olive oil, every morning
as a burnt offering.

RULES FOR THE RULER

16" 'This is what the Lord GOD says: If the
ruler gives a gift from his land to any of his
sons, that land will belong to the son and then
to the son's children. It is their property passed
down from their family. 17But if the ruler gives
a gift from his land to any of his servants, that
land will belong to the servant only until the
year of freedom. Then the land will go back to
the ruler. Only the ruler's sons may keep a gift
of land from the ruler. 18The ruler must not
take any of the people's land, forcing them out
of their land. He must give his sons some of his
own land so my people will not be scattered
out of their own land.' "

THE SPECIAL KITCHENS

19The man led me through the entrance at
the side of the gateway to the priests' holy
rooms that face north. There I saw a place at
the west end. 20The man said to me, "This is
where the priests will boil the meat of the penalty offering and sin offering and bake the
grain offering. Then they will not need to bring
these holy offerings into the outer courtyard,
because that would hurt the people."

21Then the man brought me out into the
outer courtyard and led me to its four corners.
In each corner of the courtyard was a smaller
courtyard. 22Small courtyards were in the four
corners of the courtyard. Each small courtyard
was the same size, seventy feet long and fifty-
two and one-half feet wide. 23A stone wall was
around each of the four small courtyards, and
places for cooking were built in each of the
stone walls. 24The man said to me, "These are
the kitchens where those who work in the Temple will boil the sacrifices offered by the people."

THE RIVER FROM THE TEMPLE

47
1The man led me back to the door of the
Temple, and I saw water coming out from under the doorway and flowing east. (The Temple
faced east.) The water flowed down from the
south side wall of the Temple and then south
of the altar. 2The man brought me out through
the outer north gate and led me around outside to the outer east gate. I found the water
coming out on the south side of the gate.

3The man went toward the east with a line
in his hand and measured about one-third of a
mile. Then he led me through water that came
up to my ankles. 4The man measured about
one-third of a mile again and led me through
water that came up to my knees. Then he measured about one-third of a mile again and led
me through water up to my waist. 5The man
measured about one-third of a mile again, but
it was now a river that I could not cross. The
water had risen too high; it was deep enough
for swimming; it was a river that no one could
cross. 6The man asked me, "Human, do you see
this?"

Then the man led me back to the bank of the
river. 7As I went back, I saw many trees on both
sides of the river. 8The man said to me, "This
water will flow toward the eastern areas and go
down into the Jordan Valley. When it enters the
Dead Sea, it will become fresh. 9Everywhere the

river goes, there will be many fish. Wherever
this water goes the Dead Sea will become fresh,
and so where the river goes there will be many
living things. 10 Fishermen will stand by the
Dead Sea. From En Gedi all the way to En Eglaim there will be places to spread fishing nets.
There will be many kinds of fish in the Dead
Sea, as many as in the Mediterranean Sea. 11 But
its swamps and marshes will not become fresh;
they will be left for salt. 12 All kinds of fruit trees
will grow on both banks of the river, and their
leaves will not dry and die. The trees will have
fruit every month, because the water for them
comes from the Temple. The fruit from the
trees will be used for food, and their leaves for
medicine."

WHAT'S IT MEAN?

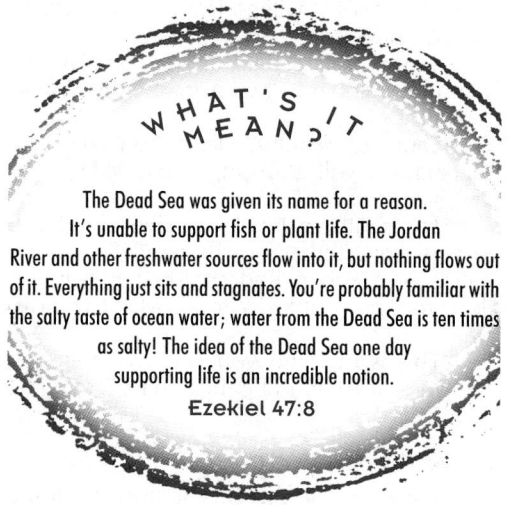

The Dead Sea was given its name for a reason. It's unable to support fish or plant life. The Jordan River and other freshwater sources flow into it, but nothing flows out of it. Everything just sits and stagnates. You're probably familiar with the salty taste of ocean water; water from the Dead Sea is ten times as salty! The idea of the Dead Sea one day supporting life is an incredible notion.

Ezekiel 47:8

BORDERS OF THE LAND

13 This is what the Lord GOD says: "These are
the borders of the land to be divided among the
twelve tribes of Israel. Joseph will have two
parts of land. 14 You will divide the land equally.
I promised to give it to your ancestors, so this
land will belong to you as family property.
15 "This will be the border line of the land:
"On the north side it will start at the Mediterranean Sea. It will go through Hethlon, toward
Lebo Hamath and on to the towns of Zedad,
16 Berothah, and Sibraim on the border between Damascus and Hamath. Then it will go
on to the town of Hazer Hatticon on the border of the country of Hauran. 17 So the border
line will go from the Mediterranean Sea east to
the town of Hazar Enan, where the land belonging to Damascus and Hamath lies on the
north side. This will be the north side of the
land.
18 "On the east side the border runs south
from a point between Hauran and Damascus.
It will go along the Jordan between Gilead and
the land of Israel and will continue to the town
of Tamar on the Dead Sea. This will be the east
side of the land.
19 "On the south side the border line will go
east from Tamar all the way to the waters of
Meribah Kadesh. Then it will run along the
brook of Egypt to the Mediterranean Sea. This
will be the south side of the land.
20 "On the west side the Mediterranean Sea
will be the border line up to a place across
from Lebo Hamath. This will be the west side
of your land.
21 "You will divide this land among the tribes
of Israel. 22 You will divide it as family property
for yourselves and for the foreigners who live
and have children among you. You are to treat
these foreigners the same as people born in
Israel; they are to share the land with the
tribes of Israel. 23 In whatever tribe the foreigner lives, you will give him some land," says
the Lord GOD.

DIVIDING THE LAND

48
1 "These are the areas of the tribes named
here: Dan will have one share at the northern
border. It will go from the sea through Hethlon
to Lebo Hamath, all the way to Hazar Enan,
where Damascus lies to the north. It will stop
there next to Hamath. This will be Dan's northern border from the east side to the Mediterranean Sea on the west side.
2 "South of Dan's border, Asher will have
one share. It will go from the east side to the
west side.
3 "South of Asher's border, Naphtali will
have one share. It will go from the east side to
the west side.
4 "South of Naphtali's border, Manasseh will
have one share. It will go from the east side to
the west side.
5 "South of Manasseh's border, Ephraim will
have one share. It will go from the east side to
the west side.
6 "South of Ephraim's border, Reuben will
have one share. It will go from the east side to
the west side.
7 "South of Reuben's border, Judah will have
one share. It will go from the east side to the
west side.
8 "South of Judah's border will be the holy
area which you are to give. It will be about
seven miles wide and as long and wide as one
of the tribes' shares. It will run from the east
side to the west side. The Temple will be in the
middle of this area.

9"The share which you will give the LORD
will be about seven miles long and three miles
wide. 10The holy area will be divided among
these people. The priests will have land about
seven miles long on the north and south sides,
and three miles wide on the west and east
sides. The Temple of the LORD will be in the
middle of it. 11This land is for the priests who
are given the holy duty of serving the LORD.
They are the descendants of Zadok who did
my work and did not leave me when Israel
and the Levites left me. 12They will have as
their share a very holy part of the holy portion
of the land. It will be next to the land of the
Levites.
13"Alongside the land for the priests, the Levites will have a share about seven miles long
and three miles wide; its full length will be
about seven miles and its full width about
three miles. 14The Levites are not to sell or trade
any of this land. They are not to let anyone else
own any of this best part of the land, because
it belongs to the LORD.

CITY PROPERTY

15"The rest of the area will be about one and
one-half miles wide and seven miles long. It
will not be holy but will belong to the city and
be used for homes and pastures. The city will
be in the middle of it. 16These are the city's measurements: the north side will be about one
mile, the south side about one mile, the east side
about one mile, and the west side about
one mile. 17The city's land for pastures will
be about four hundred thirty-seven feet on the
north, four hundred thirty-seven feet on the
south, four hundred thirty-seven feet on
the east, and four hundred thirty-seven feet on
the west. 18Along the long side of the holy area
there will be left three miles on the east and
three miles on the west. It will be used to grow
food for the city workers. 19The city workers
from all the tribes of Israel will farm this land.
20This whole area will be square, seven miles
by seven miles. You shall give to the LORD the
holy share along with the city property.
21"Land that is left over on both sides of the
holy area and city property will belong to the
ruler. That land will extend east of the holy
area to the eastern border and west of it to
the Mediterranean Sea. Both of these areas run
the length of the lands of the tribes, and they
belong to the ruler. The holy area with the
Holy Place of the Temple will be in the middle.
22The Levites' land and the city property will
be in the middle of the lands belonging to the
ruler. Those lands will be between Judah's border and Benjamin's border.

THE OTHER TRIBES' LAND

23"Here is what the rest of the tribes will receive: Benjamin will have one share. It will go
from the east side to the Mediterranean Sea on
the west side.
24"South of Benjamin's land, Simeon will
have one share. It will go from the east side to
the west side.
25"South of Simeon's land, Issachar will
have one share. It will go from the east side to
the west side.
26"South of Issachar's land, Zebulun will
have one share. It will go from the east side to
the west side.
27"South of Zebulun's land, Gad will have
one share. It will go from the east side to the
west side.
28"The southern border of Gad's land will
go east from Tamar on the Dead Sea to the
waters of Meribah Kadesh. Then it will run
along the brook of Egypt to the Mediterranean
Sea.
29"This is the land you will divide among
the tribes of Israel to be their shares," says the
Lord GOD.

THE GATES OF THE CITY

30"These will be the outside borders of the
city: The north side will measure more than
one mile. 31There will be three gates facing
north: Reuben's Gate, Judah's Gate, and Levi's
Gate, named for the tribes of Israel.
32"The east side will measure more than one
mile. There will be three gates facing east:
Joseph's Gate, Benjamin's Gate, and Dan's Gate.
33"The south side will measure more than
one mile. There will be three gates facing south:
Simeon's Gate, Issachar's Gate, and Zebulun's
Gate.
34"The west side will measure more than
one mile. There will be three gates facing west:
Gad's Gate, Asher's Gate, and Naphtali's Gate.
35"The city will measure about six miles
around. From then on the name of the city will
be The LORD Is There."

daniel

CONTENT Daniel's name means, "God Is My Judge." As you read this book that includes Daniel's life and prophecies, you can see why his name fits him. Daniel was committed to doing what was right, no matter whom it displeased as long as it pleased God. He wasn't worried about being judged by anyone else.

The Book of Daniel is a book written in a variety of styles. It has stories about stand-up kinds of guys who refused to be bullied into disrespecting God. Remember Daniel in the lions' den? Remember the fiery furnace? Those famous stories come from this book.

But the Book of Daniel isn't just a listing of true accounts. It is also a book of prophecies. Daniel was an interpreter of dreams. He could see past the reality of this world and sometimes see into the next world, the new heaven and earth.

To this very day, people read Daniel to get clues about how the end of the world as we know it will happen. The hows and whens are not always clear, but we know the event is getting closer every day.

Outline

1:1–21 .... Daniel and His Three Friends
2:1–49 .... King Nebuchadnezzar's Dream
3:1–30 .... God Rescues Shadrach, Meshach, and Abednego
4:1–37 .... Nebuchadnezzar Loses His Kingdom for Seven Years
5:1–31 .... King Belshazzar and the Writing on the Wall
6:1–28 .... God Rescues Daniel from the Den of Lions
7:1–28 .... Daniel's Vision of the Huge Animals
8:1–27 .... Daniel's Vision of the Male Sheep and the Goat
9:1–27 .... Daniel Prays for His People
10:1—12:13 .... Daniel Has a Vision Beside the Tigris River

Purpose God controls the flow of history and the circumstances of believers in pagan lands.

Theme God Controls the Destiny of All Nations

Date of writing 605–530 B.C.

"During the time of those kings, the God of heaven will set up another kingdom that will never be destroyed or given to another group of people. This kingdom will crush all the other kingdoms and bring them to an end, but it will continue forever" (2:44).

Bible Talk

A Politician, Not a Prophet

We usually think of someone who writes a book of the Bible as somebody like a pastor or a prophet. The truth is that Daniel was a politician. He grew up with a great sense of discernment and a conscience that wouldn't quit. With the opportunities afforded him because of his gifts of interpretation, he got to see his legal system work from inside the king's castle and that is where he became an influence.

Knowing that about Daniel's life reminds us that God uses people in whatever line of work they pursue. Whether it's a courtroom, a pulpit, or a governor's mansion, God works through us when we are faithful to his call.

HOW TO STAND TALL

Daniel was a prime example of a creative problem solver. When his story opens, Daniel is faced with a difficult choice. He is being offered the best food in the kingdom, but the food is off of Daniel's diet (which was prescribed by God in Leviticus). Daniel could have refused to eat, but instead he worked through the channels of authority that were already in place. He proposed a solution and it worked out.

On other occasions, though, like when Daniel was supposed to stop praying, he didn't negotiate. He simply refused.

Daniel is a good example for us. It's good to work within the current system, but when the current system won't budge, a person's got to do what a person's got to do.

DANIEL TAKEN TO BABYLON

1During the third year that Jehoiakim was king of Judah, Nebuchadnezzar king of Babylon came to Jerusalem and surrounded it with his army. 2The Lord allowed Nebuchadnezzar to capture Jehoiakim king of Judah. Nebuchadnezzar also took some of the things from the Temple of God, which he carried to Babylonia and put in the temple of his gods.

WHAT'S IT MEAN?

Let's introduce the major characters of the book. Nebuchadnezzar, the king of Babylon, led three attacks on the nation of Judah and the city of Jerusalem, capturing thousands of Jewish people in the process. Daniel was captured during the first attack, along with three of his friends—Hananiah, Mishael, and Azariah. (You may know them better as Shadrach, Meshach, and Abednego.)

Daniel 1:1, 6

3Then King Nebuchadnezzar ordered Ashpenaz, his chief officer, to bring some of the Israelite men into his palace. He wanted them to be from important families, including the family of the king of Judah. 4King Nebuchadnezzar wanted only young Israelite men who had nothing wrong with them. They were to be handsome and well educated, capable of learning and understanding, and able to serve in his palace. Ashpenaz was to teach them the language and writings of the Babylonians. 5The king gave the young men a certain amount of food and wine every day, just like the food he ate. The young men were to be trained for three years, and then they would become servants of the king of Babylon. 6Among those young men were Daniel, Hananiah, Mishael, and Azariah from the people of Judah.

7Ashpenaz, the chief officer, gave them Babylonian names. Daniel's new name was Belteshazzar, Hananiah's was Shadrach, Mishael's was Meshach, and Azariah's was Abednego.

"Ashpenaz, the chief officer, gave them Babylonian names. Daniel's new name was Belteshazzar, Hananiah's was Shadrach, Mishael's was Meshach, and Azariah's was Abednego." (Daniel 1:7)

8Daniel decided not to eat the king's food or drink his wine because that would make him unclean. So he asked Ashpenaz for permission not to make himself unclean in this way.

9God made Ashpenaz, the chief officer, want to be kind and merciful to Daniel, 10but Ashpenaz said to Daniel, "I am afraid of my master, the king. He ordered me to give you this food and drink. If you begin to look worse than other young men your age, the king will see this. Then he will cut off my head because of you."

11Ashpenaz had ordered a guard to watch Daniel, Hananiah, Mishael, and Azariah. 12Daniel said to the guard, "Please give us this test for ten days: Don't give us anything but vegetables to eat and water to drink. 13After ten days compare how we look with how the other young men look who eat the king's food. See for yourself and then decide how you want to treat us, your servants."

14So the guard agreed to test them for ten days. 15After ten days they looked healthier and better fed than all the young men who ate the king's food. 16So the guard took away the king's special food and wine, feeding them vegetables instead.

17God gave these four young men wisdom and the ability to learn many things that people had written and studied. Daniel could also understand visions and dreams.

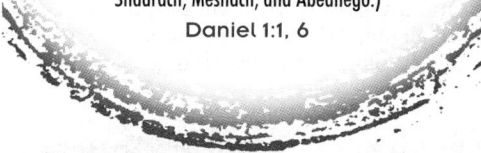

TALENTS

Who gives us our gifts? (1:17)

18At the end of the time set for them by the king, Ashpenaz brought all the young men to King Nebuchadnezzar. 19The king talked to them and found that none of the young men were as good as Daniel, Hananiah, Mishael, and Azariah. So those four young men became the king's servants. 20Every time the king asked them about something important, they showed much wisdom and understanding. They were ten times better than all the fortune-tellers and magicians in his kingdom! 21So Daniel continued to be the king's servant until the first year Cyrus was king.

NEBUCHADNEZZAR'S DREAM

2 [1]During Nebuchadnezzar's second year as
king, he had dreams that bothered him and
kept him awake at night. [2]So the king called for
his fortune-tellers, magicians, wizards, and
wise men, because he wanted them to tell him
what he had dreamed. They came in and stood
in front of the king.
[3]Then the king said to them, "I had a dream
that bothers me, and I want to know what it
means."
[4]The wise men answered the king in the
Aramaic language, "O king, live forever! Please
tell us, your servants, your dream. Then we
will tell you what it means."
[5]King Nebuchadnezzar said to them, "I
meant what I said. You must tell me the dream
and what it means. If you don't, I will have
you torn apart, and I will turn your houses
into piles of stones. [6]But if you tell me my
dream and its meaning, I will reward you with
gifts and great honor. So tell me the dream and
what it means."
[7]Again the wise men said to the king, "Tell
us, your servants, the dream, and we will tell
you what it means."

WHAT'S IT MEAN?

Because there were so many countries in the ancient Near East trying to do business with each other, they needed a common language they could use to make their lives easier. Aramaic was the language they chose. By the time Jesus was born, Aramaic had replaced Hebrew as the language spoken by most Jews. Daniel 2:4b—7:28 is written in Aramaic.

Daniel 2:4

[8]King Nebuchadnezzar answered, "I know
you are trying to get more time, because you
know that I meant what I said. [9]If you don't
tell me my dream, you will be punished. You
have all agreed to tell me lies and wicked
things, hoping things will change. Now, tell me

Promise HE PROMISES TO CONTROL HUMAN EVENTS.

[God] changes the times and the seasons of the year. He takes away the power of kings and gives their power to new kings. He gives wisdom to those who are wise and knowledge to those who understand. He makes known secrets that are deep and hidden (Dan. 2:21–22a).

Daniel praised God for being the One who both gives rulers their power and takes their power away. It's almost surprising to hear Daniel say that—when you realize the situation he was in. King Nebuchadnezzar had attacked Jerusalem. He had captured the king and taken many valuable things from God's Temple. He also captured a lot of able-bodied young men, including Daniel and some of his friends, to serve him in Babylon.

Nebuchadnezzar certainly wasn't a godly man, and Daniel could have resented all the things Nebuchadnezzar did. But he realized that the king's power came from God and that God let Nebuchadnezzar defeat Jerusalem for a reason. God had a plan that, for the time being, revolved around Nebuchadnezzar's success.

When you look at the world today, it may be hard for you to believe that God's in control. He is the One who puts leaders in their places, and he is able to change their hearts. He has all of the wisdom and knowledge they need to be good leaders. Unfortunately, not all leaders seek him. Be a person who prays for leaders. Ask God to turn their hearts toward him. Ask for his wisdom and knowledge on their behalf. God has put them in their positions because he has a plan that's invisible. He *is* in control.

SEE FOR YOURSELF:

Job 41:11; Eccl. 9:1; Is. 54:5; Jer. 10:23; 23:24; Dan. 4:35

the dream so that I will know you can tell me
what it really means!"
10The wise men answered the king, saying,
"No one on earth can do what the king asks!
No great and powerful king has ever asked the
fortune-tellers, magicians, or wise men to do
this; 11the king is asking something that is too
hard. Only the gods could tell the king this, but
the gods do not live among people."
12When the king heard their answer, he became very angry. He ordered that all the wise
men of Babylon be killed. 13So King Nebuchadnezzar's order to kill the wise men was
announced, and men were sent to look for
Daniel and his friends to kill them.
14Arioch, the commander of the king's
guards, was going to kill the wise men of Babylon. But Daniel spoke to him with wisdom
and skill, 15saying, "Why did the king order
such a terrible punishment?" Then Arioch explained everything to Daniel. 16So Daniel went
to King Nebuchadnezzar and asked for an appointment so that he could tell the king what
his dream meant.
17Then Daniel went to his house and explained the whole story to his friends Hananiah, Mishael, and Azariah. 18Daniel asked his
friends to pray that the God of heaven would
show them mercy and help them understand
this secret so he and his friends would not be
killed with the other wise men of Babylon.
19During the night God explained the secret
to Daniel in a vision. Then Daniel praised the
God of heaven. 20Daniel said:

"Praise God forever and ever,
because he has wisdom and power.
21 He changes the times and seasons of the
year.
He takes away the power of kings
and gives their power to new kings.
He gives wisdom to those who are wise
and knowledge to those who
understand.
22 He makes known secrets that are deep and
hidden;
he knows what is hidden in darkness,
and light is all around him.
23 I thank you and praise you, God of my
ancestors,
because you have given me wisdom and
power.
You told me what we asked of you;
you told us about the king's dream."

THE MEANING OF THE DREAM

24Then Daniel went to Arioch, the man King
Nebuchadnezzar had chosen to kill the wise
men of Babylon. Daniel said to him, "Don't put
the wise men of Babylon to death. Take me to
the king, and I will tell him what his dream
means."
25Very quickly Arioch took Daniel to the
king and said, "I have found a man among the
captives from Judah who can tell the king
what his dream means."
26The king asked Daniel, who was also
called Belteshazzar, "Are you able to tell me
what I dreamed and what it means?"
27Daniel answered, "No wise man, magician,
or fortune-teller can explain to the king the
secret he has asked about. 28But there is a God
in heaven who explains secret things, and he
has shown King Nebuchadnezzar what will
happen at a later time. This is your dream,
the vision you saw while lying on your bed:
29O king, as you were lying there, you thought
about things to come. God, who can tell people
about secret things, showed you what is going
to happen. 30God also told this secret to me,
not because I have greater wisdom than any
other living person, but so that you may know
what it means. In that way you will understand what went through your mind.
31"O king, in your dream you saw a huge,
shiny, and frightening statue in front of you.
32The head of the statue was made of pure
gold. Its chest and arms were made of silver. Its
stomach and the upper part of its legs were
made of bronze. 33The lower part of the legs
were made of iron, while its feet were made
partly of iron and partly of baked clay. 34While
you were looking at the statue, you saw a rock
cut free, but no human being touched the rock.
It hit the statue on its feet of iron and clay and
smashed them. 35Then the iron, clay, bronze,
silver, and gold broke to pieces at the same
time. They became like chaff on a threshing
floor in the summertime; the wind blew them
away, and there was nothing left. Then the
rock that hit the statue became a very large
mountain that filled the whole earth.
36"That was your dream. Now we will tell
the king what it means. 37O king, you are the
greatest king. God of heaven has given you a
kingdom, power, strength, and glory. 38Wher-
ever people, wild animals, and birds live, God
made you ruler over them. King Nebuchadnezzar, you are the head of gold on that statue.
39"Another kingdom will come after you,
but it will not be as great as yours. Next a third
kingdom, the bronze part, will rule over the
earth. 40Then there will be a fourth kingdom,
strong as iron. In the same way that iron
crushes and smashes things to pieces, the

fourth kingdom will smash and crush all the
other kingdoms.
41"You saw that the statue's feet and toes
were partly baked clay and partly iron. That
means the fourth kingdom will be a divided
kingdom. It will have some of the strength of
iron in it, just as you saw iron was mixed with
clay. 42The toes of the statue were partly iron
and partly clay. So the fourth kingdom will be
partly strong like iron and partly breakable like
clay. 43You saw the iron mixed with clay, but
iron and clay do not hold together. In the same
way the people of the fourth kingdom will be a
mixture, but they will not be united as one
people.
44"During the time of those kings, the God
of heaven will set up another kingdom that
will never be destroyed or given to another
group of people. This kingdom will crush all
the other kingdoms and bring them to an end,
but it will continue forever.
45"King Nebuchadnezzar, you saw a rock
cut from a mountain, but no human being
touched it. The rock broke the iron, bronze,
clay, silver, and gold to pieces. In this way the
great God showed you what will happen. The
dream is true, and you can trust this explanation."
46Then King Nebuchadnezzar fell facedown
on the ground in front of Daniel. The king
honored him and commanded that an offering
and incense be presented to him. 47Then the
king said to Daniel, "Truly I know your God is
the greatest of all gods, the Lord of all the kings.
He tells people about things they cannot know.
I know this is true, because you were able to
tell these secret things to me."
48Then the king gave Daniel many gifts plus
an important position in his kingdom. Nebuchadnezzar made him ruler over the whole
area of Babylon and put him in charge of all
the wise men of Babylon. 49Daniel asked the
king to make Shadrach, Meshach, and Abednego leaders over the area of Babylon, so the
king did as Daniel asked. Daniel himself became one of the people who stayed at the royal
court.

THE GOLD IDOL AND BLAZING FURNACE

3
1King Nebuchadnezzar made a gold statue
ninety feet high and nine feet wide and set it up
on the plain of Dura in the area of Babylon.
2Then he called for the leaders: the governors,
assistant governors, captains of the soldiers,
people who advised the king, keepers of the
treasury, judges, rulers, and all other officers in
his kingdom. He wanted them to come to the
special service for the statue he had set up. 3So
they all came for the special service and stood
in front of the statue that King Nebuchadnezzar had set up. 4Then the man who made announcements for the king said in a loud voice,
"People, nations, and those of every language,
this is what you are commanded to do: 5When
you hear the sound of the horns, flutes, lyres,
zithers,[n] harps, pipes, and all the other musical
instruments, you must bow down and worship the gold statue that King Nebuchadnezzar
has set up. 6Anyone who doesn't bow down
and worship will immediately be thrown into
a blazing furnace."
7Now people, nations, and those who spoke
every language were there. When they heard
the sound of the horns, flutes, lyres, zithers,
pipes, and all the other musical instruments,
they bowed down and worshiped the gold
statue King Nebuchadnezzar had set up.
8Then some Babylonians came up to the
king and began speaking against the men of
Judah. 9They said to King Nebuchadnezzar,
"O king, live forever! 10O king, you gave a command that everyone who heard the horns,
lyres, zithers, harps, pipes, and all the other musical instruments would have to bow down
and worship the gold statue. 11Anyone who
wouldn't do this was to be thrown into a blazing furnace. 12O king, there are some men of
Judah whom you made officers in the area of
Babylon that did not pay attention to your order. Their names are Shadrach, Meshach, and
Abednego. They do not serve your gods and do
not worship the gold statue you have set up."
13Nebuchadnezzar became very angry and
called for Shadrach, Meshach, and Abednego.
When they were brought to the king, 14Nebu-
chadnezzar said, "Shadrach, Meshach, and
Abednego, is it true that you do not serve my
gods nor worship the gold statue I have set up?
15In a moment you will again hear the sound
of the horns, flutes, lyres, zithers, harps, pipes,
and all the other musical instruments. If you
bow down and worship the statue I made, that
will be good. But if you do not worship it, you
will immediately be thrown into the blazing
furnace. What god will be able to save you
from my power then?"
16Shadrach, Meshach, and Abednego answered the king, saying, "Nebuchadnezzar, we
do not need to defend ourselves to you. 17If
you throw us into the blazing furnace, the God

3:5 zithers Musical instruments with thirty to forty strings.

we serve is able to save us from the furnace.
He will save us from your power, O king. 18But
even if God does not save us, we want you,
O king, to know this: We will not serve your
gods or worship the gold statue you have
set up."
19Then Nebuchadnezzar was furious with
Shadrach, Meshach, and Abednego, and he
changed his mind. He ordered the furnace to
be heated seven times hotter than usual.
20Then he commanded some of the strongest
soldiers in his army to tie up Shadrach, Meshach, and Abednego and throw them into the
blazing furnace.
21So Shadrach, Meshach, and Abednego
were tied up and thrown into the blazing furnace while still wearing their robes, trousers,
turbans, and other clothes. 22The king's command was very strict, and the furnace was
made so hot that the flames killed the strong
soldiers who threw Shadrach, Meshach, and
Abednego into the furnace. 23Firmly tied, Shadrach, Meshach, and Abednego fell into the
blazing furnace.
24Then King Nebuchadnezzar was so surprised that he jumped to his feet. He asked the
men who advised him, "Didn't we tie up only
three men and throw them into the fire?"
They answered, "Yes, O king."
25The king said, "Look! I see four men walking around in the fire. They are not tied up,
and they are not burned. The fourth man
looks like a son of the gods."
26Then Nebuchadnezzar went to the opening of the blazing furnace and shouted, "Shadrach, Meshach, and Abednego, come out!
Servants of the Most High God, come here!"
So Shadrach, Meshach, and Abednego
came out of the fire. 27When they came out, the
governors, assistant governors, captains of the
soldiers, and royal advisers crowded around
them and saw that the fire had not harmed
their bodies. Their hair was not burned, their
robes were not burned, and they didn't even
smell like smoke!
28Then Nebuchadnezzar said, "Praise the
God of Shadrach, Meshach, and Abednego.
Their God has sent his angel and saved his servants from the fire! These three men trusted
their God and refused to obey my command.
They were willing to die rather than serve or
worship any god other than their own. 29So I
now give this command: Anyone from any
nation or language who says anything against
the God of Shadrach, Meshach, and Abednego
will be torn apart and have his house turned
into a pile of stones. No other god can save his
people like this." 30Then the king promoted
Shadrach, Meshach, and Abednego in the area
of Babylon.

NEBUCHADNEZZAR'S DREAM OF A TREE

4
1King Nebuchadnezzar sent this letter to the
people, nations, and those who speak every
language in all the world:

I wish you peace and great wealth!

2The Most High God has done miracles and wonderful things for me that I
am happy to tell you about.
3His wonderful acts are great,
and his miracles are mighty.
His kingdom goes on forever,
and his rule continues from
now on.
4I, Nebuchadnezzar, was happy and
successful at my palace, 5but I had a
dream that made me afraid. As I was lying on my bed, I saw pictures and visions in my mind that alarmed me. 6So I
ordered all the wise men of Babylon to
come to me and tell me what my dream
meant. 7The fortune-tellers, magicians,
and wise men came, and I told them
about the dream. But they could not tell
me what it meant.

WHAT'S IT MEAN?

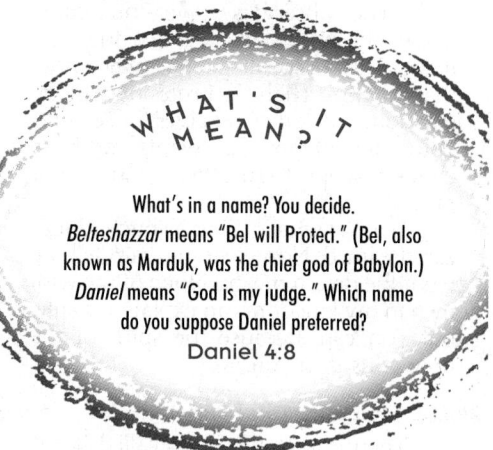

What's in a name? You decide. *Belteshazzar* means "Bel will Protect." (Bel, also known as Marduk, was the chief god of Babylon.) *Daniel* means "God is my judge." Which name do you suppose Daniel preferred?
Daniel 4:8

8Finally, Daniel came to me. (I called
him Belteshazzar to honor my god, because the spirit of the holy gods is in
him.) I told my dream to him. 9I said,
"Belteshazzar, you are the most important of all the fortune-tellers. I know that
the spirit of the holy gods is in you,
so there is no secret that is too hard for
you to understand. This was what I
dreamed; tell me what it means. 10These

are the visions I saw while I was lying in
my bed: I looked, and there in front of
me was a tree standing in the middle of
the earth. And it was very tall. 11The tree
grew large and strong. The top of the tree
touched the sky and could be seen from
anywhere on earth. 12The leaves of the
tree were beautiful. It had plenty of good
fruit on it, enough food for everyone.
The wild animals found shelter under
the tree, and the birds lived in its
branches. Every animal ate from it.

13"As I was looking at those things in
the vision while lying on my bed, I saw
an observer, a holy angel coming down
from heaven. 14He spoke very loudly
and said, 'Cut down the tree and cut off
its branches. Strip off its leaves and scatter its fruit. Let the animals under the tree
run away, and let the birds in its
branches fly away. 15But leave the stump
and its roots in the ground with a band
of iron and bronze around it; let it stay
in the field with the grass around it.

" 'Let the man become wet with dew,
and let him live among the animals and
plants of the earth. 16Let him not think
like a human any longer, but let him
have the mind of an animal for seven
years.

17" 'The observers gave this command; the holy ones declared the sentence. This is so all people may know
that the Most High God rules over every
kingdom on earth. God gives those kingdoms to anyone he wants, and he
chooses people to rule them who are not
proud.'

18"That is what I, King Nebuchadnezzar, dreamed. Now Belteshazzar,[n] tell me
what the dream means. None of the wise
men in my kingdom can explain it to me,
but you can, because the spirit of the
holy gods is in you."

DANIEL EXPLAINS THE DREAM

19Then Daniel, who was called Belteshazzar, was very quiet for a while, because his understanding of the dream
frightened him. So the king said, "Belteshazzar, do not let the dream or its
meaning make you afraid."

Then Belteshazzar answered, "My
master, I wish the dream were about
your enemies, and I wish its meaning
were for those who are against you!
20You saw a tree in your dream that grew
large and strong. Its top touched the sky,
and it could be seen from all over the
earth. 21Its leaves were beautiful, and it
had plenty of fruit for everyone to eat. It
was a home for the wild animals, and its
branches were nesting places for the
birds. 22O king, you are that tree! You
have become great and powerful, like the
tall tree that touched the sky. Your power
reaches to the far parts of the earth.

23"O king, you saw an observer, a
holy angel, coming down from heaven
who said, 'Cut down the tree and destroy it. But leave the stump and its roots
in the ground with a band of iron and
bronze around it; leave it in the field
with the grass. Let him become wet with
dew and live like a wild animal for seven
years.'

24"This is the meaning of the dream,
O king. The Most High God has commanded these things to happen to my
master the king: 25You will be forced
away from people to live among the wild
animals. People will feed you grass like
an ox, and dew from the sky will make
you wet. Seven years will pass, and then
you will learn this lesson: The Most High
God is ruler over every kingdom on
earth, and he gives those kingdoms to
anyone he chooses.

26"Since the stump of the tree and its
roots were left in the ground, your kingdom will be given back to you when
you learn that one in heaven rules your
kingdom. 27So, O king, please accept my
advice. Stop sinning and do what is
right. Stop doing wicked things and be
kind to the poor. Then you might continue to be successful."

THE KING'S DREAM COMES TRUE

28All these things happened to King
Nebuchadnezzar. 29Twelve months later
as he was walking on the roof[n] of his
palace in Babylon, 30he said, "I have built
this great Babylon as my royal home. I
built it by my power to show my glory
and my majesty."

4:18 Belteshazzar Another name for Daniel. **4:29 roof** In Bible times houses were built with flat roofs. The roof was used for drying things such as flax and fruit. And it was used as an extra room, as a place for worship, and as a cool place to sleep in the summer.

31 The words were still in his mouth
when a voice from heaven said, "King
Nebuchadnezzar, these things will happen to you: Your royal power has been
taken away from you. 32 You
will be forced away from
people. You will live with
the wild animals and
will be fed grass like
an ox. Seven years will
pass before you learn
this lesson: The Most
High God rules over
every kingdom on
earth and gives those
kingdoms to anyone he
chooses."

> **"Now I, Nebuchadnezzar, give praise and honor and glory to the King of heaven. Everything he does is right and fair, and he is able to make proud people humble."**
> **(Daniel 4:37)**

33 Immediately the words
came true. Nebuchadnezzar was forced
to go away from people, and he began
eating grass like an ox. He became wet
from dew. His hair grew long like the
feathers of an eagle, and his nails grew
like the claws of a bird.
34 At the end of that time, I, Nebuchadnezzar, looked up toward heaven, and I
could think normally again! Then I gave
praise to the Most High God; I gave honor
and glory to him who lives forever.

God's rule is forever,
and his kingdom continues for all
time.
35 People on earth
are not truly important.
God does what he wants
with the powers of heaven
and the people on earth.
No one can stop his powerful hand
or question what he does.

36 At that time I could think normally
again, and God gave back my great
honor and power and returned the glory
to my kingdom. The people who advised
me and the royal family came to me for
help again. I became king again and was
even greater and more powerful than
before. 37 Now I, Nebuchadnezzar, give
praise and honor and glory to the King
of heaven. Everything he does is right
and fair, and he is able to make proud
people humble.

5 THE WRITING ON THE WALL

1 King Belshazzar gave a big banquet for a
thousand royal guests and drank wine with
them. 2 As Belshazzar was drinking his wine, he
gave orders to bring the gold and silver cups
that his ancestor Nebuchadnezzar had taken
from the Temple in Jerusalem. This was so the
king, his royal guests, his wives, and his slave
women could drink from those cups. 3 So they
brought the gold cups that had
been taken from the Temple
of God in Jerusalem. And
the king and his royal
guests, his wives, and his
slave women drank from
them. 4 As they were
drinking, they praised
their gods, which were
made from gold, silver,
bronze, iron, wood, and
stone.
5 Suddenly the fingers of a
person's hand appeared and
began writing on the plaster of
the wall, near the lampstand in the royal palace. The king watched the hand as it wrote.
6 King Belshazzar was very frightened. His
face turned white, his knees knocked together,
and he could not stand up because his legs
were too weak. 7 The king called for the magicians, wise men, and wizards of Babylon and
said to them, "Anyone who can read this writing and explain it will receive purple clothes fit
for a king and a gold chain around his neck.

WHAT'S IT MEAN?

Who is this guy Belshazzar, and what's he doing ruling Babylon? The story is a little complicated, so hang on. After Nebuchadnezzar died, his son Evil-Merodach became king. Evil-Merodach ruled for two years before being assassinated by his brother-in-law, Nergal-Sharezer. (Got that?) Nergal-Sharezer ruled for less than three years before he died and was succeeded by his son, Labashi-Marduk. Labashi-Marduk reigned for all of two months before he was assassinated. (Still with us?) Next came Nabonidus, who may have been Nebuchadnezzar's son-in-law. In the third year of his reign, Nabonidus appointed his son as coruler of the nation. The Bible doesn't mention Nabonidus, but we know from other historical documents that he suffered from a terrible disease. As a result, he left the kingdom of Babylon in the hands of his son . . . Belshazzar. (Any questions?)

Daniel 5:1

And I will make that person the third highest ruler in the kingdom."

[8]Then all the king's wise men came in, but they could not read the writing or tell the king what it meant. [9]King Belshazzar became even more afraid, and his face became even whiter. His royal guests were confused.

[10]Then the king's mother, who had heard the voices of the king and his royal guests, came into the banquet room. She said, "O king, live forever! Don't be afraid or let your face be white with fear! [11]There is a man in your kingdom who has the spirit of the holy gods. In the days of your father, this man showed understanding, knowledge, and wisdom like the gods. Your father, King Nebuchadnezzar, put this man in charge of all the wise men, fortune-tellers, magicians, and wizards. [12]The man I am talking about is named Daniel, whom the king named Belteshazzar. He was very smart and had knowledge and understanding. He could explain dreams and secrets and could answer very hard problems. Call for Daniel. He will tell you what the writing on the wall means."

[13]So they brought Daniel to the king, and the king asked, "Is your name Daniel? Are you one of the captives my father the king brought from Judah? [14]I have heard that the spirit of the gods is in you, and that you are very smart and have knowledge and extraordinary understanding. [15]The wise men and magicians were brought to me to read this writing and to explain what it means, but they could not explain it. [16]I have heard that you are able to explain what things mean and can find the answers to hard problems. Read this writing on the wall and explain it to me. If you can, I will give you purple clothes fit for a king and a gold chain to wear around your neck. And you will become the third highest ruler in the kingdom."

[17]Then Daniel answered the king, "You may keep your gifts for yourself, or you may give those rewards to someone else. But I will read the writing on the wall for you and will explain to you what it means.

[18]"O king, the Most High God made your father Nebuchadnezzar a great, important, and powerful king. [19]Because God made him important, all the people, nations, and those who spoke every language were very frightened of Nebuchadnezzar. If he wanted someone to die, he killed that person. If he wanted someone to live, he let that person live. Those he wanted to promote, he promoted. Those he wanted to be less important, he made less important.

[20]"But Nebuchadnezzar became too proud and stubborn, so he was taken off his royal throne. His glory was taken away. [21]He was forced away from people, and his mind became like the mind of an animal. He lived with the wild donkeys and was fed grass like an ox and became wet with dew. These things happened to him until he learned his lesson: The Most High God rules over every kingdom on earth, and he sets anyone he chooses over those kingdoms.

[22]"Belshazzar, you already knew these things, because you are a descendant of Nebuchadnezzar. Still you have not been sorry for what you have done. [23]Instead, you have set yourself against the Lord of heaven. You ordered the drinking cups from the Temple of the Lord to be brought to you. Then you and your royal guests, your wives, and your slave women drank wine from them. You praised the gods of silver, gold, bronze, iron, wood, and stone that are not really gods; they cannot see or hear or understand anything. You did not honor God, who has power over your life and everything you do. [24]So God sent the hand that wrote on the wall.

[25]"These are the words that were written on the wall: 'Mene, mene, tekel, and parsin.'

[26]"This is what the words mean: Mene: God has counted the days until your kingdom will end. [27]Tekel: You have been weighed on the scales and found not good enough. [28]Parsin: Your kingdom is being divided and will be given to the Medes and the Persians."

[29]Then Belshazzar gave an order for Daniel to be dressed in purple clothes and to have a gold chain put around his neck. And it was announced that Daniel was the third highest ruler in the kingdom. [30]That very same night Belshazzar, king of the Babylonian people, was killed. [31]So Darius the Mede became the new king when he was sixty-two years old.

DANIEL AND THE LIONS

6

[1]Darius thought it would be a good idea to choose one hundred twenty governors who would rule his kingdom. [2]He chose three men as supervisors over those governors, and Daniel was one of the supervisors. The supervisors were to ensure that the governors did not try to cheat the king. [3]Daniel showed that he could do the work better than the other supervisors and governors, so the king planned to put Daniel in charge of the whole kingdom. [4]Because of this, the other supervisors and gover-

INTEGRITY

How does integrity help us? (6:4–5)

nors tried to find reasons to accuse Daniel
about his work in the government. But they
could not find anything wrong with him or
any reason to accuse him, because he was
trustworthy and not lazy or dishonest. 5Finally
these men said, "We will never find any reason
to accuse Daniel unless it is about the law of
his God."
6So the supervisors and governors went as
a group to the king and said: "King Darius, live
forever! 7The supervisors, assistant governors,
governors, the people who advise you, and the
captains of the soldiers have all agreed that
you should make a new law for everyone
to obey: For the next thirty days no one
should pray to any god or human except to
you, O king. Anyone who doesn't obey will be
thrown into the lions' den. 8Now, O king, make
the law and sign your name to it so that it
cannot be changed, because then it will be a
law of the Medes and Persians and cannot be
canceled." 9So King Darius signed the law.
10Even though Daniel knew that the new
law had been written, he went to pray in an
upstairs room in his house, which had windows that opened toward Jerusalem. Three
times each day Daniel would kneel down to
pray and thank God, just as he always had
done.

WHAT'S IT MEAN?

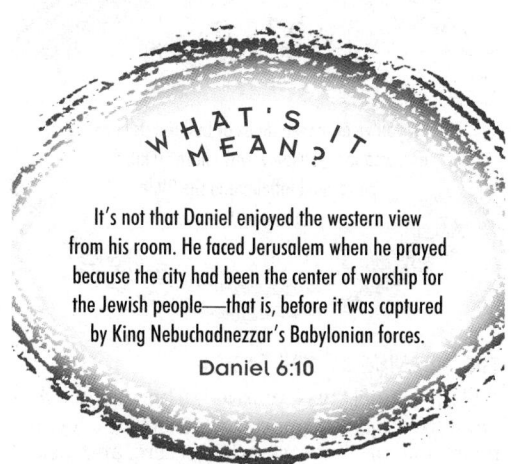

It's not that Daniel enjoyed the western view from his room. He faced Jerusalem when he prayed because the city had been the center of worship for the Jewish people—that is, before it was captured by King Nebuchadnezzar's Babylonian forces.

Daniel 6:10

11Then those men went as a group and
found Daniel praying and asking God for help.
12So they went to the king and talked to him
about the law he had made. They said, "Didn't
you sign a law that says no one may pray to
any god or human except you, O king? Doesn't
it say that anyone who disobeys during the
next thirty days will be thrown into the lions'
den?"
The king answered, "Yes, that is the law, and
the laws of the Medes and Persians cannot be
canceled."
13Then they said to the king, "Daniel, one of
the captives from Judah, is not paying attention to you, O king, or to the law you signed.
Daniel still prays to his God three times every
day." 14The king became very upset when he
heard this. He wanted to save Daniel, and he
worked hard until sunset trying to think of a
way to save him.
15Then those men went as a group to the
king. They said, "Remember, O king, the law of
the Medes and Persians says that no law or
command given by the king can be changed."
16So King Darius gave the order, and Daniel
was brought in and thrown into the lions' den.
The king said to Daniel, "May the God you
serve all the time save you!" 17A big stone was
brought and placed over the opening of the
lions' den. Then the king used his signet ring
and the rings of his royal officers to put special
seals on the rock. This ensured that no one
would move the rock and bring Daniel out.
18Then King Darius went back to his palace. He
did not eat that night, he did not have any entertainment brought to him, and he could not
sleep.
19The next morning King Darius got up at
dawn and hurried to the lions' den. 20As he
came near the den, he was worried. He called
out to Daniel, "Daniel, servant of the living
God! Has your God that you always worship
been able to save you from the lions?"
21Daniel answered, "O king, live forever!
22My God sent his angel to close the lions'
mouths. They have not hurt me, because my
God knows I am innocent. I never did anything wrong to you, O king."
23King Darius was very happy and told his
servants to lift Daniel out of the lions' den. So
they lifted him out and did not find any injury
on him, because Daniel had trusted in his God.
24Then the king commanded that the men
who had accused Daniel be brought to the
lions' den. They, their wives, and their children
were thrown into the den. The lions grabbed
them before they hit the floor of the den and
crushed their bones.
25Then King Darius wrote a letter to all people and all nations, to those who spoke every
language in the world:

I wish you great peace and wealth.

26I am making a new law for people
in every part of my kingdom. All of you
must fear and respect the God of Daniel.

Daniel's God is the living God;
he lives forever.
His kingdom will never be destroyed,
and his rule will never end.
27 God rescues and saves people
and does mighty miracles
in heaven and on earth.
He is the one who saved Daniel
from the power of the lions.

28 So Daniel was successful during the time Darius was king and when Cyrus the Persian was king.

DANIEL'S DREAM ABOUT FOUR ANIMALS

7 1 In Belshazzar's first year as king of Babylon, Daniel had a dream. He saw visions as he was lying on his bed, and he wrote down what he had dreamed.

2 "Daniel said: "I saw my vision at night. In the vision the wind was blowing from all four directions, which made the sea very rough. 3 I saw four huge animals come up from the sea, and each animal was different from the others.

4 "The first animal looked like a lion, but had wings like an eagle. I watched this animal until its wings were torn off. It was lifted from the ground so that it stood up on two feet like a human, and it was given the mind of a human.

5 "Then I saw a second animal before me that looked like a bear. It was raised up on one of its sides and had three ribs in its mouth between its teeth. It was told, 'Get up and eat all the meat you want!'

6 "After that, I looked, and there before me was another animal. This animal looked like a leopard with four wings on its back that looked like a bird's wings. This animal had four heads and was given power to rule.

7 "After that, in my vision at night I saw in front of me a fourth animal that was cruel, terrible, and very strong. It had large iron teeth. It crushed and ate what it killed, and then it walked on whatever was left. This fourth animal was different from any animal I had seen before, and it had ten horns.

8 "While I was thinking about the horns, another horn grew up among them. It was a little horn with eyes like a human's eyes. It also had a mouth, and the mouth was bragging. The little horn pulled out three of the other horns.

9 "As I looked,
thrones were put in their places,
and God, who has been alive forever,
sat on his throne.
His clothes were white like snow,
and the hair on his head was white like wool.
His throne was made from fire,
and the wheels of his throne were blazing with fire.
10 A river of fire was flowing
from in front of him.
Many thousands of angels were serving him,
and millions of angels stood before him.
Court was ready to begin,
and the books were opened.

11 "I kept on looking because the little horn was bragging. I kept watching until finally the fourth animal was killed. Its body was destroyed, and it was thrown into the burning fire. 12 (The power and rule of the other animals had been taken from them, but they were permitted to live for a certain period of time.)

13 "In my vision at night I saw in front of me someone who looked like a human being coming on the clouds in the sky. He came near God, who has been alive forever, and he was led to God. 14 He was given authority, glory, and the strength of a king. People of every tribe, nation, and language will serve him. His rule will last forever, and his kingdom will never be destroyed.

WHAT'S IT MEAN?

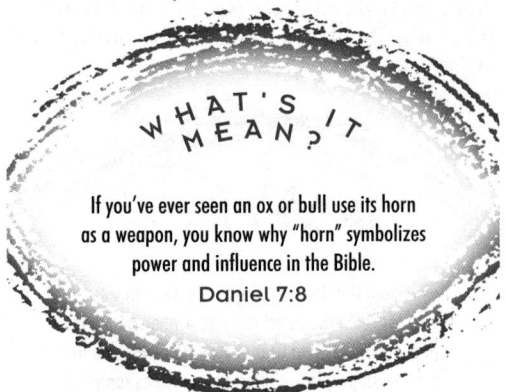

If you've ever seen an ox or bull use its horn as a weapon, you know why "horn" symbolizes power and influence in the Bible.

Daniel 7:8

THE MEANING OF THE DREAM

15 "I, Daniel, was worried. The visions that went through my mind frightened me. 16 I came near one of those standing there and asked what all this meant.

"So he told me and explained to me what these things meant: 17 'The four great animals are four kingdoms that will come from the earth. 18 But the holy people who belong to the Most High God will receive the power to rule and will have the power to rule forever, from now on.'

19 "Then I wanted to know what the fourth animal meant, because it was different from all the others. It was very terrible and had iron

teeth and bronze claws. It was the animal that
crushed and ate what it killed and then walked
on whatever was left. 20I also wanted to know
about the ten horns on its head and about the
little horn that grew there. It had pulled out
three of the other ten horns and looked greater
than the others. It had eyes and a mouth that
kept bragging. 21As I watched, the little horn
began making war against God's holy people
and was defeating them 22until God, who has
been alive forever, came. He judged in favor of
the holy people who belong to the Most High
God; then the time came for them to receive
the power to rule.

23"And he explained this to me: 'The fourth
animal is a fourth kingdom that will come on
the earth. It will be different from all the other
kingdoms and will destroy people all over the
world. It will walk on and crush the whole
earth. 24The ten horns are ten kings who will
come from this fourth kingdom. After those
ten kings are gone, another king will come. He
will be different from the kings who ruled before him, and he will defeat three of the other
kings. 25This king will speak against the Most
High God, and he will hurt and kill God's holy
people. He will try to change times and laws
that have already been set. The holy people
that belong to God will be in that king's power
for three and one-half years.

26" 'But the court will decide what should
happen. The power of the king will be taken
away, and his kingdom will be completely destroyed. 27Then the holy people who belong to
the Most High God will have the power to rule.
They will rule over all the kingdoms under
heaven with power and greatness, and their
power to rule will last forever. People from all
the other kingdoms will respect and serve them.'

28"That was the end of the dream. I, Daniel,
was very afraid. My face became white from
fear, but I kept everything to myself."

DANIEL'S VISION

8 1During the third year of King Belshazzar's
rule, I, Daniel, saw another vision, which was
like the first one. 2In this vision I saw myself in
the capital city of Susa, in the area of Elam. I
was standing by the Ulai Canal 3when I looked
up and saw a male sheep standing beside the
canal. It had two long horns, but one horn was
longer and newer than the other. 4I watched
the sheep charge to the west, the north, and the
south. No animal could stand before him, and
none could save another animal from his
power. He did whatever he wanted and became very powerful.

5While I was watching this, I saw a male
goat come from the west. This goat had one
large horn between his eyes that was easy to
see. He crossed over the whole earth so fast
that his feet hardly touched the ground.

6In his anger the goat charged the sheep
with the two horns that I had seen standing
by the canal. 7I watched the angry goat attack
the sheep and break the sheep's two horns. The
sheep was not strong enough to stop it. The
goat knocked the sheep to the ground and then
walked all over him. No one was able to save
the sheep from the goat, 8so the male goat became very great. But when he was strong, his
big horn broke off and four horns grew in
place of the one big horn. Those four horns
pointed in four different directions and were
easy to see.

WHAT'S IT MEAN?

Compare the description in this verse with the story of Alexander the Great, the first king of Greece. Alexander conquered Persia and other countries throughout Asia Minor, eventually extending his kingdom as far as modern Pakistan. In 323 B.C., Alexander died at the age of thirty-three. His empire was divided into four parts.

Daniel 8:8

9Then a little horn grew from one of those
four horns, and it became very big. It grew to
the south, the east, and toward the beautiful
land of Judah. 10That little horn grew until it
reached to the sky. It even threw some of the
army of heaven to the ground and walked on
them! 11That little horn set itself up as equal to
God, the Commander of heaven's armies. It
stopped the daily sacrifices that were offered to
him, and the Temple, the place where people
worshiped him, was pulled down. 12Because
there was a turning away from God, the people
stopped the daily sacrifices. Truth was thrown
down to the ground, and the horn was successful in everything it did.

13Then I heard a holy angel speaking. Another holy angel asked the first one, "How long
will the things in this vision last—the daily sacrifices, the turning away from God that brings
destruction, the Temple being pulled down, and
the army of heaven being walked on?"

WHAT'S IT MEAN?

The nasty little horn described in these verses may refer to a Syrian king named Antiochus Epiphanes. If you were consciously trying to make yourself an enemy of God, you probably couldn't do any better than Antiochus Epiphanes did. After the Medes and Persians conquered Babylon, Antiochus Epiphanes took control of the Temple in Jerusalem. In a disgusting act of blasphemy, he built an altar to the Greek god Zeus directly over what had been the Jewish altar of burnt offering. As if that weren't bad enough, he then sacrificed a pig on the altar. (Remember, God had declared pigs to be unclean animals.) The one good thing to come from Antiochus Epiphanes' outrageous actions was that the Jews became so enraged they revolted and overthrew the Syrian leaders. Today, the Jewish people celebrate this revolution at Hanukkah.

Daniel 8:9–12

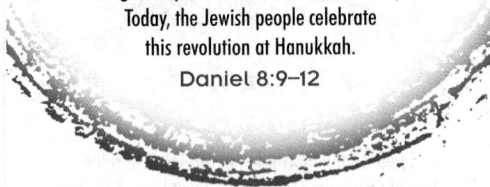

14The angel said to me, "This will happen
for twenty-three hundred evenings and mornings. Then the holy place will be repaired."
15I, Daniel, saw this vision and tried to understand what it meant. In it I saw someone
who looked like a man standing near me.
16And I heard a man's voice calling from the
Ulai Canal: "Gabriel, explain the vision to this
man."
17Gabriel came to where I was standing.
When he came close to me, I was very afraid
and bowed facedown on the ground. But Gabriel said to me, "Human being, understand
that this vision is about the time of the end."
18While Gabriel was speaking, I fell into a
deep sleep with my face on the ground. Then
he touched me and lifted me to my feet. 19He
said, "Now, I will explain to you what will
happen in the time of God's anger. Your vision
was about the set time of the end.
20"You saw a male sheep with two horns,
which are the kings of Media and Persia. 21The
male goat is the king of Greece, and the big
horn between its eyes is the first king. 22The
four horns that grew in the place of the broken
horn are four kingdoms. Those four kingdoms
will come from the nation of the first king, but
they will not be as strong as the first king.
23"When the end comes near for those kingdoms, a bold and cruel king who tells lies will
come. This will happen when many people
have turned against God. 24This king will be
very powerful, but his power will not come
from himself. He will cause terrible destruction
and will be successful in everything he does.
He will destroy powerful people and even
God's holy people. 25This king will succeed by
using lies and force. He will think that he is
very important. He will destroy many people
without warning; he will try to fight even the
Prince of princes! But that cruel king will be
destroyed, and not by human power.
26"The vision that has been shown to you
about these evenings and mornings is true. But
seal up the vision, because those things won't
happen for a long time."
27I, Daniel, became very weak and was sick
for several days after that vision. Then I got up
and went back to work for the king, but I was
very upset about the vision. I didn't understand what it meant.

DANIEL'S PRAYER

9 1These things happened during the first
year Darius son of Xerxes was king over Babylon. He was a descendant of the Medes. 2During Darius' first year as king, I, Daniel, was
reading the Scriptures. I saw that the LORD told
Jeremiah that Jerusalem would be empty ruins
for seventy years.
3Then I turned to the Lord God and prayed
and asked him for help. I did not eat any food.
To show my sadness, I put on rough cloth and
sat in ashes. 4I prayed to the LORD my God and
told him about all of our sins. I said, "Lord, you
are a great God who causes fear and wonder.
You keep your agreement of love with all who
love you and obey your commands.
5"But we have sinned and done wrong. We
have been wicked and turned against you,
your commands, and your laws. 6We did not
listen to your servants, the prophets, who
spoke for you to our kings, our leaders, our
ancestors, and all the people of the land.
7"Lord, you are good and right, but we are
full of shame today—the people of Judah and
Jerusalem, all the people of Israel, those near
and far whom you scattered among many
nations because they were not loyal to you.
8LORD, we are all ashamed. Our kings and leaders and our fathers are ashamed, because we
have sinned against you.
9"But, Lord our God, you show us mercy
and forgive us even though we have turned
against you. 10We have not obeyed the LORD
our God or the teachings he gave us through
his servants, the prophets. 11All the people of

Israel have disobeyed your teachings and have
turned away, refusing to obey you. So you
brought on us the curses and promises of
punishment written in the Teachings of Moses,
the servant of God, because we sinned against
you.
12"You said these things would happen to
us and our leaders, and you
made them happen; you
brought on us a great di-
saster. Nothing has ever
been done on earth like
what was done to
Jerusalem. 13All this
disaster came to us
just as it is written
in the Teachings of
Moses. But we have
not pleaded with the
LORD our God. We have
not stopped sinning. We
have not paid attention to
your truth. 14The LORD was
ready to bring the disaster on us, and
he did it because the LORD our God is right
in everything he does. But we still did not
obey him.
15"Lord our God, you used your power and
brought us out of Egypt. Because of that, your
name is known even today. But we have
sinned and have done wrong. 16Lord, you do
what is right, but please do not be angry with
Jerusalem, your city on your holy hill. Because
of our sins and the evil things done by our
ancestors, people all around insult and make
fun of Jerusalem and your people.
17"Now, our God, hear the prayers of your
servant. Listen to my prayer for help, and for
your sake do good things for your holy place
that is in ruins. 18My God, pay attention and
hear me. Open your eyes and see all the terrible things that have happened to us. See how
our lives have been ruined and what has happened to the city that is called by your name.
We do not ask these things because we are
good; instead, we ask because of your mercy.
19Lord, listen! Lord, forgive! Lord, hear us and
do something! For your sake, don't wait, because your city and your people are called by
your name."

"I prayed to the LORD my God and told him about all of our sins. I said, 'Lord, you are a great God who causes fear and wonder. You keep your agreement of love with all who love you and obey your commands.' "
(Daniel 9:4)

GABRIEL'S EXPLANATION

20While I was saying these things in my
prayer to the LORD, my God, confessing my
sins and the sins of the people of Israel and
praying for God's holy hill, 21Gabriel came to
me. (I had seen him in my last vision.) He came
flying quickly to me about the time of the evening sacrifice, while I was still praying. 22He
taught me and said to me, "Daniel, I have come
to give you wisdom and to help you understand. 23When you first started praying, an answer was given, and I came to tell you, because
God loves you very much. So think about the
message and understand the
vision.
24"God has ordered
four hundred ninety
years for your people
and your holy city for
these reasons: to stop
people from turning
against God; to put an
end to sin; to take
away evil; to bring in
goodness that contin-
ues forever; to bring
about the vision and
prophecy; and to appoint
a most holy place.
25"Learn and understand
these things. A command will come to rebuild
Jerusalem. The time from this command until
the appointed leader comes will be forty-nine
years and four hundred thirty-four years. Jerusalem will be rebuilt with streets and a
trench filled with water around it, but it will be
built in times of trouble. 26After the four hundred thirty-four years the appointed leader
will be killed; he will have nothing. The people
of the leader who is to come will destroy the
city and the holy place. The end of the city will
come like a flood, and war will continue until
the end. God has ordered that place to be
completely destroyed. 27That leader will make
firm an agreement with many people for seven

WHAT'S IT MEAN?

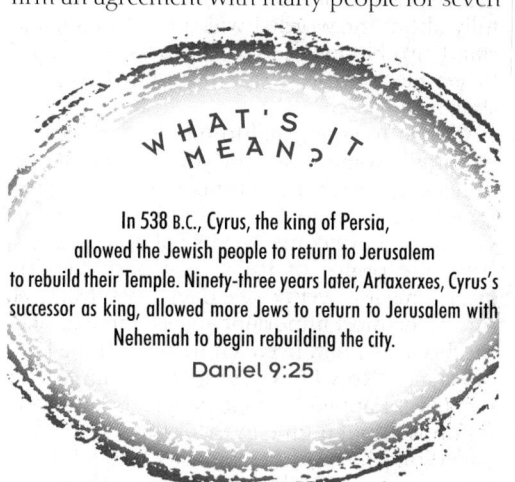

In 538 B.C., Cyrus, the king of Persia, allowed the Jewish people to return to Jerusalem to rebuild their Temple. Ninety-three years later, Artaxerxes, Cyrus's successor as king, allowed more Jews to return to Jerusalem with Nehemiah to begin rebuilding the city.

Daniel 9:25

years. He will stop the offerings and sacrifices
after three and one-half years. A destroyer will
do terrible things until the ordered end comes
to the destroyed city."

DANIEL'S VISION OF A MAN

10 1During Cyrus' third year as king of Persia,
Daniel, whose name was Belteshazzar, received
a vision about a great war. It was a true message that Daniel understood.
2At that time I, Daniel, had been very sad
for three weeks. 3I did not eat any fancy food
or meat, or drink any wine, or use any perfumed oil for three weeks.
4On the twenty-fourth day of the first
month, I was standing beside the great Tigris
River. 5While standing there, I looked up and
saw a man dressed in linen clothes with a belt
of fine gold wrapped around his waist. 6His
body was like shiny yellow quartz. His
face was bright like lightning,
and his eyes were like fire. His
arms and legs were shiny like
polished bronze, and his
voice sounded like the roar of
a crowd.

ANGELS
How impressive are angels? (10:6)

7I, Daniel, was the only
person who saw the vision. The men with me
did not see it, because they were so frightened
that they ran away and hid. 8So I was left
alone, watching this great vision. I lost my
strength, my face turned white like a dead person, and I was helpless. 9Then I heard the man
in the vision speaking. As I listened, I fell into a
deep sleep with my face on the ground.
10Then a hand touched me and set me on
my hands and knees. I was so afraid that I was
shaking. 11The man in the vision said to me,
"Daniel, God loves you very much. Think carefully about the words I will speak to you, and
stand up, because I have been sent to you."
When he said this, I stood up, but I was still
shaking.
12Then the man said to me, "Daniel, do not
be afraid. Some time ago you decided to get
understanding and to humble yourself before
your God. Since that time God has listened to
you, and I have come because of your prayers.
13But the prince of Persia has been fighting
against me for twenty-one days. Then Michael,
one of the most important angels, came to help
me, because I had been left there with the king
of Persia. 14Now I have come to explain to you
what will happen to your people, because the
vision is about a time in the future."
15While he was speaking to me, I bowed
facedown and could not speak. 16Then one
who looked like a man touched my lips, so I
opened my mouth and started to speak. I said
to the one standing in front of me, "Master, I
am upset and afraid because of what I saw in
the vision. I feel helpless. 17Master, how can I,
your servant, talk with you? My strength is
gone, and it is hard for me to breathe."
18The one who looked like a man touched
me again and gave me strength. 19He said,
"Daniel, don't be afraid. God loves you very

On the Edge

Then a hand touched me and set me on my hands and knees. I was so afraid that I was shaking. The man in the vision said to me, "Daniel, God loves you very much. Think carefully about the words I will speak to you, and stand up, because I have been sent to you" (Dan. 10:10–11a).

What a powerful story! Here we have Daniel entranced in a vision from God. When it was over, he fell down on his face and went to sleep. All of a sudden, an angel of the Lord lifted him up and told him that he was loved by God. Then several verses later, the angel said it again: "God loves you very much. Peace be with you. Be strong now; be courageous" (v. 19). And you know what? Daniel was brave and strong. You may be thinking: *If an angel of the Lord woke me up to tell me that, I'd be brave and strong, too.* Well, he already has. It's in this book. God thinks highly of *you!* He wants only the best for you. You're his child. You're his project. He wants to pour out blessings on you. God doesn't need an angel to tell you, because it's in his Word.

It doesn't matter how difficult things seem to your natural mind. You have a supernatural God! You can be brave and strong. In fact, Daniel 11:32 says that "those who know God and obey him will be *strong* and fight back" (italics added). You must realize right now that you are strong. So get out there and start doing great things for God! After all, you are loved by God. Remember, it doesn't matter what anyone else thinks of you. You're special to God. Don't forget it!

SEE FOR YOURSELF:
Deut. 31:6; Dan. 9:23; 10:18–19; 2 Tim. 1:7

much. Peace be with you. Be strong now; be
courageous."
When he spoke to me, I became stronger
and said, "Master, speak, since you have given
me strength."
[20]Then he said, "Daniel, do you know why I
have come to you? Soon I must go back to
fight against the prince of Persia. When I go,
the prince of Greece will come, [21]but I must
first tell you what is written in the Book of
Truth. No one stands with me against these enemies except Michael, the angel ruling over
your people.

11

[1]In the first year that Darius the Mede was
king, I stood up to support Michael in his fight
against the prince of Persia.

KINGDOMS OF THE SOUTH AND NORTH

[2]"Now then, Daniel, I tell you the truth:
Three more kings will rule in Persia, and then a
fourth king will come. He will be much richer
than all the kings of Persia before him and will
use his riches to get power. He will stir up
everyone against the kingdom of Greece. [3]Then
a mighty king will come, who will rule with
great power and will do anything he wants.
[4]After that king has come, his kingdom will be
broken up and divided out toward the four
parts of the world. His kingdom will not go to
his descendants, and it will not have the power
that he had, because his kingdom will be
pulled up and given to other people.
[5]"The king of the South will become strong,
but one of his commanders will become even
stronger. He will begin to rule his own kingdom with great power. [6]Then after a few years,
a new friendship will develop. The daughter of
the king of the South will marry the king of the
North in order to bring peace. But she will not
keep her power, and his family will not last.
She, her husband, her child, and those who
brought her to that country will be killed.
[7]"But a person from her family will become
king of the South and will attack the armies of
the king of the North. He will go into that king's
strong, walled city and will fight and win. [8]He
will take their gods, their metal idols, and their
valuable things made of silver and gold back to
Egypt. Then he will not bother the king of the
North for a few years. [9]Next, the king of the
North will attack the king of the South, but he
will be beaten back to his own country.
[10]"The sons of the king of the North will
prepare for war. They will get a large army together that will move through the land very
quickly, like a powerful flood. Later, that army
will come back and fight all the way to the
strong, walled city of the king of the South.
[11]Then the king of the South will become very
angry and will march out to fight against the
king of the North. The king of the North will
have a large army, but he will lose the battle,
[12]and the soldiers will be carried away. The
king of the South will then be very proud and
will kill thousands of soldiers from the northern army, but he will not continue to be successful. [13]The king of the North will gather
another army, larger than the first one. After
several years he will attack with a large army
and many weapons.
[14]"In those times many people will be
against the king of the South. Some of your
own people who love to fight will turn against
the king of the South, thinking it is time for
God's promises to come true. But they will fail.
[15]Then the king of the North will come. He will
build ramps to the tops of the city walls and
will capture a strong, walled city. The southern
army will not have the power to fight back;
even their best soldiers will not be strong
enough to stop the northern army. [16]So the
king of the North will do whatever he wants;
no one will be able to stand against him. He
will gain power and control in the beautiful
land of Israel and will have the power to destroy it. [17]The king of the North will decide to
use all his power to fight against the king of the
South, but he will make a peace agreement
with the king of the South. The king of the
North will give one of his daughters as a wife
to the king of the South so that he can defeat
him. But those plans will not succeed or help
him. [18]Then the king of the North will turn his
attention to cities along the coast of the Mediterranean Sea and will capture them. But a
commander will put an end to the pride of the
king of the North, turning his pride back on
him. [19]After that happens the king of the North
will go back to the strong, walled cities of his
own country, but he will lose his power. That
will be the end of him.
[20]"The next king of the North will send out
a tax collector so he will have plenty of money.
In a few years that ruler will be killed, although
he will not die in anger or in a battle.
[21]"That ruler will be followed by a very cruel
and hated man, who will not have the honor
of being from a king's family. He will attack the
kingdom when the people feel safe, and he will
take power by lying to the people. [22]He will
sweep away in defeat large and powerful armies and even a prince who made an agreement. [23]Many nations will make agreements
with that cruel and hated ruler, but he will lie

to them. He will gain much power, but only a few people will support him. 24The richest areas will feel safe, but that cruel and hated ruler will attack them. He will succeed where his ancestors did not. He will rob the countries he defeats and will give those things to his followers. He will plan to defeat and destroy strong cities, but he will be successful for only a short time.

25"That very cruel and hated ruler will have a large army that he will use to stir up his strength and courage. He will attack the king of the South. The king of the South will gather a large and very powerful army and prepare for war. But the people who are against him will make secret plans, and the king of the South will be defeated. 26People who were supposed to be his good friends will try to destroy him. His army will be swept away in defeat; many of his soldiers will be killed in battle. 27Those two kings will want to hurt each other. They will sit at the same table and lie to each other, but it will not do either one any good, because God has set a time for their end to come. 28The king of the North will go back to his own country with much wealth. Then he will decide to go against the holy agreement. He will take action and then return to his own country.

29"At the right time the king of the North will attack the king of the South again, but this time he will not be successful as he was before. 30Ships from the west will come and fight against the king of the North, so he will be afraid. Then he will return and show his anger against the holy agreement. He will be good to those who have stopped obeying the holy agreement.

31"The king of the North will send his army to make the Temple in Jerusalem unclean. They will stop the people from offering the daily sacrifice, and then they will set up the destroying terror. 32The king of the North will tell lies and cause those who have not obeyed God to be ruined. But those who know God and obey him will be strong and fight back.

33"Those who are wise will help the others understand what is happening. But they will be killed with swords, or burned, or taken captive, or robbed of their homes and possessions. These things will continue for many days. 34When the wise ones are suffering, they will get a little help, but many who join the wise ones will not help them in their time of need. 35Some of the wise ones will be killed. But the hard times must come so they can be made stronger and purer and without faults until the time of the end comes. Then, at the right time, the end will come.

THE KING WHO PRAISES HIMSELF

36"The king of the North will do whatever he wants. He will brag about himself and praise himself and think he is even better than a god. He will say things against the God of gods that no one has ever heard. And he will be successful until all the bad things have happened. Then what God has planned to happen will happen. 37The king of the North will not care about the gods his ancestors worshiped or the god that women worship. He won't care about any god. Instead, he will make himself more important than any god. 38The king of the North will worship power and strength, which his ancestors did not worship. He will honor the god of power with gold and silver, expensive jewels and gifts. 39That king will attack strong, walled cities with the help of a foreign god. He will give much honor to the people who join him, making them rulers in charge of many other people. And he will make them pay him for the land they rule.

40"At the time of the end, the king of the South will fight a battle against the king of the North. The king of the North will attack with chariots, soldiers on horses, and many large ships. He will invade many countries and sweep through their lands like a flood. 41The king of the North will attack the beautiful land of Judah. He will defeat many countries, but Edom, Moab, and the leaders of Ammon will be saved from him. 42The king of the North will show his power in many countries; Egypt will not escape. 43The king will get treasures of gold and silver and all the riches of Egypt. The Libyan and Nubian people will obey him. 44But the king of the North will hear news from the east and the north that will make him afraid and angry. He will go to destroy completely many nations. 45He will set up his royal tents between the sea and the beautiful mountain where the holy Temple is built. But, finally, his end will come, and no one will help him.

THE TIME OF THE END

12 1"At that time Michael, the great prince who protects your people, will stand up. There will be a time of much trouble, the worst time since nations have been on earth, but your people will be saved. Everyone whose name is written in God's book will be saved. 2Many people who have already died will live again. Some of them will wake up to have life forever, but some will wake up to find shame and disgrace forever. 3The wise people will shine like the brightness of the sky. Those who teach others to live right will shine like stars forever and ever.

4"But you, Daniel, close up the book and seal it. These things will happen at the time of the end. Many people will go here and there to find true knowledge."
5Then I, Daniel, looked, and saw two other men. One was standing on my side of the river, and the other was standing on the far side.
6The man who was dressed in linen was standing over the water in the river. One of the two men spoke to him and asked, "How long will it be before these amazing things come true?"
7The man dressed in linen, who stood over the water, raised his hands toward heaven. And I heard him swear by the name of God who lives forever, "It will be for three and one-half years. The power of the holy people will finally be broken, and then all these things will come true."
8I heard the answer, but I did not really understand, so I asked, "Master, what will happen after all these things come true?"
9He answered, "Go your way, Daniel. The message is closed up and sealed until the time
of the end. 10Many people will be made clean, pure, and spotless, but the wicked will continue to be wicked. Those wicked people will not understand these things, but the wise will understand them.
11"The daily sacrifice will be stopped. Then, after 1,290 days from that time, the destroying
terror will be set up. 12Those who wait for the end of the 1,335 days will be happy.
13"As for you, Daniel, go your way until the end. You will get your rest, and at the end you will rise to receive your reward."

DANIEL made a difference

Adults don't usually expect kids to be wise. That's why a young person with wisdom makes such an impression. Daniel proved young people can be wise. And he did it in a very difficult situation.

Daniel was taken hostage when his nation (Judah) was defeated in war. Young men were taken to Babylon to serve as slaves. But Daniel and his friends made an impression on their captors by their behavior and qualifications. They were assigned to training in the palace.

Because Daniel had already dedicated his life to God, he was faced with tough choices. He had to decide how he was going to take care of himself. For example, he chose not to eat the rich foods from the king's table. He believed that compromising his diet would lead to other compromises. But he also showed wisdom in the way he acted. His decision wasn't rude or selfish. He found a way to accomplish his goal while honoring those to whom he was responsible.

Cutting Edge

YOU can, too!

Like Daniel, refuse to do anything based on the claim that "everybody" is doing it. Those who are not willing to stand alone and be different if necessary won't make a difference with their lives, either. Even decisions about what we eat and how we work with those around us say a lot about how much we really want to honor God in the way we live. Anyone who tells you it doesn't matter how you live doesn't care about what God thinks. It's best to model your life after people who do care about his plans for them. That will help you be a better model, too, for everyone around you.

Want to know more? Read more of Daniel's early years in Daniel 1:1–21.

Hosea

CONTENT The Hebrew people struggled with idolatry throughout their whole existence. Whether they were wandering a desert, exiled in Babylon, or happy at home, they had a real problem being faithful to God. God warned them through leaders and prophets and kings, but it never failed—along would come a false god to worship and off they would go.

God used the prophet Hosea to give the people an object lesson. He asked Hosea to do something outlandish—even crazy—so the people would know how God felt about idolatry. God told Hosea to marry a prostitute, a hooker, a woman who stays with men for money. Believe it or not, Hosea did it. Her name was Gomer.

As you can guess, Gomer was not faithful to Hosea. She left him. He brought her back. She wandered away. He loved her still.

God commanded Hosea to do this because he wanted to show Hosea's people that they had treated God like Gomer treated Hosea. They wandered away, but God brought them back. They worshiped other gods, but God loved them still. God wanted them to see his love and learn to have faithful hearts.

Outline

1:1—3:5 .... Hosea's Family Is a Picture of the Lord's Unfaithful People
4:1—5:15 .... The Lord Accuses Israel, Judah, and Their Leaders
6:1—7:7 .... The People Pretend to Turn to the Lord
7:8—8:14 .... Israel Refuses to Trust the Lord
9:1-17 .... Israel Will Be Judged
10:1-15 .... Punishment for Israel
11:1-11 .... God's Love for His Faithless People
11:12—13:16 ...... Israel and Judah Are Doomed
14:1-9 .... Future Forgiveness and Blessings

Purpose God remains committed to us even when we are unfaithful to him.

Theme Return to God

Date of writing 750–720 B.C.

1
[1]The LORD spoke his word to Hosea son of
Beeri during the time that Uzziah, Jotham,
Ahaz, and Hezekiah were kings of Judah and
Jeroboam son of Jehoash was king of Israel.

HOSEA'S WIFE AND CHILDREN

[2]When the LORD began speaking through
Hosea, the LORD said to him, "Go, and marry
an unfaithful woman and
have unfaithful children, because the people in this
country have been com-
pletely unfaithful to the
LORD." [3]So Hosea mar-
ried Gomer daughter of
Diblaim, and she be-
came pregnant and gave
birth to Hosea's son.
[4]The LORD said to Ho-
sea, "Name him Jezreel, because soon I will punish the
family of Jehu for the people
they killed at Jezreel. In the future I will
put an end to the kingdom of Israel [5]and break
the power of Israel's army in the Valley of Jezreel."
[6]Gomer became pregnant again and gave
birth to a daughter. The LORD said to Hosea,
"Name her Lo-Ruhamah,[n] because I will not
pity Israel anymore, nor will I forgive them.
[7]But I will show pity to the people of Judah. I
will save them, but not by using bows or
swords, horses or horsemen, or weapons of
war. I, the LORD their God, will save them."

"Go, and marry an unfaithful woman and have unfaithful children, because the people in this country have been completely unfaithful to the LORD." (Hosea 1:2b)

WHAT'S IT MEAN?

The Israel that existed during Hosea's time was actually two separate nations. The northern kingdom, which was called Israel, had Samaria as its capital. The southern kingdom, which was called Judah, had Jerusalem as its capital. The descendants of David ruled Judah from Jerusalem, which also served as the nation's religious center.
Hosea 1:1

[8]After Gomer had stopped nursing Lo-
Ruhamah, she became pregnant again and
gave birth to another son. [9]The LORD said,
"Name him Lo-Ammi,[n] because you are not
my people, and I am not your God.

GOD'S PROMISE TO ISRAEL

[10]"But the number of the Israelites will become like the grains of sand
of the sea, which no one
can measure or count.
They were called, 'You are
not my people,' but later
they will be called 'children of the living God.'
[11]The people of Judah
and Israel will join to-
gether again and will
choose one leader for
themselves. They will
come up from the land,
because the day of Jezreel[n]
will be truly great.

2
[1]"You are to call your brothers, 'my people,'
and your sisters, 'you have been shown pity.'

GOD SPEAKS ABOUT ISRAEL

[2]"Plead with your mother.[n]
Accuse her, because she is no longer my
wife,
and I am no longer her husband.
Tell her to stop acting like a prostitute,
to stop behaving like an unfaithful wife.
[3]If she refuses, I will strip her naked
and leave her bare like the day she was
born.
I will make her dry like a desert,
like a land without water,
and I will kill her with thirst.
[4]I will not take pity on her children,
because they are the children of a
prostitute.
[5]Their mother has acted like a prostitute;
the one who became pregnant with
them has acted disgracefully.
She said, 'I will chase after my lovers,[n]
who give me my food and water,
wool and flax, wine and olive oil.'
[6]So I will block her road with thornbushes;
I will build a wall around her
so she cannot find her way.
[7]She will run after her lovers,
but she won't catch them.

1:6 Lo-Ruhamah This name in Hebrew means "not pitied." **1:9 Lo-Ammi** This name in Hebrew means "not my people." **1:11 Jezreel** This name in Hebrew means "God plants." **2:2 mother** Refers to the nation of Israel here. **2:5 lovers** Refers to the nations surrounding Israel, who led Israel to worship false gods.

She will look for them,
but she won't find them.
Then she will say, 'I will go back to my first husband,[n]
because life was better then for me than it is now.'
8 But she does not know that I was the one
who gave her grain, new wine, and oil.
I gave her much silver and gold,
but she used it for Baal.

WHAT'S IT MEAN?

Baal was the favorite god of the people who lived in Canaan before the Israelites. The Canaanites believed that Baal was responsible for making things fertile and productive, including crops, livestock, and humans. When the Israelites got to Canaan, they, too, started worshiping Baal, as well as several other Canaanite gods. Shrines to Baal were usually located on hilltops or in groves of trees. Statues of Baal were often made of gold and silver.

Hosea 2:8

9 "So I will come back and take away my grain at harvest time
and my new wine when it is ready.
I will take back my wool and linen
that covered her nakedness.
10 So I will show her nakedness to her lovers,
and no one will save her from me.
11 I will put an end to all her celebrations:
her yearly festivals, her New Moon festivals, and her Sabbaths.
I will stop all of her special feasts.
12 I will destroy her vines and fig trees,
which she said were her pay from her lovers.
I will turn them into a forest,
and wild animals will eat them.
13 I will punish her for all the times
she burned incense to the Baals.
She put on her rings and jewelry
and went chasing after her lovers,
but she forgot me!"
says the LORD.

14 "So I am going to attract her;
I will lead her into the desert
and speak tenderly to her.
15 There I will give her back her vineyards,
and I will make the Valley of Trouble a door of hope.

2:7 husband Refers to God here.

Promise

HE PROMISES YOU WILL KNOW HIM.

The LORD says, "In the future she will call me 'my husband'; no longer will she call me 'my baal.' . . . And I will make you my promised bride forever. I will be good and fair; I will show you my love and mercy. I will be true to you as my promised bride, and you will know the LORD" (Hos. 2:16, 19–20).

How do you know who God is? He says that you will know because he will give you justice, righteousness, mercy, lovingkindness, and faithfulness. He says that he will be as a husband and not as a master. In other words, he will treat you with love and tenderness and not with arrogance or harshness. He is not there to boss you around and make you work like a dog. He is there to be in love with you, to give you kindness when you don't deserve it, to be faithful to you when you aren't faithful to him, to help you live the way he wants you to, to help you reach your full potential, to know the true goodness of your heart when you do something you shouldn't, to encourage you, to understand when no one else can. It's this *unconditional love* that helps you know him.

SEE FOR YOURSELF:

2 Chr. 5:13; Ps. 91:14; Jer. 31:3; Hos. 14:4; 1 John 3:1

There she will respond as when she was young,
as when she came out of Egypt."

16 The LORD says, "In the future she will call me 'my husband';
no longer will she call me 'my baal.'[n]
17 I will never let her say the names of Baal again;
people won't use their names anymore.
18 At that time I will make an agreement for them
with the wild animals, the birds, and the crawling things.
I will smash from the land
the bow and the sword and the weapons of war,
so my people will live in safety.
19 And I will make you my promised bride forever.
I will be good and fair;
I will show you my love and mercy.
20 I will be true to you as my promised bride,
and you will know the LORD.

21 "At that time I will speak to you," says the LORD.
"I will speak to the skies,
and they will give rain to the earth.
22 The earth will produce grain, new wine, and oil;
much will grow because my people are called Jezreel.[n]
23 I will plant my people in the land,
and I will show pity to the one I had called 'not shown pity.'
I will say, 'You are my people'
to those I had called 'not my people.'
And they will say to me, 'You are our God.' "

HOSEA BUYS A WIFE

3 1 The LORD said to me again, "Go, show your
love to a woman loved by someone else, who
has been unfaithful to you. In the same way the
LORD loves the people of Israel, even though
they worship other gods and love to eat the
raisin cakes."[n]
2 So I bought her for six ounces of silver and
ten bushels of barley. 3 Then I told her, "You
must wait for me for many days. You must not
be a prostitute, and you must not have sexual
relations with any other man. I will act the
same way toward you."
4 In the same way Israel will live many days
without a king or leader, without sacrifices or
holy stone pillars, and without the holy vest or
an idol. 5 After this, the people of Israel will return to the LORD their God and follow him and
the king from David's family. In the last days
they will turn in fear to the LORD, and he will
bless them.

WHAT'S IT MEAN?

Ever had a raisin cake? If so, did you like it? In ancient times, cakes made of dried raisins were very popular. In fact, some Israelites used raisin cakes in their pagan rituals as they worshiped a goddess known as the "Queen Goddess."
Hosea 3:1

THE LORD'S WORD AGAINST ISRAEL

4 1 People of Israel, listen to the LORD's message.
The LORD has this
against you who live in the land:
"The people are not true, not loyal to God,
nor do those who live in the land even know him.
2 Cursing, lying, killing, stealing and adultery are everywhere.
One murder follows another.
3 Because of this the land dries up,
and all its people are dying.
Even the wild animals and the birds of the air
and the fish of the sea are dying.

GOD'S CASE AGAINST THE PRIESTS

4 "No one should accuse
or blame another person.
Don't blame the people, you priests,
when they quarrel with you.
5 You will be ruined in the day,
and your prophets will be ruined with you in the night.

2:16 baal Another Hebrew word for husband, but it was the same word as the false god Baal.
2:22 Jezreel This name in Hebrew means "God plants." **3:1 raisin cakes** This food was eaten in the feasts that honored false gods.

I will also destroy your mother.[n]
6 My people will be
destroyed,
because they have
no knowledge.
You have refused to learn,
so I will refuse to let
you be priests to me.
You have forgotten the
teachings of your God,
so I will forget your children.
7 The more priests there are,
the more they sin against me.
I will take away their honor
and give them shame.
8 Since the priests live off the sin offerings of
the people,
they want the people to sin more and
more.
9 The priests are as wrong as the people,
and I will punish them both for what
they have done.
I will repay them for the wrong they
have done.

DISOBEDIENCE
What if we neglect God's word? (4:6)

10 "They will eat
but not have enough;
they will have sexual relations with the
prostitutes,
but they will not have children,
because they have left the LORD
to give themselves to 11 prostitution,
to old and new wine,
which take away their ability to
understand.

GOD'S CASE AGAINST THE PEOPLE

12 "My people ask wooden idols for advice;
they ask those sticks of wood to advise
them!
Like prostitutes, they have chased after
other gods
and have left their own God.
13 They make sacrifices on the tops of the
mountains.
They burn offerings on the hills,
under oaks, poplars, and other trees,
because their shade is nice.
So your daughters become prostitutes,
and your daughters-in-law are guilty of
adultery.

14 "But I will not punish your daughters
for becoming prostitutes,
nor your daughters-in-law
for their sins of adultery.
I will not punish them,
because the men have sexual relations
with prostitutes
and offer sacrifices with the temple
prostitutes.
A foolish people will be ruined.

15 "Israel, you act like a prostitute,
but do not be guilty toward the LORD.
Don't go to Gilgal
or go up to Beth Aven.[n]
Don't make promises,
saying, 'As surely as the LORD lives . . .'
16 The people of Israel are stubborn
like a stubborn young cow.
Now the LORD will feed them
like lambs in the open country.
17 The Israelites have chosen to worship
idols,
so leave them alone.
18 When they finish their drinking,
they completely give themselves to being
prostitutes;
they love these disgraceful ways.
19 They will be swept away as if by a
whirlwind,
and their sacrifices will bring them only
shame.

GOD'S WORD AGAINST THE LEADERS

5
1 "Listen, you priests.
Pay attention, people of Israel.
Listen, royal family,
because you will all be judged.

WHAT'S IT MEAN?

In case you're not familiar with Canaanite geography, we'll tell you that Mizpah was located near Jerusalem and Mount Tabor is located in the northern part of the land, near Lake Galilee. In other words, Israel's idol worship stretched from one end of the nation to the other.

Hosea 5:1

4:5 mother Refers to the nation of Israel here. **4:15 Gilgal . . . Beth Aven** Cities in Israel where people worshiped false gods.

You have been like a trap at Mizpah
and like a net spread out at Mount Tabor.
2 You have done many evil things,
so I will punish you all.
3 I know all about the people of Israel;
what they have done is not hidden from me.
Now that Israel acts like a prostitute,
it has made itself unclean.

4 "They will not give up their deeds
and return to their God.
They are determined to be unfaithful to me;
they do not know the LORD.
5 Israel's pride testifies against them.
The people of Israel will stumble because of their sin,
and the people of Judah will stumble with them.
6 They will come to worship the LORD,
bringing their flocks and herds,
but they will not be able to find him,
because he has left them.
7 They have not been true to the LORD;
they are children who do not belong to him.
So their false worship
will destroy them and their land.

8 "Blow the horn in Gibeah
and the trumpet in Ramah.
Give the warning at Beth Aven,
and be first into battle, people of Benjamin.
9 Israel will be ruined
on the day of punishment.
To the tribes of Israel
I tell the truth.
10 The leaders of Judah are like those
who steal other people's land.
I will pour my punishment over them
like a flood of water.
11 Israel is crushed by the punishment,
because it decided to follow idols.
12 I am like a moth to Israel,
like a rot to the people of Judah.

13 "When Israel saw its illness
and Judah saw its wounds,
Israel went to Assyria for help
and sent to the great king of Assyria.
But he cannot heal you
or cure your wounds.
14 I will be like a lion to Israel,
like a young lion to Judah.
I will attack them
and tear them to pieces.
I will drag them off,
and no one will be able to save them.
15 Then I will go back to my place
until they suffer for their guilt and turn back to me.
In their trouble they will look for me."

THE PEOPLE ARE NOT FAITHFUL

6

1 "Come, let's go back to the LORD.
He has hurt us, but he will heal us.
He has wounded us, but he will bandage our wounds.
2 In two days he will put new life in us;
on the third day he will raise us up
so that we may live in his presence 3 and know him.
Let's try to learn about the LORD;
he will come to us as surely as the dawn comes.
He will come to us like rain,
like the spring rain that waters the ground."

4 The LORD says, "Israel, what should I do with you?
Judah, what should I do with you?
Your faithfulness is like a morning mist,
like the dew that goes away early in the day.
5 I have warned you by my prophets
that I will kill you and destroy you.
My justice comes out like bright light.
6 I want faithful love
more than I want animal sacrifices.
I want people to know me
more than I want burnt offerings.
7 But they have broken the agreement as Adam did;
they have been unfaithful to me.
8 Gilead is a city of people who do evil;
their footprints are bloody.
9 The priests are like robbers waiting to attack people;
they murder people on the road to Shechem[n]
and do wicked things.
10 I have seen horrible things in Israel.
Look at Israel's prostitution;
Israel has become unclean.

6:9 Shechem A city of safety where people could go for protection.

11 "Judah, I have set a harvest time for you
when I will make the lives of my people
good again.

7

1 When I heal Israel,
Israel's sin will go away,
and so will Samaria's evil.

"They cheat a lot!
Thieves break into houses,
and robbers are in the streets.
2 It never enters their minds
that I remember all their evil deeds.
The bad things they do are all around
them;
they are right in front of me.

ISRAEL'S EVIL KINGS

3 "They make the king happy with their
wickedness;
their rulers are glad with their lies.
4 But all of them are traitors.
They are like an oven heated by a
baker.
While he mixes the dough,
he does not need to stir up the fire.
5 The kings get so drunk they get sick every
day.
The rulers become crazy with wine;
they make agreements with those who
do not know the true God.
6 They burn like an oven;
their hearts burn inside them.
All night long their anger is low,
but when morning comes, it becomes a
roaring fire.
7 All these people are as hot as an oven;
they burn up their rulers.
All their kings fall,
and no one calls on me.

ISRAEL AND THE OTHER NATIONS

8 "Israel mixes with other nations;
he is like a pancake cooked only on one
side.
9 Foreign nations have eaten up his strength,
but he doesn't know it.
Israel is weak and feeble, like an old man,
but he doesn't know it.
10 Israel's pride will cause their defeat;
they will not turn back to the LORD their
God
or look to him for help in all this.
11 Israel has become like a pigeon—
easy to fool and stupid.
First they call to Egypt for help.
Then they run to Assyria.
12 When they go, I will catch them in a net,
I will bring them down like birds from
the sky;
I will punish them countless times for
their evil.
13 How terrible for them
because they left me!
They will be destroyed,
because they turned
against me.
I want to save them,
but they have spoken lies
against me.
14 They do not call to me from their hearts.
They just lie on their beds and cry.
They come together to ask for grain and
new wine,
but they really turn away from me.
15 Though I trained them and gave them
strength,
they have made evil plans against me.
16 They did not turn to the Most High God.
They are like a loose bow that can't
shoot.
Because their leaders brag about their
strength,
they will be killed with swords,
and the people in Egypt
will laugh at them.

SIN

What does God think of our sin? (7:13)

WHAT'S IT MEAN?

For a while, Israel paid "protection money"—in the form of taxes—to Assyria to keep them from attacking. When the Israelites got tired of giving their hard-earned money to a foreign king, they decided to team up with the Egyptians and fight Assyria. In 722 B.C., the Assyrians responded by attacking Samaria, the capital of the northern kingdom, and taking the people of Israel captive. The northern kingdom never recovered from the devastation.

Hosea 7:11

ISRAEL HAS TRUSTED WRONG THINGS

8

1 "Put the trumpet to your lips and give the
warning!
The enemy swoops down on the LORD's
people like an eagle.
The Israelites have broken my agreement
and have turned against my teachings.
2 They cry out to me,

'Our God, we in Israel know you!'
3 But Israel has rejected what is good,
so the enemy will chase them.
4 They chose their own kings
without asking my permission.
They chose their own leaders,
people I did not know.
They made their silver and gold into idols,
and for all this they will be destroyed.
5 I hate the calf-shaped idol of Israel!
I am very angry with the people.
How long will they remain unclean?
6 The idol is something a craftsman made;
it is not God.
Israel's calf-shaped idol will surely be smashed to pieces.

"Israel has forgotten their Maker and has built palaces; Judah has built many strong, walled cities." (Hosea 8:14a)

7 "Israel's foolish plans are like planting the wind,
but they will harvest a storm.
Like a stalk with no head of grain,
it produces nothing.
Even if it produced something,
other nations would eat it.
8 Israel is eaten up;
the people are mixed among the other nations
and have become useless to me.
9 Israel is like a wild donkey all by itself.
They have run to Assyria;
They have hired other nations to protect them.
10 Although Israel is mixed among the nations,
I will gather them together.

WHAT'S IT MEAN?

The "calf"-shaped idol was one that people worshiped in Samaria. The capital city of the northern kingdom had the dubious distinction of being the center of the nation's pagan worship. Calves and bulls were especially popular idols in ancient times. People believed the animals symbolized fertility.

Hosea 8:5

They will become weaker and weaker
as they suffer under the great king of Assyria.

11 "Although Israel built more altars to remove sin,
they have become altars for sinning.
12 I have written many teachings for them,
but they think the teachings are strange and foreign.
13 The Israelites offer sacrifices to me as gifts
and eat the meat,
but the LORD is not pleased with them.
He remembers the evil they have done,
and he will punish them for their sins.
They will be slaves again as they were in Egypt.
14 Israel has forgotten their Maker and has built palaces;
Judah has built many strong, walled cities.
But I will send fire on their cities
and destroy their strong buildings."

ISRAEL'S PUNISHMENT

9
1 Israel, do not rejoice;
don't shout for joy as the other nations do.
You have been like a prostitute against your God.
You love the pay of prostitutes on every threshing floor.
2 But the threshing floor and the winepress will not feed the people,
and there won't be enough new wine.
3 The people will not stay in the LORD's land.
Israel will return to being captives as they were in Egypt,
and in Assyria they will eat food that they are not allowed to eat.
4 The Israelites will not give offerings of wine to the LORD;
they will not give him sacrifices.
Their sacrifices will be like food that is eaten at a funeral;
it is unclean, and everyone who eats it becomes unclean.
Their food will only satisfy their hunger;
they cannot sacrifice it in the Temple.

WHAT'S IT MEAN?

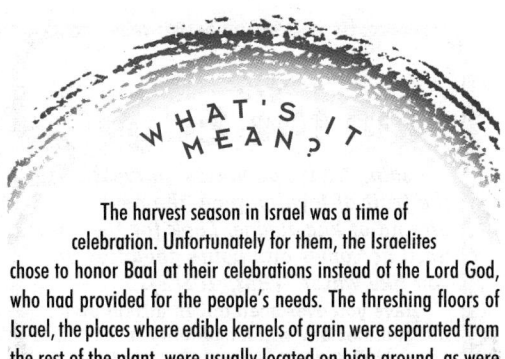

The harvest season in Israel was a time of celebration. Unfortunately for them, the Israelites chose to honor Baal at their celebrations instead of the Lord God, who had provided for the people's needs. The threshing floors of Israel, the places where edible kernels of grain were separated from the rest of the plant, were usually located on high ground, as were shrines to Baal. As you might imagine, the practices at the two sites were often combined.

Hosea 9:1

5 What will you do then on the day of
feasts
and on the day of the LORD's festival?
6 Even if the people are not destroyed,
Egypt will capture them;
Memphis[n] will bury them.
Weeds will grow over their silver treasures,
and thorns will drive them out of their
tents.
7 The time of punishment has come,
the time to pay for sins.
Let Israel know this:
You think the prophet is a fool,
and you say the spiritual person is
crazy.
You have sinned very much,
and your hatred is great.

WHAT'S IT MEAN?

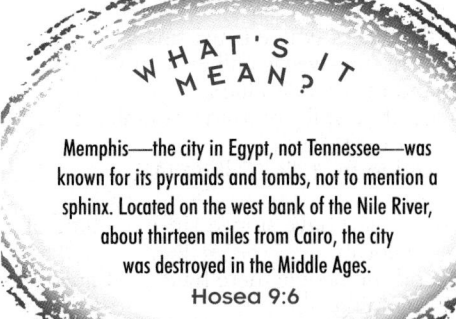

Memphis—the city in Egypt, not Tennessee—was known for its pyramids and tombs, not to mention a sphinx. Located on the west bank of the Nile River, about thirteen miles from Cairo, the city was destroyed in the Middle Ages.

Hosea 9:6

8 Is Israel a watchman?
Are God's people prophets?
Everywhere Israel goes, traps are set for
him.
He is an enemy in God's house.
9 The people of Israel have gone deep into
sin
as the people of Gibeah[n] did.
The Lord will remember the evil things
they have done,
and he will punish their sins.

10 "When I found Israel,
it was like finding grapes in the desert.
Your ancestors were like
finding the first figs on the fig tree.
But when they came to Baal Peor,
they began worshiping an idol,
and they became as hateful as the thing
they worshiped.
11 Israel's glory will fly away like a bird;
there will be no more pregnancy, no
more births, no more getting
pregnant.
12 But even if the Israelites bring up children,
I will take them all away.
How terrible it will be for them
when I go away from them!
13 I have seen Israel, like Tyre,
given a pleasant place.
But the people of Israel will soon bring
out
their children to be killed."
14 LORD, give them what they should have.
What will you give them?
Make their women unable to have
children;
give them dried-up breasts that cannot
feed their babies.

15 "The Israelites were very wicked in Gilgal,
so I have hated them there.
Because of the sinful things they have done,
I will force them to leave my land.
I will no longer love them;
their leaders have turned against me.
16 Israel is beaten down;
its root is dying, and it has no fruit.
If they have more children,
I will kill the children they love."

17 God will reject them,
because they have not obeyed him;
they will wander among the nations.

9:6 Memphis A city in Egypt famous for its tombs. **9:9 Gibeah** The sins of the people of Gibeah caused a civil war. See Judges 19–21.

ISRAEL WILL PAY FOR SIN

10 [1]Israel is like a large vine
that produced plenty of fruit.
As the people became richer,
they built more altars for idols.
As their land became better,
they put up better stone pillars to honor gods.
[2]Their heart was false,
and now they must pay for their guilt.
The LORD will break down their altars;
he will destroy their holy stone pillars.

[3]Then they will say, "We have no king,
because we didn't honor the LORD.
As for the king,
he couldn't do anything for us."
[4]They make many false promises
and agreements which they don't keep.
So people sue each other in court;
they are like poisonous weeds growing in a plowed field.
[5]The people from Israel are worried about
the calf-shaped idol at Beth Aven.
The people will cry about it,
and the priests will cry about it.
They used to shout for joy about its glory,
[6]but it will be carried off to Assyria
as a gift to the great king.
Israel will be disgraced,
and the people will be ashamed for not obeying.
[7]Israel will be destroyed;
its king will be like a chip of wood floating on the water.
[8]The places of false worship will be destroyed,
the places where Israel sins.
Thorns and weeds will grow up
and cover their altars.
Then they will say to the mountains,
"Cover us!"
and to the hills, "Fall on us!"

[9]"Israel, you have sinned since the time of Gibeah,[n]
and the people there have continued sinning.
But war will surely overwhelm them in Gibeah,
because of the evil they have done there.
[10]When I am ready,

On the Edge

I said, "Plant goodness, harvest the fruit of loyalty, plow the new ground of knowledge. Look for the LORD until he comes and pours goodness on you like water" (Hos. 10:12).

Have you ever been out in a field on a hot summer day when suddenly it started to pour rain? You got soaking wet, and felt totally refreshed! Think about this verse for a moment. It says that God will send his goodness like rain when we worship him. Are you ready for some of that rain? Do you want it to drench your friends and family? Don't you just want everybody you meet to get soaked with God's saving rain? Did you know you can be a rainmaker? When we worship the Lord, he pours out his refreshing rain! God's thunderstorms are rolling into your circumstances, ready to rain down his saving power! So the next time it starts raining outside, let that be a reminder of what God wants to do in your life.

SEE FOR YOURSELF:
Ps. 20:6; 33:20; 37:40; 109:26; Acts 3:19

WHAT'S IT MEAN?

Those who don't learn from history are destined to repeat it. To prove the point, we offer the example of Jeroboam, Solomon's son. This shortsighted king decided to have two golden calves made. These idols were then placed in Bethel and Dan to make them convenient for worshipers in the northern kingdom. If the whole golden calf thing sounds familiar, it's because Aaron made the same mistake—committed the same sin—centuries earlier while Moses was on Mount Sinai talking to God. Would it surprise you to learn that God was every bit as angry at Jeroboam and his followers as he was at Aaron and his followers?

Hosea 10:5

10:9 Gibeah The sins of the people of Gibeah caused a civil war. See Judges 19–21.

I will come to punish them.
Nations will come together against them,
and they will be punished for their
double sins.
11 Israel is like a well-trained young cow
that likes to thresh grain.
I will put a yoke on her neck
and make her work hard in the field.
Israel will plow,
and Judah will break up the ground.
12 I said, 'Plant goodness,
harvest the fruit of loyalty,
plow the new ground of knowledge.
Look for the LORD until he comes
and pours goodness on you like water.'
13 But you have plowed evil
and harvested trouble;
you have eaten the fruit of your lies.
Because you have trusted in your own
power
and your many soldiers,
14 your people will hear the noise of battle,
and all your strong, walled cities will be
destroyed.
It will be like the time King Shalman
destroyed Beth Arbel in battle,
when mothers and their children were
bashed to death.
15 The same will happen to you, people of
Bethel,
because you did so much evil.
When the sun comes up,
the king of Israel will die.

GOD'S LOVE FOR ISRAEL

11 1 "When Israel was a child, I
loved him,
and I called my son out
of Egypt.
2 But when I called the
people of Israel,
they went away from me.
They offered sacrifices to the Baals
and burned incense to the idols.
3 It was I who taught Israel to walk,
and I took them by the arms,
but they did not understand
that I had healed them.
4 I led them with cords of human kindness,
with ropes of love.
I lifted the yoke from their neck
and bent down and fed them.

GOD
Does God love his people? (11:1)

5 "The Israelites will become captives again,
as they were in Egypt,
and Assyria will become their king,
because they refuse to turn back to God.
6 War will sweep through their cities
and will destroy them
and kill them because of their wicked
plans.
7 My people have made up their minds
to turn away from me.
The prophets call them to turn to me,
but none of them honors me at all.

8 "Israel, how can I give you up?
How can I give you away, Israel?
I don't want to make you like Admah
or treat you like Zeboiim.[n]
My heart beats for you,
and my love for you stirs up my pity.
9 I won't punish you in my anger,
and I won't destroy Israel again.
I am God and not a human;
I am the Holy One, and I am among
you.
I will not come against you in anger.
10 They will go after the LORD,
and he will roar like a lion.
When he roars,
his children will hurry to him from the
west.
11 They will come swiftly
like birds from Egypt
and like doves from Assyria.
I will settle them again in their homes,"
says the LORD.

THE LORD IS AGAINST ISRAEL

12 Israel has surrounded me with lies;
the people have made evil plans.
And Judah turns against God,
the faithful Holy One.

12 1 What Israel does is as useless as chasing
the wind;
he chases the east wind all day.
They tell more and more lies
and do more and more violence.
They make agreements with Assyria,
and they send a gift of olive oil to Egypt.
2 The LORD also has some things against
Judah.
He will punish Israel for what they have
done;
he will give them what they deserve.
3 Their ancestor Jacob held on to his
brother's heel
while the two of them were being born.
When he grew to be a man,

11:8 Admah . . . Zeboiim Two other cities destroyed when God destroyed Sodom and Gomorrah.

he wrestled with God.
4 When Jacob wrestled with the angel and
won,
he cried and asked for his blessing.
Later, God met with him at Bethel
and spoke with him there.
5 It was the LORD God All-Powerful;
the LORD is his great name.
6 You must return to your God;
love him, do what is just,
and always trust in him as your God.

7 The merchants use dishonest scales;
they like to cheat people.
8 Israel said, "I am rich! I am someone with
power!"
All their money will do them no good
because of the sins they have done.

9 "But I am the LORD your God,
who brought you out of Egypt.
I will make you live in tents again
as you used to do on worship days.
10 I spoke to the prophets
and gave them many visions;
through them, I taught my lessons to
you."

11 The people of Gilead are evil,
worth nothing.
Though people sacrifice bulls at Gilgal,
their altars will become like piles of
stone
in a plowed field.
12 Your ancestor Jacob fled to Northwest
Mesopotamia
where he worked to get a wife;
he tended sheep to pay for her.
13 Later the LORD used a prophet
to bring Jacob's descendants out of
Egypt;
he used a prophet
to take care of the Israelites.
14 But the Israelites made the Lord angry
when they killed other people,
and they deserve to die for their crimes.
The Lord will make them pay
for the disgraceful things they have
done.

On the Edge

I, the LORD, have been your God since you were in the land of Egypt. You should have known no other God except me. I am the only one who saves (Hos. 13:4).

Check out the last part of this verse. Did you know that in the Hebrew, the word for "one who saves" means "Victor," "Deliverer," "Rescuer"? Since Jesus is your Savior, that means that he is your rescuer from darkness to light. You have been delivered, and you are victorious! The only way this can happen is with Jesus in your life. Jesus is the only way to God, and God is the only One who can save. In fact, Romans 10:13 says that "anyone who calls on the Lord will be saved." This word *saved*, in the Greek, is translated in several ways: "to be rescued from danger"; "to save from suffering and disease"; "to make well"; "to heal and restore to health"; "to make whole." This should get you excited! Not only is God the only One who can save you from sin, but he is the only One who can rescue you from evil. He is the only One who can save you from suffering and disease. He is the only One who can truly make you well, the only One who can heal and restore your health.

There are so many people that you rub shoulders with every day who are searching for a remedy in their lives. You have that cure, and his name is Jesus! Let them know you have the answer they've been looking for. He is the only One who saves!

SEE FOR YOURSELF:
John 6:44; Rom. 10:13; Col. 1:13

THE FINAL WORD AGAINST ISRAEL

13

1 People used to fear the tribe of Ephraim;
they were important people in Israel.
But they sinned by worshiping Baal,
so they must die.
2 But they still keep on sinning more and
more.
They make idols of their silver,
idols that are cleverly made,
the work of a craftsman.
Yet the people of Israel say to each other,
"Kiss those calf idols and sacrifice to
them."
3 So those people will be like the morning
mist;
they will disappear like the morning
dew.
They will be like chaff blown from the
threshing floor,
like smoke going out a window.

[4]"I, the LORD, have been your God
since you were in the land of Egypt.
You should have known no other God
except me.
I am the only one who saves.
[5]I cared for them in the desert
where it was hot and dry.
[6]I gave them food, and they became full
and satisfied.
But then they became too proud and
forgot me.
[7]That is why I will be like a lion to them,
like a leopard waiting by the road.
[8]I will attack like a bear robbed of her
cubs,
ripping their bodies open.
I will devour them like a lion
and tear them apart like a wild animal.

[9]"Israel, I will destroy you.
Who will be your helper then?
[10]What good is your king?
Can he save you in any of your towns?
What good are your leaders?
You said, 'Give us a king and leaders.'
[11]So I gave you a king, but only in anger,
and I took him away in my great anger.
[12]The sins of Israel are on record,
stored away, waiting for punishment.
[13]The pain of birth will come for him,
but he is like a foolish baby
who won't come out of its mother's
womb.
[14]Will I save them from the place of the
dead?
Will I rescue them from death?
Where is your sickness, death?
Where is your pain, place of death?
I will show them no mercy.
[15]Israel is doing well among the nations,
but the LORD will send a wind from the
east,
coming from the desert,
that will dry up his springs and wells of
water.
He will destroy from their treasure houses
everything of value.
[16]The nation of Israel will be ruined,
because it fought against God.
The people of Israel will die in war;
their children will be torn to pieces,
and their pregnant women will be
ripped open."

ISRAEL RETURNS TO GOD

14

[1]Israel, return to the LORD your God,
because your sins have made you fall.
[2]Come back to the LORD
and say these words to him:
"Take away all our sin
and kindly receive us,

Promise HE PROMISES TO LOVE YOU FREELY.

I will forgive them for leaving me and will love them freely, because I am not angry with them anymore (Hos. 14:4).

A father says to his son, "I've loved you for years. I've done my best. But this is it. You've gone too far this time. I want you out of my house. I don't even love you anymore. You are no longer my son." A boyfriend says to his girlfriend, "I really did love you, but now that we've had sex, it's different. I just don't feel the same. I guess it's over." A coach says to his team, "You guys better pull yourselves together. If we don't win tonight, I don't ever want to see your faces again!"

Limits. Conditions. Terms. Humans have a hard time loving without limits, so it can be hard to imagine a God who does. But that's his promise—to freely love you beyond anything you've ever experienced here on earth. He sees your scars. He's even been hurt by your sin and by the times you've rejected him. And he still loves you. He will never kick you out, never love-you-and-leave-you, never throw you off the team. We humans just can't grasp a limitless love. So you'll have to trust him. He'll prove it.

SEE FOR YOURSELF:

Ps. 36:10; Jer. 31:3; Lam. 3:22; 1 John 3:1; 4:7–11

and we will keep the promises we made to
you.
[3]Assyria cannot save us,
nor will we trust in our horses.
We will not say again, 'Our gods,'
to the things our hands have made.
You show mercy to orphans."

[4]The LORD says,
"I will forgive them for leaving me
and will love them freely,
because I am not angry with them
anymore.
[5]I will be like the dew to Israel,
and they will blossom like a lily.
Like the cedar trees in Lebanon,
their roots will be firm.
[6]They will be like spreading branches,
like the beautiful olive trees
and the sweet-smelling cedars in
Lebanon.
[7]The people of Israel will again live under
my protection.
They will grow like the grain,
they will bloom like a vine,
and they will be as famous as the wine
of Lebanon.
[8]Israel, have nothing to do with idols.
I, the LORD, am the one who answers
your prayers and watches over
you.
I am like a green pine tree;
your blessings come from me."

[9]A wise person will know these things,
and an understanding person will take
them to heart.
The LORD's ways are right.
Good people live by following
them,
but those who turn against God die
because of them.

joel

CONTENT Life pretty much seems in our control, doesn't it? If we work hard in school, we get good grades. If we get good grades, we'll get a good job one day. If we plant crops, they will grow. If we feed our dog, he will stick around. Sometimes life seems so certain and so sure that we forget how fragile it is.

That's how it was for the people of Joel's day. Things were going pretty well. There hadn't been a disaster in a while. Tragedy seemed far away. There was only one problem: The people were still not being faithful to God and, even if circumstances felt good, judgment was on its way.

Joel's message was about those consequences, and they came in the form of flying grasshopper-type insects that could strip a farmer's land in almost the time it took them to fly across it. These grasshoppers were called locusts. Joel's warning about locusts reminded his people that life is not in our control. We need God's help to face the future as well as the present. We can't just live as if God is unnecessary when any minute the locusts will be on their way.

Outline

1:1—2:17 .... Locusts and an Enemy Army
2:18–32 .... The Lord Will Bless His People
3:1–21 .... The Lord Will Punish the Nations

Purpose Repent and avoid judgment by God.

Theme The Judgment and Grace of God

Date of writing 830 or 600 B.C.

LOCUSTS DESTROY THE CROPS

1 [1]The LORD spoke his word to Joel son of
Pethuel:
[2]Older leaders, listen to this message.
Listen to me, all you who live in the
land.
Nothing like this has ever happened
during your lifetime
or during your ancestors' lifetimes.
[3]Tell your children about these things,
let your children tell their children,
and let your grandchildren tell their
children.
[4]What the cutting locusts have left,
the swarming locusts have eaten;
what the swarming locusts have left,
the hopping locusts have eaten,
and what the hopping locusts have left,
the destroying locusts[n] have eaten.

WHAT'S IT MEAN?

At first glance, the locust seems like a pretty unlikely creature of destruction. It looks like a large grasshopper with two sets of wings and a brown-colored body two to three inches long. Nothing to be worried about, right? Did we mention that locusts travel in swarms large enough to blot out the sun in the sky? An average-size swarm of locusts, numbering in the millions, can strip a field completely bare—down to its last leaf—within minutes.

Joel 1:4

[5]Drunks, wake up and cry!
All you people who drink wine, cry!
Cry because your wine
has been taken away from your
mouths.
[6]A powerful nation has come into my land
with too many soldiers to count.
It has teeth like a lion,
jaws like a female lion.
[7]It has made my grapevine a waste
and made my fig tree a stump.
It has stripped all the bark off my trees
and left the branches white.
[8]Cry as a young woman cries
when the man she was going to marry
has died.
[9]There will be no more grain or drink
offerings
to offer in the Temple of the LORD.
Because of this, the priests,
the servants of the LORD, are sad.
[10]The fields are ruined;
the ground is dried up.
The grain is destroyed,
the new wine is dried up,
and the olive oil runs out.
[11]Be sad, farmers.
Cry loudly, you who grow grapes.
Cry for the wheat and the barley.
Cry because the harvest of the field is
lost.
[12]The vines have become dry,
and the fig trees are dried up.
The pomegranate trees, the date palm
trees, the apple trees—
all the trees in the field have died.
And the happiness of the people has died,
too.
[13]Priests, put on your rough cloth and cry
to show your sadness.
Servants of the altar, cry out loud.
Servants of my God,
keep your rough cloth on all night to
show your sadness.
Cry because there will be no more grain
or drink offerings
to offer in the Temple of your God.
[14]Call for a day when no one eats food!
Tell everyone to stop work!
Bring the older leaders
and everyone who lives in the land
to the Temple of the LORD your God,
and cry out to the LORD.
[15]What a terrible day it will be!
The LORD's day of judging is near,
when punishment will come
like a destroying attack from the
Almighty.

[16]Our food is taken away
while we watch.
Joy and happiness are gone
from the Temple of our God.
[17]Though we planted fig seeds,
they lie dry and dead in the dirt.
The barns are empty and falling down.

1:4 cutting . . . locusts These are different names for an insect like a large grasshopper. The locust can quickly destroy trees, plants, and crops, and in this destruction Joel sees a warning. God will cause this type of destruction when he punishes his people.

The storerooms for grain have been
broken down,
because the grain has dried up.
18 The animals are groaning!
The herds of cattle wander around
confused,
because they have no grass to
eat;
even the flocks of sheep
suffer.
19 LORD, I am calling to you
for help,
because fire has burned up
the open pastures,
and flames have burned all
the trees in the field.
20 Wild animals also need your help.
The streams of water have dried up,
and fire has burned up the open
pastures.

"What a terrible day it will be! The LORD's day of judging is near." (Joel 1:15a)

THE COMING DAY OF JUDGMENT

2 1 Blow the trumpet in Jerusalem;
shout a warning on my holy mountain.
Let all the people who live in the land
shake with fear,
because the LORD's day of judging is
coming;
it is near.
2 It will be a dark, gloomy day,
cloudy and black.
Like the light at sunrise,
a great and powerful army will spread
over the mountains.
There has never been anything like it
before,
and there will never be anything like it
again.

WHAT'S IT MEAN?

Two questions need to be answered here: (1) Where is the holy mountain? (2) What's with the trumpet? The mountain is Mount Zion, the hill in Jerusalem where Solomon built the first Temple. The trumpet was an ancestor of the modern church bell. It was used to call people together for religious ceremonies and special festivals. Occasionally it was used to sound an alarm or to call troops to battle.

Joel 2:1

3 In front of them a fire destroys;
in back of them a flame burns.
The land in front of them is like the
garden of Eden;
the land behind them is
like an empty desert.
Nothing will escape from
them.
4 They look like horses,
and they run like war
horses.
5 It is like the noise of
chariots
rumbling over the tops of
the mountains,
like the noise of a roaring fire
burning dry stalks.
They are like a powerful army lined up for
battle.
6 When they see them, nations shake with
fear,
and everyone's face becomes pale.

7 They charge like soldiers;
they climb over the wall like warriors.
They all march straight ahead
and do not move off their path.
8 They do not run into each other,
because each walks in line.
They break through all efforts to stop
them
and keep coming.
9 They run into the city.
They run at the wall
and climb into the houses,
entering through windows like thieves.

10 Before them, earth and sky shake.
The sun and the moon become dark,
and the stars stop shining.
11 The LORD shouts out orders
to his army.
His army is very large!
Those who obey him are very strong!
The LORD's day of judging
is an overwhelming and terrible day.
No one can stand up against it!

CHANGE YOUR HEARTS

12 The LORD says, "Even now, come back to
me with all your heart.
Go without food, and cry and be sad."

13 Tearing your clothes is not enough to
show you are sad;
let your heart be broken.
Come back to the LORD your God,

because he is kind and shows mercy.
He doesn't become angry quickly,
and he has great love.
He can change his mind about doing
harm.
14 Who knows? Maybe he will turn back to
you
and leave behind a blessing for you.
Grain and drink offerings belong to the
LORD your God.

15 Blow the trumpet in Jerusalem;
call for a day when no one eats food.
Tell everyone to stop work.
16 Bring the people together
and make the meeting holy for the
LORD.
Bring together the older leaders,
as well as the children,
and even babies that still feed at their
mothers' breasts.
The bridegroom should come from his
room,
the bride from her bedroom.
17 The priests, the LORD's servants, should cry
between the altar and the entrance to
the Temple.
They should say, "LORD, have mercy on
your people.
Don't let them be put to shame;
don't let other nations make fun of
them.
Don't let people in other nations ask,
'Where is their God?'"

THE LORD RESTORES THE LAND

18 Then the LORD became concerned about
his land
and felt sorry for his people.
19 He said to them:
"I will send you grain, new wine, and
olive oil,
so that you will have plenty.
No more will I shame you
among the nations.
20 I will force the army from the north to
leave your land
and go into a dry, empty land.
Their soldiers in front will be forced into
the Dead Sea,
and those in the rear into the
Mediterranean Sea.
Their bodies will rot and stink.
The LORD has surely done a wonderful
thing!"

21 Land, don't be afraid;
be happy and full of joy,
because the LORD has done a wonderful
thing.

Promise HE PROMISES HIS SPIRIT TO EVERYONE.

After this, I will pour out my Spirit on all kinds of people. Your sons and daughters will prophesy, your old men will dream dreams, and your young men will see visions (Joel 2:28).

As you know, the Book of Joel is a book of prophecy—a book that tells what would happen in the future. Joel prophesied that a time would come on earth when God would give his Spirit to everyone. God would even use young people, Joel said, to prophesy from visions—to speak God's words and proclaim the Good News.

Joel's prophecy came true in the second chapter of Acts. The Holy Spirit fell on a group of believers and changed the world forever. The Holy Spirit lives inside of you if you are a Christian. He is not some mysterious "it." He is the third Person of the Trinity, right there beside the Father and the Son. Before Jesus died, he told his disciples that he would send them someone even better than he was—the Helper, God's Spirit of truth (see John 16:5–15). The Holy Spirit is available to you today. He is the One who helps you, who teaches you, who guides you into full truth, and who gives Jesus' message to you. The Holy Spirit is here—in your heart. He lives in you. Get to know him. He's the best friend you'll ever have!

SEE FOR YOURSELF:
Ezek. 39:29; Hag. 2:4–5; John 16:4–15; 2 Tim. 1:14; 1 John 4:13

22 Wild animals, don't be afraid,
because the open pastures have grown grass.
The trees have given fruit;
the fig trees and the grapevines have grown much fruit.
23 So be happy, people of Jerusalem;
be joyful in the LORD your God.
Because he does what is right,
he has brought you rain;
he has sent the fall rain
and the spring rain for you, as before.
24 And the threshing floors will be full of grain;
the barrels will overflow with new wine and olive oil.

THE LORD SPEAKS

25 "Though I sent my great army against you—
those swarming locusts and hopping locusts,
the destroying locusts and the cutting locusts[n] that ate your crops—
I will pay you back
for those years of trouble.
26 Then you will have plenty to eat
and be full.
You will praise the name of the LORD your God,
who has done miracles for you.
My people will never again be shamed.
27 Then you will know that I am among the people of Israel,
that I am the LORD your God,
and there is no other God.
My people will never be shamed again.

28 "After this,
I will pour out my Spirit on all kinds of people.
Your sons and daughters will prophesy,
your old men will dream dreams,
and your young men will see visions.
29 At that time I will pour out my Spirit
also on male slaves and female slaves.
30 I will show miracles
in the sky and on the earth:
blood, fire, and thick smoke.
31 The sun will become dark,
the moon red as blood,
before the overwhelming and terrible
day of the LORD comes.
32 Then anyone who calls on the LORD
will be saved,
because on Mount Zion
and in Jerusalem
there will be people
who will be saved,
just as the LORD has said.
Those left alive after the
day of punishment
are the people whom the LORD called.

SALVATION

Who can be saved? (2:32)

WHAT'S IT MEAN?

Tyre and Sidon were Mediterranean coastal cities famous for their trading business. They weren't necessarily enemies of the Israelites, but they were anxious for Jerusalem to fall so that they could take over the trade routes controlled by Judah.

Joel 3:4

PUNISHMENT FOR JUDAH'S ENEMIES

3

1 "In those days and at that time,
when I will make things better for Judah
and Jerusalem,
2 I will gather all the nations together
and bring them down into the Valley
Where the LORD Judges.
There I will judge them,
because those nations scattered my own
people Israel
and forced them to live in other nations.
They divided up my land
3 and threw lots for my people.
They traded boys for prostitutes,
and they sold girls to buy wine to drink.
4 "Tyre and Sidon and all of you regions of
Philistia! What did you have against me? Were
you punishing me for something I did, or were
you doing something to hurt me? I will very
quickly do to you what you have done to me.
5 You took my silver and gold, and you put
my precious treasures in your temples. 6 You
sold the people of Judah and Jerusalem to the

2:25 swarming . . . locusts These are different names for an insect like a large grasshopper. The locust can quickly destroy trees, plants, and crops, and in this destruction, Joel sees a warning. God will cause this type of destruction when he punishes his people.

Greeks so that you could send them far from
their land.
[7]"You sent my people to that faraway place,
but I will get them and bring them back, and I
will do to you what you have done to them. [8]I
will sell your sons and daughters to the people
of Judah, and they will sell them to the Sabean
people far away." The LORD said this.

GOD JUDGES THE NATIONS

[9] Announce this among the nations:
Prepare for war!
Wake up the soldiers!
Let all the men of war come near and attack.
[10] Make swords from your plows,
and make spears from your hooks for trimming trees.
Let even the weak person say,
"I am a soldier."
[11] All of you nations, hurry,
and come together in that place.
LORD, send your soldiers
to gather the nations.

[12] "Wake up, nations,
and come to attack in the Valley Where the LORD Judges.
There I will sit to judge
all the nations on every side.
[13] Swing the cutting tool,
because the harvest is ripe.
Come, walk on them as you would walk on grapes to get their juice,
because the winepress is full
and the barrels are spilling over,
because these people are so evil!"

[14] There are huge numbers of people
in the Valley of Decision,[n]
because the LORD's day of judging is near
in the Valley of Decision.
[15] The sun and the moon will become dark,
and the stars will stop shining.
[16] The LORD will roar like a lion from Jerusalem;
his loud voice will thunder from that city,
and the sky and the earth will shake.
But the LORD will be a safe place for his people,
a strong place of safety for the people of Israel.

[17] "Then you will know that I, the LORD your God,
live on my holy Mount Zion.
Jerusalem will be a holy place,
and strangers will never even go through it again.

WHAT'S IT MEAN?

How about a quick lesson in ancient wine making? At harvesttime, grapes were gathered in baskets and carried to the winepress. (This is where things get a little disgusting.) Barefoot workers would then stomp on the grapes, squeezing out the juice. The juice that squirted out flowed down a slope into another container. There it was collected in clay jars or wineskins and stored until it fermented and became wine. The days of harvesting and squashing the grapes were times of celebration and joy for the people of Judah and Israel.

Joel 3:13

A NEW LIFE PROMISED FOR JUDAH

[18] "On that day wine will drip from the mountains,
milk will flow from the hills,
and water will run through all the ravines of Judah.
A fountain will flow from the Temple of the LORD
and give water to the valley of acacia trees.
[19] But Egypt will become empty,
and Edom an empty desert,
because they were cruel to the people of Judah.
They killed innocent people in that land.
[20] But there will always be people living in Judah,
and people will live in Jerusalem from now on.
[21] Egypt and Edom killed my people,
so I will definitely punish them."

The LORD lives in Jerusalem!

3:14 Valley of Decision This is like the name "Valley Where the LORD Judges" in 3:2 and 3:12.

Amos

CONTENT Amos was a prophet at a time when life was good for Israel. The economy was stable. Business was booming. War was at a minimum. It was a great time to be alive for the Hebrews.

It was also a great time to be comfortable, to be complacent, and to be self-centered. Life was going so well, in general, that people really didn't want to be bothered with unpleasantness. They didn't want to think about the poor and the struggling elements of their society. They didn't want to think about obedience to God. They didn't want to have to think too much at all.

That's when Amos stepped in to say, "Do you know what God thinks of your selfish, comfortable existence? He thinks it has nothing to do with him at all. You are living apart from God and apart from people who need you. Wake up and start living a better life."

While Amos's message wasn't welcomed, it was necessary. Many poor people in his land were receiving no help from those that were better off. These same wealthy people would show up at religious services and put on a show that they were living according to God's law, but their lives were empty of compassion.

Outline

1:1—3:2 .... Crimes of the Nations Will Be Punished
3:3—6:14 .... Israel and Samaria Will Be Destroyed
7:1—9:10 .... Five Visions of Israel's Punishment
9:11–15 .... Israel's Bright Future

Purpose Immorality and injustice show a society that has lost contact with God.

Theme The Judgment of God Is About to Fall on Israel

Date of writing 760 B.C.

1These are the words of Amos, one of the
shepherds from the town of Tekoa. He saw this
vision about Israel two years before the earthquake. It was at the time Uzziah was king of
Judah and Jeroboam son of Jehoash was king
of Israel.

2Amos said,
"The LORD will roar from Jerusalem;
he will send his voice from Jerusalem.
The pastures of the shepherds will become dry,
and even the top of Mount Carmel will dry up."

ISRAEL'S NEIGHBORS ARE PUNISHED

THE PEOPLE OF ARAM

3This is what the LORD says:
"For the many crimes of Damascus,
I will punish them.
They drove over the people of Gilead
with threshing boards that had iron teeth.
4So I will send fire upon the house of Hazael
that will destroy the strong towers of Ben-Hadad.
5I will break down the bar of the gate to Damascus
and destroy the king who is in the Valley of Aven,
as well as the leader of Beth Eden.
The people of Aram will be taken
captive to the country of Kir," says the LORD.

WHAT'S IT MEAN?

Aram, or Syria, was the area northeast of Lake Galilee. It had been under Israel's control during the reign of David. Things changed when David's son, Solomon, became king. Aram, with its capital city of Damascus, united with other nations in the area against Israel. From that point on, the people of Aram and the Israelites battled each other frequently in war.

Amos 1:3

THE PEOPLE OF PHILISTIA

6This is what the LORD says:
"For the many crimes of Gaza,
I will punish them.
They sold all the people of one area
as slaves to Edom.
7So I will send a fire on the walls of Gaza
that will destroy the city's strong buildings.
8I will destroy the king of the city of Ashdod,
as well as the leader of Ashkelon.
Then I will turn against the people of the city of Ekron,
and the last of the Philistines will die,"
says the Lord GOD.

WHAT'S IT MEAN?

The Philistines lived in coastal cities along the Mediterranean Sea. Not content with merely one capital city, the Philistines boasted five: Gaza, Ashdod, Ashkelon, Gath, and Ekron. The Israelites and Philistines were long-time enemies, but their battles were especially nasty during David's lifetime.

Amos 1:6

THE PEOPLE OF PHOENICIA

9This is what the LORD says:
"For the many crimes of Tyre,
I will punish them.
They sold all the people of one area
as slaves to Edom,
and they forgot the agreement
among relatives they had made with Israel.
10So I will send fire on the walls of Tyre
that will destroy the city's strong buildings."

THE PEOPLE OF EDOM

11This is what the LORD says:
"For the many crimes of Edom,
I will punish them.
They hunted down their relatives, the
Israelites, with the sword,
showing them no mercy.
They were angry all the time
and kept on being very angry.
12So I will send fire on the city of Teman

that will even destroy the strong
buildings of Bozrah."[n]

WHAT'S IT MEAN?

The people of Ammon were actually distant relatives of the Israelites. They were descendants of Lot, the nephew of Abraham (the father of the Jews). Rabbah, the capital of ancient Ammon, is today known as Amman, the capital of Jordan.

Amos 1:13

THE PEOPLE OF AMMON

13This is what the LORD says:
"For the many crimes of Ammon,
I will punish them.
They ripped open the pregnant women in
Gilead
so they could take over that land
and make their own country larger.
14So I will send fire on the city wall of
Rabbah
that will destroy its strong buildings.
It will come during a day of battle,
during a stormy day with strong
winds.
15Then their king and leaders will be taken
captive;
they will all be taken away together,"
says the LORD.

THE PEOPLE OF MOAB

2 1This is what the LORD says:
"For the many crimes of Moab,
I will punish them.
They burned the bones of the king of
Edom into lime.
2So I will send fire on Moab
that will destroy the strong buildings of
the city of Kerioth.
The people of Moab will die in a great
noise,
in the middle of the sounds of war and
trumpets.
3So I will bring an end to the king of
Moab,
and I will kill all its leaders with him,"
says the LORD.

THE PEOPLE OF JUDAH

4This is what the LORD says:
"For the many crimes of Judah,
I will punish them.
They rejected the teachings of the LORD
and did not keep his commands;
they followed the same gods
as their ancestors had followed.
5So I will send fire on Judah,
and it will destroy the strong buildings
of Jerusalem."

ISRAEL IS PUNISHED

6This is what the LORD says:
"For the many crimes of Israel,
I will punish them.
For silver, they sell people who have done
nothing wrong;
they sell the poor to buy a pair of
sandals.
7They walk on poor people as if they were
dirt,
and they refuse to be fair to those who
are suffering.
Fathers and sons have sexual relations
with the same woman,
and so they ruin my holy name.
8As they worship at their altars,
they lie down on clothes taken from the
poor.
They fine people,
and with that money they buy wine to
drink in the house of their god.

9"But it was I who destroyed the Amorites
before them,
who were tall like cedar trees and as
strong as oaks—
I destroyed them completely.
10It was I who brought you from the land
of Egypt
and led you for forty years through the
desert
so I could give you the land of the
Amorites.
11I made some of your children to be
prophets
and some of your young people to be
Nazirites.
People of Israel, isn't this true?" says the
LORD.

1:12 Teman . . . Bozrah Since Teman was in northern Edom and Bozrah was in southern Edom, this means the whole country will be destroyed.

12 "But you made the Nazirites drink wine
and told the prophets not to prophesy.
13 Now I will make you get stuck,
as a wagon loaded with grain gets stuck.
14 No one will escape, not even the fastest
runner.
Strong people will not be
strong enough;
warriors will not be able
to save themselves.
15 Soldiers with bows and
arrows will not stand
and fight,
and even fast runners
will not get away;
soldiers on horses will
not escape alive.
16 At that time even the bravest
warriors
will run away without their armor," says
the LORD.

"The lion has roared!
Who wouldn't be afraid?
The Lord GOD has spoken.
Who will not prophesy?"
(Amos 3:8)

WARNING TO ISRAEL

3
1 Listen to this word that the LORD has spoken against you, people of Israel, against the whole family he brought out of Egypt.
2 "I have chosen only you
out of all the families of the earth,
so I will punish you
for all your sins."

3 Two people will not walk together
unless they have agreed to do so.
4 A lion in the forest does not roar
unless it has caught an animal;
it does not growl in its den
when it has caught nothing.
5 A bird will not fall into a trap
where there is no bait;
the trap will not spring shut
if there is nothing to catch.
6 When a trumpet blows a warning in a city,
the people tremble.
When trouble comes to a city,
the LORD has caused it.
7 Before the Lord GOD does anything,
he tells his plans to his servants the
prophets.
8 The lion has roared!
Who wouldn't be afraid?
The Lord GOD has spoken.
Who will not prophesy?

9 Announce this to the strong buildings of
Ashdod
and to the strong buildings of Egypt:
"Come to the mountains of Samaria,
where you will see great confusion
and people hurting others."

10 "The people don't know how to do what
is right," says the LORD.
"Their strong buildings
are filled with
treasures they took
by force from others."
11 So this is what the Lord
GOD says:
"An enemy will take over
the land
and pull down your
strongholds;
he will take the
treasures out of your
strong buildings."
12 This is what the LORD says:
"A shepherd might save from a lion's
mouth
only two leg bones or a scrap of an ear
of his sheep.
In the same way only a few Israelites in
Samaria will be saved—
people who now sit on their beds
and on their couches."
13 "Listen and be witnesses against the family of Jacob," says the Lord GOD, the God All-Powerful.
14 "When I punish Israel for their sins,
I will also destroy the altars at Bethel.

WHAT'S IT MEAN?

A devastating Assyrian attack in 722 B.C. led to the fall of Samaria, the capital of the northern kingdom of Israel. As was their custom with the territories they conquered, the Assyrians took many Israelites away as captives and brought in many foreigners to live in Canaan. It wasn't long before the Israelites who were left behind started getting involved with the new guys in town. Not only did the Israelites begin marrying and starting families with the foreigners, but they also adopted their idol worship. This mingling continued generation after generation until the distinction between the Israelites and the foreigners disappeared altogether. The descendants of these mixed marriages were known as Samaritans.

Amos 3:12

The corners of the altar will be cut off,
and they will fall to the ground.
15 I will tear down the winter house,
together with the summer house.
The houses decorated with ivory will be destroyed,
and the great houses will come to an end," says the LORD.

ISRAEL WILL NOT RETURN

4

1 Listen to this message, you cows of Bashan[n] on the Mountain of Samaria.
You take things from the poor
and crush people who are in need.
Then you command your husbands,
"Bring us something to drink!"
2 The Lord GOD has promised this:
"Just as surely as I am a holy God,
the time will come
when you will be taken away by hooks,
and what is left of you with fishhooks.
3 You will go straight out of the city
through holes in the walls,
and you will be thrown on the garbage dump," says the LORD.

WHAT'S IT MEAN?

Bethel and Gilgal were both important cities in Israel's history. Bethel was the place where Jacob had his life-changing dream of a stairway to heaven. Gilgal was the site of a memorial to God for his protection of the Israelites when they crossed the Jordan River. The people of Israel proved their lack of respect for their history by making both places centers for pagan worship.

Amos 4:4

4 "Come to the city of Bethel and sin;
come to Gilgal and sin even more.
Offer your sacrifices every morning,
and bring one-tenth of your crops every three days.
5 Offer bread made with yeast as a sacrifice
to show your thanks,
and brag about the special offerings you bring,
because this is what you love to do,
Israelites," says the Lord GOD.

6 "I did not give you any food in your cities,
and there was not enough to eat in any of your towns,
but you did not come back to me," says the LORD.
7 "I held back the rain from you
three months before harvest time.
Then I let it rain on one city
but not on another.
Rain fell on one field,
but another field got none and dried up.
8 People weak from thirst went from town to town for water,
but they could not get enough to drink.
Still you did not come back to me," says the LORD.
9 "I made your crops die from disease and mildew.
When your gardens and your vineyards got larger,
locusts ate your fig and olive trees.
But still you did not come back to me," says the LORD.
10 "I sent disasters against you,
as I did to Egypt.
I killed your young men with swords,
and your horses were taken from you.
I made you smell the stink from all the dead bodies,
but still you did not come back to me," says the LORD.
11 "I destroyed some of you
as I destroyed Sodom and Gomorrah.
You were like a burning stick pulled from a fire,
but still you did not come back to me," says the LORD.

12 "So this is what I will do to you, Israel;
because I will do this to you,
get ready to meet your God, Israel."

13 He is the one who makes the mountains
and creates the wind
and makes his thoughts known to people.
He changes the dawn into darkness
and walks over the mountains of the earth.
His name is the LORD God All-Powerful.

4:1 Bashan Amos compares the rich, lazy women of Samaria to well-fed cows from Bashan, a place known for its rich animal pastures.

ISRAEL NEEDS TO REPENT

5 [1]Listen to this funeral song that I sing
about you, people of Israel.
[2]"The young girl Israel has fallen,
and she will not rise up again.
She was left alone in her own land,
and there is no one to help her up."

[3]This is what the Lord GOD says:
"If a thousand soldiers leave a city,
only a hundred will return;
if a hundred soldiers leave a city,
only ten will return."
[4]This is what the LORD says to the nation of
Israel:
"Come to me and live.
[5] But do not look in Bethel
or go to Gilgal,
and do not go down to Beersheba.
The people of Gilgal will be taken away as
captives,
and Bethel will become nothing."
[6]Come to the LORD and live,
or he will move like fire against the
descendants of Joseph.
The fire will burn Bethel,
and there will be no one to put it out.
[7]You turn justice upside down,
and you throw on the ground what is
right.
[8]God is the one who made the star groups
Pleiades and Orion;
he changes darkness into the morning
light,
and the day into dark night.
He calls for the waters of the sea
to pour out on the earth.
The LORD is his name.
[9]He destroys the protected city;
he ruins the strong, walled city.

[10]You hate those who speak in court against
evil,
and you can't stand those who tell the
truth.
[11]You walk on poor people,
forcing them to give you grain.
You have built fancy houses of cut stone,
but you will not live in them.
You have planted beautiful vineyards,
but you will not drink the wine from
them.
[12]I know your many crimes,
your terrible sins.
You hurt people who do right,
you take money to do wrong,
and you keep the poor from getting
justice in court.
[13]In such times the wise person will keep
quiet,
because it is a bad time.

Promise HE PROMISES TO BE WITH YOU.

Try to do good, not evil, so that you will live, and the LORD God All-Powerful will be with you just as you say he is (Amos 5:14).

A lot of groups and nations claim to have God on their side. Sometimes even the opposing sides in a war both say their cause is the one God favors. But God said that this promise is conditional: He's with you *if* you stop doing the wrong thing and start doing the right thing.

Easier said than done? In fact, relying on your own ability, you'll think it's impossible. Even David failed to obey God at times. But David was quick to turn back to God when he messed up. David understood what God really wanted. "You are not pleased by sacrifices, or I would give them. You don't want burnt offerings," he told God. "The sacrifice God wants is a broken spirit. God, you will not reject a heart that is broken and sorry for sin" (Ps. 51:16–17). God wants a perfect heart, one that you constantly wash with repentance and forgiveness.

When God says you must start doing right, he's not looking for exact perfection. He's looking for someone who really wants to obey him, who will pray like David did: "Create in me a pure heart, God, and make my spirit right again" (Ps. 51:10). If that's what you want, he is definitely on your side.

SEE FOR YOURSELF:
2 Chr. 13:10–12; Ps. 118:5–9; Zech. 10:5

[14]Try to do good, not evil,
so that you will live,
and the LORD God All-Powerful will be with you
just as you say he is.
[15]Hate evil and love good;
be fair in the courts.
Maybe the LORD God All-Powerful will be kind
to the people of Joseph who are left alive.

[16]This is what the Lord, the LORD God All-Powerful, says:

"People will be crying in all the streets;
they will be saying, 'Oh, no!' in the public places.
They will call the farmers to come and weep
and will pay people to cry out loud for them.
[17]People will be crying in all the vineyards,
because I will pass among you to punish you," says the LORD.

THE LORD'S DAY OF JUDGING

[18]How terrible it will be for you who want
the LORD's day of judging to come.
Why do you want that day to come?
It will bring darkness for you, not light.
[19]It will be like someone who runs from a lion
and meets a bear,
or like someone who goes into his house
and puts his hand on the wall,
and then is bitten by a snake.
[20]So the LORD's day of judging will bring darkness, not light;
it will be very dark, not light at all.

[21]The LORD says, "I completely hate your feasts;
I cannot stand your religious meetings.
[22]If you offer me burnt offerings and grain offerings,
I won't accept them.
You bring your best fellowship offerings of fattened cattle,
but I will ignore them.
[23]Take the noise of your songs
away from me!
I won't listen to the
music of your harps.
[24]But let justice flow like a river,
and let goodness flow
like a stream that
never stops.

CHARACTER

Does God care about goodness? (5:24)

[25]"People of Israel, you did not bring me
sacrifices and offerings
while you traveled in the desert for forty years.
[26]You have carried with you
your king, the god Sakkuth,
and Kaiwan your idol,
and the star gods you have made.
[27]So I will send you away as captives
beyond Damascus,"
says the LORD, whose name is the God All-Powerful.

WHAT'S IT MEAN?

The one thing the cities listed in this verse had in common was that they were all losers in war. Calneh and Hamath were cities in Syria that had been conquered by the Assyrians. Gath had experienced its share of defeat as well.

Amos 6:2

ISRAEL WILL BE DESTROYED

6 [1]How terrible it will be for those who have
an easy life in Jerusalem,
for those who feel safe living on Mount Samaria.
You think you are the important people of
the best nation in the world;
the Israelites come to you for help.
[2]Go look at the city of Calneh,
and from there go to the great city Hamath;
then go down to Gath of the Philistines.
You are no better than these kingdoms.
Your land is no larger than theirs.
[3]You put off the day of punishment,
but you bring near the day when you
can do evil to others.
[4]You lie on beds decorated with ivory
and stretch out on your couches.
You eat tender lambs
and fattened calves.
[5]You make up songs on your harps,
and, like David, you compose songs on
musical instruments.
[6]You drink wine by the bowlful
and use the best perfumed lotions.

But you are not sad over the ruin of
Israel,
7 so you will be some of the first ones taken
as slaves.
Your feasting and lying around will
come to an end.

8The Lord GOD made this promise; the LORD
God All-Powerful says:

"I hate the pride of the Israelites,
and I hate their strong buildings,
so I will let the enemy take the city
and everything in it."

9At that time there might be only ten people
left alive in just one house, but they will also
die. 10When the relatives come to get the bodies to take them outside, one of them will call
to the other and ask, "Are there any other dead
bodies with you?"

That person will answer, "No."

Then the one who asked will say, "Hush! We
must not say the name of the LORD."

11 The LORD has given the command;
the large house will be broken into
pieces,
and the small house into bits.
12 Horses do not run on rocks,
and people do not plow rocks with
oxen.
But you have changed fairness into
poison;
you have changed what is right into a
bitter taste.
13 You are happy that the town of Lo Debar
was captured,
and you say, "We have taken Karnaim[n]
by our own strength."
14 The LORD God All-Powerful says,
"Israel, I will bring a nation against
you
that will make your people suffer from
Lebo Hamath in the north
to the valley south of the Dead Sea."

THE VISION OF LOCUSTS

7 1This is what the Lord GOD showed me: He
was forming a swarm of locusts, after the king
had taken his share of the first crop and the
second crop had just begun growing. 2When
the locusts ate all the crops in the country, I
said, "Lord GOD, forgive us. How could Israel
live through this? It is too small already!"

3So the LORD changed his mind about this.
"It will not happen," said the LORD.

THE VISION OF FIRE

4This is what the Lord GOD showed me: The
Lord GOD was calling for fire to come down
like rain. It burned up the deep water and was
going to burn up the land. 5Then I cried out,
"Lord GOD, stop! How could Israel live through
this? It is too small already."

6So the LORD changed his mind about this
too. "It will not happen," said the Lord GOD.

THE VISION OF THE PLUMB LINE

7This is what he showed me: The Lord
stood by a straight wall, with a plumb line in
his hand. 8The LORD said to me, "Amos, what
do you see?"

I said, "A plumb line."

Then the Lord said, "See, I will put a plumb
line among my people Israel to show how
crooked they are. I will not look the other way
any longer.

9 "The places where Isaac's descendants
worship will be destroyed,
Israel's holy places will be turned into
ruins,
and I will attack King Jeroboam's family
with the sword."

AMAZIAH SPEAKS AGAINST AMOS

10Amaziah, a priest at Bethel, sent this message to Jeroboam king of Israel: "Amos is making evil plans against you with the people of
Israel. He has been speaking so much that this
land can't hold all his words. 11This is what
Amos has said:

'Jeroboam will die by the sword,
and the people of Israel will be taken as
captives
out of their own country.' "

12Then Amaziah said to Amos, "Seer, go
back right now to Judah. Do your prophesying
and earn your living there, 13but don't prophesy anymore here at Bethel. This is the king's
holy place, and it is the nation's temple."

14Then Amos answered Amaziah, "I do not
make my living as a prophet, nor am I a member of a group of prophets. I make my living as
a shepherd, and I take care of sycamore trees.
15But the LORD took me away from tending the
flock and said to me, 'Go, prophesy to my people Israel.' 16So listen to the LORD's word. You
tell me,

6:13 Lo Debar . . . Karnaim These were two not especially significant cities that the Israelites had captured in war.

'Don't prophesy against Israel,
and stop prophesying against the descendants of Isaac.'
17 "Because you have said this, the LORD says:
'Your wife will become a prostitute in the city,
and your sons and daughters will be killed with swords.
Other people will measure your land and divide it among themselves,
and you will die in a foreign country.
The people of Israel will definitely be taken from their own land as captives.' "

WHAT'S IT MEAN?

Keep in mind that Jacob was also called Israel. The descendants of his twelve sons became the twelve tribes of Israel.

Amos 8:7

THE VISION OF RIPE FRUIT

8 1 This is what the Lord GOD showed me: a
basket of summer fruit. 2 He said to me, "Amos,
what do you see?"
I said, "A basket of summer fruit."
Then the LORD said to me, "An end[n] has
come for my people Israel, because I will not
overlook their sins anymore.
3 "On that day the palace songs will become
funeral songs," says the Lord GOD. "There will
be dead bodies thrown everywhere! Silence!"

4 Listen to me, you who walk on helpless people,
you who are trying to destroy the poor people of this country, saying,
5 "When will the New Moon festival be over
so we can sell grain?
When will the Sabbath be over
so we can bring out wheat to sell?
We can charge them more
and give them less,
and we can change the scales to cheat the people.
6 We will buy poor people for silver,
and needy people for the price of a pair of sandals.
We will even sell the wheat that was swept up from the floor."

7 The LORD has sworn by his name, the
Pride of Jacob, "I will never forget everything
that these people did.

8 The whole land will shake because of it,
and everyone who lives in the land will cry for those who died.
The whole land will rise like the Nile;
it will be shaken, and then it will fall
like the Nile River in Egypt."
9 The Lord GOD says:
"At that time I will cause the sun to go down at noon
and make the earth dark on a bright day.
10 I will change your festivals into days of crying for the dead,
and all your songs will become songs of sadness.
I will make all of you wear rough cloth to show your sadness;
I will make you shave your heads as well.
I will make it like a time of crying for the death of an only son,
and its end like the end of an awful day."

11 The Lord GOD says: "The days are coming
when I will cause a time of hunger in the land.
The people will not be hungry for bread
or thirsty for water,
but they will be hungry for words from the LORD.
12 They will wander from the Mediterranean Sea to the Dead Sea,
from the north to the east.
They will search for the word of the LORD,
but they won't find it.
13 At that time the beautiful young women
and the young men
will become weak from thirst.
14 They make promises by the idol in Samaria
and say, 'As surely as the god of Dan lives . . .'
and, 'As surely as the god of Beersheba[n] lives, we promise . . .'
So they will fall
and never get up again."

8:2 end The Hebrew word for "end" sounds like the Hebrew word for "summer fruit." **8:14 Dan . . . Beersheba** Dan was the city farthest north in Israel, and Beersheba was the city farthest south.

WHAT'S IT MEAN?

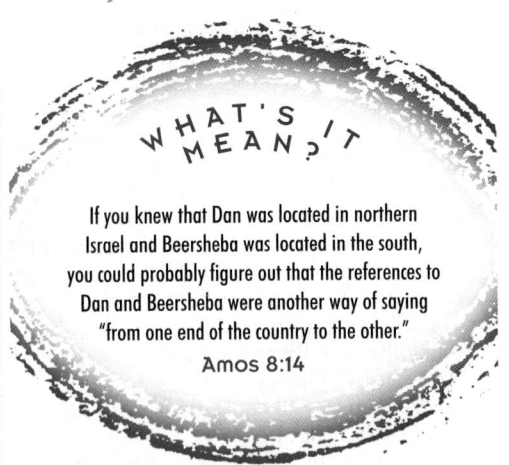

If you knew that Dan was located in northern Israel and Beersheba was located in the south, you could probably figure out that the references to Dan and Beersheba were another way of saying "from one end of the country to the other."

Amos 8:14

ISRAEL WILL BE DESTROYED

9 [1]I saw the Lord standing by the altar, and he
said:
"Smash the top of the pillars
so that even the bottom of the doors
will shake.
Make the pillars fall on the people's heads;
anyone left alive I will kill with a sword.
Not one person will get away;
no one will escape.
[2]If they dig down as deep
as the place of the
dead,
I will pull them up
from there.
If they climb up into
heaven,
I will bring them
down from there.
[3]If they hide at the top
of Mount Carmel,
I will find them and take
them away.
If they try to hide from me at the bottom
of the sea,
I will command a snake to bite them.
[4]If they are captured and taken away by
their enemies,
I will command the sword to kill them.
I will keep watch over them,
but I will keep watch to give them
trouble, not to do them good."

[5]The Lord GOD All-Powerful touches the
land,
and the land shakes.
Then everyone who lives in the land
cries for the dead.
The whole land rises like the Nile River
and falls like the river of Egypt.
[6]The LORD builds his upper rooms above
the skies;
he sets their foundations on the earth.
He calls for the waters of the sea
and pours them out on the land.
The LORD is his name.
[7]The LORD says,
"Israel, you are no different to me than the
people of Cush.
I brought Israel out of the land of Egypt,
and the Philistines from Crete,
and the Arameans from Kir.
[8]I, the Lord GOD, am watching the sinful
kingdom Israel.
I will destroy it
from off the earth,
but I will not completely destroy
Jacob's descendants," says the LORD.
[9]"I am giving the command
to scatter the nation of Israel among all
nations.
It will be like someone shaking grain
through a strainer,
but not even a tiny stone falls through.
[10]All the sinners among my people
will die by the
sword—
those who say,
'Nothing bad will
happen to us.'

"The kingdom of David is like a fallen tent, but in that day I will set it up again and mend its broken places. I will rebuild its ruins as it was before." (Amos 9:11)

THE LORD PROMISES TO RESTORE ISRAEL

[11]"The kingdom of David
is like a fallen tent,
but in that day I will
set it up again
and mend its broken
places.
I will rebuild its ruins
as it was before.
[12]Then Israel will take over what is left of
Edom
and the other nations that belong to
me,"
says the LORD,
who will make it happen.

[13]The LORD says, "The time is coming when
there will be all kinds of food.
People will still be harvesting crops
when it's time to plow again.
People will still be taking the juice from
grapes
when it's time to plant again.
Wine will drip from the mountains

and pour from the hills.
14 I will bring my people Israel back from
captivity;
they will build the ruined cities again,
and they will live in them.
They will plant vineyards and drink the
wine from them;
they will plant gardens and eat their
fruit.
15 I will plant my people on their land,
and they will not be pulled out again
from the land which I have given
them,"
says the LORD your God.

obadiah

CONTENT Obadiah's prophecy pertained to a neighboring nation. There had been a rift between Edom and Israel for many generations. It actually was more of a family feud than a rift. A few hundred years before, Israel's ancestor and Edom's ancestor were brothers. Israel cheated Edom out of the family fortune, so to speak. This created some bad vibes. As it works with bad vibes, they were passed down from generation to generation and got bigger and fiercer along the way. If Israel received blessings, then Edom booed. If Israel fell into hard times, then Edom cheered.

Finally, Obadiah, a prophet of God, stood up to say, "ENOUGH!"

While Israel was, by no means, a perfect nation, they were God's chosen people. To stand against Israel was like taking sides against God! For Edom to continue to bully and harass God's people would *not* do. Obadiah sent the message loud and clear that Edom would face the consequences for being a bully.

What were those consequences to be? Edom would die out completely as a nation. Wow!—that was pretty harsh. Was God serious?

Have you seen Edom on a map lately?

Outline

1–9 .... God's Judgment on Edom
10–14 .... Edom's Cruelty Toward Israel
15–21 .... Israel's Victory

Purpose God will judge those who harass his people.

Theme God's Judgment on Edom

Date of writing 586 B.C.

THE LORD WILL PUNISH THE EDOMITES

1 This is the vision of Obadiah.

This is what the Lord GOD says about Edom:[n]
We have heard a message from the LORD.
A messenger has been sent among the
nations, saying,
"Attack! Let's go attack Edom!"

WHAT'S IT MEAN?

There was no love lost between the Edomites, the descendants of Esau, and the Israelites, the descendants of Jacob. Apparently the sibling rivalry that existed between the two brothers was passed on to their descendants. When the Israelites were on their way to the Promised Land for the first time, the king of Edom refused to let them cross through his land. As a result, the Israelites were forced to travel through the desert. The bad feelings between the two countries continued for centuries.

Obadiah 1

THE LORD SPEAKS TO THE EDOMITES

2 "Soon I will make you the smallest of
nations.
You will be greatly hated by everyone.
3 Your pride has fooled you,
you who live in the hollow places of the
cliff.
Your home is up high,
you who say to yourself,
'No one can bring me down to the
ground.'
4 Even if you fly high like the eagle
and make your nest among the stars,
I will bring you down from there," says
the LORD.
5 "You will really be ruined!
If thieves came to you,
if robbers came by night,
they would steal only enough for
themselves.
If workers came and picked the grapes
from your vines,
they would leave a few behind.
6 But you, Edom, will really lose everything!
People will find all your hidden
treasures!
7 All the people who are your friends
will force you out of the land.
The people who are at peace with you
will trick you and defeat you.
Those who eat your bread with you now
are planning a trap for you,
and you will not notice it."

8 The LORD says, "On that day
I will surely destroy the wise people
from Edom,
and those with understanding from the
mountains of Edom.
9 Then, city of Teman, your best warriors
will be afraid,
and everyone from the mountains of
Edom will be killed.
10 You did violence to your relatives, the
Israelites,
so you will be covered with shame
and destroyed forever.
11 You stood aside without helping
while strangers carried Israel's treasures
away.
When foreigners entered Israel's city gate
and threw lots to decide what part of
Jerusalem they would take,
you were like one of them.

COMMANDS THAT EDOM BROKE

12 "Edom, do not laugh at your brother Israel
in his time of trouble
or be happy about the people of Judah
when they are destroyed.
Do not brag when cruel things are done
to them.
13 Do not enter the city gate of my people
in their time of trouble
or laugh at their problems
in their time of trouble.
Do not take their treasures
in their time of trouble.
14 Do not stand at the crossroads
to destroy those who are trying to
escape.
Do not capture those who escape alive
and turn them over to their enemy
in their time of trouble.

THE NATIONS WILL BE JUDGED

15 "The LORD's day of judging is coming soon
to all the nations.

1 Edom The Edomites were the people who came from Esau, Jacob's twin brother. They were enemies of the Israelites.

The same evil things you
did to other people
will happen to you;
they will come back
upon your own head.
16 Because you drank in my
Temple,
all the nations will drink on and on.
They will drink and drink
until they disappear.
17 But on Mount Zion some will escape the
judgment,
and it will be a holy place.
The people of Jacob will take back their land
from those who took it from them.
18 The people of Jacob will be like a fire
and the people of Joseph[n] like a flame.
But the people of Esau[n] will be like dry
stalks.
The people of Jacob will set them on fire
and burn them up.
There will be no one left of the people of
Esau."
This will happen because the LORD has
said it.

JUDGMENT

Will we reap what we sow? (15)

19 Then God's people will regain southern
Judah from Edom;
they will take back the mountains of
Edom.
They will take back the western hills
from the Philistines.
They will regain the lands of Ephraim and
Samaria,
and Benjamin will take over Gilead.
20 People from Israel who once were forced
to leave their homes
will take the land of the
Canaanites,
all the way to Zarephath.
People from Judah who once were forced
to leave Jerusalem and live in
Sepharad
will take back the cities of southern
Judah.
21 Powerful warriors will go up on Mount
Zion,
where they will rule the people living on
Edom's mountains.
And the kingdom will belong to the
LORD.

18 people of Jacob . . . Joseph The people who came from Jacob and Joseph, or the Israelites.
18 people of Esau The people who came from Esau, or the Edomites.

jonah

CONTENT Jonah is a story about the stubbornness of human nature versus the stubborn grace of God.

In one corner, you have a prophet who is so caught up in his own hate and prejudice against Nineveh that he would rather run from God than preach there. In the other corner, you have a God who loves both the delinquent prophet and the evil city and would rather give them both a hard time than let them stay the way they are.

The prophet throws the first punch by hopping a ship that's headed the opposite way from Nineveh. God counters the blow by sending a storm and big fish which, working together, give the prophet three days to evaluate his choices.

At the end of round one, Jonah does go to Nineveh.

That's the most famous part of the story, but in round two is the real knockout. Once Jonah preaches to Nineveh, the people respond beautifully. They repent of their sin and God puts off their destruction. A happy ending?

Not yet. Jonah is still so full of hate for these people that he is disappointed that they repented. Did you get that? The *prophet is disappointed* that the people *repented*.

You decide who won after you've read the rest.

Outline

1:1–17 .... Jonah Disobeys the Lord
2:1–10 .... Jonah Prays to the Lord
3:1–10 .... Jonah Goes to Nineveh, and Its People Repent
4:1–11 .... Jonah Is Angry Because the Lord Showed Mercy

Purpose We are to adopt God's gracious attitude toward all.

Theme God's Compassion for All People

Date of writing 750 B.C.

"People who worship useless idols give up their loyalty to you. But I will praise and thank you while I give sacrifices to you, and I will keep my promises to you. Salvation comes from the LORD" (2:8–9).

Bible Talk

God's Call

Sometimes we look at God's call as a scary thing. Sometimes we think that God will call us to do the one thing we just think we can't bear to do. In the case of Jonah, this was true; but, because Jonah's hate was a sin, it needed to be faced rather than run away from.

In your life, discovering God's call, or task, for you will be a process that might have scary parts and will certainly have fun parts. But you can feel certain that God does not rule our hearts, just waiting with glee until he can make us do the thing we most dread. In fact, God most often calls us to do what he has already put a passion and a dream in our hearts to do.

GOD'S GRACE FOR THE GREEDY?

If you had lived in Jonah's country in Jonah's day, his hatred for the people of Nineveh would not have seemed so unusual. Nineveh was the capital of Assyria, a cruel and warlike nation that had threatened Israel for years. Jonah had reason to be angry, fearful, and hesitant to offer himself, much less God's grace, to this city.

This brings us to the same issue that Jonah struggled with: Why should God be gracious to those who are not gracious to others? Most often, we would rather see the bad guys get beaten up in the end. If they get away with their evil, we feel disappointed. But God's grace is God's business. Jonah's story reminds us to leave judgment to God and trust him to do what is just in the end.

GOD CALLS AND JONAH RUNS

1 [1]The LORD spoke his word to Jonah son of
Amittai: [2]"Get up, go to the great city of Nineveh, and preach against it, because I see the
evil things they do."

WHAT'S IT MEAN?

The city of Nineveh was about five hundred miles away from Jonah's home. After King Sennacherib made Nineveh the capital of the Assyrian Empire, he really improved the city. In addition to many beautiful temples, Sennacherib built a seventy-one-room palace, a botanical garden, a zoo, and several parks.

Jonah 1:1–2

[3]But Jonah got up to run away from the
LORD by going to Tarshish. He went to the city
of Joppa, where he found a ship that was going
to the city of Tarshish. Jonah paid for the trip
and went aboard, planning to go to Tarshish to
run away from the LORD.
[4]But the LORD sent a great wind on the sea,
which made the sea so stormy that the ship
was in danger of breaking apart. [5]The sailors
were afraid, and each man cried to his own
god. They began throwing the cargo from the
ship into the sea to make the ship lighter.
But Jonah had gone down far inside the
ship to lie down, and he fell fast asleep. [6]The
captain of the ship came and said, "Why are
you sleeping? Get up and pray to your god!
Maybe your god will pay attention to us, and
we won't die!"
[7]Then the men said to each other, "Let's
throw lots to see who caused these troubles to
happen to us."
When they threw lots, the lot showed that
the trouble had happened because of Jonah.
[8]Then they said to him, "Tell us, who caused
our trouble? What is your job? Where do you
come from? What is your country? Who are
your people?"
[9]Then Jonah said to them, "I am a Hebrew. I
fear the LORD, the God of heaven, who made
the sea and the land."
[10]The men were very afraid, and they asked
Jonah, "What terrible thing did you do?" (They
knew he was running away from the LORD because he had told them.)
[11]Since the wind and the waves of the sea
were becoming much stronger, they said to
him, "What should we do to you to make the
sea calm down for us?"
[12]Jonah said to them, "Pick me up, and
throw me into the sea, and then it will calm
down. I know it is my fault that this great
storm has come on you."
[13]Instead, the men tried to row the ship
back to the land, but they could not, because
the sea was becoming more stormy.

On the Edge

The LORD spoke his word to Jonah son of Amittai: "Get up, go to the great city of Nineveh, and preach against it, because I see the evil things they do." But Jonah got up to run away from the LORD by going to Tarshish. He went to the city of Joppa, where he found a ship that was going to the city of Tarshish. Jonah paid for the trip and went aboard, planning to go to Tarshish to run away from the LORD (Jon. 1:1–3).

God called Jonah to go to Nineveh. Jonah was so afraid to go that he got on a ship going in the opposite direction—toward Spain. You know the rest of the story. Jonah was thrown overboard and swallowed by a big fish. Inside the fish, he decided to do what God wanted. The fish spit him up, and Jonah went to Nineveh. Why do we always think that what God wants us to do will be awful? We hear him call and we sense his leading, and then we run off to Spain trying to get away from him. Where do you think God is calling you? Are you ready? Or are you buying a ticket to Spain? Will he have to send a big fish to get your attention? God is a loving God; and while there may be hard days, he would not call you to do something you hate. You may be afraid because something is new and different, but you don't have to be afraid that God is wrong. He knows you, and he knows when you're ready for the task. So when God calls you to Nineveh—go quickly. The belly of a fish is not a cool place to start trusting God.

SEE FOR YOURSELF:
Ps. 37:4, 23–24; 40:6–8; John 4:34; Phil. 2:13

WHAT'S IT MEAN?

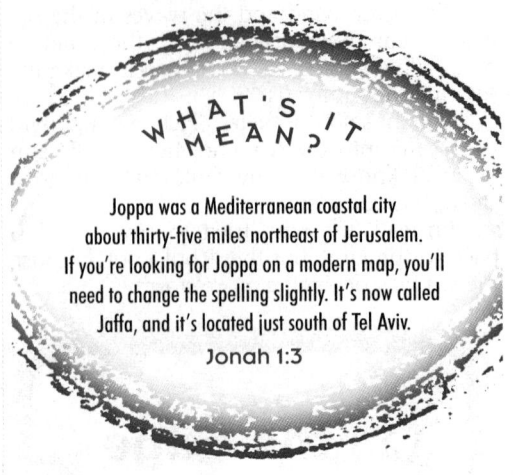

Joppa was a Mediterranean coastal city about thirty-five miles northeast of Jerusalem. If you're looking for Joppa on a modern map, you'll need to change the spelling slightly. It's now called Jaffa, and it's located just south of Tel Aviv.

Jonah 1:3

JONAH'S PUNISHMENT

14 So the men cried to the LORD, "LORD, please
don't let us die because of this man's life; please
don't think we are guilty of killing an innocent
person. LORD, you have caused all this to happen; you wanted it this way." 15 So they picked
up Jonah and threw him into the sea, and the
sea became calm. 16 Then they began to fear the
LORD very much; they offered a sacrifice to the
LORD and made promises to him.

17 The LORD caused a big fish to swallow Jonah, and Jonah was inside the fish three days
and three nights.

2 1 While Jonah was inside the fish, he prayed
to the LORD his God and said,

2 "When I was in danger,
I called to the LORD,
and he answered me.
I was about to die,
so I cried to you,
and you heard my voice.
3 You threw me into the sea,
down, down into the deep sea.
The water was all around me,
and your powerful waves flowed over
me.
4 I said, 'I was driven out of your presence,
but I hope to see your Holy Temple
again.'
5 The waters of the sea closed around my
throat.
The deep sea was all around me;
seaweed was wrapped around my head.
6 When I went down to where the
mountains of the sea start to rise,
I thought I was locked in this prison
forever,
but you saved me from the pit of death,
LORD my God.
7 "When my life had almost gone,
I remembered the LORD.
I prayed to you,
and you heard my prayers in your Holy
Temple.

8 "People who worship useless idols
give up their loyalty to you.
9 But I will praise and thank you
while I give sacrifices to you,
and I will keep my promises to you.
Salvation comes from the LORD!"

10 Then the LORD spoke to the fish, and the
fish threw up Jonah onto the dry land.

GOD CALLS AND JONAH OBEYS

3 1 The LORD spoke his word to Jonah again
and said, 2 "Get up, go to the great city Nineveh,
and preach to it what I tell you to say."
3 So Jonah obeyed the LORD and got up and
went to Nineveh. It was a very large city; just
to walk across it took a person three days.
4 After Jonah had entered the city and walked
for one day, he preached to the people, saying,
"After forty days, Nineveh will be destroyed!"

WHAT'S IT MEAN?

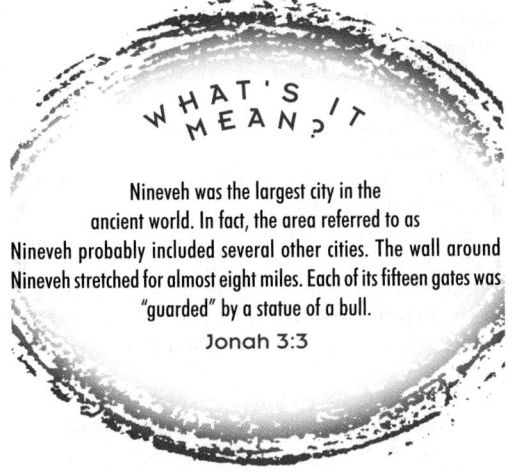

Nineveh was the largest city in the ancient world. In fact, the area referred to as Nineveh probably included several other cities. The wall around Nineveh stretched for almost eight miles. Each of its fifteen gates was "guarded" by a statue of a bull.

Jonah 3:3

5 The people of Nineveh believed God. They
announced that they would stop eating for a
while, and they put on rough cloth to show
their sadness. All the people in the city did this,
from the most important to the least important.

6 When the king of Nineveh heard this news,
he got up from his throne, took off his robe,
and covered himself with rough cloth and sat
in ashes to show how upset he was.

7 He sent this announcement through Nineveh:

By command of the king and his important men: No person or animal, herd or
flock, will be allowed to taste anything.
Do not let them eat food or drink water.
8But every person and animal should be
covered with rough cloth, and people
should cry loudly to God. Everyone must
turn away from evil living and stop doing harm all the time. 9Who knows?
Maybe God will change his mind. Maybe
he will stop being angry, and then we will
not die.

10When God saw what the people did, that
they stopped doing evil, he changed his mind
and did not do what he had warned. He did
not punish them.

GOD'S MERCY MAKES JONAH ANGRY

4 1But this made Jonah very unhappy, and he
became angry. 2He prayed to the LORD, "When
I was still in my own country this is what I
said would happen, and that is why I quickly
ran away to Tarshish. I knew that you are a
God who is kind and shows mercy. You don't
become angry quickly, and you have great
love. I knew you would choose not to cause
harm. 3So now I ask you, LORD, please kill me.
It is better for me to die than to live."
4Then the LORD said, "Do you think it is
right for you to be angry?"
5Jonah went out and sat down east of the
city. There he made a shelter for himself and
sat in the shade, waiting to see what would
happen to the city. 6The LORD made a plant
grow quickly up over Jonah, which gave him
shade and helped him to be more comfortable.
Jonah was very pleased to have the plant. 7But
the next day when the sun rose, God sent a
worm to attack the plant so that it died.
8As the sun rose higher in the sky, God sent
a very hot east wind to blow, and the sun became so hot on Jonah's head that he became
very weak and wished he were dead. He said,
"It is better for me to die than to live."
9But God said to Jonah, "Do you think it is
right for you to be angry about the plant?"
Jonah answered, "It is right for me to be
angry! I am so angry I could die!"

10And the LORD said, "You are so concerned
for that plant even though you did nothing to
make it grow. It appeared one day, and the
next day it died. 11Then shouldn't I show concern for the great city Nineveh, which has
more than one hundred twenty thousand
people who do not know right from wrong,
and many animals, too?"

micah

CONTENT Several things set Micah apart as a prophet. First, a lot of the prophets preached to either the northern kingdom, Samaria, or the southern kingdom, Judah. Micah preached to both. This is significant since there was a longtime feud between the kingdoms. It shows that Micah knew how to rise above petty human conflicts.

Second, Micah actually prophesied that Bethlehem would be the town that Jesus would be born in (psychic circuit, eat your heart out!). This is an amazing feat, since prophets of the Old Testament weren't known as people who told the future in specifics.

Third, Micah was known for being practical, down-to-earth. He talked about faith in a way that let his listeners and readers know what God expects on a day-to-day basis rather than on a Sunday-to-Sunday basis. One of the most famous passages in Micah describes the godly walk as doing right, loving kindness, and living in humble obedience to God (6:8).

The message of the Book of Micah is one that calls us to repent of our sins and to live our lives honorably. It calls us to be good people and to live out our faith, not only in how we worship God but also in how we treat other people.

Outline

1:1—2:11 .... The Lord Will Punish His People
2:12–13 .... A Promise to Rescue Israel
3:1–12 .... The Lord Will Punish Wicked Leaders and Prophets
4:1—5:15 .... A New Temple in a New Israel
6:1—7:6 .... Israel Is Declared Guilty
7:7–20 .... The Nation Turns to God

Purpose We are to be as concerned as God is with personal and social morality.

Theme Incomparability of the Compassionate Lord

Date of writing 730 B.C.

SAMARIA AND ISRAEL TO BE PUNISHED

1 [1]During the time that Jotham, Ahaz, and Hezekiah were kings of Judah, the word of the LORD came to Micah, who was from Moresheth. He saw these visions about Samaria and Jerusalem.

2 Hear this, all you nations;
listen, earth and all you who live on it.
The Lord GOD will be a witness against you,
the Lord from his Holy Temple.
3 See, the LORD is coming out of his place;
he is coming down to walk on the tops of the mountains.
4 The mountains will melt under him,
and the valleys will crack open,
like wax near a fire,
like water running down a hillside.
5 All this is because of Jacob's sin,
because of the sins of the nation of Israel.
What is the place of Jacob's sin?
Isn't it Samaria?
What is Judah's place of idol worship?
Isn't it Jerusalem?

"See, the LORD is coming out of his place; he is coming down to walk on the tops of the mountains."
(Micah 1:3)

WHAT'S IT MEAN?

During Micah's lifetime, Israel was actually split into two different nations. The northern kingdom, which was called Israel, had Samaria as its capital. The southern kingdom, which was called Judah, had Jerusalem as its capital. Both capital cities also served as the main worship centers for their nation. If you'd like to know when Micah lived, all you need to do is look at the kings he mentions in this verse. All of them reigned in Judah toward the end of the eighth century B.C.

Micah 1:1

THE LORD SPEAKS

6 "So I will make Samaria a pile of ruins in the open country,
a place for planting vineyards.
I will pour her stones down into the valley
and strip her down to her foundations.
7 All her idols will be broken into pieces;
all the gifts to her idols will be burned with fire.
I will destroy all her idols,
and because Samaria earned her money by being unfaithful to me,
this money will be carried off by others who are not faithful to me."

MICAH'S GREAT SADNESS

8 I will moan and cry because of this evil,
going around barefoot and naked.
I will cry loudly like the wild dogs
and make sad sounds like the owls do,
9 because Samaria's wound cannot be healed.
It will spread to Judah;
it will reach the city gate of my people,
all the way to Jerusalem.
10 Don't tell it in Gath.[n]
Don't cry in Acco.[n]
Roll in the dust
at Beth Ophrah.[n]
11 Pass on your way, naked and ashamed,
you who live in Shaphir.[n]
Those who live in Zaanan[n]
won't come out.
The people in Beth Ezel[n] will cry,
but they will not give you any support.
12 Those who live in Maroth[n]
will be anxious for good news to come,
because trouble will come from the LORD,
all the way to the gate of Jerusalem.
13 You people living in Lachish,[n]
harness the fastest horse to the chariot.
Jerusalem's sins started in you;
yes, Israel's sins were found in you.

1:10 Gath This name sounds like the Hebrew word for "tell." **1:10 Acco** This name sounds like the Hebrew word for "cry." **1:10 Beth Ophrah** This name means "house of dust." **1:11 Shaphir** This name means "beautiful." **1:11 Zaanan** This name sounds like the Hebrew word for "come out." **1:11 Beth Ezel** This name means "house by the side of another," suggesting help or support. **1:12 Maroth** This name sounds like the Hebrew word for "sad" or "miserable." **1:13 Lachish** This name sounds like the Hebrew word for "horses."

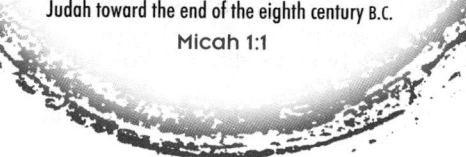

[14]So you must give farewell gifts
to Moresheth[n] in Gath.
The houses in Aczib[n] will be false help
to the kings of Israel.
[15]I will bring against you people who will
take your land,
you who live in Mareshah.[n]
The glory of Israel
will go in to Adullam.
[16]Cut off your hair to show you are sad
for the children you love.
Make yourself bald like the eagle,
because your children will be taken
away to a foreign land.

WHAT'S IT MEAN?

The Israelites liked to wear their hair and beards long. They thought it made them look attractive and manly (or womanly, depending on the sex). To them, a clean-shaven head was something to be ashamed of. Aside from priests and Levites, the only Israelite man who would have considered shaving his head was one who was going through a time of extreme sadness or mourning.

Micah 1:16

THE EVIL PLANS OF PEOPLE

2 [1]How terrible it will be for people who
plan wickedness,
who lie on their beds and make evil
plans.
When the morning light comes, they do
what they planned,
because they have the power to do so.
[2]They want fields, so they take them;
they want houses, so they take them
away.
They cheat people to get their houses;
they rob them even of their property.
[3]That is why the LORD says:
"Look, I am planning trouble against such
people,
and you won't be able to save
yourselves.
You will no longer walk proudly,
because it will be a terrible time.
[4]At that time people will make fun of you
and sing this sad song about you:
'We are completely ruined;
the LORD has taken away my people's
land.
Yes, he has taken it away from me
and divided our fields among our
enemies!' "
[5]So you will have no one from the LORD's
people
to throw lots to divide the land.

MICAH IS ASKED NOT TO PROPHESY

[6]The prophets say, "Don't prophesy to us!
Don't prophesy about these things!
Nothing to make us feel bad will
happen!"
[7]But I must say this, people of Jacob:
The LORD is becoming angry about
what you have done.
My words are welcome
to the person who does what is right.
[8]But you are fighting against my people like
an enemy.
You take the coats from people who
pass by;
you rob them of their safety;
you plan war.
[9]You've forced the women of my people
from their nice houses;
you've taken my glory
from their children forever.
[10]Get up and leave.
This is not your place of rest anymore.
You have made this place unclean,
and it is doomed to destruction.
[11]But you people want a false prophet
who will tell you nothing but lies.
You want one who promises to prophesy
good things for you
if you give him wine and beer.
He's just the prophet for you.

THE LORD PROMISES TO RESCUE HIS PEOPLE

[12]"Yes, people of Jacob, I will bring all of you
together;
I will bring together all those left alive in
Israel.
I will put them together like sheep in a
pen,
like a flock in its pasture;
the place will be filled with many
people.

1:14 Moresheth This may be a play on the word "engaged," referring to a farewell gift to a bride.
1:14 Aczib This name means "lie" or "trick." **1:15 Mareshah** This name sounds like the Hebrew word for a person who captures other cities and lands.

13 Someone will open the way and lead the
people out.
The people will break through the gate
and leave the city where they were
held captive.
Their king will go out in front of them,
and the LORD will lead them."

THE LEADERS OF ISRAEL ARE GUILTY OF EVIL

3

1 Then I said,
"Listen, leaders of the people of Jacob;
listen, you rulers of the nation of Israel.
You should know how to decide cases
fairly,
2 but you hate good and love evil.
You skin my people alive
and tear the flesh off their bones.
3 You eat my people's flesh
and skin them and break their bones;
you chop them up like meat for the pot,
like meat in a cooking pan.
4 They will cry to the LORD,
but he won't answer them.
At that time he will hide his face from them,
because what they have done is evil."
5 The LORD says this about the prophets
who teach his people the wrong way of living:
"If these prophets are given food to eat,
they shout, 'Peace!'
But if someone doesn't give them what
they ask for,
they call for a holy war against that
person.
6 So it will become like night for them,
without visions.
It will become dark for them, without
any way to tell the future.
The sun is about to set for the prophets;
their day will become dark.
7 The seers will be ashamed;
the people who see the future will be
embarrassed.
Yes, all of them will cover their mouths,
because there will be no answer from
God."

MICAH IS AN HONEST PROPHET OF GOD

8 But I am filled with power,
with the Spirit of the LORD,
and with justice and strength,
to tell the people of Jacob how they have
turned against God,
and the people of Israel how they have
sinned.
9 Leaders of Jacob and rulers of Israel,
listen to me,
you who hate fairness and twist what is
right.
10 You build Jerusalem by murdering people;
you build it with evil.
11 Its judges take money to decide who wins
in court.
Its priests only teach for pay,
and its prophets only look into the
future when they get paid.
But they lean on the LORD and say,
"The LORD is here with us,
so nothing bad will happen to us."
12 Because of you,
Jerusalem will be plowed like a field.

Promise

HE PROMISES TO BE YOUR KING.

Someone will open the way and lead the people out. The people will break through the gate and leave the city where they were held captive. Their king will go out in front of them, and the LORD will lead them (Mic. 2:13).

Sometimes, for a moment, people wonder what it would be like to be a part of a royal family—wealth, privilege, honor, and a strong heritage. You are a member of the family of God, and he promises to be your king. That makes you the son or daughter of the King. You will be honored because you belong to him. You take part in the wealth of your Father. He doesn't rule with an iron fist, but with a loving heart. It may be difficult to understand it all now, but you are truly a child of the King. Your title can never be removed, and the Lord will never be dethroned. He will reign forever.

SEE FOR YOURSELF:

Is. 33:22; Zech. 14:9; Matt. 27:37; 1 Tim. 6:15; Rev. 19:16

The city will become a pile of rocks,
and the hill on which the Temple stands
will be covered with bushes.

THE MOUNTAIN OF THE LORD

4

1 In the last days
the mountain on which the LORD's Temple stands
will become the most important of all mountains.
It will be raised above the hills,
and people from other nations will come streaming to it.
2 Many nations will come and say,
"Come, let us go up to the mountain of the LORD,
to the Temple of the God of Jacob,
so that he can teach us his ways,
and we can obey his teachings."
His teachings will go out from Jerusalem,
the word of the LORD from that city.
3 The Lord will judge many nations;
he will make decisions about strong nations that are far away.
They will hammer their swords into plow blades
and their spears into hooks for trimming trees.
Nations will no longer raise swords against other nations;
they will not train for war anymore.
4 Everyone will sit under his own vine and fig tree,
and no one will make them afraid,
because the LORD All-Powerful has said it.
5 All other nations may follow their own gods,
but we will follow the LORD our God forever and ever.
6 The LORD says, "At that time,
I will gather the crippled;
I will bring together those who were sent away,
those whom I caused to have trouble.
7 I will keep alive those who were crippled,
and I will make a strong nation of those who were sent away.
The LORD will be their king in Mount Zion
from now on and forever.

WHAT'S IT MEAN?

"The mountain of the LORD" was Mount Moriah in Jerusalem. When David was king, God selected the spot where he wanted his Temple built and even supplied the blueprints. David's son, Solomon, was the one who actually oversaw the construction of the Temple.

Micah 4:2

Promise — HE PROMISES REST AND FREEDOM FROM FEAR.

Everyone will sit under his own vine and fig tree, and no one will make them afraid, because the LORD All-Powerful has said it (Mic. 4:4).

"May your kingdom come and what you want be done, here on earth as it is in heaven" (Matt. 6:10). This is one of the things Jesus told his followers to pray for whenever they talked to God. Can you imagine what the world would be like if people on earth obeyed him as faithfully as the angels do now? There'd be no divorce, no drunk drivers, no drug deals, no car jackings. There wouldn't even be any war. It's hard to believe that could ever happen.

But Jesus wasn't telling you to pray for something impossible. That time is coming, and Micah describes it in this passage. He gives you a picture of a rest and security, not behind locked windows and doors but out in the peaceful shade. And note Micah's words of assurance: "Because the LORD All-Powerful has said it." Someday God will give rest to all of his people. Be encouraged; you're included.

SEE FOR YOURSELF:

Ps. 16:8–9; Matt. 11:28; Heb. 4:9

8 And you, watchtower of the flocks,[n] hill of
Jerusalem,
to you will come the kingdom as in the
past.
Jerusalem, the right to rule will come
again to you."

WHY THE ISRAELITES MUST GO TO BABYLON

9 Now, why do you cry so loudly?
Is your king gone?
Have you lost your helper,
so that you are in pain, like a woman
trying to give birth?
10 People of Jerusalem, strain and be in pain.
Be like a woman trying to give birth,
because now you must leave the city
and live in the field.
You will go to Babylon,
but you will be saved from that place.
The LORD will go there
and buy you back from your enemies.
11 But now many nations
have come to fight against you,
saying, "Let's destroy Jerusalem.
We will look at her and be glad we have
defeated her."
12 But they don't know
what the LORD is thinking;
they don't understand his plan.
He has gathered them like bundles of
grain to the threshing floor.

WHAT'S IT MEAN?

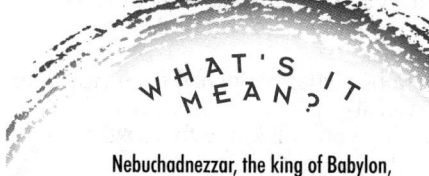

Nebuchadnezzar, the king of Babylon, was a real pain in the neck to the Jewish people. He led three different attacks against Judah, over the years taking thousands of Jews back to Babylon as prisoners. In 586 B.C., Nebuchadnezzar and his army burned down the Temple in Jerusalem.

Micah 4:10

13 "Get up and beat them, people of
Jerusalem.
I will make you strong as if you had
horns of iron
and hoofs of bronze.
You will beat many nations into small
pieces
and give their wealth to the LORD,
their treasure to the Lord of all the
earth."

5

1 So, strong city, gather your soldiers
together,
because we are surrounded and
attacked.
They will hit the leader of Israel
in the face with a club.

WHAT'S IT MEAN?

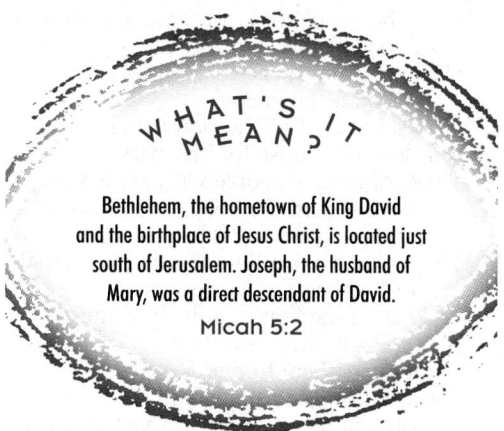

Bethlehem, the hometown of King David and the birthplace of Jesus Christ, is located just south of Jerusalem. Joseph, the husband of Mary, was a direct descendant of David.

Micah 5:2

THE RULER TO BE BORN IN BETHLEHEM

2 "But you, Bethlehem Ephrathah,
though you are too small to be among
the army groups from Judah,
from you will come one who will rule
Israel for me.
He comes from very old times,
from days long ago."

3 The LORD will give up his people
until the one who is having a baby
gives birth;
then the rest of his relatives will return
to the people of Israel.
4 At that time the ruler of Israel will stand
and take care of his people
with the LORD's strength
and with the power of the name of the
LORD his God.
The Israelites will live in safety,
because his greatness will reach all over
the earth.
5 He will bring peace.

4:8 watchtower . . . flocks This probably means a part of Jerusalem. The leaders would be like shepherds in a tower watching their sheep.

RESCUE AND PUNISHMENT

Assyria will surely come into our country
and walk over our large buildings.
We will set up seven shepherds,
eight leaders of the people.
6 They will destroy the Assyrians with their
swords;
they will conquer the land of Assyria
with their swords drawn.
They will rescue us from the Assyrians
when they come into our land,
when they walk over our borders.

7 Then the people of Jacob who are left alive
will be to other people
like dew from the LORD
or rain on the grass—
it does not wait for human beings;
it does not pause for any person.
8 Those of Jacob's people who are left alive
will be scattered among many nations
and peoples.
They will be like a lion among the animals
of the forest,
like a young lion in a flock of sheep:
As it goes, it jumps on them
and tears them to pieces,
and no one can save them.
9 So you will raise your fist in victory over
your enemies,
and all your enemies will be destroyed.

10 The LORD says, "At that time,
I will take your horses from you
and destroy your chariots.
11 I will destroy the cities in your country
and tear down all your defenses.
12 I will take away the magic charms you use
so you will have no more fortune-
tellers.
13 I will destroy your statues of gods
and the stone pillars you worship
so that you will no longer worship
what your hands have made.
14 I will tear down Asherah idols from you
and destroy your cities.
15 In my anger and rage,
I will pay back the nations that have
not listened."

WHAT'S IT MEAN?

According to the ancient Canaanites, Asherah, the goddess of fertility, was the wife of Baal, the number one god in the land. When the Israelites got to Canaan, they started worshiping Baal, Asherah, and many other pagan gods. The places where people worshiped Asherah were marked by carved wooden poles.
Micah 5:14

THE LORD'S CASE

6

1 Now hear what the LORD says:
"Get up; plead your case in front of the
mountains;
let the hills hear your story.
2 Mountains, listen to the LORD's legal case.
Foundations of the earth, listen.
The LORD has a legal case against his
people,
and he will accuse Israel."

3 He says, "My people, what did I do to
you?
How did I make you tired of me?
Tell me.
4 I brought you from the land of Egypt
and freed you from slavery;
I sent Moses, Aaron, and Miriam to
you.
5 My people, remember
the evil plans of Balak king of Moab
and what Balaam son of Beor told
Balak.
Remember what happened from Acacia to
Gilgal
so that you will know the LORD does
what is right!"

6 You say, "What can I bring with me
when I come before the LORD,
when I bow before God on high?
Should I come before him with burnt
offerings,
with year-old calves?
7 Will the LORD be pleased with a thousand
male sheep?
Will he be pleased with ten thousand
rivers of oil?
Should I give my first child for
the evil I have done?
Should I give my very
own child for my
sin?"
8 The LORD has told you,
human, what is good;

DEVOTION

What does God require of us? (6:8)

he has told you what he wants from
you:
to do what is right to other people,
love being kind to others,
and live humbly, obeying your God.

9 The voice of the LORD calls to the city,
and the wise person honors him.
So pay attention to the rod of punishment;
pay attention to the One who threatens
to punish.
10 Are there still in the wicked house
wicked treasures
and the cursed false measure?
11 Can I forgive people who cheat others
with wrong weights and scales?
12 The rich people of the city
do cruel things.
Its people tell lies;
they do not tell the truth.
13 As for me, I will make you sick.
I will attack you, ruining you because of
your sins.
14 You will eat, but you won't become full;
you will still be hungry and empty.
You will store up, but save nothing,
and what you store up, the sword will
destroy.
15 You will plant,
but you won't harvest.
You will step on your olives,
but you won't get any oil from them.
You will crush the grapes,
but you will not drink the new wine.
16 This is because you obey the laws of King
Omri
and do all the things that Ahab's family
does;
you follow their advice.
So I will let you be destroyed.
The people in your city will be laughed
at,
and other nations will make fun of you.

On the Edge

All of the faithful people are gone; there is not one good person left in this country. Everyone is waiting to kill someone; everyone is trying to trap someone else (Mic. 7:2).

You weren't born with the desire to faithfully please God and do the things he wants. No one was. Instead, you were born with the natural tendency to try to get the best for yourself and let others take the leftovers. It's not a pretty fact, but it's the truth and everybody has to come to grips with it.

Thankfully God didn't leave you at the mercy of your natural tendencies. He gave you parents and other adults—friends, teachers, grandparents, etc.—to teach you about right and wrong. There are also rules in your school and laws in your state to keep your selfish desires—and everybody else's—from wreaking havoc. You may not realize it, but these outside forces have a lot to do with the worst of your human nature not getting the best of you.

There's good news, though. The outside forces were meant to be temporary. Because you don't have a lot of faith in your own goodness—because you trust Jesus instead—God's Spirit lives inside you. Now your actions can be determined by an inside force that is constantly changing you into a different person.

SEE FOR YOURSELF:
Ps. 14:2–3; Is. 53:6; Jer. 50:6; Hos. 4:1

THE EVIL THAT PEOPLE DO

7 1 Poor me! I am like a hungry man,
and all the summer fruit has been
picked—
there are no grapes left to eat,
none of the early figs I love.
2 All of the faithful people are gone;
there is not one good person left in this
country.
Everyone is waiting to kill someone;
everyone is trying to trap someone else.
3 With both hands they are doing evil.
Rulers ask for money,
and judges' decisions are bought for a
price.
Rich people tell what they want,
and they get it.
4 Even the best of them is like a thornbush;
the most honest of them is worse than a
prickly plant.
The day that your watchmen[n] warned you
about has come.
Now they will be confused.

7:4 watchmen Another name for prophets. The prophets were like guards who stood on a city's wall and watched for trouble coming from far away.

5 Don't believe your neighbor
or trust a friend.
Don't say anything,
even to your wife.
6 A son will not honor his father,
a daughter will turn against her mother,
and a daughter-in-law will be against her mother-in-law;
a person's enemies will be members of his own family.

THE LORD'S KINDNESS

7 Israel says, "I will look to the LORD for help.
I will wait for God to save me;
my God will hear me.
8 Enemy, don't laugh at me.
I have fallen, but I will get up again.
I sit in the shadow of trouble now,
but the LORD will be a light for me.
9 I sinned against the LORD,
so he was angry with me,
but he will defend my case in court.
He will bring about what is right for me.
Then he will bring me out into the light,
and I will see him set things right.
10 Then my enemies will see this,
and they will be ashamed,
those who said to me,
'Where is the LORD your God?'
I will look down on them.
They will get walked on, like mud in the street."

"I will look to the LORD for help. I will wait for God to save me; my God will hear me." (Micah 7:7)

ISRAEL WILL RETURN

11 The time will come when your walls will be built again,
when your country will grow.
12 At that time your people will come back to you
from Assyria and the cities of Egypt,
and from Egypt to the Euphrates River,
and from sea to sea and mountain to mountain.
13 The earth will be ruined for the people who live in it
because of their deeds.

A PRAYER TO GOD

14 So shepherd your people with your stick;
tend the flock of people who belong to you.
That flock now lives alone in the forest
in the middle of a garden land.
Let them feed in Bashan and Gilead
as in days long ago.

Promise

HE PROMISES TO CONQUER OUR SINS AND THROW THEM INTO THE SEA.

You will have mercy on us again; you will conquer our sins. You will throw away all our sins into the deepest part of the sea (Mic. 7:19).

Sin can haunt you for years. Out of the blue, you may have a flashback of something you did long ago and flinch. You may wonder if God does the same thing. Does he keep a video of your sins—the oldies plus the new releases? At his leisure, he pops in your tape and reviews it? Look at Micah 7:19. It says that God conquers our sins and throws them "into the deepest part of the sea." No videos. The tapes are erased on purpose. He hurls them into the sea. He can't replay your stuff because he doesn't have it anymore. He's done what only he can do—erased your sin forever. It's totally amazing. It's totally grace. To God, forgiven means forgotten. Someone once said that God throws our sin into the sea and puts up a "No Fishing" sign. No one is allowed to go and fish them out. In your attempt to be more like God, stop playing back your sin tapes. Don't bring them up to yourself or to him. Accept his forgiveness and don't look back.

SEE FOR YOURSELF:

Is. 43:25; Jer. 31:34; Heb. 10:15–17; 1 John 1:9

WHAT'S IT MEAN?

Egypt was the first great oppressor of Israel. The Egyptians held the Israelites in slavery for several generations before the Lord used Moses to set the people free. Assyria and Babylon were the second and third great oppressors. The Assyrians destroyed Samaria, the capital of the northern kingdom of Israel, in 722 B.C. The Babylonians destroyed Jerusalem in 586 B.C. That was hardly the end of the story, though. Seventy years after Jerusalem was destroyed, a group of Jewish people were released from captivity in Babylon and allowed to return to the city to rebuild the Temple. Roughly seventy years after that, another group of Jews, this one led by Nehemiah, was allowed to return to Jerusalem to rebuild the city's walls.

Micah 7:11–12

15 "As in the days when I brought you out of
Egypt,
I will show them miracles."

16 When the nations see those miracles,
they will no longer brag about their
power.
They will put their hands over their
mouths,
refusing to listen.
17 They will crawl in the dust like a snake,
like insects crawling on the ground.
They will come trembling from their holes
to the LORD our God
and will turn in fear before you.
18 There is no God like you.
You forgive those who are guilty of
sin;
you don't look at the sins of your people
who are left alive.
You will not stay angry forever,
because you enjoy being kind.
19 You will have mercy on us again;
you will conquer our sins.
You will throw away all our sins
into the deepest part of the sea.
20 You will be true to the people of
Jacob,
and you will be kind to the people of
Abraham
as you promised to our ancestors long
ago.

Nahum

CONTENT The message of the prophet Nahum is a final showdown between good and evil. It's the promise that God would deal with the nation of Assyria, specifically with its capital city, Nineveh, once and for all.

When you think of Nineveh, think of an old western town without a sheriff. The bandits had taken over, and there was no justice to be found. It was not a place where you'd like to raise your kids or even have to ride a stagecoach through. Decency had been ridden out of this savage town before sunset a long time ago.

Nineveh had given Israel grief for hundreds of years. After Nahum's message, Assyria actually did ravage Israel, tearing the people from their homes and keeping them captive for a time.

Nahum's prophecy was a word of good news even if Nineveh had a few more years to give Israel grief. The good news was that God's cavalry was on its way, dressed in white and ready to win. Judgment would eventually, but definitely, fall on Nineveh.

Outline

1:1–6 .... The Fierce Judgment of the Lord
1:7–15 .... Assyria's Doom Brings Hope for the Lord's People
2:1—3:19 .... Nineveh, the Capital of Assyria, Will Be Destroyed

Purpose Godless nations like Assyria will surely fall.

Theme God's Judgment on the City of Nineveh

Date of writing 620 B.C.

1

1 This is the message for the city of Nineveh.[n] This is the book of the vision of Nahum, who was from the town of Elkosh.

THE LORD IS ANGRY WITH NINEVEH

2 The LORD is a jealous God who punishes;
the LORD punishes and is filled with anger.
The LORD punishes those who are against him,
and he stays angry with his enemies.
3 The LORD does not become angry quickly,
and his power is great.
The LORD will not let the guilty go unpunished.
Where the LORD goes, there are whirlwinds and storms,
and the clouds are the dust beneath his feet.
4 He speaks to the sea and makes it dry;
he dries up all the rivers.
The areas of Bashan and Carmel dry up,
and the flowers of Lebanon dry up.
5 The mountains shake in front of him,
and the hills melt.
The earth trembles when he comes;
the world and all who live in it shake with fear.
6 No one can stay alive when he is angry;
no one can survive his strong anger.
His anger is poured out like fire;
the rocks are smashed by him.

WHAT'S IT MEAN?

Nineveh was the capital of Assyria. As far as the Jewish people were concerned, the Assyrians were the biggest troublemakers on the block. The Assyrians destroyed Samaria, the capital of the northern kingdom of Israel, in 722 B.C. They also tried to conquer Judah, the southern kingdom, by surrounding Jerusalem and not allowing any food, water, or supplies to enter the city. Ultimately, they failed in their attempt, but not before causing the people of Jerusalem to suffer terribly.

Nahum 1:1

WHAT'S IT MEAN?

Is your city or town famous for anything? Bashan was known for its oak trees. Carmel was known for its breathtaking view of the Mediterranean Sea. Lebanon, a forest north of Israel, was known for its towering cedar trees.

Nahum 1:4

7 The LORD is good,
giving protection in times of trouble.
He knows who trusts in him.
8 But like a rushing flood,
he will completely destroy Nineveh;
he will chase his enemies until he kills them.

TRIALS

Where can we find protection? (1:7)

9 The LORD will completely destroy
anyone making plans against him.
Trouble will not come a second time.
10 Those people will be like tangled thorns
or like people drunk from their wine;
they will be burned up quickly like dry weeds.
11 Someone has come from Nineveh
who makes evil plans against the LORD
and gives wicked advice.
12 This is what the LORD says:
"Although Assyria is strong and has many people,
it will be defeated and brought to an end.
Although I have made you suffer, Judah,
I will make you suffer no more.
13 Now I will free you from their control
and tear away your chains."

14 The LORD has given you this command, Nineveh:
"You will not have descendants to carry on your name.
I will destroy the idols and metal images
that are in the temple of your gods.
I will make a grave for you,
because you are wicked."

1:1 Nineveh The capital city of the country of Assyria. Nahum uses Nineveh to stand for all of Assyria.

15 Look, there on the hills,
someone is bringing good news!
He is announcing peace!
Celebrate your feasts, people of Judah,
and give your promised sacrifices to God.
The wicked will not come to attack you again;
they have been completely destroyed.

NINEVEH WILL BE DEFEATED

2
1 The destroyer[n] is coming to attack you, Nineveh.
Guard the defenses.
Watch the road.
Get ready.
Gather all your strength!
2 Destroyers have destroyed God's people
and ruined their vines,
but the LORD will bring back Jacob's greatness
like Israel's greatness.

WHAT'S IT MEAN?

Chariots were a pretty scary sight to an army heading into battle. These intimidating war machines were powered by two or more horses, and usually held two or three soldiers. One person drove, while the other(s) fired arrows at the enemy. Sometimes one soldier served as a shield bearer.

Nahum 2:3–4

3 The shields of his soldiers are red;
the army is dressed in red.
The metal on the chariots flashes like fire
when they are ready to attack;
their horses are excited.
4 The chariots race through the streets
and rush back and forth through the city squares.
They look like torches;
they run like lightning.

5 He[n] calls his officers,
but they stumble on the way.
They hurry to the city wall,
and the shield is put into place.
6 The river gates are thrown open,
and the palace is destroyed.
7 It has been announced that the people of Nineveh
will be captured and carried away.
The slave girls moan like doves
and beat their breasts, because they are sad.
8 Nineveh is like a pool,
and now its water is draining away.
"Stop! Stop!" the people yell,
but no one turns back.
9 Take the silver!
Take the gold!
There is no end to the treasure—
piles of wealth of every kind.
10 Nineveh is robbed, ruined, and destroyed.
The people lose their courage, and their knees knock.
Stomachs ache, and everyone's face grows pale.

11 Where is the lions'[n] den
and the place where they feed their young?
Where did the lion, lioness, and cubs go
without being afraid?
12 The lion killed enough for his cubs,
enough for his mate.
He filled his cave with the animals he caught;
he filled his den with meat he had killed.

13 "I am against you, Nineveh,"
says the LORD All-Powerful.
"I will burn up your chariots in smoke,
and the sword will kill your young lions.
I will stop you from hunting down
others on the earth,
and your messengers' voices
will no longer be heard."

IT WILL BE TERRIBLE FOR NINEVEH

3
1 How terrible it will be for the city that has killed so many.
It is full of lies
and goods stolen from other countries.
It is always killing somebody.
2 Hear the sound of whips
and the noise of the wheels.
Hear horses galloping

2:1 destroyer The Babylonians, the Scythians, and the Medes destroyed Nineveh. **2:5 He** This probably means the king of Assyria. **2:11 lions'** The symbol of Assyria was the lion.

and chariots bouncing along!
3 Horses are charging,
swords are shining,
spears are gleaming!
Many are dead;
their bodies are piled up—
too many to count.
People stumble over the dead bodies.
4 The city was like a prostitute;
she was charming and a lover of magic.
She made nations slaves with her
prostitution
and her witchcraft.

5 "I am against you, Nineveh," says the LORD
All-Powerful.
"I will pull your dress up over your face
and show the nations your nakedness
and the kingdoms your shame.
6 I will throw filthy garbage on you
and make a fool of you.
I will make people stare at you.
7 Everyone who sees you will run away and
say,
'Nineveh is in ruins. Who will cry for
her?'
Nineveh, where will I find anyone to
comfort you?"

8 You are no better than Thebes,[n]
who sits by the Nile River
with water all around her.
The river was her defense;
the waters were like a wall around her.
9 Cush and Egypt gave her endless strength;
Put and Libya supported her.

WHAT'S IT MEAN?

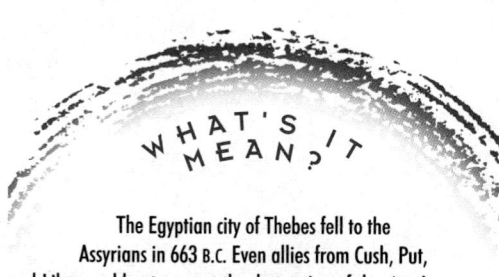

The Egyptian city of Thebes fell to the Assyrians in 663 B.C. Even allies from Cush, Put, and Libya could not prevent the destruction of the city. As you can probably tell from these verses, the Assyrians were extremely cruel to the prisoners they captured.

Nahum 3:9–10

10 But Thebes was captured
and went into captivity.
Her small children were beaten to death
at every street corner.
Lots were thrown for her important men,
and all of her leaders were put in
chains.

11 Nineveh, you will be drunk, too.
You will hide;
you will look for a place safe from the
enemy.
12 All your defenses are like fig trees with
ripe fruit.
When the tree is shaken, the figs fall into
the mouth of the eater.
13 Look at your soldiers.
They are all women!
The gates of your land
are wide open for your enemies;
fire has burned the bars of your gates.

14 Get enough water before the long war
begins.
Make your defenses strong!
Get mud,
mix clay,
make bricks!
15 There the fire will burn you up.
The sword will kill you;
like grasshoppers eating crops, the battle
will completely destroy you.
Grow in number like hopping locusts;
grow in number like swarming locusts!
16 Your traders are more than the stars in the
sky,
but like locusts, they strip the land and
then fly away.
17 Your guards are like locusts.
Your officers are like swarms of locusts
that hang on the walls on a cold day.
When the sun comes up, they fly away,
and no one knows where they have
gone.
18 King of Assyria, your rulers are asleep;
your important men lie down to rest.
Your people have been scattered on the
mountains,
and there is no one to bring them
back.
19 Nothing can heal your wound;
your injury will not heal.
Everyone who hears about you applauds,
because everyone has felt your endless
cruelty.

3:8 Thebes A great city in Egypt.

habakkuk

CONTENT The Book of Habakkuk addresses some of the same issues as the Book of Job. Remember Job? He was a good man, but he suffered. His friends tried to tell him it was his fault. All of them tried to figure out exactly why bad things happen to people who try to be good.

It's like a math equation that just doesn't compute. It seems like life should work like this:

Living a good life + being a good person = having good things happen to you.

But even if we live a good life and are good people, we can never be sure what is on the other side of the equal sign. That is what Job and his friends struggled with. That is what Habakkuk struggled with. That is what we sometimes struggle with.

In the first two chapters, Habakkuk asks God those hard questions, and God gives him some good answers. Life isn't fair, but God is just. Sometimes it takes a while to find the final equal sign. Sometimes it takes all your life. Life on earth is about learning to live a life of faith and becoming what God wants us to be in the process. Those things don't make life any more fair; they just make it worth living.

Outline
1:1—2:20 .... Habakkuk Questions God's Judgments, and the Lord Answers
3:1–19 .... Habakkuk Gives Praise to the Lord

Purpose There is no real "success" for the wicked.

Theme The Just Shall Live by Faith

Date of writing 612 B.C.

1 This is the message Habakkuk the prophet received.

HABAKKUK COMPLAINS

2 LORD, how long must I ask for help
and you ignore me?
I cry out to you about violence,
but you do not save us!
3 Why do you make me see wrong things
and make me look at trouble?
People are destroying things and hurting others in front of me;
they are arguing and fighting.
4 So the teachings are weak,
and justice never comes.
Evil people gain while good people lose;
the judges no longer make fair decisions.

WHAT'S IT MEAN?

Let's set the time frame for this conversation between Habakkuk and God. The Babylonians were on a roll, having defeated both Egypt and Assyria in battle. In 612 B.C., they destroyed the city of Nineveh, the capital of Assyria. Less than thirty years later, the Babylonians, led by King Nebuchadnezzar, would conquer the city of Jerusalem and burn down the Temple built by Solomon.

Habakkuk 1:6

THE LORD ANSWERS

5 "Look at the nations!
Watch them and be amazed and shocked.
I will do something in your lifetime
that you won't believe even when you are told about it.
6 I will use the Babylonians,
those cruel and wild people
who march across the earth
and take lands that don't belong to them.
7 They scare and frighten people.
They do what they want to do
and are good only to themselves.
8 Their horses are faster than leopards
and quicker than wolves at sunset.
Their horse soldiers attack quickly;
they come from places far away.
They attack quickly, like an eagle swooping down for food.
9 They all come to fight.
Nothing can stop them.
Their prisoners are as many as the grains of sand.
10 They laugh at kings
and make fun of rulers.
They laugh at all the strong, walled cities
and build dirt piles to the top of the walls to capture them.
11 Then they leave like the wind and move on.
They are guilty of worshiping their own strength."

HABAKKUK COMPLAINS AGAIN

12 LORD, you live forever,
my God, my holy God.
We will not die.
LORD, you have chosen the Babylonians to punish people;
our Rock, you picked them to punish.
13 Your eyes are too good to look at evil;
you cannot stand to see those who do wrong.
So how can you put up with those evil people?

On the Edge

LORD, you live forever, my God, my holy God (Hab. 1:12a).

Have you ever sat around thinking about how God created everything, and then wondered, *Yeah, but where did God come from?* Well, the answer is that he has always existed. He's everlasting—no beginning, no end. Compare Habakkuk 1:12 with Genesis 1:1. Notice that the Genesis verse says, "In the beginning God. . . ." He has always been. He was never born; he will never die. That can blow your mind. It's just too big to grasp. We are so used to a start and a finish for everything. God has no birthday, no expiration date. He always was, even before the earth was created. He is now, right where you are. He will always be, long after you and the earth have passed away (see Rev. 1:8).

SEE FOR YOURSELF:
Gen. 1:1; Is. 57:15; John 1:1; 1 Tim. 1:17; Rev. 1:8

How can you be quiet when the wicked
swallow up people who are better
than they are?
14 You treat people like fish in the sea,
like sea animals without a leader.
15 The enemy brings them in with hooks.
He catches them in his net
and drags them in his fishnet.
So he rejoices and sings for joy.
16 The enemy offers sacrifices to his net
and burns incense to worship it,
because it lets him live like the rich
and enjoy the best food.
17 Will he keep on taking riches with his net?
Will he go on destroying people without
showing mercy?

2

1 I will stand like a guard to watch
and place myself at the tower.
I will wait to see what he will say to me;
I will wait to learn how God will
answer my complaint.

THE LORD ANSWERS

2 The LORD answered me:
"Write down the vision;
write it clearly on clay tablets
so whoever reads it can run to tell
others.
3 It is not yet time for the message to come
true,
but that time is coming soon;
the message will come true.
It may seem like a long time,
but be patient and wait for it,
because it will surely come;
it will not be delayed.
4 The evil nation is very proud of itself;
it is not living as it should.
But those who are right with God will
live by trusting in him.

5 "Just as wine can trick a person,
those who are too proud will not last,
because their desire is like a grave's desire
for death,
and like death they always want more.
They gather other nations for themselves
and collect for themselves all the
countries.
6 But all the nations the Babylonians have
hurt will laugh at them.
They will make fun of the Babylonians
and say, 'How terrible it will be for the one
that steals many things.
How long will that nation get rich by
forcing others to pay them?'

7 "One day the people from whom you
have taken money will turn against
you.
They will realize what is happening and
make you shake with fear.
Then they will take everything you have.

Promise

HE PROMISES TO BE TRUTHFUL ABOUT THE FUTURE.

It is not yet time for the message to come true, but that time is coming soon; the message will come true. It may seem like a long time, but be patient and wait for it, because it will surely come; it will not be delayed (Hab. 2:3).

Everyone wants you to believe what they have to say about the future. Grocery store magazines report new predictions about the future every month or so. Late-night psychics want you to call so they can tell you about your future. And newspaper horoscopes want you to read every day to find out how this day will go. The whole business of "future-telling" is one big scam. Millions spend money because they want someone—anyone—to give them encouragement and hope. Their empty words have no value. You can only trust what God says about the future. Only his truth can guide your life. Everything else will fall short. So if you need to consult someone about a decision or life even, turn to the One who has been to the future and knows the whole story. You can trust what he says. You can build your life on his truth.

SEE FOR YOURSELF:

Josh. 21:45; Ps. 18:30; Prov. 30:5; Jer. 29:11; John 17:17

8 Because you have stolen from many
nations,
those who are left will take much from
you.
This is because you have killed many
people,
destroying countries and cities and
everyone in them.

9 "How terrible it will be for the nation that
becomes rich by doing wrong,
thinking they will live in a safe place
and escape harm.
10 Because you have made plans to destroy
many people,
you have made your own houses
ashamed of you.
Because of it, you will lose your lives.
11 The stones of the walls will cry out against
you,
and the boards that support the roof
will agree that you are wrong.

12 "How terrible it will be for the nation that
kills people to build a city,
that wrongs others to start a town.
13 The LORD All-Powerful will send fire
to destroy what those people have
built;
all the nations' work will be for nothing.
14 Then, just as water covers the sea,
people everywhere will know the LORD's
glory.

15 "How terrible for the nation that makes its
neighbors drink,
pouring from the jug of wine until they
are drunk
so that it can look at their naked
bodies.
16 You Babylonians will be filled with
disgrace, not respect.
It's your turn to drink and fall to the
ground like a drunk person.
The cup of anger from the LORD's right
hand is coming around to you.
You will receive disgrace, not respect.
17 You hurt many people in Lebanon,
but now you will be hurt.
You killed many animals there,
and now you must be afraid
because of what you did
to that land, those cities, and the people
who lived in them.

THE MESSAGE ABOUT IDOLS

18 "An idol does no good, because a human
made it;
it is only a statue that teaches lies.
The one who made it expects his own
work to help him,
but he makes idols that can't even
speak!
19 How terrible it will be for the one who
says to a wooden statue, 'Come to life!'
How terrible it will be for the one who
says to a silent stone, 'Get up!'
It cannot tell you what to do.
It is only a statue covered with gold and
silver;
there is no life in it.
20 The LORD is in his Holy Temple;
all the earth should be silent in his
presence."

HABAKKUK'S PRAYER

3 1 This is the prayer of Habakkuk the prophet,
on shigionoth.

2 LORD, I have heard the news about you;
I am amazed at what you have done.
LORD, do great things once again in our
time;
make those things happen again in our
own days.
Even when you are angry,
remember to be kind.

3 God is coming from Teman;
the Holy One comes from Mount
Paran.[n] *Selah*

WHAT'S IT MEAN?

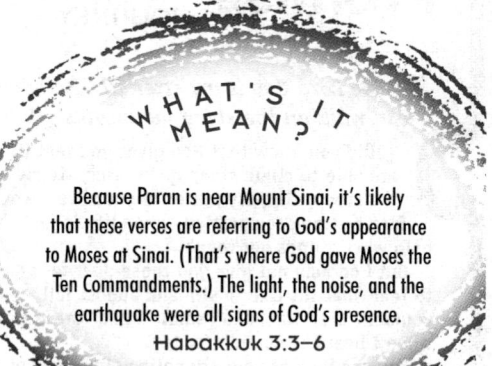

Because Paran is near Mount Sinai, it's likely that these verses are referring to God's appearance to Moses at Sinai. (That's where God gave Moses the Ten Commandments.) The light, the noise, and the earthquake were all signs of God's presence.

Habakkuk 3:3–6

3:3 Teman . . . Paran God is seen as again coming from the direction of Mount Sinai. He came from Sinai when he rescued his people from Egypt.

His glory covers the skies,
and his praise fills the earth.
4 He is like a bright light.
Rays of light shine from his hand,
and there he hides his power.
5 Sickness goes before him,
and disease follows behind him.
6 He stands and shakes the earth.
He looks, and the nations shake with fear.
The mountains, which stood for ages,
break into pieces;
the old hills fall down.
God has always done this.

7 I saw that the tents of Cushan were in trouble
and that the tents of Midian trembled.
8 LORD, were you angry at the rivers,
or were you angry at the streams?
Were you angry with the sea
when you rode your horses and chariots of victory?[n]
9 You uncovered your bow
and commanded many arrows to be brought to you. *Selah*
You split the earth with rivers.
10 The mountains saw you and shook with fear.
The rushing water flowed.
The sea made a loud noise,
and its waves rose high.
11 The sun and moon stood still in the sky;
they stopped when they saw the flash of your flying arrows
and the gleam of your shining spear.
12 In anger you marched on the earth;
in anger you punished the nations.
13 You came out to save your people,
to save your chosen one.

WHAT'S IT MEAN?

The people of Cushan are sometimes referred to as Ethiopians in the Bible. The people of Cushan and Midian were nomads, wandering tribesmen who lived in tents. When God parted the Red Sea for the Israelites, they passed from the land of Cush to the land of Midian.

Habakkuk 3:7

3:8 sea . . . victory This is probably talking about the Israelites crossing the Red Sea.

Promise

HE PROMISES TO PREPARE YOU FOR LIFE'S JOURNEY.

The Lord GOD is my strength. He makes me like a deer that does not stumble so I can walk on the steep mountains (Hab. 3:19).

Did you know that God gives you feet like a deer? Habakkuk shows us that picture—feet that are able to climb steep mountains, steady even when the path is slippery. God prepares you for the steep, slippery places in your life—when you have to cope with the tough stuff, when you face a strong temptation, when life is just hard. God gives you the strength to stand strong and bold when things get rough.

But God may not give you those deer feet automatically, like an instant miracle. You may have to feel what it's like to slip and almost fall, especially if you start up the mountain by yourself. Even Habakkuk said: "I hear these things, and my body trembles; my lips tremble when I hear the sound" (v. 16).

You can look at your stumbling steps as a gift from God. He's showing you that you can't make it without him. If you start to fall, it's a little reminder that deer feet aren't a product of your own inner strength. They come from your faith in him and in his Spirit living inside you.

SEE FOR YOURSELF:

Ps. 61:1–3; Is. 35:6; 42:16

You crushed the leader of the wicked ones
and took everything he had, from head
to toe. *Selah*
14 With the enemy's own spear you stabbed
the leader of his army.
His soldiers rushed out like a storm to
scatter us.
They were happy
as they were robbing the poor people in
secret.
15 But you marched through the sea with
your horses,
stirring the great waters.

16 I hear these things, and my body trembles;
my lips tremble when I hear the sound.
My bones feel weak,
and my legs shake.

But I will wait patiently for the day of
disaster
that will come to the people who attack
us.
17 Fig trees may not grow figs,
and there may be no
grapes on the
vines.
There may be no olives
growing
and no food growing
in the fields.
There may be no sheep in
the pens
and no cattle in the barns.
18 But I will still be glad in the LORD;
I will rejoice in God my Savior.
19 The Lord GOD is my strength.
He makes me like a deer that does not
stumble
so I can walk on the steep mountains.

For the director of music. On my stringed instruments.

ENCOURAGEMENT

Are we ever helpless? (3:17–19)

Zephaniah

CONTENT Have you ever seen a natural disaster film? Whether it's a volcano or an earthquake or a nuclear power plant gone wrong, there is always someone running around right before the explosion making one last effort to make the people understand what is about to happen. The person usually looks frazzled and wide-eyed and full of passion about his or her message.

That might have been what Zephaniah looked like. He was the last prophet to preach to Judah before judgment fell and they were taken away into captivity.

The problems Zephaniah's people faced were national problems. They had become an evil people who sacrificed their own children to false gods and spit in the face of the true God. They disrespected and disregarded everything God had done for them. As a nation, they were going to face some consequences that would change their lives forever.

The heart of Zephaniah's message, though, is personal responsibility. The problem may have been nationwide, but the solution was only as big as each person's own heart. They needed to make a choice, each of them, to obey what God told them to do.

Outline

1:1–18 .... Judah and Jerusalem Will Be Punished on the Lord's Day of Judging
2:1–3 .... Seek the Lord
2:4–15 .... The Nations Will Be Punished
3:1–20 .... Nations Will Call on the Lord

Purpose God's discipline purges evil and motivates us to return to him.

Theme The Wrath of a Loving God

Date of writing 607 B.C.

1 [1]This is the word of the LORD that came
through Zephaniah while Josiah son of Amon
was king of Judah. Zephaniah was the son of
Cushi, who was the son of Gedaliah. Gedaliah
was the son of Amariah, who was the son of
Hezekiah.

THE LORD'S JUDGMENT

[2]"I will sweep away everything
from the earth," says the LORD.
[3]"I will sweep away the people and animals;
I will destroy the birds in the air
and the fish of the sea.
I will ruin the evil people,
and I will remove human beings from the earth," says the LORD.

WHAT'S IT MEAN?

When it came to pagan gods, the Israelites weren't choosy. They worshiped just about anything. Baal was the chief god of the Canaanites, but the Israelites adopted him as their own. The followers of Molech sacrificed children as part of their worship rituals. That didn't bother the Israelites, who were eager to join in the disgusting proceedings, despite the fact that God had specifically forbidden human sacrifice. Not satisfied with merely worshiping idols, the Israelites also got involved in astrology and started worshiping the sun, the moon, and the stars. As part of their worship, they poured out drink offerings and burnt incense on their rooftops.

Zephaniah 1:4–5

THE FUTURE OF JUDAH

[4]"I will punish Judah
and all the people living in Jerusalem.
I will remove from this place
all signs of Baal, the false priests, and the other priests.
[5]I will destroy those who worship
the stars from the roofs,[n]
and those who worship and make promises
by both the LORD and the god Molech,
[6]and those who turned away from the LORD,
and those who quit following the LORD
and praying to him for direction.
[7]Be silent before the Lord GOD,
because the LORD's day for judging people is coming soon.
The LORD has prepared a sacrifice;
he has made holy his invited guests.
[8]On the day of the LORD's sacrifice,
I, the LORD, will punish the princes and the king's sons
and all those who wear foreign clothes.
[9]On that day I will punish those who worship Dagon,
those who hurt others and tell lies in the temples of their gods.

[10]"On that day," says the LORD,
"a cry will be heard at the Fish Gate.
A wail will come from the new area of the city,
and a loud crash will echo from the hills.
[11]Cry, you people living in the market area,
because all the merchants will be dead;
all the silver traders will be gone.
[12]At that time I, the LORD, will search Jerusalem with lamps.
I will punish those who are satisfied with themselves,
who think, 'The LORD won't help us or punish us.'
[13]Their wealth will be stolen
and their houses destroyed.
They may build houses,
but they will not live in them.
They may plant vineyards,
but they will not drink any wine from them.

THE LORD'S DAY OF JUDGING

[14]"The LORD's day of judging is coming soon;
it is near and coming fast.
The cry will be very sad on the day of the LORD;
even soldiers will cry.
[15]That day will be a day of anger,
a day of terror and trouble,
a day of destruction and ruin,
a day of darkness and gloom,
a day of clouds and blackness,

1:5 roofs In Bible times houses were built with flat roofs. The roof was used for drying things such as flax and fruit. And it was used as an extra room, as a place for worship, and as a cool place to sleep in the summer.

16 a day of alarms and battle cries.
'Attack the strong, walled cities!
Attack the corner towers!'
17 I will make life hard on the people;
they will walk around like the blind,
because they have sinned against the
LORD.
Their blood will be poured out like dust,
and their insides will be dumped like
trash.
18 On the day that God will show his anger,
neither their silver nor gold will save
them.
The LORD's anger will be like a fire
that will burn up the whole world;
suddenly he will bring an end, yes, an end
to everyone on earth."

WHAT'S IT MEAN?

The Philistines lived west of Israel, along the coast of the Mediterranean Sea. For some reason, the Philistines decided they needed more than one capital city in their nation. Gaza, Ashdod, Ashkelon, and Ekron were all capitals of Philistia. Actually, there had been a fifth capital, Gath, but it was under Judah's control during Zephaniah's day.

Zephaniah 2:4–5

THE LORD ASKS PEOPLE TO CHANGE

2

1 Gather together, gather,
you unwanted people.
2 Do it before it's too late,
before you are blown away like chaff,
before the LORD's terrible anger reaches
you,
before the day of the LORD's
anger comes to you.
3 Come to the LORD, all you
who are not proud,
who obey his laws.
Do what is right. Learn to
be humble.
Maybe you will escape
on the day the LORD shows his anger.

HUMILITY

Is humility important? (2:3)

PHILISTIA WILL BE PUNISHED

4 No one will be left in the city of Gaza,
and the city of Ashkelon will be
destroyed.
Ashdod will be empty by noon,
and the people of Ekron will be chased
away.
5 How terrible it will be for you who live by
the Mediterranean Sea,
you Philistines!
The word of the LORD is against you,
Canaan, land of the Philistines.

"I will destroy you
so that no one will be left."
6 The land by the Mediterranean Sea, in
which you live,
will become pastures, fields for
shepherds, and pens for sheep.
7 It will belong to the descendants of Judah
who are left alive.
There they will let their sheep eat grass.
At night they will sleep
in the houses of Ashkelon.
The LORD their God will pay attention to
them
and will make their life good again.

MOAB AND AMMON WILL BE PUNISHED

8 "I have heard the insults of the country of
Moab
and the threats of the people of
Ammon.
They have insulted my people
and have taken their land."
9 So the LORD All-Powerful, the God of
Israel, says,
"As surely as I live,
Moab will be destroyed like Sodom,

WHAT'S IT MEAN?

The people of Moab and Ammon were actually distant relatives of the Israelites. The Moabites and Ammonites were descendants of Lot, Abraham's nephew. (The Israelites, of course, were descendants of Abraham.) Despite the fact that they were "kin," the people of Moab and Ammon were enemies of Israel. The comparisons to Sodom and Gomorrah probably would have gotten people's attention. Both of those cities were destroyed by God in an awesome display of fire from heaven.

Zephaniah 2:8–9

and Ammon will be destroyed like
Gomorrah[n]—
a heap of weeds, a pit of salt,
and a ruin forever.
Those of my people who are left alive will
take whatever they want from them;
those who are left from my nation will
take their land."

10 This is what Moab and Ammon get for
being proud,
because they insulted and made fun of
the people of the LORD All-Powerful.
11 The LORD will frighten them,
because he will destroy all the gods of
the earth.
Then everyone in faraway places
will worship him wherever they are.

CUSH AND ASSYRIA WILL BE DESTROYED

12 "You Cushites also
will be killed by my sword."
13 Then the LORD will turn against the north
and destroy Assyria.
He will make Nineveh
a ruin as dry as a desert.
14 Flocks and herds will lie down there,
and all wild animals.
The owls and crows will sit
on the stone pillars.
The owl will hoot through the windows,
trash will be in the doorways,
and the wooden boards of the buildings
will be gone.
15 This is the happy and safe city
that thinks there is no one else as strong
as it is.
But what a ruin it will be,
a place where wild animals live.
All those who pass by will make fun
and shake their fists.

JERUSALEM WILL BE PUNISHED

3
1 How terrible for the wicked, stubborn city
of Jerusalem,
which hurts its own people.
2 It obeys no voice;
it can't be taught to do right.
It doesn't trust the LORD;
it doesn't worship its God.
3 Its officers are like roaring lions.
Its rulers are like hungry wolves that
attack in the evening,
and in the morning nothing is left of
those they attacked.
4 Its prophets are proud;

2:9 Sodom . . . Gomorrah Two cities God destroyed because the people were so evil.

Promise HE PROMISES TO RESTORE YOU WITH HIS LOVE.

The LORD your God is with you; the mighty One will save you. He will rejoice over you. You will rest in his love; he will sing and be joyful about you (Zeph. 3:17).

Zephaniah 3:17 is one of the most awesome verses in all the minor prophets. It shows you incredible truths about God and about yourself. It reveals such a tender and delightful side of the Lord in the middle of some hard prophecies. He rejoices and sings! People don't usually think of God rejoicing and singing, but he does! He's excited because of *you*. When you don't feel like you're worth much, remember that God is singing because of you. And on top of his rejoicing and singing, you get a blessing. He restores your life with his love. Everybody needs restoration. Life sometimes gets pretty routine and you find yourself feeling stale and soggy on the inside. You find that you can't spruce up your own heart, because God is the One who changes hearts. He promises to meet you in those stale times. He promises that you will "rest in his love." There's nothing that adds zest to life more than the breath wind of the Spirit of God blowing through your heart. It does more for you on the inside than a squirt from the garden hose on a steamy afternoon. It brings you back to life. It gives you passion again. It refuels your energy. And it stokes the fire of God that's inside of you. He does it all without thunder and lightning. He does it with such tenderness—just by his love, which touches all your deepest places. Never, ever forget that you are the one who makes God sing. And he is the One who will let you "rest in his love."

SEE FOR YOURSELF:

Ps. 23:1–3; 80:18; 147:3; Acts 3:19–21

they are people who cannot be trusted.
Its priests don't respect holy things;
they break God's teachings.
5 But the LORD is good, and he is there in
that city.
He does no wrong.
Every morning he governs the people
fairly;
every day he can be trusted.
But evil people are not ashamed of what
they do.

6 "I have destroyed nations;
their towers were ruined.
I made their streets empty
so no one goes there anymore.
Their cities are ruined;
no one lives there at all.
7 I said, 'Surely now Jerusalem will respect
me
and will accept my teaching.'
Then the place where they lived would
not be destroyed,
and I would not have to punish them.
But they were still eager
to do evil in everything they did.
8 Just wait," says the LORD.
"Some day I will stand up as a witness.
I have decided that I will gather nations
and assemble kingdoms.
I will pour out my anger on them,
all my strong anger.
My anger will be like fire
that will burn up the whole world.

A NEW DAY FOR GOD'S PEOPLE

9 "Then I will give the people of all nations
pure speech
so that all of them will speak the name
of the LORD
and worship me together.
10 People will come from where the Nile
River begins;
my scattered people will come with gifts
for me.
11 Then Jerusalem will not be ashamed
of the wrongs done against me,
because I will remove from this city
those who like to brag;
there will never be any more proud
people
on my holy mountain in Jerusalem.
12 But I will leave in the city
the humble and those who are not
proud,
and they will trust in the LORD.

On the Edge

"I will take away the sadness planned for you, which would have made you very ashamed. At that time I will punish all those who harmed you. I will save my people who cannot walk and gather my people who have been thrown out. I will give them praise and honor in every place where they were shamed. At that time I will gather you; at that time I will bring you back home. I will give you honor and praise from people everywhere when I make things go well again for you, as you will see with your own eyes," says the LORD (Zeph. 3:18–20).

There are all kinds of reasons for feeling like a misfit. Maybe you're a lot taller than everybody else you know and you stand out physically. Maybe you live in a part of town different from where most of the people you know live. Maybe you have a whole different set of values and you're labeled a "goody-goody."

For whatever reason, feeling like you don't fit in can be a painful, lonely place. For some people, the situation changes when they go to a new school or move to a new neighborhood or when they get older. Some people go all the way through their lives feeling like they don't belong.

But the truth is, you do belong. You belong to the Lord. He is in love with you. You always have a place with him. He is always glad to see you. He has such a heart for you. Seek his direction for your life. He's got a plan for you, and no one else will fit it as perfectly as you will. Ask him to bring people you can love and be loved by into your life. He is faithful. He wants you to be happy. He's there to help you.

SEE FOR YOURSELF:
Ps. 31:5; Is. 56:8; Mic. 4:7; Zeph. 3:17

13 Those who are left alive in Israel won't do
wrong or tell lies;
they won't trick people with their
words.
They will eat and lie down
with no one to make them afraid."

A HAPPY SONG

[14]Sing, Jerusalem.
Israel, shout for joy!
Jerusalem, be happy
and rejoice with all your heart.
[15]The LORD has stopped punishing you;
he has sent your enemies away.
The King of Israel, the LORD, is with you;
you will never again be afraid of being harmed.

WHAT'S IT MEAN?

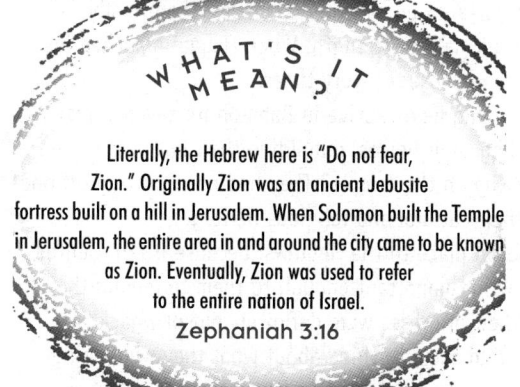

Literally, the Hebrew here is "Do not fear, Zion." Originally Zion was an ancient Jebusite fortress built on a hill in Jerusalem. When Solomon built the Temple in Jerusalem, the entire area in and around the city came to be known as Zion. Eventually, Zion was used to refer to the entire nation of Israel.
Zephaniah 3:16

[16]On that day Jerusalem will be told,
"Don't be afraid, city of Jerusalem.
Don't give up.
[17]The LORD your God is with you;
the mighty One will save you.
He will rejoice over you.
You will rest in his love;
he will sing and be joyful about you."

[18]"I will take away the sadness planned for you,
which would have made you very ashamed.
[19]At that time I will punish
all those who harmed you.
I will save my people who cannot walk
and gather my people who have been thrown out.
I will give them praise and honor
in every place where they were shamed.
[20]At that time I will gather you;
at that time I will bring you back home.
I will give you honor and praise
from people everywhere
when I make things go well again for you,
as you will see with your own eyes,"
says the LORD.

haggai

CONTENT

If you've been reading through the Bible, you are very familiar by now with the history of the Hebrews. They continued to go through these cycles of obeying God, then not obeying God, then being beaten up by other countries, then finally returning to God and regaining their natural strength. When Haggai preached his message, the Hebrews were in one of those recovery times.

They had returned home after being held captive in Babylon for seventy years. They had spent ten years rebuilding their homes, rebuilding their businesses, and starting on the Temple. Just *starting* on the Temple? They had been putting off one of the most important parts of their cultural and religious heritage!

You see, the Temple was a special place to the Hebrews, because it represented God's presence with them. If it wasn't important enough to them to rebuild the Temple (after ten years!), then their priorities were definitely out of whack.

So Haggai told them that. He told them to think about what they were doing. He told them that putting God first is the real key to getting back on track and being strong enough to face life. Those lessons would be good ones for today as well, huh?

Outline

1:1–15 .... The Command to Rebuild the Temple
2:1–19 .... The Beauty of the Temple
2:20–23 .... The Lord Chooses Zerubbabel

Purpose

Obedience to God's word brings blessings.

Theme

Rebuilding the Temple

Date of writing

520 B.C.

IT IS TIME TO BUILD THE TEMPLE

1 [1]The prophet Haggai spoke the word of the LORD to Zerubbabel son of Shealtiel, the governor of Judah, and to Joshua son of Jehozadak, the high priest. This message came in the second year that Darius was king, on the first day of the sixth month:

[2]"This is what the LORD All-Powerful says: 'The people say the right time has not come to rebuild the Temple of the LORD.'"

WHAT'S IT MEAN?

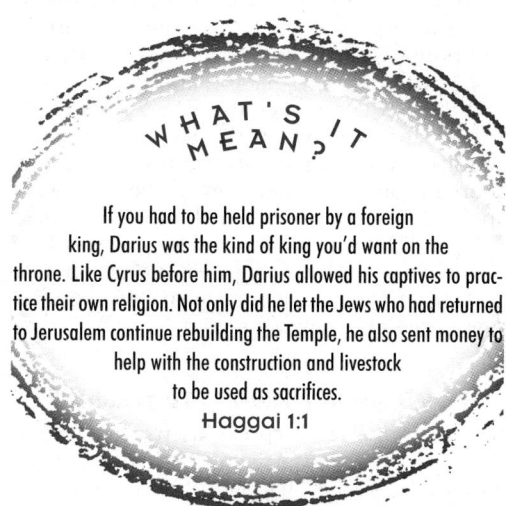

If you had to be held prisoner by a foreign king, Darius was the kind of king you'd want on the throne. Like Cyrus before him, Darius allowed his captives to practice their own religion. Not only did he let the Jews who had returned to Jerusalem continue rebuilding the Temple, he also sent money to help with the construction and livestock to be used as sacrifices.

Haggai 1:1

[3]Then Haggai the prophet spoke the word of the LORD: [4]"Is it right for you to be living in fancy houses while the Temple is still in ruins?"

[5]This is what the LORD All-Powerful says: "Think about what you have done. [6]You have planted much, but you harvest little. You eat, but you do not become full. You drink, but you are still thirsty. You put on clothes, but you are not warm enough. You earn money, but then you lose it all as if you had put it into a purse full of holes."

"Haggai, the LORD's messenger, gave the LORD's message to the people, saying, 'The LORD says, "I am with you." ' " (Haggai 1:13)

[7]This is what the LORD All-Powerful says: "Think about what you have done. [8]Go up to the mountains, bring back wood, and build the Temple. Then I will be pleased with it and be honored," says the LORD. [9]"You look for much, but you find little. When you bring it home, I destroy it. Why?" asks the LORD All-Powerful. "Because you all work hard for your own houses while my house is still in ruins! [10]Because of what you have done, the sky holds back its rain and the ground holds back its crops. [11]I have called for a time without rain on the land, and on the mountains, and on the grain, the new wine, the olive oil, the plants which the earth produces, the people, the farm animals, and all the work of your hands."

[12]Zerubbabel son of Shealtiel and Joshua son of Jehozadak, the high priest, and all the rest of the people who were left alive obeyed the LORD their God and the message from Haggai the prophet, because the LORD their God had sent him. And the people feared the LORD.

[13]Haggai, the LORD's messenger, gave the LORD's message to the people, saying, "The LORD says, 'I am with you.' " [14]The LORD stirred up Zerubbabel son of Shealtiel, the governor of Judah, and Joshua son of Jehozadak, the high priest, and all the rest of the people who were left alive. So they came and worked on the Temple of their God, the LORD All-Powerful. [15]They began on the twenty-fourth day of the sixth month in the second year Darius was king.

THE BEAUTY OF THE TEMPLE

2 [1]On the twenty-first day of the seventh month, the LORD spoke his word through Haggai the prophet, saying, [2]"Speak to Zerubbabel son of Shealtiel, governor of Judah, and to Joshua son of Jehozadak, the high priest, and to the rest of the people who are left alive. Say, [3]'Do any of you remember how great the Temple was before it was destroyed? What does it look like now? Doesn't it seem like nothing to you?' [4]But the LORD says, 'Zerubbabel, be brave. Also, Joshua son of Jehozadak, the high priest, be brave. And all you people who live in the land, be brave,' says the LORD. 'Work, because I am with you,' says the LORD All-Powerful. [5]'I made a promise to you when you came out of Egypt, and my Spirit is still with you. So don't be afraid.'

COURAGE

Why should we be confident? (2:4)

[6]"This is what the LORD All-Powerful says: 'In a short time I will once again shake the heavens and the earth, the sea and the dry land. [7]I will shake all the nations, and they will bring their wealth. Then I will fill this Temple with glory,' says the LORD All-Powerful. [8]'The silver is mine, and the gold is mine,' says the LORD All-Powerful. [9]'The new Temple will be greater than the one before,' says the LORD All-Powerful.

'And in this place I will give peace,' says the
LORD All-Powerful."
[10]On the twenty-fourth day of the ninth
month in the second year Darius was king, the
LORD spoke his word to Haggai the prophet,
saying, [11]"This is what the LORD All-Powerful
says: 'Ask the priests for a teaching. [12]Suppose
a person carries in the fold of his clothes some
meat made holy for the LORD. If that fold
touches bread, cooked food, wine, olive oil, or
some other food, will that be made holy?' "
The priests answered, "No."

WHAT'S IT MEAN?

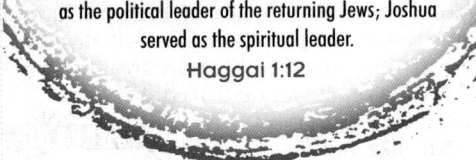

When the Jewish people returned to Jerusalem, they found some familiar faces in charge. Zerubbabel was the grandson of Jehoiakim, one of the last kings to reign in Judah before the Babylonian invasion. King Cyrus of Persia allowed Zerubbabel to lead a group of Jews back to Jerusalem to begin rebuilding the Temple. Cyrus also appointed Zerubbabel governor of Judah. Joshua was the son of Jehozadak, who was high priest when the Jewish people were deported to Babylon. Zerubbabel served as the political leader of the returning Jews; Joshua served as the spiritual leader.

Haggai 1:12

[13]Then Haggai said, "A person who touches a
dead body will become unclean. If he touches
any of these foods, will it become unclean, too?"
The priests answered, "Yes, it would become
unclean."
[14]Then Haggai answered, "The LORD says,
'This is also true for the people of this nation.
They are unclean, and everything they do with
their hands is unclean to me. Whatever they
offer at the altar is also unclean.
[15]" 'Think about this from now on! Think
about how it was before you started laying
stones on top of stones to build the Temple of
the LORD. [16]A person used to come to a pile of
grain expecting to find twenty basketfuls, but
there were only ten. And a person used to
come to the wine vat to take out fifty jarfuls,
but only twenty were there. [17]I destroyed your
work with diseases, mildew, and hail, but you
still did not come back to me,' says the LORD.
[18]'It is the twenty-fourth day of the ninth
month, the day in which the people finished
working on the foundation of the Temple of
the LORD. From now on, think about these
things: [19]Do you have seeds for crops still in
the barn? Your vines, fig trees, pomegranates,
and olive trees have not given fruit yet. But
from now on I will bless you!' "

THE LORD MAKES A PROMISE TO ZERUBBABEL

[20]Then the LORD spoke his word a second
time to Haggai on the twenty-fourth day of the
month. He said, [21]"Tell Zerubbabel, the governor of Judah, 'I am going to shake the heavens
and the earth. [22]I will destroy the foreign kingdoms and take away the power of the kingdoms of the nations. I will destroy the chariots
and their riders. The horses will fall with their
riders, as people kill each other with swords.'
[23]The LORD All-Powerful says, 'On that day I
will take you, Zerubbabel son of Shealtiel, my
servant,' says the LORD, 'and I will make you
important like my signet ring, because I have
chosen you!' says the LORD All-Powerful."

Zechariah

CONTENT Zechariah's message came to the group of Hebrews who had returned to Jerusalem and found it in ruins and inhabited by foreigners. These people wanted to reestablish their homes and rebuild the Temple, but it was really hard and discouraging.

Zechariah's message did two things. First, it was a rah-rah kind of cheer to remind the people that what they were doing was worth the effort. (You know how hard it is to work on something when you feel like you're wasting your time.)

Within Zechariah's pep rally, though, were some amazing prophecies about the coming of Christ. Part of his reasoning for rebuilding the Temple and the city was to get Jerusalem ready for the Messiah, the promise that he believed would make all this better.

Zechariah's message is a good one for us today as well. Sometimes a life of faith can feel like a losing season. Sometimes it seems like our team will never win again. Zechariah reminds us that the season isn't over until God says it is. Until then, we've got to stay in the game and get ready for Jesus' arrival on the scene.

Outline

1:1–17 .... The Vision of the Horses
1:18–21 .... The Vision of the Horns
2:1–13 .... The Vision of the Man with a Measuring Line
3:1–10 .... The Vision of the High Priest (Joshua) and Satan
4:1–14 .... The Vision of the Lampstand and the Olive Trees
5:1–4 .... The Vision of a Flying Scroll
5:5–11 .... The Vision of the Woman Inside the Basket
6:1–8 .... The Vision of the Four Chariots
6:9—8:23 .... Mourning and Celebrating
9:1—11:3 .... The Lord Will Rescue His People and Punish Their Enemies
11:4–17 .... Israel's Leaders Are Worthless Shepherds
12:1–9 .... Victory for Jerusalem
12:10—13:9 .... The People Will Mourn and Return to the Lord
14:1–21 .... The Final Battle and the Lord's Victory

Purpose God remains in control of history and will triumph.

Theme The Lord Remembers His People

Date of writing 515 B.C.

"Rejoice greatly, people of Jerusalem! Shout for joy, people of Jerusalem! Your king is coming to you. He does what is right, and he saves. He is gentle and riding on a donkey, on the colt of a donkey" (9:9).

Bible Talk

What's Everybody Waiting For?

In one way or another, all the prophets were looking toward the coming of Jesus Christ. It seems like if you talked to any of them long enough, the subject would certainly come up.

Understand that the whole identity of the Jewish people was wrapped up in the coming of the Messiah. God made the first promise about the Messiah to Adam and Eve, and the main reason for establishing the Jewish nation through Abraham was that Jesus would come through his family.

Every comfort that was given to the Hebrews as they struggled had somewhere as its message that Jesus would come and he would fix things. As we look *back* at history, Jesus' arrival seems right on time. If we had lived in 400 B.C., we might have felt differently.

PROPHECIES OF THE MESSIAH

If prophecy were a sport, like baseball, Zechariah would have been a home-run hitter.

He prophesied that Jesus would ride into Jerusalem on a donkey (9:9), which he did.

He prophesied that Judas would betray Jesus for thirty pieces of silver (11:12), which he did.

He prophesied that Jesus' side would be pierced (12:10) and that his blood would cleanse our sin (13:1), which it was and it does.

He prophesied that Jesus would have scars in his hands and side (13:6) and that he would be arrested and deserted by his disciples (13:7), which he did and he was and they did.

Zechariah also prophesied that Jesus would return a second time to reign on earth (14:4), which he will.

THE LORD CALLS HIS PEOPLE BACK

1

1In the eighth month of the second year
Darius was king, the LORD spoke his word to
the prophet Zechariah son of Berekiah, who
was the son of Iddo. The LORD said, 2"The LORD
was very angry with your ancestors. 3So tell
the people: This is what the LORD All-Powerful
says: 'Return to me, and I will return to you,'
says the LORD All-Powerful. 4Don't be like your
ancestors. In the past the prophets said to
them: This is what the LORD All-Powerful says:
'Stop your evil ways and evil actions.' But they
wouldn't listen or pay attention to me, says the
LORD. 5Your ancestors are dead, and those
prophets didn't live forever. 6I commanded my
words and laws to my servants the prophets,
and they preached to your ancestors, who
returned to me. They said, 'The LORD All-
Powerful did as he said he would. He punished
us for the way we lived and for what we did.' "

WHAT'S IT MEAN?

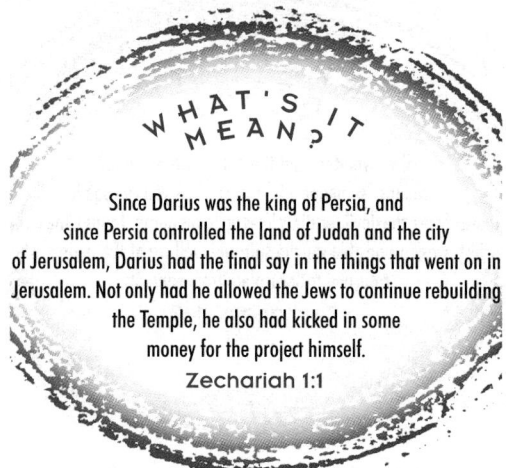

Since Darius was the king of Persia, and since Persia controlled the land of Judah and the city of Jerusalem, Darius had the final say in the things that went on in Jerusalem. Not only had he allowed the Jews to continue rebuilding the Temple, he also had kicked in some money for the project himself.

Zechariah 1:1

THE VISION OF THE HORSES

7It was on the twenty-fourth day of the
eleventh month, which is the month of Shebat,
in Darius's second year as king. The LORD
spoke his word to the prophet Zechariah son
of Berekiah, who was the son of Iddo.
8During the night I had a vision. I saw a
man riding a red horse. He was standing
among some myrtle trees in a ravine, with red,
brown, and white horses behind him.
9I asked, "What are these, sir?"
The angel who was talking with me answered, "I'll show you what they are."
10Then the man standing among the myrtle
trees explained, "They are the ones the LORD
sent through all the earth."
11Then they spoke to the LORD's angel, who
was standing among the myrtle trees. They
said, "We have gone through all the earth, and
everything is calm and quiet."
12Then the LORD's angel asked, "LORD All-
Powerful, how long will it be before you show
mercy to Jerusalem and the cities of Judah?
You have been angry with them for seventy
years now." 13So the LORD answered the angel
who was talking with me, and his words were
comforting and good.
14Then the angel who was talking to me
said to me, "Announce this: This is what the
LORD All-Powerful says: 'I have a strong love
for Jerusalem. 15And I am very angry with the
nations that feel so safe. I was only a little angry at them, but they made things worse.'
16"So this is what the LORD says: 'I will return to Jerusalem with mercy. My Temple will
be rebuilt,' says the LORD All-Powerful, 'and the
measuring line will be used to rebuild Jerusalem.'
17"Also announce: This is what the LORD
All-Powerful says: 'My towns will be rich
again. The LORD will comfort Jerusalem again,
and I will again choose Jerusalem.' "

THE VISION OF THE HORNS

18Then I looked up and saw four animal
horns. 19I asked the angel who was talking
with me, "What are these?"
He said, "These are the horns that scattered
the people of Judah, Israel, and Jerusalem."
20Then the LORD showed me four craftsmen.
21I asked, "What are they coming to do?"
He answered, "They have come to scare and
throw down the horns. These horns scattered
the people of Judah so that no one could even
lift up his head. These horns stand for the nations that attacked the people of Judah and
scattered them."

WHAT'S IT MEAN?

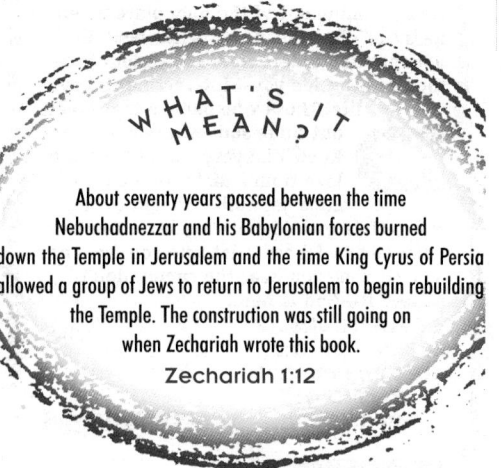

About seventy years passed between the time Nebuchadnezzar and his Babylonian forces burned down the Temple in Jerusalem and the time King Cyrus of Persia allowed a group of Jews to return to Jerusalem to begin rebuilding the Temple. The construction was still going on when Zechariah wrote this book.

Zechariah 1:12

THE VISION OF THE MEASURING LINE

2 1Then I looked up and saw a man holding a
line for measuring things. 2I asked him, "Where
are you going?"
He said to me, "I am going to measure Jerusalem, to see how wide and how long it is."
3Then the angel who was talking with me
left, and another angel came out to meet him.
4The second angel said to him, "Run and tell
that young man, 'Jerusalem will become a city
without walls, because there will be so many
people and cattle in it. 5I will be a wall of fire
around it,' says the LORD. 'And I will be the glory
within it.'
6"Oh no! Oh no! Run away from Babylon,
because I have scattered you like the four
winds of heaven," says the LORD.
7"Oh no, Jerusalem! Escape, you who live
right in Babylon." 8This is what the LORD All-
Powerful says: "After he has honored me and
sent me against the nations who took your
possessions—because whoever touches you
hurts what is precious to me— 9I will shake
my hand against them so that their slaves will
rob them."
Then you will know that the LORD All-
Powerful sent me.
10"Shout and be glad,
Jerusalem. I am coming,
and I will live among you,"
says the LORD. 11"At that time
people from many nations
will join with the LORD and
will become my people. Then I will live among
you, and you will know that the LORD All-
Powerful has sent me to you. 12The LORD will
take Judah as his own part of the holy land,
and Jerusalem will be his chosen city again.
13Be silent, everyone, in the presence of the
LORD. He is coming out of the holy place
where he lives."

ENCOURAGEMENT

Is God close to us? (2:10)

WHAT'S IT MEAN?

Ever wonder what the name *Satan* means? It means "someone who accuses." As you can see in these verses, the devil certainly lives up to his name. Joshua, the high priest, was responsible for the spiritual welfare of the people who returned to Jerusalem from captivity.

Zechariah 3:1–2

On the Edge

Be silent, everyone, in the presence of the LORD. He is coming out of the holy place where he lives (Zech. 2:13).

Somebody started this rumor about God that a lot of people seem to believe. They said, "He's up there somewhere." Some even call him "the Man upstairs." They seem to think that he's far away, beyond our reach, looking down from his comfortable throne. They must not have heard that God is here! He is "coming out of the holy place where he lives." That means he is involved. He is not shouting orders from some mountaintop. He is beside you—interacting in your life. Those who believe that God is out there somewhere must not know him very well. It's hard to love from a distance. Relationships get built through closeness and intimacy, not across a galaxy. The Lord longs to be with you, not rule you from afar. So next time you hear the rumor, don't believe it—God is here!

SEE FOR YOURSELF:
Is. 12:6; Ezek 37:27; Joel 2:27; Hab. 2:20; Zeph. 3:17; Matt. 18:20

THE VISION OF THE HIGH PRIEST

3 1Then he showed me Joshua, the high
priest, standing in front of the LORD's angel.
And Satan was standing by Joshua's right side
to accuse him. 2The LORD said to Satan, "The
LORD says no to you, Satan! The LORD who has
chosen Jerusalem says no to you! This man
was like a burning stick pulled from the fire."
3Joshua was wearing dirty clothes and was
standing in front of the angel. 4The angel said
to those standing in front of him, "Take off
those dirty clothes."
Then the angel said to Joshua, "Look, I have
taken away your sin from you, and I am giving
you beautiful, fine clothes."
5Then I said, "Put a clean turban on his
head." So they put a clean turban on his head
and dressed him while the LORD's angel stood
there.

WHAT'S IT MEAN?

The headgear worn by the high priests of Israel was unusual, to say the least. The turban was a long piece of white linen cloth that was wrapped around the head and fastened in the back. Attached to the front of the turban was a gold sign engraved with the words "Holy to the LORD."

Zechariah 3:5

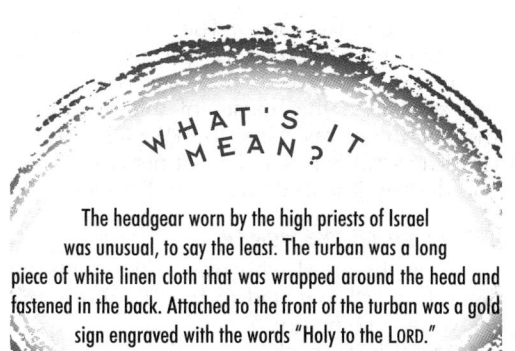

[6]Then the LORD's angel said to Joshua,
[7]"This is what the LORD All-Powerful says: 'If
you do as I tell you and serve me, you will be
in charge of my Temple and my courtyards.
And I will let you be with these angels who are
standing here.
[8]" 'Listen, Joshua, the high priest, and your
friends who are sitting in front of you. They
are symbols of what will happen. I am going
to bring my servant called the Branch. [9]Look, I
put this stone in front of Joshua, a stone with
seven sides. I will carve a message on it,' says
the LORD All-Powerful. 'And in one day I will
take away the sin of this land.'
[10]"The LORD All-Powerful says, 'In that day,
each of you will invite your neighbor to sit
under your own grapevine and under your
own fig tree.' "

THE VISION OF THE LAMPSTAND

4 [1]Then the angel who was talking with me
returned and woke me up as if I had been
asleep. [2]He asked me, "What do you see?"
I said, "I see a solid gold lampstand with a
bowl at the top. And there are seven lamps and
also seven places for wicks. [3]There are two
olive trees by it, one on the right of the bowl
and the other on the left."
[4]I asked the angel who talked with me, "Sir,
what are these?"
[5]The angel said, "Don't you know what they
are?"
"No, sir," I said.
[6]Then he told me, "This is the word of the
LORD to Zerubbabel: 'You will not succeed by
your own strength or power, but by my Spirit,'
says the LORD All-Powerful.
[7]"Who are you, big mountain? In front of
Zerubbabel you will become flat land, and he
will bring out the topmost stone, shouting, 'It's
beautiful! It's beautiful!' "
[8]Then the LORD spoke his word to me again,
saying, [9]"Zerubbabel has laid the foundation of
this Temple, and he will complete it. Then you
will know that the LORD All-Powerful has sent
me to you.
[10]"The people should not think that small
beginnings are unimportant. They will be happy when they see Zerubbabel with tools,
building the Temple.

On the Edge

Then [the angel] told me, "This is the word of the LORD to Zerubbabel: 'You will not succeed by your own strength or power, but by my Spirit,' says the LORD All-Powerful" (Zech. 4:6).

You are growing up in a time when people think they can do almost anything. Sports records are being broken every day. Scientists are discovering cures for diseases that were once considered incurable. Virtual reality can take us places we never thought we could go. It's true, technology and information have enabled humans to do a lot with their minds and bodies and abilities. But humans are still people. No matter how advanced we get, we will never even come close to being as awesome and powerful and advanced as God is.

God says that we are to depend on his Spirit. He wants us to learn to trust his Spirit instead of our own power. There are certain things that his Spirit can do that you could never do in your own strength—such as touch and change and heal a person way down deep inside. God's ways may be different from yours. When you follow his Spirit, you may need to keep your mouth shut instead of telling someone off. He may lead you to make a decision that doesn't seem to make sense; then later you realize that *not* doing it would have been devastating for you.

He leads in lots of different ways. No matter how strong or how smart you are, you can't outdo the Spirit of God. He's the One you can totally depend on.

SEE FOR YOURSELF:
Prov. 3:5–6; Is. 55:8–9; Matt. 19:26; 1 Cor. 2:10–12; Gal. 5:16–17

WHAT'S IT MEAN?

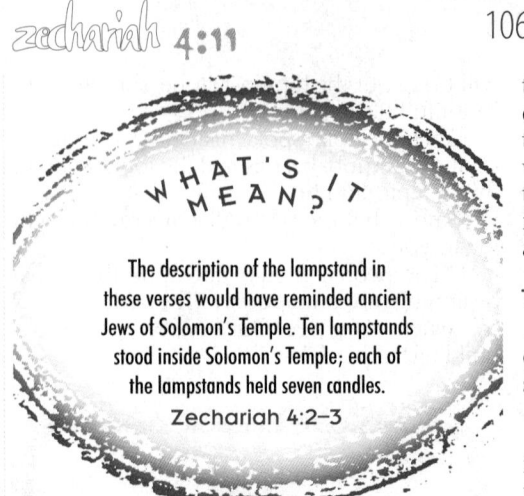

The description of the lampstand in these verses would have reminded ancient Jews of Solomon's Temple. Ten lampstands stood inside Solomon's Temple; each of the lampstands held seven candles.

Zechariah 4:2–3

"(These are the seven eyes of the LORD,
which look back and forth across the earth.)"
[11]Then I asked the angel, "What are the two
olive trees on the right and left of the lampstand?"
[12]I also asked him, "What are the two olive
branches beside the two gold pipes, from
which the olive oil flows to the lamps?"
[13]He answered, "Don't you know what they
are?"
"No, sir," I said.
[14]So he said, "They are symbols of the two
who have been appointed to serve the LORD of
all the earth."

WHAT'S IT MEAN?

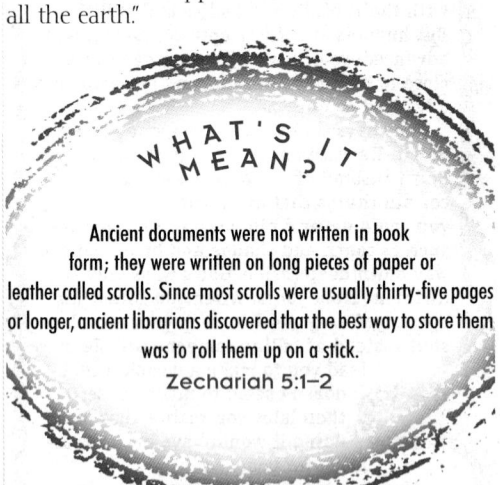

Ancient documents were not written in book form; they were written on long pieces of paper or leather called scrolls. Since most scrolls were usually thirty-five pages or longer, ancient librarians discovered that the best way to store them was to roll them up on a stick.

Zechariah 5:1–2

THE VISION OF THE FLYING SCROLL

5 [1]I looked up again and saw a flying scroll.
[2]The angel asked me, "What do you see?"
I answered, "I see a flying scroll, thirty feet
long and fifteen feet wide."
[3]And he said to me, "This is the curse that
will go all over the land. One side says every
thief will be taken away. The other side says
everyone who makes false promises will be
taken away. [4]The LORD All-Powerful says, 'I
will send it to the houses of thieves and to
those who use my name to make false promises. The scroll will stay in that person's house
and destroy it with its wood and stones.' "

THE VISION OF THE WOMAN

[5]Then the angel who was talking with me
came forward and said to me, "Look up and
see what is going out."
[6]"What is it?" I asked.
He answered, "It is a measuring basket going out." He also said, "It is a symbol of the
people's sins in all the land."
[7]Then the lid made of lead was raised, and
there was a woman sitting inside the basket.
[8]The angel said, "The woman stands for wickedness." Then he pushed her back into the basket and put the lid back down.
[9]Then I looked up and saw two women going out with the wind in their wings. Their
wings were like those of a stork, and they lifted
up the basket between earth and the sky.
[10]I asked the angel who was talking with
me, "Where are they taking the basket?"
[11]"They are going to Babylonia to build a
temple for it," he answered. "When the temple is
ready, they will set the basket there in its place."

THE VISION OF THE FOUR CHARIOTS

6 [1]I looked up again and saw four chariots
going out between two mountains, mountains
of bronze. [2]Red horses pulled the first chariot.
Black horses pulled the second chariot. [3]White
horses pulled the third chariot, and strong,
spotted horses pulled the fourth chariot. [4]I
asked the angel who was talking with me,
"What are these, sir?"
[5]He said, "These are the four spirits of heav-
en. They have just come from the presence of
the Lord of the whole world. [6]The chariot
pulled by the black horses will go to the land
of the north. The white horses will go to the
land of the west, and the spotted horses will go
to the land of the south."
[7]When the powerful horses went out, they
were eager to go through all the earth. So he
said, "Go through all the earth," and they did.
[8]Then he called to me, "Look, the horses that
went north have caused my spirit to rest in the
land of the north."

A CROWN FOR JOSHUA

[9]The LORD spoke his word to me, saying,
[10]"Take silver and gold from Heldai, Tobijah,

and Jedaiah, who were captives in Babylon. Go
that same day to the house of Josiah son of
Zephaniah, who came from Babylon. 11Make
the silver and gold into a crown, and put it on
the head of Joshua son of Jehozadak, the high
priest. 12Tell him this is what the LORD All-
Powerful says: 'A man whose name is the
Branch will branch out from where he is, and
he will build the Temple of the LORD. 13One
man[n] will build the Temple of the LORD, and
the other[n] will receive honor. One man will sit
on his throne and rule, and the other will be a
priest on his throne. And these two men will
work together in peace.' 14The crown will be
kept in the Temple of the LORD to remind Heldai, Tobijah, Jedaiah, and Josiah son of Zephaniah. 15People living far away will come and
build the Temple of the LORD. Then you will
know the LORD All-Powerful has sent me to
you. This will happen if you completely obey
the LORD your God."

THE PEOPLE SHOULD SHOW MERCY

7 1In the fourth year Darius was king, on the
fourth day of the ninth month, which is called
Kislev, the LORD spoke his word to Zechariah.
2The city of Bethel sent Sharezer, Regem-
Melech, and their men to ask the LORD a question. 3They went to the prophets and priests
who were at the Temple of the LORD All-
Powerful. The men said, "For years in the fifth
month of each year we have shown our sadness and gone without food. Should we continue to do this?"
4The LORD All-Powerful spoke his word to
me, saying, 5"Tell the priests and the people in
the land: 'For seventy years you went without
food and cried in the fifth and seventh months,

On the Edge

This is what the LORD All-Powerful says: "Do what is right and true. Be kind and merciful to each other. Don't hurt widows and orphans, foreigners or the poor; don't even think of doing evil to somebody else" (Zech. 7:9–10).

The Bible is full of advice about how God wants you to treat other people. If you'll start with the instructions here, you'll be well on your way.

These verses put some responsibility on the people who read them. Yes, you are responsible to "do what is right and true" in situations where you can. Don't let people treat others unfairly when you can speak out against it. More than that, make sure that you act fairly.

Second, you're responsible for acting with kindness and mercy. Being kind means going out of your way to help someone, sacrificing in order to share, and doing more than someone asks of you. Being merciful means that you do those things even when you think other people deserve to tough it out for themselves.

What else? "Don't hurt widows and orphans, foreigners or the poor" (v. 10). Do what you can for people who can't do things for themselves. Older people often have trouble with little things like changing lightbulbs or raking leaves. It wouldn't take long for you to do odd jobs for them and they would love it. The orphaned often just need someone to throw a football with them or take them to a movie. You can't imagine how excited they would be if you did that!

Finally, "don't even think of doing evil to somebody else" (v. 10). Pretty self-explanatory. All of these things will grow in you as you commit to walk in love.

SEE FOR YOURSELF: Deut. 6:4–5; Amos 5:21–24; Matt. 22:36–39; Phil. 1:27; 1 Pet. 2:1–3

WHAT'S IT MEAN?

The Jewish people never forgot the day their beloved Temple was destroyed by the Babylonians. In fact, while they were in captivity, the Jews fasted—they didn't eat food—during the fifth month of each year to commemorate the event. They also fasted during the seventh month of every year in remembrance of Gedaliah, the Jewish governor appointed by King Nebuchadnezzar who was murdered two months into his term.

Zechariah 7:4–5

6:13 One man This probably refers to Zerubbabel. **6:13 other** This probably refers to Joshua.

but that was not really for me. 6And when you ate and drank, it was really for yourselves. 7The LORD used the earlier prophets to say the same thing, when Jerusalem and the surrounding towns were at peace and wealthy, and people lived in the southern area and the western hills.' "

8And the LORD spoke his word to Zechariah again, saying, 9"This is what the LORD All-Powerful says: 'Do what is right and true. Be kind and merciful to each other. 10Don't hurt widows and orphans, foreigners or the poor; don't even think of doing evil to somebody else.'

CARING
How should we treat others? (7:9–10)

11"But they refused to pay attention; they were stubborn and did not want to listen anymore. 12They made their hearts as hard as rock and would not listen to the teachings of the LORD All-Powerful. And they would not hear the words he sent by his Spirit through the earlier prophets. So the LORD All-Powerful became very angry.

13" 'When I called to them, they would not listen. So when they called to me, I would not listen,' says the LORD All-Powerful. 14'I scattered them like a hurricane to other countries they did not know. This good land was left so ruined behind them that no one could live there. They had made the desired land a ruin.' "

THE LORD WILL BLESS JERUSALEM

8 1The LORD All-Powerful spoke his word, saying, 2This is what the LORD All-Powerful says: "I have a very strong love for Jerusalem. My strong love for her is like a fire burning in me."

3This is what the LORD says: "I will return to Jerusalem and live in it. Then it will be called the City of Truth, and the mountain of the LORD All-Powerful will be called the Holy Mountain."

4This is what the LORD All-Powerful says: "Old men and old women will again sit along Jerusalem's streets, each carrying a cane because of age. 5And the streets will be filled with boys and girls playing."

6This is what the LORD All-Powerful says: "Those who are left alive then may think it is too difficult to happen, but it is not too difficult for me," says the LORD All-Powerful. 7This is what the LORD All-Powerful says: "I will save my people from countries in the east and west. 8I will bring them back, and they will live in Jerusalem. They will be my people, and I will be their good and loyal God."

9This is what the LORD All-Powerful says: "Work hard, you who are hearing these words today. The prophets spoke these words when the foundation was laid for the house of the LORD All-Powerful, for the building of the Temple. 10Before that time there was no money to hire people or animals. People could not safely come and go because of the enemies; I had turned everyone against his neighbor. 11But I will not do to these people who are left what I did in the past," says the LORD All-Powerful.

12"They will plant their seeds in peace, their grapevines will have fruit, the ground will give good crops, and the sky will send rain. I will give all this to the people who are left alive. 13Judah and Israel, your names have been used as curses in other nations. But I will save you, and you will become a blessing. So don't be afraid; work hard."

"But now I will do something different. I am planning to do good to Jerusalem and Judah. So don't be afraid." (Zechariah 8:15)

14This is what the LORD All-Powerful says: "When your ancestors made me angry, I planned to punish you. I did not change my mind," says the LORD All-Powerful. 15"But now I will do something different. I am planning to do good to Jerusalem and Judah. So don't be afraid. 16These are the things you should do: Tell each other the truth. In the courts judge with truth and complete fairness. 17Do not make plans to hurt your neighbors, and don't love false promises. I hate all these things," says the LORD.

18The LORD All-Powerful spoke his word to me again. 19This is what the LORD All-Powerful says: "The special days when you give up eating in the fourth, fifth, seventh, and tenth months will become good, joyful, happy feasts in Judah. But you must love truth and peace."

20This is what the LORD All-Powerful says: "Many people from many cities will still come to Jerusalem. 21People from one city will go and say to those from another city, 'We are going to pray to the LORD and to ask the LORD All-Powerful for help. Come and go with us.' 22Many people and powerful nations will come to worship the LORD All-Powerful in Jerusalem and to pray to the LORD for help."

23This is what the LORD All-Powerful says:

On the Edge

These are the things you should do: Tell each other the truth. In the courts judge with truth and complete fairness (Zech. 8:16).

Have you ever blown it with another person? When you have, the first thing you've got to do is to be truthful with yourself. Cut yourself a big slice of humble pie, put down your pride, don't try to justify yourself—just admit it. You messed up. Whether you meant to or not, it happened. All friendships have their ups and downs. The key to great relationships is being able to work out the stuff that comes between you.

Next you've got to be honest with God. Confess your sin. Let him see that you know you've done wrong and that you're sorry. Ask him to forgive you. He'll forgive you before you finish asking. Then ask him to help you deal with your friend—to help you know what to say and how to make things right.

The hardest part may be facing your friend and admitting that you aren't perfect, that you blew it and you're sorry. Ask for your friend's forgiveness. A good Christian friend may surprise you and say "I've already forgiven you."

There are other things that will help you patch up a relationship, too. Walking in true forgiveness and grace, learning to overlook the little stuff, doing your best to love with the love that Jesus has, encouraging, supporting, having good times together—all of these things build good relationships and make it easier to work through the rough spots.

SEE FOR YOURSELF:
2 Cor. 2:7–8;
Eph. 4:25–32;
1 John 4:7

"At that time, ten men from different countries will come and take hold of a Judean by his coat. They will say to him, 'Let us go with you, because we have heard that God is with you.' "

PUNISHMENT ON ISRAEL'S ENEMIES

9 [1]This message is the word of the LORD.

The message is against the land of
Hadrach
and the city of Damascus.
The tribes of Israel and all people
belong to the LORD.
[2]The message is also against the city of
Hamath, on the border,
and against Tyre and Sidon, with their
skill.
[3]Tyre has built a strong wall for herself.
She has piled up silver like dust
and gold like the mud in the streets.
[4]But the Lord will take away all she has
and destroy her power on the sea.
That city will be destroyed by fire.
[5]The city of Ashkelon will see it and be
afraid.
The people of Gaza will shake with fear,
and the people of Ekron will lose hope.
No king will be left in Gaza,
and no one will live in Ashkelon
anymore.
[6]Foreigners will live in Ashdod,
and I will destroy the pride of the
Philistines.
[7]I will stop them from drinking blood
and from eating forbidden food.
Those left alive will belong to God.
They will be leaders in Judah,
and Ekron will become like the Jebusites.
[8]I will protect my Temple
from armies who would come or go.
No one will hurt my people again,
because now I am watching them.

THE KING IS COMING

[9]Rejoice greatly, people of Jerusalem!
Shout for joy, people of Jerusalem!
Your king is coming to you.
He does what is right, and he saves.

WHAT'S IT MEAN?

You've probably never seen a picture of a donkey being ridden into battle. Unlike horses, which were used primarily for war, donkeys were animals of peace. They were ridden by princes and kings (see Judg. 5:10; 12:14; 2 Sam. 16:1–2). When Jesus rode into Jerusalem for the last week of his earthly ministry, he was sitting on a young donkey.

Zechariah 9:9

He is gentle and riding on a donkey,
on the colt of a donkey.
10 I will take away the chariots from Ephraim
and the horses from Jerusalem.
The bows used in war will be broken.
The king will talk to the nations about
peace.
His kingdom will go from sea to sea,
and from the Euphrates River to the
ends of the earth.

11 As for you, because of the blood of the
agreement with you
I will set your prisoners free from the
waterless pit.
12 You prisoners who have hope,
return to your place of safety.
Today I am telling you
that I will give you back twice as much
as before.
13 I will use Judah like a bow
and Ephraim like the arrows.
Jerusalem, I will use your men
to fight the men of Greece.
I will use you like a warrior's sword.

14 Then the LORD will appear above them,
and his arrows will shoot like lightning.
The Lord GOD will blow the trumpet,
and he will march in the storms of the
south.
15 The LORD All-Powerful will protect them;
they will destroy the enemy with
slingshots.
They will drink and shout like drunk men.
They will be filled like a bowl
used for sprinkling blood at the corners
of the altar.
16 On that day the LORD their God will save
them
as if his people were sheep.
They will shine in his land
like jewels in a crown.
17 They will be so pretty and beautiful.
The young men will grow strong on the
grain
and the young women on new wine.

THE LORD'S PROMISES

10

1 Ask the LORD for rain during the
springtime rains.
The LORD is the one who makes the
clouds.
He sends the showers
and gives everyone green fields.
2 Idols tell lies;
fortune-tellers see false visions
and tell about false dreams.
The comfort they give is worth nothing.
So the people are like lost sheep.
They are abused, because there is no
shepherd.

3 The LORD says, "I am angry at my
shepherds,
and I will punish the leaders.
I, the LORD All-Powerful, care
for my flock, the people of Judah.
I will make them like my proud war
horses.
4 From Judah will come the cornerstone,
and the tent peg,
the battle bow,
and every ruler.
5 Together they will be like soldiers
marching to battle through muddy
streets.
The LORD is with them,
so they will fight and defeat the
horsemen.

6 "I will strengthen the people of Judah
and save the people of Joseph.
I will bring them back,
because I care about them.
It will be as though
I had never left them,
because I am the LORD their God,
and I will answer them.
7 The people of Ephraim will be strong like
soldiers;
they will be glad as when they have
drunk wine.
Their children will see it and rejoice;
they will be happy in the LORD.
8 I will call my people
and gather them together.
I will save them,
and they will grow in number as they
grew in number before.
9 I have scattered them among the nations,
but in those faraway places, they will
remember me.
They and their children will live and
return.
10 I will bring them back from the land of
Egypt
and gather them from Assyria.
I will bring them to Gilead and Lebanon
until there isn't enough room for them
all.
11 They will come through the sea of trouble.
The waves of the sea will be calm,
and the Nile River will dry up.

WHAT'S IT MEAN?

Gilead and Lebanon refer to the regions on each side of the Jordan River. Together they form the land that God originally gave to the Israelites.

Zechariah 10:10

I will defeat Assyria's pride
and destroy Egypt's power over other countries.
12 I will make my people strong,
and they will live as I say," says the LORD.

11

1 Lebanon, open your gates
so fire may burn your cedar trees.[n]
2 Cry, pine trees, because the cedar has fallen,
because the tall trees are ruined.
Cry, oaks in Bashan,
because the mighty forest has been cut down.
3 Listen to the shepherds crying
because their rich pastures are destroyed.
Listen to the lions roaring
because the lovely land of the Jordan River is ruined.

THE TWO SHEPHERDS

4 This is what the LORD my God says: "Feed
the flock that are about to be killed. 5 Their
buyers kill them and are not punished. Those
who sell them say, 'Praise the LORD, I am rich.'
Even the shepherds don't feel sorry for their

WHAT'S IT MEAN?

Can you imagine having to worry about lion attacks while you traveled? People in ancient Israel faced that danger every day. Lions were known to spring from their hiding places among the thickets near the Jordan River to pounce on people passing by. If you're planning a trip to the Holy Land, you can relax about the lions—they are long gone.

Zechariah 11:3

11:1 trees In this poem, trees, bushes, and animals stand for leaders of countries around Judah.

Promise

HE PROMISES TO STRENGTHEN YOU.

"I will make my people strong, and they will live as I say," says the LORD (Zech. 10:12).

The Lord says that he will strengthen his people because he is their Lord. He has chosen to show his power and his personality in the lives of the people who live for him. The problems you face are just opportunities for God to show his stuff. It's a chance for him to show what he can do (his awesome power) and what he will do (his incredible kindness and mercy).

In his second letter to the Christians who lived Corinth, Paul gave a long list of the difficulties he had faced. One thing in particular seemed to bother him though he didn't say what it was. He just said that he had asked the Lord three times to change things. But God answered, "My grace is enough for you. When you are weak, my power is made perfect in you" (2 Cor. 12:9). When you feel weak or overwhelmed in your life, be disciplined enough to get out your Bible and soak yourself in God's Word. Pray to him. There's strength for you in his presence.

SEE FOR YOURSELF:

Ps. 68:35; Is. 30:15; Hab. 3:19; 2 Cor. 12:9–10; Phil. 4:13

sheep. 6I don't feel sorry anymore for the people of this country," says the LORD. "I will let
everyone be under the power of his neighbor
and king. They will bring trouble to the country, and I will not save anyone from them."
7So I fed the flock about to be killed, particularly the weakest ones. Then I took two sticks;
I called one Pleasant and the other Union, and
I fed the flock. 8In one month I got rid of three
shepherds. The flock did not pay attention to
me, and I got impatient with them. 9I said, "I
will no longer take care of you like a shepherd.
Let those that are dying die, and let those that
are to be destroyed be destroyed. Let those that
are left eat each other."
10Then I broke the stick named Pleasant to
break the agreement God made with all the
nations. 11That day it was broken. The weak
ones in the flock who were watching me knew
this message was from the LORD.
12Then I said, "If you want to pay me, pay
me. If not, then don't." So they paid me thirty
pieces of silver.
13The LORD said to me, "Throw the money
to the potter." That is how little they thought I
was worth.[n] So I took the thirty pieces of silver
and threw them to the potter in the Temple of
the LORD.
14Then I broke the second stick, named
Union, to break the brotherhood between Judah and Israel.
15Then the LORD said to me, "Get the things
used by a foolish shepherd again, 16because I
am going to get a new shepherd for the country. He will not care for the dying sheep, or
look for the young ones, or heal the injured
ones, or feed the healthy. But he will eat the
best sheep and tear off their hoofs.

17 "How terrible it will be for the useless
shepherd
who abandoned the flock.
A sword will strike his arm and his right
eye.
His arm will lose all its strength,
and his right eye will go blind."

JERUSALEM WILL BE SAVED

12

1This message is the word of the LORD to
Israel. This is what the LORD says, who
stretched out the skies, and laid the foundations of the earth, and put the human spirit
within: 2"I will make Jerusalem like a cup of
poison to the nations around her. They will
come and attack Jerusalem and Judah. 3One
day all the nations on earth will come together
to attack Jerusalem, but I will make it like a
heavy rock; anyone who tries to move it will
get hurt. 4At that time I will confuse every
horse and cause its rider to go crazy," says the
LORD. "I will watch over Judah, but I will blind
all the horses of the enemies. 5Then the leaders
of Judah will say to themselves, 'The people of
Jerusalem are strong, because the LORD All-
Powerful is their God.'

WHAT'S IT MEAN?

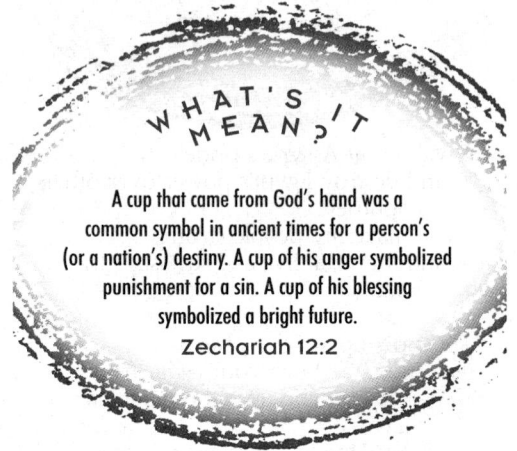

A cup that came from God's hand was a common symbol in ancient times for a person's (or a nation's) destiny. A cup of his anger symbolized punishment for a sin. A cup of his blessing symbolized a bright future.

Zechariah 12:2

6"At that time I will make the leaders of Judah like a fire burning a stack of wood or like a
fire burning straw. They will destroy all the
people around them left and right. But the
people of Jerusalem will remain safe.
7"The LORD will save the homes of Judah
first so that the honor given to David's family
and to the people of Jerusalem won't be greater
than the honor given to Judah. 8At that time
the LORD will protect the people in Jerusalem.
Then even the weakest of them will be strong
like David. And the family of David will be like
God, like an angel of the LORD in front of them.
9At that time I will go to destroy all the nations
that attack Jerusalem.

CRYING FOR THE ONE THEY STABBED

10"I will pour out on David's family and the
people in Jerusalem a spirit of kindness and
mercy. They will look at me, the one they have
stabbed, and they will cry like someone crying
over the death of an only child. They will be as
sad as someone who has lost a firstborn son.
11At that time there will be much crying in Jerusalem, like the crying for Hadad Rimmon in
the plain of Megiddo. 12The land will cry, each
family by itself: the family of David by itself
and their wives by themselves, the family of

11:13 worth This was a small amount. It was about the price paid for a slave.

Nathan by itself and their wives by themselves,
13 the family of Levi by itself and their wives by
themselves, the family of Shimei by itself and
their wives by themselves, 14 and all the rest of
the families by themselves and their wives by
themselves.

13

1 "At that time a fountain will be open for
David's descendants and for the people of Jerusalem to cleanse them of their sin and uncleanness."

2 The LORD All-Powerful says, "At that
time I will get rid of the names of
the idols from the land; no
one will remember them anymore. I will also remove the
prophets and unclean spirits
from the land. 3 If a person
continues to prophesy, his
own father and mother, the ones who gave
birth to him, will tell him, 'You have told lies
using the LORD's name, so you must die.' When
he prophesies, his own father and mother who
gave birth to him will stab him.

> **GUILT**
> How can we be made guilt-free? (13:1)

4 "At that time the prophets will be ashamed
of their visions and prophecies. They won't
wear the prophet's clothes made of hair to trick
people. 5 Each of them will say, 'I am not a
prophet. I am a farmer and have been a farmer
since I was young.' 6 But someone will ask,
'What are the deep cuts on your body?' And
each will answer, 'I was hurt at my friend's
house.'

THE SHEPHERD IS KILLED

7 "Sword, hit the shepherd.
Attack the man who is my friend,"
says the LORD All-Powerful.
"Kill the shepherd,
and the sheep will scatter,
and I will punish the little ones."
8 The LORD says, "Two-thirds of the people
through all the land will die. They will
be gone,
and one-third will be left.
9 The third that is left I will test with fire,
purifying them like silver,
testing them like gold.
Then they will call on me,
and I will answer them.
I will say, 'You are my people,'
and they will say, 'The LORD is our
God.' "

Promise — HE PROMISES TO REFINE AND TEST YOU.

The third that is left I will test with fire, purifying them like silver, testing them like gold. Then they will call on me, and I will answer them. I will say, "You are my people," and they will say, "The LORD is our God" (Zech. 13:9).

Have you ever gotten a ring that was supposed to be high quality, but made your finger turn green? You think, *This thing is cheap. It's fake.* Why? Because it isn't pure gold. It hasn't been through the refining process necessary to remove all the impurities from the metal. Maybe the ring was beautiful in the case, but it looks awful on your hand because now your finger's green. You've got a cheap ring, full of junk. It could have been beautiful, but the goldsmith didn't take the time or energy to purify the gold.

God wants you to be pure—in every way. He wants your thoughts to be pure. He wants your actions to be pure. He wants you physically, morally, spiritually, and sexually pure. He doesn't want you to just look good. He wants you to be beautiful through and through. It's a two-step process. *You* make the decision to allow the Lord to work in your life; then *he* does the purifying. He does it by renewing your mind with his word and by speaking to you by his Spirit. The process may not always be pleasant for you, but God will not leave you in the fire to burn up. He will bring you out at the perfect time and finish the process.

When a ring is put on a finger, it's put to the test. If it's pure, it's beautiful. If it isn't, almost everything it touches turns green. When you've been purified by the Lord, you will be as beautiful as pure gold.

SEE FOR YOURSELF:
Jer. 9:7; Dan. 11:35; 12:10

WHAT'S IT MEAN?

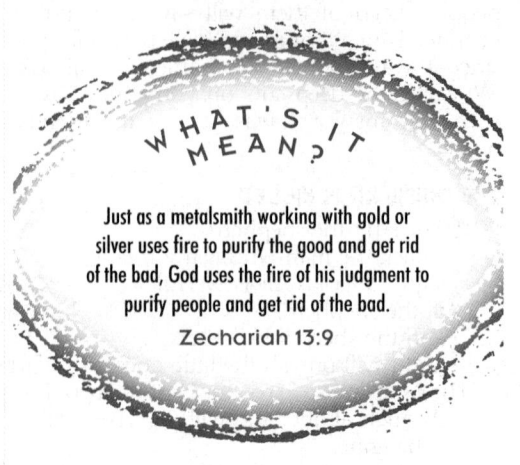

Just as a metalsmith working with gold or silver uses fire to purify the good and get rid of the bad, God uses the fire of his judgment to purify people and get rid of the bad.

Zechariah 13:9

THE DAY OF PUNISHMENT

14 [1]The LORD's day of judging is coming when
the wealth you have taken will be divided
among you.
[2]I will bring all the nations together to fight
Jerusalem. They will capture the city and rob
the houses and attack the women. Half the
people will be taken away as captives, but the
rest of the people won't be taken from the city.
[3]Then the LORD will go to war against those
nations; he will fight as in a day of battle. [4]On
that day he will stand on the Mount of Olives,
east of Jerusalem. The Mount of Olives will
split in two, forming a deep valley that runs
east and west. Half the mountain will move
toward the north, and half will move toward
the south. [5]You will run through this mountain
valley to the other side, just as you ran from
the earthquake when Uzziah was king of Judah. Then the LORD my God will come and all
the holy ones with him.
[6]On that day there will be no light, cold, or
frost. [7]There will be no other day like it, and
the LORD knows when it will come. There will
be no day or night; even at evening it will still
be light.
[8]At that time fresh water will flow from Jerusalem. Half of it will flow east to the Dead
Sea, and half will flow west to the Mediterranean Sea. It will flow summer and winter.
[9]Then the LORD will be king over the whole
world. At that time there will be only one
LORD, and his name will be the only name.
[10]All the land south of Jerusalem from Geba
to Rimmon will be turned into a plain. Jerusalem will be raised up, but it will stay in the
same place. The city will reach from the Benjamin Gate and to the First Gate to the Corner
Gate, and from the Tower of Hananel to the
king's winepresses. [11]People will live there, and
it will never be destroyed again. Jerusalem will
be safe.
[12]But the LORD will bring a terrible disease
on the nations that fought against Jerusalem.
Their flesh will rot away while they are still
standing up. Their eyes will rot in their sockets,
and their tongues will rot in their mouths. [13]At
that time the LORD will cause panic. Everybody
will grab his neighbor, and they will attack each
other. [14]The people of Judah will fight in Jerusalem. And the wealth of the nations around
them will be collected—much gold, silver, and
clothes. [15]A similar disease will strike the horses,
mules, camels, donkeys, and all the animals in
the camps.
[16]All of those left alive of the people who
came to fight Jerusalem will come back to Jerusalem year after year to worship the King, the
LORD All-Powerful, and to celebrate the Feast
of Shelters. [17]Anyone from the nations who
does not go to Jerusalem to worship the King,
the LORD All-Powerful, will not have rain fall
on his land. [18]If the Egyptians do not go to
Jerusalem, they will not have rain. Then the
LORD will send them the same terrible disease
he sent the other nations that did not celebrate
the Feast of Shelters. [19]This will be the punishment for Egypt and any nation which does not
go to celebrate the Feast of Shelters.
[20]At that time the horses' bells will have
written on them: HOLY TO THE LORD. The cooking pots in the Temple of the Lord will be like
the holy altar bowls. [21]Every pot in Jerusalem
and Judah will be holy to the LORD All-Powerful,
and everyone who offers sacrifices will be able
to take food from them and cook in them. At
that time there will not be any buyers or sellers
in the Temple of the LORD All-Powerful.

Malachi

CONTENT Have you ever been excited about something, like a family trip or a party with friends, and it turns out to be nothing like you had thought? Maybe you'd been looking forward to the trip for a long time. Maybe you had imagined how fun it was going to be and how everyone would enjoy it. But, then when reality happened, it just wasn't as bright and shiny as it was in your head.

That's how the Hebrews felt at the time when Malachi preached and wrote his message. They had struggled through some *extremely* hard times. After being exiled from their country, they returned, resettled, and rebuilt the Temple and the city walls. All of that involved years of work.

When it was done, they expected that God would bless them and their lives would be like the "good old days"—when they were happy and rich and in God's favor.

The problem was that they were still missing the point about obedience to God. They were sitting back expecting God to fix everything. They halfheartedly did what they needed to do, but they weren't *being* the people they needed to be.

Malachi addressed this with them through a series of questions and answers. See what you think.

Outline

1:1–5 .... God's Love for Israel
1:6—2:9 .... Judgment Against the Priests
2:10–16 .... Broken Agreements
2:17—3:5 .... The Lord You Are Looking for Will Come
3:6–12 .... Don't Rob God
3:13—4:6 .... The Lord Will Reward the Good and Punish the Evil

Purpose We need to check and make sure God has first place in our lives.

Theme Reassurance of God's Love and Justice

Date of writing 430 B.C.

"Suddenly, the Lord you are looking for will come to his Temple; the messenger of the agreement, whom you want, will come" (3:1b).

Bible Talk

Second Best Is Not Enough

When God originally established the customs of the Hebrews (this was back in the days of Moses), he taught them to bring their best to offer to him. This established his priority in their lives. It taught them not to put their trust in their crops or their riches, but in God.

During the days of Malachi, the people were still going through the motions of bringing sacrifices; but instead of bringing their best offerings, they were bringing their damaged goods. It was just a shadow of obedience, not the real thing.

They weren't establishing their lives around God's truth; they were fitting him in where it worked for them. This was their error. If we look, we can see that same error in our world today.

ALMOST ANONYMOUS PROPHET

malachi

We don't know much about the prophet Malachi. In fact, we don't know anything more than what is revealed in this book: He was a man who spoke out for God and who called people to serve God wholeheartedly.

It would be great, wouldn't it, to only be known for what we said for God? It would be great to be remembered for the times we spread God's word.

Malachi spoke God's truth. We don't know anything else about him, but his life can inspire us to do the same thing.

1

[1]This message is the word of the LORD given to Israel through Malachi.

GOD LOVES ISRAEL

[2]The LORD said, "I have loved you."

But you ask, "How have you loved us?"

The LORD said, "Esau and Jacob were brothers. I loved Jacob, [3]but I hated Esau. I destroyed his mountain country and left his land to the wild dogs of the desert."

WHAT'S IT MEAN?

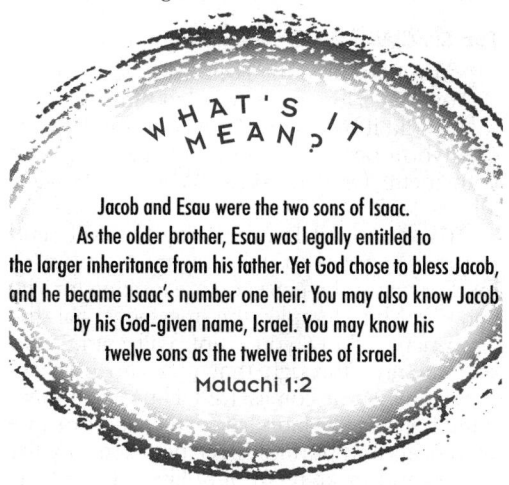

Jacob and Esau were the two sons of Isaac. As the older brother, Esau was legally entitled to the larger inheritance from his father. Yet God chose to bless Jacob, and he became Isaac's number one heir. You may also know Jacob by his God-given name, Israel. You may know his twelve sons as the twelve tribes of Israel.

Malachi 1:2

[4]The people of Edom might say, "We were destroyed, but we will go back and rebuild the ruins."

But the LORD All-Powerful says, "If they rebuild them, I will destroy them. People will say, 'Edom is a wicked country. The LORD is always angry with the Edomites.' [5]You will see these things with your own eyes. And you will say, 'The LORD is great, even outside the borders of Israel!' "

THE PRIESTS DON'T RESPECT GOD

[6]The LORD All-Powerful says, "A child honors his father, and a servant honors his master. I am a father, so why don't you honor me? I am a master, so why don't you respect me? You priests do not respect me.

"But you ask, 'How have we shown you disrespect?'

[7]"You have shown it by bringing unclean food to my altar.

"But you ask, 'What makes it unclean?'

"It is unclean because you don't respect the altar of the LORD. [8]When you bring blind animals as sacrifices, that is wrong. When you bring crippled and sick animals, that is wrong. Try giving them to your governor. Would he be pleased with you? He wouldn't accept you," says the LORD All-Powerful.

[9]"Now ask God to be kind to you, but he won't accept you with such offerings," says the LORD All-Powerful.

[10]"I wish one of you would close the Temple doors so that you would not light useless fires on my altar! I am not pleased with you and will not accept your gifts," says the LORD All-Powerful. [11]"From the east to the west I will be honored among the nations. Everywhere they will bring incense and clean offerings to me, because I will be honored among the nations," says the LORD All-Powerful.

REPUTATION

How great is God's reputation? (1:11)

[12]"But you don't honor me. You say about the Lord's altar, 'It is unclean, and the food has no worth.' [13]You say, 'We are tired of doing this,' and you sniff at it in disgust," says the LORD All-Powerful.

"And you bring hurt, crippled, and sick animals as gifts. You bring them as gifts, but I won't accept them from you," says the LORD. [14]"The person who cheats will be cursed. He has a male animal in his flock and promises to offer it, but then he offers to the Lord an animal that has something wrong with it. I am a great king," says the LORD All-Powerful, "and I am feared by all the nations.

RULES FOR PRIESTS

2

[1]"Priests, this command is for you. [2]Listen to me. Pay attention to what I say. Honor my name," says the LORD All-Powerful. "If you don't, I will send a curse on you and on your blessings. I have already cursed them, because you don't pay attention to what I say.

[3]"I will punish your descendants. I will smear your faces with the animal insides left from your feasts, and you will be thrown away with it. [4]Then you will know that I am giving you this command so my agreement with Levi will continue," says the LORD All-Powerful. [5]"My agreement for priests was with the tribe of Levi. I promised them life and peace so they would honor me. And they did honor me and fear me. [6]They taught the true teachings and spoke no lies. With peace and honesty they did what I said they should do, and they kept many people from sinning.

[7]"A priest should teach what he knows, and people should learn the teachings from him, because he is the messenger of the LORD All-Powerful. [8]But you priests have stopped obeying me. With your teachings you have caused many people to do wrong. You have broken the agreement with the tribe of Levi!" says the

LORD All-Powerful. 9"You have not been careful to do what I say, but instead you take sides
in court cases. So I have caused you to be hated and disgraced in front of everybody."

JUDAH WAS NOT LOYAL TO GOD

10We all have the same father; the same God
made us. So why do people break their promises to each other and show no respect for the
agreement our ancestors made with God?
11The people of Judah have broken their
promises. They have done something God
hates in Israel and Jerusalem: The people of
Judah did not respect the Temple that the LORD
loves, and the men of Judah married women
who worship foreign gods. 12Whoever does
this might bring offerings to the LORD All-
Powerful, but the LORD will still cut that person
off from the community of Israel.
13This is another thing you do. You cover
the LORD's altar with your tears. You cry and
moan, because he does not accept your offerings and is not pleased with what you bring.
14You ask, "Why?" It is because the LORD sees
how you treated the wife you married when
you were young. You broke your promise to
her, even though she was your partner and
you had an agreement with her. 15God made
husbands and wives to become one body and
one spirit for his purpose—so they would
have children who are true to God.

So be careful, and do not break your promise to the wife you married when you
were young.
16The LORD God of Israel
says, "I hate divorce. And I
hate people who do cruel
things as easily as they put on
clothes," says the LORD All-
Powerful.

MARRIAGE
What does God think of divorce? (2:16)

So be careful. And do not break your trust.

THE SPECIAL DAY OF JUDGING

17You have tired the LORD with your words.
You ask, "How have we tired him?"
You did it by saying, "The LORD thinks anyone who does evil is good, and he is pleased
with them." Or you asked, "Where is the God
who is fair?"

3
1The LORD All-Powerful says, "I will send
my messenger, who will prepare the way for
me. Suddenly, the Lord you are looking for will
come to his Temple; the messenger of the
agreement, whom you want, will come." 2No
one can live through that time; no one can
survive when he comes. He will be like a purifying fire and like laundry soap. 3Like someone
who heats and purifies silver, he will purify the
Levites and make them pure like gold and silver. Then they will bring offerings to the LORD
in the right way. 4And the LORD will accept the
offerings from Judah and Jerusalem, as it was

Promise HE PROMISES NOT TO CHANGE.

I the LORD do not change. So you descendants of Jacob have not been destroyed. Since the time of your ancestors, you have disobeyed my rules and have not kept them. Return to me, and I will return to you," says the LORD All-Powerful (Mal. 3:6–7a).

Athletes, even great ones, have their "off" days—days when the star basketball player can't rise above the other team and score enough points to win the game, when the best running back in the league fumbles inside the ten-yard line, when the sprinter who hasn't lost a race in seventy-six starts suddenly finds himself in second place.

You have your "off" days, too. There are days when you feel like being nice to everybody and days when you want everybody to just get out of your face. Some days it seems easy to do what God wants you to do; other days it seems hard to even care what he thinks. This moodiness is part of human nature. But God doesn't change. He is totally consistent. He's not kind one day and selfish the next. He is always faithful. He never does wrong. You can count on his power, his love, and his goodness, day in and day out.

SEE FOR YOURSELF:
Ps. 102:27; Heb. 1:12; 13:8

in the past. [5]The LORD All-Powerful says, "Then I will come to you and judge you. I will be quick to testify against those who take part in evil magic, adultery, and lying under oath, those who cheat workers of their pay and who cheat widows and orphans, those who are unfair to foreigners, and those who do not respect me.

JUDGMENT
What does God condemn? (3:5)

STEALING FROM GOD

[6]"I the LORD do not change. So you descendants of Jacob have not been destroyed. [7]Since the time of your ancestors, you have disobeyed my rules and have not kept them. Return to me, and I will return to you," says the LORD All-Powerful.

"But you ask, 'How can we return?'

[8]"Should a person rob God? But you are robbing me.

"You ask, 'How have we robbed you?'

"You have robbed me in your offerings and the tenth of your crops. [9]So a curse is on you, because the whole nation has robbed me. [10]Bring to the storehouse a full tenth of what you earn so there will be food in my house. Test me in this," says the LORD All-Powerful. "I will open the windows of heaven for you and pour out all the blessings you need. [11]I will stop the insects so they won't eat your crops. The grapes won't fall from your vines before they are ready to pick," says the LORD All-Powerful. [12]"All the nations will call you blessed, because you will have a pleasant country," says the LORD All-Powerful.

WHAT'S IT MEAN?

Here's how tithing worked in ancient times: The Israelites were commanded to give ten percent of everything they had—including crops, livestock, and money—to God. The Israelites gave their tithes to the Levites, the people who worked in the Temple. The Levites, in turn, gave ten percent of everything they received to the priests. The priests offered a sacrifice to the Lord for their tithe. The third-year tithe was given to help support the poor and needy.

Malachi 3:10

THE LORD'S PROMISE OF MERCY

[13]The LORD says, "You have said terrible things about me.

"But you ask, 'What have we said about you?'

Promise

HE PROMISES VICTORY FOR THOSE WHO HONOR HIS NAME.

But for you who honor me, goodness will shine on you like the sun, with healing in its rays. You will jump around, like well-fed calves (Mal. 4:2).

Read Malachi 4:1 and look at the contrast between the people mentioned there and the ones described in verse 2. The difference between these two groups of people begins in their hearts. The people in verse 1 are proud. They believe in themselves more than anything else. They think they deserve the best. Of course, their attitude spills over into their actions. Since they trust themselves and not God, they do some things God doesn't like. It's a way of life for them.

But the people in verse 2 have a different attitude. They know that God is better and stronger than they could ever be. They praise his greatness and feel honored that God wants to be their friend. They want to please him, and they work hard at doing the things that make him happy. Their record isn't perfect, but what God sees in their hearts makes him smile.

The day of judgment will not be a good day for proud, sinful people. But the people who honor the Lord "will jump around, like well-fed calves." In other words, peace and security await.

SEE FOR YOURSELF:

Ps. 31:19; 34:9; Eccl. 8:12

14"You have said, 'It is useless to serve God.
It did no good to obey his laws and to show
the LORD All-Powerful that we
were sorry for what we did.
15So we say that proud people
are happy. Evil people succeed. They challenge God and
get away with it.' "
16Then those who honored
the LORD spoke with each other, and the LORD
listened and heard them. The names of those
who honored the LORD and respected him
were written in his presence in a book to be
remembered.
17The LORD All-Powerful says, "They belong
to me; on that day they will be my very own.
As a parent shows mercy to his child who
serves him, I will show mercy to my people.
18You will again see the difference between
good and evil people, between those who
serve God and those who don't.

DEVOTION

What if we don't follow God? (3:14–18)

THE DAY OF THE LORD'S JUDGING

4

1"There is a day coming that will burn like a
hot furnace, and all the proud and evil people
will be like straw. On that day they will be
completely burned up so that not a root or
branch will be left," says the LORD All-Powerful.
2"But for you who honor me, goodness will
shine on you like the sun, with healing in its
rays. You will jump around, like well-fed
calves. 3Then you will crush the wicked like
ashes under your feet on the day I will do this,"
says the LORD All-Powerful.
4"Remember the teaching of Moses my servant, those laws and rules I gave to him on
Mount Sinai for all the Israelites.
5"But I will send you Elijah the prophet before that great and terrifying day of the LORD's
judging. 6Elijah will help parents love their
children and children love their parents. Otherwise, I will come and put a curse on the
land."

THE NEW TESTAMENT

Matthew

CONTENT Eventually in school you'll study "If-then" statements. It might be in a math class or a logic class or a philosophy class, but they'll come up. *If* a=b and b=c, *then* a=c. Or *if* Maggie is a four-legged animal that barks, *then* Maggie is probably a dog. "If-then" statements are the way we put together information and come to a conclusion.

The Book, or Gospel, of Matthew is an "If-then" kind of book. It is a great book to start the New Testament, because Matthew opens by referring to the Old Testament. He uses the prophecies of the Old Testament to convince his readers of one thing: Jesus is the Messiah we've been waiting for.

Matthew's point in writing his biography of Jesus' ministry is to show the connection between the promises and prophecies of the Old Testament and the life and ministry of Jesus Christ in the New Testament. Basically Matthew's message is, "*If* all these prophecies that we have studied and believed are fulfilled in this one Man, *then* Jesus of Nazareth is the Messiah!

Because of this, Matthew's Gospel is full of Old Testament prophecy. He logically and painstakingly writes Jesus' story in an effort to say, "Jesus is the One we've been waiting for! Put your trust in him."

Outline

1:1—2:23 .... The Family History and Birth of Jesus
3:1–12 .... The Work of John the Baptist
3:13—4:11 .... The Baptism and Temptation of Jesus
4:12—18:35 .... Jesus in Galilee
19:1—20:34 .... Jesus Goes from Galilee to Jerusalem
21:1—27:66 .... Jesus' Last Week: His Trial and Death
28:1–15 .... Jesus Is Alive
28:16–20 .... Jesus Appears to His Followers and Gives the Great Commission

Purpose King Jesus teaches us how to live as good citizens in his kingdom.

Themes Jesus Is the Fulfillment of Old Testament Prophecies Concerning the Messiah; His Followers Are Called to a New Agreement, to Live at a Higher Dimension Than the Old Ever Realized

Date of writing 50s or 60s A.D.

"Simon Peter answered, 'You are the Christ, the Son of the living God' " (16:16).

Bible Talk

Jesus in the Face of the Pharisees

Some of the religious leaders of Jesus' day were the Pharisees. The problem with the Pharisees was that they were hypocrites. They had their religious ideas all backwards. Instead of glorifying God, they glorified themselves. Instead of leading out of humility, they led out of pride. Instead of expecting to serve people, they expected to be served. Jesus said they looked good on the outside, but inside they were dirty (23:25). He called them whitewashed tombs (23:27) and poisonous snakes (23:33). (Okay, now tell us how you *really* feel.)

Even though the Pharisees were religious leaders, they were Jesus' biggest enemies. They didn't want to admit Jesus was the Son of God because they would lose their control over the Hebrews. They missed the point entirely.

THE REVOLUTION OF JESUS CHRIST

A lot of the passages in the Book of Matthew are famous words that we hear many times if we grow up in the church. In fact, we can hear them so often that we forget what mind-blowers these words were when Jesus first said them.

Take the Sermon on the Mount, for instance (chapters 5—7). In one simple talk, Jesus changed the whole definition of spirituality. To the people of that day, being spiritual meant obeying rules. The more rules you obeyed, the more spiritual you were. Jesus taught that the rules won't save you; your faith will save you. The rules just show you that you need God.

Jesus made a lot of people mad by saying these things. In the process, he started a revolution called Christianity.

THE FAMILY HISTORY OF JESUS

1 This is the family history of Jesus Christ. He came from the family of David, and David came from the family of Abraham.

2 Abraham was the father[n] of Isaac.
Isaac was the father of Jacob.
Jacob was the father of Judah and his brothers.
3 Judah was the father of Perez and Zerah.
(Their mother was Tamar.)
Perez was the father of Hezron.
Hezron was the father of Ram.
4 Ram was the father of Amminadab.
Amminadab was the father of Nahshon.
Nahshon was the father of Salmon.
5 Salmon was the father of Boaz.
(Boaz's mother was Rahab.)
Boaz was the father of Obed.
(Obed's mother was Ruth.)
Obed was the father of Jesse.
6 Jesse was the father of King David.
David was the father of Solomon.
(Solomon's mother had been Uriah's wife.)
7 Solomon was the father of Rehoboam.
Rehoboam was the father of Abijah.
Abijah was the father of Asa.
8 Asa was the father of Jehoshaphat.
Jehoshaphat was the father of Jehoram.
Jehoram was the ancestor of Uzziah.
9 Uzziah was the father of Jotham.
Jotham was the father of Ahaz.
Ahaz was the father of Hezekiah.
10 Hezekiah was the father of Manasseh.
Manasseh was the father of Amon.

WHAT'S IT MEAN?

More than six hundred years before Jesus was born, King Nebuchadnezzar and his Babylonian army destroyed the city of Jerusalem and carried away most of its inhabitants, forcing them to live as prisoners hundreds of miles from home in Babylon. Their captivity lasted seventy years.

Matthew 1:11

On the Edge

This is how the birth of Jesus Christ came about. His mother Mary was engaged to marry Joseph, but before they married, she learned she was pregnant by the power of the Holy Spirit. Because Mary's husband, Joseph, was a good man, he did not want to disgrace her in public, so he planned to divorce her secretly. While Joseph thought about these things, an angel of the Lord came to him in a dream. The angel said, "Joseph, descendant of David, don't be afraid to take Mary as your wife, because the baby in her is from the Holy Spirit" (Matt. 1:18–20).

In this passage, Joseph and Mary were engaged. In those days, engagements lasted one year for the purpose of proving sexual purity. During the engagement, Mary discovered that she was pregnant by God's Holy Spirit. Matthew says that Joseph was "a good man," which is why he planned to call off the wedding. He knew that Mary could have been stoned if people found out that she was pregnant during the engagement. An angel came to Joseph and told him to go ahead and marry before the engagement time was over. Joseph did what was honorable and right for Mary, and for the child, Jesus.

If your girlfriend is pregnant, it is up to you to do the honorable thing. No matter how young you are, or how afraid, you can make wise decisions with the help of the Lord, parents, and pastors. A wise decision may mean adoption. It may mean marriage. The most important thing now is that this child deserves a mother and a father who love him and are willing to care for him. Being a "good man" may mean that, for a time, you have to sacrifice your reputation, your plans, or your interests. Just keep asking yourself, "What is best for the child?" Trust the Lord to guide you. Be brave enough to do what is right.

SEE FOR YOURSELF:
Luke 1:26–28; 6:31; 2 John 5–6

1:2 father "Father" in Jewish lists of ancestors can sometimes mean grandfather or more distant relative.

Amon was the father of Josiah.
11 Josiah was the grandfather of Jehoiachin
and his brothers.
(This was at the time that the people
were taken to
Babylon.)
12 After they were taken to
Babylon:
Jehoiachin was the
father of
Shealtiel.
Shealtiel was the
grandfather of
Zerubbabel.
13 Zerubbabel was the
father of Abiud.
Abiud was the father of
Eliakim.
Eliakim was the father of
Azor.
14 Azor was the father of Zadok.
Zadok was the father of Akim.
Akim was the father of Eliud.
15 Eliud was the father of Eleazar.
Eleazar was the father of Matthan.
Matthan was the father of Jacob.
16 Jacob was the father of Joseph.
Joseph was the husband of Mary,
and Mary was the mother of Jesus.
Jesus is called the Christ.
17 So there were fourteen generations from
Abraham to David. And there were fourteen
generations from David until the people were
taken to Babylon. And there were fourteen
generations from the time when the people
were taken to Babylon until
Christ was born.

"Jesus was born in the town of Bethlehem in Judea during the time when Herod was king. When Jesus was born, some wise men from the east came to Jerusalem."
(Matthew 2:1)

THE BIRTH OF JESUS CHRIST

18 This is how the birth
of Jesus Christ came
about. His mother Mary
was engaged[n] to marry
Joseph, but before they
married, she learned she
was pregnant by the
power of the Holy Spirit.
19 Because Mary's husband,
Joseph, was a good man, he
did not want to disgrace her in
public, so he planned to divorce her secretly.
20 While Joseph thought about these things,
an angel of the Lord came to him in a dream.
The angel said, "Joseph, descendant of David,
don't be afraid to take Mary as your wife, because the baby in her is from the Holy Spirit.
21 She will give birth to a son, and you will
name him Jesus,[n] because he will save his people from their sins."
22 All this happened to bring about what the
Lord had said through the prophet: 23 "The virgin will be pregnant. She will have a son, and
they will name him Immanuel,"[n] which means
"God is with us."
24 When Joseph woke up, he did what the
Lord's angel had told him to do. Joseph took
Mary as his wife, 25 but he did not have sexual
relations with her until she gave birth to the
son. And Joseph named him Jesus.

WHAT'S IT MEAN?

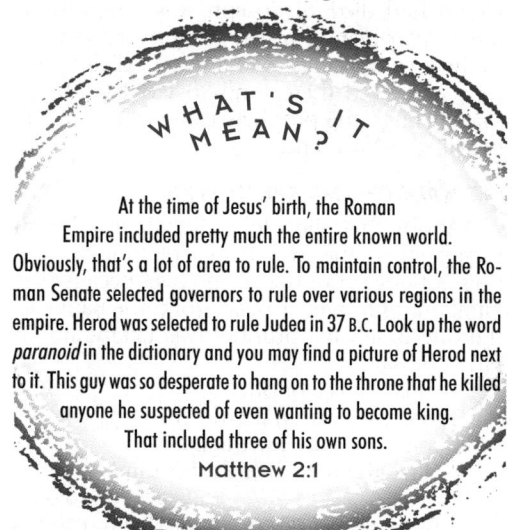

At the time of Jesus' birth, the Roman Empire included pretty much the entire known world. Obviously, that's a lot of area to rule. To maintain control, the Roman Senate selected governors to rule over various regions in the empire. Herod was selected to rule Judea in 37 B.C. Look up the word *paranoid* in the dictionary and you may find a picture of Herod next to it. This guy was so desperate to hang on to the throne that he killed anyone he suspected of even wanting to become king. That included three of his own sons.
Matthew 2:1

WISE MEN COME TO VISIT JESUS

2 1 Jesus was born in the town of Bethlehem
in Judea during the time when Herod was king.
When Jesus was born, some wise men from
the east came to Jerusalem. 2 They asked,
"Where is the baby who was born to be the
king of the Jews? We saw his star in the east
and have come to worship him."
3 When King Herod heard this, he was troubled, as well as all the people in Jerusalem.
4 Herod called a meeting of all the leading
priests and teachers of the law and asked them

1:18 engaged For the Jewish people an engagement was a lasting agreement, which could only be broken by a divorce. If a bride-to-be was unfaithful, it was considered adultery, and she could be put to death.
1:21 Jesus The name "Jesus" means "salvation." **1:23 "The virgin . . . Immanuel"** Quotation from Isaiah 7:14.

where the Christ would be born. [5]They answered, "In the town of Bethlehem in Judea.
The prophet wrote about this in the Scriptures:
[6]'But you, Bethlehem, in the land of Judah,
are important among the tribes of
Judah.
A ruler will come from you
who will be like a shepherd for my
people Israel.' " *Micah 5:2*
[7]Then Herod had a secret meeting with the
wise men and learned from them the exact
time they first saw the star. [8]He sent the wise
men to Bethlehem, saying, "Look carefully for
the child. When you find him, come tell me so
I can worship him too."
[9]After the wise men heard the king, they left.
The star that they had seen in the east went
before them until it stopped above the place
where the child was. [10]When the wise men saw
the star, they were filled with joy. [11]They came
to the house where the child was and saw him
with his mother, Mary, and they bowed down
and worshiped him. They opened their gifts
and gave him treasures of gold, frankincense,
and myrrh. [12]But God warned the wise men in
a dream not to go back to Herod, so they returned to their own country by a different way.

JESUS' PARENTS TAKE HIM TO EGYPT

[13]After they left, an angel of the Lord came
to Joseph in a dream and said, "Get up! Take
the child and his mother and escape to
Egypt, because Herod is starting to look for
the child so he can kill him. Stay in Egypt
until I tell you to return."
[14]So Joseph got up and left for Egypt during
the night with the child and his mother. [15]And
Joseph stayed in Egypt until Herod died. This
happened to bring about what the Lord had
said through the prophet: "I called my son out
of Egypt."*n*

HEROD KILLS THE BABY BOYS

[16]When Herod saw that the wise men had
tricked him, he was furious. So he gave an order to kill all the baby boys in Bethlehem and
in the surrounding area who were two years
old or younger. This was in keeping with the
time he learned from the wise men. [17]So what
God had said through the prophet Jeremiah
came true:
[18]"A voice was heard in Ramah
of painful crying and deep sadness:
Rachel crying for her children.
She refused to be comforted,
because her children are dead." *Jeremiah 31:15*

WHAT'S IT MEAN?

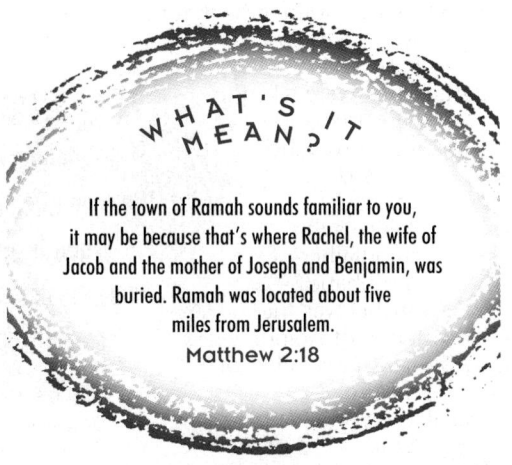

If the town of Ramah sounds familiar to you, it may be because that's where Rachel, the wife of Jacob and the mother of Joseph and Benjamin, was buried. Ramah was located about five miles from Jerusalem.

Matthew 2:18

JOSEPH AND MARY RETURN

[19]After Herod died, an angel of the Lord
spoke to Joseph in a dream while he was in
Egypt. [20]The angel said, "Get up! Take the child
and his mother and go to the land of Israel,
because the people who were trying to kill the
child are now dead."
[21]So Joseph took the child and his mother
and went to Israel. [22]But he heard that Arche-
laus was now king in Judea since his father
Herod had died. So Joseph was afraid to go
there. After being warned in a dream, he went
to the area of Galilee, [23]to a town called Nazareth, and lived there. And so what God had
said through the prophets came true: "He will
be called a Nazarene."*n*

THE WORK OF JOHN THE BAPTIST

3 [1]About that time John the Baptist began
preaching in the desert area of Judea. [2]John
said, "Change your hearts and lives because the
kingdom of heaven is near." [3]John the Baptist is
the one Isaiah the prophet was talking about
when he said:
"This is a voice of one
who calls out in the desert:
'Prepare the way for the Lord.
Make the road straight for him.' "
Isaiah 40:3
[4]John's clothes were made from camel's
hair, and he wore a leather belt around his
waist. For food, he ate locusts and wild honey.
[5]Many people came from Jerusalem and Judea

2:15 "I called . . . Egypt." Quotation from Hosea 11:1. **2:23 Nazarene** A person from the city of Nazareth, a name probably meaning "branch" (see Isaiah 11:1).

and all the area around the Jordan River to
hear John. 6They confessed their sins, and he
baptized them in the Jordan River.
7Many of the Pharisees and Sadducees
came to the place where John was baptizing
people. When John saw them, he said, "You are
all snakes! Who warned you to run away from
God's coming punishment? 8Do the things that
show you really have changed your hearts and
lives. 9And don't think you can say to yourselves, 'Abraham is our father.' I tell you that
God could make children for Abraham from
these rocks. 10The ax is now ready to cut down
the trees, and every tree that does not produce
good fruit will be cut down and thrown into
the fire.[n]

WHAT'S IT MEAN?

Think of the Pharisees and Sadducees as rival gangs. Instead of fighting with guns and knives, though, these rivals fought with words and ideas. The Pharisees were ordinary, middle-class people who emphasized the importance of obeying the Teachings God had given Moses. The Sadducees were wealthy and powerful individuals, many of whom served as priests. These two groups of Jewish scholars interpreted Scripture differently and argued over issues, such as the resurrection of the dead and the existence of angels. Members of both groups tended to take pride in themselves and to criticize others.

Matthew 3:7

11"I baptize you with water to show that
your hearts and lives have changed. But there
is one coming after me who is greater than I
am, whose sandals I am not good enough to
carry. He will baptize you with the Holy Spirit
and fire. 12He will come ready to clean the
grain, separating the good grain from the chaff.
He will put the good part of the grain into his
barn, but he will burn the chaff with a fire that
cannot be put out."[n]

JESUS IS BAPTIZED BY JOHN

13At that time Jesus came from Galilee to the
Jordan River and wanted John to baptize him.
14But John tried to stop him, saying, "Why do
you come to me to be baptized? I need to be
baptized by you!"
15Jesus answered, "Let it be this way for
now. We should do all things that are God's
will." So John agreed to baptize Jesus.

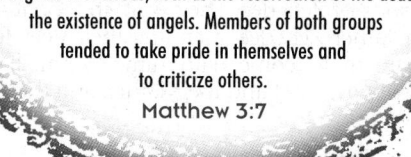

On the Edge

As soon as Jesus was baptized, he came up out of the water. Then heaven opened, and he saw God's Spirit coming down on him like a dove (Matt. 3:16).

There are two ceremonies Jesus gave for every believer to observe—communion and baptism. Why should we get baptized? Because Jesus did, and he did it publicly. Getting baptized tells the world about your faith in Jesus as your Savior. This lets people know that you mean business with God, and that you're going to live for him, with courage and excitement! Not only does God want you to profess him by being baptized in water, but he also wants you to be a witness for him by being filled daily with his Holy Spirit. Why be baptized in the Holy Spirit? Because we need the power we receive from it. Acts 1:8 says, "But when the Holy Spirit comes to you, you will receive power." We don't need to depend on our own strength and ability. God makes unlimited strength and power available to us through his Holy Spirit. As a teenager, you need that power to make a difference for him. Everyone does. Jesus is the baptizer. Let him baptize you with his power today!

SEE FOR YOURSELF:
Matt. 28:19; Acts 2:38; 8:12; Rom. 6:3–5

16As soon as Jesus was baptized, he came
up out of the water. Then heaven opened, and
he saw God's Spirit coming down on him like
a dove. 17And a voice from heaven said, "This
is my Son, whom I love, and I am very pleased
with him."

3:10 The ax . . . fire. This means that God is ready to punish his people who do not obey him.
3:12 He will . . . out. This means that Jesus will come to separate good people from bad people, saving the good and punishing the bad.

THE TEMPTATION OF JESUS

4 1Then the Spirit led Jesus into the desert to
be tempted by the devil. 2Jesus ate nothing for
forty days and nights. After this, he was very
hungry. 3The devil came to Jesus to tempt him,
saying, "If you are the Son of God, tell these
rocks to become bread."

4Jesus answered, "It is written in the Scriptures, 'A person does not live by eating only
bread, but by everything God says.' "[n]

5Then the devil led Jesus to the holy city of
Jerusalem and put him on a high place of the
Temple. 6The devil said, "If you are the Son of
God, jump down, because it is written in the
Scriptures:

'He has put his angels in charge of you.
They will catch you in their hands
so that you will not hit your foot on a
rock.' " *Psalm 91:11-12*

7Jesus answered him, "It also says in the
Scriptures, 'Do not test the Lord your God.' "[n]

8Then the devil led Jesus to the top of a very
high mountain and showed him all the kingdoms of the world and all their splendor. 9The
devil said, "If you will bow down and worship
me, I will give you all these things."

10Jesus said to the devil, "Go away from me,
Satan! It is written in the Scriptures, 'You must
worship the Lord your God and serve only
him.' "[n]

11So the devil left Jesus, and angels came
and took care of him.

WHAT'S IT MEAN?

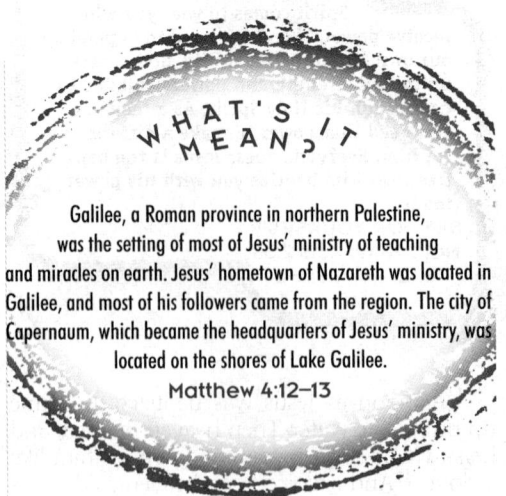

Galilee, a Roman province in northern Palestine, was the setting of most of Jesus' ministry of teaching and miracles on earth. Jesus' hometown of Nazareth was located in Galilee, and most of his followers came from the region. The city of Capernaum, which became the headquarters of Jesus' ministry, was located on the shores of Lake Galilee.

Matthew 4:12–13

JESUS BEGINS WORK IN GALILEE

12When Jesus heard that John had been put
in prison, he went back to Galilee. 13He left
Nazareth and went to live in Capernaum, a
town near Lake Galilee, in the area near Zebulun and Naphtali. 14Jesus did this to bring
about what the prophet Isaiah had said:

15"Land of Zebulun and land of Naphtali
along the sea,
beyond the Jordan River.
This is Galilee where the non-Jewish
people live.
16These people who live in darkness
will see a great light.
They live in a place covered with the
shadows of death,
but a light will shine on them." *Isaiah 9:1-2*

JESUS CHOOSES SOME FOLLOWERS

17From that time Jesus began to preach, saying, "Change your hearts and lives, because the
kingdom of heaven is near."

18As Jesus was walking by Lake Galilee, he
saw two brothers, Simon (called Peter) and his
brother Andrew. They were throwing a net
into the lake because they were fishermen.
19Jesus said, "Come follow me, and I will make
you fish for people." 20So Simon and Andrew
immediately left their nets and followed him.

21As Jesus continued walking by Lake Galilee, he saw two other brothers, James and John,
the sons of Zebedee. They were in a boat with
their father Zebedee, mending their nets. Jesus
told them to come with him. 22Immediately
they left the boat and their father, and they followed Jesus.

JESUS TEACHES AND HEALS PEOPLE

23Jesus went everywhere in Galilee, teaching
in the synagogues, preaching the Good News
about the kingdom of heaven, and healing all
the people's diseases and sicknesses. 24The
news about Jesus spread all over Syria, and
people brought all the sick to him. They were
suffering from different kinds of diseases. Some
were in great pain, some had demons, some
were epileptics,[n] and some were paralyzed.
Jesus healed all of them. 25Many people from
Galilee, the Ten Towns,[n] Jerusalem, Judea, and
the land across the Jordan River followed
him.

4:4 'A person . . . says.' Quotation from Deuteronomy 8:3. **4:7 'Do . . . God.'** Quotation from Deuteronomy 6:16. **4:10 'You . . . him.'** Quotation from Deuteronomy 6:13. **4:24 epileptics** People with a disease that causes them sometimes to lose control of their bodies and maybe faint, shake strongly, or not be able to move. **4:25 Ten Towns** In Greek, called "Decapolis." It was an area east of Lake Galilee that once had ten main towns.

JESUS TEACHES THE PEOPLE

5 1When Jesus saw the crowds, he went up
on a hill and sat down. His followers came to
him, 2and he began to teach them, saying:
3"Those people who know they have great
spiritual needs are happy,
because the kingdom of heaven belongs
to them.
4Those who are sad now are happy,
because God will comfort them.
5Those who are humble are happy,
because the earth will belong to them.
6Those who want to do right more than
anything else are happy,
because God will fully satisfy them.
7Those who show mercy to others are
happy,
because God will show mercy to them.
8Those who are pure in their thinking are
happy,
because they will be with God.
9Those who work to bring peace are happy,
because God will call them his children.
10Those who are treated badly for doing
good are happy,
because the kingdom of heaven belongs
to them.

11"People will insult you and hurt you. They
will lie and say all kinds of evil things about
you because you follow me. But when they do,
you will be happy. 12Rejoice and be glad, because you have a great reward waiting for you
in heaven. People did the same evil things to
the prophets who lived before you.

YOU ARE LIKE SALT AND LIGHT

13"You are the salt of the earth. But if the salt
loses its salty taste, it cannot be made salty
again. It is good for nothing, except to be
thrown out and walked on.
14"You are the light that gives light to the
world. A city that is built on a hill cannot be
hidden. 15And people don't hide a light under a
bowl. They put it on a lampstand so the light
shines for all the people in the house. 16In the
same way, you should be a light for other people. Live so that they will see the good things
you do and will praise your Father in heaven.

THE IMPORTANCE OF THE LAW

17"Don't think that I have come to destroy
the law of Moses or the teaching of the prophets. I have not come to destroy them but to
bring about what they said. 18I tell you the
truth, nothing will disappear from the law until heaven and earth are gone. Not even the
smallest letter or the smallest part of a letter
will be lost until everything has happened.
19Whoever refuses to obey any command and
teaches other people not to obey that command will be the least important in the kingdom of heaven. But whoever obeys the
commands and teaches other people to obey
them will be great in the kingdom of heaven.
20I tell you that if you are no more obedient
than the teachers of the law and the Pharisees,
you will never enter the kingdom of heaven.

JESUS TEACHES ABOUT ANGER

21"You have heard that it was said to our
people long ago, 'You must not murder

On the Edge

You are the salt of the earth. But if the salt loses its salty taste, it cannot be made salty again. It is good for nothing, except to be thrown out and walked on. You are the light that gives light to the world. A city that is built on a hill cannot be hidden (Matt. 5:13–14).

Jesus teaches in Matthew 5:13–14 that part of being a Christian is being salt and light to this world. Being salt means that a follower of Jesus creates a thirst for greater information. When you meet someone who is different and has superior qualities, you want to know why that person is different. Have you ever met someone who was really cool, had a great attitude even when life was hard, did nice things for no obvious reason, and later found out that he was a Christian? That explained it. That person was being salt. He made people want to know what made him different.

How about light? A light shines and gives direction. It points people toward the right path. Do you know Christians who radiate Jesus? Others are drawn to them. Their lives are examples that many want to follow. People see their goodness and know it is Jesus who lives in them. Jesus says don't hide who you are. Don't put your light under a basket where others can't see it. Go boldly into the world and give 'em Jesus. You are bound to change the place where you are when others see Jesus in you.

SEE FOR YOURSELF:
Mark 9:50; Luke 14:34; Phil. 2:15

anyone.[n] Anyone who murders another will
be judged.' 22But I tell you, if you are angry
with a brother or sister,[n] you will
be judged. If you say bad
things to a brother or sister,
you will be judged by the
council. And if you call
someone a fool, you will be
in danger of the fire of hell.

MURDER
What is the same as murder in God's eyes? (5:21–22)

23"So when you offer your
gift to God at the altar, and you remember that
your brother or sister has something against
you, 24leave your gift there at the altar. Go and
make peace with that person, and then come
and offer your gift.

WHAT'S IT MEAN?

An altar was a platform used to hold things that people offered to God. Offerings of fruit and vegetables were made by people who wanted to show their appreciation to God for a healthy herd or a good crop. Animal offerings were made as substitute payments for sin.

Matthew 5:23

25"If your enemy is taking you to court, become friends quickly, before you go to court.
Otherwise, your enemy might turn you over to
the judge, and the judge might give you to a
guard to put you in jail. 26I tell you the truth,
you will not leave there until you have paid
everything you owe.

JESUS TEACHES ABOUT SEXUAL SIN

27"You have heard that it
was said, 'You must not be
guilty of adultery.'[n] 28But I tell
you that if anyone looks at a
woman and wants to sin sexually with her, in his mind he
has already done that sin
with the woman. 29If your right
eye causes you to sin, take it out and throw it
away. It is better to lose one part of your body
than to have your whole body thrown into
hell. 30If your right hand causes you to sin, cut
it off and throw it away. It is better to lose one
part of your body than for your whole body
to go into hell.

SEX
Where do sexual sins begin? (5:27–30)

JESUS TEACHES ABOUT DIVORCE

31"It was also said, 'Anyone who divorces
his wife must give her a written divorce
paper.'[n] 32But I tell you that anyone who di-

On the Edge

He causes the sun to rise on good people and on evil people, and he sends rain to those who do right and to those who do wrong (Matt. 5:45b).

It's a fact. You *will* eventually reap what you sow. Matthew 5:45 is talking about a "rain" of blessing or cursing—good things or bad things. You've got a choice (see Deut. 30:19). Most people are ready for God to rain down his blessings upon them. But how do you get it to happen?

Simple. One way is to love your enemies. Worldly wisdom tells you to love your neighbor and hate your enemy. Jesus says we have to love our neighbor *and* our enemy. That's right, love your enemy! When you love an enemy, you are actually piling burning coals upon his or her head. In other words, God will take care of enemies with the kind of rain you don't want!

What exactly are you supposed to do for your enemies? Pray for them, feed them, give them something to drink, clothe them, and love them. By doing this, you will never be defeated by evil, but you will defeat evil with good (see Rom. 12:21). Then God can and will reward you. Remember, it's the goodness of God that leads people to ask forgiveness and turn from their sin. Start praying for your enemies right now, and let God shower you with his blessings!

SEE FOR YOURSELF:
Matt. 5:9; Luke 6:35; Rom. 12:20

5:21 You . . . anyone. Quotation from Exodus 20:13; Deuteronomy 5:17. **5:22 brother . . . sister** Although the Greek text reads "brother" here and throughout this book, Jesus' words were meant for the entire church, including men and women. **5:27 'You . . . adultery.'** Quotation from Exodus 20:14; Deuteronomy 5:18. **5:31 'Anyone . . . divorce paper.'** Quotation from Deuteronomy 24:1.

vorces his wife forces her to be guilty of adultery. The only reason for a man to divorce his
wife is if she has sexual relations with another
man. And anyone who marries that divorced
woman is guilty of adultery.

MAKE PROMISES CAREFULLY

33“You have heard that it was said to our
people long ago, ‘Don’t break your promises,
but keep the promises you make to the Lord.’[n]
34But I tell you, never swear an oath. Don’t
swear an oath using the name of heaven, because heaven is God’s throne. 35Don’t swear an
oath using the name of the earth, because the
earth belongs to God. Don’t swear an oath using the name of Jerusalem,
because that is the city of
the great King. 36Don’t
even swear by your
own head, because
you cannot make one
hair on your head be-
come white or black.
37Say only yes if you
mean yes, and no if
you mean no. If you
say more than yes or no,
it is from the Evil One.

> “When you pray, you should go into your room and close the door and pray to your Father who cannot be seen. Your Father can see what is done in secret, and he will reward you.” (Matthew 6:6)

DON’T FIGHT BACK

38“You have heard that it was said, ‘An
eye for an eye, and a tooth for a tooth.’[n] 39But I
tell you, don’t stand up against an evil person.
If someone slaps you on the right cheek, turn
to him the other cheek also. 40If someone
wants to sue you in court and take your shirt,
let him have your coat also. 41If someone
forces you to go with him one mile, go with
him two miles. 42If a person asks you for
something, give it to him. Don’t refuse to give
to someone who wants to borrow from you.

LOVE ALL PEOPLE

43“You have heard that it was said, ‘Love
your neighbor[n] and hate your enemies.’ 44But I say to you, love
your enemies. Pray for those
who hurt you. 45If you do
this, you will be true children
of your Father in heaven. He
causes the sun to rise on good
people and on evil people,
and he sends rain to those who
do right and to those who do wrong. 46If you
love only the people who love you, you will
get no reward. Even the tax collectors do that.
47And if you are nice only to your friends, you
are no better than other people. Even those
who don’t know God are nice to their friends.
48So you must be perfect, just as your Father in
heaven is perfect.

LOVE
Do we have to love our enemies? (5:43–45)

JESUS TEACHES ABOUT GIVING

6

1“Be careful! When you do good things,
don’t do them in front of people to be seen by
them. If you do that, you will have no reward
from your Father in heaven.
2“When you give to the poor, don’t be like
the hypocrites. They blow
trumpets in the syna-
gogues and on the
streets so that people
will see them and
honor them. I tell you
the truth, those hypo-
crites already have their
full reward. 3So when
you give to the poor,
don’t let anyone know
what you are doing.
4Your giving should be
done in secret. Your Father
can see what is done in secret,
and he will reward you.

JESUS TEACHES ABOUT PRAYER

5“When you pray, don’t be like the hypocrites. They love to stand in the synagogues
and on the street corners and
pray so people will see them. I
tell you the truth, they already
have their full reward. 6When
you pray, you should go into
your room and close the door
and pray to your Father who
cannot be seen. Your Father can
see what is done in secret, and he will reward
you.
7“And when you pray, don’t be like those
people who don’t know God. They continue
saying things that mean nothing, thinking that
God will hear them because of their many
words. 8Don’t be like them, because your Father knows the things you need before you ask
him. 9So when you pray, you should pray like
this:

PRAYER
Who taught the followers how to pray? (6:5–13)

5:33 ‘Don’t . . . Lord.’ This refers to Leviticus 19:12; Numbers 30:2; Deuteronomy 23:21. **5:38 ‘An eye . . . tooth.’** Quotation from Exodus 21:24; Leviticus 24:20; Deuteronomy 19:21. **5:43 ‘Love your neighbor’** Quotation from Leviticus 19:18.

'Our Father in heaven,
may your name always be kept holy.
10 May your kingdom come
and what you want be done,
here on earth as it is in heaven.
11 Give us the food we need for each day.
12 Forgive us for our sins,
just as we have forgiven those who
sinned against us.
13 And do not cause us to be tempted,
but save us from the Evil One.'
14 Yes, if you forgive others for their sins, your
Father in heaven will also forgive you for your
sins. 15 But if you don't forgive others, your Father in heaven will not forgive your sins.

WHAT'S IT MEAN?

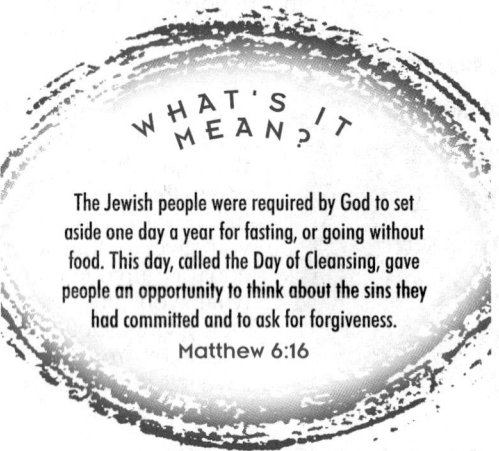

The Jewish people were required by God to set aside one day a year for fasting, or going without food. This day, called the Day of Cleansing, gave people an opportunity to think about the sins they had committed and to ask for forgiveness.

Matthew 6:16

JESUS TEACHES ABOUT WORSHIP

16 "When you give up eating,[n] don't put on a
sad face like the hypocrites. They make their
faces look sad to show people they are giving
up eating. I tell you the truth, those hypocrites
already have their full reward. 17 So when you
give up eating, comb your hair and wash your
face. 18 Then people will not know that you are
giving up eating, but your Father, whom you
cannot see, will see you. Your Father sees what
is done in secret, and he will reward you.

GOD IS MORE IMPORTANT THAN MONEY

19 "Don't store treasures for yourselves here
on earth where moths and
rust will destroy them and
thieves can break in and steal
them. 20 But store your treasures in heaven where they
cannot be destroyed by
moths or rust and where
thieves cannot break in and steal them. 21 Your
heart will be where your treasure is.

MONEY
What's most important? (6:19–20)

22 "The eye is a light for the body. If your
eyes are good, your whole body will be full of
light. 23 But if your eyes are evil, your whole
body will be full of darkness. And if the only
light you have is really darkness, then you
have the worst darkness.
24 "No one can serve two masters. The person will hate one master and love the other, or
will follow one master and refuse to follow the
other. You cannot serve both God and worldly
riches.

DON'T WORRY

25 "So I tell you, don't worry about the food
or drink you need to live, or about the clothes

On the Edge

The thing you should want most is God's kingdom and doing what God wants. Then all these other things you need will be given to you (Matt. 6:33).

No matter what the decision, you can take your advice from Matthew 6:33 and remember what Jesus said: "The thing you should want most is God's kingdom and doing what God wants." When trying to decide which option is best or what path to choose, ask yourself, "Which way would bring God glory?" If God would be honored in any decision, then choose the one you like the most. God hasn't put you on earth to make you miserable. A lot of Christians mistakenly think that the most miserable option must surely be God's will. That's not true. God has given you preferences and passions on purpose. He knows you will accomplish more for the kingdom when you are working in an area you love. If bringing God glory is your first priority, then you will always make wise decisions. They may sometimes be tough, but in the end, you will have made the right choice.

SEE FOR YOURSELF:
Josh. 6:27; Prov. 22:1; Is. 11:2; 12:6; Luke 12:31

6:16 give up eating This is called "fasting." The people would give up eating for a special time of prayer and worship to God. It was also done to show sadness and disappointment.

you need for your body. Life is more than
food, and the body is more than clothes.
26Look at the birds in the air. They don't plant
or harvest or store food in barns, but your
heavenly Father feeds them. And you know
that you are worth much more than the birds.
27You cannot add any time to your life by worrying about it.
28"And why do you worry about clothes?
Look at how the lilies in the field grow. They
don't work or make clothes for themselves.
29But I tell you that even Solomon with his
riches was not dressed as beautifully as one of
these flowers. 30God clothes the grass in the
field, which is alive today but tomorrow is
thrown into the fire. So you can be even more
sure that God will clothe you. Don't have so
little faith! 31Don't worry and say, 'What will
we eat?' or 'What will we drink?' or 'What will
we wear?' 32The people who don't know God
keep trying to get these things, and your Father
in heaven knows you need them. 33The thing
you should want most is God's kingdom and
doing what God wants. Then all these other
things you need will be given to you. 34So
don't worry about tomorrow, because tomorrow will have its own worries. Each day has
enough trouble of its own.

BE CAREFUL ABOUT JUDGING OTHERS

7 1"Don't judge other people, or you will be
judged. 2You will be judged in the same way
that you judge others, and the amount you
give to others will be given to you.
3"Why do you notice the little piece of dust in
your friend's eye, but you don't notice the big
piece of wood in your own eye? 4How can you
say to your friend, 'Let me take that little piece of
dust out of your eye'? Look at yourself! You still
have that big piece of wood in your
own eye. 5You hypocrite! First,
take the wood out of your own
eye. Then you will see clearly
to take the dust out of your
friend's eye.
6"Don't give holy things to
dogs, and don't throw your
pearls before pigs. Pigs will only
trample on them, and dogs will turn to attack
you.

DECISIONS
What do we need to do before we criticize others? (7:1–5)

ASK GOD FOR WHAT YOU NEED

7"Ask, and God will give to you. Search, and
you will find. Knock, and the door will open
for you. 8Yes, everyone who asks will receive.
Everyone who searches will find. And everyone who knocks will have the door opened.

WHAT'S IT MEAN?

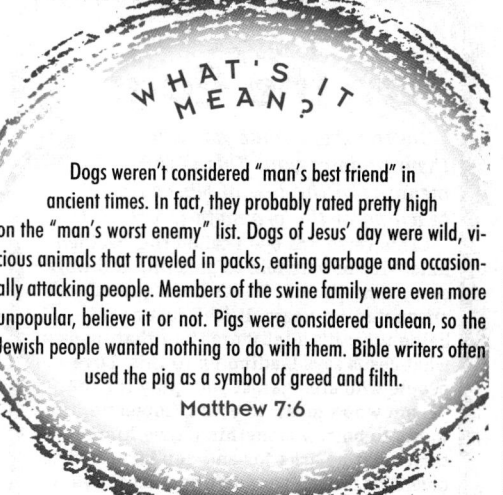

Dogs weren't considered "man's best friend" in ancient times. In fact, they probably rated pretty high on the "man's worst enemy" list. Dogs of Jesus' day were wild, vicious animals that traveled in packs, eating garbage and occasionally attacking people. Members of the swine family were even more unpopular, believe it or not. Pigs were considered unclean, so the Jewish people wanted nothing to do with them. Bible writers often used the pig as a symbol of greed and filth.
Matthew 7:6

9"If your children ask for bread, which of
you would give them a stone? 10Or if your children ask for a fish, would you give them a snake?
11Even though you are bad, you know how to
give good gifts to your children. How much
more your heavenly Father will give good
things to those who ask him!

THE MOST IMPORTANT RULE

12"Do to others what you want them to do
to you. This is the meaning of the law of Moses
and the teaching of the prophets.

THE WAY TO HEAVEN IS HARD

13"Enter through the narrow gate.
The gate is wide and the road is
wide that leads to hell, and
many people enter through
that gate. 14But the gate is
small and the road is narrow
that leads to true life. Only a
few people find that road.

HEAVEN
Will many people be allowed to enter heaven? (7:13–14)

PEOPLE KNOW YOU BY YOUR ACTIONS

15"Be careful of false prophets. They come to
you looking gentle like sheep, but they are
really dangerous like wolves. 16You will know
these people by what they do. Grapes don't
come from thornbushes, and figs don't come
from thorny weeds. 17In the same way, every
good tree produces good fruit, but a bad tree
produces bad fruit. 18A good tree cannot produce bad fruit, and a bad tree cannot produce
good fruit. 19Every tree that does not produce
good fruit is cut down and thrown into the

On the Edge

Do to others what you want them to do to you. This is the meaning of the law of Moses and the teaching of the prophets (Matt. 7:12).

This verse has been called the "Golden Rule." It's as valuable as gold and it'll work every time you use it. It's been quoted and misquoted for years. It isn't just about being nice; it's a lot more than that. Look at what Jesus says leading up to this. Love people who are against you; pray for the person who's mean to you; if someone wants to borrow something, give him more than what he asks for and don't ask him to give it back. You wouldn't dare *ask* anyone to treat you that well—you'd feel like you were using her—but you'd like it if she did, right?

Jesus isn't telling you to be a doormat. He's showing you how to follow his example. His whole life was about two things: pleasing God and helping other people. He wants you to be more concerned about others than you are about yourself. Look out for others and trust God to look out for you. Always think about how you'd want someone to treat you. That's the heart of the Golden Rule.

SEE FOR YOURSELF:
Zech. 8:16; Luke 6:31; 2 John 5–6

fire. 20 In the same way, you will know these
false prophets by what they do.
21 "Not all those who say that I am their
Lord will enter the kingdom of heaven. The
only people who will enter the
kingdom of heaven are those
who do what my Father in
heaven wants. 22 On the last
day many people will say to
me, 'Lord, Lord, we spoke for
you, and through you we
forced out demons and did
many miracles.' 23 Then I will tell them clearly,
'Get away from me, you who do evil. I never
knew you.'

ETERNAL LIFE

Who is eternal life reserved for? (7:21)

TWO KINDS OF PEOPLE

24 "Everyone who hears my words and
obeys them is like a wise man who built his
house on rock. 25 It rained hard, the floods
came, and the winds blew and hit that house.
But it did not fall, because it was built on rock.
26 Everyone who hears my words and does not
obey them is like a foolish man who built his
house on sand. 27 It rained hard, the floods
came, and the winds blew and hit that house,
and it fell with a big crash."
28 When Jesus finished saying these things,
the people were amazed at his teaching, 29 because he did not teach like their teachers of
the law. He taught like a person who had authority.

On the Edge

He did not teach like their teachers of the law. He taught like a person who had authority (Matt. 7:29).

This passage of Scripture tells us that the crowds were surprised because Jesus taught with authority. We're not talking about your basic authority; we're talking about power! There is power in the words of Jesus. Look at what Hebrews 4:12 says: "God's word is alive and working and is sharper than a double-edged sword. It cuts all the way into us, where the soul and the spirit are joined, to the center of our joints and bones. And it judges the thoughts and feelings in our hearts." Start putting the Word of God in your mind and heart today, so that when troubles come against you, you can use it like a sword.

When the devil tempted Jesus in the wilderness, what did Jesus do? He spoke the Word of God. He said, "It is written . . ." (see Matt. 4:4, 6, 10). And you know what? The devil split. We need to follow Jesus' example. John 1:1 tells us, "In the beginning there was the Word. The Word was with God, and the Word was God." Jesus is the Word, and he wants to teach you today. As you begin to study the Scriptures, you will begin to gain understanding of what the verses mean. This will help you live every day of the week and cause you to walk in victory! Remember, the Bible isn't meant to be difficult. You'll never know until you dive in. Let Jesus be *your* Teacher!

SEE FOR YOURSELF:
Matt. 4:1–11; 2 Tim. 2:15; Heb. 4:12

JESUS HEALS A SICK MAN

8 1When Jesus came down from the hill, great
crowds followed him. 2Then a man with a skin
disease came to Jesus. The man bowed down
before him and said, "Lord, you can heal me if
you will."
3Jesus reached out his hand and touched
the man and said, "I will. Be healed!" And immediately the man was healed from his
disease. 4Then Jesus said to him, "Don't tell
anyone about this. But go and show yourself
to the priest[n] and offer the gift Moses commanded[n] for people who are made well. This
will show the people what I have done."

JESUS HEALS A SOLDIER'S SERVANT

5When Jesus entered the city of Capernaum,
an army officer came to him, begging for help.
6The officer said, "Lord, my servant is at home
in bed. He can't move his body and is in much
pain."
7Jesus said to the officer, "I will go and heal
him."
8The officer answered, "Lord, I am not
worthy for you to come into my house. You
only need to command it, and my servant
will be healed. 9I, too, am a man under the
authority of others, and I have soldiers under my command. I tell one soldier, 'Go,' and
he goes. I tell another soldier, 'Come,' and he
comes. I say to my servant, 'Do this,' and my
servant does it.
10When Jesus heard this, he was amazed. He
said to those who were following him, "I tell
you the truth, this is the greatest faith I have
found, even in Israel. 11Many people will come
from the east and from the west and
will sit and eat with Abraham,
Isaac, and Jacob in the kingdom of heaven. 12But those
people who should be in the
kingdom will be thrown outside into the darkness, where
people will cry and grind their teeth with pain."
13Then Jesus said to the officer, "Go home.
Your servant will be healed just as you believed he would." And his servant was healed
that same hour.

HELL

What will the people in hell be doing? (8:12)

JESUS HEALS MANY PEOPLE

14When Jesus went to Peter's house, he saw
that Peter's mother-in-law was sick in bed
with a fever. 15Jesus touched her hand, and the
fever left her. Then she stood up and began to
serve Jesus.
16That evening people brought to Jesus
many who had demons. Jesus spoke and the
demons left them, and he healed all the sick.
17He did these things to bring about what Isaiah the prophet had said:

"He took our suffering on him
and carried our diseases." *Isaiah 53:4*

PEOPLE WANT TO FOLLOW JESUS

18When Jesus saw the crowd around him,
he told his followers to go to the other side of
the lake. 19Then a teacher of the law came to
Jesus and said, "Teacher, I will follow you any
place you go."
20Jesus said to him, "The foxes have holes to
live in, and the birds have nests, but the Son of
Man has no place to rest his head."
21Another man, one of Jesus' followers, said
to him, "Lord, first let me go and bury my father."
22But Jesus told him, "Follow me, and let the
people who are dead bury their own dead."

JESUS CALMS A STORM

23Jesus got into a boat, and his followers went
with him. 24A great storm arose on the lake so
that waves covered the boat, but Jesus was
sleeping. 25His followers went to him and woke
him, saying, "Lord, save us! We will drown!"
26Jesus answered, "Why are you afraid? You
don't have enough faith." Then Jesus got up
and gave a command to the wind and the
waves, and it became completely calm.
27The men were amazed and said, "What
kind of man is this? Even the wind and the
waves obey him!"

JESUS HEALS TWO MEN WITH DEMONS

28When Jesus arrived at the other side of the
lake in the area of the Gadarene[n] people, two
men who had demons in them met him. These
men lived in the burial caves and were so dangerous that people could not use the road by
those caves. 29They shouted, "What do you
want with us, Son of God? Did you come here
to torture us before the right time?"
30Near that place there was a large herd of
pigs feeding. 31The demons begged Jesus, "If
you make us leave these men, please send us
into that herd of pigs."
32Jesus said to them, "Go!" So the demons

8:4 show . . . priest The Law of Moses said a priest must say when a Jewish person with a skin disease was well. **8:4 Moses commanded** Read about this in Leviticus 14:1-32. **8:28 Gadarene** From Gadara, an area southeast of Lake Galilee.

left the men and went into the pigs. Then the whole herd rushed down the hill into the lake and were drowned. 33 The herdsmen ran away and went into town, where they told about all of this and what had happened to the men who had demons. 34 Then the whole town went out to see Jesus. When they saw him, they begged him to leave their area.

JESUS HEALS A PARALYZED MAN

9 1 Jesus got into a boat and went back across the lake to his own town. 2 Some people brought to Jesus a man who was paralyzed and lying on a mat. When Jesus saw the faith of these people, he said to the paralyzed man, "Be encouraged, young man. Your sins are forgiven."

3 Some of the teachers of the law said to themselves, "This man speaks as if he were God. That is blasphemy!"[n]

4 Knowing their thoughts, Jesus said, "Why are you thinking evil thoughts? 5 Which is easier: to say, 'Your sins are forgiven,' or to tell him, 'Stand up and walk'? 6 But I will prove to you that the Son of Man has authority on earth to forgive sins." Then Jesus said to the paralyzed man, "Stand up, take your mat, and go home." 7 And the man stood up and went home. 8 When the people saw this, they were amazed and praised God for giving power like this to human beings.

JESUS CHOOSES MATTHEW

9 When Jesus was leaving, he saw a man named Matthew sitting in the tax collector's booth. Jesus said to him, "Follow me," and he stood up and followed Jesus.

10 As Jesus was having dinner at Matthew's

WHAT'S IT MEAN?

The Roman Empire had a tax-happy government. The Romans taxed everything from property to imported goods to fishing rights. They even collected taxes from the Jews for worshiping at the Temple! The Romans claimed that the money was used to pay for the upkeep of the building. Some Bible experts have estimated that the average Jewish household lost as much as forty percent of its income to taxes.

Matthew 9:9

On the Edge

Jesus answered, "The friends of the bridegroom are not sad while he is with them. But the time will come when the bridegroom will be taken from them, and then they will give up eating (Matt. 9:15).

In this passage of Scripture, Jesus was foretelling that he would be taken away from his followers. In other words, the Bridegroom was getting ready to be taken out of the picture and put on a cross. Can you imagine how devastated the followers must have been?

Picture a young bride-to-be who is out getting ready for her big wedding day. One of the happiest moments of her life. She is returning from the mall where she has just picked out a beautiful wedding dress; but when she gets home, the phone rings and she hears that her bridegroom-to-be has been shot and killed on his way home from work while trying to stop a little old lady from being robbed on the subway. She cries until she has no more strength; she doesn't want anything to eat; she can't sleep that night. Suddenly at midnight she gets another phone call that tells her that her fiancé is fine and there was a mix-up in the communication. He has been at the police station giving a statement and he couldn't get away. She is thrilled because the groom is alive and *the wedding is on!*

His followers thought they had lost Jesus forever when he was put on the cross. But they were misinformed. Jesus is not dead—he is alive! He has defeated death, hell, and the grave! He is coming back for a pure bride—one without spot or wrinkle. What a wedding day that will be when we see Jesus face-to-face! Don't be misinformed. The wedding is on! Begin preparing yourself now, for he is the Bridegroom! Get ready!

SEE FOR YOURSELF:
Matt. 25:1–13;
Mark 2:20;
Luke 5:34–35

9:3 blasphemy Saying things against God or not showing respect for God.

house, many tax collectors and "sinners" came
and ate with Jesus and his followers. 11When
the Pharisees saw this, they asked Jesus' followers, "Why does your teacher eat with tax
collectors and sinners?"
12When Jesus heard them, he said, "It is not
the healthy people who need a doctor, but the
sick. 13Go and learn what this means: 'I want
kindness more than I want animal sacrifices.'[n] I
did not come to invite good people but to invite sinners."

JESUS' FOLLOWERS ARE CRITICIZED

14Then the followers
of John[n] came to Jesus
and said, "Why do we
and the Pharisees often
give up eating for a cer-
tain time,[n] but your followers don't?"
15Jesus answered, "The
friends of the bridegroom
are not sad while he is with
them. But the time will come
when the bridegroom will be taken from
them, and then they will give up eating.
16"No one sews a patch of unshrunk cloth
over a hole in an old coat. If he does, the patch
will shrink and pull away from the coat, making the hole worse. 17Also, people never pour
new wine into old leather bags. Otherwise, the
bags will break, the wine will spill, and the
wine bags will be ruined. But people always
pour new wine into new wine bags. Then both
will continue to be good."

"Jesus turned and saw the woman and said, 'Be encouraged, dear woman. You are made well because you believed.' And the woman was healed from that moment on." (Matthew 9:22)

JESUS GIVES LIFE TO A DEAD GIRL AND HEALS A SICK WOMAN

18While Jesus was saying these things, a
leader of the synagogue came to him. He
bowed down before Jesus
and said, "My daughter has
just died. But if you come
and lay your hand on
her, she will live again."
19So Jesus and his fol-
lowers stood up and
went with the leader.
20Then a woman
who had been bleeding
for twelve years came be-
hind Jesus and touched
the edge of his coat.
21She was thinking, "If I can
just touch his clothes, I will be
healed."
22Jesus turned and saw the woman and
said, "Be encouraged, dear woman. You are
made well because you believed." And the
woman was healed from that moment on.
23Jesus continued along with the leader and
went into his house. There he saw the funeral
musicians and many people crying. 24Jesus
said, "Go away. The girl is not dead, only
asleep." But the people laughed at him. 25After
the crowd had been thrown out of the house,
Jesus went into the girl's room and took hold
of her hand, and she stood up. 26The news
about this spread all around the area.

JESUS HEALS MORE PEOPLE

27When Jesus was leaving there, two blind
men followed him. They cried out, "Have mercy on us, Son of David!"
28After Jesus went inside, the blind men
went with him. He asked the men, "Do you
believe that I can make you see again?"
They answered, "Yes, Lord."
29Then Jesus touched their eyes and said,
"Because you believe I can make you see again,
it will happen." 30Then the men were able to
see. But Jesus warned them strongly, saying,

WHAT'S IT MEAN?

What's a wine bag? Good question. It was a bag used for storing liquids. Did we mention that the bag was made of the hide (or skin) of a goat or another animal? When grape juice was stored in a new wine bag, the fermentation process (the chemical changes that cause grape juice to become wine) made the wine bag stretch and swell. The older a wine bag got, the more stiff and brittle it became. When grape juice was poured into an old wine bag, often the container would break.
Matthew 9:17

9:13 'I want . . . sacrifices.' Quotation from Hosea 6:6. **9:14 John** John the Baptist, who preached to people about Christ's coming (Matthew 3, Luke 3). **9:14 give up . . . time** This is called "fasting." The people would give up eating for a special time of prayer and worship to God. It was also done to show sadness and disappointment.

"Don't tell anyone about this." 31 But the blind
men left and spread the news about Jesus all
around that area.
32 When the two men were leaving, some
people brought another man to Jesus. This
man could not talk because he had a demon in
him. 33 After Jesus forced the demon to leave the
man, he was able to speak. The crowd was
amazed and said, "We have never seen anything
like this in Israel."
34 But the Pharisees said, "The prince of demons is the one that gives him power to force
demons out."
35 Jesus traveled through all the towns and
villages, teaching in their synagogues, preaching the Good News about the kingdom, and
healing all kinds of diseases and sicknesses.
36 When he saw the crowds, he felt sorry for
them because they were hurting and helpless,
like sheep without a shepherd. 37 Jesus said to
his followers, "There are many people to harvest but only a few workers to help harvest
them. 38 Pray to the Lord, who owns the harvest, that he will send more workers to gather
his harvest."[n]

JESUS SENDS OUT HIS APOSTLES

10
1 Jesus called his twelve followers together
and gave them authority to drive out evil spirits and to heal every kind of disease and sickness. 2 These are the names of the twelve
apostles: Simon (also called Peter) and his
brother Andrew; James son of Zebedee, and his
brother John; 3 Philip and Bartholomew;
Thomas and Matthew, the tax collector; James
son of Alphaeus, and Thaddaeus; 4 Simon the
Zealot and Judas Iscariot, who turned against
Jesus.
5 Jesus sent out these twelve men with the
following order: "Don't go to the non-Jewish
people or to any town where the Samaritans
live. 6 But go to the people of Israel, who are like
lost sheep. 7 When you go, preach this: 'The
kingdom of heaven is near.' 8 Heal the sick, raise
the dead to life again, heal those who have skin
diseases, and force demons out of people. I
give you these powers freely, so help other
people freely. 9 Don't carry any money with
you—gold or silver or copper. 10 Don't carry a
bag or extra clothes or sandals or a walking
stick. Workers should be given what they need.
11 "When you enter a city or town, find some
worthy person there and stay in that home
until you leave. 12 When you enter that home,
say, 'Peace be with you.' 13 If the people there
welcome you, let your peace stay there. But if
they don't welcome you, take back the peace
you wished for them. 14 And if a home or town
refuses to welcome you or listen to you, leave
that place and shake its dust off your feet.[n] 15 I
tell you the truth, on the Judgment Day it will
be better for the towns of Sodom and
Gomorrah[n] than for the people of that town.

JESUS WARNS HIS APOSTLES

16 "Listen, I am sending you out like sheep
among wolves. So be as smart as snakes and as
innocent as doves. 17 Be careful of people, because they will arrest you and take you to
court and whip you in their synagogues. 18 Because of me you will be taken to stand before
governors and kings, and you will tell them
and the non-Jewish people about me. 19 When
you are arrested, don't worry about what to
say or how to say it. At that time you will be
given the things to say. 20 It will not really be
you speaking but the Spirit of your Father
speaking through you.
21 "Brothers will give their own brothers to
be killed, and fathers will give
their own children to be killed.
Children will fight against
their own parents and have
them put to death. 22 All people
will hate you because you follow me, but those people who
keep their faith until the end

WHAT'S IT MEAN?

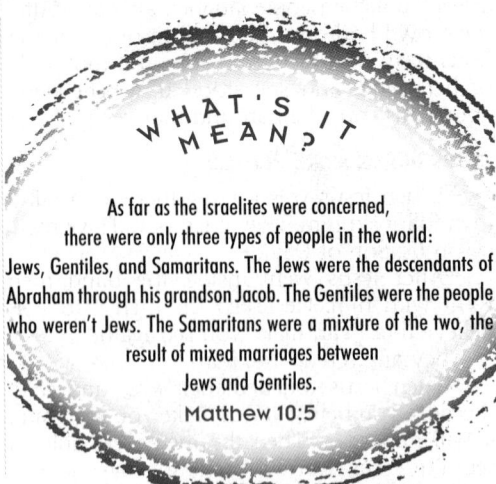

As far as the Israelites were concerned, there were only three types of people in the world: Jews, Gentiles, and Samaritans. The Jews were the descendants of Abraham through his grandson Jacob. The Gentiles were the people who weren't Jews. The Samaritans were a mixture of the two, the result of mixed marriages between Jews and Gentiles.

Matthew 10:5

HATRED

Will people ever hate me because I love Jesus? (10:22)

9:37-38 "There are . . . harvest." As a farmer sends workers to harvest the grain, Jesus sends his followers to bring people to God. **10:14 shake . . . feet.** A warning. It showed that they had rejected these people. **10:15 Sodom and Gomorrah** Two cities that God destroyed because the people were so evil.

will be saved. 23When you are treated badly in
one city, run to another city. I tell you the truth,
you will not finish going through all the cities
of Israel before the Son of Man comes.
24"A student is not better than his teacher,
and a servant is not better than his master. 25A
student should be satisfied to become like his
teacher; a servant should be satisfied to become like his master. If the head of the family is
called Beelzebul, then the other members of the
family will be called worse names!

FEAR GOD, NOT PEOPLE

26"So don't be afraid of those people, because everything that is hidden will be shown.
Everything that is secret will be made known.
27I tell you these things in the dark, but I want
you to tell them in the light. What you hear
whispered in your ear you should shout from
the housetops. 28Don't be afraid of people, who
can kill the body but cannot kill the soul. The
only one you should fear is the one who can
destroy the soul and the body in hell. 29Two
sparrows cost only a penny, but not even one
of them can die without your Father's knowing
it. 30God even knows how many hairs are on
your head. 31So don't be afraid. You are worth
much more than many sparrows.

TELL PEOPLE ABOUT YOUR FAITH

32"All those who stand before others and
say they believe in me, I will say before my
Father in heaven that they belong to me. 33But
all who stand before others and say they do
not believe in me, I will say before my Father
in heaven that they do not belong to me.
34"Don't think that I came to bring peace to
the earth. I did not come to bring peace, but a
sword. 35I have come so that

'a son will be against his father,
a daughter will be against her mother,
a daughter-in-law will be against her
mother-in-law.
36 A person's enemies will be members of
his own family.' *Micah 7:6*

37"Those who love their father or mother
more than they love me are not worthy to be
my followers. Those who love their son or
daughter more than they love me are not worthy to be my followers. 38Whoever is not willing to carry the cross and follow me is not
worthy of me. 39Those who try to hold on to
their lives will give up true life. Those who give

WHAT'S IT MEAN?

Sparrows were what people offered to God when they couldn't afford a goat or sheep. They were considered a "poor man's sacrifice."

Matthew 10:29

Promise — HE PROMISES TO TELL YOU WHAT TO SAY.

It will not really be you speaking but the Spirit of your Father speaking through you (Matt. 10:20).

Have you ever been in a situation where you just didn't know what to say? Maybe you were "smack-dab" in the middle of witnessing to someone, and suddenly you didn't know what to do? This has happened to everybody. In this verse, Jesus was telling his followers that he was sending them out to be witnesses, and he assured them they should not be worried about what to say or how to say it. Why? Because the Holy Spirit was going to give them the words to say. One of the cool parts of being a Christian is that you don't have to live on your own. Jesus is right there with you. He's never going to leave you or stand you up. He's always ready to speak to you and through you. So the next time you're sharing Jesus with a friend, or someone at school is drilling you about Christianity, remember *he* is the One who speaks. The Holy Spirit will give you the words to say. Just calm down, and let him do it. He always will, because his Word never fails!

SEE FOR YOURSELF

2 Sam. 23:2; Acts 1:16–17; Rom. 8:26

up their lives for me will hold on to true life. 40Whoever accepts you also accepts me, and whoever accepts me also accepts the One who sent me. 41Whoever meets a prophet and accepts him will receive the reward of a prophet. And whoever accepts a good person because that person is good will receive the reward of a good person. 42Those who give one of these little ones a cup of cold water because they are my followers will truly get their reward."

JESUS AND JOHN THE BAPTIST

11 1After Jesus finished telling these things to his twelve followers, he left there and went to the towns in Galilee to teach and preach.

2John the Baptist was in prison, but he heard about what Christ was doing. So John sent some of his followers to Jesus. 3They asked him, "Are you the One who is to come, or should we wait for someone else?"

4Jesus answered them, "Go tell John what you hear and see: 5The blind can see, the crippled can walk, and people with skin diseases are healed. The deaf can hear, the dead are raised to life, and the Good News is preached to the poor. 6Those who do not stumble in their faith because of me are blessed."

7As John's followers were leaving, Jesus began talking to the people about John. Jesus said, "What did you go out into the desert to see? A reed[n] blown by the wind? 8What did you go out to see? A man dressed in fine clothes? No, those who wear fine clothes live in kings' palaces. 9So why did you go out? To see a prophet? Yes, and I tell you, John is more than a prophet. 10This was written about him:

'I will send my messenger ahead of you,
  who will prepare the way for you.'

Malachi 3:1

11I tell you the truth, John the Baptist is greater than any other person ever born, but even the least important person in the kingdom of heaven is greater than John. 12Since the time John the Baptist came until now, the kingdom of heaven has been going forward in strength, and people have been trying to take it by force. 13All the prophets and the law of Moses told about what would happen until the time John came. 14And if you will believe what they said, you will believe that John is Elijah, whom they said would come. 15You people who can hear me, listen!

16"What can I say about the people of this time? What are they like? They are like children sitting in the marketplace, who call out to each other,

17'We played music for you, but you did not
  dance;
 we sang a sad song, but you did not
  cry.'

18John came and did not eat or drink like other people. So people say, 'He has a demon.' 19The Son of Man came, eating and drinking, and people say, 'Look at him! He eats too much and drinks too much wine, and he is a friend of tax collectors and sinners.' But wisdom is proved to be right by what it does."

JESUS WARNS UNBELIEVERS

20Then Jesus criticized the cities where he did most of his miracles, because the people did not change their lives and stop sinning. 21He said, "How terrible for you, Korazin! How terrible for you, Bethsaida! If the same miracles I did in you had happened in Tyre and Sidon,[n] those people would have changed their lives a long time ago. They would have worn rough cloth and put ashes on themselves to show they had changed. 22But I tell you, on the Judgment Day it will be better for Tyre and Sidon than for you. 23And you, Capernaum,[n] will you be lifted up to heaven? No, you will be thrown down to the depths. If the miracles I did in you had happened in Sodom,[n] its people

WHAT'S IT MEAN?

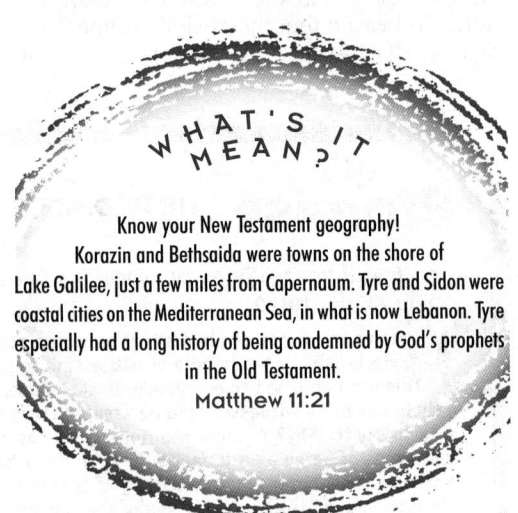

Know your New Testament geography!
Korazin and Bethsaida were towns on the shore of Lake Galilee, just a few miles from Capernaum. Tyre and Sidon were coastal cities on the Mediterranean Sea, in what is now Lebanon. Tyre especially had a long history of being condemned by God's prophets in the Old Testament.
Matthew 11:21

11:7 reed It means that John was not ordinary or weak like grass blown by the wind. **11:21 Tyre and Sidon** Towns where wicked people lived. **11:21, 23 Korazin . . . Bethsaida . . . Capernaum** Towns by Lake Galilee where Jesus preached to the people. **11:23 Sodom** A city that God destroyed because the people were so evil.

would have stopped sinning, and it would still
be a city today. 24But I tell you, on the Judgment Day it will be better for Sodom than for
you."

TRIALS

What does Christ promise us when we're dealing with trials? (11:25–30)

JESUS OFFERS REST TO PEOPLE

25At that time Jesus said, "I
praise you, Father, Lord of
heaven and earth, because
you have hidden these things
from the people who are
wise and smart. But you
have shown them to those
who are
like little children. 26Yes,
Father, this is what you
really wanted.
27"My Father has
given me all things.
No one knows the
Son, except the Father.
And no one knows
the Father, except the
Son and those whom
the Son chooses to tell.
28"Come to me, all of
you who are tired and
have heavy loads, and I
will give you rest. 29Accept
my teachings and learn from me, because
I am gentle and humble in spirit, and you will
find rest for your lives. 30The teaching that I
ask you to accept is easy; the load I give you to
carry is light."

"Come to me, all of you who are tired and have heavy loads, and I will give you rest. Accept my teachings and learn from me, because I am gentle and humble in spirit, and you will find rest for your lives." (Matthew 11:28–29)

JESUS IS LORD OF THE SABBATH

12

1At that time Jesus was walking through
some fields of grain on a Sabbath day. His followers were hungry, so they began to pick the
grain and eat it. 2When the Pharisees saw this,
they said to Jesus, "Look! Your followers are
doing what is unlawful to do on the Sabbath
day."
3Jesus answered, "Have you not read what
David did when he and the
people with him were
hungry? 4He went into
God's house, and he
and those with him
ate the holy bread,
which was lawful
only for priests to
eat. 5And have you
not read in the law
of Moses that on
every Sabbath day
the priests in the Tem-
ple break this law about
the Sabbath day? But the
priests are not wrong for doing that. 6I tell you that there is
something here that is greater than the Temple.

Promise HE PROMISES YOU REST.

Come to me, all of you who are tired and have heavy loads, and I will give you rest (Matt. 11:28).

Have you ever been hiking in the mountains with a huge backpack strapped to your back all day long? What's the first thing you did when you finally reached your destination—the top? You unstrapped that pack, stretched out on the ground, and rested, right? Oh, what a feeling! At that very moment, there was nothing better than removing that weight, lying down, and resting.

A lot of people carry around heavy backpacks every day of their lives. Now they don't carry a literal pack, but a backpack of sin, a suitcase full of guilt, or a huge load of worry. Jesus wants to give us rest. He wants to help us. It's not worth carrying around a bunch of heavy junk when all we have to do is come to Jesus and let him take the weight off our shoulders. He paid the price to carry it so we don't have to!

When he says that he will give you rest, he means it. If you can learn to rest in Jesus as a teenager, you'll be a step ahead of a lot of adults. The key is to really learn what Jesus has done for you—what burdens he bears for you—and then to let him have them. When you do what you're supposed to do and let him do what he's supposed to do, then you can rest in him.

SEE FOR YOURSELF:

Ps. 55:22; 94:13; Eccl. 10:15; Is. 14:3

[7]The Scripture says, 'I want kindness more than I want animal sacrifices.'[n] You don't really know what those words mean. If you understood them, you would not judge those who have done nothing wrong.

[8]"So the Son of Man is Lord of the Sabbath day."

WHAT'S IT MEAN?

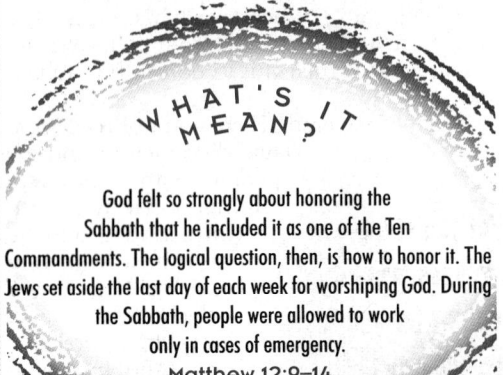

God felt so strongly about honoring the Sabbath that he included it as one of the Ten Commandments. The logical question, then, is how to honor it. The Jews set aside the last day of each week for worshiping God. During the Sabbath, people were allowed to work only in cases of emergency.
Matthew 12:9–14

JESUS HEALS A MAN'S HAND

[9]Jesus left there and went into their synagogue, [10]where there was a man with a crippled hand. They were looking for a reason to accuse Jesus, so they asked him, "Is it right to heal on the Sabbath day?"[n]

[11]Jesus answered, "If any of you has a sheep, and it falls into a ditch on the Sabbath day, you will help it out of the ditch. [12]Surely a human being is more important than a sheep. So it is lawful to do good things on the Sabbath day."

[13]Then Jesus said to the man with the crippled hand, "Hold out your hand." The man held out his hand, and it became well again, like the other hand. [14]But the Pharisees left and made plans to kill Jesus.

JESUS IS GOD'S CHOSEN SERVANT

[15]Jesus knew what the Pharisees were doing, so he left that place. Many people followed him, and he healed all who were sick. [16]But Jesus warned the people not to tell who he was. [17]He did these things to bring about what Isaiah the prophet had said:

18 "Here is my servant whom I have chosen.
I love him, and I am pleased with him.
I will put my Spirit upon him,
and he will tell of my justice to all people.
19 He will not argue or cry out;
no one will hear his voice in the streets.
20 He will not break a crushed blade of grass
or put out even a weak flame
until he makes justice win the victory.
21 In him will the non-Jewish people find hope."
Isaiah 42:1-4

On the Edge

Here is my servant whom I have chosen. I love him, and I am pleased with him. I will put my Spirit upon him, and he will tell of my justice to all people (Matt. 12:18).

A survey was recently taken to find out the priorities of the generation before World War II and of the generation after World War II. The generation before World War II listed their priorities in this order: God, family, country, etc. . . . This group listed themselves third or fourth on their priority lists.

Of the people born after World War II, around ninety-eight percent listed themselves as first on the list. In other words, more people are self-centered now than ever before. They want to serve themselves more than they want to serve others.

God has something better for us. Jesus, our Lord and example, came to serve. He was the ultimate Servant. We need to strive to be like Jesus and to work on becoming servants. What is a servant? One who will do anything for anybody with a good attitude and a willing heart. So, the next time you get asked to do something that's not so glorious or fun, smile real big (as you remember what Jesus would do), and say, "Sure, I'd be happy to!" Watch what God will do in your life. He's going to exalt you!

SEE FOR YOURSELF:
Prov. 11:2; Matt. 20:28; 23:12; Mark 9:35; 10:44; John 13:3–9; Phil. 2:3–8

12:7 'I . . . sacrifices.' Quotation from Hosea 6:6. **12:10 "Is it right . . . day?"** It was against Jewish Law to work on the Sabbath day.

JESUS' POWER IS FROM GOD

[22]Then some people brought to Jesus a man
who was blind and could not talk, because he
had a demon. Jesus healed the man so that he
could talk and see. [23]All the people were
amazed and said, "Perhaps this man is the Son
of David!"
[24]When the Pharisees heard this, they said,
"Jesus uses the power of Beelzebul, the ruler of
demons, to force demons out of people."

WHAT'S IT MEAN?

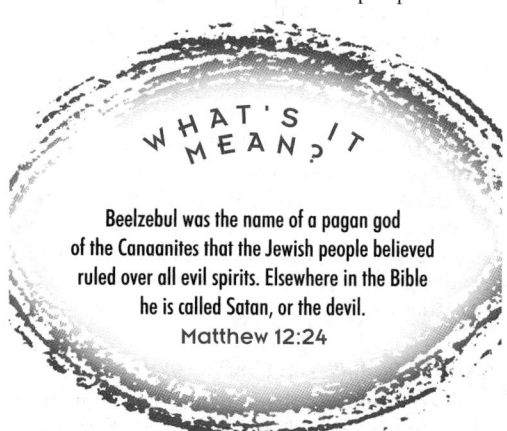

Beelzebul was the name of a pagan god of the Canaanites that the Jewish people believed ruled over all evil spirits. Elsewhere in the Bible he is called Satan, or the devil.

Matthew 12:24

[25]Jesus knew what the Pharisees were
thinking, so he said to them, "Every kingdom
that is divided against itself will be destroyed.
And any city or family that is divided against
itself will not continue. [26]And if Satan forces
out himself, then Satan is divided against himself, and his kingdom will not continue. [27]You
say that I use the power of Beelzebul to force
out demons. If that is true, then what power
do your people use to force out demons? So
they will be your judges. [28]But if I use the power of God's Spirit to force out demons, then the
kingdom of God has come to you.
[29]"If anyone wants to enter a strong
person's house and steal his things, he must
first tie up the strong person. Then he can steal
the things from the house.
[30]"Whoever is not with me is against me.
Whoever does not work with me is working
against me. [31]So I tell you, people can be forgiven for every sin and everything they say
against God. But whoever speaks against the
Holy Spirit will not be forgiven. [32]Anyone who
speaks against the Son of Man can be forgiven,
but anyone who speaks against the Holy Spirit
will not be forgiven, now or in the future.

PEOPLE KNOW YOU BY YOUR WORDS

[33]"If you want good fruit, you must make
the tree good. If your tree is not good, it will
have bad fruit. A tree is known by the kind of
fruit it produces. [34]You snakes! You are evil
people, so how can you say anything good?
The mouth speaks the things that are in the
heart. [35]Good people have good things
in their hearts, and so they say
good things. But evil people
have evil in their hearts, so
they say evil things. [36]And I
tell you that on the Judgment
Day people will be responsible
for every careless thing they
have said. [37]The words you have
said will be used to judge you. Some of your
words will prove you right, but some of your
words will prove you guilty."

JUDGMENT
Will God judge the words we speak? (12:35–37)

THE PEOPLE ASK FOR A MIRACLE

[38]Then some of the Pharisees and teachers
of the law answered Jesus, saying, "Teacher, we
want to see you work a miracle as a sign."
[39]Jesus answered, "Evil and sinful people are
the ones who want to see a miracle for a sign.
But no sign will be given to them, except the
sign of the prophet Jonah. [40]Jonah was in the
stomach of the big fish for three days and three
nights. In the same way, the Son of Man will
be in the grave three days and three nights.
[41]On the Judgment Day the people from
Nineveh[n] will stand up with you people who
live now, and they will show that you are
guilty. When Jonah preached to them, they
were sorry and changed their lives. And I tell
you that someone greater than Jonah is here.
[42]On the Judgment Day, the Queen of the
South[n] will stand up with you people who live
today. She will show that you are guilty, because she came from far away to listen to Solomon's wise teaching. And I tell you that
someone greater than Solomon is here.

PEOPLE TODAY ARE FULL OF EVIL

[43]"When an evil spirit comes out of a person, it travels through dry places, looking for a
place to rest, but it doesn't find it. [44]So the spirit
says, 'I will go back to the house I left.' When
the spirit comes back, it finds the house still
empty, swept clean, and made neat. [45]Then the
evil spirit goes out and brings seven other spirits even more evil than it is, and they go in and

12:41 Nineveh The city where Jonah preached to warn the people. Read Jonah 3. **12:42 Queen of the South** The Queen of Sheba. She traveled a thousand miles to learn God's wisdom from Solomon. Read 1 Kings 10:1-13.

live there. So the person has even more trouble
than before. It is the same way with the evil
people who live today."

JESUS' TRUE FAMILY

46While Jesus was talking to the people, his
mother and brothers stood outside, trying to
find a way to talk to him. 47Someone told Jesus,
"Your mother and brothers are standing outside, and they want to talk to you."
48He answered, "Who is my mother? Who
are my brothers?" 49Then he pointed to his followers and said, "Here are my mother and my
brothers. 50My true brother and sister and
mother are those who do what my Father in
heaven wants."

A STORY ABOUT PLANTING SEED

13 1That same day Jesus went out of the house
and sat by the lake. 2Large crowds gathered
around him, so he got into a boat and sat
down, while the people stood on the shore.
3Then Jesus used stories to teach them many
things. He said: "A farmer went out to plant his
seed. 4While he was planting, some seed fell by
the road, and the birds came and ate it all up.
5Some seed fell on rocky ground, where there
wasn't much dirt. That seed grew very fast, because the ground was not deep. 6But when the
sun rose, the plants dried up, because they did
not have deep roots. 7Some other seed fell
among thorny weeds, which grew and choked
the good plants. 8Some other seed fell on good
ground where it grew and produced a crop.
Some plants made a hundred times more,
some made sixty times more, and some made
thirty times more. 9You people who can hear
me, listen."

WHY JESUS USED STORIES TO TEACH

10The followers came to Jesus and asked,
"Why do you use stories to teach the people?"
11Jesus answered, "You have been chosen to
know the secrets about the kingdom of heaven,
but others cannot know these secrets. 12Those
who have understanding will be given more,
and they will have all they need. But those
who do not have understanding, even what
they have will be taken away from them. 13This
is why I use stories to teach the people: They
see, but they don't really see. They hear, but
they don't really hear or understand. 14So they
show that the things Isaiah said about them
are true:

'You will listen and listen, but you will not
understand.
You will look and look, but you will not
learn.
15For the minds of these people have
become stubborn.
They do not hear with their ears,
and they have closed their eyes.
Otherwise they might really understand
what they see with their eyes
and hear with their ears.
They might really understand in their
minds
and come back to me and be healed.'

Isaiah 6:9-10

16But you are blessed, because you see with
your eyes and hear with your ears. 17I tell you
the truth, many prophets and good people
wanted to see the things that you now see, but
they did not see them. And they wanted to hear
the things that you now hear, but they did not
hear them.

JESUS EXPLAINS THE SEED STORY

18"So listen to the meaning of that story
about the farmer. 19What is the seed that fell by
the road? That seed is like the person who
hears the message about the kingdom but does
not understand it. The Evil One comes and
takes away what was planted in that person's
heart. 20And what is the seed that fell on rocky
ground? That seed is like the person who hears
the teaching and quickly accepts it with joy.
21But he does not let the teaching go deep into
his life, so he keeps it only a short time. When
trouble or persecution comes because of the
teaching he accepted, he quickly gives up.
22And what is the seed that fell among the
thorny weeds? That seed is like the person
who hears the teaching but lets worries about
this life and the temptation of wealth stop that
teaching from growing. So the teaching does
not produce fruit[n] in that person's life. 23But
what is the seed that fell on the good ground?
That seed is like the person who hears the
teaching and understands it. That person
grows and produces fruit, sometimes a hundred times more, sometimes sixty times more,
and sometimes thirty times more."

A STORY ABOUT WHEAT AND WEEDS

24Then Jesus told them another story: "The
kingdom of heaven is like a man who planted
good seed in his field. 25That night, when

13:22 produce fruit To produce fruit means to have in your life the good things God wants.

everyone was asleep, his enemy came and
planted weeds among the wheat and then left.
26Later, the wheat sprouted and the heads of
grain grew, but the weeds also grew. 27Then the
man's servants came to him and said, 'You
planted good seed in your field. Where did the
weeds come from?' 28The man answered, 'An
enemy planted weeds.' The servants asked, 'Do
you want us to pull up the weeds?' 29The man
answered, 'No, because when
you pull up the weeds, you
might also pull up the
wheat. 30Let the weeds and
the wheat grow together
until the harvest time. At
harvest time I will tell the
workers, "First gather the
weeds and tie them to-
gether to be burned. Then
gather the wheat and bring it
to my barn." ' "

> "Then the good people will shine like the sun in the kingdom of their Father. You people who can hear me, listen."
> (Matthew 13:43)

STORIES OF MUSTARD SEED AND YEAST

31Then Jesus told another story: "The kingdom of heaven is like a mustard seed that a
man planted in his field. 32That seed is the
smallest of all seeds, but when it grows, it is
one of the largest garden plants. It becomes big
enough for the wild birds to come and build
nests in its branches."

33Then Jesus told another story: "The kingdom of heaven is like yeast that a woman took
and hid in a large tub of flour until it made all
the dough rise."

34Jesus used stories to tell all these things to
the people; he always used stories to teach
them. 35This is as the prophet said:

"I will speak using stories;
I will tell things that have been secret
since the world was made." *Psalm 78:2*

JESUS EXPLAINS ABOUT THE WEEDS

36Then Jesus left the crowd and went into
the house. His followers came to him and said,
"Explain to us the meaning of the story about
the weeds in the field."

37Jesus answered, "The man who planted
the good seed in the field is the Son of Man.
38The field is the world, and the good seed are
all of God's children who belong to the kingdom. The weeds are those people who belong
to the Evil One. 39And the enemy who planted
the bad seed is the devil. The harvest time is
the end of the world, and the workers who
gather are God's angels.

40"Just as the weeds are pulled up and
burned in the fire, so it will be at the end of the
world. 41The Son of Man will send out his angels, and they will gather out of his kingdom
all who cause sin and all who do evil. 42The
angels will throw them into the blazing furnace, where the people will cry and grind their
teeth with pain. 43Then the good people will
shine like the sun in the kingdom of their Father. You people who can hear me, listen.

STORIES OF A TREASURE AND A PEARL

44"The kingdom of heaven
is like a treasure hidden in a
field. One day a man found
the treasure, and then he
hid it in the field again. He
was so happy that he went
and sold everything he
owned to buy that field.

45"Also, the kingdom of
heaven is like a man looking
for fine pearls. 46When he
found a very valuable pearl, he went
and sold everything he had and bought it.

A STORY OF A FISHING NET

47"Also, the kingdom of heaven is like a net
that was put into the lake and caught many
different kinds of fish. 48When it was full, the
fishermen pulled the net to the shore. They sat
down and put all the good fish in baskets and
threw away the bad fish. 49It will be this way at
the end of the world. The angels will come and
separate the evil people from the good people.
50The angels will throw the evil people into the
blazing furnace, where people will cry and
grind their teeth with pain."

WHAT'S IT MEAN?

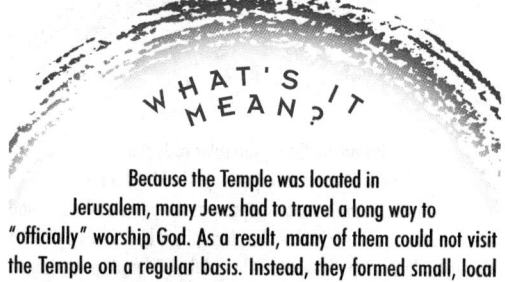

Because the Temple was located in Jerusalem, many Jews had to travel a long way to "officially" worship God. As a result, many of them could not visit the Temple on a regular basis. Instead, they formed small, local meeting places called synagogues. At first, the synagogues were simply places people met to read God's Teachings and pray together. Eventually, though, they became centers of community life.

Matthew 13:54

51Jesus asked his followers, "Do you understand all these things?"
They answered, "Yes, we understand."
52Then Jesus said to them, "So every teacher
of the law who has been taught about the
kingdom of heaven is like the owner of a
house. He brings out both new things and old
things he has saved."

JESUS GOES TO HIS HOMETOWN

53When Jesus finished teaching with these
stories, he left there. 54He went to his hometown and taught the people in the synagogue,
and they were amazed. They said, "Where did
this man get this wisdom and this power to do
miracles? 55He is just the son of a carpenter. His
mother is Mary, and his brothers are James,
Joseph, Simon, and Judas. 56And all his sisters
are here with us. Where then does this man get
all these things?" 57So the people were upset
with Jesus.
But Jesus said to them, "A prophet is honored everywhere except in his hometown and
in his own home."
58So he did not do many miracles there because they had no faith.

HOW JOHN THE BAPTIST WAS KILLED

14
1At that time Herod, the ruler of Galilee,
heard the reports about Jesus. 2So he said to
his servants, "Jesus is John the Baptist, who has
risen from the dead. That is why he can work
these miracles."
3Sometime before this, Herod had arrested
John, tied him up, and put him into prison.
Herod did this because of Herodias, who had
been the wife of Philip, Herod's brother. 4John
had been telling Herod, "It is not lawful for you
to be married to Herodias." 5Herod wanted to
kill John, but he was afraid of the people, because they believed John was a prophet.
6On Herod's birthday, the daughter of Herodias danced for Herod and his guests, and she
pleased him. 7So he promised with an
oath to give her any-
thing she wanted. 8He-
rodias told her daughter what
to ask for, so she said to Herod,
"Give me the head of John the
Baptist here on a platter." 9Al-
though King Herod was very
sad, he had made a promise, and his dinner
guests had heard him. So Herod ordered that
what she asked for be done. 10He sent soldiers
to the prison to cut off John's head. 11And they
brought it on a platter and gave it to the girl,
and she took it to her mother. 12John's followers
came and got his body and buried it. Then they
went and told Jesus.

EMBARRASSMENT

What can embarrassment lead to? (14:1–12)

WHAT'S IT MEAN?

Herod the Great, the ruler of Judea, died when Jesus was very young. His kingdom was divided among his three sons. Antipas was the name of the son who inherited the region of Galilee, the place where both Jesus and John the Baptist lived most of their adult lives. When "Herod" is mentioned later in the Gospels, it usually refers to Antipas. Not only was Antipas the one who had John the Baptist murdered, he also played a part in Jesus' trial and death.

Matthew 14:1

MORE THAN FIVE THOUSAND FED

13When Jesus heard what had happened to
John, he left in a boat and went to a lonely
place by himself. But the crowds heard about it
and followed him on foot from the towns.
14When he arrived, he saw a great crowd waiting. He felt sorry for them and healed those
who were sick.
15When it was evening, his followers came
to him and said, "No one lives in this place,
and it is already late. Send the people away so
they can go to the towns and buy food for
themselves."
16But Jesus answered, "They don't need to
go away. You give them something to eat."
17They said to him, "But we have only five
loaves of bread and two fish."
18Jesus said, "Bring the bread and the fish to
me." 19Then he told the people to sit down on
the grass. He took the five loaves and the two
fish and, looking to heaven, he thanked God
for the food. Jesus divided the bread and gave
it to his followers, who gave it to the people.
20All the people ate and were satisfied. Then the
followers filled twelve baskets with the leftover
pieces of food. 21There were about five thousand men there who ate, not counting women
and children.

JESUS WALKS ON THE WATER

22Immediately Jesus told his followers to get
into the boat and go ahead of him across the

lake. He stayed there to send the people home.
23 After he had sent them away, he went by
himself up into the hills to pray. It was late, and
Jesus was there alone. 24 By this time, the boat
was already far away from land. It was being
hit by waves, because the wind was blowing
against it.
25 Between three and six o'clock in the
morning, Jesus came to them, walking on the
water. 26 When his followers saw him walking
on the water, they were afraid. They said, "It's a
ghost!" and cried out in fear.
27 But Jesus quickly spoke to them, "Have
courage! It is I. Do not be afraid."
28 Peter said, "Lord, if it is really you, then
command me to come to you on the water."
29 Jesus said, "Come."
And Peter left the boat and walked on the
water to Jesus. 30 But when Peter saw the wind
and the waves, he became afraid and began to
sink. He shouted, "Lord, save me!"
31 Immediately Jesus reached out his hand
and caught Peter. Jesus said, "Your faith is
small. Why did you doubt?"
32 After they got into the boat, the wind became calm. 33 Then those who were in the boat
worshiped Jesus and said, "Truly you are the
Son of God!"
34 When they had crossed the lake, they
came to shore at Gennesaret. 35 When the people there recognized Jesus, they told people all
around there that Jesus had come, and they
brought all their sick to him. 36 They begged
Jesus to let them touch just the edge of his coat,
and all who touched it were healed.

OBEY GOD'S LAW

15 1 Then some Pharisees and teachers of the
law came to Jesus from Jerusalem. They asked
him, 2 "Why don't your followers obey the unwritten laws which have been handed down
to us? They don't wash their hands before they
eat."
3 Jesus answered, "And why do you refuse to
obey God's command so that you can follow
your own teachings? 4 God said, 'Honor your
father and your mother,'[n] and 'Anyone who
says cruel things to his father or mother must
be put to death.'[n] 5 But you say a person can tell
his father or mother, 'I have something I could
use to help you, but I have given it to God
already.' 6 You teach that person not to honor
his father or his mother. You rejected what God
said for the sake of your own rules. 7 You are
hypocrites! Isaiah was right when he said
about you:

8 'These people show honor to me with
words,
but their hearts are far from me.
9 Their worship of me is worthless.
The things they teach are nothing but
human rules.' " *Isaiah 29:13*

10 After Jesus called the crowd to him, he
said, "Listen and understand what I am saying.
11 It is not what people put into their mouths
that makes them unclean. It is what comes out
of their mouths that makes them unclean."

WHAT'S IT MEAN?

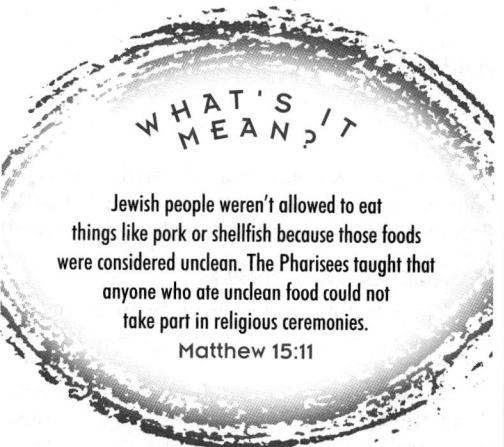

Jewish people weren't allowed to eat things like pork or shellfish because those foods were considered unclean. The Pharisees taught that anyone who ate unclean food could not take part in religious ceremonies.
Matthew 15:11

12 Then his followers came to him and
asked, "Do you know that the Pharisees are
angry because of what you said?"
13 Jesus answered, "Every plant that my Father in heaven has not planted himself will be
pulled up by the roots. 14 Stay away from the
Pharisees; they are blind leaders. And if a blind
person leads a blind person, both will fall into
a ditch."
15 Peter said, "Explain the example to us."
16 Jesus said, "Do you still not understand?
17 Surely you know that all the food that enters
the mouth goes into the stomach and then
goes out of the body. 18 But what people say
with their mouths comes from
the way they think; these are
the things that make people
unclean. 19 Out of the mind
come evil thoughts, murder,
adultery, sexual sins, stealing,
lying, and speaking evil of
others. 20 These things make
people unclean; eating with unwashed hands
does not make them unclean."

HONESTY
Where do lies come from? (15:18–20)

15:4 'Honor . . . mother.' Quotation from Exodus 20:12; Deuteronomy 5:16. **15:4 'Anyone . . . death.'** Quotation from Exodus 21:17.

JESUS HELPS A NON-JEWISH WOMAN

21Jesus left that place and went to the area of
Tyre and Sidon. 22A Canaanite woman from that
area came to Jesus and cried out, "Lord, Son of
David, have mercy on me! My daughter has a
demon, and she is suffering very much."
23But Jesus did not answer the woman. So his
followers came to Jesus and begged him, "Tell
the woman to go away. She is following us and
shouting."
24Jesus answered, "God sent me only to the
lost sheep, the people of Israel."
25Then the woman came to Jesus again and
bowed before him and said, "Lord, help me!"
26Jesus answered, "It is not right to take the
children's bread and give it to the dogs."
27The woman said, "Yes, Lord, but even the
dogs eat the crumbs that fall from their masters' table."
28Then Jesus answered, "Woman, you have
great faith! I will do what you asked." And at
that moment the woman's daughter was healed.

JESUS HEALS MANY PEOPLE

29After leaving there, Jesus went along the
shore of Lake Galilee. He went up on a hill and
sat there.
30Great crowds came to Jesus, bringing with
them the lame, the blind, the crippled, those
who could not speak, and many others. They
put them at Jesus' feet, and he healed them.
31The crowd was amazed when they saw that
people who could not speak before were now
able to speak. The crippled were made strong.
The lame could walk, and the blind could see.
And they praised the God of Israel for this.

MORE THAN FOUR THOUSAND FED

32Jesus called his followers to him and said,
"I feel sorry for these people, because they have
already been with me three days, and they
have nothing to eat. I don't want to send them
away hungry. They might faint while going
home."
33His followers asked him, "How can we get
enough bread to feed all these people? We are
far away from any town."
34Jesus asked, "How many loaves of bread
do you have?"
They answered, "Seven, and a few small
fish."
35Jesus told the people to sit on the ground.
36He took the seven loaves of bread and the
fish and gave thanks to God. Then he divided
the food and gave it to his followers, and they
gave it to the people. 37All the people ate and
were satisfied. Then his followers filled seven
baskets with the leftover pieces of food. 38There
were about four thousand men there who ate,
besides women and children. 39After sending
the people home, Jesus got into the boat and
went to the area of Magadan.

THE LEADERS ASK FOR A MIRACLE

16
1The Pharisees and Sadducees came to Jesus,
wanting to trick him. So they asked him to
show them a miracle from God.
2Jesus answered, "At sunset you say we will
have good weather, because the sky is red.
3And in the morning you say that it will be a
rainy day, because the sky is dark and red. You
see these signs in the sky and know what they
mean. In the same way, you see the things that
I am doing now, but you don't know their
meaning. 4Evil and sinful people ask for a miracle as a sign, but they will not be given any
sign, except the sign of Jonah."[n] Then Jesus left
them and went away.

GUARD AGAINST WRONG TEACHINGS

5Jesus' followers went across the lake, but
they had forgotten to bring bread. 6Jesus said
to them, "Be careful! Beware of the yeast of the
Pharisees and the Sadducees."
7His followers discussed the meaning of
this, saying, "He said this because we forgot to
bring bread."
8Knowing what they were talking about,
Jesus asked them, "Why are you talking about
not having bread? Your faith is small. 9Do you
still not understand? Remember the five loaves
of bread that fed the five thousand? And remember that you filled many baskets with the
leftovers? 10Or the seven loaves of bread that
fed the four thousand and the many baskets
you filled then also? 11I was not talking to you
about bread. Why don't you understand that?
I am telling you to beware of the yeast of the
Pharisees and the Sadducees." 12Then the followers understood that Jesus was not telling
them to beware of the yeast used in bread but
to beware of the teaching of the Pharisees and
the Sadducees.

PETER SAYS JESUS IS THE CHRIST

13When Jesus came to the area of Caesarea
Philippi, he asked his followers, "Who do people say the Son of Man is?"

16:4 sign of Jonah Jonah's three days in the fish are like Jesus' three days in the tomb. The story about Jonah is in the Book of Jonah.

14They answered, "Some say you are John
the Baptist. Others say you are Elijah, and still
others say you are Jeremiah or one of the
prophets."
15Then Jesus asked them, "And who do you
say I am?"
16Simon Peter answered, "You are the Christ,
the Son of the living God."

WHAT'S IT MEAN?

Many Jews were waiting for God to send them a special person they called the "Messiah," from a Hebrew word meaning "anointed one." (In case you're wondering, *Christ* is from the Greek for the word *Messiah.*) In Old Testament times, kings, priests, and prophets were all anointed, which means they were appointed by having oil poured on their heads to show that they were specially chosen by God. The Jews of Jesus' day believed that the Messiah would become their king and free them from the control of the Roman Empire.

Matthew 16:16

17Jesus answered, "You are blessed, Simon
son of Jonah, because no person taught you
that. My Father in heaven showed you who I
am. 18So I tell you, you are Peter.[n] On this rock
I will build my church, and the power of death
will not be able to defeat it. 19I will give you the
keys of the kingdom of heaven; the things you
don't allow on earth will be the things that
God does not allow, and the
things you allow on earth will
be the things that God allows."
20Then Jesus warned his followers not to tell anyone he
was the Christ.

"Simon Peter answered, 'You are the Christ, the Son of the living God.' " (Matthew 16:16)

JESUS SAYS THAT HE MUST DIE

21From that time on Jesus
began telling his followers that
he must go to Jerusalem, where the
older leaders, the leading priests, and the
teachers of the law would make him suffer
many things. He told them he must be killed
and then be raised from the dead on the third
day.
22Peter took Jesus aside and told him not to
talk like that. He said, "God save you from
those things, Lord! Those things will never
happen to you!"
23Then Jesus said to Peter, "Go away from
me, Satan![n] You are not helping me! You don't
care about the things of God, but only about
the things people think are important."
24Then Jesus said to his followers, "If people
want to follow me, they must give up the things
they want. They must be willing even to give up
their lives to follow me. 25Those who want to
save their lives will give up true life, and those
who give up their lives for me will have true life.
26It is worth nothing for them to have the whole
world if they lose their souls. They could never
pay enough to buy back their souls. 27The Son of
Man will come again with his Father's glory and
with his angels. At that time, he will reward them
for what they have done. 28I tell you the truth,
some people standing here will see the Son of
Man coming with his kingdom before they die."

JESUS TALKS WITH MOSES AND ELIJAH

17 1Six days later, Jesus took Peter, James, and
John, the brother of James, up on a high
mountain by themselves. 2While they watched,
Jesus' appearance was changed; his face became bright like the sun, and his clothes became white as light. 3Then Moses and Elijah[n]
appeared to them, talking with Jesus.
4Peter said to Jesus, "Lord, it is good that we
are here. If you want, I will put up three tents
here—one for you, one for Moses, and one for
Elijah."
5While Peter was talking,
a bright cloud covered them.
A voice came from the cloud
and said, "This is my Son,
whom I love, and I am very
pleased with him. Listen to
him!"
6When his followers heard
the voice, they were so frightened they fell to the ground.
7But Jesus went to them and
touched them and said, "Stand up.
Don't be afraid." 8When they looked up, they
saw Jesus was now alone.

16:18 Peter The Greek name "Peter," like the Aramaic name "Cephas," means "rock." **16:23 Satan** Name for the devil, meaning "the enemy." Jesus means that Peter was talking like Satan. **17:3 Moses and Elijah** Two of the most important Jewish leaders in the past. God had given Moses the Law, and Elijah was an important prophet.

9As they were coming down the mountain,
Jesus commanded them not to tell anyone
about what they had seen until the Son of
Man had risen from the dead.
10Then his followers asked him, "Why do the
teachers of the law say that Elijah must come
first?"
11Jesus answered, "They are right to say that
Elijah is coming and that he will make everything the way it should be. 12But I tell you that
Elijah has already come, and they did not recognize him. They did to him whatever they
wanted to do. It will be the same with the Son
of Man; those same people will make the Son
of Man suffer." 13Then the followers understood that Jesus was talking about John the
Baptist.

WHAT'S IT MEAN?

Every Jew over the age of twenty was expected to kick in some money every year to help take care of the Temple in Jerusalem, which had been built by Herod the Great. The Temple tax was nothing to sneeze at—it was about two days' wages for most Jews.

Matthew 17:24

JESUS HEALS A SICK BOY

14When Jesus and his followers came back
to the crowd, a man came to Jesus and bowed
before him. 15The man said, "Lord, have mercy
on my son. He has epilepsy[n] and is suffering
very much, because he often falls into the fire
or into the water. 16I brought him to your followers, but they could not cure him."
17Jesus answered, "You people have no faith,
and your lives are all wrong. How long must I
put up with you? How long must I continue to
be patient with you? Bring the boy here."
18Jesus commanded the demon inside the boy.
Then the demon came out, and the boy was
healed from that time on.
19The followers came to Jesus when he was
alone and asked, "Why couldn't we force the
demon out?"
20Jesus answered, "Because your faith is too
small. I tell you the truth, if your faith is as big
as a mustard seed, you can say to this mountain, 'Move from here to there,' and it will
move. All things will be possible for you." 21[n]

JESUS TALKS ABOUT HIS DEATH

22While Jesus' followers were gathering in
Galilee, he said to them, "The Son of Man will
be handed over to people, 23and they will kill
him. But on the third day he will be raised
from the dead." And the followers were filled
with sadness.

JESUS TALKS ABOUT PAYING TAXES

24When Jesus and his followers came to
Capernaum, the men who collected the Temple
tax came to Peter. They asked, "Does your
teacher pay the Temple tax?"
25Peter answered, "Yes, Jesus pays the tax."
Peter went into the house, but before he
could speak, Jesus said to him, "What do you
think? The kings of the earth collect different
kinds of taxes. But who pays the taxes—the
king's children or others?"
26Peter answered, "Other people pay the
taxes."
Jesus said to Peter, "Then the children of the
king don't have to pay taxes. 27But we don't
want to upset these tax collectors. So go to the
lake and fish. After you catch the first fish,
open its mouth and you will find a coin. Take
that coin and give it to the tax collectors for
you and me."

WHO IS THE GREATEST?

18
1At that time the followers came to Jesus
and asked, "Who is greatest in the kingdom of
heaven?"
2Jesus called a little child to him and stood
the child before his followers. 3Then he said, "I
tell you the truth, you must change and become like little children. Otherwise, you will
never enter the kingdom of heaven. 4The greatest person in the kingdom of heaven is the one
who makes himself humble like this child.
5"Whoever accepts a child in my name accepts me. 6If one of these little children believes
in me, and someone causes that child to sin, it
would be better for that person to have a large
stone tied around the neck and be drowned in
the sea. 7How terrible for the people of the

17:15 epilepsy A disease that causes a person sometimes to lose control of his body and maybe faint, shake strongly, or not be able to move. **17:21 Verse 21** Some Greek copies add verse 21: "That kind of spirit comes out only if you use prayer and give up eating."

world because of the things that cause them to
sin. Such things will happen, but how terrible
for the one who causes them to happen! [8]If
your hand or your foot causes you to sin, cut
it off and throw it away. It is better for you to
lose part of your body and live forever than to
have two hands and two feet and be thrown
into the fire that burns forever. [9]If your eye
causes you to sin, take it out and throw it
away. It is better for you to have only one eye
and live forever than to have two eyes and be
thrown into the fire of hell.

A LOST SHEEP

[10]"Be careful. Don't think these little children
are worth nothing. I tell you that they have
angels in heaven who are always with my Father in heaven. [11][n]
[12]"If a man has a hundred sheep but one of
the sheep gets lost, he will leave the other ninety-nine on the hill and go to look for the lost
sheep. [13]I tell you the truth, he is happier about
that one sheep than about the ninety-nine that
were never lost. [14]In the same way, your Father
in heaven does not want any of these little
children to be lost.

WHEN A PERSON SINS AGAINST YOU

[15]"If your fellow believer sins against you,
go and tell him in private what he did wrong.
If he listens to you, you have helped that person to be your brother or sister again. [16]But if
he refuses to listen, go to him again and take
one or two other people with you. 'Every case
may be proved by two or three witnesses.'[n] [17]If
he refuses to listen to them, tell the church. If
he refuses to listen to the church, then treat
him like a person who does not believe in God
or like a tax collector.
[18]"I tell you the truth, the things you don't
allow on earth will be the things God does not
allow. And the things you allow on earth will
be the things that God allows.
[19]"Also, I tell you that if two of you on earth
agree about something and pray for it, it will
be done for you by my Father in heaven.
[20]This is true because if two or three people
come together in my name, I am there with
them."

AN UNFORGIVING SERVANT

[21]Then Peter came to Jesus and asked, "Lord,
when my fellow believer sins against
me, how many times must I
forgive him? Should I forgive
him as many as seven times?"
[22]Jesus answered, "I tell
you, you must forgive him
more than seven times. You
must forgive him even if he
wrongs you seventy times
seven.

FORGIVENESS

How many times should I forgive someone before I stop? (18:21–35)

[23]"The kingdom of heaven is like a king who
decided to collect the money his servants owed
him. [24]When the king began to collect his
money, a servant who owed him several million dollars was brought to him. [25]But the servant did not have enough money to pay his
master, the king. So the master ordered that
everything the servant owned should be sold,
even the servant's wife and children. Then the
money would be used to pay the king what
the servant owed.
[26]"But the servant fell on his knees and
begged, 'Be patient with me, and I will pay you
everything I owe.' [27]The master felt sorry for
his servant and told him he did not have to
pay it back. Then he let the servant go free.
[28]"Later, that same servant found another
servant who owed him a few dollars. The servant grabbed him around the neck and said,
'Pay me the money you owe me!'
[29]"The other servant fell on his knees and
begged him, 'Be patient with me, and I will pay
you everything I owe.'
[30]"But the first servant refused to be patient.
He threw the other servant into prison until he
could pay everything he owed. [31]When the

WHAT'S IT MEAN?

The Romans hired local Jewish citizens to do their dirty work when it came to collecting taxes. Honesty was certainly not a requirement for the job of tax collector. Most collectors charged their fellow Jews more than they really owed and kept the extra cash for themselves. That, and the fact that they worked for the hated Romans, made Jewish tax collectors about the most unpopular people around.

Matthew 18:17

18:11 Verse 11 Some Greek copies add verse 11: "The Son of Man came to save lost people."
18:16 'Every . . . witnesses.' Quotation from Deuteronomy 19:15.

other servants saw what had happened, they were very sorry. So they went and told their master all that had happened.

32 "Then the master called his servant in and said, 'You evil servant! Because you begged me to forget what you owed, I told you that you did not have to pay anything. 33 You should have showed mercy to that other servant, just as I showed mercy to you.' 34 The master was very angry and put the servant in prison to be punished until he could pay everything he owed.

35 "This king did what my heavenly Father will do to you if you do not forgive your brother or sister from your heart."

JESUS TEACHES ABOUT DIVORCE

19 1 After Jesus said all these things, he left Galilee and went into the area of Judea on the other side of the Jordan River. 2 Large crowds followed him, and he healed them there.

3 Some Pharisees came to Jesus and tried to trick him. They asked, "Is it right for a man to divorce his wife for any reason he chooses?"

> "But Jesus said, 'Let the little children come to me. Don't stop them, because the kingdom of heaven belongs to people who are like these children.' "
> (Matthew 19:14)

4 Jesus answered, "Surely you have read in the Scriptures: When God made the world, 'he made them male and female.'[n] 5 And God said, 'So a man will leave his father and mother and be united with his wife, and the two will become one body.'[n] 6 So there are not two, but one. God has joined the two together, so no one should separate them."

7 The Pharisees asked, "Why then did Moses give a command for a man to divorce his wife by giving her divorce papers?"

8 Jesus answered, "Moses allowed you to divorce your wives because you refused to accept God's teaching, but divorce was not allowed in the beginning. 9 I tell you that anyone who divorces his wife and marries another woman is guilty of adultery. The only reason for a man to divorce his wife is if his wife has sexual relations with another man."

10 The followers said to him, "If that is the only reason a man can divorce his wife, it is better not to marry."

11 Jesus answered, "Not everyone can accept this teaching, but God has made some able to accept it. 12 There are different reasons why some men cannot marry. Some men were born without the ability to become fathers. Others were made that way later in life by other people. And some men have given up marriage because of the kingdom of heaven. But the person who can marry should accept this teaching about marriage."[n]

JESUS WELCOMES CHILDREN

13 Then the people brought their little children to Jesus so he could put his hands on them[n] and pray for them. His followers told them to stop, 14 but Jesus said, "Let the little children come to me. Don't stop them, because the kingdom of heaven belongs to people who are like these children." 15 After Jesus put his hands on the children, he left there.

A RICH YOUNG MAN'S QUESTION

16 A man came to Jesus and asked, "Teacher, what good thing must I do to have life forever?"

17 Jesus answered, "Why do you ask me about what is good? Only God is good. But if you want to have life forever, obey the commands."

18 The man asked, "Which commands?"

Jesus answered, " 'You must not murder anyone; you must not be guilty of adultery; you must not steal; you must not tell lies about your neighbor; 19 honor your father and mother;[n] and love your neighbor as you love yourself.' "[n]

20 The young man said, "I have obeyed all these things. What else do I need to do?"

21 Jesus answered, "If you want to be perfect, then go and sell your possessions and give the money to the poor. If you do this, you will have treasure in heaven. Then come and follow me."

22 But when the young man heard this, he left sorrowfully, because he was rich.

23 Then Jesus said to his followers, "I tell you the truth, it will be hard for a rich person to

19:4 'he made . . . female.' Quotation from Genesis 1:27 or 5:2. **19:5 'So . . . body.'** Quotation from Genesis 2:24. **19:12 But . . . marriage.** This may also mean, "The person who can accept this teaching about not marrying should accept it." **19:13 put his hands on them** Showing that Jesus gave special blessings to these children. **19:19 'You . . . mother.'** Quotation from Exodus 20:12-16; Deuteronomy 5:16-20. **19:19 'love . . . yourself.'** Quotation from Leviticus 19:18.

enter the kingdom of heaven. 24Yes, I tell you
that it is easier for a camel to go through the
eye of a needle than for a rich person to enter
the kingdom of God."
25When Jesus' followers heard this, they
were very surprised and asked, "Then who can
be saved?"
26Jesus looked at them and said, "This is
something people cannot do, but God can do
all things."
27Peter said to Jesus, "Look, we have left everything and followed you. So what will we
have?"
28Jesus said to them, "I tell you the truth,
when the age to come has arrived, the Son of
Man will sit on his great throne. All of you
who followed me will also sit on twelve
thrones, judging the twelve tribes of Israel.
29And all those who have left houses, brothers,
sisters, father, mother, children, or farms to follow me will get much more than they left, and
they will have life forever. 30Many who have
the highest place now will have the lowest
place in the future. And many who have the
lowest place now will have the highest place in
the future.

A STORY ABOUT WORKERS

20 1"The kingdom of heaven is like a person
who owned some land. One morning, he went
out very early to hire some people to work in
his vineyard. 2The man agreed to pay the
workers one coin[n] for working that day. Then
he sent them into the vineyard to work.
3About nine o'clock the man went to the marketplace and saw some other people standing
there, doing nothing. 4So he said to them, 'If
you go and work in my vineyard, I will pay
you what your work is worth.' 5So they went
to work in the vineyard. The man went out
again about twelve o'clock and three o'clock
and did the same thing. 6About five o'clock the
man went to the marketplace again and saw
others standing there. He asked them, 'Why did
you stand here all day doing nothing?' 7They
answered, 'No one gave us a job.' The man said
to them, 'Then you can go and work in my
vineyard.'
8"At the end of the day, the owner of the
vineyard said to the boss of all the workers,
'Call the workers and pay them. Start with the
last people I hired and end with those I hired
first.'
9"When the workers who were hired at five
o'clock came to get their pay, each received one
coin. 10When the workers who were hired first
came to get their pay, they thought they would
be paid more than the others. But each one of
them also received one coin. 11When they got
their coin, they complained to the man who
owned the land. 12They said, 'Those people
were hired last and worked only one hour. But
you paid them the same as you paid us who
worked hard all day in the hot sun.' 13But the
man who owned the vineyard said to one of
those workers, 'Friend, I am being fair to you.
You agreed to work for one coin. 14So take your
pay and go. I want to give the man who was
hired last the same pay that I gave you. 15I can
do what I want with my own money. Are you
jealous because I am good to those people?'
16"So those who have the last place now
will have the first place in the future, and those
who have the first place now will have the last
place in the future."

JESUS TALKS ABOUT HIS OWN DEATH

17While Jesus was going to Jerusalem, he
took his twelve followers aside privately and
said to them, 18"Look, we are going to Jerusalem. The Son of Man will be turned over to the
leading priests and the teachers of the law, and
they will say that he must die. 19They will give
the Son of Man to the non-Jewish people to
laugh at him and beat him with whips and
crucify him. But on the third day, he will be
raised to life again."

A MOTHER ASKS JESUS A FAVOR

20Then the wife of Zebedee came to Jesus
with her sons. She bowed before him and
asked him to do something for her.
21Jesus asked, "What do you want?"
She said, "Promise that one of my sons will
sit at your right side and the other will sit at
your left side in your kingdom."
22But Jesus said, "You don't understand
what you are asking. Can you drink the cup
that I am about to drink?"[n]
The sons answered, "Yes, we can."
23Jesus said to them, "You will drink from
my cup. But I cannot choose who will sit at my
right or my left; those places belong to those
for whom my Father has prepared them."
24When the other ten followers heard this,
they were angry with the two brothers.

20:2 coin A Roman denarius. One coin was the average pay for one day's work. **20:22 drink . . . drink** Jesus used the idea of drinking from a cup to ask if they could accept the same terrible things that would happen to him.

25 Jesus called all the followers together and
said, "You know that the rulers of the non-Jewish people love to show their power over the
people. And their important leaders love to use
all their authority. 26 But it should not be that
way among you. Whoever wants to
become great among you
must serve the rest of you like
a servant. 27 Whoever wants to
become first among you must
serve the rest of you like a
slave. 28 In the same way, the
Son of Man did not come to be
served. He came to serve others and to give his
life as a ransom for many people."

LEADERSHIP

Do leaders have to serve others? (20:26–28)

JESUS HEALS TWO BLIND MEN

29 When Jesus and his followers were leaving Jericho, a great many people followed him.
30 Two blind men sitting by the road heard that
Jesus was going by, so they shouted, "Lord, Son
of David, have mercy on us!"
31 The people warned the blind men to be
quiet, but they shouted even more, "Lord, Son
of David, have mercy on us!"
32 Jesus stopped and said to the blind men,
"What do you want me to do for you?"
33 They answered, "Lord, we want to see."
34 Jesus felt sorry for the blind men and
touched their eyes, and at once they could see.
Then they followed Jesus.

JESUS ENTERS JERUSALEM AS A KING

21

1 As Jesus and his followers were coming
closer to Jerusalem, they stopped at Bethphage
at the hill called the Mount of Olives. From
there Jesus sent two of his followers 2 and said
to them, "Go to the town you can see there.
When you enter it, you will quickly find a
donkey tied there with its colt. Untie them and
bring them to me. 3 If anyone asks you why
you are taking the donkeys, say that the Master needs them, and he will send them at once."
4 This was to bring about what the prophet
had said:
5 "Tell the people of Jerusalem,
'Your king is coming to you.
He is gentle and riding on a donkey,
on the colt of a donkey.' "

Isaiah 62:11; Zechariah 9:9

6 The followers went and did what Jesus told
them to do. 7 They brought the donkey and the
colt to Jesus and laid their coats on them, and
Jesus sat on them. 8 Many people spread their
coats on the road. Others cut branches from
the trees and spread them on the road. 9 The
people were walking ahead of Jesus and behind him, shouting,
"Praise[n] to the Son of David!
God bless the One who comes in the
name of the Lord!

Psalm 118:26

Praise to God in heaven!"
10 When Jesus entered Jerusalem, all the city
was filled with excitement. The people asked,
"Who is this man?"
11 The crowd said, "This man is Jesus, the
prophet from the town of Nazareth in Galilee."

JESUS GOES TO THE TEMPLE

12 Jesus went into the Temple and threw out
all the people who were buying and selling
there. He turned over the tables of those who
were exchanging different kinds of money, and
he upset the benches of those who were selling
doves. 13 Jesus said to all the people there, "It is
written in the Scriptures, 'My Temple will be
called a house for prayer.'[n] But you are changing it into a 'hideout for robbers.' "[n]

WHAT'S IT MEAN?

Coins with pagan symbols on them could not be used in the Temple. They had to be exchanged for acceptable coins. Likewise, only certain animals could be offered as sacrifices. People who could not afford a goat or a sheep could offer a dove as a sacrifice. Local businessmen saw these restrictions as an opportunity to make money. They set up tables in the Temple courtyard and sold approved coins and doves for outrageous prices. Believe it or not, the family of the high priest, who controlled the Temple business, were the ones raking in the profit.

Matthew 21:12

14 The blind and crippled people came to
Jesus in the Temple, and he healed them. 15 The
leading priests and the teachers of the law saw
that Jesus was doing wonderful things and
that the children were praising him in the Tem-

21:9, 15 Praise Literally, "Hosanna," a Hebrew word used at first in praying to God for help. At this time it was probably a shout of joy used in praising God or his Messiah. **21:13 'My Temple . . . prayer.'** Quotation from Isaiah 56:7. **21:13 'hideout for robbers.'** Quotation from Jeremiah 7:11.

ple, saying, "Praise[n] to the Son of David." All
these things made the priests and the teachers
of the law very angry.
16They asked Jesus, "Do you hear the things
these children are saying?"
Jesus answered, "Yes. Haven't you read in
the Scriptures, 'You have taught children and
babies to sing praises'?"[n]
17Then Jesus left and went out of the city to
Bethany, where he spent the night.

THE POWER OF FAITH

18Early the next morning, as Jesus was going
back to the city, he became hungry. 19Seeing a
fig tree beside the road, Jesus went to it, but
there were no figs on the tree, only leaves. So
Jesus said to the tree, "You will never again have
fruit." The tree immediately dried up.
20When his followers saw this, they were
amazed. They asked, "How did the fig tree dry
up so quickly?"
21Jesus answered, "I tell you the truth, if you
have faith and do not doubt, you will be able to
do what I did to this tree and even more. You
will be able to say to this mountain, 'Go, fall
into the sea.' And if you have faith, it will happen. 22If you believe, you will get anything you
ask for in prayer."

LEADERS DOUBT JESUS' AUTHORITY

23Jesus went to the Temple, and while he
was teaching there, the leading priests and the
older leaders of the people came to him. They
said, "What authority do you have to do these
things? Who gave you this authority?"
24Jesus answered, "I also will ask you a
question. If you answer me, then I will tell you
what authority I have to do these things. 25Tell
me: When John baptized people, did that come
from God or just from other people?"
They argued about Jesus' question, saying,
"If we answer, 'John's baptism was from
God,' Jesus will say, 'Then why didn't you believe him?' 26But if we say, 'It was from people,'
we are afraid of what the crowd will do
because they all believe that John was a
prophet."
27So they answered Jesus, "We don't know."
Jesus said to them, "Then I won't tell you
what authority I have to do these things.

A STORY ABOUT TWO SONS

28"Tell me what you think about this: A man
had two sons. He went to the first son and
said, 'Son, go and work today in my vineyard.'
29The son answered, 'I will not go.' But later the
son changed his mind and went. 30Then the
father went to the other son and said, 'Son, go
and work today in my vineyard.' The son answered, 'Yes, sir, I will go and work,' but he did
not go. 31Which of the two sons obeyed his
father?"
The priests and leaders answered, "The first
son."
Jesus said to them, "I tell you the truth, the
tax collectors and the prostitutes will enter the
kingdom of God before you do. 32John came to
show you the right way to live. You did not
believe him, but the tax collectors and prostitutes believed him. Even after seeing this, you
still refused to change your ways and believe him.

A STORY ABOUT GOD'S SON

33"Listen to this story: There was a man who
owned a vineyard. He put a wall around it and
dug a hole for a winepress and built a tower.
Then he leased the land to some farmers and
left for a trip. 34When it was time for the grapes
to be picked, he sent his servants to the farmers
to get his share of the grapes. 35But the farmers
grabbed the servants, beat one, killed another,
and then killed a third servant with stones.
36So the man sent some other servants to the
farmers, even more than he sent the first time.
But the farmers did the same thing to the servants that they had done before. 37So the man
decided to send his son to the farmers. He said,
'They will respect my son.' 38But when the
farmers saw the son, they said to each other,
'This son will inherit the vineyard. If we kill
him, it will be ours!' 39Then the farmers
grabbed the son, threw him out of the vineyard, and killed him. 40So what will the owner
of the vineyard do to these farmers when he
comes?"
41The priests and leaders said, "He will surely kill those evil men. Then he will lease the
vineyard to some other farmers who will give
him his share of the crop at harvest time."
42Jesus said to them, "Surely you have read
this in the Scriptures:

'The stone that the builders rejected
  became the cornerstone.
The Lord did this,
  and it is wonderful to us.' *Psalm 118:22-23*

43"So I tell you that the kingdom of God will
be taken away from you and given to people
who do the things God wants in his kingdom.
44The person who falls on this stone will be

21:16 'You . . . praises' Quotation from the Septuagint (Greek) version of Psalm 8:2.

broken, and on whomever that stone falls, that person will be crushed."[n]

45When the leading priests and the Pharisees heard these stories, they knew Jesus was talking about them. 46They wanted to arrest him, but they were afraid of the people, because the people believed that Jesus was a prophet.

A STORY ABOUT A WEDDING FEAST

22 1Jesus again used stories to teach the people. He said, 2"The kingdom of heaven is like a king who prepared a wedding feast for his son. 3The king invited some people to the feast. When the feast was ready, the king sent his servants to tell the people, but they refused to come.

4"Then the king sent other servants, saying, 'Tell those who have been invited that my feast is ready. I have killed my best bulls and calves for the dinner, and everything is ready. Come to the wedding feast.'

5"But the people refused to listen to the servants and left to do other things. One went to work in his field, and another went to his business. 6Some of the other people grabbed the servants, beat them, and killed them. 7The king was furious and sent his army to kill the murderers and burn their city.

8"After that, the king said to his servants, 'The wedding feast is ready. I invited those people, but they were not worthy to come. 9So go to the street corners and invite everyone you find to come to my feast.' 10So the servants went into the streets and gathered all the people they could find, both good and bad. And the wedding hall was filled with guests.

11"When the king came in to see the guests, he saw a man who was not dressed for a wedding. 12The king said, 'Friend, how were you allowed to come in here? You are not dressed for a wedding.' But the man said nothing. 13So the king told some servants, 'Tie this man's hands and feet. Throw him out into the darkness, where people will cry and grind their teeth with pain.'

14"Yes, many people are invited, but only a few are chosen."

IS IT RIGHT TO PAY TAXES OR NOT?

15Then the Pharisees left that place and made plans to trap Jesus in saying something wrong. 16They sent some of their own followers and some people from the group called Herodians.[n] They said, "Teacher, we know that you are an honest man and that you teach the truth about God's way. You are not afraid of what other people think about you, because you pay no attention to who they are. 17So tell us what you think. Is it right to pay taxes to Caesar or not?"

18But knowing that these leaders were trying to trick him, Jesus said, "You hypocrites! Why are you trying to trap me? 19Show me a coin used for paying the tax." So the men showed him a coin.[n] 20Then Jesus asked, "Whose image and name are on the coin?"

21The men answered, "Caesar's."

Then Jesus said to them, "Give to Caesar the things that are Caesar's, and give to God the things that are God's."

22When the men heard what Jesus said, they were amazed and left him and went away.

WHAT'S IT MEAN?

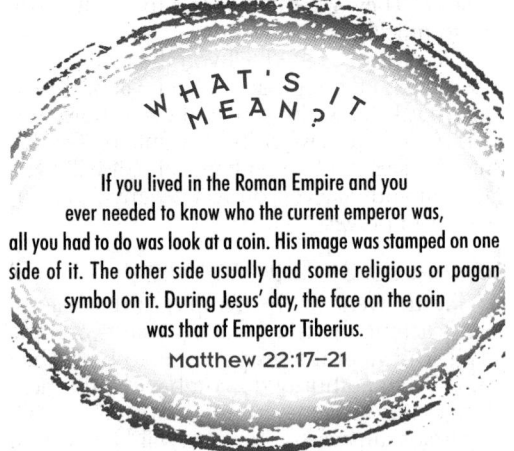

If you lived in the Roman Empire and you ever needed to know who the current emperor was, all you had to do was look at a coin. His image was stamped on one side of it. The other side usually had some religious or pagan symbol on it. During Jesus' day, the face on the coin was that of Emperor Tiberius.

Matthew 22:17–21

SOME SADDUCEES TRY TO TRICK JESUS

23That same day some Sadducees came to Jesus and asked him a question. (Sadducees believed that people would not rise from the dead.) 24They said, "Teacher, Moses said if a married man dies without having children, his brother must marry the widow and have children for him. 25Once there were seven brothers among us. The first one married and died. Since he had no children, his brother married the widow. 26Then the second brother also died. The same thing happened to the third brother and all the other brothers. 27Finally, the woman died. 28Since all seven men had married her, when people rise from the dead, whose wife will she be?"

29Jesus answered, "You don't understand,

21:44 Verse 44 Some copies do not have verse 44. **22:16 Herodians** A political group that followed Herod and his family. **22:19 coin** A Roman denarius. One coin was the average pay for one day's work.

because you don't know what the Scriptures
say, and you don't know about the
power of God. 30When peo-
ple rise from the dead, they
will not marry, nor will they
be given to someone to
marry. They will be like the
angels in heaven. 31Surely you
have read what God said to
you about rising from the dead. 32God said, 'I
am the God of Abraham, the God of Isaac, and
the God of Jacob.'[n] God is the God of the living,
not the dead."
33When the people heard this, they were
amazed at Jesus' teaching.

ANGELS

Do angels get married? (22:30)

THE MOST IMPORTANT COMMAND

34When the Pharisees learned that the Sadducees could not argue with Jesus' answers to
them, the Pharisees met together. 35One Pharisee, who was an expert on the law of Moses,
asked Jesus this question to test him: 36"Teacher,
which command in the law is the most important?"
37Jesus answered, " 'Love the Lord your God
with all your heart, all your soul, and all your
mind.'[n] 38This is the first and most important
command. 39And the second command is like
the first: 'Love your neighbor as you love
yourself.'[n] 40All the law and the writings of the
prophets depend on these two commands."

JESUS QUESTIONS THE PHARISEES

41While the Pharisees were together, Jesus
asked them, 42"What do you think about the
Christ? Whose son is he?"
They answered, "The Christ is the Son of
David."
43Then Jesus said to them, "Then why did
David call him 'Lord'? David, speaking by the
power of the Holy Spirit, said,
44'The Lord said to my Lord:
Sit by me at my right side,
until I put your enemies under your
control.' *Psalm 110:1*
45David calls the Christ 'Lord,' so how can the
Christ be his son?"
46None of the Pharisees could answer Jesus'
question, and after that day no one was brave
enough to ask him any more questions.

JESUS ACCUSES SOME LEADERS

23
1Then Jesus said to the crowds and to his
followers, 2"The teachers of the law and the
Pharisees have the authority to tell you what
the law of Moses says. 3So you should obey
and follow whatever they tell you, but their
lives are not good examples for you to follow.
They tell you to do things, but they themselves
don't do them. 4They make strict rules and try
to force people to obey them, but they are unwilling to help those who struggle under the
weight of their rules.
5"They do good things so that other people

On the Edge

"Teacher, which commandment in the law is the most important?" Jesus answered, "Love the Lord your God with all your heart, all your soul, and all your mind" (Matt. 22:36–37).

Well, this is it. This is *the* most important commandment. If you've decided to get serious about God, then this commandment is the place to start. Every element of being Christlike is built on this principle. Learning to love the Lord with your heart, soul, and mind will be a continual process that lasts your whole life. But you've got to start. So what does it look like to love the Lord with every part of you? It means that you begin to love the way God loves, think the way God thinks, act the way God acts, and hate the things God hates. If you have begun to get serious about God, don't hold back. His love for you has no limits or hesitations. You have absolutely nothing to lose and everything to gain by going for it.

Don't be disappointed if you're not an overnight sensation. Remember, this is a process—learning to spend time with him; giving and receiving grace; working on areas that don't look anything like God; forgiving and being forgiven; trusting; slowly, ever so wonderfully, looking more and more like the One you love. Imitation is the highest form of adoration. Be an imitator of God.

SEE FOR YOURSELF:
Deut. 6:5;
Mark 12:32–33;
Eph. 5:1–2

22:32 'I am . . . Jacob.' Quotation from Exodus 3:6. **22:37 'Love . . . mind.'** Quotation from Deuteronomy 6:5. **22:39 'Love . . . yourself.'** Quotation from Leviticus 19:18.

will see them. They make the boxes[n] of Scriptures that they wear bigger, and they make
their special prayer clothes very long. [6]Those
Pharisees and teachers of the law love to have
the most important seats at feasts and in the
synagogues. [7]They love people to greet them
with respect in the marketplaces, and they love
to have people call them 'Teacher.'

[8]"But you must not be called 'Teacher,' because you have only one Teacher, and you are
all brothers and sisters together. [9]And don't call
any person on earth 'Father,' because you have
one Father, who is in heaven. [10]And you
should not be called 'Master,' because you
have only one Master, the Christ. [11]Whoever is
your servant is the greatest among you.
[12]Whoever makes himself great will be made
humble. Whoever makes himself humble will
be made great.

[13]"How terrible for you, teachers of the law
and Pharisees! You are hypocrites! You close
the door for people to enter the kingdom of
heaven. You yourselves don't enter, and you
stop others who are trying to enter. [14n]

[15]"How terrible for you, teachers of the law
and Pharisees! You are hypocrites! You travel
across land and sea to find one person who
will change to your ways. When you find that
person, you make him more fit for hell than
you are.

[16]"How terrible for you! You guide the people, but you are blind. You say, 'If people swear
by the Temple when they make a promise, that
means nothing. But if they swear by the gold
that is in the Temple, they must keep that
promise.' [17]You are blind fools! Which is greater: the gold or the Temple that makes that gold
holy? [18]And you say, 'If people swear by the
altar when they make a promise, that means
nothing. But if they swear by the gift on the
altar, they must keep that promise.' [19]You are
blind! Which is greater: the gift or the altar that
makes the gift holy? [20]The person who swears
by the altar is really using the altar and also
everything on the altar. [21]And the person who
swears by the Temple is really using the Temple
and also everything in the Temple. [22]The person who swears by heaven is also using God's
throne and the One who sits on that throne.

[23]"How terrible for you, teachers of the law
and Pharisees! You are hypocrites! You give to
God one-tenth of everything you earn—even
your mint, dill, and cumin.[n] But you don't

On the Edge

But you must not be called "Teacher," because you have only one Teacher, and you are all brothers and sisters together. And don't call any person on earth "Father," because you have one Father, who is in heaven (Matt. 23:8–9).

As you learn about Jesus' life on earth, one thing you notice is that he seemed to enjoy hanging around notorious sinners more than he did the Jewish religious leaders. To thieves and prostitutes he said, "Your sins are forgiven" (Luke 7:48), but he warned the Pharisees and teachers, "How terrible for you!" (Matt. 23:16).

The Pharisees were snobs. These religious leaders actually thought they were better than the rest of the Jewish people. Because they knew a lot about Scripture and religious customs, they figured that God liked them more than he liked everybody else. Jesus could see their conceited attitude and hated it.

Jesus told his followers that God's kingdom is not made up of special people and regular people. The people who follow Jesus are all equal, and he loves each one exactly the same. If you've struggled with feelings of inferiority or insecurity, know that God never sees you as inferior to anyone. If you've gotten an attitude about how cool you are, God isn't impressed. God can peer into a high school classroom and see the most popular student in school sitting beside the biggest outcast; yet he loves them both the same. No matter how you feel, God thinks you're awesome—just as awesome as the next person. Everybody's equal with him. No one has a better chance than you do!

SEE FOR YOURSELF:
Job 34:19; 36:5;
Matt. 7:8;
Acts 13:38–39

23:5 boxes Small leather boxes containing four important Scriptures. Some Jews tied these to their foreheads and left arms, probably to show they were very religious. **23:14 Verse 14** Some Greek copies add verse 14: "How terrible for you, teachers of the law and Pharisees. You are hypocrites. You take away widows' houses, and you say long prayers so that people will notice you. So you will have a worse punishment." **23:23 mint, dill, and cumin** Small plants grown in gardens and used for spices. Only very religious people would be careful enough to give a tenth of these plants.

WHAT'S IT MEAN?

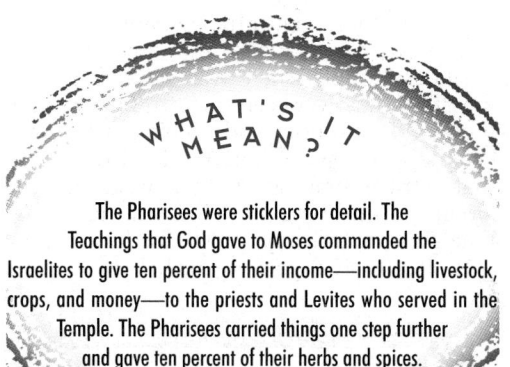

The Pharisees were sticklers for detail. The Teachings that God gave to Moses commanded the Israelites to give ten percent of their income—including livestock, crops, and money—to the priests and Levites who served in the Temple. The Pharisees carried things one step further and gave ten percent of their herbs and spices.

Matthew 23:23

obey the really important teachings of the law—justice, mercy, and being loyal. These are the things you should do, as well as those other things. 24You guide the people, but you are blind! You are like a person who picks a fly out of a drink and then swallows a camel![n]

> "Many times I wanted to gather your people as a hen gathers her chicks under her wings, but you did not let me." (Matthew 23:37b)

25"How terrible for you, teachers of the law and Pharisees! You are hypocrites! You wash the outside of your cups and dishes, but inside they are full of things you got by cheating others and by pleasing only yourselves. 26Pharisees, you are blind! First make the inside of the cup clean, and then the outside of the cup can be truly clean.

27"How terrible for you, teachers of the law and Pharisees! You are hypocrites! You are like tombs that are painted white. Outside, those tombs look fine, but inside, they are full of the bones of dead people and all kinds of unclean things. 28It is the same with you. People look at you and think you are good, but on the inside you are full of hypocrisy and evil.

PURITY

Can outward purity substitute for inner purity? (23:25–28)

29"How terrible for you, teachers of the law and Pharisees! You are hypocrites! You build tombs for the prophets, and you show honor to the graves of those who lived good lives. 30You say, 'If we had lived during the time of our ancestors, we would not have helped them kill the prophets.' 31But you give proof that you are children of those who murdered the prophets. 32And you will complete the sin that your ancestors started.

33"You are snakes! A family of poisonous snakes! How are you going to escape God's judgment? 34So I tell you this: I am sending to you prophets and wise men and teachers. Some of them you will kill and crucify. Some of them you will beat in your synagogues and chase from town to town. 35So you will be guilty for the death of all the good people who have been killed on earth—from the murder of that good man Abel to the murder of Zechariah[n] son of Berakiah, whom you murdered between the Temple and the altar. 36I tell you the truth, all of these things will happen to you people who are living now.

JESUS FEELS SORRY FOR JERUSALEM

37"Jerusalem, Jerusalem! You kill the prophets and stone to death those who are sent to you. Many times I wanted to gather your people as a hen gathers her chicks under her wings, but you did not let me.38Now your house will be left completely empty. 39I tell you, you will not see me again until that time when you will say, 'God bless the One who comes in the name of the Lord.' "[n]

THE TEMPLE WILL BE DESTROYED

24

1As Jesus left the Temple and was walking away, his followers came up to show him the Temple's buildings. 2Jesus asked, "Do you see all these buildings? I tell you the truth, not one stone will be left on another. Every stone will be thrown down to the ground."

3Later, as Jesus was sitting on the Mount of Olives, his followers came to be alone with him. They said, "Tell us, when will these things happen? And what will be the sign that it is time for you to come again and for this age to end?"

4Jesus answered, "Be careful that no one fools you. 5Many will come in my name, saying, 'I am the Christ,' and they will fool many people. 6You will hear about wars and stories

23:24 You . . . camel! Meaning, "You worry about the smallest mistakes but commit the biggest sin."
23:35 Abel . . . Zechariah In the order of the books of the Hebrew Old Testament, the first and last men to be murdered. **23:39 'God . . . Lord.'** Quotation from Psalm 118:26.

WHAT'S IT MEAN?

To make his Jewish subjects happy, Herod the Great had completely renovated the Temple in Jerusalem. Work on the Temple itself was completed in 9 B.C. The renovation of the rest of the enormous Temple complex was not completed until A.D. 64. In fact, the Temple was finished just in time for the Romans to destroy it six years later after a Jewish revolt.

Matthew 24:1

of wars that are coming, but don't be afraid.
These things must happen before the end
comes. 7Nations will fight against other nations; kingdoms will fight against other kingdoms. There will be times when there is no
food for people to eat, and there will be earthquakes in different places. 8These things are like
the first pains when something new is about to
be born.
9"Then people will arrest you, hand you
over to be hurt, and kill you. They will hate
you because you believe in me. 10At that time,
many will lose their faith, and they will turn
against each other and hate each other. 11Many
false prophets will come and cause many people to believe lies. 12There will be more and
more evil in the world, so most people will
stop showing their love for each other. 13But
those people who keep their faith until the end
will be saved. 14The Good News about God's
kingdom will be preached in all the world, to
every nation. Then the end will come.
15"Daniel the prophet spoke about 'the destroying terror.'[n] You will see this standing in
the holy place." (You who read this should understand what it means.) 16"At that time, the
people in Judea should run away to the mountains. 17If people are on the roofs[n] of their
houses, they must not go down to get anything
out of their houses. 18If people are in the fields,
they must not go back to get their coats. 19At
that time, how terrible it will be for women
who are pregnant or have nursing babies!
20Pray that it will not be winter or a Sabbath
day when these things happen and you have
to run away, 21because at that time there will
be much trouble. There will be more trouble
than there has ever been since the beginning of
the world until now, and nothing as bad will
ever happen again. 22God has decided to make
that terrible time short. Otherwise, no one
would go on living. But God will make that
time short to help the people he has chosen.
23At that time, someone might say to you,

On the Edge

Jesus answered, "Be careful that no one fools you" (Matt. 24:4).

This is a great chapter in the Bible. Jesus is foretelling some of the things that are going to happen before he comes back to the earth—wars, stories of wars, famines, earthquakes, etc. He goes on to tell us not to worry or be afraid because these things must happen before he comes back. But before he goes into all of this, he says that there will be many people who claim to be Jesus and then warns us not to be fooled by them. You've seen this already.

Remember the suicide by the cult group called "Heaven's Gate"? All of the people in that compound died because they allowed themselves to be fooled. Adam and Eve were cast out of the garden because they allowed themselves to be fooled. Esau lost his inheritance to Jacob because he allowed himself to be fooled. Samson lost his strength and his life because he allowed himself to be fooled.

You don't have to allow yourself to be fooled by some false prophet who claims to be Jesus or claims to be from God. If something doesn't line up with the Word of God, then don't believe it. There are more fruitcakes around today than ever before. This is what we call *a sign of the times.*

Jesus is coming back. No one knows exactly when, so stay tight with God and don't be fooled!

SEE FOR YOURSELF:
Matt. 7:15; 24:11, 24; Luke 21:8; 2 Pet. 2:1; 1 John 4:1

24:15 'the destroying terror' Mentioned in Daniel 9:27; 12:11 (see also Daniel 11:31). **24:17 roofs** In Bible times houses were built with flat roofs. The roof was used for drying things such as flax and fruit. And it was used as an extra room, as a place for worship, and as a cool place to sleep in the summer.

'Look, there is the Christ!' Or another person
might say, 'There he is!' But don't believe them.
24False Christs and false prophets will come
and perform great wonders and miracles. They
will try to fool even the people God has chosen, if that is possible. 25Now I have warned
you about this before it happens.

26"If people tell you, 'The Christ is in the
desert,' don't go there. If they say, 'The Christ is
in the inner room,' don't believe it. 27When the
Son of Man comes, he will be seen by everyone, like lightning flashing from the east to the
west. 28Wherever the dead body is, there the
vultures will gather.

29"Soon after the trouble of those days,
'the sun will grow dark,
and the moon will not give its light.
The stars will fall from the sky.
And the powers of the heavens will be
shaken.' *Isaiah 13:10; 34:4*

30"At that time, the sign of the Son of Man
will appear in the sky. Then all the peoples of
the world will cry. They will see the Son of
Man coming on clouds in the sky with great
power and glory. 31He will use a loud trumpet
to send his angels all around the earth, and they
will gather his chosen people from every part of
the world.

32"Learn a lesson from the fig tree: When its
branches become green and soft and new
leaves appear, you know summer is near. 33In
the same way, when you see all these things
happening, you will know that the time is near,
ready to come. 34I tell you the truth, all these
things will happen while the people of this
time are still living. 35Earth and sky will be destroyed, but the words I have said will never
be destroyed.

WHEN WILL JESUS COME AGAIN?

36"No one knows when that day or time
will be, not the angels in heaven, not even the
Son. Only the Father knows. 37When the Son
of Man comes, it will be like what happened
during Noah's time. 38In those days before the
flood, people were eating and drinking, marrying and giving their children to be married,
until the day Noah entered the boat. 39They
knew nothing about what was happening until the flood came and destroyed them. It will
be the same when the Son of Man comes.
40Two men will be in the field. One will be tak-
en, and the other will be left. 41Two women
will be grinding grain with a mill.[n] One will be
taken, and the other will be left.

42"So always be ready, because you don't
know the day your Lord will come. 43Remem-
ber this: If the owner of the house knew what
time of night a thief was coming, the owner
would watch and not let the thief break in. 44So
you also must be ready, because the Son of
Man will come at a time you don't expect him.

45"Who is the wise and loyal servant that
the master trusts to give the other servants
their food at the right time? 46When the master
comes and finds the servant doing his work,
the servant will be blessed. 47I tell you the
truth, the master will choose that servant to
take care of everything he owns. 48But suppose
that evil servant thinks to himself, 'My master
will not come back soon,' 49and he begins to
beat the other servants and eat and get drunk
with others like him? 50The master will come
when that servant is not ready and is not expecting him. 51Then the master will cut him in
pieces and send him away to be with the hypocrites, where people will cry and grind their
teeth with pain.

WHAT'S IT MEAN?

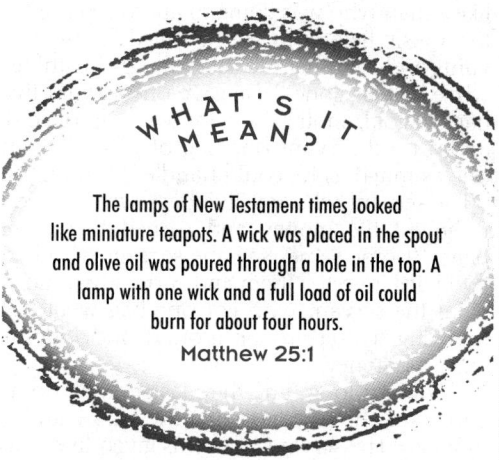

The lamps of New Testament times looked like miniature teapots. A wick was placed in the spout and olive oil was poured through a hole in the top. A lamp with one wick and a full load of oil could burn for about four hours.

Matthew 25:1

A STORY ABOUT TEN BRIDESMAIDS

25 1"At that time the kingdom of heaven will be
like ten bridesmaids who took their lamps and
went to wait for the bridegroom. 2Five of them
were foolish and five were wise. 3The five foolish bridesmaids took their lamps, but they did
not take more oil for the lamps to burn. 4The
wise bridesmaids took their lamps and more
oil in jars. 5Because the bridegroom was late,
they became sleepy and went to sleep.

6"At midnight someone cried out, 'The
bridegroom is coming! Come and meet him!'
7Then all the bridesmaids woke up and got
their lamps ready. 8But the foolish ones said to

24:41 mill Two large, round, flat rocks used for grinding grain to make flour.

the wise, 'Give us some of your oil, because
our lamps are going out.' 9The wise bridesmaids answered, 'No, the oil we have might
not be enough for all of us. Go to the people
who sell oil and buy some for yourselves.'
10"So while the five foolish bridesmaids
went to buy oil, the bridegroom came. The
bridesmaids who were ready went in with the
bridegroom to the wedding feast. Then the
door was closed and locked.
11"Later the others came back and said, 'Sir,
sir, open the door to let us in.'
12But the bridegroom an-
swered, 'I tell you the truth, I
don't want to know you.'
13"So always be ready,
because you don't know the
day or the hour the Son of
Man will come.

"So always be ready, because you don't know the day or the hour the Son of Man will come." (Matthew 25:13)

A STORY ABOUT THREE SERVANTS

14"The kingdom of heaven is
like a man who was going to another place
for a visit. Before he left, he called for his servants and told them to take care of his things
while he was gone. 15He gave one servant five
bags of gold, another servant two bags of gold,
and a third servant one bag of gold, to each
one as much as he could handle. Then he left.
16The servant who got five bags went quickly
to invest the money and earned five more
bags. 17In the same way, the servant who had
two bags invested them and earned two more.
18But the servant who got one bag went out
and dug a hole in the ground and hid the
master's money.
19"After a long time the master came home
and asked the servants what they did with his
money. 20The servant who was given five bags
of gold brought five more bags to the master
and said, 'Master, you trusted me to care for
five bags of gold, so I used your five bags to
earn five more.' 21The master answered, 'You
did well. You are a good and loyal servant. Because you were loyal with small things, I will let
you care for much greater things. Come and
share my joy with me.'
22"Then the servant who had been given
two bags of gold came to the master and said,
'Master, you gave me two bags of gold to care
for, so I used your two bags to earn two more.'
23The master answered, 'You did well. You are a
good and loyal servant. Because you were loyal with small things, I will let you care for
much greater things. Come and share my joy
with me.'
24"Then the servant who had been given
one bag of gold came to the master and said,
'Master, I knew that you were a hard man. You
harvest things you did not plant. You gather
crops where you did not sow any seed. 25So I
was afraid and went and hid your money in
the ground. Here is your bag of gold.' 26The
master answered, 'You are a wicked and lazy
servant! You say you knew that I harvest
things I did not plant and that I gather crops
where I did not sow any seed. 27So you should
have put my gold in the bank.
Then, when I came home, I
would have received my
gold back with interest.'
28"So the master told his
other servants, 'Take the bag
of gold from that servant
and give it to the servant
who has ten bags of gold.
29Those who have much
will get more, and they will
have much more than they
need. But those who do not have
much will have everything taken away from
them.' 30Then the master said, 'Throw that
useless servant outside, into the darkness
where people will cry and grind their teeth
with pain.'

THE KING WILL JUDGE ALL PEOPLE

31"The Son of Man will come again in his
great glory, with all his angels. He will be King
and sit on his great throne. 32All the nations of
the world will be gathered before him, and he
will separate them into two groups as a shepherd separates the sheep from the goats. 33The
Son of Man will put the sheep on his right and
the goats on his left.
34"Then the King will say to the people on
his right, 'Come, my Father has given you his
blessing. Receive the kingdom God has prepared
for you since the world was made. 35I was hungry, and you gave me food. I was thirsty,
and you gave me something to
drink. I was alone and away
from home, and you invited me
into your house. 36I was without clothes, and you gave me
something to wear. I was sick,
and you cared for me. I was in
prison, and you visited me.'

SICKNESS
How can believers show compassion? (25:34–40)

37"Then the good people will answer, 'Lord,
when did we see you hungry and give you
food, or thirsty and give you something to
drink? 38When did we see you alone and away
from home and invite you into our house?

When did we see you without clothes and give you something to wear? [39]When did we see you sick or in prison and care for you?'

[40]"Then the King will answer, 'I tell you the truth, anything you did for even the least of my people here, you also did for me.'

[41]"Then the King will say to those on his left, 'Go away from me. You will be punished. Go into the fire that burns forever that was prepared for the devil and his angels. [42]I was hungry, and you gave me nothing to eat. I was thirsty, and you gave me nothing to drink. [43]I was alone and away from home, and you did not invite me into your house. I was without clothes, and you gave me nothing to wear. I was sick and in prison, and you did not care for me.'

[44]"Then those people will answer, 'Lord, when did we see you hungry or thirsty or alone and away from home or without clothes or sick or in prison? When did we see these things and not help you?'

[45]"Then the King will answer, 'I tell you the truth, anything you refused to do for even the least of my people here, you refused to do for me.'

[46]"These people will go off to be punished forever, but the good people will go to live forever."

THE PLAN TO KILL JESUS

26 [1]After Jesus finished saying all these things, he told his followers, [2]"You know that the day after tomorrow is the day of the Passover Feast. On that day the Son of Man will be given to his enemies to be crucified."

[3]Then the leading priests and the older leaders had a meeting at the palace of the high priest, named Caiaphas. [4]At the meeting, they planned to set a trap to arrest Jesus and kill him. [5]But they said, "We must not do it during the feast, because the people might cause a riot."

PERFUME FOR JESUS' BURIAL

[6]Jesus was in Bethany at the house of Simon, who had a skin disease. [7]While Jesus was there, a woman approached him with an alabaster jar filled with expensive perfume. She poured this perfume on Jesus' head while he was eating.

[8]His followers were upset when they saw the woman do this. They asked, "Why waste that perfume? [9]It could have been sold for a great deal of money and the money given to the poor."

[10]Knowing what had happened, Jesus said, "Why are you troubling this woman? She did an excellent thing for me. [11]You will always have the poor with you, but you will not always have me. [12]This woman poured perfume on my body to prepare me for burial. [13]I tell you the truth, wherever the Good News is preached in all the world, what this woman has done will be told, and people will remember her."

JUDAS BECOMES AN ENEMY OF JESUS

[14]Then one of the twelve apostles, Judas Iscariot, went to talk to the leading priests. [15]He said, "What will you pay me for giving Jesus to you?" And they gave him thirty silver coins. [16]After that, Judas watched for the best time to turn Jesus in.

JESUS EATS THE PASSOVER MEAL

[17]On the first day of the Feast of Unleavened Bread, the followers came to Jesus. They said, "Where do you want us to prepare for you to eat the Passover meal?"

[18]Jesus answered, "Go into the city to a certain man and tell him, 'The Teacher says: The chosen time is near. I will have the Passover with my followers at your house.' " [19]The followers did what Jesus told them to do, and they prepared the Passover meal.

[20]In the evening Jesus was sitting at the table with his twelve followers. [21]As they were eating, Jesus said, "I tell you the truth, one of you will turn against me."

[22]This made the followers very sad. Each one began to say to Jesus, "Surely, Lord, I am not the one who will turn against you, am I?"

[23]Jesus answered, "The man who has dipped his hand with me into the bowl is the one who will turn against me. [24]The Son of Man will die, just as the Scriptures say. But how terrible it will be for the person who hands the Son of Man over to be killed. It would be better for him if he had never been born."

[25]Then Judas, who would give Jesus to his enemies, said to Jesus, "Teacher, surely I am not the one, am I?"

Jesus answered, "Yes, it is you."

THE LORD'S SUPPER

[26]While they were eating, Jesus took some bread and thanked God for it and broke it. Then he gave it to his followers and said, "Take this bread and eat it; this is my body."

[27]Then Jesus took a cup and thanked God for it and gave it to the followers. He said, "Every one of you drink this. [28]This is my

WHAT'S IT MEAN?

Bread was a major part of the Jewish diet in New Testament times. Often it was served with a stew or sauce. Several people would share one bowl of sauce, taking turns dipping their bread into it before each bite.

Matthew 26:26

blood which is the new agreement that God makes with his people. This blood is poured out for many to forgive their sins. [29]I tell you this: I will not drink of this fruit of the vine[n] again until that day when I drink it new with you in my Father's kingdom."

[30]After singing a hymn, they went out to the Mount of Olives.

JESUS' FOLLOWERS WILL LEAVE HIM

[31]Jesus told his followers, "Tonight you will all stumble in your faith on account of me, because it is written in the Scriptures:

'I will kill the shepherd,
and the sheep will scatter.' *Zechariah 13:7*

[32]But after I rise from the dead, I will go ahead of you into Galilee."

[33]Peter said, "Everyone else may stumble in their faith because of you, but I will not."

[34]Jesus said, "I tell you the truth, tonight before the rooster crows you will say three times that you don't know me."

[35]But Peter said, "I will never say that I don't know you! I will even die with you!" And all the other followers said the same thing.

JESUS PRAYS ALONE

[36]Then Jesus went with his followers to a place called Gethsemane. He said to them, "Sit here while I go over there and pray." [37]He took Peter and the two sons of Zebedee with him, and he began to be very sad and troubled. [38]He said to them, "My heart is full of sorrow, to the point of death. Stay here and watch with me."

[39]After walking a little farther away from them, Jesus fell to the ground and prayed, "My Father, if it is possible, do not give me this cup[n] of suffering. But do what you want, not what I want." [40]Then Jesus went back to his followers and found them asleep. He said to Peter, "You men could not stay awake with me for one hour? [41]Stay awake and pray for strength against temptation. The spirit wants to do what is right, but the body is weak."

[42]Then Jesus went away a second time and prayed, "My Father, if it is not possible for this painful thing to be taken from me, and if I must do it, I pray that what you want will be done."

[43]Then he went back to his followers, and again he found them asleep, because their eyes were heavy. [44]So Jesus left them and went away and prayed a third time, saying the same thing.

[45]Then Jesus went back to his followers and said, "Are you still sleeping and resting? The time has come for the Son of Man to be handed over to sinful people. [46]Get up, we must go. Look, here comes the man who has turned against me."

JESUS IS ARRESTED

[47]While Jesus was still speaking, Judas, one of the twelve apostles, came up. With him were many people carrying swords and clubs who had been sent from the leading priests and the older Jewish leaders of the people. [48]Judas had planned to give them a signal, saying, "The man I kiss is Jesus. Arrest him." [49]At once Judas went to Jesus and said, "Greetings, Teacher!" and kissed him.

[50]Jesus answered, "Friend, do what you came to do."

Then the people came and grabbed Jesus and arrested him. [51]When that happened, one of Jesus' followers reached for his sword and pulled it out. He struck the servant of the high priest and cut off his ear.

[52]Jesus said to the man, "Put your sword back in its place. All who use swords will be killed with swords. [53]Surely you know I could ask my Father, and he would give me more than twelve armies of angels. [54]But it must happen this way to bring about what the Scriptures say."

[55]Then Jesus said to the crowd, "You came to get me with swords and clubs as if I were a criminal. Every day I sat in the Temple teach-

26:29 fruit of the vine Product of the grapevine; this may also be translated "wine." **26:39 cup** Jesus is talking about the terrible things that will happen to him. Accepting these things will be very hard, like drinking a cup of something bitter.

ing, and you did not arrest me there. [56]But all these things have happened so that it will come about as the prophets wrote." Then all of Jesus' followers left him and ran away.

JESUS BEFORE THE LEADERS

[57]Those people who arrested Jesus led him to the house of Caiaphas, the high priest, where the teachers of the law and the older leaders were gathered. [58]Peter followed far behind to the courtyard of the high priest's house, and he sat down with the guards to see what would happen to Jesus.

[59]The leading priests and the whole council tried to find something false against Jesus so they could kill him. [60]Many people came and told lies about him, but the council could find no real reason to kill him. Then two people came and said, [61]"This man said, 'I can destroy the Temple of God and build it again in three days.' "

> "The leading priests and the whole council tried to find something false against Jesus so they could kill him. Many people came and told lies about him, but the council could find no real reason to kill him." (Matthew 26:59–60a)

[62]Then the high priest stood up and said to Jesus, "Aren't you going to answer? Don't you have something to say about their charges against you?" [63]But Jesus said nothing.

Again the high priest said to Jesus, "I command you by the power of the living God: Tell us if you are the Christ, the Son of God."

[64]Jesus answered, "Those are your words. But I tell you, in the future you will see the Son of Man sitting at the right hand of God, the Powerful One, and coming on clouds in the sky."

[65]When the high priest heard this, he tore his clothes and said, "This man has said things that are against God! We don't need any more witnesses; you all heard him say these things against God. [66]What do you think?"

The people answered, "He should die."

[67]Then the people there spat in Jesus' face and beat him with their fists. Others slapped him. [68]They said, "Prove to us that you are a prophet, you Christ! Tell us who hit you!"

PETER SAYS HE DOESN'T KNOW JESUS

[69]At that time, as Peter was sitting in the courtyard, a servant girl came to him and said, "You also were with Jesus of Galilee."

[70]But Peter said to all the people there that he was never with Jesus. He said, "I don't know what you are talking about."

[71]When he left the courtyard and was at the gate, another girl saw him. She said to the people there, "This man was with Jesus of Nazareth."

[72]Again, Peter said he was never with him, saying, "I swear I don't know this man Jesus!"

[73]A short time later, some people standing there went to Peter and said, "Surely you are one of those who followed Jesus. The way you talk shows it."

[74]Then Peter began to place a curse on himself and swear, "I don't know the man." At once, a rooster crowed. [75]And Peter remembered what Jesus had told him: "Before the rooster crows, you will say three times that you don't know me." Then Peter went outside and cried painfully.

JESUS IS TAKEN TO PILATE

27

[1]Early the next morning, all the leading priests and older leaders of the people decided that Jesus should die. [2]They tied him, led him away, and turned him over to Pilate, the governor.

JUDAS KILLS HIMSELF

[3]Judas, the one who had given Jesus to his enemies, saw that they had decided to kill Jesus. Then he was very sorry for what he had done. So he took the thirty silver coins back to the priests and the leaders, [4]saying, "I sinned; I handed over to you an innocent man."

The leaders answered, "What is that to us? That's your problem, not ours."

[5]So Judas threw the money into the Temple. Then he went off and hanged himself.

[6]The leading priests picked up the silver coins in the Temple and said, "Our law does not allow us to keep this money with the Temple money, because it has paid for a man's death." [7]So they decided to use the coins to buy Potter's Field as a place to bury strangers who died in Jerusalem. [8]That is why that field is still called the Field of Blood. [9]So what Jeremiah the prophet had said came true: "They took thirty silver coins. That is how little the Israelites thought he was worth. [10]They used those

On the Edge

I sinned; I handed over to you an innocent man (Matt. 27:4).

When Judas found out that the Jewish leaders intended to have Jesus executed, it was like a lightbulb came on in his head. He suddenly realized what he had done—the simple kiss that had earned him thirty silver coins was going to cost Jesus his life. Judas knew that Jesus was innocent of all the charges the Jews brought against him, and they were going to kill him anyway.

But Jesus wasn't just innocent under the man-made law of the land; he was also innocent in God's eyes. He *literally* never did anything wrong. And his innocence wasn't just a natural thing because he was God's Son. He still had to make choices. Meanwhile Satan did all he could to convince Jesus not to choose God's way. Hebrews 4:15 says, "For our high priest is able to understand our weaknesses. When he lived on earth, he was tempted in every way that we are, but he did not sin."

Because Jesus is innocent, his blood is an acceptable sacrifice to God for your sins. And because he didn't give in to temptation, he paved the way for you to stand up to Satan's tricks, because his Spirit lives in you. When you do sin, confess, repent, and ask his forgiveness and Jesus will declare you innocent, too.

SEE FOR YOURSELF:
Luke 23:14-15;
2 Cor. 5:21;
Heb. 4:15

thirty silver coins to buy the potter's field, as
the Lord commanded me."[n]

PILATE QUESTIONS JESUS

11Jesus stood before Pilate the governor, and
Pilate asked him, "Are you the king of the
Jews?"
Jesus answered, "Those are your words."
12When the leading priests and the older
leaders accused Jesus, he said nothing.
13So Pilate said to Jesus, "Don't you hear
them accusing you of all these things?"
14But Jesus said nothing in answer to Pilate,
and Pilate was very surprised at this.

PILATE TRIES TO FREE JESUS

15Every year at the time of Passover the governor would free one prisoner whom the people chose. 16At that time there was a man in
prison, named Barabbas, who was known to be
very bad. 17When the people gathered at Pilate's
house, Pilate said, "Whom do you want me to
set free: Barabbas or Jesus who is called the
Christ?" 18Pilate knew that the people turned
Jesus in to him because they were jealous.
19While Pilate was sitting there on the judge's
seat, his wife sent this message to him: "Don't
do anything to that man, because he is innocent. Today I had a dream about him, and it
troubled me very much."
20But the leading priests and older leaders
convinced the crowd to ask for Barabbas to be
freed and for Jesus to be killed.
21Pilate said, "I have Barabbas and Jesus.
Which do you want me to set free for you?"
The people answered, "Barabbas."
22Pilate asked, "So what should I do with
Jesus, the one called the Christ?"
They all answered, "Crucify him!"
23Pilate asked, "Why? What wrong has he
done?"
But they shouted louder, "Crucify him!"
24When Pilate saw that he could do nothing
about this and that a riot was starting, he took
some water and washed his hands[n] in front of
the crowd. Then he said, "I am not guilty of
this man's death. You are the ones who are
causing it!"
25All the people answered, "We and our
children will be responsible for his death."

WHAT'S IT MEAN?

Pontius Pilate was the Roman governor of Judea and Samaria from A.D. 26 to 36. Pilate lived in Samaria, so you may be wondering what he was doing in Jerusalem. He and his troops were in town for the Passover feast to prevent rioting among the thousands of Jews who had traveled to the city for the annual holiday.

Matthew 27:11–14

27:9–10 "They . . . commanded me." See Zechariah 11:12-13 and Jeremiah 32:6-9. **27:24 washed his hands** He did this as a sign to show that he wanted no part in what the people did.

26Then he set Barabbas free. But Jesus was beaten with whips and handed over to the soldiers to be crucified.

27The governor's soldiers took Jesus into the governor's palace, and they all gathered around him. 28They took off his clothes and put a red robe on him. 29Using thorny branches, they made a crown, put it on his head, and put a stick in his right hand. Then the soldiers bowed before Jesus and made fun of him, saying, "Hail, King of the Jews!" 30They spat on Jesus. Then they took his stick and began to beat him on the head. 31After they finished, the soldiers took off the robe and put his own clothes on him again. Then they led him away to be crucified.

JESUS IS CRUCIFIED

32As the soldiers were going out of the city with Jesus, they forced a man from Cyrene, named Simon, to carry the cross for Jesus. 33They all came to the place called Golgotha, which means the Place of the Skull. 34The soldiers gave Jesus wine mixed with gall[n] to drink. He tasted the wine but refused to drink it. 35When the soldiers had crucified him, they threw lots to decide who would get his clothes. 36The soldiers sat there and continued watching him. 37They put a sign above Jesus' head with a charge against him. It said: THIS IS JESUS, THE KING OF THE JEWS. 38Two robbers were crucified beside Jesus, one on the right and the other on the left. 39People walked by and insulted Jesus and shook their heads, 40saying, "You said you could destroy the Temple and build it again in three days. So save yourself! Come down from that cross if you are really the Son of God!"

41The leading priests, the teachers of the law, and the older Jewish leaders were also making fun of Jesus. 42They said, "He saved others, but he can't save himself! He says he is the king of Israel! If he is the king, let him come down now from the cross. Then we will believe in him. 43He trusts in God, so let God save him now, if God really wants him. He himself said, 'I am the Son of God.' " 44And in the same way, the robbers who were being crucified beside Jesus also insulted him.

JESUS DIES

45At noon the whole country became dark, and the darkness lasted for three hours. 46About three o'clock Jesus cried out in a loud voice, "Eli, Eli, lama sabachthani?" This means, "My God, my God, why have you rejected me?"

47Some of the people standing there who heard this said, "He is calling Elijah."

48Quickly one of them ran and got a sponge and filled it with vinegar and tied it to a stick and gave it to Jesus to drink. 49But the others said, "Don't bother him. We want to see if Elijah will come to save him."

50But Jesus cried out again in a loud voice and died.

51Then the curtain in the Temple[n] was torn into two pieces, from the top to the bottom. Also, the earth shook and rocks broke apart. 52The graves opened, and many of God's people who had died were raised from the dead. 53They came out of the graves after Jesus was raised from the dead and went into the holy city, where they appeared to many people.

54When the army officer and the soldiers guarding Jesus saw this earthquake and everything else that happened, they were very frightened and said, "He really was the Son of God!"

55Many women who had followed Jesus from Galilee to help him were standing at a distance from the cross, watching. 56Mary Magdalene, and Mary the mother of James and Joseph, and the mother of James and John were there.

JESUS IS BURIED

57That evening a rich man named Joseph, a follower of Jesus from the town of Arimathea, came to Jerusalem. 58Joseph went to Pilate and asked to have Jesus' body. So Pilate gave orders for the soldiers to give it to Joseph. 59Then Joseph took the body and wrapped it in a clean linen cloth. 60He put Jesus' body in a new tomb that he had cut out of a wall of rock, and he rolled a very large stone to block the entrance of the tomb. Then Joseph went away. 61Mary Magdalene and the other woman named Mary were sitting near the tomb.

THE TOMB OF JESUS IS GUARDED

62The next day, the day after Preparation Day, the leading priests and the Pharisees went to Pilate. 63They said, "Sir, we remember that while that liar was still alive he said, 'After three days I will rise from the dead.' 64So give

27:34 gall Probably a drink of wine mixed with drugs to help a person feel less pain. **27:51 curtain in the Temple** A curtain divided the Most Holy Place from the other part of the Temple. That was the special building in Jerusalem where God commanded the Jewish people to worship him.

the order for the tomb to be guarded closely till
the third day. Otherwise, his followers might
come and steal the body and tell people that he
has risen from the dead. That lie would be
even worse than the first one."
65 Pilate said, "Take some soldiers and go
guard the tomb the best way you know." 66 So
they all went to the tomb and made it safe
from thieves by sealing the stone in the entrance and putting soldiers there to guard it.

JESUS RISES FROM THE DEAD

28
1 The day after the Sabbath day was the first
day of the week. At dawn on the first day,
Mary Magdalene and another woman named
Mary went to look at the tomb.
2 At that time there was a strong earthquake.
An angel of the Lord came down from heaven,
went to the tomb, and rolled the stone away
from the entrance. Then he sat on the stone.
3 He was shining as bright as lightning, and his
clothes were white as snow. 4 The soldiers
guarding the tomb shook with fear because of
the angel, and they became like dead men.
5 The angel said to the women, "Don't be
afraid. I know that you are looking for Jesus,
who has been crucified. 6 He is not here. He has
risen from the dead as he said he would. Come
and see the place where his body was. 7 And go
quickly and tell his followers, 'Jesus has risen
from the dead. He is going into Galilee ahead of
you, and you will see him there.' " Then the
angel said, "Now I have told you."
8 The women left the tomb quickly. They
were afraid, but they were also very happy.
They ran to tell Jesus' followers what had happened. 9 Suddenly, Jesus met them and said,
"Greetings." The women came up to him, took
hold of his feet, and worshiped him. 10 Then
Jesus said to them, "Don't be afraid. Go and tell
my followers to go on to Galilee, and they will
see me there."

THE SOLDIERS REPORT TO THE LEADERS

11 While the women went to tell Jesus' followers, some of the soldiers who had been
guarding the tomb went into the city to tell the
leading priests everything that had happened.
12 Then the priests met with the older leaders
and made a plan. They paid the soldiers a large
amount of money 13 and said to them, "Tell the
people that Jesus' followers came during the
night and stole the body while you were
asleep. 14 If the governor hears about this, we
will satisfy him and save you from trouble."
15 So the soldiers kept the money and did as
they were told. And that story is still spread
among the people even today.

JESUS TALKS TO HIS FOLLOWERS

16 The eleven followers went to Galilee to the
mountain where Jesus had told them
to go. 17 On the mountain
they saw Jesus and wor-
shiped him, but some of
them did not believe it was
really Jesus. 18 Then Jesus
came to them and said, "All
power in heaven and on
earth is given to me. 19 So go
and make followers of all people in the world.
Baptize them in the name of the
Father and the Son and the
Holy Spirit. 20 Teach them to
obey everything that I have
taught you, and I will be
with you always, even until
the end of this age."

On the Edge

So go and make followers of all people in the world. Baptize them in the name of the Father and the Son and the Holy Spirit (Matt. 28:19).

Notice what this verse is saying. It instructs us to go and make followers—not just converts, but followers in the same way of Jesus' first twelve. We want to do more than just see people give their hearts to the Lord. We want to help them mature and grow in him. Aren't you glad that someone helped you? When you gave your heart to Jesus, God didn't just throw you out and say, "Okay, you're on your own now."

If people are going to be developed, they have to be mentored in the growth of their faith. That's where *we* come in, *showing* them as well as *telling* them how to follow Christ. That's our job—to assist in spreading the Good News, to be totally devoted to God, and to stick to him like glue. We want to see people get saved and stick with it. Let's help our friends develop and grow so they can help others!

SEE FOR YOURSELF:
Mark 16:15–16;
Luke 24:46–47;
John 20:21;
Acts 5:42

WITNESSING

Is witnessing a command? (28:16–20)

LONELINESS

Are we ever alone? (28:20)

mark

CONTENT If Mark were making a movie of Jesus' life (rather than a book of the Bible), there would have been *no* good time to go to the lobby to get popcorn. It would have been an action movie all the way. In fact, Mark is famous for using the word *immediately*. Each time a "scene" ended, Jesus *immediately* headed for the next place.

Mark was writing his version of the Jesus' story for a particular audience, the Romans. The Romans didn't grow up reading the Old Testament, so they wouldn't care that Jesus fulfilled prophecy. The Romans were conquerors and soldiers. They would care about the miracles Jesus performed and the people he helped. Mark didn't write so much about what Jesus *said* as about what Jesus *did*.

But even though Mark's movie would have been an action movie, Jesus (as the hero) was very different from our heroes today. Jesus made a difference by helping people one-on-one. Jesus didn't wreck cars (or chariots) and beat up people. He made a difference with the power of his love.

Most of the Romans in Mark's town were probably in some kind of military service. Seeing Jesus in this light would have shown them a whole new way to live and lead, which is what Jesus came to do.

Outline

1:1–8 .... The Message of John the Baptist
1:9–13 .... The Baptism and Temptation of Jesus
1:14—9:50 .... Jesus in Galilee
10:1–52 .... Jesus Goes from Galilee to Jerusalem
11:1—15:47 .... Jesus' Last Week: His Trial and Death
16:1–8 .... Jesus Is Alive
16:9–20 .... Jesus Appears to His Followers

Purpose A relationship with God calls for complete commitment to doing his will.

Theme The Suffering Son of Man Who Is, in Fact, the Son of God

Date of writing 60s A.D.

"Then Jesus called the crowd to him, along with his followers. He said, 'If people want to follow me, they must give up the things they want. They must be willing even to give up their lives to follow me' " (8:34).

Bible Talk

Why Were There Romans in Israel?

Good question. Have you ever heard of the Roman Empire? Have you heard that phrase "All roads lead to Rome"? Mark was writing at a time when Rome controlled most of the world. That included Israel. When one country controls another country, they often send soldiers there to keep an eye on everything. When they do, you call that country "occupied." Israel was an "occupied" country, and it was "occupied" by the Romans. So, in terms of government, there was a lot of Roman input.

Many of the Hebrews resented the Romans. They wanted the Romans to go back to Rome and leave them alone. It says something about Mark that he would care enough about the Romans that he would write an account of Jesus' life so they could understand the significance of it.

JESUS THE SERVANT

Mark is famous for portraying Jesus as a servant. He highlights the fact that Jesus did not come into the world to change it through power and strength, but through gentleness and love. Mark tells stories of Jesus reaching out to the outcasts of society, the people that no one would even touch or go near. Mark tells stories of Jesus spending time with people who were considered lower class. Mark wanted his readers to know that they could count on Jesus to reach out to them rather than hitting them over the head in some power-hungry frenzy.

JOHN PREPARES FOR JESUS

1 1This is the beginning of the Good News
about Jesus Christ, the Son of God,[n] 2as the
prophet Isaiah wrote:

"I will send my messenger ahead of you,
who will prepare your way." *Malachi 3:1*
3"This is a voice of one
who calls out in the desert:
'Prepare the way for the Lord.
Make the road straight for him.'" *Isaiah 40:3*

4John was baptizing people in the desert
and preaching a baptism of changed hearts
and lives for the forgiveness of sins. 5All the
people from Judea and Jerusalem were going
out to him. They confessed their sins and were
baptized by him in the Jordan River. 6John
wore clothes made from camel's hair, had a
leather belt around his waist, and ate locusts
and wild honey. 7This is what John preached
to the people: "There is one coming after me
who is greater than I; I am not good enough
even to kneel down and untie his sandals. 8I
baptize you with water, but he will baptize you
with the Holy Spirit."

JESUS IS BAPTIZED

9At that time Jesus came from the town of
Nazareth in Galilee and was baptized by John
in the Jordan River. 10Immediately, as Jesus was
coming up out of the water, he saw heaven
open. The Holy Spirit came down on him like a
dove, 11and a voice came from heaven: "You
are my Son, whom I love, and I am very
pleased with you."

12Then the Spirit sent Jesus into the desert.
13He was in the desert forty days and was
tempted by Satan. He was with the wild animals, and the angels came and took care of
him.

JESUS CHOOSES SOME FOLLOWERS

14After John was put in prison, Jesus went
into Galilee, preaching the Good News from
God. 15He said, "The right time has come. The
kingdom of God is near. Change your hearts
and lives and believe the Good News!"

16When Jesus was walking by Lake Galilee,
he saw Simon[n] and his brother Andrew
throwing a net into the lake because they were
fishermen. 17Jesus said to them, "Come follow
me, and I will make you fish for people." 18So
Simon and Andrew immediately left their nets
and followed him.

19Going a little farther, Jesus saw two more
brothers, James and John, the sons of Zebedee.
They were in a boat, mending their nets.
20Jesus immediately called them, and they left
their father in the boat with the hired workers
and followed Jesus.

JESUS FORCES OUT AN EVIL SPIRIT

21Jesus and his followers went to Capernaum. On the Sabbath day He went to the synagogue and began to teach. 22The people were
amazed at his teaching, because he taught like
a person who had authority, not like their

On the Edge

Immediately, as Jesus was coming up out of the water, he saw heaven open. The Holy Spirit came down on him like a dove, and a voice came from heaven: "You are my Son, whom I love, and I am very pleased with you" (Mark 1:10–11).

Where are you from? In what part of the world were you raised? One of the first things we ask a stranger is, "Where are you from?" Knowing where someone is from tells us a lot about him or her—why he/she has an accent, what kind of climate he/she's used to, which sports teams he/she might like the most. We can ask questions about favorite foods and whether he or she knows the one person we know from his/her city.

The Son of God is from heaven, and there is so much we can know about him because we know where he's from. He comes from the place reserved for the King of kings. He has been there with God the Father and God the Holy Spirit from the very beginning. Heaven is God's home and the place he created for those who know him. To live in heaven is an honor—a gift to those who accept Jesus here on earth.

In heaven, the Lord is continually being praised by the angels. There is no sickness or sadness there. We know that Jesus is royal, perfect, and worthy of our praise because he has come from the perfect place of heaven. He has walked among us, but he is not from around here. His righteousness and holiness give him away. He is from heaven.

SEE FOR YOURSELF:
Matt. 3:16–17; John 1:1; Acts 10:38; Rev. 21:4

1:1 the Son of God Some Greek copies omit these words. **1:16 Simon** Simon's other name was Peter.

WHAT'S IT MEAN?

The Temple, the main worship center for the Jewish people, was located in Jerusalem. The problem was that many people lived too far from Jerusalem to go to the Temple regularly. What were these people supposed to do when they wanted to worship God and hear his Word read? Many of them built synagogues, local places of worship. Jesus and his followers were no strangers to the synagogue in Capernaum. Four of his followers—Simon Peter, Andrew, James, and John—were hometown boys.

Mark 1:21

teachers of the law.[23]Just then, a man was there
in the synagogue who had an evil spirit in him.
He shouted, [24]"Jesus of Nazareth! What do you
want with us? Did you come to destroy us? I
know who you are—God's Holy One!"
[25]Jesus commanded the evil spirit, "Be quiet!
Come out of the man!" [26]The evil spirit shook
the man violently, gave a loud cry, and then
came out of him.
[27]The people were so amazed they asked
each other, "What is happening here? This man
is teaching something new, and with authority.
He even gives commands to evil spirits, and
they obey him." [28]And the news about Jesus
spread quickly everywhere in the area of Galilee.

JESUS HEALS MANY PEOPLE

[29]As soon as Jesus and his followers left the
synagogue, they went with James and John to
the home of Simon[n] and Andrew. [30]Simon's
mother-in-law was sick in bed with a fever,
and the people told Jesus about her. [31]So Jesus
went to her bed, took her hand, and helped
her up. The fever left her, and she began serving them.
[32]That evening, after the
sun went down, the people
brought to Jesus all who were
sick and had demons in them.
[33]The whole town gathered at
the door. [34]Jesus healed many
who had different kinds of

DEMONS
Can demons hurt Jesus? (1:34)

1:29 Simon Simon's other name was Peter.

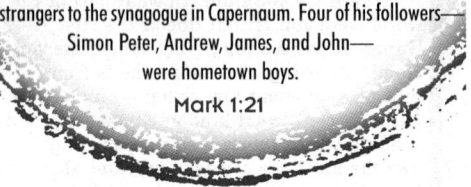

Promise HE PROMISES TO BRING GOOD NEWS.

Jesus answered, "We should go to other towns around here so I can preach there too. That is the reason I came" (Mark 1:38).

Not too long after Jesus started traveling around telling people about God's kingdom, he visited his hometown. On the Sabbath, he went to the local synagogue, where someone asked him to read from the Scriptures. He read from the Book of Isaiah: "'The Lord has put his Spirit in me, because he appointed me to tell the Good News to the poor. He has sent me to tell the captives they are free and to tell the blind that they can see again. God sent me to free those who have been treated unfairly and to announce the time when the Lord will show his kindness.' Jesus closed the book, gave it back to the assistant, and sat down. Everyone in the synagogue was watching Jesus closely. He began to say to them, 'While you heard these words just now, they were coming true!'" (Luke 4:16–21).

Jesus wanted the people to know that what seemed impossible was possible with God. When matters seemed hopeless, God was able to turn things around.

Jesus knew why he was on earth and put his whole heart into fulfilling the purpose God had given him. That's still his purpose today. What he came to earth to do then in the flesh, his Word and his Spirit continue to do today. Be serious about reading his Word. If you want to know what Jesus said when he lived on earth, read Matthew, Mark, Luke, and John. See what good news he has for you!

SEE FOR YOURSELF:
Matt. 4:23; 9:35; Luke 4:18–19; 20:1

sicknesses, and he forced many demons to
leave people. But he would not allow the demons to speak, because they knew who he
was.
[35]Early the next morning, while it was still
dark, Jesus woke and left the house. He went to
a lonely place, where he prayed. [36]Simon and
his friends went to look for Jesus. [37]When they
found him, they said, "Everyone is looking for
you!"
[38]Jesus answered, "We should go to other
towns around here so I can preach there too.
That is the reason I came." [39]So he went everywhere in Galilee, preaching in the synagogues
and forcing out demons.

JESUS HEALS A SICK MAN

[40]A man with a skin disease came to Jesus.
He fell to his knees and begged Jesus, "You can
heal me if you will."
[41]Jesus felt sorry for the man, so he reached
out his hand and touched him and said, "I will.
Be healed!" [42]Immediately the disease left the
man, and he was healed.
[43]Jesus told the man to go away at once, but
he warned him strongly, [44]"Don't tell anyone
about this. But go and show yourself to the
priest. And offer the gift Moses commanded
for people who are made well.[n] This will show
the people what I have done." [45]The man left
there, but he began to tell everyone that Jesus
had healed him, and so he spread the news
about Jesus. As a result, Jesus could not enter a
town if people saw him. He stayed in places
where nobody lived, but people came to him
from everywhere.

JESUS HEALS A PARALYZED MAN

2
[1]A few days later, when Jesus came back to
Capernaum, the news spread that he was at
home. [2]Many people gathered together so that
there was no room in the house, not even outside the door. And Jesus was teaching them
God's message. [3]Four people came, carrying a
paralyzed man. [4]Since they could not get to
Jesus because of the crowd, they dug a hole in
the roof right above where he was speaking.
When they got through, they lowered the mat
with the paralyzed man on it. [5]When Jesus saw
the faith of these people, he said to the paralyzed man, "Young man, your sins are forgiven."
[6]Some of the teachers of the law were sitting
there, thinking to themselves, [7]"Why does this
man say things like that? He is speaking as if he
were God. Only God can forgive sins."
[8]Jesus knew immediately what these teachers of the law were thinking. So he said to
them, "Why are you thinking these things?
[9]Which is easier: to tell this paralyzed man,
'Your sins are forgiven,' or to tell him, 'Stand
up. Take your mat and walk'? [10]But I will prove
to you that the Son of Man has authority on

On the Edge

Why does this man say things like that? He is speaking as if he were God. Only God can forgive sins (Mark 2:7).

Has anyone ever done something wrong to you, and instead of apologizing and making it right, he or she tried to correct his/her wrong by doing something nice for you? How did that make you feel? Really, you just wanted an apology, right?

Well, sometimes we do that to God. There are a lot of people who believe they can work their way to heaven or that God will love them more if they do enough things for him. They believe they'll be rewarded because of their good deeds. It just doesn't work that way, and these thoughts will get people into trouble. There are still others who take it to the other extreme.

These are the kind of people who believe they have to suffer just like Jesus did, so they beat themselves with whips, crawl across glass, and even hang on crosses for hours at a time in order to receive forgiveness. Both of these ways are false.

God, and God alone, is the only Person who can forgive. You can't get his forgiveness from your parents or from the people you hang out with. Sure, they can (and should) forgive your shortcomings by not holding them against you, but only God can erase them from your record permanently. All you have to do is confess your sins to him and repent and—instantly—they're gone forever.

Confess your sins to the Lord today. He's the only One who can get rid of them for you!

SEE FOR YOURSELF:
Matt. 9:6; Mark 2:10–11; Luke 5:20, 24; Eph. 2:8–9

1:44 Moses . . . well Read about this in Leviticus 14:1-32.

earth to forgive sins." So Jesus said to the paralyzed man, 11"I tell you, stand up, take your
mat, and go home." 12Immediately the paralyzed man stood up, took his mat, and walked
out while everyone was watching him.
The people were amazed and praised God.
They said, "We have never seen anything like
this!"
13Jesus went to the lake again. The whole
crowd followed him there, and he taught them.
14While he was walking along, he saw a man
named Levi son of Alphaeus, sitting in the tax
collector's booth. Jesus said to him, "Follow
me," and he stood up and followed Jesus.
15Later, as Jesus was having dinner at Levi's
house, many tax collectors and "sinners" were
eating there with Jesus and his followers. Many
people like this followed Jesus. 16When the
teachers of the law who were Pharisees saw
Jesus eating with the tax collectors and "sinners,"
they asked his followers, "Why does he eat with
tax collectors and sinners?"

WHAT'S IT MEAN?

You name it, and the Roman Empire probably charged a tax for it. The Jews expected to be taxed for everything they did, whether it was buying property or worshiping at the Temple. To collect these outrageous taxes, the Romans hired local Jewish citizens. These collectors were known for charging their fellow Jews more money than they really owed and keeping the extra cash for themselves. Because of this, and because the collectors worked for the hated Roman government, tax collectors were usually seen as traitors to their people.

Mark 2:16

17Jesus heard this and said to them, "It is not
the healthy people who need a doctor, but the
sick. I did not come to invite good people but
to invite sinners."

JESUS' FOLLOWERS ARE CRITICIZED

18Now the followers of John[n] and the Pharisees often gave up eating for a certain time.[n]
Some people came to Jesus and said, "Why do
John's followers and the followers of the Pharisees often give up eating, but your followers
don't?"
19Jesus answered, "The friends of the bridegroom do not give up eating while the bridegroom is still with them. As long as the
bridegroom is with them, they cannot give up
eating. 20But the time will come when the
bridegroom will be taken from them, and then
they will give up eating.
21"No one sews a patch of unshrunk cloth
over a hole in an old coat. Otherwise, the patch
will shrink and pull away—the new patch will

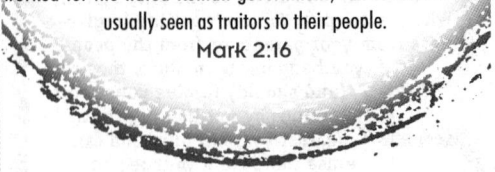

On the Edge

Jesus heard this and said to them, "It is not the healthy people who need a doctor, but the sick. I did not come to invite good people but to invite sinners" (Mark 2:17).

The Pharisees didn't understand what Jesus was all about. For one thing, he hung out with people they would have crossed the street to avoid. The Pharisees thought they were way too holy to rub elbows with those people.

What Jesus said to them is like music to your ears if you think you've done such horrible things that God could never love you. He lets you know right off the bat that he's more interested in changing sinners than in recruiting good, religious people to his cause.

But does that mean that Jesus isn't interested in you if you haven't gotten messed up in sex or drugs or haven't broken the law? Not at all. When he said he wasn't inviting "the righteous," he was talking about the attitude in people's hearts. People who consider themselves good, like the Pharisees, don't think they need Jesus. People who know they are sinners—whether their sins are obvious to everyone or the invisible sins of the heart—know they need Jesus. He welcomes them with open arms.

SEE FOR YOURSELF:
Matt. 9:12–13; Luke 5:31–32; 19:10

2:18 John John the Baptist, who preached to the Jewish people about Christ's coming (Mark 1:4-8).
2:18 gave . . . time This is called "fasting." The people would give up eating for a special time of prayer and worship to God. It was also done to show sadness and disappointment.

pull away from the old coat. Then the hole will
be worse. 22 Also, no one ever pours new wine
into old leather bags. Otherwise, the new wine
will break the bags, and the wine will be ruined
along with the bags. But new wine should be
put into new leather bags."

JESUS IS LORD OF THE SABBATH

23 One Sabbath day, as Jesus was walking
through some fields of grain, his followers began to pick some grain to eat. 24 The Pharisees
said to Jesus, "Why are your followers doing
what is not lawful on the Sabbath day?"

25 Jesus answered, "Have you never read
what David did when he and those with him
were hungry and needed food? 26 During the
time of Abiathar the high priest, David went
into God's house and ate the holy bread,
which is lawful only for priests to eat. And
David also gave some of the bread to those
who were with him."

27 Then Jesus said to the Pharisees, "The Sabbath day was made to help people; they were
not made to be ruled by the Sabbath day. 28 So
then, the Son of Man is Lord even of the Sabbath day."

JESUS HEALS A MAN'S HAND

3 1 Another time when Jesus went into a synagogue, a man with a crippled hand was there.
2 Some people watched Jesus closely to see if he
would heal the man on the Sabbath day so
they could accuse him.

3 Jesus said to the man with the crippled
hand, "Stand up here in the middle of everyone."

4 Then Jesus asked the people, "Which is lawful on the Sabbath day: to do good or to do
evil, to save a life or to kill?" But they said nothing to answer him.

5 Jesus was angry as he looked at the people,
and he felt very sad because they were stubborn. Then he said to the man, "Hold out your
hand." The man held out his hand and it was
healed. 6 Then the Pharisees left and began
making plans with the Herodians[n] about a
way to kill Jesus.

MANY PEOPLE FOLLOW JESUS

7 Jesus left with his followers for the lake,
and a large crowd from Galilee followed him.
8 Also many people came from Judea, from Jerusalem, from Idumea, from the lands across
the Jordan River, and from the area of Tyre and
Sidon. When they heard what Jesus was doing,
many people came to him. 9 When Jesus saw
the crowds, he told his followers to get a boat
ready for him to keep people from crowding
against him. 10 He had healed many people, so
all the sick were pushing toward him to touch
him. 11 When evil spirits saw Jesus, they fell
down before him and shouted, "You are the
Son of God!" 12 But Jesus strongly warned them
not to tell who he was.

JESUS CHOOSES HIS TWELVE APOSTLES

13 Then Jesus went up on a mountain and
called to him the men he wanted, and they
came to him. 14 Jesus chose twelve men and
called them apostles. He wanted them to be
with him, and he wanted to send them out to
preach 15 and to have the authority to force demons out of people. 16 These are the twelve
men he chose: Simon (Jesus named him Peter),
17 James and John, the sons of Zebedee (Jesus
named them Boanerges, which means "Sons of
Thunder"), 18 Andrew, Philip, Bartholomew,
Matthew, Thomas, James the son of Alphaeus,
Thaddaeus, Simon the Zealot, 19 and Judas Iscariot, who later turned against Jesus.

SOME PEOPLE SAY JESUS HAS A DEVIL

20 Then Jesus went home, but again a crowd
gathered. There were so many people that
Jesus and his followers could not eat. 21 When
his family heard this, they went to get him because they thought he was out of his mind.
22 But the teachers of the law from Jerusalem
were saying, "Beelzebul is living inside him! He

WHAT'S IT MEAN?

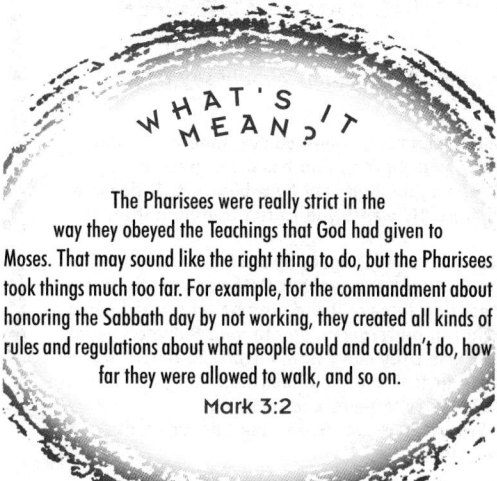

The Pharisees were really strict in the way they obeyed the Teachings that God had given to Moses. That may sound like the right thing to do, but the Pharisees took things much too far. For example, for the commandment about honoring the Sabbath day by not working, they created all kinds of rules and regulations about what people could and couldn't do, how far they were allowed to walk, and so on.

Mark 3:2

3:6 Herodians A political group that followed Herod and his family.

WHAT'S IT MEAN?

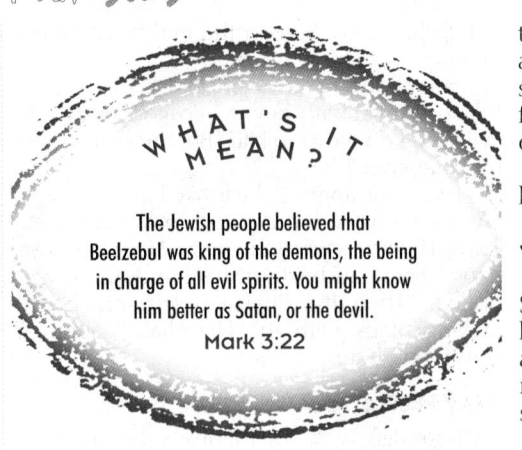

The Jewish people believed that Beelzebul was king of the demons, the being in charge of all evil spirits. You might know him better as Satan, or the devil.
Mark 3:22

uses power from the ruler of demons to force
demons out of people."
23So Jesus called the people together and
taught them with stories. He said, "Satan will
not force himself out of people. 24A kingdom
that is divided cannot continue, 25and a family
that is divided cannot continue. 26And if Satan
is against himself and fights against his own
people, he cannot continue; that is the end of
Satan. 27No one can enter a strong person's
house and steal his things unless he first ties up
the strong person. Then he can steal things
from the house. 28I tell you the truth, all sins
that people do and all the things people say
against God can be forgiven. 29But anyone who
speaks against the Holy Spirit will never be
forgiven; he is guilty of a sin that continues forever."
30Jesus said this because the teachers of the
law said that he had an evil spirit inside him.

JESUS' TRUE FAMILY

31Then Jesus' mother and brothers arrived.
Standing outside, they sent someone in to tell
him to come out. 32Many people were sitting
around Jesus, and they said to him, "Your
mother and brothers are waiting for you outside."
33Jesus asked, "Who are my mother and my
brothers?" 34Then he looked at those sitting
around him and said, "Here are my mother
and my brothers! 35My true brother and sister
and mother are those who do what God
wants."

A STORY ABOUT PLANTING SEED

4 1Again Jesus began teaching by the lake. A
great crowd gathered around him, so he sat
down in a boat near the shore. All the people
stayed on the shore close to the water. 2Jesus
taught them many things, using stories. He
said, 3"Listen! A farmer went out to plant his
seed. 4While he was planting, some seed fell by

Promise HE PROMISES ANYTHING CAN BE FORGIVEN.

I tell you the truth, all sins that people do and all the things people say against God can be forgiven (Mark 3:28).

Be encouraged! It doesn't matter what you've done in the past, where you've done it, or who you've done it with. God loves you and wants to forgive you. In fact, God has more grace than you can imagine. You may *feel* like you've blown it, and then again, you may *have* blown it. It doesn't matter. Jesus is more than ready to give you a fresh start. He wants you to run to him, not away from him!

Remember when David blew it with Bathsheba? Then he blew it again by having her husband killed. David kept messing up trying to cover his sin. God sent the prophet Nathan to confront him. David's eyes were finally opened, and he repented. God forgave David, and he later was known as the kind of man God wants (Acts 13:22). If David can be forgiven, so can you. But the key is this: David repented. He didn't just apologize. He was truly sorry in his heart. To repent means to turn from sin and go the other direction. Whatever it is that you need to be forgiven for, give it to God right now. Ask for forgiveness: Tell him you're sorry, repent, and move on.

Even good people may fall many times, but they will get back up! God is the One who will always forgive, no matter what you've done. He loves you!

SEE FOR YOURSELF:

Ps. 51; Prov. 24:16; Jer. 33:8; Ezek. 36:25–27; Titus 2:14; 1 John 1:7, 9

On the Edge

My true brother and sister and mother are those who do what God wants (Mark 3:35).

Did you know that you belong to the family of Christ? You are a brother or sister of the Lord himself; and, as a member of his family, you are royal and privileged. Because you are a brother or sister of Christ, you are perfectly cared for and protected. Your earthly family may fall short, but this family will never let you down. Some students don't know who they belong to. They aren't living like brothers and sisters of Christ, because his true brothers and sisters don't abuse their bodies, don't abuse people, and don't abuse privileges. They don't need an alternative lifestyle, because they have been promised an eternal lifestyle. Maybe you've been living like the rest of the world because you didn't know about your family—a family of grace, but a family of conviction and strong character. You are called to carry on the heritage of the family of Christ.

SEE FOR YOURSELF:
Matt. 12:48; 23:8

the road, and the birds came and ate it up.
5Some seed fell on rocky ground where there
wasn't much dirt. That seed grew very fast, because the ground was not deep. 6But when the
sun rose, the plants dried up because they did
not have deep roots. 7Some other seed fell
among thorny weeds, which grew and choked
the good plants. So those plants did not produce a crop. 8Some other seed fell on good
ground and began to grow. It got taller and
produced a crop. Some plants made thirty
times more, some made sixty times more, and
some made a hundred times more."
9Then Jesus said, "You people who can hear
me, listen!"

JESUS TELLS WHY HE USED STORIES

10Later, when Jesus was alone, the twelve
apostles and others around him asked him
about the stories.
11Jesus said, "You can know the secret about
the kingdom of God. But to other people I tell
everything by using stories 12so that:

'They will look and look, but they will not
learn.
They will listen and listen, but they will
not understand.
If they did learn and understand,
they would come back to me and be
forgiven.' " *Isaiah 6:9-10*

JESUS EXPLAINS THE SEED STORY

13Then Jesus said to his followers, "Don't
you understand this story? If you don't, how
will you understand any story? 14The farmer is
like a person who plants God's message in people. 15Sometimes the teaching falls on the road.
This is like the people who hear the teaching of
God, but Satan quickly comes and takes away
the teaching that was planted in them. 16Others
are like the seed planted on rocky ground. They
hear the teaching and quickly accept it with
joy. 17But since they don't allow the teaching to
go deep into their lives, they keep it only a
short time. When trouble or persecution comes
because of the teaching they accepted, they
quickly give up. 18Others are like the seed
planted among the thorny weeds. They hear
the teaching, 19but the worries of this life, the
temptation of wealth, and many other evil desires keep the teaching from growing and producing fruit[n] in their lives. 20Others are like the
seed planted in the good ground. They hear
the teaching and accept it. Then they grow and
produce fruit—sometimes thirty times more,
sometimes sixty times more, and sometimes a
hundred times more."

USE WHAT YOU HAVE

21Then Jesus said to them, "Do you hide a
lamp under a bowl or under a bed? No! You
put the lamp on a lampstand. 22Everything that
is hidden will be made clear and every secret
thing will be made known. 23You people who
can hear me, listen!
24"Think carefully about what you hear. The
way you give to others is the way God will give
to you, but God will give you even more.
25Those who have understanding will be given
more. But those who do not have understanding, even what they have will be taken away
from them."

JESUS USES A STORY ABOUT SEED

26Then Jesus said, "The kingdom of God is
like someone who plants seed in the ground.
27Night and day, whether the person is asleep
or awake, the seed still grows, but the person

4:19 producing fruit To produce fruit means to have in your life the good things God wants.

does not know how it grows. 28By itself the
earth produces grain. First the plant grows,
then the head, and then all the grain in the
head. 29When the grain is ready, the farmer
cuts it, because this is the harvest time."

A STORY ABOUT MUSTARD SEED

30Then Jesus said, "How can I show you
what the kingdom of God is like? What story
can I use to explain it? 31The kingdom of God is
like a mustard seed, the smallest seed you plant in
the ground. 32But when planted, this seed grows
and becomes the largest of all garden plants. It
produces large branches, and the wild birds can
make nests in its shade."

WHAT'S IT MEAN?

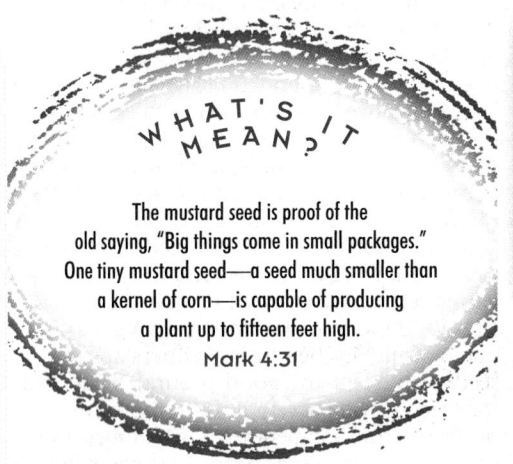

The mustard seed is proof of the old saying, "Big things come in small packages." One tiny mustard seed—a seed much smaller than a kernel of corn—is capable of producing a plant up to fifteen feet high.

Mark 4:31

On the Edge

Jesus used many stories like these to teach the crowd God's message—as much as they could understand. He always used stories to teach them (Mark 4:33–34a).

Think back to last week's sermon at church. Maybe your mind wandered for part of the time, but what made you look up and really listen? The story. Maybe it was funny, maybe tragic, but you were definitely listening. The pastor had your attention. Jesus was a great communicator. He knew that people love to listen to stories. He told the deep and incredible truths of his kingdom in the form of stories so that the people could understand what he was really saying. People listened to his stories and then retold them to their friends. Read the stories of Jesus and hear the truth he is speaking to you.

SEE FOR YOURSELF:
Matt. 13:13, 34–35

33Jesus used many stories like these to teach
the crowd God's message—as much as they
could understand. 34He always used stories to
teach them. But when he and his followers
were alone, Jesus explained everything to
them.

JESUS CALMS A STORM

35That evening, Jesus said to his followers,
"Let's go across the lake." 36Leaving the crowd
behind, they took him in the boat just as he
was. There were also other boats with them.
37A very strong wind came up on the lake. The
waves came over the sides and into the boat so
that it was already full of water. 38Jesus was at
the back of the boat, sleeping with his head on
a cushion. His followers woke him and said,
"Teacher, don't you care that we are drowning!"
39Jesus stood up and commanded the wind
and said to the waves, "Quiet! Be still!" Then the
wind stopped, and it became completely calm.
40Jesus said to his followers, "Why are you
afraid? Do you still have no faith?"
41The followers were very afraid and asked
each other, "Who is this? Even the wind and
the waves obey him!"

A MAN WITH DEMONS INSIDE HIM

5 1Jesus and his followers went to the other
side of the lake to the area of the Gerasene
people. 2When Jesus got out of the boat, instantly a man with an evil spirit came to him
from the burial caves. 3This man lived in the
caves, and no one could tie him up, not even
with a chain. 4Many times people had used
chains to tie the man's hands and feet,
but he always broke them off.
No one was strong enough to
control him. 5Day and night
he would wander around the
burial caves and on the hills,
screaming and cutting himself
with stones. 6While Jesus was
still far away, the man saw him, ran to him,
and fell down before him.

DEMONS

What can demons do to people? (5:2–5)

7The man shouted in a loud voice, "What
do you want with me, Jesus, Son of the Most
High God? I command you in God's name not
to torture me!" 8He said this because Jesus was
saying to him, "You evil spirit, come out of the
man."

[9]Then Jesus asked him, "What is your
name?"
He answered, "My name is Legion,[n] because
we are many spirits." [10]He begged Jesus again
and again not to send them out of that area.
[11]A large herd of pigs was feeding on a hill
near there. [12]The demons begged Jesus, "Send
us into the pigs; let us go into them." [13]So Jesus
allowed them to do this. The evil spirits left the
man and went into the pigs. Then the herd of
pigs—about two thousand of them—rushed
down the hill into the lake and were drowned.
[14]The herdsmen ran away and went to the
town and to the countryside, telling everyone
about this. So people went out to see what had
happened. [15]They came to Jesus and saw the
man who used to have the many evil spirits,
sitting, clothed, and in his right mind. And they
were frightened. [16]The people who saw this
told the others what had happened to the man
who had the demons living in him, and they
told about the pigs. [17]Then the
people began to beg Jesus to
leave their area.
[18]As Jesus was getting
back into the boat, the man
who was freed from the demons begged to go with
him.
[19]But Jesus would not let
him. He said, "Go home to
your family and tell them
how much the Lord has done
for you and how he has had mer-
cy on you." [20]So the man left and began to
tell the people in the Ten Towns[n] about what
Jesus had done for him. And everyone was
amazed.

> "Go home to your family and tell them how much the Lord has done for you and how he has had mercy on you."
> (Mark 5:19b)

JESUS GIVES LIFE TO A DEAD GIRL AND HEALS A SICK WOMAN

[21]When Jesus went in the boat back to the
other side of the lake, a large crowd gathered
around him there. [22]A leader of the synagogue,
named Jairus, came there, saw Jesus, and fell at
his feet. [23]He begged Jesus, saying again and
again, "My daughter is dying. Please come and
put your hands on her so she will be healed
and will live." [24]So Jesus went with him.
A large crowd followed Jesus and pushed
very close around him. [25]Among them was a
woman who had been bleeding for twelve
years. [26]She had suffered very much from
many doctors and had spent all the money she
had, but instead of improving, she was getting
worse. [27]When the woman heard about Jesus,
she came up behind him in the crowd and
touched his coat. [28]She thought, "If I can just
touch his clothes, I will be healed." [29]Instantly
her bleeding stopped, and she felt in her body
that she was healed from her disease.
[30]At once Jesus felt power go out from him.
So he turned around in the crowd and asked,
"Who touched my clothes?"
[31]His followers said, "Look at how many
people are pushing against you! And you ask,
'Who touched me?' "
[32]But Jesus continued looking around to see
who had touched him. [33]The woman, knowing
that she was healed, came and fell at Jesus' feet.
Shaking with fear, she told him the whole truth.
[34]Jesus said to her, "Dear woman, you are made
well because you believed. Go in peace; be
healed of your disease."
[35]While Jesus was still speaking, some people came from
the house of the synagogue
leader. They said, "Your
daughter is dead. There is no
need to bother the teacher
anymore."
[36]But Jesus paid no at-
tention to what they said.
He told the synagogue
leader, "Don't be afraid; just
believe."
[37]Jesus let only Peter, James,
and John the brother of James go with
him. [38]When they came to the house of the
synagogue leader, Jesus found many people
there making lots of noise and crying loudly.
[39]Jesus entered the house and said to them,
"Why are you crying and making so much
noise? The child is not dead, only asleep." [40]But
they laughed at him. So, after throwing them
out of the house, Jesus took the child's father
and mother and his three followers into the
room where the child was. [41]Taking hold of
the girl's hand, he said to her, "Talitha, koum!"
(This means, "Young girl, I tell you to stand
up!") [42]At once the girl stood right up and began walking. (She was twelve years old.)
Everyone was completely amazed. [43]Jesus gave
them strict orders not to tell people about this.
Then he told them to give the girl something to
eat.

5:9 Legion Means very many. A legion was about five thousand men in the Roman army.
5:20 Ten Towns In Greek, called "Decapolis." It was an area east of Lake Galilee that once had ten main towns.

JESUS GOES TO HIS HOMETOWN

6 [1]Jesus left there and went to his hometown,
and his followers went with him. [2]On the Sabbath day he taught in the synagogue. Many
people heard him and were amazed, saying,
"Where did this man get these teachings? What
is this wisdom that has been given to him?
And where did he get the power to do miracles? [3]He is just the carpenter, the son of Mary
and the brother of James, Joseph, Judas, and
Simon. And his sisters are here with us." So the
people were upset with Jesus.
[4]Jesus said to them, "A prophet is honored
everywhere except in his hometown and with
his own people and in his own home." [5]So
Jesus was not able to work any miracles there
except to heal a few sick people by putting his
hands on them. [6]He was amazed at how many
people had no faith.

Then Jesus went to other villages in that
area and taught. [7]He called his twelve followers
together and got ready to send them out two
by two and gave them authority over evil spirits. [8]This is what Jesus commanded them: "Take
nothing for your trip except a walking stick.
Take no bread, no bag, and no money in your
pockets. [9]Wear sandals, but take only the
clothes you are wearing. [10]When you enter a
house, stay there until you leave that town. [11]If
the people in a certain place refuse to welcome
you or listen to you, leave that place. Shake its
dust off your feet[n] as a warning to them."
[12]So the followers went out and preached
that people should change their hearts and
lives. [13]They forced many demons out and put
olive oil on many sick people and healed them.

HOW JOHN THE BAPTIST WAS KILLED

[14]King Herod heard about Jesus, because he
was now well known. Some people said, "He is
John the Baptist, who has risen from the dead.
That is why he can work these miracles."
[15]Others said, "He is Elijah."[n]

Other people said, "Jesus is a prophet, like
the prophets who lived long ago."
[16]When Herod heard this, he said, "I killed
John by cutting off his head. Now he has risen
from the dead!"
[17]Herod himself had ordered his soldiers to
arrest John and put him in prison in order to
please his wife, Herodias. She had been the wife
of Philip, Herod's brother, but then Herod had
married her. [18]John had been telling Herod, "It is
not lawful for you to be married to your
brother's wife." [19]So Herodias hated John and
wanted to kill him. But she couldn't, [20]because
Herod was afraid of John and protected him.
He knew John was a good and holy man. Also,
though John's preaching always bothered him,
he enjoyed listening to John.

WHAT'S IT MEAN?

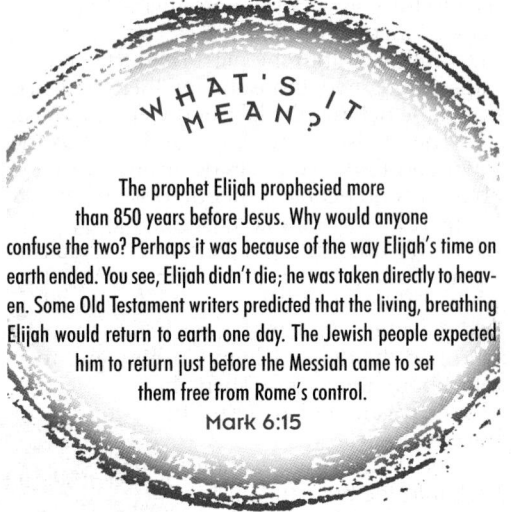

The prophet Elijah prophesied more than 850 years before Jesus. Why would anyone confuse the two? Perhaps it was because of the way Elijah's time on earth ended. You see, Elijah didn't die; he was taken directly to heaven. Some Old Testament writers predicted that the living, breathing Elijah would return to earth one day. The Jewish people expected him to return just before the Messiah came to set them free from Rome's control.

Mark 6:15

[21]Then the perfect time came for Herodias
to cause John's death. On Herod's birthday, he
gave a dinner party for the most important
government leaders, the commanders of his
army, and the most important people in Galilee.
[22]When the daughter of Herodias came in and
danced, she pleased Herod and the people eating with him.

So King Herod said to the girl, "Ask me for
anything you want, and I will give it to you."
[23]He promised her, "Anything you ask for I will
give to you—up to half of my kingdom."
[24]The girl went to her mother and asked,
"What should I ask for?"

Her mother answered, "Ask for the head of
John the Baptist."
[25]At once the girl went back to the king and
said to him, "I want the head of John the Baptist right now on a platter."
[26]Although the king was very sad, he had
made a promise, and his dinner guests had
heard it. So he did not want to refuse what she
asked. [27]Immediately the king sent a soldier to
bring John's head. The soldier went and cut off
John's head in the prison [28]and brought it back
on a platter. He gave it to the girl, and the girl
gave it to her mother. [29]When John's followers

6:11 Shake . . . feet A warning. It showed that they were rejecting these people. **6:15 Elijah** A great prophet who spoke for God and who lived hundreds of years before Christ. See 1 Kings 17.

heard this, they came and got John's body and
put it in a tomb.

MORE THAN FIVE THOUSAND FED

30The apostles gathered around Jesus and
told him about all the things they had done
and taught. 31Crowds of people were coming
and going so that Jesus and his followers did
not even have time to eat. He said to them,
"Come away by yourselves, and we will go to a
lonely place to get some rest."
32So they went in a boat by themselves to a
lonely place. 33But many people saw them
leave and recognized them. So from all the
towns they ran to the place where Jesus was
going, and they got there before him. 34When
he arrived, he saw a great crowd waiting. He
felt sorry for them, because they were like
sheep without a shepherd. So he began to
teach them many things.
35When it was late in the day, his followers
came to him and said, "No one lives in this
place, and it is already very late. 36Send the people away so they can go to the countryside and
towns around here to buy themselves something to eat."
37But Jesus answered, "You give them something to eat."

They said to him, "We would all have to
work a month to earn enough money to buy
that much bread!"
38Jesus asked them, "How many loaves of
bread do you have? Go and see."

When they found out, they said, "Five
loaves and two fish."
39Then Jesus told his followers to have the
people sit in groups on the green grass. 40So
they sat in groups of fifty or a hundred. 41Jesus
took the five loaves and two fish and, looking
up to heaven, he thanked God for the food.
He divided the bread and gave it to his followers for them to give to the people. Then he
divided the two fish among them all. 42All the
people ate and were satisfied. 43The followers
filled twelve baskets with the leftover pieces of
bread and fish. 44There were five thousand
men who ate.

JESUS WALKS ON THE WATER

45Immediately Jesus told his followers to get
into the boat and go ahead of him to Bethsaida
across the lake. He stayed there to send the
people home. 46After sending them away, he
went into the hills to pray.
47That night, the boat was in the middle of
the lake, and Jesus was alone on the land. 48He
saw his followers struggling hard to row the
boat, because the wind was blowing against
them. Between three and six o'clock in the
morning, Jesus came to them, walking on the
water, and he wanted to walk past the boat.
49But when they saw him walking on the
water, they thought he was a ghost and cried
out. 50They all saw him and were afraid. But
quickly Jesus spoke to them and said, "Have
courage! It is I. Do not be afraid." 51Then he got
into the boat with them, and the wind became
calm. The followers were greatly amazed.
52They did not understand about the miracle
of the five loaves, because their minds were
closed.
53When they had crossed the lake, they came
to shore at Gennesaret and tied the boat there.

On the Edge

They all saw him and were afraid. But quickly Jesus spoke to them and said, "Have courage! It is I. Do not be afraid" (Mark 6:50).

Here we have one of the greatest stories of all time. Can you imagine sitting in a boat with the wind and the waves beating against it? You are trying to get to the other side of the lake and not going anywhere; all of a sudden . . . "Hey, there's Jesus walking on the water!" What happened? His followers flipped out, but Jesus said, "Have courage! It is I. Do not be afraid."

When you're trying to get somewhere and it seems like you're stuck in the middle of all sorts of problems and that nothing is going your way, you don't need to flip out and get terrified. Jesus is saying, "I'm right here with you, because I'm Jesus!"

He will always show us a way out of our storms. For Peter, it was to leap out of the security of the boat and walk on the water to go to Jesus. Even when Peter began to sink Jesus was right there to help him up. Someone once said, "I'd rather be a wet water-walker than a dry boat-sitter any day!" Good advice.

You or someone you know may be sitting in the boat in the middle of a storm. Jesus is telling us not to worry because he is there with us. He is right there with you now.

SEE FOR YOURSELF:
Deut. 31:6; Josh. 1:5; Ps. 37:25, 28; Heb. 13:5

[54]When they got out of the boat, people immediately recognized Jesus. [55]They ran everywhere in that area and began to bring sick people on mats wherever they heard he was. [56]And everywhere he went—into towns, cities, or countryside—the people brought the sick to the marketplaces. They begged him to let them touch just the edge of his coat, and all who touched it were healed.

OBEY GOD'S LAW

7 [1]When some Pharisees and some teachers of the law came from Jerusalem, they gathered around Jesus. [2]They saw that some of Jesus' followers ate food with hands that were not clean, that is, they hadn't washed them. [3](The Pharisees and all the Jews never eat before washing their hands in a special way according to their unwritten laws. [4]And when they buy something in the market, they never eat it until they wash themselves in a special way. They also follow many other unwritten laws, such as the washing of cups, pitchers, and pots.)

[5]The Pharisees and the teachers of the law said to Jesus, "Why don't your followers obey the unwritten laws which have been handed down to us? Why do your followers eat their food with hands that are not clean?"

[6]Jesus answered, "Isaiah was right when he spoke about you hypocrites. He wrote,

'These people show honor to me with words,
but their hearts are far from me.
[7]Their worship of me is worthless.
The things they teach are nothing but human rules.' *Isaiah 29:13*

[8]You have stopped following the commands of God, and you follow only human teachings."

[9]Then Jesus said to them, "You cleverly ignore the commands of God so you can follow your own teachings. [10]Moses said, 'Honor your father and your mother,'[n] and 'Anyone who says cruel things to his father or mother must be put to death.'[n] [11]But you say a person can tell his father or mother, 'I have something I could use to help you, but it is Corban—a gift to God.' [12]You no longer let that person use that money for his father or his mother. [13]By your own rules, which you teach people, you are rejecting what God said. And you do many things like that."

[14]After Jesus called the crowd to him again, he said, "Every person should listen to me and understand what I am saying. [15]There is nothing people put into their bodies that makes them unclean. People are made unclean by the things that come out of them."[16n]

[17]When Jesus left the people and went into the house, his followers asked him about this story. [18]Jesus said, "Do you still not understand? Surely you know that nothing that enters someone from the outside can make that person unclean. [19]It does not go into the mind, but into the stomach. Then it goes out of the body." (When Jesus said this, he meant that no longer was any food unclean for people to eat.)

[20]And Jesus said, "The things that come out of people are the things that make them unclean. [21]All these evil things begin inside people, in the mind: evil thoughts, sexual sins, stealing, murder, adultery, [22]greed, evil actions, lying, doing sinful things, jealousy, speaking evil of others, pride, and foolish living. [23]All these evil things come from inside and make people unclean."

JESUS HELPS A NON-JEWISH WOMAN

[24]Jesus left that place and went to the area around Tyre. When he went into a house, he did not want anyone to know he was there, but he could not stay hidden. [25]A woman whose daughter had an evil spirit in her heard that he was there. So she quickly came to Jesus and fell at his feet. [26]She was Greek, born in Phoenicia, in Syria. She begged Jesus to force the demon out of her daughter.

WHAT'S IT MEAN?

Were most of the dogs of Jesus' time wild scavengers that ate garbage and caused all kinds of problems for people? (Yes.) Did Jews of that era insult Gentiles by calling them "dogs"? (Yes.) Did Jesus brutally insult the Gentile woman who came to him for help? (No.) In this verse, "dogs" refers to the household pets that would sit under the table at mealtime and eat any crumbs that fell.

Mark 7:27

7:10 'Honor . . . mother' Quotation from Exodus 20:12; Deuteronomy 5:16. **7:10 'Anyone . . . death.'** Quotation from Exodus 21:17. **7:16 Verse 16** Some Greek copies add verse 16: "You people who can hear me, listen!"

27Jesus told the woman, "It is not right to take the children's bread and give it to the dogs. First let the children eat all they want."

28But she answered, "Yes, Lord, but even the dogs under the table can eat the children's crumbs."

29Then Jesus said, "Because of your answer, you may go. The demon has left your daughter."

30The woman went home and found her daughter lying in bed; the demon was gone.

JESUS HEALS A DEAF MAN

31Then Jesus left the area around Tyre and went through Sidon to Lake Galilee, to the area of the Ten Towns.[n] 32While he was there, some people brought a man to him who was deaf and could not talk plainly. The people begged Jesus to put his hand on the man to heal him.

33Jesus led the man away from the crowd, by himself. He put his fingers in the man's ears and then spit and touched the man's tongue. 34Looking up to heaven, he sighed and said to the man, "Ephphatha!" (This means, "Be opened.") 35Instantly the man was able to hear and to use his tongue so that he spoke clearly.

36Jesus commanded the people not to tell anyone about what happened. But the more he commanded them, the more they told about it. 37They were completely amazed and said, "Jesus does everything well. He makes the deaf hear! And those who can't talk he makes able to speak."

MORE THAN FOUR THOUSAND PEOPLE FED

8

1Another time there was a great crowd with Jesus that had nothing to eat. So Jesus called his followers and said, 2"I feel sorry for these people, because they have already been with me for three days, and they have nothing to eat. 3If I send them home hungry, they will faint on the way. Some of them live a long way from here."

4Jesus' followers answered, "How can we get enough bread to feed all these people? We are far away from any town."

5Jesus asked, "How many loaves of bread do you have?"

They answered, "Seven."

6Jesus told the people to sit on the ground. Then he took the seven loaves, gave thanks to God, and divided the bread. He gave the pieces to his followers to give to the people, and they did so. 7The followers also had a few small fish. After Jesus gave thanks for the fish, he told his followers to give them to the people also. 8All the people ate and were satisfied. Then his followers filled seven baskets with the leftover pieces of food. 9There were about four thousand people who ate. After they had eaten, Jesus sent them home. 10Then right away he got into a boat with his followers and went to the area of Dalmanutha.

THE LEADERS ASK FOR A MIRACLE

11The Pharisees came to Jesus and began to ask him questions. Hoping to trap him, they asked Jesus for a miracle from God. 12Jesus sighed deeply and said, "Why do you people ask for a miracle as a sign? I tell you the truth, no sign will be given to you." 13Then Jesus left the Pharisees and went in the boat to the other side of the lake.

WHAT'S IT MEAN?

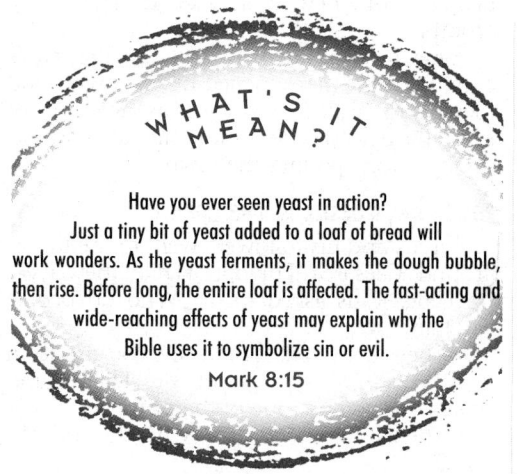

Have you ever seen yeast in action? Just a tiny bit of yeast added to a loaf of bread will work wonders. As the yeast ferments, it makes the dough bubble, then rise. Before long, the entire loaf is affected. The fast-acting and wide-reaching effects of yeast may explain why the Bible uses it to symbolize sin or evil.

Mark 8:15

GUARD AGAINST WRONG TEACHINGS

14His followers had only one loaf of bread with them in the boat; they had forgotten to bring more. 15Jesus warned them, "Be careful! Beware of the yeast of the Pharisees and the yeast of Herod."

16His followers discussed the meaning of this, saying, "He said this because we have no bread."

17Knowing what they were talking about, Jesus asked them, "Why are you talking about not having bread? Do you still not see or understand? Are your minds closed? 18You have eyes, but you don't really see. You have ears, but you don't really listen. Remember when 19I divided five loaves of bread for the

7:31 Ten Towns In Greek, called "Decapolis." It was an area east of Lake Galilee that once had ten main towns.

five thousand? How many baskets did you fill
with leftover pieces of food?"
They answered, "Twelve."
20"And when I divided seven loaves of
bread for the four thousand, how many baskets did you fill with leftover pieces of food?"
They answered, "Seven."
21Then Jesus said to them, "Don't you understand yet?"

JESUS HEALS A BLIND MAN

22Jesus and his followers came to Bethsaida.
There some people brought a blind man to
Jesus and begged him to touch the man. 23So
Jesus took the blind man's hand and led him
out of the village. Then he spit on the man's
eyes and put his hands on the man and asked,
"Can you see now?"
24The man looked up and said, "Yes, I see
people, but they look like trees walking
around."
25Again Jesus put his hands on the man's
eyes. Then the man opened his eyes wide and
they were healed, and he was able to see
everything clearly. 26Jesus told him to go home,
saying, "Don't go into the town."

PETER SAYS JESUS IS THE CHRIST

27Jesus and his followers went to the towns
around Caesarea Philippi. While they were
traveling, Jesus asked them, "Who do people
say I am?"
28They answered, "Some say you are John
the Baptist. Others say you are Elijah,[n] and
others say you are one of the prophets."
29Then Jesus asked, "But who do you say
I am?"
Peter answered, "You are the Christ."
30Jesus warned his followers not to tell anyone who he was.
31Then Jesus began to teach them that the
Son of Man must suffer many things and that
he would be rejected by the older Jewish leaders, the leading priests, and the teachers of the
law. He told them that the Son of Man must be
killed and then rise from the dead after three
days. 32Jesus told them plainly what would
happen. Then Peter took Jesus aside and began
to tell him not to talk like that. 33But Jesus
turned and looked at his followers. Then he
told Peter not to talk that way. He said, "Go
away from me, Satan![n] You don't care about
the things of God, but only about things people think are important."
34Then Jesus called the crowd to him, along
with his followers. He said, "If people want to
follow me, they must give up the things they
want. They must be willing even to give up
their lives to follow me. 35Those who want to
save their lives will give up true life. But those
who give up their lives for me and for the
Good News will have true life. 36It is worth
nothing for them to have the whole world if
they lose their souls. 37They could never pay
enough to buy back their souls. 38The people
who live now are living in a sinful and evil

On the Edge

Then Jesus asked, "But who do you say I am?" Peter answered, "You are the Christ" (Mark 8:29).

When Jesus was born, the Jews were living under the Roman government. They hated it. They had to pay ridiculously high taxes. They had no rights because they weren't Roman citizens.

Israel's prophets had said that a Messiah, God's Chosen One, would come to set the people free. Most of the Jews believed that the Messiah would appear in power and glory, maybe even raise a large army, and overthrow the Roman government that had Israel under its thumb. The Messiah would establish God's kingdom—an independent Jewish nation—on earth.

Jesus didn't exactly fit the bill. He came to set them free—from their sins, their sicknesses, and the oppression of their real enemy (Satan) rather than from the Romans. He never spoke against the Roman government and even suggested that God wanted them to pay taxes to Caesar.

But Peter recognized that Jesus was the Chosen One, even though he may not have understood (yet) that the kingdom Jesus had come to establish was not a political regime, but a kingdom of the heart and of the spirit.

Jesus is the Messiah. Let him be the ruler of your heart right now—not just in the easy places, but also in the places that may be hard for you to submit to him. Let him be the King of your whole life.

SEE FOR YOURSELF:
John 1:41; 6:69; 11:27

8:28 Elijah A man who spoke for God and who lived hundreds of years before Christ. See 1 Kings 17.
8:33 Satan Name for the devil meaning "the enemy." Jesus means that Peter was talking like Satan.

time. If people are ashamed of me and my
teaching, the Son of Man will be ashamed of
them when he comes with his Father's glory
and with the holy angels."

9 [1]Then Jesus said to the people, "I tell you the
truth, some people standing here will see
the kingdom of God come with power before
they die."

JESUS TALKS WITH MOSES AND ELIJAH

[2]Six days later, Jesus took Peter, James, and
John up on a high mountain by themselves.
While they watched, Jesus' appearance was
changed. [3]His clothes became shining white,
whiter than any person could make them.
[4]Then Elijah and Moses[n] appeared to them,
talking with Jesus.
[5]Peter said to Jesus, "Teacher, it is good that
we are here. Let us make three tents—one for
you, one for Moses, and one for Elijah." [6]Peter
did not know what to say, because he and the
others were so frightened.
[7]Then a cloud came and covered them, and
a voice came from the cloud, saying, "This is
my Son, whom I love. Listen to him!"
[8]Suddenly Peter, James, and John looked
around, but they saw only Jesus there alone
with them.
[9]As they were coming down the mountain,
Jesus commanded them not to tell anyone
about what they had seen until the Son of
Man had risen from the dead.
[10]So the followers obeyed Jesus, but they
discussed what he meant about rising from the
dead.
[11]Then they asked Jesus, "Why do the teachers of the law say that Elijah must come first?"
[12]Jesus answered, "They are right to say that
Elijah must come first and make everything
the way it should be. But why does the Scripture say that the Son of Man will suffer much
and that people will treat him as if he were
nothing? [13]I tell you that Elijah has already
come. And people did to him whatever they
wanted to do, just as the Scriptures said it
would happen."

On the Edge

Then a cloud came and covered them, and a voice came from the cloud, saying, "This is my Son, whom I love. Listen to him!" (Mark 9:7).

Jesus and God the Father are one. Think about that for a moment. When you see Jesus ministering to the poor, touching the brokenhearted, healing the sick, he is fulfilling the heart of the Father. Just like earthly sons sometimes work for their dads, Jesus works for his Father, too.

You have God living on the inside of you—the God who created this earth; the God who made every person who has ever lived on earth; the God who rules the whole universe. When you received Jesus, you received life!

Because of the price that Jesus paid for you on the cross, and because you have received him as your Lord, you have become God's very own child. Wow! Get this now—God is your Father. And the exciting thing is we inherit his characteristics.

Ever notice a father and his son? Sometimes they look a whole lot like each other; in fact, they have a lot of the same mannerisms. It's that way because they are father and son. When you accepted Jesus as your Savior, you inherited some of the same mannerisms of your heavenly Father—love, joy, and peace, to name a few (see Gal. 5:22–23).

It's amazing—the more we hang around God, the more of his ways we will pick up! When we look at people from God's perspective, we see them in a completely different light! God has given us a great heritage. We are his children. Remember: "Like Father, like son (daughter)!"

SEE FOR YOURSELF:
Luke 12:32;
Rom. 8:17;
2 Cor. 12:9–10;
Gal. 3:29; 4:7

JESUS HEALS A SICK BOY

[14]When Jesus, Peter, James, and John came
back to the other followers, they saw a great
crowd around them and the teachers of the
law arguing with them. [15]But as soon as the
crowd saw Jesus, the people were surprised
and ran to welcome him.
[16]Jesus asked, "What are you arguing
about?"
[17]A man answered, "Teacher, I brought my
son to you. He has an evil spirit in him that
stops him from talking. [18]When the spirit

9:4 Elijah and Moses Two of the most important Jewish leaders in the past. God had given Moses the Law, and Elijah was an important prophet.

attacks him, it throws him on the ground. Then
my son foams at the mouth, grinds his teeth,
and becomes very stiff. I asked your followers
to force the evil spirit out, but they couldn't."
19Jesus answered, "You people have no faith.
How long must I stay with you? How long
must I put up with you? Bring the boy to me."
20So the followers brought him to Jesus. As
soon as the evil spirit saw Jesus, it made the
boy lose control of himself, and he fell down
and rolled on the ground, foaming at the
mouth.
21Jesus asked the boy's father, "How long
has this been happening?"
The father answered, "Since he was very
young. 22The spirit often throws him into a fire
or into water to kill him. If you can do anything
for him, please have pity on us and help us."
23Jesus said to the father, "You said, 'If you
can!' All things are possible for the one who
believes."
24Immediately the father cried out, "I do believe! Help me to believe more!"
25When Jesus saw that a crowd was quickly
gathering, he ordered the evil spirit, saying,
"You spirit that makes people unable to hear or
speak, I command you to come out of this boy
and never enter him again!"
26The evil spirit screamed and caused the
boy to fall on the ground again. Then the spirit
came out. The boy looked as if he were dead,
and many people said, "He is dead!" 27But Jesus
took hold of the boy's hand and
helped him to stand up.
28When Jesus went into
the house, his followers began asking him privately,
"Why couldn't we force
that evil spirit out?"
29Jesus answered, "That
kind of spirit can only be
forced out by prayer."

JESUS TALKS ABOUT HIS DEATH

30Then Jesus and his followers left
that place and went through Galilee. He didn't
want anyone to know where he was, 31because
he was teaching his followers. He said to them,
"The Son of Man will be handed over to people, and they will kill him. After three days, he
will rise from the dead." 32But the followers did
not understand what Jesus meant, and they
were afraid to ask him.

WHO IS THE GREATEST?

33Jesus and his followers went to Capernaum. When they went into a house there, he
asked them, "What were you arguing about on
the road?" 34But the followers did not answer,
because their argument on the road was about
which one of them was the greatest.
35Jesus sat down and called the twelve
apostles to him. He said, "Whoever wants to be
the most important must be last of all and servant of all."
36Then Jesus took a small child and had him
stand among them. Taking the child in his
arms, he said, 37"Whoever accepts a child like
this in my name accepts me. And whoever accepts me accepts the One who sent me."

ANYONE NOT AGAINST US IS FOR US

38Then John said, "Teacher, we saw someone
using your name to force demons
out of a person. We told him to
stop, because he does not belong to our group."
39But Jesus said, "Don't stop
him, because anyone who
uses my name to do powerful
things will not easily say evil
things about me. 40Whoever is
not against us is with us. 41I
tell you the truth, whoever
gives you a drink of water
because you belong
to the Christ will truly get his
reward.
42"If one of these little children believes in me, and
someone causes that child
to sin, it would be better for
that person to have a large
stone tied around his neck and be drowned in
the sea. 43If your hand causes you to sin, cut it
off. It is better for you to lose part of your
body and live forever than to have two hands
and go to hell, where the fire never goes out.

WHAT'S IT MEAN?

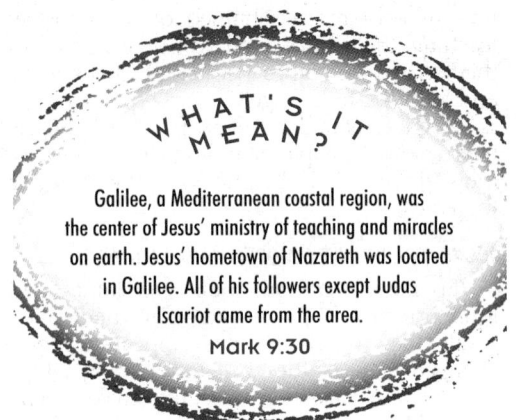

Galilee, a Mediterranean coastal region, was the center of Jesus' ministry of teaching and miracles on earth. Jesus' hometown of Nazareth was located in Galilee. All of his followers except Judas Iscariot came from the area.

Mark 9:30

"Whoever wants to be the most important must be last of all and servant of all." (Mark 9:35b)

GIVING

What is the result of giving to others? (9:41)

[44][n] [45]If your foot causes you to sin, cut it off. It
is better for you to lose part of your body and
to live forever than to have two feet and be
thrown into hell. [46][n] [47]If your eye causes you to
sin, take it out. It is better for you to enter the
kingdom of God with only one eye than to
have two eyes and be thrown into hell. [48]In
hell the worm does not die; the fire is never put
out. [49]Every person will be salted with fire.
[50]"Salt is good, but if the salt loses its salty
taste, you cannot make it salty again. So, be full
of salt, and have peace with each other."

WHAT'S IT MEAN?

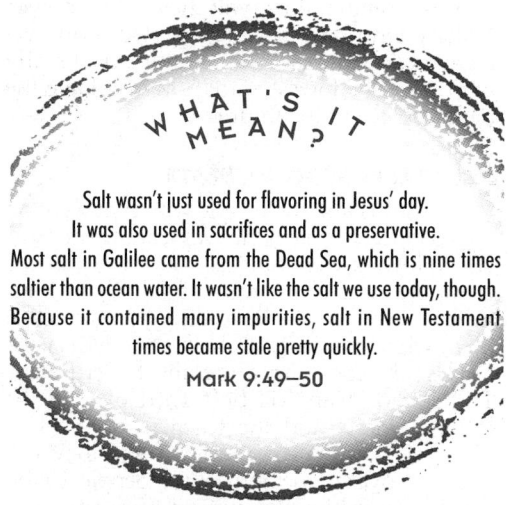

Salt wasn't just used for flavoring in Jesus' day. It was also used in sacrifices and as a preservative. Most salt in Galilee came from the Dead Sea, which is nine times saltier than ocean water. It wasn't like the salt we use today, though. Because it contained many impurities, salt in New Testament times became stale pretty quickly.

Mark 9:49–50

JESUS TEACHES ABOUT DIVORCE

10 [1]Then Jesus left that place and went into the
area of Judea and across the Jordan River.
Again, crowds came to him, and he taught
them as he usually did.
[2]Some Pharisees came to Jesus and tried to
trick him. They asked, "Is it right for a man to
divorce his wife?"
[3]Jesus answered, "What did Moses command you to do?"
[4]They said, "Moses allowed a man to write
out divorce papers and send her away."[n]
[5]Jesus said, "Moses wrote that command for
you because you were stubborn. [6]But when
God made the world, 'he made them male and
female.'[n] [7]'So a man will leave his father and
mother and be united with his wife, [8]and the
two will become one body.'[n] So there are not
two, but one. [9]God has joined the two together,
so no one should separate them."
[10]Later, in the house, his followers asked
Jesus again about the question of divorce. [11]He
answered, "Anyone who divorces his wife and
marries another woman is guilty of adultery
against her. [12]And the woman who divorces
her husband and marries another man is also
guilty of adultery."

JESUS ACCEPTS CHILDREN

[13]Some people brought their little children
to Jesus so he could touch them, but his followers told them to stop. [14]When Jesus saw
this, he was upset and said to them, "Let the
little children come to me. Don't stop them, because the kingdom of God belongs to people
who are like these children. [15]I tell you the
truth, you must accept the kingdom of God as
if you were a little child, or you will never enter
it." [16]Then Jesus took the children in his arms,
put his hands on them, and blessed them.

A RICH YOUNG MAN'S QUESTION

[17]As Jesus started to leave, a man ran to him
and fell on his knees before Jesus. The man
asked, "Good teacher, what must I do to have
life forever?"
[18]Jesus answered, "Why do you call me
good? Only God is good. [19]You know the
commands: 'You must not murder anyone.
You must not be guilty of adultery. You must
not steal. You must not tell lies about your
neighbor. You must not cheat. Honor your father and mother.'"[n]
[20]The man said, "Teacher, I
have obeyed all these things
since I was a boy."
[21]Jesus, looking at the man,
loved him and said, "There is
one more thing you need to
do. Go and sell everything
you have, and give the money
to the poor, and you will have
treasure in heaven. Then come and follow me."
[22]He was very sad to hear Jesus say this,
and he left sorrowfully, because he was rich.
[23]Then Jesus looked at his followers and
said, "How hard it will be for the rich to enter
the kingdom of God!"
[24]The followers were amazed at what Jesus
said. But he said again, "My children, it is very
hard to enter the kingdom of God! [25]It is easier
for a camel to go through the eye of a needle

MONEY
What can money do to our relationship with God? (10:17–25)

9:44 Verse 44 Some Greek copies of Mark add verse 44, which is the same as verse 48.
9:46 Verse 46 Some Greek copies of Mark add verse 46, which is the same as verse 48. **10:4 "Moses . . . away."** Quotation from Deuteronomy 24:1. **10:6 'he made . . . female.'** Quotation from Genesis 1:27. **10:7-8 'So . . . body.'** Quotation from Genesis 2:24. **10:19 'You . . . mother.'** Quotation from Exodus 20:12-16; Deuteronomy 5:16-20.

than for a rich person to enter the kingdom
of God."
[26]The followers were even more surprised
and said to each other, "Then who can be
saved?"
[27]Jesus looked at them and said, "This is
something people cannot do, but God can.
God can do all things."
[28]Peter said to Jesus, "Look, we have left
everything and followed you."
[29]Jesus said, "I tell you the truth, all those
who have left houses, brothers, sisters, mother,
father, children, or farms for me and for the
Good News [30]will get more than they left. Here
in this world they will have a hundred times
more homes, brothers, sisters, mothers, children, and fields. And with those things, they
will also suffer for their belief. But in the age
that is coming they will have life forever.
[31]Many who have the highest place now will
have the lowest place in the future. And many
who have the lowest place now will have the
highest place in the future."

JESUS TALKS ABOUT HIS DEATH

[32]As Jesus and the people with him were on
the road to Jerusalem, he was leading the way.
His followers were amazed, but others in the
crowd who followed were afraid. Again Jesus
took the twelve apostles aside and began to tell
them what was about to happen in Jerusalem.
[33]He said, "Look, we are going to Jerusalem.
The Son of Man will be turned over to the
leading priests and the teachers of the law.
They will say that he must die, and they will
turn him over to the non-Jewish people, [34]who
will laugh at him and spit on him. They will
beat him with whips and crucify him. But on
the third day, he will rise to life again."

TWO FOLLOWERS ASK JESUS A FAVOR

[35]Then James and John, sons of Zebedee,
came to Jesus and said, "Teacher, we want to
ask you to do something for us."
[36]Jesus asked, "What do you want me to do
for you?"
[37]They answered, "Let one of us sit at your
right side and one of us sit at your left side in
your glory in your kingdom."
[38]Jesus said, "You don't understand what
you are asking. Can you drink the cup that I
must drink? And can you be baptized with the
same kind of baptism that I must go
through?"[n]
[39]They answered, "Yes, we can."
Jesus said to them, "You will drink the same
cup that I will drink, and you will be baptized
with the same baptism that I must go through.
[40]But I cannot choose who will sit at my right

On the Edge

Jesus looked at them and said, "This is something people cannot do, but God can. God can do all things" (Mark 10:27).

Wow! What a promise! *God can do anything!* This Scripture should kick the limits right out of your dreams! There are plenty of things that you cannot do on your own, but with Christ *all* things are possible. Too many times we let our circumstances swallow us. We wear out, give up, and throw in the towel. We need to grab hold of this verse and realize that Jesus is the One who can do anything! You might need healing, money, help on a big test, a job, insight on how to witness to a stubborn, unsaved friend, or just a spot on the basketball team. It doesn't matter what your need is. With Christ, all things are possible. In fact, we have a promise that says that the same Spirit which raised Christ from the dead lives in you! Now that's power!

The Bible teaches us not to give up when things get tough. Hold on to God. There's a story in Mark 10:46–52 about a blind man named Bartimaeus. Bartimaeus needed a miracle, and he heard that Jesus was passing by. He began to cry out to Jesus, and the crowd told him to shut up. So he cried out even louder. Jesus stopped, turned around, and asked the man nine words that changed Bartimaeus's life forever: "What do you want me to do for you?" You know what? Bartimaeus got his miracle.

So the next time people are telling you that such-and-such will never happen, just smile with steadfast confidence in God's Word, knowing that, with him, nothing is impossible!

SEE FOR YOURSELF:
Matt. 17:20;
Mark 10:46–52;
Luke 1:37

10:38 Can you . . . through? Jesus was asking if they could suffer the same terrible things that would happen to him.

or my left; those places belong to those for whom they have been prepared."

[41]When the other ten followers heard this, they began to be angry with James and John.

[42]Jesus called them together and said, "The other nations have rulers. You know that those rulers love to show their power over the people, and their important leaders love to use all their authority. [43]But it should not be that way among you. Whoever wants to become great among you must serve the rest of you like a servant. [44]Whoever wants to become the first among you must serve all of you like a slave. [45]In the same way, the Son of Man did not come to be served. He came to serve others and to give his life as a ransom for many people."

WHAT'S IT MEAN?

The secret to Rome's success was slave labor. It's been estimated that one out of every five people in the Roman Empire was a slave. Slaves in New Testament times had very few rights. Some were treated worse than animals. The only way a slave could become a free person was to pay a certain amount of money—usually thirty pieces of silver, or about a month's earnings.

Mark 10:45

JESUS HEALS A BLIND MAN

[46]Then they came to the town of Jericho. As Jesus was leaving there with his followers and a great many people, a blind beggar named Bartimaeus son of Timaeus was sitting by the road. [47]When he heard that Jesus from Nazareth was walking by, he began to shout, "Jesus, Son of David, have mercy on me!"

[48]Many people warned the blind man to be quiet, but he shouted even more, "Son of David, have mercy on me!"

[49]Jesus stopped and said, "Tell the man to come here."

So they called the blind man, saying, "Cheer up! Get to your feet. Jesus is calling you." [50]The blind man jumped up, left his coat there, and went to Jesus.

[51]Jesus asked him, "What do you want me to do for you?"

The blind man answered, "Teacher, I want to see."

[52]Jesus said, "Go, you are healed because you believed." At once the man could see, and he followed Jesus on the road.

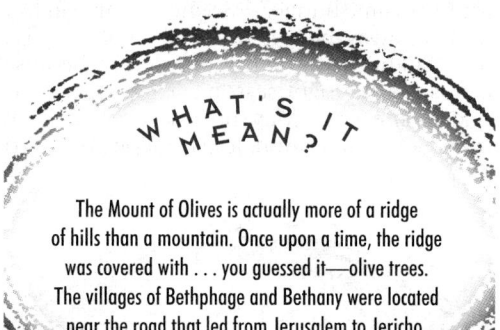

WHAT'S IT MEAN?

The Mount of Olives is actually more of a ridge of hills than a mountain. Once upon a time, the ridge was covered with . . . you guessed it—olive trees. The villages of Bethphage and Bethany were located near the road that led from Jerusalem to Jericho.

Mark 11:1

JESUS ENTERS JERUSALEM AS A KING

11

[1]As Jesus and his followers were coming closer to Jerusalem, they came to the towns of Bethphage and Bethany near the Mount of Olives. From there Jesus sent two of his followers [2]and said to them, "Go to the town you can see there. When you enter it, you will quickly find a colt tied, which no one has ever ridden. Untie it and bring it here to me. [3]If anyone asks you why you are doing this, tell him its Master needs the colt, and he will send it at once."

[4]The followers went into the town, found a colt tied in the street near the door of a house, and untied it. [5]Some people were standing there and asked, "What are you doing? Why are you untying that colt?" [6]The followers answered the way Jesus told them to answer, and the people let them take the colt.

[7]They brought the colt to Jesus and put their coats on it, and Jesus sat on it. [8]Many people spread their coats on the road. Others cut branches in the fields and spread them on the road. [9]The people were walking ahead of Jesus and behind him, shouting,

"Praise God!
God bless the One who comes in the
name of the Lord! *Psalm 118:26*
[10]God bless the kingdom of our father
David!
That kingdom is coming!
Praise[n] to God in heaven!"

11:10 Praise Literally, "Hosanna," a Hebrew word used at first in praying to God for help, but at this time it was probably a shout of joy used in praising God or his Messiah.

[11]Jesus entered Jerusalem and went into the
Temple. After he had looked at everything,
since it was already late, he went out to Bethany with the twelve apostles.
[12]The next day as Jesus was leaving Bethany, he became hungry. [13]Seeing a fig tree in leaf
from far away, he went to see if it had any figs
on it. But he found no figs, only leaves, because
it was not the right season for figs. [14]So Jesus
said to the tree, "May no one ever eat fruit
from you again." And Jesus' followers heard
him say this.

WHAT'S IT MEAN?

Coins with pagan symbols on them could not be used in the Temple. They had to be exchanged for acceptable coins. Likewise, only certain animals could be offered as sacrifices. Local businessmen saw profit potential in these restrictions. They set up tables in the Temple courtyard and sold approved coins and animals at marked-up prices. You won't believe who else benefited from this price gouging—the family of the high priest, who controlled the Temple business.

Mark 11:15

JESUS GOES TO THE TEMPLE

[15]When Jesus returned to Jerusalem, he
went into the Temple and began to throw out
those who were buying and selling there. He
turned over the tables of those who were exchanging different kinds of money, and he upset the benches of those who were selling
doves. [16]Jesus refused to allow anyone to carry
goods through the Temple courts. [17]Then he
taught the people, saying, "It is written in the
Scriptures, 'My Temple will be called a house
for prayer for people from all nations.'[n] But
you are changing God's house into a 'hideout
for robbers.'"[n]
[18]The leading priests and the teachers of the
law heard all this and began trying to find a
way to kill Jesus. They were afraid of him, because all the people were amazed at his teaching. [19]That evening, Jesus and his followers left
the city.

THE POWER OF FAITH

[20]The next morning as Jesus was passing by
with his followers, they saw the fig tree dry
and dead, even to the roots. [21]Peter remembered the tree and said to Jesus, "Teacher, look!
The fig tree you cursed is dry and dead!"
[22]Jesus answered, "Have faith in God. [23]I tell
you the truth, you can say to this mountain,
'Go, fall into the sea.' And if you have no
doubts in your mind and believe that what
you say will happen, God will do it for you.
[24]So I tell you to believe that you have received
the things you ask for in prayer, and God will
give them to you. [25]When you are praying, if
you are angry with someone, forgive him so

On the Edge

When you are praying, if you are angry with someone, forgive him so that your Father in heaven will also forgive your sins (Mark 11:25).

Jesus makes it pretty clear that Christians are to never quit forgiving. But why? Mark says that we've got to forgive other people if we want God to forgive us. Like it or not, it's the truth. If you forgive others of their wrongs, your Father will forgive you. If not, then your sins will not be forgiven. As in many other places in the Bible, God is calling us to be like him. He is a forgiving God who wants to restore relationships. He wants you to be forgiving, too. A heart that's willing to forgive is exactly like the heart of God. No matter what our sin, his forgiveness comes freely and wipes out whatever we've done. That doesn't mean you may not have to endure the consequences; it just means that God doesn't hold your sin against you. God knows, too, that unforgiveness will eat you up on the inside. It can paralyze you emotionally. Forgiving sets you free. So when a friend comes to apologize for hurting you—quickly forgive her and welcome her back into your life. God always does the same for you.

SEE FOR YOURSELF: Matt. 6:14–15; 18:21–22; Luke 6:37; 2 Cor. 2:7

11:17 'My Temple . . . nations.' Quotation from Isaiah 56:7. **11:17 'hideout for robbers.'** Quotation from Jeremiah 7:11.

that your Father in heaven will also forgive your sins." [26n]

LEADERS DOUBT JESUS' AUTHORITY

[27]Jesus and his followers went again to Jerusalem. As Jesus was walking in the Temple, the leading priests, the teachers of the law, and the older leaders came to him. [28]They said to him, "What authority do you have to do these things? Who gave you this authority?"

[29]Jesus answered, "I will ask you one question. If you answer me, I will tell you what authority I have to do these things. [30]Tell me: When John baptized people, was that authority from God or just from other people?"

[31]They argued about Jesus' question, saying, "If we answer, 'John's baptism was from God,' Jesus will say, 'Then why didn't you believe him?' [32]But if we say, 'It was from other people,' the crowd will be against us." (These leaders were afraid of the people, because all the people believed that John was a prophet.)

[33]So they answered Jesus, "We don't know."

Jesus said to them, "Then I won't tell you what authority I have to do these things."

A STORY ABOUT GOD'S SON

12

[1]Jesus began to use stories to teach the people. He said, "A man planted a vineyard. He put a wall around it and dug a hole for a winepress and built a tower. Then he leased the land to some farmers and left for a trip. [2]When it was time for the grapes to be picked, he sent a servant to the farmers to get his share of the grapes. [3]But the farmers grabbed the servant and beat him and sent him away empty-handed. [4]Then the man sent another servant. They hit him on the head and showed no respect for him. [5]So the man sent another servant, whom they killed. The man sent many other servants; the farmers beat some of them and killed others.

[6]"The man had one person left to send, his son whom he loved. He sent him last of all, saying, 'They will respect my son.'

[7]"But the farmers said to each other, 'This son will inherit the vineyard. If we kill him, it will be ours.' [8]So they took the son, killed him, and threw him out of the vineyard.

[9]"So what will the owner of the vineyard do? He will come and kill those farmers and will give the vineyard to other farmers. [10]Surely you have read this Scripture:

'The stone that the builders rejected
became the cornerstone.
[11]The Lord did this,
and it is wonderful to us.' " *Psalm 118:22-23*

[12]The Jewish leaders knew that the story was about them. So they wanted to find a way to arrest Jesus, but they were afraid of the people. So the leaders left him and went away.

IS IT RIGHT TO PAY TAXES OR NOT?

[13]Later, the Jewish leaders sent some Pharisees and Herodians[n] to Jesus to trap him in saying something wrong. [14]They came to him and said, "Teacher, we know that you are an honest man. You are not afraid of what other people think about you, because you pay no attention to who they are. And you teach the truth about God's way. Tell us: Is it right to pay taxes to Caesar or not? [15]Should we pay them, or not?"

But knowing what these men were really trying to do, Jesus said to them, "Why are you trying to trap me? Bring me a coin to look at." [16]They gave Jesus a coin, and he asked, "Whose image and name are on the coin?"

They answered, "Caesar's."

[17]Then Jesus said to them, "Give to Caesar the things that are Caesar's, and give to God the things that are God's." The men were amazed at what Jesus said.

SOME SADDUCEES TRY TO TRICK JESUS

[18]Then some Sadducees came to Jesus and asked him a question. (Sadducees believed that people would not rise from the dead.) [19]They said, "Teacher, Moses wrote that if a man's brother dies, leaving a wife but no children, then that man must marry the widow and have children for his brother. [20]Once there were seven brothers. The first brother married and died, leaving no children. [21]So the second brother married the widow, but he also died and had no children. The same thing happened with the third brother. [22]All seven brothers married her and died, and none of the brothers had any children. Finally the woman died too. [23]Since all seven brothers had married her, when people rise from the dead, whose wife will she be?"

[24]Jesus answered, "Why don't you understand? Don't you know what the Scriptures say, and don't you know about the power of God? [25]When people rise from the dead, they

11:26 Verse 26 Some early Greek copies add verse 26: "But if you don't forgive other people, then your Father in heaven will not forgive your sins." **12:13 Herodians** A political group that followed Herod and his family.

will not marry, nor will they be given to someone to marry. They will be like the angels in
heaven. [26]Surely you have read what God said
about people rising from the dead. In the book in which Moses wrote about the burning bush,[n] it says that God told Moses, 'I am the God of Abraham, the God of Isaac, and
the God of Jacob.'[n] [27]God
is the God of the living, not the dead. You Sadducees are wrong!"

> "Love the Lord your God with all your heart, all your soul, all your mind, and all your strength." (Mark 12:30)

THE MOST IMPORTANT COMMAND

[28]One of the teachers of the
law came and heard Jesus arguing with the Sadducees. Seeing that Jesus gave good answers to their questions, he asked Jesus, "Which of the commands is most important?"
[29]Jesus answered, "The most important
command is this: 'Listen, people of Israel! The
Lord our God is the only Lord. [30]Love
the Lord your God with all your heart, all your soul, all your mind, and all your
strength.'[n] [31]The second command is this: 'Love your neighbor as you love yourself.'[n] There are no commands more important than these."
[32]The man answered, "That
was a good answer, Teacher. You were right when you said God is the only Lord and there
is no other God besides him. [33]One must love
God with all his heart, all his mind, and all his strength. And one must love his neighbor as he loves himself. These commands are more important than all the animals and sacrifices we offer to God."
[34]When Jesus saw that the
man answered him wisely, Jesus said to him, "You are close to the kingdom of God." And after that, no one was brave enough to ask Jesus any more questions.
[35]As Jesus was teaching
in the Temple, he asked, "Why do the teachers of the law say that the Christ is the
son of David? [36]David himself,
speaking by the Holy Spirit, said:

'The Lord said to my Lord:
Sit by me at my right side,
until I put your enemies under your control.' *Psalm 110:1*

[37]David himself calls the Christ 'Lord,' so how
can the Christ be his son?" The large crowd listened to Jesus with pleasure.
[38]Jesus continued teaching and said, "Beware of the teachers of the law. They like to walk around wearing fancy clothes, and they love for people to greet them with respect in
the marketplaces. [39]They love to have the most
important seats in the synagogues and at
feasts. [40]But they cheat widows and steal their
houses and then try to make themselves look good by saying long prayers. They will receive a greater punishment."

LOVE

What is the most important command that God has given us? (12:29–30)

WHAT'S IT MEAN?

If Jesus' words seem familiar, it's because they come from the Old Testament Book of Deuteronomy. Jesus was quoting what's known as the Shema, which was a summary (of sorts) of the main points of the Jewish faith. The Shema is still used today to call Jewish people to worship.

Mark 12:29–30

TRUE GIVING

[41]Jesus sat near the Temple money box and
watched the people put in their money. Many
rich people gave large sums of money. [42]Then a
poor widow came and put in two small copper coins, which were only worth a few cents.
[43]Calling his followers to him, Jesus said, "I
tell you the truth, this poor widow gave more
than all those rich people. [44]They gave only
what they did not need. This woman is very poor, but she gave all she had; she gave all she had to live on."

THE TEMPLE WILL BE DESTROYED

13
[1]As Jesus was leaving the Temple, one of his
followers said to him, "Look, Teacher! How beautiful the buildings are! How big the stones are!"

12:26 burning bush Read Exodus 3:1–12 in the Old Testament. **12:26 'I am . . . Jacob.'** Quotation from Exodus 3:6. **12:30 'Listen . . . strength.'** Quotation from Deuteronomy 6:4–5. **12:31 'Love . . . yourself.'** Quotation from Leviticus 19:18.

WHAT'S IT MEAN?

It's no wonder the follower was in awe of the Temple. The building itself was a work of art, constructed over a thirty-year period on the orders of Herod the Great. The front columns stood forty feet high. Some of the marble stones used for the walls of the building were almost forty feet long! (Can you imagine how much they must have weighed?)

Mark 13:1

2Jesus said, "Do you see all these great
buildings? Not one stone will be left on another. Every stone will be thrown down to the
ground."
3Later, as Jesus was sitting on the Mount of
Olives, opposite the Temple, he was alone with
Peter, James, John, and Andrew. They asked
Jesus, 4"Tell us, when will these things happen?
And what will be the sign that they are going
to happen?"
5Jesus began to answer them, "Be careful
that no one fools you. 6Many people will come
in my name, saying, 'I am the One,' and they
will fool many people. 7When you hear about
wars and stories of wars that are coming, don't
be afraid. These things must happen before the
end comes. 8Nations will fight against other
nations, and kingdoms against other kingdoms. There will be earthquakes in different
places, and there will be times when there is no
food for people to eat. These things are like the
first pains when something new is about to be
born.
9"You must be careful. People will arrest you
and take you to court and beat you in their
synagogues. You will be forced to stand before
kings and governors, to tell them about me.
This will happen to you because you follow
me. 10But before these things happen, the Good
News must be told to all people. 11When you
are arrested and judged, don't worry ahead of
time about what you should say. Say whatever
is given you to say at that time, because it will
not really be you speaking; it will be the Holy
Spirit.
12"Brothers will give their own brothers to
be killed, and fathers will give their own children to be killed. Children will fight against
their own parents and cause them to be put to
death. 13All people will hate you because you
follow me, but those people who keep their
faith until the end will be saved.

Promise

HE PROMISES THAT THE GOOD NEWS WILL BE PREACHED TO ALL PEOPLE.

But before these things happen, the Good News must be told to all people (Mark 13:10).

One of these days, the world as you know it won't even exist. One glorious day, everyone on earth will hear the explosive blast of a trumpet and that will be the end. Whoa! Can you imagine what it's going to be like when Jesus Christ comes back to earth and sets up his kingdom? There won't be any more violence on the streets. There won't be any more cancer to kill the people you love. Even the deepest, most private pain in your own heart will be gone. The devil won't be able to torment you and cause devastation anywhere, because he'll be burning in a lake of fire.

But some things have to happen before Jesus returns to rule with perfect peace and justice. He says that "the Good News must be told to all people." Now that's something you can help with! You can go on a mission trip while you're a teen. That's the best time to go! Start to pray about it now. Ask God where he wants to send you and how you are to get the money to go. One of the conditions for Jesus' return is for the Good News to be preached in all nations. You can go and do it!

SEE FOR YOURSELF:

Matt. 24:30–31; Rev. 22:20

14“You will see ‘the destroying terror’[n] standing where it should not be.” (You who read this
should understand what it means.) “At that
time, the people in Judea should run away to
the mountains. 15If people are on the roofs[n] of
their houses, they must not go down or go inside to get anything out of their houses. 16If
people are in the fields, they must not go back
to get their coats. 17At that time, how terrible it
will be for women who are pregnant or have
nursing babies! 18Pray that these things will not
happen in winter, 19because those days will be
full of trouble. There will be more trouble than
there has ever been since the beginning, when
God made the world, until now, and nothing as
bad will ever happen again. 20God has decided
to make that terrible time short. Otherwise, no
one would go on living. But God will make that
time short to help the people he has chosen.
21At that time, someone might say to you,
‘Look, there is the Christ!’ Or another person
might say, ‘There he is!’ But don’t believe them.
22False Christs and false prophets will come and
perform great wonders and miracles. They will
try to fool even the people God has chosen, if
that is possible. 23So be careful. I have warned
you about all this before it happens.

24“During the days after this trouble comes,
‘the sun will grow dark,
and the moon will not give its light.
25The stars will fall from the sky.
And the powers of the heavens will be
shaken.’ *Isaiah 13:10; 34:4*

26“Then people will see the Son of Man coming in clouds with great power and glory.
27Then he will send his angels all around the
earth to gather his chosen people from every
part of the earth and from every part of heaven.

28“Learn a lesson from the fig tree: When its
branches become green and soft and new
leaves appear, you know summer is near. 29In
the same way, when you see these things happening, you will know that the time is near,
ready to come. 30I tell you the truth, all these
things will happen while the people of this
time are still living. 31Earth and sky will be destroyed, but the words I have said will never
be destroyed.

32“No one knows when that day or time will
be, not the angels in heaven, not even the Son.
Only the Father knows. 33Be careful! Always be
ready, because you don’t know when that time
will be. 34It is like a man who goes on a trip. He
leaves his house and lets his servants take care

13:14 ‘the destroying terror’ Mentioned in Daniel 9:27; 12:11 (cf. Daniel 11:31). **13:15 roofs** In Bible times houses were built with flat roofs. The roof was used for drying things such as flax and fruit. And it was used as an extra room, as a place for worship, and as a cool place to sleep in the summer.

Promise

HE PROMISES HIS WORDS WILL LAST FOREVER.

Earth and sky will be destroyed, but the words I have said will never be destroyed (Mark 13:31).

The earth and the sky look like the strongest, most permanent things around. In fact, if there’s one thing that most people will bet on, it’s that—cloudy or clear—the sun will come out tomorrow. It’s a lot easier to bank on the things you can see rather than on the things you can’t see.

But Jesus looked at the huge, blue sky above him and the solid, dusty earth under his feet and told his followers that the things he was saying would outlast the earth and sky. He wanted them to know that even though it might not look like it, it would be better for them to invest in things they couldn’t see—the kingdom of God that he was telling them about—rather than in things they could see.

It will be tempting for you to spend your time and your energy going after things that you can see—an education, a good job, a nice place to live, neat stuff to make your life comfortable, a family of your own eventually. There’s certainly nothing wrong with those things. But Jesus is encouraging you, even warning you, to give the best and the most of your time and energy to the things that will last forever—his Word, his kingdom, and your relationship with him.

SEE FOR YOURSELF:

Is. 40:8

of it, giving each one a special job to do. The man tells the servant guarding the door always to be watchful. 35 So always be ready, because you don't know when the owner of the house will come back. It might be in the evening, or at midnight, or in the morning while it is still dark, or when the sun rises. 36 Always be ready. Otherwise he might come back suddenly and find you sleeping. 37 I tell you this, and I say this to everyone: 'Be ready!' "

THE PLAN TO KILL JESUS

14 1 It was now only two days before the Passover and the Feast of Unleavened Bread. The leading priests and teachers of the law were trying to find a trick to arrest Jesus and kill him. 2 But they said, "We must not do it during the feast, because the people might cause a riot."

A WOMAN WITH PERFUME FOR JESUS

3 Jesus was in Bethany at the house of Simon, who had a skin disease. While Jesus was eating there, a woman approached him with an alabaster jar filled with very expensive perfume, made of pure nard. She opened the jar and poured the perfume on Jesus' head.

4 Some who were there became upset and said to each other, "Why waste that perfume? 5 It was worth a full year's work. It could have been sold and the money given to the poor." And they got very angry with the woman.

6 Jesus said, "Leave her alone. Why are you troubling her? She did an excellent thing for me. 7 You will always have the poor with you, and you can help them anytime you want. But you will not always have me. 8 This woman did the only thing she could do for me; she poured perfume on my body to prepare me for burial. 9 I tell you the truth, wherever the Good News is preached in all the world, what this woman has done will be told, and people will remember her."

JUDAS BECOMES AN ENEMY OF JESUS

10 One of the twelve apostles, Judas Iscariot, went to talk to the leading priests to offer to hand Jesus over to them. 11 These priests were pleased about this and promised to pay Judas money. So he watched for the best time to turn Jesus in.

JESUS EATS THE PASSOVER MEAL

12 It was now the first day of the Feast of Unleavened Bread when the Passover lamb was sacrificed. Jesus' followers said to him, "Where do you want us to go and prepare for you to eat the Passover meal?"

13 Jesus sent two of his followers and said to them, "Go into the city and a man carrying a jar of water will meet you. Follow him. 14 When he goes into a house, tell the owner of the house, 'The Teacher says: Where is my guest room in which I can eat the Passover meal with my followers?' 15 The owner will show you a large room upstairs that is furnished and ready. Prepare the food for us there."

16 So the followers left and went into the city. Everything happened as Jesus had said, so they prepared the Passover meal.

17 In the evening, Jesus went to that house with the twelve. 18 While they were all eating, Jesus said, "I tell you the truth, one of you will turn against me—one of you eating with me now."

19 The followers were very sad to hear this. Each one began to say to Jesus, "I am not the one, am I?"

20 Jesus answered, "It is one of the twelve—the one who dips his bread into the bowl with me. 21 The Son of Man will die, just as the Scriptures say. But how terrible it will be for the person who hands the Son of Man over to be killed. It would be better for him if he had never been born."

THE LORD'S SUPPER

22 While they were eating, Jesus took some bread and thanked God for it and broke it. Then he gave it to his followers and said, "Take it; this is my body."

23 Then Jesus took a cup and thanked God for it and gave it to the followers, and they all drank from the cup.

24 Then Jesus said, "This is my blood which is the new agreement that God makes with his people. This blood is poured out for many. 25 I tell you the truth, I will not drink of this fruit of the vine[n] again until that day when I drink it new in the kingdom of God."

26 After singing a hymn, they went out to the Mount of Olives.

JESUS' FOLLOWERS WILL LEAVE HIM

27 Then Jesus told the followers, "You will all stumble in your faith, because it is written in the Scriptures:

'I will kill the shepherd,
    and the sheep will scatter.' *Zechariah 13:7*

28 But after I rise from the dead, I will go ahead of you into Galilee."

14:25 fruit of the vine Product of the grapevine; this may also be translated "wine."

29 Peter said, "Everyone else may stumble in
their faith, but I will not."
30 Jesus answered, "I tell you the truth, tonight before the rooster crows twice you will
say three times you don't know me."
31 But Peter insisted, "I will never say that I
don't know you! I will even die with you!" And
all the other followers said the same thing.

JESUS PRAYS ALONE

32 Jesus and his followers went to a place
called Gethsemane. He said to them, "Sit here
while I pray." 33 Jesus took Peter, James, and
John with him, and he began to be very sad
and troubled. 34 He said to them, "My heart is
full of sorrow, to the point of death. Stay here
and watch."
35 After walking a little farther away from
them, Jesus fell to the ground and prayed that,
if possible, he would not have this time of suffering. 36 He prayed, "Abba,[n] Father! You can do
all things. Take away this cup[n] of suffering. But
do what you want, not what I want."
37 Then Jesus went back to his followers and
found them asleep. He said to Peter, "Simon,
are you sleeping? Couldn't you stay awake
with me for one hour? 38 Stay awake and pray
for strength against temptation. The spirit
wants to do what is right, but the body is
weak."
39 Again Jesus went away and prayed the
same thing. 40 Then he went back to his followers, and again he found them asleep, because
their eyes were very heavy. And they did not
know what to say to him.
41 After Jesus prayed a third time, he went
back to his followers and said to them, "Are
you still sleeping and resting? That's enough.
The time has come for the Son of Man to be
handed over to sinful people. 42 Get up, we
must go. Look, here comes the man who has
turned against me."

JESUS IS ARRESTED

43 At once, while Jesus was still speaking, Judas, one of the twelve apostles, came up. With
him were many people carrying swords and
clubs who had been sent from the leading
priests, the teachers of the law, and the older
Jewish leaders.
44 Judas had planned a signal for them, saying, "The man I kiss is Jesus. Arrest him and
guard him while you lead him away." 45 So Judas went straight to Jesus and said, "Teacher!"
and kissed him. 46 Then the people grabbed
Jesus and arrested him. 47 One of his followers
standing nearby pulled out his sword and
struck the servant of the high priest and cut off
his ear.
48 Then Jesus said, "You came to get me with
swords and clubs as if I were a criminal.
49 Every day I was with you teaching in the
Temple, and you did not arrest me there. But all
these things have happened to make the Scriptures come true." 50 Then all of Jesus' followers
left him and ran away.
51 A young man, wearing only a linen cloth,
was following Jesus, and the people also
grabbed him. 52 But the cloth he was wearing
came off, and he ran away naked.

JESUS BEFORE THE LEADERS

53 The people who arrested Jesus led him to
the house of the high priest, where all the leading priests, the older leaders, and the teachers
of the law were gathered. 54 Peter followed far
behind and entered the courtyard of the high
priest's house. There he sat with the guards,
warming himself by the fire.
55 The leading priests and the whole council
tried to find something that Jesus had done
wrong so they could kill him. But the council
could find no proof of anything. 56 Many people came and told false things about him,
but all said different things—none of them
agreed.
57 Then some people stood up and lied about
Jesus, saying, 58 "We heard this man say, 'I will
destroy this Temple that people made. And
three days later, I will build another Temple not
made by people.' " 59 But even the things these
people said did not agree.
60 Then the high priest stood before them
and asked Jesus, "Aren't you going to answer?
Don't you have something to say about their
charges against you?" 61 But Jesus said
nothing; he did not answer.
The high priest asked Jesus
another question: "Are you the
Christ, the Son of the blessed
God?"
62 Jesus answered, "I am.
And in the future you will see
the Son of Man sitting at the
right hand of God, the Powerful One, and coming on clouds in the sky."
63 When the high priest heard this, he tore
his clothes and said, "We don't need any more

JESUS
Will the Messiah come again? (14:61–62)

14:36 Abba Name that a Jewish child called his father. **14:36 cup** Jesus is talking about the terrible things that will happen to him. Accepting these things will be very hard, like drinking a cup of something bitter.

witnesses! 64You all heard him say these things against God. What do you think?"

They all said that Jesus was guilty and should die. 65Some of the people there began to spit at Jesus. They blindfolded him and beat him with their fists and said, "Prove you are a prophet!" Then the guards led Jesus away and beat him.

PETER SAYS HE DOESN'T KNOW JESUS

66While Peter was in the courtyard, a servant girl of the high priest came there. 67She saw Peter warming himself at the fire and looked closely at him.

Then she said, "You also were with Jesus, that man from Nazareth."

68But Peter said that he was never with Jesus. He said, "I don't know or understand what you are talking about." Then Peter left and went toward the entrance of the courtyard. And the rooster crowed.[n]

69The servant girl saw Peter there, and again she said to the people who were standing nearby, "This man is one of those who followed Jesus." 70Again Peter said that it was not true.

A short time later, some people were standing near Peter saying, "Surely you are one of those who followed Jesus, because you are from Galilee, too."

71Then Peter began to place a curse on himself and swear, "I don't know this man you're talking about!"

72At once, the rooster crowed the second time. Then Peter remembered what Jesus had told him: "Before the rooster crows twice, you will say three times that you don't know me." Then Peter lost control of himself and began to cry.

PILATE QUESTIONS JESUS

15 1Very early in the morning, the leading priests, the older leaders, the teachers of the law, and all the Jewish council decided what to do with Jesus. They tied him, led him away, and turned him over to Pilate, the governor.

2Pilate asked Jesus, "Are you the king of the Jews?"

Jesus answered, "Those are your words."

3The leading priests accused Jesus of many things. 4So Pilate asked Jesus another question, "You can see that they are accusing you of many things. Aren't you going to answer?"

5But Jesus still said nothing, so Pilate was very surprised.

PILATE TRIES TO FREE JESUS

6Every year at the time of the Passover the governor would free one prisoner whom the people chose. 7At that time, there was a man named Barabbas in prison who was a rebel and had committed murder during a riot. 8The crowd came to Pilate and began to ask him to free a prisoner as he always did.

9So Pilate asked them, "Do you want me to free the king of the Jews?" 10Pilate knew that the leading priests had turned Jesus in to him because they were jealous. 11But the leading priests had persuaded the people to ask Pilate to free Barabbas, not Jesus.

12Then Pilate asked the crowd again, "So what should I do with this man you call the king of the Jews?"

13They shouted, "Crucify him!"

14Pilate asked, "Why? What wrong has he done?"

But they shouted even louder, "Crucify him!"

15Pilate wanted to please the crowd, so he freed Barabbas for them. After having Jesus beaten with whips, he handed Jesus over to the soldiers to be crucified.

16The soldiers took Jesus into the governor's palace (called the Praetorium) and called all the other soldiers together. 17They put a purple robe on Jesus and used thorny branches to make a crown for his head. 18They began to call out to him, "Hail, King of the Jews!" 19The soldiers beat Jesus on the head many times with a stick. They spit on him and made fun of him by bowing on their knees and worshiping him. 20After they finished, the soldiers took off the purple robe and put his own clothes on him again. Then they led him out of the palace to be crucified.

JESUS IS CRUCIFIED

21A man named Simon from Cyrene, the father of Alexander and Rufus, was coming from the fields to the city. The soldiers forced Simon to carry the cross for Jesus. 22They led Jesus to the place called Golgotha, which means the Place of the Skull. 23The soldiers tried to give Jesus wine mixed with myrrh to drink, but he refused. 24The soldiers crucified Jesus and divided his clothes among themselves, throwing lots to decide what each soldier would get.

25It was nine o'clock in the morning when they crucified Jesus. 26There was a sign with this charge against Jesus written on it: THE KING OF THE JEWS. 27They also put two robbers on

14:68 And . . . crowed. A few, early Greek copies leave out this phrase.

WHAT'S IT MEAN?

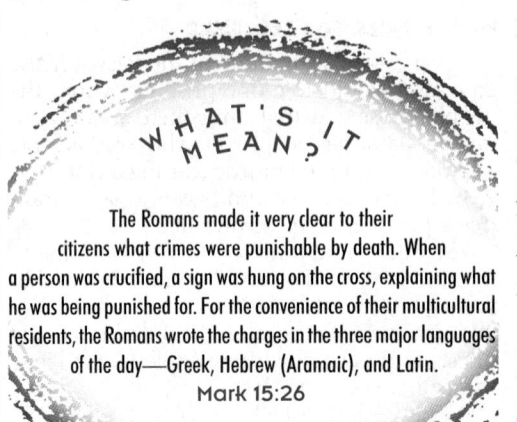

The Romans made it very clear to their citizens what crimes were punishable by death. When a person was crucified, a sign was hung on the cross, explaining what he was being punished for. For the convenience of their multicultural residents, the Romans wrote the charges in the three major languages of the day—Greek, Hebrew (Aramaic), and Latin.
Mark 15:26

crosses beside Jesus, one on the right, and the
other on the left. 28[n] 29People walked by and
insulted Jesus and shook their heads, saying,
"You said you could destroy the Temple and
build it again in three days. 30So save yourself!
Come down from that cross!"
31The leading priests and the teachers of the
law were also making fun of Jesus. They said to
each other, "He saved other people, but he can't
save himself. 32If he is really the Christ, the king
of Israel, let him come down now from the
cross. When we see this, we will believe in
him." The robbers who were being crucified
beside Jesus also insulted him.

JESUS DIES

33At noon the whole country became dark,
and the darkness lasted for three hours. 34At
three o'clock Jesus cried in a loud voice, "Eloi,
Eloi, lama sabachthani." This means, "My God,
my God, why have you rejected me?"
35When some of the people standing there
heard this, they said, "Listen! He is calling
Elijah."
36Someone there ran and got a sponge, filled
it with vinegar, tied it to a stick, and gave it to
Jesus to drink. He said, "We want to see if Elijah
will come to take him down from the cross."
37Then Jesus cried in a loud voice and died.
38The curtain in the Temple[n] was torn into
two pieces, from the top to the bottom. 39When
the army officer who was standing in front of
the cross saw what happened when Jesus died,
he said, "This man really was the Son of God!"
40Some women were standing at a distance
from the cross, watching; among them were
Mary Magdalene, Salome, and Mary the
mother of James and Joseph. (James was her
youngest son.) 41These women had followed
Jesus in Galilee and helped him. Many other
women were also there who had come with
Jesus to Jerusalem.

JESUS IS BURIED

42This was Preparation Day. (That means
the day before the Sabbath day.) That evening,
43Joseph from Arimathea was brave enough to
go to Pilate and ask for Jesus' body. Joseph, an
important member of the Jewish council, was
one of the people who was waiting for the
kingdom of God to come. 44Pilate was amazed

On the Edge

Then Jesus cried in a loud voice and died (Mark 15:37).

We hear a lot about Jesus dying for the whole world, and we know that we're included in the whole world part. But did you know that Jesus died just for *you?* Before Jesus came to earth, he knew about you. He knew what you would look like. He knew what your name and your personality would be. He even knew you would sin. Even more than knowing about you, he loved you. He loved you so much, that if you had been the *only* person to ever live on earth, he would have come to die for you. You aren't just one of many or a face in the crowd. When he hung on the cross, you were in his mind. He sacrificed his life so that you could live for eternity with him. You are the reason Jesus came, lived, died, and rose from the grave. He paid for your sin through his own death. He knows you intimately and wants you to know him—the One who died so you could live forever with him.

SEE FOR YOURSELF: Matt. 27:50; Rom. 5:6, 8, 18; 8:32

15:28 Verse 28 Some Greek copies add verse 28: "And the Scripture came true that says, 'They put him with criminals.' " **15:38 curtain in the Temple** A curtain divided the Most Holy Place from the other part of the Temple. That was the special building in Jerusalem where God commanded the Jewish people to worship him.

WHAT'S IT MEAN?

Crucifixion usually was not a quick way to die. Unless the person had been severely beaten before being crucified, he could actually survive several days on the cross! One of the most common causes of death among those who were crucified was suffocation. Because of the outstretched position, when the person became too exhausted to raise himself up to breathe, he simply suffocated.

Mark 15:44

that Jesus would have already died, so he called
the army officer who had guarded Jesus and
asked him if Jesus had already died. 45The officer told Pilate that he was dead, so Pilate told
Joseph he could have the body. 46Joseph
bought some linen cloth, took the body down
from the cross, and wrapped it in the linen. He
put the body in a tomb that was cut out of a
wall of rock. Then he rolled a very large stone
to block the entrance of the tomb. 47And Mary
Magdalene and Mary the mother of Joseph saw
the place where Jesus was laid.

JESUS RISES FROM THE DEAD

16 1The day after the Sabbath day, Mary Magdalene, Mary the mother of James, and Salome
bought some sweet-smelling spices to put on
Jesus' body. 2Very early on that day, the first
day of the week, soon after sunrise, the women
were on their way to the tomb. 3They said to
each other, "Who will roll away for us the
stone that covers the entrance of the tomb?"
4Then the women looked and saw that the
stone had already been rolled away, even
though it was very large. 5The women entered
the tomb and saw a young man wearing a
white robe and sitting on the right side, and
they were afraid.
6But the man said, "Don't be afraid. You are
looking for Jesus from Nazareth, who has been
crucified. He has risen from the dead; he is not
here. Look, here is the place they laid him.
7Now go and tell his followers and Peter, 'Jesus
is going into Galilee ahead of you, and you will
see him there as he told you before.' "
8The women were confused and shaking
with fear, so they left the tomb and ran away.
They did not tell anyone about what happened, because they were afraid.

On the Edge

Anyone who believes and is baptized will be saved, but anyone who does not believe will be punished (Mark 16:16).

God designed the world so that there would be consequences for sin. He also required that a payment be made for sin. He knew we could never pay for all our sins. Without payment, the eternal consequence is condemnation and separation from God in hell—forever. His heart was broken by that thought. The only way to save us was to send someone to be perfect, and to die the death that *we* deserved. To give us a way out of eternal damnation, he sent his perfect Son, Jesus.

Jesus lived a sinless life and then died as a sacrifice for our sins. God said that Jesus' death was enough to pay for everyone's sin. Nothing else needed to be done. Nothing else could be done. The payment has been made for all of your sin.

To receive the benefit of Jesus' death, you have to believe in him. Deciding to believe that Jesus Christ died for you is called "being saved." Believing in him saves you from being condemned and separated from God forever. Your friends may want you to be saved because they can't imagine heaven without you. Your family wants you to be saved because they don't ever want to leave you. But the Lord, more than anything, wants you to be saved because he created you, and he loves you more than you can understand. He doesn't want you to be judged and spend eternity apart from him in hell.

There are all kinds of great reasons to be saved, but the best one has to do with being with God forever. Heaven is reserved for those who decide to believe that Jesus Christ is who he said he was. You are free to choose. God will not force you to love him. Forced love is not true love. But today, if you hear his voice and know these things are true, do not harden your heart. Run to him and be saved!

SEE FOR YOURSELF:
Matt. 3:16;
John 3:16–17; 10:8–9;
Acts 3:19–20;
Rom. 6:22–23

Verses 9–20 are not included in two of the best and oldest Greek manuscripts of Mark.

SOME FOLLOWERS SEE JESUS

[9After Jesus rose from the dead early on the first day of the week, he showed himself first to Mary Magdalene. One time in the past, he had forced seven demons out of her. 10After Mary saw Jesus, she went and told his followers, who were very sad and were crying. 11But Mary told them that Jesus was alive. She said that she had seen him, but the followers did not believe her.

12Later, Jesus showed himself to two of his followers while they were walking in the country, but he did not look the same as before. 13These followers went back to the others and told them what had happened, but again, the followers did not believe them.

JESUS TALKS TO THE APOSTLES

14Later Jesus showed himself to the eleven apostles while they were eating, and he criticized them because they had no faith. They were stubborn and refused to believe those who had seen him after he had risen from the dead.

15Jesus said to his followers, "Go everywhere in the world, and tell the Good News to everyone. 16Anyone who believes and is baptized will be saved, but anyone who does not believe will be punished. 17And those who believe will be able to do these things as proof: They will use my name to force out demons. They will speak in new languages.[n] 18They will pick up snakes and drink poison without being hurt. They will touch the sick, and the sick will be healed."

19After the Lord Jesus said these things to his followers, he was carried up into heaven, and he sat at the right side of God. 20The followers went everywhere in the world and told the Good News to people, and the Lord helped them. The Lord proved that the Good News they told was true by giving them power to work miracles.]

WHAT'S IT MEAN?

The followers of Jesus were down to eleven since Judas Iscariot had committed suicide after betraying him. The remaining followers later chose a man named Matthias to replace Judas. Why? Some experts believe the number twelve had a symbolic meaning, perhaps relating to the twelve tribes of Israel.

Mark 16:14

16:17 languages This can also be translated "tongues."

Luke

CONTENT

If the Book of Mark is like an action film, then Luke is like a documentary.

Luke was a doctor: very detailed and organized. He wrote his version of the Good News that way. It was important to him to get the facts straight and to let you know exactly how things happened.

Luke's main point in writing was this: Even though Jesus was God, he was also really and truly human. He was born as a baby like we all were. He grew up as a child like we all do. He was a teenager before he was an adult. He had a human body. He had human emotions. If he cut himself, it hurt physically. If his friend let him down, it hurt emotionally.

As a doctor, Luke had spent his life understanding how humans work so that he could help fix the problems we face. It was important to him, then, to tell us that Jesus was miraculously all God and all human. That means Jesus knows even more about how humans work. He knows how it is to face life as a baby, as a child, as a teenager, as an adult. And he knows how to fix the problems that we face.

Outline

1:1–4 .... Why Luke Wrote This Book
1:5—2:52 .... The Births of John the Baptist and Jesus
3:1–20 .... The Message of John the Baptist
3:21—4:13 .... The Baptism and Temptation of Jesus
4:14—9:50 .... Jesus' Ministry in Galilee
9:51—19:27 .... Jesus Goes from Galilee to Jerusalem
19:28—23:56 ...... Jesus' Last Week: His Trial and Death
24:1–12 .... Jesus Is Alive
24:13–53 .... Jesus Appears and Is Taken to Heaven

Purpose

We are to live as Jesus did, showing concern for all.

Theme

Jesus the Savior of the World

Date of writing

Early 60s A.D.

"The Son of Man came to find lost people and save them" (19:10).

Bible Talk

John the Baptist

A lot of times before big concerts, a "front man" will go into a city and get everything ready before the singer shows up.

John the Baptist was like Jesus' front man. He prepared the way. He got the place ready.

It was not an easy job. First of all, the people of John's day were not ready to be convinced that Jesus was the Messiah. They wanted a Messiah who would lead an army and overthrow the Roman government. Instead they got a Messiah who let himself be executed. Once even John himself asked Jesus if he was really *the* One.

But John did the job he came to do. He baptized people into faith in Jesus. He even baptized Jesus. And when it came time, he was more than happy to lose his followers so they could be followers of Christ.

WOMEN IN MINISTRY

Luke mentions women in ministry more than any other book. You might already know that, when Jesus was alive, his culture didn't value women very much. Women were treated like second-class citizens—if they were treated like citizens at all.

Jesus didn't treat women like that, though. He worked side by side with women, as well as with men. There were women who supported his ministry all the way through his death, burial, and the Resurrection.

Jesus came into the world to knock down barriers—including the barriers that say "girls aren't as good as guys."

LUKE WRITES ABOUT JESUS' LIFE

1 Many have tried to report on the things that happened among us. 2 They have written the same things that we learned from others—the people who saw those things from the beginning and served God by telling people his message. 3 Since I myself have studied everything carefully from the beginning, most excellent[n] Theophilus, it seemed good for me to write it out for you. I arranged it in order 4 to help you know that what you have been taught is true.

ZECHARIAH AND ELIZABETH

5 During the time Herod ruled Judea, there was a priest named Zechariah who belonged to Abijah's group.[n] Zechariah's wife, Elizabeth, came from the family of Aaron. 6 Zechariah and Elizabeth truly did what God said was good. They did everything the Lord commanded and were without fault in keeping his law. 7 But they had no children, because Elizabeth could not have a baby, and both of them were very old.

8 One day Zechariah was serving as a priest before God, because his group was on duty. 9 According to the custom of the priests, he was chosen by lot to go into the Temple of the Lord and burn incense. 10 There were a great many people outside praying at the time the incense was offered. 11 Then an angel of the Lord appeared to Zechariah, standing on the right side of the incense table. 12 When he saw the angel, Zechariah was startled and frightened. 13 But the angel said to him, "Zechariah, don't be afraid. God has heard your prayer. Your wife, Elizabeth, will give birth to a son, and you will name him John. 14 He will bring you joy and gladness, and many people will be happy because of his birth. 15 John will be a great man for the Lord. He will never drink wine or beer, and even from birth, he will be filled with the Holy Spirit. 16 He will help many people of Israel return to the Lord their God. 17 He will go before the Lord in spirit and power like Elijah. He will make peace between parents and their children and will bring those who are not obeying God back to the right way of thinking, to make a people ready for the coming of the Lord."

18 Zechariah said to the angel, "How can I know that what you say is true? I am an old man, and my wife is old, too."

19 The angel answered him, "I am Gabriel. I stand before God, who sent me to talk to you and to tell you this good news. 20 Now, listen! You will not be able to speak until the day these things happen, because you did not believe what I told you. But they will really happen."

21 Outside, the people were still waiting for Zechariah and were surprised that he was staying so long in the Temple. 22 When Zechariah came outside, he could not speak to them, and they knew he had seen a vision in the Temple. He could only make signs to them and remained unable to speak. 23 When his time of service at the Temple was finished, he went home.

24 Later, Zechariah's wife, Elizabeth, became pregnant and did not go out of her house for five months. Elizabeth said, 25 "Look what the Lord has done for me! My people were ashamed[n] of me, but now the Lord has taken away that shame."

AN ANGEL APPEARS TO MARY

26 During Elizabeth's sixth month of pregnancy, God sent the angel Gabriel to Nazareth, a town in Galilee, 27 to a virgin. She was engaged to marry a man named Joseph from the family of David. Her name was Mary. 28 The angel came to her and said, "Greetings! The Lord has blessed you and is with you."

29 But Mary was very startled by what the angel said and wondered what this greeting might mean.

WHAT'S IT MEAN?

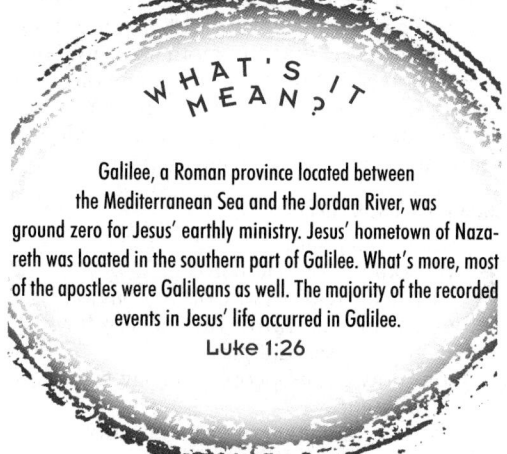

Galilee, a Roman province located between the Mediterranean Sea and the Jordan River, was ground zero for Jesus' earthly ministry. Jesus' hometown of Nazareth was located in the southern part of Galilee. What's more, most of the apostles were Galileans as well. The majority of the recorded events in Jesus' life occurred in Galilee.

Luke 1:26

1:3 excellent This word was used to show respect to an important person like a king or ruler.
1:5 Abijah's group The Jewish priests were divided into twenty-four groups. See 1 Chronicles 24.
1:25 ashamed The Jewish people thought it was a disgrace for women not to have children.

30The angel said to her, "Don't be afraid,
Mary; God has shown you his grace. 31Listen!
You will become pregnant and give birth to a
son, and you will name him Jesus. 32He will be
great and will be called the Son of the Most
High. The Lord God will give him the throne of
King David, his ancestor. 33He will rule over the
people of Jacob forever, and his kingdom will
never end."
34Mary said to the angel, "How will this
happen since I am a virgin?"
35The angel said to Mary, "The Holy Spirit
will come upon you, and the power of the
Most High will cover you. For this
reason the baby will be holy
and will be called the Son of
God. 36Now Elizabeth, your
relative, is also pregnant with
a son though she is very old.
Everyone thought she could
not have a baby, but she has
been pregnant for six months. 37God can do
anything!"

JESUS
What role does Jesus have in the Trinity? (1:35)

38Mary said, "I am the servant of the Lord.
Let this happen to me as you say!" Then the
angel went away.

MARY VISITS ELIZABETH

39Mary got up and went quickly to a town
in the hills of Judea. 40She came to Zechariah's
house and greeted Elizabeth. 41When Elizabeth
heard Mary's greeting, the unborn baby inside
her jumped, and Elizabeth was filled with the
Holy Spirit. 42She cried out in a loud voice,
"God has blessed you more than any other
woman, and he has blessed the baby to which
you will give birth. 43Why has this good thing
happened to me, that the mother of my Lord
comes to me? 44When I heard your voice, the
baby inside me jumped with joy. 45You are
blessed because you believed that what the
Lord said to you would really happen."

MARY PRAISES GOD

46Then Mary said,
"My soul praises the Lord;
47 my heart rejoices in God my Savior,
48 because he has shown his concern for his
humble servant girl.
From now on, all people will say that I am
blessed,
49 because the Powerful One has done
great things for me.
His name is holy.
50 God will show his mercy forever and ever
to those who worship and serve him.
51 He has done mighty deeds by his power.
He has scattered the people who are
proud
and think great things about themselves.
52 He has brought down rulers from their
thrones
and raised up the humble.
53 He has filled the hungry with good things
and sent the rich away with nothing.
54 He has helped his servant, the people of
Israel,
remembering to show them mercy
55 as he promised to our ancestors,
to Abraham and to his children forever."
56Mary stayed with Elizabeth for about
three months and then returned home.

THE BIRTH OF JOHN

57When it was time for Elizabeth to give
birth, she had a boy. 58Her neighbors and relatives heard how good the Lord was to her, and
they rejoiced with her.
59When the baby was eight days old, they
came to circumcise him. They wanted to name
him Zechariah because this was his father's
name, 60but his mother said, "No! He will be
named John."
61The people said to Elizabeth, "But no
one in your family has this name." 62Then
they made signs to his father to find out
what he would like to name him.
63Zechariah asked for a writing tablet and
wrote, "His name is John," and everyone was
surprised. 64Immediately Zechariah could talk
again, and he began praising God. 65All their
neighbors became alarmed, and in all the
mountains of Judea people continued talking
about all these things. 66The people who heard
about them wondered, saying, "What will this
child be?" because the Lord was with him.

ZECHARIAH PRAISES GOD

67Then Zechariah, John's father, was filled
with the Holy Spirit and prophesied:
68 "Let us praise the Lord, the God of Israel,
because he has come to help his people
and has given them freedom.
69 He has given us a powerful Savior
from the family of God's servant David.
70 He said that he would do this
through his holy prophets who lived
long ago:
71 He promised he would save us from our
enemies
and from the power of all those who
hate us.
72 He said he would give mercy to our
fathers

and that he would remember his holy
promise.
73 God promised Abraham, our father,
74 that he would save us from the power
of our enemies
so we could serve him without fear,
75 being holy and good before God as long
as we live.

76 "Now you, child, will be called a prophet
of the Most High God.
You will go before the Lord to prepare
his way.
77 You will make his people know that they
will be saved
by having their sins forgiven.
78 With the loving mercy of our God,
a new day from heaven will dawn upon
us.
79 It will shine on those who live in darkness,
in the shadow of death.
It will guide us into the path of peace."
80 And so the child grew up and became
strong in spirit. John lived in the desert until
the time when he came out to preach to Israel.

WHAT'S IT MEAN?

Ever heard of Julius Caesar? Augustus was not only his grandnephew, but he was also Caesar's chosen heir. When Julius Caesar was assassinated in 44 B.C., Augustus shared the throne of the Roman Empire with another famous figure from history, Mark Antony, and a man named Lepidus. By 27 B.C., Augustus was the sole ruler of Rome.

Luke 2:1

THE BIRTH OF JESUS

2 [1] At that time, Augustus Caesar sent an order that all people in the countries under Roman rule must list their names in a register.
[2] This was the first registration;[n] it was taken
while Quirinius was governor of Syria. [3] And
all went to their own towns to be registered.
[4] So Joseph left Nazareth, a town in Galilee,
and went to the town of Bethlehem in Judea,
known as the town of David. Joseph went
there because he was from the family of David.
[5] Joseph registered with Mary, to whom he was
engaged[n] and who was now pregnant. [6] While
they were in Bethlehem, the time came for
Mary to have the baby, [7] and she gave birth to
her first son. Because there were no rooms left
in the inn, she wrapped the baby with pieces
of cloth and laid him in a box where animals
are fed.

WHAT'S IT MEAN?

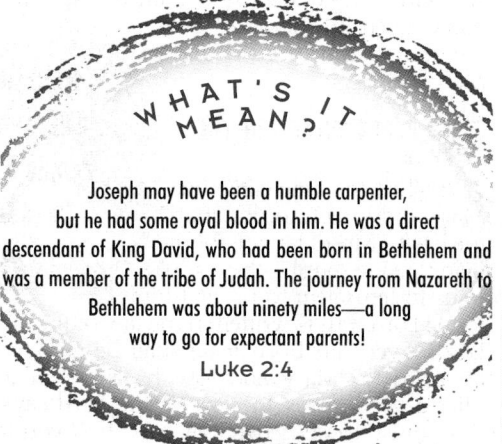

Joseph may have been a humble carpenter, but he had some royal blood in him. He was a direct descendant of King David, who had been born in Bethlehem and was a member of the tribe of Judah. The journey from Nazareth to Bethlehem was about ninety miles—a long way to go for expectant parents!

Luke 2:4

SHEPHERDS HEAR ABOUT JESUS

[8] That night, some shepherds were in the
fields nearby watching their sheep. [9] Then an
angel of the Lord stood before them. The glory
of the Lord was shining around them, and they
became very frightened. [10] The angel said to
them, "Do not be afraid. I am bringing you
good news that will be a great joy to all the
people. [11] Today your Savior was born in the
town of David. He is Christ, the Lord. [12] This is
how you will know him: You will find a baby
wrapped in pieces of cloth and lying in a feeding box."
[13] Then a very large group of angels from
heaven joined the first angel, praising God and
saying:
14 "Give glory to God in heaven,
and on earth let there be peace among
the people who please God."
[15] When the angels left them and went back
to heaven, the shepherds said to each other,
"Let's go to Bethlehem. Let's see this thing that
has happened which the Lord has told us
about."
[16] So the shepherds went quickly and found
Mary and Joseph and the baby, who was lying
in a feeding box. [17] When they had seen him,

2:2 registration Census. A counting of all the people and the things they own. **2:5 engaged** For the Jewish people, an engagement was a lasting agreement. It could only be broken by divorce.

they told what the angels had said about this
child. [18]Everyone was amazed at what the
shepherds said to them. [19]But Mary treasured
these things and continued to think about
them. [20]Then the shepherds went back to their
sheep, praising God and thanking him for
everything they had seen and heard. It had
been just as the angel had told them.
[21]When the baby was eight days old, he
was circumcised and was named Jesus, the
name given by the angel before
the baby began to grow inside
Mary.

JESUS IS PRESENTED IN THE TEMPLE

[22]When the time came for
Mary and Joseph to do what
the law of Moses taught about
being made pure,[n] they took
Jesus to Jerusalem to present him
to the Lord. [23](It is written in the law of the
Lord: "Every firstborn male shall be given to
the Lord.")[n] [24]Mary and Joseph also went to
offer a sacrifice, as the law of the Lord says:
"You must sacrifice two doves or two young
pigeons."[n]

SIMEON SEES JESUS

[25]In Jerusalem lived a man named Simeon
who was a good man and godly. He was waiting for the time when God would take away
Israel's sorrow, and the Holy Spirit was in him.
[26]Simeon had been told by the Holy Spirit that
he would not die before he saw the Christ
promised by the Lord. [27]The Spirit led Simeon
to the Temple. When Mary and Joseph brought
the baby Jesus to the Temple to do what the
law said they must do, [28]Simeon took the baby
in his arms and thanked God:

[29]"Now, Lord, you can let me, your servant,
die in peace as you said.
[30]With my own eyes I have seen your
salvation,
[31] which you prepared before all people.
[32]It is a light for the non-Jewish people to
see
and an honor for your people, the
Israelites."

[33]Jesus' father and mother were amazed at
what Simeon had said about him. [34]Then Simeon blessed them and said to Mary, "God has
chosen this child to cause the fall and rise of
many in Israel. He will be a sign from God that
many people will not accept [35]so that the
thoughts of many will be made known. And
the things that will happen will make your
heart sad, too."

ANNA SEES JESUS

[36]There was a prophetess, Anna, from the
family of Phanuel in the tribe of Asher. Anna
was very old. She had once been married for
seven years. [37]Then her hus-
band died, and she was a widow for eighty-four years.
Anna never left the Temple
but worshiped God, going
without food and praying
day and night. [38]Standing
there at that time, she thanked
God and spoke about Jesus to
all who were waiting for God
to free Jerusalem.

> **"Jesus became wiser and grew physically. People liked him, and he pleased God." (Luke 2:52)**

JOSEPH AND MARY RETURN HOME

[39]When Joseph and Mary had done
everything the law of the Lord commanded,
they went home to Nazareth, their own
town in Galilee. [40]The little child grew and
became strong. He was filled with wisdom,
and God's goodness was upon him.

JESUS AS A BOY

[41]Every year Jesus' parents went to Jerusalem
for the Passover Feast. [42]When he was twelve
years old, they went to the feast as they always
did. [43]After the feast days were over, they
started home. The boy Jesus stayed behind in
Jerusalem, but his parents did not know it.
[44]Thinking that Jesus was with them in the
group, they traveled for a whole day. Then
they began to look for him among their family
and friends. [45]When they did not find him,
they went back to Jerusalem to look for him
there. [46]After three days they found Jesus sitting in the Temple with the teachers, listening
to them and asking them questions. [47]All who
heard him were amazed at his understanding
and answers. [48]When Jesus' parents saw him,
they were astonished. His mother said to him,
"Son, why did you do this to us? Your father
and I were very worried about you and have
been looking for you."
[49]Jesus said to them, "Why were you looking for me? Didn't you know that I must be in

2:22 pure The Law of Moses said that forty days after a Jewish woman gave birth to a son, she must be cleansed by a ceremony at the Temple. Read Leviticus 12:2-8. **2:23 "Every . . . Lord."** Quotation from Exodus 13:2. **2:24 "You . . . pigeons."** Quotation from Leviticus 12:8.

my Father's house?" 50But they did not understand the meaning of what he said.

51Jesus went with them to Nazareth and was obedient to them. But his mother kept in her mind all that had happened. 52Jesus became wiser and grew physically. People liked him, and he pleased God.

THE PREACHING OF JOHN

3 1It was the fifteenth year of the rule of Tiberius Caesar. These men were under Caesar: Pontius Pilate, the ruler of Judea; Herod, the ruler of Galilee; Philip, Herod's brother, the ruler of Iturea and Traconitis; and Lysanias, the ruler of Abilene. 2Annas and Caiaphas were the high priests. At this time, the word of God came to John son of Zechariah in the desert. 3He went all over the area around the Jordan River preaching a baptism of changed hearts and lives for the forgiveness of sins. 4As it is written in the book of Isaiah the prophet:

"This is a voice of one
   who calls out in the desert:
'Prepare the way for the Lord.
   Make the road straight for him.
5Every valley should be filled in,
   and every mountain and hill should be
      made flat.
Roads with turns should be made straight,
   and rough roads should be made smooth.
6And all people will know about the
      salvation of God!' " *Isaiah 40:3-5*

7To the crowds of people who came to be baptized by John, he said, "You are all snakes! Who warned you to run away from God's coming punishment? 8Do the things that show you really have changed your hearts and lives. Don't begin to say to yourselves, 'Abraham is our father.' I tell you that God could make children for Abraham from these rocks. 9The ax is now ready to cut down the trees, and every tree that does not produce good fruit will be cut down and thrown into the fire."[n]

REPENTANCE
What effect does repentance have on our relationship with God? (3:7–9)

10The people asked John, "Then what should we do?"

11John answered, "If you have two shirts, share with the person who does not have one. If you have food, share that also."

12Even tax collectors came to John to be baptized. They said to him, "Teacher, what should we do?"

13John said to them, "Don't take more taxes from people than you have been ordered to take."

14The soldiers asked John, "What about us? What should we do?"

John said to them, "Don't force people to give you money, and don't lie about them. Be satisfied with the pay you get."

15Since the people were hoping for the Christ to come, they wondered if John might be the one.

16John answered everyone, "I baptize you with water, but there is one coming who is

On the Edge

John answered everyone, "I baptize you with water, but there is one coming who is great than I am. I am not good enough to untie his sandals. He will baptize you with the Holy Spirit and fire" (Luke 3:16).

God said that in the last days he would pour out his Spirit on all kinds of people. That means on you and me (see Joel 2:28). Just as he did in that upstairs room in Acts 2, he wants to baptize you with the Holy Spirit and with fire. This will give you a new power that you've never had before. Acts 1:8 says, "But when the Holy Spirit comes to you, you will receive power. You will be my witnesses. . . ." The word *power* comes from the Greek word *dunamis*, which is translated as *dynamite!* So the verse actually says that after the Holy Spirit comes upon you, you will receive dynamite power to be witnesses!

This is exactly what happened to Peter. The same Peter who denied Christ three times preached with dynamite power after he received the Holy Spirit and fire as told in Acts 2. In fact, he led 3,000 people to the Lord in one day. Now that's power! That's the same kind of power everyone needs. How do we get it? It's a gift. All we have to do is ask the Lord for it. He wants to baptize us with the Holy Spirit and fire today, so we can receive that dynamite power to be witnesses for him.

SEE FOR YOURSELF:
Acts 2:1–4, 14–42

3:9 The ax . . . fire. This means that God is ready to punish his people who do not obey him.

greater than I am. I am not good enough to
untie his sandals. He will baptize you with the
Holy Spirit and fire. 17He will come ready to
clean the grain, separating the good grain from
the chaff. He will put the good part of the grain
into his barn, but he will burn the chaff with a
fire that cannot be put out."[n] 18And John continued to preach the Good News, saying many
other things to encourage the people.

19But John spoke against Herod, the governor, because of his sin with Herodias, the
wife of Herod's brother, and because of the
many other evil things Herod did. 20So Herod
did something even worse: He put John in
prison.

JESUS IS BAPTIZED BY JOHN

21When all the people were being baptized
by John, Jesus also was baptized. While Jesus
was praying, heaven opened 22and the Holy
Spirit came down on him in the form of a
dove. Then a voice came from heaven, saying,
"You are my Son, whom I love, and I am very
pleased with you."

THE FAMILY HISTORY OF JESUS

23When Jesus began his ministry, he was
about thirty years old. People thought that
Jesus was Joseph's son.

Joseph was the son[n] of Heli.
24 Heli was the son of Matthat.
Matthat was the son of Levi.
Levi was the son of Melki.
Melki was the son of Jannai.
Jannai was the son of Joseph.
25 Joseph was the son of Mattathias.
Mattathias was the son of Amos.
Amos was the son of Nahum.
Nahum was the son of Esli.
Esli was the son of Naggai.
26 Naggai was the son of Maath.
Maath was the son of Mattathias.
Mattathias was the son of Semein.
Semein was the son of Josech.
Josech was the son of Joda.
27 Joda was the son of Joanan.
Joanan was the son of Rhesa.
Rhesa was the son of Zerubbabel.
Zerubbabel was the grandson of Shealtiel.
Shealtiel was the son of Neri.
28 Neri was the son of Melki.
Melki was the son of Addi.
Addi was the son of Cosam.
Cosam was the son of Elmadam.
Elmadam was the son of Er.
29 Er was the son of Joshua.
Joshua was the son of Eliezer.
Eliezer was the son of Jorim.
Jorim was the son of Matthat.
Matthat was the son of Levi.
30 Levi was the son of Simeon.
Simeon was the son of Judah.
Judah was the son of Joseph.
Joseph was the son of Jonam.
Jonam was the son of Eliakim.
31 Eliakim was the son of Melea.
Melea was the son of Menna.
Menna was the son of Mattatha.
Mattatha was the son of Nathan.
Nathan was the son of David.
32 David was the son of Jesse.
Jesse was the son of Obed.
Obed was the son of Boaz.
Boaz was the son of Salmon.
Salmon was the son of Nahshon.
33 Nahshon was the son of Amminadab.
Amminadab was the son of Admin.
Admin was the son of Arni.
Arni was the son of Hezron.
Hezron was the son of Perez.
Perez was the son of Judah.
34 Judah was the son of Jacob.
Jacob was the son of Isaac.
Isaac was the son of Abraham.
Abraham was the son of Terah.
Terah was the son of Nahor.
35 Nahor was the son of Serug.
Serug was the son of Reu.
Reu was the son of Peleg.
Peleg was the son of Eber.
Eber was the son of Shelah.
36 Shelah was the son of Cainan.
Cainan was the son of Arphaxad.
Arphaxad was the son of Shem.
Shem was the son of Noah.
Noah was the son of Lamech.
37 Lamech was the son of Methuselah.
Methuselah was the son of Enoch.
Enoch was the son of Jared.
Jared was the son of Mahalalel.
Mahalalel was the son of Kenan.
38 Kenan was the son of Enosh.
Enosh was the son of Seth.
Seth was the son of Adam.
Adam was the son of God.

3:17 He will . . . out. This means that Jesus will come to separate good people from bad people, saving the good and punishing the bad. **3:23 son** "Son" in Jewish lists of ancestors can sometimes mean grandson or more distant relative.

JESUS IS TEMPTED BY THE DEVIL

4 1Jesus, filled with the Holy Spirit, returned
from the Jordan River. The Spirit led Jesus into
the desert 2where the devil tempted Jesus for
forty days. Jesus ate nothing during that time,
and when those days were ended, he was very
hungry.
3The devil said to Jesus, "If you are the Son
of God, tell this rock to become bread."
4Jesus answered, "It is written in the Scriptures: 'A person does not live by eating only
bread.' "[n]
5Then the devil took Jesus and showed him
all the kingdoms of the world in an instant.
6The devil said to Jesus, "I will give you all
these kingdoms and all their power and glory.
It has all been given to me, and I can give it to
anyone I wish. 7If you worship me, then it will
all be yours."
8Jesus answered, "It is written in the Scriptures: 'You must worship the Lord your God
and serve only him.' "[n]
9Then the devil led Jesus to Jerusalem and
put him on a high place of the Temple. He said
to Jesus, "If you are the Son of God, jump
down. 10It is written in the Scriptures:

'He has put his angels in charge of you
to watch over you.' *Psalm 91:11*

11It is also written:

'They will catch you in their hands
so that you will not hit your foot on a
rock.' " *Psalm 91:12*

12Jesus answered, "But it also says in the
Scriptures: 'Do not test the Lord your God.' "[n]
13After the devil had tempted Jesus in every
way, he left him to wait until a better time.

JESUS TEACHES THE PEOPLE

14Jesus returned to Galilee in the power of
the Holy Spirit, and stories about him spread
all through the area. 15He began to teach in
their synagogues, and everyone praised him.
16Jesus traveled to Nazareth, where he had
grown up. On the Sabbath day he went to the
synagogue, as he always did, and stood up to
read. 17The book of Isaiah the prophet was
given to him. He opened the book and found
the place where this is written:

18"The Lord has put his Spirit in me,
because he appointed me to tell the
Good News to the poor.
He has sent me to tell the captives they are
free
and to tell the blind that they can see
again. *Isaiah 61:1*
God sent me to free those who have been
treated unfairly *Isaiah 58:6*
19 and to announce the time when the
Lord will show his kindness." *Isaiah 61:2*

On the Edge

Jesus answered, "It is written in the Scriptures: 'You must worship the Lord your God and serve only him'" (Luke 4:8).

Jesus had been in the desert praying about how to get through to men's hearts. Satan tempted him to take the easy way out—turn stones into bread instead of fasting; serve him in return for glory and power; or jump off the Temple, let the angels miraculously save him, and immediately be accepted by the people. Jesus knew that the only way to win the souls of men was to suffer and go to the cross. It was the harder way, but it was the only right way. Jesus responded to Satan by telling him that only God was to be worshiped and served.

You are going to face incredible temptation in your life. You must know that Jesus has been there. He knows the battles you face. You've got the same spiritual resources that Jesus had. You have prayer and the love of your heavenly Father. The power of the Holy Spirit was with Jesus (see 4:1), and the Holy Spirit lives in you. Jesus quoted the Word of God to Satan, and you have the complete Word in your hands. Plus, you now have Jesus in heaven, interceding on your behalf. He has dealt with the devil. And he has completely defeated him.

Satan wants to bring out the worst in us, but God can put the best in us. The next time you are up against the slick devices of Satan, quote a scripture to him and get away from the temptation. Do not play around with Satan. He knows your weakest places, and that's where he'll try to get the best of you. Stay on your toes. Keep alert. Serve God and flee the devil!

SEE FOR YOURSELF:
Deut. 10:20; Ps. 2:10–11;
Luke 3:22; 4:1–2;
James 4:7;
1 Pet. 5:8–9

4:4 'A person . . . bread.' Quotation from Deuteronomy 8:3. **4:8 'You . . . him.'** Quotation from Deuteronomy 6:13. **4:12 'Do . . . God.'** Quotation from Deuteronomy 6:16.

WHAT'S IT MEAN?

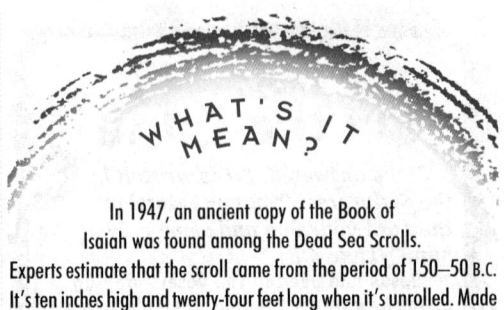

In 1947, an ancient copy of the Book of Isaiah was found among the Dead Sea Scrolls. Experts estimate that the scroll came from the period of 150–50 B.C. It's ten inches high and twenty-four feet long when it's unrolled. Made of thin leather strips sewn together, the scroll is probably very similar to the one Jesus read from.

Luke 4:17

[20]Jesus closed the book, gave it back to the
assistant, and sat down. Everyone in the synagogue was watching Jesus closely. [21]He began
to say to them, "While you heard these words
just now, they were coming true!"
[22]All the people spoke well of Jesus and
were amazed at the words of grace he spoke.
They asked, "Isn't this Joseph's son?"
[23]Jesus said to them, "I know that you will
tell me the old saying: 'Doctor, heal yourself.'
You want to say, 'We heard about the things
you did in Capernaum. Do those things here in
your own town!' " [24]Then Jesus said, "I tell you
the truth, a prophet is not accepted in his
hometown. [25]But I tell you the truth, there
were many widows in Israel during the time of
Elijah. It did not rain in Israel for three and
one-half years, and there was no food anywhere in the whole country. [26]But Elijah was
sent to none of those widows, only to a widow
in Zarephath, a town in Sidon. [27]And there
were many with skin diseases living in Israel
during the time of the prophet Elisha. But none
of them were healed, only Naaman, who was
from the country of Syria."
[28]When all the people in the synagogue
heard these things, they became very angry.
[29]They got up, forced Jesus out of town, and
took him to the edge of the cliff on which the
town was built. They planned to throw him off
the edge, [30]but Jesus walked through the crowd
and went on his way.

Promise HE PROMISES YOU FREEDOM.

The Lord has put his Spirit in me, because he appointed me to tell the Good News to the poor. He has sent me to tell the captives they are free and to tell the blind that they can see again. God sent me to free those who have been treated unfairly (Luke 4:18).

This is such an exciting verse! Did you know that *you* have been chosen to tell the Good News to the poor? The Lord has sent you to announce freedom. But not only have you been sent to announce freedom; you can have freedom as well! There is freedom in Jesus—freedom for everyone who struggles or suffers. What kind of needs do you have? What kind of needs do your friends have? You've been chosen by God, and you've also been equipped with the power of God to get free, stay free, and bring freedom to anyone and everyone who needs it! Now that's power—power over drugs, alcohol, cigarettes, lust, sex, bitterness, or whatever.

There was a movie about a man who gave up his life just to bring freedom to his people. He was beaten, tortured, and put on a chopping block. All he had to do was simply surrender his freedom, and he would live. His people would remain in bondage, but he could live. Instead, he let out a bloodcurdling cry, "Freeeeeedom!" He lost his life, but his people gained their freedom.

There is another story that hits home for all of us. Jesus died a horrible, shameful death on a cross so we could be free from sin and spend eternity with him. Don't allow yourself to be in bondage over some stupid sin—a sin that Jesus has already paid the price for. Choose freedom today, and watch God work a miracle in your life and in the lives of your friends! He is the One who sets you free!

SEE FOR YOURSELF:

Matt. 1:21; John 8:36; Rom. 6:14; 2 Cor. 3:17; Gal. 5:1, 13

JESUS FORCES OUT AN EVIL SPIRIT

[31]Jesus went to Capernaum, a city in Galilee, and on the Sabbath day, he taught the people. [32]They were amazed at his teaching, because he spoke with authority. [33]In the synagogue a man who had within him an evil spirit shouted in a loud voice, [34]"Jesus of Nazareth! What do you want with us? Did you come to destroy us? I know who you are—God's Holy One!"

[35]Jesus commanded the evil spirit, "Be quiet! Come out of the man!" The evil spirit threw the man down to the ground before all the people and then left the man without hurting him.

[36]The people were amazed and said to each other, "What does this mean? With authority and power he commands evil spirits, and they come out." [37]And so the news about Jesus spread to every place in the whole area.

JESUS HEALS MANY PEOPLE

[38]Jesus left the synagogue and went to the home of Simon.[n] Simon's mother-in-law was sick with a high fever, and they asked Jesus to help her. [39]He came to her side and commanded the fever to leave. It left her, and immediately she got up and began serving them.

[40]When the sun went down, the people brought those who were sick to Jesus. Putting his hands on each sick person, he healed every one of them. [41]Demons came out of many people, shouting, "You are the Son of God." But Jesus commanded the demons and would not allow them to speak, because they knew Jesus was the Christ.

[42]At daybreak, Jesus went to a lonely place, but the people looked for him. When they found him, they tried to keep him from leaving. [43]But Jesus said to them, "I must preach about God's kingdom to other towns, too. This is why I was sent."

[44]Then he kept on preaching in the synagogues of Judea.

JESUS' FIRST FOLLOWERS

5 [1]One day while Jesus was standing beside Lake Galilee, many people were pressing all around him to hear the word of God. [2]Jesus saw two boats at the shore of the lake. The fishermen had left them and were washing their nets. [3]Jesus got into one of the boats, the one that belonged to Simon,[n] and asked him to push off a little from the land. Then Jesus sat down and continued to teach the people from the boat.

[4]When Jesus had finished speaking, he said to Simon, "Take the boat into deep water, and put your nets in the water to catch some fish."

[5]Simon answered, "Master, we worked hard all night trying to catch fish, and we caught nothing. But you say to put the nets in the water, so I will." [6]When the fishermen did as Jesus told them, they caught so many fish that the nets began to break. [7]They called to their partners in the other boat to come and help them. They came and filled both boats so full that they were almost sinking.

[8]When Simon Peter saw what had happened, he bowed down before Jesus and said, "Go away from me, Lord. I am a sinful man!" [9]He and the other fishermen were amazed at the many fish they caught, as were [10]James and John, the sons of Zebedee, Simon's partners.

Jesus said to Simon, "Don't be afraid. From now on you will fish for people." [11]When the men brought their boats to the shore, they left everything and followed Jesus.

JESUS HEALS A SICK MAN

[12]When Jesus was in one of the towns, there was a man covered with a skin disease. When he saw Jesus, he bowed before him and begged him, "Lord, you can heal me if you will."

[13]Jesus reached out his hand and touched the man and said, "I will. Be healed!" Immediately the disease disappeared. [14]Then Jesus said, "Don't tell anyone about this, but go and show yourself to the priest[n] and offer a gift for your healing, as Moses commanded.[n] This will show the people what I have done."

[15]But the news about Jesus spread even more. Many people came to hear Jesus and to be healed of their sicknesses, [16]but Jesus often slipped away to be alone so he could pray.

JESUS HEALS A PARALYZED MAN

[17]One day as Jesus was teaching the people, the Pharisees and teachers of the law from every town in Galilee and Judea and from Jerusalem were there. The Lord was giving Jesus the power to heal people. [18]Just then, some men were carrying on a mat a man who was paralyzed. They tried to bring him in and put him down before Jesus. [19]But because there were so many people there, they could not find a way in. So they went up on the roof and

4:38; 5:3 Simon Simon's other name was Peter. **5:14 show . . . priest** The Law of Moses said a priest must say when a Jewish person with a skin disease was well. **5:14 Moses commanded** Read about this in Leviticus 14:1-32.

WHAT'S IT MEAN?

The Pharisees were obsessive about following the Teachings of Moses. They lived by a strict code of conduct, going out of their way to make sure that they honored the Sabbath and maintained their purity. They had elaborate rules about what they could and couldn't do—rules that ultimately didn't have much to do with the Spirit of God's Word. The Pharisees also had a tendency to look down on people who seemed to be careless in following the Teachings of Moses.

Luke 5:17

lowered the man on his mat through the ceiling into the middle of the crowd right before
Jesus. [20]Seeing their faith, Jesus said, "Friend,
your sins are forgiven."
[21]The Jewish teachers of the law and the
Pharisees thought to themselves, "Who is this
man who is speaking as if he were God? Only
God can forgive sins."
[22]But Jesus knew what they were thinking
and said, "Why are you thinking these things?
[23]Which is easier: to say, 'Your sins are forgiven,' or to say, 'Stand up and walk'? [24]But I
will prove to you that the Son of Man has authority on earth to forgive sins." So Jesus said
to the paralyzed man, "I tell you, stand up, take
your mat, and go home."
[25]At once the man stood up before them,
picked up his mat, and went home, praising
God. [26]All the people were fully amazed and
began to praise God. They were filled with
much respect and said, "Today we have seen
amazing things!"

LEVI FOLLOWS JESUS

[27]After this, Jesus went out and saw a tax
collector named Levi sitting in the tax
collector's booth. Jesus said to him, "Follow
me!" [28]So Levi got up, left everything, and followed him.
[29]Then Levi gave a big dinner for Jesus at his
house. Many tax collectors and other people
were eating there, too. [30]But the Pharisees and
the men who taught the law for the Pharisees

Promise — HE PROMISES TO FORGIVE YOUR SINS.

The Son of Man has authority on earth to forgive sins (Luke 5:24a).

Some schools have a wall in the school post office where they post the exam grades. Students sometimes affectionately refer to those places as "the wailing walls." One semester, a young man neglected to study for a particular exam and his test grade reflected it! They left the grades of that test up the entire semester. It was a continual reminder to him of how he had messed up. You can imagine what a happy day it was for him when they finally took down the grades at the end of the term. He could have tried covering up that exam with a black marker (which, by the way, he did). But every time he went into the school post office, there was that big black mark reminding him of his failure.

Jesus is the only One who has the right to forgive your sins. John 1:29 says that he takes them away—completely. When he forgives your sins and takes them away, it's like you never sinned at all. What freedom this understanding brings to our lives!

Sin doesn't have any more power over you! You are free from all that junk, so you don't need to let it rule over you. We are no longer required to sin, because we are free from sin. But if we do mess up, if we do fall short, if we do sin, all we have to do is confess our sins and *wham*—they're gone. God wipes them out. They're history!

So if you've been struggling with something, confess your sins to him right now. Jesus is not only going to forgive you of your sins; he is going to see to it that they are taken away! After all, he is the One who forgives, forgets, and removes!

SEE FOR YOURSELF:

Prov. 24:16; 28:13; Jer. 33:8–9; John 1:29; Rom. 8:12–18; 1 John 1:7, 9

began to complain to Jesus' followers, "Why do you eat and drink with tax collectors and sinners?"

[31]Jesus answered them, "It is not the healthy people who need a doctor, but the sick. [32]I have not come to invite good people but sinners to change their hearts and lives."

JESUS ANSWERS A QUESTION

[33]They said to Jesus, "John's followers often give up eating[n] for a certain time and pray, just as the Pharisees do. But your followers eat and drink all the time."

[34]Jesus said to them, "You cannot make the friends of the bridegroom give up eating while he is still with them. [35]But the time will come when the bridegroom will be taken away from them, and then they will give up eating."

[36]Jesus told them this story: "No one takes cloth off a new coat to cover a hole in an old coat. Otherwise, he ruins the new coat, and the cloth from the new coat will not be the same as the old cloth. [37]Also, no one ever pours new wine into old leather bags. Otherwise, the new wine will break the bags, the wine will spill out, and the leather bags will be ruined. [38]New wine must be put into new leather bags. [39]No one after drinking old wine wants new wine, because he says, 'The old wine is better.' "

JESUS IS LORD OVER THE SABBATH

6 [1]One Sabbath day Jesus was walking through some fields of grain. His followers picked the heads of grain, rubbed them in their hands, and ate them. [2]Some Pharisees said, "Why do you do what is not lawful on the Sabbath day?"

[3]Jesus answered, "Have you not read what David did when he and those with him were hungry? [4]He went into God's house and took and ate the holy bread, which is lawful only for priests to eat. And he gave some to the people who were with him." [5]Then Jesus said to the Pharisees, "The Son of Man is Lord of the Sabbath day."

JESUS HEALS A MAN'S HAND

[6]On another Sabbath day Jesus went into the synagogue and was teaching, and a man with a crippled right hand was there. [7]The teachers of the law and the Pharisees were watching closely to see if Jesus would heal on the Sabbath day so they could accuse him. [8]But he knew what they were thinking, and he said to the man with the crippled hand, "Stand up here in the middle of everyone." The man got up and stood there. [9]Then Jesus said to them, "I ask you, which is lawful on the Sabbath day: to do good or to do evil, to save a life or to destroy it?" [10]Jesus looked around at all of them and said to the man, "Hold out your hand." The man held out his hand, and it was healed.

[11]But the Pharisees and the teachers of the law were very angry and discussed with each other what they could do to Jesus.

JESUS CHOOSES HIS APOSTLES

[12]At that time Jesus went off to a mountain to pray, and he spent the night praying to God. [13]The next morning, Jesus called his followers to him and chose twelve of them, whom he named apostles: [14]Simon (Jesus named him Peter), his brother Andrew, James, John, Philip, Bartholomew, [15]Matthew, Thomas, James son of Alphaeus, Simon (called the Zealot), [16]Judas son of James, and Judas Iscariot, who later turned Jesus over to his enemies.

JESUS TEACHES AND HEALS

[17]Jesus and the apostles came down from the mountain, and he stood on level ground. A large group of his followers was there, as well as many people from all around Judea, Jerusalem, and the seacoast cities of Tyre and Sidon. [18]They all came to hear Jesus teach and to be healed of their sicknesses, and he healed those who were troubled by evil spirits. [19]All the people were trying to touch Jesus, because power was coming from him and healing them all.

[20]Jesus looked at his followers and said,
"You people who are poor are happy,
because the kingdom of God belongs to you.
[21]You people who are now hungry are happy,
because you will be satisfied.
You people who are now crying are happy,
because you will laugh with joy.

[22]"People will hate you, shut you out, insult you, and say you are evil because you follow the Son of Man. But when they do, you will be happy. [23]Be full of joy at that time, because you have a great reward waiting for you in heaven. Their ancestors did the same things to the prophets.

5:33 give up eating This is called "fasting." The people would give up eating for a special time of prayer and worship to God. It was also done to show sadness and disappointment.

24 "But how terrible it will be for you who
are rich,
because you have had your easy life.
25 How terrible it will be for you who are full
now,
because you will be hungry.
How terrible it will be for you who are
laughing now,
because you will be sad and cry.
26 "How terrible when everyone says only
good things about you, because their ancestors
said the same things about the false prophets.

LOVE YOUR ENEMIES

27 "But I say to you who are listening, love
your enemies. Do good to those who hate you,
28 bless those who curse you, pray for
those who are cruel to you.
29 If anyone slaps you on one
cheek, offer him the other
cheek, too. If someone takes
your coat, do not stop him
from taking your shirt. 30 Give
to everyone who asks you, and when someone
takes something that is yours, don't ask for it
back. 31 Do to others what you would want
them to do to you. 32 If you love only the people who love you, what praise should you get?
Even sinners love the people who love them.
33 If you do good only to those who do good to
you, what praise should you get? Even sinners
do that! 34 If you lend things to people, always
hoping to get something back, what praise
should you get? Even sinners lend to other sinners so that they can get back the same
amount! 35 But love your enemies, do good to
them, and lend to them without hoping to get
anything back. Then you will have a great reward, and you will be children of the Most
High God, because he is kind even to people
who are ungrateful and full of sin. 36 Show
mercy, just as your Father shows mercy.

CARING

Do we have to care for our enemies? (6:27–28)

LOOK AT YOURSELVES

37 "Don't judge other people, and you will
not be judged. Don't accuse others of being
guilty, and you will not be accused of being
guilty. Forgive, and you will be forgiven.
38 Give, and you will receive. You will be given
much. Pressed down, shaken together, and
running over, it will spill into your lap. The
way you give to others is the way God will
give to you."
39 Jesus told them this story: "Can a blind
person lead another blind person? No! Both of
them will fall into a ditch. 40 A student is not
better than the teacher, but the student who
has been fully trained will be like the teacher.
41 "Why do you notice the little piece of dust
in your friend's eye, but you don't notice the
big piece of wood in your own eye? 42 How can
you say to your friend, 'Friend, let me take that
little piece of dust out of your eye' when you
cannot see that big piece of wood in your own
eye! You hypocrite! First, take the wood out of
your own eye. Then you will see clearly to take
the dust out of your friend's eye.

On the Edge

Bless those who curse you, pray for those who are cruel to you. . . . But love your enemies, do good to them, and lend to them without hoping to get anything back. Then you will have a great reward, and you will be children of the Most High God, because he is kind even to people who are ungrateful and full of sin (Luke 6:28, 35).

Luke says, "Welcome to the club." People who love God have been lied about since the beginning. He also says that God will bless those who have been mistreated because of him. Proverbs 25:18–22 gives us some wisdom about friends who tell lies about us or treat us badly. The advice is to do exactly the opposite of what your friends do. Even when you're disappointed and angry, you are supposed to be Christlike. Matthew 5:11 says, "People will insult you and hurt you. They will lie and say all kinds of evil things about you because you follow me. But when they do, you will be happy" because you love Jesus. When you love a person who hurts you, it "will be like pouring burning coals on his head" (Prov. 25:22).

Wow—that's pretty tough advice. When people tell lies or spread rumors about you, your reputation gets shattered, your pride gets wounded, and your heart gets broken. And God wants you to do what? Yep, he says to love them anyway—even give food to them if they are hungry and pray for them, too. By doing so you prove the strength of your character and you overcome evil with good. God promises to reward you for that.

SEE FOR YOURSELF:
Prov. 25:18–22;
Matt. 5:11–12;
Rom. 12:21

TWO KINDS OF FRUIT

43 "A good tree does not produce bad fruit,
nor does a bad tree produce
good fruit. 44 Each tree is
known by its own fruit.
People don't gather figs
from thornbushes, and
they don't get grapes
from bushes. 45 Good
people bring good things
out of the good they
stored in their hearts. But
evil people bring evil
things out of the evil they
stored in their hearts. People speak the things that are
in their hearts.

TWO KINDS OF PEOPLE

46 "Why do you call me, 'Lord, Lord,' but do
not do what I say? 47 I will show you what
everyone is like who comes to me and hears
my words and obeys. 48 That person is like a
man building a house who dug deep and laid
the foundation on rock. When the floods
came, the water tried to wash the house away,
but it could not shake it, because the house
was built well. 49 But the one who hears my
words and does not obey is like a man who
built his house on the ground without a foundation. When the floods came, the house
quickly fell and was completely destroyed."

JESUS HEALS A SOLDIER'S SERVANT

7
1 When Jesus finished saying all these things
to the people, he went to Capernaum. 2 There
was an army officer who had a servant who
was very important to him. The servant was so
sick he was nearly dead. 3 When the officer
heard about Jesus, he sent some older Jewish
leaders to him to ask Jesus to come and heal
his servant. 4 The men went to Jesus and
begged him, saying, "This officer is worthy of
your help. 5 He loves our people, and he built
us a synagogue."
6 So Jesus went with the men. He was getting
near the officer's house when the officer sent
friends to say, "Lord, don't trouble yourself,
because I am not worthy to have you come
into my house. 7 That is why I did not come to
you myself. But you only need to command it,
and my servant will be healed. 8 I, too, am a
man under the authority of others, and I have
soldiers under my command. I tell one soldier,
'Go,' and he goes. I tell another soldier, 'Come,'
and he comes. I say to my servant, 'Do this,'
and my servant does it."
9 When Jesus heard this, he was amazed.
Turning to the crowd that was following him,
he said, "I tell you, this is the
greatest faith I have found
anywhere, even in Is-
rael."
10 Those who had
been sent to Jesus went
back to the house where
they found the servant
in good health.

JESUS BRINGS A MAN BACK TO LIFE

11 Soon afterwards
Jesus went to a town called
Nain, and his followers and a
large crowd traveled with him.
12 When he came near the town gate, he saw a

"But love your enemies, do good to them, and lend to them without hoping to get anything back. Then you will have a great reward, and you will be children of the Most High God." (Luke 6:35a)

On the Edge

Don't judge other people, and you will not be judged. Don't accuse others of being guilty, and you will not be accused of being guilty. Forgive, and you will be forgiven (Luke 6:37).

What do you do when your parents treat your brother better than they treat you? What you may want to do is scream, and pout, and whine. You may even scheme some way to get more attention than your brother gets. If good behavior won't do it, maybe rebellion will. Before you head down that path, look at Luke 6:37. Jesus is laying out some fundamental principles of the universe: Judgment leads to judgment, condemnation leads to condemnation, and forgiveness leads to forgiveness. Forgive your parents and your brother. Don't judge them and try not to be hard on them. Give this to the Lord and allow him to change your parents' hearts. He can do miracles in places you thought were hopeless. Begin to pray for your parents and forgive them daily. Consider this a challenge that you plus Jesus *can* overcome. Don't give up on them or on the Lord. He wants to restore your family and bring glory to himself in your home.

SEE FOR YOURSELF:
Prov. 10:12; 27:4;
Matt. 6:14–15;
2 John 5–6

funeral. A mother, who was a widow, had lost her only son. A large crowd from the town was with the mother while her son was being carried out. 13When the Lord saw her, he felt very sorry for her and said, "Don't cry." 14He went up and touched the coffin, and the people who were carrying it stopped. Jesus said, "Young man, I tell you, get up!" 15And the son sat up and began to talk. Then Jesus gave him back to his mother.

16All the people were amazed and began praising God, saying, "A great prophet has come to us! God has come to help his people."

17This news about Jesus spread through all Judea and into all the places around there.

WHAT'S IT MEAN?

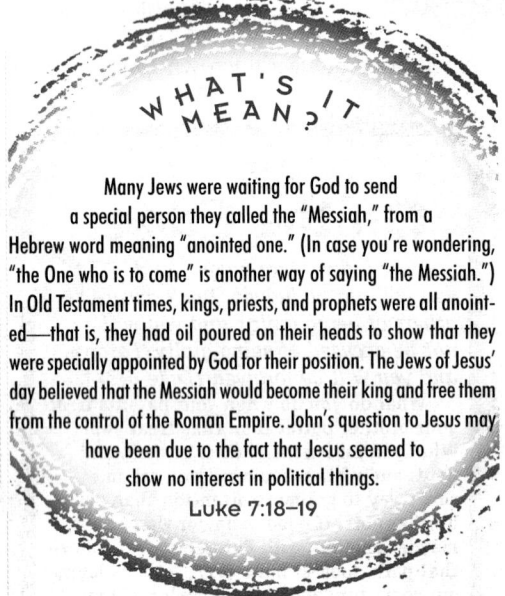

Many Jews were waiting for God to send a special person they called the "Messiah," from a Hebrew word meaning "anointed one." (In case you're wondering, "the One who is to come" is another way of saying "the Messiah.") In Old Testament times, kings, priests, and prophets were all anointed—that is, they had oil poured on their heads to show that they were specially appointed by God for their position. The Jews of Jesus' day believed that the Messiah would become their king and free them from the control of the Roman Empire. John's question to Jesus may have been due to the fact that Jesus seemed to show no interest in political things.

Luke 7:18–19

JOHN ASKS A QUESTION

18John's followers told him about all these things. He called for two of his followers 19and sent them to the Lord to ask, "Are you the One who is to come, or should we wait for someone else?"

20When the men came to Jesus, they said, "John the Baptist sent us to you with this question: 'Are you the One who is to come, or should we wait for someone else?' "

21At that time, Jesus healed many people of their sicknesses, diseases, and evil spirits, and he gave sight to many blind people. 22Then Jesus answered John's followers, "Go tell John what you saw and heard here. The blind can see, the crippled can walk, and people with skin diseases are healed. The deaf can hear, the dead are raised to life, and the Good News is preached to the poor. 23Those who do not stumble in their faith because of me are blessed!"

24When John's followers left, Jesus began talking to the people about John: "What did you go out into the desert to see? A reed[n] blown by the wind? 25What did you go out to see? A man dressed in fine clothes? No, people who have fine clothes and much wealth live in kings' palaces. 26But what did you go out to see? A prophet? Yes, and I tell you, John is more than a prophet. 27This was written about him:

'I will send my messenger ahead of you,
who will prepare the way for you.'

Malachi 3:1

28I tell you, John is greater than any other person ever born, but even the least important person in the kingdom of God is greater than John."

29(When the people, including the tax collectors, heard this, they all agreed that God's teaching was good, because they had been baptized by John. 30But the Pharisees and experts on the law refused to accept God's plan for themselves; they did not let John baptize them.)

31Then Jesus said, "What shall I say about the people of this time? What are they like? 32They are like children sitting in the marketplace, calling to one another and saying,

'We played music for you, but you did not
dance;
we sang a sad song, but you did not
cry.'

33John the Baptist came and did not eat bread or drink wine, and you say, 'He has a demon in him.' 34The Son of Man came eating and drinking, and you say, 'Look at him! He eats too much and drinks too much wine, and he is a friend of tax collectors and sinners!' 35But wisdom is proved to be right by what it does."

A WOMAN WASHES JESUS' FEET

36One of the Pharisees asked Jesus to eat with him, so Jesus went into the Pharisee's house and sat at the table. 37A sinful woman in the town learned that Jesus was eating at the Pharisee's house. So she brought an alabaster jar of perfume 38and stood behind Jesus at his feet, crying. She began to wash his feet with her tears, and she dried them with her hair, kissing them many times and rubbing them with the

7:24 reed It means that John was not ordinary or weak like grass blown by the wind.

perfume. [39]When the Pharisee who asked Jesus to come to his house saw this, he thought to himself, "If Jesus were a prophet, he would know that the woman touching him is a sinner!"

[40]Jesus said to the Pharisee, "Simon, I have something to say to you."

Simon said, "Teacher, tell me."

[41]Jesus said, "Two people owed money to the same banker. One owed five hundred coins[n] and the other owed fifty. [42]They had no money to pay what they owed, but the banker told both of them they did not have to pay him. Which person will love the banker more?"

[43]Simon, the Pharisee, answered, "I think it would be the one who owed him the most money."

Jesus said to Simon, "You are right." [44]Then Jesus turned toward the woman and said to Simon, "Do you see this woman? When I came into your house, you gave me no water for my feet, but she washed my feet with her tears and dried them with her hair. [45]You gave me no kiss of greeting, but she has been kissing my feet since I came in. [46]You did not put oil on my head, but she poured perfume on my feet. [47]I tell you that her many sins are forgiven, so she showed great love. But the person who is forgiven only a little will love only a little."

[48]Then Jesus said to her, "Your sins are forgiven."

[49]The people sitting at the table began to say among themselves, "Who is this who even forgives sins?"

[50]Jesus said to the woman, "Because you believed, you are saved from your sins. Go in peace."

THE GROUP WITH JESUS

8 [1]After this, while Jesus was traveling through some cities and small towns, he preached and told the Good News about God's kingdom. The twelve apostles were with him, [2]and also some women who had been healed of sicknesses and evil spirits: Mary, called Magdalene, from whom seven demons had gone out; [3]Joanna, the wife of Cuza (the manager of Herod's house); Susanna; and many others. These women used their own money to help Jesus and his apostles.

A STORY ABOUT PLANTING SEED

[4]When a great crowd was gathered, and people were coming to Jesus from every town, he told them this story:

[5]"A farmer went out to plant his seed. While he was planting, some seed fell by the road. People walked on the seed, and the birds ate it up. [6]Some seed fell on rock, and when it began to grow, it died because it had no water. [7]Some seed fell among thorny weeds, but the weeds grew up with it and choked the good plants. [8]And some seed fell on good ground and grew and made a hundred times more."

As Jesus finished the story, he called out, "You people who can hear me, listen!"

[9]Jesus' followers asked him what this story meant.

[10]Jesus said, "You have been chosen to know the secrets about the kingdom of God. But I use stories to speak to other people so that:

'They will look, but they may not see.
They will listen, but they may not
understand.' *Isaiah 6:9*

[11]"This is what the story means: The seed is God's message. [12]The seed that fell beside the road is like the people who hear God's teaching, but the devil comes and takes it away from them so they cannot believe it and be saved. [13]The seed that fell on rock is like those who hear God's teaching and accept it gladly, but they don't allow the teaching to go deep into their lives. They believe for a while, but when trouble comes, they give up. [14]The seed that fell among the thorny weeds is like those who hear God's teaching, but they let the worries, riches, and pleasures of this life keep them from growing and producing good fruit. [15]And the seed that fell on the good ground is like those who hear God's teaching with good, honest hearts and obey it and patiently produce good fruit.

USE WHAT YOU HAVE

[16]"No one after lighting a lamp covers it with a bowl or hides it under a bed. Instead, the person puts it on a lampstand so those who come in will see the light. [17]Everything that is hidden will become clear, and every secret thing will be made known. [18]So be careful how you listen. Those who have understanding will be given more. But those who do not have understanding, even what they think they have will be taken away from them."

JESUS' TRUE FAMILY

[19]Jesus' mother and brothers came to see him, but there was such a crowd they could not get to him. [20]Someone said to Jesus, "Your

7:41 coins Roman denarii. One coin was the average pay for one day's work.

mother and your brothers are standing outside, wanting to see you."

[21]Jesus answered them, "My mother and my brothers are those who listen to God's teaching and obey it!"

JESUS CALMS A STORM

[22]One day Jesus and his followers got into a boat, and he said to them, "Let's go across the lake." And so they started across. [23]While they were sailing, Jesus fell asleep. A very strong wind blew up on the lake, causing the boat to fill with water, and they were in danger.

WHAT'S IT MEAN?

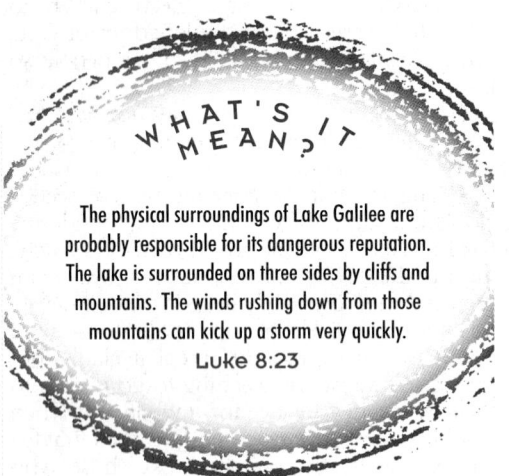

The physical surroundings of Lake Galilee are probably responsible for its dangerous reputation. The lake is surrounded on three sides by cliffs and mountains. The winds rushing down from those mountains can kick up a storm very quickly.

Luke 8:23

[24]The followers went to Jesus and woke him, saying, "Master! Master! We will drown!"

Jesus got up and gave a command to the wind and the waves. They stopped, and it became calm. [25]Jesus said to his followers, "Where is your faith?"

The followers were afraid and amazed and said to each other, "Who is this that commands even the wind and the water, and they obey him?"

A MAN WITH DEMONS INSIDE HIM

[26]Jesus and his followers sailed across the lake from Galilee to the area of the Gerasene people. [27]When Jesus got out on the land, a man from the town who had demons inside him came to Jesus. For a long time he had worn no clothes and had lived in the burial caves, not in a house. [28]When he saw Jesus, he cried out and fell down before him. He said with a loud voice, "What do you want with me, Jesus, Son of the Most High God? I beg you, don't torture me!" [29]He said this because Jesus was commanding the evil spirit to come out of the man. Many times it had taken hold of him. Though he had been kept under guard and chained hand and foot, he had broken his chains and had been forced by the demon out into a lonely place.

[30]Jesus asked him, "What is your name?"

He answered, "Legion,"[n] because many demons were in him. [31]The demons begged Jesus not to send them into eternal darkness.[n] [32]A large herd of pigs was feeding on a hill, and the demons begged Jesus to allow them to go into the pigs. So Jesus allowed them to do this. [33]When the demons came out of the man, they went into the pigs, and the herd ran down the hill into the lake and was drowned.

[34]When the herdsmen saw what had happened, they ran away and told about this in the town and the countryside. [35]And people went to see what had happened. When they came to Jesus, they found the man sitting at Jesus' feet, clothed and in his right mind, because the demons were gone. But the people were frightened. [36]The people who saw this happen told the others how Jesus had made the man well. [37]All the people of the Gerasene

On the Edge

Who is this that commands even the wind and the water, and they obey him? (Luke 8:25b).

Have you ever asked the question, "How can I avoid the storms of life?" Well, the answer is, you can't. Everybody has to go through storms, but the good news is that you don't have to go through them alone.

Jesus—the One who calmed the storms—is with you. So the next time you're experiencing a storm or difficult circumstance, and it looks like there's no way out, remember you are not alone. You can rise above your storm. If the winds and the waves obeyed Jesus, then your storm has to obey his word, too. Victory belongs to you today!

SEE FOR YOURSELF:
Ps. 23;
Mark 4:39

8:30 "Legion" Means very many. A legion was about five thousand men in the Roman army.
8:31 eternal darkness Literally, "the abyss," something like a pit or a hole that has no end.

country asked Jesus to leave, because they were all very afraid. So Jesus got into the boat and went back to Galilee.

38The man whom Jesus had healed begged to go with him, but Jesus sent him away, saying, 39"Go back home and tell people how much God has done for you." So the man went all over town telling how much Jesus had done for him.

JESUS GIVES LIFE TO A DEAD GIRL AND HEALS A SICK WOMAN

40When Jesus got back to Galilee, a crowd welcomed him, because everyone was waiting for him. 41A man named Jairus, a leader of the synagogue, came to Jesus and fell at his feet, begging him to come to his house. 42Jairus' only daughter, about twelve years old, was dying.

While Jesus was on his way to Jairus' house, the people were crowding all around him. 43A woman was in the crowd who had been bleeding for twelve years, but no one was able to heal her. 44She came up behind Jesus and touched the edge of his coat, and instantly her bleeding stopped. 45Then Jesus said, "Who touched me?"

When all the people said they had not touched him, Peter said, "Master, the people are all around you and are pushing against you."

46But Jesus said, "Someone did touch me, because I felt power go out from me." 47When the woman saw she could not hide, she came forward, shaking, and fell down before Jesus. While all the people listened, she told why she had touched him and how she had been instantly healed. 48Jesus said to her, "Dear woman, you are made well because you believed. Go in peace."

49While Jesus was still speaking, someone came from the house of the synagogue leader and said to him, "Your daughter is dead. Don't bother the teacher anymore."

50When Jesus heard this, he said to Jairus, "Don't be afraid. Just believe, and your daughter will be well."

51When Jesus went to the house, he let only Peter, John, James, and the girl's father and mother go inside with him. 52All the people were crying and feeling sad because the girl was dead, but Jesus said, "Stop crying. She is not dead, only asleep."

53The people laughed at Jesus because they knew the girl was dead. 54But Jesus took hold of her hand and called to her, "My child, stand up!" 55Her spirit came back into her, and she stood up at once. Then Jesus ordered that she be given something to eat. 56The girl's parents were amazed, but Jesus told them not to tell anyone what had happened.

JESUS SENDS OUT THE APOSTLES

9 1Jesus called the twelve apostles together and gave them power and authority over all demons and the ability to heal sicknesses. 2He sent the apostles out to tell about God's kingdom and to heal the sick. 3He said to them, "Take nothing for your trip, neither a walking stick, bag, bread, money, or extra clothes. 4When you enter a house, stay there until it is time to leave. 5If people do not welcome you, shake the dust off of your feet[n] as you leave the town, as a warning to them."

6So the apostles went out and traveled through all the towns, preaching the Good News and healing people everywhere.

HEROD IS CONFUSED ABOUT JESUS

7Herod, the governor, heard about all the things that were happening and was confused, because some people said, "John the Baptist has risen from the dead." 8Others said, "Elijah has come to us." And still others said, "One of the prophets who lived long ago has risen from the dead." 9Herod said, "I cut off John's head, so who is this man I hear such things about?" And Herod kept trying to see Jesus.

MORE THAN FIVE THOUSAND FED

10When the apostles returned, they told Jesus everything they had done. Then Jesus took them with him to a town called Bethsaida where they could be alone together. 11But the people learned where Jesus went and followed him. He welcomed them and talked with them about God's kingdom and healed those who needed to be healed.

12Late in the afternoon, the twelve apostles came to Jesus and said, "Send the people away. They need to go to the towns and countryside around here and find places to sleep and something to eat, because no one lives in this place."

13But Jesus said to them, "You give them something to eat."

They said, "We have only five loaves of bread and two fish, unless we go buy food for all these people." 14(There were about five thousand men there.)

Jesus said to his followers, "Tell the people to sit in groups of about fifty people."

9:5 shake . . . feet A warning. It showed that they had rejected these people.

15So the followers did this, and all the people
sat down. 16Then Jesus took the five loaves of
bread and two fish, and looking up to heaven,
he thanked God for the food. Then he divided
the food and gave it to the followers to give to
the people. 17They all ate and were satisfied, and
what was left over was gathered up, filling
twelve baskets.

JESUS IS THE CHRIST

18One time when Jesus was praying alone,
his followers were with him, and he asked
them, "Who do the people say
I am?"
19They answered, "Some
say you are John the Baptist.
Others say you are Elijah.[n]
And others say you are one
of the prophets from long
ago who has come back to
life."
20Then Jesus asked, "But
who do you say I am?"
Peter answered, "You are the
Christ from God."
21Jesus warned them not to tell anyone,
saying, 22"The Son of Man must suffer many
things. He will be rejected by the older Jewish
leaders, the leading priests, and the teachers of
the law. He will be killed and after three days
will be raised from the dead."
23Jesus said to all of them, "If people want to
follow me, they must give up the things they
want. They must be willing to give up their
lives daily to follow me. 24Those who want to
save their lives will give up true life. But those
who give up their lives for me will have true
life. 25It is worth nothing for them to have the
whole world if they themselves are destroyed
or lost. 26If people are ashamed of me and my
teaching, then the Son of Man will be ashamed
of them when he comes in his glory and with
the glory of the Father and the holy angels. 27I
tell you the truth, some people standing here
will see the kingdom of God before they die."

"It is worth nothing for them to have the whole world if they themselves are destroyed or lost." (Luke 9:25)

JESUS TALKS WITH MOSES AND ELIJAH

28About eight days after Jesus said these
things, he took Peter, John, and James and went
up on a mountain to pray. 29While Jesus was
praying, the appearance of his face changed,
and his clothes became shining white. 30Then
two men, Moses and Elijah,[n] were talking with
Jesus. 31They appeared in heavenly glory, talking about his departure which he would soon
bring about in Jerusalem. 32Peter and the others were very sleepy, but when they awoke fully, they saw the glory of Jesus and the two men
standing with him. 33When Moses and Elijah
were about to leave, Peter said to Jesus, "Master, it is good that we are here. Let us make
three tents—one for you, one for Moses, and
one for Elijah." (Peter did not know what he
was talking about.)
34While he was saying these things, a cloud
came and covered them, and
they became afraid as the
cloud covered them. 35A
voice came from the cloud,
saying, "This is my Son,
whom I have chosen. Listen
to him!"
36When the voice fin-
ished speaking, only Jesus
was there. Peter, John, and
James said nothing and told
no one at that time what they
had seen.

JESUS HEALS A SICK BOY

37The next day, when they came down from
the mountain, a large crowd met Jesus. 38A
man in the crowd shouted to him, "Teacher,
please come and look at my son, because he is
my only child. 39An evil spirit seizes my son,
and suddenly he screams. It causes him to lose
control of himself and foam at the mouth. The
evil spirit keeps on hurting him and almost
never leaves him. 40I begged your followers
to force the evil spirit out, but they could not
do it."
41Jesus answered, "You people have no faith,
and your lives are all wrong. How long must I
stay with you and put up with you? Bring
your son here."
42While the boy was coming, the demon
threw him on the ground and made him lose
control of himself. But Jesus gave a strong
command to the evil spirit and healed the boy
and gave him back to his father. 43All the people were amazed at the great power of God.

JESUS TALKS ABOUT HIS DEATH

While everyone was wondering about all
that Jesus did, he said to his followers, 44"Don't
forget what I tell you now: The Son of Man

9:19 Elijah A man who spoke for God and who lived hundreds of years before Christ. See 1 Kings 17.
9:30 Moses and Elijah Two of the most important Jewish leaders in the past. God had given Moses the Law, and Elijah was an important prophet.

On the Edge

Peter and the others were very sleepy, but when they awoke fully, they saw the glory of Jesus and the two men standing with him (Luke 9:32).

Can you imagine waking up and seeing Jesus in his glory? Wow! That would be something—to see the all-powerful and majestic One right there beside you when you wake up!

The fact is, we do serve a glorious God and we have the opportunity to wake up every morning and see "his glory." That's why it's so important to reach over, grab the Word of God, and meditate on it every morning. It gets our thinking headed in the right direction. If we aren't reminded of the glory and power of God every morning, it can be so easy to get caught up in our everyday affairs to the point that we forget that the "all-powerful One" is right beside us!

One thing that will bring us into the presence of his glory is to simply praise the Lord for who he is. He is so awesome, better than anyone or anything you can imagine. Even the heavens shout about his glory. The earth is filled with his glory. In fact, his Word tells us that we are crowned with his glory (see Ps. 8:5; Heb. 2:7).

Take time out right now just to praise God. He's the King of glory. He is the Alpha and Omega—the beginning and the end of everything. He's the lily of the valley, the bright and morning star. He's our safe place and our strong place. He's a tower in which we can hide from our enemy. In him we are more than winners. He's the glorious God who is more than enough.

Take time to think about the Lord's glory every day. He is the One who is glorious!

SEE FOR YOURSELF:
Ps. 8:5; 19:1; 63:6; 72:19; 92:1–2

will be handed over to people." [45]But the followers did not understand what this meant;
the meaning was hidden from them so they
could not understand. But they were afraid to
ask Jesus about it.

WHO IS THE GREATEST?

[46]Jesus' followers began to have an argument about which one of them was the greatest. [47]Jesus knew what they were thinking, so
he took a little child and stood the child beside
him. [48]Then Jesus said, "Whoever accepts this
little child in my name accepts me. And whoever accepts me accepts the One who sent me,
because whoever is least among you all is
really the greatest."

ANYONE NOT AGAINST US IS FOR US

[49]John answered, "Master, we saw someone using your name to force demons out of people.
We told him to stop, because he does not belong to our group."
[50]But Jesus said to him, "Don't stop him,
because whoever is not against you is for you."

WHAT'S IT MEAN?

To get from Judea to Galilee in New Testament times, you had to pass through Samaria or go out of your way to bypass it. The people of Samaria were not terribly popular with "pure-blooded" Jews. The reason? Samaritans were the descendants of mixed marriages between Jews and Gentiles. The Jews disliked the Samaritans not only for their mixed bloodlines, but also for their worship of pagan gods.

Luke 9:52

A TOWN REJECTS JESUS

[51]When the time was coming near for Jesus
to depart, he was determined to go to Jerusalem. [52]He sent some men ahead of him, who
went into a town in Samaria to make everything ready for him. [53]But the people there
would not welcome him, because he was set
on going to Jerusalem. [54]When James and
John, followers of Jesus, saw this, they said,
"Lord, do you want us to call fire down from
heaven and destroy those people?"[n]
[55]But Jesus turned and scolded them.
[56]Then[n] they went to another town.

9:54 Verse 54 Here, some Greek copies add: ". . . as Elijah did." **9:55-56 Verses 55-56** Some copies read: "But Jesus turned and scolded them. And Jesus said, 'You don't know what kind of spirit you belong to. [56]The Son of Man did not come to destroy the souls of people but to save them.' Then . . . ."

FOLLOWING JESUS

[57]As they were going along the road, someone said to Jesus, "I will follow you any place you go."

[58]Jesus said to them, "The foxes have holes to live in, and the birds have nests, but the Son of Man has no place to rest his head."

[59]Jesus said to another man, "Follow me!"

But he said, "Lord, first let me go and bury my father."

[60]But Jesus said to him, "Let the people who are dead bury their own dead. You must go and tell about the kingdom of God."

[61]Another man said, "I will follow you, Lord, but first let me go and say good-bye to my family."

[62]Jesus said, "Anyone who begins to plow a field but keeps looking back is of no use in the kingdom of God."

JESUS SENDS OUT THE SEVENTY-TWO

10

[1]After this, the Lord chose seventy-two[n] others and sent them out in pairs ahead of him into every town and place where he planned to go. [2]He said to them, "There are a great many people to harvest, but there are only a few workers. So pray to God, who owns the harvest, that he will send more workers to help gather his harvest. [3]Go now, but listen! I am sending you out like sheep among wolves. [4]Don't carry a purse, a bag, or sandals, and don't waste time talking with people on the road. [5]Before you go into a house, say, 'Peace be with this house.' [6]If peaceful people live there, your blessing of peace will stay with them, but if not, then your blessing will come back to you. [7]Stay in the peaceful house, eating and drinking what the people there give you. A worker should be given his pay. Don't move from house to house. [8]If you go into a town and the people welcome you, eat what they give you. [9]Heal the sick who live there, and tell them, 'The kingdom of God is near you.' [10]But if you go into a town, and the people don't welcome you, then go into the streets and say, [11]'Even the dirt from your town that sticks to our feet we wipe off against you.[n] But remember that the kingdom of God is near.' [12]I tell you, on the Judgment Day it will be better for the people of Sodom[n] than for the people of that town.

JESUS WARNS UNBELIEVERS

[13]"How terrible for you, Korazin! How terrible for you, Bethsaida! If the miracles I did in you had happened in Tyre and Sidon,[n] those people would have changed their lives long ago. They would have worn rough cloth and put ashes on themselves to show they had changed. [14]But on the Judgment Day it will be better for Tyre and Sidon than for you. [15]And you, Capernaum,[n] will you be lifted up to heaven? No! You will be thrown down to the depths!

WHAT'S IT MEAN?

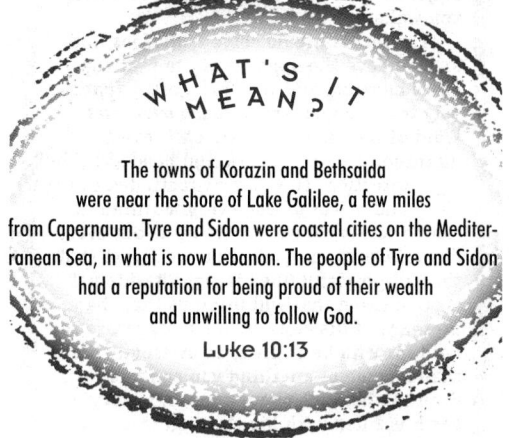

The towns of Korazin and Bethsaida were near the shore of Lake Galilee, a few miles from Capernaum. Tyre and Sidon were coastal cities on the Mediterranean Sea, in what is now Lebanon. The people of Tyre and Sidon had a reputation for being proud of their wealth and unwilling to follow God.

Luke 10:13

[16]"Whoever listens to you listens to me, and whoever refuses to accept you refuses to accept me. And whoever refuses to accept me refuses to accept the One who sent me."

SATAN FALLS

[17]When the seventy-two[n] came back, they were very happy and said, "Lord, even the demons obeyed us when we used your name!"

DEMONS
Who do demons submit to? (10:17)

[18]Jesus said, "I saw Satan fall like lightning from heaven. [19]Listen, I have given you power to walk on snakes and scorpions, power that is greater than the enemy has. So nothing will hurt you. [20]But you should not be happy because the spirits obey you but because your names are written in heaven."

10:1 seventy-two Many Greek copies read seventy. **10:11 dirt . . . you** A warning. It showed that they had rejected these people. **10:12 Sodom** City that God destroyed because the people were so evil. **10:13 Tyre and Sidon** Towns where wicked people lived. **10:13, 15 Korazin, Bethsaida, Capernaum** Towns by Lake Galilee where Jesus preached to the people. **10:17 seventy-two** Many Greek copies read seventy.

JESUS PRAYS TO THE FATHER

21Then Jesus rejoiced in the Holy Spirit and
said, "I praise you, Father, Lord of heaven and
earth, because you have hidden these things
from the people who are wise and smart. But
you have shown them to those who are like
little children. Yes, Father, this is what you really
wanted.
22"My Father has given me all things. No
one knows who the Son is, except the Father.
And no one knows who the Father is, except
the Son and those whom the Son chooses to
tell."
23Then Jesus turned to his followers and
said privately, "You are blessed to see what you
now see. 24I tell you, many prophets and kings
wanted to see what you now see, but they did
not, and they wanted to hear what you now
hear, but they did not."

THE GOOD SAMARITAN

25Then an expert on the law stood up to test
Jesus, saying, "Teacher, what must I do to get
life forever?"
26Jesus said, "What is written in the law?
What do you read there?"
27The man answered, "Love the Lord your
God with all your heart, all your soul, all your
strength, and all your mind."[n] Also, "Love your
neighbor as you love yourself."[n]
28Jesus said to him, "Your answer is right.
Do this and you will live."
29But the man, wanting to show the importance of his question, said to Jesus, "And who is
my neighbor?"
30Jesus answered, "As a man was going
down from Jerusalem to Jericho, some robbers
attacked him. They tore off his clothes, beat
him, and left him lying there, almost dead. 31It
happened that a priest was going down that
road. When he saw the man, he walked by on
the other side. 32Next, a Levite[n] came there, and
after he went over and looked at the man, he
walked by on the other side of the road. 33Then
a Samaritan[n] traveling down the road came to
where the hurt man was. When he saw the
man, he felt very sorry for him. 34The Samaritan went to him, poured olive oil and wine[n] on
his wounds, and bandaged them. Then he put
the hurt man on his own donkey and took
him to an inn where he cared for him. 35The
next day, the Samaritan brought out two
coins,[n] gave them to the innkeeper, and said,
'Take care of this man. If you spend more
money on him, I will pay it back to you when
I come again.' "
36Then Jesus said, "Which one of these three
men do you think was a neighbor to the man
who was attacked by the robbers?"
37The expert on the law answered, "The one
who showed him mercy."
Jesus said to him, "Then go and do what he
did."

MARY AND MARTHA

38While Jesus and his followers were traveling, Jesus went into a town. A woman named
Martha let Jesus stay at her house. 39Martha
had a sister named Mary, who was sitting at
Jesus' feet and listening to him teach. 40But
Martha was busy with all the work to be done.
She went in and said, "Lord, don't you care
that my sister has left me alone to do all the
work? Tell her to help me."
41But the Lord answered her, "Martha, Martha, you are worried and upset about many
things. 42Only one thing is important. Mary
has chosen the better thing, and it will never be
taken away from her."

JESUS TEACHES ABOUT PRAYER

11

1One time Jesus was praying in a certain
place. When he finished, one of his followers
said to him, "Lord, teach us to pray as John
taught his followers."
2Jesus said to them, "When you pray, say:
'Father, may your name always be kept
holy.
May your kingdom come.
3Give us the food we need for each day.
4Forgive us for our sins,
because we forgive everyone who has
done wrong to us.
And do not cause us to be tempted.' "

CONTINUE TO ASK

5Then Jesus said to them, "Suppose one of
you went to your friend's house at midnight
and said to him, 'Friend, loan me three loaves
of bread. 6A friend of mine has come into town

10:27 "Love . . . mind." Quotation from Deuteronomy 6:5. **10:27 "Love . . . yourself."** Quotation from Leviticus 19:18. **10:32 Levite** Levites were members of the tribe of Levi who helped the Jewish priests with their work in the Temple. Read 1 Chronicles 23:24-32. **10:33 Samaritan** Samaritans were people from Samaria. These people were part Jewish, but the Jews did not accept them as true Jews. Samaritans and Jews disliked each other. **10:34 olive oil and wine** Oil and wine were used like medicine to soften and clean wounds. **10:35 coins** Roman denarii. One coin was the average pay for one day's work.

to visit me, but I have nothing for him to eat.'
7Your friend inside the house answers, 'Don't
bother me! The door is already locked, and my
children and I are in bed. I cannot get up and
give you anything.' 8I tell you, if friendship is
not enough to make him get up to give you the
bread, your boldness will make him get up and
give you whatever you need. 9So I tell you, ask,
and God will give to you. Search, and you will
find. Knock, and the door will open for you.
10Yes, everyone who asks will receive. The one
who searches will find. And everyone who
knocks will have the door opened. 11If your
children ask for a fish, which of you would
give them a snake instead? 12Or, if your children ask for an egg, would you give them a
scorpion? 13Even though you are bad, you
know how to give good things to your children. How much more your heavenly Father
will give the Holy Spirit to those who ask him!"

JESUS' POWER IS FROM GOD

14One time Jesus was sending out a demon
that could not talk. When the demon came out,
the man who had been unable to speak, then
spoke. The people were amazed. 15But some of
them said, "Jesus uses the power of Beelzebul,
the ruler of demons, to force demons out of
people."

WHAT'S IT MEAN?

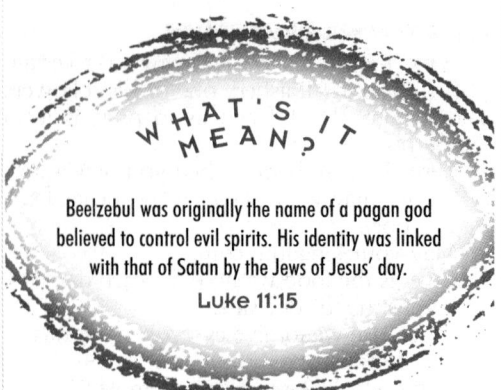

Beelzebul was originally the name of a pagan god believed to control evil spirits. His identity was linked with that of Satan by the Jews of Jesus' day.

Luke 11:15

16Other people, wanting to test Jesus, asked
him to give them a sign from heaven. 17But
knowing their thoughts, he said to them,
"Every kingdom that is divided against itself
will be destroyed. And a family that is divided
against itself will not continue. 18So if Satan is
divided against himself, his kingdom will not
continue. You say that I use the power of
Beelzebul to force out demons. 19But if I use the
power of Beelzebul to force out demons, what
power do your people use to force demons
out? So they will be your judges. 20But if I use
the power of God to force out demons, then
the kingdom of God has come to you.
21"When a strong person with many weapons guards his own house, his possessions are
safe. 22But when someone stronger comes and
defeats him, the stronger one will take away
the weapons the first man trusted and will give
away the possessions.
23"Anyone who is not with me is against me,
and anyone who does not work with me is
working against me.

On the Edge

But Jesus said, "No, happy are those who hear the teaching of God and obey it" (Luke 11:28).

"*Hear and obey* God's message." You've probably heard it said before, "It is better to obey than to sacrifice" (1 Sam. 15:22). And you know what? It's true. When we begin walking in obedience, that's when the blessings of God begin to flow. It's one thing to just hear the Word of God or to read it, but it's something else for us to start obeying it. God's Word says that if we love him, we will obey him (see John 14:15; 15:10). That's why when we seek God and his goodness first, then all these things will be added to us. As we begin to seek goodness and walk in obedience, blessings will find their way to us. You're going to become a "blessing magnet"!

If you were to go through the entire Bible and read about the men and women who were blessed with riches, fame, wisdom, etc., you'd find that most of them walked in obedience. You have to pay the price to be successful, and part of that price is obeying God's Word—doing what he says to do, and not doing what he says not to do. The choice is up to us: to be blessed or not to be blessed. Choose obedience and get out your bucket; here come the blessings of God! He is the One who blesses!

SEE FOR YOURSELF:
Deut. 5:29; Josh. 1:8; Matt. 6:33; 7:21; John 13:17; James 1:22–25

THE EMPTY PERSON

24"When an evil spirit comes out of a person, it travels through dry places, looking for a

place to rest. But when it finds no place, it says, 'I will go back to the house I left.' 25 And when it comes back, it finds that house swept clean and made neat. 26 Then the evil spirit goes out and brings seven other spirits more evil than it is, and they go in and live there. So the person has even more trouble than before."

PEOPLE WHO ARE TRULY HAPPY

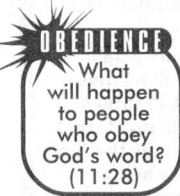

OBEDIENCE What will happen to people who obey God's word? (11:28)

27 As Jesus was saying these things, a woman in the crowd called out to Jesus, "Happy is the mother who gave birth to you and nursed you."

28 But Jesus said, "No, happy are those who hear the teaching of God and obey it."

THE PEOPLE WANT A MIRACLE

29 As the crowd grew larger, Jesus said, "The people who live today are evil. They want to see a miracle for a sign, but no sign will be given them, except the sign of Jonah.[n] 30 As Jonah was a sign for those people who lived in Nineveh, the Son of Man will be a sign for the people of this time. 31 On the Judgment Day the Queen of the South[n] will stand up with the people who live now. She will show they are guilty, because she came from far away to listen to Solomon's wise teaching. And I tell you that someone greater than Solomon is here. 32 On the Judgment Day the people of Nineveh will stand up with the people who live now, and they will show that you are guilty. When Jonah preached to them, they were sorry and changed their lives. And I tell you that someone greater than Jonah is here.

BE A LIGHT FOR THE WORLD

33 "No one lights a lamp and puts it in a secret place or under a bowl, but on a lampstand so the people who come in can see. 34 Your eye is a light for the body. When your eyes are good, your whole body will be full of light. But when your eyes are evil, your whole body will be full of darkness. 35 So be careful not to let the light in you become darkness. 36 If your whole body is full of light, and none of it is dark, then you will shine bright, as when a lamp shines on you."

JESUS ACCUSES THE PHARISEES

37 After Jesus had finished speaking, a Pharisee asked Jesus to eat with him. So Jesus went in and sat at the table. 38 But the Pharisee was surprised when he saw that Jesus did not wash his hands[n] before the meal. 39 The Lord said to him, "You Pharisees clean the outside of the cup and the dish, but inside you are full of greed and evil. 40 You foolish people! The same one who made what is outside also made what is inside. 41 So give what is in your dishes to the poor, and then you will be fully clean. 42 How terrible for you Pharisees! You give God one-tenth of even your mint, your rue, and every other plant in your garden. But you fail to be fair to others and to love God. These are the things you should do while continuing to do those other things. 43 How terrible for you Pharisees, because you love to have the most important seats in the synagogues, and you love to be greeted with respect in the marketplaces. 44 How terrible for you, because you are like hidden graves, which people walk on without knowing."

JESUS TALKS TO EXPERTS ON THE LAW

45 One of the experts on the law said to Jesus, "Teacher, when you say these things, you are insulting us, too."

46 Jesus answered, "How terrible for you, you experts on the law! You make strict rules that are very hard for people to obey, but you yourselves don't even try to follow those rules. 47 How terrible for you, because you build tombs for the prophets whom your ancestors killed! 48 And now you show that you approve of what your ancestors did. They killed the prophets, and you build tombs for them! 49 This is why in his wisdom God said, 'I will send prophets and apostles to them. They will kill some, and they will treat others cruelly.' 50 So you who live now will be punished for the deaths of all the prophets who were killed since the beginning of the world— 51 from the killing of Abel to the killing of Zechariah,[n] who died between the altar and the Temple. Yes, I tell you that you who are alive now will be punished for them all.

52 "How terrible for you, you experts on the law. You have taken away the key to learning about God. You yourselves would not

11:29 sign of Jonah Jonah's three days in the fish are like Jesus' three days in the tomb. See Matthew 12:40. **11:31 Queen of the South** The Queen of Sheba. She traveled a thousand miles to learn God's wisdom from Solomon. Read 1 Kings 10:1-3. **11:38 wash his hands** This was a Jewish religious custom that the Pharisees thought was very important. **11:51 Abel . . . Zechariah** In the Hebrew Old Testament, the first and last men to be murdered.

learn, and you stopped others from learning,
too."
[53]When Jesus left, the teachers of the law
and the Pharisees began to give him trouble,
asking him questions about many things,
[54]trying to catch him saying something wrong.

DON'T BE LIKE THE PHARISEES

12 [1]So many thousands of people had gathered that they were stepping on each other.
Jesus spoke first to his followers, saying, "Beware of the yeast of the Pharisees, because they
are hypocrites. [2]Everything that is hidden will
be shown, and everything that is secret will be
made known. [3]What you have said in the dark
will be heard in the light, and what you have
whispered in an inner room will be shouted
from the housetops.
[4]"I tell you, my friends, don't be afraid of
people who can kill the body but after that can
do nothing more to hurt you. [5]I will show you
the one to fear. Fear the one who has the power to kill you and also to throw you into hell.
Yes, this is the one you should fear.

WHAT'S IT MEAN?

Sparrows were what people offered to God when they couldn't afford to sacrifice a goat or a sheep. They were considered a "poor man's sacrifice."

Luke 12:6

[6]"Five sparrows are sold for only two pen-
nies, and God does not forget any of them.
[7]But God even knows how many hairs you
have on your head. Don't be afraid. You are
worth much more than many sparrows.

DON'T BE ASHAMED OF JESUS

[8]"I tell you, all those who stand before others and say they believe in me, I, the Son of
Man, will say before the angels of God that
they belong to me. [9]But all who stand before
others and say they do not believe in me, I will
say before the angels of God that they do not
belong to me.
[10]"Anyone who speaks against the Son of
Man can be forgiven, but anyone who speaks
against the Holy Spirit will not be forgiven.
[11]"When you are brought into the synagogues before the leaders and other powerful
people, don't worry about how to defend
yourself or what to say. [12]At that time the Holy
Spirit will teach you what you must say."

JESUS WARNS AGAINST SELFISHNESS

[13]Someone in the crowd said to Jesus,
"Teacher, tell my brother to divide with me the
property our father left us."
[14]But Jesus said to him, "Who said I should

On the Edge

Then Jesus said to them, "Be careful and guard against all kinds of greed. Life is not measured by how much one owns." Then Jesus told this story: . . . (Luke 12:15–21).

Jesus makes the point in this parable that things aren't "it." Things don't give you a relationship with God. And things don't make your walk with God any deeper. The rich man in this story thought that he would have an easy life because he had everything he could possibly ever want or need. God called him a fool, because that night when he died, his things could do nothing for him. Where are you spending most of your time? Are you worrying about the next really important "thing" you've got to have and how to get it, or are you thinking about the Lord and how to know and love him more completely?

Jesus says it's foolish to spend your time accumulating stuff that will only rust and decay in the end. God doesn't give you everything you want because first, you don't need it, and second, those things don't matter anyway. People who always get what they want are commonly known in America as "spoiled brats." They don't have the self-control or discipline it takes to be mature. God wants you to be mature, to learn what's really valuable and what isn't; to sacrifice for the good of another person, of yourself, or of the kingdom of God. He promises to provide all you need. But his focus is on the eternal—the souls of men and women. That's what really matters to God.

SEE FOR YOURSELF:
Prov. 28:22;
Luke 12:15–21;
1 Tim. 6:6–10;
James 1:10

judge or decide between you?" 15Then Jesus said to them, "Be careful and guard against all kinds of greed. Life is not measured by how much one owns."

16Then Jesus told this story: "There was a rich man who had some land, which grew a good crop. 17He thought to himself, 'What will I do? I have no place to keep all my crops.' 18Then he said, 'This is what I will do: I will tear down my barns and build bigger ones, and there I will store all my grain and other goods. 19Then I can say to myself, "I have enough good things stored to last for many years. Rest, eat, drink, and enjoy life!" '

20"But God said to him, 'Foolish man! Tonight your life will be taken from you. So who will get those things you have prepared for yourself?'

21"This is how it will be for those who store up things for themselves and are not rich toward God."

> "Your heart will be where your treasure is." (Luke 12:34)

DON'T WORRY

22Jesus said to his followers, "So I tell you, don't worry about the food you need to live, or about the clothes you need for your body. 23Life is more than food, and the body is more than clothes. 24Look at the birds. They don't plant or harvest, they don't have storerooms or barns, but God feeds them. And you are worth much more than birds. 25You cannot add any time to your life by worrying about it. 26If you cannot do even the little things, then why worry about the big things? 27Consider how the lilies grow; they don't work or make clothes for themselves. But I tell you that even Solomon with his riches was not dressed as beautifully as one of these flowers. 28God clothes the grass in the field, which is alive today but tomorrow is thrown into the fire. So how much more will God clothe you? Don't have so little faith! 29Don't always think about what you will eat or what you will drink, and don't keep worrying. 30All the people in the world are trying to get these things, and your Father knows you need them. 31But seek God's kingdom, and all the other things you need will be given to you.

DON'T TRUST IN MONEY

32"Don't fear, little flock, because your Father wants to give you the kingdom. 33Sell your possessions and give to the poor. Get for yourselves purses that will not wear out, the treasure in heaven that never runs out, where thieves can't steal and moths can't destroy. 34Your heart will be where your treasure is.

ALWAYS BE READY

35"Be dressed, ready for service, and have your lamps shining. 36Be like servants who are waiting for their master to come home from a wedding party. When he comes and knocks, the servants immediately open the door for him. 37They will be blessed when their master comes home, because he sees that they were watching for him. I tell you the truth, the master will dress himself to serve and tell the servants to sit at the table, and he will serve them. 38Those servants will be happy when he comes in and finds them still waiting, even if it is midnight or later.

39"Remember this: If the owner of the house knew what time a thief was coming, he would not allow the thief to enter his house. 40So you also must be ready, because the Son of Man will come at a time when you don't expect him!"

WHO IS THE TRUSTED SERVANT?

41Peter said, "Lord, did you tell this story to us or to all people?"

42The Lord said, "Who is the wise and trusted servant that the master trusts to give the other servants their food at the right time? 43When the master comes and finds the servant doing his work, the servant will be blessed. 44I tell you the truth, the master will choose that servant to take care of everything he owns. 45But suppose the servant thinks to himself, 'My master will not come back soon,' and he

WHAT'S IT MEAN?

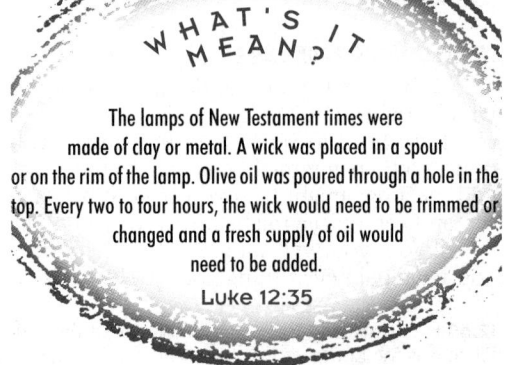

The lamps of New Testament times were made of clay or metal. A wick was placed in a spout or on the rim of the lamp. Olive oil was poured through a hole in the top. Every two to four hours, the wick would need to be trimmed or changed and a fresh supply of oil would need to be added.

Luke 12:35

begins to beat the other servants, men and
women, and to eat and drink and get drunk.
46The master will come when that servant is
not ready and is not expecting him. Then the
master will cut him in pieces and send him
away to be with the others who don't obey.
47"The servant who knows what his master
wants but is not ready, or who does not do
what the master wants, will be beaten with
many blows! 48But the servant who does not
know what his master wants and does things
that should be punished will be beaten with
few blows. From everyone who has been given
much, much will be demanded. And from the
one trusted with much, much more will be expected.

JESUS CAUSES DIVISION

49"I came to set fire to the world, and I wish
it were already burning! 50I have a baptism[n] to
suffer through, and I feel very troubled until it
is over. 51Do you think I came to
give peace to the earth? No, I
tell you, I came to divide it.
52From now on, a family with
five people will be divided,
three against two, and two
against three. 53They will be
divided: father against son
and son against father, mother
against daughter and daughter against mother,
mother-in-law against daughter-in-law and
daughter-in-law against mother-in-law."

FAMILY
Can devotion to Christ cause family division? (12:51–53)

UNDERSTANDING THE TIMES

54Then Jesus said to the people, "When
you see clouds coming up in the west, you
say, 'It's going to rain,' and it happens. 55When
you feel the wind begin to blow from the
south, you say, 'It will be a hot day,' and it
happens. 56Hypocrites! You know how to understand the appearance of the earth and sky.
Why don't you understand what is happening
now?

SETTLE YOUR PROBLEMS

57"Why can't you decide for yourselves
what is right? 58If your enemy is taking you to
court, try hard to settle it on the way. If you
don't, your enemy might take you to the judge,
and the judge might turn you over to the officer, and the officer might throw you into jail.
59I tell you, you will not get out of there until
you have paid everything you owe."

CHANGE YOUR HEARTS

13
1At that time some people were there who
told Jesus that Pilate[n] had killed some people
from Galilee while they were worshiping. He
mixed their blood with the blood of the animals they were sacrificing to God.
2Jesus answered, "Do you think
this happened to them be-
cause they were more sinful
than all others from Galilee?
3No, I tell you. But unless you
change your hearts and lives,
you will be destroyed as they
were! 4What about those eighteen people who died when the
tower of Siloam fell on them? Do you think
they were more sinful than all the others who
live in Jerusalem? 5No, I tell you. But unless
you change your hearts and lives, you will all
be destroyed too!"

REPENTANCE
What would happen to us if we didn't repent of our sin? (13:3–5)

THE USELESS TREE

6Jesus told this story: "A man had a fig tree
planted in his vineyard. He came looking for
some fruit on the tree, but he found none. 7So
the man said to his gardener, 'I have been
looking for fruit on this tree for three years, but
I never find any. Cut it down. Why should it
waste the ground?' 8But the servant answered,
'Master, let the tree have one more year to produce fruit. Let me dig up the dirt around it and
put on some fertilizer. 9If the tree produces fruit
next year, good. But if not, you can cut it
down.' "

JESUS HEALS ON THE SABBATH

10Jesus was teaching in one of the synagogues on the Sabbath day. 11A woman was
there who, for eighteen years, had an evil spirit
in her that made her crippled. Her back was
always bent; she could not stand up straight.
12When Jesus saw her, he called her over and
said, "Woman, you are free from your sickness."
13Jesus put his hands on her, and immediately
she was able to stand up straight and began
praising God.
14The synagogue leader was angry because
Jesus healed on the Sabbath day. He said to the
people, "There are six days when one has to
work. So come to be healed on one of those
days, and not on the Sabbath day."
15The Lord answered, "You hypocrites!
Doesn't each of you untie your work animals
and lead them to drink water every day—even

12:50 I . . . baptism Jesus was talking about the suffering he would soon go through. **13:1 Pilate** Pontius Pilate was the Roman governor of Judea from A.D. 26 to A.D. 36.

JESUS made a difference

People talk a lot about Jesus the baby and Jesus the man. They don't say much about Jesus the kid. What did the Son of God do when he was your age? His birth, death, and resurrection sure made a big difference—but did Jesus make a difference when he was young? Yes, he did! By the time he was twelve, Jesus knew his Bible. He could talk about it, and he understood that obeying God's Word was the key to life. When he was at church, he listened to adults and asked good questions. He amazed the teachers. He practiced obeying God by obeying his parents. That wasn't easy. He learned that life wasn't just about what he wanted to do. He had to cooperate with his parents. His decision paid off. Think about this summary of Jesus' teenage years:

Cutting Edge

"Jesus became wiser and grew physically. People liked him, and he pleased God" (Luke 2:52).

YOU can, too!

The best way to shock a teacher is to be interested! Anybody can act bored and disruptive. It takes work to learn—but the benefits are amazing. Asking questions and looking for the truth will make a big difference in at least one life—your own! Practice obeying your parents. They won't know what hit them! The description of Jesus' teenage years really can be the description of your life. It won't be long before you discover that Jesus himself will help you as you seek to live like he lived.

Want to know more? Read about Jesus and his young life in Luke 2:41–52.

JOHN THE BAPTIST made a difference

People who make a difference are themselves often different. They don't fit. They don't just go along. They stand up and stand out. Some accomplish great good; others create chaos. They are remembered both for what they did and for who they were. John the Baptist was a different person who made a difference in the best way.

God called this John into a life as a messenger, the one who announced the arrival of the Savior Jesus Christ. He understood who he was and was single-minded in pursuing his calling. He removed himself from distractions by living in the wilderness. He wore camel skins and ate desert food. But the only trend he started was a trend of guilt. He pointed out people's sinfulness. He fearlessly called people—the poor, the soldiers, a king—to repentance. He told them to get ready—to prepare a way for the Lord.

What difference did John the Baptist make? Did Jesus get the welcome he deserved? No. But there was a handful prepared for Christ. We know John made a difference because Jesus said so:

Cutting Edge

"I tell you the truth, John the Baptist is greater than any other person ever born, but even the least important person in the kingdom of heaven is greater than John" (Matt. 11:11).

YOU can, too!

John made a difference because he was different, he acted different, and he looked different. Most people get the order exactly reversed and wrong. They focus on looking different and acting different. You can tell who these people are because they often do this in groups. Being different takes more courage. Being different as God instructs and leads takes even more determination.

It's those like John, who set out to be what God has called them to be, who end up making a difference. Have you asked God to make his calling clear to you?

Want to know more? Read about this unique difference-maker in all four accounts of the Good News. He is also mentioned several times in Acts.

MARY MAGDALENE made a difference

At least six, maybe seven, distinct Marys are mentioned in the New Testament. Each one made a difference in her own way. We know very little about Mary of Magdala. Mark gives us a summary of what Jesus did for her, and Luke mentions her discipleship. All four accounts of the Good News mention her part in the crucifixion and resurrection of Jesus.

We don't know how they met, but Mary Magdalene was possessed by seven demons when Jesus entered her life. Since there was not room for both Jesus and any demons in her life, the demons naturally vacated the premises. In their place we can only imagine the gratitude that flowed from this liberated woman. Jesus transformed her life; he changed her.

Mary joined a group of seldom-mentioned women who apparently traveled with Jesus and the apostles. Several of them were wealthy enough to take care of the day-to-day traveling expenses. Luke briefly refers to their role in Luke 8:1–3. Mary's gratitude showed itself in action.

Cutting Edge

Mary's consistent faithfulness put her right in the path of honor. Wanting to anoint Jesus' body after the Cross, she was the first to see the living Christ. She became the first eyewitness to the resurrection. Did she make a difference? Her persuasive testimony was the spark that ignited the movement of people who came to be known as Christians.

YOU can, too!

Mary was trying to make a difference in one way: by honoring Jesus' buried body. God had something even greater in mind. She set out to do what was right. That put her right in God's plan and pathway. Obedience has to precede honor and fame. Honor and fame do not necessarily follow obedience, at least not on this side of eternity.

This is why it's important not only to live for God, but also to be wherever God is working, like in the church. If you are where God is acting, you may not always get to make a difference, but being there will definitely make a difference for you!

Want to know more? The clearest glimpses of Mary Magdalene can be found in **Matthew 27:55—28:11; Mark 15:40—16:11; Luke 8:1–3; 23:55—24:12; John 19:25—20:18.**

MARY AND MARTHA made a difference

One of the reasons Mary and Martha of Bethany made a difference comes from the fact that *they* were different. They were sisters, but clearly not the same. Together, they formed a hospitality team. Each had a unique personality that worked well with the other—most of the time. Mary focused on the guest. She was the conversationalist of the two. Martha busied herself with the details of entertaining. She focused on the guest's needs. Mary and Martha's hospitality was significant because their frequent guest was Jesus.

During one of Jesus' visits, a conflict arose. Martha was upset because Mary was enjoying listening to Jesus while she was having to bustle about to get a meal ready for more than a dozen men. She became flustered and frustrated. Martha finally asked Jesus to order her sister to help. Jesus' answer was an amazing example of tough and tender love: "Martha, Martha, you are worried and upset about many things. Only one thing is important. Mary has chosen the better thing, and it will never be taken away from her" (Luke 10:41–42). Jesus' point wasn't necessarily that Martha shouldn't have been busy. Rather, his point was that Martha had allowed her busy-ness to make her forget the reason she was busy. Her attention shifted from her guest to herself, which led to resentment toward her sister.

Cutting Edge

Jesus helped them work out their teamwork. The last time the sisters appear in Scripture (John 12:1–3), we see a little change in their approach. Martha is still serving (she can't help it), but there's no hint of sulking. Mary is still focused on Jesus, but she is also acting in service by pouring costly perfume on his feet. Together, each one made a difference for their guest.

YOU can, too! In any situation, you bring something very special to offer—yourself. God's intention in your design is to call you into special service. your ultimate purpose isn't to meet the expectations of anyone other than your Creator. The difference you make in life will really be determined by God. Like Mary, you will accomplish that purpose more effectively if your attention is focused on God rather than on yourself.

Want to know more? Get to know the sisters better as you read Luke 10:38–42; John 11:1–45; 12:1–3.

on the Sabbath day? [16]This woman that I healed, a daughter of Abraham, has been held by Satan for eighteen years. Surely it is not wrong for her to be freed from her sickness on a Sabbath day!" [17]When Jesus said this, all of those who were criticizing him were ashamed, but the entire crowd rejoiced at all the wonderful things Jesus was doing.

STORIES OF MUSTARD SEED AND YEAST

[18]Then Jesus said, "What is God's kingdom like? What can I compare it with? [19]It is like a mustard seed that a man plants in his garden. The seed grows and becomes a tree, and the wild birds build nests in its branches."

[20]Jesus said again, "What can I compare God's kingdom with? [21]It is like yeast that a woman took and hid in a large tub of flour until it made all the dough rise."

THE NARROW DOOR

[22]Jesus was teaching in every town and village as he traveled toward Jerusalem. [23]Someone said to Jesus, "Lord, will only a few people be saved?"

Jesus said, [24]"Try hard to enter through the narrow door, because many people will try to enter there, but they will not be able. [25]When the owner of the house gets up and closes the door, you can stand outside and knock on the door and say, 'Sir, open the door for us.' But he will answer, 'I don't know you or where you come from.' [26]Then you will say, 'We ate and drank with you, and you taught in the streets of our town.' [27]But he will say to you, 'I don't know you or where you come from. Go away from me, all you who do evil!' [28]You will cry and grind your teeth with pain when you see Abraham, Isaac, Jacob, and all the prophets in God's kingdom, but you yourselves thrown outside. [29]People will come from the east, west, north, and south and will sit down at the table in the kingdom of God. [30]There are those who have the lowest place in life now who will have the highest place in the future. And there are those who have the highest place now who will have the lowest place in the future."

JESUS WILL DIE IN JERUSALEM

[31]At that time some Pharisees came to Jesus and said, "Go away from here! Herod wants to kill you!"

[32]Jesus said to them, "Go tell that fox Herod, 'Today and tomorrow I am forcing demons out and healing people. Then, on the third day, I will reach my goal.' [33]Yet I must be on my way today and tomorrow and the next day. Surely it cannot be right for a prophet to be killed anywhere except in Jerusalem.

[34]"Jerusalem, Jerusalem! You kill the prophets and stone to death those who are sent to you. Many times I wanted to gather your people as a hen gathers her chicks under her wings, but you would not let me. [35]Now your house is left completely empty. I tell you, you will not see me until that time when you will say, 'God bless the One who comes in the name of the Lord.' "[n]

HEALING ON THE SABBATH

14 [1]On a Sabbath day, when Jesus went to eat at the home of a leading Pharisee, the people were watching Jesus very closely. [2]And in front of him was a man with dropsy.[n] [3]Jesus said to the Pharisees and experts on the law, "Is it right or wrong to heal on the Sabbath day?" [4]But they would not answer his question. So Jesus took the man, healed him, and sent him away. [5]Jesus said to the Pharisees and teachers of the law, "If your child or ox falls into a well on the Sabbath day, will you not pull him out quickly?" [6]And they could not answer him.

DON'T MAKE YOURSELF IMPORTANT

[7]When Jesus noticed that some of the guests were choosing the best places to sit, he told this story: [8]"When someone invites you to a wedding feast, don't take the most important seat, because someone more important than you may have been invited. [9]The host, who invited both of you, will come to you and say, 'Give this person your seat.' Then you will be embarrassed and will have to move to the last place. [10]So when you are invited, go sit in a seat that is not important. When the host comes to you, he may say, 'Friend, move up here to a more important place.' Then all the other guests will respect you. [11]All who make themselves great will be made humble, but those who make themselves humble will be made great."

YOU WILL BE REWARDED

[12]Then Jesus said to the man who had invited him, "When you give a lunch or a dinner, don't invite only your friends, your family, your other relatives, and your rich neighbors. At another time they will invite you to eat with

13:35 'God . . . Lord.' Quotation from Psalm 118:26. **14:2 dropsy** A sickness that causes the body to swell larger and larger.

them, and you will be repaid. [13]Instead, when
you give a feast, invite the poor, the
crippled, the lame, and the
blind. [14]Then you will be
blessed, because they have
nothing and cannot pay you
back. But you will be repaid
when the good people rise
from the dead."

CARING
Should Christians care for the needy? (14:13–14)

A STORY ABOUT A BIG BANQUET

[15]One of those at the table with Jesus heard
these things and said to him, "Happy are the
people who will share in the meal in God's
kingdom."
[16]Jesus said to him, "A man gave a big banquet and invited many people. [17]When it was
time to eat, the man sent his servant to tell the
guests, 'Come. Everything is ready.'
[18]"But all the guests made excuses. The first
one said, 'I have just bought a field, and I must
go look at it. Please excuse me.' [19]Another said,
'I have just bought five pairs of oxen; I must
go and try them. Please excuse me.' [20]A third
person said, 'I just got married; I can't come.'
[21]So the servant returned and told his master
what had happened. Then the master became
angry and said, 'Go at once into the streets and
alleys of the town, and bring in the poor, the
crippled, the blind, and the lame.' [22]Later the
servant said to him, 'Master, I did what you
commanded, but we still have room.' [23]The
master said to the servant, 'Go out to the roads
and country lanes, and urge the people there
to come so my house will be full. [24]I tell
you, none of those whom I invited first will eat
with me.' "

WHAT'S IT MEAN?

Crucifixion was an agonizing process. The person sentenced to die was beaten, then forced to carry the crossbeam to the execution site. There, his arms were fastened to the crossbeam. The crossbeam and the person were then lifted off the ground and attached to an upright wooden stake. After several hours—sometimes several days—of tremendous pain, the person would die, usually either of suffocation or exhaustion.

Luke 14:27

THE COST OF BEING JESUS' FOLLOWER

[25]Large crowds were traveling with Jesus,
and he turned and said to them, [26]"If anyone
comes to me but loves his father, mother, wife,
children, brothers, or sisters—or even life—
more than me, he cannot be my follower.
[27]Whoever is not willing to carry the cross and
follow me cannot be my follower. [28]If you
want to build a tower, you first sit down and
decide how much it will cost, to see if you have
enough money to finish the job. [29]If you don't,
you might lay the foundation, but you would
not be able to finish. Then all who would see it
would make fun of you, [30]saying, 'This person
began to build but was not able to finish.'
[31]"If a king is going to fight another king, first
he will sit down and plan. He will decide if he
and his ten thousand soldiers can defeat the
other king who has twenty thousand soldiers.
[32]If he can't, then while the other king is still far
away, he will send some people to speak to him

On the Edge

If you want to build a tower, you first sit down and decide how much it will cost, to see if you have enough money to finish the job. If you don't, you might lay the foundation, but you would not be able to finish. Then all who would see it would make fun of you, saying, "This person began to build but was not able to finish" (Luke 14:28–30).

In this passage Jesus is teaching about the element of planning in regard to following him. From his teaching we can apply the principle of financial planning to your goals for college. Like the builders of the tower, you can sit down with your folks and figure out how much it will cost to get through college. Make a plan and work the plan. Apply for scholarships, grants, and work-study programs. Begin planning a few years in advance so summer savings can go toward a college fund. There are also government loans available. Your parents may not be able to afford college, but with good planning, you will be able to get—and finish—a great education.

SEE FOR YOURSELF:
Prov. 2:7; 3:5–6; 16:3

WHAT'S IT MEAN?

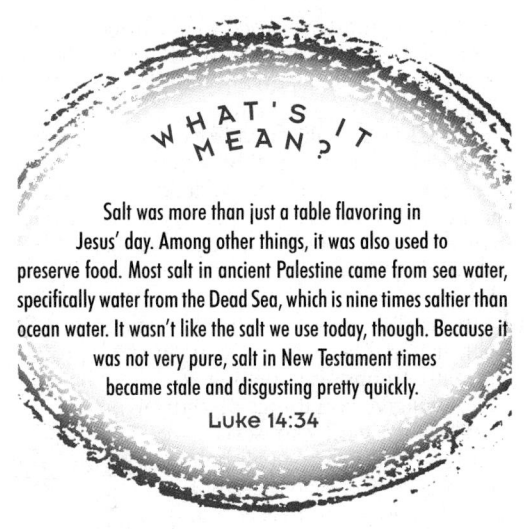

Salt was more than just a table flavoring in Jesus' day. Among other things, it was also used to preserve food. Most salt in ancient Palestine came from sea water, specifically water from the Dead Sea, which is nine times saltier than ocean water. It wasn't like the salt we use today, though. Because it was not very pure, salt in New Testament times became stale and disgusting pretty quickly.

Luke 14:34

and ask for peace. 33In the same way, you must
give up everything you have to be my follower.

DON'T LOSE YOUR INFLUENCE

34"Salt is good, but if it loses its salty taste,
you cannot make it salty again. 35It is no good
for the soil or for manure; it is thrown away.
"You people who can hear me, listen."

A LOST SHEEP, A LOST COIN

15 1The tax collectors and sinners all came to
listen to Jesus. 2But the Pharisees and the
teachers of the law began to complain: "Look,
this man welcomes sinners and even eats with
them."
3Then Jesus told them this story: 4"Suppose
one of you has a hundred sheep but loses one
of them. Then he will leave the other ninety-
nine sheep in the open field and go out and
look for the lost sheep until he finds it. 5And
when he finds it, he happily puts it on his
shoulders 6and goes home. He calls to
his friends and neighbors and
says, 'Be happy with me because I found my lost sheep.'
7In the same way, I tell you
there is more joy in heaven
over one sinner who changes
his heart and life, than over
ninety-nine good people who
don't need to change.
8"Suppose a woman has ten silver coins,[n]
but loses one. She will light a lamp, sweep the
house, and look carefully for the coin until she
finds it. 9And when she finds it, she will call her
friends and neighbors and say, 'Be happy with
me because I have found the coin that I lost.'
10In the same way, there is joy in the presence
of the angels of God when one sinner changes
his heart and life."

REPENTANCE
What do the angels do when a sinner repents? (15:7)

THE SON WHO LEFT HOME

11Then Jesus said, "A man had two sons.
12The younger son said to his father, 'Give me
my share of the property.' So the father divided
the property between his two sons. 13Then the
younger son gathered up all that was his and
traveled far away to another country. There he
wasted his money in foolish living. 14After he
had spent everything, a time came when there
was no food anywhere in the country, and the
son was poor and hungry. 15So he got a job
with one of the citizens there who sent the son
into the fields to feed pigs. 16The son was so
hungry that he wanted to eat the pods the pigs
were eating, but no one gave him anything.
17When he realized what he was doing, he
thought, 'All of my father's servants have plenty of food. But I am here, almost dying with
hunger. 18I will leave and return to my father
and say to him, "Father, I have sinned against
God and have done wrong to you. 19I am no
longer worthy to be called your son, but let me
be like one of your servants." ' 20So the son left
and went to his father.

WHAT'S IT MEAN?

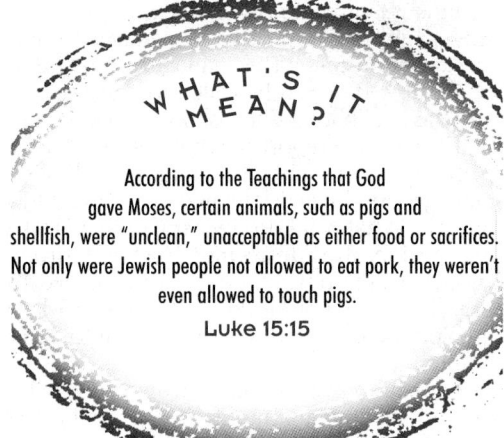

According to the Teachings that God gave Moses, certain animals, such as pigs and shellfish, were "unclean," unacceptable as either food or sacrifices. Not only were Jewish people not allowed to eat pork, they weren't even allowed to touch pigs.

Luke 15:15

"While the son was still a long way off, his
father saw him and felt sorry for his son. So
the father ran to him and hugged and kissed
him. 21The son said, 'Father, I have sinned
against God and have done wrong to you. I
am no longer worthy to be called your son.'

15:8 silver coins Roman denarii. One coin was the average pay for one day's work.

22But the father said to his servants, 'Hurry!
Bring the best clothes and put them on him.
Also, put a ring on his finger and sandals on
his feet. 23And get our fat calf and kill it so we
can have a feast and celebrate. 24My son was
dead, but now he is alive again! He was lost,
but now he is found!' So they began to celebrate.
25"The older son was in the field, and as he
came closer to the house, he heard the sound
of music and dancing. 26So he called to one of
the servants and asked what all this meant.
27The servant said, 'Your brother has come
back, and your father killed the fat calf, because
your brother came home safely.' 28The older
son was angry and would not go in to the
feast. So his father went out and begged him to
come in. 29But the older son said to his father, 'I
have served you like a slave for many years
and have always obeyed your commands. But
you never gave me even a young goat to have
at a feast with my friends. 30But your other son,
who wasted all your money on prostitutes,
comes home, and you kill the fat calf for him!'
31The father said to him, 'Son, you are always
with me, and all that I have is yours. 32We had
to celebrate and be happy because your
brother was dead, but now he is alive. He was
lost, but now he is found.' "

TRUE WEALTH

16 1Jesus also said to his followers, "Once there
was a rich man who had a manager to take
care of his business. This manager was accused
of cheating him. 2So he called the manager in
and said to him, 'What is this I hear about
you? Give me a report of what you have done
with my money, because you can't be my
manager any longer.' 3The manager thought to
himself, 'What will I do since my master is taking my job away from me? I am not strong
enough to dig ditches, and I am ashamed to
beg. 4I know what I'll do so that when I lose
my job people will welcome me into their
homes.'
5"So the manager called in everyone who
owed the master any money. He asked the first
one, 'How much do you owe?' 6He answered,
'Eight hundred gallons of olive oil.' The manager said to him, 'Take your bill, sit down quickly,
and write four hundred gallons.' 7Then the
manager asked another one, 'How much do
you owe?' He answered, 'One thousand bushels of wheat.' Then the manager said to him,
'Take your bill and write eight hundred bushels.' 8So, the master praised the dishonest manager for being smart. Yes, worldly people are
smarter with their own kind than spiritual
people are.
9"I tell you, make friends for yourselves using worldly riches so that when those riches
are gone, you will be welcomed in those
homes that continue forever. 10Whoever can be
trusted with a little can also be trusted with a
lot, and whoever is dishonest with a little is
dishonest with a lot. 11If you cannot be trusted
with worldly riches, then who will trust you
with true riches? 12And if you cannot be trusted with things that belong to someone else,
who will give you things of your own?
13"No servant can serve two
masters. The servant will hate
one master and love the other,
or will follow one master and
refuse to follow the other. You
cannot serve both God and
worldly riches."

MONEY
Can Christians serve both God and money? (16:13)

GOD'S LAW CANNOT BE CHANGED

14The Pharisees, who loved money, were
listening to all these things and made fun of
Jesus. 15He said to them, "You make yourselves
look good in front of people, but God knows
what is really in your hearts. What is important to people is hateful in God's sight.
16"The law of Moses and the writings of the
prophets were preached until John[n] came.
Since then the Good News about the kingdom
of God is being told, and everyone tries to enter it by force. 17It would be easier for heaven
and earth to pass away than for the smallest
part of a letter in the law to be changed.

DIVORCE AND REMARRIAGE

18"If a man divorces his wife and marries
another woman, he is guilty of adultery, and
the man who marries a divorced woman is
also guilty of adultery."

THE RICH MAN AND LAZARUS

19Jesus said, "There was a rich man who always dressed in the finest clothes and lived in
luxury every day. 20And a very poor man
named Lazarus, whose body was covered with
sores, was laid at the rich man's gate. 21He
wanted to eat only the small pieces of food
that fell from the rich man's table. And the
dogs would come and lick his sores. 22Later,
Lazarus died, and the angels carried him to the
arms of Abraham. The rich man died, too, and

16:16 John John the Baptist, who preached to people about Christ's coming (Matthew 3, Luke 3).

was buried. [23]In the place of the dead, he was
in much pain. The rich man saw Abraham far
away with Lazarus at his side. [24]He called, 'Father Abraham, have mercy on me! Send Lazarus to dip his finger in water and cool my
tongue, because I am suffering in this fire!'
[25]But Abraham said, 'Child, remember when
you were alive you had the good things in life,
but bad things happened to Lazarus. Now he
is comforted here, and you are suffering. [26]Be-
sides, there is a big pit between you and us, so
no one can cross over to you, and no one can
leave there and come here.' [27]The rich man said,
'Father, then please send Lazarus to my father's
house. [28]I have five brothers, and Lazarus
could warn them so that they will not come to
this place of pain.' [29]But Abraham said, 'They
have the law of Moses and the writings of the
prophets; let them learn from them.' [30]The rich
man said, 'No, father Abraham! If someone
goes to them from the dead, they would believe and change their hearts and lives.' [31]But
Abraham said to him, 'If they will not listen to
Moses and the prophets, they will not listen to
someone who comes back from the dead.' "

SIN AND FORGIVENESS

17 [1]Jesus said to his followers, "Things that
cause people to sin will happen, but how terrible for the person who causes them to happen!
[2]It would be better for you to be thrown into
the sea with a large stone around your neck
than to cause one of these little ones to sin. [3]So
be careful!

"If another follower sins, warn him, and if
he is sorry and stops sinning, forgive him. [4]If
he sins against you seven times in one day and
says that he is sorry each time, forgive him."

HOW BIG IS YOUR FAITH?

[5]The apostles said to the Lord, "Give us more
faith!"

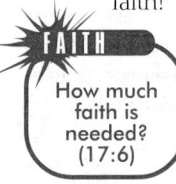

FAITH
How much faith is needed? (17:6)

[6]The Lord said, "If your faith
were the size of a mustard
seed, you could say to this
mulberry tree, 'Dig yourself
up and plant yourself in the
sea,' and it would obey you.

BE GOOD SERVANTS

[7]"Suppose one of you has a servant who
has been plowing the ground or caring for the
sheep. When the servant comes in from working in the field, would you say, 'Come in and sit

WHAT'S IT MEAN?

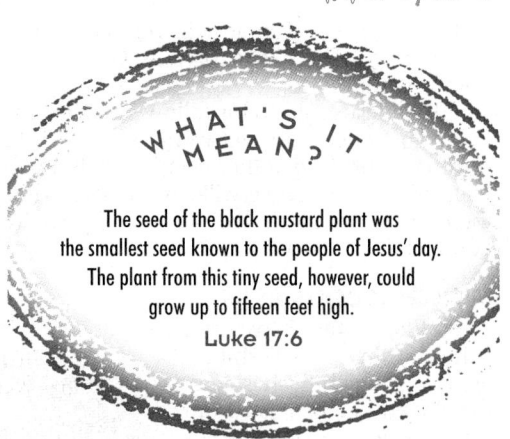

The seed of the black mustard plant was the smallest seed known to the people of Jesus' day. The plant from this tiny seed, however, could grow up to fifteen feet high.

Luke 17:6

down to eat'? [8]No, you would say to him,
'Prepare something for me to eat. Then get
yourself ready and serve me. After I finish eating and drinking, you can eat.' [9]The servant
does not get any special thanks for doing what
his master commanded. [10]It is the same with
you. When you have done everything you are
told to do, you should say, 'We are unworthy
servants; we have only done the work we
should do.' "

BE THANKFUL

[11]While Jesus was on his way to Jerusalem,
he was going through the area between Samaria and Galilee. [12]As he came into a small
town, ten men who had a skin disease met
him there. They did not come close to Jesus
[13]but called to him, "Jesus! Master! Have mercy
on us!"

[14]When Jesus saw the men, he said, "Go and
show yourselves to the priests."[n]

As the ten men were going, they were
healed. [15]When one of them saw that he was
healed, he went back to Jesus, praising God in
a loud voice. [16]Then he bowed down at Jesus'
feet and thanked him. (And this man was a
Samaritan.) [17]Jesus said, "Weren't ten men
healed? Where are the other nine? [18]Is this Samaritan the only one who came back to thank
God?" [19]Then Jesus said to him, "Stand up and
go on your way. You were healed because you
believed."

GOD'S KINGDOM IS WITHIN YOU

[20]Some of the Pharisees asked Jesus, "When
will the kingdom of God come?"

Jesus answered, "God's kingdom is coming,
but not in a way that you will be able to see

17:14 show . . . priests The Law of Moses said a priest must say when a person with a skin disease became well.

with your eyes. [21]People will not say, 'Look, here it is!' or, 'There it is!' because God's kingdom is within[n] you."

[22]Then Jesus said to his followers, "The time will come when you will want very much to see one of the days of the Son of Man. But you will not see it. [23]People will say to you, 'Look, there he is!' or, 'Look, here he is!' Stay where you are; don't go away and search.

WHEN JESUS COMES AGAIN

[24]"When the Son of Man comes again, he will shine like lightning, which flashes across the sky and lights it up from one side to the other. [25]But first he must suffer many things and be rejected by the people of this time. [26]When the Son of Man comes again, it will be as it was when Noah lived. [27]People were eating, drinking, marrying, and giving their children to be married until the day Noah entered the boat. Then the flood came and killed them all. [28]It will be the same as during the time of Lot. People were eating, drinking, buying, selling, planting, and building. [29]But the day Lot left Sodom,[n] fire and sulfur rained down from the sky and killed them all. [30]This is how it will be when the Son of Man comes again.

> "Those who try to keep their lives will lose them. But those who give up their lives will save them." (Luke 17:33)

[31]"On that day, a person who is on the roof and whose belongings are in the house should not go inside to get them. A person who is in the field should not go back home. [32]Remember Lot's wife.[n] [33]Those who try to keep their lives will lose them. But those who give up their lives will save them. [34]I tell you, on that night two people will be sleeping in one bed; one will be taken and the other will be left. [35]There will be two women grinding grain together; one will be taken, and the other will be left." [36][n]

[37]The followers asked Jesus, "Where will this be, Lord?"

Jesus answered, "Where there is a dead body, there the vultures will gather."

18

GOD WILL ANSWER HIS PEOPLE

[1]Then Jesus used this story to teach his followers that they should always pray and never lose hope. [2]"In a certain town there was a judge who did not respect God or care about people. [3]In that same town there was a widow who kept coming to this judge, saying, 'Give me my rights against my enemy.' [4]For a while the judge refused to help her. But afterwards, he thought to himself, 'Even though I don't respect God or care about people, [5]I will see that she gets her rights. Otherwise she will continue to bother me until I am worn out.' "

[6]The Lord said, "Listen to what the unfair judge said. [7]God will always give what is right to his people who cry to him night and day, and he will not be slow to answer them. [8]I tell you, God will help his people quickly. But when the Son of Man comes again, will he find those on earth who believe in him?"

BEING RIGHT WITH GOD

[9]Jesus told this story to some people who thought they were very good and looked down on everyone else: [10]"A Pharisee and a tax collector both went to the Temple to pray. [11]The Pharisee stood alone and prayed, 'God, I thank you that I am not like other people who steal, cheat, or take part in adultery, or even like this tax collector. [12]I give up eating[n] twice a week, and I give one-tenth of everything I get!'

WHAT'S IT MEAN?

To collect their taxes, the Romans hired local Jewish citizens. These collectors were known for charging their fellow Jews more money than they really owed and keeping the extra cash for themselves. Because of this and because the collectors worked for the hated Roman government, tax collectors were usually seen as traitors to their people.

Luke 18:10

17:21 within Or "among." **17:29 Sodom** City that God destroyed because the people were so evil.
17:32 Lot's wife A story about what happened to Lot's wife is found in Genesis 19:15-17, 26.
17:36 Verse 36 A few Greek copies add verse 36: "Two people will be in the field. One will be taken, and the other will be left." **18:12 give up eating** This is called "fasting." The people would give up eating for a special time of prayer and worship to God. It was also done to show sadness and disappointment.

[13]"The tax collector, standing at a distance,
would not even look up to heaven. But he beat
on his chest because he was so sad. He said,
'God, have mercy on me, a sinner.' [14]I
tell you, when this man went
home, he was right with God,
but the Pharisee was not. All
who make themselves great
will be made humble, but all
who make themselves hum-
ble will be made great."

PRAYER
What kind of attitude should we pray with? (18:9–14)

WHO WILL ENTER GOD'S KINGDOM?

[15]Some people brought even their babies to
Jesus so he could touch them. When the followers saw this, they told them to stop. [16]But
Jesus called for the children, saying, "Let the little children come to me. Don't stop them, because the kingdom of God belongs to people
who are like these children. [17]I tell you the
truth, you must accept the kingdom of God as
if you were a child, or you will never enter it."

A RICH MAN'S QUESTION

[18]A certain leader asked Jesus, "Good Teacher, what must I do to have life forever?"
[19]Jesus said to him, "Why do you call me
good? Only God is good. [20]You
know the commands: 'You
must not be guilty of adultery. You must not murder
anyone. You must not steal.
You must not tell lies about
your neighbor. Honor your
father and mother.' "[n]

ASSURANCE
Is false assurance dangerous? (18:18–30)

[21]But the leader said, "I have obeyed all
these commands since I was a boy."
[22]When Jesus heard this, he said to him,
"There is still one more thing you need to do.
Sell everything you have and give it to the
poor, and you will have treasure in heaven.
Then come and follow me." [23]But when the
man heard this, he became very sad, because
he was very rich.
[24]Jesus looked at him and said, "It is very
hard for rich people to enter the kingdom of
God. [25]It is easier for a camel to go through the
eye of a needle than for a rich person to enter
the kingdom of God."

WHO CAN BE SAVED?

[26]When the people heard this, they asked,
"Then who can be saved?"
[27]Jesus answered, "God can do things that
are not possible for people to do."
[28]Peter said, "Look, we have left everything
and followed you."
[29]Jesus said, "I tell you the truth, all those
who have left houses, wives, brothers, parents,
or children for the kingdom of God [30]will get
much more in this life. And in the age that is
coming, they will have life forever."

JESUS WILL RISE FROM THE DEAD

[31]Then Jesus took the twelve apostles aside
and said to them, "We are going to Jerusalem.
Everything the prophets wrote about the Son
of Man will happen. [32]He will be turned over
to those who are evil. They will laugh at him,
insult him, spit on him, [33]beat him with
whips, and kill him. But on the third day, he
will rise to life again." [34]The apostles did not
understand this; the meaning was hidden
from them, and they did not realize what was
said.

JESUS HEALS A BLIND MAN

[35]As Jesus came near the city of Jericho, a
blind man was sitting beside the road, begging.
[36]When he heard the people coming down the
road, he asked, "What is happening?"
[37]They told him, "Jesus, from Nazareth, is
going by."
[38]The blind man cried out, "Jesus, Son of
David, have mercy on me!"
[39]The people leading the group warned the
blind man to be quiet. But the blind man
shouted even more, "Son of David, have mercy
on me!"
[40]Jesus stopped and ordered the blind man
to be brought to him. When he came near,
Jesus asked him, [41]"What do you want me to
do for you?"
He said, "Lord, I want to see."
[42]Jesus said to him, "Then see. You are
healed because you believed."
[43]At once the man was able to see, and he
followed Jesus, thanking God. All the people
who saw this praised God.

ZACCHAEUS MEETS JESUS

19

[1]Jesus was going through the city of Jericho.
[2]A man was there named Zacchaeus, who was
a very important tax collector, and he was
wealthy. [3]He wanted to see who Jesus was, but
he was not able because he was too short to
see above the crowd. [4]He ran ahead to a place
where Jesus would come, and he climbed a
sycamore tree so he could see him. [5]When
Jesus came to that place, he looked up and said

18:20 'You . . . mother.' Quotation from Exodus 20:12-16; Deuteronomy 5:16-20.

to him, "Zacchaeus, hurry and come down! I
must stay at your house today."
6Zacchaeus came down quickly and welcomed him gladly. 7All the people saw this and
began to complain, "Jesus is staying with a sinner!"
8But Zacchaeus stood and said to the Lord,
"I will give half of my possessions to the poor.
And if I have cheated anyone, I will pay back
four times more."
9Jesus said to him, "Salvation has come to
this house today, because this man also belongs
to the family of Abraham. 10The Son of Man
came to find lost people and save them."

A STORY ABOUT THREE SERVANTS

11As the people were listening to this, Jesus
told them a story because he was near Jerusalem and they thought God's kingdom would
appear immediately. 12He said: "A very important man went to a country far away to be
made a king and then to return home. 13So he
called ten of his servants and gave a coin[n] to
each servant. He said, 'Do business with this
money until I get back.' 14But the people in the
kingdom hated the man. So they sent a group
to follow him and say, 'We don't want this man
to be our king.'
15"But the man became king. When he returned home, he said, 'Call those servants who
have my money so I can know how much
they earned with it.'
16"The first servant came and said, 'Sir, I
earned ten coins with the one you gave me.'
17The king said to the servant, 'Excellent! You
are a good servant. Since I can trust you with
small things, I will let you rule over ten of my
cities.'
18"The second servant said, 'Sir, I earned five
coins with your one.' 19The king said to this
servant, 'You can rule over five cities.'
20"Then another servant came in and said to
the king, 'Sir, here is your coin which I
wrapped in a piece of cloth and hid. 21I was
afraid of you, because you are a hard man. You
even take money that you didn't earn and
gather food that you didn't plant.' 22Then the
king said to the servant, 'I will condemn you
by your own words, you evil servant. You
knew that I am a hard man, taking money that
I didn't earn and gathering food that I didn't
plant. 23Why then didn't you put my money in
the bank? Then when I came back, my money
would have earned some interest.'
24"The king said to the men who were
standing by, 'Take the coin away from this servant and give it to the servant who earned ten
coins.' 25They said, 'But sir, that servant already
has ten coins.' 26The king said, 'Those who have
will be given more, but those who do not have
anything will have everything taken away
from them. 27Now where are my enemies who
didn't want me to be king? Bring them here
and kill them before me.' "

JESUS ENTERS JERUSALEM AS A KING

28After Jesus said this, he went on toward
Jerusalem. 29As Jesus came near Bethphage and
Bethany, towns near the hill called the Mount
of Olives, he sent out two of his followers. 30He
said, "Go to the town you can see there. When
you enter it, you will find a colt tied there,
which no one has ever ridden. Untie it and
bring it here to me. 31If anyone asks you why
you are untying it, say that the Master needs it."
32The two followers went into town and
found the colt just as Jesus had told them. 33As
they were untying it, its owners came out and
asked the followers, "Why are you untying our
colt?"
34The followers answered, "The Master
needs it." 35So they brought it to Jesus, threw
their coats on the colt's back, and put Jesus on
it. 36As Jesus rode toward Jerusalem, others
spread their coats on the road before him.
37As he was coming close to Jerusalem, on
the way down the Mount of Olives, the whole
crowd of followers began joyfully shouting
praise to God for all the miracles they had
seen. 38They said,

"God bless the king who comes in the
name of the Lord! *Psalm 118:26*
There is peace in heaven and glory to
God!"

39Some of the Pharisees in the crowd said to
Jesus, "Teacher, tell your followers not to say
these things."
40But Jesus answered, "I tell you, if my followers didn't say these things, then the stones
would cry out."

JESUS CRIES FOR JERUSALEM

41As Jesus came near Jerusalem, he saw the
city and cried for it, 42saying, "I wish you knew
today what would bring you peace. But now it
is hidden from you. 43The time is coming when
your enemies will build a wall around you and
will hold you in on all sides. 44They will destroy you and all your people, and not one
stone will be left on another. All this will hap-

19:13 coin A Greek "mina." One mina was enough money to pay a person for working three months.

WHAT'S IT MEAN?

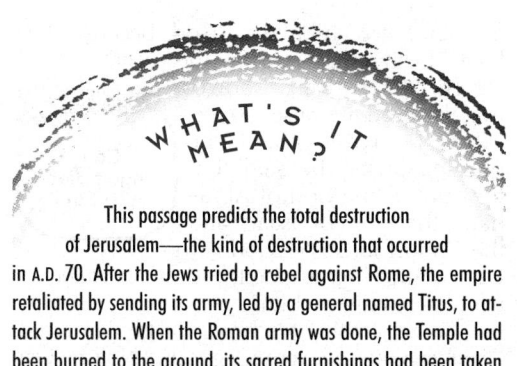

This passage predicts the total destruction of Jerusalem—the kind of destruction that occurred in A.D. 70. After the Jews tried to rebel against Rome, the empire retaliated by sending its army, led by a general named Titus, to attack Jerusalem. When the Roman army was done, the Temple had been burned to the ground, its sacred furnishings had been taken back to Rome, and the city of Jerusalem had been reduced to rubble. The Jews were no longer permitted any kind of self-rule.

Luke 19:43

pen because you did not recognize the time when God came to save you."

JESUS GOES TO THE TEMPLE

[45]Jesus went into the Temple and began to throw out the people who were selling things there. [46]He said, "It is written in the Scriptures, 'My Temple will be a house for prayer.'[n] But you have changed it into a 'hideout for robbers'!"[n]

[47]Jesus taught in the Temple every day. The leading priests, the experts on the law, and some of the leaders of the people wanted to kill Jesus. [48]But they did not know how they could do it, because all the people were listening closely to him.

JEWISH LEADERS QUESTION JESUS

20 [1]One day Jesus was in the Temple, teaching the people and telling them the Good News. The leading priests, teachers of the law, and older leaders came up to talk with him, [2]saying, "Tell us what authority you have to do these things? Who gave you this authority?"

[3]Jesus answered, "I will also ask you a question. Tell me: [4]When John baptized people, was that authority from God or just from other people?"

[5]They argued about this, saying, "If we answer, 'John's baptism was from God,' Jesus will say, 'Then why did you not believe him?' [6]But if we say, 'It was from other people,' all the people will stone us to death, because they believe John was a prophet." [7]So they answered that they didn't know where it came from.

[8]Jesus said to them, "Then I won't tell you what authority I have to do these things."

A STORY ABOUT GOD'S SON

[9]Then Jesus told the people this story: "A man planted a vineyard and leased it to some farmers. Then he went away for a long time. [10]When it was time for the grapes to be picked, he sent a servant to the farmers to get some of the grapes. But they beat the servant and sent him away empty-handed. [11]Then he sent another servant. They beat this servant also, and showed no respect for him, and sent him away empty-handed. [12]So the man sent a third servant. The farmers wounded him and threw him out. [13]The owner of the vineyard said, 'What will I do now? I will send my son whom I love. Maybe they will respect him.' [14]But when the farmers saw the son, they said to each other, 'This son will inherit the vineyard. If we kill him, it will be ours.' [15]So the farmers threw the son out of the vineyard and killed him.

"What will the owner of this vineyard do to them? [16]He will come and kill those farmers and will give the vineyard to other farmers."

When the people heard this story, they said, "Let this never happen!"

[17]But Jesus looked at them and said, "Then what does this verse mean:

'The stone that the builders rejected
became the cornerstone'?

Psalm 118:22

[18]Everyone who falls on that stone will be broken, and the person on whom it falls, that person will be crushed!"

[19]The teachers of the law and the leading priests wanted to arrest Jesus at once, because they knew the story was about them. But they were afraid of what the people would do.

IS IT RIGHT TO PAY TAXES OR NOT?

[20]So they watched Jesus and sent some spies who acted as if they were sincere. They wanted to trap Jesus in saying something wrong so they could hand him over to the authority and power of the governor. [21]So the spies asked Jesus, "Teacher, we know that what you say and teach is true. You pay no attention to who people are, and you always teach the truth about God's way. [22]Tell us, is it right for us to pay taxes to Caesar or not?"

19:46 'My Temple . . . prayer.' Quotation from Isaiah 56:7. **19:46 'hideout for robbers'** Quotation from Jeremiah 7:11.

[23]But Jesus, knowing they were trying to trick him, said, [24]"Show me a coin. Whose image and name are on it?"

They said, "Caesar's."

WHAT'S IT MEAN?

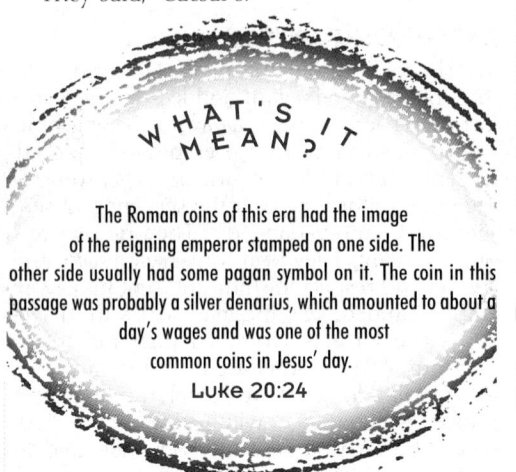

The Roman coins of this era had the image of the reigning emperor stamped on one side. The other side usually had some pagan symbol on it. The coin in this passage was probably a silver denarius, which amounted to about a day's wages and was one of the most common coins in Jesus' day.

Luke 20:24

[25]Jesus said to them, "Then give to Caesar the things that are Caesar's, and give to God the things that are God's."

[26]So they were not able to trap Jesus in anything he said in the presence of the people. And being amazed at his answer, they became silent.

SOME SADDUCEES TRY TO TRICK JESUS

[27]Some Sadducees, who believed people would not rise from the dead, came to Jesus. [28]They asked, "Teacher, Moses wrote that if a man's brother dies and leaves a wife but no children, then that man must marry the widow and have children for his brother. [29]Once there were seven brothers. The first brother married and died, but had no children. [30]Then the second brother married the widow, and he died. [31]And the third brother married the widow, and he died. The same thing happened with all seven brothers; they died and had no children. [32]Finally, the woman died also. [33]Since all seven brothers had married her, whose wife will she be when people rise from the dead?"

[34]Jesus said to them, "On earth, people marry and are given to someone to marry. [35]But those who will be worthy to be raised from the dead and live again will not marry, nor will they be given to someone to marry. [36]In that life they are like angels and cannot die. They are children of God, because they have been raised from the dead. [37]Even Moses clearly showed that the dead are raised to life. When he wrote about the burning bush,[n] he said that the Lord is 'the God of Abraham, the God of Isaac, and the God of Jacob.'[n] [38]God is the God of the living, not the dead, because all people are alive to him."

ANGELS

Can angels die? (20:36)

[39]Some of the teachers of the law said, "Teacher, your answer was good." [40]No one was brave enough to ask him another question.

IS THE CHRIST THE SON OF DAVID?

[41]Then Jesus said, "Why do people say that the Christ is the Son of David? [42]In the book of Psalms, David himself says:

'The Lord said to my Lord:
  Sit by me at my right side,
[43] until I put your enemies under your
    control.'[n] *Psalm 110:1*

[44]David calls the Christ 'Lord,' so how can the Christ be his son?"

JESUS ACCUSES SOME LEADERS

[45]While all the people were listening, Jesus said to his followers, [46]"Beware of the teachers of the law. They like to walk around wearing fancy clothes, and they love for people to greet them with respect in the marketplaces. They love to have the most important seats in the synagogues and at feasts. [47]But they cheat widows and steal their houses and then try to make themselves look good by saying long prayers. They will receive a greater punishment."

TRUE GIVING

21 [1]As Jesus looked up, he saw some rich people putting their gifts into the Temple money box.[n] [2]Then he saw a poor widow putting two small copper coins into the box. [3]He said, "I tell you the truth, this poor widow gave more than all those rich people. [4]They gave only what they did not need. This woman is very poor, but she gave all she had to live on."

THE TEMPLE WILL BE DESTROYED

[5]Some people were talking about the Temple and how it was decorated with beautiful stones and gifts offered to God.

20:37 burning bush Read Exodus 3:1–12 in the Old Testament. **20:37 'the God of . . . Jacob'** These words are taken from Exodus 3:6. **20:43 until . . . control** Literally, "until I make your enemies a footstool for your feet." **21:1 money box** A special box in the Jewish place of worship where people put their gifts to God.

On the Edge

While all the people were listening, Jesus said to his followers, "Beware of the teachers of the law. They like to walk around wearing fancy clothes, and they love for people to greet them with respect in the marketplaces. They love to have the most important seats in the synagogues and at feasts. But they cheat widows and steal their houses and then try to make themselves look good by saying long prayers. They will receive a greater punishment" (Luke 20:45–47).

More than anything else, a pastor should be a lover of God and a lover of God's people. A man can be a great fund-raiser or speaker, but if he doesn't truly love the people, everybody suffers. He should know God's Word and be able to teach in a way that is clear to you. He should be teaching truths from the Bible, and not just from his own opinion. A great pastor has compassion for sinners and love for the lost. He has the heart of a servant and the strength of a leader. A man of God listens to God. He does what he hears God tell him to do, and he goes where he senses God leads. A good pastor has honor, integrity, and a passionate devotion to Jesus.

The relationship between a pastor and his congregation can be compared to the relationship between a shepherd and his sheep. When you're looking for a pastor, think of yourself as a sheep and of him as a shepherd. Be wary of flashy and arrogant leaders. A godly pastor can be one of the most important people in your life.

SEE FOR YOURSELF:
Ps. 100:3; Is. 40:11; Jer. 23:4; Ezek. 34:11–16; Matt. 23; John 10:1–16; Acts 20:28; 1 Tim. 3:1–12; Titus 1:5–9

But Jesus said, 6"As for these things you are
looking at, the time will come when not one
stone will be left on another. Every stone will
be thrown down."
7They asked Jesus, "Teacher, when will these
things happen? What will be the sign that they
are about to take place?"
8Jesus said, "Be careful so you are not
fooled. Many people will come in my name,
saying, 'I am the One' and, 'The time has come!'
But don't follow them. 9When you hear about
wars and riots, don't be afraid, because these
things must happen first, but the end will come
later."
10Then he said to them, "Nations will fight
against other nations, and kingdoms against
other kingdoms. 11In various places there will
be great earthquakes, sicknesses, and a lack of
food. Fearful events and great signs will come
from heaven.
12"But before all these things happen, people
will arrest you and treat you cruelly. They will
judge you in their synagogues and put you in
jail and force you to stand before kings and
governors, because you follow me. 13But this
will give you an opportunity to tell about me.
14Make up your minds not to worry ahead of
time about what you will say. 15I will give you
the wisdom to say things that none of your
enemies will be able to stand against or prove
wrong. 16Even your parents, brothers, relatives,
and friends will turn against you, and they will
kill some of you. 17All people will hate you because you follow me. 18But none of these
things can really harm you. 19By continuing to
have faith you will save your lives.

WHAT'S IT MEAN?

Construction of the Temple in Jerusalem was a pet project of Herod the Great, and it showed. The ornate main building was made of cream-colored stone and gold. Some of the stones used in the construction were almost forty feet long. The main building was completed in 9 B.C. The entire structure wasn't finished until A.D. 64. (Postscript: In A.D. 70, the Romans completely destroyed the Temple once again—just six years after the construction had ended.)

Luke 21:5

JERUSALEM WILL BE DESTROYED

20"When you see armies all around Jerusalem, you will know it will soon be destroyed.
21At that time, the people in Judea should run
away to the mountains. The people in Jerusalem must get out, and those who are near the
city should not go in. 22These are the days of
punishment to bring about all that is written in

the Scriptures. 23 How terrible it will be for women who are pregnant or have nursing babies! Great trouble will come upon this land, and God will be angry with these people. 24 They will be killed by the sword and taken as prisoners to all nations. Jerusalem will be crushed by non-Jewish people until their time is over.

DON'T FEAR

25 "There will be signs in the sun, moon, and stars. On earth, nations will be afraid and confused because of the roar and fury of the sea. 26 People will be so afraid they will faint, wondering what is happening to the world, because the powers of the heavens will be shaken. 27 Then people will see the Son of Man coming in a cloud with power and great glory. 28 When these things begin to happen, look up and hold your heads high, because the time when God will free you is near!"

> "Earth and sky will be destroyed, but the words I have spoken will never be destroyed." (Luke 21:33)

JESUS' WORDS WILL LIVE FOREVER

29 Then Jesus told this story: "Look at the fig tree and all the other trees. 30 When their leaves appear, you know that summer is near. 31 In the same way, when you see these things happening, you will know that God's kingdom is near.

32 "I tell you the truth, all these things will happen while the people of this time are still living. 33 Earth and sky will be destroyed, but the words I have spoken will never be destroyed.

BE READY ALL THE TIME

34 "Be careful not to spend your time feasting, drinking, or worrying about worldly things. If you do, that day might come on you suddenly, 35 like a trap on all people on earth. 36 So be ready all the time. Pray that you will be strong enough to escape all these things that will happen and that you will be able to stand before the Son of Man."

> **DRINKING**
> Is becoming drunk dangerous? (21:34)

37 During the day, Jesus taught the people in the Temple, and at night he went out of the city and stayed on the Mount of Olives. 38 Every morning all the people got up early to go to the Temple to listen to him.

22

JUDAS BECOMES AN ENEMY OF JESUS

1 It was almost time for the Feast of Unleavened Bread, called the Passover Feast. 2 The leading priests and teachers of the law were trying to find a way to kill Jesus, because they were afraid of the people.

3 Satan entered Judas Iscariot, one of Jesus' twelve apostles. 4 Judas went to the leading priests and some of the soldiers who guarded the Temple and talked to them about a way to hand Jesus over to them. 5 They were pleased and agreed to give Judas money. 6 He agreed and watched for the best time to hand Jesus over to them when he was away from the crowd.

JESUS EATS THE PASSOVER MEAL

7 The Day of Unleavened Bread came when the Passover lambs had to be sacrificed. 8 Jesus said to Peter and John, "Go and prepare the Passover meal for us to eat."

9 They asked, "Where do you want us to prepare it?" 10 Jesus said to them, "After you go into the city, a man carrying a jar of water will meet you. Follow him into the house that he enters, 11 and tell the owner of the house, 'The Teacher says: Where is the guest room in which I may eat the Passover meal with my followers?' 12 Then he will show you a large, furnished room upstairs. Prepare the Passover meal there."

13 So Peter and John left and found everything as Jesus had said. And they prepared the Passover meal.

THE LORD'S SUPPER

14 When the time came, Jesus and the apostles were sitting at the table. 15 He said to them, "I wanted very much to eat this Passover meal with you before I suffer. 16 I will not eat another

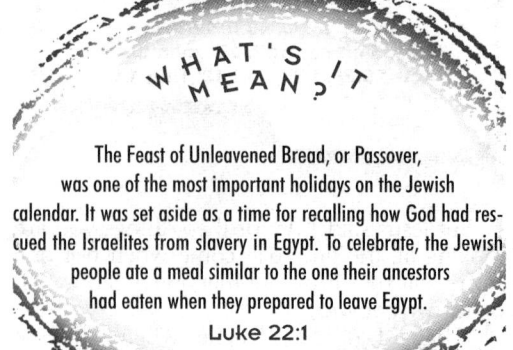

> **WHAT'S IT MEAN?**
> The Feast of Unleavened Bread, or Passover, was one of the most important holidays on the Jewish calendar. It was set aside as a time for recalling how God had rescued the Israelites from slavery in Egypt. To celebrate, the Jewish people ate a meal similar to the one their ancestors had eaten when they prepared to leave Egypt.
> Luke 22:1

Passover meal until it is given its true meaning
in the kingdom of God."
17Then Jesus took a cup, gave thanks, and
said, "Take this cup and share it among yourselves. 18I will not drink again from the fruit of
the vine[n] until God's kingdom comes."
19Then Jesus took some bread, gave thanks,
broke it, and gave it to the apostles, saying,
"This is my body, which I am giving for you.
Do this to remember me." 20In the same way,
after supper, Jesus took the cup and said, "This
cup is the new agreement that God makes with
his people. This new agreement begins with
my blood which is poured out for you.

WHO WILL TURN AGAINST JESUS?

21"But one of you will turn against me, and
his hand is with mine on the table. 22What God
has planned for the Son of Man will happen,
but how terrible it will be for that one who
turns against the Son of Man."
23Then the apostles asked each other which
one of them would do that.

BE LIKE A SERVANT

24The apostles also began to argue about
which one of them was the most important.
25But Jesus said to them, "The kings of the non-
Jewish people rule over them, and those who
have authority over others like to be called
'friends of the people.' 26But you must not
be like that. Instead, the greatest among you
should be like the youngest, and the leader
should be like the servant. 27Who is more important: the one sitting at the table or the one
serving? You think the one at the table is more
important, but I am like a servant among you.
28"You have stayed with me through my
struggles. 29Just as my Father has given me a
kingdom, I also give you a kingdom 30so you
may eat and drink at my table in my kingdom.
And you will sit on thrones, judging the twelve
tribes of Israel.

DON'T LOSE YOUR FAITH!

31"Simon, Simon, Satan has asked to test all
of you as a farmer sifts his wheat. 32I have
prayed that you will not lose your faith! Help
your brothers be stronger when you come
back to me."
33But Peter said to Jesus, "Lord, I am ready
to go with you to prison and even to die with
you!"
34But Jesus said, "Peter, before the rooster
crows this day, you will say three times that
you don't know me."

BE READY FOR TROUBLE

35Then Jesus said to the apostles, "When I
sent you out without a purse, a bag, or sandals,
did you need anything?"
They said, "No."
36He said to them, "But now if you have a
purse or a bag, carry that with you. If you
don't have a sword, sell your coat and buy
one. 37The Scripture says, 'He was treated like a
criminal,'[n] and I tell you this scripture must
have its full meaning. It was written about me,
and it is happening now."
38His followers said, "Look, Lord, here are
two swords."
He said to them, "That is enough."

JESUS PRAYS ALONE

39Jesus left the city and went to the Mount
of Olives, as he often did, and his followers
went with him. 40When he reached the place,
he said to them, "Pray for strength against
temptation."
41Then Jesus went about a stone's throw
away from them. He kneeled down and
prayed, 42"Father, if you are willing, take away
this cup[n] of suffering. But do what you want,
not what I want." 43Then an angel from heaven
appeared to him to strengthen him. 44Being full
of pain, Jesus prayed even harder. His sweat
was like drops of blood falling to the ground.
45When he finished praying, he went to his followers and found them asleep because of their
sadness. 46Jesus said to them, "Why are you
sleeping? Get up and pray for strength against
temptation."

JESUS IS ARRESTED

47While Jesus was speaking, a crowd came
up, and Judas, one of the twelve apostles, was
leading them. He came close to Jesus so he
could kiss him.
48But Jesus said to him, "Judas, are you using the kiss to give the Son of Man to his enemies?"
49When those who were standing around
him saw what was happening, they said, "Lord,
should we strike them with our swords?"
50And one of them struck the servant of the
high priest and cut off his right ear.

22:18 fruit of the vine Product of the grapevine; this may also be translated "wine." **22:37 'He . . . criminal'** Quotation from Isaiah 53:12. **22:42 cup** Jesus is talking about the painful things that will happen to him. Accepting these things will be hard, like drinking a cup of something bitter.

On the Edge

Father, if you are willing, take away this cup of suffering. But do what you want, not what I want (Luke 22:42).

A lot of people have memorized the Bible verse that tells us to obey our parents as the Lord wants—to do what they want (Eph. 6:1). Do you ever wonder, "What's the big deal?" The big deal is: God's Word says that "It is better to obey than to sacrifice"(1 Sam. 15:22). We can spend all of our time in church and put all of our money in the offering, but if we aren't walking the walk, we're missing the point of what God's Word is saying. Remember that obedience is better than a bunch of rituals. In fact, God's Word says that if we truly love him, we will really do what he says to do (see John 14:15; 15:10). When you obey God, not only does this show the world that you love him, it shows *him* that you love him!

You can study the whole Bible looking at the lives of those who obeyed God and those who didn't. You'll find that the ones who were obedient were the ones who got blessed! Abraham obeyed God. Noah obeyed God. Joseph obeyed God. Daniel obeyed God. Jesus obeyed his Father, God. Paul obeyed God. Every one of those folks reaped the benefits of obedience. Obey God today, and reap the blessings of God tomorrow!

SEE FOR YOURSELF:
Is. 1:19; John 14:15, 21; Rom. 5:19; 16:19–20

51Jesus said, "Stop! No more of this." Then he touched the servant's ear and healed him.

52Those who came to arrest Jesus were the leading priests, the soldiers who guarded the Temple, and the older leaders. Jesus said to them, "You came out here with swords and clubs as though I were a criminal. 53I was with you every day in the Temple, and you didn't arrest me there. But this is your time—the time when darkness rules."

PETER SAYS HE DOESN'T KNOW JESUS

54They arrested Jesus, and led him away, and brought him into the house of the high priest. Peter followed far behind them. 55After the soldiers started a fire in the middle of the courtyard and sat together, Peter sat with them. 56A servant girl saw Peter sitting there in the firelight, and looking closely at him, she said, "This man was also with him."

57But Peter said this was not true; he said, "Woman, I don't know him."

58A short time later, another person saw Peter and said, "You are also one of them."

But Peter said, "Man, I am not!"

59About an hour later, another man insisted, "Certainly this man was with him, because he is from Galilee, too."

60But Peter said, "Man, I don't know what you are talking about!"

At once, while Peter was still speaking, a rooster crowed. 61Then the Lord turned and looked straight at Peter. And Peter remembered what the Lord had said: "Before the rooster crows this day, you will say three times that you don't know me." 62Then Peter went outside and cried painfully.

THE PEOPLE MAKE FUN OF JESUS

63The men who were guarding Jesus began making fun of him and beating him.

64They blindfolded him and said, "Prove that you are a prophet, and tell us who hit you." 65They said many cruel things to Jesus.

JESUS BEFORE THE LEADERS

66When day came, the council of the older leaders of the people, both the leading priests and the teachers of the law, came together and led Jesus to their highest court. 67They said, "If you are the Christ, tell us."

Jesus said to them, "If I tell you, you will not believe me. 68And if I ask you, you will not answer. 69But from now on, the Son of Man will sit at the right hand of the powerful God."

70They all said, "Then are you the Son of God?"

Jesus said to them, "You say that I am."

71They said, "Why do we need witnesses now? We ourselves heard him say this."

PILATE QUESTIONS JESUS

23 1Then the whole group stood up and led Jesus to Pilate.[n] 2They began to accuse Jesus, saying, "We caught this man telling things that mislead our people. He says that we should not pay taxes to Caesar, and he calls himself the Christ, a king."

3Pilate asked Jesus, "Are you the king of the Jews?"

23:1 Pilate Pontius Pilate was the Roman governor of Judea from A.D. 26 to A.D. 36.

WHAT'S IT MEAN?

Pilate, the Roman governor of Judea and Samaria, had come to Jerusalem with his troops for the Passover feast. His purpose was to make sure that the thousands of Jews who had traveled to the city for the annual holiday did not attempt to riot or revolt. As the highest authority in the land, Pilate had the power to sentence criminals to death. The Jewish council had the authority to hand down verdicts, but did not have the authority to execute a prisoner without the okay of Roman authorities.

Luke 23:1

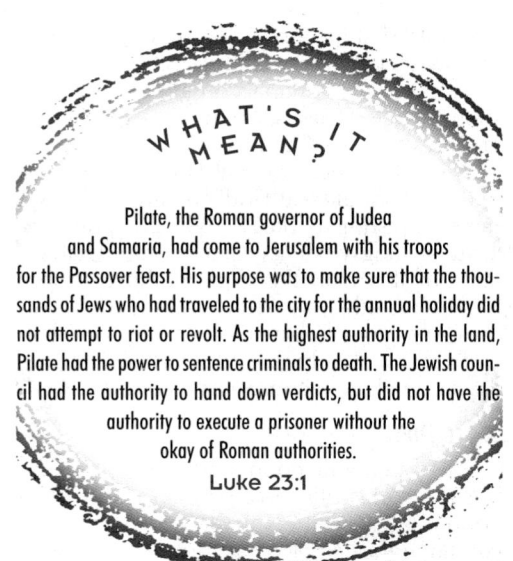

Jesus answered, "Those are your words."
[4]Pilate said to the leading priests and the
people, "I find nothing against this man."
[5]They were insisting, saying, "But Jesus
makes trouble with the people, teaching all
around Judea. He began in Galilee, and now he
is here."

PILATE SENDS JESUS TO HEROD

[6]Pilate heard this and asked if Jesus was
from Galilee. [7]Since Jesus was under Herod's
authority, Pilate sent Jesus to Herod, who was
in Jerusalem at that time. [8]When Herod saw
Jesus, he was very glad, because he had heard
about Jesus and had wanted to meet him for a
long time. He was hoping to see Jesus work a
miracle. [9]Herod asked Jesus many questions,
but Jesus said nothing. [10]The leading priests
and teachers of the law were standing there,
strongly accusing Jesus. [11]After Herod and his
soldiers had made fun of Jesus, they dressed
him in a kingly robe and sent him back to Pilate. [12]In the past, Pilate and Herod had always
been enemies, but on that day they became
friends.

JESUS MUST DIE

[13]Pilate called the people together with the
leading priests and the rulers. [14]He said to
them, "You brought this man to me, saying he
makes trouble among the people. But I have
questioned him before you all, and I have not
found him guilty of what you say. [15]Also, Herod found nothing wrong with him; he sent
him back to us. Look, he has done nothing for
which he should die. [16]So, after I punish him, I
will let him go free." [17][n]
[18]But the people shouted together, "Take this
man away! Let Barabbas go free!" [19](Barabbas
was a man who was in prison for his part in a
riot in the city and for murder.)
[20]Pilate wanted to let Jesus go free and told
this to the crowd. [21]But they shouted again,
"Crucify him! Crucify him!"
[22]A third time Pilate said to them, "Why?
What wrong has he done? I can find no reason
to kill him. So I will have him punished and set
him free."
[23]But they continued to shout, demanding
that Jesus be crucified. Their yelling became so
loud that [24]Pilate decided to give them what
they wanted. [25]He set free the man who was in
jail for rioting and murder, and he handed
Jesus over to them to do with him as they
wished.

JESUS IS CRUCIFIED

[26]As they led Jesus away, Simon, a man
from Cyrene, was coming in from the fields.
They forced him to carry Jesus' cross and to
walk behind him.
[27]A large crowd of people was following
Jesus, including some women who were sad
and crying for him. [28]But Jesus turned and said
to them, "Women of Jerusalem, don't cry for
me. Cry for yourselves and for your children.
[29]The time is coming when people will say,
'Happy are the women who cannot have children and who have no babies to nurse.' [30]Then
people will say to the mountains, 'Fall on us!'
And they will say to the hills, 'Cover us!' [31]If
they act like this now when life is good, what
will happen when bad times come?"[n]
[32]There were also two criminals led out
with Jesus to be put to death. [33]When they
came to a place called the Skull, the soldiers
crucified Jesus and the criminals—one on his
right and the other on his left. [34]Jesus said, "Father, forgive them, because they don't know
what they are doing."[n]
The soldiers threw lots to decide who
would get his clothes. [35]The people stood there
watching. And the leaders made fun of Jesus,
saying, "He saved others. Let him save himself
if he is God's Chosen One, the Christ."

23:17 Verse 17 A few Greek copies add verse 17: "Every year at the Passover Feast, Pilate had to release one prisoner to the people." **23:31 If . . . come?** Literally, "If they do these things in the green tree, what will happen in the dry?" **23:34 Verse 34** Some early Greek copies do not have this first part of the verse.

On the Edge

When they came to a place called the Skull, the soldiers crucified Jesus and the criminals—one on his right and the other on his left. Jesus said, "Father, forgive them, because they don't know what they are doing" (Luke 23:33–34).

Jesus says in the Sermon on the Mount that anyone can love someone who treats him or her well. But in order to be like God, we must love our enemies and pray for them. He says, "I say to you, love your enemies. Pray for those who hurt you. If you do this, you will be true children of your Father in heaven. . . . If you love only the people who love you, you will get no reward. Even the tax collectors do that. And if you are nice only to your friends, you are no better than other people. Even those who don't know God are nice to their friends. So you must be perfect, just as your Father in heaven is perfect" (Matt. 5:44–48). Like it or not, it's what we've got to do. All throughout the New Testament, the writers emphasize that the goal of our faith, after salvation, is to become more Christlike—to imitate God. We are instructed to love our enemies because that's what God does. Here in Luke 23:33–34, Jesus sets the example for us. He prays for the people who are killing him, and he asks God to forgive them.

Loving your enemies does not mean that you approve of what they do. It means that you love them *in spite of it*. You can pray for them, yet not participate in what they do. Sometimes you've just got to grit your teeth and determine that you will obey God. Loving when you don't feel like it, but because it's God's command—now that's love. God loves all of us, but hates our sin. Follow his example.

SEE FOR YOURSELF:
Matt. 5:43–48;
Mark 11:25;
Luke 6:27, 35

[36]The soldiers also made fun of him, coming
to Jesus and offering him some vinegar. [37]They
said, "If you are the king of the Jews, save
yourself!" [38]At the top of the cross these words
were written: THIS IS THE KING OF THE JEWS.
[39]One of the criminals on a cross began to
shout insults at Jesus: "Aren't you the Christ?
Then save yourself and us."
[40]But the other criminal stopped him and
said, "You should fear God! You are getting the
same punishment he is. [41]We are punished
justly, getting what we deserve for what we
did. But this man has done nothing wrong."
[42]Then he said, "Jesus, remember me when you
come into your kingdom."
[43]Jesus said to him, "I tell you the truth, today you will be with me in paradise."[n]

JESUS DIES

[44]It was about noon, and the whole land
became dark until three o'clock in the afternoon, [45]because the sun did not shine. The
curtain in the Temple[n] was torn in two. [46]Jesus
cried out in a loud voice, "Father, I give you my
life." After Jesus said this, he died.
[47]When the army officer there saw what
happened, he praised God, saying, "Surely this
was a good man!"
[48]When all the people who had gathered
there to watch saw what happened, they returned home, beating their chests because they
were so sad. [49]But those who were close
friends of Jesus, including the women who had
followed him from Galilee, stood at a distance
and watched.

JOSEPH TAKES JESUS' BODY

[50]There was a good and religious man
named Joseph who was a member of the
council. [51]But he had not agreed to the other
leaders' plans and actions against Jesus. He was
from the town of Arimathea and was waiting
for the kingdom of God to come. [52]Joseph
went to Pilate to ask for the body of Jesus. [53]He
took the body down from the cross, wrapped
it in cloth, and put it in a tomb that was cut out
of a wall of rock. This tomb had never been
used before. [54]This was late on Preparation
Day, and when the sun went down, the Sabbath day would begin.
[55]The women who had come from Galilee
with Jesus followed Joseph and saw the tomb
and how Jesus' body was laid. [56]Then the
women left to prepare spices and perfumes.
On the Sabbath day they rested, as the law
of Moses commanded.

23:43 paradise Another word for heaven. **23:45 curtain in the Temple** A curtain divided the Most Holy Place from the other part of the Temple, the special building in Jerusalem where God commanded the Jewish people to worship him.

WHAT'S IT MEAN?

Jesus' tomb was actually a small room carved into a large rock. A heavy stone was placed in front of the tomb, not to keep bodies from coming out, but to keep animals from getting in.

Luke 23:53

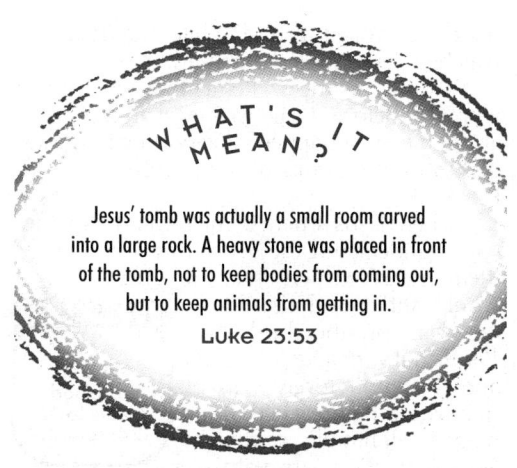

JESUS RISES FROM THE DEAD

24 1Very early on the first day of the week, at dawn, the women came to the tomb, bringing the spices they had prepared. 2They found the stone rolled away from the entrance of the tomb, 3but when they went in, they did not find the body of the Lord Jesus. 4While they were wondering about this, two men in shining clothes suddenly stood beside them. 5The women were very afraid and bowed their heads to the ground. The men said to them, "Why are you looking for a living person in this place for the dead? 6He is not here; he has risen from the dead. Do you remember what he told you in Galilee? 7He said the Son of Man must be handed over to sinful people, be crucified, and rise from the dead on the third day." 8Then the women remembered what Jesus had said.

9The women left the tomb and told all these things to the eleven apostles and the other followers. 10It was Mary Magdalene, Joanna, Mary the mother of James, and some other women who told the apostles everything that had happened at the tomb. 11But they did not believe the women, because it sounded like nonsense. 12But Peter got up and ran to the tomb. Bending down and looking in, he saw only the cloth that Jesus' body had been wrapped in. Peter went away to his home, wondering about what had happened.

JESUS ON THE ROAD TO EMMAUS

13That same day two of Jesus' followers were going to a town named Emmaus, about seven miles from Jerusalem. 14They were talking about everything that had happened. 15While they were talking and discussing, Jesus himself came near and began walking with them, 16but they were kept from recognizing him. 17Then he said, "What are these things you are talking about while you walk?"

The two followers stopped, looking very sad. 18The one named Cleopas answered, "Are you the only visitor in Jerusalem who does not know what just happened there?"

19Jesus said to them, "What are you talking about?"

They said, "About Jesus of Nazareth. He was a prophet who said and did many powerful things before God and all the people. 20Our leaders and the leading priests handed him over to be sentenced to death, and they crucified him. 21But we were hoping that he would free Israel. Besides this, it is now the third day since this happened. 22And today some women among us amazed us. Early this morning they went to the tomb, 23but they did not find his body there. They came and told us that they had seen a vision of angels who said that Jesus was alive! 24So some of our group went to the tomb, too. They found it just as the women said, but they did not see Jesus."

25Then Jesus said to them, "You are foolish and slow to believe everything the prophets said. 26They said that the Christ must suffer these things before he enters his glory." 27Then starting with what Moses and all the prophets had said about him, Jesus began to explain everything that had been written about himself in the Scriptures.

28They came near the town of Emmaus, and Jesus acted as if he were going farther. 29But they begged him, "Stay with us, because it is late; it is almost night." So he went in to stay with them.

30When Jesus was at the table with them, he took some bread, gave thanks, divided it, and gave it to them. 31And then, they were allowed to recognize Jesus. But when they saw who he was, he disappeared. 32They said to each other, "It felt like a fire burning in us when Jesus talked to us on the road and explained the Scriptures to us."

33So the two followers got up at once and went back to Jerusalem. There they found the eleven apostles and others gathered. 34They were saying, "The Lord really has risen from the dead! He showed himself to Simon."

35Then the two followers told what had happened on the road and how they recognized Jesus when he divided the bread.

JESUS APPEARS TO HIS FOLLOWERS

36While the two followers were telling this, Jesus himself stood right in the middle of them and said, "Peace be with you."

WHAT'S IT MEAN?

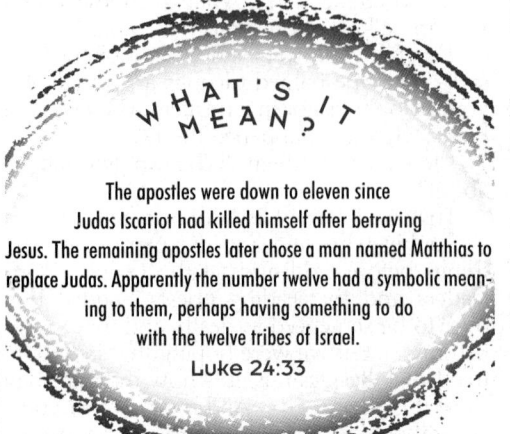

The apostles were down to eleven since Judas Iscariot had killed himself after betraying Jesus. The remaining apostles later chose a man named Matthias to replace Judas. Apparently the number twelve had a symbolic meaning to them, perhaps having something to do with the twelve tribes of Israel.
Luke 24:33

37They were fearful and terrified and
thought they were seeing a
ghost. 38But Jesus said, "Why
are you troubled? Why do
you doubt what you see?
39Look at my hands and
my feet. It is I myself!
Touch me and see, be-
cause a ghost does not
have a living body as you
see I have."
40After Jesus said this, he
showed them his hands and
feet. 41While they still could not
believe it because they were
amazed and happy, Jesus said to them, "Do
you have any food here?" 42They gave him a
piece of broiled fish. 43While the followers
watched, Jesus took the fish and ate it.
44He said to them, "Remember when I was
with you before? I said that everything written
about me must happen—everything in the law
of Moses, the books of the prophets, and the
Psalms."
45Then Jesus opened their minds so they
could understand the Scriptures. 46He said to
them, "It is written that the Christ
would suffer and rise from
the dead on the third day
47and that a change of hearts
and lives and forgiveness of
sins would be preached in his
name to all nations, starting at
Jerusalem. 48You are witnesses
of these things. 49I will send you what my Father has promised, but you must stay in Jerusalem until you have received
that power from heaven."

GOOD NEWS

Who is the Good News for? (24:46–47)

"They worshiped him and returned to Jerusalem very happy. They stayed in the Temple all the time, praising God."
(Luke 24:52–53)

JESUS GOES BACK TO HEAVEN

50Jesus led his followers
as far as Bethany, and he
raised his hands and
blessed them. 51While he
was blessing them, he was
separated from them and
carried into heaven. 52They
worshiped him and returned
to Jerusalem very happy. 53They
stayed in the Temple all the time, praising
God.

john

CONTENT The Book of John was written by one of Jesus' best friends. It's an inside look by someone who worked right beside Jesus throughout his ministry. John's account of the Good News isn't so much the story of Jesus' life. Rather, it is more like an overview of why we should believe Jesus was the Son of God.

John wasn't as concerned that we know about what Jesus did (and in what order) as he was that we know Jesus himself and that we love him as John did. John wanted us to believe the mystery of Jesus' deity—that while he was a Person, he was really and truly God.

The other three accounts of the Good News were already written by the time John sat down to have his say. John didn't need to rewrite the same things. So instead of starting with Jesus' birth or even God's promise to Abraham, John started with the creation of the world. Since Jesus was God, Jesus was there when the world was created.

It is a good thing for us that one of Jesus' best friends wrote his story. We need to know what it's like to be a friend of God so that we can learn to be one, too.

Outline

1:1–18 .... A Hymn in Praise of the Word
1:19–34 .... The Message of John the Baptist
1:35–51 .... Jesus Chooses His First Followers
2:1—12:50 .... Jesus' Seven Special Miracles
13:1—19:42 .... Jesus' Last Week: His Trial and Death
20:1–10 .... Jesus Is Alive
20:11—21:25 ...... Jesus Appears to His Followers

Purpose We can have eternal life by trusting God's Son as our Savior.

Theme Knowing God by Believing in Jesus Christ

Date of writing Late 80s or early 90s A.D.

"Jesus did many other miracles in the presence of his followers that are not written in this book. But these are written so that you may believe that Jesus is the Christ, the Son of God. Then, by believing, you may have life through his name" (20:30–31).

Bible Talk

Nicodemus and the Plan of Salvation

One of the most famous verses in the world is in the third chapter of John. You've probably heard John 3:16 many times. It says that God loved the world so much that he sent his only Son, Jesus, so that we could have eternal life by believing in him. Sound familiar?

Jesus actually said this as a part of a conversation with a man named Nicodemus. Nicodemus was a religious leader. Many of his associates were giving Jesus a hard time. Maybe that's why Nicodemus came to talk to Jesus after it was dark outside. He asked Jesus to explain all this faith and salvation and "born again" stuff to him.

Jesus did that; and, in the process, because of John's account of the Good News, he explained it to us.

CRUCIFIXION

John was actually there at the cross when Jesus was crucified. It was a gruesome sight. It must have been difficult to watch, but John was there. Jesus even talked to him from the cross. He asked John to take care of Mary, Jesus' mom.

When Jesus died on the cross, it was the single most significant moment the world had ever seen. It was God giving his life for us. It was all of our sins being forgiven in one moment.

And it was one best friend watching another best friend die like a criminal even though he was innocent. What do you think it would have been like to be John standing at the foot of the cross?

CHRIST COMES TO THE WORLD

1 [1]In the beginning there was the Word.[n] The Word was with God, and the Word was God. [2]He was with God in the beginning. [3]All things were made by him, and nothing was made without him. [4]In him there was life, and that life was the light of all people. [5]The Light shines in the darkness, and the darkness has not overpowered it.

JESUS
Is Jesus God? (1:1–5)

[6]There was a man named John[n] who was sent by God. [7]He came to tell people the truth about the Light so that through him all people could hear about the Light and believe. [8]John was not the Light, but he came to tell people the truth about the Light. [9]The true Light that gives light to all was coming into the world!

[10]The Word was in the world, and the world was made by him, but the world did not know him. [11]He came to the world that was his own, but his own people did not accept him. [12]But to all who did accept him and believe in him he gave the right to become children of God. [13]They did not become his children in any human way—by any human parents or human desire. They were born of God.

ADOPTION
Who can be called God's children? (1:12)

[14]The Word became a human and lived among us. We saw his glory—the glory that belongs to the only Son of the Father—and he was full of grace and truth. [15]John tells the truth about him and cries out, saying, "This is the One I told you about: 'The One who comes after me is greater than I am, because he was living before me.' "

[16]Because he was full of grace and truth, from him we all received one gift after another. [17]The law was given through Moses, but grace and truth came through Jesus Christ. [18]No one has ever seen God. But God the only Son is very close to the Father,[n] and he has shown us what God is like.

JOHN TELLS PEOPLE ABOUT JESUS

[19]Here is the truth John[n] told when the leaders in Jerusalem sent priests and Levites to ask him, "Who are you?"

[20]John spoke freely and did not refuse to answer. He said, "I am not the Christ."

[21]So they asked him, "Then who are you? Are you Elijah?"[n]

He answered, "No, I am not."

"Are you the Prophet?"[n] they asked.

He answered, "No."

[22]Then they said, "Who are you? Give us an answer to tell those who sent us. What do you say about yourself?"

On the Edge

In the beginning there was the Word. The Word was with God, and the Word was God (John 1:1).

This verse will knock anyone who doesn't believe in the Trinity—that God the Father, God the Son (Jesus), and the Holy Spirit are all three in one—right in the head. Verse 14 says, "The Word became a human and lived among us. We saw his glory—the glory that belongs to the only Son of the Father—and he was full of grace and truth." Jesus is the Word! That's why Hebrews 4:12 says that the Word of God is "alive and working."

If you want to get closer to God, start by spending time in his Word. Not only will you learn about him, but you'll hear from him. Jesus speaks to us through his Word more than any other way. That's why it's so important to read the Bible, study it, and memorize verses.

Did you know that as you spend time in this Book, the Word of God, your faith is being increased? It's vital that you put the Word of God in you when things are going great and you don't think you need it, so it will be there when you do need it. Remember, "Faith comes from hearing the Good News" (Rom. 10:17). That message is in the Word of God. Jesus is the Word!

SEE FOR YOURSELF:
Ps. 138:2; Rom. 10:17; 2 Tim. 2:15

1:1 Word The Greek word is "logos," meaning any kind of communication; it could be translated "message." Here, it means Christ, because Christ was the way God told people about himself. **1:6, 19 John** John the Baptist, who preached to people about Christ's coming (Matthew 3, Luke 3). **1:18 But . . . Father** This could be translated, "But the only God is very close to the Father." Also, some Greek copies say, "But the only Son is very close to the Father." **1:21 Elijah** A prophet who spoke for God. He lived hundreds of years before Christ and was expected to return before Christ (Malachi 4:5-6). **1:21 Prophet** They probably meant the prophet that God told Moses he would send (Deuteronomy 18:15-19).

23 John told them in the words of the prophet Isaiah:
"I am the voice of one
calling out in the desert:
'Make the road straight for the Lord.' "
Isaiah 40:3
24 Some Pharisees who had been sent asked
John: 25 "If you are not the Christ or Elijah or
the Prophet, why do you baptize people?"
26 John answered, "I baptize with water, but
there is one here with you that you don't
know about. 27 He is the One who comes after
me. I am not good enough to untie the strings
of his sandals."
28 This all happened at Bethany on the other
side of the Jordan River, where John was baptizing people.
29 The next day John saw Jesus coming toward him. John said, "Look, the Lamb of God,[n]
who takes away the sin of the world! 30 This is
the One I was talking about when I said, 'A
man will come after me, but he is greater than
I am, because he was living before me.' 31 Even I
did not know who he was, although I came
baptizing with water so that the people of Israel would know who he is."
32-33 Then John said, "I saw the Spirit come
down from heaven in the form of a dove and
rest on him. Until then I did not know who the
Christ was. But the God who sent me to baptize with water told me, 'You will see the Spirit
come down and rest on a man; he is the One
who will baptize with the Holy Spirit.' 34 I have
seen this happen, and I tell you the truth: This
man is the Son of God."

THE FIRST FOLLOWERS OF JESUS

35 The next day John[n] was there again with
two of his followers. 36 When he saw Jesus
walking by, he said, "Look, the Lamb of God!"[n]
37 The two followers heard John say this, so
they followed Jesus. 38 When Jesus turned and
saw them following him, he asked, "What are
you looking for?"
They said, "Rabbi, where are you staying?"
("Rabbi" means "Teacher.")
39 He answered, "Come and see." So the two
men went with Jesus and saw where he was
staying and stayed there with him that day. It
was about four o'clock in the afternoon.
40 One of the two men who followed Jesus
after they heard John speak about him was
Andrew, Simon Peter's brother. 41 The first thing
Andrew did was to find his brother Simon and
say to him, "We have found the Messiah."
("Messiah" means "Christ.")
42 Then Andrew took Simon to Jesus. Jesus
looked at him and said, "You are Simon son of
John. You will be called Cephas." ("Cephas"
means "Peter."[n])

1:29, 36 Lamb of God Name for Jesus. Jesus is like the lambs that were offered for a sacrifice to God.
1:35 John John the Baptist, who preached to people about Christ's coming (Matthew 3, Luke 3).
1:42 Peter The Greek name "Peter," like the Aramaic name "Cephas," means "rock."

Promise

HE PROMISES YOU BLESSING.

Because he was full of grace and truth, from him we all received one gift after another (John 1:16).

Check out what this verse is saying. God has given us "grace and truth." This means he's given us one blessing after another. He is the One who blesses. Notice that the verse doesn't say he *takes* from us.

A lot of people have the idea that God is out to take everything away from them, but that's not true. In fact, his Word says that he has come that we might have life "in all its fullness" (John 10:10). God isn't a taker. He's a giver, and he *wants* to give you the desires of your heart (see Ps. 37:4). So what are you going to do? Make God the joy and the delight of your life—and really mean it—and he will bring to pass your heart's desires.

What's your heart's desire? Tell God! He also says that if we will put him first and do what he wants, he will also add other things to us. What kind of things? Whatever we need. Romans 8:32 sums all of this up: "He did not spare his own Son but gave him for us all. So with Jesus, God will surely give us all things." Don't forget it: He is the One who blesses!

SEE FOR YOURSELF:

Ps. 35:27; 37:4; Matt. 6:33; James 1:17

WHAT'S IT MEAN?

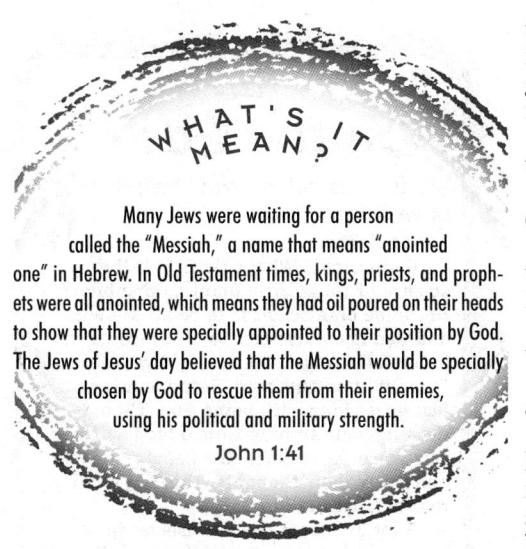

Many Jews were waiting for a person called the "Messiah," a name that means "anointed one" in Hebrew. In Old Testament times, kings, priests, and prophets were all anointed, which means they had oil poured on their heads to show that they were specially appointed to their position by God. The Jews of Jesus' day believed that the Messiah would be specially chosen by God to rescue them from their enemies, using his political and military strength.

John 1:41

43The next day Jesus decided to go to Galilee.
He found Philip and said to him, "Follow me."
44Philip was from the town of Bethsaida,
where Andrew and Peter lived. 45Philip found
Nathanael and told him, "We have found the
man that Moses wrote about in the law, and
the prophets also wrote about him. He is Jesus,
the son of Joseph, from Nazareth."
46But Nathanael said to Philip, "Can anything good come from Nazareth?"
Philip answered, "Come and see."
47As Jesus saw Nathanael coming toward
him, he said, "Here is truly an Israelite. There is
nothing false in him."
48Nathanael asked, "How do you know
me?"
Jesus answered, "I saw you when you
were under the fig tree, before Philip told you
about me."
49Then Nathanael said to Jesus, "Teacher,
you are the Son of God; you are the King of
Israel."
50Jesus said to Nathanael, "Do you believe
simply because I told you I saw you under the
fig tree? You will see greater things than that."
51And Jesus said to them, "I tell you the truth,
you will all see heaven open and 'angels of
God going up and coming down'[n] on the Son
of Man."

2

THE WEDDING AT CANA

1Two days later there was a wedding in the
town of Cana in Galilee. Jesus' mother was
there, 2and Jesus and his followers were also
invited to the wedding. 3When all the wine was
gone, Jesus' mother said to him, "They have no
more wine."
4Jesus answered, "Dear woman, why come
to me? My time has not yet come."
5His mother said to the servants, "Do whatever he tells you to do."
6In that place there were six stone water jars
that the Jews used in their washing ceremony.[n]
Each jar held about twenty or thirty gallons.
7Jesus said to the servants, "Fill the jars with
water." So they filled the jars to the top.
8Then he said to them, "Now take some out
and give it to the master of the feast."
So they took the water to the master. 9When
he tasted it, the water had become wine. He did
not know where the wine came from, but the
servants who had brought the water knew.
The master of the wedding called the bridegroom 10and said to him, "People always serve
the best wine first. Later, after the guests have
been drinking awhile, they serve the cheaper
wine. But you have saved the best wine till
now."
11So in Cana of Galilee Jesus did his first
miracle. There he showed his glory, and his
followers believed in him.

JESUS IN THE TEMPLE

12After this, Jesus went to the town of Capernaum with his mother, brothers, and followers. They stayed there for just a few days.
13When it was almost time for the Jewish Passover Feast, Jesus went to Jerusalem. 14In the
Temple he found people selling cattle,
sheep, and doves. He saw others sitting at tables, exchanging different kinds of money.
15Jesus made a whip out of
cords and forced all of them,
both the sheep and cattle, to
leave the Temple. He turned
over the tables and scattered the money of
those who were exchanging it. 16Then he said
to those who were selling pigeons, "Take these
things out of here! Don't make my Father's
house a place for buying and selling!"
17When this happened, the followers remembered what was written in the Scriptures:
"My strong love for your Temple completely
controls me."[n]
18Some of his people said to Jesus, "Show us

ANGER
What did Jesus get angry at? (2:13–17)

1:51 'angels . . . down' These words are from Genesis 28:12. **2:6 washing ceremony** The Jewish people washed themselves in special ways before eating, before worshiping in the Temple, and at other special times. **2:17 "My . . . me."** Quotation from Psalm 69:9.

a miracle to prove you have the right to do
these things."
[19]Jesus answered them, "Destroy this temple, and I will build it again in three days."
[20]They answered, "It took forty-six years to
build this Temple! Do you really believe you
can build it again in three days?"

WHAT'S IT MEAN?

It wasn't generosity that prompted Herod the Great to renovate the Temple in Jerusalem for his Jewish subjects. He wanted to keep the Jews happy with the Roman Empire so that they wouldn't get any ideas about rebelling. Specially trained priests served as advisors for the construction to make sure that the building plans matched the original floor plans that God gave to Moses. Though construction had been going on for decades, the Temple was not finished in Jesus' lifetime.

John 2:20

[21](But the temple Jesus meant was his own
body. [22]After Jesus was raised from the dead,
his followers remembered that Jesus had said
this. Then they believed the Scripture and the
words Jesus had said.)
[23]When Jesus was in Jerusalem for the Passover Feast, many people believed in him because they saw the miracles he did. [24]But Jesus
did not trust himself to them because he knew
them all. [25]He did not need anyone to tell him
about people, because he knew what was in
people's minds.

On the Edge

But Jesus did not trust himself to them because he knew them all (John 2:24).

Omniscient? What's that? Is it the science of those little Omni automobiles? No. To be omniscient is to be all-knowing and God is omniscient. In other words, he knows all things! Yep, *everything*. Nobody "taught" God anything. Being omniscient just goes along with being God. There is nothing you can hide from God. Just like in this verse, Jesus knew the people's hearts and knew their thoughts. This is a quality that belongs only to God.

A lot of people con themselves into believing that they are fooling God. You can fool your friends, your family, your youth pastor, and even your closest friend, but you'll never fool God. The good news is that no matter how crummy a day, week, month, or year you're having, God already knows. He knows exactly what you're going through. It doesn't matter if nobody on this earth understands the pain you feel, or even understands you. God does and he's on your side. Going through the tough times is a whole lot easier when you realize that he fully knows and understands what's happening and is right there with you to help. He also knows how everything is going to turn out in the end! When you get to the hard or lonely places in your life, remember—he's omniscient!

SEE FOR YOURSELF:
Ps. 135:15–17; 147:5; Is. 40:28; Rom. 11:33

NICODEMUS COMES TO JESUS

3 [1]There was a man named Nicodemus who
was one of the Pharisees and an important
Jewish leader. [2]One night Nicodemus came to
Jesus and said, "Teacher, we know you are a
teacher sent from God, because no one can do
the miracles you do unless God is with him."
[3]Jesus answered, "I tell you the truth, unless
one is born again, he cannot be in God's kingdom."
[4]Nicodemus said, "But if a person is already
old, how can he be born again? He cannot enter his mother's body again. So how can a person be born a second time?"
[5]But Jesus answered, "I tell you the truth,
unless one is born from water and the Spirit,
he cannot enter God's kingdom. [6]Human life
comes from human parents, but spiritual life
comes from the Spirit. [7]Don't be surprised
when I tell you, 'You must all be born again.'
[8]The wind blows where it wants to and you
hear the sound of it, but you don't know
where the wind comes from or where it is going. It is the same with every person who is
born from the Spirit."
[9]Nicodemus asked, "How can this happen?"
[10]Jesus said, "You are an important teacher
in Israel, and you don't understand these
things? [11]I tell you the truth, we talk about
what we know, and we tell about what we

WHAT'S IT MEAN?

The Pharisees were obsessive about following the Teachings of Moses. They lived by a strict code of conduct and had elaborate rules about what they could and couldn't do—rules that ultimately didn't have much to do with the spirit of God's Word. The Pharisees were often critical of other Jews and were reluctant to mingle with people whom they believed were not as "pure" as they were.

John 3:1–2

have seen, but you don't accept what we tell you. [12]I have told you about things here on earth, and you do not believe me. So you will not believe me if I tell you about things of heaven. [13]The only one who has ever gone up to heaven is the One who came down from heaven—the Son of Man.

[14]"Just as Moses lifted up the snake in the desert,[n] the Son of Man must also be lifted up. [15]So that everyone who believes can have eternal life in him.

[16]"God loved the world so much that he gave his one and only Son so that whoever believes in him may not be lost, but have eternal life. [17]God did not send his Son into the world to judge the world guilty, but to save the world through him. [18]People who believe in God's Son are not judged guilty. Those who do not believe have already been judged guilty, because they have not believed in God's one and only Son. [19]They are judged by this fact: The Light has come into the world, but they did not want light. They wanted darkness, because they were doing evil things. [20]All who do evil hate the light and will not come to the light, because it will show all the evil things they do. [21]But those who follow the true way come to the light, and it shows that the things they do were done through God."

> **"God did not send his Son into the world to judge the world guilty, but to save the world through him."**
> **(John 3:17)**

ETERNAL LIFE

What is required for eternal life? (3:15–16)

JESUS AND JOHN THE BAPTIST

[22]After this, Jesus and his followers went into the area of Judea, where he stayed with his followers and baptized people. [23]John was also baptizing in Aenon, near Salim, because there was plenty of water there. People were going there to be baptized. [24](This was before John was put into prison.)

[25]Some of John's followers had an argument with a Jew about religious washing.[n] [26]So they came to John and said, "Teacher, remember the man who was with you on the other side of the Jordan River, the one you spoke about so much? He is baptizing, and everyone is going to him."

[27]John answered, "A man can get only what God gives him. [28]You yourselves heard me say, 'I am not the Christ, but I am the one sent to prepare the way for him.' [29]The bride belongs only to the bridegroom. But the friend who helps the bridegroom stands by and listens to him. He is thrilled that he gets to hear the bridegroom's voice. In the same way, I am really happy. [30]He must become greater, and I must become less important.

THE ONE WHO COMES FROM HEAVEN

[31]"The One who comes from above is greater than all. The one who is from the earth belongs to the earth and talks about things on the earth. But the One who comes from heaven is greater than all. [32]He tells what he has seen and heard, but no one accepts what he says. [33]Whoever accepts what he says has proven that God is true. [34]The One whom God sent speaks the words of God, because God gives him the Spirit fully. [35]The Father loves the Son and has given him power over everything. [36]Those who believe in the Son have eternal life, but those who do not obey the Son will never have life. God's anger stays on them."

3:14 Moses . . . desert When the Israelites were dying from snake bites, God told Moses to put a brass snake on a pole. The people who looked at the snake were healed (Numbers 21:4–9). **3:25 religious washing** The Jewish people washed themselves in special ways before eating, before worshiping in the Temple, and at other special times.

On the Edge

People who believe in God's Son are not judged guilty. Those who do not believe have already been judged guilty, because they have not believed in God's one and only Son (John 3:18).

A person convicted of murder faces either justice or mercy in the courtroom. In some states and in some countries, justice requires that the convicted murderer be condemned to death. Yet the judge or the jury can treat the person with mercy if they choose to.

God has chosen mercy. Everyone deserves to be condemned to death—that's the penalty for refusing to obey God. But for those who trust in Jesus, God has set aside the sentence that justice demands. For them there is no punishment (see Rom. 8:1). The punishment for their sins was given to Jesus.

God's mercy is for everyone who has faith in his Son. Faith is not having an intellectual belief in God. It's knowing in your heart that he is real and responding with your life (the things you *do*) to the gift of mercy he gave you through his Son.

SEE FOR YOURSELF:
Neh. 13:22; Ps. 118; John 5:24; Rom. 8:1

JESUS AND A SAMARITAN WOMAN

4 1 The Pharisees heard that Jesus was making and baptizing more followers than John,
2 although Jesus himself did not baptize people, but his followers did. 3 Jesus knew that
the Pharisees had heard about him, so he left
Judea and went back to Galilee. 4 But on the
way he had to go through the country of
Samaria.
5 In Samaria Jesus came to the town called
Sychar, which is near the field Jacob gave to his
son Joseph. 6 Jacob's well was there. Jesus was
tired from his long trip, so he sat down beside
the well. It was about twelve o'clock noon.
7 When a Samaritan woman came to the well to
get some water, Jesus said to her, "Please give
me a drink." 8 (This happened while Jesus' followers were in town buying some food.)
9 The woman said, "I am surprised that you
ask me for a drink, since you are a Jewish man
and I am a Samaritan woman." (Jewish people
are not friends with Samaritans.[n])
10 Jesus said, "If you only knew the free gift
of God and who it is that is asking you for
water, you would have asked him, and he
would have given you living water."
11 The woman said, "Sir, where will you get
this living water? The well is very deep, and
you have nothing to get water with. 12 Are you
greater than Jacob, our father, who gave us this
well and drank from it himself along with his
sons and flocks?"
13 Jesus answered, "Everyone who drinks
this water will be thirsty again, 14 but whoever
drinks the water I give will never be thirsty.
The water I give will become a spring of water
gushing up inside that person, giving eternal
life."
15 The woman said to him, "Sir, give me this
water so I will never be thirsty again and will
not have to come back here to get more water."
16 Jesus told her, "Go get your husband and
come back here."
17 The woman answered, "I have no husband."
Jesus said to her, "You are right to say you
have no husband. 18 Really you have had five

WHAT'S IT MEAN?

Samaria was located in what had once been the nation of Israel. When the Assyrians conquered the northern kingdom of Israel in 722 B.C., they took many Israelites away as captives and brought in many foreigners to live in Canaan. It wasn't long before the Israelites who were left behind started getting involved with the new guys in town. Not only did the Israelites begin marrying and starting families with the foreigners, they also adopted their idol worship. This mingling continued generation after generation until the distinction between the Israelites and the foreigners disappeared altogether. The descendants of these mixed marriages were known as Samaritans.

John 4:4

4:9 Jewish people . . . Samaritans This can also be translated "Jewish people don't use things that Samaritans have used."

husbands, and the man you live with now is
not your husband. You told the truth."
[19]The woman said, "Sir, I can see that you
are a prophet. [20]Our ancestors worshiped on
this mountain, but you say that Jerusalem is
the place where people must worship."
[21]Jesus said, "Believe me, woman. The time
is coming when neither in Jerusalem nor on
this mountain will you actually
worship the Father. [22]You Samaritans worship something
you don't understand. We understand what we worship,
because salvation comes from
the Jews. [23]The time is coming
when the true worshipers will
worship the Father in spirit and truth, and
that time is here already. You see, the Father
too is actively seeking such people to worship him. [24]God is spirit, and those who
worship him must worship in spirit and
truth."
[25]The woman said, "I know that the Messiah
is coming." (Messiah is the One called Christ.)
"When the Messiah comes, he will explain
everything to us."
[26]Then Jesus said, "I am he—I, the one talking to you."
[27]Just then his followers came back from
town and were surprised to see him talking
with a woman. But none of them asked, "What
do you want?" or "Why are you talking with
her?"
[28]Then the woman left her water jar and
went back to town. She said to the people,
[29]"Come and see a man who told me everything I ever did. Do you think he might be the
Christ?" [30]So the people left the town and went
to see Jesus.
[31]Meanwhile, his followers were begging
him, "Teacher, eat something."
[32]But Jesus answered, "I have food to eat
that you know nothing about."
[33]So the followers asked themselves, "Did
somebody already bring him food?"
[34]Jesus said, "My food is to do what the One
who sent me wants me to do and to finish his
work. [35]You have a saying, 'Four more months
till harvest.' But I tell you, open your eyes and
look at the fields ready for harvest now. [36]Al-
ready, the one who harvests is being paid and
is gathering crops for eternal life. So the one
who plants and the one who harvests celebrate
at the same time. [37]Here the saying is true, 'One
person plants, and another harvests.' [38]I sent
you to harvest a crop that you did not work
on. Others did the work, and you get to finish
up their work."[n]
[39]Many of the Samaritans in that town believed in Jesus because of what the woman
said: "He told me everything I ever did."
[40]When the Samaritans came to Jesus, they
begged him to stay with them, so he stayed
there two more days. [41]And many more believed because of the things he said.
[42]They said to the woman, "First we believed in Jesus because of your speech, but
now we believe because we heard him ourselves. We know that this man really is the
Savior of the world."

JESUS

Is Jesus the Messiah? (4:21–26)

On the Edge

God is spirit, and those who worship him must worship in spirit and truth (John 4:24).

Those who worship God must be led by the Spirit. This verse isn't talking about being led by *a* spirit like the ghosts you see floating around old houses on TV. It's talking about being led by the *Holy Spirit*. The Holy Spirit is part of the Trinity: God the Father, God the Son (Jesus), and God the Holy Spirit. The Holy Spirit has been sent to guide you into all truth (see John 16:13). You are free to make your own choices, but if you're going to be successful in life, you must submit to the Holy Spirit and allow him to guide you.

That's why it's so important to listen to that still, small voice. The next time you're making an important decision or stepping out in a certain direction and you don't feel at peace about it, don't ignore it! That's the Holy Spirit. He wants to lead you. He wants to help you. He wants to see you successful in everything you do. God has given us, as his children, the opportunity and the right to be led by the Holy Spirit. Start being led by the Spirit today, and watch what God will do tomorrow!

SEE FOR YOURSELF: Ps. 32:8–9; Prov. 3:5–6; Is. 58:11; John 16:13; Rom. 8:14; Col. 3:15

4:38 I . . . their work. As a farmer sends workers to harvest grain, Jesus sends his followers out to bring people to God.

JESUS HEALS AN OFFICER'S SON

[43]Two days later, Jesus left and went to Galilee. [44](Jesus had said before that a prophet is not respected in his own country.) [45]When Jesus arrived in Galilee, the people there welcomed him. They had seen all the things he did at the Passover Feast in Jerusalem, because they had been there, too.

[46]Jesus went again to visit Cana in Galilee where he had changed the water into wine. One of the king's important officers lived in the city of Capernaum, and his son was sick. [47]When he heard that Jesus had come from Judea to Galilee, he went to Jesus and begged him to come to Capernaum and heal his son, because his son was almost dead. [48]Jesus said to him, "You people must see signs and miracles before you will believe in me."

[49]The officer said, "Sir, come before my child dies."

[50]Jesus answered, "Go. Your son will live."

The man believed what Jesus told him and went home. [51]On the way the man's servants came and met him and told him, "Your son is alive."

[52]The man asked, "What time did my son begin to get well?"

They answered, "Yesterday at one o'clock the fever left him."

[53]The father knew that one o'clock was the exact time that Jesus had said, "Your son will live." So the man and all the people who lived in his house believed in Jesus.

[54]That was the second miracle Jesus did after coming from Judea to Galilee.

JESUS HEALS A MAN AT A POOL

5

[1]Later Jesus went to Jerusalem for a special feast. [2]In Jerusalem there is a pool with five covered porches, which is called Bethzatha[n] in the Hebrew language.[n] This pool is near the Sheep Gate. [3]Many sick people were lying on the porches beside the pool. Some were blind, some were crippled, and some were paralyzed.[n] [5]A man was lying there who had been sick for thirty-eight years. [6]When Jesus saw the man and knew that he had been sick for such a long time, Jesus asked him, "Do you want to be well?"

[7]The sick man answered, "Sir, there is no one to help me get into the pool when the water starts moving. While I am coming to the water, someone else always gets in before me."

[8]Then Jesus said, "Stand up. Pick up your mat and walk." [9]And immediately the man was well; he picked up his mat and began to walk.

The day this happened was a Sabbath day. [10]So the Jews said to the man who had been healed, "Today is the Sabbath. It is against our law for you to carry your mat on the Sabbath day."

[11]But he answered, "The man who made me well told me, 'Pick up your mat and walk.' "

[12]Then they asked him, "Who is the man who told you to pick up your mat and walk?"

[13]But the man who had been healed did not know who it was, because there were many people in that place, and Jesus had left.

[14]Later, Jesus found the man at the Temple and said to him, "See, you are well now. Stop sinning so that something worse does not happen to you."

[15]Then the man left and told his people that Jesus was the one who had made him well.

[16]Because Jesus was doing this on the Sabbath day, some evil people began to persecute him. [17]But Jesus said to them, "My Father never stops working, and so I keep working, too."

[18]This made them try still harder to kill him. They said, "First Jesus was breaking the law about the Sabbath day. Now he says that God is his own Father, making himself equal with God!"

JESUS HAS GOD'S AUTHORITY

[19]But Jesus said, "I tell you the truth, the Son can do nothing alone. The Son does only what he sees the Father doing, because the Son does whatever the Father does. [20]The Father loves the Son and shows the Son all the things he himself does. But the Father will show the Son even greater things than this so that you can all be amazed. [21]Just as the Father raises the dead and gives them life, so also the Son gives life to those he wants to. [22]In fact, the Father judges no one, but he has given the Son power to do all the judging [23]so that all people will honor the Son as much as they honor the Father. Anyone who does not honor the Son does not honor the Father who sent him.

[24]"I tell you the truth, whoever hears what I say and believes in the One who sent me has

5:2 Bethzatha Also called Bethsaida or Bethesda, it is a pool of water north of the Temple in Jerusalem.
5:2 Hebrew language Or Aramaic, the language of many people in this region in the first century.
5:3 Verse 3 Some Greek copies add "and they waited for the water to move." A few later copies add verse 4: "Sometimes an angel of the Lord came down to the pool and stirred up the water. After the angel did this, the first person to go into the pool was healed from any sickness he had."

eternal life. That person will not be judged
guilty but has already left death and
entered life. 25I tell you the
truth, the time is coming and is
already here when the dead
will hear the voice of the Son
of God, and those who hear
will have life. 26Life comes
from the Father himself, and he
has allowed the Son to have life in himself as
well. 27And the Father has given the Son the
power to judge, because he is the Son of Man.
28Don't be surprised at this: A time is
coming when all who are
dead and in their graves will
hear his voice. 29Then they will
come out of their graves.
Those who did good will rise
and have life forever, but those
who did evil will rise to be
judged guilty.

ASSURANCE

What are Christians assured of? (5:24)

ETERNAL LIFE

Who receives eternal punishment? (5:28–29)

JESUS IS GOD'S SON

30"I can do nothing alone. I judge only the
way I am told, so my judgment is fair. I don't
try to please myself, but I try to please the One
who sent me.
31"If only I tell people about myself, what I
say is not true. 32But there is another who tells
about me, and I know that the things he says
about me are true.
33"You have sent people to John, and he has
told you the truth. 34It is not that I accept such
human telling; I tell you this so you can be
saved. 35John was like a burning and shining
lamp, and you were happy to enjoy his light
for a while.
36"But I have a proof about myself that is
greater than that of John. The things I do,
which are the things my Father gave me to do,
prove that the Father sent me. 37And the Father
himself who sent me has given proof about
me. You have never heard his voice or seen
what he looks like. 38His teaching does not live
in you, because you don't believe in the One
the Father sent. 39You carefully study the Scriptures because you think they give you eternal
life. They do in fact tell about me, 40but you
refuse to come to me to have that life.
41"I don't need praise from people. 42But I
know you—I know that you don't have God's
love in you. 43I have come from my Father and
speak for him, but you don't accept me. But
when another person comes, speaking only for
himself, you will accept him. 44You try to get
praise from each other, but you do not try to
get the praise that comes from the only God.
So how can you believe? 45Don't think that I
will stand before the Father and say you are
wrong. The one who says you are wrong is
Moses, the one you hoped would save you.
46If you really believed Moses, you would
believe me, because Moses wrote about me.
47But if you don't believe what Moses wrote,
how can you believe what I say?"

On the Edge

He has allowed the Son to have life in himself as well. And the Father has given the Son the power to judge, because he is the Son of Man (John 5:26b–27).

There was a young man who sat patiently before a judge waiting for his verdict. During the entire trial the young man could not keep his mind on the case, even though the outcome would mean freedom or prison. The only thing he could think about was the fact that the judge looked very familiar. Where had he seen this judge before? *I know I've seen that man before,* thought the young man. Then all of a sudden it hit him! He remembered.

When he was a child, he fell through the ice on a lake he had been playing on. He began to scream for help, and a man who saw him struggling to survive got out of his car, ran to him, and saved his life. That man was the judge! Wow! he couldn't believe it. That must have been close to fifteen years ago. Right as the judge was getting ready to read the verdict, the young man yelled out, "Your Honor! Wait, wait! Remember . . ." The young man told the judge the entire story. The judge remembered saving the boy's life; and he, too, couldn't believe that here was that same frightened boy. "Your Honor," cried the young man, "you saved me then. Won't you please save me now?!"

"I'm so sorry, young man," replied the judge. "Then I was your savior; now I am your judge."

God is a loving God who sent his only Son to die for us, so that we could have new life. Jesus is our Savior; one day he will be our Judge. If you live for him, he'll give you eternity in heaven!

SEE FOR YOURSELF: Gal. 6:7–8; Heb. 12:23; Rev. 20:11–15

MORE THAN FIVE THOUSAND FED

6 [1]After this, Jesus went across Lake Galilee (or, Lake Tiberias). [2]Many people followed him because they saw the miracles he did to heal the sick. [3]Jesus went up on a hill and sat down there with his followers. [4]It was almost the time for the Jewish Passover Feast.

[5]When Jesus looked up and saw a large crowd coming toward him, he said to Philip, "Where can we buy enough bread for all these people to eat?" [6](Jesus asked Philip this question to test him, because Jesus already knew what he planned to do.)

[7]Philip answered, "We would all have to work a month to buy enough bread for each person to have only a little piece."

[8]Another one of his followers, Andrew, Simon Peter's brother, said, [9]"Here is a boy with five loaves of barley bread and two little fish, but that is not enough for so many people."

[10]Jesus said, "Tell the people to sit down." This was a very grassy place, and about five thousand men sat down there. [11]Then Jesus took the loaves of bread, thanked God for them, and gave them to the people who were sitting there. He did the same with the fish, giving as much as the people wanted.

[12]When they had all had enough to eat, Jesus said to his followers, "Gather the leftover pieces of fish and bread so that nothing is wasted." [13]So they gathered up the pieces and filled twelve baskets with the pieces left from the five barley loaves.

[14]When the people saw this miracle that Jesus did, they said, "He must truly be the Prophet[n] who is coming into the world."

[15]Jesus knew that the people planned to come and take him by force and make him their king, so he left and went into the hills alone.

JESUS WALKS ON THE WATER

[16]That evening Jesus' followers went down to Lake Galilee. [17]It was dark now, and Jesus had not yet come to them. The followers got into a boat and started across the lake to Capernaum. [18]By now a strong wind was blowing, and the waves on the lake were getting bigger. [19]When they had rowed the boat about three or four miles, they saw Jesus walking on the water, coming toward the boat. The followers were afraid, [20]but Jesus said to them, "It is I. Do not be afraid." [21]Then they were glad to take him into the boat. At once the boat came to land at the place where they wanted to go.

THE PEOPLE SEEK JESUS

[22]The next day the people who had stayed on the other side of the lake knew that Jesus had not gone in the boat with his followers but that they had left without him. And they knew that only one boat had been there. [23]But then some boats came from Tiberias and landed near the place where the people had eaten the bread after the Lord had given thanks. [24]When the people saw that Jesus and his followers were not there now, they got into boats and went to Capernaum to find Jesus.

On the Edge

Then Jesus said, "I am the bread that gives life. Whoever comes to me will never be hungry, and whoever believes in me will never be thirsty" (John 6:35).

"Get a life." Ever heard those words? Ever said those words? Most of the time, when people say that, they mean "Go find something to do."

The life that Jesus gives is more than just enough stuff to do. It's a life beyond a beating heart and a set of breathing lungs. It's something deep that happens in your spirit when Jesus lives inside of you.

Life is living, really experiencing who you are and what happens to you. Jesus came that we might live. We're talking about really living—not just breathing and walking around, not living in a fantasyland, not living with your head in the clouds. We're talking about living to the fullest—having life not just on this earth, but forever, in the presence of God. Jesus is the bread of life. Just like God sent the Israelites manna (life-giving bread) in the wilderness, so he sent Jesus to us as the bread of abundant, eternal life!

Don't settle for second best. Live life to the fullest! That's what the Lord wants for you. That's what Jesus offers you!

SEE FOR YOURSELF: John 6:48–58; 10:10

6:14 Prophet They probably meant the prophet that God told Moses he would send (Deuteronomy 18:15-19).

JESUS, THE BREAD OF LIFE

25When the people found Jesus on the other
side of the lake, they asked him, "Teacher, when
did you come here?"
26Jesus answered, "I tell you the truth, you
aren't looking for me because you saw me do
miracles. You are looking for me because you
ate the bread and were satisfied. 27Don't work
for the food that spoils. Work for the food that
stays good always and gives eternal life. The
Son of Man will give you this food, because on
him God the Father has put his power."
28The people asked Jesus, "What are the
things God wants us to do?"
29Jesus answered, "The work God wants
you to do is this: Believe the One he sent."
30So the people asked, "What miracle will
you do? If we see a miracle, we will believe
you. What will you do? 31Our fathers ate the
manna in the desert. This is written in the
Scriptures: 'He gave them bread from heaven
to eat.' "[n]
32Jesus said, "I tell you the truth, it was not
Moses who gave you bread from heaven; it is
my Father who is giving you the true bread
from heaven. 33God's bread is the One who
comes down from heaven and gives life to the
world."
34The people said, "Sir, give us this bread always."
35Then Jesus said, "I am the bread that gives
life. Whoever comes to me will never be hungry, and whoever believes in me will never be
thirsty. 36But as I told you before, you have
seen me and still don't believe. 37The Father
gives me my people. Every one of them will
come to me, and I will always accept them. 38I
came down from heaven to do what God
wants me to do, not what I want to
do. 39Here is what the One
who sent me wants me to
do: I must not lose even one
whom God gave me, but I
must raise them all on the last
day. 40Those who see the Son
and believe in him have eternal
life, and I will raise them on the last day. This is
what my Father wants."
41Some people began to complain about
Jesus because he said, "I am the bread that
comes down from heaven." 42They said, "This is
Jesus, the son of Joseph. We know his father
and mother. How can he say, 'I came down
from heaven'?"
43But Jesus answered, "Stop complaining to
each other. 44The Father is the One who sent
me. No one can come to me unless the Father
draws him to me, and I will raise that person
up on the last day. 45It is written in the prophets, 'They will all be taught by God.'[n] Everyone
who listens to the Father and learns from him
comes to me. 46No one has seen the Father except the One who is from God; only he has
seen the Father. 47I tell you the truth, whoever

RESURRECTION
Who did Jesus promise to raise? (6:38–40)

6:31 'He gave . . . eat.' Quotation from Psalm 78:24. **6:45 'They . . . God.'** Quotation from Isaiah 54:13.

Promise

HE PROMISES NOT TO TURN YOU AWAY.

The Father gives me my people. Every one of them will come to me, and I will always accept them (John 6:37).

Some people think that they have to have their lives totally together before they turn to God. They think they need to make themselves worthy of Jesus' friendship. This is a lie that suits Satan's purposes pretty well. The problem is that *nobody* will ever be worthy of what God is offering him or her. That's a part of God's truth that's hard to swallow. And if Satan can keep people believing that they have to somehow earn God's favor—that it's even possible—he can keep them from taking the first step toward God's kingdom.

The truth is that God doesn't ask anyone to be worthy of him. If you come to him—without excuses, without trying to justify yourself, just putting your complete trust in him (like putting all of your weight in a chair)—then Jesus promises not to turn you away. He accepts you because he loves you, not because you've earned his friendship.

SEE FOR YOURSELF:

Matt. 24:24; John 6:45; 10:27–28

believes has eternal life. 48I am the bread that gives life. 49Your ancestors ate the manna in the desert, but still they died. 50Here is the bread that comes down from heaven. Anyone who eats this bread will never die. 51I am the living bread that came down from heaven. Anyone who eats this bread will live forever. This bread is my flesh, which I will give up so that the world may have life."

52Then the evil people began to argue among themselves, saying, "How can this man give us his flesh to eat?"

53Jesus said, "I tell you the truth, you must eat the flesh of the Son of Man and drink his blood. Otherwise, you won't have real life in you. 54Those who eat my flesh and drink my blood have eternal life, and I will raise them up on the last day. 55My flesh is true food, and my blood is true drink. 56Those who eat my flesh and drink my blood live in me, and I live in them. 57The living Father sent me, and I live because of the Father. So whoever eats me will live because of me. 58I am not like the bread your ancestors ate. They ate that bread and still died. I am the bread that came down from heaven, and whoever eats this bread will live forever." 59Jesus said all these things while he was teaching in the synagogue in Capernaum.

"I tell you the truth, whoever believes has eternal life." (John 6:47)

THE WORDS OF ETERNAL LIFE

60When the followers of Jesus heard this, many of them said, "This teaching is hard. Who can accept it?"

61Knowing that his followers were complaining about this, Jesus said, "Does this teaching bother you? 62Then will it also bother you to see the Son of Man going back to the place where he came from? 63It is the Spirit that gives life. The flesh doesn't give life. The words I told you are spirit, and they give life. 64But some of you don't believe." (Jesus knew from the beginning who did not believe and who would turn against him.) 65Jesus said, "That is the reason I said, 'If the Father does not bring a person to me, that one cannot come.' "

66After Jesus said this, many of his followers left him and stopped following him.

67Jesus asked the twelve followers, "Do you want to leave, too?"

68Simon Peter answered him, "Lord, where would we go? You have the words that give eternal life. 69We believe and know that you are the Holy One from God."

70Then Jesus answered, "I chose all twelve of you, but one of you is a devil."

71Jesus was talking about Judas, the son of Simon Iscariot. Judas was one of the twelve, but later he was going to turn against Jesus.

JESUS' BROTHERS DON'T BELIEVE

7 1After this, Jesus traveled around Galilee. He did not want to travel in Judea, because some evil people there wanted to kill him. 2It was time for the Feast of Shelters. 3So Jesus' brothers said to him, "You should leave here and go to Judea so your followers there can see the miracles you do. 4Anyone who wants to be well known does not hide what he does. If you are doing these things, show yourself to the world." 5(Even Jesus' brothers did not believe in him.)

6Jesus said to his brothers, "The right time for me has not yet come, but any time is right for you. 7The world cannot hate you, but it hates me, because I tell it the evil things it does. 8So you go to the feast. I will not go yet to this feast, because the right time for me has not yet come." 9After saying this, Jesus stayed in Galilee.

10But after Jesus' brothers had gone to the feast, Jesus went also. But he did not let people see him. 11At the feast some people were looking for him and saying, "Where is that man?"

12Within the large crowd there, many people were whispering to each other about Jesus. Some said, "He is a good man."

Others said, "No, he fools the people." 13But no one was brave enough to talk about Jesus

WHAT'S IT MEAN?

The Feast of Shelters, one of the major Jewish holidays, was like a national campout. Each year at harvest time, people made temporary shelters out of tree branches and stayed in those shelters for the entire eight-day holiday. Why, you ask? To remind them of the years their ancestors spent wandering in the desert and living in tents, from the time they left Egypt to the time they entered the Promised Land.

John 7:2

openly, because they were afraid of the older
leaders.

JESUS TEACHES AT THE FEAST

14 When the feast was about half over, Jesus
went to the Temple and began to teach. 15 The
people were amazed and said, "This man has
never studied in school. How did he learn so
much?"
16 Jesus answered, "The things I teach are not
my own, but they come from him who sent
me. 17 If people choose to do what God wants,
they will know that my teaching comes from
God and not from me. 18 Those who teach their
own ideas are trying to get honor for themselves. But those who try to bring honor to the
one who sent him speak the truth, and there is
nothing false in them. 19 Moses gave you the
law,[n] but none of you obeys that law. Why are
you trying to kill me?"
20 The people answered, "A demon has come
into you. We are not trying to kill you."
21 Jesus said to them, "I did one miracle, and
you are all amazed. 22 Moses gave you the law
about circumcision. (But really Moses did not
give you circumcision; it came from our ancestors.) And yet you circumcise a baby on a Sabbath day. 23 If a baby can be circumcised on a
Sabbath day to obey the law of Moses, why
are you angry at me for healing a person's
whole body on the Sabbath day? 24 Stop judging by the way things look, but judge by what
is really right."

IS JESUS THE CHRIST?

JUDGMENT
Does God ever judge by appearances? (7:24)

25 Then some of the people
who lived in Jerusalem said,
"This is the man they are trying to kill. 26 But he is teaching
where everyone can see and
hear him, and no one is trying to stop him.
Maybe the leaders have decided he really is the
Christ. 27 But we know where this man is from.
And when the real Christ comes, no one will
know where he comes from."
28 Jesus, teaching in the Temple, cried out,
"Yes, you know me, and you know where I am
from. But I have not come by my own authority. I was sent by the One who is true, whom
you don't know. 29 But I know him, because I
am from him, and he sent me."
30 When Jesus said this, the people tried to
take him. But no one was able to touch him,
because it was not yet the right time. 31 But
many of the people believed in Jesus. They
said, "When the Christ comes, will he do more
miracles than this man has done?"

THE LEADERS TRY TO ARREST JESUS

32 The Pharisees heard the crowd whispering these things about Jesus. So the leading
priests and the Pharisees sent some Temple

7:19 law Moses gave God's people the Law that God gave him on Mount Sinai (Exodus 34:29-32).

Promise HE PROMISES YOU LIVING WATER.

If anyone believes in me, rivers of living water will flow out from that person's heart, as the Scripture says (John 7:38).

Have you ever been really thirsty—like "walking-across-the-desert-in-search-of water" thirsty? Then you know that when you get that thirsty, there's nothing better than a nice, long drink of cool, refreshing water! That's the kind of water you need. When you gave your heart to Jesus, you received that refreshing, living water. The question is, What are you going to do with that water? Jesus said it flows from you, not just to you!

Have you ever been for a ride on a scalding hot summer's day, and thought you saw a shimmering image that looked like water on the street up ahead? This is called a mirage, and it happens all of the time in the desert. We've all seen it on TV—a person in need of water, crawling across the desert, spots one. Their hopes are dashed as they realize what they had thought was an oasis is really a mirage. Nothing!

That's the question: Are you going to be a mirage or an oasis of life? You have the living water that this world is searching for. Release it today!

SEE FOR YOURSELF:
Rev. 21:6; 22:17

guards to arrest him. [33]Jesus said, "I will be
with you a little while longer. Then I will go
back to the One who sent me. [34]You will look
for me, but you will not find me. And you cannot come where I am."
[35]Some people said to each other, "Where
will this man go so we cannot find him? Will
he go to the Greek cities where our people live
and teach the Greek people there? [36]What did
he mean when he said, 'You will look for me,
but you will not find me,' and 'You cannot
come where I am'?"

JESUS TALKS ABOUT THE SPIRIT

[37]On the last and most important day of the
feast Jesus stood up and said in a loud voice,
"Let anyone who is thirsty come to me and
drink. [38]If anyone believes in me, rivers of living water will flow out from that person's
heart, as the Scripture says." [39]Jesus was talking
about the Holy Spirit. The Spirit had not yet
been given, because Jesus had not yet been
raised to glory. But later, those who believed in
Jesus would receive the Spirit.

THE PEOPLE ARGUE ABOUT JESUS

[40]When the people heard Jesus' words,
some of them said, "This man really is the
Prophet."[n]
[41]Others said, "He is the Christ."
Still others said, "The Christ will not come
from Galilee. [42]The Scripture says that the
Christ will come from David's family and from
Bethlehem, the town where David lived." [43]So
the people did not agree with each other about
Jesus. [44]Some of them wanted to arrest him,
but no one was able to touch him.

SOME LEADERS WON'T BELIEVE

[45]The Temple guards went back to the leading priests and the Pharisees, who asked, "Why
didn't you bring Jesus?"
[46]The guards answered, "The words he says
are greater than the words of any other person
who has ever spoken!"
[47]The Pharisees answered, "So Jesus has
fooled you also! [48]Have any of the leaders or
the Pharisees believed in him? No! [49]But these
people, who know nothing about the law, are
under God's curse."
[50]Nicodemus, who had gone to see Jesus
before, was in that group.[n] He said, [51]"Our law
does not judge a man without hearing him and
knowing what he has done."
[52]They answered, "Are you from Galilee,
too? Study the Scriptures, and you will learn
that no prophet comes from Galilee."

Some early Greek manuscripts do not
contain 7:53—8:11.

[[53]And everyone left and went home.

THE WOMAN CAUGHT IN ADULTERY

8 [1]Jesus went to the Mount of Olives. [2]But
early in the morning he went back to the Temple, and all the people came to him, and he sat
and taught them. [3]The teachers of the law and
the Pharisees brought a woman who had been
caught in adultery. They forced her to stand
before the people. [4]They said to Jesus, "Teacher,
this woman was caught having sexual relations with a man who is not her husband. [5]The
law of Moses commands that we stone to
death every woman who does this. What do
you say we should do?" [6]They were asking this
to trick Jesus so that they could have some
charge against him.
But Jesus bent over and started writing on
the ground with his finger. [7]When they continued to ask Jesus their question, he raised up
and said, "Anyone here who has never sinned
can throw the first stone at her." [8]Then Jesus
bent over again and wrote on the ground.
[9]Those who heard Jesus began to leave one
by one, first the older men and then the others.
Jesus was left there alone with the woman

WHAT'S IT MEAN?

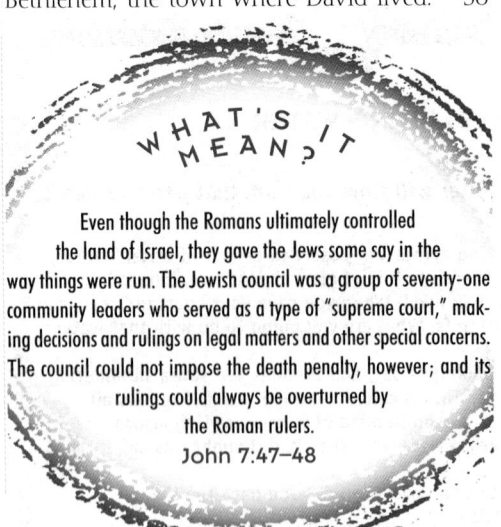

Even though the Romans ultimately controlled the land of Israel, they gave the Jews some say in the way things were run. The Jewish council was a group of seventy-one community leaders who served as a type of "supreme court," making decisions and rulings on legal matters and other special concerns. The council could not impose the death penalty, however; and its rulings could always be overturned by the Roman rulers.
John 7:47–48

7:40 Prophet They probably meant the prophet God told Moses he would send (Deuteronomy 18:15–19).
7:50 Nicodemus . . . group. The story about Nicodemus going and talking to Jesus is in John 3:1–21.

standing before him. 10Jesus raised up again and asked her, "Woman, where are they? Has no one judged you guilty?"

11She answered, "No one, sir."

Then Jesus said, "I also don't judge you guilty. You may go now, but don't sin anymore."]

JESUS IS THE LIGHT OF THE WORLD

12Later, Jesus talked to the people again, saying, "I am the light of the world. The person who follows me will never live in darkness but will have the light that gives life."

13The Pharisees said to Jesus, "When you talk about yourself, you are the only one to say these things are true. We cannot accept what you say."

14Jesus answered, "Yes, I am saying these things about myself, but they are true. I know where I came from and where I am going. But you don't know where I came from or where I
am going. 15You judge by human standards. I
am not judging anyone. 16But when I do judge,
my judging is true, because I am not alone. The
Father who sent me is with me. 17Your own law
says that when two witnesses say the same
thing, you must accept what they say. 18I am
one of the witnesses who speaks about myself, and the Father who sent me is the other witness."

19They asked, "Where is your father?"

Jesus answered, "You don't know me or my Father. If you knew me, you would know my
Father, too." 20Jesus said these things while he was teaching in the Temple, near where the money is kept. But no one arrested him, because the right time for him had not yet come.

WHAT'S IT MEAN?

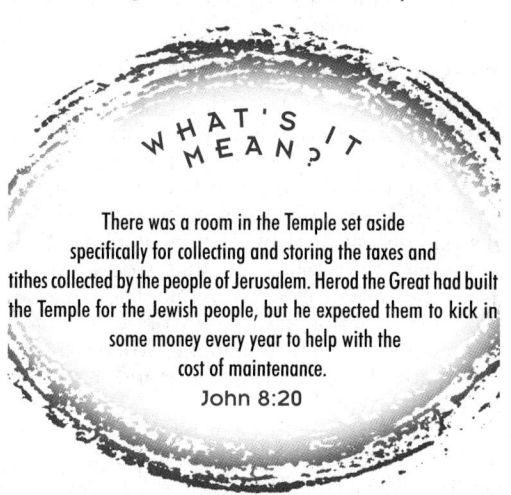

There was a room in the Temple set aside specifically for collecting and storing the taxes and tithes collected by the people of Jerusalem. Herod the Great had built the Temple for the Jewish people, but he expected them to kick in some money every year to help with the cost of maintenance.

John 8:20

THE PEOPLE MISUNDERSTAND JESUS

21Again, Jesus said to the people, "I will leave you, and you will look for me, but you will die in your sins. You cannot come where I am going."

22So the Jews asked, "Will Jesus kill himself? Is that why he said, 'You cannot come where I am going'?"

23Jesus said, "You people are from here below, but I am from above. You belong to this
world, but I don't belong to this world. 24So I
told you that you would die in your sins. Yes, you will die in your sins if you don't believe that I am he."

25They asked, "Then who are you?"

Jesus answered, "I am what I have told you
from the beginning. 26I have many things to
say and decide about you. But I tell people only the things I have heard from the One who sent me, and he speaks the truth."

27The people did not understand that he
was talking to them about the Father. 28So
Jesus said to them, "When you lift up the Son of Man, you will know that I am he. You will know that these things I do are not by my own authority but that I say only what the Father
has taught me. 29The One who sent me is with
me. I always do what is pleasing to him, so he
has not left me alone." 30While Jesus was saying
these things, many people believed in him.

FREEDOM FROM SIN

31So Jesus said to the Jews who believed in him, "If you continue to obey my teaching,
you are truly my followers.
32Then you will know the truth, and the truth will make you free."

TRUTH
What does the truth do for us? (8:31–32)

33They answered, "We are Abraham's children, and we have never been anyone's slaves. So why do you say we will be free?"

34Jesus answered, "I tell you the truth,
everyone who lives in sin is a slave to sin. 35A
slave does not stay with a family forever, but a
son belongs to the family forever. 36So if the
Son makes you free, you will be truly free. 37I
know you are Abraham's children, but you want to kill me because you don't accept my
teaching. 38I am telling you what my Father
has shown me, but you do what your father has told you."

39They answered, "Our father is Abraham."

Jesus said, "If you were really Abraham's children, you would do the things Abraham
did. 40I am a man who has told you the truth
which I heard from God, but you are trying to

On the Edge

Then you will know the truth, and the truth will make you free (John 8:32).

Jesus makes a big deal about truth because only the truth sets you free. Satan is the father of lies, a master deceiver, and he wants you to believe anything other than the teachings of Jesus. The truth is that believing in Jesus saves you from your sin and saves you for eternal life. In this verse Jesus says that the truth will set you free because Jesus frees you from your bondage to sin. Satan will whisper lies to you over and over, hoping you'll believe his tricks and get confused. Remember that confusion is not from God (see 1 Cor. 14:33).

When you feel confused or overwhelmed, return to Scripture and read the truth of the words of God. From him you will find direction and clear guidance. Meditate on those words. Let his truth come alive in your mind and in your heart.

The Bible makes a big deal about truth because lies will lead you astray. Stay focused on the truth of God's Word. Know the truth, follow the truth, tell the truth. It "will make you free"!

SEE FOR YOURSELF:
Ps. 33:4;
John 1:17; 17:17;
Eph. 4:20–21

kill me. Abraham did nothing like that. [41]So you are doing the things your own father did."

But they said, "We are not like children who never knew who their father was. God is our Father; he is the only Father we have."

[42]Jesus said to them, "If God were really your Father, you would love me, because I came from God and now I am here. I did not come by my own authority; God sent me. [43]You don't understand what I say, because you cannot accept my teaching. [44]You belong to your father the devil, and you want to do what he wants. He was a murderer from the beginning and was against the truth, because there is no truth in him. When he tells a lie, he shows what he is really like, because he is a liar and the father of lies. [45]But because I speak the truth, you don't believe me. [46]Can any of you prove that I am guilty of sin? If I am telling the truth, why don't you believe me? [47]The person who belongs to God accepts what God says. But you don't accept what God says, because you don't belong to God."

SATAN
Is Satan completely evil? (8:44)

JESUS IS GREATER THAN ABRAHAM

[48]They answered, "We say you are a Samaritan and have a demon in you. Are we not right?"

[49]Jesus answered, "I have no demon in me. I give honor to my Father, but you dishonor me. [50]I am not trying to get honor for myself. There is One who wants this honor for me, and he is the judge. [51]I tell you the truth, whoever obeys my teaching will never die."

[52]They said to Jesus, "Now we know that you have a demon in you! Even Abraham and the prophets died. But you say, 'Whoever obeys my teaching will never die.' [53]Do you think you are greater than our father Abraham, who died? And the prophets died, too. Who do you think you are?"

[54]Jesus answered, "If I give honor to myself, that honor is worth nothing. The One who gives me honor is my Father, and you say he is your God. [55]You don't really know him, but I know him. If I said I did not know him, I would be a liar like you. But I do know him, and I obey what he says. [56]Your father Abraham was very happy that he would see my day. He saw that day and was glad."

[57]They said to him, "You have never seen Abraham! You are not even fifty years old."

[58]Jesus answered, "I tell you the truth, before Abraham was even born, I am!" [59]When Jesus said this, the people picked up stones to throw at him. But Jesus hid himself, and then he left the Temple.

JESUS HEALS A MAN BORN BLIND

9 [1]As Jesus was walking along, he saw a man who had been born blind. [2]His followers asked him, "Teacher, whose sin caused this man to be born blind—his own sin or his parents' sin?"

[3]Jesus answered, "It is not this man's sin or his parents' sin that made him be blind. This man was born blind so that God's power could be shown in him. [4]While it is daytime, we must continue doing the work of the One who sent me. Night is coming, when no one can work. [5]While I am in the world, I am the light of the world."

[6]After Jesus said this, he spit on the ground and made some mud with it and put the mud on the man's eyes. [7]Then he told the man, "Go

On the Edge

Jesus answered, "I tell you the truth, before Abraham was even born, I am!" (John 8:58).

Remember when God told Moses to approach the king of Egypt and to ask him to let God's people go? How did Moses respond? He asked God, "When I go to the Israelites, I will say to them, 'The God of your fathers sent me to you.' What if the people say, 'What is his name?' What should I tell them?" Then God said to Moses, "I AM WHO I AM. . . . 'I AM sent me to you'" (Ex. 3:13–14).

I AM who? God says, "I AM your Savior. I AM your healer. I AM your deliverer. I AM your provider. I AM your help in time of trouble. I AM your friend. I AM your fortress. I AM your joy. I AM your strength. I AM all that you need me to be!" That's right, God is everything you need him to be. It doesn't matter what kind of trial you're up against—God is greater.

Just as God had spoken in the Old Testament, Jesus speaks in the New Testament. He, too, is "I AM." Jesus Christ is everything that God is. All of the power of God, all of the love of God, all of the peace of God, and all of the joy of God are in Jesus! When you find yourself doubting that he exists, remember that he said, "I AM." He wasn't just "I AM" for Bible times; he's "I AM" for your life today. He's always existed in power, in glory, and in strength. And he always will.

So the next time you're up against the wall, remember who you are, and who's on your side. He is "I AM"!

SEE FOR YOURSELF:
Ex. 3:13–14; 14:10–31

and wash in the Pool of Siloam." (Siloam means
Sent.) So the man went, washed, and came back
seeing.
8The neighbors and some people who had
earlier seen this man begging said, "Isn't this
the same man who used to sit and beg?"
9Some said, "He is the one," but others said,
"No, he only looks like him."
The man himself said, "I am the man."
10They asked, "How did you get your sight?"
11He answered, "The man named Jesus
made some mud and put it on my eyes. Then
he told me to go to Siloam and wash. So I went
and washed, and then I could see."
12They asked him, "Where is this man?"
"I don't know," he answered.

PHARISEES QUESTION THE HEALING

13Then the people took to the Pharisees the
man who had been blind. 14The day Jesus had
made mud and healed his eyes was a Sabbath
day. 15So now the Pharisees asked the man,
"How did you get your sight?"
He answered, "He put mud on my eyes, I
washed, and now I see."
16So some of the Pharisees were saying,
"This man does not keep the Sabbath day, so
he is not from God."
But others said, "A man who is a sinner
can't do miracles like these." So they could not
agree with each other.
17They asked the man again, "What do you
say about him since it was your eyes he
opened?"
The man answered, "He is a prophet."
18These leaders did not believe that he had
been blind and could now see again. So they
sent for the man's parents 19and asked them,
"Is this your son who you say was born blind?
Then how does he now see?"
20His parents answered, "We know that this
is our son and that he was born blind. 21But
we don't know how he can now see. We don't
know who opened his eyes. Ask him. He is old
enough to speak for himself." 22His parents said
this because they were afraid of the older
leaders, who had already decided that anyone
who said Jesus was the Christ would be
avoided. 23That is why his parents said, "He is
old enough. Ask him."
24So for the second time, they called the man
who had been blind. They said, "You should

WHAT'S IT MEAN?

The people of Jerusalem were drinking natural spring water long before it became a trendy thing to do. Because there were no rivers close enough to provide water for Jerusalem, the city's water supply came from a spring called Gihon, which was located just outside the city walls. A tunnel brought the water from Gihon Spring into the city, where it was collected in the Pool of Siloam.

John 9:7

give God the glory by telling the truth. We
know that this man is a sinner."
25He answered, "I don't know if he is a sinner. One thing I do know: I was blind, and
now I see."
26They asked, "What did he do to you? How
did he make you see again?"
27He answered, "I already
told you, and you didn't listen.
Why do you want to hear it
again? Do you want to be-
come his followers, too?"
28Then they insulted him
and said, "You are his follower, but we are followers
of Moses. 29We know that
God spoke to Moses, but we
don't even know where this man
comes from."
30The man answered, "This is a very strange
thing. You don't know where he comes from,
and yet he opened my eyes. 31We all know that
God does not listen to sinners, but he listens to
anyone who worships and obeys him. 32No-
body has ever heard of anyone giving sight to
a man born blind. 33If this man were not from
God, he could do nothing."
34They answered, "You were born full of sin!
Are you trying to teach us?" And they threw
him out.

"A thief comes to steal and kill and destroy, but I came to give life—life in all its fullness." (John 10:10)

SPIRITUAL BLINDNESS

35When Jesus heard that they had thrown
him out, Jesus found him and said, "Do you
believe in the Son of Man?"
36He asked, "Who is the Son of Man, sir, so
that I can believe in him?"
37Jesus said to him, "You have seen him. The
Son of Man is the one talking with you."
38He said, "Lord, I believe!" Then the man
worshiped Jesus.
39Jesus said, "I came into this world so that
the world could be judged. I came so that the
blind[n] would see and so that those who see
will become blind."
40Some of the Pharisees who were nearby
heard Jesus say this and asked, "Are you saying
we are blind, too?"
41Jesus said, "If you were blind, you would
not be guilty of sin. But since you keep saying
you see, your guilt remains."

10

THE SHEPHERD AND HIS SHEEP

1Jesus said, "I tell you the truth, the person
who does not enter the sheepfold by the door,
but climbs in some other way, is a thief and a
robber. 2The one who enters by the door is the
shepherd of the sheep. 3The one who guards
the door opens it for him. And the sheep listen
to the voice of the shepherd. He calls his own
sheep by name and leads them out. 4When he
brings all his sheep out, he goes
ahead of them, and they follow
him because they know his
voice. 5But they will never
follow a stranger. They will
run away from him because
they don't know his voice."
6Jesus told the people this
story, but they did not understand what it meant.

JESUS IS THE GOOD SHEPHERD

7So Jesus said again, "I tell you
the truth, I am the door for the sheep. 8All the
people who came before me were thieves and
robbers. The sheep did not listen to them. 9I am
the door, and the person who
enters through me will be
saved and will be able to
come in and go out and find
pasture. 10A thief comes to
steal and kill and destroy, but
I came to give life—life in all its
fullness.

LIFE
What did Jesus come to give? (10:10)

11"I am the good shepherd. The good shepherd gives his life for the sheep. 12The worker
who is paid to keep the sheep is different from
the shepherd who owns them. When the
worker sees a wolf coming, he runs away and
leaves the sheep alone. Then the wolf attacks
the sheep and scatters them. 13The man runs
away because he is only a paid worker and
does not really care about the sheep.
14-15"I am the good shepherd. I know my
sheep, as the Father knows me. And my sheep
know me, as I know the Father. I give my life
for the sheep. 16I have other sheep that are not
in this flock, and I must bring them also. They
will listen to my voice, and there will be one
flock and one shepherd. 17The Father loves me
because I give my life so that I can take it back
again. 18No one takes it away from me; I give
my own life freely. I have the right to give my
life, and I have the right to take it back. This is
what my Father commanded me to do."
19Again the leaders did not agree with each
other because of these words of Jesus. 20Many
of them said, "A demon has come into him and
made him crazy. Why listen to him?"

9:39 blind Jesus is talking about people who are spiritually blind, not physically blind.

21But others said, "A man who is crazy with
a demon does not say things like this. Can a
demon open the eyes of the blind?"

JESUS IS REJECTED

22The time came for the Feast of Dedication
at Jerusalem. It was winter, 23and Jesus was
walking in the Temple in Solomon's Porch.
24Some people gathered around him and said,
"How long will you make us wonder about
you? If you are the Christ, tell us plainly."

WHAT'S IT MEAN?

To fully understand Hanukkah, the "Feast of Dedication" mentioned in this verse, you have to know the story of a Syrian king named Antiochus Epiphanes. Years after the Greeks conquered the Middle East, Antiochus Epiphanes took control of the Temple in Jerusalem. In a disgusting act of blasphemy, he built an altar to the Greek god Zeus directly over what had been the Jewish altar of burnt offering. As if that weren't bad enough, he then sacrificed a pig on the altar. (Remember, God had declared pigs to be unclean animals.) The one good thing to come from Antiochus Epiphanes' outrageous actions was that the Jews became so enraged they revolted and overthrew the Syrian leaders. In 165 B.C., a group of Jews led by Judas Maccabeus cleansed the Temple of its desecration. The eight-day celebration of Hanukkah celebrated that cleansing.

John 10:22

25Jesus answered, "I told you already, but
you did not believe. The miracles I do in my
Father's name show who I am. 26But you don't
believe, because you are not my sheep. 27My
sheep listen to my voice; I know them, and
they follow me. 28I give them eternal life, and
they will never die, and no one can steal them
out of my hand. 29My Father gave my sheep to
me. He is greater than all, and no person can
steal my sheep out of my Father's hand. 30The
Father and I are one."
31Again some of the people picked up
stones to kill Jesus. 32But he said to them, "I
have done many good works from the Father.
Which of these good works are you killing me
for?"
33They answered, "We are not killing you
because of any good work you did, but because you speak against God. You are only a
human, but you say you are the same as God!"
34Jesus answered, "It is written in your law
that God said, 'I said, you are gods.'[n] 35This
Scripture called those people gods who received God's message, and Scripture is always
true. 36So why do you say that I speak against
God because I said, 'I am God's Son'? I am the
one God chose and sent into the world. 37If I
don't do what my Father does, then don't believe me. 38But if I do what my Father does,
even though you don't believe in me, believe
what I do. Then you will know and understand that the Father is in me and I am in the
Father."
39They tried to take Jesus again, but he escaped from them.
40Then he went back across the Jordan
River to the place where John had first baptized. Jesus stayed there, 41and many people
came to him and said, "John never did a miracle, but everything John said about this man is
true." 42And in that place many believed in
Jesus.

THE DEATH OF LAZARUS

11 1A man named Lazarus was sick. He lived in
the town of Bethany, where Mary and her sister Martha lived. 2Mary was the woman who
later put perfume on the Lord and wiped his
feet with her hair. Mary's brother was Lazarus,
the man who was now sick. 3So Mary and
Martha sent someone to tell Jesus, "Lord, the
one you love is sick."
4When Jesus heard this, he said, "This sickness will not end in death. It is for the glory of
God, to bring glory to the Son of God." 5Jesus
loved Martha and her sister and Lazarus. 6But

WHAT'S IT MEAN?

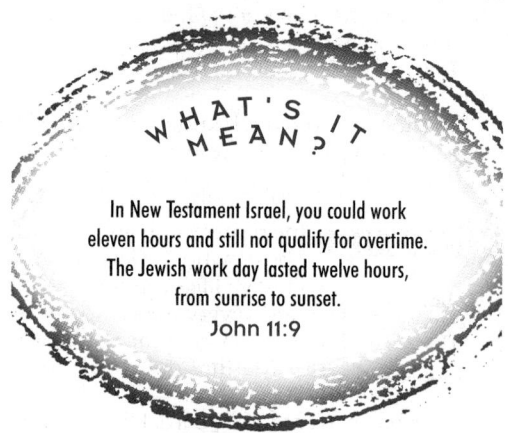

In New Testament Israel, you could work eleven hours and still not qualify for overtime. The Jewish work day lasted twelve hours, from sunrise to sunset.

John 11:9

10:34 'I . . . gods.' Quotation from Psalm 82:6.

when he heard that Lazarus was sick, he stayed
where he was for two more days. 7Then Jesus
said to his followers, "Let's go back to Judea."
8The followers said, "But Teacher, some people there tried to stone you to death only a
short time ago. Now you want to go back
there?"
9Jesus answered, "Are there not twelve
hours in the day? If anyone walks in the daylight, he will not stumble, because he can see
by this world's light. 10But if anyone walks at
night, he stumbles because there is no light to
help him see."
11After Jesus said this, he added, "Our friend
Lazarus has fallen asleep, but I am going there
to wake him."
12The followers said, "But Lord, if he is only
asleep, he will be all right."
13Jesus meant that Lazarus was dead, but
his followers thought he meant Lazarus was
really sleeping. 14So then Jesus said plainly,
"Lazarus is dead. 15And I am glad for your
sakes I was not there so that you may believe.
But let's go to him now."
16Then Thomas (the one called Didymus)
said to the other followers, "Let us also go so
that we can die with him."

JESUS IN BETHANY

17When Jesus arrived, he learned that Lazarus had already been dead and in the tomb for
four days. 18Bethany was about two miles
from Jerusalem. 19Many of the Jews had come
there to comfort Martha and Mary about their
brother.
20When Martha heard that Jesus was coming, she went out to meet him, but Mary stayed
home. 21Martha said to Jesus, "Lord, if you had
been here, my brother would not have died.
22But I know that even now God will give you
anything you ask."
23Jesus said, "Your brother will rise and live
again."
24Martha answered, "I know that he will
rise and live again in the resurrection[n] on the
last day."
25Jesus said to her, "I am
the resurrection and the life.
Those who believe in me
will have life even if they die.
26And everyone who lives
and believes in me will never
die. Martha, do you believe
this?"
27Martha answered, "Yes, Lord. I believe that

ETERNAL LIFE

What does Jesus give? (11:25)

On the Edge

And everyone who lives and believes in me will never die. Martha, do you believe this? (John 11:26).

"Do you believe this?" Jesus asked. He knew what he said sounded pretty crazy. After all, he had told his followers that he would be arrested and killed. And the apostles themselves are not still walking around telling their firsthand accounts of Jesus' life.

So what did Jesus mean when he said his followers would never really die? There's a clue in the first part of his statement: "Everyone who lives and believes in me. . ." The life that they had and that you have—and won't ever lose—isn't defined by biological functions. This life comes only from knowing Jesus. And the death that you've escaped is what Paul talked about in Ephesians 2:1: "In the past you were spiritually dead because of your sins and the things you did against God." The death you'll never taste is described in Revelation 21:8: "But cowards, those who refuse to believe, who do evil things, who kill . . . all these will have a place in the lake of burning sulfur. This is the second death." You have eternal life because of Jesus!

SEE FOR YOURSELF:
John 3:16; Rom. 6:23; Titus 1:2; 1 John 5:11

you are the Christ, the Son of God, the One
coming to the world."

JESUS CRIES

28After Martha said this, she went back and
talked to her sister Mary alone. Martha said,
"The Teacher is here and he is asking for you."
29When Mary heard this, she got up quickly
and went to Jesus. 30Jesus had not yet come
into the town but was still at the place where
Martha had met him. 31The Jews were with
Mary in the house, comforting her. When they
saw her stand and leave quickly, they followed
her, thinking she was going to the tomb to cry
there.
32But Mary went to the place where Jesus

11:24 resurrection Being raised from the dead to live again.

was. When she saw him, she fell at his feet and said, "Lord, if you had been here, my brother would not have died."

33 When Jesus saw Mary crying and the Jews who came with her also crying, he was upset and was deeply troubled. 34 He asked, "Where did you bury him?"

"Come and see, Lord," they said.

35 Jesus cried.

36 So the Jews said, "See how much he loved him."

37 But some of them said, "If Jesus opened the eyes of the blind man, why couldn't he keep Lazarus from dying?"

EMOTIONS
Did Jesus experience emotions? (11:35)

JESUS RAISES LAZARUS

38 Again feeling very upset, Jesus came to the tomb. It was a cave with a large stone covering the entrance. 39 Jesus said, "Move the stone away."

Martha, the sister of the dead man, said, "But, Lord, it has been four days since he died. There will be a bad smell."

40 Then Jesus said to her, "Didn't I tell you that if you believed you would see the glory of God?"

41 So they moved the stone away from the entrance. Then Jesus looked up and said, "Father, I thank you that you heard me. 42 I know that you always hear me, but I said these things because of the people here around me. I want them to believe that you sent me." 43 After Jesus said this, he cried out in a loud voice, "Lazarus, come out!" 44 The dead man came out, his hands and feet wrapped with pieces of cloth, and a cloth around his face.

Jesus said to them, "Take the cloth off of him and let him go."

THE PLAN TO KILL JESUS

45 Many of the people, who had come to visit Mary and saw what Jesus did, believed in him. 46 But some of them went to the Pharisees and told them what Jesus had done. 47 Then the leading priests and Pharisees called a meeting of the council. They asked, "What should we do? This man is doing many miracles. 48 If we let him continue doing these things, everyone will believe in him. Then the Romans will come and take away our Temple and our nation."

49 One of the men there was Caiaphas, the high priest that year. He said, "You people know nothing! 50 You don't realize that it is better for one man to die for the people than for the whole nation to be destroyed."

51 Caiaphas did not think of this himself. As high priest that year, he was really prophesying that Jesus would die for their nation 52 and for God's scattered children to bring them all together and make them one.

53 That day they started planning to kill Jesus. 54 So Jesus no longer traveled openly among the people. He left there and went to a place near the desert, to a town called Ephraim and stayed there with his followers.

55 It was almost time for the Passover Feast. Many from the country went up to Jerusalem before the Passover to do the special things to make themselves pure. 56 The people looked for Jesus and stood in the Temple asking each other, "Is he coming to the Feast? What do you think?" 57 But the leading priests and the Pharisees had given orders that if anyone knew where Jesus was, he must tell them. Then they could arrest him.

WHAT'S IT MEAN?

Passover was one of the most important holidays on the Jewish calendar. It was set aside as a time for recalling how God had rescued the Israelites from slavery in Egypt. To celebrate, the Jewish people ate a meal similar to the one their ancestors ate when they prepared to leave Egypt. People traveled to Jerusalem from throughout the land of Israel to celebrate this annual festival, which is still observed today.

John 12:1, 12

JESUS WITH FRIENDS IN BETHANY

12

1 Six days before the Passover Feast, Jesus went to Bethany, where Lazarus lived. (Lazarus is the man Jesus raised from the dead.) 2 There they had a dinner for Jesus. Martha served the food, and Lazarus was one of the people eating with Jesus. 3 Mary brought in a pint of very expensive perfume made from pure nard. She poured the perfume on Jesus' feet, and then she wiped his feet with her hair. And the sweet smell from the perfume filled the whole house.

4 Judas Iscariot, one of Jesus' followers who would later turn against him, was there. Judas said, 5 "This perfume was worth three hundred

coins.[n] Why wasn't it sold and the money given to the poor?" [6]But Judas did not really care about the poor; he said this because he was a thief. He was the one who kept the money box, and he often stole from it.

[7]Jesus answered, "Leave her alone. It was right for her to save this perfume for today, the day for me to be prepared for burial. [8]You will always have the poor with you, but you will not always have me."

THE PLOT AGAINST LAZARUS

[9]A large crowd of people heard that Jesus was in Bethany. So they went there to see not only Jesus but Lazarus, whom Jesus raised from the dead. [10]So the leading priests made plans to kill Lazarus, too. [11]Because of Lazarus many of the Jews were leaving them and believing in Jesus.

> **"Those who love their lives will lose them, but those who hate their lives in this world will keep true life forever." (John 12:25)**

JESUS ENTERS JERUSALEM

[12]The next day a great crowd who had come to Jerusalem for the Passover Feast heard that Jesus was coming there. [13]So they took branches of palm trees and went out to meet Jesus, shouting,

"Praise[n] God!
God bless the One who comes in the
name of the Lord!
God bless the King of Israel!" *Psalm 118:25-26*

[14]Jesus found a colt and sat on it. This was as the Scripture says,

[15]"Don't be afraid, people of Jerusalem!
Your king is coming,
sitting on the colt of a donkey." *Zechariah 9:9*

[16]The followers of Jesus did not understand this at first. But after Jesus was raised to glory, they remembered that this had been written about him and that they had done these things to him.

PEOPLE TELL ABOUT JESUS

[17]There had been many people with Jesus when he raised Lazarus from the dead and told him to come out of the tomb. Now they were telling others about what Jesus did. [18]Many people went out to meet Jesus, because they had heard about this miracle. [19]So the Pharisees said to each other, "You can see that nothing is going right for us. Look! The whole world is following him."

JESUS TALKS ABOUT HIS DEATH

[20]There were some Greek people, too, who came to Jerusalem to worship at the Passover Feast. [21]They went to Philip, who was from Bethsaida in Galilee, and said, "Sir, we would like to see Jesus." [22]Philip told Andrew, and then Andrew and Philip told Jesus.

[23]Jesus said to them, "The time has come for the Son of Man to receive his glory. [24]I tell you the truth, a grain of wheat must fall to the ground and die to make many seeds. But if it never dies, it remains only a single seed. [25]Those who love their lives will lose them, but those who hate their lives in this world will keep true life forever. [26]Whoever serves me must follow me. Then my servant will be with me everywhere I am. My Father will honor anyone who serves me.

[27]"Now I am very troubled. Should I say, 'Father, save me from this time'? No, I came to this time so I could suffer. [28]Father, bring glory to your name!"

Then a voice came from heaven, "I have brought glory to it, and I will do it again."

[29]The crowd standing there, who heard the voice, said it was thunder.

But others said, "An angel has spoken to him."

[30]Jesus said, "That voice was for your sake, not mine. [31]Now is the time for the world to be judged; now the ruler of this world will be thrown down. [32]If I am lifted up from the earth, I will draw all people toward me." [33]Jesus said this to show how he would die.

[34]The crowd said, "We have heard from the law that the Christ will live forever. So why do you say, 'The Son of Man must be lifted up'? Who is this 'Son of Man'?"

[35]Then Jesus said, "The light will be with you for a little longer, so walk while you have the light. Then the darkness will not catch you. If you walk in the darkness, you will not know where you are going. [36]Believe in the light while you still have it so that you will become

12:5 coins One coin, a denarius, was the average pay for one day's work. **12:13 Praise** Literally, "Hosanna," a Hebrew word used at first in praying to God for help, but at this time it was probably a shout of joy used in praising God or his Messiah.

children of light." When Jesus had said this, he
left and hid himself from them.

SOME PEOPLE WON'T BELIEVE IN JESUS

37 Though Jesus had done many miracles in
front of the people, they still did not believe in
him. 38 This was to bring about what Isaiah the
prophet had said:

"Lord, who believed what we told them?
Who saw the Lord's power in this?"

Isaiah 53:1

39 This is why the people could not believe: Isaiah also had said,

40 "He has blinded their eyes,
and he has closed their minds.
Otherwise they would see with their eyes
and understand in their minds
and come back to me and be healed."

Isaiah 6:10

41 Isaiah said this because he saw Jesus' glory
and spoke about him.

42 But many believed in Jesus, even many of
the leaders. But because of the Pharisees, they
did not say they believed in him for fear they
would be put out of the synagogue. 43 They
loved praise from people more than praise
from God.

44 Then Jesus cried out, "Whoever believes in
me is really believing in the One who sent me.
45 Whoever sees me sees the One who sent me.
46 I have come as light into the world so that
whoever believes in me would not stay in
darkness.

47 "Anyone who hears my words and does
not obey them, I do not judge, because I did
not come to judge the world, but to save the
world. 48 There is a judge for those who refuse
to believe in me and do not accept my words.
The word I have taught will be their judge on
the last day. 49 The things I taught were not
from myself. The Father who sent me told me
what to say and what to teach. 50 And I know
that eternal life comes from what the Father
commands. So whatever I say is what the Father told me to say."

On the Edge

I have come as a light into the world, so that whoever believes in me would not stay in darkness (John 12:46).

The light that gives light! That's what you have—light that will disperse darkness. In other words, you're like a flashlight chasing out the darkness of this world. Don't let your batteries run out, and you'd better check your bulb. The light that Christians give because of Jesus is the only light this world has.

Have you ever been in a room that was pitch black—no light, no windows, totally dark? What happened when you turned on a flashlight or struck a match? The entire room lit up. You couldn't believe how much light that one match or flashlight gave off. That's exactly the kind of effect you can have in your school and everywhere else you go. We live in a dark world, but the good news is that you are the light!

What would you do if you had a friend who was trapped in a cave with a group of people, and they couldn't get out because they couldn't find their way? Let's say that they all died and when their bodies were found, it was discovered that one of the victims had a perfectly good flashlight in his backpack that would have saved all of their lives if it had been used. Wouldn't that upset you?

You know what? You are like that same flashlight that could have saved those lives. Every day you come across the paths of people who desperately need the light of Jesus. Don't hide the light. Use it to impact someone's life forever!

SEE FOR YOURSELF:
Matt. 5:14; John 9:5

JESUS WASHES HIS FOLLOWERS' FEET

13 1 It was almost time for the Passover Feast.
Jesus knew that it was time for him to leave
this world and go back to the Father. He had
always loved those who were his own in the
world, and he loved them all the way to the
end.

2 Jesus and his followers were at the evening
meal. The devil had already persuaded Judas
Iscariot, the son of Simon, to turn against Jesus.
3 Jesus knew that the Father had given him
power over everything and that he had come
from God and was going back to God. 4 So
during the meal Jesus stood up and took off
his outer clothing. Taking a towel, he wrapped
it around his waist. 5 Then he poured water
into a bowl and began to wash the followers'
feet, drying them with the towel that was
wrapped around him.

6 Jesus came to Simon Peter, who said to
him, "Lord, are you going to wash my feet?"

7 Jesus answered, "You don't understand now
what I am doing, but you will understand later."

WHAT'S IT MEAN?

In New Testament times, people wore sandals or open shoes, and walked on dirt roads. You can imagine what their feet looked (and smelled) like after a long journey. A polite host would provide water for his guests to wash their own feet with. A wealthy host might have a slave wash his guests' feet. The idea of a host washing his guests' feet himself, though, was unheard of.

John 13:5

On the Edge

You call me "Teacher" and "Lord," and you are right, because that is what I am. If I, your Lord and Teacher, have washed your feet, you also should wash each other's feet. I did this as an example so that you should do as I have done for you (John 13:13–15).

Jesus gives his apostles a lesson in humility when he washes their feet. He tells them that they are to follow his example. And we, as followers of Christ, are to do the same. Meeting the needs of other people and sacrificing your own is the example of Jesus, and we are to be like him. Did you know that when you feel sorry for yourself, one of the best things to help you feel better is to do something good for somebody else? And if you are acting like Jesus, it may cost you something—some time, some energy, some money, maybe even your pride. Sometimes we can serve others secretly, and God gets all of the glory. Jesus came and humbled himself by being a servant to others. Being Christlike means that we humble ourselves and do the same. It's the whole point of our time here on earth—following his example, looking more and more like Jesus.

SEE FOR YOURSELF:
Matt. 16:24–26; John 12:26; Phil. 3:12–17; 1 Tim. 4:12; 6:11–12

8Peter said, "No, you will never wash my feet."

Jesus answered, "If I don't wash your feet, you are not one of my people."

9Simon Peter answered, "Lord, then wash not only my feet, but wash my hands and my head, too!"

10Jesus said, "After a person has had a bath, his whole body is clean. He needs only to wash his feet. And you men are clean, but not all of you." 11Jesus knew who would turn against him, and that is why he said, "Not all of you are clean."

12When he had finished washing their feet, he put on his clothes and sat down again. He asked, "Do you understand what I have just done for you? 13You call me 'Teacher' and 'Lord,' and you are right, because that is what I am. 14If I, your Lord and Teacher, have washed your feet, you also should wash each other's feet. 15I did this as an example so that you should do as I have done for you. 16I tell you the truth, a servant is not greater than his master. A messenger is not greater than the one who sent him. 17If you know these things, you will be happy if you do them.

18"I am not talking about all of you. I know those I have chosen. But this is to bring about what the Scripture said: 'The man who ate at my table has turned against me.'[n] 19I am telling you this now before it happens so that when it happens, you will believe that I am he. 20I tell you the truth, whoever accepts anyone I send also accepts me. And whoever accepts me also accepts the One who sent me."

JESUS TALKS ABOUT HIS DEATH

21After Jesus said this, he was very troubled. He said openly, "I tell you the truth, one of you will turn against me."

22The followers all looked at each other, because they did not know whom Jesus was talking about. 23One of the followers sitting[n] next to Jesus was the follower Jesus loved. 24Simon Peter motioned to him to ask Jesus whom he was talking about.

25That follower leaned closer to Jesus and asked, "Lord, who is it?"

26Jesus answered, "I will dip this bread into

13:18 'The man . . . me.' Quotation from Psalm 41:9.

13:23 sitting Literally, "lying." The people of that time ate lying down and leaning on one arm.

WHAT'S IT MEAN?

Bread was a major part of the Jewish diet in New Testament times. A typical meal consisted of bread served with a thin stew or sauce. Several people would share one bowl of sauce, taking turns dipping their bread into it before each bite. Often a host would feed bread to an honored guest as a token of friendship.

John 13:26

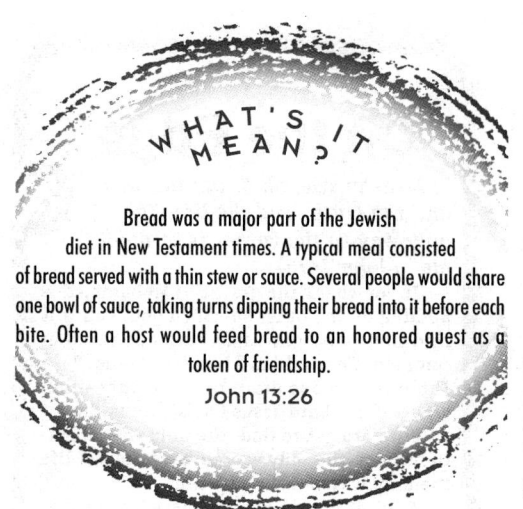

the dish. The man I give it to is the man who
will turn against me." So Jesus took a piece of
bread, dipped it, and gave it to Judas Iscariot,
the son of Simon. 27As soon as Judas took the
bread, Satan entered him. Jesus said to him,
"The thing that you will do—do it quickly."
28No one at the table understood why Jesus
said this to Judas. 29Since he was the one who
kept the money box, some of the followers
thought Jesus was telling him to buy what was
needed for the feast or to give something to the
poor.
30Judas took the bread Jesus gave him and
immediately went out. It was night.
31When Judas was gone, Jesus said, "Now
the Son of Man receives his glory, and God
receives glory through him. 32If God receives
glory through him, then God will give glory to
the Son through himself. And God will give
him glory quickly."
33Jesus said, "My children, I will be with you
only a little longer. You will look for me, and
what I told the Jews, I tell you now:
Where I am going you cannot
come.
34"I give you a new com-
mand: Love each other. You
must love each other as I have
loved you. 35All people will
know that you are my fol-
lowers if you love each other."

LOVE

Is it important for Christians to love each other? (13:34–35)

PETER WILL SAY HE DOESN'T KNOW JESUS

36Simon Peter asked Jesus, "Lord, where are
you going?"
Jesus answered, "Where I am going you
cannot follow now, but you will follow later."
37Peter asked, "Lord, why can't I follow you
now? I am ready to die for you!"
38Jesus answered, "Are you ready to die for
me? I tell you the truth, before the rooster
crows, you will say three times that you don't
know me."

JESUS COMFORTS HIS FOLLOWERS

14 1Jesus said, "Don't let your hearts be troubled. Trust in God, and trust in me. 2There are
many rooms in my Father's house; I would
not tell you this if it were not true. I am going

Promise

HE PROMISES YOU A HOME WITH HIM.

There are many rooms in my Father's house; I would not tell you this if it were not true. I am going there to prepare a place for you. After I go and prepare a place for you, I will come back and take you to be with me so that you may be where I am. You know the way to the place where I am going (John 14:2–4).

This is one of the most awesome promises in all of Scripture. Jesus has gone to heaven to prepare our home—our forever home. A room in our Father's house waits for each one of us. And then, when it is time, Jesus will return to take us there. It's the home your heart has been longing for since the day you were born. It's the place where all your wounds will be healed. All your hopes will be fulfilled. Joy will be complete. Laughter will bounce off the walls. Tears will be banned. Worry won't even be a word. Home. Home at last with Jesus. Everything you've ever thought a home should be, and more than you ever dreamed it could be. Not a day too early, but just in time, Jesus will take us home.

SEE FOR YOURSELF:
Matt. 6:19–21; Heb. 12:22–24

there to prepare a place for you. 3After I go and
prepare a place for you, I will come back and
take you to be with me so that you may be
where I am. 4You know the way to the place
where I am going."
5Thomas said to Jesus, "Lord, we don't
know where you are going. So how can we
know the way?"
6Jesus answered, "I am the way, and the
truth, and the life. The only way to the Father is
through me. 7If you really
knew me, you would know
my Father, too. But now you
do know him, and you have
seen him."
8Philip said to him, "Lord,
show us the Father. That is all
we need."
9Jesus answered, "I have been with you a
long time now. Do you still not know me, Philip? Whoever has seen me has seen the Father.
So why do you say, 'Show us the Father'?
10Don't you believe that I am in the Father and
the Father is in me? The words I say to you
don't come from me, but the Father lives in me
and does his own work. 11Believe me when I
say that I am in the Father and the Father is in
me. Or believe because of the miracles I have
done. 12I tell you the truth, whoever believes in
me will do the same things that I do. Those
who believe will do even greater things than
these, because I am going to the Father. 13And if
you ask for anything in my name, I will do it
for you so that the Father's glory will be
shown through the Son. 14If you ask me for
anything in my name, I will do it.

ETERNAL LIFE
Where can eternal life be found? (14:6)

THE PROMISE OF THE HOLY SPIRIT

15"If you love me, you will obey my commands. 16I will ask the Father, and he will give
you another Helper*n* to be with you forever—
17the Spirit of truth. The world cannot accept
him, because it does not see him or know him.
But you know him, because he lives with you
and he will be in you.
18"I will not leave you all alone like orphans;
I will come back to you. 19In a little
while the world will not see
me anymore, but you will
see me. Because I live, you will
live, too. 20On that day you
will know that I am in my Father, and that you are in me
and I am in you. 21Those who
know my commands and obey them are the
ones who love me, and my Father will love
those who love me. I will love them and will
show myself to them."
22Then Judas (not Judas Iscariot) said, "But,
Lord, why do you plan to show yourself to us
and not to the rest of the world?"
23Jesus answered, "If people love me, they
will obey my teaching. My Father will love
them, and we will come to them and make our
home with them. 24Those who do not love me
do not obey my teaching. This teaching that
you hear is not really mine; it is from my Father, who sent me.
25"I have told you all these things while I
am with you. 26But the Helper will teach you

DEATH
Who has power over death? (14:19)

On the Edge

Jesus answered, "I am the way, and the truth, and the life. The only way to the Father is through me" (John 14:6).

If you check the graves of Mohammed or Buddha or any other so-called god, you will find that those graves all have one thing in common: They all have bones in them. There is only one grave that is empty—the grave of our Lord Jesus Christ! He is the only way to get to God, the only way to get to heaven, the only way to have eternal life, the only way to have real life.

A lot of people are out there lost in the world trying to work their way into heaven. Then there are those who think they can buy their way into heaven. There are others who simply believe that as long as you try to be a good person, you'll end up in heaven. And finally there are the kind of people who just don't believe God would send anyone to hell. They believe everyone goes to heaven.

Well, here's some good news and some bad news. There really is a heaven and there really is a hell. It doesn't matter how good you may think you are, how much money you have, or how many times you've been to church. Without Jesus, you can forget it all. He is the only way. He is the only truth. He is the only life.

SEE FOR YOURSELF: Matt. 10:28; Rom. 10:13

14:16 Helper "Counselor" or "Comforter." Jesus is talking about the Holy Spirit.

everything and will cause you to remember all
that I told you. This Helper is the Holy Spirit
whom the Father will send in my name.
27“I leave you peace; my peace I give you. I
do not give it to you as the world does. So
don't let your hearts be troubled or afraid.
28You heard me say to you, 'I am going, but I
am coming back to you.' If you loved me, you
should be happy that I am going back to the
Father, because he is greater than I am. 29I have
told you this now, before it happens, so that
when it happens, you will believe. 30I will not
talk with you much longer, because the ruler of
this world is coming. He has no power over
me, 31but the world must know that I love the
Father, so I do exactly what the Father told me
to do.
“Come now, let us go.

JESUS IS LIKE A VINE

15 1“I am the true vine; my Father is the gardener. 2He cuts off every branch of mine that
does not produce fruit. And he trims and
cleans every branch that produces fruit so that
it will produce even more fruit. 3You are already clean because of the words I have spoken to you. 4Remain in me, and I will remain in
you. A branch cannot produce fruit alone but
must remain in the vine. In the same way, you
cannot produce fruit alone but must remain in
me.
5“I am the vine, and you are the branches. If
any remain in me and I remain in them, they
produce much fruit. But without me they can
do nothing. 6If any do not remain in me, they
are like a branch that is thrown away and then
dies. People pick up dead branches, throw
them into the fire, and burn them. 7If you remain in me and follow my teachings, you can

On the Edge

I am the true vine; my Father is the gardener (John 15:1).

Let's take a look at this verse. Here are some thoughts that just might jump off this page and be a great encouragement to you. The words “I am” were used in John 6:51. Jesus was talking there about being “living bread”; and in John 1:9, John referred to him as the “true Light.” Both of these relate to the verse here about Jesus being the “true vine.” The Greek word for “true vine” lets us know that he was the *original* vine. We are the branches that grow from that vine. In other words, we have life because of him.

The farmer is the one who takes care of the vineyard, and that farmer is God. He's taking care of us so we can produce good fruit. As we allow God to feed us, prune us, and care for us, we will start producing good fruit today. God is the farmer, Jesus is the vine, and you're the branch. God's on your side, and he wants to see you produce good fruit!

SEE FOR YOURSELF:
Prov. 16:3;
John 1:9; 6:32, 51

Promise

HE PROMISES TO HELP YOU BY HIS SPIRIT.

I will ask the Father, and he will give you another Helper to be with you forever (John 14:16).

Have you ever needed help? Of course you have. You may need help right now. All of us need help at some time or another. None of us is immune to the storms of life, but the good news is God sent the Holy Spirit to go with us through these storms. Not only did he come to fill us with power, but he was also sent to help us with every trial, every temptation, and every circumstance.

You may be going through something at this very moment, but you know what? The Holy Spirit is there right now ready and willing to help, even as you read this. In fact, if we will become aware of God's presence in us, there isn't anything that the devil can throw at us that we can't handle. Jesus, the greater One, lives on the inside! Nothing can stop us now! We have victory! He'll help you!

SEE FOR YOURSELF:
Ps. 33:20; 37:40; Rom. 8:26; 1 John 4:4

WHAT'S IT MEAN?

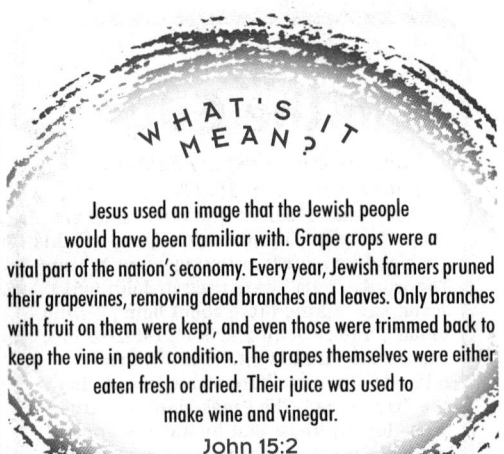

Jesus used an image that the Jewish people would have been familiar with. Grape crops were a vital part of the nation's economy. Every year, Jewish farmers pruned their grapevines, removing dead branches and leaves. Only branches with fruit on them were kept, and even those were trimmed back to keep the vine in peak condition. The grapes themselves were either eaten fresh or dried. Their juice was used to make wine and vinegar.

John 15:2

ask anything you want, and it will be given to
you. 8 You should produce much fruit and
show that you are my followers, which brings
glory to my Father. 9 I loved you as the Father
loved me. Now remain in my love. 10 I have
obeyed my Father's commands, and I remain
in his love. In the same way, if you obey my
commands, you will remain in my love. 11 I
have told you these things so that you can
have the same joy I have and so that your joy
will be the fullest possible joy.
12 "This is my command: Love each other as
I have loved you. 13 The greatest love a person
can show is to die for his friends. 14 You are my
friends if you do what I command you. 15 I no longer call
you servants, because a servant
does not know what his master is doing. But I call you friends,
because I have made known
to you everything I heard from
my Father. 16 You did not choose
me; I chose you. And I gave you this work: to
go and produce fruit, fruit that will last. Then
the Father will give you anything you ask for
in my name. 17 This is my command: Love each
other.

JESUS WARNS HIS FOLLOWERS

18 "If the world hates you, remember that it
hated me first. 19 If you belonged to the world,
it would love you as it loves its own. But I have
chosen you out of the world, so you don't belong to it. That is why the world hates you.
20 Remember what I told you: A servant is not
greater than his master. If people did wrong to
me, they will do wrong to you, too. And if they
obeyed my teaching, they will obey yours, too.
21 They will do all this to you on account of me,

FRIENDSHIP

What is friendship marked by? (15:13–15)

Promise HE PROMISES TO BE YOUR FRIEND.

You are my friends if you do what I command you. I no longer call you servants, because a servant does not know what his master is doing. But I call you friends, because I have made known to you everything I heard from my Father (John 15:14–15).

Jesus called the apostles his *friends*. That word applies to everyone who would ever become his follower. In verse 15, Jesus says, "I no longer call you servants. . . . But I call you friends."

You've probably heard a lot about being Jesus' servant. He's done so much for you! Because of him you're loved more than you can imagine. Because of him you can be strong and confident. Because of him you'll spend eternity with God. So a good response to him is, "Jesus, what can I do for you?" Of course, Jesus wants you to do your best to be a servant who pleases him. But more than that, he wants you to treat him like your friend. Jesus is a Person, and like any person, he wants a friend who loves him more than anyone or anything else. What counts is not wearing yourself out with good deeds, but turning yourself toward him and loving him with your whole heart.

Be careful not to take his friendship for granted. He isn't like your friends at school, just as imperfect as you are. He is God. While you're learning to love him as your best friend, don't ever lose sight of how awesome he is and of all the incredible gifts he gives you. Start to think of yourself as a friend of Jesus.

SEE FOR YOURSELF:

John 14:15, 21; James 2:22–23

because they do not know the One who sent
me. [22]If I had not come and spoken to them,
they would not be guilty of sin, but now they
have no excuse for their sin. [23]Whoever hates
me also hates my Father. [24]I did works among
them that no one else has ever done. If I had
not done these works, they would not be
guilty of sin. But now they have seen what I
have done, and yet they have hated both me
and my Father. [25]But this happened so that
what is written in their law would be true:
'They hated me for no reason.'*n*
[26]"I will send you the Helper*n* from the Father;
he is the Spirit of truth who comes from
the Father. When he comes, he will tell about
me, [27]and you also must tell people about me,
because you have been with me from the beginning.

16 [1]"I have told you these things to keep you
from giving up. [2]People will put you out of
their synagogues. Yes, the time is coming when
those who kill you will think they are offering
service to God. [3]They will do this because they
have not known the Father and they have not
known me. [4]I have told you these things now
so that when the time comes you will remember
that I warned you.

THE WORK OF THE HOLY SPIRIT

"I did not tell you these things at the beginning,
because I was with you then. [5]Now I am
going back to the One who sent me. But none
of you asks me, 'Where are you going?' [6]Your
hearts are filled with sadness because I have
told you these things. [7]But I tell you the truth, it
is better for you that I go away. When I go
away, I will send the Helper*n* to you. If I do not
go away, the Helper will not come. [8]When the
Helper comes, he will prove to the people of
the world the truth about sin, about being
right with God, and about judgment. [9]He will
prove to them that sin is not believing in me.
[10]He will prove to them that being right with
God comes from my going to the Father and
not being seen anymore. [11]And the Helper will
prove to them that judgment happened when
the ruler of this world was judged.
[12]"I have many more things to say to you,
but they are too much for you now. [13]But
when the Spirit of truth comes, he will lead

15:25 'They . . . reason.' These words could be from Psalm 35:19 or Psalm 69:4.
15:26; 16:7 Helper "Counselor" or "Comforter." Jesus is talking about the Holy Spirit.

Promise HE PROMISES TO SHOW YOU WHAT IS TRUE.

But when the Spirit of truth comes, he will lead you into all truth. He will not speak his own words, but he will speak only what he hears, and he will tell you what is to come (John 16:13).

Have you ever had a tough time making a decision? Everybody has. Well, the Holy Spirit has been sent to speak to you at those very moments. And this verse assures you that he will not just spout off on his own, but will only say what God says. In other words, when the Holy Spirit speaks to your heart, you can take it to the bank. You'd better go with it! He will speak to you and he's going to show you what is true. That's his job. So make sure you're listening and not ignoring him.

How do you hear the Holy Spirit speak? Second Timothy 2:15 says, "Make every effort to give yourself to God as the kind of person he will accept. Be a worker who is not ashamed and who uses the true teaching in the right way." So what do you do? Begin doing your best and studying the Bible—not just reading words, but really getting into the Word of God. Start out by just reviewing a few verses in your mind—over and over. Begin putting the Word of God inside you by memorizing a verse or two. Read Psalm 119:1–24. Notice how the psalmist felt about God's Word. Whenever you read the words *teachings, demands, rules, orders, commands,* or *word*, you can think of them as the Bible. As you begin to "feed" yourself the Word of God, you'll begin to notice that you are hearing God speak to you in ways and about things you've never heard before. Start doing it now, and let the Holy Spirit lead you "into all truth"!

SEE FOR YOURSELF:

Ps. 32:8–9; Prov. 3:5–6; Is. 58:11; John 4:24

you into all truth. He will not speak his own words, but he will speak only what he hears, and he will tell you what is to come. [14]The Spirit of truth will bring glory to me, because he will take what I have to say and tell it to you. [15]All that the Father has is mine. That is why I said that the Spirit will take what I have to say and tell it to you.

SADNESS WILL BECOME HAPPINESS

[16]"After a little while you will not see me, and then after a little while you will see me again."

[17]Some of the followers said to each other, "What does Jesus mean when he says, 'After a little while you will not see me, and then after a little while you will see me again'? And what does he mean when he says, 'Because I am going to the Father'?" [18]They also asked, "What does he mean by 'a little while'? We don't understand what he is saying."

[19]Jesus saw that the followers wanted to ask him about this, so he said to them, "Are you asking each other what I meant when I said, 'After a little while you will not see me, and then after a little while you will see me again'? [20]I tell you the truth, you will cry and be sad, but the world will be happy. You will be sad, but your sadness will become joy. [21]When a woman gives birth to a baby, she has pain, because her time has come. But when her baby is born, she forgets the pain, because she is so happy that a child has been born into the world. [22]It is the same with you. Now you are sad, but I will see you again and you will be happy, and no one will take away your joy. [23]In that day you will not ask me for anything. I tell you the truth, my Father will give you anything you ask for in my name. [24]Until now you have not asked for anything in my name. Ask and you will receive, so that your joy will be the fullest possible joy.

PRAYER
Whose name should we pray in? (16:23–24)

VICTORY OVER THE WORLD

[25]"I have told you these things, using stories that hide the meaning. But the time will come when I will not use stories like that to tell you things; I will speak to you in plain words about the Father. [26]In that day you will ask the Father for things in my name. I mean, I will not need to ask the Father for you. [27]The Father himself loves you. He loves you because you loved me and believed that I came from God. [28]I came from the Father into the world. Now I am leaving the world and going back to the Father."

[29]Then the followers of Jesus said, "You are speaking clearly to us now and are not using stories that are hard to understand. [30]We can see now that you know all things. You can answer a person's question even before it is asked. This makes us believe you came from God."

[31]Jesus answered, "So now you believe? [32]Listen to me; a time is coming when you will be scattered, each to his own home. That time is now here. You will leave me alone, but I am never really alone, because the Father is with me.

[33]"I told you these things so that you can have peace in me. In this world you will have trouble, but be brave! I have defeated the world."

COMFORT
What has Jesus defeated? (16:33)

JESUS PRAYS FOR HIS FOLLOWERS

17 [1]After Jesus said these things, he looked toward heaven and prayed, "Father, the time has come. Give glory to your Son so that the Son can give glory to you. [2]You gave the Son power over all people so that the Son could give eternal life to all those you gave him. [3]And this is eternal life: that people know you, the only true God, and that they know Jesus Christ, the One you sent. [4]Having finished the work you gave me to do, I brought you glory on earth. [5]And now, Father, give me glory with you; give me the glory I had with you before the world was made.

SALVATION
Does salvation include gaining a relationship with God? (17:1–5)

[6]"I showed what you are like to those you gave me from the world. They belonged to you, and you gave them to me, and they have obeyed your teaching. [7]Now they know that everything you gave me comes from you. [8]I gave them the teachings you gave me, and they accepted them. They knew that I truly came from you, and they believed that you sent me. [9]I am praying for them. I am not praying for people in the world but for those you gave me, because they are yours. [10]All I have is yours, and all you have is mine. And my glory is shown through them. [11]I am coming to you; I will not stay in the world any longer. But they are still in the world. Holy Father, keep them safe by the power of your name, the name you gave me, so that they will be one, just as you and I are one. [12]While I was with them, I kept them safe by the power of your name, the

name you gave me. I protected them, and only
one of them, the one worthy of destruction,
was lost so that the Scripture would come true.
13"I am coming to you now. But I pray these
things while I am still in the world so that these
followers can have all of my joy in them. 14I
have given them your teaching. And the world
has hated them, because they don't belong to
the world, just as I don't belong to the world.
15I am not asking you to take them out of the
world but to keep them safe from the Evil One.
16They don't belong to the world, just as I don't
belong to the world. 17Make them ready for
your service through your truth;
your teaching is truth. 18I have
sent them into the world, just
as you sent me into the
world. 19For their sake, I am
making myself ready to serve
so that they can be ready for
their service of the truth.

TRUTH
Is God's teaching truth? (17:17)

20"I pray for these followers, but I am also
praying for all those who will believe in me
because of their teaching. 21Father, I pray that
they can be one. As you are in me and I am in
you, I pray that they can also be one in us.
Then the world will believe that you sent me.
22I have given these people the glory that you
gave me so that they can be one, just as you
and I are one. 23I will be in them and you will
be in me so that they will be completely one.
Then the world will know that you sent me
and that you loved them just as much as you
loved me.
24"Father, I want these people that you gave
me to be with me where I am. I want them to
see my glory, which you gave me because you
loved me before the world was made. 25Father,
you are the One who is good. The world does
not know you, but I know you, and these people know you sent me. 26I showed them what
you are like, and I will show them again. Then
they will have the same love that you have for
me, and I will live in them."

JESUS IS ARRESTED

18 1When Jesus finished praying, he went with
his followers across the Kidron Valley. On the
other side there was a garden, and Jesus and
his followers went into it.
2Judas knew where this place was, because
Jesus met there often with his followers. Judas
was the one who turned against Jesus. 3So Judas came there with a group of soldiers and
some guards from the leading priests and the
Pharisees. They were carrying torches, lan-
terns, and weapons.
4Knowing everything that would happen to
him, Jesus went out and asked, "Who is it you
are looking for?"
5They answered, "Jesus from Nazareth."
"I am he," Jesus said. (Judas, the one who
turned against Jesus, was standing there with
them.) 6When Jesus said, "I am he," they moved
back and fell to the ground.
7Jesus asked them again, "Who is it you are
looking for?"
They said, "Jesus of Nazareth."
8"I told you that I am he," Jesus said. "So if
you are looking for me, let the others go." 9This
happened so that the words Jesus said before
would come true: "I have not lost any of the
ones you gave me."
10Simon Peter, who had a sword, pulled it
out and struck the servant of the high priest,
cutting off his right ear. (The servant's name
was Malchus.) 11Jesus said to Peter, "Put your
sword back. Shouldn't I drink the cup[n] the Father gave me?"

WHAT'S IT MEAN?

The Kidron Valley was east of Jerusalem and held a brook that flowed past the Temple of Jerusalem; the Garden of Gethsemane, where Jesus prayed on the night of his arrest; and the Mount of Olives. During the dry summer months, the brook was nearly nonexistent. During the rainy winter season, it turned into a steadily flowing stream.
John 18:1

JESUS IS BROUGHT BEFORE ANNAS

12Then the soldiers with their commander
and the guards arrested Jesus. They tied him
13and led him first to Annas, the father-in-law
of Caiaphas, the high priest that year. 14Caia-
phas was the one who told the Jews that it
would be better if one man died for all the
people.

18:11 cup Jesus is talking about the painful things that will happen to him. Accepting these things will be very hard, like drinking a cup of something bitter.

WHAT'S IT MEAN?

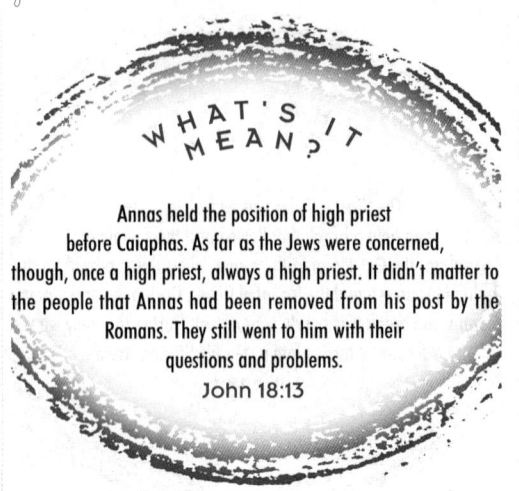

Annas held the position of high priest before Caiaphas. As far as the Jews were concerned, though, once a high priest, always a high priest. It didn't matter to the people that Annas had been removed from his post by the Romans. They still went to him with their questions and problems.

John 18:13

PETER SAYS HE DOESN'T KNOW JESUS

15 Simon Peter and another one of Jesus' followers went along after Jesus. This follower knew the high priest, so he went with Jesus into the high priest's courtyard. 16 But Peter waited outside near the door. The follower who knew the high priest came back outside, spoke to the girl at the door, and brought Peter inside. 17 The girl at the door said to Peter, "Aren't you also one of that man's followers?"

Peter answered, "No, I am not!"

18 It was cold, so the servants and guards had built a fire and were standing around it, warming themselves. Peter also was standing with them, warming himself.

WHAT'S IT MEAN?

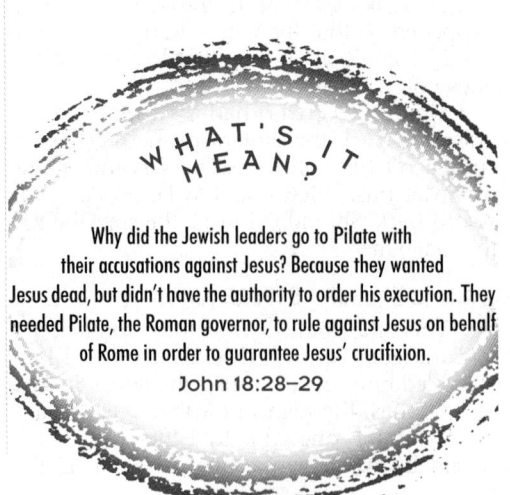

Why did the Jewish leaders go to Pilate with their accusations against Jesus? Because they wanted Jesus dead, but didn't have the authority to order his execution. They needed Pilate, the Roman governor, to rule against Jesus on behalf of Rome in order to guarantee Jesus' crucifixion.

John 18:28–29

THE HIGH PRIEST QUESTIONS JESUS

19 The high priest asked Jesus questions about his followers and his teaching. 20 Jesus answered, "I have spoken openly to everyone. I have always taught in synagogues and in the Temple, where all the Jews come together. I never said anything in secret. 21 So why do you question me? Ask the people who heard my teaching. They know what I said."

22 When Jesus said this, one of the guards standing there hit him. The guard said, "Is that the way you answer the high priest?"

23 Jesus answered him, "If I said something wrong, then show what it was. But if what I said is true, why do you hit me?"

24 Then Annas sent Jesus, who was still tied, to Caiaphas the high priest.

PETER SAYS AGAIN HE DOESN'T KNOW JESUS

25 As Simon Peter was standing and warming himself, they said to him, "Aren't you one of that man's followers?"

Peter said it was not true; he said, "No, I am not."

26 One of the servants of the high priest was there. This servant was a relative of the man whose ear Peter had cut off. The servant said, "Didn't I see you with him in the garden?"

27 Again Peter said it wasn't true. At once a rooster crowed.

JESUS IS BROUGHT BEFORE PILATE

28 Early in the morning they led Jesus from Caiaphas's house to the Roman governor's palace. They would not go inside the palace, because they did not want to make themselves unclean;[n] they wanted to eat the Passover meal. 29 So Pilate went outside to them and asked, "What charges do you bring against this man?"

30 They answered, "If he were not a criminal, we wouldn't have brought him to you."

31 Pilate said to them, "Take him yourselves and judge him by your own law."

"But we are not allowed to put anyone to death," the Jews answered. 32 (This happened so that what Jesus said about how he would die would come true.)

33 Then Pilate went back inside the palace and called Jesus to him and asked, "Are you the king of the Jews?"

34 Jesus said, "Is that your own question, or did others tell you about me?"

35 Pilate answered, "I am not one of you. It

18:28 unclean Going into the Roman palace would make them unfit to eat the Passover Feast, according to their Law.

was your own people and their leading priests who handed you over to me. What have you done wrong?"

36Jesus answered, "My kingdom does not belong to this world. If it belonged to this world, my servants would fight so that I would not be given over to the Jews. But my kingdom is from another place."

37Pilate said, "So you are a king!"

Jesus answered, "You are the one saying I am a king. This is why I was born and came into the world: to tell people the truth. And everyone who belongs to the truth listens to me."

38Pilate said, "What is truth?" After he said this, he went out to the crowd again and said to them, "I find nothing against this man. 39But it is your custom that I free one prisoner to you at Passover time. Do you want me to free the 'king of the Jews'?"

40They shouted back, "No, not him! Let Barabbas go free!" (Barabbas was a robber.)

19 1Then Pilate ordered that Jesus be taken away and whipped. 2The soldiers made a crown from some thorny branches and put it on Jesus' head and put a purple robe around him. 3Then they came to him many times and said, "Hail, King of the Jews!" and hit him in the face.

4Again Pilate came out and said to them, "Look, I am bringing Jesus out to you. I want you to know that I find nothing against him." 5So Jesus came out, wearing the crown of thorns and the purple robe. Pilate said to them, "Here is the man!"

6When the leading priests and the guards saw Jesus, they shouted, "Crucify him! Crucify him!"

But Pilate answered, "Crucify him yourselves, because I find nothing against him."

7The leaders answered, "We have a law that says he should die, because he said he is the Son of God."

8When Pilate heard this, he was even more afraid. 9He went back inside the palace and asked Jesus, "Where do you come from?" But Jesus did not answer him. 10Pilate said, "You refuse to speak to me? Don't you know I have power to set you free and power to have you crucified?"

11Jesus answered, "The only power you have over me is the power given to you by God. The man who turned me in to you is guilty of a greater sin."

12After this, Pilate tried to let Jesus go. But some in the crowd cried out, "Anyone who makes himself king is against Caesar. If you let this man go, you are no friend of Caesar."

13When Pilate heard what they were saying, he brought Jesus out and sat down on the judge's seat at the place called The Stone Pavement. (In the Hebrew language[n] the name is Gabbatha.) 14It was about noon on Preparation Day of Passover week. Pilate said to the crowd, "Here is your king!"

15They shouted, "Take him away! Take him away! Crucify him!"

Pilate asked them, "Do you want me to crucify your king?"

The leading priests answered, "The only king we have is Caesar."

16So Pilate handed Jesus over to them to be crucified.

JESUS IS CRUCIFIED

The soldiers took charge of Jesus. 17Carrying his own cross, Jesus went out to a place called The Place of the Skull, which in the Hebrew language[n] is called Golgotha. 18There they crucified Jesus. They also crucified two other men, one on each side, with Jesus in the middle. 19Pilate wrote a sign and put it on the cross. It read: JESUS OF NAZARETH, THE KING OF THE JEWS. 20The sign was written in Hebrew, in Latin, and in Greek. Many of the people read the sign, because the place where Jesus was crucified was near the city. 21The leading priests said to Pilate, "Don't write, 'The King of the Jews.' But write, 'This man said, "I am the King of the Jews." ' "

WHAT'S IT MEAN?

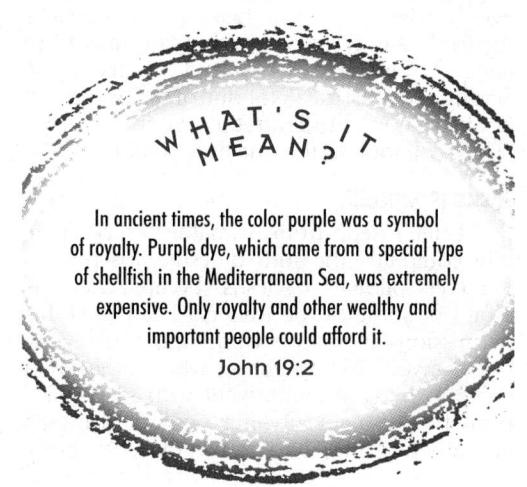

In ancient times, the color purple was a symbol of royalty. Purple dye, which came from a special type of shellfish in the Mediterranean Sea, was extremely expensive. Only royalty and other wealthy and important people could afford it.

John 19:2

19:13, 17 Hebrew language Or Aramaic, the language of many people in this region in the first century.

22Pilate answered, "What I have written, I
have written."
23After the soldiers crucified Jesus, they took
his clothes and divided them into four parts,
with each soldier getting one part. They also
took his long shirt, which was all one piece of
cloth, woven from top to bottom. 24So the soldiers said to each other, "We should not tear
this into parts. Let's throw lots to see who will
get it." This happened so that this Scripture
would come true:

> "They divided my clothes among them,
> and they threw lots for my clothing."
>
> *Psalm 22:18*

So the soldiers did this.
25Standing near his cross were Jesus' mother, his mother's sister, Mary the wife of Clopas,
and Mary Magdalene. 26When Jesus saw his
mother and the follower he loved standing
nearby, he said to his mother, "Dear woman,
here is your son." 27Then he said to the follower, "Here is your mother." From that time on,
the follower took her to live in his home.

JESUS DIES

28After this, Jesus knew that everything had
been done. So that the Scripture would come
true, he said, "I am thirsty."[n] 29There was a jar
full of vinegar there, so the soldiers soaked a
sponge in it, put the sponge on a branch of a
hyssop plant, and lifted it to Jesus' mouth.
30When Jesus tasted the vinegar, he said, "It is
finished." Then he bowed his head and died.

WHAT'S IT MEAN?

The hyssop was a sweet-smelling plant that had been used in religious ceremonies since Old Testament times. Perhaps its most famous appearance in the Bible was as the instrument the Israelites used to mark their doors with blood during the first Passover, when they escaped from Egypt. The angel of death passed over the houses that were marked with blood when he took the lives of all the firstborn sons of the Egyptians.

John 19:29

WHAT'S IT MEAN?

According to the Teachings that God gave Moses, touching a dead body made a person unclean, which meant he was considered unfit to take part in any religious ceremonies. Uncleanness wasn't a permanent condition, though. A person was considered clean again after a certain amount of time had passed and certain cleansing rituals had been performed. Joseph of Arimathea and Nicodemus wanted to finish the burial so that they could complete the necessary cleansing rituals before the Sabbath day began.

John 19:42

31This day was Preparation Day, and the
next day was a special Sabbath day. Since the
religious leaders did not want the bodies to
stay on the cross on the Sabbath day, they
asked Pilate to order that the legs of the men be
broken[n] and the bodies be taken away. 32So the
soldiers came and broke the legs of the first
man on the cross beside Jesus. Then they broke
the legs of the man on the other cross beside
Jesus. 33But when the soldiers came to Jesus
and saw that he was already dead, they did not
break his legs. 34But one of the soldiers stuck
his spear into Jesus' side, and at once blood
and water came out. 35(The one who saw this
happen is the one who told us this, and whatever he says is true. And he knows that he tells
the truth, and he tells it so that you might believe.) 36These things happened to make the
Scripture come true: "Not one of his bones will
be broken."[n] 37And another Scripture says,
"They will look at the one they stabbed."[n]

JESUS IS BURIED

38Later, Joseph from Arimathea asked Pilate
if he could take the body of Jesus. (Joseph was
a secret follower of Jesus, because he was
afraid of some of the leaders.) Pilate gave his
permission, so Joseph came and took Jesus'
body away. 39Nicodemus, who earlier had
come to Jesus at night, went with Joseph. He
brought about seventy-five pounds of myrrh
and aloes. 40These two men took Jesus' body

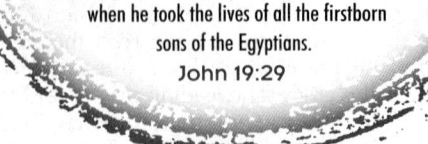

19:28 "I am thirsty." Read Psalms 22:15; 69:21. **19:31 broken** The breaking of their bones would make them die sooner. **19:36 "Not one . . . broken."** Quotation from Psalm 34:20. The idea is from Exodus 12:46; Numbers 9:12. **19:37 "They . . . stabbed."** Quotation from Zechariah 12:10.

and wrapped it with the spices in pieces of
linen cloth, which is how they bury the
dead. [41]In the place where Jesus was crucified,
there was a garden. In the garden was a new
tomb that had never been used before. [42]The
men laid Jesus in that tomb because it was
nearby, and they were preparing to start their
Sabbath day.

JESUS' TOMB IS EMPTY

20
[1]Early on the first day of the week, Mary
Magdalene went to the tomb while it was still
dark. When she saw that the large stone had
been moved away from the tomb, [2]she ran to
Simon Peter and the follower whom Jesus
loved. Mary said, "They have taken the Lord
out of the tomb, and we don't know where
they have put him."
[3]So Peter and the other follower started
for the tomb. [4]They were both running, but
the other follower ran faster than Peter and
reached the tomb first. [5]He bent down and
looked in and saw the strips of linen cloth
lying there, but he did not go in. [6]Then following him, Simon Peter arrived and went
into the tomb and saw the strips of linen lying there. [7]He also saw the cloth that had
been around Jesus' head, which was folded
up and laid in a different place from the
strips of linen. [8]Then the other follower, who
had reached the tomb first, also went in. He
saw and believed. [9](They did not yet understand from the Scriptures that Jesus must rise
from the dead.)

JESUS APPEARS TO MARY MAGDALENE

[10]Then the followers went
back home. [11]But Mary stood
outside the tomb, crying. As
she was crying, she bent
down and looked inside
the tomb. [12]She saw two
angels dressed in white, sitting where Jesus' body had
been, one at the head and
one at the feet.
[13]They asked her, "Woman,
why are you crying?"
She answered, "They have taken away
my Lord, and I don't know where they have
put him." [14]When Mary said this, she turned
around and saw Jesus standing there, but she
did not know it was Jesus.
[15]Jesus asked her, "Woman, why are you
crying? Whom are you looking for?"
Thinking he was the gardener, she said to
him, "Did you take him away, sir? Tell me
where you put him, and I will get him."
[16]Jesus said to her, "Mary."
Mary turned toward Jesus and said in
Hebrew,[n] "Rabboni." (This means Teacher.)
[17]Jesus said to her, "Don't hold on to me,
because I have not yet gone up to the Father.
But go to my brothers and tell them, 'I am going back to my Father and your Father, to my
God and your God.' "
[18]Mary Magdalene went and said to the followers, "I saw the Lord!" And she told them
what Jesus had said to her.

JESUS APPEARS TO HIS FOLLOWERS

[19]When it was evening on the first day of
the week, the followers were together. The
doors were locked, because they were afraid of
the older leaders. Then Jesus came and stood
right in the middle of them and said, "Peace be
with you." [20]After he said this, he showed them
his hands and his side. The followers were
thrilled when they saw the Lord.
[21]Then Jesus said again, "Peace be with you.
As the Father sent me, I now send you." [22]After
he said this, he breathed on them and said,
"Receive the Holy Spirit. [23]If you forgive anyone his sins, they are forgiven. If you don't forgive them, they are not forgiven."

JESUS APPEARS TO THOMAS

[24]Thomas (called Didymus), who was one
of the twelve, was not with them when Jesus
came. [25]The other followers kept telling Thomas, "We saw the Lord."
But Thomas said, "I will
not believe it until I see the
nail marks in his hands
and put my finger where
the nails were and put my
hand into his side."
[26]A week later the fol-
lowers were in the house
again, and Thomas was
with them. The doors were
locked, but Jesus came in and
stood right in the middle of
them. He said, "Peace be with you."
[27]Then he said to Thomas, "Put your finger here,
and look at my hands. Put your hand here in
my side. Stop being an unbeliever and believe."
[28]Thomas said to him, "My Lord and my
God!"
[29]Then Jesus told him, "You believe because

> **"Then Jesus told him, 'You believe because you see me. Those who believe without seeing me will be truly happy.' " (John 20:29)**

20:16 Hebrew language Or Aramaic, the language of many people in this region in the first century.

you see me. Those who believe without seeing
me will be truly happy."

WHY JOHN WROTE THIS BOOK

[30]Jesus did many other miracles in the presence of his followers that are not written in this
book. [31]But these are written so that you may
believe that Jesus is the Christ, the Son of God.
Then, by believing, you may have life through
his name.

WHAT'S IT MEAN?

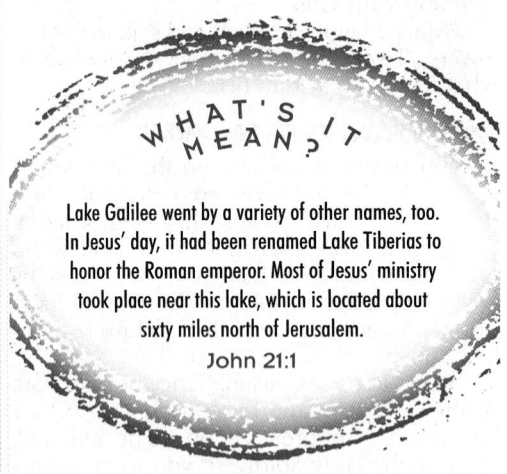

Lake Galilee went by a variety of other names, too. In Jesus' day, it had been renamed Lake Tiberias to honor the Roman emperor. Most of Jesus' ministry took place near this lake, which is located about sixty miles north of Jerusalem.

John 21:1

JESUS APPEARS TO SEVEN FOLLOWERS

21

[1]Later, Jesus showed himself to his followers
again—this time at Lake Galilee.[n] This is how
he showed himself: [2]Some of the followers
were together: Simon Peter, Thomas (called
Didymus), Nathanael from Cana in Galilee, the
two sons of Zebedee, and two other followers.
[3]Simon Peter said, "I am going out to fish."
The others said, "We will go with you." So
they went out and got into the boat. They
fished that night but caught nothing.
[4]Early the next morning Jesus stood on the
shore, but the followers did not know it was
Jesus. [5]Then he said to them, "Friends, did you
catch any fish?"
They answered, "No."
[6]He said, "Throw your net on the right side
of the boat, and you will find some." So they
did, and they caught so many fish they could
not pull the net back into the boat.
[7]The follower whom Jesus loved said to Peter, "It is the Lord!" When Peter heard him say
this, he wrapped his coat around himself. (Peter
had taken his clothes off.) Then he jumped into
the water. [8]The other followers went to shore in
the boat, dragging the net full of fish. They
were not very far from shore, only about a
hundred yards. [9]When the followers stepped
out of the boat and onto the shore, they saw a
fire of hot coals. There were fish on the fire,
and there was bread.
[10]Then Jesus said, "Bring some of the fish
you just caught."
[11]Simon Peter went into the boat and pulled
the net to the shore. It was full of big fish, one
hundred fifty-three in all, but even though
there were so many, the net did not tear. [12]Jesus
said to them, "Come and eat." None of the followers dared ask him, "Who are you?" because
they knew it was the Lord. [13]Jesus came and
took the bread and gave it to them, along with
the fish.
[14]This was now the third time Jesus showed
himself to his followers after he was raised
from the dead.

JESUS TALKS TO PETER

[15]When they finished eating, Jesus said to
Simon Peter, "Simon son of John do you love
me more than these?"
He answered, "Yes, Lord, you know that I
love you."
Jesus said, "Feed my lambs."
[16]Again Jesus said, "Simon son of John do
you love me?"
He answered, "Yes, Lord, you know that I
love you."
Jesus said, "Take care of my sheep."
[17]A third time he said, "Simon son of John
do you love me?"
Peter was hurt because Jesus asked him the
third time, "Do you love me?" Peter said, "Lord,
you know everything; you know that I love
you!"
He said to him, "Feed my sheep. [18]I tell you
the truth, when you were younger, you tied
your own belt and went where you wanted.
But when you are old, you will put out your
hands and someone else will tie you and take
you where you don't want to go." [19](Jesus said
this to show how Peter would die to give glory
to God.) Then Jesus said to Peter, "Follow me!"
[20]Peter turned and saw that the follower
Jesus loved was walking behind them. (This
was the follower who had leaned against Jesus
at the supper and had said, "Lord, who will turn
against you?") [21]When Peter saw him behind
them, he asked Jesus, "Lord, what about him?"
[22]Jesus answered, "If I want him to live until
I come back, that is not your business. You follow me."

21:1 Lake Galilee Literally, "Sea of Tiberias."

[23]So a story spread among the followers that this one would not die. But Jesus did not say he would not die. He only said, "If I want him to live until I come back, that is not your business."

[24]That follower is the one who is telling these things and who has now written them down. We know that what he says is true.

[25]There are many other things Jesus did. If every one of them were written down, I suppose the whole world would not be big enough for all the books that would be written.

Acts

CONTENT Have you ever watched one of those shows where an actress is supposed to be having a baby? Remember all the pain and the yelling and the not-pushing and then the pushing. Then, there the baby is; and everybody in the room is all smiles and happy tears. That process is called labor and delivery. It's a lot of work for everyone involved.

Reading the Book of Acts is like watching a baby being born. The baby, though, is the church. Before Jesus came and revolutionized the world's thinking, people went to churches called temples. There they learned, worshiped, gave offerings, and offered sacrifices.

With Christ's death and resurrection, though, church meant something different. Church was no longer a place to go to meet with God. Instead, it was the group of people who made up the family of God and the body of Christ.

When Christ was here on earth, he was God in a human body. Then he left; and now we, the church, are God in human bodies. Making that transition was and is a lot of work for everyone involved: apostles, followers, church members, missionaries, pastors, and so on. Here's how it all began.

Outline

1:1—8:4 .... Telling the Good News in Jerusalem
8:5—12:25 .... The Good News in Judea and Samaria
13:1—14:28 .... Paul's First Journey to Tell the Good News
15:1-35 .... An Important Decision in Jerusalem
15:36—18:22 ...... Paul's Second Journey to Tell the Good News
18:23—21:16 ...... Paul's Third Journey to Tell the Good News
21:17—23:22 ...... Paul's Arrest in Jerusalem
23:23—26:32 ...... Paul Is Taken to Caesarea
27:1—28:31 .... Paul Is Taken to Rome

Purpose The message of the Good News is to be carried to the whole world.

Theme The Work of the Holy Spirit in the Early History of Christianity

Date of writing Early 60s A.D.

"But when the Holy Spirit comes to you, you will receive power. You will be my witnesses—in Jerusalem, in all of Judea, in Samaria, and in every part of the world" (1:8).

Bible Talk

The Early Church: A Commune?

The early church wasn't exactly a commune. They didn't live in the same building or anything. But they did function as a serious community. The people who had money shared with those who didn't. The Bible says there was no poverty in the early church because they took care of each other.

Think of what it was like to walk in their shoes. Jesus had just turned their world upside down. With their very own eyes, they had watched him go back into heaven. They knew for real that this world was not their home—that heaven was—so they didn't feel ownership over things and money and houses. They shared everything.

How do you think that would work for the church today?

A PERSECUTOR, THEN A MISSIONARY

Paul was one of the most famous people in the New Testament church. Our first glimpse of him is in Acts. His name was Saul, and he was searching out and killing Christians. One day in his travels he was confronted by Jesus, who had already ascended into heaven. "Why are you persecuting me?" Jesus asked. (The church is considered the body of Christ, so when Saul/Paul destroyed the church, he was destroying Christ's body all over again.)

Within a few days, Saul became Paul; and he focused his energy in an entirely different direction. Instead of destroying the church, he became a missionary and started churches in every place that he could.

That's how it works when you face Jesus. You can't stay the same.

LUKE WRITES ANOTHER BOOK

1To Theophilus.
The first book I wrote was about everything Jesus began to do and teach 2until the
day he was taken up into heaven. Before this,
with the help of the Holy Spirit, Jesus told the
apostles he had chosen what they should do.
3After his death, he showed himself to them
and proved in many ways that he was alive.
The apostles saw Jesus during the forty days
after he was raised from the dead, and he
spoke to them about the kingdom of God.
4Once when he was eating with them, he told
them not to leave Jerusalem. He said, "Wait
here to receive the promise from the Father
which I told you about. 5John baptized people
with water, but in a few days you will be baptized with the Holy Spirit."

JESUS IS TAKEN UP INTO HEAVEN

6When the apostles were all together, they
asked Jesus, "Lord, are you now going to give
the kingdom back to Israel?"
7Jesus said to them, "The Father is
the only One who has the authority to decide dates and
times. These things are not for
you to know. 8But when the
Holy Spirit comes to you, you
will receive power. You will be
my witnesses—in Jerusalem, in
all of Judea, in Samaria, and in every part of the
world."
9After he said this, as they were watching,
he was lifted up, and a cloud hid
him from their sight. 10As he
was going, they were looking
into the sky. Suddenly, two
men wearing white clothes
stood beside them. 11They
said, "Men of Galilee, why are
you standing here looking into the sky?
Jesus, whom you saw taken up from you
into heaven, will come back in the same way
you saw him go."

HOLY SPIRIT

What does the Holy Spirit empower us to be? (1:8)

WITNESSING

What are Christians called to do? (1:8)

WHAT'S IT MEAN?

Jesus' followers had expected him to wrest control of Israel from the Roman Empire, which had been in charge of the land since 63 B.C.

Acts 1:6

On the Edge

"But when the Holy Spirit comes to you, you will receive power. You will be my witnesses—in Jerusalem, in all of Judea, in Samaria, and in every part of the world." After he said this, as they were watching, he was lifted up, and a cloud hid him from their sight (Acts 1:8–9).

Just think of it—your favorite teacher calls a class meeting. He or she says, "This is the last time you will ever see me. I'm leaving for heaven in a matter of minutes. Before I go, I have one last thing to say to you." You listen intently. Nothing else matters at this moment. How long will you remember your teacher's last words to you? Probably until the day you die.

That's what's happening here. Jesus leaves his followers with this final word. He tells them that the Holy Spirit is coming after him. The Holy Spirit is going to give them power. He'll give them the strength they need to do everything Jesus wants them to do.

As a Christian, you have that same power. The Holy Spirit lives inside of you to give you the power you need to do everything Jesus wants you to do. One thing you know is that he wants you to go out and spread the Good News about his love and forgiveness. He's the power for shaky voices, weak knees, butterflies in your stomach. He's the giver of abundant life, the supplier of words, the revealer of truth, and the protector of courageous hearts. He's the One who always loves you and will never leave you. He gives you comfort and good advice. He gives you the power to know what to do in every situation. That's power!

SEE FOR YOURSELF:
Joel 2:28–29; Luke 9:1–2; John 14:15–31; Acts 2:38–39; Rom. 15:13, 19; 1 Cor. 2:4; Eph. 3:7

On the Edge

Judas bought a field with the money he got for his evil act. But he fell to his death, his body burst open, and all his intestines poured out. Everyone in Jerusalem learned about this so they named the place Akeldama. In their language Akeldama means "Field of Blood" (Acts 1:18–19).

Mike started telling his friends that he didn't have anything to live for. Nothing was fun to him anymore. He wanted to stay in bed all day. He talked a lot about a girl from school who had killed herself. He was so serious all the time. He began to give some of his clothes and stuff away. He withdrew from everybody. He didn't want to go out or to ball games. He seemed depressed. His family thought it was a phase and overlooked it. His friends thought he needed some space and left him alone. He died in his parents' car in their garage one afternoon after school. The note he left said he was just too lonely. Life was too hard. No one seemed to care.

If your friend mentions suicide, talks about not having anything to live for, distances himself/herself from everyone, or shows any other suspicious behavior, take that person seriously. Always take suicide threats seriously. Your friend needs help—quick. Talk to his or her parents, your pastor, a teacher, or counselor until you find someone who cares about your friend and is willing to help. Your job as a friend is to get qualified help. Don't try to handle this one alone. Whatever you do, believe that your friend is hurting, pray for him or her and for wisdom, and get help immediately.

SEE FOR YOURSELF:
Ps. 46:1; Prov. 19:8;
1 Thess. 5:17;
Heb. 4:16;
James 1:5

A NEW APOSTLE IS CHOSEN

12 Then they went back to Jerusalem from
the Mount of Olives. (This mountain is about
half a mile from Jerusalem.) 13 When they entered the city, they went to the upstairs room
where they were staying. Peter, John, James,
Andrew, Philip, Thomas, Bartholomew, Matthew, James son of Alphaeus, Simon (known
as the Zealot), and Judas son of James were
there. 14 They all continued praying together
with some women, including Mary the mother
of Jesus, and Jesus' brothers.
15 During this time there was a meeting of
the believers (about one hundred twenty of
them). Peter stood up and said, 16-17 "Brothers
and sisters,[n] in the Scriptures the Holy Spirit
said through David something that must happen involving Judas. He was one of our own
group and served together with us. He led
those who arrested Jesus." 18 (Judas bought a
field with the money he got for his evil act. But
he fell to his death, his body burst open, and
all his intestines poured out. 19 Everyone in
Jerusalem learned about this so they named
this place Akeldama. In their language Akeldama means "Field of Blood.") 20 "In the Book of
Psalms," Peter said, "this is written:

'May his place be empty;
leave no one to live in it.' *Psalm 69:25*

And it is also written:

'Let another man replace him as leader.' *Psalm 109:8*

21-22 "So now a man must become a witness
with us of Jesus' being raised from the dead. He
must be one of the men who were part of our
group during all the time the Lord Jesus was
among us—from the time John was baptizing
people until the day Jesus was taken up from
us to heaven."
23 They put the names of two men before
the group. One was Joseph Barsabbas, who
was also called Justus. The other was Matthias.
24-25 The apostles prayed, "Lord, you know the
thoughts of everyone. Show us which one of
these two you have chosen to do this work.
Show us who should be an apostle in place of
Judas, who turned away and went where he
belongs." 26 Then they used lots to choose between them, and the lots showed that Matthias
was the one. So he became an apostle with the
other eleven.

THE COMING OF THE HOLY SPIRIT

2 1 When the day of Pentecost came, they
were all together in one place. 2 Suddenly a
noise like a strong, blowing wind came from
heaven and filled the whole house where they
were sitting. 3 They saw something like flames
of fire that were separated and stood over each

1:16-17 Brothers and sisters Although the Greek text says "Brothers" here and throughout this book, the words of the speakers were meant for the entire church, including men and women.

person there. 4They were all filled with the
Holy Spirit, and they began to speak different
languages[n] by the power the Holy Spirit was
giving them.
5There were some religious Jews staying in
Jerusalem who were from every country in the
world. 6When they heard this noise, a crowd
came together. They were all surprised, because
each one heard them speaking in his own language. 7They were completely amazed at this.
They said, "Look! Aren't all these people that
we hear speaking from Galilee? 8Then how is it
possible that we each hear them in our own
languages? We are from different places:
9Parthia, Media, Elam, Mesopotamia, Judea,
Cappadocia, Pontus, Asia, 10Phrygia, Pamphylia, Egypt, the areas of Libya near Cyrene, Rome
11(both Jews and those who had become Jews),
Crete, and Arabia. But we hear them telling in
our own languages about the great things God
has done!" 12They were all amazed and confused, asking each other, "What does this
mean?"
13But others were making fun of them, saying, "They have had too much wine."

PETER SPEAKS TO THE PEOPLE

14But Peter stood up with the eleven apostles, and in a loud voice he spoke to the crowd:
"My fellow Jews, and all of you who are in
Jerusalem, listen to me. Pay attention to what I
have to say. 15These people are not drunk, as
you think; it is only nine o'clock in the morning! 16But Joel the prophet wrote about what is
happening here today:
17'God says: In the last days
I will pour out my Spirit on all kinds of people.
Your sons and daughters will prophesy.

WHAT'S IT MEAN?

The countries listed in this passage were all neighbors of Israel. Today, this list would include Iran, Turkey, Egypt, and Saudi Arabia. Crete is an island in the Mediterranean. Many of the Jews who had been deported by the conquering Babylonians and Assyrians in Old Testament times never returned to their homeland. Their descendants did, though—even if it was only to celebrate the Feast of Pentecost. The Temple in Jerusalem was the only place Jewish people could participate in the special sacrifices and worship services that went along with the Pentecost celebration.

Acts 2:9–12

2:4 languages This can also be translated "tongues."

Promise

HE PROMISES TO SAVE YOU.

Then anyone who calls on the Lord will be saved (Acts 2:21).

Salvation is a one-time thing. You make the decision to *become* a Christian one time. You make decisions to *live* like a Christian daily—sometimes even moment by moment. Sometimes people are insecure about their salvation. They keep wondering if they "did it right" the first time. So they wind up raising their hand to accept Christ every time the offer is made.

Jesus promises that when you call out to him and ask him to save you, he does. It's that simple. You give your heart to him, ask him to forgive your sins, and make him the Lord and Savior of your life. You are saved from that moment until forever. So nail it down. If you've accepted Jesus Christ as your Savior, then you are saved. It's time to move on and grow up in Christ. If you are still unsure, then turn to Acts 16:30–31 and find out what you need to do in order to be saved. Salvation isn't a tricky thing. The Lord sees your heart and knows your sincerity. The right attitude is more important than the right words. Jesus' promise is strong—call out to him, and you will be saved.

SEE FOR YOURSELF:

Mark 16:16; John 10:28; Acts 16:30–31

Your young men will see visions,
and your old men will dream dreams.
18 At that time I will pour out my Spirit
also on my male slaves and female
slaves,
and they will prophesy.
19 I will show miracles
in the sky and on the earth:
blood, fire, and thick smoke.
20 The sun will become dark,
the moon red as blood,
before the overwhelming and glorious
day of the Lord will come.
21 Then anyone who calls on the Lord will
be saved.' *Joel 2:28–32*

22 "People of Israel, listen to these words:
Jesus from Nazareth was a very special man.
God clearly showed this to you by the miracles, wonders, and signs he did through Jesus.
You all know this, because it happened right
here among you.
23 Jesus was given to you, and
with the help of those who don't know the
law, you put him to death by nailing him to a
cross. But this was God's plan which he had
made long ago; he knew all this would happen.
24 God raised Jesus from the dead and set
him free from the pain of death, because death
could not hold him.
25 For David said this
about him:

'I keep the Lord before me always.
Because he is close by my side,
I will not be hurt.
26 So I am glad, and I rejoice.
Even my body has hope,
27 because you will not leave me in the
grave.
You will not let your
Holy One rot.
28 You will teach me how
to live a holy
life.
Being with you will
fill me with joy.' *Psalm 16:8–11*

29 "Brothers and sisters,
I can tell you truly that
David, our ancestor, died
and was buried. His grave is
still here with us today.
30 He was
a prophet and knew God had promised him that he would make a person
from David's family a king just as he was.[n]
31 Knowing this before it happened, David
talked about the Christ rising from the dead.
He said:

'He was not left in the grave.
His body did not rot.'

32 So Jesus is the One whom God raised from
the dead. And we are all witnesses to this.
33 Jesus was lifted up to heaven and is now at
God's right side. The Father has given the Holy
Spirit to Jesus as he promised. So Jesus has
poured out that Spirit, and this is what you
now see and hear.
34 David was not the one
who was lifted up to heaven, but he said:

'The Lord said to my Lord,
"Sit by me at my right side,
35 until I put your enemies under your
control." '[n] *Psalm 110:1*

36 "So, all the people of Israel should know
this truly: God has made Jesus—the
man you nailed to the cross—
both Lord and Christ."

37 When the people heard
this, they felt guilty and asked
Peter and the other apostles,
"What shall we do?"
38 Peter said to them,
"Change your hearts and lives
and be baptized, each one of you, in
the name of Jesus Christ for
the forgiveness of your sins.
And you will receive the gift
of the Holy Spirit.
39 This
promise is for you, for your
children, and for all who are
far away. It is for everyone the
Lord our God calls to himself."

SALVATION
What must we do when we receive salvation? (2:37–38)

REPENTANCE
Is repentance essential for the Holy Spirit to work? (2:38)

40 Peter warned
them with many other words.
He begged them, "Save yourselves from the evil of
today's people!"
41 Then
those people who accepted
what Peter said were bap-
tized. About three thou-
sand people were added to
the number of believers
that day.
42 They spent their
time learning the apostles'
teaching, sharing, breaking
bread,[n] and praying together.

"So, all the people of Israel should know this truly: God has made Jesus—the man you nailed to the cross—both Lord and Christ." (Acts 2:36)

THE BELIEVERS SHARE

43 The apostles were doing many miracles
and signs, and everyone felt great respect for

2:30 God . . . was See 2 Samuel 7:13; Psalm 132:11. **2:35 until . . . control** Literally, "until I make your enemies a footstool for your feet." **2:42 breaking bread** This may mean a meal as in verse 46, or the Lord's Supper, the special meal Jesus told his followers to eat to remember him (Luke 22:14–20).

God. 44All the believers were together and shared everything. 45They would sell their land and the things they owned and then divide the money and give it to anyone who needed it. 46The believers met together in the Temple every day. They ate together in their homes, happy to share their food with joyful hearts. 47They praised God and were liked by all the people. Every day the Lord added those who were being saved to the group of believers.

MONEY
Should we share the resources that God has blessed us with? (2:42–45)

GIVING
What does giving help others to do? (2:44–45)

PETER HEALS A CRIPPLED MAN

3 1One day Peter and John went to the Temple at three o'clock, the time set each day for the afternoon prayer service. 2There, at the Temple gate called Beautiful Gate, was a man who had been crippled all his life. Every day he was carried to this gate to beg for money from the people going into the Temple. 3The man saw Peter and John going into the Temple and asked them for money. 4Peter and John looked straight at him and said, "Look at us!" 5The man looked at them, thinking they were going to give him some money. 6But Peter said, "I don't have any silver or gold, but I do have something else I can give you. By the power of Jesus Christ from Nazareth, stand up and walk!" 7Then Peter took the man's right hand and lifted him up. Immediately the man's feet and ankles became strong. 8He jumped up, stood on his feet, and began to walk. He went into the Temple with them, walking and jumping and praising God. 9-10All the people recognized him as the crippled man who always sat by the Beautiful Gate begging for money. Now they saw this same man walking and praising God, and they were amazed. They wondered how this could happen.

PETER SPEAKS TO THE PEOPLE

11While the man was holding on to Peter and John, all the people were amazed and ran to them at Solomon's Porch. 12When Peter saw this, he said to them, "People of Israel, why are you surprised? You are looking at us as if it were our own power or goodness that made this man walk. 13The God of Abraham, Isaac, and Jacob, the God of our ancestors, gave glory to Jesus, his servant. But you handed him over to be killed. Pilate decided to let him go free, but you told Pilate you did not want Jesus. 14You did not want the One who is holy and good but asked Pilate to give you a murderer[n] instead. 15And so you killed the One who gives life, but God raised him from the dead. We are witnesses to this. 16It was faith in Jesus that made this crippled man well. You can see this man, and you know him. He was made completely well because of trust in Jesus, and you all saw it happen!

JESUS
Who is the One who gives life? (3:15)

17"Brothers and sisters, I know you did those things to Jesus because neither you nor your leaders understood what you were doing. 18God said through the prophets that his Christ would suffer and die. And now God has made these things come true in this way. 19So you must change your hearts and lives! Come back to God, and he will forgive your sins. Then the Lord will send the time of rest. 20And he will send Jesus, the One he chose to be the Christ. 21But Jesus must stay in heaven until the time comes when all things will be made right again. God told about this time long ago when he spoke through his holy prophets. 22Moses said, 'The Lord your God will give you a prophet like me, who is one of your own people. You must listen to everything he tells you. 23Anyone who does not listen to that prophet will die, cut off from God's people.'[n] 24Samuel, and all the other prophets who spoke for God after Samuel, told about this time now. 25You are descendants of the prophets. You have received the agreement God made with your ancestors. He said to your father Abraham, 'Through your descendants all the nations on the earth will be blessed.'[n] 26God has raised up his servant Jesus and sent him to you first to bless you by turning each of you away from doing evil."

PETER AND JOHN AT THE COUNCIL

4 1While Peter and John were speaking to the people, priests, the captain of the soldiers that guarded the Temple, and Sadducees came up to them. 2They were upset because the two apostles were teaching the people and were preaching that people will rise from the dead through

3:14 murderer Barabbas, the man the crowd asked Pilate to set free instead of Jesus (Luke 23:18). **3:22-23 'The Lord . . . people.'** Quotation from Deuteronomy 18:15, 19. **3:25 'Through . . . blessed.'** Quotation from Genesis 22:18; 26:4.

the power of Jesus. 3The older leaders grabbed
Peter and John and put them in jail. Since it
was already night, they kept them in jail until
the next day. 4But many of those who had
heard Peter and John preach believed the
things they said. There were now about five
thousand in the group of believers.
5The next day the rulers, the older leaders,
and the teachers of the law met in Jerusalem.
6Annas the high priest, Caiaphas, John, and
Alexander were there, as well as everyone from
the high priest's family. 7They made Peter and
John stand before them and then asked them,
"By what power or authority did you do this?"

WHAT'S IT MEAN?

The Sanhedrin, a council made up of seventy men plus the high priest, was the highest Jewish court in the land. The council met regularly to settle disputes among the Jewish people. Caiaphas had been selected by the Romans to replace his father-in-law, Annas, as high priest. Annas, though, was considered to be high priest emeritus and was the highest-ranking member of the Sanhedrin.

Acts 4:6

8Then Peter, filled with the Holy Spirit, said
to them, "Rulers of the people and you older
leaders, 9are you questioning us about a good
thing that was done to a crippled man? Are
you asking us who made him well? 10We want
all of you and all the people to know that this
man was made well by the power of Jesus
Christ from Nazareth. You crucified him, but
God raised him from the dead. This man was
crippled, but he is now well and able to stand
here before you because of the power of Jesus.
11Jesus is

'the stone[n] that you builders rejected,
which has become the cornerstone.'

Psalm 118:22

12Jesus is the only One who can save people.
His name is the only power in the world that
has been given to save people. We must be
saved through him."
13The leaders saw that Peter and John were
not afraid to speak, and they understood that
these men had no special training or education. So they were amazed. Then they realized
that Peter and John had been with Jesus. 14Be-
cause they saw the healed man standing
there beside the two apostles, they could say
nothing against them. 15After the leaders ordered them to leave the meeting, they began
to talk to each other. 16They said, "What shall
we do with these men? Everyone in Jerusalem
knows they have done a great miracle, and we
cannot say it is not true. 17But to keep it from
spreading among the people, we must warn
them not to talk to people anymore using that
name."
18So they called Peter and John in again and
told them not to speak or to teach at all in the
name of Jesus. 19But Peter and John answered
them, "You decide what God would want.
Should we obey you or God? 20We cannot
keep quiet. We must speak about what we
have seen and heard." 21The leaders warned the
apostles again and let them go free. They could
not find a way to punish them, because all the
people were praising God for what had been
done. 22The man who received the miracle of
healing was more than forty years old.

THE BELIEVERS PRAY

23After Peter and John left the meeting of
leaders, they went to their own group and told
them everything the leading priests and the
older leaders had said to them. 24When the believers heard this, they prayed to God together,
"Lord, you are the One who made the sky, the
earth, the sea, and everything in them. 25By the
Holy Spirit, through our father David your
servant, you said:

'Why are the nations so angry?
Why are the people making useless
plans?
26The kings of the earth prepare to fight,
and their leaders make plans together
against the Lord
and his Christ.'

Psalm 2:1-2

27These things really happened when Herod,
Pontius Pilate, and some of the people all came
together against Jesus here in Jerusalem. Jesus
is your holy servant, the One you made to be
the Christ. 28These people made your plan
happen because of your power and your will.
29And now, Lord, listen to their threats. Lord,
help us, your servants, to speak your word
without fear. 30Help us to be brave by showing
us your power to heal. Give proofs and make

4:11 stone A symbol meaning Jesus.

WHAT'S IT MEAN?

Let's introduce two of the judges in Jesus' trial. Herod was the ruler of the Jewish people in Galilee and Perea. Pilate was the Roman governor of Judea and Samaria. Because Jesus was from Galilee and the charges against him were made in Jerusalem, his trial fell under the jurisdiction of both men. It's interesting to note that neither man found Jesus guilty, yet both allowed him to be crucified.

Acts 4:27

miracles happen by the power of Jesus, your holy servant."

31After they had prayed, the place where they were meeting was shaken. They were all filled with the Holy Spirit, and they spoke God's word without fear.

THE BELIEVERS SHARE

32The group of believers were united in their hearts and spirit. All those in the group acted as though their private property belonged to everyone in the group. In fact, they shared everything. 33With great power the apostles were telling people that the Lord Jesus was truly raised from the dead. And God blessed all the believers very much. 34No one in the group needed anything. From time to time those who owned fields or houses sold them, brought the money, 35and gave it to the apostles. Then the money was given to anyone who needed it.

36One of the believers was named Joseph, a Levite born in Cyprus. The apostles called him Barnabas (which means "one who encourages"). 37Joseph owned a field, sold it, brought the money, and gave it to the apostles.

ANANIAS AND SAPPHIRA DIE

5 1But a man named Ananias and his wife Sapphira sold some land. 2He kept back part of the money for himself; his wife knew about this and agreed to it. But he brought the rest of the money and gave it to the apostles. 3Peter said, "Ananias, why did you let Satan rule your thoughts to lie to the Holy Spirit and to keep for yourself part of the money you received for the land? 4Before you sold the land, it belonged to you. And even after you sold it, you could have used the money any way you wanted. Why did you think of doing this? You lied to God, not to us!" 5-6When Ananias heard this, he fell down and died. Some young men came in, wrapped up his body, carried it out, and buried it. And everyone who heard about this was filled with fear.

7About three hours later his wife came in, but she did not know what had happened. 8Peter said to her, "Tell me, was the money you got for your field this much?"

Sapphira answered, "Yes, that was the price."

9Peter said to her, "Why did you and your husband agree to test the Spirit of the Lord? Look! The men who buried your husband are at the door, and they will carry you out." 10At that moment Sapphira fell down by his feet and died. When the young men came in and saw that she was dead, they carried her out and buried her beside her husband. 11The whole church and all the others who heard about these things were filled with fear.

WHAT'S IT MEAN?

Why were the young men in such a hurry to bury Ananias? Actually, quick burials were a necessity in the ancient Middle East. The hot climate caused the corpses to decay (and stink) pretty quickly. The bodies of wealthy and powerful people were placed in tombs cut out of rocky hillsides. A stone was then placed in front of the tomb to protect the body from scavenging animals.

Acts 5:5–6

THE APOSTLES HEAL MANY

12The apostles did many signs and miracles among the people. And they would all meet together on Solomon's Porch. 13None of the others dared to join them, but all the people respected them. 14More and more men and women believed in the Lord and were added to the group of believers. 15The people placed their sick on beds and mats in the streets, hoping that when Peter passed by at least his shadow might fall on them. 16Crowds came from all the towns around Jerusalem, bringing their sick and those who were bothered by evil spirits, and all of them were healed.

LEADERS TRY TO STOP THE APOSTLES

[17]The high priest and all his friends (a group called the Sadducees) became very jealous. [18]They took the apostles and put them in jail. [19]But during the night, an angel of the Lord opened the doors of the jail and led the apostles outside. The angel said, [20]"Go stand in the Temple and tell the people everything about this new life." [21]When the apostles heard this, they obeyed and went into the Temple early in the morning and continued teaching.

When the high priest and his friends arrived, they called a meeting of the leaders and all the important older men. They sent some men to the jail to bring the apostles to them. [22]But, upon arriving, the officers could not find the apostles. So they went back and reported to the leaders. [23]They said, "The jail was closed and locked, and the guards were standing at the doors. But when we opened the doors, the jail was empty!" [24]Hearing this, the captain of the Temple guards and the leading priests were confused and wondered what was happening.

[25]Then someone came and told them, "Listen! The men you put in jail are standing in the Temple teaching the people." [26]Then the captain and his men went out and brought the apostles back. But the soldiers did not use force, because they were afraid the people would stone them to death.

[27]The soldiers brought the apostles to the meeting and made them stand before the leaders. The high priest questioned them, [28]saying, "We gave you strict orders not to continue teaching in that name. But look, you have filled Jerusalem with your teaching and are trying to make us responsible for this man's death."

[29]Peter and the other apostles answered, "We must obey God, not human authority! [30]You killed Jesus by hanging him on a cross. But God, the God of our ancestors, raised Jesus up from the dead! [31]Jesus is the One whom God raised to be on his right side, as Leader and Savior. Through him, all people could change their hearts and lives and have their sins forgiven. [32]We saw all these things happen. The Holy Spirit, whom God has given to all who obey him, also proves these things are true."

"We must obey God, not human authority!" (Acts 5:29b)

WHAT'S IT MEAN?

Though Gamaliel was a highly respected member of the Jewish council and an extremely well-educated Pharisee, he is perhaps best known as the teacher of the apostle Paul.
Acts 5:34

[33]When the leaders heard this, they became angry and wanted to kill them. [34]But a Pharisee named Gamaliel stood up in the meeting. He was a teacher of the law, and all the people respected him. He ordered the apostles to leave the meeting for a little while. [35]Then he said, "People of Israel, be careful what you are planning to do to these men. [36]Remember when Theudas appeared? He said he was a great man, and about four hundred men joined him. But he was killed, and all his followers were scattered; they were able to do nothing. [37]Later, a man named Judas came from Galilee at the time of the registration.[n] He also led a group of followers and was killed, and all his followers were scattered. [38]And so now I tell you: Stay away from these men, and leave them alone. If their plan comes from human authority, it will fail. [39]But if it is from God, you will not be able to stop them. You might even be fighting against God himself!"

The leaders agreed with what Gamaliel said. [40]They called the apostles in, beat them, and told them not to speak in the name of Jesus again. Then they let them go free. [41]The apostles left the meeting full of joy because they were given the honor of suffering disgrace for Jesus. [42]Every day in the Temple and in people's homes they continued teaching the people and telling the Good News—that Jesus is the Christ.

SEVEN LEADERS ARE CHOSEN

6 [1]The number of followers was growing. But during this same time, the Greek-speaking followers had an argument with the other

5:37 registration Census. A counting of all the people and the things they own.

followers. The Greek-speaking widows were
not getting their share of the food that was
given out every day. 2The twelve apostles
called the whole group of followers together
and said, "It is not right for us to stop our work
of teaching God's word in order to serve tables.
3So, brothers and sisters, choose seven of your
own men who are good, full of the Spirit and
full of wisdom. We will put them in charge of
this work. 4Then we can continue to pray and
to teach the word of God."

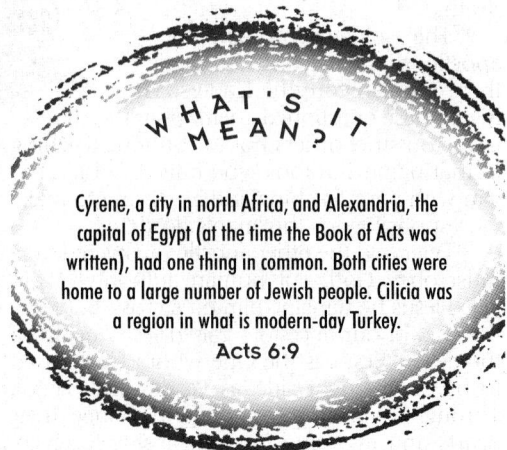

WHAT'S IT MEAN?

The "Greek-speaking followers" were people of Jewish descent who were raised in the Greek culture, outside of Israel. Most spoke Greek. The Jews who were raised in Israel, and who spoke the native Aramaic language, tended to look down on them, believing that they had abandoned their Jewish heritage and culture.

Acts 6:1

5The whole group liked the idea, so they
chose these seven men: Stephen (a man with
great faith and full of the Holy Spirit), Philip,[n]
Procorus, Nicanor, Timon, Parmenas, and Nic-
olas (a man from Antioch who had become a
follower of the Jewish religion). 6Then they put
these men before the apostles, who prayed and
laid their hands[n] on them.
7The word of God was continuing to
spread. The group of followers in Jerusalem
increased, and a great number of the Jewish
priests believed and obeyed.

STEPHEN IS ACCUSED

8Stephen was richly blessed by God who
gave him the power to do great miracles and
signs among the people. 9But some people were
against him. They belonged to the synagogue of
Free Men[n] (as it was called), which included
people from Cyrene, Alexandria, Cilicia, and
Asia. They all came and argued with Stephen.
10But the Spirit was helping him to speak
with wisdom, and his words were so strong
that they could not argue with him. 11So they
secretly urged some men to say, "We heard Stephen speak against Moses and against God."
12This upset the people, the older leaders,
and the teachers of the law. They came and
grabbed Stephen and brought him to a meeting of the leaders. 13They brought in some people to tell lies about Stephen, saying, "This man
is always speaking against this holy place and
the law of Moses. 14We heard him say that
Jesus from Nazareth will destroy this place and
that Jesus will change the customs Moses gave
us." 15All the people in the meeting were watching Stephen closely and saw that his face
looked like the face of an angel.

STEPHEN'S SPEECH

7 1The high priest said to Stephen, "Are these
things true?"
2Stephen answered, "Brothers and fathers,
listen to me. Our glorious God appeared to
Abraham, our ancestor, in Mesopotamia before he lived in Haran. 3God said to Abraham,
'Leave your country and your relatives, and go
to the land I will show you.'[n] 4So Abraham left
the country of Chaldea and went to live in Haran. After Abraham's father died, God sent him
to this place where you now live. 5God did not
give Abraham any of this land, not even a foot
of it. But God promised that he would give this
land to him and his descendants, even before
Abraham had a child. 6This is what God said

WHAT'S IT MEAN?

Cyrene, a city in north Africa, and Alexandria, the capital of Egypt (at the time the Book of Acts was written), had one thing in common. Both cities were home to a large number of Jewish people. Cilicia was a region in what is modern-day Turkey.

Acts 6:9

6:5 Philip Not the apostle named Philip. **6:6 laid their hands** The laying on of hands had many purposes, including the giving of a blessing, power, or authority. **6:9 Free Men** Jewish people who had been slaves or whose fathers had been slaves, but were now free. **7:3 'Leave . . . you.'** Quotation from Genesis 12:1.

WHAT'S IT MEAN?

If you're looking for Mesopotamia on an ancient map, focus your attention on the area between the Tigris and Euphrates Rivers. Abraham's hometown of Ur was located in the land of the Chaldeans (later the Babylonians), near the Persian Gulf. Haran, Abraham's temporary home before he headed for the Promised Land, was about 450 miles northwest of Ur.

Acts 7:2

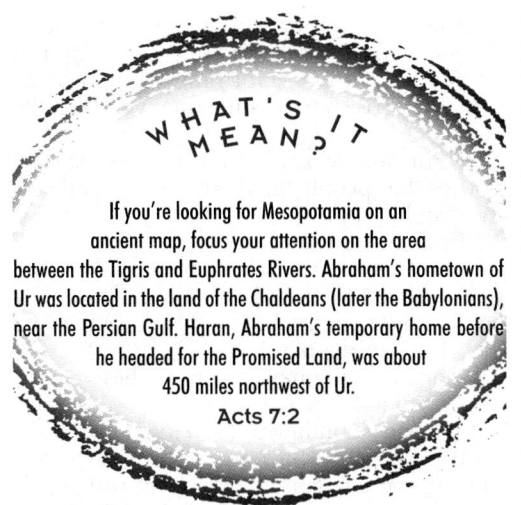

to him: 'Your descendants will be strangers in a
land they don't own. The people there will
make them slaves and will mistreat them for
four hundred years. [7]But I will punish the nation where they are slaves. Then your descendants will leave that land and will worship me
in this place.'[n] [8]God made an agreement with
Abraham, the sign of which was circumcision.
And so when Abraham had his son Isaac,
Abraham circumcised him when he was eight
days old. Isaac also circumcised his son Jacob,
and Jacob did the same for his sons, the twelve
ancestors[n] of our people.

JEALOUSY

What kind of actions can jealousy lead to? (7:9)

[9]"Jacob's sons became jealous
of Joseph and sold him to be a
slave in Egypt. But God was
with him [10]and saved him
from all his troubles. The king
of Egypt liked Joseph and respected him because of the
wisdom God gave him. The
king made him governor of Egypt and put him
in charge of all the people in his palace.

GOD'S WILL

Can God turn something bad into good? (7:9–10)

[11]"Then all the land of
Egypt and Canaan became so
dry that nothing would grow,
and the people suffered very
much. Jacob's sons, our ancestors, could not find anything to eat. [12]But when Jacob
heard there was grain in
Egypt, he sent his sons there. This
was their first trip to Egypt. [13]When they went
there a second time, Joseph told his brothers
who he was, and the king learned about
Joseph's family. [14]Then Joseph sent messengers
to invite Jacob, his father, to come to Egypt
along with all his relatives (seventy-five persons altogether). [15]So Jacob went down to
Egypt, where he and his sons died. [16]Later their
bodies were moved to Shechem and put in a
grave there. (It was the same grave Abraham
had bought for a sum of money from the sons
of Hamor in Shechem.)

[17]"The promise God made to Abraham was
soon to come true, and the number of people
in Egypt grew large. [18]Then a new king, who
did not know who Joseph was, began to rule
Egypt. [19]This king tricked our people and was
cruel to our ancestors, forcing them to leave
their babies outside to die. [20]At this time Moses
was born, and he was very beautiful. For three
months Moses was cared for in his father's
house. [21]When they put Moses outside, the
king's daughter adopted him and raised him as
if he were her own son. [22]The Egyptians taught
Moses everything they knew, and he was a
powerful man in what he said and did.

[23]"When Moses was about forty years old,
he thought it would be good to visit his own
people, the people of Israel. [24]Moses saw an
Egyptian mistreating one of his people, so he
defended the Israelite and punished the Egyptian by killing him. [25]Moses thought his own
people would understand that God was using
him to save them, but they did not. [26]The next
day when Moses saw two men of Israel fighting, he tried to make peace between them. He
said, 'Men, you are brothers. Why are you
hurting each other?' [27]The man who was hurting the other pushed Moses away and said,
'Who made you our ruler and judge? [28]Are
you going to kill me as you killed the Egyptian
yesterday?'[n] [29]When Moses heard him say this,
he left Egypt and went to live in the land of
Midian where he was a stranger. While Moses
lived in Midian, he had two sons.

[30]"Forty years later an angel appeared to
Moses in the flames of a burning bush as he
was in the desert near Mount Sinai. [31]When
Moses saw this, he was amazed and went near
to look closer. Moses heard the Lord's voice
say, [32]'I am the God of your ancestors, the God
of Abraham, Isaac, and Jacob.'[n] Moses began
to shake with fear and was afraid to look.
[33]The Lord said to him, 'Take off your sandals,
because you are standing on holy ground. [34]I

7:6-7 'Your descendants . . . place.' Quotation from Genesis 15:13–14 and Exodus 3:12. **7:8 twelve ancestors** Important ancestors of the people of Israel; the leaders of the twelve tribes of Israel. **7:27-28 'Who . . . yesterday?'** Quotation from Exodus 2:14. **7:32 'I am . . . Jacob.'** Quotation from Exodus 3:6.

have seen the troubles my people have suffered in Egypt. I have heard their cries and
have come down to save them. And now, Moses, I am sending you back to Egypt.'[n]
[35]"This Moses was the same man the two
men of Israel rejected, saying, 'Who made you
a ruler and judge?'[n] Moses is the same man
God sent to be a ruler and savior, with the help
of the angel that Moses saw in the burning
bush. [36]So Moses led the people out of Egypt.
He worked miracles and signs in Egypt, at the
Red Sea, and then in the desert for forty years.
[37]This is the same Moses that said to the people of Israel, 'God will give you a prophet like
me, who is one of your own people.'[n] [38]This is
the Moses who was with the gathering of the
Israelites in the desert. He was with the angel
that spoke to him at Mount Sinai, and he was
with our ancestors. He received commands
from God that give life, and he gave those
commands to us.
[39]"But our ancestors did not want to obey
Moses. They rejected him and wanted to go
back to Egypt. [40]They said to Aaron, 'Make us
gods who will lead us. Moses led us out of
Egypt, but we don't know what has happened
to him.'[n] [41]So the people made an idol that
looked like a calf. Then they brought sacrifices
to it and were proud of what they had made
with their own hands. [42]But God turned
against them and did not try to stop them from
worshiping the sun, moon, and stars. This is
what is written in the book of the prophets:
God says,

'People of Israel, you did not bring me
sacrifices and offerings
while you traveled in the desert for forty
years.
[43]You have carried with you
the tent to worship Molech
and the idols of the star god Rephan
that you made to worship.
So I will send you away beyond Babylon.'

Amos 5:25-27

[44]"The Holy Tent where God spoke to our
ancestors was with them in the desert. God
told Moses how to make this Tent, and he
made it like the plan God showed him. [45]Later,
Joshua led our ancestors to capture the lands
of the other nations. Our people went in, and
God forced the other people out. When our
people went into this new land, they took with
them this same Tent they had received from
their ancestors. They kept it until the time of
David, [46]who pleased God and asked God to
let him build a house for him, the God of Jacob. [47]But Solomon was the one who built the
Temple.
[48]"But the Most High does not live in
houses that people build with their hands. As
the prophet says:

[49]'Heaven is my throne,
and the earth is my footstool.
So do you think you can build a house for
me? says the Lord.
Do I need a place to rest?
[50]Remember, my hand made all these
things!' "

Isaiah 66:1-2

[51]Stephen continued speaking: "You stubborn people! You have not given your hearts
to God, nor will you listen to him! You are always against what the Holy Spirit is trying to
tell you, just as your ancestors were. [52]Your ancestors tried to hurt every prophet who ever
lived. Those prophets said long ago that the
One who is good would come, but your ancestors killed them. And now you have turned
against and killed the One who is good. [53]You
received the law of Moses, which God gave
you through his angels, but you haven't
obeyed it."

STEPHEN IS KILLED

[54]When the leaders heard this, they became
furious. They were so mad they were grinding
their teeth at Stephen. [55]But Stephen was full of
the Holy Spirit. He looked up to heaven and
saw the glory of God and Jesus standing at
God's right side. [56]He said, "Look! I see heaven
open and the Son of Man standing at God's
right side."
[57]Then they shouted loudly and covered
their ears and all ran at Stephen. [58]They took
him out of the city and began to throw stones
at him to kill him. And those who told lies
against Stephen left their coats with a
young man named Saul. [59]While
they were throwing stones,
Stephen prayed, "Lord Jesus,
receive my spirit." [60]He fell on
his knees and cried in a loud
voice, "Lord, do not hold this
sin against them." After Stephen said this, he died.
8 [1]Saul agreed that the killing of Stephen was
good.

DEATH
What does the death of Christians bring? (7:55–59)

7:33-34 'Take . . . Egypt.' Quotation from Exodus 3:5-10. **7:35 'Who . . . judge?'** Quotation from Exodus 2:14. **7:37 'God . . . people.'** Quotation from Deuteronomy 18:15. **7:40 'Make . . . him.'** Quotation from Exodus 32:1.

SOME FOLLOWERS SEE JESUS

[[9]After Jesus rose from the dead early on the
first day of the week, he showed himself first to
Mary Magdalene. One time in the past, he had
forced seven demons out of her. [10]After Mary
saw Jesus, she went and told his followers,
who were very sad and were crying. [11]But
Mary told them that Jesus was alive. She said
that she had seen him, but the followers did
not believe her.

[12]Later, Jesus showed himself to two of his
followers while they were walking in the
country, but he did not look the same as before. [13]These followers went back to the others
and told them what had happened, but again,
the followers did not believe them.

JESUS TALKS TO THE APOSTLES

[14]Later Jesus showed himself to the eleven
apostles while they were eating, and he criticized them because they had no faith. They
were stubborn and refused to believe those
who had seen him after he had risen from the
dead.

[15]Jesus said to his followers, "Go everywhere in the world, and tell the Good News to
everyone. [16]Anyone who believes and is baptized will be saved, but anyone who does not
believe will be punished. [17]And those who
believe will be able to do these things as proof:
They will use my name to force out demons.
They will speak in new languages.[n] [18]They will
pick up snakes and drink poison without being hurt. They will touch the sick, and the sick
will be healed."

[19]After the Lord Jesus said these things to his
followers, he was carried up into heaven, and
he sat at the right side of God. [20]The followers
went everywhere in the world and told the
Good News to people, and the Lord helped
them. The Lord proved that the Good News
they told was true by giving them power to
work miracles.]

WHAT'S IT MEAN?

The followers of Jesus were down to eleven since Judas Iscariot had committed suicide after betraying him. The remaining followers later chose a man named Matthias to replace Judas. Why? Some experts believe the number twelve had a symbolic meaning, perhaps relating to the twelve tribes of Israel.

Mark 16:14

16:17 languages This can also be translated "tongues."

WHAT'S IT MEAN?

Crucifixion usually was not a quick way to die. Unless the person had been severely beaten before being crucified, he could actually survive several days on the cross! One of the most common causes of death among those who were crucified was suffocation. Because of the outstretched position, when the person became too exhausted to raise himself up to breathe, he simply suffocated.

Mark 15:44

that Jesus would have already died, so he called
the army officer who had guarded Jesus and
asked him if Jesus had already died. 45The officer told Pilate that he was dead, so Pilate told
Joseph he could have the body. 46Joseph
bought some linen cloth, took the body down
from the cross, and wrapped it in the linen. He
put the body in a tomb that was cut out of a
wall of rock. Then he rolled a very large stone
to block the entrance of the tomb. 47And Mary
Magdalene and Mary the mother of Joseph saw
the place where Jesus was laid.

JESUS RISES FROM THE DEAD

16
1The day after the Sabbath day, Mary Magdalene, Mary the mother of James, and Salome
bought some sweet-smelling spices to put on
Jesus' body. 2Very early on that day, the first
day of the week, soon after sunrise, the women
were on their way to the tomb. 3They said to
each other, "Who will roll away for us the
stone that covers the entrance of the tomb?"
4Then the women looked and saw that the
stone had already been rolled away, even
though it was very large. 5The women entered
the tomb and saw a young man wearing a
white robe and sitting on the right side, and
they were afraid.
6But the man said, "Don't be afraid. You are
looking for Jesus from Nazareth, who has been
crucified. He has risen from the dead; he is not
here. Look, here is the place they laid him.
7Now go and tell his followers and Peter, 'Jesus
is going into Galilee ahead of you, and you will
see him there as he told you before.' "
8The women were confused and shaking
with fear, so they left the tomb and ran away.
They did not tell anyone about what happened, because they were afraid.

On the Edge

Anyone who believes and is baptized will be saved, but anyone who does not believe will be punished (Mark 16:16).

God designed the world so that there would be consequences for sin. He also required that a payment be made for sin. He knew we could never pay for all our sins. Without payment, the eternal consequence is condemnation and separation from God in hell—forever. His heart was broken by that thought. The only way to save us was to send someone to be perfect, and to die the death that *we* deserved. To give us a way out of eternal damnation, he sent his perfect Son, Jesus.

Jesus lived a sinless life and then died as a sacrifice for our sins. God said that Jesus' death was enough to pay for everyone's sin. Nothing else needed to be done. Nothing else could be done. The payment has been made for all of your sin.

To receive the benefit of Jesus' death, you have to believe in him. Deciding to believe that Jesus Christ died for you is called "being saved." Believing in him saves you from being condemned and separated from God forever. Your friends may want you to be saved because they can't imagine heaven without you. Your family wants you to be saved because they don't ever want to leave you. But the Lord, more than anything, wants you to be saved because he created you, and he loves you more than you can understand. He doesn't want you to be judged and spend eternity apart from him in hell.

There are all kinds of great reasons to be saved, but the best one has to do with being with God forever. Heaven is reserved for those who decide to believe that Jesus Christ is who he said he was. You are free to choose. God will not force you to love him. Forced love is not true love. But today, if you hear his voice and know these things are true, do not harden your heart. Run to him and be saved!

SEE FOR YOURSELF:
Matt. 3:16;
John 3:16–17; 10:8–9;
Acts 3:19–20;
Rom. 6:22–23

Verses 9-20 are not included in two of the best and oldest Greek manuscripts of Mark.

vision in which a man named Ananias comes
to him and lays his hands on him. Then he is
able to see again."
13But Ananias answered, "Lord, many people have told me about this man and the terrible things he did to your holy people in
Jerusalem. 14Now he has come here to Damascus, and the leading priests have given him the
power to arrest everyone who worships you."
15But the Lord said to Ananias, "Go! I have
chosen Saul for an important work. He must
tell about me to those who are not Jews, to
kings, and to the people of Israel. 16I will show
him how much he must suffer for my name."
17So Ananias went to the house of Judas. He
laid his hands on Saul and said, "Brother Saul,
the Lord Jesus sent me. He is the one you saw
on the road on your way here. He sent me so
that you can see again and be filled with the
Holy Spirit." 18Immediately, something that
looked like fish scales fell from Saul's eyes, and
he was able to see again! Then Saul got up and
was baptized. 19After he ate some food, his
strength returned.

SAUL PREACHES IN DAMASCUS

Saul stayed with the followers of Jesus in
Damascus for a few days. 20Soon he began to
preach about Jesus in the synagogues, saying,
"Jesus is the Son of God."
21All the people who heard him were
amazed. They said, "This is the man who was
in Jerusalem trying to destroy those who trust
in this name! He came here to arrest the followers of Jesus and take them back to the leading priests."
22But Saul grew more powerful. His proofs
that Jesus is the Christ were so strong that his
own people in Damascus could not argue with
him.
23After many days, they made plans to kill
Saul. 24They were watching the city gates day
and night, but Saul learned about their plan.
25One night some followers of Saul helped him
leave the city by lowering him in a basket
through an opening in the city wall.

SAUL PREACHES IN JERUSALEM

26When Saul went to Jerusalem, he tried to
join the group of followers, but they were all
afraid of him. They did not believe he was
really a follower. 27But Barnabas accepted Saul
and took him to the apostles. Barnabas explained to them that Saul had seen the Lord on
the road and the Lord had spoken to Saul.
Then he told them how boldly Saul had
preached in the name of Jesus in Damascus.
28And so Saul stayed with the followers, going everywhere in Jerusalem, preaching boldly
in the name of the Lord. 29He would often talk
and argue with the Jewish people who spoke
Greek, but they were trying to kill him. 30When
the followers learned about this, they took Saul
to Caesarea and from there sent him to Tarsus.
31The church everywhere in Judea,
Galilee, and Samaria had
a time of peace and be-
came stronger. Respect-
ing the Lord by the way they
lived, and being encouraged
by the Holy Spirit, the group
of believers continued to grow.

ENCOURAGEMENT

Who is our source of encouragement? (9:31)

PETER HEALS AENEAS

32As Peter was traveling through all the area,
he visited God's people who lived in Lydda.
33There he met a man named Aeneas, who was
paralyzed and had not been able to leave his
bed for the past eight years. 34Peter said to him,
"Aeneas, Jesus Christ heals you. Stand up and
make your bed." Aeneas stood up immediately.
35All the people living in Lydda and on the
Plain of Sharon saw him and turned to the
Lord.

PETER HEALS TABITHA

36In the city of Joppa there was a follower
named Tabitha (whose Greek name was Dor-
cas). She was always doing good deeds and
kind acts. 37While Peter was in Lydda, Tabitha
became sick and died. Her body was washed
and put in a room upstairs. 38Since Lydda is
near Joppa and the followers in Joppa heard
that Peter was in Lydda, they sent two messengers to Peter. They begged him, "Hurry, please
come to us!" 39So Peter got ready and went
with them. When he arrived, they took him to
the upstairs room where all the widows stood

WHAT'S IT MEAN?

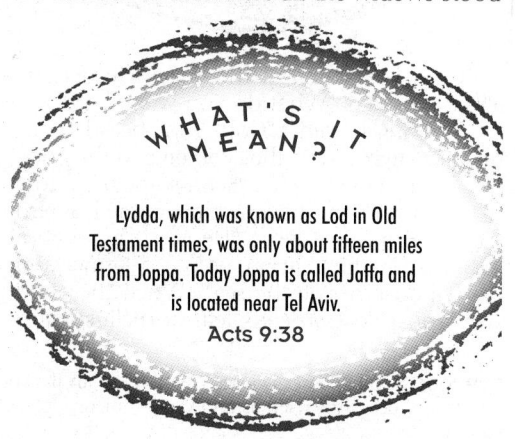

Lydda, which was known as Lod in Old Testament times, was only about fifteen miles from Joppa. Today Joppa is called Jaffa and is located near Tel Aviv.

Acts 9:38

around Peter, crying. They showed him the
shirts and coats Tabitha had made when she
was still alive. [40]Peter sent everyone out of the
room and kneeled and prayed. Then he turned
to the body and said, "Tabitha, stand up." She
opened her eyes, and when she saw Peter, she
sat up. [41]He gave her his hand and helped her
up. Then he called the saints and the widows
into the room and showed them that Tabitha
was alive. [42]People everywhere in Joppa
learned about this, and many believed in the
Lord. [43]Peter stayed in Joppa for many days
with a man named Simon who was a tanner.

PETER TEACHES CORNELIUS

10 [1]At Caesarea there was a man named Cornelius, an officer in the Italian group of the Roman army. [2]Cornelius was a religious man. He
and all the other people who lived in his house
worshiped the true God. He gave much of his
money to the poor and prayed to God often.
[3]One afternoon about three o'clock, Cornelius
clearly saw a vision. An angel of God came to
him and said, "Cornelius!"

WHAT'S IT MEAN?

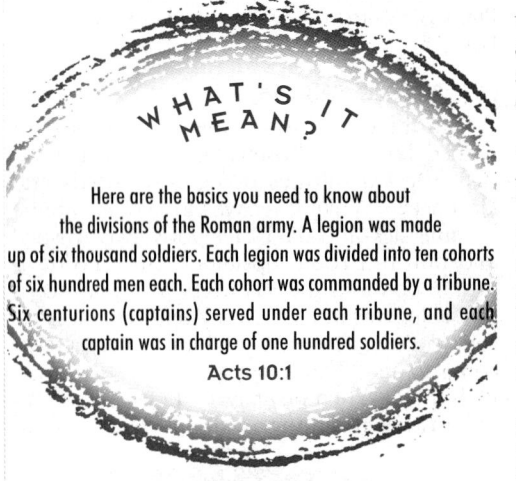

Here are the basics you need to know about the divisions of the Roman army. A legion was made up of six thousand soldiers. Each legion was divided into ten cohorts of six hundred men each. Each cohort was commanded by a tribune. Six centurions (captains) served under each tribune, and each captain was in charge of one hundred soldiers.

Acts 10:1

[4]Cornelius stared at the angel. He became
afraid and said, "What do you want, Lord?"
The angel said, "God has heard your
prayers. He has seen that you give to the poor,
and he remembers you. [5]Send some men now
to Joppa to bring back a man named Simon
who is also called Peter. [6]He is staying with a
man, also named Simon, who is a tanner and
has a house beside the sea." [7]When the angel
who spoke to Cornelius left, Cornelius called
two of his servants and a soldier, a religious
man who worked for him. [8]Cornelius explained everything to them and sent them to
Joppa.
[9]About noon the next day as they came
near Joppa, Peter was going up to the roof[n] to
pray. [10]He was hungry and wanted to eat, but
while the food was being prepared, he had a
vision. [11]He saw heaven opened and something coming down that looked like a big sheet
being lowered to earth by its four corners. [12]In
it were all kinds of animals, reptiles, and birds.
[13]Then a voice said to Peter, "Get up, Peter; kill
and eat."
[14]But Peter said, "No, Lord! I have never eat-
en food that is unholy or unclean."
[15]But the voice said to him again, "God has
made these things clean so don't call them 'unholy'!" [16]This happened three times, and at
once the sheet was taken back to heaven.
[17]While Peter was wondering what this vision meant, the men Cornelius sent had found
Simon's house and were standing at the gate.
[18]They asked, "Is Simon Peter staying here?"
[19]While Peter was still thinking about the
vision, the Spirit said to him, "Listen, three men
are looking for you. [20]Get up and go downstairs. Go with them without doubting, because I have sent them to you."
[21]So Peter went down to the men and said,
"I am the one you are looking for. Why did
you come here?"
[22]They said, "A holy angel spoke to Cornelius, an army officer and a good man; he worships God. All the people respect him. The
angel told Cornelius to ask you to come to his
house so that he can hear what you have to
say." [23]So Peter asked the men to come in and
spend the night.
The next day Peter got ready and went with
them, and some of the followers from Joppa
joined him. [24]On the following day they came
to Caesarea. Cornelius was waiting for them
and had called together his relatives and close
friends. [25]When Peter entered, Cornelius met
him, fell at his feet, and worshiped him. [26]But
Peter helped him up, saying, "Stand up. I too
am only a human." [27]As he talked with Cornelius, Peter went inside where he saw many
people gathered. [28]He said, "You people understand that it is against our law for Jewish people to associate with or visit anyone who is not
Jewish. But God has shown me that I should

10:9 roof In Bible times houses were built with flat roofs. The roof was used for drying things such as flax and fruit. And it was used as an extra room, as a place for worship, and as a cool place to sleep in the summer.

not call any person 'unholy' or 'unclean.'
29That is why I did not argue when I was asked
to come here. Now, please tell me why you
sent for me."
30Cornelius said, "Four days ago, I was
praying in my house at this same time—three
o'clock in the afternoon. Suddenly, there was a
man standing before me wearing shining
clothes. 31He said, 'Cornelius, God has heard
your prayer and has seen that you give to the
poor and remembers you. 32So send some men
to Joppa and ask Simon Peter to come. Peter is
staying in the house of a man, also named
Simon, who is a tanner and has a house beside
the sea.' 33So I sent for you immediately, and it
was very good of you to come. Now we are all
here before God to hear everything the Lord
has commanded you to tell us."
34Peter began to speak: "I really understand
now that to God every person is the same. 35In
every country God accepts anyone who worships him and does what is
right. 36You know the message that God has sent
to the people of Israel is
the Good News that
peace has come through
Jesus Christ. Jesus is the
Lord of all people! 37You
know what has hap-
pened all over Judea,
beginning in Galilee after
John[n] preached to the
people about baptism. 38You
know about Jesus from Naza-
reth, that God gave him the Holy Spirit and
power. You know how Jesus went everywhere
doing good and healing those who were ruled
by the devil, because God was with him. 39We
saw what Jesus did in Judea and in Jerusalem,
but the Jews in Jerusalem killed him by hanging him on a cross. 40Yet, on the third day, God
raised Jesus to life and caused him to be seen,
41not by all the people, but only by the witnesses God had already chosen. And we are
those witnesses who ate and drank with him
after he was raised from the dead. 42He told us
to preach to the people and to tell them that he
is the one whom God chose to be the judge of
the living and the dead. 43All the prophets say
it is true that all who believe in Jesus will be
forgiven of their sins through Jesus' name."
44While Peter was still saying this, the Holy
Spirit came down on all those who were listening. 45The Jewish believers who came with Peter were amazed that the gift of the Holy Spirit
had been given even to the nations. 46These
believers heard them speaking in different languages[n] and praising God. Then Peter said,
47"Can anyone keep these people from being
baptized with water? They have received the
Holy Spirit just as we did!" 48So Peter ordered
that they be baptized in the name of Jesus
Christ. Then they asked Peter to stay with them
for a few days.

> "I really understand now that to God every person is the same. In every country God accepts anyone who worships him and does what is right."
> (Acts 10:34b–35)

PETER RETURNS TO JERUSALEM

11 1The apostles and the believers in Judea
heard that some who were not Jewish had accepted God's teaching too. 2But when Peter
came to Jerusalem, some people argued with
him. 3They said, "You went into the homes of
people who are not circumcised and ate with
them!"
4So Peter explained the whole story to them.
5He said, "I was in the city of
Joppa, and while I was
praying, I had a vision. I
saw something that looked
like a big sheet being lowered from heaven by its
four corners. It came very
close to me. 6I looked inside it and saw animals,
wild beasts, reptiles, and
birds. 7I heard a voice say
to me, 'Get up, Peter. Kill
and eat.' 8But I said, 'No, Lord!
I have never eaten anything
that is unholy or unclean.' 9But the voice
from heaven spoke again, 'God has made these
things clean, so don't call them unholy.' 10This
happened three times. Then the whole thing
was taken back to heaven. 11Right then three
men who were sent to me from Caesarea came
to the house where I was staying. 12The Spirit
told me to go with them without doubting.
These six believers here also went with me, and
we entered the house of Cornelius. 13He told us
about the angel he saw standing in his house.
The angel said to him, 'Send some men to Joppa and invite Simon Peter to come. 14By the
words he will say to you, you and all your
family will be saved.' 15When I began my
speech, the Holy Spirit came on them just as he
came on us at the beginning. 16Then I remembered the words of the Lord. He said, 'John
baptized with water, but you will be baptized

10:37 John John the Baptist, who preached to people about Christ's coming (Luke 3).
10:46 languages This can also be translated "tongues."

with the Holy Spirit.' [17]Since God gave them the
same gift he gave us who believed in the Lord
Jesus Christ, how could I stop the work of
God?"

[18]When the believers heard this, they
stopped arguing. They praised God and said,
"So God is allowing even other nations to turn
to him and live."

THE GOOD NEWS COMES TO ANTIOCH

[19]Many of the believers were scattered
when they were persecuted after Stephen was
killed. Some of them went as far as Phoenicia,
Cyprus, and Antioch telling the message to
others, but only to Jews. [20]Some of these believers were people from Cyprus and Cyrene.
When they came to Antioch, they spoke also
to Greeks, telling them the Good News about
the Lord Jesus. [21]The Lord was helping the believers, and a large group of people believed
and turned to the Lord.

[22]The church in Jerusalem heard about all
of this, so they sent Barnabas to Antioch.
[23-24]Barnabas was a good man, full of the Holy
Spirit and full of faith. When he reached Antioch and saw how God had blessed the people,
he was glad. He encouraged all the believers in
Antioch always to obey the Lord with all their
hearts, and many people became followers of
the Lord.

[25]Then Barnabas went to the city of Tarsus
to look for Saul, [26]and when he found Saul, he
brought him to Antioch. For a whole year Saul
and Barnabas met with the church and taught
many people there. In Antioch the followers
were called Christians for the first time.

WHAT'S IT MEAN?

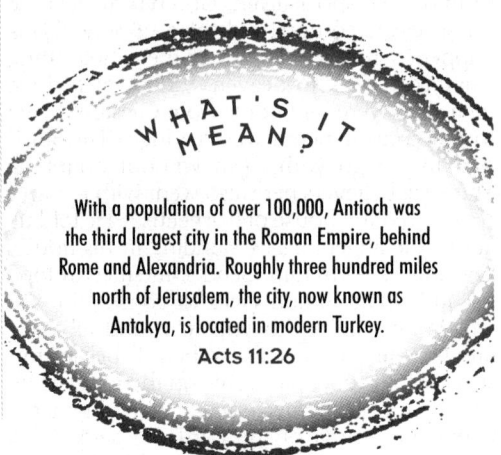

With a population of over 100,000, Antioch was the third largest city in the Roman Empire, behind Rome and Alexandria. Roughly three hundred miles north of Jerusalem, the city, now known as Antakya, is located in modern Turkey.

Acts 11:26

[27]About that time some prophets came
from Jerusalem to Antioch. [28]One of them,
named Agabus, stood up and spoke with the

On the Edge

And when he [Barnabas] had found Saul, he brought him to Antioch. For a whole year Saul and Barnabas met with the church and taught many people there. In Antioch the followers were called Christians for the first time (Acts 11:26).

After Jesus returned to heaven, the apostless and other followers became known as Christians. It literally means "belonging to the party of Jesus." At a restaurant, you may wait with a group until the host calls "table for the Smith party." Everyone who is with your group gets up to be seated. Each one of you is different, but you all belong together. You are recognized as a distinct group. Your party is separate from all the other people in the restaurant. In Antioch, the followers of Christ had become recognized as a separate group of people who belonged together. Followers today are still called Christians, meaning that we belong with all the others who believe in Christ. It is a high privilege to carry the banner of Christ along with those who have gone before us.

SEE FOR YOURSELF:
Acts 26:28;
1 Pet. 4:16

help of the Holy Spirit. He said, "A very hard
time is coming to the whole world. There will
be no food to eat." (This happened when Claudius ruled.) [29]The believers all decided to help
the followers who lived in Judea, as much as
each one could. [30]They gathered the money
and gave it to Barnabas and Saul, who brought
it to the elders in Judea.

HEROD AGRIPPA HURTS THE CHURCH

12
[1]During that same time King Herod began to
mistreat some who belonged to the church.
[2]He ordered James, the brother of John, to be
killed by the sword. [3]Herod saw that some of
the people liked this, so he decided to arrest
Peter, too. (This happened during the time of
the Feast of Unleavened Bread.)

[4]After Herod arrested Peter, he put him in
jail and handed him over to be guarded by
sixteen soldiers. Herod planned to bring Peter
before the people for trial after the Passover

Feast. 5So Peter was kept in jail, but the church
prayed earnestly to God for him.

PETER LEAVES THE JAIL

6The night before Herod was to bring him
to trial, Peter was sleeping between two soldiers, bound with two chains. Other soldiers
were guarding the door of the jail. 7Suddenly,
an angel of the Lord stood there, and a light
shined in the cell. The angel struck Peter on the
side and woke him up. "Hurry! Get up!" the
angel said. And the chains fell off Peter's hands.
8Then the angel told him, "Get dressed and put
on your sandals." And Peter did. Then the angel
said, "Put on your coat and follow me." 9So Peter followed him out, but he did not know if
what the angel was doing was real; he thought
he might be seeing a vision. 10They went past
the first and second guards and came to the
iron gate that separated them from the city.
The gate opened by itself for them, and they
went through it. When they had walked down
one street, the angel suddenly left him.
11Then Peter realized what had happened.
He thought, "Now I know that the Lord really
sent his angel to me. He rescued me from Herod and from all the things the people thought
would happen."
12When he considered this, he went to the
home of Mary, the mother of John Mark.
Many people were gathered there, praying.
13Peter knocked on the outside door, and a servant girl named Rhoda came to answer it.
14When she recognized Peter's voice, she was so
happy she forgot to open the door. Instead, she
ran inside and told the group, "Peter is at the
door!"
15They said to her, "You are crazy!" But she
kept on saying it was true, so they said, "It
must be Peter's angel."
16Peter continued to knock, and when they
opened the door, they saw him and were
amazed. 17Peter made a sign with his hand to
tell them to be quiet. He explained how the
Lord led him out of the jail, and he said, "Tell
James and the other believers what happened."
Then he left to go to another place.
18The next day the soldiers were very upset
and wondered what had happened to Peter.
19Herod looked everywhere for him but could
not find him. So he questioned the guards and
ordered that they be killed.

THE DEATH OF HEROD AGRIPPA

Later Herod moved from Judea and went to
the city of Caesarea, where he stayed. 20Herod
was very angry with the people of Tyre and
Sidon, but the people of those cities all came in
a group to him. After convincing Blastus, the
king's personal servant, to be on their side,
they asked Herod for peace, because their
country got its food from his country.
21On a chosen day Herod put on his royal
robes, sat on his throne, and made a speech to
the people. 22They shouted, "This is the voice of
a god, not a human!" 23Because Herod did not
give the glory to God, an angel of the Lord
immediately caused him to become sick, and
he was eaten by worms and died.
24God's message continued to spread and
reach people.
25After Barnabas and Saul finished their
task in Jerusalem, they returned to Antioch,
taking John Mark with them.

BARNABAS AND SAUL ARE CHOSEN

13

1In the church at Antioch there were these
prophets and teachers: Barnabas, Simeon (also
called Niger), Lucius (from the city of Cyrene),
Manaen (who had grown up with Herod, the
ruler), and Saul. 2They were all worshiping the
Lord and giving up eating for a certain time.[n]
During this time the Holy Spirit said to them,
"Set apart for me Barnabas and Saul to do a
special work for which I have chosen them."
3So after they gave up eating and prayed,
they laid their hands on[n] Barnabas and Saul
and sent them out.

BARNABAS AND SAUL IN CYPRUS

4Barnabas and Saul, sent out by the Holy
Spirit, went to the city of Seleucia. From there
they sailed to the island of Cyprus. 5When they
came to Salamis, they preached the Good
News of God in the synagogues. John Mark
was with them to help.
6They went across the whole island to Pa-
phos where they met a magician named Bar-
Jesus. He was a false prophet 7who always
stayed close to Sergius Paulus, the governor
and a smart man. He asked Barnabas and Saul
to come to him, because he wanted to hear the
message of God. 8But Elymas, the magician,
was against them. (Elymas is the name for Bar-
Jesus in the Greek language.) He tried to stop

13:2 giving up . . . time This is called "fasting." The people would give up eating for a special time of prayer and worship to God. It was also done sometimes to show sadness and disappointment. **13:3 laid their hands on** The laying on of hands had many purposes, including the giving of a blessing, power, or authority.

On the Edge

They were all worshiping the Lord and giving up eating for a certain time. During this time the Holy Spirit said to them, "Set apart for me Barnabas and Saul to do a special work for which I have chosen them" (Acts 13:2).

In the Book of Acts, we see the followers looking to the Lord for instruction and guidance. They needed direction about how to spread the message of Christ. In this passage, the Holy Spirit speaks to them about sending out Barnabas and Saul. The Lord still gives clear instruction and direction to believers. The Holy Spirit still guides us through the will of God. The church in Acts worshiped, fasted, and waited for God to give instruction. They actively sought the Lord about what to do. Do you actively seek the Lord about the direction of your life and activities? We must follow the example of the apostles and pursue him. We hear from God when we listen for him to speak. If you want God to speak to you, then spend time with him, worshiping, fasting, and praying. If you will be faithful to listen, then he will speak.

SEE FOR YOURSELF:
Job 37:4–5;
Ezek. 1:25–28;
Matt. 10:20;
John 10:27;
Rev. 3:20

the governor from believing in Jesus. [9]But Saul,
who was also called Paul, was filled with the
Holy Spirit. He looked straight at Elymas [10]and
said, "You son of the devil! You are an enemy
of everything that is right! You are full of evil
tricks and lies, always trying to change the
Lord's truths into lies. [11]Now the Lord will
touch you, and you will be blind. For a time
you will not be able to see anything—not even
the light from the sun."
Then everything became dark for Elymas,
and he walked around, trying to find someone
to lead him by the hand. [12]When the governor
saw this, he believed because he was amazed
at the teaching about the Lord.

WHAT'S IT MEAN?

If you're confused about the apostle's two names, remember this: Saul was his Jewish name, and Paul was the Greek translation of it. When the apostle was in his Jewish surroundings, he used the name Saul. When he was ministering to the Gentiles, he used the name Paul. Using the Greek version of his name would have helped Paul identify with the people he was teaching about Jesus.

Acts 13:9

PAUL AND BARNABAS LEAVE CYPRUS

[13]Paul and those with him sailed from Pa-
phos and came to Perga, in Pamphylia. There
John Mark left them to return to Jerusalem.
[14]They continued their trip from Perga and
went to Antioch, a city in Pisidia. On the Sabbath day they went into the synagogue and sat
down. [15]After the law of Moses and the writings of the prophets were read, the leaders of
the synagogue sent a message to Paul and Barnabas: "Brothers, if you have any message that
will encourage the people, please speak."
[16]Paul stood up, raised his hand, and said,
"You Israelites and you who worship God,
please listen! [17]The God of the Israelites chose
our ancestors. He made the people great during the time they lived in Egypt, and he
brought them out of that country with great
power. [18]And he was patient with them for
forty years in the desert. [19]God destroyed
seven nations in the land of Canaan and gave
the land to his people. [20]All this happened in
about four hundred fifty years.
"After this, God gave them judges until the
time of Samuel the prophet. [21]Then the people
asked for a king, so God gave them Saul son of
Kish. Saul was from the tribe of Benjamin and
was king for forty years. [22]After God took him
away, God made David their king. God said
about him: 'I have found in David son of Jesse
the kind of man I want. He will do all I want
him to do.' [23]So God has brought Jesus, one of
David's descendants, to Israel to be its Savior,
as he promised. [24]Before Jesus came, John[n]
preached to all the people of Israel about a

13:24 John John the Baptist, who preached to people about Christ's coming (Luke 3).

baptism of changed hearts and lives. 25When
he was finishing his work, he said, 'Who
do you think I am? I am not the Christ. He is
coming later, and I am not worthy to untie his
sandals.'
26"Brothers, sons of the family of Abraham,
and others who worship God, listen! The news
about this salvation has been sent to us.
27Those who live in Jerusalem and their leaders
did not realize that Jesus was the Savior. They
did not understand the words
that the prophets wrote,
which are read every Sab-
bath day. But they made
them come true when they
said Jesus was guilty.
28They could not find any
real reason for Jesus to be
put to death, but they
asked Pilate to have him
killed. 29When they had done
to him all that the Scriptures
had said, they took him down
from the cross and laid him in a tomb. 30But
God raised him up from the dead! 31After
this, for many days, those who had gone with
Jesus from Galilee to Jerusalem saw him. They
are now his witnesses to the people. 32We tell
you the Good News about the promise God
made to our ancestors. 33God has made this
promise come true for us, his children, by raising Jesus from the dead. We read about this also
in Psalm 2:

> 'You are my Son.
> Today I have become your Father.'
>
> *Psalm 2:7*

34God raised Jesus from the dead, and he will
never go back to the grave and become dust.
So God said:

> 'I will give you the holy and sure blessings
> that I promised to David.' *Isaiah 55:3*

35But in another place God says:

> 'You will not let your Holy One rot.'
>
> *Psalm 16:10*

36David did God's will during his lifetime.
Then he died and was buried beside his ancestors, and his body did
rot in the grave. 37But the
One God raised from
the dead did not rot in the
grave. 38-39Brothers, understand what we are telling you:
You can have forgiveness of
your sins through Jesus. The law
of Moses could not free you from your sins.
But through Jesus everyone who believes is free
from all sins. 40Be careful! Don't let what the
prophets said happen to you:

> 41'Listen, you people who doubt!
> You can wonder, and then die.
> I will do something in your lifetime
> that you won't believe even when you
> are told about it!' " *Habakkuk 1:5*

42While Paul and Barnabas were leaving the
synagogue, the people asked them to tell them
more about these things on the
next Sabbath. 43When the
meeting was over, many
people with those who had
changed to worship God
followed Paul and Barna-
bas from that place. Paul
and Barnabas were per-
suading them to continue
trusting in God's grace.
44On the next Sabbath
day, almost everyone in the
city came to hear the word of
the Lord. 45Seeing the crowd, the
Jewish people became very jealous and said
insulting things and argued against what Paul
said. 46But Paul and Barnabas spoke very
boldly, saying, "We must speak the message of
God to you first. But you refuse to listen. You
are judging yourselves not worthy of having
eternal life! So we will now go to the people of
other nations. 47This is what the Lord told us to
do, saying:

> 'I have made you a light for the nations;
> you will show people all over the world
> the way to be saved.' "
>
> *Isaiah 49:6*

48When those who were not Jewish heard
Paul say this, they were happy and gave honor
to the message of the Lord. And the people
who were chosen to have life forever believed
the message.
49So the message of the Lord was spreading
through the whole country. 50But the Jewish
people stirred up some of the important religious women and the leaders of the city. They
started trouble against Paul and Barnabas and
forced them out of their area. 51So Paul and
Barnabas shook the dust off their feet[n] and
went to Iconium. 52But the followers were filled
with joy and the Holy Spirit.

"Brothers, sons of the family of Abraham, and others who worship God, listen! The news about this salvation has been sent to us." (Acts 13:26)

FORGIVENESS
Who can receive forgiveness? (13:38–39)

14

PAUL AND BARNABAS IN ICONIUM

1In Iconium, Paul and Barnabas went as
usual to the synagogue. They spoke so well

13:51 shook . . . feet A warning. It showed that they had rejected these people.

that a great many Jews and Greeks believed. 2But some people who did not believe excited the others and turned them against the believers. 3Paul and Barnabas stayed in Iconium a long time and spoke bravely for the Lord. He showed that their message about his grace was true by giving them the power to work miracles and signs. 4But the city was divided. Some of the people agreed with the Jews, and others believed the apostles.

5Some who were not Jews, some Jews, and some of their rulers wanted to mistreat Paul and Barnabas and to stone them to death. 6When Paul and Barnabas learned about this, they ran away to Lystra and Derbe, cities in Lycaonia, and to the areas around those cities. 7They announced the Good News there, too.

PAUL IN LYSTRA AND DERBE

8In Lystra there sat a man who had been born crippled; he had never walked. 9As this man was listening to Paul speak, Paul looked straight at him and saw that he believed God could heal him. 10So he cried out, "Stand up on your feet!" The man jumped up and began walking around. 11When the crowds saw what Paul did, they shouted in the Lycaonian language, "The gods have become like humans and have come down to us!" 12Then the people began to call Barnabas "Zeus"[n] and Paul "Hermes,"[n] because he was the main speaker. 13The priest in the temple of Zeus, which was near the city, brought some bulls and flowers to the city gates. He and the people wanted to offer a sacrifice to Paul and Barnabas. 14But when the apostles, Barnabas and Paul, heard about it, they tore their clothes. They ran in among the people, shouting, 15"Friends, why are you doing these things? We are only human beings like you. We are bringing you the Good News and are telling you to turn away from these worthless things and turn to the living God. He is the One who made the sky, the earth, the sea, and everything in them. 16In the past, God let all the nations do what they wanted. 17Yet he proved he is real by showing kindness, by giving you rain from heaven and crops at the right times, by giving you food and filling your hearts with joy." 18Even with these words, they were barely able to keep the crowd from offering sacrifices to them.

19Then some evil people came from Antioch and Iconium and persuaded the people to turn against Paul. So they threw stones at him and dragged him out of town, thinking they had killed him. 20But the followers gathered around him, and he got up and went back into the town. The next day he and Barnabas left and went to the city of Derbe.

WHAT'S IT MEAN?

If you're not up on your Greek mythology, you should know that Zeus was believed to be the father of gods and the ruler of heaven. Hermes, the Greek god of science and business, was thought to serve as the messenger of the gods.

Acts 14:12

WHAT'S IT MEAN?

What do Derbe, Iconium, Lystra, and Antioch have in common? They're all found in modern Turkey.

Acts 14:20–21

THE RETURN TO ANTIOCH IN SYRIA

21Paul and Barnabas told the Good News in Derbe, and many became followers. Paul and Barnabas returned to Lystra, Iconium, and Antioch, 22making the followers of Jesus stronger and helping them stay in the faith. They said, "We must suffer many things to enter God's kingdom." 23They chose elders for each church, by praying and giving up eating for a certain time.[n] These elders had trusted the Lord, so Paul and Barnabas put them in the Lord's care.

14:12 "Zeus" The Greeks believed in many false gods, of whom Zeus was most important.
14:12 "Hermes" The Greeks believed he was a messenger for the other gods. **14:23 giving . . . time** This is called "fasting." The people would give up eating for a special time of prayer and worship to God. It was also done sometimes to show sadness and disappointment.

[24]Then they went through Pisidia and came
to Pamphylia. [25]When they had preached the
message in Perga, they went down to Attalia.
[26]And from there they sailed away to Antioch
where the believers had put them into God's
care and had sent them out to do this work.
Now they had finished.
[27]When they arrived in Antioch, Paul and
Barnabas gathered the church together. They
told the church all about what God had done
with them and how God had made it possible
for those who were not Jewish to believe.
[28]And they stayed there a long time with the
followers.

THE MEETING AT JERUSALEM

15 [1]Then some people came to Antioch from
Judea and began teaching the non-Jewish believers: "You cannot be saved if you are not
circumcised as Moses taught us." [2]Paul and
Barnabas were against this teaching and argued with them about it. So the church decided to send Paul, Barnabas, and some others to
Jerusalem where they could talk more about
this with the apostles and elders.

WHAT'S IT MEAN?

Circumcision was an important ritual in Jewish tradition. The removal of the foreskin from the male sex organ was a physical sign that the Jews belonged to God. Any male who desired to convert to Judaism had to be circumcised.

Acts 15:5

[3]The church helped them leave on the trip,
and they went through the countries of Phoenicia and Samaria, telling all about how the
other nations had turned to God. This made all
the believers very happy. [4]When they arrived
in Jerusalem, they were welcomed by the
apostles, the elders, and the church. Paul, Barnabas, and the others told about everything
God had done with them. [5]But some of the
believers who belonged to the Pharisee group
came forward and said, "The non-Jewish believers must be circumcised. They must be told
to obey the law of Moses."
[6]The apostles and the elders gathered to
consider this problem. [7]After a long debate, Peter stood up and said to them, "Brothers, you
know that in the early days God chose me
from among you to preach the Good News to
the nations. They heard the Good News from
me, and they believed. [8]God, who knows the
thoughts of everyone, accepted them. He
showed this to us by giving them the Holy
Spirit, just as he did to us. [9]To God, those people are not different from us. When they believed, he made their hearts pure. [10]So now
why are you testing God by putting a heavy
load around the necks of the non-Jewish believers? It is a load that neither we nor our ancestors were able to carry. [11]But we believe that
we and they too will be saved by the grace of
the Lord Jesus."
[12]Then the whole group became quiet. They
listened to Paul and Barnabas tell about all the
miracles and signs that God did through them
among the people. [13]After they finished speaking, James said, "Brothers, listen to me. [14]Simon
has told us how God showed his love for
those people. For the first time he is accepting
from among them a people to be his own.
[15]The words of the prophets agree with this
too:

[16]'After these things I will return.
The kingdom of David is like a fallen
tent.
But I will rebuild its ruins,
and I will set it up.
[17]Then those people who are left alive may
ask the Lord for help,
and the other nations that belong to me,
says the Lord,
who will make it happen.
[18]And these things have been known for a
long time.' *Amos 9:11-12*

[19]"So I think we should not bother the other

WHAT'S IT MEAN?

Eating rare meat was a no-no, according to the law that God gave to Moses. Drinking blood or eating meat before the blood had been drained was forbidden. Why, you ask? Because blood, like sexual orgies, was associated with the worship of idols and pagan gods.

Acts 15:20

people who are turning to God. [20]Instead, we should write a letter to them telling them these things: Stay away from food that has been offered to idols (which makes it unclean), any kind of sexual sin, eating animals that have been strangled, and blood. [21]They should do these things, because for a long time in every city the law of Moses has been taught. And it is still read in the synagogue every Sabbath day."

LETTER TO NON-JEWISH BELIEVERS

[22]The apostles, the elders, and the whole church decided to send some of their men with Paul and Barnabas to Antioch. They chose Judas Barsabbas and Silas, who were respected by the believers. [23]They sent the following letter with them:

> From the apostles and elders, your brothers.
>
> To all the non-Jewish believers in Antioch, Syria, and Cilicia:
>
> Greetings!
>
> [24]We have heard that some of our group have come to you and said things that trouble and upset you. But we did not tell them to do this. [25]We have all agreed to choose some messengers and send them to you with our dear friends Barnabas and Paul— [26]people who have given their lives to serve our Lord Jesus Christ. [27]So we are sending Judas and Silas, who will tell you the same things. [28]It has pleased the Holy Spirit that you should not have a heavy load to carry, and we agree. You need to do only these things: [29]Stay away from any food that has been offered to idols, eating any animals that have been strangled, and blood, and any kind of sexual sin. If you stay away from these things, you will do well.
>
> Good-bye.

[30]So they left Jerusalem and went to Antioch where they gathered the church and gave them the letter. [31]When they read it, they were very happy because of the encouraging message. [32]Judas and Silas, who were also prophets, said many things to encourage the believers and make them stronger. [33]After some time Judas and Silas were sent off in peace by the believers, and they went back to those who had sent them. [34][n]

[35]But Paul and Barnabas stayed in Antioch and, along with many others, preached the Good News and taught the people the message of the Lord.

PAUL AND BARNABAS SEPARATE

[36]After some time, Paul said to Barnabas, "We should go back to all those towns where we preached the message of the Lord. Let's visit the believers and see how they are doing."

[37]Barnabas wanted to take John Mark with them, [38]but he had left them at Pamphylia; he did not continue with them in the work. So Paul did not think it was a good idea to take him. [39]Paul and Barnabas had such a serious argument about this that they separated and went different ways. Barnabas took Mark and sailed to Cyprus, [40]but Paul chose Silas and left. The believers in Antioch put Paul into the Lord's care, [41]and he went through Syria and Cilicia, giving strength to the churches.

TIMOTHY GOES WITH PAUL

16 [1]Paul came to Derbe and Lystra, where a follower named Timothy lived. Timothy's mother was Jewish and a believer, but his father was a Greek.

[2]The believers in Lystra and Iconium respected Timothy and said good things about him. [3]Paul wanted Timothy to travel with him, but all the people living in that area knew that Timothy's father was Greek. So Paul circumcised Timothy to please his mother's people. [4]Paul and those with him traveled from town to town and gave the decisions made by the apostles and elders in Jerusalem for the people to obey. [5]So the churches became stronger in the faith and grew larger every day.

PAUL IS CALLED OUT OF ASIA

[6]Paul and those with him went through the areas of Phrygia and Galatia since the Holy Spirit did not let them preach the Good News in the country of Asia. [7]When they came near the country of Mysia, they tried to go into Bithynia, but the Spirit of Jesus did not let them. [8]So they passed by Mysia and went to Troas. [9]That night Paul saw in a vision a man from Macedonia. The man stood and begged, "Come over to Macedonia and help us." [10]After Paul had seen the vision, we immediately prepared to leave

GOD'S WILL
Can we trust God with the events in our lives? (16:6–7)

15:34 Verse 34 Some Greek copies add verse 34: ". . . but Silas decided to remain there."

for Macedonia, understanding that God had
called us to tell the Good News to those
people.

LYDIA BECOMES A CHRISTIAN

11We left Troas and sailed straight to the island of Samothrace. The next day we sailed to
Neapolis.[n] 12Then we went by land to Philippi,
a Roman colony[n] and the leading city in that
part of Macedonia. We stayed there for several
days.

WHAT'S IT MEAN?

In ancient times, the color purple was a symbol of royalty. Purple dye came from a special type of shellfish in the Mediterranean Sea. About two hundred fifty thousand of them were needed to make one ounce of dye. As you may have guessed, the dye, which was used to color clothing, was extremely expensive. Only royalty and other wealthy and important people could afford it.

Acts 16:14

13On the Sabbath day we went outside the
city gate to the river where we thought we
would find a special place for prayer. Some
women had gathered there, so we sat down
and talked with them. 14One of the listeners
was a woman named Lydia from the city of
Thyatira whose job was selling purple cloth.
She worshiped God, and he
opened her mind to pay attention to what Paul was saying.
15She and all the people in
her house were baptized.
Then she invited us to her
home, saying, "If you think I
am truly a believer in the
Lord, then come stay in my
house." And she persuaded us
to stay with her.

" 'Men, what must I do to be saved?' They said to him, 'Believe in the Lord Jesus and you will be saved.' "
(Acts 16:30b–31a)

PAUL AND SILAS IN JAIL

16Once, while we were going to the place for
prayer, a servant girl met us. She had a special
spirit[n] in her, and she earned a lot of money
for her owners by telling fortunes. 17This girl
followed Paul and us, shouting, "These
men are servants of the Most
High God. They are telling
you how you can be saved."
18She kept this up for
many days. This bothered
Paul, so he turned and said to
the spirit, "By the power of
Jesus Christ, I command you to come out of
her!" Immediately, the spirit came out.

DEMONS

Who can drive out demons? (16:16–18)

19When the owners of the servant girl saw
this, they knew that now they could not use
her to make money. So they grabbed Paul and
Silas and dragged them before the city rulers in
the marketplace. 20They brought Paul and Silas
to the Roman rulers and said, "These men are
Jews and are making trouble in our city. 21They
are teaching things that are not right for us as
Romans to do."
22The crowd joined the attack against them.
The Roman officers tore the clothes of Paul
and Silas and had them beaten with rods.
23Then Paul and Silas were thrown into jail,
and the jailer was ordered to guard them carefully. 24When he heard this order, he put them
far inside the jail and pinned their feet down
between large blocks of wood.
25About midnight Paul and Silas were praying and singing songs to God as the other prisoners listened. 26Suddenly, there was a strong
earthquake that shook the foundation of the
jail. Then all the doors of the jail broke open,
and all the prisoners were freed from their
chains. 27The jailer woke up and saw that the
jail doors were open. Thinking
that the prisoners had already
escaped, he got his sword
and was about to kill
himself.[n] 28But Paul shouted,
"Don't hurt yourself! We are
all here."
29The jailer told someone
to bring a light. Then he ran
inside and, shaking with
fear, fell down before Paul
and Silas. 30He brought them
outside and said, "Men, what
must I do to be saved?"
31They said to him, "Believe in the Lord Jesus
and you will be saved—you and all the people

16:11 Neapolis City in Macedonia. It was the first city Paul visited on the continent of Europe.
16:12 Roman colony A town begun by Romans with Roman laws, customs, and privileges.
16:16 spirit This was a spirit from the devil, which caused her to say she had special knowledge.
16:27 kill himself He thought the leaders would kill him for letting the prisoners escape.

On the Edge

He brought them outside and said, "Men, what must I do to be saved?" They said to him, "Believe in the Lord Jesus and you will be saved—you and all the people in your house" (Acts 16:30–31).

Tommy thought that since his family went to church every Sunday and he knew the words to the hymns that he must be saved. Alexa goes to a church where they don't talk about being saved. She's heard other people talk about it, but she's confused. Every night she begs God to take her to heaven if she dies in her sleep. Every time she thinks about this "saved" thing, she gets scared. No one has ever explained it to her, and she's too proud to ask. Joey heard from a friend that God loves everybody, and that God would let everyone into heaven. Sounds great.

Tommy, Alexa, and Joey aren't saved. Here's the answer for them and for you: "Believe in the Lord Jesus and you will be saved." When you decide that you believe in God and in his Son, Jesus, and in the fact that Jesus died on a cross for you, then you are saved from an eternity away from God. That's salvation. Your faith in Jesus saves you. Nothing more. Nothing less. It's a matter of believing so much that you commit your life to him.

Are you unsure of your salvation? Then nail it down once and for all. Tell the Lord that you love him, that you believe that Jesus died for you, and that you want him to be in charge of your life. Ask him to forgive you of your sins. Ask him to show you how to live what you have decided to believe. He is waiting to be invited into your life. He is waiting for you to choose him. Long ago—way before you were born—he chose you. He loves you and wants to spend forever with you.

SEE FOR YOURSELF:
Mark 16:16;
John 3:16–18; 10:9;
Acts 2:21;
Rom. 10:9

in your house." 32So Paul and Silas told the message of the Lord to the jailer and all the people in his house. 33At that hour of the night the jailer took Paul and Silas and washed their wounds. Then he and all his people were baptized immediately. 34After this the jailer took Paul and Silas home and gave them food. He and his family were very happy because they now believed in God.

35The next morning, the Roman officers sent the police to tell the jailer, "Let these men go free."

36The jailer said to Paul, "The officers have sent an order to let you go free. You can leave now. Go in peace."

37But Paul said to the police, "They beat us in public without a trial, even though we are Roman citizens.[n] And they threw us in jail. Now they want to make us go away quietly. No! Let them come themselves and bring us out."

38The police told the Roman officers what Paul said. When the officers heard that Paul and Silas were Roman citizens, they were afraid. 39So they came and told Paul and Silas they were sorry and took them out of jail and asked them to leave the city. 40So when they came out of the jail, they went to Lydia's house where they saw some of the believers and encouraged them. Then they left.

PAUL AND SILAS IN THESSALONICA

17 1Paul and Silas traveled through Amphipolis and Apollonia and came to Thessalonica where there was a synagogue. 2Paul went into the synagogue as he always did, and on each Sabbath day for three weeks, he talked with his fellow Jews about the Scriptures. 3He explained and proved that the Christ must die and then rise from the dead. He said, "This Jesus I am telling you about is the Christ." 4Some of them were convinced and joined Paul and Silas, along with many of the Greeks who worshiped God and many of the important women.

5But some others became jealous. So they got some evil men from the marketplace, formed a mob, and started a riot. They ran to Jason's house, looking for Paul and Silas, wanting to bring them out to the people. 6But when they did not find them, they dragged Jason and some other believers to the leaders of the city. The people were yelling, "These people have made trouble everywhere in the world, and now they have come here too! 7Jason is keeping them in his house. All of them do things against the laws of Caesar, saying there is another king, called Jesus."

16:37 Roman citizens Roman law said that Roman citizens must not be beaten before they had a trial.

WHAT'S IT MEAN?

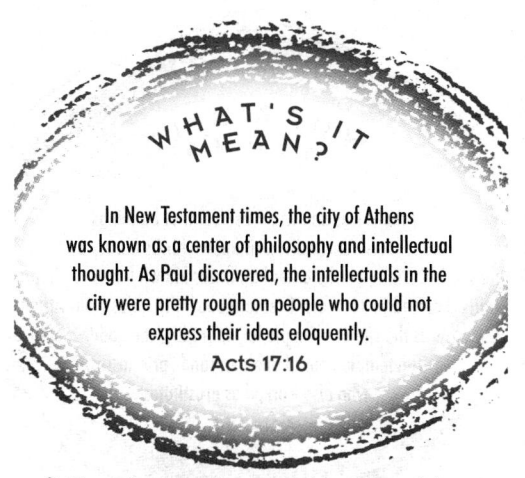

In New Testament times, the city of Athens was known as a center of philosophy and intellectual thought. As Paul discovered, the intellectuals in the city were pretty rough on people who could not express their ideas eloquently.

Acts 17:16

8When the people and the leaders of the city
heard these things, they became very upset.
9They made Jason and the others put up a sum
of money. Then they let the believers go free.

PAUL AND SILAS GO TO BEREA

10That same night the believers sent Paul
and Silas to Berea where they went to the synagogue. 11These people were more willing to
listen than the people in Thessalonica. The Be-
reans were eager to hear what Paul and Silas
said and studied the Scriptures every day to
find out if these things were true. 12So, many of
them believed, as well as many important
Greek women and men. 13But the people in
Thessalonica learned that Paul was preaching
the word of God in Berea, too. So they came
there, upsetting the people and making trouble.
14The believers quickly sent Paul away to the
coast, but Silas and Timothy stayed in Berea.
15The people leading Paul went with him to
Athens. Then they carried a message from Paul
back to Silas and Timothy for them to come to
him as soon as they could.

PAUL PREACHES IN ATHENS

16While Paul was waiting for Silas and Timothy in Athens, he was troubled because he
saw that the city was full of idols. 17In the synagogue, he talked with the Jews and the Greeks
who worshiped God. He also talked every day
with people in the marketplace.
18Some of the Epicurean and Stoic philosophers[n] argued with him, saying, "This man
doesn't know what he is talking about. What is
he trying to say?" Others said, "He seems to be
telling us about some other gods," because Paul
was telling them about Jesus and his rising
from the dead. 19They got Paul and took him
to a meeting of the Areopagus,[n] where they
said, "Please explain to us this new idea you

17:18 Epicurean and Stoic philosophers Philosophers were those who searched for truth. Epicureans believed that pleasure, especially pleasures of the mind, were the goal of life. Stoics believed that life should be without feelings of joy or grief. **17:19 Areopagus** A council or group of important leaders in Athens. They were like judges.

Promise HE PROMISES TO HELP YOU BE WHO YOU ARE.

We live in him. We walk in him. We are in him. . . . (Acts 17:28).

Ever feel like you're expected to be somebody you're not? Straight-A student? Club president? Perfect little angel? Sure, there are times when you need to venture out of your comfort zone and expect more of yourself than what comes easily for you. And God has given you natural, inborn abilities that (as you begin to spot them) will shape the person you are. He didn't just bundle up a bunch of leftovers and throw them in your direction. He knew what he wanted to do in you, what he wanted you to accomplish, what he wanted you to be good at. And he knew exactly what you'd need in order to pull it off.

He's placed spiritual gifts in you, unique and powerful tools that shape the way you serve him and relate to others—as a peacemaker, an encourager, a leader.

You're not an afterthought, but a complete package of Christlike potential, waiting to be discovered and put into practice. And you can start living it today. Right where you are. With the people right around you. You'll be miserable being anybody else.

SEE FOR YOURSELF:

Rom. 12:6; 1 Cor. 12:7; Eph. 2:10

have been teaching. [20]The things you are saying are new to us, and we want to know what
this teaching means." [21](All the people of Athens and those from other countries who lived
there always used their time to talk about the
newest ideas.)
[22]Then Paul stood before the meeting of the
Areopagus and said, "People of Athens, I can
see you are very religious in all things. [23]As I
was going through your city, I saw the objects
you worship. I found an altar that had these
words written on it: TO A GOD WHO IS NOT
KNOWN. You worship a god that you don't
know, and this is the God I am telling you
about! [24]The God who made the whole world
and everything in it is the Lord of the land and
the sky. He does not live in temples built by
human hands. [25]This God is the One who
gives life, breath, and everything else to people.
He does not need any help from them; he has
everything he needs. [26]God began by making
one person, and from him came all the different people who live everywhere in the world.
God decided exactly when and where they
must live. [27]God wanted them to look for him
and perhaps search all around for him and
find him, though he is not far from any of us:
[28]'We live in him. We walk in him. We are in
him.' Some of your own poets have said: 'For
we are his children.' [29]Since we are God's children, you must not think that God is like
something that people imagine or make from
gold, silver, or rock. [30]In the past, people did
not understand God, and he ignored this. But
now, God tells all people in the world to
change their hearts and lives. [31]God has set a
day that he will judge all the world with fairness, by the man he chose long ago. And God
has proved this to everyone by raising that
man from the dead!"
[32]When the people heard about Jesus being
raised from the dead, some of them laughed.
But others said, "We will hear more about this
from you later." [33]So Paul went away from
them. [34]But some of the people believed Paul
and joined him. Among those who believed
was Dionysius, a member of the Areopagus, a
woman named Damaris, and some others.

PAUL IN CORINTH

18 [1]Later Paul left Athens and went to Corinth.
[2]Here he met a Jew named Aquila who had
been born in the country of Pontus. But Aquila
and his wife, Priscilla, had recently moved to
Corinth from Italy, because Claudius[n] commanded that all Jews must leave Rome. Paul
went to visit Aquila and Priscilla. [3]Because they
were tentmakers, just as he was, he stayed with
them and worked with them. [4]Every Sabbath
day he talked with the Jews and Greeks in the
synagogue, trying to persuade them to believe
in Jesus.
[5]Silas and Timothy came from Macedonia
and joined Paul in Corinth. After this, Paul
spent all his time telling people the Good
News, showing them that Jesus is the Christ.
[6]But they would not accept Paul's teaching and
said some evil things. So he shook off the dust
from his clothes[n] and said to them, "If you are
not saved, it will be your own fault! I have
done all I can do! After this, I will go only to
other nations." [7]Paul left the synagogue and
moved into the home of Titius Justus, next to
the synagogue. This man worshiped God.
[8]Crispus was the leader of that synagogue, and
he and all the people living in his house believed in the Lord. Many others in Corinth also
listened to Paul and believed and were baptized.
[9]During the night, the Lord told Paul in a
vision: "Don't be afraid. Continue talking to
people and don't be quiet. [10]I am with you, and
no one will hurt you because many of my people are in this city." [11]Paul stayed there for a year
and a half, teaching God's word to the people.

PAUL IS BROUGHT BEFORE GALLIO

[12]When Gallio was the governor of the
country of Southern Greece, some people came

WHAT'S IT MEAN?

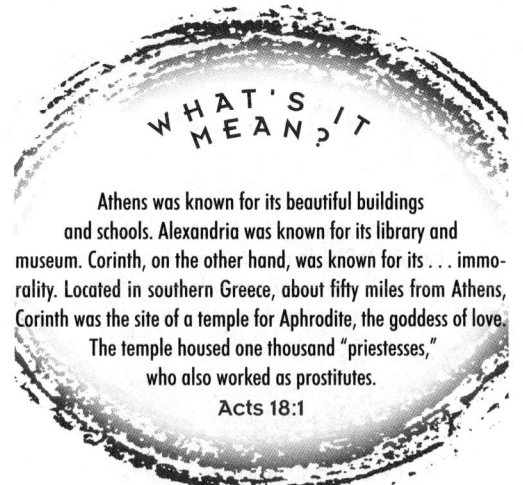

Athens was known for its beautiful buildings and schools. Alexandria was known for its library and museum. Corinth, on the other hand, was known for its . . . immorality. Located in southern Greece, about fifty miles from Athens, Corinth was the site of a temple for Aphrodite, the goddess of love. The temple housed one thousand "priestesses," who also worked as prostitutes.

Acts 18:1

18:2 Claudius The emperor (ruler) of Rome, A.D. 41–54. **18:6 shook . . . clothes** This was a warning to show that Paul was finished talking to the people in that city.

together against Paul and took him to the court. 13They said, "This man is teaching people to worship God in a way that is against our law."

WHAT'S IT MEAN?

Corinth was located in Achaia, the region of southern Greece. Gallio ruled the entire area.
Acts 18:12

14Paul was about to say something, but Gallio spoke, saying, "I would listen to you if you were complaining about a crime or some wrong. 15But the things you are saying are only questions about words and names—arguments about your own law. So you must solve this problem yourselves. I don't want to be a judge of these things." 16And Gallio made them leave the court.

17Then they all grabbed Sosthenes, the leader of the synagogue, and beat him there before the court. But this did not bother Gallio.

PAUL RETURNS TO ANTIOCH

18Paul stayed with the believers for many more days. Then he left and sailed for Syria, with Priscilla and Aquila. At Cenchrea Paul cut off his hair,[n] because he had made a promise to God. 19Then they went to Ephesus, where Paul left Priscilla and Aquila. While Paul was there, he went into the synagogue and talked with the people. 20When they asked him to stay with them longer, he refused. 21But as he left, he said, "I will come back to you again if God wants me to." And so he sailed away from Ephesus.

22When Paul landed at Caesarea, he went and gave greetings to the church in Jerusalem. After that, Paul went to Antioch. 23He stayed there for a while and then left and went through the regions of Galatia and Phrygia. He traveled from town to town in these regions, giving strength to all the followers.

WHAT'S IT MEAN?

Alexandria was second only to Rome as the largest city in the Roman Empire. Founded by Alexander the Great (yes, he named the city after himself), Alexandria was considered an important cultural center, with a world-class library and museum.
Acts 18:24

APOLLOS IN EPHESUS AND CORINTH

24A Jew named Apollos came to Ephesus. He was born in the city of Alexandria and was a good speaker who knew the Scriptures well. 25He had been taught about the way of the Lord and was always very excited when he spoke and taught the truth about Jesus. But the only baptism Apollos knew about was the baptism that John[n] taught. 26Apollos began to speak very boldly in the synagogue, and when Priscilla and Aquila heard him, they took him to their home and helped him better understand the way of God. 27Now Apollos wanted to go to the country of Southern Greece. So the believers helped him and wrote a letter to the followers there, asking them to accept him. These followers had believed in Jesus because of God's grace, and when Apollos arrived, he helped them very much. 28He argued very strongly with the Jews before all the people, clearly proving with the Scriptures that Jesus is the Christ.

BIBLE
What does the Bible reveal? (18:28)

PAUL IN EPHESUS

19

1While Apollos was in Corinth, Paul was visiting some places on the way to Ephesus. There he found some followers 2and asked them, "Did you receive the Holy Spirit when you believed?"

They said, "We have never even heard of a Holy Spirit."

3So he asked, "What kind of baptism did you have?"

They said, "It was the baptism that John taught."

18:18 cut . . . hair Jews did this to show that the time of a special promise to God was finished.
18:25 John John the Baptist, who preached to people about Christ's coming (Luke 3).

4 Paul said, "John's baptism was a baptism of changed hearts and lives. He told people to believe in the one who would come after him, and that one is Jesus."

5 When they heard this, they were baptized in the name of the Lord Jesus. 6 Then Paul laid his hands on them,[n] and the Holy Spirit came upon them. They began speaking different languages[n] and prophesying. 7 There were about twelve people in this group.

8 Paul went into the synagogue and spoke out boldly for three months. He talked with the people and persuaded them to accept the things he said about the kingdom of God. 9 But some of them became stubborn. They refused to believe and said evil things about the Way of Jesus before all the people. So Paul left them, and taking the followers with him, he went to the school of a man named Tyrannus. There Paul talked with people every day 10 for two years. Because of his work, every Jew and Greek in the country of Asia heard the word of the Lord.

> **"So in a powerful way the word of the Lord kept spreading and growing." (Acts 19:20)**

THE SONS OF SCEVA

11 God used Paul to do some very special miracles. 12 Some people took handkerchiefs and clothes that Paul had used and put them on the sick. When they did this, the sick were healed and evil spirits left them.

13 But some people also were traveling around and making evil spirits go out of people. They tried to use the name of the Lord Jesus to force the evil spirits out. They would say, "By the same Jesus that Paul talks about, I order you to come out!" 14 Seven sons of Sceva, a leading priest, were doing this.

15 But one time an evil spirit said to them, "I know Jesus, and I know about Paul, but who are you?"

DEMONS

Do demons have power? (19:16)

16 Then the man who had the evil spirit jumped on them. Because he was so much stronger than all of them, they ran away from the house naked and hurt. 17 All the people in Ephesus—Jews and Greeks—learned about this and were filled with fear and gave great honor to the Lord Jesus. 18 Many of the believers began to confess openly and tell all the evil things they had done. 19 Some of them who had used magic brought their magic books and burned them before everyone. Those books were worth about fifty thousand silver coins.[n]

20 So in a powerful way the word of the Lord kept spreading and growing.

21 After these things, Paul decided to go to Jerusalem, planning to go through the countries of Macedonia and Southern Greece and then on to Jerusalem. He said, "After I have been to Jerusalem, I must also visit Rome." 22 Paul sent Timothy and Erastus, two of his helpers, ahead to Macedonia, but he himself stayed in Asia for a while.

TROUBLE IN EPHESUS

23 And during that time, there was some serious trouble in Ephesus about the Way of Jesus. 24 A man named Demetrius, who worked with silver, made little silver models that looked like the temple of the goddess Artemis.[n] Those who did this work made much money. 25 Demetrius had a meeting with them and some others who did the same kind of work. He told them, "Men, you know that we make a lot of money from our business. 26 But look at what this man Paul is doing. He has convinced and turned away many people in Ephesus and in almost all of Asia! He says the gods made by human hands are not real. 27 There is a danger that our business will lose its good name, but there is also another danger: People will begin to think that the temple of the great goddess Artemis is not important. Her greatness will be destroyed, and Artemis is the goddess that everyone in Asia and the whole world worships."

28 When the others heard this, they became very angry and shouted, "Artemis, the goddess of Ephesus, is great!" 29 The whole city became confused. The people grabbed Gaius and Aristarchus, who were from Macedonia and were traveling with Paul, and ran to the theater. 30 Paul wanted to go in and talk to the crowd, but the followers did not let him. 31 Also, some

19:6 laid his hands on them The laying on of hands had many purposes, including the giving of a blessing, power, or authority. **19:6 languages** This can also be translated "tongues." **19:19 fifty thousand silver coins** Probably drachmas. One coin was enough to pay a worker for one day's labor. **19:24 Artemis** A Greek goddess that the people of Asia Minor worshiped.

EUTYCHUS made a difference

Eutychus left a mark not so much because of what he did as because of what happened to him. He fell asleep in a meeting. That in itself wasn't that unusual. The meeting was long and late at night. The unusual part of the story turned out to be the location of Eutychus's seat. He was perched on a windowsill in a third-floor room. He had one of those falling dreams, which in his case turned out to be true! He fell out of the window. This might be a good time to point out that Eutychus's name means "Lucky."

There was a doctor in the house—Luke—and he immediately recognized that the fall had been fatal. The apostle Paul offered not so much a second opinion as an alternative treatment. He held the dead boy and prayed. Eutychus lived! The miracle in his life, Luke notes, affected everyone in such a way that

"they . . . were greatly comforted" (Acts 20:12).

Cutting Edge

YOU can, too!

In spite of Eutychus's story, falling asleep in church tends to create negative impressions. Perhaps a better lesson to take from Eutychus has to do with the effect changes in a young person's life have on others. Adults tend to have a stereotypical view of youth. They need to receive a good, healthy shock once in a while.

You want to make a difference in your church? Speak up about what God is doing in your life. If God has gotten hold of you, that is no less a miracle than Eutychus being revived on the lawn. But even little lessons will make a difference. Find out how many people know about Eutychus. Tell them the story. You'll be amazed at what a difference it will make to others when they find out God is making a difference in your Life.

Want to know more? Luke recorded Eutychus's brief but exciting episode in Acts 20:7–12.

leaders of Asia who were friends of Paul sent him a message, begging him not to go into the theater. 32 Some people were shouting one thing, and some were shouting another. The meeting was completely confused; most of them did not know why they had come together. 33 They put a man named Alexander in front of the people, and some of them told him what to do. Alexander waved his hand so he could explain things to the people. 34 But when they saw that Alexander was a Jew, they all shouted the same thing for two hours: "Great is Artemis of Ephesus!"

WHAT'S IT MEAN?

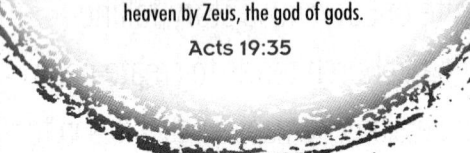

The Greek goddess Artemis had a much more alluring Roman name—Diana. The temple built in her honor in Ephesus was one of the seven wonders of the ancient world. The temple boasted more than one hundred columns, each five stories tall. Inside the temple was an image of Artemis/Diana, carved into a stone that many scholars believe was a meteorite. Worshipers of the goddess claimed that the stone had been sent from heaven by Zeus, the god of gods.

Acts 19:35

35 Then the city clerk made the crowd be quiet. He said, "People of Ephesus, everyone knows that Ephesus is the city that keeps the temple of the great goddess Artemis and her holy stone[n] that fell from heaven. 36 Since no one can say this is not true, you should be quiet. Stop and think before you do anything. 37 You brought these men here, but they have not said anything evil against our goddess or stolen anything from her temple. 38 If Demetrius and those who work with him have a charge against anyone they should go to the courts and judges where they can argue with each other. 39 If there is something else you want to talk about, it can be decided at the regular town meeting of the people. 40 I say this because some people might see this trouble today and say that we are rioting. We could not explain this, because there is no real reason for this meeting." 41 After the city clerk said these things, he told the people to go home.

PAUL IN MACEDONIA AND GREECE

20 1 When the trouble stopped, Paul sent for the followers to come to him. After he encouraged them and then told them good-bye, he left and went to the country of Macedonia. 2 He said many things to strengthen the followers in the different places on his way through Macedonia. Then he went to Greece, 3 where he stayed for three months. He was ready to sail for Syria, but some evil people were planning something against him. So Paul decided to go back through Macedonia to Syria. 4 The men who went with him were Sopater son of Pyrrhus, from the city of Berea; Aristarchus and Secundus, from the city of Thessalonica; Gaius, from Derbe; Timothy; and Tychicus and Trophimus, two men from the country of Asia. 5 These men went on ahead and waited for us at Troas. 6 We sailed from Philippi after the Feast of Unleavened Bread. Five days later we met them in Troas, where we stayed for seven days.

PAUL'S LAST VISIT TO TROAS

7 On the first day of the week,[n] we all met together to break bread,[n] and Paul spoke to the

WHAT'S IT MEAN?

The Feast of Unleavened Bread was part of the annual Passover celebration. In case you're wondering, unleavened bread does not have yeast in it. Why would people make bread without yeast, the ingredient that makes it rise? When Moses and the Israelites left Egypt, they were in a hurry. There was no time for them to prepare food or to wait for bread to rise. Today unleavened bread is called matzo.

Acts 20:6

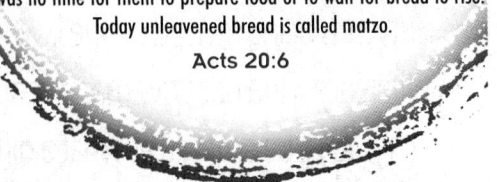

19:35 holy stone Probably a meteorite or stone that the people thought looked like Artemis.
20:7 first day of the week Sunday, which for Jews began at sunset on our Saturday. But if in this part of Asia a different system of time was used, then the meeting was on our Sunday night. **20:7 break bread** Probably the Lord's Supper, the special meal that Jesus told his followers to eat to remember him (Luke 22:14-20).

group. Because he was planning to leave the
next day, he kept on talking until midnight.
[8]We were all together in a room upstairs, and
there were many lamps in the room. [9]A young
man named Eutychus was sitting in the window. As Paul continued talking, Eutychus was
falling into a deep sleep. Finally, he went sound
asleep and fell to the ground from the third
floor. When they picked him up, he was dead.
[10]Paul went down to Eutychus, knelt down,
and put his arms around him. He said, "Don't
worry. He is alive now." [11]Then Paul went upstairs again, broke bread, and ate. He spoke to
them a long time, until it was early morning,
and then he left. [12]They took the young man
home alive and were greatly comforted.

THE TRIP FROM TROAS TO MILETUS

[13]We went on ahead of Paul and sailed for
the city of Assos, where he wanted to join us
on the ship. Paul planned it this way because
he wanted to go to Assos by land. [14]When he
met us there, we took him aboard and went to
Mitylene. [15]We sailed from Mitylene and the
next day came to a place near Kios. The following day we sailed to Samos, and the next
day we reached Miletus. [16]Paul had already
decided not to stop at Ephesus, because he did
not want to stay too long in the country of
Asia. He was hurrying to be in Jerusalem on
the day of Pentecost, if that were possible.

THE ELDERS FROM EPHESUS

[17]Now from Miletus Paul sent to Ephesus
and called for the elders of the church. [18]When
they came to him, he said, "You know about
my life from the first day I came to Asia. You
know the way I lived all the time I was with
you. [19]The evil people made plans against me,
which troubled me very much. But you know I
always served the Lord unselfishly, and I often
cried. [20]You know I preached to you and did
not hold back anything that would help you.
You know that I taught you in public and in
your homes. [21]I warned both Jews and Greeks
to change their lives and turn to God and believe in our Lord Jesus. [22]But now I must obey
the Holy Spirit and go to Jerusalem. I don't
know what will happen to me there. [23]I know
only that in every city the Holy Spirit tells me
that troubles and even jail wait for me. [24]I don't
care about my own life. The most important
thing is that I complete my mission, the work
that the Lord Jesus gave me—to tell people the
Good News about God's grace.

[25]"And now, I know that none of you
among whom I was preaching the kingdom of
God will ever see me again. [26]So today I tell
you that if any of you should be lost, I am not
responsible, [27]because I have told you everything God wants you to know. [28]Be careful for
yourselves and for all the people the Holy
Spirit has given to you to care for. You must be
like shepherds to the church of God,[n] which he
bought with the death of his own son. [29]I
know that after I leave, some people will come
like wild wolves and try to destroy the flock.
[30]Also, some from your own group will rise up
and twist the truth and will lead away followers after them. [31]So be careful! Always remember that for three years, day and night, I never
stopped warning each of you, and I often cried
over you.

[32]"Now I am putting you in the care of God
and the message about his grace. It is able to
give you strength, and it will give you the
blessings God has for all his holy people.
[33]When I was with you, I never wanted
anyone's money or fine clothes. [34]You
know I always worked to take
care of my own needs and the
needs of those who were with
me. [35]I showed you in all
things that you should work
as I did and help the weak. I
taught you to remember the
words Jesus said: 'It is more blessed to give
than to receive.' "

GIVING
What's better than getting gifts? (20:35)

[36]When Paul had said this, he knelt down
with all of them and prayed. [37-38]And they all
cried because Paul had said they would never
see him again. They put their arms around him
and kissed him. Then they went with him to the
ship.

PAUL GOES TO JERUSALEM

21
[1]After we all said good-bye to them, we
sailed straight to the island of Cos. The next
day we reached Rhodes, and from there we
went to Patara. [2]There we found a ship going
to Phoenicia, so we went aboard and sailed
away. [3]We sailed near the island of Cyprus,
seeing it to the north, but we sailed on to Syria.
We stopped at Tyre because the ship needed to
unload its cargo there. [4]We found some followers in Tyre and stayed with them for seven
days. Through the Holy Spirit they warned
Paul not to go to Jerusalem. [5]When we finished
our visit, we left and continued our trip. All the
followers, even the women and children, came

20:28 of God Some Greek copies say, "of the Lord."

outside the city with us. After we all knelt on
the beach and prayed, 6we said good-bye and
got on the ship, and the followers went back
home.
7We continued our trip from Tyre and arrived at Ptolemais, where we greeted the believers and stayed with them for a day. 8The
next day we left Ptolemais and went to the city
of Caesarea. There we went into the home of
Philip the preacher, one of the seven helpers,[n]
and stayed with him. 9He had four unmarried
daughters who had the gift of prophesying.
10After we had been there for some time, a
prophet named Agabus arrived from Judea.
11He came to us and borrowed Paul's belt and
used it to tie his own hands and feet. He said,
"The Holy Spirit says, 'This is how evil people
in Jerusalem will tie up the man who wears
this belt. Then they will give him to the older
leaders.' "
12When we all heard this, we and the people
there begged Paul not to go to Jerusalem. 13But
he said, "Why are you crying and making me
so sad? I am not only ready to be tied up in
Jerusalem, I am ready to die for the Lord Jesus!"
14We could not persuade him to stay away
from Jerusalem. So we stopped begging him
and said, "We pray that what the Lord wants
will be done."
15After this, we got ready and started on our
way to Jerusalem. 16Some of the followers from
Caesarea went with us and took us to the
home of Mnason, where we would stay. He
was from Cyprus and was one of the first followers.

PAUL VISITS JAMES

17In Jerusalem the believers were glad to see
us. 18The next day Paul went with us to visit
James, and all the elders were there. 19Paul
greeted them and told them everything God
had done among the other nations through
him. 20When they heard this, they praised God.
Then they said to Paul, "Brother, you can see
that many thousands of our people have become believers. And they think it is very important to obey the law of Moses. 21They have
heard about your teaching, that you tell our
people who live among the nations to leave
the law of Moses. They have heard that you
tell them not to circumcise their children and
not to obey customs. 22What should we do?
They will learn that you have come. 23So we
will tell you what to do: Four of our men have
made a promise to God. 24Take these men with
you and share in their cleansing ceremony.[n]
Pay their expenses so they can shave their
heads.[n] Then it will prove to everyone that
what they have heard about you is not true
and that you follow the law of Moses in your
own life. 25We have already sent a letter to the
non-Jewish believers. The letter said: 'Do not
eat food that has been offered to idols, or
blood, or animals that have been strangled. Do
not take part in sexual sin.' "
26The next day Paul took the four men and
shared in the cleansing ceremony with them.
Then he went to the Temple and announced
the time when the days of the cleansing ceremony would be finished. On the last day an
offering would be given for each of the men.
27When the seven days were almost over,
some of his people from Asia saw Paul at the
Temple. They caused all the people to be upset
and grabbed Paul. 28They shouted, "People of
Israel, help us! This is the man who goes everywhere teaching against the law of Moses,
against our people, and against this Temple.
Now he has brought some Greeks into the
Temple and has made this holy place unclean!"
29(They said this because they had seen Trophimus, a man from Ephesus, with Paul in Jerusalem. They thought that Paul had brought
him into the Temple.)
30All the people in Jerusalem became upset.
Together they ran, took Paul, and dragged him
out of the Temple. The Temple doors were
closed immediately. 31While they were trying
to kill Paul, the commander of the Roman

WHAT'S IT MEAN?

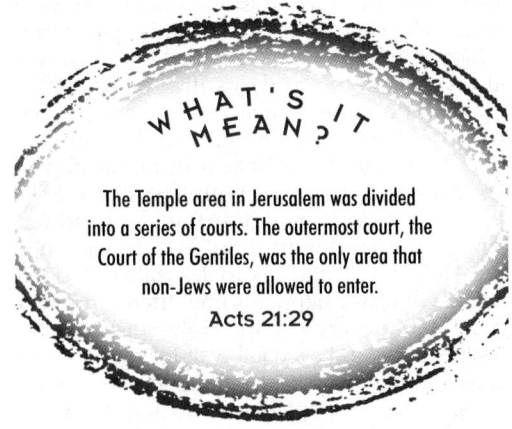

The Temple area in Jerusalem was divided into a series of courts. The outermost court, the Court of the Gentiles, was the only area that non-Jews were allowed to enter.

Acts 21:29

21:8 helpers The seven men chosen for a special work described in Acts 6:1–6. Sometimes they are called "deacons." **21:24 cleansing ceremony** The special things Jews did to end the Nazirite promise. **21:24 shave their heads** Jews did this to show that their promise was finished.

army in Jerusalem learned that there was trouble in the whole city. 32Immediately he took some officers and soldiers and ran to the place where the crowd was gathered. When the people saw them, they stopped beating Paul. 33The commander went to Paul and arrested him. He told his soldiers to tie Paul with two chains. Then he asked who he was and what he had done wrong. 34Some in the crowd were yelling one thing, and some were yelling another. Because of all this confusion and shouting, the commander could not learn what had happened. So he ordered the soldiers to take Paul to the army building. 35When Paul came to the steps, the soldiers had to carry him because the people were ready to hurt him. 36The whole mob was following them, shouting, "Kill him!"

37As the soldiers were about to take Paul into the army building, he spoke to the commander, "May I say something to you?"

The commander said, "Do you speak Greek? 38I thought you were the Egyptian who started some trouble against the government not long ago and led four thousand killers out to the desert."

39Paul said, "No, I am a Jew from Tarsus in the country of Cilicia. I am a citizen of that important city. Please, let me speak to the people."

40The commander gave permission, so Paul stood on the steps and waved his hand to quiet the people. When there was silence, he spoke to them in the Hebrew language.

PAUL SPEAKS TO THE PEOPLE

22

1Paul said, "Friends, fellow Jews, listen to my defense to you." 2When they heard him speaking the Hebrew language,[n] they became very quiet. Paul said, 3"I am a Jew, born in Tarsus in the country of Cilicia, but I grew up in this city. I was a student of Gamaliel,[n] who carefully taught me everything about the law of our ancestors. I was very serious about serving God, just as are all of you here today. 4I persecuted the people who followed the Way of Jesus, and some of them were even killed. I arrested men and women and put them in jail. 5The high priest and the whole council of older leaders can tell you this is true. They gave me letters to the brothers in Damascus. So I was going there to arrest these people and bring them back to Jerusalem to be punished.

6"About noon when I came near Damascus, a bright light from heaven suddenly flashed all around me. 7I fell to the ground and heard a voice saying, 'Saul, Saul, why are you persecuting me?' 8I asked, 'Who are you, Lord?' The voice said, 'I am Jesus from Nazareth whom you are persecuting.' 9Those who were with me did not hear the voice, but they saw the light. 10I said, 'What shall I do, Lord?' The Lord answered, 'Get up and go to Damascus. There you will be told about all the things I have planned for you to do.' 11I could not see, because the bright light had made me blind. So my companions led me into Damascus.

" 'Who are you, Lord?' The voice said, 'I am Jesus from Nazareth.' " (Acts 22:8)

12"There a man named Ananias came to me. He was a religious man; he obeyed the law of Moses, and all the Jews who lived there respected him. 13He stood by me and said, 'Brother Saul, see again!' Immediately I was able to see him. 14He said, 'The God of our ancestors chose you long ago to know his plan, to see the Righteous One, and to hear words from him. 15You will be his witness to all people, telling them about what you have seen and heard. 16Now, why wait any longer? Get up, be baptized, and wash your sins away, trusting in him to save you.'

17"Later, when I returned to Jerusalem, I was praying in the Temple, and I saw a vision. 18I saw the Lord saying to me, 'Hurry! Leave Jerusalem now! The people here will not accept the truth about me.' 19But I said, 'Lord, they know that in every synagogue I put the believers in jail and beat them. 20They also know I was there when Stephen, your witness, was killed. I stood there agreeing and holding the coats of those who were killing him!' 21But the Lord said to me, 'Leave now. I will send you far away to the other nations.' "

22The crowd listened to Paul until he said this. Then they began shouting, "Kill him! Get him out of the world! He should not be allowed to live!" 23They shouted, threw off their coats,[n] and threw dust into the air.[n]

22:2 Hebrew language Or Aramaic, the language of many people in this region in the first century.
22:3 Gamaliel A very important teacher of the Pharisees, a Jewish religious group (Acts 5:34).
22:23 threw off their coats This showed that the people were very angry with Paul. **22:23 threw dust into the air** This showed even greater anger.

24 Then the commander ordered the soldiers
to take Paul into the army building and beat
him. He wanted to make Paul tell why the people were shouting against him like this. 25 But as
the soldiers were tying him up, preparing to
beat him, Paul said to an officer nearby, "Do
you have the right to beat a Roman citizen[n]
who has not been proven guilty?"
26 When the officer heard this, he went to
the commander and reported it. The officer
said, "Do you know what you are doing? This
man is a Roman citizen."
27 The commander came to Paul and said,
"Tell me, are you really a Roman citizen?"
He answered, "Yes."
28 The commander said, "I paid a lot of
money to become a Roman citizen."
But Paul said, "I was born a citizen."
29 The men who were preparing to question
Paul moved away from him immediately. The
commander was frightened because he had already tied Paul, and Paul was a Roman citizen.

PAUL SPEAKS TO LEADERS

30 The next day the commander decided to
learn why the Jews were accusing Paul. So he
ordered the leading priests and the council to
meet. The commander took Paul's chains off.
Then he brought Paul out and stood him before their meeting.
23 1 Paul looked at the council and said,
"Brothers, I have lived my life without guilt
feelings before God up to this day." 2 Ananias,[n]
the high priest, heard this and told the men
who were standing near Paul to hit him on the
mouth. 3 Paul said to Ananias, "God will hit
you, too! You are like a wall that has been
painted white. You sit there and judge me, using the law of Moses, but you are telling them
to hit me, and that is against the law."
4 The men standing near Paul said to him,
"You cannot insult God's high priest like that!"
5 Paul said, "Brothers, I did not know this
man was the high priest. It is written in the
Scriptures, 'You must not curse a leader of your
people.' "[n]
6 Some of the men in the meeting were Sadducees, and others were Pharisees. Knowing
this, Paul shouted to them, "My brothers, I am
a Pharisee, and my father was a Pharisee. I am
on trial here because I believe that people will
rise from the dead."
7 When Paul said this, there was an argument between the Pharisees and the Sadducees, and the group was divided. 8 (The Sadducees do not believe in angels or spirits or that
people will rise from the dead. But the Pharisees believe in them all.) 9 So there was a great
uproar. Some of the teachers of the law, who
were Pharisees, stood up and argued, "We find
nothing wrong with this man. Maybe an angel
or a spirit did speak to him."
10 The argument was beginning to turn into
such a fight that the commander was afraid
some evil people would tear Paul to pieces. So
he told the soldiers to go down and take Paul
away and put him in the army building.
11 The next night the Lord came and stood
by Paul. He said, "Be brave! You have told people in Jerusalem about me. You must do the
same in Rome."

WHAT'S IT MEAN?

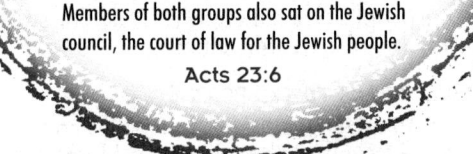

What's the difference between a Pharisee and a Sadducee? Pharisees were drawn mostly from the middle class and emphasized the importance of obeying the Teachings God had given Moses. Sadducees were wealthy and powerful individuals, many of whom served as priests. These two groups of Jewish scholars interpreted Scripture differently and argued over issues, such as the resurrection of the dead and the existence of angels. Because they knew so much about Scripture, members of both groups tended to take pride in themselves and to criticize others. Members of both groups also sat on the Jewish council, the court of law for the Jewish people.

Acts 23:6

12 In the morning some evil people made a
plan to kill Paul, and they took an oath not to
eat or drink anything until they had killed him.
13 There were more than forty men who made
this plan. 14 They went to the leading priests
and the older leaders and said, "We have taken
an oath not to eat or drink until we have killed
Paul. 15 So this is what we want you to do: Send
a message to the commander to bring Paul out
to you as though you want to ask him more
questions. We will be waiting to kill him while
he is on the way here."

22:25 Roman citizen Roman law said that Roman citizens must not be beaten before they had a trial.
23:2 Ananias This is not the same man named Ananias in Acts 22:12. **23:5 'You . . . people.'** Quotation from Exodus 22:28.

16But Paul's nephew heard about this plan
and went to the army building and told Paul.
17Then Paul called one of the officers and said,
"Take this young man to the commander. He
has a message for him."
18So the officer brought Paul's nephew to the
commander and said, "The prisoner, Paul,
asked me to bring this young man to you. He
wants to tell you something."
19The commander took the young man's
hand and led him to a place where they could
be alone. He asked, "What do you want to
tell me?"
20The young man said, "The Jews have decided to ask you to bring Paul down to their
council meeting tomorrow. They want you to
think they are going to ask him more questions. 21But don't believe them! More than
forty men are hiding and waiting to kill Paul.
They have all taken an oath not to eat or drink
until they have killed him. Now they are waiting for you to agree."
22The commander sent the young man
away, ordering him, "Don't tell anyone that
you have told me about their plan."

PAUL IS SENT TO CAESAREA

23Then the commander called two officers
and said, "I need some men to go to Caesarea.
Get two hundred soldiers, seventy horsemen,
and two hundred men with spears ready to
leave at nine o'clock tonight. 24Get some
horses for Paul to ride so he can be taken to
Governor Felix safely." 25And he wrote a letter
that said:

> 26From Claudius Lysias.
> To the Most Excellent Governor Felix:
> Greetings.
> 27Some of the Jews had taken this
> man and planned to kill him. But I
> learned that he is a Roman citizen, so I
> went with my soldiers and saved him. 28I
> wanted to know why they were accus-
> ing him, so I brought him before their
> council meeting. 29I learned that these
> people said Paul did some things that
> were wrong by their own laws, but no
> charge was worthy of jail or death.
> 30When I was told that some of them
> were planning to kill Paul, I sent him to
> you at once. I also told them to tell you
> what they have against him.

31So the soldiers did what they were told
and took Paul and brought him to the city of
Antipatris that night. 32The next day the horsemen went with Paul to Caesarea, but the other
soldiers went back to the army building in Jerusalem. 33When the horsemen came to Caesarea and gave the letter to the governor, they
turned Paul over to him. 34The governor read
the letter and asked Paul, "What area are you
from?" When he learned that Paul was from
Cilicia, 35he said, "I will hear your case when
those who are against you come here, too."
Then the governor gave orders for Paul to be
kept under guard in Herod's palace.

WHAT'S IT MEAN?

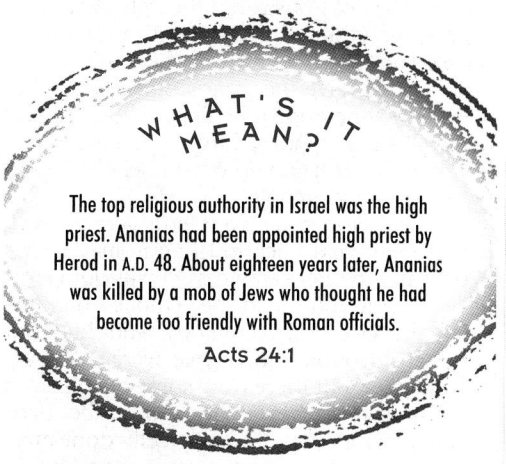

The top religious authority in Israel was the high priest. Ananias had been appointed high priest by Herod in A.D. 48. About eighteen years later, Ananias was killed by a mob of Jews who thought he had become too friendly with Roman officials.

Acts 24:1

PAUL IS ACCUSED

24
1Five days later Ananias, the high priest,
went to the city of Caesarea with some of the
older leaders and a lawyer named Tertullus.
They had come to make charges against Paul
before the governor. 2Paul was called into the
meeting, and Tertullus began to accuse him,
saying, "Most Excellent Felix! Our people enjoy
much peace because of you, and many wrong
things in our country are being made right
through your wise help. 3We accept these
things always and in every place, and we are
thankful for them. 4But not wanting to take
any more of your time, I beg you to be kind
and listen to our few words. 5We have found
this man to be a troublemaker, stirring up his
people everywhere in the world. He is a leader
of the Nazarene group. 6Also, he was trying to
make the Temple unclean, but we stopped
him.[n] 8By asking him questions yourself, you
can decide if all these things are true." 9The

24:6 Verse 6 Some Greek copies add 6b-8a: "And we wanted to judge him by our own law. 7But the officer Lysias came and used much force to take him from us. 8And Lysias commanded those who wanted to accuse Paul to come to you."

others agreed and said that all of this was true.

[10]When the governor made a sign for Paul to speak, Paul said, "Governor Felix, I know you have been a judge over this nation for a long time. So I am happy to defend myself before you. [11]You can learn for yourself that I went to worship in Jerusalem only twelve days ago. [12]Those who are accusing me did not find me arguing with anyone in the Temple or stirring up the people in the synagogues or in the city. [13]They cannot prove the things they are saying against me now. [14]But I will tell you this: I worship the God of our ancestors as a follower of the Way of Jesus. The others say that the Way of Jesus is not the right way. But I believe everything that is taught in the law of Moses and that is written in the books of the Prophets. [15]I have the same hope in God that they have—the hope that all people, good and bad, will surely be raised from the dead. [16]This is why I always try to do what I believe is right before God and people.

[17]"After being away from Jerusalem for several years, I went back to bring money to my people and to offer sacrifices. [18]I was doing this when they found me in the Temple. I had finished the cleansing ceremony and had not made any trouble; no people were gathering around me. [19]But there were some people from the country of Asia who should be here, standing before you. If I have really done anything wrong, they are the ones who should accuse me. [20]Or ask these people here if they found any wrong in me when I stood before the council in Jerusalem. [21]But I did shout one thing when I stood before them: 'You are judging me today because I believe that people will rise from the dead!' "

[22]Felix already understood much about the Way of Jesus. He stopped the trial and said, "When commander Lysias comes here, I will decide your case." [23]Felix told the officer to keep Paul guarded but to give him some freedom and to let his friends bring what he needed.

PAUL SPEAKS TO FELIX AND HIS WIFE

[24]After some days Felix came with his wife, Drusilla, who was Jewish, and asked for Paul to be brought to him. He listened to Paul talk about believing in Christ Jesus. [25]But Felix became afraid when Paul spoke about living right, self-control, and the time when God will judge the world. He said, "Go away now. When I have more time, I will call for you." [26]At the same time Felix hoped that Paul would give him some money, so he often sent for Paul and talked with him.

[27]But after two years, Felix was replaced by Porcius Festus as governor. But Felix had left Paul in prison to please the Jews.

PAUL ASKS TO SEE CAESAR

25

[1]Three days after Festus became governor, he went from Caesarea to Jerusalem. [2]There the leading priests and the important leaders made charges against Paul before Festus. [3]They asked Festus to do them a favor. They wanted him to send Paul back to Jerusalem, because they had a plan to kill him on the way. [4]But Festus answered that Paul would be kept in Caesarea and that he himself was returning there soon. [5]He said, "Some of your leaders should go with me. They can accuse the man there in Caesarea, if he has really done something wrong."

[6]Festus stayed in Jerusalem another eight or ten days and then went back to Caesarea. The next day he told the soldiers to bring Paul before him. Festus was seated on the judge's seat [7]when Paul came into the room. The people who had come from Jerusalem stood around him, making serious charges against him, which they could not prove. [8]This is what Paul said to defend himself: "I have done nothing wrong against the law, against the Temple, or against Caesar."

[9]But Festus wanted to please the people. So he asked Paul, "Do you want to go to Jerusalem for me to judge you there on these charges?"

[10]Paul said, "I am standing at Caesar's judgment seat now, where I should be judged. I have done nothing wrong to them; you know this is true. [11]If I have done something wrong and the law says I must die, I do not ask to be saved from death. But if these charges are not true, then no one can give me to them. I want Caesar to hear my case!"

[12]Festus talked about this with his advisers.

WHAT'S IT MEAN?

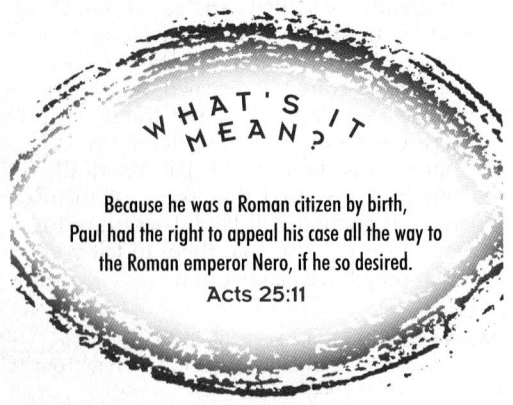

Because he was a Roman citizen by birth, Paul had the right to appeal his case all the way to the Roman emperor Nero, if he so desired.

Acts 25:11

Then he said, "You have asked to see Caesar, so
you will go to Caesar!"

PAUL BEFORE KING AGRIPPA

13A few days later King Agrippa and Bernice
came to Caesarea to visit Festus. 14They stayed
there for some time, and Festus told the king
about Paul's case. Festus said, "There is a man
that Felix left in prison. 15When I went to Jerusalem, the leading priests and the older leaders
there made charges against him, asking me to
sentence him to death. 16But I answered, 'When
a man is accused of a crime, Romans do not
hand him over until he has been allowed to
face his accusers and defend himself against
their charges.' 17So when these people came
here to Caesarea for the trial, I did not waste
time. The next day I sat on the judge's seat and
commanded that the man be brought in.
18They stood up and accused him, but not of
any serious crime as I thought they would.
19The things they said were about their own
religion and about a man named Jesus who
died. But Paul said that he is still alive. 20Not
knowing how to find out about these questions, I asked Paul, 'Do you want to go to Jerusalem and be judged there?' 21But he asked to
be kept in Caesarea. He wants a decision from
the emperor.[n] So I ordered that he be held until
I could send him to Caesar."

22Agrippa said to Festus, "I would also like
to hear this man myself."

Festus said, "Tomorrow you will hear him."

23The next day Agrippa and Bernice appeared with great show, acting like very important people. They went into the judgment
room with the army leaders and the important
men of Caesarea. Then Festus ordered the soldiers to bring Paul in. 24Festus said, "King
Agrippa and all who are gathered here with us,
you see this man. All the people, here and in
Jerusalem, have complained to me about him,
shouting that he should not live any longer.
25When I judged him, I found no reason to
order his death. But since he asked to be
judged by Caesar, I decided to send him.
26But I have nothing definite to write the emperor about him. So I have brought him before all of you—especially you, King Agrippa. I
hope you can question him and give me something to write. 27I think it is foolish to send a
prisoner to Caesar without telling what
charges are against him."

PAUL DEFENDS HIMSELF

26

1Agrippa said to Paul, "You may now speak
to defend yourself."

Then Paul raised his hand and began to
speak. 2He said, "King Agrippa, I am very happy to stand before you and will answer all the
charges the evil people make against me. 3You
know so much about all the customs and the
things they argue about, so please listen to me
patiently.

4"All my people know about my whole life,
how I lived from the beginning in my own
country and later in Jerusalem. 5They have
known me for a long time. If they want to, they
can tell you that I was a good Pharisee. And
the Pharisees obey the laws of my tradition
more carefully than any other group. 6Now I
am on trial because I hope for the promise that
God made to our ancestors. 7This is the promise that the twelve tribes of our people hope to
receive as they serve God day and night. My
king, they have accused me because I hope for
this same promise! 8Why do any of you people
think it is impossible for God to raise people
from the dead?

9"I, too, thought I ought to do many things
against Jesus from Nazareth. 10And that is
what I did in Jerusalem. The leading priests
gave me the power to put many of God's people in jail, and when they were being killed, I
agreed it was a good thing. 11In every synagogue, I often punished them and tried to
make them speak against Jesus. I was so angry
against them I even went to other cities to find
them and punish them.

12"One time the leading priests gave me permission and the power to go to Damascus.
13On the way there, at noon, I saw a light from
heaven. It was brighter than the sun and
flashed all around me and those who were
traveling with me. 14We all fell to the ground.
Then I heard a voice speaking to me in the
Hebrew language,[n] saying, 'Saul, Saul, why are
you persecuting me? You are only hurting
yourself by fighting me.' 15I said, 'Who are you,
Lord?' The Lord said, 'I am Jesus, the one you
are persecuting. 16Stand up! I have chosen you
to be my servant and my witness—you will
tell people the things that you have seen and
the things that I will show you. This is why I
have come to you today. 17I will keep you safe
from your own people and also from the others. I am sending you to them 18to open their

25:21 emperor The ruler of the Roman Empire, which was almost all the known world.
26:14 Hebrew language Or Aramaic, the language of many people in this region in the first century.

eyes so that they may turn away from darkness to the light, away from the power of Satan
and to God. Then their sins can be forgiven,
and they can have a place with those people
who have been made holy by believing in me.'
19"King Agrippa, after I had this vision from
heaven, I obeyed it. 20I began telling people that
they should change their hearts and lives and
turn to God and do things to show they really
had changed. I told this first to those in Damascus, then in Jerusalem, and in every part of
Judea, and also to the other people. 21This is
why the Jews took me and
were trying to kill me in the
Temple. 22But God has
helped me, and so I stand
here today, telling all
people, small and great,
what I have seen. But I
am saying only what
Moses and the prophets
said would happen—
23that the Christ would
die, and as the first to rise
from the dead, he would
bring light to all people."

> "Stand up! I have chosen you to be my servant and my witness—you will tell people the things that you have seen and the things that I will show you." (Acts 26:16)

PAUL TRIES TO PERSUADE AGRIPPA

24While Paul was saying these things to defend himself, Festus said loudly, "Paul, you are
out of your mind! Too much study has driven
you crazy!"
25Paul said, "Most excellent Festus, I am not
crazy. My words are true and sensible. 26King
Agrippa knows about these things, and I can
speak freely to him. I know he has heard about
all of these things, because they did not happen
off in a corner. 27King Agrippa, do you believe
what the prophets wrote? I know you believe."
28King Agrippa said to Paul, "Do you think
you can persuade me to become a Christian in
such a short time?"
29Paul said, "Whether it is a short or a long
time, I pray to God that not only you but every
person listening to me today would be saved
and be like me—except for these chains I have."
30Then King Agrippa, Governor Festus, Bernice, and all the people sitting with them stood
up 31and left the room. Talking to each other,
they said, "There is no reason why this man
should die or be put in jail." 32And Agrippa said
to Festus, "We could let this man go free, but he
has asked Caesar to hear his case."

PAUL SAILS FOR ROME

27
1It was decided that we would sail for Italy.
An officer named Julius, who served in the
emperor's[n] army, guarded Paul and some other
prisoners. 2We got on a ship that was from the
city of Adramyttium and was about to sail to
different ports in the country of Asia. Aristarchus, a man from the city of Thessalonica in
Macedonia, went with us. 3The next day we
came to Sidon. Julius was very good to Paul
and gave him freedom to go visit his friends,
who took care of his needs. 4We left Sidon and
sailed close to the island of
Cyprus, because the wind
was blowing against us.
5We went across the sea
by Cilicia and Pamphylia
and landed at the city of
Myra, in Lycia. 6There the
officer found a ship from
Alexandria that was go-
ing to Italy, so he put us
on it.
7We sailed slowly for
many days. We had a hard
time reaching Cnidus be-
cause the wind was blowing
against us, and we could not go any farther. So
we sailed by the south side of the island of
Crete near Salmone. 8Sailing past it was hard.
Then we came to a place called Fair Havens,
near the city of Lasea.
9We had lost much time, and it was now
dangerous to sail, because it was already after
the Day of Cleansing.[n] So Paul warned them,
10"Men, I can see there will be a lot of trouble
on this trip. The ship, the cargo, and even our
lives may be lost." 11But the captain and the
owner of the ship did not agree with Paul, and
the officer believed what the captain and owner of the ship said. 12Since that harbor was not
a good place for the ship to stay for the winter,
most of the men decided that the ship should
leave. They hoped we could go to Phoenix and
stay there for the winter. Phoenix, a city on the
island of Crete, had a harbor which faced
southwest and northwest.

THE STORM

13When a good wind began to blow from
the south, the men on the ship thought, "This is
the wind we wanted, and now we have it." So
they pulled up the anchor, and we sailed very

27:1 emperor The ruler of the Roman Empire, which was almost all the known world. **27:9 Day of Cleansing** An important Jewish holy day in the fall of the year. This was the time of year that bad storms arose on the sea.

close to the island of Crete. 14But then a very strong wind named the "northeaster" came from the island. 15The ship was caught in it and could not sail against it. So we stopped trying and let the wind carry us. 16When we went below a small island named Cauda, we were barely able to bring in the lifeboat. 17After the men took the lifeboat in, they tied ropes around the ship to hold it together. The men were afraid that the ship would hit the sandbanks of Syrtis,[n] so they lowered the sail and let the wind carry the ship. 18The next day the storm was blowing us so hard that the men threw out some of the cargo. 19A day later with their own hands they threw out the ship's equipment. 20When we could not see the sun or the stars for many days, and the storm was very bad, we lost all hope of being saved.

21After the men had gone without food for a long time, Paul stood up before them and said, "Men, you should have listened to me. You should not have sailed from Crete. Then you would not have all this trouble and loss. 22But now I tell you to cheer up because none of you will die. Only the ship will be lost. 23Last night an angel came to me from the God I belong to and worship. 24The angel said, 'Paul, do not be afraid. You must stand before Caesar. And God has promised you that he will save the lives of everyone sailing with you.' 25So men, have courage. I trust in God that everything will happen as his angel told me. 26But we will crash on an island."

27On the fourteenth night we were still being carried around in the Adriatic Sea.[n] About midnight the sailors thought we were close to land, 28so they lowered a rope with a weight on the end of it into the water. They found that the water was one hundred twenty feet deep. They went a little farther and lowered the rope again. It was ninety feet deep. 29The sailors were afraid that we would hit the rocks, so they threw four anchors into the water and prayed for daylight to come. 30Some of the sailors wanted to leave the ship, and they lowered the lifeboat, pretending they were throwing more anchors from the front of the ship. 31But Paul told the officer and the other soldiers, "If these men do not stay in the ship, your lives cannot be saved." 32So the soldiers cut the ropes and let the lifeboat fall into the water.

33Just before dawn Paul began persuading all the people to eat something. He said, "For the past fourteen days you have been waiting and watching and not eating. 34Now I beg you to eat something. You need it to stay alive. None of you will lose even one hair off your heads." 35After he said this, Paul took some bread and thanked God for it before all of them. He broke off a piece and began eating. 36They all felt better and started eating, too. 37There were two hundred seventy-six people on the ship. 38When they had eaten all they wanted, they began making the ship lighter by throwing the grain into the sea.

THANKFULNESS

Who should we thank for what we have? (27:35)

THE SHIP IS DESTROYED

39When daylight came, the sailors saw land. They did not know what land it was, but they saw a bay with a beach and wanted to sail the ship to the beach if they could. 40So they cut the ropes to the anchors and left the anchors in the sea. At the same time, they untied the ropes that were holding the rudders. Then they raised the front sail into the wind and sailed toward the beach. 41But the ship hit a sandbank. The front of the ship stuck there and could not move, but the back of the ship began to break up from the big waves.

42The soldiers decided to kill the prisoners so none of them could swim away and escape. 43But Julius, the officer, wanted to let Paul live and did not allow the soldiers to kill the prisoners. Instead he ordered everyone who could swim to jump into the water first and swim to land. 44The rest were to follow using wooden boards or pieces of the ship. And this is how all the people made it safely to land.

PAUL ON THE ISLAND OF MALTA

28

1When we were safe on land, we learned that the island was called Malta. 2The people who lived there were very good to us. Because it was raining and very cold, they made a fire and welcomed all of us. 3Paul gathered a pile of sticks and was putting them on the fire when a poisonous snake came out because of the heat and bit him on the hand. 4The people living on the island saw the snake hanging from Paul's hand and said to each other, "This man must be a murderer! He did not die in the sea, but Justice[n] does not want him to live." 5But Paul

27:17 Syrtis Shallow area in the sea near the Libyan coast. **27:27 Adriatic Sea** The sea between Greece and Italy, including the central Mediterranean. **28:4 Justice** The people thought there was a god named Justice who would punish bad people.

WHAT'S IT MEAN?

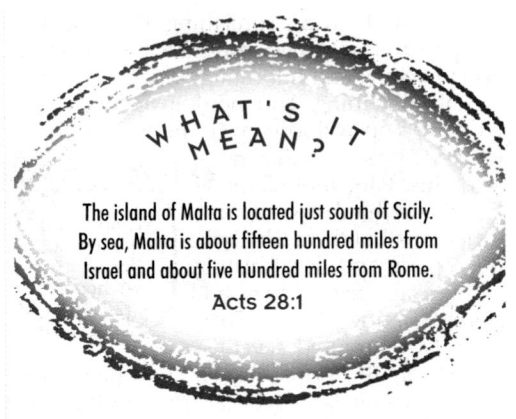

The island of Malta is located just south of Sicily.
By sea, Malta is about fifteen hundred miles from
Israel and about five hundred miles from Rome.
Acts 28:1

shook the snake off into the fire and was not
hurt. 6The people thought that Paul would
swell up or fall down dead. They waited and
watched him for a long time, but nothing bad
happened to him. So they changed their minds
and said, "He is a god!"
7There were some fields around there
owned by Publius, an important man on the
island. He welcomed us into his home
and was very good to us for
three days. 8Publius' father
was sick with a fever and
dysentery.[n] Paul went to him,
prayed, and put his hands on
the man and healed him. 9Af-
ter this, all the other sick peo-
ple on the island came to Paul, and he healed
them, too. 10-11The people on the island gave us
many honors. When we were ready to leave,
three months later, they gave us the things we
needed.

GIVING
Who should we be mindful to support? (28:7–10)

PAUL GOES TO ROME

We got on a ship from Alexandria that had
stayed on the island during the winter. On the
front of the ship was the sign of the twin gods.[n]
12We stopped at Syracuse for three days.
13From there we sailed to Rhegium. The next
day a wind began to blow from the south, and
a day later we came to Puteoli. 14We found
some believers there who asked us to stay with
them for a week. Finally, we came to Rome.
15The believers in Rome heard that we were
there and came out as far as the Market of
Appius[n] and the Three Inns[n] to meet us. When
Paul saw them, he was encouraged and
thanked God.

PAUL IN ROME

16When we arrived at Rome, Paul was allowed to live alone, with the soldier who
guarded him.
17Three days later Paul sent for the leaders
there. When they came together, he said,
"Brothers, I have done nothing against our
people or the customs of our ancestors. But I
was arrested in Jerusalem and given to the Romans. 18After they asked me many questions,
they could find no reason why I should be
killed. They wanted to let me go free, 19but the
evil people there argued against that. So I had
to ask to come to Rome to have my trial before
Caesar. But I have no charge to bring against
my own people. 20That is why I wanted to see
you and talk with you. I am bound with this
chain because I believe in the hope of Israel."
21They answered Paul, "We have received
no letters from Judea about you. None of our
Jewish brothers who have come from there
brought news or told us anything bad about
you. 22But we want to hear your ideas, because
we know that people everywhere are speaking
against this religious group."
23Paul and the people chose a day for a
meeting and on that day many more of the
Jews met with Paul at the place he was staying.
He spoke to them all day long. Using the law of
Moses and the prophets' writings, he explained
the kingdom of God, and he tried to persuade
them to believe these things about Jesus.
24Some believed what Paul said, but others did
not. 25So they argued and began leaving after
Paul said one more thing to them: "The Holy
Spirit spoke the truth to your ancestors through
Isaiah the prophet, saying,
26'Go to this people and say:
You will listen and listen, but you will not
understand.
You will look and look, but you will not
learn,
27because these people have become
stubborn.
They don't hear with their ears,
and they have closed their eyes.
Otherwise, they might really understand
what they see with their eyes
and hear with their ears.
They might really understand in their
minds
and come back to me and be healed.'

Isaiah 6:9-10

28:8 dysentery A sickness like diarrhea. **28:10-11 twin gods** Statues of Castor and Pollux, gods in old Greek tales. **28:15 Market of Appius** A town about twenty-seven miles from Rome.
28:15 Three Inns A town about thirty miles from Rome.

28 "I want you to know that God has also
sent his salvation to all nations, and they will
listen!" 29 [n]
30 Paul stayed two full years in his own rented
house and welcomed all people who came to
visit him. 31 He boldly preached about the kingdom of God and taught about the Lord Jesus
Christ, and no one tried to stop him.

28:29 Verse 29 Some late Greek copies add verse 29: "After Paul said this, the Jews left. They were arguing very much with each other."

Romans

CONTENT Do you know what a primer is? It is the most basic handbook you can find. When you learned to read, you probably used a primer of some kind. It is a book that explains a big concept in simple, small pieces. It is an outline of the fundamentals.

The Book of Romans is a kind of primer. It is a primer to the Christian life. Paul wrote it to the Romans so that they would have an introduction to him and to his beliefs before he came to visit them. He wanted to make the most of his trip there, so the more he could explain to them ahead of time, the better. He could answer their questions when he arrived.

The basic message of Romans is this: You are saved by God's grace through faith, not by the good things you do. None of us deserves salvation. It is God's free gift through Jesus.

Life gets complicated sometimes—trying to figure out what to do and what not to do. Romans takes us back to the basics so that we can find our way to God and then figure out life in light of his love.

Outline

1:1–17 .... Paul and His Message of Good News
1:18—3:20 .... Everyone Is Guilty
3:21—4:25 .... Made Right with God by Faith
5:1—8:39 .... A New Life in Christ for God's People
9:1—11:36 .... What About the People of Israel?
12:1—15:13 .... How to Live a Transformed Life of Love
15:14—16:27 ...... Paul's Plans and Personal Greetings

Purpose God declares us right with himself and helps us to live that way.

Theme The Goodness of God in the Good News of Christ

Date of writing Spring A.D. 57

"I am proud of the Good News, because it is the power God uses to save everyone who believes—to save the Jews first, and also to save those who are not Jews" (1:16).

Bible Talk

Faith: A New Concept?

We are used to talking about faith. It doesn't seem like a difficult concept. We hear songs about it on the radio. We hear the word at least three times every time we go to church. Why does it seem to be such a new thought to the early Christians?

Before Christ's life and death, God was worshiped through sacrifices and rituals. People still had to have faith, but it was faith that *one day* God would send a savior. They still depended on their sacrifices to keep them right with God.

Once Jesus came, he made the one true sacrifice. No one had to do all those rituals to keep themselves right with God anymore. They just had to have faith in Jesus' sacrifice for their sins. In that way, faith was a very new concept.

WANTED: DEAD OR ALIVE

In Paul's letter to the Romans, he makes one bold statement in a lot of different ways: Before we come to believe in Christ and his sacrifice, we are dead in our sins. We are spiritual corpses. Our bodies might be carrying on, but our spirits have no breath in them. We don't function. We can't do the things that we were created to do like spill over with joy and kindness and patience and abundant life.

But when we accept Christ's sacrifice for our sins and put our faith in *his* goodness rather than our own, then we come to life. The Holy Spirit breathes his life into us, and our spirits come alive and dance and sing in the light of God's love.

1 From Paul, a servant of Christ Jesus. God called me to be an apostle and chose me to tell the Good News.

2 God promised this Good News long ago through his prophets, as it is written in the Holy Scriptures. 3-4 The Good News is about God's Son, Jesus Christ our Lord. As a man, he was born from the family of David. But through the Spirit of holiness he was appointed to be God's Son with great power by rising from the dead. 5 Through Christ, God gave me the special work of an apostle, which was to lead people of all nations to believe and obey. I do this work for him. 6 And you who are in Rome are also called to belong to Jesus Christ.

> **"First I want to say that I thank my God through Jesus Christ for all of you, because people everywhere in the world are talking about your faith."**
> **(Romans 1:8)**

7 To all of you in Rome whom God loves and has called to be his holy people:

Grace and peace to you from God our Father and the Lord Jesus Christ.

WHAT'S IT MEAN?

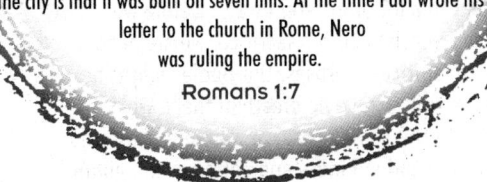

As you may have guessed from the name, the capital of the Roman Empire was Rome. Apparently, the city was a pretty good choice for a capital because the country of Italy is using it today. During New Testament times, the population of Rome was about eight hundred thousand, including about ten thousand Jews. One of the most unusual features of the city is that it was built on seven hills. At the time Paul wrote his letter to the church in Rome, Nero was ruling the empire.

Romans 1:7

A PRAYER OF THANKS

8 First I want to say that I thank my God through Jesus Christ for all of you, because people everywhere in the world are talking about your faith. 9 God, whom I serve with my whole heart by telling the Good News about his Son, knows that I always mention you 10 every time I pray. I pray that I will be allowed to come to you, and this will happen if God wants it. 11 I want very much to see you, to give you some spiritual gift to make you strong. 12 I mean that I want us to help each other with the faith we have. Your faith will help me, and my faith will help you. 13 Brothers and sisters,[n] I want you to know that I planned many times to come to you, but this has not been possible. I wanted to come so that I could help you grow spiritually as I have helped the other non-Jewish people.

14 I have a duty to all people—Greeks and those who are not Greeks, the wise and the foolish. 15 That is why I want so much to preach the Good News to you in Rome.

EMBARRASSMENT
Is the Good News a source of embarrassment? (1:16)

16 I am proud of the Good News, because it is the power God uses to save everyone who believes—to save the Jews first, and also to save those who are not Jews. 17 The Good News shows how God makes people right with himself—that it begins and ends with faith. As the Scripture says, "But those who are right with God will live by trusting in him."[n]

ALL PEOPLE HAVE DONE WRONG

HOMOSEXUALITY
Will homosexuals be held accountable for their actions? (1:18–32)

18 God's anger is shown from heaven against all the evil and wrong things people do. By their own evil lives they hide the truth. 19 God shows his anger because some knowledge of him has been made clear to them. Yes, God has shown himself to them. 20 There are things about him that people cannot see—his eternal power and all the things that make him God. But since the beginning of the world those things have been easy to understand by what God has made. So people have no excuse for the bad things they do. 21 They knew God, but they did not give glory to God or thank him. Their thinking be-

1:13 Brothers and sisters Although the Greek text says "Brothers" here and throughout this book, Paul's words were meant for the entire church, including men and women. **1:17 "But those . . . him."** Quotation from Habakkuk 2:4.

came useless. Their foolish minds were filled with darkness. 22They said they were wise, but they became fools. 23They traded the glory of God who lives forever for the worship of idols made to look like earthly people, birds, animals, and snakes.

24Because they did these things, God left them and let them go their sinful way, wanting only to do evil. As a result, they became full of sexual sin, using their bodies wrongly with each other. 25They traded the truth of God for a lie. They worshiped and served what had been created instead of the God who created those things, who should be praised forever. Amen.

26Because people did those things, God left them and let them do the shameful things they wanted to do. Women stopped having natural sex and started having sex with other women. 27In the same way, men stopped having natural sex and began wanting each other. Men did shameful things with other men, and in their bodies they received the punishment for those wrongs.

28People did not think it was important to have a true knowledge of God. So God left them and allowed them to have their own worthless thinking and to do things they should not do. 29They are filled with every kind of sin, evil, selfishness, and hatred. They are full of jealousy, murder, fighting, lying, and thinking the worst about each other. They gossip 30and say evil things about each other. They hate God. They are rude and conceited and brag about themselves. They invent ways of doing evil. They do not obey their parents. 31They are foolish, they do not keep their promises, and they show no kindness or mercy to others. 32They know God's law says that those who live like this should die. But they themselves not only continue to do these evil things, they applaud others who do them.

YOU PEOPLE ALSO ARE SINFUL

2 1If you think you can judge others, you are wrong. When you judge them, you are really judging yourself guilty, because you do the same things they do. 2God judges those who do wrong things, and we know that his judging is right. 3You judge those who do wrong, but you do wrong yourselves. Do you think you will be able to escape the judgment of God? 4He has been very kind and patient, waiting for you to change, but you think nothing of his kindness. Perhaps you do not understand that

Promise

HE PROMISES EVERYONE WHO HAS FAITH WILL LIVE.

The Good News shows how God makes people right with himself—that it begins and ends with faith. As the Scripture says, "But those who are right with God will live by trusting in him" (Rom. 1:17).

Most people want to do something so that God will like them. They think that if they're really good, if they do everything—or most things—right, then God will accept them. It makes people feel really good to think there's something so neat about them that they can earn a spot in heaven.

The truth is that no one can be *that* good. There's something special about every single person on earth, but there's some junk in everyone, too. God doesn't accept anyone's goodness as good enough to get into heaven.

But that's not the end of the story. "The Good News shows how God makes people right with himself—that it begins and ends with faith." In other words, God accepts those who come to him in faith. Now *that's* good news. It's not being good that gets God to accept you; it's having faith in his Son. You don't have to settle for some mealy-mouthed, lip-service faith. You can have a faith so strong, so alive that you can't wait to commit your whole life to Jesus. Then, as Romans 1:17 says, you will live—not just physically, but live with strength and power because you're trusting in him.

Keep renewing your mind with God's Word. That's how you build faith. Do your best to live the way God wants you to just because you love him and you want to please him. Faith sets you free from the vicious cycle of constantly trying to work your way into God's good graces.

SEE FOR YOURSELF:

Hab. 2:4; Rom. 5:18–19; Gal. 3:9, 26–27; Heb. 11

God is kind to you so you will change your
hearts and lives. 5But you are stubborn and
refuse to change, so you are making your own
punishment even greater on the day he shows
his anger. On that day everyone will see God's
right judgments. 6God will reward or punish
every person for what that person has done.
7Some people, by always continuing to do
good, live for God's glory, for honor, and for
life that has no end. God will give them life
forever. 8But other people are selfish. They refuse to follow truth and, instead, follow evil.
God will give them his punishment and anger.
9He will give trouble and suffering to everyone
who does evil—to the Jews first and also to
those who are not Jews. 10But he will give glory,
honor, and peace to everyone who does
good—to the Jews first and also to those who
are not Jews. 11For God judges all people in the
same way.

12People who do not have the law and who
are sinners will be lost, although they do not
have the law. And, in the same way, those who
have the law and are sinners will be judged by
the law. 13Hearing the law does not make people right with God. It is those who obey the
law who will be right with him. 14(Those who
are not Jews do not have the law, but when
they freely do what the law commands, they
are the law for themselves. This is true even
though they do not have the law. 15They show
that in their hearts they know what is right
and wrong, just as the law commands. And
they show this by their consciences. Sometimes their thoughts tell them they did wrong,
and sometimes their thoughts tell them they
did right.) 16All these things will happen on the
day when God, through Christ Jesus, will judge
people's secret thoughts. The Good News that I
preach says this.

THE JEWS AND THE LAW

17What about you? You call yourself a Jew.
You trust in the law of Moses and brag that
you are close to God. 18You know what he
wants you to do and what is important, because you have learned the law. 19You think
you are a guide for the blind and a light for
those who are in darkness. 20You think you
can show foolish people what is right and
teach those who know nothing. You have the
law; so you think you know everything and
have all truth. 21You teach others, so why don't
you teach yourself? You tell others not to steal,
but you steal. 22You say that others must not
take part in adultery, but you are guilty of that
sin. You hate idols, but you steal from temples.
23You brag about having God's law, but you
bring shame to God by breaking his law, 24just
as the Scriptures say: "Those who are not Jews
speak against God's name because of you."[n]

WHAT'S IT MEAN?

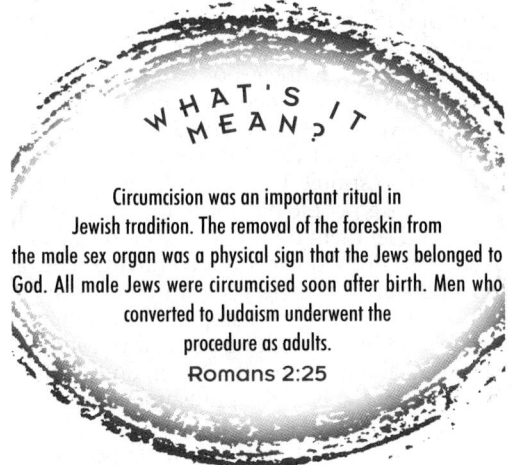

Circumcision was an important ritual in Jewish tradition. The removal of the foreskin from the male sex organ was a physical sign that the Jews belonged to God. All male Jews were circumcised soon after birth. Men who converted to Judaism underwent the procedure as adults.

Romans 2:25

25If you follow the law, your circumcision
has meaning. But if you break the law, it is as if
you were never circumcised. 26People who are
not Jews are not circumcised, but if they do
what the law says, it is as if they were circumcised. 27You Jews have the written law and circumcision, but you break the law. So those
who are not circumcised in their bodies, but
still obey the law, will show that you are guilty.
28They can do this because a person is not a
true Jew if he is only a Jew in his physical
body; true circumcision is not only on the outside of the body. 29A person is a Jew only if he
is a Jew inside; true circumcision is done in the
heart by the Spirit, not by the written law. Such
a person gets praise from God rather than
from people.

3 1So, do Jews have anything that other people do not have? Is there anything special
about being circumcised? 2Yes, of course, there
is in every way. The most important thing is
this: God trusted the Jews with his teachings.
3If some Jews were not faithful to him, will that
stop God from doing what he promised? 4No!
God will continue to be true even when every
person is false. As the Scriptures say:

"So you will be shown to be right when
you speak,
and you will win your case." *Psalm 51:4*

5When we do wrong, that shows more

2:24 "Those . . . you." Quotation from Isaiah 52:5; Ezekiel 36:20.

clearly that God is right. So can we say that
God is wrong to punish us? (I am talking as
people might talk.) 6No! If God could not punish us, he could not judge the world.
7A person might say, "When I lie, it really
gives him glory, because my lie shows God's
truth. So why am I judged a sinner?" 8It would
be the same to say, "We should do evil so that
good will come." Some people find fault with us
and say we teach this, but they are wrong and
deserve the punishment they will receive.

ALL PEOPLE ARE GUILTY

9So are we Jews better
than others? No! We have
already said that Jews
and those who are not
Jews are all guilty of sin.
10As the Scriptures say:

"There is no one who
always does
what is right,
not even one.
11There is no one who
understands.
There is no one who
looks to God for help.
12All have turned away.
Together, everyone has
become useless.
There is no one who does
anything good;
there is not even one."
Psalm 14:1-3
13"Their throats are like
open graves;
they use their tongues for telling lies."
Psalm 5:9
"Their words are like snake poison." *Psalm 140:3*
14"Their mouths are full of cursing
and hate." *Psalm 10:7*
15"They are always ready to kill people.
16Everywhere they go they cause ruin and
misery.
17They don't know how to live in peace."
Isaiah 59:7-8
18"They have no fear of God." *Psalm 36:1*

19We know that the law's commands are for
those who have the law. This stops all excuses
and brings the whole world under God's judgment, 20because no one can be made right with
God by following the law. The law only shows
us our sin.

HOW GOD MAKES PEOPLE RIGHT

21But God has a way to make people right
with him without the law, and he has now
shown us that way which the law and the
prophets told us about. 22God makes people
right with himself through their faith in Jesus
Christ. This is true for all who believe
in Christ, because all people are
the same: 23All have sinned
and are not good enough for
God's glory, 24and all need to
be made right with God by
his grace, which is a free gift.
They need to be made free from
sin through Jesus Christ. 25God gave him as a
way to forgive sin through
faith in the blood of Jesus'
death. This showed that
God always does what
is right and fair, as in
the past when he was
patient and did not
punish people for their
sins. 26And God gave
Jesus to show today
that he does what is
right. God did this so
he could judge rightly
and so he could make right
any person who has faith in
Jesus.
27So do we have a reason to brag about
ourselves? No! And why not? It is the way of
faith that stops all bragging, not the way of trying to obey the law. 28A person is made right
with God through faith, not through obeying
the law. 29Is God only the God of the Jews? Is
he not also the God of those who are not Jews?
30Of course he is, because there is only one
God. He will make Jews right with him by their

SIN
Can God tolerate sin? (3:23)

"All have sinned and are not good enough for God's glory, and all need to be made right with God by his grace, which is a free gift. They need to be made free from sin through Jesus Christ." (Romans 3:23–24)

GUILT
Are all people guilty of sin? (3:9–12)

WHAT'S IT MEAN?

Under the Teachings that God gave to Moses, when a person had sinned, an animal had to be sacrificed, meaning killed on an altar. Usually it was a sheep whose blood was offered as payment for the sin. Jesus put an end to that old system of sacrifice when he became the ultimate sacrifice. Jesus' death paid for the sins of the entire world, once and for all. God accepted his blood as the only offering that would ever need to be made.
Romans 3:25–26

faith, and he will also make those who are not
Jews right with him through their faith. [31]So do
we destroy the law by following the way of
faith? No! Faith causes us to be what the law
truly wants.

THE EXAMPLE OF ABRAHAM

4 [1]So what can we say that Abraham,[n] the
father of our people, learned about faith? [2]If
Abraham was made right by the things he did,
he had a reason to brag. But this is not God's
view, [3]because the Scripture says, "Abraham
believed God, and God accepted Abraham's
faith, and that faith made him right with God."[n]
[4]When people work, their pay is not given
as a gift, but as something earned. [5]But people
cannot do any work that will make them right
with God. So they must trust in him, who makes
even evil people right in his sight. Then God
accepts their faith, and that makes them right
with him. [6]David said the same thing. He said
that people are truly blessed when God, without paying attention to good deeds, makes people right with himself.

[7]"Happy are they
whose sins are forgiven,
whose wrongs are pardoned.
[8]Happy is the person
whom the Lord does not consider
guilty." *Psalm 32:1-2*

[9]Is this blessing only for those who are circumcised or also for those who are not circumcised? We have already said that God
accepted Abraham's faith and that faith made
him right with God. [10]So how did this happen?
Did God accept Abraham before or after he
was circumcised? It was before his circumcision. [11]Abraham was circumcised to show that
he was right with God through faith before he
was circumcised. So Abraham is the father of
all those who believe but are not circumcised;
he is the father of all believers who are accepted as being right with God. [12]And Abraham is
also the father of those who have been circumcised and who live following the faith that
our father Abraham had before he was circumcised.

GOD KEEPS HIS PROMISE

[13]Abraham[n] and his descendants received
the promise that they would get the whole
world. He did not receive that promise

4:1, 13 Abraham Most respected ancestor of the Jews. Every Jew hoped to see Abraham.
4:3 "Abraham . . . God." Quotation from Genesis 15:6.

Promise

HE PROMISES TO TREAT YOU BETTER THAN YOU DESERVE.

All need to be made right with God by his grace, which is a free gift. They need to be made free from sin through Jesus Christ (Rom. 3:24).

Hate to break it to you this way. You're a pretty good kid and all. But unfortunately, your situation leaves no other choice. Pockets of sin have been discovered in numerous places on your body—some leading all the way down to your heart—and your track record certainly bears out the fact that you do indeed have a serious problem.

So . . .your file's being turned over to the justice department. Been nice knowing you.

However, if it will make you feel better, you should know that you're in good company. In fact, in all the time that God's been handling this, only one Person has ever been cleared of the death sentence on the first try. Just one. Fellow from Nazareth by the name of Jesus. But ever since then, before these cases can be properly executed, convicted lawbreakers like you have the right to pursue one final route of appeal.

It goes something like this. If you'll deliver an honest confession to God that your personal performance has been a dismal failure, and that you are willing to let Jesus' innocence stand in the place of all your hard work and effort at passing the grade . . .well, let's just say no one has ever been turned down yet.

Are you ready to exercise your option? Go for it!

SEE FOR YOURSELF:

Dan. 9:9; Eph. 2:8–9; Titus 3:4–7

On the Edge

Abraham was circumcised to show that he was right with God through faith before he was circumcised. So Abraham is the father of all those who believe but are not circumcised; he is the father of all believers who are accepted as being right with God (Rom. 4:11).

In the Bible, Abraham is famous for his faith. He packed up and left his home when God told him to, even though he had no clue where God was taking him. (Basically, the Lord said, "I'll tell you when you get there.") Later, he obeyed when God told him to sacrifice his only son, Isaac—the one he had waited 100 years to have and the one God had promised him. Abraham's faith in God was so strong that he even raised a knife to kill Isaac as a sacrifice to the Lord. And then an angel of the Lord commanded him to stop. Abraham sinned many times, but his enormous faith made him acceptable to God.

The Jews were so proud of being Abraham's descendants that they went around calling themselves children of Abraham. Everyone wanted to be a child of Abraham because of the great blessings those children were promised. Read about those blessings in Genesis 17. Paul writes that the real children of Abraham are not the people who can write his name at the base of their family tree. The children of Abraham are the people who have the same kind of faith that he had—faith that proves itself by actions.

You are a child of Abraham if you have real, active faith in Jesus. It's your faith that makes you acceptable to God, not your bloodline.

SEE FOR YOURSELF:
Gen. 17; Matt. 3:9; Rom. 4:9–13; Gal. 3:7, 29

through the law, but through being right with
God by his faith. 14If people could receive what
God promised by following the law, then faith
is worthless. And God's promise to Abraham is
worthless, 15because the law can only bring
God's anger. But if there is no law, there is
nothing to disobey.
16So people receive God's promise by having faith. This happens so the promise can be a
free gift. Then all of Abraham's children can
have that promise. It is not only for those who
live under the law of Moses but for anyone
who lives with faith like that of Abraham, who
is the father of us all. 17As it is written in the
Scriptures: "I am making you a father of many
nations."[n] This is true before God, the God
Abraham believed, the God who gives life to
the dead and who creates something out of
nothing.

WHAT'S IT MEAN?

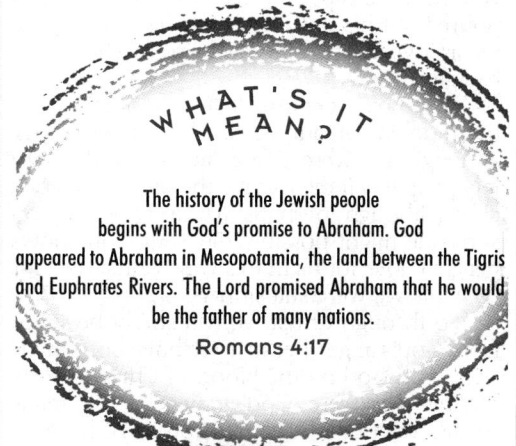

The history of the Jewish people begins with God's promise to Abraham. God appeared to Abraham in Mesopotamia, the land between the Tigris and Euphrates Rivers. The Lord promised Abraham that he would be the father of many nations.

Romans 4:17

18There was no hope that Abraham would
have children. But Abraham believed God and
continued hoping, and so he became the father
of many nations. As God told him, "Your descendants also will be too many to count."[n]
19Abraham was almost a hundred years old,
much past the age for having children, and
Sarah could not have children. Abraham
thought about all this, but his faith in God did
not become weak. 20He never doubted that
God would keep his promise, and he never
stopped believing. He grew stronger in his faith
and gave praise to God. 21Abraham felt sure
that God was able to do what he had promised. 22So, "God accepted Abraham's faith, and
that faith made him right with God."[n] 23Those
words ("God accepted Abraham's faith") were
written not only for Abraham 24but also for us.
God will accept us also because we believe in
the One who raised Jesus our Lord from the
dead. 25Jesus was given to die for our sins, and

4:17 "I . . . nations." Quotation from Genesis 17:5. **4:18 "Your . . . count."** Quotation from Genesis 15:5. **4:22 "God . . . God."** Quotation from Genesis 15:6.

he was raised from the dead to make us right
with God.

RIGHT WITH GOD

5 1Since we have been made right with God
by our faith, we have peace with God. This
happened through our Lord Jesus Christ, 2who
has brought us into that blessing of God's
grace that we now enjoy. And we are happy
because of the hope we have of sharing God's
glory. 3We also have joy with our troubles, because we know that these troubles produce
patience. 4And patience produces character,
and character produces hope. 5And this hope
will never disappoint us, because God has
poured out his love to fill our hearts. He gave
us his love through the Holy Spirit, whom God
has given to us.
6When we were unable to help ourselves, at
the moment of our need, Christ died for us,
although we were living against God. 7Very
few people will die to save the life of someone
else. Although perhaps for a good person
someone might possibly die. 8But God shows
his great love for us in this way: Christ died for
us while we were still sinners.
9So through Christ we will surely be saved
from God's anger, because we have been made
right with God by the blood of Christ's death.
10While we were God's enemies, he made
friends with us through the death of his Son.
Surely, now that we are his friends, he will save
us through his Son's life. 11And not only that,
but now we are also very happy in God
through our Lord Jesus Christ. Through him
we are now God's friends again.

On the Edge

Since we have been made right with God by our faith, we have peace with God. This happened through our Lord Jesus Christ (Rom. 5:1).

Now that you are a believer, the battle for your spirit is over. You chose the path of victory when you chose Jesus. When you trusted him, God gave you peace. Are you enjoying the peace you have, or are you trying to fight a battle that's already been won? God wants to come into your life and bring calm to the chaos. He wants you to let him be the light that shatters your darkest storm. A lot of people give their hearts to Jesus and then keep on fighting the same old way they used to. With the peace of God, you can let go of some of your anxiety about grades, college, finances, family, whatever. Do everything you know to do and trust God. You don't have to manipulate decisions and worry about things you can't see. You don't have to go through life by yourself anymore. Rest in the peace God brings. Maybe, if we could hear him, he would be saying, "Stop fighting that battle. I've already done that for you. Be still. Rest. Open your eyes. My love for you has cast out all fear. Look at what I've done. Stop wringing your hands in worry. I love you. I want you to experience the peace I've given you."

SEE FOR YOURSELF:
John 14:27; Col. 3:15; 2 Thess. 3:16

WHAT'S IT MEAN?

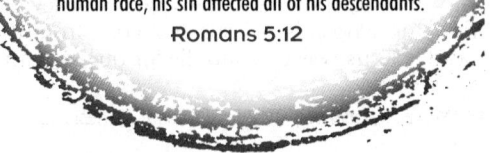

After God created Adam, he placed him in the Garden of Eden. The place was paradise—literally. The law of the land was pretty simple, too: Eat from any tree in the garden except the tree of the knowledge of good and evil. That's it. That's the only rule Adam and his wife Eve had to remember and obey. Guess what? They chose to disobey God and eat the fruit from the forbidden tree. Because Adam represented the entire human race, his sin affected all of his descendants.

Romans 5:12

ADAM AND CHRIST COMPARED

12Sin came into the world because of what
one man did, and with sin came death. This is
why everyone must die—because everyone
sinned. 13Sin was in the world before the law
of Moses, but sin is not counted against us as
breaking a command when there is no law.
14But from the time of Adam to the time of
Moses, everyone had to die, even those who
had not sinned by breaking a command, as
Adam had.
Adam was like the One who was coming in
the future. 15But God's free gift is not like
Adam's sin. Many people died because of the
sin of that one man. But the grace from God
was much greater; many people received God's

gift of life by the grace of the one man, Jesus
Christ. 16After Adam sinned once, he was
judged guilty. But the gift of God is different.
God's free gift came after many sins, and it
makes people right with God. 17One man
sinned, and so death ruled all people because
of that one man. But now those people who
accept God's full grace and the great gift of being made right with him will surely have true
life and rule through the one man, Jesus Christ.
18So as one sin of Adam brought the punishment of death to all people, one good act
that Christ did makes all people right with
God. And that brings true life for all. 19One
man disobeyed God, and many became sinners. In the same way, one man obeyed God,
and many will be made right. 20The law came
to make sin worse. But when sin grew worse,
God's grace increased. 21Sin once used death to
rule us, but God gave people more of his grace
so that grace could rule by making people right
with him. And this brings life forever through
Jesus Christ our Lord.

DEAD TO SIN BUT ALIVE IN CHRIST

6 1So do you think we should continue sinning so that God will give us even more grace?
2No! We died to our old sinful lives, so how
can we continue living with sin? 3Did you forget that all of us became part of Christ when
we were baptized? We shared his death in our
baptism. 4When we were baptized, we were
buried with Christ and shared his death. So,
just as Christ was raised from the dead by the
wonderful power of the Father, we also can
live a new life.
5Christ died, and we have been joined with
him by dying too. So we will also be joined
with him by rising from the dead as he did.
6We know that our old life died with Christ on
the cross so that our sinful selves would have
no power over us and we would not be slaves
to sin. 7Anyone who has died is made free
from sin's control.
8If we died with Christ, we know we will
also live with him. 9Christ was raised from the
dead, and we know that he cannot die again.
Death has no power over him now. 10Yes,
when Christ died, he died to defeat the power
of sin one time—enough for all time. He now
has a new life, and his new life is with God.
11In the same way, you should see yourselves
as being dead to the power of sin and alive
with God through Christ Jesus.
12So, do not let sin control your life here on
earth so that you do what your sinful self
wants to do. 13Do not offer the parts of your
body to serve sin, as things to be used in doing
evil. Instead, offer yourselves to God as people
who have died and now live. Offer the parts of
your body to God to be used in doing good.
14Sin will not be your master, because you are
not under law but under God's grace.

BE SLAVES OF RIGHTEOUSNESS

15So what should we do? Should we sin
because we are under grace and not under
law? No! 16Surely you know that when you
give yourselves like slaves to obey someone,
then you are really slaves of that person. The
person you obey is your master. You can follow sin, which brings spiritual death, or you
can obey God, which makes you right with

On the Edge

So do you think we should continue sinning so that God will give even more grace? No! We died to our old sinful lives, so how can we continue living with sin? (Rom. 6:1–2).

Paul went around preaching that people couldn't do anything to earn God's friendship. When he told them that the only way they could know God and go to heaven one day was by having faith and trusting in God's kindness (grace), he probably knew that some people were going to say, "Cool. Then we can do anything we want because it doesn't matter, right?"

Knowing that the question would come up, Paul included something incredible in this letter: "We died to our old sinful lives." That doesn't sound right. How can Paul say that you're dead to sin when you know that you mess up and sin all the time? Well, Paul wasn't just making that up. He explains it this way: "When we were baptized, we were buried with Christ and shared his death. So, just as Christ was raised from the dead by the wonderful power of the Father, we also can live a new life" (6:4).

Paul was explaining that, because you've put your trust in Jesus, sin only has power over you when you let it. Keep being transformed by God's Word. Keep making the effort to walk in love, forgiveness, and purity before the Lord.

SEE FOR YOURSELF:
Rom. 6; Eph. 2:1–9; Col. 2:11–14

him. [17]In the past you were slaves to sin—sin
controlled you. But thank God, you fully
obeyed the things that you were taught. [18]You
were made free from sin, and now you are
slaves to goodness. [19]I use this example because this is hard for you to understand. In the
past you offered the parts of your body to be
slaves to sin and evil; you lived only for evil. In
the same way now you must give yourselves
to be slaves of goodness. Then you will live
only for God.

WHAT'S IT MEAN?

The comparison between sin and slavery probably hit home to many of the people who read Paul's letter. In New Testament times, one out of every four people in the Roman Empire was a slave. People who were captured in battle, whether they were soldiers or civilians, usually became slaves. People who could not afford to pay their debts also became slaves to work off what they owed.

Romans 6:19

[20]In the past you were slaves to sin, and
goodness did not control you. [21]You did evil
things, and now you are ashamed of them.
Those things only bring death. [22]But now you
are free from sin and have become
slaves of God. This brings you
a life that is only for God, and
this gives you life forever.
[23]When people sin, they earn
what sin pays—death. But
God gives us a free gift—life
forever in Christ Jesus our Lord.

DEATH

What does sin earn us? (6:23)

AN EXAMPLE FROM MARRIAGE

7 [1]Brothers and sisters, all of you understand
the law of Moses. So surely you know that the
law rules over people only while they are alive.
[2]For example, a woman must stay married to
her husband as long as he is alive. But if her
husband dies, she is free from the law of
marriage. [3]But if she marries another man
while her husband is still alive, the law says
she is guilty of adultery. But if her husband
dies, she is free from the law of marriage. Then
if she marries another man, she is not guilty of
adultery.

[4]In the same way, my brothers and sisters,
your old selves died, and you became free
from the law through the body of Christ. This
happened so that you might belong to someone else—the One who was raised from the
dead—and so that we might be used in service
to God. [5]In the past, we were ruled by our sinful selves. The law made us want to do sinful
things that controlled our bodies, so the things
we did were bringing us death. [6]In the past, the
law held us like prisoners, but our old selves
died, and we were made free from the law. So
now we serve God in a new way with the Spirit, and not in the old way with written rules.

OUR FIGHT AGAINST SIN

[7]You might think I am saying that sin and
the law are the same thing. That is not true. But
the law was the only way I could learn what
sin meant. I would never have known what it
means to want to take something belonging to
someone else if the law had not said, "You
must not want to take your neighbor's things."[n]
[8]And sin found a way to use that command
and cause me to want all kinds of things I
should not want. But without the law, sin has
no power. [9]I was alive before I knew the law.
But when the law's command came to me,
then sin began to live, [10]and I died. The command was meant to bring life, but for me it
brought death. [11]Sin found a way to fool me
by using the command to make me die.

[12]So the law is holy, and the command is
holy and right and good. [13]Does this mean that
something that is good brought death to me?
No! Sin used something that is good to bring
death to me. This happened so that I could see
what sin is really like; the command was used
to show that sin is very evil.

THE WAR WITHIN US

[14]We know that the law is spiritual, but I am
not spiritual since sin rules me as if I were its
slave. [15]I do not understand the things I do. I do
not do what I want to do, and I do the things I
hate. [16]And if I do not want to do the hated
things I do, that means I agree that the law is
good. [17]But I am not really the one who is doing these hated things; it is sin living in me that
does them. [18]Yes, I know that nothing good
lives in me—I mean nothing good lives in the
part of me that is earthly and sinful. I want to

7:7 "You . . . things." Quotation from Exodus 20:17.

do the things that are good, but I do not do
them. 19I do not do the good things I want to
do, but I do the bad things I do not want to do.
20So if I do things I do not want to do, then I am
not the one doing them. It is sin
living in me that does those
things.
21So I have learned this
rule: When I want to do
good, evil is there with me.
22In my mind, I am happy
with God's law. 23But I see
another law working in
my body, which makes war
against the law that my mind
accepts. That other law working in my body is the law of sin,
and it makes me its prisoner. 24What a miserable man I am! Who will save me from this
body that brings me death? 25I thank God for
saving me through Jesus Christ our Lord!

So in my mind I am a slave to God's law,
but in my sinful self I am a slave to the law of
sin.

BE RULED BY THE SPIRIT

8
1So now, those who are in Christ Jesus are
not judged guilty. 2Through Christ Jesus the
law of the Spirit that brings life made me free
from the law that brings sin and death. 3The
law was without power, because the law was
made weak by our sinful selves. But God did
what the law could not do. He sent his own
Son to earth with the same human life that
others use for sin. By sending his Son to be an
offering for sin, God used a human life to destroy sin. 4He did this so that we could be the
kind of people the law correctly wants us to be.
Now we do not live following our sinful selves,
but we live following the Spirit.
5Those who live following their sinful selves
think only about things that their sinful selves
want. But those who live following the Spirit
are thinking about the things the Spirit wants
them to do. 6If people's thinking is controlled
by the sinful self, there is death. But if their
thinking is controlled by the Spirit, there is life
and peace. 7When people's thinking is controlled by the sinful self, they are against God,
because they refuse to obey God's law and
really are not even able to obey God's law.
8Those people who are ruled by their sinful
selves cannot please God.
9But you are not ruled by your sinful
selves. You are ruled by the Spirit, if that
Spirit of God really lives in you. But the person who does not have the Spirit of Christ
does not belong to Christ. 10Your body will
always be dead because of sin. But if Christ is
in you, then the Spirit gives you life, because
Christ made you right with God. 11God raised
Jesus from the dead, and if
God's Spirit is living in you,
he will also give life to your
bodies that die. God is the
One who raised Christ from
the dead, and he will give
life through his Spirit that
lives in you.
12So, my brothers and
sisters, we must not be
ruled by our sinful selves
or live the way our sinful
selves want. 13If you use your
lives to do the wrong things your
sinful selves want, you will die spiritually. But
if you use the Spirit's help to stop doing the
wrong things you do with your body, you will
have true life.

"But now you are free from sin and have become slaves of God. This brings you a life that is only for God, and this gives you life forever." (Romans 6:22)

On the Edge

The true children of God are those who let God's Spirit lead them (Rom. 8:14).

When you put your faith in God's Son, his Spirit became part of your life. God knew that you would need his Spirit to help you live the way he wants you to live. People who haven't trusted Jesus don't have God's Spirit. They have no choice but to live life to please themselves or to get on the good side of other people. But you don't have to live that way. You can let God's Spirit choose the road you're going to take. Living that way pleases God. And it has a fringe benefit for you, too. "If people's thinking is controlled by the sinful self, there is death. But if their thinking is controlled by the Spirit, there is life and peace" (8:6).

In order for your mind to be ruled by his Spirit, you've got to stay tight with God. Spend time in prayer, in worship, and in his Word. Really work these things into your life—so much that they become a part of you. Then you'll know when the Spirit is leading you, and you'll be able to follow.

SEE FOR YOURSELF:
Is. 63:11–14;
Rom. 8:14–17;
2 Cor. 2:14; Gal. 5:16

14The true children of God are those who let God's Spirit lead them. 15The Spirit we received does not make us slaves again to fear; it makes us children of God. With that Spirit we cry out, "Father."[n] 16And the Spirit himself joins with our spirits to say we are God's children. 17If we are God's children, we will receive blessings from God together with Christ. But we must suffer as Christ suffered so that we will have glory as Christ has glory.

OUR FUTURE GLORY

18The sufferings we have now are nothing compared to the great glory that will be shown to us. 19Everything God made is waiting with excitement for God to show his children's glory completely. 20Everything God made was changed to become useless, not by its own wish but because God wanted it and because all along there was this hope: 21that everything God made would be set free from ruin to have the freedom and glory that belong to God's children.

22We know that everything God made has been waiting until now in pain, like a woman ready to give birth. 23Not only the world, but we also have been waiting with pain inside us. We have the Spirit as the first part of God's promise. So we are waiting for God to finish making us his own children, which means our bodies will be made free. 24We were saved, and we have this hope. If we see what we are waiting for, that is not really hope. People do not hope for something they already have. 25But we are hoping for something we do not have yet, and we are waiting for it patiently.

26Also, the Spirit helps us with our weakness. We do not know how to pray as we should. But the Spirit himself speaks to God for us, even begs God for us with deep feelings that words cannot explain. 27God can see what is in people's hearts. And he knows what is in the mind of the Spirit, because the Spirit speaks to God for his people in the way God wants.

TRIALS

Does God know what he is doing with our lives? (8:28)

28We know that in everything God works for the good of those who love him. They are the people he called, because that was his plan. 29God knew them before he made the world, and he decided that they would be like his Son so that Jesus would be the firstborn[n] of many brothers. 30God planned for them to be like his Son; and those he planned to be like his Son, he also called; and those he called, he also made right with him; and those he made right, he also glorified.

GOD'S LOVE IN CHRIST JESUS

31So what should we say about this? If God is with us, no one can defeat us. 32He did not

On the Edge

He did not spare his own Son but gave him for us all. So with Jesus, God will surely give us all things (Rom. 8:32).

God is a giver. That's true. A lot of people are under the impression that God is a taker—always wanting something from them—but this is not true. Check out John 10:10, "A thief comes to steal and kill and destroy, but I came to give life—life in all its fullness." God wants you blessed with a full life. Satan is the thief who comes to steal everything you've got.

Not only does God want to meet all of your needs; he also wants to give you the desires of your heart. Psalm 37:4 states, "Enjoy serving the LORD, and he will give you what you want." Does that mean that you can dream up some horrible thing and make it your heart's desire and expect God to let you have it? No! It means that God will put desires in your heart. When you're going after him with everything you've got, he'll begin to put his desires in your heart. As you begin to understand how good and how right his desires for you are, they'll become your desires, too. It may be your desire to be a lawyer, play pro baseball, go to college, have a car, or simply get a good grade on a test. Do what the Lord wants, and he will give you your heart's desires.

Let the Lord help you identify what he wants for you. Let him help you figure out how your current desires fit into his plan. Let him know what you want, and don't be afraid to ask. He's ready, willing, and able to give you what you need. Just ask him today.

SEE FOR YOURSELF: Ps. 2:8; John 14:14

8:15 "Father" Literally, "Abba, Father." Jewish children called their fathers "Abba." **8:29 firstborn** Here this probably means that Christ was the first in God's family to share God's glory.

WHAT'S IT MEAN?

If there was one thing the Jewish people knew about, it was sheep. From their earliest days, the Israelites were known as a nation of wandering herdsmen. Throughout the Bible, people are compared to sheep, though usually not in a good way. You see, sheep are pretty helpless creatures. That's why Jesus is often described as the Good Shepherd who protects his flocks from danger.

Romans 8:36

spare his own Son but gave him for us all. So
with Jesus, God will surely give us all things.
[33]Who can accuse the people God has chosen?
No one, because God is the One who makes
them right. [34]Who can say God's people are
guilty? No one, because Christ Jesus died, but
he was also raised from the dead, and now he
is on God's right side, begging God for us.
[35]Can anything separate us from the love
Christ has for us? Can troubles or problems or
sufferings or hunger or nakedness or danger
or violent death? [36]As it is written in the Scriptures:

"For you we are in danger of death all the
time.
People think we are worth no more
than sheep to be killed." *Psalm 44:22*

[37]But in all these things we have full victory
through God who showed his love for us. [38]Yes,
I am sure that neither death, nor life, nor angels,
nor ruling spirits, nothing now, nothing in the
future, no powers, [39]nothing above us, nothing
below us, nor anything else in the whole world
will ever be able to separate us from the love of
God that is in Christ Jesus our Lord.

On the Edge

Can anything separate us from the love Christ has for us? Can troubles or problems or sufferings or hunger or nakedness or danger or violent death? As it is written in the Scriptures: "For you we are in danger of death all the time. People think we are worth no more than sheep to be killed." But in all these things we have full victory through God who showed his love for us. Yes, I am sure that neither death, nor life, nor angels, nor ruling spirits, nothing now, nothing in the future, no powers, nothing above us, nothing below us, nor anything else in the whole world will ever be able to separate us from the love of God that is in Christ Jesus our Lord (Rom. 8:35–39).

Feelings and truth rarely have very much in common. No matter how you feel, the truth is that you are completely loved by God and that nothing can ever separate you from his love. We sometimes compare God's love to the love we know here on earth. The love we know here can be conditional, based on your performance as a friend, a student, or even a child. But God's love has no conditions and nothing you could ever do can remove his constant devotion to you. There is nothing you can do to make God stop loving you. You can't run away from his love. You can't hide from his love. You can only decide to accept or reject it. You are loved perfectly and completely by the Creator of everything. You have his word on that.

SEE FOR YOURSELF: Ps. 91:14; 136:1; 139:13–14; Zeph. 3:17; Eph. 3:14–19

GOD AND THE JEWISH PEOPLE

9 [1]I am in Christ, and I am telling you the
truth; I do not lie. My conscience is ruled by
the Holy Spirit, and it tells me I am not lying. [2]I
have great sorrow and always feel much sadness. [3]I wish I could help my Jewish brothers
and sisters, my people. I would even wish that
I were cursed and cut off from Christ if that
would help them. [4]They are the people of Israel, God's chosen children. They have seen the
glory of God, and they have the agreements
that God made between himself and his people. God gave them the law of Moses and the
right way of worship and his promises. [5]They
are the descendants of our great ancestors, and
they are the earthly family into which Christ
was born, who is God over all. Praise him
forever![n] Amen.

9:5 born . . . forever! This can also mean "born. May God, who rules over all things, be praised forever!"

On the Edge

But in all these things we have full victory through God who showed his love for us (Rom. 8:37).

Your team just won the state championship. What a season! You worked hard and it really paid off. The whole city is celebrating. It's so exciting. The great feeling seems like it'll carry you forever. Every time you think about that win you grin from ear to ear. Your team is the best! That feeling does carry you for a while, maybe for the rest of the year, and even on into the next season. But eventually, someone else wins. Your glory fades a little. Every year the light grows a little dimmer. Your trophy gets pushed aside by newer things. Your sweet victory becomes a sweet memory. It doesn't sustain you anymore. It doesn't inspire you to push harder. Now you used to be a winner.

Who says winning is everything? Paul says there's more. He says that being loved by Christ makes you more than a winner. Believers get to share in the victory for eternity. In Christ, victory lasts forever. The celebration never ends. His glory never grows dim. Because of him, you'll be more than a conqueror, always victorious, with a prize that lasts forever.

SEE FOR YOURSELF:
1 Cor. 15:57;
2 Cor. 2:14

6It is not that God failed to keep his promise
to them. But only some of the people of Israel
are truly God's people,[n] 7and only some of
Abraham's[n] descendants are true children of
Abraham. But God said to Abraham: "The descendants I promised you will be from Isaac."[n]
8This means that not all of Abraham's descendants are God's true children. Abraham's true
children are those who become God's children
because of the promise God made to Abraham. 9God's promise to Abraham was this: "At
the right time I will return, and Sarah will have
a son."[n] 10And that is not all. Rebekah's sons
had the same father, our father Isaac. 11-12But
before the two boys were born, God told Rebekah, "The older will serve the younger."[n] This
was before the boys had done anything good
or bad. God said this so that the one chosen
would be chosen because of God's own plan.
He was chosen because he was the one God
wanted to call, not because of anything he did.
13As the Scripture says, "I loved Jacob, but I
hated Esau."[n]

WHAT'S IT MEAN?

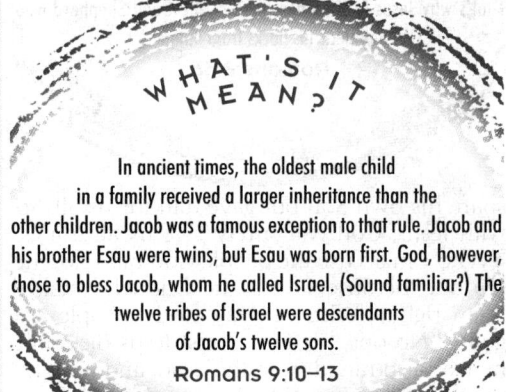

In ancient times, the oldest male child in a family received a larger inheritance than the other children. Jacob was a famous exception to that rule. Jacob and his brother Esau were twins, but Esau was born first. God, however, chose to bless Jacob, whom he called Israel. (Sound familiar?) The twelve tribes of Israel were descendants of Jacob's twelve sons.

Romans 9:10–13

14So what should we say about this? Is God
unfair? In no way. 15God said to Moses, "I will
show kindness to anyone to whom I want to
show kindness, and I will show mercy to anyone to whom I want to show mercy."[n] 16So
God will choose the one to whom he decides
to show mercy; his choice does not depend on
what people want or try to do. 17The Scripture
says to the king of Egypt: "I made you king for
this reason: to show my power in you so that
my name will be talked about in all the earth."[n]
18So God shows mercy where he wants to
show mercy, and he makes stubborn the people he wants to make stubborn.

19So one of you will ask me: "Then why
does God blame us for our sins? Who can fight
his will?" 20You are only human, and human
beings have no right to question God. An object should not ask the person who made it,
"Why did you make me like this?" 21The potter

9:6 God's people Literally, "Israel," the people God chose to bring his blessings to the world.
9:7 Abraham Most respected ancestor of the Jews. Every Jew hoped to see Abraham. **9:7 "The descendants . . . Isaac."** Quotation from Genesis 21:12. **9:9 "At . . . son."** Quotation from Genesis 18:10, 14. **9:11-12 "The older . . . younger."** Quotation from Genesis 25:23. **9:13 "I . . . Esau."** Quotation from Malachi 1:2-3. **9:15 "I . . . mercy."** Quotation from Exodus 33:19. **9:17 "I . . . earth."** Quotation from Exodus 9:16.

can make anything he wants to make. He can
use the same clay to make one thing for special
use and another thing for daily use.
[22]It is the same way with God. He wanted to
show his anger and to let people see his power.
But he patiently stayed with those people he
was angry with—people who were made
ready to be destroyed. [23]He waited with patience so that he could make known his rich
glory to the people who receive his mercy. He
has prepared these people to have his glory,
[24]and we are those people whom God called.
He called us not from the Jews only but also
from those who are not Jews. [25]As the Scripture says in Hosea:

"I will say, 'You are my
people'
to those I had called
'not my people.'
And I will show my
love
to those people I did
not love." *Hosea 2:1, 23*

[26]"They were called,
'You are not my
people,'
but later they will be called
'children of the living
God.' " *Hosea 1:10*

[27]And Isaiah cries out about Israel:
"The people of Israel are many,
like the grains of sand by the sea.
But only a few of them will be saved,
[28] because the Lord will quickly and
completely punish the people on the
earth." *Isaiah 10:22-23*

[29]It is as Isaiah said:
"The Lord All-Powerful
allowed a few of our descendants to live.
Otherwise we would have been
completely destroyed
like the cities of Sodom and
Gomorrah."[n] *Isaiah 1:9*

[30]So what does all this mean? Those who
are not Jews were not trying to make themselves right with God, but they were made
right with God because of their faith. [31]The
people of Israel tried to follow a law to make
themselves right with God. But they did not
succeed, [32]because they tried to make themselves right by the things they did instead of
trusting in God to make them right. They
stumbled over the stone that causes people to
stumble. [33]As it is written in the Scripture:

"I will put in Jerusalem a stone that causes
people to stumble,
a rock that makes them fall.
Anyone who trusts in him will never be
disappointed." *Isaiah 8:14; 28:16*

10 [1]Brothers and sisters, the thing I want most
is for all the Jews to be saved. That is my
prayer to God. [2]I can say this about them:
They really try to follow God, but they do not
know the right way. [3]Because they did not
know the way that God makes people right
with him, they tried to make themselves right in
their own way. So they did not accept God's
way of making people right.
[4]Christ ended the law so that
everyone who believes in
him may be right with God.
[5]Moses writes about be-
ing made right by following
the law. He says, "A person
who obeys these things will
live because of them."[n] [6]But
this is what the Scripture
says about being made right
through faith: "Don't say to
yourself, 'Who will go up into
heaven?' " (That means, "Who will go
up to heaven and bring Christ down to earth?")
[7]"And do not say, 'Who will go down into the
world below?' " (That means, "Who will go
down and bring Christ up from the dead?")
[8]This is what the Scripture says: "The word is
near you; it is in your mouth and in
your heart."[n] That is the teaching of faith that we are telling.
[9]If you use your mouth to say,
"Jesus is Lord," and if you believe in your heart that God
raised Jesus from the dead,
you will be saved. [10]We believe
with our hearts, and so we are made right with
God. And we use our mouths to say that we
believe, and so we are saved. [11]As the Scripture
says, "Anyone who trusts in him will never be
disappointed."[n] [12]That Scripture says "anyone"
because there is no difference between those
who are Jews and those who are not. The same
Lord is the Lord of all and gives many blessings
to all who trust in him, [13]as the Scripture says,
"Anyone who calls on the Lord will be saved."[n]

"If you use your mouth to say, 'Jesus is Lord,' and if you believe in your heart that God raised Jesus from the dead, you will be saved." (Romans 10:9)

SALVATION
Is our salvation personal? (10:8–10)

9:29 Sodom and Gomorrah Two cities that God destroyed because the people were so evil.
10:5 "A person . . . them." Quotation from Leviticus 18:5. **10:6-8 Verses 6-8** Quotations from Deuteronomy 9:4; 30:12-14; Psalm 107:26. **10:11 "Anyone . . . disappointed."** Quotation from Isaiah 28:16.
10:13 "Anyone . . . saved." Quotation from Joel 2:32.

[14]But before people can ask the Lord for
help, they must believe in him; and before they
can believe in him, they must hear about him;
and for them to hear about the Lord, someone
must tell them; [15]and before someone can go
and tell them, that person must be sent. It is
written, "How beautiful is the person who
comes to bring good news."[n] [16]But not all the
Jews accepted the good news. Isaiah said,
"Lord, who believed what we told them?"[n] [17]So
faith comes from hearing the Good News, and
people hear the Good News when someone
tells them about Christ.
[18]But I ask: Didn't people hear the Good
News? Yes, they heard—as the Scripture says:

"Their message went out through all the
world;
their words go everywhere on
earth." *Psalm 19:4*

[19]Again I ask: Didn't the people of Israel understand? Yes, they did understand. First, Moses
says:

"I will use those who are not a nation to
make you jealous.
I will use a nation that does not
understand to make you
angry." *Deuteronomy 32:21*

[20]Then Isaiah is bold enough to say:

"I was found by those who were not
asking me for help.
I made myself known to people who
were not looking for me." *Isaiah 65:1*

[21]But about Israel God says,

"All day long I stood ready to accept
people who disobey and are
stubborn." *Isaiah 65:2*

GOD SHOWS MERCY TO ALL PEOPLE

11 [1]So I ask: Did God throw out his people?
No! I myself am an Israelite from the family of
Abraham, from the tribe of Benjamin. [2]God
chose the Israelites to be his people before they
were born, and he has not thrown his people
out. Surely you know what the Scripture says
about Elijah, how he prayed to God against the
people of Israel. [3]"Lord," he said, "they have
killed your prophets, and they have destroyed
your altars. I am the only prophet left, and
now they are trying to kill me, too."[n] [4]But what
answer did God give Elijah? He said, "But I
have left seven thousand people in Israel who
have never bowed down before Baal."[n] [5]It is the
same now. There are a few people that God

10:15 "How . . . news." Quotation from Isaiah 52:7. **10:16 "Lord, . . . them?"** Quotation from Isaiah 53:1. **11:3 "They . . . too."** Quotation from 1 Kings 19:10, 14. **11:4 "But . . . Baal."** Quotation from 1 Kings 19:18.

Promise HE PROMISES THAT ANYONE CAN BE SAVED.

If you use your mouth to say, "Jesus is Lord," and if you believe in your heart that God raised Jesus from the dead, you will be saved. We believe with our hearts, and so we are made right with God. And we use our mouths to say that we believe, and so we are saved. As the Scripture says, "Anyone who trusts in him will never be disappointed." That Scripture says "anyone" because there is no difference between those who are Jews and those who are not. The same Lord is the Lord of all and gives many blessings to all who trust in him, as the Scripture says, "Anyone who calls on the Lord will be saved" (Rom. 10:9–13).

Know any people who think they're too far gone for Jesus? Maybe they think their sins are too big or their lives too ugly. They think God couldn't possibly save them. They think God's probably mad or that he's given up on them by now or that he's too holy to want them around.

Well, this passage is for the hopeless. God delights in saving the unlovable and the lost and the ones who think they could never be saved. To think that God couldn't save you because you're too far gone is to say, "I'm bigger than God. I can do something so evil that he can't forgive me. I have more power than God." The truth is that *everyone* is hopelessly lost without him and every sin is repulsive to him. But Jesus died for everybody—no exceptions. Anyone who calls out to him will be saved.

SEE FOR YOURSELF:

John 3:16–18; Rom. 1:16; Gal. 3:7–9, 26–27

WHAT'S IT MEAN?

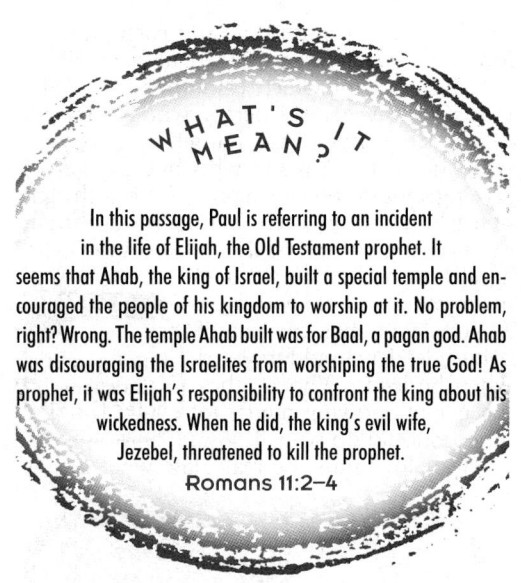

In this passage, Paul is referring to an incident in the life of Elijah, the Old Testament prophet. It seems that Ahab, the king of Israel, built a special temple and encouraged the people of his kingdom to worship at it. No problem, right? Wrong. The temple Ahab built was for Baal, a pagan god. Ahab was discouraging the Israelites from worshiping the true God! As prophet, it was Elijah's responsibility to confront the king about his wickedness. When he did, the king's evil wife, Jezebel, threatened to kill the prophet.

Romans 11:2–4

has chosen by his grace. [6]And if he chose them
by grace, it is not for the things they have
done. If they could be made God's people by
what they did, God's gift of grace would not
really be a gift.
[7]So this is what has happened: Although
the Israelites tried to be right with God, they
did not succeed, but the ones God chose did
become right with him. The others were made
stubborn and refused to listen to God. [8]As it is
written in the Scriptures:

"God gave the people a dull mind so they
could not understand." *Isaiah 29:10*
"He closed their eyes so they could not see
and their ears so they could not hear.
This continues until today." *Deuteronomy 29:4*

[9]And David says:

"Let their own feasts trap them and cause
their ruin;
let their feasts cause them to stumble
and be paid back.
[10]Let their eyes be closed so they cannot see
and their backs be forever weak from
troubles." *Psalm 69:22-23*

[11]So I ask: When the Jews fell, did that fall
destroy them? No! But their mistake brought
salvation to those who are not Jews, in order
to make the Jews jealous. [12]The Jews' mistake
brought rich blessings for the world, and the
Jews' loss brought rich blessings for the non-
Jewish people. So surely the world will receive
much richer blessings when enough Jews become the kind of people God wants.

[13]Now I am speaking to you who are not
Jews. I am an apostle to those who are not
Jews, and since I have that work, I will make
the most of it. [14]I hope I can make my own
people jealous and, in that way, help some of
them to be saved. [15]When God turned away
from the Jews, he became friends with other
people in the world. So when God accepts the
Jews, surely that will bring them life after
death.
[16]If the first piece of bread is offered to God,
then the whole loaf is made holy. If the roots of
a tree are holy, then the tree's branches are
holy too.
[17]It is as if some of the branches from an
olive tree have been broken off. You non-Jewish people are like the branch of a wild olive
tree that has been joined to that first tree. You
now share the strength and life of the first tree,
the Jews. [18]So do not brag about those
branches that were broken off. If you brag, remember that you do not support the root, but
the root supports you. [19]You will say,
"Branches were broken off so that I could be
joined to their tree." [20]That is true. But those
branches were broken off because they did not
believe, and you continue to be part of the tree
only because you believe. Do not be proud,
but be afraid. [21]If God did not let the natural
branches of that tree stay, then he will not let
you stay if you don't believe.
[22]So you see that God is kind and also very
strict. He punishes those who stop following
him. But God is kind to you, if you continue
following in his kindness. If you do not, you
will be cut off from the tree. [23]And if the Jews
will believe in God again, he will accept them
back. God is able to put them back where they
were. [24]It is not natural for a wild branch to be
part of a good tree. And you who are not Jews
are like a branch cut from a wild olive tree and
joined to a good olive tree. But since those Jews
are like a branch that grew from the good tree,
surely they can be joined to their own tree
again.
[25]I want you to understand this secret,
brothers and sisters, so you will understand
that you do not know everything: Part of Israel
has been made stubborn, but that will change
when many who are not Jews have come to
God. [26]And that is how all Israel will be saved.
It is written in the Scriptures:

"The Savior will come from Jerusalem;
he will take away all evil from the
family of Jacob.[n]

11:26 Jacob Father of the twelve family groups of Israel, the people God chose to be his people.

27 And I will make this agreement with those
people
when I take away their sins."
Isaiah 59:20-21; 27:9

28 The Jews refuse to accept the Good News,
so they are God's enemies. This has happened
to help you who are not Jews. But the Jews are
still God's chosen people, and he loves them
very much because of the promises he made to
their ancestors. 29 God never changes his mind
about the people he calls and the things he
gives them. 30 At one time you refused to obey
God. But now you have received mercy, because those people refused to obey. 31 And now
the Jews refuse to obey, because God showed
mercy to you. But this happened so that they
also can receive mercy from him. 32 God has
given all people over to their stubborn ways so
that he can show mercy to all.

PRAISE TO GOD

33 Yes, God's riches are very great, and his
wisdom and knowledge have no end! No one
can explain the things God decides or understand his ways. 34 As the Scripture says,
"Who has known the mind of the Lord,
or who has been able to give him
advice?" *Isaiah 40:13*
35 "No one has ever given God anything
that he must pay back." *Job 41:11*
36 Yes, God made all things, and everything
continues through him and for him. To him be
the glory forever! Amen.

GIVE YOUR LIVES TO GOD

12 1 So brothers and sisters, since God has
shown us great mercy, I beg you to offer your
lives as a living sacrifice to him. Your offering
must be only for God and pleasing to him,
which is the spiritual way for you to worship.
2 Do not change yourselves to be like the people of this world, but be changed within by a
new way of thinking. Then you will be able to
decide what God wants for you; you will
know what is good and pleasing to
him and what is perfect. 3 Because God has given me a special gift, I have something to
say to everyone among you.
Do not think you are better
than you are. You must decide
what you really are by the
amount of faith God has
given you. 4 Each one of us has
a body with many parts, and these parts all
have different uses. 5 In the same way, we are
many, but in Christ we are all one body. Each
one is a part of that body, and each part belongs to all the other parts. 6 We all have different gifts, each of which came because of the
grace God gave us. The person who has the gift
of prophecy should use that gift in agreement
with the faith. 7 Anyone who has the gift of
serving should serve. Anyone who has the gift
of teaching should teach. 8 Whoever has the gift
of encouraging others should encour-
age. Whoever has the gift of giving to others should give freely.
Anyone who has the gift of
being a leader should try hard
when he leads. Whoever has
the gift of showing mercy to
others should do so with joy.
9 Your love must be real. Hate what is evil,

MIND

What should a Christian's thoughts be characterized by? (12:2)

HATRED

What should Christians hate? (12:9)

On the Edge

Since God has shown us great mercy, I beg you to offer your lives as a living sacrifice to him. Your offering must be only for God and pleasing to him, which is the spiritual way for you to worship (Rom. 12:1).

Under the old agreement that God had made with the Jewish people, there were two kinds of sacrifices. One sacrifice was for people's sins; the other sacrifice was an offering of worship. Both sacrifices involved killing an animal, usually a goat or a lamb that didn't have any flaws.

Jesus' death on the cross made a new agreement between God and anyone who has faith in him. Under that new agreement, Jesus is the once-for-all sacrifice for sin. People don't have to offer lambs or goats to make up for sin. But what do you do about the sacrifice of worship?

Just as *God* chose to make Jesus the sacrifice for sin, *you* choose to make the sacrifice of worship. Instead of offering an animal, you offer your own life to God. You dedicate your life to doing what he wants. That's why it's called a *living* sacrifice. Paul says that living a life that's pure and pleasing to God is the best way to serve him—to worship him. In other words, living the way God wants you to is your way of saying to him, "You're awesome and I want everything about me to worship you!"

SEE FOR YOURSELF:
John 12:26; Rom. 1:9; 1 Pet. 2:5

On the Edge

Each one of us has a body with many parts, and these parts all have different uses. In the same way, we are many, but in Christ we are all one body. Each one is a part of that body, and each part belongs to all the other parts (Rom. 12:4–5).

You have a destiny that God has designed for you. He wants you to live in a way that honors him, to be part of his plan to bring other people to know him, and eventually to have the same character traits that Jesus has. But part of God's plan is that you wouldn't be able to accomplish any of this by yourself. Of course, you need his Spirit, and he's given you that. But you also need other people.

God wants his people to care about each other and to be able to depend on each other. Your strengths and weaknesses are different from another person's. That person may be able to help you with an area of your life that gives you a lot of trouble. Or you may be able to help someone else see clearly in a situation that is really confusing to him.

Everyone has to trust Jesus as an individual. But once you become a Christian, your life and your relationship with God is connected to other people. You need other Christians! And they need you.

SEE FOR YOURSELF:
Rom. 12:4–8;
1 Cor. 12:12; Col. 1:18

and hold on to what is good. [10]Love each other like brothers and sisters. Give each other more honor than you want for yourselves. [11]Do not be lazy but work hard, serving the Lord with all your heart. [12]Be joyful because you have hope. Be patient when trouble comes, and pray at all times. [13]Share with God's people who need help. Bring strangers in need into your homes.

"Love each other like brothers and sisters. Give each other more honor than you want for yourselves. Do not be lazy but work hard, serving the Lord with all your heart." (Romans 12:10–11)

[14]Wish good for those who harm you; wish them well and do not curse them. [15]Be happy with those who are happy, and be sad with those who are sad. [16]Live in peace with each other. Do not be proud, but make friends with those who seem unimportant. Do not think how smart you are.

[17]If someone does wrong to you, do not pay him back by doing wrong to him. Try to do what everyone thinks is right. [18]Do your best to live in peace with everyone. [19]My friends, do not try to punish others when they wrong you, but wait for God to punish them with his anger. It is written: "I will punish those who do wrong; I will repay them,"[n] says the Lord. [20]But you should do this:

> "If your enemy is hungry, feed him;
> if he is thirsty, give him a drink.
> Doing this will be like pouring burning
> coals on his head." *Proverbs 25:21-22*

[21]Do not let evil defeat you, but defeat evil by doing good.

CHRISTIANS SHOULD OBEY THE LAW

13 [1]All of you must yield to the government rulers. No one rules unless God has given him the power to rule, and no one rules now without that power from God. [2]So those who are against the government are really against what God has commanded. And they will bring punishment on themselves. [3]Those who do right do not have to fear the rulers; only those who do wrong fear them. Do you want to be unafraid of the rulers? Then do what is right, and they will praise you. [4]The ruler is God's servant to help you. But if you do wrong, then be afraid. He has the power to punish; he is God's servant to punish those who do wrong. [5]So you must yield to the government, not only because you might be punished, but because you know it is right.

OBEDIENCE
Should Christians obey the government? (13:1–4)

[6]This is also why you pay taxes. Rulers are working for God and give their time to their work. [7]Pay everyone, then, what you owe. If you owe any kind of tax, pay it. Show respect and honor to them all.

12:19 "I . . . them" Quotation from Deuteronomy 32:35.

On the Edge

So you must yield to the government, not only because you might be punished, but because you know it is right. This is also why you pay taxes. Rulers are working for God and give their time to their work. Pay everyone, then, what you owe. If you owe any kind of tax, pay it. Show respect and honor to them all (Rom. 13:5–7).

God is very clear about respecting authority and the rulers who govern us. Even when we disagree with their decisions, we are to obey. God is not surprised by the elections every few years. The laws made by Congress do not upset his plans. He is completely in charge and working through the authority over us to do his will. So, it matters that we drive the speed limit, pay our taxes, and abide by the laws. We obey God when we obey the authority he has allowed to govern us. In the same way, you obey God when you obey the authorities at your school and when you obey your parents. Authority keeps things from going totally out of control. Work with it.

SEE FOR YOURSELF:
Matt. 22:17–21;
Mark 12:14–17;
Luke 20:22–25;
Col. 3:20

LOVING OTHERS

8Do not owe people anything, except always owe love to each other, because the person who loves others has obeyed all the law.
9The law says, "You must not be guilty of adultery. You must not murder anyone. You must
not steal. You must not want to take your
neighbor's things."[n] All these commands and all
others are really only one rule: "Love your
neighbor as you love yourself."[n] 10Love never
hurts a neighbor, so loving is obeying all the
law.
11Do this because we live in an important
time. It is now time for you to wake up from
your sleep, because our salvation is
nearer now than when we first
believed. 12The "night"[n] is almost finished, and the "day"[n]
is almost here. So we should
stop doing things that belong
to darkness and take up the
weapons used for fighting in
the light. 13Let us live in a right
way, like people who belong to the day. We
should not have wild parties or get drunk.
There should be no sexual sins of any kind, no
fighting or jealousy. 14But clothe yourselves
with the Lord Jesus Christ and forget about
satisfying your sinful self.

DRINKING
Is drunkenness appropriate for a Christian? (13:11–14)

WHAT'S IT MEAN?

The Roman government liked to tax its citizens. The Romans taxed everything from property to imported goods to fishing rights. They even collected taxes from the Jews for worshiping at the Temple! The Romans claimed that the money was used to pay for the upkeep of the building. Some scholars have estimated that as much as forty percent of the income from an average Jewish household went to taxes.
Romans 13:6

DO NOT CRITICIZE OTHER PEOPLE

14 1Accept into your group someone who is
weak in faith, and do not argue about opinions. 2One person believes it is right to eat all
kinds of food.[n] But another, who is weak, believes it is right to eat only vegetables. 3The one
who knows that it is right to eat any kind of
food must not reject the one who eats only
vegetables. And the person who eats only vegetables must not think that the one who eats
all foods is wrong, because God has accepted
that person. 4You cannot judge another
person's servant. The master decides if the servant is doing well or not. And the Lord's ser-

13:9 "You . . . things." Quotation from Exodus 20:13–15, 17. **13:9 "Love . . . yourself."** Quotation from Leviticus 19:18. **13:12 "night"** This is used as a symbol of the sinful world we live in. This world will soon end. **13:12 "day"** This is used as a symbol of the good time that is coming, when we will be with God. **14:2 all . . . food** The Jewish law said there were some foods Jews should not eat. When Jews became Christians, some of them did not understand they could now eat all foods.

vant will do well because the Lord helps him
do well.
[5]Some think that one day is more important
than another, and others think that every day
is the same. Let all be sure in their own mind.
[6]Those who think one day is more important
than other days are doing that for the Lord.
And those who eat all kinds of food are doing
that for the Lord, and they give thanks to God.
Others who refuse to eat some foods do that
for the Lord, and they give thanks to God. [7]We
do not live or die for ourselves. [8]If we live, we
are living for the Lord, and if we die, we are
dying for the Lord. So living or dying, we belong to the Lord.

On the Edge

If we live, we are living for the Lord, and if we die, we are dying for the Lord. So living or dying, we belong to the Lord (Rom. 14:8).

As you've gotten older, you've started making choices for yourself rather than letting your parents choose for you. After all, you're an adult now (or almost an adult) and it's your life, not your parents', right?

Well, not exactly. Have you considered the fact that it's not "your life" anymore? It's true that you now have the responsibility of making some decisions that your parents used to make. But since you're a Christian, you belong to the Lord. The decisions you make have to fit in with his plans. You need to be thinking about what he wants, not what you want. Paul says, "So each of us will have to answer to God" (Rom. 14:12). You belong to him, and he *treasures* you. He values you so much that he went to great lengths to establish a friendship with you. So whatever you do, do it for him, remembering how much he loves you.

SEE FOR YOURSELF:
Mark 9:41; 1 Cor. 3:23; Gal. 3:26–29

[9]The reason Christ died and rose from the
dead to live again was so he would be Lord
over both the dead and the living. [10]So why do
you judge your brothers or sisters in Christ?
And why do you think you are better than
they are? We will all stand before God to be
judged, [11]because it is written in the Scriptures:

" 'As surely as I live,' says the Lord,
'Everyone will bow before me;
everyone will say that I am God.' "

Isaiah 45:23

[12]So each of us will have to answer to God.

DO NOT CAUSE OTHERS TO SIN

[13]For that reason we should stop judging
each other. We must make up our minds not to
do anything that will make another Christian
sin. [14]I am in the Lord Jesus, and I know that
there is no food that is wrong to eat. But if a
person believes something is wrong, that thing
is wrong for him. [15]If you hurt your brother's
or sister's faith because of something you eat,
you are not really following the way of love.
Do not destroy someone's faith by eating food
he thinks is wrong, because Christ died for
him. [16]Do not allow what you think is good to
become what others say is evil. [17]In the kingdom of God, eating and drinking are not important. The important things are living right
with God, peace, and joy in the Holy Spirit.
[18]Anyone who serves Christ by living this way
is pleasing God and will be accepted by other
people.
[19]So let us try to do what makes peace and
helps one another. [20]Do not let the eating of
food destroy the work of God. All foods are all
right to eat, but it is wrong to eat food that
causes someone else to sin. [21]It is better not to
eat meat or drink wine or do anything that will
cause your brother or sister to sin.
[22]Your beliefs about these things should be
kept secret between you and God. People are
happy if they can do what they think is right
without feeling guilty. [23]But those who eat
something without being sure it is right are
wrong because they did not believe it was
right. Anything that is done without believing
it is right is a sin.

15

[1]We who are strong in faith should help the
weak with their weaknesses, and not please
only ourselves. [2]Let each of us please our
neighbors for their good, to help them be
stronger in faith. [3]Even Christ did not live to
please himself. It was as the Scriptures said:
"When people insult you, it hurts me."[n] [4]Every-
thing that was written in the past was written
to teach us. The Scriptures give us patience and
encouragement so that we can have hope. [5]Pa-
tience and encouragement come from God.
And I pray that God will help you all agree

15:3 "When . . . me." Quotation from Psalm *69:9*.

On the Edge

Patience and encouragement come from God. And I pray that God will help you all agree with each other the way Christ Jesus wants (Rom. 15:5).

Galatians 5:22–23 lists the fruit or qualities of God's Spirit: love, joy, peace, patience, kindness, goodness, faithfulness, gentleness, self-control. Do you ever look at that list and think, *No way!* Or maybe you think, *Well, three out of nine isn't too bad.* Trying to measure up to this list can be kind of intimidating.

But Paul gives you some good news here: "I pray that God will help you all agree with each other." The key to seeing God make things happen in your life is to commit yourself to being open to the changes he wants to make in your heart. Prove your commitment by seriously studying God's Word and putting it into practice. Pray and meditate on Bible verses, especially verses that are relevant to areas you're weak in. God will honor your efforts and make things happen for you.

SEE FOR YOURSELF:
Gal. 5:22–23;
Col. 1:9–12;
2 Thess. 3:5

with each other the way Christ Jesus wants.
[6]Then you will all be joined together, and you
will give glory to God the Father of our Lord
Jesus Christ. [7]Christ accepted you, so you
should accept each other, which will bring glory to God. [8]I tell you that Christ became a servant of the Jews to show that God's promises
to the Jewish ancestors are true. [9]And he also
did this so that those who are not Jews could
give glory to God for the mercy he gives to
them. It is written in the Scriptures:

"So I will praise you among the non-
Jewish people.
I will sing praises to your name."

Psalm 18:49

[10]The Scripture also says,

"Be happy, you who are not Jews, together
with his people." *Deuteronomy 32:43*

[11]Again the Scripture says,

"All you who are not Jews, praise the Lord.
All you people, sing praises to him."

Psalm 117:1

[12]And Isaiah says,

"A new king will come from the family of
Jesse.[n]
He will come to rule over the non-
Jewish people,
and they will have hope because of him."

Isaiah 11:10

[13]I pray that the God who gives hope will
fill you with much joy and peace while you
trust in him. Then your hope will overflow by
the power of the Holy Spirit.

PAUL TALKS ABOUT HIS WORK

[14]My brothers and sisters, I am sure that
you are full of goodness. I know that you have
all the knowledge you need and that you are
able to teach each other. [15]But I have written to
you very openly about some things I wanted
you to remember. I did this because God gave
me this special gift: [16]to be a minister of Christ
Jesus to those who are not Jews. I served God
by teaching his Good News, so that the non-
Jewish people could be an offering that God
would accept—an offering made holy by the
Holy Spirit.

[17]So I am proud of what I have done for
God in Christ Jesus. [18]I will not talk about anything except what Christ has done through me
in leading those who are not Jews to obey
God. They have obeyed God because of what I
have said and done, [19]because of the power of
miracles and the great things they saw, and because of the power of the Holy Spirit. I
preached the Good News from Jerusalem all
the way around to Illyricum, and so I have
finished that part of my work. [20]I always want

WHAT'S IT MEAN?

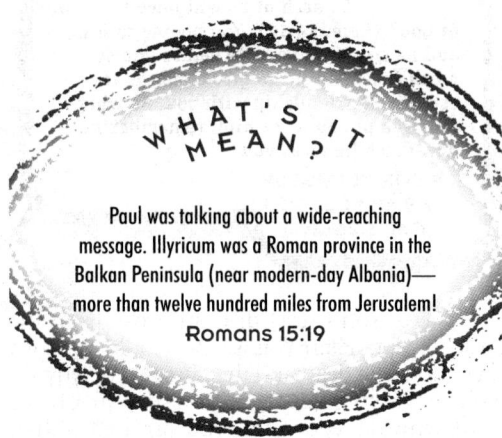

Paul was talking about a wide-reaching message. Illyricum was a Roman province in the Balkan Peninsula (near modern-day Albania)—more than twelve hundred miles from Jerusalem!
Romans 15:19

15:12 Jesse Jesse was the father of David, king of Israel. Jesus was from their family.

to preach the Good News in places where people have never heard of Christ, because I do
not want to build on the work someone else
has already started. 21But it is written in the
Scriptures:

"Those who were not told about him will
see,
and those who have not heard about
him will understand." *Isaiah 52:15*

PAUL'S PLAN TO VISIT ROME

22This is the reason I was stopped many
times from coming to you. 23Now I have finished my work here. Since for many years I
have wanted to come to you, 24I hope to visit
you on my way to Spain. After I enjoy being
with you for a while, I hope you can help me
on my trip. 25Now I am going to Jerusalem to
help God's people. 26The believers in Macedonia and Southern Greece were happy to give
their money to help the poor among God's
people at Jerusalem. 27They were happy to do
this, and really they owe it to them. These who
are not Jews have shared in the Jews' spiritual
blessings, so they should use their material
possessions to help the Jews. 28After I am sure
the poor in Jerusalem get the money that has
been given for them, I will leave for Spain and
stop and visit you. 29I know that when I come
to you I will bring Christ's full blessing.

30Brothers and sisters, I beg you to help me
in my work by praying to God for me. Do this
because of our Lord Jesus and
the love that the Holy Spirit
gives us. 31Pray that I will
be saved from the non-
believers in Judea and
that this help I bring to
Jerusalem will please
God's people there.
32Then, if God wants me
to, I will come to you
with joy, and together
you and I will have a time
of rest. 33The God who gives
peace be with you all. Amen.

GREETINGS TO THE CHRISTIANS

16
1I recommend to you our sister Phoebe,
who is a helper[n] in the church in Cenchrea. 2I
ask you to accept her in the Lord in the way
God's people should. Help her with anything
she needs, because she has helped me and
many other people also.

WHAT'S IT MEAN?

Priscilla and Aquila were originally from Rome. When the Emperor Claudius decided he wanted all of the Jews out of Rome, the couple moved to Corinth, a city in Greece, and worked with Paul there. They also helped Paul in Ephesus, a city across the Aegean Sea from Corinth, before moving back to Rome.

Romans 16:3

3Give my greetings to Priscilla and Aquila,
who work together with me in Christ Jesus
4and who risked their own lives to save my life.
I am thankful to them, and all the non-Jewish
churches are thankful as well. 5Also, greet for
me the church that meets at their house.

Greetings to my dear friend Epenetus, who
was the first person in the country of Asia to
follow Christ. 6Greetings to Mary, who worked
very hard for you. 7Greetings to Andronicus
and Junia, my relatives, who were in prison
with me. They are very important apostles.
They were believers in Christ before I was.
8Greetings to Ampliatus, my
dear friend in the Lord.
9Greetings to Urbanus, a
worker together with me
for Christ. And greetings
to my dear friend Sta-
chys. 10Greetings to
Apelles, who was tested
and proved that he truly
loves Christ. Greetings to
all those who are in the
family of Aristobulus.
11Greetings to Herodion,
my fellow citizen. Greetings
to all those in the family of
Narcissus who belong to the
Lord. 12Greetings to Tryphena and Tryphosa,
women who work very hard for the Lord.
Greetings to my dear friend Persis, who also
has worked very hard for the Lord. 13Greetings
to Rufus, who is a special person in the Lord,
and to his mother, who has been like a mother
to me also. 14Greetings to Asyncritus, Phlegon,

"All the believers have heard that you obey, so I am very happy because of you. But I want you to be wise in what is good and innocent in what is evil."
(Romans 16:19)

16:1 helper Literally, "deaconess." This might mean the same as one of the special women helpers in 1 Timothy 3:11.

Hermes, Patrobas, Hermas, and all the brothers
who are with them. 15Greetings to Philologus
and Julia, Nereus and his sister, and Olympas,
and to all God's people with them. 16Greet each
other with a holy kiss. All of Christ's churches
send greetings to you.
17Brothers and sisters, I ask you to look out
for those who cause people to be against each
other and who upset other people's faith. They
are against the true teaching you learned, so
stay away from them. 18Such people are not
serving our Lord Christ but are only doing
what pleases themselves. They use fancy talk
and fine words to fool the minds of those who
do not know about evil. 19All the believers
have heard that you obey, so I am very happy
because of you. But I want you to be wise in
what is good and innocent in what is evil.
20The God who brings peace will soon defeat Satan and give you power over him.
The grace of our Lord Jesus be with you.
21Timothy, a worker together with me,
sends greetings, as well as Lucius, Jason, and
Sosipater, my relatives.
22I am Tertius, and I am writing this letter
from Paul. I send greetings to you in the Lord.
23Gaius is letting me and the whole church
here use his home. He also sends greetings to
you, as do Erastus, the city treasurer, and our
brother Quartus. 24[n]
25Glory to God who can make you strong
in faith by the Good News that I tell people
and by the message about Jesus Christ. The
message about Christ is the secret that was
hidden for long ages past but is now made
known. 26It has been made clear through the
writings of the prophets. And by the command
of the eternal God it is made known to all nations that they might believe and obey.
27To the only wise God be glory forever
through Jesus Christ! Amen.

WHAT'S IT MEAN?

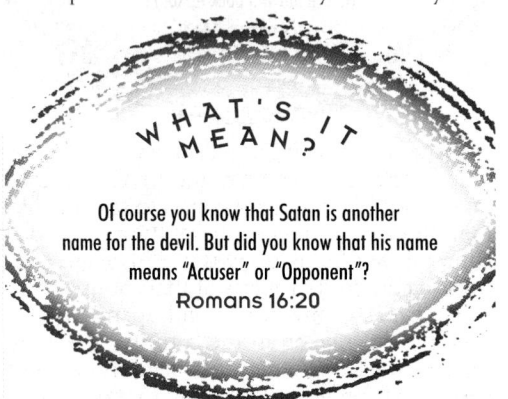

Of course you know that Satan is another name for the devil. But did you know that his name means "Accuser" or "Opponent"?

Romans 16:20

16:24 Verse 24 Some Greek copies add verse 24: "The grace of our Lord Jesus Christ be with all of you. Amen."

1 Corinthians

CONTENT Paul helped start the church in Corinth. He loved the people there, and he believed in them. But when he got a letter from one of the church members telling him that everyone was picking on and fighting with each other, he got a little ticked. In fact, when he wrote them the letter that we call 1 Corinthians, he said he was writing with tears in his eyes. He was disappointed, and he was angry.

But you have to give the Corinthians some credit. They could have read that first letter and ignored Paul's advice. After all, he wasn't even there to check up on them, and who *was* the tattletale anyway?

That's not what they did, though. Instead, they took Paul's words to heart. They changed from nit-picking church members to generous partners in ministry.

Outline

1:1–9 .... Paul's Greeting and Prayer
1:10—4:21 .... A Call for Unity
5:1—7:40 .... Problems in Relationships
8:1—11:1 .... Honoring God Instead of Idols
11:2—14:40 .... Guidance for Worship and Church Life
15:1–58 .... Christ's Victory Over Death
16:1–4 .... An Offering for the Poor
16:5–12 .... Paul's Travel Plans
16:13–24 .... Personal Concerns and Greetings

Purpose We are to resolve the differences that divide us.

Theme Resolving Doctrinal and Practical Church Problems and Growth of a Church in Christ

Date of writing Spring A.D. 56

"You were bought by God for a price. So honor God with your bodies" (6:20).

Bible Talk

Immorality

Corinth was one of the wickedest and wildest cities of its day. Idol worship was everywhere to bizarre extremes. There were actual prostitutes in the temples of the goddess, Venus. If you wanted to do something morally wrong, Corinth certainly had a lot to offer.

Now that you know this, think about what kind of challenges faced the church at Corinth. Somehow they were supposed to stay true to God's commands in a place where no one even pretended to care about God's commands. It's one thing to be tempted in a place where everyone knows sin is wrong. What would it be like to be tempted to sin in a place where no one cared if you did it . . . except God . . . and your friends at church?

IT'S A GIFT!

One of the things that Paul wrote to the Corinthians about was their gifts. He told them that the church is like a body. Everybody has their own job to do. When everyone does their job the body works well. The feet carry it places. The mouth talks on the phone. The hands reach out to give a hug.

Paul tells the Corinthians to find their role and then to be happy in that role instead of wishing they were doing something else.

Paul's words teach us about the church today. We each have a gift to use at church. When we all work together our gifts make us into the body of Christ.

[1]From Paul. God called me to be an apostle
of Christ Jesus because that is what God wanted.
Also from Sosthenes, our brother in Christ.
[2]To the church of God in Corinth, to you
who have been made holy in Christ Jesus. You
were called to be God's holy people with all
people everywhere who pray in the name of
the Lord Jesus Christ—their Lord and ours:
[3]Grace and peace to you from God our Father and the Lord Jesus Christ.

WHAT'S IT MEAN?

The word *apostle* means "messenger," but that definition doesn't begin to cover who the apostles of the New Testament were. These were men who had talked with Jesus personally and who had been given—by him—the responsibility of continuing his ministry of preaching and healing. His original twelve followers were the first apostles. Others who met with Jesus after he rose from the dead were called apostles as well. Paul's encounter with Jesus, though, was unique. Paul was called to be a messenger when Jesus spoke to him from heaven while Paul was traveling on the road to Damascus.

1 Corinthians 1:1

On the Edge

God, who has called you to share everything with his Son, Jesus Christ our Lord, is faithful (1 Cor. 1:9).

Paul says that God chose you to "share everything" with Jesus, to be his partner. Being his partner is an honor you don't deserve, but neither does anyone else. But God, because of his kindness and love, chose you for the job even though you aren't qualified for it.

What does it mean to be Jesus' partner? Partners work together toward a common goal. Think about what that goal might be for you and Jesus. Don't just think about your own life—Jesus isn't your genie-in-a-bottle helping you get the things you want. Instead, think about other people. Ask yourself, What does Jesus want to do in my sister's life, my dad's life? What does he want to do for my friends? Ask Jesus those questions, too, and ask him what you can do to make that happen. He'll answer you.

It's an awesome privilege to be chosen as Jesus' partner, to work with him to change the lives of people you care about—and maybe even some people you haven't met yet. Make up your mind to be the kind of partner Jesus can be proud of.

SEE FOR YOURSELF:
John 15:4; Rom. 8:16–17; Eph. 2:6; Col. 3:1

PAUL GIVES THANKS TO GOD

[4]I always thank my God for you because of
the grace God has given you in Christ Jesus. [5]I
thank God because in Christ you have been
made rich in every way, in all your speaking
and in all your knowledge. [6]Just as our witness
about Christ has been guaranteed to you, [7]so
you have every gift from God while you wait
for our Lord Jesus Christ to come again. [8]Jesus
will keep you strong until the
end so that there will be no
wrong in you on the day our
Lord Jesus Christ comes again.
[9]God, who has called you to
share everything with his
Son, Jesus Christ our Lord, is
faithful.

"God, who has called you to share everything with his Son, Jesus Christ our Lord, is faithful."
(1 Corinthians 1:9)

PROBLEMS IN THE CHURCH

[10]I beg you, brothers and
sisters,[n] by the name of our Lord
Jesus Christ that all of you agree with each
other and not be split into groups. I beg that
you be completely joined together by having
the same kind of thinking and
the same purpose. [11]My
brothers and sisters, some
people from Chloe's family
have told me quite plainly
that there are quarrels
among you. [12]This is what I
mean: One of you says, "I
follow Paul"; another says,
"I follow Apollos"; another
says, "I follow Peter"; and another says, "I follow Christ."

1:10 brothers and sisters Although the Greek text says "brothers" here and throughout this book, Paul's words were meant for the entire church, including men and women.

[13]Christ has been divided up into different
groups! Did Paul die on the cross for you? No!
Were you baptized in the name of Paul? No! [14]I
thank God I did not baptize any of you except
Crispus and Gaius [15]so that now no one can
say you were baptized in my name. [16](I also
baptized the family of Stephanas, but I do not
remember that I baptized anyone else.) [17]Christ
did not send me to baptize people but to
preach the Good News. And he sent me to
preach the Good News without using words
of human wisdom so that the cross[n] of Christ
would not lose its power.

WHAT'S IT MEAN?

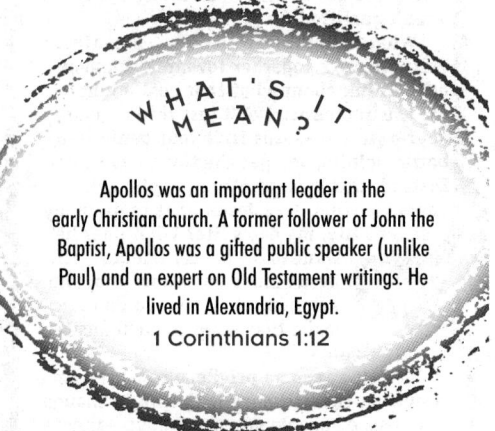

Apollos was an important leader in the early Christian church. A former follower of John the Baptist, Apollos was a gifted public speaker (unlike Paul) and an expert on Old Testament writings. He lived in Alexandria, Egypt.

1 Corinthians 1:12

CHRIST IS GOD'S POWER AND WISDOM

[18]The teaching about the cross is foolishness to those who are being lost, but to us who
are being saved it is the power of God. [19]It is
written in the Scriptures:

"I will cause the wise men to lose their
wisdom;
I will make the wise men unable to
understand." *Isaiah 29:14*

[20]Where is the wise person? Where is the
educated person? Where is the skilled talker of
this world? God has made the wisdom of the
world foolish. [21]In the wisdom of God the
world did not know God through its own wisdom. So God chose to use the message that
sounds foolish to save those who believe.
[22]The Jews ask for miracles, and the Greeks
want wisdom. [23]But we preach a crucified
Christ. This is a big problem to the Jews, and it
is foolishness to those who are not Jews. [24]But
Christ is the power of God and the wisdom of
God to those people God has called—Jews and
Greeks. [25]Even the foolishness of God is wiser
than human wisdom, and the weakness of
God is stronger than human strength.

[26]Brothers and sisters, look at what you
were when God called you. Not many of you
were wise in the way the world judges wisdom. Not many of you had great influence.
Not many of you came from important families. [27]But God chose the foolish things of the
world to shame the wise, and he chose the
weak things of the world to shame the strong.
[28]He chose what the world thinks is unimportant and what the world looks down on and
thinks is nothing in order to destroy what the
world thinks is important. [29]God did this so
that no one can brag in his presence. [30]Because
of God you are in Christ Jesus, who has become for us wisdom from God. In Christ we
are put right with God, and have been made
holy, and have been set free from sin. [31]So, as
the Scripture says, "If someone wants to brag,
he should brag only about the Lord."[n]

WHAT'S IT MEAN?

The Greeks were more interested in intellectual discussions ("wisdom") than in the story of Jesus' death on the cross. Subjects such as architecture, art, literature, philosophy, politics, and science were easy for the Greeks to talk about. Something as brutal as a crucifixion would have been a difficult topic for them to understand.

1 Corinthians 1:22

THE MESSAGE OF CHRIST'S DEATH

2
[1]Dear brothers and sisters, when I came to
you, I did not come preaching God's
secret with fancy words or a
show of human wisdom. [2]I
decided that while I was with
you I would forget about
everything except Jesus Christ
and his death on the cross. [3]So
when I came to you, I was
weak and fearful and trem-

WISDOM
How is God's wisdom different from human wisdom? (2:1–16)

1:17 cross Paul uses the cross as a picture of the Good News, the story of Christ's death and rising from the dead for people's sins. The cross, or Christ's death, was God's way to save people. **1:31 "If . . . Lord."** Quotation from Jeremiah 9:24.

bling. 4My teaching and preaching were not
with words of human wisdom that persuade
people but with proof of the power that the
Spirit gives. 5This was so that your faith would
be in God's power and not in human wisdom.

GOD'S WISDOM

6However, I speak a wisdom to those who
are mature. But this wisdom is not from this
world or from the rulers of this world, who are
losing their power. 7I speak God's secret wisdom,
which he has kept hidden. Before the world began, God planned this wisdom for our glory.
8None of the rulers of this world understood it.
If they had, they would not have crucified the
Lord of glory. 9But as it is written in the Scriptures:

"No one has ever seen this,
and no one has ever heard about it.
No one has ever imagined
what God has prepared for those who
love him." *Isaiah 64:4*

10But God has shown us these things
through the Spirit.

The Spirit searches out all things, even the
deep secrets of God. 11Who knows the
thoughts that another person has? Only a
person's spirit that lives within him knows his
thoughts. It is the same with God. No one
knows the thoughts of God except the Spirit of
God. 12Now we did not receive the spirit of the
world, but we received the Spirit that is from
God so that we can know all that God has
given us. 13And we speak about these things,
not with words taught us by human wisdom
but with words taught us by the Spirit. And so
we explain spiritual truths to spiritual people.
14A person who does not have the Spirit does
not accept the truths that come from the Spirit
of God. That person thinks they are foolish
and cannot understand them, because they
can only be judged to be true by the Spirit.
15The spiritual person is able to judge all things,
but no one can judge him. The Scripture says:

16"Who has known the mind of the Lord?
Who has been able to teach him?"
Isaiah 40:13

But we have the mind of Christ.

FOLLOWING PEOPLE IS WRONG

3
1Brothers and sisters, in the past I could not
talk to you as I talk to spiritual people. I had to
talk to you as I would to people without the
Spirit—babies in Christ. 2The teaching I gave
you was like milk, not solid food, because you
were not able to take solid food. And even
now you are not ready. 3You are still not spiritual, because there is jealousy and quarreling
among you, and this shows that you are not
spiritual. You are acting like people of the
world. 4One of you says, "I belong to Paul," and

On the Edge

Brothers and sisters, in the past I could not talk to you as I talk to spiritual people. I had to talk to you as I would to people without the Spirit—babies in Christ. The teaching I gave you was like milk, not solid food, because you were not able to take solid food. And even now you are not ready. You are still not spiritual, because there is jealousy and quarreling among you, and this shows that you are not spiritual. You are acting like people of the world (1 Cor. 3:1–3).

Little kids fight over a toy because they're little kids. They are babies. Immature. They both think that the world revolves around them. They both think that their pleasure is the most important. Some little kids grow up, become Christians, lay down their toys, and find other things to fight about. The reason is still the same. On the outside they look like adults, but on the inside they're still babies. Still immature. Still believing that their ideas count more and that their pleasure matters most. Paul says in this passage that they are acting like the rest of the world. You can hardly blame the world when they act selfish, because without God, they've only got themselves.

But Christians should know better. Christians who argue and are jealous with each other are babies in their faith. They do not understand the teachings of Christ or they would act differently. Becoming a Christian is about more than getting to heaven. What happens in your heart when Jesus comes to live there should begin to transform your attitude and your actions. When the world looks at you, do they see Jesus, or do they see a reflection of themselves? Growing up in Jesus means looking less like the world and more like him.

SEE FOR YOURSELF:
Rom. 12:2;
Gal. 5:16–18;
Heb. 5:12–13

another says, "I belong to Apollos." When you
say things like this, you are acting like people
of the world.
[5]Is Apollos important? No! Is Paul important? No! We are only servants of God who
helped you believe. Each one of us did the work
God gave us to do. [6]I planted the seed, and
Apollos watered it. But God is the One who
made it grow. [7]So the one who plants is not
important, and the one who waters is
not important. Only God,
who makes things grow, is
important. [8]The one who
plants and the one who waters have the same purpose,
and each will be rewarded for
his own work. [9]We are God's
workers, working together; you
are like God's farm, God's house.

> **WITNESSING**
> Can Christians make other people's faith grow? (3:5–9)

[10]Using the gift God gave me, I laid the
foundation of that house like an expert builder.
Others are building on that foundation, but all
people should be careful how they build on it.
[11]The foundation that has already been laid is
Jesus Christ, and no one can lay down any
other foundation. [12]But if people build on that
foundation, using gold, silver, jewels, wood,
grass, or straw, [13]their work will be clearly
seen, because the Day of Judgment[n] will make
it visible. That Day will appear with fire, and
the fire will test everyone's work to show what
sort of work it was. [14]If the building that has
been put on the foundation still stands, the
builder will get a reward. [15]But if the building is
burned up, the builder will suffer loss. The
builder will be saved, but it will be as one who
escaped from a fire.
[16]Don't you know that you are God's temple and that God's Spirit lives in you? [17]If anyone destroys God's temple, God will destroy
that person, because God's temple is holy and
you are that temple.
[18]Do not fool yourselves. If you think you
are wise in this world, you should become a
fool so that you can become truly wise, [19]be-
cause the wisdom of this world is foolishness
with God. It is written in the Scriptures, "He
catches those who are wise in their own clever
traps."[n] [20]It is also written in the Scriptures, "The
Lord knows what wise people think. He knows
their thoughts are just a puff of wind."[n] [21]So you
should not brag about human leaders. All
things belong to you: [22]Paul, Apollos, and Peter;
the world, life, death, the present, and the future—all these belong to you. [23]And you belong
to Christ, and Christ belongs to God.

APOSTLES ARE SERVANTS OF CHRIST

4 [1]People should think of us as servants of
Christ, the ones God has trusted with his secrets. [2]Now in this way those who are trusted
with something valuable must show they are
worthy of that trust. [3]As for myself, I do not
care if I am judged by you or by any human
court. I do not even judge myself. [4]I know of
no wrong I have done, but this does not make
me right before the Lord. The Lord is the One
who judges me. [5]So do not judge before the
right time; wait until the Lord comes. He will
bring to light things that are now hidden in
darkness, and will make known the secret purposes of people's hearts. Then God will praise
each one of them.

> ## On the Edge
>
> ***We are fools for Christ's sake, but you are very wise in Christ. We are weak, but you are strong. You receive honor, but we are shamed (1 Cor. 4:10).***
>
> **Like everybody else, Christians can sometimes act dumb. They come in all shapes and sizes—Bible-thumpers, Scripture-screamers, unforgivers, grace-stealers—the kind of people you wouldn't want to be in a group with because they're ruining it for the rest of us. But there's a whole category of Christians that Paul calls "fools for Christ's sake." The apostles were laughed at and thought of as fools. Their relationship with Christ was so real, but so unusual, that some people laughed at them. Is it possible that some of the "nerds" get ridiculed because they really are trying to live like Jesus—pursuing purity and holiness, giving grace? If that's the case, sign us all up. Let people call you anything as long as God calls you faithful.**
>
> **SEE FOR YOURSELF:**
> **Job 12:4; Ps. 22:7–10; Matt. 5:10**

3:13 Day of Judgment The day Christ will come to judge all people and take his people home to live with him. **3:19 "He . . . traps."** Quotation from Job 5:13. **3:20 "The Lord . . . wind."** Quotation from Psalm 94:11.

6 Brothers and sisters, I have used Apollos
and myself as examples so you could learn
through us the meaning of the saying, "Follow
only what is written in the Scriptures." Then
you will not be more proud of one person
than another. 7 Who says you are better than
others? What do you have that was not given
to you? And if it was given to you, why do you
brag as if you did not receive it as a gift?
8 You think you already have everything
you need. You think you are rich. You think
you have become kings without us. I wish you
really were kings so we could be kings together
with you. 9 But it seems to me that God has put
us apostles in last place, like those sentenced to
die. We are like a show for the whole world to
see—angels and people. 10 We are fools for
Christ's sake, but you are very wise in Christ.
We are weak, but you are strong. You receive
honor, but we are shamed. 11 Even to this very
hour we do not have enough to eat or drink or
to wear. We are often beaten, and we have no
homes in which to live. 12 We work hard with
our own hands for our food. When people
curse us, we bless them. When they hurt us, we
put up with it. 13 When they tell evil lies about
us, we speak nice words about them. Even today, we are treated as though we were the garbage of the world—the filth of the earth.
14 I am not trying to make you feel ashamed.
I am writing this to give you a warning as my
own dear children. 15 For though you may have
ten thousand teachers in Christ, you do not
have many fathers. Through the Good News I
became your father in Christ Jesus, 16 so I beg
you, please follow my example. 17 That is why I
am sending to you Timothy, my son in the
Lord. I love Timothy, and he is faithful. He will
help you remember my way of life in Christ
Jesus, just as I teach it in all the churches everywhere.
18 Some of you have become proud, thinking that I will not come to you again. 19 But I
will come to you very soon if the Lord wishes.
Then I will know what the proud ones do, not
what they say, 20 because the kingdom of God
is present not in talk but in power. 21 Which do
you want: that I come to you with punishment
or with love and gentleness?

WICKEDNESS IN THE CHURCH

5
1 It is actually being said that there is sexual
sin among you. And it is a kind that does not
happen even among people who do not know
God. A man there has his father's wife. 2 And
you are proud! You should have been filled
with sadness so that the man who did this
should be put out of your group. 3 I am not
there with you in person, but I am with you in
spirit. And I have already judged the man who
did that sin as if I were really there. 4 When you
meet together in the name of our Lord Jesus,
and I meet with you in spirit with the power of
our Lord Jesus, 5 then hand this man over to
Satan. So his sinful self[n] will be destroyed, and
his spirit will be saved on the day of the Lord.
6 Your bragging is not good. You know the
saying, "Just a little yeast makes the whole
batch of dough rise." 7 Take out all the old yeast
so that you will be a new batch of dough
without yeast, which you really are. For Christ,
our Passover lamb, has been sacrificed. 8 So let
us celebrate this feast, but not with the bread
that has the old yeast—the yeast of sin and
wickedness. Let us celebrate this feast with the
bread that has no yeast—the bread of goodness and truth.
9 I wrote you in my earlier letter not to associate with those who sin sexually. 10 But I did
not mean you should not associate with those
of this world who sin sexually, or with the
greedy, or robbers, or those who worship
idols. To get away from them you would have
to leave this world. 11 I am writing to tell you
that you must not associate with those who
call themselves believers in Christ but who sin
sexually, or are greedy, or worship idols, or
abuse others with words, or get drunk, or
cheat people. Do not even eat with people like
that.
12-13 It is not my business to judge those
who are not part of the church. God will judge
them. But you must judge the people who are
part of the church. The Scripture says, "You
must get rid of the evil person among you."[n]

JUDGING PROBLEMS AMONG CHRISTIANS

6
1 When you have something against another
Christian, how can you bring yourself to go
before judges who are not right with God?
Why do you not let God's people decide who is right? 2 Surely you
know that God's people will
judge the world. So if you are
to judge the world, are you
not able to judge small cases
as well? 3 You know that in the
future we will judge angels, so

ANGELS
Who will judge the angels? (6:3)

5:5 sinful self Literally, "flesh." This could also mean his body. **5:12-13 "You . . . you."** Quotation from Deuteronomy 17:7; 19:19; 22:21, 24; 24:7.

surely we can judge the ordinary things of this
life. 4If you have ordinary cases that must be
judged, are you going to appoint people as
judges who mean nothing to the church? 5I say
this to shame you. Surely there is someone
among you wise enough to judge a complaint
between believers. 6But now one believer goes
to court against another believer—and you do
this in front of unbelievers!

7The fact that you have lawsuits against
each other shows that you are already defeated. Why not let yourselves be wronged?
Why not let yourselves be cheated? 8But you
yourselves do wrong and cheat, and you do
this to other believers!

9-10Surely you know that the people who
do wrong will not inherit God's kingdom. Do
not be fooled. Those who sin sexually, worship
idols, take part in adultery, those who are male
prostitutes, or men who have sexual relations
with other men, those who steal, are greedy, get
drunk, lie about others, or rob—these people
will not inherit God's kingdom. 11In the past,
some of you were like that, but you were
washed clean. You were made holy, and you
were made right with God in the name of the
Lord Jesus Christ and in the Spirit of our God.

USE YOUR BODIES FOR GOD'S GLORY

12"I am allowed to do all things," but all
things are not good for me to do. "I am allowed to do all things," but I will not let anything make me its slave. 13"Food is for the
stomach, and the stomach for food," but God
will destroy them both. The body is not for
sexual sin but for the Lord, and the Lord is for
the body. 14By his power God has raised the
Lord from the dead and will also raise
us from the dead. 15Surely you
know that your bodies are
parts of Christ himself. So I
must never take the parts of
Christ and join them to a
prostitute! 16It is written in the
Scriptures, "The two will become one body."n So you should know that
anyone who joins with a prostitute becomes
one body with the prostitute. 17But the one
who joins with the Lord is one spirit with the
Lord.

18So run away from sexual sin. Every other
sin people do is outside their bodies, but those
who sin sexually sin against their own bodies.
19You should know that your body is a temple
for the Holy Spirit who is in you. You have
received the Holy Spirit from God. So you do
not belong to yourselves, 20because you were
bought by God for a price. So honor God with
your bodies.

SEX

Can sex be casual? (6:13–20)

On the Edge

You should know that your body is a temple for the Holy Spirit who is in you. You have received the Holy Spirit from God. So you do not belong to yourselves (1 Cor. 6:19).

A temple is a place where God is worshiped. God says that your body is a temple for him. Think about what you do to your body. If you could see God dwelling inside you, would you treat your body the same? Doing drugs turns the temple into a haunted house. Not only are you tearing down the place God lives, you're making a mockery of his home and his creation. Would you go to an actual temple and mess it all up? No. Neither should you throw trash into your own temple, turn it into a house of prostitution, or cover it with graffiti.

The God who loves you deserves better than a crack house for a temple. He wants to glorify himself in you. Drugs are stupid and kill. You already know that. But did you know that Satan uses drugs to destroy as many temples as possible? Don't do drugs. Practice self-control and keep your temple pure and holy and healthy. Ask God to dwell richly in you and commit to being a good temple for him.

SEE FOR YOURSELF:
Rom. 6:12;
1 Cor. 3:16;
2 Cor. 6:16

ABOUT MARRIAGE

7

1Now I will discuss the things you wrote
me about. It is good for a man not to have
sexual relations with a woman. 2But because
sexual sin is a danger, each man should have
his own wife, and each woman should have
her own husband. 3The husband should give
his wife all that he owes her as his wife. And
the wife should give her husband all that she
owes him as her husband. 4The wife does not
have full rights over her own body; her husband shares them. And the husband does not

6:16 "The two . . . body." Quotation from Genesis 2:24.

have full rights over his own body; his wife
shares them. 5Do not refuse to give your bodies to each other, unless you both agree to stay
away from sexual relations for a time so you
can give your time to prayer. Then come together again so Satan cannot tempt you because of a lack of self-control. 6I say this to give
you permission to stay away
from sexual relations for a time.
It is not a command to do so.
7I wish that everyone were
like me, but each person has
his own gift from God. One
has one gift, another has another gift.
8Now for those who are
not married and for the widows I say this: It is good for
them to stay unmarried as I am.
9But if they cannot control themselves, they
should marry. It is better to marry than to
burn with sexual desire.
10Now I give this command for the married
people. (The command is not from me; it is
from the Lord.) A wife should not leave her
husband. 11But if she does leave, she must not
marry again, or she should make up with her
husband. Also the husband should not divorce his wife.
12For all the others I say this (I am saying
this, not the Lord): If a Christian man has a
wife who is not a believer, and she is happy to
live with him, he must not divorce her. 13And if
a Christian woman has a husband who is not
a believer, and he is happy to live with her, she
must not divorce him. 14The husband who is
not a believer is made holy through his believing wife. And the wife who is not a believer is
made holy through her believing husband. If
this were not true, your children would not be
clean, but now your children are holy.
15But if those who are not believers decide
to leave, let them leave. When this happens, the
Christian man or woman is free. But God
called us to live in peace. 16Wife, you don't
know; maybe you will save your husband.
And husband, you don't know; maybe you
will save your wife.

LIVE AS GOD CALLED YOU

17But in any case each one of you should
continue to live the way God has given you to
live—the way you were when God called you.
This is a rule I make in all the churches. 18If a
man was already circumcised when he was
called, he should not undo his circumcision. If
a man was without circumcision when he was
called, he should not be circumcised. 19It is not
important if a man is circumcised or not. The
important thing is obeying God's commands.
20Each one of you should stay the way you
were when God called you. 21If you were a
slave when God called you, do not let that
bother you. But if you can be free, then make
good use of your freedom.
22Those who were slaves
when the Lord called them
are free persons who belong
to the Lord. In the same
way, those who were free
when they were called are
now Christ's slaves. 23You all
were bought at a great price,
so do not become slaves of
people. 24Brothers and sisters,
each of you should stay as you
were when you were called, and stay there
with God.

"You all were bought at a great price, so do not become slaves of people." (1 Corinthians 7:23)

QUESTIONS ABOUT GETTING MARRIED

25Now I write about people who are not
married. I have no command from the Lord
about this; I give my opinion. But I can be
trusted, because the Lord has shown me mercy. 26The present time is a time of trouble, so I
think it is good for you to stay the way you
are. 27If you have a wife, do not try to become
free from her. If you are not married, do not try
to find a wife. 28But if you decide to marry, you
have not sinned. And if a girl who has never
married decides to marry, she has not sinned.
But those who marry will have trouble in this
life, and I want you to be free from trouble.
29Brothers and sisters, this is what I mean:

WHAT'S IT MEAN?

First-century Rome was a dangerous place for Christians. In fact, people throughout the entire Roman Empire were turning against Christians. The emperor Claudius kicked all Jews and Christians out of the city of Rome. Other believers were tortured and killed for their faith in the Lord. Paul knew firsthand about the persecution of Christians. Before he was called to be an apostle of Jesus, Paul himself was a notorious Christian hunter.

1 Corinthians 7:26

We do not have much time left. So starting
now, those who have wives should live as if
they had no wives. 30Those who are crying
should live as if they were not crying. Those
who are happy should live as if they were not
happy. Those who buy things should live as if
they own nothing. 31Those who use the things
of the world should live as if they were not
using them, because this world in its present
form will soon be gone.
32I want you to be free from worry. A man
who is not married is busy with the Lord's
work, trying to please the Lord. 33But a man
who is married is busy with things of the
world, trying to please his wife. 34He must
think about two things—pleasing his wife and
pleasing the Lord. A woman who is not married or a girl who has never married is busy
with the Lord's work. She wants to be holy in
body and spirit. But a married woman is busy
with things of the world, as to how she can
please her husband. 35I am saying this to help
you, not to limit you. But I want you to live in
the right way, to give yourselves fully to the
Lord without concern for other things.
36If a man thinks he is not doing the right
thing with the girl he is engaged to, if she is
almost past the best age to marry and he feels
he should marry her, he should do what he
wants. They should get married. It is no sin.
37But if a man is sure in his mind that there is
no need for marriage, and has his own desires
under control, and has decided not to marry
the one to whom he is engaged, he is doing the
right thing. 38So the man who marries his girl
does right, but the man who does not marry
will do better.
39A woman must stay with her husband as
long as he lives. But if her husband dies, she is
free to marry any man she wants, but she must
marry in the Lord. 40The woman is happier if
she does not marry again. This is my opinion,
but I believe I also have God's Spirit.

ABOUT FOOD OFFERED TO IDOLS

8 1Now I will write about meat that is sacrificed to idols. We know that "we all have
knowledge." Knowledge puffs you up with
pride, but love builds up. 2If you think you
know something, you do not yet know anything as you should. 3But if any person loves
God, that person is known by God.
4So this is what I say about eating meat sacrificed to idols: We know that an idol is really
nothing in the world, and we know there is
only one God. 5Even though there are things
called gods, in heaven or on earth (and there
are many "gods" and "lords"), 6for us there is
only one God—our Father. All things came
from him, and we live for him. And there is
only one Lord—Jesus Christ. All things were
made through him, and we also were made
through him.
7But not all people know this. Some people
are still so used to idols that when they eat
meat, they still think of it as being sacrificed to
an idol. Because their conscience is weak, when
they eat it, they feel guilty. 8But food will not
bring us closer to God. Refusing to eat does not
make us less pleasing to God, and eating does
not make us better in God's sight.
9But be careful that your freedom does not
cause those who are weak in faith to fall into
sin. 10You have "knowledge," so you eat in an
idol's temple.[n] But someone who is weak in
faith might see you eating there and be encouraged to eat meat sacrificed to idols while
thinking it is wrong to do so. 11This weak believer for whom Christ died is ruined because
of your "knowledge." 12When you sin against
your brothers and sisters in Christ like this and
cause them to do what they feel is wrong, you
are also sinning against Christ. 13So if the food
I eat causes them to fall into sin, I will never eat
meat again so that I will not cause any of them
to sin.

PAUL IS LIKE THE OTHER APOSTLES

9 1I am a free man. I am an apostle. I have
seen Jesus our Lord. You people are all an example of my work in the Lord. 2If others do
not accept me as an apostle, surely you do,
because you are proof that I am an apostle in
the Lord.
3This is the answer I give people who want
to judge me: 4Do we not have the right to eat
and drink? 5Do we not have the right to
bring a believing wife with us when we travel as do the other apostles and the Lord's
brothers and Peter? 6Are Barnabas and I the
only ones who must work to earn our living?
7No soldier ever serves in the army and pays
his own salary. No one ever plants a vineyard
without eating some of the grapes. No person
takes care of a flock without drinking some of
the milk.
8I do not say this by human authority;
God's law also says the same thing. 9It is written in the law of Moses: "When an ox is working in the grain, do not cover its mouth to keep

8:10 Idol's temple Building where a god is worshiped.

it from eating."[n] When God said this, was he thinking only about oxen? No. 10He was really talking about us. Yes, that Scripture was written for us, because it goes on to say: "The one who plows and the one who works in the grain should hope to get some of the grain for their work." 11Since we planted spiritual seed among you, is it too much if we should harvest from you some things for this life? 12If others have the right to get something from you, surely we have this right, too. But we do not use it. No, we put up with everything ourselves so that we will not keep anyone from believing the Good News of Christ. 13Surely you know that those who work at the Temple get their food from the Temple, and those who serve at the altar get part of what is offered at the altar. 14In the same way, the Lord has commanded that those who tell the Good News should get their living from this work.

15But I have not used any of these rights. And I am not writing this now to get anything from you. I would rather die than to have my reason for bragging taken away. 16Telling the Good News does not give me any reason for bragging. Telling the Good News is my duty—something I must do. And how terrible it will be for me if I do not tell the Good News. 17If I preach because it is my own choice, I have a reward. But if I preach and it is not my choice to do so, I am only doing the duty that was given to me. 18So what reward do I get? This is my reward: that when I tell the Good News I can offer it freely. I do not use my full rights in my work of preaching the Good News.

19I am free and belong to no one. But I make myself a slave to all people to win as many as I can. 20To the Jews I became like a Jew to win the Jews. I myself am not ruled by the law. But to those who are ruled by the law I became like a person who is ruled by the law. I did this to win those who are ruled by the law. 21To those who are without the law I became like a person who is without the law. I did this to win those people who are without the law. (But really, I am not without God's law—I am ruled by Christ's law.) 22To those who are weak, I became weak so I could win the weak. I have become all things to all people so I could save some of them in any way possible. 23I do all this because of the Good News and so I can share in its blessings.

24You know that in a race all the runners run, but only one gets the prize. So run to win! 25All those who compete in the games use self-control so they can win a crown. That crown is an earthly thing that lasts only a short time, but our crown will never be destroyed. 26So I do not run without a goal. I fight like a boxer who is hitting something—not just the air. 27I treat my body hard and make it my slave so that I myself will not be disqualified after I have preached to others.

WHAT'S IT MEAN?

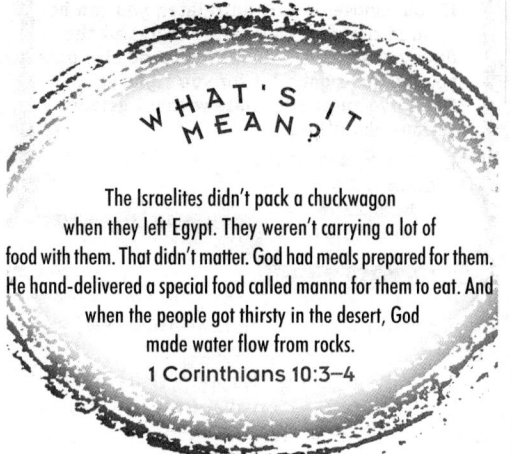

Paul's reference to running and boxing would have had special significance to the people of Corinth. Every two years, their city hosted the Isthmian Games, an ancient predecessor to our Summer Olympics. Fans traveled for miles to watch athletic contests of strength and skill.

1 Corinthians 9:24–26

WARNINGS FROM ISRAEL'S PAST

10 1Brothers and sisters, I want you to know what happened to our ancestors who followed Moses. They were all under the cloud and all went through the sea. 2They were all baptized as followers of Moses in the cloud and in the sea. 3They all ate the same spiritual food, 4and all drank the same spiritual drink. They drank from that spiritual rock that followed them, and that rock was Christ. 5But God was not

WHAT'S IT MEAN?

The Israelites didn't pack a chuckwagon when they left Egypt. They weren't carrying a lot of food with them. That didn't matter. God had meals prepared for them. He hand-delivered a special food called manna for them to eat. And when the people got thirsty in the desert, God made water flow from rocks.

1 Corinthians 10:3–4

9:9 "When an ox . . . eating." Quotation from Deuteronomy 25:4.

On the Edge

You know that in a race all the runners run, but only one gets the prize. So run to win! All those who compete in the games use self-control so they can win a crown. That crown is an earthly thing that lasts only a short time, but our crown will never be destroyed. So I do not run without a goal. I fight like a boxer who is hitting something—not just the air. I treat my body hard and make it my slave so that I myself will not be disqualified after I have preached to others (1 Cor. 9:24–27).

In this passage Paul compares life to a race. The goal for believers is to run the whole race and finish well. If life is a race, it is a marathon, not a sprint. An athlete prepares his body for the long distance because he knows it will be grueling at times. The believer has to be prepared as well. You can't wait until you are older to get serious about God for several reasons.

First, you don't know how long your race is. You may already be nearing the end. Second, the blessing is in the race, not back at the concession stand—God gets blessings from a life that honors him, and he blesses you for a job well done. And third, the race began the minute you arrived. You can jump in now, pace yourself, and finish well, or you can blow it off, hoping your little sprint at the end will count for something. If you choose to wait until later, you can be assured that you will deeply regret all the days you sat and watched everyone else pass you by. God's got a lot for you right now. Don't live another minute without getting serious about him.

SEE FOR YOURSELF:
Luke 12:35–36;
Acts 22:16;
Heb. 10:37

pleased with most of them, so they died in the
desert.
[6]And these things happened as examples
for us, to stop us from wanting evil things as
those people did. [7]Do not worship idols, as
some of them did. Just as it is written in the
Scriptures: "They sat down to eat and drink,
and then they got up and sinned sexually."[n]
[8]We must not take part in sexual sins, as some
of them did. In one day twenty-three thousand of them died because of their sins. [9]We
must not test Christ as some of them did; they
were killed by snakes. [10]Do not complain as
some of them did; they were killed by the angel
that destroys.
[11]The things that happened to those people
are examples. They were written down to
teach us, because we live in a time when all
these things of the past have reached their goal.
[12]If you think you are strong, you should be
careful not to fall. [13]The only temptation that
has come to you is that which everyone has.
But you can trust God, who will not permit
you to be tempted more than you can stand.
But when you are tempted, he will also give
you a way to escape so that you will be able to
stand it.

WHAT'S IT MEAN?

Not only was Jesus' final meal with his disciples his "last supper" on earth, it was also a ceremony he wanted his followers to repeat on a regular basis. This ceremony, called the Lord's Supper or Communion, involves eating a piece of bread and drinking wine or grape juice. The bread symbolizes Jesus' body, and the wine or juice symbolizes his blood. Jesus wanted his followers to remember his death on the cross—his sacrifice for them.

1 Corinthians 10:16

[14]So, my dear friends, run away from the
worship of idols. [15]I am speaking to you as to
intelligent people; judge for yourselves what I
say. [16]We give thanks for the cup of blessing,[n]
which is a sharing in the blood of Christ. And
the bread that we break is a sharing in the
body of Christ. [17]Because there is one loaf of
bread, we who are many are one body, because we all share that one loaf.
[18]Think about the Israelites: Do not those
who eat the sacrifices share in the altar? [19]I do
not mean that the food sacrificed to an idol is

10:7 "They . . . sexually." Quotation from Exodus 32:6. **10:16 cup of blessing** The cup of the fruit of the vine that Christians thank God for and drink at the Lord's Supper.

important. I do not mean that an idol is anything at all. [20]But I say that what is sacrificed to
idols is offered to demons, not to God. And I
do not want you to share anything with demons. [21]You cannot drink the cup of the Lord
and the cup of demons also. You cannot share
in the Lord's table and the table of demons.
[22]Are we trying to make the Lord jealous? We
are not stronger than he is, are we?

HOW TO USE CHRISTIAN FREEDOM

[23]"We are allowed to do all things," but all
things are not good for us to do. "We are allowed to do all things," but not all things help
others grow stronger. [24]Do not look out only
for yourselves. Look out for the good of others
also.

[25]Eat any meat that is sold in the meat market. Do not ask questions to see if it is meat you
think is wrong to eat. [26]You may eat it, "because
the earth belongs to the Lord, and everything
in it."[n]

[27]Those who are not believers may invite
you to eat with them. If you want to go, eat
anything that is put before you. Do not ask
questions to see if you think it might be wrong
to eat. [28]But if anyone says to you, "That food
was offered to idols," do not eat it. Do not eat it
because of that person who told you and because eating it might be thought to be wrong.
[29]I don't mean you think it is wrong, but the
other person might. But why, you ask, should
my freedom be judged by someone else's conscience? [30]If I eat the meal with thankfulness,
why am I criticized because of something for
which I thank God?

[31]The answer is, if you eat or drink, or if you
do anything, do it all for the glory of God.
[32]Never do anything that might hurt others—
Jews, Greeks, or God's church— [33]just as I, also,
try to please everybody in every way. I am not
trying to do what is good for me but what is
good for most people so they can be saved.

11 [1]Follow my example, as I follow the example of Christ.

BEING UNDER AUTHORITY

[2]I praise you because you remember me in
everything, and you follow closely the teachings just as I gave them to you. [3]But I want you
to understand this: The head of every man is
Christ, the head of a woman is the man,[n] and

10:26 "because . . . it" Quotation from Psalms 24:1; 50:12; 89:11. **11:3 the man** This could also mean "her husband."

Promise

HE PROMISES NOT TO LET YOU BE TEMPTED MORE THAN YOU CAN STAND.

If you think you are strong, you should be careful not to fall. The only temptation that has come to you is that which everyone has. But you can trust God, who will not permit you to be tempted more than you can stand. But when you are tempted, he will also give you a way to escape so that you will be able to stand it (1 Cor. 10:12–13).

Before there's heavy breathing and a backseat, there's a door. A way out. Before there's a friend's test paper to cheat off of, there's a window to study by.

Temptations can sometimes get too hot for you to handle on your own, but only because you've passed up a long line of escape hatches along the way—places where God was warning you to turn back, to trust him, to bail out with his parachute of protection.

If you can learn to avoid temptation when it's just a sprinkle, before it builds into a driving rain that hits you from all sides, you'll find life a lot easier, guilt a lot rarer, and the warm, safe feeling of living under God's umbrella.

He always gives you a way out, over and over again, far in advance of the 40-foot drop-off at the end. And even up there, when you're hanging on by your fingernails—if you'll call on him to help you and if you'll stop trying to grit your teeth and fight the battle in your own strength, he'll be right there to put you back on solid ground.

SEE FOR YOURSELF:
Matt. 6:13; Heb. 2:18; 2 Pet. 2:9

the head of Christ is God. 4Every man who
prays or prophesies with his head covered
brings shame to his head. 5But every woman
who prays or prophesies with her head uncovered brings shame to her head. She is the
same as a woman who has her head shaved.
6If a woman does not cover her
head, she should have her hair cut
off. But since it is shameful for a
woman to cut off her hair or to
shave her head, she should
cover her head. 7But a man
should not cover his head,
because he is the likeness and
glory of God. But woman is
man's glory. 8Man did not
come from woman, but wom-
an came from man. 9And man
was not made for woman, but
woman was made for man. 10So
that is why a woman should have a
symbol of authority on her head, because of
the angels.
11But in the Lord women are not independent of men, and men are not independent of
women. 12This is true because woman came
from man, but also man is born from woman.
But everything comes from God. 13Decide this
for yourselves: Is it right for a woman to pray
to God with her head uncovered? 14Even
nature itself teaches you that wearing long hair
is shameful for a man. 15But long hair is a
woman's glory. Long hair is given to her as a
covering. 16Some people may still want to argue
about this, but I would add that neither we nor
the churches of God have any other practice.

THE LORD'S SUPPER

17In the things I tell you now I do not praise
you, because when you come together you do
more harm than good. 18First, I hear that when
you meet together as a church you are divided,
and I believe some of this. 19(It is necessary to
have differences among you so that it may be
clear which of you really have God's approval.) 20When you come together, you are not
really eating the Lord's Supper.[n] 21This is because when you eat, each person eats without
waiting for the others. Some people do not get
enough to eat, while others have too much to
drink. 22You can eat and drink in your own
homes! You seem to think God's church is not
important, and you embarrass those who are
poor. What should I tell you? Should I praise
you? I do not praise you for doing this.

23The teaching I gave you is the same teaching I received from the Lord: On the night
when the Lord Jesus was handed over to be
killed, he took bread 24and gave thanks for it.
Then he broke the bread and said, "This is my
body; it is for you. Do this to remember me."
25In the same way, after
they ate, Jesus took the
cup. He said, "This cup
is the new agreement
that is sealed with
the blood of my
death. When you
drink this, do it
to remember me."
26Every time you eat
this bread and drink
this cup you are tell-
ing others about the
Lord's death until he
comes.

> "So a person who eats the bread or drinks the cup of the Lord in a way that is not worthy of it will be guilty of sinning against the body and the blood of the Lord."
> (1 Corinthians 11:27)

27So a person who eats the bread or
drinks the cup of the Lord in a way that is not
worthy of it will be guilty of sinning against
the body and the blood of the Lord. 28Look
into your own hearts before you eat the bread
and drink the cup, 29because all who eat the
bread and drink the cup without recognizing
the body eat and drink judgment against
themselves. 30That is why many in your group
are sick and weak, and many have died. 31But if
we judged ourselves in the right way, God
would not judge us. 32But when the Lord
judges us, he punishes us so that we will not
be destroyed along with the world.
33So my brothers and sisters, when you
come together to eat, wait for each other.
34Anyone who is too hungry should eat at
home so that in meeting together you will not
bring God's judgment on yourselves. I will tell
you what to do about the other things when I
come.

GIFTS FROM THE HOLY SPIRIT

12 1Now, brothers and sisters, I want you to
understand about spiritual gifts. 2You know
the way you lived before you were believers.
You let yourselves be influenced and led away
to worship idols—things that could not speak.
3So I want you to understand that no one who
is speaking with the help of God's Spirit says,
"Jesus be cursed." And no one can say, "Jesus is
Lord," without the help of the Holy Spirit.
4There are different kinds of gifts, but they
are all from the same Spirit. 5There are different

11:20 Lord's Supper The meal Jesus told his followers to eat to remember him (Luke 22:14–20).

ways to serve but the same Lord to serve. [6]And there are different ways that God works through people but the same God. God works in all of us in everything we do. [7]Something from the Spirit can be seen in each person, for the common good. [8]The Spirit gives one person the ability to speak with wisdom, and the same Spirit gives another the ability to speak with knowledge. [9]The same Spirit gives faith to one person. And, to another, that one Spirit gives gifts of healing. [10]The Spirit gives to another person the power to do miracles, to another the ability to prophesy. And he gives to another the ability to know the difference between good and evil spirits. The Spirit gives one person the ability to speak in different kinds of languages[n] and to another the ability to interpret those languages. [11]One Spirit, the same Spirit, does all these things, and the Spirit decides what to give each person.

THE BODY OF CHRIST WORKS TOGETHER

[12]A person's body is only one thing, but it has many parts. Though there are many parts to a body, all those parts make only one body. Christ is like that also. [13]Some of us are Jews, and some are Greeks. Some of us are slaves, and some are free. But we were all baptized into one body through one Spirit. And we were all made to share in the one Spirit.

WHAT'S IT MEAN?

The secret to Rome's success was slave labor. A large segment of the Roman population was made up of slaves. What's more, those slaves served a variety of purposes in Roman society. Some were used for extremely difficult and dangerous work. Others were put in charge of businesses. Still others taught Roman children.

1 Corinthians 12:13

[14]The human body has many parts. [15]The foot might say, "Because I am not a hand, I am not part of the body." But saying this would not stop the foot from being a part of the body. [16]The ear might say, "Because I am not an eye, I am not part of the body." But saying this would not stop the ear from being a part of the body. [17]If the whole body were an eye, it would not be able to hear. If the whole body were an ear, it would not be able to smell. [18-19]If each part of the body were the same part, there would be no body. But truly God put all the parts, each one of them, in the body as he wanted them. [20]So then there are many parts, but only one body.

[21]The eye cannot say to the hand, "I don't need you!" And the head cannot say to the foot, "I don't need you!" [22]No! Those parts of the body that seem to be the weaker are really necessary. [23]And the parts of the body we think are less deserving are the parts to which we give the most honor. We give special respect to the parts we want to hide. [24]The more respectable parts of our body need no special care. But God put the body together and gave more honor to the parts that need it [25]so our body would not be divided. God wanted the different parts to care the same for each other. [26]If one part of the body suffers, all the other parts suffer with it. Or if one part of our body is honored, all the other parts share its honor.

[27]Together you are the body of Christ, and each one of you is a part of that body. [28]In the church God has given a place first to apostles, second to prophets, and third to teachers. Then God has given a place to those who do miracles, those who have gifts of healing, those who can help others, those who are able to govern, and those who can speak in different languages.[n] [29]Not all are apostles. Not all are prophets. Not all are teachers. Not all do miracles. [30]Not all have gifts of healing. Not all speak in different languages. Not all interpret those languages. [31]But you should truly want to have the greater gifts.

LOVE IS THE GREATEST GIFT

And now I will show you the best way of all.

13 [1]I may speak in different languages[n] of people or even angels. But if I do not have love, I am only a noisy bell or a crashing cymbal. [2]I may have the gift of prophecy. I may understand all the secret things of God and have all knowledge, and I may have faith so great I can move mountains. But even with all these things, if I do not have love, then I am nothing. [3]I may give away everything I have, and I may

12:10, 28; 13:1 languages This can also be translated "tongues."

On the Edge

Love is patient and kind. Love is not jealous, it does not brag, and it is not proud. Love is not rude, is not selfish, and does not get upset with others. Love does not count up wrongs that have been done (1 Cor. 13:4–5).

A wise mom once said, "Take it as a compliment that other girls think your guy is great, too." Be secure enough to acknowledge their good taste. If your relationship is about love, then jealousy can't be part of it. Paul spends this whole chapter defining love. He is clear to point out that true love is not jealous. Somehow we've confused this and begun to think that if you love someone, you are supposed to act jealous and possessive. Love is about serving, selflessness, and caring. Arrogance and jealousy are for the insecure. Have faith in Jesus. He will bring the perfect mate for you. Learning to love and trust someone means that you don't worry about who he talks to, or who he's in the same room with. If your guy isn't trustworthy, then he's definitely not the one for you. Don't even start a romantic relationship with him. Start making friendships instead of dating. That way you can spend time with different people until you find the one who lines up with your beliefs and values, the one you have fun with, the one you love, the one you trust completely.

The possibility for boyfriends and girlfriends will come and go. Don't give in to the "gotta have a date" mentality. Commit to having holy courtships and let God bring the one he has chosen for you. When it's really about love, jealousy will lose out and trust will win.

SEE FOR YOURSELF:
2 Cor. 1:12; 2:7–8; Eph. 5:2

even give my body as an offering to be burned.[n] But I gain nothing if I do not have love.

4Love is patient and kind. Love is not jealous, it does not brag, and it is not proud. 5Love is not rude, is not selfish, and does not get upset with others. Love does not count up wrongs that have been done. 6Love is not happy with evil but is happy with the truth. 7Love patiently accepts all things. It always trusts, always hopes, and always remains strong.

8Love never ends. There are gifts of prophecy, but they will be ended. There are gifts of speaking in different languages, but those gifts will stop. There is the gift of knowledge, but it will come to an end. 9The reason is that our knowledge and our ability to prophesy are not perfect. 10But when perfection comes, the things that are not perfect will end. 11When I was a child, I talked like a child, I thought like a child, I reasoned like a child. When I became a man, I stopped those childish ways. 12It is the same with us. Now we see a dim reflection, as if we were looking into a mirror, but then we shall see clearly. Now I know only a part, but then I will know fully, as God has known me. 13So these three things continue forever: faith, hope, and love. And the greatest of these is love.

LOVE
Does true love ever quit? (13:4–8)

DESIRE SPIRITUAL GIFTS

14

1You should seek after love, and you should truly want to have the spiritual gifts, especially the gift of prophecy. 2I will explain why. Those who have the gift of speaking in different languages[n] are not speaking to people; they are speaking to God. No one understands them; they are speaking secret things through the Spirit. 3But those who prophesy are speaking to people to give them strength, encouragement, and comfort. 4The ones who speak in different languages are helping only themselves, but those who prophesy are helping the whole church. 5I wish all of you had the gift of speaking in different kinds of languages, but more, I wish you would prophesy. Those who prophesy are greater than those who can only speak in different languages—unless someone is there who can explain what is said so that the whole church can be helped.

6Brothers and sisters, will it help you if I come to you speaking in different languages? No! It will help you only if I bring you a new truth or some new knowledge, or prophecy, or teaching. 7It is the same as with lifeless things that make sounds—like a flute or a harp. If they do not make clear musical notes, you will not know what is being played. 8And in a war, if the trumpet does not give a clear sound, who will prepare for battle? 9It is the same with you.

13:3 Verse 3 Other Greek copies read: "hand over my body in order that I may brag."
14:2 languages This can also be translated "tongues."

Unless you speak clearly with your tongue, no one can understand what you are saying. You will be talking into the air! [10]It may be true that there are all kinds of sounds in the world, and none is without meaning. [11]But unless I understand the meaning of what someone says to me, I will be a foreigner to him, and he will be a foreigner to me. [12]It is the same with you. Since you want spiritual gifts very much, seek most of all to have the gifts that help the church grow stronger.

[13]The one who has the gift of speaking in a different language should pray for the gift to interpret what is spoken. [14]If I pray in a different language, my spirit is praying, but my mind does nothing. [15]So what should I do? I will pray with my spirit, but I will also pray with my mind. I will sing with my spirit, but I will also sing with my mind. [16]If you praise God with your spirit, those persons there without understanding cannot say amen[n] to your prayer of thanks, because they do not know what you are saying. [17]You may be thanking God in a good way, but the other person is not helped.

[18]I thank God that I speak in different kinds of languages more than all of you. [19]But in the church meetings I would rather speak five words I understand in order to teach others than thousands of words in a different language.

[20]Brothers and sisters, do not think like children. In evil things be like babies, but in your thinking you should be like adults. [21]It is written in the Scriptures:

"With people who use strange words and
    foreign languages
  I will speak to these people.
But even then they will not listen to me,"

Isaiah 28:11-12

says the Lord.

[22]So the gift of speaking in different kinds of languages is a proof for those who do not believe, not for those who do believe. And prophecy is for people who believe, not for those who do not believe. [23]Suppose the whole church meets together and everyone speaks in different languages. If some people come in who do not understand or do not believe, they will say you are crazy. [24]But suppose everyone is prophesying and some people come in who do not believe or do not understand. If everyone is prophesying, their sin will be shown to them, and they will be judged by all that they hear. [25]The secret things in their hearts will be made known. So they will bow down and worship God saying, "Truly, God is with you."

MEETINGS SHOULD HELP THE CHURCH

[26]So, brothers and sisters, what should you do? When you meet together, one person has a song, and another has a teaching. Another has a new truth from God. Another speaks in a

WHAT'S IT MEAN?

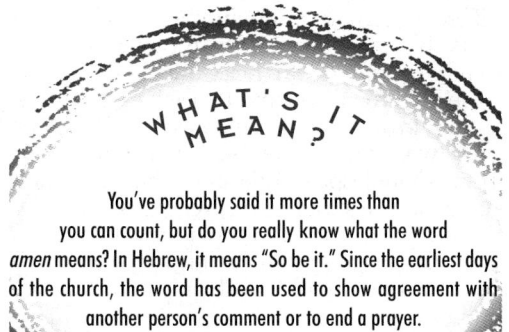

You've probably said it more times than you can count, but do you really know what the word *amen* means? In Hebrew, it means "So be it." Since the earliest days of the church, the word has been used to show agreement with another person's comment or to end a prayer.

1 Corinthians 14:16

On the Edge

Now we see a dim reflection, as if we were looking into a mirror, but then we shall see clearly. Now I know only a part, but then I will know fully, as God has known me (1 Cor. 13:12).

Life seems unfair because we don't see the whole picture. Paul says in this passage that we can only see a dim picture of God. We do not know everything he is doing. We only have earthly eyes that see little parts and earthly minds that understand tiny pieces of God's very big plan. Limited vision requires great faith and trust. The God who created you knows exactly what he is doing. Sometimes we understand later why things happened that at first seemed so unfair. Paul says though, that we won't completely understand everything until we are with God in heaven.

SEE FOR YOURSELF: Ps. 119:169; Phil. 4:6; Col. 2:2–3

14:16 amen To say amen means to agree with the things that were said.

different language,[n] and another person interprets that language. The purpose of all these things should be to help the church grow strong. [27]When you meet together, if anyone speaks in a different language, it should be only two, or not more than three, who speak. They should speak one after the other, and someone else should interpret. [28]But if there is no interpreter, then those who speak in a different language should be quiet in the church meeting. They should speak only to themselves and to God.

[29]Only two or three prophets should speak, and the others should judge what they say. [30]If a message from God comes to another person who is sitting, the first speaker should stop. [31]You can all prophesy one after the other. In this way all the people can be taught and encouraged. [32]The spirits of prophets are under the control of the prophets themselves. [33]God is not a God of confusion but a God of peace.

As is true in all the churches of God's people, [34]women should keep quiet in the church meetings. They are not allowed to speak, but they must yield to this rule as the law says. [35]If they want to learn something, they should ask their own husbands at home. It is shameful for a woman to speak in the church meeting. [36]Did God's teaching come from you? Or are you the only ones to whom it has come?

[37]Those who think they are prophets or spiritual persons should understand that what I am writing to you is the Lord's command. [38]Those who ignore this will be ignored by God.

[39]So my brothers and sisters, you should truly want to prophesy. But do not stop people from using the gift of speaking in different kinds of languages. [40]But let everything be done in a right and orderly way.

THE GOOD NEWS ABOUT CHRIST

15 [1]Now, brothers and sisters, I want you to remember the Good News I brought to you. You received this Good News and continue strong in it. [2]And you are being saved by it if you continue believing what I told you. If you do not, then you believed for nothing.

[3]I passed on to you what I received, of which this was most important: that Christ died for our sins, as the Scriptures say; [4]that he was buried and was raised to life on the third day as the Scriptures say; [5]and that he was seen by Peter and then by the twelve apostles. [6]After that, Jesus was seen by more than five hundred of the believers at the same time. Most of them are still living today, but some have died. [7]Then he was seen by James and later by all the apostles. [8]Last of all he was seen by me—as by a person not born at the normal time. [9]All the other apostles are greater than I am. I am not even good enough to be called an apostle, because I persecuted the church of God. [10]But God's grace has made me what I am, and his grace to me was not wasted. I worked harder than all the other apostles. (But it was not I really; it was God's grace that was with me.) [11]So if I preached to you or the other apostles preached to you, we all preach the same thing, and this is what you believed.

WE WILL BE RAISED FROM THE DEAD

[12]Now since we preached that Christ was raised from the dead, why do some of you say that people will not be raised from the dead? [13]If no one is ever raised from the dead, then Christ has not been raised. [14]And if Christ has not been raised, then our preaching is worth nothing, and your faith is worth nothing. [15]And also, we are guilty of lying about God, because we testified of him that he raised Christ from the dead. But if people are not raised from the dead, then God never raised Christ. [16]If the dead are not raised, Christ has not been raised either. [17]And if Christ has not been raised, then your faith has nothing to it; you are still guilty of your sins. [18]And those in Christ who have already died are lost. [19]If our hope in Christ is for this life only, we should be pitied more than anyone else in the world.

RESURRECTION
What is the foundation of Christianity? (15:12–21)

[20]But Christ has truly been raised from the dead—the first one and proof that those who sleep in death will also be raised. [21]Death has come because of what one man did, but the rising from death also comes because of one man. [22]In Adam all of us die. In the same way, in Christ all of us will be made alive again. [23]But everyone will be raised to life in the right order. Christ was first to be raised. When Christ comes again, those who belong to him will be raised to life, [24]and then the end will come. At that time Christ will destroy all rulers, authorities, and powers, and he will hand over the kingdom to God the Father. [25]Christ must rule until he puts all enemies under his control. [26]The last enemy to be destroyed will be death. [27]The Scripture says that God put all things

14:26 language This can also be translated "tongue."

under his control.[n] When it says "all things" are under him, it is clear this does not include God himself. God is the One who put everything under his control. 28After everything has been put under the Son, then he will put himself under God, who had put all things under him. Then God will be the complete ruler over everything.

29If the dead are never raised, what will people do who are being baptized for the dead? If the dead are not raised at all, why are people being baptized for them?

30And what about us? Why do we put ourselves in danger every hour? 31I die every day. That is true, brothers and sisters, just as it is true that I brag about you in Christ Jesus our Lord. 32If I fought wild animals in Ephesus only with human hopes, I have gained nothing. If the dead are not raised, "Let us eat and drink, because tomorrow we will die."[n]

WHAT'S IT MEAN?

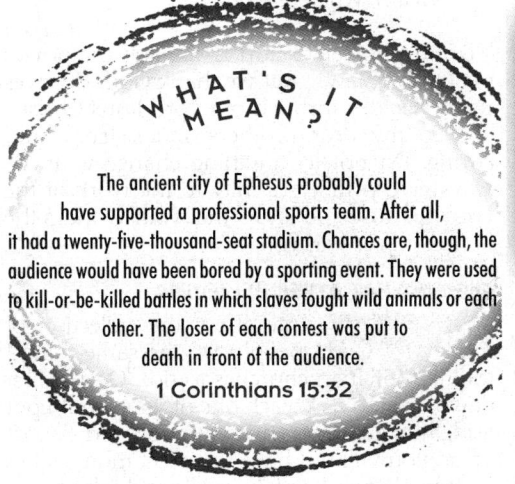

The ancient city of Ephesus probably could have supported a professional sports team. After all, it had a twenty-five-thousand-seat stadium. Chances are, though, the audience would have been bored by a sporting event. They were used to kill-or-be-killed battles in which slaves fought wild animals or each other. The loser of each contest was put to death in front of the audience.

1 Corinthians 15:32

On the Edge

Do not be fooled: "Bad friends will ruin good habits" (1 Cor. 15:33).

Parents know that sooner or later you begin to look and act like the people you hang out with. You start wearing the same kind of clothes, speaking the same lingo, hanging out at the same places, doing the same things. Eventually your friends begin to give you advice. If your friends are wise and make wise decisions, then everything's cool. It's the foolish friends that get you into trouble. Proverbs 13 affirms that in verse 20, "Spend time with the wise and you will become wise, but the friends of fools will suffer." Your parents care who your friends are because they care so much about you.

They want everything to go well with your life. They want the absolute best for you. They love you. Don't get so uptight the next time they ask about a friend. It would be smart to take their advice and choose wisely. Those who hang out with fools eventually blend right in.

SEE FOR YOURSELF:
Prov. 1:8–19; 13:20; 23:25; 27:9

33Do not be fooled: "Bad friends will ruin good habits." 34Come back to your right way of thinking and stop sinning. Some of you do not know God—I say this to shame you.

WHAT KIND OF BODY WILL WE HAVE?

35But someone may ask, "How are the dead raised? What kind of body will they have?" 36Foolish person! When you sow a seed, it must die in the ground before it can live and grow. 37And when you sow it, it does not have the same "body" it will have later. What you sow is only a bare seed, maybe wheat or something else. 38But God gives it a body that he has planned for it, and God gives each kind of seed its own body. 39All things made of flesh are not the same: People have one kind of flesh, animals have another, birds have another, and fish have another. 40Also there are heavenly bodies and earthly bodies. But the beauty of the heavenly bodies is one kind, and the beauty of the earthly bodies is another. 41The sun has one kind of beauty, the moon has another beauty, and the stars have another. And each star is different in its beauty.

42It is the same with the dead who are raised to life. The body that is "planted" will ruin and decay, but it is raised to a life that cannot be destroyed. 43When the body is "planted," it is without honor, but it is raised in glory. When the body is "planted," it is weak, but when it is raised, it is powerful. 44The body that is "planted" is a physical body. When it is raised, it is a spiritual body.

There is a physical body, and there is also a spiritual body. 45It is written in the Scriptures:

15:27 God put . . . control. From Psalm 8:6. **15:32 "Let us . . . die."** Quotation from Isaiah 22:13; 56:12.

"The first man, Adam, became a living person."[n]
But the last Adam became a spirit that gives
life. 46The spiritual did not come first, but the
physical and then the spiritual. 47The first man
came from the dust of the earth. The second
man came from heaven. 48People who belong
to the earth are like the first man of earth. But
those people who belong to heaven are like the
man of heaven. 49Just as we were made like
the man of earth, so we will also be made like
the man of heaven.
50I tell you this, brothers and sisters: Flesh
and blood cannot have a part in the kingdom
of God. Something that will ruin cannot have a
part in something that never ruins. 51But look!
I tell you this secret: We will not all sleep in
death, but we will all be changed. 52It will take
only a second—as quickly as an eye blinks—
when the last trumpet sounds. The trumpet
will sound, and those who have died will be
raised to live forever, and we will all be
changed. 53This body that can be destroyed
must clothe itself with something that can never
be destroyed. And this body that dies must
clothe itself with something that can never die.
54So this body that can be destroyed will clothe
itself with that which can never be destroyed,
and this body that dies will clothe itself with
that which can never die. When this happens,
this Scripture will be made true:

"Death is destroyed forever in victory."

Isaiah 25:8

55"Death, where is your victory?
Death, where is your pain?"

Hosea 13:14

56Death's power to hurt is sin, and the power
of sin is the law. 57But we thank God! He gives
us the victory through our Lord Jesus Christ.
58So my dear brothers and sisters, stand
strong. Do not let anything change you. Always give yourselves fully to the work of the
Lord, because you know that your work in the
Lord is never wasted.

THE GIFT FOR OTHER BELIEVERS

16 1Now I will write about the collection of
money for God's people. Do the same thing I
told the Galatian churches to do: 2On the first
day of every week, each one of you should put
aside money as you have been blessed. Save it
up so you will not have to collect money after
I come. 3When I arrive, I will send whomever
you approve to take your gift to Jerusalem. I
will send them with letters of introduction,
4and if it seems good for me to go also, they
will go along with me.

PAUL'S PLANS

5I plan to go through Macedonia, so I will
come to you after I go through there. 6Perhaps
I will stay with you for a time or even all winter. Then you can help me on my trip, wherever I go. 7I do not want to see you now just in
passing. I hope to stay a longer time with you
if the Lord allows it. 8But I will stay at Ephesus
until Pentecost, 9because a good opportunity
for a great and growing work has been given

On the Edge

The first man came from the dust of the earth. The second man came from heaven. People who belong to the earth are like the first man of earth. But those people who belong to heaven are like the man of heaven (1 Cor. 15:47–48).

Call it amazing. God takes a handful of dirt and makes a man. Very humble beginnings for people who think so highly of themselves. Have you felt jealous of anyone lately? Do you think you deserve more than you have? Are you mad at God because your family doesn't have some of the comforts other families do? Maybe it's time to remember where you came from—dust. Yep, you (and all the people you're jealous of) are just a bunch of dust.

Your life is a gift. It's a blessing to be on earth and to be able to enjoy life. You've got the freedom to choose what you're going to do with your life. The point is to make something out of the gifts God has given you. Your body, mind, emotions, and personality are specially crafted by God for his purpose. God wants you to use the time you've got on earth and the gifts you've been given to glorify him. Your glory comes later. Paul says that everyone in heaven will have a body like the glorified Christ. There's a lot to do between now and the time you get to heaven, so get that old, dusty body in gear. God has great things for you!

SEE FOR YOURSELF:
Gen. 2:7; 3:19;
Is. 40:6–7

15:45 "The first . . . person." Quotation from Genesis 2:7.

WHAT'S IT MEAN?

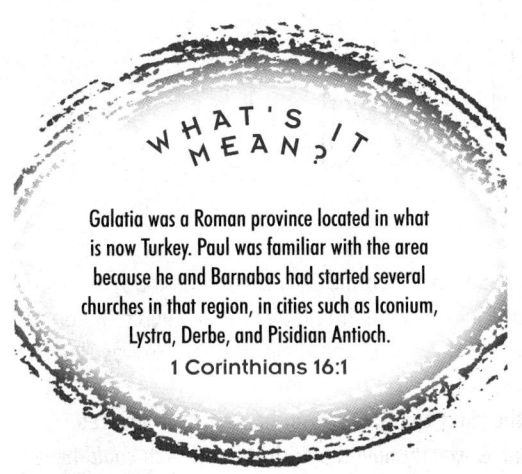

Galatia was a Roman province located in what is now Turkey. Paul was familiar with the area because he and Barnabas had started several churches in that region, in cities such as Iconium, Lystra, Derbe, and Pisidian Antioch.

1 Corinthians 16:1

to me now. And there are many people working against me.

[10]If Timothy comes to you, see to it that he has nothing to fear with you, because he is working for the Lord just as I am. [11]So none of you should treat Timothy as unimportant, but help him on his trip in peace so that he can come back to me. I am expecting him to come with the brothers.

[12]Now about our brother Apollos: I strongly encouraged him to visit you with the other brothers. He did not at all want to come now; he will come when he has the opportunity.

PAUL ENDS HIS LETTER

[13]Be alert. Continue strong in the faith. Have courage, and be strong. [14]Do everything in love.

[15]You know that the family of Stephanas were the first believers in Southern Greece and that they have given themselves to the service of God's people. I ask you, brothers and sisters, [16]to follow the leading of people like these and anyone else who works and serves with them.

[17]I am happy that Stephanas, Fortunatus, and Achaicus have come. You are not here, but they have filled your place. [18]They have refreshed my spirit and yours. You should recognize the value of people like these.

[19]The churches in the country of Asia send greetings to you. Aquila and Priscilla greet you in the Lord, as does the church that meets in their house. [20]All the brothers and sisters here send greetings. Give each other a holy kiss when you meet.

[21]I, Paul, am writing this greeting with my own hand.

[22]If anyone does not love the Lord, let him be separated from God—lost forever!

Come, O Lord!

[23]The grace of the Lord Jesus be with you.

[24]My love be with all of you in Christ Jesus.

WHAT'S IT MEAN?

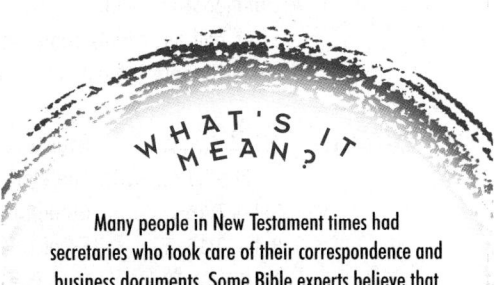

Many people in New Testament times had secretaries who took care of their correspondence and business documents. Some Bible experts believe that Paul needed a secretary to write his letters for him because he had very poor eyesight.

1 Corinthians 16:21

2 Corinthians

CONTENT You can't really understand how amazing 2 Corinthians is without knowing why Paul wrote 1 Corinthians. When Paul wrote his first letter to the church in Corinth, he was telling them off a little bit. He was setting them straight. He was "letting them have it."

It's difficult enough to do the right thing. It's even harder when you get defensive and hardheaded. That is exactly how the Corinthian church *could* have responded to Paul's correction—but they didn't.

In fact, by the time Paul wrote them the letter that we know as 2 Corinthians he was bragging about their giving spirits. He was complimenting them. He was commending them.

As bad as it feels sometimes to be confronted about stuff we do wrong, we are better people if we'll stop and listen. Second Corinthians reminds us of that.

Outline

1:1–11 .... Paul Gives Thanks to God
1:12—2:17 .... The Work of an Apostle for God's People
3:1—7:16 .... Guided by the Love of Christ
8:1—9:15 .... Excel in Giving
10:1—13:10 .... Paul Is a True Apostle
13:11–14 .... Final Greetings

Purpose We are to have ministries under the new agreement.

Theme Powerful Ministry Through Weak Vessels

Date of writing Fall A.D. 56

"If anyone belongs to Christ, there is a new creation. The old things have gone; everything is made new!" (5:17)

Bible Talk

Paul's Physical Problems

We don't know what Paul's problems were that caused him such physical suffering, but we know from his letters to the Corinthians that there was something about Paul that he wanted to change. This thing held him back. It made his life harder, and he thought it made him less effective for Christ.

While we don't know exactly what Paul was talking about, we all know what it is to wish we could change something about ourselves. It's okay to ask God to change that thing. Paul asked God more than once to remove his problem. But he also didn't let it hold him back from doing what God wanted.

GETTING MAD AT THE TRUTH

We have a lot to learn from the Corinthians about hearing the truth and responding to it. It's so easy to want to be right, whether we really *are* right or not. It's often a matter of pride. When someone tells us something that shows us we are wrong, we want to defend ourselves at all costs.

It's often at church or when we read the Bible that God confronts us about the sin in our lives. When he does, we have to make the choice that the Corinthians had to make with Paul. We can get mad and defensive, or we can listen and let God make us into better people. It's not worth trying to be right instead of just being humble and letting God make us right.

1 [1]From Paul, an apostle of Christ Jesus. I am an apostle because that is what God wanted. Also from Timothy our brother in Christ.

To the church of God in Corinth, and to all of God's people everywhere in Southern Greece:

[2]Grace and peace to you from God our Father and the Lord Jesus Christ.

PAUL GIVES THANKS TO GOD

[3]Praise be to the God and Father of our Lord Jesus Christ. God is the Father who is full of mercy and all comfort. [4]He comforts us every time we have trouble, so when others have trouble, we can comfort them with the same comfort God gives us. [5]We share in the many sufferings of Christ. In the same way, much comfort comes to us through Christ. [6]If we have troubles, it is for your comfort and salvation, and if we have comfort, you also have comfort. This helps you to accept patiently the same sufferings we have. [7]Our hope for you is strong, knowing that you share in our sufferings and also in the comfort we receive.

COMFORT
Are hurting people important to God? (1:3–11)

[8]Brothers and sisters,[n] we want you to know about the trouble we suffered in Asia. We had great burdens there that were beyond our own strength. We even gave up hope of living. [9]Truly, in our own hearts we believed we would die. But this happened so we would not trust in ourselves but in God, who raises people from the dead. [10]God saved us from these great dangers of death, and he will continue to save us. We have put our hope in him, and he will save us again. [11]And you can help us with your prayers. Then many people will give thanks for us—that God blessed us because of their many prayers.

THE CHANGE IN PAUL'S PLANS

[12]This is what we are proud of, and I can say it with a clear conscience: In everything we have done in the world, and especially with you, we have had an honest and sincere heart from God. We did this by God's grace, not by the kind of wisdom the world has. [13-14]We write to you only what you can read and understand. And I hope that as you have understood some things about us, you may come to know everything about us. Then you can be proud of us, as we will be proud of you on the day our Lord Jesus Christ comes again.

1:8 Brothers and sisters Although the Greek text says "Brothers" here and throughout this book, Paul's words were meant for the entire church, including men and women.

Promise HE PROMISES YOU COMFORT.

Praise be to the God and Father of our Lord Jesus Christ. God is the Father who is full of mercy and all comfort. He comforts us every time we have trouble, so when others have trouble, we can comfort them with the same comfort God gives us (2 Cor. 1:3–4).

Trouble can come in all sizes. There's the kind you get yourself into, like staying out too late or tossing water balloons at passing cars. There's the kind that other people cause for you, like when somebody tells somebody else something you said when you said something totally different. And there's also the kind that just sort of hits you out of the blue, like when your best friend gets hurt in a car wreck or your grandmother dies on an operating table.

But God's comfort comes in colors to match every problem. It fits every hole left behind by someone you love. It soothes every wound that's opened by the daggers of jealousy and anger. It covers every sin with the hope that Christ's blood can forgive completely—and his discipline can keep you from ever visiting this awful place again.

God's comfort—so real, so refreshing—can appear in a Bible verse, a mom's tender arm around your shoulder, a series of events. But it's always there. And it's always yours. And it's always God.

SEE FOR YOURSELF:
Ps. 23:4; Is. 49:13; 2 Thess. 2:16–17

15I was so sure of all this that I made plans to visit you first so you could be blessed twice. 16I planned to visit you on my way to Macedonia and again on my way back. I wanted to get help from you for my trip to Judea. 17Do you think that I made these plans without really meaning it? Or maybe you think I make plans as the world does, so that I say yes, yes and at the same time no, no.

18But if you can believe God, you can believe that what we tell you is never both yes and no. 19The Son of God, Jesus Christ, that Silas and Timothy and I preached to you, was not yes and no. In Christ it has always been yes. 20The yes to all of God's promises is in Christ, and through Christ we say yes to the glory of God. 21Remember, God is the One who makes you and us strong in Christ. God made us his chosen people. 22He put his mark on us to show that we are his, and he put his Spirit in our hearts to be a guarantee for all he has promised.

23I tell you this, and I ask God to be my witness that this is true: The reason I did not come back to Corinth was to keep you from being punished or hurt. 24We are not trying to control your faith. You are strong in faith. But we are workers with you for your own joy.

2 1So I decided that my next visit to you would not be another one to make you sad. 2If I make you sad, who will make me glad? Only you can make me glad—particularly the person whom I made sad. 3I wrote you a letter for this reason: that when I came to you I would not be made sad by the people who should make me happy. I felt sure of all of you, that you would share my joy. 4When I wrote to you before, I was very troubled and unhappy in my heart, and I wrote with many tears. I did not write to make you sad, but to let you know how much I love you.

On the Edge

Our offering to God is this: We are the sweet smell of Christ among those who are being saved and among those who are being lost. To those who are lost, we are the smell of death that brings death, but to those who are being saved, we are the smell of life that brings life. So who is able to do this work? (2 Cor. 2:15–16).

When you do what God wants instead of acting like all the people around you, Paul says that you are, figuratively speaking, a perfume. For some people that perfume smells wonderful. These people are inspired by your relationship with Jesus. If they haven't met him, they see the peace you have, the way it really makes you happy to follow him, and they want what you have. If they do know Jesus, your example encourages them to keep getting closer to him.

Unfortunately, there are others who think your life really stinks. The fact that you do things they wouldn't do—stand up for someone who everyone else is picking on, stay straight-faced when you hear a dirty joke, refuse to drink at a party—that bugs them a lot. They can make things pretty unpleasant for you, but they're hurting themselves more than they hurt you and they don't even realize it. By giving you a hard time, they're pushing away Jesus—and knowing him is the whole reason they were born!

SEE FOR YOURSELF: Matt. 5:13–14; 28:19–20

FORGIVE THE SINNER

5Someone there among you has caused sadness, not to me, but to all of you. I mean he caused sadness to all in some way. (I do not want to make it sound worse than it really is.) 6The punishment that most of you gave him is enough for him. 7But now you should forgive him and comfort him to keep him from having too much sadness and giving up completely. 8So I beg you to show that you love him. 9I wrote you to test you and to see if you obey in everything. 10If you forgive someone, I also forgive him. And what I have forgiven—if I had anything to forgive—I forgave it for you, as if Christ were with me. 11I did this so that Satan would not win anything from us, because we know very well what Satan's plans are.

PAUL'S CONCERN IN TROAS

12When I came to Troas to preach the Good News of Christ, the Lord gave me a good opportunity there. 13But I had no peace, because I did not find my brother Titus. So I said goodbye to them at Troas and went to Macedonia.

VICTORY THROUGH CHRIST

14But thanks be to God, who always leads us in victory through Christ. God uses us to spread his knowledge everywhere like a sweet-smelling perfume. 15Our offering to God is this:

We are the sweet smell of Christ among those
who are being saved and among those who
are being lost. 16To those who are lost, we are
the smell of death that brings death, but to
those who are being saved, we are the smell of
life that brings life. So who is able to do this
work? 17We do not sell the word of God for a
profit as many other people do. But in Christ
we speak the truth before God, as messengers
of God.

SERVANTS OF THE NEW AGREEMENT

3 1Are we starting to brag about ourselves
again? Do we need letters of introduction to
you or from you, like some other people? 2You
yourselves are our letter, written on our hearts,
known and read by everyone. 3You show that
you are a letter from Christ sent through us.
This letter is not written with ink but with the
Spirit of the living God. It is not written on
stone tablets[n] but on human hearts.

On the Edge

We can say this, because through Christ we feel certain before God (2 Cor. 3:4).

People who didn't know Paul might have listened to what he said or read his letters and thought that he was pretty conceited. When he talked to people, he spoke with authority. He let them know that they had better listen to what he had to say. He was pretty sure that he was right.

But Paul wasn't conceited. He didn't consider himself a great person. His confidence was in Jesus, not in himself. "It is God who makes us able to do all that we do," he writes. "He made us able to be servants of a new agreement from himself to his people. This new agreement is not a written law, but it is of the Spirit. The written law brings death, but the Spirit gives life" (3:5–6). He spoke boldly because he knew that his words came from Jesus. He was so sure of what Jesus had done for him that he could stand in God's presence without being afraid—because of *Christ*.

You can have the same kind of confidence and boldness that Paul had. Because of Jesus, you can be sure in God's presence. You can stand before him as a totally innocent person. Your faith in Jesus—not anything you did or didn't do—has made you acceptable to God.

SEE FOR YOURSELF:
Heb. 6:19–20; 7:25

WHAT'S IT MEAN?

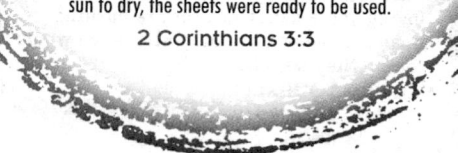

Most letters in New Testament times were written on an early form of paper called papyrus. The papyrus plant is a large reed that grows in shallow water. The reed was sliced into very thin, broad strips, which were then pressed together using a muddy, gluelike substance. After being left out in the sun to dry, the sheets were ready to be used.

2 Corinthians 3:3

4We can say this, because through Christ we
feel certain before God. 5We are not saying that
we can do this work ourselves. It is God who
makes us able to do all that we do. 6He made
us able to be servants of a new agreement from
himself to his people. This new agreement is
not a written law, but it is of the Spirit. The
written law brings death, but the Spirit gives
life.
7The law that brought death was written in
words on stone. It came with God's glory,
which made Moses' face so bright that the Israelites
could not continue to look at it. But
that glory later disappeared. 8So surely the
new way that brings the Spirit has even more
glory. 9If the law that judged people guilty of
sin had glory, surely the new way that makes
people right with God has much greater glory.
10That old law had glory, but it really loses its
glory when it is compared to the much greater
glory of this new way. 11If that law which disappeared
came with glory, then this new way
which continues forever has much greater
glory.
12We have this hope, so we are very bold.
13We are not like Moses, who put a covering
over his face so the Israelites would not see it.
The glory was disappearing, and Moses did
not want them to see it end. 14But their minds
were closed, and even today that same covering
hides the meaning when they read the old

3:3 stone tablets Meaning the Law of Moses that was written on stone tablets (Exodus 24:12; 25:16).

agreement. That covering is taken away only
through Christ. 15Even today, when they read
the law of Moses, there is a covering over their
minds. 16But when a person changes and follows the Lord, that covering is taken away.
17The Lord is the Spirit, and where the Spirit of
the Lord is, there is freedom. 18Our faces, then,
are not covered. We all show the Lord's glory,
and we are being changed to be like him. This
change in us brings ever greater glory, which
comes from the Lord, who is the Spirit.

WHAT'S IT MEAN?

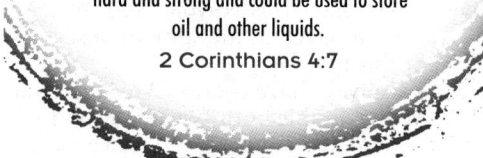

How much do you know about ancient pottery? Maybe it's time you learned a thing or two. Clay jars were used to hold oil and grain. Before the clay could be shaped by a potter, stones and other large objects had to be removed from it. After the clay was shaped, the potter had two options for drying it: Let the sun do it or stick it in a kiln. A sun-dried jar could hold grain, but it would collapse if it were filled with liquid. A jar heated in a kiln—at temperatures above 900 degrees Fahrenheit—became hard and strong and could be used to store oil and other liquids.

2 Corinthians 4:7

PREACHING THE GOOD NEWS

4 1God, with his mercy, gave us this work to
do, so we don't give up. 2But we have turned
away from secret and shameful ways. We use
no trickery, and we do not change the teaching
of God. We teach the truth plainly, showing
everyone who we are. Then they can know in
their hearts what kind of people we are in
God's sight. 3If the Good News that we preach
is hidden, it is hidden only to those who are
lost. 4The devil who rules this world has blinded the minds of those who do not believe.
They cannot see the light of the Good News—
the Good News about the glory of Christ, who
is exactly like God. 5We do not preach about
ourselves, but we preach that Jesus Christ is
Lord and that we are your servants for Jesus.
6God once said, "Let the light shine out of the
darkness!" This is the same God who made his
light shine in our hearts by letting us know the
glory of God that is in the face of Christ.

SPIRITUAL TREASURE IN CLAY JARS

7We have this treasure from God, but
we are like clay jars that hold the treasure. This shows that the great
power is from God, not from
us. 8We have troubles all
around us, but we are not
defeated. We do not know
what to do, but we do not
give up the hope of living. 9We
are persecuted, but God does not leave us.
We are hurt sometimes, but we are not destroyed. 10We carry the death of Jesus in our

WORRY

Does God care about our stress? (4:8–12)

On the Edge

We have this treasure from God, but we are like clay jars that hold the treasure. This shows that the great power is from God, not from us (2 Cor. 4:7).

Did you know that God stores his treasure inside of you? That's right! God has given you special qualities that nobody else has. You are God's treasure, filled with unique talents and abilities. It doesn't matter if your parents have referred to you as "mommy's little terror," or if your friends have said you will never amount to anything. It really doesn't matter, because before you were ever born God chose you and formed you and placed his gifts and treasures inside you!

You are special in God's eyes, and somehow or another, he is going to pull that treasure out of you. He's just looking for someone who is willing to be used for his glory. He has great plans for you; he wants to bless you with a future filled with hope—a future of success, not suffering! (Check out Jeremiah 29:11.)

Remember, you are already filled with God's treasure and with his power! They go beyond your own ability and strength. They come from God. Just as if you would bust open a clay pot with a hammer and pull out a treasure, so it is with you and God. He wants to open you up and see you blossom into what he wants you to be. Realize God's treasures are inside of you, and watch what he can do with you.

SEE FOR YOURSELF:
Ps. 37:4; Prov. 16:3; Jer. 1:5; 29:11

own bodies so that the life of Jesus can also be
seen in our bodies. 11 We are alive, but for Jesus
we are always in danger of death so that the
life of Jesus can be seen in our bodies that die.
12 So death is working in us, but life is working
in you.

On the Edge

We know that our body—the tent we live in here on earth—will be destroyed. But when that happens, God will have a house for us. It will not be a house made by human hands; instead, it will be a home in heaven that will last forever. But now we groan in this tent. We want God to give us our heavenly home (2 Cor. 5:1–2).

Your body is just a temporary home. That's right, it's just like a tent—a place for the real you, your spirit, to live. It's important to exercise, eat right, and take care of your body, but someday your tent is going to check out of here. That's just the natural cycle of life. Your body cannot live forever, but, thank God, death is not the end. You're on your way to a much greater place—a place where there's no more sadness, a place we've all heard about, a place called heaven!

Your body may be like a tent down here on earth, but someday you're going to live in a home that God himself has prepared just for you. Just think—he made the whole world in seven days, but he's still working on your eternal home. Your mind can't even imagine how awesome that place will be! So don't be discouraged with your home here on earth. It won't be long, and you'll be walking those streets of gold!

SEE FOR YOURSELF:
John 14:2; 2 Cor. 4:18; Rev. 21:18–21

13 It is written in the Scriptures, "I believed,
so I spoke."[n] Our faith is like this, too. We believe, and so we speak. 14 God raised the Lord
Jesus from the dead, and we know that God
will also raise us with Jesus. God will bring us
together with you, and we will stand before
him. 15 All these things are for you. And so the
grace of God that is being given to more and
more people will bring increasing thanks to
God for his glory.

LIVING BY FAITH

16 So we do not give up. Our physical body
is becoming older and weaker, but our spirit
inside us is made new every day. 17 We have
small troubles for a while now, but they are
helping us gain an eternal glory that is much
greater than the troubles. 18 We set our eyes not
on what we see but on what we cannot see.
What we see will last only a short time, but
what we cannot see will last forever.

5 1 We know that our body—the tent we live
in here on earth—will be destroyed. But when
that happens, God will have a house for us. It
will not be a house made by human hands;
instead, it will be a home in heaven that will
last forever. 2 But now we groan in this tent. We
want God to give us our heavenly
home, 3 because it will clothe
us so we will not be naked.
4 While we live in this body,
we have burdens, and we
groan. We do not want to be
naked, but we want to be
clothed with our heavenly
home. Then this body that dies will be fully
covered with life. 5 This is what God made us
for, and he has given us the Spirit to be a guarantee for this new life.

DEATH
Will life in heaven be better than life on earth? (5:1–8)

6 So we always have courage. We know that
while we live in this body, we are away from
the Lord. 7 We live by what we believe,
not by what we can see. 8 So I
say that we have courage. We
really want to be away from
this body and be at home
with the Lord. 9 Our only goal
is to please God whether we
live here or there, 10 because we
must all stand before Christ to be
judged. Each of us will receive what we should
get—good or bad—for the things we did in the
earthly body.

JUDGMENT
Will Christians be judged for their actions? (5:10)

BECOMING FRIENDS WITH GOD

11 Since we know what it means to fear the
Lord, we try to help people accept the truth
about us. God knows what we really are, and I
hope that in your hearts you know, too. 12 We
are not trying to prove ourselves to you again,
but we are telling you about ourselves so you
will be proud of us. Then you will have an
answer for those who are proud about things

4:13 "I . . . spoke." Quotation from Psalm 116:10.

On the Edge

If anyone belongs to Christ, there is a new creation. The old things have gone; everything is made new! (2 Cor. 5:17).

The Bible talks a lot about God's power. There are lots of stories about how he wiped out armies, cured diseases, and brought dead people back to life. Here, Paul is talking about one of God's less spectacular miracles. It's an invisible thing, but it's very real. When you let your life belong to Jesus, he makes you a new creation—a new person. What happens is this: Your *spirit*—the real you—is made new. Your mind and body are not. They are your responsibility. Once you make Jesus your Lord, your job is to renew your mind with his Word and to practice purity and self-control in your body. The real you, your spirit, loves God and you tell your mind and body what to do in order to line up with that love.

Here's another miracle: *The past is forgotten*. It's like all the bad things you ever did and all the things that hurt you *never happened*. You don't have to define yourself by things that have happened in the past; instead, you can define yourself by what God says about you. He made you to be happy, confident, and complete. The old junk passes away and you become a brand-new person. He makes you new so that you can live to your fullest potential!

SEE FOR YOURSELF:
Ezek. 36:26;
Gal. 6:15;
Eph. 4:23–24

that can be seen rather than what is in the
heart. [13]If we are out of our minds, it is for
God. If we have our right minds, it is for you.
[14]The love of Christ controls us, because we
know that One died for all, so all have died.
[15]Christ died for all so that those who live
would not continue to live for themselves. He
died for them and was raised from the dead so
that they would live for him.

[16]From this time on we do not think of anyone as the world does. In the past we thought
of Christ as the world thinks, but we no longer
think of him in that way. [17]If anyone belongs
to Christ, there is a new creation. The old
things have gone; everything is made new!
[18]All this is from God. Through Christ, God
made peace between us and himself, and God
gave us the work of telling everyone about the
peace we can have with him. [19]God
was in Christ, making peace
between the world and himself. In Christ, God did not
hold the world guilty of its
sins. And he gave us this message of peace. [20]So we have
been sent to speak for Christ. It is
as if God is calling to you through us. We
speak for Christ when we beg you to be at
peace with God. [21]Christ had no sin, but God
made him become sin so that in Christ we
could become right with God.

WITNESSING
What has God entrusted us with? (5:18–21)

6
[1]We are workers together with God, so we
beg you: Do not let the grace that you received
from God be for nothing. [2]God says,

"At the right time I heard your prayers.
On the day of salvation I helped you."

Isaiah 49:8

I tell you that the "right time" is now, and the
"day of salvation" is now.

[3]We do not want anyone to find fault with
our work, so nothing we do will be a problem
for anyone. [4]But in every way we show we are
servants of God: in accepting many hard
things, in troubles, in difficulties, and in great
problems. [5]We are beaten and thrown into
prison. We meet those who become upset with
us and start riots. We work hard, and sometimes we get no sleep or food. [6]We show we
are servants of God by our pure lives, our understanding, patience, and kindness, by the
Holy Spirit, by true love, [7]by speaking the
truth, and by God's power. We use our right
living to defend ourselves against everything.
[8]Some people honor us, but others blame us.
Some people say evil things about us, but others say good things. Some people say we are
liars, but we speak the truth. [9]We are not
known, but we are well known. We seem to be
dying, but we continue to live. We are punished,
but we are not killed. [10]We have much sadness,
but we are always rejoicing. We are poor, but
we are making many people rich in faith. We
have nothing, but really we have everything.

[11]We have spoken freely to you in Corinth
and have opened our hearts to you. [12]Our feelings of love for you have not stopped, but you
have stopped your feelings of love for us. [13]I
speak to you as if you were my children. Do to
us as we have done—open your hearts to us.

WARNING ABOUT NON-CHRISTIANS

[14]You are not the same as those who do not
believe. So do not join yourselves to them.

WHAT'S IT MEAN?

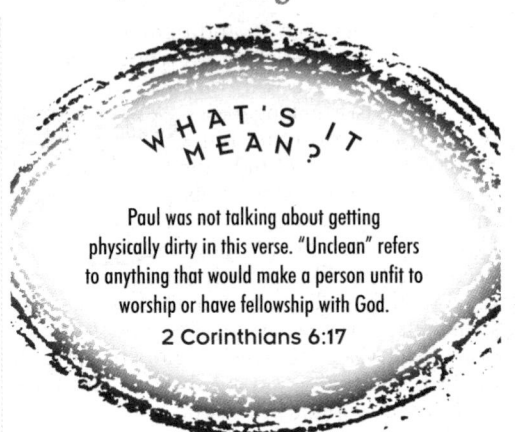

Paul was not talking about getting physically dirty in this verse. "Unclean" refers to anything that would make a person unfit to worship or have fellowship with God.

2 Corinthians 6:17

Good and bad do not belong together. Light
and darkness cannot share together. 15How
can Christ and Belial, the devil, have any agreement? What can a believer have together with
a nonbeliever? 16The temple of God cannot
have any agreement with idols, and we are the
temple of the living God. As God said: "I will
live with them and walk with them. And I will
be their God, and they will be my people."[n]

17"Leave those people,
and be separate, says the Lord.
Touch nothing that is unclean,
and I will accept you."
Isaiah 52:11; Ezekiel 20:34, 41

18"I will be your father,
and you will be my sons and daughters,
says the Lord Almighty."
2 Samuel 7:14

7 1Dear friends, we have these promises from
God, so we should make ourselves pure—free
from anything that makes body or soul unclean. We should try to become holy in the
way we live, because we respect God.

PAUL'S JOY

2Open your hearts to us. We have not done
wrong to anyone, we have not ruined the faith
of anyone, and we have not cheated anyone. 3I
do not say this to blame you. I told you before
that we love you so much we would live or die
with you. 4I feel very sure of you and am very
proud of you. You give me much comfort, and
in all of our troubles I have great joy.

5When we came into Macedonia, we had
no rest. We found trouble all around us. We
had fighting on the outside and fear on the inside. 6But God, who comforts those who are
troubled, comforted us when Titus came. 7We
were comforted, not only by his coming but
also by the comfort you gave him. Titus told us
about your wish to see me and that you are
very sorry for what you did. He also told me
about your great care for me, and when I
heard this, I was much happier.

8Even if my letter made you sad, I am not

6:16 "I . . . people." Quotation from Leviticus 26:11-12; Jeremiah 32:38; Ezekiel 37:27.

Promise HE PROMISES TO COMFORT PEOPLE IN NEED.

But God, who comforts those who are troubled, comforted us when Titus came (2 Cor. 7:6).

Paul is so honest. He wasn't always standing on a spiritual mountaintop, and he doesn't mind admitting it. He spends a lot of time in this book talking about his suffering, worry, tears, and broken heart. He doesn't try to pretend that just because he loves Jesus, nothing hard ever happens. He admits to his struggles and hardships. He talks about the troubles he's faced. He is real and vulnerable.

Somehow over time, Christians have lost sight of Paul's example. Somehow we've replaced honesty with pretending. Too many Christians pretend that their lives are happy and suffer in total silence. They won't admit to their own needs and weaknesses, yet wonder why God doesn't do something. God will bring cheer and comfort to those who are in need. Do you need God to comfort you? Do you need some cheering up? Then talk to the Lord. Be honest with some people who are close to you. Be brave enough to say, "I love God, but life is tough right now." God may use the Holy Spirit, or the body of believers, or the truth of his Word—but he will bring cheer to people in need.

SEE FOR YOURSELF:
Ps. 16:11; John 14:1–24

WHAT'S IT MEAN?

Titus was Paul's assistant. (You may recognize his name from the letter Paul wrote to him, a letter that just happens to be the fifty-sixth book of the Bible.) Paul had asked Titus to deliver his first letter to the Corinthians—a letter that had very few good things to say about the Christian church in Corinth. Paul was especially disappointed by the way the Corinthians had ignored the sins of a sexually immoral church member. Paul had expected to meet Titus in Troas to find out how the church responded to the letter, but the two didn't hook up until the apostle got to Macedonia.

2 Corinthians 7:6

sorry I wrote it. At first I was sorry, because it
made you sad, but you were sad only for a
short time. 9Now I am happy, not because you
were made sad, but because your sorrow
made you change your lives. You became sad
in the way God wanted you to, so you were
not hurt by us in any way. 10The kind of sorrow God wants makes people change their
hearts and lives. This leads to salvation, and
you cannot be sorry for that. But the kind of
sorrow the world has brings death. 11See what
this sorrow—the sorrow God wanted you to
have—has done to you: It has made you very
serious. It made you want to prove you were
not wrong. It made you angry and afraid. It
made you want to see me. It made you care. It
made you want the right thing to be done. You
proved you were innocent in the problem. 12I
wrote that letter, not because of the one who
did the wrong or because of the person who
was hurt. I wrote the letter so you could see,
before God, the great care you have for us.
13That is why we were comforted.

Not only were we very comforted, we were
even happier to see that Titus was so happy.
All of you made him feel much better. 14I
bragged to Titus about you, and you showed
that I was right. Everything we said to you was
true, and you have proved that what we
bragged about to Titus is true. 15And his love
for you is stronger when he remembers that
you were all ready to obey. You welcomed him
with respect and fear. 16I am very happy that I
can trust you fully.

CHRISTIAN GIVING

8 1And now, brothers and sisters, we want
you to know about the grace God gave the
churches in Macedonia. 2They have been tested
by great troubles, and they are very poor. But
they gave much because of their great joy. 3I
can tell you that they gave as much as they
were able and even more than they could afford. No one told them to do it. 4But they
begged and pleaded with us to let them share
in this service for God's people. 5And they gave
in a way we did not expect: They first gave
themselves to the Lord and to us. This is what
God wants. 6So we asked Titus to help you finish this special work of grace since he is the
one who started it. 7You are rich in everything—in faith, in speaking, in knowledge, in
truly wanting to help, and in the love you

On the Edge

You know the grace of our Lord Jesus Christ. You know that Christ was rich, but for you he became poor so that by his becoming poor you might become rich (2 Cor. 8:9).

Jesus had it all. In heaven, he had angels singing his praises all day long. He'd been sitting at God's right hand ever since the beginning of time. He ruled the whole universe and walked on streets of gold—comfortable, adored, worshiped. Then, one day, it was decision time. Someone had to go to earth. God loved his people so much that he couldn't stand to watch them suffer and wander. The humans needed someone like them to explain God's plan and purpose. So God sent Jesus to be like the people and to live among them on earth. He poured his glorious body into one like ours, gave up all the magnificence of heaven just to help us learn how to live and be right with God. He became poor so that we could know the riches of heaven—joy in a busted world, love when hearts are broken, peace when chaos is reigning, and other blessings. Jesus said that his riches have become ours by our faith in him. That's great news—you're rich!

SEE FOR YOURSELF:
Rom. 8:17; 1 Cor. 4:8; 1 Tim. 6:17; James 2:5

learned from us. In the same way, be strong
also in the grace of giving.
[8]I am not commanding you to give. But I
want to see if your love is true by comparing
you with others that really want to help. [9]You
know the grace of our Lord Jesus Christ. You
know that Christ was rich, but for you he became poor so that by his becoming poor you
might become rich.

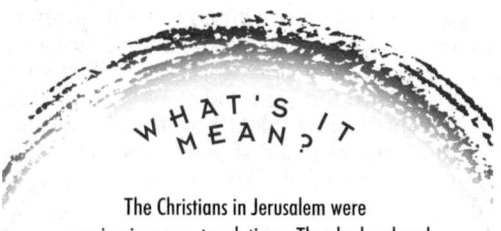

WHAT'S IT MEAN?

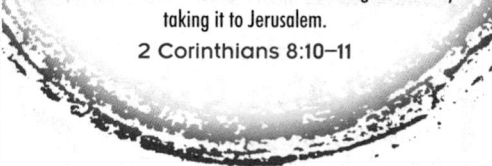

The Christians in Jerusalem were experiencing some tough times. They had endured two earthquakes and a severe famine. Christian churches in other cities offered to give their own money to help their brothers and sisters in Christ. Paul and Barnabas were collecting the money and taking it to Jerusalem.

2 Corinthians 8:10–11

[10]This is what I think you should do: Last
year you were the first to want to give, and
you were the first who gave. [11]So now finish
the work you started. Then your "doing" will
be equal to your "wanting to do." Give from
what you have. [12]If you want to give, your gift
will be accepted. It will be judged by what you
have, not by what you do not have. [13]We do
not want you to have troubles while other
people are at ease, but we want everything to
be equal. [14]At this time you have plenty. What
you have can help others who are in need.
Then later, when they have plenty, they can
help you when you are in need, and all will be
equal. [15]As it is written in the Scriptures, "The
person who gathered more did not have too
much, nor did the person who gathered less
have too little."[n]

TITUS AND HIS COMPANIONS HELP

[16]I thank God because he gave Titus the
same love for you that I have. [17]Titus accepted
what we asked him to do. He wanted very
much to go to you, and this was his own idea.
[18]We are sending with him the brother who is
praised by all the churches because of his service in preaching the Good News. [19]Also, this
brother was chosen by the churches to go with
us when we deliver this gift of money. We are
doing this service to bring glory to the Lord
and to show that we really want to help.
[20]We are being careful so that no one will
criticize us for the way we are handling this
large gift. [21]We are trying hard to do what the
Lord accepts as right and also what people
think is right.
[22]Also, we are sending with them our
brother, who is always ready to help. He has
proved this to us in many ways, and he wants
to help even more now, because he has much
faith in you.
[23]Now about Titus—he is my partner who
is working with me to help you. And about the
other brothers—they are sent from the
churches, and they bring glory to Christ. [24]So
show these men the proof of your love and the
reason we are proud of you. Then all the
churches can see it.

HELP FOR FELLOW CHRISTIANS

9 [1]I really do not need to write you about this
help for God's people. [2]I know you want to
help. I have been bragging about this to the
people in Macedonia, telling them that you in
Southern Greece have been ready to give since
last year. And your desire to give has made
most of them ready to give also. [3]But I am
sending the brothers to you so that our bragging about you in this will not be empty
words. I want you to be ready, as I said you
would be. [4]If any of the people from Macedonia come with me and find that you are not
ready, we will be ashamed that we were so
sure of you. (And you will be ashamed, too!)
[5]So I thought I should ask these brothers to go
to you before we do. They will finish getting in
order the generous gift you promised so it will
be ready when we come. And it will be a generous gift—not one that you did not want to
give.
[6]Remember this: The person who plants a
little will have a small harvest, but the person
who plants a lot will have a big harvest. [7]Each
one should give as you have decided in your
heart to give. You should not be sad when you
give, and you should not give because you feel
forced to give. God loves the person who gives
happily. [8]And God can give you more blessings than you need. Then you will always have
plenty of everything—enough to give to every
good work. [9]It is written in the Scriptures:
"He gives freely to the poor.

8:15 "The person . . . little." Quotation from Exodus 16:18.

The things he does are right and will
continue forever." *Psalm 112:9*
10God is the One who gives seed to the farmer
and bread for food. He will give you all the
seed you need and make it grow so there will
be a great harvest from your goodness. 11He
will make you rich in every way so that you
can always give freely. And your giving
through us will cause many to give thanks to
God. 12This service you do not only helps the
needs of God's people, it also brings many
more thanks to God. 13It is a proof of your
faith. Many people will praise God because
you obey the Good News of Christ—the gospel you say you believe—and because you
freely share with them and with all others.
14And when they pray, they will wish they
could be with you because of the great grace
that God has given you. 15Thanks be to God
for his gift that is too wonderful for words.

PAUL DEFENDS HIS MINISTRY

10
1I, Paul, am begging you with the gentleness
and the kindness of Christ. Some people say
that I am easy on you when I am with you and
bold when I am away. 2They think we live in a
worldly way, and I plan to be very bold with
them when I come. I beg you that when I come
I will not need to use that same boldness with
you. 3We do live in the world, but we do not
fight in the same way the world fights. 4We fight
with weapons that are different from those the
world uses. Our weapons have power from
God that can destroy the enemy's strong
places. We destroy people's arguments 5and
every proud thing that raises itself against the
knowledge of God. We capture every thought
and make it give up and obey Christ. 6We are
ready to punish anyone there who does not
obey, but first we want you to obey fully.
7You must look at the facts before you. If
you feel sure that you belong to Christ, you
must remember that we belong to Christ just
as you do. 8It is true that we brag freely about
the authority the Lord gave us. But this authority is to build you up, not to tear you down. So
I will not be ashamed. 9I do not want you to
think I am trying to scare you with my letters.
10Some people say, "Paul's letters are powerful
and sound important, but when he is with us,
he is weak. And his speaking is nothing."
11They should know this: We are not there
with you now, so we say these things in letters.
But when we are there with you, we will show
the same authority that we show in our letters.

On the Edge

I, Paul, am begging you with the gentleness and the kindness of Christ. Some people say that I am easy on you when I am with you and bold when I am away (2 Cor. 10:1).

Paul modeled his ministry after Jesus. Jesus was gentle. The world sometimes mistakes gentleness for weakness; but for Jesus, gentleness was a strength. A gentle spirit comes from loving others more than you love yourself. Jesus was able to calmly handle the wrongs done to him because he was a gentle Man. He didn't rant and rave, or fuss and fume. He was stronger than that. Paul wanted to be like him, and so should we. As you grow in maturity, other-centeredness replaces selfish ambitions, short tempers become hearts that are slow to anger, and genuine love replaces jealousy and envy. A gentle spirit is a treasure. When you meet a gentle person, you can know that you have met someone who is strong in heart and in character. You have met someone like Jesus.

SEE FOR YOURSELF:
Ps. 143:10; Is. 42:3; Matt. 11:29; John 13:1–17

12We do not dare to compare ourselves
with those who think they are very important.
They use themselves to measure themselves,
and they judge themselves by what they themselves are. This shows that they know nothing.
13But we will not brag about things outside the
work that was given us to do. We will limit our
bragging to the work that God gave us, and
this includes our work with you. 14We are not
bragging too much, as we would be if we had
not already come to you. But we have come to
you with the Good News of Christ. 15We limit
our bragging to the work that is ours, not what
others have done. We hope that as your faith
continues to grow, you will help our work to
grow much larger. 16We want to tell the Good
News in the areas beyond your city. We do not
want to brag about work that has already been
done in another person's area. 17But, "If someone wants to brag, he should brag only about
the Lord."[n] 18It is not those who say they are

10:17 "If . . . Lord." Quotation from Jeremiah 9:24.

good who are accepted but those who the Lord thinks are good.

PAUL AND THE FALSE APOSTLES

11 [1]I wish you would be patient with me even when I am a little foolish, but you are already doing that. [2]I am jealous over you with a jealousy that comes from God. I promised to give you to Christ, as your only husband. I want to give you as his pure bride. [3]But I am afraid that your minds will be led away from your true and pure following of Christ just as Eve was tricked by the snake with his evil ways. [4]You are very patient with anyone who comes to you and preaches a different Jesus from the one we preached. You are very willing to accept a spirit or gospel that is different from the Spirit and Good News you received from us.

[5]I do not think that those "great apostles" are any better than I am. [6]I may not be a trained speaker, but I do have knowledge. We have shown this to you clearly in every way.

[7]I preached God's Good News to you without pay. I made myself unimportant to make you important. Do you think that was wrong? [8]I accepted pay from other churches, taking their money so I could serve you. [9]If I needed something when I was with you, I did not trouble any of you. The brothers who came from Macedonia gave me all that I needed. I did not allow myself to depend on you in any way, and I will never depend on you. [10]No one in Southern Greece will stop me from bragging about that. I say this with the truth of Christ in me. [11]And why do I not depend on you? Do you think it is because I do not love you? God knows that I love you.

> "But, 'If someone wants to brag, he should brag only about the Lord.' It is not those who say they are good who are accepted but those who the Lord thinks are good."
> (2 Corinthians 10:17–18)

[12]And I will continue doing what I am doing now, because I want to stop those people from having a reason to brag. They would like to say that the work they brag about is the same as ours. [13]Such men are not true apostles but are workers who lie. They change themselves to look like apostles of Christ. [14]This does not surprise us. Even Satan changes himself to look like an angel of light.[n] [15]So it does not surprise us if Satan's servants also make themselves look like servants who work for what is right. But in the end they will be punished for what they do.

SATAN
How does Satan disguise himself? (11:14)

PAUL TELLS ABOUT HIS SUFFERINGS

[16]I tell you again: No one should think I am a fool. But if you think so, accept me as you would accept a fool. Then I can brag a little, too. [17]When I brag because I feel sure of myself, I am not talking as the Lord would talk but as a fool. [18]Many people are bragging about their lives in the world. So I will brag too. [19]You are wise, so you will gladly be patient with fools! [20]You are even patient with those who order you around, or use you, or trick you, or think they are better than you, or hit you in the face. [21]It is shameful to me to say this, but we were too "weak" to do those things to you!

But if anyone else is brave enough to brag, then I also will be brave and brag. (I am talking as a fool.) [22]Are they Hebrews?[n] So am I. Are they Israelites? So am I. Are they from Abraham's family? So am I. [23]Are they serving Christ? I am serving him more. (I am crazy to talk like this.) I have worked much harder than they. I have been in prison more often. I have been hurt more in beatings. I have been near death many times. [24]Five times the Jews have given me their punishment of thirty-nine lashes with a whip. [25]Three different times I was beaten with rods. One time I was almost stoned to death. Three times I was in ships that wrecked, and one of those times I spent a night and a day in the sea. [26]I have gone on many travels and have been in danger from rivers, thieves, my own people, the Jews, and those who are not Jews. I have been in danger in cities, in places where no one lives, and on the sea. And I have been in danger with false Christians. [27]I have done hard and tiring work, and many times I did not sleep. I have been hungry and thirsty, and many times I have been without food. I have been cold and with-

11:14 angel of light Messenger from God. The devil fools people so that they think he is from God.
11:22 Hebrews A name for the Jews that some Jews were very proud of.

WHAT'S IT MEAN?

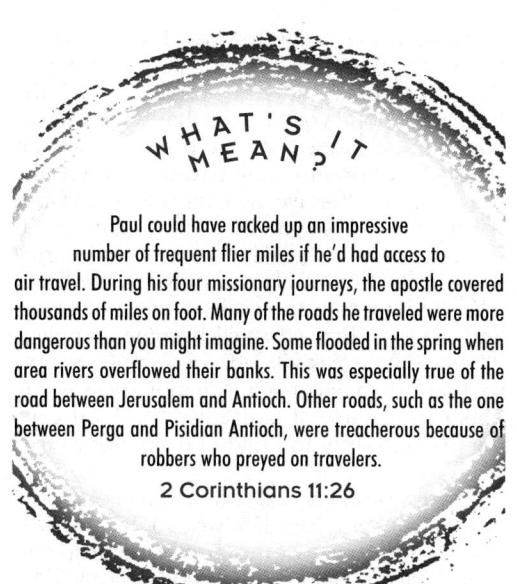

Paul could have racked up an impressive number of frequent flier miles if he'd had access to air travel. During his four missionary journeys, the apostle covered thousands of miles on foot. Many of the roads he traveled were more dangerous than you might imagine. Some flooded in the spring when area rivers overflowed their banks. This was especially true of the road between Jerusalem and Antioch. Other roads, such as the one between Perga and Pisidian Antioch, were treacherous because of robbers who preyed on travelers.

2 Corinthians 11:26

out clothes. 28Besides all this, there is on me
every day the load of my concern for all the
churches. 29I feel weak every time someone is
weak, and I feel upset every time someone is
led into sin.

30If I must brag, I will brag about the things
that show I am weak. 31God knows I am not
lying. He is the God and Father of the Lord
Jesus Christ, and he is to be praised forever.
32When I was in Damascus, the governor under King Aretas wanted to arrest me, so he put
guards around the city. 33But my friends lowered me in a basket through a hole in the city
wall. So I escaped from the governor.

A SPECIAL BLESSING IN PAUL'S LIFE

12 1I must continue to brag. It will do no good,
but I will talk now about visions and
revelations[n] from the Lord. 2I know a man in
Christ who was taken up to the third heaven
fourteen years ago. I do not know whether the
man was in his body or out of his body, but
God knows. 3-4And I know that this man was
taken up to paradise.[n] I don't know if he was in
his body or away from his body, but God
knows. He heard things he is not able to explain, things that no human is allowed to tell.
5I will brag about a man like that, but I will not
brag about myself, except about my weaknesses. 6But if I wanted to brag about myself, I
would not be a fool, because I would be telling
the truth. But I will not brag about myself. I do
not want people to think more of me than
what they see me do or hear me say.

7So that I would not become too proud of
the wonderful things that were shown to me, a
painful physical problem[n] was given
to me. This problem was a
messenger from Satan, sent to
beat me and keep me from
being too proud. 8I begged
the Lord three times to take
this problem away from me.
9But he said to me, "My grace
is enough for you. When you
are weak, my power is made perfect in you." So
I am very happy to brag about my weaknesses.
Then Christ's power can live in me. 10For this
reason I am happy when I have weaknesses,
insults, hard times, sufferings, and all kinds of
troubles for Christ. Because when I am weak,
then I am truly strong.

SICKNESS Who had sickness that God would not heal? (12:7–10)

PAUL'S LOVE FOR THE CHRISTIANS

11I have been talking like a fool, but you
made me do it. You are the ones who should
say good things about me. I am worth nothing,
but those "great apostles" are not worth any
more than I am!

12When I was with you, I patiently did the
things that prove I am an apostle—signs, wonders, and miracles. 13So you received everything that the other churches have received.
Only one thing was different: I was not a burden to you. Forgive me for this!

14I am now ready to visit you the third time,
and I will not be a burden to you. I want nothing from you, except you. Children should not
have to save up to give to their parents. Parents
should save to give to their children. 15So I am
happy to give everything I have for you, even
myself. If I love you more, will you love me
less?

16It is clear I was not a burden to you, but
you think I was tricky and lied to catch you.
17Did I cheat you by using any of the messengers I sent to you? No, you know I did not. 18I
asked Titus to go to you, and I sent our brother
with him. Titus did not cheat you, did he? No,
you know that Titus and I did the same thing
and with the same spirit.

19Do you think we have been defending
ourselves to you all this time? We have been
speaking in Christ and before God. You are our
dear friends, and everything we do is to make

12:1 revelations Revelation is making known a truth that was hidden. **12:3-4 paradise** Another word for heaven. **12:7 painful physical problem** Literally, "thorn in the flesh."

you stronger. [20]I am afraid that when I come, you will not be what I want you to be, and I will not be what you want me to be. I am afraid that among you there may be arguing, jealousy, anger, selfish fighting, evil talk, gossip, pride, and confusion. [21]I am afraid that when I come to you again, my God will make me ashamed before you. I may be saddened by many of those who have sinned because they have not changed their hearts or turned from their sexual sins and the shameful things they have done.

FINAL WARNINGS AND GREETINGS

13 [1]I will come to you for the third time. "Every case must be proved by two or three witnesses."[n] [2]When I was with you the second time, I gave a warning to those who had sinned. Now I am away from you, and I give a warning to all the others. When I come to you again, I will not be easy with them. [3]You want proof that Christ is speaking through me. My proof is that he is not weak among you, but he is powerful. [4]It is true that he was weak when he was killed on the cross, but he lives now by God's power. It is true that we are weak in Christ, but for you we will be alive in Christ by God's power.

[5]Look closely at yourselves. Test yourselves to see if you are living in the faith. You know that Jesus Christ is in you—unless you fail the test. [6]But I hope you will see that we ourselves have not failed the test. [7]We pray to God that you will not do anything wrong. It is not important to see that we have passed the test, but it is important that you do what is right, even if it seems we have failed. [8]We cannot do anything against the truth, but only for the truth. [9]We are happy to be weak, if you are strong, and we pray that you will become complete. [10]I am writing this while I am away from you so that when I come I will not have to be harsh in my use of authority. The Lord gave me this authority to build you up, not to tear you down.

[11]Now, brothers and sisters, I say good-bye. Try to be complete. Do what I have asked you to do. Agree with each other, and live in peace. Then the God of love and peace will be with you.

[12]Greet each other with a holy kiss. [13]All of God's holy people send greetings to you.

[14]The grace of the Lord Jesus Christ, the love of God, and the fellowship of the Holy Spirit be with you all.

13:1 "Every . . . witnesses." Quotation from Deuteronomy 19:15.

galatians

CONTENT Have you ever tried to explain something to someone over and over and over and just when you think they're about to get it—you realize they don't even know what you are talking about?

That's how Paul felt about the Galatians. Paul had spent time with the churches in Galatia teaching them the basics of Christianity. He thought they had finally gotten the fact that Christ's sacrifice on the cross changed everything. Righteousness (being made right with God) was no longer a by-product of rules and regulations followed to a "T". Righteousness now came from faith in Christ's one-time sacrifice of himself. Compared to the kind of life people had faced under Jewish law, this new understanding of righteousness was pure freedom.

Paul got exasperated with the Galatians because, even though he had taught them this new way of thinking, they had reverted back to trying to earn their righteousness by obeying the Jewish law. Paul was irritated. So he sat down and wrote them a letter to try to get them back on the right track. That is how we got the Book of Galatians in the Bible.

Because of all this, some people call the Book of Galatians the spiritual Declaration of Independence.

Outline

1:1–10 .... A True Apostle and the True Message
1:11–24 .... God Chose Paul to Be an Apostle
2:1–21 .... Paul Defends His Message
3:1—4:31 .... Blessing Comes Only by Faith
5:1—6:10 .... Guided by the Spirit and Love
6:11–18 .... Final Warnings

Purpose We are saved and we live "by faith."

Theme Made Right with God by Faith Alone

Date of writing A.D. 48

"I was put to death on the cross with Christ, and I do not live anymore—it is Christ who lives in me. I still live in my body, but I live by faith in the Son of God who loved me and gave himself to save me" (2:20).

Bible Talk

Judaizers

When the Galatians fell back into legalism (believing you could be made right with God by obeying the law), they did it with a little help. There was a group of people called "Judaizers" who came to Galatia and began to influence the church there. The Judaizers believed that anyone who wanted to be a Christian should obey the Jewish customs including circumcision.

Now the Jewish customs were a product of years of traditions passed down from family to family from generation to generation. It would have been a lot for anyone to take, not to mention that Christ had freed the people from those customs. The Judaizers ignored the grace that God offered through Christ. This is why Paul could not ignore their influence.

CHRISTIAN FRUIT

One of the famous passages in Galatians says we should bear fruit. In fact, there are several places in the Bible where Christians are compared to growing things like grapevines and fruit-bearing trees. Do you think being a Christian is like being a tree?

In some ways it is. The purpose of an apple tree is to bear apples. The way you know whether that tree is doing what it is supposed to do is when you pick an apple and take a bite. That's how we are as Christians. The test of whether we are growing spiritually is the fruit we produce. Galatians says our fruit is love, joy, peace, patience, kindness, goodness, faithfulness, gentleness, and self-control (see 5:22–23). What kind of fruit do people pick off your branches?

1
1From Paul, an apostle. I was not chosen
to be an apostle by human beings, nor was I
sent from human beings. I was made an apostle through Jesus Christ and God the Father
who raised Jesus from the dead. 2This letter is
also from all those of God's family[n] who are
with me.
To the churches in Galatia:[n]
3Grace and peace to you from God our Father and the Lord Jesus Christ. 4Jesus gave himself for our sins to free us from this evil world
we live in, as God the Father planned. 5The
glory belongs to God forever and ever. Amen.

THE ONLY GOOD NEWS

6God, by his grace through Christ, called
you to become his people. So I am amazed that
you are turning away so quickly and believing
something different than the Good News.
7Really, there is no other Good News. But some
people are confusing you; they want to change
the Good News of Christ. 8We preached to you
the Good News. So if we ourselves, or even an
angel from heaven, should preach to you
something different, we should be judged
guilty! 9I said this before, and now I say it
again: You have already accepted the Good
News. If anyone is preaching something different to you, he should be judged guilty!
10Do you think I am trying to make people
accept me? No, God is the One I am trying to
please. Am I trying to please people? If I still
wanted to please people, I would not be a servant of Christ.

PAUL'S AUTHORITY IS FROM GOD

11Brothers and sisters,[n] I want you to know
that the Good News I preached to you was not
made up by human beings. 12I did not get it
from humans, nor did anyone teach it to me,
but Jesus Christ showed it to me.
13You have heard about my past life in the
Jewish religion. I attacked the church of God
and tried to destroy it. 14I was becoming a
leader in the Jewish religion, doing better than
most other Jews of my age. I tried harder than
anyone else to follow the teachings handed
down by our ancestors.
15But God had special plans for me and set
me apart for his work even before I was born.
He called me through his grace 16and showed
his son to me so that I might tell the Good
News about him to those who are not Jewish.
When God called me, I did not get advice or
help from any person. 17I did not go to Jerusalem to see those who were apostles before I
was. But, without waiting, I went away to Arabia and later went back to Damascus.
18After three years I went to Jerusalem to
meet Peter and stayed with him for fifteen
days. 19I met no other apostles, except James,
the brother of the Lord. 20God knows that
these things I write are not lies. 21Later, I went
to the areas of Syria and Cilicia.

WHAT'S IT MEAN?

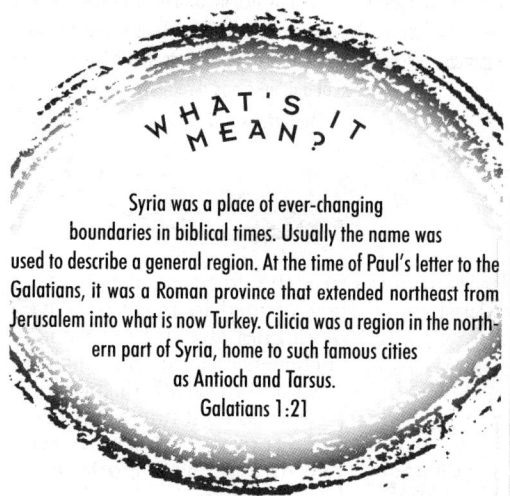

Syria was a place of ever-changing boundaries in biblical times. Usually the name was used to describe a general region. At the time of Paul's letter to the Galatians, it was a Roman province that extended northeast from Jerusalem into what is now Turkey. Cilicia was a region in the northern part of Syria, home to such famous cities as Antioch and Tarsus.
Galatians 1:21

22In Judea the churches in Christ had never
met me. 23They had only heard it said, "This
man who was attacking us is now preaching
the same faith that he once tried to destroy."
24And these believers praised God because of
me.

OTHER APOSTLES ACCEPTED PAUL

2
1After fourteen years I went to Jerusalem
again, this time with Barnabas. I also took Titus
with me. 2I went because God showed me I
should go. I met with the believers there, and
in private I told their leaders the Good News
that I preach to the non-Jewish people. I did
not want my past work and the work I am
now doing to be wasted. 3Titus was with me,
but he was not forced to be circumcised, even
though he was a Greek. 4We talked about this
problem because some false believers had
come into our group secretly. They came in like

1:2 those . . . family The Greek text says "brothers." **1:2 Galatia** Probably the same country where Paul preached and began churches on his first missionary trip. Read the Book of Acts, chapters 13 and 14.
1:11 Brothers and sisters Although the Greek text says "Brothers" here and throughout this book, Paul's words were meant for the entire church, including men and women.

WHAT'S IT MEAN?

Barnabas lived quite an interesting life. Before he became a Christian, he was a wealthy Jew living on the island of Cyprus. After he became a Christian, he sold his property and gave the money to the followers in Jerusalem. Later, he took on the role of Paul's traveling companion. Titus, who accompanied Paul and Barnabas on their trips, had his own claim to fame. He was one of the first non-Jews to become a Christian. Titus worked as Paul's assistant, delivering the apostle's messages to various churches in need of guidance and direction.

Galatians 2:1

spies to overturn the freedom we have in
Christ Jesus. They wanted to make us slaves.
5But we did not give in to those false
believers for a minute. We
wanted the truth of the Good
News to continue for you.
6Those leaders who
seemed to be important did
not change the Good News
that I preach. (It doesn't matter
to me if they were "important" or not. To God
everyone is the same.) 7But these leaders saw
that I had been given the work of telling the
Good News to those who are not Jewish, just
as Peter had the work of telling the Jews. 8God
gave Peter the power to work as an apostle for
the Jewish people. But he also gave me the
power to work as an apostle for those who are
not Jews. 9James, Peter, and John, who seemed
to be the leaders, understood that God had
given me this special grace, so they accepted
Barnabas and me. They agreed that they would
go to the Jewish people and that we should go
to those who are not Jewish. 10The only thing
they asked us was to remember to help the
poor—something I really wanted to do.

JEALOUSY

Is envying other Christians wise? (2:6)

WHAT'S IT MEAN?

One of the best ways to determine whether a person is Jewish or not is to ask this question: "Are you a Jew?" If the person says yes, he or she is a Jew. Jewish people in Paul's day set themselves apart from non-Jews by following the customs and rules of the Old Testament, particularly the Teachings that God gave to Moses.

Galatians 2:8

PAUL SHOWS THAT PETER WAS WRONG

11When Peter came to Antioch, I challenged
him to his face, because he was wrong. 12Peter

On the Edge

I was put to death on the cross with Christ, and I do not live anymore—it is Christ who lives in me. I still live in my body, but I live by faith in the Son of God who loved me and gave himself to save me (Gal. 2:20).

Obviously, you're still breathing and your heart's still beating. And Paul was certainly still alive when he wrote this letter. So what did he mean when he said, "I was put to death on the cross with Christ, and I do not live anymore—it is Christ who lives in me"?

Like he did so many times, Paul was describing something that was not *physically* true but *spiritually* true. When you put your faith in Jesus, something changes inside you. The old you—the old spirit—dies and a new spirit is born in you. You become Christ-centered instead of self-centered. You have a new life in Christ and it's totally different from your old life without him. You've got a new reason to live.

Before you gave your heart to Jesus, you were on your own. Now you've got the King of Kings with you all the time—loving you, forgiving you, guiding you, inspiring you.

When your old self dies and Christ lives fully in you, all that's left is what God planned for you in the first place. Nothing could be better or more satisfying than that.

SEE FOR YOURSELF:

Ps. 110:1;

Col. 3:1

ate with the non-Jewish people until some
Jewish people sent from James came to Antioch. When they arrived, Peter
stopped eating with those who
weren't Jewish, and he separated himself from them. He
was afraid of the Jews. [13]So
Peter was a hypocrite, as
were the other Jewish believers who joined with him.
Even Barnabas was influ-
enced by what these Jewish
believers did. [14]When I saw they
were not following the truth of the
Good News, I spoke to Peter in front of them
all. I said, "Peter, you are a Jew, but
you are not living like a Jew.
You are living like those who
are not Jewish. So why do
you now try to force those
who are not Jewish to live
like Jews?"

[15]We were not born as
non-Jewish "sinners," but as
Jews. [16]Yet we know that a
person is made right with
God not by following the law,
but by trusting in Jesus Christ. So
we, too, have put our faith in Christ Jesus, that
we might be made right with God because we
trusted in Christ. It is not because we followed
the law, because no one can be made right
with God by following the law.

[17]We Jews came to Christ, trying to be made
right with God, and it became clear that we are
sinners, too. Does this mean that Christ encourages sin? No! [18]But I would really be wrong to
begin teaching again those things that I gave
up. [19]It was the law that put me to death, and I
died to the law so that I can now live for God.
[20]I was put to death on the cross with Christ,
and I do not live anymore—it is Christ who
lives in me. I still live in my body, but I live by
faith in the Son of God who loved me and gave
himself to save me. [21]By saying these things I
am not going against God's grace. Just the opposite, if the law could make us right with God,
then Christ's death would be useless.

"I was put to death on the cross with Christ, and I do not live anymore—it is Christ who lives in me." (Galatians 2:20a)

On the Edge

Tell me this one thing: How did you receive the Holy Spirit? Did you receive the Spirit by following the law? No, you received the Spirit because you heard the Good News and believed it (Gal. 3:2).

This passage of Scripture shows you that you have God's Spirit by faith in Christ. How did you get saved? It happened by putting your faith in Christ. So how did you receive his Spirit? It was the same way, by putting your faith in Christ. When you received Christ, you received his Spirit.

Paul goes on to say that God will complete the work that he has started in you, and that God gives you his Spirit and works miracles in you (see 3:3–5). Paul was trying to get a point across. He was asking if all these things happen because of obedience to rules, or because of faith in Christ.

After reading this entire passage, you'll see that God's Spirit moves because of faith in Christ. Of course, you have to exercise your faith. Jesus says in Mark 9:23, "All things are possible for the one who believes." Hebrews 11:6 tells us that "without faith no one can please God." It's faith that saves us, faith that fills us with God's Holy Spirit, faith that heals us. In fact, every promise God has ever given us must be received by faith. Thank God today that you have his Spirit by faith.

SEE FOR YOURSELF:
Mark 9:23;
Eph. 1:13; Heb. 11:6

BLESSING COMES THROUGH FAITH

3 [1]You people in Galatia were told very clearly about the death of Jesus Christ on the cross.
But you were foolish; you let someone trick
you. [2]Tell me this one thing: How did you receive the Holy Spirit? Did you receive the Spirit
by following the law? No, you received the
Spirit because you heard the Good News and
believed it. [3]You began your life in Christ by
the Spirit. Now are you trying to make it complete by your own power? That is foolish.
[4]Were all your experiences wasted? I hope not!
[5]Does God give you the Spirit and work miracles among you because you follow the law?
No, he does these things because you heard
the Good News and believed it.

[6]The Scriptures say the same thing about
Abraham: "Abraham believed God, and God
accepted Abraham's faith, and that faith made
him right with God."[n] [7]So you should know

3:6 "Abraham . . . God." Quotation from Genesis 15:6.

that the true children of Abraham are those
who have faith. 8The Scriptures, telling what
would happen in the future, said that God
would make the non-Jewish people right
through their faith. This Good News was told
to Abraham beforehand, as the Scripture says:
"All nations will be blessed through you."[n] 9So
all who believe as Abraham believed are
blessed just as Abraham was. 10But those who
depend on following the law to make them
right are under a curse, because the Scriptures say, "Anyone will be cursed who does
not always obey what is written in the Book
of the Law."[n] 11Now it is clear that no one can
be made right with God by the law, because
the Scriptures say, "Those who are right with
God will live by trusting in him."[n] 12The law
is not based on faith. It says, "A person who
obeys these things will live because of
them."[n] 13Christ took away the curse the law
put on us. He changed places with us and
put himself under that curse. It is written in
the Scriptures, "Anyone whose body is displayed on a tree[n] is cursed." 14Christ did this so
that God's blessing promised to Abraham
might come through Jesus Christ to those who
are not Jews. Jesus died so that by our believing we could receive the Spirit that God promised.

THE LAW AND THE PROMISE

15Brothers and sisters, let us think in human
terms: Even an agreement made between two
persons is firm. After that agreement is accepted by both people, no one can stop it or add
anything to it. 16God made promises both to
Abraham and to his descendant. God did not
say, "and to your descendants." That would
mean many people. But God said, "and to your
descendant." That means only one person; that
person is Christ. 17This is what I mean: God
had an agreement with Abraham and promised to keep it. The law, which came four hundred thirty years later, cannot change that
agreement and so destroy God's promise to
Abraham. 18If the law could give us Abraham's
blessing, then the promise would not be necessary. But that is not possible, because God
freely gave his blessings to Abraham through
the promise he had made.

19So what was the law for? It was given to
show that the wrong things people do are
against God's will. And it continued until the
special descendant, who had been promised,

3:8 "All . . . you." Quotation from Genesis 12:3 and 18:18. **3:10 "Anyone . . . Law."** Quotation from Deuteronomy 27:26. **3:11 "Those . . . him."** Quotation from Habakkuk 2:4. **3:12 "A person . . . them."** Quotation from Leviticus 18:5. **3:13 displayed on a tree** Deuteronomy 21:22–23 says that when a person was killed for doing wrong, the body was hung on a tree to show shame. Paul means that the cross of Jesus was like that.

Promise

HE PROMISES THAT YOU ARE HIS CHILD BY FAITH.

This means that you are all children of God through faith in Christ Jesus (Gal. 3:26–27b).

You are God's child, and he is your Father. But how? Because you put your faith in Jesus. What is faith? Belief without proof. Hebrews 11:1 says, "Faith means being sure of the things we hope for and knowing that something is real even if we do not see it." Even though you've never seen God, you know he exists. Because you know he exists, you put your faith in him.

God cares for you the same way an earthly father takes care of his children, only better. God is concerned with every detail of your life. He wants to give you good things. He wants to see you grow up and be everything he's designed you to be. He really wants you to know him—deeply and powerfully. How can you get to know your Father better? By spending time with him in prayer and by studying his Word.

You're God's child. You're a prince or a princess in his kingdom because the King is your Dad! He loves you so much that he's adopted you as his very own. By faith, take your place as a child of God.

SEE FOR YOURSELF:

Matt. 7:11; John 1:12–13; Rom. 8:15–16; 1 John 3:1

came. The law was given through angels who
used Moses for a mediator[n] to give the law to
people. 20But a mediator is not needed when
there is only one side, and God is only one.

THE PURPOSE OF THE LAW OF MOSES

21Does this mean that the law is against
God's promises? Never! That would be true
only if the law could make us right. But God
did not give a law that can bring life. 22Instead,
the Scriptures showed that the whole world is
bound by sin. This was so the promise would
be given through faith to people who believe
in Jesus Christ.
23Before this faith came, we were all held
prisoners by the law. We had no freedom until
God showed us the way of faith that was coming. 24In other words, the law was our guardian leading us to Christ so that we could be
made right with God through faith. 25Now the
way of faith has come, and we no longer live
under a guardian.
26-27You were all baptized into Christ, and
so you were all clothed with Christ.
This means that you are all
children of God through faith
in Christ Jesus. 28In Christ,
there is no difference between
Jew and Greek, slave and free
person, male and female. You
are all the same in Christ Jesus.
29You belong to Christ, so you
are Abraham's descendants. You will inherit all
of God's blessings because of the promise God
made to Abraham.

HATRED
Is the salvation of all Christians equal? (3:28–29)

4

1I want to tell you this: While those who
will inherit their fathers' property are still children, they are no different from slaves. It does
not matter that the children own everything.
2While they are children, they must obey those
who are chosen to care for them. But when the
children reach the age set by their fathers, they
are free. 3It is the same for us. We were once
like children, slaves to the useless rules of this
world. 4But when the right time came, God
sent his Son who was born of a woman and
lived under the law. 5God did this so he could
buy freedom for those who were under the
law and so we could become his children.
6Since you are God's children, God sent the
Spirit of his Son into your hearts, and the Spirit
cries out, "Father."[n] 7So now you are not a slave;
you are God's child, and God will give you the
blessing he promised, because you are his
child.

WHAT'S IT MEAN?

Slaves may have been considered second-class citizens in New Testament times, but that didn't stop their masters from entrusting their kids to the slaves' care. Slaves regularly supervised the education of their master's children. According to the custom of the day, most girls received their education at home. Boys, on the other hand, attended school, where they learned to read and write.

Galatians 4:1–2

PAUL'S LOVE FOR THE CHRISTIANS

8In the past you did not know God. You
were slaves to gods that were not real. 9But
now you know the true God. Really, it is God
who knows you. So why do you turn back to
those weak and useless rules you followed before? Do you want to be slaves to those things
again? 10You still follow teachings about special days, months, seasons, and years. 11I am
afraid for you, that my work for you has been
wasted.
12Brothers and sisters, I became like you, so
I beg you to become like me. You were very
good to me before. 13You remember that it was
because of an illness that I came to you the
first time, preaching the Good News. 14Though
my sickness was a trouble for you, you did not
hate me or make me leave. But you welcomed
me as an angel from God, as if I were Jesus
Christ himself! 15You were very happy then,
but where is that joy now? I am ready to testify
that you would have taken out your eyes and
given them to me if that were possible. 16Now
am I your enemy because I tell you the truth?
17Those people[n] are working hard to persuade you, but this is not good for you. They
want to persuade you to turn against us and
follow only them. 18It is good for people to
show interest in you, but only if their purpose
is good. This is always true, not just when I am

3:19 mediator A person who helps one person talk to or give something to another person.
4:6 "Father" Literally, "Abba, Father." Jewish children called their fathers "Abba." **4:17 Those people** They are the false teachers who were bothering the believers in Galatia (Galatians 1:7).

with you. [19]My little children, again I feel the
pain of childbirth for you until you truly become like Christ. [20]I wish I could be with you
now and could change the way I am talking to
you, because I do not know what to think
about you.

WHAT'S IT MEAN?

Sarah and Hagar both gave birth to a son of Abraham. The difference between the two women is that Sarah was Abraham's wife and Hagar was Sarah's slave. Before you get the wrong idea about Abraham, you should know that his encounter with Hagar was Sarah's idea. God had promised Abraham and Sarah that they would have a son. Sarah realized that she was too old to have a child, so she thought the next best thing would be for her servant to have Abraham's son. And that's what happened. Hagar gave birth to a son named Ishmael. God, however, made it clear that Ishmael was not the son he had promised. Despite the fact that she was ninety years old, Sarah herself became pregnant and gave birth to a son named Isaac—the one God had promised.

Galatians 4:23

THE EXAMPLE OF HAGAR AND SARAH

[21]Some of you still want to be under the
law. Tell me, do you know what the law says?
[22]The Scriptures say that Abraham had two
sons. The mother of one son was a slave woman, and the mother of the other son was a free
woman. [23]Abraham's son from the slave
woman was born in the normal human way.
But the son from the free woman was born
because of the promise God made to Abraham.
[24]This story teaches something else: The two
women are like the two agreements between
God and his people. One agreement is the law
that God made on Mount Sinai,[n] and the people who are under this agreement are like
slaves. The mother named Hagar is like that
agreement. [25]She is like Mount Sinai in Arabia
and is a picture of the earthly Jewish city of
Jerusalem. This city and its people, the Jews, are
slaves to the law. [26]But the heavenly Jerusalem,
which is above, is like the free woman. She is
our mother. [27]It is written in the Scriptures:

"Be happy, Jerusalem.
    You are like a woman who never gave
        birth to children.
Start singing and shout for joy.
    You never felt the pain of giving birth,
but you will have more children
    than the woman who has a husband."

Isaiah 54:1

[28]My brothers and sisters, you are God's
children because of his promise, as Isaac was
then. [29]The son who was born in the normal

On the Edge

We have freedom now, because Christ made us free. So stand strong. Do not change and go back into the slavery of the law (Gal. 5:1).

Being entangled with "the slavery of the law" means that "religious things" have become more important to you than your relationship with Christ. What kinds of things sometimes replace fellowship with God? Well, carrying a Bible that rarely gets opened, just so people can see it. Trying to fool people with a bunch of churchy words you don't mean. Showing up for every church service, prayer meeting, concert, or special event just so everyone will think you're so committed.

Those things are bondage. They're about law and not about Christ. Being involved in Christian activities is not the same as being involved with Jesus. He says you are free. You're free not to pretend anymore; free to say no to sex before marriage; free not to hang out with friends who always get you in trouble; free to *really* pray—just "real talk" with God; free from sin and sinful habits; free to follow God's leading; free to not care what everyone else thinks; free, free, free!

Worldly success is so temporary. What matters most is that you have a relationship with God and that you do what he tells you to do. The other stuff will burn. Only eternal things matter. And you are free to live for those eternal things. Love God and be free in him.

SEE FOR YOURSELF:
John 8:32;
2 Cor. 3:17;
Gal. 5:13

4:24 Mount Sinai Mountain in Arabia where God gave his Law to Moses (Exodus 19 and 20).

way treated the other son badly. It is the same
today. [30]But what does the Scripture say?
"Throw out the slave woman and her son. The
son of the slave woman should not inherit
anything. The son of the free woman should
receive it all."[n] [31]So, my brothers and sisters, we
are not children of the slave woman, but of the
free woman.

KEEP YOUR FREEDOM

5 [1]We have freedom now, because Christ
made us free. So stand strong. Do not change
and go back into the slavery of the law. [2]Listen,
I Paul tell you that if you go back to the law by
being circumcised, Christ does you no good.
[3]Again, I warn every man: If you allow yourselves to be circumcised, you must follow all
the law. [4]If you try to be made right with God
through the law, your life with Christ
is over—you have left God's
grace. [5]But we have the true
hope that comes from being
made right with God, and by
the Spirit we wait eagerly for
this hope. [6]When we are in
Christ Jesus, it is not important
if we are circumcised or not. The important
thing is faith—the kind of faith that works
through love.

SALVATION
Can we be saved by keeping the law? (5:1–6)

[7]You were running a good race. Who
stopped you from following the true way?
[8]This change did not come from the One who
chose you. [9]Be careful! "Just a little yeast makes
the whole batch of dough rise." [10]But I trust in
the Lord that you will not believe those different ideas. Whoever is confusing you with such
ideas will be punished.
[11]My brothers and sisters, I do not teach
that a man must be circumcised. If I teach circumcision, why am I still being attacked? If I
still taught circumcision, my preaching about
the cross would not be a problem. [12]I wish the
people who are bothering you would castrate[n]
themselves!
[13]My brothers and sisters, God called you
to be free, but do not use your freedom as an
excuse to do what pleases your sinful self.
Serve each other with love. [14]The whole law is
made complete in this one command: "Love
your neighbor as you love yourself."[n] [15]If you
go on hurting each other and tearing each
other apart, be careful, or you will completely
destroy each other.

On the Edge

Our sinful selves want what is against the Spirit, and the Spirit wants what is against our sinful selves. The two are against each other, so you cannot do just what you please (Gal. 5:17).

God's Word tells us to love the Lord with all of our heart, with all of our soul, and with all of our strength (see Deut. 6:4–5). When you first got saved, you gave your heart to Jesus first. You didn't give him your soul or your strength first. You gave him your heart.

Satan will always counterfeit what God does, and do the exact opposite. He'll always go after your mind first, because he knows that if he can get something into your mind and get you to think continually about it, then he can get you to do it. That's why it's so important to realize that you can control your thoughts and desires.

Sin always starts in the mind. It's not sin to have an evil thought—that's temptation; but it is wrong to dwell on and entertain those thoughts. To make it simpler: A bird can lay an egg on your head, but only you can let him build a nest in your hair!

James 1:13–15 reminds us that if we think about sin long enough, we'll desire to sin. If we want to sin, we will eventually sin. After sin is done, it will leave us dead. That's why it's so important to walk in the Spirit and feed your mind with the Word of God.

Paul sums it up in Galatians 5:24–25: "Those who belong to Christ Jesus have crucified their own sinful selves. They have given up their old selfish feelings and the evil things they wanted to do. We get our new life from the Spirit, so we should follow the Spirit." His Spirit helps you overcome evil desires!

SEE FOR YOURSELF:
2 Cor. 10:4–6;
James 1:13–15

THE SPIRIT AND HUMAN NATURE

[16]So I tell you: Live by following the Spirit.
Then you will not do what your sinful selves
want. [17]Our sinful selves want what is against

4:30 "Throw . . . all." Quotation from Genesis 21:10. **5:12 castrate** To cut off part of the male sex organ. Paul uses this word because it is similar to "circumcision." Paul wanted to show that he is very upset with the false teachers. **5:14 "Love . . . yourself."** Quotation from Leviticus 19:18.

the Spirit, and the Spirit wants what is against
our sinful selves. The two are against each
other, so you cannot do just
what you please. [18]But if the
Spirit is leading you, you are
not under the law.
[19]The wrong things the
sinful self does are clear:
being sexually unfaithful,
not being pure, taking part
in sexual sins, [20]worship-
ing gods, doing witchcraft,
hating, making trouble, being jealous, being angry, being
selfish, making people angry
with each other, causing divisions among
people, [21]feeling envy, being drunk, having
wild and wasteful parties, and doing other
things like these. I warn you
now as I warned you be-
fore: Those who do these
things will not inherit
God's kingdom. [22]But the
Spirit produces the fruit of
love, joy, peace, patience,
kindness, goodness, faithfulness, [23]gentleness, self-
control. There is no law
that says these things are
wrong. [24]Those who belong
to Christ Jesus have crucified
their own sinful selves. They have
given up their old selfish feelings and the evil
things they wanted to do. [25]We get our new life
from the Spirit, so we should follow the Spirit.
[26]We must not be proud or make trouble with
each other or be jealous of each other.

"We must not become tired of doing good. We will receive our harvest of eternal life at the right time if we do not give up." (Galatians 6:9)

On the Edge

But the Spirit produces the fruit of love, joy, peace, patience, kindness, goodness, faithfulness, gentleness, self-control. There is no law that says these things are wrong. Those who belong to Christ Jesus have crucified their own sinful selves. They have given up their old selfish feelings and the evil things they wanted to do. We get our new life from the Spirit, so we should follow the Spirit (Gal. 5:22–25).

The Spirit of God lives in each believer and is the agent of change. He brings power to our lives that we would otherwise be without. Because he is in us, we have the ability to change and become more Christ-like. Verses 22 and 23 list some of the areas that the Holy Spirit can change in your life. In which of these areas could you use some help? Find a specific Scripture and use it to renew your mind. Memorize it; meditate on it; say it in your sleep! Then pray for the Holy Spirit to begin working. The most important part is that you cooperate with the Holy Spirit when he reminds you to be gentle instead of whining. It's called obedience. Eventually, little by little, the whining will be replaced and you will have begun to make some changes in your life.

SEE FOR YOURSELF:
Prov. 3:5–6;
13:10;
Matt. 6:33

HELP EACH OTHER

6 [1]Brothers and sisters, if someone in your
group does something wrong, you who are
spiritual should go to that person and gently
help make him right again. But be careful, because you might be tempted to sin, too. [2]By
helping each other with your troubles, you truly obey the law of Christ. [3]If anyone thinks he is
important when he really is not, he is only fooling himself. [4]Each person should judge his own
actions and not compare himself with others.
Then he can be proud for what he himself has
done. [5]Each person must be responsible for
himself.
[6]Anyone who is learning the teaching of
God should share all the good things he has
with his teacher.

LIFE IS LIKE PLANTING A FIELD

[7]Do not be fooled: You cannot cheat God.
People harvest only what they plant. [8]If they
plant to satisfy their sinful selves, their sinful
selves will bring them ruin. But if they plant to
please the Spirit, they will receive eternal life
from the Spirit. [9]We must not become tired of
doing good. We will receive our harvest of
eternal life at the right time if we do not give
up. [10]When we have the opportunity to help
anyone, we should do it. But we should give
special attention to those who are in the family
of believers.

PAUL ENDS HIS LETTER

[11]See what large letters I use to write this
myself. [12]Some people are trying to force you

WHAT'S IT MEAN?

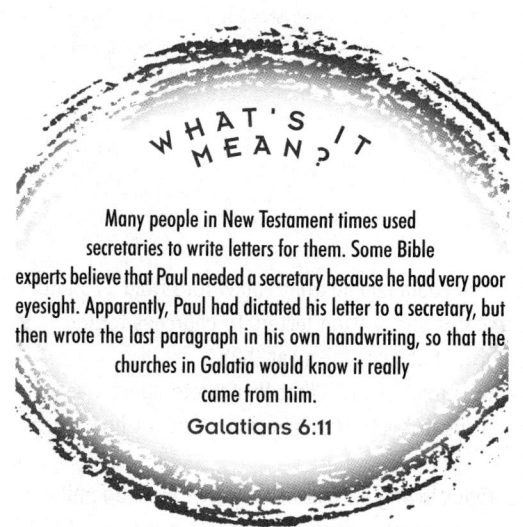

Many people in New Testament times used secretaries to write letters for them. Some Bible experts believe that Paul needed a secretary because he had very poor eyesight. Apparently, Paul had dictated his letter to a secretary, but then wrote the last paragraph in his own handwriting, so that the churches in Galatia would know it really came from him.

Galatians 6:11

to be circumcised so the Jews will accept them.
They are afraid they will be attacked if they
follow only the cross of Christ.[n] 13Those who
are circumcised do not obey the law themselves, but they want you to be circumcised so
they can brag about what they forced you to
do. 14I hope I will never brag about things like
that. The cross of our Lord Jesus Christ is my
only reason for bragging. Through the cross of
Jesus my world was crucified, and I died to the
world. 15It is not important if a man is circumcised or uncircumcised. The important thing is
being the new people God has made. 16Peace
and mercy to those who follow this rule—and
to all of God's people.

17So do not give me any more trouble. I
have scars on my body that show[n] I belong to
Christ Jesus.

18My brothers and sisters, the grace of our
Lord Jesus Christ be with your spirit. Amen.

6:12 cross of Christ Paul uses the cross as a picture of the Good News, the story of Christ's death and rising from the dead to pay for our sins. The cross, or Christ's death, was God's way to save us. **6:17 that show** Many times Paul was beaten and whipped by people who were against him because he was teaching about Christ. The scars were from these beatings.

ephesians

CONTENT The Book of Ephesians is a letter of encouragement that Paul wrote from . . . jail? Yes that's right, Paul is sitting in chains and writing letters to churches telling them to be strong and keep the faith. That's commitment, huh?

So what *does* someone write about from prison? What Paul wrote about was God's unending love. Almost half of his letter to the Ephesians is about how much God loves them.

The last half of Paul's letter is about loving each other whether we are family members or church members or work associates. Paul makes the connection between God's love in us pouring out to those around us.

There's a lot of good advice in Paul's letter to the Ephesians. Advice about being patient and loving and forgiving and honest. It's amazing, isn't it, that a prisoner could write a letter to a church in the first century that has so much to do with the life we are living today?

Outline

1:1–2 .... Greetings
1:3—3:21 .... Christ Gives Spiritual Blessings
4:1—6:20 .... A New Life in Unity with Christ
6:21–24 .... Final Greetings

Purpose Christians are to love and serve one another.

Theme The Glorious Church

Date of writing A.D. 60

"I mean that you have been saved by grace through believing. You did not save yourselves; it was a gift from God. It was not the result of your own efforts, so you cannot brag about it" (2:8–9).

Bible Talk

Suiting Up for War

If you are going to play football for a team, you suit up. You wear protective gear on every joint and a helmet for your head. If you are going to go scuba diving, you suit up as well. You carry tanks and you wear flippers. For almost anything we do, there are uniforms and some gear attached.

It's no different for the Christian walk. In Ephesians, Paul describes how we suit up spiritually and what kind of gear we need to carry. Among other things, he describes our shield of faith and our helmet of salvation (6:11–17). It makes sense, doesn't it, that we would be able to equip ourselves for something so important as the ultimate battle between good and evil?

GIFTS

Do you realize that God has gifted you? Do you realize that he has given you a certain set of skills that allow you to minister to other people? Ephesians 4 gives one of several lists of gifts in the New Testament.

Some people feel like they don't have any gifts at all, but they're wrong. Everyone has a gift from God. Sometimes we get so used to our own gifts that we don't even notice them. We tend to notice the gifts that are different from our own.

If you don't know what your gifts are, start noticing what comes easy to you and what you enjoy the most. Those might be your best clues.

1
1From Paul, an apostle of Christ Jesus. I am
an apostle because that is what God wanted.
To God's holy people living in Ephesus, believers in Christ Jesus:
2Grace and peace to you from God our Father and the Lord Jesus Christ.

SPIRITUAL BLESSINGS IN CHRIST

3Praise be to the God and Father of our
Lord Jesus Christ. In Christ, God has given us
every spiritual blessing in the heavenly world.
4That is, in Christ, he chose us before the world
was made so that we would be his holy people—people without blame before him. 5Be-
cause of his love, God had already decided to
make us his own children through Jesus Christ.
That was what he wanted and what pleased
him, 6and it brings praise to God because of his
wonderful grace. God gave that grace to us
freely, in Christ, the One he loves. 7In Christ we
are set free by the blood of his death, and so
we have forgiveness of sins. How rich is God's
grace, 8which he has given to us so fully and
freely. God, with full wisdom and understanding, 9let us know his secret purpose. This was
what God wanted, and he planned to do it
through Christ. 10His goal was to carry out his
plan, when the right time came, that all things
in heaven and on earth would be joined together in Christ as the head.
11In Christ we were chosen to be God's people, because from the very beginning God had
decided this in keeping with his plan. And he is
the One who makes everything agree with
what he decides and wants. 12We are the first
people who hoped in Christ, and we were
chosen so that we would bring praise to God's
glory. 13So it is with you. When you heard the
true teaching—the Good News about your salvation—you believed in Christ. And in Christ,
God put his special mark of ownership on you
by giving you the Holy Spirit that he had
promised. 14That Holy Spirit is the guarantee
that we will receive what God promised for his
people until God gives full freedom to those
who are his—to bring praise to God's glory.

PAUL'S PRAYER

15That is why since I heard about your faith
in the Lord Jesus and your love for all God's
people, 16I have not stopped giving thanks to
God for you. I always remember you in my
prayers, 17asking the God of our Lord Jesus
Christ, the glorious Father, to give you a spirit
of wisdom and revelation so that you will
know him better. 18I pray also that you will
have greater understanding in your heart so
you will know the hope to which he has called
us and that you will know how rich and glorious are the blessings God has promised his
holy people. 19And you will know that God's
power is very great for us who believe. That
power is the same as the great strength 20God
used to raise Christ from the dead and put him
at his right side in the heavenly world. 21God
has put Christ over all rulers, authorities, powers, and kings, not only in this world but also
in the next. 22God put everything under his
power and made him the head over everything
for the church, 23which is Christ's body. The
church is filled with Christ, and Christ fills
everything in every way.

On the Edge

That Holy Spirit is the guarantee that we will receive what God promised for his people until God gives full freedom to those who are his—to bring praise to God's glory (Eph. 1:14).

God is a God of promise. Here, he's promised to pour out everything that he has been saving for you. He wants to bless you with good things! He doesn't want to hold one thing back! As you begin to walk in the Spirit by allowing him to lead and guide you into God's perfect will, then the blessings of God will start being poured into your lap.

Look at Bartimaeus in Mark 10:46–52. He was a blind beggar who sat outside of God's blessings his entire life. One day, he heard that Jesus was coming down the road. He knew that healing had been stored up for him, so he began crying out, "Jesus, Son of David, have mercy on me!" The crowd told him to knock it off, but he cried out even louder. What happened? He got Jesus' attention! Jesus stopped and called for him. Jesus asked Bartimaeus, "What do you want me to do for you?" Of course, Bartimaeus wanted his sight and he got it! Healing had been stored up for him, and he was finally set free. God wants to do the same for us. The Holy Spirit "is the guarantee that we will receive what God promised"—the guarantee that God's other promises will happen!

SEE FOR YOURSELF:
Prov. 28:20;
Mark 10:46–52;
2 Cor. 1:20;
Eph. 1:3

WE NOW HAVE LIFE

2 1In the past you were spiritually dead because of your sins and the things you did
against God. 2Yes, in the past you lived the way
the world lives, following the ruler of the evil
powers that are above the earth. That same
spirit is now working in those who refuse to
obey God. 3In the past all of us lived like them,
trying to please our sinful selves and doing all
the things our bodies and minds wanted. We
should have suffered God's anger because of
the way we were. We were the same as all
other people.
4But God's mercy is great, and he loved us
very much. 5Though we were spiritually dead
because of the things we did against God, he gave
us new life with Christ. You have been saved by
God's grace. 6And he raised us up with Christ
and gave us a seat with him in the heavens. He
did this for those in Christ Jesus 7so that for all
future time he could show the very great riches
of his grace by being kind to us in Christ Jesus.
8I mean that you have been saved by
grace through believing. You did
not save yourselves; it was a gift
from God. 9It was not the result
of your own efforts, so you
cannot brag about it. 10God has
made us what we are. In Christ
Jesus, God made us to do good
works, which God planned in advance for us to
live our lives doing.

WORK Can eternal life be earned? (2:8–9)

ONE IN CHRIST

11You were not born Jewish. You are the
people the Jews call "uncircumcised."*n* Those

On the Edge

But God's mercy is great . . . he gave us new life with Christ. You have been saved by God's grace. And he raised us up with Christ and gave us a seat with him in the heavens (Eph. 2:4–6).

A prince is tragically separated from his parents at birth. For years they search for him, sending out soldiers to every region to look for the one who belongs to them. Finally, the boy is found, living in poverty, robbing for food, and acting like a savage. A soldier tells the boy about his father. His father is king of the entire country. In an instant, the beggar child has a new position. He is the son of a king. The one who thought he had no family has become royalty. He has a new life, new power, and a new home. He even has a place to sit beside his father's throne. You, too, are the child of a King. God has been merciful. He knew that you were dead in your sins, ruled by selfish desires, and destined for eternal punishment. He loved you and graciously gave you new life. With your new life has come new power and a new home with Christ in heaven.

SEE FOR YOURSELF:
John 14:1–4; 2 Cor. 5:1–2; Phil. 3:20

On the Edge

I mean that you have been saved by grace through believing. You did not save yourselves; it was a gift from God (Eph. 2:8).

Being saved means receiving the forgiveness of sins that God offers you because of Jesus' death and resurrection. It takes faith. You have to believe that God loves you. You have to believe that Jesus is God's Son. You have to believe that Jesus' death on the cross made up for everybody's sins. That's why Paul wrote, "You have been saved by grace through believing."

In verse 10, Paul added, "God has made us what we are. In Christ Jesus, God made us to do good works, which God planned in advance for us to live our lives doing." God definitely wants you to do what's right, and the person who has real faith and love will want to do what pleases him. In fact, your actions say a lot about just how deep your faith goes (read James 2:17). Paul's point is that what you *do* doesn't save you. It's human nature to try to get on God's good side by doing good things, but all the good deeds in the world will not impress him. The only thing that pleases God is faith.

SEE FOR YOURSELF:
Rom. 10:9; Gal. 3:7, 29; James 2:17

2:11 uncircumcised People not having the mark of circumcision as the Jews had.

WHAT'S IT MEAN?

In New Testament times, if a man was not a Jew, he probably wasn't circumcised. Circumcision was an important ritual in Jewish tradition. The removal of the foreskin from the male sex organ, a surgical procedure usually performed eight days after birth, was a physical sign that the Jews belonged to God. It also set them apart from other people. Many Jews of Paul's time looked down on Gentiles because they weren't circumcised.

Ephesians 2:11

who call you "uncircumcised" call themselves
"circumcised." (Their circumcision is only
something they themselves do on their bodies.)
12Remember that in the past you were without
Christ. You were not citizens of Israel, and you
had no part in the agreements[n] with the promise that God made to his people. You had no
hope, and you did not know God. 13But now
in Christ Jesus, you who were far away from
God are brought near through the blood of
Christ's death. 14Christ himself is our peace. He
made both Jewish people and those who are
not Jews one people. They were separated as if
there were a wall between them, but Christ
broke down that wall of hate by giving his
own body. 15The Jewish law had many commands and rules, but Christ ended that law.
His purpose was to make the two groups of
people become one new people in him and in
this way make peace. 16It was also Christ's purpose to end the hatred between the two

WHAT'S IT MEAN?

The Temple area in Jerusalem was divided into a series of courts. The outermost court was the only area of the Temple that non-Jews were allowed to enter.

Ephesians 2:14

2:12 agreements The agreements that God gave to his people in the Old Testament.

Promise HE PROMISES TO HAVE A PLAN FOR YOU.

God has made us what we are. In Christ Jesus, God made us to do good works, which God planned in advance for us to live our lives doing (Eph. 2:10).

Most days just seem to go by like every other day. Same old stuff. Same old everything. Blah blah blah. One day runs into another one. You close your eyes and wake up to do it all over again.

Doesn't seem like much of a plan, does it?

Maybe not. But God has an exciting plan for your life—a plan that will give you purpose and fulfillment beyond your wildest dreams. Following God's plan takes commitment from you. You don't just accidentally fulfill what he's planned for you to do. You've got to seek God and ask him to reveal his plan to you and to give you understanding about how you can fulfill it. Then, you've got to determine to make every day count for him and for his plan.

Pay attention to every decision you face—even the ones that seem so insignificant. Take seriously every person you meet—even the ones you don't like. Embrace every situation you find yourself in—even the ones that seem to make no sense at all. They're shaping you, molding you, preparing you for the next decision, the next person, the next situation.

Lose yourself in doing what God wants with every aspect of your life. Live your life in light of his plan!

SEE FOR YOURSELF:

Matt. 25:34; John 15:16; Eph. 1:4

groups, to make them into one body, and to
bring them back to God. Christ did all this with
his death on the cross. [17]Christ came and
preached peace to you who were far away
from God, and to those who were near to God.
[18]Yes, it is through Christ we all have the right
to come to the Father in one Spirit.

[19]Now you who are not Jewish are not foreigners or strangers any longer, but are citizens
together with God's holy people. You belong
to God's family. [20]You are like a building that
was built on the foundation of the apostles
and prophets. Christ Jesus himself is the most
important stone[n] in that building, [21]and that
whole building is joined together in Christ. He
makes it grow and become a holy temple in
the Lord. [22]And in Christ you, too, are being
built together with the Jews into a place where
God lives through the Spirit.

PAUL'S WORK IN TELLING THE GOOD NEWS

3 [1]So I, Paul, am a prisoner of Christ Jesus for
you who are not Jews. [2]Surely you have heard
that God gave me this work through his grace
to help you. [3]He let me know his secret by
showing it to me. I have already written a little
about this. [4]If you read what I wrote then, you
can see that I truly understand the secret about
the Christ. [5]People who lived in other times
were not told that secret. But now, through the
Spirit, God has shown that secret to his holy
apostles and prophets. [6]This is that secret: that
through the Good News those who are not
Jews will share with the Jews in God's blessing.
They belong to the same body, and they share
together in the promise that God made in
Christ Jesus.

[7]By God's special gift of grace given to me
through his power, I became a servant to tell
that Good News. [8]I am the least important of
all God's people, but God gave me this gift—to
tell those who are not Jews the Good News
about the riches of Christ, which are too great
to understand fully. [9]And God gave me the
work of telling all people about the plan for his
secret, which has been hidden in him since the
beginning of time. He is the One who created
everything. [10]His purpose was that through the
church all the rulers and powers in the heavenly world will now know God's wisdom,
which has so many forms. [11]This agrees with
the purpose God had since the beginning of
time, and he carried out his plan through
Christ Jesus our Lord. [12]In Christ we can come
before God with freedom and without fear. We
can do this through faith in Christ. [13]So I ask
you not to become discouraged because of the
sufferings I am having for you. My sufferings
are for your glory.

THE LOVE OF CHRIST

[14]So I bow in prayer before the Father
[15]from whom every family in heaven and on
earth gets its true name. [16]I ask the Father in his
great glory to give you the power to be strong
inwardly through his Spirit. [17]I pray that Christ

2:20 most important stone Literally, "cornerstone." The first and most important stone in a building.

Promise — HE PROMISES YOU BOLDNESS AND CONFIDENCE.

In Christ we can come before God with freedom and without fear. We can do this through faith in Christ (Eph. 3:12).

Because of the work of Christ, all believers are given the confidence and boldness to come to God. Before you knew Jesus, you were like a stranger to the family of God. You may have even been afraid to talk to God or be in his presence. Through Christ, you have become a member of the family. In a family you can run to your father at anytime. You do not have to beg for his time, or be afraid of his presence. He loves you. He knows you. You are his child. Do not be afraid to run to your heavenly Father. He expects you to come to him when you have doubts, or questions, or need comfort. You do not have to be timid. You belong to him, and you can boldly turn to him with every need.

SEE FOR YOURSELF:

Ps. 119:28; 2 Cor. 3:4; Heb. 4:16; 10:19

will live in your hearts by faith and that your
life will be strong in love and be built on love.
[18]And I pray that you and all God's holy people will have the power to understand the
greatness of Christ's love—how wide and how
long and how high and how deep that love is.
[19]Christ's love is greater than anyone can ever
know, but I pray that you will be able to know
that love. Then you can be filled with the fullness of God.
[20]With God's power working in us, God can
do much, much more than anything we can
ask or imagine. [21]To him be glory in the church
and in Christ Jesus for all time, forever and
ever. Amen.

THE UNITY OF THE BODY

4 [1]I am in prison because I belong to the
Lord. God chose you to be his people, so I urge
you now to live the life to which God called
you. [2]Always be humble, gentle, and patient,
accepting each other in love. [3]You are joined
together with peace through the Spirit, so make
every effort to continue together in this way.
[4]There is one body and one Spirit, and God
called you to have one hope. [5]There is one
Lord, one faith, and one baptism. [6]There is one
God and Father of everything. He rules everything and is everywhere and is in everything.
[7]Christ gave each one of us the special gift
of grace, showing how generous he is. [8]That is
why it says in the Scriptures,

"When he went up to the heights,
he led a parade of captives,
and he gave gifts to people." *Psalm 68:18*

[9]When it says, "He went up," what does it
mean? It means that he first came down to the
earth. [10]So Jesus came down, and he is the
same One who went up above all the heaven.
Christ did that to fill everything with his presence. [11]And Christ gave gifts to people—he
made some to be apostles, some to be prophets, some to go and tell the Good News, and
some to have the work of caring for and teaching God's people. [12]Christ gave those gifts to
prepare God's holy people for the work of
serving, to make the body of Christ stronger.
[13]This work must continue until we are all
joined together in the same faith and
in the same knowledge of the
Son of God. We must become
like a mature person, growing
until we become like Christ
and have his perfection.
[14]Then we will no longer
be babies. We will not be
tossed about like a ship that
the waves carry one way and then another. We
will not be influenced by every new teaching
we hear from people who are trying to fool us.
They make plans and try any kind of trick to
fool people into following the wrong path.
[15]No! Speaking the truth with love, we will
grow up in every way into Christ, who is the

On the Edge

When you talk, do not say harmful things, but say what people need—words that will help others become stronger. Then what you say will do good to those who listen to you. . . . Do not be bitter or angry or mad. Never shout angrily or say things to hurt others. Never do anything evil (Eph. 4:29, 31).

These verses aren't just talking about filthy words. They're talking about letting anything evil come out of your mouth. Proverbs 18:21 tells us words can bring death or life. You've heard the slogan: "Sticks and stones may break my bones, but words will never hurt me!" This may be true physically, but spiritually, words can be very destructive. Hurtful words can do a lot of damage to people and leave them wounded and bitter. We need to learn to put a guard over our mouths. Our mouths can get us in trouble more than almost anything else. That's why we are commanded to be quick to listen and slow to speak.

We've all had opportunity to get upset and "pop off" at the mouth. When we do, we end up saying things we wish we hadn't, and the worst thing is that we can't take them back. God forgives and forgets, but people usually hang on to those kind of things. So the next time someone rubs you the wrong way, don't rip into that person. Stop and think before you speak. The same is true when we hurt ourselves physically. The next time you hit your thumb with a hammer, or you drop something on your toe, remember . . . don't let anything filthy come out of your mouth! Be clean inside and out. Begin to praise God instead, and watch what God will do.

SEE FOR YOURSELF:
Prov. 12:18; 15:1–2, 4; 18:21

EDUCATION

Should Christians ever stop learning about God? (4:14–15)

head. 16The whole body depends on Christ,
and all the parts of the body are joined and
held together. Each part does its own work to
make the whole body grow and be strong with
love.

THE WAY YOU SHOULD LIVE

17In the Lord's name, I tell you this. Do not
continue living like those who do not believe.
Their thoughts are worth nothing. 18They do
not understand, and they know nothing, because they refuse to listen. So they cannot have
the life that God gives. 19They have lost all feeling of shame, and they use their lives for doing
evil. They continually want to do all kinds of
evil. 20But what you learned in Christ was not
like this. 21I know that you heard about him,
and you are in him, so you were taught the
truth that is in Jesus. 22You were taught to leave
your old self—to stop living the evil way you
lived before. That old self becomes worse, because people are fooled by the evil things they
want to do. 23But you were taught to be made
new in your hearts, 24to become a new person.
That new person is made to be like God—
made to be truly good and holy.
25So you must stop telling lies. Tell
each other the truth, because we
all belong to each other in the
same body.[n] 26When you are
angry, do not sin, and be sure
to stop being angry before the
end of the day. 27Do not give
the devil a way to defeat you.
28Those who are stealing must stop stealing and
start working. They should earn an
honest living for themselves.
Then they will have something
to share with those who are
poor.
29When you talk, do not
say harmful things, but say
what people need—words that
will help others become stronger. Then what you say will do
good to those who listen to you.
30And do not make the Holy Spirit sad. The
Spirit is God's proof that you belong to him.
God gave you the Spirit to show that God will
make you free when the final day comes. 31Do
not be bitter or angry or mad. Never shout
angrily or say things to hurt others. Never do
anything evil. 32Be kind and loving to each
other, and forgive each other just as God forgave you in Christ.

ANGER

Can anger be sinful? (4:26–27)

WHAT'S IT MEAN?

Few things are as offensive to God as idol worship. Throughout the Bible, God warned his people not to worship pagan deities. Unfortunately, his people rarely heeded his warnings. The Israelites were always quick to adopt the gods and idols of their pagan neighbors. In Paul's day, however, the word *idol* took on a broader meaning. It came to refer not only to statues and pagan gods, but to anything that was more important than God in a believer's life.

Ephesians 5:5

LIVING IN THE LIGHT

5 1You are God's children whom he
loves, so try to be like him.
2Live a life of love just as
Christ loved us and gave himself for us as a sweet-smelling
offering and sacrifice to God.
3But there must be no sexual sin among you, or any
kind of evil or greed. Those
things are not right for God's holy people.
4Also, there must be no evil talk among you,
and you must not speak foolishly or tell evil
jokes. These things are not right for you. Instead, you should be giving thanks to God.
5You can be sure of this: No one
will have a place in the kingdom of Christ and of God who
sins sexually, or does evil
things, or is greedy. Anyone
who is greedy is serving a false
god.
6Do not let anyone fool
you by telling you things that
are not true, because these
things will bring God's anger on
those who do not obey him. 7So have
nothing to do with them. 8In the past you were
full of darkness, but now you are full of light in
the Lord. So live like children who belong to
the light. 9Light brings every kind of goodness, right living, and truth. 10Try to learn
what pleases the Lord. 11Have nothing to do
with the things done in darkness, which are
not worth anything. But show that they are

SEX

Is sexual immorality improper for Christians? (5:1–3)

"So do not be foolish but learn what the Lord wants you to do." (Ephesians 5:17)

4:25 Tell . . . body. Quotation from Zechariah 8:16.

WHAT'S IT MEAN?

Believe it or not, praise choruses are not a modern church innovation. Music has been a part of worship for a long, long time. Worship services in the original Temple in Jerusalem included a four-thousand-member choir and an orchestra. The New Testament tells of Christians singing hymns together and even records portions of their songs.

Ephesians 5:19

wrong. 12It is shameful even to talk about
what those people do in secret. 13But the
light makes all things easy to see, 14and everything that is made easy to see can become light.
This is why it is said:
"Wake up, sleeper!
Rise from death,
and Christ will shine on you."
15So be very careful how you live.
Do not live like those who are
not wise, but live wisely. 16Use
every chance you have for
doing good, because these are
evil times. 17So do not be
foolish but learn what the
Lord wants you to do. 18Do
not be drunk with wine,
which will ruin you, but be filled with the Spirit. 19Speak to each other with psalms, hymns,
and spiritual songs, singing and making music in
your hearts to the Lord. 20Always give thanks to
God the Father for everything, in the name of our
Lord Jesus Christ.

DRINKING

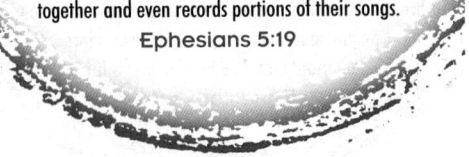

Is drunkenness associated with foolishness? (5:17–18)

WIVES AND HUSBANDS

21Yield to obey each other because you respect Christ.
22Wives, yield to your husbands, as you do
to the Lord, 23because the husband is the head
of the wife, as Christ is the head of the church.
And he is the Savior of the body, which is the
church. 24As the church yields to Christ, so you
wives should yield to your husbands in everything.
25Husbands, love your wives as Christ
loved the church and gave himself for it 26to
make it belong to God. Christ used the word to
make the church clean by washing it with water. 27He died so that he could give the church
to himself like a bride in all her beauty. He died
so that the church could be pure and without
fault, with no evil or sin or any other wrong
thing in it. 28In the same way, husbands should
love their wives as they love their own bodies.
The man who loves his wife loves himself.
29No one ever hates his own body, but feeds
and takes care of it. And that is what Christ
does for the church, 30because we are parts of
his body. 31The Scripture says, "So a man will
leave his father and mother and be united with
his wife, and the two will become one body."[n]
32That secret is very important—I am talking

On the Edge

The husband is the head of the wife, as Christ is the head of the church. And he is the Savior of the body (Eph. 5:23).

Your brain controls everything that your body does. If you want to walk across the room, your brain tells your feet to go and they go. If your shoulder itches, your brain tells your fingers to scratch, and they do it. If your foot moves when your brain doesn't tell it to, you call that a spasm. If your brain tells your hand to make a fist and your hand lies still, you know you've got a problem—something isn't right. The brain is the boss.

Paul talked a lot about the church—Christians—being the body of Christ. Everyone plays a different part, has a different function. Jesus is the head—the brain. That means that everything you do—as a part of his body—needs to be directed by Jesus. If you do something without him, it's spastic and useless. And if he tells you to do something and you don't or can't, you know that something in your relationship needs attention.

All the parts functioning independently can turn into chaos (picture a chicken with its head cut off). Jesus brings all the parts together in a way that makes sense.

SEE FOR YOURSELF:
1 Cor. 12:12–31;
Eph. 1:22–23;
Col. 1:18

5:31 "So . . . body." Quotation from Genesis 2:24.

On the Edge

Children, obey your parents as the Lord wants, because this is the right thing to do. The command says, "Honor your father and mother." This is the first commandment that has a promise with it—"Then everything will be well with you, and you will have a long life on the earth" (Eph. 6:1–3).

God gave you to your parents so that they could raise you. He chose them especially to care for you. The promise in Ephesians 6:3 says that if you obey your father and your mother, "everything will be well with you, and you will have a long life on the earth." Also, when you honor the authority that God has put over you, you get his blessing. Kids who choose to rebel and disobey miss the instructions God has for them through their parents. As a result, things go poorly for them. They make bad choices and life becomes difficult. We would be hard pressed to find an adult in a counselor's office boasting, "I rebelled against my parents as a child, disobeyed their every word, and worried them sick. It was the right thing to do. My life is so much better because I always broke their rules." More common are the adults who live in regret under a pile of guilt because they were so ugly to their parents. God is the Master Designer and this is his design: Obedience leads to right choices and a good life, but rebellion leads to regret.

SEE FOR YOURSELF:
Prov. 15:31–32;
Col. 3:20

about Christ and the church. [33]But each one of
you must love his wife as he loves himself, and
a wife must respect her husband.

CHILDREN AND PARENTS

6 [1]Children, obey your parents as the Lord
wants, because this is the right thing to do.
[2]The command says, "Honor your father and
mother."[n] This is the first command that has
a promise with it— [3]"Then everything will be
well with you, and you will have a long life on
the earth."[n]

[4]Fathers, do not make your children angry,
but raise them with the training and teaching of
the Lord.

SLAVES AND MASTERS

[5]Slaves, obey your masters here on earth
with fear and respect and from a sincere heart,
just as you obey Christ. [6]You must do this not
only while they are watching you, to please
them. With all your heart you must do what
God wants as people who are obeying Christ.
[7]Do your work with enthusiasm. Work as if
you were serving the Lord, not as if you were
serving only men and women. [8]Remember
that the Lord will give a reward to everyone,
slave or free, for doing good.
[9]Masters, in the same way, be good to your
slaves. Do not threaten them. Remember that
the One who is your Master and their Master is
in heaven, and he treats everyone alike.

WHAT'S IT MEAN?

Paul spent so much time under arrest, chained to soldiers, that he had excellent opportunities to consider their battle dress. Roman foot soldiers wore armor and carried shields for protection. The armor was made of thick leather or of metal. Helmets came in all shapes and sizes. Some covered the entire head with metal, except for a protective screen for the face.

Ephesians 6:11–13

WEAR THE FULL ARMOR OF GOD

[10]Finally, be strong in the Lord and in his
great power. [11]Put on the full armor of God so
that you can fight against the devil's evil tricks.
[12]Our fight is not against people on earth but
against the rulers and authorities and the powers of this world's darkness, against the spiritual powers of evil in the heavenly world.
[13]That is why you need to put on God's full
armor. Then on the day of evil you will be able
to stand strong. And when you have finished
the whole fight, you will still be standing. [14]So

6:2 "Honor . . . mother." Quotation from Exodus 20:12; Deuteronomy 5:16. **6:3 "Then . . . earth."** Quotation from Exodus 20:12; Deuteronomy 5:16.

stand strong, with the belt of truth tied around
your waist and the protection of right living on
your chest. 15On your feet wear the Good
News of peace to help you stand strong. 16And
also use the shield of faith with which you can
stop all the burning arrows of the Evil One.
17Accept God's salvation as your helmet, and
take the sword of the Spirit, which is the word
of God. 18Pray in the Spirit at all times with
all kinds of prayers, asking for everything you
need. To do this you must always be ready
and never give up. Always pray for all God's
people.
19Also pray for me that when I speak, God
will give me words so that I can tell the secret
of the Good News without fear. 20I have been
sent to preach this Good News, and I am doing
that now, here in prison. Pray that when I
preach the Good News I will speak without
fear, as I should.

FINAL GREETINGS

21I am sending to you Tychicus, our
brother whom we love and a faithful servant
of the Lord's work. He will tell you everything that is happening with me. Then you
will know how I am and what I am doing. 22I
am sending him to you for this reason—so
that you will know how we are, and he can
encourage you.
23Peace and love with faith to you from
God the Father and the Lord Jesus Christ.
24Grace to all of you who love our Lord Jesus
Christ with love that never ends.

Philippians

CONTENT

Have you ever written a thank-you note? If you have, someone probably had given you something or had done something nice for you. Then one of your parents probably made you sit down and write a short note saying "thank you."

That is actually part of the reason that Paul wrote the Philippians. He wanted to thank them for supporting his ministry and for their love and friendship.

If there is any word that describes this book, it's "joy." That's a pretty amazing fact since Paul wrote it from jail. But even though he was in jail, he shared his joy about everything from his life in Christ to his friends in Philippi.

There are several keys to being joyful. Paul seemed to understand each one of them. Paul could focus on his blessings even when he had chains on his hands and feet. Somehow he knew that life is more than the difficult moments.

So if you need a pick-me-up, Philippians is the book to read. Maybe we should subtitle it "Philippians: looking up when everything looks down."

Outline

1:1–11 .... Greetings and a Prayer
1:12–30 .... What Life Means to Paul
2:1–18 .... Christ's Example of True Humility
2:19–30 .... News About Paul's Friends
3:1—4:9 .... All for Christ
4:10–20 .... Paul Thanks the Philippians
4:21–23 .... Final Greetings

Purpose

Joy is experienced by those who live a truly Christian life.

Theme

Joy in Christ

Date of writing

A.D. 61

"To me the only important thing about living is Christ, and dying would be profit for me" (1:21).

Bible Talk

An Apostle Jailbird

When you look at all the books of the Bible that Paul wrote while he was in jail, you realize that he was in jail a *lot*.

Paul was in and out of jail because he believed that obeying Jesus was the most important thing he could do. That scared the government. If Paul obeyed Jesus instead of the government and got away with it, then *everybody* might start obeying God rather than the government. That didn't feel really good to the authorities, so they kept telling Paul not to preach. Of course, he kept preaching and they kept putting him in jail.

Since Paul was really focused on spreading the Good News, jail seemed like as good a place as any to do this. Guards and inmates were his "captive" audience.

JOY

There's a big difference between joy and happiness. Happiness is what you feel when circumstances in your life go right. If you make good grades and get what you want for your birthday—those kinds of things make you happy. Because happiness is related to circumstances, it comes and goes with the good times in life.

Joy, on the other hand, is more than an emotion. It is a perspective, a way of looking at life. We have joy when we feel secure inside that, no matter how our circumstances might change, God is still in control. That's why Paul could write a letter about gratitude and joy in a yucky place like prison. He might not have been happy, but in the end he knew that God was in control of his life.

1
1From Paul and Timothy, servants of Christ
Jesus.
To all of God's holy people in Christ Jesus
who live in Philippi, including your elders and
deacons:
2Grace and peace to you from God our Father and the Lord Jesus Christ.

PAUL'S PRAYER

3I thank my God every time I remember
you, 4always praying with joy for all of you. 5I
thank God for the help you gave me while I
preached the Good News—help you gave
from the first day you believed until now.
6God began doing a good work in you, and I
am sure he will continue it until it is finished
when Jesus Christ comes again.
7And I know that I am right to think like
this about all of you, because I have you in my
heart. All of you share in God's grace with me
while I am in prison and while I am defending
and proving the truth of the Good News. 8God
knows that I want to see you very much, because I love all of you with the love of Christ
Jesus.
9This is my prayer for you: that your love
will grow more and more; that you will have
knowledge and understanding with your love;
10that you will see the difference between good
and bad and will choose the good; that you
will be pure and without wrong for the coming of Christ; 11that you will do many good
things with the help of Christ to bring glory
and praise to God.

WHAT'S IT MEAN?

Talk about a slow judicial system! Paul lived under house arrest in Rome for two years while he waited for Caesar to hear his case. Since electronic monitoring devices weren't available in Paul's day, he had soldiers guarding him day and night. The guards worked four-hour shifts, with at least one person handcuffed to Paul at all times. Even though he was officially a prisoner, Paul was allowed to receive visitors. That gave him an opportunity to share the message of Christ not only with the people who came to see him, but with the soldiers as well.

Philippians 1:7

PAUL'S TROUBLES HELP THE WORK

12I want you brothers and sisters[n] to know
that what has happened to me has helped to
spread the Good News. 13All the palace guards
and everyone else knows that I am in prison
because I am a believer in Christ. 14Because I
am in prison, most of the believers have become more bold in Christ and are not afraid to
speak the word of God.
15It is true that some preach about Christ
because they are jealous and ambitious, but

1:12 brothers and sisters Although the Greek text says "brothers" here and throughout this book, Paul's words were meant for the entire church, including men and women.

Promise HE PROMISES TO FINISH A GOOD WORK IN YOU.

God began doing a good work in you, and I am sure he will continue it until it is finished when Jesus Christ comes again (Phil. 1:6).

Have you heard? Jesus is coming back again. No, really. It may seem highly unlikely from where you're sitting. But one day, in some heart-pounding way where no one in the world will have to wonder what's happening, he's going to step back in here and finish some business. One of those little unfinished matters . . . is you.

Don't sweat it though. If you're one of his, he won't be coming back to pull the curtain down on your performance, but to raise the blinds and allow you to see what he's been doing in your life. And one day—one great, big, glorious day—he'll let you know what was going on.

God finishes what he starts. Give him permission to get started with you.

SEE FOR YOURSELF:

Ps. 139:16; John 17:24; Acts 20:24

others preach about Christ because they want to help. [16]They preach because they have love, and they know that God gave me the work of defending the Good News. [17]But the others preach about Christ for selfish and wrong reasons, wanting to make trouble for me in prison.

[18]But it doesn't matter. The important thing is that in every way, whether for right or wrong reasons, they are preaching about Christ. So I am happy, and I will continue to be happy. [19]Because you are praying for me and the Spirit of Jesus Christ is helping me, I know this trouble will bring my freedom. [20]I expect and hope that I will not fail Christ in anything but that I will have the courage now, as always, to show the greatness of Christ in my life here on earth, whether I live or die. [21]To me the only important thing about living is Christ, and dying would be profit for me. [22]If I continue living in my body, I will be able to work for the Lord. I do not know what to choose—living or dying. [23]It is hard to choose between the two. I want to leave this life and be with Christ, which is much better, [24]but you need me here in my body. [25]Since I am sure of this, I know I will stay with you to help you grow and have joy in your faith. [26]You will be very happy in Christ Jesus when I am with you again.

LIFE
What is the reason for life? (1:21)

HEAVEN
Is heaven better than earth? (1:23)

[27]Only one thing concerns me: Be sure that you live in a way that brings honor to the Good News of Christ. Then whether I come and visit you or am away from you, I will hear that you are standing strong with one purpose, that you work together as one for the faith of the Good News, [28]and that you are not afraid of those who are against you. All of this is proof that your enemies will be destroyed but that you will be saved by God. [29]God gave you the honor not only of believing in Christ but also of suffering for him, both of which bring glory to Christ. [30]When I was with you, you saw the struggles I had, and you hear about the struggles I am having now. You yourselves are having the same kind of struggles.

2

[1]Does your life in Christ give you strength? Does his love comfort you? Do we share together in the spirit? Do you have mercy and kindness? [2]If so, make me very happy by having the same thoughts, sharing the same love, and having one mind and purpose. [3]When you do things, do not let selfishness or pride be your guide. Instead, be humble and give more honor to others than to yourselves. [4]Do not be interested only in your own life, but be interested in the lives of others.

BE UNSELFISH LIKE CHRIST

[5]In your lives you must think and act like Christ Jesus.

[6]Christ himself was like God in everything.
But he did not think that being equal
with God was something to be used
for his own benefit.

On the Edge

And when he was living as a man, he humbled himself and was fully obedient to God, even when that caused his death—death on a cross (Phil. 2:8).

For a great story about how humble Jesus was, look at John 13:1–17. It's a fascinating story about humility. Can you imagine sitting in the same room as Jesus only to have him come up to you and wash your feet? Your feet . . . the ugliest and smelliest part of your body! Wow! Jesus displayed the ultimate act of servanthood in this illustration. We need to serve others in the same way.

What does it really mean to be humble? It means that someone will do anything asked and will do it with a willing heart and a good attitude. It means that you put down the wonderful things about yourself just to love and serve other people. If you know anything about the life and ministry of Jesus, then you know that he was a humble servant. He even said that he didn't come to be served but to serve (see Matt. 20:28). If that was Jesus' attitude, how much more should it be ours? From now on, work on being humble enough to serve others rather than being served yourself. You've heard that pride comes before a fall. If we are humbled before him as servants, we are imitating Christ—and that's what our Christian walk is all about.

SEE FOR YOURSELF:
Prov. 11:2;
Matt. 20:28; 23:12;
John 13:3–15

7 But he gave up his place with God and
made himself nothing.
He was born to be a man
and became like a servant.
8 And when he was living as a man,
he humbled himself and was fully
obedient to God,
even when that caused his death—death
on a cross.
9 So God raised him to the highest place.
God made his name greater than every
other name
10 so that every knee will bow to the name
of Jesus—
everyone in heaven, on earth, and under
the earth.
11 And everyone will confess that Jesus
Christ is Lord
and bring glory to God the Father.

BE THE PEOPLE GOD WANTS YOU TO BE

12 My dear friends, you have always obeyed
God when I was with you. It is even more important that you obey now while I am away
from you. Keep on working to complete your
salvation with fear and trembling, 13 because
God is working in you to help you want to do
and be able to do what pleases him.
14 Do everything without complaining or
arguing. 15 Then you will be innocent and
without any wrong. You will be God's children
without fault. But you are living with crooked
and mean people all around you, among
whom you shine like stars in the dark world.
16 You offer the teaching that gives life. So when
Christ comes again, I can be happy because
my work was not wasted. I ran the race and
won.
17 Your faith makes you offer your lives as a
sacrifice in serving God. If I have to offer my
own blood with your sacrifice, I will be happy
and full of joy with all of you. 18 You also
should be happy and full of joy with me.

TIMOTHY AND EPAPHRODITUS

19 I hope in the Lord Jesus to send Timothy
to you soon. I will be happy to learn how you
are. 20 I have no one else like Timothy, who truly cares for you. 21 Other people are interested
only in their own lives, not in the work of
Jesus Christ. 22 You know the kind of person
Timothy is. You know he has served with me
in telling the Good News, as a son serves his
father. 23 I plan to send him to you quickly
when I know what will happen to me. 24 I am
sure that the Lord will help me to come to you
soon.
25 Epaphroditus, my brother in Christ,
works and serves with me in the army of
Christ. When I needed help, you sent him to
me. I think now that I must send him back to
you, 26 because he wants very much to see all
of you. He is worried because you heard that
he was sick. 27 Yes, he was sick, and nearly died,
but God had mercy on him and me too so that
I would not have more sadness. 28 I want very
much to send him to you so that when you see
him you can be happy, and I can stop worrying about you. 29 Welcome him in the Lord
with much joy. Give honor to people like him,
30 because he almost died for the work of
Christ. He risked his life to give me the help
you could not give in your service to me.

THE IMPORTANCE OF CHRIST

3
1 My brothers and sisters, be full of joy in
the Lord. It is no trouble for me to write the
same things to you again, and it will help you
to be more ready. 2 Watch out for those who do
evil, who are like dogs, who demand to cut[n]
the body. 3 We are the ones who are truly circumcised. We worship God through his Spirit,
and our pride is in Christ Jesus. We do not put
trust in ourselves or anything we can do, 4 although I might be able to put trust in myself. If
anyone thinks he has a reason to trust in himself, he should know that I have greater reason
for trusting in myself. 5 I was circumcised eight
days after my birth. I am from the people of

WHAT'S IT MEAN?

Paul wasn't talking about loyal household pets in this verse. He was talking about packs of wild, vicious canines that roamed the Near East, eating anything they could find—including garbage—and attacking people. "Dog" was popular among Jews as an insulting name for non-Jews. Paul turned the insult around in this verse. The people he called dogs were those who insisted that circumcision was necessary for Christians.

Philippians 3:2

3:2 cut The word in Greek is like the word "circumcise," but it means "to cut completely off."

Israel and the tribe of Benjamin. I am a Hebrew, and my parents were Hebrews. I had a
strict view of the law, which is why I became a
Pharisee. [6]I was so enthusiastic I tried to hurt
the church. No one could find fault with the
way I obeyed the law of Moses. [7]Those things
were important to me, but now I think they are
worth nothing because of Christ. [8]Not only
those things, but I think that all things are
worth nothing compared with the greatness of
knowing Christ Jesus my Lord. Because of him,
I have lost all those things, and now I know
they are worthless trash. This allows me to
have Christ [9]and to belong to him. Now I am
right with God, not because I followed the law,
but because I believed in Christ. God uses my
faith to make me right with him. [10]I want to
know Christ and the power that raised him
from the dead. I want to share in his sufferings
and become like him in his death. [11]Then I
have hope that I myself will be raised from the
dead.

On the Edge

But our homeland is in heaven, and we are waiting for our Savior, the Lord Jesus Christ, to come from heaven (Phil. 3:20).

Young women sleep with their boyfriends thinking they will help them feel satisfied. They don't. Maybe having a baby will fill the void? Nope, it's worse than before. Some of us search all our lives for something or someone to fill us up and keep us fulfilled. The truth is that our souls were created to live with God. From time to time you will wrestle with dissatisfaction. Let your feelings remind you that your heart is longing for heaven. Rejoice in knowing that one day you will stand complete and full in the presence of your Savior, never to feel incomplete again.

SEE FOR YOURSELF:
Ps. 91:14; Zeph. 3:17; Rom. 8:35–39; Eph. 3:16–19

WHAT'S IT MEAN?

The Pharisees were a political and religious group within the Jewish community. They studied the Scriptures constantly and insisted on strict obedience to God's Old Testament laws. Most Jewish people respected the Pharisees' dedication and knowledge. In turn, the Pharisees tended to look down on anyone who didn't meet their standards.

Philippians 3:5

CONTINUING TOWARD OUR GOAL

[12]I do not mean that I am already as God
wants me to be. I have not yet reached that
goal, but I continue trying to reach it and to
make it mine. Christ wants me to do that,
which is the reason he made me his. [13]Brothers
and sisters, I know that I have not yet reached
that goal, but there is one thing I always do.
Forgetting the past and straining toward what
is ahead, [14]I keep trying to reach the goal and
get the prize for which God called me through
Christ to the life above.
[15]All of us who are spiritually mature
should think this way, too. And if there are
things you do not agree with, God will make
them clear to you. [16]But we should continue
following the truth we already have.
[17]Brothers and sisters, all of you should try
to follow my example and to copy those who
live the way we showed you. [18]Many people
live like enemies of the cross of Christ. I have
often told you about them, and it makes me
cry to tell you about them now. [19]In the end,
they will be destroyed. They do whatever their
bodies want, they are proud of their shameful
acts, and they think only about earthly things.
[20]But our homeland is in heaven, and we are
waiting for our Savior, the Lord Jesus Christ, to
come from heaven. [21]By his power to rule all
things, he will change our simple bodies and
make them like his own glorious body.

WHAT THE CHRISTIANS ARE TO DO

4 [1]My dear brothers and sisters, I love you
and want to see you. You bring me joy and
make me proud of you, so stand strong in the
Lord as I have told you.
[2]I ask Euodia and Syntyche to agree in the
Lord. [3]And I ask you, my faithful friend, to
help these women. They served with me in
telling the Good News, together with Clement

and others who worked with me, whose names are written in the book of life.[n]

4Be full of joy in the Lord always. I will say
again, be full of joy.
5Let everyone see that you are
gentle and kind. The Lord is
coming soon. 6Do not worry
about anything, but pray and
ask God for everything you
need, always giving thanks.
7And God's peace, which is so
great we cannot understand it,
will keep your hearts and minds in Christ Jesus.

WORRY
What can help when we are worried? (4:4–9)

8Brothers and sisters, think about the things
that are good and worthy of praise. Think
about the things that are true and honorable
and right and pure and beautiful and respected.
9Do what you learned and received from me,
what I told you, and what you saw me do. And
the God who gives peace will be with you.

On the Edge

Brothers and sisters, think about the things that are good and worthy of praise. Think about the things that are true and honorable and right and pure and beautiful and respected (Phil. 4:8).

Mom is probably more concerned with the lyrics of the songs than the style of music. So put your CD collection through the Philippians 4:8 test. Do any of the lyrics oppose the teaching of Paul in verse 8? If what you are listening to makes you think about things that are impure, wrong, or immoral, it fails the test. What you put into your mind simmers there and eventually comes back out. So throw out the stuff that's trash and let Mom know that you've cleaned out the music she's been worried about. Wailing guitar riffs may still make Mom's head throb, but a good pair of headphones should bring her some relief. Next time you buy a CD, give it the "4:8" test and ask yourself if God would be pleased.

SEE FOR YOURSELF:
Rom. 12:2; Eph. 4:20–24; Col. 3:1–2

On the Edge

I can do all things through Christ, because he gives me strength (Phil. 4:13).

Paul had a rough time. He had been thrown in jail, beaten up, and had rocks thrown at him. He'd been robbed, lived through a shipwreck, and gone hungry. At times he barely had enough clothes to keep him warm. So Paul wasn't just blowing smoke when he told the Philippians, "I can do all things through Christ, because he gives me strength."

You have the same kind of strength in you. It doesn't matter if you can't relate to Paul. It doesn't matter if you aren't an apostle or a missionary living in the jungle. It doesn't matter if you think you'll never have to face the stuff Paul did. The truth is that Paul was strong because Jesus lived inside of him, and the same Jesus lives in you.

That means that, just like Paul, you can face *anything*. You can face a really tough exam. You can face your parents when you need to apologize to them. You can face your friends when doing what God wants isn't cool with them. You can face the future even when you have no idea what's going to happen. Just don't try to do it by yourself. The strength to face all those things comes only from Jesus. He'll make you strong.

SEE FOR YOURSELF:
Ps. 68:35; Jer. 15:20; Hab. 3:19; Eph. 3:12

PAUL THANKS THE CHRISTIANS

10I am very happy in the Lord that you
have shown your care for me again. You continued to care about me, but there was no way
for you to show it. 11I am not telling you this
because I need anything. I have learned to be
satisfied with the things I have and with everything that happens. 12I know how to live when
I am poor, and I know how to live when I have
plenty. I have learned the secret of being happy
at any time in everything that happens, when I
have enough to eat and when I go hungry,
when I have more than I need and when I do
not have enough. 13I can do all things through
Christ, because he gives me strength.

4:3 book of life God's book that has the names of all God's chosen people (Revelation 3:5; 21:27).

WHAT'S IT MEAN?

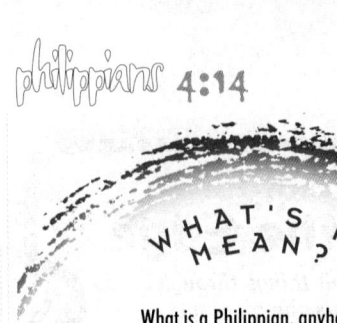

What is a Philippian, anyhow? A Philippian was a person who lived in Philippi, a city in Macedonia (modern-day Greece). When Paul visited Philippi during his second missionary journey, the people of the city gave him money to continue his ministry in Thessalonica, a seaport about eighty miles west of Philippi.

Philippians 4:15–16

14 But it was good that you helped me when
I needed it. 15 You Philippians remember when I
first preached the Good News there. When I
left Macedonia, you were the only church that
gave me help. 16 Several times you sent me
things I needed when I was in Thessalonica.
17 Really, it is not that I want to receive gifts
from you, but I want you to have the good
that comes from giving. 18 And now I have
everything, and more. I have all I need, because
Epaphroditus brought your gift to me. It is like
a sweet-smelling sacrifice offered to God, who
accepts that sacrifice and is pleased with it.
19 My God will use his wonderful riches in
Christ Jesus to give you everything you need.
20 Glory to our God and Father forever and
ever! Amen.

21 Greet each of God's people in Christ.
Those who are with me send greetings to you.
22 All of God's people greet you, particularly
those from the palace of Caesar.

23 The grace of the Lord Jesus Christ be with
you all.

A BOY WITH A LUNCH made a difference

One boy in the Bible lived by a motto that turned out to make quite a difference: Lunch—don't leave home without it. That boy was among the crowd of thousands following Jesus around Lake Galilee to hear him teach. Not knowing how long he would be gone, the boy had with him a simple meal: five loaves and two fish. That was probably enough for several snacks for a young boy. When it turned out to be the only food on hand for the huge crowd, it looked pretty insignificant.

But that little lunch was turned over to Jesus. He prayed and multiplied the contents of the meal so that it served everyone, and there were leftovers! The boy himself gave up his meal, but got at least as much in return, not to mention the thrill of Jesus' miracle.

Cutting Edge

The boy's act of generosity was mentioned by all four writers of the Good News.

What seemed to the apostles to be proof of how impossible it was to meet the need Jesus took and used to meet the need. The apostles concluded that they only had five loaves and two fish. They momentarily overlooked the obvious fact that they also had Jesus. He made the difference. Even a little boy's lunch gift was more than enough in Jesus' hands.

YOU can, too! You may be convinced that you have little to offer Christ. Measured against the needs of the world around you, you may well be right. The choice you must make is between trying to make a difference on your own and placing what little you are and have into God's hands and expecting him to make a difference in you and through you. What you choose willl make a difference!

Want to know more? You can find this story in

Matthew 14:13–21; Mark 6:30–44; Luke 9:10–17; John 6:1–14.

JOHN MARK made a difference

Can someone still make a difference after they have made a big mistake? John Mark may have failed twice before he finally realized what discipleship in Jesus Christ is all about. Actually, that record is probably better than average. John Mark gives us a good example of the fact that people don't make a difference for Christ when they fall, but when they keep getting up by God's grace!

We know John Mark best by his second name, which identifies the account of the Good News he probably wrote, using Peter as one of his sources. In his account, he gives a subtle glimpse of his own uncertain discipleship on the night Jesus was betrayed. He mentions a young follower who fled in such fear that he ran right out of his clothes (see Mark 14:51–52).

Cutting Edge

Later, when Paul and Barnabas were setting out on their first missionary journey, they chose John Mark as their traveling assistant. He quit during the adventure. On the next mission, Barnabas wanted to give Mark another try, but Paul refused. The two giants split. Barnabas helped Mark grow up in the faith. Later, Paul realized that Mark had become a real asset to the cause of Christ. It took a while, but Mark made a difference.

YOU can, too! Everybody makes mistakes. All of them have consequences—some bad; some good. If and when you decide to follow Jesus, you will find the need to grow through your failures. The journey to maturity—the way to making a difference—takes you right through the middle of mistakes. Remember John Mark; keep getting up by God's grace!

Want to know more? Follow the ups and downs for Mark's journey in these passages: Acts 12:25—13:13; 15:36–40; Colossians 4:10–11; 2 Timothy 4:11; Philemon 23–24; 1 Peter 5:13.

RHODA made a difference

People don't find out how much they really believe in prayer until one of God's answers comes knocking at the door! Rhoda was a young believer caught up in exciting days that followed Jesus' resurrection. At first, it may have looked like everyone would turn to the risen Christ. Then came the backlash. Ugly confrontations, imprisonment, and even death were used to resist the wildfire of the Good News. No one was safe.

Rhoda participated in a fervent prayer meeting, asking God for the safe release of Peter who had been imprisoned. While they were praying, God was working. An angel broke Peter out of his confinement. Once the angel left him on the street, Peter made his way to the house where Rhoda and the others were still in prayer. He knocked on the outer door, and Rhoda went to answer. She recognized Peter's voice and got so excited that she rushed back into the house to tell the news. During the next confusing minutes, Peter was left standing out in the street. At first, the others in the house didn't believe Rhoda's report. But someone finally decided that the best way to check her story was to open the door. They found to their surprise and delight that God had answered their prayers. Rhoda had the right attitude; she just forgot an item that would have easily persuaded others—Peter himself. We may chuckle over Rhoda's oversight, but it reminds us how easily we fall into the error of praying for what we don't really expect God to provide. God will not be bound by our prayers, but he often answers them with a precision we miss because we aren't paying close enough attention.

Cutting Edge

YOU can, too!

We pray to make a difference. We pray to put ourselves in a place where we can see God make a difference. When we pray for rain, we ought to carry our umbrellas with us. Sometimes, when we are surprised by God's answer, we end up giving an unclear report. When God's answers come knocking, open the door. That will make a big difference!

Want to know more? Read about Rhoda's small adventure in Acts 12:1–17.

JAMES, Jesus' little brother, made a difference

James must have felt that having Jesus as a big brother was a mixed blessing. Did James ever hear his mother say, "Why can't you be more like your big brother?" Now there is an intimidating comparison! James probably had some good reasons to consider his big brother unique and amazing, but the Bible tells us he had a hard time accepting his big brother as his Savior. It took a while. In fact, it took Jesus' death and resurrection to finally convince James that Jesus was much more than his brother. Paul tells us (1 Cor. 15:7) that Jesus paid his little brother a personal visit after his resurrection. That must have been quite a reunion!

James had always watched Jesus. How can you ignore a famous brother? When he finally realized the identity of his brother, James's faith took a great leap forward. Everything he had heard his brother say and had seen his brother do suddenly made sense. All the shapes and colors were there; faith brought the picture into sharp focus. James became a leader in the church almost overnight. He grew up!

Cutting Edge

Even though James was a late bloomer, God used him in several crucial ways. He provided key wisdom in the early days of the church. He also wrote the Book of James, probably the most down-to-earth, practical, how-to manual for the Christian life. Every time someone reads that book, James makes a difference again.

YOU can, too!

Fortunately, you can respond in faith to Jesus at any point in your Life. Late bloomer or not, it's never too late to begin applying the lessons James learned and passed on in his book. In fact, one way to think about the Book of James is to describe it as a book written for believers who really want to make a difference for Christ in their lives.

Want to know more? As you read the accounts of the Good News, think about what it must have been like as Jesus' little brother to see and hear what Jesus was doing. James is mentioned directly in John 7:1–5; Acts 15:1–29; 1 Corinthians 15:7; and in his own letter, James.

Colossians

CONTENT Paul wrote to the church at Colossae because they had fallen prey to some heretics (false teachers). There were people in the Colossian church that were teaching that Christianity was just too easy. Righteousness *couldn't* be as simple as faith in Christ. There had to be more to it than that.

Paul wrote to say, "Let's go over it again. There's no more to it. If you add more to it, then you are wrong. Faith in Christ is all there is."

Because of this, Colossians is a good book to read to review the basics of Christianity. At the bottom of it all, the message of Christ is simple and clear. Humans needed to be righteous (made right) in order to relate to God. Christ gave his life to provide that righteousness for us. When we put our faith in Christ's sacrifice, God sees us through Christ's righteousness.

There is nothing we can do to add to that. If we think we can, then we need to read the Book of Colossians and let Paul set us straight.

Outline

1:1–2 .... Greetings
1:3–8 .... A Prayer of Thanks
1:9—2:19 .... The Person and Work of Christ
2:20—4:6 .... New Life with Christ
4:7–18 .... Final Greetings

Purpose Faith is to be lived out daily.

Theme The Supremacy and Sufficiency of Christ

Date of writing A.D. 60

"Since you were raised from the dead with Christ, aim at what is in heaven, where Christ is sitting at the right hand of God. Think only about the things in heaven, not the things on earth" (3:1–2).

Bible Talk

Do You Have an Apostle Paul in Your Life?

Paul was so important to the early church. He set church members straight when they drifted from the truth. He encouraged them when they were overwhelmed. He was like a big brother and a teacher rolled into one.

Do you have a Paul in your life? If you don't, look around. Find someone who trusts God and has lived the Christian life for a long time. Find someone you can trust to help you decide what to believe and what to stand against. Find someone who will tell you the truth even when it hurts and even when it may disappoint you.

HOW TO DECIDE IF IT'S HERESY

Several of Paul's letters were written to correct some heresy that had slipped into the church. Do you know when something is heresy and when it is not? Here are some tests:

1. Does this way of thinking honor Christ as the one true God?
2. Does this way of thinking require anything more than faith to be righteous?
3. Does this way of thinking help me to be more obedient to God or less?

Be wise and ask questions about what you are taught. Don't let someone fool you into believing a lie.

Colossians

1 From Paul, an apostle of Christ Jesus. I am
an apostle because that is what God wanted.
Also from Timothy, our brother.
2 To the holy and faithful brothers and
sisters[n] in Christ that live in Colossae:
Grace and peace to you from God our Father.
3 In our prayers for you we always thank
God, the Father of our Lord Jesus Christ, 4 because we have heard about the faith you have
in Christ Jesus and the love you have for all of
God's people. 5 You have this faith and love because of your hope, and what you hope for is
kept safe for you in heaven. You learned about
this hope when you heard the message about
the truth, the Good News 6 that was told to
you. Everywhere in the world that Good News
is bringing blessings and is growing. This has
happened with you, too, since you heard the
Good News and understood the truth about
the grace of God. 7 You learned about God's
grace from Epaphras, whom we love. He works
together with us and is a faithful servant of
Christ for us. 8 He also told us about the love
you have from the Holy Spirit.

What's It Mean?

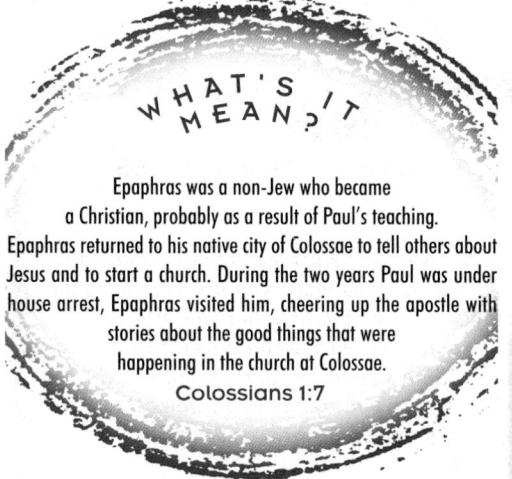

Epaphras was a non-Jew who became a Christian, probably as a result of Paul's teaching. Epaphras returned to his native city of Colossae to tell others about Jesus and to start a church. During the two years Paul was under house arrest, Epaphras visited him, cheering up the apostle with stories about the good things that were happening in the church at Colossae.

Colossians 1:7

On the Edge

Live the kind of life that honors and pleases the Lord in every way. . . . God will strengthen you with his own great power so that you will not give up when troubles come, but you will be patient (Col. 1:10–11).

Remember the story in Luke 8:42–48 about the woman who had been bleeding for twelve years? Talk about enduring. This woman had endured patiently for twelve years trying to get well. Luke reports that she had spent all of her money on doctors. They helped her the best they could, but she still couldn't get well. In fact, she just got worse and worse. Finally, she heard that Jesus was passing by. She knew that if she could just touch him, that she would be whole. It happened! Do you think she was happy? You bet she was!

The apostle Paul is telling us here that we have been given the power to endure anything. Anything! It doesn't matter what your circumstances look like. As you begin to tap into the power of God, it will produce patience, and that patience will give you the ability to endure anything. And after the storm blows over and you've endured it, the rainbow will come out and there will be joy beyond your wildest thoughts! It's what we do during the storm that will make the difference.

If anyone knew endurance, it was Paul. He was beaten many times, shipwrecked, bitten by a poisonous snake, stoned, and put in jail. That's some rough stuff! But you know what? Paul made it through all of that junk, and if anyone was happy, he was. He's the one who wrote to "be full of joy in the Lord always" (Phil. 4:4), and he wrote that while he was stuck in prison! Don't give up. You're going to make it through life's storms. God gives you the power to endure, and he's going to make you truly happy someday!

SEE FOR YOURSELF:
Rom. 5:3–4;
2 Cor. 6:4–5

9 Because of this, since the day we heard
about you, we have continued praying for
you, asking God that you will know fully what
he wants. We pray that you will also have great
wisdom and understanding in spiritual things
10 so that you will live the kind of life that honors and pleases the Lord in every way. You will
produce fruit in every good work and grow in
the knowledge of God. 11 God will strengthen
you with his own great power so that you will
not give up when troubles come, but you will
be patient. 12 And you will joyfully give thanks

1:2 brothers and sisters Although the Greek text says "brothers" here and throughout this book, Paul's words were meant for the entire church, including men and women.

to the Father who has made you able to have a
share in all that he has prepared for his people
in the kingdom of light. 13God has freed us
from the power of darkness, and he brought
us into the kingdom of his dear Son. 14The Son
paid for our sins, and in him we have forgiveness.

THE IMPORTANCE OF CHRIST

15No one can see God, but Jesus Christ is
exactly like him. He ranks higher than everything that has been made. 16Through
his power all things were
made—things in heaven and
on earth, things seen and unseen, all powers, authorities,
lords, and rulers. All things
were made through Christ and
for Christ. 17He was there be-
fore anything was made, and all things continue because of him. 18He is the head of the body,
which is the church. Everything comes from
him. He is the first one who was raised from
the dead. So in all things Jesus has first place.
19God was pleased for all of himself to live in
Christ. 20And through Christ, God has brought
all things back to himself again—things on
earth and things in heaven. God made peace
through the blood of Christ's death on the
cross.

JESUS
Did Jesus create the world? (1:15–16)

21At one time you were separated from
God. You were his enemies in your minds, and
the evil things you did were against God. 22But
now God has made you his friends again. He
did this through Christ's death in the body so
that he might bring you into God's presence as
people who are holy, with no wrong, and with
nothing of which God can judge you guilty.
23This will happen if you continue strong and
sure in your faith. You must not be moved
away from the hope brought to you by the
Good News that you heard. That same Good
News has been told to everyone in the world,
and I, Paul, help in preaching that Good News.

PAUL'S WORK FOR THE CHURCH

24I am happy in my sufferings for you.
There are things that Christ must still suffer
through his body, the church. I am accepting,
in my body, my part of these things that must
be suffered. 25I became a servant of the church
because God gave me a special work to do that
helps you, and that work is to tell fully the
message of God. 26This message is the secret
that was hidden from everyone since the beginning of time, but now it is made known to

Promise — HE PROMISES TO PRESENT YOU GUILTLESS IN HIS SIGHT.

At one time you were separated from God. You were his enemies in your minds, and the evil things you did were against God. But now God has made you his friends again. He did this through Christ's death in the body so that he might bring you into God's presence as people who are holy, with no wrong, and with nothing of which God can judge you guilty. This will happen if you continue strong and sure in your faith. You must not be moved away from the hope brought to you by the Good News that you heard. That same Good News has been told to everyone in the world, and I, Paul, help in preaching that Good News (Col. 1:21–23).

It seems like people are always dividing up. Teams, clubs, cliques, or groups. With everyone taking sides, there are a lot of ways you can be left out. Your grades might keep you from the Honor Society or your first-choice college. Lack of skill keeps you off the basketball team. Your friends plan a party and forget to call you. Being left out will happen for all kinds of reasons for the rest of your life. But Jesus promises that, one day in heaven, he will call your name, and you will never be left out again. You won't have to watch while everyone else has all the fun. You won't have to congratulate everyone else on their great accomplishments. Because of Christ, you will be made perfect enough to stand with him—holy, sinless, and free from the guilt of your sin. You'll be first-team, first-pick, forever included with Jesus and all the saints of heaven.

SEE FOR YOURSELF:

2 Cor. 3:4; Eph. 1:4; Heb. 6:19; 7:25

God's holy people. 27God decided to let his
people know this rich and glorious secret
which he has for all people. This secret is
Christ himself, who is in you. He is our only
hope for glory. 28So we continue to preach
Christ to each person, using all wisdom to
warn and to teach everyone, in order to bring
each one into God's presence as a mature person in Christ. 29To do this, I work and struggle,
using Christ's great strength that works so
powerfully in me.

2 1I want you to know how hard I work for
you, those in Laodicea, and others who have
never seen me. 2I want them to be strengthened and joined together with love so that they
may be rich in their understanding. This leads
to their knowing fully God's secret, that is,
Christ himself. 3In him all the treasures of wisdom and knowledge are safely kept.
4I say this so that no one can fool you by
arguments that seem good, but are false.
5Though I am absent from you in my body,
my heart is with you, and I am happy to see
your good lives and your strong faith in Christ.

CONTINUE TO LIVE IN CHRIST

6As you received Christ Jesus the Lord, so
continue to live in him. 7Keep your roots deep
in him and have your lives built on him. Be
strong in the faith, just as you were taught, and
always be thankful.
8Be sure that no one leads you away with
false and empty teaching that is only human,
which comes from the ruling spirits of this
world, and not from Christ. 9All of God lives in
Christ fully (even when Christ was on earth),
10and you have a full and true life in Christ,
who is ruler over all rulers and powers.
11Also in Christ you had a different kind of
circumcision, a circumcision not done by
hands. It was through Christ's circumcision,
that is, his death, that you were made free from
the power of your sinful self. 12When you were
baptized, you were buried with Christ, and
you were raised up with him through your
faith in God's power that was shown when he

WHAT'S IT MEAN?

Built on the banks of the Lycus River in what is today Turkey, Laodicea was known for its wealth in New Testament times. Other passages in the Bible seem to suggest that the Christians in Laodicea had lost their enthusiasm for and commitment to the things of God.

Colossians 2:1

Promise

HE PROMISES TO CANCEL THE DEBT AGAINST YOU.

God made you alive with Christ, and he forgave all our sins. He canceled the debt, which listed all the rules we failed to follow (Col. 2:13b–14a).

We think we're pretty slick with our big-screen TVs and surround-sound systems. But wonder what God's got in store for the day of judgment, when every person who's ever lived has to stand before him and give account of their lives?

This is just a wild guess—highly unproven—but can't you just imagine some gigantic movie screen, out in the middle of this huge mass of people, playing surveillance camera footage of their secret sins, their bad thoughts, their evil intentions—right there in front of their mamas and everybody?

If that scenario is even remotely true, what do you think would be on your tape? The time you let your sister's pet mouse loose? The day you got mad and told your dad you hated him—and thought something worse?

If you've asked Christ into your heart, your own personal private showing will have been somehow, mysteriously erased . . . deleted from memory by a nail-scarred hand.

SEE FOR YOURSELF:

Is. 43:25; Rom. 3:24

raised Christ from the dead. [13]When you were
spiritually dead because of your sins and because you were not free from the power of
your sinful self, God made you alive with
Christ, and he forgave all our sins. [14]He canceled the debt, which listed all the rules we
failed to follow. He took away that record with
its rules and nailed it to the cross. [15]God
stripped the spiritual rulers and powers of
their authority. With the cross, he won the victory and showed the world that they were
powerless.

WHAT'S IT MEAN?

In the days of the Roman Empire, any time a Roman general returned home after a successful military campaign, he was honored with a special ceremony called a triumph. A parade was thrown in his honor, with the general leading the way in his chariot and prisoners of war following along behind it. Those prisoners were then divided into two groups: those who would be executed and those who would become slaves of the Roman Empire.

Colossians 2:15

DON'T FOLLOW PEOPLE'S RULES

[16]So do not let anyone make rules for you
about eating and drinking or about a religious
feast, a New Moon Festival, or a Sabbath day.
[17]These things were like a shadow of what was
to come. But what is true and real has come
and is found in Christ. [18]Do not let anyone disqualify you by making you humiliate yourself
and worship angels. Such people enter into visions, which fill them with foolish pride because of their human way of thinking. [19]They
do not hold tightly to Christ, the head. It is
from him that all the parts of the body are
cared for and held together. So it grows in the
way God wants it to grow.
[20]Since you died with Christ and were made
free from the ruling spirits of the world, why
do you act as if you still belong to this world
by following rules like these: [21]"Don't eat this,"
"Don't taste that," "Don't even touch that
thing"? [22]These rules refer to earthly things that
are gone as soon as they are used. They are
only man-made commands and teachings.
[23]They seem to be wise, but they are only part
of a man-made religion. They make people
pretend not to be proud and make them punish their bodies, but they do not really control
the evil desires of the sinful self.

On the Edge

Since you were raised from the dead with Christ, aim at what is in heaven, where Christ is sitting at the right hand of God (Col. 3:1).

Paul says that because you have a new life in Christ, you are to set your heart and mind on what is in heaven. He isn't saying that you should lose your sense of reality because your head is always somewhere else, but that life in this world will be better if it is lived with the power that comes from heaven. You will handle success, failure, and disappointment with maturity and poise when you have an eternal perspective. An eternal perspective means that you look at today's events in light of eternity.

Does today's "crisis" have any bearing on eternity? Will it matter when you get to heaven? Will it even matter in 100 years? Is it worth all the anxiety, worry, and pain?

An eternal perspective lets you give others a lot of grace. You'll be more patient with people and events when you realize that, because of Christ, some things are not a big deal. Since you have been raised to life with Christ, then think about things with a heavenly mind-set. Let the truth of eternity guide your decisions and reactions about the world.

SEE FOR YOURSELF:
Ps. 110:1; Gal. 2:20

YOUR NEW LIFE IN CHRIST

3 [1]Since you were raised from the dead with
Christ, aim at what is in heaven, where Christ
is sitting at the right hand of God. [2]Think only
about the things in heaven, not the things on
earth. [3]Your old sinful self has died, and your
new life is kept with Christ in God. [4]Christ is
our life, and when he comes again, you will
share in his glory.
[5]So put all evil things out of your life: sexual
sinning, doing evil, letting evil thoughts control
you, wanting things that are evil, and greed.
This is really serving a false god. [6]These things

make God angry.[n] 7In your past, evil life you also did these things.

8But now also put these things out of your life: anger, bad temper, doing or saying things to hurt others, and using evil words when you talk. 9Do not lie to each other. You have left your old sinful life and the things you did before. 10You have begun to live the new life, in which you are being made new and are becoming like the One who made you. This new life brings you the true knowledge of God. 11In the new life there is no difference between Greeks and Jews, those who are circumcised and those who are not circumcised, or people who are foreigners, or Scythians.[n] There is no difference between slaves and free people. But Christ is in all believers, and Christ is all that is important.

12God has chosen you and made you his holy people. He loves you. So always do these things: Show mercy to others, be kind, humble, gentle, and patient. 13Get along with each other, and forgive each other. If someone does wrong to you, forgive that person because the Lord forgave you. 14Do all these things; but most important, love each other. Love is what holds you all together in perfect unity. 15Let the peace that Christ gives control your thinking, because you were all called together in one body[n] to have peace. Always be thankful. 16Let the teaching of Christ live in you richly. Use all wisdom to teach and instruct each other by singing psalms, hymns, and spiritual songs with thankfulness in your hearts to God. 17Everything you do or say should be done to obey Jesus your Lord. And in all you do, give thanks to God the Father through Jesus.

YOUR NEW LIFE WITH OTHER PEOPLE

18Wives, yield to the authority of your husbands, because this is the right thing to do in the Lord.

19Husbands, love your wives and be gentle with them.

20Children, obey your parents in all things, because this pleases the Lord.

21Fathers, do not nag your children. If you are too hard to please, they may want to stop trying.

22Slaves, obey your masters in all things. Do not obey just when they are watching you, to gain their favor, but serve them honestly, because you respect the Lord. 23In all the work you are doing, work the best you can. Work as if you were doing it for the Lord, not for

WHAT'S IT MEAN?

A large segment of the Roman population—anywhere from one-fourth to one-half—was made up of slaves. Slaves in New Testament times had very few rights. Some were treated worse than animals. The only way a slave could become a free person was to buy his freedom.

Colossians 3:22

MUSIC

Why should we make music? (3:16)

On the Edge

Children, obey your parents in all things, because this pleases the Lord (Col. 3:20).

In his wisdom, the Lord has put people in places of authority over you. When you are a student, the Lord calls you to obey your parents, your teachers, coaches, and leaders at your church. Even as an adult you will still be under the rule of government, and called to submit to the leadership of church elders. God works out his will in your life through the authority that he has allowed. By obeying your parents or other leaders, you are obeying God. God says that it pleases him when you obey your parents. So even when you disagree with them, or feel frustrated, remember that obedience to them is a gift that you are giving to God.

SEE FOR YOURSELF:
Prov. 15:21, 31;
Rom. 13:5–7;
Eph. 6:1–13

3:6 These . . . angry Some Greek copies add: "against the people who do not obey God."
3:11 Scythians The Scythians were known as very wild and cruel people. **3:15 body** The spiritual body of Christ, meaning the church or his people.

people. 24Remember that you will receive your
reward from the Lord, which he promised to
his people. You are serving the Lord Christ.
25But remember that anyone who does wrong
will be punished for that wrong, and the Lord
treats everyone the same.
4 1Masters, give what is good and fair to your
slaves. Remember that you have a Master in
heaven.

WHAT THE CHRISTIANS ARE TO DO

2Continue praying, keeping alert, and always thanking God. 3Also pray for us that God
will give us an opportunity to tell people his
message. Pray that we can preach the secret
that God has made known about Christ. This
is why I am in prison. 4Pray that I can speak in
a way that will make it clear, as I should.
5Be wise in the way you act with people
who are not believers, making
the most of every opportunity. 6When you talk, you
should always be kind and
pleasant so you will be able to
answer everyone in the way
you should.

WITNESSING

What does our speech reflect? (4:6)

NEWS ABOUT THE PEOPLE WITH PAUL

7Tychicus is my dear brother in Christ and a
faithful minister and servant with me in the
Lord. He will tell you all the things that are
happening to me. 8This is why I am sending
him: so you may know how we are and he
may encourage you. 9I send him with Onesimus, a faithful and dear brother in Christ, and
one of your group. They will tell you all that
has happened here.
10Aristarchus, a prisoner with me, and
Mark, the cousin of Barnabas, greet you. (I
have already told you what to do about Mark.
If he comes, welcome him.) 11Jesus, who is
called Justus, also greets you. These are the
only Jewish believers who work with me for
the kingdom of God, and they have been a
comfort to me.
12Epaphras, a servant of Jesus Christ, from
your group, also greets you. He always prays for
you that you will grow to be spiritually mature
and have everything God wants for you. 13I
know he has worked hard for you and the people in Laodicea and in Hierapolis. 14Demas and
our dear friend Luke, the doctor, greet you.

On the Edge

Continue praying, keeping alert, and always thanking God (Col. 4:2).

What is prayer? Prayer is simply communication with God—just talking and listening to him. You see, prayer moves the hand of God, and the hand of God moves the world! He wants us to come to him in prayer. There's not a right or wrong way to pray. All you have to do is talk to God like you would with your best friend.

A lot of people have the idea that prayer is only talking to God. That's only half of it. You really can't communicate with someone without another important activity—listening. Prayer is a two-way street. Not only does God want you to talk to him; he also wants to talk to you. How can God talk to you? Through his Word.

Try it right now. Whatever need you have, go to God in prayer, and then pick this Bible back up and let God speak to you from his Word. But don't just get in a habit of praying when you're in a bind. God wants you to be in continual prayer, talking to him throughout the day. Start every day with a quiet time—moments that are reserved for you and God. Prayer can only happen when the two of you are spending time together. If you were to only talk to a close friend once in a while, what would happen? Your friendship wouldn't be that close. If we expect our relationship with Christ to be strong, we must never stop praying. Kick it up a notch today!

SEE FOR YOURSELF:
Matt. 21:22; 26:41; John 15:7; Rom. 12:12; 1 Thess. 5:17

WHAT'S IT MEAN?

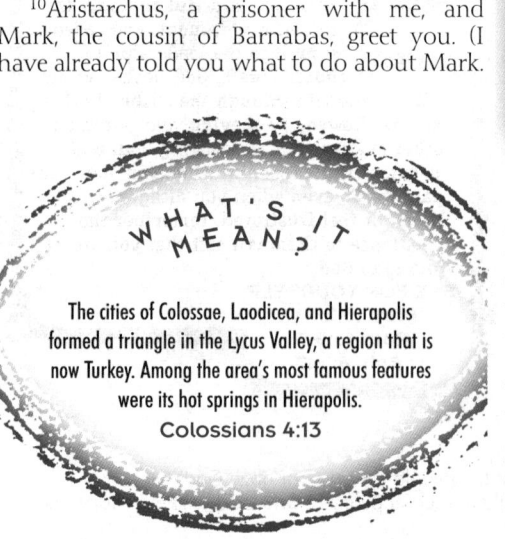

The cities of Colossae, Laodicea, and Hierapolis formed a triangle in the Lycus Valley, a region that is now Turkey. Among the area's most famous features were its hot springs in Hierapolis.
Colossians 4:13

[15]Greet the brothers in Laodicea. And greet
Nympha and the church that meets in her
house. [16]After this letter is read to you, be sure
it is also read to the church in Laodicea. And
you read the letter that I wrote to Laodicea.
[17]Tell Archippus, "Be sure to finish the work the
Lord gave you."

[18]I, Paul, greet you and write this with my
own hand. Remember me in prison. Grace be
with you.

1 Thessalonians

CONTENT

If there's one thing you can say about the church at Thessalonica, it's that they had a lot of questions about Jesus' second coming. For one thing, they wanted to know what would happen to the people who had already died when Christ returns. Paul wrote 1 Thessalonians, in part, to answer this specific question.

Because the people of Thessalonica had so many questions, we know a lot more about what will happen when Christ returns. Did you know he'll return in the sky? Did you know that the people who have already died will meet him first? Did you know that there will be a shout and a trumpet?

Some of the most famous verses about Christ's second coming are found in 1 Thessalonians. It's a message of hope, particularly if you've lost someone you love in death. This book tells us, "Don't worry, death isn't the end of everything. You'll see them again."

Outline

1:1–3 .... Greetings
1:4—3:13 .... The Thessalonians' Faith and Example
4:1–12 .... Live to Please God Even More
4:13—5:11 .... What to Expect When the Lord Returns
5:12–28 .... Final Instructions and Greetings

Purpose

Live godly lives while waiting for Jesus to return.

Theme

The Twin Comforts of Past Ministry and the Future Return of the Lord

Date of writing

A.D. 51

"May the Lord make your love grow more and multiply for each other and for all people so that you will love others as we love you. May your hearts be made strong so that you will be holy and without fault before our God and Father when our Lord Jesus comes with all his holy ones" (3:12–13).

Bible Talk

Waiting and Watching

Jesus really could come back during your lifetime. Many of the prophecies of the Old and New Testament have come true just in the last century. Whether he does or doesn't return while you are alive, live your life so that you are ready to go to heaven at any moment.

It's okay to think that maybe you would like to grow up first or pass some other mile marker in your life. God gave us this life to enjoy. The point is that we keep our lives as clear of sin as possible and continue to grow in our relationship with God. If we do that, then when Christ returns, we will be ready.

JESUS COMES TO EARTH

People have been looking forward to Jesus' coming to earth since the beginning of time. Even in the garden of Eden God promised Someone would come eventually and take care of that evil snake that got Adam and Eve into a pickle. In Old Testament times, people were waiting for Christ's *first* trip to earth.

Since Jesus died and went to heaven, though, we have been waiting for his next trip to earth. In the first trip, he came as a Servant to die for our sins. At the next trip, he'll come as a triumphant King who will change life as we know it.

W are not a lot different from people back in Bible days. We are still waiting for God's promise to be revealed. Jesus is coming!

[1]From Paul, Silas, and Timothy.
To the church in Thessalonica, the church
in God the Father and the Lord Jesus Christ:
Grace and peace to you.

THE FAITH OF THE THESSALONIANS

[2]We always thank God for all of you and
mention you when we pray. [3]We continually
recall before God our Father the things you
have done because of your faith and the work
you have done because of your love. And we
thank him that you continue to be strong because of your hope in our Lord Jesus Christ.
[4]Brothers and sisters,[n] God loves
you, and we know he has
chosen you, [5]because the
Good News we brought to
you came not only with
words, but with power, with
the Holy Spirit, and with sure
knowledge that it is true. Also
you know how we lived
when we were with you in order
to help you. [6]And you became like us and like
the Lord. You suffered much, but still you accepted the teaching with the joy that comes
from the Holy Spirit. [7]So you became an example to all the believers in Macedonia and
Southern Greece. [8]And the Lord's teaching
spread from you not only into Macedonia and
Southern Greece, but now your faith in God
has become known everywhere. So we do
not need to say anything about it. [9]People

GOOD NEWS
How does believing in the Good News affect a person? (1:4–5)

WHAT'S IT MEAN?

If you're trying to keep track of Paul's journeys, here's what you need to know. Thessalonica was the capital of Macedonia, a region in the north of what is now Greece. Speaking of Greece, in Paul's day its southern part was known as Achaia. The city of Athens was located in Achaia. Paul visited Thessalonica and Athens on his second missionary journey.
1 Thessalonians 1:7

1:4 Brothers and sisters Although the Greek text says "Brothers" here and throughout this book, Paul's words were meant for the entire church, including men and women.

Promise HE PROMISES TO SAVE US FROM GOD'S ANGRY JUDGMENT.

People everywhere are telling . . . how you stopped worshiping idols and began serving the living and true God. And you wait for God's Son, whom God raised from the dead, to come from heaven. He is Jesus, who saves us from God's angry judgment that is sure to come (1 Thess. 1:9–10).

The return of Jesus is an incredible source of hope for all believers! We have hope for many reasons, but the one Paul mentions here is that Jesus will save us from God's angry judgment.

God is love and he loves all people and wants them to be saved (see 1 John 4:8–10). But the day will come when God will pour out his anger on those who have not believed. The great white throne judgment will be a specific time of anger (see Rev. 20:11–15), and the great tribulation (see Rev. 6—19) will be another. The anger of God is also poured out on earth, where unbelievers live without the Holy Spirit and without the power and presence of God. Their lives have fallen under the power of Satan.

As a Christian, you can rest in the promise that Jesus saves you from God's anger over sinful human rebellion. You will be kept from it because you are covered with the blood of Jesus. That is, because Jesus is the Lord of your life and you have accepted his work on the cross, God's anger is satisfied. Thank Jesus today for sparing you from God's anger on the day of judgment.

SEE FOR YOURSELF:
John 3:36; Rom. 1:18; 1 John 4:8–10; Rev. 6—19; 20:11–15

everywhere are telling about the way you accepted us when we were there with you. They tell how you stopped worshiping idols and began serving the living and true God. 10And you wait for God's Son, whom God raised from the dead, to come from heaven. He is Jesus, who saves us from God's angry judgment that is sure to come.

WHAT'S IT MEAN?

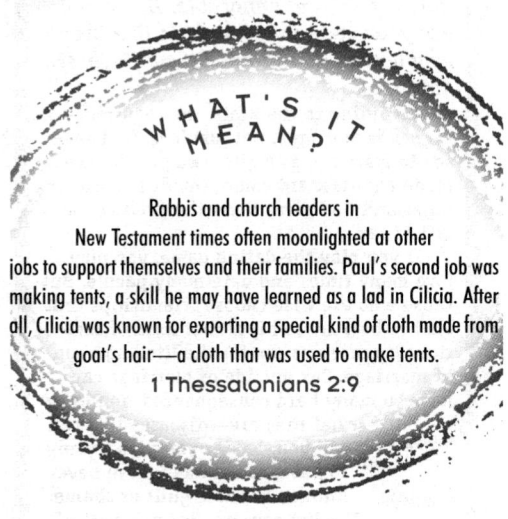

Rabbis and church leaders in New Testament times often moonlighted at other jobs to support themselves and their families. Paul's second job was making tents, a skill he may have learned as a lad in Cilicia. After all, Cilicia was known for exporting a special kind of cloth made from goat's hair—a cloth that was used to make tents.

1 Thessalonians 2:9

PAUL'S WORK IN THESSALONICA

2 1Brothers and sisters, you know our visit to you was not a failure. 2Before we came to you, we suffered in Philippi. People there insulted us, as you know, and many people were against us. But our God helped us to be brave and to tell you his Good News. 3Our appeal does not come from lies or wrong reasons, nor were we trying to trick you. 4But we speak the Good News because God tested us and trusted us to do it. When we speak, we are not trying to please people, but God, who tests our hearts. 5You know that we never tried to influence you by saying nice things about you. We were not trying to get your money; we had no selfishness to hide from you. God knows that this is true. 6We were not looking for human praise, from you or anyone else, 7even though as apostles of Christ we could have used our authority over you.

But we were very gentle with you, like a mother caring for her little children. 8Because we loved you, we were happy to share not only God's Good News with you, but even our own lives. You had become so dear to us! 9Brothers and sisters, I know you remember our hard work and difficulties. We worked night and day so we would not burden any of you while we preached God's Good News to you.

10When we were with you, we lived in a holy and honest way, without fault. You know this is true, and so does God. 11You know that we treated each of you as a father treats his own children. 12We encouraged you, we urged you, and we insisted that you live good lives for God, who calls you to his glorious kingdom.

13Also, we always thank God because when you heard his message from us, you accepted it as the word of God, not the words of humans. And it really is God's message which works in you who believe. 14Brothers and sisters, your experiences have been like those of God's churches in Christ that are in Judea.[n] You suffered from the people of your own country, as they suffered from the Jews, 15who killed both the Lord Jesus and the prophets and forced us to leave that country. They do not please God and are against all people. 16They try to stop us from teaching those who are not Jews so they may be saved. By doing this, they are increasing their sins to the limit. The anger of God has come to them at last.

PAUL WANTS TO VISIT THEM AGAIN

17Brothers and sisters, though we were separated from you for a short time, our thoughts were still with you. We wanted very much to see you and tried hard to do so. 18We wanted to come to you. I, Paul, tried to come more than once, but Satan stopped us. 19You are our hope, our joy, and the crown we will take pride in when our Lord Jesus Christ comes. 20Truly you are our glory and our joy.

WHAT'S IT MEAN?

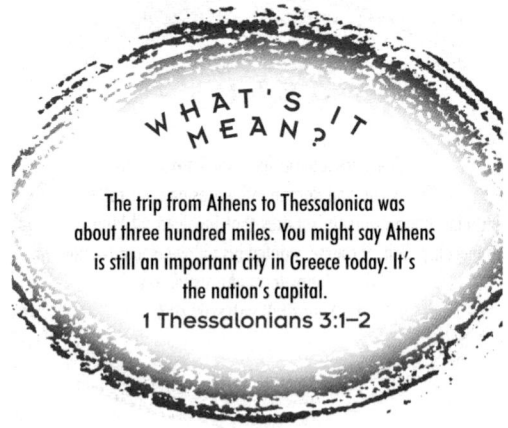

The trip from Athens to Thessalonica was about three hundred miles. You might say Athens is still an important city in Greece today. It's the nation's capital.

1 Thessalonians 3:1–2

2:14 Judea The Jewish land where Jesus lived and taught and where the church first began.

3 1When we could not wait any longer, we
decided it was best to stay in Athens alone
2and send Timothy to you. Timothy, our
brother, works with us for God and helps us
tell people the Good News about Christ. We
sent him to strengthen and encourage you in
your faith 3so none of you would be upset by
these troubles. You yourselves know that we
must face these troubles. 4Even when we were
with you, we told you we all would have to
suffer, and you know it has happened. 5Be-
cause of this, when I could wait no longer, I
sent Timothy to you so I could learn about
your faith. I was afraid the devil had tempted
you, and then our hard work would have been
wasted.

6But Timothy now has come back to us
from you and has brought us good news
about your faith and love. He told us that you
always remember us in a good way and that
you want to see us just as much as we want to
see you. 7So, brothers and sisters, while we
have much trouble and suffering, we are encouraged about you because of your faith.
8Our life is really full if you stand strong in the
Lord. 9We have so much joy before our God
because of you. We cannot thank him enough
for all the joy we feel. 10Night and day we continue praying with all our heart that we can see
you again and give you all the things you need
to make your faith strong.

11Now may our God and Father himself
and our Lord Jesus prepare the way for us to
come to you. 12May the Lord make your love
grow more and multiply for each other and for
all people so that you will love others as we
love you. 13May your hearts be made strong so
that you will be holy and without fault before
our God and Father when our Lord Jesus
comes with all his holy ones.

On the Edge

He wants each of you to learn to control your own body in a way that is holy and honorable. Don't use your body for sexual sin like the people who do not know God (1 Thess. 4:4–5).

According to the Bible, the requirement for sex is *marriage*, not just love. God gave sex to marriage as a gift. Two people have made a permanent commitment to each other and God gives them the privilege and gift of sex.

If you play the dating game, you may love many times and date many people. But those who are wise choose friendships that lead to holy courtships. That kind of relationship reserves sex for the lifelong bond of marriage. Sex outside of marriage can have so many hard consequences. You know what they are—diseases that can kill you, babies you aren't ready to have, stress like you've never known, horrible guilt or shame. The list goes on. Sex as a part of marriage is good and blessed.

Don't have sex with the person you're dating because dating is not marriage. There is no commitment. There is no blessing from God. The consequences could be damaging and even deadly. God's advice is perfect and it's perfectly right and good for you. Take his advice and wait. You'll be so glad you did.

SEE FOR YOURSELF:
1 Cor. 6:18;
1 Thess. 4:3

WHAT'S IT MEAN?

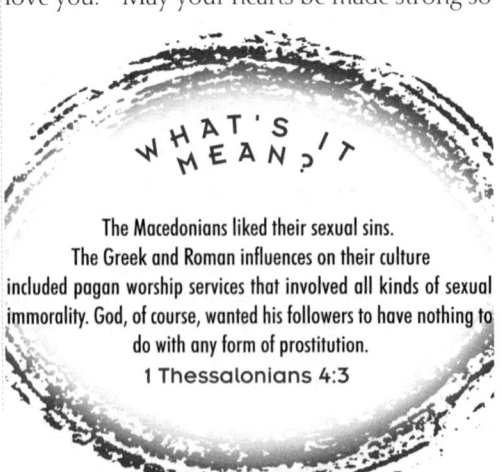

The Macedonians liked their sexual sins. The Greek and Roman influences on their culture included pagan worship services that involved all kinds of sexual immorality. God, of course, wanted his followers to have nothing to do with any form of prostitution.

1 Thessalonians 4:3

A LIFE THAT PLEASES GOD

4 1Brothers and sisters, we taught you how to
live in a way that will please God, and you are
living that way. Now we ask and encourage
you in the Lord Jesus to live that way even
more. 2You know what we told you to do by
the authority of the Lord Jesus. 3God wants
you to be holy and to stay away from sexual
sins. 4He wants each of you to learn to control
your own body[n] in a way that is holy and
honorable. 5Don't use your body for sexual sin

4:4 learn . . . body This might also mean "learn to live with your own wife."

like the people who do not know God. [6]Also,
do not wrong or cheat another Christian in
this way. The Lord will punish people who do
those things as we have already told you and
warned you. [7]God called us to be holy and
does not want us to live in sin. [8]So the person
who refuses to obey this teaching is disobeying God, not simply a human teaching. And
God is the One who gives us his Holy Spirit.
[9]We do not need to write you about having
love for your Christian family, because God
has already taught you to love each other.
[10]And truly you do love the Christians in all of
Macedonia. Brothers and sisters, now we encourage you to love them even more.
[11]Do all you can to live a peaceful life. Take
care of your own business, and do your own
work as we have already told you. [12]If you do,
then people who are not believers will respect
you, and you will not have to depend on others for what you need.

THE LORD'S COMING

[13]Brothers and sisters, we want you to
know about those Christians who have died so
you will not be sad, as others who
have no hope. [14]We believe
that Jesus died and that he
rose again. So, because of
him, God will raise with Jesus
those who have died. [15]What
we tell you now is the Lord's
own message. We who are
living when the Lord comes
again will not go before those
who have already died. [16]The Lord himself will
come down from heaven with a loud command, with the voice of the archangel,[n] and
with the trumpet call of God. And those who
have died believing in Christ will rise first.
[17]After that, we who are still alive will be gathered up with them in the clouds to meet the
Lord in the air. And we will be with the Lord
forever. [18]So encourage each other with these
words.

PAIN

How should Christians treat each other in times of pain? (4:13–18)

BE READY FOR THE LORD'S COMING

5
[1]Now, brothers and sisters, we do not need
to write you about times and dates. [2]You know
very well that the day the Lord comes again
will be a surprise, like a thief that comes in the
night. [3]While people are saying, "We have
peace and we are safe," they will be destroyed
quickly. It is like pains that come quickly to a
woman having a baby. Those people will not

On the Edge

You are all people who belong to the light and to the day. We do not belong to the night or to darkness (1 Thess. 5:5).

Are you more concerned about someone stealing your car or breaking into your house during the day or at night? Something like that can happen anytime, but you're on the lookout for it more at night. People looking to do something illegal are prone to choose night because the darkness hides their actions. In the daytime they're more likely to get caught.

In John 3, Jesus told Nicodemus that some people didn't like the light because they didn't want their evil deeds exposed (see John 3:20). But Paul says because you're a Christian, you can have a different attitude. You belong to the light. You don't mind if people know what's going on with you. Your life can be an open book because your conscience is clean. Even your mistakes and failures don't have to embarrass you because you know that Jesus has taken care of all that. Belonging to the light gives you incredible freedom!

SEE FOR YOURSELF:
Matt. 5:14–16;
John 12:36;
Eph. 5:8

WHAT'S IT MEAN?

The protective gear that Roman soldiers wore wasn't like the suits of armor you see in medieval castles. Roman armor did not cover the soldier's entire body. Instead, the soldier wore pieces of metal or thick leather to protect his most vital organs. Roman helmets came in all shapes. Some covered the entire head, with a screen covering the face that allowed the warrior to breathe and see clearly.

1 Thessalonians 5:8

4:16 archangel The leader among God's angels or messengers.

escape. 4But you, brothers and sisters, are not
living in darkness, and so that day will not
surprise you like a thief. 5You are all people
who belong to the light and to the day. We do
not belong to the night or to darkness. 6So we should not be like
other people who are sleeping, but we should be alert
and have self-control.
7Those who sleep, sleep at
night. Those who get
drunk, get drunk at night.
8But we belong to the day,
so we should control our-
selves. We should wear faith
and love to protect us, and
the hope of salvation should be
our helmet. 9God did not choose
us to suffer his anger but to have salvation
through our Lord Jesus Christ. 10Jesus died for
us so that we can live together with him,
whether we are alive or dead when he comes.
11So encourage each other and give each other
strength, just as you are doing now.

"Always be joyful. Pray continually, and give thanks whatever happens. That is what God wants for you in Christ Jesus." (1 Thessalonians 5:16–18)

FINAL INSTRUCTIONS AND GREETINGS

LAZINESS
Who should we encourage to work? (5:12–14)

12Now, brothers and sisters,
we ask you to appreciate
those who work hard among
you, who lead you in the Lord
and teach you. 13Respect them
with a very special love because of the work they do.
Live in peace with each other. 14We ask you,
brothers and sisters, to warn those who do not
work. Encourage the people who are afraid.
Help those who are weak. Be patient with
everyone. 15Be sure that no
one pays back wrong for
wrong, but always try to do
what is good for each other
and for all people.
16Always be joyful.
17Pray continually, 18and
give thanks whatever hap-
pens. That is what God
wants for you in Christ
Jesus.
19Do not hold back the
work of the Holy Spirit. 20Do
not treat prophecy as if it were
unimportant. 21But test everything. Keep what
is good, 22and stay away from everything that
is evil.
23Now may God himself, the God of peace,
make you pure, belonging only to him. May
your whole self—spirit, soul, and body—be
kept safe and without fault when our Lord
Jesus Christ comes. 24You can trust the One
who calls you to do that for you.
25Brothers and sisters, pray for us.
26Give each other a holy kiss when you
meet. 27I tell you by the authority of the Lord
to read this letter to all the believers.
28The grace of our Lord Jesus Christ be
with you.

2 Thessalonians

CONTENT The church at Thessalonica took what Paul said to heart. In fact, some of them maybe took it too much to heart.

In Paul's first letter to this church, he had written that they needed to live their lives in anticipation of Christ's return. Later, he found out that some of them had responded to this by quitting their jobs and literally just *hanging out* waiting for Christ to come back.

These people who were hanging out began to do what anyone does when they hang out too much: They got bored, which led to gossiping, which led to nit-picking, which led to arguing, which led to the same church problems it always leads to.

Paul wrote his second letter to this church to remind them that waiting for Christ's return is a way of living. It *is not* standing in the yard all day and looking at the sky. It *is* living holy lives and connecting with God every day.

Outline

1:1–2 .... Greetings
1:3–12 .... The Lord's Return Will Bring Justice
2:1–12 .... The Lord Has Not Returned Yet
2:13–17 .... Stand Fast
3:1–15 .... Pray and Work
3:16–18 .... A Final Prayer

Purpose Until Jesus does return, live disciplined, godly lives.

Theme The Return of the Lord—Advance Indicators and Lifestyle in the Meanwhile

Date of writing A.D. 51

"May the Lord lead your hearts into God's love and Christ's patience. Brothers and sisters, by the authority of our Lord Jesus Christ we command you to stay away from any believer who refuses to work and does not follow the teaching we gave you" (3:5–6).

Bible Talk

Gossip in the Church

Gossip can seem very harmless when you are sitting with your friend, laughing at someone else and talking about them. At first, it doesn't seem like it will hurt anyone. Of course, there's always the chance that the person you are gossiping about will hear you or hear about what you said; but if you're careful, that won't happen, will it?

Maybe not, but that's not really the point. When we gossip about each other, we disrespect each other. We forget that we are all a part of the body of Christ. When we disrespect someone, we become like a cancer destroying the very body that we are a part of. It is a big deal. That's why Paul made a big deal about it.

ANY EARTHLY GOOD

Have you ever heard that expression about being too heavenly minded to be any earthly good? When someone says that, they are usually talking about someone who has faith, but it's not a practical faith that makes a difference in the everyday details of life. That's also sort of what Paul was writing about in his second letter to the church at Thessalonica.

The people in Thessalonica were doing something that *sounded* good. They were looking for Christ's return. But they forgot that, while Christ's return is important, it isn't the *only* thing God told us to do. He also told us to do good deeds in this life and to be kind to other people. He told us to make a living and to spend time with family.

Be careful whenever you find yourself obeying one of God's commands without thinking about all the other ones.

1

1From Paul, Silas, and Timothy.
To the church in Thessalonica in God our
Father and the Lord Jesus Christ:
2Grace and peace to you from God the Father and the Lord Jesus Christ.

PAUL TALKS ABOUT GOD'S JUDGMENT

3We must always thank God for you,
brothers and sisters.[n] This is only right, because your faith is growing more and more,
and the love that every one of you has for each
other is increasing. 4So we brag about you to
the other churches of God. We tell them about
the way you continue to be strong and have
faith even though you are being treated badly
and are suffering many troubles.
5This is proof that God is right in his judgment. He wants you to be counted worthy of
his kingdom for which you are suffering. 6God
will do what is right. He will give trouble to
those who trouble you. 7And he will give rest
to you who are troubled and to us also when
the Lord Jesus appears with burning fire from
heaven with his powerful angels. 8Then he will
punish those who do not know God and who
do not obey the Good News about our Lord
Jesus Christ. 9Those people will be punished
with a destruction that continues forever. They
will be kept away from the Lord and from his
great power. 10This will happen on the day
when the Lord Jesus comes to receive glory because of his holy people. And all the people
who have believed will be amazed at Jesus. You
will be in that group, because you believed
what we told you.
11That is why we always pray for you, asking our God to help you live the kind of life he
called you to live. We pray that with his power
God will help you do the good things you

WHAT'S IT MEAN?

Paul was in the middle of a very busy missionary journey when he wrote this second letter to the church in Thessalonica. Apparently, Paul was writing from Corinth, where he was staying after preaching in Athens, Berea, and Thessalonica. Silas and Timothy are mentioned because they were with Paul when he started the church in Thessalonica.

2 Thessalonians 1:1

1:3 brothers and sisters Although the Greek text says "brothers" here and throughout this book, Paul's words were meant for the entire church, including men and women.

Promise

HE PROMISES TO GIVE YOU REST FROM YOUR TROUBLES.

God will do what is right. He will give trouble to those who trouble you. And he will give rest to you who are troubled and to us also when the Lord Jesus appears with burning fire from heaven with his powerful angels. Then he will punish those who do not know God and who do not obey the Good News about our Lord Jesus Christ (2 Thess. 1:6–8).

Been laughed at lately? Taken any jabs for being a Christian? Been made fun of because you did the right thing? Take heart, because relief is on its way. When Jesus comes, he promises to give you rest from your troubles. You won't have to fight anymore. Jesus will take over with his powerful angels and a flaming fire. He will take care of your enemies and all who would persecute you. Sometimes the battle is bigger than you are. The trouble seems overwhelming. Be courageous enough to know which battles belong to the Lord, and leave them for him to fight.

SEE FOR YOURSELF:

Jer. 29:11; 31:13; Lam. 3:22–23; Eph. 3:14–19

want and perform the works that come from
your faith. [12]We pray all this so that the name
of our Lord Jesus Christ will have glory in you,
and you will have glory in him. That glory
comes from the grace of our God and the Lord
Jesus Christ.

EVIL THINGS WILL HAPPEN

2 [1]Brothers and sisters, we have something to
say about the coming of our Lord Jesus Christ
and the time when we will meet together with
him. [2]Do not become easily upset in your
thinking or afraid if you hear that the day of
the Lord has already come. Someone may say
this in a prophecy or in a message or in a letter
as if it came from us. [3]Do not let anyone fool
you in any way. That day of the Lord will not
come until the turning away[n] from God happens and the Man of Evil, who is on his way to
hell, appears. [4]He will be against and put himself above anything called God or anything
that people worship. And that Man of Evil will
even go into God's Temple and sit there and
say that he is God.

WHAT'S IT MEAN?

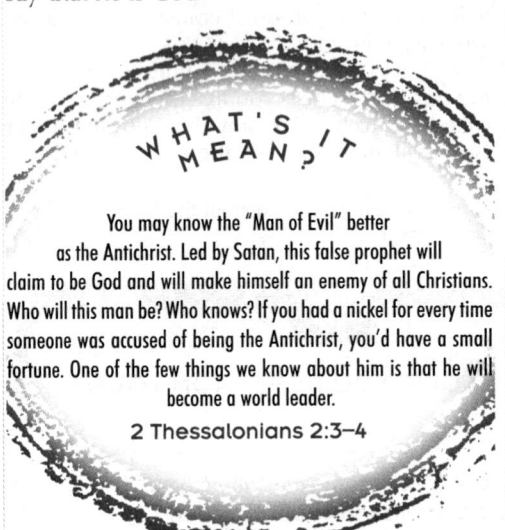

You may know the "Man of Evil" better as the Antichrist. Led by Satan, this false prophet will claim to be God and will make himself an enemy of all Christians. Who will this man be? Who knows? If you had a nickel for every time someone was accused of being the Antichrist, you'd have a small fortune. One of the few things we know about him is that he will become a world leader.

2 Thessalonians 2:3–4

On the Edge

Brothers and sisters, whom the Lord loves, God chose you from the beginning to be saved. So we must always thank God for you. You are saved by the Spirit that makes you holy and by your faith in the truth (2 Thess. 2:13).

When you gave your heart to Jesus, you became a new person—"a new creation" (see 2 Cor. 5:17). The old you disappeared, and you were transformed from darkness to light—from death to life! Now God wants you to be changed into his likeness, and he has equipped you to do this by his Spirit. The Holy Spirit puts in you the desire not to sin—not just the desire, but also the ability. Sin doesn't have authority over you anymore. You are free! We all need to submit ourselves to God, by remaining set apart for him. As you begin to do this, it will become easier to walk in his will.

Walking in God's will is nothing more than walking in obedience to him and to his Word. That's when the true blessings of God will begin to flow in your life. When Paul writes you are chosen to be "saved by the Spirit that makes you holy," he is telling you that the Holy Spirit has given you the power to live a holy life. In fact, Titus 2:12 says grace "teaches us not to live against God nor to do the evil things the world wants to do. Instead, that grace teaches us to live now in a wise and right way and in a way that shows we serve God." You have the power to walk in holiness—not only power to get free, but power to stay free. He is the One who makes you holy!

SEE FOR YOURSELF:
Rom. 12:1–2;
2 Cor. 5:17

[5]I told you when I was with you that all this
would happen. Do you not remember? [6]And
now you know what is stopping that Man of
Evil so he will appear at the right time. [7]The
secret power of evil is already working in the
world, but there is one who is stopping that
power. And he will continue to stop it until he
is taken out of the way. [8]Then that Man of Evil
will appear, and the Lord Jesus will kill him
with the breath that comes from his mouth
and will destroy him with the glory of his
coming. [9]The Man of Evil will come by the
power of Satan. He will have great power, and
he will do many different false miracles, signs,
and wonders. [10]He will use every kind of evil
to trick those who are lost. They will die, because they refused to love the truth. (If they
loved the truth, they would be saved.) [11]For
this reason God sends them something powerful that leads them away from the truth so they

2:3 turning away Or "the rebellion."

will believe a lie. 12So all those will be judged
guilty who did not believe the truth, but enjoyed doing evil.

YOU ARE CHOSEN FOR SALVATION

13Brothers and sisters, whom the Lord loves,
God chose you from the beginning to be
saved. So we must always thank God for you.
You are saved by the Spirit that makes you
holy and by your faith in the truth. 14God used
the Good News that we preached to call you to
be saved so you can share in the glory of our
Lord Jesus Christ. 15So, brothers and sisters,
stand strong and continue to believe the teachings we gave you in our speaking and in our
letter.
16-17May our Lord Jesus Christ himself and
God our Father encourage you and strengthen
you in every good thing you do and say. God
loved us, and through his grace he gave us a
good hope and encouragement that continues
forever.

WHAT'S IT MEAN?

Apparently, some impostors had been sending out letters full of false teachings and then signing Paul's name to them. To make sure that the people in Thessalonica knew this was a genuine letter, Paul signed his name to it. You may be wondering why Paul only signed it, as opposed to writing the letter himself. Some Bible experts believe that Paul suffered from an eye disease that made it necessary for him to use a secretary to write the letters he dictated.

2 Thessalonians 3:17

PRAY FOR US

3 1And now, brothers and sisters, pray for us
that the Lord's teaching will continue to spread
quickly and that people will give honor to
that teaching, just as happened with you. 2And
pray that we will be protected from stubborn and evil people, because not all people
believe.
3But the Lord is faithful and will give you
strength and will protect you from the Evil
One. 4The Lord makes us feel sure that you are
doing and will continue to do the things we
told you. 5May the Lord lead your hearts into
God's love and Christ's patience.

On the Edge

But you, brothers and sisters, never become tired of doing good (2 Thess. 3:13).

"So why have I kept my heart pure? Why have I kept my hands from doing wrong?" (Ps. 73:13). Can you relate to this person's frustration? You tell the truth, even when it costs you, because you trust God to reward you for it. You help other people to try to make their lives better. Those are good reasons, but sometimes you just don't see those things happening. It's enough to make you want to give up.

Paul says you *must not* give up. How can you keep from getting tired of doing the right thing when it seems like it's getting you nowhere? Well, it takes some faith. You have to believe that God's going to do what he promised he would—even when his timetable is different from yours (and it usually is). You also have to continually fill up with God's Spirit. If you don't do that, you're like a car that's about to run out of gas. He keeps you going—you can't do it yourself.

Finally, you have to have your priorities straight. Ask yourself: Am I doing this to get results or am I doing it to please God? The answer makes all the difference.

SEE FOR YOURSELF:
Gal. 6:9

THE DUTY TO WORK

6Brothers and sisters, by the authority of
our Lord Jesus Christ we command you to stay
away from any believer who refuses to work
and does not follow the teaching we
gave you. 7You yourselves know
that you should live as we live.
We were not lazy when we
were with you. 8And when
we ate another person's food,
we always paid for it. We
worked very hard night and
day so we would not be an
expense to any of you. 9We
had the right to ask you to help
us, but we worked to take care of
ourselves so we would be an example for you
to follow. 10When we were with you, we gave

LAZINESS

Should lazy people be allowed to take advantage of other people? (3:10)

you this rule: "Anyone who refuses to work should not eat."

[11]We hear that some people in your group refuse to work. They do nothing but busy themselves in other people's lives. [12]We command those people and beg them in the Lord Jesus Christ to work quietly and earn their own food. [13]But you, brothers and sisters, never become tired of doing good.

[14]If some people do not obey what we tell you in this letter, then take note of them. Have nothing to do with them so they will feel ashamed. [15]But do not treat them as enemies. Warn them as fellow believers.

FINAL WORDS

[16]Now may the Lord of peace give you peace at all times and in every way. The Lord be with all of you.

[17]I, Paul, end this letter now in my own handwriting. All my letters have this to show they are from me. This is the way I write.

[18]The grace of our Lord Jesus Christ be with you all.

1 Timothy

CONTENT Have you ever gotten a letter or an e-mail from someone older who is really important to you? How do you read it? Do you skip over parts or maybe not even finish? Probably not. Probably you read every word and maybe even read some of them twice.

That might have been how it was for Timothy when he got letters from Paul. Timothy was like a son to Paul. Paul loved him and took him on trips and talked to him about things that mattered. Paul really invested in Timothy's life.

Timothy had a lot to learn. Paul had a lot to teach. We get to read a lot of truth because of that. God used their relationship to teach us about following Christ and being the church.

Outline

1:1–2 .... Greetings
1:3—3:13 .... Instructions for Church Life
3:14—4:10.......... Be Faithful to Your Calling
4:11—6:21.......... Paul's Advice to Timothy

Purpose Young adults have a significant role to play in Christ's church.

Themes Removal of False Doctrine, Preservation of Public Worship, and Proper Leadership in the Church

Date of writing Fall A.D. 62

"Fight the good fight of faith, grabbing hold of the life that continues forever. You were called to have that life when you confessed the good confession before many witnesses" (6:12).

Bible Talk

What Kind of Leader Leads a Church?

Paul wrote to Timothy about the kind of people who should be leading the church. We still depend on Paul's requirements for leadership today. It's not that the leaders of the church are any better than anyone else in the church, but they do have more responsibilities than other church members.

Paul said that the leaders of the church should be respected and have self-control. He also said they should be good family members and family leaders. How do you think the leaders in your church measure up? How do you think you'll measure up as a church leader?

WHEN YOU ARE YOUNG

One of the neat things about Paul's letter to Timothy was that Paul was writing to a young person. When you read about the people God used in the Bible, a lot of times those people are old people. Some of them are having babies even when they are too old to have babies. Some of them are teaching and preaching.

Paul's letters to Timothy remind us that God uses people of all ages. He can use us no matter how old or young we are, as long as we are willing to have faith and love others.

Timothy

1

1From Paul, an apostle of Christ Jesus, by
the command of God our Savior and Christ
Jesus our hope.
2To Timothy, a true child to me because you
believe:

Grace, mercy, and peace
from God the Father and
Christ Jesus our Lord.

MERCY
Is Jesus merciful? (1:2)

WARNING AGAINST FALSE TEACHING

3I asked you to stay longer
in Ephesus when I went into Macedonia so
you could command some people there to
stop teaching false things. 4Tell them not to
spend their time on stories that are not true
and on long lists of names in family histories.
These things only bring arguments; they do
not help God's work, which is done in faith.
5The purpose of this command is for people to
have love, a love that comes from a pure heart
and a good conscience and a true faith. 6Some
people have missed these things and turned to
useless talk. 7They want to be teachers of the
law, but they do not understand either what
they are talking about or what they are sure
about.

WHAT'S IT MEAN?

How much do you know about your family tree? Do you know the name of your great-grandfather? How about your great-great-grandfather? Do you have any famous ancestors? The Jewish leaders of New Testament times could have answered these questions with no problem. Apparently, they took great pride in being able trace their ancestors all the way back to Abraham. We're talking about genealogies that stretched back over two thousand years!

1 Timothy 1:4

8But we know that the law is good if someone uses it lawfully. 9We also know that the
law is not made for good people but for those
who are against the law and for those who
refuse to follow it. It is for people who are
against God and are sinful, who are not holy
and have no religion, who kill their fathers and
mothers, who murder, 10who take part in sexual sins, who have sexual relations with people
of the same sex, who sell slaves, who tell lies,
who speak falsely, and who do anything
against the true teaching of God. 11That teaching is part of the Good News of the blessed
God that he gave me to tell.

On the Edge

So, I want the men everywhere to pray, lifting up their hands in a holy manner, without anger and arguments (1 Tim. 2:8).

Your best friend tells you she'll call tonight at 8:00. You wait around the house most of the evening, because you care about your friend and you'd love to talk to her. The time goes by so quickly when you two are on the phone. You wait and wait but she never calls. At school, she promises again to call the next night. Still nothing. This goes on for a week and you become incredibly disappointed. You had hoped that your friend would want to spend time with you. She eventually calls a few weeks later, apologizing that she's had too much going on, but really needs you to help her do something.

You love your friend so you forgive her and help her out. The Lord is waiting for those who love him to pray to him. We shove our time with him under the pile of everything else, eventually running back when we need him. He loves us and so he waits, but he hopes for more. He is happy when people pray.

SEE FOR YOURSELF:
Ps. 134; Prov. 15:8; Eph. 6:18

THANKS FOR GOD'S MERCY

12I thank Christ Jesus our Lord, who gave
me strength, because he trusted me and gave
me this work of serving him. 13In the past I
spoke against Christ and persecuted him and
did all kinds of things to hurt him. But God
showed me mercy, because I did not know
what I was doing. I did not believe. 14But the
grace of our Lord was fully given to me, and
with that grace came the faith and love that are
in Christ Jesus.
15What I say is true, and you should fully
accept it: Christ Jesus came into the world to
save sinners, of whom I am the worst. 16But I
was given mercy so that in me, the worst of all

sinners, Christ Jesus could show that he has
patience without limit. His patience with me
made me an example for those who would believe in him and have life forever. 17To the King
that rules forever, who will never die, who
cannot be seen, the only God, be honor and
glory forever and ever. Amen.
18Timothy, my child, I am giving you a
command that agrees with the prophecies that
were given about you in the past. I tell you this
so you can follow them and fight the good
fight. 19Continue to have faith and do what
you know is right. Some people have rejected
this, and their faith has been shipwrecked.
20Hymenaeus and Alexander have done that,
and I have given them to Satan so they will
learn not to speak against God.

SOME RULES FOR MEN AND WOMEN

2
1First, I tell you to pray for all people, asking
God for what they need and being thankful to
him. 2Pray for rulers and for all who have authority so that we can have quiet and peaceful
lives full of worship and respect for God. 3This
is good, and it pleases God our Savior, 4who
wants all people to be saved and to know the
truth. 5There is one God and one way human
beings can reach God. That way is through Christ
Jesus, who is himself human. 6He gave himself
as a payment to free all people. He is proof that
came at the right time. 7That is why I was chosen to tell the Good News and to be an apostle. (I
am telling the truth; I am not lying.) I was chosen
to teach those who are not Jews to believe and to
know the truth.
8So, I want the men everywhere to pray, lifting up their hands in a holy manner, without
anger and arguments.
9Also, women should wear proper clothes
that show respect and self-control, not using
braided hair or gold or pearls or expensive
clothes. 10Instead, they should do good deeds,
which is right for women who say they worship God.
11Let a woman learn by listening quietly and
being ready to cooperate in everything. 12But
I do not allow a woman to teach or to have
authority over a man, but to listen quietly,
13because Adam was formed first and then
Eve. 14And Adam was not tricked, but the
woman was tricked and became a sinner. 15But
she will be saved through having children if
they continue in faith, love, and holiness, with
self-control.

WHAT'S IT MEAN?

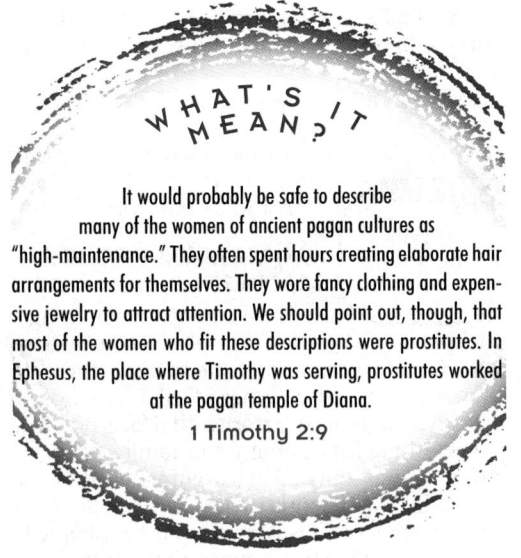

It would probably be safe to describe many of the women of ancient pagan cultures as "high-maintenance." They often spent hours creating elaborate hair arrangements for themselves. They wore fancy clothing and expensive jewelry to attract attention. We should point out, though, that most of the women who fit these descriptions were prostitutes. In Ephesus, the place where Timothy was serving, prostitutes worked at the pagan temple of Diana.

1 Timothy 2:9

ELDERS IN THE CHURCH

3
1What I say is true: Anyone wanting to become an elder desires a good work. 2An elder
must not give people a reason to criticize him,
and he must have only one wife. He must be
self-controlled, wise, respected by others,
ready to welcome guests, and able to teach. 3He
must not drink too much wine or like to fight,
but rather be gentle and peaceable, not loving
money. 4He must be a good family leader, having children who cooperate with full respect.
5(If someone does not know how to lead the
family, how can that person take care of God's
church?) 6But an elder must not be a new believer, or he might be too proud of himself and
be judged guilty just as the devil was. 7An elder
must also have the respect of people who are
not in the church so he will not be criticized by
others and caught in the devil's trap.

DEACONS IN THE CHURCH

8In the same way, deacons must be respected by others, not saying things they do not
mean. They must not drink too much wine or
try to get rich by cheating others. 9With a clear
conscience they must follow the secret of the
faith that God made known to us. 10Test them
first. Then let them serve as deacons if you find
nothing wrong in them. 11In the same way,
women[n] must be respected by others. They
must not speak evil of others. They must be
self-controlled and trustworthy in everything.
12Deacons must have only one wife and be

3:11 women This might mean the wives of the deacons, or it might mean women who serve in the same way as deacons.

good leaders of their children and their own families. [13]Those who serve well as deacons are making an honorable place for themselves, and they will be very bold in their faith in Christ Jesus.

THE SECRET OF OUR LIFE

[14]Although I hope I can come to you soon, I am writing these things to you now. [15]Then, even if I am delayed, you will know how to live in the family of God. That family is the church of the living God, the support and foundation of the truth. [16]Without doubt, the secret of our life of worship is great:

He was shown to us in a human body,
proved right in spirit,
and seen by angels.
He was preached to those who are not Jews,
believed in by the world,
and taken up in glory.

"[God] was shown to us in a human body." (1 Timothy 3:16b)

A WARNING ABOUT FALSE TEACHERS

4 [1]Now the Holy Spirit clearly says that in the later times some people will stop believing the faith. They will follow spirits that lie and teachings of demons. [2]Such teachings come from the false words of liars whose consciences are destroyed as if by a hot iron. [3]They forbid people to marry and tell them not to eat certain foods which God created to be eaten with thanks by people who believe and know the truth. [4]Everything God made is good, and nothing should be refused if it is accepted with thanks, [5]because it is made holy by what God has said and by prayer.

SATAN
Who does Satan work through? (4:1–2)

BE A GOOD SERVANT OF CHRIST

[6]By telling these things to the brothers and sisters,[n] you will be a good servant of Christ Jesus. You will be made strong by the words of the faith and the good teaching which you have been following. [7]But do not follow foolish stories that disagree with God's truth, but train yourself to serve God. [8]Training your body helps you in some ways, but serving God helps you in every way by bringing you blessings in this life and in the future life, too. [9]What I say is true, and you should fully accept it. [10]This is why we work and struggle: We hope in the living God who is the Savior of all people, especially of those who believe.

[11]Command and teach these things. [12]Do not let anyone treat you as if you are unimportant because you are young. Instead, be an example to the believers with your words, your actions, your love, your faith, and your pure life. [13]Until I come, continue to read the Scriptures to the people, strengthen them, and teach them. [14]Use the

On the Edge

Do not let anyone treat you as if you are unimportant because you are young. Instead, be an example to the believers with your words, your actions, your love, your faith, and your pure life (1 Tim. 4:12).

If you've never given your parents reason to distrust you, they probably trust you more than you know. It's everyone else they worry about. Really. If you've broken your parents' trust and want to restore it, read Proverbs 23:22–25. Look at the things that make parents proud: truth, wisdom, self-control, and understanding. Developing these qualities in your life will help you learn to set a good example—for your parents and for other people. Begin to work on these areas of your life and, though it may take some time, watch your parents' doubt turn to trust. You don't have to transform overnight, just work on one thing at a time. For instance, if you say you'll be home at midnight, be there. Rolling in at 12:10 with a lame excuse doesn't make you trustworthy. After you get the "on-time thing" down, start working on something else.

Even though they're the parents and you're the child, you can still set an example for them. You can still earn their respect. They're watching you more closely than you think!

SEE FOR YOURSELF: Prov. 23:22–25

4:6 brothers and sisters Although the Greek text says "brothers" here and throughout this book, Paul's words refer to the entire church, including men and women.

WHAT'S IT MEAN?

Based on Paul's words in this verse, how old do you suppose Timothy was? Obviously, people weren't taking him seriously because they thought he was too young to know anything important. Do you suppose he was twenty-one? Eighteen? Younger? Actually, Timothy could have been in his thirties! In Bible times, people under forty were considered too young to have gained true wisdom.

1 Timothy 4:12

gift you have, which was given to you through
prophecy when the group of elders laid their
hands on[n] you. [15]Continue to do those things;
give your life to doing them so your progress
may be seen by everyone. [16]Be careful in your
life and in your teaching. If you continue to
live and teach rightly, you will save both yourself and those who listen to you.

RULES FOR LIVING WITH OTHERS

5 [1]Do not speak angrily to an older man, but
plead with him as if he were your father. Treat
younger men like brothers, [2]older women like
mothers, and younger women like sisters. Always treat them in a pure way.
[3]Take care of widows who are truly wid-

WHAT'S IT MEAN?

If you think it was Paul's idea for Christians to help widows, orphans, and others in need, think again. He was merely repeating the command that God had given to Moses centuries earlier. A widow usually lived with her husband's family or with one of her children. However, if she had no family to live with, the church was responsible for taking care of her.

1 Timothy 5:3

On the Edge

But if a widow has children or grandchildren, let them first learn to do their duty to their own family and to repay their parents or grandparents. That pleases God (1 Tim. 5:4).

The most wonderful thing you can give your grandparents is your time. That shows them that they are important to you. They are already so proud of you. They would love to get to know you better, to be seen with you, to be listened to by you. Making time for your grandparents lets them know that you appreciate all the sacrifices they've made and all the love they have shown. One of the best ways you can honor them is to ask questions and learn from them. Senior adults complain that one of the hardest things about growing older is not feeling useful anymore. Let your grandparents know that they are still needed, they are valuable, and they are greatly loved. You hold such a tender place in their hearts—your grandparents will consider their time with you a treasure.

SEE FOR YOURSELF:
Lev. 19:32; Prov. 17:6

ows. [4]But if a widow has children or grandchildren, let them first learn to do their duty
to their own family and to repay their parents
or grandparents. That pleases God. [5]The true
widow, who is all alone, puts her hope in God
and continues to pray night and day for God's
help. [6]But the widow who uses her life to
please herself is really dead while she is alive.
[7]Tell the believers to do these things so that no
one can criticize them. [8]Whoever does not care
for his own relatives, especially his own family
members, has turned against the faith and
is worse than someone who does not believe
in God.
[9]To be on the list of widows, a woman must
be at least sixty years old. She must have been
faithful to her husband. [10]She must be known
for her good works—works such as raising her
children, welcoming strangers, washing the feet
of God's people, helping those in trouble, and
giving her life to do all kinds of good deeds.

4:14 laid their hands on The laying on of hands had many purposes, including the giving of a blessing, power, or authority.

11But do not put younger widows on that
list. After they give themselves to Christ, they
are pulled away from him by their physical
needs, and then they want to marry again.
12They will be judged for not doing what they
first promised to do. 13Besides that, they learn
to waste their time, going from house to house.
And they not only waste their time but also
begin to gossip and busy themselves with
other people's lives, saying things they should
not say. 14So I want the younger widows to
marry, have children, and manage their homes.
Then no enemy will have any reason to criticize them. 15But some have already turned
away to follow Satan.
16If any woman who is a believer has widows in her family, she should care for them
herself. The church should not have to care for
them. Then it will be able to take care of those
who are truly widows.
17The elders who lead the church well
should receive double honor, especially those
who work hard by speaking and teaching,
18because the Scripture says: "When an ox is
working in the grain, do not cover its mouth to
keep it from eating,"[n] and "A worker should be
given his pay."[n]
19Do not listen to someone who accuses an
elder, without two or three witnesses. 20Tell
those who continue sinning that they are
wrong. Do this in front of the whole church so
that the others will have a warning.
21Before God and Christ Jesus and the chosen angels, I command you to do these things
without showing favor of any kind to anyone.

On the Edge

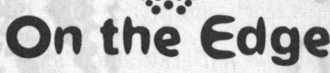

Serving God does make us very rich, if we are satisfied with what we have (1 Tim. 6:6).

Becoming a Christian doesn't mean you have to be poor for the rest of your life. Nor does it mean that the bright red sports car you've been dreaming of will appear in your driveway if you give all your money to the church. Christianity does make you rich, Paul says, by teaching you to look at things in a new way. The reason that a relationship with Jesus makes you content with what you have is that the more you get to know him, the less your stuff matters. It's fine to enjoy driving a sports car or wearing nice clothes, but what makes you truly, deeply happy is really knowing Jesus and being a part of what he is doing in the world around you. Get preoccupied with his plan for you.

If that isn't you right now, don't give up. Repent. Go after God with everything you've got. Tell him, "I'm sorry I settled for the stuff of this world and for superficial happiness." Determine to make his work your passion. Use your energy building his kingdom and you won't even notice what kind of stuff you have or don't have because, then, you will be content.

SEE FOR YOURSELF: Phil. 4:11; Heb. 13:5

WHAT'S IT MEAN?

Can you imagine being told to drink wine for a stomachache? In New Testament times, before antibiotics or other medicines were developed, wine was used as the cure-all. If you had wounds that needed healing, you poured wine on them. If you needed a sedative or painkiller, you drank wine.

1 Timothy 5:23

22Think carefully before you lay your hands
on[n] anyone, and don't share in the sins of others. Keep yourself pure.
23Stop drinking only water, but drink a little
wine to help your stomach and your frequent
sicknesses.
24The sins of some people are easy to see
even before they are judged, but the sins of
others are seen only later. 25So also good deeds
are easy to see, but even those that are not easily seen cannot stay hidden.
6 1All who are slaves under a yoke should
show full respect to their masters so no one
will speak against God's name and our teaching. 2The slaves whose masters are believers
should not show their masters any less respect

5:18 "When . . . eating." Quotation from Deuteronomy 25:4. **5:18 "A worker . . . pay."** Quotation from Luke 10:7. **5:22 lay your hands on** The laying on of hands had many purposes, including the giving of a blessing, power, or authority.

because they are believers. They should serve
their masters even better, because they are
helping believers they love.
You must teach and preach these things.

FALSE TEACHING AND TRUE RICHES

3Anyone who has a different teaching does
not agree with the true teaching of our Lord
Jesus Christ and the teaching that shows the
true way to serve God. 4This person is full of
pride and understands nothing, but is sick with
a love for arguing and fighting about words.
This brings jealousy, fighting, speaking against
others, evil mistrust, 5and constant quarrels
from those who have evil minds and have lost
the truth. They think that serving God is a way
to get rich.
6Serving God does make us very rich, if we
are satisfied with what we have. 7We brought
nothing into the world, so we can take nothing
out. 8But, if we have food and clothes, we will
be satisfied with that. 9Those who want to become rich bring temptation to themselves and
are caught in a trap. They want many foolish
and harmful things that ruin and destroy people. 10The love of money causes all kinds of
evil. Some people have left the faith, because
they wanted to get more money, but they have
caused themselves much sorrow.

SOME THINGS TO REMEMBER

11But you, man of God, run away from all
those things. Instead, live in the right way, serve
God, have faith, love, patience, and gentleness.
12Fight the good fight of faith, grabbing hold of
the life that continues forever. You were called
to have that life when you confessed the good
confession before many witnesses. 13In the
sight of God, who gives life to everything, and
of Christ Jesus, I give you a command. Christ
Jesus made the good confession when he
stood before Pontius Pilate. 14Do what you
were commanded to do without wrong or
blame until our Lord Jesus Christ comes again.
15God will make that happen at the right time.
He is the blessed and only Ruler, the King of all
kings and the Lord of all lords. 16He is the only
One who never dies. He lives in light so bright
no one can go near it. No one has ever seen
God, or can see him. May honor and power
belong to God forever. Amen.

WHAT'S IT MEAN?

Pontius Pilate was the governor of Judea, the site of Jesus' trial. As the highest authority in the land, Pilate had the power to sentence criminals to death. After questioning Jesus, though, Pilate declared him innocent of all charges. That didn't sit well with the crowd that had gathered outside. Fearing that the Jewish leaders would incite a revolt, Pilate went along with their plan and allowed Jesus to be executed.

1 Timothy 6:13

17Command those who are rich with things
of this world not to be proud. Tell them to
hope in God, not in their uncertain riches. God
richly gives us everything to enjoy. 18Tell the
rich people to do good, to be rich in doing
good deeds, to be generous and ready to share.
19By doing that, they will be saving a treasure
for themselves as a strong foundation for the
future. Then they will be able to have the life
that is true life.
20Timothy, guard what God has trusted to
you. Stay away from foolish, useless talk and
from the arguments of what is falsely called
"knowledge." 21By saying they have that
"knowledge," some have missed the true faith.
Grace be with you.

2 Timothy

CONTENT Even as important as Paul was to Timothy on a regular day, this last letter must have been particularly important. Paul was in jail when he wrote. This second letter was the last thing Paul wrote before he died.

Wow. It's pretty amazing that we can read Paul's final words to somebody he loved so much. Remember to hang on every word, just like Timothy probably did when he read this letter the first time. Remember to not just read, but to understand. Remember to ask yourself, *What should I do about this?* And then do it.

That's what Timothy did. He became a leader and put into practice all the things Paul and his mom and his grandmom had taught him. When he did that, he not only pleased God; he also honored the people who taught him about God.

Outline

1:1–2 .... Greetings and Prayer for Timothy
1:3–18 .... Do Not Be Ashamed of the Lord
2:1–26 .... How to Be a Good Soldier of Jesus Christ
3:1–9 .... Perilous Times Are Coming
3:10—4:8 .... Keep Being Faithful
4:9–22 .... Personal Instructions and Final Greetings

Purpose Commitment to Scripture and holy living is essential.

Theme The Commitment to Ministry

Date of writing Fall A.D. 67

"Share in the troubles we have like a good soldier of Christ Jesus" (2:3).

Bible Talk

Who are your mentors?

Timothy had three important influences in his life (that we know of). One was his grandmother. Her name was Lois. Another was his mom, Eunice. The third was Paul.

As you grow up, it becomes more and more important to be independent and to do things your own way. That doesn't mean you don't need mentors, though. Everyone needs help getting through life. Everyone needs to hear from someone wiser sometimes.

Think about who can be mentors to you. Visit with them. Ask them questions. Trust them to help you make good decisions. Be somebody's Timothy and let somebody be your Paul.

PAUL, AS A JAILBIRD

Paul was in jail several times in his life. He wrote more than one book of the Bible while he was in jail. It seems like Paul would have been discouraged sitting in jail for doing something good: sharing the Good News. Paul had an understanding, though, that helped him not be discouraged.

Paul believed that God was in control of his life. So if he was in jail, he figured that God must need him there. He looked for opportunities to serve God while he was in prison. One of those ways was to write the letters that are now part of the New Testament.

Sort of gives you a new perspective on accepting where you are in life, doesn't it?

1 1From Paul, an apostle of Christ Jesus by the
will of God. God sent me to tell about the
promise of life that is in Christ Jesus.
2To Timothy, a dear child to me:
Grace, mercy, and peace to you from God
the Father and Christ Jesus our Lord.

ENCOURAGEMENT FOR TIMOTHY

3I thank God as I always mention you in
my prayers, day and night. I serve him, doing
what I know is right as my ancestors did. 4Re-
membering that you cried for me, I want very
much to see you so I can be filled with joy. 5I
remember your true faith. That faith first lived
in your grandmother Lois and in your mother
Eunice, and I know you now have that same
faith. 6This is why I remind you to keep using
the gift God gave you when I laid my hands
on[n] you. Now let it grow, as a small flame
grows into a fire. 7God did not give us a spirit
that makes us afraid but a spirit of power and
love and self-control.

8So do not be ashamed to tell people about
our Lord Jesus, and do not be ashamed of me,
in prison for the Lord. But suffer with me for
the Good News. God, who gives us the
strength to do that, 9saved us and made us his
holy people. That was not because of anything
we did ourselves but because of God's purpose
and grace. That grace was given to us through
Christ Jesus before time began, 10but it is now
shown to us by the coming of our Savior
Christ Jesus. He destroyed death, and through
the Good News he showed us the way to have
life that cannot be destroyed. 11I was chosen to
tell that Good News and to be an
apostle and a teacher. 12I am
suffering now because I tell
the Good News, but I am not
ashamed, because I know
Jesus, the One in whom I have
believed. And I am sure he is
able to protect what he has
trusted me with until that day.[n]
13Follow the pattern of true teachings that you
heard from me in faith and love, which are in
Christ Jesus. 14Protect the truth that you were
given; protect it with the help of the Holy Spirit
who lives in us.

ASSURANCE

Will God ever disappoint his children? (1:12)

On the Edge

God did not give us a spirit that makes us afraid but a spirit of power and love and self-control (2 Tim. 1:7).

The Spirit of God lives in believers. He gives us strength so that we do not have to be afraid anymore. When an adult acts inappropriately toward you, tell the adult, "I am offended by your actions. You have really made me feel uncomfortable and I want you to stop it now!" Then immediately report this person to your parents or to another adult you respect. There are sick adults who choose to mistreat kids because they think kids will be too timid to report them. The Spirit of God gives you power because he lives inside of you. Do not be afraid. Do the right thing and be confident that God will protect you and go before you. Evil must be revealed where you find it or else it will just grow stronger, hurting you and maybe even others.

SEE FOR YOURSELF:
Jer. 15:20; Phil. 4:13

WHAT'S IT MEAN?

Paul wasn't referring to the ancient Chinese or Japanese when he said the people of Asia had rejected him. Asia was the name of a Roman province located in what is now Turkey. At the time Paul wrote this letter, Nero, the Roman emperor, was stepping up his persecution of Christians throughout the empire.

2 Timothy 1:15

15You know that everyone in the country of
Asia has left me, even Phygelus and Hermoge-
nes. 16May the Lord show mercy to the family
of Onesiphorus, who has often helped me and
was not ashamed that I was in prison. 17When
he came to Rome, he looked eagerly for me

1:6 laid my hands on The laying on of hands had many purposes, including the giving of a blessing, power, or authority. **1:12 day** The day Christ will come to judge all people and take his people to live with him.

until he found me. [18]May the Lord allow
him to find mercy from the Lord on that day.
You know how many ways he helped me in
Ephesus.

A LOYAL SOLDIER OF CHRIST JESUS

2 [1]You then, Timothy, my child, be strong in
the grace we have in Christ Jesus. [2]You should
teach people whom you can trust the things
you and many others have heard me say. Then
they will be able to teach others. [3]Share in the
troubles we have like a good soldier of Christ
Jesus. [4]A soldier wants to please the enlisting
officer, so no one serving in the army wastes
time with everyday matters.
[5]Also an athlete who takes
part in a contest must obey
all the rules in order to win.
[6]The farmer who works
hard should be the first
person to get some of the
food that was grown.
[7]Think about what I am
saying, because the Lord
will give you the ability to
understand everything.
[8]Remember Jesus Christ, who
was raised from the dead, who is from the
family of David. This is the Good News I
preach, [9]and I am suffering because of it to the
point of being bound with chains like a criminal. But God's teaching is not in chains. [10]So I
patiently accept all these troubles so that those
whom God has chosen can have the salvation
that is in Christ Jesus. With that salvation
comes glory that never ends.
[11]This teaching is true:

If we died with him, we will also live with
him.
[12]If we accept suffering, we will also rule
with him.
If we refuse to accept him, he will refuse to
accept us.
[13]If we are not faithful, he will still be
faithful,
because he cannot be false to himself.

"If we died with him, we will also live with him. If we accept suffering, we will also rule with him." (2 Timothy 2:11–12a)

WHAT'S IT MEAN?

Many people in Paul's day were sports fans. They would have appreciated and understood his references to athletics. The Isthmian Games, a forerunner to our modern Olympics, were held every two years in the Greek city of Corinth. People came from all around to see these athletic contests.

2 Timothy 2:5

A WORKER PLEASING TO GOD

[14]Continue teaching these things, warning
people in God's presence not to argue about
words. It does not help anyone, and it ruins
those who listen. [15]Make every
effort to give yourself to God
as the kind of person he will
accept. Be a worker who is
not ashamed and who uses
the true teaching in the
right way. [16]Stay away from
foolish, useless talk, because that will lead people
further away from God.
[17]Their evil teaching will
spread like a sickness inside
the body. Hymenaeus and Phile-
tus are like that. [18]They have left the true
teaching, saying that the rising from the dead
has already taken place, and so they are destroying the faith of some people. [19]But God's
strong foundation continues to stand. These
words are written on the seal: "The Lord
knows those who belong to him,"*n* and "Everyone who wants to belong to the Lord must
stop doing wrong."
[20]In a large house there are not only things
made of gold and silver, but also things made of
wood and clay. Some things are used for special
purposes, and others are made for ordinary
jobs. [21]All who make themselves clean from
evil will be used for special purposes. They will
be made holy, useful to the Master, ready to do
any good work.
[22]But run away from the
evil young people like to do.
Try hard to live right and to
have faith, love, and peace, together with those who trust in
the Lord from pure hearts.
[23]Stay away from foolish and
stupid arguments, because you
know they grow into quarrels. [24]And a servant
of the Lord must not quarrel but must be kind
to everyone, a good teacher, and patient. [25]The

TEMPTATION

What should we do when faced with temptation? (2:22)

2:19 "The Lord . . . him" Quotation from Numbers 16:5.

On the Edge

But run away from the evil young people like to do. Try hard to live right and to have faith, love, and peace, together with those who trust in the Lord from pure hearts. Stay away from foolish and stupid arguments, because you know they grow into quarrels (2 Tim. 2:22–23).

Run. Mentally run back to the truths of this passage, "Run away from the evil young people like to do . . . Stay away from foolish and stupid arguments." Ask God to give you the courage to stand up to your friends and question their choices. If they still decide to do something you don't feel right about, then leave. Get out of Dodge. Hit the road. Call somebody. Run if you have to, but physically separate yourself from the temptation of your friends' bad decisions. If you hang around, even if you don't participate, you could become a victim of their circumstances. God is a just God, and eventually there will be consequences. Sometimes we are more afraid of losing friends than we are of the consequences of our sin. The truth is that doing the right thing takes incredible strength and strong people attract lots of friends—maybe even better ones.

SEE FOR YOURSELF:
Matt. 6:33;
Gal. 5:22–25

Lord's servant must gently teach those who
disagree. Then maybe God will let them
change their minds so they can accept the
truth. [26]And they may wake up and escape
from the trap of the devil, who catches them to
do what he wants.

THE LAST DAYS

[1]Remember this! In the last days there will
be many troubles, [2]because people will love
themselves, love money, brag, and be proud.
They will say evil things against others and
will not obey their parents or be thankful or be
the kind of people God wants. [3]They will not
love others, will refuse to forgive, will gossip,
and will not control themselves. They will be
cruel, will hate what is good, [4]will turn against
their friends, and will do foolish things without thinking. They will be conceited, will love

WHAT'S IT MEAN?

If you don't recognize the names of Jannes and Jambres, don't be surprised. They're not mentioned in the Old Testament. According to Jewish tradition, Jannes and Jambres were the names of the Egyptian king's court magicians. When Moses was trying to persuade the king of Egypt to let the Israelites go, he performed a series of miracles to demonstrate God's power. Believe it or not, Jannes and Jambres were actually able to copy some of the miracles. However, when the time came to reverse them, they couldn't do it.

2 Timothy 3:8

pleasure instead of God, [5]and will act as if they
serve God but will not have his power. Stay
away from those people. [6]Some of them go
into homes and get control of silly women
who are full of sin and are led by many evil
desires. [7]These women are always learning
new teachings, but they are never able to understand the truth fully. [8]Just as Jannes and
Jambres were against Moses, these people are
against the truth. Their thinking has been ruined, and they have failed in trying to follow
the faith. [9]But they will not be successful in
what they do, because as with Jannes and Jambres, everyone will see that they are foolish.

WHAT'S IT MEAN?

If you'd like to visit the modern equivalents of Antioch, Iconium, and Lystra, head for Turkey. As far as city authorities were concerned, Paul overstayed his welcome in each city he visited. When people began responding to the message Paul preached in Antioch, city officials ran him out of town. His next stop was Iconium. When the people there started converting to Christianity, Paul was forced to leave out of fear for his life. His next stop was Lystra, Timothy's hometown.

2 Timothy 3:11

On the Edge

Since you were a child you have known the Holy Scriptures which are able to make you wise. And that wisdom leads to salvation through faith in Christ Jesus. All Scripture is given by God and is useful for teaching, for showing people what is wrong in their lives, for correcting faults, and for teaching how to live right. Using the Scriptures, the person who serves God will be capable, having all that is needed to do every good work (2 Tim. 3:15–17).

The Bible is an awesome book. It's full of answers and advice and wisdom. It's full of war and deceit and natural disasters and family squabbles. It tells you how to live and be successful, and it tells you what to look out for. It's the richest piece of literature ever written.

But beyond all of that, the Bible is the Word of God. It's the letter that God has personally written to you. God's got some things to say and they're all together in this one incredible book. When Jesus lived on earth, he prayed to God one day and said, "Make them ready for your service through your truth; your teaching is truth" (John 17:17). Are you a follower of Jesus? Then this prayer is for you. Jesus says that God's Word is truth. And what does truth do for you? It makes you free (see John 8:32). The Bible has the power to give you freedom from whatever has got you down—family, school, depression, confusion, guilt, stress, frustration, bad self-image, loneliness, lack of direction, apathy, boredom. You name it. The truth of God's Word can make you free.

The Bible is like a lot of other things. You can't experience it just because it's there. You've got to pick it up and read it. You've got to spend time in it. You've got to get it into your head and into your heart. Of all the stuff you can do in your life, getting serious about God's Word is the very best. Nothing else will make you free.

SEE FOR YOURSELF:
Ps. 119:11, 105; Prov. 30:5; Is. 40:8; John 1:1–18; 8:31–32; 17:17; Heb. 4:12; 1 John 1:1–4

OBEY THE TEACHINGS

10But you have followed what I teach, the
way I live, my goal, faith, patience, and love.
You know I never give up. 11You know how I
have been hurt and have suffered, as in Antioch, Iconium, and Lystra. I have suffered, but
the Lord saved me from all those troubles.
12Everyone who wants to live as God desires,
in Christ Jesus, will be hurt. 13But people who
are evil and cheat others will go from bad to
worse. They will fool others, but they will also
be fooling themselves.
14But you should continue following the
teachings you learned. You know they are true,
because you trust those who taught you.
15Since you were a child you have known the
Holy Scriptures which are able to make you
wise. And that wisdom leads to salvation
through faith in Christ Jesus. 16All Scripture is
given by God and is useful for teaching, for
showing people what is wrong in their lives,
for correcting faults, and for teaching how to
live right. 17Using the Scriptures, the person
who serves God will be capable, having all that
is needed to do every good work.

4 1I give you a command in the presence of
God and Christ Jesus, the One who will judge
the living and the dead, and by his coming and
his kingdom: 2Preach the Good News. Be ready
at all times, and tell people what they need to do.
Tell them when they are wrong. Encourage them
with great patience and careful teaching, 3because the time will come when people will not
listen to the true teaching but will find many
more teachers who please them by saying the
things they want to hear. 4They will stop listening to the truth and will begin to follow false
stories. 5But you should control yourself at all
times, accept troubles, do the work of telling
the Good News, and complete all the duties of
a servant of God.
6My life is being given as an offering to
God, and the time has come for me to leave
this life. 7I have fought the good fight, I have
finished the race, I have kept the faith. 8Now, a
crown is being held for me—a crown for being
right with God. The Lord, the judge who judges
rightly, will give the crown to me on that
day[n]—not only to me but to all those who
have waited with love for him to come again.

PERSONAL WORDS

9Do your best to come to me as soon
as you can, 10because Demas, who loved
this world, left me and went to Thessalonica.

4:8 day The day Christ will come to judge all people and take his people to live with him.

WHAT'S IT MEAN?

New Testament documents were written either on papyrus or on long pieces of leather called scrolls. Since scrolls could be twenty-five feet long or more, people discovered that the best way to store them was to roll them around a stick.

2 Timothy 4:13

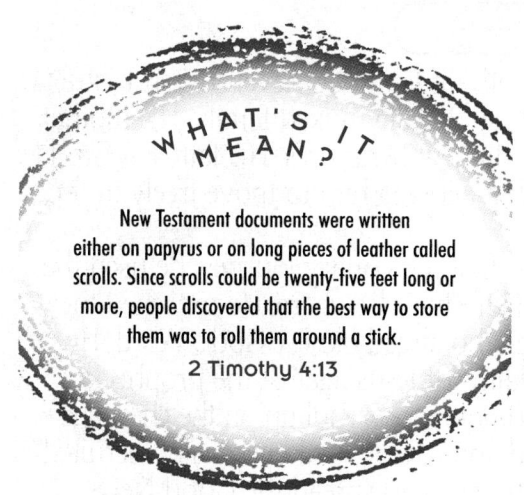

Crescens went to Galatia, and Titus went to
Dalmatia. [11]Luke is the only one still with me.
Get Mark and bring him with you when you
come, because he can help me in my work
here. [12]I sent Tychicus to Ephesus. [13]When I
was in Troas, I left my coat there with Carpus.
So when you come, bring it to me, along with
my books, particularly the ones written on
parchment.[n] [14]Alexander the metalworker did
many harmful things against me. The Lord will
punish him for what he did. [15]You also should
be careful that he does not hurt you, because
he fought strongly against our teaching.

[16]The first time I defended myself, no one
helped me; everyone left me. May they be forgiven. [17]But the Lord stayed with me and gave
me strength so I could fully tell the Good News
to all those who are not Jews. So I was saved
from the lion's mouth. [18]The Lord will save me
when anyone tries to hurt me, and he will
bring me safely to his heavenly kingdom. Glory forever and ever be the Lord's. Amen.

FINAL GREETINGS

[19]Greet Priscilla and Aquila and the family
of Onesiphorus. [20]Erastus stayed in Corinth,
and I left Trophimus sick in Miletus. [21]Try as
hard as you can to come to me before winter.

Eubulus sends greetings to you. Also Pu-
dens, Linus, Claudia, and all the brothers and
sisters in Christ greet you.

[22]The Lord be with your spirit. Grace be
with you.

4:13 parchment A writing paper made from the skins of sheep.

TIMOTHY made a difference

What would have happened to Timothy if Paul had never visited Lystra, his hometown? He had been raised in a racially mixed family. His mother, a Jewess, had taught him the Old Testament Scriptures. His father, a Greek, gave him at least a social position that allowed him to move freely in the Roman world.

When Paul came through on his first missionary journey, he used the approach in Lystra that had proven effective elsewhere. He preached the Good News of Jesus Christ to those who already knew God's Word. He challenged them to check out the claims of Jesus against the prophecies and promises of the Old Testament. Timothy took Paul up on the challenge and became convinced Jesus is Lord and Savior. Paul eventually recruited Timothy as a member of his team, traveling to spread the Good News.

Cutting Edge

Timothy served Paul in various capacities: companion, scribe, and messenger. Although he represented the apostle in places like Thessalonica, Corinth, and Ephesus, he was apparently never comfortable in the spotlight. Paul constantly encouraged Timothy to rely on God for boldness. Paul's other counsel to Timothy indicates that the young follower struggled with youthful temptations (see 2 Tim. 2:22) and the tendency to be ashamed of the Good News (see 2 Tim. 1:8).

Yet, in spite of his youth and weaknesses, Timothy made a difference in Paul's life. Paul wrote of his unique loyalty. He also continues to make a direct difference in lives today as people are influenced by the letters he helped Paul write or find themselves in situations similar to the ones Timothy faced when Paul wrote the two letters to his closest companion.

YOU can, too! Timothy had a powerful model and mentor in his life. Paul may have even been somewhat intimidating to Timothy. You can benefit greatly from the examples and teaching of older Christians. They often know more and they have definitely lived more than you have. Your growth can have some definite positive direction under their influence. Ask God to lead you to other believers who can guide and encourage you. Get familiar with Timothy, too.

Want to know more? Timothy enters the Bible in Acts 16. Several of Paul's letters mention him, and two were addressed to him.

titus

CONTENT Do you know what a "stereotype" is? It is when people in a certain group get a reputation for being a certain way. If you know someone is an athlete, you might assume they'll act like a jock. Or, if you know a girl is a cheerleader, you might assume she'll be really perky.

Titus was the young pastor of the churches on the island of Crete (south of Greece). People from Crete definitely were stereotyped. They were stereotyped as pirates and scoundrels. When most people thought about Crete, they thought of the integrity-challenged. If ever there was a pastor who needed and deserved a letter of instruction from the apostle Paul, it was Titus.

Titus was a Gentile Christian and had been one of Paul's traveling companions. On several occasions he had proven himself to be a good problem solver. Maybe that's why he was given a pastor's job in this particular place.

Understandably, Paul had a lot to say to Titus about the kinds of leadership he should choose for his churches. He also wrote about civil obedience (obeying the law). We might not be as mischievous as Titus's parishioners, but we can still learn a lot from Paul's instructions.

Outline

1:1–4 .... Greetings and a Prayer for Titus
1:5–16 .... Instructions for Church Officials
2:1—3:11 .... Instructions for Church People
3:12–15 .... Personal Advice and Final Greetings

Purpose Grace creates believers whose good works honor God.

Theme Setting the Church at Crete in Order

Date of writing A.D. 64

1

1From Paul, a servant of God and an apostle
of Jesus Christ. I was sent to help the faith of
God's chosen people and to help them know
the truth that shows people how to serve God.
2That faith and that knowledge come from the
hope for life forever, which God promised to
us before time began. And God cannot lie. 3At
the right time God let the world know about
that life through preaching. He trusted me with
that work, and I preached by the command of
God our Savior.

4To Titus, my true child in the faith we
share:

Grace and peace from God the Father and Christ Jesus our Savior.

WHAT'S IT MEAN?

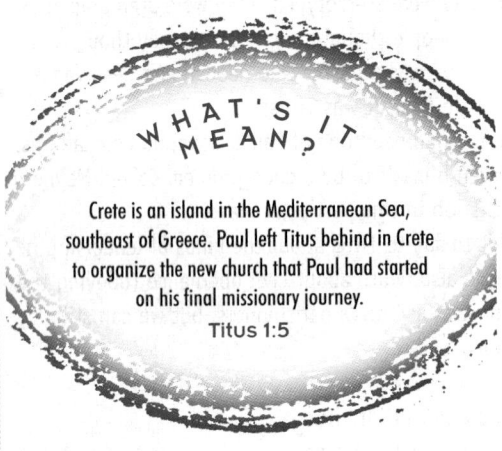

Crete is an island in the Mediterranean Sea, southeast of Greece. Paul left Titus behind in Crete to organize the new church that Paul had started on his final missionary journey.

Titus 1:5

TITUS' WORK IN CRETE

5I left you in Crete so you could finish doing
the things that still needed to be done and so
you could appoint elders in every town, as I
directed you. 6An elder must not be
guilty of doing wrong, must
have only one wife, and must
have believing children. They
must not be known as children who are wild and do not
cooperate. 7As God's manager, an elder must not be guilty
of doing wrong, being selfish,
or becoming angry quickly.
He must not drink too much
wine, like to fight, or try to get rich by cheating
others. 8An elder must be ready to welcome
guests, love what is good, be wise, live right,
and be holy and self-controlled. 9By holding
on to the trustworthy word just as we teach it,
an elder can help people by using true teaching, and he can show those who are against
the true teaching that they are wrong.

CHARACTER

What type of people need to be extra careful to be filled with integrity? (1:7)

10There are many people who refuse to cooperate, who talk about worthless things and
lead others into the wrong way—mainly those
who say all who are not Jews must be circumcised. 11These people must be stopped, because
they are upsetting whole families by teaching
things they should not teach, which they do to
get rich by cheating people. 12Even one of their
own prophets said, "Cretans are always liars,
evil animals, and lazy people who do nothing
but eat." 13The words that prophet said are true.
So firmly tell those people they are wrong so
they may become strong in the faith, 14not accepting Jewish false stories and the commands
of people who reject the truth. 15To those who
are pure, all things are pure, but to those who
are full of sin and do not believe, nothing is
pure. Both their minds and their consciences
have been ruined. 16They say they know God,
but their actions show they do not accept him.
They are hateful people, they refuse to obey,
and they are useless for doing anything good.

FOLLOWING THE TRUE TEACHING

2

1But you must tell everyone what to do to
follow the true teaching. 2Teach older men to
be self-controlled, serious, wise, strong in faith,
in love, and in patience.

3In the same way, teach older women to be
holy in their behavior, not speaking against
others or enslaved to too much wine, but
teaching what is good. 4Then they can teach
the young women to love their husbands, to
love their children, 5to be wise and pure, to be
good workers at home, to be kind, and to yield
to their husbands. Then no one will be able to
criticize the teaching God gave us.

6In the same way, encourage young men to
be wise. 7In every way be an example of doing
good deeds. When you teach, do it with honesty and seriousness. 8Speak the truth so that
you cannot be criticized. Then those who are
against you will be ashamed because there is
nothing bad to say about us.

9Slaves should yield to their own masters at
all times, trying to please them and not arguing
with them. 10They should not steal from them
but should show their masters they can be fully trusted so that in everything they do they
will make the teaching of God our Savior attractive.

11That is the way we should live, because
God's grace that can save everyone has come.
12It teaches us not to live against God nor to do
the evil things the world wants to do. Instead,
that grace teaches us to live now in a wise and
right way and in a way that shows we serve

TITUS made a difference

For one who made such a difference, Titus is, in large part, a mystery to us. He was a Greek believer in Jesus who joined Paul's traveling band of messengers of the Good News. His effectiveness as a representative of Paul is evident from the way the apostle trusted Titus with difficult and important tasks. Titus served as Paul's example of what God could do in the life of a non-Jewish person. When the Jerusalem church debated whether Gentiles could be called true followers of Jesus without first becoming Jewish converts, Paul presented Titus as proof of Gentile believers.

Titus came from a Greek background, and yet his faith in Jesus was undeniable. His character paved the way for other Gentiles to enter the church. The Good News was emphasized as a universal invitation based partly on people like Titus in the early church. Yes, Titus made a difference.

Cutting Edge

Like Timothy, Titus served Paul in official capacities. He was involved in his most difficult assignment, on the island of Crete, when Paul wrote him the letter that bears his name. Titus reminds us that the Good News and the work of the church must be intentionally passed from one generation to another. The process isn't automatic. It is both spiritual and relational. Those who are further along must take responsibility for those who are coming along. Titus received the torch of the Good News and passed it on faithfully. He made a difference.

YOU can, too! Few believers are too young to begin thinking of those who are younger. Adolescent believers can have a powerful influence on their peers and on younger children. Kids will often listen more attentively to a teenager share his or her faith than they will to an adult. Those who are younger offer you opportunities right now to make a difference for Christ. Have you helped with or led a children's Sunday school class? Explore other possibilities with your pastor.

Want to know more? Outside the letter that bears his name, Titus is mentioned in the following places:

2 Corinthians 2:13; 7:6–16; 8:6, 16–24; 12:18; Galatians 2:1–5; 2 Timothy 4:10.

God. 13We should live like that while we wait
for our great hope and the coming of the glory
of our great God and Savior Jesus Christ. 14He
gave himself for us so he might pay the price to
free us from all evil and to make us pure people who belong only to him—people who are
always wanting to do good deeds.
15Say these things and encourage the people
and tell them what is wrong in their lives, with
all authority. Do not let anyone treat you as if
you were unimportant.

THE RIGHT WAY TO LIVE

3 1Remind the believers to yield to the authority of rulers and government leaders, to
obey them, to be ready to do good, 2to speak
no evil about anyone, to live in peace, and to
be gentle and polite to all people.
3In the past we also were foolish. We did
not obey, we were wrong, and we were slaves
to many things our bodies wanted
and enjoyed. We spent our
lives doing evil and being
jealous. People hated us, and
we hated each other. 4But
when the kindness and love
of God our Savior was
shown, 5he saved us because
of his mercy. It was not because of good deeds
we did to be right with him. He saved us
through the washing that made us new people
through the Holy Spirit. 6God poured out richly upon us that Holy Spirit through Jesus
Christ our Savior. 7Being made right with God
by his grace, we could have the hope of receiving the life that never ends.
8This teaching is true, and I want you to be
sure the people understand these things. Then
those who believe in God will be careful to use
their lives for doing good. These things are
good and will help everyone.

WHAT'S IT MEAN?

Paul's reference to family histories has to do with the obsession of certain Jewish leaders with being able to trace their family tree all the way back to Abraham. Apparently, knowing the name of one's great-great-great-great-great-great-great-great-great-grandfather was a big deal to some people in New Testament times.

Titus 3:9

ETERNAL LIFE

What does eternal life give us? (3:4–7)

Promise

HE PROMISES TO PURIFY YOU.

[Jesus Christ] gave himself for us so he might pay the price to free us from all evil and to make us pure people who belong only to him—people who are always wanting to do good deeds (Titus 2:14).

Sometimes people think that God's grace is nothing more than the forgiveness of sins. It would be enough if that's all there was to it—just the forgiveness of every sin in your whole life—even the ones you won't commit for another twenty or thirty years.

But God knows you need more than just a clean slate to become all he wants you to be. You also need a heart that's tender toward him, a mind that can be made to think like his, and a soul that yields its will to the wishes of his Spirit. This verse tells you that he "gave himself for us so he might pay the price to free us . . . and to make us pure people who belong only to him. . . ." You're included.

But gentle and patient to the end, he's also allowed your heart to be tested. He's also given you the power to stand up to temptation. Anything that doesn't agree with God or his Word is temptation. Know his Word so well that you are quick to recognize temptation. When you see it, run.

Your pure heart can feel impure sometimes. If it does, get clean. Ask God's forgiveness and receive it. His forgiveness purifies you.

He's changed your heart forever. Go and live like you believe it.

SEE FOR YOURSELF:

Matt. 5:8; Heb. 9:14; 1 Pet. 1:22

WHAT'S IT MEAN?

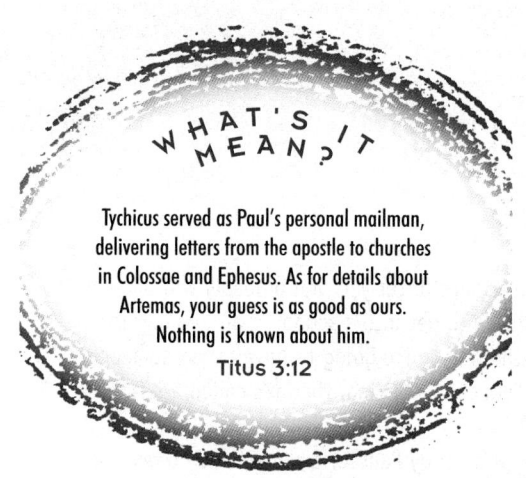

Tychicus served as Paul's personal mailman, delivering letters from the apostle to churches in Colossae and Ephesus. As for details about Artemas, your guess is as good as ours. Nothing is known about him.

Titus 3:12

9But stay away from those who have foolish arguments and talk about useless family
histories and argue and quarrel about the law.
Those things are worth nothing and will not
help anyone. 10After a first and second warning, avoid someone who causes arguments.
11You can know that such people are evil and
sinful; their own sins prove them wrong.

SOME THINGS TO REMEMBER

12When I send Artemas or Tychicus to you,
make every effort to come to me at Nicopolis,
because I have decided to stay there this winter. 13Do all you can to help Zenas the lawyer
and Apollos on their journey so that they have
everything they need. 14Our people must learn
to use their lives for doing good deeds to provide what is necessary so that their lives will
not be useless.
15All who are with me greet you. Greet
those who love us in the faith.

Grace be with you all.

philemon

CONTENT

If you haven't had to ask for a reference letter yet, you probably will one day. It might be to get a job. It might be to get into a school or an extracurricular program. But somewhere along the way you're going to have to ask someone to vouch for you. If they put that "vouch" in writing, then it's called a reference letter.

Philemon is a reference letter written by Paul for a slave named Onesimus (o-NES-i-muss). In those days, people who were broke or bankrupt had the option of "selling" themselves as servants or slaves. That way they could get work experience and pay off their debts. Usually, at some point in time, they could then choose either to stay servants or move on as free persons.

Onesimus was a slave, but he had run away and so had not kept up his end of the bargain. Then Onesimus met Paul and became a Christian. He needed to go back and make his actions right. In order to pave the way for him, Paul wrote this letter asking Philemon (the owner) to forgive Onesimus and to accept him back into Philemon's home.

Outline

1–3 .... Greetings to Philemon
4–22 .... Paul's Appeal to Philemon About Onesimus
23–25 .... Final Greetings and a Prayer

Purpose

Coming to know Christ transforms interpersonal relationships.

Theme

Brotherly Love

Date of writing

A.D. 60

"Have him back forever—no longer as a slave, but better than a slave, as a loved brother. I love him very much, but you will love him even more, both as a person and as a believer in the Lord. So if you consider me your partner, welcome Onesimus as you would welcome me" (15b–17).

Bible Talk

Philemon's Perspective

From Philemon's perspective he had the right to be angry. His servant had run off and had taken money, too. When Paul wrote this letter asking Philemon to forgive, he wasn't just asking Philemon to do what Philemon already knew he should do. No, Paul was asking Philemon to do something that was totally unexpected.

That's hard to take sometimes. When people wrong us or let us down, there's nothing wrong with holding them accountable—but not every time. Sometimes God calls us to lay down our rights, to give them a very undeserved break. Sometimes God calls us to do for them what he has done for us—forgive and let it go.

ONESIMUS'S PERSPECTIVE

How hard do you think it was for Onesimus to return to the scene of his crime? How hard do you think it was for him to face the man he had robbed and abandoned? How much courage do you think it took for him to travel back to the captivity he had known?

It probably took a lot out of him, but he did it because his life had changed. He had put his faith in God. He had accepted God's forgiveness. That meant he couldn't live the same as he had before. Things had to change. The first change was facing up to some consequences.

That's what happens to us, too, when we receive God's love and forgiveness.

1From Paul, a prisoner of Christ Jesus, and
from Timothy, our brother.
To Philemon, our dear friend and worker
with us; 2to Apphia, our sister; to Archippus, a
worker with us; and to the church that meets
in your home:
3Grace and peace to you from God our Father and the Lord Jesus Christ.

WHAT'S IT MEAN?

Home Bible studies are nothing new. In fact, people met together in their houses to read Scripture and pray long before there were any church buildings as we know them today—places set aside specifically for Christian worship and Bible study—which were not common until the third century. So when you see the word *church* in the Bible, it's referring to a group of Christ's followers in a certain place.

Philemon 2

PHILEMON'S LOVE AND FAITH

4I always thank my God when I mention
you in my prayers, 5because I hear about the
love you have for all God's holy people and
the faith you have in the Lord Jesus. 6I pray
that the faith you share may make you understand every blessing we have in Christ. 7I have
great joy and comfort, my brother, because the
love you have shown to God's people has refreshed them.

ACCEPT ONESIMUS AS A BROTHER

8So, in Christ, I could be bold and order you
to do what is right. 9But because I love you, I
am pleading with you instead. I, Paul, an old
man now and also a prisoner for Christ Jesus,
10am pleading with you for my child Onesimus,
who became my child while I was in prison.
11In the past he was useless to you, but now he
has become useful for both you and me.
12I am sending him back to you, and with
him I am sending my own heart. 13I wanted to
keep him with me so that in your place he

WHAT'S IT MEAN?

Onesimus was living dangerously when he ran away from Philemon, his master. In the Roman Empire, slaves were considered to be nothing more than property. They were bought, sold, and used as their masters saw fit. The punishment for a runaway slave was a severe beating or, in some cases, crucifixion.

Philemon 10

might help me while I am in prison for the
Good News. 14But I did not want to do anything without asking you first so that any
good you do for me will be because you want
to do it, not because I forced you. 15Maybe
Onesimus was separated from you for a short
time so you could have him back forever—
16no longer as a slave, but better than a slave,
as a loved brother. I love him very much, but
you will love him even more, both as a person
and as a believer in the Lord.
17So if you consider me your partner, welcome Onesimus as you would welcome me.
18If he has done anything wrong to you or
if he owes you anything, charge that to me.
19I, Paul, am writing this with my own hand. I
will pay it back, and I will say nothing about
what you owe me for your own life. 20So, my
brother, I ask that you do this for me in the
Lord: Refresh my heart in Christ. 21I write this
letter, knowing that you will do what I ask you
and even more.
22One more thing—prepare a room for me
in which to stay, because I hope God will
answer your prayers and I will be able to come
to you.

FINAL GREETINGS

23Epaphras, a prisoner with me for Christ
Jesus, sends greetings to you. 24And also Mark,
Aristarchus, Demas, and Luke, workers together
with me, send greetings.
25The grace of our Lord Jesus Christ be with
your spirit.

ONESIMUS made a difference

God often makes a difference through unexpected people. Onesimus was a runaway slave. He and the apostle Paul found each other in Rome. Perhaps they had met previously in the house of Philemon in Colossae when Paul had visited. But this time, Onesimus himself became a believer in Jesus.

Eventually Paul and Onesimus decided the slave must return to the master. Paul's letter to Philemon included the apostle's effort to reintroduce the former runaway to his master as a fellow believer. In an almost humorous way, Paul is certain that Philemon will give Onesimus a good welcome.

Through Onesimus's experience we are reminded that we cannot run away from God. Onesimus's experience also reminds us that when we run away from problems God often works things out so that we have to return to the scene of our departure as part of our training. So Onesimus went home. It is possible that Onesimus eventually became a leader of the church in Colossae. But he didn't make a difference by running away. It wasn't until he met Christ and then returned home that he was in a position to be truly "useful," which is what his name means.

Cutting Edge

YOU can, too!

If one of your problem-solving approaches is to run away, you can learn a lot from Onesimus. His escape was only temporary. In the meantime, God did reach and change him. God can certainly make that kind of difference in your Life.

Perhaps you can think of places and people from which you have run. Are there broken relationships and situations that still need to be resolved in your life? God wants to help. Other believers can help, too. Ask God to lead you to a Paul who can give you wisdom and who can run interference during your return.

Want to know more? Onesimus is mentioned briefly in Colossians 4:9 and several times in Philemon.

hebrews

CONTENT Have you ever read Cliffs Notes? These are small paperback books that tell you, in shortened form, the story of famous classics (like Shakespeare's *Romeo and Juliet*). They help you understand the highlights of the plot and the significance of the different story lines. Cliffs Notes were not meant to be substituted for reading the classic; they are meant to supplement it.

Hebrews is like Cliffs Notes for the whole Bible. The writer of Hebrews walked back through the whole history of the Hebrews starting with their earliest and most famous ancestors, Abraham and Moses. The Hebrews were a people with a strong, *strong* sense of tradition. To say that they thought highly of their ancestors is putting it mildly. The whole point for walking back through this history in the Book of Hebrews was to point out that Jesus was greater than any of their ancestors.

Now if you say to a Hebrew that someone is greater than Moses, you are making a bold statement—a statement worth fighting over—so you'd better be sure. The writer of Hebrews was sure. He was trying to convince his Hebrew readers that Jesus was, indeed, the Messiah that all their ancestors had pointed them toward.

Outline

1:1–4 .... The Greatness of God's Son
1:5—2:18 .... Jesus Is Greater Than Angels
3:1—4:13 .... Jesus Is Greater Than Moses and Joshua
4:14—7:28 .... Jesus Is Our High Priest
8:1—9:22 .... Jesus Brings a New Agreement
9:23—10:39 .... Jesus' Sacrifice Is Once and for All
11:1–40 .... Some of God's People Who Had Great Faith
12:1—13:17 .... Follow Jesus' Example
13:18–25 .... Final Prayers and Greetings

Purpose Jesus provides all we need for a vital personal relationship with God.

Theme The Superiority of Jesus Christ over the Old Agreement

Date of writing Before A.D. 64

"We have around us many people whose lives tell us what faith means. So let us run the race that is before us and never give up. We should remove from our lives anything that would get in the way and the sin that so easily holds us back" (12:1).

Bible Talk

The Law

The writer of Hebrews talks a lot about "the Law." One definition of the law is "the first five books of the Bible" (Genesis, Exodus, Leviticus, Numbers, and Deuteronomy). The Hebrews looked to these books for every law that they needed. Another definition of the law is "all the laws that the Jews had written *based on* the first five books of the Bible." As humans will do, the Hebrews had analyzed the laws until they had expanded them to include every possible scenario. For instance, if the law said that you weren't supposed to work on the Sabbath, the Hebrews wrote laws explaining what "work" actually was, when the "Sabbath" actually was, and how many steps a person had to take before they were actually "working." You can imagine that it got a little confusing.

A BETTER LAW

The revolution of Jesus' life is that the law got simplified. Instead of counting your steps to see if you had broken the Sabbath, Jesus told people that they needed to love God with everything they had and to love each other. Period.

This didn't feel good to the Hebrews. How would they know if they were living a good life if they didn't have the specifics of the law to show them when they messed up? They had put their faith in the law to make them righteous. Now they needed to put their faith in Jesus and *he* would make them righteous. It was a whole new way of thinking for the Hebrews, which is why there is a whole book dedicated to explaining it to them.

GOD SPOKE THROUGH HIS SON

1 [1]In the past God spoke to our ancestors
through the prophets many times and in many
different ways. [2]But now in these last days God
has spoken to us through his Son. God has
chosen his Son to own all things, and through
him he made the world. [3]The Son reflects the
glory of God and shows exactly what God is
like. He holds everything together with his
powerful word. When the Son made people
clean from their sins, he sat down at the right
side of God, the Great One in heaven. [4]The Son
became much greater than the angels, and God
gave him a name that is much greater than
theirs.

WHAT'S IT MEAN?

Angels enjoyed great popularity in the first century. Pagans, Jews, and Christians all placed a tremendous amount of importance on these heavenly beings. Some groups may even have gone so far as to worship angels. Others mistakenly believed that Jesus himself was an angel because of the miracles he performed.

Hebrews 1:4

[5]This is because God never said to any of
the angels,

"You are my Son.
Today I have become your Father."
Psalm 2:7

Nor did God say of any angel,

"I will be his Father,
and he will be my Son."
2 Samuel 7:14

[6]And when God brings his
firstborn Son into the world,
he says,

"Let all God's angels
worship him."[n]
Psalm 97:7

[7]This is what God said about
the angels:

"God makes his angels become
like winds.
He makes his servants become like
flames of fire."
Psalm 104:4

[8]But God said this about his Son:

"God, your throne will last forever and
ever.
You will rule your kingdom with
fairness.
[9]You love right and hate evil,
so God has chosen you from among
your friends;
he has set you apart with much joy."
Psalm 45:6-7

[10]God also says,

"Lord, in the beginning you made the
earth,
and your hands made the skies.
[11]They will be destroyed, but you will
remain.
They will all wear out like clothes.
[12]You will fold them like a coat.
And, like clothes, you will change them.
But you never change,
and your life will never end."
Psalm 102:25-27

[13]And God never said this to an angel:

"Sit by me at my right side
until I put your enemies under your
control."[n]
Psalm 110:1

[14]All the angels are spirits
who serve God and are sent
to help those who will receive
salvation.

HELP
How do angels help Christians? (1:14)

OUR SALVATION IS GREAT

2 [1]So we must be more careful to
follow what we were taught. Then we will not
stray away from the truth. [2]The teaching God
spoke through angels was shown to be true,
and anyone who did not follow it or obey it
received the punishment that was earned. [3]So
surely we also will be punished if we ignore
this great salvation. The Lord himself first told about this salvation, and it was proven true to
us by those who heard him.
[4]God also proved it by using
wonders, great signs, many
kinds of miracles, and by giving people gifts through the
Holy Spirit, just as he wanted.

"Lord, in the beginning you made the earth, and your hands made the skies." (Hebrews 1:10)

CHRIST BECAME LIKE HUMANS

[5]God did not choose angels to
be the rulers of the new world that

1:6 "Let . . . him." These words are found in Deuteronomy 32:43 in the Septuagint, the Greek version of the Old Testament, and in a Hebrew copy among the Dead Sea Scrolls. **1:13 until . . . control** Literally, "until I make your enemies a footstool for your feet."

was coming, which is what we have been talking about. 6 It is written in the Scriptures,

"Why are people important to you?
Why do you take care of human beings?
7 You made them a little lower than the angels
and crowned them with glory and honor.
8 You put all things under their control."

Psalm 8:4-6

When God put everything under their control,
there was nothing left that they did not rule.
Still, we do not yet see them ruling over everything. 9 But we see Jesus, who for a short time
was made lower than the angels. And now he is
wearing a crown of glory and honor because
he suffered and died. And by God's grace, he
died for everyone.

10 God is the One who made all things, and
all things are for his glory. He wanted to have
many children share his glory, so he made the
One who leads people to salvation perfect
through suffering.

11 Jesus, who makes people holy, and those
who are made holy are from the same family.
So he is not ashamed to call them his brothers
and sisters.[n] 12 He says,

"Then, I will tell my fellow Israelites about
you;
I will praise you in the public meeting."

Psalm 22:22

13 He also says,

"I will trust in God." *Isaiah 8:17*

And he also says,

"I am here, and with me are the children
God has given me." *Isaiah 8:18*

14 Since these children are people with physical bodies, Jesus himself became like them. He
did this so that, by dying, he could destroy the
one who has the power of death—the devil—
15 and free those who were like slaves all their
lives because of their fear of death. 16 Clearly, it

WHAT'S IT MEAN?

Before Jesus' death on the cross, the high priest was responsible for offering the sacrifice every year that provided forgiveness for the Israelites' sins. The blood of the sacrifice was the payment necessary in God's eyes for all of the sins the people had committed in the previous year.

Hebrews 2:17

2:11 brothers and sisters Although the Greek text says "brothers" here and throughout this book, the writer's words were meant for the entire church, including men and women.

Promise

HE PROMISES TO AID WHEN YOU ARE TEMPTED.

And now he can help those who are tempted, because he himself suffered and was tempted (Heb. 2:18).

It's not unusual to hear somebody excuse personal faults by saying, "Well, that's just the way I am"—as if it would be unfair to expect anything better out of him or her. It's true that everybody has flaws and everyone is susceptible to some temptations. Some people have a hard time being nice when things aren't going well for them; some people are tempted to cheat because they're so driven to make a good grade; some people are sucked in by the buzz they get from drinking or drugs. That's the way they are.

But Jesus never said that it was okay to do wrong because you have a weakness. He told people to do the right thing anyway. He wasn't being heartless. He wasn't looking down from some ivory tower shouting, "You must resist temptation." He was flesh and blood, just like you. He knew what it was like to be tempted. He isn't leaving you to overcome your weaknesses all by yourself. He's right there with you, giving you the strength to make the right choice. He's saying, "You can do it!" He's God. He's given you the strength to overcome and he knows you can!

SEE FOR YOURSELF:

Rom. 8:37; 1 Cor. 10:13; Heb. 4:15–16; James 1:13–15

is not angels that Jesus helps, but the people
who are from Abraham.[n] [17]For this reason
Jesus had to be made like his brothers in every
way so he could be their merciful and faithful
high priest in service to God. Then Jesus could
bring forgiveness for their sins. [18]And now he
can help those who are tempted, because he
himself suffered and was tempted.

JESUS IS GREATER THAN MOSES

3 [1]So all of you holy brothers and sisters, who
were called by God, think about Jesus, who
was sent to us and is the high priest of our
faith. [2]Jesus was faithful to God as Moses was
in God's family. [3]Jesus has more honor than
Moses, just as the builder of a house has more
honor than the house itself. [4]Every house is
built by someone, but the builder of everything is God himself. [5]Moses was faithful in
God's family as a servant, and he told what
God would say in the future. [6]But Christ is
faithful as a Son over God's house. And we are
God's house if we keep on being very sure
about our great hope.

WE MUST CONTINUE TO FOLLOW GOD

[7]So it is as the Holy Spirit says:
"Today listen to what he says.
[8]Do not be stubborn as in the past
when you turned against God,
when you tested God in the desert.
[9]There your ancestors tried me and tested me
and saw the things I did for forty years.
[10]I was angry with them.
I said, 'They are not loyal to me
and have not understood my ways.'
[11]I was angry and made a promise,
'They will never enter my rest.' "[n]

Psalm 95:7-11

[12]So brothers and sisters, be careful that
none of you has an evil, unbelieving heart that
will turn you away from the living God. [13]But
encourage each other every day while it is
"today."[n] Help each other so none of you will
become hardened because sin has tricked you.

On the Edge

But encourage each other every day while it is "today." Help each other so none of you will become hardened because sin has tricked you (Heb. 3:13).

Most of us feel insecure when we are in a new place, doing new things, or meeting new people. Somehow we forget everything that is good and strong about ourselves. We can only see our weaknesses and think about our failures. You may have a friend who needs some encouragement in this area.

Verse 13 says she may need it every day. That's what being in the body of Christ is all about. Christians are supposed to encourage one another and remind each other that they are children of a loving God—empowered by his strength and covered by his grace. It's your official job as a Christian to encourage your friend. Be there when she needs you and cheer her on. Give her a big hug and tell her how wonderful she is. There will come a day when you'll be the one who needs those things. Your friend will be happy to return the favor.

SEE FOR YOURSELF:
2 Cor. 1:3–4;
Gal. 6:9–10;
1 Thess. 5:14

WHAT'S IT MEAN?

Though there is no address on the letter, the Book of Hebrews apparently was written to Jewish Christians who were being persecuted by the Roman Empire for their beliefs. Here's the problem they faced. As Jews, they had been safe, since Judaism was recognized by the empire as a legitimate religion and was therefore protected under the law. When those Jews became Christians, however, they put themselves in danger. Christianity was not a recognized religion. As a result, new Christians faced harassment not only from Rome, but also from other Jews who were upset with them for leaving the Jewish faith. As you might imagine, some Jewish Christians were seriously considering leaving their Christian faith and going back to Judaism.

Hebrews 3:14

2:16 Abraham Most respected ancestor of the Jews. Every Jew hoped to see Abraham. **3:11 rest** A place of rest God promised to give his people. **3:13 "today"** This word is taken from verse 7. It means that it is important to do these things now.

14We all share in Christ if we keep till the end
the sure faith we had in the beginning. 15This is
what the Scripture says:

"Today listen to what he says.
Do not be stubborn as in the past
when you turned against God." *Psalm 95:7-8*

16Who heard God's voice and was against
him? It was all those people Moses led out of
Egypt. 17And with whom was God angry for
forty years? He was angry with those who
sinned, who died in the desert. 18And to whom
was God talking when he promised that they
would never enter his rest? He was talking to
those who did not obey him. 19So we see they
were not allowed to enter and have God's rest,
because they did not believe.

4 1Now, since God has left us the promise
that we may enter his rest, let us be very careful so none of you will fail to enter. 2The Good
News was preached to us just as it was to
them. But the teaching they heard did not help
them, because they heard it but did not accept
it with faith. 3We who have believed are able to
enter and have God's rest. As God has said,

"I was angry and made a promise,
'They will never enter my rest.' " *Psalm 95:11*

But God's work was finished from the time he
made the world. 4In the Scriptures he talked
about the seventh day of the week: "And on the
seventh day God rested from all his works."[n]
5And again in the Scripture God said, "They
will never enter my rest."

6It is still true that some people will enter
God's rest, but those who first heard the way
to be saved did not enter, because they did not
obey. 7So God planned another day, called "today." He spoke about that day through David a
long time later in the same Scripture used before:

"Today listen to what he says.
Do not be stubborn." *Psalm 95:7-8*

8We know that Joshua[n] did not lead the people
into that rest, because God spoke later about
another day. 9This shows that the rest[n] for

WHAT'S IT MEAN?

When Moses died, he left some pretty big sandals to fill. After all, he had led the Israelites out of Egypt and through the wilderness for almost forty years. Joshua was the man God chose to succeed Moses. As Israel's spiritual and military leader, Joshua marched the people into the land God had promised them and directed them in the wars they fought against the enemies of God. The Israelites spent years in battle with various tribes throughout the land.

Hebrews 4:8

On the Edge

For our high priest is able to understand our weaknesses. When he lived on earth, he was tempted in every way that we are, but he did not sin (Heb. 4:15).

A weakness is an area of life that's hard to control. It takes concentration and extra effort to avoid a weakness—once you're in the habit of giving in to it. Weaknesses come in all shapes and sizes—jealousy, drugs, alcohol, being irresponsible, manipulation, food, anger, laziness, reckless driving, pornography, or money. You name it, and it's probably a weakness for someone.

When we ask the Lord for strength to overcome a weakness, we can be sure that we are talking to Someone who understands. When Jesus became a man, he took on the weaknesses that people have to deal with. He's walked in your shoes. He's lived on the earth as a boy, a teenager, and a man. He's felt the temptations you feel, but he showed us how to live a life that doesn't give in. His time here made him sympathetic toward you. He understands the trials you face, and he knows how hard temptation can be.

You can talk to him and count on him to provide the strength you need to overcome the things that are hard to control. He's already dealt with the tough places you'll face in life. Determine right now in your heart that you *will not give in*. He's there to help you overcome!

SEE FOR YOURSELF:
Is. 53:3–5; John 14:16; Rom. 8:26; 2 Cor. 5:21

4:4 "And . . . works." Quotation from Genesis 2:2. **4:8 Joshua** After Moses died, Joshua became leader of the Jewish people and led them into the land that God promised to give them. **4:9 rest** Literally, "sabbath rest," meaning a sharing in the rest that God began after he created the world.

God's people is still coming. [10]Anyone who enters God's rest will rest from his work as God did. [11]Let us try as hard as we can to enter God's rest so that no one will fail by following the example of those who refused to obey.

[12]God's word is alive and working and is sharper than a double-edged sword. It cuts all the way into us, where the soul and the spirit are joined, to the center of our joints and bones. And it judges the thoughts and feelings in our hearts. [13]Nothing in all the world can be hidden from God. Everything is clear and lies open before him, and to him we must explain the way we have lived.

JESUS IS OUR HIGH PRIEST

[14]Since we have a great high priest, Jesus the Son of God, who has gone into heaven, let us hold on to the faith we have. [15]For our high priest is able to understand our weaknesses. When he lived on earth, he was tempted in every way that we are, but he did not sin. [16]Let us, then, feel very sure that we can come before God's throne where there is grace. There we can receive mercy and grace to help us when we need it.

> **JESUS**
> Has Jesus ever sinned? (4:15)

5 [1]Every high priest is chosen from among other people. He is given the work of going before God for them to offer gifts and sacrifices for sins. [2]Since he himself is weak, he is able to be gentle with those who do not understand and who are doing wrong things. [3]Because he is weak, the high priest must offer sacrifices for his own sins and also for the sins of the people.

[4]To be a high priest is an honor, but no one chooses himself for this work. He must be called by God as Aaron[n] was. [5]So also Christ did not choose himself to have the honor of being a high priest, but God chose him. God said to him,

"You are my Son.
Today I have become your Father."
Psalm 2:7

[6]And in another Scripture God says,
"You are a priest forever,
a priest like Melchizedek."[n] *Psalm 110:4*

[7]While Jesus lived on earth, he prayed to God and asked God for help. He prayed with loud cries and tears to the One who could save him from death, and his prayer was heard because he trusted God. [8]Even though Jesus was the Son of God, he learned obedience by what he suffered. [9]And because his obedience was perfect, he was able to give eternal salvation to all who obey him. [10]In this way God made Jesus a high priest, a priest like Melchizedek.

On the Edge

He learned obedience by what he suffered. And because his obedience was perfect, he was able to give eternal salvation to all who obey him (Heb. 5:8b–9).

Flip back a couple of pages and read Hebrews 2:18. You'll see that Jesus experienced suffering and temptation. But how did that make him perfect? He made the right choices in the midst of his suffering and temptation. Now he is the perfect One to save and strengthen you.

Jesus is perfect, but that does not distance him from you. He became a man, remained perfect, and died for your sin, so that he could get to know you. He wants a relationship with you. He wants to be there for you in your suffering. He can carry you through it. His strength is perfect when all your strength is gone. His perfection enables him to minister to you. He can anticipate your needs. And because he is perfect, he knows all the answers. He knows when you're empty. He knows when to send in the troops. You benefit from the perfection of Christ. He is a perfect Savior for the lost, a perfect intercessor for the needy, a perfect friend for everybody.

SEE FOR YOURSELF:
Heb. 2:10, 18; 9:14;
1 Pet. 1:18–19

WARNING AGAINST FALLING AWAY

[11]We have much to say about this, but it is hard to explain because you are so slow to understand. [12]By now you should be teachers, but you need someone to teach you again the first lessons of God's message. You still need the teaching that is like milk. You are not ready for solid food. [13]Anyone who lives on milk is still a baby and knows nothing about right teaching. [14]But solid food is for those who are

5:4 Aaron Aaron was Moses' brother and the first Jewish high priest. **5:6 Melchizedek** A priest and king who lived in the time of Abraham. (Read Genesis 14:17-24.)

grown up. They have practiced in order to
know the difference between good and evil.

6 [1]So let us go on to grown-up teaching. Let
us not go back over the beginning lessons we
learned about Christ. We should not again start
teaching about faith in God and about turning
away from those acts that lead to death. [2]We
should not return to the teaching about
baptisms,[n] about laying on of hands,[n] about
the raising of the dead and eternal judgment.
[3]And we will go on to grown-up teaching if
God allows.

[4]Some people cannot be brought back
again to a changed life. They were once in
God's light, and enjoyed heaven's gift, and
shared in the Holy Spirit. [5]They found out how
good God's word is, and they received the
powers of his new world. [6]But they fell away
from Christ. It is impossible to bring them back
to a changed life again, because they are nailing the Son of God to a cross again and are
shaming him in front of others.

[7]Some people are like land that gets plenty of
rain. The land produces a good crop for those
who work it, and it receives God's blessings.
[8]Other people are like land that grows thorns
and weeds and is worthless. It is in danger of
being cursed by God and will be destroyed by
fire.

[9]Dear friends, we are saying this to you, but
we really expect better things from you that
will lead to your salvation. [10]God is fair; he will
not forget the work you did and the love you
showed for him by helping his people. And he
will remember that you are still helping them.
[11]We want each of you to go on with the same
hard work all your lives so you will surely get
what you hope for. [12]We do not want you to
become lazy. Be like those who through faith
and patience will receive what God has promised.

[13]God made a promise to Abraham. And as
there is no one greater than God, he used himself when he swore to Abraham, [14]saying, "I
will surely bless you and give you many
descendants."[n] [15]Abraham waited patiently for

6:2 baptisms The word here may refer to Christian baptism, or it may refer to the Jewish ceremonial washings. **6:2 laying on of hands** The laying on of hands had many purposes, including the giving of a blessing, power, or authority. **6:14 "I . . . descendants."** Quotation from Genesis 22:17.

Promise

HE PROMISES TO TELL THE TRUTH.

God wanted to prove that his promise was true to those who would get what he promised. And he wanted them to understand clearly that his purposes never change, so he made an oath. These two things cannot change: God cannot lie when he makes a promise, and he cannot lie when he makes an oath. These things encourage us who came to God for safety. They give us strength to hold on to the hope we have been given (Heb. 6:17–18).

Do you ever doubt God? Maybe you doubt the whole thing—God, the Bible, and all the Jesus stuff. Do you think that everyone who believes must be out to lunch? Maybe you do believe in God, but aren't sure that he's really going to come through for you. Hebrews says that the hope of Christ is right in front of you—"the hope we have been given." You are holding a record of the promises God has made to you. He has told the truth. He has kept his promises. His vows have never changed. Be encouraged to run to him because he never lies. You've got to make up your mind to believe that and you've got to decide that you are going to believe his Word. Until you've made that commitment, you'll constantly struggle with doubt.

The truth of his Word will replace your doubt. John 8:32 says "the truth will make you free." So immerse yourself in these pages. Commit to do more than just slide your eyes over the words. Really concentrate and study the Bible prayerfully. Read about how God has kept his promises. Read about the incredibly deep and powerful love he has for you. Read about his longing to know you and to be with you forever. Get these words into your heart and into your mind. Pretty soon, all your doubts will be replaced with the absolute certainty of God and of his truth.

SEE FOR YOURSELF:

John 1:14; 8:32; 14:6, 17; 2 Tim. 3:15–17

this to happen, and he received what God
promised.
[16]People always use the name of someone
greater than themselves when they swear. The
oath proves that what they say is true, and this
ends all arguing. [17]God wanted to prove that
his promise was true to those who would get
what he promised. And he wanted them to
understand clearly that his purposes never
change, so he made an oath. [18]These two
things cannot change: God cannot lie when he
makes a promise, and he cannot lie when he
makes an oath. These things encourage us who
came to God for safety. They give us strength
to hold on to the hope we have been given.
[19]We have this hope as an anchor for the soul,
sure and strong. It enters behind the curtain in
the Most Holy Place in heaven, [20]where Jesus
has gone ahead of us and for us. He has become the high priest forever, a priest like
Melchizedek.[n]

WHAT'S IT MEAN?

In ancient times, six towns in Israel were set aside as "cities of safety." In order to understand the purpose of cities of safety, you have to understand the law of the land in Old Testament times. "An eye for an eye" was the rule of the day. If a person killed someone else—even accidentally—legally, he himself could be killed in retaliation. That's why cities of safety were important. If a person accidentally killed another person, he could run to the nearest city of safety to escape vengeance-seeking family members of the person he killed. Once the person reached a city of safety, no one was allowed to harm him until a fair trial could be conducted. If the killing was found to be accidental, the person on trial was allowed to live in the city of safety with full protection from those who wanted to kill him.

Hebrews 6:18

THE PRIEST MELCHIZEDEK

7 [1]Melchizedek[n] was the king of Salem and a
priest for God Most High. He met Abraham
when Abraham was coming back after defeating the kings. When they met, Melchizedek
blessed Abraham, [2]and Abraham gave him a
tenth of everything he had brought back from
the battle. First, Melchizedek's name means
"king of goodness," and he is king of Salem,
which means "king of peace." [3]No one knows
who Melchizedek's father or mother was,[n]
where he came from, when he was born, or
when he died. Melchizedek is like the Son of
God; he continues being a priest forever.

WHAT'S IT MEAN?

What do we know about Melchizedek? First, we know that in the Book of Genesis, he is described as the king of Salem, a city in Canaan. (Salem may be the city that later became known as Jerusalem.) Second, we know that Melchizedek was a priest of God, as well as a king. Third, we know that Abraham ran into Melchizedek on his way back from rescuing his nephew Lot from the kings who had kidnapped him. Fourth, we know that Abraham recognized something in Melchizedek that caused him to give ten percent of everything he had seized in battle to the king-priest.

Hebrews 7:1

[4]You can see how great Melchizedek was.
Abraham, the great father, gave him a tenth of
everything that he won in battle. [5]Now the law
says that those in the tribe of Levi who become
priests must collect a tenth from the people—
their own people—even though the priests and
the people are from the family of Abraham.
[6]Melchizedek was not from the tribe of Levi,
but he collected a tenth from Abraham. And he
blessed Abraham, the man who had God's
promises. [7]Now everyone knows that the more
important person blesses the less important
person. [8]Priests receive a tenth, even though
they are only men who live and then die. But
Melchizedek, who received a tenth from Abraham, continues living, as the Scripture says.
[9]We might even say that Levi, who receives a
tenth, also paid it when Abraham paid Melchizedek a tenth. [10]Levi was not yet born, but
he was in the body of his ancestor when Melchizedek met Abraham.
[11]The people were given the law[n] based on
a system of priests from the tribe of Levi, but

6:20; 7:1 Melchizedek A priest and king who lived in the time of Abraham. (Read Genesis 14:17–24.)
7:3 No . . . was Literally, "Melchizedek was without father, without mother, without genealogy."
7:11 The . . . law This refers to the people of Israel who were given the Law of Moses.

they could not be made perfect through that
system. So there was a need for another priest
to come, a priest like Melchizedek, not Aaron.
[12]And when a different kind of priest comes,
the law must be changed, too. [13]We are saying
these things about Christ, who belonged to a
different tribe. No one from that tribe ever
served as a priest at the altar. [14]It is clear that
our Lord came from the tribe of Judah, and
Moses said nothing about priests belonging to
that tribe.

JESUS IS LIKE MELCHIZEDEK

[15]And this becomes even more clear when
we see that another priest comes who is like
Melchizedek.[n] [16]He was not made a priest by
human rules and laws but through the power
of his life, which continues forever. [17]It is said
about him,

"You are a priest forever,
a priest like Melchizedek." *Psalm 110:4*

[18]The old rule is now set aside, because it
was weak and useless. [19]The law of Moses
could not make anything perfect. But now a
better hope has been given to us, and with this
hope we can come near to God. [20]It is important that God did this with an oath. Others became priests without an oath, [21]but Christ
became a priest with God's oath. God said:

"The Lord has made a promise
and will not change his mind.
'You are a priest forever.' " *Psalm 110:4*

[22]This means that Jesus is the guarantee of a
better agreement[n] from God to his people.
[23]When one of the other priests died, he
could not continue being a priest. So there
were many priests. [24]But because Jesus lives
forever, he will never stop serving as priest.
[25]So he is able always to save those who come
to God through him because he always lives,
asking God to help them.
[26]Jesus is the kind of high priest we need. He
is holy, sinless, pure, not influenced by sinners,
and he is raised above the heavens. [27]He is not
like the other priests who had to offer sacrifices
every day, first for their own sins, and then for
the sins of the people. Christ offered his sacrifice only once and for all time when he offered
himself. [28]The law chooses high priests who
are people with weaknesses, but the word of
God's oath came later than the law. It made
God's Son to be the high priest, and that Son
has been made perfect forever.

JESUS IS OUR HIGH PRIEST

8 [1]Here is the point of what we are saying: We
have a high priest who sits on the right side of
God's throne in heaven. [2]Our high priest
serves in the Most Holy Place, the true place of
worship that was made by God, not by humans.
[3]Every high priest has the work of offering
gifts and sacrifices to God. So our high priest

On the Edge

Jesus is the kind of high priest we need. He is holy, sinless, pure, not influenced by sinners, and he is raised above the heavens (Heb. 7:26).

Jesus, the most honored Person in heaven, sits beside God and tells him what it's like to be human. He prays the prayers we don't know how to pray. He sympathizes with us. He talks to God for us. He represents us well before the Father. He is honored because of his perfect life, suffering, death, and resurrection. He is honored because he became the sacrifice that saves us forever. He is holy and innocent.

In a time when people are worshiping and honoring angels, the earth, and all kinds of spirits, it's important to remember that Jesus is honored above everything else. All the heavenly beings—saints and angels—are praising and worshiping God, thanking him for his Son, Jesus. Only Jesus offers salvation. Only Jesus made it possible for people to even get to heaven in the first place. That's why he's honored above heavenly beings. That's why he's higher than the angels. No angel will ever be able to do for you what Jesus Christ can do—and has done.

Does Jesus have a place of honor in your life? Give him the glory he deserves. Thank him for the unending mercy and compassion he gives you day after day. Thank him for giving his life for you. Worship him with your day. Honor him with your life.

SEE FOR YOURSELF:
John 3:31; 5:23; Eph. 1:20; Phil. 2:9; Heb. 6:20

7:15 Melchizedek A priest and king who lived in the time of Abraham. (Read Genesis 14:17–24.)
7:22 agreement God gives a contract or agreement to his people. For the Jews, this agreement was the Law of Moses. But now God has given a better agreement to his people through Christ.

must also offer something to God. [4]If our high
priest were now living on earth, he would not
be a priest, because there are already priests
here who follow the law by offering gifts to
God. [5]The work they do as priests is only a
copy and a shadow of what is in heaven. This
is why God warned Moses when he was ready
to build the Holy Tent: "Be very careful to make
everything by the plan I showed you on the
mountain."[n] [6]But the priestly work that has
been given to Jesus is much greater than the
work that was given to the other priests. In the
same way, the new agreement that Jesus
brought from God to his people is much greater than the old one. And the new agreement is
based on promises of better things.
[7]If there had been nothing wrong with the
first agreement,[n] there would have been no
need for a second agreement. [8]But God found
something wrong with his people. He says:

"Look, the time is coming, says the Lord,
when I will make a new agreement
with the people of Israel
and the people of Judah.
[9]It will not be like the agreement
I made with their ancestors
when I took them by the hand
to bring them out of Egypt.
But they broke that agreement,
and I turned away from them, says the
Lord.
[10]This is the agreement I will make
with the people of Israel at that time,
says the Lord.
I will put my teachings in their minds
and write them on their hearts.
I will be their God,
and they will be my people.
[11]People will no longer have to teach their
neighbors and relatives
to know the Lord,
because all people will know me,
from the least to the most
important.
[12]I will forgive them for the wicked things
they did,
and I will not remember their sins
anymore." *Jeremiah 31:31-34*

[13]God called this a new agreement, so he
has made the first agreement old. And anything that is old and worn out is ready to disappear.

8:5 "Be . . . mountain." Quotation from Exodus 25:40. **8:7 first agreement** The contract God gave the Jewish people when he gave them the Law of Moses.

Promise HE PROMISES YOU BETTER THINGS.

The new agreement that Jesus brought from God to his people is much greater than the old one. And the new agreement is based on promises of better things (Heb. 8:6b).

Because of Jesus, things are much better for us than they were for our ancestors. We've got a new high priest, a new place of worship, and a new agreement with God. The priests of our ancestors were sinful and wicked. Their sin kept them from representing the people well before God. Jesus is our new High Priest. His perfection has replaced the old priests, making him the only way to God the Father.

The old Meeting Tent of worship is now just a shadow of the real one in heaven. The new place of worship is where Jesus sits with the Father. Having a new place of worship means that we can worship God straight out of our own hearts. Our worship isn't dictated by ritual, but by relationship. We worship out of our love for Jesus. The new agreement that God has made through Jesus replaces the one he made with our ancestors. The old agreement didn't work because there was no cure for the people's sinfulness. It promises that, through Jesus Christ, we will belong to the Lord forever and he will belong to us as our God (see Jer. 31:31–34). The new agreement promises to forgive the sins of those who trust in Christ. Because of Christ, we can pray and fellowship directly with the Lord. We can personally ask for the forgiveness of our sins. We can sense his leading and compassion in our lives.

God has promised us better things. He's given us the best gift—a better relationship with him—through the work of Jesus and the Holy Spirit.

SEE FOR YOURSELF:
Jer. 31:31–34; Heb. 7:22

THE OLD AGREEMENT

9 [1]The first agreement[n] had rules for worship and a man-made place for worship. [2]The Holy Tent was set up for this. The first area in the Tent was called the Holy Place. In it were the lamp and the table with the bread that was made holy for God. [3]Behind the second curtain was a room called the Most Holy Place. [4]In it was a golden altar for burning incense and the Ark covered with gold that held the old agreement. Inside this Ark was a golden jar of manna, Aaron's rod that once grew leaves, and the stone tablets of the old agreement. [5]Above the Ark were the creatures that showed God's glory, whose wings reached over the lid. But we cannot tell everything about these things now.

[6]When everything in the Tent was made ready in this way, the priests went into the first room every day to worship. [7]But only the high priest could go into the second room, and he did that only once a year. He could never enter the inner room without taking blood with him, which he offered to God for himself and for sins the people did without knowing they did them. [8]The Holy Spirit uses this to show that the way into the Most Holy Place was not open while the system of the old Holy Tent was still being used. [9]This is an example for the present time. It shows that the gifts and sacrifices offered cannot make the conscience of the worshiper perfect. [10]These gifts and sacrifices were only about food and drink and special washings. They were rules for the body, to be followed until the time of God's new way.

THE NEW AGREEMENT

[11]But when Christ came as the high priest of the good things we now have, he entered the greater and more perfect tent. It is not made by humans and does not belong to this world. [12]Christ entered the Most Holy Place only once—and for all time. He did not take with him the blood of goats and calves. His sacrifice was his own blood, and by it he set us free from sin forever. [13]The blood of goats and bulls and the ashes of a cow are sprinkled on the people who are unclean, and this makes their bodies clean again. [14]How much more is done by the blood of Christ. He offered himself through the eternal Spirit[n] as a perfect sacrifice to God. His blood will make our consciences pure from useless acts so we may serve the living God.

[15]For this reason Christ brings a new agreement from God to his people. Those who are called by God can now receive the blessings he has promised, blessings that will last forever. They can have those things because Christ died so that the people who lived under the first agreement could be set free from sin.

[16]When there is a will,[n] it must be proven that the one who wrote that will is dead. [17]A will means nothing while the person is alive; it can be used only after the person dies. [18]This is why even the first agreement could not begin without blood to show death. [19]First, Moses told all the people every command in the law. Next he took the blood of calves and mixed it with water. Then he used red wool and a branch of the hyssop plant to sprinkle it on the book of the law and on all the people. [20]He said, "This is the blood that begins the Agreement that God commanded you to obey."[n] [21]In the same way, Moses sprinkled the blood on the Holy Tent and over all the things used in worship. [22]The law says that almost everything must be made clean by blood, and sins cannot be forgiven without blood to show death.

CHRIST'S DEATH TAKES AWAY SINS

[23]So the copies of the real things in heaven had to be made clean by animal sacrifices. But the real things in heaven need much better sacrifices. [24]Christ did not go into the Most Holy Place made by humans, which is only a copy of the real one. He went into heaven itself and is there now before God to help us. [25]The high priest enters the Most Holy Place once every year with blood that is not his own. But Christ did not offer himself many times. [26]Then he would have had to suffer many times since the world was made. But Christ came only once and for all time at just the right time to take away all sin by sacrificing himself. [27]Just as everyone must die once and be judged, [28]so Christ was offered as a sacrifice one time to take away the sins of many people. And he will come a second time, not to

DEATH
What should our spiritual life be in preparation of? (9:27–28)

9:1 first agreement The contract God gave the Jewish people when he gave them the Law of Moses. **9:14 Spirit** This refers to the Holy Spirit, to Christ's own spirit, or to the spiritual and eternal nature of his sacrifice. **9:16 will** A legal document that shows how a person's money and property are to be distributed at the time of death. This is the same word in Greek as "agreement" in verse 15. **9:20 "This . . . obey."** Quotation from Exodus 24:8.

On the Edge

So, brothers and sisters, we are completely free to enter the Most Holy Place without fear because of the blood of Jesus' death. We can enter through a new and living way that Jesus opened for us. It leads through the curtain—Christ's body (Heb. 10:19–20).

The Temple the Israelites built had a special room called the Most Holy Place (Heb. 9:3–8). The door of this room was covered by a thick, heavy curtain because God's presence lived in the room. Because the presence of the Lord is so awesome, the people had to be separated from it. They were sinful and sin cannot stand in the presence of God's love and holiness. Only the high priest could go through the curtain, and he could do it only once a year. At that time, the high priest had to make one sacrifice for sins he and his family had committed and another sacrifice for the sins of the whole nation. The blood of the sacrifice took away the people's sins for the next year (see Lev. 16).

At the moment Jesus died on the cross, the curtain in front of the Most Holy Place was torn from top to bottom (see Matt. 27:51). God's presence was made available to everyone! It's like God had been sitting behind a locked door for years and years; and only the high priest had the key. Then Jesus came along and unlocked that door for everyone. His blood takes away the sins of everyone who trusts in him. Now he's the High Priest. Because of his death—because the curtain is torn—you can go into the place where God is. You don't need another person as a go-between. You don't have to go to a temple. And you don't have to make another sacrifice next year. Jesus made it possible for you to go into God's presence—personally, freely, as often as you want.

SEE FOR YOURSELF:
Matt. 27:51; 2 Cor. 3:4; Col. 1:21–23; Heb. 6:19

offer himself for sin, but to bring salvation to those who are waiting for him.

10

1The law is only an unclear picture of the
good things coming in the future; it is not
the real thing. The people under the law offer
the same sacrifices every year, but these sacrifices can never make perfect those who come
near to worship God. 2If the law could make
them perfect, the sacrifices would have already
stopped. The worshipers would be made clean,
and they would no longer have a sense of sin.
3But these sacrifices remind them of their sins
every year, 4because it is impossible for the
blood of bulls and goats to take away sins.

5So when Christ came into the world, he
said:

"You do not want sacrifices and offerings,
but you have prepared a body for me.
6You do not ask for burnt offerings
and offerings to take away sins.
7Then I said, 'Look, I have come.
It is written about me in the book.
God, I have come to do what you
want.' " *Psalm 40:6-8*

8In this Scripture he first said, "You do not
want sacrifices and offerings. You do not ask
for burnt offerings and offerings to take away
sins." (These are all sacrifices that the law commands.) 9Then he said, "Look, I have come to
do what you want." God ends the first system
of sacrifices so he can set up the new system.
10And because of this, we are made holy
through the sacrifice Christ made in his body
once and for all time.

11Every day the priests stand and do their
religious service, often offering the same sacrifices. Those sacrifices can never take away sins.
12But after Christ offered one sacrifice for sins,
forever, he sat down at the right side of God.
13And now Christ waits there for his enemies
to be put under his power. 14With one sacrifice
he made perfect forever those who are being
made holy.

15The Holy Spirit also tells us about this.
First he says:

16"This is the agreement[n] I will make
with them at that time, says the Lord.
I will put my teachings in their hearts
and write them on their minds."
Jeremiah 31:33

17Then he says:

"Their sins and the evil things they do—
I will not remember anymore."
Jeremiah 31:34

18Now when these have been forgiven, there is
no more need for a sacrifice for sins.

10:16 agreement God gives a contract or agreement to his people. For the Jews, this agreement was the Law of Moses. But now God has given a better agreement to his people through Christ.

CONTINUE TO TRUST GOD

[19]So, brothers and sisters, we are completely free to enter the Most Holy Place without fear because of the blood of Jesus' death. [20]We can enter through a new and living way that Jesus opened for us. It leads through the curtain—Christ's body. [21]And since we have a great priest over God's house, [22]let us come near to God with a sincere heart and a sure faith, because we have been made free from a guilty conscience, and our bodies have been washed with pure water. [23]Let us hold firmly to the hope that we have confessed, because we can trust God to do what he promised.

WHAT'S IT MEAN?

The Most Holy Place in the Meeting Tent, the place only the high priest was allowed to enter, was separated from the rest of the Meeting Tent by an embroidered curtain or veil.
Hebrews 10:19–20

[24]Let us think about each other and help each other to show love and do good deeds. [25]You should not stay away from the church meetings, as some are doing, but you should meet together and encourage each other. Do this even more as you see the day[n] coming.

[26]If we decide to go on sinning after we have learned the truth, there is no longer any sacrifice for sins. [27]There is nothing but fear in waiting for the judgment and the terrible fire that will destroy all those who live against God. [28]Anyone who refused to obey the law of Moses was found guilty from the proof given by two or three witnesses. He was put to death without mercy. [29]So what do you think should be done to those who do not respect the Son of God, who look at the blood of the agreement that made them holy as no different from others' blood, who insult the Spirit of God's grace? Surely they should have a much worse punishment. [30]We know that God said, "I will punish those who do wrong; I will repay them."[n] And he also said, "The Lord will judge his people."[n] [31]It is a terrible thing to fall into the hands of the living God.

[32]Remember those days in the past when you first learned the truth. You had a hard struggle with many sufferings, but you continued strong. [33]Sometimes you were hurt and attacked before crowds of people, and sometimes you shared with those who were being treated that way. [34]You helped the prisoners. You even had joy when all that you owned was taken from you, because you knew you had something better and more lasting.

[35]So do not lose the courage you had in the past, which has a great reward. [36]You must hold on, so you can do what God wants and receive what he has promised. [37]For in a very short time,

"The One who is coming will come
  and will not be delayed.
[38]The person who is right with me
  will live by trusting in me.
But if he turns back with fear,
  I will not be pleased with him."

Habakkuk 2:3-4

[39]But we are not those who turn back and are lost. We are people who have faith and are saved.

WHAT IS FAITH?

[1]Faith means being sure of the things we hope for and knowing that something is real even if we do not see it. [2]Faith is the reason we remember great people who lived in the past.

FAITH
What is the definition of faith? (11:1)

[3]It is by faith we understand that the whole world was made by God's command so what we see was made by something that cannot be seen.

[4]It was by faith that Abel offered God a better sacrifice than Cain did. God said he was pleased with the gifts Abel offered and called Abel a good man because of his faith. Abel died, but through his faith he is still speaking.

[5]It was by faith that Enoch was taken to heaven so he would not die. He could not be found, because God had taken him away. Before he was taken, the Scripture says that he was a man who truly pleased God. [6]Without faith no one can please God. Anyone who comes to God must believe that he is real

10:25 day The day Christ will come to judge all people and take his people to live with him.
10:30 "I . . . them." Quotation from Deuteronomy 32:35. **10:30 "The Lord . . . people."** Quotation from Deuteronomy 32:36; Psalm 135:14.

On the Edge

Without faith no one can please God. Anyone who comes to God must believe that he is real and that he rewards those who truly want to find him (Heb. 11:6).

The Bible talks a lot about having faith and about people who had faith. In the world, you don't often see much faith. In fact, some people are negative almost all the time. Any time you present them with a big idea, they start rattling off reasons that it won't work. That's not faith.

In order to please God, you've got to have faith. You've got to be sure of "the things we hope for" (see Heb. 11:1) and to believe in what you can't see. God does give people dreams and ideas; and most of the time they'll seem bigger than your abilities and resources. He wants you to be absolutely confident that he can make it happen.

Start by believing the Bible. Faith can really grow as you begin to get confident in his Word. Don't just memorize some verses. Get them into your heart. Try them and let God show you that he means business. He's good for his Word. Believing him is crucial, and no one else can do it for you. You have to develop your own faith and determine not to be shaken. You'll see it work and God will be pleased.

SEE FOR YOURSELF:
Hab. 2:4; Matt. 9:22; Mark 11:22; Luke 7:50; Rom. 4:9; 12:3; 1 Cor. 16:13; 2 Cor. 5:7; 2 Thess. 1:3; 1 Tim. 6:12; Heb. 11

and that he rewards those who truly want to
find him.
7It was by faith that Noah heard God's
warnings about things he could not yet see. He
obeyed God and built a large boat to save his
family. By his faith, Noah showed that the
world was wrong, and he became one of those
who are made right with God through faith.
8It was by faith Abraham obeyed God's call
to go to another place God promised to give
him. He left his own country, not knowing
where he was to go. 9It was by faith that he
lived like a foreigner in the country God promised to give him. He lived in tents with Isaac
and Jacob, who had received that same promise from God. 10Abraham was waiting for the
city[n] that has real foundations—the city planned
and built by God.
11He was too old to have children, and Sarah could not have children. It was by faith that
Abraham was made able to become a father,
because he trusted God to do what he had
promised. 12This man was so old he was
almost dead, but from him came as many
descendants as there are stars in the sky. Like
the sand on the seashore, they could not be
counted.

WHAT'S IT MEAN?

Sarah wasn't just past the age of childbearing when she gave birth to her son Isaac; she was past the age of most life spans. Isaac was born when Sarah was ninety! If that weren't incredible enough, her husband Abraham was one hundred! Isaac's son Jacob had twelve sons of his own. Their descendants became the twelve tribes of Israel.

Hebrews 11:11–12

13All these great people died in faith. They
did not get the things that God promised his
people, but they saw them coming far in the
future and were glad. They said they were like
visitors and strangers on earth. 14When people
say such things, they show they are looking
for a country that will be their own. 15If they
had been thinking about the country they had
left, they could have gone back. 16But they
were waiting for a better country—a heavenly
country. So God is not ashamed to be called
their God, because he has prepared a city for
them.
17It was by faith that Abraham, when God
tested him, offered his son Isaac as a sacrifice.
God made the promises to Abraham, but
Abraham was ready to offer his own son as a
sacrifice. 18God had said, "The descendants I
promised you will be from Isaac."[n] 19Abraham
believed that God could raise the dead, and

11:10 city The spiritual "city" where God's people live with him. Also called "the heavenly Jerusalem." (See Hebrews 12:22.) **11:18 "The descendants . . . Isaac."** Quotation from Genesis 21:12.

really, it was as if Abraham got Isaac back from
death.
20It was by faith that Isaac blessed the future of Jacob and Esau. 21It was by faith that
Jacob, as he was dying, blessed each one of
Joseph's sons. Then he worshiped as he leaned
on the top of his walking stick.
22It was by faith that Joseph, while he was
dying, spoke about the Israelites leaving Egypt
and gave instructions about what to do with
his body.
23It was by faith that Moses' parents hid
him for three months after he was born. They
saw that Moses was a beautiful baby, and they
were not afraid to disobey the king's order.
24It was by faith that Moses, when he grew
up, refused to be called the son of the king of
Egypt's daughter. 25He chose to suffer with
God's people instead of enjoying sin for a short
time. 26He thought it was better to suffer for the
Christ than to have all the treasures of Egypt,
because he was looking for God's reward. 27It
was by faith that Moses left Egypt and was not
afraid of the king's anger. Moses continued
strong as if he could see the God that no one
can see. 28It was by faith that Moses prepared
the Passover and spread the blood on the
doors so the one who brings death would not
kill the firstborn sons of Israel.
29It was by faith that the people crossed the
Red Sea as if it were dry land. But when the
Egyptians tried it, they were drowned.
30It was by faith that the walls of Jericho fell
after the people had marched around them for
seven days.
31It was by faith that Rahab, the prostitute,
welcomed the spies and was not killed with
those who refused to obey God.
32Do I need to give more examples? I do not
have time to tell you about Gideon, Barak,
Samson, Jephthah, David, Samuel, and the
prophets. 33Through their faith they defeated
kingdoms. They did what was right, received
God's promises, and shut the mouths of lions.
34They stopped great fires and were saved from
being killed with swords. They were weak, and
yet were made strong. They were powerful in
battle and defeated other armies. 35Women received their dead relatives raised back to life.
Others were tortured and refused to accept
their freedom so they could be raised from the
dead to a better life. 36Some were laughed at
and beaten. Others were put in chains and
thrown into prison. 37They were stoned to
death, they were cut in half, and they were
killed with swords. Some wore the skins of
sheep and goats. They were poor, abused, and
treated badly. 38The world was not good
enough for them! They wandered in deserts
and mountains, living in caves and holes in the
earth.
39All these people are known for their faith,
but none of them received what God had
promised. 40God planned to give us something
better so that they would be made perfect, but
only together with us.

FOLLOW JESUS' EXAMPLE

12
1We have around us many people whose
lives tell us what faith means. So let us run the
race that is before us and never give up. We

On the Edge

Think about Jesus' example. He held on while wicked people were doing evil things to him. So do not get tired and stop trying (Heb. 12:3).

Life can be tough sometimes—even for a person who has made up his mind to follow Jesus, to be his friend, and to live the way he wants. The person who wrote this letter knew that, and wanted to be sure that these Christians (and you, too) would keep going even when times were tough.

The answer for your hard times is to focus on Jesus. You've got to choose to replace your negative thoughts with thoughts about the hope and grace the Lord has for you. Don't dwell on how awful your life is. That's called self-pity, and it's not good for you. Don't worry about how much harder things might get. Don't waste time being concerned about what other people think of you. Concentrating on these things is just a recipe for depression.

Instead, get your mind on Jesus. He has a solution for you! When other things try to distract you, push your thoughts back to him. Think about the way he lived—his gentleness, his joy, his mercy, his patience with people who didn't deserve it. Think about the way he died—the incredible sacrifice he made for you. Praise him for his goodness, his awesomeness. Thank him for the love he pours out on you. In the face of things like that, it's hard to stay discouraged. He will help you!

SEE FOR YOURSELF:
Eph. 4:23–24;
Phil. 2:5; 4:8

should remove from our lives anything that would get in the way and the sin that so easily holds us back. [2]Let us look only to Jesus, the One who began our faith and who makes it perfect. He suffered death on the cross. But he accepted the shame as if it were nothing because of the joy that God put before him. And now he is sitting at the right side of God's throne. [3]Think about Jesus' example. He held on while wicked people were doing evil things to him. So do not get tired and stop trying.

GOD IS LIKE A FATHER

[4]You are struggling against sin, but your struggles have not yet caused you to be killed. [5]You have forgotten the encouraging words that call you his children:

"My child, don't think the Lord's discipline
is worth nothing,
and don't stop trying when he corrects
you.
[6]The Lord disciplines those he loves,
and he punishes everyone he accepts as
his child." *Proverbs 3:11-12*

[7]So hold on through your sufferings, because they are like a father's discipline. God is treating you as children. All children are disciplined by their fathers. [8]If you are never disciplined (and every child must be disciplined), you are not true children. [9]We have all had fathers here on earth who disciplined us, and we respected them. So it is even more important that we accept discipline from the Father of our spirits so we will have life. [10]Our fathers on earth disciplined us for a short time in the way they thought was best. But God disciplines us to help us, so we can become holy as he is. [11]We do not enjoy being disciplined. It is painful, but later, after we have learned from it, we have peace, because we start living in the right way.

BE CAREFUL HOW YOU LIVE

[12]You have become weak, so make yourselves strong again. [13]Live in the right way so that you will be saved and your weakness will not cause you to be lost.

[14]Try to live in peace with all people, and try to live free from sin. Anyone whose life is not holy will never see the Lord. [15]Be careful that no one fails to receive God's grace and begins to cause trouble among you. A person like that can ruin many of you. [16]Be careful that no one takes part in sexual sin or is like Esau and never thinks about God. As the oldest son, Esau would have received everything from his father, but he sold all that for a single meal. [17]You remember that after Esau did this, he wanted to get his father's blessing, but his father refused. Esau could find no way to change what he had done, even though he wanted the blessing so much that he cried.

[18]You have not come to a mountain that can be touched and that is burning with fire. You have not come to darkness, sadness, and storms. [19]You have not come to the noise of a trumpet or to the sound of a voice like the one the people of Israel heard and begged not to hear another word. [20]They did not want to hear the command: "If anything, even an animal, touches the mountain, it must be put to

On the Edge

We do not enjoy being disciplined. It is painful, but later, after we have learned from it, we have peace, because we start living in the right way (Heb. 12:11).

God has given every parent the difficult task of disciplining their children (see Prov. 22:6). For example, it may seem like your parents are too strict when it comes to going out. The truth is that the world just isn't as safe as it once was. Parents have a good reason to be concerned for your safety. They're not being jerks; they're looking out for you. Maybe you think your parents are a lot tougher on you than your friends' parents are on them. This may be because you live in a time when a lot of parents have checked out on raising their children. Kids get to raise themselves in a lot of homes, and they aren't doing a very good job.

While the process may be frustrating and hard at times, be thankful that you have parents who love you and want to do what God has called them to do. Believe it or not, when you look back on these years, you will thank your parents for caring so much about you. Try to learn from their correction. More freedom is always given to those who become responsible. Begin to apply these lessons and see what happens!

SEE FOR YOURSELF:
Prov. 3:12; 22:6; 23:13–14; Eph. 6:4; Col. 3:21

death with stones."[n] 21What they saw was so terrible that Moses said, "I am shaking with fear."[n]

22But you have come to Mount Zion,[n] to the city of the living God, the heavenly Jerusalem. You have come to thousands of angels gathered together with joy. 23You have come to the meeting of God's firstborn[n] children whose names are written in heaven. You have come to God, the judge of all people, and to the spirits of good people who have been made perfect. 24You have come to Jesus, the One who brought the new agreement from God to his people, and you have come to the sprinkled blood[n] that has a better message than the blood of Abel.[n]

25So be careful and do not refuse to listen when God speaks. Others refused to listen to him when he warned them on earth, and they did not escape. So it will be worse for us if we refuse to listen to God who warns us from heaven. 26When he spoke before, his voice shook the earth, but now he has promised, "Once again I will shake not only the earth but also the heavens."[n] 27The words "once again" clearly show us that everything that was made—things that can be shaken—will be destroyed. Only the things that cannot be shaken will remain.

28So let us be thankful, because we have a kingdom that cannot be shaken. We should worship God in a way that pleases him with respect and fear, 29because our God is like a fire that burns things up.

13 1Keep on loving each other as brothers and sisters. 2Remember to welcome strangers, because some who have done this have welcomed angels without knowing it. 3Remember those who are in prison as if you were in prison with them. Remember those who are suffering as if you were suffering with them.

SEX

When is sex honorable and pure? (13:4)

4Marriage should be honored by everyone, and husband and wife should keep their marriage pure. God will judge as guilty those who take part in sexual sins. 5Keep your lives free from the love of money, and be satisfied with what you have. God has said,

"I will never leave you;
I will never forget you." *Deuteronomy 31:6*

6So we can be sure when we say,

"I will not be afraid, because the Lord is
my helper.
People can't do anything to me." *Psalm 118:6*

7Remember your leaders who taught God's message to you. Remember how they lived and died, and copy their faith. 8Jesus Christ is the same yesterday, today, and forever.

9Do not let all kinds of strange teachings lead you into the wrong way. Your hearts should be strengthened by God's grace, not by obeying rules about foods, which do not help those who obey them.

10We have a sacrifice, but the priests who serve in the Holy Tent cannot eat from it. 11The high priest carries the blood of animals into the Most Holy Place where he offers this blood for sins. But the bodies of the animals are burned outside the camp. 12So Jesus also suffered outside the city to make his people holy with his own blood. 13So let us go to Jesus outside the camp, holding on as he did when we are abused.

14Here on earth we do not have a city that lasts forever, but we are looking for the city that we will have in the future. 15So through Jesus let us always offer to God our sacrifice of praise, coming from lips that speak his name. 16Do not forget to do good to others, and share with them, because such sacrifices please God.

17Obey your leaders and act under their authority. They are watching over you, because they are responsible for your souls. Obey them so that they will do this work with joy, not sadness. It will not help you to make their work hard.

18Pray for us. We are sure that we have a clear conscience, because we always want to do the right thing. 19I especially beg you to pray so that God will send me back to you soon.

20-21I pray that the God of peace will give you every good thing you need so you can do what he wants. God raised from the dead our Lord Jesus, the Great Shepherd of the sheep, because of the blood of his death. His blood began the eternal agreement that God made with his people. I pray that God will

12:20 "If . . . stones." Quotation from Exodus 19:12-13. **12:21 "I . . . fear."** Quotation from Deuteronomy 9:19. **12:22 Mount Zion** Another name for Jerusalem, here meaning the spiritual city of God's people. **12:23 firstborn** The first son born in a Jewish family was given the most important place in the family and received special blessings. All of God's children are like that. **12:24 sprinkled blood** The blood of Jesus' death. **12:24 Abel** The son of Adam and Eve, who was killed by his brother Cain (Genesis 4:8). **12:26 "Once . . . heavens."** Quotation from Haggai 2:6, 21.

do in us what pleases him, through Jesus Christ, and to him be glory forever and ever. Amen.

22My brothers and sisters, I beg you to listen patiently to this message I have written to encourage you, because it is not very long. 23I want you to know that our brother Timothy has been let out of prison. If he arrives soon, we will both come to see you.

24Greet all your leaders and all of God's people. Those from Italy send greetings to you.

25Grace be with you all.

James

CONTENT

Have you ever known anyone who said they wanted to be your friend, but then they didn't act like a friend? Maybe they talked about you behind your back. Maybe they found another friend and left you behind. Whatever they did, their actions didn't match their words. When people's actions don't match their words, which do we usually believe?

Their actions.

The Book of James is about that kind of concept. It's about making the faith that you confess with your words match the way you act. James even goes so far as to say that if your actions don't match your faith, then your faith is worthless.

Whew. That's a little harsh, don't you think? It's the truth, though. What good is it to God or our family or ourselves, or to a world that needs to see a real Christian, if we say a lot of good stuff but don't live according to it?

James is one of those where-the-rubber-meets-the-road kinds of books. It reminds us that we are playing with holy fire when we say we believe. It reminds us that, when we say we believe, we are making a promise that will change everything we do.

Outline

1:1 .... Greetings
1:2–18 .... A Life of Faith and Wisdom
1:19–27 .... Hearing and Obeying God's Message
2:1–13 .... Don't Favor the Rich and Powerful
2:14–26 .... Faith and Good Works
3:1–18 .... Words and Wisdom
4:1—5:6 .... Warning Against Friendship with the World
5:7–20 .... Patience, Kindness, and Prayer

Purpose

Authentic faith produces an authentic Christian lifestyle.

Theme

Faith That Works

Date of writing

Mid-40s A.D.

"My dear brothers and sisters, always be willing to listen and slow to speak. Do not become angry easily, because anger will not help you live the right kind of life God wants" (1:19–20).

Bible Talk

Caution! Caution! Caution!

James is famous for giving us a warning about one of the most dangerous forces known to man. It has the violent nature of a forest fire and a power greater than a wild animal. Know what it is?

The force that James warns about is the human tongue. It's not that the tongue itself has so much power. It's that we use our tongues to speak. When we speak, we use words. When we use words, we hold the power to hurt or to heal, and we are stuck with the outcome. Words are hard to take back.

So when James warns us to learn to control our tongues, he's really saying that we should control our wills and our brains and our mouths and all the words that we say.

TEMPTATION

James tells us some very important facts about temptation. He tells us that God will never tempt us with evil. That means when you are wanting to do something you know you shouldn't, God is not testing your will. According to James, more likely that temptation comes from the fact that we humans are evil at best, and we want to do what is wrong.

So when we are tempted, it is not that some force outside of ourselves is trying to get us to sin. We are just getting a snapshot of what is inside of us. That snapshot should send us running to God, the only One who can make us better than we naturally are.

1

1From James, a servant of God and of the Lord Jesus Christ.

To all of God's people who are scattered everywhere in the world:

Greetings.

FAITH AND WISDOM

2My brothers and sisters,[n] when you have many kinds of troubles, you should be full of joy, 3because you know that these troubles test your faith, and this will give you patience. 4Let your patience show itself perfectly in what you do. Then you will be perfect and complete and will have everything you need. 5But if any of you needs wisdom, you should ask God for it. He is generous and enjoys giving to all people, so he will give you wisdom. 6But when you ask God, you must believe and not doubt. Anyone who doubts is like a wave in the sea, blown up and down by the wind. 7-8Such doubters are thinking two different things at the same time, and they cannot decide about anything they do. They should not think they will receive anything from the Lord.

TRUE RICHES

9Believers who are poor should be proud, because God has made them spiritually rich. 10Those who are rich should be proud, because God has shown them that they are spiritually poor. The rich will die like a wild flower in the grass. 11The sun rises with burning heat and dries up the plants. The flower falls off, and its beauty is gone. In the same way the rich will die while they are still taking care of business.

TEMPTATION IS NOT FROM GOD

12When people are tempted and still continue strong, they should be happy. After they have proved their faith, God will reward them with life forever. God promised this to all those who love him. 13When people are tempted, they should not say, "God is tempting me." Evil cannot tempt God, and God himself does not tempt anyone. 14But people are tempted when their own evil desire leads them away and traps them. 15This desire leads to sin, and then the sin grows and brings death.

16My dear brothers and sisters, do not be fooled about this. 17Every good action and every perfect gift is from God. These good gifts come down from the Creator of the sun, moon, and stars, who does not change like their shifting shadows. 18God decided to give us life through the word of truth so we might be the most important of all the things he made.

LISTENING AND OBEYING

19My dear brothers and sisters, always be willing to listen and slow to speak. Do not become angry easily, 20because anger will not help you live the right kind of life God wants. 21So put out of your life every evil thing and every kind of wrong. Then in gentleness accept God's teaching that is planted in your hearts, which can save you.

22Do what God's teaching says; when you only listen and do nothing, you are fooling yourselves. 23Those who hear God's teaching and do nothing are like people who look at themselves in a mirror. 24They see their faces and then go away and quickly forget what they looked like. 25But the truly happy people are those who carefully study God's perfect law that makes people free, and they continue to study it. They do not forget what they heard, but they obey what God's teaching says. Those who do this will be made happy.

BLESSING
What brings us blessing (happiness)? (1:25)

THE TRUE WAY TO WORSHIP GOD

26People who think they are religious but say things they should not say are just fooling themselves. Their "religion" is worth nothing. 27Religion that God accepts as pure and without fault is this: caring for orphans or widows who need help, and keeping yourself free from the world's evil influence.

LOVE ALL PEOPLE

2

1My dear brothers and sisters, as believers in our glorious Lord Jesus Christ, never think some people are more important than others. 2Suppose someone comes into your church meeting wearing nice clothes and a gold ring. At the same time a poor person comes in wearing old, dirty clothes. 3You show special attention to the one wearing nice clothes and say, "Please, sit here in this good seat." But you say to the poor person, "Stand over there," or, "Sit on the floor by my feet." 4What are you doing? You are making some people more important than others, and with evil thoughts you are deciding that one person is better.

1:2 brothers and sisters Although the Greek text says "brothers" here and throughout this book, James's words were meant for the entire church, including men and women.

5Listen, my dear brothers and sisters! God
chose the poor in the world to be rich with
faith and to receive the kingdom God promised to those who love him. 6But you show no
respect to the poor. The rich are always trying
to control your lives. They are the ones who
take you to court. 7And they are the ones who
speak against Jesus, who owns you.
8This royal law is found in the Scriptures:
"Love your neighbor as you love yourself."[n] If
you obey this law, you are doing right. 9But if
you treat one person as being more important
than another, you are sinning. You are guilty of
breaking God's law. 10A person who follows all
of God's law but fails to obey even one command is guilty of breaking all the commands in
that law. 11The same God who said, "You must
not be guilty of adultery,"[n] also said, "You must
not murder anyone."[n] So if you do not take
part in adultery but you murder someone, you
are guilty of breaking all of God's law. 12In
everything you say and do, remember that
you will be judged by the law that makes people free. 13So you must show mercy to others,
or God will not show mercy to you when he
judges you. But the person who shows mercy
can stand without fear at the judgment.

FAITH AND GOOD WORKS

14My brothers and sisters, if people say they
have faith, but do nothing, their faith is worth
nothing. Can faith like that save them? 15A

WHAT'S IT MEAN?

It's said that couples who have children later in life appreciate the parenting experience more than young parents do. If that's true, Abraham and Sarah may have been the most appreciative parents in history. When their son Isaac was born, Abraham was one hundred years old and Sarah was ninety. Years later, God tested Abraham's appreciation—and his faith—by asking him to kill Isaac as a sacrifice. Even after waiting a century for the son God had promised him, Abraham didn't hesitate to obey. Just when Abraham was ready to kill Isaac, the Lord stopped him and sent a ram to sacrifice instead.

James 2:21

2:8 "Love . . . yourself." Quotation from Leviticus 19:18. **2:11 "You . . . adultery."** Quotation from Exodus 20:14 and Deuteronomy 5:18. **2:11 "You . . . anyone."** Quotation from Exodus 20:13 and Deuteronomy 5:17.

Promise

HE PROMISES THAT YOU WILL INHERIT HIS KINGDOM.

Listen, my dear brothers and sisters! God chose the poor in the world to be rich with faith and to receive the kingdom God promised to those who love him (James 2:5).

Maybe you'll find a lot of money, or stumble onto a fortune, or marry into royalty. Most people spend all of their lives trying to build a kingdom or to win one. They haven't heard the news that we're already heirs to a kingdom—the eternal kingdom of God—the one that doesn't rot, or fade away, or go broke.

Where are you spending your time? Building a kingdom on earth, or building the kingdom of heaven. Think for a moment. Do you know your grandmother's name? Easy? How about your great-grandmother's name? Harder, but okay. Now, what's your great-great-grandmother's name? Stumped? It's the sad truth. In about three or four generations, no one will remember your name either. Oh, it'll be written down somewhere, but you'll be long gone. Your earthly kingdom won't matter anymore. If you're a Christian, you'll be with Jesus, sharing in the kingdom he has for you. There, you'll matter forever.

SEE FOR YOURSELF:

Luke 6:20; 2 Thess. 1:5; Heb. 12:28

brother or sister in Christ might need clothes
or food. 16If you say to that person, "God be
with you! I hope you stay warm and get plenty
to eat," but you do not give what that person
needs, your words are worth nothing. 17In the
same way, faith that is alone—that does nothing—is dead.
18Someone might say, "You have faith, but I
have deeds." Show me your faith without doing anything, and I will show you my faith by
what I do. 19You believe there is one God.
Good! But the demons believe that, too, and
they tremble with fear.

WHAT'S IT MEAN?

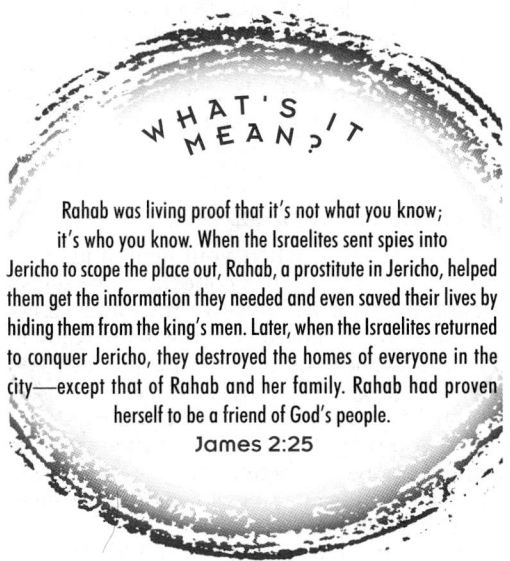

Rahab was living proof that it's not what you know; it's who you know. When the Israelites sent spies into Jericho to scope the place out, Rahab, a prostitute in Jericho, helped them get the information they needed and even saved their lives by hiding them from the king's men. Later, when the Israelites returned to conquer Jericho, they destroyed the homes of everyone in the city—except that of Rahab and her family. Rahab had proven herself to be a friend of God's people.

James 2:25

20You foolish person! Must you be shown
that faith that does nothing is worth nothing?
21Abraham, our ancestor, was made right with
God by what he did when he offered his son
Isaac on the altar. 22So you see that Abraham's
faith and the things he did worked together.
His faith was made perfect by what he did.
23This shows the full meaning of the Scripture
that says: "Abraham believed God, and God
accepted Abraham's faith, and that faith made
him right with God."[n] And Abraham was
called God's friend.[n] 24So you see that people
are made right with God by what they do, not
by faith only.
25Another example is Rahab, a prostitute,
who was made right with God by something
she did. She welcomed the spies into her home
and helped them escape by a different road.
26Just as a person's body that does not have
a spirit is dead, so faith that does nothing is
dead!

CONTROLLING THE THINGS WE SAY

3 1My brothers and sisters, not many of you
should become teachers, because you know
that we who teach will be judged more strictly.
2We all make many mistakes. If people never
said anything wrong, they would be perfect
and able to control their entire selves, too.
3When we put bits into the mouths of horses
to make them obey us, we can control their
whole bodies. 4Also a ship is very big, and it is
pushed by strong winds. But a very small rud-
der controls that big ship, making it go wherever the pilot wants. 5It is the same with the
tongue. It is a small part of the body, but it
brags about great things.
A big forest fire can be started with only a
little flame. 6And the tongue is like a fire. It is a
whole world of evil among the parts of our
bodies. The tongue spreads its evil through the
whole body. The tongue is set on fire by hell,
and it starts a fire that influences all of life.
7People can tame every kind of wild animal,
bird, reptile, and fish, and they have tamed
them, 8but no one can tame the tongue. It is
wild and evil and full of deadly poison. 9We
use our tongues to praise our Lord and Father,
but then we curse people, whom God made
like himself. 10Praises and curses come from
the same mouth! My brothers and sisters, this
should not happen. 11Do good and bad water

WHAT'S IT MEAN?

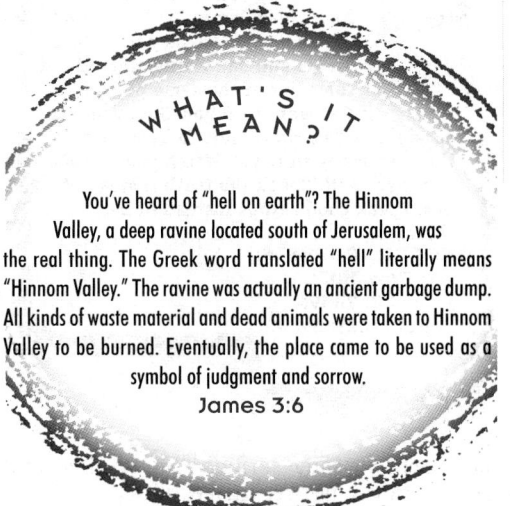

You've heard of "hell on earth"? The Hinnom Valley, a deep ravine located south of Jerusalem, was the real thing. The Greek word translated "hell" literally means "Hinnom Valley." The ravine was actually an ancient garbage dump. All kinds of waste material and dead animals were taken to Hinnom Valley to be burned. Eventually, the place came to be used as a symbol of judgment and sorrow.

James 3:6

2:23 "Abraham . . . God." Quotation from Genesis 15:6. **2:23 God's friend** These words about Abraham are found in 2 Chronicles 20:7 and Isaiah 41:8.

On the Edge

We all make many mistakes. If people never said anything wrong, they would be perfect and able to control their entire selves, too. . . . It is the same with the tongue. It is a small part of the body, but it brags about great things. A big forest fire can be started with only a little flame. And the tongue is like a fire. It is a whole world of evil among the parts of our bodies. The tongue spreads its evil through the whole body. The tongue is set on fire by hell, and it starts a fire that influences all of life (James 3:2, 5–6).

At the time, gossip can seem so harmless—a few words about a friend, information that nobody else knew. You felt big. Everyone paid attention to you and seemed to be impressed. And then, a few days pass. Your friend hears that you told her secrets. You gossiped. She's pretty upset and she's really hurt. You're ashamed, so you try to cover your tracks with lies. But it's too late. She already knows. What a mess.

James says that your tongue gets out of control and causes evil (see v. 8). In other words, your mouth can get you into big trouble. Words are powerful, like "deadly poison" (v. 8). They can ruin somebody's day or somebody's life. They can also save somebody's life. They can hurt or they can heal. Read James 3:10–12. You'll see that praises and curses (good words and bad words) should not come out of the same person. So if you want to follow God, you can't gossip. Besides, who wants to be known as the best gossip in town? Watch your words. Use them well. Speak the truth instead of lies. Speak good things instead of bad things.

SEE FOR YOURSELF:
Prov. 11:13; 16:28; 20:19; Eph. 4:29; 5:4

flow from the same spring? [12]My brothers and
sisters, can a fig tree make olives, or can a
grapevine make figs? No! And a well full of
salty water cannot give good water.

TRUE WISDOM

[13]Are there those among you who are truly
wise and understanding? Then they should
show it by living right and doing good things
with a gentleness that comes from wisdom.
[14]But if you are selfish and have bitter jealousy
in your hearts, do not brag. Your bragging is a
lie that hides the truth. [15]That kind of "wisdom"
does not come from God but from the world.
It is not spiritual; it is from the devil. [16]Where
jealousy and selfishness are, there will be confusion and every kind of evil. [17]But the wisdom
that comes from God is first of all pure, then
peaceful, gentle, and easy to please. This wisdom is always ready to help those who are
troubled and to do good for others. It is always
fair and honest. [18]People who work for peace
in a peaceful way plant a good crop of right-
living.

GIVE YOURSELVES TO GOD

4 [1]Do you know where your fights and arguments come from? They come from the selfish
desires that war within you. [2]You want things,
but you do not have them. So you are ready to
kill and are jealous of other people, but you
still cannot get what you want. So you argue
and fight. You do not get what you want, because you do not ask God. [3]Or when you ask,
you do not receive because the reason you ask
is wrong. You want things so you can use them
for your own pleasures.
[4]So, you are not loyal to God! You should
know that loving the world is the same as hating God. Anyone who wants to be a friend of
the world becomes God's enemy. [5]Do you
think the Scripture means nothing that says,
"The Spirit that God made to live in us wants
us for himself alone"?[n] [6]But God gives us even
more grace, as the Scripture says,

"God is against the proud,
but he gives grace to the humble."

Proverbs 3:34

[7]So give yourselves completely to God.
Stand against the devil, and the devil will run
from you. [8]Come near to God, and
God will come near to you.
You sinners, clean sin out of
your lives. You who are trying
to follow God and the world
at the same time, make your
thinking pure. [9]Be sad, cry,
and weep! Change your laugh-
ter into crying and your joy into sadness.

WORSHIP
When does God come near to us? (4:8)

4:5 "The Spirit . . . alone." These words may be from Exodus 20:5.

10 Don't be too proud in the Lord's presence,
and he will make you great.

YOU ARE NOT THE JUDGE

11 Brothers and sisters, do not tell evil lies
about each other. If you speak against your fellow believers or judge them, you are judging
and speaking against the law they follow. And
when you are judging the law, you are no
longer a follower of the law. You have become
a judge. 12 God is the only Lawmaker and
Judge. He is the only One who can save and
destroy. So it is not right for you to judge your
neighbor.

LET GOD PLAN YOUR LIFE

13 Some of you say, "Today or tomorrow we
will go to some city. We will stay there a year,
do business, and make money." 14 But you do
not know what will happen tomorrow! Your
life is like a mist. You can see it for a short time,
but then it goes away. 15 So you should say, "If
the Lord wants, we will live and do this or
that." 16 But now you are proud and you brag.
All of this bragging is wrong. 17 Anyone who
knows the right thing to do, but does not do it,
is sinning.

A WARNING TO THE RICH

5
1 You rich people, listen! Cry and be very sad
because of the troubles that are coming to you.
2 Your riches have rotted, and your clothes
have been eaten by moths. 3 Your gold and silver have rusted, and that rust will be a proof
that you were wrong. It will eat your bodies
like fire. You saved your treasure for the last
days. 4 The pay you did not give the workers
who mowed your fields cries out against you,

WHAT'S IT MEAN?

Moths are mentioned several times in the Bible as symbols of destruction and the foolishness of putting one's hope in material things. Here's how the little critters are able to do so much damage. Female moths often lay their eggs in clothing. When the eggs hatch, the newborn larvae eat the fibers of the material. Because the larvae chew quietly, the owner of the clothing may not know that damage is being done until it's too late.

James 5:2

Promise

HE PROMISES TO HONOR HUMBLE PEOPLE.

But God gives us even more grace, as the Scripture says, "God is against the proud, but he gives grace to the humble." . . . Don't be too proud in the Lord's presence, and he will make you great (James 4:6, 10).

The way up with God, the way toward honor, is to be humble. God is looking for young men and women who will be genuinely humble. He doesn't want a fake humility that says, "I'm really a nothing," but is conceited and arrogant on the inside. Some people think that humility means really believing that you are a nothing. No way. *True humility is knowing and recognizing who God is and who you are.* God says that, through Christ, you can do all things (see Phil. 4:13). He rejoices and sings because of you (see Zeph. 3:17). You are not a nothing!

Being humble does not mean acting like a doormat. It means that you know for certain that you are strong through Jesus Christ. It means that you are secure enough to serve others and not care what people think. You're strong enough to be seen with people who aren't popular. You're secure enough to really care about someone who often gets left out—and you show it.

Pride and arrogance have no place with God. Jesus measures strength not by how cool you act, but by your humility. Look at John 13:3–17. You'll see a great picture of Jesus' humility. Working on humility in your life will help you be more like him. And that's what it's all about.

SEE FOR YOURSELF:

Ps. 149:4; Prov. 3:34; Dan. 10:12; Matt. 23:12; John 13:3–17; Phil. 2:8

On the Edge

Anyone who is having troubles should pray. Anyone who is happy should sing praises (James 5:13).

Did you know that grades in school are not very good indicators of how successful a person will be in life? Success comes to people who never quit trying. Failure may shake them up, but it doesn't stop them. You've got to jump right back in and try again when you fail. Don't let a failing grade beat you up. Failing a class doesn't make you a failure in life!

It's important to constantly pursue excellence in every area of your life. But the fact is, you will fall short somewhere along the way. Learn from your mistakes and take all your anxieties to the Lord. One of the cruel things about failure is that it can make you afraid. Some people get so afraid of failing again that they refuse to try. So pray, pray, pray, and ask the Lord for strength to face the challenge again. Ask him to provide a clear path for you to walk through—removing the obstacles that tripped you up before. Each time you think about your failure, talk to God about it. Give him the burden of it, thank him for the great success you are to him, and listen as he whispers to you, "Never, never give up!"

SEE FOR YOURSELF:
Deut. 28:6; Ps. 103:5; John 14:16; Heb. 4:16

On the Edge

Confess your sins to each other and pray for each other so God can heal you. When a believing person prays, great things happen (James 5:16).

Real accountability keeps you growing and keeps you honest. Meeting regularly with some friends who love you and who love Jesus will strengthen you as a Christian. As you confess your sins to each other, pray together, and grow closer as friends, you'll begin to pull for one another.

Kate and Rachel are accountability partners. Kate is an early bird, but Rachel is a sleepyhead. Kate calls Rachel every morning and they pray together. Kate's had a hard time getting her prayer life going, so her morning prayer time with Rachel not only helps Rachel roll out of bed; it also helps Kate develop her prayer life.

A high-school senior asks his youth pastor to pray with him before he goes on dates. Praying with someone reminds him to commit the date to the Lord, to respect his date, and to honor God with his behavior. He also knows that his youth pastor will ask him later how the time went, and he wants to be able to give a good report.

Accountability can help you conquer areas you've been struggling with. People who have real accountability in their lives seem to grow faster than people who don't. They work as a team and as a family to become more like Jesus. The Lord is pleased with relationships like that.

SEE FOR YOURSELF:
Prov. 27:6, 17; Rom. 14:12; Heb. 4:13

and the cries of the workers have been heard
by the Lord All-Powerful. 5Your life on earth
was full of rich living and pleasing yourselves with everything you wanted. You
made yourselves fat, like an animal ready to be
killed. 6You have judged guilty and then murdered innocent people, who were not against
you.

BE PATIENT

7Brothers and sisters, be patient until the
Lord comes again. A farmer patiently waits for
his valuable crop to grow from the earth and
for it to receive the autumn and spring rains.
8You, too, must be patient. Do not give up
hope, because the Lord is coming soon.
9Brothers and sisters, do not complain against
each other or you will be judged guilty. And
the Judge is ready to come! 10Brothers and sisters, follow the example of the prophets who
spoke for the Lord. They suffered many hard
things, but they were patient. 11We say they are
happy because they did not give up. You have
heard about Job's patience, and you know the
Lord's purpose for him in the end. You know
the Lord is full of mercy and is kind.

BE CAREFUL WHAT YOU SAY

12My brothers and sisters, above all, do not
use an oath when you make a promise. Don't
use the name of heaven, earth, or anything else

to prove what you say. When you mean yes, say only yes, and when you mean no, say only no so you will not be judged guilty.

THE POWER OF PRAYER

[13]Anyone who is having troubles should pray. Anyone who is happy should sing praises. [14]Anyone who is sick should call the church's elders. They should pray for and pour oil on the person[n] in the name of the Lord. [15]And the prayer that is said with faith will make the sick person well; the Lord will heal that person. And if the person has sinned, the sins will be forgiven. [16]Confess your sins to each other and pray for each other so God can heal you. When a believing person prays, great things happen. [17]Elijah was a human being just like us. He prayed that it would not rain, and it did not rain on the land for three and a half years! [18]Then Elijah prayed again, and the rain came down from the sky, and the land produced crops again.

SAVING A SOUL

[19]My brothers and sisters, if one of you wanders away from the truth, and someone helps that person come back, [20]remember this: Anyone who brings a sinner back from the wrong way will save that sinner's soul from death and will cause many sins to be forgiven.

5:14 pour oil on the person Oil was used in the name of the Lord as a sign that the person was now set apart for God's special attention and care.

1&2 peter

CONTENT The letters that Peter wrote to the early church were like survival manuals. These churches faced danger every day. They were written at the time when Nero was actually throwing Christians to the lions. They were written at a time when even admitting what you believed was a dangerous thing. They were written to help people survive both physically and spiritually.

In Peter's first letter, he wrote to the Christians who were being persecuted by people outside of the church. These Christians faced torture and death because of what they believed. Peter wrote to help them gain some perspective in the midst of the struggle to survive. He encouraged their faith even if it endangered their lives. He knew that if their faith stayed strong, they might be in physical danger but their souls would be safe.

In Peter's second letter, he warned the Christians to watch out for traitors *inside* the church. These persecutors took the form of false teachers who taught doctrines that would weaken faith rather than build it up. Paul knew that, for these Christians, even though their bodies weren't in physical danger, their souls were in a precarious position.

Outline 1 Peter:

1:1–2 .... Greetings and Prayer
1:3–12 .... God's Mercy and Living Hope
1:13—2:17 .... Living as God's Holy Priesthood
2:18–25 .... The Example of Christ's Suffering
3:1—4:19 .... Being a Christian and Suffering
5:1–11 .... Advice for Church Leaders
5:12–14 .... Final Greetings

Purpose We can triumph over suffering as we follow Jesus.

Theme Suffering as a Christian

Date of writing A.D. 64

Outline 2 Peter:

1:1–2 .... Greetings and Prayer
1:3–15 .... How the Lord's Followers Should Live
1:16–21 .... The Glory of Christ
2:1–22 .... False Prophets and Teachers
3:1–18 .... The Lord's Return Is Certain

Purpose We dare not set our hearts on worldly things.

Theme Remaining True to the Biblical Faith

Date of writing A.D. 65

"No prophecy ever came from what a person wanted to say, but people led by the Holy Spirit spoke words from God" (2 Pet. 1:21).

Bible Talk

Why Endure Persecution?

History has taught us that persecution does not deter Christianity. In fact, Christianity has often grown in countries that threatened death to people who declared faith in God. Why do you think that is true?

Part of it is because true faith is true, no matter what. If God is God and if he is active in your life, then that is true, no matter how much people might harass you or intimidate you.

Part of it is because when faith is put to the test, it grows the strongest. Faith in a fire shines the brightest.

And when you think about it, if Christianity is not real, then why should governments and nations and armies go to such great lengths to stamp it out? If Christianity is just an empty custom with no power, what is the big deal after all?

WHAT IS "HERESY" ANYWAY?

Peter warned against false teachers inside of the church. The question is, at what point do you stop saying people have different opinions and start saying they are teaching heresy?

Just about everyone you ask will give you a different answer for that question. We care about our faith, and we work hard to understand it. When someone disagrees with us, it's sometimes hard to feel okay about it.

That doesn't mean that every difference of opinion should result in a disagreement. Real heresy focuses on who Jesus is. If someone is telling you that Jesus is not *really* God in the flesh, then you have some heresy going on. That doesn't mean you have to be angry or even loud-mouthed, but it does mean you have to stand up for the truth.

1 [1]From Peter, an apostle of Jesus Christ.
To God's chosen people who are away from
their homes and are scattered all around the
countries of Pontus, Galatia, Cappadocia, Asia,
and Bithynia. [2]God planned long ago to choose
you by making you his holy people, which is
the Spirit's work. God wanted you to obey him
and to be made clean by the blood of the death
of Jesus Christ.
Grace and peace be yours more and more.

WHAT'S IT MEAN?

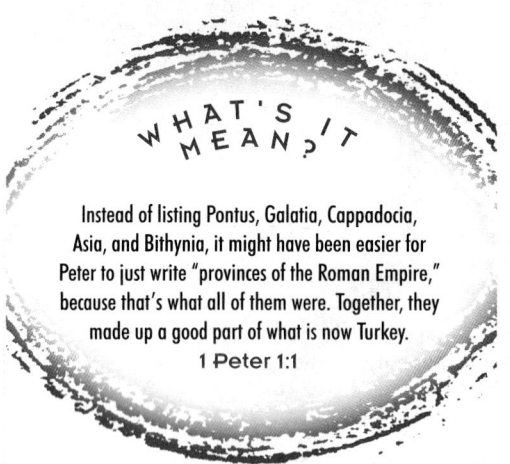

Instead of listing Pontus, Galatia, Cappadocia, Asia, and Bithynia, it might have been easier for Peter to just write "provinces of the Roman Empire," because that's what all of them were. Together, they made up a good part of what is now Turkey.

1 Peter 1:1

WE HAVE A LIVING HOPE

[3]Praise be to the God and Father of our
Lord Jesus Christ. In God's great mercy he has
caused us to be born again into a living hope,
because Jesus Christ rose from the dead. [4]Now
we hope for the blessings God has for his children. These blessings, which cannot be destroyed or be spoiled or lose their beauty, are
kept in heaven for you. [5]God's power protects
you through your faith until salvation is
shown to you at the end of time. [6]This makes
you very happy, even though now for a short
time different kinds of troubles may make you
sad. [7]These troubles come to prove that your
faith is pure. This purity of faith is worth more
than gold, which can be proved to be pure by
fire but will ruin. But the purity of your faith
will bring you praise and glory and honor
when Jesus Christ is shown to you. [8]You have
not seen Christ, but still you love him. You
cannot see him now, but you believe in him.
So you are filled with a joy that cannot be explained, a joy full of glory. [9]And you are receiving the goal of your faith—the salvation of
your souls.
[10]The prophets searched carefully and tried
to learn about this salvation. They prophesied
about the grace that was coming to you. [11]The
Spirit of Christ was in the prophets, telling in
advance about the sufferings of Christ and
about the glory that would follow those sufferings. The prophets tried to learn about what
the Spirit was showing them, when those
things would happen, and what the world
would be like at that time. [12]It was shown
them that their service was not for themselves
but for you, when they told about the truths
you have now heard. Those who preached the
Good News to you told you those things with
the help of the Holy Spirit who was sent from
heaven—things into which angels desire to
look.

A CALL TO HOLY LIVING

[13]So prepare your minds for service and
have self-control. All your hope should be for
the gift of grace that will be yours when Jesus
Christ is shown to you. [14]Now that you are
obedient children of God do not live as you
did in the past. You did not understand, so you
did the evil things you wanted. [15]But be holy in
all you do, just as God, the One who called
you, is holy. [16]It is written in the Scriptures:
"You must be holy, because I am holy."[n]

WHAT'S IT MEAN?

Gold is rarely found by itself. Usually it's mined with many other rocks and substances. So how did ancient miners separate the valuable from the worthless? They put everything into a large container and then set the container over a very hot flame. As the rocks heated, the impurities melted and separated from the gold. As the substance cooled, the impurities formed a crust that could be scraped off. The purifying process greatly increased the value of the gold.

1 Peter 1:7

[17]You pray to God and call
him Father, and he judges
each person's work equally.
So while you are here on
earth, you should live with respect for God. [18]You know
that in the past you were

SALVATION

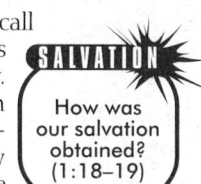

How was our salvation obtained? (1:18–19)

1:16 "You must be . . . holy." Quotation from Leviticus 11:45; 19:2; 20:7.

living in a worthless way, a way passed down
from the people who lived before you. But you
were saved from that useless life. You were
bought, not with something that ruins like gold
or silver, [19]but with the precious blood of
Christ, who was like a pure and perfect lamb.
[20]Christ was chosen before the world was
made, but he was shown to the world in these
last times for your sake. [21]Through Christ you
believe in God, who raised Christ from the
dead and gave him glory. So your faith and
your hope are in God.
[22]Now that you have made your souls pure
by obeying the truth, you can have true love
for your Christian brothers and sisters.[n] So
love each other deeply with all your heart.
[23]You have been born again, and this new life
did not come from something that dies, but
from something that cannot die. You were
born again through God's living message that
continues forever. [24]The Scripture says,

"All people are like the grass,
and all their glory is like the flowers of
the field.
The grass dies and the flowers fall,
25 but the word of the Lord will live
forever." *Isaiah 40:6-8*

And this is the word that was preached to you.

JESUS IS THE LIVING STONE

2 [1]So then, rid yourselves of all evil, all lying,
hypocrisy, jealousy, and evil speech. [2]As
newborn babies want milk, you should want
the pure and simple teaching. By it you can
grow up and be saved, [3]because you have
already examined and seen how good the
Lord is.
[4]Come to the Lord Jesus, the "stone"[n] that
lives. The people of the world did not want this
stone, but he was the stone God chose, and he
was precious. [5]You also are like living stones,
so let yourselves be used to build a spiritual
temple—to be holy priests who offer spiritual
sacrifices to God. He will accept those sacrifices
through Jesus Christ. [6]The Scripture says:

"I will put a stone in the ground in
Jerusalem.
Everything will be built on this
important and precious rock.
Anyone who trusts in him
will never be disappointed." *Isaiah 28:16*

[7]This stone is worth much to you who believe.
But to the people who do not believe,

"the stone that the builders rejected
has become the cornerstone." *Psalm 118:22*

[8]Also, he is

"a stone that causes people to stumble,
a rock that makes them fall." *Isaiah 8:14*

On the Edge

But you are a chosen people, royal priests, a holy nation, a people for God's own possession. You were chosen to tell about the wonderful acts of God, who called you out of darkness into his wonderful light (1 Pet. 2:9).

When you don't know many other people who want to follow Jesus, sometimes it's easy to think it's just the two of you—you and Jesus strolling down the road of life together. But God doesn't intend for things to stay that way. He has something in mind for all the people who love him, not just as individuals, but as a group. All of us together are his holy nation—just like when the nation of Israel belonged to him in Old Testament times.

What that means to you is that you're not alone. You're part of a group of people known as Christians and they're available to help you, to be your friends, and to serve the Lord along with you. If you're feeling lonely, look for other people your age who really want to know God and do what he says. And don't stop there. God's holy nation is made up of adults and children, too. Find some grown-ups who have won out over some of the challenges you're facing now. Keep an eye out for little kids who might need to know what you had to learn the hard way. Make friends with elderly people whose eyes sparkle with the love of Jesus, and listen to what they have to say.

As a person, you are so incredibly valuable to God. You are also *part* of something valuable to him—the holy nation that consists of the people who love him. Let it be important to you, too.

SEE FOR YOURSELF:
Ex. 19:5–6; Deut. 4:20; 14:2; Is. 43:20–21; Titus 2:14

1:22 brothers and sisters Although the Greek text says "brothers" here and throughout this book, Peter's words were meant for the entire church, including men and women. **2:4 "stone"** The most important stone in God's spiritual temple or house (his people).

They stumble because they do not obey what
God says, which is what God planned to happen to them.
9But you are a chosen people, royal priests,
a holy nation, a people for God's own possession. You were chosen to tell about the wonderful acts of God, who called you out of
darkness into his wonderful light. 10At one
time you were not a people, but now you are
God's people. In the past you had never received mercy, but now you have received
God's mercy.

LIVE FOR GOD

11Dear friends, you are like foreigners and
strangers in this world. I beg you to avoid the
evil things your bodies want to do that fight
against your soul. 12People who do not believe
are living all around you and might say that
you are doing wrong. Live such good lives that
they will see the good things you do and will
give glory to God on the day when Christ
comes again.

YIELD TO EVERY HUMAN AUTHORITY

13For the Lord's sake, yield to the people
who have authority in this world: the king,
who is the highest authority, 14and the leaders
who are sent by him to punish those who do

On the Edge

Dear friends, you are like foreigners and strangers in this world. I beg you to avoid the evil things your bodies want to do that fight against your soul (1 Pet. 2:11).

Sometimes you can feel like a foreigner or even an alien on this earth (or in your world) because you love Jesus. You feel like a foreigner who doesn't really belong here. A temporary resident. And foreigners can be rejected because their beliefs are different from those of most people around them. If you're trying to live for Jesus, you may have already felt that way.

Do you pray before your meals in public? If you do, then you know that almost no one else does. Do you tell your friends "no thanks" when they invite you to an out-of-control party? Maybe you don't even get invited anymore because they know it's not your scene. Have you been dumped by someone because you chose not to have sex before marriage? You made the right choice, but it may have made you feel like an alien.

Peter says that a part of being Christlike is continually holding yourself back from the "evil things"—the sinful pulls of the world. When you hold back or stand apart, then you've become the foreigner or stranger Peter is talking about. Take comfort though. Even when you are living here on earth, it is not your home. You have a home in heaven that is so far beyond the beauty and comfort of this world. You'll never feel like a stranger there. You'll be known and loved and respected. You'll be among friends.

SEE FOR YOURSELF:
1 Cor. 2:12; Phil. 3:20;
Heb. 11:13

On the Edge

A person might have to suffer even when it is unfair, but if he thinks of God and stands the pain, God is pleased. If you are beaten for doing wrong, there is no reason to praise you for being patient in your punishment. But if you suffer for doing good, and you are patient, then God is pleased (1 Pet. 2:19–20).

Your world can be really cruel sometimes. You do the absolute most right thing, and they laugh, or snicker behind your back, or leave you out. They treat you that way out of their own insecurity. The light of Christ in you shines on their dark lives and they probably feel ashamed. Don't let their attitudes hinder your loyalty to Christ. Keep loving him visibly.

These verses say that your loyalty to God counts for something with him. He notices when people make fun of you because of him. Trust him and ask him to make you strong. Keep doing the right thing, and keep the faith that God will bless all your right choices. Maybe your friends will grow up. Maybe they won't. Either way, you must know that God is so proud of you. He commends your actions. He sees the battles you fight because of him. He will never turn away from you.

SEE FOR YOURSELF:
Ps. 119:157;
Matt. 5:10;
Rom. 12:14;
2 Tim. 3:12

wrong and to praise those who do right. [15]It is
God's desire that by doing good you should stop
foolish people from saying stupid things about
you. [16]Live as free people, but do not use your
freedom as an excuse to do evil. Live as servants of God. [17]Show respect for all people:
Love the brothers and sisters of God's family,
respect God, honor the king.

FOLLOW CHRIST'S EXAMPLE

[18]Slaves, yield to the authority of your masters with all respect, not only those who are
good and kind, but also those who are dishonest. [19]A person might have to suffer even when
it is unfair, but if he thinks of God and stands
the pain, God is pleased. [20]If you are beaten for
doing wrong, there is no reason to praise you
for being patient in your punishment. But if
you suffer for doing good, and you are patient,
then God is pleased. [21]This is what you were
called to do, because Christ suffered for you
and gave you an example to follow. So you
should do as he did.

[22]"He had never sinned,
and he had never lied." *Isaiah 53:9*

[23]People insulted Christ, but he did not insult
them in return. Christ suffered, but
he did not threaten. He let God,
the One who judges rightly,
take care of him. [24]Christ carried our sins in his body on
the cross so we would stop
living for sin and start living
for what is right. And you
are healed because of his
wounds. [25]You were like
sheep that wandered away, but
now you have come back to the Shepherd and
Protector of your souls.

REVENGE
Whose life should we look to when we are tempted to get revenge on someone? (2:21–23)

WIVES AND HUSBANDS

3
[1]In the same way, you wives should yield to
your husbands. Then, if some husbands do
not obey God's teaching, they will be persuaded to believe without anyone's saying a word
to them. They will be persuaded by the way
their wives live. [2]Your husbands will see the
pure lives you live with your respect for God.
[3]It is not fancy hair, gold jewelry, or fine
clothes that should make you beautiful. [4]No,
your beauty should come from within you—
the beauty of a gentle and quiet spirit that will
never be destroyed and is very precious to
God. [5]In this same way the holy women who
lived long ago and followed God made themselves beautiful, yielding to their own husbands. [6]Sarah obeyed Abraham, her husband,
and called him her master. And you women
are true children of Sarah if you always do
what is right and are not afraid.
[7]In the same way, you husbands should live
with your wives in an understanding way,
since they are weaker than you. But show
them respect, because God gives them the
same blessing he gives you—the grace that
gives true life. Do this so that nothing will stop
your prayers.

SUFFERING FOR DOING RIGHT

[8]Finally, all of you should be in agreement,
understanding each other, loving each other as

On the Edge

It is not fancy hair, gold jewelry, or fine clothes that should make you beautiful. No, your beauty should come from within you—the beauty of a gentle and quiet spirit that will never be destroyed and is very precious to God (1 Pet. 3:3–4).

Peter says that beauty has more to do with your inside than your outside. God cares about your heart and your attitude more than the shape of your face or the color of your eyes. If you ask him, God will reveal to you the beauty he created in you. He created you for a purpose. Your life gives him such pleasure. He thinks you're beautiful. You are precious to him. Can you see what he sees?

If you feel like God created you for something more than beauty contests, then begin to search and pray for his purpose. Ask him to show you your strengths and help you use them. The most attractive people in the world are the ones who are confident about their purpose. They know what their life is supposed to be about, and they are hard at work to fulfill God's plan for them.

If you can't stand the way you look, then ask God to show you what he has in mind for you. Ask him to make you into a person who looks into the mirror and likes the reflection. Focus on the awesome things he has built into you. Ask him to replace your insecurity with his purpose.

SEE FOR YOURSELF:
Is. 43:3–4; Zeph. 3:17; 1 Tim. 2:8–9

family, being kind and humble. 9 Do not do
wrong to repay a wrong, and do not insult to
repay an insult. But repay with a blessing, because you yourselves were called to do this so
that you might receive a blessing. 10 The Scripture says,

"A person must do these things
to enjoy life and have many happy
days.
He must not say evil things,
and he must not tell lies.
11 He must stop doing evil and do good.
He must look for peace and work for it.
12 The Lord sees the good people
and listens to their prayers.
But the Lord is against
those who do evil." *Psalm 34:12-16*

13 If you are trying hard to do good, no one
can really hurt you. 14 But even if you suffer for
doing right, you are blessed.

"Don't be afraid of what they fear;
do not dread those things." *Isaiah 8:12-13*

15 But respect Christ as the holy Lord in your
hearts. Always be ready to answer everyone
who asks you to explain about the hope you
have, 16 but answer in a gentle way and with
respect. Keep a clear conscience so that those
who speak evil of your good life in Christ will
be made ashamed. 17 It is better to suffer for
doing good than for doing wrong if that is
what God wants. 18 Christ himself suffered for
sins once. He was not guilty, but he suffered
for those who are guilty to bring you to God.
His body was killed, but he was made alive in
the spirit. 19 And in the spirit he went and
preached to the spirits in prison 20 who refused
to obey God long ago in the time of Noah.
God was waiting patiently for them while
Noah was building the boat. Only a few people—eight in all—were saved by water. 21 And
that water is like baptism that now saves
you—not the washing of dirt from the body,
but the promise made to God from a good
conscience. And this is because Jesus Christ
was raised from the dead. 22 Now Jesus has
gone into heaven and is at God's right side ruling over angels, authorities, and powers.

CHANGE YOUR LIVES

4 1 Since Christ suffered while he was in his
body, strengthen yourselves with the same
way of thinking Christ had. The person who
has suffered in the body is finished with sin.
2 Strengthen yourselves so that you will live
here on earth doing what God wants, not the
evil things people want. 3 In the past you wasted too much time doing what nonbelievers
enjoy. You were guilty of sexual sins, evil

Promise HE PROMISES TO LISTEN TO YOU.

The Lord sees the good people and listens to their prayers. But the Lord is against those who do evil (1 Pet. 3:12).

Maybe you've picked up your Bible today hoping it'll make a little sense out of what you're going through, give you a reason to think God cares whether you live or die.

You've tried praying. But you've wondered if it does any good. You feel like you're just launching words into dead air and thinking they'll magically make a difference.

Why talk when no one's listening?

The guy who wrote this particular book knew the feeling. Rough-and-tumble Peter, sidekick to a mysterious traveling man from Nazareth named Jesus, saw everything he dreamed about blow up in his face as his Lord was led away to die. This is what he gave up a good-paying job for? Ridicule? Embarrassment? Maybe even the end of his life?

"Why me, God?" he must have cried into the heavens. His words seemed to clank against an iron sky and landed back at his feet with an empty thud.

But God *was* listening—and doing something more loving than an easy answer would have done. He was letting Peter do some searching, giving him room to stretch beyond his own strength, to prove to himself that his faith was in God and not in his blessings.

Your ceiling may seem dark and silent. But God *is* watching. And listening. And waiting. And working. And one day, you'll wonder why you thought he wasn't.

SEE FOR YOURSELF:

Ps. 5:3; John 11:42

desires, drunkenness, wild and drunken parties, and hateful idol worship. [4]Nonbelievers
think it is strange that you do not do the many
wild and wasteful things they do, so they insult
you. [5]But they will have to explain this to God,
who is ready to judge the living and the dead.
[6]For this reason the Good News was preached
to those who are now dead. Even though they
were judged like all people, the Good News
was preached to them so they could live in the
spirit as God lives.

WHAT'S IT MEAN?

Hospitality was a way of life in biblical times. Throughout the Bible, God's people are commanded to show kindness to visitors. In the early days of Christianity, people were constantly traveling from town to town to share the message about Jesus and to encourage fellow believers. The apostles and preachers of that time depended on the kindness of strangers for food, housing, and even protection from angry mobs who didn't want them teaching about Jesus.

1 Peter 4:9

USE GOD'S GIFTS WISELY

[7]The time is near when all things will end.
So think clearly and control yourselves so you
will be able to pray. [8]Most importantly, love
each other deeply, because love will cause
many sins to be forgiven. [9]Open your homes
to each other, without complaining. [10]Each of
you has received a gift to use to serve others.
Be good servants of God's various gifts of
grace. [11]Anyone who speaks should speak
words from God. Anyone who serves should
serve with the strength God gives so that in
everything God will be praised through Jesus
Christ. Power and glory belong to him forever
and ever. Amen.

SUFFERING AS A CHRISTIAN

[12]My friends, do not be surprised at the terrible trouble which now comes to test you. Do
not think that something strange is happening
to you. [13]But be happy that you are sharing in
Christ's sufferings so that you will be happy
and full of joy when Christ comes again in
glory. [14]When people insult you because you
follow Christ, you are blessed, because the glorious Spirit, the Spirit of God, is with you. [15]Do
not suffer for murder, theft, or any other crime,
nor because you trouble other people. [16]But if
you suffer because you are a Christian, do not
be ashamed. Praise God because you wear that
name. [17]It is time for judgment to begin with
God's family. And if that judging begins with
us, what will happen to those people who
do not obey the Good News of God?

[18]"If it is very hard for a good person to be
saved,

On the Edge

Each of you has received a gift to use to serve others. Be good servants of God's various gifts of grace (1 Pet. 4:10).

Peter says "each of you" has something he or she does well—a gift. You might have a hard time believing that. Maybe you think you don't have anything to offer because, as people say, you're "just a teenager." Maybe you think you can't give much because you still have a lot to learn. Maybe self-confidence just isn't your thing. But Peter isn't just telling you what he thinks here; he's telling you what God thinks. So even if you think, *Well, that's not for me*, you can buy it because it's God's Word.

In verse 11, Peter gives two examples of God's gifts. Paul listed others in his letters to various churches (see Rom. 12:6–8; 1 Cor. 12:7–11; Eph. 4:11). It might not be a good idea, though, to comb through the lists to look for a label to pin on yourself. Instead, pay attention to the opportunities God brings your way.

Do everything he wants you to do. Pretty soon you'll discover what gift he's given you. Whatever your gift is, give it all you've got. Don't do it looking for a pat on the back. Peter says to use your gift to "serve others." In other words, do what you do to make life better for other people. Do it because you love God. Do it because—in your heart—you really want to help and serve the people God loves. Be available for him to love them through you.

SEE FOR YOURSELF:
1 Cor. 12:27–31;
1 Tim. 4:14;
2 Tim. 1:6–7;
James 1:17

On the Edge

Give all your worries to him, because he cares about you (1 Pet. 5:7).

Have you ever felt like nobody cared? Maybe you feel like that now. Well, the good news is that Jesus *does* care! It doesn't matter what kind of situation you are going through, or what anyone else says. God is concerned with your problems. Not only that, God is concerned with *everything* about you. He is the One who created you, and he knows what makes you tick better than you do. So let go of your worries by giving them to him.

Paul tells us in Philippians 4:6–7 not to worry, but to pray about everything. After you pray, start thanking God for answering those prayers. He goes on to tell us that, after we do this, God will bless us with peace. If you need peace in the midst of a situation, all you need to do is go to him in prayer. Look carefully at the last words of 1 Peter 5:7, "because he cares about you." God cares in your place. He cares so you don't have to. He does it *because of you.* So let him have your concerns. He'll do a better job with them than you will!

SEE FOR YOURSELF:
Ps. 50:15; 118:6;
Matt. 6:31–32;
Luke 12:25–26

the wicked person and the sinner will
surely be lost!"[n]
19So those who suffer as God wants should
trust their souls to the faithful Creator as they
continue to do what is right.

THE FLOCK OF GOD

5 1Now I have something to say to the elders
in your group. I also am an elder. I have seen
Christ's sufferings, and I will share in the glory
that will be shown to us. I beg you to 2shep-
herd God's flock, for whom you are responsible. Watch over them because you want to, not
because you are forced. That is how God
wants it. Do it because you are happy to serve,
not because you want money. 3Do not be like a
ruler over people you are responsible for, but
be good examples to them. 4Then when Christ,
the Chief Shepherd, comes, you will get a glorious crown that will never lose its beauty.
5In the same way, younger people should
be willing to be under older people. And all of
you should be very humble with each other.

"God is against the proud,
but he gives grace to the humble."

Proverbs 3:34

6Be humble under God's powerful hand so
he will lift you up when the right time comes.
7Give all your worries to him, because he cares
about you.
8Control yourselves and be careful! The
devil, your enemy, goes around like a
roaring lion looking for someone to eat. 9Refuse to give in
to him, by standing strong in
your faith. You know that
your Christian family all over
the world is having the same
kinds of suffering.

SATAN
Who are Satan's enemies? (5:8)

10And after you suffer for a short time, God,
who gives all grace, will make everything right.
He will make you strong and support you and
keep you from falling. He called you to share in
his glory in Christ, a glory that will continue
forever. 11All power is his forever and ever.
Amen.

FINAL GREETINGS

12I wrote this short letter with the help of
Silas, who I know is a faithful brother in Christ.
I wrote to encourage you and to tell you that
this is the true grace of God. Stand strong in
that grace.
13The church in Babylon, who was chosen
like you, sends you greetings. Mark, my son in
Christ, also greets you. 14Give each other a kiss
of Christian love when you meet.
Peace to all of you who are in Christ.

4:18 "If . . . lost!" Quotation from Proverbs 11:31 in the Septuagint, the Greek version of the Old Testament.

1From Simon Peter, a servant and apostle of
Jesus Christ.
To you who have received a faith as valuable as ours, because our God and Savior Jesus
Christ does what is right.
2Grace and peace be given to you more and
more, because you truly know God and Jesus
our Lord.

GOD HAS GIVEN US BLESSINGS

3Jesus has the power of God, by which he
has given us everything we need to live and to
serve God. We have these things because we
know him. Jesus called us by his glory and
goodness. 4Through these he gave us the very
great and precious promises. With these gifts
you can share in being like God, and the world
will not ruin you with its evil desires.
5Because you have these blessings, do your
best to add these things to your lives: to your
faith, add goodness; and to your goodness, add
knowledge; 6and to your knowledge, add self-
control; and to your self-control, add patience;
and to your patience, add service for God; 7and
to your service for God, add kindness for your
brothers and sisters in Christ; and to this kindness, add love. 8If all these things are in you and
are growing, they will help you to be useful and
productive in your knowledge of our Lord
Jesus Christ. 9But anyone who does not have
these things cannot see clearly. He is blind and
has forgotten that he was made clean from his
past sins.
10My brothers and sisters,[n] try hard to be
certain that you really are called and chosen
by God. If you do all these things, you will
never fall. 11And you will be given a very great
welcome into the eternal kingdom of our Lord
and Savior Jesus Christ.
12You know these things, and you are very
strong in the truth, but I will always help you
remember them. 13I think it is right for me to
help you remember as long as I am in this
body. 14I know I must soon leave this body, as
our Lord Jesus Christ has shown me. 15I will
try my best so that you may be able to remember these things even after I am gone.

WE SAW CHRIST'S GLORY

16When we told you about the powerful
coming of our Lord Jesus Christ, we were not
telling just smart stories that someone invented. But we saw the greatness of Jesus with our
own eyes. 17Jesus heard the voice of God, the
Greatest Glory, when he received honor and
glory from God the Father. The voice said,

On the Edge

Because you have these blessings, do your best to add these things to your lives: to your faith, add goodness; and to your goodness, add knowledge; and to your knowledge, add self-control; and to your self-control, add patience; and to your patience, add service for God; and to your service for God, add kindness for your brothers and sisters in Christ; and to this kindness, add love. If all these things are in you and are growing, they will help you to be useful and productive in your knowledge of our Lord Jesus Christ (2 Pet. 1:5–8).

This passage is talking about improving your faith. When you improve your faith by adding the qualities in these verses, you're developing character. You develop character one step at a time, one day at a time, one decision at a time. It's like building a house by putting one brick on top of another. A lot of Christians are running themselves ragged doing things *for* God, but they may not be doing anything in their walk *with* God. They may not be adding anything to their faith. They just keep doing what they've always done—going to church, reading a devotion, praying before meals.

Peter challenges us to add some things to our faith—things that develop godly character. Faith is great, but it's got to grow. And you've got to add to your faith in order to grow. Part of improving your faith is finding ways to express it. You can do that with goodness, knowledge, self-control, patience, service to God, kindness, and love (vv. 5–7). You won't master these overnight, but you can commit to working on them. Character will develop in you and your faith will grow. You'll have substance and credibility in your life. You'll begin to look more and more like Jesus.

SEE FOR YOURSELF:
Gal. 5:22–23;
Eph. 4:15–16;
2 Pet. 1:2; 3:18

1:10 brothers and sisters Although the Greek text reads "brothers" here and throughout this book, Peter's words were meant for the entire church, including men and women.

WHAT'S IT MEAN?

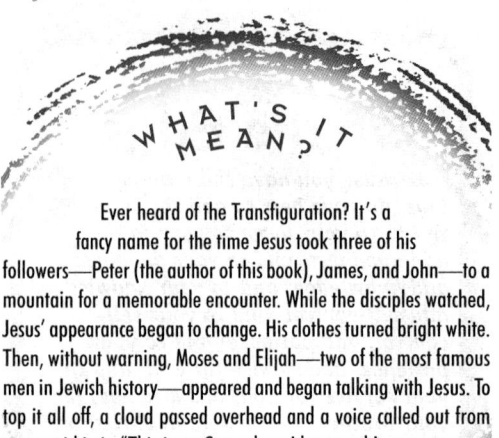

Ever heard of the Transfiguration? It's a fancy name for the time Jesus took three of his followers—Peter (the author of this book), James, and John—to a mountain for a memorable encounter. While the disciples watched, Jesus' appearance began to change. His clothes turned bright white. Then, without warning, Moses and Elijah—two of the most famous men in Jewish history—appeared and began talking with Jesus. To top it all off, a cloud passed overhead and a voice called out from within it, "This is my Son, whom I love, and I am very pleased with him. Listen to him!" (Matt. 17:5).

2 Peter 1:18

"This is my Son, whom I love, and I am very pleased with him." [18]We heard that voice from heaven while we were with Jesus on the holy mountain.

[19]This makes us more sure about the message the prophets gave. It is good for you to follow closely what they said as you would follow a light shining in a dark place, until the day begins and the morning star rises in your hearts. [20]Most of all, you must understand this: No prophecy in the Scriptures ever comes from the prophet's own interpretation. [21]No prophecy ever came from what a person wanted to say, but people led by the Holy Spirit spoke words from God.

FALSE TEACHERS

2 [1]There used to be false prophets among God's people, just as you will have some false teachers in your group. They will secretly teach things that are wrong—teachings that will cause people to be lost. They will even refuse to accept the Master, Jesus, who bought their freedom. So they will bring quick ruin on themselves. [2]Many will follow their evil ways and say evil things about the way of truth. [3]Those false teachers only want your money, so they will use you by telling you lies. Their judgment spoken against them long ago is still coming, and their ruin is certain.

[4]When angels sinned, God did not let them go free without punishment. He sent them to hell and put them in caves of darkness where they are being held for judgment. [5]And God punished the world long ago when he brought a flood to the world that was full of people who were against him. But God saved Noah, who preached about being right with God, and seven other people with him.

DISOBEDIENCE

What happened to the angels who followed Satan? (2:4)

[6]And God also destroyed the evil cities of Sodom and Gomorrah[n] by burning them until they were ashes. He made those cities an example of what will happen to those who are against God. [7]But he saved Lot from those cities. Lot, a good man, was troubled because of the filthy lives of evil people. [8](Lot was a good man, but because he lived with evil people every day, his good heart was hurt by the evil things he saw and heard.) [9]So the Lord knows how to save those who serve him when troubles come. He will hold evil people and punish them, while waiting for the Judgment Day. [10]That punishment is especially for those who live by doing the evil things their sinful selves want and who hate authority.

These false teachers are bold and do anything they want. They are not afraid to speak against the angels. [11]But even the angels, who are much stronger and more powerful than false teachers, do not accuse them with insults before the Lord. [12]But these people speak against things they do not understand. They are like animals that act without thinking, animals born to be caught and killed. And, like animals, these false teachers will be destroyed. [13]They have caused many people to suffer, so they themselves will suffer. That is their pay for what they have done. They take pleasure in openly doing evil, so they are like dirty spots and stains among you. They delight in trickery while eating meals with you. [14]Every time they look at a woman they want her, and their desire for sin is never satisfied. They lead weak people into the trap of sin, and they have taught their hearts to be greedy. God will punish them! [15]These false teachers left the right road and lost their way, following the way Balaam went. Balaam was the son of Beor, who loved being paid for doing wrong. [16]But a donkey, which cannot talk, told Balaam he was sinning. It spoke with a man's voice and stopped the prophet's crazy thinking.

[17]Those false teachers are like springs without water and clouds blown by a storm.

2:6 Sodom and Gomorrah Two cities God destroyed because the people were so evil.

A place in the blackest darkness has been kept
for them. [18]They brag with words that mean
nothing. By their evil desires they lead people
into the trap of sin—people who are just beginning to escape from others who live in error.
[19]They promise them freedom, but they themselves are not free. They are slaves of things that
will be destroyed. For people are slaves of anything that controls them. [20]They were made free
from the evil in the world by knowing our Lord
and Savior Jesus Christ. But if they return to evil
things and those things control them, then it is
worse for them than it was before. [21]Yes, it
would be better for them to have never known
the right way than to know it and to turn away
from the holy teaching that was given to them.
[22]What they did is like this true saying: "A dog
goes back to what it has thrown up,"[n] and, "After a pig is washed, it goes back and rolls in the
mud."

WHAT'S IT MEAN?

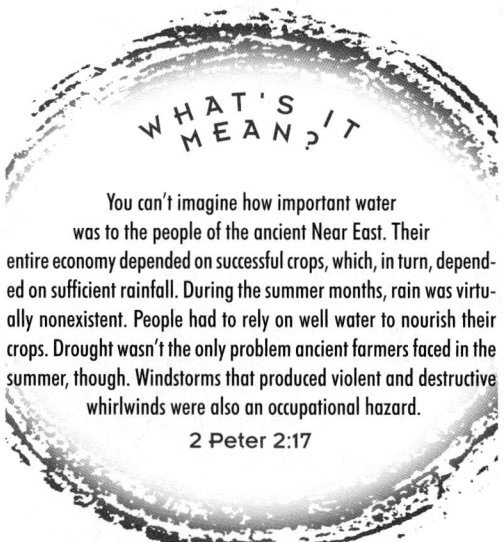

You can't imagine how important water was to the people of the ancient Near East. Their entire economy depended on successful crops, which, in turn, depended on sufficient rainfall. During the summer months, rain was virtually nonexistent. People had to rely on well water to nourish their crops. Drought wasn't the only problem ancient farmers faced in the summer, though. Windstorms that produced violent and destructive whirlwinds were also an occupational hazard.

2 Peter 2:17

JESUS WILL COME AGAIN

3
[1]My friends, this is the second letter I have
written you to help your honest minds remember. [2]I want you to think about the words
the holy prophets spoke in the past, and remember the command our Lord and Savior
gave us through your apostles. [3]It is most important for you to understand what will happen in the last days. People will laugh at you.
They will live doing the evil things they want
to do. [4]They will say, "Jesus promised to come
again. Where is he? Our fathers have died, but
the world continues the way it has been since
it was made." [5]But they do not want to remember what happened long ago. By the word of
God heaven was made, and the earth was
made from water and with water. [6]Then the
world was flooded and destroyed with water.
[7]And that same word of God is keeping heaven
and earth that we now have in order to be
destroyed by fire. They are being kept for the
Judgment Day and the destruction of all who
are against God.

[8]But do not forget this one thing, dear
friends: To the Lord one day is as a thousand
years, and a thousand years is as one day. [9]The
Lord is not slow in doing what he promised—
the way some people understand slowness.
But God is being patient with you. He does not
want anyone to be lost, but he wants all people
to change their hearts and lives.

[10]But the day of the Lord will come like a
thief. The skies will disappear with a loud
noise. Everything in them will be destroyed by
fire, and the earth and everything in it will be
burned up.[n] [11]In that way everything will be
destroyed. So what kind of people should you
be? You should live holy lives and serve God,
[12]as you wait for and look forward to the coming of the day of God. When that day
comes, the skies will be destroyed with fire, and everything in them will melt with
heat. [13]But God made a promise to us, and we are waiting
for a new heaven and a new
earth where goodness lives.

HEAVEN
Where is the home of goodness? (3:13)

[14]Dear friends, since you are
waiting for this to happen, do your best to be
without sin and without fault. Try to be at
peace with God. [15]Remember that we are
saved because our Lord is patient. Our dear
brother Paul told you the same thing when he
wrote to you with the wisdom that God gave
him. [16]He writes about this in all his letters.
Some things in Paul's letters are hard to understand, and people who are ignorant and weak
in faith explain these things falsely. They also
falsely explain the other Scriptures, but they
are destroying themselves by doing this.

[17]Dear friends, since you already know
about this, be careful. Do not let those evil
people lead you away by the wrong they do.
Be careful so you will not fall from your strong
faith. [18]But grow in the grace and knowledge of
our Lord and Savior Jesus Christ. Glory be to
him now and forever! Amen.

2:22 "A dog . . . up" Quotation from Proverbs 26:11.
3:10 will be burned up Many Greek copies say, "will be found." One copy says, "will disappear."

1, 2 & 3 John

CONTENT You know how sometimes you struggle to learn something, like a math problem or a foreign language? Then, something will "click" and you'll "get it"? It often takes one big concept and then we are on our way to a whole new level of understanding. For the apostle John (who once was called a "Son of Thunder"), that concept was love.

In his account of the Good News, many believe that John defined himself by the fact that Jesus loved him. It is no surprise that when he wrote to the church, the body of Christ, he most often wrote about love.

We can't really categorize John's letters as "love letters" because when we think of a "love letter" we think of a mushy kind of thing. John's letters weren't mushy. In fact, they were so strong that they have some of the most famous verses in the Bible.

In John's first letter he explores the doctrine of love. He basically expands on John 3:16 (possibly THE most famous verse in the Bible). In his second letter he encourages the church. In his third letter he encourages a friend.

John understood that when Christ came he showed us a whole new way to love God and to love each other. Understanding this kind of love turned John's life inside out. It can do the same for us.

Date of writing A.D. 90 for 1, 2 and 3 John

Outline

1 John:
1:1–4 .... The Word of Life
1:5—2:6 .... God Is Light and Christ Is Our Example
2:7–17 .... The Old/New Command
2:18—3:10 .... The Enemies of Christ and God's Children
3:11—4:21 .... God's Love and Our Love
5:1–21 .... Jesus Overcomes the World

Purpose To live in fellowship with God, obey his Word, and love his children.

Theme Jesus Is the Son of God. Those Who Follow Him Must Do What Is Right

Outline

2 John:
1–3 .... Greetings and Prayer
4–11 .... Follow the Way of Truth and Love
12–13 .... Final Greetings

Purpose Truth is based on the fact that Jesus was both human and divine.

Theme Warning About False Teachers

Outline

3 John:
1–4 .... Greetings to Gaius
5–12 .... The Importance of Working Together
13–15 .... Final Greetings

Purpose Total devotion to the truth of the Good News is the key to the Christian life.

Theme Practicing Hospitality Toward Genuine Christian Teachers

> "We announce to you what we have seen and heard, because we want you also to have fellowship with us. Our fellowship is with God the Father and with his Son, Jesus Christ" (1 John 1:3).

Bible Talk

Loving God

John teaches us a lesson. It's something we really should know anyway. We already understand this lesson when we are talking about loving each other. If someone says they love you but they treat you like dirt, you don't really believe they love you, do you? What if they say they love you, but they constantly do things that annoy you and even upset you? Do you really believe they love you?

John teaches us that we show our love for God by our obedience to him. If we say we love God but we treat him like he doesn't matter or constantly do things that upset him, do we really love him?

That's why obedience matters in love.

LOVING OTHERS

John doesn't just tell us to love people. He tells us why.

He doesn't tell us to love people because they are always lovable. They aren't. He doesn't tell us to love people just because God tells us to. He could have. He doesn't tell us to love people because they love us. Sometimes they don't.

What he tells us to do is to love people because God loved us. He even tells us to love people *the way* God loves us. The message God sent through John is simple: Obeying God means loving people—they go hand in hand.

1 1We write you now about what has always
existed, which we have heard, we have seen
with our own eyes, we have looked at, and we
have touched with our hands. We write to you
about the Word[n] that gives life. 2He who gives
life was shown to us. We saw him and can give
proof about it. And now we announce to you
that he has life that continues forever. He was
with God the Father and was shown to us. 3We
announce to you what we have seen and
heard, because we want you also to have
fellowship with us. Our fellowship is with
God the Father and with his Son, Jesus Christ.
4We write this to you so you can be full of joy
with us.

GOD FORGIVES OUR SINS

5Here is the message we have heard from
Christ and now announce to you: God is
light,[n] and in him there is no darkness at all.
6So if we say we have fellowship with God, but
we continue living in darkness, we are liars
and do not follow the truth. 7But if we live in
the light, as God is in the light, we can share
fellowship with each other. Then the blood of
Jesus, God's Son, cleanses us from every sin.
8If we say we have no sin, we are fooling
ourselves, and the truth is not in us. 9But if we
confess our sins, he will forgive our sins, because we can trust God to do what is right. He
will cleanse us from all the wrongs we have
done. 10If we say we have not sinned, we make
God a liar, and we do not accept God's teaching.

JESUS IS OUR HELPER

2 1My dear children, I write this letter to you
so you will not sin. But if anyone does sin, we
have a helper in the presence of the Father—
Jesus Christ, the One who does what is right.
2He is the way our sins are taken away, and not
only our sins but the sins of all people.
3We can be sure that we know God if we
obey his commands. 4Anyone who says, "I
know God," but does not obey God's commands is a liar, and the truth is not in that
person. 5But if someone obeys God's teaching,
then in that person God's love has truly
reached its goal. This is how we can be sure we
are living in God: 6Whoever says that he lives
in God must live as Jesus lived.

THE COMMAND TO LOVE OTHERS

7My dear friends, I am not writing a new
command to you but an old command you
have had from the beginning. It is the teaching
you have already heard. 8But also I am writing
a new command to you, and you can see its
truth in Jesus and in you, because the darkness
is passing away, and the true light is already
shining.

1:1 Word The Greek word is "logos," meaning any kind of communication. Here, it means Christ, who was the way God told people about himself. **1:5 light** Here, this word is used as a symbol of God's goodness or truth.

Promise HE PROMISES TO BE YOUR HELPER.

My dear children, I write this letter to you so you will not sin. But if anyone does sin, we have a helper in the presence of the Father—Jesus Christ, the One who does what is right (1 John 2:1).

There's a certain sick feeling that comes after you've done something you shouldn't have done. Maybe it's dread or anger or guilt or shame or all of the above—and more—rolled into one big downer of depressing disgust.

All you want to do is hide from God, to wait until the feeling passes, to go listen to some music or watch some TV and let your mind just go to mush. That's too bad, because Jesus is just waiting for you to call for help. He's waiting to pick you up with one nail-scarred hand, and hold the other one out before his Father—to show that the price has been paid, the debt has been canceled, the way of forgiveness has been paved with cleansing blood.

That's what Jesus does as our Helper with the Father. He's our counsel for the defense. Call him up. He's ready and waiting right now.

SEE FOR YOURSELF:
Rom. 8:34; Heb. 4:16; 7:25

9Anyone who says, "I am in the light,"[n] but
hates a brother or sister,[n] is still in the darkness.
10Whoever loves a brother or sister lives in the
light and will not cause anyone to stumble in
his faith. 11But whoever hates a brother or sister is in darkness, lives in darkness, and does
not know where to go, because the darkness
has made that person blind.

12I write to you, dear children,
because your sins are
forgiven through
Christ.
13I write to you, parents,
because you know the
One who existed
from the beginning.
I write to you, young
people,
because you have
defeated the Evil One.
14I write to you, children,
because you know the Father.
I write to you, parents,
because you know the One who existed
from the beginning.
I write to you, young people,
because you are strong;
the teaching of God lives in you,
and you have defeated the Evil One.

"The Father has loved us so much that we are called children of God. And we really are his children." (1 John 3:1a)

15Do not love the world or the things in the
world. If you love the world, the love of the
Father is not in you. 16These are the ways of
the world: wanting to please our sinful selves,
wanting the sinful things we see, and being too
proud of what we have. None of these come
from the Father, but all of them come from the
world. 17The world and everything that people
want in it are passing away, but
the person who does what
God wants lives forever.

REJECT THE ENEMIES OF CHRIST

18My dear children, these
are the last days. You have
heard that the enemy of
Christ is coming, and now
many enemies of Christ are
already here. This is how we
know that these are the last days.
19These enemies of Christ were in our fellowship, but they left us. They never really belonged to us; if they had been a part of us, they
would have stayed with us. But they left, and
this shows that none of them really belonged
to us.
20You have the gift[n] that the Holy One gave
you, so you all know the truth. 21I do not write

2:9 light Here, this word is used as a symbol of God's goodness or truth. **2:9 brother or sister** Although the Greek text says "brother" here and throughout this book, the writer's words were meant for the entire church, including men and women. **2:20 gift** This might mean the Holy Spirit, or it might mean teaching or truth as in verse 24.

Promise

HE PROMISES THAT YOU WILL HAVE LIFE FOREVER.

And this is what the Son promised to us—life forever (1 John 2:25).

Here is the most awesome promise in all of Scripture. Jesus Christ has promised us life forever (eternal life). Could anyone else keep that promise besides the Lord God himself? Would you believe anyone else if they promised you the same thing? The magnificent truth is that no one else, living or dead, can offer you eternal life. Some other religions claim multiple lives or reincarnation for their followers, but where are their resurrected sons? There are none. The Resurrection of Christ is proof that he holds the power over death. The Resurrection is the basis of our faith and the proof that this promise is real. Only Jesus Christ gives eternal life. Your faith in him will be rewarded. The reward is all the fellowship, love, and joy of heaven. Commit your heart and life to Christ. Decide that you're going to stick with him—no matter what. Don't miss out on the best that God has for you. He'll change your life, your stuff, your circumstances; but best of all, he'll change you forever.

SEE FOR YOURSELF:
John 3:16; Titus 1:2; 1 John 5:9, 20

to you because you do not know the truth but
because you do know the truth. And you
know that no lie comes from the truth.
22Who is the liar? It is the person who does
not accept Jesus as the Christ. This is the enemy
of Christ: the person who does not accept the
Father and his Son. 23Whoever does not accept
the Son does not have the Father. But whoever
confesses the Son has the Father, too.
24Be sure you continue to follow the teaching you heard from the beginning. If you continue to follow what you heard from the
beginning, you will stay in the Son and in the
Father. 25And this is what the Son promised to
us—life forever.
26I am writing this letter about those people
who are trying to lead you the wrong way.
27Christ gave you a special gift that is still in
you, so you do not need any other teacher. His
gift teaches you about everything, and it is
true, not false. So continue to live in Christ, as
his gift taught you.
28Yes, my dear children, live in him so that
when Christ comes back, we can be without
fear and not be ashamed in his presence. 29If
you know that Christ is all that is right, you
know that all who do right are God's children.

WE ARE GOD'S CHILDREN

3 1The Father has loved us so much that we
are called children of God. And we really are
his children. The reason the people in the world
do not know us is that they have not known
him. 2Dear friends, now we are children of God,
and we have not yet been shown what we will
be in the future. But we know that when Christ
comes again, we will be like him, because we
will see him as he really is. 3Christ is pure, and
all who have this hope in Christ keep themselves pure like Christ.
4The person who sins breaks God's law. Yes,
sin is living against God's law. 5You know that
Christ came to take away sins and that there is
no sin in Christ. 6So anyone who lives in Christ
does not go on sinning. Anyone who goes on
sinning has never really understood Christ and
has never known him.
7Dear children, do not let anyone lead you
the wrong way. Christ is all that is
right. So to be like Christ a person must do what is right.
8The devil has been sinning
since the beginning, so anyone who continues to sin belongs to the devil. The Son of
God came for this purpose: to
destroy the devil's work.

SATAN

How did Jesus destroy Satan's work? (3:7–8)

9Those who are God's children do not continue sinning, because the new life from God
remains in them. They are not able to go on
sinning, because they have become children of
God. 10So we can see who God's children are
and who the devil's children are: Those who
do not do what is right are not God's children,
and those who do not love their brothers and
sisters are not God's children.

On the Edge

The Father has loved us so much that we are called children of God. And we really are his children. The reason the people in the world do not know us is that they have not known him (1 John 3:1).

You might hear a preacher tell people they need to "make a decision" for Christ. It almost makes it sound like people can turn themselves into God's children. But John says something different. *God* is the One who makes you his child. He wanted you and chose you—even before you were born.

Now that might have you scratching your head. Didn't you "make a decision" for Christ? Didn't you decide to ask him to forgive you of your sins and come to live in your heart? Yes, you did. You had to come to the place where you wanted to be a follower of Jesus. But the words you use to express your faith in Jesus and ask for God's forgiveness are not some kind of magic spell and now—poof!—you're a child of God. It isn't a formula that you repeat three times and then you're saved.

No, there was nothing you did that made you God's child. Instead, when he looked inside your heart and saw real faith, *he* made you his child. He did it because he said he would. He did it because that's what he wanted to do all along.

SEE FOR YOURSELF:
Rom. 8:16; Gal. 4:4–5; Eph. 1:5

WE MUST LOVE EACH OTHER

11This is the teaching you have heard from
the beginning: We must love each other. 12Do
not be like Cain who belonged to the Evil One
and killed his brother. And why did he kill

him? Because the things Cain did were evil, and
the things his brother did were good.
13Brothers and sisters, do not be surprised
when the people of the world hate you. 14We
know we have left death and have come into
life because we love each other. Whoever does
not love is still dead. 15Everyone who hates a
brother or sister is a murderer,[n] and you know
that no murderers have eternal life in them.
16This is how we know what real love is: Jesus
gave his life for us. So we should give our lives
for our brothers and sisters. 17Suppose someone has enough to live and sees a brother or
sister in need, but does not help. Then God's
love is not living in that person. 18My children,
we should love people not only with words
and talk, but by our actions and true caring.
19-20This is the way we know that we belong
to the way of truth. When our hearts make us
feel guilty, we can still have peace before God.
God is greater than our hearts, and he knows
everything. 21My dear friends, if our hearts do
not make us feel guilty, we can come without
fear into God's presence. 22And God gives us
what we ask for because we obey God's commands and do what pleases him. 23This is what
God commands: that we believe in his Son,
Jesus Christ, and that we love each other, just as
he commanded. 24The people who obey God's
commands live in God, and God lives in them.
We know that God lives in us because of the
Spirit God gave us.

WARNING AGAINST FALSE TEACHERS

4 1My dear friends, many false prophets have
gone out into the world. So do not believe
every spirit, but test the spirits to see if they are
from God. 2This is how you can know God's
Spirit: Every spirit who confesses that Jesus
Christ came to earth as a human is from God.
3And every spirit who refuses to say this about
Jesus is not from God. It is the spirit of the
enemy of Christ, which you have heard is
coming, and now he is already in the world.
4My dear children, you belong to God and
have defeated them; because God's Spirit, who
is in you, is greater than the devil, who is in the
world. 5And they belong to the world, so what
they say is from the world, and the world listens to them. 6But we belong to God, and those
who know God listen to us. But those who are
not from God do not listen to us. That is how
we know the Spirit that is true and the spirit
that is false.

LOVE COMES FROM GOD

7Dear friends, we should love each other,
because love comes from God. Everyone who
loves has become God's child and knows God.
8Whoever does not love does not know God,
because God is love. 9This is how God showed
his love to us: He sent his one and only Son
into the world so that we could have life
through him. 10This is what real love is: It is
not our love for God; it is God's love for us in
sending his Son to be the way to take away our
sins.
11Dear friends, if God loved us that much

On the Edge

Whoever does not love does not know God, because God is love (1 John 4:8).

If you say you love your friend, but spread rumors behind her back, then everyone else knows that you didn't really love her. Love is loyal. A dad may tell his kids that he loves them, but divorces their family and moves hundreds of miles away. No one in that family will feel very loved.

Love doesn't run when the going gets hard. You can tell the whole world that you love, but if no one can feel it or see it, then it probably doesn't exist. God is love. If you have a relationship with him, then you will possess the love of God. Others will know that you are in love with God because his love will flow through you as you grow in him. You will love others freely. You will forgive with grace. You'll be kind and gentle and merciful. When you have God, you have love because he *is* love. Verses 17 and 18 tell us that there is nothing to be afraid of. You don't have to fear the judgment or punishment of God because you belong to him. So go for it—love the world like God loves you. There is nothing to lose and everything to gain. Relax and let him love *you*. Others will trust in Christ and come to know him because they have seen his love through you.

SEE FOR YOURSELF:
1 Cor. 13; Gal. 5:22–23; Eph. 2:4–7; 1 John 4:7

3:15 Everyone . . . murderer If one person hates a brother or sister, then in the heart that person has killed that brother or sister. Jesus taught about this sin to his followers (Matthew 5:21-26).

we also should love each other. [12]No one has
ever seen God, but if we love each other, God
lives in us, and his love is made perfect in us.
[13]We know that we live in God and he lives
in us, because he gave us his Spirit. [14]We have
seen and can testify that the Father sent his
Son to be the Savior of the world. [15]Whoever
confesses that Jesus is the Son of God has God
living inside, and that person lives in God.
[16]And so we know the love that God has for
us, and we trust that love.
God is love. Those who live in love live in
God, and God lives in them. [17]This is how love
is made perfect in us: that we can be without
fear on the day God judges us, because in this
world we are like him. [18]Where God's love is,
there is no fear, because God's perfect love
drives out fear. It is punishment that makes a
person fear, so love is not made perfect in the
person who fears.
[19]We love because God first loved us. [20]If
people say, "I love God," but hate their brothers
or sisters, they are liars. Those who do not love
their brothers and sisters, whom they have
seen, cannot love God, whom they have never
seen. [21]And God gave us this command: Those
who love God must also love their brothers
and sisters.

On the Edge

We love because God first loved us. If people say, "I love God," but hate their brothers or sisters, they are liars. Those who do not love their brothers and sisters, whom they have seen, cannot love God, whom they have never seen. And God gave us this command: Those who love God must also love their brothers and sisters (1 John 4:19–21).

Brothers and sisters can really test your ability to love. They know you so well. They know what makes you cringe and what makes you cry. They can understand you (sometimes) better than anyone else. They can irritate you to no end, but God says that if you love him you *have* to love them. He says that if you don't, you're a liar. If you don't love the people you can see (the ones who share your bathroom, eat the last of your favorite snacks, and go through your things), then God says you can't possibly love him, the One you haven't seen. Getting along with your brothers and sisters means you'll get lots of practice at forgiveness. The best thing that could happen is that you'll become really good friends with the people God put right in your home. He can do anything. So love and just watch him!

SEE FOR YOURSELF:
Lev. 19:18; Matt. 22:39; Gal. 5:13; Eph. 4:1–3; 1 Pet. 4:8; 2 John 5–6

WHAT'S IT MEAN?

Christ is not Jesus' last name. It's from the Greek translation of the Hebrew word for "Messiah" or "Anointed One." In Old Testament times, kings, priests, and prophets were all anointed, which means they had olive oil poured on their heads to show that they were specially appointed by God. The Jews of Jesus' day believed that the Messiah would become their king and free them from the control of the Roman Empire. Jesus, however, came as a spiritual leader who would free the world from the effects of sin.

1 John 5:1

FAITH IN THE SON OF GOD

5 [1]Everyone who believes that Jesus is the
Christ is God's child, and whoever loves the
Father also loves the Father's children. [2]This is
how we know we love God's children: when
we love God and obey his commands. [3]Loving
God means obeying his commands. And God's
commands are not too hard for us, [4]because
everyone who is a child of God conquers the
world. And this is the victory that conquers the
world—our faith. [5]So the one who wins against
the world is the person who believes that Jesus
is the Son of God.
[6]Jesus Christ is the One who came by
water[n] and blood.[n] He did not come by water
only, but by water and blood. And the Spirit
says that this is true, because the Spirit is the

5:6 water This probably means the water of Jesus' baptism. **5:6 blood** This probably means the blood of Jesus' death.

On the Edge

And this is the boldness we have in God's presence: that if we ask God for anything that agrees with what he wants, he hears us. If we know he hears us every time we ask him, we know we have what we ask from him (1 John 5:14–15).

If your job is getting the best of your homework, and you have to keep your job, then you need a God-solution. It's time to ask God for direction. You can be confident that he will listen. He does care about the details of your life.

In fact, your prayers have already been answered. Begin to pray specifically about what to do. Pray through the different options as they come up. Watch for God's answer. It may be a solution you haven't thought of before. It may require you to be more disciplined or more efficient. It may require more sacrifices. It may just mean you've got to rearrange your time. When you see where God is working, and where he is leading, then follow. Go with him and praise him for his interest in your life.

SEE FOR YOURSELF:
Deut. 28:6; Ps. 103:6; John 14:16; Heb. 4:16

truth. [7]So there are three witnesses that tell us
about Jesus: [8]the Spirit, the water, and the
blood; and these three witnesses agree. [9]We
believe people when they say something is
true. But what God says is more important,
and he has told us the truth about his own
Son. [10]Anyone who believes in the Son of God
has the truth that God told us. Anyone who
does not believe makes God a liar, because that
person does not believe what God told us
about his Son. [11]This is what God told us: God
has given us eternal life, and this life is in his
Son. [12]Whoever has the Son has life, but whoever does not have the Son of God does not
have life.

WE HAVE ETERNAL LIFE NOW

[13]I write this letter to you who believe in the
Son of God so you will know you have eternal
life. [14]And this is the boldness we have in
God's presence: that if we ask God for anything that agrees with what he wants, he hears
us. [15]If we know he hears us every time we ask
him, we know we have what we ask from him.
[16]If anyone sees a brother or sister sinning
(sin that does not lead to eternal death), that
person should pray, and God will give the sinner life. I am talking about people whose sin
does not lead to eternal death. There is sin that
leads to death. I do not mean that a person
should pray about that sin. [17]Doing wrong is
always sin, but there is sin that does not lead to
eternal death.
[18]We know that those who are God's children do not continue to sin. The Son of God
keeps them safe, and the Evil One cannot
touch them. [19]We know that we belong to God,
but the Evil One controls the whole world.
[20]We also know that the Son of God has come
and has given us understanding so that we can
know the True One. And our lives are in the
True One and in his Son, Jesus Christ. He is the
true God and the eternal life.
[21]So, dear children, keep yourselves away
from gods.

[1]From the Elder.[n]

To the chosen lady[n] and her children:

I love all of you in the truth,[n] and all those who know the truth love you. [2]We love you because of the truth that lives in us and will be with us forever.

[3]Grace, mercy, and peace from God the Father and his Son, Jesus Christ, will be with us in truth and love.

[4]I was very happy to learn that some of your children are following the way of truth, as the Father commanded us. [5]And now, dear lady, this is not a new command but is the same command we have had from the beginning. I ask you that we all love each other. [6]And love means living the way God commanded us to live. As you have heard from the beginning, his command is this: Live a life of love.

LOVE

What should Christians be known for? (5–6)

[7]Many false teachers are in the world now who do not confess that Jesus Christ came to earth as a human. Anyone who does not confess this is a false teacher and an enemy of Christ. [8]Be careful yourselves that you do not lose everything you have worked for, but that you receive your full reward.

[9]Anyone who goes beyond Christ's teaching and does not continue to follow only his teaching does not have God. But whoever continues to follow the teaching of Christ has both the Father and the Son. [10]If someone comes to you and does not bring this teaching, do not welcome or accept that person into your house. [11]If you welcome such a person, you share in the evil work.

[12]I have many things to write to you, but I do not want to use paper and ink. Instead, I hope to come to you and talk face to face so we can be full of joy. [13]The children of your chosen sister[n] greet you.

WHAT'S IT MEAN?

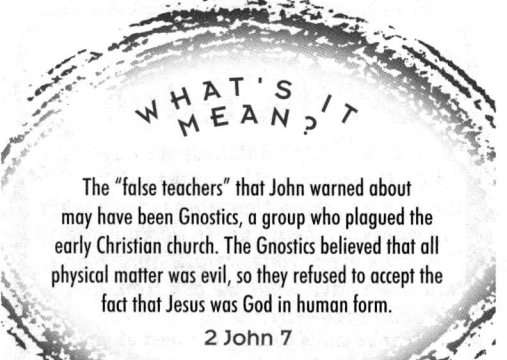

The "false teachers" that John warned about may have been Gnostics, a group who plagued the early Christian church. The Gnostics believed that all physical matter was evil, so they refused to accept the fact that Jesus was God in human form.

2 John 7

1 Elder "Elder" means an older person. It can also mean a special leader in the church (as in Titus 1:5). **1 lady** This might mean a woman, or in this letter it might mean a church. If it is a church, then "her children" would be the people of the church. **1 truth** The truth or "Good News" about Jesus Christ that joins all believers together. **13 sister** Sister of the "lady" in verse 1. This might be another woman or another church.

JOHN THE APOSTLE made a difference

A fisherman one day, John was called by Jesus to become a fisher of men the next. He walked with and watched Jesus for three years. He alone of the disciples stood at the cross as Jesus died. He was among the first to see the risen Christ. Jesus made a difference in John's life; that's why John made such a difference in so many other lives.

John was probably the youngest of the original Twelve. He lived the longest. We owe him for five New Testament books: John, 1 John, 2 John, 3 John, and Revelation. God chose John to write about the greatest theme of all: God's love. John tells us God is love. He knew God's love firsthand. And the goal of John's writing was to convince readers about Jesus and help them to experience, through him, God's love. "The Father has loved us so much that we are called children of God. And we really are his children" (1 John 3:1a).

Cutting Edge

The love he experienced in Jesus Christ transformed John. It made such a difference in his life that he made a difference in the lives of countless others. Think for a moment about how many lives have been changed by these simple words first penned by John: "God loved the world so much that he gave his one and only Son so that whoever believes in him may not be lost, but have eternal life" (John 3:16).

YOU can, too! If John could speak to you right now, he would undoubtedly ask if you have ever personalized that verse you just read. Have you ever realized how far God's love went in sending Jesus? Have you believed that gift was for you? Have you accepted forgiveness and eternal life from him? If you have, the biggest possible difference has begun in your Life. It will last beyond time.

Make sure you offer that difference-making message to others.

Want to know more? Read about John and the Jesus he loved in the Book of John as well as in his other writings and the other accounts of the Good News.

1 From the Elder.[n]
To my dear friend Gaius, whom I love in the
truth:[n]
2 My dear friend, I know your soul is doing
fine, and I pray that you are doing well in every way and that your health is good. 3 I was
very happy when some brothers and sisters[n]
came and told me about the truth in your life
and how you are following the way of truth.
4 Nothing gives me greater joy than to hear that
my children are following the way of truth.
5 My dear friend, it is good that you help the
brothers and sisters, even those you do not
know. 6 They told the church about your love.
Please help them to continue their trip in a way
worthy of God. 7 They started out in service to
Christ, and they have been accepting nothing
from nonbelievers. 8 So we should help such
people; when we do, we share in their work
for the truth.
9 I wrote something to the church, but Diotrephes, who loves to be their leader, will not
listen to us. 10 So if I come, I will talk about
what Diotrephes is doing, about how he lies
and says evil things about us. But more than
that, he refuses to accept the other brothers
and sisters; he even stops those who do want
to accept them and puts them out of the
church.
11 My dear friend, do not follow what is bad;
follow what is good. The one who does good
belongs to God. But the one who does evil has
never known God.
12 Everyone says good things about Demetrius, and the truth agrees with what they say.
We also speak well of him, and you know
what we say is true.
13 I have many things I want to write you,
but I do not want to use pen and ink. 14 I hope
to see you soon and talk face to face. 15 Peace to
you. The friends here greet you. Please greet
each friend there by name.

WHAT'S IT MEAN?

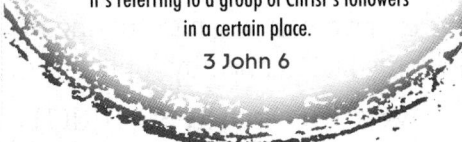

The "church" John describes in this verse is not the same kind of church you're used to. Church buildings as we know them today—places set aside specifically for Christian worship and Bible study—were not common until the third century. Before then, people met together in their homes to study Scripture and pray. Traveling teachers and missionaries moved from city to city, relying on the kindness of local Christians for food, housing, and other necessities. When you see the word *church* in the Bible, it's referring to a group of Christ's followers in a certain place.

3 John 6

1 Elder "Elder" means an older person. It can also mean a special leader in the church (as in Titus 1:5).
1 truth The truth or "Good News" about Jesus Christ that joins all believers together. **3 brothers and sisters** Although the Greek text says "brothers" here and throughout this book, the writer's words were meant for the entire church, including men and women.

jude

CONTENT

Have you ever read a "letter to the editor" in the newspaper? Sometimes regular, everyday people (which means, not reporters) will write letters to the newspaper. They usually do this when they feel strongly about an issue and they want everyone to know how they feel. The Book of Jude is like one of those letters.

Jude was a man with a mission. Even though Christianity hadn't been around a long time (and maybe *because* of that), there were lots of people twisting and turning the truth of the Good News to mean something totally different. Some were saying that Christianity was too simple, that there must be more to the Good News than Jesus' life and death. Others were saying that Christianity was too hard, that with God's grace we didn't really have to worry at all anymore about obeying the law. There were so many fake stories out there that it was difficult to know who was telling the truth.

Jude had no patience for that kind of trickery and lying. He wrote his letter to the church to straighten out these kinds of deceptions and to remind them that what we do matters to God.

Outline

1–2 .... Greetings
3–23 .... Defending the Faith Against False Teachers
24–25 .... Final Prayer

Purpose

Insulate yourselves from false teaching by growing in the faith.

Theme

Contending for the Faith

Date of writing

Early 60s A.D.

1 From Jude, a servant of Jesus Christ and a brother of James.

To all who have been called by God. God the Father loves you, and you have been kept safe in Jesus Christ:

2 Mercy, peace, and love be yours richly.

GOD WILL PUNISH SINNERS

3 Dear friends, I wanted very much to write you about the salvation we all share. But I felt the need to write you about something else: I want to encourage you to fight hard for the faith that was given the holy people of God once and for all time. 4 Some people have secretly entered your group. Long ago the prophets wrote about these people who will be judged guilty. They are against God and have changed the grace of our God into a reason for sexual sin. They also refuse to accept Jesus Christ, our only Master and Lord.

> "I felt the need to write you . . . I want to encourage you to fight hard for the faith that was given the holy people of God once and for all time."
> (Jude 3b)

5 I want to remind you of some things you already know: Remember that the Lord saved his people by bringing them out of the land of Egypt. But later he destroyed all those who did not believe. 6 And remember the angels who did not keep their place of power but left their proper home. The Lord has kept these angels in darkness, bound with everlasting chains, to be judged on the great day. 7 Also remember the cities of Sodom and Gomorrah[n] and the other towns around them. In the same way they were full of sexual sin and people who desired sexual relations that God does not allow. They suffer the punishment of eternal fire, as an example for all to see.

HELL

What kind of place is hell? (6–7)

8 It is the same with these people who have entered your group. They are guided by dreams and make themselves filthy with sin. They reject God's authority and speak against the angels. 9 Not even the archangel[n] Michael, when he argued with the devil about who would have the body of Moses, dared to judge the devil guilty. Instead, he said, "The Lord punish you." 10 But these people speak against things they do not understand. And what they do know, by feeling, as dumb animals know things, are the very things that destroy them. 11 It will be terrible for them. They have followed the way of Cain, and for money they have given themselves to doing the wrong that Balaam did. They have fought against God as Korah did, and like Korah, they surely will be destroyed. 12 They are like dirty spots in your special Christian meals you share. They eat with you and have no fear, caring only for themselves. They are clouds without rain, which the wind blows around. They are autumn trees without fruit that are pulled out of the ground. So they are twice dead. 13 They are like wild waves of the sea, tossing up their own shameful actions like foam. They are like stars that wander in the sky. A place in the blackest darkness has been kept for them forever.

14 Enoch, the seventh descendant from Adam, said about these people: "Look, the Lord is coming with many thousands of his holy angels to 15 judge every person. He is coming to punish all who are against God for all the evil they have done against him. And he will punish the sinners who are against God for all the evil they have said against him."

16 These people complain and blame others,

WHAT'S IT MEAN?

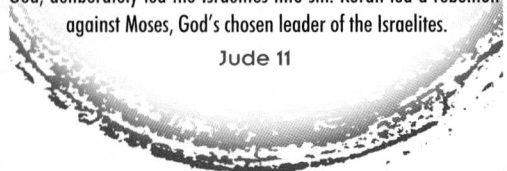

What did a person have to do to make this biblical "Hall of Shame"? Cain chose to worship God in his own way, rather than to follow the Lord's instructions. When his brother, Abel, received God's approval for his worship, Cain got jealous and killed Abel. Balaam, who had once been a prophet of God, deliberately led the Israelites into sin. Korah led a rebellion against Moses, God's chosen leader of the Israelites.

Jude 11

7 Sodom and Gomorrah Two cities God destroyed because they were so evil. **9 archangel** The leader among God's angels or messengers.

doing the evil things they want to do. They brag about themselves, and they flatter others to get what they want.

A WARNING AND THINGS TO DO

17Dear friends, remember what the apostles of our Lord Jesus Christ said before. 18They said to you, "In the last times there will be people who laugh about God, following their own evil desires which are against God." 19These are the people who divide you, people whose thoughts are only of this world, who do not have the Spirit.

20But dear friends, use your most holy faith to build yourselves up, praying in the Holy Spirit. 21Keep yourselves in God's love as you wait for the Lord Jesus Christ with his mercy to give you life forever.

22Show mercy to some people who have doubts. 23Take others out of the fire, and save them. Show mercy mixed with fear to others, hating even their clothes which are dirty from sin.

PRAISE GOD

24God is strong and can help you not to fall. He can bring you before his glory without any wrong in you and can give you great joy. 25He is the only God, the One who saves us. To him be glory, greatness, power, and authority through Jesus Christ our Lord for all time past, now, and forever. Amen.

Promise HE PROMISES TO HELP YOU PRAY.

But dear friends, use your most holy faith to build yourselves up, praying in the Holy Spirit (Jude 20).

How's your prayer life? Stumbling, fumbling, falling asleep? Don't quite know where to start or how to end? Don't let your lack of practice keep you from spending time with Jesus. The Lord God promises to help you pray through the power of the Holy Spirit.

God is not impressed with big, long prayers or Bible-sounding words. He sees right through all that stuff, clear down to the bottom of your heart. He wants to know how you really feel. You can be totally honest with him. (He already knows the truth anyway.) He won't be distracted, won't spread rumors, won't act like your stuff is stupid. He loves to hear from you, so speak to him with reverence, in truth, and according to his will.

Try using the acrostic PRAY to guide your prayer time. *P* stands for *praise*. Spend the first part of your time with the Lord in praise and worship. You may pray through some verses in the Book of Psalms. You might sing some praise choruses. Be creative with your worship. The Holy Spirit will lead you. *R* is for *repent*. The next part of your prayer time is repentance. Tell God about your sin and ask him for forgiveness. Talk to him about turning from your sin and the habits you've fallen into. Ask him for strength and character. Ask him for the power to overcome temptation. *A* is *ask anything for anybody*. When Jesus prayed for other people, he prayed boldly. You can follow his example and pray boldly for your friends and family. Finally, *Y* is for *yourself*. Bring your concerns and needs to the Lord. Talk through your day and your plans. Ask him to reveal his will for you today. Ask him to go before you; then expect him to be there.

Remember that the acrostic is PRAY, not YARP—the order is important. No matter how you choose to pray, the Holy Spirit promises to help you. Know that your prayers are important, and you will always be heard by the Father.

SEE FOR YOURSELF:

Rom. 8:26–27; Eph. 6:18; Heb. 7:24–25

revelation

CONTENT If we could see the Book of Revelation instead of reading it, it would be a special effects extravaganza. Revelation is a book by John, the disciple, cataloguing a vision he was given of the end of the world. He describes heavenly things in earthly terms. Sometimes it gets pretty bizarre trying to imagine what a whole other dimension of life will look like.

Some of the images in Revelation are a mystery to this day. We won't recognize them until we see them for ourselves in the new heaven and new earth. But we do recognize enough of Revelation's message to know this: For now, God gives Satan and human evil some leeway in this world. There will come a day, though, when God will say, "Enough," and we all will be judged according to our faith and our works.

Revelation also teaches us that in the end, those who have their faith in Christ's goodness will be invited into God's presence forever and Satan will be banished from the kingdom. It's a real and true happily-ever-after kind of story.

Outline

1:1–7 .... A Prophecy from John
1:8–20 .... A Vision of the Living Lord
2:1—3:22 .... Letters to the Seven Churches
4:1–11 .... A Vision of Worship in Heaven
5:1—6:17 .... A Scroll with Seven Seals
7:1–17 .... Worship in Front of God's Throne
8:1—11:19 .... Seven Trumpets
12:1—13:18 .... A Dragon and Two Beasts
14:1—15:8 .... Visions of God's Judgment
16:1–21 .... Seven Bowls of God's Anger
17:1—20:10 .... God's Enemies Are Defeated
20:11–15 .... The Final Judgment
21:1–8 .... A New Heaven and a New Earth
21:9—22:5 .... The New Jerusalem
22:6–21 .... Christ Will Soon Return

Purpose God will surely judge sin and provide heaven for believers.

Theme The Lord Our God the Almighty Reigns

Date of writing A.D. 96

"So write the things you see, what is now and what will happen later" (1:19).

Bible Talk

The Rapture

The Bible teaches us that, at some point during the last years of the earth, Christ will return and we will be caught up with him into the heavens. Most people call this the "rapture" even though most Bibles don't use that word.

We don't know exactly how the rapture will happen. Will our clothes be left in a pile on the floor? Will our bodies disappear? Will it be so quick that no one will notice?

The rapture and the other "end times" events can seem frightening sometimes. There is so much we don't know and even the things we do know lead us to more questions.

We have to remember, though, that God will take care of us. When it all happens, it will seem just right to us because God will be handling things.

SHOULD I TRY TO GUESS WHEN JESUS WILL RETURN?

You should be anticipating Christ's return. That means you should live your life so that you are ready to face him at any moment. But the Bible clearly tells us that there is no way to figure out when Jesus will come back to earth. We may enjoy paying close attention to the prophecies of the Bible and the news headlines to see if we can spot when a prophecy is fulfilled. That's okay as long as we realize that some new information may come along that will force us to rethink the prophecy's meaning and fulfillment.

JOHN TELLS ABOUT THIS BOOK

1 1This is the revelation[n] of Jesus Christ,
which God gave to him, to show his servants
what must soon happen. And Jesus sent his
angel to show it to his servant John, 2who has
told everything he has seen. It is the word of
God; it is the message from Jesus Christ. 3Hap-
py is the one who reads the words of God's
message, and happy are the people who hear
this message and do what is written in it. The
time is near when all of this will happen.

JESUS' MESSAGE TO THE CHURCHES

4From John.
To the seven churches in the country of
Asia:
Grace and peace to you from the One who
is and was and is coming, and from the seven
spirits before his throne, 5and from Jesus
Christ. Jesus is the faithful witness, the first
among those raised from the dead. He is the
ruler of the kings of the earth.
He is the One who loves us, who made us
free from our sins with the blood of his death.
6He made us to be a kingdom of priests who
serve God his Father. To Jesus Christ be glory
and power forever and ever! Amen.
7Look, Jesus is coming with the clouds, and
everyone will see him, even those who stabbed
him. And all peoples of the earth will cry loudly because of him. Yes, this will happen! Amen.
8The Lord God says, "I am the Alpha and
the Omega.[n] I am the One who is and was and
is coming. I am the Almighty."
9I, John, am your brother. All of us share
with Christ in suffering, in the kingdom, and in
patience to continue. I was on the island of
Patmos,[n] because I had preached the word of
God and the message about Jesus. 10On the
Lord's day I was in the Spirit, and I heard a
loud voice behind me that sounded like a
trumpet. 11The voice said, "Write what you see
in a book and send it to the seven churches: to
Ephesus, Smyrna, Pergamum, Thyatira, Sardis,
Philadelphia, and Laodicea."
12I turned to see who was talking to me.
When I turned, I saw seven golden lampstands
13and someone among the lampstands who
was "like a Son of Man."[n] He was dressed in a
long robe and had a gold band around his
chest. 14His head and hair were white like
wool, as white as snow, and his eyes were like
flames of fire. 15His feet were like bronze that
glows hot in a furnace, and his voice was like
the noise of flooding water. 16He held seven
stars in his right hand, and a sharp double-
edged sword came out of his mouth. He
looked like the sun shining at its brightest time.
17When I saw him, I fell down at his feet like
a dead man. He put his right hand on me
and said, "Do not be afraid. I am the First and
the Last. 18I am the One who lives; I was dead,
but look, I am alive forever and ever! And I
hold the keys to death and to the place of the
dead. 19So write the things you see, what is
now and what will happen later. 20Here is the
secret of the seven stars that you saw in my
right hand and the seven golden lampstands:
The seven lampstands are the seven churches,
and the seven stars are the angels of the seven
churches.

WHAT'S IT MEAN?

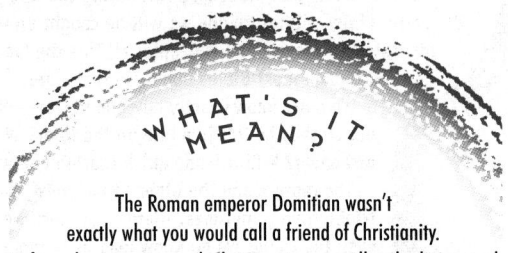

The Roman emperor Domitian wasn't exactly what you would call a friend of Christianity. As far as he was concerned, Christianity was an illegal religion, and those who practiced it were asking for persecution. Tradition has it that the apostle John was sentenced to live on the island of Patmos for eighteen months because he refused to stop preaching about Jesus. Don't assume that island life on Patmos was easy, either. People sentenced to the small, rocky island (about thirty-five miles off the coast of what is now Turkey) were forced to work in mines and quarries.

Revelation 1:9

TO THE CHURCH IN EPHESUS

2 1"Write this to the angel of the church in
Ephesus:
"The One who holds the seven stars in his
right hand and walks among the seven golden
lampstands says this: 2I know what you do,
how you work hard and never give up. I know
you do not put up with the false teachings of
evil people. You have tested those who say
they are apostles but really are not, and you

1:1 revelation Making known truth that has been hidden. **1:8 Alpha and the Omega** The first and last letters of the Greek alphabet. This means "the beginning and the end." **1:9 Patmos** A small island in the Aegean Sea, near the coast of Asia Minor (modern Turkey). **1:13 "like . . . Man"** "Son of Man" is a name Jesus called himself.

WHAT'S IT MEAN?

Any list of the major cities of the ancient world would have to include Ephesus. This bustling seaport city boasted a population of two hundred fifty thousand, a thriving business community, and an active religious culture—not to mention one of the seven wonders of the ancient world. The temple dedicated to the Roman goddess Diana was truly an architectural marvel. It also symbolized the pagan worship that went on in the city. The apostle Paul had started a church in Ephesus, and the apostle John had worked in the city for almost thirty years before being shipped off to Patmos.

Revelation 2:1

On the Edge

You have patience and have suffered troubles for my name and have not given up. But I have this against you: You have left the love you had in the beginning (Rev. 2:3–4).

Jesus was talking to some people who had done great things for him. They had worked hard and persevered; but in all of that, they somehow lost their first love for him. You probably know people like that. They go to church all the time, wear Christian T-shirts, and scream "Jesus" really loud at concerts. But they're missing a passion for him.

The Lord wants you to be known as a person who loves him. He'd rather have you be known as a gentle, humble lover of God than as the most eloquent preacher who just sounds good. All kinds of things will tempt you to love them more than you love Jesus, but don't give in. Hold on tight to your love for him. When other people walk away from an encounter with you, they should know one thing—that you have a passionate, fervent, fiery love for God that will not quit. You don't want them to know all the great things you've done for God. You want them to know that you know and love him, that you're connected to him, that he is number one in your life.

If you've gotten caught up in doing a bunch of stuff in the name of the Lord, slam on the brakes. Run into his presence. Pray and worship him. Start listening to him and hearing his voice. Let him melt your heart again. Ask him to rekindle your fire for him. Your service is made great because your love for him is great. Keep your passion burning for him!

SEE FOR YOURSELF:
Deut. 6:4–6, 14–15; Josh. 23:11; Matt. 22:36–37

found they are liars. [3]You have patience and
have suffered troubles for my name and have
not given up.
[4]"But I have this against you: You have left
the love you had in the beginning. [5]So remember where you were before you fell. Change
your hearts and do what you did at first. If you
do not change, I will come to you and will take
away your lampstand from its place. [6]But there
is something you do that is right: You hate
what the Nicolaitans[n] do, as much as I.
[7]"Every person who has ears should listen
to what the Spirit says to the churches. To
those who win the victory I will give the right
to eat the fruit from the tree of life, which is in
the garden of God.

TO THE CHURCH IN SMYRNA

[8]"Write this to the angel of the church in
Smyrna:
"The One who is the First and the Last, who
died and came to life again, says this: [9]I know
your troubles and that you are poor, but really
you are rich! I know the bad things some people say about you. They say they are Jews, but
they are not true Jews. They are a synagogue
that belongs to Satan. [10]Do not be afraid of
what you are about to suffer. I tell you, the
devil will put some of you in prison to test
you, and you will suffer for ten days. But be
faithful, even if you have to die, and I will give
you the crown of life.
[11]"Everyone who has ears should listen to
what the Spirit says to the churches. Those
who win the victory will not be hurt by the
second death.

TO THE CHURCH IN PERGAMUM

[12]"Write this to the angel of the church in
Pergamum:

2:6 Nicolaitans This is the name of a religious group that followed false beliefs and ideas.

WHAT'S IT MEAN?

Would you believe that some citizens of the Roman Empire thought so much of their emperor that they actually worshiped him? Smyrna, a large harbor city about forty miles north of Ephesus, was the home of a temple built to honor the emperor Tiberius. The city became a center of emperor worship. Christians who chose not to join the pagan worship were severely persecuted. Today the city, which is located in Turkey, is known as Izmir.

Revelation 2:8

"The One who has the sharp, double-edged
sword says this: 13 I know where you live. It is
where Satan has his throne. But you are true to
me. You did not refuse to tell about your faith
in me even during the time of Antipas, my
faithful witness who was killed in your city,
where Satan lives.
14 "But I have a few things against you: You
have some there who follow the teaching of
Balaam. He taught Balak how to cause the
people of Israel to sin by eating food offered to
idols and by taking part in sexual sins. 15 You
also have some who follow the teaching of the

WHAT'S IT MEAN?

Pergamum was the capital of Asia—not the continent of Asia, but the Roman province of the same name. The city, located about fifty miles north of Smyrna, was known for its cultural and scientific communities. Pergamum boasted a library of about two hundred thousand volumes and a famous medical center. The city also offered a wide variety of pagan worship opportunities. In addition to its three temples dedicated to the Roman emperors, Pergamum was home to temples for the pagan goddess Athena and the god Zeus.

Revelation 2:12

Nicolaitans.[n] 16 So change your hearts and lives.
If you do not, I will come to you quickly and
fight against them with the sword that comes
out of my mouth.
17 "Everyone who has ears should listen to
what the Spirit says to the churches.
"I will give some of the hidden manna to
everyone who wins the victory. I will also give
to each one who wins the victory a white
stone with a new name written on it. No one
knows this new name except the one who receives it.

WHAT'S IT MEAN?

Purple was the color of choice for the citizens of Thyatira. The city, located about twenty miles southeast of Pergamum, was famous for the purple dye and cloth that was produced there. Because of Thyatira's focus on business and manufacturing, a number of trade unions were located there. We get the impression that when members of the union weren't discussing business in their meetings, they were usually worshiping pagan gods or committing sexual sins.

Revelation 2:18

TO THE CHURCH IN THYATIRA

18 "Write this to the angel of the church in
Thyatira:
"The Son of God, who has eyes that blaze
like fire and feet like shining bronze, says this:
19 I know what you do. I know about your love,
your faith, your service, and your patience. I
know that you are doing more now than you
did at first.
20 "But I have this against you: You let that
woman Jezebel spread false teachings. She says
she is a prophetess, but by her teaching she
leads my people to take part in sexual sins and
to eat food that is offered to idols. 21 I have
given her time to change her heart and turn
away from her sin, but she does not want to
change. 22 So I will throw her on a bed of suffering. And all those who take part in adultery
with her will suffer greatly if they do not turn
away from the wrongs she does. 23 I will also
kill her followers. Then all the churches will

2:15 Nicolaitans This is the name of a religious group that followed false beliefs and ideas.

know I am the One who searches hearts and
minds, and I will repay each of you for what
you have done.
24"But others of you in Thyatira have not
followed her teaching and have not learned
what some call Satan's deep secrets. I say to
you that I will not put any other load on you.
25Only continue in your loyalty until I come.
26"I will give power over the nations to
everyone who wins the victory and continues
to be obedient to me until the end.
27'You will rule over them with an iron rod,
as when pottery is broken into pieces.'

Psalm 2:9

28This is the same power I received from my
Father. I will also give him the morning star.
29Everyone who has ears should listen to what
the Spirit says to the churches.

WHAT'S IT MEAN?

Sardis was what you might call a "recovering" city. Located about fifty miles east of Smyrna, the city of Sardis was destroyed by an earthquake in A.D. 17. The Roman emperor Tiberius helped rebuild the city. The citizens were so grateful that they built temples in his honor and made Sardis one of the centers for emperor worship in the Near East.

Revelation 3:1

TO THE CHURCH IN SARDIS

3 1"Write this to the angel of the church in
Sardis:
"The One who has the seven spirits and the
seven stars says this: I know what you do.
People say that you are alive, but really you are
dead. 2Wake up! Make yourselves stronger before what you have left dies completely. I have
found that what you are doing is less than
what my God wants. 3So do not forget what
you have received and heard. Obey it, and
change your hearts and lives. So you must
wake up, or I will come like a thief, and you
will not know when I will come to you. 4But
you have a few there in Sardis who have kept
their clothes unstained, so they will walk with
me and will wear white clothes, because they
are worthy. 5Those who win the victory will be
dressed in white clothes like them. And I will
not erase their names from the book of life, but
I will say they belong to me before my Father
and before his angels. 6Everyone who has ears
should listen to what the Spirit says to the
churches.

WHAT'S IT MEAN?

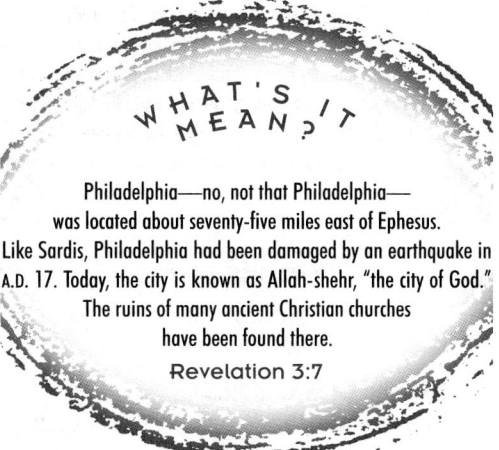

Philadelphia—no, not that Philadelphia—was located about seventy-five miles east of Ephesus. Like Sardis, Philadelphia had been damaged by an earthquake in A.D. 17. Today, the city is known as Allah-shehr, "the city of God." The ruins of many ancient Christian churches have been found there.

Revelation 3:7

TO THE CHURCH IN PHILADELPHIA

7"Write this to the angel of the church in
Philadelphia:
"This is what the One who is holy and true,
who holds the key of David, says. When he
opens a door, no one can close it. And when
he closes it, no one can open it. 8I know what
you do. I have put an open door before you,
which no one can close. I know you have a
little strength, but you have obeyed my teaching and were not afraid to speak my name.
9Those in the synagogue that belongs to Satan
say they are Jews, but they are not true Jews;
they are liars. I will make them come before
you and bow at your feet, and they will know
that I have loved you. 10You have obeyed my
teaching about not giving up your faith. So I
will keep you from the time of trouble that will
come to the whole world to test those who live
on earth.
11"I am coming soon. Continue strong in
your faith so no one will take away your
crown. 12I will make those who win the victory
pillars in the temple of my God, and they will
never have to leave it. I will write on them the
name of my God and the name of the city of
my God, the new Jerusalem,[n] that comes down
out of heaven from my God. I will also write
on them my new name. 13Everyone who has

3:12 Jerusalem This name is used to mean the spiritual city God built for his people. See Revelation 21–22.

WHAT'S IT MEAN?

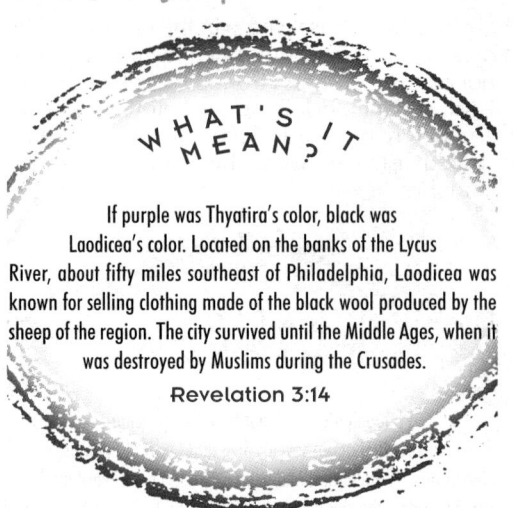

If purple was Thyatira's color, black was Laodicea's color. Located on the banks of the Lycus River, about fifty miles southeast of Philadelphia, Laodicea was known for selling clothing made of the black wool produced by the sheep of the region. The city survived until the Middle Ages, when it was destroyed by Muslims during the Crusades.

Revelation 3:14

ears should listen to what the Spirit says to the
churches.

TO THE CHURCH IN LAODICEA

14"Write this to the angel of the church in
Laodicea:
"The Amen,[n] the faithful and true witness,
the beginning of all God has made, says this:
15I know what you do, that you are not hot or
cold. I wish that you were hot or cold! 16But
because you are lukewarm—neither hot, nor
cold—I am ready to spit you out of my mouth.
17You say, 'I am rich, and I have become
wealthy and do not need anything.' But you do
not know that you are really miserable, pitiful,
poor, blind, and naked. 18I advise you to buy
from me gold made pure in fire so you can be
truly rich. Buy from me white clothes so you
can be clothed and so you can cover your
shameful nakedness. Buy from me medicine to
put on your eyes so you can truly see.
19"I correct and punish those whom I love.
So be eager to do right, and change your hearts
and lives. 20Here I am! I stand at the door and
knock. If you hear my voice and open the door,
I will come in and eat with you, and you will
eat with me.
21"Those who win the victory will sit with
me on my throne in the same way that I won
the victory and sat down with my Father on
his throne. 22Everyone who has ears should
listen to what the Spirit says to the churches."

4

JOHN SEES HEAVEN

1After the vision of these things I looked,
and there before me was an open door in
heaven. And the same voice that spoke to me
before, that sounded like a trumpet, said,
"Come up here, and I will show you what must
happen after this." 2Immediately I was in the
Spirit, and before me was a throne in heaven,
and someone was sitting on it. 3The One who
sat on the throne looked like precious stones,
like jasper and carnelian. All around the throne
was a rainbow the color of an emerald.
4Around the throne there were twenty-four
other thrones with twenty-four elders sitting
on them. They were dressed in white and had
golden crowns on their heads. 5Lightning
flashes and noises and thundering came from
the throne. Before the throne seven lamps were
burning, which are the seven spirits of God.
6Also before the throne there was something
that looked like a sea of glass, clear like crystal.
In the center and around the throne were
four living creatures with eyes all over them, in
front and in back. 7The first living creature was
like a lion. The second was like a calf. The third
had a face like a man. The fourth was like a
flying eagle. 8Each of these four living creatures
had six wings and was covered all over with
eyes, inside and out. Day and night they never
stop saying:

"Holy, holy, holy is the Lord God
Almighty.
He was, he is, and he is coming."

WHAT'S IT MEAN?

This isn't the first time these four bizarre creatures are mentioned in the Bible. The Old Testament prophet Ezekiel saw a very similar vision. Notice that each of the four looks like one of the most powerful creatures on earth—a man, a lion, a bull (the calf), and an eagle. Think about it. Human beings rule over every creature on earth. The lion is the king of the jungle. Bulls are the strongest tame animals. Eagles are the fastest, strongest birds.

Revelation 4:7

9These living creatures give glory, honor,
and thanks to the One who sits on the throne,
who lives forever and ever. 10Then the twenty-
four elders bow down before the One who sits

3:14 Amen Used here as a name for Jesus; it means to agree fully that something is true.

on the throne, and they worship him who
lives forever and ever. They put their crowns
down before the throne and say:
11 "You are worthy, our Lord and God,
to receive glory and honor and power,
because you made all things.
Everything existed and was made,
because you wanted it."

5 1 Then I saw a scroll in the right hand of the
One sitting on the throne. The scroll had writing on both sides and was kept closed with
seven seals. 2 And I saw a powerful angel calling in a loud voice, "Who is worthy to break
the seals and open the scroll?" 3 But there was
no one in heaven or on earth or under the
earth who could open the scroll or look inside
it. 4 I cried hard because there was no one who
was worthy to open the scroll or look inside.
5 But one of the elders said to me, "Do not cry!
The Lion[n] from the tribe of Judah, David's descendant, has won the victory so that he is
able to open the scroll and its seven seals."

WHAT'S IT MEAN?

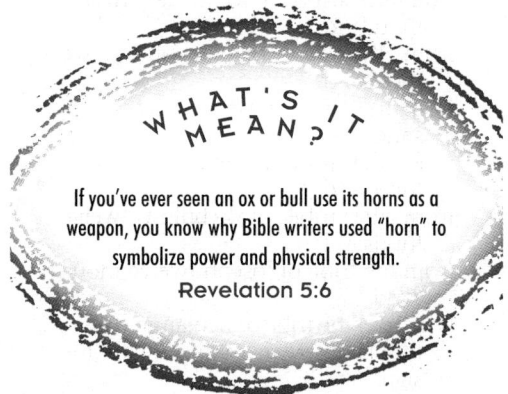

If you've ever seen an ox or bull use its horns as a weapon, you know why Bible writers used "horn" to symbolize power and physical strength.
Revelation 5:6

6 Then I saw a Lamb standing in the center
of the throne and in the middle of the four
living creatures and the elders. The Lamb
looked as if he had been killed. He had seven
horns and seven eyes, which are the seven
spirits of God that were sent into all the world.
7 The Lamb came and took the scroll from the
right hand of the One sitting on the throne.
8 When he took the scroll, the four living creatures and the twenty-four elders bowed down
before the Lamb. Each one of them had a harp
and golden bowls full of incense, which are the
prayers of God's holy people. 9 And they all
sang a new song to the Lamb:
"You are worthy to take the scroll
and to open its seals,
because you were killed,
and with the blood of your death you
bought people for God
from every tribe, language, people, and
nation.
10 You made them to be a kingdom of priests
for our God,
and they will rule on the earth."
11 Then I looked, and I heard the voices of
many angels around the throne, and the four
living creatures, and the elders. There were
thousands and thousands of angels, 12 saying
in a loud voice:
"The Lamb who was killed is worthy
to receive power, wealth, wisdom, and
strength,
honor, glory, and praise!"
13 Then I heard all creatures in heaven and
on earth and under the earth and in the sea
saying:
"To the One who sits on the throne
and to the Lamb
be praise and honor and glory and power
forever and ever."
14 The four living creatures said, "Amen," and
the elders bowed down and worshiped.

6 1 Then I watched while the Lamb opened the
first of the seven seals. I heard one of the four
living creatures say with a voice like thunder,
"Come!" 2 I looked, and there before me was a
white horse. The rider on the horse held a bow,
and he was given a crown, and he rode out,
determined to win the victory.
3 When the Lamb opened the second seal, I
heard the second living creature say, "Come!"
4 Then another horse came out, a red one. Its
rider was given power to take away peace
from the earth and to make people kill each
other, and he was given a big sword.
5 When the Lamb opened the third seal, I
heard the third living creature say, "Come!" I
looked, and there before me was a black horse,
and its rider held a pair of scales in his hand.
6 Then I heard something that sounded like a
voice coming from the middle of the four living creatures. The voice said, "A quart of wheat
for a day's pay, and three quarts of barley for a
day's pay, and do not damage the olive oil and
wine!"
7 When the Lamb opened the fourth seal, I
heard the voice of the fourth living creature
say, "Come!" 8 I looked, and there before me
was a pale horse. Its rider was named death,
and Hades[n] was following close behind him.
They were given power over a fourth of the
earth to kill people by war, by starvation, by

5:5 Lion Here refers to Christ. **6:8 Hades** The unseen world of the dead.

WHAT'S IT MEAN?

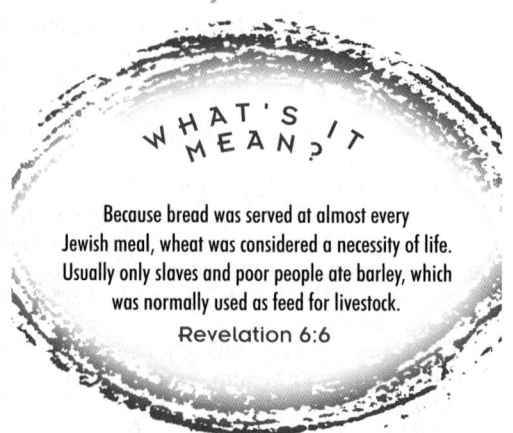

Because bread was served at almost every Jewish meal, wheat was considered a necessity of life. Usually only slaves and poor people ate barley, which was normally used as feed for livestock.

Revelation 6:6

disease, and by the wild animals of the earth.
9 When the Lamb opened the fifth seal, I saw under the altar the souls of those who had been killed because they were faithful to the word of God and to the message they had received. 10 These souls shouted in a loud voice, "Holy and true Lord, how long until you judge the people of the earth and punish them for killing us?" 11 Then each one of them was given a white robe and was told to wait a short time longer. There were still some of their fellow servants and brothers and sisters[n] in the service of Christ who must be killed as they were. They had to wait until all of this was finished.

12 Then I watched while the Lamb opened the sixth seal, and there was a great earthquake. The sun became black like rough black cloth, and the whole moon became red like blood. 13 And the stars in the sky fell to the earth like figs falling from a fig tree when the wind blows. 14 The sky disappeared as a scroll when it is rolled up, and every mountain and island was moved from its place.

15 Then the kings of the earth, the rulers, the generals, the rich people, the powerful people, the slaves, and the free people hid themselves in caves and in the rocks on the mountains. 16 They called to the mountains and the rocks, "Fall on us. Hide us from the face of the One who sits on the throne and from the anger of the Lamb! 17 The great day for their anger has come, and who can stand against it?"

THE 144,000 PEOPLE OF ISRAEL

7 1 After the vision of these things I saw four angels standing at the four corners of the earth. The angels were holding the four winds of the earth to keep them from blowing on the land or on the sea or on any tree. 2 Then I saw another angel coming up from the east who had the seal of the living God. And he called out in a loud voice to the four angels to whom God had given power to harm the earth and the sea. 3 He said to them, "Do not harm the land or the sea or the trees until we mark with a sign the foreheads of the people who serve our God." 4 Then I heard how many people were marked with the sign. There were one hundred forty-four thousand from every tribe of the people of Israel.

5 From the tribe of Judah twelve thousand were marked with the sign,
from the tribe of Reuben twelve thousand,
from the tribe of Gad twelve thousand,
6 from the tribe of Asher twelve thousand,
from the tribe of Naphtali twelve thousand,
from the tribe of Manasseh twelve thousand,
7 from the tribe of Simeon twelve thousand,
from the tribe of Levi twelve thousand,
from the tribe of Issachar twelve thousand,
8 from the tribe of Zebulun twelve thousand,
from the tribe of Joseph twelve thousand,
and from the tribe of Benjamin twelve thousand were marked with the sign.

THE GREAT CROWD WORSHIPS GOD

9 After the vision of these things I looked, and there was a great number of people, so many that no one could count them. They were from every nation, tribe, people, and language of the earth. They were all standing before the throne and before the Lamb, wearing white robes and holding palm branches in their hands. 10 They were shouting in a loud voice, "Salvation belongs to our God, who sits on the throne, and to the Lamb." 11 All the angels were standing around the throne and the elders and the four living creatures. They all bowed down on their faces before the throne and worshiped God, 12 saying, "Amen! Praise, glory, wisdom, thanks, honor, power, and

6:11 brothers and sisters Although the Greek text says "brothers" here and throughout this book, both men and women would have been included.

WHAT'S IT MEAN?

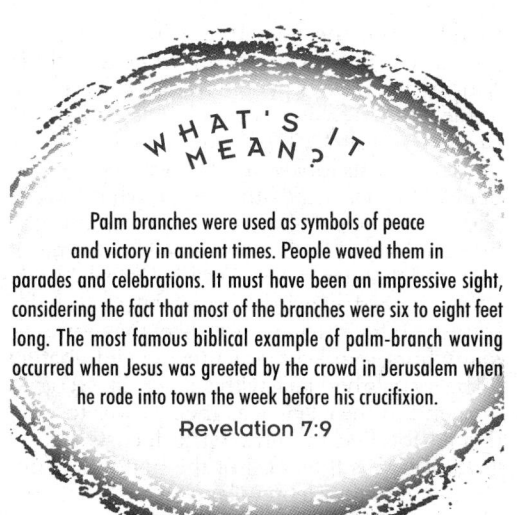

Palm branches were used as symbols of peace and victory in ancient times. People waved them in parades and celebrations. It must have been an impressive sight, considering the fact that most of the branches were six to eight feet long. The most famous biblical example of palm-branch waving occurred when Jesus was greeted by the crowd in Jerusalem when he rode into town the week before his crucifixion.

Revelation 7:9

strength belong to our God forever and ever. Amen!"

13Then one of the elders asked me, "Who are these people dressed in white robes? Where did they come from?"

14I answered, "You know, sir."

And the elder said to me, "These are the people who have come out of the great distress. They have washed their robes[n] and made them white in the blood of the Lamb. 15Because of this, they are before the throne of God. They worship him day and night in his temple. And the One who sits on the throne will be present with them. 16Those people will never be hungry again, and they will never be thirsty again. The sun will not hurt them, and no heat will burn them, 17because the Lamb at the center of the throne will be their shepherd. He will lead them to springs of water that give life. And God will wipe away every tear from their eyes."

> **"Amen! Praise, glory, wisdom, thanks, honor, power, and strength belong to our God forever and ever. Amen!" (Revelation 7:12)**

HEAVEN

What will the focus of our attention be in heaven? (7:17)

8

THE SEVENTH SEAL

1When the Lamb opened the seventh seal, there was silence in heaven for about half an hour. 2And I saw the seven angels who stand before God and to whom were given seven trumpets.

3Another angel came and stood at the altar, holding a golden pan for incense. He was given much incense to offer with the prayers of all God's holy people. The angel put this offering on the golden altar before the throne. 4The smoke from the incense went up from the angel's hand to God with the prayers of God's people. 5Then the angel filled the incense pan with fire from the altar and threw it on the earth, and there were flashes of lightning, thunder and loud noises, and an earthquake.

THE SEVEN ANGELS AND TRUMPETS

6Then the seven angels who had the seven trumpets prepared to blow them.

7The first angel blew his trumpet, and hail and fire mixed with blood were poured down on the earth. And a third of the earth, and all the green grass, and a third of the trees were burned up.

8Then the second angel blew his trumpet, and something that looked like a big mountain, burning with fire, was thrown into the sea. And a third of the sea became blood, 9a third of the living things in the sea died, and a third of the ships were destroyed.

10Then the third angel blew his trumpet, and a large star, burning like a torch, fell from the sky. It fell on a third of the rivers and on the springs of water. 11The name of the star is Wormwood.[n] And a third of all the water became bitter, and many people died from drinking the water that was bitter.

12Then the fourth angel blew his trumpet, and a third of the sun, and a third of the moon, and a third of the stars were struck. So a third of them became dark, and a third of the day was without light, and also the night.

13While I watched, I heard an eagle that was flying high in the air cry out in a loud voice, "Trouble! Trouble! Trouble for those who live on the earth because of the remaining sounds of the trumpets that the other three angels are about to blow!"

7:14 washed their robes This means they believed in Jesus so that their sins could be forgiven by Christ's blood. **8:11 Wormwood** Name of a very bitter plant; used here to give the idea of bitter sorrow.

WHAT'S IT MEAN?

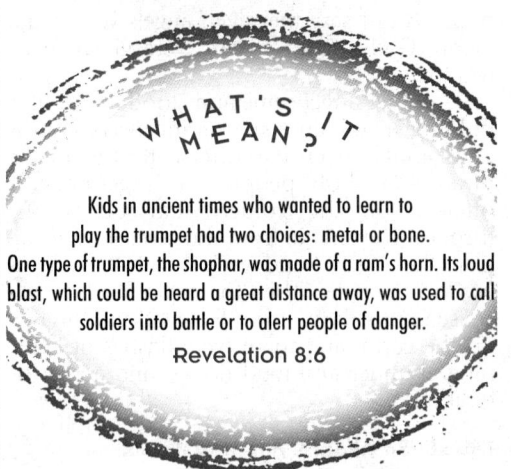

Kids in ancient times who wanted to learn to play the trumpet had two choices: metal or bone. One type of trumpet, the shophar, was made of a ram's horn. Its loud blast, which could be heard a great distance away, was used to call soldiers into battle or to alert people of danger.

Revelation 8:6

9

1Then the fifth angel blew his trumpet, and I
saw a star fall from the sky to the earth. The
star was given the key to the deep hole that
leads to the bottomless pit. 2Then it opened up
the hole that leads to the bottomless pit, and
smoke came up from the hole like smoke from
a big furnace. Then the sun and sky became
dark because of the smoke from the hole.
3Then locusts came down to the earth out of
the smoke, and they were given the power to
sting like scorpions.[n] 4They were told not to
harm the grass on the earth or any plant or
tree. They could harm only the people who did
not have the sign of God on their foreheads.
5These locusts were not given the power to kill
anyone, but to cause pain to the people for five
months. And the pain they felt was like the
pain a scorpion gives when it stings someone.
6During those days people will look for a way
to die, but they will not find it. They will want
to die, but death will run away from them.
7The locusts looked like horses prepared for
battle. On their heads they wore what looked
like crowns of gold, and their faces looked like
human faces. 8Their hair was like women's
hair, and their teeth were like lions' teeth. 9Their
chests looked like iron breastplates, and the
sound of their wings was like the noise of
many horses and chariots hurrying into battle.
10The locusts had tails with stingers like scorpions, and in their tails was their power to hurt
people for five months. 11The locusts had a
king who was the angel of the bottomless pit.
His name in the Hebrew language is Abaddon
and in the Greek language is Apollyon.[n]
12The first trouble is past; there are still two
other troubles that will come.

WHAT'S IT MEAN?

At first glance, the locust seems like a pretty unlikely creature of destruction. It looks like a large grasshopper with two sets of wings and a brown-colored body two to three inches long. Nothing to be worried about, right? Wrong. Locusts travel in swarms large enough to blot out the sun in the sky! An average-size swarm of locusts, numbering in the millions, can strip a field completely bare—down to its last leaf—within minutes.

Revelation 9:3

WHAT'S IT MEAN?

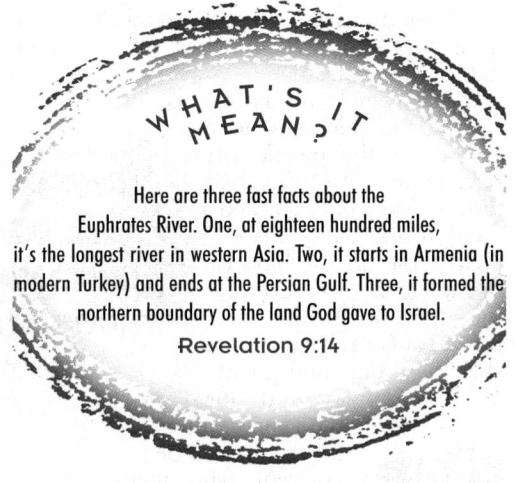

Here are three fast facts about the Euphrates River. One, at eighteen hundred miles, it's the longest river in western Asia. Two, it starts in Armenia (in modern Turkey) and ends at the Persian Gulf. Three, it formed the northern boundary of the land God gave to Israel.

Revelation 9:14

13Then the sixth angel blew his trumpet,
and I heard a voice coming from the horns on
the golden altar that is before God. 14The voice
said to the sixth angel who had the trumpet,
"Free the four angels who are tied at the great
river Euphrates." 15And they let loose the four
angels who had been kept ready for this hour
and day and month and year so they could kill
a third of all people on the earth. 16I heard how
many troops on horses were in their army—
two hundred million.
17The horses and their riders I saw in the
vision looked like this: They had breastplates
that were fiery red, dark blue, and yellow like

9:3 scorpions A scorpion is an insect that stings with a bad poison. **9:11 Abaddon, Apollyon** Both names mean "Destroyer."

sulfur. The heads of the horses looked like
heads of lions, with fire, smoke, and sulfur
coming out of their mouths. 18A third of all the
people on earth were killed by these three terrible disasters coming out of the horses'
mouths: the fire, the smoke, and the sulfur.
19The horses' power was in their mouths and
in their tails; their tails were like snakes with
heads, and with them they hurt people.
20The other people who were not killed by
these terrible disasters still did not change their
hearts and turn away from what they had
made with their own hands. They did not stop
worshiping demons and idols made of gold,
silver, bronze, stone, and wood—things that
cannot see or hear or walk. 21These people did
not change their hearts and turn away from
murder or evil magic, from their sexual sins or
stealing.

THE ANGEL AND THE SMALL SCROLL

10 1Then I saw another powerful angel coming
down from heaven dressed in a cloud with a
rainbow over his head. His face was like the
sun, and his legs were like pillars of fire. 2The
angel was holding a small scroll open in his
hand. He put his right foot on the sea and his
left foot on the land. 3Then he shouted loudly
like the roaring of a lion. And when he shouted, the voices of seven thunders spoke. 4When
the seven thunders spoke, I started to write.
But I heard a voice from heaven say, "Keep
hidden what the seven thunders said, and do
not write them down."
5Then the angel I saw standing on the sea
and on the land raised his right hand to heav-
en, 6and he made a promise by the power of
the One who lives forever and ever. He is the
One who made the skies and all that is in them,
the earth and all that is in it, and the sea and all
that is in it. The angel promised, "There will be
no more waiting! 7In the days when the seventh angel is ready to blow his trumpet, God's
secret will be finished. This secret is the Good
News God told to his servants, the prophets."
8Then I heard the same voice from heaven
again, saying to me: "Go and take the open
scroll that is in the hand of the angel that is
standing on the sea and on the land."
9So I went to the angel and told him to give
me the small scroll. And he said to me, "Take
the scroll and eat it. It will be sour in your
stomach, but in your mouth it will be sweet as
honey." 10So I took the small scroll from the
angel's hand and ate it. In my mouth it tasted
sweet as honey, but after I ate it, it was sour in
my stomach. 11Then I was told, "You must
prophesy again about many peoples, nations,
languages, and kings."

THE TWO WITNESSES

11 1I was given a measuring stick like a rod, and
I was told, "Go and measure the temple of God
and the altar, and count the people worshiping
there. 2But do not measure the yard outside the
temple. Leave it alone, because it has been given
to those who are not God's people. And they
will trample on the holy city for forty-two
months. 3And I will give power to my two witnesses to prophesy for one thousand two hundred sixty days, and they will be dressed in
rough cloth to show their sadness."

WHAT'S IT MEAN?

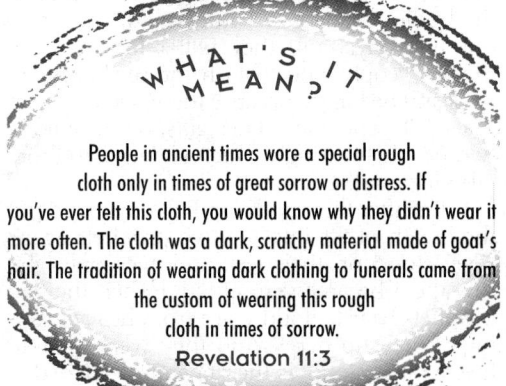

People in ancient times wore a special rough cloth only in times of great sorrow or distress. If you've ever felt this cloth, you would know why they didn't wear it more often. The cloth was a dark, scratchy material made of goat's hair. The tradition of wearing dark clothing to funerals came from the custom of wearing this rough cloth in times of sorrow.

Revelation 11:3

4These two witnesses are the two olive trees
and the two lampstands that stand before the
Lord of the earth. 5And if anyone tries to hurt
them, fire comes from their mouths and kills
their enemies. And if anyone tries to hurt them
in whatever way, in that same way that person
will die. 6These witnesses have the power to
stop the sky from raining during the time they
are prophesying. And they have power to
make the waters become blood, and they have
power to send every kind of trouble to the
earth as many times as they want.
7When the two witnesses have finished telling their message, the beast that comes up
from the bottomless pit will fight a war against
them. He will defeat them and kill them. 8The
bodies of the two witnesses will lie in the street
of the great city where the Lord was killed. This
city is named Sodom[n] and Egypt, which has a
spiritual meaning. 9Those from every race of

11:8 Sodom City that God destroyed because the people were so evil.

WHAT'S IT MEAN?

The double-barreled reference to Sodom and Egypt says a lot about the "great city." Sodom was one of the cities destroyed by God because of the wickedness of its citizens. Egypt was the place the Israelites were held as slaves until God told Moses to lead them to the land he promised to give them.

Revelation 11:8

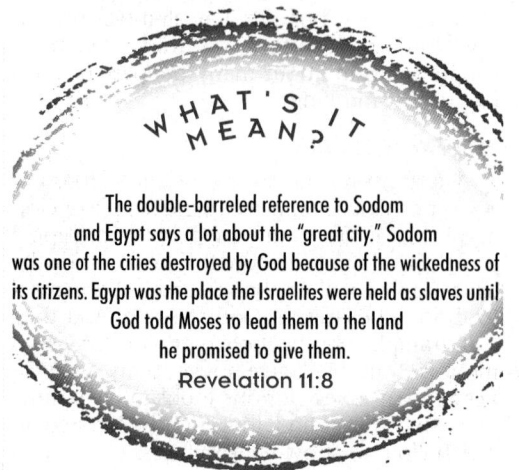

people, tribe, language, and nation will look at the bodies of the two witnesses for three and one-half days, and they will refuse to bury them. [10]People who live on the earth will rejoice and be happy because these two are dead. They will send each other gifts, because these two prophets brought much suffering to those who live on the earth.

[11]But after three and one-half days, God put the breath of life into the two prophets again. They stood on their feet, and everyone who saw them became very afraid. [12]Then the two prophets heard a loud voice from heaven saying, "Come up here!" And they went up into heaven in a cloud as their enemies watched.

[13]In the same hour there was a great earthquake, and a tenth of the city was destroyed. Seven thousand people were killed in the earthquake, and those who did not die were very afraid and gave glory to the God of heaven.

[14]The second trouble is finished. Pay attention: The third trouble is coming soon.

THE SEVENTH TRUMPET

[15]Then the seventh angel blew his trumpet. And there were loud voices in heaven, saying:

"The power to rule the world now belongs
to our Lord and his Christ,
and he will rule forever and ever."

[16]Then the twenty-four elders, who sit on their thrones before God, bowed down on their faces and worshiped God. [17]They said:

"We give thanks to you, Lord God
Almighty,
who is and who was,
because you have used your great power
and have begun to rule!
[18]The people of the world were angry,
but your anger has come.
The time has come to judge the dead,
and to reward your servants the
prophets
and your holy people,
all who respect you, great and small.
The time has come to destroy those who
destroy the earth!"

[19]Then God's temple in heaven was opened. The Ark that holds the agreement God gave to his people could be seen in his temple. Then there were flashes of lightning, noises, thunder, an earthquake, and a great hailstorm.

THE WOMAN AND THE DRAGON

12 [1]And then a great wonder appeared in heaven: A woman was clothed with the sun, and the moon was under her feet, and a crown of twelve stars was on her head. [2]She was pregnant and cried out with pain, because she was about to give birth. [3]Then another wonder appeared in heaven: There was a giant red dragon with seven heads and seven crowns on each head. He also had ten horns. [4]His tail swept a third of the stars out of the sky and threw them down to the earth. He stood in front of the woman who was ready to give birth so he could eat her baby as soon as it was born. [5]Then the woman gave birth to a son who will rule all the nations with an iron rod. And her child was taken up to God and to his throne. [6]The woman ran away into the desert to a place God prepared for her where she would be taken care of for one thousand two hundred sixty days.

[7]Then there was a war in heaven. Michael[n] and his angels fought against the dragon, and the dragon and his angels fought back. [8]But the dragon was not strong enough, and he and his angels lost their place in heaven. [9]The giant dragon was thrown down out of heaven. (He is that old snake called the devil or Satan, who tricks the whole world.) The dragon with his angels was thrown down to the earth.

[10]Then I heard a loud voice in heaven saying:

"The salvation and the power and the
kingdom of our God
and the authority of his Christ have
now come.
The accuser of our brothers and sisters,
who accused them day and night before
our God,
has been thrown down.

12:7 Michael The archangel—leader among God's angels or messengers (Jude 9).

11 And our brothers and sisters defeated him
by the blood of the Lamb's death
and by the message they preached.
They did not love their lives so much
that they were afraid of death.
12 So rejoice, you heavens
and all who live there!
But it will be terrible for the earth and the sea,
because the devil has come down to you!
He is filled with anger,
because he knows he does not have much time."

13 When the dragon saw he had been
thrown down to the earth, he hunted for the
woman who had given birth to the son. 14 But
the woman was given the two wings of a great
eagle so she could fly to the place prepared for
her in the desert. There she would be taken
care of for three and one-half years, away from
the snake. 15 Then the snake poured water out
of its mouth like a river toward the woman so
the flood would carry her away. 16 But the earth
helped the woman by opening its mouth and
swallowing the river that came from the
mouth of the dragon. 17 Then the dragon was
very angry at the woman, and he went off to
make war against all her other children—those
who obey God's commands and who have the
message Jesus taught.

18 And the dragon stood on the seashore.

THE TWO BEASTS

13 1 Then I saw a beast coming up out of the
sea. It had ten horns and seven heads, and
there was a crown on each horn. A name
against God was written on each head. 2 This
beast looked like a leopard, with feet like a
bear's feet and a mouth like a lion's mouth.
And the dragon gave the beast all of his power
and his throne and great authority. 3 One of the
heads of the beast looked as if it had been
killed by a wound, but this death wound was
healed. Then the whole world was amazed and
followed the beast. 4 People worshiped the
dragon because he had given his power to the
beast. And they also worshiped the beast, asking, "Who is like the beast? Who can make war
against it?"

5 The beast was allowed to say proud words
and words against God, and it was allowed to
use its power for forty-two months. 6 It used its
mouth to speak against God, against God's
name, against the place where God lives, and
against all those who live in heaven. 7 It was
given power to make war against God's holy
people and to defeat them. It was given power
over every tribe, people, language, and nation.
8 And all who live on earth will worship the
beast—all the people since the beginning of
the world whose names are not written in the
Lamb's book of life. The Lamb is the One who
was killed.

9 Anyone who has ears should listen:
10 If you are to be a prisoner,
then you will be a prisoner.
If you are to be killed with the sword,
then you will be killed with the sword.

This means that God's holy people must have
patience and faith.

11 Then I saw another beast coming up out
of the earth. It had two horns like a lamb, but it
spoke like a dragon. 12 This beast stands before
the first beast and uses the same power the
first beast has. By this power it makes everyone living on earth worship the first beast,
who had the death wound that was healed.
13 And the second beast does great miracles so
that it even makes fire come down from heaven to earth while people are watching. 14 It
fools those who live on earth by the miracles it
has been given the power to do. It does these
miracles to serve the first beast. The second
beast orders people to make an idol to honor
the first beast, the one that was wounded by
the deadly sword but sprang to life again.
15 The second beast was given power to give life
to the idol of the first one so that the idol could
speak. And the second beast was given power
to command all who will not worship the image of the beast to be killed. 16 The second beast
also forced all people, small and great, rich and
poor, free and slave, to have a mark on their
right hand or on their forehead. 17 No one
could buy or sell without this mark, which is
the name of the beast or the number of its
name. 18 This takes wisdom. Let the one who
has understanding find the meaning of the
number, which is the number of a person. Its
number is six hundred sixty-six.

THE SONG OF THE SAVED

14 1 Then I looked, and there before me was the
Lamb standing on Mount Zion.[n] With him
were one hundred forty-four thousand people
who had his name and his Father's name written on their foreheads. 2 And I heard a sound
from heaven like the noise of flooding water
and like the sound of loud thunder. The sound

14:1 Mount Zion Another name for Jerusalem; here meaning the spiritual city of God's people.

I heard was like people playing harps. [3]And they sang a new song before the throne and before the four living creatures and the elders. No one could learn the new song except the one hundred forty-four thousand who had been bought from the earth. [4]These are the ones who did not do sinful things with women, because they kept themselves pure. They follow the Lamb every place he goes. These one hundred forty-four thousand were bought from among the people of the earth as people to be offered to God and the Lamb. [5]They were not guilty of telling lies; they are without fault.

THE THREE ANGELS

[6]Then I saw another angel flying high in the air. He had the eternal Good News to preach to those who live on earth—to every nation, tribe, language, and people. [7]He preached in a loud voice, "Fear God and give him praise, because the time has come for God to judge all people. So worship God who made the heavens, and the earth, and the sea, and the springs of water."

[8]Then the second angel followed the first angel and said, "Ruined, ruined is the great city of Babylon! She made all the nations drink the wine of the anger of her adultery."

[9]Then a third angel followed the first two angels, saying in a loud voice: "If anyone worships the beast and his idol and gets the beast's mark on the forehead or on the hand, [10]that one also will drink the wine of God's anger, which is prepared with all its strength in the cup of his anger. And that person will be put in pain with burning sulfur before the holy angels and the Lamb. [11]And the smoke from their burning pain will rise forever and ever. There will be no rest, day or night, for those who worship the beast and his idol or who get the mark of his name." [12]This means God's holy people must be patient. They must obey God's commands and keep their faith in Jesus.

WHAT'S IT MEAN?

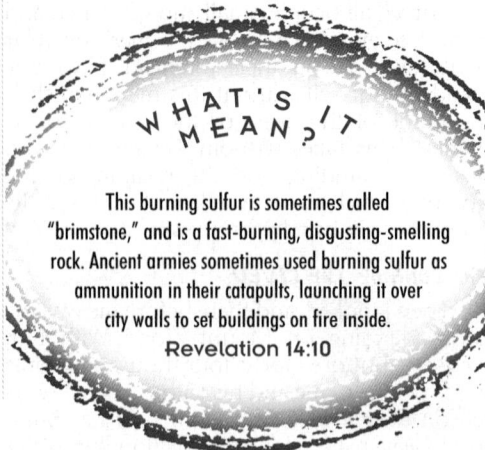

This burning sulfur is sometimes called "brimstone," and is a fast-burning, disgusting-smelling rock. Ancient armies sometimes used burning sulfur as ammunition in their catapults, launching it over city walls to set buildings on fire inside.
Revelation 14:10

[13]Then I heard a voice from heaven saying, "Write this: Happy are the dead who die from now on in the Lord."

The Spirit says, "Yes, they will rest from their hard work, and the reward of all they have done stays with them."

THE EARTH IS HARVESTED

[14]Then I looked, and there before me was a white cloud, and sitting on the white cloud was One who looked like a Son of Man.[n] He had a gold crown on his head and a sharp sickle[n] in his hand. [15]Then another angel came out of the temple and called out in a loud voice to the One who was sitting on the cloud, "Take your sickle and harvest from the earth, because the time to harvest has come, and the fruit of the earth is ripe." [16]So the One who was sitting on the cloud swung his sickle over the earth, and the earth was harvested.

[17]Then another angel came out of the temple in heaven, and he also had a sharp sickle. [18]And then another angel, who has power over the fire, came from the altar. This angel called to the angel with the sharp sickle, saying, "Take your sharp sickle and gather the bunches of grapes from the earth's vine, because its grapes are ripe." [19]Then the angel swung his sickle over the earth. He gathered the earth's grapes and threw them into the great winepress of God's anger. [20]They were trampled in the winepress outside the city, and blood flowed out of the winepress as high as horses' bridles for a distance of about one hundred eighty miles.

THE LAST TROUBLES

15 [1]Then I saw another wonder in heaven that was great and amazing. There were seven angels bringing seven disasters. These are the last disasters, because after them, God's anger is finished.

[2]I saw what looked like a sea of glass mixed with fire. All of those who had won the victory over the beast and his idol and over the

14:14 Son of Man "Son of Man" is a name Jesus called himself. **14:14 sickle** A farming tool with a curved blade. It was used to harvest grain.

number of his name were standing by the sea
of glass. They had harps that God had given
them. 3They sang the song of Moses, the servant of God, and the song of the Lamb:

"You do great and wonderful things, *Psalm 111:2*
Lord God Almighty. *Amos 3:13*
Everything the Lord does is right and true, *Psalm 145:17*
King of the nations.
4Everyone will respect you, Lord, *Jeremiah 10:7*
and will honor you.
Only you are holy.
All the nations will come
and worship you, *Psalm 86:9-10*
because the right things you have done
are now made known." *Deuteronomy 32:4*

5After this I saw that the temple (the Tent of
the Agreement) in heaven was opened. 6And
the seven angels bringing the seven disasters
came out of the temple. They were
dressed in clean, shining linen
and wore golden bands tied
around their chests. 7Then
one of the four living creatures gave to the seven
angels seven golden bowls
filled with the anger of
God, who lives forever
and ever. 8The temple was
filled with smoke from the
glory and the power of God,
and no one could enter the
temple until the seven disasters
of the seven angels were finished.

"You do great and wonderful things, Lord God Almighty. Everything the Lord does is right and true, King of the nations." (Revelation 15:3b)

THE BOWLS OF GOD'S ANGER

16 1Then I heard a loud voice from the temple
saying to the seven angels, "Go and pour out
the seven bowls of God's anger on the earth."
2The first angel left and poured out his bowl
on the land. Then ugly and painful sores came
upon all those who had the mark of the beast
and who worshiped his idol.
3The second angel poured out his bowl on
the sea, and it became blood like that of a dead
man, and every living thing in the sea died.
4The third angel poured out his bowl on the
rivers and the springs of water, and they became blood. 5Then I heard the angel of the waters saying:

"Holy One, you are the One who is and
who was.
You are right to decide to punish these
evil people.
6They have poured out the blood of your
holy people and your prophets.
So now you have given them blood to
drink as they deserve."

7And I heard a voice coming from the altar
saying:

"Yes, Lord God Almighty,
the way you punish evil people is right
and fair."

8The fourth angel poured out his bowl on
the sun, and he was given power to burn the
people with fire. 9They were burned by the
great heat, and they cursed the name of God,
who had control over these disasters. But the
people refused to change their hearts and lives
and give glory to God.
10The fifth angel poured out his bowl on the
throne of the beast, and darkness covered its
kingdom. People gnawed their tongues because of the pain. 11They also cursed the God
of heaven because of their pain and the sores
they had, but they refused to change their
hearts and turn away from the
evil things they did.
12The sixth angel poured
out his bowl on the great
river Euphrates so that the
water in the river was dried
up to prepare the way for
the kings from the east to
come. 13Then I saw three
evil spirits that looked like
frogs coming out of the
mouth of the dragon, out
of the mouth of the beast,
and out of the mouth of the
false prophet. 14These evil spirits
are the spirits of demons, which have power to
do miracles. They go out to the kings of the
whole world to gather them together for the
battle on the great day of God Almighty.
15"Listen! I will come as a thief comes! Happy

WHAT'S IT MEAN?

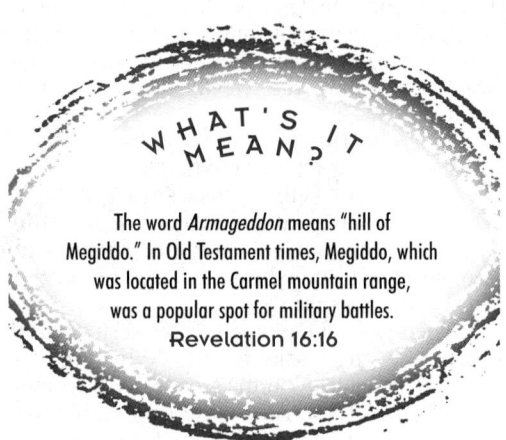

The word *Armageddon* means "hill of Megiddo." In Old Testament times, Megiddo, which was located in the Carmel mountain range, was a popular spot for military battles.
Revelation 16:16

are those who stay awake and keep their
clothes on so that they will not walk around
naked and have people see their shame."
[16]Then the evil spirits gathered the kings together to the place that is called Armageddon
in the Hebrew language.
[17]The seventh angel poured out his bowl
into the air. Then a loud voice came out of the
temple from the throne, saying, "It is finished!"
[18]Then there were flashes of lightning, noises,
thunder, and a big earthquake—the worst
earthquake that has ever happened since people have been on earth. [19]The great city split
into three parts, and the cities of the nations
were destroyed. And God remembered the sins
of Babylon the Great, so he gave that city the
cup filled with the wine of his terrible anger.
[20]Then every island ran away, and mountains
disappeared. [21]Giant hailstones, each weighing
about a hundred pounds, fell from the sky
upon people. People cursed God for the disaster of the hail, because this disaster was so
terrible.

THE WOMAN ON THE ANIMAL

17 [1]Then one of the seven angels who had the
seven bowls came and spoke to me. He said,
"Come, and I will show you the punishment
that will be given to the great prostitute, the
one sitting over many waters. [2]The kings of the
earth sinned sexually with her, and the people
of the earth became drunk from the wine of
her sexual sin."
[3]Then the angel carried me away by the
Spirit to the desert. There I saw a woman
sitting on a red beast. It was covered with
names against God written on it, and it had
seven heads and ten horns. [4]The woman was
dressed in purple and red and was shining
with the gold, precious jewels, and pearls she
was wearing. She had a golden cup in her hand,
a cup filled with evil things and the uncleanness of her sexual sin. [5]On her forehead a title
was written that was secret. This is what was
written:

THE GREAT BABYLON
MOTHER OF PROSTITUTES
AND OF THE EVIL THINGS OF THE EARTH

[6]Then I saw that the woman was drunk
with the blood of God's holy people and with
the blood of those who were killed because of
their faith in Jesus.
When I saw the woman, I was very amazed.
[7]Then the angel said to me, "Why are you
amazed? I will tell you the secret of this woman
and the beast she rides—the one with seven
heads and ten horns. [8]The beast you saw was
once alive but is not alive now. But soon it will
come up out of the bottomless pit and go away
to be destroyed. There are people who live on
earth whose names have not been written in
the book of life since the beginning of the
world. They will be amazed when they see the
beast, because he was once alive, is not alive
now, but will come again.
[9]"You need a wise mind to understand this.
The seven heads on the beast are seven mountains where the woman sits. [10]And they are
seven kings. Five of the kings have already
been destroyed, one of the kings lives now, and
another has not yet come. When he comes, he
must stay a short time. [11]The beast that was
once alive, but is not alive now, is also an
eighth king. He belongs to the first seven kings,
and he will go away to be destroyed.
[12]"The ten horns you saw are ten kings who
have not yet begun to rule, but they will receive power to rule with the beast for one
hour. [13]All ten of these kings have the same
purpose, and they will give their power and
authority to the beast. [14]They will make war
against the Lamb, but the Lamb will defeat
them, because he is Lord of lords and King of
kings. He will defeat them with his called, chosen, and faithful followers."
[15]Then the angel said to me, "The waters
that you saw, where the prostitute sits, are
peoples, races, nations, and languages. [16]The
ten horns and the beast you saw will hate the
prostitute. They will take everything she has
and leave her naked. They will eat her body
and burn her with fire. [17]God made the ten
horns want to carry out his purpose by agreeing to give the beast their power to rule, until
what God has said comes about. [18]The woman
you saw is the great city that rules over the
kings of the earth."

BABYLON IS DESTROYED

18 [1]After the vision of these things, I saw another angel coming down from heaven. This
angel had great power, and his glory made the
earth bright. [2]He shouted in a powerful voice:
"Ruined, ruined is the great city of Babylon!
She has become a home for demons
and a prison for every evil spirit,
and a prison for every unclean bird and
unclean beast.
[3]She has been ruined, because all the
peoples of the earth
have drunk the wine of the desire of her
sexual sin.
She has been ruined also because the
kings of the earth

have sinned sexually with her,
and the merchants of the earth
have grown rich from the great wealth
of her luxury."

4 Then I heard another voice from heaven
saying:

"Come out of that city, my people,
so that you will not share in her sins,
so that you will not receive the disasters
that will come to her.
5 Her sins have piled up as high as the sky,
and God has not forgotten the wrongs
she has done.
6 Give that city the same as she gave to
others.
Pay her back twice as much as she did.
Prepare wine for her that is twice as strong
as the wine she prepared for others.
7 She gave herself much glory and rich
living.
Give her that much suffering and
sadness.
She says to herself, 'I am a queen sitting
on my throne.
I am not a widow; I will never be sad.'
8 So these disasters will come to her in one
day:
death, and crying, and great hunger,
and she will be destroyed by fire,
because the Lord God who judges her is
powerful."

9 The kings of the earth who sinned sexually
with her and shared her wealth will see the
smoke from her burning. Then they will cry
and be sad because of her death. 10 They will
be afraid of her suffering and stand far away
and say:

"Terrible! How terrible for you, great city,
powerful city of Babylon,
because your punishment has come in
one hour!"

11 And the merchants of the earth will cry
and be sad about her, because now there is no
one to buy their cargoes— 12 cargoes of gold,
silver, jewels, pearls, fine linen, purple cloth,
silk, red cloth; all kinds of citron wood and all
kinds of things made from ivory, expensive
wood, bronze, iron, and marble; 13 cinnamon,
spice, incense, myrrh, frankincense, wine, olive
oil, fine flour, wheat, cattle, sheep, horses, carriages,
slaves, and human lives.

14 The merchants will say,

"Babylon, the good things you wanted are
gone from you.
All your rich and fancy things have
disappeared.
You will never have them again."

15 The merchants who became rich from selling
to her will be afraid of her suffering and will
stand far away. They will cry and be sad 16 and
say:

"Terrible! How terrible for the great city!
She was dressed in fine linen, purple
and red cloth,
and she was shining with gold, precious
jewels, and pearls!
17 All these riches have been destroyed in
one hour!"

Every sea captain, every passenger, the sailors,
and all those who earn their living from
the sea stood far away from Babylon. 18 As they
saw the smoke from her burning, they cried out
loudly, "There was never a city like this great
city!" 19 And they threw dust on their heads and
cried out, weeping and being sad. They said:

"Terrible! How terrible for the great city!
All the people who had ships on the sea
became rich because of her wealth!
But she has been destroyed in one hour!
20 Be happy because of this, heaven!
Be happy, God's holy people and
apostles and prophets!
God has punished her because of what
she did to you."

21 Then a powerful angel picked up a large
stone, like one used for grinding grain, and
threw it into the sea. He said:

"In the same way, the great city of Babylon
will be thrown down,
and it will never be found again.
22 The music of people playing harps and
other instruments, flutes, and
trumpets,
will never be heard in you again.
No workman doing any job
will ever be found in you again.
The sound of grinding grain
will never be heard in you again.
23 The light of a lamp
will never shine in you again,
and the voices of a bridegroom and bride
will never be heard in you again.
Your merchants were the world's great
people,
and all the nations were tricked by your
magic.
24 You are guilty of the death of the prophets
and God's holy people
and all who have been killed on earth."

19

PEOPLE IN HEAVEN PRAISE GOD

1 After this vision and announcement I
heard what sounded like a great many people
in heaven saying:

"Hallelujah![n]
Salvation, glory, and power belong to our God,
2 because his judgments are true and right.
He has punished the prostitute
who made the earth evil with her sexual sin.
He has paid her back for the death of his servants."
3Again they said:
"Hallelujah!
She is burning, and her smoke will rise forever and ever."
4Then the twenty-four elders and the four
living creatures bowed down and worshiped
God, who sits on the throne. They said:
"Amen, Hallelujah!"
5Then a voice came from the throne, saying:
"Praise our God, all you who serve him
and all you who honor him, both small and great!"
6Then I heard what sounded like a great
many people, like the noise of flooding water,
and like the noise of loud thunder. The people
were saying:
"Hallelujah!
Our Lord God, the Almighty, rules.
7 Let us rejoice and be happy
and give God glory,
because the wedding of the Lamb has come,
and the Lamb's bride has made herself ready.
8 Fine linen, bright and clean, was given to her to wear."
(The fine linen means the good things done by God's holy people.)

WHAT'S IT MEAN?

Linen, which was handwoven from the fibers of the hemp plant, was considered to be the highest quality fabric in the ancient world. For the most part, only people of great wealth or power wore linen. Priests and those who served in the Temple were the exception. They, too, wore linen. Throughout the Bible, white linen symbolizes purity.

Revelation 19:8

9And the angel said to me, "Write this:
Happy are those who have been invited to the
wedding meal of the Lamb!" And the angel
said, "These are the true words of God."
10Then I bowed down at the angel's feet to
worship him, but he said to me, "Do not worship me! I am a servant like you and your
brothers and sisters who have the message of
Jesus. Worship God, because the message
about Jesus is the spirit that gives all prophecy."

THE RIDER ON THE WHITE HORSE

11Then I saw heaven opened, and there before me was a white horse. The rider on the
horse is called Faithful and True, and he is right
when he judges and makes war. 12His eyes are
like burning fire, and on his head are many
crowns. He has a name written on him, which
no one but himself knows. 13He is dressed in a
robe dipped in blood, and his name is the
Word of God. 14The armies of heaven, dressed
in fine linen, white and clean, were following
him on white horses. 15Out of the rider's
mouth comes a sharp sword that he will use to
defeat the nations, and he will rule them with a
rod of iron. He will crush out the wine in the
winepress of the terrible anger of God the Almighty. 16On his robe and on his upper leg
was written this name: KING OF KINGS AND
LORD OF LORDS.
17Then I saw an angel standing in the sun,
and he called with a loud voice to all the birds
flying in the sky: "Come and gather together
for the great feast of God 18so that you can eat
the bodies of kings, generals, mighty people,
horses and their riders, and the bodies of all
people—free, slave, small, and great."
19Then I saw the beast and the kings of the
earth. Their armies were gathered together to
make war against the rider on the horse and his
army. 20But the beast was captured and with
him the false prophet who did the miracles for
the beast. The false prophet had used these miracles to trick those who had the mark of the
beast and worshiped his idol. The false prophet
and the beast were thrown alive into the lake of
fire that burns with sulfur. 21And their armies
were killed with the sword that came out of the
mouth of the rider on the horse, and all the
birds ate the bodies until they were full.

THE THOUSAND YEARS

20 1I saw an angel coming down from heaven.
He had the key to the bottomless pit and a
large chain in his hand. 2The angel grabbed the

19:1 Hallelujah This means "praise God!"

On the Edge

On his robe and on his upper leg was written this name:* KING OF KINGS AND LORD OF LORDS *(Rev. 19:16).

Wow. Can you imagine seeing Jesus? Can you imagine really, finally coming face-to-face with the One you've been in love with all your life? What would you think when you saw his robe and read the words "KING OF KINGS AND LORD OF LORDS"? A lot of Christians have been tossing that description of Jesus around for ages. But do you get it?

There are kings and lords all over the earth—have been for hundreds of years. You've heard about them in history class—King David, King Saul, King Louis XIV, King Henry VIII. You've heard about them in literature class—Alfred, Lord Tennyson, and George Gordon, Lord Byron.

Kings and lords are known primarily for their power, their wealth, their military might, and their positions as rulers over groups of people. Jesus Christ puts it all to shame. You talk about power. His power can raise the dead. You talk about wealth. His Father owns the cattle on a thousand hills (see Ps. 50:10). You talk about military might. He's raising up an army that will someday defeat the raging forces of Satan. You talk about a ruler. He rules the whole world. Philippians 2:10 says that "every knee will bow to the name of Jesus—everyone in heaven, on earth, and under the earth." Think of it: *Everyone* will bow at just the mention of his name.

He is the King of all the kings who have ever ruled and the Lord of every lord. Go ahead. Enthrone him in your heart. You'll never find a more loving, merciful, gracious King.

SEE FOR YOURSELF:
1 Tim. 6:15;
Rev. 17:14

dragon, that old snake who is the devil and
Satan, and tied him up for a thousand years.
3Then he threw him into the bottomless pit,
closed it, and locked it over him. The angel did
this so he could not trick the people of the
earth anymore until the thousand years were
ended. After a thousand years he must be set
free for a short time.

4Then I saw some thrones and people sitting on them who had been given the power to
judge. And I saw the souls of those who had
been killed because they were faithful to the
message of Jesus and the message from God.
They had not worshiped the beast or his idol,
and they had not received the mark of the
beast on their foreheads or on their hands.
They came back to life and ruled with Christ
for a thousand years. 5(The others that were
dead did not live again until the thousand
years were ended.) This is the first raising of the
dead. 6Happy and holy are those who share in
this first raising of the dead. The second death
has no power over them. They will be priests
for God and for Christ and will rule with him
for a thousand years.

7When the thousand years are over, Satan
will be set free from his prison. 8Then he will
go out to trick the nations in all the earth—
Gog and Magog—to gather them for battle.
There are so many people they will be like
sand on the seashore. 9And Satan's army
marched across the earth and gathered around
the camp of God's people and the city God
loves. But fire came down from heaven and
burned them up. 10And Satan, who tricked
them, was thrown into the lake of burning sulfur with the beast and the false prophet. There
they will be punished day and night forever
and ever.

PEOPLE OF THE WORLD ARE JUDGED

11Then I saw a great white throne and the
One who was sitting on it. Earth and sky ran
away from him and disappeared. 12And I saw
the dead, great and small, standing before the
throne. Then books were opened, and the
book of life was opened. The dead were judged
by what they had done, which was written in
the books. 13The sea gave up the dead who
were in it, and Death and Hades[n] gave up the
dead who were in them. Each person was
judged by what he had done. 14And Death and
Hades were thrown into the lake of fire. The
lake of fire is the second death. 15And anyone
whose name was not found written in the
book of life was thrown into the lake of fire.

THE NEW JERUSALEM

21 1Then I saw a new heaven and a new earth.
The first heaven and the first earth had disappeared, and there was no sea anymore. 2And
I saw the holy city, the new Jerusalem,[n] coming down out of heaven from God. It was

20:13 Hades The place of the dead. **21:2 new Jerusalem** The spiritual city where God's people live with him.

prepared like a bride dressed for her husband.
3And I heard a loud voice from the throne,
saying, "Now God's presence is with people,
and he will live with them, and they will be his
people. God himself will be with them and will
be their God. 4He will wipe away every tear
from their eyes, and there will be no
more death, sadness, crying, or
pain, because all the old ways
are gone."
5The One who was sitting
on the throne said, "Look! I
am making everything new!"
Then he said, "Write this, be-
cause these words are true and can be trusted."
6The One on the throne said to me, "It is
finished. I am the Alpha and the Omega,[n] the
Beginning and the End. I will give free water
from the spring of the water of life to anyone
who is thirsty. 7Those who win the victory will
receive this, and I will be their God, and they
will be my children. 8But cowards, those who
refuse to believe, who do evil things, who kill,
who sin sexually, who do evil magic, who
worship idols, and who tell lies—all these will
have a place in the lake of burning sulfur. This
is the second death."
9Then one of the seven angels who had the seven bowls
full of the seven last troubles
came to me, saying, "Come
with me, and I will show
you the bride, the wife of the
Lamb." 10And the angel carried me away by the Spirit to
a very large and high mountain. He showed me the holy
city, Jerusalem, coming down out
of heaven from God. 11It was shining with
the glory of God and was bright like a very
expensive jewel, like a jasper, clear as crystal.
12The city had a great high wall with twelve
gates with twelve angels at the gates, and on
each gate was written the name of one of the
twelve tribes of Israel. 13There were three gates
on the east, three on the north, three on the
south, and three on the west. 14The walls of the
city were built on twelve foundation stones,
and on the stones were written the names of
the twelve apostles of the Lamb.
15The angel who talked with me had a measuring rod made of gold to measure the city, its
gates, and its wall. 16The city was built in a
square, and its length was equal to its width.
The angel measured the city with the rod. The
city was twelve thousand stadia[n] long, twelve
thousand stadia wide, and twelve thousand
stadia high. 17The angel also measured the wall.
It was one hundred forty-four cubits[n] high, by
human measurements, which the angel was
using. 18The wall was made of
jasper, and the city was made of
pure gold, as pure as glass.
19The foundation stones of
the city walls were decorated
with every kind of jewel.
The first foundation was jasper, the second was sapphire,
the third was chalcedony,
the fourth was emerald, 20the
fifth was onyx, the sixth was
carnelian, the seventh was chrysolite, the eighth was beryl, the ninth
was topaz, the tenth was chrysoprase, the eleventh was jacinth, and the twelfth was amethyst.
21The twelve gates were twelve pearls, each gate
having been made from a single pearl. And the
street of the city was made of pure gold as clear
as glass.
22I did not see a temple in the city, because
the Lord God Almighty and the Lamb are the
city's temple. 23The city does not need the sun
or the moon to shine on it, because the glory
of God is its light, and the Lamb is the city's
lamp. 24By its light the people of the world will
walk, and the kings of the earth will bring their

HEAVEN

Will there be sadness in heaven? (21:4)

WHAT'S IT MEAN?

Alpha and Omega are the first and last letters of the Greek alphabet. The Greeks learned to use the alphabet from the Phoenicians, a group of sea traders who lived in what is now Lebanon. In turn, the Greeks passed on their alphabet knowledge to the Romans.

Revelation 21:6

"The first heaven and the first earth had disappeared, and there was no sea anymore." (Revelation 21:1b)

21:6 Alpha and the Omega The first and last letters of the Greek alphabet. This means "the beginning and the end." **21:16 stadia** One stadion was a distance of about two hundred yards; about one-eighth of a Roman mile. **21:17 cubits** A cubit is about half a yard, the length from the elbow to the tip of the little finger.

glory into it. 25The city's gates will never be
shut on any day, because there is no night
there. 26The glory and the honor of the nations
will be brought into it. 27Nothing unclean and
no one who does shameful things or tells lies
will ever go into it. Only those whose names
are written in the Lamb's book of life will enter
the city.

22 1Then the angel showed me the river of the
water of life. It was shining like crystal and was
flowing from the throne of God and of the
Lamb 2down the middle of the street of the city.
The tree of life was on each side of the river. It
produces fruit twelve times a year, once each
month. The leaves of the tree are for the healing of all the nations. 3Nothing that God judges
guilty will be in that city. The throne of God
and of the Lamb will be there, and God's servants will worship him. 4They will see his face,
and his name will be written on their foreheads. 5There will never be night again. They
will not need the light of a lamp or the light of
the sun, because the Lord God will give them
light. And they will rule as kings forever and
ever.

6The angel said to me, "These words can be
trusted and are true." The Lord, the God of the
spirits of the prophets, sent his angel to show
his servants the things that must happen soon.

7"Listen! I am coming soon! Happy is the
one who obeys the words of prophecy in this
book."

8I, John, am the one who heard and saw
these things. When I heard and saw them, I
bowed down to worship at the feet of the angel who showed these things to me. 9But the
angel said to me, "Do not worship me! I am a
servant like you, your brothers the prophets,
and all those who obey the words in this book.
Worship God!"

10Then the angel told me, "Do not keep secret
the words of prophecy in this book, because
the time is near for all this to happen. 11Let
whoever is doing evil continue to do evil. Let
whoever is unclean continue to be unclean.
Let whoever is doing right continue to do right.
Let whoever is holy continue to be holy."

12"Listen! I am coming soon! I will bring my
reward with me, and I will repay each one of
you for what you have done. 13I am the Alpha
and the Omega,[n] the First and the Last, the Beginning and the End.

14"Happy are those who wash their robes[n]
so that they will receive the right to eat the fruit

22:13 Alpha and the Omega The first and last letters of the Greek alphabet. This means "the beginning and the end." **22:14 wash their robes** This means they believed and obeyed Jesus so that their sins could be forgiven by Christ's blood. The "washing" may refer to baptism (Acts 22:16).

Promise HE PROMISES TO COME SOON.

Jesus, the One who says these things are true, says, "Yes, I am coming soon." Amen. Come, Lord Jesus! (Rev. 22:20).

What if you were God? What if you'd spent years inspiring the Bible, making sure that the people who read it would have access to everything you wanted them to know? What would you tell them at the very end? Would you let your book just fizzle out with some kind of lame ending? Or would you let the whole work build up to one exciting, crucial climax?

God chose to end his Book with a thought that thrills some people and terrifies others. The end of the story is this: Jesus is coming back. And he's coming back soon. Christians should be the ones who are thrilled by this knowledge. It gives you so much hope! It gives you courage to live the challenging days you're living through right now. It gives you powerful motivation to get serious about answering God's call for your life. You want to be ready. You want to have your life right with God when the last trumpet sounds. You can't know the exact moment when he will arrive; you just know it's going to be soon.

Make your prayer the words of Revelation 22:20, "Amen. Come, Lord Jesus!" Do your part to be ready—be excited about his return. Get your heart tender and right before him. Share the news with those who don't know. It'll be the most awesome, most glorious moment the world has ever seen.

SEE FOR YOURSELF:

Heb. 10:37; James 5:8; Rev. 1:7; 22:12

from the tree of life and may go through the
gates into the city. 15Outside the city are the evil
people, those who do evil magic, who sin
sexually, who murder, who worship idols, and
who love lies and tell lies.

16"I, Jesus, have sent my angel to tell you
these things for the churches. I am the descendant from the family of David, and I am
the bright morning star."

17The Spirit and the bride say, "Come!" Let
the one who hears this say, "Come!" Let whoever is thirsty come; whoever wishes may have
the water of life as a free gift.

18I warn everyone who hears the words of
the prophecy of this book: If anyone adds
anything to these words, God will add to that
person the disasters written about in this book.
19And if anyone takes away from the words of
this book of prophecy, God will take away that
one's share of the tree of life and of the holy
city, which are written about in this book.

20Jesus, the One who says these things are
true, says, "Yes, I am coming soon."

Amen. Come, Lord Jesus!

21The grace of the Lord Jesus be with all.
Amen.

Reading Plans

Okay, so you think that reading the Bible is a good idea—but where should you start? The Bible is a BIG book—make that a *library*—of sixty-six books. Should you just start on page 1 and read every page? Sure you could; that's a great way. But there are other ways, too. You might pick a book of the Bible and read it (many people like to start with the Book of John). But if you're looking for other options, here are a few ideas for you.

30 DAYS WITH JESUS

Ever ask yourself, *I wonder what Jesus would do?* Here's how you can find out. Take a month and read the story of Jesus.

60 DAYS WITH PAUL

You've probably heard of the apostle Paul. He's the guy who wrote most of the New Testament. After you read Jesus' story, this is a good place to learn what it means to be a follower of Jesus.

90-DAY OVERVIEW OF THE BIBLE

This plan takes you through the major events of the Bible without your reading the entire book.

365 DAYS THROUGH THE WHOLE BIBLE

Ready for the biggest challenge of all? Why not read through the entire Bible in a year? This plan will take you through every verse of the Bible in one year.

No matter how you decide to read, stick with it. It's normal to skip a day here and there. Don't get discouraged. Just pick up where you left off and read this amazing Book.

30 Days with Jesus

1. John 1:1-51
2. Luke 2:1–52
3. Mark 1:1–11
4. Luke 4:1–44
5. John 3:1–36
6. Luke 5:1–39
7. John 4:1–54
8. Luke 6:1–49
9. Luke 7:1–50
10. Luke 8:1–56
11. Mark 8:1–38
12. Luke 10:1–42
13. Matthew 5:1–48
14. Matthew 6:1–34
15. Matthew 7:1–29
16. Luke 14:1–35
17. Luke 15:1–32
18. Luke 16:1–31
19. John 8:1–59
20. Luke 17:1–37
21. Luke 18:1–43
22. John 9:1–41
23. Luke 19:1–48
24. Luke 20:1–47
25. John 10:1–42
26. John 11:1–57
27. Mark 13:1–37
28. Luke 22:1–71
29. Matthew 27:1–66
30. Luke 24:1–53

60 Days with Paul

1. Romans 1:16–32
2. Romans 2:1–16
3. Romans 3:21–31
4. Romans 4:1–25
5. Romans 5:12–21
6. Romans 6:1–23
7. Romans 7:1–25
8. Romans 8:18–39
9. Romans 10:1–21
10. Romans 12:1–21
11. Romans 13:1–14
12. Romans 14:1—15:6
13. 1 Corinthians 1:10–31
14. 1 Corinthians 2:1–16
15. 1 Corinthians 3:1–23
16. 1 Corinthians 7:1–24
17. 1 Corinthians 7:25–40
18. 1 Corinthians 9:19—10:13
19. 1 Corinthians 12:1–31
20. 1 Corinthians 13:1–13
21. 1 Corinthians 15:1–28
22. 2 Corinthians 1:3–14
23. 2 Corinthians 1:15—2:11
24. 2 Corinthians 4:1–18
25. 2 Corinthians 5:1—6:2
26. 2 Corinthians 6:14—7:1
27. 2 Corinthians 8:1–15
28. Galatians 2:11–21
29. Galatians 3:19—4:7
30. Galatians 5:1–26
31. Galatians 6:1–10
32. Ephesians 1:3–14
33. Ephesians 1:15—2:10
34. Ephesians 5:1–20
35. Ephesians 5:21—6:9
36. Ephesians 6:10–20
37. Philippians 1:3–26
38. Philippians 1:27—2:18
39. Philippians 3:1–16
40. Philippians 3:17—4:9
41. Philippians 4:10–23
42. Colossians 1:15–23
43. Colossians 2:6–23
44. Colossians 3:1–17
45. Colossians 3:18—4:6
46. 1 Thessalonians 1:1–10
47. 1 Thessalonians 4:1–18
48. 1 Thessalonians 5:1–28
49. 2 Thessalonians 2:1–17
50. 2 Thessalonians 3:1–15
51. 1 Timothy 2:1–15
52. 1 Timothy 3:1–16
53. 1 Timothy 4:1–16
54. 1 Timothy 5:1–22
55. 1 Timothy 6:3–21
56. 2 Timothy 1:3–18
57. 2 Timothy 2:1—3:9
58. 2 Timothy 4:1–8
59. Titus 1:1–16
60. Titus 2:1—3:11

90-Day Overview of the Bible

1. Genesis 1:1—2:3
2. Genesis 3:1–24
3. Genesis 6:9—7:24
4. Genesis 8:1—9:17
5. Genesis 17:1–22
6. Genesis 22:1–19
7. Genesis 25:19–34
8. Genesis 27:1—28:9
9. Genesis 37:1–36
10. Genesis 41:1–57
11. Genesis 45:1–28
12. Exodus 1:8—2:15
13. Exodus 3:1—4:17
14. Exodus 5:1—6:13
15. Exodus 12:1–42
16. Exodus 13:17—14:31
17. Exodus 20:1–21
18. Numbers 13:1–33
19. Joshua 2:1–24
20. Joshua 6:1–27
21. Judges 16:4–31
22. 1 Samuel 1:1–28
23. 1 Samuel 3:1–21
24. 1 Samuel 10:1–27
25. 1 Samuel 16:1–13
26. 1 Samuel 17:1–58
27. 1 Samuel 24:1–22
28. 2 Samuel 11:1—12:25
29. 1 Kings 3:1–28
30. 1 Kings 17:8–24
31. 1 Kings 18:1–46
32. 2 Kings 2:1–18
33. 2 Kings 4:8–37
34. 2 Chronicles 35:20—36:23
35. Esther 2:1–23
36. Esther 6:1—8:8
37. Job 1:1—2:13; 42:1–17
38. Psalm 23:1–6
39. Psalm 51:1–19
40. Psalm 100:1–5
41. Psalm 121:1–8
42. Psalm 145:1–21
43. Proverbs 4:1–27
44. Ecclesiastes 11:9—12:14
45. Isaiah 53:1–12
46. Daniel 1:1–21
47. Daniel 3:1–30
48. Daniel 6:1–28
49. Jonah 1:1—4:11
50. Matthew 1:18—2:23
51. Matthew 5:1–16; 6:1—7:12
52. Matthew 14:13–36
53. Matthew 21:1–17
54. Matthew 26:47–75
55. Matthew 27:15–66
56. Matthew 28:1–20
57. Mark 1:1–20
58. Mark 4:1–20
59. Luke 1:26–56; 2:1–20
60. Luke 10:25–42; 14:25–35
61. Luke 15:1–32
62. Luke 22:1–23
63. Luke 24:13–53
64. John 1:1–18
65. John 3:1–21
66. John 4:1–42
67. John 8:1–11
68. John 11:1–44
69. John 14:1–31
70. Acts 1:1–11
71. Acts 2:1–47
72. Acts 8:26–40
73. Acts 9:1–31
74. Acts 11:1–18
75. Acts 16:11–40
76. Romans 3:1–31
77. Romans 8:1–39
78. Romans 12:1–21
79. 1 Corinthians 13:1–13
80. 1 Corinthians 15:1–58
81. Ephesians 2:1–22; 6:10–20
82. Philippians 3:1—4:9
83. Colossians 3:1—4:1
84. 1 Thessalonians 4:1–18
85. Hebrews 11:1–40
86. James 1:1–27
87. James 3:1–18
88. 1 Peter 1:3–25
89. 1 John 1:1—2:17
90. Revelation 21:1—22:21

365 Days Through the Whole Bible

DATE	REFERENCE
January 1	Genesis 1:1—3:24
January 2	Genesis 4:1—5:32
January 3	Genesis 6:1—8:22
January 4	Genesis 9:1—11:32
January 5	Genesis 12:1—14:24
January 6	Genesis 15:1—17:27
January 7	Genesis 18:1—20:18
January 8	Genesis 21:1—23:20
January 9	Genesis 24:1—28:9
January 10	Genesis 28:10—30:43
January 11	Genesis 31:1—36:43
January 12	Genesis 37:1—41:57
January 13	Genesis 42:1—45:28
January 14	Genesis 46:1—50:26
January 15	Exodus 1:1—4:31
January 16	Exodus 5:1—7:13
January 17	Exodus 7:14—12:30
January 18	Exodus 12:31—18:27
January 19	Exodus 19:1—24:18
January 20	Exodus 25:1—31:18
January 21	Exodus 32:1—34:35
January 22	Exodus 35:1—40:38
January 23	Leviticus 1:1—7:38
January 24	Leviticus 8:1—10:20
January 25	Leviticus 11:1—17:16
January 26	Leviticus 18:1—22:33
January 27	Leviticus 23:1—25:55
January 28	Leviticus 26:1—27:34
January 29	Numbers 1:1—4:49
January 30	Numbers 5:1—10:10
January 31	Numbers 10:11—14:45
February 1	Numbers 15:1—21:35
February 2	Numbers 22:1—25:18
February 3	Numbers 26:1—31:54
February 4	Numbers 32:1—34:29
February 5	Numbers 35:1—36:13
February 6	Deuteronomy 1:1—5:33
February 7	Deuteronomy 6:1—11:32
February 8	Deuteronomy 12:1—16:17
February 9	Deuteronomy 16:18—20:20
February 10	Deuteronomy 21:1—26:19
February 11	Deuteronomy 27:1—30:20
February 12	Deuteronomy 31:1—34:12
February 13	Joshua 1:1—5:12
February 14	Joshua 5:13—8:35

DATE	REFERENCE
February 15	Joshua 9:1—12:24
February 16	Joshua 13:1—19:51
February 17	Joshua 20:1—24:33
February 18	Judges 1:1—3:6
February 19	Judges 3:7—8:35
February 20	Judges 9:1—12:15
February 21	Judges 13:1—16:31
February 22	Judges 17:1—21:25
February 23	Ruth 1:1—4:22
February 24	1 Samuel 1:1—3:21
February 25	1 Samuel 4:1—7:17
February 26	1 Samuel 8:1—12:25
February 27	1 Samuel 13:1—15:35
February 28	1 Samuel 16:1—17:58
March 1	1 Samuel 18:1—20:42
March 2	1 Samuel 21:1—26:25
March 3	1 Samuel 27:1—31:13
March 4	2 Samuel 1:1—4:12
March 5	2 Samuel 5:1—7:29
March 6	2 Samuel 8:1—10:19
March 7	2 Samuel 11:1—12:31
March 8	2 Samuel 13:1—14:33
March 9	2 Samuel 15:1—20:26
March 10	2 Samuel 21:1—24:25
March 11	1 Kings 1:1—4:34
March 12	1 Kings 5:1—8:66
March 13	1 Kings 9:1—11:43
March 14	1 Kings 12:1—16:34
March 15	1 Kings 17:1—19:21
March 16	1 Kings 20:1—22:53
March 17	2 Kings 1:1—8:15
March 18	2 Kings 8:16—10:36
March 19	2 Kings 11:1—13:25
March 20	2 Kings 14:1—17:41
March 21	2 Kings 18:1—21:26
March 22	2 Kings 22:1—25:30
March 23	1 Chronicles 1:1—9:44
March 24	1 Chronicles 10:1—12:40
March 25	1 Chronicles 13:1—17:27
March 26	1 Chronicles 18:1—21:30
March 27	1 Chronicles 22:1—27:34
March 28	1 Chronicles 28:1—29:30
March 29	2 Chronicles 1:1—5:1
March 30	2 Chronicles 5:2—9:31
March 31	2 Chronicles 10:1—14:1

DATE	REFERENCE
April 1	2 Chronicles 14:2—16:14
April 2	2 Chronicles 17:1—21:3
April 3	2 Chronicles 21:4—24:27
April 4	2 Chronicles 25:1—28:27
April 5	2 Chronicles 29:1—32:33
April 6	2 Chronicles 33:1—35:27
April 7	2 Chronicles 36:1-23
April 8	Ezra 1:1—2:70
April 9	Ezra 3:1—6:22
April 10	Ezra 7:1—8:36
April 11	Ezra 9:1—10:44
April 12	Nehemiah 1:1—2:10
April 13	Nehemiah 2:11—3:32
April 14	Nehemiah 4:1—7:73
April 15	Nehemiah 8:1—10:39
April 16	Nehemiah 11:1—13:31
April 17	Esther 1:1—2:23
April 18	Esther 3:1—4:17
April 19	Esther 5:1—10:3
April 20	Job 1:1—2:13
April 21	Job 3:1—14:22
April 22	Job 15:1—21:34
April 23	Job 22:1—31:40
April 24	Job 32:1—37:24
April 25	Job 38:1—41:34
April 26	Job 42:1-17
April 27	Psalms 1:1—4:8
April 28	Psalms 5:1—8:9
April 29	Psalms 9:1—12:8
April 30	Psalms 13:1—16:11
May 1	Psalms 17:1—20:9
May 2	Psalms 21:1—24:10
May 3	Psalms 25:1—28:9
May 4	Psalms 29:1—32:11
May 5	Psalms 33:1—36:12
May 6	Psalms 37:1—41:13
May 7	Psalms 42:1—45:17
May 8	Psalms 46:1—49:20
May 9	Psalms 50:1—53:6
May 10	Psalms 54:1—56:13
May 11	Psalms 57:1—59:17
May 12	Psalms 60:1—62:12
May 13	Psalms 63:1—65:13
May 14	Psalms 66:1—68:35
May 15	Psalms 69:1—72:20
May 16	Psalms 73:1—75:10
May 17	Psalms 76:1—78:72
May 18	Psalms 79:1—81:16
May 19	Psalms 82:1—84:12
May 20	Psalms 85:1—89:52
May 21	Psalms 90:1—92:15
May 22	Psalms 93:1—95:11
May 23	Psalms 96:1—98:9
May 24	Psalms 99:1—101:8
May 25	Psalms 102:1—104:35
May 26	Psalms 105:1—106:48
May 27	Psalms 107:1—109:31
May 28	Psalms 110:1—112:10
May 29	Psalms 113:1—115:18
May 30	Psalms 116:1—118:29
May 31	Psalm 119:1-176
June 1	Psalms 120:1—124:8
June 2	Psalms 125:1—129:8
June 3	Psalms 130:1—134:3
June 4	Psalms 135:1—137:9
June 5	Psalms 138:1—140:13
June 6	Psalms 141:1—144:15
June 7	Psalms 145:1—150:6
June 8	Proverbs 1:1-33
June 9	Proverbs 2:1-22
June 10	Proverbs 3:1-35
June 11	Proverbs 4:1-27
June 12	Proverbs 5:1-23
June 13	Proverbs 6:1-35
June 14	Proverbs 7:1-27
June 15	Proverbs 8:1-36
June 16	Proverbs 9:1-18
June 17	Proverbs 10:1-32
June 18	Proverbs 11:1-31
June 19	Proverbs 12:1-28
June 20	Proverbs 13:1-25
June 21	Proverbs 14:1-35
June 22	Proverbs 15:1-33
June 23	Proverbs 16:1-33
June 24	Proverbs 17:1-28
June 25	Proverbs 18:1-24
June 26	Proverbs 19:1-29
June 27	Proverbs 20:1-30
June 28	Proverbs 21:1-31
June 29	Proverbs 22:1-29
June 30	Proverbs 23:1-35
July 1	Proverbs 24:1-34
July 2	Proverbs 25:1-28
July 3	Proverbs 26:1-28
July 4	Proverbs 27:1-27
July 5	Proverbs 28:1-28
July 6	Proverbs 29:1-27
July 7	Proverbs 30:1-33
July 8	Proverbs 31:1-31
July 9	Ecclesiastes 1:1—2:26
July 10	Ecclesiastes 3:1—5:20
July 11	Ecclesiastes 6:1—8:17
July 12	Ecclesiastes 9:1—12:14
July 13	Song of Solomon 1:1—8:14
July 14	Isaiah 1:1—6:13
July 15	Isaiah 7:1—12:6
July 16	Isaiah 13:1—18:7
July 17	Isaiah 19:1—23:18
July 18	Isaiah 24:1—27:13
July 19	Isaiah 28:1—31:9
July 20	Isaiah 32:1—35:10
July 21	Isaiah 36:1—39:8

DATE	REFERENCE
July 22	Isaiah 40:1—48:22
July 23	Isaiah 49:1—52:12
July 24	Isaiah 52:13—55:13
July 25	Isaiah 56:1—59:21
July 26	Isaiah 60:1—66:24
July 27	Jeremiah 1:1—6:30
July 28	Jeremiah 7:1—10:25
July 29	Jeremiah 11:1—15:21
July 30	Jeremiah 16:1—20:18
July 31	Jeremiah 21:1—24:10
August 1	Jeremiah 25:1—29:32
August 2	Jeremiah 30:1—33:26
August 3	Jeremiah 34:1—38:28
August 4	Jeremiah 39:1—45:5
August 5	Jeremiah 46:1—52:34
August 6	Lamentations 1:1—5:22
August 7	Ezekiel 1:1—3:27
August 8	Ezekiel 4:1—11:25
August 9	Ezekiel 12:1—17:24
August 10	Ezekiel 18:1—24:27
August 11	Ezekiel 25:1—32:32
August 12	Ezekiel 33:1—39:29
August 13	Ezekiel 40:1—48:35
August 14	Daniel 1:1—3:30
August 15	Daniel 4:1—6:28
August 16	Daniel 7:1—12:13
August 17	Hosea 1:1—3:5
August 18	Hosea 4:1—5:15
August 19	Hosea 6:1—10:15
August 20	Hosea 11:1—14:9
August 21	Joel 1:1—2:27
August 22	Joel 2:28—3:21
August 23	Amos 1:1—2:16
August 24	Amos 3:1—6:14
August 25	Amos 7:1—9:15
August 26	Obadiah 1-21
August 27	Jonah 1:1—2:10
August 28	Jonah 3:1—4:11
August 29	Micah 1:1—2:13
August 30	Micah 3:1—5:15
August 31	Micah 6:1—7:20
September 1	Nahum 1:1—3:19
September 2	Habakkuk 1:1—3:19
September 3	Zephaniah 1:1—3:20
September 4	Haggai 1:1—2:23
September 5	Zechariah 1:1—8:23
September 6	Zechariah 9:1—14:21
September 7	Malachi 1:1—4:6
September 8	Matthew 1:1—4:25
September 9	Matthew 5:1-48
September 10	Matthew 6:1-34
September 11	Matthew 7:1-29
September 12	Matthew 8:1—10:42
September 13	Matthew 11:1—13:52
September 14	Matthew 13:53—15:39
September 15	Matthew 16:1—18:35

DATE	REFERENCE
September 16	Matthew 19:1—20:34
September 17	Matthew 21:1—23:39
September 18	Matthew 24:1—25:46
September 19	Matthew 26:1—28:20
September 20	Mark 1:1—3:35
September 21	Mark 4:1—7:23
September 22	Mark 7:24—9:1
September 23	Mark 9:2—10:52
September 24	Mark 11:1—12:44
September 25	Mark 13:1-37
September 26	Mark 14:1—16:20
September 27	Luke 1:1—4:13
September 28	Luke 4:14—6:49
September 29	Luke 7:1—9:50
September 30	Luke 9:51—10:42
October 1	Luke 11:1-54
October 2	Luke 12:1-59
October 3	Luke 13:1—14:35
October 4	Luke 15:1—16:31
October 5	Luke 17:1—19:27
October 6	Luke 19:28—21:38
October 7	Luke 22:1-71
October 8	Luke 23:1-56
October 9	Luke 24:1-53
October 10	John 1:1—2:12
October 11	John 2:13—3:36
October 12	John 4:1-45
October 13	John 4:46—6:71
October 14	John 7:1—10:42
October 15	John 11:1—12:50
October 16	John 13:1—14:31
October 17	John 15:1—17:26
October 18	John 18:1—19:42
October 19	John 20:1—21:25
October 20	Acts 1:1—4:37
October 21	Acts 5:1—7:60
October 22	Acts 8:1—12:24
October 23	Acts 12:25—15:35
October 24	Acts 15:36—18:23
October 25	Acts 18:24—21:16
October 26	Acts 21:17—28:31
October 27	Romans 1:1—3:20
October 28	Romans 3:21—5:21
October 29	Romans 6:1—8:39
October 30	Romans 9:1—11:36
October 31	Romans 12:1—16:27
November 1	1 Corinthians 1:1—4:21
November 2	1 Corinthians 5:1—6:20
November 3	1 Corinthians 7:1-40
November 4	1 Corinthians 8:1—11:1
November 5	1 Corinthians 11:2—14:40
November 6	1 Corinthians 15:1—16:24
November 7	2 Corinthians 1:1—2:11
November 8	2 Corinthians 2:12—7:16
November 9	2 Corinthians 8:1—9:15
November 10	2 Corinthians 10:1—13:14

DATE	REFERENCE
November 11	Galatians 1:1—2:21
November 12	Galatians 3:1—4:31
November 13	Galatians 5:1—6:18
November 14	Ephesians 1:1—3:21
November 15	Ephesians 4:1—6:24
November 16	Philippians 1:1–30
November 17	Philippians 2:1–30
November 18	Philippians 3:1—4:1
November 19	Philippians 4:2–23
November 20	Colossians 1:1—2:23
November 21	Colossians 3:1—4:18
November 22	1 Thessalonians 1:1—3:13
November 23	1 Thessalonians 4:1—5:28
November 24	2 Thessalonians 1:1—2:17
November 25	2 Thessalonians 3:1–18
November 26	1 Timothy 1:1–20
November 27	1 Timothy 2:1—3:16
November 28	1 Timothy 4:1—6:21
November 29	2 Timothy 1:1—2:26
November 30	2 Timothy 3:1—4:22
December 1	Titus 1:1–16
December 2	Titus 2:1–15
December 3	Titus 3:1–15
December 4	Philemon 1–25
December 5	Hebrews 1:1—2:18
December 6	Hebrews 3:1—4:13

DATE	REFERENCE
December 7	Hebrews 4:14—7:28
December 8	Hebrews 8:1—10:18
December 9	Hebrews 10:19—13:25
December 10	James 1:1–27
December 11	James 2:1—3:12
December 12	James 3:13—5:20
December 13	1 Peter 1:1—2:10
December 14	1 Peter 2:11—4:19
December 15	1 Peter 5:1–14
December 16	2 Peter 1:1–21
December 17	2 Peter 2:1–22
December 18	2 Peter 3:1–18
December 19	1 John 1:1—2:27
December 20	1 John 2:28—4:21
December 21	1 John 5:1–21
December 22	2 John 1—3 John 15
December 23	Jude 1–25
December 24	Revelation 1:1—3:22
December 25	Revelation 4:1—5:14
December 26	Revelation 6:1—8:5
December 27	Revelation 8:6—11:19
December 28	Revelation 12:1—14:20
December 29	Revelation 15:1—16:21
December 30	Revelation 17:1—20:15
December 31	Revelation 21:1—22:21

Extreme Index

APPEARANCE

ATTITUDE

AUTHORITY

BAPTISM

BIBLE

BLESSING

Extreme Notes

This section is provided for you to write in your Bible . . . yes, that's right. . . . We want you to write in your Bible! Jot down things that are important to you, things you want to remember, things to pray for, and things that touch your heart as you study your Bible and live life in the Extreme!

PRAYER REQUESTS People and situations you want to pray for:

PRAYER REQUESTS

PRAISE REPORTS Examples of answered prayer in your life and in the lives of your family, friends, church, etc.:

PRAISE REPORTS

FAVORITE VERSES Scriptures that speak to you:

FAVORITE VERSES

SERMON NOTES Too good to forget!

SERMON NOTES

BLESSINGS IN MY LIFE

God touches lives in big and small ways and shares his love in both the obvious and the subtle. Who and what do you count as blessings in your life?

BLESSINGS IN MY LIFE

Addresses

Frequently Used Websites

Website	Web Address

Website	Web Address

Website	Web Address

People & Places

A B

1566

NOPQ

TUV